JURAN'S
QUALITY CONTROL
HANDBOOK

Other McGraw-Hill Reference Books of Interest

Handbooks

Avallone and Baumeister · MARKS' STANDARD HANDBOOK FOR MECHANICAL ENGINEERS

Brady and Clauser · MATERIALS HANDBOOK

Carrubba and Gordon · PRODUCT ASSURANCE PRINCIPLES

Considine · PROCESS INSTRUMENTS AND CONTROLS HANDBOOK

Crosby · QUALITY IS FREE

Crosby · QUALITY WITHOUT TEARS

Feigenbaum · TOTAL QUALITY CONTROL

Fink and Beaty · STANDARD HANDBOOK FOR ELECTRICAL ENGINEERS

Fink and Christiansen · ELECTRONICS ENGINEER'S HANDBOOK

Gerelle and Stark · INTEGRATED MANUFACTURING

Harrington · THE IMPROVEMENT PROCESS

Higgins and Morrow · MAINTENANCE ENGINEERING HANDBOOK

Hradesky · PRODUCTIVITY AND QUALITY IMPROVEMENT

Ireson and Coombs · HANDBOOK OF RELIABILITY ENGINEERING AND MANAGEMENT

Juran · MANAGERIAL BREAKTHROUGH

Juran and Gryna · QUALITY PLANNING AND ANALYSIS

Lubben · JUST-IN-TIME MANUFACTURING

Maynard · INDUSTRIAL ENGINEERING HANDBOOK

Ott · PROCESS QUALITY CONTROL

Perry and Green · PERRY'S CHEMICAL ENGINEERS' HANDBOOK

Ross · TAGUCHI TECHNIQUES FOR QUALITY ENGINEERING

Shinskey · PROCESS CONTROL SYSTEMS

Taylor · QUALITY CONTROL SYSTEMS

Woodson · HANDBOOK OF HUMAN FACTORS ENGINEERING DATA

Encyclopedias

CONCISE ENCYCLOPEDIA OR SCIENCE AND TECHNOLOGY
ENCYCLOPEDIA OF ELECTRONICS AND COMPUTERS
ENCYCLOPEDIA OF ENERGY
ENCYCLOPEDIA OF ENGINEERING
ENCYCLOPEDIA OF PHYSICS

Dictionaries

DICTIONARY OF SCIENTIFIC AND TECHNICAL TERMS
DICTIONARY OF MECHANICAL AND DESIGN ENGINEERING
DICTIONARY OF ELECTRONICS AND COMPUTER TECHNOLOGY
DICTIONARY OF ENGINEERING

*For more information about other McGraw-Hill materials,
call 1–800–2–MCGRAW in the United States. In other
countries, call your nearest McGraw-Hill office.*

JURAN'S
QUALITY CONTROL
HANDBOOK

J. M. Juran Editor-in-Chief

Founder and Chairman Emeritus, Juran Institute, Inc.
Wilton, Connecticut

Frank M. Gryna Associate Editor

Vice President, Juran Institute, Inc.
Wilton, Connecticut
Distinguished Professor of Industrial Engineering
Emeritus, Bradley University

FOURTH EDITION

McGRAW-HILL BOOK COMPANY

New York   St. Louis   San Francisco   Auckland   Bogotá
Hamburg   London   Madrid   Mexico   Milan
Montreal   New Delhi   Panama
Paris   São Paulo   Singapore
Sydney   Tokyo   Toronto

Library of Congress Cataloging-in-Publication Data

Juran's quality control handbook / J. M. Juran, editor-in-chief, Frank
  M. Gryna, associate editor. — 4th ed.
      p.   cm.
    Rev. ed. of: Quality control handbook. 3rd ed. 1974.
    Includes bibliographies and indexes.
    ISBN 0-07-033176-6
      1. Quality control—Handbooks, manuals, etc.   I. Juran, J. M.
  (Joseph M.), 1904-   . II. Gryna, Frank M.   III. Quality control
  handbook.   IV. Title: Quality control handbook.
  TS156.J87   1988
  658.5′62—dc19   88-4002
                                                                          CIP

    34567890   DOC/DOC   93210

ISBN 0-07-033176-6

*The editors for this book were Betty Sun and Lester Strong and the
production supervisor was Richard Ausburn. It was set in Times Roman
by University Graphics, Inc.*

Printed and bound by R. R. Donnelley & Sons Company.

*For more information about other McGraw-Hill materials,
call 1–800–2–MCGRAW in the United States. In other
countries, call your nearest McGraw-Hill office.*

CONTENTS

List of Contributors   ix
Preface to the Fourth Edition   xi

1. HOW TO USE THE HANDBOOK 1.1
   J. M. Juran

2. THE QUALITY FUNCTION 2.1
   J. M. Juran

3. QUALITY AND INCOME 3.1
   J. M. Juran

4. QUALITY COSTS 4.1
   Frank M. Gryna

5. QUALITY POLICIES AND OBJECTIVES 5.1
   J. M. Juran

6. COMPANYWIDE PLANNING FOR QUALITY 6.1
   J. M. Juran

7. ORGANIZING FOR QUALITY 7.1
   J. M. Juran

8. UPPER MANAGEMENT AND QUALITY 8.1
   J. M. Juran

9. QUALITY ASSURANCE 9.1
   Frank M. Gryna

10. MANAGING HUMAN PERFORMANCE 10.1
    Edward M. Baker

11. TRAINING FOR QUALITY 11.1
    Frank M. Gryna

12. FIELD INTELLIGENCE 12.1
    Frank M. Gryna

13. PRODUCT DEVELOPMENT 13.1
Frank M. Gryna

14. SOFTWARE DEVELOPMENT 14.1
Patrick J. Fortune

15. SUPPLIER RELATIONS 15.1
Frank M. Gryna

16. MANUFACTURING PLANNING 16.1
Frank M. Gryna

17. PRODUCTION 17.1
Frank M. Gryna

18. INSPECTION AND TEST 18.1
Joseph J. Zeccardi

19. MARKETING 19.1
Frank M. Gryna

20. CUSTOMER SERVICE 20.1
Frank M. Gryna

21. ADMINISTRATIVE AND SUPPORT OPERATIONS 21.1
Frank M. Gryna

22. QUALITY IMPROVEMENT 22.1
Frank M. Gryna

23. BASIC STATISTICAL METHODS 23.1
Edward J. Dudewicz

24. STATISTICAL PROCESS CONTROL 24.1
Dorian Shainin and Peter D. Shainin

25. ACCEPTANCE SAMPLING 25.1
Edward G. Schilling and Dan J. Sommers

26. DESIGN AND ANALYSIS OF EXPERIMENTS 26.1
J. Stuart Hunter, with Mary G. Natrella, E. Harvey Barnett, William G. Hunter, and
Truman L. Koehler

27. COMPUTERS AND QUALITY 27.1
F. I. Orkin

28. PROCESS INDUSTRIES 28.1
R. S. Bingham, Jr., and Clyde H. Walden

29. ELECTRONICS COMPONENTS INDUSTRIES 29.1
A. Blanton Godfrey and Robert E. Kerwin

30. ASSEMBLY INDUSTRIES 30.1
J. Douglas Ekings

31. COMPLEX INDUSTRIES 31.1
H. Dean Voegtlen

32. JOB SHOP INDUSTRIES 32.1
Leonard A. Seder

33. SERVICE INDUSTRIES 33.1
Charles D. Zimmerman, III, and John W. Enell

34. QUALITY AND SOCIETY 34.1
J. M. Juran

35A. QUALITY AND THE NATIONAL CULTURE 35A.1
J. M. Juran

35B. QUALITY IN DEVELOPING COUNTRIES 35B.1
Lennart Sandholm

35C. QUALITY IN FRANCE 35C.1
Jean-Marie Gogue

35D. QUALITY IN THE FEDERAL REPUBLIC OF GERMANY 35D.1
Ernst Schlötel

35E. QUALITY IN GREAT BRITAIN 35E.1
Wilfred R. Thoday

35F. QUALITY IN JAPAN 35F.1
Yoshio Kondo

35G. QUALITY IN THE UNITED STATES OF AMERICA 35G.1
J. M. Juran

35H. QUALITY IN SOCIALIST COUNTRIES 35H.1
F. Egermayer

APPENDIX I—Glossary **AI.1**

APPENDIX II—Tables and Charts **AII.1**

**APPENDIX III—Selected Quality Standards, Specifications, and Related
Documents** **AIII.1**

APPENDIX IV—Quality Systems Terminology **AIV.1**

Name Index
Subject Index

CONTRIBUTORS

Dr. Edward M. Baker
Director, Total Quality Planning, Consulting, and Statistical Methods, Ford Motor Company, World Headquarters, Dearborn, MI
SECTION 10, MANAGING HUMAN PERFORMANCE

E. Harvey Barnett
Research Associate, Statistics, Corning Glass Works Corning, NY
SECTION 26, DESIGN AND ANALYSIS OF EXPERIMENTS

Richard S. Bingham, Jr.
Consultant, Wisconsin Rapids, WI
SECTION 28, PROCESS INDUSTRIES

Dr. Edward J. Dudewicz
Professor, Department of Mathematics, and Chairman, University Statistical Council, Syracuse University, Syracuse, NY
SECTION 23, BASIC STATISTICAL METHODS

Professor F. Egermayer, RN Dr., Dr. Sc.
Department of Industrial Engineering, Faculty of Mechanical Engineering, Czech Technical College, Prague, Czechoslovakia
SECTION 35H, QUALITY IN SOCIALIST COUNTRIES

J. Douglas Ekings
Manager, Customer Satisfaction, Xerox Corporation, Stamford, CT
SECTION 30, ASSEMBLY INDUSTRIES

John W. Enell, Eng.Sc.D.
Vice President, Research, Juran Institute, Inc., Wilton, CT
SECTION 33, SERVICE INDUSTRIES

Dr. Patrick Fortune
President, Parenteral Products Division, Baxter Healthcare Corporation, Deerfield, IL
SECTION 14, SOFTWARE DEVELOPMENT

A. Blanton Godfrey, Ph.D.
Chairman and CEO, Juran Institute, Inc., Wilton, CT
SECTION 29, ELECTRONIC COMPONENTS INDUSTRIES

Jean-Marie Gogue
President, Mast, Inc., Paris, France
SECTION 35C, QUALITY IN FRANCE

Dr. Frank M. Gryna
Vice President, Juran Institute, Inc., Wilton, CT
SECTION 4, QUALITY COSTS; SECTION 9, QUALITY ASSURANCE; SECTION 11, TRAINING FOR QUALITY; SECTION 12, FIELD INTELLIGENCE; SECTION 13, PRODUCT DEVELOPMENT; SECTION 15, SUPPLIER RELATIONS; SECTION 16, MANUFACTURING PLANNING; SECTION 17, PRODUCTION; SECTION 19, MARKETING; SECTION 20, CUSTOMER SERVICE; SECTION 21, ADMINISTRATIVE AND SUPPORT OPERATIONS; SECTION 22, QUALITY IMPROVEMENT

Dr. J. Stuart Hunter
Consultant, Princeton, NJ
SECTION 26, DESIGN AND ANALYSIS OF EXPERIMENTS

William G. Hunter
Director, Center for Quality and Productivity Improvement; Professor, Statistics and Engineering, University of Wisconsin, Madison, WI
SECTION 26, DESIGN AND ANALYSIS OF EXPERIMENTS

Dr. J. M. Juran
Founder and Chairman Emeritus, Juran Institute, Inc., Wilton, CT
SECTION 1, HOW TO USE THE HANDBOOK; SECTION 2, QUALITY FUNCTION; SECTION 3, QUALITY AND INCOME; SECTION 5, QUALITY POLICIES AND OBJECTIVES; SECTION 6, COMPANYWIDE PLANNING FOR QUALITY; SECTION 7, ORGANIZATION FOR QUALITY; SECTION 8, UPPER MANAGEMENT AND QUALITY; SECTION 34, QUALITY AND SOCIETY; SECTION 35A, QUALITY AND THE NATIONAL CULTURE; SECTION 35G, QUALITY IN THE UNITED STATES OF AMERICA

Dr. Robert Kerwin
Technology Management Director, AT&T, Berkeley Heights, NJ
SECTION 29, ELECTRONIC COMPONENTS INDUSTRIES

Truman L. Koehler
Vice President, Sandoz Corporation, East Hanover, NJ
SECTION 26, DESIGN AND ANALYSIS OF EXPERIMENTS

Dr. Yoshio Kondo
Professor Emeritus, Kyoto University, Kyoto, Japan
SECTION 35F, QUALITY IN JAPAN

Mary G. Natrella
Guest Worker, National Bureau of Standards, Gaithersburg, MD
SECTION 26, DESIGN AND ANALYSIS OF EXPERIMENTS

Fredric I. Orkin
Vice President, General Manager, Multiplex Systems Division of Baxter Healthcare Corporation, Round Lake, IL
SECTION 27, COMPUTERS AND QUALITY

Dr. Lennart Sandholm
Management Consultant, Bjorklund and Sandholm, Djursholm, Sweden
SECTION 35B, QUALITY IN DEVELOPING COUNTRIES

Dr. Edward G. Schilling
Paul A. Miller Distinguished Professor and Chairman of the Graduate Statistics Department, Rochester Institute of Technology Center for Quality and Applied Statistics, Rochester, NY
SECTION 25, ACCEPTANCE SAMPLING

Dipl.-Ing. Ernst Schlötel
Lecturer & Consultant in Quality Matters, Bad Homburg, Federal Republic of Germany
SECTION 35D, QUALITY IN THE FEDERAL REPUBLIC OF GERMANY

Leonard A. Seder
Leonard A. Seder and Associates, Lexington, MA
SECTION 32, JOB SHOP INDUSTRIES

Dorian Shainin, CMC
Shainin Consultants, Inc., Manchester, CT
SECTION 24, STATISTICAL PROCESS CONTROL

Peter D. Shainin, PE
Shainin Consultants, Inc., Burlington, WA
SECTION 24, STATISTICAL PROCESS CONTROL

Dan J. Sommers
Manager, New Product Quality, General Electric Company, Cleveland, OH
SECTION 25, ACCEPTANCE SAMPLING

Wilfred R. Thoday, Ph.D.
Vice President, Institute of Quality Assurance, London, England
SECTION 35E, QUALITY IN GREAT BRITAIN

H. Dean Voegtlen
Consultant, Inglewood, CA, Formerly Director, Product Cost Effectiveness, Hughes Aircraft Company
SECTION 31, COMPLEX INDUSTRIES

Clyde H. Walden, Ph.D.
Consultant, Piedmont, CA
SECTION 28, PROCESS INDUSTRIES

Joseph J. Zeccardi
Vice President, Customer Service Logistics, Unisys Corporation, Blue Bell, PA
SECTION 18, INSPECTION AND TEST

Charles D. Zimmerman, III
Vice President, Human Resources, United States Fidelity & Guaranty Co., Baltimore, MD
SECTION 33, SERVICE INDUSTRIES

PREFACE TO THE FOURTH EDITION

Over four decades have passed since *Quality Control Handbook* (now *Juran's Quality Control Handbook*) was first in gestation. (The contract to produce it was signed in 1945; the First Edition was published in 1951.) In the intervening years it has attained the status of the leading international reference work on the subject. Including its various translations, the first three editions have exceeded 350,000 copies, cumulatively.

A parallel development has been a remarkable growth in the importance of quality to society generally. Much of this growth is due to the phenomenon of "Life behind the Quality Dikes." The industrial society provides its citizenry with the marvelous benefits of technology. However it also makes the continuity of that life style depend absolutely on the quality of the goods and services which are the base of an industrial society.

In addition there has been a growth of competition in quality. This has become especially intense on the international level. Quality is now a critical element in international trade, in defense capability, in human safety and health, in maintaining the environment.

Industrial companies have been responding to this growth in importance of the quality function. This response is evident in a number of ways:

1. The scope of "quality" has increasingly been broadened to include:

   Manufacturing support activities

   Business processes

   The needs of internal customers

2. Planning for quality has increasingly been evolving into a formalized, structured approach involving extensive internal participation as well as joint planning with clients and suppliers.

3. Upper managers are increasingly taking charge of managing for quality. This trend is evident from such movements as:

   Evolution of the concept of companywide quality management (total quality control, etc.)

   Creation of high-level quality councils

   Enlargement of the business plan to include annual quality improvement

   Establishment of corporate quality goals, measures of performance, and upper management reviews

4. Training in managing for quality has increasingly been extended into all functions, including general management.

In addition various organs of society—government, academia, professional societies, etc.—have increasingly become involved with managing for quality in ways such as:

   Government sponsorship of national quality motivation programs

   Creation of national awards for quality

Promulgation of laws to protect safety, health, and the environment

Proliferation of training courses and consultancies oriented to various aspects of managing for quality

The Fourth Edition has recognized the emerging massive changes through extensive revisions in structure as well as through updating. A major change has been the construction of a new conceptual approach to managing for quality—the Trilogy of processes through which quality is managed: quality planning; quality control; quality improvement. This Trilogy has established itself as a tested framework on which to build a cohesive, unified approach to managing for quality.

The organizational structure of the Third Edition met with a distinctly favorable reception from users. In consequence I have retained much of that structure. It consists mainly of:

1. A series of 12 sections setting out the various managerial concepts and tools associated with achieving quality

2. Another series of 10 sections which follow the product through its life cycle

3. Four sections devoted to the statistical tools associated with attaining quality

4. Six sections which exemplify application of concepts, methods, and tools in important industries

5. Nine sections which examine the ways of managing quality in various national cultures

Many of the sections retain the same titles they had in the Third Edition, but the user should not be deceived. No section has escaped extensive revision. It is doubtful that as much as 20 percent of the Third Edition was incorporated into the Fourth Edition.

All this growth and change have enlarged the editorial burdens as well. As a result I am most grateful to those whose collaboration has made this Fourth Edition possible.

Dr. F. M. Gryna has for the third time served as associate editor while enlarging his role as author. He collaborated fully in planning the revision, and he carried the major burden of enlisting the contributing authors and critiquing their outlines and manuscripts. Collectively all this was an extensive undertaking.

Another debt is owed to the authors—managers, educators, and specialists—who took time from full schedules to share their knowledge and experience with their international counterparts. These contributions are the very heart of the handbook. Supporting these authors are the numerous secretaries, staff members, and librarians (as well as family members) who assisted in the exacting preparation of the technical manuscripts. All of us deeply appreciate the dedication behind this essential support.

I am indebted to the Literary Executor of the late Sir Ronald A. Fisher, F.R.S., to Dr. Frank Yates, F.R.S., and to Oliver and Boyd, Edinburgh, for permission to reprint Table III from their book *Statistical Tables for Biological, Agricultural and Medical Research.*

In the planning stages of this edition, the editors were fortunate to receive advice from a number of highly experienced professionals. These included W. Edwards Deming, J. Douglas Ekings, Ralph A. Evans, H. James Harrington, Lloyd S. Nelson, Naomi J. McAfee, Arnold O. Putnam, John S. Ramberg, and Edward A. Reynolds.

Many practitioners contributed examples and advice in specific areas. Particularly helpful were Roger W. Berger, Roger L. Bollenbacher, J. Douglas Ekings, Donald N. Ekvall, Ronald Follett, Richard A. Freund, Derek S. Gryna, Gerald J. Hahn, John A. Keane, James F. Leonard, Dana B. Loson, Joseph M. Mazzeo, David A. McGaughy, Fredric I. Orkin, Joseph J. Pignatiello, Jr., Lawrence J. Schrader, R. M. Smith, Ronald D. Snee, James L. Thresh, Joseph J. Tsiakals, H. DeanVoegtlen, and Harrison M. Wadsworth.

John W. Enell, Al C. Endres, and Harris M. Brokke contributed significantly to the review and editing of manuscripts. In the final preparation of all sections, Randolph Warren provided editorial assistance while acting as liaison with the publisher's Production Department.

Our administrative assistants at the Juran Institute, Inc., particularly Judith A. Schalick, Marilyn M. Schmid, and Sharon Davis, were most helpful in preparing the manuscripts and conducting related researches, as well as maintaining correspondence with authors and others. Additional participants included Laura A. Sutherland and Margaret Cutrona at Juran Institute and Willie Luscher and Rita Borwick at Bradley University.

Dr. Gryna continues to be amazed by the support from his wife Dee, and her infinite patience and understanding.

Finally, I acknowledge the moral support provided by my wife of 62 years standing. This Fourth Edition is the only edition for which she did not personally prepare the bulk of the manuscript. As befits a gallant lady, her patience and encouragement have not wavered. I am once more deeply grateful to her.

One last note: Recognizing as we do the important and growing role of women in business and industry, every effort has been made to use gender-neutral language in this book. However, we have retained terms such as "ombudsman," "workmanship," and "craftsmanship," for which no generally agreed-upon gender-neutral equivalents exist; likewise in historical discussions we have not changed the terms "master" and "journeyman," which had technical meanings within the guild systems of the medieval era; and we have not altered terminology used in direct quotations from other sources. In all those instances, the words should be taken in a purely generic sense, intended to apply to women as well as to men.

J. M. JURAN

SECTION 1
HOW TO USE THE HANDBOOK

J. M. Juran

INTRODUCTION 1.1

USES OF THE HANDBOOK . . . 1.2

ORGANIZATION OF THE
HANDBOOK 1.2

   Managing the Quality
    Function 1.2

   Statistical Methods 1.3

   Industries 1.3

HOW TO FIND IT 1.3

   Tables of Contents 1.3

   Use of the Index 1.3

   Cross-References 1.4

   Main Road and Side Roads 1.4

ADAPTING TO USE 1.5

INTRODUCTION

This is a reference book for all who are involved with "fitness for use" of products and services. "All who are involved" includes:

The various departmental functions, e.g., product development, purchasing, manufacture, inspection, sales, customer service, and various support functions

The various levels of management, from top executives through supervisors

The various staff specialties associated with policies, objectives, planning, organizing, and improving and controlling quality

Practitioners in a variety of industries and processes, e.g., chemical, metallurgical, mechanical, electronic, job shop, service, etc.

It is a mistake to assume that the sole purpose of the book is to serve the needs of quality managers and quality specialists. The purpose of the book is to serve the entire quality function, and this includes participation from every major department of the organization.

While there is a great deal of know-how in this book, it takes skill and a bit of determination to learn how to find and make use of it. This first section of the book has therefore been designed to help the reader to find and apply those contents of the handbook which relate to the problem at hand.

USES OF THE HANDBOOK

Practitioners make a wide variety of uses of the *Quality Control Handbook*. A survey conducted as part of the planning for the Fourth Edition showed that usage is dominated by the following principal motives:

1. To study the narrative material as an aid to solving problems
2. To find structured answers in tables, charts, formulas, etc.
3. To review for specific self-training
4. To secure material for the teaching or training of others

Beyond these four most frequent uses, there is a longer list of less frequent uses:

To review for personal briefing prior to attending a meeting

To cross-check one's approach to tackling a problem

As references for instructors and students during training courses

To indoctrinate the boss

To train new employees

To help sell ideas to others, based on (1) the information in the handbook and (2) the authoritative status of the handbook

Usage appears to be more frequent during times of change, e.g., while developing new programs, working on new contracts and projects, reassigning functions, or trying out new ideas.

Irrespective of intended use, the information is very likely there. The problem for the practitioner becomes one of (1) knowing where to find it and (2) adapting the information to his or her specific needs.

ORGANIZATION OF THE HANDBOOK

Knowing "where to find it" starts with understanding how the handbook is structured. The handbook consists of several broad groupings, outlined below, of quality control know-how.

Managing the Quality Function.   This Management Group of handbook sections (i.e., chapters) is devoted to the attainment of quality in *any* industry, product, or process. Some of the sections in this group follow the "management sequence" as applied to the quality function: policy formation, goal setting, planning, organizing, training, etc. Other sections of this Management Group follow the "product progression sequence": new-product development, purchasing, manufacture, test, marketing, customer service, etc. Still other sections deal with broad problems of a coordinating nature, e.g., quality costs and quality improvement. Collectively, the Management Group consists of 33 sections and subsections (Sections 2 through 22, 27, 34 through 35H, and Appendices III and IV), and constitutes about 60 percent of the contents of the handbook.

Statistical Methods.   This Statistical Group shows how to make use of most of the statistical tools which are available for controlling and improving quality. This group is made up of the following:

1. Sections 23 through 26, each of which deals with one or more of these statistical tools
2. The Glossary of Symbols (Appendix I)
3. The supplemental statistical tables and charts (Appendix II)

Collectively, the Statistical Group makes up about 20 percent of the handbook.

Industries.   This Industry Group summarizes how quality is attained and maintained in each of a number of leading industries. These may be product-based (e.g., Assembly Industries) or process-based (e.g., Process Industries). This group (Sections 28 through 32) constitutes about 20 percent of the handbook. The growing service sector is represented by its own section, 33.

HOW TO FIND IT

There are three main roads for locating information in the handbook:

1. Tables of Contents
2. The Index
3. Cross-references

In addition, there are supplemental devices to aid in securing elaboration.

Note that the handbook follows a *dual system of numbering,* consisting of the section number followed by page number, figure number, or table number. For example, page number 16.7 is the seventh page in Section 16. Figure or table number 12.4 is in Section 12, and it is the fourth figure or table in that section.

Tables of Contents.   There is a hierarchy of these. At the top is the list of 42 *section and subsection headings,* each of which describes, in the broadest terms, the contents of that section.

Next there is the *list of contents* that appears on the first page of each section. Each item in any section's list of contents becomes a *major heading* within that section.

Next, under each of these major headings, there may be one or more *minor headings,* each descriptive of its bundle of contents. Some of these bundles may be broken down still further by alphabetic or numeric lists of subtopics.

In a good many cases, it will suffice merely to follow the hierarchy of tables of contents to find the information sought. In many other cases it will not. For such cases, an alternative approach is to use the Index.

Use of the Index.   A great deal of effort has gone into preparing the Index so that, through it, the reader can locate *all* the handbook material bearing on a subject. For example, the topic "self-control" is found in several sections (e.g., 16, Manufacturing Planning; 17, Production, etc.). The Index entry for "self-control" assembles *all* uses of the self-control concept and shows the numbers of the pages on which they may be found.

The fact that information about a single topic is found in more than one section (and even in many sections) gives rise to criticisms of the organization of the handbook, i.e., Why can't all the information on one subject be brought together in one place? The answer is that we require multiple and interconnected uses of knowledge, and hence these multiple appearances cannot be avoided. In fact, what must be done to minimize duplication is to make one and only one exhaustive explanation at some logical place and then to use cross-referencing elsewhere. In a sense, all the information on one subject *is* brought together—in the Index.

Some key words and phrases may be explained in several places in the handbook. However, there is always one passage which constitutes the major explanation or definition. In the Index, the word "defined" is used to identify this major definition, for example, "Evolutionary Operation, defined."

The Index also serves to assemble all case examples or applications under one heading for easy reference. For example, Section 22 deals with the general approach to quality improvement and includes numerous examples of the application of this approach. However, additional examples are found in other sections, notably Sections 21, and 28 through 33. The Index enables the reader to find these additional examples readily, since the page numbers are given.

Cross-References. The handbook makes extensive use of cross-references in the text in order to (1) guide the reader to further information on a subject and (2) avoid duplicate explanations of the same subject matter. The reader should regard these cross-references, wherever they occur, as extensions of the text.

Cross-referencing is to either (1) specific major headings in various sections or (2) specific figure numbers or table numbers. Study of the referenced material will provide further illumination.

A Note on Abbreviations. Abbreviations of names or organizations are usually used only after the full name has previously been spelled out, e.g., American Society for Quality Control (ASQC). In any case, all such abbreviations are listed and defined in the Index.

Main Road and Side Roads. The text of the handbook emphasizes the "main road" of quality control know-how, i.e., the comparatively limited number of usual situations which nevertheless occupy the bulk of the time and attention of practitioners. Beyond the main road are numerous "side roads," i.e., less usual situations which are quite diverse and which require special solutions.

(The term "side road" is not used in any derogatory sense. The practitioner who faces an unusual problem must nevertheless find a solution for it.)

As to these side roads, the handbook text, while not complete, nevertheless points the reader to available solutions. This is done in several ways:

Citations. The handbook cites numerous papers, books, and other bibliographic references. In most cases these citations also indicate the nature of the special contribution made by the work cited in order to help the reader to decide whether to go to the original source for elaboration.

Special Bibliographies. Some sections provide supplemental lists of bibliographical material for further reference. The editors have attempted to restrict the contents of these lists to items which (1) bear directly on the subject matter discussed in the text or (2) are of uncommon interest to the practitioner. A special bibliography in Appendix III lists quality standards and specifications.

Literature Search. Papers, books, and other references cited in the handbook contain further references which can be hunted up for further study. Use can be made of available abstracting and indexing services. A broad abstracting service in the engineering field is Engineering Index, Inc., 345 E. 47 St., New York, NY

10017. A specialized abstracting service in quality control and applied statistics is Executive Sciences Institute, Inc., 1005 Mississippi Ave., Davenport, IA 52803. In addition, various other specialized abstracting services are available on such subjects as reliability, statistical methods, research and development, etc.

In searching the literature, the practitioner is well advised to make use of librarians. To an astonishing degree, library specialists have devised tools for locating literature on any designated subject: special bibliographies, abstracting services, indexes by subject and author, etc. Librarians are trained in the use of these tools, and they maintain an effective communication network among themselves.

Author Contact. The written book or paper is usually a condensation of the author's knowledge; i.e., what he or she wrote is derived from material which is one or two orders of magnitude more voluminous than the published work. In some cases it is worthwhile to contact the author for further elaboration. Most authors have no objection to being contacted, and some of these contacts lead not only to more information but also to visits and enduring collaboration.

Other Sources. Resourceful people are able to find still other sources of information relating to the problem at hand. They contact the editors of journals to discover which companies have faced similar problems, so that they may contact these companies. They contact suppliers and customers to learn if competitors have found solutions. They attend meetings—such as courses, seminars, and conferences of professional societies—at which there is discussion of the problem. There is hardly a problem faced by any practitioner which has not already been actively studied by others.

ADAPTING TO USE

In many cases a practitioner is faced with adapting, to a special situation, knowledge derived from a totally different technology, i.e., industry, product, process. Making this transition requires that he or she identify the commonality, i.e., the common principle to which both the special situation and the derived knowledge correspond.

Often the commonality is managerial in nature and is comparatively easy to grasp. For example, the concept of self-control is a management universal and is applicable to any person in the company.

Commonality of a statistical nature is even easier to grasp, since so much information is reduced to formulas which are indifferent to the nature of the technology involved.

Even in technological matters, it is possible to identify commonalities despite great outward differences. For example, concepts such as process capability apply not only to manufacturing processes, but to administrative and support processes as well. (See Section 21 under Process Development.) In like manner, the approaches used to make quality improvements by discovering the causes of defects have been classified into specific categories which exhibit a great deal of commonality despite wide differences in technology. (See Section 22 under Diagnosis.)

In all these situations, the challenge to practitioners is to establish a linkage between their own situations and those from which the know-how was derived. This linkage is established by discovering the commonality which makes them both members of one species.

SECTION 2
THE QUALITY FUNCTION

"QUALITY" DEFINED **2.2**

Product 2.2

Product Feature 2.2

Customer 2.2

Customer Needs 2.3

Product Satisfaction 2.3

Conformance to
Specification; also,
Conformance to
Requirements 2.3

Product Deficiency 2.3

Product Dissatisfaction . . 2.3

Product Satisfaction and
Product Dissatisfaction
Are Not Opposites . . . 2.4

Definitions in the Literature 2.4

THE QUALITY FUNCTION . . . **2.4**

*HOW TO THINK ABOUT
QUALITY* **2.5**

The Financial Analogy . . 2.5

The Quality Trilogy 2.6

The Juran Trilogy 2.7

FITNESS FOR USE **2.8**

Product Features and
Quality Characteristics . 2.8

Parameters of Fitness for
Use 2.9

Additional Terminology . . 2.11

*BUSINESS, MANAGEMENT, AND
TECHNOLOGY* **2.11**

*STANDARDIZATION OF
TERMINOLOGY IN THE QUALITY
FUNCTION* **2.12**

A Wistful Postscript 2.13

REFERENCES **2.13**

This section is devoted to some fundamental concepts which underlie the subject of quality: what is meant by the word "quality"; how to think about quality, i.e., the organization of the subject. To explain these concepts requires definition of what is meant by the associated key words, e.g., "product," "customer." Those definitions will be provided at the first use of such key words.

"QUALITY" DEFINED

The word quality has multiple meanings. Two of those meanings dominate the use of the word:

1. Quality consists of those product features which meet the needs of customers and thereby provide product satisfaction.
2. Quality consists of freedom from deficiencies.

To explain these dominant meanings it is first necessary to define the key words.

Product. "Product" is the output of any process. It consists mainly of goods, software, and services. "Goods" are physical things: pencils, color television sets, office buildings. "Software" has more than one meaning. A major meaning is instruction programs for computers. Another major meaning is information generally: reports, plans, instructions, advice, commands. "Service" is work performed for someone else. Entire industries are established to provide services in such forms as central energy, transportation, communication, entertainment, etc.

Product Feature. A "product feature" is a property which is possessed by a product and which is intended to meet certain customers' needs. Product features may be technological in nature, e.g., fuel consumption of a vehicle, dimension of a mechanical component, viscosity of a chemical, uniformity of the voltage of an electric power supply. Product features may also take other forms, e.g., promptness of delivery, ease of maintenance, courtesy of service.

Hierarchy of Product Features. Products exist in a sort of hierarchical or pyramidal organization. At the apex is the overall product or system. Below the apex are multiple layers made up of subsystems, components, etc. At each layer the products have features which must be defined by specifications and procedures. In the bottom layer are numerous bits of the whole, e.g., tasks in a procedure, properties of materials or piece parts. For such tasks or properties, the product features consist of elemental definitions, e.g., the temperature of the oven, the diameter of the shaft. Such product features are often referred to as "quality characteristics."

Customer. A customer is someone who is impacted by the product. Customers may be external or internal.

External Customers. These are impacted by the product but are not members of the company (or other institution) which produces the product. External customers include clients who buy the product, government regulatory bodies, the public (which may be impacted because of unsafe products or damage to the environment), etc.

Internal Customers. Within any company there are numerous situations in which departments and persons supply products to each other. The recipients are often called "customers" despite the fact that they are not customers in the dictionary sense, i.e., they are not clients.

Users.   Users are customers who carry out positive actions with respect to the product. Users include processors who buy the product as an input to their process, merchants who resell the product, and consumers who carry out the ultimate use of the product.

Customer Needs.   All customers have needs to be met, and the product features should be responsive to those needs. This applies to both external and internal customers. In the case of external customers, the response determines product satisfaction, and in consequence, product salability. In the case of internal customers, the response determines the company's competitiveness in productivity, quality, etc., as well as the state of morale among internal departments.

Product Satisfaction.   Product features which do respond to customer needs are said to provide "product satisfaction," a state of affairs which is decisive as to salability of the product. In competitive markets there are multiple suppliers of product features. The resulting variation leads to degrees of product satisfaction, and to associated differences in market share for the respective suppliers.

Grade.   A popular name for degrees of product satisfaction is "grade," sometimes called "quality of design." Products whose features are perceived as meeting customer needs to a superior degree are called "higher-grade" products. Sometimes these grades are established formally, as in hotel services or cuts of meat.

Conformance to Specification; also, Conformance to Requirements.   Some people define quality as consisting of conformance to some standard, e.g., conformance to specifications, procedures, or requirements. Such definitions can be helpful in clarifying the quality responsibilities of workers and supervisors. At those levels the personnel may lack full knowledge of what are the needs of the numerous external and internal customers. Yet these same workers and supervisors need clear definitions of their responsibilities with respect to quality. Such needs can be met through stating the responsibilities in terms of conformance. However, none of these conformance definitions adequately defines the quality responsibility of the company. For the company, the definition should be stated in terms of (1) meeting customer needs, and (2) freedom from deficiencies.

Product Deficiency.   The second major definition of quality is "freedom from deficiencies." Product deficiencies take such forms as late deliveries, field failures of goods, errors in invoices, factory scrap or rework, and design changes. Each of such events is the result of some deficiency in a product or process. Each makes trouble for customers.

Product Dissatisfaction.   A consequence of product deficiencies is that customers are dissatisfied. External customers express their dissatisfaction in such forms as field complaints, returns, and claims. If the response to these dissatisfactions is inadequate, or if the extent of dissatisfaction is too high, the external customers may stop buying the product. These reactions by external customers impact the supplier through a combination of lower sales, higher costs, fewer on-time deliveries, lower productivity, etc.

Product deficiencies can also impact internal customers. These internal customers then express their dissatisfaction in the form of internal complaints. If the response is inadequate, or if the level of dissatisfaction is too high, the consequences are a deterioration in the cooperation between departments, mutual blame, poor morale, etc. Such consequences likewise contribute to lower sales, high cost, fewer on-time deliveries, lower productivity, etc.

Product Satisfaction and Product Dissatisfaction Are Not Opposites. For the most part, the two concepts are unrelated. Product satisfaction has its origin in product features, and is why clients buy the product. Product dissatisfaction has its origin in nonconformances, and is why customers complain. There are many products which give little or no dissatisfaction; the products do what the supplier said they would do. Yet the products are not salable because some competing product provides greater product satisfaction.

Definitions in the Literature. ANSI/ASQC Standard A3-1987 (draft) recognizes that the word "quality" has multiple meanings. The meaning adopted in the standard is: "The totality of features and characteristics of a product or service that bear on its ability to satisfy stated or implied needs."

The European Organization for Quality Control Glossary (1981) has the following definition for quality: "The totality of features and characteristics of a product or service that bear on its ability to satisfy a given need. N.B. with manufactured products quality is mainly determined by quality of design and quality of manufacture."

The Soviet encyclopedia defines quality as follows: "Quality of Products, the aggregate of properties of a product determining its ability to satisfy the needs it was built to satisfy."

For some detailed views on whether quality is conformance to standard or fitness for use, see Groocock (1980), Zaludova (1981), Thoday (1981), Seghezzi (1981), and Groocock (1981).

THE QUALITY FUNCTION

Any organization produces and distributes its products through a series of specialized activities carried out by specialized departments. In industrial companies these specialized departments include product development, process development, production, marketing, etc. Figure 2.1, the Spiral of progress in quality, depicts a typical progression of activities as carried out in industrial companies. This figure will be referred to as the "Spiral."

Each specialized department is given the responsibility to carry out its assigned special function. In addition, each specialized department is also assigned a share of the responsibility of carrying out certain companywide functions such as human relations, finance, and *quality*.

A companywide quality function arises from the fact that product quality is the resultant of the work of all departments around the Spiral. Each of those specialized departments has not only the responsibility to carry out its special function; it also has the responsibility to do its work correctly—to make its products fit for use. In this way, each department has a quality-oriented activity to carry out along with its main function. (These departmental quality-oriented activities are supplemented by other quality-oriented activities carried out by staff departments and by upper management.)

It is convenient to have some short name to represent the activities, departmental and companywide, which collectively result in product quality. In this handbook that short name is the "quality function."

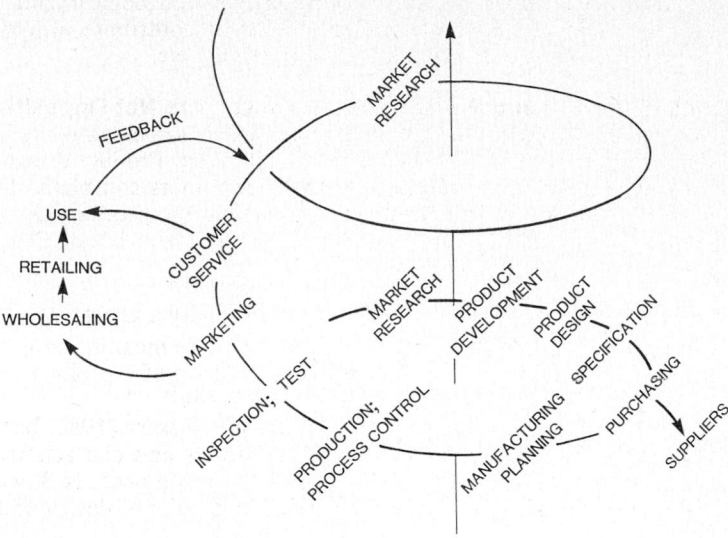

FIG. 2.1 The Spiral of progress in quality.

The quality function is the entire collection of activities through which we achieve fitness for use, no matter where these activities are performed.

HOW TO THINK ABOUT QUALITY

Individuals performing any important function have a need to think through and define the universal concepts which underlie the activity's very existence as a function. In addition the language describing the function needs to evolve and be standardized so that the key concepts can be communicated and understood.

In the case of the quality function, identification of the universal concepts has followed an erratic course. The concept of inspection and test is thousands of years old, as is the concept of measurement. Application of statistical methodology to the quality function is largely a twentieth century phenomenon. Significant efforts to identify the managerial processes inherent in the quality function did not get under way until the second half of the twentieth century.

There are a number of alternative ways for organizing the subject of how to think about quality. A major criterion for choosing from these alternatives is the ease of explaining the quality function to nonexperts, and especially to upper managers. In the author's experience, these upper managers have most readily understood the subject when it is presented to them in the form of a trilogy of managerial processes—the same managerial processes which have long served as the basis for organizing the subject of finance.

The Financial Analogy.   The finance function has been under intense study for centuries. That study has evolved various alternative ways for organizing the subject—how to think about finance. The dominant alternative is now to think of attaining good financial results through three managerial processes: planning, control, and improvement.

Financial Planning. This planning is centered on preparation of the annual financial budget. In turn, this preparation involves a companywide process which starts by defining the deeds to be done in the year ahead. These deeds are then translated into money equivalents. Such translation permits summary and analysis to determine the financial consequences of doing all those deeds. After revisions, the final result sets the financial goals for the company and its various divisions and departments.

Financial Control. This well-known process is used to aid managers in reaching the established financial goals. The process consists of evaluating actual financial performance, comparing this with financial goals, and taking action on the difference—the "variance." There are numerous subprocesses for financial control: cost control, expense control, inventory control, etc.

Financial Improvement. This process takes many forms: cost reduction projects, purchase of new facilities to improve productivity, development of new products to increase sales, acquisition of other companies, etc.

The Quality Trilogy. Managing for quality is done by use of the same three managerial processes of planning, control, and improvement. The conceptual approaches are identical with those used to manage for finance. However, the procedural steps are special, and the tools used are also special.

Quality Planning. This is the activity of developing the products and processes required to meet customers' needs. It involves a series of universal steps:

1. Determine who are the customers.
2. Determine the needs of the customers.
3. Develop product features which respond to customers' needs.
4. Develop processes which are able to produce those product features.
5. Transfer the resulting plans to the operating forces.

For an elaboration of the quality planning process, see Section 6, Companywide Planning for Quality. See also Juran (1988).

Quality Control. This process is used by the operating forces as an aid to meeting the product and process goals. It is based on the feedback loop, and consists of the following steps:

1. Evaluate actual operating performance
2. Compare actual performance to goals
3. Act on the difference

Section 6, Companywide Planning for Quality, elaborates on the use of the feedback loop for quality control. Many sections of this handbook provide examples of use of the control process. Section 24 discusses use of statistical tools as part of the control process; Section 9 elaborates on the use of the control process for quality assurance.

Quality Improvement. This third member of the quality trilogy aims to attain levels of performance which are unprecedented—levels which are significantly better than any past level. The methodology consists of a process—an unvarying series of steps. These are set out in detail in Section 22, Quality Improvement.

The Juran Trilogy.   The three processes of the quality trilogy are interrelated. Figure 2.2, the Juran Trilogy, shows this interrelationship.

The Juran Trilogy is a graph with time on the horizontal axis and cost of poor quality (quality deficiencies) on the vertical axis. The initial activity is quality planning. The planners determine who are the customers and what their needs are. The planners then develop product and process designs which are able to respond to those needs. Finally, the planners turn the plans over to the operating forces.

The job of the operating forces is to run the processes and produce the products. As operations get under way, it becomes evident that product deficiencies abound. In the company represented in Figure 2.2, the products produced are deficient in various ways, resulting in a total of 20 percent deficiency. Why are the products deficient? Most usually, the deficiencies are traceable to the planning process. That planning process, for whatever reasons, has resulted in that high level of product deficiencies. This waste then becomes chronic because *the operating process was planned that way.*

Under conventional responsibility patterns the operating forces are unable to get rid of that planned chronic waste. What they do instead is to carry out *quality control*—to prevent things from getting worse. Control includes putting out the fires, such as that sporadic spike in Figure 2.2.

But the chart also shows that in due course the chronic waste was driven down to a level far below that planned originally. That gain was achieved by the third process in the trilogy—*quality improvement.* In effect, it was realized that the chronic waste was also an opportunity for improvement. So steps were taken to seize that opportunity.

In most companies there exists a widespread situation in which:

1. Numerous operating processes are deficient. Each is an opportunity for quality improvement through the project by project approach, as described in Section 22, Quality Improvement.
2. The approach to quality planning is also deficient. This deficiency is the root cause of most of those deficient operating processes. That same deficient planning process continues to create new wasteful operating processes. The remedy is to improve the planning process.

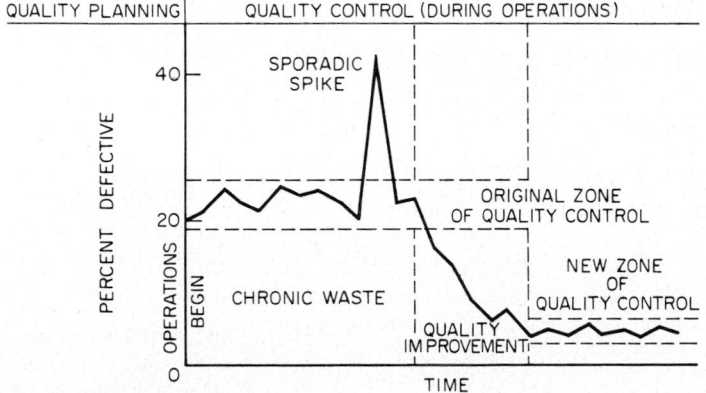

FIG. 2.2   The Juran Trilogy.

To improve the quality planning process requires several major changes:

1. A revision in priorities so that the planners are given enough time and resources to do a more thorough job of quality planning.
2. A more structured approach to quality planning, as set out in Section 6, Companywide Planning for Quality.
3. A broader data base for quality planners, derived from "lessons learned," i.e., feedback from problems encountered and solved during the control process, and especially during the improvement process. The concept of "lessons learned" is discussed in Section 6.

FITNESS FOR USE

It would be most convenient to have some short phrase which is universally accepted as a comprehensive definition of quality, i.e., so that it includes the product features which lead to product satisfaction, and in addition includes freedom from deficiencies. Various such phrases have been proposed by practitioners but none has achieved universal acceptance.

Nevertheless, in a handbook such as this it is most convenient to standardize on a short definition of the word "quality." In the preceding Third Edition, quality was defined as "fitness for use." This definition has in fact attained wide acceptance. In view of this, this Fourth Edition will also adopt the definition "quality is fitness for use," realizing that the definition has not achieved universal acceptance.

Product Features and Quality Characteristics.   Human needs are extremely diverse, and this has led to a corresponding proliferation of product features and quality characteristics. This proliferation extends to multiple human disciplines, as in the following examples:

Technological: Hardness, inductance, acidity, etc.

Psychological: Taste, beauty, status, etc.

Time-oriented: Reliability, maintainability, etc.

Contractual: Guarantee provisions, etc.

Ethical: Courtesy of sales personnel, honesty of service shops, etc.

The concept of "quality characteristics" is as old as the human species (the entire biological world is responsive to the concept). Moreover, there has been a long-range trend to quantify these characteristics. Technological characteristics, notably properties of materials, were extensively quantified beginning several centuries ago with the accelerated growth of instrumentation. The twentieth century has seen a similar movement to quantify the remaining types of characteristics.

Service industry quality characteristics, while including all of the above subspecies, are dominated by the psychological and ethical. In addition, the service industries generally regard promptness of service as a quality characteristic, whereas the manufacturing industries generally do not. Instead, manufacturing companies regard promptness (i.e., timely delivery of products to customers in accordance with promised date) as a parameter very different from "quality." The distinction is so sharp that there is a separate organization (Materials Management) to set standards for delivery time (schedules), measure performance, and stimulate compliance.

Parameters of Fitness for Use.   Beyond those product features which bear directly on product satisfaction there are additional aspects of the product which also contribute to fitness for use. These additional aspects are often called "parameters" of quality. An example is the time-related "abilities."

For products which are consumed promptly (food, fuel, many services) fitness for use is determined by (1) the adequacy of the product design and (2) the extent to which the product originally conforms to that design. For long lived products, some new time-oriented factors come into play: availability, reliability, and maintainability. These abilities are closely interrelated and are vital to fitness for use.

Availability.   Continuity of life in the industrial society depends absolutely on the continuity of service from sources of energy, communication, transport, water, etc. To provide this continuity, much effort has been devoted to discovering how to minimize the failure rates of products and how to restore service promptly in case of failure. One element of this effort has been to recognize continuity of service as a parameter of fitness for use and to set up to measure it. The name given to this parameter is "availability." It is time-related and is measured by the extent to which the user can secure service when he or she wants it.

A product is said to be available when it is in an operative state. The total time in the operative state (also called uptime) is the sum of the time spent (1) in active use and (2) in standby state.

The total time in the nonoperative state (also called downtime) is the sum of the time spent (3) under active repair (i.e., diagnosis and remedy), and (4) waiting for spare parts, paperwork, etc.

Availability is expressed mathematically by the ratio:

$$\frac{\text{Uptime}}{\text{Uptime} + \text{downtime}}$$

In equivalent terminology, availability is also expressed by the ratio:

$$\frac{\text{Mean time between failures (MTBF)}}{\text{MTBF} + \text{mean time to repair (MTTR)}}$$

Other terms used as equivalents of availability are "operational readiness" and "percent uptime."

Reliability.   If products never failed, availability would be 100 percent. However, products do fail, so that an essential subparameter of availability is freedom from failure, for which the accepted technical term is "reliability." The classic definition is "the probability of a product performing without failure a specified function under given conditions for a specified period of time" (AGREE, 1957).

Architects and designers have for millennia tried to design structures and products for long life. What is now new is the movement to quantify reliability. It is a movement similar to, and probably as important as, the movement several centuries ago to quantify properties of materials. Once we are able to quantify reliability, we can more scientifically do many other things about reliability: predict, apportion, plan, achieve, test, control, improve, etc.

The probability of performing without failure can be converted readily to other measures, such as mean time between failures, failure rate, etc. For simple systems the calculations are comparatively simple. However, for complex systems they become extremely complex. This has given rise to a huge literature on the methods for quantifying reliability.

Reliability is determined largely by the quality of design. The attainable reliability inherent in the design is called "intrinsic reliability." However, the achieved reliability is usually less than this because of unanticipated environments during use, lapses in quality of conformance, inadequacies in maintenance, etc.

The term "operational reliability" is sometimes used to distinguish attained reliability from intrinsic reliability.

Reliability is not to be confused with conformance to product specification (as evidenced by test of conformance) or even with reliability estimates based on life tests in the laboratory. The evaluation of achieved reliability requires actual use of product over a period of time plus collection and interpretation of data on performance and failures during that time.

For a discussion of quantifying reliability, see Section 13 under Planning for Time-Oriented Performance.

Maintainability.   The need for continuity of service has also stimulated much effort to improve the maintenance of long-life products. This maintenance takes place in two major ways:

1. Preventive or scheduled maintenance consisting of tests and checkouts to detect potential failures, scheduled servicing (e.g., lubrication), and planned overhauls plus replacement of worn or failure-prone parts
2. Unscheduled maintenance consisting of restoring service in the event of failure

The term "maintainability" has been adopted as an expression of the ease with which maintenance can be conducted.

Attempts to quantify maintainability soon encounter the fact that multiple measures are involved. Maintenance requires the time of technicians, spare parts, expendable supplies, and other costs. Hence multiple measures of maintenance have been developed to correspond to these multiple factors. Of these measures, those that are time-oriented are regarded as most important, because so much human activity remains disturbed until service is restored.

The measures of maintainability actually in use include:

Mean time to repair

Probability of restoring service in the time period specified

Mean time for scheduled maintenance (this is often subdivided between the inspecting and the servicing)

An emerging practice is to establish standards for the various repetitive time-consuming elements of maintenance.

Effectiveness of maintenance is strongly influenced by the supporting technology: design for easy access and modular replacement at the users' premises, special instruments for easy diagnosis of causes of failure, special repair tools, and technical information about the product and its use. Providing this supporting technology is generally regarded as a part of the subject matter of maintainability.

Effectiveness of maintenance is also strongly influenced by the availability of spare parts, sometimes called "logistical support." Providing this logistical support is regarded by some practitioners as part of the subject matter of maintainability.

Terminology associated with maintainability is still in a state of evolution. Some practitioners separate maintainability into two categories: (1) the ease of conducting scheduled inspections and servicing, called "serviceability," and (2) the ease of restoring service after failure, called "repairability."

In the case of maintenance of aircraft, recent studies have led to extensive revisions in the concept of maintenance. From the earliest days of flying, maintenance of aircraft engines was done under the concept of "overhaul"—a scheduled complete disassembly of the engine, followed by inspection of all parts, repair or replacement as needed, and finally reassembly. During the last several decades the airlines enlarged their data systems so that they could go beyond the needs of restoring service, and could reexamine long standing practices. One stunning finding was that of the items in the product, *89 percent exhibited failure patterns which were not age-related.* Hence such items could not benefit from the overhaul concept. The findings have led to new concepts, e.g., "on-condition" maintenance. They have also led to fundamental improvements in engine performance and availability through feedback to engine design, manufacture, and test. (For an extensive discussion, see Nowlan and Heap, 1978).

Producibility (or Manufacturability). This parameter measures the extent to which the product design can be readily produced with the facilities and process available to the operating forces. Producibility has no direct relation to fitness for use of external customers, but is obviously of great importance to internal customers.

Additional Terminology. The search for a short phrase to describe "everything"—product features and freedom from deficiencies—has stimulated a variety of local dialects. For example, in certain complex systems industries (military, aerospace), terms such as "system effectiveness," "product performance," or "product effectiveness" have been tested out. Sometimes such special terminology finds acceptance in specific industries, and may endure for some years before being revised. However, the special nature of the industry makes the terms not acceptable to other industries, e.g., the word "system" is too elaborate to be applied to production of simple products.

BUSINESS, MANAGEMENT, AND TECHNOLOGY

The activities needed to achieve fitness for use (Figure 2.1) can also be classified in terms of the basic disciplines employed. Three of these are of major concern:

1. *Business or entrepreneurship:* This is concerned with taking the risks associated with doing business at all and with the circumstances under which risks are taken. It includes judging the economic climate, choosing which markets to enter, financing the enterprise, taking specific investment risks, etc.
2. *Management:* This is the process through which people are mobilized to achieve designated goals. When applied to the quality function, management consists of the three elements of the quality trilogy: quality planning, quality control, and quality improvement. The leaders who preside over these managerial processes are generally called "managers." What distinguishes managers from other individuals is that the managers must secure results through the efforts of other people.

3. *Technology:* This is concerned with harnessing the forces and materials of nature for the benefit of human beings. Technological quality matters include designs, specifications, processes, instruments, tests, and failure analysis.

Many quality problems are traceable to the fact that top managers live in the world of business and management, whereas the quality specialists live in the world of technology. The higher that people climb the managerial hierarchy, the more time they devote to business and managerial problems. Top management's attention to quality activities is almost exclusively devoted to managerial matters. When we ask company presidents "What does the word 'quality' mean to you?" they usually answer in business terminology, e.g., "Quality is what we sell. It's what our customers want. Our reputation is built on quality." Seldom is the answer in technological terms, e.g., tolerances, control charts, gage laboratories, etc.

These same differences are evident in the setting of quality goals and in planning to meet those goals. Company goals and plans are usually in business and managerial terms, whereas departmental goals and plans are usually in technological terms. In this handbook, the sections dealing with business and management make little distinction as to industry involved, since these two disciplines apply to all industries with little variation in application.

STANDARDIZATION OF TERMINOLOGY IN THE QUALITY FUNCTION

The search for universal concepts and principles in the quality function is a relatively recent phenomenon. In consequence, standardization of terminology is still in the formative stages. Many words and phrases are used in special meanings which differ from the dictionary meanings. In view of this state of affairs, this handbook attempts to define key words and phrases as they appear (or define them through cross-referencing). In addition, the Index identifies, for each key word or phrase, the location of the principal definition.

Despite these efforts, the reader is urged to keep in mind that there remains much confusion in the language of quality. Some words or phrases are used in special meanings which have not yet found their way into the dictionaries. Other words have multiple meanings, e.g., "quality." It is quite common for participants in meetings to be forced to ask each other: In what sense are you using that word? To illustrate, in a meeting of managers the question arises: Does higher quality cost more or does it cost less? The resulting discussion may well yield no agreement. The reason is that some participants have in mind quality in the sense of grade, in which case higher quality usually does cost more. Other participants have in mind quality in the sense of freedom from deficiencies, in which case higher quality usually does cost less. So each is right, but there is no meeting of the minds.

Much has been done within specific organizations to establish local glossaries. In addition, some professional societies have evolved glossaries of quality-related terms. A major glossary of terms is the European Organization for Quality Control (EOQC) *Glossary of Terms Used in Quality Control* (1981). This compilation lists 398 terms and defines them in English. In addition, the compilation shows, for 14 other languages (13 European plus Arabic), the equivalents of these 398 terms (but not equivalent definitions). This glossary was prepared by the Glossary Committee of EOQC. It is available from the European Organization for Quality Control, Secretariat, P.O. Box 2613, CH-3001, Berne, Switzerland.

Additional glossaries are available in several American National Standards, as follows:

ANSI/ASQC A1-1987, *Definitions, Symbols, Formulas and Tables for Control Charts*

ANSI/ASQC A2-1987, *Terms, Symbols and Definitions for Acceptance Sampling*

ANSI/ASQC A3-1987 (draft), *Quality Systems Terminology*

All of these are available from the American Society for Quality Control, 310 West Wisconsin Ave., Milwaukee.

A Wistful Postscript. It would be wonderful if all managers and practitioners were to standardize on the terminology used to describe concepts, deeds, and meanings. Such a paradise is far away, since there are some very active obstacles to standardization. These obstacles are mainly the following:

The differences in the technology, dialect, and cultural history of the various industries

The rapidly changing ingredients of fitness for use

The deliberate efforts of human beings to create and use terminology to secure benefits for their organizations and for themselves

The prime need is to discover the realities under the labels, i.e., the deeds, activities, or things which the other person is talking about. Once these are understood, accurate communication can take place whether the labels are agreed on or not. In contrast, if communication is purely through labels, it is easy to be deluded into believing there is an understanding despite the fact that each of the parties literally does not know what the other is talking about.

REFERENCES

AGREE (1957). This is the historic report, *Reliability of Military Electronic Equipment,* by the Advisory Group on Reliability of Electronic Equipment, Office of the Assistant Secretary of Defense (R&D), June 1957.

European Organization for Quality Control (1981). *Glossary of Terms Used in Quality Control,* 5th ed. Berne, Switzerland.

Groocock, J. M. (1980). "Conformance or Fitness for Use?" *EOQC Quality,* vol. 2, pp. 3–6.

Groocock, J. M. (1981). "Conformance or Fitness for Use? (II)." *EOQC Quality,* vol. 4. pp. 5–7.

Juran, J. M. (1988). *Juran on Planning for Quality.* The Free Press, New York.

Nowlan, F. Stanley and Heap, Howard F. (1978). *Reliability-Centered Maintenance.* Available from National Technical Information Service, Springfield, VA 22161. (Catalog no. ADA 066579.)

Seghezzi, H. D. (1981). "What is Quality? Conformance with Requirements or Fitness for the Intended Use?" *EOQC Quality,* vol. 4, pp. 3–4.

Thoday, W. R. (1981). "Additional Reflections on Quality Terminology." *EOQC Quality,* vol. 1, p. 11.

Zaludova, A. H. (1981). "Some Reflections on Quality Terminology." *EOQC Quality,* vol. 1, pp. 3–10.

SECTION 3
QUALITY AND INCOME

J. M. Juran

QUALITY AND ECONOMICS . . 3.2

MAJOR ECONOMIC INFLUENCES 3.3

National Affluence and
Organization 3.3

Life Behind the Quality
Dikes 3.3

Voluntary Obsolescence . . 3.4

Involuntary Obsolescence . 3.4

CONTRAST IN VIEWS:
CUSTOMER AND SUPPLIER . . . 3.5

The Spectrum of Affluence 3.5

Stated Needs and Real
Needs 3.5

Reasons Behind the Stated
Needs 3.6

Differences in Language . . 3.6

Nonfunctional Needs . . . 3.6

Definition of Quality . . . 3.6

DEGREES OF USER KNOWLEDGE 3.7

Fitness for Use 3.8

QUALITY AND PRICE 3.9

Consumer Products 3.9

Price Differences 3.10

Quality and Value 3.10

Efforts to Quantify Value . 3.10

Industrial Products 3.10

Product Differences 3.11

Commodity versus
Specialty or System . . . 3.11

The Bundled Price 3.12

The Macroeffect of Pricing
Strategy 3.12

QUALITY AND SHARE OF
MARKET 3.12

Effect of Quality Superiority 3.12

Consumer Preference and
Share of Market 3.15

Industrial Products and
Share of Market 3.17

QUALITY LEADERSHIP AND
BUSINESS STRATEGY 3.17

Building Quality Leadership 3.18

The "Market Leader"
Concept 3.19

Carryover of Failure-Prone
Features 3.20

LIFE CYCLE COSTING 3.20

Steps in Life Cycle Cost
Analysis 3.21

Breadth of Application . . 3.22

Application to Consumer
Products 3.23

Application to Industrial
Products 3.25

Application to Defense
Industries 3.25

Cultural Resistance 3.26

Contracts Based on
Amount of Use 3.26

PERFECTIONISM **3.27**
  Perfectionism in Quality of
    Design 3.27
  Perfectionism in Quality of
    Conformance 3.28
  Perfectionism in the
    "Abilities" 3.28
  Perfectionism in Field
    Service 3.28

  Perfectionism by
    Government Regulators   3.28
  The Perfectionists 3.28
  Defenses against
    Perfectionism 3.29

REFERENCES **3.30**

QUALITY AND ECONOMICS

Quality affects a supplier's economics in two principal ways:

1. *The effect on costs:* With respect to its effect on costs, the word "quality" is used in the sense of freedom from deficiencies, or the degree of conformance to standards, goals, specifications, etc. In this sense "higher quality" means greater freedom from deficiencies, and hence also lower costs. That subject of the effect of quality on costs is discussed in Section 5, Quality Costs.

2. *The effect on income:* As used here, "income" refers to such things as the sales of an industrial company; the appropriations received by a government agency; the tuition, grants, etc., received by an educational institution. Income also refers to the gross receipts, not to the surplus or profit. With respect to its effect on income, the word "quality" is used here in the sense of the features of the product which respond to customer needs. Those features make the product salable and provide "product satisfaction" to customers. The subject of the effect of quality on income is discussed in this section. The section discusses the forces through which quality affects income and the methods in use for studying the cause-effect relationships.

Closely related to this subject of quality and income are several other sections of the handbook:

Section 12—Field Intelligence

Section 19—Marketing

Section 20—Customer Service

The above two effects of quality—on costs and on income—interact with each other. Product deficiencies which directly affect a company's clients will often result in higher costs in such forms as complaints, claims, etc. In addition, news of those deficiencies reaches the ears of those who make the purchase decisions. The result may be lower sales income for the guilty supplier.

Product deficiencies found internally by the manufacturer can also have an effect on income. There is always a high correlation between the level of these product deficiencies and the level of product deficiencies reported by customers. In addition, success in reducing deficiencies through quality improvement is a form of cost reduction. The resulting improvement in cost competitiveness is an aid to securing higher share of market.

In recent decades there has been much study of the effect of quality on costs, especially on the costs of poor quality. (See generally, Section 5, Quality Costs). In contrast, study of the effect of quality on income has lagged. This imbalance is all the more surprising since in the view of upper managers the effect of quality on income is the more important of the two effects. This same imbalance presents an opportunity for creative and imaginative invention of new ways to study the effect of quality on income.

MAJOR ECONOMIC INFLUENCES

The ability of an industrial company to secure income is strongly influenced by the economic climate and by the cultural habits which the various economies have evolved. These overriding influences affect product quality as well as other elements of commerce.

National Affluence and Organization.   The form of a nation's economy and its degree of affluence strongly influence the approach to its quality problems.

Subsistence Economies.   In such economies the numerous impoverished users have little choice but to devote their income to basic human needs. Their protection against poor quality is derived more from collective political power than from their collective economic power. Most of the world's population remains in a state of subsistence economy.

Planned Economies.   In all countries there are some socialized industries, i.e., government monopolies for specific products or services. In some countries the entire economy is so organized. These monopolies limit the choice of the user to those qualities which result from the national planning and its execution. For elaboration, see Section 35A, Quality and National Culture.

Shortages and Surpluses.   In all economies, a shortage of goods (a "sellers' market") results in a relaxing of quality standards. Because the demand for goods exceeds the supply, users take what they can get (and bid up the price to boot). In contrast, a buyers' market results in a tightening of quality standards.

Life Behind the Quality Dikes.   As societies industrialize they revise their life-style in order to secure the benefits of technology. These benefits consist of numerous varieties of goods and services. Collectively these goods and services have greatly improved the quality of life, but they have also created a new dependence. In the industrial societies, great masses of human beings place their safety, health, and even their daily well-being behind numerous protective dikes of quality control.

For example, the daily safety and health of the citizenry now depend absolutely on the quality of manufactured products: drugs, food, aircraft, automobiles, elevators, tunnels, bridges, etc.

The very continuity of our daily lives is built around the continuity of numerous vital services: power, transport, communication, water, waste removal, and many others. We have structured our society on the premise that these services will continue without interruption. A major power failure paralyzes the lives of millions of people.

Not only individuals but also nations and their economies live dangerously behind the dikes of quality control. National productivity relies on automated processes. National defense relies on complex weaponry. The national income depends on the marketability of products. The growth of the national economy is keyed to the reliability of its systems for energy, communication, transport, etc.

In such situations, users (whether individuals or nations) are willing to pay for good dikes. (For elaboration of this theme, see Juran, 1969.)

Voluntary Obsolescence.   As customers acquire affluence, the industrial companies increasingly bring out new products (and new models of old products) which they urge prospective users to buy. Many of the users who buy these new models do so while possessing older models which are still in working order. This practice is regarded by some economists and reformers as a reprehensible economic waste.

In their efforts to put an end to this waste, the reformers have attacked the industrial companies who bring out these new models and who promote their sale. Using the term "planned obsolescence," the reformers imply (and state outright) that the large companies, by their clever new models and their powerful sales promotion, break down the resistance of the users. Under this theory, the responsibility for the waste lies with the industrial companies who create the new models.

In the experience and judgment of the author, this theory of planned obsolescence is mostly nonsense. The simple fact, obvious both to manufacturers and consumers, is that *the consumer makes the decision* (of whether to discard the old product and buy the new). Periodically this fact is dramatized by some massive marketing failure.

For example, in March 1971, E. I. Du Pont de Nemours & Co., Inc. (Du Pont) announced its plans to discontinue the manufacture and sale of "Corfam," a synthetic material invented to compete with leather for shoe uppers (and other applications). Corfam, though costly, possessed excellent properties for shoe uppers: durability, ease of care, shape retention, scuff resistance, water repellency, and ability to "breathe." Although Du Pont became a major supplier of shoe uppers materials, it withdrew from the business because Corfam "never attained sufficient sales volume to show a profit."

Industry observers felt that the high durability of Corfam was an irrelevant property because of rapid style obsolescence; i.e., the life of the shoes was determined not by the inherent technological properties but by style obsolescence. Du Pont's investment in Corfam may have exceeded $100 million.

In the Corfam case, a large corporation undertook a program which was antagonistic to obsolescence, but the users decided against it. In a miscalculation involving an even larger investment, the Ford Motor Company's Edsel automobile failed to gain consumer acceptance despite possessing numerous innovations and being promoted by an extensive marketing campaign.

Involuntary Obsolescence.   Quite a different situation is the case in which long-life products contain components which will not last for the life of the product. The life of these components is determined by the manufacturer. As a result, even though the user decides to have the failed component replaced (to keep the product in service), *the manufacturer makes the real decision* because the design determines the life of the component.

This situation is at its worst when the original manufacturer had designed the product in such a way that the supplies, spare parts, etc., are nonstandard, so that, in effect, the sole source for these needs is the original manufacturer. In such a situation, the user is locked in to a single source of supply. Collectively, these cases have lent themselves to a good deal of abuse and have contributed to the consumerism movement.

For elaboration, see Juran, 1970.

CONTRAST IN VIEWS: CUSTOMER AND SUPPLIER

Industrial companies derive their income from the sale of their products. These sales are made to "customers," but customers vary as to their function. Customers may be merchants, processors, ultimate users, etc. These variations in function result in variations in customer needs. Such a response must be preceded by an understanding of what are the needs of customers.

Human needs cover a wide spectrum. To meet these needs suppliers evolve a correspondingly wide spectrum of products and product features. Moreover, human needs are complex. They extend beyond technological matters into social, artistic, status, and other seemingly intangible areas. Suppliers are nevertheless obliged to understand these seeming intangibles in order to be able to provide product responses.

The Spectrum of Affluence. In all economies the affluence of the population varies across a wide spectrum. Suppliers respond to this spectrum by developing variations in product features. These variations are often called "grades." For example, hotels all offer the basic service of overnight sleeping accommodations. Beyond this basic function hotels vary remarkably in the range of services offered, and the grades (deluxe, etc.) reflect this variation. In like manner any model of automobile provides the basic function of point-to-point transportation. However, there are multiple grades of automobiles. The higher grades supply services beyond pure transportation, including higher levels of appearance, comfort, status, etc.

Stated Needs and Real Needs. Customers state their needs as seen by them, and in their language. Suppliers are then faced with understanding the real needs and also translating those needs into suppliers' language. For example, travelers need transportation. They may state their needs in such forms as:

> I wish to buy a bicycle.
>
> I wish to rent a bicycle.
>
> I wish to buy a bus ticket.

It is quite common for customers to state their needs in the form of goods when their real needs are for the services provided by these goods. Some manufacturers are careful to make this distinction in their sales promotion. They emphasize the service provided by the goods. For example:

Manufacturer's goods	Emphasis of the sales promotion
Grinding wheels	Metal removal
Nuts and bolts	Fastening systems
Toothpaste	Clean teeth, sweet breath, improved social life
Aluminum siding	Maintenance-free exteriors

In contrast, preoccupation with the concept of selling goods can divert attention from the real needs of customers. For example, two hairnet manufacturers were in competition. They devoted much energy to improving the qualities of the product and to strengthening their marketing techniques. They were both made extinct when someone developed a hair spray which gave the user a better way of holding hair in place. (Private communication to J. M. Juran.)

(For elaboration, see the classic, widely read paper "Marketing Myopia" by Theodore Levitt, 1960.)

Reasons behind the Stated Needs. These reasons may become evident through in-depth discussions with users. An interesting example is narrated by Charles A. Lindbergh (Lindbergh, 1970, pp. 517–620). He was interviewing combat fliers to secure inputs for aircraft design. He found it quite important to understand the reasons behind the pilots' recommendations.

Differences in Language. Often the stated needs are real needs but stated in the language of the buyer. In such cases it is necessary to translate those needs into the language of the supplier. For a case example involving paper towels, see Mottle and Shiah (1974).

Nonfunctional Needs. For many products, customer needs extend beyond the pure function of the product; the needs include matters of a psychological nature. Such intangible needs apply to both goods and services.

To illustrate: A man in need of a haircut has the option of going to (1) a barbershop inhabited by barbers or (2) a "salon" inhabited by "hair stylists." The end result is the same. Either way he is shorn by a skilled artisan. Either way he emerges with the same outward appearance. What differs is (*a*) his remaining assets and (*b*) his sense of well-being.

What applies to services also applies to physical goods.

There are factories in which chocolate-coated candies are carried by a belt to the packaging department. At the end of the belt are two teams of packagers. One of these teams packs the chocolates into modest cardboard boxes destined for budget-priced merchant shops. The other team packs the chocolates into satin-lined wooden boxes destined to be sold in deluxe shops. The resulting price for a like amount of chocolate can differ by several fold. The respective purchasers encounter other differences as well: the decor, the extent of service, the box. However, the chocolates are identical. In fact, when any chocolate reaches the packers it has no way of predicting whether it will end up in the budget shops or in the deluxe shop.

Nonfunctional needs take such forms as securing attention, courteous treatment, prompt service, pleasant surroundings, and sense of importance. Despite their detachment from the technological functions of the product, these needs are very real to the customers and hence to the income of the suppliers.

Definition of Quality. The differences in viewpoints (of customers and suppliers) can readily extend to a difference in the definition of what is quality. Any such difference is an invitation to trouble.

To most customers, quality means those features of the product which respond to customer needs. In addition, quality means freedom from deficiencies, as well as good customer service if deficiencies do occur. One comprehensive definition for the above is "fitness for use." (There are of course some exceptions. In the nuclear energy industry the regulatory bodies tend to reserve to themselves the determination of fitness for use, leaving to the manufacturers the more limited function of conformance to specification.)

In contrast, many manufacturers of goods had for years tended to equate quality with conformance to specification at the time of final product test. This form of definition of quality gave inadequate attention to numerous factors which influenced quality as defined by customers: packaging, storage, transport, installation, reliability, maintainability, customer service, etc.

Table 3.1 tabulates some of the differences in viewpoint as applied to long-life goods.

TABLE 3.1   Contrasting Views: Customers and Suppliers

	Principal views	
Aspects	Of customers	Of manufacturers
What is bought	A service needed by the customer	Goods made by the manufacturer
Definition of quality	Fitness for use during the life of the product	Conformance to specification on final test
Cost	Cost of use, including Purchase price Operating costs Maintenance Downtime Depreciation Loss on resale	Cost of manufacture
Responsibility for keeping in service	Over the entire useful life	During the warranty period
Spare parts	A necessary evil	A profitable business

The ongoing revolution in quality has consisted in part of revising the manufacturers' definition of quality to be more nearly in accord with the customers' definition.

Cost of Use.   For consumable products the purchase price paid by the customer is quite close to the total cost of using (consuming) the product. However, for long-lived products the cost of use can diverge considerably from the purchase price because of added factors such as operating costs, maintenance costs, downtime, depreciation, etc.

The centuries-old emphasis on purchase price has tended to obscure the subsequent costs of use. One consequence has been a practice of suboptimization, i.e., manufacturers optimize their costs rather than the combined costs of manufacturers and customers.

The concept of life cycle costing offers a solution to this problem, and progress is being made in adopting this concept. (See Life Cycle Costing, below.)

DEGREES OF USER KNOWLEDGE

In a competitive market, customers for products have multiple sources of supply. In choosing from these alternatives, product quality is an obvious consideration. However, prospective customers vary considerably as to their ability to evaluate quality, especially prior to purchase. Table 3.2 summarizes the extent of customer knowledge and strength in the market place as related to quality matters.

TABLE 3.2   Customer Influences on Quality

Aspects of the problem	Original equipment manufacturers (OEM)	Dealers and repair shops	Consumers
Makeup of the market	A few very large customers	Some large customers plus many smaller ones	Very many very small customers
Economic strength of any one customer	Very large, cannot be ignored	Modest or low	Negligible
Technological strength of customer	Very high; has engineers and laboratories	Low or nil	Nil; requires technical assistance
Political strength of customer	Modest or low	Low to nil	Variable, but can be very great collectively
Fitness for use is judged mainly by	Qualification testing	Absence of consumer complaints	Successful usage
Quality specifications dominated by	Customers	Manufacturer	Manufacturer
Use of incoming inspection	Extensive test for conformance to specification	Low or nil for dealers; in-use tests by repair shops	In-use test
Collection and analysis of failure data	Good to fair	Poor to nil	Poor to nil

The broad conclusions which can be drawn from Table 3.2 are as follows:

1. Original equipment manufacturers (OEMs) can protect themselves through their technological and/or economic power as much as through contract provisions.
2. Merchants and repair shops must rely mainly on contract provisions supplemented by some economic power.
3. Small users have very limited knowledge and protection. The situation of the small user requires some elaboration.

Fitness for Use.   With few exceptions, small users are devoid of understanding of the technological nature of the product. The user does have sensory recognition of some aspects of fitness for use: the bread smells fresh-baked; the radio set has clear reception; the shoes are good-looking. Beyond such sensory judgments, and especially concerning the long-life performance of the product, the small user must rely mainly on prior personal experience with the manufacturer or merchant. Lacking such prior experience, the small user must choose from the propaganda of competing manufacturers plus other available inputs (neighbors, merchants, independent laboratories, etc.).

To the extent that the user does understand fitness for use, the effect on the manufacturer's income is somewhat as follows:

As seen by the user, product or service is	Resulting income to the producer is
Not fit for use	None, or in immediate jeopardy
Fit for use but noticeably inferior to competitive products	Low because of need for lowering prices
Fit for use and competitive	At market prices
Noticeably superior to competitive products	High because of premium prices or greater share of market

In the foregoing, the terms "fitness for use," "inferior," "competitive," and "superior" all relate to the situation *as seen by the user.* (The foregoing table is valid as applied to both large customers and small users.)

QUALITY AND PRICE

There is general awareness that product price bears some rational relationship to product quality. However, researches on the subject have often reported confused relationships, some of which appear to run contrary to logical reasoning. To interpret these researches it is useful to separate the subject as between consumer products and industrial products.

Consumer Products.   Numerous researches have tried to quantify the correlation between product quality and product price. See, for example, Reisz (1979); also Morris and Bronson (1969). A major data base for these researches has been the journal *Consumer Reports,* a publication of Consumer Union, a nonprofit supplier of information and advice to consumers. The specific information used in the researches consisted of *Consumer Reports'* published quality ratings of products, along with the associated prevailing market prices.

The researches generally concluded that there is little positive correlation between quality ratings and market prices. For a significant minority of products the correlation was negative. Such conclusions were reached as to foods, both convenience and nonconvenience (Reisz, 1979). Similar conclusions were reached as to other consumable products, household appliances, tools, and other long-life products (Morris and Bronson, 1969).

Researchers offer various theories to explain why so many consumers seem to be acting contrary to their own best interests:

1. The quality ratings are based solely on evaluations of the functional features of the products—the inherent quality of design. The ratings do not evaluate various factors which are known to influence consumer behavior. These factors include *service* in such forms as attention, courtesy, and promptness; also *decor* in such forms as pleasant surroundings and attractive packaging.
2. Consumers generally possess only limited technological literacy, and most are unaware of the quality ratings.

3. Lacking objective quality information, consumers give weight to the image projected by manufacturers and merchants through their promotion and advertising.
4. The price itself is perceived by many consumers as a quality rating. There appears to be a widespread belief that a higher-priced product is also a higher-quality product. Some companies have exploited this belief as a part of their marketing and pricing strategy ("Pricing of Products Is Still an Art," 1981).

Price Differences.   Premium priced products most usually run about 10 to 20 percent higher than other products. For example, branded products often are priced in this range relative to generic products. However, there are many instances of much greater price differences.

Haircuts given in some "salons" sell at several times the price prevailing in "barbershops."

Chocolates packaged in elegant boxes and sold in deluxe shops may sell for several times the price of the identical chocolates packaged in simple boxes and sold in budget shops.

Restaurant meal prices can vary by an order of magnitude.

Many branded drugs regularly sell for several times the price of generic drugs asserted to be therapeutically equivalent.

A price premium based on perceived quality differences is constantly under threat from competitors who look for ways to wipe out those quality differences. For a case example (washing machines), see "The Problem of Being Premium" (1978).

Quality and Value.   What emerges is that for many consumers, perception of the quality-price relationship is derived from unique interpretations of the terms used:

Quality is interpreted as including factors which go beyond the inherent functional features of the product.

Price is interpreted as relating to "value" and is paid for those added factors, along with the inherent functional features.

Efforts to Quantify Value.   These efforts are generally restricted to inherent functional properties of products. For example, the U.S. Department of Transportation evaluated and published the performance of automobile tires for several qualities, notably tread wear. Quantifying the amount of tread wear under standard test conditions made it possible to estimate the cost per unit of distance traveled ("Consumer Guide on Tires," 1980). Consumers Union periodically undertakes such evaluations for consumer products. For an example, see "Dishwashing Liquids" (1984).

Such evaluations clearly can be useful to consumers. However, the impact of such information is limited because of consumer unawareness and because consumer perceptions are based on broader concepts of what constitutes quality and value.

Industrial Products.   These products employ the concepts of quality, price, and value in much the same way as consumer products. However, industrial buyers are generally much better informed as to the significance of these concepts. In addition, industrial buyers are better provided with the technological and economic information needed to make rational decisions.

Product Differences. In the competitive marketplace product differences abound. These differences create problems in applying the principle of "standard product, market price."

For example, a company making standard power tools improved the reliability of the tools, but the marketing manager resisted increasing the prices on the ground that they were standard tools and market share would be lost if prices were raised. A field study disclosed that the high-reliability tools greatly reduced the costs of the (industrial) users in maintenance and especially in downtime. This information then became the means of convincing users to accept a price increase (of $500,000 per year).

When product differences are obvious (e.g., additional features or functions) both suppliers and buyers are open to establishing price differences. Now the problem becomes: How much difference? Suppliers and buyers both are faced with (1) making product comparisons to identify the differences and (2) establishing price differences in accordance with the product differences. In some markets a great many different products may be involved.

An early approach, involving several thousands of products, made use of two concepts:

1. A "percentage of desirability" determined by comparing the quality of design of company products to those of competitors
2. A "competitive price index" determined by dividing the price ratio by the percentage of desirability

For details, see MacGowan (1957).

Commodity versus Specialty or System. An important question in much industrial buying is whether the product being bought is a commodity or something broader. The greater breadth may involve a specialty or a system of which the commodity is a part, but which includes other attributes of special value to the buyer.

Commodities are typically bought at market prices, and the price tends to dominate the purchasing decisions. Any perceived quality superiority tends to be translated into higher share of market rather than into a price differential. In contrast, specialties are not standard. What is being bought includes additional attributes which result in premium prices, the premium being paid for the additional attributes.

The additional attributes which make premium prices possible are numerous. Some of these attributes are widely prevalent: predictable uniformity of product, promptness of delivery, technological advice and service, assistance in training buyers' personnel, prompt assistance in trouble shooting, and product innovation. Still other influences in the pricing decision include prestige of the supplier, mutual confidences established, sharing of inspection and test data, personal relationships established, joint quality planning, and joint projects for quality improvement. For a case example of a joint quality improvement project involving Aluminum Company of America and Eastman Kodak, see Kegarise and Miller (1986) and Kegarise et al. (1987) in *The Juran Report,* no. 6 and no. 8, respectively.

There is no known, agreed method for quantifying the extent to which those additional attributes contribute to the pricing decision. What can be done is to secure buyers' subjective estimates of the relative importance of the respective attributes. These estimates can then be used as inputs to marketing strategy and as a basis for allocating resources.

For an interesting research on pricing in the chemicals industry, along with an approach to evaluation of the "additional attributes," see Gross (1978). See also Section 12, under Examples of Field Studies.

The Bundled Price. When products are sold as specialties or as part of a system, the price is often "bundled." Bundled prices provide no breakdown of price as between the goods (commodities) and the associated services.

Bundled prices are an advantage to the manufacturer as long as the product remains a specialty and requires the associate technical services. However, if wide use of the specialty products results in standardization, the need for the technical services diminishes. In such cases it is common for competitors to offer the standard product at lower prices but without the technical services. This is a form of "unbundling" the price.

The Macroeffect of Pricing Strategy. Companies whose products are in the high-quality category have the option of seeking their reward through either higher price, or higher share of market (or both). Generally companies' strategy has been to opt for higher price.

A report, *Pricing High Quality Products* (PIMS, 1978), raises questions concerning this strategy. According to the report the market is willing to pay premium prices for high quality products. However, if the premium price is not demanded, the market responds by awarding so high an increase in market share that the supplier ends up with a return on investment greater than that resulting solely from premium pricing.

QUALITY AND SHARE OF MARKET

Once a product is actively on the market it attains some "share of market," i.e., a proportion of all sales by all suppliers of that type of product. The size of the attained market share is of great economic importance. Greater market share means higher sales volume. In turn, higher sales volume results in disproportionately higher return on investment due to the nature of the breakeven chart (Figure 3.1).

In Figure 3.1, an increase of 20 percent in sales creates an increase of 50 percent in profit, since no increase in "constant" costs is involved. (Actually, constant costs do vary with volume, but not at all in proportion.) There is little risk involved in such an increase, since the technology, production facilities, market, etc., are already in existence and of proved effectiveness. In contrast, to increase sales by creating a new product line involves much investment in market research, technology, facilities, and personnel. In addition, the venture is far more risky than greater share of market in an existing product line. In this way, a dollar of sales gained through quality superiority is commonly much more valuable than a dollar of sales gained through investment in a new venture.

Effect of Quality Superiority. Quality superiority can usually be translated into higher share of market but it may require special effort to do so. Much depends on the degree of superiority and on the ability of the buyer to perceive the difference and its significance.

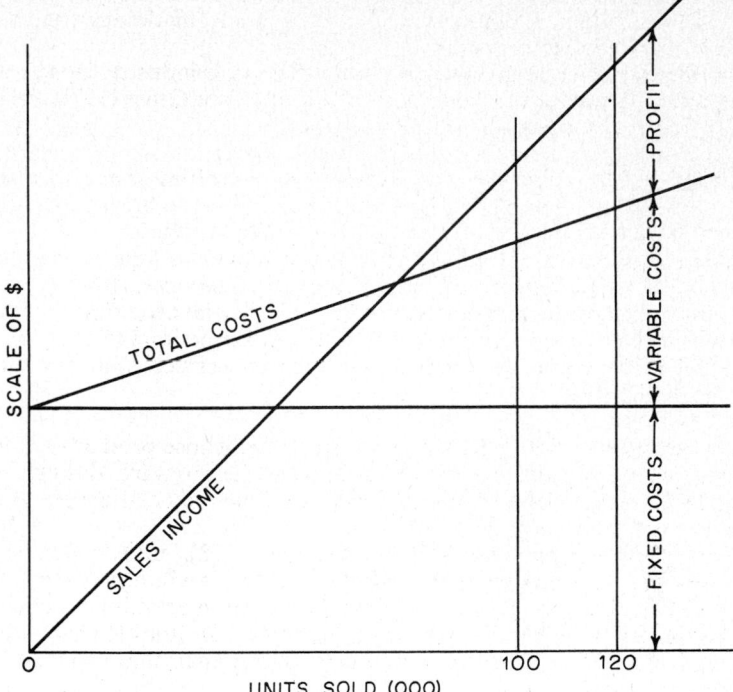

FIG. 3.1 Break-even chart.

Quality Superiority Obvious to the Buyer. In such cases the obvious superiority can be translated into higher share of market. This concept is fully understood by marketers, and they have from time immemorial urged product developers to come up with product features which can then be used to secure higher share of market. Examples of such cases are legion.

Quality Superiority Translatable into Users' Economics. Some products are out-wardly "alike" but have unlike performances. Obvious examples are the electric power consumption of an appliance or the fuel consumption of an automobile. In these and similar examples it is feasible to translate the technological superi-ority into the language of money. Such a translation makes it easier for those who lack technological expertise to understand the significance of the quality superiority.

The power tool case (p. 3.11) is to the same effect. In that case the superior reliability was translated into the language of money to secure a price premium. It could instead have been used to secure higher share of market. Cases such as tire wear (p. 3.10) can similarly be translated into the language of money.

The initiative to translate may also be taken by the buyer. For example, some users of abrasive grinding wheels keep records on wheel life. This is then trans-lated into money—grinding wheel cost per 1000 pieces processed. Such a measure makes it unnecessary for the buyer to become expert in the technology of abrasives.

Collectively, cases such as the above can be generalized as follows:

There is in fact a quality difference among competing products.

This difference is technological in nature so that its significance is not understood by many users.

It is possible, by appropriate data collection in the field, to translate the technological difference into the language of money or into other meaningful forms.

To stimulate action by users the results must be presented in terms of the users' system of values, not the manufacturers'.

Quality Superiority Minor but Demonstrable. In some cases product superiority can be used to secure addded share of market even though the "inferior" product meets customer needs. For example, a manufacturer of antifriction bearings had refined his processes to such an extent that his products were more precise than those of his competitors. As it happened, the competitors' products were entirely fit for use, so no price differential was feasible. Nevertheless, the fact of greater precision was a forceful selling tool and resulted in increased share of market.

In the case of consumer products, even a small product difference can be translated into an increased share of market if the consumers are adequately sensitized. For example, a manufacturer of candy-coated chocolates seized on the fact that its product did not create chocolate smudge marks on consumers' hands. The company dramatized this in television advertisements by contrasting the appearance of children's hands after eating its own and competitors' (uncoated) chocolate. The company's share of market rose dramatically.

Quality Superiority Accepted on Faith. It has been amply demonstrated that buyers can be persuaded to accept on faith, assertions of product superiority which the buyers themselves are unable to verify. A dramatic example involved an ingenious market research on electric razors. The sponsoring company (Schick) employed an independent test laboratory to conduct the tests. During the research, consumer panelists shaved themselves twice, using two electric razors one after the other. On one day the Schick razor was used first and a competing razor immediately after. On the next day the sequence was reversed. In all tests the contents of the second razor were weighed precisely. The data assertedly showed that when the Schick was second, its weighed contents were more than those of competitors. The implication was that Schick razors gave a cleaner shave. Within a few months the Schick share of market rose as follows:

September	8.3 percent
December	16.4 percent

The most striking feature of the above case is the fact that the consumer had *no way to verify* the validity of the published account. They had the choice of accepting it on faith, or not. Many accepted it on faith.

No Quality Superiority. Where there is no demonstrable quality superiority, share of market is determined by the marketing skills. These take such forms as persuasive propaganda, attractive packaging, etc. (See Section 19, Marketing, under Emotional Stimuli.) Price reductions in various forms provide only temporary increases in share of market, since competitors usually move promptly to take similar action.

Consumer Preference and Share of Market.   The willingness of consumers to respond to qualities and to differences they can sense has resulted in much study to:

1. Develop objective methods for measuring consumer preference and other forms of consumer response. A large body of literature is now available setting out the types of sensory tests, the methods for conducting them, and the interpretation of the resulting data. (See Section 18, under Sensory Testing.)
2. Use these methods to aid in making decisions. While much of this application has been for process control and product acceptance decisions (see Section 18), there is a growing use of these methods for market testing, product development, advertising, and marketing of products.

For some products it is easy to secure a measure of consumer preference through "forced choice" tests. For example, a table is set up in a department store and passersby are invited to taste two cups of coffee, A and B, and to express their preference. Or pairs of swatches of carpet may be shown to panels of potential buyers with the request that they indicate their preferences. For comparatively simple consumer products, these preference tests can secure good data on consumer preference. In turn, these data can be used to make sound marketing decisions.

The value of consumer preference data is greatly multiplied through correlation with data on share of market. Figure 3.2 shows such a correlation for 41 different packaged consumer products. This was an uncommonly important analysis and deserves careful study.

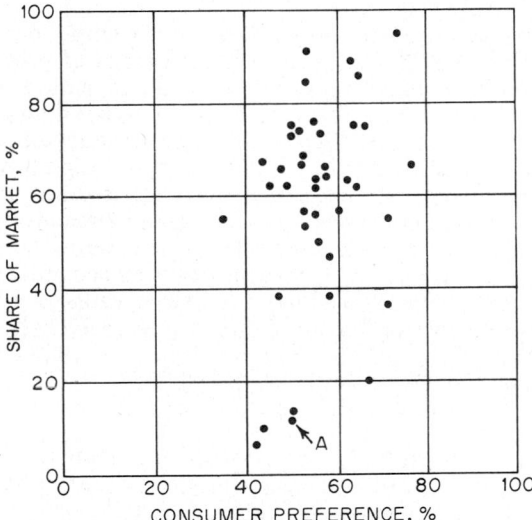

FIG. 3.2   Consumer preference versus share of market.

Each dot on Figure 3.2 represents a food product sold on supermarket shelves. It competes these with other products for shelf space. The competing products sell for identical prices and are packaged in identically sized boxes containing identical amounts of product. What may influence the buyer are:

1. The marketing skills, i.e., attractiveness of the package, the appeal of the prior advertising, the reputation of the manufacturer, etc.
2. The contents of the package as judged by the buyer's senses and usage, which may cause her or him to prefer A to B

On Figure 3.2 the horizontal scale shows consumer preference over the leading competitor as determined by statistically sound preference testing. The vertical scale shows the share of market versus the leading competitor, considering the two as constituting 100 percent.

It is evident that in no instance did any product exhibit a consumer preference below 25 percent (or above 75 percent). This phenomenon is undoubtedly related to the fact that a consumer quality preference above 75 percent means that the product is so superior that three out of four users can detect that superiority. Since all other factors are essentially equal, the product which is so overwhelmingly preferred takes over the entire market while its competition disappears.

In contrast to the vacant areas on the horizontal scale of consumer preference, the vertical scale of share of market has data along the entire spectrum. One product (marked A on Figure 3.2) lies squarely on the 50 percent consumer preference line, which probably means (under forced choice testing) that the users are guessing as to whether they prefer that product or its competition. Yet this product has only 10 percent share of market and its competitor 90 percent. Not only that, this inequality in share of market has persisted for years. The reason is that the 90 percent company had pioneered in that product, acquired a "prior franchise," and retained its position through good promotion thereafter.

The conclusion is that when competing products are quite similar in consumer preference, any effect of such small quality differentials is obscured by the effect of the marketing skills. In consequence, it is logical to conclude that when quality preferences are clearly evident to the user, such quality differences are decisive in share of market, all other things being equal. When quality preferences are slight, the decisive factor in share of market is the marketing skills.

As a corollary, it appears that companies are well advised to undertake quality improvements which will result in either (1) bringing them from a clearly weak to an acceptable preference or (2) bringing them from an acceptable preference to a clearly dominant preference. However, companies are not well advised to undertake quality improvements which will merely move them from one acceptable level to another, since the dominant role in share of market in such cases is played by the marketing skills. For elaboration, see Juran (1959).

It is easy for technologists to conclude that what they regard as important in the product is also of prime concern to the user. In the carpet industry, the engineers devote much effort to improving wear qualities and other technological aspects of fitness for use. However, a market survey established that consumers' reasons for selecting carpets were primarily sensory, i.e.,

Color	56 percent
Pattern	20 percent
Other sensory	6 percent
Nonsensory	18 percent

For more complex consumer products it would seem feasible, in theory, to study the relation of quality to share of market by securing quantitative data on (1) actual changes in buying patterns of consumers and (2) states of quality which may have brought about these changes.

In practice, it is soon discovered that such data are difficult to acquire and that it is also very difficult to conclude, in any one instance, why the purchase was of model A rather than B. What does emerge are some "demographic" patterns, i.e., age of buyers, size of family, etc., which favor model A rather than B. In addition, there emerge some "negatives," i.e., what not to do.

Industrial Products and Share of Market.   Industrial products are sold much more on technological performance than on sensory qualities. However, the principle of preference is still present, and there is need to find ways of relating quality to customer preference and to share of market.

One approach is that of sales analysis, as described in Section 12, under Analysis of Available Field Intelligence: Decline in Sales. For the vital few large accounts, such analyses can be made individually. For the numerous small accounts, sampling is adequate.

Another approach is to analyze the company's performance during its bidding for contracts. The practice of competitive bidding is widespread. Most government agencies are required by law to secure competitive bids before awarding large contracts. Industrial companies require their purchasing managers to do the same. The usual factors of price, delivery date, and quality enter the bidding process, as do the marketing skills. Quality includes the usual parameters of fitness for use plus the important factor of quality reputation of the manufacturer.

The ratio of awards received to bids made is of great significance. The volume of sales and profit depends importantly on this ratio. In addition, the cost of preparing bids is substantial; for large systems the cost of bid preparation is itself large. Finally, the ratio affects the morale of the people involved. (Members of a winning team fight their competitors; members of a losing team fight with each other.)

It is feasible to analyze the record of prior bids in an effort to improve the award percentage. Table 3.3 shows such an analysis involving 20 unsuccessful bids. The installation price turned out to be the biggest influencing factor. This led to a revision of the process for estimating the installation price, and an improvement in the bidding success ratio.

QUALITY LEADERSHIP AND BUSINESS STRATEGY

Among marketers there has always been a school of thought which gave quality the highest weight among the factors which determine marketability. A survey (Hopkins and Bailey, 1971) of 125 senior marketing executives as to their first preference for their own product superiority showed the following:

Form of product superiority	Percent of marketing executives giving first preference to this form
Superior quality	40
Lower price (or better value)	17
More features, options, or uses	12
All others	31

TABLE 3.3 Analysis of Unsuccessful Bids*

Contract proposal	Bid not accepted due to				
	Quality of design	Product price	Installation price†	Reciprocal buying	Other
A 1	...	×	×	...	×
A 2	...		× ×		
A 3	× ×	×			
A 4	× ×	...	×		
A 5	× ×				
A 6	× ×				
A 7	...	× ×			
A 8	...	× ×			
A 9	...	...	× ×		
A 10	...	...	× ×		
B 1	×	...	×		
B 2	...	...	...	× ×	
B 3	...	...	...	× ×	
B 4	...	...	...	× ×	
B 5	...	×	×		
B 6	...	×	× ×		
B 7	× ×				
B 8	...	×	×		
B 9	...	...	...	×	
B 10	×	×	×		
Totals	7	8	10 (of 14)	4	1

*× = Contributing reason; × × = main reason.
†Only 14 bids were made for installation.

Such opinions are supported by the PIMS study (Schoeffler, Buzzell, and Heany, 1974). That study, involving 521 businesses, undertook (among other things) to relate (1) competitiveness in quality with (2) share of market. The findings can be expressed as follows:

Quality vs. competitors	Number of businesses in these zones of share of market		
	Under 12%	12–26%	Over 26%
Inferior	79	58	35
Average	51	63	53
Superior	39	55	88
Total	169	176	176

Building Quality Leadership. Quality leadership is usually the result of an original quality superiority which gains what the marketers call a "prior franchise." Once gained, this franchise can be maintained through continuing product improvement and effective market promotion.

Companies which have attained quality leadership have usually done so based on one of two principal strategies:

1. Let nature take its course. In this approach, companies apply their best efforts, confident that in time these efforts will be recognized.
2. Help nature out by adopting a positive policy, i.e., establish leadership as a formal goal and then set out to reach that goal.

Those who decide to make quality leadership a formal goal soon find that they must answer also the question, "Leadership in what?" Quality leadership can exist in any of the multiple aspects of fitness for use, but the structure of the company will differ significantly depending on which aspect is chosen.

If quality leadership is to consist of	*The company must emphasize*
Superior quality of design	Product development, systems development
Superior quality of conformance	Manufacturing quality controls
Availability	Reliability and maintainability programs
Guarantees, field service	Field service capability

Once attained, quality leadership endures until there is significant cumulative evidence that some competitor has overtaken the leader. Lacking such evidence, the leadership can endure for decades and even centuries.

However, quality leadership can also be lost through some catastrophic change. For example a leading brewing company was reported to have changed its beer brewing formulation in an effort to reduce costs. Within several years its share of market had declined dramatically. The original formula was subsequently restored but the market share did not recover. (See "The Perils of Cutting Quality," 1982.)

In some cases the quality reputation is built not around a specific company but around an association of companies. In that event this association adopts and publicizes some mark or symbol. The quality reputation becomes identified with this symbol, and the association goes to great lengths to protect this reputation.

The medieval guilds imposed strict specifications and quality controls on their members, including "export" (i.e., beyond the city) controls on the finished goods. Such export controls are common in some industrial countries today.

The growth in competition in quality has stimulated the expansion of strategic business planning to include planning for quality and quality leadership. See Section 6, under Companywide Quality Management.

The "Market Leader" Concept.   One approach to quality leadership is through development of product in collaboration with the leading user (or users) of such products. The term "leading user" here has a meaning of influential in the market, and hence likely to be followed. For example, in the medical field, a leading user might be one who is "internationally renowned; a chairman of several scientific societies; is invited to congresses as speaker or chairman; writes numerous scientific papers" (Ollson, 1986, pp. 62, 63).

Determining who is the leading user requires some analysis. (In some respects the situation is similar to the marketer's problem of discovering who within the client company is the most influential in the decision to buy.) Ollson lists ten leader types, each serving a different function.

Carryover of Failure-Prone Features.   A widespread form of loss of quality leadership is through perpetuating failure-prone features of predecessor products. The guilty features are well known; the field service force is busy restoring service because of the product failures resulting from these features. Nevertheless there has been an extensive practice of carryover of those same features into new models. At the least, this practice of carryover perpetuates a sales detriment and a cost burden. At its worst it is a cancer which can destroy market share leadership of seemingly healthy product lines.

A widely publicized example was the small "tabletop" copier machine. In that case the "top ten" list of field failure modes remained essentially identical, model after model. A similar phenomenon prevailed for years in the automobile industry.

The reasons behind this carryover have much in common with the chronic internal wastes which abound in so many companies:

1. The alarm signals are disconnected. The wastes get incorporated into the budgets, and the departments are meeting their budgets.

2. It is no one's responsibility to take the initiative to get rid of the wastes.

There are also other factors. The product and process developers of course have the technological capability to eliminate much of the carryover. However, those developers are usually occupied with bringing new models to market, i.e., developing new product and process features. In addition, they share a distaste for spending their time on cleaning up old problems. In their culture there is greater social prestige in developing the new.

The surprising result can be that each department is carrying out its assigned responsibilities and yet the product line is dying. Seemingly nothing short of upper management intervention can break up the impasse.

LIFE CYCLE COSTING

In its simplest form, a sales contract is based on a purchase price for a specific product (goods or services), e.g., X cents for a glass of milk; Y dollars for a bus ticket. For simple consumable products, the purchase price is also the cost of using the product. Consuming the milk or taking the bus ride normally involves no cost for the user, beyond the original purchase price. Expressed in simple terms,

$$\text{Purchase price} = \text{cost of use}$$

As products grow in complexity and especially as they are used over long periods of time, this simple equation is no longer valid. Purchase price expands to include such factors as cost of capital invested, installation cost, deductions for resale value, etc. Cost of use expands to include costs of operation and maintenance. Even "simple" consumer products are impacted. For some articles of clothing the cumulative costs of cleaning and maintenance can easily exceed the original purchase price. (The famous comedian Ed Wynn is said to have worn the same $3.50 shoes throughout his long career in vaudeville, radio, and television. They cost him $3000 in repairs.)

The basic concept of life cycle costing is one of finding the optimum—finding that set of conditions which (1) meets the needs of both supplier and customer, and (2) minimizes their combined costs.

Life cycle cost is only one of many names given to this concept of an optimum. Other names include:

Cost of ownership

Cost of use (or usage)

Mission cost

Lifetime cost

Cost effectiveness

The life cycle cost concept can be applied to any product. The concept can be defined in models which identify the factors to be considered, the data to be acquired, and the equations to be used in arriving at life cycle costs. The slow pace to date in adopting the concept is not due to difficulty in setting up the models. Instead, the slow pace is due mainly to inadequacies in the needed data and especially to cultural resistance to adopting the life cycle cost concept.

Steps in Life Cycle Cost Analysis.   The literature has gone far to organize the subject of conducting life cycle cost analyses. The steps set out below represent a typical organized approach. For elaboration on various organized approaches, see Brook and Barasia (1977), Ebenfelt and Ogren (1974), Stokes and Stehle (1968), Toohey and Calvo (1980), and Wynholds and Skratt (1977).

Identify the Life Cycle Phases.   Optimizing life cycle cost requires striking a balance among numerous costs, some of which are antagonistic to others. The starting point is to identify the phases or activities through which the product goes during its life cycle. These activities are usually mapped out in a flow diagram as an aid to group understanding. Typical sequences of such activities include:

Product research.

Product development. (In some complex systems there may be several subphases of product development.)

Product design.

Manufacturing planning.

Production.

Installation.

Provision of spares.

Operation.

Maintenance.

Support services.

Modifications.

Disposal.

Identify the Cost Structure.   Once the phases of activity are defined the next step is to identify the cost structure associated with each phase. For example, operating costs for civilian aircraft include (Rose and Phelps, 1979):

Maintenance labor and material

Delay/flight interruptions

Administrative

Insurance

Spares holding

Training

Flight operation (crew, aircraft and traffic servicing, fuel and oil)

For an example from the Tennessee Valley Authority, see Duhan and Catlin (1973).

Acquire the Cost Data. This step can be a formidable obstacle. At best, the prevailing accounting systems provide only part of the essential cost information. The rest must be acquired by special study, by estimate, or by restructuring the accounting system. The work involved can be reduced by concentrating the detailed efforts on the vital few cost categories. These are normally the largest in amount. However close attention must also be given to those categories which are highly sensitive, i.e., they are leveraged to respond to small changes in other factors—the "cost drivers."

Analyze Relationships. This step undertakes to quantify the interrelationship among the cost factors. Such analysis goes far beyond organizing the figures in various ways. The main part of the analysis is to quantify the interrelationships of the activities which generate costs. For example, a comparatively simple analysis establishes that for automotive vehicles, tire wear correlates mainly with distance traveled and speed of travel. For aircraft, the tire wear correlates mainly with number of landings and takeoffs.

However, many analyses are far more complex. A common example is the relationship of designed mean time between failures (MTBF) and mean time to repair (MTTR) to the subsequent costs of operation and maintenance. For some products (e.g., certain military categories) repair and maintenance (R&M) costs over the life of the product run to many multiples of the original purchase price. These R&M costs are highly sensitive to the designed MTBF and MTTR. However, efforts to quantify the interrelationship run into complex estimates bounded by a wide range of error. For a case example involving military avionics, see Toohey and Calvo (1980).

Formulate Aids to Decision Making. The purpose of these analyses is to aid decision making. Typically the decision maker first establishes what categories of cost are to be included in the decison-making process. Then, based on the analysis, equations are set up to arrive at the life cycle cost in terms of those same established cost categories. For example, the State of Virginia arrived at the following equation for estimating cost per hour for a certain class of highway machinery:

> Cost per hour equals initial price, plus repair parts, plus foregone interest, less resale value, all divided by operating hours (Doom, 1969, p. 25).

Breadth of Application. Ideally the life cycle cost analysis should provide aid to sweeping decisions on grand strategy of optimizing costs. In practice this is feasible only for rather simple products. For the most part, life cycle cost analyses are being used as aids to decision making on a more limited scope; for example, see state government purchase of room air-conditioners (Doom, 1969); optimum

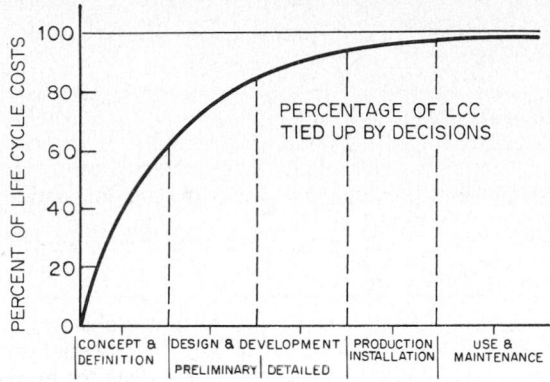

FIG. 3.3 Phases affecting life cycle cost. *(Adapted from Björklund, 1981, p. 3.)*

inventory levels (Dushman, 1970); repair level strategy, i.e., discard, base repair, or depot repair (Henderson, 1979); effect of test system requirements of operation and support costs (Gleason, 1981); optimization of number of thermal cycles (Shumaker and DuBuisson, 1976).

Probably the widest application has been in the area of industrial products. (See below under Application to Industrial Products.)

Irrespective of area of application, most investigators have concluded that the decisions which determine life cycle cost are concentrated in the early stages of the product life cycle. Figure 3.3 is a typical model. It shows that life cycle cost is determined mainly by decisions made during the very early phases of the life cycle. Such a concentration makes clear the need for providing the product researchers, developers, and designers with a good data base on the subsequent costs of production, installation, operation, and maintenance.

Application to Consumer Products. In a classic study, Gryna (1970) found that for various household appliances and television sets the ratio of life cycle costs to original price ranged from 1.9 to 4.8. (See Table 3.4.)

TABLE 3.4 Life Cycle Costing: Consumer Products

Product	Original price, $	Cost of operation plus maintenance, $	Total cost, $	Ratio, life cycle cost to original price
Room air conditioner	200	465	665	3.3
Dishwasher	245	372	617	2.5
Freezer	165	628	793	4.8
Range, electric	175	591	766	4.4
Range, gas	180	150	330	1.9
Refrigerator	230	561	791	3.5
TV (black and white)	200	305	505	2.5
TV (color)	560	526	1086	1.9
Washing machine	235	617	852	3.6

Source: Gryna, 1970.

A study, *Consumer Appliances: The Real Cost* (MIT, 1974), found the following proportions of life cycle costs to prevail during the year 1972 for color TV sets and household refrigerators:

Elements of life cycle cost	Color TV sets	Household refrigerators
Purchase price	53	36
Power	12	58
Service	35	6
Total	100	100

Lund (1978) provides some supplemental information based on a followup study.

Fody (1977) reported on how a U.S. government agency made its first application of the life cycle cost concept to the procurement of room air conditioners. The suppliers made their bids based on original price. However, the agency considered in addition the expected electric power cost based on certified energy efficiency rates. The basis for awarding the contracts then became the lowest life cycle costs rather than the lowest bid price.

Life cycle costs for automobiles have been studied in depth. Table 3.5 shows life cycle costs for intermediate size cars driven 120,000 mi (192,000 km) in 12 years.

TABLE 3.5 Life Cycle Costs, Automobiles

Original price	$10,320
Additional "ownership" costs	
Accessories	198
Registration	240
Titling	516
Insurance	6,691
Scheduled maintenance	1,169
Nonoperating taxes	33
Subtotal	$ 8,847
Operation and maintenance costs	
Gasoline	$ 6,651
Unscheduled maintenance	4,254
Tires	638
Oil	161
Gasoline tax, federal	514
Gasoline tax, other	771
Sales taxes	130
Parking, tolls	1,129
Subtotal	$14,248
Grand total	$33,415

Source: Federal Highway Administration, 1984.

Although data on life cycle cost of consumer products have become increasingly available, consumer use of such data has lagged. The major reasons include:

1. Cultural resistance (see below)
2. The economics of administering numerous small long-life contracts
3. The complexities created by multiple ownership

The most notable example of the last problem is passenger automobiles, which, in the United States, usually go through multiple ownership before being scrapped. Even under short-term guarantees, the transfer of ownership creates severe problems of administering guarantee contracts. Existing practice usually imposes a charge for transfer of short-term guarantees between successive owners. For contracts over the useful life of the product, this problem would become considerably more complicated.

Application to Industrial Products. In terms of broad decision making, this is probably the area of greatest progress. A major example is seen in the airlines' evolution of life cycle costing strategy for aircraft engine maintenance. A critical element has been establishment of an adequate data system relative to field operation and maintenance. Data analysis then resulted in a change in grand strategy for maintenance, from the overhaul concept to the concept of on-condition maintenance. In addition, the data analysis resulted in a superior feedback to product designers and manufacturers. For a well-documented explanation, see Nowlan and Heap (1978).

Part of the competition to sell industrial equipment consists of convincing prospective buyers that their operation and maintenance costs will be low. In some cases this conviction is created by guaranteeing the operating costs, or by offering low-cost maintenance contracts. Some manufacturers provide record-keeping aids to enable users to accumulate data on competitive products as an aid to future purchasing decisions. Some industrial users build up data banks on cost of downtime for various types of industrial equipment as an input to future decision making.

The approach to making decisions to acquire capital equipment follows generally the steps set out above under the heading Steps in Life Cycle Cost Analysis. Kaufman (1969) gives an explanation of methodology along with case examples of application.

Application to Defense Industries. During the twentieth century many governments greatly expanded their acquisition of military weaponry, both in volume and in complexity. Mostly the governments acquired these weapons by purchase rather than by expansion of government arsenals and shipyards. It was most desirable that the life cycle cost concept be applied to such weapons. However a major obstacle was the deeply rooted practice of buying based on the lowest bid price.

Starting in about the 1960s the U.S. Department of Defense organizations stepped up their efforts to make the life cycle cost concept effective in procurement contracts. Directives were issued to define the new emphasis and to clear away old obstacles. However, as events unfolded it became evident that to apply the concept to government procurement was more difficult than for comparable situations in civilian procurement. The differences have their origin in such factors as the nature of the respective missions, the system of priorities, the organization for decision making and the extent of public scrutiny. For a more detailed discussion of these differences, see Gansler (1974); also Pedrick (1968); also Bryan (1981).

The urge for applying the life cycle concept to military products has stimulated an extensive literature. Most of the published papers relate to division of the subject and to the structure of models. See, for example, Barasia and Kiang (1978), Peratino (1968), and Ryan (1968).

There are also numerous papers on application. These are mainly directed at subsystems, e.g., optimizing inventory levels. Alternatively, the applications are directed at lower level components. A published example relates to standardization of electronic modules (Laskin and Smithhisler, 1979). Another example deals with standardization of test equipment (Rosenberg and Witt, 1976). See also Eustis (1977); also Gallagher and Knobloch (1971). Application to subsystems or lower level components obviously runs the risk of suboptimizing unless care is taken to examine the impact of any proposed change on related subsystems or components.

Cultural Resistance.   This is a major force holding back the application of the life cycle cost concept. Purchase based on original price has dominated commercial practice for thousands of years. The skills, habit patterns and status of many persons—product designers, purchasing managers, marketers—have long been built around the original purchase price concept. To change over to a life cycle cost concept demands a considerable change in habit patterns with associated risks of damage to long-standing skills and status.

The most deeply rooted habits are probably those of consumers—small buyers for personal use. They keep few records on costs of operation and maintenance, and tend to underestimate the amounts. For less-than-affluent consumers the purchase of a costly product is obscured by the fact that they may lack the capital needed even for the original price and hence must borrow part of it. In addition, the laws of sales are well worked out as applied to original price contracts but are still in evolution as applied to life cycle cost contracts.

Obviously, makers of consumer goods cannot abandon marketing on original price when such is the cultural pattern. What they can do is to experiment by offering some optional models designed for lower cost of usage as a means of gaining experience and time for the day when life cycle costing comes into wide use.

Makers of industrial products also face cultural resistance in trying to use life cycle costing as a business opportunity. However, with good data they can make out a persuasive case and strike responsive chords in buyers who see in these data a way to further the interests of their company and themselves.

Contracts Based on Amount of Use.   An alternative approach to life cycle costing is through sales contracts which are based on the amount of use. Such contracts shift all the life cycle costs to the supplier, who then tends to redesign the system in a way which optimizes the cost of providing service.

The public utilities—e.g., telephone, power—are long-standing examples. These utilities do not sell a product nor do they often even lease a product; they sell only the service (e.g., watthours of electricity, message units of telephone service). In such cases the ownership of the equipment remains with the utility, which also has the responsibility of keeping the equipment maintained and repaired. The consequence is that the income of the utility is directly bound up with keeping the equipment in service. There are numerous other instances; e.g., the "U-drive" car is rented based on the actual mileage driven; laundromat machines are rented based on minutes of use.

Sale of goods can sometimes be converted into a sale of use. It is common practice for vehicle fleets to buy tires based on mileage. Airlines buy engines based on hours of use. There is much opportunity for innovation in the use of this concept.

For consumer products, the metering of actual use adds many complications. Common practice is therefore to use elapsed time as an approximation of amount of use.

PERFECTIONISM

The human being exhibits an instinctive drive for precision, beauty, and perfection. When unrestrained by economics, this drive has created the art treasures of the ages. In the arts and in esthetics, this timeless human instinct still prevails.

In the industrial society there are many situations in which this urge for perfection coincides with technological needs. In food and drug preparation, certain organisms must be completely eliminated or they will multiply and create health hazards. Nuclear reactors, underground mines, aircraft, and other structures susceptible to catastrophic destruction of life require a determined pursuit of perfection to minimize dangers to human safety. So does the mass production of hazardous products.

However, there are numerous other situations in which the pursuit of perfection is antagonistic to society, since it consumes materials and energy without adding to fitness for use, either technologically or esthetically. This wasteful activity is termed "perfectionism" because it adds cost without adding value.

Perfectionism in Quality of Design.   This is often called "overdesign." Common examples are:

Long life for products which will become obsolete before they wear out.

Costly finishes on nonvisible surfaces.

Tolerances or features added beyond the needs of fitness for use. (The military budget reviewers call this "gold-plating.")

Some cases of overdesign are not simple matters of yes or no. For example, in television reception there are "fringe areas" which give poor reception with conventional circuit design. For such areas, supplemental circuitry is needed to attain good quality of image. However, this extra circuitry is for most areas an overdesign and a waste. The alternative of designing an attachment to be used only in fringe areas creates other problems, since these attachments must be installed under nonfactory conditions.

It is best to prevent overdesign during design review, while the design is still fluid. Those who understand the economics of manufacture, marketing, use, and maintenance can then challenge any design features which do not contribute to fitness for use and which therefore will add to costs without adding to income. Some systems of design review provide for classification of characteristics, e.g., essential, desirable, unessential. The unessential then become candidates for removal on the ground of perfectionism.

Overdesign is one of the targets of value analysis. See Section 13, Product Development, under Value Engineering.

Perfectionism in Quality of Conformance.   Typical examples are:

Insistence on conformance to specification despite long-standing successful use of nonconforming product

Setting of appearance standards to levels beyond those sensed by users

Generally, perfectionism in quality of conformance can be held in check by separating two decisions which are all too often confounded: (1) the decision on whether product conforms to specification and (2) the decision on whether nonconforming product is fit for use. Decision (1) may be delegated to the bottom of the hierarchy. Decision (2) should be made only by people who have knowledge of fitness for use.

Perfectionism in the "Abilities."   Some of the examples encountered are these:

"Worst case" designs in which provision is made to anticipate the worst combination of adverse conditions which might converge to cause a failure, even when the odds against such a combination are fantastically high. Such designs can be justified in critical situations but not necessarily in noncritical situations.

Use of unduly large factors of safety.

Use of high-duty or high-precision components for products which will be subjected to conventional usage.

Because such instances have their origin in design, the remedies are through design reviews such as are discussed above under Perfectionism in Quality of Design.

Perfectionism in Field Service.   To date there has been little of this; more commonly the service has been inadequate.

Perfectionism by Government Regulators.   There is an uncomfortable degree of this, though with more experience the practice tends to moderate.

Some of this perfectionism is undoubtedly influenced by the pressures to which regulators are subjected from reformers, special pleaders, and zealots. Public officials cannot readily defend themselves against all such pressures.

The Perfectionists.   It is possible to categorize the people most often contributing to perfectionism, and the more usual forms in which their proposals are presented. Table 3.6 shows this relationship.

Those who advocate perfectionism often do so with the best intentions and always for reasons which seem logical to them. The resulting proposals are nevertheless of no benefit to users for one of several common reasons:

The added perfection has no value to the user. (The advocate is not aware of this.)

TABLE 3.6   Perfectionists

Basis for perfectionism	Usual guilty parties
"Superiority" which does not add to fitness for use	Top management, marketing managers
Urge to comply with the specification despite clear evidence of fitness for use	Government regulators, industrial quality managers
Belief that tighter specifications assure greater fitness for use	Researchers; designers; theoreticians
Belief that humans can be motivated to make no errors	Enthusiasts and fanatics behind misguided motivational programs
Contention that failure to conform is proof of unfitness for use	Reformers, politicians, journalists, publicity seekers
Adverse publicity given to isolated failures	Muckrakers, publicity seekers

The added perfection has value to the user, but not enough to make up for the added cost. (The advocate is unaware of the extent of the costs involved.)

The added perfection is proposed not to benefit the user but to protect the personal position of the advocate (e.g., he or she has responsibility for conformance but not for cost), or to make a hero of the advocate in the eyes of some bloc.

The weaknesses of these proposals are all related back to costs: e.g., ignorance of the costs, no responsibility for costs, indifference to costs due to preoccupation with something else. Those who do have responsibility for the costs should quantify them and then dramatize the results in order to provide the best challenge.

Defenses against Perfectionism.   There are several of these: quantifying the economics; dramatizing the feedback of fitness for use; use of the concept that "the customer is right."

Quantifying the Economics.   A major defense against perfectionism is to quantify and dramatize the costs. Precision, reliability, or conformance can always be improved, but the cost of improvement can rise spectacularly as we approach perfection.

Dramatizing Fitness for Use.   Originally, evidence of fitness for use is derived from product development and test information. Then, as the product is marketed, new evidence comes from the marketplace in the form of repeat orders, absence of complaints, absence of orders for spare parts, etc. This growing feedback should be embodied into the decision-making process, e.g., material review board decisions, deviation practices, design changes.

"The Customer Is Right."   Use can also be made of the concept that "the customer is right," not only as to things customers can sense but also as to things customers cannot sense.

REFERENCES

Barasia, R. K. and Kiang, T. D. (1978). "Development of a Life Cycle Management Cost Model." *Proceedings, Annual Reliability and Maintainability Symposium.* IEEE, New York, pp. 254–260.

Björklund, O. (1981). "Life Cycle Costs; An Analysis Tool for Design, Marketing, and Service." *Q-Bulletin* of Alfa-Laval, no. 2, pp. 1–4.

Brook, Cyril and Barasia, Ramesh (1977). "A Support System Life Cycle Cost Model." *Proceedings, Annual Reliability and Maintainability Symposium.* IEEE, New York, pp. 297–302.

Bryan, N. S. (1981). "Contracting for Life Cycle Cost to Improve System Affordability." *Proceedings, Annual Reliability and Maintainability Symposium.* IEEE, New York, pp. 342–345.

"Consumer Guide on Tires Is Issued by U.S. Agency" (1980). *New York Times,* Dec. 31, p. 6.

"Dishwashing Liquids" (1984). *Consumer Reports,* July, pp. 412–414.

Doom, I. F. (1969). *Total Cost Purchasing Applied to Heavy Equipment Procurement.* Virginia Highway Research Council, Charlottesville.

Duhan, Stanley and Catlin, John C., Sr. (1973). "Total Life Cost and the 'Ilities'." *Proceedings, Annual Reliability and Maintainability Symposium.* IEEE, New York, pp. 491–495.

Dushman, Allan (1970). "Effect of Reliability on Life Cycle Inventory Cost." *Proceedings, Annual Reliability and Maintainability Symposium.* IEEE, New York, pp. 549–561.

Ebenfelt, Hans and Ogren, Stig (1974). "Some Experiences from the Use of an LCC Approach." *Proceedings, Annual Reliability and Maintainability Symposium.* IEEE, New York, pp. 142–146.

Eustis, G. E. (1977). "Reduced Support Costs for Shipboard Electronic Systems." *Proceedings, Annual Reliability and Maintainability Symposium.* IEEE, New York, pp. 316–319.

Fody, Theodore, J. (1977). "The Procurement of Window Air Conditioners Using Life Cycle Costing." *Proceedings, Annual Reliability and Maintainability Symposium.* IEEE, New York, pp. 81–88.

Gallagher, B. M. and Knobloch, W. H. (1971). "Helicopter Auxiliary Power Unit Cost of Ownership." *Proceedings, Annual Symposium on Reliability.* IEEE, New York, pp. 285–291.

Gansler, J. S. (1974). "Application of Life Cycle Costing to the DOD System Acquisition Decision Process." *Proceedings, Annual Reliability and Maintainability Symposium,* IEEE, New York, pp. 147–148.

Gleason, Daniel (1981). "The Cost of Test System Requirements." *Proceedings, Annual Reliability and Maintainability Symposium.* IEEE, New York, pp. 108–113.

Gross, Irwin (1978). "Insights from Pricing Research." In *Pricing Practices and Strategies,* ed. E. L. Bailey. The Conference Board, New York, pp. 34–39.

Gryna, F. M., Jr. (1970). "User Costs of Poor Product Quality." Doctoral dissertation, University of Iowa, Iowa City. For additional data and discussion, see Gryna, F. M., Jr. (1970). "Quality Costs: User vs. Manufacturer." *Quality Progress,* June 1977, pp. 10–13.

Henderson, J. T. (1979). "A Computerized LCC/ORLA Methodology." *Proceedings, Annual Reliability and Maintainability Symposium.* IEEE, New York, pp. 51–55.

Hopkins, David S. and Bailey, Earl (1971). "New Product Pressures." *The Conference Record,* June. pp. 16–24.

Juran, J. M. (1959). "A Note on Economics of Quality." *Industrial Quality Control,* February, pp. 20–23.

Juran, J. M. (1969). "Mobilizing for the 1970s." *Quality Progress,* August, pp. 8–17.

Juran, J. M. (1970). "Consumerism and Product Quality." *Quality Progress,* July, pp. 18–27.

Kaufman, R. J. (1969). "Life Cycle Costing: Decision-Making Tool for Capital Equipment Acquisitions." *Journal of Purchasing,* August, pp. 16–31.

Kegarise, R. J. and Miller, G. D. (1986). "An Alcoa-Kodak Joint Team." *The Juran Report,* no. 6, pp. 29–34.

Kegarise, R. J., Heil, M., Miller, G. D., and Miller, G. (1987). "A Supplier/Purchaser Project: From Fear to Trust." *The Juran Report,* no. 8, pp. 284–252.

Laskin, R. and Smithhisler, W. L. (1979). "The Economics of Standard Electronic Packaging." *Proceedings, Annual Reliability and Maintainability Symposium.* IEEE, New York, pp. 67–72.

Levitt, Theodore (1960). "Marketing Myopia." *Harvard Business Review,* July–August, pp. 26–28ff.

Lindbergh, Charles A. (1970). *The Wartime Journals of Charles A. Lindbergh.* Harcourt Brace Jovanovich, New York.

Lund, Robert T. (1978). "Life Cycle Costing: A Business and Societal Instrument." *Management Review,* April, pp. 17–23.

MacGowan, T. G. (1957). *Competitive Pricing.* National Industrial Conference Board Studies in Business Policies, no. 84, New York, pp. 116–119.

MIT (1974). *Consumer Appliances: The Real Cost.* Prepared jointly by the Massachusetts Institute of Technology Center for Policy Alternatives with the Charles Stark Draper Laboratory, Inc. Sponsored by the National Science Foundation. Available from RANN Document Center, National Science Foundation, Washington, DC 20550.

Morris, Ruby Turner and Bronson, Claire Sekulski (1969). "The Chaos of Competition Indicated by Consumer Reports." *Journal of Marketing,* July, pp. 26–34.

Mottl, N. J. and Shiah, P. M. (1974). "Prepared Consumer Standards." *ASQC Technical Conference Transactions,* Milwaukee, pp. 218–222.

Nowlan, F. S. and Heap, H. F. (1978). *Reliability Centered Maintenance.* Document ADA066579, Defense Documentation Center, Alexandria, VA.

Ollson, John Ryding (1986). "The Market-Leader Method; User-Oriented Development." *Proceedings, 30th EOQC Annual Conference,* pp. 59–68.

Pedrick, P. C. (1968). "Survey of Life Cycle Costing Practices of Non-Defense Industry." *Proceedings, Annual Symposium on Reliability.* IEEE, New York, pp. 188–192.

Peratino, G. S. (1968). "Air Force Approach to Life Cycle Costing." *Proceedings, Annual Symposium on Reliability.* IEEE, New York, pp. 184–187.

"The Perils of Cutting Quality" (1982). *New York Times,* Aug. 22.

PIMS (1978). "Pricing High-Quality Products." *The PIMSletter.* The Strategic Planning Institute, Cambridge, MA.

"Pricing of Products Is Still an Art." (1981). *Wall Street Journal,* Nov. 25, pp. 25, 33.

"The Problem of Being Premium" (1978). *Forbes,* pp. 56, 57.

Riesz, Peter C. (1979). "Price-Quality Correlations for Packaged Food Products," *Journal of Consumer Affairs.*

Rose, John and Phelps, E. L. (1979). "Cost of Ownership Application to Airplane Design." *Proceedings, Annual Reliability and Maintainability Symposium.* IEEE, New York, pp. 47–50.

Rosenberg, H. and Witt, J. H. (1976). "Effects on LCC of Test Equipment Standardization." *Proceedings, Annual Reliability and Maintainability Symposium.* IEEE, New York, pp. 287–292.

Ryan, W. J. (1968). "Procurement Views of Life Cycle Costing." *Proceedings, Annual Symposium on Reliability.* IEEE, New York, pp. 164–168.

Schoeffler, Sidney, Buzzell, Robert D., and Heany, Donald F. (1974). "Impact of Strategic Planning on Profit Performance." *Harvard Business Review,* March–April, pp. 137–145.

Shumaker, M. J. and DuBuisson, J. C. (1976). "Tradeoff of Thermal Cycling vs Life Cycle Costs." *Proceedings, Annual Reliability and Maintainability Symposium.* IEEE, New York, pp. 300–305.

Stokes, R. G. and Stehle, F. N. (1968). "Some Life-Cycle Cost Estimates for Electronic Equipment: Methods and Results." *Proceedings, Annual Reliability and Maintainability Symposium.* IEEE, New York, pp. 169–183.

Toohey, Edward F. and Calvo, Alberto B. (1980). "Cost Analyses for Avionics Acquisition." *Proceedings, Annual Reliability and Maintainability Symposium.* IEEE, New York, pp. 85–90.

Wynholds, Hans W. and Skratt, John P. (1977). "Weapon System Parametric Life Cycle Cost Analysis." *Proceedings, Annual Reliability and Maintainability Symposium.* IEEE, New York, pp. 303–309.

SECTION 4
QUALITY COSTS[1]

Frank M. Gryna

EVOLUTION OF THE QUALITY COST CONCEPT **4.2**

   Lessons Learned 4.2

CATEGORIES OF COST OF POOR QUALITY **4.4**

   Internal Failure Costs . . . 4.5

   External Failure Costs . . . 4.5

   Appraisal Costs 4.5

   Prevention Costs 4.6

   Example 4.9

CONTROVERSIAL COST CATEGORIES **4.9**

MAKING THE INITIAL COST STUDY **4.12**

   Special Problems Encountered in Data Collection 4.14

PRESENTATION OF INITIAL FINDINGS TO MANAGEMENT . . **4.14**

   Use of the Grand Total to Demonstrate Need For Quality Improvement . . 4.14

   Relating the Grand Total to Business Measures . . . 4.15

   Interrelation of Categories 4.16

GAINING APPROVAL FOR THE QUALITY IMPROVEMENT PROGRAM **4.17**

DISCOVERING THE OPTIMUM . . **4.17**

   Analyzing the Categories of Costs of Poor Quality . . 4.18

   Economic Models of Quality of Conformance 4.19

   Cost Balance Different in Certain Circumstances . 4.21

SCOREBOARD ON THE COST OF POOR QUALITY **4.22**

   Defining the Cost of Poor Quality 4.23

   Collecting and Summarizing the Data . 4.23

   Bases for Comparison . . . 4.25

   Reporting the Results . . . 4.25

OTHER APPLICATIONS OF THE QUALITY COST CONCEPT . . . **4.26**

WHY QUALITY COST PROGRAMS FAIL **4.28**

COMPANY COSTS AND USER COSTS **4.28**

ROAD MAP FOR INTRODUCING A SYSTEM FOR REPORTING THE COST OF POOR QUALITY . . . **4.28**

REFERENCES **4.29**

---

[1]In the Third Edition, the section on Quality Costs was prepared by Daniel M. Lundvall and J. M. Juran.

EVOLUTION OF THE QUALITY COST CONCEPT

All organizations make use of the concept of identifying the costs needed to carry out the various functions—product development, marketing, personnel, production, etc. Until the 1950s this concept had not been extended to the quality function, except for the departmental activities of inspection and test. There were, of course, many other quality-related costs, but they were scattered among various accounts, especially "overhead" accounts.

During the 1950s there evolved numerous quality-oriented staff departments. The heads of these new departments were faced with "selling" their activities to the company managers. Because the main language of those managers was money, there emerged the concept of studying quality-related costs as a means of communication between the quality staff departments and the company managers.

Over the decades as the staff quality specialists extended their studies, some surprises emerged:

The quality-related costs were much larger than had been shown in the accounting reports. For most companies these costs ran in the range of 20 to 40 percent of sales.

The quality costs were not simply the result of factory operation; the support operations were also major contributors.

The bulk of the costs were the result of poor quality. Such costs had been buried in the standards, but they were in fact avoidable.

While the costs of poor quality were avoidable, there was no clear responsibility for action to reduce them. Neither was there any structured approach for doing so.

These findings emerged slowly, amid a good deal of confusion. At the outset many quality specialists took their companies into vague quality cost "programs" without being clear on the objectives. Gradually the objectives emerged in two main forms:

1. Estimate the costs of poor quality as a "one-shot" study, and then use the findings to identify specific projects for improvement.
2. Expand the accounting system to quantify quality costs, and then publish the results as a continuing scoreboard. The expectation was that the published figures would stimulate managers to take action to reduce the costs.

It has turned out that these two objectives are interrelated. Some companies which opted for objective 1 did use the estimates to identify improvement projects, after which they actually made improvements. Having done so, they found that to hold the gains they needed controls, including financial controls. Those financial controls were then established based on quantifying the pertinent quality costs. While there is a logic behind both objectives 1 and 2, getting actual cost reductions solely through publication has turned out to be illusory. By themselves, the published figures do *not* stimulate action unless the company sets up a structured process for quality improvement. (See generally, Section 22 on Quality Improvement.) Identifying the specific projects is a necessary step in that structured approach, but it is not sufficient. The full structure must be set up.

Lessons Learned.   Since those early decades a great deal of experience has been accumulated, leading to some useful lessons learned.

The Meaning of "Quality Costs." The term "quality costs" had different meanings to different people. Some equated "quality costs" with the costs of attaining quality. Others equated the term with the costs of running the Quality Department. The emerging interpretation of the quality specialists has been to equate "quality costs" with the cost of poor quality (mainly the costs of finding and correcting defective work).

The trend has been to adopt the interpretation of the quality specialists. Increasingly, when managers use the term "quality costs" they mean the cost of poor quality. In this handbook, the term "quality costs" means the *cost of poor quality.*

Objectives of Evaluation. The accumulated experience has also identified the main objectives which lead companies to go into programs of evaluating quality costs. The primary objectives are:

1. *Quantify the size of the quality problem in language that will have impact on upper management:* The language of money improves communication between middle managers and upper managers. In some companies the need to improve communications on quality-related matters has been so acute as to become a major objective for embarking on a study of the costs of poor quality.

Some managers say: "We don't need to spend time to translate the defects into dollars. We realize that quality is important and we already know what the major problems are." Typically when the study is made, these managers are surprised by two results. First, the quality costs turn out to be much higher than had been realized. In many industries they are in excess of 20 percent of sales. Second, while the distribution of the quality costs confirms some of the known problem areas, it also reveals other problem areas that had not previously been recognized.

2. *Identify major opportunities for cost reduction:* Costs of poor quality do not exist as a homogeneous mass. Instead, they are the result of some specific segments, each traceable to some specific cause. These segments are unequal in size, and a relative few of the segments account for the bulk of the costs. A major byproduct of evaluation of costs of poor quality is identification of these vital few segments.

3. *Identify opportunities for reducing customer dissatisfaction and associated threats to produce salability:* Some costs of poor quality are the result of product failures which take place after sale. In part, these costs are paid by the manufacturer in the form of warranty charges, claims, etc. But whether the costs are paid by the manufacturer or not, the failures add to customers' costs due to downtime and other forms of disturbance. Analysis of the manufacturer's costs, supplemented by marketing research into customers' costs of poor quality, can identify the vital few areas of high costs. These areas then lead to problem identification.

While the above have turned out to be the primary objectives of evaluation, there have been secondary objectives as well:

4. *Expand budgetary and cost controls:* Most companies establish financial controls on a basis which parallels the departmental organization. The resulting budgets and cost controls have included the costs of inspection and test since these costs are incurred by a recognized department—Inspection and Test. However, most companies have not established financial controls on such costs as scrap, rework, and field failures which cut across departmental lines. As a result, one objective of evaluating quality costs is to expand budgetary and cost controls to cover the nondepartmental costs of poor quality.

5. *Stimulate improvement through publication:* Some companies have undertaken to evaluate costs of poor quality in the belief that publication of the cost data will stimulate the responsible managers to take action to reduce the costs. The realities are that publication alone is not enough. As noted above, this seemingly logical objective has not been borne out in practice. Publication alone makes no provision for identifying projects, establishing clear responsibilities, providing resources, and taking other essential steps. (See generally, Section 22 on Quality Improvement.)

Scoreboards, if properly designed, can be a healthy stimulus to competition among departments, plants, and divisions. To work effectively, the scoreboard must be supplemented by a structured improvement program. In addition, scoreboards must be designed to take into account inherent differences in operations among various organizational units. Otherwise, comparisons made will become a source of friction.

The Language of Money Is Essential.   Another lesson learned is the soundness of the concept of using money as a language. Money *is* the basic language of upper management. Despite the prevalence of estimates, the figures have provided upper managers with information showing:

The overall size of the quality costs

Their prevalence in areas beyond manufacture

The major areas for potential improvement

Without the estimated quality cost figures, the communication of such information to upper managers would have been slower and less effective.

Why High Quality Costs Have Persisted.   Most companies have for years made various forms of cost reduction: e.g., improvement budgets, management by objectives, and structured annual improvement programs. For the most part, these efforts have addressed "conventional" areas of cost reduction: product redesign to reduce cost of materials and manufacture; methods improvement to reduce labor costs; automation; new facilities to increase productivity; and improved materials management to reduce costs of material handling, warehousing, distribution, and inventories. These same efforts did not address the "unconventional" quality-related costs which were largely buried in the overheads. The fact that these costs could not readily be allocated to specific departments was a further and serious limitation.

A related lesson learned has been that new organization machinery is needed to attack and reduce the high costs of poor quality. The nature of this organization machinery is discussed in Section 22, Quality Improvement.

Some Quality Cost "Programs" Have Failed.   There have been numerous efforts by companies to use quality cost information as a basis for making improvements. Many of these efforts have failed. The reasons are mostly those discussed later in this section, under the heading Why Quality Cost Programs Fail.

CATEGORIES OF COST OF POOR QUALITY

Many companies summarize these costs into four broad categories. These categories and examples of typical subcategories are discussed below. (A useful reference that includes details of these four categories is ASQC, 1986. A reference that applies these same categories to a service industry, banking, is Aubrey and Zimbler, 1982.)

Internal Failure Costs. These are costs associated with defects that are found prior to transfer of the product to the customer. They are costs that would disappear if no defects existed in the product prior to shipment. Examples of subcategories are:

Scrap: The labor, material, and (usually) overhead on defective product that cannot economically be repaired. The titles are numerous—scrap, spoilage, defectives, etc.

Rework: The costs of correcting defectives to make them fit for use.

Failure analysis: The costs of analyzing nonconforming product to determine causes.

Scrap and rework—supplier: The costs of scrap and rework due to nonconforming product received from suppliers.

One hundred percent sorting inspection: The costs of finding defective units in product lots which contain unacceptably high levels of defectives.

Reinspection, retest: The costs of reinspection and retest of products that have undergone rework or other revision.

Avoidable process losses: The cost of losses that occur even with conforming product. For example, "overfill" of containers (going to customers) due to excessive variability in filling and measuring equipment.

Downgrading: The difference between the normal selling price and the reduced price due to quality reasons.

External Failure Costs. These are costs associated with defects that are found after product is shipped to the customer. These costs also would disappear if there were no defects. Examples are:

Warranty charges: The costs involved in replacing or making repairs to products that are still within the warranty period

Complaint adjustment: The costs of investigation and adjustment of justified complaints attributable to defective product or installation

Returned material: The costs associated with receipt and replacement of defective product received from the field

Allowances: The costs of concessions made to customers due to substandard products accepted by the customer as is or to conforming product that does not meet fitness-for-use needs.

Appraisal Costs. These are the costs incurred to determine the degree of conformance to quality requirements. Examples are:

Incoming inspection and test: The costs of determining the quality of purchased product, whether by inspection on receipt, by inspection at the source, or by surveillance

In-process inspection and test: The costs of in-process evaluation of conformance to requirements

Final inspection and test: The costs of evaluation of conformance to requirements for product acceptance

Product quality audits: The costs of performing quality audits on in-process or finished products

Maintaining accuracy of test equipment: The costs of keeping measuring instruments and equipment in calibration

Inspection and test materials and services: The costs of materials and supplies in inspection and test work (e.g., x-ray film) and services (e.g., electric power) where significant

Evaluation of stocks: The costs of testing products in field storage or in stock to evaluate degradation

In collecting appraisal costs, what is decisive is the kind of work done and not the department name (the work may be done by chemists in the laboratory, by sorters in Production, by testers in Inspection, or by an external firm engaged for the purpose of testing).

Prevention Costs.   These are costs incurred to keep failure and appraisal costs to a minimum. Examples are:

Quality planning: This includes the broad array of activities which collectively create the overall quality plan and the numerous specialized plans. It includes also the preparation of procedures needed to communicate these plans to all concerned.

New-products review: The costs of reliability engineering and other quality-related activities associated with the launching of new designs.

Process planning: The costs of process capability studies, inspection planning, and other activities associated with the manufacturing process.

Process control: The costs of in-process inspection and test to determine the status of the process (rather than for product acceptance).

Quality audits: The costs of evaluating the execution of activities in the overall quality plan.

Supplier quality evaluation: The costs of evaluating supplier quality activities prior to supplier selection, auditing the activities during the contract, and associated effort with suppliers.

Training: The cost of preparing and conducting quality-related training programs. As in the case of appraisal costs, some of this work may be done by personnel who are not on the payroll of the Quality Department. The decisive criterion is again the type of work, not the name of the department performing the work.

The costs of poor quality are a collection of costs that are incurred by many departments in a company. An example ("Quality Costs," 1975) for one company is shown in Table 4.1.

Although many organizations have found it useful to divide the overall cost into the internal failure, external failure, appraisal, and prevention categories, the structure is not a panacea. In defining the costs of poor quality for a given organization, the following points should be kept in mind:

1. The definitions should be tailor-made for each organization. The usual approach is to review the literature and select those detailed categories which apply to the organization. The titles used should be those of the organization, not the literature. This selected list is then discussed with the various functions to

TABLE 4.1 Quality Cost Matrix

	Prevention	Appraisal	Failure
Design	1. Design reviews 2. Design checking	1. Prototype inspection 2. Design evaluation tests 3. Qualification tests	1. Redesign efforts 2. Scrap, rework, warranty, unplanned purchases, and lost-time costs due to design deficiencies
Purchasing	1. Supplier capability surveys 2. Purchase order tech data review and control 3. Supplier product inspection and test planning	1. Source surveillance 2. Incoming inspection and test 3. First article inspection and test 4. Qualification test	1. Evaluation, disposition, corrective action, and repurchasing efforts for supplier product rejects. 2. Scrap, rework, lost time, and warranty costs due to defective purchased material
Production	1. Machine and process capability studies 2. Tool inspection and control 3. Preventive maintenance 4. Process control and inspection and test planning 5. Inspection and test equipment design 6. Prevention training programs 7. Quality audits and administration 8. Customer inspection liaison	1. Product inspection and test 2. Process control measurements 3. Pack and ship inspection 4. Stock room audits 5. Calibration and maintenance of measurement equipment 6. Production environmental tests	1. Review, disposition, and corrective action efforts for nonconforming material 2. Scrap, rework, lost time, and warranty costs due to deficient workmanship, tooling, maintenance, and operator instructions 3. Rework or redesign costs for deficient manufacturing plans, procedures, and tooling

Source: "Quality Costs," 1975.

4.7

identify additional categories, refine the wording, and decide on broad groupings, if any, for the costs. The resulting definitions are "right" for the organization. Whether they conform to the literature is not critical. It is far more important that the definition within an organization be based on local needs.

(It would be useful if all organizations defined the cost of poor quality in the same way. This would then permit comparisons among organizations and eventually lead to the development of typical values by type of industry. The difficulties of accomplishing such standardization are so formidable that all attempts have been unsuccessful.)

2. The key categories are the failure cost elements because these provide the major opportunity for reduction in costs and for removal of the causes of customer dissatisfaction. These are the costs that should be attacked first. Appraisal costs are also an area for reduction, especially if the causes of the failures are identified and removed so as to reduce the need for appraisal. The compilation of prevention costs can be initially important because it highlights the small investment made in prevention activities and suggests the potential for an increase in prevention costs with the aim of reducing failure costs.

Experience suggests, however, that continuing measurement of prevention costs can often be excluded in order to (a) focus on the major opportunity, i.e., failure costs and (b) avoid the time spent discussing what should be counted as prevention costs.

(Strictly defined, the "cost of poor quality" is the sum of the internal and external failure cost categories. This assumes that those elements of appraisal costs— e.g., 100 percent sorting inspection—necessitated by inadequate processes are classified under internal failures. Some practitioners use the four broad categories but refer to the failure categories as resultant costs and the appraisal and prevention categories as controllable costs.)

3. Agreement should be reached on the categories of cost to be included before any data are collected. Upper management should be a party to this agreement. Initially, summarized data on scrap and rework can gain management's attention and stimulate the need for a full study. Such summaries can be an impetus for management to become personally involved by calling and chairing the meetings to discuss a draft definition of the costs of poor quality. The draft should be prepared jointly by the quality specialist and the accountant with inputs from all areas.

4. The costs of poor quality have in the past been associated with costs that directly involve the product, e.g., scrap, inspection, etc. However, the trend is to broaden the concept; i.e., poor quality is increasingly being viewed as applying to any activity in the company. Thus, any work that must be discarded or repeated is viewed as a cost of poor quality. Some of these costs can be readily identified and should be included in an overall study. An example is the cost incurred when a customer receives an incorrect shipment.

5. Certain costs routinely incurred in a company may have been accepted as inevitable but are really part of the costs of poor quality. Examples are the costs of redesigning the product due to deficiencies in fitness for use and the costs of changing manufacturing processes because of an inability to meet product specifications. If the original design and original manufacturing plans had been adequate, these costs would not have occurred. Typically, these costs have been accepted as normal operating costs, but should be viewed as opportunities for improvement and subsequent cost reduction.

Ten "scenarios" describing issues in defining and using quality costs are given by Gryna (1978).

Example. An example of a study for a tire manufacturer is shown in Table 4.2. This example resulted in some conclusions that are typical in these studies:

1. The total of almost $900,000 per year is large.

2. Most (79.1 percent) of the total is concentrated in failure costs, specifically in "waste-scrap" and consumer adjustments.

3. Failure costs are about five times the appraisal costs. Failure costs must be attacked first.

4. A small amount (4.3 percent) is spent on prevention.

5. There are some consequences of poor quality that could not be conveniently quantified, e.g., "customer ill will" and "customer policy adjustment." Here, the factors were listed as a reminder of their existence.

As a result of this study, management decided to increase the budget for prevention activities. Three engineers were assigned to identify and pursue specific quality improvement projects.

CONTROVERSIAL COST CATEGORIES

As the detailed categories of the cost of poor quality are identified, there are some that will be controversial. Much of the controversy centers around the point:

TABLE 4.2 Annual Quality Cost—Tire Manufacturer

1. Cost of quality failures—losses		
a. Defective stock	$ 3,276	0.37
b. Repairs to product	$ 73,229	8.31
c. Collect scrap	$ 2,288	0.26
d. Waste-scrap	$187,428	21.26
e. Consumer adjustments	$408,200	46.31
f. Downgrading products	$ 22,838	2.59
g. Customer ill will	Not counted	
h. Customer policy adj.	Not counted	
Total	$697,259	79.10%
2. Cost of appraisal		
a. Incoming inspection	$ 32,655	2.68
b. Inspection 1	$ 32,582	3.70
c. Inspection 2	$ 25,200	2.86
d. Spot-check inspection	$ 65,910	7.37
Total	$147,347	16.61%
3. Cost of prevention		
a. Local plant Quality control engineering	$ 7,848	0.89
b. Corporate Quality control engineering	$ 30,000	3.40
Total	$ 37,848	4.29%
Grand total	$882,454	100.00%

"These are not quality-related costs but costs that are part of normal operating expenses and therefore should not be included." Examples are:

1. Inclusion of overhead on top of direct labor and direct material costs of scrap and rework. (One approach is to include variable overhead but exclude fixed overhead costs.)
2. Unavoidable manufacturing waste. These are not defective parts, but trim removed from the beginning of a coil of wire, excess material surrounding a molded plastic part, spillage of a chemical loaded into a process. It is argued that this is a normal part of operating a process.
3. Profit lost on scrapped product.
4. Product liability costs.
5. Depreciation on measuring equipment.
6. Preventive maintenance. (Many of the controversial categories are classified as prevention costs. Ironically, prevention usually accounts for less than 5 percent of the total quality cost.)
7. Tool maintenance.
8. Production delays due to a high scrap rate.
9. Loss in customer good will and sales.
10. Loss in morale.

Arguments about including such categories can result in the downfall of the entire study. If the numbers are included without prior agreement, then doubt is cast on the entire study because it is claimed that the controversial costs were included in order to increase the total.

In most companies, the cost of poor quality is a large sum, frequently larger than the company's profits. This is true even when the controversial categories are not included, so it seems prudent to omit these categories and avoid the controversy in order to focus attention on the major areas of potential cost reduction. Numerous efforts to quantify quality costs have failed because of tenacious insistence by some specialists that certain controversial categories be included. A useful guide is to ask: "Suppose all defects disappeared. Would the cost in question also disappear?" A "yes" answer means that the cost is associated with quality problems and therefore should be included. A "no" answer means that the category should not be included in the cost of poor quality.

At the minimum, controversial categories should be separated out of the totals so that attention will be directed to the main issues.

Another controversy concerns the categorization of cost items. Some examples are:

1. Should 100 percent inspection costs be included as part of appraisal costs or internal failure costs? If the 100 percent inspection was performed in order to improve an unsatisfactory quality level, then it is part of an internal failure cost. If the quality level is satisfactory but 100 percent inspection is performed because of a requirement by the customer or management, then the cost is an appraisal cost.
2. Should the costs of investigating and correcting the causes of failures be included as part of prevention costs or failure costs? The point is made that the investigations will prevent future defects. As the investigations were initiated because of actual failures, we believe that such efforts should be included

as failure costs. Design reviews and other activities connected with the evaluation of new designs would be classified as prevention.

Such controversies should be settled quickly (even if arbitrarily) and not permitted to divert attention from the main target—the failure costs.

There are also costs incurred that may result in understating the costs of poor quality. These "hidden" costs include:

1. Potential lost sales.

2. Costs of redesign due to quality reasons.

3. Costs of changing manufacturing processes due to inability to meet quality requirements.

4. Costs of software changes due to quality reasons.

5. Costs included in standards because history shows that a certain level of defects is inevitable and allowances should be included in standards:

> *a. Extra material purchased:* The purchasing agent orders 5 percent more than the production quantity needed.
>
> *b. Allowances for scrap and rework during production:* History shows that 3 percent is "normal" and accountants have built this into the cost standards. One accountant said, "Our scrap cost is zero. We make about 3 percent defective and have built this into our standard cost system. The production departments are able to stay within this 3 percent and therefore the scrap cost is zero."
>
> *c. Allowances in time standards for scrap and rework:* One manufacturer allows 9.6 percent in the time standard for certain operations to cover scrap and rework.

In such cases, the alarm signals ring only when the standard value is exceeded. However, even when operating within those standards, the costs should be a part of the cost of poor quality. They represent opportunities for improvement.

6. Extra manufacturing costs due to defects. These include additional costs for space, inventory charges, and overtime.

7. Scrap not reported. This may mean scrap that is never reported because of fear of reprisals, or scrap that is charged to a general ledger account without an identification as scrap.

8. Excess process costs for acceptable product. For example, a process for filling packages with a dry soap mix meets requirements for label weight on the contents. However, the process aim is set above label weight to account for the variability in the filling process. If the variability is "large" then the aim must be set far enough above the minimum to accomodate the variability. A reduction in variability could mean setting the aim closer to the minimum and thus reduce the average amount of overfill.

9. Cost of errors made in support operations such as order filling, production control, etc.

10. Costs of poor quality within a supplier's plant. These costs are included in the selling price.

These hidden costs can accumulate to a large amount. (Brown and Kane, 1978, report a multiplier effect of 3 or 4 times the reported failure cost.) Where agreement can be reached to include some of these costs, and where credible data or estimates are available, then they should be included in the initial study on the cost of poor quality. Otherwise, they should be left for future exploration.

The results of research on difficulties in complementation of quality cost concepts are summarized by Dale and Plunkett (1986). Hagan (1985) traces some evolution of quality costs and proposes certain changes in the definition and use.

MAKING THE INITIAL COST STUDY

It would seem logical that a study on the cost of poor quality would be made by the accountant, but the usual approach follows a different scenario. A quality manager learns about the quality cost concept and speaks with the accountant about making a study. The accountant responds that "the books are not kept that way." The accountant does provide numbers on scrap, rework, or certain other categories, but is not convinced to take the initiative to prepare and define a complete list of categories and collect the data. The quality manager decides that the study should be made and follows one of two routes: (1) unilaterally prepares a definition of the categories and collects data or (2) presents the limited data provided by the accountant to upper management with a recommendation that a full study be made using the resources of Accounting, Quality, and other functions. To assure acceptance of the results of the study, the second approach is preferred.

A recommended approach is this:

1. Present to management whatever information is readily available to show that the quality problem is potentially big. This information has maximum impact if it is in the language of money.
2. Recommend that someone in management chair a task force to determine the costs of poor quality. The task force should include personnel from Accounting and major line functions. More simply, the operating committee of the plant can act as the task force, the study being regarded as an agenda item for their meetings.
3. Propose a list of categories comprising the costs of poor quality. The list can be prepared in a short time by the quality manager using the literature plus inputs from Accounting and other functions.
4. Recommend that upper management finalize the definitions and assign responsibilities, with a schedule for data collection.

This approach provides an opportunity for upper management to demonstrate leadership on quality, and it also assures the involvement of functions so that the study receives priority and the results are recognized as credible. Without leadership by upper management, the study will likely be made by the Quality manager with minimum input from others. The risk is that the results will be viewed with skepticism because they were prepared by someone with a biased viewpoint.

Next comes the problem of obtaining the figures. There are two main approaches:

1. *By estimate:* This is the practical approach. It involves only a modest amount of effort. It can, in a few days or weeks, find out enough about quality related costs to tell:

   Whether there is a major cost reduction opportunity or not

   Where this opportunity is concentrated

2. *By enlarging the accounting system:* This is a more elaborate approach. It requires a lot of effort from various departments, especially Accounting and Quality. It also takes a lot of time, running into months and even years.

In the early stages of quality improvement, the estimates are good enough. They involve less work and they provide answers in far less time. The study in Table 4.2 required only 3 weeks and it was conducted in an Industrial Engineering Department by personnel who had no prior knowledge of quality costs.

Many companies have chosen to embark on programs of enlarging the accounting system—setting up to compute and publish "quality costs." All too often these programs have run into maddening delay due to the time required to define the accounting categories, argue out the classifications, set up the data systems, etc. Still more delay has resulted from preoccupation with a level of accuracy not needed for managerial decision making.

To illustrate, the cost of defect X in an electronics company was $3 million per year. That figure was an estimate. The real figure might have been as high as $3.5 million or as low as $2.5 million. Had the accuracy of the estimates been challenged, the managers' response would have been: "All three figures are too high, so let's go after the cost reduction." Over a wide range of estimate, managerial decisions are identical. In the initial study, estimates within 20 percent are sufficient for taking action.

The initial study collects cost data from different sources:

1. *Established accounts:* Examples are appraisal activities conducted by an Inspection Department and warranty expenses to respond to customer problems.

2. *Analysis of ingredients of established accounts:* For example, an account called "customer returns" may report the cost of all goods returned. However, returns are made to reduce inventories as well as to send back defective product. Hence, it may be necessary to go back to the basic return documents to separate the quality costs from the rest.

3. *Basic accounting documents:* For example, some product inspection is done by Production Department employees. By securing their names and the associated payroll data, it is feasible to quantify these quality costs.

4. *Estimates:* Several approaches may be needed.

    a. *Temporary records:* For example, some production workers spend part of their time repairing defective product. It may be feasible to arrange with their supervisor to create a temporary record so as to evaluate the repair time and thereby the repair cost. This cost can then be extrapolated for the time period to be covered by the study.

    b. *Work sampling:* In another approach, random observations of activities are taken and the percent of time spent in each of a number of predefined categories can then be estimated. (See Salvendy, 1982, chapter 4.6.)

    c. *Allocation:* For example, in one of the engineering departments, some of the engineers are engaged part time in making product failure analyses. However, the department makes no provision for charging engineering time to multiple accounts. Ask each engineer to make an estimate of time spent on product failure analysis.

    d. *Standard costs data:* Examples include scrap, rework, and replacement of field samples. Note that such data may be based on history that is obsolete.

    e. *Opinions of knowledgeable personnel:* Examples are design review, training, etc.

Special Problems Encountered in Data Collection. A special problem is whether all of the defective product is reported. This problem can occur if there is no procedure for recording the defectives. It can also occur for an ominous reason. Organizations that have "drives" on quality may create a fear that results in people hiding the scrap:

The defective valves under a pile of snow in the far corner of the parking lot

The poor grade paint buried in the ground

The defective rubber product kept in transit between plants

An approach that can be used to estimate the total amount of scrap follows an "input-output" analysis of material. A manufacturer of molded plastic parts followed this approach:

1. Determine (from inventory records) the pounds of raw material placed in the manufacturing process.
2. Determine the pounds of finished goods shipped. If necessary, convert shipments from units to pounds.
3. Calculate the overall loss as step 1 minus step 2.
4. Make subtractions for work in process and finished goods inventory.

The result is the amount of raw material unaccounted for and is presumably due to defective product (or other unknown reasons). A comparison of this result and the recorded amount of defectives provides a practical check on the recorded number of defectives.

Another special problem is the rare but large cost. Examples are liability costs, or a sales order lost because of customer dissatisfaction with previous quality. When they occur, these can be significant costs, but including them in a study may present a distorted picture. Such costs can be handled in two ways:

1. Report the cost in a special category separating it from the total for the other categories. (Financial reports use this approach to handle unusual transactions such as the sale of a portion of a company.)
2. Use an average of the cost over, say, a 5-year period of history. As a refinement of this approach, calculate an expected cost as the product of the probability of occurrence of the unlikely event and the cost if the event does occur. (See Vaughn, 1975.)

In most cases, the first approach is preferable.

PRESENTATION OF INITIAL FINDINGS TO MANAGEMENT

The results can have a striking impact on management if the presentation shows the size of the total cost and identifies areas for improvement.

Use of the Grand Total to Demonstrate Need for Quality Improvement. The most significant figure in a quality cost study is the total of the quality costs. The total may be so small as to fail to compete for managerial priority. For example, in a confectionery company the avoidable quality costs totaled

$44,500 per year. The managers decided that any program to reduce these costs would have to wait, since numerous other problems had higher priority.

More usually, managers are stunned by the size of the total—they had no idea the amount was so big. One memorable example was a leading manufacturer of aircraft engines. When the total quality costs were made known to the managing director, he promptly convened his senior executives to discuss a broad plan of action.

Those presenting the report should be prepared for the report to be greeted with skepticism. The cost may be such that it will not be believed. This can be avoided if management has previously agreed to the definitions of the cost categories and if the accounting function has either collected the data or has been a party to the data collection process.

Relating the Grand Total to Business Measures.   Interpretation of the total is aided by relating total quality costs to other figures with which managers are familiar. The relationships which have the greatest impact on upper management are:

1. *Quality costs as a percent of sales:*   The financial reports to upper managers and even to shareholders make extensive use of sales as a basis for comparison. When quality costs are similarly related to sales, it becomes easier for upper management to grasp the significance of the numbers.

2. *Quality costs compared to profit:*   It comes as a shock to managers to learn that quality costs exceed the company's profit (which often they do). A component manufacturer with a strong reputation for quality reported direct costs of scrap and rework of $7.5 million versus a profit of $1.5 million.

3. *Quality costs compared to the magnitude of current problems:*   While money is the universal language of upper management, there are additional ways of conveying significance to these managers.

(Two universal languages are spoken in the company. At the "bottom" the language is that of things and deeds: square meters of floor space, schedules of 400 tons per week, rejection rates of 3.6 percent. At the "top" the language is that of money: sales, profit, taxes, investment. The middle managers and the technical specialists must be *bilingual.* They must be able to talk to the "bottom" in the language of things and to the "top" in the language of money.)

In one company which was preoccupied with meeting delivery schedules, the quality costs were translated into equivalent added production. Since this coincided with the chief current goals of the managers, their interest was aroused. In another company, the total quality costs of $76 million per year for the company were shown to be equivalent to one of the company plants employing 2900 people, occupying 1.1 million ft^2 of space and requiring $6 million of in-process inventory. These latter three figures in turn meant the equivalent of one of their major plants making 100 percent defective work every working day of the year. This company is the quality leader in its industry.

Other relationships include:

4. *Dollars per share of common stock outstanding*

5. *Dollars as a percent of cost of goods sold*

6. *Dollars as a percent of total manufacturing cost*

7. *Effect of quality costs on the breakeven point*

(See Grimm, 1974; see also below under Scoreboard on the Cost of Poor Quality.)

Interrelation of Categories.   Additional useful comparisons are available from the interrelationship among the subtotals of the quality costs for the major categories. In many companies the appraisal costs have been budgeted and hence have long been a subject for discussion. However, the typical quality cost study will show that the previously underemphasized failure costs are several times the appraisal costs. This comes as a surprise to most managers and forces them to reconsider their emphasis.

In like manner, when managers discover that prevention costs are pitifully low in relation to the total, their instinctive reaction is to look more attentively at the possibilities of increasing preventive efforts. The relationship between internal failure costs and external failure costs likewise has significance. The former generally point to the need for programs involving manufacturing planning and production, whereas the latter generally point to programs involving product design and field service.

An example, using data for 8 months, is shown in Table 4.3. Here, for each product, the failure costs are over 80 percent of the total, failure costs are at least six times the appraisal costs, and prevention costs are less than 2 percent of the total. The implications are clear:

1. To achieve any significant cost reduction, the failure costs must be attacked first. This will have more impact than reducing the inspection (appraisal) costs.
2. An increase in prevention costs could reap a return in terms of lower failure costs.
3. The largest opportunity for cost reduction is with product A. Note that using "quality cost to shipments" and "total quality cost per machine" results in highlighting product C. This is because of the product mix.
4. Product A is generating scrap and rework internally but there are also field (external) problems. For products B and C, the problem centers more on internal scrap and rework.

A simulation model is useful in studying the interrelation of categories of quality costs. Krishnamoorthi (1986) supplies a computer program and presents results of simulations.

TABLE 4.3   Quality Cost Statement by Product Line

	Product A	Product B	Product C
Prevention, $	5,698	1,569	1,908
Appraisal, $	37,676	10,384	9,206
Internal failures, $	119,107	60,876	63,523
External failures, $	133,168	12,625	15,755
Grand total, $	295,649	85,454	90,392
Shipments, $	8,165,000	1,750,000	840,000
Ratio—quality to shipments, %	3.62	4.88	10.76
Machines, number of	71	14	14
Total quality cost per machine, $	4,165	6,104	6,456

GAINING APPROVAL FOR THE QUALITY IMPROVEMENT PROGRAM

Those presenting the results of the cost study should be prepared to answer this question from management: "What action must we take to reduce the cost of poor quality?"

The control of quality in many companies has followed a recognizable pattern—as defects increase take action in the form of more inspection. This approach has failed because it usually does not remove the causes of defects, i.e., it is detection but not prevention. To achieve a significant and lasting reduction in costs requires a structured process for attacking the main sources of loss—the failure costs. Such an attack requires proceeding on a project-by-project basis. These projects in turn will require resources of various types (see Section 22 under Organizing for Projects).

To launch such an attack requires resources, and these must be justified by the expected benefits. Several justifications are possible.

1. Establish that the costs are large enough to justify action (see, for example, Table 4.2).

2. Use a successful case history (a "bellwether" project) of quality improvement in the company to justify a broader program.

3. Show the opportunities presented by a reasonable goal for cost reduction coupled with identification of projects. A typical goal for a structural program on quality improvement is to cut the cost of poor quality in half within 5 years. An important tool in identifying projects is the Pareto analysis which distinguishes between the "vital few" and the "useful many" elements of quality cost. This concept and other aids in identifying projects is covered in Section 22 under The Project Concept.

4. Compare the return on investment from reducing cost of poor quality with the return from investment in added sales.

5. Calculate the improvement in return on investment resulting from improvement in quality.

6. Show the effect of quality improvement on sales income. Although an increase in sales income may be difficult to estimate, it is an intangible factor that can help to justify a quality improvement program.

Justification is essential for an effective program of quality improvement. The approaches listed above are discussed in more detail in Section 22 under Proof of the Need.

DISCOVERING THE OPTIMUM

When cost summaries on quality are first presented to managers, one of the usual questions is: "What are the right costs?" The managers are looking for a standard ("par") against which to compare their actual costs so that they can make a judgment on whether there is a need for action.

Unfortunately, few credible data are available. Companies almost never publish such data. Attempts to conduct research on these costs have encountered several obstacles. (See "Quality Cost Survey," 1980, and Gilmore, 1983.) First, the cost data are confidential and most companies will not release the information. Second, the definition of quality costs varies by company. For example, some companies include unavoidable manufacturing waste as a part of the cost of poor quality, while other companies do not; some companies add overhead to the direct cost of labor and material on scrap and rework, while other companies do not. The wide ranges in published examples are a grim reminder of the risk in comparing quality cost in one company with so-called industry averages. Three conclusions do stand out: The total costs are higher for complex industries, failure costs are the largest percent of the total, and prevention costs are a small percent of the total.

Analyzing the Categories of Costs of Poor Quality.   Analysis of how quality costs are distributed among the various categories can shed further light on the significance of the cost of poor quality. When such analysis is carried out over a period of time it can help to guide the direction of the overall improvement program. An example showing how the costs are distributed over a period of time is shown in Table 4.4. This table shows that the distribution of the total cost changed as the improvement program evolved. At the start of the program, 82 percent of the total cost was in the failure categories. As the program proceeded, the costs shifted from the failure categories into prevention and appraisal. The improvement efforts were successful, since the overall cost (quality cost as percent of sales) dropped from 4.5 percent of sales to 1.5 percent. In this case, the strong initial concentration of costs in the failure categories highlighted the opportunity to reduce the cost of internal and external failures. The shifting of the costs showed the progress of the improvement program.

TABLE 4.4   History of Quality Costs at an Allis-Chalmers Plant

	1967	1968	1969	1970	1971	1972	1973	1974
Prevention, %	5	9	18	20	24	27	27	26
Appraisal, %	13	20	30	30	31	32	33	35
Internal failure, %	36	34	32	35	35	25	29	33
External failure, %	46	37	20	15	10	16	11	6
Quality cost as %								
of sales	4.5	3.9	2.0	1.9	1.7	1.8	1.7	1.5

Source: Kolacek, O. G. (1976). "Quality Cost—A Place for Financial Impact." *Transactions of the 1976 Annual Conference of ASQC,* Milwaukee, p. 131.

Noz, Redding, and Ware (1983) explain a technique in which knowledge of the phase of an improvement program can be combined with "opportunity dollars" to establish a priority matrix for optimizing quality costs.

Economic Models of Quality of Conformance.   The study of the distribution of quality costs over the major categories can be further explored using models as shown in Figure 4.1 *a* and *b*.

Each model shows three curves:

1. *The failure costs:*   These equal zero when the product is 100 percent good, and rise to infinity when the product is 100 percent defective. (Note that the vertical scale is *cost per good unit* of product. At 100 percent defective, the number of good units is zero, and hence the cost per good unit is infinity.)

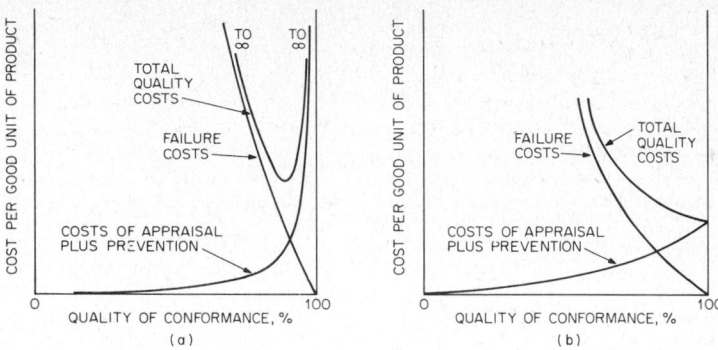

FIG. 4.1 Model for optimum quality costs: (*a*) traditional processes, (*b*) emerging processes.

2. *The costs of appraisal plus prevention:* These costs are zero at 100 percent defective, and rise as perfection is approached. However, the amount of rise differs for the two models.

3. *The sum of curves 1 and 2:* This third curve is marked "total," and represents the total cost of quality per good unit of product.

The model in part *a* of Figure 4.1 represents the conditions which prevailed widely during much of the twentieth century. "Appraisal plus prevention" consisted of much appraisal and little prevention. Moreover, most appraisal was carried out by fallible human beings who are unable to maintain attention 100 percent of the time, are unable to exert muscular energy 100 percent of the time, etc. This human fallibility effectively limits the efforts to attain perfection at finite costs. Hence the model shows the curve "costs of appraisal plus prevention" rising to infinity as perfection is approached. In consequence the "total cost" curve also rises to infinity.

The model in part *b* of Figure 4.1 represents conditions as they evolved in the late twentieth century. Priorities on prevention became higher. New technology reduced the inherent failure rates of materials and products. Robotics and other forms of automation reduced human error during production. Automated inspection and testing reduced the human error of appraisal. (Automated processes do not have lapses in attention, do not get tired, etc.) Collectively these developments have resulted in an ability to achieve perfection at finite costs.

While perfection is obviously the goal for the long run, it does not follow that perfection is the most economic goal for the short run, or for every situation. In the left-hand model (Figure 4.1*a*) the total cost curve reaches a minimum at a level short of perfection. That minimum has had practical meaning and application, as shown in Figure 4.2.

Figure 4.2 divides the total quality cost curve of Figure 4.1*a* into three zones. The zone a company is in can usually be identified from the prevailing ratios of the quality costs in the principal categories, as follows:

Quality Improvement Zone. This is the left-hand portion of Figure 4.2. The usual distinguishing features are that failure costs constitute over 70 percent of the total quality costs, while prevention costs are under 10 percent of the total. In such cases, there are opportunities to reduce total quality costs by improving the quality of conformance. The approach is to identify specific improvement projects and pursue them to improve the quality of conformance and thereby reduce the costs of poor quality, especially the failure costs.

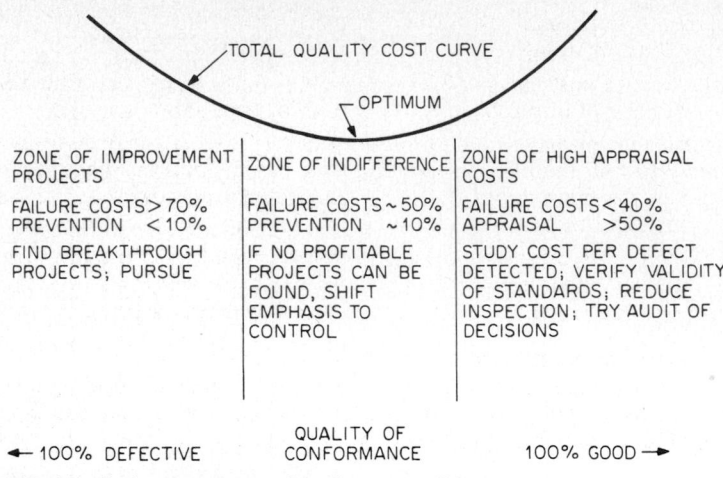

FIG. 4.2 Optimum segment of quality cost model.

High Appraisal Cost Zone. This is the right-hand zone of Figure 4.2 and is usually characterized by the fact that appraisal costs exceed failure costs. In such cases there are also opportunities to reduce costs. This may be done in ways such as:

1. Compare the cost of detecting defects to the damage done if they are not detected. For example, a company had long engaged in detailed inspection for quality characteristic X. The detailed inspection had been started at a time when defect X was widespread. Meanwhile over the years, the process had been improved to a point where defect X was now a rare occurrence—only 15 defects per million parts. However, the detailed inspection went on and on. A study showed that it was costing the company about $2.80 to find each of the defects, yet the sales price of the product was about 5 cents each.

2. Review the quality standards to see if they are realistic in relation to fitness for use.

3. See if it is feasible to reduce the amount of inspection through sampling based on knowledge of process capability and order of manufacture.

4. See if it is feasible to avoid duplication of inspection through use of audit of decisions.

Indifference Zone. This is the central zone of Figure 4.2. In this zone the failure costs are usually about half of the quality costs while prevention costs are about 10 percent of the quality costs. In the indifference zone the optimum has been reached in terms of worthwhile quality improvement projects to pursue. Further improvement may be possible, but the projects are competing against other worthwhile projects, projects which are not yet at optimum levels.

Several concepts need to be stressed in relation to Figures 4.1 and 4.2.

1. The models are conceptual and illustrate the importance of an optimum value of quality of conformance for many industries. In practice, data are not available to construct the curves shown.

2. Improving the quality of conformance results in a reduction of total costs over

most of the horizontal spectrum. This is contrary to the belief that higher "quality" results in higher costs.

3. A reduction in cost can be achieved by moving toward the optimum from either the zone of improvement or the zone of high appraisal costs.

4. Companies which have not yet engaged extensively in quality improvement are likely to find their processes mainly in the improvement zone. For such companies, the main opportunities for cost reduction are through projects for improving conformance.

5. The hidden costs of poor quality (see above under Controversial Cost Categories) are not included in the model. If the data were available, the effect would be to move the optimum toward 100 percent conformance.

The most important criterion for evaluating whether quality improvement has reached the economic limit is to compare the benefits possible from specific projects with the costs involved in achieving these benefits. When no justifiable projects can be found, the optimum has been reached.

Cost Balance Different in Certain Circumstances. The models shown in Figures 4.1 and 4.2 apply to a wide variety of industries. However, there are exceptions:

1. *Industries producing goods that have a critical impact on human safety:* Examples include generation of nuclear power, or manufacture of pharmaceuticals. Such industries are subject to societal pressures to achieve perfect quality at almost any cost.

2. *Highly automated industries:* Here, it is often possible to achieve a low level of defects by proper planning of the manufacturing process to assure that processes are capable of meeting specifications. In addition, automated inspection often makes it economically feasible to perform 100 percent inspection to find all the defects.

3. *Companies selling to affluent clients:* These customers are often willing to pay a premium price for perfect quality to avoid even a small risk of a defect.

4. *Companies striving to optimize the user's cost:* The models depicted in Figure 4.1a and b show the concept of an optimum from the viewpoint of the producer. When the user's costs due to product failure are added to such models, the optimum point moves toward perfection. The same result occurs if lost sales income to the manufacturer is included in the failure cost. (See below for a discussion of the contrast between company costs and user costs.)

Such exceptions to the models of Figures 4.1 and 4.2 can make it economic to produce at 100 percent conformance. The reason is that the added sales value of perfect product more than offsets the added cost of attaining 100 percent conformance. This has already approached realization in products such as electrical refrigerators and color television sets. The prospect is that the trend to 100 percent conformance will extend to more and more products of greater and greater complexity.

For additional discussion relative to the models (Figures 4.1a, b and 4.2), see:

Kume (1985): This paper discusses quality economics and makes the point (among others) that "From a management perspective quality economics is more important than quality cost."

Letters to the editor of *Quality Progress* relative to the Kume paper, by Caplan,

Johnson, Ortwein, and Kume, all in *Quality Progress,* February 1986, pp. 6, 8; also by Juran, in *Quality Progress,* April 1986, p. 10.

Schneiderman (1986); also Juran (1987), relative to Schneiderman's paper.

SCOREBOARD ON THE COST OF POOR QUALITY

Some companies use periodic reporting on the cost of poor quality in the form of a scoreboard. Such a scoreboard can be put to certain constructive uses. However, creating and maintaining the scoreboard requires a considerable expenditure of time and effort. Before undertaking such an expenditure the company should look beyond the assertions of the advocates; it should look also at the realities derived from experience. (Many companies have constructed quality cost scoreboards and have then abandoned them as not achieving the results promised by the advocates.) Whether or not to have such a scoreboard involves a number of issues, which are summarized in Table 4.5.

TABLE 4.5 Issues Concerning Scoreboard on Costs of Poor Quality

Assertions	Realities
1. Publication of the cost figures will stimulate cost reduction.	Publication alone will not result in cost reduction unless the company is well set up to identify projects, organize for improvement, etc.
2. Knowledge of these costs enables us to transfer charges to the guilty departments, thereby stimulating improvement.	True, provided (*a*) we really know who is guilty and (*b*) the company is well organized to identify and carry out improvement projects.
3. We need a financial scoreboard for these costs just as we do for any other kind of costs.	A valid reason, but the choice of standards is critical. The standards for these costs should be the levels reached *after* a quality improvement program has brought the costs down. Otherwise the cost controls will help perpetuate the high level of costs.
4. A financial scoreboard is needed to help hold the gains resulting from the quality improvement program.	Usually correct. Of course, such a scoreboard is created after the costs have been reduced. In this way, control is applied to the improved level.
5. The figures are needed to identify the smaller projects which cannot be identified through broad estimates.	A valid reason if we have already made some of the big gains.
6. The figures are needed for contract reasons, e.g., to bid for business, or because a major client asks to see them.	These are persuasive reasons.
7. The conferences and published papers report how other companies have gotten good results from quantifying these costs.	Seldom an adequate reason. Published reports are biased. (People do not report their failure stories.)

Once there has been a decision to go forward with such a cost scoreboard, the planning must include:

Finalizing the cost categories
Collecting and summarizing the data
Establishing bases for comparison
Reporting the results

Defining the Cost of Poor Quality. For the scoreboard to be useful, the line departments must agree with the choice of categories of costs of poor quality. The categories used in the literature can serve as a starting point. For example, many companies include the four broad categories in their initial study but restrict the scoreboard to those categories of failure costs which represent the opportunities for improvement.

Collecting and Summarizing the Data. The data collection system must provide for accumulating basic data in various units of measure, converting these to monetary units, and charging the proper accounts. A basic step is to provide code numbers to facilitate data recording on the source documents and also to simplify the subsequent data processing. Code numbers are assigned to the accounts, departments, products, components, operations, dates, machine classes, types of defects, job orders, suppliers, customers, workers, etc. The many types of source records include a time card, material requisition, inspection report, scrap ticket, repair ticket, field service report, complaint report, and Material Review Board report. Increasing use is being made of automated data collection system (for example, see Adamek, 1979).

There are multiple ways of summarizing the cost data. The most basic ways are:

1. *By product, process, component, defect type, or other likely defect concentration pattern:* Such summaries make it easy to prepare a Pareto analysis to identify the vital few contributors to the cost.

2. *By organizational unit:* Such summaries are by division, department, or other convenient organizational unit. These summaries not only evaluate the performance of specific organization units; they tend to be regarded as a form of personal scoreboard by the managers of the respective organization units.

Many companies also prepare such summaries for outside suppliers. The results are then used as a basis for action, whether relative to specific suppliers or to suppliers generally.

3. *By category of cost of poor quality:* These summaries are useful for study of the cost relationships among categories. For example, to apply the model of Figure 4.2 requires information on the makeup of quality costs by category. In addition, the trends of the respective costs by category are informative as to the progress of efforts to reduce costs.

4. *By time:* Summaries of cost data by calendar periods provide information on trends and progress in improvement efforts. To help spotlight trends, it is useful to plot the current data and also a moving average. An example of this is shown in Figure 4.3 where monthly data on internal failure costs are plotted along with a 6-month moving average. Each average is based on 6 months of data. (As the data become available for a new month, data for the oldest month are discarded and then the "moving average" is recalculated for the most recent six values.)

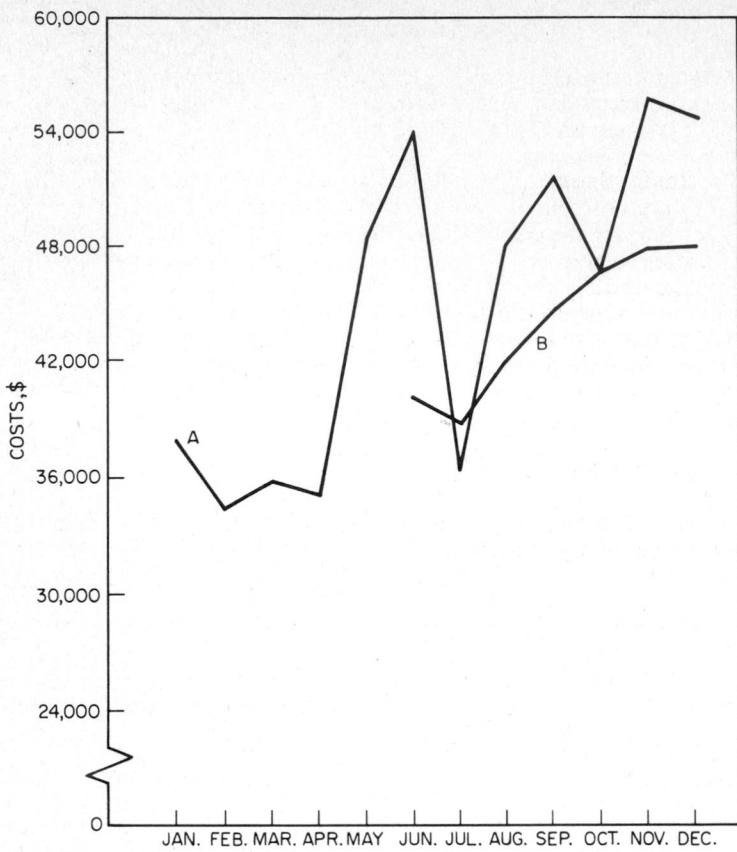

FIG. 4.3 Internal failures costs. *A*, monthly costs curve; *B*, moving averages curve.

TABLE 4.6 Measurement Bases for Quality Costs

Base	Advantages	Disadvantages
Direct labor hour	Readily available and understood	Can be drastically influenced by automation
Direct labor dollars	Available and understood; tends to balance any inflation effect	Can be drastically influenced by automation
Standard manufacturing cost dollars	More stability than above	Includes overhead costs both fixed and variable
Value-added dollars	Useful when processing costs are important	Not useful for comparing different types of manufacturing departments
Sales dollars	Appeals to higher management	Sales dollars can be influenced by changes in prices, marketing costs, demand, etc.
Product units	Simplicity	Not appropriate when different products are made unless "equivalent" item can be defined

Often, the published summaries involve combinations of these different ways. Table 4.3 summarizes data by product and by category of quality cost along with several indices based on the amount of production.

Bases for Comparison.   When managers use a scoreboard on the cost of poor quality, they are not content to look at the gross dollar figures. They want, in addition, to compare the costs with some base which is an index of the opportunity for creating these costs. A summary of some widely used bases, along with the advantages and disadvantages of each, is presented in Table 4.6. The base used can greatly influence the interpretation of the cost data.

It is best to start with several bases and then, as managers gain experience with the reports, retain only the most meaningful. The literature stresses that quality costs be stated as percent of sales income. This is a useful base for some, but not all, purposes (see Table 4.6).

Reporting the Results.   The specific matters requiring decision include:

1. *Format:* The most widely used formats are tabular, graphic, and narrative. An example of a graphical report is given in Figure 4.4. Note that (*a*) the

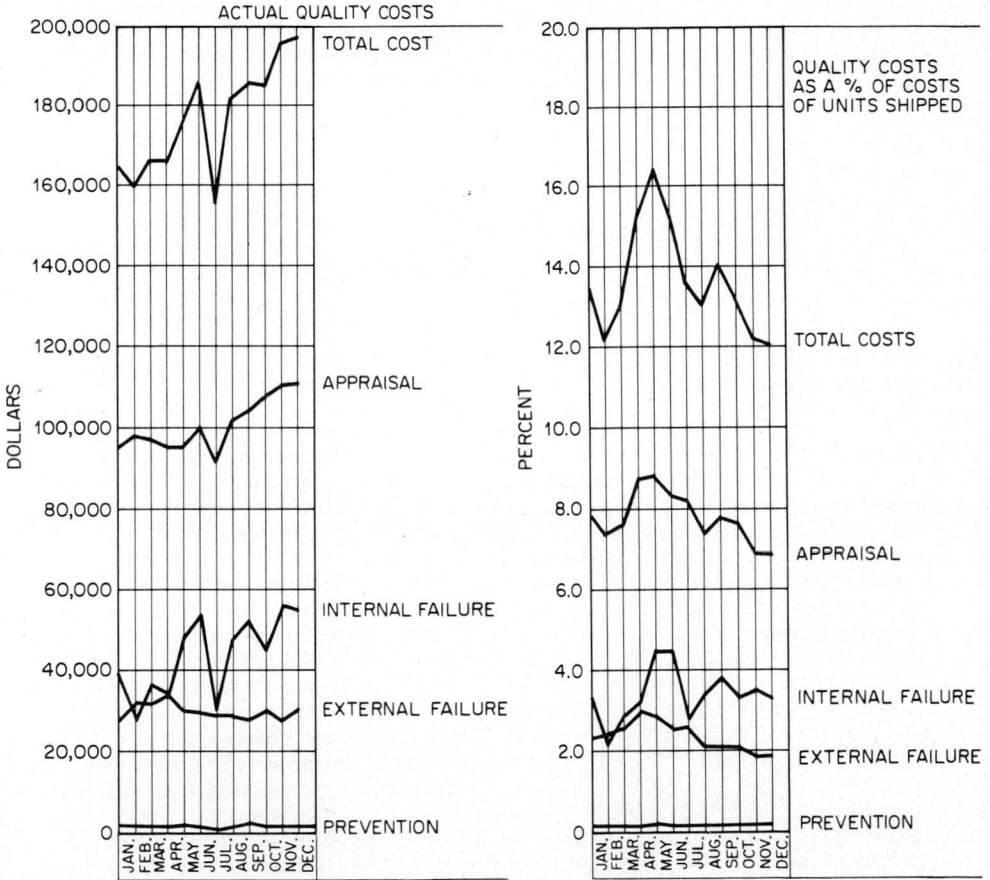

FIG. 4.4 Graphs of quality cost data. *(ASQC, 1977, pp. 18, 20.)*

interpretation of the data is influenced by the base chosen and (*b*) prevention costs are essentially constant during the period studied.

Another means of "publication" involves the display of information at a computer terminal (see Tsiakals, 1983). The data are presented on a color graphic screen in the form of graphs which can be selected by the manager from a "menu" offered on the screen. (Paper copy output is also available.) The cost data for the entire plant can be viewed and then, if desired, the manager can examine layers of intermediate information providing greater detail. In a 1-h session, about 20 graphs can be generated and examined from many thousands of combinations available. The graphs have a time base so that all data are presented in trend chart form. Users may select monthly or year-to-date data; dollars, dollars divided by the value of production, or dollars divided by machine hour. Summaries can also be presented in ratio form such as prevention cost/internal failure cost, product A/product B.

2. *Frequency:*   Here again, the regular cost control reporting system will provide guidelines. Reports to upper management are quarterly and monthly. Reports to middle and lower management are typically more frequent.

Reports on improvement projects are normally quarterly, since change proceeds slowly. Of course, the minutes of the team meetings provide more detail of what is happening, and with greater frequency.

3. *Distribution:*   All levels of management receive quality cost reports, but they do not all receive the same data. The basic quality data are common to all reports. To provide the assorted summaries from common data sources requires a well organized data network and a modular concept of report preparation.

4. *Responsibility for publication:*   This responsibility is best carried out as a joint venture between Accounting and Quality. The planning has, of course, been done jointly to assure that the end result meets the needs of the line managers. Carrying out the plan is commonly done by giving Accounting the responsibility for basic cost data collection, data processing, and preparation of the summaries. Such an approach utilizes Accounting's extensive experience in such matters while reducing jurisdictional disputes. This same approach adds credibility to the figures, since upper management looks to Accounting for unbiased financial reporting.

OTHER APPLICATIONS OF THE QUALITY COST CONCEPT

The costs of poor quality are present not only in production operations, but also in many other company operations. For example, Schrader (1986) describes the measurement of quality costs in a product development organization. The application to finance, personnel, and other "white-collar" areas is discussed by Harrington (1986). Nickell (1985) describes how a marketing organization identified opportunities including one to reduce the percent of cancelled sales orders. Juran and Gryna (1980, pp. 18, 349) present examples from gage control and auditing activities.

In selected activities of an organization, quantifying the costs of errors can draw attention to the seriousness of a problem and identify specific problem areas (Groocock, 1977).

WHY QUALITY COST PROGRAMS FAIL

A number of "Quality Cost Systems" have failed to get useful results. The major reasons for failure are summarized in Table 4.7.

TABLE 4.7   Reasons Why Quality Cost Systems Fail

Reason	Preferred approach
1. Accounting Department is ignored because of its lack of cooperation.	Work with Accounting to whatever degree it is willing to participate.
2. Quality Department insists that certain controversial costs be included.	Agree to exclude or at least separately identify any such costs.
3. Corporate Quality Department issues one quality cost procedure without giving each plant the opportunity to review before issuance.	Provide time for plants to comment. Allow enough flexibility to care for plant differences.
4. Reports fail to talk the different languages needed at various management levels.	Use different units of measure for various levels. Try out a sample report before finalizing the system.
5. No provision is made for investing additional funds in prevention activities.	Tell management the amount and type of resources needed to achieve a defined saving.
6. Role of top management in quality improvement.	Propose numerical goals and identify specific projects. Ask management to provide necessary resources and assign responsibility to line departments.
7. No provision is made to obtain the facts needed to diagnose causes of problems.	Propose some organizational mechanism that will be responsible for diagnosis of causes.
8. Cost data are presented in categories that are too broad to be useful.	Provide detail to the level needed.
9. System is instituted for all products and departments at one time.	Try it out for one product to obtain a successful case history.
10. Divisiveness caused by unfair comparisons of results among plants.	Recognize that plants are different. Make comparisons of planned action programs.
11. Assumption that publication alone will achieve an improvement in quality.	Structured program of improvement with responsibility and resources assigned.
12. Arguments occur about "transfer of charges."	Agree on some arbitrary way to settle the assignment of charges.
13. Undue emphasis is placed on precision in the figures.	Emphasis should be on identification of problem areas. This does not require extreme precision.
14. System is personalized. It is associated with an individual who is a strong advocate and sponsor.	Quality cost system should be depersonalized. Tie it in with a structured program of quality improvement that has the support of middle and upper management.
15. Quality Department regards the system as "its own" to maintain.	Turn over data collection and issuance of reports to Accounting. Quality Department should concentrate on analysis of the data.

The failures have been primarily due to losing sight of the key objective: show the size of the quality problem and identify the projects for improvement.

COMPANY COSTS AND USER COSTS

The costs of poor quality affect two parties—the manufacturer and the user. This section discusses the impact on the manufacturer. Poor quality also increases the costs of the user of the product in the form of repair costs after the warranty period, various losses due to downtime, etc. Gryna (1977) presents a methodology with case examples of user costs of poor quality. The extent of these user costs clearly affects future purchasing decisions of the user. This in turn influences the sales income of the manufacturer. This section stresses the potential for profit improvement by reducing manufacturer costs. The effects of quality on sales income is even more important. See Section 3, under Quality and Sales Income.

ROAD MAP FOR INTRODUCING A SYSTEM FOR REPORTING THE COST OF POOR QUALITY

The sequence of events needs to be tailored for each company. However, the following have application to most companies:

1. Review the literature on quality costs. Consult others in similar industries who have had experience with installing a program.
2. Select one organizational unit of the company to serve as a pilot run. This unit may be one plant, one large department, one product line, etc.
3. Discuss the objectives of the study with the controller in the organization. The objectives should stress determining the size of the quality problem and identification of specific projects for improvement.
4. Collect whatever cost data are conveniently available from the accounting system and use this information to gain the support of management in making a full cost study.
5. Make a proposal to management for a full study. The proposal should provide for participation of all concerned parties to develop the list of categories. The proposal should include setting up a task force to gain agreement on the definition of the costs of poor quality.
6. Publish a draft of the categories defining the cost of poor quality. Secure comments and revise as needed.
7. Finalize the definitions and secure management approval.
8. Secure agreement on responsibility for data collection and report preparation.
9. Collect and summarize the data. Ideally, this should be done by Accounting.
10. Present the cost results to management along with a report of a successful "bellwether" quality improvement project (if available). Request authorization to proceed with a broader companywide program of measuring the costs and pursuing projects.
11. If needed, first conduct the several trial projects and then propose a companywide program.

12. Based on the initial experiences, review the need for simplification or other revision of the cost categories.

13. Extend the program of cost measurement and project improvement to other departments.

14. Consider the need for a corporate scoreboard on the costs of poor quality.

Harrington (1986) provides further elaboration on the steps involved in implementation of a "poor-quality cost system."

REFERENCES

Adamek, Kenneth C. (1979). "Automated Collective Analysis of Scrap and Rework." *ASQC Technical Conference Transactions,* Milwaukee, pp. 190–199.

ASQC (1977). *Guide for Reducing Quality Costs,* American Society for Quality Control, Milwaukee, pp. 18, 20.

ASQC (1986). *Principles of Quality Costs,* American Society for Quality Control, Milwaukee.

Aubrey, C. A., III and Zimbler, D. A. (1982). "A Banking Quality Cost Model: Its Uses and Results." *ASQC Quality Congress Transactions,* Milwaukee, pp. 195–201.

Brown, F. X. and Kane, R. W. (1978). "Quality Cost and Profit Performance." *ASQC Technical Conference Transactions,* Milwaukee, pp. 505–514.

Caplan, Frank (1986). Letter to editors. *Quality Progress,* February, p. 6.

Dale, B. G. and Plunkett, J. J. (1986). "The Determination and Use of Quality Related Costs in Manufacturing Industry." *EOQC Quality,* March, pp. 3–6.

Gilmore, Harold L. (1983). "Consumer Product Quality Control Costs Revisited." *Quality Progress,* April, pp. 28–32.

Grimm, A. F. (1974). "Quality Costs: Where Are They in the Accounting Process?" *ASQC Technical Conference Transactions,* Milwaukee, pp. 190–200.

Groocock, J. M. (1977). "Quality Costs and No Failure Costs." *Quality,* vol. 2, p. 9.

Gryna, Frank M. (1977). "Quality Costs: User vs. Manufacturer." *Quality Progress,* June, pp. 10–15.

Gryna, Frank M. (1978). "Quality Costs—What Does Management Expect?" *ASQC Technical Conference Transactions,* Milwaukee, pp. 210–217.

Hagan, John T. (1985). "Quality Cost II—The Economics of Quality Improvement." *Quality Progress,* October, pp. 48–51.

Harrington, H. James (1986). *Poor-Quality Cost.* ASQC Quality Press, Milwaukee, and Marcel Dekker, New York.

Johnson, Michael (1986). Letter to editors. *Quality Progress,* February, p. 6.

Juran, J. M. and Gryna, Frank M. (1980). *Quality Planning and Analysis.* McGraw-Hill, New York.

Juran, J. M. (1986). Letter to editors. *Quality Progress,* April, p. 10.

Juran, J. M. (1987). Letter to editors. *Quality Progress,* April, pp. 7, 9.

Krishnamoorthi, K. S. (1986). "Predicting Quality Cost Changes Using Regression." *ASQC Quality Congress Transactions,* Milwaukee, pp. 406–410.

Kume, Hitoshi (1985). "Business Management and Quality Cost: The Japanese View." *Quality Progress,* May, pp. 13–18.

Kume, Hitoshi (1986). Reply to letters to editors. *Quality Progress,* February, p. 8.

Nickell, Warren L. (1985). "Quality Improvement in Marketing," *The Juran Report,* no. 4 (winter), pp. 29–35.

Noz, William C., Jr., Redding, Bradley F., and Ware, Paul A. (1983). "The Quality Manager's Job: Optimize Costs." *ASQC Quality Congress Transactions,* Milwaukee, pp. 301–306.

Ortwein, W. J. (1986). Letter to editors. *Quality Progress,* February, pp. 6, 8.

"Quality Costs: The Real Measurement of Performance." (1975). *Quality Management and Engineering,* January, Hitchcock Publishing Company.

"Quality Cost Survey." (1980). *Quality,* July, pp. 16–17.

Salvendy, Gavriel (1982). *Handbook of Industrial Engineering.* John Wiley & Sons, New York.

Schneiderman, Arthur M. (1986). "Optimum Quality Costs and Zero Defects: Are they Contradictory Concepts?" *Quality Progress,* November, pp. 28–31.

Schrader, Lawrence J. (1986). "An Engineering Organization's Cost of Quality Program." *Quality Progress,* January, pp. 29–34.

Tsiakals, Joseph J. (1983). "Management Team Seeks Quality Improvement from Quality Costs." *Quality Progress,* April, pp. 26–27.

Vaughn, T. C. (1975). "Zubits: Regular $18.50-Liability Extra." *Quality Progress,* February, p. 16.

SECTION 5

QUALITY POLICIES AND OBJECTIVES[1]

J. M. Juran

THE NEED FOR QUALITY
POLICIES **5.2**

The Urge for Written
Quality Policies 5.2

Recent Massive Forces . . 5.2

Advantages of Written
Policies 5.3

Disadvantages of Written
Policies 5.3

CORPORATE QUALITY POLICIES **5.4**

Summary Statement . . . 5.4

Definition of Quality . . . 5.5

Other Elaborations 5.5

Additional Subject Matter 5.7

DIVISIONAL QUALITY POLICIES **5.7**

Policies on Improvement . 5.7

QUALITY POLICIES FOR
FUNCTIONS **5.8**

New Product Introduction 5.8

Supplier Relations 5.8

Manufacturing Planning . . 5.9

Production 5.9

Marketing; Customer
Service 5.10

Quality Assurance 5.11

Administrative and Support
Functions 5.11

QUALITY POLICIES FOR
SPECIFIC PARAMETERS **5.12**

Product Safety 5.12

Reliability 5.12

FORMULATION OF QUALITY
POLICIES **5.13**

The "Right" Policies . . . 5.13

The Policy Formulation
Process 5.13

Policies: Holy Ground? . . 5.14

Publication of Quality
Policies 5.14

ADHERENCE TO POLICIES . . . **5.14**

QUALITY OBJECTIVES **5.15**

Objectives Compared to
Policies . . . .

Objectives Compared to
Standards 5.15

Subject Matter of Quality
Objectives 5.15

AN OBJECTIVE SHOULD BE— . **5.17**

---

[1]*Note:* This section contains many extracts from company manuals on quality, but the identities of the companies are not always disclosed. Companies are well advised to secure, where feasible, copies of the quality manuals of other companies.

**THE BASES FOR ESTABLISHING
QUALITY OBJECTIVES** **5.18**

History as a Basis 5.18

Engineering Study as a
    Basis 5.18

The Market as a Basis . . . 5.19

**OBJECTIVES FOR
BREAKTHROUGH OR CONTROL** **5.20**

Objectives for Breakthrough 5.20

Objectives for Control . . . 5.21

**ZERO DEFECTS AS AN
OBJECTIVE** **5.21**

**ESTABLISHING QUALITY
OBJECTIVES** **5.22**

**STRATEGIC QUALITY
OBJECTIVES** **5.22**

REFERENCES **5.23**

THE NEED FOR QUALITY POLICIES

All organizations have in mind (or in writing) some principles, creeds, beliefs, etc., which are their broad guides to managerial conduct. These guides rest on a philosophical and ethical base. They concern important issues, are the result of much reflection, and are intended to have long life, i.e., to act as a stabilizer. In this handbook such principles, etc., are designated as "policies."

(Note that the word "policy" is not standardized as to meaning. In many companies the organization charts and the procedures for control are assembled into a manual which is called the "policy manual" or "policy and procedures manual.")

In tiny organizations where one person makes all the decisions, these guides to conduct are literally "in mind." The one person operates in accordance with an unwritten code of conduct. Anyone who wants to discover that code must deduce it from the observed deeds.

For example, the master of a small shop adheres to the (unwritten) policy of making good on any defects in shop products. The townspeople discover this policy from the shop owner's deeds and "publish" the policy by word-of-mouth.

As organizations grow, more and more managers are engaged in making significant decisions. These decisions affect numerous people inside and out of the organization, including the managers themselves. Unless there is consistency in these decisions, there is no predictability; neither insiders nor outsiders know what to expect. An impersonal way of creating this predictability is to think through, write down, and publish the policies which then become the basis for consistent conduct.

The Urge for Written Quality Policies. Behavior of large organizations is not determined by the decisions and actions of some one individual. Many individuals take actions on behalf of the organization, and it becomes easy for the organization to present multiple and inconsistent faces to outsiders. Within the organizations, behavior in some functional areas can be antagonistic to the long-range goals of the organization. As the unwelcome incidents accumulate, there arises a growing urge to think through, write out, and publish quality policies to serve as guides to managerial action.

Recent Massive Forces. Until the 1950s, published quality policy statements were rare. The exceptions were usually the result of requirements by government agencies that their contractors prepare written manuals for review and approval.

During the last half of the twentieth century some massive new forces came over the horizon:

A "population explosion" of consumer products with a resulting spectacle of millions of consumers depending for day-to-day health and convenience on products they own but are unable to repair or even understand ("Life behind the quality dikes")

A public awakening to the problems of pollution, many of which have their origin in the operation of manufactured products

An erosion of traditional manufacturers' defenses in matters of safety and product liability

The emergence of very complex apparatus—aerospace systems, automated factories, defense systems, and computers

A consumerism movement directed at protecting the small user from misleading advertising and from failures without recourse

A growing invasion by government regulation not only into the traditional fields of human health and safety but also into consumer economics, i.e., integrity of guarantee, product labeling, etc.

A new, intense level of international competition in quality, resulting in large scale shifts of shares of market and trade balances, with associated severe impacts on employment in the impacted industries.

Each of the above forces was in the nature of a revolutionary change in the existing order, and has required a revolutionary response. A part of that response has consisted of communicating to all concerned the nature of the new changes and the associated guides to company action. In part, this communication has been through published quality policies. For elaboration, see Juran (1969 and 1970).

That same list of massive forces also sheds light on the stability of quality policies. If well thought through, policies are quite stable. They seldom require change from year to year. However, in our industrial societies, quality policies do require changes from decade to decade.

Advantages of Written Policies.   Organizations which have undertaken to prepare written quality policies generally report that the benefits have been worth the effort. They point to certain specific advantages of the undertaking:

1. It provides insiders and outsiders with a new, superior form of predictability, i.e., a *written* guide to managerial action.
2. It forces the organization to think about quality problems to a depth never before achieved. "Before you can write it down, you must first think it out."
3. It establishes legitimacy and can be communicated in an authoritative, uniform manner. Policies which are not established at high levels may, by default, be established at low levels.
4. It provides a basis for management by agreed policies agreed upon rather than by crisis or opportunism.
5. It permits practice to be audited against that policy.

Disadvantages of Written Policies.   The major disadvantage is the work involved. In the great majority of organizations, quality policies must be approved at the very highest levels of organization. These top officials understandably want to avoid being drawn into the detailed work of sitting in meetings to evolve and refine the drafts. One way of avoiding this work is to insist that the final draft bear the approval of all subordinate organizations. Since many diverse interests are involved, it takes many meetings and a great deal of time to reach full agreement on the drafts.

Beyond the work involved, there is a feeling among some managers that written policies tend to restrict innovation and to narrow the range of action available to adapt to changing conditions. There is merit in this contention. Policies are intended to be a guide as to what *not* to do, as well as what to do. However, in most organizations the policies are regarded as guides, and there is awareness that conditions may arise requiring departure from established policies.

CORPORATE QUALITY POLICIES

As a company grows to an extent which involves it in multiple markets and products, it becomes evident that no one set of quality policies can fit all company activities. This problem is solved by creating several levels of quality policy. One of these levels is corporate quality policy, which consists of the following:

1. A statement of those policies which are companywide in their effect and hence binding on all company organization units. This corporate policy statement usually sets out:

   a. The purpose of writing and publishing quality policies

   b. A brief statement of corporate intent as to quality (the "motherhood" statement)

   c. The minimal actions to be taken by company divisions with respect to quality (see below)

   d. Interdivisional relationships concerning quality

   e. Quality standards policies for overlapping markets

   f. Provision for corporate audit of compliance with quality policies

   g. Relationship of quality policies to other company policies

2. A delegation of authority to subordinate company organization units (usually the "profit centers" known as "divisions") to establish subsidiary quality policies appropriate to their needs. This delegation is needed because the divisions are commonly engaged in different businesses—each involving different markets, laws, traditions, technology, etc.—which require different policies.

Summary Statement. Virtually all published statements of corporate quality policy contain a brief declaration which summarizes the company's position. For example:

> It is the policy of the company to provide products and services of a quality that meet the initial and continuing needs and expectations of customers in relation to the price paid and to the nature of competitive offerings, and in doing so, to be the leader in product quality reputation.
>
> To achieve and sustain a reputation for quality at competitive prices in the National and International markets for our entire product range.

To provide a product which satisfies the performance, quality, reliability, and safety requirements of our customers at a fair market price.

To provide products and services which consistently meet the needs and expectations of our customers and of users within the company.

No one quarrels with such statements. However, they are regarded by most managers as too vague to provide guides for conduct. (Hence the name "motherhood" policies; i.e. everyone is in favor of motherhood.) To be useful, quality policies should provide specific guides to action for specific, important matters. Such guides help the insiders to understand what is expected of them and the outsiders to understand what to expect from the company managers.

Increasingly the emerging policy statements do provide such specifics. Usually these specifics are contained in the functional level policies. (See below.) However, some specifics are elaborations of corporate quality policy.

Definition of Quality.   Usually these definitions are built around quality parameters such as safety, performance, reliability, economy, appearance, "user friendliness," etc. Alternatively the definitions relate to such aspects as quality of market research, quality of design, quality of conformance, etc.

Other Elaborations.   The subject matter of elaboration varies from company to company. The choice is no doubt influenced by the specific pressures present at the time the policy drafts are in preparation. The subjects most frequently elaborated include those discussed below.

Importance of Quality.   In many companies, the top priority prior to the 1980s was *not* on quality. The top priority was on delivery dates, cost, or other parameters. The emerging forces then required raising the priority given to quality. This new need then gave rise to quality statements such as:

Leadership in quality has top priority.

Quality shall be given equal priority to costs and delivery.

Managerial decisions must give equal consideration to quality as well as to aspects of cost and schedule.

Quality Competitiveness.   Quality policy statements usually refer to competitiveness, whether in the short summary or in elaborations. The various wordings in general state that the company's products shall:

Equal or exceed competitive quality

Be of the highest quality

Have quality excellence

Be best in class

Provide unmatched value

Attain world leadership

Customer Relations.   Here the elaboration often identifies specific customer needs to be met; e.g., the company's products should:

Provide customer satisfaction

Meet customer perceptions of good quality

Be useful, reliable, maintainable

Provide value

A typical comprehensive statement reads:

> Assure that customer needs are identified and that our products meet these needs.

Internal Customers. There has been a growing trend to widen the meaning of the word "customers" to include internal persons and organizations who are impacted by the product. This trend is reflected in quality policy statements such as:

> We regard the receivers of our work results as "customers" whose needs are important to understand and satisfy.
>
> Quality should extend to all phases of the business.
>
> Processes should be established at high yields and process capability.
>
> Product designs should be producible.

Work Force Involvement. A special case of internal customers is the work force—the nonsupervisors in factories, offices, warehouses, etc. Some quality policy elaborations aim to emphasize the role of the work force, along with related aspects of work force involvement. Typical statements include:

> Our policy is to foster a spirit of pride among employees regarding the company's quality performance.
>
> Our policy is to stimulate our co-workers' creativity, initiative, and sense of responsibility.
>
> Our policy is to provide current skills training and promote open communications to maximize employee contributions.
>
> No employee of this company will ever be called upon to do anything in the line of duty that is morally, ethically, or legally wrong.

Quality Improvement. This activity has expanded enormously starting in the early 1980s. This expansion is reflected in quality policy elaborations such as:

> Resources will be allocated primarily to the prevention of defects, and corrective action will be focused on root-cause identification and elimination.
>
> Preventive quality actions and correction of quality deficiencies shall be given priority.
>
> The quality assurance program should be designed to emphasize preventive techniques coupled with aggressive investigation and corrective action programs.

Planning and Organization. Many published statements of quality policy include declarations which actually relate to other managerial matters, e.g., planning and organization. In this handbook such matters are discussed in their respective sections.

Additional Subject Matter. The above examples of subject matter for corporate quality policies are widely applicable. However, some organizations face special quality questions which may require formulation of quality policy. Examples of such questions include:

Is the aim to sell standard goods (commodities) or to sell a broad service in which the goods are only one element?

Is the aim to sell on the basis of life cycle costing or on the basis of initial price?

Which part of the spectrum of affluence is to be the target for the company's products?

Questions such as these have an impact on all major functions of the organization, including the quality function. It can be useful to the managers to have answers in the form of written policy. Whether the resulting declarations are included among the quality policy statements or elsewhere is not critical.

DIVISIONAL QUALITY POLICIES

In large companies it is common for the corporation to require that the divisions establish divisional quality policies as needed, and within the framework of corporate policies. It is also common to require the divisions to:

Prepare a formal plan for quality assurance, including minimal contents such as formal systems for design reviews, supplier qualification, process control, inspection and test, and field feedback.

Publish a quality manual which includes the formal plans, the definitions of responsibility, the organization charts, the procedures, etc.

Conduct audits to determine the extent to which the plans are adequate and are being carried out. (Copies of the audit reports are sometimes required to be submitted to the corporate offices.)

The delegation to divisions may also impose limitations. For example, some multinational companies conduct manufacturing operations in multiple facilities, and then market the resulting goods in multiple countries. In such situations the corporation may mandate product uniformity. One such mandate is worded as follows:

The same design shall be used in all factories making a specific product.
Quality of design and quality of conformance for a specific product shall be the same in all markets.

In certain industries the company divisions are organized around specific "programs" such as major government defense contracts or major construction projects. In such cases the customers typically make extensive use of mandated quality policies and regulations. These mandates then apply to all contractors who, in turn, must apply them to subcontractors.

Policies on Improvement. The acute need for quality improvement has also been reflected in quality policy formation. Increasingly the corporate policies emphasize allocating efforts to eliminate quality problems at their source rather than detecting and correcting them afterward. An example of such a policy declaration is as follows:

> Resources will be allocated primarily to the prevention of defects, and corrective action will be focused on root-cause identification and elimination.

QUALITY POLICIES FOR FUNCTIONS

Many of these policies are prepared to provide guidance to managers in specific functional departments such as product development, manufacture, and marketing. Additional policies relate to activities of an interdepartmental nature such as the process for developing, making, and marketing new products. Still other functional policies focus on specific quality parameters and their impact, whether departmental or interdepartmental. Examples are product safety and product reliability.

The written functional policy statements may be assembled into a comprehensive policy manual which includes corporate quality policies as well. Alternatively, the functional policy statements are published as part of a departmental manual which includes other departmental information, e.g., planning and organization.

New Product Introduction.   Quality policies in this vital area often mandate the use of specified managerial processes. A common example is the phase system. Under this system a sequence of milestones is established. As each milestone is reached, a business decision must be made to determine whether work should proceed on the next phase in the sequence. A simple example of a sequence of milestones is design completion, prototype release, release for production, and release for shipment.

Within the phase system there may be further mandated processes such as engineering change control and design reviews and audits. For example, the following is a policy statement mandating design reviews:

> Design reviews shall be conducted that cover the compliance of the design with customer market and regulatory body requirements for function, quality, reliability, and safety.

For additional discussion, see Section 13, Product Development, under Basic Concepts: Design Review.

Supplier Relations.   Quality policy formation in this area has been active due to an emerging change from an adversary relationship to a teamwork relationship. An early example of this trend is seen in extracts from the Johnson & Johnson policy on supplier relations:

> To place, whenever possible, the facilities of our research, development, and technical services at the disposal of our suppliers in order to help them with any problems they may encounter in supplying materials to our specifications and to aid them in developing better means for production and quality improvement
>
> To encourage exchange visiting by our suppliers' technical personnel and our technical personnel to observe our respective plant operations, thereby promoting a better understanding of mutual problems and objectives

Some recent policy statements exemplify the trend to a teamwork relationship:

> We will work cooperatively with our suppliers to assure that their materials meet the same standards as our products.
>
> We will assure that our requirements are accurately specified and communicated to suppliers.
>
> We seek to establish long-term, open relations with our suppliers.

See Section 15, Supplier Relations, for further discussion.

Manufacturing Planning.   This function (also called "process engineering") has recently been heavily impacted by the concept of process capability and the associated statistical methodology. One result of this impact has been the emergence of quality policy declarations relative to manufacturing process capability. Here are some examples:

> Manufacturing process capability must be verified during the product development cycle.
>
> Manufacturing equipment shall be able to meet quality requirements with sufficient margin and at the lowest cost.
>
> Process variability and capability must be understood, and operating procedures clearly specified.

The increased emphasis on quality-oriented parameters has intensified some earlier policy questions relative to manufacturing planning. Examples include:

Should the quality-oriented portion of manufacturing planning be done by quality specialists, or should the manufacturing planners be trained in the necessary skills and techniques?

Should design reviews for producibility be mandated?

Should formal planning for safety, reliability, maintainability, etc., be applied to the manufacturing process as well as to the product?

For additional discussion, see Section 16, Manufacturing Planning.

Production.   This function has also been impacted by the increased use of statistical methodology. In addition, there has been a trend to enlarge worker participation in the affairs of the company and of their own jobs. The two principal forms of such participation have been:

1. Increasing the role of workers in data collection, analysis, and feedback.
2. Use of Quality Circles for making improvements in performance. (See Section 10, Managing Human Performance, under Team Performance: Quality Circles.)

The above two trends of increased use of statistical methodology and enlarged worker participation have been especially strong in the production function and have stimulated much development of relevant policy. Here are some policy examples:

> It is the policy to foster involvement and a spirit of pride among employees by encouraging ideas and resolutions regarding the company's quality performance.

Each employee must accept responsibility for maintaining, and where possible, improving product quality within the scope of the employee's job assignment.

All managers are responsible for providing an environment reflecting quality as the top priority objective, including clearly defined expectations which provide each employee the maximum opportunity to contribute.

Looming behind such policy statements is the broader question of whether to retain the Taylor system of separating planning from execution. The major premise of the Taylor system was that the work force lacked the technological literacy needed to do planning. (That same premise applied to many of the first-line supervisors of that day.) Since then a remarkable growth in education levels has made Taylor's premise obsolete and hence has brought the current validity of the system into question.

Once a consensus emerges on what is to replace the Taylor system, it will be necessary to formulate new policy statements to guide the changeover process. Some sensitive issues will need to be addressed. Increased worker participation in planning can affect long-standing "management prerogatives" such as the right to "stop the line," the right to decide which topics are to have priority on the management agenda, and the right of workers to take over work formerly performed by engineers or supervisors.

For additional discussion, see Section 17, Production.

Marketing; Customer Service.   These functions have been impacted by recent major forces which include:

Growing dependence of continuity of customers' operations on the reliability of processes, goods, and services provided by suppliers

Growth of life cycle costing with its need for information on product performance and user costs over the life of the product

Growth of competition in quality, requiring continuing improvement to remain competitive

Response to such forces has required increased emphasis on information from the field, especially with respect to:

1. Market research to determine customers' needs and competitive performance
2. Feedback of field information on product performance and users' costs over the life of the product

In part this response is reflected in policy statements. Such statements are usually included in the marketing/customer service sections of the policy manual, since in many companies these functions have major responsibilities for interface with clients and users.

Examples of pertinent policy statements include:

Marketing shall create only such customer expectations as can realistically be met.

Systems must be developed and maintained to provide accurate and current information on product quality performance and customer acceptance.

When specified, data on products shipped to customers will be transmitted to them for their assistance in determining the usability of the product.

Service operations shall be conducted so as to minimize customers' shutdowns.

Managers involved in customer interface must assure that performance expectations are clearly defined and that their employees are qualified to meet those expectations.

Quality Assurance.   It is common for corporate policy statements to mandate the creation and "independence" of a quality assurance function. For example:

> Each division is to maintain a Quality Assurance department which:
>
> 1. Will report to divisional top management
> 2. Will not be subordinate to the production function
>
> There shall be a clearly defined Quality organization with sufficient, well-defined responsibility and organization freedom to identify and evaluate quality problems and to initiate, recommend, or provide solutions.

Until the 1980s the Quality Assurance departments played major roles in managing the quality affairs of the companies. Those roles are bound to undergo extensive change due to the recent growth of emphasis on quality. This change of emphasis will require development of new policies relative to the quality assurance function, but this development has been proceeding slowly.

The earliest expressions of the new policies have been in such broad forms as:

> Quality has top priority.
>
> Quality is everyone's job.
>
> Prevention, not detection.

These are well-meaning expressions of intent but they generally have not been accepted by subordinates as guides to action. The statements are very general, whereas the prior responsibilities have been very specific, and there has been no discernible change in responsibilities, or in evaluation of performance, or in the nature of the reward system.

To put those broad expressions into effect requires extensive changes such as:

> Revisions in the planning process so that quality-oriented planning will be largely carried out by line managers and specialists rather than by quality specialists
>
> A revolutionary growth in the effort allocated by line organizations to quality improvement
>
> Massive training of line managers and specialists to be able to carry out their new quality-oriented responsibilities

There is much need here for policy formulation. However, the resulting statements must be much more specific than the vague declarations which dominated the scene during the early 1980s.

Administrative and Support Functions.   This is usually shortened to A&S functions. A basic policy question is whether the company's formal approach to managing for quality should include the quality of A&S operations. To illustrate, should the concept of "quality" include such matters as:

The extent to which the invoicing process produces correct invoices

The promptness of service provided to internal customers, e.g., recruitment done by the employment department

The accuracy of the sales forecast relative to subsequent realities

Historically such matters were *not* regarded as related to "quality" since they did not directly impact the goods or services sold. However, the emerging trends are clear and in the direction of enlarging the concept of quality to include A&S operations. Upper managers, in particular, have readily accepted this enlarged concept.

As of the early 1980s the needed policy formulations had not kept pace with this trend. This deficiency remains to be remedied. Otherwise there will be delays in establishing the infrastructure needed to improve the quality of A&S operations—infrastructure such as means for setting quality objectives and processes for planning, controlling, and improving quality.

QUALITY POLICIES FOR SPECIFIC PARAMETERS

This has been a growth area for quality policy formation. The most active parts of this area have related to product safety and reliability.

Product Safety.   Starting in the 1960s there emerged a great expansion of government regulation relative to the impact of products on safety, health, and the environment. In addition there has been an explosive growth in lawsuits and the associated awards for product liability. All this has had its effect on quality policy, leading to statements such as:

Our products shall be free from unacceptable properties that cause damage, and shall meet applicable standards and regulations.

All products must comply with applicable health, safety, and environmental laws and regulations, and with Corporate policy relating to health, safety, and the environment.

All available evidence indicates that this emphasis will continue, even to the extent of spending huge sums of money to undo the accumulated damage of the past.

For additional discussion, see Section 35, Impact of Quality on Society.

Reliability.   This is widely recognized as a parameter of the highest importance. It is already a major basis for marketplace competition and is destined to remain so. This importance is reflected in some company policy statements:

Reliability goals shall be established in the early stages of product design.

The reliability of any new product must be at least equal to that of the product it replaces, and at least equal to that of leading competitive models.

Each division shall identify the organization responsible for reliability functions applicable to the products and services of the division. The Reliability organization shall have sufficient, well-defined responsibility, authority, and organizational freedom to identify and evaluate Reliability problems and to initiate, recommend, or provide solutions.

For additional discusssion, see Section 13, Product Development, under Planning for Time-Oriented Performance (Reliability).

FORMULATION OF QUALITY POLICIES

Policies are approved at the highest levels of organization. The chief executives logically require, prior to this approval, that their subordinate executives review the drafts. In this way the key managers all participate in the formulation of quality policies.

The "Right" Policies.   Managers often wonder whether the "right" policies can be found somewhere in the literature. The answer is that there are no "right" policies other than for a few rather obvious questions. Instead, policy decisions must be made to measure. Each company is unique in its history, management, and state of development. The deliberating managers must identify that uniqueness and structure their policies to fit it.

The Policy Formulation Process.   The process of formulating policies requires that the key managers have the opportunity for participation but without the burden of performing the detailed staff work. One way to do this is to assign to a specialist the job of securing from these key managers:

1. Their nominations for what should be the subject matter contained in quality policies
2. Their judgments as to what should be the direction of the company with respect to these subjects

Through this method it is possible to discover the consensus among these key managers for the various subjects. A draft prepared in the light of this consensus then contains the basis for a meeting of the minds, even on abstract matters.

For example, in one company it became important to establish a policy on a number of quality matters including the elusive question of quality leadership. The individual assigned to interview the key managers included in the questions a choice of quality leadership levels, i.e., should the company aim to be:

1. The recognized quality leader of the industry ("sole leadership")?
2. One of the top group of companies ("shared leadership")?
3. Competitive with the average of the industry ("respectability")?
4. Adequate as to quality so as to secure minimal costs and charge minimal prices ("adequacy")?

The 26 managers interviewed opted as follows:

Sole leadership	3
Shared leadership	22

Respectability   1
Adequacy   0

This consensus resolved a long-standing debate.

Policies: Holy Ground?   In many companies there is little initiative from lower or middle management to propose policies. In some cases this is the result of an unfavorable climate created by previous or present top managements. In other cases there is lack of awareness by middle management that their proposals are an expected and useful contribution. Some of this lack of awareness is the result of a mistaken belief that company policies are "holy ground." The belief stems from reasoning as follows: since only top management can approve company policies, only top management can venture on such ground.

In most companies this reasoning is not well founded. The road to final approval of policies is somewhat as follows:

	Usual roles	
Activities in formulating policies	Middle management	Upper management
Identify need and nominate	X	X
Draft proposal	X	
Review		X
Redraft	X	
Review		X
Approve		X

It is evident that middle management has a very real role to play.

Publication of Quality Policies.   Until the 1960s, examples of written quality policy were rare. Such publication as took place was for internal use and usually restricted to the upper levels of the hierarchy.

All this has changed radically. Many companies have written out comprehensive quality policies. Publication to insiders is now extensive. The short declarations are widely publicized down to the work force.

Publication now also extends to outsiders, on a selective basis. Appropriate portions of the policy are made available to customers, suppliers, the media, government regulators, etc. In some cases quality policy statements have been included in the annual report to stockholders.

ADHERENCE TO POLICIES

Before a policy is published, it is well to face realistically the question, "Do we intend to adhere to this policy?" If there is doubt about this, the policy should not be published.

In the long run, insiders and outsiders alike draw their conclusions about company policy from the deeds. If the company's products continue to show innovation, observers conclude that the company has a policy of design leadership. If the company adjusts quality complaints promptly and fairly, the observers conclude that the company has a policy of ethical dealing on quality.

If, in addition, there is a written policy and it conforms to the deeds, the written policy gains credibility. If, however, the written policy says one thing and the deeds say something else, what is believed is the deeds. Not only does the written policy lose its credibility, but other pronouncements of the company become suspect as well.

So important is the need for adherence to published policy that most companies establish audits to provide a feedback on how well the policies are being followed.

QUALITY OBJECTIVES

An objective is an aimed-at target—an achievement toward which effort is expended. A quality objective is an aimed-at quality target. The word "goal" is a synonym for "objective."

The concept of objectives is in wide use, and this use extends broadly into managing for quality. Under this concept, managers establish objectives which then are reduced to writing and become the basis of planning for results. The concept is effective because well-defined objectives:

Help to unify the thinking of all concerned

Have the power within themselves to stimulate action

Are a necessary prerequisite for operating on a planned basis rather than on a crisis to crisis basis

Permit a subsequent comparison of performance against objectives

Objectives Compared to Policies.   The two concepts differ widely. Table 5.1 sets out the major differences.

Objectives Compared to Standards.   As used in this handbook, a standard is a model to be followed. It is often mandated by external sources.

Standards differ from objectives in ways which are set out in Table 5.2. However, the distinction is often blurred in practice. There is no confusion when the standard is mandated by outside forces, e.g., government regulations or industry codes. However, some mandates originate with internal sources, e.g., product tolerances published by the Design Department. In such cases it is common for the operating departments to look upon them as continuing objectives.

Subject Matter of Quality Objectives.   Quality objectives are in use throughout the entire organization hierarchy.

At the worker level the objectives usually take such forms as conformance to specific product features or to specific process features.

Above the worker levels it becomes necessary to widen the objectives. Much of this is done by creating groupings such as multiple product features and multiple process features. The groupings become progressively broader at progressively higher levels of organization.

In the supervisory levels the groupings of quality features may be based on product families. The resulting quality objectives are expressed in such terms as

TABLE 5.1   Objectives Compared to Policies

Features	Objectives	Policies
Subject matter	Wide range of activities	Broad, managerial
Formulation by	Many levels of organization	Middle managers, specialists
Language	Usually in numbers; often with associated schedule	Narrative
Approval at	Many levels	Highest levels
Duration	Limited; often revised annually	Lengthy; extends for years, even decades

error rates in type X insurance policies, or assembly repair rates for type Y color television sets.

At middle management levels the objectives are stated in terms such as:

To reduce the cost of poor quality for the X product line by 50 percent over the next 5 years

To reduce the cancellation rate of sales contracts by 50 percent over the next 2 years

In many cases the functions and the organization units which perform the functions are coextensive. For example, the function of filling customer orders may be carried out by a Customer Order Department which has no other function. In such cases the quality objective for the function can also serve as a goal for the organization unit and thereby as an objective for the manager of that unit.

In other cases function and organization unit are not coextensive. Some organization units carry out multiple functions; some functions are carried out by

TABLE 5.2   Objectives Compared to Standards

Features	Objectives	Standards
Usual origin	Internal decisions	Outside forces
Usual range of application	Local, to originating organizations	Wide, to many organizations
Voluntariness	Often preceded by internal participation, negotiation	Often mandated by law or powerful economic forces
Purpose: improvement versus control	Often requires improvement	Largely limited to control
Effort demanded	Often requires extra effort	Usually requires only holding status quo
Attainability	Often unproven	Usually proven
Stability	Often revised annually	Stable over long periods

multiple organization units. Where function and organization are not coextensive, it is common to evolve objectives for the organization units as well as for the functions.

At the highest level are the strategic corporate goals for quality. These goals are properly an extension of the business goals of the corporation. Here are some examples:

> On-time arrivals must attain a level of 80 percent by the end of the next year [an airline].

> Our product performance must at least be equal to that of our three principal competitors.

> During the next 5 years our objective is to bring the cost of poor quality down to 6 percent of sales.

> During the next 5 years we should cut by a third the time required to bring new products to market.

AN OBJECTIVE SHOULD BE—

From long experience we have evolved a list of criteria to be met by those who establish quality objectives.

An objective should be:

Measurable: Objectives which are stated in numbers can be communicated with precision.

Optimal as to overall results: Objectives which "suboptimize" performance of various activities can easily damage overall performance.

All-inclusive: Activities for which objectives have been set tend to have high priority but at the expense of the remaining activities.

Maintainable: Objectives should be designed in modular fashion so that elements can be revised without extensive teardown.

Economic: The value of meeting the objectives should be clearly greater than the cost of setting and administering them.

No less important is the list of criteria as perceived by those who are faced with meeting the objectives. To these operating forces, objectives should be:

Legitimate: Objectives should have undoubted official status.

Understandable: They should be stated in clear, simple language—ideally in the language of those who are faced with meeting the objectives.

Applicable: The objectives should fit the conditions of use or should include the flexibility to adapt to conditions of use.

Worthwhile: Meeting the objective should be regarded as benefiting those who do the added work as well as benefiting the organization which established the objective.

Attainable: It should be possible for "ordinary" people to meet the objectives by applying reasonable effort.

Equitable: Since performance against objectives is frequently used for merit rating of individuals, the objectives should be reasonably alike as to difficulty of attainment.

THE BASES FOR ESTABLISHING QUALITY OBJECTIVES

There are various bases for setting quality objectives, for example, history, engineering study, the market, and mandates. Each of these (and others) has its merits and deficiencies.

History as a Basis.   Historical performance is widely used as a basis for quality objectives. In manufacturing areas we make use of historical data (on scrap, rework, etc.) for planning the amount of material to order, how much machinery to provide, how many workers, etc. In the field service department we make similar use of historical field failure data for planning the size of the field service force and the inventories of spare parts. In the functional departments we use historical data on error rates as an input to next year's planning. In preparing the annual budget we take notice of historical levels of performance such as cost of poor quality.

The historical basis for an objective has much appeal for the operating forces who face the problem of meeting that objective in the future. A major reason is that such an objective meets the criterion of attainability. It has already been attained; hence it is attainable. Historical bases are also a source of stability and predictability since they demand no departure from established practice. In addition they are also economic—the data base is largely in existence.

All those benefits of historical bases can easily hide a serious weakness—we may be perpetuating a poor level of performance. This has in fact taken place on a huge scale. Many companies have lost their quality leadership by perpetuating failure-prone product designs, incapable manufacturing processes, error-prone clerical processes, or high costs of poor quality. The quality leadership was taken over by companies which moved aggressively into planning to improve on historical performance.

Engineering Study as a Basis.   By engineering study we mean scientific collection and analysis of data. This approach has long been used for activities such as design of technological goods and processes. The resulting quality objectives (often called standards) are expressed in technological units of measure and take the form of limiting tolerances: maxima, minima, ranges. Products and processes based on such engineering studies have in general greatly outperformed those which are empirically based.

Despite the inherent superiority of the scientific approach, we continue to encounter severe problems when we try to meet the quality objectives established by engineering study. Some of these problems are traceable to weaknesses in our use of the scientific approach. However, the bulk of them seem to be traceable to weaknesses in our organizational and managerial structure.

These organizational and managerial weaknesses usually arise from the fact that two categories of people are often involved ("two worlds"):

Those who establish the quality objectives: systems analysts, researchers, product developers, designers, etc.

Those who are impacted by the resulting quality objectives: the end users, the intermediate users, the operating forces who have the responsibility of meeting the objectives

Where there is a strict organizational separation between these categories it is easy to end up with quality objectives which are:

Not applicable: The objectives were evolved under "laboratory" conditions, not under operating conditions.

Not attainable: For the same reason.

The "laboratory" world is characterized by distinct features:

Conditions of use are simulated, not real.

Many environmental conditions are deliberately controlled in order to keep out extraneous variables.

The personnel are trained in the associated technology.

The basic mission is to attain "structural integrity."

Major emphasis is on external customers and end use. Other customers, including "those faced with meeting the quality objectives," receive lower priority.

In contrast, the "real" world of the customers and operating forces exhibits a different set of features:

The conditions of use are "actual," including misuse.

The environment is subject to entry of extraneous variations.

The personnel are not necessarily trained in the associated technology. (In the case of consumers there is extensive ignorance of the technology.)

There are multiple users, many of whom are not end users.

The basic mission is to meet operating objectives and/or fitness for end use.

Many of our quality problems have their origin in the separation between these two worlds. To minimize these problems we must provide connecting bridges. Chief of these is the participation concept. Under that concept the operating forces and other customers are brought into the process of establishing the quality objectives.

The Market as a Basis.   Another major basis for setting quality objectives is "the market." We define the market as the composite of performances in a competitive society.

There are some persuasive reasons for using the market as one of the bases for setting quality objectives:

The market objective is *attainable under operating conditions.* The proof is that others are already attaining it.

It we are not meeting the market level of quality our clients will in due course discover this. (We may already be in trouble.)

We should have early warning of lack of competitiveness so we have time to take remedial action.

It can be a lot of work to discover what is the level of market quality. We must acquire information on competitive products, in a variety of ways. The more usual ways include:

Physical inspection and test: This may require that we buy or borrow competitors' products and conduct the necessary programs of inspection and test.

Acquisition of field performance data: We may need to put competing products into service to secure such data. Alternatively we can buy the data from ultimate users, maintenance shops, etc. We can even contract to do maintenance service for ultimate users with a view of securing the performance data as a major byproduct.

Marketing research to discover customers' perceptions: For the methods used, see Section 12, Field Intelligence, under Analysis of Available Field Intelligence: Data from Customers.

The concept of market-based quality objectives applies to all levels in the company, from the general manager to the nonsupervisors.

OBJECTIVES FOR BREAKTHROUGH OR CONTROL

A major decision in setting objectives is whether to go for a breakthrough (an improvement to unprecedented levels of performance) or to hold the status quo. In popular terminology, control aims to do things right whereas improvement aims to do the right things.

Objectives for Breakthrough. There are many reasons why managers create objectives for breakthrough. Among the more usual are:

1. The managers wish to attain or hold quality leadership. (Even to hold quality leadership requires continuing breakthrough because competitors are ever closing the gap.) They may launch innovative product designs, offer superior service, provide more complete technical assistance, etc.

2. They have identified some opportunities to improve income through superior fitness for use. For example, one company improved the reliability of its products and found from field studies that the users' costs of maintenance, and especially of downtime, were sharply reduced thereby. In consequence, the company was able to increase its prices without losing customers.

3. They are losing share of market through lack of competitiveness. For example, a company making abrasive cloth found that although its products met specification, the users' "cost per hundred pieces polished" was greater than when using competitive cloth.

4. They have too many field troubles—failures, complaints, returns—and wish to reduce these as well as cutting the external costs resulting from guarantee charges, investigation expense, product discounts, etc. Solution may require new test programs, product redesign, training manuals for users, etc.

5. They have identified some projects which offer internal cost-reduction opportunities, e.g., improvement of process yields or reduction of scrap, rework inspection, or testing.

6. They have a poor image with customers, suppliers, the public, or other groups of outsiders.

7. There is internal dissension and a need to improve motivation and morale.

Objectives for breakthrough are not limited to "hardware," or to things which can be counted, e.g., income, cost. Objectives for breakthrough can include projects such as a reliability training program for designers, a supplier rating plan, a complaint investigation manual, a reorganization for the quality control staff, or a new executive report on quality.

Objectives for Control. Managers have many reasons for avoiding breakthrough. In such cases the objectives are to hold the status quo, i.e., maintain control at present levels. The more usual reasons for choosing control in specific situations are:

1. The managers believe that improvement is uneconomic; i.e., the cost of trying for breakthrough would not be recovered.
2. Present performance is competitive. Many managers regard "the market" as a sound standard since it embodies the breakthrough efforts of competitors.
3. There are few alarm signals—e.g., few complaints or internal flareups—to suggest the need for breakthrough.
4. There is need for breakthrough, but it is not timely to undertake breakthrough because (*a*) there has been no agreement on the specific projects to be tackled or (*b*) the climate for quality breakthrough is unfavorable (e.g., too many other programs going; some key manager is not convinced; the breakthrough would require risky technological research).

The more usual objectives for control include holding the materials, processes, and products to specification; holding the field failures, complaints, returns, and other external performance measures to current levels; holding costs of inspection, test, scrap, rework, and other internal costs to current levels; and holding the gains achieved by recent breakthrough projects.

ZERO DEFECTS AS AN OBJECTIVE

This topic is awash in confusion arising from the two major meanings of the term "zero defects":

1. Defect-free product, which is the literal meaning
2. A slogan to be used during "drives" to improve quality

Defect-Free Product. This concept has value as a long-range objective, since it implies the need for never-ending improvement. The concept rejects the idea that we can relax our efforts short of perfection.

In contrast, if we decree defect-free product as a short-range objective, such a goal is in the great majority of cases not attainable. In such cases the risk is that the decree will be counterproductive by shutting off efforts to reach attainable goals.

Zero Defects as a Slogan. In this meaning the term is adopted as a kind of banner to fly during a company "drive" to improve quality. In its best usage this is comparable to adopting an appealing brand name to help sell a product. In such cases much depends on the substance behind the drive. If the drive is well conceived (i.e., a "good" product), then a good brand name is an aid to selling it to the internal customers. If the drive is ill-conceived (e.g., an attempt to solve the company's quality problems by exhorting the work force), then it will fail no matter how clever is the slogan.

ESTABLISHING QUALITY OBJECTIVES

Objectives for control are usually self-evident from the mandates, specification, procedures, etc., issued by the various sources. Objectives for improvement are not so self-evident. Even where the need is evident, it takes some effort to translate that need into an official, legitimate quality objective.

Until the 1980s objectives for control were dominant. Under the prevailing priorities, neither quality nor quality improvement had top priority. The urge for quality improvement usually came from two main sources:

1. Specific quality crises, either external or internal
2. Specific projects urged by conscientious middle managers, often quality managers

The 1980s ushered in a climate much more favorable to establishment of objectives for quality improvement. This same climate stimulated ways to identify what were the needed improvements and to list them as official quality objectives. The methods for identifying potential quality improvement projects are quite similar to those used in broad undertakings to improve quality. (See Section 22, Quality Improvement, under The Project Concept: Nominations for Projects. That same section also discusses approaches used for establishing priorities for improvement projects, and for quantifying proposals for improvement into the language of money—the major language of upper managers.)

Experience has shown that upper managers' approval of proposals for quality objectives is strongly influenced by three vital criteria:

1. Objectives for improvement are preferred over objectives for control.
2. Objectives which have a clear orientation to business or managerial matters (e.g., sales, growth, manager development) are preferred over objectives which are oriented to technology or technique.
3. Objectives which are quantified in money are preferred over objectives which are not.

STRATEGIC QUALITY OBJECTIVES

As companies acquire experience in companywide quality management (See Section 6, under Companywide Quality Management), there arises the concept of enlarging the strategic business plan to include *strategic quality planning.* Under that concept, broad quality objectives are established at corporate and division levels. These broad objectives are then "deployed" to lower levels of management. The middle managers then have the responsibility to do the quality planning—to identify what actions need to be taken to meet the objectives and what resources will be required. The approach is entirely analogous to the approach long used for carrying out other types of strategic objectives.

The methodology behind strategic quality planning is described in Section 6. However it is well to note here that before a company embarks on strategic quality planning, *all* levels of management should have acquired substantial training and experience in managing for quality. This training and experience should extend to all the processes of the quality trilogy: quality planning, quality control, and quality improvement.

REFERENCES

Juran, J. M. (1969). "Mobilizing for the 1970s." *Quality Progress,* August, pp. 8–17.

Juran, J. M. (1970). "Consumerism and Product Quality." *Quality Progress,* July, pp. 18–27.

SECTION 6

COMPANYWIDE PLANNING FOR QUALITY[1]

J. M. Juran

DIVISION OF THE SUBJECT . . . **6.2**

THE QUALITY PLANNING CONCEPT **6.3**

THE QUALITY PLANNING ROAD MAP **6.3**

Identification of Customers   6.4

Discovery of Customer Needs 6.6

Translation into Suppliers' Language 6.10

Product Development . . . 6.11

Optimizing Product Design   6.12

Process Development . . . 6.15

Transfer to Operations . . 6.17

APPLICATION OF THE QUALITY PLANNING ROAD MAP **6.18**

Application to Supervisory and Worker Levels . . . 6.19

Application to Functional Levels 6.21

Application to Multifunctional Systems   6.21

Application to Major Programs 6.23

COMPANYWIDE QUALITY MANAGEMENT (CWQM) **6.23**

Purposes of CWQM 6.24

Disadvantages of CWQM . 6.24

Establishing Strategic Quality Goals 6.24

Deployment of Corporate Quality Goals 6.25

Providing Resources . . . 6.25

Organization for CWQM . 6.26

Assurance of Performance against Objectives 6.26

APPLICATION TO SMALL COMPANIES **6.26**

How Small Is Small? . . . 6.26

Inherent Features 6.26

Separation of Planning from Execution 6.27

Extent of Formality in Quality Planning 6.27

Advantages and Limitations of Informality 6.27

LESSONS LEARNED **6.28**

Application to Multifunctional Processes   6.28

The Log of Problems . . . 6.28

The Consequences of Time   6.28

---

[1] In the Third Edition, the section on quality planning was prepared by Richard J. Pierce.

The Forms of Improvement 6.29

Organization for Historical
  Review 6.29

Application to Functional
  Processes 6.29

PLANNING FOR CONTROL . . . **6.31**

QUALITY CONTROL **6.31**

On-line and Off-line
  Quality Control 6.32

Self-Control 6.32

THE FEEDBACK LOOP **6.32**

The Control Subject 6.33

Control Stations 6.34

Unit of Measure 6.35

The Sensor 6.35

Data Collection and
  Processing 6.36

Analysis for Decision
  Making 6.36

Control Reports 6.38

Corrective Action 6.38

Application to Upper-
  Management Control . . 6.38

**PLANNING FOR QUALITY
IMPROVEMENT** **6.40**

THE QUALITY MANUAL **6.40**

Terminology 6.40

Evolution of the Manual . . 6.40

Contents of the Manual . . 6.41

Distribution of the Manual 6.43

Provision for Audit 6.44

Limitations of Quality
  Manuals as Predictors of
  Good Quality 6.44

**GENERIC STANDARDS;
INFLUENCE ON QUALITY
PLANNING** **6.45**

Mandated and Advisory
  Generic Standards . . . 6.45

Purposes of Generic
  Standards 6.45

Evolution of Generic
  Quality Standards 6.45

Adaptation to Diversity . . 6.46

Certification; Accreditation 6.46

WHO PLANS FOR QUALITY? . . **6.47**

Influence of the Scope of
  the Planning 6.47

Allocation of
  Responsibilities 6.48

Future Trends 6.48

**TOOLS FOR QUALITY
PLANNERS** **6.48**

Training in Use of the
  Tools 6.49

**TRAINING FOR QUALITY
PLANNERS** **6.49**

Common Subject Matter . 6.49

Specialized Subject Matter 6.49

Training for Suppliers . . . 6.50

Training for Clients 6.50

The Quality School 6.50

REFERENCES **6.50**

DIVISION OF THE SUBJECT

The subject of quality planning can be divided in a variety of ways, such as by subsystems, functions, hierarchical levels, and tools used. Any extensive treatment of the subject inevitably requires discussion of every one of those ways, but not necessarily in the same sequence. The choice of sequence involves making some judgmental decisions.

A popular method has been to divide the subject on the basis of subsystems (e.g., product development, supplier relations, measurement, human relations). This method has been followed by Caplan (1980, 1984), Cound (1965), Kolacek (1978), Lewis (1964), and Wilhelm (1980). Other methods have been followed by Kofoed (1982), Olsbro (1970), Scanlon and Hagan (1982), and Taguchi (1978).

In this section the first division of the subject has been based on the universal sequence of steps taken during planning for quality. Thereafter the remaining topics are treated, the sequence being generally that which is encountered by planners as their work impacts operations.

THE QUALITY PLANNING CONCEPT

Quality planning is one of the three basic processes used in managing for quality. (See Section 2, under The Quality Trilogy, for a discussion of the three processes.) In its broadest sense quality planning is the process of establishing quality objectives and developing the means (plans) for meeting those objectives.

The terminology associated with quality planning is not well standardized. Objectives are all aimed-at targets, but they may be called "goals," "requirements," "missions," "visions," and so on. Plans may be called "systems," "procedures," "processes," "programs," and so forth. In specific applications the terminology may also become specific. For example, in manufacture of goods, the objective may be called the "specification" or "tolerance." The plan may be called a "production process."

Section 5, under Quality Objectives and the headings that follow, sets out certain fundamentals relative to quality objectives. It is shown there that quality objectives exhibit wide variation in nature and scope. They may be intended for breakthrough or for control. They can be departmental, companywide, or intercompany in scope. They can deal with matters of great importance or with numerous matters of limited importance. The resulting permutations of kind and scope of quality objectives call for a corresponding assortment of quality plans. Table 6.1 lists the more usual quality objectives and the types of quality plan which have been evolved in response to the various objectives.

THE QUALITY PLANNING ROAD MAP

Within any organization the quality plans are closely interrelated. At the top of the organization, the broad quality objectives require broad-based plans. Such broad-based plans then require establishment of subobjectives, each of which requires a subplan. In large organizations this subdivision can involve many layers of objectives and plans.

Irrespective of level in the hierarchy, quality planning involves meeting the quality needs of customers. To meet these quality needs, a universal series of actions must be taken. This series is shown graphically in Figure 6.1 as the quality planning road map. It consists of a structured, coherent sequence of steps. Each step is an activity whose output becomes an input to the next step in the sequence. The quality planning road map is described in detail in the training manual *Planning for Quality* (Juran, 1986), published in hardback under the title Juran on Planning for Quality (Juran, 1988), and in the videocassette series *Juran on Quality Planning* (Juran Institute, 1988).

TABLE 6.1 Types of Quality Plan

Objectives	Associated forms of quality planning	Discussed under
Establish self-control	Triple-role concept; feedback loop	Self-control; The Triple-Role concept; The Feedback Loop
Maintain quality for repetitive activities	Quality manual; feedback loop	The Quality Manual; The Feedback Loop
Launch numerous small changes	Multiuse procedures; quality manual	The Quality Manual
Launch major changes, programs	Central quality planning; program management; quality planning road map	Application to Multifunctional Systems; Application to Major Programs; The Quality Planning Road Map
Review execution versus plans	Quality reports; quality audits	Control Reports; Quality Assurance (see Section 9)
Eliminate existing chronic quality problems	Project-by-project improvement	Quality Improvement (see Section 22)
Avoid creation of new chronic quality programs	Quality planning road map	The Quality Planning Road Map
Attain quality for new major products, programs	Central quality planning; program management; quality planning road map	Application to Multifunctional Systems; Application to Major Programs; The Quality Planning Road Map
Establish and meet broad corporate quality goals	CWQM; strategic quality planning as part of business plan	Companywide Quality Management (CWQM)

Identification of Customers. The first step is to identify the "customers." The word "customer" is used here in the sense of anyone who is impacted by the product or process. Customers can be "external" or "internal" (see Section 2, under Customer).

A fundamental planning tool for identifying customers is the flow diagram (Figure 6.2). The flow diagram is a graphic means for depicting the steps or activities which constitute a process. The flow diagram is constructed from standardized symbols (Figure 6.3).

In many cases the customers are numerous. In addition, what appears to be one customer may actually be an entire cast of characters. For example, a hospital supply company has customers in the form of hospitals. However, the supplies sold to the hospital impact a large number of persons in a large number of departments: purchasing managers; pharmacists; heads of test laboratories; physicians; nurses; and of course, patients.

Where customers are numerous, it is useful to apply the Pareto principle and to classify the customers between the two categories of the vital few and the useful many. Such classification helps to assure that the allocation of planning resources is concentrated in the areas of major importance.

Some classes of useful many customers are so numerous that the class is treated as one of the vital few. Examples are consumers and the internal work force.

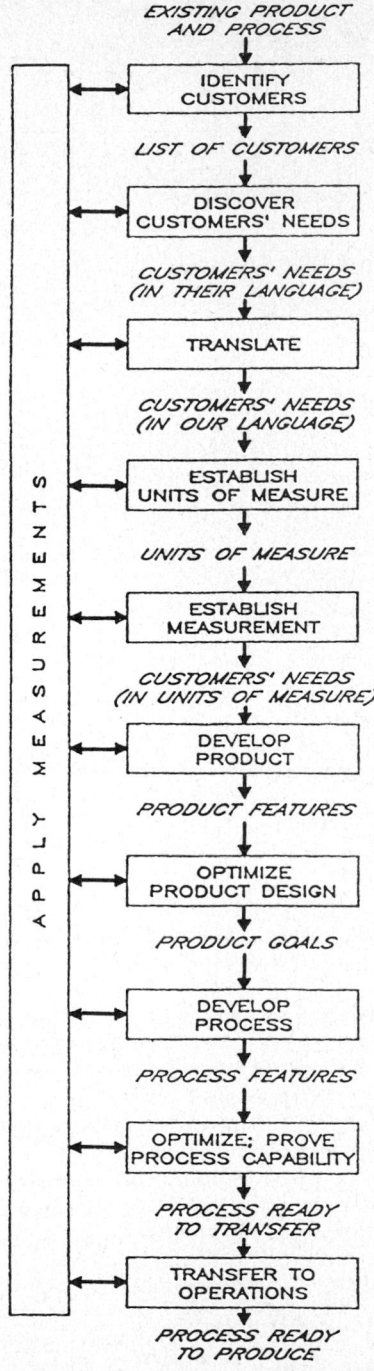

FIG. 6.1 The quality planning road map.

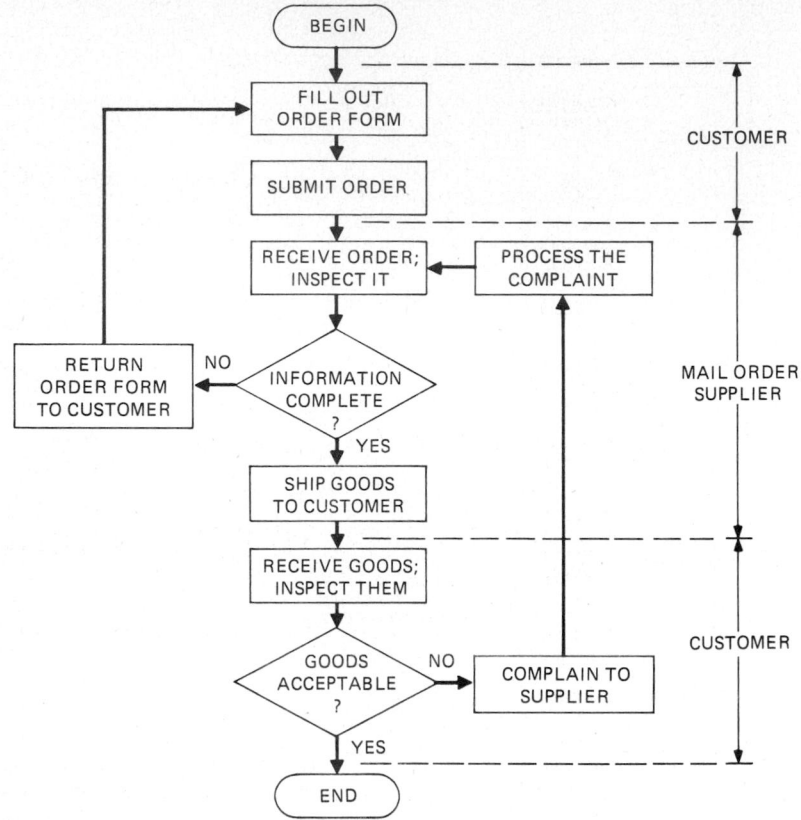

FIG. 6.2 The flow diagram.

Discovery of Customer Needs.

Customers state their needs from their own viewpoints and (often) in their own language. However, much may lie below the surface.

Real needs may differ from stated needs. Stated needs for goods are often a popular way of expressing needs for services. For instance, the stated need may be a color television set, whereas the real need may be entertainment.

Customers' perceptions of needs often differ from those of suppliers. Industrial buyers may mandate that suppliers provide extensive documentation or keep statistical control charts which the suppliers feel are merely adding cost without adding value. Consumers may pay a premium price for identical products in order to shop amid handsome decor and attentive service. Customers' use (and misuse) of products can differ from suppliers' intended use.

Customers (especially internal customers) may resist introduction of some new product or process because it carries some unwelcome social consequence or threat.

Proliferation of Customer Needs.

Customer needs tend to proliferate into very large numbers. A basic need such as transportation breaks down into primary needs such as safety, economy, dependability, and comfort. The primary need of

BASIC SYMBOLS

Most flow diagrams are built up out of a few basic symbols:

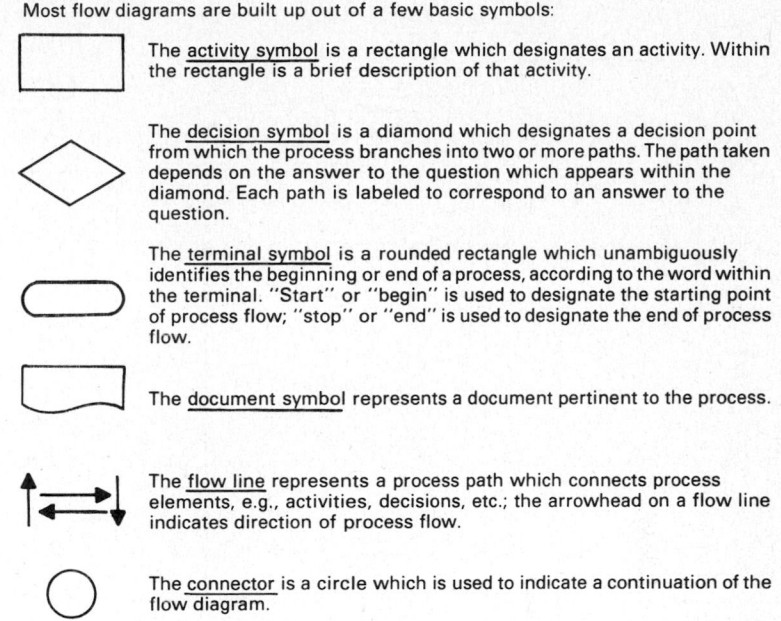

The <u>activity symbol</u> is a rectangle which designates an activity. Within the rectangle is a brief description of that activity.

The <u>decision symbol</u> is a diamond which designates a decision point from which the process branches into two or more paths. The path taken depends on the answer to the question which appears within the diamond. Each path is labeled to correspond to an answer to the question.

The <u>terminal symbol</u> is a rounded rectangle which unambiguously identifies the beginning or end of a process, according to the word within the terminal. "Start" or "begin" is used to designate the starting point of process flow; "stop" or "end" is used to designate the end of process flow.

The <u>document symbol</u> represents a document pertinent to the process.

The <u>flow line</u> represents a process path which connects process elements, e.g., activities, decisions, etc.; the arrowhead on a flow line indicates direction of process flow.

The <u>connector</u> is a circle which is used to indicate a continuation of the flow diagram.

FIG. 6.3 Standard symbols for flow diagrams.

economy (for a consumer-owned vehicle) then breaks down into secondary needs such as low purchase price, low financing cost, low operating and maintenance cost, high resale value, and high trade-in value. In turn, low operating and maintenance cost breaks down into tertiary needs such as warranty coverage, fuel efficiency, dependability, and adequacy of service. This proliferation continues on down the hierarchy of products to the properties of bits and pieces of goods, and to the basic tasks inherent in services.

To deal with this proliferation, in an organized, orderly way, quality planners make use of quality planning spreadsheets (Figures 6.4, 6.5, and 6.6). These spreadsheets are discussed below. See also Section 13 under Planning for Basic Functional Requirements.

Spreadsheets do not provide the planners with answers. However, spreadsheets do serve to organize the planning information in ways which permit easy reference and self-checking. Such organization is an obvious aid to the planners and to the other participants in the planning process.

Methods for Discovering Customer Needs. The major methods consist of:

Being a customer

Communicating with customers

Simulating customers' needs

Planners who acquire experience in use of products thereby learn much about the needs of external customers for those products. Similarly, planners who undergo training in various phases of product progression learn much about the

CUSTOMER'S NEED	SENSOR	PRODUCT FEATURE A	PRODUCT FEATURE B	...	COMPONENT PACKAGING	SOLDERED JOINTS	...
MECHANICALLY STRONG CONNECTIONS	VIBRATION TEST					**	
ELECTRICAL CONTINUITY	CONTINUITY TEST					**	
EASY COMPONENT INSERTION	INSERTION PROCESS				**		

Column group heading: PRODUCT FEATURE (spanning PRODUCT FEATURE A, PRODUCT FEATURE B, ..., COMPONENT PACKAGING, SOLDERED JOINTS, ...)

KEY: **STRONG RELATIONSHIP

FIG. 6.4 Quality planning spreadsheet: customer needs and product features. (The product is an electronic circuit board.)

PRODUCT FEATURE	GOAL	PROCESS FEATURE 1	PROCESS FEATURE 2	...	WAVE SOLDER	AUTOMATED INSERTION	...
PRODUCT FEATURE A							
PRODUCT FEATURE B							
COMPONENT PACKAGING	100% AUTOMATED INSERTION					**	
SOLDERED JOINTS	100% ELECTRICAL CONTINUITY				**		

Column group heading: PROCESS FEATURE (spanning PROCESS FEATURE 1, PROCESS FEATURE 2, ..., WAVE SOLDER, AUTOMATED INSERTION, ...)

KEY: ** STRONG RELATIONSHIP

FIG. 6.5 Quality planning spreadsheet: product features and process features. (The product is an electronic circuit board.)

PROCESS CONTROLS

PROCESS FEATURE	CONTROL SUBJECT	SENSOR	GOAL	MEASURE-MENT FREQUENCY	SAMPLE SIZE	CRITERION	RESPONS-IBILITY
PROCESS FEATURE 1							
PROCESS FEATURE 2							
. . .							
WAVE SOLDER	SOLDER TEMPER-ATURE	THERMO-COUPLE	505°F	CONTIN-UOUS	N/A	≥510°F, DECREASE HEAT; 500°F, INCREASE HEAT	OPERATOR
	CONVEYOR SPEED	FT/MIN METER	4.5 FT/MIN	1/HOUR	N/A	>5 FT/MIN, REDUCE SPEED; ≤4 FT/MIN, INCREASE SPEED	OPERATOR
	ALLOY PURITY	LAB. CHEM. ANALYSIS	1.5% MAX TOTAL CONTAMIN-ANTS	1/MONTH	15 GRAMS	≥1.5%, DRAIN BATH, REPLACE SOLDER	PROCESS ENGINEER

FIG. 6.6 Quality planning spreadsheet: process features and process control features. (The product is an electronic circuit board.)

6.9

needs of internal customers as well as those of external customers. Some companies establish training courses in order to expose planners to customer needs. During this training the planners *make* the product in factory departments; they *sell* the product in merchant shops; they *service* the product in repair shops.

Communication with customers is the most widely used method of discovering customer needs. Some of this communication is initiated by customers through complaints, claims, returns, and other manifestations of dissatisfaction. Other communication is at the initiative of suppliers and usually relates to product satisfaction and salability of the product. Such supplier-initiated communication makes extensive use of the tools of marketing research. (See generally, Section 12, under Summary of Marketing Research Tools and Techniques.)

A third method for discovering customer needs is simulation. Customer needs can, in part, be simulated in the laboratory. In the laboratory it is possible to exclude unwanted variables, to measure with precision, and otherwise to secure pertinent technological information. However, simulation does not fully reproduce operating conditions and hence cannot by itself provide complete answers relative to customer needs.

Translation into Suppliers' Language.   Customers' needs may be stated in any of several languages: customers' language, suppliers' language, and a common language. If the needs are stated in customers' language, it becomes necessary to translate those needs into suppliers' language.

The translation process is handicapped because of vague terminology and multiple dialects, even within the same company. These differences become magnified when the relationships involve multiple companies, industries, and countries.

Tools for Translation.   A number of tools have been evolved to aid in translation and communication of customer needs.

The "glossary" is a sort of dictionary—a list of key terms along with agreed definitions for each.

"Samples" take such forms as textile swatches, colored chips, and audiocassettes. They are often used as specifications for sensory product features (e.g., feel, color, sound).

"Standardization" is a tool widely used to improve communication at various levels: intracompany, intraindustry, interindustry, and international. Official standards organizations are available to coordinate the efforts. The pace is painfully slow, but without standardization the modern industrial societies would be seriously handicapped.

"Measurement systems" are the means of "saying it in numbers"—the most effective means known for precise communication. These systems require agreement on (1) units of measure and (2) means (sensors) to carry out the measurement.

"Special organization" to translate is used when other tools are unavailable or inadequate. An example of such an organization is "order editing." It receives purchase orders from clients and then produces a translated version for use within the supplier company.

Translation for Managerial Products.   A critical problem in translation is "products" of a managerial nature. These include policies, objectives, reviews, incentives, and audits. The customers are mainly internal, across all functions and all levels. The problem is to assure that these internal customers interpret these products in ways intended by the internal suppliers. In turn, there is the problem of assuring that the responses are made in ways which minimize misunderstanding.

Tools for translation of managerial products consist mainly of the glossary, standardization, and measurement systems. Often these are assembled and published in the quality manual (see below, under Quality Manual).

Product Development. This step on the quality planning road map determines the product features required to meet customer needs. In competitive situations, product development is subject to constraints—the product features should comply with the following criteria:

Meet the needs of the customers

Meet the needs of the suppliers

Be competitive

Optimize the combined costs of the customers and suppliers

Quality planning is a part of the product development activity. The quality planning may be done by product designers, quality specialists, operating personnel, or some combination of personnel in all these categories. Irrespective of who does the quality planning, the preceding criteria should all be met.

The activity of product development faces squarely the proliferation of needs as the development proceeds down the product hierarchy. The numerous customer needs demand numerous responses in the form of numerous product features. To deal with all those numbers, it is necessary to employ a structured, systematic approach in which the spreadsheet (Figure 6.4) plays a central role.

In Figure 6.4, the first of three key spreadsheets used in planning for quality, each horizontal row relates to a particular customer need. The vertical columns are used to accumulate information pertinent to the product features which will provide the means of meeting those customer needs. The remaining two key spreadsheets are Figures 6.5 and 6.6.

The Role of Measurement. Measurement plays an extensive role throughout the entire quality planning process; thus Figure 6.1 shows measurement as applying to all steps of the quality planning road map.

The most obvious use of measurement is seen during product development for physical goods, since this so often demands journeys into technology. However, measurement and other, less precise forms of evaluation all play important roles in product development for nontechnological features as well. Objectives of all sorts are quantified, and this requires that the associated planning also make use of measurement and evaluation.

Tools for Product Developers. Numerous tools have been evolved to assist quality planning during product development. These tools are described in the following paragraphs.

The Spreadsheet.   The spreadsheet can assemble a great deal of information into condensed, convenient form (see Figure 6.4).

The Phase System.   Under this concept (also called the "stage system"), the product development cycle is divided into phases. Each phase is defined in terms of the activities to be carried out and the results to be achieved. The definitions include criteria to be satisfied for completion of the phase.

Criticality Analysis.   This analysis is used to identify the "vital few" product features so that they will receive priority of attention and resources. Product features may be classified as critical for reasons such as: essential to human safety, legislated mandates, essential to salability, demanding as to investment, demanding as to continuity of performance (reliability, failure rate, uptime, maintainability, etc.), and long lead time.

Some of these reasons for criticality (e.g., continuity of performance) can be so demanding that they require as much product development effort as the conventional technological product features. The extent of criticality analysis may require construction of a separate spreadsheet as an aid.

Competitive Analysis. This analysis compares product features with those offered by competitors. The obvious reason is that customers make such comparisons. An example on a major scale was that undertaken by Ford Motor Company during the quality planning for the Taurus/Sable line of motor vehicles. The analysis involved 400 key product features, and the objective was to be "best in class" throughout (Veraldi, 1985).

Salability Analysis. This analysis attempts to establish relationships between product quality and product salability. Customer *behavior* can be studied to determine which products customers buy, which they do not buy, and why. Demand for nonstandard product features—options, or "specials"—can also be studied. The analysis can be extended to the process of bidding for business, i.e., why bids are successful or unsuccessful. (See Section 3, under Industrial Products and Share of Market.)

Customer *perceptions and opinions* can also be analyzed, using the methods of marketing research. See Section 12, under Summary of Marketing Research Tools and Techniques, for discussion of the methods used.

Yet another approach is to study competitive product differences and their impact on share of market. See Section 3, under Quality and Share of Market, for an extended discussion, with examples.

Value Analysis. This tool is an aid to identifying the functions to be performed by the product and to providing those functions at minimum cost. See Section 13, under Planning to Minimize Cost; Value Engineering.

Systematic Obstacles. These abound in the product development area. A widespread example is failure-prone features which are carried over from prior models to new models. In such cases the vulnerability for failure is usually well known and even notorious. However, the "solution" has been to make customer service available in the event of failure. Such a solution perpetuates the problem by disconnecting the alarm signals. Of course, customers do not regard the problem as solved. The real solution is to bring these failure-prone features to the surface and place them on the product development agenda along with the new features required to meet customer needs.

A second widespread systematic obstacle is inadequacy of early warning to product designers, resulting in future problems for customers, especially internal customers. The remedy is through systems of participation and design review (see below, under Optimizing Product Design).

Optimizing Product Design. This step on the quality planning road map is intended to "optimize" the product design. The optimum is defined as the result which meets the needs of customer and supplier alike and minimizes their combined costs. The resulting product features become the objectives or goals to be met.

Between customers and external suppliers, the ideal approach for optimization is joint quality planning. Lacking this, the need is for open communication and mutual trust. Failing these the result is pursuit of local goals. This pursuit of local goals is known as suboptimizing. The result of suboptimization is usually a detriment to one of the parties, or more usually, to both parties.

Suboptimization also takes place within companies, that is, between internal customers and internal suppliers. The major causes of internal suboptimization are (1) monopolies on issuance of documents and (2) merit rating systems which encourage strict adherence to local goals.

Monopolies on Issuance of Documents. For certain critical documents (e.g., product specifications, purchase orders, sales contracts), it is necessary to provide all concerned with the means of knowing whether such documents have official status. To this end there is widespread use of internal monopolies. Under the monopoly concept the documents are valid only if they have been signed by certain designated persons in designated departments.

These internal monopolies are very useful for establishing clear responsibility as to whose signature renders a document legitimate. In addition, the monopolies help to minimize any confusion as to whether a specific document is official. However, in many cases these monopolies spread into other areas, notably:

A monopoly on the choice of the inputs and criteria which then become the basis for decision making

A monopoly on decision making, i.e., to have the last word in the event of a difference of opinion

For instance, virtually all companies give their product design departments a clear monopoly on approval of product designs. No product design has official status until it is approved by that department. However, in many of these same companies the product design department has over the years acquired a monopoly on choice of inputs and criteria, and on decision making. The latter two monopolies have been a source of much discord and damage. They have often resulted in designs of products which are uneconomic to produce, difficult to test, unreliable in service, difficult to maintain, and so on. In effect, one activity (product development) has used its monopoly to unilaterally create problems for other activities. They key to avoidance of such damage and discord is *participation* in such forms as design review.

Emphasis on Departmental Goals. A further source of internal suboptimization is the merit rating system. Many companies establish departmental goals and then use the merit rating system to stimulate department managers to meet the goals. These systems generally do stimulate attainment of goals. However, they also invite the risk that high attainment in one department will unilaterally reduce attainment in other departments. A major tool for reducing this risk is again participation among departments.

Participation. The participation concept is inherently a team approach. The team membership includes customers and suppliers, whether between companies or within companies. The team members use their experience and expertise to make contributions such as those described in the following paragraphs.

Early Warning of Upcoming Problems. "If you plan it this way, here is the problem I will face."

Data to Aid in Finding the Optimum. The various customers are frequently in a position to provide data in the form of costs which will be incurred, process capability of facilities, and so on. Such data are of obvious value for optimizing overall performance.

Challenge to Theories. Specialist departments are typically masters of their own specialty but seldom masters of the specialties of other departments. In the absence of participation by those other departments the risk is that unproven theories or unwarranted beliefs will prevail. Participation by the customers provides an informed challenge.

Resolving Differences.   Securing participation requires a detailed understanding of the forces which favor suboptimization. In the case of external customers these forces are mainly of a technological and economic nature. In the case of internal customers, some additional forces of a behavioral nature are present.

Essential Inputs.   Discovery of the optimum requires certain inputs which are not needed by the forces of suboptimization. Examples in the area of product design include competitive analysis, salability analysis, value analysis, and life cycle costing.

Technological Analysis.   Many problems in product design involve the convergence of numerous variables. Discovery of the optimum combination of these variables can require sophisticated design of experiments and equally sophisticated analysis of the resulting data. The major forms of such designs are discussed in Section 26, Design and Analysis of Experiments.

Behavioral Obstacles.   These obstacles prevail widely within companies. Often they arise from a departmental claim of exclusive jurisdiction over some area of broad subject matter. The claim may be stated in such forms as: "We are responsible for quality" (or for cost, schedule, etc). Actually, any broad subject matter has broad impacts, so that numerous departments are "responsible." The real purpose of the claim is often to guard a status (real or imagined) which is derived from exclusive jurisdiction over an essential area of subject matter.

To deal with claims of exclusive jurisdiction, it is necessary to identify the specific decisions and actions which are at issue. Managers can usually agree as to who should be responsible for making specific decisions or taking specific actions. Managers can seldom agree as to who should have responsibility for broad abstractions. For an example of such an analysis as applied to who is responsible for quality on the factory floor, see Section 17, under Quality Responsibilities on the Factory Floor.

Authority of Expertise.   With respect to some critical matters, it is necessary to rely on the judgment of acknowledged experts, or even to give the experts a monopoly on making such judgments (e.g., a license to practice). For example, regarding matters of potential safety hazards, reliance is placed on the design engineer to determine the safety factor needed for structural integrity. Regarding structural integrity, the engineer is given the benefit of the doubt and the last word.

In applying this principle of authority of expertise, it is necessary to distinguish carefully between the areas of expertise and the broad planning of which they are a part. Companies do look to the product designer to provide the expertise needed to attain structural integrity. They do not give the product designer the last word on whether to go to market with the product—that is a business decision.

Methodologies.   Practicing managers and behavioral scientists have given much thought to ways to resolve differences. One of these ways was described in a classic paper (Coonley and Agnew, 1941). Relative to the problem at hand (a national standard for cast-iron pipe), the method was as follows:

1. They must identify their areas of agreement and their areas of disagreement: "That is, they must first agree upon the exact point at which the road began to fork." When this was done, it was found that a major point of disagreement concerned the validity of a certain formula.

2. "They must agree on why they disagreed. . . . " They concluded that the known facts were inadequate to decide whether the formula was valid.

3. "They must decide what they were going to do about it." The decision was to raise a fund to conduct the research needed to establish the necessary facts. "With the facts at hand, the controversies disappeared."

A second method for resolving differences is proposed by Follett (1941). This is the method of "constructive conflict." Under this concept, the parties, working together, use their ingenuity to devise unprecedented ways to arrive at an optimum. This approach contrasts with "dominance" and "compromise"—methods which arrive at decisions but leave some parties dissatisfied.

Section 22, under Resistance to Change, describes another method for resolving differences.

Process Development.   Once the product goals have been established the next planning step is process development or process planning. (The terminology is not well standardized.) In this handbook, process planning is the activity of providing the operating forces with the means of producing products which can meet customers' needs. The end result of process planning includes:

1. The process design, which defines the specific means to be used. This definition covers (*a*) the necessary physical facilities; (*b*) the associated software (the brain and the nervous system of the equipment; and (*c*) information on how to operate, control, and maintain the facilities.

2. Provision of the facilities.

Review of Product Goals.   Ideally, the product goals should have been established with the participation of the process planners and the operating forces. Where this prior participation has been deficient, it is useful for the process planners to review the product goals with the product planners. The purpose of the review is to identify such obstacles to process planning as unrealistic goals or incomplete product information. The earlier these obstacles are identified, the wider is the range of potential solutions.

Operating Realities.   A critical consideration in process planning is what the operating realities will be. These realities include:

The training and skills of those who will use the process.

The environments of use—these can differ radically from the "laboratory" environment in which process development takes place.

The manner of actual use (and misuse)—this can differ from intended use.

Process planners learn about these operating realities from various sources: prior experience in operations, study of operating conditions, and participative meetings with operating personnel. The more complete the planners' knowledge, the less the risk that the resulting process plan will be unrealistic under operating conditions.

Carryover of Prior Process Designs.   A good deal of process design consists of carryover of prior designs. Such carryover may unwittingly include unwelcome, uninvited guests—chronic quality problems which have never been solved. Process designers should inform themselves as to the prior performance of the potential carryover. Once informed, they are faced with alternatives: reject, revise, or adopt as is.

Optimizing Process Designs.   As in the case of product design, there is need to optimize the process design. The methods are quite similar to those described above for product design—joint planning, participation, and so on.

Tools for Process Planners.   These tools are numerous. Those which are strongly quality-oriented include the concept of dominance, the concept of anatomy of the process, process capability quantification, and the spreadsheet.

Concept of Dominance.   Operating processes harbor numerous variables, but these follow the Pareto principle of the vital few and useful many. Often one variable is more important than all the rest collectively—it is the dominant variable. If quality planners are able to identify which is the dominant variable, they can, with confidence, assign top priority to acquiring mastery over that variable.

In the case of manufacturing processes, the more usual forms of dominance include setup-dominant, time-dominant, component-dominant, worker-dominant, and information-dominant. (See Section 17, under Process Control Tools, for extended discussion.)

Concept of Anatomy of the Process.   Processes assume various forms: autonomous, assembly tree, procession, and still others. The *autonomous* department, such as in manufacturing, receives basic materials and fabricates them into finished products, all within a self-contained department. In the *assembly tree* form, numerous suppliers or in-house departments make parts or components, and these then converge to be assembled in other departments. In the *procession* form, products progress sequentially through numerous in-house departments (with occasional supplier departments), each performing some operation which contributes to the final result. See Juran (1988) for further discussion of the anatomy of the process. See also Section 16 under Responsibility for Manufacturing Planning.

Choice of anatomy of the process can strongly influence the level of attained quality. For example, an assembly line (a procession) is converted to an autonomous process in which one worker assembles a unit of product complete from bits and pieces. The effect on quality is almost always to improve it. A major reason is that workers now have a much clearer understanding of the quality needs of the various steps in the assembly process; thus, over and over again, workers are their own customers.

Process Capability Quantification.   This is one of the most useful of all process planning tools. For a detailed discussion, see Section 16 under Process Capability: The Concept.

The potential benefits of process capability quantification are impressive. They include:

An ability to evaluate process capability in numbers and in standardized form (usually six standard deviations of the frequency distribution)

An aid to early warning during design review

A means of specifying what is an acceptable process capability (usually in the form of a ratio of six standard deviations to the product tolerance)

An aid to comparing the capability of alternative processes

The Spreadsheet.   This tool helps planners to organize their work in a systematic manner. Applied to process planning, the spreadsheet (Figure 6.5) shows the product features in the horizontal rows. It then accumulates in the vertical columns the process features needed to produce the product features and meet the product goals.

Process Control.   Quality planning includes the activity of establishing process control—the means of maintaining the process in its planned state. All control is based on the feedback loop. The general approach to control is described later in this section under the heading Planning for Control. What follows now relates to the application of the control principle to planning for process control.

Who Plans for Process Control?   Generally the responsibility is related to criticality of the process. For processes which present potential· serious dangers to human safety or to the environment, it is common to assign the responsibility to the process planners. For other processes, it is usual to assign the responsibility to the operating managers.

Critical Processes.   Processes are "critical" if they involve serious risks to human safety, to the environment, to large sums of money, and so on. To reduce these risks, special features are built into the process control system, features such as:

Criteria for selection, training and qualification of control personnel

Redundancy in the various elements of the feedback loop

Independent audits to assure compliance with specified procedures

Followup of critical incidents to determine and eliminate root causes

These and other special provisions are vital parts of the control system for critical processes. Experience with such processes suggests that disasters and near disasters are often attributable to failures in the operating controls rather than to the failures of the physical facilities.

The Feedback Loop.   In process control, this follows closely the general approach described below, under Planning for Control. The control subjects (features to be controlled) include process features as well as product features. For each control subject it is necessary to provide means to measure or evaluate actual performance. Actual performance is then compared to goals, whether by technological or by human methods. Means must also be provided to close the loop— to take remedial action in the event performance does not conform to goals.

The Spreadsheet.   The third spreadsheet (Figure 6.6) is organized with process features in the horizontal rows. Then as planning for control progresses, the vertical columns accumulate the process control features required to run the process and meet the operating goals.

Transfer to Operations.   This transfer is the final step in the quality planning process. It usually involves a complete shift of responsibility, since the planners soon become fully occupied with the next planning project.

Proof of Process Capability.   The ideal proof is a demonstration of capability under operating conditions. For established processes, such proof may be available from previous performance. In the absence of such proof, other forms of demonstration are needed. One such form is the "dry run," in which a small-scale operation is conducted solely to demonstrate process capability. Another form is the "pilot run"—the first full-scale operation, during which special arrangements are made to evaluate the process capability.

In some industries proof of process capability is mandated under the name "process validation." A guideline drafted by the Food and Drug Administration defines the term as follows:

> Process validation is a documented program which provides a high degree of assurance that a specific process will consistently produce a product meeting its predetermined specifications and quality attributes.

In some cases, proof of process capability must be based on simulation in the "laboratory" or on mathematical models. Such forms of proof require extrapolation from the world of the laboratory to the world of operations. These two worlds differ in several important respects: the respective missions, the technology, the scale of operations, and the training and motivation of the personnel. Such differences require that extrapolation from laboratory findings be based on input from both worlds. The technologists are quite competent to interpret what happened in the laboratory. However, they are not necessarily able to extrapolate—to predict what will happen in the world of operations—unless they have adequate knowledge of how life is lived in that world. Lacking such knowledge, they must acquire it from inhabitants of the world of operations through such team efforts as joint planning, design review, and by other means.

Proof of Process Controllability. This is the proof that means have been provided to enable the operating forces to carry out the activities within the feedback loop. These means include such process features as measurement reproducibility, information on the relationship between process variables and product results, process stability, and maintainability. Providing these means should not be left for the last (on the theory that planning for control will then be done by the operating forces). Instead, planning to provide these means should be done concurrently with process planning, and done jointly with the operating forces.

Transfer of Know-How. This transfer always includes the process specifications which set out the process goals to be met. Ideally, the transfer should also include a database in the form of procedures, cautions, and lessons learned during the planning. Such a database has value for training operating personnel and for reference.

Some companies make a practice of organizing briefing meetings to facilitate the transfer. These may include training sessions in which planners participate as instructors. Such training is vital in the case of radically new processes. These briefing meetings also establish a reverse flow of information—the planners learn from the feedback.

For additional discussion relative to transfer to operations, see Bemesderfer (1979) relative to manufacturing processes and Norton and Mason (1987) relative to nuclear projects.

APPLICATION OF THE QUALITY PLANNING ROAD MAP

This road map (Figure 6.1) is universal in nature. It is applicable to quality planning throughout the economy. It is applicable to all industries (e.g., service, manufacture, defense), at all levels (e.g., corporate, division, department, job), to all functions (e.g., product development, production, marketing, finance), and to all organization forms (e.g., functional, matrix, project-oriented). Some of these applications are elaborated below.

Application to Supervisory and Worker Levels. At the bottom of the hierarchy, work consists of operations or tasks—definable types of activity. Obvious examples are edit, assemble, and transport. Each employee is given responsibility to perform one or more tasks. When the assigned responsibility occupies any person on a full-time basis, it is usually called a "job."

A great many tasks and jobs in the lower levels of organization require quality planning. These jobs do not remain static—they continue to change and hence require replanning. The resulting volume of needed quality planning has stimulated interest in training the lower levels of supervision so that they can do the quality planning or replanning for their departments. In some cases this training is extended to selected nonsupervisors to enable them to plan their own jobs.

Quality planning at these levels makes use of a few helpful concepts and tools, as described in the following paragraphs.

The Concept of Self-Control. Ideally, the quality planning for any job should put the employee into a state of self-control. When work is organized in a way which enables a person to have full mastery over the attainment of planned results, that person is said to be in a state of self-control and can therefore properly be held responsible for the results. Self-control is a universal concept, applicable to the general manager responsible for running a company division at a profit, the plant manager responsible for meeting the various goals set for that plant, the machinist running a lathe, and others. (Closely related to the concept of self-control is the triple role concept; see the Triple-Role Concept below.)

To put people into a state of self-control, several fundamental criteria must be met. People must be provided with:

1. Knowledge of what they are supposed to do, e.g., the budgeted profit, the schedule, and the specification.
2. Knowledge of what they are doing, e.g., the actual profit, the delivery rate, the extent of conformance to specification.
3. Means for regulating what they are doing in the event that they are failing to meet the goals. These means must always include the authority to regulate and the ability to regulate by varying either (*a*) the process under the person's authority or (*b*) the person's own conduct.

If all the foregoing parameters have been met, the person is said to be in a state of self-control and can properly be held responsible for any deficiencies in performance. If any parameter has not been met, the person is not in a state of self-control and, to the extent of the deficiency, cannot properly be held responsible.

The application of the concept of self-control can be seen in detail in Section 17, under Concept of Controllability.

The Triple-Role Concept. This concept is shown graphically in Figure 6.7. Under this concept any job requires the job holder to carry out three roles:

As a *customer* who receives inputs from suppliers

As a *processor* who converts these inputs into products

As a *supplier* who delivers the resulting products to customers

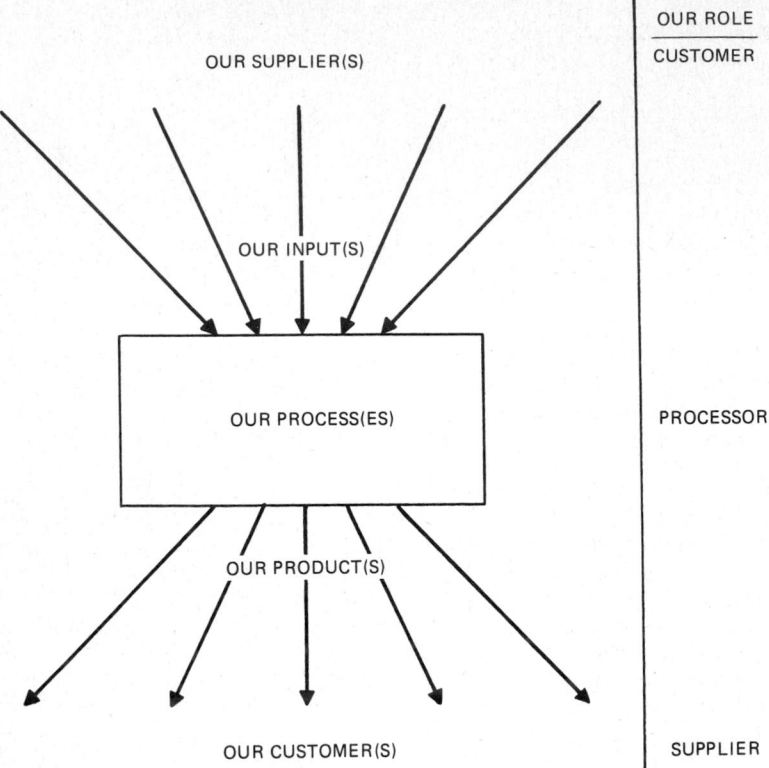

FIG. 6.7   The triple role.

(Actually, the concept operates in reverse as well, since each customer provides feedback to suppliers.)

The triple-role concept helps the quality planning to proceed in its natural progression. It starts at the base of Figure 6.7 by analysis of who the customers are and what their needs are. The analysis then proceeds on to the product, the process, and the inputs to the process.

The Tools of Analysis.   These are general-use tools—they are not unique to quality planning at the supervisory and worker levels. The tools include:

The flow diagram: This diagram maps out the process flow in detail and helps to make clear who is impacted. For examples, see Figures 16.3, 28.6, 28.9, 28.13, 28.14, 29.7, 30.9, and 30.21 in their respective sections of this handbook.

The Pareto principle: This principle is employed to identify the "vital few," whether customers, customer needs, product features, process features, or inputs. Identification of the vital few helps to assure that resources and attention are concentrated where they will do the most good.

Process capability analysis: This analysis quantifies the inherent ability of a process to meet the demands of quality objectives.

Basic statistical tools: These include tally sheets, frequency distributions, control charts, and sampling. These simple tools go far to solve many problems. The mid-1980s witnessed a resurgence of interest in these tools, with a corresponding growth in statistical literacy.

The need for job planning goes beyond quality planning. It extends to planning for productivity, costs, human relations, and still other parameters. Each of these areas has a degree of uniqueness which demands "professional" planning, that is, use of special planning tools and skills, as well as special application of general-use tools. If supervisors or workers are to carry out quality planning in a professional way they must be trained in use of the associated concepts and tools.

Application to Functional Levels. These levels relate to broad functions such as product development, purchasing, and manufacture. Planning for such functions is often done by the functional managers in collaboration with full-time planners. The planning is normally done for multiple parameters, but with major emphasis on the core responsibility of the function. For example, planning for the purchasing function places major emphasis on the defined role of the purchasing department.

For such functions the managers and planners tend to be "professionals" with respect to the core responsibility, but not with respect to the quality parameter. Regarding the quality parameter, they are usually experienced amateurs who lack expertise in the special skills and tools of planning for quality.

The major alternative (to use of experienced amateurs) has been to assign planning for quality to quality specialists (e.g., quality engineers, reliability engineers). This has been the major alternative in the United States.

A second alternative is to help the experienced amateurs to become professional through training in the skills and tools of planning for quality. This has been the trend in Japan for some years. More recently such a trend has become evident in the United States.

As a further aid to functional planners, the emerging literature is identifying the key element of quality planning for various functions. Some examples are:

Writing technical specifications (Livni, 1985)

Manufacturing engineering (Müller, 1971)

Information systems (Hill and Sorrell, 1985)

For additional discussion as applied to support operations, see Section 21, Administrative and Support Operations.

Application to Multifunctional Systems. Examples of such systems include new-product development and launch, the system of human relations, and the management information system. Such systems are all-pervasive. They demand inputs from all major functions. The quality of the systems depends importantly on the quality of those inputs. The systems represent large commitments which can be jeopardized by inadequate quality planning. In the discussion which follows, the system for new product development will be used to illustrate the approach to multifunctional quality planning.

Central Quality Planning. For any new product, there is need for some degree of central planning. This central planning establishes the overall objectives for such parameters as:

The performance features of the finished product

The cost target for the finished product

The overall schedule

The budget for the work of product development and launch

To meet these overall objectives, considerable planning, including quality planning, is necessary. Some of this planning must be done with central coordination, since the final result is a composite of many elements. This central planning may be carried out by various methods:

A team (or committee) of functional managers

A similar team, with the assistance of quality specialists

A Project Management Department

The Quality Assurance Department

A complicating factor is that the needed planning involves not only quality planning but also planning for other parameters. If the planners lack expertise in quality planning, the quality planning will be done by "experienced amateurs."

Functional Quality Planning.   Beyond the central quality planning there is need for functional quality planning. Here again there is a range of choice. Functional quality planning may be done by:

The same organization form which does the central planning

The respective functional department managers

Quality specialists, e.g., quality engineers, reliability engineers

No matter which organization form is chosen, the responsibility should be made clear. The quality planning tasks should be defined, and there should be clear assignment of who is to perform which tasks. (The quality planning tasks associated with various functions are generally described in Sections 12 through 21 of this handbook.)

Allocation of the quality planning tasks is often linked to the phased system of product development. Under that system, the progression of events is divided into logical stages or phases, such as market evaluation, research and development, product design, process design, materials acquisition, production, test, marketing, and field service. (For elaboration, see Section 13, Product Development.) The quality planning tasks are then identified and assigned to the appropriate planners. Where these assignments are made to various functional departments, it is feasible to publish a matrix showing which planning tasks are assigned to which department (see, e.g., George, 1977).

Coordination of Functional Quality Planning.   This coordination may be supplied through centralized forms such as a project management department or a multifunctional committee of managers. If no specific provision is made for coordination, the risk is that every function will be on its own. For example, one approach to product development has been the "procession." According to that approach, product development progresses sequentially from one functional department to the next, each then carrying out its assigned functional responsibility. This arrangement then makes it tempting for the functional departments to meet their schedules and budgets by shortcutting the needed coordination with their internal customers. In some industries there has been considerable damage done by this shortcutting.

Application to Major Programs. The term "major program" is used here in the sense of a costly undertaking such as a military weapon system, a nuclear power plant, or an ocean oil-drilling platform. Each such program has so great a degree of complexity and uniqueness as to require the quality planning to be specially designed for the program.

Quality planning for major programs is nearly always subject to some extensive restraints:

The clients (Department of Defense, electric utilities, etc.) impose mandated quality plans which are extensive in scope

The organization for planning is usually in the form of a Program Management Department

The organization for quality planning is often closely linked to the Program Management Department

In these major programs it is common for clients to incorporate, in the purchase contract, the mandated quality plans as well as the product performance specification and numerous auxiliary specifications. The contractor then supplements these as needed or required. However, on critical performance matters the role of the contractor is one of conformance to mandated plans and specifications, since the critical decisions on product performance are reserved by the client.

The principle underlying the preceding approach is that the contractor must not only deliver the product under contract but also *provide the assurance* that the quality is according to contract. In this way, the client is not forced to create a large organization to duplicate much of the work done by the contractor, with resulting added cost and delay.

The contractor provides assurance to the client in a number of ways, such as:

Submitting the quality plans for review by the client

Providing the client with access to information of all sorts: logs of actions taken, test reports, essential correspondence, etc.

Conducting independent quality audits and providing the client with access to the audit reports

The amount of this documentation can be extensive, and this is often a source of contention between contractors and clients. Many contractors sincerely believe that much of the documentation could be eliminated without any detriment to quality. However, many clients are equally sincere in feeling that the documentation is essential to providing assurance of quality as well as serving other purposes within the client organizations and the regulatory bodies (e.g., traceability, defense against lawsuits).

For elaboration on the documentation problem, see Juran, "Quality and Its Assurance—an Overview" (1977).

COMPANYWIDE QUALITY MANAGEMENT (CWQM)

A major application of the quality planning concept is "strategic quality planning," sometimes called "companywide quality management" (CWQM). CWQM is, in effect, an extension of the company's business planning to include planning for quality. The nature of CWQM is readily understood by looking at the makeup of strategic business planning. Strategic business planning consists of a sequence of activities somewhat as follows:

Establish broad business goals

Determine the deeds needed to meet the goals

Organize—assign clear responsibility for doing those deeds

Provide the resources needed to meet those responsibilities

Provide the needed training

Establish the means to evaluate actual performance against goals

Establish a process for periodic review of performance against goals

Establish a reward system which relates rewards to performance

CWQM applies this same sequence to managing for quality. While the sequence is the same, the application to quality requires special organization design, skills, tools, training, and so on. In addition, CWQM requires the upper managers to become personally involved in the setting and meeting of broad quality goals.

Purposes of CWQM.   Traditionally, planning for quality has been delegated to the functional departments. Each department has been responsible for establishing and meeting quality goals for its function. Despite the presence of various means for coordination, in many companies this approach has failed to optimize company performance relative to quality. In addition, there are indications that adoption of CWQM (notably by some major Japanese companies) has contributed to quality superiority.

The advocates of CWQM point out that adoption of the concept makes it easier to broaden the concept of quality to include all company processes—not just manufacture. The advocates also point out that optimizing company performance demands increased teamwork between upper management and the functional departments, as well as among the functional departments. This teamwork then persists beyond the planning stages and into the subsequent operations. [For additional discussion, see Juran (1988), *Juran on Planning for Quality*, chapters 11 and 13; see also Bhote (1985).]

Disadvantages of CWQM.   For a company to adopt CWQM requires establishing a high-level organization (e.g., a Quality Council) to coordinate quality at the highest level. CWQM also requires establishing the organization structure needed to prepare the quality equivalent of the financial budget and the financial reports. (See below, under Organization for CWQM.)

Adoption of CWQM invariably adds to the workload of the uppper managers—people who usually are already quite busy. Introduction of CWQM also invades some of the prior autonomy of the company divisions and departments. Those organizations resist such invasion. Finally, there is no proof that CWQM will, in fact, improve results in a specific company until it has been tried out. In some companies these disadvantages have impeded the adoption of CWQM until the concept has been tested out in some division of the company.

Establishing Strategic Quality Goals.   The general nature of quality goals is discussed in Section 5, under Quality Objectives, and subsequent headings. Establishment of specific quality objectives (or goals) starts with focus on the "driving forces" which significantly impact quality. Some of these forces are of a broad political, social, and economic nature. Other forces are very specific with respect to the company's operations: activities of competitors, trends in technology, relations with suppliers, and internal cooperation. [For further discussion, see Kohoutek (1983).]

It is relatively easy to list the "driving forces." However, such a list is of little help to managers unless action is taken to evaluate those forces and their impact on quality. Such evaluation requires data and data analysis.

Some essential data are readily available as a byproduct of operations. Examples of such data are presented in a number of sections of this handbook. (See, for example, Section 12, Field Intelligence, under Organization for Field Intelligence; Data Sources; also Section 8, Upper Management and Quality, under Executive Reports on Quality.) However, CWQM also requires the creation and analysis of additional data sources. Generally these additional sources require a review of history in order to develop "lessons learned."

Deployment of Corporate Quality Goals. Broad objectives do not lead directly to results; they must first be "deployed." Such deployment consists of:

   Division and subdivision of the objectives until they identify specific deeds to be done

   Allocation of responsibility for doing the deeds

   Provision of the needed resources

Such deployment involves communication both up and down the hierarchy. Corporate quality goals may be proposed at the top. The lower levels then identify the deeds which, if done, will collectively meet the goals. The lower levels also submit the bill: To perform these deeds, we need the following resources. The subsequent negotiations then arrive at an optimum which balances the value of meeting the goals against the cost of doing so. [For a case example, see Brunetti (1986).]

While deployment usually follows the hierarchical organization (corporation to division to functional department) there are many goals which are inherently multidivisional or multifunctional in nature. For such goals, deployment generally must go down to project *teams.*

Corporate goals often originate through nomination from below. Managers at lower levels may identify needs which should be met but which require corporate participation owing to such features as extensive resources required, multidivisional impact, and major precedents to be set. As experience is acquired in setting and deploying corporate quality goals, the organization becomes progressively more comfortable in upward communication as well.

Once responsibility has been assigned, quality planning to carry out the deeds then follows the planning processes described earlier in this section.

Providing Resources. Many well-meaning efforts to attain and improve quality have been defeated by failure to provide the needed resources. This failure has been notorious in the case of efforts applied to quality improvement projects. To bring such projects to completion, various resources are required: time for project team members to guide the projects, support from technicians and specialists, and training in several directions. With the exception of some aspects of training, these resources seldom have been provided adequately. In turn, lack of the resources has thwarted many efforts to improve quality on a scale which offered major benefits.

The CWQM approach, which is tied into companywide business planning, offers a way to overcome this deficiency. Companywide business planning has long included a positive approach to bring out into the open the resources required to meet the corporate business goals. Those who are apprehensive about "corporate interference" (see below) should note that CWQM provides a channel for dealing with the problem of securing resources.

Organization for CWQM. To adopt CWQM requires setting up special organizational machinery similar to that widely used for companywide business planning. The major components of this special organization consist of:

1. *A companywide quality committee (CWQC):* Committee members are high-level upper managers, and membership is a part-time assignment. This committee proposes the broad quality objectives. It also approves the final objectives and the associated resources. In addition, the committee carries out a broad control through review of performance against objectives and through high-level quality audits. The committee responsibilities generally parallel those of the Finance Committee with respect to finance. See also Section 8, under Quality Audits by Upper Managers.

2. *A full-time, quality management department:* This department has a coordination responsibility relative to deployment of objectives, preparation of the final list of objectives, and provision of the associated resources. The department also has the responsibility to prepare reports of performance against objectives and to assist in the conduct of high-level quality audits. These responsibilities relative to quality parallel those of the financial controller relative to finance.

Assurance of Performance against Objectives. This assurance is carried out mainly through review of reports of performance against objectives (see Section 8, under Executive Reports on Quality) and quality audits (see Section 9, under Quality Audits.)

APPLICATION TO SMALL COMPANIES

Many elements of quality planning are applicable to small companies as well as large ones. However, a significant difference in size tends to become difference in kind and hence results in differences in behavior, including approaches to quality planning. Small companies operate with less formality and system than do large companies. The reasons proceed logically from the difference in size.

How Small Is Small? The dividing line is quite arbitrary. In the United States the Small Business Administration defines small business as companies which are profit-seeking, have 500 or fewer employees, and are not dominant in their field. In a study in Ireland, the boundary was drawn at 100 (Roche and Sheil, 1984). Regardless of the boundary, small companies abound. Even at a boundary of 500, over 95 percent of all companies are "small."

Many large companies include autonomous divisions which, if independent, would be classified as small companies. Such autonomous divisions tend to follow practices in quality planning similar to those used by independent small companies.

Inherent Features. Small companies possess certain features which tend to shape the approach to quality planning:

The business scope is limited to a niche involving a relatively narrow product line. The actions of any manager thereby impact fewer customers.

The organization has fewer functional departments. Much multifunctional planning takes place within the minds of individuals.

The organization has fewer layers in the hierarchy. The upper managers are closer to the actions which take place at the work level.

The total number of managers is fewer, thus simplifying the work of communication and coordination.

Separation of Planning from Execution. Those same inherent features of small companies require a close linkage between planning and execution. Quality planning is, therefore, carried out largely by operating personnel, and this includes the work force. The craft workers concept is widely retained. Workers undergo a form of apprenticeship under the guidance of supervisors or of experienced workers. For example, at Steinway and Sons Piano Company, workers progress upward within three crafts: woodworker, machinist, and tuner (Karabatsos, 1983). Anchor Brewing Company employs 14 full-time and 7 part-time employees. The management system involves extensive delegation to the work force. In turn, the work force is able to accept extensive delegation because of prior indoctrination and training (Maytag, 1986.)

In small companies the concept of quality planning by operating personnel applies also to multifunctional projects such as new product launching. Hartz (1982) describes such an approach using multifunctional "working groups."

For small projects within large companies, the quality planning may assume hybrid forms. Lange (1978) gives examples in which multifunctional teams are aided by specialized quality planners and by adapting the company's standard practices as needed.

Extent of Formality in Quality Planning. This topic was researched by Roche and Sheil (1984). The study extended to 591 small companies and 380 large companies; the size criterion was 100 employees. Both groups made wide use of product inspection and test. However, there were significant differences in use of such planned control methods as formal supplier evaluation and such tools as statistical methodology.

Such differences in formality are generally known to large buyers whose suppliers include small companies. Some of those large buyers recognize the differences when buying from small companies. The approach is usually to classify purchase contracts according to importance. Contracts of high levels of importance require the supplier to establish a full array of formal quality systems and procedures. Contracts of lower levels of importance require fewer and less formal systems and procedures.

Military buyers formalize these distinctions by publishing several levels of military or defense standards defining quality assurance systems [for further details, see Heslop (1981) and below, under Generic Standards].

Advantages and Limitations of Informality. By avoiding formality, small companies also avoid the costs of preparing written systems and procedures, as well as the associated documentation. Instead, the information is in the memories of the experienced personnel. However, this arrangement renders the company vulnerable to the loss of essential information in the event of employee turnover.

The absence of a quality planning function also creates a risk that the small company will remain isolated and static—will fail to keep its planning methods up to date. One proposed solution is to establish quality audits which utilize expertise available in the local community, such as managers from other companies and university professors [for details, see Willborn (1978)].

LESSONS LEARNED

A simple example is seen in the world of sports. Some sports teams arrange for videotaping of their games. Collectively, such tapes present a history which can be analyzed to provide inputs to the quality planning process. Analysis of the history can identify opportunities for improvements such as change of strategy, training to reduce the incidence of predominant errors, revision of the signaling system, and redesign of the equipment.

The lessons-learned concept is applicable to general management as well as to the various functions. An example relative to general management is the post-project appraisals conducted by British Petroleum (BP). BP maintains a full-time postproject appraisal (PPA) organization unit to conduct appraisals of the conduct of large undertakings: acquisitions, joint ventures, and major construction projects. In its first 9 years the unit appraised over 80 such undertakings. The lessons learned from the appraisals include:

How to formulate investment proposals more accurately

How to approve the proposals more objectively

How to execute the undertakings more efficiently

For a detailed explanation, see Gulliver (1987).

Application to Multifunctional Processes.   The lessons-learned concept has wide application to multifunctional processes. An important example is the process for developing and launching new products. Such a launching progresses through numerous phases or stages. In some industries it continues for several years. A significant portion of this time is devoted to rework. This rework is caused by chronic deficiencies in the new-product launching system. The outward symptoms of the deficiencies include engineering change orders, process redesigns, and product recalls.

The Log of Problems.   For such multifunctional processes, a useful approach to lessons learned is the "historical review." A historian is appointed to review the history of a number of prior cycles of launchings. A part of this review consists of preparing a log of problems encountered in prior launchings. For each such problem, the log specifies the outward symptoms, the causes which were discovered to have been the sources of the symptoms, the remedies to solve the problem, and the estimated amount of damage done (if substantial).

In a sense, the preceding review is a study of the "cost of poor quality" as applied to the product development process. However, some of these costs are quite different from those encountered in manufacture of products. Product development necessarily tries out new ideas, and this inevitably creates problems which are inherent in risk taking. The historical review takes account of this feature of product development problems by studying the consequences of the *time* of discovery of the problems.

The Consequences of Time.   This step in the historical review determines, for each problem: at what stage it was first discovered, at what stage it could have been discovered, and what could have been done to discover the problem earlier (or to have avoided the problem altogether).

Kano (1984) makes use of a "T-type matrix" for comparing the actual stage at which problems are found with the stage at which they could have been found. Ingram (1984) describes a history review process comprising five steps—historical setup, grouping and review, creation of a problem log, cause analysis, and remedial action.

The Forms of Improvement.   Most of the improvements consist of new or improved tools for the planners. For example, in the automotive industry a major recurring problem in new-product development has been the inability of the factory processes to meet product tolerance criteria established a year or two earlier during product design. The movement to quantify process capability of manufacturing processes has enabled designers and manufacturing planners to secure early warning of such problems and thus reduce their frequency.

The specific new or improved tools include databases, early warning reviews, procedures, countdowns, and foolproofing measures. Collectively, these tools can significantly improve future launchings. Some problems become extinct—they will not appear at all in future launchings. Other problems will be discovered earlier, so that they will cost less to remedy and will create less delay. Perhaps the most attractive gain is a substantial reduction in the time required to go to market. A company making industrial sewing machines is reported to have cut that time in two, in a space of 5 years.

Organization for Historical Review.   This organization consists of (1) the guidance function and (2) the historian(s).

Guidance is provided by a multifunctional team of managers. Their responsibilities include defining the mission, determining the questions to which answers are needed, providing resources and assistance to the historian, and acting on the findings. The team also takes steps to abolish any atmosphere of blame, in order to assure the objectivity of the historical review.

The historian conducts the detailed review by drawing on various sources: minutes of meetings, correspondence, reports, test results, change notices, and logs. All this is supplemented by interviews with those who actually participated in prior launchings. These interviews are needed to fill in gaps and to clear up biases and vagueness.

A company making process control equipment used the historical review approach to analyze 15 previous projects. The review revealed that certain decisions were being made at too low a level. This, in turn, resulted in improving the performance of certain specific functions, but not in optimizing overall company performance. A second conclusion was that more thorough verification was needed to assure that design changes would, indeed, correct the problems for which the changes were instituted.

Goree and Musson (1984) describe a structured "case study analysis" of a sample of defense products. The analysis used 26 specific elements to review the historical performance in management, contracting, design, test, and evaluation.

For additional discussion and examples, see Section 22 under Diagnosis—General; Diagnosis of Failures in Broad Systems.

Application to Functional Processes.   The lessons-learned concept has been widely applied in all functions. An example in the service function is related by Heskett (1987). The example concerns Hartford Steam Boiler Inspection & Insurance Company (HSB). HSB insures industrial equipment, especially steam boilers. As part of its activity, HSB has compiled a database on the performance of the key types of equipment. This database then serves multiple purposes such as an actuarial base for insurance rates, a source of operating and maintenance data for clients, and a source of information enabling HSB's engineers to provide consulting assistance to clients.

An example in the supplier relations function is a historical review of problems encountered in prior supply contracts (Table 6.2). In this case the frequency of problems in each category of cause helps to identify the vital few areas which should have priority of attention.

TABLE 6.2   Study of Problems in Supply Contracts

Major factors	Totals
Preaward surveys	
Q history (marginal/bad)	13
Contract requirements	
Poorly written	28
Deficient specs and/or drawings	72
Inadequate Q requirements	22
Postaward	
Inadequate conference	5
First article	
Inadequate evaluation	10
First article failure	5
Contract management	
Contractor Q program not viable	76
Contractor financial assets inadequate	29
Contractor physical assets inadequate	13
Contractor CA not sustained	41
Inadequate and/or unqualified contractor personnel	40
Excessive scrap	12
Control of suppliers and subcontractors	6
Miscellaneous factors	
Contractor commitments not met	36
PQAP did not detect problem cause	23
PCO inaction	27
Lack of PCO-Contractor coordination with ACO-QAR	1
Total	459

The concept of historical review has been applied to a great variety of functional problems, such as cancellation of sales contracts, data feedback on field performance, and maintenance of physical facilities. The variety is so great as to suggest that the concept has universal application.

In many cases the benefits of lessons learned can be extended beyond the planners. A common example is the owners' manuals for consumer products. Some of these manuals include tables showing, for various potential problems: the outward symptoms, the likely causes, and the likely remedies. Such tables enable many owners to conduct their own diagnosis and remedy.

The same concept is widely applied to industrial products. See, for example, a table of cause and correction relative to use of industrial grinding wheels ("Grinding Wheel Quality Improvement Hints," 1977).

PLANNING FOR CONTROL

Once planning is complete, the plans are put into operation. The responsibility of the operating personnel is mainly to meet the established goals. They do this through a planned system of quality "control." Control is largely directed at meeting goals and preventing adverse change. This is in contrast to "improvement," which is directed largely at creating beneficial change.

Much human energy is devoted to control. Biologically, this consists of maintaining the body temperature, the blood count, and other physiological functions. Industrially it takes the form of meeting goals: delivery according to schedule, expenses according to budget, and quality according to specification. This control "process" consists of a universal series of steps which, when applied to problems of quality, can be listed as follows:

1. Choosing the control subject, i.e., selecting what is to be regulated
2. Choosing a unit of measure
3. Establishing a goal for the control subject, i.e., specifying the target value for operating performance
4. Creating a sensor—a means of evaluating actual performance in terms of the unit of measure
5. Evaluating actual performance
6. Interpreting the difference between actual performance and goal
7. Taking action on the difference

This series of steps is the regulatory process by which we control anything: in other words, if you know how to control, you can control anything.

The preceding definition of "control" as a process is very different from the meaning given in some European countries to a word of the same pronunciation. The European word, spelled variously as "control," "controle," "Kontrola," "Kontroll," or (Cyrillic) "КОНТРОЛ," is often used in the narrow sense of product inspection. (For an extensive discussion of this universal process, see Juran, *Managerial Breakthrough,* chapters 12 through 20.)

QUALITY CONTROL

The term "quality control" has multiple meanings. In this handbook:

> *Quality control is the regulatory process through which we measure actual quality performance, compare it with quality goals, and act on the difference.*

The other definitions of quality control include:

1. A part of the regulatory process, e.g., product inspection.
2. The name of a department which is devoted full-time to the quality function. In this usage, the term is capitalized, i.e., Quality Control.
3. The tools, skills, or techniques through which some or all of the quality function is carried out.

The term "quality control" has had a short but lively history. Early in the twentieth century, it began to be used as a synonym for "defect prevention" (in contrast to the widely prevailing after-the-fact inspection). However, during the 1940s and 1950s there was a wave of enthusiasm (and overenthusiasm) for the use of statistical methods in quality control. The proponents of this movement coined the phrase "statistical quality control" (SQC) and publicized it so widely that many managers gained the impression that quality control consisted of the use of statistical methods in industry. As a consequence, the SQC movement weakened the use of "quality control" as an accepted term for the regulatory process.

In subsequent decades, various other terms emerged to erode the use of "quality control" as an all-inclusive term for the regulatory process. The term "total quality control" implied that anything else was only partial quality control. Reliability engineers contended that quality control as practiced had been limited to internal quality matters. Advocates of exhortation drives invented new terminology (e.g., "zero defects") to be used as a central slogan. Managers invented terms to represent conduct of the entire quality function (e.g., quality assurance, product assurance). During the mid-1980s there emerged a revival of keen interest in statistical methodology, this time under the name "statistical process control." The end is not in sight.

It would be helpful to agree on a single term for the regulatory process. However, it is difficult to secure such agreement. Most people tend to structure their glossary in a way which affirms their beliefs on organization structure, priority of technique, and other aspects. There have been enough instances in which choice of terminology was decisive in settling jurisdictional disputes to cause people to use terminology as a weapon in such contests. It is not merely a matter of aggression; there are many sincere human beings who feel that broadly standardized terminology is a detriment to their company needs (or personal aspirations) and that, therefore, new, local terminology must be coined to respond to these needs.

On-Line and Off-Line Quality Control.   These terms are used to distinguish (1) the application of the feedback loop to "production line" activities from (2) the progression of events on the quality planning road map. "On-line quality control" is readily visible and even dramatic in appearance. However, "off-line quality control," while less conspicuous, is much more influential in attaining quality. [For elaboration, see Taguchi (1978).]

Self-Control.   This term is applied to situations in which a person is provided with all the means needed to conform to planned goals (for details, see the Concept of Self-Control above).

Quality control is greatly simplified when operating people are in a state of self-control.

THE FEEDBACK LOOP

The universal series of steps (listed under Planning for Control) takes place within a system called the "feedback loop." Figure 6.8 shows in simplified form the flow of events in the feedback loop.

The nucleus of the loop is the control subject—the thing being regulated. A goal or standard is established as the intended value of the control subject. A sensor measures the actual value (performance). A collator compares actual per-

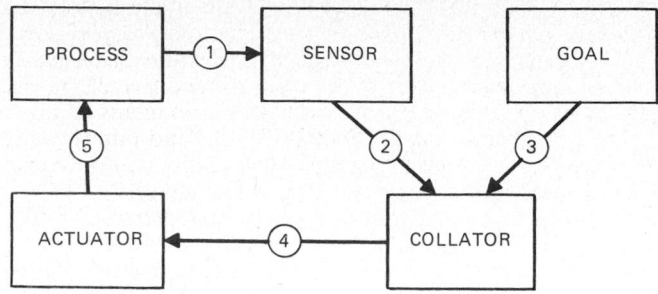

FIG. 6.8 The feedback loop.

formance to goal. When actual performance differs from goal by more than a predetermined tolerance, the loop is closed, actuating the means for restoring the status quo.

The evolution of the modern computer has stimulated the growth of computerized on-line systems of self-control. These computerized systems are used not only in factories but also widely in service industries, as well as in administrative and support operations.

In fully automated processes, the steps of the feedback loop may all be carried out without human intervention. In cases of self-control, the steps may all be carried out by one individual. Lacking self-control, the steps are carried out by multiple individuals. In such cases it is necessary to define with precision who is responsible for carrying out which step.

The Control Subject. Control subjects exist in very large numbers. At the technological level, there are many quality characteristics of the products being produced: components, units, subsystems, and systems. There are also quality characteristics of the processing conditions (e.g., time cycle, temperature) and the processing facilities. In addition, there are quality characteristics of the input materials and services. Still more control subjects are imposed by external forces: clients, government regulations, and standardization bodies.

Beyond technological quality control subjects are the managerial quality control subjects. These are mainly the performance goals for organization units and the associated managers. Managerial goals extend to nontechnological matters such as customer relations, financial trends (e.g., progress in reducing cost of poor quality), employee relations, and community relations. For elaboration on control subjects at upper management levels, see Section 8, Upper Management and Quality, under Executive Reports on Quality.

The Control Pyramid. Despite the large numbers of control subjects, relatively few human beings are needed to carry out the necessary controls. They do so by extensive use of the principle of self-control. A great deal of this self-control is built into the technology through use of foolproofing and automated processes which require no human intervention.

Additional self-control is created through job design in ways which meet the criteria of self-control. Such job designs enable the supervisors to delegate most of the burden of human control to the work force. Such delegation enables the supervisors to limit their control activities to the vital few control subjects.

This plan of delegation can be depicted as a control pyramid (Figure 6.9). The bulk of the control is carried out without human intervention. Another large seg-

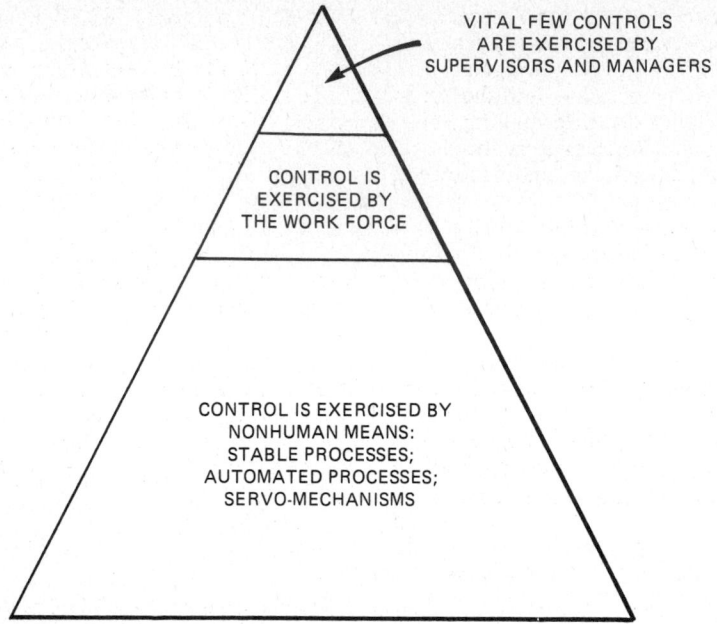

FIG. 6.9   The control pyramid.

ment is carried out by the work force. The remaining vital few controls are carried out by the supervisors and managers.

Control Stations.   In organizing for control it is useful to establish a limited number of centers or control stations. Each such control station then is given the responsibility for carrying out the steps of the feedback loop for a selected list of control subjects. A review of numerous control stations discloses that they are usually located in one of several principal ways:

1. At changes of jurisdiction, to protect the recipients: between stages of major projects (e.g., design review), at movement of products between companies or between major departments, and prior to delivery to finished goods store or to the customer

2. Before embarking on an irreversible path: setup approval before production, product approval before completing a costly operation (e.g., laboratory test before pouring a heat of steel), and product approval before diffusion of a uniform stream

3. After creation of a critical quality

4. At dominant process variables, i.e., the vital few

5. At natural "windows," for economical control

Choice of control stations is aided by preparation of a flow diagram which shows the progression of events through which the product is produced. For examples of flow diagrams, see Figures 16.3, 28.6, 28.9, 28.13, 28.14, 29.7, 30.9, and 30.21 in their respective sections of this handbook. Flow diagrams help planners to visualize the overall process and thereby to do a more logical job of grouping control features into control stations.

Definition of Work.   For each control station, it is necessary to define the work to be done: which quality features are to be measured, the goals and standards to be met, the governing regulations and procedures, the instruments to be used, the data to be recorded, and the decisions to be made. It is also necessary to provide criteria for decision making, such as seriousness classification, sample sizes, and tolerances. Such criteria should be provided by the planners if the control station personnel lack the qualifications to do so.

Assignment of Responsibility.   Often there are a number of people associated with each control station. For example, in a factory department the work of quality control may be shared by setup workers, machine operators, inspectors, supervisors, and process engineers. In such cases it is not possible to determine who is responsible for quality until there has been identification of the actions and decisions needed to attain quality. For details of such identification, see Section 17, under Quality Responsibilities on the Factory Floor.

Unit of Measure.   Communication of quality-related features is best done through numbers. In order to "say it in numbers," it is necessary to create a system of measurement consisting of:

A unit of measure: A defined amount of some quality feature which permits evaluation of that feature in numbers

A sensor: A method or instrument which can carry out the evaluation and state the findings in numbers in terms of the unit of measure.

Units of measure for product and process performance are usually expressed in technological terms; for example, fuel efficiency is measured in terms of distance traveled per volume of fuel; timeliness of service is expressed in minutes (or hours, days, etc.) required to provide service.

Units of measure for product deficiency usually take the form of a fraction:

$$\frac{\text{Number of occurrences}}{\text{Opportunity for occurrences}}$$

The numerator may be in such terms as number of defective units of product, number of field failures, and cost of warranty charges. The denominator may be in such terms as number of units produced, dollar volume of sales, number of units in service, and length of time in service.

Supervisory and managerial controls usually require data in the form of summaries. Preparation of such summaries often requires use of units of measure such as indexes and ratios.

Figure 6.10 shows the interrelation of units of measure at various organization levels.

The Sensor.   Most sensors are designed to provide information in terms of units of measure. At the bottom of the pyramid (Figure 6.10) the sensors are usually technological instruments or human beings employed as instruments (e.g., inspectors, auditors). In the upper layers of the pyramid the sensors are data systems.

There has been a continuing trend to provide sensors with additional functions of the feedback loop: data recording, data processing, comparison of performance with standards, and initiating corrective action in the process. For a discussion of precision, accuracy and maintenance of sensors, see Section 18, under Sensory Qualities.

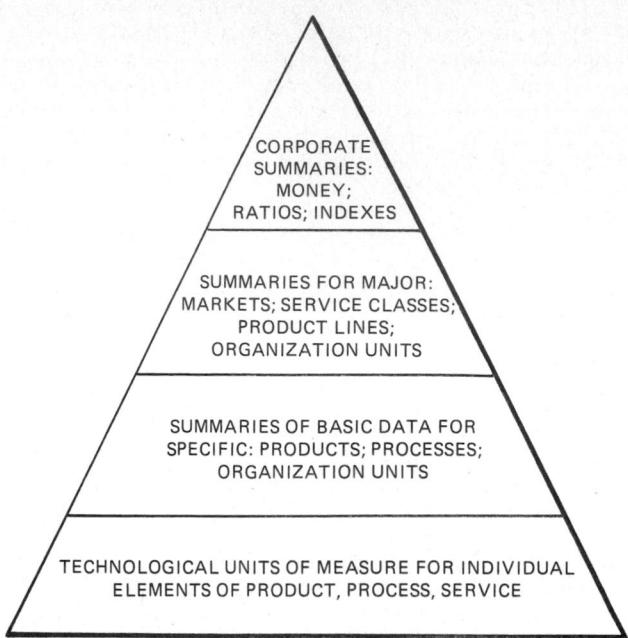

FIG. 6.10   Interrelation of units of measure.

Human Sensing.   Much sensing is done by human beings. Human sensing is subject to a variety of errors. Remedies have been evolved for these error types. Table 6.3 summarizes the principal types of human error and the associated remedies. For elaboration, see Juran (1988), *Juran on Planning for Quality,* chapter 6, under Human Errors.

Data Collection and Processing.   Additional steps in the feedback loop include data collection by sensors, data entry, and data processing. These steps have all been revolutionized by recent advances in electronic data processing. Sensed data can be entered directly, without the use of paper. The speed of data processing permits real-time display of the processed data. The systems can be programmed to display control charts and summaries in various forms. The systems can also be programmed to carry out analyses, such as identification of the "vital few" problems, and to display these. See generally, Section 27, Computers and Quality.

Analysis for Decision Making.   In its most primitive form, this analysis consists of comparing the sensed performance with the quality goals. The observed difference must then be interpreted in terms of its significance. If the difference is "significant," decisions must then be made as to what to do about (1) the deviant process and/or (2) the deviant product.

"Significance" includes statistical significance and economic significance. They are very different in nature.

Statistical Significance; Control Charts.   The problem here is to separate false alarms from the real thing. An observed difference between performance and goals can be the result of (1) a real difference or (2) an apparent difference arising from chance variation.

TABLE 6.3 Types and Remedies of Human Error

Type	Remedy
Misinterpretation	Precise definition; glossary
	Checklists
	Examples
Inadvertent errors	Aptitude testing
	Reorganization of work to reduce fatigue and monotony
	Fail-safe designs
	Redundancy
	Foolproofing (errorproofing)
	Automation; robotics
Lack of technique	Discovery of knack of successful workers
	Revision of technology to incorporate the knack
	Retraining
Conscious errors	
Coloration	Design review of data collection plan
Bias	Removal of atmosphere of blame
Futility	Action on reports, or explanation of why not
	Depersonalize orders
	Establish accountability
	Provide balanced emphasis on goals
	Conduct quality audits
	Create competition, incentives
	Reassign the work

A major tool for separating false alarms from the real thing is the Shewhart control chart. This chart is designed to show graphically the limits of variation due to specified chance odds, for instance, 19 to 1. Differences which fall within these limits are then assumed to be due to chance since they could readily have been caused by chance. Differences which fall outside these limits are assumed to be real since the odds against chance causation are so high. For a detailed discussion of the Shewhart control chart, see Section 24.

Starting in about 1980 there emerged in the United States a new wave of interest in the use of statistical tools for quality control. This movement, often called "statistical process control" (SPC), concentrated on use of the Shewhart control chart to distinguish statistically significant variations from those which were not statistically significant. This same movement included extensive training of supervisors and workers in basic statistical tools, with a resulting increase in statistical literacy.

Observed variations which are not statistically significant rarely are acted on because the cause is so often due to chance and hence not "findable." Variations which do have statistical significance become candidates for action (see below, under Economic Significance).

Trend Analysis; Leading Indicators. A useful aid to decision making is trend analysis. The purpose is to create "leading indicators" which help to predict future events. A common example is cumulative forms of data summary. For example, cumulative sum charts have greater sensitivity for identifying trends than do the conventional Shewhart control charts. (See Section 24, under Types of Control Charts, for further discussion.) In like manner, cumulative data on field returns (or field service calls) help to predict the ultimate levels of returns. Similarly, cumulative data on early failures during life testing can facilitate prediction of ultimate failure rates. [For elaboration, see Section 13 under Planning for Time-Oriented Performance (Reliability); Reliability Tests.]

Other Analyses.   There are many varieties of analysis. Data can be organized to separate the vital few problems from the rest. Correlation analysis can be used to discover relationships among variables. Examples of these and other forms of analysis are common in quality improvement projects as well as within the feedback loop. See generally, Section 22, Quality Improvement.

Control Reports.   Most reporting on quality is done by instruments which provide real-time information directly to operating personnel (production workers, office clerks, airline pilots, etc.). Beyond such real-time feedbacks, summarized reports are prepared to enable supervisors and middle managers to become informed and to take action as needed.

Table 6.4 lists some typical subjects for control reports, along with the usual units of measure, sources of data, standards, format, and frequency of reporting.

Upper management levels also require control reports on quality. These are discussed in Section 8, Upper Management and Quality. See especially, Tables 8.1 through 8.4 and associated discussions.

Corrective Action.   The final step in closing the feedback loop is to actuate a change which restores a state of conformance with quality goals.

The term "corrective action" has been loosely applied to two very different conditions:

1. Elimination of *chronic* sources of deficiency. The feedback loop is *not* a suitable means for dealing with such chronic problems. Instead, the need is to employ the quality improvement process as described in Section 22.
2. Elimination of *sporadic* sources of deficiency. The feedback loop is well designed for this purpose.

In such sporadic cases the cardinal issue is what changes caused the sporadic difference to arise. Discovery of those changes, plus action to restore control, can usually be carried out by the unaided local operating supervision (see Section 22, under Troubleshooting).

Economic Significance.   The fact that a nonconformance is statistically significant does not mean that there will be corrective action. In some companies nonconformances are so numerous that the personnel cannot apply corrective action to all of them. In such cases it is customary to establish priorities based on economic significance and related parameters. If the economic significance of some nonconformance is at a very low level, corrective action may not be taken for a long time.

In situations where nonconformances are numerous it is customary to formalize the corrective action process. The cases are documented, and organization machinery is created for decision-making, (e.g., Material Review Boards). See Section 18, under Judgment of Fitness for Use.

Application to Upper-Management Control.   A special and vital application of the feedback loop is for quality control at the upper levels of the company. This application is discussed in Section 8, under Quality Assurance for Upper Managers.

TABLE 6.4 Matrix of Reports on Quality

Control subjects	Typical units of measure	Usual data source	Typical standard	Typical format	Typical frequency*
Product conformance	Parts (defective) per million; average performance	Inspection; test	Engineered; historical	Tabulation; charts	D, W
Outgoing quality based on product audit	Demerits per unit	Product audit	Historical	Charts; narrative	M
Rework	Rework hours per 100 total hours	Accounting; quality	Historical	Tabulation; charts	W, M
Field failures					
Complaints	Number of complaints per 100 units; per $000 of sales	Customer service; accounting	Historical	Tabulation; narrative	M
Returns	Value of returns per $000 of sales	Customer service; accounting	Historical	Tabulation; narrative	M
Warranty charges	Cost per 1000 units under warranty	Customer service; accounting	Historical	Tabulation; charts	M, Q
Service calls	Number per 1000 units under warranty; cost per 1000 units under warranty	Customer service; accounting	Historical	Tabulation; narrative	M, Q
Product reliability	Failure rate; mean time between failures	Quality; customer service	Historical; engineered	Charts; narrative	M, Q
Suppliers' quality performance	Cost of poor quality per $000 of purchases; % of shipments nonconforming	Incoming inspection; accounting	Historical	Tabulation; narrative	Q

*Legend: D = daily; W = weekly; M = monthly; Q = quarterly.

6.39

PLANNING FOR QUALITY IMPROVEMENT

The approach used depends on what kind of quality is to be improved. The two major forms of "quality" consist of:

1. Quality in the sense of "those product features which meet the needs of customers and thereby provide product satisfaction." In general, improvement of this form of quality is done by following the quality planning road map as set out in this section. In effect, the quality improvement results from replanning.
2. Quality in the sense of freedom from deficiencies. In general, improvement of this form of quality is done by the process set out in Section 22, Quality Improvement.

For elaboration of the distinction between the two kinds of quality, see Section 2, under "Quality" Defined.

THE QUALITY MANUAL

A great deal of planning for quality is done with the aid of formal repetitive-use plans often called *systems* or *procedures*. Such procedures are thought out, written out, approved formally, and published to become the authorized, legitimate way of conducting the company's affairs relative to planning for quality. The subject matter of these quality plans ranges over the entire spectrum of the activities through which companies manage for quality. In many companies these plans are published collectively in a document known as a "quality manual" (also "quality assurance manual," "quality management requirements," etc.).

The basic objectives of such manuals are to provide the organization with plans which exhibit certain useful features:

Optimal: The plans are the result of multifunctional discussion and agreement.

Repetitive use: The plans reduce the need for repeated replanning.

Official: The plans are approved at the highest levels of organization.

Readily findable: The plans are assembled into a well-known reference source rather than being scattered among many memoranda, oral agreements, reports, minutes, etc.

Stable: The plans survive despite lapses in memory and employee turnover.

Terminology. Multiple-use plans are designated by various names. Quality plans for major multifunctional activities are sometimes called quality "systems" or "subsystems." Military and other governmental bodies have favored the term "program." At functional levels the plans may be called "methods," "procedures," or "routines." For major projects requiring tailor-made, single-use plans, the term may be "project plan." For informal plans, the term may be "practice."

Evolution of the Manual. The predecessors of an organized manual are a wide assortment of memoranda, instructions, marked prints, and other bits of information. These have multiple origins and end up in desk drawers, filing cabinets, people's heads, and wastebaskets. As these things multiply, so does the job of finding authoritative information. Finally a state is reached where the company concludes that a more orderly approach is needed.

The moving force for the first quality manual is usually the quality manager. In consequence, the first manual also tends to be mainly departmental in nature and to emphasize procedures for improving the effectiveness of the Quality Department rather than for optimizing company performance. However, as evolution proceeds, the manual tends to expand into all activities which affect managing for quality.

For some companies, the decisive factor in moving from a narrow-based to a broad-based manual has been a determined customer. One such customer has been the military. For example, the military specification MIL-Q-9585A, *Quality Program Requirements,* includes a provision as follows:

> "3.3 Work Instructions. The quality program shall insure that all work affecting quality . . . shall be prescribed in clear and complete documented instructions. . . . "

This specification is elaborated by setting out various specific requirements and criteria to be met by the quality plans. Other government buying and/or regulatory bodies similarly require that quality plans meet certain specified criteria, some of which are quite demanding.

During the 1980s some major industrial customers undertook to improve their quality in response to increased competition. As a part of their efforts to improve, they demanded improved quality from their suppliers. Those demands went beyond the quality of the products being purchased; the demands extended to the quality *plans* used by the suppliers. A widespread requirement was that the suppliers make use of statistical tools during their process controls (SPC). However, some major buyers established a broad array of requirements to be met by suppliers' quality plans, including use of SPC.

As the company grows and breaks up into divisions which are themselves autonomous businesses, the bulk of the quality plans are contained in divisional manuals. However, there evolves a corporate quality manual which contains corporate quality policies, corporate organization, interdivisional quality procedures, and other matters of a corporate or interdivisional nature.

A second moving force for evolution of a quality manual is a gathering dissatisfaction with quality planning which has been relying on all those scattered memoranda, oral agreements, and so on. Such dissatisfactions in due course culminate in an initiative (often by a quality manager) to create order by organizing an official quality manual.

For some case examples of evolution of a quality manual, see Murray (1976); also Holt (1976).

Contents of the Manual. The manual is usually organized into modular sections. Such an organization simplifies the job of maintaining the manual as well as providing for selective distribution of the modules.

General Sections. These deal with broad administration of the manual along with aids to its use. General sections include:

1. A statement by the general manager (or other high official). The statement includes a message relative to the significance of the manual. It sometimes makes some specific assignments of responsibility. It includes the signatures which confer legitimacy.

2. The purpose and the intended use of the manual and how to use it.

3. The table of contents.

4. The pertinent company (or divisional, etc.) quality policies. Often these may be incorporated by reference to the policy document. (See, in this connection, Section 5, under Quality Policies.)

5. The organization charts and tables of responsibility relative to the quality function. (See, in this connection, Section 7, Organization for Quality.)

6. The authorized distribution list for copies of the various modules.

7. Provision for keeping the manual up to date, e.g., periodic audits and scheduled reviews.

8. Supplementary aids for use of the manual. These may include a glossary of terms, a list of acronyms and their meanings, a list of materials referenced, and a bibliography. In some companies the manual includes sample copies of the principal forms cited by the manual, along with instructions for their use.

9. An index.

Managerial Sections. These sections, sometimes called "subsystems," exhibit a good deal of similarity from one company to another. Most manuals include a selection from the following:

Customer relations: Product safety, liability, recall; competitive quality evaluations; preparation of quality-oriented portions of bids for business; order entry process. (See Section 20, Customer Service.)

New-product "cradle to grave" quality planning: Phases or stages; product goals—reliability, mean time between failures, mean time to repair, warranties, etc; design review; model construction and test; software development and test; specifications; qualification testing; configuration and engineering change control. Management for software quality has emerged as a major new area requiring extensive data collection, analysis, and feedback. (See Section 13, Product Development.)

Manufacture: Producibility analysis, equipment specification and procurement, process capability analysis, prove-in of processes, pilot production runs, provisions for traceability. The expanded use of statistical process control (SPC) has expanded the use of quantified process capability as a basis for making decisions relative to manufacturing processes. (See Sections 16, Manufacturing Planning; 17, Production; and 24, Statistical Process Control.)

Supplier relations: Supplier surveys, qualification; quality provisions in purchase agreements; assistance to suppliers, feedback; incoming inspection, test; conversion to "just in time"; supplier rating; certification. (See Section 15, Supplier Relations.)

Inspection and test: Incoming, in-process, and final; visual and other sensory standards; feedback. (See Section 18, Inspection and Test.)

Test equipment: Design, procurement, reproducibility, checkout, calibration, maintenance. (Section 18.)

Nonconforming material: Identification; segregation; Material Review Board; corrective action. (See Section 18.)

Postmanufacture: Identification, packing, storage, transport, installation, checkout. (See Section 20, Customer Service.)

Field service: Service instructions; equipment, tools, manuals; evaluation of use, misuse; visits to dealers, users; analysis of returns, complaints, warranty charges, field failures; administration of warranties; spare-parts provision. (See Section 20.)

Quality assurance: Product audits; competitive ratings; audits of organization, plans (methods, procedures); audit of conformance to plans. (For elaboration, see Section 9, Quality Assurance; also Section 8, Upper Management and Quality.)

Quality-related costs: Classification of costs, collection of cost data (by estimate or from the accounting structure), analysis to find opportunities, reports on trends (see Section 4, Quality Costs).

Quality information system: Information requirements; data sources; data recording, summary, analysis, reporting.

Statistical methodology: Areas of application; statistical tools. (See Sections 23, 24, 25, and 26.)

Corrective action (for sporadic quality problems):   Identification of deviations, diagnosis of causes, restoring the status quo (see Section 22 under Troubleshooting).

Quality improvement (for chronic quality problems):   Project identification, diagnosis of causes, provision of remedies (see Section 22, Quality Improvement).

Human relations: Recruitment, selection; training, qualification, certification. (See Section 10, Managing Human Performance.)

Motivation for quality: Quality awareness, priority; participation in planning, problem identification, problem solving; responsibility for quality planning, control, improvement. (See Section 10.)

Technological Sections.   These deal with the numerous materials, processes, components, products, tests, and other elements which are special to the company. Usually these sections are intradepartmental in nature, and often the publications are not in the company manual but in separate departmental manuals.

"White-Collar" Processes.   Traditionally, quality and quality planning have been regarded as associated with factory-produced goods and factory processes. As a result, the quality manuals of the past have emphasized planning of processes directly associated with design and manufacture of goods.

During the 1980s there emerged a strong trend toward widening the concept of "quality" to include quality of services sold by service companies (see Section 33). This same trend has been extended to include the quality of the administrative and support operations (see Section 21) which contribute to a company's quality image: accuracy of invoices, adequacy of response to customers' inquiries (promptness, courtesy, satisfaction), and so on.

This trend appears to be irreversible. It can, therefore, be expected that quality manuals will increasingly devote attention to quality of administrative and support operations and will assume broader roles in service companies.

Distribution of the Manual.   If the manual is of a modular design, it becomes feasible to make distribution on a selective basis. Tables are prepared showing which organization units are to receive which modules.

Some companies design portions of the quality manual in ways which make them suitable for distribution to outsiders. For example, the module on supplier relations may be designed in a way which is suitable for distribution to suppliers. Other companies design a "showpiece" version of the quality manual to be sent to clients and prospective clients as a sales promotion device.

Provision for Audit.   Any well-designed plan includes provisions for reviewing results to determine whether the execution follows the plan. Sometimes these provisions are written into the plans themselves; for instance, the quality manual may stipulate that there shall be an annual review of execution versus plan. More usually, there is a separate "plan" for audit, sometimes informal, sometimes formal.

The term "audit" has multiple meanings. Applied to quality planning, two of these meanings are vital: (1) audit to determine whether the quality plans are adequate to achieve the quality goals of the company and (2) audit to determine whether the execution follows the plans. (For elaboration, see Section 9, Quality Assurance.)

Limitations of Quality Manuals as Predictors of Good Quality.   Quality manuals are a form of repetitive-use plans. When well prepared, they are the result of participation by those in interest and hence are likely to represent an optimum approach to planning for quality. Companies which prepare such manuals are likely to be armed with better plans, procedures, and so on than are companies which lack such manuals.

These proven values of quality manuals have stimulated many large buyers and regulators to establish criteria to be met by quality plans and procedures. These criteria are mandated in contracts with suppliers. Surveys (or assessments) are conducted to assure that the criteria are met by the conditions in suppliers' facilities and by the provisions in suppliers' quality manuals. Successful compliance is formally recognized—the successful supplier receives a documented status. This status puts the supplier on a favored list.

In some countries there are national standards which establish the criteria to be met by quality plans (e.g., in Great Britain BS 5750). In addition, there are officially designated agencies to conduct the assessments. In such situations a status of having successfully "passed" an assessment can become prerequisite to qualifying as a bidder for certain classes of contracts, such as military contracts. Aggressive promotion by the official assessment agencies can make this status so influential that companies are stimulated to undergo assessment for public relations purposes as well as for the inherent merits.

It does not follow that companies which score well in the assessment will surely deliver high-quality products. A company's top priority may be on some parameter other than quality, such as meeting the delivery schedule. The facilities may be inadequate to produce good quality. Employee training may be inadequate. Human relations, internal and/or external, may be adversarial amid an atmosphere of blame. In still other ways, companies with admirable plans and manuals may fail to deliver good quality. Conversely, there are many companies, with long records of having delivered good quality, whose quality manual, if any, would fail to pass an assessment. See Section 9 under Questions for Quality Surveys; Reference Standards for Surveys.

The assessments do evaluate the state of the procedures and of the written manual. However, there has been no well-researched study to discover the extent to which the results of the assessments correlate with the quality of the subsequent products. [One such research project revealed no correlation; see Brainard (1966).] For this reason, managers should be wary of assuming that the assessments are proven predictors of subsequent quality of product. As in the prediction of creditworthiness, the principal predictor of a supplier's quality is probably that supplier's previous quality performance on similar products.

GENERIC STANDARDS; INFLUENCE ON QUALITY PLANNING

The second half of the twentieth century witnessed an outpouring of generic standards for quality planning. Most of these standards were prepared and published by:

Large industrial buyers (e.g., original equipment manufacturing companies).

Large government buying agencies (e.g., defense departments). One such standard is the well-known MIL-Q-9858A.

Industry associations.

Standardization bodies. Examples of such standards are the U.S. American National Standards Institute standard ANSI Z1.15/1979 and the British standard BS5750.

Government regulatory bodies, usually those oriented to safety, health, and the environment.

Mandated and Advisory Generic Standards.   Some generic standards make compliance a prerequisite to the marketing of products. Generally, the generic standards published by large buyers and by government regulators are mandatory.

Advisory generic standards are "guidelines." They do not require compliance. However, in some cases failure to comply makes the product unmarketable, such as use of nonstandard voltages on appliances. In other cases, compliance becomes commercially necessary because compliance has become a tool for marketing.

Purposes of Generic Standards.   Generic standards evolve for much the same reasons as quality manuals (see the Quality Manual, above). There are some additonal reasons. Generic standards can be designed to serve the broader standardization needs inherent within industries, national economies, and multinational economies. Usually these broad-based generic standards are developed by broad-based committees which are able to enlist the experience and know-how of experts from the various impacted organs of society. The resulting published consensus is more likely to be accepted as a goal and as a reference base for any subsequent surveys (assessments) and the associated certification.

Evolution of Generic Quality Standards.   The evolutionary process begins with recognition of the need for a generic standard. A committee (or subcommittee, task force, working group, etc.) is formed to develop a standard in response to the need. In the case of standardization bodies, the committee is broad-based—it includes representatives from producers, users, government, and public-interest groups.

The working group prepares a draft which later is reviewed by the organization hierarchy of committees, agencies, and so on. In the case of government standards, the drafts are usually published, following which public hearings are held. The final draft is formally approved at the highest levels and is published as the official standard.

Adaptation to Diversity.   Standards can be designed to be generic, but the areas of application are quite diverse. One way of adapting to this diversity is to design multiple generic standards, each at a different "level" of requirements. For example, the U.S. Department of Defense publishes two such generic standards:

> MIL-Q-9858A, *Quality Program Requirements*
>
> MIL-I-45208A, *Inspection Systems Requirements*

The Canadian Standards Association Z299 series, *Quality Program Standards,* is published in four levels:

> CAN3-Z299.1-1985 *Quality Assurance Program—Category 1*
>
> CAN3-Z299.2-1985 *Quality Assurance Program—Category 2*
>
> CAN3-Z299.3-1985 *Quality Assurance Program—Category 3*
>
> CAN3-Z299.4-1985 *Quality Assurance Program—Category 4*

(See also Appendix III, "Selected Quality Standards, Sepcifications, and Related Documents.")

In practice, the buyers incorporate into the purchase contracts that level of generic standards judged to be appropriate for the specific application.

An additional way of dealing with diversity is through administrative regulations. For example, contracts involving relatively modest sums of money are often exempted from many of the requirements imposed on large contracts. [For a discussion, see Aboud (1980).]

A further approach is to "tailor" or adapt the requirements to the special nature of the contract. This tailoring is logically arrived at by discussion between buyer and contractor and can involve revision or waiver of provisions in the generic standards. [For elaboration, see Todt (1979) and Bell and Nicholson (1981).]

Adaptation is aided if there is a clear understanding of the markets and "environments" to be served. [For a discussion, see Marquardt (1982).]

Certification; Accreditation.   Many purchase contracts and regulations specify suppliers' compliance with generic quality standards. To assure compliance with such standards, use is made of various forms of assurance:

> Audit (assessment, survey, review) of the supplier's quality manual to assure that it corresponds adequately to the contract or the regulation
>
> Audit of operations to assure that they conform to the terms of the standards

These audits may be carried out by the buying organization, the regulatory organization, or some third party to whom the audits are subcontracted.

If the audits find that compliance is adequate, some written report or certificate is issued to formalize that finding.

Reliance on such audits requires assurance that the auditing process itself is adequate. To this end, many organizations establish an auditing manual which specifies the auditing procedures to be followed. Such procedures help to assure the completeness and uniformity of the audits. However, much must be left to the resourcefulness and judgment of the auditor.

The latter fact brings up an additional need—how to assure that the human auditors are qualified. Much of this assurance is based on informal criteria such as extent of education, length of experience, and extent of special training. In some cases, formal systems of accreditation are established, requiring successful completion of training courses and examinations. Such accreditation may be extended to suppliers' personnel under controlled conditions of certification.

For further elaboration, including third-party audits, see Section 9 under Quality Surveys.

WHO PLANS FOR QUALITY?

Prior to the rise of the Taylor system (see Juran, 1973), virtually all planning for operations in the United States, including planning for quality, was done by the operating managers, supervisors, and workers. The Taylor system (introduced early in the twentieth century) brought about a revolutionary separation of planning from execution. In due course this revolution spread to the quality function and resulted in the creation of quality specialists, principally in two specialist categories: (1) quality engineers, whose functions were associated with product quality in the factory, and (2) reliability engineers, whose functions were associated with product quality in the field.

These quality specialists did much to evolve concepts and tools which are essential aids to managing for quality. However, the operating managers and line specialists (design engineers, process engineers) were slow to adopt these aids. This lack of adoption was traceable in part to that same separation of planning from execution.

Meanwhile, during the second half of the twentieth century, Japanese industries surprised the Western world by taking over quality leadership in many important product lines. A distinguishing feature of the Japanese quality revolution was their approach to quality planning:

They assigned responsibility for quality planning mainly to the operating managers and line specialists.

They carried out massive training programs to enable the operating managers and line specialists to understand and use the new quality concepts and tools.

The Japanese results caused Western companies to reexamine their assignment of responsibility for quality planning. These companies then began to shift increasing amounts of this responsibility to the operating managers and line specialists, while providing the training needed to support such a change.

Influence of the Scope of the Planning.   The options for assigning responsibility for quality planning are influenced by the scope of the planning, mainly according to whether the planning is *inter*departmental or *intra*departmental in scope.

Interdepartmental Processes.   These processes link together various intradepartmental processes. Planning of an interdepartmental process requires some sort of interdepartmental organization. The forms most widely used are:

A team of line managers, called a "task force," "committee," etc.

A separate planning (or "staff") function which has responsibility to prepare a plan and then secure approval from the line managers

Intradepartmental Processes.   These processes involve multidepartmental tasks or operations. Responsibility for planning of such departmental processes is usually assigned to one or a combination of the following:

The same process planning office which has responsibility for planning of the interdepartmental process

A departmental process planner

The departmental supervision

Tasks and Operations.   Tasks and operations make up the base of the hierarchy of processes. At this level of the hierarchy the responsibility for process planning is usually assigned to one or a combination of the following:

A departmental process planner

A local supervisor

The work force

Allocation of Responsibilities.   When quality planning is done by staff specialists, it is common for the operating forces to be involved through some form of participation, such as design review. In addition, it is usual for the operating forces to have the final word as to the adequacy of the plan before it becomes effective. The arrangment can be depicted as follows:

	Operating forces	Staff specialists
Prepare the quality plan	X	X
Execute the plan	X	
Audit execution versus plan		X

Future Trends.   The trend is to delegate an increasing amount of the quality planning function to the operating people. The trend has been growing and is probably irreversible.

A major premise of the Taylor system was that the supervisors and workers of that day lacked the technological education needed to do planning. That premise was valid in Taylor's time, but it has since become invalid because of the dramatic rise in education levels. That rise has provided the operating forces with the educational base needed to accept increased responsibility for quality planning. However, the transfer of responsibility must be preceded by training in the concepts, skills, and tools of quality planning.

TOOLS FOR QUALITY PLANNERS

Quality planners have developed numerous tools through which the planning becomes economical as well as effective. Some of the major tools have been discussed as major topics in this section (e.g., the quality planning road map, the feedback loop, the quality manual). Subsidiary important tools include the flow digram (e.g., Figure 6.2), the quality planning spreadsheet (e.g., Figures 6.4, 6.5, and 6.6), and the responsibility matrix (e.g., Table 7.3). Additional tools are discussed in other sections of this handbook (e.g., design review, Section 13; process capability analysis, Section 16; project-by-project improvement, Section 22; quality cost analysis, Section 4; supplier surveys, Section 15).

Training in Use of the Tools. Whoever is to participate in quality planning should be trained in use of the quality planning tools. This training should go beyond education; the training should include solution of actual quality problems with the aid of the tools. For example, training in use of the feedback loop should include planning the work of some control station.

TRAINING FOR QUALITY PLANNERS

Historically, planning for quality was done by people (planners, operating managers, etc.) whose planning responsibility extended to multiple parameters, such as schedule, cost, and safety. Generally these people lacked expertise in how to plan for quality—they had never undergone special training in the subject. In some companies they had access to quality specialists (reliability engineers, quality engineers) who did have special training and expertise in planning for quality.

Since the early 1980s, the trend has been to increase the expertise of the planners and operating personnel by training them in how to plan for quality. This training has been taking place at all levels of the hierarchy.

Division of the subject matter into specific training courses (or modules) has varied among companies. An emerging pattern has been somewhat as described below.

Common Subject Matter. Certain elements of subject matter have been regarded as applicable to all categories of managers and specialists. These elements include the following: what is quality, effect of quality on sales, effect of quality on costs, external and internal customers, customer needs, the quality planning road map, the feedback loop for control, the universal sequence for quality improvement, measures of quality, quality cost analysis, basic problem-solving tools, quality audits, employee participation, and motivation for quality.

Specialized Subject Matter. Beyond the commonalities there are topics which are usually special to specific categories of personnel:

Upper management: Companywide quality management (CWQM), quality goals, deployment of quality goals, multifunctional planning to meet goals, allocation of resources, organizing for quality, broad measures of quality, motivation for quality.

Product development: Phase system; customer needs, competitive quality; safety analysis; failure-mode and effect analysis; reliability and maintainability analysis; value analysis; life cycle costing; design of experiment; producibility analysis, process capability, measurement capability; design review; lessons learned.

Process development: Design review; process environment; process capability; measurement capability, adjustment capability; design of experiment; feedback loop; statistical process control; self-control; human error, errorproofing.

Materials management: Supplier survey, selection; supplier relations; process capability; preproduction evaluation; data feedback, quality rating; just-in-time method; quality audit.

Production: Design review; process capability; measurement capability; adjustment capability; controllability (management or worker); feedback loop;

statistical process control; self-control; human error, errorproofing; trouble-shooting.

Marketing: Field intelligence, field performance, competitive performance, complaint analysis, warranty analysis, product liability, life cycle cost, phase system of product development, design review.

Customer service: Field environment; product safety; field operation, economy; field maintenance; customer use, misuse; data feedback.

Quality assurance: All the above; quality manuals, quality audits, quality reports.

Training for Suppliers. In general, suppliers to large clients must eventually train their personnel to the same level of expertise as is done by those clients for their internal sources of supply. However, there is a time lag. Clients who feel that new levels of training are needed will first train their own people. Subsequently, they urge similar training for suppliers' personnel.

In critical cases this urge is a mandate—the specifications require the use of certificated personnel. In less than critical cases the supplier survey may include evaluation of the state of training as an essential parameter.

An approach short of a mandate has been to offer "scholarships" for suppliers' personnel to attend training courses conducted by the client company. This approach emerged during the growth period of "statistical process control."

Training for Clients. This training has long been done with respect to use of the product. In part, this is carried out by the product literature: owners' manuals and instructions for operation and maintenance. In part, the training is done during product installation and maintenance. Still other forms are training courses and seminars conducted by marketing and customer service personnel with backup by experts in the technology.

An emerging trend is to provide a consulting service to assist clients in efficient use of the product. In many companies such consulting is already being done by technical representatives and/or customer service representatives, but on an informal basis. To expand such consulting (and use it as a marketing tool), it is necessary to summarize the knowledge acquired through prior customer contact and identify the "lessons learned." These lessons learned then become the basis for enlarged consultation, seminars, and other forms of training.

The Quality School. In very large companies it is customary to maintain an in-house capability—a "school"—for training of all sorts. During the 1980s these schools were faced with responding to a rapidly growing demand for training in managing for quality. Some of the schools responded to the demand by creating a special quality-oriented school to establish the needed curricula and to offer courses to company personnel.

REFERENCES

Aboud, George M., Sr. (1980). "DoD Procurement Quality Requirements (ASPR)." *ASQC Technical Conference Transactions,* Milwaukee, pp. 771–782.

Bell, L. Ferris and Nicholson, Richard H. (1981). "Tailoring Quality Systems for Program Requirements." *ASQC Quality Congress Transactions,* Milwaukee, pp. 263–278.

Bemesderfer, John L. (1979). "Approving a Process for Production." *Journal of Quality Technology,* January, pp. 1–12.

Bhote, Keki R. (1985). "C.W.Q.C.: A New Horizon for American Management." *ASQC Quality Congress Transactions,* Milwaukee, pp. 552–557.

Brainard, Edgar H. (1966). "Just How Good Are Vendor Surveys?" *Quality Assurance,* August, pp. 22–25.

Brunetti, Wayne (1986). "Policy Development—A Corporate Roadmap," *The Juran Report,* No. 8, pp. 20–29.

Caplan, Frank (1980). *The Quality System,* Chilton, Radnor, PA

Caplan, Frank (1984). "Managing for Success through the Quality System." *ASQC Quality Congress Transactions,* Milwaukee, pp. 10–21.

Coonley, Howard and Agnew, P. G. (1941). *The Role of Standards in the System of Free Enterprise.* American National Standards Institute, New York.

Cound, Dana M. (1965). "Quality System Analysis—Key to Recurring Cost Reduction." *ASQC Technical Conference Transactions,* Milwaukee, pp. 109–115.

Follett, Mary Parker (1941). Report in Metcalf, H. C. and Urwick, L. (Eds.), *Dynamic Administration.* Harper & Row, New York.

George, William W. (1977). "Task Teams for Rapid Growth." *Harvard Business Review,* March-April, pp. 71–80.

Goree, Paul F. and Musson, Thomas A. (1984). "DOD/Industry—R&M Case Study Analysis." *Proceedings, Annual Reliability and Maintainability Symposium.* IEEE, New York, pp. 91–98.

"Grinding Wheel Quality Improvement Hints." (1977). *Quality,* April, p. 44.

Gulliver, Frank R. (1987). "Post-Project Appraisals Pay." *Harvard Business Review,* March-April, pp. 128–132.

Hartz, Ove (1982). "Quality Management and Cooperation in Small Firms." *Quality Progress,* April, pp. 18–21.

Heskett, James L. (1987). "Lessons in the Service Sector." *Harvard Business Review,* March-April 1987, pp. 118–126.

Heslop, S. (1981). "Practical Experience in Implementing Quality Assurance in a Small Business." *Quality Assurance,* vol. 7, no. 1, March, pp. 10–14.

Hill, Hubert M. and Sorrell, D. Lynn (1985). "Designing a Quality Assurance System for Information Systems." *ASQC Quality Congress Transactions,* Milwaukee, pp. 416–421.

Holt, J. (1976). "Elaboration and Implementation of a Quality Control System in Nordisk Ventilator Co. A/S." *EOQC Proceedings, Copenhagen.* EOQC, Berne, Switzerland, pp. 65–75.

Ingram, Gary E. (1984). "Historical Processes for Quality Project Management." *Project Management Institute Proceedings,* Philadelphia, pp. 1–3.

Juran, J. M. (1964). *Managerial Breakthrough.* McGraw-Hill, New York.

Juran, J. M. (1988). *Juran on Planning for Quality.* Free Press, New York.

Juran, J. M. (1973). "The Taylor System and Quality Control." A series of articles in *Quality Progress,* May 1973 through December 1973 (listed under "Mangement Interface").

Juran, J. M. (1977). "Quality and Its Assurance—an Overview." *Second NATO Symposium on Quality and Its Assurance.* North Atlantic Treaty Organization, London.

Juran, J. M. (1986). *Planning for Quality.* Juran Institute, Wilton, CT.

Juran Institute (1987). *Juran on Quality Planning* (videocassette series). Juran Institute, Wilton, CT.

Kano, Noriaki (1984). "Problem Solving in New Product Development—Application of T-Typed Matrix." *World Quality Congress Proceedings,* vol. 3. EOQC, Berne, Switzerland, pp. 45–55.

Karabatsos, Nancy (1983). "Quality is Instrumental at Steinway." *Quality,* October, pp. 19–22.

Kofoed, Carl A. (1982). "The Integration Phase." *ASQC Quality Congress Transactions,* Milwaukee, pp. 433–440.

Kohoutek, Henry J. (1983). "Commitment to Quality through a Strategic Plan." *ASQC Quality Congress Transactions,* Milwaukee, pp. 82–86.

Kolacek, O. G. (1978). "So, You Are Going to Have A Quality Assurance Department!" *Proceedings, ICQC '78.* Japanese Union of Scientists and Engineers, Tokyo, pp. C1-45 through C1-50.

Lange, Henry N. (1978). "QA for Small Programs in a Large Industry." *ASQC Technical Conference Transactions,* Milwaukee, pp. 314–320.

Lewis, Wyatt H. (1964). "Design of a Quality System for a Business." *ASQC Convention Transactions,* Milwaukee, pp. 257–259.

Livni, Haim (1985). "Quality Assurance of Technical Specifications." *ASQC Quality Congress Transactions,* Milwaukee, pp. 523–528.

Marquardt, Donald W. (1982). "Comparison of Multi-Level and Generic Standards." *ASQC Quality Congress Transactions,* Milwaukee, pp. 244–248.

Maytag, Fritz (1986). "The Joys of Keeping the Company Small." *Harvard Business Review,* July-August, pp. 6–14 and ES14.

Müller, A. (1971). "Quality Assurance during Manufacturing Engineering Phase." *Quälitat und Zuverlässigkeit,* vol. 16, no. 2, February, pp. 27–32.

Murray, David J. (1976). "The Introduction of a Quality Manual in a Multi-Factory Paint Company." *EOQC Proceedings, Copenhagen.* EOQC, Berne, Switzerland, pp. 207–215.

Norton, Chris E. and Mason, Don L. (1987). "Quality during Transition Construction to Operation." *ASQC Energy Division Newsletter,* Milwaukee, March, pp. 3, 4.

Olsbro, Bertil (1976). "Quality Assurance System for Telephone Equipment." *EOQC Proceedings, Copenhagen.* EOQC, Berne, Switzerland, pp. 169–177.

Roche, J. G. and Sheil, J. (1984). "Quality Practices in Small Manufacturing Firms." *1984 World Quality Congress.* EOQC, Berne, pp. 346–361.

Scanlon, Frank and Hagan, John T. (1982). "Improved Productivity through Quality Management." *ASQC Quality Congress Transactions,* Milwaukee, pp. 491–505.

Taguchi, Genichi (1978). "Off-Line and On-Line Quality Control Systems." *Proceedings, ICQC '78.* Japanese Union of Scientists and Engineers, Tokyo, pp. B4-1 through B4-5.

Todt, Howard C. (1979). "Tailored Requirements for Quality Programs." *ASQC Technical Conference Transactions,* Milwaukee, pp. 608–613.

Veraldi, L. C. (1985). "The Team Taurus Story," MIT Conference paper, Chicago, Aug. 22. Center for Advanced Engineering Study, MIT, Cambridge, MA.

Wilborn, Walter (1978). "Quality Audits in Support of Small Business." *ASQC Technical Conference Transactions,* Milwaukee, pp. 179–185, 979–980.

Wilhelm, W. C. (1980). "Quality Program Modeling for Cost Effective Tailoring." *ASQC Technical Conference Transactions,* Milwaukee, pp. 648–655.

SECTION 7
ORGANIZING FOR QUALITY

J. M. Juran

**BUILDING THE ORGANIZATION
STRUCTURE** 7.2

**QUALITY MANAGEMENT WORK
ELEMENTS AND JOBS** 7.3

Assignment of
Responsibility 7.5

Structuring Jobs 7.5

A Major Trend in
Assignment of
Responsibility 7.6

**NONTRADITIONAL QUALITY-
ORIENTED WORK ELEMENTS** . . 7.7

Commonalities 7.7

Another Major Trend . . . 7.8

Impact on Job Structure . . 7.8

**EVOLUTION OF THE QUALITY
MANAGEMENT HIERARCHY** . . 7.8

A Humble Origin 7.9

Organization for Inspection 7.9

Organization for Prevention 7.9

Organization for Assurance 7.10

Proliferation of Quality
Function Activities . . . 7.10

THE QUALITY MANAGER . . . 7.13

The Plant Quality Manager 7.13

The Division Quality
Manager 7.16

The Corporate Quality
Manager 7.18

Why Quality Managers Fail 7.21

**COORDINATION OF THE
QUALITY FUNCTION** 7.21

The Common Boss 7.22

Self-Coordination 7.22

Committees 7.22

Written Procedure 7.22

Precedent 7.23

Staff Departments 7.23

Project Manager 7.23

The "Owner" 7.23

Matrix Organizations . . . 7.23

Crisis-by-Crisis
Coordination 7.23

Tools for Coordination . . 7.24

**COORDINATION AMONG
DIVISIONS** 7.24

Responsibility Matrix . . . 7.25

STAFF QUALITY ACTIVITIES . . 7.25

Examples of Staff Quality
Activities 7.25

Life Cycle of a Staff Quality
Activity 7.28

STAFF QUALITY DEPARTMENTS 7.28

Quality Control
Engineering 7.28

Reliability Engineering . . 7.29

Interface among Staff
Quality Specialties . . . 7.29

Other Specialties; Staff-Staff
Conflicts 7.30

ADMINISTRATION OF THE
QUALITY STAFF SPECIALTY . . **7.30**
   Perceptions 7.30
   Transfers from Staff to Line 7.31
   Budgeting 7.31
   Reports on Staff Quality
      Activities 7.31

Introducing Change 7.32
Other Staff-Line
   Relationships 7.32
Careers, Training, and
   Professionalism for
   Quality Staff Specialists . 7.32
REFERENCES **7.33**

"Organizing" as used in this section is the process of getting work done by human beings. The organizing process consists of two major activities:

1. Designing the organization *structure*—defining the work to be done and the hierarchical responsibility for doing it. This activity is the subject of this section.
2. Recruiting, training, and motivating the personnel—the inhabitants of the structure. This activity is discussed in Section 10, Managing Human Performance, and Section 11, Training for Quality.

BUILDING THE ORGANIZATION STRUCTURE

The basic building block of the organization is the operation (also called "function," "task," "work element," etc.). An operation is an identifiable type of activity such as edit, assemble, or transport. Many operations are carried out by human beings; others are carried out by nonhuman means. Collectively, the operations carried out by human beings make up the human "work pile."

The organizing process consists of six basic steps:

1. Identify the operations which need to be performed.
2. Assign responsibility for doing these operations, whether to internal or external agencies.
3. Divide the total work pile into logical parcels of work, called "jobs." In general, a job consists of a collection of one or more operations, so chosen that it is feasible to recruit or train people to carry out that collection.
4. Define the responsibilities and authorities associated with each job.
5. Define the relationships of each job to other jobs. These relationships include:
   a. The hierarchical relationship, i.e., the chain of command
   b. The communication and coordination patterns through which interdepartmental activities join to carry out specific purposes
6. Orchestrate the work of the internal and external agencies so that the company's mission is carried out in an optimum manner.

QUALITY MANAGEMENT WORK ELEMENTS AND JOBS

Many of the operations performed in the company directly impact the salability of the company's goods and services. The literature of managing for quality has often referred to these operations as "quality control work elements." In view of the trends in use of the word "control," these operations will be referred to as "quality management work elements."

Some of these work elements have traditionally been carried out by the various functional "line" departments:

Work element	Assigned to
Choose design tolerance	Product Design
Establish process capable of meeting tolerance	Process Engineering
Measure product to determine whether production process is in control	Production
Remedy field failure of products under warranty	Customer Service

This table represents only a small sample. Additional such work elements are discussed in the various functional Sections 12 through 21 of this handbook.

In the United States, other quality management work elements have traditionally been assigned to special departments which are oriented full-time to the quality function. (Such departments are variously called "Quality Management," "Quality Assurance," "Quality Control," etc.) The following list includes those principal work elements which have usually been assigned to such departments.

1. *Broad administration of the quality function.* This involves the following tasks:
   a. Draft quality policies.
   b. Develop major quality objectives.
   c. Develop plans for meeting quality objectives.
   d. Develop the organization structure for carrying out the plans.
   e. Design the system of product quality rating, quality audits, and summarized reports needed to provide quality assurance to upper management.
   f. Conduct quality audits; prepare and issue summarized reports on quality.
2. *Launching new products.* This involves the following tasks:
   a. Study customer needs for quality-oriented parameters.
   b. Review previous performance of similar products to identify chronic problems in manufacture, test, and usage.
   c. Conduct reliability analysis. (This consists of a whole array of work elements: modeling, apportionment, prediction, etc.)
   d. Conduct design review for various quality-oriented purposes: producibility, maintainability, etc.
   e. Establish test programs to evaluate materials, processes, and products.
   f. Conduct inspections and tests of trial production.
   g. Estimate quality costs for bid proposals and for new designs.

3. *Supplier quality relations.*   This involves the following tasks:
   a. Prepare the supplier relations quality manual: policies, methods, and procedures.
   b. Prepare the plan for conducting supplier quality surveys.
   c. Conduct surveys of prospective suppliers to judge quality capability.
   d. Maintain quality surveillance of suppliers.
   e. Assist suppliers through seriousness classifications, measurement cross-check, training, etc.
   f. Conduct inspection and test of supplier shipments; provide data feedback.
4. *Manufacture.*   This involves the following tasks:
   a. Evaluate quality capability of processes.
   b. Design plans for process control: choice of control stations, definition of control activities, data feedback system, etc.
   c. Conduct process surveillance.
   d. Analyze out-of-control conditions; follow up to secure corrective action.
   e. Design methods for evaluating quality performance of production units.
   f. Prepare and publish quality ratings.
5. *Inspection and test.*   This involves the following tasks:
   a. Design the inspection and test plan; choose control stations; define work to be done at each station.
   b. Prepare supplementary standards and criteria as needed, e.g., standards for sensory qualities; standardize test procedures.
   c. Prepare inspection manuals, systems, and procedures.
   d. Prepare inspection job specifications; recruit, select, and train inspectors.
   e. Conduct inspections and tests in accordance with the plan.
   f. Investigate causes of sporadic defects; report findings; follow up for corrective action.
   g. Initiate action to dispose of nonconforming product.
   h. Prepare and report summaries of results of inspection in appropriate ways: by product, by component, by process, by department responsible, by operator, etc.
   i. Provide for measurement of inspector accuracy.
6. *Metrology.*   This involves the following tasks:
   a. Design gages, instruments, and test equipment.
   b. Construct or purchase measuring equipment.
   c. Maintain calibration of measuring equipment.
   d. Design and administer systems for ensuring maintenance of precision of measuring equipment.
7. *Customer relations.*   This involves the following tasks:
   a. Test finished products. Evaluate adequacy for customer needs.
   b. Evaluate effect of activities which follow final product test: packing, shipping, transport, and storage.
   c. Analyze customer quality complaints, warranty charges, and returns; recommend corrective action.

   d. Evaluate customer experience with product performance; identify the opportunities presented.

   e. Analyze competitors' products relative to customer needs.

   f. Identify customer needs for quality-oriented assistance; develop responsive plans.

8. *Consulting and training services.* This involves the following tasks:

   a. Analyze costs of poor quality; identify major opportunities for improvement.

   b. Stimulate creation of companywide approaches to quality improvement.

   c. Provide consulting services: analysis of chronic quality problems, reliability analysis, data collection and analysis, and design of experiments.

   d. Design and conduct training courses in various quality-oriented skills and tools.

Published lists of quality management work elements are usually limited to brief statements of each element. However, some lists provide good elaboration of what is meant by the brief statements. The list published by the American Society for Quality Control (1961) is oriented toward a concept of a "profession" of quality engineering, and this orientation has influenced the choice of elements to enter the list.

Assignment of Responsibility. The quality management work elements may be assigned to various categories of organization units:

1. Functional "line" departments such as Product Development, Manufacture, and Customer Service.

2. Inspection and Test Departments. These departments carry out much of the work of product inspection and test.

3. Quality "staff" departments. The work elements of these departments are mainly planning, analysis, and assurance, and are assigned to quality specialists such as Quality Engineers.

4. Outside agencies. Some work elements are assigned to be performed by suppliers, customers, third-party auditors, and still others.

Choice of which organization unit is to receive which assignment depends on:

1. The extent to which these units have been trained (or are willing to be trained) to perform the work elements.

2. The prior record of initiative or resistance of these units in responding to new ways.

3. The traditions with respect to separating planning from execution and the use of staff versus line. These traditions have a built-in momentum and vary remarkably among companies, industries, and nations.

4. The volume of work. As the company grows in size and complexity, the staff activities tend to proliferate.

Structuring Jobs. A job is the "bundle of work" assigned to one person. The bundle may consist solely of a single quality-related work element (e.g., inspect, test). In such cases the job title usually is descriptive of the work element being performed (e.g., Inspector, Tester).

In other cases the job consists solely of a mixture of quality-related work elements. Such jobs carry a broader title (e.g., Quality Engineer).

In most cases the job consists of multiple work elements of which only a minority are quality-oriented. In such cases the job title reflects the core responsibilities of the jobholder (e.g., Product Designer, Process Engineer, Customer Service Representative, Order Entry Clerk, Machinist).

While jobs are structured with a view toward stability and toward fitting into a career pattern, the elements which make up the job are not stable. The advance of technology creates new elements and renders old ones obsolete. In addition, elements are frequently transferred from one job to another. For instance, with the development of a simplified instrument, a test which once could be performed only by specialists in a laboratory may be conducted by production workers. The task of computing mean time between failures, previously performed by reliability engineers, may be assigned to designers following a training program.

Because of the mobility and mortality of work elements, there are constant discussions on how to make the assignment. For example, the work element "design test equipment" might logically be assigned to a line manager (Inspection Supervisor), an existing staff specialist (Quality Engineer), or a new staff specialist (Test Equipment Engineer). The choice depends as much on the record of each department in carrying out its assignments to date as on organization theory. Managers tend to give assignments to persons who have demonstrated the ability to achieve results. As a corollary, managers do not assign new duties to persons whose records are mediocre, no matter how "logical" it would appear on the organization chart. If necessary, related duties will be divided, new departments created, and organization charts distorted rather than giving important new duties to persons who have a record of poor performance.

A Major Trend in Assignment of Responsibility.   During the 1980s there emerged in the United States a major trend toward assigning quality management work elements to the functional line departments rather than the Quality Departments. For example:

> Responsibility for reliability analysis began to shift from Reliability Engineers (in the Quality Department) to Design Engineers in Product Development.

> Responsibility for evaluation of process capability began to shift from quality engineers (in the Quality Department) to Process Engineers, Production Supervisors, and production workers in quality control circles.

> Responsibility for design of experiments and analysis of variance began to shift from engineers in the Quality Department to engineers in the functional line departments.

Necessarily, such shifts in responsibility must be preceded by training to qualify the line personnel to be able to perform the newly assigned work. This training has, in fact, also emerged as a major trend.

This trend is a result of the need to increase the expertise used in carrying out the quality-related work elements. Generally the line personnel lacked this expertise because of lack of training. The Quality Department personnel generally had the expertise but lacked the authority to apply it. A joint effort was needed, but some formidable obstacles stood in the way:

> Not being trained or experienced in the use of quality-oriented skills and tools, line personnel lacked awareness of the potential aid to their own traditional responsibilities such skills and tools can provide.

The functional line departments were faced with meeting multiple parameters (schedule, cost, productivity, etc.) in addition to quality. Hence they perceived the quality specialists as special pleaders and advocates for just one of those parameters.

The careers of line personnel were linked to their traditional core discipline (e.g., metallurgy, machine tools) and not to expertise in quality-related skills and tools.

The prevailing merit rating system enforced this same career orientation.

As of the late 1980s, this trend (to assign quality management work elements to the line personnel) has been gaining in momentum and has probably become irreversible.

NONTRADITIONAL QUALITY-ORIENTED WORK ELEMENTS

Few operations directly impact product salability; however, they do impact customers, both external and internal. (*Every* operation produces products of some sort and sends these products on to customers of some sort.)

For example, the process for producing invoices impacts clients as well as internal customers. If invoices are incorrect, the clients endure additional expense and irritation. They publicize the errors not only to the producing company but also to the community, the press, the regulators, and others. The errors may not significantly impact the company's sales, but they damage the company's image as a "quality house." In addition, the errors are costly. It takes work to resolve them, and payment of the invoices is delayed in the process.

In other cases the operations impact clients indirectly. For example, a product design has salable product features but turns out to lack producibility—the available processes are unable to meet the tolerances. In such a case the operation (product design) has produced a product—a design—which does not meet the needs of internal customers. In addition, there are side effects: The resulting delay may cause the loss of some of the potential market, the added costs reduce the profit margin, internal harmony is disrupted, and so on.

In still other cases the operations do not impact external customers at all but do impact internal customers. Examples are the operations which produce employee records or various internal control reports.

Commonalities. All the preceding examples have certain commonalities:

The operations are regular company operations.

The resulting products are not sold to produce the company's income.

Some of the products are deficient.

The deficiencies do not necessarily impact company income.

The deficiencies do cause damage in various forms: higher costs, delays, and irritation.

The deficiencies also damage the company's quality image.

During the 1980s there emerged a new awareness relative to the extent of these deficiencies. It became evident that the damage done by these deficiencies was huge—as large as that associated with factory operations. In response to this finding, much analysis was done to discover the causes of the deficiencies. (See, generally, Section 22, Quality Improvement; also Section 21, Administrative and Support Operations.)

To a large extent the causes were found to be traceable to the original planning of the operations. In turn, the original planning was found to be deficient largely because of the lack of quality planning expertise on the part of the functional department planners. The needed remedies paralleled those for improving quality planning for the "conventional" quality management work elements. (See above, under A Major Trend in Assignment of Responsibility.)

Another Major Trend.   From the findings described above, a dramatic shift in viewpoint and assignment of responsibility for those nontraditional quality work elements has begun to emerge. The shift in viewpoint is to apply the word "quality" to describe the performance of those nontraditional work elements and the resulting products, such as quality of the invoicing process and quality of the invoices. This same shift has widened the perception of the scope of "quality."

The reasons for this shift are rooted in two massive trends: (1) the growing importance of quality to society generally (see Section 34, Impact of Quality on Society) and (2) the intensified competition in quality.

The word "quality" has long had the connotation of something which is good; with the increasing importance of the quality function, the word "quality" has become a useful banner as well. Companies which want to introduce some important change are aided if they can introduce the change under the banner of quality.

Impact on Job Structure.   The main method chosen to upgrade quality for the nonconventional work elements has been to train the functional department personnel in the skills and tools of managing for quality. This approach parallels the trend in progress with respect to the conventional work elements, but with a difference—there is nothing to undo. Previously, the central quality departments were not involved with the nontraditional work elements.

The needed increases in quality expertise have an impact on the job descriptions for the functional line planners. The job requirements expand to include training and experience in quality-oriented skills and tools. The training needs are correspondingly impacted, as are the criteria for qualification. In addition, the merit rating systems are revised to give greater weight to the quality parameter.

In some companies the need to increase quality-related expertise has resulted in creation of new posts within the functional departments (e.g., Director of Quality for the Marketing Department or for the Customer Service Department). These new posts are intended to provide, for those functional departments, the same array of services that quality managers have traditionally provided for the company in general: quality planning, consulting, training, and auditing.

EVOLUTION OF THE QUALITY MANAGEMENT HIERARCHY

Any major industrial function acquires recognition in the form of status on the organization chart and leadership from a member of the management team. During the twentieth century, the quality function attained this status through an evolution which is still in progress.

A Humble Origin. The quality function has emerged from humble origins. From time immemorial, human activity has had the responsibility of meeting multiple needs, including the quality needs of customers. Village crafts people had this responsibility. With the rise of factories, the production departments had this same responsibility.

Under the influence of the Taylor system (Juran, 1973), the emphasis on the productivity parameter increased at the expense of the emphasis on quality. In response, the upper managers created the central Inspection Department which later became the nucleus of a separate quality function.

Organization for Inspection. The early Inspection Department was oriented to quality of goods and of factory processes. It consisted mainly of a hierarchy of inspection supervisors to direct the work of the scattered inspectors. The hierarchy of these supervisors ascended to the new post of Chief Inspector, whose authority also extended to auxiliary activities such as the measurement laboratory and the disposition of nonconforming products.

With the creation of the Inspection Department, it was also necessary to address the issue of whom the Inspection Department should report to. The usual solution was to make it responsible to the factory manager, although there were variations in detail.

In the United States, the concept of the central Inspection Department was widely adopted in the two decades following World War I. By the early 1940s, the majority of industrial companies had adopted it.

For additional discussion, see Section 18, Inspection and Test, under Organization for Inspection and Test.

Organization for Prevention. World War II required industry to make a drastic shift from civilian to military production. Many companies encountered problems in meeting delivery schedules, and a major obstacle was failure to meet quality specifications. It became dramatically evident that what was missing was the means for preventing defects from occurring in the first place.

Quality Control Engineering. After some experimentation, in the 1950s a new department was created to conduct quality planning and analysis, especially for defect prevention. This department came to be known as Quality Control Engineering.

It became necessary to locate the new department somewhere on the organizational tree. To do this, there was created a new post of Quality Manager (or Quality Control Manager) to which the Chief Inspector, the new department (Quality Control Engineering), and the associated services now reported.

The process industries evolved differently. In these industries, inspection for nonfunctional qualities (e.g., appearance) had commonly been done by inspectors responsible to the Production Department. However, the functional testing and the process controls had commonly been done by a laboratory which was responsible to the Technical Department. In consequence, when the new departments of Quality Control Engineering were created in the process industries, they were located in the Technical Department, the precise location being either (1) reporting to the manager of Process Development or (2) reporting to a newly created post of Quality Manager, to whom the traditional laboratory also reported.

Reliability Engineering. During the 1950s a number of companies were faced with new problems of designing and building complex systems to levels of reliability well beyond the usual practice. Traditional approaches to product development and design soon proved inadequate—the field failure rates were unacceptable. One consequence was the rise of a new type of specialist known as a "reliability engineer." These engineers recommended that a separate department be created for them, and the managers usually accepted this recommendation. The activities of this department are discussed below, under Staff Quality Departments.

Organization for Assurance. The term "assurance" is used here in the limited sense of determining with confidence that the company's quality mission is being well carried out.

The managers of small enterprises secured this assurance from personal contact, such as personal examination of the products and processes. As the enterprises grew, this personal contact was delegated to intermediate supervisors and to inspectors, thereby depriving the upper managers of "assurance through personal observation." For many years, the upper managers derived their assurance from their confidence in these supervisors and inspectors, but without creating a substitute for the former "independent" assurance (through personal observation). However, it became progressively evident that some form of independent assurance was essential, so a search began for new forms of such assurance.

One form of such assurance now in wide use requires prior preparation of detailed quality plans plus subsequent reviews and audits to establish that the plans are (1) adequate and (2) being followed. The organization structure through which this is accomplished is as follows:

| | | Staff quality departments | |
Activities	Line departments	Quality planning	Quality assurance
Prepare the quality plans	X	X	
Execute the plans	X		
Audit to determine whether the execution follows the plans			X

Use of this plan of delegation retains for the line departments the full command of their personnel while providing for independent reviews of plans and execution.

For additional discussion, see generally Section 9, Quality Assurance, and Section 8, Upper Management and Quality, under Quality Audits by Upper Managers and under Executive Reports on Quality.

Figure 7.1 shows one of the forms of organizational structure widely adopted during the 1950s.

Proliferation of Quality Function Activities. Once established, the Inspection Department and its successor, the Quality Department, began to acquire an increasing number of functions. The actual assignments have varied remarkably from company to company. Table 7.1 lists a typical sequence of evolution of activities assigned to quality departments.

Some distinct trends are evident from Table 7.1. These trends are summarized in Table 7.2.

TABLE 7.1 Activities Assigned to Quality Departments

Activities	Usual responsibility							See Section
	Analysis	Planning	Consulting	Coordinating	Execution	Audit	Assurance	
Inspection of factory goods: final; in process; supplier		X			X			18
Measurement control		X			X			18
Factory process control		X			X			17
Statistical process control		X			X			24
Inspection planning		X			X			18
Analysis of causes of defects	X		X					22
Field complaint analysis	X		X					20
Supplier surveillance	X	X			X		X	15
Self-control by workers	X	X						17
Self-inspection by workers		X				X		17
Analysis of cost of poor quality	X			X				4
Defect prevention		X	X	X				22
New-product reviews	X		X					13

TABLE 7.1 Activities Assigned to Quality Departments (*Continued*)

Activities	Analysis	Planning	Consulting	Coordinating	Execution	Audit	Assurance	See Section
				Usual responsibility				
Motivation for quality	X		X					10
Quality assurance		X			X			9
Product safety; liability	X			X		X		34
Environmental impact	X		X			X		34
Consumerism movement	X		X					34
Government regulation	X		X			X		34
Impact of quality on sales income	X		X					3
Annual quality improvement		X		X			X	22
Companywide quality management		X		X			X	6
Executive reports on quality		X		X			X	8
Training for quality	X	X	X					11

TABLE 7.2 Trends Relative to Quality-Oriented Activities

Early orientation	Trends in orientation
Inspection; detection	Planning; prevention
Factory goods	Goods and services
Conformance to specification	Fitness for customer use
Factory processes	All processes
Empiricism	Statistical methodology
Separation of planning from execution	Participation
Adversary relationship with suppliers	Teamwork relationship
Training of quality specialists	Training for all
Technology	Business: sales, costs
Clients	All customers: external; internal
Factorywide	Companywide

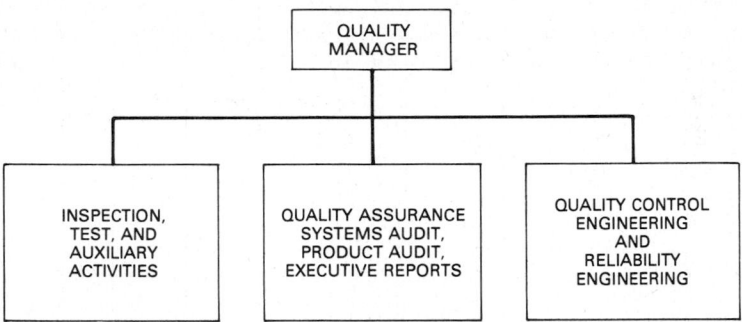

FIG. 7.1 Organization form widely adopted during the 1950s.

THE QUALITY MANAGER

The proliferation of quality-oriented activities has also given rise to a proliferation in job titles and associated responsibilities for persons appointed to head quality-oriented activities. A common generic title is Quality Manager, but there are other titles as well, such as Director of Quality. These Quality Managers are found at various levels in the hierarchy. During the 1980s Quality Managers also began to emerge in such functions as marketing and customer service.

The Plant Quality Manager. The term "Plant Quality Manager" refers to a Quality Manager who is resident in a plant (a factory) which, in turn, is part of a multiplant division. (In a single-plant division it is usual for the same person to serve as both Plant Quality Manager and Division Quality Manager.)

The Conformance Role. The basic role of the Plant Quality Manager is to determine product conformance to specification. To this end the manager establishes the laboratories and facilities needed for product inspection and test. The manager also recruits and trains inspectors and technicians to evaluate the product and make the conformance decisions. Borderline and debatable issues come to the manager for resolution. This role of determining conformance applies to all stages of progression of the product within the plant: incoming, in-process, and final.

Under appropriate conditions the work of determining conformance to specification can be delegated to production personnel. See Section 17, Production, under Self-Inspection.

The Role in Cases of Nonconformance.   Each nonconformance requires a new decision: what the disposition of that nonconforming product should be. Decisions to repair or scrap are usually within the jurisdiction of the Plant Quality Manager. However, the optimum disposition may be to use as is: That is, the product may be fit for use despite the nonconformance. [For further discussion, see Sears (1983).]

The Plant Quality Manager participates in the fitness-for-use decision by providing such information as the nature of the nonconformance, the amount of product involved, and the cost of scrap or rework. However, the manager is normally *not* provided with the personnel needed to collaborate with other departments to study such issues as what the client's use of the product will be, what the dangers to society are, and what the urgency is. More usually these matters are studied by divisional personnel, after which they inform the plant of their decisions.

Some buyers mandate the use of material review boards for dealing with nonconforming products. In such cases the Plant Quality Manager is usually a member of the Material Review Board.

In some regulated industries (e.g., nuclear, pharmaceutical) the regulations mandate that nonconformances be recorded and reported to the authorities.

Chronic cases of nonconformance can result in severe pressures on quality managers. The causes of such chronic cases are usually in the system, that is, the product-process planning is inadequate. As a result, Production is unable to produce conforming product. Yet there are schedules to be met and costs to be held down. Such cases call for organization of prevention effort. The Plant Quality Manager can play a constructive role in such effort. (See below.)

The Data Feedback Role.   The Plant Quality Manager also has the role of providing data on product quality to suppliers and to production personnel. Mostly, this data feedback is designed to identify abnormalities, specifically, sporadic outbreaks of quality troubles. The manager also assists in troubleshooting through discovering the precise failure mode, contributing theories as to the causes, and assisting in finding remedies.

Modern electronic data systems have revolutionized the data feedback process. This revolution has made it possible to provide real-time feedback as well as summaries in preanalyzed forms. See Section 27, Computers and Quality.

The Quality Improvement Role.   Companies which set out to improve quality on a systematic basis usually establish quality improvement councils to direct the effort. Some of these councils are at the plant level. The Plant Quality Manager is invariably a member of such a plant council. The manager may also become active in some of the quality improvement projects as a member of the respective project teams.

In addition, the manager is able to assist the quality improvement teams by theorizing as to causes, collecting and providing pertinent data, stimulating remedial action, and evaluating remedial action.

The Training Role. During the 1980s there was increased interest in quality improvement. This, in turn, stimulated a demand for training in quality-oriented skills and tools such as the quality improvement process, team building, and statistical process control. Many Plant Quality Managers accepted responsibility as trainers in these skills and tools.

The Police Image. Some of the roles described above are perceived by production personnel as police roles. Under this interpretation the Plant Quality Manager is viewed as a chief of police, engaged in checking for violations of the law and in reporting offenders to the authorities. This view is deplored and resented by such managers, yet it is really quite a logical analogy from the perspective of the production personnel.

Many quality managers would like to eliminate this police image. The method they commonly employ is logical reasoning. They try to demonstrate by logic that it is important to establish control, test the product, and provide data feedback. This exercise in logical reasoning is normally completely futile—the deeds are more convincing than the words.

The best way to end the police image is to engage in "positive" work. (This positive work is *in addition to,* not instead of, the "negative" work of control.) The most eloquent form of positive work is quality improvement and cost reduction. The improvement process requires creation of teams in which personnel from multiple departments jointly tackle chronic quality problems. The resulting team spirit then carries over into the traditional responsibilities and helps to offset the police image. The Plant Quality Manager who becomes identified with a successful record of "positive" work loses the police image even though the role of "chief of police" remains.

Plant managers have employed additional ways of offsetting the police image:

Being a proponent for resources needed by other departments to improve their quality performance

Periodically "making the rounds" to understand the needs and perceptions of other departments

Helping to establish the conditions which make it possible to delegate greater autonomy to Production, e.g., self-control and self-inspection

Stimulating, within the quality department, an attitude of service to others.

The Qualifications. Qualifications for the job of Plant Quality Manager are mainly of a technological nature. Most job descriptions call for specialized degrees such as in food technology, electronic engineering, and microbiology. Most also require experience in the industry. In recruitment from outside the company there is a universal demand for prior experience as a quality manager. However, within the same company it is not unusual to fill the job of Quality Manager by lateral transfer from other departments. What is seldom demanded in the case of Plant Quality Managers is business training and experience.

The Boss. The Plant Quality Manager normally reports to either the local plant manager or the Division Quality Manager. Life is lived successfully both ways, and there is no clear evidence that the performance of one method exceeds that of the other. Either way, the division quality office participates in establishing the control plan and in audits of plant performance.

An important influence is the criticality of quality with respect to human safety and health and to the environment. In critical cases the upper managers as well as the external regulators tend to mandate that the Plant Quality Manager report to upper management through a separate chain of command.

The Division Quality Manager. The word "division" usually refers to an autonomous organization unit—a profit center—supervised by a general manager. In manufacturing companies, most of such profit centers have been organized in ways which include a Division Quality Manager.

The word "division" has also been used to designate major functional organization units such as Marketing and Customer Service. Previously, Divisional Quality Managers for such organization units were rare. Starting in the 1980s, some major companies established Division Quality Managers in such functional divisions.

An additional new development, also starting in the 1980s, was the movement by companies in the service industries to give higher priority to quality. One feature of this movement was the creation of Quality Managers. Some of these were for profit centers. Others were for functional divisions, or at the corporate level.

Roles of the Division Quality Manager. These roles vary from one company to another but typically consist of a selection from the following list:

1. *Fitness for use:* This involves collecting the information needed for disposition of nonconforming products and then ensuring that the appropriate decision-makers determine the disposition. (The conformance decisions are made at the plant level.)

2. *Quality planning:* Traditionally, this planning focused on the factory process controls and product controls. The trend has been to broaden the areas of quality planning to include essential processes such as the new-product launch cycle, especially the creation of early warning systems to detect potential quality troubles ahead. In some companies the Division Quality Manager's planning role now extends to all phases of activity, including general management of the business, specifically, divisionwide planning for quality.

3. *Quality improvement:* The Division Quality Manager is an essential member of the division quality improvement council. In this capacity the manager shares in the planning and coordination of the quality improvement effort. In addition, the Division Quality Manager is able, through the specialized know-how of the Quality Department, to provide specific assistance to the council and the quality improvement teams in such forms as identifying vital few chronic quality problems, estimating costs of poor quality both overall and in specific areas of concentration, providing the quality improvement teams with data pertinent to their projects, and providing training in quality-oriented skills and tools.

4. *Consulting service:* At the division level the Quality Department usually employs quality specialists who have acquired training and experience in the use of numerous problem-solving tools. This same training and experience can assist in solution of a wide variety of quality problems throughout the division. In consequence, these specialists are able to provide consulting services throughout the division.

5. *Quality assurance:* The Division Quality Manager conducts audits, prepares reports, and in other ways provides an independent source of quality assurance to other divisional managers, including the General Manager. The scope of these forms of quality assurance is described in Section 9, Quality Assurance, and in Section 8, Upper Management and Quality, under Quality Audits by Upper Managers.

The Change to Business Orientation. The growing emphasis on quality has increasingly caused companies to consider managing for quality as an extension of the business plan and to view quality problems as business problems rather than as problems in technology. (See, generally, Section 6, under Companywide Quality Management.)

Many divisions are profit centers, each of which is a near-autonomous business. The General Manager's role is one of business manager, not technologist. (Often the General Manager lacks a technological background.) Of course, some of the subordinate departments (such as Technical, Manufacture, Quality) have a high technological content. Yet the managers of such departments can best help the General Manager by (1) understanding the business mission and (2) directing the resources of their departments toward that mission.

Most Quality Managers have an educational background in technology. Much of their experience has been acquired from the technological departments of the company: the testing laboratories, the factory floor, and the engineering design offices. Their exposure to the business departments (e.g., Marketing, Finance) has been limited. For such Quality Managers, a change to business orientation is a major change. [For elaboration, see Smith (1978).]

To participate in such a change, Division Quality Managers must acquire training and experience in business management—the process of establishing business goals and planning how to meet them. In addition, the division Quality Departments must take steps to transfer many of their technology-oriented activities to other departments. Such transfers must, in turn, be preceded by training those departments in the necessary skills and tools and by establishing means to assure that those departments give continuing priority to the quality goals.

An aid to change in orientation is "making the rounds"—a form of internal marketing research. The Quality Manager visits with each key manager to raise questions such as:

What, in your opinion, are the three company quality problems most in need of solution?

Where lie our best opportunities for improving sales through better quality?

Which are our best opportunities for quality cost reduction?

What major quality threats do we face in the decade ahead?

What are our most urgently needed changes in quality policies, goals, plans, and organization?

Collectively, the responses are revealing (and often full of surprises). They broaden the outlook of the Quality Manager and stimulate the process of change in orientation.

The Boss. During the early stages of evolution the Division Quality Managers were assigned to report to either the Manufacturing Manager or the Technical Manager. The trend has been to make the Division Quality Manager report directly to the Division General Manager. A typical organization chart is shown in Figure 7.2. Since the late 1970s, this organizational form has become the major form in the United States. This same trend in organization form is consistent with the trend toward business orientation of the quality function.

The Department Name. The name has undergone extensive evolution. The first name—Inspection Department—was so descriptive of what the members did that it achieved ready acceptance and standardization.

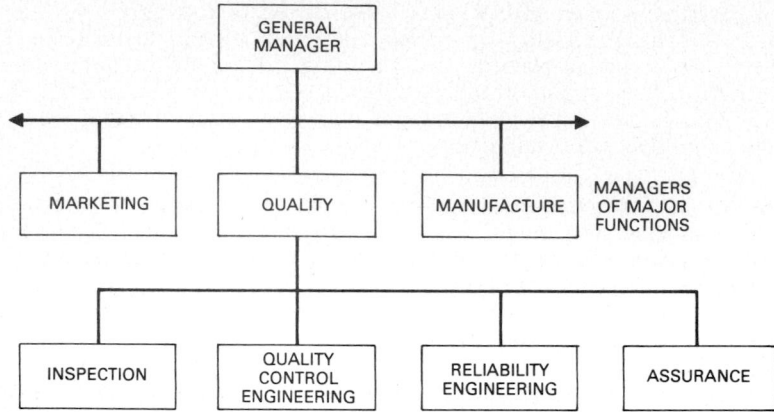

FIG. 7.2 Typical organization for quality-related activities.

When the function of quality control engineering was added, new names were devised to recognize the broader responsibility. These names competed with each other until some consensus emerged. The name "Quality Control Department" became the most widely adopted replacement for the name "Inspection Department."

In due course the word "control" was "downgraded" from its earlier broad connotation. This led to a search for words with broader implications. One name which met with wide acceptance was "Quality Assurance Department."

This evolution of names continues apace. The shift to business orientation probably calls for a change in the department name. The emerging name will likely include the word "quality"—society at large regards quality as a "good" word. A probable name for the future is Quality Management Department, or simply Quality Department.

(The name Quality Assurance Department has been a source of confusion. In some companies the name is intended to mean broad responsibility over the entire quality function. In other companies the term "quality assurance" is used in a narrower sense—to designate the specialized activities of conducting audits and preparing summarized reports for managers. These activities are discussed in Section 9, Quality Assurance.)

The Corporate Quality Manager.   Some large corporations establish a corporate quality office to provide quality-related services to various internal and external customers. Generally these corporate quality offices are found in multidivisional and/or multinational corporations within which the divisions are linked by some commonality (in markets, products, technology, etc.). The corporate quality office is a service center, not a profit center. It is usually located physically at the corporate headquarters. The corporate Quality Manager is often a vice president and may report directly to the company President or through an intermediate staff Vice President.

The functions of the corporate quality office vary from company to company but usually include the functions listed below. [For a lengthy list, see Robert (1967).]

Assistance to Corporate Management.   This assistance takes such forms as developing corporate quality policies, coordinating the preparation of annual quality goals, preparation of the corporate quality manual, audit of divisional performance, and preparation and publication of reports to management. The trend toward companywide quality management will likely expand the use of corporate quality offices to aid in planning and reporting. Such activities are undertaken only with the clear support of (or mandate from) corporate management. During the 1970s there was much mandating of corporate audits with respect to such matters as product safety and liability.

Assistance to Divisional Management.　One form of this assistance is a consulting service. Some corporate quality offices include specialists who can provide consulting assistance. For many problems, an in-house consulting service has advantages over use of outside consultants.

A second form of assistance is training. For certain training courses, it is more efficient to use a corporate capability than to establish self-sufficiency in the divisions.

In some companies, certain quality-oriented services are centralized in order to gain specific efficiencies. An example is a service for conducting supplier surveys and audits. Another example is the laboratory for field failure analysis. When such services are centralized, one option for managing the service is the Corporate Quality Department.

Criteria for Invitation.　In general, the central quality office provides services to the divisions only when invited to do so. (The exceptions are in such forms as quality audits mandated by corporate management.) Experience has shown that in issuing such invitations, Division General Managers require that the corporate personnel be

1. Knowledgeable about business matters to an extent which commands the respect of the Division General Manager.
2. Knowledgeable about quality matters to an extent which commands the respect of the Division Quality Manager.
3. Sufficiently personable to minimize the stresses and abrasion which can develop out of such a relationship.

Corporate Quality Managers are well advised to keep these criteria in mind when recruiting their staffs.

Professional Development.　The corporate quality office is often the corporate center for collecting and disseminating information on quality methodology. The collection takes place through means such as attending conferences, reading literature, and visiting organizations which are conducting innovative programs. (These organizations may well include divisions within the corporation.)

The resulting information is then disseminated in a number of ways:

Preparation of training programs with associated structured courses and text materials. (Some of the best test materials available in the United States have been prepared by corporate quality offices.)

Publication of success stories through internal news letters or journals.

Organization of internal conferences on quality, with associated committee work, project reports, and discussion of future planning.

Some of those "innovative programs" may be judged to have useful application within the corporation. In such cases the corporate quality office tries to stimulate some division to test them out.

Another form of professional development relates to personnel appraisal.

Many companies require multiple appraisals of their managers. The Corporate Quality Manager is well situated to provide such appraisals with respect to Division Quality Managers and their assistants. (In some companies the Corporate Quality Manager participates in those deliberations which precede filling a vacancy for a post of Division Quality Manager.)

External Relations.   The corporation has numerous relationships on quality matters with outside organizations such as government regulatory agencies, industry associations, standardization bodies, and professional societies. The corporate quality office is often given key roles with respect to such relationships.

Figure 7.3 shows graphically the organization relationship of the corporate quality office to the divisions.

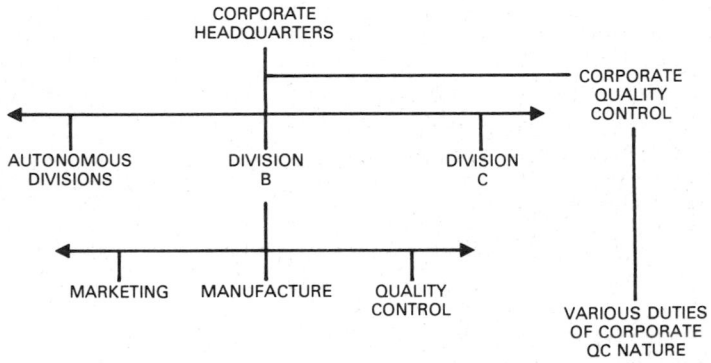

FIG. 7.3 Organization in multidivision companies, featuring corporate quality staff.

The Life Cycle of Corporate Quality Offices.   The preceding list of activities for a quality manager would seem to be a persuasive argument for establishing a corporate quality office. However, there is a cost, without any known measure of return on investment. As a result, the actual establishment usually awaits a favorable financial climate—a time when business is expanding and budgets are liberal. The exceptions have been times of crisis such as the wave of product safety legislation of the 1960s, or the more recent wave of loss of market share to foreign imports, due largely to quality differences.

Once created, it takes a year or two for the corporate quality office to identify the needs of its customers and to arrange to meet those needs. Thereafter the office must survive by earning the support of the Division General Managers.

As viewed by some divisions, the merits of the corporate services are debatable. The costs are quantifiable and real, since in many companies the divisions are "charged" for these costs in the form of mandated overhead burdens. However, the benefits are not quantifiable. As a result, evaluation of the merits of the corporate services are based mainly on the judgment of the Division General Managers.

The real test comes during a time of financial troubles. When business declines and budgets are tight, it is common for the corporate heads to demand a review of each "nonproductive" service to determine whether its continued existence is justified. This review includes securing the judgments of the clients who have been "paying" for the services, specifically, the Division General Managers. At such a time the General Managers do not need to prove that the service has not been worth the overhead charges it imposes on the divisions; their judgments become decisive. The lesson is that *the corporate quality office must earn the support of the divisions before the crisis comes.*

The ups and downs of the business cycle have contributed to a shocking mortality rate of corporate quality offices. In some companies there has actually been a cyclical creation and dismantling of a corporate quality office about once every decade. An added, important variable is the caliber of the corporate quality personnel—to what extent they meet the criteria listed above, under the heading Criteria for Invitation. In too many cases these criteria have not been met, and this has contributed to the mortality rate of the departments.

The emerging trend toward companywide quality management is a new force favoring a role for a corporate quality office. (See generally, Section 6, under Companywide Quality Management.)

Why Quality Managers Fail.　　Some fail for reasons unrelated to quality, such as lack of leadership skills and poor rapport with peers. (Such reasons can cause any manager to fail.) However, some failures are attributable to quality-related factors such as:

Preoccupation with conformance:　　This is understandable at the plant or laboratory level. However, at the division level the emphasis should be on meeting the needs of customers.

Emphasis on technology versus business:　　Here again there is a difference due to level. The plant or laboratory is a technological facility, but the division is a business.

Emphasis on departmental goals:　　Every Quality Manager has departmental goals and should, of course, meet them. In addition, the Quality Manager is concerned with a broad function which impacts all departments. The quality goals of the division and corporation are much broader than those of the Quality Department. These broader goals impose a broader role on the Quality Manager.

Unfamiliarity with the culture:　　An obvious example is the case of the Quality Manager who moves from defense-oriented industries to the civilian goods industries. They are two very different worlds with different cultures. The defense world is dominated by an extensive, complex array of mandated specifications and quality plans. It takes much time and effort just to learn what is in those plans and where to apply them. The civilian world also has some mandated specifications and plans, but the dominant force is the competitive marketplace. It places great stress on fitness for use as well as on such parameters as cost and productivity. Quality Managers who move from one such culture to another are in grave danger of failure unless they grasp at the very outset the remarkable change in emphasis.

COORDINATION OF THE QUALITY FUNCTION

"Coordination" as used here is the process of orchestrating all quality-oriented activities so as to attain optimum company results. In the absence of some recognized organization mechanism for assuring coordination, it is easy for departments to emphasize departmental results, to the detriment of company results.

There is a range of alternatives for coordination. While there is a good deal of flexibility in the choice, the most important need is to provide a positive mechanism for coordination rather than leaving it to chance.

The principal forms used for coordination are discussed below.

The Common Boss.   In small companies this is a natural and effective method. Through knowledge of the general needs of the business, the boss can identify the quality needs (objectives) and determine how these needs should be met (plans). Through direct access to all employees, the boss can issue orders to perform those deeds which carry out the plans. Then through this same access, the boss can observe to determine whether the orders have been executed and whether the results have been obtained.

As the company grows, its size and complexity reach a stage such that the common boss can no longer maintain this intimate personal contact with all the people and deeds. Nevertheless, the boss can continue to coordinate personally, provided the company:

Creates special tools analogous to those used for coordinating the finance function (budgets, periodic reports, audits)

Trains the General Manager and subordinate managers in use of these tools

These criteria are central to the concept of companywide quality management discussed in Section 6. If these criteria are not met, the boss lacks the tools for coordination, and coordination must be done by other means.

Self-Coordination.   Where there is no organized provision for coordination, the resulting vacuum may be filled by self-coordination among the various managers. This is certainly what happens when some sporadic trouble flares up. The impacted managers converge on the scene to put out the fire. However, chronic problems tend to go on and on because they lack alarm signals.

An essential ingredient in all forms of coordination is a spirit of teamwork. This is especially necessary if reliance is placed on self-control. Some industry external relationships have long been on an adversary basis: relations with suppliers and relations with unions. Adversary relations can also be present internally; in that event they are a fatal obstacle to self-coordination.

Committees.   Committees (also task forces, teams, etc.) are widely used for coordination. They are at their best when they are closely focused on specific subject matter such as design review, material review boards, and quality improvement projects. For broader matters, the committees can encounter severe jurisdictional complications with line department responsibilities.

In some cases, the committee membership consists of the upper managers themselves. An example is the Quality Improvement Council, the council which directs companywide quality management. In such cases the committee can be effective in a broad undertaking since the members also have line department jurisdiction over the subject matter.

Written Procedure.   This approach is widely used to provide official, repetitive-use plans. (See Section 6, under the Quality Manual.) The result is a form of law and order—a predictable, impersonal means of coordination.

The stabilizing aspect of written procedure can also become an obstacle to progress. Written procedures are intended to provide a predictable, stable plan of action—the precise opposite of improvement. Even worse, in very large organizations (bureaucracies), the procedure can become the end rather than the means.

Precedent. Precedent serves as an informal, unwritten manual of procedure. Despite fallible memories, it is quite useful in small organizations for whom formal, written procedure is too great a burden. Like written procedure, it can also hinder progress.

Staff Departments. This is the main road chosen by companies in the United States. See below, under Staff Quality Departments.

Project Manager. Large, unique projects require extensive planning and coordination, involving multiple major functions. (See Section 6, under Application to Major Programs.) Many such projects are coordinated by a full-time Project Management Department headed by a Project Manager (also called "Program Manager"). Such Project Managers then coordinate for all parameters, including quality.

The "Owner." Many business processes consist of a series of steps, each of which contributes to a final result. Any department head who has command over one of those steps is widely referred to as the "owner" of that part of the process. However, in many cases there is no one in clear command of the entire process, since it progresses through multiple major functions. Some companies have tried to improve the coordination for such processes by assigning each to some manager who then becomes the owner despite not having full command over the process.

Although the owner lacks full command, the designation of "owner" confers certain rights. These rights help the owner to organize informal teams and in other ways establish the means for coordination. The companies are aware of the limitations of informality, so they try to designate, as owners, selected managers whose status and personality are appropriate to give leadership to the coordination effort.

There are variations on the ownership concept. In some companies, each quality improvement project is assigned to a "champion" who is usually a member of the Quality Improvement Council. A project team which encounters a serious organization obstacle can use its access to the project champion to help clear that obstacle.

Matrix Organizations. Matrix organizations exist in various forms. They are used to coordinate for multiple parameters, including quality. What the various forms have in common is the concept of superimposing a team culture on functional departments in order to improve business performance. Team membership is a part-time assignment. The full-time responsibilities of the members are in the business and functional departments.

Experience with matrix organizations suggests that they are at their best in coordination to meet short-range business goals. Such short-range business goals have usually had higher priority than quality goals of a more fundamental nature, such as improving quality on a project-by-project basis and improving the quality planning process.

For an analysis of the matrix organization concept in its various forms, see Cleland (1981a, 1981b).

Crisis-by-Crisis Coordination. This is the coordination of last resort. It takes place when a fire breaks out and all managers rush to do the firefighting. It is also the most expensive form of coordination.

Tools for Coordination. Coordination is aided by use of various tools of quality management: quality policies, objectives and plans to meet them, executive reports, quality surveys, and audits. These tools are the result of coordinated effort, and, once in use, they provide further coordination by the fact of use.

COORDINATION AMONG DIVISIONS

In some multidivisional companies there is much community of interest because the divisions (1) sell their products in the same or overlapping markets, (2) sell under the same company name or brand name, (3) produce components which will enter the same final product, and (4) employ common technology.

In such cases there are obvious needs for coordination with respect to quality. However, any organization for coordination must accommodate the tendency of the divisions to resist invasion of their autonomous status. The more usual forms of coordination include:

1. *An informal council of quality managers:* In this form the various divisional quality managers establish a network of communication by all available means: telephone, correspondence, and meetings. They identify problems of mutual interest and try to establish action programs to deal with these problems. They are, however, handicapped by lack of official recognition (legitimacy) and lack of personnel needed to carry out the numerous associated details.

2. *A formal council of quality managers:* The informal council may succeed in obtaining an official status. This conversion into a formal council provides legitimacy. Now the council has the clear right to call meetings, request data, conduct studies, and recommend action. This same legitimacy also simplifies the problem of securing the personnel and other resources needed to relieve busy quality managers of some of the associated detailed work. For a case example, see Comish (1983).

3. *An international quality office:* This form is widely used in multinational companies. The International Quality Manager typically reports to a corporate staff officer who has broad responsibilities for coordination of foreign subsidiaries, including coordination for quality. Figure 7.4 shows a typical organization form.

The International Quality Manager may be assigned any one or all of the following usual responsibilities:

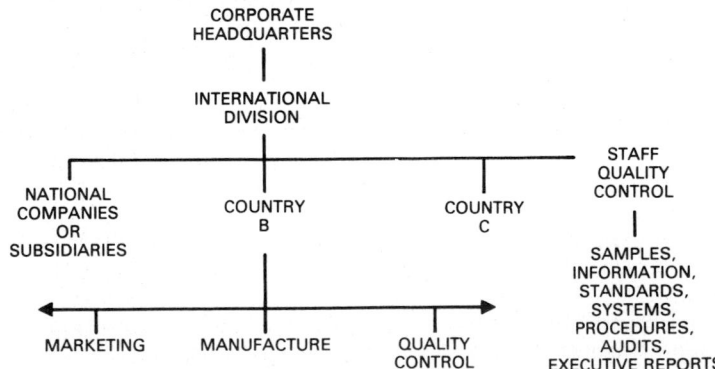

FIG. 7.4 Organization for coordination through an international quality office.

Provide information and assistance to the subsidiaries in such forms as standards, systems, and procedures.

Receive samples for comparative testing.

Receive data for analysis and comparative reporting.

Assist in interchange of information on projects in progress and on results attained.

Convene international conferences on quality-related matters.

Conduct audits of quality performance, including surveillance visits.

4. *A corporate quality office:* This formal office is not attached to any profit center—it reports to corporate management. It has multiple responsibilities, including coordination, as discussed above, under The Corporate Quality Manager.

In the case of conglomerate companies there is little commonality among divisions (other than financial); hence there is little need for quality coordination among divisions.

In some cases the activities to be coordinated are divided among multiple companies. The need for coordination is especially severe in large, complex systems requiring extensive subcontracting. In such cases the prime contractor engages various subcontractors to design and build the subsystems which are to enter the total system.

For such undertakings, the work of coordination is so extensive that conventional collaboration among the companies does not do the job. Instead, there is need to create a new organization whose main job is coordination. This organization, often called "Program Management," is discussed in Section 31, under the Program Management Function.

Responsibility Matrix. Organization charts are effective for defining the chain of command. However, the charts are not effective for showing the interrelationships needed for coordination. One way of showing this interrelation is through a responsibility matrix.

Table 7.3 is an example of a responsibility matrix. The horizontal elements consist of specific decisions or actions to be taken. The vertical columns show the various organization units involved. The intersections bear code letters to define the extent of responsibility, whether primary (R) or contributory (C).

STAFF QUALITY ACTIVITIES

In this handbook, the "line" (or "operating") activities are those without which an enterprise cannot exist at all, such as marketing and manufacture. "Staff" activities are those which, while not vital to the existence of the enterprise, are essential to its efficient operation.

Examples of Staff Quality Activities. Staff quality activities exist in several varieties. The most common are listed in Table 7.4, along with examples in the quality function.

Staff quality activities may be performed at the outset by a staff Quality Department. However, many such activities will in due course be performed by the line departments. This change takes place through a natural, evolutionary life cycle of any staff specialty.

TABLE 7.3 Responsibility Matrix (R—primary responsibilities; C—contributing responsibilities)

Areas of responsibility	General manager	Marketing	Program manager	Engineering	Manufacturing	QC&T*	Finance
Product quality level for business	R	C	C			C	
Initiate program plan, schedules, and budgets		C	R	C	C	C	C
Issue work statement		R	C				
Customer quality requirements		C	R	C		C	
Prepare quality plan						R	
Establish engineering standards				R			
Establish quality standards						R	
Establish product design capability			C	R			
Provide reliability apportionment			C	R			
Prepare design specifications			C	R	C	C	
Perform design review			C	R	C	C	
Accomplish make/buy decision			C	C	R	C	C
Provide drawing and change control			C	R	C	C	

7.26

Task			
Implement production process designs		R	
Implement new design control by reviewing engineering and manufacturing designs against quality standards	C	C	R
Engineering standards	C	R	C
Configuration definition	C	R	
Produce product to design specifications	R		R
Configuration verification			R
Implement incoming material	C	C	R
Design major items of test equipment which require significant design effort		R	C
Design all other test equipment and fixtures and procure all test equipment and fixtures for QC&T, plant and field use; provide QC requirements for engineering designs		C	R

*Quality control and test.

TABLE 7.4   Staff Quality Activities

Types of staff activity	Examples in quality function
Planning—establishing goals and devising ways to reach goals	Preparation of quality manuals; reliability planning; companywide quality planning
Control—ensuring that execution conforms to plan	Product inspection and test; quality audits
Advisory services	Consulting in statistical methodology; design review
Utility services	Data collection and analysis; laboratory test services

Life Cycle of a Staff Quality Activity.   A new staff activity has its origin in some new tool (concept, method, technique, etc). Examples in the quality function have included Shewhart control charts, reliability quantification, and quality cost analysis.

The subsequent events are in the nature of a life cycle for the staff activity:

The new tool is tried out in limited areas and it secures good results.

The results are publicized and attract the attention of managers in other areas. These managers want similar results, so they also try out the new tools.

In due course the cumulative results come to the attention of journalists and conference organizers. They propagandize the results and tools through mass media.

The extensive applications build up a body of experience and expertise among the specialists and managers. This expertise is further refined by an evolving literature.

The scholars and philosophers develop models for standardizing the new tools. They also evolve simplified procedures to enable nonprofessionals to apply the tools.

Training is given to the line people so that they can use the simplified tools and procedures to make additional applications on their own.

The staff specialists move to other problems, but they may retain an audit on the line applications as well as providing a consulting service.

STAFF QUALITY DEPARTMENTS

These departments first emerged on a wide scale during the 1940s. Three forces converged to stimulate a rapid growth: a need for improving quality of production of goods required during World War II, a sudden and extensive growth of interest in the use of statistical methodology to aid quality control, and formation of an American Society for Quality Control (ASQC).

Quality Control Engineering.   The original emphasis of these staff Quality Departments was on employing the statistical tools. However, it soon became clear that a broader approach was needed. This broader approach required assignment of the bulk of the staff quality activities to engineers (rather than to statisticians). As a result, the emerging dominant title for the personnel became Quality Control Engineer. Correspondingly, the dominant title for the staff Quality Department became Quality Control Engineering.

In due course the Quality Control Engineers became involved with a broad list of quality work elements (see Quality Management Work Elements and Jobs, above). Through this involvement they impacted most of the functions being carried out. For example:

Work elements	*Functions impacted*
Field complaint analysis	Sales; customer service
Quality cost analysis	Accounting
Supplier surveillance	Purchasing
Motivation for quality	Human relations

This same broadening of the scope of quality control engineering also resulted in a broadening of the titles. The title Quality Engineer became more popular than the title Quality Control Engineer.

The one major area not invaded by the Quality Control Engineers was that of launching of new products. When the need arose for modernizing this activity to meet the needs of the computer, defense, and aerospace industries, a new specialty—reliability engineering—was created.

Reliability Engineering. In response to the urging of these new specialists, many companies, notably in the defense and aerospace industries, created new departments for reliability engineering (rather than expanding the scope of the Quality Control Engineering Departments). In some companies a single staff department was retained but was renamed (e.g., Quality Control and Reliability Engineering). The growing competition in reliability of civilian goods then expanded the role of Reliability Engineers into many civilian industries.

The activities associated with the reliability "movement" actually involve two sets of tools: (1) *technological* tools for reliability modeling and quantification throughout the product hierarchy and (2) *managerial* tools to formalize the approach and to assure that it is used. See generally, Section 13, under Planning for Time-Oriented Performance (Reliability).

Interface among Staff Quality Specialties. Establishment of those two categories of quality-oriented engineering also required establishment of jurisdictional boundaries. Generally, the responsibilities of reliability engineering were focused on the launching of new product designs and evaluation of reliability performance throughout all stages of the product life cycle. The responsibilities of quality control engineering related to the remaining quality work elements.

While the areas of responsibility differ, the skills and tools have much in common. Both categories of engineers should have:

An educational background in basic science and in applied science

Understanding of the nature of quality and the processes by which it is attained

Training and experience in using the tools: technological, statistical, and managerial

The respective areas of knowledge do not overlap fully; there are differences as well. Theoretically, it is possible for one person to be qualified to carry out both specialties. (Some individuals hold ASQC certifications both as Quality Engineer and Reliability Engineer.) However, industry practice has largely been to recognize the two categories as separate.

Other Specialties; Staff-Staff Conflicts. In organizations which employ many quality staff specialists there is a tendency for the work to specialize further and for the titles to proliferate. Examples of such titles have been: Maintainability Engineer, Material Review Engineer, Salvage Engineer, Configuration Control Engineer, Systems Engineer, and still others. In addition, there are "non-quality" specialists whose area of responsibility overlaps that of the quality specialists. Examples are Industrial Engineer, Value Analyst, Operations Research Analyst, Statistician, Standardization Engineer, and Project Engineer.

The presence of multiple specialties with overlapping areas of responsibility sometimes leads to lively conflicts—the respective specialists tend to try to expand their areas of jurisdiction. Running through such staff-staff conflicts is the risk of "rediscovery of scientific management." Once a new, narrow specialty succeeds in obtaining results, it is tempting for those involved to use these results as the basis for securing a broad charter plus associated budget. This is sometimes done by phrasing the specialty in such broad language as to encompass the entire concept of "scientific management." Some of the definitions put forward for operations research, value analysis, systems engineering, and so on have been precisely of this nature.

Managers should be on the alert for this tendency to draft broad staff charters since they are a breeding ground for staff-staff conflicts. Preparing the charter for a new department is similar to launching a new design—in this case, for organizational structure. This design should be subject to close "design review" by all who will be asked to live with it, both line and staff.

ADMINISTRATION OF THE QUALITY STAFF SPECIALTY

This administration is best performed if there is a prior understanding of the perceptions of the major parties in interest.

Perceptions. The line departments perceive the staff services as a mixture of benefit and detriment. Auxiliary services are often welcomed, but controls are usually resented as imposing delays and interfering with autonomy. The costs are often transferred to the line in the form of overhead burdens. The individual specialists may exhibit abrasive personalities.

The staff Quality Departments view their specialty as vital to the health of the enterprise. However, this view is somewhat self-serving. A staff department is a cost center, not a profit center. The costs are readily quantifiable, but the benefits are not. Such a situation is inherently insecure. To the specialists a possible additional source of security is to convert the specialty into a profession—an essential service to society, with practice limited to licensed professionals. (For further discussion, see Section 11, under Professionalism.)

The managers who preside over both line and staff would like to attain efficient operations at optimum cost and with minimal friction. One attractive solution is to minimize the use of staff quality specialists by transferring staff quality activities to line departments.

Transfer from Staff to Line. A major form of this transfer can come from close attention to the concept of the "product life cycle" of staff quality activities. (See Life Cycle of a Staff Quality Activity above.) According to that concept, a staff department is able to live on and on despite continuing transfer of its activities to line departments. The solution is a continuing development of new products—updating the product line.

For the staff to turn activities over to the line people sounds like economic suicide, and it might well be the case in a static society. However, new problems are continuously arising. These problems require new tools for solution and provide a basis for the staff specialists to modernize their "product line" as they turn the old, matured tools over to the line departments. To continue "doing business at the old stand," in other words, working on solved problems, is the surest way to decay and death of the staff department.

Another method of transfer is to reorganize major functions to provide them with more complete "ownership" of their mission. In a reported case example, a new department—Procurement Engineering—was created within the procurement function. The procurement engineers were trained to provide the procurement function with the technical support previously provided by several staff departments, including the staff Quality Department. For further details, see Brown (1974).

Any method of transfer requires training line specialists to undertake work previously done by quality staff specialists. An example is training product designers in reliability modeling and reliability quantification, as well as in design of experiments.

Budgeting. Budgets for staff Quality Departments are set up to correspond to the types of activity conducted, somewhat as follows:

Activity	*Basis of budget*
Quality improvement	Project-by-project
Planning	Anticipated extent of new products, processes, etc., requiring quality planning
Consulting; control; audits	Previous history, adjusted for expected growth

In their own interest as well as that of their superiors, staff Quality Departments should propose budgets which are dominated by improvement projects. Most of these projects are justifiable on the basis of return on investment. This has strong appeal to upper management as well as to the line departments.

Reports on Staff Quality Activities. Because the bulk of staff work is long range, the frequency of reporting should be infrequent—normally quarterly. Each quarterly report shows the progress made during the last quarter and lists plans for the quarter ahead. The annual report (every fourth quarter) contains the next annual plan as well.

Completed projects are reported on at the time of completion.

In reporting financial results the staff is well advised to enlist the aid of the company's Accounting Department. Upper management gives more credibility to financial figures if they have been "certified" by the Accounting Department.

Much of the content of staff Quality Department reports consists of progress reports on projects of a multidepartmental nature. In such projects the staff Quality Department often plays essential roles in such forms as data collection and analysis or application of quality-oriented expertise. In reporting the results of such projects, the staff people are well advised to lean over backward to give maximum credit to line supervisors. Some staff specialists draft reports on finished projects in the form of joint reports (with the line departments involved).

For a discussion of the contents of managerial reports on quality, see Section 8, Upper Management and Quality, under Executive Reports on Quality.

Introducing Change.   In its creative and project work, the staff department is trying to change the existing order. On the surface, the proposed changes are technological in character. However, any technological change is a potential threat to the "cultural pattern" of those who have a vested interest in the existing order. As a result, a distinct phase in introducing change is dealing with cultural resistance—resistance to the "social" consequences of technological change.

For an extensive discussion as applied to quality improvement projects, see Section 22, Quality Improvement, under Resistance to Change.

Other Staff-Line Relationships.   It is almost universal that responsibility for results of operations rests with the line managers, not the staff managers. For this reason the line managers are given the discretion to either accept or reject the advice of staff specialists. (They do either at their own peril.) This is a good rule. If managers are to be held responsible for results, they should have authority over the means for obtaining those results. To require them to accept staff advice is equivalent to transferring part of that authority to the staff (a form of authority without responsibility).

This very real responsibility of line managers renders the authority of the staff specialist illusory. To be sure, the staff department has status on the organization chart. It has a budget, a table of duties, and other outward symbols of authority. These symbols certainly do confer legitimacy in some important ways—the right to secure information, attend meetings, and present proposals. However, the real authority, that is, the ability to secure action, is not derived from the rank of the staff managers. It is derived from their knowledge, their proved competence in assisting line managers in improving their results, and their individual personalities. The matter of personality is surprisingly important. Although personality by itself solves no problems, it avoids some severe problems by converting the conflicts inherent in the staff-line relationships into innocent rivalries or even good-natured collaboration.

Aside from the conflicts inherent in introducing change, there are others inherent in planning and controlling. Of these, the problem of "two bosses" is probably the most common. The problem arises when staff specialists prepare plans to be executed by line departments. For example, a plant laboratory "reports" to the Plant Manager. However, the Division Quality (staff) Department is a major force in preparing the quality plans to be used and in auditing to ensure that the execution follows the plans. The organization chart itself reflects a dualism. A solid line runs from the laboratory to the Plant Manager. However, a dotted or dashed line runs from the laboratory to the Division Quality Manager.

The solution lies in the fact that the plant laboratory has only one personal boss (the Plant Manager) but numerous impersonal bosses, of which the quality plan is but one. (Others include the personnel manual, the budget, the safety regulations, etc.) As long as there is only one personal boss, the plant laboratory head has a place for appeal to secure the final word.

Careers, Training, and Professionalism for Quality Staff Specialists.   These topics are pertinent to administration of the quality staff specialty. They are discussed in Section 11, under the respective headings.

REFERENCES

American Society for Quality Control (1961). *The Basic Elements of Quality Control Engineering.* ASQC, Milwaukee.

Brown, Arthur W. (1974). "Procurement Engineering." *ASQC Technical Conference Transactions,* Milwaukee, pp. 161–168.

Cleland, David I. (1981*a*). "The Cultural Ambience of the Matrix Organization." *Management Review,* November, pp. 25–28, 37–39.

Cleland, David I. (1981*b*). "Matrix Management (Part II): A Kaleidoscope of Organizational Systems." *Management Review,* December, pp. 48–56.

Comish, John W. (1983). "Managing a Multidivisional Quality Function." *ASQC Quality Congress Transactions,* Milwaukee, pp. 268–271.

Juran, J. M. (1977). "Quality and Its Assurance, An Overview." *Second NATO Symposium on Quality and its Assurance,* London.

Juran, J. M. (1973). "The Taylor System and Quality Control." A series of articles in *Quality Progress,* May 1973 through December 1973 (listed under "Management Interface").

Robert, Paul A. (1967). "Quality Control Management at the Corporate Level." *ASQC Technical Conference Transactions,* Milwaukee, pp. 3–5.

Sears, James A. (1983). "Changing Role of the Quality Inspection Function." *Quality Progress,* July, pp. 12–17.

Smith, Martin R. (1978). "Why QC Need PR." *Industry Week,* October 30, pp. 37–39.

SECTION 8
UPPER MANAGEMENT AND QUALITY

J. M. Juran

INTRODUCTION; BACKGROUND 8.2

Response through
  Comprehensive Structure 8.3

Response through Upper-
  Management
  Participation 8.3

**PARTICIPATION BY UPPER
MANAGEMENT** 8.3

Establish a Quality Council 8.4

Serve on the Quality
  Council 8.4

Establish Quality Policies . 8.4

Establish Quality Goals . . 8.4

Deploy the Goals 8.5

Provide the Resources . . . 8.5

Provide Problem-Oriented
  Training 8.5

Serve on Quality
  Improvement Teams . . 8.6

Review Progress 8.6

Stimulate Improvement . . 8.6

Give Recognition 8.6

Revise the Reward System 8.7

**UPPER-MANAGEMENT
RESISTANCE TO
PARTICIPATION** 8.7

Selective Participation . . . 8.8

**QUALITY ASSURANCE FOR
UPPER MANAGERS** 8.8

**EXECUTIVE REPORTS ON
QUALITY** 8.8

Control Subjects 8.10

Executive Controls and
  Operational Controls . . 8.11

Units of Measure 8.12

Data Collection and
  Summary 8.14

Standards of Comparison . 8.14

The Executive Report
  Battery 8.15

Format 8.16

Publication 8.17

Interpretation 8.17

A Universal Measure for
  Quality 8.19

**QUALITY AUDITS BY UPPER
MANAGERS** 8.20

Why Quality Audits by
  Upper Managers? 8.20

Subject Matter of Upper-
  Management Audits . . . 8.21

Organization for Quality
  Audits by Upper
  Managers 8.23

**TRAINING FOR UPPER
MANAGERS** 8.24

REFERENCES 8.24

INTRODUCTION; BACKGROUND

"Upper management" as used here refers to the highest leadership posts of an enterprise. Applied to a corporation, upper management includes the president (or chief executive officer) plus the corporate vice presidents. Applied to an autonomous division, upper management includes the general manager and the directly subordinate managers.

Previously, in tiny organizations the chief executive personally directed all activities in the organization, including managing for quality. As organizations grew in size, the volume of activity outgrew the capacity of the chief executive to manage by personal direction. It became necessary to delegate.

A major form of this delegation was through the craft concept. Apprentices were trained in the craft and qualified by examination to become craftsmen. The chief executive—the master—then delegated much of the managing for quality to the craftsmen, subject to inspection and audit by the master.

Growth of organization was sharply accelerated by the Industrial Revolution, which opened the way to mass marketing and mass production. The resulting large enterprises required organization into functional departments. The chief executives delegated to each functional department head the responsibility for managing that function, including the responsibility for quality—for performing the function correctly.

With the growth of technology, products and processes became increasingly complex. To deal with these complexities, many industries adopted the principle of separating planning from execution. Planning of the various functions was delegated to trained planners, leaving to the supervisors and the work force the job of executing the plans. This separation of planning from execution had several major consequences:

A decline in use of the craftsmanship concept

A dramatic rise in productivity

A dispersion of the responsibility of managing for quality among still more organization units

A further distancing of upper management from the job of managing for quality

[For elaboration on the Taylor System of separating planning from execution, and its effect on quality, see Juran (1973).]

The progressive removal of upper management from managing for quality produced negative effects on quality. To offset these effects, various organization devices were adopted. (See generally, Section 7, Organizing for Quality.) Nevertheless, numerous instances arose in which product performance fell short of customer needs. In addition, the companies accumulated huge chronic costs of poor quality.

Despite these quality deficiencies, many companies remained profitable because their competitors had similar problems. This equilibrium was then upset by two major forces: (1) the growing impact of quality on society (see Section 34, Impact of Quality on Society) and (2) the emergence of a new level of competition, notably from Japan.

These new forces severely impacted many companies. The impacted companies then responded in various ways, and with varying results. By the 1980s it had become abundantly clear that those major forces required major responses. It was not enough to make adjustments to the existing approach; it was necessary to go back to fundamentals—to question the premises behind the then-existing approach.

One of those premises was that managing for quality could successfully be delegated to the functional managers (and then on to their subordinates). A second premise was that once managing for quality had been delegated to the subordinate hierarchy, it would no longer be necessary for upper managers to participate personally in managing for quality. These premises had become deeply rooted in Western industrial culture. Many managerial practices, organization designs, areas of responsibility, and even careers had been built around these premises. However, by the 1980s it had become clear that these premises were no longer valid as applied to many of the industries impacted by those major forces. As a corollary, the needed responses from those industries required:

1. A comprehensive, companywide approach to managing for quality
2. Extensive personal participation by upper managers in both the design of the companywide approach and its operation thereafter.

Response through Comprehensive Structure.   One form of response of the impacted industries was to design a more broadly structured approach to managing for quality. In its broadest form, managing for quality is conducted through a structured approach which employs all the processes of the Trilogy: planning, controlling, and improving. This approach is designed to serve the needs of all customers, internal as well as external. It is applied to business processes as well as to technological processes. It parallels closely the way in which companies manage for finance. (For elaboration, see Section 2, the Quality Function, under How to Think about Quality.)

In this handbook, such a comprehensive, structured approach to managing for quality is referred to as companywide quality management (CWQM). It is described in Section 6, under the heading Companywide Quality Management.

Response through Upper-Management Participation.   A second form of response by the impacted companies was through enlisting the personal participation of the upper managers. This participation has ranged across a broad spectrum. At one extreme the upper managers have personally taken full charge of managing for quality. At the other extreme the upper managers have exhorted all personnel to do better, to "do it right the first time," but have limited their own role to such activities as lecturing, blaming, and stimulating others.

PARTICIPATION BY UPPER MANAGEMENT

There is no way known for defining upper-management participation through use of such broad words as "commitment" and "involvement." Instead, it is necessary to define, with precision:

Which specific decisions are to be made by upper managers

Which specific actions are to be taken by upper managers

The more usual decisions and actions which collectively represent upper managers' options for personal participation in CWQM are discussed in the following paragraphs. The actual participation is usually a selection from this list of topics.

For some of these topics, the upper managers' participation is carried out by the upper managers collectively. For other topics the upper managers participate within their respective individual spheres of responsibility.

Establish a Quality Council. This council (also called "committee," etc.) plays the central role in directing and coordinating the company's efforts to manage for quality. When established at the corporate level, the council plays a role in the quality function analogous to the role played by the Finance Committee with respect to the finance function. If the aim is to establish CWQM, then a corporate quality council is indispensable.

Ideally, CWQM is designed to become a part of the business planning of the company. Such a design is feasible because of the similarity in concept—both business planning and CWQM involve establishing goals, providing the means to meet the goals, reviewing progress against goals, and so on. Where CWQM does, in fact, become an extension of business planning, corporate quality council functions so extensively overlap those of the corporate management committee that the quality council may lose its identity.

In large companies it is common to establish quality subcouncils for major organization segments, such as divisions or functional departments. It is also common to establish councils for major managerial undertakings, such as quality improvement. When subcouncils are established, it is usual to "network" them; that is, members of higher level councils are appointed to be the chairpersons of lower-level councils.

Serve on the Quality Council. The membership of the council should be in keeping with the scope of the council's mission. Membership on the quality council exposes the members to essential inputs relative to the quality problems requiring solution, the resources needed, and other issues. The council is seldom effective if the members lack decision-making power over the subject matter. In addition, the rank of the council membership sends a message to the rest of the organization regarding the priority of the subject matter.

Establish Quality Policies. As used in this handbook, policies are guides to managerial action. Once formulated, they are approved at the highest levels of organization. Section 5, under various headings, presents many examples of published quality policy statements at various levels and for various functions.

Upper managers participate in quality policy formation in several ways:

1. *Identifying the need for policies:* Major evidence of need for policies is found in repeated questions raised at lower levels, asking for directions on broad issues. In many cases the lower levels of management take the initiative in identifying the need for quality policies.

2. *Assigning responsibility for preparing a draft:* Policy formation usually requires securing inputs from multiple sources—a time-consuming process. In the absence of clear responsibility it is unlikely that a draft will be prepared.

3. *Reviewing, revising, and approving:* Because policies must be approved at the highest levels, the upper managers must personally review the draft.

Establish Quality Goals. At upper-management levels the quality goals (also objectives, etc.) are quite broad. See, for examples, Section 5, under the heading Subject Matter of Quality Objectives.

Broad quality goals are properly oriented to the *results* needed by the organization, not to the means used for getting the results. To illustrate, a broad quality goal may be to reduce the cost of poor quality by 50 percent in 5 years. Attainment of such a goal may require raising awareness, training in statistical process control, and other measures. However, at the upper-management level the goal is results-oriented, not technique-oriented or tool-oriented. In general, efforts to improve quality are headed for disappointment if the goals are tool-oriented rather than results-oriented.

Quality goals should be expressed in numbers and should include a time frame—the time during which the goals are to be reached. Lacking such quantification, it is difficult to agree on issues such as what is meant by the goals, what resources are needed, and how to evaluate performance against goals.

Deploy the Goals. Broad goals are merely "wish lists" until they are "deployed." The deployment process consists of allocating the goals to lower levels of organization. These lower levels then propose specific deeds which, if done, will collectively result in meeting the goals. The lower levels also present a list of the resources needed to meet the goals: personnel, facilities, money, and so on. There follows a negotiation process to balance the value of reaching the goals against the resources needed. This negotiation process then arrives at a final list of deeds and resources. During this process the original goals may well have been modified.

Provide the Resources.   A major failing of upper managers has been the failure to provide the resources needed to carry out the "list of deeds." Such a failure sends a negative message to the lower levels.

In part the needed resources relate to added burdens placed on subordinates, such as the time required to do the deeds. In part, the resources relate to establishing the supporting infrastructure. For example, major goals for quality improvement may require setting up new organization entities in such forms as a quality improvement council and numerous teams to carry out specific improvement projects. This, in turn, may require setting up a supporting infrastructure which includes a process for choosing projects, a process for making project-by-project improvement, training of facilitators, and training of teams. (See, generally, Section 22, Quality Improvement.)

The resources are a price to be paid for meeting the goals. If the resources are not provided, the perception in the lower levels is that the goals lack priority relative to those goals for which resources are provided.

Provide Problem-Oriented Training.   Training is a special form of resource and is a vital element of response to those major forces. It is also a resource which upper managers have generally been willing to provide. However, the upper managers have generally not personally involved themselves with the issue of what training is needed.

The lack of personal involvement by upper managers has led to a good deal of unbalance in training for quality. Until the 1980s, training for quality was largely confined to personnel in the Quality Departments. The emerging quality crisis then stimulated extensive training, principally:

Training for workers in Quality Circles, emphasizing basic problem-solving tools

Training for production supervision and managers, emphasizing statistical tools—"statistical process control"

Training for managerial personnel emphasizing exhortation to do better

Training for managerial personnel emphasizing project-by-project quality improvement

Each of those directions had value, some more than others. In the judgment of the author, the training efforts would have been much better directed and more effective had the upper managers participated in the list of activities set out above. Through such participation the upper managers would have been much better able to identify the quality problems, and thereby to assure that the training activities would be oriented to the solution of those problems. They also would have been better able to judge their personal needs for quality-oriented training.

Serve on Quality Improvement Teams.   There are some persuasive reasons for this form of upper-management participation:

It is a form of leadership by example—the highest form of leadership.

It enables upper managers to understand what they are asking their subordinates to do. In most companies the number of needed improvements runs into hundreds of specific projects, each demanding time of subordinates as well as various resources. There is no better way to understand the nature of these demands than to participate personally in some improvement projects.

Some projects by their very nature require upper managers' membership on the project teams.

Review Progress.   Reviews of progress are an essential part of assuring that goals are being met. The very fact that upper managers do review progress sends a message to the rest of the organization as to the priority given to the quality goals.

Reviews are carried out in two major ways: (1) summarized reports on actual quality performance (see Executive Reports on Quality below) and (2) audits of the processes being used to attain quality (see Executive Quality Audits below).

In conducting reviews it is necessary for upper managers to maintain a constructive approach. The basic purpose of such reviews is, of course, to inform the upper managers of the actual state of affairs. If actual performance falls short of goals, the need is to discover and remove the causes. It is risky, and damaging to morale, to blame subordinates when the cause is not known; often the cause is the system or even the upper managers.

Stimulate Improvement.   One byproduct of review of progress is identification of opportunities for improvement. This is especially true with respect to chronic quality problems. Unlike sporadic problems, chronic quality problems usually originate in the initial planning. The remedy is often to replan, and this is a time-consuming process which is best done as part of a broad undertaking to improve quality. (See, generally, Section 22, Quality Improvement.)

Give Recognition.   The word "recognition" as used here relates to ceremonial actions taken to publicize meritorious performance. These ceremonial actions are typically nonfinancial in nature. They usually focus on activities of an improvement nature rather than on the conduct of operations. In contrast, the reward systems for successful conduct of operations employ such devices as performance appraisal or merit rating and focus on the supervisor–subordinate relationship.

Response to the "major forces" (see Introduction; Background above), requires doing much more than meeting traditional goals; it requires setting and meeting unconventional goals. In turn, to meet these unconventional goals requires extensive revisions in prior practice—virtually a change in culture.

Such a change in culture is accelerated if upper managers give recognition to teams and individuals who make specific contributions to the change. For example, it is common practice for upper managers to preside at ceremonial awards of certificates or plaques to persons who have completed training courses. In some companies, upper managers personally and prominently participate in dinner meetings specifically organized to honor teams who have completed their quality improvement projects. Similar meetings are organized to recognize outstanding contributions made by suppliers. Still other companies establish special awards for teams or individuals whose contributions are judged to be outstanding. These awards are made by upper managers at ceremonial occasions and are publicized through various media such as the company's newsletter, the bulletin boards, and the local press. For case examples, see Gibson (1987) and Onnias (1986).

Revise the Reward System. Many companies employ reward systems in which the rewards include money as well as progress in job grade. In such systems the extent of the rewards depends importantly on the adequacy of performance against operating goals. These goals include quality as well as others (schedule, cost standard, etc.).

For such reward systems, a response to the "major forces" may consist of revising the weight given to the quality component. For example, a large company in the automotive industry revised the merit rating system of its customer service organization by raising to 50 percent (out of 100 percent) the weight given to quality.

Another form of response is to add new parameters to the existing list. Some companies which have undertaken quality improvement on a large scale have added the parameter "performance on quality improvement" to the existing list.

UPPER-MANAGEMENT RESISTANCE TO PARTICIPATION

Many upper managers have exhibited resistance to adding so extensively to their own work loads. In their view they were already quite busy with their traditional responsibilities. In addition, they tended to feel that their contribution could be made by conventional delegation, that is, by establishing the goals and then urging their subordinates to meet those goals. Such conventional delegation was carried out in many companies; it resulted in widespread disappointments. The desired results were not achieved. The lack of results fostered an atmosphere of blame and divisiveness.

The failures to obtain results took the upper managers by surprise. The concept of delegation is vital to all managerial activity. The ability to delegate is an essential attribute of a good manager. However, analysis of a number of the failures shows that there were some serious weaknesses in the delegation strategy:

The new policy of raising quality to a position of top priority was too revolutionary a change to be achieved by a simple act of delegation.

The upper managers were not sufficiently knowledgeable about the subject matter to be able to define the quality goals with adequate precision. Their stated goals (e.g., "Do it right the first time") were too vague to convey to subordinates "What to do differently."

Such vague goals could not compete in priority with the traditional clearly defined goals of meeting specifications, schedules, budgets, etc.

There was no accompanying change in the system of evaluating the performance of subordinates. Hence it was logical for subordinates to conclude that despite the upper-management pronouncements, nothing had really changed. Such a conclusion is especially likely if the company regularly mounts "drives" which come and go with little residual effect.

Despite these serious weaknesses, some companies made significant progress in improving quality. Usually they did so in specific areas where determined middle managers took the initiative, and found ways to supply what the upper managers had failed to supply. Some upper managers feel that such is precisely what the middle managers should do. However, the latter have difficulty in doing so when the former limit their participation to setting broad goals and making broad delegations.

Selective Participation. The upper managers may participate selectively on the basis of perceived specific needs. For example, in some companies upper management has taken the initiative to establish a teamwork relationship with suppliers (to replace the prevailing adversary relationship). Such a change requires support from upper managers in the supplier companies as well, as a result of deeply rooted practices and cultural resistance.

Another example of selective management participation relates to product reliability. The outward evidence is a policy requiring that no new product go to market unless its reliability is at least equal to that of (1) the product it replaces and (2) the product of leading competitors. This policy is then enforced by independent audit.

QUALITY ASSURANCE FOR UPPER MANAGERS

Upper managers have various needs to know what is going on with respect to quality. One of these needs is for *assurance* that all is well with respect to quality. (If not, that need expands into specifics.)

The general nature of quality assurance is described in Section 9, Quality Assurance. The principles and methods discussed there apply widely. However, the application to upper management's needs involves special designs of reports and audits. These special designs are discussed below.

In small companies it is feasible for upper managers to maintain personal contact with all activities in the organization and thereby to secure firsthand assurance as to the state of quality. As the organization grows, the ability to maintain personal contact shrinks. The resulting gap must then be filled by some system of quality assurance. This system consists largely of quality reports and audits.

EXECUTIVE REPORTS ON QUALITY

A major form of quality assurance for upper managers is derived from a battery of executive reports. (The word "executive" as used here is synonymous with the term "upper manager.")

Executive reports on quality have much in common with the feedback loop used at lower levels, such as control subjects, units of measure, data collection systems, and means for summary and analysis. (Table 6.4 shows some examples of the feedback loop as applied to control reports.) The prime difference is the choice of control subject. In turn, choice of control subject affects the other elements of the feedback loop.

Early forms of executive reports on quality tended to be limited to summaries of factory quality information, plus summaries of negative field reports. Table 8.1 lists some typical control subjects and associated units of measure. In large companies such summaries were often prepared by major groupings, such as by factory or by product line.

TABLE 8.1   Early Executive Reports on Quality

Control subjects	Units of measure
Factory quality	
First-time yield	Percent of product accepted on test
Scrap	Percent of material issued
Rework	Percent of direct labor-hours
Field performance	
Rejections by customer	Percent to shipments
Claims	Percent of sales
Complaints	Number
Warranty charges	Cost

With the growth of special quality-oriented departments, various additions and refinements were made to these early forms of reports. A major trend was to enlarge the use of money as the unit of measure for product deficiencies. A second trend was to improve field feedback in order to be able to discover causes of poor quality and identify opportunities for improvement. The availability of electronic data processing greatly simplified data summary and analysis as well as timely reporting. There were also numerous refinements in such forms as: seriousness classification systems, rating systems, and charting to show trends. The Pareto principle was employed to highlight the top few quality problems. Table 8.2 illustrates the nature of executive reports which include these additions and refinements.

TABLE 8.2   Revisions in Executive Reports on Quality

Control subjects	Units of measure
Factory quality deficiencies	Cost of poor quality relative to sales
Finished goods quality	Parts (defective) per million; demerits per unit; demerits per $1000 of sales; demerits per 1000 possible errors
Field quality performance	Percent uptime; maintenance hours per 1000 operating hours
Field quality deficiencies	Cost relative to sales; cost per 1000 units under warranty
Suppliers' quality	Cost of poor quality as a percent of purchases
Top 10 quality problems	Narrative listing
Significant events	Narrative listing

The 1980s accelerated additional trends. Executive reports on quality were increasingly extended to quality performance of business systems. The growing activity in quality improvement required progress reports. The emergence of CWQM necessitated special reporting. An emerging national concern with slow growth in productivity required linking of reports on quality with reports on productivity. The trend toward use of personal computers by upper managers demanded that report systems be "networked" to these personal computers.

Table 8.3 illustrates some of the ways in which executive reports on quality have been influenced by such developments.

TABLE 8.3   Influence of Recent Developments on Executive Reports on Quality

Control subject	Unit of measure
Promptness of service	Days; percent of responses within target goals
Competitiveness in quality	Performance versus top three competitors
Avoidable changes in engineering drawings, purchase orders, etc.	Percent of all changes
Document quality	Percent of pages defective
Software quality	Errors per 1000 lines of code; cost to correct errors
Invoicing errors	Percent in error; cost of correction
Quality improvement	Project data: undertaken, in progress, completed; results of projects collectively; status of major projects individually; percent of managers assigned to projects
Companywide quality management— progress against strategic quality goals	Various

Control Subjects.   The feedback loop is centered on the control subject. Tables 8.1, 8.2, and 8.3 show that the list of control subjects has been undergoing extensive changes. These changes have demanded that upper managers review performance with respect to certain control subjects which previously had been delegated to lower levels. Some of these control subjects are common to many industries: reliability in the field, time required to provide customer service, time required to place new products on the market, parts per million defective, and cost of poor quality. Other control subjects are unique to specific industries: software quality, maintenance hours per 1000 operating hours, and inspection escapes.

Since all control is built around specific control subjects, the choice of these subjects is the most critical element in the entire control system. If a vital control subject is omitted, the managers will lack a vital instrument on their instrument panel. If an unimportant control subject is included, it will receive undue attention while the attention given to more important matters will be diluted.

Because of continuing change in technology, competition, and other factors, it is necessary periodically to update the list of control subjects—to discard those which have outlived their usefulness and add new subjects which have become more important. One way to carry out such updating is through a multifunctional team. Such a team secures from the upper managers their views and nominations for revision. The consensus of these inputs provides the basis for a revised draft of a battery of executive reports. Following review by upper managers, this draft is revised. The "final" design then becomes the executive report battery until the next such updating several years later.

Alternatively, the work of updating is assigned to some individual (usually the quality manager). This individual then makes the rounds, secures inputs, and so on.

Executive Controls and Operational Controls. Because the total number of control subjects is fantastically large, a hierarchy of controls as depicted in Figure 6.9 (the control pyramid) is used. For discussion, see Section 6, under The Feedback Loop.

Table 8.4 shows how the major elements which make up the control systems apply to both operational and upper-management levels. It is evident that although the two control systems rest largely on a common base, they end up as virtually two separate worlds.

Leading and Lagging Indicators. A further distinction in controls is whether they provide information before, during, or after operations. Operational controls are obviously designed to assist in the conduct of day-to-day operations (Table 8.4).

Executive control reports are regarded as lagging indicators because the reports appear weeks or even months after the operations have been performed. Such reports are nevertheless of great value in showing trends, identifying substantial failures to meet goals, measuring performance of managers, and so forth.

The degree of lag varies considerably. The summarized scrap or rework reports

TABLE 8.4 Operational Quality Controls versus Executive Quality Controls

Element	Application to operational quality controls	Application to executive quality controls
Control subjects	Physical, chemical, specification requirements	Summarized performance for product lines, departments, etc.
Units of measure	Natural physical, chemical (ohms, kilograms, etc.)	Various: money; indexes; ratios (see Tables 8.1 through 8.3)
Sensing devices	Physical instruments, human senses	Summaries of data
Who collects the sensed information	Operators, inspectors, clerks, automated instruments	Various statistical departments
When the sensing is done	During current operations	Days, weeks, or months after current operations
Standards used for comparison	Engineered specifications; specified procedures	History; the market; the plan
Who acts on the information	Servomechanisms, nonsupervisors, first-line supervisors	Managers
Action taken	Process regulation, repair, sorting	Replanning; quality improvement; motivation

may lag only one month behind the day-to-day events. However, warranty charges may lag several months behind the date of manufacture and years behind the date of product development.

In contrast, some executive reports are leading indicators. Market research on quality may lead product development by months. Design review is a leading indicator of failure rates. Product audit lags behind date of manufacture but is a leading indicator of quality as received by the user.

The well-balanced system of executive reports makes use of leading indicators ("early warning signals") as well as summaries which lag behind operations.

Onnias (1986) describes how Texas Instruments, Inc. makes use of leading, concurrent, and lagging indicators in its *Quality Blue Book,* which is the central report on progress in quality.

For elaboration on control subjects, see Juran (1964), chapter 13, "Choosing the Control Subject."

Control Subjects which Lack Units of Measure.   Ideally, every process should have generally accepted means for evaluating its quality. However, there are many processes for which such means for evaluation are at best in a primitive state. In such cases it is usually easy enough to nominate control subjects but difficult to reach agreement, and even more difficult to work out suitable units of measure.

Table 8.5 lists some examples of functions along with nominations for evaluations which would be useful to managers. When such nominations are made, the lack of ready agreement on units of measure tends to discourage efforts to proceed further.

Actually, control subjects and units of measure follow an evolutionary path. A control subject is proposed. Ideas for units of measure are brainstormed, and a short list is agreed on. For example, a short list for "worker involvement" might emerge as follows:

Percent of workers who have undergone training in statistical process control

Percent of eligible workers who have achieved a self-inspection status

Percent of workers who are active participants on problem-solving teams

Data systems are then designed to collect the information needed to test out the short list. On the basis of the test results, some units of measure are discarded; others are retained and refined. In due course this process of evolution through experience arrives at units of measure which simply could not have been discovered solely by logical reasoning at the outset.

Units of Measure.   There are two basic meanings of the word "quality": (1) product features which provide product satisfaction and (2) freedom from defi-

TABLE 8.5   Nominations for Evaluation of Quality Performance

Functions	Nominations for control subjects
Product development	Producibility of designs; avoidable engineering changes
Manufacturing planning	Process capability of processes provided
	Adequacy of technology transfer
Purchasing	Avoidable purchase orders
Production	Worker involvement in quality

ciencies. (For elaborations, see Section 2, under "Quality" Defined.) Each of these two kinds of quality has its own forms of units of measure.

Freedom from Deficiencies. This aspect of quality is most often evaluated in the form of a fraction. The numerator is a number which expresses the *frequency* of deficiencies minus the number of defects, demerits, field failures, returns, hours of rework, dollars spent in rework, and so on. The denominator is a number expressing the *opportunity* for deficiencies, e.g., the number of units of product manufactured, units of product in service, dollars of sales, and so on. The resulting fractions take such forms as percent defective, demerits per unit, failure rate, percent returned, warranty dollars per 1000 units in service, and so forth.

Note that the above fractions are all in inverse form—the extent of deficiencies rather than freedom from deficiencies. Sometimes the direct form is used, for example, percent yield rather than percent defective, or percent uptime rather than percent downtime.

Product Features. For this aspect of quality, there is no convenient universal fraction. Instead, there is an extensive array of technological and related control subjects (diameter, speed, etc.) evaluated in technological units of measure (millimeters, revolutions per minute, etc.) by technological instruments (micrometer, tachometer, etc.) Nevertheless, there is a sort of universal rule which applies to units of measure for product features: the units of measure should include the customers' units of measure. To illustrate, suppliers who sell components to an assembler usually include, as a unit of measure, the time required to attach that component to the customer's assembly. Similarly, suppliers of equipment usually include, as units of measure: percent uptime, maintenance hours per 1000 operating hours and other parameters. Yet another application of this universal rule is seen in cases where the internal merit rating system fails to reflect customers' key units of measure. In some companies, merit ratings for the quality parameter are based on demerits per unit found during product audit. Yet the product may be unsalable because of unacceptable field failure rates.

Summaries of Unlike Units of Measure. The executive report, which is a summary, usually deals with items which are not homogeneous. In consequence, it is necessary to create new units of measure which permit summary of unlike items. There are several ways of doing this:

1. *Arbitrary weighting:* For example, defects are classified as to seriousness and each class is assigned a weight (demerits). This makes it possible to use demerits per unit of product as new unit of measure.

2. *Conversion into a common natural unit:* A well-known example is the use of money as a common measure of scrap, rework, service work, etc., despite wide differences in products and processes. Another example is the concept of "opportunities for failure" used as the denominator of indexes of performance. Wilson (1967) developed a measure in terms of demerits per possible error. Brainard (1974) proposed summations in the form of defects per 100 (labor) hours and defects per $1000 (labor). Some companies use failures per million dollars (of sales) as a universal unit of measure across multiple product lines.

3. *Conversion into statistical equivalents:* In this approach, the historical performance in natural units is equated to 100 percent (for example). A 10 percent departure from this level becomes a score of 90 percent, regardless of what the natural unit is. This method also permits preparation of composite scores for several performances by weighting.

For elaboration on units of measure, see Juran (1964), Chapter 14, "The Unit of Measure."

Data Collection and Summary. Preparation of executive reports on quality requires a good deal of precise coordination among the data sources in order to:

Standardize terminology such as names of defects, parts, and other names which enter the data system.

Standardize the code numbers which are used to translate this terminology into the language of the computer. See, for example, Noyes (1979).

Standardize the calendar dates for defining time intervals (weeks, months) and for meeting report deadlines.

Agree on the form of delivery of information to minimize the problems of preparation of the final executive reports.

Define the respective responsibilities of all departments associated in this cooperative venture.

It is also important to note the distinction between the deeds and the data (which are only the evidence of the deeds). The realities are the deeds, and the surest control is through personal observation of the deeds: "I don't care what the report says—the bins are empty."

The successive layers of summary and the creation of unnatural units of measure all carry the risk that the data will fail to reflect the deeds because of coloration, statistical quirks, and just plain mistakes. Careful checking and auditing are needed to maintain the full connection between deeds and data.

Data processing has been revolutionized by the computer, with dramatic improvements in accuracy and timeliness of reports. See generally, Section 27, Computers and Quality; see also Munro (1982).

Standards of Comparison. The system of executive reports should provide standards against which to compare performance. In the absence of standards, it is easy for managers to overreact to individual complaints or to other alarm signals.

At the technological level the standards are engineered and are embodied into the material, process, and product specifications. Other engineered standards include material usage and labor usage. Next are the historical standards in which current performance is compared with the past. A further standard is the market, that is, what other people do when faced with similar problems. Competitive performance is the most usual market standard for quality. A fourth standard is the plan, such as the budget, quota, and schedule. The plan is established by human judgment after the other inputs—technology, history, and market—are considered.

The recent growth of competition in quality has broadened the use of competitive standards as a basis for judging product performance. This in turn has intensified efforts to discover what is the level of competitive quality. Sources of competitive data include:

1. Customers who purchase from competing sources. Often they are willing to prepare comparative data, although without identifying competitors.

2. Trade associations who become a database, again preserving anonymity.

3. Independent laboratories who publish comparative test results, often naming the competitors.

4. Government regulatory bodies who publish test results, sometimes naming names.

5. Professional society research studies.

To go beyond these sources requires special studies in the form of marketing research. Some of these can be conducted in the laboratory; others require studies in the field. See Section 12 for elaboration.

History as a standard for comparison has long been popular. The data are available, and the standard is known to be attainable. However, use of an historical standard includes a risk of perpetuating poor performances such as high costs of poor quality or carryover of failure-prone designs. This risk can be reduced by judicious design of audits which look for opportunities and threats as well as conformance to standards. For elaboration, see Section 9, Quality Assurance, under Quality Survey. See also Quality Audit by Upper Managers below.

For a broad discussion of standards of comparison, see Juran (1964), chapter 15, "The Standard."

The Executive Report Battery.   The growth of upper-management involvement with quality has demanded creation of a battery of reports specially designed to meet the needs of upper management. This battery of reports is variously called the "executive report battery," "the executive instrument panel," etc. Such special design has been an essential element of CWQM.

Texas Instruments, an electronics manufacturer, has used the *Quality Blue Book* since 1981 as the basis of reports to divisional upper managers. The book was deliberately designed to parallel the company's financial reporting system, down to the color of the cover (blue). The report battery is organized into (1) leading indicators (e.g., quality of purchased components), (2) concurrent indicators (e.g., product test results, process conditions, service to customers), (3) lagging indicators (e.g., data feedback from customers, returns), and (4) data on cost of poor quality.

The report is issued monthly and is the basis for annual performance appraisal for managers' contribution to quality. For elaboration, see Onnias (1986).

General Dynamics Corporation, a defense contractor, undertook a form of corporate quality improvement, starting in the early 1980s. One element of the approach is a report battery. The reports deal with numerous parameters, of which 12 are corporate—they are common to all divisions of the corporation. The corporate parameters are as follows:

Avoidable engineering changes

Deviations/waivers

First-time yield

Scrap (labor-hour content)

Scrap (material value content)

Repair and/or rework (labor-hour content)

On-time delivery by Production

Purchased item acceptability

Service report response time

Material review actions

Inspection escapes

Overtime

For elaboration, see Talley (1986).

In 1981, Florida Power & Light (FPL), a public utility, undertook to develop a form of CWQM. Its executive report battery features over 20 parameters, including:

Operating and maintenance cost per customer

Customers per employee

Overtime percent

Extension costs per new service account

Efficiency

Vehicle utilization

Credit memos per 1000 customers

Public Service Commission inquiries

Work-load factor

Service unavailability

Service interruptions

Under its companywide approach, FPL's corporate goals include broad quality improvement goals. These broad goals are then deployed to lower levels for action by project teams. For elaboration, see Brunetti (1987); for additional information concerning the FPL approach, see McDonald (1987), Walden (1987), and Sterett (1987).

For additional discussion concerning the executive report battery and its use for decision-making, see Juran (1964), chapter 17, "Mobilizing for Decision Making." See also Section 20 under Executive Reports on Field Performance.

Opportunities and Threats. Conventional executive reports are designed neither to disclose opportunities available to the organization nor to identify threats which are converging on the organization. These limitations have long been present in financial reporting and have been carried over into reports on quality. Nevertheless, the opportunities and threats are there. What is lacking in many companies is a positive means for identifying them.

One such means is the audit. It is feasible to design the system of audits to provide for identifying opportunities and threats. See Quality Audits by Upper Managers below; see also Section 9, Quality Assurance, under Quality Surveys.

Format. Executive reports should be designed to read at a glance to permit easy concentration on the exceptional matters requiring executive attention.

Tabulations of data are the most primitive format. Some of these consist of forbidding stacks of pages from a computer printout or from a statistical department. These masses of data are an imposition on busy executives, who are, in effect, being asked to do the summarizing which someone else should have done.

Summarized tabulations are a long step in the right direction. They do not give a perspective in time, but they do tabulate the three essential current figures: standard, actual, and variance. In some companies the significant deficiencies or improvements are marked in a distinctive way to simplify the job of reading the tabulation.

Graphic presentation requires added work by the reporting departments but greatly simplifies interpretation by the executive. Blake (1978) dramatizes this principle by producing a single page containing 18 charts, each of which shows the performance trend for some important aspect of operations.

Recent computer development has also enabled managers to display data and graphics on personal computer terminals. The early applications were generally to aid quality managers and engineers (Clements, 1979). However, the trend may well be to provide upper managers with such facilities (Rockart, 1979).

Another approach to visual display is through a "visibility center." Under this concept a special room is fitted with wall charts which are updated monthly. These charts are then viewed and discussed by convening managers. The same room is also used for ceremonial awards. For details, see Frankovich (1978).

Graphic presentation ideally displays a full perspective with respect to time, as shown in Figure 8.1. Typically, a left-hand segment shows some recent history (e.g., several years) on a condensed time scale. The main part of the graph shows current performance against goals (e.g., on a month-by-month basis). The goals are then extended into the near future to show the anticipated results.

Charting technique has been studied exhaustively and is available in the literature. An excellent early reference availably in some engineering libraries is *Time Series Charts—A Manual of Design and Construction,* American Standard Z15.2-1938. (A photocopy of this out-of-print document may be obtained from Engineering Societies Library, 345 E. 47th St., New York, NY 10017.)

When numerous charts are needed, it is feasible to make use of a standardized format to create a coordinated "executive instrument panel." In the absence of such standardization, the managers are faced with a problem of frequent "tuning in and out" because of the variety of format. As a result, their reviews are delayed and the opportunities for error increased.

Publication.   It is useful to assemble the principal executive reports on quality into a comprehensive package which is published regularly and can eventually earn status as the authoritative source of essential information on quality (i.e., an official executive instrument panel). To reach such status requires years of dedicated reporting using unquestioned objectivity, good format, and careful attention to the needs of the executives who are the users.

Interpretation.   The editor of the executive reports can provide useful illumination of the facts through the inclusion of supplemental information which does the following:

Identifies the vital few quality problems. Preferably, this list does not exceed 10 items.

Reports on the status of major quality programs under way; results achieved, work in progress; what the next move is and who is to take it; and need, if any, for action by upper management.

Summarizes the findings of audits and surveys, whether in-house or of suppliers.

Discusses major developments which are taking place with respect to quality as a result of industry programs, government action, competitor action, consumer organizations, and other outside forces.

Previews proposals which will be presented for upper-management consideration.

The editor of the reports must also take pains to avoid the common errors which lead to loss of confidence in the reports. These include:

Failure to distinguish between important and unimportant issues.

Too many false alarms, resulting from failure to check the alarm signals.

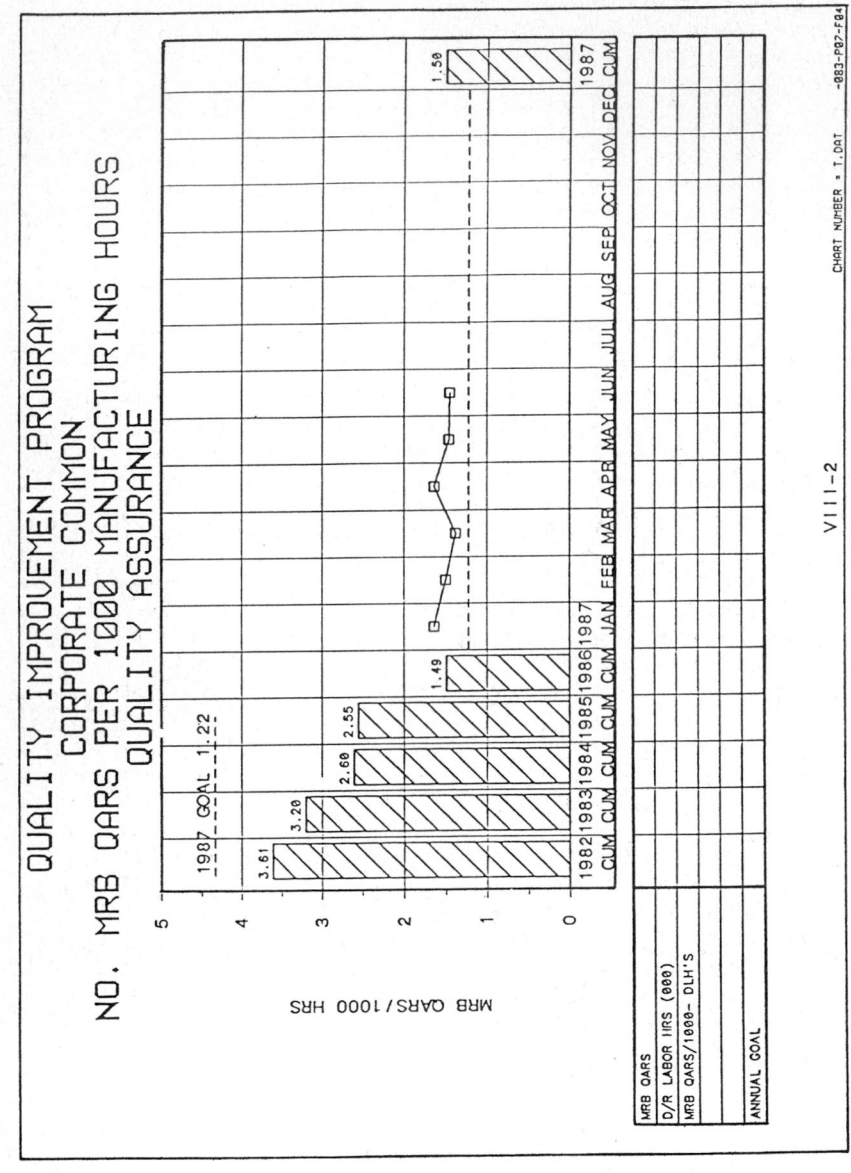

FIG. 8.1 Example of chart format for executive report. *(Courtesy General Dynamics Corp.)*

8.18

An atmosphere of "blame" in the reports, rather than one of constructive search for remedy and improvement.

"Overkill" in its various forms. This is always easier to understand when someone else does it, e.g., government regulators.

A Universal Measure for Quality. In some economies, universal measures have been developed for such social phenomena as gross national product, cost of living, unemployment, and crime. It would obviously be most useful if a corresponding universal measure could be evolved for quality.

As of the 1980s there existed neither such a universal measure for quality nor a generally accepted model which could become the basis for such a universal measure.

For quality in the sense of freedom from deficiencies, a universal measure is theoretically feasible—the model exists. It would require enlarging the accounting systems in order to evaluate how much less the costs would be if there were no deficiencies—in effect, to evaluate the cost of poor quality.

For quality in the sense of product features (which render the product salable), there is no such generally accepted comprehensive model. For certain parameters of this aspect of quality, models do exist (e.g., life cycle costing, product audit based on a system of demerits). However, the parameters are numerous, and many lack models. In addition, efforts to composite the parameters into a single measure requires extensive empirical judgment as to the weights to be assigned to the respective parameters.

Nevertheless, there are forces which press for such comprehensive measures. A growing number of countries have established national awards for quality. The establishment of such awards requires evaluation of the quality performance of companies, as well as their products and the processes they employ. It would be helpful to consumers, many of whom lack technological sophistication, if product quality could be expressed in some simple measure. Many chief executives have urged, "Give me some simple measure for quality, much as I now have for profit or safety."

Qualimetry. Socialist economies have a special need for solving this problem. These economies include a good deal of central planning, and the planners are handicapped in their work if they are unable to quantify so important a factor in the economy as quality. Lacking this quantification, they have greater difficulty in establishing pricing structures for the products, allocating investments for quality, judging what broad programs to undertake, and so on.

Starting in the late 1960s the All-union Research Institute for Standardization of the Soviet Union undertook a project to develop means for evaluating quality. The term "qualimetry" was adopted as a name for the science of evaluating quality (Derbisher, 1971).

Glichev (1985) has summarized the subsequent events under the title "15 Years of Qualimetry: Problems and Prospects." According to Glichev, progress has been made in design of algorithms and models and also in identification of quality parameters. However, practical application has lagged because of various limitations, such as evaluation of sensory qualities, evaluation of long-life parameters, variations in product use and environments, and consumer perceptions.

Future directions appear to involve reliance on market research to secure consumers' evaluations of consumer goods, use of panels of qualified experts to evaluate quality of commercial goods, and computerized data collection and analysis.

Productivity as a Measure.   In general terms, productivity is the ratio of output to input, where input consists of labor, material, capital, and services. Methods for evaluation of productivity are in a more advanced state than methods for evaluation of quality. As a result, data on national and industry productivity are widely compiled and published. In turn, the published data are the focus of attention of political leaders, economists, industrial leaders, and others.

To a degree, productivity and quality are interrelated. Projects to reduce cost of poor quality almost invariably improve productivity as well. Attainment of "just-in-time" objectives requires, as a prerequisite, the solution of quality-related problems. However, there are also some important differences. Some of the ingredients of high productivity are not quality-related; some of the ingredients of quality are not productivity-related. The respective planners typically come from different disciplines, for example, industrial engineering as opposed to quality engineering. Improvement of productivity is regarded with suspicion in some quarters as a source of unemployment. In contrast, improvement of quality is universally regarded as a benefit to society.

The overlap between productivity and quality has led to the suggestion that measures of quality be expressed in productivity terms (Midas, 1982). In the judgment of the author, the two measures should be kept separate despite the overlap.

QUALITY AUDITS BY UPPER MANAGERS

Section 9, Quality Assurance, deals extensively with three major forms of quality assurance: quality audits, quality surveys, and product audits. Those forms of quality assurance are typically carried out by full-time quality auditors, sometimes supplemented by middle managers. (The summarized findings are often reviewed at higher levels as well.)

The present topic, quality audits by upper managers, deals with special forms of quality audit in which the upper managers personally participate in conduct of the audits.

Why Quality Audits by Upper Managers?   In general, such audits are not undertaken as isolated activities. Instead, they are part of a broader effort to improve performance with respect to quality. The stimulus for such broader effort may come from a threat, such as loss of sales due to lack of quality competitiveness in the marketplace. Alternatively, the stimulus may come from the urge to gain quality leadership and the associated benefits.

The earliest widespread use of such audits was in Japan. Shortly after World War II, many Japanese companies had difficulty selling their goods to the West. A major reason was poor quality. To make matters worse, the long-standing perception of the West had been that Japanese goods were chronically poor. To render the goods salable and to reverse the national quality reputation demanded changes of a revolutionary nature—changes which could be accomplished only through the personal leadership of upper managers. One element of that personal leadership was quality audits conducted by upper managers.

Several decades later, many companies in the West also faced a need for making revolutionary changes in their approach to quality. The needed changes were not merely a matter of improving conformance to policies and goals; what was needed most was revision in policies and goals—revisions in areas which required decisions by upper managers.

The upper managers were then faced with (1) determining what changes were needed, (2) ordering these changes to be made, and (3) assuring that the changes went into effect and remained in effect.

In simplified form, the resulting upper-management participation is as follows:

	Subordinate managers and below	Upper managers
Establish revised policies, goals, plans	X	X
Carry out the plans; meet the goals	X	
Audit		X

The audit is in part a review of results versus goals. However, the personal participation of the upper managers establishes direct contact with various personnel and direct exposure to various realities. These contacts and exposures provide the upper managers with additional vital inputs for decision-making—inputs which are not found in reports of performance versus goals.

Ishikawa (1987) lists the following as benefits of upper-management quality audits when led by the president:

Increased understanding by the president of the state of affairs

Greater objectivity of information coming to the president

Improved human relations with subordinates

Greater stimulus to subordinates through personal participation by the president

Subject Matter of Upper-Management Audits. A useful preview of the emerging content of such audits is provided by the Japanese experience during the decades since World War II. For example, Komatsu Ltd., a manufacturer of construction equipment, conducts audits which serve also as the basis for quality awards to subsidiaries, subcontractors, distributors, and dealers. Figure 8.2 lists the subject matter of these audits along with the weights assigned. For elaboration, see Shimoyamada (1987).

An additional preview is provided by the list of criteria used for awarding the Deming Application Prize in Japan. (The first award was in 1951.) The parameters include:

Policies and objectives

Organization and its operation

Education and its dissemination

Information flow and utilization

Product and process quality

Standardization

Control and management

Quality assurance of functions, systems, and methods

Results

Future plans

For elaboration, see Ishikawa (1987).

Classification / Evaluation item	Domestic Subsidiaries		Subcontractors	Distributors	Dealers
	Production and sales	Mainly sales			
1	Company policy and overall control system	30	30	30	30	30
2	Quality assurance	30	30	30	30	30
3	Product development and technical development	20	20	(30)		
4	Cost control	20		30		
5	Delivery control	10		10		
6	Sales control	20	40		40	30
7	Training, safety, and environment	10	10	10	10	10
8	Priority execution items			30		
	Total	140	130	140 (170)	110	100
	Eagerness and understanding of top management	100		100	100	100

FIG. 8.2 Example of subject matter and weights used in upper management audits. *Note:* Numbers show weights assigned; parentheses around numbers indicate they are for specialized manufacturers only.

The preceding lists are generally applicable to companies in developed countries and, to a degree, to all companies. For companies whose quality revolution is still young, special emphasis is warranted with respect to (1) the functional processes and (2) opportunities and threats.

Functional Processes. These include the processes which determine the quality contributions of such major functions as product development, purchasing, and marketing. They also include numerous business processes of a multifunctional nature, such as launching new products, filling customers' orders, and preparing invoices.

For the major functions, the broad responsibility is clear, but there are inherent weaknesses. For example, in such functions the quality planning has traditionally been done by functional experts who lack expertise in the quality function. It is feasible for the audits to find ways to help overcome such weaknesses. For examples of questions to be raised, see Section 9, Quality Assurance, under Questions for Quality Surveys; Functional Areas.

In the case of multifunctional processes, a major weakness is lack of "ownership." For each step in such processes, there is clear responsibility. However, there is no such clear responsibility for the overall process; the process is supervised by some impersonal procedure or manual which tends to remain static and to acquire inflexibility. Audits by upper managers offer an additional avenue for dealing with weaknesses in such processes.

Opportunities. A major emphasis of the upper-management audit should be on quality improvement. In most companies the pace of creating new quality problems has for years exceeded the pace of solution. The result has been an increasing accumulation of chronic problems which are seriously counterproductive to operations. It takes a determined effort, guided by upper management, to reverse this trend. (See Section 22, Quality Improvement, for details of the improvement process.) A key element is to estimate the cost of poor quality.

Where such accumulation has been continuing for years, it takes years to eliminate it. Nothing short of personal intervention by upper management can supply the necessary leadership. The concept of CWQM includes provision for annual quality improvement. See Section 6, Companywide Quality management; see also Brunetti (1987).

"Opportunities" include the various management movements which are continually emerging over the horizon. Some of these are meritorious; others are cults, or worse. It is sometimes difficult at the outset to tell which is which. One solution is to conduct a tryout at some test site to determine whether the concept has useful application in the company.

Threats. Threats are a leading indicator of trouble ahead. The upper-management audit should include looking ahead in various directions, such as demographic trends, emerging social forces, trends in legislation, and trends in the marketplace.

Threats can also be internal. A new product under development can, because of lack of early warnings, threaten to create problems for those who will be required to produce the design, or to maintain it. Lack of employee participation may fester into human relations problems. Such internal threats can seldom be sensed from conventional reports. They require personal exposure to the realities.

The Social Responsibility Audit. "Social responsibility" is a broad term relating to the impact of business on society generally. Widely publicized examples include product safety and damage to the environment, but there are many other impacts as well.

Some of the problems created by such impacts came to a head during the 1960s and spawned new legislation relative to environmental protection, product safety, consumerism, and other issues. In addition, there emerged the concept of a special "social responsibility audit" as an early warning device to assist upper managers in their strategic business planning (see, e.g., Humble, 1973).

A quality audit by upper managers necessarily has some overlap with the concept of a social responsibility audit. The design of the quality audit should consider the degree to which it should extend into the area of social responsibility.

Organization for Quality Audits by Upper Managers. Normally a quality audit by upper managers is part of a broader effort to improve quality performance. Usually a high-level quality council (committee, etc.) has been created to guide the broad effort. Members of this council typically conduct the audits.

Upper-management audits are preceded by collection and analysis of information pertinent to the subject matter of the audits. This preparatory work is done by subordinate managers in collaboration with staff personnel. The frequency is semiannual or annual. For examples, see Shimoyamada (1987) and Brunetti (1987); see also section 35F, Quality in Japan, under Internal QC Audit by Top Management.

The President's Quality Audit. In some major Japanese companies the president personally participates in the audit. In such cases it is called "the president's quality audit." For a description of the workings of the president's quality audit, see Section 35F, Quality in Japan, under Internal QC Audit by Top Management; see also Shimoyamada (1987) and Ishikawa (1987).

Third-Party Audits. Some types of quality audit are subcontracted to third parties for various reasons, such as expertise, economy, and independence. Usually such subcontracting must be authorized by upper managers. In turn, the resulting reports are reviewed by upper managers.

The concept of third-party audits is in wide use. An extensive form is independent test laboratories. Previously these laboratories provided only testing services for goods; some of them now provide auditing services as well. For a discussion of the rationale for this, see Rennie, Morris, and Blackburn (1978).

The growth of the field has attracted other sources of such audits. Standardization bodies in some countries have increasingly organized to provide such services.

An important consideration in employing such services is the independence of the third party. In some cases this independence is the major consideration. (The Deming Application Prize is awarded by an independent committee of experts.)

TRAINING FOR UPPER MANAGERS

A company can undertake a major revision in managing for quality only if its upper managers are trained in the design and supervision of such an undertaking. The needed training is derived from multiple sources, including:

Training "by the book," i.e., through courses and seminars. See, generally, Section 11, Training for Quality, especially under Training for Various Categories of Personnel; Upper Management.

Membership on the quality council. Such membership requires upper managers to address many of the problems faced by the company relative to managing for quality.

Membership on quality audit teams. Such membership brings upper managers into direct contact with many subordinates and the realities faced by them.

REFERENCES

Blake, Geroge B. (1978). "Ideas for Action." *Harvard Business Review,* March-April, pp. 6–8, 12.

Brainard, E. H. (1974). "Quality Measurement and Reporting as Related to Management Cybernetics." *ASQC Technical Conference Transactions,* Milwaukee, pp. 208–217.

Brunetti, Wayne (1987). "Policy Deployment—A Corporate Roadman." *The Juran Report,* No. 8, pp. 20–29.

Clements, John A. (1979). "Interactive Graphics in New Product Quality Assurance Programs." *Quality Progress,* February, pp. 14–16; abstract, Executive Sciences Institute, 1980, pp. 61–62.

Derbisher, A. (1971). "Qualimetry—A New Scientific Discipline." Abstract, Executive Sciences Institute, pp. 939–940.

Frankovich, Jim (1978). "Quality Awareness." *Quality Progress,* vol. 11, no. 2, February, pp. 22–24.

Gibson, Thomas C. (1987). "Looking Back on Three Years of QI." *The Juran Report,* No. 8, pp. 43–49.

Glichev, A. V. (1985). "15 Years of Qualimetry. Problems and Prospects." *Proceedings, EOQC Conference Quality & Development,* vol. 2, pp. 259–269.

Humble, John (1973). *Social Responsibility Audit.* AMACOM, A Division of American Management Associations, New York.

Ishikawa, Kaoru (1987). "The Quality Control Audit." *Quality Progress,* January, pp. 39–41.

Juran, J. M. (1964). *Managerial Breakthrough.* McGraw-Hill, New York.

Juran, J. M. (1973). "The Taylor System and Quality Control." A series of articles in *Quality Progress,* May through December 1973 (listed under "Management Interface").

McDonald, Marshall (1987). "Why FPL Pursued Quality Improvement." *The Juran Report,* No. 8, pp. 17–19.

Midas, Michael, Jr. (1982). "A Measure." *Quality,* August, pp. Q9–Q10.

Munro, Bruce (1982). "The Quality Information System." *ASQC Quality Congress Transactions,* Milwaukee, pp. 327–334.

Noyes, Richard J. (1979). "Quality Measurement System." *ASQC Technical Conference Transactions,* Milwaukee, pp. 434–437.

Onnias, Arturo (1986). *"The Quality Blue Book." The Juran Report,* No. 6, pp. 127–131.

Rennie, D., Morris, W., and Blackburn, K. (1978). "Quality Assurance: The Modern Concept of the Third Party Inspection." *International Conference on Quality Control.* Japanese Union of Scientists and Engineers, Tokyo, pp. C1-27 through C1-32.

Rockart, John F. (1979). "Chief Executives Define Their Own Data Needs." *Harvard Business Review,* March-April, pp. 81–93.

Shimoyamada, Kaoru (1987). "The President's Audit: QC Audits at Komatsu." *Quality Progress,* January, pp. 44–49.

Sterett, W. Kent (1987). "Commitment and Involvement: Vital Components in a Successful Quality Improvement Program." *The Juran Report,* No. 8, pp. 35–37.

Talley, D. J. (1986). "The Quest for Sustaining Quality Improvement." *The Juran Report,* No. 6, pp. 188–192.

Walden, James C. (1987). "Integrating Customer Satisfaction into Daily Work." *The Juran Report,* No. 8, pp. 30–34.

Wilson, Myron F. (1967). "The Quality Your Customer Sees." *ASQC Journal of the Electronics Division,* July, pp. 3–16.

SECTION 9
QUALITY ASSURANCE[1]

Frank M. Gryna

INTRODUCTION **9.2**
Concept of Quality
    Assurance 9.2
Quality Audit: General . . 9.4
AUDIT OF QUALITY PLANS . . . **9.5**
Subject Matter 9.5
Reference Standards for
    Auditing 9.6
AUDIT OF EXECUTION VERSUS
PLANS **9.6**
PLANNING AND PERFORMING
AUDITS **9.7**
Audit Initiation 9.7
Audit Planning 9.7
Audit Implementation . . . 9.10
Audit Reporting 9.12
Report Publication 9.13
Audit Completion 9.14
Quality Assurance of Audits 9.14
QUALITY SURVEYS **9.14**
QUESTIONS FOR QUALITY
SURVEYS **9.17**
Companywide Issues . . . 9.17
Functional Areas 9.18

Summary of Quality Status 9.20
Third-Party Audit or
    Survey 9.20
Reference Standards for
    Surveys 9.21
PRODUCT AUDITING **9.22**
Definition and Purposes . . 9.22
Stage of Evaluation 9.22
Designing the Audit Plan . 9.23
Reporting the Results of
    Product Auditing 9.24
ACTION ON DISCREPANCIES . . **9.26**
Effect of Product Audit on
    Clarifying Quality
    Standards 9.27
PERSONNEL FOR QUALITY
ASSURANCE **9.27**
Upper Management 9.27
Middle Managers 9.27
Audit Teams 9.28
External Auditors 9.28
Full-Time Auditors 9.28
Product Auditors 9.29
REFERENCES **9.29**

[1]In the Third Edition, material on quality assurance was prepared by J. M. Juran.

INTRODUCTION

In this handbook, "quality assurance" is the activity of providing the evidence needed to establish confidence, among all concerned, that the quality function is being effectively performed.

While such is the meaning given in this handbook, the term "quality assurance" has other meanings as well. Confusion regarding this important term can lead to serious misunderstandings. For example, the capitalized term "Quality Assurance" often means the title of a broad-based department which is concerned with many quality-related activities, such as quality planning, quality control, quality improvement, quality audit, and reliability.

This section discusses three forms of companywide quality assurance: quality audits, quality surveys, and product audit. Additional forms of assurance are performed within functional departments. Table 9.1 lists some important departmental assurance activities. Additional examples of assurance can be found in the industry sections of this handbook (see Sections 28 and 29, under The Control Plan; Section 30, under Audit Plan; Section 31, under Critical Tasks; and Section 33, under Quality Audits; see also Section 5, under Quality Policies for Functions; Quality Assurance, and Section 17, under Audit of Production Quality).

Concept of Quality Assurance. Quality assurance provides protection against quality problems through early warnings of trouble ahead. Such early warnings play an important role in the prevention of both internal and external problems. The assurance is provided from objective evidence, but the type of evidence differs widely according to the persons requiring the assurance and the nature of the product.

For natural products, quality assurance is attained through direct sensory examination of the product—for example, freshness of vegetables in the village marketplace. For manufactured products of a simple, short-lived nature, the sensory evidence must usually be supplemented by laboratory testing. Those who lack test facilities must rely on the word of the manufacturer or on feedback from use testing.

For longer-life products, more elaborate testing (environmental, life) is needed, but most merchants and users lack such test facilities. Hence they must secure their added assurance from such forms as the manufacturer's quality reputation, tests by independent laboratories, or warranties.

For complex products, even data obtained from sophisticated environmental and life tests do not provide full quality assurance, since they fail to guard against inadequate product designs, process designs, and quality planning. They also fail to deal with those aspects of quality performance which show up after final testing (e.g., packing, transport, storage, usage, and maintenance).

To meet these added needs for quality assurance, the manufacturer must not only produce the product but also prepare and make available to the customer the proof that the product is fit for use.

In complex products this proof usually consists of:

1. A formal plan which spells out, for all phases of product progression "from cradle to grave," how fitness for use will be achieved

2. A system of reviews to verify that the plan, if followed, will result in fitness for use

3. A system of audits to verify that the plans are actually being followed

4. A system to provide data on the quality achieved

TABLE 9.1　Examples of Departmental Assurance Activities

Department/assurance activity	Reference pages
Marketing	
Product evaluation by a test market	19.8
Controlled use of product	12.11
Product monitoring	12.11
Captive service activity	12.11
Special surveys	12.12
Competitive evaluations	12.17
Product development	
Design review	13.7
Reliability analysis	13.21
Maintainability analysis	13.43
Safety analysis	13.50
Human factors analysis	13.55
Manufacturing, inspection, and transportation analysis	16.5
Value engineering	13.63
Self-control analysis	13.70
Supplier relations	
Qualification of supplier design	15.12
Qualification of supplier process	15.13
Evaluation of initial samples	15.25
Evaluation of first shipments	15.26
Production	
Design review	16.5
Process capability analysis	16.25
Preproduction trials	16.41
Preproduction runs	16.42
Failure mode, effect, and criticality analysis for processes	16.42
Review of manufacturing planning (checklist)	16.44
Evaluation of proposed process control tools	16.50
Self-control analysis	17.4
Audit of production quality	17.26
Inspection and test	
Interlaboratory tests	18.69
Measuring inspector accuracy	18.94
Customer service	
Audit of packaging, transportation, and storage	20.2
Evaluation of maintenance services	20.10

The foregoing concept has some similarity to the concept of the financial audit, which provides assurance of financial integrity by establishing, through "independent" audit, that the plan of accounting is (1) such that, if followed, it will correctly reflect the financial condition of the company and (2) actually being followed. Today independent financial auditors (certified public accountants) have become an influential force in the field of finance.

The deeds used to provide the evidence for quality assurance masquerade under a variety of names such as "audit," "survey," "surveillance," and "assessment." In the topics which follow, these deeds and their definitions are discussed in detail.

Quality Audit: General.   A quality audit is an independent review conducted to compare some aspect of quality performance with a standard for that performance. The term "independent" is critical and is used in the sense that the reviewer (called the "auditor") is neither the person responsible for the performance under review nor the immediate supervisor of that person. An independent audit provides an unbiased picture of performance.

Quality audits are used mainly by companies to evaluate their own quality performance and the performance of their suppliers, licensees, agents, and others and by regulatory agencies to evaluate the performance of organizations which they are assigned to regulate.

The usual purposes of quality audits are to provide independent assurance that:

Plans for attaining quality are such that, if followed, the intended quality will, in fact, be attained

Products are fit for use and safe for the user

Laws and regulations are being followed

There is conformance to specifications

Procedures are adequate and are being followed

The data system provides accurate and adequate information on quality to all concerned

Deficiencies are identified and corrective action is taken

Opportunities for improvement are identified and the appropriate personnel alerted

Farrow (1987) explains how audits also assist in management decision making, allocation of resources, and improving morale.

The subject matter of quality audits extends across the entire spectrum of the quality function, but the bulk of auditing is performed under several well-established categories:

1. *Audits of policies and objectives:*   This review is conducted at the highest level of company operations and hence is normally done by upper management.

2. *Audit of performance against company objectives:*   Because company objectives are quite broad, this review is also conducted by upper management and is based largely on the data presented by the executive reports on quality.

3. *Audits of plans, systems, and procedures:*   These measures are reviewed to judge their adequacy for enabling the company to meet its quality policies and objectives. This includes audits of computerized systems to detect errors in computer programs. Willborn (1987) discusses the effects of computerization on auditing.

4. *Audit of execution:*   This audit is conducted to determine whether execution follows the plans, systems, and procedures. The term "quality system audit" is often used in contrast to "product audit" described below.

5. *Product audit:*   This audit is conducted to determine whether the product meets specifications and the needs of fitness for use.

Audit categories 1 and 2 are discussed in Section 8, under Quality Audit by Upper Managers. Categories 3, 4, and 5 are discussed below.

Plum (1987) discusses an 11-week implementation plan for an audit program. Ishikawa (1987) identifies four categories of audit by "outsiders" and four categories of audit "from within." Sayle (1981) provides additional detail on many of the steps covered below on conducting audits.

AUDIT OF QUALITY PLANS

The term "audit of quality plans" refers to review of the entire family of elements of quality planning to judge their adequacy for meeting the quality mission of the company. The more complex the product, the greater the need to review the quality plans, systems, procedures, and other measures to judge their adequacy.

Subject Matter. The scope of these audits covers a wide range: all functions affecting quality, a single function (e.g., product development), a broad process (e.g., handling of complaints), or a single activity (e.g., calibration of measuring equipment). Since quality-related activities are numerous, priorities must be determined.

Priorities should emphasize (1) activities impacting on fitness for use and/or contractual requirements and then (2) activities which affect the cost of poor quality. In setting priorities, attention should focus on the opportunity for improvement versus the cost of performing the audit. Thus, as audits identify and help to correct a problem, audit resources should be switched to other areas, or the frequency of audit for the improved areas should be reduced.

Defining clearly just what is the subject matter of specific audits is usually done by:

1. *Identifying the broad areas of quality activity:* Kane (1984) discusses an example which identifies 23 elements (see Table 9.2) for auditing at a manufacturer of refrigeration equipment.

2. *Establishing, for each chosen subject, a detailed checklist of the features to be studied and the questions to be raised:* Checklists benefit both the auditor and auditee (see Sayle, 1981, chapter 8).

TABLE 9.2 Quality Program Requirements

1. Quality policy	13. Purchases and subcontracts
2. Organization	14. Manufacturing activities
3. Quality program documentation	15. Material identification and control
4. Personnel selection and qualification	16. Examination, inspection, and test
5. Document control	17. Nonconformances
6. Measuring and test equipment	18. Special processes
7. Records	19. Handling, storage, and shipping
8. Performance feedback	20. Deliverable software
9. Quality costs	21. Installation and service
10. Corrective action	22. Audits
11. Marketing activities	23. Performance improvement
12. Design assurance	

Source: Kane, 1984, p. 264.

Many checklists have been published and are available in the literature. Hayes and Romig (1977) provide samples of checklists for 10 broad activities. For example, a checklist for "Fabrication" lists 21 elements to be audited, with audit items listed for each element. Element 3, under "Fabrication," is "Adequacy of fabrication work instruction or traveler that denotes and details the job." Recommended items to be audited for this one element are as follows: (1) the function to be performed; (2) sequence of operations; (3) inspection points; (4) setups, equipment, and tools; (5) speeds, feeds, and processes; (6) drawing numbers and revisions; (7) sketches and working drawings; (8) specifications; and (9) raw material, type and size.

Checklists based on the concept of self-control can also be useful (see Section 13, under Concept of Self-Control in Product Development, and Section 17, under Concept of Controllability). Each company, however, should prepare its own checklists.

Reference Standards for Auditing.   Audit of quality plans requires reference standards against which to judge the adequacy of the plans. (Failing this, the audit becomes heavily subjective.) The reference standards normally available include:

The written policies of the company as they apply to quality

The stated objectives in the budgets, programs, contracts, etc.

The customer and company quality specifications

The pertinent government specifications and handbooks

The company, industry, and other pertinent quality standards on product, processes, and computer software

The published guides for conduct of quality audits

The pertinent quality departmental instructions

The general literature on auditing

AUDIT OF EXECUTION VERSUS PLANS

This form of audit is for the purpose of determining whether the conduct of operations is in accordance with the plans, procedures, specifications, and so on. The activities reviewed may be broad (control and improvement of quality costs, response to quality alarm signals) or highly specific (calibration of measuring instruments, documentation of engineering changes).

Audit of execution versus plans reveals a wide variety of activities that are deficient in execution. Some of the more common ones are:

Feedback of inspection data to operating personnel is inadequate.

Quality cost data are not collected.

Chronic quality problems are not identified and pursued.

Obsolete specification documents are used during manufacturing.

Inadequate quality requirements are included in specifications to suppliers.

Test equipments with expired calibration dates are in use.

Detailed process instructions or inspection instructions are inadequate or nonexistent.

Personnel are performing critical operations without being certified in those operations.

In cases where supplier relations are conducted under a plan of assurance rather than incoming inspection, the review of execution versus plan is used widely; this review is often called "surveillance." The customer's representative is extensively engaged in assuring that the supplier is following the agreed-on plan (see Section 15, under Supplier Surveillance).

An important stimulus to audit of execution versus plan has been the growing extent of government regulation of products. As the regulatory agencies gain experience, they turn to the concept of audit as a means of covering maximum ground with the available personnel. When these audits turn up discrepancies which create unwelcome attention and publicity for the companies, the companies respond, in part, by creating or strengthening their own audits (self-audits). A striking illustration of the scope of government audits is the concept of "prudence" audits applied in the utility industry. These audits are retrospective reviews of the decisions, actions, and events involved in the creation of nuclear power plants. From these reviews, state utility commissions have disallowed hundreds of millions of dollars of plant investment from utility rate bases (Charnoff, 1986).

PLANNING AND PERFORMING AUDITS

ANSI/ASQC (1986) identify the main steps in performing audits as initiation, planning, implementation, reporting, and completion. A flowchart describing these steps is shown in Figure 9.1 (adapted from ANSI/ASQC, 1986, pp. 9–13). [Wilborn (1983) abstracts and summarizes existing standards and guidelines for auditing.]

Audit Initiation. The basic right to conduct audits is derived from the "charter" which has been approved by upper management, following participation by all concerned.

A specific audit is initiated by the manager of the activity to be audited either by request or through approval of a program of audits. It is preferable that an audit be conducted only on request of the manager of the activity.

Audit Planning. An audit plan should be prepared to inform the manager of the activity being audited and the participating auditors regarding the details of the impending audit. Vital elements of the plan include a definition of the scope and objectives of the audit, identification of the area to be audited, identification of the auditor(s), a schedule including the expected start and completion time for the audit, reference to any relevant standards or procedures, and audit documentation.

Several areas of audit planning warrant highlighting here.

Scheduling. Most auditing is done on a scheduled basis. This enables all concerned to organize workloads, assign personnel, and conduct other necessary activities in an orderly manner. It also minimizes the irritations that are inevitable when auditors are unannounced. (There are, however, some situations, e.g., bank audits, where the need to avoid "coverup" may require surprise audits.)

Areas to be Audited. The amount of execution of plans is simply enormous, and priorities must be determined (see above, under Audit of Quality Plans). Conse-

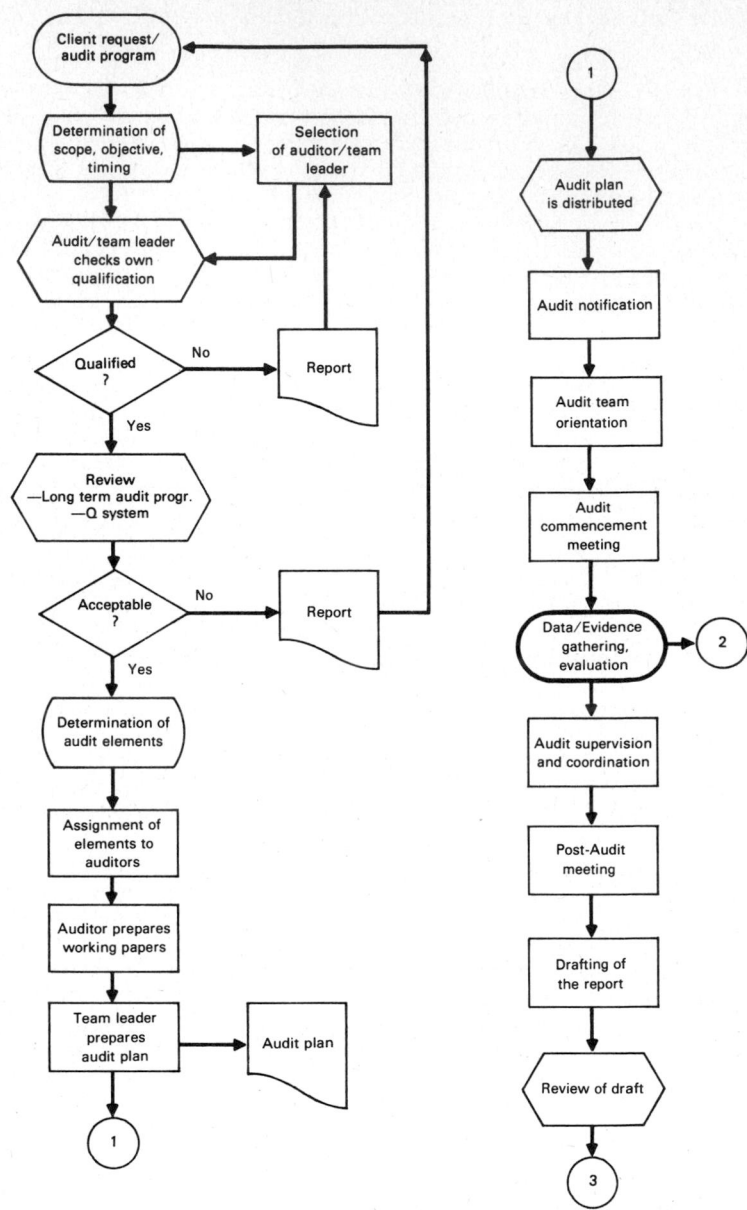

FIG. 9.1 Flow chart for quality audit. *(Adapted from ANSI/ASQC, 1986, pp. 9–13.)*

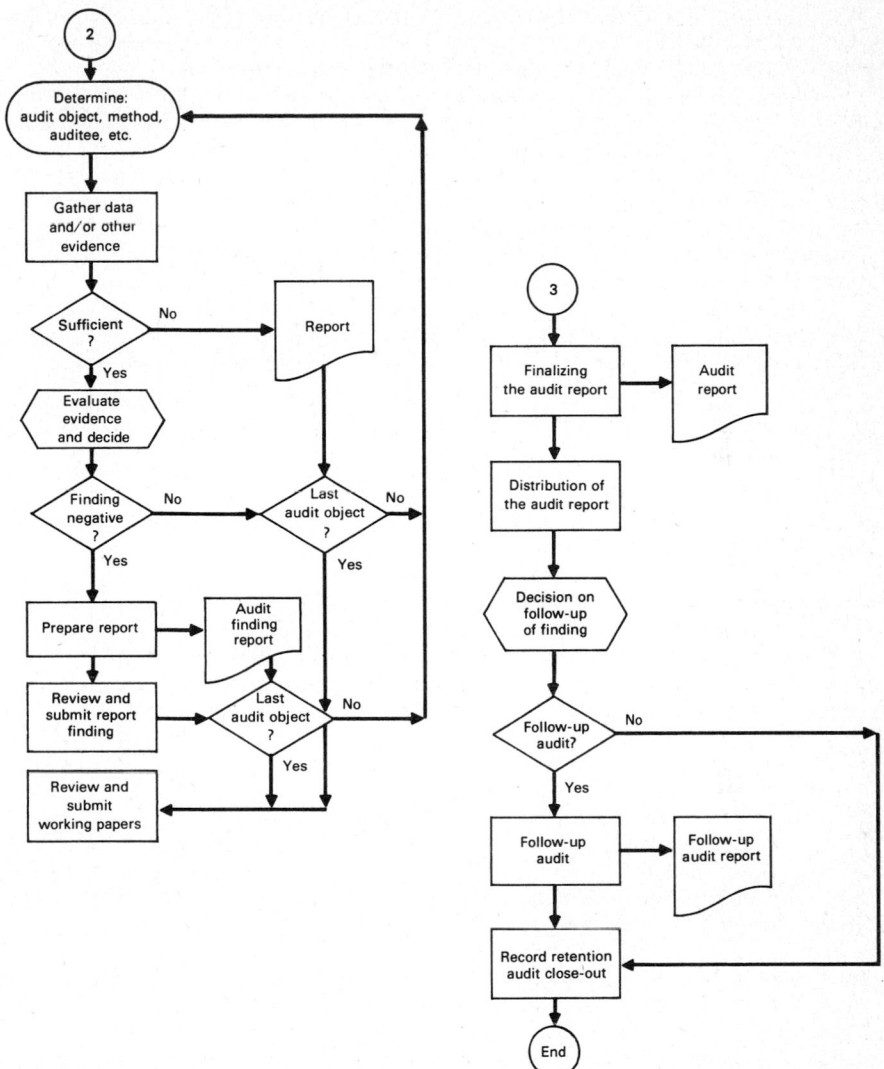

FIG. 9.1 (*Continued*)

quently, the audit of execution must be based on sampling; even the choice of sampling methods turns out to be an intricate problem. (In contrast, the "sampling" for audit of plans is fairly simple. Plans change slowly, so that periodic audits, even every 2 or 3 years, are adequate.)

In one large electronics company the audit of divisional practice (conducted by corporate staff auditors) employs a plan of sampling based on selected combinations of (1) the product lines made by the company, (2) the functional activities engaged in (e.g., design, production), and (3) the subject matter within these products and activities (e.g., instrument accuracy, recordkeeping).

This sampling approach replaced the former approach of auditing a specific product line within a specific division and reporting the results with recommendations for action (Purcell, 1968).

Another form of audit sampling is by product control centers. In this approach a group of related product control stations is regarded as a center for sampling purposes. Each month or so a sample of about 100 decisions is chosen at random and checked for adequacy. On the basis of the findings, the center is allowed to proceed, the sample is extended, or a product audit is instituted.

Documentation. The necessary "working papers" for the audit should be identified and/or created. These are all the documents required for an effective audit, including flowcharts, checklists, the auditing approach, forms for reporting observations, and results of previous audits.

Objectivity. The auditor is expected to be objective. Where objective standards are available, there is less need for the auditor to make a subjective judgment and thereby less opportunity for wide differences of opinion. Provision should be made, however, for challenge of the standard itself.

Discovery of Causes. In many companies the auditor is expected to investigate major deficiencies in an effort to determine the cause. This investigation then becomes the basis for the auditor's recommendation. In other companies the auditor is expected to leave such investigations to the line people; the auditor's recommendations will include proposals that such investigations be made.

Competence of Auditors. The basic education and experience of the auditors should be sufficient to enable them to learn in short order the technological aspects of the operations they are to audit. Lacking this background, they will be unable to earn the respect of the operations personnel. In addition, they should receive special training in the human relations aspects of auditing. In 1987 the American Society for Quality Control embarked on a program for the certification of quality auditors. Stenecker (1982) discusses the elements of certification.

Audit Implementation. The heart of this phase is the collection, analysis, and evaluation of factual information and the drawing of conclusions from these facts. Sayle (1981, chapter 6) proposes that four elements be covered in auditing an activity: (1) person, (2) item, (3) equipment, and (4) documentation.

In making observations, it is important to include a representative sample; for instance, if several shifts are involved, all operating shifts should be at least partially audited.

The information collected in practice consists of a combination of both documented evidence and information obtained through interviews of various personnel.

As a guide, the audit information collected is considered sufficient when it can be seen that the analysis of the evidence by some other qualified person who had not collected the information would reach essentially the same conclusions.

Human Relations. In theory, the audit is a sort of instrument plugged into the operations to secure an independent source of information. Where it is a physical instrument (e.g., the propeller speed indicator on the bridge of a ship), there is no problem of clash of personalities. Auditors, however, are human beings, and in practice, their relationships with those whose work is audited can become quite prickly. Deficiencies revealed by the audit may be resented because of the implied criticism. Recommendations in the audit may be resented as an invasion of responsibilities. In the reverse direction, auditors may regard slow responses to requests for information as a form of grudging collaboration. These realities warrant extensive discusison and, in addition, indoctrination of both auditors and auditees with respect to the following:

1. *The reasons behind the audits:* These reasons may have been well discussed with the managers. There is also need to explain to the supervisors and non-supervisors the "why" of the audits. (It is not sufficient to explain that upper management wants audits.) It can be made clear that the managers, customers, regulators, and others concerned likewise require assurance. Ideally, the manager of the activity being audited should be the one who explains the purposes of the audit to the subordinates engaged in the activity.

2. *Avoiding an atmosphere of blame:* A sure way to cause deterioration of human relations is to look for whom to blame rather than how to achieve improvement. Line managers as well as auditors can fall into this trap. An atmosphere of blame not only breeds resentment; it dries up the sources of information. The audit reports and recommendations should be problem-oriented rather than person-oriented.

There are other advantages to being sensitive to the human relationships involved in auditing. For example, it is useful for the supervisor in an area being audited to accompany the auditor during the audit. This helps to eliminate arguments later as to what was really observed during an audit. For audits running several days or longer, interim reviews of the audit with the auditees are helpful to show the information that has been gathered and what conclusions are being drawn, at least in a preliminary manner. This provides an opportunity to test some of those conclusions.

A self-audit and an independent audit can be combined to provide a "two-tier" audit. Goldstein (1983) describes how the two audits each have an audit plan, execution, and report. The advantages include using the expertise of the person responsible for the function, assuring objectivity with an independent auditor, and minimizing some of the human relationship issues.

The aim of both the self-audit and the independent audit is to build an atmosphere of trust based on the prior reputation of the auditors, the approach used during the audit, and the emphasis on being helpful to the activity audited. Even such small matters as the title of the audit process should be carefully considered. Occasionally people try to avoid the use of the term "audit" when, indeed, what will be done *is* an observation and evaluation. Also, audits may be hidden as part of a company education program. Such subterfuges detract from the trust that must be developed in order for audits to be effective and useful to all concerned.

Burr (1987) provides specific suggestions on overcoming resistance to audits. Sayle (1981, chapter 14) identifies 25 "tactics" to guide auditors in behavioral matters.

Post-Audit Meeting. An important part of the implementation phase is the post-audit meeting that is held with the manager of the audited activity. At this meeting the audit observations are presented so that the manager can plan for corrective action. In addition, the manager can point out to the auditor any mistakes with respect to the facts that have been collected.

Audit Reporting. Audit results should be documented in a report and a draft should be reviewed (preferably at the post-audit meeting) with the management of the activity that was audited. The report may be jointly issued by the auditor and auditee. For a report to be viewed as credible, it should be balanced in perspective and be depersonalized.

Balance in Reporting. An audit which reports only deficiencies may be factual as far as it goes. Yet it will be resented, because nothing is said about the far greater number of elements of performance which are well done. Some companies require the auditors to begin their reports with "commendable observations." Others have evolved overall summaries or ratings which consider not only deficiencies but also the opportunities for deficiencies (see below, under Units of Measure).

One serious and common criticism of audit reports is the tendency for the report to emphasize deficiencies that are minor in nature (at least in the opinions of those who were audited). For audits to be viewed as useful and constructive, the relative importance of the deficiencies reported should be analyzed. Such an analysis must be based on determining what the impact of the deficiency is on other activities (see below, under Seriousness Classification).

Depersonalizing the Report. In many companies auditors derive much influence from the fact that their reports are reviewed by upper management. Auditing departments should be careful to avoid misusing this influence. The ideal is to depersonalize the reports and recommendations. The real basis of the recommendations should be the facts rather than the opinion of the auditor. (Some auditors follow a practice of noting in the report when a statement is an impression or opinion, without a factual basis.) Where there is room for a difference of opinion, auditors have the right and the duty to offer their opinions as an input to the decision-making process. However, any position of undue advocacy should be avoided, as this tends to reduce the auditor's credibility as an objective observer. (The ultimate responsibility for results rests on the line managers, not on the auditors.) A practice commonly followed to help to depersonalize is to omit the names of any individuals involved, and instead to report the facts on the situation.

The report should include the following items:

Purpose and scope of the audit.

Details of the audit plan, including audit personnel, dates, the activity that was audited (personnel contacted, material reviewed, number of observations made, etc.). Details should be placed in an appendix.

Standards, checklist, or other reference documents that were used during the audit.

Audit observations, including supporting evidence, conclusions, and recommendations.

Recommendations for improvement opportunities.

Recommendations for followup on the corrective action that is to be proposed and implemented by line management, along with subsequent audits if necessary.

Distribution list for the audit report.

Summarizing Audit Data.   In an audit most elements of performance are found to be adequate, while some are found to be discrepant. Reporting of these findings requires two different levels of communication:

1. Reports of each discrepancy to secure corrective action. These reports are made promptly to the responsible operating personnel, with copies to some of the managerial levels.

2. A report of the overall status of the subject matter under review. To meet these requirements, the report should:

    a. Evaluate overall quality peformance in ways which provide answers to the major questions raised by upper managers—for instance: Is the product safe? Are we complying with legal requirements? Is the product fit for use? Is the product marketable? Is the performance of the department under review adequate?

    b. Provide evaluations of the status of the major subdivisions of the overall performance—the quality systems and subsystems, the divisions, the plants, the procedures, etc.

    c. Provide some estimate of the frequency of discrepancies in relation to the number of opportunities for discrepancies (see below, under Units of Measure).

    d. Provide some estimate of the trend of this ratio (of discrepancies found to discrepancies possible) and of the effectiveness of programs to control the frequency of occurrence of discrepancies.

Seriousness Classification.   Some of the audit programs make use of seriousness classification of discrepancies. This is quite common in the case of product audits, where defects found are classified in terms such as critical, major, and minor, each with some "weight" in the form of demerits. These systems of seriousness classification are highly standardized (see Section 18, under Seriousness Classification).

Some audit programs also apply seriousness classification to discrepancies found in planning, in procedures, in decision making, data recording, and so on. The approach parallels that used for product audits. Definitions are established for such terms as "serious," "major," and "minor"; demerit values are assigned; and total demerits are computed (see, e.g., Thresh, 1984, pp. 3–18).

Units of Measure.   For audits of plans, procedures, documentation, and so forth, it is desirable to compare the discrepancies found against some estimate of the opportunities for discrepancies. Some companies provide for this by an actual count of the opportunities, such as the number of criteria or check points called out by the plans and procedures. Another form is to count the discrepancies per audit with a correction factor based on the length of time consumed by the audit. The obvious reason is that more time spent in auditing means more ground covered and more discrepancies found.

Report Publication.   Agreement is reached on report format, responsibility for editing, lists of which managers are to receive what reports, and so on. In some organizations, the report is given only to the manager of the activity that was audited. A followup audit (on progress) can be distributed to upper management. Design of the audit reports is often modular to permit selective distribution. The report should be issued as soon as possible, but no later than 1 month after the post-audit meeting.

Audit Completion.   The audit is completed when the report is submitted to the client, except in those circumstances when the verification of corrective action is to be part of the audit assignment and plan.

Responsibility for Corrective Action.   Auditors are commonly told to avoid becoming involved in designing remedies and making them effective. Operations managers are required to respond in writing as to what they plan to do with respect to discrepancies found or recommendations made. (Operations managers are not obligated to follow the recommendations. They may conclude not to follow them, in which case they must state why not.) This formality helps to assure that quality audits have a high priority of managerial attention. Auditors are expected to follow up recommendations to assure that some action is taken; thus the recommendation is accepted or is considered and then rejected.

A special situation exists when an auditor documents the symptom of a problem but is unable, during the audit, to identify the cause. Here, the audit report should be directed to the manager of the audited activity even though the underlying cause may rest within that activity or be elsewhere. The report should state steps required to determine the underlying causes.

When deficiencies reported in an audit are serious, the auditor may recommend that a subsequent audit be held to assure that the necessary corrective action has been taken.

Finally, a wrap-up of the audit involves deciding which records from the audit should be retained, for what period of time, and how access should be provided to authorized personnel who need to review such audit documents.

Quality Assurance of Audits.   The audit process itself can benefit from the concept of quality assurance. Evaluation of a sample of audits can include examination of the competence and training of auditors, maintenance of auditor independence, documentation of factual information during audits, usefulness of audit reports, handling of human relations problems, and retention of audit records. One approach is to obtain feedback from managers whose activities were audited. Thresh (1984, Appendix) lists 21 questions that examine the fairness, objectivity, audit methods, and usefulness of the audit results—all from the viewpoint of the auditee.

QUALITY SURVEYS

The audits as described above are concerned almost exclusively with conformance of various sorts: conformance of plans to standards of good planning and conformance of execution to plan. Such audits provide answers to some vital questions and must be regarded as an essential element of quality assurance. These audits are, however, not sufficient to provide full assurance to upper management that all is well with respect to quality, since they commonly are not concerned with such matters as:

Relative standing in the marketplace with regard to quality

Analysis of users' situations with respect to cost, convenience, etc. over the life of the product

Opportunities for reducing costs of poor quality

Challenge to product development, design engineering, and other "monopolistic" departments on quality adequacy, perfectionism, cost, etc.

Challenge to top management itself with respect to policies, goals, premises, and axiomatic beliefs

Employee perceptions on quality

To provide such missing elements of quality assurance requires a broader view than the structured audit. The broader review is often called a "quality survey," a "quality assessment," or a "companywide audit." In this section, the word "audit" implies the existence of established criteria against which the plans and execution can be checked. In contrast, the word "survey" implies the inclusion of matters not covered by agreed criteria. (In a sense, the audit discovers discrepancies and alarm signals; the survey goes further and also discovers opportunities and unexpected threats.)

An early form of quality survey was that used by the Bell System in reviewing the adequacy of its approach to quality. These surveys were conducted by personnel engaged full-time in quality matters. The Bell System survey brought together information from six related investigations, as follows:

1. An examination of the product design specifications from the standpoint of product fitness for use, completeness, and freedom from ambiguity

2. An examination of the manufacturing specifications and procedures, for similar reasons

3. A review of customer quality complaints and the action taken in diagnosis and remedy

4. A review of product audit data and shop performance data to appraise the state of product quality and process controls

5. A study of inspection performance, inspector accuracy, test equipment accuracy, and other aspects of inspection integrity

6. An examination into the quality performance and understanding of the shop personnel

The detailed investigations were conducted by full-time staff specialists, and their findings were reviewed by the managers who were members of a survey committee. The resulting reports and followups received the attention of upper management as well as local management.

Another example of a quality survey is that conducted by the Japanese Deming Prize Committee in its examination of companies nominated for this prize. The principal elements examined are as follows: the company's quality policies; organization and management; training in and dissemination of quality control ideas and practices; collection, feedback, and utilization of information; analysis of information data; active utilization of statistical methods; standardization; process control; quality assurance; results attained; and future planning (Mizuno,

1968). The Deming Prize is the most prestigious quality status attainable by a Japanese company.

As an example of a broad survey, a consultant was engaged to evaluate the operations of one division of a large processing company. The objectives of the survey were stated in broad terms:

1. To discover where the company wants to be with respect to quality
2. To discover where the company is now with respect to quality
3. To recommend plans and policies which can economically move the company closer to its objectives

Operations were studied in six different plants, various data were reviewed, and discussions were conducted with plant personnel and with personnel in manufacturing and nonmanufacturing functions at the division level.

The consultant reached five conclusions:

1. The division was generally well equipped to do a good quality job in terms of adequate processes, modern technology, capable personnel, and a favorable organizational climate.
2. Personnel were doing a good job on meeting the quality policies as interpreted by them.
3. Personnel interpretation of policy, however, did not match that of most division executives.
4. A considerable amount of money was being wasted as quality losses, without anyone having a clear idea how much this was or how much of it was readily avoidable.
5. There was a good chance for worthwhile cost reduction, while at the same time improving outgoing quality.

The consultant then presented 14 specific recommendations in areas such as quality policy, losses due to poor quality, machine capability studies, responsibility for deciding whether machines may run, supplier relations plans, measuring outgoing quality, measures of customer complaints and other forms of executive reports on quality, evaluation of the usefulness of process control charts, and evaluation of the effectiveness of lot acceptance plans.

In a different type of survey, a consultant was asked to define specific task responsibilities in the quality program for all major departments of a health care company. The consultant used five questions to interview the department managers:

1. What tasks in your department affect quality?
2. Should any additional quality-related tasks be performed in your department?
3. Should any additional quality-related tasks be performed anywhere else in the company?
4. What quality-related tasks have unclear responsibility?
5. What quality-related tasks currently done in your department require more definitive written procedures?

The consultant summarized the findings as follows: (1) the quality program consisted of 178 tasks performed in 26 functional areas; (2) responsibility was not clearly defined for 19 tasks; and (3) for 27 quality-related tasks, the managers expressed concern about the clarity of the task.

The report included detailed comments on the overall scope of the quality program, key tasks requiring improvement, organization for quality, and the role of upper management.

Some organizations identify the key elements of an overall quality program and evaluate each of these key elements. For example, 23 specific elements of a program are identified in Table 9.2. For each element, a scoring guideline provides a maximum of 100 possible points, allocated equally into four categories: required procedures exist, procedures meet requirements, procedures and practice agree, and results are effective.

The Allis Chalmers Company certifies each of its plants with respect to quality ("We Can, Allis-Chalmers Has," 1981). Ten major elements of "total quality assurance" are evaluated at each plant: management of the quality system, product quality and reliability development, product and process quality planning, supplier quality assurance, product and process quality evaluation and control, special quality studies, quality information feedback, quality measurement equipment, quality training and work force development, and field quality evaluation and control.

Freund and Trulli (1982) explain a method of summarizing the state of an overall quality program through the use of flowcharts, cause-and-effect diagrams, and other inputs. The method evaluates quality parameters that affect the customer. Useful checklists for conducting quality surveys are given by Dobbins (1981), Miller (1982), and White (1983).

QUESTIONS FOR QUALITY SURVEYS

The questions presented in the following subsections, based on a list originally prepared by J. M. Juran, cover companywide issues and issues for functional areas.

Companywide Issues. Questions relating to companywide issues may be categorized as those addressing issues of (1) responsibility to society or (2) quality management.

Responsibility to Society. Questions in this category are:

To what extent is the quality of your product related to human safety and health? To the environment? To regulation by governmental bodies?

Have these responsibilities to society generated any significant problems? What are the three main problems?

How are you organized to prevent these problems from occurring in the first place?

Quality Management. Questions pertaining to this category include:

Are policies, plans, and procedures such that, if followed, quality will be competitive in the marketplace?

To what extent are quality planning, coordination, and so on at the discretion of the Quality Department as opposed to the line managers?

What is the climate for training line managers and supervisors to assume some of these functions now being carried out by specialists in the Quality Department?

Has an estimate been made of the cost of poor quality?

Is the organizational machinery in place to identify and pursue opportunities for increasing sales income and/or reducing costs?

Is the concept of internal customers understood and acted on by all units involved?

Is there an effective system for having early warnings of potential quality problems?

What are your ways for judging the motivation of the personnel (managers, supervisors, workers) with respect to quality in relation to other parameters (productivity, delivery date, cost, etc.)?

On the basis of these ways, what is the adequacy of the present motivation?

How comfortable is the relationship between the management and the work force?

How willing would some of the work force be to receive training in problem-solving and then undertake projects for solution?

Functional Areas. Questions relating to functional areas may be categorized as (1) questions common to all functional areas and (2) specific questions pertaining to selected areas:

Questions Common to All Functional Areas. Questions in this category include:

What measures are used to judge the quality of the output? What is the performance, as reflected in these measures?

Have the resources spent in detecting and correcting quality-related problems been estimated?

To what extent are the quality-related responsibilities understood by the personnel?

To what extent have the personnel been trained in the quality disciplines?

To what extent has the capability of key processes been quantified?

Does the data system meet the needs of the personnel?

Questions for Selected Areas

Customer Relations. Questions pertaining to customer relations are:

Is quality delivered to the customer an asset or a liability to the sales force?

Which qualities are of prime importance to your customers?

How does your quality compare to that of your competitors?

Does field performance meet users' needs?

What are the 10 quality problems most in need of solution from a customer relations viewpoint?

How do you know the answers to the preceding questions: from which sources (complaints, tests, marketing research, etc.)?

What are the leading causes of field failures (product design, purchased components, manufacturing errors, etc.)?

Where do you strike the balance between design for low initial selling price and low life cycle cost?

What part of your profit is derived from sale of spare parts?

Product Development. Questions addressing product development issues are:

What has been the record in launching new designs?

Do specifications originate with the customers? If not, how do you determine what qualities are needed to achieve fitness for use by subsequent processors, merchant chain, ultimate user, and maintenance shops?

How adequate is the system of early warning to detect problems which new products will create elsewhere in the organization or in the field?

To what extent are new and changed designs reviewed by specialists from other departments to evelute producibility, reliability, and maintainability?

What are the top 10 quality problems today? What were the top 10 two years ago? Three years ago? (To what degree are problems carried over from model to model?)

To what extent do product designers become involved in nonconformance questions which affect only internal factory economics?

Supplier Relations. Questions in this category include:

Are factory costs or field failures classified in ways which permit separating out the supplier-related problems?

What is the basic philosophy of supplier relations? Emphasis on contract preparation and enforcement? Less formality but not sharing all information? Teamwork? What is the extent of joint efforts with suppliers on quality planning? On quality improvement?

What is the basis for choosing suppliers in the first place? For allocating purchases among suppliers?

Manufacture. Questions relating to manufacture are:

What is the first-time yield of key manufacturing processes?

Who does the manufacturing planning (technical specialists, production supervisors, workers, etc.)?

Where is the main emphasis placed for manufacturing good products (foolproofing the processes, supervisory attention, motivation of work force, inspection and test following production, etc.)?

Who designs the system of quality controls used on the factory floor (manufacturing engineers, production supervision, workers themselves, quality control engineers, etc.)?

Customer Service.   Questions pertaining to customer service include:

Are field deficiencies acted on?

To what extent is the field service report adequate for providing field intelligence feedback (on quality) to Design, Manufacture, Purchasing, Quality, etc.?

Quality.   Questions in this category include:

What activities are assigned to be conducted by the Quality Department?

To what extent is the Quality Department regarded as a constructive contributor to quality (rather than as a police force)?

Are the line departments making use of the data feedback from the Quality Department?

Do the line departments make use of the specialized know-how of the Quality Department?

Upper Management.   Questions pertaining to upper-management issues are:

What active participation does upper management have on quality-related matters?

To what extent are there policies specifically quality-related?

To what extent does the system of Management by Objectives (formal or informal) include quality-related objectives?

What kind of information regarding quality performance does upper management receive?

Summary of Quality Status.   An overall view of quality status can be obtained by collecting information on three aspects:

1. *The cost of poor quality:*   This represents the internal losses that a company is experiencing due to poor quality. Methodology for estimating such losses is given in Section 4, under Categories of Cost of Poor Quality.

2. *The quality status of the company relative to competition:*   Some methodology for obtaining this information is given in Section 12, under Competitive Evaluations by Field Studies.

3. *Employee perceptions on quality.*   One approach for understanding the culture on quality involves the use of a questionnaire that is distributed to employees. Ryan and Wong (1984) present an example consisting of 14 questions. Wilson Learning Corporation and E. I. Du Pont de Nemours (1986) have prepared a list of 82 questions making up a "Quality Orientation Profile."

These three inputs plus the results from the above questions for quality surveys would provide an overall assessment on quality.

Third-Party Audit or Survey.   Two parties are involved in the purchase of products: the purchaser and the supplier. In the past, the purchaser evaluated the quality from the supplier. Purchasers are now increasingly using the concept of a "third party" to evaluate supplier quality. The third party (a person or an organization) performs the evaluation service for the purchaser but is independent of the purchaser and the supplier. This relieves the purchaser of maintaining a staff with the necessary skills. A third party can either inspect the product, evaluate the quality system, or both.

The concept of third-party inspection is not new. For example, the surveying of ships by the Lloyd's Register of Shipping began over two centuries ago. Rennie, Morris, and Blackburn (1979) describe how the approach has changed from one of primarily witnessing tests and examining components at prescribed stages of manufacture, to one which couples an evaluation of the quality system with periodic inspections of the final product. Underwriters Laboratories performs third-party evaluation by testing products, materials, and systems for public safety (Berman, 1980). The British Standards Institution (BSI) offers a service of assessing the conformance of an organization's quality system to BS 5750, *Quality Systems (The National Standard for Quality Systems in Great Britain).*

Evaluation by a third party is often associated with formal "certification" and is sometimes coupled with a listing of approved sources, or the issuance of a symbol or mark. For example, an evaluation by the British Standards Institution showing that a firm complies with BS 5750 entitles the firm to use a special symbol in their company literature and to have its name appear in the BSI *Buyers' Guide* for potential buyers of products.

When a really fundamental examination is to be made, the managers guiding the survey should be aware that they are part of the problem. To provide assurance against their own biases, they should have recourse to outsiders who have the independence and competence to identify those problems and causes which have their origin in upper management itself. Most third-party audits, however, are evaluations of product and/or quality systems to some given standard.

A further need is to take note of new forces and phenomena to which traditional programs have not given weight. For example, in previous decades product liability, government regulation, higher levels of customer expectation, competition—both nationally and internationally—on both low price and high quality, increased consumer demands for better servicing of product, the impact of computer software, and still other quality-related problems were not regarded as major factors to be considered in quality policies, objectives, and plans. Subsequently, each of these issues became recognized as a major problem. Those companies who had foreseen some of this through their long-range planning thereby gained important head starts over their competitors. The use of consultants, educators, selected dealers, and other "outsiders" can be useful in assessing the current and expected future status of a company with regard to quality.

Reference Standards for Surveys.   In evaluation of an overall quality system, use is often made of reference standards issued by regulatory bodies or by contracting bodies. Examples are MIL-Q-9858A (*Quality Program Requirements*), BS 5750 (*Quality Systems*), and ISO 9000 series (*Quality Systems*).

Such standards provide important benefits. They help to define the activities that are needed to achieve quality objectives, provide criteria for evaluation and thereby increase the objectivity of audits, and are useful during bidding on contracts by providing a common understanding of the activities required of all bidders.

Some cautions, however, must be noted. Most important, it has not been proved that surveys based on such standards are good predictors of subsequent quality performance. (The surveys do, however, provide objective information on the presence or absence of tangible facilities, written procedures, etc.) The best predictor of product quality is the quality performance on similar products in the past. Of course, high quality can be delivered with excessive internal costs. It is important, therefore, to evaluate not only final results but also the activities by which those results were achieved. As another caution, some standards omit such important elements as process capability, training, fitness for use considerations, quality of previous products delivered, etc. Finally, Juran (1977) traces the evolution of quality assurance and discusses the influence of the cultural pattern in different countries on the form of assurance.

If a reference standard is to be used but has not been specified, one must be selected. Pereira (1987) explains how five evaluation factors can help to decide which standard to employ.

PRODUCT AUDITING

Definition and Purposes.   Product auditing is an independent evaluation of product quality to determine its fitness for use and conformance to specification. Product auditing takes place after inspections have been completed. The purposes of product auditing include:

1. Estimating the quality level as delivered to customers
2. Evaluating the effectiveness of the inspection decisions in determining conformance to specifications
3. Providing information useful in improving the outgoing product quality level and improving the effectiveness of inspection
4. Providing additional assurance beyond routine inspection activities

There are often telltale signs indicating the need for product audit. Such signs include:

1. Nonconforming product being received by customers after 100 percent inspection has been performed
2. Damage to product after 100 percent inspection, but before receipt by a customer
3. Product inadequacies that are not evaluated in 100 percent inspection, and so forth

Diggs (1979) discusses some of the indicators of the need for product audit.

Stage of Evaluation.   Ideally, the product audit should compare actual service performance with users' service needs. This ideal is so difficult and costly to administer that most product auditing consists of an approximation (see Table 9.3).

For many simple, stable products, the approximation of test results versus specification is a useful and economic way of conducting the product audit. Even for products not so simple, the majority of quality characteristics identifiable by the user are also completely identifiable while the product is still at the factory. Thus, product characteristics which are essential to use are properly evaluated at some appropriate stage, whether in the factory or in some more advanced stage of progression.

As products become increasingly complex, the product auditing is conducted increasingly at several of the stages shown in Table 9.3. The bulk of the characteristics may be evaluated at the most economical stage, that is, shortly after factory inspection. However, the remaining (and usually more sophisticated) characteristics may be evaluated at other stages.

A useful adjunct to a product audit is a "tear-down" of the product. Cameron (1977) describes how a winding operator on a quality audit team pointed out that

TABLE 9.3 Potential Stages for Product Auditing

Stage at which product auditing is conducted	Pro and cons of using this stage
After acceptance by inspectors	Most economical, but does not reflect effect of packing, shipping, storage, or usage
After packing but before shipment to fields	Requires unpacking and repacking, but evaluates effect of original packing
On receipt by dealers	Difficult to administer at such multiple locations, but reflects effect of shipping and storage
On receipt by users	Even more difficult to administer, but evaluated the added effects of dealer handling and storage plus effects of shipment to user and unpacking
Performance in service	The ideal, but also the most difficult to administer because of the number and variety of usages; can be simplified through sampling

his incoming supplies included two types of diode in the same box. Since the diodes were identical in appearance, the wrong diode could be easily selected and inserted. The action taken: mark each diode with a red or green dot and place them in separate boxes.

In conducting product auditing after shipment to the field, there are further alternatives. If the product consists of small, stable units, it may be feasible to send samples back to a central laboratory for evaluation. If the product consists of large units, it may be more economical to send an audit team out to the field. For example, in the graphic arts industry, a supplier of coated paper may send a team out to the field to observe (1) product in customer warehouses and (2) actual running of the paper on the customer's presses, such as printing of magazines.

Product audit can also be applied at stages during manufacture. "In-line audit" or "work in process audit" are the terms commonly used. Such audits evaluate the effectiveness of previous inspections to detect nonconformances. Thresh (1984) discusses in-line product audits.

A special case of product auditing is that for new products. Love (1982) describes how an audit of new products can facilitate evaluation of the product development program and what went wrong on new product launches and can alert management of the nonconforming product that might be in the distribution system.

Designing the Audit Plan. Because the plan has a wide impact on executive decision making, it is essential that the design be made with the full participation of the departments affected. The usual approach is to designate an interdepartmental committee to guide the preparation of the plan, leaving it to the Quality Assurance Department to do the detailed work in the interim between meetings. (As product auditing becomes accepted, there often evolves a procedures manual to guide the auditors.)

Scope of the Audit. Lacking broad-based participation in designing the plan, the practical burdens of making product audits that depict the quality as the customer receives it often result in less than satisfactory plans.

As one example, the plant manager of an electronics manufacturing firm received a rating of 98 percent on a product audit from the plant. For this rating, the plant received an award for quality. When the mean time between failures of that same product was measured in the field, a value of only 200 hours was experienced. This was a known reason for customer complaints, but such matters were not evaluated by the product audit.

In another case, a vehicle manufacturer had a system of taking a product audit sample weekly from production. A comparison of separate marketing research results with the internal product audit was devastating. Only 18 percent of the characteristics that customers claimed were important to them were being checked in the product audit.

Sampling for Product Audit. When the purpose of the audit remains one of assurance rather than control, the sample size is arbitrary and reflects a balance between the cost of large samples and the unreliability of small samples. The selection of units within a sample should be based on the concepts of random sampling (see Section 25, under Random Sampling).

For products manufactured by mass production, sample sizes for product audit can often be determined using conventional statistical methods. These methods determine the sample size required for stated degrees of risk (see Section 23, under Confidence Internal Estimates). Thresh (1984, section 7) applies these methods to quality audit. Sample sizes for product audit determined by these methods when applied to mass production still represent a small fraction of the product that needs to be sampled. In contrast, for products manufactured as large units or in small quantity, the conventional concepts of statistical sampling are prohibitively costly. In such cases sample sizes are often arbitrary and they seem small from the viewpoint of probability considerations. For example, a vehicle manufacturer uses a product of audit sample consisting of 2 percent of production per shift with a minimum of five vehicles—whichever number is larger. Even though the number of vehicles sampled may be small, the total number of characteristics that are sampled may be quite large. For these vehicles, 380 items are checked on each vehicle and the product audit test includes a 17-mi (27.2-km) road test. In some cases of highly homogeneous production, a sample of one unit taken from batch production can be adequate for product audit. Thresh (1984) recommends a minimum of three units.

Hsiang and Gordon (1982) have proposed a method of determining the sample size that is based on the amount of production, the likelihood that current production is substandard, the cost of correcting problems in the field, the cost of audit sampling, and present quality standards. Unfortunately, the formulas include certain numerical values that must be calculated for particular products.

An allied consideration is the frequency for product audit (daily, weekly, by shift, etc.). Again, practical considerations such as changes in the design, suppliers, production methods, and other factors play an important role.

Reporting the Results of Product Auditing. Most product auditing is done under a broader concept of preparing a continuing score or "rating" of quality. This running score is then used as one of the inputs for the executive reports on quality.

Seriousness Classification. The results of product audit appear in the form of presence or absence of defects, failures, and other factors. Because these discrepancies are unequal in importance, a simple summary such as percent defective is not acceptable to the managers involved. In consequence, several levels of seriousness are chosen (e.g., critical, major, minor, incidental). The details of establishing a system of "seriousness classification for defects" are discussed in Section 12, under Seriousness Classification.

Weighting. It is comparatively easy to assign weights to each class to quantify the seriousness. Usually a weight of 100 "demerits" is arbitrarily assigned to the most serious defect class and weights then assigned to the other classes; for instance:

Seriousness classification	Weight or demerit value
A (critical)	100
B (major)	35–75
C (minor)	10–25
D (incidental)	1–10

Summary. In summarizing, defects are converted to demerits to arrive at a composite demerits per unit. For example, the results of product audit on one product line for 1 month were:

Defect class	Weight	Number of defects found	Total demerits
A (critical)	100	2	200
B (major)	50	7	350
C (minor)	10	28	280
D (incidental)	1	26	26
Total			856

Since there were 2500 units of product audited during the month, the demerits per unit totaled $856 \div 2500 = 0.34$.

For mass production products, the unit of product may be a simple concept (e.g., lamps, gallons, tons). When the product line is miscellaneous in nature, it is necessary to find some common index which expresses the extent of opportunities for defects (e.g., number of electrical connections, weight of airframe, number of quality characteristics, "possible error count"). Use of such a common index facilitates comparison with previous history, with competitors, across product lines, and so on.

The scoreboard in terms of demerits per unit is by no means universally accepted. Managers in some industries want ready access to the figures on critical and major defects, feeling that these are the real problems no matter what the figure of demerits per unit is.

It is often useful to summarize the product audit results in other languages. A manufacturer of consumer products classifies defects at a product audit as visual (V), electrical (E), and performance (P) and then predicts service costs on products in the field. This is done by first establishing classes for each type of defect in terms of the probability of receiving a field complaint, (e.g., a class II visual defect has a 60 percent probability). Service call costs are then combined with the audit data. For example, Table 9.4 shows the results for an audit of 50 units. The expected cost is the product of the probability, the number of defects, and the cost per service call. The expected service cost per unit is then estimated as $269 \div 50 = \$5.38$. Alternatively, as indicated in Table 9.4, the expected number of service calls is the product of the probability and the number of defects. The expected number of service calls per unit is then estimated as $10.8 \div 50 = 0.22$, or about 22 out of every 100 products delivered to the field is expected to have a service call.

TABLE 9.4   Audit Data

Class of defect	Probability	Number of defects revealed by audit	Cost per service call, $	Expected cost, $	Expected number of service calls
V1	1.00	1	15.00	15.00	1.00
V2	0.60	3	15.00	27.00	1.80
E1	1.00	3	30.00	90.00	3.00
E2	0.60	4	30.00	72.00	2.40
P1	1.00	1	25.00	25.00	1.00
P2	0.60	2	25.00	30.00	1.20
P3	0.20	2	25.00	10.00	0.40
Totals				269.00	10.80

In addition to summarizing the defects found (both number and relative seriousness), the audit results can be tallied by functional responsibility (i.e., design, purchasing, production).

Audit results can also be summarized to show the effectiveness of the previous inspection activities. Typically, a simple ratio is used such as the percentage of total defects which are detected by inspection. For example, if the previous inspection revealed a total of 45 defects in a sample of N pieces and if the product audit inspection revealed 5 additional defects, the inspection effectiveness would be $45 \div 50 \times 100$, or 90 percent.

Standard for Comparison.   To be meaningful, the score on demerits per unit (or the conversion thereof) must be compared with some "standard." The usual standard is previous practice; the managers want to see whether quality is improving or worsening.

To quantify past practice, the auditors conduct the product audit over a sufficient number of months to acquire stable data. This period is known as the *base period*. In calculating the base period, it is usual to exclude known abnormalities such as new-product troubles and the effect of temporary crises. The resulting "refined" base period then becomes a basis for comparison, much as previous years' costs or expenses.

Alternatively, the standard for comparison may be "market quality." In such cases, the product audit plan is applied to competitive products in the same way that it is applied to the company's own products. The methods of securing competitive products follow the practices discussed in Section 12, under Competitive Evaluations.

Action on Discrepancies.   When a product audit reveals defects or discrepancies, the line supervisors are notified for two reasons:

1. To secure their verification of the factual situation so that the subsequent quality rating is based on established facts
2. To alert them to the alarm signals inherent in the presence of defects in the product which has already been approved for shipment to customers

When the product audit sampling reveals critical or major defects, the audit procedures normally provide for documenting these cases fully, just as is done for any other discovery of a serious internal or field failure. A discrepancy form is executed to put corrective action machinery into motion.

Effect of Product Audit on Clarifying Quality Standards.   Introduction of product auditing invariably has a beneficial effect on clarifying quality standards. This effect is the result of:

1. The inevitable discussions between the auditors and the line organizations who contest some of the findings of the auditors.
2. The differences in viewpoint attributable to differences in emphasis. The product audit is specifically set up to reflect the user's viewpoint, whereas the line organizations have a strong tradition of emphasizing conformance to specification.
3. The use of product audit results to provide a running scoreboard of product performance. Such a continuing scoreboard requires that the quality standards be consistent from month to month.

A consequence of the need for clear, uniform standards is that the quality auditors play a role, sometimes the dominant role, in defining quality standards from the viewpoint of the user.

PERSONNEL FOR QUALITY ASSURANCE

Multiple categories of personnel for auditors are generally used, primarily in response to the different types of audits and surveys which must be conducted.

Upper Management.   The role of upper management in conducting company-wide (and other) types of quality audit is discussed in Section 8, under Quality Audit by Upper Managers.

Middle Managers.   A significant number of companies make use of teams of middle managers to conduct quality audits on a part-time basis. These teams include not only quality managers but also managers from other functions as well (e.g., production, personnel, marketing, purchasing). There are advantages as well as limitations to the use of middle managers as auditors.

The Advantages.   Managers have a broader outlook than conventional auditors do and are more likely to consider activities from the viewpoint of the company mission, the needs of users, and the impact on society. The managers do not feel bound by existing plans and are more open to the idea that the plans may need to be revised. They are more likely to identify opportunities (e.g., cost reduction) or threats (e.g., increasing foreign competition) and are more imaginative in recommendations for action. In addition, when a team of managers is seen to be moving from department to department to audit quality, that fact conveys a message to the supervision and the work force.

The Disadvantages.   Managers tend to be undisciplined auditors. They are reluctant to be bound by detailed checklists, so that some aspects of operation are not audited at all. They lack the time to thoroughly analyze their findings; this results in some degree of overreaction, with wear and tear on all concerned. In addition, managers have difficulty in adhering to the schedules for auditing—they are busy people, and their time is subject to being preempted by crises.

A combined approach is to use conventional auditors to conduct the detailed audit. Following this, a team of managers makes a supplemental, broader review and prepares a report for distribution to upper management. Such a combined approach was used by the Bell System for years and was known as the quality "survey" (see above, under Quality Surveys).

Audit Teams.   Sometimes, teamwork is useful. Cameron (1977) describes an audit team for electric power systems. The team consists of nine people: unit assembler and assembly supervisor, unit tester, unit inspector and supervisor, winding operator and winding supervisor, methods engineer, manufacturing engineer, project engineer and production liaison engineer, product support engineer, quality engineer, and customer representatives. The audit centers around a tear-down inspection (see above, under Stage of Evaluation).

Two work units within the same company may audit each other ("mutual audits"). For example, a manufacturing process and the process following it may exchange teams to audit each other's quality performance (Ishikawa, 1987).

A steel manufacturer has audit teams of middle managers—one from the Corporate Quality Assurance Department, one from the general manager's staff of the plant being audited, and one from another plant in the company.

Some organizations have established an audit group with a strong customer orientation. This audit group can veto the release of a new design or block the release of daily production of a product.

External Auditors.   Quality audits are also conducted by persons external to the company. An extensive example is the audits conducted by clients in the form of supplier surveys and surveillance (see Section 15, under Evaluating Supplier Capability). Section 8, under Organization for Quality Audits by Upper Managers; Third-Party Audits, discusses the role of outside consultants.

Full-Time Auditors.   The use of full-time auditors greatly improves the competence of the auditing. The auditing job exposes the personnel to a wide variety of company activities so that they undergo intensive training and development, especially during the first 2 years or so of their assignments. As a result, the auditors soon become well-trained professionals. They participate in discussions of quality specifications, standards, procedures, and peripheral "nonquality" matters which nevertheless have a bearing on quality. Their resulting broad exposure also increases their capacity to assume added responsibilities. They are aware of this to such an extent that they become restive after several years. One approach for dealing with this personnel problem is to reassign the person at the end of 3 years or so to a new job which takes advantage of the experience gained on the auditing job.

The common situation of locating a quality audit group within a Quality Assurance Department provides professional supervision, but it can sometimes result in a conflict of interest. This refers to the role of the audit group in identifying weaknesses within a quality system and the typical role of a Quality Assurance Department of attempting to gain acceptance of a variety of techniques for improving quality throughout an organization. An auditor who becomes a strong advocate for certain activities to be performed may unconsciously lose some objectivity and, in turn, damage the credibility of the audit function. Locating the audit function within the Quality Assurance Department can be workable as long as the manager of that department is particularly cautious to stress the objectivity and independence of the audit function.

Product Auditors.   Product auditing is usually a full-time job; often the product auditor remains full-time on the same product line year after year.

The general practice is to fill these posts from the ranks of inspectors who have considerable experience and have demonstrated a high level of objectivity and integrity and also have certain special skills required, such as in evaluating the taste of food or drivability of an automobile.

REFERENCES

ANSI/ASQC (1986). *Generic Guidelines for Auditing of Quality Systems.* American Society for Quality Control, Milwaukee.

Berman, Harvey S. (1980). "Quality Assurance in UL's Follow-Up Program." *Quality Progress,* January, pp. 14–17.

Burr, John T. (1987). "Overcoming Resistance to Audits." *Quality Progress,* January, pp. 15–18.

Cameron, R. D. (1977). "Up Your Quality with Show and Tell." *Quality,* May, pp. 24–25.

Charnoff, Gerald (1986). "An Evaluation of the Prudence Consultants Retained by State Commissions and Consumer Counsel." Paper presented at Winter Meeting, American Nuclear Society, Washington, DC (no page numbers).

Diggs, E. J. (1979). "Why Have Outgoing Quality Audits?" *ASQC Technical Conference Transactions,* Milwaukee, pp. 506–512.

Dobbins, Richard K. (1981). "Your Quality Posture—A Profit/Survival Challenge." *ASQC Quality Congress Transactions,* Milwaukee, pp. 485–490.

Farrow, John H. (1987). "Quality Audits: An Invitation to Management." *Quality Progress,* January, pp. 11–13.

Freund, R. A. and Trulli, H. B. (1982). "Quality Assurance Review Technique." *Quality Assurance,* vol. 8, no. 1, March, pp. 17–22.

Goldstein, Raymond (1983). "The Two-Tier Audit System." *ASQC Quality Congress Transactions,* Milwaukee, pp. 14–16.

Hayes, Glenn E. and Romig, Harry G. (1977). *Modern Quality Control.* Bruce (a division of Benzigh Bruce and Glencoe, Inc.), Collier Macmillan, New York, pp. 706–723.

Hsiang, Thomas C. and Gordon, John J. (1982) "New Statistical Methodologies in a QA Audit System." *ASQC Quality Congress Transactions,* Milwaukee, pp. 335–342.

Ishikawa, Kaoru (1987) "The Quality Control Audit." *Quality Progress,* January, pp. 39–41.

Juran, J. M. (1977). "Quality and Its Assurance—an Overview." *Second NATO Symposium on Quality and Its Assurance.* North Atlantic Treaty Organization, London.

Kane, Roger W. (1984). "Fitness Reviews: Key to a Total Quality Program." *ASQC Quality Congress Transactions,* Milwaukee, pp. 263–267.

Love, Kenneth S. (1982). "Quality Auditing of New Products." *ASQC Quality Congress Transactions,* Milwaukee, pp. 534–537.

Marash, Stanley A. (1982) "Conducting an Audit." *Medical Device and Diagnostic Industry,* December, pp. 31–35.

Miller, Ervin F. (1982). "Corporate Quality Audit/Survey." *ASQC Quality Congress Transactions,* Milwaukee, pp. 538–545.

Mizuno, Shigeru (1968). "Quality Systems in Japan." *Reports of Statistical Applications and Research,* Japanese Union of Scientists and Engineers, vol. 15, no. 1, pp. 32–44.

Pereira, Armando Lopes (1987). "Quality Audits and International Standards." *Quality Progress,* January, pp. 27–29.

Plum, Kathryn S. (1987). "A Success Story." *Quality Progress,* January, pp. 32–34.

Purcell, Warren R. (1968). "Sampling Techniques in Quality Systems Audits." *Quality Progress,* October, pp. 13–16.

Rennie, D., Morris W., and Blackburn, K. (1979). "Quality Assurance: Inspection." *Quality Assurance,* September, pp. 71–74.

Riggs, E. J. (1979). "Why Have Outgoing Quality Audits?" *ASQC Technical Conference Transactions,* Milwaukee, pp. 506–512.

Ryan, J. M. and Wong, H. Y. S. (1984). "Breaking Down the Barriers." *Quality,* April, pp. 40–41.

Sayle, A. J. (1981). *Management Audits.* McGraw-Hill Book Company (U.K.), London.

Stenecker, Robert G. (1982). "Proposed ASQC Quality Auditor Certification Program." *ASQC Quality Congress Transactions,* Milwaukee, pp. 830–834.

Thresh, James L. (1984). *How to Conduct, Manage, and Benefit from Effective Quality Audits.* MGI Management Institute, Harrison, NY, pp. 5–7.

Wachniak, R. (1979). "Ten Commandments for Quality Auditors." *Quality,* November, pp. 36–37.

"We Can, Allis-Chalmers Has." (1981). *Quality,* May, pp. 34–40.

White, Bruce (1983). "Measuring the Status of Quality, Part I." *Quality,* August, pp. 63, 64.

Willborn, Walter (1983). *Compendium of Audit Standards.* American Society for Quality Control, Milwaukee.

Willborn, Walter (1987). "Software Quality Auditing." *Quality Progress,* January, pp. 36–37.

Wilson Learning Corporation and E. I. Du Pont de Nemours Company (1986). *Quality Orientation Profile.* John Wiley, New York; Du Pont, Wilmington, DE.

SECTION 10

MANAGING HUMAN PERFORMANCE[1]

Edward M. Baker, Ph.D

INTRODUCTION **10.2**

*THE TAYLOR SYSTEM OF
MANAGEMENT* **10.3**

*THEORIES OF MOTIVATION AND
IMPLICATIONS FOR
MANAGEMENT* **10.4**

   Theories X and Y 10.4

   Theory X or Y? 10.7

*JAPANESE HUMAN RESOURCE
MANAGEMENT PRACTICES* . . **10.7**

   Western Influences on
    Japan 10.8

   Quality Circles 10.9

   Project Teams 10.10

   Consensus Decision
    Making 10.10

   Self-Control 10.10

   Social and Cultural
    Controls 10.11

   Economic Controls 10.11

   Recruitment, Selection,
    Education, and Training 10.11

   Japanese Operations in the
    United States 10.12

*AMERICAN HUMAN RESOURCE
MANAGEMENT PRACTICES* . . **10.12**

   Predominantly American
    Approaches 10.12

   Transplanted Japanese
    Techniques 10.14

MANAGEMENT'S ROLE **10.16**

   Lessons from and for Japan 10.16

   Defining and Creating a
    Responsive Corporate
    Culture 10.17

   Management's Task:
    Applying the Knowledge 10.20

ROLE OF THE LABOR UNION . .**10.21**

THE PROCESSING SYSTEM . . .**10.23**

   Internal Supplier–Customer
    Network 10.23

   System Components . . . 10.23

*WORKER PARTICIPATION IN
PROCESS MANAGEMENT* . . .**10.25**

   Process Control and
    Improvement Cycles . . 10.25

   Process Management and
    Worker Self-Control . . . 10.27

*DIAGNOSING WORKER
PERFORMANCE* **10.31**

   Execution Deficiencies . . . 10.31

   Motivation (Consequence)
    Deficiencies 10.31

   Combination of Execution
    and Motivation
    Deficiencies 10.32

---

[1]In the Third Edition, the section on motivation was prepared by J. M. Juran.

*MANAGING THE
CONSEQUENCES OF
PERFORMANCE* **10.33**

Reinforcement and
Punishment: Definitions   10.33

Planning and Administering
Performance
Consequences 10.34

Performance Appraisal . . 10.36

PROCESSING SYSTEM DESIGN   **10.37**

Job Characteristics 10.37

Horizontal Job
Enlargement 10.37

Vertical Job Enlargement . 10.38

Job Enlargement, both
Vertical and
Horizontal 10.38

Autonomous Work
Groups 10.39

Self-Inspection 10.40

Job Design: The
Investigation 10.40

High Technology and Work
Redesign. 10.40

*TEAM PERFORMANCE: A
PROCESSING SYSTEM
VIEWPOINT* **10.41**

Organization Barriers to
Teamwork 10.42

Teamwork: Linking
Customer and Supplier
Requirements 10.42

Effective Team
Functioning: The
Behavior of Groups . . . 10.43

Quality Circles: Processes,
Tools, Administration . . 10.45

QUALITY CAMPAIGNS **10.48**

Prerequisites 10.49

Phase I: Prelaunch Planning
and Preparation 10.49

Phase 2: The Launch . . . 10.53

Phase 3: Implementation . 10.54

Improvement Projects . . . 10.55

ACKNOWLEDGMENT **10.55**
REFERENCES **10.55**
*SUPPLEMENTAL BIBLIOGRAPHY
AND RESOURCES* **10.60**

American Periodical
Publications 10.60

Publications (in English) of
the Japanese Union of
Scientists and Engineers
(JUSE) 10.61

Other Japanese English-
Language Publications. . 10.61

American Experiences with
Quality Circles 10.61

INTRODUCTION

This section of the handbook reviews the factors which influence the amount and type of worker participation and contribution to the planning, control, and improvement of quality. A key dimension of the management process is the establishment and maintenance of a work climate that encourages and makes it possible for workers to behave in ways that contribute to effective individual and organization performance. Only management can create the conditions which enable workers to control the processes over which they preside and to participate with management in projects that seek to achieve breakthrough to new quality levels. In turn, the work must provide meaningful rewards to each worker.

Since the advent of mass production, Western management systems have defined narrow roles for workers. Worker contributions typically have been limited to executing tasks as directed. Worker involvement in work planning, process management, and improvement efforts generally have been limited to providing information when requested. Alternative approaches to human resource management are emerging under a variety of names such as "quality of work life," "work redesign," "sociotechnical systems," "quality circles," "employee involvement," and "participative management." These efforts have goals related to quality and productivity improvement, worker job satisfaction, union-management cooperation, reduction of conflict, and building of trust. These approaches are evolving especially in the United States, from three interrelated influences: (1) behavioral scientists who, with management's support, are attempting to find ways to make work more meaningful for workers and productive for the business, (2) union leaders who are trying to bring to the workplace the same democratic rights and privileges existing in the larger society, and (3) managers who are attempting to apply worker-related management practices which Japanese companies appear to have used to help produce high-quality products and achieve other successful business outcomes.

THE TAYLOR SYSTEM OF MANAGEMENT

Many of the obstacles to meaningful worker contributions to quality performance are rooted in the philosophy, values, and beliefs and their manifestations—the management control systems—developed under the leadership of Frederick W. Taylor. Taylor was a mechanical engineer who joined a factory as a lathe hand, became head of the lathe gang, and then became manager of the machine shop. It was in the late nineteenth century, when factories were beginning their conversion from "many laborers and few machines" to "many machines and few laborers." Taylor concluded that the foremen and workers of those days lacked the educational qualifications to decide how work should be done, what constituted a day's work, or how to select and train workers.

Taylor undertook to remedy all this by changing the shop organization. He created industrial engineers to plan the work methods and to establish standards of a day's work. In other words, he turned the work planning over to the various specialists, leaving to the foremen and workers only the job of executing plans prepared by someone else. Workers had virtually no discretion as to how the work was done. Worker motivation was viewed as an all-or-none situation; workers either were or were not motivated. It was believed that once the proper piecework incentive was established (based on well-defined job tasks), the workers would be motivated to meet the standards of a day's work. Establishment of the proper incentive scheme would eliminate the worker as a source of variation and free the engineers to work on improving the machines, materials, and methods contributing to the operation's efficiency.

Taylor's approach resulted in substantial increases in productivity. These results were publicized by Taylor in his writings (see the compilation of his papers in Taylor, 1947), and they attracted wide attention. This concept of separation of planning from execution became and remains the norm for the practice of management in the United States. In the decades after World War II, when the industrial companies greatly expanded their work of quality planning, they continued to follow the Taylor concept of separating planning from execution. They did so by creating new specialist positions (quality control engineers, reliability engineers, etc.) to do the planning and analysis, leaving it to the line supervisors, operators, and inspectors to execute the plan.

Taylor's approach to efficient mass production in the early 1900s was innovative in many areas including:

Development of concepts and methods for measuring work and analyzing jobs into simple task elements

Recognition of the need to match workers' abilities to jobs through selection and training

The concept that incentives will be most effective if contingent on good performance and provided soon after the work has been completed

Recognition of the need for goals to be specific and clearly understood by all involved in their attainment

However, as workers' economic and education levels increased and job mobility expanded, the dissatisfaction inherent in simple, repetitive tasks that provided only money as a reward with little worker input into planning of daily activities (in contrast with activities outside of work), began to be expressed in various ways: Worker absenteeism and turnover increased; collective bargaining and adversarial union-management relations became the norm.

The unions, when emerging, had two options, according to Cole (1979, pp. 104–105): They could struggle to increase the amount of worker discretion over how the job was to be done; or they could accept the existing power framework and struggle to make quantitative improvements in worker rewards. Faced with management and government power and the lack of worker support, they chose to gain control over job opportunities by working to replace incentive pay schemes (which management preferred) with standard rate structures. The mutual interest of union and management in tight and narrow job definitions reinforced and deepened the division of labor. The union accepted industrial engineering as a way to unambiguously define jobs, thereby institutionalizing seniority as the basis for allocating jobs and pay.

THEORIES OF MOTIVATION AND IMPLICATIONS FOR MANAGEMENT

Since the late 1920s, when behavioral scientists at Western Electric's Hawthorne plant (Roethlisberger and Dickson, 1939) began to investigate the factors affecting worker job satisfaction, there has been a proliferation of theories and research on the subject. A common characteristic of the approaches—and the most significant—is the focus on the work processes, including the social, psychological climate, rather than on economic incentives as a source of satisfaction.

Maslow (1954) postulated that people will work to satisfy needs, but in a hierarchical order of importance, with each lower-level need to be satisfied partially before working to satisfy a higher-level need. Maslow's model has been taught to many managers and has provided the rationale for contemporary approaches to quality motivation. It is restated in Table 10.1 along with some of the usual forms of quality motivation.

Another scheme to understand human performance was proposed by Herzberg (Herzberg, 1971, and Herzberg et al., 1959). Motivating factors exist in the work itself, e.g., challenging work, growth and learning, identification with groups, and responsibility for planning. These provide job satisfaction but will not stimulate superior performance unless the work provides adequate working conditions,

TABLE 10.1   Hierarchy of Human Needs and Usual Forms of Quality Motivation

Maslow's list of human needs	Usual forms of quality motivation
Physiological needs, i.e., food, shelter, basic survival. In an industrial economy this translates into minimum subsistence earnings.	Opportunity to increase earnings by bonus for good work.
Safety needs, i.e., to remain employed at a subsistence level, once it is achieved.	Appeal to job security, e.g.: quality makes sales, sales make jobs.
Social needs, i.e., to belong to a group and be accepted.	Appeal to the employee as a team member not to let the team down.
Ego needs, i.e., self-respect and the respect from others.	Appeal to pride of workmanship, to achieving a good score. Recognition through awards, publicity, etc.
Self-fulfillment needs, i.e., creativity and self-expression.	Opportunity to propose creative ideas and to participate in creative planning.

wages, and other "hygiene" factors. Inadequacy in these hygiene factors is a source of dissatisfaction. Once adequate, they are accepted as normal. They are prerequisites but do not stimulate performance. Instead, "motivators" must be used.

Theories X and Y.   McGregor (1960) described the beliefs and assumptions about workers under the titles "Theory X" and "Theory Y."

Theory X.   The major beliefs underlying the operation of the Taylor management system are:

Labor is a commodity which can be purchased as needed, like other materials.

Work is inherently distasteful to most people and will be avoided if possible; what people do at work is less important than what they get paid for doing it.

Workers must be influenced to perform in the desired manner with monetary incentives for meeting standards and with penalties for failure.

Few workers want or can handle work which requires creativity, self-direction, or self-control.

Under Theory X, workers are assumed to have no interest in quality. The job of management and supervision is to counter this negative attitude with incentives for meeting standards and penalties for failure, supervise closely, and directly control workers. Tasks must be broken down into specific, simple, repetitive, easily learned operations, which workers are expected to follow. Detailed work routines and procedures have to be established and enforced. Product quality is achieved through use of a separate cadre of inspectors and quality engineers.

Theory Y.   McGregor proposed that management adopt an alternative set of assumptions about employees—Theory Y—which could lead to greater organization efficiency and effectiveness. Under this approach:

Workers are viewed as the most important asset of the organization.

The work itself is viewed as a potential source of satisfaction to workers if it provides opportunities for successful accomplishments.

Most workers are viewed as able and willing to exercise self-control and self-direction.

Workers are assumed to have an internal drive for accomplishment and derive satisfaction from producing results of craftlike quality. The organization, however, gives workers meaningless, monotonous jobs which stifle their natural drive.

Workers become frustrated because they cannot attain the satisfaction they want from the job. Management's job is to create the conditions under which workers can contribute meaningfully to the work and exercise self-control.

Table 10.2 compares the quality control approaches of two shops, one operating under Theory X beliefs, the other operating under Theory Y beliefs. Some of the more usual differences in approaches to control of quality are listed. While some aspects of shop operation are alike under both theories (e.g., specifications, processes, inspection, instruments), there are great differences in the design of jobs, i.e., how the work gets done and by whom. To oversimplify, Theory X management does not trust the people and hence relies on the external control system. Theory Y management does trust the people, and exhibits this trust through wider

TABLE 10.2   Shop Operation under Theory X versus Theory Y

Operation under Theory X	Operation under Theory Y
Extensive use of piecework rates and other financial incentives to meet the standard.	Less emphasis on financial incentives; greater use of supervisory leadership.
Emphasis on wage-penalty clauses or disciplinary measures to punish poor quality performance.	Emphasis on the "why" and "how" to improve poor quality performance.
Reliance mainly on inspection personnel for tool control.	Reliance mainly on production personnel for tool control.
Reliance placed mainly on patrol inspectors to see that setups are correct.	Reliance mainly on operators and setup people for correctness of setup.
Reliance on inspection personnel to detect defects.	Reliance on operator self-inspection for process control to prevent defects.
Debates on the factory floor center on authority to shut down machines, and on fixing blame for problems.	Debates on the factory floor center on the interpretation of specifications and measurements, and on fixing problems.
Relationships between operators and inspectors tense, often hostile and acrimonious.	Relationships between operators and inspectors businesslike, often good-natured.
Upper-management response to high scrap in the form of criticism of Inspection and Production.	Upper-management response to high scrap in the form of problem-probing questions to Production and Support Systems.
Operators do not exhibit interest or desire to do a quality job.	Operators do exhibit interest and desire to do a quality job.
Operators largely ignored as a source of ideas for improvement.	Operators frequently consulted for ideas and involved in improvement efforts.

delegation of responsibility and reliance on employee self-control. Berman and Mase (1983) compare management styles for staff jobs.

Theory X or Y?   Examples of Theory Y managment are described in Peters and Waterman (1982). There is widespread belief that organizations operating under Theory Y have superior human relations. There is evidence (see Sherwood and Hoylman, 1977) that group participative problem-solving and decision-making processes (e.g., quality circles)—a key aspect of Theory Y operation—can produce higher quality solutions and decisions (as defined by an internal criterion or standard) and a high level of worker commitment to the proper execution of those decisions. However, to date, there has been no exhaustive research study which establishes that one of these theories outperforms the other in terms of the major measures of quality: fitness for customer use, cost of poor quality, etc. Ancedotal cases can be cited to support either theory. The essential management issue is whether employees are able to contribute to quality at each stage of the quality spiral (see Section 2 under The Quality Function). There is nothing inherent in Theory Y which provides for worker involvement in the cross-departmental activities required to carry a product from its inception, through design, development, manufacture, sales, and service. Participative work environments cannot themselves guarantee massive worker contributions to quality breakthrough if workers are not able to work on the system's improvement. Organizations where worker participation in problem solving has led to quality and productivity improvement usually have a means (e.g., a hierarchy of committees, as described by Donnelly, 1977) to pass upward problems requiring management attention.

JAPANESE HUMAN RESOURCE MANAGEMENT PRACTICES

Japanese successes in export product quality and market penetration have focused the attention of Western management on the human (as well as the technical) resource management techniques used by Japanese businesses. The most visible techniques (quality circles, bottom-up consensus decision making, self-inspection, job rotation) are studied by management in order to transplant them to their own companies with the hope of reaping quality improvement. Viewed from a traditional Western business perspective, it is often difficult to determine what to copy, especially to improve quality (see Deming, 1982, and Juran, 1979). What is usually overlooked—or unobservable to the uneducated spectator—are the social, cultural, and economic controls on people's behavior that enable the techniques to work. The techniques work because they are consistent with the values and norms of Japanese society and business life. Many American attempts to utilize the techniques for quality and productivity improvment have not been successful because of a failure to take a total system ("organic") perspective. Rather than assuring that the transplant would be accepted by the organization, typically it is introduced in a programmatic, mechanistic manner akin to installing new equipment. When it is incompatible or in conflict with the rest of the system, it is rejected. Many researchers (e.g., Cole, 1979, Nosow, 1984, Ouchi, 1981, Schein, 1981, and Sethi et al., 1984) have tried to understand the social, cultural, and economic conditions which have made possible worker contributions to quality and productivity improvement in Japan. Their findings have provided a basis for analyzing the successes and failures of these techniques in American companies.

Western Influences on Japan.   Japanese management practices—on the surface—appear consistent with Theory Y precepts and values. In fact, Maslow, McGregor, Herzberg, and other American behavioral scientists have been cited as providing the rationale for instituting contemporary participative management practices (e.g., Kobayashi and Burke, 1976, and Kondo, 1975, 1976, 1977) and job redesign (Takezawa, 1976). Cole (1979, pp. 130–132) notes that the Japanese were interested in the implications of modern Western motivation theories and conducted experiments in the 1960s to redesign jobs, humanize work, and increase worker responsibility. Much of this was done before or at the same time as (but independent of) American efforts.

Takezawa (1976) observed that Japanese managers tend to accept Western behavioral science (Theory Y) models as an idealized goal which is consistent with their own orientation. They are often surprised when they discover that in practice American management fits the scientific management (Theory X) model better than the Theory Y model. Cole explains that the American engineering and managerial professions became locked into the scientific management solution for raising worker productivity. Japanese versions of scientific management allowed for innovation based on modern social science approaches. The history of Japanese industrialization in the twentieth century is one of adapting external methods to fit into the existing culture. Cole (1979, chapter 4) contrasts Japanese and U.S. approaches to scientific management. Taylor's *Principles of Scientific Management* was translated into Japanese soon after its publication in 1911 under the title, *The Secret of Saving Lost Motion*. (It is said to have sold 1.5 million copies.) Much of the effort during this period focused on standardizing work procedures rather than doing time and motion studies. For example, teams of railroad workers conducted a thorough analysis of railcar maintenance operations. Detailed work schedules were developed by the workers, enabling the reduction of repair time. The wage systems in most Japanese industries during this period were not geared toward individual achievement. The Taylor principle of high wages for high efficiency was ignored. Wages were determined by seniority rather than on job determined rates. During the 1920s and 1930s, time and motion studies were applied under a government thrust to overcome worldwide economic depression. These were abandoned in the 1940s as too resource-consuming. In the 1940s, a legal ruling on wage increases prevented the tying of wage rates directly to individual work performance.

Cole notes that the emphasis on paternalism grew in parallel with the rise of scientific management. When first introduced, the principles of scientific management were adapted to complement practices of permanent employment, and pay and promotion according to seniority. Time and motion studies were used primarily to determine "correct" job procedures and played a minor role in wage determination. Management was concerned with motivating workers to look at cost reduction and other management goals as a personal challenge. Thus, even though the Japanese had every chance to incorporate Western-style scientific management, they did it in a way consistent with existing social practices, values, and labor market characteristics.

Cole observed also that the interplay of union and management interests and demands that led to the sharp demarcation of jobs in the United States had exactly the opposite outcome in Japan. Since wages were based historically on seniority rather than specific jobs, there was no model of job control to be adopted by the emerging unions. Management had and still has the prerogative, without union interference, to decide on work assignments, job demarcation, and restructuring to meet changing technology. In order to guarantee employment until retirement, management has the flexibility to meet economic upturns and downturns with transfers and reassignments. Downgrading or undesirable assignments are tolerated because they are viewed as a temporary condition. This is changing (see Sethi et al., 1984, chapter 10).

The major processes through which workers contribute to quality and the underlying social and economic controls are described below.

Quality Circles.   Circles are quality improvement and self-improvement study groups. A circle usually is composed of workers (no more than 10) and their supervisor who functions as leader. The emergence of circles was a natural consequence of a top-down process of statistical and quality management education that began with senior executives and worked its way down the organization pyramid to the engineers, supervisors, and shop-floor foremen. Often cited milestones are Deming's seminar in 1950 (Deming, 1951) and Juran's 1954 lectures. The first circle was registered with JUSE (Japanese Union of Scientists and Engineers) in 1962. See the JUSE publications listed in this section's Supplemental Bibliography for the history, philosophy, and operating methods of circles in Japan. Circles in the United States are discussed later under Quality Circles: Processes, Tools, Administration.

Circles usually are the shop-floor manifestation of a broad range of activities called companywide quality control (CWQC) which gives every employee responsibility for quality. This stems from a philosophy that views each person as having unrealized potential that can be realized through education and study. Improvement of the individual will enable the company to improve. Workers, therefore, are more than a commodity—they are an asset to be developed. The circle process also helps supervisors develop leadership skills.

A primary contribution of quality circles in Japan according to Juran (1967a, 1980) has been in improving workers' knowledge and skills and developing interest in the job by providing opportunities for planning and decision making not present in the daily routine. Circle projects enable workers to interface with management (e.g., through project selection, conduct of studies, presentation of results) which help to prepare some workers for supervisory and managerial responsibilities. As circles gain experience and competence, members may form subcircles (sometimes called "minicircles") and elect a coworker to lead each group. The scope of the group may be expanded to include such topics as cost reduction, safety, absenteeism, delivery, facility planning, jigs and tools, and production control. Circles have spread from the shop floor to the warehouse, from the plant to the office, and from manufacturing to the service sector (see *Quality Control Circles at Work,* in the Supplemental Bibliography). A coalition of two or more circles in an internal supplier-customer relationship may form a joint circle, e.g., production with maintenance or with the warehouse.

Worker participation is supposed to be "voluntary," but that is a relative term given the amount of social control that exists. The supervisor is supposed to have the leadership skills necessary to encourage worker participation. The worker's desire to participate comes from a mix of the supervisor's personal enthusiasm, informing the worker of the need to contribute to the common good of the group and the company (Yamamoto, 1980), and building worker confidence. Confidence is built by proper training, success in tackling projects workers can handle, and recognition of efforts to improve.

Cole (1980, 1981) also has observed that even in Japanese plants recognized as having the best circle efforts, management must continually work at revitalizing circle activities so they do not degenerate into ritualistic behavior, e.g., people attending meetings because participation is expected. Cole (1979, p. 166) reports that one company's morale survey showed 30 percent of workers felt that quality circles were a burden because of competition between groups and pressures to submit suggestions. Circles are not necessarily self-sustaining. Some management techniques to maintain interest are intercompany visits by circle members, conventions within Japan, passing of customer complaints to the circles, and even the goal of helping the company win the Deming prize (Cole, 1979, p. 167). Cole emphasizes that Japanese managers told him they do not have all of the answers to sustaining employee interest and participation. The JUSE has done its part to stimulate quality circle activities by selecting outstanding projects for publication and presentation outside of Japan.

In the opinion of Juran and others (see Cole, 1980, Gryna, 1981, and Sandholm, 1983), quality circles themselves have not been the source of the major upturn in Japanese quality because the members have been limited to working on the "useful many" day-to-day problems within the department. Breakthroughs in quality come mainly from working on the management-controllable systems problems. These require interfaces across departments (see Project Teams below). Cole (1979, pp. 163–167) feels that it is difficult to separate the effect of quality circles from job redesign (discussed later in this section) and technological improvements.

While circles may have contributed directly to only about 10 percent of quality improvement, their efforts have indirectly made possible a great deal of the improvement in management-controllable areas by freeing the engineers and managers to work on the vital few system problems. For example, a number of years ago Toyota discovered that of the quality problems accounting for warranty losses, 50 percent were due to 120 big problems. The other 50 percent of losses came from 4000 small problems. The big 120 were assigned to the engineers while the 4000 were assigned to the circles (see Juran, 1980, "Quality Sagging?" 1972, and Rubinstein, 1973).

Project Teams.   These are cross-functional teams created by management to identify, analyze, and solve chronic problems which usually are beyond the scope of the circle. Sometimes the problem is surfaced by a circle. A team often is composed of circle leaders, supervisors, and engineers. In some cases, it may be necessary for the team first to solve the broader problem after which the circle can work on its more narrow project (see Juran, 1966, 1967a, 1967b). Unlike circles which are intended to be permanent, teams usually are formed to work on specific problems or objectives and then disband. (Project team approaches in the United States are discussed later in the section under Team Performance: A Processing System Viewpoint, and in Section 22, Quality Improvement.)

Consensus Decision Making.   This is a bottom-up process whereby desired changes to the system (e.g., procedures, methods) can be originated at any level and submitted upward and laterally for approval. This tends to be a time-consuming method, but it brings about understanding from all concerned members of the organization, eliminates surprises, and provides for elimination of disagreements at each organization level. Each higher-level manager can be sure that subordinates endorse fully the recommendations the manager is being asked to approve. (See Sethi et al., 1984, pp. 34–41.)

Self-Control.   In the narrow sense, this means the inspection of output by the individual who produces it rather than by an inspector from the quality control department. In the broad sense, it means that the worker participates in the planning (process design, scheduling, etc.) of the work and exercises autonomy and discretion in the way the work is executed. (The conditions necessary for self-control are discussed later in this section.) Self-control pertains to work on individual tasks, as well as involvement in group activities.

There are a number of social, cultural, and economic factors that interact in a complex way to assure that workers will learn and abide by the standards, values, and goals of the company. They create a common viewpoint which guides the behavior of each individual. Ishikawa (1981) has contrasted Japanese and Western cultural values. In his view, one major difference between the two societies is its view of humanity. Whereas the East views people as inherently good and trustworthy, the West views people as inherently evil and not to be trusted. This could be a prime reason why the Taylor system, with all of its external controls, has become institutionalized in Western industry and why the Japanese had little trouble creating systems that institutionalize each individual's responsibility for quality. Schein (1981) has observed that most American students of Japanese management approaches fail to see the subtle way in which self-control is acquired by employees. The system makes it possible for workers to learn the goals of the company, what it is trying to achieve, and its values for how to do things. This provides the worker with a set of criteria regarding what is appropriate behavior in an ambiguous situation. The worker can figure out what to do without asking or waiting for direction from the supervisor. Kondo (1975) notes, for example, that the shop manual is for reference only and not a set of step-by-step procedures workers should follow without question.

Social and Cultural Controls.   Employees do what society and the organization expects them to do. In order to do what one's superiors would approve of, one must determine what they are thinking. Not to do so would violate the hierarchical authority structure. The consensus decision-making process reflects a societal and business culture which values overt conformity of viewpoint with one's superiors and the avoidance of conflict. Relationships should be harmonious. The consensus process enables one to learn what others think and feel about an issue so as not to take action that would violate the superiors' expectations and organization norms.

People participate in quality circles (see Cole, 1979, 1980, 1981), contribute suggestions, and do whatever else is expected of them. Failure to do so can lead to social ostracism and the resulting loss of face. The identity and status of workers and their families are gained through the group; there is no identity apart from the identity of the group. Discharge from the company means loss of the social status derived through employment in the company. (See Sethi et al., 1984, chapters 2 and 3.)

Economic Controls.   The economic consequences of failing to meet the expectations of the hierarchy are also disastrous. A worker can lose favor to the point of being discharged (lifetime employment exists for about 40 percent of employees in a firm). If some are fortunate enough to obtain jobs with other firms, the seniority-based wage system starts them at the low end of the wage scale.

Lifetime employment, and compensation and promotion by seniority, are intended to promote cooperation, teamwork, and accomplishment of group and company goals. Employees are supposed to recognize that as tenure increases and the company is successful, they will share in the rewards. The lack of external mobility combined with the consequences of having one's internal mobility blocked puts enormous pressures on the individual to conform and participate.

Recruitment, Selection, Education, and Training.   Interviews and extensive testing prior to employment assure consistency of the candidate's views with those of the company. Job rotational assignments develop a broad base of technical skills and teach workers how the company philosophy and values guide behavior in the various organizations. They give workers a better understanding of the jobs and needs of other company functions. This facilitates communication and cooperation across departments. At the managerial level, rotational assignments develop managers into generalists with a broad understanding of the business and a network of friendships necessary for developing consensus. Job rotation develops competent workers who are valued for the skills they have rather than the job they are doing at any particular time. This helps develop the individual's concern for the company as a whole rather than any particular unit.

These indoctrination and learning experiences are not intended to teach blind conformity, but rather the exercise of judgment guided by organization goals and values. They are intended to create individual self-control and minimize the need for supervision. The role of the supervisor is less one of issuing direct orders and more one of teacher. Cole's research has led him to conclude (1979, pp. 222–223) that worker-related management practices in Japan reflect a belief that human nature can be perfected, thus the willingness to invest in education and training, career development, and quality circles, and to apply the ideas and findings of behavioral scientists.

Japanese Operations in the United States.   The research of the Japan External Trade Organization, JETRO (1981), has provided the data base for many of the opinions about the form and effectiveness of Japanese management practices applied to their operations located in the United States. JETRO surveyed 230 firms in the United States with varying degrees of Japanese financial interest (most were predominately Japanese-owned) and mix of Japanese and American employees.

Sethi et al. (1984, chapter 8), based in part on their analysis of the JETRO data, found that management strategies ranged from the rigid intact transplanting of the systems and people from Japan to a more flexibile approach with attempts, over time, to acculturate the American workers to the Japanese systems.

Based on his own analysis of the JETRO data, Nosow (1984) concluded the following: (1) The most critical attribute of Japanese companies in the United States is the development of an internal homogeneity that binds all members of the enterprise into a corporate family, (2) development of a corporate family requires commonly understood and shared cultural values, and (3) the specific techniques needed to improve organization performance are not rigidly predetermined, but adaptively selected. Nosow's analysis showed, as an example, that only about 20 percent of the Japanese firms were using quality circles (at the time of the JETRO survey) in the United States, largely because management focused initially on changing relationships and ways of thinking.

AMERICAN HUMAN RESOURCE MANAGEMENT PRACTICES

In recent years, American management practices and systems have been taking two paths, one deriving from predominantly American traditions with some recent adaptations of Japanese techniques and one predominantly a transplant of Japanese techniques.

Predominantly American Approaches.   American approaches are characterized by a growing working relationship between management and human resource development specialists. The historic roots date back to the period 1924–

1932. During that time, studies were conducted at the Western Electric Company, Hawthorne (Chicago) manufacturing plant (Roethlisberger and Dickson, 1939). In a departure from usual industrial practice, management collaborated with behavioral scientists to investigate the effects of various working conditions, e.g., illumination, number of rest periods, length of workday, and time of day on productivity and quality. Experiments were conducted with workers in small groups (there were about five people in a group, compared to the approximately 100 people on the shop floor). Although the experiments were conducted in simulated shop-floor conditions, a number of unusual features were introduced such as asking operators to work at a comfortable pace and discussing changes with them before they were made. It was found that rejects decreased and productivity increased during the early studies as favorable changes were made, e.g., better illumination, more and longer rest periods, and a shorter workday. The improvement continued even after the researchers reversed the changes and brought conditions back to the initial levels. The favorable results were attributed to the improved human relations atmosphere that surrounded the studies, particularly the unusual management attention.

During the following decades, studies continued in various firms. Selection and training systems developed during World War II were implemented as the behavioral scientists turned their attention back to industry. The period beginning with the 1950s has seen a large number of attempts at work improvement, e.g., job enrichment, work redesign, sociotechnical systems, participative management, quality of work life (QWL), and worker involvement. (Quality circles may be one form of group participation in a broader QWL or worker involvement effort.) QWL has been viewed as a process for changing an organization (see Rosow, 1982, for the process steps) from Theory X (with its technological and control systems, and associated beliefs, values, attitudes, behaviors, and relationships) to one consistent with Theory Y. QWL also has been viewed as an outcome of the change process, its success being measured in terms of employee attitudes and work satisfaction. These efforts have been led by behavioral scientists, but with influences from some American union leaders who were trying to bring about "social democracy" in the workplace, as well as influences from European industrial democracy efforts. For more on these efforts see, for example, Burck (1981), "The New Industrial Relations" (1981), Davis (1983–1984), Guest (1979), and Walton (1979). The union's role and issues surrounding union-management collaboration are discussed later in this section under Role of the Labor Union and in Batt and Weinberg (1978), Bluestone (1977), Burck (1981), Lawler and Ozley (1979), and Rubinstein (1982).

An assumption implicit in some QWL approaches is that job satisfaction is a prerequisite for high-quality, productive work. An alternate view is that job satisfaction is a result of–not a condition for–quality performance. Satisfaction comes when management removes the obstacles and provides the processes that enable workers to perform well. Good performance brings satisfaction and pride.

A trend now emerging appears to be one of integrating fully the human resources management expertise (the managers and specialists) into the business management team. The human resource development function is being elevated to the status of a key business system requiring strategic planning and a long-range outlook encompassing culture change rather than a simple technique or programmatic orientation (Golden and Ramanujam, 1985, and Tichy, 1983). Human resource specialists are taking a broader systems perspective, learning more about the business and the ways in which their approaches can contribute to business success (especially quality). The specialists previously had focused on the quality of work life or worker involvement process as an end in itself, with quality and productivity a desirable by-product. There is now growing awareness that quality is also a desirable focus since it (1) is necessary for business health and (2) will require greater worker involvement and self-control. Conversely, line managers are acquiring more of the human resource development knowledge, skills, and roles formerly delegated to the personnel function. This is a development parallel to the shifting of *other* key quality functions from the quality control department to line management.

Certainly there have been false starts and setbacks due to attempts to play "catch-up" to the Japanese and compress the time needed to build a collaborative relationship with the union and bring about the necessary changes. There have also been some dramatic demonstrations of worker contributions to improved product and process design when management shared its prerogatives with the workers, and the union relaxed work rules (see Main, 1983). Longer-term views are beginning to prevail as well as recognition of the need to better integrate human resource management systems and technological innovations (automation, scheduling, inventory controls, etc.) into a coherent work system.

Sethi et al. (1984) list a number of companies—some of which are on Peters and Waterman's (1982) list of "excellent" companies—which have a history of human resource management practices similar to those associated with Japanese companies. These companies devote a great deal of energy to creating a work environment in which workers can closely identify their interests with those of their employers. There is heavy emphasis on product quality, innovation, and customer satisfaction. Features of these organizations include sharing of financial rewards at all levels in the organization, no layoffs, a largely salaried rather than hourly based wage system, above-average compensation, worker training, promotion from within, and a genuine interest in all aspects of employee welfare.

Ouchi (1981) has observed the similarity of these practices—which he calls Type Z—to those of companies in Japan. He has cited Type Z companies to support his view that Japanese management practices can be applied successfully in the United States. Sethi et al. (1984, pp. 221–223, 265–271) and Nosow (1984) argue that the practices of these Type Z companies derive from a uniquely American social, cultural, and political environment. Sethi and his colleagues, based on their own research and that of others (e.g., Bruce-Briggs, 1982, and Sullivan, 1983), believe that traditional Western business organizations will have difficulty developing quickly into a Type Z organization. They also note (with criticism of the authors' methodology) the performance decline of some of the Peters and Waterman "excellent" companies since publication of their book in 1982. Much of the success of these companies was attributed to progressive human resource management practices and entrepreneurial type leadership (see also "Who's Excellent Now?" 1984).

American approaches will be discussed in more detail in subsections to follow such as Processing System Design.

Transplanted Japanese Techniques. U.S. management interest in quality circles was stimulated primarily by Juran's (e.g., 1967*a*, 1967*b*) observations of circle operations in Japan as well as by Rubinstein's (1971) efforts during the 1960s to involve operators—in small groups—in quality improvement. Circles were introduced to American business in the early to middle 1970s through use of adapted JUSE training materials and guidelines (for more history see the ASQC 1976 and 1983 references in the Supplemental Bibliography). During the following 10 years, there was a proliferation of research, consultants, training materials, convention presentations, papers, and books. (Circles also spread to Western Europe and South America.) The New York Stock Exchange study, *People and*

Productivity (Epstein and Freund, 1984), showed 44 percent of all U.S. companies with more than 500 employees had quality circle programs. Nearly three out of four started after 1980. Lawler and Mohrman (1985) estimate that over 90 percent of the Fortune 500 companies have quality circle programs. Circles have been applied on the shop floor and in the offices, in manufacturing, and in service industries (see, for example, Ingle and Ingle, 1983).

Sethi and his associates (1984) characterized the use of quality circles by some U.S. companies as "cosmetic." These companies are usually midsized and have market share niches that partially protect them from intensive competition. Their approach usually has the following features:

Introduction is accompanied by a tremendous fanfare in the in-house magazines and the local media. The emphasis is on conveying an image to employees and community that the company is forward-looking in its industrial relations and willing to experiment with new modes to improve productivity and worker relations. But the principal organization concept of top-down management remains unchanged.

Programs are directed by the personnel or public relations departments, and there is little real top management involvement or commitment.

There is inadequate resource allocation, and once the program is initiated, there is insufficient follow-through.

The new practices are too often introduced without enough prior training for the involved workers and plant supervisors as to what is expected of them and how the circles are supposed to function. There is greater attention to form than to substance.

The program often is consultant-driven. A convincing sales presentation leads management to expect great results. In the experience of this author, many (although not all) of the consultants have little expertise beyond delivering training. They do not work with top management to remove inhibitors to meaningful worker participation.

Circles implemented under these conditions usually have a life of 9 months to 2 years. Their growth and decline follow a characteristic pattern (see Cole and Tachiki, 1984, and Lawler and Mohrman, 1985). The program runs into trouble when management is required to go beyond words and become involved personally, for example in face-to-face meetings with workers to listen to a project proposal and a request for management support. While some local problems may be solved, management itself does not form its own circles to address systems issues surfaced by workers. Nor do the circles lead to other forms of participation (e.g., cross-functional project teams) where workers can work with management on systems improvement. (See discussion of improvement project teams in Section 22 as well as: Deming, 1982, pp. 84–86, 107–110, and Gryna, 1981.) Worker enthusiasm is replaced with frustration, and participation fades. When management expectations for results are not met, a scapegoat (e.g., the union, the method) is found for the failure. Morale and trust are worse than before the circle program.

Sethi et al. (1984) have identified a category of companies which follow an approach they call "exploitation." Quality and productivity improvements are sought *through* rather than *in collaboration* with workers. Most of the firms taking this approach have no union. Characteristics are:

The management strategy toward worker relations is essentially authoritarian in character, combined with a large measure of paternalism.

The machine aspects of production rather than the human aspects of management are emphasized.

A great deal of emphasis is placed on the measurement of individual worker productivity, and the reward system emphasizes individual production versus group output.

The primary mode of worker motivation for participating in group activity—whether it involves quality control or increased production—is fear. The highly paternalistic management orientation ensures that this fear is never brutally exercised or overtly manifested, but cooperation and acquiescence on the part of workers is expected and taken for granted.

Management makes every effort to keep as large a share of the gains from productivity as possible. The workers' share is often minimal, grudgingly given, and carries a large measure of acclaimed management generosity.

Management keeps itself insulated from the work force. Top-down communication consists of requests for information, not suggestions or opinions. Bottom-up communication is one of providing the facts. Management does what is minimally required to get workers involved without delegating any of its authority and prerogatives. The primary focus is on things that can be accomplished on the shop floor, and involves streamlining production processes and reducing the number of workers rather than increasing the intellectual contributions of workers.

Companies using this approach still have in place the bureaucratic, autocratic, Theory X management systems. Management does not want worker participation because it fears loss of its own authority. Workers do not trust management. Thus, the system does not encourage meaningful worker participation nor provide mechanisms for it. Quality circles, when used, are viewed strictly from an engineering rather than a human relations perspective. Results are periodically evaluated to see if the costs are justified.

MANAGEMENT'S ROLE

Lessons from and for Japan.   The Japanese successes in application of the various techniques—as has been shown—were made possible because they were consistent and supported by the social, cultural, and economic environment. Western failures to reap fully the benefits of these practices occur when the prerequisites for success do not exist or the organization does not create the personnel systems and work climate to encourage, enable, and reward workers for contributing their energies and ideas. The importance of these environmental controls in sustaining worker-related management practices was made evident by the Japanese over the history of their industrialization, and particularly since 1950. The importance of these factors is being demonstrated today in Japan, but in a different way. In a number of companies—particularly high technology—the slowdown of economic growth has reduced management's ability to reciprocate worker loyalty and dedication to the company with guarantees of jobs for life and built-in promotions and salary increases. Sethi et al (1984, chapter 10) describe a weakening of the foundation upon which past Japanese successes were built resulting from cost competition from other Asian producers (e.g., Korea and Taiwan), requirements to compete in high-technology markets requiring innovation and fast response, and internal cultural changes (e.g., role of women).

Thus, under cost and technological competitive pressures, worker-related management practices of a number of Japanese companies are becoming more like those of some American companies, with similar disastrous results on worker attitudes and loyalties. Younger workers with high technology skills have greater mobility than before and are less willing to accept a system that requires conformity or does not compensate them adequately.

Defining and Creating a Responsive Corporate Culture. Worker-related management systems and practices should enable the business to be responsive and flexibile in anticipating and meeting customer needs and requirements under changing market, economic, political, social, and government-regulatory conditions. The recent experiences of American and Japanese companies suggest that workers cannot and will not contribute fully if the company operates in a manner that is inconsistent with workers' abilities, needs, values, and expectations which have been conditioned by the larger society. (In a sense, workers as internal customers of the company's management systems have user input requirements.)

The nature of work and the work force is changing in a way that requires management to evaluate explicitly how its systems and practices affect the loyalty, dedication, and commitment of employees (all levels) to the company and whether they promote or inhibit the full contribution of employee skills, knowledge, and creativity. The research of Yankelovich and Immerwahr (1983) has documented a widening "commitment gap" between employees' perception of their ability to perform and their actual performance. For example: 75 percent of those surveyed felt they could be much more effective; 63 percent felt they had a great deal of discretion over the quality of their work, but 44 percent reported giving only the minimum amount of effort required. As technology continues to change jobs, even on the shop floor, to predominantly high-discretion, information-processing, knowledge work, then employee discretion and capability to contribute to the control and improvement of quality will increase (see Davis, 1983–1984, Howard, 1984, Miller, 1984, and Sethi et al., 1984, especially chapter 11). Management should look closely to see whether traditional organization characteristics ranging from rewards, punishments, and compensation practices, to forms of involvement in planning and decision making are consistent with the ability of the company to be competitive in quality and productivity.

Workers are better educated than their predecessors, both technically and in financial aspects of the business. They want the democratic freedoms, rights, and responsibilities they exercise in private life extended to the workplace. Sethi et al. (1984), Miller (1984), and others contend that Western business organizations cannot meet future demands by copying the techniques of currently successful companies, American or Japanese. Harmonious relations, a spirit of cooperation, and worker loyalty cannot be created by imposing groupism. Rather, American management practices are best based on American traditions and culture which place great value on the individual's freedom of choice, particularly in the participation in various activities and selection of one's associates. In a high-discretion environment, imposition of tight controls would not produce more than the minimum contribution. Workers need to feel that management is reasonable, is competent to make the request, and that the worker will benefit. Juran (1964, chapter 21) has observed that freedom is a relative term. People do consent to the imposition of organization controls in return for various rewards. There is always a tradeoff. Extreme individualists are out of place if they join bureaucratic organizations, or if they do, they are best placed in jobs of high autonomy, e.g., researcher.

Schein (1981) suggests that a key role of management is to know when individual contributions are needed and when team contributions are needed in order to create the norms and reward systems that will produce appropriate forms of behavior as required. This is much like the job of a sports team coach who has to create a team effort while maximizing the contribution of individual player talents. In addition, this must be done in a way that maintains individual responsibility and accountability. Accountability requires self-control.

Companies will compete successfully if they have created a system of values, beliefs, and behaviors (individual and team)—a culture—necessary for that success. Miller (1984) observes that typically top management develops financial, market, and product strategies without asking if the work environment will enable and encourage people to accomplish these company plans. In the future, management will need to define and create the culture necessary to optimize business performance. The achievement of the desired culture requires planning. Miller has identified eight primary (general) values which promote worker loyalty, productivity, and innovation in American companies—purpose, consensus, excellence, unity, performance, empiricism, intimacy, and integrity. His ideas are representative of the thinking of a growing number of behavioral scientists and managers regarding the new roles facing management. (See, for example, Berman and Mase, 1983; Kanter, 1983; Myers, 1981, chapter 7; Peters and Waterman, 1982; Sethi et al., 1984, chapter 11; and Yankelovich and Immerwahr, 1983.) Many of these ideas are not new. Decades ago Juran (1956) proposed that the anthropologists' concepts of culture could be applied to business organizations by managers desiring to create beneficial change. Miller's eight values, summarized below, provide a framework to define the existing culture, the desired culture, and develop a plan for change.

Purpose. The goals of the company are stated, not in accounting terms (e.g., return on investment, or ROI), but in terms of product or service and benefit to the customer. Miller talks about "power of purpose," the energizing effects of working toward a worthy cause, a noble goal, a vision. It gives meaning to people's efforts.

Consensus. Organizations, according to Miller, should broaden the available forms of decision making beyond the traditional top-down command styles. How and by whom problems are solved, decisions are made and carried out should be determined by what will produce the highest quality results. Miller describes three forms of managerial decision-making styles that can be matched to the particular situations:

1. *Command:* The individual manager makes the decision without discussion with subordinates or peers. This is used for short-term operating decisions where it would be inappropriate to disrupt or take the time of others. It also may be appropriate in crisis situations where there is no time to get the ideas of others.

2. *Consultative:* The individual manager makes the decision after discussion, either one-on-one or in a small group, with others who have knowledge or interests related to the decision.

3. *Consensus:* A group of the manager's subordinates or peers who have the necessary knowledge and information and who will be affected by the decision participate in the discussion until a decision is reached which they all agree to support.

A more detailed discussion of the range of decision-making styles, levels of employee involvement, and the criteria for their selection is given by Baker (1982), Sherwood and Hoylman (1977), and Tannenbaum and Schmidt (1973). (Individual self-control where, in a sense, the individual manages a process, will be discussed later.)

Excellence. Management's job is not to promote satisfaction with the way things are but to create dissatisfaction with the way things are and could be. Closing this gap would be energizing. Management can create an environment of intellectual inquiry in which the pursuit of knowledge becomes the norm by (1) demanding and rewarding individual initiative and improvement, (2) publicly recognizing those who excel, and (3) designing the systems and organization structures that cause individuals to feel they can control their own destinies in a way that promotes acceptance of responsibility. (Juran's "breakthrough" sequence and Deming's continuous improvement cycle, discussed later, are processes to help accomplish these ends.)

Unity. In a theme consistent with the views of Juran (1964), Deming (1982), Myers (1981), Sethi et al. (1984), some union leaders (e.g., Bluestone, 1977), and others, Miller feels that companies must try to return to earlier American craft traditions for their workers. Ownership and identity with the work and the product were a source of pride. Personal ownership, replaced by the alienation of impersonal mass production systems, can again be made possible by information technologies that change the nature of work from doing to thinking. Workers are prepared to accept new relationships and responsibilities. The bureaucratic divisions that separate manager as thinker from worker as doer are barriers to competitive quality and productivity and can be overcome by management practices which are directed at creating harmony of purpose and creation of common interests. Miller (1984, chapter 5) describes a number of plants where management increased its power to perform effectively by delegating to employees more self-control for day-to-day decisions. To accomplish this, he concludes that management should:

> Design an organization structure to eliminate unnecessary layers and give greatest possible responsibility to lowest possible levels.
>
> Redesign compensation systems to create a common concern rather than accentuating distinctions between management and labor (e.g., hourly versus salaried employees).
>
> Seek the greatest possible degree of involvement from people at all levels.
>
> Exhibit through personal style and example, the trust and unity they feel with employees.

The unification of people, processes, and organization unit is discussed in detail later under the subsections The Processing System, Worker Participation in Process Management, and Team Performance: A Processing System Viewpoint.

Performance. Performance will matter to the individual if rewards are dependent on performance. Financial rewards are part of a total array of positive consequences for performance. Performance measurement can serve to let individuals know how they are doing. Evaluation can be made against the individual's or group's prior performance rather than against arbitrary and artificial standards. (See the topic Managing the Consequences of Performance later in this section.)

Empiricism. Effective organization performance is promoted by the use of scientific logic, the encouragement of intellectual curiosity and questioning of why something is known and the reliance on statistical thinking that provides a common basis for the interpretation of data. Employees at all levels will perform measurably better if they know how they are performing. This was clearly demonstrated to this writer in a discussion with an operator in an automotive plant. In describing the resolution of some problems, the operator pointed to the statistical process control chart and said: "This chart is great. I can't remember what I had for dinner last night, but I can see what this process was doing 3 months ago." He went on to describe how the chart was like a scoreboard which helped him see his contributions (physical and mental) to the control and improvement of the process.

Intimacy. This relates to the ability of individuals to share ideas, feelings, and needs in an open, trusting manner, without fear of punishment. The business relies less on procedures, forms, and technology and more upon the cohesiveness of its people.

Integrity. Action is based on what is ethical, not just legal. Deeds are consistent with words. Managers are role models of integrity that inspire their subordinates to believe the purpose of the organization is right, just, and worth sacrificing for. Management's role is to create and manage a culture consistent with the organization behaviors needed to execute the business plan.

Management's Task: Applying the Knowledge. The application of behavioral science knowledge often is a difficult task. Even if one believes that a Theory Y approach is a more effective (and ethical) way to manage human resources, it is not easy to translate the behavioral scientist's concepts, principles, and research findings into action. A major source of difficulty is the abstract language used to explain why people behave as they do in complex industrial organizations. Discussions typically focus on internal events within the individual. Rather than dealing with factors the manager can observe, measure, and influence, the subject matter is one of internal "psychological" events, e.g., motives, attitudes, needs. These abstractions need to be transformed into concrete actions a manager can use.

Organization effectiveness does not depend solely on good people management systems or good technology management systems, but rather on the interaction of all business systems. It may be useful to view business performance as dependent on three related categories of systems:

Technical processing systems: Employee technical skills and knowledge, equipment, technologies, methods, etc.

Social/cultural systems: Beliefs, values, and preferred modes of behaving; reward systems; willingness of people to contribute and cooperate.

Process management systems: Concepts, methods, tools to integrate the social/cultural and technical systems in order to control and improve processes and properly link them across the areas of the business.

Deficiencies in any of these areas can degrade quality and jeopardize competitive viability. The approach to applying human performance management techniques will be described later within a process management framework.

ROLE OF THE LABOR UNION

Irving Bluestone, a former United Auto Workers vice-president, has discussed (reported in Yankelovich and Immerwahr, 1983) the need for management and the union to overcome traditional relationships that are preventing cooperation on issues of mutual concern. There are factors on both sides that label efforts to cooperate as "collusion," "being in bed with the enemy," etc. Cooperation is viewed by union militants as selling out to the company. It is viewed by certain managers as giving away the company to the union. The economic challenge has made the health of the business a common concern. A process is needed to enable appropriate adversarial roles to be exercised while finding ways to work together for mutual benefit.

Trade unions, in the tradition of their craft guild predecessors, have prepared their members to exercise the self-control implicit in their jobs. Long apprenticeships teach the knowledge and skills to bring equipment and facilities to a state of fitness for use (or to specification). Industrial unions, on the other hand, have not traditionally focused on self-control, but have defined their primary roles as one of establishing equitable pay systems. To the extent that mutual trust could be established with management, and the union and its members could benefit, the union has collaborated on quality-of-worklife projects. Some of these efforts have given workers wide latitude in how work is accomplished. However, there have been setbacks when the union felt that management had not generalized its open, cooperative approach beyond the specific quality-of-work-life projects and consulted with the union.

The Yankelovich and Immerwahr study found that blue-collar workers, particularly union members, have the least discretion of all of those surveyed. The union faces new challenges in helping its members close this "commitment gap." Unions and management must find a process to undo many of the features of the Taylor system and turn over some of the specialist functions to the operator.

Joint labor-management committees have provided a way for both parties to cooperate outside of the labor contract. They have been especially successful in business and industries facing an economic threat. Some of the gain-sharing plans offer a model for providing an institutionalized basis for cooperation in matters of quality and productivity (e.g., see Rubinstein, 1982). According to Batt and Weinberg (1978), Scanlon gain-sharing plans (although not widespread) have proven successful as a cooperative effort because:

The plan does not depend on the support of any individual union official or manager who is subject to change. Everyone has a visible, measurable stake in its continuation—the monthly bonus check.

This plan is agreed to voluntarily by union and management, outside the contract, with the acceptance of a majority of employees. Final adoption is decided after a 1-year trial period.

The benefits reach everyone immediately.

There is a continuing incentive for communications to improve in all directions. The monthly bonus provides immediate feedback on company performance. Everyone comes to realize that the success of each person and group depends on the success of the enterprise.

Based on his research, Schuster (1984) attributes a good deal of the plan's success to the management philosophy necessary to establish employee participation, information sharing, and mutual trust.

Although union-management collaboration in work environment improvements does not replace the fundamental adversarial relationship of both parties, there is a mutual willingness to explore new forms of cooperation. For example:

A provision of the 1982 Ford and General Motors collective bargaining agreement authorized mutual growth forums (Katz, 1982).

AT&T and the Communications Workers of America have created "common interest forums" to discuss long-range employment efforts of new telecommunications technologies (Hanlon, 1985).

The 1983 agreement between the Steelworkers of America and the major steel companies established labor-management participation teams. Teams work on any area of mutual interest not specifically excluded by or in violation of the contract (Rubinstein, 1984).

General Motors and the United Auto Workers in 1983 set up a joint committee to study the social, technical, and management system requirements for a new automobile manufacturing organization. This resulted in the formation of the Saturn Corporation, a General Motors subsidiary (Ephlin, 1985).

This type of union-management cooperation is associated with quality and productivity improvement, although the specific linkages are not well understood (Hanlon, 1985). These efforts tend to improve communication and trust to a level where the union is flexible in its acceptance of innovative human resource management practices, (e.g., self-managing work teams) and new technologies. In turn, management accepts the union's job security provisions. Such companies are characterized by effective group problem solving, innovative employee suggestions, and low rates of grievances, disciplinary actions, absenteeism, and turnover.

Reisman and Compa (1985) take the opposite view. They believe that the adversarial character of American labor-management relations is organic to an economic system propelled by hard-driving managers seeking to maximize profits. Both the historical roots of American unionism and the underlying pressures that drive management suggest that those who recommend a new spirit of labor-management cooperation are asking for a cultural revolution that has no basis in industrial reality. The "new era" in labor-management cooperation is a repeat of the cycle of "new eras" that has existed for as long as unions have existed. They maintain that the traditional adversarial relationship is better for both sides than one based on cooperation. Adversarialism is a positive concept. It includes room for give and take in solving shop (or office) problems, in improving quality and productivity, and in meeting workers' needs. From the union's viewpoint, economic progress and shop-floor autonomy are best achieved by having labor and management negotiate from opposite sides of the table where both sides are conscious of inherent differences and respectful of each other's interests, and where the strength of each side serves to check the reach of the other.

The history of some cooperative efforts can reinforce this skepticism. Schuster (1984), Rubinstein (1984), and Cohen-Rosenthal and Burton (1986) acknowledge that the failures have occurred, but the causes were more in process implementation than in philosophical differences or profit motives. Difficulties were found to stem from high management mobility, competitive and adversarial relationships between management functions as well as between operating management and technical staffs, weak union leadership, and absence of expert consultants and practitioners skilled in implementing change in union settings. These writers describe methods for successfully overcoming these obstacles.

THE PROCESSING SYSTEM

Any business organization can be viewed as a network of interdependent functions working to accomplish the organization's purpose. This is done through a diffusion of goals and objectives horizontally and vertically throughout the organization. Most of the individuals, however, may not understand how what they do relates to that higher purpose, and how they affect the ability of other organization members to contribute to that purpose. The processing system concept described below represents a synthesis of various systems approaches to analyzing human performance in organizations (e.g., see Brethower, 1982, Connellan, 1978, Kast and Rosenzweig, 1979, Lawler, 1976, Myers, 1981, and Rummler, 1981). A systems perspective can provide a useful framework for understanding and managing the factors that affect people's performance in any line, service, or administrative and staff work—at any level in the hierarchy. It applies to the production of hardware and to "software" (information, ideas, etc.). If the primary purpose of the enterprise is defined as the production of goods and services that satisfy customers' needs and expectations, the concept of fitness for use may be extended throughout the entire enterprise. It may be useful for each suborganization to view its own purpose as one of satisfying internal customer requirements. These ideas have their origins in the same kinds of systems thinking that gave rise to Japanese companywide quality control practices (see, for example, Ishikawa, 1985, Juran, 1964, Kogure, 1970, and Suzuki, 1978). See also Section 6 under The Triple Role Concept.

Internal Supplier–Customer Network.   Figure 10.1 shows three stages of a larger processing system that produces goods (e.g., parts manufacturing or assembly) or services (e.g., accounts payable, scheduling). Activities at each stage transform inputs to outputs of greater value. Each stage is a supplier to subsequent stages and customer of previous stages. Each individual employee, as "process manager," plays these two roles of customer and supplier.

System Components.   The system components necessary for quality performance are illustrated in Figure 10.2 for a single supplier-customer interface and are described below.

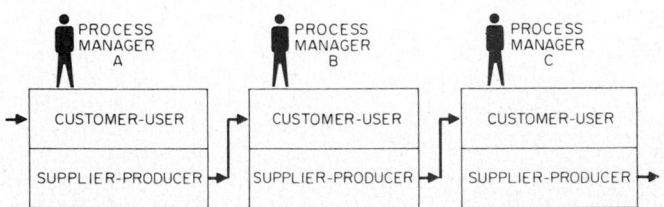

FIG. 10.1   Dual roles of the process manager in the network of supplier-customer interfaces.

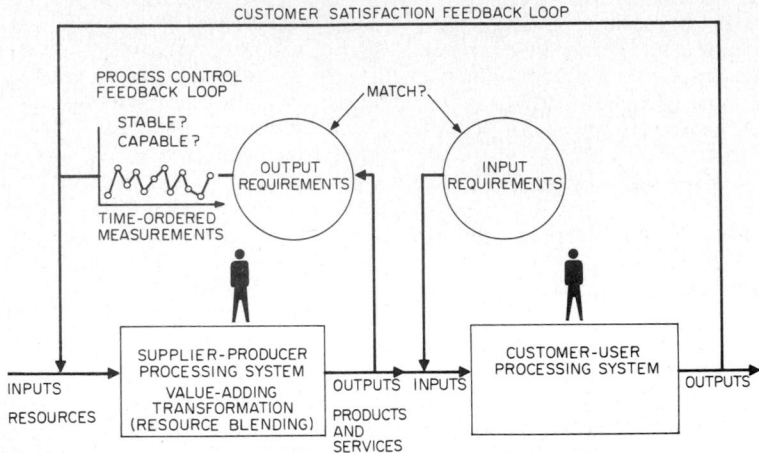

FIG. 10.2   Processing system components necessary for quality performance. *Note*: User's input requirements derived from own output requirements established to satisfy subsequent customers.

Supplier (Producer) Processing System.   The "supplier (producer) processing system" can represent the job of the individual worker who, although not a manager in the traditional sense of managing subordinates, can be viewed as presiding over a process, managing the resources at his or her disposal. "Presiding" is a relative term. It can mean that individual simply follows procedures and executes tasks as told; or it can have a broader definition where the worker exercises discretion and self-control over how the work is done and participates in all of the management control functions for that job. The individual uses personal efforts, skills, knowledge, and intellect to blend the other input resources (process sheets and other "how-to" documents, equipment and tools, materials, etc.) to create outputs of value to the organization.

The person illustrated above each processing system box can represent a production operator or tradesperson on the shop floor, an engineer, production control specialist, finance analyst, secretary—any nonsupervisory professional, technical, or clerical employee. Inside each box are the tasks and related process activities which could be detailed by a process flow diagram. This framework also may be used to depict the processing system of any higher-level employee—supervisor, manager, etc. A manager's system contains the processing systems that contribute to the products and services provided by his or her organization. This could include staff, service, support, and administrative functions which do not report to the manager. This concept is explained further in a subsequent subsection, Team Performance: A Processing System Viewpoint.

Outputs.   These are the products and services. The output of plant engineering, for example, could be "serviced machines"; of material control, "delivered parts"; of accounts payable, "paid invoices." It is the vital few important characteristics of the output—the *critical outcomes*—which are measured. As one moves up the organization hierarchy from microlevel processing systems to macrosystems presided over by middle- and higher-level managers, the process output measurements change in the frequency with which they are generated and in their complexity. Measurements are taken less often and tend to be indexes and composites.

Inputs. These are resources that, for convenience, can be summarized into five categories: people—their knowledge, skills, intellect, creativity, and energy; equipment—machines and tools; methods—e.g., process sheets, shop manuals, instructions; materials and information; environment—the psychological and social as well as the physical. Inputs function in two ways. There are those which *do* the transforming and may be consumed (oil burns off, tools wear, people get tired). The inputs *to be* transformed are *throughputs* to the system. Rather than being consumed, they emerge as outputs with greater value than when they entered (e.g., raw materials to become functioning parts, equipment to be rehabilitated, people to be trained or advised, invoices to be paid, management reports to be acted upon).

Output Requirements. The measured value or values (target, aim, standard, objective, specification, etc.) for the outputs that the processing system—as supplier—intends to achieve.

Customer (User) Processing System. Any system is in a customer role when it uses a supplier's outputs as inputs to its own processes. Each customer becomes the producer for subsequent users.

Customer Input Requirements. These are the types and characteristics of inputs the processing system—as customer—needs from the supplier to perform effectively (i.e., to meet the customer's own output requirements). Value added by the supplier can be evaluated in terms of how well the customer's requirements have been met.

Supplier's External Feedback Loop: Customer Satisfaction. This is information about how well the supplier's outputs are meeting customer requirements. The information may be used for decisions affecting output (e.g., what characteristics to measure and control) or process (e.g., what can be changed to reduce processing time or output variability).

Supplier's Internal Feedback Loop: Process Control. This is information about process stability (repeatability) and output uniformity needed for process regulation. (See Juran, 1964, for a detailed discussion of the manager's feedback loop for control; see also Section 6 under The Feedback Loop.)

WORKER PARTICIPATION IN PROCESS MANAGEMENT

There are two distinct, but intertwined, sets of process management activities necessary to produce quality products and services continuously:

Process control: the prevention of adverse, undesired change; maintenance of the status quo, of a stable state

Process improvement: planning and creating beneficial, desired change

Process Control and Improvement Cycles. A four-stage cycle for each set of activities is shown in Figure 10.3. An early version of the cycle was introduced to Japan by Deming (1951) in his statistical quality control lectures in 1950. Deming (personal communication) derived the cycle from Shewhart's three-stage cycle of activities necessary to manage a production process: specify, produce, inspect. Shewhart (1939, pp. 44–49) observed that these activities were analogous to the

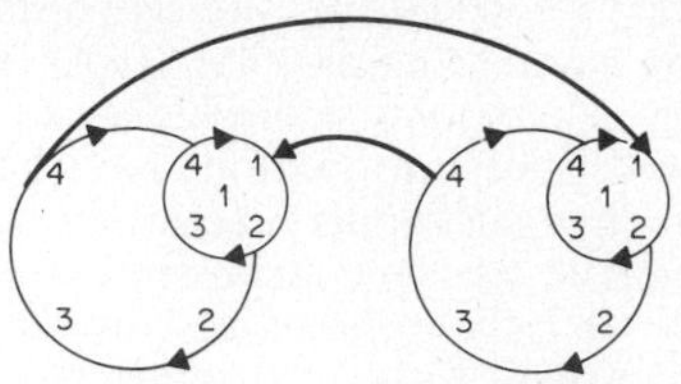

	CONTROL	IMPROVEMENT
1. PLAN	Define internal customer requirements Develop output requirements and measures Establish feedback loops and other control plan elements Inform suppliers of input requirements Plan the work (process sheets, etc.)	Form project team Identify improvement opportunity as gap between current and desired situation Plan the change (e.g., on-line or off-line experiment)
2. DO	Execute plan Collect process data (observations, measurements)	Make the change Collect data
3. CHECK	Analyze data Decide on actions (do nothing; identify and remove assignable causes of sporadic variation; adjust)	Analyze results Observe effects of the change Assess what was learned
4. ACT	Take action determined in Step 3 Go to Step 1 of control cycle or to Step 1 of improvement cycle to remove chronic problems	Go to Step 1 of control cycle to hold gains or to Step 1 above to continue the investigation

FIG. 10.3 Plan-do-check-act (PDCA) processing system management cycle.

steps of the scientific method for acquiring knowledge: hypothesize, experiment, test the hypothesis. The cycle, hence, is a process for learning and improving. The stages have been labeled "plan-do-check-action" by the Japanese (see Ishikawa, 1985, and Kondo, 1977) and for convenience will be referred to as the PDCA cycle. The cycles are similar to the universal control and breakthrough sequences developed by Juran (1964).

According to Shewhart and Deming, a process must be stable before it can be improved. Without statistical control there is no consistently reproducing process. Stable performance requires a process control feedback loop. A PDCA cycle is shown within the planning stage, indicating that the planning for control and improvement also requires a series of activities such as identifying intended suppliers and customers who can form teams to work on process control and improvement. This will be discussed in subsequent subsections.

When Western industry organized for mass production with its dependence on large quantities of unskilled labor, it separated the "doing" from the rest of the cycle. Prior to mass production, most—if not all—functions were integrated within the same individual. The worker was both producer and entrepreneur, carrying out all of the activities of the management cycle from the planning and design of product and process, to the manufacture and sale of the goods. The controls on the worker's behavior came directly from feedback from the customer in the marketplace. Income and reputation required making goods fit for use. In order to stay in business, resources had to be managed efficiently with little waste. The individual had the control and flexibility needed to make the necessary decisions and tradeoffs between internal costs and market forces in order to produce a decent return (see Juran and Gryna, 1980, p. 138).

In most Western industrial organizations (which are based on the Taylor model of functional specialization), the steps of the control cycle are carried out by different people. Managers and engineers plan the work and design the process and tell workers the "right way" to do the work. Workers follow the prescribed methods and inspectors check their work. It is assumed that when things are going well it is because of the system. Since management, not workers, designed the process and set the goals, management, not workers, deserves the credit. Workers are being paid, and that, it is thought, is sufficient. When problems occur, e.g., scrap or rework, workers receive feedback (negative) from supervisors, inspectors, and others. Feedback is used in an attempt to restore control, not maintain control. It takes the form of warnings of what will happen if the worker does not follow procedures. Unfortunately, this approach usually induces overcontrol producing process instability, greater product variability, and high defect rates along with conflict, finger pointing, defensiveness, and other dysfunctional human behavior.

The management systems put in place for mass production may have done three things for workers:

1. Reduced their effectiveness by not giving them the information they need (feedback) to regulate and maintain control of the process
2. Made the work itself essentially meaningless by also removing the planning and other activities needed to give the work continuity, a clear purpose, and provide a sense of accomplishment
3. Precluded participation in planned improvement projects to breakthrough to new quality levels

In this writer's opinion, many white-collar jobs have the same characteristics. Whether in engineering, accounting, or other areas, white-collar work often is characterized by limited positive feedback to employees when results are good, abundant negative feedback when results are poor, and a limited employee role in planning, goal setting, and decision making.

Process Management and Worker Self-Control

Self-Control in Sports and Recreation. A number of writers (Connellan, 1980, Kondo, 1976, Myers, 1981, and Miller, 1978), trying to better understand the factors affecting human behavior, have been intrigued by the willingness of people to participate and try to do well in sports, games, and other leisure and recreational activities, under conditions that they would not tolerate at work. The authors ask, for example:

Why do people who are fatigued at work find energy the same evening to play three sets of tennis or two games of racquetball?

Why do people get up at 5:30 in the morning to play golf in the rain?

Would golf be as much fun if it were part of work and the boss directed the employee to shoot an 80?

Why do people voluntarily play cards or bingo when it is usually done in smoky, noisy, poorly lighted rooms at night after working all day?

Would bowling be as much fun if the bowler could not see what happens to the pins after the ball was launched; or if one had to wait until the end of the evening (or end of the season) to find out the score?

It is obvious why people play a Las Vegas "one-armed bandit"; but why will they pay to play an electronic "pinball machine," and do this hour after hour even when there is no monetary payoff?

The answers to these types of questions can shed light on why work is "work" and play is "fun," and provide an understanding of the essential elements of jobs that encourage ("motivate") people to expend effort, try to improve, and make it possible for them to improve the results of their efforts.

Analysis of these activities indicates that people engaged in sports or recreation have the means for self-control:

1. They know what they are supposed to do. Goals and targets are visible. The relationship (contingency) between performance and reward is known.

2. They know what they are doing. Output is measurable (the score) and there is immediate feedback on performance (the scoreboard). The cheers and encouragement of the other participants provide additional feedback and social recognition that is positively reinforcing and causes effort to be maintained or increased; scores do not have to be related to money or other material rewards to reinforce behavior.

The knowledge that one has achieved the goal also is a source of positive reinforcement.

3. They have the ability to regulate. The method of doing the task is not tightly specified; people can do it in a way that is comfortable for them.

Feedback of results and knowledge of goals makes it possible to change one's own behavior if desired results are not being achieved.

Participation in the sport (which includes selecting ones associates and leaders) and the setting of one's own goals is voluntary; achievement of goals which people have set for themselves is usually more rewarding than achieving someone else's goals.

The freedom afforded individuals causes their creativity, intelligence, and skill to be challenged.

Self-Control in Processing Systems.   When employees, whether on the shop floor or in the offices, are not provided with the means for self-control, they cannot be held accountable for failure to achieve the desired results. Deficiencies may exist in the process itself, e.g., equipment design, work organization and layout, tools, and job aids; or they may exist in the feedback loops (e.g., cannot communicate with supplier or customer) or in the consequences of performance. These affect the worker's knowledge of "supposed to do," "is doing," and ability to regulate (take action), summarized below.

See the following related discussions: Section 17 under Concept of Controllability explains the concept of self-control and includes checklists applicable to the production function. Section 13 under Improving the Effectiveness of Product Development discusses the application to product development (see particularly Table 13.17); see also Juran and Gryna, 1980, chapters 5, 13, 14; May, 1978; and Myers, 1981, chapter 3. The effect of broader responsibility for planning and organizing on the meaningfulness of work is discussed later in this section under Work Redesign.

In a state of self-control, workers follow the PDCA cycle to manage their own processes.

Knowledge of "Supposed to Do."   Workers know (and may have been involved in establishing) the intended outcomes of the process from engineering specifications, budgets, sales quotas, delivery schedules, or other statements of process aim, target or objective, etc. There also is knowledge of how to do the work. This can come from training, instructions, job aids, shop manuals, etc. According to Kondo (1977), the "how to" is described in a way that does not restrict the worker's freedom to exercise judgment in the accomplishment of the process aim. Specification of method is detailed and restrictive only where fitness for customer use is at stake, as for example, in areas of worker and customer safety. The reasons for the restrictions are explained to workers. Within these limitations, workers are encouraged to do the work in ways best suited for each of them. Manuals and other "how to" instructions are for reference only. Workers, for example, are able to:

Refer to product specifications, product sample, or other definition of the end result to be obtained

State the critical (vital few) quality characteristics and why they are important to customers, i.e., describe how the outputs of the process are used

Describe what to do with defective raw material or defective output

Knowledge of "Is Doing."   Workers are able to determine the relationship between their own behavior and the outcomes the process is producing. This requires feedback. (Guidelines for developing performance feedback systems are provided by Fairbank and Prue, 1982.) Feedback is provided in the three ways described below (see Figure 10.2).

During the Process Operation.   Information is continuously provided to the workers through their senses directly or through the mediation of measuring instruments. This helps workers regulate their behavior on a continuous basis to "home in" on the target while creating the output (see Pettigrew, 1983). Obviously the accuracy, repeatability, and ease of use of the instruments are critical.

Direct Feedback after Output Production.   On the shop floor, control charts can provide information on process stability (statistical methods for process control are reviewed in Section 24 of the handbook). They tell the worker when to leave the process alone, when to adjust, and when to seek assistance from management. It is preferable that this information be provided directly to the worker without intervention from the supervisor or other "experts" who may exercise pressure to "do something" when the chart provides no evidence that quality can be improved by employee regulatory actions.

The responsibility of management and supervision for understanding control charts has been discussed by Deming (1982). Inability to "read" a chart and failure to abide by the statistical decision rules will produce overadjustment, increase the variability of outputs, and increase the proportion of defectives. Charts provide a guide to appropriate action for workers and for management. A process in statistical control and capable of meeting specifications can not do better unless a change is made in the system. Only management actions, not operator adjustments, can improve the capability. Management can provide the worker with a significant role in improvement, for example, by participating in breakthrough projects. This is discussed later in this section under the topic Quality Campaigns and in Section 22, Quality Improvement.

Feedback from Customers.   Feedback from customers directly or through others (e.g., supervisor) can show workers the importance of their work to overall product quality. Feedback from internal customers such as may be obtained in worker group problem-solving sessions can lead to recommendations to management for changes to improve process capability or modify internal customer requirements. Periodic feedback discussions with supervisors, particularly regarding process performance shown on the control charts, can provide opportunities for the supervisor to positively reinforce workers for their work in maintaining process control. This is discussed in more detail under Managing the Consequences of Performance.

Ability to Regulate.   Workers have both the authority and means to take action when there is evidence (e.g., on the control chart) that an unplanned change has occurred. Some companies provide criteria to guide worker actions in such cases. A change can be sporadic or sustained. The worker has the diagnostic skills to identify the causes and respond with adjustments or other actions to correct the situation. It may be necessary on occasion to summon additional help, e.g., supervision or engineering. If a sporadic change was in the direction of improvement, e.g., a reduction in defects by the occurrence of a special (assignable) cause, management should be informed so that this condition can be made to happen all of the time, i.e., become a common cause. Workers may not be able to regulate the process because of the design of the equipment, tools, job aids, workspace, or organization of the work. These types of factors are discussed extensively in a number of human factor engineering books (see, for example, Harris and Chaney, 1969, and McCormick and Sanders, 1982).

Feedback and Self-Control at Hawthorne.   The classic "Hawthorne effect" can be better understood in terms of the availability of performance feedback and consequences. This milestone research was reviewed four decades after the original studies, by H. M. Parsons (1980), who also interviewed one of the workers who participated in the studies. He and other behavioral scientists (Connellan, 1978, pp. 160–163; Miller, 1978, pp. 368–369) emphasized the importance of feedback on the workers' ability to control their own behavior. Unlike conditions on the shop floor, the experiment procedure provided frequent feedback on group productivity. Incentive pay was based on the amount by which the group exceeded production standards. Since each group consisted of five employees (rather than 100), each individual could better relate payment to individual efforts. This provided workers the opportunity to set production targets for themselves. Feedback on group performance was available throughout the day. It informed workers how well they were doing with respect to the targets and the payment which followed.

Division of Responsibility.   When a process has changed, e.g., entry of a new supplier of materials or installation of new equipment, it is management's responsibility to bring the process into statistical control. Self-control enables the worker to maintain the quality only at the level which the process is capable of achieving. It does not guarantee defect-free performance. It is up to management to create the policies and procedures in all of the business systems, e.g., purchasing, maintenance, training, etc., so that variation due to materials, equipment, people, etc., will be small relative to the targets, specifications, etc.

Workers also have a responsibility to bring to their management's attention situations in which they do not have the means for self-control. It sometimes happens, when workers attempt to inform management of deficiencies in these areas, they are ignored, told they are making excuses, etc. That discourages them from further attempts to communicate with management.

Self-control gives each employee, management and non-management, a reasonable (vital few) number of things to regulate. It makes possible broad spans of management control.

DIAGNOSING WORKER PERFORMANCE

People are an integral part of processing systems in which they work. What they do, or fail to do to produce quality goods and services depends on:

1. The capability of the system in which they operate and the extent to which they are given self-control, as described previously.

2. What actually happens to them as a result of their performance, i.e., the consequences from output quality (or quantity, cost, schedule, etc.), or from how and what they did to produce those outputs—their behavior. These consequences greatly influence future performance. Deficiencies in worker contributions to processing system performance are classified below.

Execution Deficiencies.   Even when workers want to perform well, they cannot. They do not have the skills, knowledge, abilities, information, communication links, or other process resources (performance antecedents) needed to achieve performance goals. The process is not capable. These deficiencies are correctable by management through better systems of selection, training, information (feedforward, e.g., process sheets, and feedback), equipment, design, etc. Tools and machines, for example, can be designed to be compatible with abilities and limitations of the operators and maintenance personnel—the users of the equipment (see McCormick and Sanders, 1982).

Motivation (Consequence) Deficiencies.   Even though the process is technically capable of achieving objectives, i.e., the people and equipment are able to do things correctly, the performance is degraded because people have little or no reason to do the right things, or in fact may have reason to avoid doing the right things.

Most of these kinds of behaviors are rational worker responses to the organization's reward system. People tend to behave in ways that help them achieve positive consequences and avoid negative ones. Whereas execution deficiencies place limits on how well an individual *can* perform, consequence deficiencies place limits on how well an individual *will* perform. The vast majority of these motivational deficiencies are correctable by the proper management of consequences to workers (discussed below), and through leadership that inspires people to work toward a goal whose achievement is reward in itself. There will be instances, however, where the nature of the work does not provide the worker with sufficient challenges or other rewards to elicit the desired performance. This can be remedied through better design of selection systems.

An operator, for example, may find that taking the time to monitor and regulate the process (make proper adjustments, call for maintenance to help remove an assignable cause of variation, etc.) does not bring supervisor praise for these quality-oriented actions. The supervisor may, in fact, say nothing about the defective items that could result from improper regulation, and criticize the operator for jeopardizing production counts. The operator quickly *learns* that life will be a lot more pleasant if the production goals are met. The supervisor in turn, who is responding to his or her own reward system, suffers no negative consequences for failing to service the equipment. The equipment is serviced between shifts or by the next shift supervisor who has to keep the equipment running to meet production goals. The supervisor in turn is responding to his or her reward system which has established accountability for production volume only with no negative consequences for defect rates or running equipment into the ground. The consequences reinforce undercontrol of the process.

Combination of Execution and Motivation Deficiencies.   Many worker performance problems are difficult to diagnose because they result from a combination of execution and motivation deficiencies. When workers, for example, do not have the necessary information, proper equipment, and discretion to act, they can become frustrated and discouraged to the point that they no longer want to contribute beyond the minimum required, if that. Even highly motivated individuals eventually will be demotivated by the failures which an incapable process forces them to experience. For example: Equipment may be poorly designed; grease, oil, or metal filings piled on the floor may make it a difficult and unpleasant task to get to the controls; it may be inconvenient to contact the supervisor or engineers to discuss the problem. It may just not be worth the effort to deal with the problem in comparison to the potentially few negative consequences for failing to act.

The use of process overcontrol can also be used to illustrate the interactive nature of execution and motivation deficiencies. There may be the best intentions to reduce product variation and prevent output from exceeding specifications. Lack of knowledge (execution deficiency) of the phenomenon of natural process variation (see Section 24, Statistical Process Control) can lead to overreaction to output fluctuation. In order to avoid negative consequences for producing defective parts or for standing by and doing nothing, the operator will feel pressured to "do something." Statistical theory and practice tells us that reacting to random piece-to-piece variation as if it had an assignable cause will, in fact, increase variation and increase the number of defectives. A vicious cycle develops of frustration and anger whereby more action is taken and more people become involved (perhaps the parts supplier, tool engineer, middle management) with behaviors focused on avoiding blame.

The capability of the processing system to repeatedly accomplish its goals and objectives, meet the product specifications, etc., is management controllable. It is common experience to hear of a quality problem diagnosed as worker "laziness," "carelessness," or "lack of concern." Resolution is sought through pleas for better performance, e.g., through use of motivational posters, or by fixing blame and warning of dire consequences if things do not improve. It automatically puts the burden of responsibility for improvement on subordinates without diagnosing the higher management-controllable causes. It forces people into a no-win situation because they do not have the means to change the system. This can be said of all employees, at every level in the hierarchy. Managers are part of the system like everyone else and there are factors affecting their performance which are beyond their own direct control and require upward and lateral communication.

People's performance can be improved by following the improvement cycle shown in Figure 10.3. Techniques for diagnosing problem sources (deficiencies of execution, motivation, or both), as well as identifying solutions, are described by Connellan (1978, 1980), Gilbert (1982), Miller (1978, chapter 11), and Zemke and

Kramlinger (1982). See also Section 22 under Test of Theories of Worker-Controllable Errors.

MANAGING THE CONSEQUENCES OF PERFORMANCE

People tend to behave in ways that enable them to achieve positive consequences and avoid negative ones. Consequences can be positive, negative, or neutral depending on the individual employee, and the circumstances. Whether a consequence is positive or negative for an individual cannot be assumed in advance. For example, a worker may not want the additional responsibility of self-inspection, particularly if it is hard to do with the present process design. Thus, what is positive and what is negative for workers can best be determined by asking workers or by observing the effects on their performance.

Reinforcement and Punishment: Definitions. A *positive reinforcer* is a desirable consequence that causes people to maintain or increase their level of contribution (of physical and mental energy). The individual performs because the outcome will produce a desirable consequence, e.g., peer or supervisor recognition for solving a problem or keeping a process in control. A *negative reinforcer* is an undesirable consequence. It also maintains or increases employee behavior, but the type of behavior that enables the individual to avoid the consequence. Examples are: an employee returns to the desk or machine after lunch to avoid losing pay or being reprimanded; an employee consistently turns in reports late rather than on time, since on-time reports are returned for correction and additional explanation, while late reports are rarely returned for rework; a manager does not report savings that brings the department in under budget in order to avoid losing that amount in the next budget; work is done a certain way to avoid unpleasant or potentially harmful consequences (shock, bruises, fatigue, etc.) from the equipment or environment.

Punishment results when the employee fails to avoid a negative consequence. Its effect is to reduce the tendency of the employee to behave in the way that brought the punishment, e.g., after a reprimand for coming to work late, the employee comes in on time; after the department has been charged with the cost of errors, the supervisor warns workers that their performance reviews will be downgraded if errors continue. Punishment, however, only temporarily reduces or eliminates the occurrence of the undesired behavior (not following guidelines, omitting information, coming in late, etc.) which reappears when the punisher leaves, or punishment is not administered, or can be avoided in other ways. (Once the employee behaves in ways to avoid the punishment, that negative consequence becomes a reinforcer of avoidance behavior.) Although punishment is usually a quick short-term solution, it is not a viable way of bringing about long-term behavior change for two major reasons: (1) it typically depends on external control of someone else, usually the boss, who must spend an exorbitant amount of time being a police officer. (2) The persons delivering the punishment stand a good chance of being punished in return by the worker (e.g., equipment sabotaged, critical information omitted from reports, no meaningful participation in problem-solving meetings when led by the same supervisor who delivers the punishment).

The most effective way to manage consequences (particularly to instill self-control) is through the identification and administration of positive reinforcers. Positive reinforcement makes people feel good about themselves and feel like winners. Reliance on aversive consequences by punishment or negative reinforcement as a control mechanism is an "I gotcha" mentality. It betrays lack of trust of the person to do the job without being watched, and makes people feel like losers. It creates fear, inhibits risk-taking, creativity, and innovation. People behave in a way that enables them to avoid negative consequences, and no more. Chambers (in Deming, 1982, pp. 208–210) describes a case where the defect rates reported on the control chart fluctuated below the manager's quality objective. The chart itself displayed an unnatural tight pattern of variation "hugging" the central line. Interviews of the inspector who maintained the charts revealed that the unusual pattern of variation shown on the chart was "fudged" because of worker fear of punishment for failure to meet management's quality goals and did not reflect actual process performance.

Planning and Administering Performance Consequences. The way consequences are used to control worker behavior communicates to workers how much trust and confidence management has in their abilities to take on greater responsibility. Control by negative consequences will induce fear in workers. It will make it difficult, if not impossible, to establish self-control and will discourage worker involvement in improvement efforts. Most organizations seem to rely on negative consequences. For example, people may come to work on time not because of the positive consequences for that effort, but to avoid negative consequences such as reprimand or loss of pay. The use of negative reinforcement puts a limit on improvement. People generally will do no more than is minimally necessary to avoid the negative consequences. There is no incentive to do better. Positive consequences, on the other hand, seem to be a consistent and efficient (in terms of the manager's time) means for establishing and maintaining process stability through self-control and for eliciting contributions to quality improvement.

Balance of Consequences. A person desiring to change the behavior of others (superiors, subordinates, coworkers) can look at the effects of consequences as a net ledger balance after subtracting debits (negative consequences) from credits (positive consequences) or as a balance scale with weights accumulating on the positive and negative sides. The tendency of people to act in certain ways is affected by that balance.

Determining Which Consequences Are Positive. It has been stated previously that positive consequences can best be defined for each employee through investigation. In a sense, workers are the customers of the person for whom they work. Thus, some "market research" by supervisors most likely will be necessary to determine the kinds of things the workers value and will work to achieve. This can be done in a number of ways:

> Ask them directly what they like about the job or what they like to do off the job.
>
> Questionnaire survey.
>
> Listen to what people discuss among themselves.
>
> Trial and error.

Potential Positive Consequences. One of the most powerful consequences for workers is positive feedback regarding how they are doing with respect to goals which they participated in establishing. Knowledge that one has accomplished the goal, or at least is moving in that direction, is a positive consequence that can accompany the feedback provided by the control chart, or feedback from fellow workers (i.e., from the next customer and from discussions with the supervisor regarding performance).

Examples of consequences which workers may find positive are:

Self-control and increased job responsibility, e.g., opportunity to schedule own work, flexible working hours.

Recognition for job well done, e.g., sincere and thorough praise, being listened to, having ideas used, public acknowledgement of contributions, more interesting work, training for a better job, time off when work is complete. Daniels and Rosen (1983, p. 91) present research findings indicating that managers and supervisors may overestimate how often they provide workers with recognition for good work.

Personal growth, e.g., being sent to a trade show, professional association meeting, or seminar; participation in goal-setting or in problem-solving groups.

Economic gains, e.g., bonus, stock options, stock ownership—a stake in the company, merit pay, fringe benefits (especially "cafeteria" style where workers are able to choose benefits appropriate to their needs combined with a sharing in savings resulting from use of the plan). The effect of pay on performance has been widely studied (e.g., Lawler, 1976). Pay may be an incentive only when it is dependent on performance. (See Reinforcement Contingencies below.) Generally when people do what is necessary to avoid losing pay, rather than working to achieve it, pay is a negative reinforcer. Thus, even though one may believe that people are "paid to work," that is not the case unless pay is tied to performance. Compensation and profit sharing must depend on worker performance to have an incentive effect.

Group incentive programs which reward the performance of organization units (a profit-sharing plan rewards on basis of entire company's profits). The Scanlon, Rucker, and Improshare plans are the best known of the hundreds of methods and formulas to define and distribute incentives. Many plans emphasize quality, e.g., returns will be charged as costs against the plan. See the following references: Bullock and Lawler (1984), Ross and Hauck (1984); see Majerus (1984) for a union leader's viewpoint.

Positive Reinforcement Contingencies.   A positive consequence is not necessarily a reinforcer of behavior. The consequence, whether provided for the behavior (how the work is done) or the outcome (what is produced), will maintain performance only if it depends on the occurrence of the performance. There must be an "if–then" time relationship between the performance and the consequence:

If the performance occurs, then the consequence follows.

If the performance does not occur, the consequence does not follow.

Connellan (1978, p. 31) notes that managers often reverse this sequence, e.g., "You can have this afternoon off if you will do it correctly tomorrow."

A contingency (based on positive consequences) can be established when workers have the means for self-control: They know the targets, goals, standards (the "supposed to do") that constitute the "if," part of the "if–then" relationship; they know the "then"—the consequences—and these must occur according to the expectations created.

Intermittent Reinforcement.   In general, positive consequences are most effective when given on an intermittent basis, i.e., occasionally rather than continuously. Usually, it is not feasible to provide a positive consequence every time the desired performance occurs. The supervisor would have to spend all the time observing the workers to "catch" them doing the right thing. Constant supervision contradicts the self-control concept and undoubtedly will be negative for most workers. Intermittent reinforcement is feasible and lets the workers know that rewards will be forthcoming for good performance, even though they may not occur at the time of performance. The length of time between reinforcement can be relatively short, e.g., every few hours, every morning at the start-of-shift meeting, or longer, as with formal performance appraisals.

Additional discussion on the subject of consequences management with examples and supporting evidence is provided in the following references: Connellan (1978, 1980), Daniels and Rosen (1982), Frederiksen (1982), O'Brien et al. (1982), and Miller (1978).

Performance Appraisal.   Unlike coaching, counseling, and other forms of frequent feedback which focus on a specific task performance, the performance appraisal is a general review of results achieved and the activities (process) which produced those results.

The appraisal can provide an opportunity for supervisor and subordinate to work together to improve the worker's—and hence the supervisor's—performance as an individual contributor and as a member of the organization team. It typically is underutilized for this purpose. Following the cycle shown in Figure 10.3, the improvement process could include the following activities:

Planning.   Identifying a gap between current and desired performance; planning of a method to identify and remedy execution and motivation deficiencies producing that gap.

It is extremely helpful to avoid characterizing performance with abstractions and generalities, e.g., "lazy," "not aggressive," "terrible" which imply that the worker is at fault and could do the job if only there was the desire. This approach deflects the responsibility for improvement away from management. Focusing on the specific behaviors and outcomes (upon which the abstraction was based) will help point the way to improvement.

Doing.   Collecting existing data and records as well as interviewing the worker's suppliers and customers.

Checking.   Analyzing the sources of improvement.

Acting.   Better supervisor use of positive reinforcement; more worker training; better cooperation from others (suppliers and customers) in the organization.

In the latter case, for example, a plan (step 1) to gain that cooperation would need to be developed and the improvement cycle repeated. The "interlocking objectives process," described in a subsequent subsection, is one way of helping the individual's performance by strengthening teamwork.

Performance evaluation is a process that—as with any process—needs to be controlled. The rater must have proper training, instructions, rating formats and information. Without this, worker ratings can be as much a function of poor evaluation as actual performance. Baker and Schuck (1975) offer theory and evidence to show that a rater can be affected by factors unrelated to the worker's performance.

Additional discussion of performance appraisals is provided by Deming (1982, chapter 10), Juran (1964, pp. 247–249), Latham and Wexley (1981), Myers (1981, pp. 234–244), and Scherkenbach (1985).

PROCESSING SYSTEM DESIGN

Under the precepts of Taylor, manufacturing production operations have been organized into a series of tasks with some being performed at each sequential processing station. This concept has been carried over to administrative and service areas, particularly where a large volume of transactions occur. Engineering and other support functions often show signs of the Taylor influence where workers are responsible for only a small part of the total product or service and do not understand how they contribute to the larger organization mission. Often they do not know their internal suppliers, the customers who receive the output of their efforts, and how it is used. There are, however, many forms of job (process) design which can provide workers with greater self-control and sense of purpose, and contribute to individual and organizational effectiveness.

Job Characteristics. Hackman and Oldham (1980) describe five characteristics of jobs which they have found contribute to the meaning and satisfaction workers derive from the work. Jobs that are high in these characteristics are sometimes referred to as "enriched." Table 10.3 summarizes these job characteristics and the management actions that can be taken to enrich jobs in these characteristics. A number of approaches which have been used to redesign jobs are described in more detail below.

Horizontal Job Enlargement. Workers are given a greater number of production tasks, but requiring the same skill level. For example, an assembly line of 40 workers can be redesigned to consist of five lines of eight workers each. While this

TABLE 10.3 Job Enrichment Characteristics and Management Actions (Based on Work of Hackman and Oldham, 1980)

Characteristic	Definition	Action
1. Skill variety	Degree to which the job has a sufficient variety of activities to require a diversity of employee skills and talents	Combine sequential tasks to produce larger work modules (horizontal enlargement)
2. Task identity	Extent to which work requires doing a job from beginning to end and results in a completed visible unit of output	Arrange work into meaningful groups, e.g., by customer, by product
3. Task significance	Extent to which the job impacts internal and external customers	Provide means for direct communication and personal contact with customer
4. Autonomy	Amount of employee self-control in planning and doing the work	Provide employee greater self-control for decision making (vertical enlargement)
5. Feedback	Degree to which direct knowledge of results is provided to employee	Create feedback systems to provide employees information directly from doing the job

gives each worker greater variety, it may not make work more satisfying and meaningful if all the tasks are inherently boring. Some of the other job enrichment characteristics will also have to be incorporated such as enabling workers to see how their efforts contribute to an identifiable product. In the extreme examples of horizontal enlargement, the assembly line is eliminated and each worker assembles the complete product unit. Examples of quality improvements resulting from horizontal job enlargement are given by Huse and Beer (1971) and Tuggle (1969). An alternate approach to horizontal job enlargement is to train each member of a unit to do all the jobs with tasks assigned on a rotating basis (this may require a higher pay rate).

Vertical Job Enlargement.   The job can be vertically enlarged by giving the work unit responsibilities previously restricted to the supervisor, e.g., assigning the work, scheduling breaks, establishing work rules, and interviewing and hiring job applicants. Production operators may be given the added duties of product inspection, tool control, inventory control, recordkeeping, etc. The individual becomes a "minimanager" for that work station.

In one case (Maher et al., 1969), the job of process inspectors was enlarged by adding unconventional duties such as trouble-shooting, disposition of nonconforming product, conducting process capability studies, planning production station quality control criteria, establishing prevention programs, and assisting in design reviews.

Myers (1981, p. 97) provides additional examples of vertical enlargement:

1. Assemblers on a radar assembly line are given information on customer contract commitments in terms of price, quality specifications, delivery schedules, and company data on material and personnel costs, break-even performance, and potential profit margins. Assemblers and engineers work together in methods and design improvements. Assemblers inspect, adjust, and repair their own work, help test completed units, and receive copies of customer inspection reports.

2. Electronic assemblers involved in intricate assembling, bonding, soldering, and welding operations are given training in methods improvement and encouraged to make suggestions for improving manufacturing processes. Natural work groups of 5 to 20 assemblers each elect a "team captain" for a term of 6 months. In addition to normal duties, the captain collects work-improvement ideas from team members, describes them on a standard form, credits the suggestors, presents the recommendations to their supervisor and superintendent at the end of the week, and gives the team feedback on idea utilization. Though most job operations remain the same, vertical job enlargement is achieved by providing workers increased opportunity for planning, reorganizing, and controlling their work.

Job Enlargement, both Vertical and Horizontal.   Myers (1981, p. 97) describes two examples of jobs incorporating both horizontal and vertical characteristics:

1. Jobs are enlarged horizontally in a clad metal rolling mill by qualifying operators to work interchangeably on breakdown rolling, finishing rolling, slitter, pickler, and abrader operations. After giving the operators training in methods improvement and basic metallurgy, jobs are enlarged vertically by involving them with engineering and supervisory personnel in problem-solving sessions for increasing production yields.

2. Jobs in a large employee insurance section are enlarged horizontally by qualifying insurance clerks to work interchangeably in filing claims, mailing checks,
enrolling and orienting new employees, checking premium and enrollment
reports, adjusting payroll deductions, and interpreting policies to employees.
Vertical enlargement involves clerks in insurance program planning meetings
with personnel directors and carrier representatives, authorizes them to sign
disbursement requests, attend a paperwork systems conference, recommend
equipment replacements, and to rearrange their work layout.

Hackman and Oldham (1980) describe the redesign of keypunch operator jobs
in a large insurance company. Before the change, operators were strictly limited
to keypunch tasks. They were isolated from their customers by assignment clerks
who distributed the work in batches that could be completed in 1 hour. The operators did not know who was their customer or the impact of their work on the
customer. Since the supervisors reviewed their work for errors and assigned corrections to someone other than the original operator, there was no opportunity
for feedback. The performance situation was characterized by high error rates,
missed schedules, high costs, and absenteeism. This situation was dramatically
improved after introduction of the following changes:

1. Each operator was given the responsibility for all of the work for a number of
accounts. In addition to keypunching, the operators planned and scheduled
their work.

2. Operators interfaced directly with their customers. They personally inspected
incoming work for corrections and legibility. Any customer concerns were discussed with the operator who had the freedom to correct errors without checking with the supervisor.

3. Operators kept their own records which were used for regular performance
reviews.

Juran and Gryna (1980, p. 161) cite a case where the telephone company
revised the job of preparing telephone directories for publication. Each step of the
21 steps of the process previously was done by one or more different workers. The
revised approach allowed each worker to assemble an entire directory, i.e., to perform all 21 operations. There was a dramatic reduction in turnover, absenteeism,
and errors.

Autonomous Work Groups.   A work team may become self-managing by taking over some of the PDCA control functions usually performed by a supervisor.
Teams are also referred to as semiautonomous since they are constrained by the
organization's control systems. Creation of autonomous work teams will not
guarantee improved performance if the team structure is imposed on workers and
they have to operate in a tight top-down environment without the opportunity
for significant decisionmaking (see Bluestone, 1977). Juran and Gryna (1980, pp.
160–161) describe the case of a Swedish company which redesigned its process to
enable a team of approximately 10 employees to assemble the entire engine. The
team decides which members perform the various operations. The team also performs some of the administrative and service functions related to materials supply, tool maintenance, inspection, and recordkeeping. Self-managing groups may
be a local effort or part of a broad organization work restructuring effort. See the
following for additional studies and bibliographies: Gyllenhammar (1978), Ketchum (1984), Tichy (1976), and Woodman and Sherwood (1977).

Self-Inspection.   Responsibility for in-process inspection of their own work can be given to the production operators. Kondo et al. (1982) report an increase in operator motivation, a decrease in time for corrective action, and 40 percent decrease in defects. This can also help the operator close the feedback loop to "upstream" operations. (See Production, Section 17 of this handbook.)

Job Design: The Investigation.   Hackman and Oldham (1980) recommend a cautious approach be taken to job redesign. There are definite differences between employees as to how much freedom and complexity they want, or have the ability to take on. Most, but not all, people want a more demanding, challenging job. Putting employees in jobs for which they are not trained or otherwise suited can cause them to fail. Investigation should be conducted to assess the appropriate types of job design. All persons directly affected or whose support will be needed to conduct the investigation and help in the change should be involved. This includes management and supervisors, union leaders, and workers. Without their participation and education, changes could be perceived as threatening, and result in overt or covert resistance (see also Myers, 1981, pp. 108–114).

Hackman and Oldham (1980) recommend six criteria that can be used in deciding if and how to redesign jobs. In summary, job design is appropriate where:

1. Job design solves an existing problem or takes advantage of an opportunity.
2. The problem or opportunity involves work effectiveness (quality and quantity of output), motivation, or satisfaction.
3. Job design appears to be a solution, rather than supervisor training, or change in the reward system.
4. The five job enrichment characteristics which redesign is to address have been identified.
5. Workers are enthusiastic about the change.
6. The organization is receptive to the needed changes.

High Technology and Work Redesign.   The implications of high technology for effective worker performance have been discussed by Davis (1983–1984). Manufacturing systems are becoming more automated through the use of robots and the linking of individual machines into complex, computer-controlled, integrated systems where failures in any part of the system can have serious consequences for the entire system. In this arrangement, the worker no longer has simple repetitive tasks. The job is one of monitoring, diagnosing, and correcting the causes of instability. The diagnostic and correction process is complex, due to the multiplicity of potential failure modes. It is not sufficient to train workers in advance to deal with a limited number of potential assignable causes of instability. Workers need a broad repertoire of skills and knowledge to deal with failure modes that are hard to anticipate. In addition, they need to have the flexibility and self-control to respond rapidly and decide where, whether, and when to intervene without having to take the time to get permission from supervision or engineering.

Davis (1983–1984) cites the Three Mile Island nuclear plant near-disaster of 1979 to illustrate the results of failure of organizations to recognize the demands technology places on an organization and its personnel. The series of events leading to the disaster involved a combination of conditions which made it impossible to correct the malfunction promptly, e.g.:

Control room deficiencies.

Lack of clarity in operating procedures.

Operator training deficiencies: no worker or engineer knew how to operate more than a small segment of the total system.

Negotiated work rules precluded a quick response. Engineers were not allowed to do the operator's work of turning knobs or moving levers; workers were prohibited from doing any "engineering calculations."

In Davis's view, the use of the single approaches such as job enrichment, incentives, and profit sharing do not promote the degree of organizational adaptability and flexibility of response as does an integrated approach that matches the technical and social system requirements. Sociotechnical systems have been implemented in a number of new plants beginning in the 1970s. Common characteristics are (Davis, 1983–1984, p. 13):

Little or no plant middle management

Self-regulation of process by work teams

Workers with wide repertoires of skills and no specific jobs or job descriptions

Localized planning and decision making

Open flow of information across and between all levels of the organization

Weekly team meetings to review progress and difficulties, and plan and solve problems

Fairly open job progression

Wage schemes based on payment for knowledge and skills

Work team representatives who sit on plantwide committees and participate in the selection of new employees

The performance of these new plants was superior to other plants in the same company operating under more traditional systems. They had higher product quality, lower costs, fewer grievances, lower worker turnover, and less reported dissatisfaction.

TEAM PERFORMANCE: A PROCESSING SYSTEM VIEWPOINT

A spirit of teamwork (as well as substantive individual contributions) can be built when people recognize that it is in the best interests of themselves and their organization to cooperate with others. Obviously, cooperation is easier when one knows with whom to cooperate, as in groups with a special identity and common purpose (e.g., autonomous work groups, quality circles, quality breakthrough project teams, ad hoc task forces). When the common purpose and mutual dependencies of the members are not obvious to each member, there is no team.

Organization Barriers to Teamwork. The entire enterprise can be viewed as a network of people in interdependent supplier (producer)–customer (user) relationships as illustrated in Figures 10.1 and 10.2. These relationships typically are not well understood, either by employees at the lower organization levels or by middle and higher level managers. This is especially true of hierarchical, bureaucratic organizations whose structures and management systems make it difficult for people to see how they contribute to the common good. Juran (1964, pp. 131–133) pointed out years ago the impediment of "provincialism" to quality improvement. Deming (1982) calls it "departmental barriers." Ishikawa (1985, pp. 107–109, 125) describes his attempts years ago in Japan to resolve hostility between production areas by having each worker view the next process as a customer. Similar attempts were made to reduce "sectionalism" between staff and line employees.

This separateness produces the phenomenon of organization suboptimization. Department or functional objectives are not linked in a coherent way that is in the best interests of the overall business purpose and goals. Hence, even though people meet their individual objectives, the enterprise as a whole fails to fully accomplish its larger mission. Organization effectiveness is diminished by the costs associated with waste, inefficiencies, rework, in-fighting, and other dysfunctional behaviors. Engineering, for example, may release drawings to meet manufacturing schedules, even though all engineering and test work has not been completed. Subsequent inevitable engineering changes have cost and quality ramifications throughout the organization. Sales, for example, may promise customers option combinations and quantities that exceed the plant's production capability. Then the orders are submitted to the plant with insufficient information or errors that require the order to be returned to Sales. Conversely, the plant may give Sales unrealistic production schedules or fail to inform them of planned shutdowns.

Barriers between organizations can be made even more impenetrable by the special languages of each function and the failure to work at establishing common understandings [see Juran (1964, pp. 212–213) and Deming (1982, chapter 15 on Operational Definitions)]. In addition, communication across organizations may occur at managerial levels well above the employees who need or provide the information.

Teamwork: Linking Customer and Supplier Requirements. The establishment of process output requirements—specifications, objectives, schedules, quotas, budgets, etc.—can be viewed as a two-way street that considers both the customer's needs and the supplier's capability. Admonishing people to cooperate and help each other will not bring about the intended results. Teamwork requires: (1) a process that will overcome bureaucratic complexities and barriers, and (2) a system of rewards that reinforces use of the process.

This is being accomplished in Japanese business through companywide quality control. Using a variety of techniques and activities known as "quality function deployment," the critical interdependencies between the organization's processing systems are identified (e.g., see Kogure, 1984, Kogure and Akao, 1983, and Sullivan, 1986). The mutual requirements—supplier to customer and customer to supplier—are established in a way that coherently links the processes to each other and to the requirements of the final customer.

Various approaches to overcoming the barriers imposed by traditional hierarchical, functionally separated organization structures are emerging outside of Japan. These are not attempts to copy Japanese companywide quality control.

They derive, however, from the same kind of systems thinking that recognizes the need to meaningfully integrate people, units, and processes within the enterprise in order to generate the responsiveness and innovativeness to anticipate rapidly changing customer demands. Hermann and Baker (1985) describe an "interlocking objectives" process to link individual and unit objectives across the plant and to the objectives and goals of the plant manager. Pettigrew (1983) used a "process intent" approach to link operators in an automotive assembly plant. Brethower (1982) describes application of this concept to help a plant manager and sales manager—each of whom are suppliers to and customers of the other—establish mutually supporting objectives. Efforts to build teamwork by linking internal customers and suppliers in administrative and service processes such as accounts receivable, document distribution, and marketing are described by Baker and Artinian (1985), Kane (1986), Melan (1985), and Nickell (1985). Kotter (1985) describes the manager's role and approaches to managing cross-functional relationships and interfaces within the political realities of organization life.

Effective Team Functioning: The Behavior of Groups.   A team is a group of individuals each with specific skills and knowledge and interests that enable the members to contribute to the accomplishment of a common purpose. (See, for example, the team approach to quality improvement taken by the Florida Power and Light Company, 1982.) The team's purpose may be accomplished in a relatively short time after which the team is disbanded; or, it may have a longer-term purpose requiring ongoing activity. Whether participation is voluntary or mandatory depends on the purpose, who is needed, and the time available. Team leaders typically are from supervision and management, although a nonsupervisory employee may be elected by the group when appropriate. The team may be composed of people from the same local organization unit (e.g., a quality circle of operators reporting to the same supervisor; an autonomous work group) or formed within a given function (e.g., electricians, accountants). Cross-functional teams are formed where expertise and a vested interest in the outcome rests in a number of different organization units, departments, or functions. (Numerous team approaches to quality improvement are described in the *Juran Report*—see Supplemental Bibliography.) A team may have members from the same organization level (e.g., all operators, supervisors, or managers), from a vertical slice within the organization or function, or a diagonal slice of organization levels and functions. In some cases, e.g., joint union-management quality of work life committees, a special structure may have to be created to accommodate the new roles and relationships (see Carlson, 1978, Rubinstein, 1982, and Stein and Kanter, 1980). Finally, the team may be characterized by the scope of its purpose and amount of its discretion to gather information, make decisions, and take action.

Teams may be formed, as needed (perhaps on an ad hoc basis) to fight fires and solve local problems (remove assignable causes) to maintain process control. On the other hand, with the support of higher management, a team may work on improving the system (e.g., a quality "breakthrough" project) by working on management-controllable issues, but where discretion has been delegated to the group and the means have been provided to develop and recommend a change, and perhaps implement the change (e.g., Davidson, 1982, and Kondo, 1981). A team formed of internal customers and suppliers, working through the control and improvement cycles (Figure 10.3), can constitute a powerful force for positive change. Moehlenbrock (1985) contrasts control teams with breakthrough teams. Each manager can set the stage for effective teamwork by guiding subordinates through the planning activities needed to identify critical supplier-customer interfaces. An early step, usually done at the department level, is the development of processing system flow diagrams. This is done first at a macrolevel of analysis to identify supplying and using organization units or functions. Then each individual can develop a microflow which details specific tasks and pinpoints specific individuals who are suppliers and customers. It is an iterative process (a PDCA at the planning stage, as illustrated in Figure 10.3) because additional information usually needs to be gathered. In addition, there often are differences of opinion within the department regarding the process flow that have to be reconciled. Then arrangements can be made for people to meet with their customers and suppliers. Table 10.4 provides an idea of the kinds of questions that need to be answered and can serve as a guide for supplier-customer discussions (they may interview each other). This can help the team identify improvement areas, particularly in components of the system, e.g., poor or nonexistent feedback loops.

A team is a processing system producing outputs (problem solutions, decisions, recommendations, strategic plans, policy statements, engineering drawings, repaired equipment, etc.) for a user, e.g., a manager, another team, its own members. High-quality outputs (innovative solutions) are likely because the idea generating and evaluation processes used by groups (e.g., Sink, 1983) can produce results usually not possible by simply combining the ideas and efforts of people working alone. This synergy of ideas is supported by the energy created by the positive reinforcement inherent in working for a worthy goal and the ability of individuals to see that the group's success depends on each person's contribution and cooperation.

The behavior of people in groups can be more difficult to manage than their behavior as individuals. The strength of the group comes from the diversity of viewpoints, backgrounds, and special knowledge of the individual members. These differences can be a source of disfunction unless there are controls to guide

TABLE 10.4   Guide to Help Identify Processing System Components Necessary for Teamwork

---

1. Processing system as supplier (producer).
   a. What products and services are produced?
   b. For whom? (List your customers—individuals, units, functions; be as specific as possible.)
   c. What is the value to customers of these output products and services?
      • What is their purpose? Why are they needed?
      • How are they used? Under what conditions?
      • What are the customers' usage (input) requirements?
   d. How do you know if you are meeting these requirements? (Are you capable?)
      • Do you find out? When? How Often?
      • Do your own output requirements (standards, goals, targets) relate to your customers' input requirements?
      • What do you measure, and why? Are you your own customer?
   e. How do you evaluate output fluctuation and deviations from targets? Do you have a statistical definition of process stability?
2. Processing system as customer (user).
   a. What inputs (material, information, tools, other resources) do you receive?
   b. From whom? (List your suppliers.)
   c. Do they know your input requirements?
   d. Do you communicate with your suppliers? When (e.g., only when there is a problem)? How (e.g., face-to-face, mediation by someone else)?

---

people's behavior in the same direction. The following conditions will contribute to effective group functioning:

The group's purpose is clearly understood and supported by all members.

There is a process for establishing and prioritizing goals and objectives to the vital few that can be accomplished. The roles and responsibilities of each member for specific tasks or functions are clear and agreed upon by all members. This is especially true of the leader's role.

Individual accountability is established for the accomplishment of specific, measurable outcomes.

Feedback to individuals, e.g., from the leader or other team members, is specific and nonpersonal so individuals can evaluate the effect of their behavior on the group performance.

A process (e.g., procedures, guidelines, rules, etc.) exists for getting the work done. This includes a method for assigning work to individuals, coordination of efforts, exchange of information, discussion, and problem-solving and decision-making processes.

Rubin et al. (1978) have found that most of the conflict, mistrust, and counterproductive behaviors of people in groups are symptoms of failure to clarify and agree upon goals, roles, and procedures—in that order. A great deal of literature is available describing the principles, processes, and techniques of effective group and team functioning. Examples are Fisher (1980), Rubin et al. (1978), Zander (1983), and the *Handbook for Group Facilitators* (updated each year, it provides a compendium of concepts and tools—see the Supplemental Bibliography). Prince (1970, 1972) describes a process for stimulating creative and innovative ideas.

Juran (1956) observed that blind opposition often faces the proponent of change who fails to properly understand and deal with the concerns of others who will be affected by the change. Opposition may be expressed in many ways, e.g., "We tried that before and it didn't work." Connellan (1980, pp. 104–105) lists dozens of "killer phrases" which can arise in team discussions which will prevent ideas from budding. He recommends the learning of a new vocabulary of "booster phrases" which can help team members positively reinforce each other's generation of creative ideas.

Quality Circles: Processes, Tools, Administration.   The likelihood of success will be increased greatly if management thinks through what it hopes to accomplish with this form of worker involvement and develops a common understanding regarding a number of related issues:

Will circles constitute a stand-alone program—a separate appendage to the organization—guided and promoted only by the manufacturing or quality control departments? Or will they be a logical consequence of a business strategy that integrates human resources management planning into the overall business process in a context analogous to companywide quality control?

Is the purpose of the circles to solve local quality problems (typically sporadic) or to work with management and other circles on chronic, systems problems?

Is the purpose equally to improve work relationships between workers, management, and the union?

What is the state of union-management relations? Can circles be undertaken as a cooperative effort? Can structures, e.g., union-management committees, be created to jointly manage the effort? Is preparatory work needed to build union-management relations? What is the risk in proceeding without an active union role?

What will be the role of middle and top management?

Is this intended to be a short-term or ongoing effort? Is the purpose consistent with the planned or likely duration of circles in the organization?

See Barra (1983), Gryna (1981), Ingle (1982), Ishikawa (1985), Shea (1986), and the Supplemental Bibliography for more on these and other quality circle issues discussed in this subsection. The role of management and the functions of a steering committee are discussed in the next subsection, Quality Campaigns. The participation of the union is discussed in a previous subsection, Role of the Labor Union.

Circles are composed of workers reporting to the same supervisor. As discussed in early subsections, this limits their ability to directly tackle and influence chronic systems problems which typically requires cross-functional collaboration, as with project teams.

The circle leader usually is the supervisor. If a circle is subdivided into mini-circles (of three to five workers), one of the members is elected to be leader. Worker presence may be mandated (depending on labor contract provisions if workers are represented), but worker involvement cannot be ordered or achieved through coercion. Worker commitment to the process has been found to be best achieved through voluntary participation based on an understanding of the circle's purpose and benefits. Circles usually meet about 1 hour per week on regular time. If there is a need to meet more frequently, this may occur on regular time or overtime. Practice varies. Additional time is often needed to work on the project, attend training, study, etc.

Coordination and facilitation functions may be assumed by the same individuals. Large plants and multidivision plants may have two or more facilitators. In many cases, facilitators report to a line manager—even the plant manager—with a dotted-line relationship with a division coordinator. Practice varies. In the discussion below, both functions will be treated as the responsibility of a single individual or individuals with the title of facilitator. In joint union-management efforts, these roles are often shared by a union member and nonunion employee.

The facilitator's primary roles are those of change agent, counselor, promotor, and trainer with additional administrative tasks, e.g., recordkeeping and scheduling. The following attributes are necessary for facilitator effectiveness:

1. Good interpersonal and communications skills to interact with people at all levels of the organization, resolve conflict, and break down resistance to change
2. Trust and respect of union, management, and workers
3. Sufficient knowledge of the organization's processes and products to speak the language, follow up, etc.
4. Technical knowledge of circle processes, e.g., PDCA cycle, tools, management presentation techniques
5. Administrative skills for self-management and circle management (e.g., develop and follow up plans and monitor progress, provide timely feedback)

The facilitator is a critical vertical and lateral link, particularly during the period of introduction of circles to the organization and during the first 6 to 9 months of any circle. It is common for the facilitator to participate as an active member of the organization steering committee.

Quality circles use statistical tools and related graphical techniques to provide input to various stages of the PDCA cycle (Figure 10.3). For example:

Checksheets are used to record observations and measurements made during the *do* stage. These data are inputs to the *check* stage where they are summarized and transformed into Pareto diagrams, control charts, or graphs.

Control charts developed in the *check* stage provide information to the *act* stage where actions are taken depending on the sporadic or chronic nature of the process variation and whether improvements are locally controllable.

Pareto diagrams provide input to the *plan* stage to help prioritize the efforts and allocation of resources according to improvement potential.

Flow diagrams provide input to the *plan* stage by describing how process resources—people, parts materials, information, paperwork, etc.—move through the system, who acts on them, and interacts with them. This tool helps identify improvement opportunities by showing where waste, cost, redundancy, rework, and scrap can be reduced or eliminated.

Cause-effect diagrams, and their variants, e.g., "why-why," "how-how," "interrelationship" diagrams (see also Fukuda's, 1983, modification, "CEDAC" or cause-effect diagrams with the addition of cards), are used to surface potential problem causes or process improvement sources which can be used to *plan* a study, test, or experiment.

These and other basic tools and recommendations for training in their use are discussed in Barra (1983), Ingle (1982), Ishikawa (1983), and the JUSE and other quality circle references in the Supplemental Bibliography; see also this handbook, Sections 22, Quality Improvement; 23, Basic Statistical Methods; and 24, Statistical Process Control. More sophisticated methods, e.g., design of experiments, are used less frequently (see papers of I. Kusaba and T. Sugimoto in *Reports of Statistical Applications Research,* Japanese Union of Scientists and Engineers, vol. 25, no. 2).

Management can support and sustain circle activities in a number of ways, including:

1. Recognizing and rewarding (not necessarily monetarily) workers' efforts, even if recommendations are not adopted. Giving workers increased discretion and self-control to act on their own recommendations is an excellent reward.

2. Offering monetary rewards through the suggestion program (which may have to be modified to accommodate joint submission by circle members).

3. Providing sufficient training to expand worker skills to take on more complex projects.

4. Establishing a system for circles to expand into cross-functional teams when it appears to be a logical step. Circles may become "fatigued" when they feel they have accomplished about all they can by themselves and see the need to work with their internal suppliers and customers.

5. Training of middle managers in circle tools and techniques so they can ask their subordinates the "right questions" and not be "outsiders." These tools are also useful for the managers' own processes.

6. Addressing middle management resistance when diagnosed. Typically, management is concerned about a loss of authority and control.

7. Measuring effectiveness by focusing on the quality of the process—e.g., the training, the group discussion process, the interpersonal relationships, supervisory leadership style—rather than outcomes (e.g., reduction of scrap and

costs). If the process is right, the outcomes will be also and that will reinforce employee involvement, as well as management commitment.

QUALITY CAMPAIGNS

Intensive drives and campaigns sometimes are used in an effort to bring about quick improvements in quality. The kind of management thinking that seeks remedy in short-term programs is usually the kind of thinking that brought about the poor quality performance in the first place. When a campaign is sought, what is actually needed is a change in management systems that will enable people to consistently produce high levels of quality. This requires a "breakthrough" approach, of the type described by Juran (1964; see also Section 22 of this handbook), in which the organization transition to improved processes and systems is guided by the results of planned experimentation and investigation.

The pressures for immediate quality improvements do occur, however. They may result from poor performance in a number of areas, e.g., competitive quality position, field failures, warranty costs, waste, and other internal costs, with urging of the customer to "do something" to turn around. The "zero defects" campaigns of the 1960s in the defense and aerospace industries resulted primarily from the insistence by government officials that suppliers undertake such campaigns.

Campaigns typically are initiated by top executives who are responding to a high-visibility problem. The campaign, therefore, should be viewed as an opportunity to begin to put in place needed changes which can be instituted on a long-term basis when the campaign ends. In the campaign, the needed resources usually are made available, the usual red tape and other obstacles disappear, and there is a chance to try out new approaches.

Some grievous errors have been made in quality campaigns which have left the organization in worse shape, with less performance capability than before the campaign, even when the stated objectives of the campaign were met and short-term results obtained. The major assumption underlying most short-term programs is that deficient quality performance (errors, defects, etc.) results from an unwillingness of workers to pay attention to the details necessary for quality. Hence, the thrust of the campaign is to convince workers to take greater care and pride in their work without providing a method to improve. This was characteristic of many of the "zero defects" programs of the 1960s—lots of hype, but little substance.

These asumptions of worker inattention were made without adequate diagnosis. They also are unsound from the viewpoint of behavioral psychology, and unsupported by the facts. The majority of defects are inherent in the system and, therefore, only management can create the conditions for improvement. This is true even where defects are attributed to causes within the worker such as "lack of concern," "unwillingness" to put forth the best effort, and even behaviors that seem to be worker-controllable. In most cases, the root cause of worker behavior of this type can be traced to heavy management reliance on punishment or to setting of poor examples with regard to quality. Thus, even most "conscious" errors are management-controllable (see Section 22 under Test of Theories of Worker-Controllable Errors for more on types of human errors).

Improvements that came out of zero-defects type campaigns can be explained better, not by "increased motivation and attitude," but by changes actually made in the way work was done, e.g., use of checklists that were not used before. Often product inspection was increased. This may have improved short-term outgoing quality but also added cost and did little to improve the production process.

In addition to the propaganda, campaigns need a roadmap for improvement. If not, after the excitement of the campaign—with its banners, posters, pins, and management speeches—has passed, there most likely will be a great letdown and loss in worker morale. Workers may recognize that the blame for poor quality and the responsibility for its improvement was placed with them, but without adequate means to produce the improvement and without meaningful management involvement. Management, on the other hand, may become frustrated and angry at the work force when their high expectations for success have not been realized. A possible result is a management decision to impose tighter external controls and establish other conditions which provide no basic improvements.

The opportunity to build a base for longer-term positive change can be enhanced by treating the program as a "breakthrough" effort with three phases:

1. Prelaunch planning and preparation of communications to inform people about the "why" and promote the effort (the motivation component), and of the "how"—the necessary training, communications, and project methodologies to bring about improvement (the execution/prevention component)
2. Launch
3. Implementation

Prerequisites.   The conditions which favor a successful campaign are mainly as follows:

1. The company has already done a respectable job of reducing management-controllable defects and hence is coming to the worker body with clean hands.
2. The worker-controllable defects are substantial enough, for economic or usage reasons, to warrant a serious effort of this type.
3. The extent of mutual confidence between management and workers and union leadership is such that worker participation in a campaign is likely to be genuine.
4. The top managers are willing to show personal interest, especially to set an example by changing their priority of emphasis on quality in relation to other company goals.
5. The intermediate supervision is sufficiently openminded to be willing to listen seriously to the ideas and suggestions of the workers.
6. Management is willing to provide the staff people needed to conduct the numerous detailed studies (discovering the knack of superior operators, investigating worker proposals, etc.; see Juran, 1966).

Phase 1: Prelaunch Planning and Preparation.   The following steps are recommended before getting workers and managers actively involved in quality campaigns:

Form a Steering Committee.   This is a corporate-level committee which provides overall guidance, direction, and review. The committee demonstrates management's involvement and support of the effort by participation in review meetings, plant visits, awards dinners, and other activities that provide opportunities for direct communication to workers and recognition of their accomplishments. The committee is chaired by a senior executive, preferably the chief executive officer, and includes key executives from the major line and staff organizations. The top union official may be invited to participate as a member. The union may have a consultative role. If the program was initiated as a joint union-management effort, the senior labor relations executive and top union officer may co-chair the committee. A full-time administrator also is needed.

Form Subcommittees.   In large companies, it is necessary to create division and plant subcommittees, similarly constituted, with people from these organizations who are responsible for local planning and implementation. Part-time coordinators may have to be appointed from the divisions and plants. The line departments (production, marketing, design, etc.) need representation, since their people will take the bulk of the action. In addition, staff department representation is needed. The campaign will give each participant an opportunity to improve their own performance, as well as enabling them to contribute needed skills and talents to the overall effort. For example:

> Advertising can help in designing the publicity, exhibits, etc., to have high positive impact on workers.

> Personnel and public relations can provide communications through the existing company media (bulletin boards, newspapers, etc.) and design new means of communication internally and outside the company.

> Quality engineering can provide guidance to the corporate steering committee and line organizations regarding the tools and methods of investigation used for the diagnosis of quality problems.

> The corporate steering committee and subcommittees can provide a model of cooperation and clarity of goals by defining overall program goals, their own committee goals, roles, tasks of their members, and working relationships.

Budget.   There are three categories of costs to be considered.

1. Promotion and training materials.
2. Salary of the full-time administrator.
3. Time spent by all employees including managers and supervisors in coordinating, recordkeeping, and diagnostic activities

   Budget planning is done in advance of the implementation phase to assure that the necessary resources will be allocated to the program and not be in conflict with other objectives and commitments. The same budget planning subsequently becomes an aid to evaluation of the program. Cost-benefit analysis may be difficult, since improvements in working relationships may take a while to be reflected in performance measures.

Communication Plan, Worker Recognition Methods, Training Manuals, and Information Materials.   These are given attention by subcommittees and the steering committee to assure consistency with program objectives, corporate culture, and external image. Information review by various disciplines, e.g., product and quality engineering, industrial relations, will help ensure that a sound quality message is conveyed to the public. For example, some published advertisements stress the extensive use of quality control inspectors to assure quality. The risk is that the public will question whether the company is using good production methods if its product needs all that inspection, and wonder who is really paying for that inspection.

Education and Training

Awareness. The same pressures that initiated the campaign often produce a desire to launch the program promptly without taking the time to have a top-down educational process. However, it is unrealistic to think that workers will accept the program if supervisors and managers do not understand and believe in the program's merits. Managers and supervisors, as well as union representatives, need the opportunity to learn the details of the program, their respective roles, and to discuss the benefits and their concerns. Many early quality circle efforts failed in the United States because the educational process bypassed middle management (Gryna, 1981).

Manager and Supervisor Skill Development. Success will be promoted by training in the following participative management skills: managing team goal-setting; group dynamics; group leadership; positive reinforcement, for individuals and its use in groups; delivering feedback; PDCA cycle tools (e.g., graphs, control charts, Pareto charts) for planning, monitoring, and evaluating process changes.

Schedules. Accomplishment of tasks will be facilitated with benchmark dates established for the prelaunch, launch, and implementation phases.

Goals and Accountability. It has been universal for campaigns to set improvement goals. Goals at the local department and unit level can be set jointly by workers and supervision, based on analysis of what is achievable at their level. During the period immediately after launch, accountability for proper implementation process will assure that the right things are done; for example: interpersonal, planning and problem-solving skills are learned; positive reinforcement and recognition are used; support groups provide assistance as needed; meetings are held on schedule; workers are provided adequate and timely responses to their suggestions.

Prior Publicity. Proper interpretation internally and by the public of the need for the program can be addressed when considering publicity approaches. Sources of publicity are local newspapers, TV and radio, house organs, payroll envelope inserts, information booklets, and teasers that something is going to happen.

Measurement of Performance. The usual quality measures can be used to evaluate shop floor performance, e.g., reduction in percent defective (or increase in percent conforming), reduction in error rate, or reduction in variation around a target value. However, since the programs are companywide, the need to measure goes beyond the "hardware" departments involved in production; it extends to the "software" departments performing support activities—engineering, accounting, data processing, finance, marketing, material control, etc. While all these departments have quality problems, not all of them have a quantified measure of quality. It may be necessary to develop new units of measure for this purpose. In some cases it may be necessary to resort to a universal measure such as errors per 100 worker-hours. When measurement of outputs is not feasible, audits of the process, e.g., of materials handling, can be conducted and points awarded for positive accomplishment. It is always better, however, from the point of view of objective measurement and employee participation, if each work team, nonproduction as well as production, defines what it wants to measure and how it will be done. Improvement can be evaluated by the graphs, control charts, Pareto charts, or other statistical methods. Guidelines can be developed which describe proper ways to measure performance and how to provide positive reinforcement for doing the right things (good process) even if objectives are not accomplished fully.

Posting of work team or department performance charts can help maintain a positive spirit. Clear depiction of current performance can provide positive reinforcement for movement toward the goals and encourage discussion about how the individual members are doing (see Leek and Riley, 1978). Since the products, processes, etc., differ between groups, the basis of competition can be in terms of universal measures such as percent improvement for the month. A statistical basis for evaluation will help assure that meaningful improvement is recognized. If the "best" performing group is there by chance, then recognition awards are nothing more than a lottery (see Deming, 1982, pp. 219–220). Obviously, each week or month someone will be on top and someone at the bottom. It is incumbent on management to make sure the performance being recognized is really at a new level. If not, recognition can be provided for the positive things the group has done, e.g., cooperation. If "chance" performance is rewarded, there is risk of a letdown during the next period if the low side of the chance distribution occurs and performance "appears" to have worsened.

Awards to groups are plaques or trophies which stay in the possession of the winning group for a month and then travel to the next winning group. Certificates may be awarded to individual members to be retained permanently.

Individual Performance.   Programs may also recognize individual workers. The cautions discussed for group performance also apply here. Companies generally avoid publication of the performance of individuals other than in the exceptional cases when an award is to be given. Praise of individuals may be in public, but criticism is best given in private.

Awards to individuals are made by an awards committee on recommendation of the supervisor. In some companies, individual recognition may be granted by financial rewards such as cash prizes, paid holiday, trips, and merchandise prizes. Other companies provide nonfinancial recognition: designation of crafts worker of the day, badges or plaques, special parking privileges. Care must be taken not to use an award that "cheapens" the accomplishments. Whether financial or nonfinancial, the awards are made at a ceremonial presentation. Pictures and narratives appear in the house organ, in the public press, on the local television, or on the "wall of fame." Commendation letters, sometimes sent to the worker's home, are used.

Extension to Include Suppliers.   Some companies believe that suppliers should be included in the program in view of the impact of supplier quality on the final product. The question of whether it is "right" for a company to "shove the program down the supplier's throat" is resolved by applying the same rule as is applied to workers—it should be voluntary on the part of the supplier. The conventional approach to suppliers parallels that used for workers, but scaled up to size. The activities usually include:

Informing the suppliers of the company's action in launching a quality improvement campaign

Sending each supplier copies of the materials used to indoctrinate the company's supervisors

Structuring means for measuring supplier performance

Organizing seminars for suppliers to discuss supplier relations problems and solutions

Creating a principal award, e.g., quality supplier of the month (do not make this a lottery)

Creating subsidiary awards, e.g., outstanding supplier

Making ceremonial awards and publicizing these to all suppliers

Preparing and distributing periodic summaries on the company's progress in supplier relations

Choice of a Name for the Program.   The name can be chosen in a way which merely describes the program contents. However, because these programs require selling to many people and have customer relations implications, it is usual for companies to derive added benefits by choosing a name which:

Takes advantage of currently favorable publicity

Responds to the wishes of important customers

Provides a catchy slogan to improve the salability to workers

In the absence of some currently favorable publicity, it is usual for companies to build a name around their usual sales slogans or public relations image. Alternatively, a theme is invented specially for the program, and the name relates to this theme.

Phase 2: The Launch.   The dramatic launch has for centuries been used by leaders to convey to followers the nature and importance of a new campaign. In several ways, the dramatic launching can be of aid to the program.

It constitutes a spectacle—a memorable occasion—and thereby gives the program significance and importance.

It convenes a host of people, proposes a meritorious cause, and provides opportunity for membership in this meritorious cause.

It assembles the recognized leadership and shows them to be actively behind the program.

It introduces and legitimizes the individuals designated to guide the program, i.e., the committees and the administrator.

It pledges the managers to a new level of conduct on some matters which have in the past been obstacles to motivation, e.g., action on ideas for improvement.

Collectively these are forceful reasons for conducting the dramatic launching— so forceful that any excess of advertising can detract from the value of the meeting.

The meeting may be convened in any large hall, or outdoors, or even via closed-circuit television if several locations are involved. The dignitaries include the senior executive of the company, national and local political leaders, the union head, an important customer, a guest of honor who is a well-publicized figure. Speeches are made explaining and supporting the program. The committee and the administrator are introduced. Films are shown. Pledge cards are usually used and the first ones are signed (by the senior executive and the union head). The messages can establish clearly that:

Top management regards quality as one of its highest priorities and will play an active role.

Worker involvement is a key element of the program—it cannot succeed without the voluntary participation of workers (the program is not optional for supervision and management).

Quality is a key factor in sales—and hence in jobs; management also will play an active part.

Program identity typically is established through use of slogans, banners, posters, pins, etc. Care must be taken not to cheapen the effort, insult workers, or put the responsibility for improvement solely on workers (pledge cards often do the latter). To the extent that publicity information provides guidance on ways to do things better rather than simply stating goals, management will have demonstrated its intention to provide the means to improve.

Phase 3: Implementation.   Management operating through the corporate and local steering committees provides workers with the means and desire to contribute to quality improvement through individual and team effort. Activities are directed at reducing worker-controllable defects and management-controllable defects. After the launch, communications activities become an integral part of the implementation phase, both to increase worker awareness of the company products and inform them about their own role in the quality of those products, as described below.

Product Exhibits and Demonstrations.   The purpose is to help workers understand how the product is used, what will happen if the product fails, and how their work relates to all this. In some cases, simple exhibits can be set up to demonstrate product use. In other cases, special effort is needed. For example, in an automotive parts plant, the managers were faced with showing the metal finishers in the "white" stage the unfinished component (an automobile hood) adjacent to the corresponding finished component. The left side of each hood had various defects; the right side had none. The display made it very easy to see the real damage done by the process defects. The same approach can be taken by placing competitive products side by side so that similarities and differences can be contrasted. Where exhibits are not feasible, they may be approximated through visual presentations: posters, pictures, videotapes, etc.

Worker Participation in Company Advertising.   Advertisements in which workers describe their contributions to quality can be combined into a package (television or printed media) and shown to fellow workers.

Usage Information.   The impact of quality on customers and users can be shown in various ways: arranging visits to customer locations; inviting customers to come to the plant; display of customer letters resulting from good work (repeat orders) or from bad work (complaints). Well-known users, e.g., athletic stars and TV celebrities, may be invited for memorable occasions. Visits can be made to supplier and customer plants to "close the feedback loop."

Communications also serve to inform workers about program status, provide feedback about the effectiveness of their efforts toward improved quality levels ("scoreboard"), maintain a spirit of positive competition, and provide recognition for individual and group accomplishments (reduction of worker and management-controllable defects resulting from worker suggestions).

Communications vehicles may include newsletters, bulletin boards, quality visibility centers (Leek and Riley, 1978), awards dinners, periodic meetings (weekly, monthly, etc.), and letters of recognition.

Improvement Projects. Quality campaigns, by themselves, do not result in lasting improvements in quality. Potential benefits in quality and work climate are realized through improvement projects. The process of identifying organizing, and executing these projects is disucssed in Section 22, Quality Improvement.

ACKNOWLEDGMENT

The author thanks one of his major suppliers, Carol Gestwicki, for her expert transformation of the manuscript to meet the publisher's requirements.

REFERENCES

Baker, E. M. (1982). "Managing for Quality through Employee Involvement." *ASQC Quality Congress Transactions,* Milwaukee, pp. 282–284.

Baker, E. M. and Artinian, H. L. M. (1985). "The Deming Philosophy of Continuing Improvement in a Service Organization: The Case of Windsor Export Supply." *Quality Progress,* vol. 18, no. 6, pp. 61–69.

Baker, E. M. and Schuck, J. R. (1975). "Theoretical Note: Use of Signal Detection Theory to Clarify Problems of Evaluating Performance in Industry." *Organization Behavior and Human Performance,* vol. 13, pp. 307–317.

Barra, R. (1983). *Putting Quality Circles to Work.* McGraw-Hill, New York.

Batt, W. L., Jr., and Weinberg, E. (1978). "Labor-Management Cooperation Today." *Harvard Business Review,* vol. 56, no. 1, pp. 96–104.

Berman, D. L. and Mase, H. (1983). "The Key to the Productivity Dilemma: 'The Performance Manager.'" *Human Resource Management,* vol. 22, no. 3, pp. 275–286.

Bluestone, I. (1977). "Creating a New World of Work." *International Labour Review,* vol. 115, no. 1, pp. 1–10.

Brethower, D. M. (1982). "The Total Performance System." In O'Brien, Richard M. et al. (eds.). *Industrial Behavior Modification: A Management Handbook.* Pergamon, New York, pp. 340–369.

Bruce-Briggs, B. (1982). "The Dangerous Folly Called Theory Z." *Fortune,* May 17, p. 44.

Bulock, R. J. and Lawler, E. E. (1984). "Gainsharing: A Few Questions, and Fewer Answers." *Human Resource Management,* vol. 23, no. 1, pp. 23–40.

Burck, C. G. (1981). "What's in It for the Unions." *Fortune,* August 24, pp. 88–92.

Carlson, H. C. (1978). "The Parallel Organization Structure at General Motors." *Personnel,* July–August, pp. 64–69.

Cohen-Rosenthal, E. and Burton, C. (1986). *Mutual Gains: A Practical Guide to Union-Management Cooperation.* Praeger, New York.

Cole, R. E. (1979). *Work Mobility and Participation: A Comparative Study of American and Japanese Industry.* University of California Press, Berkeley, CA.

Cole, R. E. (1980). "Will QC Circles Work in the US?" *Quality Progress,* vol. 13, no. 6, pp. 30–33.

Cole, R. E. (1981). "Common Misconceptions of Japanese QC Circles." *ASQC Quality Congress Transactions,* Milwaukee, pp. 188–189.

Cole, R. E. and Tachiki, D. S. (1984). "Forging Institutional Links: Making Quality Circles Work in the U.S." *National Productivity Review,* vol. 3, no. 4, pp. 417–429.

Connellan, T. K. (1978). *How to Improve Human Performance: Behaviorism in Business and Industry.* Harper and Row, New York.

Connellan, T. K. (1980). *How to Grow People into Self-Starters.* The Achievement Institute, Ann Arbor, MI.

Daniels, A. C. and Rosen, T. A. (1983). *Performance Management: Improving Quality and Productivity through Positive Reinforcement.* Performance Publications, Atlanta, GA.

Davidson, W. H. (1982). "Small Group Activity at Musashi Semiconductor Works. *Sloan Management Review,* vol. 23, no. 3, pp. 3–14.

Davis, L. E. (1983–1984). "Workers and Technology: the Necessary Joint Basis for Organizational Effectiveness." *National Productivity Review,* vol. 3, no. 1, pp. 7–14.

Deming, W. E. (1951). *Elementary Principles of the Statistical Control of Quality.* Nippon Kagaku Gijutsu Remmei, Tokyo, Japan.

Deming, W. E. (1982). *Quality Productivity and Competitive Position.* MIT Center for Advanced Engineering Study, Cambridge, MA.

Donnelly, J. F. (1977). "Participative Management at Work." *Harvard Business Review,* vol. 55, no. 1, pp. 117–127.

Ephlin, D. F. (1985). "Launching Saturn: The UAW Perspective on Quality." *Quality Progress,* vol. 18, no. 4, pp. 55–57.

Epstein, E. and Freund, W. C. (1984). *People and Productivity: The New York Stock Exchange Guide to Financial Incentives and the Quality of Work Life.* Dow Jones–Irwin, Homewood, IL.

Fairbank, J. A. and Prue, D. M. (1982). "Developing Performance Feedback Systems." In Frederiksen, L. W. (ed.). *Handbook of Organizaitonal Behavior Management.* John Wiley & Sons, New York, pp. 281–299.

Florida Power and Light Company (1982). *FPL Quality Improvement Program.* Miami, FL.

Fisher, B. A. (1980). *Small Group Decision Making: Communication and the Group Process.* McGraw-Hill, New York.

Frederiksen, L. W. (ed.) (1982). *Handbook of Organization Behavior Management.* John Wiley & Sons, New York.

Fukuda, R. (1983). *Managerial Engineering.* Productivity, Inc., Stamford, CT.

Gilbert, T. F. (1982). "Analyzing Productive Performance." In Frederiksen, L. W. (ed.). *Handbook of Organizational Behavior Management.* John Wiley & Sons, New York, pp. 117–144.

Golden, K. A. and Ramanujam, V. (1985). "Between a Dream and a Nightmare: On the Integration of the Human Resource Management and Strategic Business Planning Processes." *Human Resource Management,* vol. 24, no. 4, pp. 429–452.

Gryna, F. M., Jr. (1981). *Quality Circles, a Team Approach to Problem Solving.* AMACOM, American Management Association, New York.

Guest, R. H. (1979). "Quality of Work Life—Learning from Tarrytown." *Harvard Business Review,* 57, July–August, pp. 76–87.

Gyllenhammar, P. G. (1978). *People at Work.* Addison-Wesley, Reading, MA.

Hackman, J. R. and Oldham, G. R. (1980). *Work Redesign.* Addison-Wesley, Reading, MA.

Hanlon, M. D. (1985). "Unions, Productivity, and the New Industrial Relations: Strategic Considerations." *Interfaces,* vol. 15, no. 3, pp. 41–53.

Harris, D. and Chaney, F. B. (1969). *Human Factors in Quality Assurance.* John Wiley & Sons, New York.

Hermann, J. A. and Baker, E. M. (1985). "Teamwork Is Meeting Internal Customer Needs." *Quality Progress,* vol. 18, no. 7, pp. 12–16.

Herzberg, F. (1971). "An Interview with Frederick Herzberg." *The Management Review,* July, pp. 2–15.

Herzberg, F., Mausman, B., and Snyderman, B. (1959). *The Motivation to Work,* 2nd ed. John Wiley & Sons, New York.

Howard, R. (1984). "High Technology and the Reenchantment of the Work Place." *National Productivity Review,* vol. 3, no. 3, pp. 255–264.

Huse, E. F. and Beer, M. (1971). "Eclectic Approach to Organizational Development." *Harvard Business Review,* September–October, pp. 103–112.

Ingle, S. (1982). *Quality Circles Master Guide.* Prentice-Hall (Spectrum), Englewood Cliffs, NJ.

Ingle, S. and Ingle, N. (1983). *Quality Circles in Service Industries.* Prentice-Hall (Spectrum), Englewood Cliffs, NJ.

Ishikawa, K. (1981). "Company-Wide Quality Control—Revolution—Management." *ASQC Quality Congress Transactions,* Milwaukee, pp. 124–131.

Ishikawa, K. (1983). *Guide to Quality Control.* Asian Productivity Organization, Tokyo, Japan. Distributed by UNIPUB, New York.

Ishikawa, K. (1985). *What is Total Quality Control? The Japanese Way.* Prentice-Hall, Englewood Cliffs, NJ.

Japan External Trade Organization, JETRO (1981). *Japanese Manufacturing Operations in the United States,* September, Toyko, Japan.

Juran, J. M. (1956). "Improving the Relationship between Line and Staff." *Personnel,* May.

Juran, J. M. (1964). *Managerial Breakthrough.* McGraw-Hill, New York.

Juran, J. M. (1966). "Quality Problems, Remedies and Nostrums." *Industrial Quality Control,* vol. 22, no. 12, pp. 647–653.

Juran, J. M. (1967a). "The QC Circle Phenomenon." *Industrial Quality Control,* vol. 23, no. 7, pp. 329–336.

Juran, J. M. (1967b). "The Japanese QC Circle: Questions and Answers." *Quality,* summer, no. 2, pp. 37–38.

Juran, J. M. (1979). "Japanese and Western Quality—A Contrast." *Quality,* Part I: vol. 18, no. 1, pp. 8–12; Part II: vol. 18, no. 2, pp. 12–14.

Juran, J. M. (1980). "International Significance of the QC Circle." *Quality Progress,* vol. 13, no. 11, pp. 18–22.

Juran, J. M. and Gryna, F. M., Jr. (1980). *Quality Planning and Analysis,* 2nd ed. McGraw-Hill, New York.

Kane, E. J. (1986). "IBM's Quality Focus on the Business Process." *Quality Progress,* vol. 19, no. 4, pp. 24–33.

Kanter, R. M. (1983). *The Change Masters.* Simon and Schuster, New York.

Kast, F. E. and Rosenzweig, J. E. (1979). *Organization and Management: A Systems and Contingency Approach.* McGraw-Hill, New York.

Katz, H. C. (1982). "Assessing the New Auto Labor Agreements." *Sloan Management Review,* vol. 23, no. 4, pp. 57–63.

Ketchum, L. D. (1984). "How Redesigned Plants Really Work." *National Productivity Review,* vol. 3, no. 3, pp. 246–254.

Kobayashi, M. K. and Burke, W. W. (1976). "Organization Development in Japan." *Columbia Journal of World Business,* summer, pp. 113–123.

Kogure, M. (1970). "On the Systems Approach in Japan's Quality Control." *ASQC Technical Conference Transactions,* Milwaukee, pp. 429–439.

Kogure, M. (1984). "Quality Control in the Japanese Service Industry." *Reports of Statistical Applications and Research,* Japanese Union of Scientists and Engineers, vol. 31, no. 4, pp. 15–27.

Kogure, M. and Akao, Y. (1983). "Quality Function Deployment and CWQC in Japan." *Quality Progress,* vol. 16, no. 10, pp. 25–29.

Kondo, I., Wakimoto, K., and Hanawa, N. (1982). "Operator Inspection at a Japanese Steelmaker." *Quality Progress,* vol. 15, no. 12, pp. 14–16.

Kondo, Y. (1975). "Human Motivation and Quality Control." *Joint Conference Proceedings, European Organization for Quality Control—International Association for Quality,* Venice, vol. 1, pp. 139–150.

Kondo, Y. (1976). "The Roles of Manager in QC Circle Movement." *Reports of Statistical Applications Research,* Japanese Union of Scientists and Engineers, vol. 23, pp. 71–81.

Kondo, Y. (1977). "Creativity in Daily Work." *ASQC Technical Conference Transactions,* Milwaukee, pp. 430–439.

Kondo, Y. (1981). "Participation and Leadership." *ASQC Technical Conference Transactions,* Milwaukee, pp. 110–117.

Kotter, J. P. (1985). *Power and Influence.* Free Press, Macmillian, New York.

Latham, G. P. and Wexley, K. N. (1981). *Increasing Productivity through Performance Appraisal.* Addison-Wesley, Reading, MA.

Lawler, E. E., III (1976). "Control Systems in Organizations." In Dunnette, M. D. (ed.). *Handbook of Industrial and Organizational Psychology.* Rand McNally College Publishing Company, Chicago, pp. 1247–1291.

Lawler, E. E., III, and Mohrman, S. A. (1985). "Quality Circles after the Fad." *Harvard Business Review,* vol. 63, no. 1, pp. 65–71.

Lawler, E. E., III, and Ozley, L. (1979). "Winning Union-Management Cooperation on Quality of Worklife Projects." *The Management Review,* March, pp. 19–24.

Leek, J. W. and Riley, F. H. (1978). "Product Quality Improvement through Visibility." *ASQC Technical Conference Transactions,* Milwaukee, pp. 229–236.

Maher, J., Overbach, W., Palmer, G., and Persol, D. (1969). "Enriched Jobs Mean Better Inspection Performance." *Quality Assurance,* November, pp. 23–26.

Main, J. (1983). "Ford's Drive for Quality." *Fortune,* April 18, pp. 62–70.

Majerus, R. E. (1984). "Workers Have a Right to Share Profits." *Harvard Business Review,* vol. 62, no. 5, pp. 42–50.

Maslow, A. H. (1954). *Motivation and Personality.* Harper and Bros., New York.

May, E. (1978). "Operator Participation in Quality Control, Also Called Self-Control." *Proceedings of the International Conference on Quality Control, Tokyo.* Section A4, pp. 17–22.

McCormick, E. J. and Sanders, M. S. (1982). *Human Factors in Engineering and Design,* 5th ed. McGraw-Hill, New York.

McGregor, D. N. (1960). *The Human Side of Enterprise.* McGraw-Hill, New York.

Melan, E. H. (1985). "Process Management in Service and Administrative Operations." *Quality Progress,* vol. 18, no. 6, pp. 52–60.

Miller, L. M. (1978). *Behavior Management.* John Wiley & Sons, New York.

Miller, L. M. (1984). *American Spirit: Visions of a New Corporate Culture.* William Morrow, New York.

Moehlenbrock, M. (1985). "Control Teams Contrasted with Breakthrough Teams." *The Juran Report: Proceedings of Annual Conference (IMPRO 84) on Quality Improvement,* winter, no. 4, pp. 175–179.

Myers, M. S. (1981). *Every Employee a Manager,* 2nd ed. McGraw-Hill, New York.

"The New Industrial Relations." (1985). *Business Week,* May 11, pp. 85–93.

Nickell, W. L. (1985). "Quality Improvement in a Marketing Organization." *Quality Progress,* vol. 18, no. 6, pp. 46–51.

Nosow, S. (1984). "A Lesson for American Managers: Learning from Japanese Experiences in the U.S." *National Productivity Review,* vol. 3, no. 4, pp. 407–416.

O'Brien, R. M., Dickinson, A. M., and Rosow, M. P. (1982). *Industrial Behavior Modification: A Management Handbook.* Pergamon, New York.

Ouchi, W. G. (1981). *Theory Z: How American Business Can Meet the Japanese Challenge.* Addison-Wesley, Reading, MA.

Parsons, H. M. (1974). "What Happened at Hawthorne." *Science,* vol. 183, pp. 922–930.

Peters, T. J. and Waterman, R. A., Jr. (1982). *In Search of Excellence.* Harper and Row, New York.

Pettigrew, T. J. (1983). *Process Quality Control: The New Approach to the Management of Quality in Ford.* SAE Australasia Seminar on Development Trends in Automotive Quality Control, April.

Prince, G. M. (1970). *The Practice of Creativity.* Harper and Row, New York.

Prince, G. M. (1972). "Creative Meetings through Power Sharing." *Harvard Business Review,* vol. 50, no. 4, pp. 47–54.

"Quality Sagging? Workers Depressed? Try these Ideas." (1972). *Iron Age,* vol. 210, no. 23, p. 29.

Reisman, B. and Compa, L. (1985). "The Case for Adversarial Unions." *Harvard Business Review,* vol. 63, no. 3, pp. 22–36.

Roethlisberger, F. J. and Dickson, W. J. (1939). *Management and the Worker.* Harvard University Press, Cambridge, MA.

Rosow, M. P. (1982). "Quality of Working Life: A Behavioral Process for Organizational Change." In O'Brien, Richard M. et al. (eds.). *Industrial Behavior Modification: A Management Handbook.* Pergamon, New York, pp. 335–349.

Ross, T. L. and Hauck, W. C. (1984). "Gainsharing in the United States." *Industrial Management,* vol. 26, March–April, pp. 9–14.

Rubin, I. M., Plovnick, M. S., and Fry, R. E. (1978). *Task Oriented Team Development.* McGraw-Hill, New York.

Rubinstein, S. P. (1971). "Participative Quality Control." *Quality Progress,* vol. 4, no. 1, pp. 24–27.

Rubinstein, S. P. (1973). "Engineering Management Attitudes and U.S. Productivity Challenges." *Professional Engineer,* vol. 43, no. 7, pp. 37–39.

Rubinstein, S. P. (1982). "Labor Management Quality Systems." *ASQC Quality Congress Transactions,* Milwaukee, pp. 674–682.

Rubinstein, S. P. (1984). "Quality Control Requires a Social and Technical System." *Quality Progress,* vol. 17, no. 8, pp. 22–27.

Rummler, G. A. (1981). *A View of the Management Process.* The Rummler Group, Summit, NJ.

Sandholm, L. (1983). "Japanese Quality Circles—A Remedy for the West's Quality Problems?" *Quality Progress,* vol. 16, no. 2, pp. 20–23.

Schein, E. H. (1981). "Does Japanese Management Style Have a Message for American Managers?" *Sloan Management Review,* vol. 23, no. 1, pp. 55–68.

Scherkenbach, W. W. (1985). "Performance Appraisal and Quality: Ford's New Philosophy." *Quality Progress,* vol. 18, no. 4, pp. 40–46.

Schuster, M. (1984). "Cooperation and Change in Union Settings: Problems and Opportunities." *Human Resource Management,* vol. 23, no. 2, pp. 145–160.

Sethi, S. P., Namiki, N., and Swanson, C. L. (1984). *The False Promise of the Japanese Miracle.* Pitman, Marshfield, MA.

Shea, G. P. (1986). "Quality Circles: The Danger of Bottled Change." *Sloan Management Review,* vol. 27, no. 3, pp. 33–46.

Sherwood, J. J. and Hoylman, F. M. (1977). *Utilizing Human Resources: Individual versus Group Approaches to Problem-Solving and Decision-Making.* Paper No. 621, Institute for Research in the Behavioral, Economic, and Management Sciences, Krannert Graduate School of Management, Purdue University, West Lafayette, IN.

Shewhart, W. A. (1939). *Statistical Method from the Viewpoint of Quality Control.* Lancaster Press, Lancaster, PA.

Sink, D. S. (1983). "Using the Nominal Group Technique Effectively." *National Productivity Review,* spring, pp. 173–184.

Stein, B. A. and Kanter, R. M. (1980). "Building the Parallel Organization: Creating Mechanisms for Permanent Quality of Work Life." *Journal of Applied Behavioral Science,* pp. 371–386.

Sullivan, J. J. (1983). "A Critique of Theory Z." *Academy of Management Review,* vol. 8, no. 1, p. 133.

Sullivan, L. P. (1986). "Quality Function Deployment." *Quality Progress,* vol. 19, no. 6, pp. 39–50.

Suzuki, T. (1978). "Quality Function and Industrial Cybernetics." *Proceedings of the International Conference on Quality Control, Tokyo,* Section B4, pp. 39–43.

Takezawa, S. (1976). "The Quality of Working Life: Trends in Japan." *Labour and Society,* vol. 1, pp. 29–48.

Tannenbaum, R. and Schmidt, W. H. (1973). "How to Choose a Leadership Pattern." *Harvard Business Review*, vol. 51, no. 3, pp. 162–173.

Taylor, F. W. (1947). *Scientific Management*. Harper and Bros., New York.

Tichy, N. M. (1976). "When Does Work Restructuring Work? Organizational Innovation at Volvo and GM." *Organizational Dynamics*, vol. 5, no. 1.

Tichy, N. M. (1983). *Managing Strategic Change: Technical, Political, and Cultural Dynamics*. John Wiley & Sons, New York.

Tuggle, G. (1969). "Job Enlargement." *Industrial Engineering*, February, pp. 26–31.

Walton, R. E. (1979). "Work Innovations in the United States." *Harvard Business Review*, vol. 57, pp. 88–98.

"Who's Excellent Now?" (1984). *Business Week*, Nov. 5, pp. 76–86.

Woodman, R. W. and Sherwood, J. J. (1977). "A Comprehensive Look at Job Design." *Personnel Journal*, August, pp. 384–418.

Yamamoto, M. (1980). "The Japanese—Homogeneity Promotes 'Ikigai.'" *Quality Progress*, vol. 13, no. 9, pp. 18–21.

Yankelovich, D. and Immerwahr, J. (1983). *Putting the Work Ethic to Work*. The Public Agenda Foundation, New York.

Zander, A. (1983). *Making Groups Effective*. Jossey-Bass, San Francisco, CA.

Zemke, R. and Kramlinger, T. (1982). *Figuring Things Out*. Addison-Wesley, Reading, MA.

SUPPLEMENTAL BIBLIOGRAPHY AND RESOURCES

American Periodical Publications

Harvard Buisness Review. Published bimonthly by the Graduate School of Business, Harvard University, Boston, MA 02163.

Handbook for Group Facilitators. Published annually by University Associates, 8517 Production Avenue, San Diego, CA. It is a source of ideas and techniques for managing group meetings and team performance.

Human Resource Management. Published quarterly (for the University of Michigan Graduate School) by John Wiley & Sons, 605 Third Avenue, New York, NY 10158.

Juran Report. Published by the Juran Institute, 88 Danbury Rd., Wilton, CT 06897. Contains proceedings of Annual Quality Conferences—IMPRO—which describe project team approaches to quality improvement.

Management Review. Published monthly by the American Management Association, 135 West 50th Street, New York, NY 10020.

National Productivity Review. Published quarterly by Executive Enterprises Publications Co., 33 West 60th Street, New York, NY 10023.

Organization Dynamics. Published quarterly by AMACOM Division of the American Management Associations, 135 West 50th Street, New York, NY 10020.

Performance Management Magazine. Published quarterly by Performance Management Publications, 3531 Habersham at Northlake, Tucker, GA 30084.

Productivity Newsletter. Published by Productivity, Inc., P.O. Box 16722, Stamford, CT 06905.

Quality Progress. Published monthly by the American Society for Quality Control, 230 West Wells Street, Milwaukee, WI 53203.

Sloan Management Review. Published quarterly by the Sloan Management Review Association, Alfred P. Sloan School of Management, Massachusetts Institute of Technology, 50 Memorial Drive, Cambridge, MA 02139.

Training and Development Journal. Published monthly by the American Society for Training and Development, Suite 305, 600 Maryland Avenue S.W., Washington, DC 20024.

Publications (in English) of the Japanese Union of Scientists and Engineers (JUSE).

Available from JUSE, 5-10-11 Sendagaya, Shibuya-ku, Tokyo 151, Japan (additional materials are cited in the References):

Reports of QC Circle Activities. Published annually since 1968. Each booklet contains numerous reports of Japanese quality circle projects presented in the West. JUSE also publishes *Reports of QC Circle Activities in Japan.* These contain quality circle team presentations given within Southeast Asia.

International QC Circle Convention Proceedings. Contains reports of Japanese and foregin quality circle activities presented in Japan.

Reports of Statistical Applications Research. This quarterly journal sometimes includes descriptions of quality circle projects. Volume 21, no. 4 (December 1974) was reprinted as the booklet, *Training for Foremen and QC Circle Leaders.* Volume 25, no. 2 (June 1978) contains a listing of statistical courses for quality circle members, supervision, and management, within the context of companywide quality control.

Ishikawa, Kaoru (ed.) (1983). *QC Circle Activities.* A comprehensive history and description of the quality circle movement.

QC Circle Koryo: General Principles of the QC Circle (1980). A translation of the original Japanese book.

Other Japanese English-Language Publications

Ishikawa, Kaoru (1983). *Guide to Quality Control.* Asian Productivity Organization, Tokyo, Japan. Distributed by UNIPUB, New York.

Jishu Kanri Activities in the Japanese Steel Industry (1971). Japan Iron and Steel Federation, Tokyo.

Quality Control Circles at Work: Cases from Japan's Manufacturing and Service Sectors (1984). Asian Productivity Organization, Tokyo. Distributed by UNIPUB, New York.

American Experiences with Quality Circles

American Society for Quality Control (1976). *QC Circles Applications, Tools, and Theory* [Amsden, R. T. and Amsden, D. M. (eds.)]. Available from ASQC, 310 West Wisconsin Avenue, Milwaukee, WI 53203.

American Society for Quality Control (1982). *Quality Circles and Quality of Work Life—Directory of Resources.* Available from ASQC (includes extensive bibliography).

American Society for Quality Control (1983). *Quality Circle Papers: A Compilation.* Available from ASQC.

The Quality Circles Journal. Published quarterly by the International Association of Quality Circles, 801-B West Eighth Street, Suite 301, Cincinnati, OH 45203.

SECTION 11
TRAINING FOR QUALITY[1]

Frank M. Gryna

INTRODUCTION **11.2**

PREMISES AND GUIDELINES . . **11.3**

Effect of Massive Training
for Line Departments . . 11.3

Major Issues to be
Considered 11.3

PLANNING THE TRAINING
PROGRAM **11.4**

Example of a Companywide
Program 11.4

Who Plans? 11.4

Corporate Plan or Not? . . 11.5

Example of Planning a
Quality Training Program 11.5

ANALYSIS OF TRAINING NEEDS **11.9**

WHY QUALITY TRAINING
PROGRAMS FAIL **11.9**

MEANS OF PROVIDING
TRAINING **11.10**

Job Experience 11.10

Rotational Job Experience 11.11

Classroom Training 11.12

Self-Instruction 11.12

Supplements to Formal
Training Approaches . . 11.12

TRAINING FOR VARIOUS
CATEGORIES OF PERSONNEL . **11.13**

Upper Management 11.13

Quality Managers 11.15

Other Middle Managers . . 11.15

Specialists 11.16

First-Line Supervisors . . . 11.19

Nonsupervisors 11.20

Support Areas 11.21

Service Industries 11.21

Outsiders 11.21

Training for Course Leaders 11.22

CLASSROOM TRAINING
METHODS **11.24**

Application to Company
Problems 11.24

Case Examples 11.24

Role Playing 11.25

Simulation 11.25

INSTRUCTIONAL TECHNOLOGY **11.25**

Textbooks: Broad
Orientation 11.25

Textbooks: Statistical
Orientation 11.25

Books: General 11.26

Journals 11.26

Audio-Visual Systems . . . 11.27

Computer Interactive
Instruction 11.27

Training Films 11.27

Home Study Instruction . . 11.28

Teaching Aids 11.28

---

[1] In the Third Edition, the material on training was prepared by J. M. Juran.

Facilities and Operational
Matters for Courses . . . 11.30

EVALUATION OF TRAINING
PROGRAMS 11.31

Implementation of
Concepts. 11.31

Feedback 11.31

Examinations 11.31

CAREERS IN THE QUALITY
FUNCTION 11.32

Professionalism. 11.32

UNIVERSITY-LEVEL TRAINING IN
QUALITY. 11.33

Individual Courses . . . 11.34

Two-Year Degree Programs 11.34

Four-Year Degree
Programs 11.34

Graduate Programs 11.34

NATIONAL APPROACHES TO
TRAINING 11.34

Japan 11.34

The United States. . . . 11.36

Other Countries 11.36

BUDGETS FOR TRAINING IN
QUALITY. 11.37

SCHEDULES FOR TRAINING . .11.37

REFERENCES 11.38

INTRODUCTION

All companies organize their activities along functional lines. Each of the resulting functional departments trains its members in the concepts and tools needed to carry out the departmental function. One such functional department is called the Quality Department (or similar name). Its members are exclusively engaged in quality-related activities. In consequence these members are extensively trained in quality-related concepts and tools. Other departments engage in quality-related activities to only a limited degree, and hence their members have had only limited training in quality-related concepts and tools. For many years, the practice of functional training was sufficient to enable companies to make products of a quality which could compete successfully in the marketplace. For some products this is still the case, but it is no longer the case for sophisticated modern products.

The need is to extend training in quality-related matters to personnel in all functions. To help explain this need it is useful to resort to an analogy with finance. There is a considerable body of finance-related concepts and tools: budgets, cost controls, balance sheets, etc. In some companies only members of the finance department have been trained in these concepts and tools. In other companies such training has been provided to the entire management team. This difference in training strongly influences the respective financial performances.

In like manner, companies differ in their extent of training in quality-related concepts and tools. Companies in the west have traditionally concentrated such training in the Quality Department. In contrast, many Japanese companies have extended this training to all departments. This difference in extent of training has strongly influenced the respective performances with respect to quality. The same difference in training has also contributed to a quality crisis in Western countries, and the crisis has led to a revision in Western training policy. The underlying premises for this revision are set out below.

PREMISES AND GUIDELINES

The need for the West to revise its approach to training for quality is based on the following premises:

1. There is a body of quality-related knowledge which is an essential element of modern competition in quality. This body of knowledge will be called the "quality disciplines." These disciplines consist of quality-related concepts, tools, techniques, etc. A listing of most of these disciplines is given in Table 11-1.

TABLE 11.1   The Quality Disciplines

Major managerial concepts	Errorproofing
Fitness for use	Design of experiments
The quality function	Computer controls
Parameters of quality	Self-control
Quality specifications and standardization	Self-inspection
Quality planning	Troubleshooting
Quality control	Inspection and test
Quality assurance	Inspection planning
Quality improvement	Inspector accuracy
Reliance on the laws of nature	Classification of characteristics
The factual approach	Classification of defects
Quantification	Reproducibility of measurements
Tools for functional areas	Sensory tests
Sales	Calibration systems
Marketing research for quality	Field performance
Product development	Complaint procedures
Design review	Analysis of field data
Errorproofing	Preventive maintenance
Failure mode and effects analysis	Quality improvement
Fault tree analysis	Sporadic versus chronic problems
Quantification of reliability,	Pareto concept
maintainability, availability, and safety	Project concept
Weibull analysis of data	Diagnosis
Design of experiments	Management-controllable defects
Setting tolerances	Worker-controllable defects
Supplier relations	Quality circles
Supplier surveys	Broad management of the quality function
Quality requirements	Policies
Quality planning	Objectives
Supplier surveillance	Quality cost
Incoming inspection	Company-wide planning
Audit of decisions	Organizing
Data banks	Coordination
Supplier rating	Motivation
Manufacture	Recruiting and training personnel
Manufacture planning	Quality and society
Process capability	Data collection and analysis
Tolerances for interacting dimensions	Planning for data collection
Statistical control charts	Statistical tools

2. These quality disciplines apply to all activities and at all levels of the company. (This is identical to the finance-oriented disciplines.)

3. In companies in the West, training in the quality disciplines has largely been concentrated in one specialized department—the "Quality Department" (or similar name).

4. In companies in Japan, training in the quality disciplines has largely been companywide rather than concentrated in one specialized department.

5. The evidence is overwhelming that the Western approach of concentrating this training only in the Quality Department is unable to compete with the approach of companywide training in the quality disciplines. Line personnel in the West, and especially in the United States, have access to assistance from well-trained quality specialists. However, experience has shown that the line people make only limited use of this assistance. *Unless the tools are put into the hands of the line people, the amount of this use will remain limited.* As a result, many quality-related activities are poorly performed and some are not performed at all.

6. Hence, the West is now faced with undertaking a massive program of company training in the quality disciplines, much as was undertaken by the Japanese starting in the early 1950s. (To fully understand the impact of the training effort in Japan, it is useful to visit Japan and witness at first hand the knowledge that has been acquired by all personnel.)

Effect of Massive Training for Line Departments.   Such "massive training" for line people has a profound effect on organization for quality. A preview of this effect is seen in the conduct of quality-related activities in Japan. There the line specialists (e.g., product designers and manufacturing planners) perform most of the work of quality planning and analysis which in the United States is done by reliability engineers and quality engineers. The line supervisors do most of the planning of quality systems, and make them work. The line supervisors are also active in initiating and carrying out projects for improving quality and reducing quality-related costs. In addition, millions of workers in the quality circles are active in devising control plans and in finding ways to improve quality and reduce costs. This training in the quality disciplines and the associated experience has made the line people more self-sufficient in quality matters and hence better able to meet future competition.

There is much cultural resistance to accepting such training, and especially to the consequences of using it. The former resistance comes from line people who have long conducted their affairs without training in the quality disciplines. The latter resistance comes from Quality Departments and quality specialists who see a threat to their vested interests. Collectively all this resistance can delay and even defeat the training program. It follows that companies should understand the nature and extent of this cultural resistance before embarking on any program which is to extend throughout the hierarchy. The conclusion may be that such a broad program is premature and that what is needed at the outset is selective training which responds to the more obvious and urgent company needs.

Major Issues to be Considered.   Training must be specially tailored to each company's needs. Each company has a uniqueness due to:

1. The quality problems and challenges faced by the company.

2. The knowledge and skills needed to solve these problems and meet these challenges. The purposes of training can be designed to provide an awareness of the significance of the quality issue, to provide problem-solving tools to correct

current problems, and to show individuals how quality can be integrated into their own positions. The skills may be technological, managerial, or statistical. These skills must be identified on a job-by-job basis; i.e., for each job, it is necessary to determine what skills are required to perform the quality-oriented tasks contained within that job.

3. The knowledge and skills actually possessed by the jobholders. To understand this requires that an inventory be taken to discover the prevailing levels of knowledge and state of skill.

4. The training facilities and processes already in existence. These may include apprentice schools, on-the-job training by supervisors, self-training through manuals, company Training Department courses, collaboration with local university extention services, etc. These existing forms are supported by vested interests, and the organizer of any new program is well advised to secure the use of their services.

5. The prevailing climate for training, based on the record of past programs.

6. "What is different?" Most personnel believe that they are already doing what is needed to achieve the desired quality. The critical question in the minds of the people being trained is: "What do you want me to do different in my job that I am currently doing today?" The training program should provide specific responses to that question.

PLANNING THE TRAINING PROGRAM

Example of a Companywide Program.   Table 11.2 is an extract from the training program for a Japanese company.

It is evident that this program goes from top to bottom in the organization and covers managerial, technological, and statistical subjects. It also provides training that is at the awareness level in addition to training that will enable people to perform specific quality-related activities.

For Western companies, a program of companywide training in the quality disciplines is a radical departure from the past. Clearly, such a program is more likely to become successful if there is careful planning beforehand. Planning is needed to answer these questions:

Who is to be trained?

Training in what?

Where will we get the training materials?

How will we secure leaders to do the training?

Should we train in-house or elsewhere?

How much will it cost?

How long will it take?

What should be the schedules and priorities?

Many of these questions are discussed in this section of the handbook.

Who Plans?   A widely used approach is to create a broad-based task force to do the planning. Such a task force includes:

Several managers from major line departments, e.g., Product Development, Manufacture, Marketing

TABLE 11.2 Training Program in Matsushita Electric Industries Co.

Title of course	Held for	No. of persons	Hours	Contents
Management Course	President and directors	8	21	Introduction to QC, statistical way of thinking, quality assurance, development of new products, organization and administration of QC
Course for Chiefs of Departments	1. Factory manager, Chiefs of departments at head office	22	18	Same as above top management course
	2. Sales managers	15	6	Introduction to QC, market survey
Middle Management Course	Chiefs of departments at factories, chiefs of sections (out of 200 persons, 60 persons attended QC:MC course held by JUSE)	200	6	How to introduce and promote QC
Engineer's Course	QC engineers OR workers			Attended the courses held outside the company
Intermediate	People in charge of design and research	60	144	QC application method, statistical method, control chart method, sampling inspection method, sampling, etc.
Introductory Course	Engineers in general (out of 260 persons, 20 persons attended the courses held outside the company) (this course has been held five times)	260	36	Received the training under the course corresponding to introductory course held by JUSE
Foreman Course (Primary)	Foremen	200	12	Foremen's QC text (A) used
Foreman Course (Secondary)	Foremen picked up from those getting primary course	80	30	Foremen's QC text (B) used

Source: Ishikawa, K. (1969). "Education of Quality Control in Japanese Industry." *Reports of Statistical Applications and Research,* Japanese Union of Scientists and Engineers, vol. 16, no. 3, p. 21.

11.6

Several managers from major service departments, e.g., Finance, Industrial, Engineering

A manager from Management Development or Training

A manager from Quality

A major appliance manufacturer established a high-level management team to do the broad planning for the training program. This team first took a 30-h training course covering managerial, statistical, and technological topics. At the start of the course, presented by this author, the president announced that the purpose was (1) to provide knowledge for upper management and (2) to help upper management decide what elements of the training should be provided to the various departments. Then, at the end of the course, the president asked each of the managers for recommendations on training for quality.

The broad-based task force can lay out the training program in general terms. However, there is also a need for much detailed planning. The detailed planning can be done either by the central training department or it can be decentralized to various organization units: division, functions, offices, plants.

Corporate Plan or Not?   The practice varies. Some large companies have left it to each division to work up its own plan of approach, with only limited coordination by corporate headquarters. Smaller companies tend to do the planning on a corporate basis, with participation by the divisions (or plants).

Where broad corporate planning is used, it tends to concentrate on broad matters:

Coordination with other active programs (e.g., productivity improvement, participative management).

Training for upper managers

The budget for major expenditures

Development of training materials which are applicable to multiple divisions

Development of leaders for the seed courses

Example of Planning a Quality Training Program.   Hill and McClaskey (1980) described the approach used at the Tennessee Eastman Company. The approach consisted of the following steps:

1. *Define the purpose:*   Their discussions resulted in a list of nine alternative purposes. The one selected was "To make each level of management aware of its quality responsibilities." The Development and Control departments for several areas were selected as a target group for the training program. Management was defined to include all members of the Development and Control departments, from workers to department superintendents.

2. *Identify alternatives that will achieve the purposes:*   Brainstorming was used, and several dozen alternatives were generated. These were narrowed to a list of seven:

    a. Set up a company system to develop, evaluate, and certify quality control programs

    b. Prepare written quality plans for every product

    c. Require position guides that include quality responsibilities

    d. Teach about quality responsibilities

    e. Have standard administrative procedures that assign quality responsibilities

    f. Establish improved communication among various groups

    g. Have a central quality organization responsible for the coordination of quality program development and knowledge dissemination

  3. *Analyze the alternatives:* The seven alternatives were compared using five criteria with weights assigned, as follows:

Criteria	Weight
Chance of implementation	9
Completeness	8
Flexibility of format	4
Levels of management reached	3
Probability of reducing cost of internal and external failures	2

    Each alternative was given a raw score which was multiplied by the weight for each criterion. These weighted scores were then added and the sum used as a score for each alternative. The alternative with the highest score was "teach about quality responsibilities."

  4. *Design the actual program:* The following design criteria were developed for planning the individual courses. The criteria stated that courses should:

    a. Create awareness of quality responsibility

    b. Cover total learning needs in quality awareness

    c. Be modifiable to meet specific needs

    d. Be designed for intended audience

    e. Be used only by people requiring the knowledge

    f. Be limited in content to fill a specific need

    g. Be developed so that specific curricula can be selected for individual needs

    h. Be usable by individuals or small groups at random times

    i. Have a maximum length of 2 hours

    j. Be portable and usable near work area

    k. Be used just before knowledge is needed

    l. Have pre and post tests

    m. Have the development costs monitored

    n. Be reviewed for quality, consistency of terminology, and accomplishment of objectives

    The personnel were surveyed to identify course needs. The survey form listed 40 potential courses and 13 different job categories. The courses covered management, quality engineering, quality assurance, operations, and statistical methodology. An analysis of the survey results revealed the need for 16 new courses.

  5. *Implement the solution:* The task force decided that the 16 courses should be developed in house. A company "expert" was selected to develop each course, and a steering committee reviewed the outline, drafts of the course material, and the final script and slides. To track the cost of developing each course, a set of charge codes was established and expenses were accumulated.

6. *Evaluate the results:* For each course the transfer of knowledge was evaluated by the use of pre and post tests.

ANALYSIS OF TRAINING NEEDS

The analysis to determine training needs should not be left in the hands of a quality specialist, but instead should be under the direction of a broad based task force planning the training program. One approach to obtaining input is to "make the rounds" of all the managers who will be sending people to the training program. Each manager should be asked to describe those quality-related problems which require response in the training program. With that information as a base, discussions should then be held with specialists to decide which tools and techniques to incorporate into the training program.

Some companies find it useful to create a matrix relating subject matter of training to the types of personnel to be trained. To construct such a matrix, potential training topics (e.g., the items in Table 11.1) are listed vertically. Then columns are identified with headings for various personnel (e.g., the categories listed later in this section under Training for Various Personnel). The matrix is completed by checking the topics needed for each category of personnel.

One large company (IBM) has identified five major elements of education for quality, as follows:

1. Quality awareness
2. Quality truths
3. Attitude change through case studies
4. Quality science, i.e., tools and methodology
5. Implementation

WHY QUALITY TRAINING PROGRAMS FAIL

Training programs are often conducted to change the attitude or to change the behavior of personnel. If these changes do not take place, the training program has failed. Experience has uncovered several reasons:

1. *Cultural resistance by line managers:* Often, line managers believe that they and their people have all the information necessary to do "a quality job." They see no need for additional training, and many regard it as a waste of time that could better be spent on other activities. Some remedies are (a) present factual information describing the need for such training, (b) secure the full support of upper management, and (c) start the training at upper management levels.

2. *Doubt as to the usefulness of the training:* An approach to overcome this doubt is to develop some case examples within the company. These examples can then be included in the training course. One "inside" example can work wonders.

3. *Lack of participation by line managers:* Line managers clearly have an interest in these training programs. The hours their subordinates spend on training are hours deducted from productive time. The line managers face the realities of quality-related problems and hence are an essential source of inputs to planning the training. As a minimum, the views of these managers should be solicited. Better yet, some of the line managers should be members of the task force which designs the training program.

4. *Technique versus problem orientation:* Many courses on quality have been designed around specific techniques rather than around the quality problems which require solution. Making the rounds of line managers to collect the list of quality-related problems can help ensure that the course will be problem-oriented.

5. *Inadequacies of leaders:* When a large amount of training is undertaken, one of the key decisions is the selection and preparation of leaders. These leaders should not only be competent teachers; they should also have high credibility as professionals in the area of knowledge of the course.

6. *Mixing of levels of participants:* In some companies, if the same "class" includes "students" from several ranks in the hierarchy, the effect can be to inhibit discussion. Ideally, the students in a class should be in the same or similar levels of rank.

7. *Lack of application during the course:* The ideal approach is to design the course so that the participants must apply the training during the course. One of the best learning experiences is the application of the material being taught. This was successfully done during World War II in the area of work-simplification programs. More recently, value engineering seminars often have a project included as part of the seminar. Quality circles also use the concept. In the first half of a circle meeting, the leader instructs the members in a new problem-solving technique. During the remainder of the meeting, the technique is applied to the problem currently pursued by the circle.

8. *Language too complex:* Some courses fail because the language used is too complicated for the audiences. This has been particularly so in the area of statistical techniques. What the statistician considers as a "simple" technique may be too complex for some people. The remedy is not only careful preparation and aids to presentation, but preferably a test run of the material before a small pilot group.

9. *Lack of participation by the training function:* Large companies often have a training department with people who are knowledgeable about the design and execution of training programs. These people are not necessarily knowledgeable about specific quality-related techniques, but they can provide excellent inputs into the overall design, execution, and evaluation of training programs. Their expertise should be utilized.

10. *Operational and logistical deficiencies:* Some courses fail because of poor physical environment and facilities. These matters involve control of environment (e.g., noise), space available for each student, audio-visual facilities, luncheon arrangement, and a myriad of other details. Again, a corporate training department can be helpful based on their experience in conducting many courses.

To avoid some of these pitfalls, allow sufficient time for thorough planning and for a pilot run of the course.

MEANS OF PROVIDING TRAINING

The classroom is not the only method of providing training. The other methods include:

Job Experience.   One of the most effective ways of acquiring knowledge is from experience in work situations. This can be a useful form of training at all levels. For example, as upper managers become more involved in quality matters, they need to acquire knowledge of quality issues and methodologies. One way to acquire such knowledge is through conduct of quality audits. (See Section 9 under Quality Audits.) At each of these audits, managers in some area of the company are asked to respond to a structured list of questions concerning quality issues and activities in their area. These audits are conducted by members of upper management and hence become a part of their training. At a different level, a quality specialist is assigned a specific problem to solve, such as locating the cause of rejects on a particular operation or preparing an inspection plan for a new product. The experience acquired in executing these projects is an important method of training the quality engineer (Reynolds, 1979).

For production workers, training is often a major responsibility of the supervisor. To an important degree, the supervisor personally is the trainer in:

1. Job induction, when the employee first starts on a new task
2. Job rotation, when the employee is assigned to a variety of tasks
3. Self-teaching, when the employee must study the procedures and other documentation as part of the preparation for doing the job

A special form of on-the-job training is "vestibule training." Here, employees are taught their particular operations by building product in a special classroom before they are sent out to the production line. For example, a manufacturer of disk drives for computer systems requires that all new production employees receive vestibule training before they ever see the real assembly line. The training ranges from several days to several weeks depending on the nature of the job. Before an employee joins the assembly line, dozens of disk drives will have been built under the supervision of an instructor. By the end of the first week, the trainee is able to build a complete disk drive. This company reports that in the final test in assembly areas, yield by untrained employees was about 75 to 80 percent. After trained employees joined the line, the yield rose to over 90 percent ("Vestibule Training," 1981).

Rotational Job Experience. The concept here is that employees will perform better if they are aware of the effects of their activity on other activities in the company, or on the performance of the product. An example of this is the practice followed by the Matsushita Company in their training program for design engineers. The young graduate undergoes a 1-year indoctrination program before being assigned to a specific design activity. For the first 3 months, the engineer works full time at a dealer's facility. Here, knowledge is gained on how the sets are sold, the needs of customers, and typical field service problems. The engineer then spends an additional 9 months full time in the production shops working at production stations, learning the manufacturing processes, and helping to introduce new designs into manufacturing processes. Later steps in the overall training program require formal classroom work and a second round of field experience for those being considered for promotion. In the United States, designers at the Maytag Company spend 6 months in the factory before going on to their engineering assignments. Similarly, one division of the Westinghouse Company assigns new designers for 6 to 12 months on the factory floor as training prior to design. Many Quality Departments provide rotational experience to broaden the knowledge of various quality specialists, e.g., staff people are assigned full time to line operations in order to "live" the problems of the line. Such experiences can be sobering and invaluable in the development of the staff specialist.

There are many opportunities for applying the rotational experience concept, but it does require a plan and the determination to follow the plan.

Classroom Training. This widely used training form has broad application to training programs in quality. Effective use of the classroom requires care in dealing with several elements of the learning process:

> A training content which links the quality mission of the company, the unsolved quality problems, and the role of the trainee in solving those problems
>
> A clear course outline plus prepared text material, so that the trainee can see what will be coming up and can do some advance preparation
>
> Competent instructors, both as to the subject matter and as to ability to communicate
>
> Well-designed teaching aids

In addition, it is well to do some judicious screening so that trainees do not get into courses for which they are seriously overqualified or underqualified.

The classroom training may consist of courses designed and conducted by company personnel, public courses, or courses provided on-site by outside consultants. Several organizations have extensive activities in presenting public and on-site seminars. These organizations include the Education and Training Institute of the American Society for Quality Control, the American Management Association, Juran Institute, and Philip Crosby Associates.

Self-Instruction. This can be accomplished through:

1. *Video cassettes:* Here, the knowledge is presented through a series of video cassettes that are usually supplemented with a workbook. Typically, the cassettes are viewed by a group of people who discuss each cassette and the potential applications within their own company.
2. *Training films:* There are increasingly available a wide variety of films ranging from quality awareness topics to metrology, statistical methods, reliability and maintainability, and other topics.
3. *Programmed instruction:* In this form, written materials are prepared and designed to present successive "frames" or small segments of information for self-study. The design further permits immediate feedback to the student to judge the absorption of the knowledge.

Further details on each of these three methods are presented under Instructional Technology, below.

Supplements to Formal Training Approaches. These include:

1. *The quality control manual:* These manuals are used for reference when procedural questions arise and for the induction of new people into jobs. Well-prepared manuals can help an employee learn a good deal about the new job. In special situations, the manual can be used as a text for training seminars.
2. *Visits to other companies:* Such visits can be to customers, suppliers, or other companies. Not only can specific knowledge be acquired, but viewing quality activities in other companies can help to change attitudes and broaden horizons.
3. *Membership in professional societies:* Attendance at monthly society meetings can be a source of new knowledge from outside speakers and also from the contacts made with local people at the meetings. Some professional societies reserve one of their evening meetings for programs specially designed for

managers. This can be part of the program for training managers in quality. Some sections of the American Society for Quality Control present a variety of courses each year to meet the needs of the local member (for an example, see Rado, 1976).

4. *Publications:* Books and journal articles make wide use of case histories showing how some companies have solved quality problems. Making this information available within a company can be part of the overall training program. With the enormous amount of literature available, it can be helpful to subscribe to an abstracting service. Such services exist for quality. One service is *Quality Control and Applied Statistics,* an international literature digest published by Executive Sciences Institute, Whippany, NJ 07981.

The service provides abstracts of articles taken from journals all over the world.

TRAINING FOR VARIOUS CATEGORIES OF PERSONNEL

Upper Management. Ideally, the quality training program in a company should include the entire managerial and supervisory hierarchy, *starting at the top.* Such a proposal was, until the 1980s, seldom welcomed by upper managers. Their instinctive belief was that upper managers already know what needs to be done and that training is for others—the work force, the middle managers, the engineers. The present atmosphere of crisis in some countries is forcing a reexamination of this belief.

The training for upper management should include a broad coverage of all of the quality activities in the company, but more importantly should show exactly what role upper management should take in the overall program.

Course Leadership. Experience in conducting training courses for upper managers has generated some feedback:

Upper managers regard themselves as business managers. Hence, the training should establish a clear linkage to business goals.

Upper managers are results-oriented—they are measured by business results. Hence the training should be oriented to results, not techniques.

Upper managers are usually aware that they themselves may be a part of the problem. Hence they look for answers to the question: What should I be doing different that I am doing now?

Upper managers strongly prefer to be in training meetings with other upper managers. They feel that no one else understands the problem faced by upper managers.

As a consequence of the foregoing, upper managers are reluctant to accept insiders or subordinates as instructors. Instead, their preference is to listen to outsiders. These outsiders may be upper managers from other companies. Alternatively, the outsiders may be consultants who appear to be:

Knowledgeable in quality-oriented matters.

Able to convey this knowledge in ways which relate squarely to the business realities faced by upper managers.

Able to provide answers to the question: What should I do different than I am doing now?

Outlines of Some Courses.   The Japanese Union of Scientists and Engineers has provided a course for upper management since 1957. The outline for the 1980 version of the course is shown in Table 11.3.

A 1-day seminar presented by Juran Institute consists of the topics shown in Table 11.4.

The outline for a top management course at IBM is shown in Table 11.5.

TABLE 11.3   Course for Upper Management (Japanese Union of Scientists and Engineers)

Topic	Hours
Role of top management in implementing QC	1.5
QC in new product development	2.0
Statistical methods	3.5
Management of QC	3.5
QC in manufacture	3.5
QC in purchasing and sales	3.5
Quality assurance	3.5
QC in Japan and in the world	3.5
Group discussions on promoting QC in the companies	3.0
Reports of group discussions	3.0
Total	30.5

TABLE 11.4   Topics of 1-Day Seminar for Upper Management*

The job of upper management	Training for quality
Annual quality improvement	Motivation for quality
Audit of departmental activities	The Japanese quality revolution
Audit of coordination for quality	Epilogue

*Presented by the Juran Institute.

TABLE 11.5   Top Management Course Outline*

1. Quality awareness
   - Fundamentals of quality
   - Worldwide quality challenge
   - Quality's impact on productivity
   - White collar and blue collar quality
2. Assessment of IBM's quality status
   - IBM's goals for the 1980s
   - Worldwide computer performance
   - Corporate quality direction
   - Corporate quality staff strategy
3. Life cycle quality costs
4. IBM managers' role in quality
   - Behavior change
   - Requirements setting

   - Measure of quality performance
   - Setting and improving quality goals
5. Overview of quality programs across IBM
   - Software
   - Manufacturing
   - Marketing
   - Service
   - Finance
   - Administration
6. Quality tools
   - Statistics
   - Managing breakthrough
   - Problem analysis methods
   - Special tools

*Presented at IBM.

Quality Managers. Many quality managers have risen to their positions through experience in inspection, quality engineering, product development, manufacturing, or field service. For these managers, there is often a need for formal training in the management of the broad quality function, i.e., the business orientation.

Course Leadership. For large corporations, it may be economic to establish in-house courses for quality managers. The courses can be conducted by corporate personnel or by outside consultants. What is critical is that the leaders have high credibility for their knowledge of the managerial and business aspects of the overall quality function.

Outline of a Course. The outline for a 4-day course on Management of Quality presented by Juran Institute is shown in Table 11.6.

TABLE 11.6 Management of Quality*

The quality mission	Worker errors
Quality and sales	Motivation for quality
Product development	Quality cost analysis
Supplier relations	Policies, objectives, planning
Manufacture	Organizing: role of upper management
Inspection and test	The quality manager
Field performance	Quality assurance
Improvement: projects	Quality and society
Improvement: organizing	The quality disciplines
Improvement: diagnosis	Training and quality
Improvement: remedy	The decade ahead

*Four-day course presented by Juran Institute.

Other Middle Managers. The role of "middle manager" covers a wide spectrum of responsibility. In large companies, the training program for middle managers who are at the high end of this spectrum will have much in common with the program set out above for upper management. At the lower end of the spectrum the training program will tend to overlap that used for first line supervisors. Since companies vary widely in size and systems of delegation, the planning task force may be well advised to look beyond simplistic labels such as "middle management" and examine the responsibility pattern as well.

A major question for the planning task force is whether to offer a single standardized training program for middle managers broadly, or to design special programs for the various categories of middle managers. There are persuasive reasons for specializing the courses. Middle managers operate at various levels of responsibility, in different functional activities, in different types of business, markets, product lines. However, it takes a lot of work to agree on the special needs, prepare the specialized training materials, train the leaders, etc.

Course Leadership. All managers are results-oriented. However, middle managers also have departmental responsibilities. In large companies these departmental responsibilities can dominate the attention of middle managers; i.e., they are judged based on measures of departmental performance. This same domination will have its effect on such wide-spectrum training programs as annual improvement. In such programs these middle managers will strongly prefer that case examples and illustrative improvement projects come from their specialty.

All of this has its effect on the content of the training materials and on the choice and development of leaders. There may well be need for multiple leaders, i.e., some to deal with the broader companywide matters and others to deal with specialties.

Outline of Some Courses.   If it is decided to offer a single standardized training program for middle managers, then an adaptation of an outline such as the one given in Table 11.6 is appropriate. If it is decided to offer special courses then separate outlines may be required for courses for managers of product development, purchasing, manufacturing, field service, and other functional areas.

Training for Quality Improvement.   An important part of the training program is that directed at quality improvement. Section 22, Quality Improvement, explains the project-by-project approach to improvement. This approach makes use of cross-functional teams working on selected problems. Implementation of the project approach requires that upper management, middle management, first-line supervisors, professional specialists, and selected line personnel be trained in the improvement process.

Various levels of middle management and line and staff specialists comprise the membership of most of the project teams. As membership on a team is drawn from several functions, the importance of having members work effectively together must be recognized in the training. In addition, the tools of problem solving (see Section 22 under Diagnosis) must be provided in the training. The training, therefore, includes the project approach, conducting team meetings, group dynamics, and problem solving. Table 11.7 shows the relative emphasis of these four areas for team leaders, team members, and facilitators. An outline of a video cassette course providing the methodology for the project approach is presented in Table 11.8.

Specialists.   In the United States, many quality specialists have received an extensive amount of training. This training has been concentrated in areas such as statistical methodology, quality costs, quality audit, reliability engineering, and other subjects.

There is also a need to train the line specialists such as design engineers and manufacturing engineers.

As of the early 1980s such training was largely on a voluntary basis. The subject matter was dominated by statistical methods, but there was much variation by industry and function. Specialists in the chemical industries exhibited much interest in advanced statistical tools such as evolutionary operation and response

TABLE 11.7   Training for Project Teams

	Project approach	Conduct meetings	Group dynamics	Problem solving
Leaders	P	P	P	P
Members	S	...	P	P
Facilitators	P	P	P	S

Note: P = primary; S = secondary.

TABLE 11.8 Video Cassette Course on Quality Improvement*

Proof of the need
Project identification
Projects to improve product salability
Organizing for improvement
Organizing for diagnosis: the diagnostic journey
Operator-controllable errors
The diagnostic tools
The remedial journey
Motivation for quality
Holding the gains

---

*Courtesy, Juran Institute.

surface methodology, whereas product designers were more interested in reliability-oriented training.

Despite the availability of these courses the volunteers were few. As a result, use of the quality-oriented tools required collaboration between:

1. The line managers and specialists whose work would benefit by use of the tools

2. The quality specialists who were trained in use of the tools

In most companies this collaboration was limited—so limited as to warrant the conclusion that *the tools will be used only if the line people are trained in their use.*

Starting in the early 1980s there evolved a trend to make such training courses mandatory for line specialists.

It is feasible to take soundings on the extent to which some of the quality-oriented tools are used by or even known to the line specialist. An example of a census form is shown in Table 11.9.

Course Leadership. In some large companies, qualified trainers are available in the form of internal consultants from corporate service departments such as Corporate Quality Assurance. Such departments have been an important source of training materials and training expertise for in-house use.

In those companies where in-house sources are not available it is necessary to use outside sources at the outset. Potential trainers can be chosen and sent to outside courses. Alternatively, outside trainers are brought in to conduct the seed courses. (Some training materials are specially designed to simplify use by in-house trainers.)

In small companies it is seldom economic to develop in-house training at this level. Hence outside sources are used, e.g., training at outside courses, use of consultants, etc.

Professional organizations are a source of courses useful for members and others interested. For example, the American Society for Quality Control presents courses and seminars on a variety of quality-related topics. (See Table 11.19 for a list of offerings of ASQC.)

Outline for Some Courses. An outline of topics for a statistical quality control course developed by the General Electric Company and aimed at manufacturing engineering, shop operations, and quality department personnel is shown in Table

TABLE 11.9 Census on Diagnostic Tools

In my organization the status of these tools is about as follows:

Diagnostic tools	Degree of our understanding			Extent of our use		
	Well understood	Not well understood	Unknown	Often	Seldom	None
Data sheets						
Frequency distribution						
Average and standard deviation						
Frequency histogram						
Process capability analysis						
Pareto analysis						
Orderly arrangement of theories						
Process dissection						
Time-to-time analysis						
Cumulative failure analysis						
Weibull analysis						
Concentration diagrams						
Correlation analysis						
Experimental designs						

TABLE 11.10 Applied Statistics in Manufacturing

Course topics	
Achieving parts per million defect levels	Process control charting
Process variability concept	np X, R
Measuring variability	p $\tilde{X}, R$
Sample size requirements	c $\overline{X}, R$
Process capability analysis	u
	Control chart implementation
	Getting the process into control

Note: $\tilde{X}$ is the median value of X.

11.10. In this video-based course, participants apply techniques by interacting with a computer simulation of a manufacturing process.

Applying training to specific industries, products, processes, etc., often requires specialized training materials and leadership. For example, a discussion of training needs for microcontamination control is given in Trimble (1983). Another example in the area of handling of hazardous waste is Coop (1982).

First-Line Supervisors. This category has long been exposed to training courses. Traditionally the course content has emphasized elements of supervision, work planning, job technology, cost control, etc. Until recently the quality-oriented content has been minimal. Then, in the early 1980s there came a shift in emphasis due to the growth in competition in quality plus the explosive interest in quality circles. This shift in emphasis has in turn resulted in a growth in quality-oriented training courses for first-line supervisors, notably production supervisors.

Course Leadership. In large companies the number of first-line supervisors is also large. Such members require the development of in-house facilities and leaders. The seed courses may be provided from the outside, along with training of those who are to be the in-house leaders. Thereafter the in-house leaders take over.

At this level, some of training will relate to the company's broad approach to quality: quality policies, goals, planning, organization, systems, procedures. In many companies the Training (or Management Development) Department includes specialists who are qualified to conduct in-house training in such matters. Similarly, when training requires interplay among trainees (as in project teams for quality improvement), there is need for leadership with skills in group dynamics. Such leadership is commonly available on an in-house basis in the form of trainers or "facilitators" from the Training Department.

Another substantial area of training is at the technique level. Leaders for training in techniques can be developed on an in-house basis, either from the Quality Department or from the Training Department.

Outlines for Some Courses. In Japan the training courses for first-line supervisors have become well standardized, and deal with the subjects listed in Table 11.11. A basic textbook in the foregoing topics is Ishikawa (1972).

The Japanese training materials have been translated into many languages. In most countries these translations, with local modifications, have become the dominant training materials used in courses for first-line supervisors.

The topics for a typical course for inspection and test supervision are shown in Table 11.12.

TABLE 11.11   Course for First-Line Supervisors

What is quality control?	Binomial probability paper
Role of the supervisor	Process improvement and control
Pareto diagram	Sampling concepts
Ishikawa cause-and-effect diagram	Application
The statistical viewpoint	Quality circle activities
Control charts	Quality assurance

Nonsupervisors.   Quality-oriented courses for nonsupervisors had their origin in Japan in 1962. Since then millions of Japanese workers have undergone such training as part of the QC circle movement. (A basic text, translated from the Japanese, is *QC Circle Koryo,* 1980.) Part of the course is "by the book," and this book portion consists largely of the technique portion of the production supervisors course. After the training in techniques, the circles study improvement projects which have been successfully carried out by other Circles. (See, for example, *Quality Control Circles at Work,* 1984.) Such projects show how the techniques were applied in actual work situations. Finally, the circle undertakes improvement projects to be worked out by its own members.

During the late 1970s the quality circle movement became popular in the United States. The training courses were based on translations of Japanese materials.

Course Leadership.   In the United States, wide use is made of consultants who specialize in quality circle training. These consultants conduct the seed courses for leaders, facilitators and even for the pioneering quality circle members. With the growth of a demand of quality circle training (during the early 1980s) there have emerged courses which offer to train leaders directly from the training materials.

Outlines for Some Courses.   A typical training program for quality circles consists of 10 modules. An example, from the Harley-Davidson Company, is shown in Table 11.13. Many circles teach a technique in the first half of the circle meeting and then apply the technique to the circle project in the last half of the meeting. Some companies also give an advanced course primarily of statistical tools, such as sampling, control charts, and scatter diagrams.

Specialized courses have been developed for nonsupervisors. See Overturf (1977). This example makes use of audio and video cassettes, modules, workbooks, pocket guides, and sample bottles with a suitable measuring gage. For training of technicians, see Hromi (1980).

TABLE 11.12   Course for Inspection and Test Supervisors

Supervision	Conformance
Job technology	Troubleshooting
Measurement	Inspection and test
Statistical methodology	data

TABLE 11.13 Typical Modules for Quality Circle Training

Introduction to quality circles	Histograms
	Check sheets
Brainstorming	Case study
Cause-and-effect diagrams	Graphs
Pareto diagrams	Presentations

Support Areas. Increasingly, attention has been given to the effect on quality of activities in support areas such as materials handling, production control, order filling, and accounting. In some companies, efforts have been made to train supervisors of support areas by including them in training courses being held for the manufacturing and product design functions. The approach has not been successful. The applications discussed here are oriented to design and manufacturing activities, and many personnel in support areas find it difficult to make the transition.

It is likely that separate courses will have to be developed for the support areas. These courses will need to stress two issues:

1. What is the effect of the activities in the support area on the quality of the outgoing product or service?
2. How can the quality of activities in the support area be improved?

When mistakes are made in a support area, the work is repeated and the "rework" absorbed as part of the regular workday. However, the rework is a part of the cost of poor quality and represents an opportunity for cost reduction and quality improvement. Training courses should address that potential.

The emergence of quality circles of hourly workers and also quality improvement teams of personnel at higher levels has included projects in support areas. Experiences with these projects can provide case examples for training programs.

Service Industries. Managers in the service industries have traditionally felt that their business is "different." In consequence they have rejected training in courses based on materials oriented to manufacturing industries.

Starting in the early 1980s, training courses specially oriented to service industries began to come on the market. (A pioneering example is Quality Improvement for Services, Juran Institute, 88 Danbury Road, Wilton, CT 06897.)

This trend will likely continue until courses are developed to be applicable to any and all industries.

Outsiders. Training in quality-related matters must also extend to people outside of the company. This includes suppliers, clients, and others.

Suppliers. Some companies make extensive use of outside suppliers, contractors, and subcontractors. Quality-oriented training for these outsiders is clearly as necessary as for inside sources of supply.

In a major construction company, one of the vice-presidents has been largely occupied with preparing and conducting training courses for subcontractors on the subject of attaining and improving quality. As a byproduct of this training it became possible to organize multitrade teams of supervisors and tradesmen to tackle projects for solving some long-standing quality problems. The teams were so effective that their results came to the attention of the respective presidents of the subcontracting companies. These presidents, in turn, organized multicompany teams to tackle still other projects which were beyond the scope of the lower-level teams.

An outline for a 1-day training seminar for suppliers for an appliance manufacturer is given in Table 11.14.

TABLE 11.14 Supplier Seminar

Introduction
Concept of variability
Improvement of quality of current products
Prevention of quality problems—product engineering
Prevention of quality problems—manufacturing engineering
Role of upper management

Clients.   In some cases it is the supplier who is large and whose clients include numerous small companies with limited training in the quality disciplines. In such cases, training of clients may be a means of increasing share of market for the supplier. Such training becomes an extension of conventional technical service.

Others.   The Japanese have introduced the concepts of quality circles into the consumer area. (See Takahashi, 1981.)

Others can also include government regulators, independent auditors, union officials, and the media. They may be invited to attend regular courses. They may also be invited to attend special briefings organized to provide them with a depth of understanding of quality-related matters which they could never acquire solely through official contacts.

Training for Course Leaders.   In the foregoing the approach to training of leaders has included:

1. Use of consultants.
2. Use of outside training courses.
3. Self-training from specially designed training materials.
4. "Leader train leader." During each course the leader identified those trainees who might be good candidates to become leaders for future courses.
5. Learn from new trainees. Any idea that the learning is all in one direction is naive. The trainees have extensive experience in the realities of the subject matter. They bring up cases for discussion. They raise pertinent questions. They challenge the course materials and the assertions of the leader. All these constitute inputs for improving the content of the training materials and the knowhow of the leader. In this way, a training course may be launched with the awareness that it will be "debugged" during the first several classes!

Many organizations have reported that there is need for improving the training of leaders of quality circles. Such training should include the following:

Group dynamics: The leader is trained to conduct circle meetings so that the decisions are made more by consensus than by a majority vote.

Motivation: The concept of motivation coming from within individuals is emphasized, and this is illustrated by showing how quality circles can contribute to self-motivation, leadership, and communication. The importance of communication as an expression of leadership style is emphasized. Several barriers to communication are described and applied to conducting problem-solving discussions in circle meetings.

Problem-solving tools: These were discussed above, under the heading "Nonsupervisors."

The aim of training circle leaders is to show them how to function as coach, coordinator, and trainer in the quality circle. The agenda for a leader-training program at 3M is given in Table 11.15 (Gryna, 1981).

TABLE 11.15   Agenda for Quality Circle Leader Training at 3M

January 15

8:00	a.m.	Introduction—Meet each other
		History
		Training materials
		(Audiovisual) Introduction to
		quality circles
		Why quality circles?
		Brainstorming—Quality circle objectives
9:30		Break
9:45		Group dynamics (wilderness exercise)
10:45		Cause and effect I
11:30		Morning summary
11:45		Lunch
12:30	p.m.	Motivation
1:15		Pareto
2:00		Break
2:15		Starting, training, and operating your circle
3:15		Group discussion
4:15		Training assignments and summary

January 16

12:30	p.m.	Review
1:00		Brainstorming (leader teach)
1:45		"What circles are doing"
2:15		Break
2:30		Cause and effect II (leader teach)
3:15		Histograms (leader teach)
4:00		Summary

January 17

8:00	a.m.	Review
8:15		Communications and leadership
9:00		Graphs (leader teach)
9:30		Break
9:45		Check Sheets (leader teach)
10:30		Case Study (leader teach)
11:00		Management presentation (leader teach)
11:45		Lunch
12:00	p.m.	Management presentation (continued)
1:15		Group discussion
1:30		Simulation
4:00		Summary

CLASSROOM TRAINING METHODS

For training in the industrial setting, the straight lecture approach is not enough. Among the means of supplementing the lectures are the following.

Application to Company Problems. For a course given within a single company, the instructor asks the attendees to apply specific training topics to specific company problems. For example, small groups can be assigned to problems such as drafting specific quality policies, identification of quality improvement projects, or development of a design review checklist. On an individual basis, participants can be asked to rate the company with respect to specific activities covered in the lecture. A rating form for evaluating the elements of a quality improvement program is given in Table 11.16. This census form can be filled out by each person. The class results are then summarized on a transparency, followed by a discussion of the strengths and weaknesses of the company. Similar census forms can be developed for other aspects of the quality program.

Case Examples. It is essential that an abundant supply of case examples be included in classroom training. Where possible, the examples should come from the company and preferably be presented by the individuals who did the work. In the industrial setting it is best to present a series of cases first and then generalize later. Case examples can be presented by the instructor or they can be

TABLE 11.16 Census of Company Practices in Quality Improvement

(Do not sign your name)
In my company the effectiveness in quality improvement is about as follows:

Elements of quality improvement	Strong	Adequate	Weak	No opinion
Atmosphere for breakthrough activity				
Proof of the need				
Use of the language of management				
Use of Pareto analysis				
Establishment of clear priorities for projects				
Clear responsibility for guiding projects				
Clear responsibility for diagnosis				
Use of controllability concept				
Diagnostic competence				
Overcoming resistance to change				
Action on the findings				
Control at the new level				

assigned as exercises for the students. Some textbooks have case examples for the students. For example, one source of case examples for students, along with suggested solutions, can be found in the instructor's manual for *Quality Planning and Analysis* (Juran and Gryna, 1980). Another source is Heldt (1975).

Role Playing. Role playing can be an effective way to demonstrate concepts. (For a description of four scenarios, see Heldt and Pinschmidt, 1977.) At several ASQC conferences, role-playing has been staged for supplier relations problems. The concept has also been applied to product liability (see Mundel, 1982).

Simulation. Simulation, particularly using a computer, can be an effective way to liven up the classroom. The United States Air Force Institute of Technology has made extensive application of the simulation technique in the areas of quality and reliability training. Two specific areas are:

Reliability management simulation: The student is required to make decisions comparable to those which arise in the development, production, testing, and field usage of a system. (See Rehg, 1969.)

Product life cycle: Random number generators are explained and then used to produce simulated data on equipment failure times, repair times, results after repair, lead times for inventory replacement, personnel availability, and other related processes. All of this is put together in a life cycle cost model (see Rehg, 1973).

INSTRUCTIONAL TECHNOLOGY

The technology available has expanded beyond written material and now includes audio-visual material, films, and teaching aids.

Textbooks: Broad Orientation

Feigenbaum, A. V. (1983). *Total Quality Control,* 3rd ed. McGraw-Hill, New York.

Hayes, Glenn E. and Romig, Harry G. (1982). *Modern Quality Control.* Bruce, Benziger & Glencoe, 17337 Ventura Boulevard, Encino, CA 91316.

Juran, J. M. (1981). *Management of Quality,* 4th ed. Juran Institute, 88 Danbury Road, Wilton, CT 06897.

Juran, J. M. (1982). *Upper Management and Quality,* 4th ed. Juran Institute, 88 Danbury Road, Wilton, CT 06897.

Juran, J. M. and Gryna, Frank M., Jr. (1980). *Quality Planning and Analysis,* 2nd ed. McGraw-Hill, New York.

Textbooks: Statistical Orientation. The more basic books include the following:

Charbonneau, Harvey and Webster, Gordon L. (1978). *Industrial Quality Control.* Prentice-Hall, Englewood Cliffs, NJ.

Grant, E. L. and Leavenworth, R. S. (1979). *Statistical Quality Control,* 5th ed. McGraw-Hill, New York.

Moroney, M. J. (1969). *Facts From Figures,* 3rd ed. Penguin Books, Baltimore.

Ott, E. R. (1975). *Process Quality Control.* McGraw-Hill, New York.

Small, Bonnie B. et al. (1956). *Statistical Quality Control Handbook.* Western Electric Company, New York.

Books on advanced statistical methodology include:

Box, G. E. P. et al (1978). *Statistics for Experimenters.* John Wiley & Sons, New York.

Daniel, C. (1976). *Applications of Statistics to Industrial Experimentation.* John Wiley & Sons, New York.

Duncan, A. J. (1974). *Quality Control and Industrial Statistics.* Richard D. Irwin, Homewood, IL.

Johnson, N. L. and Leone, F. C. (1977). *Statistics and Experimental Design in Engineering and the Physical Sciences,* 2nd ed. Wiley-Interscience, New York.

Miller, I. and Freund, J. E. (1977). *Probability and Statistics for Engineers,* 2nd ed. Prentice-Hall, Englewood Cliffs, NJ.

Schilling, Edward G. (1982). *Acceptance Sampling in Quality Control.* Marcel Dekker, New York.

Books: General

Carruba, Eugene R. et al. (1975). *Assuring Product Integrity.* Lexington Books, Lexington, MA.

Crosby, Philip B. (1979). *Quality is Free.* McGraw-Hill, New York.

Juran, J. M. (1988). *Quality Control Handbook,* 4th ed. McGraw-Hill, New York.

Simmons, David A. (1970). *Practical Quality Control.* Addison-Wesley, Reading, MA.

Smith, Martin (1980). *Quality Sense.* American Management Association, 135 West 50th Street, New York, NY 10020.

Journals

Quality Progress, a journal of the American Society for Quality Control (ASQC), 310 West Wisconsin Avenue, Milwaukee, WI 53203.

Journal of Quality Technology, a journal of ASQC.

Technometrics, a journal sponsored by ASQC and the American Statistical Association.

Annual Conference Transactions, the papers presented at the National Conference of ASQC.

IEEE Proceedings, Annual Reliability and Maintainability Symposium, published by the Institute of Electrical and Electronic Engineers, 345 East 47th Street, New York, NY 10017. (Also serves as the Journal of the Electronics Division of ASQC.)

Quality, published by Hitchcock Publishing Company, Box 3002, Wheaton, IL 60187.

Quality Assurance, journal of the Institute of Quality Assurance, 8110 Grosvenor Gardens, London SW1, England.

EOQC Quality, journal of the European Organization for Quality Control, P.O. Box 2516, CH-3001 Berne, Switzerland.

In the area of quality circles, written and audio-visual material is available from consultants.

Audio-Visual Systems. Video cassettes appear to be emerging as the dominant form for instructional systems. One example is *Juran on Quality Improvement:* This is a series of 16 color video cassettes on the subject of quality improvement and reduction of quality-related costs published by Juran Institute, 88 Danbury Road, Wilton, CT 06897. These cassettes are available in nine languages.

Other video cassettes are oriented to statistical methodology and reliability.

Dr. J. Stuart Hunter's course on Design of Experiments: A comprehensive series of 32 cassettes on experimental design by a leading authority, with Dr. George E. P. Box as technical consultant. Available from: Office of Continuing Education and Training, 779 Anderson Hall, University of Kentucky, Lexington, KY 40506. Also available on film.

Statistics in Quality, Productivity, and Problem Solving: This is a series of 11 color video cassettes prepared by Dr. Lloyd S. Nelson. Available from MIT Video Courses, Massachusetts Institute of Technology, 77 Massachusetts Avenue, Room 9-234, Cambridge, MA 02139; telephone (617) 253-7444.

Dr. Sanford Thayer's courses: There are several of these, each involving 10 cassettes. Available from ERG Director, Colorado State University, Fort Collins, CO 80523; also from Massachusetts Institute of Technology, Center for Advanced Engineering Study, Cambridge, MA 02139.

Computer Interactive Instruction. The increased capabilities of computer hardware and software combined with a decrease in computation costs have broadened the interest in computer interactive instruction. Commercials extol the use of computers in classrooms. For example, children are portrayed at computer terminals at which they learn elementary spelling and arithmetic. The reported benefits stemming from such instruction, e.g., self-paced instruction, increased enthusiasm, or the ability to summarize individual students' problem areas, have provided the impetus for expanding application areas to industry.

One corporation has used computer interactive instruction to train engineers in problem-solving skills. Instruction is conducted via personal computer, video disk player, and a monitor. After a particular topic is played on the video monitor, the computer guides the engineer. If the engineer answers correctly, the presentation continues. If the answer is not correct, the computer cues back the relevant video instruction segment, and then the engineer is asked to choose another answer.

Training Films. Motion picture films, strips, and transparencies are among the media available for in-house training or for training through local university and professional society sections. There are numerous distribution houses which offer such films for sale or rental. Some of these films are general or motivational in nature. Others deal with specifics, e.g., metrology, statistical methods.

In 1974 ASQC turned its films over to one such distribution house (ROA Films, 1969 North Astor Street, Milwaukee, WI 53202).

Another approach makes use of the "talk-back television" concept. In one example, 1-day workshops were conducted (in various locations) in discussions by means of two-way communication. Attendees received workbooks, and graduate students were available at each location to aid participants in understanding the material. (See "Oklahomians," 1977.)

Home Study Instruction.   The American Society for Quality Control has prepared quality assurance training material for use by individuals or groups on a home study basis. Examples of courses are statistical methods and nondestructive testing. The courses are designed to permit students to evaluate their progress on specific topics before proceeding on with the next material. Leader guides are available. (See Leaman, 1975 and 1979.)

Teaching Aids.   Presentations can be enlivened by some ingenious teaching aids. They include:

1. *Attribute sampling demonstrators:*   These consist of a supply of wooden beads, some of which are colored to represent defects. Pitted paddles are thrust into the bead pile to collect a sample in the pits (Fig. 11.1). This sampling can be done by each member of the class, and the results can then be tabulated and analyzed.

A typical proportion of colors is as follows:

Color A	1 percent	Color D	8 percent
Color B	2 percent	Color E	16 percent
Color C	4 percent	Natural	69 percent

By adding various combinations, a percent defective anywhere from 1 to 31 percent can be simulated.

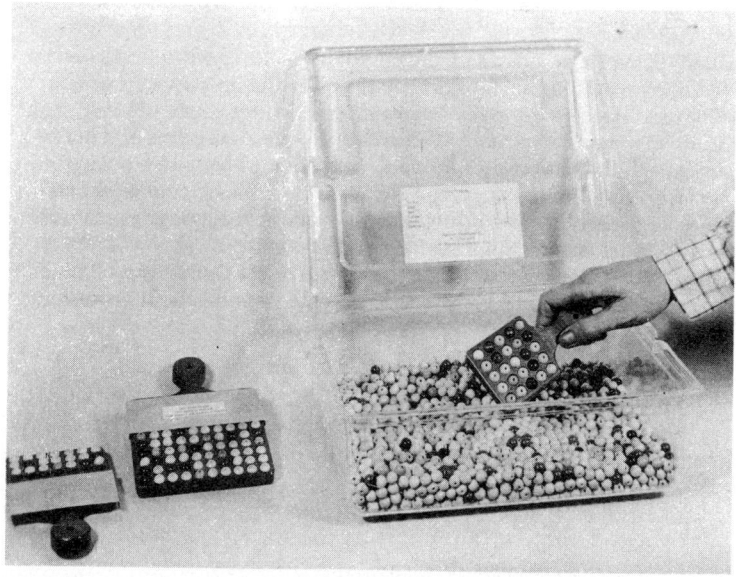

FIG. 11.1   Attribute sampling demonstrator.

2. *Galton's quincunx:* This creates frequency distributions by letting beads tumble over multiple rows of pins. At each row the bead can fall to the right or the left of the pin. After a random journey over numerous rows of pins, the bead drops into a vertical slot. When many beads are dropped, the result is a frequency distribution (Fig. 11.2).

The device makes it easy to simulate a manufacturing process in the classroom. Each bead becomes a unit of product which can be "manufactured" and measured before the eyes of the audience. As a series of units is measured, the frequency distribution takes shape. The central tendency and dispersion can then be calculated, the latter representing process capability.

In addition, the device can be used to demonstrate the nature of the control chart for averages and ranges. Limit lines for the "process" are calculated and drawn on the blackboard. Samples generated by the device represent process subgroups. The averages and ranges for these subgroups can be plotted to test for out-of-control, both when the process is undisturbed and when it is deliberately changed. (Some devices are designed to permit ready change of average; the others can only be tilted.)

3. *Statistical tolerancing simulator:* This device consists of several sets of blocks, each simulating a set of components waiting to be assembled. The purpose is to demonstrate that as random assembly takes place, the extremes will seldom

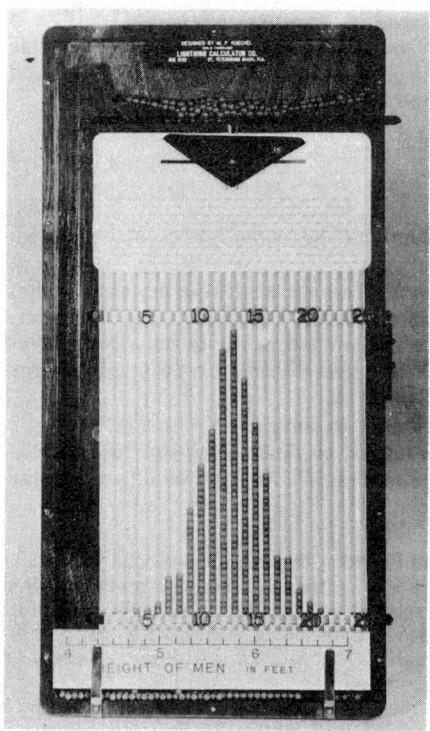

FIG. 11.2 Galton's quincunx.

TABLE 11.17 Simulator for Statistical Tolerancing*

Size, in	Silver	Black	Red	Blue	Orange	Total
0.500						
0.600					1	1
0.700		1	1	1	1	4
0.800	1	3	2	1	2	9
0.900	5	6	4	3	4	22
1.000	8	6	6	5	4	29
1.100	5	3	4	5	4	21
1.200	1	1	2	3	2	9
1.300			1	1	1	3
1.400				1	1	2
1.500						
Totals	20	20	20	20	20	100
$s =$	0.095	0.116	0.145	0.163	0.192	

*The maximum assembly is 6.5 in and the minimum is 3.5 in. However, since s of the composite of all five distributions figures out to be 0.327, further calculation shows that only about 2 of 100 assemblies will actually be outside of $\pm$ 0.750 around the average of 5.0.

come together. A typical set of blocks is described in Table 11.17. The class participates in assembling the "parts" at random and demonstrates the difficulty of reaching the worst-case dimensions.

Lacking the more sophisticated teaching aids, the instructor can resort to use of ordinary six-faced dice, coin tossing, and still other simple devices.

Sometimes the classroom must be brought to the field. An automobile manufacturer constructed a mobile facility completely equipped as a classroom for training dealer personnel. The facility was moved to different locations for presenting a 1-day course. Technicians from several nearby dealers were brought to one location thus saving expenses and providing an opportunity to exchange experiences. The local dealer furnished a car to provide for hand-on work (see "Datsun's Mobile Training Vehicle," 1977).

Facilities and Operational Matters for Courses. These are matters that must be planned by experienced people—not well-intentioned amateurs. They include:

1. Size and physical layout of the room. Particularly, if the course is to be longer than one day, people must have sufficient space to sit comfortably. Tables are preferable (to spread out course materials) and each person needs about 3 ft of table space.
2. Control of room temperature.
3. Proper audio-visual aids and lighting.
4. Provisions for taking phone messages.
5. Location off-site or on the company site.
6. Provisions for meals and coffee breaks.

Although such matters are details, they can make the difference between a successful and unsuccessful course. The corporate training department is an excellent source of advice.

EVALUATION OF TRAINING PROGRAMS

The ultimate measure of the value of training is the degree of success in applying the concepts. Although there is no known way to evaluate the return on investment, it is feasible to evaluate some of the aspects of the training.

Implementation of Concepts. A potential source of evaluation is a newsletter to collect and disseminate results which are traceable in part to the training programs. The newsletter may be a new medium specially established to serve the needs of quality-oriented programs. Alternatively, some existing media (e.g., a company newspaper or bulletin board) may establish a special supplement for quality-related information.

Contents of such a newsletter typically include:

Case examples of how the training helped to secure improvements in quality, costs, etc. Such case examples become a supplemental source of training materials, including postgraduate training for those who have completed the course work.

New uses for the training course, e.g., to help improve supplier performance, to inform clients of efforts toward continued improvement.

Pictures and conventional news stories (e.g., interviews) relative to trainees, leaders, etc.

Messages from senior managers, major clients, other important people.

These and other contents not only help to maintain a lively interest; they constitute a deeply appreciated form of recognition for those who are active in securing results.

Feedback. All instructors need feedback. Provisions must be made to obtain the feedback in specific terms (e.g., most and least useful subjects, duration of the training, instructors, physical facilities). Again, a corporate training department is an important source of experience.

The United States Army, through a "quality control division" at one of the training centers, has a program for evaluating the basic combat training provided to recruits. Through a series of four formal test programs, the knowledge acquired by the soldiers is evaluated, problem areas identified, and formal feedback given to the instructors in the program. (See Binstock, 1977.) For a description of a program involving seminars and factory visits along with results of the evaluation, see Stephens (1982).

Examinations. To date, companies have avoided the use of examinations and certificates with respect to courses for managers. It is in fact difficult to write examination questions on managerial subject matter, i.e., to secure objectivity in questions or answers. In addition, managers have exhibited considerable cultural resistance to being examined. They prefer to be judged by results on the job.

At nonmanagerial levels (specialists, first-line supervisors, the work force), much of the course content consists of techniques and tools. These do permit objectivity in questions and answers. In addition, there is less cultural resistance. Hence some companies do conduct examinations with purposes in mind such as:

To evaluate the trainees' grasp of the subject matter

To provide a form of recognition to those who are successful in the examination

CAREERS IN THE QUALITY FUNCTION

The growing importance of the quality function has required that industrial companies establish major quality-related departments. Whether such departments can provide a lifetime career depends largely on the activities assigned to them.

In the United States, many companies have established large central Quality departments which include numerous full-time inspectors and staff specialists. In such departments a lifetime career in quality is entirely feasible. Inspectors can progress horizontally into higher inspection and test grades. Through added education and experience, they can progress into engineering grade work. Alternatively, they can progress vertically into supervisory and managerial posts. In like manner, quality engineers and reliability engineers can progress horizontally into such posts as product designer or field engineer. Alternatively, they can progress vertically into the supervisory and managerial hierarchy, whether in Quality or some other department, e.g., Production.

Any job is a mixture of management and technology, the proportions changing over the years. Figure 11.3 is a reminder that as the job shifts the incumbent must shed the technological and grasp the managerial.

In many U.S. companies the quality manager reports directly to the division general manager. Such an organizational link makes the quality manager one of the competitors for the post of general manager. Any such promotion obviously has considerable significance to persons who contemplate a career in the quality function. (The fact of such promotion is propagandized to aid in recruitment and retention of employees.)

In companies which use different organization forms the career pattern can differ. An electronics engineer may be assigned full time to activities of a reliability engineering nature. In the United States the title would usually be "reliability

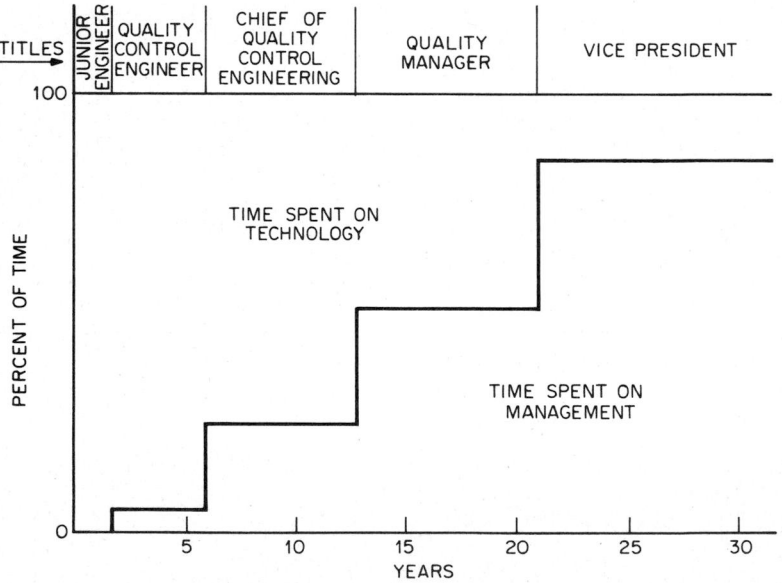

FIG. 11.3 Job progression management and technology.

engineer." In many European companies the engineer continues to use the title of "electronics engineer." The reason is that he or she regards electronics engineering as a better recognized and more secure career than reliability engineering.

Although large, central Quality Assurance departments have been widely established in the United States, the mid-1980s saw the beginnings of a trend toward the Japanese concept of organization for quality. Under that concept, line engineers receive extensive training in the quality disciplines, thereby reducing the need for quality engineers and reliability engineers. In addition, the Japanese companies have less need for inspectors as a result of their revolutionary rate of quality improvement. Moreover, the full-time inspectors are not part of the Quality Department; they are part of the Manufacturing Department. (Audit inspectors reside in the Quality Department.)

If the trend toward the Japanese concept of organization were to grow to large proportions, it would obviously have a major impact on the extent to which the quality function can provide a lifetime career.

Professionalism. In the United States the growing numbers of quality specialists and managers have stimulated interest in attaining the status of a recognized "profession" for the quality function. (The outstanding example of a recognized profession is medicine. For a discussion of the "components" of several professions, see Hoppmann et al., 1980.) Numerous collective actions have been taken in the direction of establishing a professional status.

The American Society for Quality Control (ASQC) was formed in 1946. By June 1987 it had over 54,000 members.

Much has been done to evolve an organized, special body of knowledge (books, papers, standards, etc.) to serve as the basis for training in the quality profession.

Training courses have been established to enable persons who enter the field to acquire this special body of knowledge.

Many states require continuing education for various professions. As of 1979, Iowa was the only state with such a requirement for engineers. (See Courter, 1980.)

Examinations have been evolved to provide a basis for certificated recognition of the acquisition of this special knowledge. By April 1986 there were about 2000 certified reliability engineers, and 12,000 certified quality engineers.

As of 1980 none of the states in the United States had authorized a license and a monopoly for the practice of quality engineering. No such action is likely during the 1980s. One state (California) has established an examination and certificate for the *title* of Quality Engineer. However, this confers a monopoly only as to the use of the title. Anyone may do the work.

The outward evidences of steps toward professionalism have been most obvious in the United States. (See Juran, 1976.)

However, some of the European societies have been considering the matter of certification. (Virtually all European countries have created a national society for quality and have evolved literature and training courses relative to the quality function.)

UNIVERSITY-LEVEL TRAINING IN QUALITY

At the university level, training is provided either in individual courses, 2-year programs, 4-year degree programs, or graduate programs.

Individual Courses. Courses are usually located in departments of Industrial Engineering, Business Management, Industrial Technology, or Statistics. The majority of these courses emphasize statistical quality control as applied to manufacturing. Some schools have courses in reliability engineering, maintainability engineering, engineering statistics, and the management of quality control. Quality-related topics are often included as a part of other courses, e.g., a course in production management in a college of business. (See LaForge, 1981.) Some courses and seminars are given on a credit basis; others are on a noncredit basis.

Two-Year Degree Programs. These programs aim primarily at training quality technicians, although they have been useful for others in the quality function. The programs, which lead to an associate degree, consist of about 35 percent general education, 30 percent quality and related disciplines, 25 percent science and mathematics, and 10 percent business. As of 1985, 67 colleges reported having a 2-year degree program in quality. The state of California is one of the leaders in the development of 2-year programs. In addition to these degree programs, 44 institutions reported having a 1-year certification program.

Four-Year Degree Programs. As of 1985 there were eight colleges that provided a 4-year degree program in quality. The programs follow a curriculum similar to that described for the 2-year programs but with additional courses in each area. Universities have been reluctant to make the investments for new 4-year programs which they regard as overly specialized—such as a program in quality. Overcoming this reluctance has usually required the strong moral and tangible support of local industry.

Many industrial engineering programs provide an excellent background for quality engineers because of the emphasis on the cost, schedule, and quality parameters. The typical program includes general education, mathematics, pure science, engineering science, computer science, communication skills, and problem-solving courses. Courses in statistical methods are required, and some schools require courses in quality control. Some offer elective courses in reliability, advanced statistics, design of experiments, and other areas useful to the quality engineer.

Graduate Programs. These degrees lead to a master's degree in applied statistics, business administration, or engineering. The programs in business administration and engineering follow a basic graduate program with elective courses taken in quality disciplines. There are also nontraditional degree programs that grant credit for job experience and combine it with formal classes. (See Land and Heldt, 1981.)

The American Society for Quality Control has cooperated with universities to develop educational programs. (See Constable, 1983; also Leaman, 1981.)

NATIONAL APPROACHES TO TRAINING

The Japanese have made the greaest strides in training, but other countries have also been active.

Japan. After World War II, the Japanese industrial leaders decided that until their quality of products was raised to levels which could compete in the international market, Japan would remain a developing nation. In consequence, the leaders took bold steps to create a revolution in quality. One of the major steps taken was a massive training program in quality.

The Japanese training in management of quality *started at the top* with seminars for company presidents.

That was only the beginning. Two Japanese professional societies—the Japanese Union of Scientists and Engineers (JUSE) and Japan Standards Association (JSA) designed followup on courses. Over the years courses in quality management and/or methodology were widely given to presidents, directors, managers, superintendents, supervisors, engineers, etc. (see Table 11.18). In a sense, all managers in the hierarchy concluded that they could put their training to better use if their subordinates were similarly trained. The result was that all levels of the hierarchy in all company functions received training in quality management and/or methodology appropriate to their roles. Much of the training was done in courses sponsored by JUSE and JSA. In addition, large companies established in-house training, usually for the lower levels of the hierarchy. In the case of supervisors, training courses were also offered on the national radio. Beyond the supervisors, training was provided to hourly workers through the concept of Quality

TABLE 11.18   JUSE Education and Training Courses (1985)

Quality Control
  Basic Course
  Middle Management Course
  Top Management Course
  Introductory Course
  Executive Course
  Basic Course for Foremen
  Course for Sales Department
  Course for Purchasing Department
  Correspondence Course
  Circle Instructor Course
  Circle Top Management Course
  Basic Course for Group Leaders
  Introductory Course for Sales Department
    (Osaka)
  Instructor Course
  Course for GMP (Pharmaceutical)
  Circle Leader Course
  Circle Course for Clerical Work
  Introductory Course for Executives
    and Managers
  Introductory Course for Purchasing Dept.
  Introductory Course for Sales Department
    (Tokyo)
  Introductory Course for Service Ind.
  Introductory Course for New 7 Tools for TQC
Reliability
  Basic Course
  Introductory Course
  Management Course
  Course on FMEA-FTA
  Course on Design Review
  Six-Day Course (Osaka)
  Course on Probability Paper
  Course on Test
  Course on Failure Analysis

Design of Experiment
  Basic Course
  Osaka Course
  Introductory Course
Multivariate Analysis
  Advanced Course
  Seminar (Osaka)
  Basic Course
Operations Research
  Basic Course
  Corporate Strategy, Manager Course
  Corporate Strategy, Executive Course
Industrial Engineering
  Basic Course
  Basic Course for Foremen
Marketing
  Seminar
Sensory Test
  Sensory Inspection Seminar
Product Liability
  Prevention Introductory Course
Other Management Techniques
  Statistical Application Seminar for Clinical
    Test
  Finite Element Method Seminar for Fluid
    Mechanics
  Software Production Control Seminar
  Cost Reduction Seminar
  Numerical Analysis in Geotechnical
    Engineering
  VE Basic Course for Foremen

Circles. The Japanese have also extended their training programs to developing countries. (See Mizuno and Kume, 1978.)

The United States. Most training in the United States is done by industrial companies, consultants, professional societies, and universities. Some organizations (e.g., AT&T, IBM, TRW, and Westinghouse) have extensive programs in training for quality. The American Society for Quality Control through its Education and Training Institute presents a variety of courses throughout the country (Table 11.19). Until recently, the emphasis in the United States has been on training quality specialists. This is in contrast to Japan where the training is companywide.

Other Countries. The affiliate organizations of the European Organization for Quality Control (EOQC) also sponsor quality courses.

Since 1973 the United Nations Industrial Development Organization (UNIDO) has provided training for engineers in about two dozen countries. (See Sandholm, 1976.) The program, consisting of 10 weeks in Sweden and 2 weeks in the developing countries, has the following structure:

A theoretical portion lasting 4 weeks covering statistics, metrology, inspection, and reliability

A practical study session in industry of 1 week

A second theoretical portion lasting 2 weeks and covering management topics

A second practical stage of 1 week in which the participants study quality control in a company similar to their own

A final 2-week seminar dealing with a variety of management topics

The Japanese, under the auspices of the Association for Overseas Technical Scholarships, also provide a course for developing countries. The course is held in Japan and consists of a curriculum of 6 weeks:

First week: Orientation and introductory lectures on Japanese management systems, history, characteristics of quality control in Japan, and concept of quality control

TABLE 11.19 List of ASQC Courses (1986)

Fundamentals of Quality Control
Basic Statistical Quality Control
Statistical Process Quality Control
Quality Audit-Development and Administration
Design of Industrial Experiments
Reliability Engineering
Quality Engineering by Design—The Taguchi Approach
Quality Engineering
Software Quality Assurance
Managing for Quality
Quality Management for Supervisors
Managing Quality for Profits
Managing the Inspection Function
Introduction to Quality Costs
Quality in the Service Industries

Second, third, and fourth weeks: Fundamental quality control techniques through lectures, classroom, and in-plant participation

Fifth and sixth weeks: Lectures, factory visits, and discussions on topics such as vendor-vendee relations, QC promotion system, quality circles, and the human aspects of quality control.

West (1981) reports experiences of an American organization that provided training in quality for a developing country.

Training on quality prevails throughout other countries. For an example from Turkey, see Stephens (1982). For an example from India, see Gopal et al. (1981).

BUDGETS FOR TRAINING IN QUALITY

There is no consensus on what constitutes a "right" budget for quality-oriented training. A few quality managers have proposed use of a budget equal to 10 percent of the cost of poor quality. That proposal has a degree of logic behind it but there is no experience to back it up. Until some experience is acquired, the approach must be to plan the training, translate the plans to money, and judge whether the total is reasonable in relation to other priorities.

Such a budgeting process is quite straightforward. The planning team can:

Design training courses which are appropriate for the various categories of persons to be trained

Estimate the class hours consumed by in-house courses and thereby the hours of time required from leaders, attendees, and facilities

Estimate the cost of preparing or buying the training materials

Estimate the cost of outside course fees along with the travel and living expenses

The budgeting is also influenced by the scheduling. The programs will likely extend over a span of several years (see below) so that the annual budget will be only a fraction of the total.

SCHEDULES FOR TRAINING

A program to train the entire company hierarchy in the quality disciplines cannot be carried out in a single year. Such a pace is beyond the digestive capacity of company training facilities and leaders. For large companies such a program will likely need to be spread over a range of 5 to 10 years. Accordingly, the planning team is faced with establishing schedules and priorities. The variables to be considered in setting priorities are:

Multiple businesses, i.e., divisions, profit centers, major contracts

Multiple levels of managers

Multiple types of technical specialty

Multiple locations (plants, laboratories, offices)

Multiple functional departments

Some groups wish to be among the first to be trained; others wish to be among the last.

For the longer range the planning team should bear in mind that after a few years there will arise a "maintenance" level of training. With cumulative turnover, promotions, transfers, etc., there will be need for a program to maintain the training at the new level.

REFERENCES

Binstock, S. L. (1977). "Quality Control in Combat Training." *Quality Progress*, May, pp. 10–12.

Constable, Gordon K. (1983). "The Role of ASQC in Academic Programs." *ASQC Quality Technology Program Accreditation Update*, pp. 49–53.

Coop, Philip G. (1982). "Training as a Key to Hazardous Waste Compliance." *ASQC Quality Congress Transactions*, Milwaukee, pp. 653–658.

Courter, Sandra Shaw (1980). "Continuing Education: A Growth Industry." *Quality Progress*, April, pp. 16–21.

"Datsun's Mobile Training Vehicle" (1977). *Quality*, September, p. 47.

Gopal, Krishan, Rai, Suresh, Aggarwarl, K. K., Gupta, J. S. (1981). "Reliability Education in India, Present and Future." *Institute of Electrical and Electronic Engineers Transactions on Reliability*, vol. I-30, no. 1, April, pp. 4–7.

Grant, E. L. and Leavenworth, R. S. (1979). *Statistical Quality Control*, 5th ed. McGraw-Hill, New York.

Gryna, Frank M., (1981). "Quality Circles—A Team Approach to Problem Solving." *AMACOM Journal*, pp. 57–58.

Heldt, John (1975). *Quality and Reliability Cases, Projects and Exercises*. Published by the DeAnza College Book Store, Los Altos Hills, CA.

Heldt, John J. and Pinschmidt, Robert J. (1977). "Learning by Doing." *Quality Progress*, August, pp. 30–32.

Hill, Hubert M. and McClaskey, David J. (1980). "Developing Awareness of Quality Responsibilities." *ASQC Technical Conference Transactions*, Milwaukee, pp. 160–167.

Hoppmann, W. H., II, Liu, James C. C., and Rivello, J. Roberto (1980). "Models of Professions: Law, Medicine, and Engineering." *Mechanical Engineering*, May, pp. 44–49.

Hromi, John D. (1980). Training Quality Control Technicians." *Quality Progress*, October, pp. 35–37.

Ishikawa, K. (1972). *Guide To Quality Control*. English language translation available from UNIPUB, 345 Park Avenue South, New York, NY 10010.

Juran, J. M. (1976). "Emerging Professionalism in Quality Assurance." *Quality Assurance*, vol. 2, no. 3, September, pp. 71–77.

Juran, J. M. and Gryna, Frank M., Jr. (1980). *Quality Planning and Analysis*, 2nd ed. McGraw-Hill, New York.

LaForge, R. Lawrence (1981). "Education." *Quality Progress*, June, pp. 13–15.

Land, William E. and Heldt, John J. (1981). "New Dimensions in Quality Education." *Quality Progress*, July, pp. 20–22.

Leaman, David C. (1975 and 1979). "Education and Training" column of *Quality Progress*, November 1975, p. 34, and December 1979, p. 5.

Leaman, David C. (1981). "Quality Technology Program Accreditation Update." *Quality Progress*, May, pp. 4, 5, and June, pp. 4, 5.

Mizuno, Shigeru, and Kume, Hitoshi (1978). "Development of Education and Training in Quality Control." *Reports of Statistical Applications and Research*, Japanese Union of Scientists and Engineers, vol. 25, no. 2, June, pp. 36–59.

Mundel, August B. (1982). "Product Liability Trial." *ASQC Quality Congress Transactions,* Milwaukee, pp. 791–793.

"Oklahomians Learn about Quality Assurance via Talk Back Television." (1977). *Quality Progress,* February, p. 9.

Overturf, George (1977). "Roll On Bottle Closures." *Quality Progress,* November, pp. 12–16.

QC Circle Koryo, 3rd ed. (1980). Japanese Union of Scientists and Engineers. Available from the American Society for Quality Control.

Quality Control Circles at Work (1984). Asian Productivity Organization, Tokyo (in English).

Rado, Leonard G. (1976). "Status Report: Quality Training." *Quality Progress,* March, p. 25.

Rehg, Virgil (1973). "A Computer Simulation of the Life Cycle." *Institute of Electronic and Electrical Engineers Transactions on Reliability and Quality Control.* IEEE, New York, pp. 564–675.

Rehg, Virgil (1969). "Reliability Management Simulation Exercise." *Institute of Electronic and Electrical Engineers Transactions on Reliability and Quality Control.* IEEE, New York, pp. 68–71.

Reynolds, Edward A. (1979). "The Value of 'Hands On' Training for the Quality Engineer." *Quality Progress,* May, pp. 34, 35.

Sandholm, Lennart (1976). "United Nations Training Programmes in Quality Control." *Quality,* vol. 20, no. 2, pp. 8–11.

Stephens, Kenneth S. (1982). "Quality Control in Turkey," *Quality Progress,* January, pp. 16–21.

Takahashi, Hiroyuki (1981). "QC Education for Consumer's Opinion Leader." *ASQC Quality Congress Transactions,* Milwaukee, pp. 703–708.

Trimble, John M. (1983). "It's Time to Assess Your Training Needs." *Microcontamination,* June-July, pp. 52–55.

"Vestibule Training." (1981). *Quality,* January, p. 57.

West, Andrew H. (1981). "Transferring Q.C. Technology to Developing Nations." *ASQC Quality Congress Transactions,* Milwaukee, pp. 359–364.

SECTION 12
FIELD INTELLIGENCE[1]

Frank M. Gryna

CONCEPT OF FIELD
INTELLIGENCE 12.2

Needs and Sources of Field
Intelligence Information   12.2

Feedback on Performance
of Current Products . . .   12.2

Limitations Inherent in
Feedback of Information
on Current Products . .   12.4

ANALYSIS OF AVAILABLE FIELD
INTELLIGENCE 12.5

Decline in Sales 12.5

Field Complaints 12.6

Salespersons' Reports . . .   12.6

Sale of Spare Parts 12.7

Data from Customers . . .   12.7

Government Reports . . .   12.8

Independent Laboratories .   12.8

ORGANIZATION FOR FIELD
INTELLIGENCE 12.8

Team Approach 12.8

Specific Assignment for
Coordination 12.9

Special Field Intelligence
Department 12.9

Planning for Field
Intelligence. 12.9

The Data Plan 12.10

Data Sources 12.10

The Sampling Concept . . 12.12

SOME SIMPLE TOOLS FOR
COLLECTING FIELD
INTELLIGENCE 12.12

Warranty Cards 12.12

Telephone Calls to the
Customers 12.12

Visits to Individual
Customers 12.13

Mail Surveys 12.14

Special Arrangements
with Individual
Customers 12.14

Focus Groups 12.14

COMPETITIVE EVALUATIONS . . 12.16

Laboratory Evaluations . . 12.16

COMPETITIVE EVALUATIONS
BY FIELD STUDIES 12.16

Examples of Field
Studies 12.17

DISCOVERING MARKETING
OPPORTUNITIES 12.20

Analyze the Present Use of
the Product by the
Customer 12.20

Analyze the Total System of
Use of the Product . . . 12.23

Strategic Planning for
Quality 12.24

REFERENCES 12.24

---

[1]In the Third Edition, material on Field Intelligence was prepared by J. M. Juran.

CONCEPT OF FIELD INTELLIGENCE

This section of the handbook is mainly devoted to the first step on the Spiral of Quality (Figure 2.1). That step is called marketing research.

Marketing research for the quality parameter is needed for (1) developing new products and (2) monitoring the performance of current products.

All companies collect a variety of information for new and current products, but the information related to product quality often has serious weaknesses. It concentrates on "product dissatisfaction" information, i.e., complaint data. Also, the planning for collection of the information is often minimal and leads to results that have low credibility. To be competitive on fitness for use, organizations must have a clear understanding of user needs. Often, the information needed is not available in the form or depth required and additional information must be captured through marketing research.

The term "field intelligence" will be used as the label for all information on product use whether relating to in-house use (other departments, sister divisions) or external use (merchants, processors, ultimate users). It includes information about product performance and the impact of that performance on all concerned—the merchant chain, users, service shops, society, government, the press, and the advocates.

This section of the handbook concentrates on that field intelligence needed for use in the next step on the Spiral—product development. Other sections of the handbook cover additional subjects that are allied to field intelligence. The section on Quality and Sales Income discusses the broad issue of the effect of product quality on sales income; Section 19 on Marketing covers quality issues during the process of marketing the product; Section 20 on Customer Service discusses the significance and processing of customer complaints; see also Section 8 under Quality Audits by Upper Managers.

Needs and Sources of Field Intelligence Information.   To develop and market its products, an organization requires information about quality in the marketplace. Some of this information is readily available in the form of feedback from customers. This feedback may include complaints from individual customers or changes in market share due to product quality or other parameters. Such information is not only used to monitor the performance of current products but also serves as input to the development of future products. Table 12.1 summarizes the principal needs for field intelligence and the sources for obtaining the knowledge.

Feedback on Performance of Current Products.   The feedback on current products provides an important source of information both for designing future products and for monitoring the performance of current products. This feedback often provides alarm signals that must be acted on to maintain good customer relations. The main effect of an individual alarm signal (a complaint from one customer) is to stimulate action that provides satisfaction to the customer. Collectively, these signals supply one measure of overall customer dissatisfaction. However, they are a poor measure of product quality, since many quality failures do not result in alarm signals. (See, in this connection, Section 20 under Quality Complaints.)

Loss of customers due to quality failures is another form of alarm signal, and sometimes the signal can be quite dramatic (see Table 12.2). This case involves a consumer product in which four models are sold to one major distributor. The letters in the table indicate the source of supply for each model by year. In 1979

TABLE 12.1 Needs and Sources of Field Intelligence on Quality

Needs for market quality information	Forcibly brought to company attention by "alarm signals"	Readily available but requires analysis	Not readily available; must be created by special studies
Individual dissatisfactions of customers	Complaints, returns, failure reports, claims Loss of customers Reports of Sales and Service personnel Safety and liability cases Supplier ratings		Study of failures beyond guarantee period Study of users' quality costs Interviews with users
Widespread customer dissatisfactions	Loss of customers Guarantee account charges	Pareto analysis of complaints, returns Pareto analysis of sales reports Analysis of decline in share of market Analysis of sale of spare parts	
Relative priorities of customers			Study of quality versus other parameters; study of quality-related attributes
Competitive quality status		Ratings from customers Ratings from consumer journals Government reports Share of market reports Salesforce reports	Laboratory test of competing products Usage test of competing products by customers and consumers
Opportunities for improving income through quality	Pareto analyses to identify major causes of dissatisfaction Projects to eliminate these causes	Summary of above analyses; projects for improvement based on these summaries	Special studies to study use of product Purchase of performance data Use of product by company personnel Projects based on above

12.3

TABLE 12.2   Change in Suppliers of Product*

Model	1979	1980	1981	1982
High price	A	C	C	C
Middle price	B	B	C	C
Low price	C	C	C	C
Special model	B	B	B	C

*A, B, C indicates suppliers.

Company B was the supplier for two of the four models, but by 1982 they had lost all of the business to Company C. Analysis revealed that Company B was competitive on price, delivery, and product features, but lost the business because of poor quality.

The situation does not have to become such a disaster before the alarm signals sound a warning. See below under Competitive Evaluations and also Section 20 under Data Analysis Techniques.

Limitations Inherent in Feedback of Information on Current Products. Routine feedback from current customers can provide valuable input, but it can also be completely silent on other areas that are critical. There are several such areas.

1. Dissatisfied Customers who Silently Switch to a Competitor's Product. Current customers are certainly a main source of business for the future, but those customers will switch to a competing product if they believe that the other product is superior. Often, the customer has no complaint about the product currently in use, but discovers a competing product that has superior performance or value. Thus the customer will quietly buy the other brand, and the original company will miss the problem until enough customers switch to cause a broad decrease in sales. The product probably conforms to specifications but it simply is not competitive with respect to fitness for use. Here are some examples:

A semiconductor manufacturer supplied parts to another manufacturer and the parts met specifications. However, the customer reported that the parts simply did not work as well in the printed circuit board as did parts from another manufacturer. The customer changed suppliers.

A manufacturer of surgical needles noticed a significant decline in market share from some major customers. Again the product met all specifications. Discussions with the customers revealed that a competitor had created a sharper needle that did not become dull as fast and performed more effectively during surgery. The original manufacturer changed the design of the needle, but several years later was still trying to regain the market loss.

A manufacturer of abrasive cloth, competitive on price and conformance to specification, gradually lost a significant market share to a competitor. Investigation revealed that the competitor had developed an abrasive cloth which cut the user's costs significantly. (The user measured fitness for use based on "cost per 100 pieces polished" and had compiled data for each supplier of cloth.)

In all three examples the product met specifications and there was no product dissatisfaction. Customers simply changed to another brand because of greater product satisfaction—a superiority in fitness for use. The lack of alarm signals underscores the need for field intelligence on fitness for use.

Absence of product dissatisfaction is sometimes confused with fitness for use. Some managers reason that if no one is dissatisfied then everyone must be satisfied. The fallacy is a subtle one: *Product dissatisfaction and product satisfaction are not opposites.*

2.   Noncustomers.   A major gap is information on the needs and attitudes of people who are not customers. Intelligence is needed to learn why they are not customers, and what it would take to cause them to purchase the product.

3.   Product Dissatisfaction beyond the Warranty Period.   All companies have extensive systems for keeping track of product performance during the warranty period. However, the warranty period is usually between 10 and 20 percent of the actual product life expected by the customer. Once the warranty period is passed, the feedback of information from the customer to the company becomes sporadic at best, and thus the company lacks information about the complete history of the product. As fitness for use applies for the life of the product, field intelligence information is needed over the lifetime.

ANALYSIS OF AVAILABLE FIELD INTELLIGENCE

The raw data for some types of field intelligence are readily available (see Table 12.1), but full use is not made of the data for two reasons: (1) the data are not recognized as valuable in planning for future products; and (2) the data are not in a form useful to product development and other functions.

Decline in Sales.   All companies have data systems to compute the volume and trend of sales. Seldom are these sales analyses structured to permit evaluation of the effect of quality on sales. The concepts for arriving at such an evaluation are clear enough. At periodic intervals, the sales summaries are published. These summaries show which accounts and/or product types have gone up in volume and which have declined. It is then feasible to analyze individually those which have undergone a significant change. These analyses require going into the individual accounts and product types to see whether volume changes were due to quality or other reasons. However, in practice it is not a simple matter to draw conclusions. The analyses require a joint effort among marketing, quality, and other departments to draw the proper conclusions. A discussion of the effect of quality on sales income is provided in Section 3, Quality and Sales Income.

A further indicator of the effect of quality on sales is a change in the price premium connected with a product. A change in price premium can be due to a number of factors including product quality. For example, a chemical manufacturer noted that the amount of a price premium had declined on a product, but the reason was not obvious. A marketing research study showed that product quality was one of the key reasons for the decline. (See below under Competitive Evaluations by Field Studies.)

Another source of information is the company's performance during its bidding for contracts. Table 12.3 shows an analysis involving 20 unsuccessful bids. Quality of design was a major contributor in the pattern. From knowledge of the users' specific objections to the designs and other users' preferences in successful

TABLE 12.3 Analysis of Unsuccessful Bids

Contract proposal	Quality of design	Product price	Installation price*	Reciprocal buying	Other
			Bid not accepted because of		
A 1	...	X†	X	...	X
A 2	...	...	XX	...	...
A 3	XX†	X	...	...	...
A 4	XX	...	X	...	...
A 5	XX	...	...	...	...
A 6	XX	...	...	...	...
A 7	...	XX	...	...	...
A 8	...	XX	...	...	...
A 9	...	...	XX	...	...
A 10	...	...	XX	...	...
B 1	X	...	X	...	...
B 2	...	...	...	XX	...
B 3	...	...	...	XX	...
B 4	...	...	...	XX	...
B 5	...	X	X	...	...
B 6	...	X	XX	...	...
B 7	XX	...	...	...	...
B 8	...	X	X	...	...
B 9	...	...	...	X	...
B 10	X	X	X	...	...
Totals	7	8	10 (of 14)	4	1

*Only 14 bids were made for installation.
†X = contributing reason; XX = main reason.

bids, the needed remedies emerged much more clearly than was evident merely from the memory of the managers involved.

Field Complaints.   Most organizations have systems of collecting and analyzing information on customer complaints. (For a discussion of these systems see Section 20 under Processing of Complaints.) A Pareto analysis of field failures, complaints, product returns, etc., serves to identify the vital few quality problems to be addressed in both current and future products. This type of analysis is in wide use. Table 12.4 shows a Pareto analysis of field complaints on fuel nozzles using several different indices. A conventional Pareto analysis would rank the various types of complaints according to the frequency of occurrence; but when those complaints are evaluated on an economic basis, the ranking changes. Note also that there are several possible economic indices such as warranty costs or effect on the user. The priorities for future product development can be quite different depending on the measure used in the Pareto analysis.

Salespersons' Reports.   Salespeople, distributors, and other people in the marketing process are a natural, though imperfect, field intelligence system. Their reports on quality usually deal with troubles which jeopardize current customer relations. In addition, the salespeople report on competitive products which are

TABLE 12.4 Pareto Analysis of Complaints on Fuel Nozzles

Failure mode	Ranking based on various measures		
	Frequency	Warranty charges	Effect on user
G	1	4	3
A	2	1	6
D	3	2	1
F	4	5	4
N	5	7	8
L	6	3	2
P	7	6	5
R	8	8	7

creating difficulties for them. Although such input is clearly part of the field intelligence system, the emphasis is understandably on those aspects which will aid in meeting marketing departmental goals such as sales volume and sales expense. As a result, the amount of factual information on quality matters is often limited. There are too many cases in which input from the marketing department on quality matters has such low credibility with technical people that it is ignored. In the worst case, complaints from marketing personnel about poor quality are viewed as an excuse for failure to meet sales quotas. Such episodes illustrate the need for marketing, product development, and quality personnel to work jointly together to agree on what facts need to be collected.

Sale of Spare Parts.   These sales are often regarded as a benefit to the company because of the contribution to sales income. In many cases, customers have become accustomed to the routine replacement of certain parts, and it occurs without any complaints. From the customer's point of view, the need for spare parts not only means the additional cost of the parts but also the time and expense to install those parts. (In some cases an additional element is an expensive cost of equipment downtime.) Despite the fact that many users put up with these replacements as a necessary evil, the manufacturers should analyze the sales of spare parts to identify major field problems from the viewpoint of the customer. The high usage of a certain part for replacement as spares may indicate a need for new product development to search for alternatives that would reduce the requirement for spare parts. This would of course reduce the sales income from the sale of spare parts. However, it would guard against losing the entire business to competitors who come up with products of higher reliability.

Data from Customers.   Information from customers not only consists of complaints but can include other information on quality.

A simple form of this information consists of warranty cards returned by customers upon receipt of the product. These cards can provide some information about the customer's perception of product quality upon delivery. They can also record the approximate date that the product was placed in operation (a useful input for later reliability analyses).

A broader type of information is provided in the form of supplier rating data (see Section 15 under Supplier Quality Rating). The customer keeps track of quality and other data from suppliers and summarizes the information in the form of comparative ratings. These ratings are often sent to the suppliers to stimulate action, and the effect can be dramatic. Generally supplier names are coded, but an individual company will be told its ranking relative to competitors.

Purchasers of expensive equipment usually have detailed data systems for recording maintenance and repair work. Examples include construction, transportation, and manufacturing processing equipment. These data systems become a gold mine of information for the manufacturers of the equipment. The challenge is to work out arrangements with the customers to obtain the performance data in a form that will be useful for future product development. Contracts to buy such data are not unusual.

Government Reports. Governments are increasingly involved in product evaluation, mainly in their capacity as regulators but also in their capacity as purchasers. Sometimes the data on performance of companies are published in aggregate form, but in other cases data are given on the performance of products from individual companies. Whatever the form of the information, it is a valuable input for product development. An example of such information is the reporting on tests conducted to evaluate the safety of automotive vehicles.

Independent Laboratories. These include consumer journals, standardization organizations, and still others. Some of these laboratories make comparative tests for competing lines of products. They then publish the results for the benefit of their subscribers as an aid to making purchasing decisions.

There is some confusion about interpreting the comparative analyses published in consumer journals. Generally, these journals publish analyses based on tests of only one or a few items from each supplier of a product. These analyses provide factual information about the *design* of the product and often draw some conclusions about the adequacy of the design for fulfilling typical consumer needs. The journals point out that because of the limited sample size, they are unable to draw conclusions about the ability of the manufacturer to produce, in volume, products that meet the design specifications. This distinction between quality of design and quality of conformance is often not understood by the consumer. Thus, a consumer may buy a product that was rated high in a consumer journal and then be dissatisfied with the product because of conformance defects.

Manufacturers do not always agree with the ratings given in consumer journals, but the evaluations are publicly available and do influence consumer perceptions. Hence they are properly one more input for new product development.

ORGANIZATION FOR FIELD INTELLIGENCE

Team Approach. Normally there exists no separate department whose basic activity is one of collecting and analyzing field intelligence. Instead, this activity is dispersed among several departments: sales, customer service, quality assurance, complaint investigation, technical service. Under this typical form of organization, the field intelligence activity suffers through lack of effective leadership and coordination. One solution to the problem is to create a team of members from the pertinent departments—those who need field intelligence and those who can provide it. Such a team can take on the job of identifying what are the needs for field intelligence and what means should be used for satisfying the needs.

Specific Assignment for Coordination.   A second approach is to assign coordination of field intelligence to some specific, designated department. Such an assignment increases accountability for getting action. In addition, it gives the field intelligence function a sponsor who has a legitimate place in the hierarchy.

In clarifying who is responsible for doing what, it is useful to create a matrix of responsibilities. A chemical company prepared such a matrix for one area of field intelligence, i.e., the determination of fitness-for-use needs for new products (see Table 12.5).

TABLE 12.5 Responsibility Matrix for Analyzing Fitness-for-Use Needs

Actions	Marketing	Technical service	Production	Development and control	Research
Contact customer to learn needs	R	C			
Identify critical properties		C		C	R
Learn process capability			R	C	
Identify critical measurements			C	R	
Determine if measurements reflect fitness for use	C	R			
Collect cost information		C	R	C	
Integrate all information and finalize specifications		C	C	R	

Note: R: primary responsibility; C: contributing responsibility.

Special Field Intelligence Department.   A third form of organization is to create a separate department whose prime responsibility relates to field intelligence. This form is quite useful if the company needs an aggressive revision of its approach. Such a department, when first created, is not content with the available sources and methods for securing field intelligence. Instead, it comes up with proposals for developing new sources such as creation of dealer councils or in-depth interviews with a sample of users.

Planning for Field Intelligence.   As noted in Table 12.1, the main needs are to:

1. Discover customer dissatisfactions not evident from complaints or other alarm signals.
2. Discover the relative priority of quality versus other product parameters.
3. Discover the status of quality in relation to competitors.
4. Determine the specific fitness-for-use needs of customers.
5. Identify opportunities for improving income by improving fitness for use.

Such broad needs make it necessary to carefully plan the approach to data collection.

The Data Plan. Field intelligence can be useful to the manufacturer in various ways—to improve product designs, processes, tests, field service, marketing strategy. The wide range of purposes served makes clear that no single department can identify the company's needs for field intelligence. An interdepartmental team is able to come up with a list of needs such as:

The vital few quality characteristics on which information is needed

Product performance with respect to those vital few characteristics, expressed in agreed units of measure

Information on users' costs and satisfaction as well as dissatisfaction

Failure information, including exact failure modes

Environments of use, both for successful use and for failures

The team can, in addition, usefully face up to the problem of data communications—preparation of a glossary of terms and a system of code numbers to facilitate data entry to computers, and other matters to improve field feedback.

Data Sources. In addition to using the available sources of field intelligence previously discussed, other approaches to data collection may be necessary.

1.   Natural Field Contacts. Every company has some employees who are in direct contact with the field: the sales force, complaint investigators, technical service specialists, service shop personnel. It is feasible to secure some field intelligence through these contacts, but only if certain special steps are first taken:

Prepare a detailed plan setting out just what information is wanted.

Provide the time and assistance needed for acquiring the information.

Motivate the employees to accept responsibility for acquiring the planned field intelligence as part of their job.

The last step is usually the most difficult. When the "regular" job is something else (e.g., service calls), then field intelligence is incidental and is not readily accepted as part of the job.

2.   Controlled Use. In some cases a company makes enough use of its own products to serve as a significant data base on product performance. In such cases it is feasible to design a data plan and to acquire useful field intelligence. In other cases the need may be to create an outside data base, as by placing household appliances in employee homes or by sending packages of food to a consumer panel. The users get free use of the product but they pay in data through keeping a complete log on quality-related performance.

3.   Purchase of Data. Contracts may be made to buy data from users of the product. The arrangements specify the data plan to be followed. They also provide for such associated features as training of personnel, audit of validity of data, and return of failed samples. For example, one automobile manufacturer agreed to pay all of the repair expenses for its cars at a car rental agency in return for getting complete detailed data on the repairs. In another case, a manufacturer designed a repair information system for its customers and provided the service of analyzing the data and presenting summaries to the customers. This analysis was done not only for the manufacturer's product but also for competitors. In such cases, the manufacturers participate in the design of the data plan so that the joint needs for data are given.

4. Product Monitoring. There is a growing technology which enables the "health" of products to be monitored during operation. An example is the in-flight instrumentation used to monitor aircraft engine performance. Periodic spectroscopic analysis of the engine oil is a related example. In another case, an independent entrepreneur developed instruments to monitor the performance of computers. Users were asked to install the instruments as a means of collecting data on error rates. The data were then *(a)* used by clients to compare competing systems and *(b)* sold to manufacturers of the computers.

5. Captive Service Center. Some consumer product companies maintain service centers throughout the country at which repair work on their products is performed. Thus, information on product performance, failure modes, and the cost of repairs is accumulated as part of the process of providing the repair service. The acquisition of field intelligence from such operations does not occur automatically. Repair organizations view their objective as providing the repair service to customers, and not as collecting data and writing reports. There must be explicit cooperation between that repair service and product development in order to obtain the field intelligence needed. In one company there was great difficulty in achieving this cooperation, and an unusual approach was developed. A sample of customers were told to send any products requiring repair to the Quality Control Department. The department performed the repair work and returned the products to the customers. However, as part of their repair work they collected the kind of information needed for future product planning.

6. Maintaining the Product for the Customer. A variation of the captive service center is the mobile service center. In this form, a field force of repair people visits the customer's site and performs all preventive and corrective maintenance work on the product. Examples include computers and office equipment.

7. Following Progression of the Product on Site. In this approach a company "staples itself" to its product and observes how the customer uses the product. The idea is to identify opportunities for improving fitness for use. For a further discussion of this, see Discovering Market Opportunities, below.

8. Special Surveys and Studies. These are special marketing research studies conducted on an infrequent basis to obtain evaluations of quality versus competition, answer specific questions about a product, or learn about customer perceptions of the relative priority of quality versus other product parameters. Examples of such studies are discussed below under Competitive Evaluations by Field Studies.

9. Continuing Measurements to Obtain Customer Perception on Quality. Increasingly, companies are trying to identify measures that can be continuously used to evaluate how customers feel about quality. For example, a division of one of the large electronics companies developed a six-point program for quality improvement. One of the six points was to create quality and reliability "experience measures" that measured performance throughout the complete product life cycle. In an organization making copier and duplicator products, a series of competitive benchmarks were developed that became the basis for establishing quality, cost, and delivery targets. These benchmarks were incorporated in both the annual operating plan and the 5-year business plan. Their experience showed that many of the prior measurements used did not reflect the realities of the marketplace (Pipp, 1983).

The Sampling Concept.   A common and fatal error in the pursuit of field intelligence is to go after 100 percent of the data. Normally a well-chosen sample will provide adequate field intelligence, and at a cost which is reasonable rather than prohibitive.

For example, a vehicle maker tried to secure complete field data from its 5000 dealers. The data quality was poor and the cost was high. The company then changed its approach. It concentrated on data from a sample of 35 dealers who were well distributed geographically and who accounted for 5 percent of the sales. The result was a more prompt feedback of a better basis for decision making, and at a much lower cost.

Section 23 under Statistical Estimation discusses methodology for determining the sample size required.

SOME SIMPLE TOOLS FOR COLLECTING FIELD INTELLIGENCE

Like certain statistical tools, the simpler marketing research tools seem almost trite, but can be surprisingly effective.

Warranty Cards.   Upon the purchase of the product, the customer is asked to return a card showing the customer's name, address, date, and source of purchase, and the condition of the product when it was received by the customer. The information is limited, but it is one snapshot of the product, taken by the customer.

Telephone Calls to the Customers.   Here, customers are called and asked for impressions on the quality of the item they purchased. The information gained can provide a general impression of quality, but it can also lead to important contacts for obtaining more information. Two examples will illustrate this tool.

The Sales Department in a high-technology company complained that "about 20 percent of the customers say quality is poor, and this is making it difficult for us to get repeat orders—no wonder we're having trouble meeting our sales goals." The design and manufacturing departments were amazed because they had recently taken steps that they believed had resulted in superior quality. The Quality Control Department contacted some customers, and they heard a different story. Problems had occurred with early units of a new model, but the problems had been corrected and, said the customers, "Your overall quality record is really fine." Thus, the salespeople heard about problems but not about good performance and had therefore concluded that quality was poor.

Contacting the customers resulted in clarification of customer perception, but it also led to positive action. First, the salespeople were given information on product quality to make them believers of the superior quality level, and they highlighted this information in their selling efforts. Second, the positive reaction of customers resulted in Sales giving additional customer names to the Quality Department and encouraging them to contact customers on a planned basis.

Customers appreciate being asked their views about product performance. One customer offered to give the manufacturer the log of all events that occurred during the initial usage of the product. The offer was accepted with enthusiasm; imagine the usefulness of that information to the product development and manufacturing functions.

In another example, phone calls were made to 192 housewives who were asked about the performance of their washing machines. The owners of brand B were delighted, but brand A was another story. Many owners of brand A complained that the clothes got tangled during washing. The manufacturer stated that the tangling problem had been corrected in a new model. Unfortunately, records showed that the source of complaints on the tangling problem included owners of the "improved" model. A change had been made but it just did not solve the tangling problem. The change reduced the amount of tangling and the manufacturer rationalized that the problem was corrected, but the housewives said the clothes still got tangled. (Their friends used other brands that didn't tangle the clothes.) Of brand A's present customers, 10.5 percent said they would not buy brand A again (because of the tangling and other quality problems), while only 1.1 percent of brand B owners planned to switch brands. Some simple marketing research on the improved model would have given a warning that the redesign was not adequate. Thus, the inadequacy would have been discovered before the "improved" model was released for full production (Gryna, 1970).

Visits to Individual Customers. Another form of research is the periodic visit to major customers by a marketing or engineering representative of the company. These visits are not made in response to complaints but are designed to learn about customer experiences with the product. These visits should be structured to provide answers to specific questions. (In practice, the visits are often not structured and are only partially successful in collecting useful information.)

In one example, a manufacturer of disposable medical items for hospitals was investigating a decline in market share. For the product involved it was usual for a hospital to use the product for about a year and then make a decision on a long-term purchase contract.

Historically, about 65 to 70 percent of customers became regular customers after the trial period, but for product X only about 40 to 50 percent were signing up with the company. To learn why, visits were made to some of the hospitals that rejected a long-term arrangement. Prior to the research there had been pressure on the manufacturing function to improve quality in four key areas. As a result of the visits to customers, two of the four areas were confirmed as needing improvement, the other two were shown not to need improvement, and there were three new reasons for dissatisfaction that had not been previously revealed. These additional reasons centered around the product design.

In another case, a manufacturer of car wax held discussions with customers to learn how customers evaluated quality of wax. Within the company, high priority was attached to the "gloss" properties of the wax. The research revealed that the customers did not associate this property with car wax (although it was associated with house paint). Even when the term "gloss" was brought up for discussion it generated little reaction by the customer. What the customers did talk about was the "beading" property of the wax. Customers described beading as "when the water rolls off the surface." About 82 percent of the respondents indicated that they used "water beading" as a measure of continued wax performance. This study led to a change in priorities for the manufacturer and even influenced the selection of a name for the wax.

Mail Surveys.   Still another means of collecting field intelligence is the questionnaire. For example, a manufacturer of programmable controllers makes an annual customer survey by sending a questionnaire consisting of the following questions:

Model number used

Approximate date of installation

Other programmable calculators used

How would you rate:

  The quality/reliability of our controller?

  The quality/reliability of our controller versus other manufacturers?

  The quality of the documentation you have received from us?

  The quality of hardware service you have received at your site?

  The response time on service?

  The quality of application programs support you have received?

  The training provided (separately on hardware and program logic training)?

  The quality of the sales support you have received?

  The repair turnaround?

  The quality of the repaired units?

Are there any other comments or suggestions you would like to make?

To most of the questions the customer is asked to respond by checking off excellent, very good, good, fair, or poor. These responses are converted to a numerical scale and the results are summarized in quantitative form.

Kukla (1981) explains how a questionnaire was used for transmission and axle customers of an equipment company. This questionnaire asks for responses on an absolute basis, a comparison to competition, and also the relative importance of the attribute being evaluated.

Special Arrangements with Individual Customers.   A simple but effective approach for gaining field intelligence is to establish a special arrangement with a few customers to obtain information in depth. An electronics manufacturer does this with two or three key customers in each of several industries. The manufacturer offers, with the help of the customer (the "quality partner"), to maintain detailed records on the performance of the equipment in the customer's plant. The records benefit the manufacturer by relating performance to specific applications and environments rather than to assumed conditions. The customer benefits by having a direct link to the manufacturing and engineering operations of the manufacturer.

Focus Groups.   In order to better understand customer perceptions of their company's products, a food company sponsors meetings of small groups of customers to discuss product requirements. (The company holds an average of one such meeting per day.) The technique is called a focus group. A focus group consists of about eight to ten current or potential customers who meet for a few hours to discuss a product. Here are some key features:

1. The discussion can focus on current products, proposed products, or future products.

2. A moderator who is skilled in group dynamics guides the discussion.

3. The moderator has a clear goal as to the information needed and a plan for guiding the discussion.

4. Often company personnel observe and listen in an adjacent room shielded by a one-way mirror.

Focus groups can discuss many facets of a product or can discuss quality only. A discussion on quality can be broad (e.g., obtaining views on what are the factors comprising fitness for use) or can have a narrower scope (e.g., determining customer sensitivity to various degrees of surface imperfections on silverware).

Depending on the goals, the participants in a focus group may be average customers, noncustomers, or special customers. Sometimes the participants are a special segment of society: For example, a toy manufacturer assembles a focus group of youngsters and provides them with a variety of toys for use in the group session. The children are observed to see which toys command the most attention and what kind of abuse the toys must take. The parents get their chance to talk in a separate focus group. A manufacturer of hospital supplies uses focus groups of nurses who apply products under simulated hospital conditions and offer comments while the product designers are observing and listening behind a one-way mirror. The designers translate the comments of nurses as wisdom based on experience, while the feedback of company marketing personnel is viewed as gossip.

Focus groups provide information quickly and at low cost. Calder (1977) provides some incisive views on focus groups. Some marketing research specialists are concerned that the technique may be viewed as a cure-all. Focus groups can pinpoint problems, obtain specific information on quality matters, and identify issues that need to be explored with quantitative or other techniques.

The following example illustrates the use of questionnaires and focus groups. An annual mail survey of automobile customers revealed a significant number of complaints on "fit of doors." Within the company this term meant problems of "margin" and "flushness." Margin is the space between the front door and fender, or between the front and rear doors. Sometimes the margin was not uniform, e.g., a different amount of space at the top as compared to space at the bottom of the door. Flushness refers to the smoothness of fit of the door with the body of the car after the door is shut. The manufacturer took action, but it was doomed to failure. Steps were taken during processing and assembly to correct the margin and flushness problems, but the action didn't correct the problem—a later survey again reported a problem on fit of doors.

Fortunately, there was other marketing research input. The company also held periodic focus group meetings in which a group of people were paid to attend a meeting where they answered a questionnaire and also discussed issues in detail. The questionnaire listed fit of doors as one category of problems, and some customers in the clinic checked it. On the spot they were asked, "What do you mean by fit of doors?" Their answer was not margin or flushness but two other matters. First, fit meant the amount of effort required to close the door. They complained that they had to "slam the door hard in order to get it to close completely the first time." Second, fit meant sound. As the door was shut they wanted to hear a solid "businesslike" sound instead of the metallic, loose sound they heard (telling them the door was not closed) as they walked away from the car. The marketing research gave a better understanding of the symptom, and then the company pursued the right problem, which required changes in the product design and the manufacturing process. The company had long realized that fit of doors was important, but the first time the company acted, it solved the wrong problem.

A method similar to a focus group is a council of consumer advisors. Such a council is a relatively permanent group and meets periodically to discuss issues of concern to the manufacturer.

COMPETITIVE EVALUATIONS

An important part of field intelligence is to learn where a company stands on quality with respect to competition. In some cases, the necessary knowledge can be learned from laboratory testing. In other cases it is necessary to conduct field studies.

Laboratory Evaluations. These provide useful technical data at modest expense. In some companies, competitive studies are part of the annual product planning program. A manufacturer of floor tiles made an annual comparison with competition (see Table 12.6). From such a comparison, the planners can consider whether characteristics T and U, now below market, should be improved. In the case of characteristic R and S, where the company now excels, they can consider whether this excellence can be sold or whether it should become the basis of a cost reduction. This program worked out so successfully that it is now performed on a semiannual basis and is one of the key inputs for a semiannual visit by corporate management to each plant.

TABLE 12.6 Comparison of Competitive Products

Characteristics of the product	Home Co.	Competitors			
		A Co.	B Co.	C Co.	D Co.
P	3	2	1	4	5
Q	2	4	3	1	5
R	1	3	2	5	4
S	1	5	3	4	2
T	5	2	3	1	4
U	4	1	2	5	3

Many companies purchase competing products and not only test them but disassemble them to evaluate the design concepts. For products not involving destructive tests it may be feasible to inspect and test such products at some friendly dealer. Carpets and watches are examples of products for which competitive evaluations have been made without purchase. (In the carpet example, a traveling laboratory was set up so that the examinations were performed in the storage warehouse.)

COMPETITIVE EVALUATIONS BY FIELD STUDIES

The ultimate evaluation of quality is made by the user under the conditions of the marketplace. The field intelligence gathered on these evaluations must be based on factual inputs and not on hearsay. These evaluations aim to discover the users' viewpoint on fitness for use, and also to provide a comparison to competitors. The distinguishing feature of the field studies is that the user is the prime source of data.

Such studies should not be planned by any one department but by a team involving members from marketing, product development, quality, manufacturing, and other areas as needed. This team must agree beforehand on what questions need to be answered by the field study. The types of questions which should be considered are:

1. What is the relative importance of various product qualities as seen by the user?
2. For each of the key qualities, how does our product compare with competitors' products, as seen by the users?
3. What is the effect of the quality differences on user costs, well-being, and other aspects of fitness for use?
4. What are users' problems about which they do not complain but which our product might nevertheless be able to remedy?
5. What ideas do users have that might be useful in new-product development?

Examples of Field Studies. In a case involving an industrial product, a field study was made as part of a strategic planning analysis. Although both failure costs and customer complaints were low, the product had been losing market share for several years. Quality was one of five areas of strategic planning that was studied in order to improve market share. (See Utzig, 1980 and 1981.)

Table 12.7 shows a summary of the results. The six attributes studied were collectively a measure of fitness for use. On a scale of 1 to 10, customers were asked for two responses—the relative importance of each attribute and a perceived performance rating versus two key competitors. The average score for General Electric was lowest—not just for one attribute but for all of them. These unpleasant findings were not believed. (After all, the failure costs were at an acceptable level and complaints were few.) The study was repeated. It was repeated again. Three geographical areas, covering all types of customers, were studied before the results were believed. The details revealed that customers not only wanted fewer failures; they also wanted to improve their own productivity, and this meant purchasing products with higher efficiency, durability, and better maintainability and serviceability. The desire for improved service was a surprise.

TABLE 12.7   Customer-Based Measurements

Product attribute	Mean importance rating	Competitor performance ratings		
		GE	A	B
Reliable operation	9.7	8.1	9.3	9.1
Efficient performance	9.5	8.3	9.4	9.0
Durability/life	9.3	8.4	9.5	8.9
Easy to inspect and maintain	8.7	8.1	9.0	8.6
Easy to wire and install	8.8	8.3	9.2	8.8
Product service	8.8	8.9	9.4	9.2

Source: Utzig, 1980, p. 150. Copyright 1980, American Society for Quality Control. Reprinted by permission.

The company thought they were the leader on service (because theirs was a comprehensive service organization). However, the customers reported that the speed and quality of service were not equal to that of the competition. All of this led to the development of a plan including actions in product design, the manufacturing processes, product service, and the quality assurance system.

In another example, a manufacturer of equipment was also going through an era of declining market share. Complaints about "quality" led to a proposal to "beef up the inspection." Discussions within the company revealed uncertainty about the nature of the complaints, so it was decided to conduct a field study to learn more about customer view. A team was formed to plan and conduct the study. Visits were made to about 50 customers.

In one part of the study, five attributes were identified and customers were asked to rate the company as superior, competitive, or inferior to competition on each of the attributes (see Table 12.8). The results were stunning. The hardware problems were confirmed, but the study revealed the presence of both design and manufacturing causes. Also, documentation and field repair service were identified as weak areas (these were surprises to the company involved). The action taken was dramatic. A broad approach to quality was created, starting in initial design and continuing throughout the Spiral of all activities affecting fitness for use. This was in stark contrast to the original proposal of adding inspectors. The study required about seven worker-months of effort, including the planning, customer visits, analysis of results, and preparation of a report—a small price to pay to develop a proper strategy.

An example from a chemical company involves a specialty product that is used exclusively in one industry (Gross, 1978). The product had been granted a premium price by the market but the amount of the premium was declining. The study investigated the relationship of price and product attributes. For each of six attributes, customers were questioned. An analysis of the responses provided information on:

The relative importance of each attribute (the study referred to this as "value")

The relative rating of the product versus competition on each attribute ("perception")

The contribution to the price premium for each attribute

TABLE 12.8 Heavy Equipment Case

Parameter	Comparison to competition, %		
	Superior	Competitive	Inferior
Analysis of customer needs			
Preparation of quality requirements and purchase order			
Preparation of specifications and technical documentation			
Quality of equipment			
Quality and availability of spare parts			
Quality of field repair service			

Source: Private communication.

Some of the results are shown in Table 12.9. The relative importance ("value") numbers were determined by means of a trade-off analysis. Two realistic levels of performance for each attribute were defined. For the quality attribute, a high level was defined as impurities of less than 1 part per million (ppm.); a low level was defined as impurities of less than 10 ppm.

> The respondent was told, first, to consider an offering with all of the attributes at the high level; and, next, to suppose that the company making the offering was faced with increasing costs and, rather than raise the price, was considering sacrificing performance on one of the attributes by reducing it to the lower level. The respondent was then given a pair of attributes (such as product quality and speed of delivery) and asked which he would rather see kept at the higher level, and the degree of his preference. (A number of additional pairs of attribute sacrifices were given for similar ranking.) Finally he assigned dollar values to the price difference he would tolerate to retain the higher level of performance on each attribute. As a result of this questioning, and the use of statistical analysis, we were able to construct a scale of the relative dollar value of each attribute for each respondent. (Gross, 1978, pp. 35, 37)

The average results are shown in the "Value" column of Table 12.9. To no one's surprise, the quality attribute was regarded as the most valuable. Somewhat surprisingly, product innovation was second on the value list. The other four attributes trailed far behind the first two. Note that although quality was the most valued attribute, it was not the largest contributor to the price premium. The detailed responses revealed that the customers perceived quality to be about equal to that of its principal competitor—equal but not superior. The results of this study provided the company with an opportunity for making certain changes to protect the price premium.

TABLE 12.9 Research on a Speciality Product

Attribute	Value, $	Perceived performance				Contribution to price premium, $
		DuPont	A	B	C	
Quality	108					1.70
Innovation	105					2.00
System	103					0.80
Service	102					0.25
Delivery	101					0.15
Retraining	101					0.40
						5.30

Source: Gross, 1978, p. 39.

Studies of this type often reveal differences between the customers' perceived performance of some product attribute and the actual performance of that attribute. In some cases, customers may perceive the level of an attribute as poor when in reality the performance of that attribute is good. In such cases, the need is to take action to change the perception of the customers. In other cases the level may be correctly perceived as poor. This then requires an improvement in the level of performance rather than a change in the perception of the customer.(For further discussion of perceived quality, see Goble et al., 1981.)

A final example of a field study on competitive quality comes from a manufacturer of health products. This was also a "multiattribute study" in which customers were asked to consider several product attributes and indicate both the relative importance and a competitive rating. The results for one product are shown in Table 12.10. Note that an overall score is obtained for each manufacturer by multiplying the relative importance by the score for that attribute and then adding up these products. (For an extension to include costs, see Gryna, 1983.)

In generalizing about these examples, it should first be observed that all were based on a study of customers who were experienced in using the product involved. The studies determined both the relative importance of a number of attributes and a competitive rating for each of those attributes. Also note that the attributes involved can encompass quality as well as other business factors or be restricted to quality-related issues. For example, the chemical example was general in the sense that quality was just one of a number of business attributes, whereas the example of an industrial product was more specific with respect to quality as each of the attributes listed was a facet of fitness for use. It is useful to make multiattribute studies from both a general point of view and a more specific point of view. Most studies are general, but additional studies at a more detailed level will provide valuable information to product development, manufacturing, customer service, and other functions. (See also Utzig, 1981.)

DISCOVERING MARKETING OPPORTUNITIES

The search for ideas to achieve a unique position in the marketplace is perpetual. (Market quality is a moving target.) One important avenue is to seek ideas for the improvement of fitness for use. The broad steps are: analyze the present use of the product, analyze the total system of use, and strategically plan for quality.

Analyze the Present Use of the Product by the Customer.   This includes:

Collect and Analyze All Available Information on Current Product Usage.   (See, generally, Section 20, Customer Service.)

Visit the Scene of Action.   That is, go to the places where the product is used. There is no substitute for "stapling ourselves to the product." The observation on site provides information about:

1. Conditions of Use.   Actual conditions of use can differ markedly from those assumed by the product designer, but field conditions are the realities.

2. Problems Reported by the User.   These problems can be of several types. One type of problem involves inconvenience during use. One instrument manufacturer learned from customers that it was difficult to read the scale on an instrument through the normal 3-in.-high window ("Beckman Gets Customers to Design," 1974). The design was changed to provide a 6-in window. A second type of problem relates to the effects of a product failure. The effects of downtime due to failures can be significant, but there may be other consequences as well. A manufacturer of process control devices learned from a study that the devices were so unreliable that they represented the single biggest maintenance problem of the customer. A third type of problem is a disagreeable chore imposed on the user. An example is the disposal of garbage created by the product. The early instant cameras made use of a peel-back film that required the user to peel off a surface from the photo and then dispose of it. In a later model of the camera, the peel-back feature was eliminated.

TABLE 12.10 Multiattribute Study

Attribute	Relative importance, %	Company X		Competitor A		Competitor B	
		Rating	Weighted rating	Rating	Weighted rating	Rating	Weighted rating
Safety	28	6	168	5	140	4.5	126
Performance	20	6	120	7	140	6.5	130
Quality	20	6	120	7	140	4	80
Field service	12	4	48	8	96	5	60
Ease of use	8	4	32	6	48	5	40
Company image	8	8	64	4	32	4	32
Plant service	4	7.5	30	7.5	30	5	20
Total			582		626		488

Source: Private communication.

3. *Problems Not Reported by the User.* Sometimes the user reports being perfectly happy with a product when in reality a problem exists. As part of a field intelligence network for a television manufacturer, company executives visited the homes of consumers. Although the consumers were satisfied with the picture, the executives realized that the picture was not as good as what had been engineered in the laboratory. The problem was a lack of fine adjustment by the owners. The company had been working on an improved tuning system, but the intelligence led to establishing a high priority for developing single-button tuning. It was on the market within a few months. (See Reavey, 1973.)

4. *Remedial Steps Already Taken by the User (or Contemplated by the User) to Improve the Product.* This source of ideas for product changes even includes some built-in field testing.

5. *Needs for Which the User Sees No Present Solution.* These needs represent an opportunity for the product development function to create a new design that would be unique in the marketplace.

Visits to the customer sites need not require a large amount of resources; a sample of customers is sufficient. However, before the visits are made, a plan must spell out the questions to be answered and the procedures to be followed to collect the information. One company has a built-in mechanism for continuously obtaining knowledge on conditions of use, problems of the user, and any special steps taken by the user. This company manufactures tools for automobile mechanics and has its marketing function literally in a truck. As sales are made at the customer site, the salesperson observes the conditions of use and learns about any customer dissatisfaction.

Quantify the User's View of the Product. This includes:

1. Information on the costs to the user of operating and maintaining the product throughout its life. Data of this nature become targets for the product development function to beat through future product designs.

2. Information on the amount of employee training required to operate the product. To the extent that future designs can reduce the training, the design will be superior.

3. Information on the amount of technical service required to support the product. An example includes the amount of diagnosis and maintenance work required to repair product failures.

An electronics company now has a product that can be linked by telephone from the user's site to diagnostic equipment at the factory. For certain types of products, such self-diagnosis can solve 90 percent of the service problems. Another example involves the setup of equipment. Traditionally, some computers and terminals have been considered too complex to be set up by the user. However, the advent of self-testing diagnostic capabilities now provides an opportunity to design new products that can be set up and installed by the user (see Richardson, 1981).

The study of the user's operation can be aided by dissecting the process of use. This is done by documenting all of the steps, analyzing them, and identifying opportunities for new-product development. Such information is valuable input to the product development function as that group embarks on a new design project. Section 13 under Planning for Basic Functional Requirements shows an example using a functional flow diagram and a requirements allocation sheet. In another application, a certain clamp controlled the amount of flow of fluid from an external source to a patient during a dialysis process. An analysis showed that the proposed clamp was excellent in controlling the flow of fluid, but it was inconvenient in a later step that required the patient to wear the product under clothing. The original focus was on performance of the product, but the block diagram pinpointed a later problem of inconvenience to the patient.

The opportunities for improvement span the full range of customer use from initial receipt through operation. The primary stages and examples of ideas for improving fitness for use are given in Table 12.11.

TABLE 12.11 Opportunities for Improving Fitness for Use of an Industrial Product

Stage	Opportunities
Receiving inspection	Provide data so incoming inspection can be eliminated
Material storage	Design product and packaging for case of identification and handling
Processing	Do preprocessing of material (e.g., ready mixed concrete); design product to maximize productivity when it is used in customer's manufacturing operation
Finished goods storage warehouse and field	Design product and packaging for ease of identification and handling
Installation, alignment, and checkout	Use modular concepts and other means to facilitate setups by customer rather than manufacturer
Maintenance, preventive	Incorporate preventive maintenance in product (e.g., self-lubricated bearings)
Maintenance, corrective	Design product to permit self-diagnosis by user

Analyze the Total System of Use of the Product.   To a degree, fitness for use can be improved by refining the steps in the current use of the product. However, the most spectacular historical benefits have come not from such refinements but rather from discarding the existing progression entirely in favor of some new concept of serving the user. The term "systems approach" is here used to designate any approach which tries to improve fitness for use by restudying the entire progression rather than by accepting the present progression and refining the elements within it.

There have been a number of examples of the systems approach that enable us to identify some distinct categories:

Transfer of decentralized processing to a central process facility (e.g., frozen food, instant photography)

Modular concepts (e.g., prefabricated housing modules)

Elimination of user maintenance (e.g., self-lubricated bearings, aluminum exteriors)

New centralized service (e.g., centrally generated gas for heating, a central computer center into which various terminals feed)

Extending the shelf life of a product—e.g., by making a basic change in the manufacturing process, the shelf life of a brand of potato chips was increased from 2 months to 1 year (Vanderwicken, 1974)

Making a product compatible with other products (e.g., linking of products to a computer)

A listing of the main steps in the progression of an industrial product and examples of potential areas of improvement are shown in Table 12.11. The benefits to the user may take the form of:

Eliminating some of the users' work entirely

Transferring work from the user to some other stage in the progression of events at which it can be done more easily

Improving the effectiveness of such work as still remains

Strategic Planning for Quality. Companywide strategic planning focuses on the opportunities and threats that lie in the future and the subsequent decision making that defines organizational aims, policies, and plans. An important element of strategic planning is to differentiate the product in a way that will result in a competitive advantage. One strategy is to differentiate on the basis of cost; another strategy is to differentiate on the basis of quality. A discussion of the many issues involved is provided in the section on Quality and Sales Income. For a discussion of the key questions involved in strategic planning, see South, 1981. An example of strategic planning using quality as part of the strategy is given in Utzig, 1980.

REFERENCES

"Beckman Gets Customers to Design its Product." (1974). *Business Week,* Aug. 17, p. 54.

Calder, Bobby J. (1977). "Focus Groups and the Nature of Qualitative Marketing Research." *Journal of Marketing Research,* August, pp. 353–364.

Goble, J., Gruska, G. S., and Bajaria, H. (1981). "Perceived Quality." *ASQC Quality Congress Transactions,* Milwaukee, pp. 639–645.

Gross, Irwin (1978). "Insights for Pricing Research." In Bailey, E. L. (ed.), *Pricing Practices and Strategies.* The Conference Board, New York, pp. 34–39.

Gryna, Frank M., Jr. (1983). "Marketing Research and Product Quality." *ASQC Quality Transactions,* Milwaukee, 385–392.

Gryna, Frank M., Jr. (1970). *User Costs of Poor Product Quality.* Doctoral dissertation, University of Iowa, Iowa City.

Kukla, Robin (1981). "How Do We Rate in the Market Place?" *Quality Progress,* May, pp. 18–20.

Pipp, Frank J. (1983). "Management Commitment to Quality: Xerox Corp." *Quality Progress,* August, pp. 12–17.

Reavey, Edward P., Jr. (1973). "Motorola Executives Call on Consumers in Their Homes." *Harvard Business Review,* November–December, pp. 6–7.

Richardson, Hugh (1981). "Designing for Customer Set-up." *Quality,* October, pp. 62–65.

South, Stephen E. (1981). "Competitive Advantage: The Cornerstone of Strategic Thinking." *The Journal of Business Strategy,* Spring, pp. 15–25.

Utzig, Lawrence (1981). "Customer Based Measurements Close the Loop." *ASQC Technical Conference Transactions,* Milwaukee, pp. 673–683.

Utzig, Lawrence (1980). "Quality Reputation—A Precious Asset." *ASQC Technical Conference Transactions,* Milwaukee, pp. 145–154.

Vanderwicken, Peter (1974). "P & G's Secret Ingredient." *Fortune,* pp. 76–77.

SECTION 13

PRODUCT DEVELOPMENT[1]

Frank M. Gryna

INTRODUCTION **13.2**

    Importance of Product
       Development 13.3

    Traditional and Modern
       Products 13.3

BASIC CONCEPTS **13.4**

    Cost-Effectiveness Concept 13.4

    The Phase Concept of
       Product Development . . 13.4

    Early Warning Concept and
       Design Assurance 13.7

    Design Review 13.7

POLICY ISSUES **13.11**

    Level of Quality of Design 13.11

    Carryover of Failure-Prone
       Designs 13.11

    Design for Intended Use
       versus Design for Actual
       Use 13.11

    Design for High Reliability
       and Design for
       Maintainability 13.12

    Quantification of Reliability
       and Other Parameters . . 13.12

    The Learning Curve as
       Inevitable 13.12

    Jurisdiction in Product
       Specifications 13.12

    Requirement of a Formal
       Product Development
       Process 13.12

    Release of Design Prior to
       Production Capability
       Verification 13.13

    Breaking the Monopoly of
       Designers 13.13

PLANNING FOR BASIC
FUNCTIONAL REQUIREMENTS . **13.13**

PLANNING FOR TIME-ORIENTED
PERFORMANCE (RELIABILITY) . **13.17**

    Definition of Reliability . . 13.18

    Reliability Program 13.18

    Quantification of Reliability 13.19

    Establishing the
       Requirements 13.19

    Apportionment of
       Reliability 13.21

    Reliability Prediction and
       Analysis 13.21

    Parts Selection and Control 13.27

    Failure Mode, Effect, and
       Criticality Analysis: Fault
       Tree Analysis 13.28

    Other Analysis Techniques 13.31

    Evaluating Designs by Tests 13.31

    Reliability Tests 13.34

---

[1] In the Third Edition, this section was prepared by H. D. Voegtlen.

Reliability Data Systems . . 13.36
Reliability Improvement . 13.38
Reliability Growth 13.40
**PLANNING FOR
MAINTAINABILITY** **13.40**
Maintainability Concepts
and Terms 13.41
Maintainability Program
Elements. 13.43
Maintainability Modeling
and Allocation 13.43
Maintainability Prediction 13.44
Failure Mode, Effect, and
Criticality Analysis . . . 13.46
Design Aids for
Maintainability 13.46
Maintainability
Demonstration 13.48
Maintainability Data
Systems 13.48
PLANNING FOR SAFETY **13.48**
The Organized Safety
Program 13.48
Quantification of Safety . . 13.49
General Approach to Safety
Analysis 13.50
Tools of Safety Analysis . . 13.51
Improving Safety through
Design. 13.53
**PLANNING FOR HUMAN
FACTORS (ERGONOMICS)** . . . **13.55**

**PLANNING FOR
MANUFACTURING, INSPECTION,
AND TRANSPORTATION** **13.55**
Planning for Manufacturing 13.55
Planning for Inspection and
Test 13.62
Planning for Packaging,
Transportation, and
Storage 13.62
PLANNING TO MINIMIZE COST **13.63**
Value Engineering 13.63
Other Cost-Related
Approaches 13.66
**CONFIGURATION
MANAGEMENT** **13.66**
Configuration Identification 13.67
Configuration Control . . . 13.67
**IMPROVING THE
EFFECTIVENESS OF PRODUCT
DEVELOPMENT** **13.70**
Concept of Self-Control in
Product Development . . 13.70
**IMPROVING THE
EFFECTIVENESS OF INDIVIDUAL
DESIGNERS**. **13.70**
Design Experience
Retention 13.70
Training for Designers. . . 13.72
Staff Specialist Organization 13.73
REFERENCES **13.74**

INTRODUCTION

This step on the Spiral of quality activities concerns the process of translating the needs of the user, learned from field intelligence, into a set of product design requirements for manufacturing. The activity is often called product development, research and development, engineering, or design.

In this handbook, the business aspects of launching new products are discussed in Section 3, Quality and Income, and Section 19, Marketing. The broad planning approach for quality is discussed in Section 6, Companywide Planning for Quality. Section 12, Field Intelligence, discusses the collection of information needed as inputs to initiate the product development process. The present section concentrates on the managerial and technological steps needed during product development to assure that the user needs are reflected in the product design.

Importance of Product Development. There is increasing evidence that many fitness-for-use problems can be traced to the design of the product.

In a classic study of 850 field failures of relatively simple electronic equipment, 43 percent of the failures were due to engineering design (Juran and Gryna, 1980).

In a study of seven space programs, 35.2 percent of component failures were due to design or specification error (Juran and Gryna, 1970).

During a typical period of 11 months at a chemical plant, 42 percent of the rework dollars were traced to research and development (consulting experience of the author).

In a study of "quality calamities" by the British Institute of Management, 36 percent were due to lack of proving new designs, materials, or processes and 16 percent were due to lack of or wrong specifications (Belbin, 1970).

In one chemical company, a startling 50 percent of the product shipped was out of specification. Fortunately the product was fit for use. A review concluded that many of the specifications were obsolete and had to be changed (consulting experience of the author).

For mechanical and electronics products of at least moderate complexity, it is the author's opinion that errors during product development cause about 40 percent of the fitness-for-use problems. Where Product Development is responsible for both creating the formulation (design) of the product and also responsible for developing the manufacturing process, as in chemicals, about 50 percent of the problems are due to development.

The amount of activity within product development to correct deficiencies in products can be surprisingly high. In one typical year, an electronics organization determined that the cost of design changes was about 67 percent of the operating profit. Some of these changes were initiated by the customer but over 80 percent of the changes were related to design deficiencies.

Traditional and Modern Products. Times have changed, products have changed. A comparison of traditional and modern products is shown in Table 13.1. The traditional product is shoes, a garden tool, bread, or an aspirin. The modern product is a printed circuit board, an electronic computer, or a nuclear reactor. In practice, products are on a continuous spectrum from traditional to modern. Some products move on that spectrum. For example, the earliest automobiles and telephones were traditional in simplicity but now are modern in complexity; the advent of microwave cooking has changed the stove industry from traditional to modern; requirements on lead-free chemicals have changed some chemical companies from traditional to modern. The change from traditional to modern products is often gradual and can mask the need for new approaches in product development.

Two processes are needed for launching new products: (1) the traditional process for traditional products and (2) a revolutionary process for modern products. Traditional methods are not adequate to launch modern products. They were tried and they failed. As a corollary, the fact that revolutionary ways are available does not mean that they should be used for traditional products as well. For many traditional products the traditional ways are adequate and the use of modern ways is uneconomic.

All products, traditional and modern, have two types of requirements: "functional performance" requirements and other, fitness-for-use requirements such as

TABLE 13.1 Traditional versus Modern Products

Aspects of products	Traditional	Modern
Simplicity	Simple, static	Complex, dynamic
Precision	Low	High
Need for interchangeability	Limited	Extensive
Consumables or durables	Mainly consumables	Mainly durables
Environment in which used	Natural	Unnatural
User understanding of product	High	Low
Importance to human health, safety and continuity of life	Seldom important	Often important
Life cycle cost to user	Similar to purchase price	Much greater than purchase price
Life of a new design	Long; decades and even centuries	Short; less than a decade
Scientific basis of design	Largely empirical	Largely scientific
Basis of reliability, maintainability, etc.	Vague: "best effort"	Quantified
Volume of production	Usually low	Often high
Usual cause of field failures	Manufacturing errors	Design weaknesses

reliability, maintainability, and safety. For traditional products, the design work done to achieve the performance requirements is usually sufficient to meet the other parameters. Modern products have more exacting needs that require additional managerial methods and technological tools.

BASIC CONCEPTS

Cost-Effectiveness Concept. For modern products, attainment of fitness for use involves a balance among competing parameters and costs. The aggregation of these parameters and costs, from the inception of the design to the end of the operational life is called the cost-effectiveness concept (Figure 13.1). Zaludova (1981) discusses a similar model and gives examples of individual characteristics of the effectiveness features. Many of the technical and economical parameters in the model are discussed in this section of the handbook.

The Phase Concept of Product Development. The broad concept of cradle-to-grave quality planning is discussed in Section 6, Companywide Planning for Quality. The reader is urged to study this broad planning in conjunction with the present topic.

A major segment of the cradle-to-grave quality planning is "product development." This segment logically breaks down into a number of recognized phases.

1. *Concept and feasibility phase:* In this phase the known or anticipated need for a product is studied in enough detail to determine if it is feasible to design and

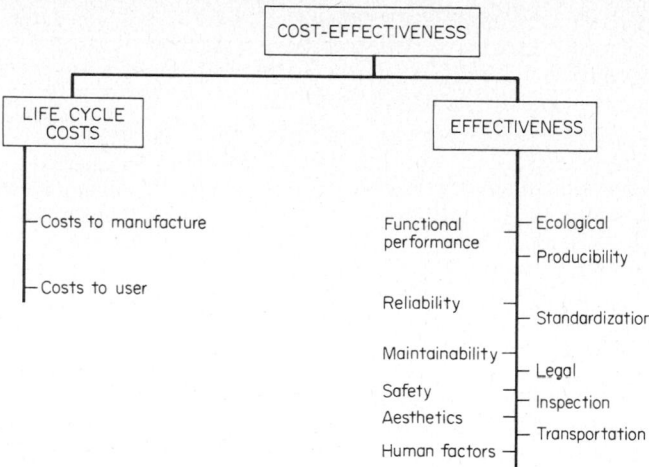

FIG. 13.1 Cost-effectiveness.

manufacture a product responsive to the need. An important element of this feasibility is the expected cost to the company and to the customer. This phase culminates in a conclusion that it is feasible (or not feasible) to continue with the project. This conclusion recommends one or more design concepts that appear to be promising to explore in the future.

2. *Detailed design phase:* In this phase, the alternative design concepts are evaluated, the most promising one is selected, and the product is designed in sufficient detail to prepare purchasing specifications for parts and materials and to plan the manufacture of products for prototype testing. For complex products, the detailed design phase may consist of two major subphases: (1) a more detailed exploration of several design concepts uncovered in the feasibility stage (these explorations may be conducted simultaneously or sequentially), and (2) selection of a final design concept followed by a full, detailed design.

There is always the possibility that during or after the detailed design phase, the design concept selected may prove to be poor and may have to be discarded. The cycle then starts all over. (The detailed design phase may also include major work in new-component development and may go beyond and include fabrication of hardware to evaluate the design proposed on paper.)

3. *Prototype phase:* In this phase, the first essentially complete units of the product are built and tested. The tests may evaluate such factors as basic design capability, effects of extreme environments, and reliability for extended periods of operation. The units built may not be complete, but are complete enough to test the adequacy of the basic design approach. The prototype tests should indicate that the initial design approach can be adopted and completed in detail. If not, "back to the drawing board."

Ideally, prototype units are built using the manufacturing procedures and equipment planned for full-scale production, but this is sometimes not possible. In such cases, the test results may not be completely representative of what the production units will do. However, the prototype phase is a valuable means for the designer to evaluate the adequacy of his or her design approach ("technical feasibility") and to revise the design prior to setting up manufacturing procedures.

In this phase, some companies sell the product on a limited basis (a "test market") to measure potential sales performance and identify weaknesses in the product or in the marketing plan. (See Section 19 under Role of the Marketing Department During the Launching of New Products.)

4. *Preproduction demonstration:* In this phase a "production design" is prepared and is evaluated for producibility and performance.

The production design differs from the prototype design, due to design changes made for a variety of reasons: to simplify manufacturing processes, cut the cost of materials, standardize for greater interchangeability with existing products, utilize present production facilities, etc.

Next, a preproduction lot of product is made according to the production design, using the production equipment. (See Section 16 under Preproduction Trials and Preproduction Runs.) This "pilot run" is then tested, sometimes under simulated-use environments (proving grounds) and sometimes by selected customers under conditions of actual use.

Based on the results of the tests and the experience of manufacture, the design is either released for full-scale production or sent back to be reworked.

5. *Full-scale production:* This is the regular production for sale and delivery to customers.

6. *Design changes:* Based on experience gained in production, marketing, and use of the product, design changes are made to improve product performance and to eliminate field failures which showed up under the conditions of use. These design changes go through one or more of the previous phases of the life cycle.

7. *Customer use:* This is the entire period of product useful life, including the warranty interval (if provided) and all service and repair until the product is discarded, traded in, or replaced.

There are other methods of dividing the cradle-to-grave progression into logical phases. For example, some practitioners divide the prototype phase into three subphases, i.e., prototype design, prototype construction, and prototype testing. There is no single method which fits all companies or even all projects within a single company. Renna and Howard (1979) discuss the phases of a development cycle for a television camera and identify some of the quality-related tasks that are needed.

The need for careful evolution of a new product is not restricted to products having complex hardware. The evolution of a new antiperspirant is an example (*Wall Street Journal,* 1978). It started with a formal market research study that established the need for a new product, one that "did not go on wet and make you wait to get dressed." First, a volatile silicone was used as a substitute for water, but the silicone dissolved part of the applicator. The next model corrected the problem but was "too oily." The next model looked promising until it became a rock-hard gel that could not be removed from the package. The next model had several problems: (1) The product leaked out of most containers, (2) the new dispenser was too confusing, and (3) users felt the product was too dry on application and, therefore, they were not sure that the product was working properly. After other futile attempts to develop a new applicator (including one with a clicking noise to assure users that it was working), a conventional applicator was chosen and the new product was released for production. The cost of this development was $18 million over a 2-year period—and the product was a simple one with just a few moving parts. Hammel (1974) describes the development effort for a new line of dolls. This involved 5 years of research, much trial and error, and worldwide searches for sources of materials, manufacture, and skilled labor.

Early Warning Concept and Design Assurance. The frequency and severity of problems caused by design has stimulated companies to develop more and better forms of early warning on impending troubles. These early warnings are available in a variety of forms (Table 13.2). All companies make use of some combination of these alternatives, the specific choice being tailored to the unique conditions present in the company. In addition, much has been done to evolve special quality-oriented tools to help evaluate the designs and to improve the design process itself. Collectively these early warnings and quality-oriented tools provide added assurance that the new designs will not create undo trouble as they progress around the Spiral. Many of these forms of early warning are administered by reliability, maintainability, and other specialists. The timing of their inputs is critical. Early timing can provide constructive help; late timing causes resistance to the early warnings and often creates an atmosphere of blame.

The forms of early warning can be enhanced by other steps taken to improve the overall effectiveness of the product development function (see later in this section under Improving the Effectiveness of Product Development).

Design Review. During the development cycle, the product undergoes several reviews. One form is a business review in which the results to date of the development effort are summarized and a decision is made whether or not to proceed further. Another type of review is technical in nature and is usually called design review.

Design review is a technique for evaluating a proposed design to assure that the design (1) will perform successfully during use, (2) can be manufactured at low cost, and (3) is suitable for prompt, low-cost field maintenance. Design review is not new. For traditional products the design review is carried out by the head of the enterprise, by the head of the technical department, by a new-products com-

TABLE 13.2 Forms of Early Warning of New-Product Problems

Phases of new-product progression	Forms of early warning of new-product troubles
Concept and feasibility study	Concept review
Prototype design	Design review, reliability and maintainability prediction, failure mode, effect, and criticality analysis, safety analyses, value engineering
Prototype construction	Prototype test, environmental test, overstressing
Preproduction	Pilot production lots, evaluation of tolerances
Early full-scale production	In-house testing (e.g., kitchen, road), consumer use panels, limited marketing area
Full-scale production, marketing, and use	Employees as test panels, special provisions for prompt feedback
All phases	Failure analysis, data collection and analysis

mittee, or by manufacturing planning specialists. For these products, an informal review is sufficient.

Modern products require a more structured program. The characteristics of a program include:

1. Design reviews are made mandatory, either through customer demand or through upper-management policy declaration.

2. The design reviews are conducted by a team of specialists who are not directly associated with the development of the design. These specialists must be highly experienced and bring with them the reputation of objectivity. Table 13.3 (derived from Jacobs, 1967) shows the possible membership and responsibilities of a design review team for three phases of design review. Special members could include an industrial designer, a representative from a university, or the technical press.

3. The ultimate decision on inputs from the design review rests with the designer. The designer must listen to the inputs, but on matters of structural integrity and other creative aspects of the design, the designer retains the monopoly on decisions. The control and publication of the specification remains with the designer.

4. Design reviews are formal. They are planned and scheduled like any other legitimized activity. The meetings are built around prepared agendas and documentation sent out in advance. Minutes of meetings are prepared and circulated. Follow-ups for action are likewise formalized.

5. The parameters can include reliability, performance, maintainability, producibility, testability, interchangeability, installation, safety, ergonomics, appearance, and cost and value. Other special parameters can also be included when needed for a particular product. Alternatively, design review can be restricted to just several of the parameters cited.

6. As much as possible, design reviews are made to defined criteria. Such criteria may include customer requirements, industry standards, government regulations, and checklists based on experience with previous products. The computer can help in the capture, recording, and retrieval of previous experience. (For an example, see Section 27 under New Product Quality Design Review.)

7. Design reviews are conducted at several phases of the progression of the design, such as design concept, prototype design and test, and final design. Reviews are made at several levels of the product hierarchy, such as system and subsystem.

The adoption of the design review concept takes place in several ways. These include: by mandate from upper management in response to an undue extent of field troubles traceable to inadequacies in designs; through pressure from outsiders (e.g., clients, regulators, or insurance companies, who want assurances with respect to public safety or health); and through internal evolution (designers gradually become aware that useful inputs can be obtained from specialists such as reliability and maintainability engineers). Acceptance of the concept is best gained by having a successful case example of design review within the company. A design review that identifies potential problems and results in design changes carries more weight than a discussion of the logic of design review. Another approach is to try out a retrospective design review, on several previous designs. For each design, a list of problems that required design changes is prepared. This list is evaluated and the question asked: "Suppose we had a design review, would the review have detected this problem?" If many of the problems are detected,

TABLE 13.3   Design Review Team Membership and Responsibility

Group member	Responsibilities	Type of design review* PDR	IDR	FDR
Chairperson	Calls, conducts meetings of Group, and issues interim and final reports	X	X	X
Design Engineer(s) (of product)	Prepares and presents design and substantiates decisions with data from tests or calculations	X	X	X
Reliability Manager or Engineer	Evaluates design for optimum reliability consistent with goals	X	X	X
Quality Manager or Engineer	Ensures that the functions of inspection, control, and test can be efficiently carried out		X	X
Manufacturing Engineer	Ensures that the design is producible at minimum cost and schedule		X	X
Field Engineer	Ensures that installation, maintenance, and user considerations were included in the design		X	X
Procurement Representative	Assures that acceptable parts and materials are available to meet cost and delivery schedules		X	
Materials Engineer	Ensures that materials selected will perform as required		X	
Tooling Engineer	Evaluates design in terms of the tooling costs required to satisfy tolerance and functional requirements		X	
Packaging and Shipping Engineer	Assures that the product is capable of being handled without damage, etc.		X	X
Marketing Representative	Assures that requirements of customers are realistic and fully understood by all parties	X		
Design Engineers (not associated with unit under review)	Constructively reviews adequacy of design to meet all requirements of customer	X	X	X
Consultants, Specialists on components, value, human factors, etc., (as required)	Evaluates design for compliance with goals of performance, cost, and schedule	X	X	X
Customer Representative (optional)	Generally voices opinion as to acceptability of design and may request further investigation on specific items			X

*P = Preliminary; I = Intermediate; F = Final.
Source: Jacobs, 1967.

this suggests that design review should be tried on future designs. This approach can enlist the support of personnel from manufacturing, field service, marketing, and other areas.

The track record on formal design review is mixed. Many companies have tried design review, but only a minority report success. Sometimes the remark is heard that "a designer who is a good salesperson can often sell a poor design during the design review process." The ingredients for a successful design review include:

1. *An emphasis on constructive input to designers, rather than criticism:* A universal obstacle to design review has been the cultural resistance of the design department. It has been common practice for this department to hold a virtual monopoly on design decisions; i.e., these decisions have historically been immune from challenge unless actual product trouble was being encountered. With such a background, it was not surprising that the designers have resisted the use of design reviews to challenge their designs. Some people believe that the designer's resistance to design review borders on arrogance. However, a review is interpreted by the designer as a criticism of the design work. Designers, like other human beings, are sensitive to criticism—particularly if it is presented to management. One approach that has been tried is the concept of a "peer walk-through." These are a series of meetings in which technical specialists provide input to the designers without any management people being present. This identifies potential problems and allows time for design changes before the formal design review is held.

2. *Avoiding any competition at the technological level that results in the designer feeling that there are others competing for the role of designing the product:* The resistance to design review is aggravated when reliability engineers propose competing designs. The designers resist the idea of competitors even more than they resist the idea of design review.

3. *Realistic schedules:* If the review is held close to the time of design release, there will not be sufficient time to investigate a potential weakness and change the design. The reaction then is: "Why didn't you tell us this sooner?" This can be minimized by scheduling several stages of design review (e.g., preliminary, intermediate, and final design reviews).

4. *Sufficient resources:* The team membership must provide the knowledge needed to cover the many parameters of fitness for use. (Of course, to facilitate discussions the number of members should be kept to a minimum.) Members must have enough time to prepare for and follow up on meetings. In addition, they must have a high level of competence and credibility. Such people are in great demand and it is easier to assign others who do not have sufficient knowledge and experience. The result may be marginal inputs to the design review—and rejection by the designers.

5. *Adequate planning for design review meetings:* The responsibilities of team members should be made clear (Table 13.3). Also, prior to meetings, documentation should be collected and sent out to the design review members for study. Such material includes specifications and design review checklists. Lawlor (1978) provides examples of checklists for several product development stages. Either before or during the design review meetings, other analyses can be presented including failure mode effect, and criticality analysis, reliability predictions, and results of reliability tests.

6. *Focusing on the unproven and untried features of a design.*

7. *Sufficient structure in the design review process:* This assures that design weaknesses are identified, documented, and provision for follow-up and resolution is made. Generally the chairperson of the design review team is someone from the line design function that was responsible for creating the design, e.g., the project engineer. This helps to promote implementation of inputs from the design reviews. (In other organizations, the project manager chairs the reviews.) Much of the success, however, of design review depends on the planning for review meetings and on the follow-up after the meetings—a role for the quality and reliability specialist. Some companies have found it useful to conduct a training course in design review.

8. *A realization that the design review may uncover some interdepartmental conflicts:* Means should be available to resolve these conflicts.

9. *Management directive:* Management must formalize the design-review process to make it clear to all concerned that resources, time, and priorities must reflect the importance of the activity.

Burgess (1985) identifies some common problems encountered in design review and explains how these can be overcome.

POLICY ISSUES

There are basic issues in product development that deserve deliberation and decision making by management. Where such issues are not explicitly faced, policies are developed by default at lower levels of the organization. These policy issues go beyond technology; they can involve legal, financial, and marketing matters as well. Such matters are normally beyond the designer's training and experience.

Level of Quality of Design.   Several alternative quality strategies exist for new-product development—quality superior to competition, quality equal to the average of competition, and quality at a minimal acceptable level so that cost and other parameters can receive higher priority. Many organizations have evolved an unwritten policy from past experience. In other organizations, however, product development personnel receive little guidance from either past experience or a policy from management.

Carryover of Failure-Prone Designs.   New models of a product often use design features of previous models. If such design features are failure-prone, these weaknesses are carried over into the new model. Such a condition can be revealed by summarizing past history in a matrix. The columns of the matrix are product models listed in chronological order; the rows of the matrix are the failure-prone features. Of course, the solution to the design weakness may be unknown, or known but not economically feasible. The problem of carryover is intensified by pressures for new models, along with a preference by designers to work on new models rather than to correct deficiencies on old models. The policy issue is the relative priority of correcting carryover weaknesses versus developing new features. Concentrating on new features runs the risk that competition will develop a product free of the carryover weaknesses and thereby have a competitive advantage.

Design for Intended Use versus Design for Actual Use.   Actual use of a product can differ from what the designer regards as the intended use. The difference can be due to variations in environment and other conditions of use. In addition, some users will misapply or misuse the product (in liability cases, juries and judges have been notoriously unsympathetic to defense contentions that the products have been misused). The policy question is: Should the design be based on how the product is intended to be used, or based on how the product will actually be used (and misused)? In most companies this question has never been placed before upper management for decision. Hence, by default, designers make the decision.

Design for High Reliability and Design for Maintainability.   For complex products, reliability and maintainability are important parameters of fitness for use. The policy issue is: What should be the relative priorities of reliability and maintainability? Evaluation of this issue requires consideration of the effect on costs (both to the manufacturer and the user), trade-off analyses for uptime, and the relative importance of reliability and maintainability as perceived by customers. Helland (1978) reports two examples involving office reproduction equipment.

Quantification of Reliability and Other Parameters.   Traditionally, performance parameters (power generated, pH temperature rise, parts per million of impurities) have been quantified during design; other fitness-for-use parameters (reliability and maintainability) have not been quantified in many companies. Designers understand that reliability and maintainability are important, but without quantification, these parameters do not receive the same degree of formal evaluation as performance parameters. The policy issue is whether reliability, maintainability, and similar parameters should be quantified. Quantification means establishing numerical requirements, evaluating the design before release to see if those requirements have been met, and measuring field performance. Staff specialists can recommend quantification, but it will not be effective without management affirmation. In one organization with such specialists, management made the decision to quantify—but only after a serious failure of a new model due to poor reliability.

The Learning Curve as Inevitable.   The process of developing a new product design often consists of many trials before the "learning curve" results in an acceptable design. In manufacturing operations, a large amount of rework on product is viewed as a deficiency, and attempts are made to identify the causes and take action. In product development, however, there often is not that same sense of urgency because the learning curve is accepted as inevitable. The policy issue is whether to let learning take place fortuitously, or to take the initiative— to formally study product development as a process and learn from the past in order to improve the process for the future. See Section 6 under Lessons Learned and Section 22 under Diagnosis—General.

Jurisdiction in Product Specifications.   Usually, product specifications are issued and any changes are made by the product development function. Many specification characteristics affect fitness for use, but there are other characteristics that do not—they only provide internal manufacturing information. The policy question is whether the production function should be allowed to set and change specifications on those characteristics that do not affect fitness for use. More realistic specifications could be the result.

Requirement of a Formal Product Development Process.   The simplicity of traditional products permits product development to be done with a modest amount of effort. The complexity of modern products and the consequences of releasing deficient designs can mean that product development must be structured with phases (see above under The Phase Concept of Product Development) to assure that the designs released are adequate. The establishment of a formal product development process is a policy decision for management.

Release of Design Prior to Production Capability Verification. History is replete with designs that were released and then caused many problems during manufacturing. For example, the specifications on a chemical product are based on a few laboratory results, minimal input on customer needs, and no information on process variability. Such a situation breeds future problems and costly changes. The policy issue is whether the capability to manufacture should be formally verified before the design is released.

Breaking the Monopoly of Designers. The ultimate responsibility for the design of a product rests with the product development function. With modern products, it is virtually impossible for individual designers to possess all the knowledge needed on all of the attributes of fitness for use. Thus it becomes necessary that the designer's knowledge be supplemented with the knowledge of specialists in other areas such as reliability, maintainability, and producibility. What is needed is a policy decision on whether an independent evaluation of the design will be performed before the design is relased for full production.

Examination of these and other policy issues can be a part of an audit of product development by upper managers. See Section 8 under Quality Audit by Upper Managers.

PLANNING FOR BASIC FUNCTIONAL REQUIREMENTS

Examples of basic functional requirements are weight, power consumption, and speed. The achievement of these requirements, the heart of the product development task, rests on a foundation of technological disciplines such as chemistry, electrical engineering, and mechanical engineering. Product development efforts to achieve the functional requirements are related to fitness for use:

1. Fitness for use includes the functional requirements. Unless these are provided at some adequate level, there is no product to market.
2. Designing for functional capability can result in high complexity. High complexity, in turn, is a breeding ground for problems in reliability and maintainability—important parameters of fitness for use. Trade-offs may need to be evaluated bctween additional functional capability and the effects on other fitness-for-use parameters.

Product development translates customer expectations on functional requirements into specific engineering and quality characteristics. For traditional products, this process is not complicated and can be achieved by experienced design engineers without using any special techniques. For modern products, it is useful to document and analyze the design logic. This means starting with the desired product attributes and then identifying the necessary characteristics for raw materials, parts, assemblies, and process steps. Such an approach goes under a variety of names such as systems engineering, functional analysis systems, technique, structured product/process analysis, and product quality deployment.

One example of this approach is shown in Figure 13.2 [Kogure and Akao (1983)]. This figure shows a matrix of customer requirements ("required quality")

				REQUIRED QUALITY					
STAGE	No.	Primary	No.	Secondary	No.	Tertiary	Importance	Thickness	Weight
STAGE OF SEWING	1	Easy to sew	11	Easy to stitch and cut	111	Light	C		0
					112	Does not stick	B		
			12		121	Easy to work on sewing machine	B		
					122	Surface coating does not fall off	B		
			13	Can use adhesives	131	Withstands organic solvent	C		
STAGE OF USAGE	2	Protect passengers	21	Does not let rain seep	211	No hole, no tear	A		
			22	No change in atmospheric pressure in tunnel	221	Airtight (no pinhole)	A		
			23	Does not tear under pressure	231	No tear under air pressure	A		
					232	No tear from poking from inside	A		
					233	No tear from shocks of starting or stopping	A		

FIG. 13.2   Matrix of required quality and counterpart characteristics.

COUNTERPART CHARACTERISTICS				
Tensile strength	Tear strength	Extension ratio	Anticrumple strength	Water pressure resistance
				●
●	●		●	
●	●	●		
●	●	●		

and product quality characteristics ("counterpart characteristics") developed for the hood that connects railroad cars of a train. The left-hand side of the matrix shows customer requirements in terms of primary, secondary, and tertiary needs, along with importance ratings of A, B, or C; the right-hand side of the matrix shows the technological characteristics that are needed to achieve the requirements. Thus the design value of tensile strength can be determined by considering requirements 231, 232, and 233. Traditionally the strength would have been determined by a design engineer based on prior experience. This matrix approach provides a more methodical way of converting customer needs into product characteristics. When this is done for all customer needs, specific responsibilities can then be assigned for the various characteristics ("deployment of the quality function").

Vinson and Heany (1977) describe the development process for a new fluorescent lamp starting with customer expectations and proceeding through design logic and the creation of product and process characteristics.

Baxter Healthcare Corporation, a manufacturer in the health care field, uses the following approach:

1. Prepare a functional flow block diagram to show the normal flow of manufacturing and use for the product. Figure 13.3 contains a partial reproduction of a functional flow diagram.
2. Assign requirements to each block of the diagram (an example of this for one subfunction is shown in Figure 13.3). Each design requirement is allocated to one or more components.
3. Sort the requirements by component and prepare a separate requirements document for each component.
4. Add nonfunctional requirements such as quality verification methods to each component specification.
5. Generate the basic product system specification capturing system requirements and references to the component specifications.

The company cites the following benefits:

1. It provides a disciplined approach to defining requirements—particularly helpful to less experienced design project leaders.
2. Analyses made can be used during the development of new products using the same or similar components. This saves much labor and paperwork. In addition, the approach provides a methodical way to establish test methods to assure verification of requirements.
3. The approach starts with customer expectations and emphasizes customer use of the product.
4. The potential for interface problems between design groups is reduced by the analysis and documentation.
5. A means is provided to communicate and manage mandatory versus desirable marketing issues.
6. The approach provides a trail to allow a designer to determine what other components may be affected by a design change.
7. From the analysis, the specification is able to define not just functional requirements but all other requirements of fitness for use.

In planning for a new product model, an automotive manufacturer identified

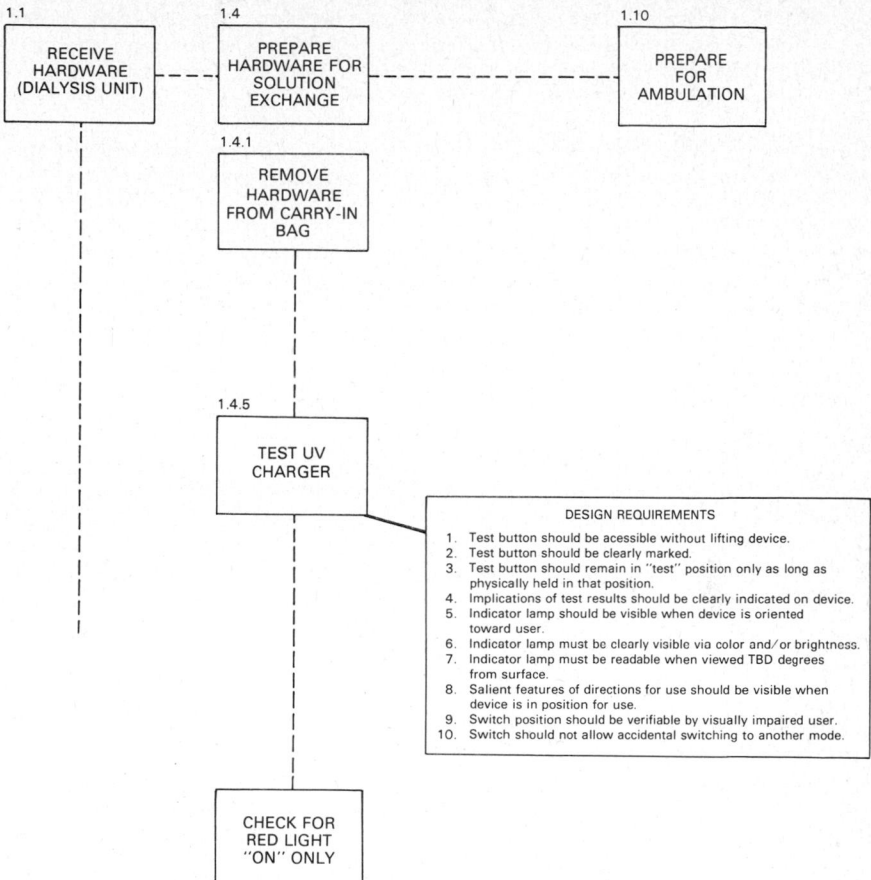

FIG. 13.3 Requirements allocation sheet.

over 400 characteristics of fitness for use (see Veraldi, 1985). For each character-istic, (1) marketing research was conducted to learn the current status relative to competition and (2) targets were set, also relative to competition, for the new model. Product development then proceeded.

Sullivan (1986) describes a system of quality function deployment that trans-lates customer requirements into technical requirements for each stage of product development and production. See also Section 6 under the Quality Planning Roadmap.

PLANNING FOR TIME-ORIENTED PERFORMANCE (RELIABILITY)

From time immemorial engineers recognized that a product should have a long service life and that during this life it should give service with few failures. As products became more complex, there were increasing problems with failures over time. Traditional efforts of design, although necessary, were not sufficient to achieve both the functional performance requirements and a low rate of failures with time. What has evolved is a collection of tools called "reliability engineering." Some of the tools are old, some are new.

Definition of Reliability.   Reliability is the probability that an item will perform a required function under stated conditions for a stated period of time.

This definition has four key elements:

1. *The quantification of reliability in terms of a probability.*

2. *A statement defining the required product performance:*   As the function is defined in detail, it becomes more clear which product failures impair the success of the mission and which do not.

3. *A statement of the required operating time between failures:*   (Otherwise, the probability is a meaningless number for time-oriented products.)

4. *A statement defining the environmental conditions in which the equipment must operate:*   Numerous product failures are traceable to a lack of meeting of the minds on what the real environments are to be; e.g., the designer designed the product to operate at 180°C, but in some applications the temperatures rise to 200°C. One of the contributions of the reliability "movement" has been to force all parties to dig deeper in order to discover what the real environment will be.

To achieve a required level of reliability, certain tasks are necessary. The collection of tasks is called the reliability program.

Reliability Program.   An example of the typical tasks in a reliability program for a complex product is given in Table 13.4 [from MIL-STD-785B (1980)]. The Standard explains the degree of applicability by program phase (concept, demonstration and validation, full-scale engineering development, and production). Many of the tasks listed are discussed in this section. (Appendix III, Selected

TABLE 13.4   Reliability Tasks

Reliability program plan
Monitor/control of subcontractors and suppliers
Program reviews
Failure reporting, analysis, and corrective action system (FRACAS)
Failure review board (FRB)
Reliability modeling
Reliability allocations
Reliability predictions
Failure mode, effect, and criticality analysis (FMECA)
Sneak circuit analysis (SCA)
Electronic parts/circuits tolerance analysis
Parts program
Reliability critical items
Effects of functional testing, storage, handling, packaging, transportation, and maintenance
Environmental stress screening (ESS)
Reliability qualification test (RQT) program
Production reliability acceptance test (PRAT) program

Source: MIL-STD-785B, 1980.

Quality Standards, Specifications, and Related Documents, includes reliability documentation.)

The tasks in the reliability program span many company functions. A program requires positive, formal planning if the deeds are to be done and done on time. Moreover, since many departments and individuals are involved, it is useful to have a written list of the tasks to be performed, who is to do them, the timetable, procedures for performing the tasks, and procedure for evaluating the status and control of each task. Often such a written definition is missing. Someone should "make the rounds" of all company functions and help get agreement on tasks and responsibilities. This definition helps to clarify "who is responsible for doing what" and to assure that adequate resources are available.

Before embarking on a discussion of reliability tasks, a remark on the application of the tasks is in order:

1. Many of these tasks are clearly not warranted for simple products. However, products that were originally simple are now becoming more complex. When this is the case, the various reliability tasks should be examined to see which, if any, might be justified to use.

2. These techniques apply both to products that the company markets and to complex manufacturing equipment that a company purchases, e.g., numerically controlled machines in the metalworking industries and processing equipment in the chemical industries.

Quantification of Reliability.   A major new tool is the quantification of reliability. The process of reliability quantification involves four phases:

Establishment of reliability requirements or objectives: The process of determining the overall reliability that is needed for the product

Apportionment (or budgeting):   The process of allocating the overall reliability objective to the elements which collectively make up the total product

Prediction: The estimation of overall reliability based on prior reliability data of components

Analysis: Identification of the strong and weak portions of the design to serve as a basis for improvements, trade-offs, and similar actions

Fundamental to the quantification process are some statistical concepts that are described in Section 23 under Reliability. The reader is urged to study that discussion to more fully understand the quantification process.

Establishing the Requirements.   The definition of reliability as a probability of performing a function for a specified time interval provides one way of stating a reliability requirement. In practice, a reliability requirement is usually stated in simpler language. A summary of common indices (often called figures of merit) is presented in Table 13.5.

Examples of reliability indices and goals are:

1. For a telephone system, the downtime of each switching center should be a maximum of 24 h per 40 years.

2. For an engine manufacturer, 70 percent of the engines produced should pass through the warranty period without generating a claim. The number of failures per failed engine should not exceed 1.

3. For a consumer product manufacturer, the percent failure shall be a maximum

TABLE 13.5 Reliability Figures of Merit

Figure of merit	Meaning
Mean time between failures (MTBF)	Mean time between successive failures of a repairable product
Failure rate	Number of failures per unit time
Mean time to failure (MTTF)	Mean time to failure of a nonrepairable product or mean time to first failure of a repairable product
Mean life	Mean value of life ("life" may be related to major overhaul, wear-out, etc.)
Mean time to first failure (MTFF)	Mean time to first failure of a repairable product
Mean time between maintenance (MTBM)	Mean time between a specified type of maintenance action
Longevity	Wear-out time for a product
Availability	Operating time expressed as a percentage of operating and repair time
System effectiveness	Extent to which a product achieves the requirements of the user
Probability of success	Same as reliability (but often used for "one-shot" or non-time-oriented products)
b_{10} life	Life during which 10% of the population would have failed
b_{50} life	Median life, or life during which 50% of the population would have failed
Repairs/100	Number of repairs per 100 operating hours

of 5.7 percent "dead on arrival," 6.4 percent during the first month, an average of 2.0 percent/month during the first year, and an average of 1.2 percent during the 5-year service life.

4. For a locomotive manufacturer (Emphrain and Hamilton, 1973, p. 6):

Reliability goals: These will be normally expressed as a failure rate in terms of a multiple of warranty periods. For example, a 3 percent failure rate in two warranty periods is expressed as

$$W2 = 3\%$$

Service conditions:

a. Locomotive to have 95 percent availability, and therefore, to have a total operating time of 8350 h/year.

b. Additional details on service conditions included numerical statements on the time spent at each throttle notch, outside ambient temperature, throttle changes per hour, and percent of operating time run at various speeds.

Note that all of these examples quantify reliability.

Setting overall reliability goals requires a meeting of the minds on (1) reliability as a number, (2) the environmental conditions to which the numbers apply, and (3) a definition of successful product performance. This is not easily accomplished. However, the act of requiring designers to define with precision both environmental conditions and successful product performance forces the designer to understand the design in greater depth.

Designers should be alert to the precise wording of the reliability requirements portion of the product specification:

1. For a time-oriented performance, a statement of product reliability purely in percentage is meaningless. For example, a reliability is specified as 95 percent. However, the buyer has in mind mission times of 1.5 h whereas the supplier has in mind mission times of 1.1 h.

2. In some cases, specifications have included a confidence level; e.g., "The MTBF shall be at least 100 h at the 90 percent confidence level." This means that the meantime between failures (MTBF) shall be at least 100 h and *that tests shall be conducted* and analyzed to show that the lower one-sided 90 percent confidence limit is at least 100 h. In such cases, the MTBF needed to meet the demonstration requirement may be many times the MTBF number specified. For further discussion, see Section 23 under Statistical Estimation.

A further critical wording is the definition of what constitutes a failure. This definition can readily be decisive as to whether the product meets the test. It is important to determine and specify any exceptions to the failure definition early, particularly with respect to periodic maintenance, e.g., replacement prior to wearout. In consumer products, the definition of failure is critical to the provisions of the warranty; e.g., was the product serviced in accordance with the provisions of the service manual? [MIL-STD-721C (1981) defines eight types of failures: catastrophic, critical, dependent, independent, intermittent, nonchargeable, nonrelevant, and random.]

Apportionment of Reliability.　This phase of quantification is illustrated in the top two sections of Table 13.6.

In the top section of the table, an overall reliability requirement of 95 percent for 1.45 h is apportioned to the six subsystems of a missile. The second section of the table apportions the budget for the explosive subsystem to the three units within the subsystem. The allocation for the fusing circuitry is 0.998 or, in terms of mean time between failures, 725 h.

Apportionment combines engineering judgment with knowledge of (1) the interrelationships of various subsystems (i.e., is everything in series or are there some redundant elements?), (2) reliability experience of subsystems used on previous products, (3) relative complexity of subsystems, and (4) relative criticality of subsystems. The apportionment process provides numerical objectives for each portion of the design. Kapur and Lamberson (1977) discuss five methods of reliability apportionment.

Reliability Prediction and Analysis.　Inherent in the establishment of reliability requirements is the need to estimate or predict reliability in advance of manufacturing the product. This prediction is a continuing process which takes place at several stages of the progression from design through usage. (See Table 13.7.) At the outset the predictions are "on paper," based on design information, e.g., number of components, plus past failure rate experience. In the final stages, the predictions become measurement based on data from field use of the product.

While the visible result of the prediction procedure is to quantify the reliability numbers, the process of prediction is usually as important as the resulting numbers. This is so because the prediction cannot be made without obtaining rather detailed information on product missions, environments, critical component his-

TABLE 13.6 Establishment of Reliability Objectives

System breakdown

Subsystem	Type of operation	Reliability	Unre-liability	Failure rate per hour	Reliability objective*
Air frame	Continuous	0.997	0.003	0.0021	483
Rocket motor	One-shot	0.995	0.005		1/200 operations
Transmitter	Continuous	0.982	0.018	0.0126	80.5 h
Receiver	Continuous	0.988	0.012	0.0084	121 h
Control system	Continuous	0.993	0.007	0.0049	207 h
Explosive system	One-shot	0.995	0.005		1/200 operations
System		0.95	0.05		

Explosive subsystem breakdown

Unit	Operating mode	Reliability	Unreliability	Reliability objective
Fusing circuitry	Continuous	0.998	0.002	725 h
Safety and arming mechanism	One-shot	0.999	0.001	1/1000 operations
Warhead	One-shot	0.998	0.022	2/1000
Explosive subsystem		0.995	0.005	

Unit breakdown

Fusing circuitry component part classification	Number used, n	Failure rate per part, λ, %/1000 h	Total part failure rate, $n\lambda$, %/1000 h
Transistors	93	0.30	27.90
Diodes	87	0.15	13.05
Film resistors	112	0.04	4.48
Wirewound resistors	29	0.20	5.80
Paper capacitors	63	0.04	2.52
Tantalum capacitors	17	0.50	8.50
Transformers	13	0.20	2.60
Inductors	11	0.14	1.54
Solder joints and wires	512	0.01	5.12
			71.51

$$\text{MTBF} = \frac{1}{\text{failure rate}} = \frac{1}{\Sigma \, n\lambda} = \frac{1}{0.0007151} = 1398 \text{ h}$$

Source: Adapted by F. M. Gryna from G. N. Beaton (1959). "Putting the R&D Reliability Dollar to Work." *Proceedings of the Fifth National Symposium on Reliability and Quality Control.* IEEE, New York, p. 65.
*For a mission time of 1.45 h.

TABLE 13.7 Stages of Reliability Analysis and Prediction*

	1 Start of design	2 During detailed design	3 At final design	4 From system tests	5 From customer usage
Basis	Prediction based on approximate part counts and part failure rates from previous product usage; little knowledge of stress levels, redundancy, etc.	Prediction based on quantities and types of parts, redundancies, stress levels, etc.	Prediction based on types and quantities of parts failure rates for expected stress levels, redundancies, external environments, special maintenance practices, special effects of system complexity, cycling effects, etc.	Measurement based on the results of tests of the complete system. Approximate reliability indexes are calculated from the number of failures and operating time	Same as step 4 except calculations are based on customer usage data
Primary uses	*a.* Evaluate feasibility of meeting a proposed numerical requirement *b.* Help in establishing a reliability goal for design	*a.* Evaluate overall reliability *b.* Define problem areas	*a.* Evaluate reliability *b.* Define problem areas	*a.* Evaluate overall reliability *b.* Define problem areas	*a.* Measure achieved reliability *b.* Define problem areas *c.* Obtain data for future designs

*Note: System tests in steps 4 and/or 5 may reveal problems that result in a revision of the "final" design. Such changes can be evaluated by repeating steps 3 to 5.
Source: From Juran, J. M. and Gryna, F. M. (1980). *Quality Planning and Analysis*, 2nd ed. McGraw-Hill, New York. p. 179.

tories, etc. Acquiring this information often gives the designer knowledge previously not available. Even if the designer is unable to secure the needed information, this inability nevertheless identifies the areas of ignorance in which the designer is forced to work.

The following steps make up a reliability prediction method which analyzes the design as well as arriving at the reliability numbers (ARINC, 1962):

1. Define the product. The system, subsystems, and units must be precisely defined in terms of their functional configurations and boundaries. This precise definition is aided by preparation of a functional block diagram (Figure 13.4) which shows the subsystems and lower-level products, their interrelation, and the interfaces with other systems. For large systems it may be necessary to prepare block diagrams for several levels of the product hierarchy.

Given a functional block diagram and a well-defined statement of the functional requirements of the product, the conditions which constitute failure or unsatisfactory performance can be defined. The functional block diagram also makes it easier to define the boundaries of each unit and to assure that important items are neither neglected nor considered more than once. For example, a switch used to connect two units must be classified as belonging to one or the other (or as a separate unit).

2. Draw a reliability block diagram. The reliability block diagram (Figure 13.5) is similar to the functional block diagram, but it is modified to emphasize those aspects which influence reliability. The diagram shows, in sequence, those elements which must function for successful operation of each unit. Redundant paths and alternative modes should be clearly shown. Elements which are not essential to successful operation need not be included, e.g., decorative escutcheons. Also, because of the many thousands of individual parts that constitute a complex product, it is necessary to exclude from the calculation those classes of parts which are used in mild applications. The contribution of such parts to product unreliability is relatively small. Examples of items that can generally be disregarded are terminal strips, knobs, chassis, and panels.

3. List factors relevant to reliability. For each critical part, it is necessary to list all factors which are relevant to reliability. These factors include part function, part ratings, internal environments and stresses, expected external environments and stresses, and duty ("on" time) cycle. This detailed information makes it possible to perform a stress analysis which will not only provide information on the appropriate adjustments to standard input data but also serve to uncover weak or questionable areas in the design. Parts with dependent failure probabilities should be grouped together into modules so that the assumptions upon which the prediction is based are satisfied.

4. Select part reliability data. The required part data consist of information on catastrophic failures and on tolerance variations with respect to time under known operating and environmental conditions. Acquiring these data is a major problem for the designer, since there is no single reliability data bank comparable to handbooks such as those which are available for physical properties of materials. Instead, the designer (or supporting technical staff) must either build up a data bank or use reliability data secured from a variety of sources:

Field performance studies conducted under controlled conditions

Specification life tests

Data from parts manufacturers or industry associations

Customers' part-qualification and inspection tests

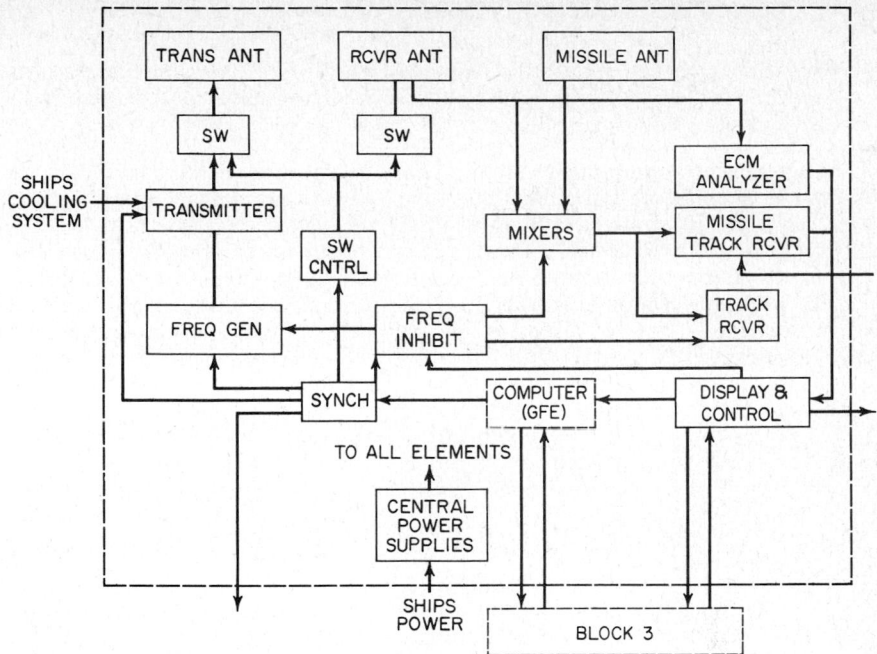

FIG. 13.4 Functional block diagram. *(From Handbook of Reliability Engineering, NAVAIR 00-65-502, courtesy the Commander, Naval Air Systems Command.)*

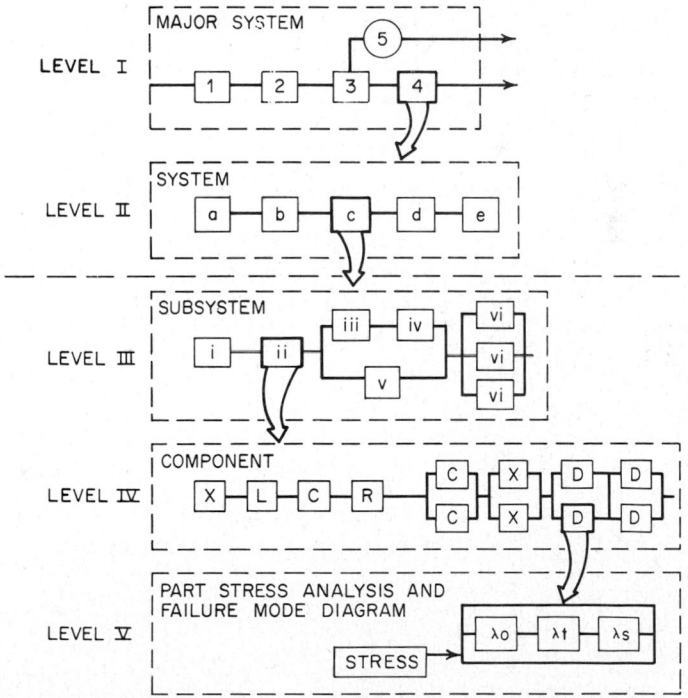

FIG. 13.5 Reliability block diagram. *(From Handbook of Reliability Engineering, NAVAIR 00-65-502, courtesy the Commander, Naval Air Systems Command.)*

Government agency data banks such as MIL-HDBK-217D, which contains a large amount of failure-rate data together with stress analysis procedures essential to its use

5. Determine appropriate reliability relationships for each part, part class, or module in the product. Basic reliability data such as are acquired in step 4 are in the form of curves or tables (e.g., Table 13.8) which show the relationship of reliability to various stress levels, e.g., failure rates versus temperature (T) under various ratios of operating to rated electrical stress (S). Applying these tables to the specific units, applications, and environments provides the reliability numbers which become the basis of summing up failure rates in step 6, below.

In the absence of basic reliability data, it may be feasible to make reasonably

TABLE 13.8 Base Failure Rates, λ_b, Related to Temperature T and Stress S

MIL-S-19500 transistors, group III, unijunction, in failures per 10^6 h

T, °C	.1	.2	.3	.4	.5	.6	.7	.8	.9	1.0
					S					
0	.0064	.0088	.011	.015	.019	.024	.031	.039	.052	.073
10	.0079	.010	.013	.017	.022	.028	.036	.047	.064	.095
20	.0097	.012	.016	.020	.026	.033	.043	.058	.083	.13
25	.010	.013	.017	.022	.028	.036	.047	.064	.095	.15
30	.011	.015	.019	.024	.031	.039	.052	.073	.11	
40	.013	.017	.022	.028	.036	.047	.064	.095	.15	
50	.016	.020	.026	.033	.043	.058	.083	.13		
55	.017	.022	.028	.036	.047	.064	.095	.15		
60	.019	.024	.031	.039	.052	.073	.11			
65	.020	.026	.033	.043	.058	.083	.13			
70	.022	.028	.036	.047	.064	.095	.15			
75	.024	.031	.039	.052	.073	.11				
80	.026	.033	.043	.058	.083	.13				
85	.028	.036	.047	.064	.095	.15				
90	.031	.039	.052	.073	.11					
95	.033	.043	.058	.083	.13					
100	.036	.047	.064	.095	.15					
105	.039	.052	.073	.11						
110	.043	.058	.083	.13						
115	.047	.064	.095	.15						
120	.052	.073	.11							
125	.058	.083	.13							
130	.064	.095	.15							
135	.073	.11								
140	.083	.13								
145	.095	.15								
150	.11									
155	.13									
160	.15									

Source: MIL-HDBK-217D (1982), p. 5.1.3.3-2.

accurate estimates based on past experience with similar part types. Lacking such experience, it becomes necessary to perform part evaluation tests to secure the data.

6. Determine block and unit failure rates. The failure data of step 5 are added up to obtain failure rates for higher-level product units. (See Table 13.6 and associated discussion.) Pertinent subsystem or assembly correction factors, such as those taking into account the effects of maintenance, can be applied at this point. Block and unit rates are in turn combined to give subsystem and system failure rates.

7. Determine the appropriate reliability unit of measure. This is the choice of reliability index or "figure of merit" as listed in Table 13.5, e.g., MTBF and failure rate.

8. Apply the resulting predictions. The predictions not only indicate the expected reliability of the product, but also point up the weak areas, the extent of improvement needed, and likely opportunities for securing improvement.

An example of a reliability prediction is given in the bottom portion of Table 13.6. In this case, all parts are critical for operation of the fusing circuitry so the failure rates are added up to yield a prediction of the overall failure rate. The reciprocal of the failure is then calculated to yield a mean time between failures of about 1400 h. The 1400 h is greater than the apportionment of 725 h, and the proposed design is therefore acceptable. The prediction technique provides a quantitative evaluation of a design and also identifies design areas having the largest potential for reliability improvement. In this example, the transistors, diodes, and tantalum capacitors account for about 70 percent of the total failure rate.

Reliability predictions and reliability analyses are more effective by making use of software. Such software not only handles the detailed calculations but makes it feasible to identify and assess many alternatives before finalizing a design. The "Directory of Software" published periodically in *Quality Progress* includes a description of software for reliability.

Parts Selection and Control.   Table 13.6 illustrates how system reliability rests on a base of reliability of the component parts.

The vital role played by part reliability has resulted in programs for thorough selection, evaluation, and control of parts. These programs include mainly:

1. *Parts application study:*   The specification and design information supplied by parts manufacturers generally provides guidelines for application. If previous history is available from parts used in similar products, this history becomes an essential input. New applications must be subjected to qualification tests, including overstress, to determine safety factors. The analyses include derating (see below), stress analysis, thermal analysis, and other forms appropriate to each product.

2. *Approved parts list:*   Preliminary component-parts lists are reviewed as early in the design phase as possible to:

Verify that proved parts (i.e., proved in previous usage) are being utilized wherever possible

Verify that unproved or questionable parts are actually capable of meeting reliability or environmental ratings

Compare ratings or qualification test data with anticipated environmental (life) stresses

3. *Critical components list:* A component part is considered "critical" if any of the following conditions apply:

It has a high population in the equipment.

It has a single source of supply.

It must function to special, tight limits.

It has not been proved to the reliability standard, i.e., no test data, insufficient usage data.

The critical components list should be prepared early in the design effort. It is common practice to formalize these lists, showing, for each critical component, the nature of the critical features, the plan to quantify reliability, the plan for improving reliability, etc. The list becomes the basic planning document for (*a*) test programs to qualify parts, (*b*) design guidance in application studies and techniques, and (*c*) design guidance for application of redundant parts, circuits, or subsystems.

4. *Derating practice:* Derating is the assignment of a product to operate at stress levels below its normal rating; e.g., a capacitor rated at 300 V is used in a 200-V application. For many components, data are available showing failure rate as a function of stress levels. The conservative designer will use such data to achieve reliability by using the parts at low power ratios and low ambient temperatures.

Some companies have established internal policies with respect to derating. Derating is a form of quantifying the factor of safety and hence lends itself to setting guidelines as to the margins to be used. Derating may be considered as a method of determining more scientifically the factor of safety which engineers have long provided on an empirical basis. For example, if the calculated load was 20 tons, the engineers might design the structure to withstand 100 tons as a protection against unanticipated loads, misuse, hidden flaws, deterioration, etc.

Failure Mode, Effect, and Criticality Analysis; Fault Tree Analysis.   These techniques provide a methodical way to examine a proposed design for possible ways in which failure can occur. In the failure mode, effect, and criticality analysis (FMECA), potential failures are first identified in terms of failure modes. For each mode, the effect on the total system is then studied. Finally, a review is made of the action being taken (or planned) to minimize the probability of failure or to minimize the effect of failure. Figure 13.6 shows a portion of an FMECA for a traveling lawn sprinkler. Each hardware item is listed on a separate line. Note that the failure "mode" is the symptom of the failure, as distinct from the cause of failure, which consists of the proved reasons for the existence of the symptoms. A generalization of the FMECA form is provided in Figure 13.7 (Bajaria, 1983). Dussault (1984) discusses the basic technique (and variations) with a focus on a computerized approach.

Various approaches are used to show the criticality of the failure modes. In Figure 13.7, a risk priority number is calculated as the product of ratings on frequency of occurrence, severity, and likelihood of detection. The risk priority number establishes priorities for further investigations of different failure modes. MIL-STD-1629A (1980) provides a more precise quantification of criticality using data on the probability of mission loss due to the failure mode, the part failure rate, the ratio that a particular failure mode has of the total part failure rate, and the duration of the applicable mission phase.

1 = Very low (<1 in 1000)
2 = Low (3 in 1000)
3 = Medium (5 in 1000)
4 = High (7 in 1000)
5 = Very high (>9 in 1000)

T = Type of failure
P = Probability of occurrence
S = Seriousness of failure to system
H = Hydraulic failure
M = Mechanical failure
W = Wear failure
C = Customer abuse

Product	HRC-1
Date	Jan. 14, 1987
By	S.M.

Component part number	Possible failure	Cause of failure	T	P	S	Effect of failure on product	Alternatives
Worm bearing 4224	Bearing worn	Not aligned with bottom housing	M	1	4	Spray head wobble or slowing down	Improve inspection
Zytel 101		Excessive spray head wobble	M	1	3	DITTO	Improve worm bearing
Bearing stem 4225	Excessive wear	Poor bearing/ material combination	M	5	4	Spray head wobbles and loses power	Change stem material
Brass		Dirty water in bearing area	M	5	4	DITTO	Improve worm seal area
		Excessive spray head wobble	M	2	3	DITTO	Improve operating instructions
Thrust washer 4226	Excessive wear	High water pressure	M	2	5	Spray head will stall out	Inform customer in instructions
Fulton 404		Dirty water in washers	M	5	5	DITTO	Improve worm seal design
Worm 4527	Excessive wear in bearing area	Poor bearing/ material combination	M	5	4	Spray head wobbles and loses power	Change bearing stem material
Brass		Dirty water in bearing area	M	5	4	DITTO	Improve worm seal design
		Excessive spray head wobble	M	2	3	DITTO	Improve operating instructions

FIG. 13.6   Failure mode, effect, and criticality analysis.

Block diagrams which illustrate the operation, interrelationships, and inter-dependencies of functional parts to the system are a useful adjunct to the failure mode, effect, and criticality analysis. These diagrams provide the ability for tracing failure mode-effects throughout all levels of the equipment. Both functional and reliability block diagrams are required to show the functional flow sequence and the series dependence or independence of functions and operations. Raheja (1981) provides examples showing the value of block diagrams in these analyses.

The FMECA can be elaborated to include effects of other matters such as safety, downtime, access to hardware items, maintenance planning, and inspection planning.

Fault tree analysis is another method of studying the potential failures in a system. A fault tree analysis differs from failure mode, effect, and criticality analysis in three respects. First, fault tree analysis studies only those negative outcomes of a product that are considered serious enough to warrant further analysis; FMECA studies all potential modes of failures. Second, the fault tree analysis can analyze situations in which the negative event will not occur unless several sub-events first occur. Third, the fault tree analysis does a more explicit job of showing the relationships between events that have an interaction with each other.

In fault tree analysis, the starting point is the list of failure modes (or other undesired events) for which the designer must provide some solution. Each event on the list then becomes a failure mode requiring analysis. The analysis considers

Failure Mode and Effects Analysis

(1) Item _____   (2) Analysis Engineer

_____

Date

_____

(3) Function _____

_____

Mode of Failure	Mechanism and Cause of Failure	Effects of Failure	Frequency of Occurrence 1-10	Degree of Severity 1-10	Chance of Direction 1-10
(4)	(5)	(6)	(7)	(8)	(9)

Risk Priority Number 1-1000	Design Action	Design Validation
(10) = (7) × (8) × (9)	(11)	(12)

Failure Mode and Effects Analysis Form Entry Explanation —

1. Item — Item to which analysis applies.

2. Analysis Engineer — an engineer in charge of design project.

3. Function — Function of the item as user perceives it. This description should be as broad as possible.

4. Mode of Failure — A mode in which the item will fail as perceived by user.

5. Mechanism and Cause of Failure — What caused failure to occur?

6. Effects of Failure — What effects this failure will have on the user or nearby person or nearby property?

7. Frequency of Occurrence (1-10) — How often is this failure expected to occur? This column is subjectively rated on 1 to 10 basis.
 1 — Rare occurrence
 10 — Almost certain occurrence

8. Degree of Severity (1-10) — How severe is the effect of this failure on the user or anything else? This column is subjectively rated on 1 to 10 basis.
 1 — Insignificant loss to user
 10 — Product inoperable or major replacement cost or safety hazard

9. Degree of Detection (1-10) — Can problem be detected by the user before it does the damage? This column too is subjectively rated on 1 to 10 basis.

 1 — Certain detection before failure
 10 — No detection possible before failure

10. Risk Priority Number (1-1000) — Order of problem-solving priority is given by multiplying numbers in columns 7, 8, and 9.

11. Design Action — Action to reduce risk priority number.

12. Design Validation — Method to verify the design motion.

FIG. 13.7 Generalized failure mode, effect, and criticality analysis.

the possible direct causes that could lead to the event. Next, it looks for the origins of these causes. Finally, it looks for ways to avoid these origins and causes. The branching out of origins and causes is what gives the technique the name "fault tree" analysis. The approach is the reverse of failure mode, effect, and criticality analysis, which starts with origins and causes and looks for any resulting bad effects. Fault tree analysis can be useful in studying potential failures for reliability analysis and also potential failures that result in damages or injuries. An example of fault tree analysis will be presented later in this section under Planning for Safety.

Other Analysis Techniques.   Other techniques have been developed to aid in analyzing product effectiveness during design. The *Transactions on Reliability* of the Institute of Electrical and Electronics Engineers is a good source of information on such techniques. Two of these techniques, worst-case analysis and sneak-circuit analysis, will be mentioned here.

The "worst-case" analysis technique is a detailed electrical analysis often made in conjunction with computer programs. The purpose is to verify the ability of the circuits to perform in an acceptable manner under all anticipated extremes of electrical and physical environments and in the presence of degradation of parts with time and environment. The worst-case approach can be used either by taking all absolute values of the parameters in their extreme condition or by using a probabilistic approach which studies the outcomes for highly probable combinations of parameter values. MIL-STD-785B (1980) provides further discussion.

Another technique is called "sneak-circuit analysis." This is usually a computer-aided technique used to identify latent paths in a circuit which could cause occurrence of unwanted functions or could result in desired functions being inhibited even though all components are functioning properly. In contrast to other analysis techniques, it is not based on failed items. A further description is given in MIL-STD-785B (1980).

The broad area of computer-aided design (CAD) makes use of computers to translate a product's specific requirements into the final physical product. Thus it is useful in doing much of the detailed design and analysis work. Computer-aided design makes it possible for the designer to consider many alternative designs and then select the one that comes closest to having the optimum values. Although this could be done without the use of computers, the time required would be prohibitive. Computer-aided design is now being extended to reliability and other fitness-for-use parameters:

Reliability: Thermal design of equipment for improved reliability at lower operating temperatures (Berger and Jenkins, 1984)

Maintainability: Graphical analysis of work positions, reach, and other human requirements associated with a design (Cahill and Davids, 1984)

Testability: Analysis of overall testing requirements to integrate test planning during the design process (Fennell and Nicolino, 1984)

Mitsuya (1977) discusses the application of an automatic designing and drawing system using a computer and drafting machine for the design of elevator equipment. The application reported improvements in quality due to the standardization of drawings and elimination of mistakes by means of computer checking.

Evaluating Designs by Tests.   Although reliability prediction, design review, failure mode, effect, and criticality analysis, and other techniques are valuable as early warning devices, they cannot be a substitute for the ultimate proof, i.e., use of the product by the customer. However, field experience comes too late and must be preceded by a substitute—various forms of testing the product to simulate field use. A summary of types of tests for evaluating a design is given in Table 13.9. Sometimes, a number of tests can be integrated so that one type of test can serve several purposes, e.g., evaluation of both performance and environmental capabilities. Brach and Phaller (1980) describe how an electronics manufacturer reviewed the test programs on a variety of projects and developed an integrated test philosophy (Table 13.10). Stevens (1978) discusses the planning and execution of integrated test programs under operational conditions.

TABLE 13.9 Summary of Tests Used to Evaluate a Design

Type of test	Purpose
Performance	Determine ability of product to meet basic performance requirements
Environmental	Evaluate ability of product to withstand defined environmental levels; determine internal environments generated by product operation; verify environmental levels specified
Stress	Determine levels of stress that a product can withstand in order to determine the safety margin inherent in the design; determine modes of failure that are not associated with time
Reliability	Determine product reliability and compare to requirements; monitor for trends
Maintainability	Determine time required to make repairs and compare to requirements
Life	Determine wear-out time for a product, and failure modes associated with time or operating cycles
Pilot run	Determine if fabrication and assembly processes are capable of meeting design requirements; determine if reliability will be degraded.

Some Problems in Testing.   A widely used form of early warning is through construction and test of product models. The model may be a single mechanical or electrical product unit (or part thereof). It may be chemical in nature—all the way from the test tube level to the pilot plant. The test may be a simulation in the laboratory or a large-scale trial lot sent out for field use. All such cases provide some degree of design assurance. They also involve a risk of being led astray. The principal sources of this risk are as follows:

   1. *Intended use versus actual use:*   The designer typically aims to attain fitness for intended use. However, actual use can differ from the designer's concept due to variations in environments and other conditions of use. In addition some users will misapply or misuse the product.

   The solution is for the designer to understand what will be the actual conditions of use and misuse. Field visits will provide this understanding. Alternatively, the design can be reviewed by someone who does have direct knowledge of conditions of use.

   2. *Model construction versus subsequent production:*   Models are usually built by skilled specialists under the supervision of the designers. The subsequent production is carried out by less skilled factory workers under supervisors who must meet standards of productivity as well as quality. In addition, the factory processes seldom possess the adaptive flexibility available in the model shop.

   As before, the solution is for the designer to have enough direct knowledge of the factory conditions and processes to understand how they correlate with model shop conditions. The alternative is for the design to be reviewed by people who do have such understanding.

   3. *Variability due to small numbers:*   The number of models built is usually small. (Often there is only one.) Yet tests on these small numbers are used to judge the adequacy of the design for making many production units, sometimes running into the thousands and even millions.

   The need here is for the designer to understand the extent to which test results on small numbers of models can be relied on to predict the performance of the

TABLE 13.10 Typical Test Program

Test program	Test level*	Purpose	Environment*	Typical test hours
Engineering development tests	SRU/LRU	1. Design verification 2. Design feasibility 3. Overstress test 4. Exploratory environmental tests	Temp. cycle Humidity Vibration	500–1500
	System	1. LRU integration 2. Pre-qual. env. tests 3. Software evaluation 4. System performance verification 5. Maintainability design verification	Temp. cycle Humidity Vibration Lab-bench	1000–3000 ±
Formal environmental qualification	LRU/system	1. Verify design integrity under specified environmental conditions 2. Test for endurance limits of hardware	Temp./alt. Humidity Vibration Salt-fog Dust/sand EMI/EMC Explosive atmosphere	200–300
Preproduction and production tests	SRU/LRU/ system	1. In-line environmental test for quality reliability control 2. Burn-in 3. Acceptance test	Temp. cycle Vibration Bench-lab	1. 25–50 h/syst. 2. Depends on level 3. 10–50 h/syst.
Reliability tests	LRU/system	1. Growth-induced failures caused by wear, design, quality, and workmanship	Temp. cycle Vibration (CERT)	1000 up—depends on program
		2. Qualification-reliability demonstration for spec. compliance	Temp. cycle Vibration MIL-STD-781	Depends on MTBF—test plan, etc.
		3. Acceptance—sample test	Temp. cycle Vibration (CERT) MIL-STD-781	Depends on MTBF—test plan, etc.
		4. Assurance—all equipments test—PRVT	Temp. cycle Vibration (CERT) MIL-STD-781	20–50 h/syst.
Flight test	System	1. Aircraft/system integration 2. Initial R/M assessment 3. Engineering measurement	Aircraft operating environment	100–300

Note: SRU = shop replaceable unit; LRU = line replaceable unit; EMI = electromagnetic interference; EMC = electromagnetic compatibility; CERT = combined environment reliability test; PRVT = production reliability verification test.
Source: Brach and Phaller, 1980, p. 243.

more numerous production units. This understanding is best derived from statistical quantification of the respective variations and of the "confidence limits" which apply to the numbers of models tested. If the designer is not personally knowledgeable in such matters, the alternative is to enlist the assistance of specialists who do have such knowledge (usually the quality engineers).

4. *Evaluation of test results:* Pressures to release a design for production can result in test plans and evaluations that do not objectively evaluate conformance to performance requirements (let alone complete fitness for use). One organization studied the process of qualifying a new design by having an independent review team analyze a sample of "qualification test" results on designs that had been approved for release. Two conclusions were:

a. Pressures to release designs caused design approvals that later resulted in field problems. The situation was traced to (*i*) inadequate initial testing or (*ii*) lack of verification of design changes made to correct failures that surfaced on the initial test.

b. Over 50 percent of the approved test results were rejected because the *test procedure* was unable to evaluate the requirements set by Product Development.

Stern action was taken. All test procedures and test results were submitted to a group independent of Product Development for approval.

Reliability Tests.   MIL-STD-785B (1980) identifies four areas of testing:

1. *Environmental stress screening:*   These are tests conducted at lower levels of the product to identify early failures due to weak parts, workmanship defects, and other reasons for nonconformance. Environmental stress tests can also be combined with life testing to help identify weak points in new designs. Bailey and Gilbert (1982) describe a program that combines both stress and life testing.

2. *Reliability development/growth tests:*   This testing is performed before the final release of the design to improve product reliability through the identification, analysis, and correction of failures and the verification of the corrective action.

3. *Reliability qualification tests:*   These tests are conducted on product which is representative of the approved production configuration. The tests provide assurance that the production articles will meet the formal reliability requirements.

4. *Production reliability acceptance tests:*   These tests provide periodic evaluations of reliability of production hardware, particularly when any changes have been made in design, tooling, processes, parts, or other characteristics. MIL-STD-781C (1981) is used as the basis of planning the tests.

Tests for reliability focus on three elements: performance requirements, environmental conditions during use, and time requirements.

Performance requirements are defined uniquely for each product, e.g., the kilowatt output of a generator. During the performance, the product is subjected to stresses, and these stresses vary (e.g., a tractor works in sandy soil on one day and in rocky soil the next day). Hence stress must be viewed as a distribution rather than as a single value. Similarly, strength varies from one unit of product to the next and hence must also be viewed as a distribution. Obtaining the data needed to construct these distributions can be so costly that shortcuts have to be taken, e.g., sampling actual use of the product by typical customers. An alternative is to simulate customer use, e.g., in the company "proving ground." The resulting data disclose the stress levels being encountered. Tests must then be conducted to verify that the product can withstand the expected stress levels for the required time period.

Environmental conditions (e.g., temperature, humidity, vibration) are critical to many products. Here again, the problem is twofold: (a) discovering the expected environmental levels and (b) testing to verify that the product can meet them. By skillful design of test programs, it may be feasible to meet both of these needs simultaneously.

Time requirements are the third element of reliability testing. Testing one item of product to failure, then repairing it and testing again to failure, through several cycles, may provide good information on that particular item. It may also provide useful data on product wear-out, but it will not necessarily reveal the variability that occurs among many items of the same product due to part and production variability. However, testing many items of product for a shorter period of time will produce test data and failure data which do show many effects of part and production variability. Bringing these test data to a state of statistical significance may result in cost problems with both test facilities and "appraisal." In addition, such testing is not necessarily complete; it may still fail to disclose critical early wear-out characteristics of the product.

Interpretation of time-oriented test data is aided greatly by use of the Weibull form of data plotting. (See Section 23 under Predictions with Weibull Distributions.) These plots usually approximate a straight line and simplify the extrapolation process. They are also useful for comparing the results of accelerated testing (see below) with results of testing under normal operating conditions. *This tool is a "must" for the designer.*

Accelerated testing is a common form of securing reliability test data at reduced testing cost. In this form of testing, the products are made to perform at abnormally high levels of stress and/or environments in order to make them fail sooner. (Earlier failures mean less test equipment, lower testing costs, and earlier answers.) Extrapolation is then used to convert the short life under severe conditions into the expected life under normal conditions. Great care is needed to assure that the accelerated test time is properly correlated to normal use time to avoid overstating the expected life. A further problem is that accelerated testing can introduce new failure modes which do not occur during normal product use. Taking such failure modes seriously has sometimes led to major redesigns which provided no benefit from the standpoint of the original product requirements. While the benefits from accelerated testing can be substantial, there are serious risks of being misled. It is obviously essential to apply engineering judgment in such tests.

The accelerated-testing concept can be combined with probability-paper analysis to relate test results with field results. Stanton (1974) describes how this was done for two models of room air conditioners. The field data and data from accelerated tests were plotted on Weibull probability paper as shown in Figure 13.8. As the lines were essentially parallel, it was concluded that the basic mode of failure was the same on the test as in the field. In Figure 13.8 the field data are plotted in *years* of service. The test data are plotted in *tens of days.* The 5-year warranty period is represented by a heavy vertical line. If one follows this line to the point where it intersects the field data line and then horizontally from the field data line to the lines for the accelerated test data, the accelerated time equivalent

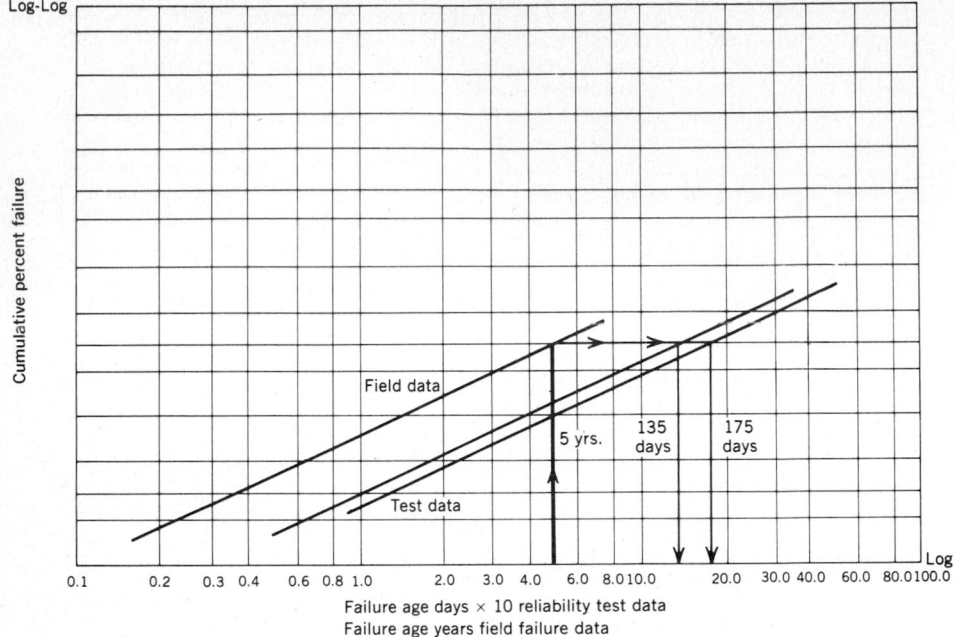

FIG. 13.8 Superposed plot of field failure data over test data for two air conditioner models.

to the 5-year period can be read. For example, on one model the cumulative per-cent failed in 135 days of accelerated testing is equivalent to 5 years of field use. On the other model, the equivalent accelerated test time is 175 days.

Behind all testing is detailed test planning that includes the identification of the key characteristics for testing; deciding on the level of test in terms of going to specification limits or beyond; planning the environment for the test; planning the statistical aspects of the test including sample sizes and other matters; and making provisions for control of the test methods including equipment, calibra-tion, documentation, action in case of failures, and other matters. Stevens (1978) discusses the overall planning of test programs.

Section 23 of this handbook provides the basic tools of statistical methods and Section 26 provides a discussion of the statistical aspects of planning experiments and tests. Nelson (1982) discusses the statistical analysis of life testing. Frank (1982) provides guidelines on maintaining documentation of test data.

Reliability Data Systems.   Reliability data serve several important purposes:

1. To detect current reliability problems and assist in their solution. An example is the use of the data feedback loop shown in Figure 13.9. This loop operates in the conventional way: Failures are detected and reported, analyses are made for causes, remedies are devised and applied.

2. To provide managers with quantitative information on product performance and on the status of problems. This feedback should not be limited to infor-mation on current problems; it should include also summaries in the form of executive reports, as discussed in Section 8 under Executive Reports on Quality.

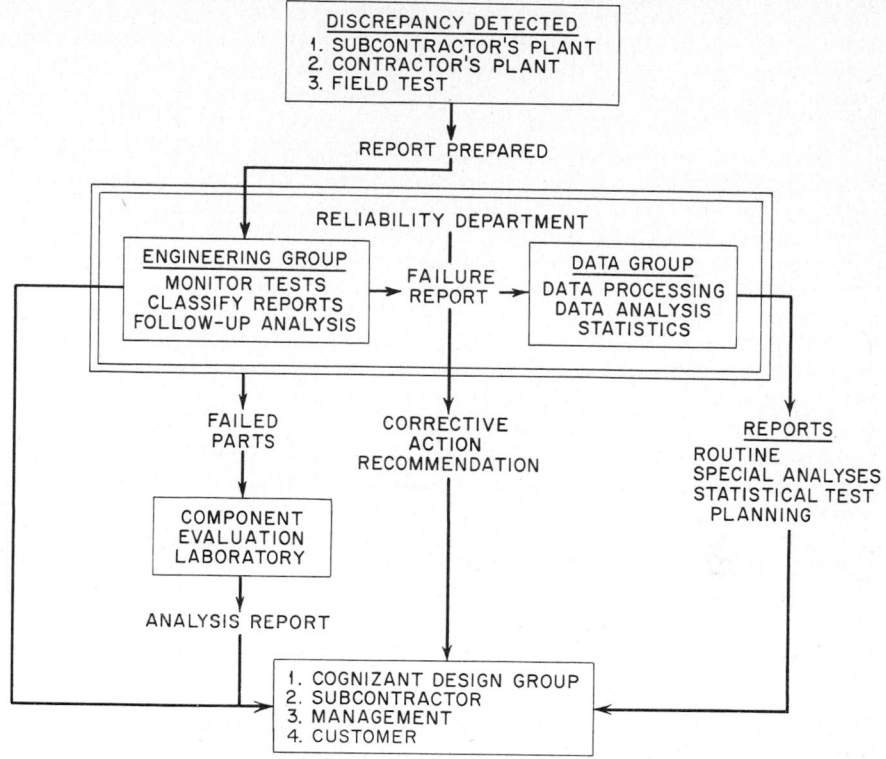

FIG. 13.9 Failure reporting, analysis, and feedback.

3. To assist in reliability improvement programs. (See below, under Reliability Improvement.)

4. To provide failure history and other reference data for use in product changes and in future products. This is the "data bank" concept. It serves the needs of reliability in a manner analogous to that served by handbooks of properties of materials (when one is choosing materials for specific applications).

Reliability Data Banks. The term "data bank" implies an organized approach to data collection, classification, analysis, summary, and retrieval. Despite the seeming advantages of such an organized approach, it is difficult and costly to execute. In practice, companies make only limited use of the available data. These data originate from:

1. *Engineering, preproduction, production, or special tests (e.g., test track, test kitchen) under the manufacturer's control:* These tests are usually conducted on the premises, but may include "captive" usage tests, e.g., employee homes, consumer panels, captive sales outlets.

2. *Suppliers and major subcontractors:* Increasingly these companies are organizing their test data in forms which can be readily used by their customers for product design purposes.

3. *Field performance data, including customer returns:* While these data have an obvious dramatic effect on practical people, they are suspect in many ways: the sources of the data are notoriously difficult to control; the data are frequently incomplete and of dubious validity; coverage (e.g., the spectrum of environments) is incomplete. For a more extensive discussion, see Section 20 under Quality Complaints: General.

4. *Independent data banks:* These are springing up in recognition of the fact that basic failure data can be used by many companies. For such multiple use, it may be more economic to maintain a central data bank instead of numerous duplicating company data banks. (See below under Public data banks.) In addition, there are laboratories devoted mainly to testing products for safety, and these laboratories develop test data which have wide application.

Acquisition of data is only the first step in creating a working data bank. There must be summaries to permit evaluation of trends and identification of the more important problems. Then the data must be analyzed to assist specialists in finding causes and remedies. See Section 22 under Diagnosis.

5. *Public data banks:* An example is the Government Industry Data Exchange Program (GIDEP), a cooperative activity between the U.S. government and industry. The program provides a means of exchanging technical data in the area of research, design, development, production, and the operational phases of various products. Management and funding of the program is handled by the U.S. government. Participants in the program are expected to contribute information from their own company to the data bank. This then entitles them to access all of the information in the data bank. Participants in GIDEP are presently provided access to four major data interchanges: engineering, reliability-maintainability, metrology, and failure experience.

Special GIDEP services include a system for notifying participants of problem areas (ALERT System); a system which allows a GIDEP participant to query all other GIDEP participants on specific problems (the urgent data request or UDR System); a system for providing rapid responses to participants on queries related to test equipment and measurement (this is the Metrology Information Service, or MIS). Arnitz (1981) provides a description of the GIDEP program. Herrold (1976) discusses the application of GIDEP data to solving reliability problems.

Reliability Improvement. The general approach to quality improvement (Section 22, Quality Improvement) is widely applicable to reliability improvement as far as the economic analysis and the managerial tools are concerned. The differences are in the technological tools used for diagnosis and remedy. Projects can be identified through reliability prediction, design review, failure mode, effect and criticality analysis, and other reliability evaluation techniques.

Action to improve reliability during the design phase is best taken by the designer. The reliability engineer can help by defining areas needing improvement and by assisting in the development of alternatives. The following actions indicate some approaches to improving a design:

1. Review the users' needs to see if the function of the unreliable parts is really necessary to the user. If not, eliminate those parts from the design. Alternatively, look to see if the reliability index (figure of merit) correctly reflects the real needs of the user. For example, availability (see below) is sometimes more meaningful than reliability. If so, a good maintenance program might improve availability and hence ease the reliability problem.

2. Consider trade-offs of reliability for other parameters, e.g., functional performance, or weight. Here again it may be found that the customers' real needs may be better served by such a trade-off.

3. Use redundancy to provide more than one means for accomplishing a given task in such a way that all the means must fail before the system fails. This is discussed in Section 23 under System Reliability.

There are several types of redundancy, a common form being parallel redundancy. A familiar example is the multiengined aircraft, which is so designed that even if one engine fails, the aircraft will still be able to continue on to a safe landing.

Under conditions of independent failures, the overall reliability for parallel redundancy is expressed by the formula

$$P_s = 1 - (1 - P_i)^n$$

where P_s = reliability of the system
P_i = reliability of the individual elements in the redundancy
n = number of identical redundant elements

Figure 13.10 shows some simple examples of series-parallel and parallel-series redundancies and calculates the system reliability versus that prevailing for the case of no redundancy.

4. Review the selection of any parts that are relatively new and unproven. Use standard parts whose reliability has been proven by actual field use. (However, be sure that the conditions of previous use are applicable to the new product.)

5. Use derating to assure that the stresses applied to the parts are lower than the stresses the parts can normally withstand.

6. Use "robust" design methods that enable a product to handle unexpected environments.

7. Control the operating environment to provide conditions that yield lower failure rates. Common examples are (a) potting electronic components to protect them against climate and shock, and (b) use of cooling systems to keep down ambient temperatures.

8. Specify replacement schedules to remove and replace low-reliability parts before they reach the wear-out stage. In many cases the replacement is made contingent on the results of checkouts or tests which determine whether degradation has reached a prescribed limit.

9. Prescribe screening tests to detect infant-mortality failures and to eliminate substandard components. The tests take various forms—bench tests, "burn in," accelerated life tests. Ekings and Sweetland (1978) discuss how machine

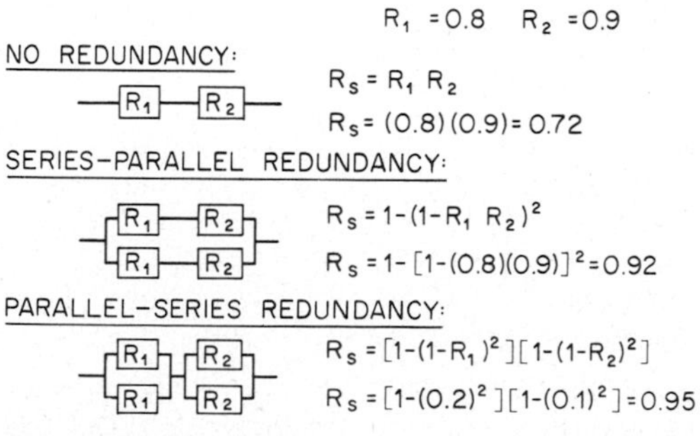

$R_1 = 0.8 \quad R_2 = 0.9$

NO REDUNDANCY:

$R_s = R_1 R_2$
$R_s = (0.8)(0.9) = 0.72$

SERIES–PARALLEL REDUNDANCY:

$R_s = 1 - (1 - R_1 R_2)^2$
$R_s = 1 - [1 - (0.8)(0.9)]^2 = 0.92$

PARALLEL–SERIES REDUNDANCY:

$R_s = [1 - (1 - R_1)^2][1 - (1 - R_2)^2]$
$R_s = [1 - (0.2)^2][1 - (0.1)^2] = 0.95$

FIG. 13.10 Redundancy.

burn-in decision criteria were used in a reliability assurance program for office copier machines.

10. Conduct research and development to attain an improvement in the basic reliability of those components which contribute most of the unreliability. While such improvements avoid the need for subsequent trade-offs, they may require advancing the state of the art and hence an investment of unpredictable size. Research in failure mechanisms has created a body of knowledge called the physics of failure, or reliability physics. *Proceedings of the Annual Meeting on Reliability Physics,* sponsored by the Institute of Electrical and Electronic Engineers, Inc., is an excellent reference.

Although none of the foregoing actions provides a perfect solution, the range of choice is broad. In some instances the designer can arrive at a solution single-handedly. More usually it means collaboration with other company specialists. In still other cases the customer and/or the company management must concur because of the broader considerations involved.

Reliability Growth. A technique for predicting future performance from tests and early field data is the concept of growth curves. The concept assumes that the product involved is one that is undergoing continuous improvements in design and refinements in operating and maintenance procedure. Thus the product performance will improve ("grow") with time. An early reliability growth model is that proposed by Duane (1964):

The Duane reliability growth model is given by:

$$\lambda_t = k(t)^{-b}$$

where λ_t = accumulative failure rate
  t = accumulative time
  b = slope of the growth curve
  k = a constant which depends on equipment complexity, design margins and design factors

Reiff (1978) shows how test data collected during four design phases were used for a reliability growth analysis based on the Duane model.

When such a model has been proven to apply to a class of products, early field data can be plotted on log-log paper and a line drawn using the slope based on previous similar products. The extrapolation of the line then provides a prediction of future performance. This has several uses, including the monitoring of actual progress toward meeting some requirement.

The Duane model can be adapted for measures of use other than time. For example, a manufacturer of duplicating machines uses it to predict failure rates for new products by plotting failure rate versus cumulative number of copies run. Peacord (1975) presents examples of the application of the Duane model. Jayachandran and Moore (1976) describe a simulation study made to compare four growth models. Willard (1979) discusses the approach for developing reliability growth curves for office equipment. MIL-HDBK-189 (1981) discusses reliability growth principles and techniques including 17 growth models.

PLANNING FOR MAINTAINABILITY

Maintainability refers to the ease with which preventive and corrective maintenance on a product can be achieved. ANSI/ASQC Standard A3 (ANSI, 1978) defines maintainability more formally as the ability of an item under stated conditions to be retained in, or restored to, within a given period of time, a specified state in which it can perform its required functions when maintenance is performed under stated conditions and while using prescribed procedures and resources.

Like reliability, maintainability is a fitness-for-use parameter that design engineers have recognized during the creation of new designs. These efforts resulted in many advances, e.g., aluminum siding, maintenance-free batteries, self-lubricating bearings, longer times between oil changes, fewer hours to change an engine on a jet aircraft.

As products have moved from the simple to the complex, the problems of maintainability have increased manyfold. For many electronic military products, the annual maintenance costs are typically several times the original cost of the equipment. As a result of critical needs on military products, some government agencies created specifications for programs of maintainability for contractors. These specifications required the development of goals on maintainability, prediction, and analysis of maintainability during the design process, and demonstration that maintainability goals had been achieved.

The evolution of a maintainability discipline gave rise to the creation of a maintainability specialist. These specialists tried to work with designers to develop maintainability goals and follow through with the analysis, prediction, and demonstration of maintainability. Like the reliability specialist, the maintainability specialist ran into resistance from the designers, and the record of accomplishment was varied.

Maintainability Concepts and Terms.   Users want products that are ready for use when they need them. This fitness-for-use parameter is called "availability." Availability is the ability of an item to perform its designated function when required for use. The availability of a product depends on how often failures occur (reliability), how long it takes to fix any failures (maintainability), and the amount of maintenance support provided. The total time in the operative state (also called uptime) is the sum of the time spent (1) in active use and (2) in the standby state. The total time in the nonoperative state (also called downtime) is the sum of the time spent (3) under active repair, and (4) waiting for spare parts, paperwork, etc. These categories are illustrated in Figure 13.11.

Availability is calculated as the ratio of operating time to operating time plus downtime. However, downtime can be viewed in two ways:

1. *Total downtime:*   This includes the active repair time (diagnosis and repair), preventive maintenance time, and logistics time (time spent waiting for personnel, spare parts, etc.). When total downtime is used, the resulting ratio is called operational availability (A_o).

2. *Active repair time:*   When active repair time is used, the resulting ratio is called "intrinsic availability" (A_i).

Under certain conditions, the availability can be calculated as

$$A_o = \frac{\text{MTBF}}{\text{MTBF} + \text{MDT}} \quad \text{and} \quad A_i = \frac{\text{MTBF}}{\text{MTBF} + \text{MTTR}}$$

where MTBF = mean time between failures
MDT = mean downtime
MTTR = mean time to repair

This is known as the "steady-state formula for availability."

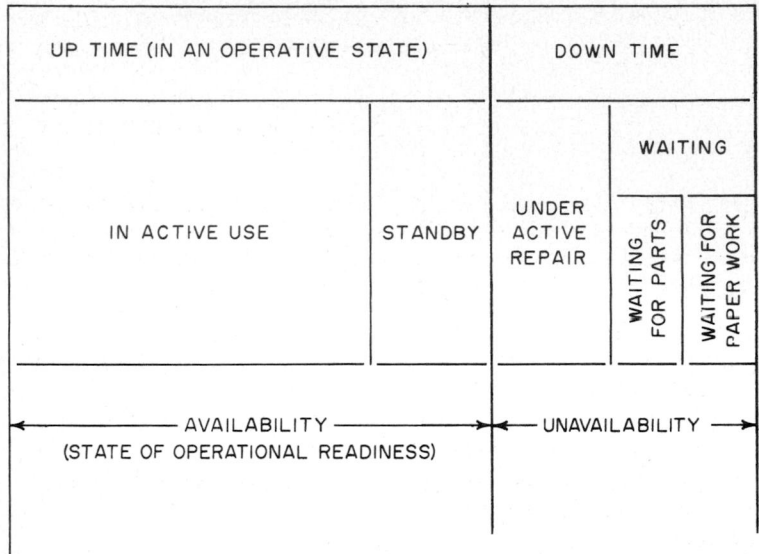

FIG. 13.11   Ingredients of availability.

Garrick and Mulvihill (1974) present data on certain subsystems of a mecha-nized bulk mail system (see Table 13.11). If estimates of reliability and maintain-ability can be made during the design process, availability can be evaluated before the design is released for production.

The steady-state formula for availability has the virtue of simplicity. However, the formula has several assumptions that are not always met in the real world. The assumptions are:

1. The product is operating in the constant-failure-rate period of the overall life. Thus, the failure time distribution is exponential.

2. The downtime or repair time distribution is exponential.

3. Attempts to locate system failures do not change the overall system failure rate.

4. No reliability growth occurs. (Such growth might be due to design improve-ments or through debugging of bad parts.)

5. Preventive maintenance is scheduled outside the time frame included in the availability calculation.

TABLE 13.11   Availability Data for Mail System Equipment

Equipment	MTBF, h	MTTR, h	Availability, %
Sack sorter	90	1.620	98.2
Parcel sorter	160	0.8867	99.4
Conveyor, induction	17,900	1.920	100.0
Deflector, traveling	3,516	3.070	99.9

More precise formulas for calculating availability depend on operational conditions and statistical assumptions. These formulas are discussed by Locks (1973).

Availability analysis has also been applied to developing chemical processes. Such analysis applied the steady-state availability formula to processes involving a series of operations (Cherry et al., 1978).

Maintainability Program Elements. Formal maintainability programs start with the premise that maintainability can be programmed in the same way as parameters such as product performance or reliability. The program consists of three stages:

1. *Program surveillance and control:* This stage consists of defining all of the tasks required in the maintainability program, and monitoring and reviewing those tasks as they are executed.
2. *Design and analysis:* During product design, maintainability goals are set and analyses and predictions are made.
3. *Evaluation and test:* The key element here is a demonstration that maintainability goals have been achieved.

An example of maintainability tasks during a product development program is illustrated in Table 13.12. (MIL-STD-470A, 1983.) The Standard explains the degree of application of each task from the design concept stage to the final operating system development. Many of these tasks are discussed below.

Maintainability Modeling and Allocation. There is a trend toward specifying maintainability in quantitative form. A summary of some common figures of merit for maintainability is given in Table 13.13. [MIL-STD-721C (1981) lists 11 different figures of merit based on the mean time concept.]

Wellborn and Lawson (1978) report a case of extensive quantitative maintainability requirements (e.g., mean time between maintenance) for an engine to be furnished to the U.S. Army. In addition to the quantitative requirements there were 15 qualitative requirements, such as "the engine shall be modular."

When product complexity or importance warrants it, a formal model for maintainability can be created. The term "model" here is used to mean a systematic, analytical process that will predict maintainability. The complexity of the model may range from a simple flow or block diagram to a mathematical relationship

TABLE 13.12   MIL-STD-470A (1983) Maintainability Tasks

Maintainability program plan
Monitor/control of subcontractors and suppliers
Program reviews
Data collection, analysis, and corrective action system
Maintainability modeling
Maintainability allocations
Maintainability predictions
Failure modes and effects analysis (FMEA), maintainability information
Maintainability analysis
Maintainability design criteria
Preparation of inputs to detailed maintenance plan and logistics support analysis (LSA)
Maintainability demonstration (MD)

TABLE 13.13 Maintainability Figures of Merit

Figure of merit	Meaning
Mean time to repair (MTTR)	Mean time to correct a failure
Mean time to service	Mean time to perform an act to keep a product in operating condition
Mean preventive maintenance time	Mean time for scheduled preventive maintenance
Repair hours per 100 operating hours	Number of hours required for repairs per 100 product operating hours
Rate of preventive maintenance actions	Number of preventive maintenance actions required per period of operative or calendar hours
Downtime probability	Probability that a failed product is restored to operative condition in a specified downtime
Maintainability index	Score for a product design based on evaluation of defined maintainability features
Rate of maintenance cost	Cost of preventive and corrective maintenance per unit of operating or calendar time

that predicts maintainability as a function of system parameters. A key purpose of the model is to determine the effect of the change in one variable on the cost and/or maintainability performance characteristics. MIL-STD-470A (1983) provides further discussion of maintainability modeling.

Another task in the maintainability program is the allocation of the maintainability goal. The task consists of apportioning the overall maintainability goal to provide designers with goals for individual items and thereby make maintainability a design parameter. The allocation process combines experience on similar products with engineering judgment. An example of the allocation of a mean corrective maintenance time requirement of 0.5 h is given in Table 13.14 (Blanchard and Fabrycky, 1981). Reliability estimates are provided in columns 2 through 5. An assumed maintainability allocation is given in column 6. (Items with a high contribution to total failures are allocated a low maintenance time.) The calculations show an overall time of 0.485. As this is within the 0.5 requirement, the allocation given in column 6 is accepted. MIL-STD-470A (1983) and Blanchard and Fabrycky (1981) provide further discussion on maintainability allocation.

Maintainability Prediction. Maintainability prediction provides a quantitative tool for (1) evaluating a proposed design for maintainability and (2) identifying areas of the design requiring improvement.

Three main approaches can be used:

1. Secure data of past experience on similar equipment, and extrapolate to make predictions on the new design.
2. Break down the maintenance task into elemental tasks needed to carry out maintenance at the various product levels. Then acquire data representing "standard" times to accomplish these tasks. These standards can then be used to build up a predicted total maintainability time in much the same way as reliability is built up from elemental failure rates or as time for manufacturing

TABLE 13.14 Maintainability Allocation for System *XYZ*

1 Item	2 Quantity of items per system (Q)	3 Failure rate $(\lambda) \times 1000$ h	4 Contribution of total failures $C_f = (Q)(\lambda)$	5 Percent contribution $C_p = C_f/\Sigma C_f \times 100$	6 Average corrective maint. time $\overline{M}ct$,h	7 Contribution of total corrective maint. time $C_t = (C_f)(\overline{M}ct)$
1. Unit *A*	1	0.246	0.246	11%	0.9	0.221
2. Unit *B*	1	1.866	1.866	84%	0.4	0.746
3. Unit *C*	1	0.110	0.110	5%	1.0	0.110
Total			$\Sigma C_f = 2.222$	100%		$\Sigma C_t = 1.077$

$$\overline{M}ct \text{ for system } XYZ = \frac{\Sigma C_t}{\Sigma C_f} = \frac{1.077}{2.222} = 0.485 \text{ h (requirement: 0.5 h)}$$

Source: Blanchard and Fabrycky, 1981, p. 392.

operations is built up from standard elemental times. An example from Blan-chard and Fabrycky (1981) is given in Table 13.15.

3. Employ a regression equation that predicts maintainability as a function of key characteristics of the proposed design. Detailed checklists are used to establish a score for the design on each of these characteristics. These scores are inserted into the equation to develop an estimate of the total maintenance time. (Miller, 1971, explains a simpler technique that provides a comparative, rather than absolute, measure of maintainability. Checklists are used to score the design on maintainability characteristics. The total number of points is the measure of maintainability.)

The methodology of maintainability prediction and analysis is going through a period of development. Discussions of advanced techniques can be found in the various issues of the Institute of Electrical and Electronics Engineers publication *Transactions on Reliability*. See particularly the August 1981 issue which was devoted primarily to maintainability.

Failure Mode, Effect, and Criticality Analysis.   The concept of failure mode, effect, and criticality analysis discussed under Reliability can also be applied to evaluating maintainability (Kimble, 1982). The steps are:

1. List the failure modes for the proposed design.
2. For each failure mode, state the effect on other components or on the overall system.
3. For each failure mode, rate the likelihood of occurrence, accessability, detec-tibility, and labor hours to service or replace the part. The "service value" is the product of these ratings. The higher the number, the more serious is the mode of serviceability or failure. The analysis also takes into account the types of routine servicing required by the design.

Design Aids for Maintainability.   To attain a proper balance between main-tainability and other parameters requires that the product designer give consid-eration to various alternatives and trade-offs, such as the following:

Reliability versus maintainability: For example, given an availability requirement, should the response be an improvement in reliability or in maintainability?

Modular versus nonmodular construction: Modular design requires added design effort but reduces the time required for diagnosis and remedy in the field. The fault need only be localized to the module level, after which the defective module is unplugged and replaced. This concept is being rapidly extended to consumer products such as television sets.

Repair versus throwaway: For some products or modules, the cost of field repair exceeds the cost of making new units in the factory. In such cases, design for throwaway is an economic improvement in maintainability.

Built-in versus external test equipment: Built-in test features reduce diagnos-tic time but usually at an added investment.

Person versus machine: For example, should the operation/maintenance function be highly engineered with special instrumentation and repair facili-ties, or should it be left to skilled technicians with general-use equipment?

Beyond such widely prevailing questions, there are numerous design features

TABLE 13.15 Maintainability Prediction Worksheet*

Part category	λ	N	$(N)(\lambda)$	Maintenance times, h							$(N)(\lambda)(\text{Mct}_i)$
				Loc	Iso	Acc	Ali	Che	Int	Mct_i	
Part A	0.161	2	0.322	0.02	0.08	0.14	0.01	0.01	0.11	0.370	0.119
Part B	0.102	4	0.408	0.01	0.05	0.12	0.01	0.02	0.12	0.330	0.134
Part C	0.021	5	0.105	0.03	0.04	0.11	$\cdots$	0.01	0.14	0.330	0.034
Part D	0.084	1	0.084	0.01	0.03	0.10	0.02	0.03	0.11	0.300	0.025
Part E	0.452	9	4.060	0.02	0.04	0.13	0.02	0.03	0.08	0.320	1.299
Part F	0.191	8	1.520	0.01	0.02	0.11	0.01	0.02	0.07	0.240	0.364
Part G	0.022	7	0.154	0.02	0.05	0.15	$\cdots$	0.05	0.15	0.420	0.064
Total			6.653								2.039

*N = quantity of parts; λ = failure rate; Loc = localization; Iso = isolation; Acc = access; Ali = alignment; Che = check-out; Int = interchange; Mct_i = maintenance cycle time. For determination of MMHc, enter worker-hours for maintenance times.

Source: Blanchard and Fabrycky, 1981, p. 405.

which have been identified as contributing to good maintainability. NAVSHIP (1972) has identified design criteria for improved maintainability.

Maintainability Demonstration. For complex equipment, MIL-STD-471A (1983) provides detailed maintainability demonstration procedures. It provides approaches for evaluating maintainability during design by identifying three phases—verification, demonstration, and evaluation. In the verification phase, the objectives are to (1) verify and update the maintainability model that has evolved from a design analysis, (2) correct any design deficiencies with respect to maintainability, and (3) provide assurance that the maintainability requirements can be achieved. In the demonstration phase, tests or analyses are conducted to determine if the formal maintainability requirements have been achieved. Finally, the evaluation phase has three purposes: (1) evaluate the operational, maintenance, and support environment on maintainability parameters, (2) evaluate the correction of any deficiencies that were found in previous phases, and (3) demonstrate maintainability at the depot level.

Demonstration of qualitative requirements consists of evaluating the design using certain design checklists for maintainability. For quantitative maintainability requirements, demonstration consists of conducting certain maintainability tasks, timing them, and comparing the results to the maintainability time requirements.

Maintainability Data Systems. Maintainability data are collected throughout the entire life cycle of a product. The sources of such data include maintainability analyses during design, engineering tests, maintainability demonstration tests, mock-ups, field evaluation of the product, and operational use. Such data are ultimately useful in determining compliance of a product with maintainability requirements and in identifying problem areas requiring corrective action. However, maintainability data have other uses that go beyond determining conformance with specifications. These uses include providing information for spare parts, determining personnel requirements, providing information for technical manuals, test equipment and training, and establishing repair time data for use in prediction on new designs.

Data collection systems for maintainability (and reliability) are essential if designers are to be provided with feedback to help them on future designs. Such feedback is essential during the product development phase of the product life cycle in order to provide insight into areas of the design that may be deficient in maintainability.

PLANNING FOR SAFETY

The wave of new legislation and court decisions of the 1960s and 1970s has greatly intensified emphasis on product safety. Nowhere is this emphasis greater than during product design. The mood of society has been one of putting responsibility for human safety overwhelmingly on manufacturers, and hardly at all on the users of the products.

The Organized Safety Program. Organized, companywide approaches to product safety have taken one of two main roads:

1. *A company product safety committee to coordinate activities of all company* *departments:* This approach is discussed in Section 34 under Product Liability.

2. *A concept of product safety engineering and management which is based in the Product Design Department:* This approach has been fostered by the military agencies (and others) and is discussed below.

Safety Program Objectives. An example of the military approach is seen in MIL-STD-882 (1969) which is frequently specified on government contracts. This standard identifies the following as objectives for safety programs:

Safety should be designed into the product to a degree consistent with mission requirements.

Hazards associated with each product (and its components and units) are to be identified, eliminated, or controlled to an acceptable level.

Control is to be established over hazards that cannot be eliminated, so as to protect personnel, equipment, and property.

Risks involved in the use of new materials, production techniques, or testing techniques are to be minimized.

Safety Tasks. The organized program identifies specific tasks to be performed during the various phases of new-product development. These tasks are principally as follows:

During concept formulation phase: Conduct concept safety studies; perform preliminary hazard analysis; define product safety performance "envelope"; select product safety effectiveness measures, i.e., figure of merit.

During contract definition phase (A:) Prepare a proposed safety plan; update the preliminary hazard analysis; identify which are the safety requirements in the specification; include safety considerations in trade-off studies. It is becoming common practice for safety-sensitive specification requirements to be marked with a special symbol. This symbol then carries through to suppliers, manufacturing processes, test specifications, etc.

During contract definition phase (B): Implement approved contract definition safety plan; complete preliminary hazards analysis; identify safety decisions to be made before the development phase; establish a firm safety plan for the development phase, including a breakdown of safety tasks.

During development phase: Implement program approved in definition phase; provide design criteria and evaluate product design through hazard analysis and safety studies; establish test requirements; participate in program reviews and in trade-off studies.

During subsequent phases: Help maintain safety precautions throughout, including audit of engineering changes.

Quantification of Safety. Generally, quantification of safety has been time-related. Industrial injury rates are quantified on the basis of lost-time accidents per million labor-hours of exposure. (Note that this expresses the frequency of occurrence but does not indicate the severity of the accidents.) Motor vehicle injury rates are on the basis of injuries per 100 million miles. School injury rates are on the basis of injuries per 100 thousand student-days.

Product designers have tended to quantify safety in two ways:

1. *Hazard frequency:* Hazard is any combination of parts, components, conditions, or changing set of circumstances which present an injury potential. Hazard frequency takes the form of frequency of occurrence of an unsafe event and/or injuries per unit of time, e.g., per million hours of exposure. MIL-STD-882A (1977), *System Safety Program Requirements,* has established categories of probability levels for hazards ranging from "frequent" to "impossible." Such probabilities are sometimes referred to as "risk."

2. *Hazard severity:* MIL-STD-882A recognizes four levels of severity:

    Category I—Catastrophic: May cause death or system loss

    Category II—Critical: May cause severe injury, severe occupational illness, or minor system damage

    Category III—Marginal: May cause minor injury, minor occupational illness, or minor system damage

    Category IV—Negligible: Will not result in injury, occupational illness, or system damage

General Approach to Safety Analysis.   The steps are:

1.   Review available historical data on safety of similar and predecessor products. These data obviously should include complaints, claims, and lawsuits. In addition, data are available from regulators, independent laboratories, and still other sources.

2.   Study the ways in which the product has actually been used and misused. This study is especially important for products which are used by a wide spectrum of the population, e.g., consumer products or those military products which are used directly by the "foot soldier." Such a wide spectrum of humanity inevitably misuses products or finds uses for which the products were never designed. The ordinary household ladder includes a small platform for holding tools, a can of paint, etc. The platform is "obviously" too flimsy to support the weight of a person. Yet enough people do stand on it and are injured by the resulting fall to suggest that the platform may need to be designed to hold a person's weight.
Products for children (or to which children have access) are a special case because of the inexperience of youngsters and because "logic" becomes academic when injured childern are displayed before a jury. A child's building block has a high reliability. Yet the child may fall and get injured on a corner of the block; the child may throw the block and injure another child. Manufacturers may turn to the use of plastic foam for making the blocks, but now new questions arise: Could a child bite off a piece and choke on it? Would the material be toxic? Obviously, a child is misusing a block when biting off a piece. Yet the standards on electric lamp cords have been revised to minimize the danger to a child who may bite through the insulation.

3.   Assess the likelihood that damage will actually occur. This likelihood is the resultant of several probabilities:

    a.   That the product will fail in a way which creates a hazard (this probability may be available through failure-rate analysis)

    b.   That the existence of the hazard will result in damage

    c.   That despite no failures in the product, it will be misused so as to result in damage

4. Quantify the exposure (time, cycles, etc.) of the product and the users to hazardous conditions.

5. Determine the severity of the effect of hazards on product or user.

While safety analyses are of long standing, the empirical, qualitative approaches of the past are giving way to more formalized, quantitative studies, as discussed below.

Tools of Safety Analysis.   Henley (1979) discusses some of the numerous techniques of safety analysis. Only the most complex products, involving detailed human-product interrelationships, will require so wide an array of techniques. Usually a few widely used techniques will supply the bulk of the analysis needed.

The most fundamental technique is the hazard analysis. This is similar to the failure mode, effect, and criticality analysis (Figure 13.6). Three forms of hazard analysis can be prepared: the preliminary hazard analysis for use during the conceptual design phase; the operation of procedure hazard analysis for identifying hazards created by operating the system; fault hazard analysis for identifying hazardous conditions as a result of hardware failure. RADC (1983) discusses these several forms of hazard analysis. Hammer (1980) shows a preliminary analysis (Figure 13.12) for a household coffee mill.

The hazard analysis technique presents a thorough and logical analysis of all potential hazards in the system. Like the failure mode, effect, and criticality analysis, the technique is exhaustive but it is also costly and time-consuming.

A second technique is the fault tree analysis. This "top-down" approach starts by supposing that an accident takes place. It then considers the possible direct causes which could lead to this accident. Next, it looks for the origins of these causes. Finally, it looks for ways to avoid these origins and causes. The branching out of origins and causes is what gives the technique the name of "fault tree" analysis. The approach is the reverse of the failure mode, effect, and criticality analysis, which starts with origins and causes and looks for any resulting bad effects.

The general procedure for fault tree analysis consists of the following seven steps as defined by RADC (1983):

1. Define the system, ground rules, and any assumptions to be used in the analysis.

2. Develop a simple block diagram of the system showing inputs, outputs, and interfaces.

3. Define the top event (ultimate failure effect) of interest.

4. Construct the fault tree for the top event using the rules of formal logic.

5. Analyze the completed fault tree.

6. Recommend any corrective actions for design changes.

7. Document the analysis and its results.

Hammer (1980) presents a fault tree analysis for an interlock safety circuit (Figure 13.13).

Fault tree diagrams make use of a standard set of symbols. For example, in Figure 13.13, the spadelike symbol with a straight bottom is an "and gate," meaning the output occurs if all input events below it occur. The spade symbol with the curved bottom is an "or gate," meaning the output occurs if one or more of the input events below it occur.

The basic analysis can be extended by adding estimates of probability of occur-

PRODUCT: Electrically operated rotary coffee mill for household use.

Hazard	Occurrence (Cause) Description	Effect	Probability (with No Safeguard)	Possible Safeguard	Remarks and References
Flying object injury	1. Rotating blade assembly is a device which could come apart at high operating speeds, especially if a hard object is put in mill by mistake. 2. Operating mill without cover could permit beans or ground coffee to be thrown out by centrifugal force.	Parts or fragments of mill thrown out at high speed could injure user. Coffee beans or ground coffee thrown out at high velocity and hitting eye could cause severe damage.	Reasonably probable	1. a. Design to positively secure blade so it will not come off during operation. b. Ensure that stresses due to rotational speeds will not be greater than strength. c. Make case and cover strong enough to hold any parts or fragments thrown off.	Normally, the person operating the mill will be holding it and therefore in close proximity. Flying fragments and parts will therefore have a good probability of hitting someone.
High temperature	Electrical power loss or mechanical motion can create high temperatures.	Burns to personnel who contact a hot surface.	1. Metal surfaces: Reasonably probable 2. Plastic material: Remote	1. a. Keep power and friction losses as low as possible. b. Cool mill if there is still a high source of heat. c. Provide insulation to keep outer surfaces at safe temperature.	

FIG. 13.12 Preliminary hazard analysis—coffee mill.

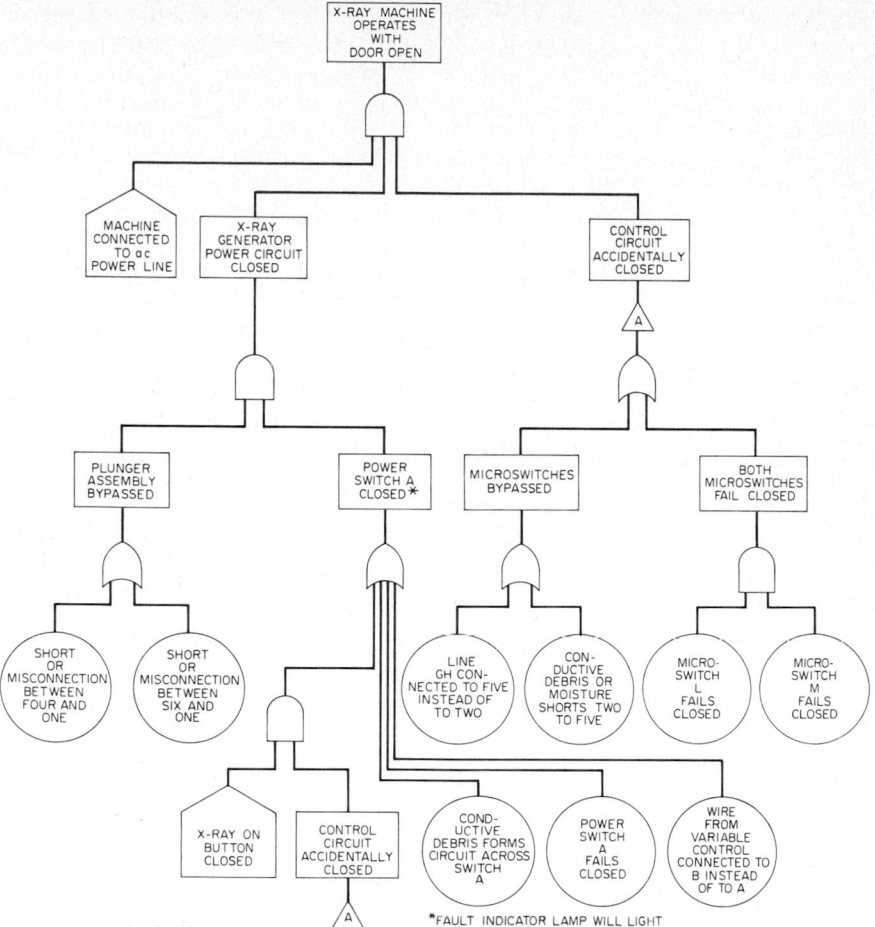

FIG. 13.13   Fault-tree analysis of an interlock safety circuit.

rence to each event on the fault tree. A computer program can then be used to calculate probabilities for various paths and establish priorities for further safety analyses.

Improving Safety through Design.   The following are some examples of means used by designers to reduce the hazard levels of products.

1. *Elimination of hazard:*   For example, a pneumatic or hydraulic system might be used instead of an electrical system, where there is a possiblity of fire, explosion, shock, or undesirable heating. Fluidic control systems are being applied more and more for these reasons.

2. *Hazard-level limitation:*   The product can be made intrinsically safe by limiting the energy level of the potential hazard. Electricity may be essential for a system and cannot be eliminated, but use of solid-state devices—operating at low power levels—can eliminate possibilities of fire, shock, or excessive heating.

3. *Lockouts, lockins, and interlocks:*   Isolating transformers in a vault minimizes the possibility of electrocuting personnel. Explosion-proof equipment keeps flame in electrical lines, fittings, and machinery from igniting a flammable environment which surrounds it. Pushbutton switches that must be operated in a specific sequence (if a mishap is to be avoided) can be interlocked.

4. *Fail-safe designs:*   These may be fail-passive, fail-operational, or fail-active. A fuse or circuit breaker is a fail-passive device that opens when a dangerous situation occurs, deenergizing and "safing" an electrical system. Admitting water under the disk of a boiler inlet value, instead of over, is a fail-operational arrangement; if the disk separates from the value stem, it is raised by the flowing water so the boiler will continue to operate safely. A destruct system on an air-to-air missile is a fail-active device; if the missile misses its target and does not detonate within a set time, the destruct system blows the missile apart to halt its flight and limit the damage that an armed warhead or entire missile could cause by hitting the ground.

Microprocessors can be incorporated into a design so that single circuit component failures can be detected before the effects produce a hazard to the user. See Section 27 under Computer Integration into Product Design.

While most accidents are caused by failures (of material or personnel), others are the result of hazards inherent in the product; e.g., a color television set may produce an excellent picture and sound but still generate harmful radiation. Minimizing these inherent hazards involves a further list of methods available to the designer:

5. *Monitors:*   These are devices which detect dangerous conditions or potential failures so that corrective action can be taken before an accident or failure occurs. Typical examples are temperature and pressure gages, radiation counters, infrared indicators to detect hot spots or flames, and even personnel paired in a buddy-system arrangement to guard each other's well-being in a dangerous situation.

6. *Warnings:*   Generally, warnings are made to personnel, but the signals generated by the monitoring systems used for warnings can also be directed to take corrective actions automatically.

7. *Minor loss acceptance:*   A restricted amount of product damage may be accepted to assure that major damage is avoided. For example, blowout panels in oil and gas furnaces give way in the event of an explosion and overpressurization from delayed ignition of accumulated fuel vapors. This prevents damage to furnace walls, boiler tubes, and other equipment and structures.

8. *Escape and survival:*   Procedures, equipment, and means must be provided to personnel to enable them to leave the scene of an accident to avoid injury, and to survive in the new location. An ejection seat permits escape of a pilot from a disabled aircraft: the parachute is necessary for survival after leaving the aircraft.

9. *Rescue:*   Personnel may be incapacitated or trapped in a vehicle or structure where they may be subjected to further injury. It is therefore necessary to provide devices, equipment, and procedures that others can use for their rescue.

10. *Isolation:*   Not all hazards can be eliminated. Frequently, control of those hazards which remain is lost, and an accident occurs. It is therefore necessary to provide safeguards to minimize injury or damage that could result. Isolation is not only a means of avoiding accidents, but can also be used to avoid or minimize damaging effects.

Mihalasky (1980) examines the part that human beings play in safety problems. This discussion includes a consideration of the conditions under which machines or human beings are more effective, some of the reasons why human beings make mistakes, and methods to detect and reduce error opportunities involving human beings.

PLANNING FOR HUMAN FACTORS (ERGONOMICS)

As products have become more complex, the interaction of the product with the human being operating the product has assumed increasing importance. The evaluation of the design of a product to assure compatibility with the capabilities of human beings is referred to as "ergonomics" or "human engineering."

The interaction between person and product has two impacts on fitness for use:

1. *The effect that the design has on the ease with which the user can install, operate, and maintain the product:* For example, extensive work has been done applying ergonomics principles to visual display terminals and computer keyboards. This involves the analysis of physical attributes and capabilities to relieve problems of eyestrain, aches and pains, excessive fatigue, and stress (McQuade, 1984).

2. *The effect of the design on the reliability of the performance of the human being using the product:* Some failures of a product are due to mistakes made by the user. Other product failures are due to designs that make human errors more likely. One example concerns the connection for an instrument box on an aircraft. Failures were reported after only 200 to 300 flight hours, but when the "faulty" boxes were returned for repair they operated satisfactorily. Investigation revealed that the boxes would in effect unplug from the plane because of loose connections—an apparent human error. The cause of the loose connection was traced to the position of the boxes in the plane; i.e., it was physically impossible for technicians to apply enough force on the box to lock it firmly in place. The corrective action was a design change to move the location of the boxes. A similar scenario is reported for loose bolts on vehicles. Loose bolts are often viewed as due to improper torquing by an assembly operator. The reason for the improper torquing may be a design that makes it impossible to properly insert a torque tool. Either the design must be changed to gain access or a special tool must be developed.

The early applications of ergonomics were heavily in the aerospace industry. Other applications now include telephones, cameras, sewing machines, and bowling balls. Eastman Kodak Company (1983) has prepared a useful reference that provides principles and guidelines for designing products for human use.

PLANNING FOR MANUFACTURING, INSPECTION, AND TRANSPORTATION

As the product design is the foundation for later steps on the Spiral, planning for these steps should start during product development.

Planning for Manufacturing. All industries are replete with examples illustrating how the lack of thorough consideration of producibility during product development resulted in serious problems during manufacturing.

In one company, a new chemical was developed to provide an economical substitute for another product. Laboratory trials confirmed the savings. Pressure to realize these savings led to a decision to proceed with large-scale manufacture without going through a scaled-up trial or pilot plant. Unfortunately, many problems occurred. An analysis revealed that the "successful" laboratory trials treated some technical factors as insignificant and used oversimplified assumptions. The product was abandoned.

An essential need is to improve the understanding of the relationship of process variables to product results. With such an understanding, designers can then identify in specifications the product characteristics (and their limits) that must be controlled during manufacturing in order to achieve fitness for use. This will be useful to:

1. *Improve the launching of new products:* For example, lighter automobiles require that castings be made with thinner cross sections. In turn, these demands on castings require closer controls on materials and manufacturing processes. However, making such controls effective requires that engineers, supervisors, and workers know which process variables to control and how to control them. In due course, this knowledge is gradually acquired through experience, experiments, and other means. However, during the time of acquiring that knowledge much scrap and rework is endured and often some product recalls are necessary.

2. *Improve the current yield of the manufacuring processes:* Where the relationship is not clearly understood, the costs of scrap, rework, and excessive inspection are high—much higher than the cost of acquiring the new knowledge needed to understand the relationships.

3. *Provide information which can be used to train supervisors and workers:* Job turnover is destroying the old concept of training by experienced supervisors and workers. What is needed is to learn these important relationships, incorporate them into manufacturing planning documents, and train the manufacturing personnel in the use of those relationships.

In understanding the relationship of process variables to product results, experimental design techniques can be useful (see Section 16 under Application of Experimental Design to Optimize Process Variables).

Tolerancing. The selection of tolerances has a dual effect on the economics of quality. The tolerance affects:

1. Fitness for use and hence the saleability of the product
2. Costs of manufacturer (facilities, tooling, productivity) and quality costs (equipment, inspection, scrap, rework, material review, etc.)

Most tolerances are established by methods which, in varying degrees, are less than scientific, The principal methods include:

1. *By precedent:* There is much merit to use of past practice (which has stood the test of time), provided the practice is sound. As will be seen, past practice includes a serious bias toward tight tolerances.
2. *By bargaining:* When proposed tolerances are challenged on the ground of high costs, it is often easier to reach an agreement by bargaining than to undergo the costs of a thorough investigation.

3. *From tolerance systems:* There has been a great deal of standardization of methods of dimensioning and tolerancing, at company, industry, national, and international levels. The published standards become the basis of design and shop practice except for those tolerances which require special consideration. Many companies use preprinted notes on drawings stating, for example, "Unless otherwise specified, all dimensions shown are to be held to ± 0.015 in." Even more basic is the approach to always use shop standards and have the designer put tolerances only on characteristics for which shop standards are inadequate. This approach results in realistic tolerances than can be rigidly enforced.

In theory, the designer should, by scientific study, establish the proper balance between the value of precision and the cost of precision. In practice, the designer is unable to do this for each tolerance—there are too many quality characteristics. As a result, only a minority of tolerances are set scientifically. Scientific tools for tolerancing include:

1. *Regression studies:* For example, a thermostat may be required to turn on and shut off a power source at specified low and high temperature values, respectively. A number of thermostat elements are built and tested. The prime recorded data are (*a*) turn on temperature, (*b*) shut off temperature, and (*c*) physical characteristics of the thermostat elements. These data permit scatter diagrams to be prepared and regression equations (see Section 23 under Regression) to be computed to aid in establishing critical component tolerances on a basis which is scientific within the confidence limits for the numbers involved.

In Figure 13.14, the performance limits are located on the vertical axis and extended horizontally until the regression line is intersected. The tolerance limits on the critical dimension can then be read on the horizontal axis. Shainin (1976, 1978) discusses this concept along with the effect of gage variability.

2. *Statistical analysis of development data:* Designers often must set tolerance limits with only a few measurements from the process (or more likely from the development tests conducted under laboratory conditions). In developing a

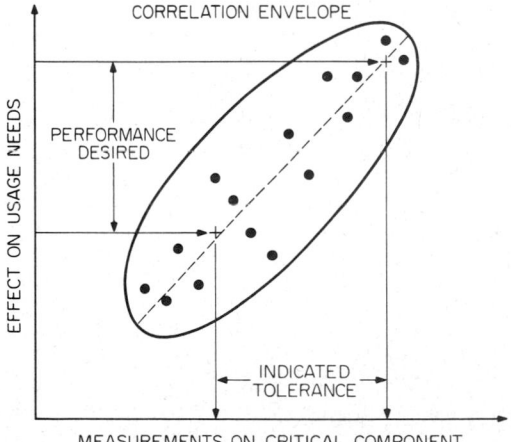

FIG. 13.14 Scatter diagram for setting tolerances.

paint formulation, the following values of gloss were obtained: 76.5, 75.2, 77.5, 78.9, 76.1, 78.3, and 77.7. A group of chemists were asked where they would set a minimum specification limit. Their answer was 75.0—a reasonable answer for those without statistical knowledge. Figure 13.15 shows a plot of the data on normal probability paper (see Section 23 under Predictions with Normal Distributions). If the line is extrapolated to 75.0, the plot predicts that about 11 percent of the population with fall below 75.0—even though all of the sample data exceeds 75.0. Of course, a larger sample size is preferred and further statistical analyses could be made, but the plot provides a simple tool to evaluate a small sample of data.

Another technique for dealing with small samples consists of combining data from different development tests. Suppose the development process investigated several alternative design concepts in order to find a satisfactory design. For each of these concepts, a few tests were run to evaluate the design. Although the different concepts may have yielded much different results on the *average* value, the amount of *variation* about the different average values may be the same. If this is proven statistically to be true, then the data on *variation* within each design can be combined to provide a larger sample size for setting tolerance limits for the chosen design. This approach requires judgment, but it can help when the designer is forced to set limits based on only a few measurements.

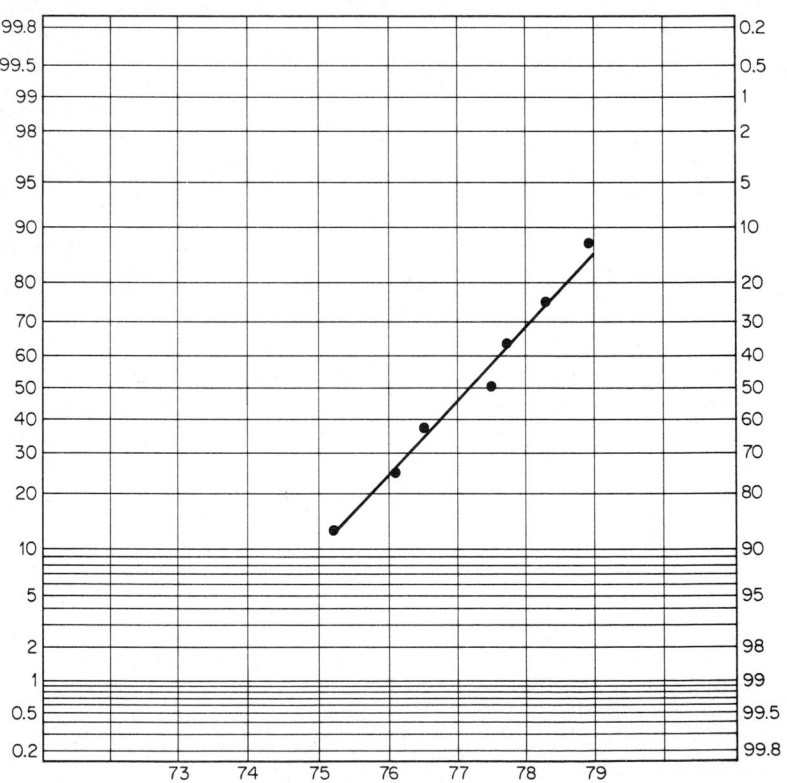

FIG. 13.15   Probability plot of development data.

3. *Tolerances for interacting dimensions:* Numerous designs involve "interacting dimensions." An electronic circuit may consist of 11 elements in series; a mechanical assembly may consist of a buildup of 8 elements; a single complex part may include a chain of 10 dimensions, starting from a base line. What these designs have in common is the existence of interaction among these elements or dimensions. Each element of dimension has its own tolerances. However, the variation of the composite (the circuit, the assembly, or the chain) will be related to the variations of the elements according to the laws of probability; i.e., it is unlikely that all the extremes will come together simultaneously.

This unlikelihood makes it possible to establish wider tolerances on elements of such designs without significantly increasing the extent of nonconformance. The scientific approach to this is discussed in Section 23 under Tolerance Limits for Interacting Dimensions. The formula involved requires certain assumptions that have been studied by Bender (1975). He provides suggestions on how to combine "probability and experience" in applying the formula.

4. *Computer simulation of interacting dimensions:* In a series of three papers, Evans (1975) discusses four methods of statistical tolerancing covering both linear and nonlinear cases. One of the methods is a Monte Carlo simulation.

Simulation is one of the most useful of the techniques of operations research and is directly applicable to the problem of statistical tolerancing. It is particularly useful when the component distributions are nonnormal and the relationship between the components and the final result is complex and difficult to analyze with conventional statistical methods.

A simulation is usually made using a computer model. The distribution of each component is defined in terms of the form of the distribution and numerical parameters, e.g., a normal distribution with a mean of 2.000 and standard deviation of 0.004 or an exponential distribution with a mean of 1.000. The relationship between the components and the final result is then expressed in a model equation. This may be a simple or complex combination of component dimensions.

In a Monte Carlo simulation, the computer uses a "random-number generator" to draw values at random from each component distribution and combine them (using the model equation) to obtain a simulated value of the overall result. This process is repeated many times and represents a simulation of what would happen if many assemblies were made at random from components having the characteristics described in the simulation model. The simulated assembly dimensions can then be summarized in a histogram or other form, and used to set assembly tolerances or to evaluate previously defined assembly tolerances. With a simulation model, component distributions can be changed and the effect on the overall result immediately predicted by running additional simulation runs.

Holmes and Michalek (1982) present some examples of the simulation technique as applied in the automotive industry. Rimondi, Tavazza, and Turello (1976) discuss the application to vulcanization and structural problems in rubberlike products.

5. *Concept of position tolerance:* This concept is important where the function and interchangeability of mating parts are vital. It can result in (1) larger tolerances than those possible from conventional tolerancing, and (2) more efficient inspection techniques. Further discussion can be found in Frank (1977) and Shaffer (1982).

6. *Tolerances for nonquantifiable characteristics:* An important subset of quality characteristics are "sensory" features such as surface blemishes, color, and others. These cannot be quantified and measured through conventional technology. If limits on these characteristics are not adequately defined during product development, they will be defined by default by the manufacturing and inspection personnel.

An organized approach to setting sensory standards is discussed in Section 18 under Sensory Qualities.

Peach (1980) discusses a procedure for setting limits of acceptability for characteristics of consumer products.

Unrealistic Tolerances Loosely Enforced. In most companies the accumulated specifications contain an extensive array of unduly tight tolerances, i.e., tolerances not really needed to achieve fitness for use. This accumulation is a natural result of the historical forces to which the design department has been subjected:

1. The designers had clear responsibility for assuring that the product was fit for use and had only vague responsibility for assuring that the product could be made economically.

2. The designer had facilities for testing whether the design would be fit for use, but lacked facilities for testing whether the design could be produced economically.

3. When the resulting tight tolerances created shop troubles, the shop often responded by exceeding the tolerances in order to meet delivery dates. Then, when many of the products performed satisfactorily, the shop drew the conclusion that the designers were needlessly tight. However, there were also cases in which exceeding the tolerances resulted in field failures. From these cases the designers drew the conclusion that the shop could not be trusted fully. One reaction of designers was to set still closer limits in order to neutralize the expected overruns. This game was detected or suspected by the shop, so that the mistrust became mutual.

Recent trends have been in the direction of reducing the biases of both the designers and the shops. However, there remains an accumulation of "unrealistic tolerances loosely enforced" which all concerned would like to convert into a situation of "realistic tolerances rigidly enforced." This conversion cannot be accomplished by the "legitimate" process of making engineering investigations and issuing engineering change orders. There are too many investigations, and the issuance of engineering change orders is too elaborate a process.

The conversion must be restricted to selected tolerances which are creating the bulk of the cost problem. The selection may be made from the "high dollar loss list" of the quality cost studies, the list of products for which 100 percent inspection is being conducted, the list of nonconforming products which has come before the material review board, and the list of changes requested by suppliers.

Once the list of suspect tolerances has been identified, there are a number of ways in use for minimizing the conversion effort:

1. Establish an order of priority for the "vital few" and deal with them through the regular engineering change procedure.

2. For tolerances of less than vital importance, create a "short loop" for changes; i.e., designate a team (e.g., designer and quality control engineer) to make changes without going through full documentation, e.g., marking up local drawings. Later, when some other reason arises for making an engineering change, the incompletely documented cases will be included.

3. Alternatively, if the tolerance is discovered to be too tight, leave the specification unchanged, but revise the sampling plans to accept a wider dispersion of product. In most companies, changes in sampling plans are accomplished with minimal documentation.

4. Adopt the rule that three material review board waivers of the same defect constitutes a permanent waiver.

A broad solution consists of devising a new system of tolerancing and enforcement for all new product lines so that they will be launched on a basis of "realistic tolerances rigidly enforced." (This will mean that there will be two systems of tolerancing and enforcement in the company simultaneously.) Then as the older designs phase out, only the new system will remain in force.

Providing Aids to Designers.   Any evolutionary solution to unrealistic tolerances must include ways to minimize the bias of the designers. An essential need is to provide designers with tools which can assist them in understanding the cost consequences of proposed tolerances. Several of these tools are available.

1. *Process capability data:*   As data on process capability are worked up and made available for ready reference (see Section 16 under Process Capability: Application), it becomes feasible to train designers in the significance and use of these data.

2. *Data on cost of precision:*   A further step is to quantify the actual cost of achieving various levels of precision, e.g., how the cost in dollars increases as the tolerance in millimeters decreases. Surprisingly, the data for preparing tables or charts of these relationships are often already available in the labor standards used to measure production and inspection productivity. What has not been done generally is to convert these data into tables of cost versus precision. For one example, see Section 16, Manufacturing Planning, Table 16.4, and associated discussion.

3. *Seriousness classification:*   Generally, the most important characteristics also call for the greatest precision. In consequence, use of seriousness classification of characteristics is also a broad guide to tolerancing. See Section 18 under Seriousness Classification for the methodology employed.

4. *Value analysis:*   See the discussion in this section.

5. *Sensory qualities:*   See Section 18 under Sensory Qualities.

Rating of Designs for Ease of Manufacture and Other Factors.   Phillips (1980) has created a "design quality index" for evaluating proposed designs of an automobile. The numerical value of the index is the sum of the demerits received from checklists of design features which make quality difficult to achieve during manufacture. One checklist covers finish, fit, and function. Typical examples from the checklist along with the number of demerits are given below:

Surface quality: A joint requiring weld, braze, solder, or plastic filler receives one demerit for each 25 mm.

Complexity: Count the number of surface planes, gaps, and joints that have to be matched. If a vertical match is required, this receives one demerit for each feature counted.

Electrical: Each connector not self-ejecting receives one demerit.

The overall quality index is obtained by summing up all of the demerits and subtracting from 145. The result is called the "design quality index."

Fischer (1984) discusses seven principles of designing for assembly. Gager (1986) describes a software system which uses a quantitative approach to analyze a design for efficiency of assembly.

Planning for Inspection and Test.   Complex products increasingly require that planning of inspection and test be done concurrently with design and involve the designer. Jefferson (1974) describes how designers traditionally were asked to create a design and also a factory test specification. A separate department then developed the test. For some designs, test access to the product was difficult. The company now requires the designer to provide an associated debugged test statement (in appropriate automatic test equipment language) which will drive the instrumentation on the shop floor, along with a proven test interface box. In this way, due account is taken of test access, buffering, and measurement capability before designs become too heavily committed. The test statements are evaluated by running formal tests on prototype equipments.

RACD (1982) dicusses approaches for evaluating testability throughout all phases of a major project. Appropriate checklists, design guidelines, and testability engineering techniques are provided.

Designers should identify all quality characteristics in the early design stages and should rate the criticality of characteristics (see below) in order to establish inspection priorities.

Functional and Nonfunctional Characteristics.   The distinction between functional and nonfunctional is set out in Section 18 under Seriousness Classification. The distinctions are clear enough, but industrial practice can intervene to complicate matters. When both kinds of characteristics are published in the same document (as often happens), there is confusion unless it is clearly designated which is which. A major reason for clear designation is the difference in jurisdiction over waivers of nonconformance cases. Generally, the Design Department must be a party to any waiver of functional requirements, but not as to nonfunctional requirements. (Design also has the major voice in deciding what is functional and what is not.)

The trend is toward making clear which characteristics are functional. This is done in any of several ways:

1. Use of separate documents to carry the functional requirements
2. Designation of functional requirements by special code letters
3. Seriousness classifications of characteristics (see Section 18 under Seriousness Classification)

Planning for Packaging, Transportation, and Storage.   Products must be protected from the time they leave the factory to the time they are in the hands of the ultimate user. During that time, the product is exposed to environment in both the transportation mode and the storage mode. Clearly it is important to know what these various environments will be and to plan for them both in the design of the product itself and in the design of the packaging and other protective material used with the product. Planning of the protective material should be done as concurrently as possible with the design of the product. Some of the approaches used to plan for these various environments are discussed in Section 20 on Customer Service under Packaging, Transportation, and Storage.

PLANNING TO MINIMIZE COST

Designing for reliability, maintainability, safety, and other parameters must be done with a simultaneous objective of minimizing cost. Formal techniques to achieve an optimum balance between performance and cost include both quantitative and qualitative approaches. The quantitative approach makes use of a ratio relating performance and cost. Such a ratio tells "what we get for each dollar we spend." The ratio is particularly useful in comparing alternative design approaches for accomplishing a desired function. A comparison of the cost-effectiveness of four alternative designs is shown in Table 13.16. Note that design 3 is the optimum design even though design 4 has higher availability.

Two approaches for achieving a balance between performance and cost, Value Engineering and Design to Cost, are discussed below.

Value Engineering. Value engineering (often called "value analysis") is a technique for evaluating the *design* of a product to assure that the *essential functions* are provided at minimum overall cost to the manufacturer and user. Value engineering tries to assure that the design provides only the essential functions and nothing else that can result in higher costs. Although the aim of value engineering is cost driven, the elimination of nonessential functions can result in improved reliability due to a reduction in product complexity. The steps in a value engineering study are:

1. Collect information on the product.
   a. Define what the customer really wants (e.g., performance, size, weight, appearance, durability, etc.).
   b. Collect design and manufacturing information (e.g., design concepts, preliminary cost estimates, etc.).
   c. Collect cost data and, if appropriate, define the new cost goal to be achieved to meet profitability targets.
   d. Collect information on (b) and (c) above for competing products.

TABLE 13.16 Cost-Effectiveness Comparison of Alternative Designs

	Design			
	1	2	3	4
Mean time between failures (MTBF)	100	200	500	500
Mean downtime (MDT)	18	18	15	6
Availability	0.847	0.917	0.971	0.988
Life-cycle cost, $	51,000	49,000	50,000	52,000
Number of effective hours	8470	9170	9710	9880
Cost/effective hour, $	6.02	5.34	5.15	5.26

$$\text{Availability} = \frac{\text{MTBF}}{\text{MTBF} + \text{MDT}}$$

Number of effective hours = 10,000 h of life $\times$ availability

2. Define the functions of the product.
   a. Define the total function of the product and then define functions for the lower levels of hardware.
   b. Distinguish between basic and secondary functions.
   c. Define each function in terms of a verb and noun.
   d. Evaluate the relationship between functions.
   e. Determine the current cost of accomplishing each function.
   f. Establish a value target for each function. Possible bases for value are (*i*) the least expensive way of accomplishing the function described by the verb and noun or (*ii*) the estimated cost of accomplishing the same function in a competitor's product.
   g. Analyze the ways competing products accomplish each function.
3. Develop alternative design approaches for accomplishing the function at lower cost.
   a. Establish an atmosphere of open thinking about alternatives and use knowledge from all sources.
   b. Use creative thinking techniques.
   c. Use checklists based on experience within or outside the company.
4. Compare the alternative design approaches and select one for further development and refinement.
   a. Consider using a quantitative rating scheme to compare the alternatives for the various performance factors.
   b. Estimate the cost for each function and compare this to present costs and the target defined in step 2*f.*
   c. Evaluate by comparison of alternatives and search for ways to combine the best ideas from different alternatives.
   d. Estimate the total cost of the selected design approach and determine if this is acceptable for product pricing.
   e. Submit the proposed approach for management approval.
5. Develop the detailed design for the selected design approach.
   a. Use value engineering checklists.
   b. Use knowledge from all sources of information.
   c. Consider using a value engineering team to coordinate the effort.
   d. Prepare a summary report on the old and new designs and submit to management.
   e. Provide for follow-up to determine actual costs.

Some of these steps are illustrated below. Two useful references on concepts and techniques are Miles (1972) and Mudge (1971). Beeck (1985) discusses the interrelation of value engineering and quality.

Tools of Analysis.   The heart of the value engineering approach is the evaluation of function. A product has higher-order functions (the desired function), basic functions, and secondary functions. Allocation of assets should concentrate on the essential functions rather than secondary functions.

The functions can be listed and classified in tabular or graphical form. One graphical tool is the function analysis system technique (FAST) diagram. Figure 13.16 shows a FAST diagram for a truck torsion bar front anchor. The higher-order function on the left-hand side of the diagram is the desired function (in this case, "support vehicle"). Between the two dotted "scope" lines are shown all of the functions required to achieve the higher-order function. The diagram is constructed by working from left to right while asking the question, "How do I achieve the function listed on the left?" In Figure 13.16, the function of "support vehicle" is achieved by "transmit force" which is a basic function. Every FAST diagram has a horizontal critical path of functions going through the center of the diagram. On this path lie the higher-order function, the basic function, required secondary functions, and the "assumed" function. (The assumed function is some activity which is required as input to the basic product itself.)

Required secondary functions appear inside the scope lines but off the critical path. Any function that happens at the same time as a critical path function appears below it and is connected by a vertical line to the critical path function. A function that happens all the time or at the same time as two or more critical path functions is called an "all the time function" and appears in the upper right-hand corner of the diagram (e.g., "fasten parts"). Design objectives or requirements are listed in dotted line boxes above the critical path (e.g., "lab test").

In evaluating the necessity of secondary and basic functions, the diagram is read from right to left while the question is continually asked, "Why do I perform the function to the right of this point?"

A cost analysis revealed that two functions, "fasten parts" and "resist deformation", accounted for 55.5 percent of the total cost. These two functions are not on the critical path of the FAST diagram and thus represent opportunities for cost reduction by redesign.

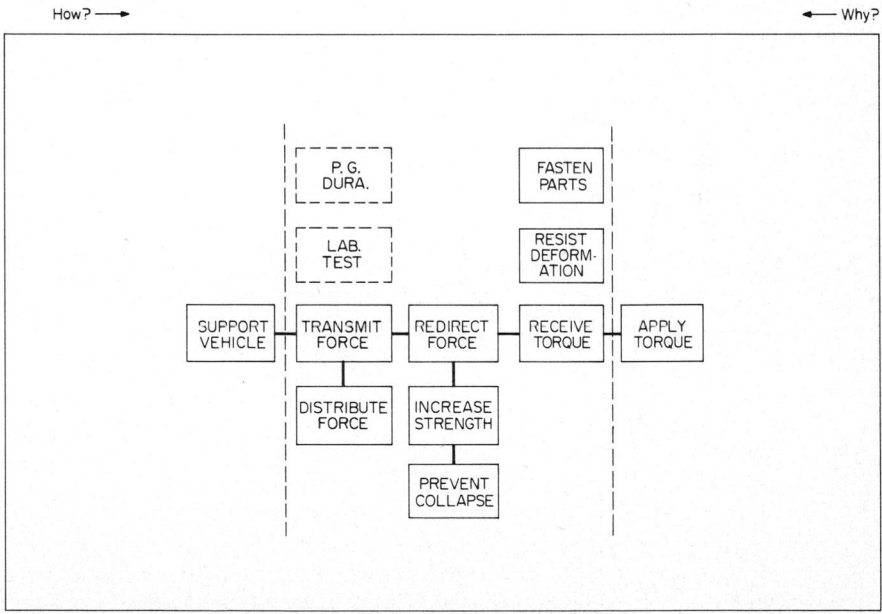

FIG. 13.16 FAST diagram.

Other Cost-Related Approaches. Two other approaches are related to the objectives of value analysis—the life cycle cost approach and the design-to-cost (DTC) approach. Life cycle cost is discussed in Section 3 under Life Cycle Costing. In the DTC approach, the starting point is a life cycle cost target and a statement of the overall function desired. No design approach is specified. Alternative design concepts are then developed and evaluated keeping in mind that the cost target must be met. This is in contrast to the conventional approach of creating a design and then estimating the cost of that design.

The DTC approach establishes cost as a parameter equal in importance to technical and field support requirements and delivery schedules. DTC parameters are identified and addressed throughout the product development cycle. The following steps are adapted from MIL-STD-449A (1961):

1. Review technical requirements for feasibility.
2. Translate essential mission requirements into product functions and subfunctions.
3. Define hardware and software characteristics for functions.
4. Evaluate design alternatives for cost.
5. Formulate product requirements.
6. Identify major high-cost elements.
7. Relate high-cost elements to operations, performance, support parameters, and form, fit, and function design characteristics. This requires sensitivity analyses to learn the effect on cost of changes in parameters and characteristics.
8. Perform trade-off analyses to adjust parameters and characteristics to meet DTC targets.
9. Incorporate parameters and characteristics in development specifications and establish firm DTC targets.

To assist in the analyses, computer programs that perform the calculations for life cycle cost are available for specific products (e.g., helicopters, ammunition, and missile systems).

CONFIGURATION MANAGEMENT

Configuration refers to the physical and functional characteristics of a product, including both hardware and software. Ideally, design and development concludes with a design that is "frozen." In practice, design changes are often made after production has started. The collection of activities needed to accomplish these changes is called configuration management. Three elements are involved:

1. *Configuration identification:* This is the process of defining and identifying every element of the product.
2. *Configuration control:* This is a series of actions which manages a design change from the time of the original proposal for change through implementation of approved changes.
3. *Configuration accounting:* This is the process of recording the status of proposed changes and the implementation status of approved changes. Configuration identification and configuration control are discussed below. Configuration accounting is discussed in Section 20 under Configuration Management.

Configuration Identification.   A configuration established at a particular point in time is called a base line. The base line is used as a basis of reference from which all future changes are controlled. Configuration identification consists of three levels of base line: (1) the functional base line, which defines the general requirements of an entire product; (2) the allocated base line, which defines the general requirements for a major item in the overall product; and (3) the product base line, which defines the detailed requirements of an item. Additional base lines can be set up if needed.

The base line documents include drawings, specifications, test procedures, standards, and any other information which defines the physical and functional characteristics. In some companies, a configuration base line includes facts such as the following:

1. The physical item conforms to issue 04 of the engineering drawing.

2. The steel was purchased from Feric Steel Furnace on Purchase Order Number 230656, dated 3/27/71, was made on Heat Number WX 37791, and conforms to ASTM 176-61T.

3. The welding was done by operator number 29991 using TIG process 10-721 during April 1981, at which time the operator's license to weld was still in force.

4. The bracket on the item was rejected on April 28, 1981, because the 2.176-in (5.53-cm)-diameter hole was off location (2.719 in instead of 2.705 in ± 0.010), after which acceptance "as is" was authorized by Engineer Joe Jensen on May 6, 1981.

This broader definition of configuration obviously includes also the identification of the pertinent materials, processes, personnel, etc., which have collectively created the product, plus the data which proves that the resulting product conforms to specifications. Some identification may be marked on the product, but mainly the identification and proof of adequacy are achieved through chains of documentation. The documents consist of engineering drawings, specifications, in-process inspection reports, acceptance inspection and test results, special test results, etc. These inputs are summarized in Figure 13.17 along with some of the resulting outputs.

Configuration Control.   This element of configuration management starts at the time of the original proposal for a change and ends with the implementation of approved changes. Configuration control involves the technical evaluation, costing, and determination of which specific products ("serial numbers") will have the change incorporated (called the "effectivity" of the change).

Companies vary widely in their approach to assigning responsibility for configuration control. At one extreme, the real decisions of whether and what to change all rest with the designers, and the "processing" of engineering changes consists solely of assuring that the documentation and products are changed to conform to the intent of the engineers' designs. At the other extreme, processing the engineering change becomes a highly formalized, closely coordinated activity in which the coordinating agency carries a good deal of weight in the decisions of whether and what to change.

The trend has been toward the more formalized, coordinated approach. The reason is that as products have become more complex, the effect of an engineering change has multiplied in complexity and in cost. Since more is at stake and the change for error is multiplied, the companies have made their review structure

Inputs	Documentation system	Outputs and uses
Configuration data		Corrective action loops
Contracts		Discrepancy identification
Product development data	Forms	Failure analysis
Design specifications		Corrective action
Process, other specifications	Procedures	
Engineering changes		Configuration management
	Data recording	Engineering change control
		Traceability
Inspection and test data from:	Data processing	
Receiving inspection	Manual	Improvement programs
Vendor surveillance	Electronic	Quality cost analysis
Process control	Other	Quality improvement
Final inspection, test		
Field performance results	Distribution	Executive reports by time
		Product, responsibility, etc.
	Filing	Vendor performance
Discrepancy data	Retention	In-house performance
Vendor failures	Retrieval	Field performance
Process out of control		Cost results
Scrap rework		Improvement projects
Field complaints, claims		
Warranty charges		Quality assurance to:
Product safety claims		Management
		Customers
		Regulators
		Etc.

FIG. 13.17   Model of documentation system.

more elaborate in order to guard against unneeded or unwise changes and against errors in introducing needed changes.

Special organization machinery is set up to coordinate the engineering changes. This machinery consists of some combination of the following:

1. *A published procedure which defines the role of each department:* Action is taken by the line departments and coordination is done according to the procedure. This approach is sometimes the sole engineering change machinery, e.g., in small companies for noncritical changes or in any company for situations in which there is a continuing procession of many small changes.

2. *A project engineer plus "sign off" by the line departments, usually Design, Manufacture, and Quality Control:* Here the project engineer provides coordination.

3. *A Configuration Control Board set up to review all proposed changes:* The board has representatives from engineering, quality, field engineering, purchasing, manufacturing, and the customer. Usually, the chairman has the authority to make a decision on the change (the decision may be appealed through normal channels). The quality representative may often be in the position of justifying the importance of a change.

4. *A Project Change Administrator who prepares plans, secures approvals, publishes reports, expedites, etc.:* Use of such Administrators tends to be limited to cases where engineering changes are complex and costly.

Classes of Change. A convenient aid for configuration management is to classify the changes as to priority. Companies which use only two classes define them as follows:

> *Class A changes:* These are changes ordered by the customer or changes intended to provide remedies for product safety hazards, deficiencies in field usage, high costs, late deliveries, inadequate field interchangeability, and retrofits in the field.
>
> *Class B changes:* These are any changes not included in Class A, e.g., minor improvements, phasing out of obsolete products.

In companies using such systems of classifying changes, the class of change is decisive as to:

1. The choice of organization to be used in coordinating the change— e.g., for Class A changes, the combination of committee and administrator may be used, but not for Class B changes.
2. The extent to which the change will be made effective in various categories of product—in field service, in the finished-goods pipeline, in process of manufacture. etc.

Formalized Review Procedure. As the formalized coordination concept takes hold, there evolves a structured review procedure. A sequence of essential tasks is established and forms are designed to require that all changes go through this sequence. Marguglio (1971) presents a thorough discussion of the entire design change control process.

In the formalized reviews, close attention is paid to clear definition of the base line, i.e., the intended design. (During the various phases of product development, there are several design stages.) Unless this base line is clear, the reviews and actions will become confused and will work at cross-purposes.

Once the baseline and the intended changes are clear, the effect of the change is determined. This requires "tracking" the changes through assembly "trees," parts lists, processes, tools, instruments, etc. This tracking must be done through the entire hierarchy of product: system, subsystems, units, components, etc. Increasingly, computers are used to perform most of the tracking in the case of complex products.

As it becomes clear just what aspects of the product are affected, it becomes possible to evaluate the cost and the benefit of the change. For this purpose it is also necessary to secure an inventory of the physical products which will be affected by the change: i.e., how many there are in field use, how many in the pipeline, how many in a semifinished state. There many also be an effect on maintenance support, i.e., on spare parts, repair parts, diagnostic instruments, and repair tools.

Control over this array of information and action is maintained by assigning a project number to each change and establishing for that project the same array of controls as goes with any complex project: list of activities, schedules, cost estimates, cost accounting, status reports, and documentation. This is done over the entire life cycle of the change, from design concept through being made fully effective.

In situations involving sizable, complex inventories, the effectivity of the change likewise becomes complex. If the units of product are serially numbered, then these serial numbers are used to define effectivity, e.g., serial numbers under 450 will undergo no change; serial numbers 451 to 620 will undergo change J only;

serial numbers 621 and over will undergo changes J and K. Where serial numbers are not used, an alternative is to base the effectivity on status of the product in the pipeline, e.g., product already sold will undergo no change; product in finished goods or spare parts inventories will undergo change J; product in process will undergo changes J and K.

Provision is made for countdown, i.e., checking with all affected departments and verifying all critical elements affected.

Marguglio (1971) provides a list of the quality-related factors to be considered during each phase of a change, starting with the change proposal phase and ending with the product verification phase. Berke (1977) discusses methods of monitoring changes during design including the use of a "quality assurance drawing controller." McCarthy (1975) explains how the principles of configuration management can be applied to computer software.

IMPROVING THE EFFECTIVENESS OF PRODUCT DEVELOPMENT

Product development is a "process" which requires the activities of planning, measurement, feedback, and corrective action similar to those required for the manufacturing process, the purchasing process, and other processes. In maximizing the contribution of product development to product quality, the concept of self-control, improving the effectiveness of individual designers, and the role of staff specialists should be examined. These issues are discussed below.

Kano (1984) discussed the use of a "T-typed matrix" for evaluating the capability of an organization to find problems at the early rather than late stages of product development.

Ingram (1984) describes a historical process comprising five steps—historical set-up, grouping and review, creation of a problem log, course analysis, and remedial action.

Gust (1985) describes how the breakthrough sequence for quality improvement (see Section 22, Quality Improvement) was applied to the product development system of a films company.

Concept of Self-Control in Product Development.   Section 17 under Concept of Worker Self-Control presents three criteria which must be met before workers can be held responsible for controlling the quality of their activities. These same criteria are also applicable to product development. Table 13.17 shows a checklist of sample questions to help apply the criteria to product development.

IMPROVING THE EFFECTIVENESS OF INDIVIDUAL DESIGNERS

Implementation of reliability and maintainability techniques is best achieved by bringing designers to a state of self-sufficiency. This is done in two main ways: (1) design experience retention and (2) training.

Design Experience Retention.   All design managers agree that experience is an essential requirement for a good designer. To supplement the designer's own

TABLE 13.17 Self-Control as Applied to Product Development

I. Have designers been provided with the means of knowing what they should be doing?
  A. Do they know the variety of applications for the product?
    1. Do they have complete information on operating environments?
    2. Do they have access to the user to discuss applications?
    3. Do they know the potential field misuses of the product?
  B. Do they have a clear understanding of product requirements on performance, life, warranty period, reliability, maintainability, accessibility, availability, safety, operating costs, and other product features?
    1. Have nonquantitative features been defined in some manner?
    2. Do designers know the level of product sophistication suitable for the user involved?
  C. Are adequate design guidelines, standards, handbooks, and catalogs available?
  D. Do designers understand the interaction of their part of the design with the remainder of the design?
  E. Do they understand the consequences of a failure (or other inadequacy) of their design on: (1) the functioning of the total system? (2) warranty costs? (3) user costs?
  F. Do they know the relative importance of various components and characteristics within components?
  G. Do they know what are the manufacturing process capabilities relative to the design tolerances?
  H. Do they derive tolerances based on functional needs or just use standard tolerances?
  I. Do they know the shop and field costs incurred because of incomplete design specifications or designs requiring change?
II. Have designers been provided with the means for knowing what they are doing?
  A. Do they have the means of testing their design in regard to the following:
    1. Performance, reliability, and other tests?
    2. Tests for unknown design interactions or effects?
    3. Mock-up or pilot run?
  B. Is there an independent review of the design?
  C. Have the detail drawings been checked?
  D. Are designers required to record the analyses for the design?
  E. Do they receive adequate feedback from development tests, manufacturing tests, proving ground tests, acceptance tests, and user experience?
    1. Are the results quantified where possible, including severity and frequency of problems and costs to the manufacturer and user?
    2. Does failure information contain sufficient technical detail on causes?
    3. Have designers visited the user site when appropriate?
  F. Are designers aware of material substitutions, or process changes?
  G. Do they receive notice when their design specifications are not followed in practice?
III. Have designers been provided with the means of regulating the design process?
  A. Are they provided with information on new alternative materials or design approaches? Do they have a means of evaluating these alternatives?
  B. Have they been given performance information on previous designs?
  C. Are the results of research efforts on new products transmitted to designers?
  D. Are designers' approvals required to use products from new suppliers?
  E. Do designers participate in defining the criteria for shipment of products?
  F. May designers propose changes involving trade-offs between functional performance, reliability, and maintainability?
  G. Are designers told of changes to their designs before they are released?
  H. Have causes of design failures been determined by thorough analysis?
  I. Do designers have the authority to follow their designs through the prototype stage and make design changes where needed?
  J. May designers initiate design changes?
  K. Are field reports reviewed with designers before making decisions on design changes?
  L. Do designers understand the procedures and chain of command for changing a design?

experience, it is common to summarize the experience of other designers as well. This "experience retention" is achieved through several widely used tools:

1. *Design Standards Manual:*   This book accumulates the departmental standards derived from experience, along with referencing the outside standards which have been adopted. The manual is supplemented by notes, memoranda, and other "standards in the making." In large companies there is an Engineering Standards Department which prepares and maintains these standards manuals.

2. *Checklists:*   These lists are a form of "countdown" to be checked out by the designer as he or she proceeds with the project. For example, the checklist on fire hazard would typically include the following:

   - What could cause a break in the fuel line or oil line?
   - What could cause a fuel or oil leak?
   - Could there be a source of ignition?
   - What is combustible?
   - How can a fire be detected?
   - How can the fuel be turned off?
   - What is the escape route for personnel?

3. *Usage and Failure Data Banks:*   The performance of the product under conditions of actual use constitutes the most important single source of experience data. A data bank to collect and summarize such information becomes one of the most useful sources of design experience.

4. *Tools for Economic Analysis:*   These include charts and tables showing the relationship of cost to precision (see, for example, Section 16, Table 16.4), tables of process capability, and comparative costs of alternative designs.

Training for Designers.   To attain self-sufficiency, designers also need training. In part, this is training to use the design experience retention and, in part, to become proficient in the use of tools which have had their origin in other disciplines. These tools include:

1. *Quantification of reliability:*   The basic reliability models, formulas, and procedures are well known and have been organized into standardized training courses. It is comparatively easy to train designers in the use of these basic formulas and procedures (which have wide application). For more complex situations, there must be access to reliability specialists.

2. *Other quantification:*   Training courses have been worked up in maintainability and safety, but to a lesser degree. However, enough is available to offer a useful indoctrination to designers.

3. *Design of experiments:*   The increased complexity of products and the greater demand for statistical significance in test results has required that test programs be designed in a way which holds costs of testing to a minimum while yielding maximum information. Courses in design of experiments and the associated analysis of the resulting data have been standardized at several levels of sophistication and are widely available.

4. *Process capability:*   The concept of process capability as an input in the setting of tolerances is important and can be taught to designers.

5. *Problem-solving methodology:*   Quality improvement concepts (see Section 22, Quality Improvement) apply to product development as well as to other

functions on the Spiral. The diagnostic journeys from symptom to cause and cause to remedy are defined and can be taught to designers.

Training courses work best when the student is required to apply the training as part of the course ("learning by doing"). For example, in value engineering seminars, students conduct a value engineering analysis on actual hardware; in quality improvement seminars, students work on a team project while viewing video tapes on problem solving.

Experimentation in training techniques should be encouraged. Crothers (1971) describes using training workshops as a means of conducting audits on activites. In one case, a circuit analysis workshop was held to evaluate the lack of compatibility between circuit analyses performed by designers and those performed by reliability analysts. Ironically, the initial goal of the workshop was to "educate" designers regarding the value of the work from the reliability analysis group. As a result of the workshop, however, it was concluded that the output of the reliability analysts should be changed to present designers with information in a more useful form. This included revising the work on worst-case analysis criteria, thermo analysis goals, and traditional reliability analysis methods using computer aids.

Beyond the specific material presented in formal training courses there is a need for designers to understand more fully the demands which will be made on the product through its life cycle. A Japanese maker of color television sets uses a combination of on-the-job training and classroom training to achieve this goal. Prospective designers are required to undergo training in the following areas:

1. *In the marketplace:* Part of this 3-month training is in the merchant shops, meeting clients, selling the product, and learning of the problems of marketing. In addition, the trainee makes service calls to learn about the conditions of use, the problems of field maintainability, supply of spare parts, etc.

2. *In the factory:* This 9-month training program provides the trainee with knowledge about factory conditions, the factory work stations, the training and outlook of the factory personnel, the capabilities of the processes, etc. In addition, the future designer becomes familiar with the special assembly line used to test out new models.

3. *In statistical methodology:* This 144-h training course enables the designer to become familiar with the mathematical tools. (This training is not given to a new designer, but it is a prerequisite for promotion to the level of "lead designer.")

A designer who possesses the foregoing bodies of knowledge will obviously be more effective than one who lacks them. As an alternative the designer can collaborate with those who do have the knowledge (as in the design review meetings). Failing such collaboration, the designs will be deficient due to the absence of useful knowledge and tools.

Staff Specialist Organization.   A prickly problem in organizing for new-product design is that of using "new" disciplines such as reliability engineering, maintainability engineering, and safety engineering. While the discussion which follows will concentrate on reliability, the principles involved apply generally to all these specialties.

The time required to introduce a new discipline is usually shortened if a new specialty department is created for it and if the head of the specialty understands his or her role. This role is ideally one of analyzing the projects, using the tools of the new specialty, and making the results of the analysis available to the "regular line" departments. All of this must be done in a way that emphasizes that *the responsibility for achieving fitness for use in the product design rests with the line departments—not the staff specialty.*

The track record on the use of specialist departments has been mixed. Usually, the specialist evaluates the design for reliability or maintainability and provides comments to the designer. Unfortunately, these reviews often occur too late. Nothing is more aggravating than to have suggestions made on a design after the design is finalized and manufacturing is waiting for the design to be released. Reliability inputs must be made available early during the design process if they are to be acted upon.

Ultimately, implementation of the new techniques can best be accomplished by training designers to use them as an integral part of the design process. Steps must then be taken by the staff department to gradually transfer the associated responsibilities to the line designers. Jefferson (1974) explains how one company evolved an approach where a designer is required to produce a design, a test specification, a test package, a reliability prediction, and a repair chart. Bajaria (1979, 1980) discusses the relative role of specialists and line designers along with other issues involved in motivating design engineers to use techniques for reliability.

REFERENCES

Advisory Group on Reliability of Electronic Equipment (1957). *Reliability of Military Electronic Equipment.* Office of the Assistant Secretary of Defense (R & D), U. S. Government Printing Office, Washington, DC.

Allen, Martin (1980). "CAD/CAM and the Third Industrial Revolution." Paper presented at the American Society of Mechanical Engineers, 101st Winter Annual Meeting, New York.

ANSI (1978). *Quality Systems Terminology.* American National Standard A-3. Available from American Society for Quality Control, 310 West Wisconsin Avenue, Milwaukee, WI 53202.

ARINC Research Corporation (1962). *Reliability Theory and Practice.* A training program developed by ARINC, Washington, DC.

Arnitz, William E. (1981). "GIDEP Can Improve Productivity through Information Exchange." *Proceedings, Annual Reliability and Maintainability Symposium.* IEEE, New York, pp. 128–131.

Bailey, R. A. and Gilber, R. A. (1982). "Strife Testing." *Quality,* November, pp. 53–55.

Bajaria, H. J. (1979). "Motivating Line Engineers for Reliability, Part I." *ASQC Technical Conference Transactions,* Milwaukee, pp. 767–773.

Bajaria, H. J. (1980). "Motivating Line Engineers for Reliability, Part II." *ASQC Technical Conference Transactions,* Milwaukee, pp. 168–176.

Bajaria, H. J. (1983). *Integration of Reliability, Maintainability and Quality Parameters in Design.* Paper SP-533, Society of Automotive Engineers, Warrendale, PA.

Beeck, W. O. (1985). "Quality and Value Analysis—Engineering, the Ideal Marriage." *Proceedings of the Conference of Quality and Development.* European Organization for Quality Control, Berne, vol. 3, pp. 299–312.

Belbin, R. M. (1970). *Quality Calamities and their Management Implications.* OPN8, British Institute of Management, London.

Bender, Art (1975). "Statistical Tolerancing as it Relates to Quality Control and the Designer." *Automotive Division Newsletter of ASQC,* April, p. 12.

Berger, Robert L. and Jenkins, Larry C. (1984). "Electronic Equipment Thermal Management." *Proceedings, Annual Reliability and Maintainability Symposium.* IEEE, New York, pp. 17–22.

Berke, Howard L. (1977). "To Assure Quality Productivity, Monitor the Design." *ASQC Technical Conference Transactions,* Milwaukee, pp. 590–593.

Blanchard, Benjamin S. and Fabrycky, Wolter J. (1981). *Systems Engineering and Analysis.* Prentice-Hall, Englewood Cliffs, NJ, pp. 391–406.

Brach, J. P., Jr. and Phaller, L. J. (1980). "Integrated Test—A Must for Reliability Achievement." *Proceedings, Annual Reliability and Maintainability Symposium.* IEEE, New York, pp. 242–247.

Burgess, John A. (1985). "Design Reviews for All Seasons." *ASQC Quality Congress Transactions,* Milwaukee, pp. 451–455.

Cahill, Hugh E. and Davids, Richard C. (1984). "Adam—A Computer Aid to Maintainability Design." *Proceedings, Annual Reliability and Maintainability Symposium.* IEEE, New York, pp. 12–16.

Cherry, D. H., Grogan, J. C., Holmes, W. A., and Perris, F. A. (1978). "Availability Analysis for Chemical Plants." *Chemical Engineering Process,* January, pp. 172–185.

Crothers, D. H. (1971). "Workshop Techniques for Programmed Audits." *Proceedings, Annual Symposium on Reliability.* IEEE, New York, pp. 139–144.

Duane, J. T. (1964). "Learning Curve Approach to Reliability Monitoring." *IEEE Transactions on Aerospace,* vol. 2, no. 2, pp. 563–566.

Dussault, Heather B. (1984). "Automated FMEA—Status and Future." *Proceedings, Annual Reliability and Maintainability Symposium.* IEEE, New York, pp. 1–5.

Eastman Kodak Company (1983). *Ergonomic Designs for People at Work,* vol. I, Human Factors Section. Lifetime Learning Publications, Division of Wadsworth Publishing Company, Belmont, CA.

Ekings, J. Douglas and Sweetland, Robert L. (1978). "Burn-In Forever? There Must Be a Better Way." *Proceedings, Annual Reliability and Maintainability Symposium.* IEEE, New York, pp. 286–293.

Emphrain, M., Jr. and Hamilton, A. B. (1973). *Locomotive Reliability.* Paper 73-DGP-14, Diesel and Gas Engine Power Division, American Society of Mechanical Engineers, New York.

Erhardt, C. C. (1980). "Economic Advantages of True Position Tolerancing." *ASQC Technical Conference Transactions,* Milwaukee, pp. 559–564.

Evans, David H. (1975). "Statistical Tolerancing: The State of the Art, Part I: Background; Part II: Methods for Estimating Moments; Part III: Shifts and Drifts." *Journal of Quality Technology,* January, vol. 6, no. 4; April, vol 7, no. 1; October, vol. 7, no. 2.

Fennell, Thomas L. and Nicolino, Thomas A. (1984). Computer Aided Testability." *Proceedings, Annual Reliability and Maintainability Symposium.* IEEE, New York, pp. 6–11.

Fischer, W. Robert (1984). "Design for Assembly." *Proceedings, Annual Reliability and Maintainability Symposium.* IEEE, New York, pp. 409–411.

Frank, Norman C. (1982). "Ten Commandments for Laboratory Notebooks." *Quality Progress,* November, pp. 40–41.

Frank, G. R. (1977). "Tolerance Challenge." *ASQC Technical Conference Transactions,* Milwaukee, pp. 72–78.

Gager, Russ (1986). "Designing for Productivity Saves Millions." *Appliance Manufacturer,* January.

Garrick, B. John and Mulvihill, Robert J. (1974). "Reliability and Maintainability of Mechanized Bulk Mail Systems." *Proceedings, Annual Reliability and Maintainability Symposium.* IEEE, New York.

Goree, Paul F. and Musson, Thomas A. (1984). "DOD/Industry—R&M Case Study Analysis." *Proceedings, Annual Reliability and Maintainability Symposium,* IEEE, New York, pp. 91–98.

Gust, Lawrence J. (1985). "Non-Manufacturing Quality Improvement." *The Juran Report,* No. 4, Winter, pp. 112–120.

Hammel, Lisa (1974). "Five Years and a Large Sum of Money Later, A New Line of Dolls." *The New York Times,* Feb. 18, p. 20.

Hammer, Willie (1980). *Product Safety Management and Engineering.* Prentice-Hall, Englewood Cliffs, NJ.

Hellend, Kris L., Jr. (1978). "Motivating Management on Maintainability." *Proceedings, Annual Reliability and Maintainability Symposium.* IEEE, New York, pp. 32–37.

Henley, Ernest J. (1979). "Analytical Methods in Risk and Safety Assessment." *ASQC Technical Conference Transactions,* Milwaukee, pp. 717–725.

Herrold, George R. (1976). "GIDEP Data Aids Technical Problem Solving." *Proceedings, Annual Reliability and Maintainability Symposium.* IEEE, New York, pp. 46–51.

Hill, John S. and Still, Richard R. (1984). "Adapting Products to LDC Tastes." *Harvard Business Review,* March–April, pp. 92–101.

Holmes, Richard K. and Michalek, Joseph M. (1982). "Optimizing Quality through Variation Simulation." *ASQC Quality Congress Transactions,* Milwaukee, pp. 382–390.

Ingram, Gary E. (1984). "Historical Processes for Quality Project Management." *Project Management Institute Proceedings,* Philadelphia, pp. 1–3.

Jacobs, Richard M. (1967). "Implementing Formal Design Review." *Industrial Quality Control,* February, pp. 398–404.

Jayachandran, Toke and Moore, Louis R. (1976). "A Comparison of Reliability Growth Models." *IEEE Transactions on Reliability,* vol. R-25, no. 1, April, pp. 49–51.

Jefferson, G. R. (1974). "Establishing Quality at the Design and Development Phase." *Joint Conference of the Defense Quality Assurance Board and the Defense Industry Quality Assurance Panel.* University of Kent, Canterbury, England, September, pp. 11–17.

Juran, J. M. and Gryna, Frank M. (1970). *Quality Planning and Analysis,* 1st ed. McGraw-Hill, New York, p. 613.

Juran, J. M. and Gryna, Frank M. (1980). *Quality Planning and Analysis,* 2nd ed. McGraw-Hill, New York, p. 106.

Kano, Noriaki (1984). "Problem Solving in New Product Development—Application of T-Typed Matrix." *World Quality Congress.* European Organization for Quality Control, Berne, pp. 45–55.

Kapur, K. C., and Lamberson, L. R. (1977). *Reliability in Engineering Design.* John Wiley & Sons, New York, pp. 405–423.

Kimble, Roger G. (1982). "Serviceability Analysis." *Proceedings of the Quality in Electronics Conference.* ASQC, Milwaukee, pp. 79–81.

Kogure, Masao and Akao, Yogi (1983). "Quality Function Deployment and CWQC in Japan." *Quality Progress,* October, pp. 25–29.

Lawlor, A. J. (1978). "Quality Assurance in Design and Development." *Quality Assurance,* vol. 4, no. 3, September, pp. 87–91.

Locks, Mitchell O. (1973). *Reliability, Maintainability, and Availability Assesment.* Hayden, Rochelle Park, NJ.

Lowry, Daniel W. (1970). "Maintainability Demonstration Test Performed on a Computer System." *Proceedings, Annual Reliability and Maintainability Symposium.* IEEE, New York.

Marguglio, B. W.(1971). "Quality Factors to be Considered in Implementing Design Changes." *ASQC Technical Conference Transactions,* Milwaukee, pp. 189–191.

McCarthy, Rita (1975). "Configuration Management and Software Reliability." *Transactions of the American Society for Quality Control,* Mikwaukee, pp. 49–55.

McQuade, Walter (1984). "Easing Tensions between Man and Machine." *Fortune,* March, pp. 58–66.

Mihalasky, John (1980). "The Human Factor in Product Safety." *ASQC Technical Conference Transactions,* Milwaukee, pp. 33–40.

MIL-HDBK-189 (1981). *Reliability Growth Management.* U.S. Department of Defense, Naval Publications and Forms Center, Philadelphia.

MIL-HDBK-217D (1982). *Reliability Stress and Failure Data for Electronic Equipment.* U.S. Department of Defense, Naval Publications and Forms Center, Philadelphia.

MIL-STD-449A (1961). *Engineering Management.* Defense Document Distribution Center, Washington, DC.

MIL-STD-470A (1983). *Maintainability Program Requirements for System and Equipment.* U.S. Department of Defense, Naval Publications and Forms Center, Philadelphia.

MIL-STD-471A (1973). *Maintainability Verification/Demonstration/Evaluation.* U.S. Department of Defense, Naval Publications and Forms Center, Philadelphia.

MIL-STD-721C (1981). *Definitions of Terms for Reliability and Maintainability.* U.S. Department of Defense, Naval Publications and Forms Center, Philadelphia.

MIL-STD-785B (1980). *Reliability Program for Systems and Equipment Development and Production.* U.S. Department of Defense, Naval Publications and Forms Center, Philadelphia.

MIL-STD-882 (1969). *Requirements for System Safety Programs for Systems and Associated Subsystems and Equipment.* U.S. Department of Defense, Naval Publications and Forms Center, Philadelphia.

MIL-STD-882A (1977). *System Safety Program Requirements.* U.S. Department of Defense, Naval Publications and Forms Center, Philadelphia.

MIL-STD-1629A (1980). *Procedures for Performing a Failure Mode, Effects and Criticality Analysis.* U.S. Department of Defense, Naval Publications and Forms Center, Philadelphia.

Miles, L. D. (1972). *Techniques of Value Analysis and Engineering,* 2nd ed. McGraw-Hill, New York.

Miller, E. W. (1971). *Maintenance Index—A Design Tool.* SAE Paper 710680, Society of Automotive Engineers, Detroit.

Mitsuya, Chikao (1977). "Automatic Designing and Drafting System of Elevators." *Reports of Statistical Applications and Research,* Japanese Union of Scientists and Engineers, vol. 24, no. 2, June, pp. 18–27.

Mudge, A. E. (1971). *Value Engineering.* McGraw-Hill, New York.

NAVSHIP (1972). *Maintainability Design Criteria Handbook for Designers of Shipboard Electronic Equipment.* NAVSHIP Document 0967-312-8010, July, Department of the Navy, Naval Publications and Forms Center, Philadelphia.

Nelson, Wayne (1982). *Applied Life Data Analysis.* John Wiley & Sons, New York.

Peach, Robert W. (1980). "Defining Hard to Define Customer Quality Expectations." *Quality Progress,* December, pp. 14–16.

Peacore, E. J. (1975). "Reliability Developments—AWACS." *Proceedings, Annual Reliability and Maintainability Symposium.* IEEE, New York, pp. 383–389.

Phillips, G. P. (1980). *Design Quality Index.* Internal Document of the Cadillac Motor Car Division, Detroit.

RADC, Rome Air Development Center (1983). *The Evolution and Practical Applications of Failure Modes and Effects Analyses.* Copy can be obtained from the National Technical Information Service, Department of Commerce, 5285 Port Royal Rd., Springfield, VA 22151. The document number is ADA131-358.

RADC, Rome Air Development Center (1982). *RADC Testability Notebook.* Copy can be obtained from the National Technical Information Service, Department of Commerce, 5285 Port Royal Rd., Springfield, VA 22151. The document number is AD-A118881L.

Raheja, Dev (1981). "Failure Mode and Effects Analysis—Uses and Misuses." *ASQC Quality Congress Transactions,* Milwaukee, pp. 374–379.

Reiff, Henry E. (1978). "Practical Application of the Duane Reliability Growth Model." *Automotive Division Newsletter, American Society for Quality Control,* January, pp. 5–7.

Renna, Vincent F. and Howard, Harry P. (1979). "New Product Development—Quality Assurance System Approach." *ASQC Technical Conference Transactions,* Milwaukee, pp. 848–856.

Rimondi, G., Tavazza, G., and Turello, U. (1976). "Numerical Simulation Techniques in the Tolerance Settlement of Product Qualitative Characteristics." *EOQC Quality,* vol. 20, no. 5, pp. 4–8.

Schrader, Lawrence J. (1986). "An Engineering Organization's Cost of Quality Program." *Quality Progress,* January, pp. 29–36.

Shaffer, James (1982). "Project Your Production." *Quality,* April, pp. 33–35.

Shainin, Dorian (1976). *Tool and Manufacturing Engineers Handbook.* Edited by Society of Manufacturing Engineers, McGraw-Hill, New York, pp. 31-6 to 31-10.

Shainin, Dorian (1978). "Test: Tolerances and Measuring—Both Vitally Weak in Q.C." *ASQC Technical Conference Transactions,* Milwaukee, pp. 39–43.

Stanton, Burr (1974). "Consumer Appliance Reliability: Closing the Feedback Loop." *Proceedings, Annual Reliability and Maintainability Symposium.* IEEE, New York, pp. 30–34.

Stevens, Roger T. (1978). *Operational Test and Evaluation: A Systems Engineering Process.* John Wiley & Sons, New York.

Sullivan, L. P. (1986). "Quality Function Deployment." *Quality Progress,* June, pp. 39–50.

Taylor, William R. (1981). "Quality Assured in New Products via Comprehensive Systems Approach." *Industrial Engineering,* March, pp. 28–32.

Veraldi, L. C. (1985). "The Team Taurus Story." Paper presented at MIT conference, Chicago, Aug. 22.

Vinson, William D. and Heany, Donald F. (1977). "Is Quality Out of Control?" *Harvard Business Review,* November–December, pp. 114–122.

Wall Street Journal (1978). "Sweating it Out." November 17, p. 1.

Wellborn, John M. and Lawson, G. W. (1978). "Maintainability by Design." *Proceedings, Annual Reliability and Maintainability Symposium.* IEEE, New York, pp. 478–485.

Willard, Irving E. (1979). "Reliability Growth Curves." *ASQC Technical Conference Transactions,* Milwaukee, pp. 321–328.

Yamada, Katsuyoshi (1977). "Reliability Activities at Toyota Motor Company." *Reports of Statistical Applications and Research,* Japanese Union of Scientists and Engineers, vol. 24, no. 3, September, pp. 22–39.

Zaludova, A. H. (1981). "Some Reflections on Quality Terminology." *EOQC Quality,* vol. 25, no. 1, pp. 3–10.

SECTION 14
SOFTWARE DEVELOPMENT

Patrick J. Fortune, Ph.D.

INTRODUCTION 14.1

BASIC CONCEPTS 14.2

SYSTEMS ENGINEERING 14.5

SOFTWARE ENGINEERING . . . 14.6

    Requirements Analysis . . 14.9

    Preliminary Design 14.11

    Detailed Design 14.12

    Coding 14.14

    Testing 14.16

    Maintenance 14.18

MANAGEMENT ISSUES 14.19

    Configuration Management 14.19

VALIDATION 14.20

IMPLICATIONS OF SYSTEM SIZE
AND RISK 14.22

PROTOTYPING 14.23

CONCLUSIONS AND SUMMARY 14.23

REFERENCES 14.24

INTRODUCTION

Over the past 50 years, the computer has had a more significant impact on commercial enterprises than any other single new technology. Starting as extensions of punched card processing that automated a variety of routine financial operations, the breadth of computer applications has expanded significantly. Today, this includes sophisticated monitoring, analysis, and control processing in medicine, defense, and industry as well as a significant expansion of computer usage in what may be termed "business data processing."

In 1972, to mark the 25th anniversary of computing, the Association of Computing Machinery developed a list of computer applications. (See "Perspectives," 1980.) The list numbered 1400, and while already large, it has certainly expanded since then. With the advent of microcomputers, personal computers, and relatively inexpensive software, computer power is within economic reach of essentially all commercial enterprises and a large number of individuals. This can be expected to lead to further growth in the types and complexity of applications.

The economic significance of computer usage is staggering. Within manufacturing companies, annual expenditures on computer-based processing approximate 0.5 to 1.5 percent of revenues. For service companies, which tend to be somewhat more information-intensive than manufacturing companies, this rate rises to 3.0 to 7.0 percent of revenues. Assuming an average of 1 percent among manufacturing companies, the total average annual investment in computer-related information processing among the 500 largest U.S. industrial corporations exceeds $16 billion ("Introduction," 1983). Like the number of applications, the level of investment continues to grow. It is likely that engineering applications are growing faster than traditional commercial applications, due to the increasing complexity of products and the quality and productivity improvement opportunities that computer usage supports. The rapid growth of computer-aided design, computer-aided manufacturing, and computer-based process control are cases in point. It follows that while business data processing has received little attention from formal quality control proponents, expansion to areas more directly related to products and manufacturing processes ensures that this situation will be short-lived.

From a business point of view, cost is the attribute of computer usage that has been and continues to be primary. In the early days of computing, hardware was extremely expensive, so that operating efficiency of both systems and applications programs was crucial. Today, however, system effectiveness and reliability as cost drivers have stepped to the fore. This has occurred for several reasons. First, maximal utilization of hardware is less important as the cost of hardware declines. Second, the applications themselves are involved with processing of data that can be impossible or at least very expensive to repair or replace once corrupted or destroyed. Third, as computers become more involved with designing products, controlling their manufacture, and generally ensuring product quality, the consequences of failures within computer systems can represent costly failures indeed.

This section introduces the concepts of computer system quality in general and the development of computer software quality in particular. (Section 27, Computers and Quality, discusses the application of the computer to various activities within the quality function throughout an organization.) The standard quality assurance terms of "verification," "validation," and "reliability" will be defined with respect to software. Procedures and processes by which quality of software may be realized will be discussed.

Appendix III, Selected Quality Standards, Specifications, and Related Documents, includes documents on software development and software quality assurance.

BASIC CONCEPTS

The central question is: How does one assure that a computer system does what it is supposed to do? To understand the approaches used to achieve such assurance requires an understanding of certain characteristics of computers and computer systems. If we look at a computer system from the point of view of the software, it is clear that all computer systems share certain structural characteristics. In particular, a structure like that in Figure 14.1 is appropriate. Formally, a computer system is defined as an external environment combined with a collection of (often complex) interacting pieces of hardware and software components assembled to solve or address a specific problem. The environment interacts with the hardware and software through a series of inputs and outputs (I/Os).

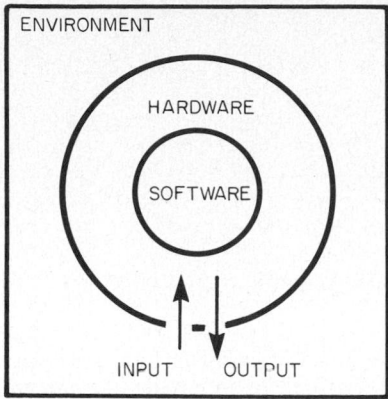

FIG. 14.1 Computer system model.

The environment includes the physical environment and process environment. The physical environment is specified by such parameters as required
power, temperature, humidity, etc. The process environment includes all I/O
variables with which the computer system must deal. A list of components in
typical computer systems is given in Table 14.1. This table serves by example to
define the boundaries of the environment and the system. It is noteworthy that
the software includes procedures and documentation as well as computer programs. Proper attention to these two areas is critical in assuring system quality.

While the model in Figure 14.1 provides a general view of a computer system,
system quality assurance requires a more detailed structure. The implementation
of a computer system solution assumes that the system components have been
combined into a suitable architecture. By "system architecture," we mean the
arrangement of system components comprising the decisions to relegate certain
functions to hardware and software and subfunctions to modules. This is illustrated in Figure 14.2.

Based on the above, two issues related to system performance and quality are
immediately clear. These might be termed capability and complexity.

"Capability" refers to the fact that we clearly know/understand the problem
that we are trying to solve and that we have selected a configuration capable of

TABLE 14.1 System Components*

Hardware	Software
Sensors	Operating systems
Signal conditioners	Telecommunication systems
A/D, D/A converters	Data base management systems
Control actuators	Language processors
Central processors	File systems
Peripheral processors	Application programs
Peripheral devices	Procedures
Timers	Documentation
Annunciator panels	

*This is a partial list.

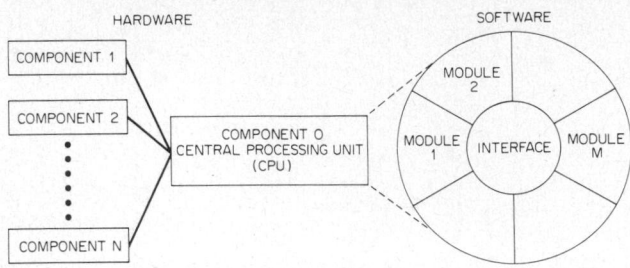

FIG. 14.2 "Internal" computer system structure.

dealing with it. For example, if a parameter to be sensed is represented by a voltage of −5.0 to +5.0 V and if it is necessary to measure it with a precision of ± 5 mV, the analog-to-digital (A/D) converter must have at least 10 bits plus sign. That is, from 0 to +5.0 V, there are five intervals. Each of these must be divided into 200 parts to get the ± 5-mV precision. Thus, we must be able to represent at least 1000 different values. A 10-bit A/D converter is capable of representing $2^{10} − 1 = 1023$ different values. By adding the sign bit, the range from −5.0 to 0 V is also taken care of. Similarly, if the signal to be processed must be sampled at a rate of 100 times per second, the A/D converter and central processing unit must be capable of supporting this bandwidth. To address this point properly requires that the disciplines of signal processing, computer engineering, computer science, etc., are well understood.

The second factor, system "complexity," refers to the degree of complication of a system or system component as determined by such factors as the size, the number and intricacy of special conditions, the degree of nesting in the software, the types of data structures and languages used, and other system characteristics. [Here, "nesting" refers to the extent to which one module (or segregatable instruction sequence) is contained within or referenced by other modules.] These attributes are determined in part by the problem and in part by the design decisions made in order to arrive at the final solution. Clearly, selection of architecture involves a large number of trade-offs. For example, relegating particular functions to specific software modules leads, in general, to greater simplicity within each module. Thus, it is easier to write the programs that comprise each module, and the quality of those modules will be easier to assure. On the other hand, depending on the problem, the number of module interfaces may increase. Thus, the resultant complexity of the total system may be increased (relative to an alternative architecture), leading to difficulties in assuring quality. As system complexity increases, the problem of ensuring reliability becomes more difficult. Here, "reliability" (numerical) refers to the ability of an item to perform a required function under stated conditions for a stated period of time (ANSI/ASQC A3-1987). (See IEEE, 1983b.) Thus, a key thrust in developing high-quality computer systems involves the use of techniques which reduce system complexity.

In the foregoing discussion, hardware and software have been treated in the same manner. It is, however, worthwhile to note some differences, especially as they relate to performance over time in context of the above definition of reliability.

One key difference between hardware and software in relation to quality assurance is that hardware reliability involves not only initial verification and validation but also ongoing indication of failure-free status. Software reliability also involves initial verification and validation. However, the logical components of software are durable. Put another way, software failure results from design/implementation errors only. Since any errors in the software are there until specifically removed and are "encountered" only when the "right" input arises, mean time between failure (MTBF) does not by definition directly apply.

It is possible to construct software reliability models in which MTBF becomes a predicted property of the system. These, however, usually involve the assumption of some probability distribution that describes the probability of encountering a software error between times t_0 and t. To the extent that this assumption is valid, MTBF calculations are straightforward. (See, for example, Sukert, 1977.) Within these models, it is theoretically possible to reduce the software errors to zero at which time the software MTBF approaches infinity. Because of the nonzero probability of hardware failures, the same is not true of hardware.

This difference in durability must be clearly understood as we adapt the usual concepts of verification and validation to software and as policies and procedures are put in place to help assure quality on an ongoing basis. Failure to recognize this can lead to unnecessary, unproductive, and, therefore, overly expensive quality assurance procedures. Worse, it may lead to a failure to address the issues that are truly critical.

Before dealing further with the process of developing quality systems and assuring that quality, the concepts of verification and validation need to be explicitly defined. "Verification" is the process by which a hardware component or software module is shown to meet its specification. Thus, in verification, the specifications (i.e., requirements) are not challenged. "Validation," on the other hand, is the process by which an assembly of hardware components and/or software modules are shown to function properly in a total systems environment (IEEE, 1983b). Here, "function properly" implies that an evaluation of the specification with respect to the problem being addressed is explicit.

Within the set of technologies applied to assuring quality in computer systems, verification and validation attempt to increase system reliability through elimination of errors in elucidation of requirements, as well as elimination of errors in design or implementation. Other techniques are also available as a complement to these. Fault-tolerant and fail-soft design and implementation techniques attempt to introduce mechanisms that permit a system to continue to function properly in spite of the presence of errors, failures, or inputs that are out of range, etc. Hardware and software redundancy are examples of these techniques. Treatment of the fault-tolerant approach will not be included further here.

SYSTEMS ENGINEERING

The problem of determining requirements, implementing a computer-based solution to those requirements, and validating that solution is amenable to an engineering approach. This approach is herein termed "systems engineering." For the purposes of the present discussion, systems engineering may be defined as the systematic, hierarchical approach to the development, operation, maintenance, and retirement of computer systems. Embedded in this definition is the usual association of systems engineering with the process of taking a total (i.e., systems) view of a problem and its solution. From an implementation point of view, systems engineering is supported by a systems engineering process. This process may be defined as the structured series of steps that breaks down a system into its conceptual, functional, and technical operating components so as to reduce complexity and support the effectiveness and efficiency of implementation. This approach clearly applies to any complex problem in general, and to the development of computer systems in particular.

The essence of the systems engineering process is to first separate the problem into digestible subsets and then to distinguish clearly between *what* is to be done within each subset and *how* it is to be done. This ensures that the problem to be solved is clearly defined and that it is broken down into natural units that can be addressed more easily, with solutions implemented more efficiently.

To be sure, the idea of "engineering" a solution to a problem is not novel. Further, to some extent, the systems engineering approach has been applied to the development of computer systems from the outset. This has been particularly true of the hardware parts of a system. Presumably, this is a natural extension of the engineering practices applied to hardware solutions of a mechanical or analog nature to digital computer system engineering. Software, on the other hand, was (and often still is) approached differently, at least partly, because "code" is relatively easy to change. For example, changing a hardware module may involve the use of new parts, significant changes to wiring, changes to board layouts, changes to power requirements, changes to edge connector assignments, etc. A software module can, however, be changed relatively easily by altering a few lines of code, recompiling, linkage editing, and running. Worse, individual machine instructions can be "zapped" or "patched" into stored execution modules with a few manipulations from the system console. In the early days of computer usage, this procedure was seen as an efficient way to develop or fix software. This was partly because early computer applications were not as complex as current and emerging ones and partly because programming as a distinct discipline had not yet developed. In fact, it was felt that as people wrote more programs, the tendency to error would naturally decrease. That a separate discipline of programming was actually required was not recognized clearly until the 1960s; that the development of software systems was actually an engineering process was not recognized until even later.

As computer solutions were applied to more complex problems, the ease of software modification became more of a problem than a boon. This is because the ease of change led to reduced focus on design steps, since the final product could so "easily" be changed. At present levels of complexity, the engineering of the software solution has become critical. Indeed, since a large number of computer applications today are implemented on existing hardware, software is the dominant issue. The remainder of this section deals primarily with the issue of software and software engineering. Conceptually, the extension of the structured approach to problems other than software is direct.

SOFTWARE ENGINEERING

In parallel to the definitions of the previous section, software engineering can be defined as the systematic, hierarchical approach to the development, operation, maintenance, and retirement of computer software. The engineering process used for software development is the structured process that breaks down a system into its conceptual, functional, and technical operating components in order to reduce complexity and support the effectiveness and efficiency of implementation. (Section 27 under Managing Computer Projects discusses the planning, organization, and control of projects to automate manual quality-related activities.)

From a formal point of view, the software engineering process is guided by a software development life cycle (SDLC). For our purposes, an SDLC can be broken down into some six phases.

1. Requirements analysis
2. Preliminary design
3. Detailed design
4. Coding
5. Test and installation
6. Maintenance

Not all formal SDLCs are broken down into six phases; nor do all SDLCs define the phases in precisely the way it is done here. All such SDLCs are, however, functionally equivalent, and in this sense the SDLC discussed here can be considered to be a prototype.

Before proceeding with a discussion of each phase separately, it is worthwhile to look at how the resource requirements in a typical software project breaks down with respect to these phases. For the above prototypical life cycle this breakdown is presented in Table 14.2. The amount of effort spent on maintenance is most striking. The size of the maintenance effort is the main reason why maintenance is explicitly included in the above definitions. It is also why high-quality, cost-effective software by definition must be maintainable and why change control proves to be a critical process. It follows that maintainability must be designed into the system from the beginning, not as an afterthought in the coding phase.

At present, much software development for all types of systems is done by professional systems staffs on behalf of a user group. While this can be expected to change as computers become adapted as tools by the users themselves, it is likely that large data processing, process control, and other real-time systems will continue to involve systems professionals (this includes highly educated and aware users) for the foreseeable future. It is reasonable then to ask what the users' role is in a process such as that outlined above. To be most effective, the group responsible for development of systems should formally include "users" along with systems people. Different people then play different roles in each of the above steps and underlying individual tasks. For example, the requirements definition involves more user time than systems time (say 80 percent versus 20 percent). Coding involves more systems time than user time (say 90 percent versus 10 percent), and testing is approximately a 50-50 proposition. Maintenance involves integration of ongoing user feedback with systems development staff as needed. It follows from this that software is most effectively and efficiently devel-

TABLE 14.2 Typical Resource Requirements for Phases of an SDLC

	Total effort, %	Development effort, %
Requirements definition	3	9
Preliminary design	3	9
Detailed design	5	15
Coding	7	21
Test and installation	15	46
Maintenance	67	

oped by appropriately organized and managed teams of users and systems people. The issue of feedback from users to the development team then makes little sense, since these groups are (or ought to be) synonymous.

In Table 14.2 the relative amount of time (percent of effort) for each of the development phases is also exhibited. If we treat the first three phases as the software design process, we see that testing is the largest consumer of development resources, design second, and coding last. This not only points out the criticality of testing but also illustrates that coding (or programming) is (or ought to be) the least resource-intensive. The use of high-level languages, problem-oriented languages, and specialized packages that permit generation of application programs from libraries and specifications (application generators) are developments in programming technology that help reduce the proportion of time spent on coding. A *well-planned* SDLC is a system engineering development that will ensure that proper resources are dedicated to the upstream processes.

Another perspective on the relative importance of the requirements analysis and design steps is gained from being aware of the incidence of errors in development and the associated costs. Such data are presented in Table 14.3. Here, the logic and syntax errors refer to corresponding types of errors in the programming steps. Design errors not only predominate in number, but also represent an even larger fraction of the total cost of errors. This arises because the later that errors are detected, the greater is the associated cost, due to the need to modify parts of the existing design and the need to change the code in modules outside of those in which the errors actually occurred. It is evident that for software to be cost-effective and reliable, proper effort devoted to the design phases is a necessary condition. The temptation to proceed quickly to coding must be strenuously resisted.

From a management point of view, a cost profile such as that shown in Table 14.3 for any particular software development group will provide the most compelling reason why software quality assurance must be addressed early in the development process. Program managers, quality managers, and others involved in defining projects, estimating costs, and allocating resources must be aware that experience (and to some extent theory) indicates that attempting to assure quality only by inspection of the final product will generally lead to considerably higher costs.

A formal SDLC is most beneficial when applied to large development projects. From a mechanical point of view, small projects or individual programs can utilize a subset of the full SDLC. Conceptually, it is more important that proper attention be paid to the segregation of the design, code, test, and maintenance phases in small projects, or these projects can result in a merry-go-round of continual modification.

A common misconception exists that certain applications, particularly real-time applications, are not appropriate targets for an SDLC, but that a formal

TABLE 14.3 Nature, Number, and Costs of Errors

Error type	Total errors, %	Relative severity	Total cost of error, %
Design	68	2.5	>83
Logic	16	1.0	>8
Syntax	16	1.0	>8

Source: Alberts, 1976, p. 438.

SDLC applies only to "business data processing." Since an SDLC seeks only to partition and structure the steps involved in an engineering approach to systems development, the treatment of real-time systems as an exception is incorrect. To be sure, in the design phases there may have to be an explicit, detailed evaluation of hardware and software timing in order to ensure that an architecture and components are sufficiently *capable*. However, the use of structured systems development techniques serves to mitigate the *complexity* of even real-time systems. In fact, outputs of the various SDLC phases can be tailored to enhance various development steps including emulation, simulation, and design review. The coding and testing phases must readdress any timing requirements noted during design. However, even this can be aided by some of the (graphical) documentation techniques outlined below. Clearly, some of the techniques used in real-time system development do not apply to other types of systems. All types, however, benefit from the spirit and form of the structured approach.

Requirements Analysis.   As its name implies, the requirements analysis (or requirements definition) phase seeks to clearly spell out *what* a system is required to do. Thus, the main thrust is to provide for the effectiveness of the system. Not surprisingly, this phase is the newest and least developed in terms of tools and techniques. The problem (e.g., in a narrative form) here is a difficult one in that the requirements must be first understood and then written down or represented in some other way. Moreover, the representation of the requirements and requirements themselves interact. That is, continued evaluation of the list (i.e., representation) of the requirements in design review steps leads to elucidation of holes and refinement of the requirements themselves. Thus, to be effective, the representation should itself be modular to promote review, understanding, and modification. To support this end, the output of the requirements analysis phase generally consists of five parts:

1. Clear, meaningful statement of the problem scope
2. Explanation of how the problem is presently addressed
3. A statement of deficiencies of the present approach
4. A statement of constraints and added features which, if included, would materially enhance the present system
5. A cost-benefit analysis of the system broken out by system feature

To illustrate these steps, consider the problem of building a system to track the value of manufacturing process parameters, quality control test results, and measures of product quality. Here, a problem statement will include delineation of the specific process steps to be covered, a listing of the parameters to be collected and tracked, the type of analysis to be done on them, expandability requirements, timing of analysis and feedback, etc. Here, feedback can be intrashift feedback, end-of-shift feedback, or periodic reporting. It is also necessary to describe the current system and its deficiencies (e.g., handles too few parameters, feedback to operations is not sufficiently frequent, analysis is error prone, etc.). The requisite timing, calculation requirements (method, accuracy, and precision), and total parameter list in this case define the added features. The cost-benefit analysis helps to identify whether computerization is necessary or cost-effective. It also provides a basis by which individual features can be dropped or modified to simplify the system and reduce its cost.

It is clear that at this stage the target system is subject to considerable change before it is actually implemented. Thus, the system must be specified in a manner that supports the review and the change processes that will occur as the project proceeds.

It is helpful to use graphic techniques such as data flow diagrams (DFD) which show how a data element is created and used, how it must be processed, and where it goes. A data flow diagram consists of four elements: data flows (edges), processing nodes, reference data storage files, and data sources/sinks. An example of a data flow diagram for part of the problem noted above is illustrated in Figure 14.3.

A graphical representation such as this for the requirements of a subset of the monitoring process is easily reviewed and modified. Each process step can be broken down further using similar diagrams. That is, process step 1.1 can be decomposed into 1.11, 1.12, and 1.13; 1.12 can be decomposed into 1.121, 1.122, 1.123, etc. This segregation of function into process steps and decomposition into lower levels of detail as the requirements are developed is referred to as "hierarchical decomposition." Notwithstanding the utility of DFDs, system requirements have historically been represented in a narrative form. This clearly has a number of problems associated with it. One such problem is that the requirements for even a moderate system may take hundreds of pages to describe. Recalling a specific system need and understanding its implications over several pages can be difficult. Resolving ambiguities of the language itself is a further problem. As a partial resolution, both graphical tools and hierarchical decomposition of requirements are useful in the requirements development, the design reviews, and especially in support of system maintenance. The use of graphical tools minimizes ambiguity; hierarchical decomposition facilitates comprehension. The requirements document for a complex system should be partitioned into groups that are meaningful and that are of a sufficiently small size to promote easy understanding and review. These groups are then networked to form the complete requirement. Using the hierarchical numbering approach described above, the requirement is represented in a structured fashion with a progression from less detail (higher level of abstraction) to more detail. Thus, it is not necessary to review a total 100-page specification in one step, but each level is reviewed separately. Since each level of the specification is small (a few pages), self-contained, and concise, it is easier to understand and review. The ease of understanding is a key requirement in reducing the cost of maintenance, since maintaining a system requires educating new staff as well as refreshing the memories of old staff as the need for changes arise. [De Marco (1978) provides an excellent introduction to the various techniques

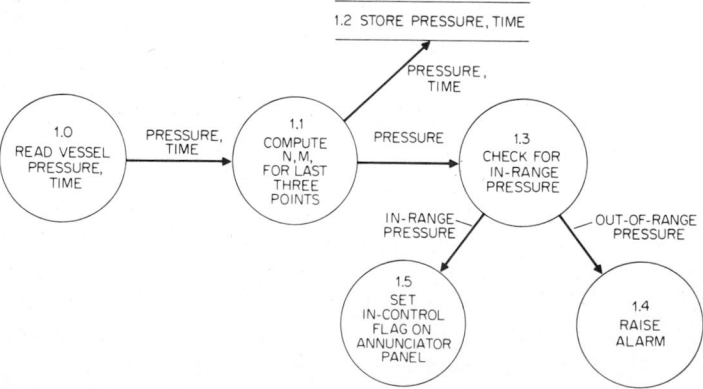

FIG. 14.3 Data flow diagram.

used to express system requirements, including data flow diagrams and structure charts.]

It is noteworthy that the use of a structured specification and an easily understood representation is an aid in promoting the inclusion of users on the systems development team, as discussed earlier. In the above example, a process engineer or quality engineer can easily be involved in both the definition of the requirements and the specification review without being a programmer or without being knowledgable in computer or systems architecture and design. In this way, as the requirements specification documents are used as input to the next SDLC phase (preliminary design), the ultimate user of the system is in a position to certify that what is specified is what is needed.

Preliminary Design. The preliminary design phase proceeds directly from the requirements definition. Here, the various functions represented in the requirements specifications are assigned to logical modules and these modules are characterized from the external, or user, point of view. That is, they specify how the user will view and interact with the final system. This includes preparation of a dictionary of all critical data, all reports, and all screens. The modules themselves are described by an expression of their input, output, and some description of processing done. To the extent that a system function chart or a data flow diagram has been prepared in the requirements definition, the preliminary design step is a refinement of that diagram and is a further expression of what processing will be done with each element of data.

The data dictionary is one of the most critical parts of the documentation prepared during the preliminary design. Actually, the phrase "data dictionary" presently has two different meanings. The first (not of interest here) is "a piece of software that is used to manage the logical and physical data resource of a group of operational systems." Packages to do this are commercially available. The second meaning (and the one of interest here) is, simply, "a collection of information that describes the data that are important to a system." The data dictionary used in structured design defines the data elements that flow in the system and identifies the processes involved with using or modifying it. Other operational parameters may also be included. For example, the definition of a data element may include its security requirements, its frequency of use, the identification of the update modules that use it, how many bytes in the data, etc. These data attributes evolve as the system is specified in more and more detail. It is evident that the data dictionary and data flow diagrams go hand in hand in describing the structure of a system. The data flow diagram specifies how the data are manipulated from process step to process step, while the data dictionary is a repository of information about the characteristics of that data. This, in turn, helps clarify the process steps.

The system functions are explicitly defined using a function chart technique, e.g., Warnier-Orr diagrams (De Marco, 1978) or an input-process-output (IPO) technique. Warnier-Orr diagrams combine the use of hierarchical data structures and functional requirements (Orr, 1981). The use of IPO techniques is older and less powerful but easier to understand, and will be used here to illustrate the intent. IPO approaches attempt to explicitly add more information to that available in data flow diagrams. Here, the functions are arrayed as blocks that have associated input and output defined. The processing requirements are summarized by brief descriptions within the blocks. Further processing information as well as information on procedures and control is included in the specification either as text associated with each processing block or as appended material [IBM (1974)]. Note that the user's view of data entry and report requirements are automatically provided for, and it follows that user involvement and sign-off are critical here.

The detailed characteristics of the techniques used to represent the preliminary design specification are less important than the use of a structured hierarchical approach in refinement of the system design. The use of an IPO technique is not new, and will be familiar to engineers that have dealt with the development and simulation of manufacturing processes. The important point here is that the same technique can be useful in development of computer systems. Within any given organization, techniques from a variety of alternatives can be chosen to fit that organization's needs at a particular point in time. Where appropriate, structured analysis packages can aid in fostering standard practices throughout an organization. (A review of some of the issues and choices can be found in Colter, 1984.)

One of the key activities undertaken during the preliminary design phase is the search for a commercial application package to solve the problem, instead of in-house-developed software. That is, the system requirements and user view of the system are understood in the later stages of the preliminary design. These requirements can, therefore, be compared to the features of a commercial package to see if the degree of fit is sufficient to justify acquisition. The search for a package also can refine and validate the in-house specification by comparison of that specification to existing systems that purport to fulfill a similar function. Both needed and extraneous functions can be identified in this manner. For example, if the application is relatively common, a reasonable degree of fit of the requirements with the package should be expected. If the degree of fit is (surprisingly) low, the requirements need to be reviewed to see if they are really *requirements.* As a practical matter, many projects tend to confuse "wants" with "needs," so that the system has specified features that are not cost-justified. The candidate packages may be used as foils in ensuring that this does not occur.

Because of the above confusion between needs and wants and the high cost of subsequent life cycle phases, it is often of interest to try to change the business process to enable usage of a "vanilla" package. In this way, needs can be met at the lowest possible costs. In cases where some customization is truly needed to gain business benefit, the customization should be designed as an add-on (e.g., via new report or analysis modules) rather than a modification of the source code in the package. It is worth remembering that the main cost of a system is incurred as maintenance. If an unmodified package can be used, the supplier incurs the cost of maintenance. If add-on modules are used (as opposed to package source code modifications), at least the in-house maintenance costs will be minimized.

In the use of packages, SDLC phases subsequent to preliminary system design are also modified. The extent of modification depends on the degree of fit between package and requirements. For example, coding may be eliminated and in-house (unit) testing reduced.

Detailed Design.   The detailed design phase takes the output of the preliminary design phase and converts it to detailed specifications that are sufficient to permit development of physical data bases and files, and coding of the actual programs. The focus of this phase is in the internal design—design, that is, from the computer's point of view.

The data dictionary serves as the basis for construction of the actual data bases and files used within the system. File descriptions, data element length, and security requirements go into detailed descriptions of the file and data base layouts.

When using a formal data base management system (DBMS), construction of the data bases will depend on the DBMS used. The detailed data base specifications involve definitions of relationships among data elements. These may be hierarchical relationships, network relationships, or formal relations. Transactions that add an item, delete an item, or update an item must be identified, and access keys must be specified. Overall properties of the data base structure that affect maintainability and expandability are also taken into account. One such property is normalization. Normalization is a formal approach that examines the data and groups data elements together in a structure that is more adaptable to future changes (see Martin, 1983). Tools to automate the actual normalization process are being developed, and can be expected to greatly aid this process in the future.

The previously developed module specifications are the inputs to this stage. The programming specifications should be developed in a manner that enhances system design review by project participants who are themselves not programmers. There are a number of techniques by which this can be done. One example is the use of pseudocode (see Page-Jones, 1980).

"Pseudocode" is a semiformal language that converts *what* is to be done into *how* the logic will flow in actually doing it. The primitive structures in the pseudolanguage are a balance between the logical constructs required in the programs (IF-THEN-ELSE, DO-WHILE, SEQUENTIAL EXECUTION) and the characteristics of the target programming language to be used in the implementation. The closer the language is to English, the greater is the ease of design review by nonprogrammers, but the more ambiguous the description may be. The closer the pseudolanguage is to the target language, the easier the final programming step is. Besides enhancing the design review steps, the use of pseudolanguages permits the programmer to concentrate separately on the program logic versus the syntax and semantics of the target language. That is, the detailed logic flow is spelled out in pseudocode followed by transliteration of the pseudocode into the target language. There are no generally accepted, standard pseudolanguages, but working examples are readily constructed.

To view the use of pseudocode, consider an example of a module to control temperature in a manufacturing process. Part of the module would be coded in pseudolanguage as follows:

```
READ PROCESS TEMPERATURE:
    COMPARE TO LOW-SET-POINT;
        IF LESS THAN LOW-SET-POINT
            THEN PROCESS HEAT-CYCLE:

    COMPARE TO HI-SET-POINT;
        IF GREATER THAN HI-SET-POINT
            THEN PROCESS COOLING-CYCLE
END;
```

The I/O process and heating-cooling cycles would be specified by other pseudocoded modules. It should be clear from this example that dialects of pseudolanguages are simply definable. The above dialect is useful if the target language is a higher-level language like FORTRAN or even if it is an assembler language. Note that the indentation of pseudocode and resulting source code can help improve structure and understanding.

The use of pseudocode as a specification technique is useful independent of the size of the project. Even if the "project" involves writing a single program, pseudocode will aid in getting the program right the first time. In addition, module pseudocode serves as excellent program documentation.

Design Reviews. During the requirements analysis, the preliminary system design, and the detailed design phases, the process is punctuated by a number of design reviews. These reviews may be conducted among the design team itself (including user personnel) or may include outside reviewers (formal quality reviewers, peer reviewers, etc.). The challenges put to the system in these reviews include what-if scenarios, fault tree analysis, etc. The design review process throughout these phases represents a large part of the static testing (or desk checking) to which the system is subjected. "Static" refers to the fact that the system being tested is not executed on a machine as part of the test process. Nonetheless, the static tests must be formally planned and executed if design errors are to be minimized.

Coding. The coding, or programming, phase is the first of the two implementation phases. In this phase, the detailed programming specifications are converted to a form executable by a computer. This includes source language development, job control language development, compilation, linkage editing (i.e., linking all modules of the system together into a single load module), and execution. At this point, the design is essentially frozen, but may be changed as errors are discovered. The cost of uncovering design errors at this late point is excessive, as already noted (see Table 14.3).

In addressing the role of the coding process in relation to software quality, the same issues that impacted design will be considered here. Namely, the key way to improve the reliability of the original product as well as its maintainability is to reduce the complexity of the programs. This is done in three ways: First, the programs should be developed from well-written, clear specifications of a properly structured system. Second, the internal structure of the programs should be streamlined and the control should, as much as possible, flow cleanly from start to finish. Third, the language used should be as high a level as possible; that is, it should be as far from machine language and the idiosyncrasies of the hardware as practical, given the problem.

The first point above speaks to the structure of the overall system. By the time the coding phase is reached, this level of structure is largely fixed. The second point, on the other hand, addresses the internal structure of the programs, which, at this point, is only partially set (assuming that well-structured pseudocode is used to produce final program specifications). The approach to programming that incorporates top-down design and top-down control flow implementation and that focuses on the use of explicitly defined data types and on the use of a restricted set of control primitives to improve the structure is called "structured programming." While a rigorous definition would restrict the control primitives to the set DO-WHILE, IF-THEN-ELSE, plus sequential statement execution, for our purposes the definition can be broadened. Within structured programming, we include any approach by which the control flows are simplified via restriction of entry and exit points, segregation of program subfunctions into blocks, and use of a control flow that moves generally from program start to program end. Each of these restrictions helps to reduce complexity, improve clarity, and facilitate maintenance.

To further develop the concept of structured programming (used here very broadly), we can consider some illustrative practices that ought to be followed in programming. For example, all intents should be made explicit. That is, variables ought to be typed explicitly (e.g., REAL, INTEGER, PICTURE, DOUBLE PRECISION, etc.), vector and array sizes ought to be specified explicitly, and legitimate variable ranges should be checked explicitly. Further, variable names should be meaningful. A mnemonic such as PRESSR is more meaningful than X as a variable that represents pressure. All of these points increase the "structure" of the data used within a program.

As a second example, the sections of a program that implement functions within a program should be grouped in explicit program blocks or subroutines. The program blocks should be separated from each other using features of the implementation language (e.g., BEGIN. . . .END in PL/1) or through the use of comments (e.g., in FORTRAN or assembler languages). The use of subroutines will automatically support this functional segregation. The programs themselves should be heavily commented to promote understanding of program intent. As noted earlier, simple techniques (such as indenting source code) further convey structure and promote understanding.

The logical flow in a program should as much as possible be unidirectional with as little branching back to earlier program statements as possible. This implication of structured programming has led to a situation in which GOTO-less programming and structured programming are taken as synonymous. As can be seen from the above, the latter concept is much broader (see also Knuth, 1974, and Dahl et al., 1972).

The techniques of structured programming seek to impact the structure of both data and the program instruction sequences that manipulate that data. Consistent with the general theme of this discussion, the imposition of structure within programs decreases complexity, thereby improves clarity and understanding, and leads to improved quality. It is worth repeating that this is a consequence of the fact that use of structured approaches involves thinking on successively lower levels of abstraction, such that at any point only features relevant to that level are considered. Irrelevant issues then tend not to impact the quality or speed of problem solution. (See Dahl et al., 1972.)

Some programming languages contain features that permit data and logic structure to be more easily implemented than others. It follows then that within some limits, system developers can affect quality by the choice of programming language and programming standards. By definition, the closer a given programming language is to English, the higher level it is said to be. The set of language options available for a particular project is restricted to the set that the selected hardware can support and to a lesser extent by the parameters of the problem itself. Modern hardware tends to support a variety of languages: Assembler language, FORTRAN, and PASCAL is a language sequence (in order of increasing level) available on most hardware today.

In certain applications such as programs that directly control the operation of a device such as a printer disk or communication line, or in cases where high speed is required, low-level (i.e., assembler) languages are often used. More recently, however, optimizing compilers for high-level languages resolves the need for execution speed without recourse to the assembler level. Language extensions such as the Instrument Society of America version of FORTRAN permit device level manipulations within a high-level language.

The current direction of program language development is toward a higher level. The use of languages that are designed to solve a specific class of problems is one approach. These languages are called problem-oriented languages in that the basic verbs or other constructs used are most suited to solving particular types of problems. Report generation (e.g., RAMIS and FOCUS), statistical analysis (SAS), and graphics (SASGRAPH, TELEGRAPH) are examples.

An approach to formally defining the interaction among language level, program volume (i.e., "size"), and complexity to predict the effort required to write a given program in a given language is embedded in the discipline of software science (see Fitzsimmons and Love, 1978, and Halstead, 1977). Mean language levels (λ) computed by comparing implementations of various programs written in these languages have been developed with the following results (Fitzsimmons and Love, 1978, p. 6):

Language	Mean level (λ)
English prose	2.16
PL/1	1.53
ALGOL 68	1.21
FORTRAN	1.14
ASSEMBLER	0.88

Since software science predicts that the effort to create or understand a program (to implement a given algorithm) varies like λ^{-2}, the effort required in creating (understanding) a PL/1 program is 1.8 times less than that for a FORTRAN program and 3.0 times less than that for an assembler language program (Fitzsimmons and Love, 1978). This is because of the reduced complexity of the programming task in these respective languages. Thus, one can conclude that an average programming project will, in general, proceed faster in PL/1 than in FORTRAN or in assembler. Results of using PASCAL would be expected to be similar for these with PL/1. These comparisons assume all alternatives are equally reasonable choices; that is, that no choice is eliminated because of specific problem characteristics. Software science, therefore, quantitatively corroborates the intuition of programmers familiar with these languages. These data illustrate the impact that the proper choice of programming language can have on the simplicity and therefore (presumably) the quality of a system.

Testing.   As pointed out in Table 14.2, the testing phase is the most resource-intensive of all the development phases. As discussed above, static or desk checking takes place during the design phases of the system development cycle. In addition, there is the widely used concept of program testing—or, more correctly, dynamic testing.

In a structured testing approach, dynamic testing is broken down into several subphases such as:

1. Unit testing
2. String testing
3. System testing
4. Stress testing

Unit Testing.   "Unit testing" is targeted toward the testing of each module individually. In this process, the data to be used for exercising the module is selected by a careful examination of the source code for that module. Since the details of program internals are critical in this process, this type of testing is called "white-box" testing.

One of the key success factors in a sound unit test is the extent to which the test data challenge the software. This, in turn, is driven by how well the test data exercise the execution paths of the program. One way of ensuring that unit testing is properly stressful of the program is to ensure that each branch of the program is traversed when executed using the test data as input. Placement of counters in each execution path can facilitate this (see Myers, 1979; and Huang, 1975). Since each well-written program should first check for legitimate inputs, this approach guarantees that at least one point outside the acceptable range, one point on or near the boundary, and one point in the acceptable range execute properly.

By acceptable range, we mean the collection of ranges for each of the program variables (including input and output data) for which the program is supposed to produce good results. An example of an out-of-range condition for an input variable in a subroutine that computes $f(x) = 1/(1 - x)$ is $x = 1$, since $f(x)$ has a discontinuity at $x = 1$.

As programs become complex, the number of branches can become impractically large as a basis for testing. In this case, the test data should be selected by examination of acceptable input ranges and by a consideration of potential internal failure modes. In all cases, one point outside the accepted range for input variables, one point near the boundary, and one point inside is a minimal requirement. Other inside points should be selected based on examination of the program itself.

If a package is used, the source code should be inspected as to structure and comments. However, rerunning the unit test on supplier-provided software may not be worthwhile. It may suffice to audit and validate the testing approaches used by the supplier. Local modifications are then unit-tested, and the linkages to the package are tested during the string and systems test.

String Testing.   In the second subphase of testing, "string testing," one begins to put the particular programs together. Since this may involve the use of programs developed by other programmers that have not as yet made their final programs available, stub programs can be useful. "Stub programs" are dummy programs that either generate calls to the tested program or accept or check output from the tested program. As the remainder of the programs become available to the programmers (usually by being added to a project library), the stub programs can be replaced in subsequent testing.

Since unit testing and string testing use a "white-box" approach, most of the testing in these phases is done by the individuals who developed the programs. In addition, since the test data are developed by looking at source code, no explicit evaluation of requirements is performed. Thus, these subphases actually test whether the sets of instructions (i.e., programs) that the programmers put together execute the way the programmers intended. Accordingly, unit test and string test are actually verification techniques. The result of a verified program, however, may differ from what the user intended the system to do. For example, a program to compute a standard deviation can be checked to see if it correctly computes standard deviations. Whether the standard deviation is the correct variable to compute to solve the problem is a separate question. This problem is one of validation and is addressed during system testing.

System Testing.   "System testing" refers to testing of the integrated hardware and software *system* to ensure that all *system* requirements are met. Several attributes are implied by this definition. First, data used should be developed from an evaluation of the actual requirements of the system. Second, the data selection and test output evaluation lies more in the end-user domain rather than that of the system developers. In fact, the system test process in many cases is best carried out by members of an organization other than the one that developed the system (Myers, 1979). Third, from the point of view of the code itself, system testing is a "black-box" process. System test data are most appropriately selected by examination of the written systems specifications. The system structure charts, data flow diagrams, data dictionary, etc. developed during the design phases are useful sources. In addition to these approaches, the user documentation is also useful in performing the systems test. During system test execution, user documentation may be particularly useful in understanding ways in which the system may be *misused.* Avoidance of problems that promote misuse is, of course, an implied system requirement. Common examples of problems that promote misuse include output that is difficult to read, error messages that are hard to understand, options that are redundant or unnecessary, and sequences of operations that are cumbersome.

The development of a sound system test is a difficult and creative process for which a consistent general methodology does not appear to exist. One useful alternative to a general methodology is to separate the systems test into test categories and then ensure that no category has been omitted in the test protocol (Myers, 1979). One such category is stress testing. Whether one treats this as an element of system testing or as a separate phase is immaterial as long as it is done.

Stress Testing. By "stress testing," we mean stresses exerted in both volume and time. That is, systems may fail because arrays or files run out of allotted space or the physical capacity of tapes, disks, buffers, etc. are exceeded. Volume testing subjects the system to an amount of data sufficient to test this type of failure mode. Systems may also fail because the volume is nominal, but it arrives in a very short period of time. Short-term buffer capacities may be exceeded, temporary arrays may overflow, etc. This class of error can be a problem in real-time data acquisition and control systems, or collections of batch systems that must turn around within a fixed time period and can have time-based stress failures if the execution time in any given period is too great.

Before leaving the subject of testing, the issue of "debugging" warrants some discussion. Intuitively, the process of debugging is closely related to that of testing. This arises because bugs are often identified through a testing process, and subsequently removed. Testing, as defined herein, is a concept broader than debugging in that the latter concept is usually a "dynamic test" activity only. Further, the limits of testing and debugging need to be clearly recognized inasmuch as, with either approach, one does not show that a piece of software works but actually highlights when and where it does not.

The process of actively showing that software works (as opposed to showing instances in which it does not) is embodied in the concept of "proof of correctness." This technique relies on the development of correctness statements or assertions as statements that must be correct or true if the program is correct (see Anderson, 1979). These assertions can be checked by hand, using flow charts or graphs, or they can actually be inserted in the programs and checked for "truth" during execution. Proof-of-correctness approaches, at the present time, continue to be a subject of research in mathematics and computer science, and it would appear to be sometime before this technique is practically applicable to a broad class of real life problems.

Maintenance.   System maintenance includes all the ongoing activities required to ensure that the system continues to function properly even as the problem that the system was designed to address changes over time. Further, notwithstanding careful adherence to a formal SDLC, it is possible for certain errors to remain undetected during all testing work. These errors can remain in the system for long periods of time. Maintenance then also includes fixing such errors as they are discovered.

Since both new requirements and elimination of errors may require either major or minor system modifications, the logic involved in the first five phases of the SDLC should be reapplied as the need for modification is perceived and as the modifications are defined and implemented. In many instances, maintenance activities are routine and the reapplication of the SDLC is done implicitly without the detail described earlier (except for coding and testing of course). In other cases, especially as the system ages, the most economical approach is to redo the entire system. One then proceeds with the full SDLC in detail, including analysis of the cost and benefits of repair versus reconstruction.

MANAGEMENT ISSUES

As with other engineering processes, systems development must be managed properly to ensure quality results. Project organization and staff selection consistent with the requirements of the systems development life cycle are mandatory. One organizational approach that has been used successfully is the concept of a chief–programmer team. The team itself consists of a small group of specialists organized to do a specific project or set of tasks. These specialists are led by an experienced developer/programmer/analyst, etc., and the rest of the team consists of sufficient numbers of other developers/programmers/analysts at appropriate skill levels. The team also has the services of a clerical person (librarian) who assists the rest of the team in job setup, documentation preparation, project time reporting, cost tracking, etc. The key here is to target a *team* toward a particular part of a project. Team members help each other in design reviews, structured walk-throughs, desk checks, and other types of processes that help assure quality. The team approach is useful to the extent that it helps overcome the individual egos that can interfere with project success (Anderson, 1979).

In addition to techniques that focus on software development technology, techniques such as development of software quality assurance units (SQAU) are also being tried. The unit may be an organizational element separate from the systems department or project team. The SQAU is responsible for reviewing the project outputs on a phase-by-phase basis with respect to a formal software quality assurance plan. The plan is actually an outline of documentation requirements relating to both the system product and development process. The scope of the plan covers all issues from system purpose to configuration management and maintenance procedures. (An outline of a prototypical software quality assurance plan may be found in IEEE, 1982.)

Although we have not indicated it directly above, some people may define quality software as that which not only meets functional requirements, but also is implemented on time and on budget. The engineering management techniques of program evaluation and review technique (PERT) and critical path method (CPM) are useful in this connection. However, the use of standard forms-driven SDLCs, project history tracking, and data bases of errors commonly made within a given shop are all useful in preparing accurate estimates to be used with PERT or CPM. In addition, data bases of errors and design lessons learned can be useful in defining training opportunities. Schulmeyer and McManus (1987) discuss concepts and techniques of software quality assurance.

Configuration Management. The last general area of management interest to be covered here is that of configuration management. The financial impact of configuration management was noted in Table 14.2: 67 percent of the cost of a system is incurred after the system goes into production. It should be clear from the foregoing general discussion that documentation requirements are tailored to each phase of the development life cycle. This includes standards for exposition of clear requirements, concise specifications, unambiguous and uncluttered design descriptions, meaningful program specifications, properly documented source code, and properly prepared test cases, test case results, and user documentation. These items taken together with all other items (hardware and software) that comprise the system may be termed the "system configuration."

Proper control of the quality and cost of system maintenance is supported via the system configuration management plan. This plan provides the outline and detail that defines each configuration end item, and provides definitions of the processes by which these items will be changed, by which the changes will be released, and by which changes are requested, recorded, effected, and audited. (An outline of a configuration management plan may be found in IEEE, 1983a. A further discussion of the general management issues overviewed here can be found in Grinath and Vess, 1983.)

The process-of-change management is supported by the use of software libraries. Many computing problems reappear in a number of forms. Mathematical subroutines are a case in point. Once programs that help solve these problems are written and validated, they can be added to a library for use by a number of people within the same organization. The repeated developing and testing of these particular programs is, therefore, avoided. Equally important, however, is the fact that each user has available a valid implementation of an acceptable algorithm for a particular application.

In using in-house developed libraries, it is useful to employ different software classes as approved for problems with different levels of risk. For example, one class may be approved for use at one's own risk and another may be unconditionally certified. Between these two is a continuum of classes. The configuration management process and software quality assurance activity must then support the classification and certification process.

VALIDATION

An essential step in software development is assurance that the computer system does what it is supposed to do. This is important not only from the point of view of developing software engineering techniques but also in ascertaining whether evaluation schemes can be defined to assess software quality in an after-the-fact fashion. As was evident during the above discussion of software engineering, computer systems cannot be validated using simple testing procedures.

To validate a computer system in any meaningful way, one must begin by looking closely at the process by which it was developed. This evaluation must be keyed to an evaluation of the input to and output from each phase of the SDLC. It must, therefore, be conducted on a phase-by-phase basis. To the extent that the process was properly structured, each phase can be examined individually with consideration of how the output of one phase is guaranteed to be consistent with the input of the next.

Source code review plays a special role in the assessment of system validity. Examination of source code for a system of any significant size cannot be done at a level of detail that adds much to the assurance of system quality (beyond that done in unit testing). Rather, the internal quality control process, the nature of the program specifications, and the scope, structure, and output of the various testing phases are more useful targets for examination. To assess the validity of the system in a maintenance environment, the configuration management approach should also be examined.

As indicated above, while the idea of validation "runs" makes little sense, the concept of a "test for record" does. In such a test, the system is executed using the user documentation to determine what steps to take, what the results should be, and how to interpret the output. The test for record differs from a system test in that fewer data are required and the user actually executes the test. Thus the systems test may obviate the need for a test for record. It must be recognized that the result of the test for record is an assessment of how the system can be misused rather than as a testimony of total system validity. As a corollary, and in view of the detailed discussion of the structured testing approach presented above, the full complement of tests (from unit test through systems test) is a far more robust challenge to the system than that associated with a test for record. Further, in absence of the type of analysis and data preparation done in structured testing, there is no way to document the extent to which the data used in the test for record adequately challenges the system. By contrast, audit of the unit test through system test protocols can provide an assessment of the extent of the challenge to which the system was subjected. This audit is therefore a better basis for drawing conclusions with respect to system validity.

There is one exception to the use of the SDLC-based validation process. This exception arises in the large number of instances in which old systems must be evaluated with respect to validity. Here, a structured SDLC may not have been used in systems development, so that many of the procedures discussed above do not directly apply. In this case, top-down analysis can still be performed to permit a validity assessment to be made. To maintain perspective, it is important here to recall what the mission is: Systems validation aims to ensure that the system solves the problem of concern and that it operates at the requisite level of reliability. In order to address these issues with respect to old systems, the structured approach outline throughout this discussion can still be used as a foundation for the type of analysis of system function and performance that must be made.

Although validation of the development process may not be possible for an existing system, system history may obviate the need for certain analysis steps normally done. To illustrate, consider the requirements definition. The purpose of this step is to ensure that the problem is sufficiently well understood and described to permit a solution to be developed. If a system has been operating for some time, the extent to which it solves the problem under consideration ought to be clear. That is, by system performance history, one can *inductively* determine the extent to which the problem is solved. The *deductive* process is used in new development.

If system history shows that some question exists as to the ability of the system to solve the problem, several steps can be taken. First, the requirements as currently (as opposed to originally) defined must be formally understood. Based on these requirements, data for a systems test can be prepared and critical failure modes can be identified and specifically tested for. Second, if the system is expected to require modification over the period of use, the architecture must be understood. Here, the modules and data structures used, mapped to required functions, can also be developed. This provides a basis for determination of the forms of systems modifications necessary to realize given functional changes. Where appropriate, this description can also be used to assess the viability of an existing architecture with respect to adaptability as well as with respect to acceptable operating costs. Based on the results of this analysis, a decision to scrap an old system or parts of it can be made. Note that this is tantamount to the review processes that occur in the preliminary and detailed design steps, and as such increases the level of assurance that the function of the system is clearly understood.

The third step that can be taken involves review of the program specifications and program documentation. The source code can be evaluated with respect to comments and clarity. The program and user documentation should be evaluated to ensure that the function described is consistent with the program specifications. If special concerns arise, the source code can be evaluated in detail by desk checking and unit testing. Data range checks can usually be added to programs relatively easily without impacting the main program flows.

It is worth repeating that some measure of system validity can be inferred from the length of time the system has been in operation without error. Prolonged error-free operation is implicitly equivalent to the desk checking and unit testing that goes on during the structured development process.

Each instance of establishing the validity of an old system must be looked at on a case-by-case basis. The effort expended should be balanced with respect to current knowledge of the system, the cost of additional validation, and the risk associated with system failure. Certain occasions may arise in which it becomes cheaper to rewrite the old system or parts of it than try to revalidate it, especially if risks are high and modifications are expected to be frequent.

Proper validation of an existing system does not depart from the structured approach advocated throughout this discussion. It requires instead that one elucidate the necessary validation requirements assuming that a structured development process had been followed; use system performance history and existing documentation as appropriate to show equivalence between conclusions based on that history and specific validation requirements; and perform the validation steps that are not obviated by consideration of historical performance in some meaningful way.

IMPLICATIONS OF SYSTEM SIZE AND RISK

The foregoing discussion has been concerned mainly with the recommended engineering approach for development of large-scale systems. Actually, the concepts presented apply equally to all types of systems, but the necessary level of documentation and formal control varies with the size and risk associated with the system. For example, systems which control manufacturing processes, process corporate payrolls, or take customer orders on-line have high financial risks associated with failure modes. Accordingly, a great deal of effort is expended in the control of system development, documentation, and maintenance.

Other applications such as reports and analyses written to meet specific departmental needs or other (intact) systems that are small, light-duty, and stand alone do not require a similarly rigorous approach. In fact, these types of applications are often developed exclusively by people who are not professional analysts, designers, or programmers. Alternatively, these systems, especially departmental reports, may be developed using report writer software applied to existing data via an approach known as "prototyping" using a combination of end users and systems professionals. In these instances, the documentation and control required is not as extensive as that for high-risk systems. The level that is required should be determined based on the nature of use, expected lifetime, and attendant risks, and should be judged on a case-by-case basis. Nonetheless, the implication of maintenance costs in large systems should be extrapolated to smaller ones, and requisite documentation, testing, and control practices adopted accordingly.

PROTOTYPING

The general subject of prototyping is one of growing interest. (See Mason and Cary, 1983.) Prototyping is a development process by which part of the requirements definition and preliminary design phases are abbreviated via a trial-and-error approach. The idea here is that much of the cost of system design arises through the iterative process required to communicate users' needs to system developers. In developing a prototype, less time is spent in a formal requirements definition, but enough information is provided to permit a systems developer to get "close" to what the user needs. The system is then implemented using a very high level language in which changes are easy to make. Users are then in a position to review the system and indicate clearly their likes or dislikes. This feedback is converted into a series of required changes. Trade-offs between wants and complexity are easy to identify, and decisions as to what is a true need and what is merely a want become easier to make. Only a few iterations through this process are usually required to arrive at a finished product.

Once the prototype system is in place, the user can exercise it and elucidate the need for further refinement. When the prototype becomes more or less static, a decision can be made to keep it as a prototype or rewrite it in some other programming language. One might wish, for example, to do such rewriting for reasons of operational efficiency. Note that in this case, the final prototype becomes the pseudocode representation of the system specification. Thus, when the rewritten system is delivered, it is what the user needs. Based on the nature of the problem and the tools used, systems development costs and development time may be reduced by 50 percent or more. System quality is assured, since the system delivered is the right one.

CONCLUSION AND SUMMARY

Software engineering is a relatively new discipline and is now one of the key focuses of computer systems engineering. Its birth occurred during the late 1960s to early 1970s and it continues to be developed and refined. Underlying the techniques of development and refinement is the fundamental concept of minimizing complexity by proper structuring of the overall process into phases, as well as structuring the process within each phase. A variety of tools and techniques are available to support the "engineering" content of each phase of the software development life cycle. The tools, techniques, and processes outlined in this discussion constitute the best demonstrated practice for software development defined to date.

High-quality, verified, and validated computer systems result from a well-planned, structured development process using the set of tools, techniques, and controls most appropriate for a given problem in a given organization at a given time. Documentation at each step of the process is critical. The form and substance should be adjusted to the particular phase being documented. Forms-driven methodologies can be of significant help; standards within a given organization help further.

The use of a formal system development life cycle applies (with proper adjustment) to all types of systems projects, including those which rely on package software, maintenance and support projects, and real-time systems projects. The detailed form of an SDLC is less important than its use as a guideline in the development process.

Project management practices, organizational approaches, and configuration management are also applicable. Software quality assurance groups, quality audits, and team building are examples. Validation of the product is intimately tied to validation of the process. As the field of software engineering continues to develop, new tools and techniques will be introduced to improve software quality and reliability. However, the rate at which these are recognized and adopted by organizations as a whole will remain the critical issue.

REFERENCES

Alberts, D. S. (1976). "Economics of Software Quality Assurance." *NCC Conference Proceedings,* vol. 45. National Computer Conference, New York. AFIPS Press, Montvale, NJ.

Anderson, R. D. (1979). *Proving Programs Correct.* John Wiley & Sons, New York.

Beizer, B. (1983). *Software Testing Techniques.* Van Nostrand, New York.

Colter, M. (1984). "A Comparative Examination of Systems Analysis Techniques." *MIS Quarterly,* vol. 8, pp. 51–66.

De Marco, T. (1978). *Structured Analysis and System Specification.* Yourdan Press, New York.

Dahl, O. J., Dijsktra, E. W., and Hoare, C. A. R. (1972). *Structured Programming.* Academic Press, London.

Fitzsimmons, A. and Love, T. (1978). "A Review and Evaluation of Software Science." *Computing Surveys,* vol. 10, pp. 3–17.

Grinath, A. C. and Vess, P. H. (1983). "Making SQA Work: The Development of a Software Quality System." *Quality Progress,* July, pp. 18–23.

Halstead, M. H. (1977). *Elements of Software Science,* North Holland, New York.

"Introduction to the Fortune 500." (1983). *Fortune,* May 2, p. 227.

Huang, J. C. (1975). "An Approach to Program Testing." *Computing Surveys,* vol. 7, pp. 113–128.

IBM (1974). *HIPO—A Design Aid and Documentation Tool.* IBM Publication 6C20–1851, White Plains, NY.

IEEE (1982). *Standard for Software Quality Assurance Plans.* IEEE, Piscataway, NJ.

IEEE (1983a). *Standard for Software Configuration Management Plans.* IEEE, Piscataway, NJ.

IEEE (1983b). *Standard Glossary of Software Engineering Terminology.* IEEE, Piscataway, NJ.

Knuth, D. E. (1974). "Structured Programming with 6070 Statements." *Computing Surveys,* vol. 6, pp. 261–301.

Martin, J. (1983). *Managing the Data Base Environment.* Prentice-Hall, Englewood Cliffs, NJ.

Mason, R. and Cary, T. (1983). "Prototyping Interactive Information Systems." *Communications of the ACM,* vol. 26, May, pp. 347–354.

Myers, G. J. (1979). *The Art of Software Testing.* Wiley-Interscience, New York.

Orr, K. (1981). *Structured Requirements Definition.* Ken Orr & Associates, Topeka, KS.

Page-Jones, M. (1980). *Practical Guide to Structure Systems Design.* Prentice-Hall, Englewood Cliffs, NJ.

"Perspectives in Business Data Processing." (1980). *Computer,* November, pp. 84–99.

Schulmeyer, G. G. and McManus, J. I. (1987). *Handbook of Software Quality Assurance.* Van Nostrand Reinhold, New York.

Sukert, A. N. (1977). "An Investigation of Software Reliability Models." *1977 Proceedings, Annual Reliability and Maintainability Symposium.* IEEE, New York, pp. 478–484.

Weinberg, G. (1971). *The Psychology of Computer Programming.* Van Nostrand Reinhold, New York.

Zelkowitz, N. V., Shaw, A. C., and Gannon, J. D. (1979). *Principles of Software Engineering and Design.* Prentice-Hall, Englewood Cliffs, NJ.

SECTION 15
SUPPLIER RELATIONS[1]

Frank M. Gryna

INTRODUCTION **15.2**

Importance of Supplier
Quality 15.2

Supplier Relations:
Objectives and Activities 15.3

*SUPPLIER RELATIONS QUALITY
POLICY* **15.4**

Basic Relationship between
Buyer and Supplier . . . 15.4

Relative Emphasis of
Quality in Purchasing
Decisions 15.5

Multiple Suppliers versus
Single Source 15.6

Internal versus External
Suppliers 15.6

Long-Term Relationship or
Not 15.6

Providing Technical
Assistance to Suppliers . 15.6

Published Quality Policy . . 15.7

*ORGANIZING FOR SUPPLIER
RELATIONS* **15.7**

PRECONTRACT PLANNING . . . **15.9**

Models for Supplier Quality
Programs 15.9

Requirements for a
Supplier Reliability
Program 15.11

*EVALUATING SUPPLIER
CAPABILITY* **15.12**

Qualification of the
Supplier Design 15.12

Qualification of the
Supplier Manufacturing
Process 15.13

Approved Supplier Lists . . 15.18

SUPPLIER SELECTION **15.18**

Total Cost of a
Purchase 15.19

JOINT QUALITY PLANNING . . **15.20**

Joint Economic Planning . 15.20

Joint Technological
Planning 15.21

Joint Managerial
Planning 15.23

*COOPERATION WITH
SUPPLIERS DURING EXECUTION
OF CONTRACT* **15.25**

Evaluation of Initial
Samples of Product . . . 15.25

Evaluation of First
Production Shipments . . 15.26

Two-Way Communication 15.26

Supplier Surveillance . . . 15.27

Use of On-Site Inspection
Personnel 15.28

---

[1]In the Third Edition, the section on vendor relations was prepared by Robert G. Fitzgibbons and J. M. Juran.

EVALUATING DELIVERED
PRODUCT **15.28**

   Evaluation of Supplier
   Product by Incoming
   Inspection 15.29

   Economics of Incoming
   Inspection 15.30

   Use of Supplier Data . . . 15.30

   Use of Histogram Analysis
   on Supplier Data 15.30

CERTIFICATION **15.32**

   Certificates 15.32

   Supplier Certification . . . 15.32

   Preferred Supplier Program 15.34

   Other Meanings of
   Certification 15.34

IMPROVEMENT OF SUPPLIER
QUALITY **15.34**

   Stimulating the Supplier to
   Take Action 15.35

   Pareto Analysis 15.35

   Providing Technical
   Assistance to the
   Supplier 15.36

   Role of Upper
   Management 15.37

SINGLE-SOURCE SUPPLIERS . . **15.38**

TRAINING OF SUPPLIERS **15.38**

SUPPLIER QUALITY RATING . . **15.40**

   Measures in Use 15.41

   Using Supplier Ratings . . 15.42

SPECIAL BUSINESS
PROBLEMS **15.43**

   Legal Problems 15.43

   Ethical Problems 15.44

   Counterfeit Product 15.44

REFERENCES **15.44**

INTRODUCTION

This step on the Spiral of Quality activities concerns the purchase of products (goods or services from suppliers, or "vendors"). Purchases are of two types: (1) those which become a part of the product marketed by the buyer and (2) non-product purchases such as equipment used for plant services, supplies for plant operations, and office supplies and equipment. The concepts discussed in this section apply to all purchases. Juran (1968) presents an overview of supplier relations activities.

Importance of Supplier Quality. The quality of purchased items has become increasingly important for several reasons:

1. *Amount of purchased product:* For many original equipment manufacturers, at least half of the materials embodied in their products is purchased from other companies or from divisions of the parent company. Manufacturers of products such as automobiles and office equipment now design the total product, manufacture a chassis or frame, and then purchase and assemble most of the remaining items going into the product.

2. *High costs associated with poor quality supplier items:* For one home appliance manufacturer, 75 percent of all the warranty claims were traced to purchased items.

3. *Interdependence of buyers and suppliers:* Some buyers are highly integrated with the facilities of the supplier. For example, a beer producer obtains the beer cans from a supplier whose plant is literally next door to the brewery. A can manufactured by the supplier at 7:00 a.m. is transported to the customer, filled with beer, and shipped by 10:00 a.m.

Other cases of interdependency involve technological skills. The buyer may be completely dependent on the knowledge of the supplier in designing and manufacturing the item. But the supplier is also dependent on the buyer—for complete information on how the supplier product needs to function in the buyer's product.

4. *Other internal factors at the buyer's organization:* One example is inventory reduction. The "just-in-time" inventory concept aims to receive items from suppliers only in the quantity and at the exact time that they are needed for production. Such tight scheduling makes it imperative that the purchased products meet quality requirements. If a portion of the purchased product is defective, then a major disruption may occur at the buyer's plant because of the lack of sufficient backup inventory. Under conventional purchasing, supplier quality problems can be hidden by excess inventory and bringing material in early. Heckel (1984) describes the case of a supplier who sent poor quality material for 4 years. Under the just-in-time concept, the supplier was replaced.

A second example is control of internal costs for the buyer, e.g., incoming inspection costs.

Supplier relations are worthy of review by upper management (see Section 8 under Quality Audits by Upper Managers).

Supplier Relations: Objectives and Activities. The overall objective is to create a relationship with a supplier that assures that the product will meet fitness-for-use needs with a minimum of incoming inspection or corrective action. The primary activities necessary are:

1. Define product and program quality requirements
2. Evaluate alternative suppliers
3. Select suppliers
4. Conduct joint quality planning
5. Cooperate with the supplier during the execution of the contract
6. Obtain proof of conformance to requirements
7. Certify qualified suppliers
8. Conduct quality improvement programs as required
9. Create and utilize supplier quality ratings

The degree that these activities are needed depends on the type of product being purchased, from the simple commodity item to the complex technological marvel. With respect to planning for quality, the spectrum of purchases can be divided into three categories:

1. *Standard materials and hardware.* Examples include fasteners, valves, resistors, simple chemicals, and supplies. For these kinds of purchases, industry specifications have usually been prepared. Generally the supplier relations program for quality is a minimal one.

2. *Minor components and materials:* Examples include gears, bearings, diodes, and relays. The specifications may be unique to each supplier or may be industrywide, or they may be prepared by the buyer. The supplier relations program usually requires some level of each activity previously mentioned.

3. *Major components:* These are often relatively complex items such as electronic assemblies, special purpose chemicals, and mechanical or electrome-

TABLE 15.1 Supplier Relations Activities

	Type of purchase*		
Activity	Standard material and hardware	Minor component	Major component
Definition of requirements	⋯	M	H
Supplier evaluation	⋯	M	H
Supplier selection	⋯	H	H
Joint planning	⋯	M	H
Cooperation during contract	⋯	M	H
Proof of conformance	M	H	H
Certification	H	H	II
Quality improvement	⋯	H	H
Supplier rating	M	H	H

*H = high level of effort; M = moderate level of effort.

chanical assemblies. Design responsibility may reside with either the supplier or the buyer. Such purchases require a complete supplier relations program.

Table 15.1 shows the relative emphasis of the primary activities for the three types of purchases. Simple products require only a minimal quality program. For major components, the consequences of poor supplier quality on the buyer's product justify a complete program. Some highly traditional industries fail to see the need for in-depth quality planning because they view their products as basically simple. Many of these products have now changed and require a higher level of technology; e.g., mechanical products make increasing use of electronics, many paints must be lead-free, and kitchen stoves now use microwave technology. The movement from simplicity to complexity for a product is often gradual, so the need for more intensive quality planning can be overlooked until a disaster occurs. Quality planning in such an environment cannot be done in a vacuum. Other factors must be considered to develop overall strategies for purchasing management. Kraljic (1983) discusses such strategies for several classifications of purchases.

Often it is assumed that supplier relations activities are primarily aimed at external suppliers. In practice, many companies report that their most difficult quality problems rest with suppliers who are "sister divisions" in the same corporation. This section discusses supplier relations both for external and internal suppliers.

SUPPLIER RELATIONS QUALITY POLICY

The general nature of quality policies is set out in Section 5, Quality Policies and Objectives. When supplier relations are studied, the following major problems emerge that require policy decisions:

Basic Relationship between Buyer and Supplier. The relationship varies from "adversarial" to "teamwork," with several variations in between. In the adversarial relationship the supplier is viewed with suspicion—as someone who tries to sneak a bad product past the receiving inspection activity of the buyer. Low bid price is emphasized, and each party presses for short-term advantages even if this results in terminating the relationship. Mutual suspicion precludes mutual assistance, joint planning, and other forms of close collaboration. In some companies, the adversarial relationship extends to both external and internal suppliers.

In the teamwork relationship, the buyer and the supplier work together as if both were part of the same company. This is a planned, continuing relationship based on mutual confidence, joint planning, mutual visits, and assistance—no secrets. The supplier is regarded as an extension of the buyer's factory.

The 1980s have witnessed some dramatic changes in supplier relations, including some changes of a policy nature. Chief of these was a shift from the prevailing adversarial relationship toward a teamwork relationship. This shift was necessitated by the need to secure quality improvement from suppliers. A company whose product includes a heavy extent of purchased components needs improved quality in those components in order to fully improve their final product. Securing such quality improvement from suppliers is obviously more readily done in a teamwork environment.

To create such a teamwork environment has required some policy changes which many suppliers had long wanted, mainly:

Long-term purchase agreements rather than year to year or batch to batch. The long-term contracts (usually several years) encourage suppliers to invest in improvements. There has, in fact, been a considerable shift to long-term contracts.

Fewer suppliers, thereby increasing the share of market of the survivors. During the period 1980–1985, some large buyers in fact reduced their list of suppliers by about one-third.

In turn, some large buyers have established new or strengthened criteria for judging supplier adequacy:

"Full service," meaning that the supplier is expected to make positive contributions in product design, process design, cost reduction, etc.

Positive programs of quality improvement

Training in quality-related methodology

Miller and Kegaris (1986) describe how the Kodak and Alcoa companies used the teamwork approach to improve the quality of lithoplate materials.

The teamwork relationship gives full recognition to the interdependence of the buyer and the supplier of modern purchases. This interdependence takes three major forms: technological, economic, and managerial. Effective use of the forms is discussed under Joint Quality Planning below. An important element is strong lines of communication between technical specialists to replace the restrictive lines imposed by many companies.

For purchases of moderate to high level of product complexity the teamwork policy is essential to achieve fitness-for-use needs. For purchases of standard materials, the importance of working closely together is at a minimum.

Relative Emphasis of Quality in Purchasing Decisions.   The selection of suppliers must assure that the desired product is fit for use, delivered on time, and has low cost. The relative importance of these three criteria is set by the company's middle and upper management. Some companies have traditionally awarded contracts on the basis of the lowest bid price; other companies have traditionally assigned highest priority to quality. Those who select suppliers understand the importance of quality but often are not provided with information which discriminates clearly among suppliers. In such cases it is quite understandable why buyers select suppliers. The tradition of buying primarily by price is an ingrained practice in many companies and will not be changed without a clear policy direction.

One electronics organization separates its purchases into two categories. The first category consists of items in which the quality level has been well established for many suppliers. For this type, purchasing managers are permitted to bargain with suppliers to obtain the lowest price. Items in the second category are more unique, and the quality depends greatly on the suppliers chosen. For these latter purchases, buyers are instructed to award contracts to the supplier who has the highest reputation for quality—even if a premium price must be paid.

Multiple Suppliers versus Single Source.   Multiple sources of supply have advantages: competition can result in better quality, lower costs, better service, and minimum disruption of supply due to strikes or other catastrophes.

A single source of supply also has advantages: the size of contract given to a single source will be larger than with multiple sources, and the supplier may attach more significance to the contract. However, if there are no alternative sources of supply, the monopoly secured by the supplier can have negative effects. With a single source, communications are simplified, and this can foster a team relationship. The most dramatic examples of single source are multidivisional companies in which some divisions are suppliers to others.

The policy decision determines how far the use of multiple suppliers should be carried. During the late 1970s, Toyota Motor Car Company had about 200 suppliers in contrast to large American manufacturers who had many thousands of suppliers.

For those products which require a teamwork relationship, a small number of suppliers provides more time for exchange visits and other forms of technological cooperation.

Internal versus External Suppliers.   Many companies are partly or wholly "integrated," i.e., some divisions are suppliers to others. In such companies it is quite common for the buying divisions to use external suppliers as additional sources of supply. This multiple sourcing provides a comparison of the quality of internal versus external sources.

There are obvious advantages to using the available internal sources: better employee relations, use of existing capacity, financial benefits, etc. However, some managers report that the internal suppliers are the biggest source of supplier quality problems. If such internal problems cannot be resolved, the superiority in quality by external suppliers may become the determining factor when deciding whether to buy from internal or external suppliers.

Long-Term Relationship or Not.   For those types of purchases which require a teamwork relationship, it is important that the supplier be assured of a relatively long-term contract. Otherwise there will be little incentive for that supplier to participate in teamwork. In some companies such a long-term relationship represents a policy change from past practices of annual rebidding of contracts. For an example of the actions taken by a company to promote long-term relationships, see Itoh (1978).

Providing Technical Assistance to Suppliers.   Technical assistance takes multiple forms: provision of training materials; scholarships for training courses; reliability engineering assistance, e.g., in reliability prediction; quality engineering assistance, e.g., in process capability studies; consulting assistance in technology, e.g., metrology. The policy decision is whether to provide such resources or to require the supplier to seek other resources.

Published Quality Policy. A good deal of unwritten supplier quality policy exists in the form of long-standing industry practices, sanctioned by the laws governing sales. There exist also some elements of written policy contained here and there in company supplier relations manuals. (For some examples of published supplier quality policy, see Section 5 under Quality Policies for Functions; Supplier Relations.) As interdependence grows, the need for published policy grows with it. Commonly the resulting published policy is embodied in a supplier relations manual, along with other information of importance and use to suppliers.

On a more comprehensive scale, the U.S. Department of Defense makes wide use of MIL-Q-9858A (1985) as a document to govern quality relations with contractors. This document includes some quality policy matters.

A policy statement specifically oriented to supplier relations is the "Ten Principles for Vendor-Vendee Relationships" evolved by a research committee of the Japanese Union of Scientists and Engineers. In paraphrased form, these principles include:

Mutual respect and cooperation

Prior contractual understanding

Agreed methods of evaluation

Agreed plans for settling disputes

Exchange of essential information

Adequate performance in related functions, e.g., inventory control

Supplier responsible to deliver good product and supporting data

Consumers' interests preeminent

ORGANIZING FOR SUPPLIER RELATIONS

In many companies, a controversial question often arises: Who is responsible for supplier quality? Discussions on so broad a subject are usually futile. Instead, it is better to identify the specific actions and decisions which collectively constitute supplier relations. Then, as these specifics are discussed individually, it is usually easy to agree on most of them. That narrows the area of controversy to a few specific items which require resolution. Table 15.2 shows a typical list, with responsibilities as assigned in one company.

In Table 15.2, most of the effort concerning supplier quality resides in the Quality Department. In an alternative approach, the Purchasing Department carries the ultimate responsibility for supplier quality and executes some of the detailed activities. (This is analogous to shifting the responsibility for quality internally from a Quality Department to the Manufacturing Department.) Under the concept, purchasing managers become familiar with quality requirements, supplier capabilities, and the effects of poor supplier quality. The objectives of such delegation include improvement of supplier selection and unification of responsibility for supplier quality relations.

One aerospace organization decided to place the primary responsibility for

TABLE 15.2 Responsibility Matrix—Supplier Relations

	Participating departments*		
Activity	Product Development	Purchasing	Quality Control
1. Establish a supplier quality policy	X	X	XX
2. Use multiple suppliers for major procurements		XX	
3. Evaluate quality capability of potential suppliers	X	X	XX
4. Specify requirements for suppliers	XX		X
5. Conduct joint quality planning	X		XX
6. Conduct supplier surveillance		X	XX
7. Evaluate delivered product	X		XX
8. Conduct improvement programs	X	X	XX
9. Use supplier quality ratings in selecting suppliers		XX	X

*XX = principal responsibility, X = collateral responsibility.

supplier quality in the Purchasing Department. A published statement listed the following responsibilities for Purchasing:

1. Evaluate the relative capability of suppliers to deliver products that will satisfy quality requirements and utilize the evaluation results as a major factor in procurement.
2. Provide terms and conditions in procurement documents that establish supplier responsibility for compliance with quality requirements and that permit adequate control of supplier performance.
3. Administer procurement contracts and exercise control of supplier performance adequate to assure the delivery of products that satisfy requirements.
4. Provide aggressive follow-up and obtain supplier corrective action when improvement is required.

There are significant resource implications that result from this organizational approach. At a minimum, it requires purchasing personnel to be trained to understand the quality disciplines as they apply to suppliers. It may also require the Purchasing Department to add personnel who are quality specialists. All of this significantly diminishes the role of the Quality Department in supplier matters.

On a related organizational matter, some multiplant organizations are experimenting with the concept of centralized responsibility for supplier quality on a product basis. Under this concept, the responsibility for supplier quality on all purchases of product X is assigned to one of the plants. That plant then becomes a coordinator for all plants who buy product X, and for all the suppliers who supply product X. For example, the plant responsible for procuring product X becomes responsible for specifications, contracts, and quality assurance. The coordinating plant receives inputs from the individual plants and handles all negotiations with suppliers both before and during the contract. This centralized approach is intended to assure that suppliers are presented with consistent requirements from any of the corporation's different plants. It is also intended to provide the buyer with more stature in obtaining resolution of quality problems.

Norquist (1983) describes some of the attitudes of Quality and Purchasing personnel and suggests appropriate responsibilities for each function. For an example of how a team is formed to administer the quality related aspects of major subcontracts, see Ziegler and Diggs (1982). This paper shows specific responsibilities of Engineering, Manufacturing, and Quality department members of a team both during the preaward phase and the post award phase of a subcontract.

PRECONTRACT PLANNING

Precontract planning is largely devoted to securing a mutual understanding sufficient to reach a decision on whether to contract or not. In this exchange the supplier needs to understand the use requirements and specifications of what is to be met; how the system will make use of the purchased component; what the interface requirements are; what the main requirements are for performance, reliability, maintainability, safety, etc.; what the meaning is of key words and phrases. The buyer, in turn, needs to understand just what capabilities the supplier is able to muster to meet all these requirements. Quality surveys can be used to assess prospective suppliers' capabilities.

In the precontract stage there are two types of inputs for specifications.

1. Performance specifications defining what the product is to do, i.e., fitness for use. These specifications are essential.

2. Specifications defining the quality activities the supplier is expected to conduct. Increasingly, buyers are mandating quality systems for suppliers.

The second type of specification is a departure from the traditional practice of the buyer refraining from telling a supplier "how to run the plant." Defining required activities within a supplier's plant is sometimes necessary to assure that a supplier does have the expertise to conduct the full program needed to create a satisfactory product. For some products, government regulations require that a buyer impose certain processing requirements (e.g., keeping special records for traceability; maintaining a locked storeroom as a hold area for nonconforming products) on suppliers. For other products, such as a complex mechanical or electronic subsystem, the overall system requirements may result in a need for a supplier to meet a numerical reliability or maintainability requirement and to conduct certain activities (see Section 13 under Planning for Time-Oriented Performance—Reliability) to assure that such a requirement is met.

Models for Supplier Quality Programs. Documents defining adequate quality programs exist in several models:

ANSI/ASQC Z-1.15-1979 (1979). *Generic Guidelines for Quality Systems*

MIL-Q-9858A (1985). *Quality Program Requirements*

AQAP-1 (1985). *NATO Quality Control System Requirements for Industry* 3rd ed.

NHB 5300.4 (1B) (1969). *Quality Program Provisions for Aeronautical and Space Systems Contractors*

See Appendix III, Selected Quality Standards, Specifications, and Related Documents, for the sources of these documents. Appendix III also lists additional documents.

Some industrial buyers have prepared documents describing quality program requirements for suppliers (see below). An example is the Q-101 *Quality System Standard* issued by the Ford Motor company (1983). This standard is aimed at defect prevention during the manufacturing phase of the product life cycle. The standard starts with an introduction and a glossary giving definitions for 41 terms. Next, the standard presents requirements that apply to all products:

Advanced Quality planning—control plans
Incoming (subcontracted) products
    Approved materials
    Control of subcontracted products
Manufacturing process capability
    Process potential studies
    Process capability studies
Statistical process control
Ongoing verification and testing
    Inspection and laboratory test instructions
    Measuring and inspecting equipment
    Engineering specification test performance requirements
    Product qualification
    Indication of product status
    Periodic layout inspections
    Repaired products
    Returned product analysis
    Internal audits
    Heat-treated parts and fasteners
Documentation
    Procedures
    Drawing and change control
    Deviation control
    Records
    Changes in manufacturing process
Interface with Ford on quality related matters
    Initial samples and first production shipment approvals
    Requirements for new suppliers
    Requirements for initial samples
    Requirements for first production shipments
Ford supplier quality assurance surveys

There are additional requirements that apply to "control items." Control items are parts which can affect either compliance with government regulations or safe vehicle operations. The additional requirements are:

Preproduction
    Feasibility
    Failure mode and effects analysis (FMEA)
    Control plan
Manufacturing process capability

First production shipment approval
Documentation
   Document identification
   Product identification
   Certification of control items
   Lot traceability
   Process changes
   Heat-treated parts
Critical items

The standard describes the quality system survey, process capability, testing, documentation, approval procedures, and other requirements.

Requirements for a Supplier Reliability Program. For complex products it may be necessary to identify the reliability engineering activities that a supplier is expected to conduct. One company listed the following required activities:

Validation of reliability requirements received from customer
Preparation of mathematical model for reliability
Apportionment of the reliability requirement to phases of the mission and to elements of the system
Design criteria for reliability
Evaluation of design for reliability
   Reliability estimate
   Design review
Reliability tasks during manufacturing
   Manufacturing and procurement criteria
   Evaluation of manufacturing methods
Reliability activities during shipping, storage, and use
Test program
   Integration of reliability with other tests
   Reliability demonstration plan
Data system
   Requirements for malfunction reports
   Distribution of malfunction reports
   Problem status summary
   Equipment operating time records
Organization for reliability
   Program review and monitoring

The following reliability inputs are also required in proposals submitted to the buyer:

Preliminary estimate of reliability
Reliability features of the equipment

Preliminary analysis showing effects of failures

Design review

Approach to measurement and demonstration of reliability

Preventing degradation of reliability during manufacture and operational use of the product

Integration of reliability efforts with the design efforts

Integration of reliability with the test program

Management philosophy on achieving reliability

Proposed method of reliability program control

Schedule of major reliability tasks

Personnel resources to be assigned

The time spent in precontract planning for quality has several benefits. First, the supplier is made aware of product requirements and program requirements. Conformance to these requirements can then be monitored and problem areas identified before noncomforming product is produced. Second, precontract planning can assure that all suppliers are bidding on the contract on the same basis. If a supplier is not aware of all of the activities necessary, the resources will not be included in the budget and the activities will probably never be performed.

EVALUATING SUPPLIER CAPABILITY

Evaluating supplier capability has two facets:

1. Qualifying the supplier's design through the evaluation of product samples
2. Qualifying the supplier's capability to meet quality requirements on production lots

Qualification of the Supplier Design.   In some purchases, the buyer provides the supplier with a description of the desired function of the product and asks the supplier to create a design and produce the items. The first phases, then, of supplier qualification is an evaluation of the design to assure that it can meet performance and other requirements.

The supplier prepares samples based on the proposed design. The samples are tested either by the buyer or by the supplier who submits the results to the buyer. Numerous performance tests are conducted, often under a variety of environments including temperature, vibration, humidity, and other conditions. Reliability, maintainability, and other parameters of use are also evaluated, but, because of the limited number of samples and test time, to a much lesser degree. For these latter parameters, the supplier can be required to submit other analyses such as a reliability prediction or a failure mode, effect, and criticality analysis (see Section 13 under Planning for Time-Oriented Performance—Reliability).

An important variable in the qualification test of a design is the extent to which the sample is representative of future production. For a new design, the sample items are usually made in an engineering or development shop. In such cases, the results of a qualification test of a design provide little if any information about the ability of the supplier to conform to the design under production conditions. The qualification test results, however, do show whether the supplier understood the basic performance requirements and created a design meeting those requirements.

Qualification of the Supplier Manufacturing Process. Separate steps must be taken to evaluate the ability of the supplier to conform to the design in production quantities. This evaluation of manufacturing capability can take several forms: prior product performance, process capability analysis, and evaluation of the supplier's quality system.

Prior Product Performance. The best predictor of future product quality is the supplier's past quality for the same or similar products. This prior experience can include:

1. *Experience in the buyer's organization with the same supplier:* In many cases, the experience has been codified into a formal rating of the supplier (see below under Supplier Quality Rating).
2. *Experience pooled from multiple plants within the same corporation:* An example of this is the General Motors Source Performance Evaluation and Reporting (SPEAR) system. This is a data bank that pools information on supplier quality surveys, performance reports, and defective material reports.
3. *Data from government data banks:* One example of this is Government Industry Data Exchange Program (GIDEP). The information in the data bank includes engineering evaluation test reports, reliability and maintainability data, metrology data and procedures, and manufacturing test data. Military and other government agencies and industrial organizations make up the primary participants. The program is centrally managed and funded by the U.S. government. The contact is: Director, GIDEP Operations Center, Corona, CA 91720.
4. *Data banks serving a specific industry:* An example is the Coordinating Agency for Supplier Evaluation (CASE). This data bank was set up to reduce redundant surveys of suppliers. Survey data are available to members of the Association (Sheppard, 1977).

Process Capability Analysis. A process capability study is based on measurements collected from the manufacturing process to determine the inherent uniformity of a process, and thereby whether or not the process is capable of meeting the specification. (See Section 16 under Process Capability.) Ford Motor Company requires suppliers to conduct either a process potential study or a process capability study.

The process potential study provides a preliminary assessment of the process. These studies are of short duration and are not intended to measure long-term process capability. Typically a sample of at least 30 units is taken from a production run of at least 300 units. A control chart on average and range is run (see Section 24 under Types of Control Charts; Variables Data). If the chart shows no points out of control and no evidence of trends of an adverse nature, then the data is used to calculate the process potential. The process potential is acceptable if the measured process average ± 4 standard deviations is within the bilateral specifications or on the favorable side of a unilateral specification.

In the process capability study, the control charts are continued from the process potential study until all factors likely to contribute to process variation are reflected in the data. These factors include raw material, personnel, environment, tool wear, and other factors. The study often requires at least 30 days. Again, if the control charts show a state of statistical control, then the capability can be calculated in the manner discussed in Section 16 under Process Capability Management. For a capability study using variables data, Ford requires that the measured process average ± 3 standard deviations be within specification limits. For attributes data, average performance must be at least 99.73 percent conforming to specifications. When this is not met, 100 percent inspection must be used along with a program of analysis to improve the process.

Evaluation of process capability is required by Ford on all "control items" (parts which affect either compliance with government regulations or safety) and other significant product characteristics.

The supplier can also be asked to prepare a failure mode, effect, and criticality analysis. See Section 13 under Failure Mode, Effect, and Criticality Analysis. This analysis is not based on process measurements, but it provides some assurance that the supplier has analyzed the proposed process and identified potential problems.

Evaluation of the Supplier System through a Quality Survey. A supplier quality survey is based on a plant visit to evaluate a supplier's ability to meet quality requirements on production lots. The usual steps in making a survey are:

1. Assemble available information on prior experience with the supplier. This can help to identify areas to highlight during the survey.

2. Send a presurvey questionnaire to the supplier. The information collected can help to plan the visit itself and save time during the visit. Doing this homework prior to the visit makes it possible to focus the visit on potential problems that may arise during the contract.

3. Organize the survey team. Membership varies and may include specialists from Purchasing, Manufacturing, Engineering, and Quality.

4. Conduct the survey. The survey generally takes one to several days at the supplier's plant. It starts with an opening conference at which the purpose of the survey, the kind of information desired, and a proposed schedule for the visit are discussed. The most usual points of concentration during the survey are:

   a. Management capabilities: These relate mainly to such matters as:
   Policies: Is the supplier willing to be "on the team," i.e., operate on the basis of exchange of visits, no secrets, joint planning, mutual technical assistance, etc.? Does the supplier engage actively in quality improvement and cost reduction?
   Organization: Have the activities essential to attainment of quality been identified and described? Are these activities clearly assigned to the various departments in a logical relationship?
   Personnel: Have the managers, specialists, and work force been trained in modern ways as evidenced by attendance at structured courses and certificates of qualification? Are there clear evidences of high motivation for quality in relation to other parameters (cost, delivery, etc.)?

   b. Technological capabilities: Here the emphasis is on matters such as: the facilities and equipment in the supplier's plant, plus their up-to-dateness and condition; the ability of the process to meet product specifications; the degree of understanding of the relationship between process variables and product results; and the adequacy of the measuring equipment.

   c. Quality discipline capabilities: Here the emphasis is typically on quality-oriented systems and procedures. These include systems for process control, product inspection and test, data recording and summary, documentation, maintenance of equipment, etc. In addition, this part of the survey looks for the existence and completeness of quality manuals as well as provision for audit of conformance to systems and procedures. But systems need to be applied to the specific product. For example, to assure that planning for process control has occurred, a useful technique is to require the supplier to prepare a flow chart showing the proposed inspection stations and process control points for the product.

From the presurvey questionnaire or checklists used during the visit, detailed information can be collected. This can include:

Management: philosophy, quality policies, organization structure, indoctrination, commitment to quality

Design: organization, systems in use, caliber of specifications, orientation to modern technique, attention to reliability, engineering change control, development laboratories

Manufacture: physical facilities, maintenance, special processes, process capability, production capacity, caliber of planning, lot identification and traceability

Purchasing: specifications, supplier relations, procedures

Quality assurance: organization structure, availability of quality control and reliability control and reliability engineers, quality planning (materials, in-process, finished goods, packing, storage, shipping, usage, field service), audit of adherence to plan

Inspection and test: laboratories, special tests, instruments, measurement control

Quality coordination: organization for coordination, order analysis, control over subcontractors, quality cost analysis, corrective action loop, disposition of nonconforming product

Data systems: facilities, procedures, effective use, reports

Personnel: indoctrination, training, motivation

Quality results: performance attained, self-use of product, prestigious customers, prestigious subcontractors

The evaluation of various quality activities can be quantified by a scoring system. For example, in surveys made by the Ford Motor Company, 20 areas of the supplier program are evaluated. Each area is rated on a scale of 0 to 10. A rating of 5 is required for each area and a total of 140 is needed overall.

A scoring system that includes importance weights for activities is illustrated in Table 15.3. This system is used by a manufacturer of electronic assemblies. In this case, the importance weights (W) vary from 1 to 4 and are designed to total to 25 for each of the three areas surveyed. The weights show the relative importance of the various activities in the overall index. The actual ratings (R) of the activities observed are assigned as follows:

10: The specific activity is satisfactory in every respect (or does not apply).

8: The activity meets minimum requirements, but improvements could be made.

0: The activity is unsatisfactory.

Scoring schemes can be made simpler (see ASQC, 1976, *Procurement Quality Control—A Handbook of Recommended Practices*), or more complicated as illustrated by a probabilistic approach described by Shilliff and Bodis (1975).

After the survey is completed there is usually a closing conference at which the team presents an oral and sometimes a brief written summary of their observa-

TABLE 15.3 Scoring of a Supplier Quality Survey

Activity	Receiving inspection			Manufacturing			Final inspection		
	R^*	W	$R \times W$	R	W	$R \times W$	R	W	$R \times W$
1. Quality management	8	3	24	8	3	24	8	3	24
2. Quality planning	8	4	32	8	4	32	10	4	40
3. Inspection equipment	10	3	30	10	3	30	10	3	30
4. Calibration	0	3	0	10	3	30	0	3	0
5. Drawing control	0	3	0	10	2	20	10	2	20
6. Corrective action	10	3	30	8	3	24	8	3	24
7. Handling rejects	10	2	20	8	2	16	10	3	30
8. Storage and shipping	10	1	10	10	1	10	10	1	10
9. Environment	8	1	8	8	1	8	8	1	8
10. Personnel experience	10	2	20	10	3	30	10	2	20
			Area total = 174†			Area total = 224			Area total = 206

$*R$ = rating; W = weight.
†Interpretation of area totals:
    Fully approved: Each of the three area totals is 250.
    Approved: None of the three area totals is less than 200.
    Conditionally approved: No single area total is less than 180.
    Unapproved: One or more of the area totals is less than 180.

tions and conclusions. Some companies require the supplier to sign the written report indicating that it has been presented to the supplier. Later the team prepares a final report summarizing the visit and recommending whether or not the supplier should become an approved source.

Supplier Surveys in Practice.   Supplier surveys have been used extensively for many years, and a large body of experience has been collected. One of the few published studies is that by Brainard (1966). In the study 151 supplier surveys were made and a recommendation made in each case to purchase or not purchase. In all 151 cases the company did purchase from the supplier (even if the recommendation was against such action). The results of the study indicated that in 77 of the 151 cases, the survey correctly predicted the quality of the product as subsequently found at incoming inspection. In the remaining 74 cases, the survey incorrectly predicted the subsequent quality. The study raised doubts as to the predictive value of the surveys, and led to changes in the survey approach.

Collective experience suggests that supplier surveys have both merits and limitations:

Merits.   All surveys provide some extent of objective information. The most obvious concerns the physical facilities—what type, how many, what condition, etc. Where certain essential facilities are not in evidence, e.g., a special type of test equipment, the buyer is alerted as to the extent of delays which might result.

The survey may turn up additional findings of an objective nature—the presence or absence of essential training programs, traceability provisions, data feedbacks, etc. Such findings also give early warnings as to the time and effort required for the supplier to meet the provisions of the contract.

The survey also has the merit of opening up communications between buyer and supplier, and even within the supplier organization. There have been numerous instances in which survey findings have stimulated supplier upper management action on matters which the supplier's own quality manager had been unable to communicate to the top. ⌐

Limitations. Supplier surveys as conducted in the United States have not proved to be useful predictors of future quality performance of suppliers. It is possible that a change in emphasis would improve this. The U.S. emphasis has been on organization, procedures, documentation, etc., whereas the Japanese emphasis has been on the capability of the process, the adequacy of the process controls, the training and qualifications of the work force, etc. (If the survey finds the procedures to be inadequate, they can be changed in a matter of weeks. However, it takes months and even years to remedy inadequate processes or lack of essential training.)

This same U.S. approach has tended to concentrate attention on conformance to procedural specifications rather than on product fitness for use. The procedural emphasis is not on the supplier's general plan of approach, but on specific products or processes.

Multiple Assessment. In the early days of supplier surveys, suppliers were willing to make themselves available for the visit. However, as the number of customers requesting surveys increased, the survey teams became a burden and many suppliers objected to the time required. Repeat surveys of the same supplier are referred to as multiple assessment. Attempts are being made to reduce the amount of multiple assessment. The "assessment" that is referred to is the initial assessment of the supplier to determine capability. It does not refer to monitoring of the supplier during the execution of a contract. Thoday (1983) discusses four elements necessary to reduce the amount of multiple assessment.

1. A standard specification of the element of a quality system
2. Individual assessors who are trained and qualified by a competent body
3. An independent third party to operate a service of supplier assessment
4. The publication of details of the firms who have been successfully appraised

In England, BSI Document BS5750, *Quality Systems,* or BSI *Handbook 22 Quality Assurance* (British Standards Institution, 1979 and 1981), are used to define a quality system. The Institute of Quality Assurance provides training and examinations to qualify assessors. The British Standards Institution (BSI) provides the service of supplier assessment. A register of assessed firms is published by a Stationery Office of the British government.

In the United States, the CASE data bank of supplier surveys (see above under Prior Product Performance) has been effective in reducing multiple assessments.

Third-Party Assessment. This term refers to supplier evaluation by someone other than the supplier or buyer. The forces behind such external audits have been mainly:

1. Large buyers demanding quality assurance beyond that supplied by the supplier
2. Insurance companies demanding independent quality certification as a prerequisite to carrying the risks
3. Government departments engaged in administering regulations oriented to safety, health, and the environment

More recently there has been an added and growing demand for "independent" sources of quality-oriented information relative to consumer economics. An example is the pressure from consumer organizations for independent information to assist consumers in determining which among the competing products offers the best value for the money.

Collectively, these trends in the field of quality bear a striking resemblance to the history of independent audits in the field of finance.

The BSI has created a service of making an independent assessment of the quality program of an organization. The survey is made in comparison to publication BS5750, *Quality Systems,* a 1979 publication that defines the basic elements of a quality program. The BSI provides, on a contract basis, an assessment of a supplier.

Approved Supplier Lists.   A supplier may be listed as "qualified" in two broad respects:

1. Business matters—integrity, financial capability, prompt payment, etc.
2. Product quality (design and manufacturing capability)

The qualification process involves two separate evaluations. The results are often formalized into approved supplier lists—one for business matters in general and one for quality on specific products. Qualification of a supplier on business matters does not automatically qualify the supplier on quality for any product. A "preferred suppliers list" is slightly different, and is discussed below under Certification.

SUPPLIER SELECTION

The selection of suppliers starts with the decision whether to make or buy. This decision requires an analysis of factors such as the skills and facilities needed, plant capacity, ability to meet delivery schedules, expected costs of "make" or "buy," and other matters.

The process of obtaining bids can sometimes reveal excessive design requirements. One electronics company decided to permit purchases externally even though capability was available in-house. Surprisingly, many suppliers submitted bid prices much higher than expected. The suppliers claimed that the prices were necessary in order to meet all requirements. These same requirements had been used internally but the costs had simply been distributed over many products. A review of the requirements revealed that some of them were unnecessary.

At the outset, when there is no prior experience with a supplier, the selection must be pieced together using:

The reputation of the supplier

Information derived from buyers who have had experience with this supplier on similar products

Qualification tests of the supplier's design

Survey of the supplier's manufacturing facility

Information from data banks

Collectively all these inputs still leave doubts as to what will be the subsequent actual performance of the supplier. Many buying companies respond to these doubts by placing new suppliers in a provisional category until the subsequent deliveries remove these doubts. At that time the supplier is placed on a list of approved suppliers. Admittance to this "club" confers on the supplier some useful advantages over other suppliers who are not on the list. These advantages can include a higher share of the available business and longer-term contracts.

Supplier selection is not based solely on quality; it must include consideration of prices, delivery against schedules, and still other parameters. The purchasing manager (or the project manager) has the responsibility for coordinating the competing demands behind these parameters.

Total Cost of a Purchase.   The total cost of purchased products is the purchase price plus the added costs due to scrap, rework, delays, field failures, and other consequences of poor supplier quality. These added costs sometimes exceed greatly the savings due to buying from the lowest bidder. It is easy in such cases to accuse the purchasing managers of buying solely based on the lowest price.

Purchasing managers generally agree that the purchasing decision should be based on all costs—not just the purchase price. However, they point out that they lack data adequate to specify the added quality-related costs; they also point out that they are not in a position to evaluate them. Instead, such evaluation must be made by other departments, e.g., Quality, Accounting.

In theory it is feasible to quantify these added costs by enlarging the accounting system to identify and evaluate all quality-related costs of supplier origin. Many companies have tried this. In practice it is found that these costs follow the Pareto principle of vital few and useful many. For the vital few, it is decidedly worthwhile to evaluate the added costs. For the useful many, the work of tracking the needed data becomes formidable and hence difficult to justify. The way out of this dilemma is to deal with the vital few cases individually and the useful many collectively, e.g., through sampling evaluation.

Some organizations have developed a quality cost index for the vital few cases of procurement. This index is defined as the supplier quality cost plus the purchase price, all divided by the purchase price. The supplier quality cost is the cost associated with quality problems on supplier items. To trace this cost completely would require an extensive record-keeping system. What can be done is to identify the main categories of this cost and to collect actual cost data for those categories. For example, one company identified the categories as:

The cost of processing lot rejections: This can be estimated as the cost of processing the paperwork and handling other matters for each rejected lot.

Cost of complaint investigations: This is the cost involved in resolving quality problems that have arisen on supplier items.

Cost of receiving inspection: This is an estimate of the receiving inspection cost for the particular item and the particular supplier. Depending on the reputation of the supplier, the amount of receiving inspection can vary greatly.

Cost of nonconforming product identified after receiving inspection: This is the cost incurred if a nonconforming product is not identified until later assembly or field use of the product.

The supplier quality cost index can be used to estimate the total cost of future purchases by multiplying the bid price by the index of a similar product from the same supplier. If data on these indices can be given to purchasing managers for the vital few products and suppliers, the managers will be better able to select suppliers on the basis of lowest total cost instead of lowest bid price. ASQC (1980) provides a discussion of this index.

The importance of carefully evaluating the supplier's bid price is emphasized by Itoh (1978). The Toyota Motor Company does not blindly accept an offer based on an unusually low bid. Toyota feels that if the price is unrealistic, serious business problems may arise. That in turn can result in less attention paid to quality matters. Their policy stresses that the supplier should receive a fair price to help maintain a proper quality system and make a fair profit. This helps to develop long-term business relationships with their suppliers.

Products requiring special development efforts may require special types of contracts. Hayes and Romig (1977) discuss seven types of contracts along with the issues involved with respect to quality.

Some organizations keep track of supplier performance and identify certain suppliers as "preferred." Such suppliers have a favored position in source selection and may receive other benefits. The concept is discussed below under Certification.

JOINT QUALITY PLANNING

The finalization and execution of the contract between supplier and buyer requires detailed quality planning covering three elements: economic, technological, and managerial.

Joint Economic Planning.   The economic aspects of joint quality planning concentrate on two major approaches:

1. *Buying value rather than conformance to specification:*   The technique used is to analyze the value of what is being bought and to try to effect an improvement (see Section 13 under Value Engineering). Applied to supplier quality relations, value engineering looks for excessive costs due to:

   a. *Overspecification for the use to which the product will be put (e.g., special products ordered when a standard product would do:*   One example concerns an outboard motor crankshaft seal. A fluoroelastomer costing 20 times as much as the previously used nitrile rubber was chosen for this seal. As a result of a design analysis the metallic seal component was strengthened and a reduced amount of the expensive elastomer was needed to provide the seal. The result was a new design with less cost and no loss in quality (Cooper, 1980).

   b. *Emphasis on original price rather than on cost of use over the life of the product:*   For some products, the cost of use can be at least three times the original price.

   c. *Emphasis on conformance to specification, not fitness for use:*   A tire manufacturer purchased valves from several suppliers, all of whom met specifications. All valves were fit for use by the ultimate user—the vehicle operator. However, there was an added use for the valves. They were used to inflate and deflate the tires during the vulcanization process. The valves which had the largest hole diameter resulted in the shortest cycle time for the vulcanization process, resulting in higher productivity for the manufacturer of the tires. (Each supplier was permitted to set the hole diameter.)

2. *Optimizing quality costs:*   To the purchase price the buyer must add a whole array of quality-related costs: incoming inspection, material review, production delays, downtime, extra inventories, etc. However, the supplier also has a set of costs to be optimized. Both the buyer and seller should put together the data needed to understand their life-cycle costs, or the cost of use, and then work cooperatively toward joint optimization. For example, a heavy-equipment manufacturer bought castings from several suppliers. It was decided to calculate the "total cost of the purchased casting" as the original purchase price

plus incoming inspection costs plus the costs of rejections detected later in assembly. The unit purchase price on a contract given to the lowest bidder was $19.00. The inspection and rejection costs amounted to an additional $2.11. The variation among bid prices was $2.00.

Some buyers require successful performance of the purchased item before payment is authorized. One chemical manufacturer accepts two types of purchase agreements. One is the conventional type in which the buyer performs incoming inspection of the supplier item and then authorizes payment. In the second type of contract, payment is not authorized until the product performs satisfactorily in the buyer's process. Other buyers authorize payment upon initial receipt but later submit a claim to the supplier if the product performs poorly in the buyer's process.

Joint Technological Planning.   The more usual elements of such planning include:

1. *Agreement on the meaning of performance requirements in the specifications:*   Sometimes requirements are inadvertently omitted (e.g., a requirement for edgewise bending of copper strips for the frame size associated with a certain type of motor). In other cases, the need is for clarification on how the product will be used. For example, in investigating cracks on a forged round, it was learned that the supplier was never told that the rounds would receive further forging by upsetting as bars. Given that information, the supplier would have used a higher quality of ingot to prevent the cracks developing (Rau, 1981).

2. *Quantification of reliability and maintainability requirements:*   A supplier was given a contract to provide an air-conditioning system with a mean time between failures of at least 2000 h. As part of joint planning, the supplier was required to submit a detailed reliability program early in the design phase. The program write-up was submitted and included a provision to impose the same 2000-h requirement on each supplier of parts for the system. This revealed a complete lack of understanding by the supplier of the multiplication rule (see Section 23 under Reliability).

3. *Definition of reliability and maintainability tasks to be conducted by the supplier.*

4. *Preparation of a process control plan for the manufacturing process:*   The supplier can be asked to submit a plan summarizing the specific activities that will be conducted during the manufacture of the product. Plans can be required for all products or only for critical items. An example is shown in Figure 15.1.

5. *Definition of special tasks required of the supplier:*   These may include activities to assure that sanitary and other aspects of "good manufacturing practices" are met, special documentation requirements, and special analyses to be prepared for critical items. An example of a special analysis to be submitted by the supplier is the process failure mode effect and criticality analysis (see Section 13 under Failure Mode, Effect, and Criticality Analysis).

6. *Seriousness classification of defects:*   This is intended to help the supplier understand where to concentrate his or her efforts (see Section 18 under Quality Standards).

7. *Establishment of sensory standards:*   This is indicated for those qualities which require use of the human being as an instrument (see Section 18 under Sensory Standards). For example, the federal government was faced with the problem of defining the limits of color on a military uniform. The solution was

PRO FORMA CONTROL PLAN Ongoing

Part Number: ∇E2EB-9A889-BA		Part Name: Switch Assembly—Headlight				Supplier: Able Switch Company

Significant Characteristics:

A. Terminal Blade Thickness
B. Terminal Blade Width
C. Mounting Bushing Threads
D. Terminal Alignment
E. Continuity—All Circuits(∇)
F. Millivolt Drop—Circuit Number 321

	Characteristics Affected	Part Detail	Frequency*	Sample Size*	Analysis Methods	Reaction Program if Out-of-Control Conditions are Encountered***
Incoming Inspection	A	stock thickness	every shipment	· · ·	review control charts provided with each lot	impound lot—contact supplier for resolution
In-Process Inspection						
• Press Area	A	thickness after coining	every 1000 parts	2 pieces	micrometers/$\bar{X}$ and R chart	correct process
	B	width after stamping	every 10,000 parts	5 pieces	micrometers/median chart	correct process
	C	threads after forming	every 4 hours	75 pieces	tapered ring gage/p chart	correct process
• Assembly Area	D	alignment after staking	hourly	30 pieces	special gage/p chart	correct process
	E	complete assembly	chart hourly	100%	automatic tester/u chart	repair by responsible operator
Outgoing Inspection**	F	complete assembly	hourly	20 pieces	automatic tester/$\bar{X}$ and s chart	correct process
	C, D, E	complete assembly	each lot	50 pieces	complete visual inspection plus gages and test stand/c chart	reject lot and sort for identified nonconformance

*The frequencies and sample sizes are determined from an initial study of the stability of each process. They are periodically reviewed and updated as required.

**After 6 months production experience, the process control and inspection records will be reviewed with Ford SOA to determine if outgoing inspection can be reduced.

***If any nonconforming products are found in process control samples, 100% inspect all products produced since the last in control point.

SUBMITTED BY:

Plant Manager—Smalltown Plant
Able Switch Company

APPROVED BY: _____

Ford SOA Representative

FIG. 15.1 Form Q-101. (*Ford Motor Company, 1983.*)

to prepare physical samples of the lightest and darkest acceptable colors. Standards were sent to the field with the provision of replacing the standards periodically because of color fading.

8. *Standardization of test methods and test conditions between supplier and buyer to assure their compatibility:* A carpet manufacturer complained about yarn weight to the yarn supplier. When the supplier visited the customer to verify the test methods, the mechanics of the methods were found to be alike. An impartial testing lab was hired and the tests at the carpet plant were verified. Finally, the mystery was solved. The supplier was spinning (and measuring) the yarn at bone-dry conditions, but the carpet manufacturer measured it at standard conditions. During this period, $62,000 more was spent for yarn than if it had been purchased at the standard weight.

9. *Establishment of quality levels:* In the past, suppliers were often given "acceptable quality levels" (AQL). The AQL value was an abbreviation of the "operating characteristic" curve that described the risks associated with sampling plans. A typical AQL value might be 2.0 percent. Many suppliers interpreted this to mean that product which included 2 percent defective was to be acceptable. It is best to make clear to the supplier through the contract that all product submitted is expected to meet specifications and that any product which is nonconforming may be returned for replacement.

10. *Establishment of a system of lot identification and traceability:* This concept has long been used in some industries, e.g., heat numbers of steel, lot numbers of pharmaceutical products. More recently, with intensified attention to product reliability, use of this concept has been expanded to simplify localization of trouble, to reduce the volume of product recall, and to fix responsibility. Traceability systems, although demanding some extra effort to preserve the order of manufacture and to identify the product, can be helpful in many ways. For critical products they are usually mandated.

11. *Establishment of a system of timely response to alarm signals resulting from defects:* In many contracts, the buyer and supplier are yoked to a common timetable for completion of the final product. Usually, a separate department called Production Control (or Materials Management, etc.) presides over major aspects of scheduling. However, the upper management properly looks to the people associated with the quality function to set up alarm signals to detect quality failures and to act positively on these signals to avoid deterioration, whether in quality, cost, or delivery.

Joint Managerial Planning. Achieving the economic and technological goals requires use of the conventional management tools of planning. Ideally these should be applied on a joint basis, as though buyer and supplier were all part of the same management team. The more usual elements of this planning include:

Definition of Responsibility: Buyer versus Supplier. When multiple departments of both companies are involved in a joint effort, it becomes important to clear up the assignment of duties between buyer and supplier. The assignments are spelled out partly in the contracts, partly in the supplier relations manual, and partly in the conferences and other communications between the parties.

In modern products some innocent-looking tasks turn out to be quite demanding, e.g., those associated with achieving reliability. These tasks should be clearly defined, and should be clearly assigned as to responsibility, before the contract is signed.

Definition of Responsibility: Within Buyer. Responsibilities within the buying organization are often more difficult to straighten out than those between buyer and supplier. Table 15.2 shows a typical assignment of some common responsibilities. In practice, this needs to be expanded to cover greater detail.

Documentation and Reporting. In many contracts the supplier is required to provide documented proof that the product conforms to specification and is fit for use. The buyer can then use these proofs in lieu of incoming inspection of the product.

Achieving compatibility on such reporting requires that a whole array of details be made compatible, details such as designs of forms, code numbers for defects, seriousness classification, data processing systems, terminology, target dates for reports, computer programs, and still other aspects of systems and procedures.

All this compatibility is used for other essential purposes as well, e.g., data feedback, quality certifications, and audits.

Multiple Communication Channels. The need for multiple forms of joint planning can be met only by setting up multiple channels of communications: designers must communicate directly with designers, quality specialists with quality specialists, etc. These multiple channels are a drastic departure from the single channel (buyer's purchasing department and supplier's sales department) which is the method in common use for purchase of traditional products. The multiple channels also create a risk of confusion unless coordination is provided. One form of such coordination is to provide Purchasing and Sales with copies of all letters, minutes, etc. However, in many cases this is not enough and needs to be supplemented with conferences at which members from the key departments of both companies are present. It is easier to arrive at necessary understandings and trade-offs through such conferences than through multiple isolated channels.

Media for Written Plans. When the parties reduce their planning to written contracts, there are several ways of putting the quality planning into the official documents:

1. Write the provisions into the purchase order.
2. Incorporate some provisions, e.g., seriousness classification of characteristics, into the product specifications.
3. Prepare a separate quality/reliability specification, and reference this in the purchase orders.
4. Include some quality provisions (e.g., incoming inspection procedures) in a supplier relations manual, and reference this manual in the purchase order.

Of the foregoing methods, numbers 1 and 2 are applicable for specific products, whereas 3 and 4 are more convenient to application to families of products.

Supplier Relations Manual. Typically, the contents of a supplier relations manual include:

1. A statement or preamble dealing with the company's quality policies and with supplier relations generally.
2. A description of the company's operations and the role played by product quality.

3. The general plan of organization with respect to quality and especially the role of the key supplier relations departments, usually Purchasing and Quality. The duties of specific categories of employees are sometimes set out in detail to help the supplier understand what can be expected from whom.

4. An explanation of the nature of the company's quality specifications, standards, and other means of expressing the product requirements, including seriousness classification.

5. An explanation of the procedures used to evaluate supplier product.

6. Copies of the quality data and report forms used by the buyer.

7. Explanation of the buyer's plan of supplier surveys.

8. Actions expected of the supplier (these may be listed as instructions or as recommendations):

   a. Submission of samples

   b. Preparation of quality plans

   c. Specific inspection and test programs needed

   d. Specific reliability programs needed

   e. Procedure used for disposition of nonconforming material

   f. Records and reports kept

   g. Procedure for making engineering changes effective

9. A glossary of the terms used by the buyer.

Publication of the manual (or a revision) is commonly an occasion for holding seminars for suppliers to explain the manual and to provide other indoctrination.

Joint quality planning may be illustrated by activities in the automobile industry. Every new model of automobile is quite an exercise in teamwork, since both buyer and supplier must meet a severe timetable. The crux of it is a joint venture on several fronts: engineers work directly with engineers; other specialists work directly with their opposite numbers. The manufacturing planning is a joint venture in providing an adequate process, machines, and tools. The quality planning is a joint venture, down to avoiding duplication of gages. The first samples go through a prove-in procedure which includes assembly into prove-out vehicles. Through such joint planning and execution, not only is the preparation intrinsically better done; the personnel of the two companies are brought to work together face to face. The confidence born of such relationships can often outperform the most precisely drawn procedures.

COOPERATION WITH SUPPLIERS DURING EXECUTION OF CONTRACT

The cooperation usually concentrates on the following activities:

Evaluation of Initial Samples of Product.   Under many circumstances, it is important that the supplier submit test results of initial samples produced from production tooling. The conditions that warrant such a procedure are:

Purchase of a product from a new supplier

The first shipment of a new product

The first shipment following a change in design, manufacturing process, or manufacturing location

Usually the size of the sample is small (less than 10 units) but submission of an initial sample can provide evidence that the buyer fully understands the specifications.

Evaluation of First Production Shipments. An evaluation of a sample from the first production shipment is also in order before the full shipment is made. The evaluation can be accomplished by having a buyer representative visit the supplier's plant and observe the inspection of a random sample selected from the first production lot. A review can also be made of process capability or process control type data from that lot.

Two-Way Communication. With the end of the planning stage there arises a need for providing continual two-way communication during the execution of the contract. The purpose of this communication is to supply essential information, provide performance data, identify troubles which arise, stimulate corrective action, and improve the ability of the parties to work together. For some special problems in dealing with overseas suppliers, see Doty (1982).

Design Information and Changes. Industry has made great strides in learning how to communicate design information at the beginning of a contract, but the record on communicating design changes is less impressive.

Design changes may take place at the initiative of either the buyer or the supplier. Either way, there is need to treat the supplier like an in-house department in the procedures for processing design changes and in configuration control (see Section 13 under Configuration Management). This need is especially acute for modern products, where design changes can affect products, processes, tools, instruments, stored materials, procedures, etc. Failure to provide adequate design change information to suppliers has been a distinct obstacle to good supplier relations.

Whether the design was originally prepared by the supplier or the buyer, the supplier should be encouraged to make recommendations for changes in the design. Often, the supplier is in a better position to identify needed design changes that can improve overall fitness for use and at the same time reduce costs. Such changes in the design must be submitted to the buyer for approval.

Deviations. During the performance of the contract there will arise instances of nonconformance. These may be on the product itself or on process requirements or procedural requirements. Steps must be established to resolve these deviations. For example, a material review board (see Section 18 under Judgment of Fitness for Use) is one mechanism for assuring proper inputs and decisions on nonconforming product.

Product Unfitness for Use. Cases may be discovered through product testing, material review board decisions, field complaints, service calls, returns, etc. The impact on the manufacturer is direct and severe, since the ability to sell the product is jeopardized. Despite the importance of these feedbacks, the manufacturer may have difficulty in relaying the necessary alarm signals of unfitness for use to the supplier. Some of this difficulty is technological; i.e., there are problems in securing samples to identify the suppliers involved, in acquiring adequate field data, and in working out the data processing needed to separate out the information required by the various suppliers. However, some of the inadequacies in communication have been due to lack of buyer awareness of the usefulness of good feedback to the suppliers.

Corrective Action.   Communications to the supplier on nonconformance must include precise description of the symptoms of the defects. The best description is in the form of samples, but if this is not possible, the supplier should have the opportunity to visit the site of the trouble. There are numerous related questions: What disposition is to be made of the defectives? Who will sort or repair? Who will pay the costs? What were the causes? What steps are needed to avoid a recurrence? These questions are outside the scope of pure defect detection; they require joint discussion among departments within each company and further joint discussions between buyer and supplier. On modern products it is no longer feasible to settle these matters through the single communication link of purchasing agent and sales person. Instead, conferences are held and attended by those who can make the main contribution to the problem at hand.

A final note concerns "positive communication." Buyers usually quickly communicate to suppliers the data defining nonconformance, unfitness for use, and other troubles encountered. In contrast, the supplier is usually not given product data when the situation is trouble-free. When communication is limited to reports of a negative nature, the atmosphere for constructive improvement can also become negative. There is increasing awareness of this problem. Positive communication can include letters of praise, supplier awards, and recognition in supplier ratings. When successfully done, it can help change the supplier's attitude from a defensive one to constructive cooperation on a problem needing quality improvement.

The general approach to quality improvement (see Section 22, Quality Improvement) also applies to suppliers. The Pareto analysis to identify the vital few problems is particularly important as an alternative to broad attempts to tighten up all procedures on a supplier.

Supplier Surveillance.   For many modern products only the supplier has sufficient product knowledge, inspection skills, and facilities to evaluate the final product. In these cases the contract may require the supplier to present (1) a written plan for controlling quality and (2) proof that the plan has been followed.

The contracts permit the buyer to exercise a "surveillance" over all the supplier activities to achieve conformance to specifications and fitness for use. This surveillance includes procedural, process, and product audits, as well as product inspection conducted by the buyer. Surveillance can take place through periodic visits to the supplier's plant. Alternatively, the buyer may maintain a resident auditor at the supplier's plant to provide for a continuing surveillance. This same auditor may also conduct source inspection, although this is not universal. For suppliers who must do considerable design and development, the surveillance may include periodic reviews of the reliability engineering efforts.

The approaches used in a surveillance program (Burgess, 1981) can take a number of forms including:

Program auditing: Here the buyer audits elements of the supplier quality program.

In-process surveillance: This consists of monitoring the manufacturing practices of the supplier.

Witnessing of key events: The events include specific operations, inspections, or tests. An example is the initial sample inspection or the first production lot inspection.

Supplementing receiving inspection: This consists of performing or witnessing specific inspections or tests on critical characteristics.

Acceptance of product: Inspections or tests are performed by the buyer and used as a basis for acceptance.

Troubleshooting: To identify underlying causes, investigations of quality and related problems are conducted.

Supplier surveillance can provide the buyer (and the supplier) with an early warning of problems prior to product nonconformance or unfitness for use. However, surveillance is difficult to administer to the satisfaction of both parties. The buyer emphasis must be on whether or not the product is fit for use rather than on minor product deviations, process deviations, or procedural deviations. Concurrently, the supplier must understand the need for the buyer to insist on a level of documentation that may go beyond the ordinary needs of the supplier. Bruewer and Zaworski (1981) discuss the setting up and functioning of a surveillance program.

Use of On-Site Inspection Personnel.   For important supplier contracts, it is useful for the buyer to have personnel residing at the supplier's plant. On-site capability can improve communications between the two organizations and expedite product acceptance and other decision making. LaBarre (1978) describes one company's field resident program covering the entire United States. The capability does not necessarily have to reside in the buyer's organization. There are now independent services available that will perform many aspects of supplier surveillance for the buyer ("Contract Representative Service," 1981). In another approach the buyer selects someone within the supplier's organization to act as a representative for the buyer. This "certified supplier representative" witnesses inspections and tests and keeps an accurate log of all activities performed. The representative is usually selected from the buyer's organization by a field quality representative who has had contact with personnel in the buyer's organization ("Quality Representative—Certified Vendor Representative," 1981).

EVALUATING DELIVERED PRODUCT

The evaluation of supplier product can assume several forms:

1. *100 percent inspection:*   Every item in the lot is inspected for some or all of the specification requirements.
2. *Sampling inspection:*   A portion of each lot is inspected and a decision made on the entire lot (see Section 25, Acceptance Sampling).
3. *Identity check:*   The lot is examined to determine if the correct product has been received. No inspections for conformance to requirements are made.
4. *No inspection:*   The lot is directly sent to a storeroom or a processing department.
5. *Use of supplier data:*   The supplier provides a copy of the results of outgoing inspection and test at the supplier's plant and this is used in place of incoming

inspection at the buyer's plant. The general concept is explained below under Supplier Certification.

Weaver (1978) discusses an example of how cost reduction efforts at incoming inspection brought about by adverse economic conditions can result in a quality deterioration of purchased product.

Evaluation of Supplier Product by Incoming Inspection. A difficult problem at incoming inspection is distributing the limited inspection resources available over the large number of parts and suppliers. Generally, the resources are not sufficient for 100 percent inspection on all parts or even sampling inspection of all lots, using sample sizes from the conventional sampling tables. Judgments must then be made on how to allocate the inspection effort to part numbers and suppliers. The factors to be considered include:

1. Prior quality history on the part and supplier.
2. Criticality of the part on overall system performance.
3. Criticality on later manufacturing operations.
4. Warranty or use history.
5. Supplier process capability information.
6. Nature of the manufacturing process. For example, a press operation primarily depends on the adequacy of the setup. Information on the first few pieces and last few pieces in a production run is usually sufficient to draw conclusions about the entire run.
7. Product homogeneity. For example, fluid product is homogeneous and reduces the need for large sample sizes.
8. Availability of required inspection skills and equipment.

Often the volume of part numbers and suppliers is so large that judgments on the amount of inspection are made in a cursory manner, resulting in a inefficient distribution of effort at incoming inspection. A balance must be reached between a simple incoming inspection system and one that formally recognizes the factors listed.

At the recommendation of the author, a spare-parts distribution center reviewed its approach to incoming inspection. Inspection ranged from 100 percent to almost no inspection. Special sampling tables had been created because the conventional tables required sample sizes that were judged to be uneconomically large. Prior history of suppliers was documented but only periodically used to determine the amount of inspection. Also, it was felt that all lots should have some inspection and, therefore, the minimum size was one unit.

Seven years of data were readily available (stored in a computer) on lot decisions by supplier and part number, but no continuous system was used to evaluate the data and adjust the amount of inspection. A preliminary analysis revealed:

1. Forty-five percent of the supplier/part number combinations had not had a single lot rejected in 20 or more consecutive lots.
2. Most of the rejected lots were on part numbers with recent lot rejections, i.e., 93 percent of rejected part numbers had four or fewer accepted lots since the last rejected lot.

A system was devised to provide inspection personnel with updated pertinent information to properly allocate inspection effort. History on each supplier/part number combination was compiled using an arbitrary scoring system:

Lot rejection: 20 points

Rejection discovered later: 10 points

Borderline acceptance: 5 points

Dealer complaint: 10 points

Warranty claim: 10 points

The score for a part number was the sum of the points. Each accepted lot resulted in a subtraction of 8 points. Other adjustments restricted the range of the score to 0 to 50.

The sampling tables are now related to the current score, thereby providing inspection personnel with a simple way to reallocate effort on the basis of product history. The system also contains provisions for critical parts in other special situations. Under the new system, 30 percent of inspection hours were saved initially with additional savings expected later. In some cases inspection was eliminated (except for an audit inspection), but in other cases inspection was increased to provide more protection on troublesome part numbers or suppliers.

Allocation of incoming inspection effort is usually done with oversimplified procedures having high or unknown risks. The future need is to develop reasonably simple procedures that incorporate pertinent information, including prior supplier history and the effect of poor product entering the buyer's production process.

Economics of Incoming Inspection.   In deciding the amount of incoming inspection, the cost of performing the inspection is compared to the possible damage resulting from no inspection. The approach generally follows that outlined in Section 25 under Sampling Risks and Parameters; Selection of a Numerical Value of The Quality Index. Boudreault (1975) also discusses the concept of the economic aspects of testing.

Use of Supplier Data.   Incoming inspection has some drawbacks. These include costs, time delays, added inventories, and the necessity to build up appropriate skills and equipment. An alternative is to eliminate incoming inspection and rely on the inspection already performed by the supplier. The concept is known as audit of decisions or ship to stock, and is discussed below under Supplier Certification.

Use of Histogram Analysis on Supplier Data.   A useful tool for learning about a supplier's process and comparing several suppliers' manufacturing product to the same specification is the histogram (see Section 16 under Process Capability: The Concept, and Section 23 under Descriptive Statistics for Summarizing Data). A random sample is selected from a lot, and measurements are made on the selected quality characteristics. The data are charted as frequency histograms. The analysis consists of comparing the histograms to the specification limits.

An application of histograms to evaluating the hardenability of a particular grade of steel from four suppliers is shown in Figure 15.2. The specification was a maximum Rockwell C reading of 43 measured at Jominy position J8. Histo-

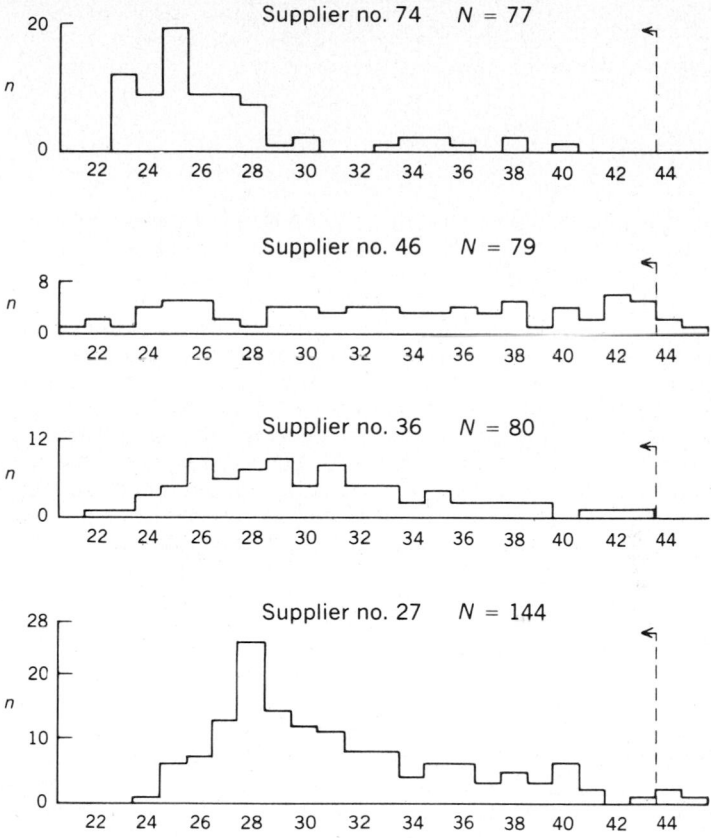

FIG. 15.2   Histograms on hardenability.

grams were also prepared for carbon, manganese, nickel, and chromium content. Analysis revealed:

1. Supplier 46 had a process without any strong central tendency. The histogram on nickel for this supplier was also rectangular in shape, indicating a lack of control of the nickel content and resulting in several heats of steel with excessively high Rockwell values.

2. Supplier 27 had several heats above the maximum, although the process had a central value of about 28. The histograms for manganese, nickel, and chromium showed several values above and apart from the main histogram.

3. Supplier 74 showed much less variability than the others. Analysis of other histograms for this supplier suggested that about half of the original heats of steel had been screened out and used for other applications.

Note how these analyses can be made without visiting the supplier plants, i.e., the "product tells on the process."

The lot plot is a sampling plan that uses histograms to make acceptance and rejection decisions on lots. Section 25 under Variables Sampling discusses this plan.

CERTIFICATION

The terms "certificate" and "certification" have multiple meanings in usage, and these varied meanings have resulted in extensive confusion.

Certificates.   Various forms include the following.

Certificate of Test.   This term is used in the sense of evidence that testing was done. The evidence is embodied in a formal document called a "certificate of test." The document, issued by a test laboratory, states that certain product was tested for certain qualities. The product is identified by description, amount, lot number, etc. Test data are given, along with the conclusion on conformance or nonconformance to specification. The document is signed by a designated official.

The laboratory may be an independent test laboratory or a captive laboratory, i.e., the supplier's laboratory. (There are many situations in which there is recourse to an independent test laboratory.)

The distinguishing characteristic of the certificate of test is the objective evidence it presents—data which are the result of positive, reproducible tests performed to determine the quality of the product.

Certificate of Compliance.   The document asserts that product conforms to specification. A typical wording is: "To whom it may concern: This certifies that to the best of our knowledge the material delivered under this contract is in accord with the terms of the contract." The contract makes no clear identification of the product, makes no statement that tests were conducted, provides no test data. The certificates are often preprinted, including signatures, to serve as an inexpensive way of complying with the wishes of a customer who insists on having them.

Certificates of compliance do not provide any assurance to the buyer that is not already present by the act of shipment. The courts have long held that when the supplier ships the product there is implied certification that the product conforms with the specifications referenced in the purchase contract. *Certificates of test do* provide additional assurance in the form of test data.

Supplier Certification.   "Supplier certification" is the process of evaluating the performance of a supplier, with respect to product quality, with the view of authorizing the supplier to self-certify shipments (if the evaluation concludes that the supplier's performance justifies such authorization).

The process is illustrated by the steps taken by one manufacturer (summarized from information provided by M. E. Noakes of General Motors, Harrison Radiator Division):

1. The buyer invites proposals for self-certification from prospective suppliers. The response from the supplier must include a "failure prevention analysis" along with the supplier's quality plan for the item.
2. The buyer evaluates the failure prevention analysis and the quality plan submitted by the supplier.
3. Conclusions are drawn about supplier capability. This may require a visit to

the supplier's plant. If the capability is acceptable, discussions are held with the supplier to assure that all quality requirements are understood and there is agreement on the quality plan.

4. The supplier starts production and sends a sample shipment along with data to document process capability. If process capability data are not available an estimate of the capability, based on similar processes, must be submitted.

5. The buyer inspects the sample shipment and compares the results to the supplier quality data to determine if the supplier can be relied on to make good product conformance decisions. If the comparison is favorable and if the parts conform to specifications, the supplier is authorized to make a pilot shipment.

6. If the pilot shipment is acceptable, then production shipments are authorized. Data are included with each shipment.

7. After a number of these production shipments have been approved, the supplier becomes "certified" for that item. This means that the supplier is to self-certify all future shipments and keep process data on file for possible review by the buyer. Inspection by the buyer is restricted to sample inspection audits and periodic plant visits to review the supplier's quality program.

Self-certification is sometimes called "audit of decisions" because such is the end result. In conventional inspection of supplier's product (by the buyer) the purpose is to answer the question: Is this lot of product good or not? After supplier self-certification, the buyer's purpose in inspecting the supplier's product is to answer the question: Does the supplier continue to make good decisions? Hence the name "audit of decisions."

Companies that contemplate use of the concept of audit of decisions are always concerned about what to do when the audit check shows an incorrect decision by the supplier's laboratory. Usually, these companies insist that means be set up for tracing the identity and rechecking of all lots not tested by the buyer since the previous audit check. This is quite a sensible requirement and calls for joint planning that will establish clear lot identification and traceability.

Possible differences in supplier and buyer results due to sampling can be analyzed using special evaluation procedures (Office of the Assistant Secretary of Defense, 1960).

Christensen (1975) describes the certification process followed and the savings in receiving inspection costs that were achieved in one company. LaFord and Steers (1979) discuss the steps in a "ship to stock" program for electronics equipment.

Berman (1983) describes a system of international certification for electronic components. Evolved from earlier systems called "Tripartite" (England, France, Germany), and "Cenel" (Europe), this system provides for formal approval of manufacturers, independent test laboratories, and independent distributors. An organization can seek approval in two areas: facilities and specific electronic components. Participating countries have a "national supervising inspectorate" which provides evaluations within that country. When facility approvals are granted, the name of the organization is entered on a list of approved manufacturers, distributors, and test laboratories. When certification is sought for a component, the certification organization observes the testing conducted by the manufacturer. These tests cover both lot-by-lot and periodic testing. Observations of the testing cover test procedures, accuracy and precision of the test equipment, and the range of values for the components being tested. When the tests have been satisfactorily completed, the manufacturer is eligible to ship the components with a "certificate of conformity." The certifying organization conducts periodic surveys during future production. If problems are identified, the manufacturer is instructed to stop using the certificate of conformity until the problem is corrected.

Preferred Supplier Program.   The Ford Motor Company has a program called the "Preferred Quality Supplier Program." To become preferred, a supplier must meet the following criteria:

1. Adequacy of the supplier's system to control product quality including the use of statistical process control on selected product characteristics or process parameters that are significant to part function, fit, durability, or appearance (for appearance items only)
2. High success rate on initial sample and first production shipment evaluations
3. Outstanding ongoing performance at the Ford using location
4. An absence of significant field problems
5. The commitment and act of support of the supplier's management to pursuing never-ending improvement in quality
6. The ability and willingness to conduct manufacturing feasibility studies during the design process for parts within the supplier's area of expertise

The main benefit that the supplier receives is a preferred position in new part development programs and in future purchasing decisions. In addition, a preferred supplier is exempt from certain requirements ordinarily required of Ford suppliers (e.g., on-site reviews by Ford of initial samples and first production shipments, submission of quality plans and other documentation to Ford, and routine Ford supplier surveys).

Other Meanings of Certification.   The term "certification" is used in other contexts:

Personnel Certification.   This refers to the common practice of requiring that supplier (or other) personnel performing critical operations, e.g., those doing welding critical to human safety should first undergo a course of training and pass a qualifying examination. A certificate of qualification is issued as part of the formal procedure.

Lot Certification.   This is the process of associating homogeneous lots with certificates of test so that multiple buyers are spared the expense of testing. An old application of this is the use of heat numbers in the metals industry. A more recent application is in centralized testing of electronic parts. Berman (1983) discusses a system for lot testing leading to international certification.

Supplier Accreditation.   The term "accreditation" is sometimes used to denote the process of evaluating the overall quality system of a supplier as contrasted to evaluating a specific product (see Mundel, 1972).

IMPROVEMENT OF SUPPLIER QUALITY

The general approach to handling chronic supplier problems follows the approach to quality improvement in Section 22, Quality Improvement. For supplier items certain aspects deserve elaboration.

Stimulating the Supplier to Take Action. Frequently there have been extensive discussions between the buyer and the supplier (internal or external) on chronic quality problems. Promises are made, but often with no results. What is needed is for the supplier to become convinced of the importance of the problem to the *supplier's organization.* This is often best accomplished with factual information.

One approach is to show the supplier the effect of poor quality on supplier costs and sales income. Specifically, the buyer can show the supplier how to calculate the costs of poor quality within the supplier's organization. (For many suppliers, the number has never been determined.) In addition, the effect on sales income of the buyer and the supplier can be dramatized by presentation of data on competitive quality from the marketplace.

Some buyers take a penalizing approach. In one electronics organization any supplier with a lot acceptance rate of less than 95 percent for the prior quarter is placed on probation. The supplier must submit a corrective action plan within 2 weeks. If 95 percent lot acceptance rate is not achieved within 3 months, the supplier is subject to disqualification and cancellation of all open orders. A supplier with a lot acceptance rate less than 95 percent for the prior two quarters is disqualified. Disqualified suppliers are not given any future business until a satisfactory corrective action plan is submitted and accepted by the buyer. Hopefully, the negative tone of such an approach is balanced by technical assistance offered by the buyer.

Pareto Analysis. Supplier improvement programs can fail because the vital few problems are not identified and attacked. Instead, the programs consist of broad attempts to tighten up all procedures. The Pareto analysis (see Section 22 under Pareto Concept) can take a number of forms:

1. *Analysis of losses (or nonconformities, lot rejections, etc.) by material number or part number:* Such analysis serves a useful purpose as applied to catalog numbers involving substantial or frequent purchases.

2. *Analysis of losses by product family:* This identifies the vital few product families present in small but numerous purchases of common product families, e.g., fasteners, resistors, paints.

3. *Analysis of losses by process:* That is, classifying the defects or lot rejections in terms of the process to which they relate, e.g., plating, swaging, coil winding, etc.

4. *Analysis by supplier across the entire spectrum of purchases:* This can help to identify weaknesses in the supplier's managerial approach as contrasted to the technological, which more usually is correlated with products and processes. In one company there were 222 suppliers on the active list. Of these, 38 (or 17 percent) accounted for 53 percent of the lot rejections and 45 percent of the bad parts.

5. *Analysis by cost of the products:* In one company, 37 percent of the product numbers purchased accounted for only 5 percent of the total dollar volume of purchases, but for a much higher percent of the total incoming inspection cost. The conclusion was that these "useful many" products should be purchased from the best suppliers, even at top prices. The alternative of relying on incoming inspection would be even more costly.

6. *Analysis by system weakness:* This technique is used to discover major weaknesses in the management system. For example, some studies disclose multiple instances of working to the wrong issue of the specification. In such cases, the

system used for specification revision should be reexamined. If value analysis discovers multiple instances of overspecification, the design procedures for choosing components should be reexamined. These analyses can reveal how the buyer is contributing to his or her own problems.

Bowers (1978) describes an application to printed circuit boards. A study was made of 1092 lots received over 11 months from the five suppliers supplying the boards. Overall, 45.1 percent of the lots were rejected, and this varied, by supplier, from 39.0 percent to 68.8 percent. The cost to process the rejected lots totaled $19,680. A Pareto analysis of the results at receiving inspection is shown in Table 15.4.

Of 27 requirements checked, 7 accounted for 70.4 percent of the defects. For many requirements (e.g., hole size and board dimensions) a large percent of defects were finally accepted as a deviation to the specification. Based on an engineering review, certain specifications were changed. The study was instrumental in alerting management to the size of the supplier problem, defining a main cause, and returning product to suppliers that was not fit for use.

Providing Technical Assistance to the Supplier.   The main supplier quality problems are intercompany in nature and can therefore best be solved by joint analysis and action rather than separately. Each of the parties has experiences and know-how, both in management and technology, which can be of aid in the problem at hand. These aids may consist of:

Access to experts in the technological specialty which underlies the problem

Equipment and instrumentation of a special character

Experience in solving similar problems with other buyers or suppliers

Expertise in problem solving generally

The general approach must be on a project-by-project basis and make use of improvement teams with representatives from both organizations. Miller and Kegarise (1986) describe how it may be necessary to share proprietary information on a "need-to-know" basis.

TABLE 15.4   Pareto Analysis of Incoming Inspection

Requirement	Pareto distribution			Defects accepted under deviation	
	Number of defects	Percent defective	Cumulative percent	Number accepted	Percent accepted
Hole size	165	19.0	19.0	150	90.9
Board dimensions	110	12.7	31.7	96	87.3
Cond. defects	79	9.1	40.8	23	29.1
Cold thickness	69	8.0	48.8	31	44.9
Plating visual	66	7.6	56.4	31	50.8
Cold visual	61	7.0	63.4	27	44.3
PTH thickness	61	7.0	70.4	10	16.4
20 other	257	29.6	100.0	158	61.4
	868			526	60.6

In some cases, supplier problems are due to a design specified by the buyer. Lacking diagnosis based on facts, the buyer initially blames the supplier's manufacturing process. An aura or disagreement then prevails. A manufacturer of electronic components had an incoming rejection rate of 9 percent. Surprisingly, 68 percent of the rejections were classified "use as is." This suggested that the design requirements (set by the buyer) needed either clarification or revision. Investigation revealed this to be the case.

In another case, a rubber drive belt that had been trouble-free for 7 years suddenly experienced problems. The rubber mix used by the supplier was identified as the cause. In order to solve a problem for another client, the supplier had changed the mix. As there was no requirement for the supplier to have a dedicated process for producing the item, the supplier was free to change that process. The proprietary nature of the process and the lack of a teamwork relationship between the organizations complicated the process of achieving improvement.

In another case, a supplier reviewed the inspection process used to evaluate incoming supplier products. Based on an analysis of actual quality results, it was decided to reduce the inspection work force. Some of the inspectors were retrained in problem-solving techniques and assigned to work full time with problem suppliers. Percent defective on incoming product was reduced from 4 percent to 0.5 percent. (These three cases are from the consulting experience of the author.)

Role of Upper Management. Sometimes upper management must provide the leadership to obtain action from suppliers. One company used this approach in the following manner:

1. Data on failure rate and failure costs were summarized for each supplier. Of the buyer's warranty costs, 75 percent were due to supplier items.
2. A team from the buyer organization met individually with a team from each of the 10 key suppliers. The teams consisted of the president and the heads of Product Engineering, Purchasing, Production, and Quality Assurance from both organizations. The warranty data were presented, the program of quality improvement explained, and a goal set for a 50 percent reduction in warranty costs over a 5-year period. Each supplier was asked to develop a quality improvement program.
3. A quality improvement training session was held for the president and key staff members of the 10 key suppliers. (The outline is presented later in this Section under Training of Suppliers.)
4. Follow-up meetings were held to review the supplier quality improvement plans. Again the participants were the presidents and key staff members.
5. Semiannual followup meetings were held at which the buyer presented the newest data and the suppliers presented the latest data on laboratory test results and other activities to improve quality.
6. A system of supplier recognition awards was set up.
7. Purchasing practices were changed to transfer business to those suppliers who achieved the highest levels of quality and reliability. Sometimes this meant selecting the supplier with the highest bid price, but this was more than offset by a reduction in warranty costs.

The result has been a decline in service calls from 41 calls per 100 products to 13 calls per 100 products and a saving of $16 per unit in the cost of warranty—a significant improvement for the product involved.

SINGLE-SOURCE SUPPLIERS

Some purchased items can be procured from only one source. The reasons are many: another division of the same company makes the item; a customer specifies a supplier; only one supplier exists; the quantity involved is small.

A serious problem arises if a single-source supplier provides poor quality, has been notified, but takes little or no action. The question then is what further steps can be taken to obtain action. Presenting the problem in a form that shows the effect on the supplier is important. With the single-source supplier, the potential effect on future sales is not a strong impetus to spur action. However, showing how to calculate the costs of poor quality in the supplier's organization can help stimulate the supplier to take action.

In addition there are some specific alternatives that can be pursued:

1. Show the supplier what use is made of the product. It may turn out that the supplier can meet the needs of fitness for use despite an inability to conform to specification.

2. Classify the quality characteristics as to their seriousness. This helps the supplier to concentrate efforts on the relatively few critical and major qualities.

3. Provide technical assistance to the supplier, e.g., set up joint quality improvement teams.

4. Provide financial assistance, e.g., to buy an essential machine or instrument.

Beyond the above possibilities for assisting the supplier, there are alternatives for self-solution or for bypassing the supplier:

5. Add an in-house test to sort the good product from the bad.

6. Add an in-house operation to bring the supplier's product into compliance.

7. Make, not buy.

8. Offer the contract to a competing supplier who can solve the problem.

9. Find an alternative design which eliminates the need for what this supplier is supplying.

Finally, there are possibilities for use of broad forms of persuasion:

10. Enlist the support of sister divisions which may be giving profitable business to this supplier.

11. Enlist the support of the (buyer's) client who may also be a client of the supplier.

12. See if the supplier's upper management is responsive to a teamwork policy as a basis for continuity in relationship.

TRAINING OF SUPPLIERS

In many cases, the supplier wishes to improve but is not certain what steps are necessary. The knowledge required by the supplier can be acquired in several ways:

1. *Inviting the supplier to participate in quality training sessions sponsored by the buyer:* Sessions should start with the supplier's upper management. One appliance manufacturer sponsored an 8-hour training course for upper management of the 10 key suppliers. The outline is given in Table 15.5. The training, given by this author, was held after the president's team in the buyer's organization met with each supplier president's team to discuss the significance of the quality problem. Concepts, tools, and techniques were discussed, and each participant was given a copy of a text book.

Training programs can also be sponsored by the buyer for specific elements of the quality disciplines. Examples are courses in statistical quality control techniques, a structured project-by-project approach to quality improvement, use of

TABLE 15.5 Condensed 8-h Training Course

1. Introduction
   a. Fitness for use
   b. Quality function, systems
   c. Quality cost
2. Concept of variability
   a. Basic statistical indices
   b. Patterns of variability
   c. Probability paper
3. Improvement of quality on current products
   a. Distinction between chronic and sporadic problems
   b. Breakthrough sequence for solving problems
   c. Defining the size of the problem and identifying specific projects
   d. Organizing for breakthrough
   e. Distinction between management controllable and operator controllable defects
   f. Diagnosis of management controllable defects
   g. Subspecies of operator controllable defects
4. Prevention of quality problems—product engineering
   a. Quantification of reliability
   b. Selection of tolerances
   c. Formal design review
   d. Failure mode and effects analysis
   e. Reliability testing
   f. Improving reliability during design
   g. Safety analysis
5. Prevention of quality problems—manufacturing
   a. Manufacturing planning for quality
   b. Meeting the criteria for operator control
   c. Process capability evaluation
   d. Failure mode and effects analysis for processes
   e. Selecting tolerance limits for discrete parts
   f. Selecting tolerance limits for interacting dimensions
   g. Concepts of dominance
   h. Process control techniques
   i. Defining responsibility for quality in manufacturing
   j. Process quality audits
6. Role of upper management
   a. Quality policies and objectives
   b. Directing quality improvement
   c. Companywide training for quality
   d. Defining responsibility for quality

reliability techniques during product design, process capability, and other manufacturing planning techniques.

2. *Recommendations to suppliers concerning other training courses:* The buyer can help suppliers by sharing knowledge on the variety of training materials and training courses available in the quality disciplines.

3. *Joint quality improvement teams:* An effective way to learn is to learn by doing. Quality improvement teams formed with members from both organizations can be particularly helpful if the buyer's organization is following a structured approach to quality improvement of chronic problems (see Section 22, Quality Improvement). Not only will problems be solved, but the supplier can benefit generally by applying the improvement process to other products.

SUPPLIER QUALITY RATING

The "rating" of quality of work done by the supplier can take on a variety of forms. "Component rating" shows performance properties of an individual component. "Lot rating" summarizes the quality of incoming lots. "Supplier quality rating" is an overall assessment of supplier quality performance and is used to assist in making decisions of the broadest nature, e.g., whether or not to continue to do business with this supplier. Supplier quality rating has several purposes including:

To provide objective, quantified measures of supplier performance

To aid in arriving at a balanced judgment of supplier performance for all categories of buyer needs

To provide both buyer and supplier with common factual information on overall performance

To minimize the risk of being stampeded by isolated instances of failure

To identify troublesome areas so that corrective action can be concentrated

The extensive literature on supplier quality rating schemes makes clear that differences in products and in purchasing patterns require differences in rating plans. For products whose qualities are clearly identified at incoming inspection, a plan based on summarizing results of incoming inspection is adequate. For purchased components which create substantial excess processing costs, the plan should reflect the existence of these costs. For purchased components which affect the buyer's warranty and service costs, the supplier rating plan should (ideally) reflect these field troubles as well. Dobbins (1980) presents guidelines for developing a plan.

Supplier rating measures and formulas cover the spectrum from the simple to the highly complex. For example, one measure is the ratio of the number of parts accepted to the total number of parts received; a more complex formula includes factors such as the criticality of the nonconformities and the value of the parts.

To create a single numerical quality score is difficult because there are several units of measure, such as:

1. The quality of multiple lots expressed as lots rejected versus lots inspected
2. The quality of multiple parts expressed as percent nonconforming

3. The quality of specific characteristics, expressed in numerous natural units, e.g., ohmic resistance, percent active ingredient, mean time between failures, etc.

4. The economic consequences of bad quality, expressed in dollars

Because these units of measure vary in importance among different companies, the published rating schemes differ markedly in emphasis.

Measures in Use.   Supplier quality rating plans are based on one or more of the following measures:

1. *Product percent nonconforming:*   This is a ratio of the amount of defective items received to the total number of items received. On a lot-by-lot basis, the formula is number of lots rejected divided by number of lots received; on an individual piece basis, the formula is number of individual pieces rejected divided by the number of individual pieces received. If individual pieces are used, the formula can be adjusted to assign demerits to the different types of defects observed.

2. *Disposition of lots:*   This plan summarizes supplier performance by using a weighted analysis of the action taken on lots that were nonconforming. The rating is determined by multiplying the percent of nonconforming lots received (for each of three action categories) by a weighting factor. The products are then totaled and subtracted from 100 percent (see Table 15.6). A rating of 95 through 100 percent is considered excellent, 90 to 94.9 percent is acceptable, and below 90 percent unacceptable (Admiral Corporation, 1976).

3. *Economic analysis:*   This type of plan compares suppliers on the total dollar cost for specific purchases. The total dollar cost includes the quoted price plus quality costs associated with defect prevention, detection, and correction. An example of this was given previously in this section under Supplier Selection. Other formulas based on cost define total cost as the quoted price plus quality costs, plus additional cost in connection with deliveries and other matters (Dobbins, 1980).

4. *Composite plan:*   Supplier performance is not limited to quality. It includes delivery against schedule, price, and still other performance categories. These multiple needs suggest that supplier rating should include overall supplier performance rather than just supplier quality performance. The purchasing department is a strong advocate of this principle and has valid grounds for this advocacy.

TABLE 15.6   Supplier Rating Example

Action on lots	Number of lots*	% of lots	Weight	% weight
Use "as is"	2	2/50 = 4	1	4
Sort/rework	1	1/50 = 2	5	10
Reject and return	1	1/50 = 2	2	4
Supplier rating = 100 − 18 = 82%				18

*Number of lots received during period from supplier: 50

The National Association of Purchasing Management (1967) has recommended several types of supplier rating plans. In one of these plans the three areas of supplier performance are combined into a supplier rating with a weighting that depends on market conditions. For example:

Factor	Unit of measure	Weight
Quality	Percent of lots accepted	40
Price	Low price ÷ net price	35
Service	Percent of promises kept	25

Caplan (1980) describes a supplier rating system based on an evaluation of quality, delivery, and service. The plan uses detailed criteria for each of these three parameters and then combines the data into one overall rating. ASQC (1976) also presents a composite supplier rating formula. This formula reflects incoming inspection results, support documentation, delivery, price, service, and the effect of problems on production and field operations.

Using Supplier Ratings.   It is possible, through the use of arbitrary weightings, to summarize the various types of supplier data into a single index. However, there is no known way of ending up with a single index on which all can agree. If an arbitrary method is used and mandated, the original purpose of supplier rating is lost. Supplier ratings should be used as a servant, not as a master for decision making. The single index hides important details; the decision maker should understand what is hidden. The single index, being numerical, has a pseudoprecision, but the decision maker should not be deceived. The decision maker should understand the fringe around the numbers. The purpose should be kept clearly in mind—product rating (for which the specification is usually the standard) should not be confused with supplier rating (for which other suppliers may be the standard). Supplier rating is an important defect prevention device if it is used in an atmosphere of interdependence betweeen supplier and customer. This means that the customer must:

1. Make the investment of time, effort, and special skills to help the suppliers to improve.
2. Be willing to change the specification when warranted. In some companies, 20 to 40 percent of rejected purchases can be used without any quality compromise. The customer must search for these situations and change the specifications.

Some organizations use a periodic supplier rating to determine the share of future purchases given to each supplier. The rating system and effect on share of market is fully explained to suppliers. The approach has been used successfully by both automotive and appliance manufacturers to highlight the importance of quality to their suppliers.

Finally, in the cases of consistently poor performance by suppliers who seem unable to respond to help, the supplier rating highlights them as candidates to be dropped as suppliers.

SPECIAL BUSINESS PROBLEMS

When an organization purchases products from external sources some special problems arise.

Legal Problems.   The legal basis of supplier relations is the Uniform Commercial Code (UCC). With respect to quality, the legal aspects include such matters as the formalization of product requirements in contracts, matters concerning authorization to ship, separation of goods into separate lots, and inspection and acceptance of goods. Johnson and Webber (1985) discuss legal ramifications of supplier contracts.

One legal aspect is the product warranty. Even if there are no express warranties documented by purchase orders or specifications, the law implies certain warranties based solely on the actions of the parties involved:

1. The warranty of "merchantability," i.e., a warranty that the product is suitable for the general purposes for which products of the same description are used, and that the product is thereby suitable for moving in the channels of trade

2. A warranty of fitness for intended use, in those cases where the supplier knows the specific use the buyer will make of the product

Suppose a product conforms to specification but is not fit for use. Is the supplier responsible for the failure to meet fitness for use? The answer depends on what information is originally conveyed to the supplier. If the supplier is given only a specification, then the supplier is legally responsible only for meeting that specification. However, if the supplier is given knowledge (whether in writing or not) of the fitness needs of the product, then the supplier is responsible for meeting those needs. Hodge (1977) discusses aspects of warranty provisions as they affect quality.

Another issue is liability. Suppose that a supplier component is incorporated in a system, use of the system results in an injury, and the cause of the injury is traced to the supplier component. Who is responsible for damages to the injured person? The injured person has the right (and usually exercises it) to proceed against everyone who is involved, including certainly the manufacturer of the system and the supplier of the component. If damages are awarded, the plaintiff collects from whom he or she chooses. The multiple defendants then contest with each other on how to share the burden.

Another legal matter is the requirement that the buyer select certain suppliers on a contract. For example, on certain military contracts. the prime contractor must select suppliers from four countries (McClure, 1979). Another example is Public Law 95-507 which requires that "small business concerns and small businesses owned and controlled by socially and economically disadvantaged individuals shall have the maximum practicable opportunity to participate in the performance of contracts let by any federal agency." A relatively small supplier may not have the skills and knowledge to conduct a thorough quality program. The implication of the law is that the buyer will need to help such small suppliers so that they do become acceptable suppliers and thereby are able to compete for contracts. Ziegler (1981) discusses the impact of Public Law 95-507 on supplier quality.

Ethical Problems.   In dealing with suppliers, there is a continuing need to establish a relationship that is built on mutual trust and respect and ethical conduct. With respect to quality matters some of the issues that must be faced are:

Suppliers must be completely honest and objective in informing the customer of the quality status of delivered item; e.g., certifications that fail to indicate deviations from specifications will be interpreted as lack of good faith.

Buyers should appraise the supplier's quality and make the supplier aware of this appraisal. Preferably the appraisal should show the comparative quality position of the supplier with respect to other suppliers.

Generally the supplier should on request permit representatives from the buyer to observe inspections or tests performed by the supplier and to review the resulting data.

Both supplier and buyer should respect proprietary information.

Rudelius and Buchholz (1979) discuss the ethical problems involved in purchasing generally.

Counterfeit Product.   Some unscrupulous suppliers knowingly describe product in a false way. Instances of such "counterfeit" product have occurred for both consumer and industrial products.

A supplier manufactures a copy of a product and sells it using the label of a national well-known manufacturer. The product is sold through regular distribution chains at the full price commanded by the well-known manufacturer. The well-known manufacturer is not a party to this and is deprived of the income involved. Such counterfeit product may have poor quality, and damages the reputation of the well-known manufacturer because the buyer is not aware that the product is counterfeit.

In addition, there has been false upgrading of products. For example, a manufacturer produces some off-specification product and sells it to an outside source. The source relabels it to claim full grade quality and then sells the product for full price.

The counterfeiting can take several forms: i.e., upgrading a reliability code, changing a production date code, or even changing an identity number. In some cases the counterfeiting is so well done that only an internal microscopic inspection of the product can detect the situation. Abbott (1977) discusses examples and suggested approaches to taking action.

REFERENCES

American Society for Quality Control (1976). *Procurement Quality Control—A Handbook of Recommended Practices,* 2nd ed. Milwaukee, pp. 65–68.

American Society for Quality Control (1977). *How to Conduct a Supplier Survey.* Milwaukee.

American Society for Quality Control (1980). *Guide for Managing Vendor Quality Costs.* Milwaukee, pp. 9–10.

Abbott, Robert A. (1977). "The Cost of Honest Quality." *Quality Progress,* February, p. 4.

Admiral Corporation (1976). *Supplier Quality Control Manual.* Galesburg, IL.

Berman, Harvey S. (1983). "International Certification for Electronic Components." *Quality Progress,* November, pp. 12–15.

Boudreault, Art (1975). "Component Integrity—A Key Factor in Optimum Design." *Quality,* June, pp. 20–22.

Bowers, Virgil L. (1978). "Procurement Quality Assurance of PC Boards." *ASQC Technical Conference Transactions,* Milwaukee, pp. 62–69.

Brainard, Edgar H. (1966). "Just How Good Are Vendor Surveys?" *Quality Assurance,* August, pp. 22–25.

British Standards Institution (1979). *Quality Systems,* Parts 1–6. BSI Document BS5750, London, England.

British Standards Institution (1981). *Quality Assurance.* BSI Handbook 22, London, England.

Bruewer, Henry F. and Zaworski, Richard A. (1981). "Initiation of a Supplier Surveillance Program." *ASQC Quality Congress Transactions,* Milwaukee, pp. 992–995.

Burgess, J. A. (1981). "Supplier Surveillance." *Quality,* August, pp. Q4–Q7 (reprint).

Caplan, Frank (1980). *The Quality System.* Chilton Book Co., Radnor, PA, pp. 100–108.

Christensen, K. L. (1975). "Certification Program Reduces Costs." *Quality,* August, pp. 14–16.

"Contract Representative Service." (1981). *Quality,* August, p. Q4 (reprint).

Cooper, James (1980). "Total Quality—Design and Conformance." *Quality,* October, pp. 24–25.

Dobbins, Richard K. (1980). "Designing an Effective Procurement Rating System." *ASQC Technical Conference Transactions,* Milwaukee, pp. 488–494.

Doty, Alan L. (1982). "Far East Sourcing." *ASQC Quality Congress Transactions,* Milwaukee, pp. 217–224.

Ford Motor Company (1983). *Q-101 Quality System Standard.* Ford Product Quality Office. Dearborn, MI.

Hayes, Glenn E. and Romig, Harry G. (1977). *Modern Quality Control.* Bruce Publishing Co., Encino, CA, pp. 538–545.

Heckel, Jim (1984). "Purchasing Considerations under the JIT Concept." *Quality,* February, p. 36.

Hodge, Jack H. (1977). "Vendor Relations and Recovery." *ASQC Technical Conference Transactions,* Milwaukee, pp. 214–221.

Itoh, Wasuro (1978). "Upbringing of Component Suppliers Surrounding Toyota." *International Conference on Quality Control.* Japanese Union of Scientists and Engineers, Tokyo, Japan, pp. B1-29 through B1-34.

Johnson, Ross and Webber, Richard (1985). *Buying Quality.* Watts Publications, New York.

Juran, J. M. (1968). "Vendor Relations—An Overview." *Quality Progress,* July, pp. 10–16.

Kraljic, Peter (1983). "Purchasing Must Become Supply Management." *Harvard Business Review,* September–October, pp. 109–117.

LaBarre, Kenneth C. (1978). "Building a Field Resident Quality Program." *Quality Progress,* October, pp. 24–27.

LaFord, Richard J. and Steers, Robert R. (1979). "Receiving Inspection or Ship to Stock, Parts I and II." *ASQC Technical Conference Transactions,* Milwaukee, pp. 69–78.

McClure, J. Y. (1979). "Procurement Quality Control within the Multinational Environment." *ASQC Technical Conference Transactions,* Milwaukee, pp. 643–654.

Miller, G. D. and Kegaris, Ronald J. (1986). "An Alcoa-Kodak Joint Team." *The Juran Report,* no. 6, pp. 29–34.

MIL-Q-9858A (1985). *Quality Program Requirements.* Naval Publications and Forms Center, Philadelphia.

Mundel, August B. (1972). "Vendor-Vendee Accreditation." *ASQC Technical Conference Transactions,* Milwaukee, pp. 408–416.

National Association of Purchasing Agents (1967). *Evaluation of Supplier Performance.* New York.

Norquist, Warren E. (1983). "Improving Quality/Purchasing Teamwork." *ASQC Quality Congress Transactions,* Milwaukee, pp. 136–141.

Office of the Assistant Secretary of Defense (1960). *Statistical Procedures for Determining Validity of Supplier's Attributes Inspection.* Handbook 109, Naval Publications and Forms Center, Philadelphia.

"Quality Representative—Certified Vendor Representative." (1981). *Quality,* August, pp. Q3–Q4 (reprint).

Rau, Sri Y. R. (1981). "Development of Vendor Quality Control." *BHEL Quality Journal* (Bharat Heavy Electricals, Limited, New Delhi), pp. 3–6.

Rudelius, William and Buchholz, Rogene A. (1979). "Ethical Problems of Purchasing Managers." *Harvard Business Review,* March–April, pp. 8–14.

Sheppard, John W. (1977). "CASE Is Now 12 Years Old." *Quality Progress,* November, pp. 38–39.

Shilliff, Karl A. and Bodis, Milan (1975). "How to Pick the Right Vendor." *Quality Progress,* January, pp. 12–14.

Thoday, Wilfred R. (1983). "A Solution to Multiple Assessment." *ASQC Quality Congress Transactions,* Milwaukee, pp. 653–655.

Weaver, Henry (1978). "Quality Deterioration (Economic Marketplace)." *Quality Progress,* February, pp. 28–30.

Ziegler, August H. (1981). "Vendor Quality's New Challenge, Public Law 95-507." *ASQC Quality Congress Transactions,* Milwaukee, pp. 281–286.

Ziegler, August H. and Diggs, James (1982). "An Integrated Approach to Subcontract Support." *ASQC Quality Congress Transactions,* Milwaukee, pp. 947–954.

SECTION 16

MANUFACTURING PLANNING[1]

Frank M. Gryna

INTRODUCTION **16.2**

RESPONSIBILITY FOR
MANUFACTURING PLANNING . **16.3**

DESIGN REVIEW **16.5**

RELATIVE IMPORTANCE OF
PRODUCT CHARACTERISTICS . **16.6**
   Identification of Critical
     Items 16.6
   Classification of
     Characteristics 16.6
   Cost of Tolerances 16.8

INITIAL PLANNING FOR
QUALITY **16.9**
   Process Diagrams 16.9
   Correlation of Process
     Variables with Product
     Results 16.9
   Predicting Adequacy of
     Processes 16.14

PROCESS CAPABILITY: THE
CONCEPT **16.14**
   Basic Definitions 16.14
   Process Patterns 16.15
   Product Mixture 16.17
   Standardized Formula . . . 16.17
   Relation to Product
     Tolerance 16.18

PROCESS CAPABILITY
MEASUREMENT **16.21**
   Measuring Present Process
     Performance 16.21
   Measuring Inherent
     Capability 16.25
   Application of
     Experimental Design to
     Optimize Process
     Variables ("Off-Line
     Quality Control") 16.30
   Steps in Evaluating
     Proposed Complex
     Processes 16.32
   Planning for the Process
     Capability Study 16.32

PROCESS CAPABILITY:
APPLICATIONS **16.33**
   Choice among Alternative
     Processes 16.33
   Purchase of Machinery . . 16.34
   Interrelation of Sequential
     Processes 16.34
   Other Uses of Capability
     Data 16.35

ERROR-PROOFING THE
PROCESS **16.35**
   Methods of Error-Proofing 16.35
   Error-Prone Systems . . . 16.36

---

[1] In the Third Edition, this section was prepared by Donald N. Ekvall and J. M. Juran.

*OTHER ELEMENTS OF
EQUIPMENT AND WORK
METHODS PLANNING* **16.37**

   Providing for Adjustments
   to Processes 16.37

   Preventive Maintenance . . 16.38

*PLANNING OF PERSONNEL
REQUIREMENTS* **16.38**

*PLANNING FOR PROTECTION
AND TRACEABILITY OF
MATERIAL* **16.38**

   Traceability 16.39

   Batch Control 16.39

   Continuous Production,
   Low Unit Value 16.39

   Continuous Production,
   High Unit Value 16.39

*PLANNING OF PROCESS
ENVIRONMENT* **16.40**

*OVERALL REVIEW OF
MANUFACTURING PLANNING* . **16.41**

   Preproduction Trials . . . 16.41

   Preproduction Runs . . . 16.42

   Failure Mode, Effect, and
   Criticality Analysis for
   Processes 16.42

   Checklist for Review of
   Manufacturing
   Planning 16.44

   Role of Quality Assurance
   in Review of
   Manufacturing Planning 16.45

Use of a "Lessons Learned"
System in Reviewing
Plans 16.47

PLANNING PROCESS CONTROLS **16.48**

   Control Criteria 16.49

   Relation to Product
   Controls 16.49

   Control Systems and the
   Concept of Dominance . 16.50

   Evaluation of Proposed
   Control Tools 16.50

*PLANNING FOR EVALUATION OF
PRODUCT* **16.52**

*QUALITY INFORMATION
EQUIPMENT* **16.52**

AUTOMATED MANUFACTURING **16.53**

   Benefits to Product Quality 16.53

   Key Functions of Computer
   Integrated Manufacturing 16.54

   Group Technology 16.54

   Flexible Manufacturing
   System 16.55

   Quality Planning for
   Automated Processes . . 16.56

REFERENCES **16.57**

INTRODUCTION

The word "manufacture" as used in this handbook encompasses two areas:

1. *Manufacturing planning:* This is the collection of activities through which the factory is put into a state of readiness to meet quality and other standards. The quality-related aspects of manufacturing planning are discussed in this section.

2. *Production:* This is the execution of the plan; i.e., use of the machines, methods, etc., to make finished products out of purchased materials and components. Quality-related activities of production are covered in Section 17, Production. The role of statistical methods during production is discussed in Section 24, Statistical Process Control. Policy issues are discussed in Section 5 under Quality Policies for Functions

Manufacturing planning begins with the examination of the design concept to identify alternative approaches to manufacture. It ends when all is in readiness for the factory personnel to take over and produce.

Several recent developments make it essential that the quality parameter be an integral part of manufacturing planning:

1. *The increasing complexity of both products and processes:* Many products have become complex because of additional mechanical and electronic design features; many processes must meet "good manufacturing practices" and other forms of government regulation of manufacturing processes.

2. *The emphasis on reduced inventory levels during manufacture:* Under the "just-in-time" (JIT) production system, the concept of large lot sizes is challenged by reducing setup time, redesigning processes, and standardizing jobs. The results can be smaller lot sizes and substantial reductions in inventory. JIT is often run in combination with a production control information system called "kanban" (a card). With the kanban system, cards accompany the work in process and serve to indicate the use of a part in a subsequent operation and the need for production to replace the part. The aim is to have no inventory or buffer stock. If there are disruptions in the system, the causes are investigated and steps taken to reduce the buffer stock even further. Such a system relies on a process that is capable of meeting quality requirements because little or no inventory exists to replace defective product. Thus, JIT is not viable unless product quality is acceptable. Schonberger (1982) explains JIT, kanban, and the impact of these systems on product quality.

3. *Impact of computer-aided manufacture (CAM):* Computer aided manufacturing has the potential of improving the quality of products by providing more consistent equipment operation than is possible with human beings. However, the presence of the human being is an advantage when a process develops special problems. With CAM, the planning for quality must anticipate and make provisions for reacting to such problems.

Putting the factory into a state of readiness for production requires that the planners carry out a series of planning activities such as is shown in Table 16.1. This table shows also the results of the planning and the departments mainly responsible. A major objective of these activities is defect prevention.

RESPONSIBILITY FOR MANUFACTURING PLANNING

A major decision in manufacturing planning for quality is the division of the planning work among major departments. In the mechanical and the electronic industries, the work is usually performed within the manufacturing function by a specialist department (e.g., manufacturing engineering, methods engineering, process engineering). In the process industries, the work is usually divided into two parts. Broad planning (e.g., type of manufacturing process) is done within the research and development function; detailed planning is executed within the manufacturing function. Meal (1984) discusses sequential levels of planning starting at the corporate level and proceeding to the level of plant manager and shop superintendent.

TABLE 16.1   Manufacturing Planning

Planning activity	Planning principally performed by	End result of planning
Review design for clarity of specifications and for producibility; recommend changes	Manufacturing Engineering	Producible design; revised product specification
Choose process for manufacture: operations, sequences	Manufacturing Engineering	Economic, feasible process; process specification
Provide machines and tools capable of meeting tolerances	Manufacturing Engineering and Quality Engineering	Capable machines and tools
Provide instruments with accuracy adequate to control the process	Manufacturing Engineering	Capable instrumentation
Provide manufacturing information: methods, procedures, cautions	Manufacturing Engineering	Operation sheets
Provide system of quality controls: data collection, feedback, adjustment	Quality Engineering and Production	Control stations equipped to provide feedback
Define responsibilities for agreed pattern of quality	Production Supervision	Responsibilities
Select and train Production personnel	Production Supervision	Qualified production workers
Prove adequacy of planning; tryouts, trial lots	Manufacturing Engineering	Proof of adequacy
Provide protection for material during handling and storage	Material Control	Control of material
Provide proper environment	Plant Engineering	Controlled manufacturing conditions
Provide system for disposition of nonconforming product	Quality Engineering	Decision making at proper levels

A further decision in manufacturing planning for quality is the division of planning work among:

Staff planners who operate across departments

Planners within each department

Production supervisors

Production nonsupervisors

The main factors influencing the decision on responsibility are: the complexities of the products being made, the anatomy of the manufacturing process, the technological literacy of the work force, and the managerial philosophy of reliance on systems versus reliance on people.

Some industrialized countries delegate little of the job of manufacturing planning to the departmental supervision or to the work force. In the United States, this situation is largely a residue of the Taylor system of separating manufacturing planning from execution (Taylor, 1947). This system gave rise to separate departments for manufacturing planning.

The Taylor system was proposed early in the twentieth century, at a time when the educational level of the work force was low, while at the same time products and manufacturing technology were becoming more complex. The system was so successful in improving productivity that it was widely adopted in the United States. It took firm root and remains as the dominant approach to manufacturing planning, not only interdepartmentally but departmentally as well.

Times have changed. A major premise of the Taylor system, i.e., technological illiteracy of the work force, is obsolete because of the dramatic increase in the educational levels of the work force. Many companies recognize that extensive job knowledge resides in the work force, and are taking steps to utilize that knowledge. Manufacturing planning should ideally be a collaborative effort in which the work force has the opportunity to contribute input to the planning effort. In the United States, this collaboration is slow-moving because of the widespread adoption of the Taylor system and the vested interests that have been created by that approach.

Some companies are taking dramatic organizational steps to integrate quality matters into manufacturing planning. In one case, a separate quality department was eliminated, and the personnel and their activity were merged within the research and engineering department (Kearney, 1984). A formal "manufacturing plan of control" was established for each operation by analyzing the material and process variables which affected key product properties. This document was prepared by a team of people from Research and Engineering, Manufacturing, and Quality. The responsibility of the team member from Quality was to lead in the development of the plan of quality control.

DESIGN REVIEW

The general approach to design review is discussed in Section 13, under Design Review. The emphasis in that section is on the evaluation of the product design for the adequacy of field performance. Design review must also include an evaluation of producibility to cover the following matters:

1. Clarity of all requirements
2. Relative importance of product characteristics (see below)
3. Effect of tolerances on manufacturing economics (see below)
4. Availability of processes to meet tolerances
5. Tolerance buildup to give excessive clearance or interference
6. Ability to meet special requirements on surface finishes, fits, and other characteristics
7. Identification of special needs for handling, transportation, and storage during manufacture
8. Availability of measurement processes to evaluate requirements
9. Ease of access for measurement
10. Special skills required of manufacturing personnel

Specific criteria should be developed for each of these matters. This review of the *product* design must be supplemented by a review of the *process* design, which is discussed later in this section. These reviews provide an early warning to anticipate the difficulties during manufacture. The manufacturing engineer and the quality engineer, as members of a design review team, have a responsibility to identify these potential troubles and to contribute constructive ideas for possible solutions.

RELATIVE IMPORTANCE OF PRODUCT CHARACTERISTICS

Planners are better able to allocate available time and money where they will do the most good when they are well informed about the relative importance of the diverse characteristics of the product. Two useful techniques are the identification of critical items and the classification of characteristics of the product.

Identification of Critical Items.   Critical items are those features of a product which require a high level of attention to assure that all requirements are achieved. At one company, part of a procedure to identify "quality sensitive parts" uses specific criteria (Table 16.2). For each such part, special planning for quality is undertaken, e.g., supplier involvement before and during the contract, process capability studies, reliability verification, and other activities.

TABLE 16.2   Criteria for Quality-Sensitive Parts

Item	Criteria
Long lead items	25 weeks or longer
Tools and molds	$5000 or greater
Complex items	Multiple/complex operations
Reliability	Parts with predictable high failure rates
Safety items	Potentially hazardous parts
Proprietary items	Company-sensitive technology
Spare parts	Extended volume/special tooling
SMO	Critical processes/materials
New parts	Significant configuration/material changes
Critical specifications	Parts with greater than 20 percent critical design specifications

Source: Private communication.

Classification of Characteristics.   Under this system, the relative importance of individual features or properties of a product are determined and indicated on drawings and other documents. The classification can be simply "functional" or "nonfunctional" or can include several degrees of importance. An example of the latter is a system (Deere and Co., 1983) featuring three classes of seriousness, and criteria based on the impact of the quality characteristic on safety, operating failure, performance, service, and manufacture. (See Table 16.3.) The input data are derived from study of the part and its application, field and test data, reliability design analysis, warranty experience, and past experience on similar designs.

The classifications should be made by personnel with sufficient background in the functioning of the product. For most products, this must include technical

TABLE 16.3 Classification of Characteristics—Definition Product Classification if Characteristic Tolerance Is Increased by Evaluation Criteria*

Class	Safety	Operating failure	Performance	Service	Manufacturing
Critical (C—●)	Condition can create a risk of personal injury (see note below)	Certain failure. Probable failure not readily corrected at point of use.	Critical classification of performance, service, or manufacturing not defined because the characteristic becomes a critical safety or operating failure or a major performance, service, or manufacturing classification.		
Major (M—◐)	Not defined—use next higher classification	Probable failure which can be readily corrected at point of use. Possible failure not readily corrected at point of use.	Cause of substandard performance difficult to locate and/or to correct at point of use	Frequency of repair, cost of repair, time to repair, will be excessive, requiring dealer shop service	Will probably cause disruption of production
Minor (N—○)	Not defined—use next higher classification	Possible failure readily corrected at point of use.	Cause of substandard performance easily located and/or corrected at point of use	Frequency of repair, time to repair will be minimal and readily corrected at point of use	Possibly cause disruption of production
Incidental		The general classification assigned when no higher classification judgment results from application of the evaluation criteria			

*Note: Characteristics classified critical for safety reasons should be reviewed by the Product Safety Committee. (Courtesy Deere and Company.)

16.7

personnel from the product development function. However, they frequently voice two objections to spending time on classifying characteristics:

1. *"All of the characteristics are critical":* However, the realities are that the multitude of characteristics inevitably requires setting priorities for manufacturing and inspection efforts. Setting these priorities requires knowledge of the relative importance of characteristics. If this knowledge is not provided by the development engineer, the decisions will by default be made by others who have less background on the design.

2. *"The size of the tolerance range already provides a classification of relative importance":* One company responds by explaining that the classification is based on the effect of a change in the tolerance range. The design engineer is asked to classify the characteristic assuming that the product variation was twice the stated tolerance. A factor of 2.0 provides a significant enough step for the engineer to form an opinion on the importance of the characteristic.

A classification approach can also be applied to the manufacturing process using the process capability ratio as a criterion (see below under Process Capability: The Concept). Product-process combinations can then be studied to identify high-risk areas, e.g., critical-critical, critical-major, major-critical.

The classification of characteristics often leads to a useful dialogue between Product Development and Manufacturing Planning before the start of production. For example, a characteristic was classified by the designer as "incidental" but required a costly process to meet the tolerance range. After discussions, the design engineer increased the tolerance range and also decided to reclassify the characteristic. The expanded tolerance permitted the substitution of a less costly process. For further discussion of classifying characteristics, see Section 18 under Quality Standards.

Cost of Tolerances. Discussion of tolerances is an extensive activity during design review. To aid these discussions, it is useful to prepare quantitative data on the cost of holding various tolerances. An example for several levels of surface finish is shown in Table 16.4. The cost varies widely with the precision demanded. Data of this type can sometimes be compiled from industrial engineering studies conducted to set work standards.

TABLE 16.4   Relative Costs of Surface Finishes

Surface symbol designation	Surface roughness, μ in	Approximate cost, %
Cast and other unmachined	500	100
Rough machining	250	250
Ordinary machining	125	500
Fine machining or rough ground	63	1100
Very fine machining or ordinary grinding	32	1800
Fine grinding, shaving, or honing	16	3500
Very fine grinding, shaving, honing, or lapping	6	6000

Source: Martin Marietta Corporation.

INITIAL PLANNING FOR QUALITY

Planning starts with understanding the overall manufacturing process, and correlating process variables with product results.

Process Diagrams. Understanding the process can be aided by laying out the overall process in a flow or logic diagram. Several types are helpful. Vinson and Heaney (1977) show a quality map (Figure 16.1) that relates customer needs with manufacturing steps for a fluorescent lamp. The map describes some important relationships; i.e., the amount of light depends in part on phosphor surface purity which in turn is affected by five factors. One of these factors, "oven temperature at exhaust," is a process variable that must be closely controlled. If each customer expectation is identified and analyzed, the resulting quality map shows the relationships among customer expectations, raw materials, and the process variables. Although not shown in Figure 16.1 for proprietary reasons, the product and product specifications can in practice be added to the quality map.

Another example is the "process control map" used by a steel manufacturer (Jones and Laughlin Co., 1984). This map (Figure 16.2) has three elements:

Control area: This is a geographic area or a major function.

Control point: This is a function or activity within a control area.

Control element: This is the specific process variable which must be controlled.

A cause-and-effect diagram (see Section 13 under Formulation of Theories) is also helpful in initial planning. Fukuda (1981) describes a system of using cause-and-effect diagrams to transmit new knowledge about a process to all workers. The diagram is posted and, as experience is gained with the process, the engineers and workers attach index cards which contain information on process conditions and technical know-how to prevent defects.

A further type of diagram is a flow diagram showing the paths followed by the materials through their progression into finished product. Planners use such a diagram to divide the flow into logical sections called work stations. For each work station they prepare a formal document listing such items as operations to be performed, sequence of operations, facilities and instruments to be employed, and the process conditions to be maintained. This formal document becomes the plan to be carried out by the production supervision and work force. It serves as the basis for control activities by the inspectors. It also becomes the standard against which the process audits are conducted. An example of a flow diagram for a coating process is shown in Figure 16.3 (Siff, 1984). Venn (1971) discusses the creation of process flowcharts for quality control purposes.

Correlation of Process Variables with Product Results. A critical aspect of planning during manufacture is to discover, by data collection and analysis, the relationships between process variables or parameters and product results. Such knowledge enables the planner to specify various controls on the variables in order to achieve the specified product results. In Figure 16.3, process variables are shown in a rectangle attached to the circle representing the operation; product characteristics are listed in a rectangle between operations, at the point where conformance can be verified. Some characteristics (e.g., coat weight) are both a process variable and a product characteristic. Determining the optimal settings and

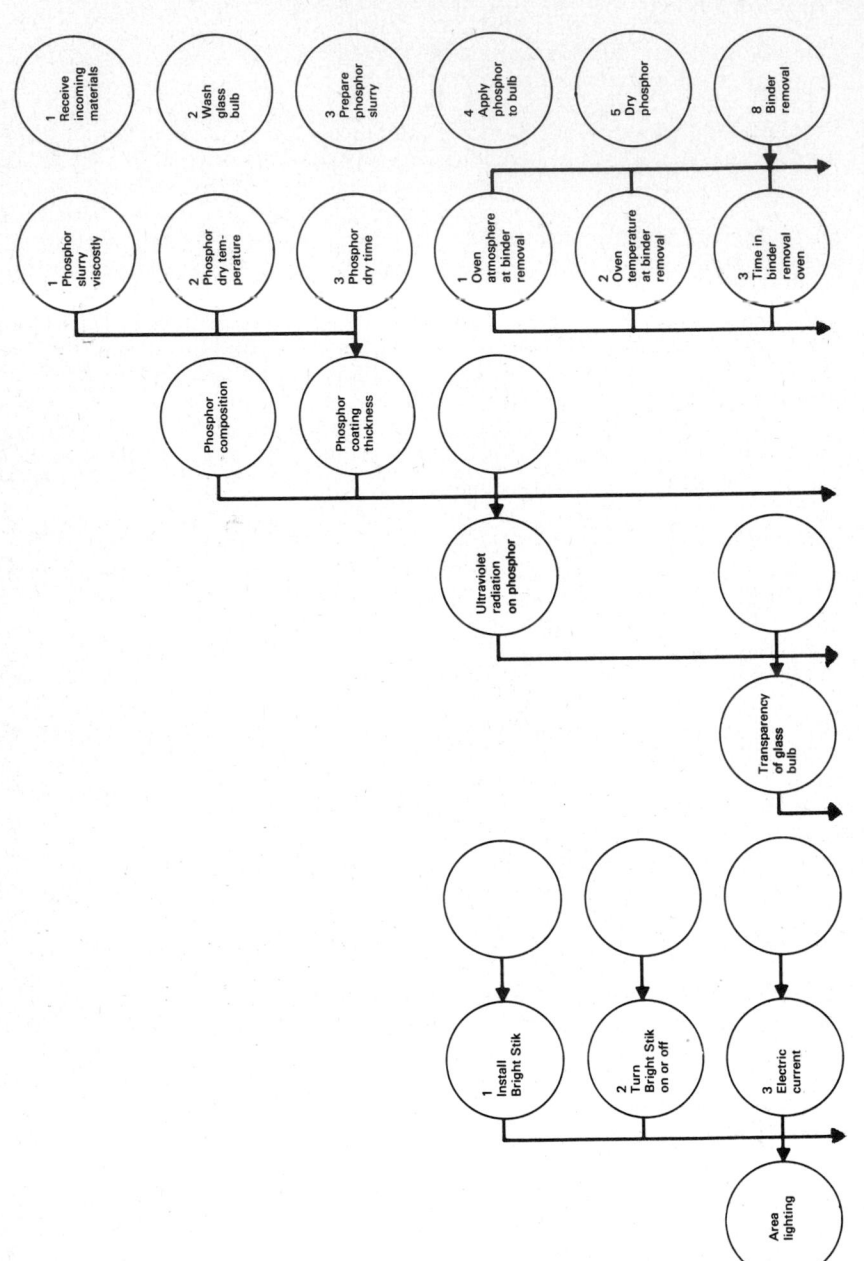

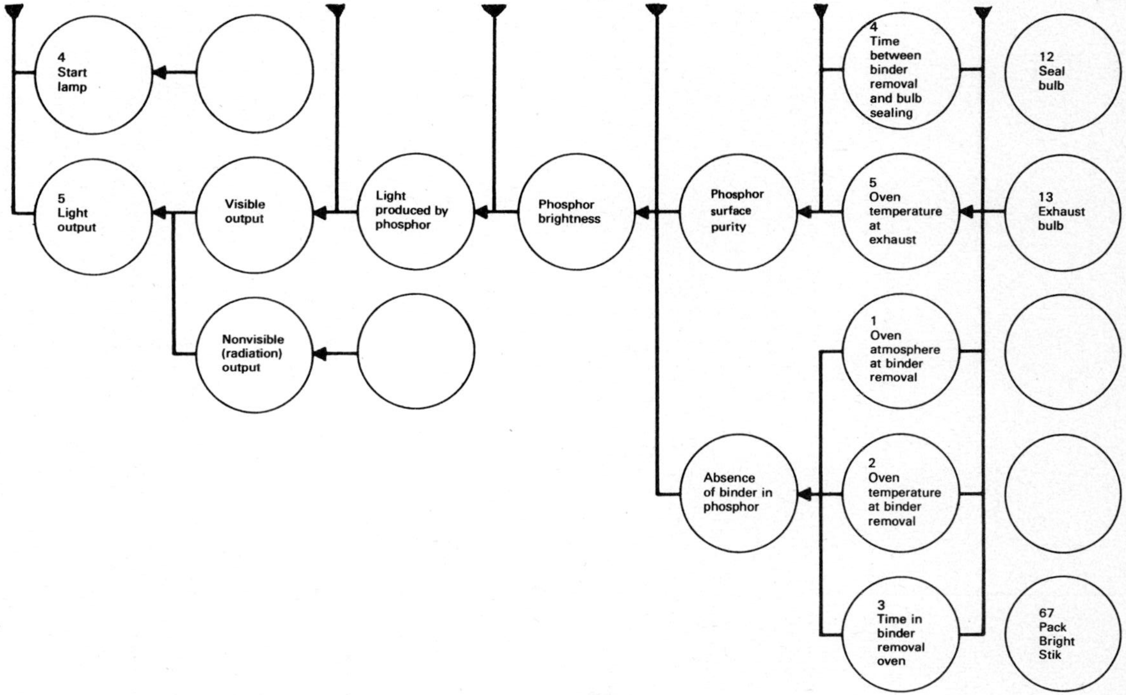

FIG. 16.1 Product design logic.

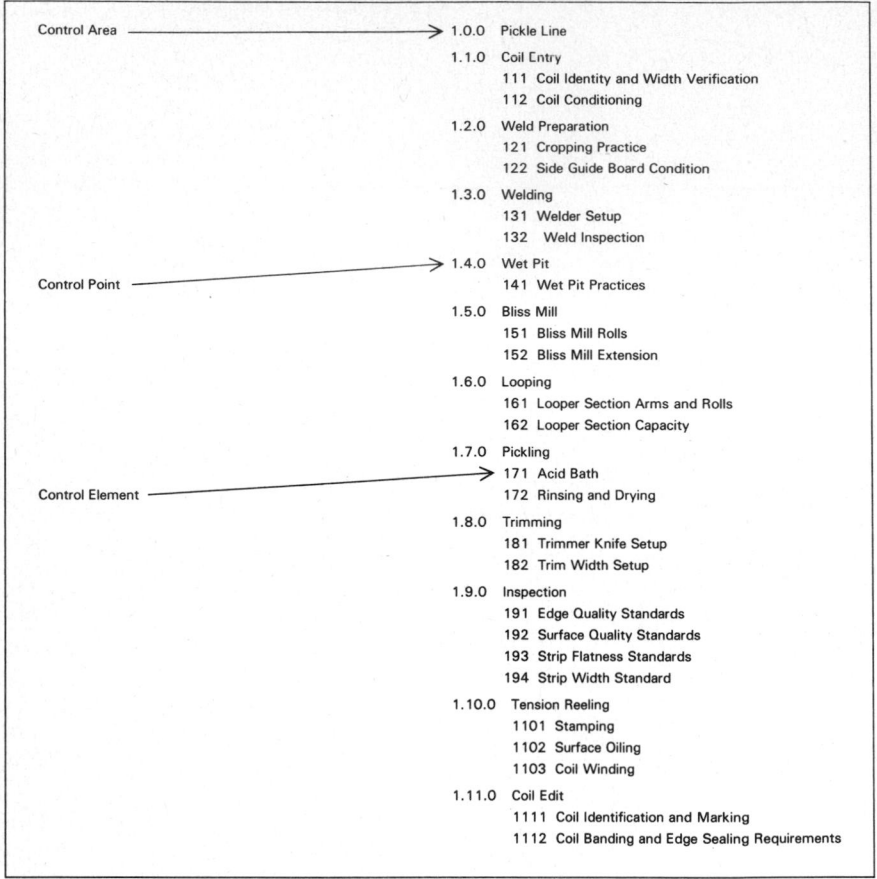

FIG. 16.2   Process control map.

tolerances for process variables sometimes requires much data collection and analysis. Carpenter (1982) discusses a case which required a statistical analysis of data on 33 parameters in order to pinpoint the key process variables in a copper ore roasting operation.

Many companies have not studied the relationships between process variables and product results. The need is especially acute in those industries where the product goes sequentially through a series of processes and accumulates the effect of many variables. In practice, process engineers conduct only such studies as are sufficient to attain product conformance to specification with competitive yields because:

1. They have no time. The priorities are on bringing new products into production and there is no end to the procession of new products.
2. They lack proficiency in the use of the quality disciplines, notably design of experiments and analysis of variance. Lacking such proficiency, they try to get answers by more intense use of their technological specialty (e.g., organic chemistry, metallurgy), but this is not enough.

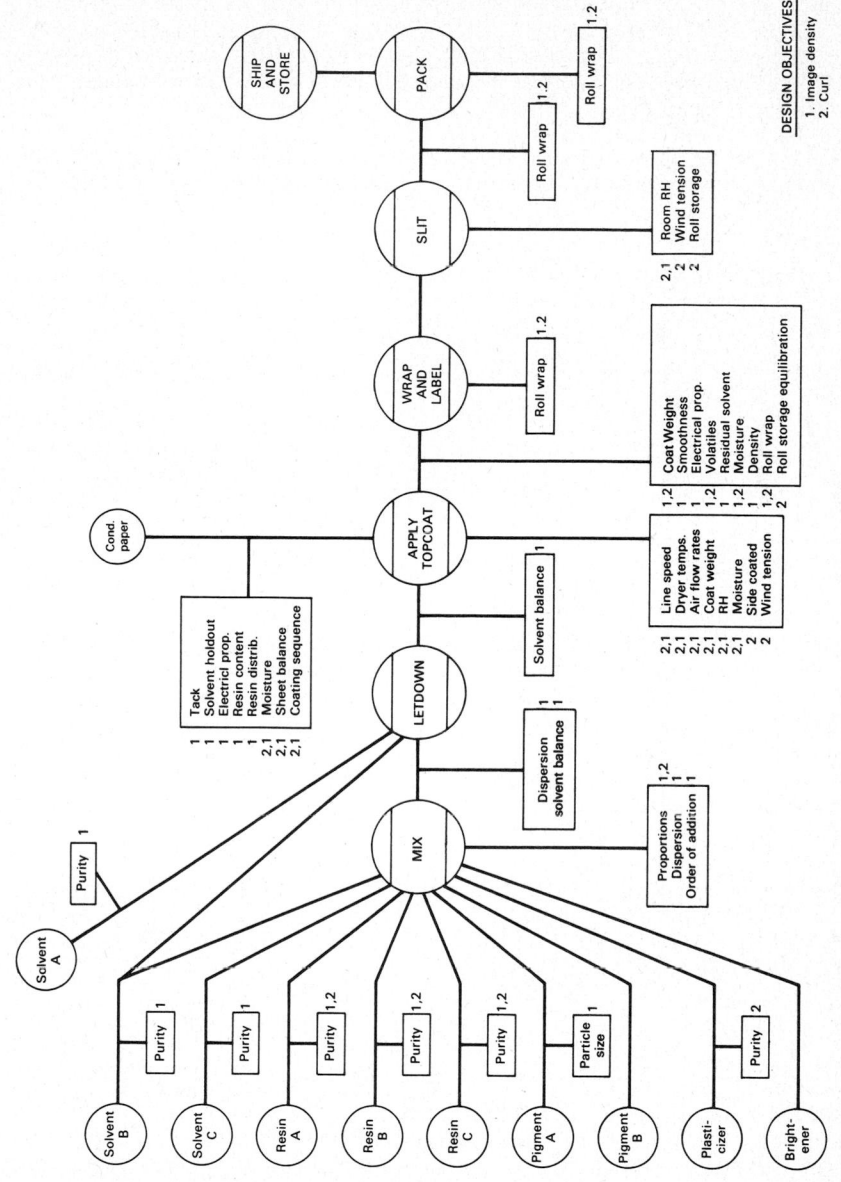

FIG. 16.3 Strategic plan of control. Product and process analysis chart (P-PAC).

The consequences of this lack of knowledge (of the relationship between process variables and product results) can be severe. In the electronic component manufacturing industry some yields are shockingly low and will likely remain that way until the process variables are studied in depth. In all industries the imposition of new quality demands (e.g., reduction in weight of automotive components) can cause a sharp rise in scrap (and hence in costs) because not enough is known about the process variables to adapt promptly to the new demands.

Only upper management can supply the missing essentials, which consist of:

1. The budget for personnel needed full time to assist by analyzing existing data, determining the need for additional studies, designing the experiments, collecting the new data, analyzing, etc.
2. The budget for training in the quality disciplines. The full-time analysts should, of course, have this training in depth. In addition, it is quite helpful for the process engineers to become knowledgeable as well. The necessary training programs are widely available.

The return on these investments is in the form of higher yields, higher productivity, lower costs, and better quality.

Some industries must meet explicit government regulations concerning manufacturing practices, and these must be recognized during manufacturing planning. An example is the good manufacturing practices (GMP) regulations in health-related industries.

Predicting Adequacy of Processes. The planner should know in advance whether the process will be able to turn out products which are fit for use. One of the necessary ingredients is knowledge of the adequacy of the process.

There are several ways of evaluating adequacy of equipment. In one approach, measurements are made on the process rather than the product. For example, in the manufacture of machine tools it is common to place dial gages, test mandrels, spirit levels, and other instruments in appropriate mountings, in order to measure the trueness of the machine. Also, sterilization chambers are checked with thermocouples to assure that all areas can be brought up to the minimal temperature needed to kill off unwanted organisms. Such measurements are part of the overall evaluation of equipment. However, a complete evaluation requires measurements on the *product* through "process capability studies."

PROCESS CAPABILITY: THE CONCEPT

Process capability is the measured, inherent reproducibility of the product turned out by a process.

Basic Definitions. Each key word in this definition must itself be clearly defined, since the concept of capability has an enormous extent of application and since nonscientific terms are inadequate for communication within the industrial community.

Process: This refers to some unique combination of machine, tools, methods, materials, *and people* engaged in production. It is often feasible to separate and quantify the effect of the variables entering this combination. Such separation can be illuminating.

Capability: This word is used in the sense of a competence, based on tested performance, to achieve measurable results.

Measured: This refers to the fact that process capability is quantified from data which, in turn, are the results of measurement of work performed by the process.

Inherent reproducibility: This refers to the product uniformity resulting from a process which is in a state of statistical control, i.e., in the absence of time-to-time "drift" or other assignable causes of variation. "Instantaneous reproducibility" is a synonym.

Product: The measurement is made on the product because it is product variation which is the end result.

Machine capability versus process capability: Some practitioners distinguish between these two terms. Machine capability refers to the reproducibility under one set of process conditions (e.g.: one operator, homogeneous raw material, uniform manufacturing practice). Process capability refers to the reproducibility over a long period of time with normal changes in workers, material, and other process conditions.

Process capability as defined above is a measurable property of the process (much as volume in liters is a measurable property of a container). The resulting measure is expressed in terms of 6σ of variation (see below) and is unrelated to the product tolerance; i.e., "the process doesn't know what the tolerance is." However, the capability measurement is compared to the tolerance in order to judge the adequacy of the process.

Process Patterns. The concept of process capability can be better understood by an examination of the usual process patterns encountered. A useful technique for making this examination is to measure a sample, summarize the data in a histogram, and compare the result to the specification limits.

Typical histograms and the usual meaning of each are shown in Figure 16.4. The examination has a three-part focus:

The centering of the histogram: This defines the aim of the process.

Width of the histogram: This defines the variability about the aim.

The shape of the histogram: For most characteristics, a normal or bell-shaped curve is expected. Any significant deviation from the normal pattern has a cause which, once determined, can shed much light on the variability in the process. For example, histograms with two or more peaks reveal that multiple "populations" have been mixed together. These populations may be different mold cavities, different spindles, different heads on a machine, different suppliers, and so forth.

Histograms and chronological plots of process data indicate several reasons why some processes are not capable of holding tolerances. These are:

1. *The inherent variability of the process is too large for the proposed tolerance:* Assuming the process is in statistical control, the only courses of action are to revise the process, to expand the tolerances, or to live with a certain level of defectives.

2. *The process is misdirected:* Here the planner must provide the operating forces with the means to evaluate the extent of misdirection and to make compensating adjustments in the process.

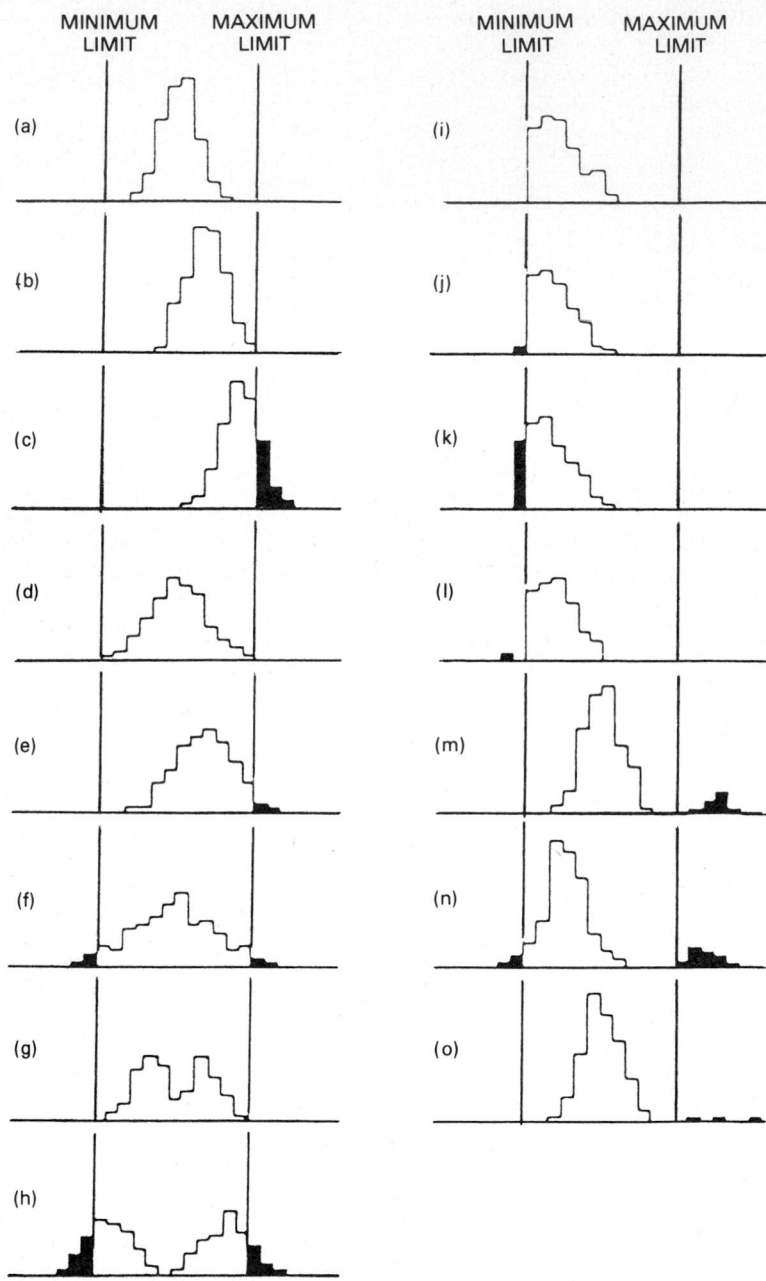

FIG. 16.4 Histogram distribution patterns. *(Adapted from Armstrong, G. R. and Clarke, P. C. (1946). "Frequency Distribution vs. Acceptance Table." Industrial Quality Control. vol. 3, no. 2, September, pp. 22–27.)*

3. *The instrumentation is inadequate.*

4. *There is process drift:*   Here the need is to quantify the amount of drift in a given period of time and to provide means for resetting the process to compensate for this drift.

5. *There are cyclical changes in the process:*   The need is to identify the underlying cause and either remove it or reduce the effect on the process.

6. *The process is erratic:*   Sudden changes can take place in processes. As the capability studies quantify the size of these changes and help to discover the reasons for them, appropriate planning action can be taken:

   a. Temporary phenomena (e.g., cold machine coming up to operating temperature) can be dealt with by scheduling warming periods plus checks at the predicted time of stability.

   b. More enduring phenomena (e.g., change due to new material supply) can be dealt with by specifying setup reverification at the time of introducing such change.

Product Mixture.   A common obstacle to utilizing the inherent capability of a process is that, for reasons of productivity, products from several processes are commingled at the time of manufacture. Examples of this are widespread: multicavity plastic molding, multiple unit film deposition for electronic components, multiple head filling of containers, etc. What these processes have in common is a multiplicity of "machines" mounted on a single frame. The multiple character of these producing sources superimposes a stream-to-stream variation which materially affects the ability of the process to meet the specifications.

In such cases, any conventional sampling of product ends up with data which are a composite of two different sources of variation:

1. The stream-to-stream variation, traceable to differences in the mold cavities, spindles, heads, etc.

2. The within-stream variation, which characterizes a single "pure" process

To quantify the stream-to-stream variation requires that the product from different streams (cavities, spindles, molds, heads) can be segregated. Once segregated, the data for each stream can be treated in the conventional manner. Figure 16.5 is an example of such segregation and quantification for a multiple spindle screw machine. Tarver (1984) presents procedures for process capability studies of multiple stream processes.

Standardized Formula.   The most widely adopted formula for process capability is

$$\text{Process capability} = 6\sigma$$

where σ = the standard deviation of the process under a state of statistical control, i.e., under no drift and no sudden changes.

If the process is centered at the nominal specification and follows a normal probability distribution, 99.73 percent of production will fall within $\pm 3\sigma$ of the nominal specification.

Some industrial processes do operate under a state of statistical control. For such processes, the computed process capability of 6σ can be compared directly to specification tolerances, and judgments of adequacy can be made. However, the majority of industrial processes do exhibit drift and do exhibit sudden

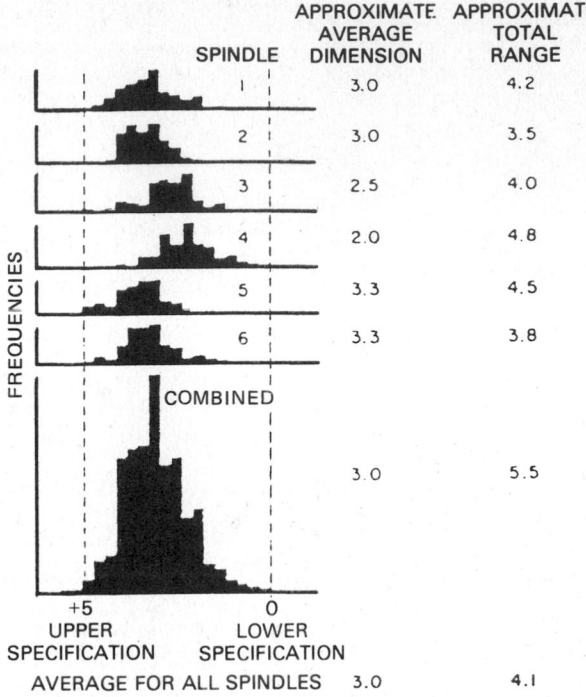

FIG. 16.5 Separating multiple streams, multiple spindle machine.

changes. These departures from the ideal are a fact of life, and the practitioner must deal with them.

Nevertheless, there is great value in standardizing on a formula for process capability based on a state of statistical control. Under this state, the product variations are the resultant of numerous small variables (rather than being the effect of a single large variable) and hence have the character of random variation. It is most helpful for planners to have such limits in quantified form.

The standardized formula (process capability = 6σ) assumes a normal probability distribution. This is often the case, but it is not universally true. For example, dimensions that are close to a physical limit, such as the amount "out of round" (where a value of zero is desired), tend to show "skewed" distributions. In such cases, $\pm 3\sigma$ does not include 99.73 percent of the population. However, it is possible to use the log normal or Weibull distribution to derive a measure of process capability. This can be most conveniently done by using probability paper (see below).

Relation to Product Tolerance.   A major reason for quantifying process capability is to be able to compute the ability of the process to hold product tolerances. For processes which are in a state of statistical control, a comparison of the variation of 6σ to the tolerance limits permits ready calculation of percent defective by conventional statistical theory. (See Section 23, under Continuous Probability Distributions.)

Capability Ratio. In most processes, not only are there departures from a state of statistical control but the process is not necessarily being operated to secure optimum yields, e.g., the average of the process is not centered between the upper and lower tolerance limits. To allow for these realities, planners try to select processes with the 6σ process capability well within the tolerance width. The two factors are expressed in a capability ratio:

$$\text{Capability ratio} = \frac{\text{tolerance width}}{\text{process capability}}$$

Some companies define the ratio as the reciprocal. Some industries now express defect rates in terms of parts per million. A defect rate of 1 part per million requires a capability ratio (tolerance width over process capability) of about 1.63.

The comparison of process capability to tolerances leads to some broad plans of action:

1. If the process capability is inadequate to meet the tolerance:

   a. Try to shift the job to another process with more adequate capability. If the order already is completed, make provisions for proper assignment when the job occurs again.

   b. Try to improve the capability. This is particularly advisable if the value obtained differs markedly from that of a similar process. The process may require overhauling or the tooling may need to be reviewed. For multispindle machines, the causes for spindle-to-spindle differences may need to be pinpointed. Control chart analysis may be helpful. If the process is in a state of statistical control, a major change such as an overhaul will be required to improve the capability. If the process is not in statistical control, the assignable causes should be identified for the out-of-control points, and removal of these causes can result in improved capability.

   c. Try to get a review of the tolerance. The availability of specific information showing what tolerance can be achieved may soften the engineer's attitude on liberalizing the tolerance.

2. If the process capability is equal to the tolerance, this usually should be treated as in item 1 above, since it means that process must be set exactly at the nominal point and gives no allowance for factors such as tool wear. However, if such factors are negligible or where a small percentage of parts just outside the tolerance can be tolerated, this should be treated as in item 3 below.

3. If the process capability is adequate to meet the tolerance:

   a. If the capability is of the order of two-thirds to three-fourths of the tolerance or less, it is the acceptable situation. The process should produce practically all good work over a long period of time if periodic samples are taken to check the setting of the process.

   b. If the capability is less than one-half of the tolerance, do nothing unless reducing the tolerance will achieve some gain. The ability to tighten the tolerance on one part in an assembly may permit loosening a difficult tolerance on another part. Closer guarantee of tolerances may also have competitive sales advantage.

   c. One hundred percent inspection of the product is not needed and a sampling procedure should be considered.

Kane (1986) discusses the use of a "Performance Index" C_{pk} which reflects the current process mean's proximity to either the upper specification limit USL or lower specification limit LSL. C_{pk} is estimated by:

$$\hat{C}_{pk} = \min \left[\frac{\overline{X} - \text{LSL}}{3s}, \frac{\text{USL} - \overline{X}}{3s} \right]$$

For Kane's example where

$$\text{USL} = 20 \qquad \overline{X} = 16$$
$$\text{LSL} = 8 \qquad s = 2$$

the standard capability ratio is estimated as

$$\frac{\text{USL} - \text{LSL}}{6\sigma} = \frac{20 - 8}{12} = 1.0$$

which implies that, *if* the process were centered between the specification limits (at 14), then only a small proportion (about 0.27 percent) of product would be defective.

However, when we calculate C_{pk}, we obtain

$$\hat{C}_{pk} = \min \left[\frac{16 - 8}{6}, \frac{20 - 16}{6} \right] = 0.67$$

which alerts us that the process mean is *currently* nearer the USL. (Note that if the process were centered at 14, the value of C_{pk} would be 1.0.) An acceptable process will require reducing the standard deviation and/or centering the mean.

There can be circumstances in which product uniformity around a target value is more important than the percent of product that meets specifications. Sullivan (1984) describes a case of two company facilities making the same television set (Figure 16.6). The San Diego plant had no product outside specifications but the

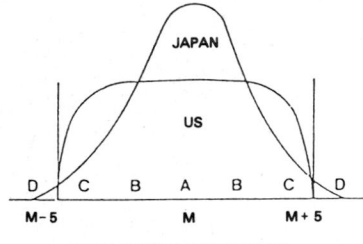

SONY'S case (cited from the Asahi, April 17, 1979):
Color density of TV set
Assumption: repairing cost A = 4 ($)
Loss function:

$$L = \frac{4}{5^2} \sigma^2 = 0.16\sigma^2$$

San Diego: $L = 0.16 \times \left(\frac{10}{\sqrt{12}} \right)^2 = 1.33$

Japan: $L = 0.16 \times \left(\frac{10}{6} \right)^2 = 0.44$

JAPAN

US

D C B A B C D

M − 5   M   M + 5

TYPES OF DISTRIBUTION IN THE ASAHI

Factory location	Type of distribution (approx.)	Percent out of spec., %	Standard deviation	Loss per unit, $	Difference in quality, $
San Diego	Uniform	Almost nil	$\frac{10}{\sqrt{12}}$	1.33	− 0.89
Japan	Normal	0.3	$\frac{10}{6}$	0.44	

FIG. 16.6 Uniformity and production quality in Japan and the United States. *(From Sullivan, 1984, p. 19.)*

distribution was virtually rectangular, with a large percent of product close to the specification limits. In contrast, the plant in Japan did have some product outside of specification limits, but the distribution was normal and was concentrated around the target value. Field experience revealed that product near the specification limits generated complaints from customers. This and other reasons led to a higher loss per unit at San Diego even though that plant was superior in meeting the specification.

Sometimes the relationship of process variation to process economics can be evaluated to determine the most profitable target value for a process. Hunter and Kartha (1977) have developed a technique for determining the best target value for a process with a single specification limit that simultaneously produces (1) product conforming to specification, (2) product not conforming but which can be sold at a lower selling price, and (3) product that results in a "giveaway" cost, as when a minimum weight specification is exceeded and product is given away. Nelson (1978) presents an approximating function for the Hunter and Kartha technique.

PROCESS CAPABILITY MEASUREMENT

"Process capability" refers to the variation in a process about some target value. This is illustrated in Figure 16.7. The two processes have equal capabilities because 6σ is the same for the two, as indicated by the widths of the distribution curves. The process aimed at μ_2 is producing defectives because the aim is off center, not because of the inherent variation about the aim (i.e., the capability).

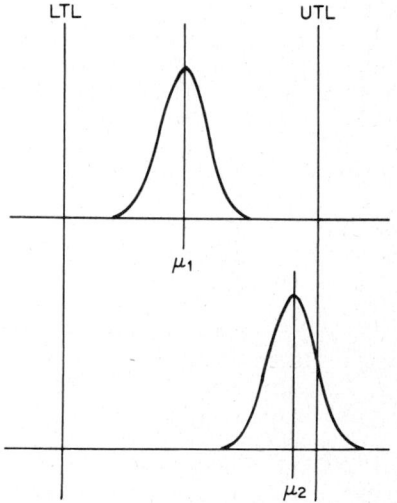

Two categories of techniques are involved:

1. Techniques that measure the present process performance, i.e., what the process is doing
2. Techniques that estimate the inherent process capability, i.e., what the process can do under certain conditions

If a process is in statistical control, then the measure of process performance results also in determining process capability. Several of the techniques described below for determining process performance use the

FIG. 16.7 Processes with equal process capability but different aim.

same calculations as techniques described later for process capability. (The difference involves the assumption of statistical control as explained below.) Mentch (1980) provides a further breakdown of process analysis into four categories and presents methods and examples for each.

Measuring Present Process Performance. Specific tools for this type of study include the frequency distribution and histograms, probability paper, the mini-capability study, plot of individual measurements, and attributes data analysis. It is highly preferable to use variables rather than attributes data, i. e., numerical measurements rather than accept-reject information.

Frequency Distribution and Histogram. In this type of study, a sample of about 50 consecutive units is taken, during which time no adjustments are made on the machines or tools. The units are all measured, the data are tallied in frequency distribution form, and the standard deviation is calculated and used as an estimate of σ. The characteristic is assumed to follow a normal probability distribution where ± 3 standard deviations includes 99.73 percent of the population. Process performance is then defined as $\pm 3\sigma$ or 6σ.

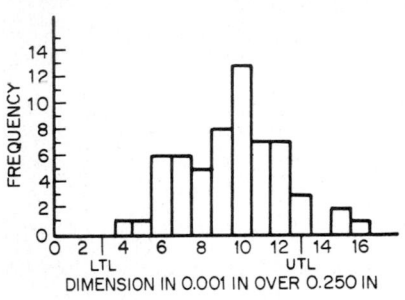

For example, the histogram for a sample of 60 measurements is shown in Figure 16.8 (machine N-5). Analysis of the 60 measurements yielded:

FIG. 16.8 Histogram of measurement.

$$\overline{X} = 9.6 \qquad s = 2.5$$

Computer programs are available to calculate the average and standard deviation, develop and plot the histogram, and make various checks on the assumption of a normal probability distribution. The process capability is calculated $\pm 3(2.5)$ or ± 7.5, or a total of 15.0.

Probability Paper. Normal probability paper (see Section 23 under Predictions with Normal Distributions) can be used to graphically determine process performance. For example, a sample of 100 measurements on total indicator reading (T.I.R.) was grouped into a frequency distribution of 10 cells. The frequencies were then plotted on normal probability paper (Figure 16.9).The measurements are plotted and are observed to follow a straight line (indicating that the population is normally distributed). The left vertical scale shows the cumulative percent of the population under a value of T.I.R.; the right vertical scale shows the cumulative percent over a value of T.I.R. and also the number of standard deviations from the mean. The upper and lower horizontal grid lines represent $\pm 3\sigma$, respectively. When the plotted line is extended to intersect the grid lines for $\pm 3\sigma$, the values of 0.01 and 0.059 are read, indicating that 99.73 percent of the population will fall between 0.01 and 0.059. The $\pm 3\sigma$ capability is then calculated as 0.059 − 0.01, or 0.058. As the specification range is 0.060, the performance is satisfactory.

By extending the plotted line to intersect the specification limits (shown as vertical lines), the percent of nonconforming product can be predicted. Essentially, zero percent will fall under the lower specification limit or over the upper specification limit.

The mean value can also be quickly estimated from the plot. Enter the vertical axis on the 50 percent line. This line intersects the diagonal at 0.030 on the horizontal scale.

Some examples of probability plots as applied to process analysis are given in Figure 16.10. Weibull probability paper (see Section 23 under Predictions with Weibull Distributions) is available for nonnormal distributions.

Plots of Individual Measurements. A simple plot of individual measurements, in order of production, can be surprisingly revealing.

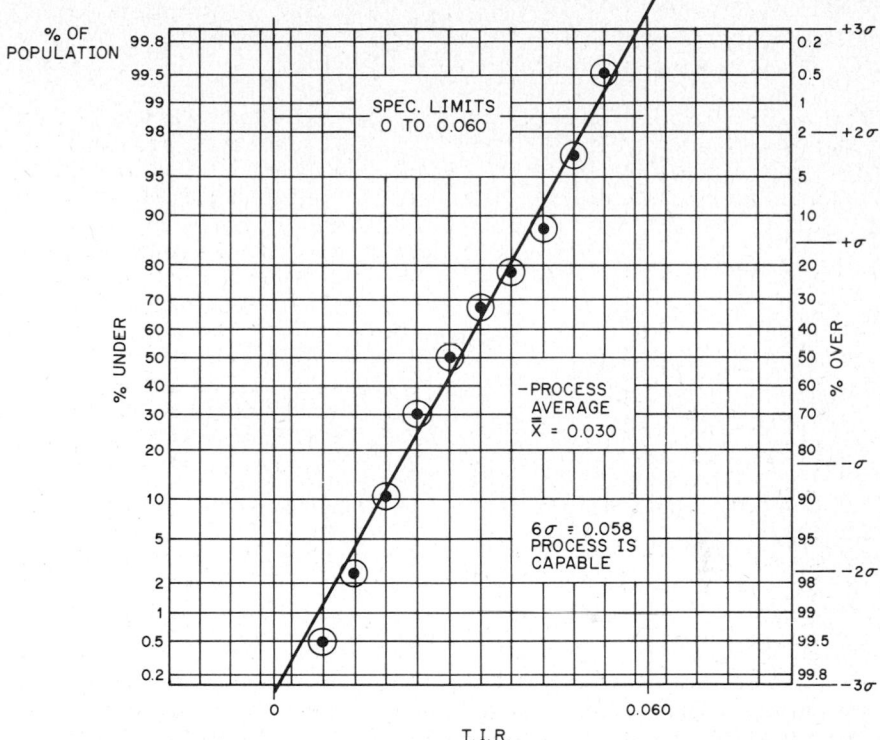

FIG. 16.9 Capability analysis on probability paper. *(Adapted from Amsden, Butler, and Amsden, 1986, p. 137.)*

In a classic study of a lathe process for making watch parts, each piece was measured for each of five quality characteristics. The resulting measurements were then plotted in chronological order on a chart which also showed the five sets of tolerances. The study demonstrated that the process was capable of meeting the specification limits. The study also showed that the poor performance (12 percent nonconforming product) was due to the inadequacy of the instruments provided to the work force. Provision of adequate instruments reduced the defect level to 2 percent and made possible a sharp reduction in the amount of gaging done by inspectors (consulting experience of J. M. Juran).

Minicapability Study. This study provides a quick, but highly approximate, estimate of "capability." Ten measurements are taken and the range (maximum-minimum values) is determined. "Capability" (defined as 6σ) is then calculated as twice the range of the sample. The rationale for this simple method is explained later in this section under Determination of Process Capability from a Control Chart Analysis. The method requires that the sample size be 10 and that the characteristic be normally distributed.

Special Studies. Some processes, notably in the process industries, do not readily submit to conventional forms of analysis, and therefore require specially designed studies. Sahrmann (1979) describes a study of the variation of weight of coating applied to a moving web by reverse roll coating. Processes of this type

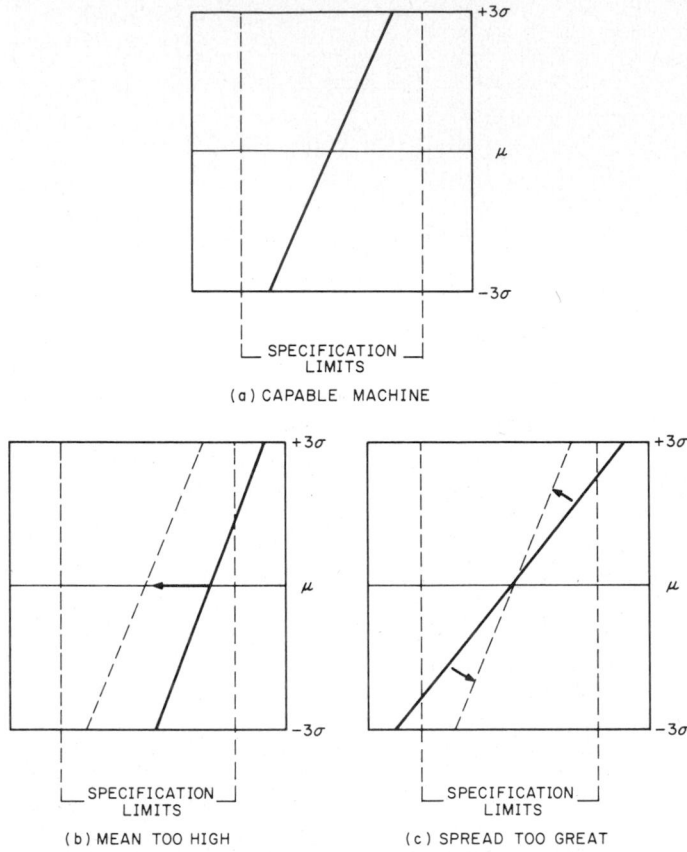

FIG. 16.10 Interpreting the results.

often show a significant amount of cyclical variation with high-low values occurring at regular intervals. (Figure 16.11). Regression analysis and other techniques helped to identify the sources of cyclical variation and measure their relative contribution to overall process variation. This led to a reduction in the total variation, thereby permitting a lower target value. The benefits were reduction in raw material "give-away" and better product uniformity for the customer.

Attributes Data Analyses.   The methods discussed above assume that numerical measurements are available from the process. This is the preferable type of data for a capability study. Sometimes, however, the only data available are in attribute form, i.e., the number defective and the number acceptable. Attributes data require large sample sizes and should be used only where variable measurement is impractical.

  Since shifts in the process average are not revealed by attributes data, the sample taken should be randomly selected over as long a time period as possible to assure that the study includes the long-term variability of the process. For attributes data, the Ford Motor Company required a minimum sample size of 250 measurements with none outside of specifications. With this criterion, about 99.73 percent of the products will be within the specified tolerances. In general,

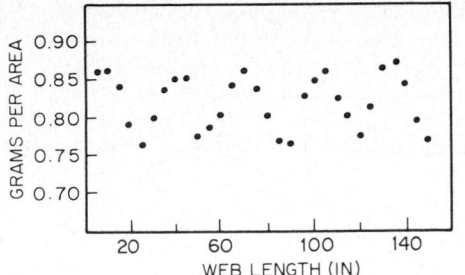

FIG. 16.11 Variations in coating weight applied by reverse roll coating.

where zero products are outside of specification limits the "capability" percentage can be determined as follows:

$$\text{Capability \%} = 100(0.5)^{1/(N+1)}$$

where N is the sample size.

If there are one or more failures to meet specifications, then

$$\text{Capability \%} = 100 \left(1 - \frac{F + 0.7}{N} \right)$$

where F is the numbers of failures.

Attributes control charts can also be used in capability studies (Mentch, 1980).

Limitations of Histograms and Probability Paper Analysis. These methods of evaluating process performance do not necessarily evaluate the inherent capability of the process. The data may include measurements from several populations (as in Figure 16.5). There may be time-to-time changes such as solutions becoming dilute or tools becoming worn. Such process conditions result in observed dispersions which are wider than the inherent capability of the process. To evaluate that inherent capability requires use of other, more precise methods of evaluation.

Measuring Inherent Capability. Specific tools for this type of study include the control chart, prediction from data on process elements, computer simulation, and tools for complex processes.

The Control Chart. A control chart is a graphic comparison of process performance data to statistical control limits, not specification limits. The performance data consists of groups of measurements ("rational subgroups") selected in regular sequence of production while preserving the order. The statistical control limits help to evaluate capability by first evaluating whether the process is operating at its minimum inherent variation.

Process variations are traceable to two kinds of causes: (1) random, i.e., due solely to chance, and (2) assignable, i.e., due to specific "findable" causes. Ideally, only random causes should be present in a process, because this represents the minimum possible amount of variation with the given set of process conditions. A process that is operating without assignable causes of variation is said to be "in a state of the statistical control." A control chart analysis should be made and assignable causes eliminated from the process prior to calculating 6σ as a measure of process capability. When this is done, 6σ then represents the inherent process capability. If 6σ is calculated without first making a control chart analysis, the 6σ will probably be inflated. Many control chart analyses reveal the presence of assignable causes even though production people profess that the process is operating with the minimum possible variation. A description of control chart methodology, including formulas and procedures, is given in Section 24, Statistical Process Control.

A state of statistical control is not an end point to process improvement. The use of experimental design techniques makes it possible to reduce process variation even further. A state of statistical control is related to the given set of process conditions including the process variables that are being controlled to yield the product results. The identification and control of other important process variables can result in less product variation. To achieve such improvement requires the use of a variety of techniques. See, for example, Section 26, Design and Analysis of Experiments, and below under Application of Experimental Design to Optimize Process Variables.

For process capability analyses using variables data, a control chart for sample averages and sample ranges is applied. Figure 16.12 shows a control chart for coded T.I.R. readings. Calculations for the control limits are explained in Section 24 under Control Chart for Average and Range. The upper chart, a plot of sample averages of five measurements each, traces the aim of the process. The lower chart, a plot of sample ranges (maximum-minimum in the sample), shows the

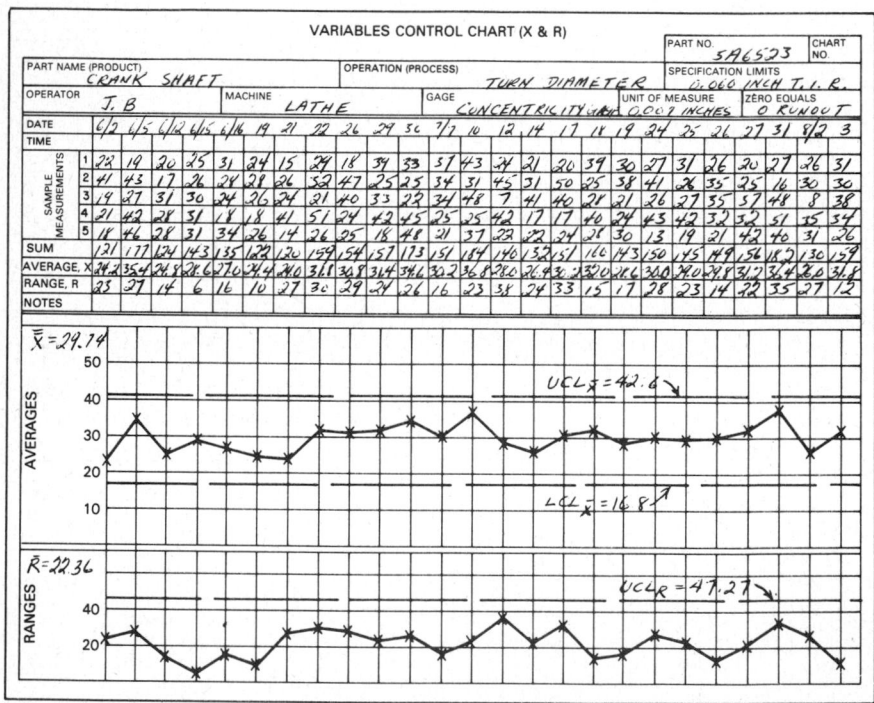

FIG. 16.12   Control Chart for averages and ranges. (*Amsden, Butler, and Amsden, 1986, p. 134.*)

inherent piece to piece variability about the process aim. As both plots fall within the respective statistical control limits, it is concluded that the process is operating in statistical contol. A calculation for process capability then represents the inherent capability.

Determination of Process Capability from a Control Chart Analysis. If, and only if, a process is in statistical control, the following relationship holds:

$$\text{Estimate of } \sigma = s = \frac{\overline{R}}{d_2}$$

Table A in Appendix II provides values of d_2. Knowing the standard deviation, process capability limits can be set at $\pm 3s$ and this used as an estimate of 3σ. (This calculation converts $\overline{R}$ to a standard deviation of *individual* values. Control limits represent 3 standard deviations of samples *averages*.)

For the data of Figure 16.12,

$$s = \frac{\overline{R}}{d_2} = \frac{22.4}{2.326} = 9.63$$

and

$$\pm 3s = \pm 3(9.63) = 28.9 \text{ (or 0.029 in original readings)}$$

or

$$6s = 57.8 \text{ (or 0.058 in original readings)}$$

Note a special case of the $s = \overline{R}/d_2$ calculation. When $n = 10$, $d_2 = 3.078$. Then

$$3s = \frac{3\overline{R}}{3.078} = \text{approximately } 1\overline{R}$$

or the 6σ process is about $2\overline{R}$. If it were necessary to make a quick approximation of process capability, a single sample of 10 could be measured, the range calculated, and process capability estimated at $2R$. (This is described previously under Minicapability Study.) Of course, this loses the advantage of the control chart.

The Assumption of Statistical Control and Its Effect on Process Capability. All statistical predictions assume a stable population. In a statistical sense, a stable population is one which is repeatable, that is, a population that is in a state of statistical control. The statistician rightfully insists that this be the case before predictions can be made. The manufacturing engineer also insists that the process conditions (feeds, speeds, etc.) be fully defined.

In practice, the original control chart analysis will often show the process to be out of statistical control. (It may or may not be meeting product specifications.) However, an investigation may show that the causes cannot be economically eliminated from the process. In theory, a process capability prediction should not be made until the process is in statistical control. However, in practice, some kind of comparison of capability to product tolerances is needed. The danger in delaying the comparison is that the assignable causes may never be eliminated from the process. The resulting indecision will thereby prolong interdepartmental bickering on whether "the tolerance is too tight" or "manufacturing is too careless."

A good way to start is by plotting individual measurements against tolerance limits (see Plots of Individual Measurements above). This may show that the process can meet the product tolerances even with assignable causes present. If a process has assignable causes of variation, but is able to meet the product tolerances, usually no economic problem exists. The statistician can properly point out that a process with assignable variation is unpredictable. This point is well taken; but in establishing priority of quality improvement efforts, processes that are meeting tolerances are seldom given high priority.

If a process is out of control and the causes cannot be economically eliminated, the standard deviation and process capability limits can nevertheless be computed (with the out-of-control points included). These limits will be inflated because the process will not be operating at its best. In addition, the instability of the process means that the prediction is approximate.

It is important to distinguish between a process in a state of statistical control and a process that is meeting specifications. A state of statistical control does *not* necessarily mean that the product from the process conforms to specifications. Statistical control limits on sample averages *cannot* be directly compared to specification limits because the control limits refer to individual units. For some processes which are not in control, the specifications are being met and no action is required; other processes are in control but the specifications are not being met and action is needed. Section 12 under Special Situation of Taking Action When Control Charts Are Used discusses the more usual permutations.

Statistical Prediction of Process Capability from Data on Process Elements. Process capability can sometimes be predicted before any product is manufactured. This may be possible if the process can be divided into elements for which previous data are available. The data are combined statistically to yield an estimate of capability for the new process.

The U.S. Department of Transportation (1982) describes how the approach can be used in ship building:

1. Identify the specific processes that contribute to some final product characteristic.

2. Provide detailed work instructions for executing each of these processes.

3. Obtain data on the mean and variance of each process step from the prior construction of other ships. (As a result of this, tables of data are now available for various work processes.)

4. Statistically predict the result of a final product characteristic on a new product:

    a. Mean value: Add or subtract mean values of the process steps according to the geometry of the dimensions.

    b. Variance: Add the variances of the contributing processes to estimate the variance of the final product characteristic. This is identical to the approach used in the statistical merger of tolerances (see Section 23 under Statistical Method of Relating Tolerances on Interacting Dimensions). Independence of the contributing processes and normality of each of the process characteristics is assumed.

5. Predict the percent of the product outside the specification limits by finding the area under the normal curve (see Section 23 under Predictions with Normal Distributions).

6. If the process is not capable, review the calculations to decide which of the contributing processes must be reduced in variability, and then plan an improvement program.

McCubbin (1971) reports on research to predict capability as a function of manufacturing variables. One mathematical model predicts capability from values of depth of cut, feed, length of cut, material hardness, and dimension size for metal working operations. A second model predicts tool wear as a function of material hardness, depth of cut, and machine dimension.

Computer Simulation of Process Capability.   This technique is useful when (1) several component parts or manufacturing steps contribute to a final result, (2) the distributions are nonnormal, and (3) the relationship between the component and the final result is difficult to analyze with conventional statistical methods. A mathematical model is first created to express the result as a function of the contributing variables. The distribution of each component or each process step is then defined—for example, a normal distribution with a mean of 2.000 and standard deviation of 0.004 or an exponential distribution with a mean of 1.000. Simulated values of the final result are generated by means of a random number generator which draws values at random from each component distribution and combines them in the model. By repeating this process many times, the result is a simulation of what would happen if many products were made at random from components or process steps having the characteristics described in the simulation model. The simulated values can be summarized in a distribution, and the average, standard deviation, and other measures computed. With the simulation model, component distributions can be changed and the effect on the overall result predicted by running additional simulations. In this way, different approaches can be tried before finalizing the manufacturing plans. Michalek and Holmes (1981) apply this technique to analyze manufacturing steps in the automotive industry.

In a communication to the author, Dr. Ronald D. Snee suggests a similar approach for predicting process capability in the process industries. First, a mathematical model is developed which relates the response characteristic (Y) to a set of control variables (X, X_2, ... ,X_p). This would probably require formally designed experiments to identify the control variables, and regression analysis to develop the mathematical model. Next, distributions of each of the control variables are developed from past experience. Finally, a computer simulation is run to generate values of the response Y from values of each of the control variables randomly generated by the simulation. The resultant Y values are summarized in a distribution, and the capability calculated as 6σ.

Measuring Potential Capability of Complex Processes.   As the process becomes complex, the analysis to measure process capability also becomes complex. As noted, the product lots are in reality composed of multiple streams, each of which can exhibit time-to-time drift and other changes. In addition, even at instantaneous time, there are piece-to-piece and within-piece variations.

Several methods of analysis are available to assist the planner in quantifying these components of total variations.

Graphic analysis: An example is the Multi-Vari graph discussed in Section 22 under Test of Theories of Management-Controllable Problems.

Span plan: This is a structured approach to analysis and is likewise discussed in Section 22 under Test of Theories of Management-Controllable Problems.

Design of experiment and analysis of variance: This is a generalized approach, with flexibility to fit any combination of variables. For each such combination, there is prepared a tailor-made "design of experiment" for collecting the data which will permit resolution of the composite variation into its components. The resulting data are analyzed by the technique of "analysis of variance," which provides, in standardized format, the determination of significance of the variables under experiment as well as their interaction. (See Section 26, Design and Analysis of Experiments.)

Response surface methodology: This sophisticated planning device has been increasingly used in the chemical process industries and some others to study the effects of multiple variables on yields or other desired characteristics and to find the combination which optimizes the final result. (See Section 26 under Response Surface Methodology.)

Evolutionary operation (EVOP): This analytical approach is aimed at securing data from manufacturing operations (as distinguished from laboratory or pilot plant experiments). Successive lots are made under process conditions which vary from one lot to another. The EVOP method goes a step further by deliberately creating some variation which will provide needed data without jeopardizing the product. Special analysis techniques then derive the relationships which form the basis of product improvement. (See Section 26 under Evolutionary Operation.)

Application of Experimental Design to Optimize Process Variables ("Off-Line Quality Control").   Taguchi (1978) has developed a method for determining the optimum values of process variables which will minimize the variation in a process while keeping a process mean on target. Phadke et al. (1983) describe an application of this approach to manufacturing planning for integrated circuits. The example concerns the dimensions on the contact window of a large-scale integrated chip. Windows that are not open or are too small result in a loss of contact to the devices, while excessively large windows lead to shorted device features. The steps in window forming and the factors critical in each step are shown in Table 16.5.

Levels of each of the nine critical factors were selected. Six of the factors have three levels each; three of the factors have only two levels each. A full factorial experiment to explore all possible factor-level combinations would require 3 raised to the 6th power times 2 raised to the 3rd power, or 5832 observations. (There were 12 experiments originally planned.) Instead, a fractional factorial design was chosen to investigate 18 combinations (with a total of 34 measurements). Three dimensions were measured on each window. Transformed variables instead of the absolute values were used in the data analysis. The variables selected were the mean and the signal-to-noise ratio (s/n). The signal-to-noise ratio is defined as:

$$s/n = \log_{10}\left(\frac{\text{mean}}{\text{standard deviation}}\right)$$

The problem was to determine the factor levels that yield a maximum signal to noise ratio while keeping the mean on target. Two steps were needed:

1. Determine the factors which have a significant effect on the signal-to-noise ratio. These are the factors that control the process variability and are referred to as control factors. For each control factor, the level chosen is that with the highest signal-to-noise ratio, thus maximizing the overall ratio.

2. Select from the control factors one that has the smallest effect on the signal-to-noise ratio. This factor is called a signal factor. The levels of the factors that are neither control factors nor signal factors are set at the nominal levels prior to the experiment. Finally, the level of the signal factor is set so that the mean response is on target.

TABLE 16.5 Fabrication Steps and Critical Factors in Window Forming

Fabrication step	Critical factors
Apply photo resist	Photo resist viscosity (B) and spin speed (C)
Bake	Bake temperature (D) and bake time (E)
Expose	Mask dimension (A), aperture (F) and exposure time (G)
Develop	Developing time (H)
Plasma etch	Etch time (I)
Remove photo resist	Does not affect window size

The analysis of variance revealed the control factors to be factors A, B, C, F, G, and H. Based on an analysis of the data, and engineering judgment, the signal factor was chosen to be exposure time.

The levels selected for each of the factors are shown in Table 16.6. Using these levels a sample of chips was manufactured. The resulting benefits were:

	Old conditions	Optimum conditions
Standard deviation	0.29	0.14
Visual defects (window per chip)	0.12	0.04

After observing these improvements, the process engineers eliminated a number of in-process checks, thereby reducing the overall time spent by the wafers in photolithography by a factor of 2.

Byrne and Taguchi (1986) discuss a case study where the objective was to maximize the force required to separate a small assembly. The October 1985 issue of the *Journal of Quality Technology* is primarily devoted to papers explaining the Taguchi approach.

TABLE 16.6 Optimum Factor Levels

Label	Factors' names	Standard levels	Optimum levels
A	Mask dimension μm	2.0	2.5
B	Viscosity	204	204
C	Spin speed r/min	3000	4000
D	Bake temperature °C	105	105
E	Bake time, min	30	30
F	Aperture	2	2
G	Exposure, PEP setting	Normal	Normal
H	Developing time, s	45	60
I	Plasma etch time, min	13.2	13.2

Source: Phadke et al., 1983, p. 1303.

Steps in Evaluating Proposed Complex Processes. Bemesderfer (1979) describes an eight-point program for the evaluation of new processes prior to production:

1. Develop a process description using quantitative mathematical equations describing the effects of each process variable on the final quality characteristic. A useful tool for doing this is response surface methodology (see Section 26 under Response/Surface Methodology).

2. Determine the optimum values for each process variable to meet quality requirements. For complex processes, this often requires statistically designed experiments (see Section 26, Design and Analysis of Experiments). Bemesderfer reports an experiment to *(a)* identify the key variables and *(b)* determine optimum machine settings for the drilling of holes using a laser beam. Five process variables were identified, the optimum settings determined, and the results presented in tables giving the "recipe" of settings for various values of hole diameter and material thickness. Each line of the table presents a recipe of the machine settings for drilling a particular size hole.

3. Determine the process capability. Complex processes often involve a variety of operating conditions, and the capability may vary considerably throughout the region of different conditions. The approach to process capability then often involves a formal planned experiment with the data analyzed by analysis of variance (see the previous discussion of the Taguchi method for an example of a specific technique).

4. Determine the capability of the measurement process. This is discussed in Section 18 under Error of Measurement.

5. Evaluate potential side effects. In one situation, a plating process was developed to provide protection against salt air corrosion. The process was defined in the specification, but a corrosion test was not required. After much discussion it was decided to hold up the process until a corrosion test was performed. A suitable test was defined, the parts failed, and the process had to be abandoned.

6. Make sure that each product characteristic has at least one process variable that can be used to adjust it. For example, a fluid temperature control was added to equipment because experiments proved that temperatures affected several product characteristics.

7. Prepare process specifications. The specifications must include one or more variables that can define the process including the means of setting, adjustment, and control.

8. Communicate the process information to production personnel. The means of communicating can run the gamut from manufacturing instructions to a formal course explaining in detail how the process must be run.

Bemesderfer reports that the eight steps have helped to prevent major problems on processes where it was applied, whereas a number of severe problems had been encountered in earlier processes.

Planning for the Process Capability Study. Prior to data collection, the following steps should be taken:

1. Choose the machine(s) to be used to establish capability. If the results of a study on one screw machine are to be used to define capability of all screw

machines of that type, the machine selected must be representative. In addition, a "machine" may actually consist of several machines within it; i.e., a machine with multiple spindles often shows different results for supposedly identical spindles.

2. Define the process conditions. For mechanical processes, examples are machine feeds and speeds, coolant, and cycle time; and for chemical processes, examples are temperature and pressure. Process capability numbers are meaningless unless they are related to a defined set of conditions that will repeat in the future.

3. Select a representative production worker. Where variability depends mainly on the worker, the study may really be one of worker variability.

4. Provide sufficient raw material for an uninterrupted study. A sample of about 50 units is preferred. Smaller samples are sometimes necessary, but they may not clearly show the statistical distribution of the characteristic under study.

5. Provide adequate gauging and a defined measurement method.

6. Make provisions for preserving the order in which the units are made.

7. Use materials or parts which are representative of normal production or shipments during the study.

8. To measure the inherent capability, avoid making adjustments during the study.

9. Measure to a minimum precision of one-tenth the specification tolerance, and use calibrated gauges.

10. Avoid unnecessary interruptions during the study.

11. Observe production under any abnormal conditions which might contribute to product variation.

12. Use tooling that is representative of production conditions.

13. Make sure the process is operating under its normal operating conditions unless the study is also investigating abnormalities (e.g., warmup during startup).

Ford Motor Company (1980) provides further detail on planning a study.

PROCESS CAPABILITY: APPLICATIONS

The most obvious use of process capability data during manufacturing planning is to predict whether the design tolerances can be met with the available processes. In addition there are other uses.

Choice among Alternative Processes. When capability data are available for several alternative processes, it becomes feasible to conduct cost analysis as a means of judging relative cost-effectiveness (see the discussion earlier in this section under Cost of Tolerances). This helps the design engineer to set specifications on a more rational basis; it also helps the manufacturing planner to assign equipment best suited to make particular products. Gibbons (1982) explains the statistical aspects of ranking several processes and identifying the best one.

Purchase of Machinery. In some industries process capability (in terms of 6σ) is sometimes specified in purchase orders for machinery. The follow-through consists of two phases:

1. A demonstration of capability at the equipment manufacturer's facility. When the equipment is ready for shipment, the manufacturer invites the customer to observe a small production of parts which are used to demonstrate capability. The customer must approve this demonstration before shipment is authorized.

2. A capability demonstration at the customer's facility. This demonstration uses customer personnel and customer operating conditions. Payment is authorized after this final demonstration is approved.

The two phases serve important purposes. The first phase provides some early assurance on capability. It also prevents shipment of equipment with marginal capability. (Equipment, once delivered, tends to move into routine production even if performance is marginal.) The second phase assures that the equipment meets capability requirements under typical operating conditions.

Interrelation of Sequential Processes. There are numerous situations in which several operation stages are interrelated. In such cases the planner must prepare a virtual product design for each stage of the operation (since the functional design defines only the end product). To prepare these intermediate designs means, for example, specifying how much material to provide for subsequent removal, uniformity of locating surfaces, etc. In such cases, knowledge of the capability of the respective operations greatly facilitates the planning.

Figure 16.13 shows an example of studies of related rough and finishing operations. The data make clear how much material is removed in finishing and what the final uniformity of the product is. With this knowledge and with knowledge of the final product specification, the prior operation can be planned with confidence. (In Figure 16.13, the rough process is more uniform than the finishing process for the charted characteristic. However, the finishing process is performed to

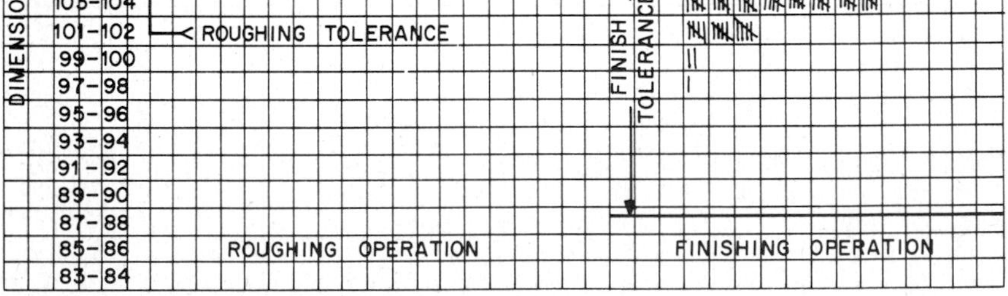

FIG. 16.13 Relation of sequential operations.

achieve high precision on a different characteristic. To do so, it must remove material.)

Other Uses of Capability Data. Knowledge of process variation provided by capability data can yield still other applications. These include the evaluation of machine setup, establishing control limits, selection of workers, and determining the economic aim of a process. Feigenbaum (1983) discusses these applications.

ERROR-PROOFING THE PROCESS

An important element of manufacturing planning is the concept of designing the process to be error-free through "error-proofing." Where this type of design is economic, it can:

Prevent defects or nonconformities which fallible human beings would otherwise make through inadvertence

Make effective a knack which would otherwise require retraining many workers

Prevent defects or nonconformities resulting from carelessness, indifference, and similar reasons

Bypass complex analysis for causes, by finding a solution even though the cause of defects remains a mystery

Methods of Error-Proofing. Some of the more usual forms are summarized below.

Fail-Safe Devices These consist of

1. *Interlocking sequences:* For example, to ensure that operation A is performed, the subsequent operation B locates from a hole which only operation A creates.

2. *Alarms and cutoffs:* These are used to signal depletion of material supply, broken threads, or other abnormalities. The alarms are also fail-safe, i.e., they are silent only if all is well. If there is doubt, they sound anyhow.

3. *All-clear signals:* These are designed to signal only if all remedial steps have been taken.

4. *Foolproof fixtures:* These serve not only as fixtures but also as instruments to check the quality of work from preceding operations.

5. *Limiting mechanisms:* For example, a slipping-type torque wrench to prevent overtightening.

Magnification of Senses. Examples are:

1. Locating indexes and fixtures to outperform human muscle in precision of position

2. Optical magnification to improve visibility

3. Remote-control viewing (closed circuit television) to permit viewing of the process despite distance, heat, fumes, etc.

4. Multiple signals to improve likelihood of recognition and response, e.g., simultaneously ringing of bells and flashing of lights; audiovisual systems

5. Use of pictures in place of numbers (e.g., cards on the hood of a car undergoing assembly, to show pictorially the equipment needed for that car)

Redundancy. This consists of extra work performed purely as a quality safeguard. Examples are:

1. *Multiple-identity codings:* These are intended to prevent product mixups, e.g., color codes or other recognition schemes on drug labels, tool steel, aluminum sheet, etc.

2. *Redundant actions and approvals:* For example, the drug industry requires that formulation of recipes be prepared and approved by two registered pharmacists working independently.

3. *Audit review and checking procedures:* These are widely used to assure that the plans are being followed.

4. *Design for verification:* The product may include specially designed provision for verification (holes for viewing, coupons for test, etc). It also includes the rapidly growing use of nuclear tracers.

5. *Multiple test stations:* For example, a can-filling line may provide checks for empty cans through height gages, weighing scales, and air jets (for blowing empties off the conveyer).

Countdowns. These are arranged by structuring sensing and information procedures to parallel the operating procedures so that the operational steps are checked against the sensing and informational needs. A dramatic example is the elaborate countdown for the launching of a space vehicle. Surgical operations require countdowns, accounting for all materials and tools used (sponges, surgical instruments, etc.). A useful principle is to use an active rather than passive form of countdown. For example, a welder counts all welds *aloud* in progressing from spot to spot. When the count reaches 17 the last weld has been made—just as called for by the specification.

A useful principle in errorproofing is that of providing feedback to the worker, i.e., *the performance of the work conveys a message to the worker.* For example, a worker at a control panel pushes a switch and receives three feedbacks: the *feel* of the shape of the switch handle; the *sound* of an audible click signaling that the switch went all the way; the *sight* of a visual illumination of a specific color and shape.

In a classic study, Nakajo and Kume (1985) discuss five fundamental principles of errorproofing developed from an analysis of about 1000 examples collected mainly from assembly lines. The principles are elimination, replacement, facilitation, detection, and mitigation (see Table 16.7).

Error-Prone Systems. Beyond the errorproofing of individual operations, there may be need to errorproof entire systems which are error-prone. In one classic example, a naval vessel was almost lost due to conflict in standards for hydraulic versus electrical systems. A hydraulic valve increases energy when turned counterclockwise; an electrical valve does the opposite. A technician who had been upgraded from the hydraulics section of the ship to the electronics section became confused during an emergency and reverted back to the hydraulic standard, causing a near disaster.

Identifying such error-prone systems is seldom done from ordinary analysis.

TABLE 16.7 Summary of Errorproofing Principles

Principle	Objective	Example
Elimination	Eliminate the possibility of error	Redesign the process or product so that the task is no longer necessary
Replacement	Substitute a more reliable process for the worker	Use robotics (e.g., in welding or painting)
Facilitation	Make the work easier to perform	Color code parts
Detection	Detect the error before further processing	Develop computer software which notifies the worker when a wrong type of keyboard entry is made (e.g., alpha versus numeric)
Mitigation	Minimize the effect of the error	Utilize fuses for overloaded circuits

More usually, it requires a feedback from actual problems encountered, so that some analyst can find a common cause. At the least, the planner should keep informed on the failures which are occurring and on the causes and remedies. To an important degree, the new ideas for planning have their origin in remedies found during troubleshooting and especially during breakthroughs.

OTHER ELEMENTS OF EQUIPMENT AND WORK METHODS PLANNING

Planning for equipment goes beyond making a process capability study. Other factors include providing for process adjustments and for preventive maintenance.

Providing for Adjustments to Processes. Many processes require periodic adjustments. Manufacturing planners should (1) identify the process variables that must be monitored for possible adjustment, (2) provide rules for determining when an adjustment is necessary, (3) provide instructions for determining the amount of adjustment, and (4) provide a convenient physical means for making the adjustment.

Each product characteristic should have a process variable that can be used to adjust it. As corollaries to this principle, Bemesderfer (1979) proposes:

1. A single process variable should correspond to a single characteristic.
2. The degree of adjustment required during the process for a given change in the characteristic should be constant.
3. The range of possible adjustments must be consistent with the range of application need.
4. The setting accuracy must be consistent with the product tolerance requirements.
5. The controlling accuracy, once the process is set, must be consistent with the product tolerance requirements.

To the degree that these aims cannot be achieved, the process will be difficult for a worker to control.

Preventive Maintenance. Maintenance of equipment is generally recognized as essential, but pressures for production can result in delaying the scheduled preventive maintenance. Sometimes the delay is indefinite, the equipment breaks down, and the maintenance becomes corrective instead of preventive.

The planning should determine how often preventive maintenance is necessary, what form it should take, and how processes should be audited to assure that preventive maintenance schedules are followed.

In the event of objections to the proposed plan for preventive maintenance on the grounds of high cost, data on the cost of poor quality from the process can help to justify the maintenance plan.

PLANNING OF PERSONNEL REQUIREMENTS

This planning should identify the skills required during manufacturing and should provide criteria for selecting and training personnel to assure that those skills are provided. If the skills required are simple, the selection and training of personnel can be handled in ordinary ways; if the skills are complex, special approaches are needed. Examples of the latter include the skills required for welding, heat treatment wire bonding for integrated circuits, and other processes.

Critical processes often justify a program to formally "certify" workers. The certification program consists first of training workers in the specific skills required and then requiring them to demonstrate those skills in the manufacture of product. If the demonstration is satisfactory the worker becomes certified for that skill, e.g., welding. Periodic recertification is often required. Certification programs for workers are typically conducted by companies but are sometimes conducted by labor unions.

The training of workers should include thorough communication of any special process requirements or procedures. For simple processes the training can be done in conventional ways; for complex processes special approaches may be necessary. Bemesderfer (1979) describes how a 20-h course on an electrochemical machining process was given to a group of managers, professional personnel, and production workers as part of their training for using the process.

PLANNING FOR PROTECTION AND TRACEABILITY OF MATERIAL

The processing, transportation, and storage of product from raw materials through finished goods are potential sources of degradation of quality. Caplan (1980) discusses the prevention activities needed during receipt of purchased material, production operations, and post production. These include tasks to protect product from handling damage, environmental effects, transportation damage, and deterioration. In addition, nonconforming product should be segregated from good product throughout all phases. Finally, provision should be made for traceability.

Traceability.   The process design must provide for "traceability," i.e., the ability to preserve the identify of the product and its origins. Traceability is needed principally to:

1. Assure that only materials and components of adequate quality enter the final product, e.g., sterility in drug materials, adequate metallurgical composition and heat treatment in structural components.
2. Provide obvious identification to avoid mixup of products which otherwise look alike (these cases abound).
3. Permit recall of suspected product on a precise basis. Many of the huge recalls of automobiles in the 1960s were the result of inadequate traceability. The defective cars were only a small fraction of the total recalled.
4. Localize causes of failure and take remedial action at minimal cost.

There are still other uses of traceability—in inventory control, scheduling, etc. Some of these uses also affect quality. For example, use of materials on a first-in, first-out basis reduces the risk of quality deterioration due to perishable materials.

Batch Control.   The materials entering a batch are measured out in accordance with the recipe or formula. A lot number is assigned and a set of batch documents bearing that lot number is created. The "genealogy" of the input materials is recorded in the batch documents, as are the processing data and the product test data. For complex or critical products (e.g., aerospace vehicles, drugs) the batch documents may become a formidable collection. When the finished product is packaged, the lot number is imprinted on the individual containers and on the mass containers, i.e., cartons, drums, skids, etc. Subsequently, when the product is sold, it may be necessary to maintain a record of customers' names through the entire distribution chain.

Continuous Production, Low Unit Value.   In this form there is no natural lot, since materials of various genealogical origins keep entering the process at irregular intervals. In consequence, the designation for traceability becomes a *date code* and is based on the calendar dates of the occurrence of some cardinal event, e.g., packaging, final test, final assembly. The choice of time span is arbitrary, e.g., a week's production. (This arbitrary amount of production may still be called a "lot.") See Section 18, under The Nature of Lots of Product.

The documentation system for this arbitrary lot is quite similar to that used for the batch. Provision is made to record the history of the input materials, the process conditions prevailing during fabrication, and the test results. Due to the inherent nature of continuous production, traceability is now incomplete, since cutoff dates for introduction of new material batches or for process changes cannot be identified with precision. In consequence, any subsequent recalls or investigations must provide for this margin of error.

For some products, it may be feasible to show the date code (lot number) directly on the product. More usually, for reasons of cost (and available space), the date code appears only on the containers.

Continuous Production, High Unit Value.   In this form, the distinguishing feature is the unique designation of each unit of product by serial number. The documentation is then keyed to individual serial number or blocks of numbers.

The serial number is widely used in the manufacture of consumer goods as well as industrial equipment. Household appliances and home entertainment electronics use serial numbers, and the system of guarantees is keyed to these. Larger units (e.g., motor vehicles) may employ serial numbers for major subsystems (e.g., engines) as well as for the vehicle itself.

Traceability requires the coding of products. Among the methods in use are dating of products, "bar-code" symbols which appear as parallel bars and spaces on packages and which are read by computers, and laser coding which marks a code into virtually any material.

Attaining complete traceability for complex products (made of many materials and components and employing numerous processes) can be a formidable job, involving extensive paperwork, records, bonded stock rooms, physical markings on the products, etc. Yet this is actually done for many products in the drug, aerospace, and nuclear industries.

In commercial products complete traceability is limited to safety-oriented qualities and to those components which are decisive in achieving overall fitness for use. For example, in one semiconductor product line the component chiefly responsible for final product quality was the semiconducting wafer. The company therefore structured the traceability system around the wafer lot numbers. The finished products were then coded with the wafer lot number rather than with a weekly dating code, which might involve the same code number for products made from multiple wafer lots (Staffiery, 1975).

Caplan (1980, pp. 118–120) identifies five techniques used in a material tracking program which has much in common with traceability. See also the discussion in Section 20 under Configuration Management.

PLANNING OF PROCESS ENVIRONMENT

For simple products the necessary process environment can be achieved by good housekeeping. Without adequate housekeeping there can be catastrophies, e.g., mating parts abnormally wearing because of foreign material in a lubricant, or fumes during processing causing discoloration of products.

Complex products are more sensitive to environmental conditions that can cause contamination of product by chlorides, acids, shop grit, microscopic skin particles, nonvolatile residues, fibers from work sheet papers, and other conditions. For example, some companies must control airborne particles such that products are free from particles that are larger than 20 millionths of an inch. Also, rigid control of temperature and humidity in electronics manufacture can be critical in order to control electrostatic discharge (Downer, 1983).

The techniques of assuring a clean environment include a cleaning of air, selection of tools, flooring, containers, paper and paint, special clothing for personnel, and other methods. For example, in the control of electrostatic discharge, simple tools such as pliers and side cutters can be a problem if they are not equipped with plastic handles.

The control of environmental conditions is often referred to as a "clean-room" program. Harrington (1981) recommends that the following items be included in a clean-room specification for an electronics plant:

1. Contamination level
2. Temperature range
3. Humidity level

4. Pressure differential—positive pressure out of the clean room
5. Dressing area adjacent to the clean room with sink, disposal
6. Ceiling tile
7. Types of paper used in the room

Harrington further recommends that the certification procedure for a clean room include:

1. Complete air flow measurments
2. Leak testing of all filters
3. Measurement of temperature and humidity throughout the area
4. Differential pressure measurements
5. Initial janitorial cleaning accomplished according to a separate specification
6. Complete particle count measurements conducted in all areas, to numerical requirements
7. Deviations corrected and verified by measurement
8. Complete data recorded for all of the above steps

The pharmaceutical and other industries must meet stringent government regulations ("good manufacturing practice") to control the manufacturing environment.

Marguglio (1981) discusses the role of the quality function in compliance with environmental program requirements.

OVERALL REVIEW OF MANUFACTURING PLANNING

Review of the proposed process can most effectively be accomplished through preproduction trials and runs. Techniques such as failure mode, effect, and criticality analysis can provide an even earlier warning before any product is made. Checklists for review of proposed processes can also be useful. These approaches are discussed below.

Preproduction Trials.   Because the manufacturing plan starts as a mental concept, it will be "scaled up" many orders of magnitude if it goes into large-scale production. There is great risk in going directly into production from the conceptual plan primarily because of the risk of quality failures. To reduce this risk, companies make use of trial production lots (called "pilot plant production," "preproduction," etc.) to discover deficiencies in the planning and to remedy them before going into full-scale production. In some industries this concept is formalized into regular phases of scaling up.

The scaling up of production is actually a continuation of the scaling up which takes place from product design concept to prototype or model construction and test. The adequacy of the full-scale manufacturing plan cannot be judged from the record of models made in the model shop. In the model shop the basic purpose is to prove engineering feasibility; in the production shop the purpose is to meet standards of quality, cost, and delivery. The model-shop machinery, tools, personnel, supervision, motivation, etc., are all different from the corresponding situations in the production shop.

Tool Tryout   At the work-station level, as new tools are completed, they are subjected to a tryout procedure which, in most companies, is highly formalized. The tryout consists of producing enough product from the new tool to demonstrate that it can meet quality standards under shop conditions.

These formalized tryouts conclude with the execution of a formal document backed up by supporting data, which always include the quality data. The release of the tool for full-scale production is contingent on the approval of this tryout document.

Limited Trial Lots.   Beyond the tryouts at individual work stations, there is need for collective tryouts. These require trial production lots, which must be scheduled for the prime purpose of proving in the manufacturing process. The trial lot is usually made in the regular production shop and provides an extensive preview of the problems which will be encountered in large-scale production. In the process industries the equivalent intermediate scaling up is the "pilot plant." It is widely used to provide the essential information (on quality, costs, productivity, etc.) needed to determine whether and how to go into full-scale production.

Software Verification.   Software used with a process requires a tryout just like new tools—with the same degree of formality and approval process.

Experimental Lots.   The trial lot concept provides opportunities for planners to test out alternatives, and they often combine the concept of experimentation with that of proving in the nonexperimental portion of the trial.

Attainment of good process yields is one of the most important purposes of experimental lots. These experiments can make use of all the techniques discussed in Section 26, Design and Analysis of Experiments, and in the various statistical sections.

Preproduction Runs.   Ideally, product lots should be put through the entire system, with the deficiencies found and corrected before going into full-scale production. In practice, companies usually make some compromises with this ideal approach. The "preproduction" may be merely the first of the regular production, but with special provision for prompt feedback and correction of errors as found. Alternatively, the preproduction may be limited to those features of product and process design which are so new that prior experience cannot reliably provide a basis for good risk taking. While some companies do adhere to a strict rule of proving in the product and process through preproduction lots, the more usual approach is one of flexibility, in which the use of preproduction lots depends on:

1. The extent to which the product embodies new or untested quality features
2. The extent to which the design of the manufacturing process embodies new or untried machines, tools, etc.
3. The amount and value of product which will be out in the field before there is conclusive evidence of the extent of process, product, and use difficulties

These trials sometimes include "production validation tests" to ensure that the full-scale process can meet the design intent. Figure 16.14 shows an example from Ford Motor Company (1972).

Failure Mode, Effect, and Criticality Analysis for Processes.   A failure mode, effect, and criticality analysis is useful in analyzing the proposed design of a product (see Section 13 under Failure Mode, Effect, and Criticality Analysis).

PRODUCTION VALIDATION PLAN AND REPORT #3   1.14-21812-A   PAGE 1 OF 3

SYSTEM 1.00 Body   ASSEMBLY Door Latch-Diab.   PROGRAM ____   DES. ENGR. S. Martin

SUBSYSTEM 1.14 Locks Handles & Mechs.   COMP N/A   DES LEVEL AA   CONC'R W.R.

TEST NAME SOURCE	ACCEPTANCE CRITERIA	TEST RESULTS	DES.	S/SIZE		REL. ACCEP. CRIT.		TIMING		REMARKS
				REQ.	TEST	REQ.	ACTUAL	SCH.	ACTUAL	
Life Cycle ES-Diab-652181 AB	35,000 cycles minimum at 650# rebound and 250#	21 completed 120,000 cycles	AA	21	21	$P_{.90} = .90$	$P_{.90} = .90$	7-15-71	7-20-71	
Static Strength FMVSS (ES)	Prim. Sec. longitude 3000 2250 transverse 4000 2700	-3σ greater than min. strength req'd (see Problem Plots)	AA	60	60	$-3\sigma>$ req't.	$-3\sigma>$ req't.	7-24-71	7-20-71	
Corrosion Resistance (ES) 48-hour salt spray	Operating efforts must not increase 25% over drawing specifications	$+3\sigma$ less than max. effort allowed (see Problem Plots)	AA	40	40	$+3\sigma<$ req't.	$+3\sigma<$ req't.	7-30-71	8-15-71	

FIG. 16.14 Product validation plan and report.

The same technique can dissect the potential failure modes and their effects on a proposed process. Ishiyama (1977) discusses the application of the failure mode and effects analysis technique to both product design and manufacturing processes in the automobile industry.

The fault tree analysis technique is also useful in analyzing a design (see Section 13 under Fault Tree Analysis). Proposed manufacturing processes can be analyzed with this same technique. Raheja (1982) discusses this approach. Fault tree analysis can help to identify areas of a process that require errorproofing.

Checklist for Review of Manufacturing Planning.   The review of manufacturing planning for quality should be made in accordance with previously defined criteria. An example for a complex electronics manufacturing facility is discussed below (Harrington, 1981).

The review takes place at four stages or levels. At Level I, a product is being considered for capitalization. Parts from the process will not be shipped to customers. Qualification at this level requires the following:

1. Controlled engineering documents.
2. The process plan must demonstrate good manufacturing and quality practices including:
   a. The development pilot line description and process instructions must be released and the change level controlled.
   b. All changes in process activity and documentation must be reviewed by Quality Assurance.
   c. Quality must certify the functional level tester for each component and subassembly.
   d. Inspectors from the Quality Department must verify the results of all final functional tests on a piece-by-piece basis.
   e. An evaluation by Quality Assurance indicates that there are no major problems that cannot be resolved.

Level II is also a development pilot line qualification, but the parts may later be classified as customer shippable. Level II certification requires:

1. All engineering documents must be formally released and controlled.
2. The following additional process controls beyond Level I are required:
   a. Manufacturing is to avoid any large dollar commitment on tool design and procurement negotiation because the parts design is still under review.
   b. Formal release process routings are available and controlled.
   c. Each operation must be certified by Quality Assurance.
   d. Critical development manufacturing tools and test equipment must be certified.
   e. Certain components used will be classified as customer shippable.
   f. Development level product standards must be identified and controlled.
   g. Incoming components and materials must be processed through receiving inspection.
   h. An in-process quality assurance audit plan must be available.

3. A series of qualification lots must be processed through the development pilot line with the following preconditions:

a. All supporting documents must have completed the sign-off cycle.

b. Operators must be trained.

c. Yield targets must be established and documented.

d. Lot size must be large enough to get an adequate evaluation of process yields.

e. Equipment must be calibrated.

f. Head and disk development level standards must be used with supporting documentation.

g. Purchased parts must be inspected to specification.

In a Level III situation a manufacturing production facility is set up to produce mass quantities. The requirements here are shown in Figure 16.15. A qualification lot is also required.

Whereas Level III qualifies a single production line, Level IV qualifies a complete manufacturing facility. The qualification consists of process certification, qualification lots, and evaluation of "technical exposures" (conditions that could impact on performance).

The requirements for process certification include:

1. Documentation, including engineering software, maintenance procedures, quality program plan, and inspection specification and training requirements

2. Test/process equipment, equipment accepted by maintenance, long-term precision drift evaluations completed, extremes of settings evaluated, manufacturing training program implemented, equipment certification and correlation

3. Process capability studies completed, process variation analysis completed, process controls totally implemented, in-process audit inspection and control program implemented, quality reporting system implemented, process compatibility assessment completed

4. Process yields progressing, process quality goals being achieved, first customer ship performance target levels being measured, reliability and environmental testing performed, outgoing quality levels being met

A Level IV qualification lot is processed with requirements similar to those under Level III, and the results at the two levels are compared.

Finally, an independent audit is made of the quality and manufacturing programs to identify any outstanding issues related to product performance, process variation, manufacturability assessment, and process stability.

Role of Quality Assurance in Review of Manufacturing Planning. Bell (1983) describes the role of a quality assurance function in reviewing the quality-related aspects of manufacturing planning for an electronics manufacturing facility. Prior to instituting a formal system of review, 7 percent of the manufacturing planning was defective (based on a page count of planning documentation). Some of the problems were essentially documentation errors, but other errors could result in defective product. A 40-h training program for reviewers was developed to make the reviews effective (Table 16.8).

LIII PROCESS CERTIFICATION CHECKLIST

ACTIVITY

I. DOCUMENTATION

1. All Development documents released to Manufacturing
2. All Manufacturing documents released
3. All Quality documents released
4. Manufacturing training requirements released
5. Four-way signoff in practice
6. Software documented
7. Test equipment and tool prints complete
8. Workmanship standards released
9. Outgoing quality levels documented
10. Critical components list complete
11. Quality inspector training requirements released
12. Stress test specifications released
13. Process compatibility plan complete
14. Quality plan updated
15. Rework procedures complete
16. In-process quality defect targets established

LIII PROCESS CERTIFICATION CHECK LIST

ACTIVITY

II. TESTS/PROCESS EQUIPMENT

1. Equipment evaluated by Manufacturing engineer and Test engineer
2. Quality certified equipment
3. Calibration intervals established
4. Maintenance and calibration program in place and working
5. Equipment testing to specifications
6. Safety approval on all major equipment
7. Products standards supported by the products standard lab
8. Added control over art effects standards
9. Receiving inspection tool and certified
10. Test equipment software level control
11. Process that manufactures special tools is certified

III. MANUFACTURING OPERATIONS

1. Qualified operators and inspectors used to mfg. product
2. Operators are following the documentation
3. Adequacy of the manufacturing procedures and documents have been evaluated by Quality Assurance

LIII PROCESS CE

ACTIVITY

III. MANUFACTURING OPERATIONS Contin.

4. Tools were built to print
5. Brass tag tools and equipment are on the recall cycle
6. Only mfg. tools & equipment used on the mfg. floor
7. Nonconforming materials controls in place
8. Class room operating to specification
9. Hard tooling requirements and documented & understood
10. Controls over water, air, temperature, humidity, etc., are adequate
11. Shipping containers & packaging containers have been evaluated
12. Adequate controls over materials used in mfg. are in place
13. Mfg. data system is adequate to report defects and yields
14. Quality engineering, process inspection, and control program implemented
15. Mfg. process is stable
16. Clean controls in place
17. Quality Assurance failure analysis system working
18. Added controls over experiment and sent-ahead orders

FIG. 16.15 Process certification checklist.

As a result of the review activity, the errors in manufacturing planning dropped to 3 percent and defects due to poor planning were eliminated.

An important but often missing element in manufacturing planning is the input of line production personnel. A steel company (Jones and Laughlin Company, 1984) obtains this input through a formal meeting in which manufacturing personnel review the preliminary draft of a process control standards handbook. The meeting, which is held off site, is chaired by a department superintendent. Included on the agenda are a videotape presentation on the review process, small group discussions on the proposed process, and preparation of revisions.

See also Section 8 under Quality Audit by Upper Managers.

RTIFICATION CHECKLIST

	LIII PROCESS CERTIFICATION CHECKLIST			
ACTIVITY		**COMMENTS**	**VERIFIED BY:**	**DATE**
IV. PRODUCT				
1. No Q. level components used				
2. Traceability system in place				
3. Incoming parts controlled and purchased from approved vendors				
4. Product meeting performance specification				
5. Product meeting quality and yield levels				

FIG. 16.15 (*Continued*)

Use of a "Lessons Learned" System in Reviewing Plans.

As applied to manufacturing planning, this system captures and documents past problems in a readily retrievable form to use in the review of plans for a new process. The documentation of each lesson includes key words, a problem description, actions taken along with results, and references for further details.

Sources of problems include production activities, complaints, product holds and recalls, and test results which reveal cause-effect relationships or identify important product or process parameters. Criteria are defined for deciding if a problem should be entered in the system.

To use the system, the planner reviews the key word index and selects those

TABLE 16.8 Quality Planning Review

1st Day	*3rd Day (cont.)*
Introduction	Tool order to engineering drawing
Background—purpose	verification
Government requirements	Manufacturing aids
Division requirements	Other
Planning manual—overview	Special requirements
Types of planning (planning levels)	Controlled components
Planning formats	Traceability
Content of complete planning package	Lot-date codes
	Serialization
2nd Day	
Configuration verification	*4th Day*
Drawing change	Detailed review—continued: visual aids
Specification change	Verification of clarity
Parts list—alternative parts	Compliance with engineering design
Planning change control	Adequacy for level of personnel
Traceability—history jackets	Nonambiguous
Verification of change	Traceability of specific operations
Effect on next use application	Control—change authority
Manufacturing change orders	Planning change requests
	How initiated
3rd Day	When planning changes required
Detailed review techniques	Effect of shop liaison requests
Specific operations	Quality assurance role
Logical sequence	
Adequacy	*5th Day*
Sequence of inspection operations	Planning review documentation
No. of inspection operations (too	Need for objective evidence
many/too few)	Data collection
Test requirements	Reporting/charting
Customer requirements	Trend evaluation
Customer inspection/witness	Review/feedback to planning
Referenced items	department
Workmanship standards	Corrective action
Manufacturing process standards	Effectiveness evaluation
Equipment operation instructions	Post review audits
Test procedures	Final critique
Tooling/fixtures	

words which seem relevant. Next, the data base is searched for entries with the selected key words, and the references are obtained from the listed originators.

    Werner and Zetzsche (1982) discuss the concept of an "experience-return flow-store" as a means of using past experiences in starting up and operating large chemical plants. The technique uses catalogs and notched cards to document about 50,000 items of information.

PLANNING PROCESS CONTROLS

The process specification, procedures, and instruction sheets prepared by the planners are the software of manufacturing planning. Their purpose is to inform the production people how to set up, run, and regulate the processes so that the result will be good product. Conversely, the production people should follow these plans. Otherwise, good product might not be the result.

Many companies institute process controls to provide assurance that the plans will in fact be followed. There are several kinds of these controls, and they are established by some combination of manufacturing engineers, quality engineers, production supervisors, and workers. The precise combination varies widely from company to company.

Process control is based on the feedback loop as discussed in Section 6 under The Feedback Loop. The steps for planning manufacturing process controls follow closely the universal approach for use of the feedback loop.

Control Criteria.   While execution of the control plan is typically delegated to the work force, it is common to impose criteria to be met before the process is allowed to run. These criteria are imposed in three main areas:

1. *Setup criteria:*   For some processes the start of production must await meeting setup criteria (e.g., five pieces in a row must test "good"). In critical cases this form of early warning assurance may require that a supervisor or inspector independently approve the setup.

2. *Running criteria:*   For many processes there is need to check the running periodically to decide whether the process should continue to run or should stop for readjustment. The criteria here relate to such things as frequency of check, size of sample, manner of sample selection, tests to be made, tolerances to be met.

3. *Equipment maintenance criteria:*   In some processes the equipment itself must be closely controlled if quality is to be maintained. This type of control is preventive in nature and is quite different in concept from repair of equipment breakdowns. This preventive form of equipment maintenance includes a carefully drawn set of criteria which define the essential performance characteristics of the equipment. Then, on a scheduled basis (strictly adhered to), the equipment is checked against these criteria. In the United States this aspect of equipment maintenance is not well developed, and there is need to take positive steps to strengthen it.

Relation to Product Controls.   Process controls are sometimes confused with product controls but there is a clear difference. Process controls are associated with the decision: Should the process run or stop? Product controls are associated with the decision: Does the product conform to specification? Usually both of these decisions require input derived from sampling and measuring the product. (It is seldom feasible to measure the process directly.) However, the method of selecting the samples is often different. Production usually makes the "process run or stop" decision and tends to sample in ways which tell the most about the process. Inspection usually (in the United States) makes the product conformance decision and tends to sample in ways which tell the most about the product.

This difference in sampling can easily result in different conclusions on the "same" product. Production commonly does its sampling on a scheduled basis and at a time when the product is still traceable to specific streams of the process. Inspection often does its sampling on a random basis and at a time when traceability has begun to blur.

Despite the different purposes being served, it is feasible for the two departments to do joint planning. Usually they are able to establish their respective controls so that both purposes are well served and so that the respective data reinforce each other.

Control Systems and the Concept of Dominance. Specific systems for controlling characteristics can be related to the underlying factors that dominate a process. The main categories of dominance include those discussed below.

1. *Setup-dominant:* Such processes have high reproducibility and stability for the entire length of the batch to be made. Hence the control system emphasizes verification of the setup before production proceeds. Examples of such processes are drilling, labeling, heat sealing, printing, and presswork.

2. *Time-dominant:* Such a process is subject to progressive change with time (wear of tools, depletion of reagent, machine heating up). The associated control system will feature a schedule of process checks with feedback to enable the worker to make compensatory changes. Screw machining, volume filling, wood carding, and papermaking are examples of time-dominant processes.

3. *Component-dominant:* Here the quality of the input materials and components is the most influential. The control system is strongly oriented toward supplier relations along with incoming inspection and sorting of inferior lots. Many assembly operations and food formulation processes are component-dominant.

4. *Worker-dominant:* For such processes quality depends mainly on the skill and knack possessed by the production worker. The control system emphasizes such features as training courses and certification for workers, errorproofing, and worker and quality rating. Workers are dominant in processes such as welding, painting, and order picking.

5. *Information-dominant:* These are usually processes in which the job information undergoes frequent change. Hence the control system places emphasis on the accuracy and up-to-dateness of the information provided to the worker (and everyone else). Examples include order editing and "travelers" used in job shops.

The different types of dominance differ also in the tools used for process control. Table 16.9 lists the forms of process dominance along with the usual tools used for process control. Additonal discussion of control tools as related to precess dominance is included in Section 17 under Ability to Regulate.

Evaluation of Proposed Control Tools. Proposed control tools need to be evaluated for both deficiencies and excesses. One health care manufacturer uses "process failure analysis" to analyze proposed control tools. A flowchart is first prepared to identify the elements of the manufacturing system and the output. Possible failure mechanisms are listed and the control system is analyzed in terms of:

1. *The failure:* probability of occurrence, criticality, effects, etc.

2. *The measurement:* method, frequency, documentation, etc.

3. *The standard of comparison:* selection, limits, etc.

4. *The feedback:* method, content, speed

The proposed control for each failure mechanism is analyzed and classified as deficient, appropriate, or excessive.

TABLE 16.9 Control Tools for Forms of Process Dominance

Setup-dominant	Time-dominant	Component-dominant	Worker-dominant	Information-dominant
Inspection of process conditions	Periodic inspection	Supplier rating	Acceptance inspection	Computer generated information
First piece inspection	$\overline{X}$ chart	Incoming inspection	p chart	"Active" checking of documentation
Lot plot	Median chart	Prior operation control	c chart	Barcodes and electronic entry
Precontrol	$\overline{X}$ and R chart	Acceptance inspection	Operator scoring	Process audits
Narrow limit gaging	Precontrol	Mockup evaluation	Recertification of workers	
Attribute visual inspection	Narrow-limit gaging		Process audits	
	p chart			
	Process variables check			
	Automatic recording			
	Process audits			

PLANNING FOR EVALUATION OF PRODUCT

The planning must recognize the need for formal evaluation of product to determine its suitability for the marketplace. Three activities are involved:

1. Measuring the product for conformance to specifications
2. Taking action on the nonconforming product
3. Communicating information on the disposition of nonconforming product

These activities are discussed in Section 18 under Inspection and Test. However, these activities impinge on the manufacturing planning process. For example, several alternatives are possible for determining conformance, i.e., to have it done by production workers, by an independent inspection force, or by a combination of both. Second, the disposition of nonconforming product involves participation by production personnel, in such forms as segregation of product in the shop, and documentation. Finally, the communication of the decisions should include feedback to Production.

QUALITY INFORMATION EQUIPMENT

The term "quality information equipment" (QIE), as used here, designates the physical apparatus which makes measurements of products and processes, processes the information, and feeds the information back for decision making.

The development cycle for the QIE must plan for product effectiveness parameters including:

1. Reliability
2. Maintainability (calibration, repair, preventive maintenance, and so forth)
3. Accuracy and precision
4. Human factors aspects (ease of use, errorproofing to prevent errors)
5. Interfaces of the QIE with the product being measured to assure swift, sure connections and disconnect
6. Design of the QIE to withstand use environments
7. Safety
8. Skill levels available versus requirements of the QIE
9. Modes on input and output
10. Procedures for formal evaluation of the QIE (e.g., acceptance tests of hardware and software)
11. Operating instructions and training of personnel
12. Tie-in of the QIE with the overall data processing system

The extensive interdepartmental effect of QIE makes it evident that the planner must follow the QIE project through to the end. The design must meet exacting, complex criteria; the construction must be responsive to that design. Most important, the design must then be proved out in trials conducted under actual use conditions.

The evolution of the automated process (see below) and the numerically controlled machine has required corresponding evolution in QIE.

AUTOMATED MANUFACTURING

In many manufacturing facilities, the computer is leading the march to automation. Several terms have become important:

Computer-integrated manufacturing (CIM):   This is the process of applying the computer in a planned fashion from design through manufacturing and shipping of the product. CIM has a broad scope.

Computer-aided manufacturing (CAM):   This is the process in which the computer is used to plan and control the work of specific equipment.

Computer-aided design (CAD):   This is the process by which the computer assists in the creation or modification of a design.

Some useful references are available. The June 1984 issue of *Quality Progress* describes the "factory of the future." An introductory book by Harrington (1979) discusses conventional manufacturing, CAD, CAM, application of the computer to scheduling and control, and other topics. Krouse (1982) provides an introduction to some of the technologies of CAD/CAM including geometric modeling, finite analysis, machine tool controls, and artificial intelligence. Goldhar and Jelinek (1983) explain how CAM can automate not only high-volume operations on a few products but also low-volume requirments on many products. Wilson (1983) describes an automated manufacturing planning system for aircraft production and how quality assurance inputs are integrated in the planning. Section 27 under New-Process Quality discusses the role of the computer in process planning and control.

Benefits to Product Quality.   Automation may provide as large an increase in factory productivity as did the introduction of electric power. Product quality will benefit in several ways:

1. Automation can eliminate some of the monotonous or fatiguing tasks that cause errors by human beings. For example, when a manual seam welding operation was turned over to a robot, the scrap rate plunged from 15 percent to zero (Kegg, 1985).
2. Process variation can be reduced by the automatic monitoring and continuous adjustment of process variables.
3. An important source of process troubles can be reduced, i.e., the number of machine setups.
4. Machines can not only automatically measure product, but can record, summarize, and display the data for line production operators and staff personnel. Feedback to the worker can be immediate, thus providing an early warning of impending troubles.
5. With cellular manufacture (see below), tracing a part to its origin is simplified, and this facilitates accountability for quality.
6. With CAD, the quality engineer can provide inputs early in the design stage. When a design is placed in the computer, the quality engineer can review that design over and over again and keep abreast of design changes.

Achieving these benefits requires a spectrum of concepts and techniques. Three of these are discussed below: the key functions of CIM, group technology, and flexible manufacturing systems.

Key Functions of Computer Integrated Manufacturing. To integrate the computer from design through shipping involves a network of functions and associated computer systems. Willis and Sullivan (1984) describe this in terms of eight functions (Table 16.10). Such a CIM system rests on a foundation of data bases covering both manufacturing data and product data.

Group Technology. Group technology is the process of examining all items manufactured by a company to identify those with sufficient similarity that a common design or manufacturing plan can be used. The aim is to reduce the number of new designs or new manufacturing plans. In addition to the savings in resources, group technology can improve both the quality of design and the quality of conformance by using proven designs and manufacturing plans. Gunn (1982, p. 121) reports that in many companies "only 20 percent of the parts initially thought to require new designs actually need them; of the remaining new

TABLE 16.10   Eight Key CIMS Functions

Function	Description	Typical hardware
1. Design and drafting (CAD/CAM)	Automated design and drafting of products and computer-aided manufacturing	Minicomputer, mainframe
2. Production scheduling and control	Master scheduling coupled with material management and requirements planning from procurement to shipment	Host mainframe
3. Process automation	Direct numerical control of processes, inspection and testing; utilization of robotics, flexible manufacturing systems, and other automated equipment to perform certain processes and direct shop floor activities	Programmable controller, minicomputer, mainframe
4. Process control	Sensing of equipment activities and reporting of conditions that require operator intervention	Programmable controller
5. Material handling and storage	Automated storage and retrieval of finished and purchased parts based on picking schedules and requisitions	Minicomputer
6. Maintenance scheduling and control	Preventive maintenance scheduling and reporting of equipment downtime by cause; spare parts inventory management and usage reporting	Host mainframe
7. Distribution management	Order processing, sales reporting, and invoicing coupled with warehousing and transportation	Host mainframe
8. Finance and accounting	Reporting of operating results, forecasting of future results, and analysis of costs	Host mainframe

Source: Willis and Sullivan, 1984, p. 32.

parts 40 percent could be built from an existing design and the other 40 percent could be created by modifying an existing design."

Each item is coded according to a variety of characteristics such as shape, material, tolerances, finish, and required production operations. After coding, parts with similar characteristics are sorted into groups. Phillipp (1982) shows an example of an 18-digit coding system:

Form	4 digits
Dimensions	4 digits
Tolerances	2 digits
Material	2 digits
Machine	2 digits
Process	2 digits
Inspection	2 digits

The process planner for a new part can retrieve a list of old parts that have some of the same characteristics. Planning for the new part can then simply specify the process for an old part with any differences noted.

Location of the production machines can also benefit from the group technology concept. Machines are grouped according to the parts they make and can be sorted into cells of machines, each cell producing one or several part families (thus "cellular manufacture").

Flexible Manufacturing System. A flexible manufacturing system (FMS) is a group of several computer controlled machine tools linked by a materials handling system and a mainframe computer to completely process a group of parts. The FMS can be programmed to suit varying production requirements and can be reprogrammed to accommodate design changes or new parts. This is in contrast to a fixed automation system which follows a preordained sequence.

Kegg (1984) summarizes the evolution of a flexible system in six steps:

1. The basic elements are a machine and an operator. Adjustments to the process are continually made by the operator.
2. Electronic intelligence is added in the form of computer control. This involves programming ("numerically controlling") the machine tools. A complicated series of operations can be repeated with the push of a single button.
3. Automatic devices for tool changing and workpiece loading and unloading are added.
4. Sensing devices are added to the machine that allow adjustments to be made automatically. Batch operations can then be performed continuously without human intervention.
5. The work cell is linked with other areas of the plant which supply workpieces, tooling, and other materials and information. The operator becomes a manager of a computer controlled system.
6. Finally, integration of all of the functions from design and manufacturing planning to inventory control, scheduling, and shop floor control is achieved by having all of the systems communicate with each other automatically.

Typically, the individual machines are robots or other types of numerically controlled machine tools, each of which is run by a microcomputer. Several of these numerically controlled tools are linked by a minicomputer and then several of these minicomputers tie into the mainframe computer. Gunn (1982, p. 128) shows an example of a flexible manufacturing system.

Quality Planning for Automated Processes. Planning for automated processes requires special precautions:

1. Changes in the product design may be necessary to facilitate automated manufacture. For example, robots have difficulty picking up a randomly oriented part in a bin, but a redesign of the part may solve the problem.
2. Automated manufacturing equipment is complex and has the reliability and maintainability problems of most complex products. Design planning and evaluation tools (see Section 13, Product Development) should be a part of the design process for automated equipment.
3. All software must be thoroughly tested (see Section 14, Software Development). In a survey of problems with numerically controlled tapes, Flavell (1983) classified the reasons for changes in the computer programs (Table 16.11). Note that 24.1 percent of the changes were due to programming technique or program errors.

TABLE 16.11   Analysis of Problems with Numerical Control Programs

Reason for program change	Percentage of changes
Dimensional error	19.4
Programming technique	18.1
Tooling problems	12.1
Speeds and feeds	9.1
Setup problems	8.4
Machine function errors	7.8
Stock allowance	7.7
Miscellaneous program errors	6.0
Engineering change	3.5
Routing change	2.5
Miscellaneous	4.7
Total	100.0

4. Knowledge of process capability, precise setup of equipment, and preventive maintenance are essential.
5. When feasible, on-line automatic inspection should be integrated with the operation. With manual operation of a process, the worker can observe a defect and take action. Automated processes can have mechanical, programming, or other problems that can create a disaster if not detected early.
6. Special provisions are necessary for measurement. This includes the need for rugged gages, cleaning of the measured and measuring surfaces, reliability of gages, and adherence to calibration schedules.
7. Some personnel will have greater responsiblity under automated manufacture. This is particularly so as we give minicomputers and microcomputers to workers for data entry and process control. All of this means training.

The potential benefits of the automated factory will require significant time and resources for planning.

REFERENCES

Amsden, R. T., Butler, H. E., and Amsden, D. M. (1986). *SPC Simplified; Practical Steps to Quality.* UNIPUB, Whiteplains, NY.

Bell, L. Ferris (1983). "Quality Verification of Manufacturing Planning." *ASQC Quality Congress Transactions,* Milwaukee, pp. 70–75.

Bemesderfer, John L. (1979). "Approving a Process for Production." *Journal of Quality Technology,* vol. 11, no. 1, pp. 1–12.

Byrne, Diane M. and Taguchi, Shin (1986). "The Taguchi Approach to Parameter Design." *ASQC Quality Congress Transactions,* Milwaukee, pp. 168–177.

Caplan, Frank (1980). *The Quality System.* Chilton Book Company, Radnor, PA.

Carpenter, Ben H. (1982). "Control of Copper Ore Roasting Exit Gas Quality." *ASQC Quality Congress Transactions,* Milwaukee, pp. 748–755.

Caswell, A. R. and Zimmer, J. D. (1979). "Flow Chart Analysis of Pharmaceutical Products." *ASQC Technical Conference Transactions,* Milwaukee, pp. 161–167.

Deere and Company (1983). *Classification of Characteristics.* John Deere Standard JDE-D46, Moline, IL.

Downer, Winston C. (1983). "Management's Commitment to QA Includes ESD Control." *ASQC Quality Congress Transactions,* Milwaukee, pp. 76–81.

Feigenbaum, Armand V. (1983). *Total Quality Control,* 3rd ed. McGraw-Hill, New York.

Flavell, Norman L. (1983). "Error Rate of First Run NC Programs." *20th Annual Meeting and Technical Conference,* Numerical Control Society, Cincinnati, pp. 34–46.

Ford Motor Company (1972). *Reliability Methods—Manufacturing Planning for Reliability—Module XX.* Dearborn, MI, p. 11.

Ford Motor Company (1980). *Study and Analysis of Machine, Equipment and Process Capability.* Manufacturing Procedure VII-b-3, Dearborn, MI.

Ford Motor Company (1980). *Machine Capability Studies.* Booklet 80-01-250, Dearborn, MI.

Fukuda, Ryuji (1981). "Introduction to the CEDAC." *Quality Progress,* November, pp. 14–19.

Gibbons, Jean D. (1982). "Methods for Selecting the Best Process." *Journal of Quality Technology,* vol. 14, no. 2, pp. 80–88.

Goldhar, Joel D. and Jelinek, Mariann (1983). "Plan for Economies of Scope." *Harvard Business Review,* November–December, pp. 141–148.

Gunn, Thomas G. (1982). "The Mechanization of Design and Manufacturing," *Scientific American,* September, p. 121.

Harrington, H. James (1981). *Process Qualification—Manufacturing's Insurance Policy.* IBM Technical Report 02.901, San Jose, CA.

Harrington, Joseph, Jr. (1979). *Computer Integrated Manufacturing.* Robert E. Krieger, Huntington, NY.

Hunter, William G. and Kartha, C. P. (1977). "Determining the Most Profitable Target Value for a Production Process." *Journal of Quality Technology,* vol. 9, no. 4, October, pp. 176–181.

Ishiyama, Takayuki (1977). "On System for Applying FMEA, An Outline of Its Application." *Reports of Statistical Applications and Research,* Japanese Union of Scientists and Engineers, vol. 24, no. 3, pp. 40–50.

Jones and Laughlin Company (1984). *The Integrated Quality System: How to Develop a Process Control Map of Key Control Variables.* Pittsburgh.

Kane, Victor E. (1986). "Process Capability Indices." *Journal of Quality Technology,* vol. 18, no. 1, January, pp. 41–52.

Kaneko, Hiromi (1977). "Plant Reliability Improvement." *Reports of Statistical Applications and Research,* Japanese Union of Scientists and Engineers, vol. 24, no. 3, pp. 68–77.

Kearney, Francis J. (1984). "Management of Product Quality without A Quality Department." *ASQC Quality Congress Transactions,* Milwaukee, pp. 249–252.

Kegg, Richard L. (1985). "Quality and Productivity in Manufacturing Systems." *Annals of the CIRP* (International Association for Production Research), Rivis, vol. 34, no. 2, pp. 531–534.

Kegg, Richard L. (1984). "Quality and Productivity in Manufacturing Systems." *Second Bi-Annual Machine Tool Technical Conference.* National Machine Tool Builders Association, Gaithersburg, MD, pp. 9-71 to 9-86.

Kinnucan, Paul (1983). "Flexible Systems Invade the Factory." *High Technology,* July, pp. 32–42.

Krouse, John (1982). *What Every Engineer Should Know about Computer-Aided Design and Computer-Aided Manufacturing.* Marcel Dekker, New York.

Marguglio, B. W. (1981). "Environmental Compliance and Universal Quality Assurance." *Quality Progress,* September, pp. 14–18.

McCubbin, Robert E. (1971). "Machine Tool Information System." *ASQC Technical Conference Transactions,* Milwaukee, pp. 235–243.

Meal, Harlan C. (1984). "Putting Production Decisions Where They Belong." *Harvard Business Review,* March-April, pp. 102–111.

Mentch, C. C. (1980). "Manufacturing Process Quality Optimization Studies." *Journal of Quality Technology,* vol. 12, no. 3, pp. 119–129.

Michalek, Joseph M. and Holmes, Richard K. (1981). *Quality Engineering Techniques in Product Design/Process.* Society of Automotive Engineers Paper 810392, Detroit.

Nakajo, Takeshi and Kume, Hitoshi (1985). "The Principles of Foolproofing and Their Application in Manufacturing." *Reports of Statistical Application Research,* Union of Japanese Scientists and Engineers, vol. 32, no. 2, June, pp. 10–29.

Nelson, Lloyd S. (1978). "Best Target Value for a Production Process." *Journal of Quality Technology,* vol. 10, no. 2, April, pp. 88–89.

Phadke, M. S., Kackar, R. R., Speeny, D. V., and Grieco, M. J. (1983). "Off-Line Quality Control in Integrated Circuit Fabrication Using Experimental Design." *The Bell System Technical Journal,* vol. 62, no. 5, pp. 1273–1309.

Phillipp, Thomas J. (1982). "Quality System Concepts in the CAD/CAM Era." *ASQC Quality Congress Transactions,* Milwaukee, pp. 569–573.

Raheja, Dev (1982). "Fault Tree Analysis—How Are We Doing?" *ASQC Quality Congress Transactions,* Milwaukee, pp. 355–359.

Remboldt, Ulrich, Seth, Mahesh K., and Weinstein, Jeremy (1977). *Computers in Manufacturing.* Marcel Dekker, New York.

Sahrmann, Herman (1979). "Set-Up Assurance through Time Series Analysis." *Journal of Quality Technology,* vol. 11, no. 7, pp. 105–115.

Schonberger, Richard J. (1982). *Japanese Manufacturing Techniques.* Free Press, New York.

Siff, Walter C. (1984). "The Strategic Plan of Control—A Tool for Participative Management." *ASQC Quality Congress Transactions,* Milwaukee, pp.384–390.

Staffiery, Richard A. (1975). "A Semiconductor Traceability Plan That Avoids Confusion." *Quality Management and Engineering,* April, pp. 20, 21.

Sullivan, L. P. (1984). "Reducing Variability: A New Approach to Quality." *Quality Progress,* July, pp. 15–21.

Taguchi, G. (1978). "Off-Line and On-Line Quality Control Systems." *International Conference on Quality Control,* Japanese Union of Scientists and Engineers, Tokyo, pp. B4-1 through B4-5.

Tarver, Mae-G. (1984). "Multistation Process Capability—Filling Equipment." *ASQC Quality Congress Transactions,* Milwaukee, pp. 281–288.

Taylor, F. W. (1947). *Scientific Management.* Harper & Brothers, New York.

U.S. Department of Transportation (1982). "Process Analysis via Accuracy Control." *The National Ship Building Research Program,* Washington, DC.

Venn, B. (1971). "Standardization of Flow Charts for Process Quality Control Systems." *EOQC Quality,* vol. 25, no. 2, pp. 35–39.

Vinson, William D. and Heany, Donald F. (1977). "Is Quality Out of Control?" *Harvard Business Review,* vol. 55, no. 6, November-December, pp. 114–122.

Werner, G. W. and Zetzsche, E. (1982). "Working Methods and Means of Quality and Reliability Assurance in Large Industrial Plants." *EOQC Quality,* vo. 26, no. 5, pp. 8–13.

Willis, Roger G. and Sullivan, Kevin H. (1984). "CIMS in Perspective: Costs, Benefits, Timing, Payback Periods Are Outlined." *Industrial Engineering,* February, vol. 16, no. 2, pp. 23–36.

Wilson, Lawrence A. (1983). "Generative Quality Assurance Planning." *ASQC Quality Congress Transactions,* Milwaukee, pp. 95–100.

SECTION 17
PRODUCTION[1]

Frank M. Gryna

NATURE OF PRODUCTION . . . **17.2**

Scope of Activity 17.2

QUALITY RESPONSIBILITIES ON THE FACTORY FLOOR **17.2**

Principal Decision and Action Categories 17.2

Pattern of Departmental Responsibilities 17.3

Pattern of Individual Responsibilities 17.3

CONCEPT OF CONTROLLABILITY; SELF-CONTROL **17.4**

KNOWLEDGE OF "SUPPOSED TO DO" **17.6**

Product Specifications . . . 17.6

Process Specifications . . . 17.7

Checklist 17.11

KNOWLEDGE OF "IS DOING" . . **17.12**

Measurement Inherent in the Process 17.12

Measurements by Workers 17.12

Measurements by Inspectors 17.13

Feedback to Supervisors . . 17.16

Automated Quality Information 17.17

Checklist 17.18

ABILITY TO REGULATE **17.18**

Process Control Tools . . . 17.19

Checklist 17.21

QUALITY AND PRODUCTION FLOOR CULTURE **17.21**

SELF-INSPECTION **17.23**

Criteria for Self-Inspection 17.24

Cautions to be Observed under Self-Inspection 17.25

Sequence for Instituting Self-Inspection Concept 17.25

Audit of Decisions . . . 17.26

Results of Self-Inspection 17.26

AUDIT OF PRODUCTION QUALITY **17.26**

Systems Audit 17.26

Product Audit 17.29

TROUBLESHOOTING **17.29**

Responsibility for Troubleshooting . . . 17.29

TRAINING OF PRODUCTION PERSONNEL **17.30**

REFERENCES **17.31**

---

[1]In the Third Edition, the section on production was prepared by J. M. Juran.

NATURE OF PRODUCTION

"Production," as the term is used here, designates the activity of running the processes, machines, and tools, and of performing the associated mental and manual operations to make products from basic materials and components. Production is part of the broader activity of manufacture, which includes also manufacturing planning; see Section 16, Manufacturing Planning. As the term is commonly used, production involves the use of manufacturing "processes" to change the physical raw material into products. Other areas of an organization also make use of a variety of "processes" which do not involve the changing of a raw material. Many of these other processes are discussed in Section 21, Administrative and Support Operations.

Statistical techniques useful in process control are discussed in Section 24, Statistical Process Control; behavioral aspects on the production floor and throughout an organization are covered in Section 10, Managing Human Performance. Policy issues are discussed in Section 5 under Quality Policies for Functions.

Scope of Activity.   Production as an activity must be distinguished from the capitalized word "Production," meaning a department of that name. The Production Department is often given duties beyond those of performing direct production activities. These added duties vary widely from one company to another, depending on product and process complexity, volume of production, management philosophy, training of supervisors, and national tradition.

Company response to these factors has resulted in divergent forms of organization. At one extreme the department called Production has wide responsibilities for manufacturing planning, machine maintenance, and product inspection. At the other extreme, the department has a narrow scope of activity—that of executing the plans which others have prepared. Competitive forces of the 1980s have fostered some useful experiments in organizing and conducting production operations. From these experiments are emerging new approaches that would have been considered heretical just a decade earlier. Stone and Guith (1985) describe an example for an automobile plant.

QUALITY RESPONSIBILITIES ON THE FACTORY FLOOR

"Responsibility" is never clear unless it is stated in terms of decisions or actions. A question in the form, "Who is responsible for approving setups?" admits of an unequivocal answer.

The factory floor is the scene of myriad decisions which affect quality. Several categories of these decisions are so highly repetitive that companies should make crystal clear who is to make which decisions.

Principal Decision and Action Categories.   The most frequent categories are the following:

Setup Approval.   The "setup" consists of assembling the proper machines, tools, instruments, and material and adjusting them so that the resulting product will conform to specification. This setup is prepared either by the production worker or by a setup specialist. Once the setup has been prepared, a decision must be made: "Should this process be allowed to commence production?" This decision is known as "setup approval."

Running Approval.   Once the process is running, there is need for periodic checks to see if the process is still producing product which conforms to specification. The decision to be made is: "Should the process continue to run or should it stop?" This decision is known as "running approval."

Product Approval.   As product is completed, there is a periodic need to decide whether the product conforms to specification. This decision is called "product approval," as contrasted with the preceding two decisions, which together constitute process approval.

Decision on Fitness for Use.   As a result of the product approval procedure, some nonconforming product may be found. A further decision is then necessary on the disposition of the nonconforming product.

Pattern of Departmental Responsibilities.   In the United States, the *departmental* assignment for making these decisions has usually been as follows:

Decision	*Usually assigned to*
Setup approval	Production, but sometimes jointly with Inspection
Running approval	Production
Product approval	Inspection
Fitness-for-use decision	Committee of representatives from various departments

There is also the further question of how these departmental responsibilities are to be assigned to the categories of job classes on the factory floor. To answer this question, it is convenient to make use of a responsibility matrix to reach agreement on who should make which decisions.

Pattern of Individual Responsibilities.   Unless the managers decide who may make what decisions, the people on the work floor must work out among themselves who is to decide what. Some of these local agreements are an unpleasant surprise to managers once they are discovered.

Managers can quite readily work out an agreed pattern of decision making by using a responsibility matrix. Cognizant supervisors meet to discuss the problem. At this meeting the blank matrix is first drawn on the blackboard. The members then agree on what decisions and actions they will talk about. These are listed in the left-hand column to become the headings for the horizontal rows of the matrix. Next, the members agree on who is available on the factory floor to make these decisions. These potential decision makers become the headings for the vertical columns of the matrix.

Next, the matrix is reproduced and a copy is given to each conferee to indicate who should make which decision and take which action. These filled-in copies (sometimes executed anonymously) are collected and all the marks are transferred to the blackboard to show the composite belief of the membership.

The summary enables the members to identify their collective agreements and the extent of their differences. These differences can be talked out until agreement is complete. This agreement can then be reduced to a written procedure, formally approved and published.

An example of the results of this approach is given in Table 17.1. Inputs were collected on five decisions—the four already mentioned and an additional decision on product sorting. The beliefs on current responsibility came from four

TABLE 17.1 Divergence of Views on Responsibility

Plant	W*	S	I	E	W	S	I	E
	Setup acceptance				Running acceptance			
A	1	4	2	0	5	1	2	0
B	4	2	7	0	7	4	3	0
C	0	0	1	7	2	1	5	0
D	3	0	5	0	2	1	7	2
	Conformance				Fitness for use			
A	1	5	2	0	1	3	4	0
B	3	5	7	0	2	6	6	1
C	0	1	6	1	0	2	4	2
D	3	1	5	2	2	1	10	0
	Sorting							
A	0	4	3	0				
B	4	2	6	0				
C	0	1	4	0				
D	0	0	5	4				

*W = worker; S = supervisor; I = inspector; E = engineer.

plants (A, B, C, D) within the company. Lack of agreement on who was responsible for the decisions was a clear conclusion from the study. Disagreement existed within every plant on each of the five decisions. Clarification was essential.

Managers often ask, "Is there a right way to organize?" The answer is no. The pattern of responsibility must be designed to fit the local conditions. In one department it is convenient to assign to the same person the jobs of setup and operate; in another department setup is best done by a special setup person. In one department the process is so stable that the original setup will endure for the length of the lot; in another department the setup requires check and readjust during the life of the lot. There are differences in the extent of training, the level of morale, etc., of the work force. The permutations of these and other differences make each department unique and require a made-to-measure design of responsibility for decision making.

It is instructive to study the approach to responsibility for quality on the production floor in Japan. Here a heavy emphasis is placed on having many decisions and actions under the control of the production workers themselves. Schonberger (1982) discusses the emphasis on responsibility of the workers in Japan. See also Section 35F, Quality in Japan.

CONCEPT OF CONTROLLABILITY; SELF-CONTROL

Creating a state of self-control for a human being requires that we meet several essential criteria. We must provide people with a means for:

1. Knowing what they are supposed to do

2. Knowing what they are actually doing

3. Regulating the process

May (1978) divides the criteria into seven categories, all of which are incorporated and discussed below for the three criteria stated.

The three basic criteria for self-control make possible a separation of defects into categories of "controllability," of which the most important are:

1. *Worker-controllable:*   A defect or nonconformity is worker-controllable if all three criteria for self-control have been met.

2. *Management-controllable:*   A defect or nonconformity is management-controllable if one or more of the critera for self-control have not been met.

The theory behind these categories is that only the management can provide the means for meeting the criteria for self-control. Hence any failure to meet these criteria is a failure of management, and the resulting defects are therefore beyond the control of the workers. This theory is not 100 percent sound. Workers commonly have the duty to call management's attention to deficiencies in the system of control, and sometimes they do not do so. (Sometimes they do, and it is management who fails to act.) However, the theory is much more right than wrong.

Whether the defects or nonconformities in a plant are mainly management-controllable or worker-controllable is a fact of the highest order of importance. To reduce the former requires a program in which the main contributions must come from the managers, supervisors, and technical specialists. To reduce the latter requires a different kind of program in which much of the contribution comes from the workers. The great difference between these two kinds of programs suggests that managers should quantify their knowledge of the state of controllability before embarking on major programs.

An example of controllability study is given in Table 17.2. A diagnostic team was set up to study scrap and rework reports in six machine shop departments for 17 working days. The defect cause was entered on each report by a quality engineer who was assigned to collect the data. When the cause was not apparent,

TABLE 17.2   Controllability Study in a Machine Shop, %

Management-controllable	
Inadequate training	15
Machine inadequate	8
Machine maintenance	8
Other process problems	8
Materials handling	7
Tool, fixture, gage (TFG) maintenance	6
TFG inadequate	5
Wrong material	3
Operation run out of sequence	3
Miscellaneous	5
Total	68
Worker-controllable	
Failure to check work	11
Improperly operated	11
Other (e.g., piece mislocated)	10
Total	32

the team reviewed the defect and, when necessary, contacted other specialists (who had been alerted by management about the priority of the project) to identify the cause. The purpose of the study was to resolve a lack of agreement on the causes of chronically high scrap and rework. It did the job. The study was decisive in obtaining agreement on the focus of the improvement program. In less than 1 year over $2 million was saved and important strides were made in reducing production backlogs.

Controllability can also be evaluated by posing specific questions for each of the three criteria of self-control. (Typical questions that can be posed are presented below.) Although this approach does not yield a quantitative evaluation of management-controllable and worker-controllable defects, it does show whether the defects are primarily management-controllable or worker-controllable.

In the experience of the editors, defects are about 80 percent management-controllable. This figure does not vary much from industry to industry, but varies greatly among processes. Other investigators, in Japan, Sweden, the Netherlands, and Czechoslovakia, have reached similar conclusions.

While the available quantitative studies make clear that defects are mainly management-controllable, many industrial managers do not know this, or are unable to accept the data. Their long-standing beliefs are that most defects are the result of worker carelessness, indifference, and even sabotage. Such managers are easily persuaded to embark on worker-motivation schemes which, under the usual state of facts, aim at a small minority of the problems and hence are doomed to achieve minor results at best. The issue is not whether quality problems *in industry* are management-controllable. The need is to determine the answer *in a given plant*. This cannot be answered authoritatively by opinion, but requires solid facts, preferably through a controllability study of actual defects, as in Table 17.2.

The concept of self-control draws attention to the importance of manufacturing planning. Manufacturing planning for quality (see Section 16) is the means of *prevention* of both management- and worker-controllable defects on the manufacturing floor.

The three main criteria for self-control are discussed below.

KNOWLEDGE OF "SUPPOSED TO DO"

This knowledge commonly consists of the following:

1. The product standard, which may be a written specification, a product sample, or other definition of the end result to be attained
2. The process standard, which may be a written process specification, written process instructions, an oral instruction, or other definition of "means to an end"
3. A definition of responsibility, i.e., what decisions to make and what actions to take (discussed earlier in this section)

Product Specifications.   The ideal source of knowledge is the use required by the user. In most situations this is translated into a product specification. In developing these product specifications, some essential precautions must be observed.

Provide Unequivocal Information.   Two obstacles to proper knowledge can exist:

1. The specification may be vague. For example, when fiberglass tanks are transported in vehicles, the surface of the supporting cradles should be smooth. It

was recognized that weld spatter would be deposited on the cradle surface, so an operation was specifed to scrape the surface "smooth." However, there was no definition of "how smooth," and many rejections resulted.

2. There may be conflicting specifications. The supervisor's "black book" has had a long, durable career. Changes in specifications may fail to be communicated, especially when there is a constant parade of changes. In one instance, an inspector rejected product which lacked an angle cut needed for clearance in assembly. It was discovered that the inspector was using drawing revision D, the production floor had used revision B, and the design office had issued revision E just 3 days before.

Provide Information on Seriousness. All specifications contain multiple characteristics, and these are not equally important. When workers are informed of the vital few characteristics, their emphasis is better placed.

Explain the "Why." Explanation of the purposes served by the product and by the specification enlarges the knowledge of "supposed to do" and provides motivation through the resulting feeling of participation.

For example, a specification on weight called for a nominal value of 40.0 g with a tolerance of $\pm$ 0.5 g. Although the total tolerance of 1.0 was being met, most of the tolerance range was being used up, and this created some problems later in assembly. A process capability study showed that the process capability was 0.10 g—far better than the tolerance of 1.0 g. But why was most of the tolerance range being used? Discussion revealed that (1) workers had not been told of the impact of inconsistent weights on later assembly, and (2) workers had not been instructed on centering the process to the nominal specification value.

Provide Standards. In those cases where the specification cannot be quantitative, physical or photographic standards should be provided. There is an extensive array of needs here, especially on widely prevailing characteristics such as product appearance. (For years, enormous numbers of electrical connections were soldered in the absence of clear standards for an acceptable soldered connection.) If these standards are not provided by the managers and engineers, then, by default, the standards will be set by the inspectors and workers.

Train the Workers. The general aspects of worker training for quality are discussed in Section 11, Training for Quality. Beyond this general training are the special training needs of specific jobs. For example, some welding operations affect human safety. It is common practice to require that workers undergo a training program, including welding of specimen pieces, to qualify for the job. A qualification examination is then held, including test of the specimen pieces. Workers who pass the examination are given a license to perform the operation for a stated interval of time. In some cases the license remains in effect until there is evidence of poor work or until the worker becomes inactive for several months. In such cases, requalification is required.

Process Specifications.
Work methods and process conditions (e.g., temperature, pressure, time cycles) must be unequivocally clear.

Howell (1981) states that six factors are important in developing a statement of a work method:

1. Provide only the information needed to accomplish the task.
2. Make sure abbreviations are understood.
3. Do not make written instructions too wordy.

4. Use photographs and visual aids, where possible.

5. Make sure assembly instructions are consistent with the specified engineering configuration.

6. Make sure that on-the-job instructions are consistent with formal training program instruction.

LTV Steel

INTEGRATED PROCESS CONTROL
Standard Procedures
Process Control

Plant __Indiana Harbor__

Dept __No. 3 Sheet Mill__

File No ___716-2.2.2___

Date Orig Issue __3/83__

Revision No __1__

Date Revised __9/83__

Control Area	Control Point	Control Element	No
Tandem Mill	Rolling	Rolling Solutions	2.2.2

Control Task
To maintain rolling solution characteristics at the proper levels.

Responsible for Control
Solution Attendant

Process Standard
- Oil concentration must be 2.5% to 3.5%
- Solution temperature must be 110°F - 120°F
- SAP value must be above 120
- Iron fines must be less that 600 ppm

Reason for Control
- To provide the correct lubricity between work rolls and strip for reduced roll wear and control of strip temperature. This helps control strip flatness and avoids friction scratches.

Measurement
Tools/Equipment - Standard chem. test set-up
Frequency - Twice/turn
By - Solution Attendant

Routine Reporting of Data
Form/Form No. -
Solution Attendant's Report
By - Solution Attendant

Control Chart Yes | No
X |

Type - X & Moving Range
By - Solution Att.

Corrective Action
- Solution concentration approaching limits - add rolling oil or water.
- Solution temp. approaching limits - adjust temperature control.
- SAP reading between 100 & 120, skim solution tank and add new oil. SAP reading below 100, retest immediately and contact Operating Supervisor. If retest below 100, shutdown mill and switch to alternative solution tank.
- Iron fines approaching limit, skim tank for 2 hours and add 100 gallons oil. Retest after 30 minutes second time, repeat procedure if still near or above limit.

Operating Procedure

See attached sheet

Disposition of Non-Compliant Product
Identify coil(s) for special surface evaluation. Notify Metallurgical Supervisor.

Review Procedure
Once per turn the Operating Supervisor will:
- Check Solution Attendant's Report
- Visually check temperature of solution

Developed By: _Robert Goedken_
IPC Coordinator

Richard H. Berry

Approved: _DT Ziol_
Department Superintendent/Manager

Dale H. Dick Jr.
Manager - Quality Control

R. Voth
General Superintendent/ Plant Manager

FIG. 17.1 Process Control standard procedure. *(From LTV Steel pamphlet, Integrated Process Control.)*

A steel manufacturer uses a highly structured system of identifying key process variables, defining process control standards, communicating the information to the work force, monitoring performance, and accomplishing diagnosis when problems arise. The process specification is a collection of process control standard procedures (Figure 17.1.) A procedure is developed for controlling each of the key process variables (variables that must be controlled in order to meet specification limits on the product). The procedure answers the following questions:

1. What the process standards are
2. Why control is needed
3. Who is responsible for control
4. How to measure
5. Whcn to measure
6. How to report routine data
7. Who is responsible for data reporting
8. How to audit
9. Who is responsible for audit
10. What to do with product out of compliance
11. Who developed the standard

Often, detailed process instructions are not known until workers have become experienced with the process. Updating of process instructions based on job experience can be conveniently accomplished by posting a cause-and-effect diagram in the production department and attaching index cards to the diagram (Fukuda, 1981). Each card states additional process instructions based on recent experience.

Confusion of Process Control Tolerances with Product Accept Tolerances.   Process control tolerances apply to characteristics of the process; product acceptance tolerances apply to characteristics of the product. Table 17.3 distinguishes between these two kinds of tolerances.

In some operations the units of measure for the process are dramatically different from those used on the product. For example, in hardening of steel, the process variables are bath temperature, cycle time, etc. In contrast, the product is measured in terms of grain size, degrees of hardness, etc. In such a case the responsibility of the hardening furnace worker is clearly one of meeting the process tolerances, not the product tolerances.

In other operations, the units of measure for process and product are identical. A common example is the millimeter or inch used as a unit of measure in metal cutting. This is used both for controlling the process and accepting the product.

Confusion of Mandatory with Advisory Process Tolerances.   Many process specifications contain two different kinds of tolerances:

1. *Mandatory tolerances:*   These are specified to assure fitness for use, make the product more marketable, achieve high reliability, etc.
2. *Advisory tolerances:*   These are specified for the convenience of production, e.g., to help reduce the amount of cut and try in running the process. For example, the process for cooking fish sticks (for frozen food marketing) includes requirements that (*a*) the cooking cycle shall be x degrees for y minutes and

TABLE 17.3 Distinction between Tolerances

	Process control	Product acceptance
Purpose of the tolerances:	To provide a basis for making decisions on the process	To provide a basis for making decisions on the product
Tolerances published in:	Process specification	Product specification
Specification usually issued by:	Process Engineering Department	Product Design Department
Tolerances concern:	Process conditions	Product qualities
Instrumentation is usually:	An integral part of the process	Not an integral part of the process
Usual measurement to discover compliance is by:	Production Department for advisory tolerances; Inspection Department for mandatory tolerances*	Inspection Department
Decisions on whether there is compliance made usually by:	Production Department for advisory tolerances, Inspection Department for mandatory tolerances	Inspection Department
Deviation from specification usually authorized by:	Production Department for advisory tolerances, Process Engineering Department for mandatory tolerances	Inspection Department for nonfunctional tolerances, Product Design Department for functional tolerances

*Advisory tolerances are supplied to workers for manufacturing convenience. Mandatory process tolerances must be met as a means of supplying essential product qualities, i.e., long life, safety, etc., when there is no immediate economic test for the product quality.

also that (*b*) the cooked product shall have a golden brown color. The latter is regarded as mandatory for marketing the product; the former is advisory. For most input materials (fish), the specified temperature and time will produce the proper color. However, the materials vary, and Production is authorized to vary the cooking cycle to suit.

Some process specifications contain many tolerances without designating which are mandatory and which are advisory. Lacking this knowledge, Production tends to regard them all as advisory, whereas Inspection tends to regard them all as mandatory. The answer, "of course," is to designate which is which. The problem is to induce busy technical departments to take the time to do the designating. Where they are unable to take the time, the quality manager may be driven to make his or her own determination.

Confusion When Control Charts Are Introduced into a Process. Control charts are discussed in Section 24, Statistical Process Control. To the quality specialists, control charts serve as a sensitive device for detecting process changes. To the production force the charts are complex and confusing. Table 17.4 shows the initial impact on the production worker.

TABLE 17.4 Operator Action Table

	Sources of worker's information or decision		
	Before introduction of control charts; worker responsible for meeting:		
Type of information or decision needed	Process specification	Product specification	After introduction of control charts
1. Information on what the process should be doing	Direct from process specification	Direct from product specification	From the control chart
2. Information on what the process actually is doing	From process instruments or inspectors	From measurements on the product	From the control chart
3. Decision on whether "is doing" differs from "should be doing" by an amount great enough to warrant process adjustment	From worker experience	From worker experience	From the control chart
4. Decision on extent of process adjustment needed	From worker experience	From worker experience	From worker experience

Since the earliest applications (and into the 1980s), some pertinent questions were raised about the status of the control chart:

1. What is the official status of the control chart? Is it merely an informal suggestion by the quality engineer, or is it a "legitimate" impersonal boss, like the specification, the collective bargaining agreement, etc.? Workers react to non-conforming product because specification limits have been law in the shop. Workers do not react in the same way to control charts, because legitimacy has not been fully established.

2. Is the control to be used in addition to or instead of the specification?

3. If "in addition to," what of the cases where there is conflict; e.g., control chart requires more frequent adjustment, process is not capable, etc.?

4. If the control chart is to be used instead of the specification, why is this not legitimized; i.e., why is there no formal order relieving the worker of the responsibility for meeting specifications?

Unless these questions are answered, confusion will result and the charts will be doomed to the grave of a file cabinet.

Checklist. The above discussion covers the first criterion of self-control: people must have the means for knowing what they are supposed to do. To evaluate adherence to this criterion, a checklist of questions can be created, including the following:

1. Are there written product specifications, process specifications, and work instructions? If written in more than one place, do they all agree? Are they legible? Are they conveniently accessible to the worker?
2. Does the specification define the relative importance of different quality characteristics? Are advisory tolerances on a process distinguished from mandatory tolerances on a product? If control charts or other control techniques are to be used, is it clear how these relate to product specifications?
3. Are standards for visual defects displayed in the work area?
4. Are the written specifications given to the worker the same as the criteria used by inspectors? Are deviations from the specification often allowed?
5. Does the worker know how the product is used?
6. Has the worker been adequately trained to understand the specification and perform the steps needed to meet the specification? Has the worker been evaluated by test or other means to see if he or she is qualified?
7. Does the worker know the effect on future operations and product performance if the specification is not met?
8. Does the worker receive specification changes automatically and promptly?
9. Does the worker know what to do with defective raw material and defective finished product?
10. Have responsibilities in terms of decisions and actions been clearly defined?

KNOWLEDGE OF "IS DOING"

This is the second criterion for self-control. For self-control, people must have the means of knowing whether their performance conforms to standard. This conformance applies to:

1. The product in the form of specifications on product characteristics
2. The process in the form of specifications on process variables

The knowledge is secured from three primary sources: measurements inherent in the process, measurements by production workers, and measurements by inspectors.

Measurement Inherent in the Process.   Many processes are engineered to include much instrumentation. The resulting information provides a feedback to enable the worker to close the loop. Even where the feedback is into an automated system, the data are usually available to human workers acting as monitors.

Measurements by Workers.   Where the worker is to use the instruments, it is necessary to provide training in how to measure, what sampling criteria to use, how to record, how to chart, and what kinds of corrective action to take. The difficulty of motivating the workers to follow these instructions is so widespread a problem that many companies go to great lengths to minimize the need for worker action by providing instruments which require little or no human effort to measure, record, and control.

When these instruments are provided to workers, it is also necessary to ensure that these instruments are compatible with those used by inspectors and in other operations later in the progression of events.

On one construction project, the "form setters" were provided with carpenter levels and rulers to set the height of forms prior to the pouring of concrete. The inspectors were provided with a complex optical instrument. The differences in measurement led to many disputes.

Control of the process is strengthened if the worker is provided with the type of gage that provides numerical measurements on a characteristic rather than providing accept-reject information.

A problem arises when the measurement necessary to control a process must be made in a laboratory off the production floor. The time required to send a sample to the laboratory, to have the analysis made, and to have the data relayed back to production can result in a delay to proper control of a process. One solution is the development of auxiliary measuring devices that can be used on the production floor by the worker and thereby provide immediate feedback. An example comes from a process used to control the concentration of chloride in a corn product derivative. Traditionally the raw material undergoes centrifuging, a sample of the product is sent to a laboratory for analysis, the test results are forwarded to Production, and any necessary changes are then made in the centrifugal loads. (Chloride level, for the most part, is dependent on the load size of crystallized liquor being spun in the centrifugals.) Under the new setup, the worker takes a spot sample at the surge bin, and analyzes the product for parts per million chloride on an ion analyzer, and thereby directly regulates the process. Total time between processing a batch and obtaining a measurement plunges from 90 to 20 min. As a result, the amount of inferior product due to delayed process adjustment is greatly reduced.

Parker (1981) describes how the use of on-line gages overcame problems in obtaining adequate sampling of product at a paper mill.

Measurements by Inspectors.   When Inspection makes measurements which are to serve as a basis for action by Production, the division of work is as follows:

Activity	Usually performed by
Measure the product or process	Inspection
Record and publish the data	Inspection
Analyze the data for significance	Both
Decide on a course of action	Production
Take the action	Production

Where this form persists for any length of time, it is common for the responsibility for achievement of quality to pass from Production to Inspection. Once this has happened, it is a long road back.

Methods of Closing the Feedback Loop.   The choice of ways of closing the loop is influenced partly by technology, but more often by the prevailing pattern of human relations.

Loop Closed by Inspector.   At one extreme, the inspector is under orders to stop the process when there is evidence of failure to conform. This form is used in cases where the management has become unwilling to entrust the production workers with the responsibility for closing the loop.

Personal Feedback to Workers.   In this form the inspector tells the worker of the results of measurement, and advises on the change needed. In some companies it is virtually mandatory for the workers to act on this advice. Usually, however, the worker decides whether to take the advice or not.

Personal Feedback to Supervisor. In some companies the rule is that the inspector may not communicate directly with the worker but, instead, must take feedback to the supervisor.

Where the worker is in a state of self-control, feedback through the supervisor slows up the signal and may distort it as well. Usually it is better to communicate directly with the workers, provided that the feedback avoids the implication of being an order.

Impersonal Feedback. One way of directing the feedback to the worker without implying an order is through depersonalizing the feedback. A special reporting format is needed for this purpose (e.g., charts, signal lights) as discussed under Timeliness of Feedback (see below).

In some cases it is feasible to provide feedback of deeds rather than data. Numerous applications of closed-circuit television are used to permit observation of processes which are distant or which are conducted in an environment hostile to human comfort, e.g., heat, fumes, noise.

The opportunity to view the deeds has the added advantage of being a "real-time" feedback; i.e., the deeds and the signals are simultaneous. The response of workers to such realities tends to be more wholehearted than their response to after-the-fact data.

Timeliness of Feedback. Once defects are discovered, prompt feedback is needed to avoid continuing production of defects. Depending on the process, various ways have been devised for providing this prompt feedback.

Multiple Machines. Where the process consists of numerous machines all producing independently (e.g., textile looms, lathes), signals are designed to identify those machines which are in need of attention. For example, signal lamps may be mounted to each machine. Green lights show that the product from those machines is under control. A red light signals that the machine is in trouble. These signals are turned on and off by Inspection. There are numerous other forms of such signals at machines: colored tags, swiveling red hands, etc. Denissoff (1980) describes a process control system that classifies each process into one of four levels of quality performance. Color codes are used for identification. Different process control approaches are used for the four levels.

Large Assembly Lines. One form of feedback has been the large chart mounted in the assembly area so as to be widely visible. The chart is a matrix with vertical columns representing hours of the shift and horizontal rows representing various assembly defects. The results of inspection are posted hourly, so that any one square of the matrix shows how many instances of that type of defect were found in that hour. These feedbacks can be provided by instantaneous electronic readout.

Criteria for Good Feedback to Workers. The needs of production workers (as distinguished from supervisors or technical specialists) require that the data feedback read at a glance, deal only with the few important defects, deal only with worker-controllable defects, provide prompt information about symptom and cause, and provide enough information to guide corrective actions. Criteria of good feedback are:

1. *Read at a glance:* The pace of events on the factory floor is swift. Workers should be able to review the feedback in stride.

Where the worker needs information about process performance over time, charts can provide an excellent form of feedback, provided they are designed to be consistent with the assigned responsibility of the worker (Table 17.5). It is useful to use visual displays to highlight recurrent problems. A problem described as "outer hopper switch installed backwards" displayed on a wall chart in large block letters has much more impact than the same message buried away as a marginal note in a work folder. Carlisle (1981) describes the effectiveness of such a system.

2. *Deal only with the few important defects:* Overwhelming workers with data on all defects will result in diverting attention from the vital few.

3. *Deal only with worker-controllable defects:* Any other course provides a basis for argument which will be unfruitful.

4. *Provide prompt information about symptom and cause:* Timeliness is a basic test of good feedback; the closer the system is to "real time" signaling, the better.

5. *Provide enough information to guide corrective action:* The signal should be in terms which make it easy to decide on remedial action.

Feedback Related to Worker Action.   The worker needs to know what kind of *process* change to make to respond to a *product* deviation. Sources of the knowledge are:

1. From the process specification (see Figure 17.1 under "corrective action")
2. From cut-and-try experience by the worker
3. From the fact that the units of measure for product and process are identical

Lacking all these, the workers can only cut and try further or stop the process and sound the alarm.

Sometimes it is feasible for the data feedback to be converted into a form which makes easier the worker's decision about what action to take on the process.

For example, a copper cap had six critical dimensions. It was easy to measure the dimensions and to discover the nature of product deviation. However, it was difficult to translate the product data into process changes. To simplify this translation, use was made of a position-dimension (*P-D*) diagram. The six measurements were first "corrected" (i.e., coded) by subtracting the thinnest from all the

TABLE 17.5 Worker Responsibility versus Chart Design

Responsibility of the worker is to	Chart should be designed to show
1. Make individual units of product meet a product specification	The measurements of individual units of product compared to product specification limits
2. Hold process conditions to the requirements of a process specification	The measurements of the process conditions compared with the process specification limits
3. Hold averages and ranges to specified statistical control limits	The averages and ranges compared to the statistical control limits
4. Hold percent nonconforming below some prescribed level	Actual percent nonconforming compared to the limiting level

others. These corrected data were then plotted on a *P-D* diagram as shown in Figure 17.2. Such diagrams provided a way of analyzing the tool setup.

Feedback to Supervisors.   Beyond the need for feedback at the work stations, there is need to provide supervisors with short-term summaries. These take several forms.

Matrix Summary.   A common form of matrix is workers versus defects; i.e., the vertical columns are headed by worker names and the horizontal rows by the names of defect types. The matrix makes clear which defect types predominate, which workers have the most defects, and what the interaction is. Other matrices include machine number versus defect type, defect type versus calendar week, etc.

When the summary is published, it is usual to circle the matrix cells to highlight the vital few situations which call for attention.

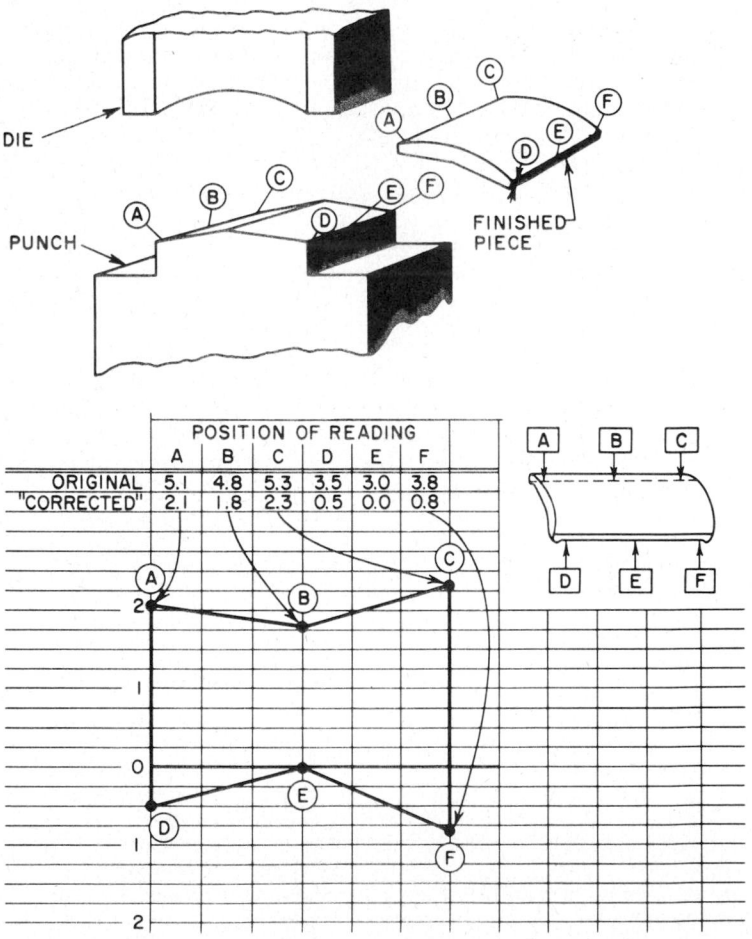

FIG. 17.2 Method of drawing *P-D* diagram.

An elaboration of the matrix is to split the cell diagonally, permitting the entry of two numbers, e.g., number defective and number produced.

Pareto Analysis. Some companies prefer to minimize the detail and provide information on the total defects for the day plus a list of the top three (or so) defects encountered, and how many of each.

In some industries, a "chart room" displays performance by product and by department, against goals.

Computer Data Analysis and Reporting. Production volume and complexity are important factors in determining the role of the computer. Burgess (1982) describes a simple manual reporting system for a low-volume, labor-intensive operation. Blumenthal (1978) discusses a system of greater complexity that is useful for moderate- to high-volume operations. Section 27, Computers and Quality, explains the role of computers in analyzing and reporting data during production and other phases of the product life cycle.

Automated Quality Information. Some situations justify the mechanization of both the recording of data and the analysis of data. Direct feedback can even include printing of summaries at typewriters located in the offices of the supervisors involved. Fisher (1983) describes a system (Figure 17.3) for using a mini-computer to control the net weight in a food-filling operation. The quality station has a cathode ray tube (CRT) and a scale; the supervisor's office has a CRT and a hard copy machine; a modem connects corporate headquarters with each plant's computer setup.

As weight data are obtained and entered at the weight station, the computer forms the data into samples (five weights in each sample), and when the final net weight in each sample is obtained, the CRT instantly displays an average and range control chart. Touch another key and a histogram is the output. All graphs and charts are in real time and are updated automatically after each subgroup. Although the computer is graphing only subgroup averages and ranges, it is internally checking each individual reading against a minimum allowable value. If this value is not met, the CRT locks out until the worker acknowledges the low reading. In addition, a terminal in the supervisor's office beeps in response to an out-

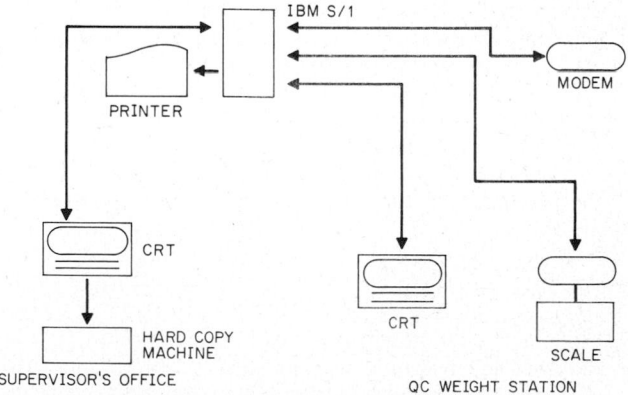

FIG. 17.3 Gerber computerized net weight system.

of-control situation. This beeping continues until the supervisor clears the terminal, signalling recognition of the problem. The system enables the supervisor to monitor the line without leaving the office.

Entry of data through the use of computer terminals on production floors is now common. Kassarda (1980) describes the versatility of these shop floor terminals. Many varieties of software are now available for analyzing, processing, and presenting quality information collected on the production floor. See Section 24 under Software for Statistical Process Control.

Checklist.   A checklist to evaluate the second criterion of self-control includes questions such as:

1. Are gages provided to the worker? Do they provide numerical measurements rather than sort good from bad? Are they precise enough? Are they regularly checked for accuracy?
2. Is the worker told how often to sample work? Is sufficient time allowed?
3. Is the worker told how to evaluate measurements to decide when to adjust the process and when to leave it alone?
4. Is there a check to see that the worker does follow instructions on sampling work and making process adjustments?
5. Are inspection results provided to the worker, and are these results reviewed by the supervisor with the worker?

ABILITY TO REGULATE

This is the third criterion for self-control. Regulating the process depends on a number of management-controllable factors, including:

1. *The process must be capable of meeting the tolerances:* (see Section 16 under Process Capability).

2. *The process must be responsive to the regulatory action in a predictable cause-and-effect relationship:* In a process for making polythelyne film, the workers were required to meet multiple product parameters. The equipment had various regulatory devices, each of which could vary performance with respect to one or more parameters. However, the workers could not "dial in" a predetermined list of settings which would meet all parameters. Instead, it was necessary to cut and try in order to meet all parameters simultaneously. During the period of cut and try, the machine produced nonconforming product to an extent which interfered with meeting standards for productivity and delivery. The workers were unable to predict how long the cut-and-try process would go on before full conformance was achieved. In consequence it became the practice to stop "cut and try" after a reasonable amount of time, and to let the process run, whether in conformance or not.

3. *The worker must be trained in how to use the regulating mechanisms and procedures:* This training should cover the entire spectrum of action—under what conditions to act, what kind and extent of changes to make, how to use the regulating devices, and why these things need to be done.

Of three qualified workers on a food process, only one operated the process every week and became proficient. The other two workers were used when the primary worker was on vacation or was ill, and thus they never became proficient.

Continuous training of the relief people was considered uneconomical, and agreements with the union prohibited their use except under the situations cited above. This problem is management-controllable; i.e., additional training or a change in union agreements is necessary.

4. *The act of adjustment should not be personally distasteful to the worker, e.g., should not require undue physical exertion:* In a plant making glass bottles, one adjustment mechanism was located next to a furnace area. During the summer months this area was so hot that workers tended to keep out as much as possible.

When the regulation consists of varying the human component of the operation, the question of process capability arises in a new form: Does the worker have the capability to regulate? This important question is discussed in Section 22 under Technique Errors, which includes some examples of discovering worker "knack."

Process Control Tools.   Section 16, under Planning Process Controls, discusses how manufacturing planning should include the development of specific process control tools. The tools selected are often related to one of five forms of dominance in a process.

Setup-Dominant Operations.   When the setup is the dominant cause of poor quality, the process setup should be formally approved before production starts. The evaluation of a process setup can vary from a first-piece inspection for a simple mechanical operation to an evaluation of a pilot plant for a complex chemical process. (See Section 16 under Overall Review of Manufacturing Planning.)

Setup acceptance criteria have historically been based on rule-of-thumb methods, exemplified by first-piece inspection. Here the process is set up and the first piece produced is inspected. If acceptable, the setup is approved and production begins. Unfortunately, one measurement provides little information on the *centering* of the process and no information on the variation of the process.

A limited sample of measurements can lead to incorrect decisions. One error can be to disapprove a correct setup; another error can be to approve an incorrect setup. The risks associated with these errors can be controlled by using tools such as lot plot, variables sampling plans, attributes sampling plans (see Section 25, Acceptance Sampling), PRE-Control (see Section 24, under PRE-Control), and tests of hypotheses (see Section 23 under Tests of Hypotheses).

Cyclical variation presents a further complication. Sahrmann (1979) discusses the evaluation of setups for a coating weight process that exhibits significant cyclical variation.

Time-Dominant Operations.   Time-dominant processes undergo a continuing time-to-time change (e.g., depletion of reagents, wear of tools, heat buildup) of such magnitude that nonconforming product will eventually be made. To prevent this, provision must be made for a periodic check and adjustment. This is often called "patrol inspection," of which there are numerous forms:

1. Preserve the order of manufacture. For example, the machine discharges its production into a small container called a "pan." The production worker periodically empties the entire pan into one of three larger containers:
   a. A "junk" box if the parts are junk.
   b. A "doubtful" box if the parts are questionable or are mixed good and bad.
   c. A "tray" if the parts are presumably good. The patrol inspector periodically checks product in the tray—either the most recent pieces or a random sam-

ple. Based on this check, the product in the tray goes to the junk box, the doubtful box, or a "good" box. The good box goes on to the next operation. Only the inspector may dispose of the tray, and only the inspector may place any product in the good box. The doubtful box is gone over by a sorter, who makes the final disposition.

2. This method is similar to that described in item 1 above, but the inspection data from the last few pieces are posted to a control chart (see Section 24, Statistical Process Control). If the process remains in control, all product made since the last check is accepted.

3. The accumulated product is sampled at random using a standard sampling plan, and acceptance is based on the sampling criteria (see Section 25, Acceptance Sampling).

4. The process variables are checked against a process specification, and product is accepted provided the process conforms to specification. This method is usually restricted to cases in which there is to be a direct check on the product at later stages. Checks of process variables can be supplemented with checks on other process conditions (see Systems Audit later in this section).

Worker-Dominant Operations.   When the worker is the dominant cause, feedback can be presented to supervisors and workers using the methods discussed earlier in this section.

Performance can also be presented in control-chart form using one of the following indices:

1. *Percent nonconforming:*   This method is used in attributes cases when the product is either good or bad.

2. *Number of nonconformities:*   This method is used for more elaborate products in which multiple errors can occur on a single unit of product, e.g., a television set or a large roll of woven carpeting.

3. *Nonconformities per opportunity:*   Each job is given a rating, prior to production based on its complexity, or on the "number of opportunities for a non-conformity." In electronics assembly work, for example, the rating is the sum of all components, solder connections, hardware insertions, etc., for the operations to be performed by a given worker. The worker's error rate is then the actual number of nonconformities found in a sample divided by the total number of opportunities for a nonconformity (i.e., units inspected times opportunities per unit for the job). This denominator more nearly puts all workers on the same basis, so that fair comparisons can be made between them.

4. *Nonconformities per characteristic:*   For mechanical parts or assemblies, "opportunities for a nonconformity" may more conveniently be defined as the total number of quality characteristics for a given operation. This is used as the denominator. Such a scoring method is readily adapted to cumulative "pyramiding" for higher-management reporting.

Control charts for fraction nonconforming or number of nonconformities are often plotted without statistical control limits. When such charts are installed on a worker-dominant process, a dramatic and quick improvement in quality sometimes occurs. There can be several reasons for such an improvement. First, the chart may demonstrate management's concern about quality and thereby bring increased worker vigilance on the process. Second, the chart may provide the worker with useful time-related information that was not available before.

Another technique for worker-dominated processes is the system audit (discussed later in this chapter).

Component-Dominant Operations. In component-dominant operations, the prime cause of poor quality is in the input materials to the operations. Defects may occur in epidemics (a lot of wrong material or out-of-specification material) or they may occur at random (a lot containing partially defective material). Assembly and subassembly, many chemical and food-processing operations, and packaging operations are typical examples.

Means of worker regulation are usually limited to notifying supervisors of the incoming materials' problems, and screening out the defective material.

Information-Dominant Operations. In information-dominant processes, the main cause of poor quality is in the data, instructions, and other forms of information provided to supervisors and workers. Such information may relate either to the product or to the process. Problems are often associated with products or processes that are subject to frequent changes, e.g., job shop operations (see Section 32, Job Shop Industries).

As in component-dominant operations, the worker has limited means of direct regulation. Problem areas, however, can be brought to the attention of supervision or reported through other corrective action channels such as Engineering Change Requests.

Special Situation of Taking Action When Control Charts Are Used. Limits on statistical control charts are different from engineering specification limits. In some situations, a process is not in statistical control, but may not require action since the product tolerances are being easily met; in other situations a process is in statistical control but the product tolerances are not being met. Table 17.6 shows the more usual permutations encountered and provides suggestions on the type of action to be taken.

Checklist. A checklist to evaluate the third criterion of self-control typically includes such questions as the following:

1. Has the quality capability of the process been measured to include both inherent variability and variability due to time? Is the capability periodically checked?
2. Has the worker been told how often to reset the process or how to evaluate measurements to decide when the process should be reset?
3. Is there a process adjustment that the worker can make to eliminate defects? Under what conditions should the worker adjust the process? When should the worker shut down the machine and seek more help? Whose help?
4. Have the worker actions which cause defects, and the necessary preventive action, been given to the worker, preferably in the written form?
5. Is there an adequate preventive maintenance program on the process?
6. Is there a hidden "knack" possessed by some workers that needs to be discovered and transmitted to all workers?

QUALITY AND PRODUCTION FLOOR CULTURE

Meeting the criteria of self-regulation is necessary but not sufficient. Even if all three criteria are initially met (they rarely are), two problems remain:

1. Worker errors may occur. The causes of some of those errors can be corrected

TABLE 17.6 Action to Be Taken

	Product meets tolerances		Product does not meet tolerances	
	Process variation small relative to tolerances*	Process variation large relative to tolerances*	Process variation small relative to tolerances	Process variation large relative to tolerances
Process is in control.	Consider cost reduction through less precise process; consider value to designer of tighter tolerances.	Generally no action.	Process is "misdirected" to wrong average. Generally easy to correct permanently.	Process may be misdirected and also too scattered. Correct misdirection. Consider economics of more precise process versus wider tolerances versus sorting the product.
Process is out of control.	Process is erratic and unpredictable. Investigate causes of lack of control. Decision to correct based on economics of corrective action.		Process is misdirected or erratic or both. Correct misdirection. Discover cause for lack of control. Consider economics of more precise process versus wider tolerances versus sorting the product.	

*As a rule of thumb, a process variation (sometimes called natural tolerance = 6σ) less than a third of tolerance is small; more than two-thirds of tolerance is large.

by the workers themselves (see Section 22, under Test of Theories of Worker-Controllable Problems).

2. Conditions change and result in violations of the criteria of self-control: e.g., a specification becomes obsolete, a gage is out of calibration, equipment deteriorates due to a reduction in preventive maintenance.

To handle these problems, production management and the work force must be determined to remove the causes by directly taking action or by having others take action. Such determination requires a strong quality ethic on the production floor. For some companies, this entails a revolution.

An important step is to determine if the production floor culture does foster quality. Examples are legion to suggest that not only is a positive culture on qualtiy lacking, but negative actions are often taken in order to achieve other objectives such as production quotas. Worse yet, such actions are hidden from management, such as in the following three ways.

1. *Not reporting the nonconforming product:* Examples include burying nonconforming paint in the ground, storing defective tires in railroad cars that are kept in transit, and disguising nonconforming parts as spare parts and shipping them with a finished vehicle. A variation is to "delay reporting" nonconforming items, i.e., report only the allowable percent of nonconforming needles in a given week and hold back any excess until a "good week" occurs.

2. *Finessing the inspector:* One form of this approach is for the worker to ignore the fact that defectives are occurring and wait until a patrol inspector discovers the situation. In another ploy, the worker purposely creates a minor defect and makes an obvious correction in order to draw attention away from another defect, e.g., roughs up a surface and smooths it over, hoping that an inspector will overlook some rivets that are out of line (possibly reducing the strength).

3. *Charging rework operations as part of basic manufacturing costs.*

To survive in a culture that stresses production quotas or other priorities, people devise ways to meet these priorities. Clearly, a culture having the symptoms described above needs significant change. Two steps are required:

1. *Acertain the culture for quality on the production floor:* Some of the conditions described can be discovered with special data collection and analysis. Also, a carefully planned attitude survey on quality for various levels of production supervision and workers can be a sobering and revealing study. See Section 9 under Summary of Quality Status.

2. *Take the steps necessary to change the culture:* The road will be lengthy and difficult. A change in culture must be led by upper management. (Often enough the supervisors and managers have known about the goings-on and done nothing, or have even set bad examples.) Before that happens, management must understand (*a*) the extent of the problem and (*b*) that the conditions of the past have changed and new conditions demand a new culture. Section 10 under Management's Role discusses the role of management in creating the proper culture.

SELF-INSPECTION

Once product has been produced, there arises the question: Does this product conform to specification? In the United States, the responsibility for making this decision has generally rested with full-time inspectors who are members of a separate Inspection Department. These inspectors measure the product and decide whether it conforms to specification.

Under the concept of self-inspection, the worker who made the product also measures the product and decides whether it conforms to specification.

Note that the worker is *not* given the responsibility for determining the disposition of any nonconforming product. Also, self-inspection does *not* involve transfer of full-time inspectors to the Production Department. It involves abolishing the jobs of full-time inspectors and having the inspection done on a part-time basis by the production workers. Provision is made for an audit (see below under Audit of Decisions).

Self-inspection has decided advantages over the traditional delegation of inspection to a separate department:

1. Production workers are made to feel more responsible for the quality of their work.
2. Feedback on performance is immediate, thereby facilitating process adjustments. Traditional inspection also has the psychological disadvantage of using an "outsider" to report the defects to a worker.
3. The costs of a separate Inspection Department can be reduced.
4. The job enlargement that takes place by adding inspection to the production activity of the worker helps to reduce the monotony and boredom that are inherent in many jobs.
5. Elimination of a specific station for inspecting all products reduces the total manufacturing cycle time.

Criteria for Self-Inspection.   Before self-inspection can be adopted, some essential criteria must be met:

1. Quality must be the number 1 priority within an organization. If this is not clear, the worker may succumb to schedule and cost pressures and classify, as acceptable, products that should be rejected.
2. Mutual confidence is necessary. Managers must have sufficient confidence in the work force to be willing to entrust to them the responsibility of deciding whether the product conforms to specification. In turn, workers must have enough confidence in the management to be willing to accept this responsibility.
3. The criteria for self-control must be met. Failure to eliminate the management-controllable causes of defects suggest that management does not view quality as a high priority, and this may bias the workers during inspections.
4. Workers must be trained to understand the specifications and perform the inspection.
5. Specifications must be unequivocally clear.
6. Workers should understand the use that will be made of their products (internally and externally) in order to grasp the importance of a conformance decision.
7. The process must be of a nature which permits assignment of clear responsibility for decision making. An easy case for application is the worker running a lathe, since there is clear responsibility for making both the product and the product-conformance decision. In contrast, the long assembly line or the

numerous steps in a chemical process make it difficult to assign clear responsibility. Application to such multistep processes is best deferred until experience is gained with simple processes.

Whittingham (1982) describes the operation of self-inspection at an electronics plant. A "keypoint card" placed at the work station shows what inspections must be made, including the frequency interval and the method of inspection. Feedback to supervisors from an audit inspection summarizes the defects missed by each worker.

Cautions to Be Observed under Self-Inspection.   Note the following:

1. Training costs can be high, particularly with high turnover. It may take months for a worker to perform confidently the inspection of a complex electronic product.
2. The time needed for inspection may significantly reduce the time for doing productive work.
3. There may be potential conflicts in interpretation of specifications between workers and auditors.
4. Union agreements may require strict job specialization.
5. Workers may feel that the added responsibility of inspection requires additional compensation (and they may be correct).
6. There must be agreement on who is to perform any reinspection of a lot if an audit sample discovers nonconformities. (A "clean-up" to go back over prior lots can involve products already shipped to the customer.)
7. Some regulators oppose such delegations to the work force.
8. The reasons for instituting self-inspection must be explained to everyone so that the change is not interpreted as lowering the priority on quality.

Sequence for Instituting Self-Inspection Concept.   If workers are to be given the product-conformance decision, it is necessary to decide whether the responsibility should be given to all workers or only to those who have demonstrated their ability to make good decisions. The latter approach is highly preferable and should proceed as follows:

1. Train the workers in how to make product-conformance decisions.
2. Set up the necessary system of product indentification and preserving the order to assure that product decisions can be traced readily back to the worker who made them.
3. Institute a trial period during which workers make conformance decisions while duplicate decision making is done by inspectors. The purpose of this duplication is to discover, through data, which workers consistently make good product-conformance decisions.
4. Issue "licenses" (for making product-conformance decisions) only to those workers who demonstrate their competence. (This is analogous to qualification for certain manufacturing skills such as welding.)
5. For the licensed workers, institute an audit of decisions (see below). For the workers who do not qualify, retain the regular inspection.
6. Based on the results of the audits, continue or suspend the licenses.
7. Periodically conduct new trials in an effort to qualify the unlicensed workers.

Audit of Decisions.   During the trial period the inspection is conducted for two purposes:

1. Product approval, lot by lot
2. Comparison of inspector results with worker results

As the comparison establishes validity of the worker's decisions, the duplicate inspections are reduced in frequency until their prime purpose is to determine whether the worker continues to make good decisions. (Hence the name "audit of decisions.") At this stage any knowledge of the product is incidental. If an audit reveals that wrong decisions were made by the workers, then the product evaluated since the last audit is suspect and must be investigated.

Results of Self-Inspection.   Castagna (1983) reports results of applying the self-inspection concept at a rework facility for military aircraft. The number of in-process nonconformities decreased 31.8 percent in 1 year.

In a coning operation of textile yarn, the traditional method of inspection often resulted in finished cones sitting for several days in the inspection department, thereby delaying any feedback to production. Under the self-inspection, the worker received immediate feedback and could more promptly get machines repaired and setups improved. Overall, the program reduced nonconformities from 8 to 3 percent. An audit inspection of the products that were classified by the workers as "good" showed that virtually all of them were correctly classified. In this company workers can also classify product as "doubtful." In one analysis, worker inspections classified 3 percent of the product as doubtful, after which an independent inspector reviewed the doubtful product and classified 2 percent as acceptable, and 1 percent as nonconforming.

Wittingham (1982) and Noonan (1984) describe self-inspection in the electronics industry, including some unusual approaches to the audit inspection. Sanders (1974) discusses the ingredients for success and the results achieved at an aircraft plant. Kolinka (1984) traces the evolution of self-inspection for a computer manufacturer.

AUDIT OF PRODUCTION QUALITY

A quality audit is an independent evaluation of various aspects of quality performance for the purpose of providing information to those in need of assurance with respect to that performance. A full discussion of quality audit is given in Section 9 generally. See also Section 8 under Quality Audits by Upper Managers.

Application to manufacturing has been extensive and includes both audit of activities (systems audits) and audit of product (product audit).

Systems Audit.   Systems audits can be conducted for any activity that can affect final product quality.

The audit (as contrasted to a broad survey) is usually made on a specific activity, such as the system for calibrating measuring equipment. The checklists presented earlier in this section for the three criteria of self-control can suggest useful specific subjects for audits. Priority should be assigned to subjects that affect fitness for use. Adherence to existing procedures is often emphasized, but systems audits often uncover situations of inadequate or nonexistent procedures.

Dedhia (1985) describes an audit system for an electronics manufacturer. The audit consists of 14 subsystems each having an audit checklist (see Figure 17.4). Routine audits are performed by quality audit personnel on a scheduled basis. For selected activities, annual audits are conducted by a team from manufacturing, quality engineering, test engineering, purchasing, and other disciplines. The system includes a numerical audit rating based on classifying each discrepancy as major or minor. A rating below 90 percent requires an immediate corrective action response. A discussion of systems audit for an assembly manufacturer is given by Zeccardi and Radigan (1976). Freund and Trulli (1982) describe a comprehensive approach that incorporates flowcharts, cause-and-effect diagrams, and detailed check sheets.

Who Performs the Audits. There are several categories of personnel to whom systems audits may be delegated:

Production Management. In this situation, the middle or upper Production managers undertake the audit of execution versus plan. Because most production activities are highly visible, skilled observers can learn much from shop tours. Generally, Production managers possess these skills and, in addition, put a high value on direct observation.

The strength of these audits is that the managers believe and respond to their own senses more vigorously than to an auditor's report. The weaknesses are that the managers lack the time and skills to be thorough auditors. They seldom get fully into the data and documentation or into other matters not evident from shop observation. The fact that they are busy people limits the completeness of the audit and even the adherence to the audit schedule. There is also a risk that they will overreact to the shop observations. Finally, they do not document their findings adequately, so that for long-range solutions the follow-up can be poor.

Inspectors. Some inspections are conducted not to measure the product but to observe the process (see, for example, the patrol beat, Section 18 under Inspection at Inspection Stations; Patrol Inspection). Such observations are themselves a review of execution versus plan. It is often feasible to extend these patrol inspections to review other aspects of execution.

The advantages of using inspectors are the economy of avoiding a separate auditor and the regularity inherent in use of patrol inspectors. The disadvantages arise from the fact that the patrol inspector is not sufficiently detached and not sufficiently "independent." Findings are less likely to come to the attention of the middle or upper supervision than those of the independent auditor who is on the scene only occasionally.

Independent Auditors. For critical work the auditing should preferably be done by those who are not a part of the Inspection Department. Usually such auditors review the practices of inspectors as well as production workers.

The independent audit tends to be more completely planned than an audit by Production management or by inspectors. In addition, the entire concept of the independent audit has the support of upper management, which receives the audit reports for review.

Special Audit Teams. Some organizations create a team of supervisory, professional, and production workers to audit the process. Wirkus (1982) describes a program in which the department supervisor, an area manufacturing engineer, a quality control engineer, workers, and inspectors form a team to perform audits. Ashby and Hines (1982) discuss a concept of auditing as applied to "quality clusters" or areas of activity on a production floor. Here the audit team includes production supervision, a statistical quality engineer, and cluster auditors.

The audit of decisions discussed previously requires a regular examination of

Audit Type

1. **Equipment / tester / tools control**
   Calibration control/schedule
   Monitoring activity
   Certification status
   Maintenance status
   Data integrity/verification
   Standards check
   Availability of tools
   Startup/shutdown procedure
   Correlation verification

2. **Operator**
   Qualification status
   Compliance with procedure
   Output (quality) verification/operator capability
   Data recording verification
   Rework verification
   Observation for conformance to procedures
   Product handling
   Workmanship

3. **Documentation**
   • Line documents (availability, readability, accessibility, document content, level)
       MPI
       PCN
   • Document adherence
   • Quality documents
       Inspection instructions
       Inspection tools
       Applicable test procedures
       Routings/flow chart/traveller
   • Maintenance documents
   • Training documents
   • Experimental procedures
   • Records/log books
   • Off-specs

Audit Type

4. **Parts / Assembly**
   Conformance to spec.
   EC level
   Handling/packaging/storage/shipping
   Data availability
   Scrap/M.E. hold/MRB parts (nonconforming parts)
   Traceability
   Inprocess product
   Finished product
   Nonconforming product control and disposition

5. **Process Control Status**
   Process control instructions/actions
   Control chart status
   Check corrective actions
   Verify manufacturing data

6. **Environment**
   Cleanliness of the work area
   Particle count verification
   Humidity recording
   Temperature recording
   General housekeeping (safety, etc.)

7. **Calibration / standards audits**
   Calibration evidence
   Overdue for calibration
   Monitor standards

8. **Chemicals / materials control**
   Shelf life labeling
   Receiving inspection status
   Handling/storage
   Shelf life
   Nonconforming chemicals/materials control and disposition
   Relationship to work instructions

Audit Type

9. **Software system**
   Software control
   Data integrity/verification

10. **Q.A. Self-Audits**
    Inspection data verification
    Housekeeping
    Inspector training/qualification

11. **Production Control Crib**
    • Finished product control
       Storage/handling
       Receiving inspection status
       EC level
    • Raw material control
       Storage/handling
       Receiving inspection status
       EC level

12. **Rework**
    • Procedures
    • Product quality
    • Product disposition

13. **System Audit**
    • General administration
    • Product development
    • Product qualification
    • Functional testing
    • Field performance
    • Personnel training

14. **MRB Audit**

FIG. 17.4 Audit checklist guidelines. *(Adapted from Dedhia, 1985, pp. 170–172.)*

product conformance along with the associated documentation. This cannot readily be done by the independent auditors who are on the scene so infrequently. Instead it is assigned to a special category of auditor created at the time of delegating conformance decisions to production workers.

Product Audit.   This form of audit provides information on the extent of product conformance to specification and fitness for use. See Section 9 under Product Audit.

TROUBLESHOOTING

Factory quality troubles exist in two different forms: chronic and sporadic.

Chronic troubles go on and on because no way has ever been found to eliminate them. For example, a factory process has for years operated at 10 percent nonconforming. No one has succeeded in reducing this level, so the factory has learned to live with it.

Sporadic troubles are the result of some sudden adverse change. For example, a process which is usually at 10 percent nonconforming suddenly goes to 25 percent. Such a change sets off a number of alarm signals which demand prompt action to restore the status quo (to go back to the usual 10 percent).

"Troubleshooting" (also "firefighting") is the process of dealing with the sporadic and restoring quality to the original level. Section 22, Quality Improvement, discusses a structured approach for dealing with chronic problems.

Responsibility for Troubleshooting.   Production personnel have quite a clear responsibility for restoring the status quo. Sometimes this responsibility is specifically written out. In other cases it is implied from the more basic responsibility of meeting the goals for quality, productivity, schedule, etc. Those goals cannot be met unless the sporadic trouble is eliminated.

To carry out this responsibility requries that Production:

Discover the cause (make the journey from symptom to cause).

Remove the cause. This action also makes the journey from cause to remedy— i.e., removing the cause will result in restoring the status quo.

Diagnosing the cause requires a problem-solving process of the kind described in Section 22 under Troubleshooting. This process focuses on *discovering what has changed.* Production personnel, by virtue of extensive presence on the factory floor, can contribute valuable theories of causes and can in addition evaluate the likely validity of theories.

While Production Department responsibility for troubleshooting is fairly clear, the ability to carry out this responsibility varies. The main variables are:

The complexity of the adverse change

The extent to which Production personnel are trained in the tools of diagnosis

A complex adverse change can require an extent of data collection and analysis which goes beyond the training and experience of Production personnel. That same complexity can also require extensive time for data collection and analysis—time which is not available to Production supervisors.

In such complex cases a team approach may be needed. The team is usually drawn from the following:

Production personnel to supply theories and authorize data collection

Technicians to carry out data collection

Diagnosticians to design the data plan and to analyze the subsequent data

"Outsiders" as the needs arise

The responsibility for creating such a team rests with Production.

The ideal approach is to train Production personnel to become self-sufficient in troubleshooting. If nonsupervisors are trained to do troubleshooting within their own work areas, the supervisors will have more time to participate on the cross-functional project teams that are typically needed for chronic troubles. The training needed is common to that needed by Production personnel for dealing with quality problems generally. The problem-solving training provided to quality circles is useful (see Section 11 under Training for Nonsupervisors).

TRAINING OF PRODUCTION PERSONNEL

The general subject of training for quality is treated in Section 11, and includes those aspects of training which relate to production.

The training required for Production supervisors and other personnel depends on the responsibilities assigned (see the discussion earlier in this section). Major areas of training are:

1. *Job skills:*   This is the minimal training. Such training must include provisions for updating, as knowledge on "special knacks" or other process information becomes available. Critical skills such as welding should have formal skills testing to certify that personnel can apply their training to make product that meet specifications. Passing these tests becomes a requirement for this job. Instances of falsification of tests have occurred, and steps must be taken to ensure valid results.

2. *Problem-solving tools:*   Depending on the responsibilities assigned to Production, training in problem solving may be needed. A notable example is the training provided to quality circles (data collection, cause-and-effect diagrams, Pareto analysis, histograms and other graphic techniques, etc.).

3. *Process control tools:*   Increasingly, production workers are receiving training in statistical control charts and other analysis techniques for routine control of a process.

4. *Importance of meeting specifications:*   It is useful periodically to reinforce the importance of meeting all specifications. In one chemical company, visits are made by workers to customer sites. Immediately after each visit, the workers hold a "reflections meeting" to discuss their observations and to decide how to get the message to the rest of the work force.

Training given in order to change the practices of personnel must unequivocally answer the question, "What do you want me to do differently?"

REFERENCES

Asby, Carl C. III and Hines, James E. (1982). "Quality Clusters, a New Concept in Quality Control." *Proceedings, Quality in Electronics Conference.* ASQC, Milwaukee, pp. 89–94.

Blumenthal, Irvin R. (1978). "Fabrication Information System." *ASQC Technical Conference Transactions,* Milwaukee, pp. 661–668.

Burgess, John A. (1982). "Measuring In-Process Quality Performance," *ASQC Quality Congress Transactions,* Milwaukee, pp. 70–76.

Carlisle, Rodney (1981). "Shirt-Sleeve Quality." *Quality,* March, pp. 48–49.

Castagna, Edward (1983). "Well Done." *Quality,* March, pp. 50–51.

Dedhia, Navin S. (1985). "Process Audit System Effectiveness." *European Organization for Quality Control Annual Conference, 1985.* EOQC, Berne, Switzerland, pp. 159–173.

Denissoff, Basile A. (1980). "Process Control Management." *Quality Process,* June, pp. 14–16.

Emmons, Sidney L. (1977). "Auditing for Profit and Productivity." *ASQC Technical Conference Transactions,* Milwaukee, pp. 206–212.

Fisher, James R. (1983). "Computer Assisted Net Weight Control." *Quality Progress,* June, pp. 22–25.

Freund, R. A. and Trulli, H. B. (1982). "Quality Assurance Review Technique." *Quality Assurance,* vol. 8, no. 1, March, pp. 17–22.

Fukuda, Ryuji (1981). "Quality Control Factor in Methods Engineering." *ASQC Quality Congress Transactions,* Milwaukee, pp. 268–273.

Howell, Vincent W. (1981). "Quality Control Factor in Methods Engineering." *ASQC Quality Congress Transactions,* Milwaukee, pp. 268–273.

Kassarda, John B. (1980). " Shop Floor Control Must Be Able to Provide Real-Time Status and Control." *Industrial Engineering,* pp. 74–78, 96.

Kolinka, Edward (1984). "Zero Inspectors—Is It Attainable?" *ASQC Quality Congress Transactions,* Milwaukee, pp. 152–156.

May, E. (1978). "Operator Participation in Quality Control, Also Called Self-Control." *Proceedings, International Convention on QC Circle,* Tokyo, pp. A4-17 through A4-22.

Noonan, Martin (1984). "Operator Quality Control." *EOQC Quality,* November, pp. 7–11.

Parker, H. V. (1981). "A Paper Mill Solves a Quality Control Problem with Process Control Data." *Quality Progress,* March, pp. 18–22.

Sahrmann, Herman (1979). "Set-Up Assurance through Time Series Analysis." *Journal of Quality Technology,* July, pp. 105–115.

Sanders, George (1974). "Total Process Control." *Quality Progress,* January, pp. 22–25.

Schonberger, Richard J. (1982). "Production Workers Bear Major Quality Responsibility in Japanese Industry." *Industrial Engineering,* December, pp. 34–40.

Stone, Herbert D. and Guith, T. A. (1984). "Buick City: Strategy for Quality and Productivity." *Quality Progress,* April, pp. 34–38.

Whittingham, P. R. B. (1982). "Practical Operator Control." *Quality Assurance,* December, pp. 99–102.

Wirkus, Stephen R. (1982). "Quality Awareness—Control Where It Counts." *ASQC Quality Congress Transactions,* Milwaukee, pp. 225–229.

Zeccardi, J. J. and Radigan, R. A. (1976). "Auditing Systems which Affect Product Quality: Increasing the Management Visibility of Quality Systems Performance." *ASQC Technical Conference Transactions,* Milwaukee, pp. 323–329.

SECTION 18
INSPECTION AND TEST[1]

Joseph J. Zeccardi

INTRODUCTION **18.4**

INSPECTION AND TEST
PLANNING **18.7**

Who Plans? 18.7

The Flow Diagram 18.8

Inspection Stations 18.8

List of Characteristics . . . 18.9

Interpretation of the
Specification 18.9

Written Inspection
Instructions 18.10

INSPECTION MANUAL **18.15**

Inspection Procedures
Manual 18.17

Product and Process
Inspection Manuals . . . 18.17

THREE DECISIONS **18.17**

The Conformance Decision 18.17

The Fitness-for-Use
Decision 18.18

The Communication
Decision 18.18

PRODUCT CONFORMANCE . . .**18.19**

The Nature of Product . 18.19

The Nature of Lots of
Product 18.20

Product Conformance
Criteria 18.20

HOW MUCH INSPECTION?
EFFECT OF PRIOR KNOWLEDGE **18.21**

Prior Conformance
Decisions on the Same
Lot 18.21

Prior Knowledge of the
Process 18.24

Product Fluidity **18.24**

Prior Successful Usage . . . 18.24

Cost Impact 18.24

Product Inspection 18.24

Securing the Prior
Knowledge 18.24

HOW MUCH INSPECTION? THE
ALTERNATIVES **18.25**

No Inspection 18.25

Small Samples 18.25

Large Samples 18.25

ONE HUNDRED PERCENT
INSPECTION **18.25**

OTHER TYPES OF
CONFORMANCE INSPECTION . .**18.26**

Simulation 18.26

Management by Exception 18.26

---

[1]In the Third Edition, the section on Inspection and Test was prepared by J. M. Juran and Hardy M. Cook, Jr.; the section on Measurement was prepared by J. M. Juran.

Automated Inspection . . . 18.26
Computer-Aided Inspection 18.28

**INSPECTION AT INSPECTION
STATIONS** **18.28**
Incoming Inspection . . . 18.28
Process Inspection 18.29
Setup Inspection 18.29
Patrol Inspection 18.29
Tollgate Inspection 18.31
Finished Goods Inspection 18.31

**JUDGMENT OF FITNESS FOR
USE** **18.31**
Methods of Decision
Making on Fitness for
Use 18.32
Material Review Board . . 18.32
Multiple Delegation 18.33
Organized Material
Reviews 18.34
Steps Preceding Review . . 18.34
Inputs for Fitness-for-Use
Decisions 18.34
Effect of Multiple Product
Usage 18.35
Disposition of Unfit
Product 18.36
Physical Control of the
Product 18.37

QUALITY STANDARDS . . . **18.38**
Seriousness Classification . 18.38
Number of Levels or Strata 18.40
Definitions for the Classes 18.40
Classifying the Defects . . 18.41
Classification of
Characteristics 18.44
Who Classifies? 18.45

SENSORY QUALITIES **18.45**
Discovery of Sensory
Characteristics Required
for Fitness for Use . . . 18.46
Consumer Likes and
Dislikes 18.46
Consumer Preference
Testing 18.48

Consumer Sensitivity
Testing 18.48
Visual Quality
Characteristics 18.49
Visual Inspection Standards 18.50
Standardizing the
Conditions of Inspection 18.50
Design of Products to
Achieve Sensory Effects . 18.51
Providing Standards for
Sensory Qualities . . . 18.51
Judgment of Conformance
to Sensory Standards . . 18.52
Panels for Sensory Testing 18.52
Sensory Tests: Design and
Analysis 18.54
Creating New Instruments
to Measure Sensory
Qualities 18.56

**MEASUREMENT—AN
INTRODUCTION** **18.57**

UNITS OF MEASURE **18.58**
Metrication 18.58
SI System 18.58
Nonmeasurable
Characteristics 18.60

MEASUREMENT STANDARDS . **18.60**
Primary Reference
Standards 18.60
Hierarchy of Standards . . 18.61

ERROR OF MEASUREMENT . . **18.63**
Accuracy 18.63
Precision 18.64
Sources of Error 18.65
Effect of Measurement
Error on Acceptance
Decisions 18.68
Programs to Reduce Error 18.68

MEASUREMENT TECHNOLOGY **18.69**
Measurement of Length . . 18.69
Obsolescence of Fixed-
Limit Gages 18.69

New Technological
  Principles 18.70
Electronic Measurement . . 18.70
Pneumatic Measurement . 18.70
Optical Measurement . . . 18.70
Nondestructive Testing . . 18.71
Emergence of New
  Functions Associated
  with Measurement . . . 18.71
CALIBRATION CONTROL **18.76**
New-Equipment Control . . 18.76
Inventory and Classification 18.78
Calibration Schedules . . . 18.78
Adherence to Schedule . . 18.79
Calibration Practice 18.80
Record and Analysis of
  Results 18.80
Organization for
  Calibration Control . . . 18.81
HUMAN FACTORS IN
INSPECTION **18.81**
Machine Vision 18.81
Vigilance Problem 18.82
Drift Problem 18.84
INSPECTOR ERRORS **18.84**
Technique Errors 18.84
Remedies for Technique
  Errors 18.85
Inadvertent Inspector
  Errors 18.86
Remedies for Inadvertent
  Inspector Errors 18.87
Procedural Errors 18.89
Conscious Inspector Errors:
  Management-Initiated . . 18.90
Conscious Inspector Errors:
  Inspector-Initiated . . . 18.91
Measures of Inspector
  Accuracy 18.94
FEEDBACK OF INSPECTION
DATA **18.97**
Feedback to Production . . 18.97
Data Feedback to
  Management 18.98

Feedback to Inspection . . 18.98
Data "Feedforward" to the
  Market 18.98
Data System 18.98
ORGANIZATION FOR
INSPECTION AND TEST **18.98**
Emergence of the Inspector 18.99
Emergence of the Central
  Inspection Department 18.100
Inspection Department
  Structure 18.100
Purchased Material
  Inspection 18.100
Process Inspection . . . 18.101
Finished Goods Inspection 18.101
Evolution of Inspection
  Support Activities . . . 18.103
Noninspection Operations
  Performed by Inspectors 18.104
INSPECTION DEPARTMENT
MANAGEMENT **18.105**
Laboratory Management . 18.105
Inspection by Production
  Departments 18.106
INSPECTION PERSONNEL
MANAGEMENT **18.107**
PRODUCTIVITY IN INSPECTION
AND TEST **18.108**
Loss Productivity Factors 18.108
Measuring Inspectors'
  Productivity 18.108
BUDGETING FOR INSPECTION **18.108**
Inspection Cost Reduction 18.108
Defect Prevention . . . 18.109
Census of Inspection Costs 18.109
Contract Inspection . . . 18.109
Industrial Engineering
  Studies 18.110
Quality Engineering Studies 18.110
Interdepartmental Studies 18.111
The Budgetary Process . 18.111
SUMMARY **18.114**
REFERENCES **18.115**

INTRODUCTION

The word "inspection" has so many meanings that precise definition must precede any critical discussion. As used in this handbook, "inspection" always involves evaluating the quality of some characteristic in relation to a standard. This evaluation may be described as the "inspection act" and consists of the following actions applied to each quality characteristic (Juran, 1945, p. 23):

1. Interpretation of the specification
2. Measurement of the quality of the characteristic
3. Comparing 1 with 2
4. Judging conformance
5. Disposing of conforming cases
6. Disposing of nonconforming cases
7. Recording the data obtained

Every key word in the foregoing is itself subject to much variation. The word "specification" is used in the generic sense as the *standard* for the characteristic. It may consist of a written description, a drawing, a photograph, a physical sample, an oral instruction, a hazy memory.

The term "measurement" is used in the generic sense of *evaluation,* and it has its own dialect:

When the measurement is done	*The word commonly used to describe it is*
By the unaided human being	Inspection (this is a second meaning for the word used in the title of this section)
With the aid of mechanical measuring instruments	Gaging or calipering
With the aid of electronic measuring instruments	Testing
With the aid of chemical or metallurgical measuring instruments	Testing or assaying

The main purpose of inspection is to determine whether products conform to specification. This purpose is often called "acceptance inspection," or "product acceptance." However, there are other purposes as well, the more important being listed in Table 18.1. The present section is concerned primarily with acceptance inspection, but it deals also with those purposes of inspection which are closely allied to acceptance inspection, e.g., rating of accuracy of inspectors.

The persons engaged full time in inspection work commonly carry the title "inspector." (The title is sometimes used to describe persons not concerned with industrial products, processes, or services, e.g., safety inspectors, health inspectors, etc. These categories are outside the scope of this section.) Other titles include "tester, " "gager," "chemist," "metallurgist," "technician." Persons engaged only part time in inspection commonly carry a job title which reflects their major activities, e.g., "machine operator," "adjuster," etc.

Since the 1960s there has been a worldwide trend toward returning some of the responsibility for product acceptance to production operators. Details of this

TABLE 18.1 The Purposes of Inspection* (*Continued*)

Purpose	Usually called	Distinguishing features
a. To distinguish good lots from bad lots.	Acceptance sampling or sampling inspection; also called:	Prime purpose is to classify lots of product as to whether they are acceptable or nonacceptable. Results of the sampling are used to make this classification. Data from sampling usually made available to producing department.
	Supplier (or incoming) inspection	If done by purchaser on material bought from another company.
	Process inspection	If done between departments of the same company.
	Final inspection	If done by seller prior to shipment of finished goods to the customer.
b. To distinguish good pieces from bad pieces.	Detail inspection, 100% inspection, or sorting; also called:	Prime purpose is to sort the product between good pieces and bad. Any data are incidental but are usually made available to producer.
	Classification	If process is inadequate to meet tolerances.
		If process is adequate, but shop difficulties have created defects "needlessly."
c. To determine if the process is changing. See Section 24.	Control sampling	Prime purpose is to see if the process is changing. Usually done through Shewhart control charts which compare averages of samples to statistical limit lines. Detects the entrance of significant causes of variation. Any classification of product is incidental.
d. To determine if the process is approaching the specification limits. See Section 24.	PRE-Control	Prime purpose is to see if the trend of change within the process is such that there is danger of producing defective

18.5

TABLE 18.1 The Purposes of Inspection* (*Continued*)

Purpose	Usually called	Distinguishing features
		product. Usually done through charts which compare measurements on individual units of product to narrowed specification limits.
e. To rate the quality of product. See Section 9, under Product Auditing.	Product auditing or quality rating	Prime purpose is to "photograph" the quality of product. Usually the seriousness of defects is recognized by assigning demerits or weights depending on the severity of defects. Results are usually charted as demerits per unit of product.
f. To rate the accuracy of inspectors. See in this section, under Measure of Inspector Accuracy.	Accuracy inspection, or overinspection, or accuracy rating, or check inspection	Prime purpose is to measure the effectiveness of inspectors in finding defects. Comparison is made between (1) defects found by the inspector and, (2) defects which should have been found by the inspector. The ratio of (1) to (2) is the accuracy of the inspector.
g. To measure the precision of the measuring instrument. See in this section, under Error of Measurement.		Prime purpose is to measure the ability of the instrument to reproduce its own readings under like conditions. Usually involves repeat checks by the same instrument on the same unit of product. May involve checks by more than one instrument on the same unit of product.
h. To secure product-design information.	Qualification testing	Prime purpose is to judge the service capability of the product. Sometimes involves tests of increased severity.
i. To measure process capability. See Section 16, under Process Capability Measurement.	Process-capability measurement	Quantifies inherent variation of process.

*Inspection includes, in all instances (1) interpretation of the specification, (2) measurement of the product, and (3) comparison of (1) with (2). Inspection also includes additional elements depending on the purpose (as noted).

18.6

are discussed in Section 11, under Self-Inspection. See also Sears (1982) for a discussion on how this trend will provide the inspection function the opportunity to improve its effectiveness through more specialized testing.

Appendix III, Selected Quality Standards, Specifications, and Related Documents, includes documents on inspection and test methods.

INSPECTION AND TEST PLANNING

As products have grown complex and the job of making them has been divided among many departments, the job of inspection has also become complex and divided. Most inspection is now done by inspectors who lack full understanding of fitness for use. For this more complex work, it has been found necessary to engage in formal inspection planning, i.e., preparing a written plan of what to inspect for and how to do it (see also American Society for Quality Control and American National Standards Institute, 1984).

The approach to inspection planning follows closely the principles of quality planning as set out in Section 6. Application of these principles to the inspection job has been extensively studied, and good tools are available to facilitate inspection planning.

Who Plans? It depends on the work situation. Table 18.2 lists some usual inspection and test activities and the identity of the usual planner. The unifying concept within Table 18.2 is that inspection planning can be done by anyone who understands the fitness for use of the product being inspected.

Where planning is done by a staff planner, it is usual to require that his or her proposal be accepted by the inspection supervision before the plan becomes effective. The staff planner also is assigned a scope of responsibility to work within. This scope determines which aspects of inspection planning are to be covered: inspecton instructions, instrumentation, cost estimates, space and workplace design, documentation, etc. In large organizations the planning is sometimes divided among specialists rather than being assigned by project.

TABLE 18.2 Who Does the Inspection Planning?

Products requiring inspection and test planning	Inspector	Inspection supervisor	Quality control staff planner
		Usual planner	
Components completed within single department, small series production	X		
Components completed within single department, large series production		X	
Simple components and services, purchased or in-house (casting, plating)		X	
Complex units, small series production (machine tools)		X	
Components produced by progression through multiple departments			X
Subsystem test, interdependent units			X

The Flow Diagram. The more complex the product, the greater the need to prepare a flow diagram showing the various materials, components, and processes which collectively or sequentially turn out the final product. Figure 6.5 (in Section 6) is an example of a flow diagram prepared to aid inspection planning.

To prepare the flow diagram, the planner visits the various locations, interviews the key people, observes the activities, and records findings. The planner simplifies the picture by good use of symbols. The most usual symbols are:

○ OPERATION	ᴰ DELAY
⇨ TRANSPORTATION	▽ STORAGE
☐ INSPECTION	◑ COMBINED ACTIVITY

In addition, the planner prepares proposals for improvement, sends copies of the diagram to all concerned, and then is ready to convene them for discussion of the diagram and the proposals.

Inspection Stations. Selection of inspection stations follows closely the criteria for selection of control stations set out in Section 6. Applied to inspection, the stations are usually placed:

At movement of goods between companies, usually called "supplier inspection"

Before starting a costly or irreversible operation, usually called "setup inspection"

At movement of goods between departments, usually called "process inspection"

Upon completion of the product, usually called "finished goods inspection"

For complex products, such as missile systems, acceptance may require tests of mechanical compatibility, electrical mating, vehicle performance under specified environmental conditions, and final configuration. These are usually called "systems tests."

These general rules do not decide all questions of inspection stations. Complex supplier relations may require an inspection station at the supplier's plant. Some process operations may require a "station" in which the inspector patrols a large area. Other process operations may be sufficiently well in hand so that no inspection stations are used between departments; instead, there is a station after completion of all operations. In assembly lines, inspection stations may be located on the line as well as at the end of the line. (See Section 30, under In-Line Assembly Inspection.) In still other situations, there may be an added station after packing or at the customer's premises.

For each inspection station, instruct the inspector what to inspect for and how to do it:

Just what the mission of that inspection station is, i.e., which qualities to check

How to determine whether a unit of product conforms to standard or not

How to determine whether a lot of product is acceptable or not ("lot criteria")

What to do with conforming and nonconforming products

What records to make

While these categories of instruction are quite similar from one job to another, the degree of detail varies enormously.

In allocating the inspection work among the various inspection stations, the planner should be alert to the presence of "self-policing" operations. Some oversize parts will not enter tools or fixtures for further processing, or cannot be assembled. Some parts are subjected to greater stresses during manufacture than during usage. Some electrical circuit tests identify deficient components. Oil-pressure tests identify some undersize parts. [Refer to Trippi (1975) for a discussion on the optimal allocation of inspection resources; Ballou and Pazer (1982) for the optimal placement of inspection stations; and Eppen and Hurst (1974) for the optimal location of inspection stations in multistage production processes.]

List of Characteristics.   For each inspection station, the planner lists the quality characteristics to be checked. To determine these, the planner considers the various sources of pertinent product information:

The needs of fitness for use

The product and process specifications as published by the engineers

The customer's order, which references the product specification but may call for modifications

The pertinent industry standards, shop standards, and other general use sources

The presence of such multiple sources of information poses a question which should be faced squarely: Should the job of finding, interpreting, and reconciling these sources be left to the inspector, or should the planner do it? The answer will depend on the situation, but it should be clear.

Interpretation of the Specification.   The specification information is seldom sufficient for the inspector to meet the realities to be faced. The inspection planner can help to bridge this gap in several ways:

1. *Clear up the meaning of the words used:*   Terminology for describing sensory qualities is often confusing. In one company, the term "beauty defects" was used generally to describe blemishes on the product. Some of these blemishes (scratches in the focal plane of an optical instrument) made the product unfit for service. Other blemishes, though nonfunctional, could be seen by the customers and were objectionable for esthetic reasons. Still other nonfunctional blemishes could be seen by the company inspectors but not by consumers. However, because the multiple meanings of the term "beauty defect" had not been clarified, the inspectors rejected all blemishes. Data analysis showed that most of the blemishes were both nonfunctional and nonoffensive to customers. Hence, new terminology was created to make the distinctions needed to describe the effect of blemishes. The clarification of terminology improved yields and opened the way to improvement in manufacturing processes as well. [Based on the consulting experience of J. M. Juran. For some added examples, see Juran (1952).]

2. *Provide supplemental information:*   Make it available on matters for which the specification is vague or silent, e.g., workmanship. Usually this can be done for entire commodity or component classes, with minimum individual analysis. The greatest needs for supplemental standards arise in new and rapidly changing technology; in such cases it is common to find that vague standards are provided to the inspectors. Vague standards create confusion among departments as well as among companies. Refer to Miller (1975) for a discussion on specifying test methods and specifications.

3. *Classify the characteristics for seriousness:* This will help place the emphasis on the most important features of the product. (See Seriousness Classification, later in this section.) In the case of process characteristics, make use of the Concept of Dominance, as discussed in Section 16.

4. *Provide samples, photographs, or other reference aids:* This will help explain the meaning of the specification. The greatest single need is for visual standards (see below).

5. *Review clarity of specifications in general:* Periodically, the inspection planners should take time out from product-by-product planning to review with the specification writers the recurring, chronic problems of interpretation. Such reviews have historically been the means for making major strides in clarifying specifications, e.g., serious classification of characteristics; quantifying widely used characteristics such as torque required to turn knobs; standardization of surface finishes; sample reference file, etc.

Written Inspection Instructions. The final results of inspection planning are reduced to writing in one of several ways:

Inspection and Test Procedure. This is a tailor-made plan for a specific component or product type. It always lists the characteristics to be checked, the method of check (e.g., visual, gage, etc.), and the instruments to be used. It may, in addition, include the seriousness classification of characteristics; tolerances and other piece criteria; list of applicable standards; sequence of inspection operations; frequency of inspection; sample size, allowable number of defects, and other lot criteria; and inspection stamps to be applied.

Inspection and test procedures are very widely used in industry. In companies making complex systems or undergoing frequent design changes, these procedures become very numerous and consume extensive staff manpower to prepare them.

For some simple examples of inspection and test procedures, see Figure 13.11 and Table 29.1, in Sections 13 and 29, respectively.

Patrol Beat. For many types of process inspection, the inspection stations require less than the full time of an inspector—often much less. A usual practice is to collect such stations into a "patrol beat" so designed that it will occupy the full time of one person. Table 18.3 is an example of such a patrol beat.

Patrol beats usually involve multiple production and inspection departmental areas. In addition, the inspection findings are reported to several departments for information and action, e.g., Production, Inspection, Quality Control.

In consequence, the planner should assure that these and other departments affected participate in the design of the patrol beat.

"Work sampling" is a useful concept in patrol inspection. Under this concept, the inspectors make *random* visits to the inspection stations. The resulting data are analyzed and become the basis for supervisory action. [Refer to Cooper (1977) for further discussion.]

Finished Goods Acceptance Procedure. There are actually a number of levels of "finished goods": materials, parts, components, subassemblies, assembled units, subsystems, systems. Each of these can be a completed product to some company or department, and thereby "finished goods" acceptance is performed at all these levels. System tests are most elaborate, not merely because of the problems of mating subsystems but because of the many complex environmental tests needed for modern apparatus.

The acceptance procedure should certainly provide inspection for new defects created by the progression of the product into higher levels of assembly and finishing operations. In addition, acceptance testing may be designed to provide redundancy against failure to detect defects missed at earlier stages of progression.

Much of the previous and current inspection literature uses the term "defect" to mean a deviation from the specification of a particular quality characteristic. Clearly a deviation from a specification does not automatically mean a product is unfit for use (see later in this section under Three Decisions). Thus, some recent terminology has used the term "nonconforming" to describe a deviation from a specification. For simplicity, the terms "defect" and "defective" will be used in this section.

The planner should be especially alert to discover duplications between what is done at final inspection and elsewhere. When field troubles show up as a result of ineffective controls prior to final inspection, field engineers and higher management all may be indifferent to the niceties of inspection stations and may urge multiple checks as a temporary measure. These bits of work can take firm root, accumulate, and endure beyond the reasons which gave them birth. The planner is in a good position to discover such out-of-date duplications and to root them out.

In conveyor assembly and test lines, the planning is usually for an entire inspection and test *team*. Sometimes the team is housed in a separate test area, the product being conveyed in and out. In other cases, the team is largely stationed on the main assembly line, the inspection stations being located amid production stations.

Planning of such team activities requires close collaboration among the industrial neighbors involved in the common work flow. It also requires a balancing of the work load among the team members through ingenious design of test equipment, handling equipment, and work assignments.

Nonproduction Operations. The planner should be alert to the need for locating inspection stations at such operations as material handling, storage, packing, and shipping. The fact that the departments doing these operations are not a part of production is of no consequence if product quality is affected.

Aspects which may require inspection planning include:

Internal handling: Use of correct containers and other handling facilities; product protection against corrosion, contamination, etc.

Internal storage: Adequate identity and traceability

Packing: Product identification, lot numbers, traceability; protection against adverse environments; protection against damage due to handling, shipping and unpacking; presence of incidental small parts and information circulars

Shipping: Care in loading; special markings required by customers

Once the planner has prepared the procedure, the interested departmental supervisors can be convened to reach agreement on who is to carry out that part of the inspection plan.

Inspection Data Planning. The planner also determines the data-recording needs for each inspection station. In many cases, the standard inspection report forms will meet the recording needs. For finished products, a special test document is usually provided. In addition, the planner makes provision for any special recording needed for frequency distribution, control charts, certification, traceability, etc. (See also Feedback of Inspection Data, below.)

TABLE 18.3 Patrol Beat

No.	Test	Sampling		Testing	How results are used
		Where	Frequency	Where	
		Acid manufacturing process			
1	% SO$_2$ gas test TAPPI 603 M-45	From gas line off coolers	Once every two hours	Acid plant	This test is used for checking the automatic Leeds and Northrup SO$_2$ recorders.
2	Temperature of gas, strong tower and weak tower M & O method		Once per hour	Acid plant	The acid maker controls the temperature of the gas, the strong tower, and the weak tower to regulate the speed of the gas absorption in the acid-making process.

3	Acid test, total, free, and combined SO_2 TAPPI 640 M-45	From strong and weak towers	Once per hour	Acid plant	This test tells the acid maker how much lime rock to use. The amount of water and gas going to the towers is adjusted with this information.
4	Baumé on acid in strong tower and acid in weak tower M & O method	From strong tower and weak tower	Once per hour	Acid plant	The acid maker controls the strength of his acid in the towers with these test results. They tell the concentration of the acid.
		Digester cooking process			
5	Chip moisture M & O method	Sample taken in chip bin	Once per cook	Chip room	The cook adjusts the volume of the chips put in the digesters with this information.

Source: Carter, C. W. (1958). "Audit Testing," Industrial Quality Control, March, pp. 8–11.

Extent of Planning.   The concept of separating inspection planning from execution has great value if properly applied. If planning is underapplied, there is increased risk of catastrophic product failure. If overapplied, the result is excess cost and much internal friction. Striking a sound balance requires periodic reappraisal of the major forces in contention as well as analysis of the conventional alarm signals, e.g., rising staff costs, abrasion between departments. In addition, the changing job situations influence the extent of formal planning needed, notably (1) the education, experience, and training of the work force; (2) the stability of the processes; and (3) the severity of the product requirements.

Recognition of Profound Changes.   Planners should be on the alert to identify revolutionary changes in quality criteria and to provide correspondingly revolutionary procedures dealing with these changes. To cite several examples:

1. Assembly of nuclear reactors and space vehicles requires a level of care far beyond that exercised in conventional assembly. The Enrico Fermi reactor at Lagoona Beach, MI, was badly damaged in October 1966, evidently because of a foreign object blocking the flow of sodium coolant. Pumps in nuclear reactors have been badly damaged by a loose nut being pumped through the system. Complex missiles have failed in their mission because of comparatively simple defects on mechanical components. In such situations the penalties for undetected defects rise so high that elaborate countdowns and checkouts must be instituted.

2. When the U.S. Navy undertook procurement of materials and components to build nuclear submarines, it encountered a widespread failure to adhere to specifications and sharply criticized the contractors for the nonconformances. Actually, the contractors were doing what they had always done—shipping nonconforming products which experience had shown to be fit for use. The big change was that the new species of submarines required rigid compliance with specifications which had been unrealistic in respect to previous applications. In addition, there was a clash between two cultures: (*a*) the contractors, who took too long to discover that loose enforcement had no place in the nuclear submarine program, and (*b*) a new breed of Navy engineers, who were unaware that loose enforcement had long been used to neutralize the effect of unrealistic specifications. [See also Juran (1969) and Ramaswamy (1981).]

3. Soon after the Motor Vehicle Safety Act of 1966 became law, the government regulators found that a significant number of vehicle components failed to comply to standards which "industry itself" (i.e., committees of industry engineers) had set before there was legislation on the subject. Here the two cultures involved (industry regulation and government regulation) represented different levels of enforcement, the one based on fitness for use and the other based on the concept that each instance of nonconformance now constituted a "federal case."

These cases of "massive change" can be multiplied widely. Failure to recognize their existence sets the stage for a shocking, expensive confrontation which damages many innocent people as well as the guilty (see also Paul, 1982).

Errorproofing.   The planner faces two responsibilities related to inspection error: (1) avoiding built-in sources of error and (2) providing positive means of foolproofing the inspection against error. See, for a detailed discussion, Inadvertent Inspector Errors, under Inspector Errors, below.

Overplanning.   In some companies, the writing of inspection plans is extensively done. New customer orders, new product designs, new process changes, new regulations, etc., are all occasions for scrutiny by the quality engineers, who issue inspection plans accordingly. As this goes to extremes, the cost of planning rises, and the excess formality increases the training time for inspectors, the attention to trivia, the documentation, and the control effort generally. Error rates tend to increase, with adverse effects on inspection costs and inspector morale.

Dealing with excess planning costs takes several forms. One is to do the planning by computer or by other means of mechanizing much of what the engineers otherwise do manually.

A second approach is to minimize the amount of tailor-made planning by extending the use of inspection and test manuals which have broad application. See Inspection Manual, below.

A third approach is to delegate some of the planning itself to the inspection supervisors and the inspectors. To do this usually requires preparation of a manual on inspection planning plus training the inspection force to do the planning for all except the vital few characteristics, which are reserved for the staff planners.

Still another device is to agree, case by case, on the amount of detailed planning needed.

Human, Machine, and System.   A major decision in all planning is the extent to which tasks will be assigned to people versus machines, and the related decision regarding delegation of tasks to people versus systems.

Machines are superior for doing deeds which can be clearly defined and which require exacting attention to repetitive detail. (Contrary to popular belief, machines cannot think for humans; rather, humans must do the thinking for the machines. Thereafter, the machines follow the prescribed programs.)

Table 18.4 is a list contrasting intellectual activities, and proposes a division between person and machine as applied to inspection and test. (See also Thompson and Reynolds, 1964.)

The study of the interrelationship of people, machines, and system masquerades under a variety of names: human factors; biomechanics; human engineering; ergonomics; industrial psychology. Industrial managers, including quality managers, are commonly amateurs in the understanding of human capacities and especially human behavior. The behavioral scientists are the "professionals," but the subject is as yet hardly a science. In addition, communication between the practicing managers and the behavioral scientists is severely limited by differences in dialect and, especially, cultural background.

INSPECTION MANUAL

This manual elaborates the work of the Inspection Department and includes much information of general interest to all company departments with respect to inspection practice. (The inspection manual is a part of the overall quality manual. See Section 6.) It consists of:

1. A manual of inspection procedures common to all products and processes
2. Supplemental manuals for specific products and processes

TABLE 18.4   Assignment to Machines versus People

Lower intellectual activities	Higher intellectual activities
1. Things that can be expressed exactly.	Things that cannot be expressed exactly.
2. Decisions that can be made in advance.	Decisions that cannot be made in advance.
3. Arithmetic, algebraic, and chesslike symbolic logic.	Pattern recognition, judgment, creativity, foresight, leadership, and such thinking.
4. Highly repetitive and, therefore, menial.	Random, having many degrees of freedom, never exactly the same.
5. Can be reduced to logic and, therefore, programmed exactly into a machine.	Cannot be programmed exactly but can use heuristic approximations as an aid.
6. Those a small machine can handle completely, faster, and more positively.	A machine cannot handle completely and it becomes excessively large and uneconomical in attempting to do so.
7. Design and programming require a high level of intelligence but, once done, the mental activity need not be repeated.	This problem is never exactly the same and it must be reconsidered, that is, rethought out for each new decision.
8. Involves decisions as to what is right or wrong. The person guesses and the machine monitors to prevent him or her from making a mistake. It does this positively enough for use in safety systems.	People use the display which is driven by the machine and possibly a separate computer to assist them in making the choice type of decisions as to what is best, using the most advanced mathematical techniques.
9. Requires a high degree of orderliness.	Takes care of matters which cannot be arranged into any sort of orderly procedures.
10. Includes the decisions which must be made rapidly by the machine in periods of congestions and in emergencies.	Involves situations that develop more slowly, that will, sooner or later, require a considered decision.

Inspection Procedures Manual.   The contents of this manual are quite similar from one company to another and consist typically of:

The statement of legitimacy and purpose, approved by the responsible manager.

The table of contents of the manual.

The organization section, including inspection organization charts, job descriptions, and statements of responsibilities.

The general concept of inspection as used in the company.

The plan for seriousness classification of defects. (The actual classifications of defects are in the supplemental product manuals.)

The standard plans for sampling inspection: bulk sampling, tables for random sampling, continuous sampling, narrow-limit sampling.

The standard plans for use of control charts.

Supplier inspection procedures.

In-process inspection procedures.

Finished goods inspection procedures.

Measurement control procedures, including the schedule of checking intervals for general-use equipment.

Copies of all the inspection forms used and instructions for data recording and documentation.

Product identification procedure.

Procedure for issuance and control of inspection stamps.

Feedback of data to Production; procedure for corrective action.

Procedure for dealing with nonconforming material.

Index and glossary.

Product and Process Inspection Manuals.   These specialized supplemental manuals, though dealing with a variety of products, are organized under similar outlines, typically:

The materials section, which includes material specification

The process section which includes:

   Process specifications

   Formulation control criteria

   Patrol beats and associated criteria

The product section, which includes:

   Product specifications and associated technical data

   Product samples where feasible, e.g., textile swatches, color samples

   Lists of defects, classified for seriousness

   Sample sizes, frequencies, AQLs, and acceptance criteria

The test section, which includes test specifications—both internal and industrial standards

THREE DECISIONS

A major purpose of inspection is to determine the disposition of a product based on its quality. This disposition involves three cardinal decisions (Juran and Gryna, 1980):

Conformance decision	To judge whether the product conforms to specification
Fitness-for-use decision	To decide whether nonconforming product is fit for use
Communication decision	To decide what to communicate to outsiders and insiders

The Conformance Decision.   Except in small companies, the number of conformance decisions made per year is simply huge. There is no possibility for the supervisory body to become involved in the details of so many decisions. Hence the work is so organized that the inspectors or production workers can make these decisions. To this end they are trained to understand the products, the standards, and the instruments. Once trained, they are given the job of making the inspections and of judging conformance. (In many cases the delegation is to automated instruments.)

Associated with the conformance decision is the disposition of conforming product; the inspector is authorized to identify the product ("stamp it up") as an acceptable product. This identification then serves to inform the packers, shippers, etc., that the product should proceed to its next destination (further processing, storeroom, customer). Strictly speaking, this decision to "ship" is made not by the inspectors but by the management. With some exceptions, a product that conforms to specification is also fit for use. Hence the company procedures (which are established by the managers) provide that conforming products should be shipped as a regular practice.

The Fitness-for-Use Decision.   In the case of nonconforming products, a new question arises: Is this nonconforming product fit for use or unfit? In some cases the answer is obvious—the nonconformance is so severe as to make the product clearly unfit. Hence it is scrapped or, if economically repairable, brought to a state of conformance. However, in many cases the answer as to fitness for use is not obvious. In such cases, if enough is at stake, a study is made to determine fitness for use. This study involves securing inputs such as those shown in Table 18.5.

Once all the information has been collected and analyzed, the fitness-for-use decision can be made. If the amount at stake is small, this decision will be delegated to a staff specialist, to the quality manager, or to some continuing decision-making committee such as a Material Review Board. If the amount at stake is large, the decision will usually be made by a team of upper managers.

The Communication Decision.   Inspection serves not only to make decisions on the product, but also to generate data which provide essential information for a wide variety of purposes, such as those listed in Table 18.1. The conformance and fitness-for-use decisions likewise are a source of essential information, although some of this is not well communicated.

Data on nonconforming products are usually communicated to the producing departments to aid them in preventing a recurrence. In more elaborate data collection systems there may be periodic summaries to identify "repeaters" or "top 10," which then become the subject of special studies.

TABLE 18.5   Inputs Required for Fitness-for-Use Decision

Input	Usual sources
Who will be the user?	Marketing
How will the nonconforming product be used?	Marketing, client
Are there risks to human safety or structural integrity?	Product research and design
What is the urgency?	Marketing, client
What are the company's and the users' economics?	All departments, client
What are the users' measures of fitness for use?	Market research, marketing, client

When nonconforming products are sent out as fit for use, there arises the need for two additional categories of communication:

1. *Communication to "outsiders":* They (usually customers) have a right and a need to know. All too often, the manufacturing companies neglect to inform their customers when shipping nonconforming products. This may be as a result of bad experience, i.e., some customers will seize on such nonconformances to secure a price discount despite the fact that use of the product will not add to their costs. More usually, the neglect indicates a failure even to face the question of what to communicate. A major factor here is the design of the forms used to record the decisions. With rare exceptions, these forms lack provisions which force those involved to make recommendations and decisions on (*a*) whether to inform the outsiders, and (*b*) what to communicate to them.

2. *Communication to insiders:* When nonconforming goods are shipped as fit for use, the reasons are not always communicated to the inspectors and especially not to the production workers. The resulting vacuum of knowledge has been known to breed some bad practices. When the same type of nonconformance has been shipped several times, an inspector may conclude (in the absence of knowing why) that it is just a waste of time to report such nonconformances in the first place. Yet in some future case, the special reasons (which were the basis of the decision to ship the nonconforming goods) may not be present. In like manner, a production worker may conclude that it is a waste of time to exert all that effort to avoid some nonconformance which will be shipped anyway. Such reactions by well-meaning employees can be minimized if the company faces squarely the question: what shall we communicate to the insiders?

PRODUCT CONFORMANCE

The principal decision making assigned to inspectors is to determine whether product conforms to standard. (See also Three Decisions, discussed above, and under Feedback to Production below, for a discussion of decision making to determine whether the process conforms to standard.) When the words "product" and "standard" are examined closely, it becomes evident that some careful distinctions be made.

The Nature of Product. "Product" takes multiple forms. When submitted to Inspection for decision on conformance to standard, product may consist either of (*a*) single elements of product or (*b*) lots of product. Single elements exhibit one of two main forms:

Discrete Units of Product. These are separate entities such as bolts, teacups, refrigerators. The term "discrete" refers to the fact that the product is made, tested, and used as a separate unit. The approach to these activities is simplified through prior knowledge of how the product will be used.

Specimens from a Coalesced Mass. These are samples from batches, such as a melt of steel or from continuous processes such as petroleum refining. These situations lack the common base of knowledge of the discrete units, since the product is made as a coalesced mass, tested as a specimen, and used in numerous forms not fully predictable at the time of test.

The Nature of Lots of Product.   Usually the product submitted for decision on conformance to standard consists of a "lot." The true lot is an aggregation of product made under a common system of causes. When this ideal is met, the lot possesses an *inherent uniformity derived from the common system of causes.* The extent to which the lot conforms to this ideal greatly influences the approach to the product conformance decision and especially the kind and extent of sampling.

In its simplest form, the true lot emerges from one machine run by one operator processing one material batch, all under a state of statistical control, e.g., a single formulation of a drug product or a run of screw machine parts turned from one piece of rod on one machine. A great deal of industrial production consists of true lots.

However, a great deal of other production consists of product mixtures which, in varying degrees, fall short of the ideal lot definition. Product made from several material batches, or on several machines, or by several operators, may be dumped into a common container. In shop language, this mixture is a "lot," but in precise language it is only a mixture. In continuous processes or in conveyor production, the process may well be common and constant, but the input materials may not be.

For precise and economic product conformance decisions, it is most helpful to "preserve the order." This means that product is kept segregated in true lots or at least identified as to common cause. In addition, for those processes which exhibit a time-to-time variation or "drift" (e.g., the solution gradually becomes dilute, the tool gradually wears), preserving the order includes preserving the time sequence during which various portions of the lot were made. Any loss of order of manufacture becomes also a loss of some prior knowledge as to inherent uniformity. (See Section 17, under Product and Process Relationship, for a discussion of preserving the order as an important aid to process regulation.)

Some products are naturally fluid and develop a homogeneity through this fluidity. Homogeneity from this new cause can also qualify the product as a true lot, with important implications for the sampling process.

When several true lots are combined for the purposes of acceptance, the combination is known as a "grand lot" (a term believed to have been first used by L. E. Simon). Such mixtures are very common, e.g., product from multiple cavities of molding operations or from multiple spindles of screw machine operations.

The two categories of single elements of product (discrete units and specimens) have their counterparts in two categories of lots:

The Lot as a Collection of Discrete Units.   Here the lot consists of numerous bolts, teacups, or refrigerators, each one of which is governed by the product specification. In batch production, the lot is usually determined by the obvious boundaries of the batch. In continuous production, the lot is usually defined as an arbitrary amount of production, or as the amount produced during an arbitrary time span, e.g., a shift, a week.

The Lot as a Coalesced Mass.   Here the lot may also consist of a batch, e.g., the melt of steel. In continuous production, the lot is again based on some arbitrary selection, e.g., 1 ton, a day's production.

Product Conformance Criteria.   Table 18.6 shows the criteria used for judging product conformance to standard, both for product elements and for lots, whether of discrete units or coalesced. It is evident that there are profound differences which affect decisions on how to inspect and which even affect the way of thinking about inspection.

Criteria for Discrete Units. Table 18.6 shows that criteria for judging conformance of discrete units to standard are contained in the product specifications and in the supplemental interpretations provided by the inspection planning (see Interpretation of the Specification, above). Inspection planners are greatly aided in setting these criteria because of the consistency inherent in the discrete unit concept—it is made, tested, and used as a unit. Knowledge of product usage is obtainable and can be put to work in developing added criteria for judging conformance.

Criteria for Specimens. Coalesced products usually lack the consistency among manufacture, test, and usage which characterizes discrete units of product. Quite often it is not known, at the time of testing the specimen, what the future use of the product will be. As a result, criteria for judging the conformance of a specimen to its specification must include much discussion and common consent among the parties of interest. This is precisely what has happened, and a great deal has been done to evolve industry standards which define the specimen and prescribe how to test it.

Criteria for Lots (Collections of Discrete Units). For these lots, the lot criteria consist of rules for lot formation, sample sizes, and allowable number of defects. These criteria are not provided in the design specifications. In consequence, they are provided as part of the inspection planning process.

Criteria for Lots (Coalesced). For some of these products the lot criteria are set up in a manner similar to that used for lots of discrete units, treating each specimen as though it were a discrete unit of product. Coalesced products exhibit *defects* but not defective units *(defectives)*. Discrete units of products can exhibit either defects or defectives.

Increasingly, the lot criteria are being established by setting limits on the product mass in the form of (1) plus and minus tolerances on the average and (2) a maximum on the standard deviation. When the lot limits are in this form, the data on the various specimens are pooled together on a variables basis to permit judgement of conformance.

Sampling Criteria for Lots. Two major considerations guide the sampling plans to be established for lot acceptance:

1. The extent of knowledge available from sources other than sampling the lot. This is discussed below, under How Much Inspection?
2. The statistical principles governing sampling. These are discussed in Section 25.

HOW MUCH INSPECTION? EFFECT OF PRIOR KNOWLEDGE

The usual starting point is an awareness that product conformance decisions must be based on product knowledge and that this product knowledge is available from multiple sources:

Prior Conformance Decisions on the Same Lot. In some cases, the concept of "audit of decisions" has been put to work so that suppliers, independent lab-

TABLE 18.6 Criteria for Judging Conformance of Product in Units and Lots

Aspects of conformance	Product consists of discrete units		Product consists of a coalesced mass	
	Individual unit of product	Lot = collection of discrete units	Specimen from mass	Lot = coalesced mass
Usual name of subject matter of inspection:	Part, unit, component, assembly, product, etc.	Lot	Specimen	Lot, mass
Standard usually consists of:	Product specification, plus supplemental criteria in inspection plan	Sampling plan	Material specification	Sampling plan
Standard usually published by:	Product Design Department and Inspection Planning	Quality Control Department	Product Design Department	Product Design or Quality Control Department
Standard usually expressed in terms of:	Natural units of measure	Percent defective	Natural units of measure	Percent conforming

Tolerance usually expressed as:	Maximum and minimum measurements	Allowable defects in sample	Maximum and minimum measurements	Maximum and minimum on averages; maximum on dispersion
Information on conformance usually derived from:	Measuring instruments	Sampling data plus prior knowledge of process (capability, order of manufacture, etc.)	Measuring instruments	Sampling data; inherent fluidity; prior knowledge of process
Criteria for judging conformance are:	Measurement versus tolerance	Actual defects versus allowable evidence of process behavior	Measurement versus tolerance	Averages and dispersion versus tolerances; prior data

oratories, workers, etc., have been qualified as able to give reliable product conformance decisions and in addition have accepted this very lot. In such cases, no further product inspection is necessary (beyond that inherent in "audit of decisions"). See, in this connection, Section 15, under Audit of Decisions; also Section 17, under Self-Inspection.

Prior Knowledge of the Process.   To illustrate, a press operation stamps out 10,000 pieces. If the first and last pieces contain certain specified holes of correct size and location, it follows that the intervening 9998 pieces also carry holes of correct size and in correct locations. Such is the inherent nature of the press dies. In statistical language, the sample size is two pieces and the number of allowable defects is zero. Yet despite the tiny sample size, this is a sound way to do the inspection for these characteristics in the example given.

The press example is rather simple. In more complex cases there is need to measure process capability and to arrange specially to take the samples with knowledge of the order of production. One organized form of this is the conventional control chart method used for process control (see Section 24 generally). For product conformance, the approach is less well organized (see, however, Section 25, under Bayesian Procedures).

Prior knowledge of the "process" as used here includes knowledge of the qualifications of the suppliers, workers, etc., who run the process. Workers who have qualified for licenses require less rigorous inspection of their work than operators who have not qualified. Suppliers who have established a record of good deliveries need not be checked as severely as suppliers who lack such a record.

Product Fluidity.   When the product is a fluid, this fluidity contributes to homogeneity. The extent of this homogeneity can be established by taking multiple specimens and computing the dispersion (another form of study of process capability). The presence of uniformity through fluidity greatly reduces the need for random sampling and thereby greatly reduces the sample sizes.

Even when the product is a solid, the inspection planner should be alert to the possibility that it possesses homogeneity through former fluidity. For example, a centrifugal casting process was used to cast metal cylinders which were then destroyed during testing for strength. However, it was then found that the dispersion of several strength tests all made on one ring was not different from the ring-to-ring dispersion. This discovery made it possible to reduce the amount of product destroyed during test.

Prior Successful Usage.   Where product, though nonconforming, has nevertheless been successfully used, this fact is a proper consideration in the question of how much inspection.

Cost Impact.   When it is important to allocate limited testing resources to those parts which cost the most to replace, unique testing strategies can be designed that utilize past test, line, and field history. (See Wambach and Anthony, 1977, for a discussion of this application for reliability critical parts.)

Product Inspection.   To the extent that the foregoing sources of knowledge are not adequate to make product-acceptance decisions, the gap must be filled by inspection and test of the product.

Securing the Prior Knowledge.   The "prior knowledge" does not automatically come to the inspection planner or the inspector. Some of this knowledge is already in existence as a by-product of other activities and hence can be had for the procedural cost of retrieval. Other knowledge is not in existence, and must be created by additional effort. However, this added effort is usually a one-time study, whereas the benefits then go on and on.

HOW MUCH INSPECTION? THE ALTERNATIVES

It is evident that a determination of "How much inspection?" should be made only after there has been an evaluation of the other inputs to product knowledge. This evaluation can then dictate any of several levels of inspection:

No Inspection. There is already adequate evidence that the product conforms, and hence no further inspection is needed.

Small Samples. There is a high degree of prior knowledge, requiring only small *stratified* samples so chosen as to verify the continuing validity of this prior knowledge, e.g., control charts, audit of decisions, preserving the order. In the absence of prior knowledge, such small sample sizes would be absurd, i.e., lots 20 or 30 percent defective could easily escape detection. See Section 25, under Sampling Plans Based on Prior Information, for the statistical approaches; and see also Babcombe (1970) for a discussion on quality control for small lots.

Large Samples. Where there is little or no prior knowledge and no product fluidity, the main source of product knowledge becomes product inspection through *random* sampling. The amount of this inspection can be determined "scientifically" once the tolerable level of defects in accepted product has been clearly defined. However, choice of these levels—using the sampling parameters AQL (acceptable quality level), AOQL (average outgoing quality level), etc.—is largely arbitrary and is usually determined by negotiation. In theory, the sampling parameters can be determined from economic considerations, i.e., the cost of detecting unsatisfactory lots versus the cost of failing to detect them. In practice, the "cost of detecting" is fairly easy to determine, but the cost of "failing to detect" is difficult to determine. For intangibles such as customer goodwill, there is no way known to make the determination with any useful precision.

ONE HUNDRED PERCENT INSPECTION

This alternative is usually used for final test of critical or complex products. In very critical cases, it is used to provide redundancy against the unreliability of 100 percent inspection. In these cases the amount may be 200 percent or over. In cases where "zero defects" is the objective or requirement, 100 percent automated inspection is required (see Nygaard, 1981, and the discussion on machine-vision systems later in this section). In some cases, 100 percent inspection is required to satisfy legal or political requirements (see Walsh, 1974). In other cases 100 percent inspection is the most cost-effective approach. (See Walsh et al., 1976 and 1978, for examples where 100 percent inspection is the cost-effective alternative in high-volume production and in testing hardness of finished steel wheels.)

One hundred percent inspection may also be used when process capability is inherently too poor to meet product specifications. Sampling is of no avail in such cases, since the accepted lots are usually no better than the rejected lots, i.e., the difference is merely the result of statistical variations in the respective samples. This does not apply in cases where the process is highly erratic so that some lots are truly conforming and others are not merely the result of statistical accidents. For such processes, sampling can be a useful way to separate the conforming lots from the nonconforming ones.

Whatever the motivation for selecting the 100 percent alternative, effective implementation goes beyond choosing the inspection methodology or test equipment. Physical arrangements and personnel procedures must be changed. In many cases, attitudes of in-house and vendor personnel must be changed through reeducation. (See Walsh et al., 1979b.)

With the advent of computer-based testing, 100 percent inspection is becoming more practical (see Schweber, 1982). However, it is not clear that it is cost-effective in all cases, even if the technology is readily available (see Walsh et al., 1979a). This is especially true if the total costs of quality are considered. (See Gunter, 1983.)

OTHER TYPES OF CONFORMANCE INSPECTION

Faced with the objective to minimize (inspection) costs and achieve maximum (quality) control, management must be sensitive to nontraditional types of conformance decision-making inspection.

Simulation. With the advancement of the digital computer, system-simulation techniques are used as an alternative to the experimental or analytical approach (see Wang et al., 1981). Examples of application:

Receiving inspection simulation

Printed circuit board assembly inspection simulation

Camera subassembly and final inspection simulation

Management by Exception. This employs the principle of *no inspection* described in How Much Inspection? above. The variation, described by Moburg (1968) employs the Pareto concept to focus the major conformance-decision resources on the "relatively few" lots that had rejects in them. This approach is also feasible within the lot with the advent of new automated technology. (See Keller et al., 1975, for a discussion of exception inspection through automated video techniques.)

Automated Inspection. The first large-scale applications of automated testing were very likely done by the Western Electric Company during the 1920s. Current developments in the microcomputer, artifical intelligence (AI), integrated computer-aided manufacturing (ICAM), robotics, and software are making automated inspection practical and cost-effective. (See "An Outlook for 3D Vision," 1984, and "ASD's Quality Assurance Program Rates in Top 10," 1984; also the discussion on 100 percent inspection above, and that on Machine Vision, in Human Factors in Inspection, below.)

Automated inspection and testing are used to reduce costs, improve precision, shorten time intervals, alleviate labor shortages, and avoid inspection monotony among other advantages. In some industries the labor problems now seem insoluble in the absence of automated inspection. Already in widespread use, automated inspection is still expanding, with no end in sight.

The economics of automation involve a substantial investment in special equipment to secure a reduction in operating costs. The crux of justifying the investment lies in the amount of repetitive work the equipment will be called on to perform. This estimate of the anticipated volume of testing should therefore be checked out with great care.

A common starting point in discovering opportunities for automated inspection is to make a Pareto analysis of the kinds of inspections and tests being conducted. The vital few types are identified. Estimates are then made of the personnel, costs, and other current problems associated with these tests. The economics of automation are then estimated, and the comparable figures are an aid in deciding on the feasibility of successful conversion.

For complex equipments involving depot storage and field maintenance, the question of use of automated testing is itself highly complex and requires a tailormade study of some magnitude.

Technologically, the "machine" poses many problems. It is less adaptable than the human being it replaces, so some changes may need to be made in the product to offset this rigidity. For example, the machine may hold the units to be tested by grasping certain surfaces whose dimensions were previously unimportant. Now these surfaces may need to be held to close dimensions because the machine is not as adaptable as the human inspector. Alternatively, the product design may need to be changed to provide for adequate location.

Beyond the work of original design, construction, and prove-in, the machine must be set up specially for each job. (See generally Section 16, under Quality Information Equipment.) However, modular construction, master test pieces, and taped programs have considerable reduced setup time while improving reproducibility. Reliability has generally been high, and use of printed circuit cards and other modular components has so reduced the "mean time to repair" that downtime is generally below 5 percent for well-designed machines.

Automated gaging and testing is extensively used in the mechanical industries. It is also widely used in the electronics industries, especially for electronic components (see Section 29, under Automated Test and Data Processing), where the problem of making connections to the automated test equipment is so severe that the original product design must provide specially for this.

In the chemical industries, the corresponding development has been the "autoanalyzer." This has already made possible some extensive cost reductions and solutions of otherwise forbidding problems of recruitment of laboratory technicians.

The autoanalyzer makes use of some equipment common to all tests—sensors, transducers, recorders, and computers. However, each type of analysis has its unique procedure for converting the material under test into a form suitable for sensing.

The advent of numerically controlled (NC) machines has required development of new inspection techniques which likewise use the NC principle. Since the machine is controlled by a tape, the validity of that tape is critical. One form of inspection control is through certifying the tapes. Once certified, the tapes become an important stabilizer in the process capability of the NC machine. (See "Tape Controlled Machines," 1970.)

Inspection of NC product can make use of the properties of the machines by substituting a stylus for the cutter. The measurements made by the stylus can be checked against the master tape. A further approach is to use coordinate-measuring machines, also tape-controlled, to check the NC-produced components. Still another approach is to make and measure a full-scale picture. (See Kirwan, 1972, Woods and Zeiss, 1981, and Karabatsos, 1983.)

Computer-Aided Inspection.   The marriage of computers and inspectors takes the form of (*a*) providing information and/or (*b*) providing assistance to enhance the conformance decision for almost any inspection situation. This is especially applicable to inspecting precision machine parts and assembly inspection (see Holmes, 1974, and Linn, 1981, for further discussion). The selective use of computer-aided inspection (CAI) techniques can minimize the more mental, repetitive inspection tasks and direct the human resource (the inspector) to preventative quality control.

Voice Entry.   Antother unique enhancement of computer-aided technology is the voice-data-entry system (VDES), which has at least these practical benefits (see "Voice Entry System Gives Quality Inspectors a Hand," 1973):

1. Saves money
2. Eliminates manual entry
3. Reduces labor requirements
4. Speeds management information
5. Has instant response time
6. Accepts all speakers
7. Permits on-line, real-time control
8. Has flexible and expandable capabilities
9. Allows remote control
10. Accepts off-line telephone input
11. Has verification-correction capability

INSPECTION AT INSPECTION STATIONS

Inspection stations are usually staffed by full-time inspectors responsible to the Inspection Department. This is by no means universal. Some final inspection stations are staffed by full-time inspectors responsible to Production. Many process inspection stations are staffed by Production workers whose principal job is production.

Incoming Inspection.   The extent of inspection of products received from suppliers depends largely on the extent of prior planning for supplier quality control (see Section 15, under Joint Quality Planning). In the extreme case of using surveillance and audit of decisions (see Section 15, under Audit of Decision), there is virtually no incoming inspection except for identity. At the other extreme, many "conventional" products are bought under an arrangement which relies primarily on incoming inspection for control of supplier quality.

The inspectors and their facilities are housed in the receiving area to provide ready collaboration with other supplier-related activities, i.e., materials receiving, weighing, counting, storage. Depending on the physical bulk and tonnage of product, entire shipments or just samples are brought to the inspection floor. The documentation routines provide the inspectors with copies of the purchase orders and specifications, which are filed by supplier name.

Inspection planning is conventional, as discussed under Inspection Planning, above. However, there is usually a lack of prior knowledge of process capability, order of manufacture, etc. In consequence, the sampling plans involve random and (often) large samples, employing standard random inspection tables (see generally Section 25, Acceptance Sampling). Randomness becomes a severe problem in the case of large shipments, whether bulk or not. However, special arrangements can be made with the supplier. (See Section 15, under Joint Quality Planning: Joint Technolgoical Planning.) Setting AQLs has been a troublesome problem to such an extent that some industry standards have been worked up. In the absence of such standards, the AQLs are established based on precedent, past performance, or just arbitrarily. Then, as instances of rejection arise, the negotiations with vendors result in adjustment of the AQLs.

Data feedback to vendors follows conventional feedback practice. (In this connection, see also Section 15, under Two-Way Communication; Deviations.)

Process Inspection.   This commonly serves two purposes simultaneously:

1. To provide data for making decisions on the *product;* i.e., does the product conform to specification?

2. To provide data for making decisions on the *process;* i.e., should the process run or stop?

Because of the interrelation between process and product variables, process inspection involves observation of process variables as well as inspection of the product. These observations and inspections are made by both Production and Inspection personnel. The resulting interplay is discussed in Section 17, Production of Quality, under Product and Process Relationship.

Product acceptance of work in process may be done in any of several stages or by a combination of them. These stages include:

Setup Inspection.   Some processes are inherently so stable that if the setup is correct, the entire lot will be correct, within certain limits of lot size. For such processes the setup approval can also be used as the lot approval. Where a good deal is at stake, it is usual to formalize the setup inspection and to require that the process may not run until the inspector has formally approved the setup, e.g., by signing off, by stamping the first pieces, etc. (See Garfinkel and Clodfelter, 1984.) Some of the setup criteria make use of narrow limit or PRE-control techniques as discussed in Section 24.

Patrol Inspection.   For processes which will not remain stable for the duration of the lot, it is usual to provide for periodic sampling to be conducted during the progression of the lot, making use of various techniques described in Section 24. The numerous plans in use consist mainly of variations of the following four types:

1. Preserve the order of manufacture under an arrangement such as is depicted in Figure 18.1. In this example, the machine discharges its production into a small container called a "pan." The production operator periodically empties the pan into one of three larger containers:

    a. Into the junk box if the parts are junk

    b. Into the reject box if the parts are questionable or are mixed good and bad

    c. Into the "tray" if the parts are presumably good

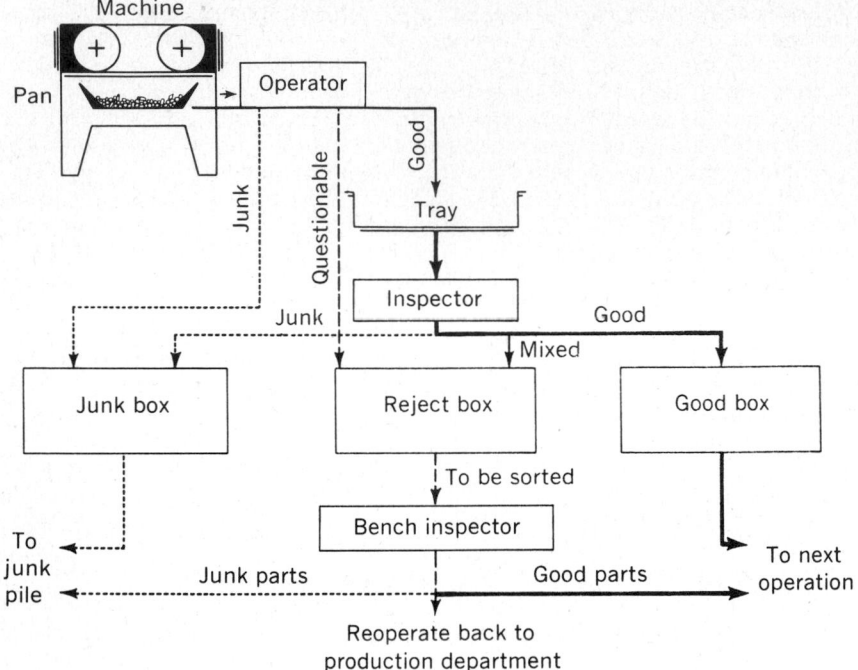

FIG. 18.1   Patrol inspection plan based on preserving the order.

The patrol inspector comes to the machine and checks the last few pieces being made. (He or she may also sample the tray.) Based on this check, the tray is disposed of in one of three ways:

    a. Into the junk box if the parts are junk.

    b. Into the reject box if the parts are questionable or are mixed good or bad.

    c. Into the "good" box if the parts are acceptable. The good box goes on to the next operation.

Only the inspector may dispose of the tray, and only the inspector may place any product in the good box.

The reject box is gone over by a sorter, who makes three dispositions:

    a. Junk to junk department

    b. Reoperate back to production department

    c. Good parts on to next operation

   2. This method is similar to the first, but the inspection data from the last few pieces are posted to a control chart. If the process remains in control, all product made since the last check is accepted.

   3. The accumulated product (e.g., in the tray of Figure 18.1) is sampled at random using some standard sampling plan, and acceptance is based on the sampling criteria.

   4. The process variables are checked against a process specification, and the product is accepted provided the process conforms to specification. This method is usually restricted to cases in which there is to be a direct check on the product at later stages.

Tollgate Inspection. This is a lot-by-lot product acceptance procedure. Commonly it is done after a production department has concluded its operations. Sometimes the product is moved physically to an inspection area, where it waits its turn to be inspected. Sampling is at random, using standard sampling tables.

Tollgate inspection reduces congestion at the machines and clarifies departmental responsibility. The price paid is in added material handling, added floor space, loss of order of production, and greater difficulty in fixing individual responsibility.

Finished Goods Inspection. Most finished products are tested 100 percent for minimal simulation of use. Tests are often automated, as are the data recordings. Testing may be done either at inspection stations on the production line or in separate inspection areas.

JUDGMENT OF FITNESS FOR USE

Knowledge of *conformance to specification* is needed to:

Provide protection to the user when usage experience is not yet available

Provide working criteria to those who lack knowledge of fitness for use

Create an atmosphere of law and order

Protect innocents from unwarranted blame

In contrast, *knowledge of fitness* for use is needed to:

Protect the user

Preserve marketability of the product

Avoid excesses of perfectionism

A trained inspector, if provided with the specification, the product, and the instruments, can readily judge conformance to the specification. However, possession of these facilities is not enough to enable him or her to judge fitness for use. This second judgment requires added knowledge, as discussed below.

When inspection determines that the product conforms to specification, the product is routinely assumed to be fit for use; i.e., if the answer to the conformance question is yes, the fitness-for use is not even raised. (There are occasional exceptions to this. Field reports of unfitness for use are enough to hold up deliveries even if the product under test conforms to specification.) The routines are structured to ship the product accordingly. It is only when product fails to conform to specification that there arises the second question: Is the (nonconforming) product fit for use?

What is significant is that much nonconforming product is actually fit for use and that this fact is known to many people in middle and lower management. Unless the authorized routines provide for legitimate ways for dealing with this practical problem, the unauthorized ways will take over, with unpredictable results. Where the Quality Department is poorly supported, there will be unauthorized shipment of nonconforming product, including some which is unfit for use. Where the Quality Department is well supported, there may be unnecessary waste due to failure to accept nonconforming product which is fit for use.

The hazards of delegation by default have led many companies to establish an organized approach for review of nonconforming products. The most popular form of this organized approach is the Material Review Board.

Methods of Decision Making on Fitness for Use.   There have been several methods for providing answers to this:

1. Assume that all nonconforming product is unfit for use. Under this assumption, all nonconforming lots are scrapped, repaired, sorted, etc., but not shipped as is. A great deal of waste has resulted from this assumption, since many designs are unrealistically strict and many nonconforming products are in fact fit for use.

2. Create an agency for decision making, e.g., a Material Review Board, and give this agency the responsibility to determine fitness for use of all nonconforming product. This arrangement is fairly practical if there is very little nonconforming material, but tends to require an elaborate apparatus for disposing of numerous small matters (as well as for the vital few cases where the elaborate appartus is clearly warranted).

3. Create a system of multiple delegation for making decisions on fitness for use. Under such a system, the "vital few" decisions are reserved to a formal Material Review Board. The remaining decisions are delegated to other people. This is the emerging solution.

Material Review Board.   The basic function of a Material Review Board (MRB) is to (*a*) review material that does not conform to standard, (*b*) determine what its disposition should be, and (*c*) drive the development of effective corrective action to prevent recurrence.

The MRB is a broad-based reviewing agency whose membership usually consists minimally of representatives from:

Engineering: The cognizant designer is often the representative.

Quality Assurance: The representative is often from Quality Control Engineering.

Customers: The representative may be from the customer's organization (e.g., the government inspector) or from Marketing.

Bond (1983) discusses board composition, philosophy, and problem documentation.

In some companies, the role of the Material Review Board is solely one of judging fitness for use of nonconforming products. Such was the scope of the boards when they were first set up (by the military procurement services). However, other companies broaden the scope of the MRB so that it includes:

Decision on disposition of unfit lots internally—by scrap, repair, sorting, etc.; fixing responsibility for the losses incurred

Periodic analysis of the accumulated waiver investigations to identify quality improvement projects

As MRBs conduct their affairs, they tend to work out some delegations of the more routine cases to individual members to act without taking up the time of the full Board. The main form of this delegation is in fact finding, which is usually delegated to the Quality Engineer. However, there may be added delegations, e.g., to the Product Designer for memorandum or marked print waivers in certain cases; to the Quality Engineer for guiding internal disposition of product, etc.

The MRB works to a formal agenda and keeps minutes of its deliberations and actions. A universal rule is that acceptance of nonconforming material requires *unanimous concurrence* of all members of the MRB.

Multiple Delegation. In some companies the delegation for decision making is based on a system of classification to separate the "vital few" nonconformances from the rest. One such system involves classifying defects (and/or quality characteristics) into categories of seriousness. (See Seriousness Classification, below.) If such classification is available it simplifies the problem of delegating the fitness-for-use decision. The vital few cases are decided by the upper managers. The less serious cases are delegated to lower levels.

Another such system is based on classifying quality characteristics as to whether they are functional or nonfunctional. (The term "nonfunctional" is not to be confused with appearance or other esthetic qualities. For some products, esthetic qualities are quite essential to fitness for use.) Where such classification is available, it becomes feasible to assign decisions on functional characteristics to the upper levels of the organizations, leaving the rest to the lower levels.

With multiple delegation in a large company, uncertainty can arise as to placement of authority. The way out of such vagueness is to establish a table of delegation which fits the unique situation of the company. Table 18.7 shows an example of such a table of delegation for a specific company.

TABLE 18.7   Responsibility for Making Decisions on Fitness for Use*

Effect of nonconformance is on:	Amount of product or money at stake is:	
	Small	Large
Internal economics only	Department head directly involved; quality engineer	Plant managers involved; quality manager
Economic relations with Supplier	Supplier; purchasing agent; quality engineer	Supplier, manager
Economic relations with client	Client; salesperson; quality engineer	Client; for Marketing, Manufacturing, Technical, Quality
Field performance of the product	Product designer; salesperson; quality engineer	Client; managers for Technical, Manufacturing, Marketing Quality
Risk of damage to society or of nonconformance to government regulations	Product design manager; compliance officer; lawyer; quality manager	General manager and team of upper managers

*For those industries whose quality mission is really one of conformance to specification (e.g., atomic energy, space), the real decision maker on fitness for use is the client or the government regulator.

Organized Material Reviews.   In any case, decision making on nonconforming products should be done on an organized basis, through recognized, legitimate channels. Lacking an organized approach there arises a "delegation by default." In one company (consulting experience of J. M. Juran) there existed five sources of waivers in actual use by inspection:

1. Written authority from Engineering
2. Written authority from Sales
3. Long-standing practice for which there existed no written authority
4. Measurement variations added to product tolerances
5. Inspector judgment on sensory qualities not clearly defined in the specifications

Steps Preceding Review.   Some elements of the preparation for review of non-conforming material are virtually alike for all companies:

1. The inspector prepares a nonconformance report identifying the product involved, the nature of the defects, and related factual data. These reports are serially numbered (for some examples of the documentation, see Section 19).
2. The inspector "red-tags" the product, thereby creating an automatic "hold for disposition." Often the product is moved to a special "hold area" to get it out of the regular stream of production.
3. An investigator (often a Quality Engineer) is assigned to collect information pertinent to disposition of the impounded material. This information includes:
   Value of the product
   Cost of scrap, repair. or sort
   Possibility of use in various ways: "as is," with modifications, through concessions to customer, etc.
4. Based on the analysis and on the prevailing pattern of delegation of authority, the investigator takes or recommends action. One of these recommendations may be to accept the material as fit for use.
5. To recommend acceptance "as is" despite nonconformance, the investigator prepares a formal waiver request to a reviewing agency.

Inputs for Fitness-for-Use Decisions.   Factual answers to several questions are useful in arriving at fitness-for-use decisions:

1. *Who will be the user?*   A technologically sophisticated user may be able to deal successfully with the nonconformance; a consumer may not. A nearby user may have easy access to field service; a distant or international user may lack such easy access.
2. *How will this product be used?*   For many materials and standard products the specifications are broad enough to cover a variety of possible uses, and it is not known at the time of manufacture just what will be the actual use to which the product will be put. For example, sheet steel may be cut up to service as decorative plates or as structural members; the television receiver may be stationed at a comfortable range or at an extreme range; chemical intermediates may be employed in numerous formulas.
3. *Are there risks to human safety or to structural integrity?*   Where such risks are significant, all else is academic.

4. *What is the urgency?* For some applications, clients cannot wait, because the product in question is critical to putting some broader system into operation. Hence they may demand delivery now, and make repairs in the field. Thus for the review process, facts are needed on:

   a. The schedule requirements for the part(s) or material

   b. The lead time to replace or rework the part(s) or material

5. *What are the company's and the user's economics?* For some nonconformances the economics of repair are so forbidding that the product must be used as is, although at a price discount. In some industries, e.g., textiles, the price structure formalizes this concept by use of a separate grade—"seconds." Among the facts needed for the review of the economics are:

   a. The minimum rework required to make the part(s) or material usable, and the cost of this rework

   b. The cost of scrapping and replacing the part(s) or material

6. *What are the users' measures of fitness for use?* These may differ significantly from those available to the manufacturer. For example, a manufacturer of abrasive cloth used a laboratory test to judge the ability of the cloth to polish metal; a major client evaluated the cost per 1000 pieces polished.

These and other inputs may be needed at several levels of fitness for use, i.e., the effects on the economics of subsequent processors, the marketability requirements of the merchants, and the qualities that determine fitness for the ultimate user, and the qualities that influence field maintenance.

The job of securing such inputs is often assigned to a staff specialist, e.g., a quality engineer. This person "makes the rounds," contacting the various departments which are able to provide pertinent information. There may be need to contact the customer, and even to conduct an actual tryout.

Effect of Multiple Product Usage. Fitness for use is often complicated by the multiple usage for the products under investigation. For the coalesced products, multiple forms of usage are widespread. In consequence, the study of fitness for use involves an inquiry as to how this impounded lot will be used. The resulting waiver may very well be restricted, e.g., for this specific customer or application only.

Product in discrete units likewise involves multiple usages, and the same principles hold. Sometime the technological usage may be identical, but the circumstances of usage create the difference. An example is seen in many kinds of interchangeable components. These serve a multiplicity of uses:

1. To be shipped to original equipment manufacturers (OEM) to be assembled into apparatus

2. To be shipped to OEM to be sold or used by them as spare parts

3. To be assembled into apparatus by the component maker itself

4. To be shipped, through intermediate merchants, to repair shops who use the components as spare parts for repair of products in the hands of the general public

At the time these components are made, it is seldom known to which of these destinations they will be shipped. However, when the OEM customer orders (1) and (2) are filled, the practice is to follow strict product acceptance procedures, since the OEM customer has great economic importance, backed up by competent engineers and inspectors who in turn operate out of well-equipped laboratories.

In contrast, components used for purposes 3 and 4 may include those which failed to make the OEM grade. In the company's own assembly department, the operators often have tools which permit them to adjust for nonconforming components. Failing this, they put the poor parts aside and use others. In the case of spare parts to be sold to the general public (through merchants and repair shops), there are opportunities for abuses due to the technological ignorance of everyone involved, and some of these abuses take place. (See generally Juran, 1970.) Some highly ethical companies flatly require that nonconforming components be used only in their own assembly areas and never be shipped out as spare parts.

Disposition of Unfit Product. Product which is unfit for use is disposed of in a number of ways: scrap, sort, rework, return to supplier, sell at a discount, etc. Mainly these alternatives involve internal economics within the manufacturing company, and hence they can be quantified sufficiently to arrive at a logical economic balance. However, no matter what the disposition is, money is lost, schedules are disrupted, and people are blamed. In such an atmosphere it is important to establish rules of conduct which minimize the costs, disruptions, and human abrasion.

When purchased products are involved, the rule should be to find that disposition which creates the minimum total loss to the parties. Adherence to this rule reduces the amount at stake so that there is less to argue about. In turn, this makes it easier to bargain how to share this loss. It is also well to write the purchase contract in a way which makes clear how to handle the various elements of cost which arise because of unfit product.

For self-made products, the rule should still be the same—to find that disposition which results in the minimum total loss. On the face of it this should be obvious, e.g., any sorting of product should be done by that department which can do it at the lowest total cost to the company. However, this logic can be frustrated by other considerations, e.g., labor shortages or cultural resistance.

A major obstacle to "logical" solutions is the presence of an atmosphere of "blame" in the company, e.g., an official requirement that responsibility for errors should be discovered and allocated (often with associated "charging" of the departments responsible). In such an atmosphere the disposition of unfit products is hampered at every turn by the reluctance of supervisors to agree to actions which might be construed as admissions of guilt.

A policy of charging back all cases of error pays a high price for dubious results. The price is not only the cost of analysis but also—and even greater—the effect on supervisory time and morale. The other extreme of regarding everything as indeterminate is no better. The middle ground is to concentrate the analysis on the chronic, vital few defects which go on and on, since these account for the bulk of the losses. For the sporadic "useful many" errors, analysis to fix blame is seldom warranted. The local supervision is in the best position to study these and to find ways to minimize their recurrence.

For the vital few errors there remains a question of transfer of charges to the department responsible once responsibility is clear. As a matter of good accounting practice, the department responsible should be charged. However, much depends on how the budgets were prepared in the first place. If charging is to be inaugurated, the setting up of future budgets should take this into account. In addition, a look should be taken to assure that the costs of analysis and accounting are low in relation to the amounts at stake.

An undue atmosphere of blame can infect the nonsupervisory levels as well.

Here the effect is often to conceal the evidence of defects by hiding the scrap, scrapping products which may be repairable, "forgetting" to execute the scrap or repair tickets, etc. See, in this connection, Section 22 under Test of Theories of Worker-Controllable Problems.

Disposition of unfit product by sorting may involve external as well as internal economics. Several sorting situations are common:

1. The product in question is processed further within the same company, e.g., resistors wired into circuits. In such cases it is usually feasible to evaluate:

a. The cost of finding a defect through inspection. This is approximately equal to the inspection cost per unit divided by the fraction defective.

b. The cost of not finding a defect, i.e., the added costs incurred by further processing until the defect is found in later testing. This can be estimated.

Under these circumstances (and assuming 100 percent accuracy of sorting) it is economic to sort the product when the fraction defective is more than the ratio of *a* to *b* (see Taguchi, 1970).

2. The product in question goes to the user. Here it is still feasible to evaluate the cost of finding a defect. However, it is now more difficult to estimate the cost of not finding a defect and virtually impossible to estimate the intangible damage done to goodwill. Nevertheless, when the cost of finding a defect is *compared* to the *value of the product,* managers seem to be able to make a practical judgment. Commonly, managers will conclude that they are not willing to spend as much to find a defect as the sales value of the product.

For example, a line of consumer products sells for $5 each. A major defect has an incidence of one per thousand. The cost of testing to find the defect is $10 per thousand, so it costs $10 to find one defect. Most managers would not be willing to spend $10 to find a defective $5 product.

3. The product in question contains defects which are known to be a safety or health hazard. The cost of finding the defect can still be figured, but the managers make their decision almost exclusively on the fact that the hazard is present. (There is risk of civil and criminal lawsuits.) Somehow the hazard will be eliminated or neutralized.

Physical Control of the Product.   The majority of companies apply rigid controls to movement of finished goods. Inspection approval is required before goods enter the (locked) finished goods storeroom (or are shipped to a customer). Packers, counters, and storekeepers are under strict orders to assure that inspection approval is present before finished goods move on to their destination. To a lesser degree, similar controls apply to finished components entering the assembly storeroom.

Control of nonconforming product is likewise rigid. The containers are red-tagged and usually are moved out of the stream of production to avoid mixups.

For parts, components, and intermediate products moving between Production departments, the practice varies widely. At one extreme, physical control is entirely in the hands of production people until the final product is presented to Inspection for acceptance as finished goods. At the other extreme, movement from any Production department is always to an Inspection area (before dispatch to the next Production department) and then only after an Inspection-approved "move ticket" has been executed.

A further form of inspection control is through approval stamps applied directly to the product during various stages of operation and especially at final test. Some stamps are coded to show the condition of the product. Stamps commonly identify the inspector to establish traceability as well as to fix responsibility.

For complex apparatus a dossier is invariably prepared to collect the history of the product, the inspection log books, calibration curves, and other matters of significance. Copies of pertinent results go to the customer as well. Seals or locks may be used to minimize unauthorized tampering with the product.

The need for elaborate control systems is obvious when a mixup could be catastrophic (e.g., for pharmaceuticals). However, some companies use these elaborate systems largely because the managers do not trust the work force. Such mistrust is always mutual, and the long-range solution lies in resolving this mistrust, not in retaining elaborate systems.

Another source of elaboration of system is the human drive for self-sufficiency in floor space, equipment, etc. This drive can be accentuated by departmental loyalties and interdepartmental conflicts. Managers should be alert to distinguish cases requiring elaborate systems due to the nature of the product from those created by human beings for reasons of status, departmental loyalty, etc. For example, creation of separate Inspection areas can greatly increase the total time interval for manufacture, the process inventory, and the amount of paperwork. As far as possible, the inspector should be brought to the product rather than the other way around. This principle is illustrated by patrol inspectors, assembly line inspectors, resident inspectors at supplier plants, etc. It has been applied to conveyorized production by establishing inspection stations at the conveyor. It has even been applied where, for reasons of identity and certification, a physical fence separates the Production and Inspection departments; i.e., a conveyor moves the product into and out of the inspection cage through windows cut for the purpose.

A similar principle is used where strict certification of inspected parts is essential. The only entrance to the fenced-in storeroom is through a fenced-in inspection area.

QUALITY STANDARDS

The cornerstone of quality control is the specfication. Specifications embody the minimum and maximum values. (See also Bader, 1980.) However, they are usually *incomplete*. They tend to ignore *visual quality characteristics,* or they treat characteristics labeled as *workmanship* superficially. (Refer to the discussion of visual quality characteristics below; and see also Dodds, 1967, and Alaimo, 1969, for further discussion on workmanship standards.)

Seriousness Classification.   Some quality characteristics and defects are very important to fitness for use; others are not. The village craftsperson and the small-shop proprietor, with their firsthand knowledge of fitness for use, are able to concentrate their efforts on the most important qualities. In modern, large, complex organizations, the workmen, inspectors, and many of the supervisors lack complete knowledge of fitness for use and thereby are not fully clear on where to place their emphasis and how to make their decisions.

For example, one company studying the fabrication and inspection of machine parts classified the quality characteristics into four classes. Table 18.8 shows the effect of this classification on product tolerances and on the number of dimensions checked. The inspection time was reduced from 215 to 120 min. In addition, there were greater savings through lower rework costs, lower tooling costs, and lower engineering costs for disposition of nonconforming product. (See also Allen, 1959.)

To provide such missing knowledge on a broad scale, there has evolved a concept of formal seriousness classification, both for quality characteristics and for defects. The quality characteristics list comes from the specifications; the list of defects comes from evidences of failures during use (e.g., service reports) and from evidence of nonconformance during manufacture (e.g., inspection reports). When these two lists are classified for seriousness, the former is used mainly for quality planning while the latter is used mainly for inspection planning and for product auditing. (See Section 8; also El Gabry, 1972.)

These two lists differ in their content, though the overlap is often great. A single quality characteristic, e.g., shaft diameter 1.000 ± 0.001, gives rise to two defects, oversize and undersize. These defects may be assigned different degrees of seriousness depending on the extent of nonconformance. Some extensive defect lists, e.g., the list for glass bottles, have little resemblance to the list of characteristics set out in the specifications.

Some companies use the same system of classification both for characteristics and defects. However, there is enough uniqueness about each of the two lists to suggest that adoption of a single system should be preceded by a positive examination of the nature of the two lists. For example, the effect of seriousness classification on design decisions can be quite different from the effect on inspection decisions, as is evident from Table 18.8.

Formal systems of seriousness classification were originally evolved to serve specialized purposes. (The Bell System pioneered by developing a system to permit rating of quality of finished product. The U.S. Armed Services developed systems to simplify the administration of acceptance of goods purchased from contractors.) However, as the systems came into being, they were found to have application in the entire progression of product from design through usage: in quality specification, manufacturing planning, supplier relations, tooling, produc-

TABLE 18.8 Results of Seriousness Classification of Characteristics

Characteristic classification	Effect of classification on design tolerance	Effect of classification on amount of inspection	Number of dimensions checked	
			Before classification	After classification
Critical	None.	None.	154	154
Major	None.	None.	110	110
Minor A	Tolerance was increased by a specified amount (doubled, etc.) provided the part assembled satisfactorily.	Inspection was made normally, but to wider tolerances.	66	15
Minor B	Tolerance was ignored provided the part assembled satisfactorily.	Inspection was eliminated.	352	0
Total			682	279

tion, salvage, product auditing, and executing reporting. Vital qualities could now be identified with greater confidence, and it also became feasible to delegate class decisions and actions on a broad scale. For example, all class C defects could be assigned a common sampling plan, thereby avoiding the need for publishing numerous individual plans.

The multiple uses of seriousness classification systems make it desirable that the job of developing such a system be guided by an interdepartmental committee which has the responsibility for drafting a plan, modifying it, and recommending it for adoption. Such a committee has a series of tasks:

1. Determining the number of strata or classes of seriousness to use
2. Defining each class
3. Classifying each defect into one of the classes

Number of Levels or Strata.   In theory, the number may be large, e.g., a defect may have any weight from 1000 down to 1. In practice, such a large number of weights is too complex to administer. The actual plans in use consist of only several classes. While choice of the actual number of classes is arbitrary, extensive experience has shown that three or four classes suffice for a wide variety of situations.

Definitions for the Classes.   These will differ with the nature of the product, process, etc. However, plans in existence tend to show striking similarity in definition, the result in part of the influence of the Bell System classification plan (see also Dodge, 1928, and Dodge and Torrey, 1956). Not only was this pioneering plan uncommonly well reasoned out; the men who devised it were later consultants to some of the U.S. Armed Services during World War II, and their thinking influenced the classification plans adopted by these services. These plans, in turn, influenced the plans adopted by the contractors to the armed services.

The standard definitions adopted by the Bell System (see also Dodge and Torrey, 1956) are shown in Table 18.9. Study of these definitions discloses that there is an inner pattern common to the basic definitions (Table 18.10).

A composite of definitions used in food industry companies is shown in Table 18.11. It is evident that there are industry-to-industry differences in products, markets, etc., which require a tailor-made wording for each industry. In addition, the lists are not static. The growth of government regulation has further influenced the definition, as has the problem of repairs and guarantees for long-life products.

It is also evident that the classifications must simultaneously take into account multiple considerations such as functional performance, user awareness, and financial loss. For example, the effects and awareness of a radio receiver's defects may be as follows:

Defect	Effect on functional performance	Consumer awareness
Open circuit in power supply	Set is inoperative	Fully aware
Short circuit in resistor	Excess power consumption	Seldom aware
Poor exterior finish	No effect	Usually aware
Poor dress or internal wiring	No effect	Seldom aware

TABLE 18.9   Serious Classification of Defects (Bell System)

Class A—very serious (demerit value, 100)

a. Will surely cause an operating failure of the unit in service which cannot be readily corrected in the field, e.g., open relay winding; or

b. Will surely cause intermittent operating trouble, difficult to locate in the field, e.g., loose connection; or

c. Will render unit totally unfit for service, e.g., dial finger wheel does not return to normal after operation; or

d. Liable to cause personal injury or property damage under normal conditions of use, e.g., exposed part has sharp edges.

Class B—serious (demerit value, 50)

a. Will probably cause an operating failure of the unit in service which cannot be readily corrected in the field, e.g., protective finish missing from coaxial plug; or

b. Will surely cause an operating failure of the unit in service which can be readily corrected in the field, e.g., relay contact does not make; or

c. Will surely cause trouble of a nature less serious than an operating failure, such as substandard performance, e.g., protector block does not operate at specified voltage; or

d. Will surely involve increased maintenance or decreased life, e.g., single contact disk missing.

e. Will cause a major increase in installation effort by the customer, e.g., mounting holes in wrong location; or

f. Defects of appearance or finish that are extreme in intensity, e.g., finish does not match finish on other parts—requires refinishing.

Class C—moderately serious (demerit value, 10)

a. May possibly cause an operating failure of the unit in service, e.g., contact follow less than minimum; or

b. Likely to cause trouble of a nature less serious than an operating failure, such as substandard performance, e.g., ringer does operate within specified limits; or

c. Likely to involve increased maintenance or decreased life, e.g., dirty contact; or

d. Will cause a minor increase in installation effort by the customer, e.g., mounting bracket distorted; or

e. Major defects of appearance, finish, or workmanship, e.g., finish conspicuously scratched, designation omitted or illegible.

Class D—not serious (demerit value, 1)

a. Will not affect operation, maintenance, or life of the unit in service (including minor deviations from engineering requirements), e.g., sleeving too short; or

b. Minor defects of appearance, finish, or workmanship, e.g., slightly scratched finish.

Classifying the Defects.   This essential task is time-consuming, since there are always many defects to be classified. If the class definitions have been well drawn, the task becomes much easier.

During classifying, much confusion is cleared up. It is found that the seriousness of important visual defects depends not so much on whether the inspector can see it as on whether the consumer can see it. It is found that some words describing defects must be subdivided; i.e., a "stain" may be placed in two or

TABLE 18.10 Inner Pattern—Seriousness Classification System

Defect class	Demerit weight	Cause personal injury	Cause operating failure	Cause intermittent operating trouble difficult to locate in field	Cause substandard performance	Involve increased maintenance or decreased life	Cause increase in installation effort by customer	Appearance, finish, or workmanship defects
A	100	Liable to	Will surely*	Will surely				
B	50		Will surely† Will probably		Will surely	Will surely	Major increase	Major
C	10		May possibly		Likely to	Likely to	Minor increase	Minor
D	1		Will not		Will not	Will not		

*Not readily corrected in the field.
†Readily corrected in the field.

18.42

TABLE 18.11 Composite Definitions for Seriousness Classification in Food Industry

Defect	Effect on consumer safety	Effect on usage	Consumer relations	Loss to company	Effect on conformance to government relations
Critical	Will surely cause personal injury or illness	Will render the product totally unfit for use	Will offend consumer's sensibilities because of odor, appearance, etc.	Will lose customers and will result in losses greater than value of product	Fails to conform to regulations for purity, toxicity, identification
Major A	Very unlikely to cause personal injury or illness	May render the product unfit for use and may cause rejection by the user	Will likely be noticed by consumer, and will likely reduce product salability	May lose customers and may result in losses greater than the value of the product; will substantially reduce production yields	Fails to conform to regulations on weight, volume, or batch control
Major B	Will not cause injury or illness	Will make the product more difficult to use, e.g., removal from package, or will require improvisation by the user; affects appearance, neatness	May be noticed by some consumers, and may be an annoyance if noticed	Unlikely to lose customers; may require product replacement; may result in loss equal to product value	Minor nonconformance to regulations on weight, volume, or batch control, e.g., completeness of documentation
Minor	Will not cause injury or illness	Will not affect usability of the product; may affect appearance, neatness	Unlikely to be noticed by consumers, and of little concern if noticed	Unlikely to result in loss	Conforms fully to regulations

18.43

three classes depending on severity and location. In many ways, the work of classifying defects is rewarding through clearing away misconceptions and through giving a fresh view to all who participate.

Classification of Characteristics.   In some companies the formal "seriousness" classification is not of defects but of characteristics in the specifications. The classification may be in any of several alternatives:

   1. *Functional or nonfunctional:*   Where a single set of drawings carries both functional ("end use") requirements and nonfunctional ("means to an end") requirements, it is important to make clear which is which. (This is not to be confused with mechanical, chemical, or electrical functioning. In products such as jewelry or textiles, the most important functional requirement is *appearance.*) The purposes served by these two classes are generally alike throughout industry:

Functional requirements are intended to	*Nonfunctional requirements are intended to*
Ensure performance for intended use	Inform the shop as to method of manufacture
Ensure long, useful life	Reduce cost of manufacture
Minimize accident hazards	Facilitate manufacture
Protect life or property	Provide interchangeability in the shop
Provide interchangeability in the field	Provide information to toolmakers
Provide competitive sales advantage	

   "Which is which" becomes important because it directs the priorities of process design and many aspects of economics of manufacture, as well as the jurisdiction over waivers.

   When the engineers make this classification, they commonly add a designation such as E (for Engineering) to the functional characteristics. All others are then assumed to be nonfunctional.

   A comparable situation prevails in process specifications, where the need is to distinguish mandatory from advisory requirements, which correspond roughly to functional and nonfunctional requirements as applied to the product. However, the process specifications seldom make this distinction. (For further discussion, see Section 17, in Process Specifications, under Knowledge of "Supposed to Do.")

   2. *Seriousness classification:*   When this method is used, it parallels closely the classification into critical, major, and minor as used for classification of defects. (The contention is often raised that the tolerances on the specifications are an automatic form of seriousness classification, i.e., anything with assigned tolerances must be met and is "therefore" critical. An alternative contention is that the closeness of the tolerances is a key to seriousness classification, i.e., the narrowest tolerances are assigned to the most critical characteristics. When these contentions are examined more closely, they are found to contain too many exceptions to serve as firm rules for classifications.)

   The resulting classifications then become a supplement to the specification or are shown on the drawings themselves by some code designation, for example:

   Critical—   ⊕
   Major A—   ⊖
   Major B—   ◯
   Minor—not marked

One large automotive company differentiates between regulatory and nonregulatory critical characteristics by the use of two different symbols.

3. *Segregation of functional requirements:* Place in a separate document, such as an "engineering specification" or a "test specification."

4. *Shop practice tolerances versus special tolerances:* This method is based on preparation of a shop practice manual which sets out general use tolerances derived from the process capability of general use machines and tools. Once published, these shop practice tolerances govern all characteristics not specially toleranced.

Who Classifies?   For defect classification, an interdepartmental committee is the ideal choice. This provides each department with the benefits derived from the process of active review, and it also produces a better final result (sometimes the committee goes further and establishes a plan for product rating, including demerit weights for each class; see Section 8, under Product Auditing). However, some companies assign a staff specialist to prepare a proposed classification, which is then reviewed by all interested departments. The specialist is usually a quality control engineer.

When the classification is limited to specified characteristics, e.g., functional versus nonfunctional, the designer usually prepares the draft.

SENSORY QUALITIES

"Sensory qualities" are those for which we lack technological measuring instruments and for which the senses of human beings must be used as measuring instruments. (For some special purposes, e.g., tests of toxicity, the test panel may consist of animals.) Sensory qualities may involve:

Technological performance of the product, e.g., adhesion of a protective coating; friction of a sliding fit

Esthetic characteristics of consumer products, e.g., taste of food, odor of perfume, appearance of carpets, noise of room air conditioners

In common with other qualities, sensor qualities require:

1. Discovery of which characteristics, and in what degree, are required to meet the needs of fitness for use
2. Design of products which will possess these characteristics
3. Establishment of product and process standards, and of tests which will simulate fitness for use
4. Judgment of conformance to the product and process standards

This multiplicity of tasks requires a corresponding multiplicity in type of sensory test panel used, choice of test design, etc. It is easy to become confused, since the conventional terminology does not reflect the great differences needed in the approaches. Table 18.12 lists some of the main problems requiring use of sensory testing and shows the resulting differences in subject matter of test, choice of test panel, environment, statistical design, etc.

Discovery of Sensory Characteristics Required for Fitness for Use.   For technological sensory qualities, this determination is made using mainly the conventional methods of product development, laboratory testing, field tryouts, etc., as discussed in Section 13. Commonly it is feasible to set up, in the laboratory, test criteria which simulate field usage. Such simulation greatly simplifies discovery of the needed characteristics of the product.

Esthetic sensory qualities present a more difficult problem and pose several questions as to fitness for use:

Do consumers like or dislike the esthetic quality in question, and to what degree? (The term "consumer" commonly applies to the user of products made for sale and use by individuals, as distinguished from enterprises. More broadly, most commercial products are also "used" by individuals, e.g., the operator running a lathe, the programmer running a computer, the employee using the cafeteria. The collective views of these industrial users become an important input to decisions on esthetic qualities for commerical products.)

Of two or more competing products (exhibiting the same sensory quality), which do consumers prefer?

At what threshold level of an esthetic quality do consumers notice its presence?

On the face of it, manufacturing company employees (managers, sales persons, engineers, inspectors) are qualified to answer these questions, since they are also members of the consuming public. However, in practice, these employees exhibit strong biases due to close association with the product, vested departmental interests, and undue sensitivity arising from intimate knowledge. Some costly instances of marketing failure and of perfectionism have been directly traceable to biased judgments of consumer preference made by company employees. The safe course is to secure answers to these questions not from company employees but from consumers (or potential consumers) in the marketplace. The cost of the market research may restrict this approach to the important qualities. (The very question of which are the important qualities is likewise best answered by consumers in the marketplace.)

The upper half of Table 18.12 deals with these same three questions and notes that to get objective answers, we:

Employ panel members who are representative of consumers in the marketplace. The resulting data are more likely to predict actual market response to the product.

Avoid training of the panelists. The potential and actual consumers represent a mixture of people in varying degrees of product knowledge.

Conduct the study under conditions of regular use, not in a laboratory environment. Only in this way can the data reflect the future results of actual usage.

Consumer Likes and Dislikes.   One approach to prediction of consumer acceptance of a new product is to secure data on consumer likes or dislikes. For example, a food company may be interested in securing market reaction to a new ingredient (e.g., passion fruit). A new food formulation containing the ingredient under test is submitted to numerous users. Their responses are secured on a "hedonic" scale, e.g., (1) like very much, (2) like, (3) neither like nor dislike, (4) dislike, (5) dislike very much.

The consumer panel may consist of a "standing panel" of several hundred families to whom samples are sent "free." (Such panels are usually contacted not

TABLE 18.12 Uses of Sensory Tests

Problem	Products under test—what is being measured	Panel selected from	Criteria for selection of panel members	Prior training of panel members	Test environment desired	Type of test	Results of test
To discover consumer likes and dislikes	Experimental products containing new or changed qualities	Potential consumers	Should be representative of consumers in the market	None	Conditions of regular use of the product	Quality evaluation	Rating of product on a "hedonic scale" of how well liked
To discover consumer preferences	Two (or more) different products, for the same quality	Consumers	Should be representative of consumers in the market	None	Conditions of regular use of the product	Preference test	Percent and degree of preference of product A versus product B
To discover consumer sensitivity	A controlled selection of products varying across the range under study	Consumers	Should be representative of consumers in the market	None	Conditions of regular use of the product	Special	Basis for decision on product tolerances
To discover effect, on a sensory quality, of material and process changes (for design of products and processes)	A controlled selection of products varying across the range under study	Laboratory or other company personnel	Proved ability to discriminate with respect to the quality under study	Experience with testing and with qualities under test	Controlled laboratory conditions	Various	Relationship of material and process variables to effect on quality characteristic under study
Process regulation	Samples of intermediate or finished product	Quality control laboratory or other company personnel	Proved ability to discriminate	Experience with testing and with qualities under test	Controlled laboratory conditions	Duo-trio, triangle, etc.	Basis for decision on whether to change process
Product (batch or lot) acceptance	Finished products	Quality control laboratory	Proved ability to discriminate	Experience with testing and with qualities under test	Controlled laboratory conditions	Duo-trio, triangle, etc.	Basis for decision on acceptance of product

by the food company but by an intermediate research company, so as to avoid any associations with the name of the food company.) The "payment" is in data on the extent to which the family (adults, children, pets) liked or disliked the product. Alternatively, the panel may consist of other groups, e.g., passersby at a booth rented in a department store.

The data on the hedonic scale are summarized in conventional ways. As experience is gained in the response patterns to such tests, the decisions on whether to proceed further with the new product can be made with greater and greater confidence.

Consumer Preference Testing. The aim of this test is to discover consumer preferences, e.g., our product versus competitors' products, new designs versus current designs, etc. In competitive markets, such preference tests can give useful guides to decisions on product marketability, pricing, etc.

For preference testing, the submission to the consumer panel always consists of two or more samples. The responses may be "forced choice," i.e., prefer A or prefer B. Another form involves degrees of preference, e.g., strongly prefer A, prefer A, no preference, prefer B, strongly prefer B.

Figure 3.2 (in Section 3, Quality and Income) is an example showing the results of consumer preference testing of 41 products plotted against share of market. The great concentration of data along the horizontal axis suggests strongly that products with consumer preference test results of less than 30 percent are unable to survive in a competitive market, all other things being equal.

Consumer Sensitivity Testing. In this form of test, the purpose is to discover the "threshold" level at which consumers can detect the presence of sensory qualities. The qualities under test may be "desirable." For example, if an expensive ingredient is used in a product blend, it is very useful to know the threshold concentration level which ensures consumer recognition of the ingredient. The qualities under test may also be "undesirable." For example, a product exhibits varying degrees of visual blemish. It is very useful to know the threshold degree of defectiveness which makes the consumer respond negatively to the product.

In consumer-sensitivity testing, a graduated set of samples is prepared, each exhibiting a progressively greater extent of the quality or deficiency under investigation. These samples are submitted to a consumer panel as part of an organized study.

For example, in two companies—one making sterling silverware and the other making costume jewelry—studies were conducted to discover consumer sensitivity to visual defects. In both companies, a committee of key people (from Marketing, Design, Manufacture, and Quality) structured a plan of study as follows:

1. An assortment of product was chosen to reflect the principal visual defects, the principal products in the product line, and the principal price levels.

2. These samples were inspected in the factory by the regular inspectors to determine the severity of the defects as judged by the frequency with which the inspectors rejected the various units of product.

3. The assortment of products was then shown to a number of consumer panels chosen from those segments of the buying public which constituted important customer classes, e.g., suburban women, college students, etc. These panels reviewed the products under conditions which simulated use of the product, e.g., silverware in place settings on a dining room table. The consumers were instructed (by printed card) somewhat as follows: "Assume you have previously bought these products and they have been delivered to you. Naturally,

you will want to look them over to see that the merchandise is satisfactory. Will you be good enough to look it over, and if you see anything which is objectionable to you, will you please point it out to us?"

The resulting data showed that the consumer panels were highly sensitive to some defects. For such defects the strict visual standards were retained. For certain other defects the consumer sensitivity was far less than factor-inspector sensitivity. For such defects the standards were relaxed. In still other instances, some operations had deliberately been omitted, but the consumers proved to be insensitive to the effect of the omission. As a result, the operations were abolished.

Consumer-sensitivity testing is an extension of the principle that "the consumer is right." This principle may be subdivided as follows:

1. The consumer is right as to qualities he or she can sense. As to such qualities, the manufacturer is justified in taking action to make such qualities acceptable to the consumer.

2. The consumer is also right as to qualities he or she *cannot* sense. The manufacturer is not justified in adding costs to create an esthetic effect not sensed by the consumer.

3. Where, for a given quality, the customer is sensitive to a limited level but not beyond, the manufacturer should take action to make the quality to that level but not beyond.

The intermediate marketing chain sometimes interferes with these principles. Sales clerks are proficient in emphasizing product differences, whether important or not. In turn, dealers are alert to seize on such differences to wring concessions out of competing manufacturers. A frequent result is that all manufacturers are driven to adopt wasteful standards, resulting in a needlessly high cost, e.g., finishes on nonworking or nonvisible surfaces. Elimination of such perfectionism commonly requires that the manufacturer secure data direct from consumers and then use the data to convince the distribution chain. These same data may be needed to convince other nonconsumers who exhibit perfectionist tendencies: upper management, designers, salespeople, inspectors, etc.

Visual Quality Characteristics.   These are a special category of sensory qualities. (Visual inspection remains the largest single form of inspection activity.) For these characteristics, the written specifications seldom describe completely what is wanted, and often inspectors are left to make their own interpretation. In such cases, inspectors are really making two judgments simultaneously:

1. What is the meaning of this visual characteristic of the specification, e.g., what is the standard?

2. Does this unit of product conform to the standard?

Where inspectors understand fitness for use, they are qualified to make both these judgments. If a particular inspector lacks this knowledge, he or she is qualified only to make judgment 2, no matter how long on the job. Extensive experience has shown that inspectors who lack this knowledge differ widely when setting standards and, in addition, do not remain consistent. (As an example, from the consulting experience of J. M. Juran, in an optical company, study of the methods used by 18 different inspectors, engineers, etc., disclosed the existence of six methods of counting the number of "fringes of irregularity.")

Several methods are available to planners to clarify the standard for visual characteristics.

Visual Inspection Standards. The most elementary form of visual standard is the limit sample—a unit of product showing the worst condition acceptable. In using this standard the inspector is aided in two ways:

1. The Sample conveys a more precise meaning than does a written specification.
2. The inspection is now made by comparison, which is well known to give more consistent results than judgment in the absence of comparison.

A more elaborate form of visual standards involves preparation of an exhibit of samples of varying degrees of defects, ranging from clearly defective to clearly acceptable. See, for an example involving solder connections, Leek (1975 and 1976), who describes how the companies Martin Marietta and Northrup support series or "ranges" to provide manufacturing latitude in processing material, while at the same time identifying minimum and maximum limits on visual attributes. This exhibit is used to secure the collective judgments of all who have a stake in the standard—consumers, supervisors, engineers, inspectors. Based on these judgments, standards are agreed on and limit samples are chosen. (It is also feasible to estimate, by sampling, what would be the yield of the process, and thereby the cost of defects, for any one of the various degrees of defectiveness.)

In products sold for esthetic appeal, appearance becomes a major element of fitness for use and commonly a major element of cost as well. In such cases, an exhibit of samples of various degrees of defects intermingled with perfect units of product becomes a means of measuring consumer sensitivity (or insensitivity) to various defects. Use of consumer panels to judge such mixtures of product invariably confirms some previous concepts but also denies some long-standing beliefs held by the managers as well as by the inspectors.

In the sterling silverware case, above, consumers were quite sensitive to several types of defect—they held out 22 percent of the defects present. However, for the bulk of defects, the consumers were quite insensitive and found only 3 percent of such defects. The salespeople generally found twice as many defects as consumers but still considerable less than factory inspectors.

A further use of samples of various defects is to establish *grades* of defects. The concept of different grades is vital when a plant makes products which, while outwardly similar, are used in widely different applications, e.g., ball bearings used for precision instruments and those used for roller skates, lenses for precision apparatus and lenses for simple magnifiers, sterling silverware and plated silverware. Unless the grades are well defined and spelled out in authoritative form, the risk is that the inspectors will apply one standard to all grades.

Once limit samples have been agreed on, there remains a problem of providing working standards to the inspection force. Sometimes it is feasible to select duplicates for inspection use while retaining the official standard sample in the laboratory. An alternative is to prepare photographs (sometimes stereoscopic) of the approved standards and to distribute these photographs instead. (See also Schilling, 1982.)

Standardizing the Conditions of Inspection. Visual inspection results are greatly influenced by the type, color, and intensity of illumination, by the angle of viewing, by the viewing distance, etc. Standardizing these conditions is a long step in the direction of securing uniform inspection results.

In the case of esthetic visual qualities, the guiding rule for conditions of inspection is to simulate the conditions of use, but with a factor of safety.

Establish a "fading distance." In some products the variety of visual defects is so great and the range of severity so wide that the creation of visual standards becomes prohibitively complex. An alternative approach is to standardize the conditions of inspection and then to establish a *fading distance* for each broad defect class. The definition for a defect becomes "anything which can be seen at the fading distance." [This technique appears to have been evolved in 1951 by N. O. Langenborg of St. Regis Paper Company. See also Riley (1979).]

Design of Products to Achieve Sensory Effects.   The approach to this product design parallels closely the general approach set out in Section 13, Product Development. What is special is the absence of agreed units of measure and of instruments which can measure in terms of those units. Lacking these tools, the methods of sensory testing must be applied to the new designs, using both laboratory panels and consumer panels. Experiments involving substitution of materials, changes in process, reformulation, etc., all require sensory evaluations if cause and effect relationships are to be established. The laboratory panels provide the judgment on which these relationships can be based. The consumer panels are used to confirm the acceptability of the design in the marketplace.

The fourth row of Table 18.12 traces the use of sensory testing to discover the effect of material and process changes on sensory qualities. It is seen that the testing is done by a laboratory panel, specially selected and trained and working under controlled laboratory conditions.

Providing Standards for Sensory Qualities.   Once the laboratory and consumer panels have provided the technological and marketing data, respectively, there remains a problem of setting standards to serve as a future basis for judging conformance. Setting these standards can be done by an organized approach which also considers factory yields and economics. This organized approach includes the following:

1. Definition of various levels of sensory quality along a "scale of measurement," i.e., a hedonic scale or a degree of defect severity as judged by panels.

2. Estimation of cost of meeting these various levels based on studies of process yields, need for added refinements in the process, etc.

3. Consideration of the effect of the various levels on product marketability based on consumer-sensitivity data, competitive product analysis, etc. (See Figure 18.2.)

4. Decision on the level to be adopted as the standard. This decision should be made with full participation of all departments in interest.

5. Executive approval of the standards. This approval should be formalized. The signature of the responsible executive(s) should appear on the approved samples (or on the document evidencing the approval). This formality serves to clear the air on decision making as well as to identify the samples unmistakably. These standards take any of numerous forms: physical samples of product for visual comparison, feel, texture, etc.; photographs; sound recordings; formulation of taste and smell; and still others.

6. Duplication of the standard for shop use. For *stable* products, the sensory standard can be filed like any other master reference standard. Duplicates can be prepared for everyday use, and these duplicates can be checked against the master under a scheduled maintenance plan. For *unstable* products, new masters must regularly be prepared, at intervals shorter than the rate of deterioration. Sometimes special storage or preservatives can help to stabilize the master.

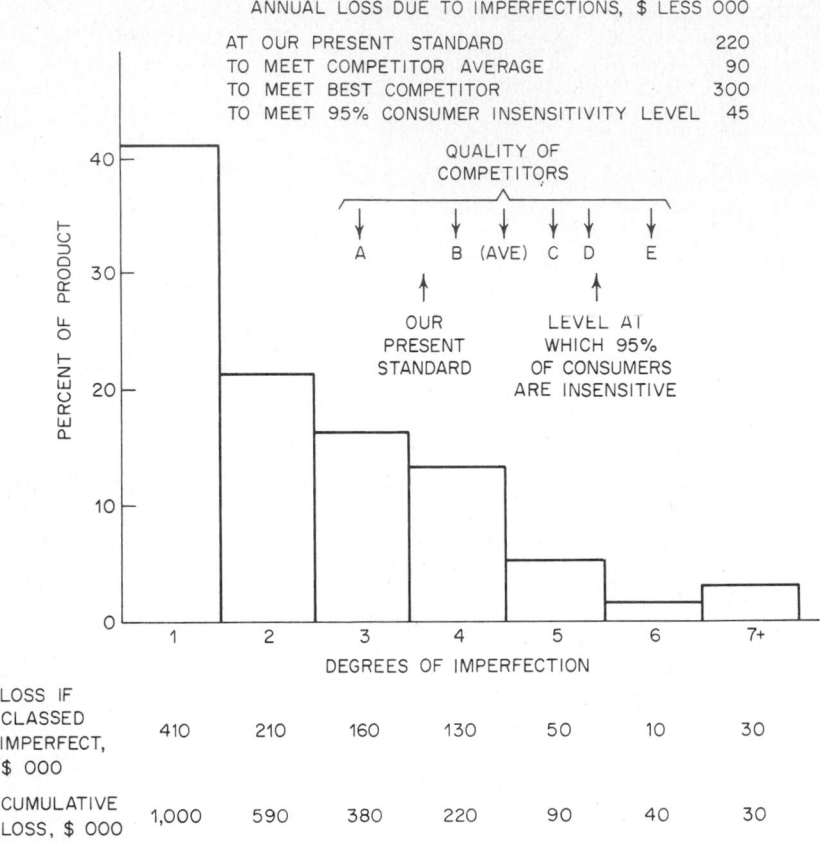

ANNUAL LOSS DUE TO IMPERFECTIONS, $ LESS 000

AT OUR PRESENT STANDARD	220
TO MEET COMPETITOR AVERAGE	90
TO MEET BEST COMPETITOR	300
TO MEET 95% CONSUMER INSENSITIVITY LEVEL	45

	1	2	3	4	5	6	7+
LOSS IF CLASSED IMPERFECT, $ 000	410	210	160	130	50	10	30
CUMULATIVE LOSS, $ 000	1,000	590	380	220	90	40	30

FIG. 18.2 Summary for executive decision on sensory standards.

Judgment of Conformance to Sensory Standards. The lowest two rows in Table 18.12 elaborate this problem. It is evident that there are conformance problems both as to process regulation and as to product acceptance. Laboratory panels are used throughout, under controlled laboratory conditions, employing various types of sensory tests and making use of the approved standards for reference purposes.

Panels for Sensory Testing. Panels are composed of two very different populations, and these must not be confused.

Consumer Panels. These serve to provide information on fitness for use in its various aspects (consumer likes and dislikes, preferences, sensitivity). The prime qualification for such a panel is to be representative of the consumers in the market. Since this precludes prior selection for ability to discriminate, it follows that a proportion of the panel members will lack the ability to make discriminations (e.g., color blindness). Training is also precluded because it introduces bias. Controlled test environments are also precluded; the conditions must be those of normal usage. These restrictions combine to make consumer panels numerically large. Often they run to hundreds of people. As a corollary, the time to conduct a test is lengthy—it can readily run to weeks and even months.

Laboratory Panels. These serve to judge conformance to standards and to provide product and process research data. Here the need is to make prompt, low-cost judgments. Selection of panel members for this purpose is based on tested ability to discriminate, and this ability is then sharpened by training. The work of these panels is carried out under controlled laboratory conditions, hence the name "laboratory panels." These features make it possible for small panels to provide prompt, low-cost data of measurable precision.

Selection of Laboratory Panels. In this selection it is first necessary to distinguish the candidate's (1) inherent ability to sense from (2) the ability to translate what is sensed into a judgment. For example, in color classification, the distinguishing terms are color blindness and color ignorance. Ability to sense differs in humans, and this difference is discoverable by selection tests; i.e., tests for visual acuity, taste perception, etc. If the candidate lacks the ability to sense, it is normally not feasible nor economic to awaken this ability. If, however, the candidate has the sensory ability, then he or she can be trained to use this ability to render judgments.

The overwhelming source of laboratory panelists is company employees. The company makes clear its needs for panelists and invites employees to volunteer to be tested for qualification. Responses are generally good, so that there is little difficulty in selecting and training enough panelists to provide for attrition in existing panels. The job of panelist is almost always a part-time job and consitutes a welcome change from the regular job (bottling line or whatever).

Tests used for screening prospective panelists are designed to discover (1) *sensitivity,* i.e., ability to detect the stimulus under study, and (2) *consistency,* i.e., ability to reproduce results on repeated testing. (For an early, pioneering study, see Helm and Trolle, 1946.) The paper reports extensive studies made at Carlsberg Breweries, Copenhagen, Denmark, and shows results for various categories of personnel. [See also Louis (1981) for a later discussion on testing by Jos. Schlitz Brewing Company.] These tests make use of various statistical designs as discussed in Sensory Tests: Design and Analysis, below. To execute these designs, test samples are prepared to possess known concentrations or degrees of the characteristics under study. (For products made as discrete units, the examination may be based on a preselected lot of graded samples. For coalesced products, special samples, in varying degrees of concentration, are commonly prepared.) The ability of the prospective panelist to judge the samples correctly is the decisive element in the panel-selection process. (For many years, industries such as brewing, food, and candy had put their confidence in a taste "expert." When, in due course, these experts were tested under statistical designs, some of the companies underwent a good deal of shock.)

Environment for Laboratory Panels. The laboratory panels conduct their work under controlled laboratory conditions to minimize the effect of extraneous variables, reduce the sample sizes needed, and increase the precision of results. See, for example, Figure 18.3, which shows the environment of a taste-test panel. In such an environment, unwanted variables can be stratified or randomized, design of experiments can be scientific, and cost of experimentation can be held to a minimum for a given precision.

Of course, laboratory testing is not conclusive as to consumer acceptability, which is properly determined by actual use by consumers (hence "kitchen-tested," "road-tested," etc.); it is still only an approximation. Simulated service

FIG. 18.3 Sensory test panel. *(Courtesy Schenley Distillers, Inc., Cincinnati, OH.)*

testing is an approximation further removed. Materials test data (to predict *potential* service results) are an approximation still further removed.

Selecting Inspectors for Sensory Tests. It is important for the inspector to have a *feel* for the end use of the product. He or she can then not only categorize the material or product but make more intelligent decisions in borderline circumstances (Chebookjian, 1980). However, four elements are needed to conduct a sensory or *cosmetic* inspection program in order to avoid too much product being rejected. They are documented cosmetic criteria, proper viewing and lighting conditions, methods to monitor inspection results, and formal training for inspectors who have decision-making authority (Davidson, 1982). The above four elements are most effective if those inspectors are selected who have the highest abilities to discriminate sensory characteristics. Evaluation techniques are rooted in common statistical methods (see Geidel, 1978), and they range from geometrical methods (Ohta and Kase, 1980) to the use of the *indifference zone approach* (Shimoda and Miyazaki, 1981).

Sensory Tests: Design and Analysis. There are numerous designs of sensory tests, some of them quite complex. Some of the basic forms are described below.

Tests for Differences or Similarities. These include:

1. *The paired-comparison test:* Product is submitted to members of a panel in pairs of samples. One sample is identified to each panelist as the standard or

"control"; the other is the test sample. The panelist is asked to judge and record the difference on a scale of differences (such as no difference, slight difference; pronounced difference). Some of the pairs have no difference; i.e., both are "controls."

2. *The triangle test:* The panelist is asked to identify the odd sample in a group of three, two of which are alike. He or she may also be asked to estimate the degree of difference and to describe the difference between the odd sample and the two like samples.

3. *The duo-trio test:* The panelist is asked to identify which of two samples is like the "control" to which she or he has previously been subjected. For example, in liquor manufacture, the aim is to make each batch indistinguishable in taste from past batches. The duo-trio test is used as a product-acceptance test. Each panelist tastes the "control," which he or she is told comes from previous product. Then each panelist tastes the two remaining samples, one of which is "control" and the other the batch under test. However, the panelists are not told which is which. If the data make clear that the panel cannot distinguish the new batch from the control, the batch is accepted. Otherwise, it is reblended.

4. *Ranking test:* Coded samples are submitted to each panelist, who is asked to rank them in the order of concentration.

Tests for Quality Description. The panelist is asked to judge the absence, presence, or intensity of various suspected quality characteristics in the sample. A usual form is "profile" testing, in which the characteristics to be judged are listed in advance and the panelist is used as an instrument for qualitative and quantitative analysis, i.e., to "prepare a profile."

Descriptive tests are also used to identify the seeming nature of unknown qualities ("it smells like lilac").

Tests for Quality Preference or Acceptance. These are aimed at judging marketability and therefore make use of consumer panels. The most usual forms are:

1. Hedonic scale tests, which rank the product anywhere between limits, e.g., from "like very much" down to "dislike very much."

2. "Home use" testing done by a "standing" panel of consumers to whom products and instructions are delivered. The panel sends its data in return. Emphasis is on *use* testing at the point of use.

3. "Store testing" done by a sample of the stream of people flowing through a store. Data are recorded by a trained observer. Emphasis is on *preference* testing at the point of *sale.* (See Brandt, 1963.)

Analysis of sensory test data is mainly by conventional statistical significance tests. [See generally Section 23 under Tests of Hypotheses. However, a specialized literature has also evolved. Methods for dealing with paired comparisons were prepared by Scheffe (1952).] An early use of the duo-trio test was by Peryam (1950), who used 2.26 as the boundary for significance, in accordance with the formula:

$$\sigma_p = \left(\frac{pq}{n}\right)^{1/2}$$

TABLE 18.13 Rating Table for Sensory Testing

Total judgments	Number correct	Percent correct	SE distance from 50% (σ_p rating)	Percent area between 50% and this point	Percent area beyond this point
20	10	50.0	0.0	0.0	50.0
20	11	55.0	0.4	15.6	34.4
20	12	60.0	0.9	31.6	18.4
20	13	65.0	1.3	40.3	9.7
20	14	70.0	1.8	46.4	3.6
20	15	75.0	2.2	48.6	1.4
20	16	80.0	2.7	49.7	0.3
20	17	85.0	3.1	49.9	0.1
20	18	90.0	3.6	50.0—	Very small
20	19	95.0	4.0	50.0—	Very small
20	20	100.0	4.5	50.0—	Very small
30	18	60.0	1.1	36.4	13.6
30	19	63.3	1.5	43.3	6.7
30	20	66.7	1.8	46.4	3.6
30	21	70.0	2.2	48.6	1.4
30	22	73.3	2.6	49.6	0.4
30	23	76.7	2.9	49.8	0.2
30	24	80.0	3.3	50.0—	Very small

where p = fraction correct identification of the unknown with standard
q = fraction incorrect = $(1 - p)$
n = number of samples in the series

At this level of significance, the probability is 0.014 that the lot is actually at standard despite the ratings of the panelists to the contrary. Peryam's table for sample sizes of 20 and 30 is reproduced as Table 18.13.

A comparison of operating characteristic curves for the pair, duo-trio, and triangle tests is provided by Fortuin and Van Beek (1960).

Creating New Instruments to Measure Sensory Qualities. Many sensory qualities formerly judged by human perception are now measured by instruments. This development of new instrumentation goes on apace, using essentially the following approach (based on a procedure set out by Dr. Amihud Kramer, 1952; see also Hains, 1978):

1. Define precisely what is meant by the quality characteristic under discussion. This must be done with participation of all interested parties.
2. Discover, through analytical study, the subcharacteristics, and define them in a way which permits, in theory, measurement by some inanimate instrument.
3. Search the literature to become informed on methods already in existence or under development for measuring these subcharacteristics. This search will disclose a number of such possible measurement methods.
4. Choose or create product samples which vary widely for the subcharacteristics. Test a limited number (10 to 50) of samples with each of the various

measurement methods, and correlate these tests with evaluation by panels of human testers. The human evaluation here aims not to measure personal preferences but to rate the degree to which the samples possess the variable under study. Hence the main requirement of the panel is that it be able to discriminate the subcharacteristics under study. Discard those measurement methods which lack precision or which fail to reflect human evaluation.

5. For the remaining, more promising measurement methods, conduct tests on a larger number of samples (100 to 1000) also chosen to reflect the entire range of quality variation. In addition, conduct tests of duplicate samples using evaluation by human test panels.

6. Correlate the results of measurement against the human test panel evaluation; select that method which gives a high, outstanding correlation. (Multiple correlation methods may be necessary.)

7. Improve and simplify the selected measurement method through further test and correlation.

8. Establish a scale of grades through use of a human sensory test panel. At this stage, the prime purpose of the human test panel is *to state preferences* along the scale of measure. Hence the main requirement of this panel is that it be representative of the producers and users of the product.

9. Weigh the various subcharacteristics in accordance with their rated performance (see also Montville, 1983, and Papadopoulos, 1983).

10. Develop the sampling procedures needed to apply the resulting method of measurement.

MEASUREMENT—AN INTRODUCTION

Conduct of the quality function depends heavily on quantification of product and process characteristics. This quantification is done through a systematic approach involving:

1. Definition of standardized units called "units of measure" which permit conversion of abstractions (e.g., length, mass) into a form capable of being quantified (e.g., meter, kilogram).

2. *Instruments* which are calibrated in terms of these standardized units of measure.

3. Use of these instruments to quantify or *measure* the extent to which the product or process possesses the characteristic under study. This process of quantification is called "measurement."

The word "measurement" has multiple meanings, these being principally:

1. The *process* of quantification, e.g., "the measurement was done in the laboratory"

2. The resulting number, e.g., "the measurement fell within the tolerances"

Measurement rests on a highly organized, scientific base called "metrology," i.e., the science of measurement. This science underlies the entire systematic approach through which we quantify quality characteristics.

UNITS OF MEASURE

The concept of quantifying bigness and smallness is thousands of years old. At first, units of measure were in terms of parts of the human body. For example, the ancient Egyptian unit of measure for length was the royal cubit, which was defined as the length of the forearm of the reigning pharaoh.

With the expansion of commerce, and especially of international commerce, the metrologists evolved systems of international units of measure, the chief systems being the metric and the English. The metric system is entirely based on decimal notation and primarily uses units of measure which scientists developed in the nineteenth and twentieth centuries. The English system is only partially based on decimal notation, and includes units of measure which antedate the industrial revolution.

Metrication. The existence of multiple systems of measurement is a serious handicap to international commerce. During the twentieth century there has been extensive adoption of the metric system by countries previously using the English or other systems. At the beginning of the 1970s, all industrialized countries with the single exception of the United States had either adopted the metric system or had decided to do so. In the United States, resistance to the metric system arises from a heavy investment in the English system coupled with a low ratio of volume of international trade to total size of the economy. However, those industries which are strongly exposed to international trade have largely adopted dual systems or have converted to metric. On purely technological grounds, the metric system is widely regarded as preferable to the English. (For further discussion see Sharp, 1976, and Darby, 1970.)

Despite the lack of a positive national plan for converting to metric, the United States is in a slow conversion process. The gradual conversion, if continued, will likely become virtually complete in about a century, whereas a planned program would reduce the conversion time to a decade or two. (For further discussion, see De Simone, 1971.)

Conversion costs in specific cases vary widely. Dual reading scales for instruments or dual reading dials for machines may involve less than $100 per instance. In contrast, new digital readout systems for machine tools may run to several thousand dollars per axis (Blaufuss, 1972).

Aside from conversion of machine tools, instruments, and small tools, there are other costs (De Simone, 1972):

Revision of specifications, standards, and other documentation

Provision of dual sets of spare parts during the conversion process

Retraining of personnel

SI System. More recently there has been evolved a fully coherent international system, the Système International d'Unités (SI). This SI system consists of:

1. Seven fundamental units of measure—for length, mass, time, electric current, temperature, light intensity, and amount of substance
2. Two supplemental units for plane and solid angles
3. A long list of units derived from 1 and 2
4. A standardized terminology for multiples and subdivisions of all units of measure

TABLE 18.14 SI System Units of Measure

Characteristic	Unit of measure	Symbol	Formula
	Fundamental units		
Length	Meter	m	
Mass	Kilogram	kg	
Time	second	s	
Electric current	ampere	A	
Thermodynamic temperature	Kelvin	K	
Luminous intensity	candela	cd	
Amount of substance	Mole	mol	
	Supplementary units		
Plane angle	radian	rad	
Solid angle	steradian	sr	
	Derived units		
Area	square meter	m^2	
Volume	cubic meter	m^3	
Frequency	hertz	Hz	(s^{-1})
Density	kilogram per cubic meter	kg/m^3	
Velocity	meter per second	m/s	
Angular velocity	radian per second	rad/s	
Acceleration	meter per second squared	m/s^2	
Angular acceleration	radian per second squared	rad/s^2	
Force	newton	N	(kg/ms)
Pressure	newton per sq meter	N/m^2	
Kinematic viscosity	sq meter per second	m^2/s	
Dynamic viscosity	newton-second per sq meter	$N \cdot s/m^2$	
Work, energy, quantity of heat	joule	J	(N/m)
Power	watt	W	(J/s)
Electric charge	coulomb	C	(A/s)
Voltage, potential difference, electromotive force	volt	V	(W/A)
Electric field strength	volt per meter	V/m	
Electric resistance	ohm	Ω	(V/A)
Electric capacitance	farad	F	(A/s/V)
Magnetic flux	weber	Wb	(V/s)
Inductance	henry	H	(V/s/A)
Magnetic flux density	tesla	T	(Wb/m^2)
Magnetic field strength	ampere per meter	A/m	
Magnetomotive force	ampere	A	
Luminous flux	lumen	lm	(cd/sr)
Luminance	candela per sq meter	cd/m^2	
Illumination	lux	lx	(lm/m^2)

Table 18.14 lists the fundamental, supplemental, and derived units of the SI system along with the symbols used and the derivation formulas. (See Griffin, 1980, and McNish, 1966.) Table 18.15 lists the terms used for multiples and subdivisions of these units of measure. (See also "SI—Systeme International Rationale," 1972.)

TABLE 18.15   SI System Multiples and Subdivisions

Multiple or subdivision	Prefix	Symbol
1 000 000 000 000 = 10^{12}	tera	T
1 000 000 000 = 10^{9}	giga	G
1 000 000 = 10^{6}	mega	M
1 000 = 10^{3}	kilo	k
100 = 10^{2}	hecto*	h
10 = 10^{1}	deca*	da
0.1 = 10^{-1}	deci*	d
0.01 = 10^{-2}	centi*	c
0.001 = 10^{-3}	milli	m
0.000 001 = 10^{-6}	micro	μ
0.000 000 001 = 10^{-9}	nano	n
0.000 000 000 001 = 10^{-12}	pico	p
0.000 000 000 000 001 = 10^{-15}	femto	f
0.000 000 000 000 000 001 = 10^{-18}	atto	a

*Use is discouraged.

The SI system is fully compatible with the metric system, though it supersedes some earlier units (e.g., liter, calorie). The SI system is not fully compatible with the English system of feet, pounds, etc., though conversion factors are, of course, available.

Nonmeasurable Characteristics.   For many characteristics there are as yet no agreed units of measure. Nevertheless, useful evaluations can be made of such characteristics by:

1. *Sensory testing:*   Here no instrument is available for sensing, and the sensing is done by human sense organs (taste, feel, smell, etc.). For a full discussion, see Section 18, under Sensory Qualities.
2. *Instrument testing:*   An example is the "nondestructive" testing performed to detect weaknesses in metal components (see below, under Nondestructive Testing).

Development of new units of measure and of new sensing instruments is a continuing process. All today's units of measure were evolved to replace qualitative evaluations. Presumably all today's qualitative evaluations will, at some time in the future, be susceptible of measurement using agreed units of measure.

MEASUREMENT STANDARDS

The seven fundamental units of the International System (SI) are defined as shown in Table 18.16. It is seen that except for the kilogram, all units are defined in terms of natural phenomena. (The kilogram is defined as the mass of a specific object.)

Primary Reference Standards.   In all industrialized countries there exists a national bureau of standards whose functions include construction and maintenance of "primary reference standards." These standards consist of copies of the

TABLE 18.16 Definitions of Fundamental Units of the SI System

Unit	Definition
Meter, m	1/650 763.73 Wavelengths in vacuo of the unperturbed transition 2_{p10}—$5d_5$ in ^{86}Kr
Kilogram, kg	Mass of the international kilogram at Sevres, France
Second, s	1/31 556 925 974 7 of the tropical year at 12^h ET, 0 January 1900, supplementarily defined in 1964 in terms of the cesium F, 4; M, 0 to F, 3; M, 0, transition, the frequency assigned being 9 192 631 770 Hz
Kelvin, K	Defined in the thermodynamic scale by assigning 273.16 K to the triple point of water (freezing point, 273.15 K = 0°C)
Ampere, A	The constant current which, if maintained in two straight parallel conductors of infinite length, of negligible circular sections, and placed 1 m apart in a vacuum, will produce between these conductors a force equal to 2×10^{-7} mks unit of force per meter of length.
Candela, cd	1/60 of the intensity of 1 cm^2 of a perfect radiator at the temperature of freezing platinum.
Mole, mol	An amount of substance whose weight in grams numerically equals the molecular formula weight.

International Kilogram plus measuring systems which are responsive to the definitions of the fundamental units (Table 18.16 and to the derived units of Table 18.14).

In addition, professional societies, (e.g., American Society for Testing and Materials) have evolved standardized test methods for measuring many hundreds of quality characteristics not listed in Table 18.13. These standard test methods describe the test conditions, equipment, procedure, etc., to be followed. The various national bureaus of standards, as well as other laboratories, then develop primary reference standards which embody the units of measure corresponding to these standard test methods.

Primary reference standards have a distinct legal status, since commercial contracts usually require that "measuring and test equipment shall be calibrated . . . utilizing reference standards . . . whose calibration is certified as being traceable to the National Bureau of Standards." (This wording is from MIL-STD-45662, *Military Specification—Calibration System Requirements.*) In practice it is not feasible for the U.S. National Bureau of Standards to calibrate and certify the accuracy of the enormous volume of test equipment in use in the shops and test laboratories. Instead, resort is had to a hierarchy of secondary standards and laboratories, along with a system of documented certification of accuracy.

Hierarchy of Standards. The primary reference standards are the apex of an entire hierarchy of reference standards (Figure 18.4). At the base of the hierarchy there stands the huge array of "test equipment" (the terminology varies; for a discussion, see Section 16, under Quality Information Equipment), i.e., instruments used by laboratory technicians, workers and inspectors to control processes and products. These instruments are calibrated against "working standards" which are used solely to calibrate these laboratory and shop instruments. In turn, the working standards are related to the primary reference standards through one or more intermediate secondary reference standards or "transfer standards." Each

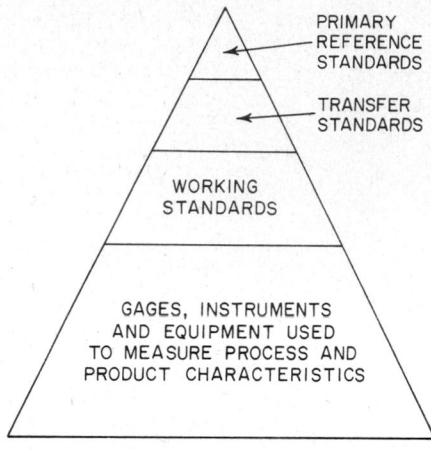

FIG. 18.4   Hierarchy of standards.

of these levels in the hierarchy serves to "transfer" accuracy of measurement to the next lower level in the hierarchy.

Within the hierarchy of standards there are differences both in the physical construction of the standards and in their precision. The primary reference standards are used by a relatively few highly skilled metrologists, and their skills are a vital contribution to the high precision attained by these standards. As we progress down the hierarchy, the number of technicians increases with each level, until at the base there are millions of workers, inspectors, and technicians using test equipment to control product and process. Because of the wide variation in the training, skills, and dedication among these millions, the design and construction of test equipment must feature ruggedness, stability, and foolproofing so as to minimize errors contributed by the human beings using the equipment.

Precision of measurement differs widely among the various levels of the hierarchy of standards. At the level of primary reference standards, the precision is determined by the state of the art. For example, Figure 18.5 shows the precision

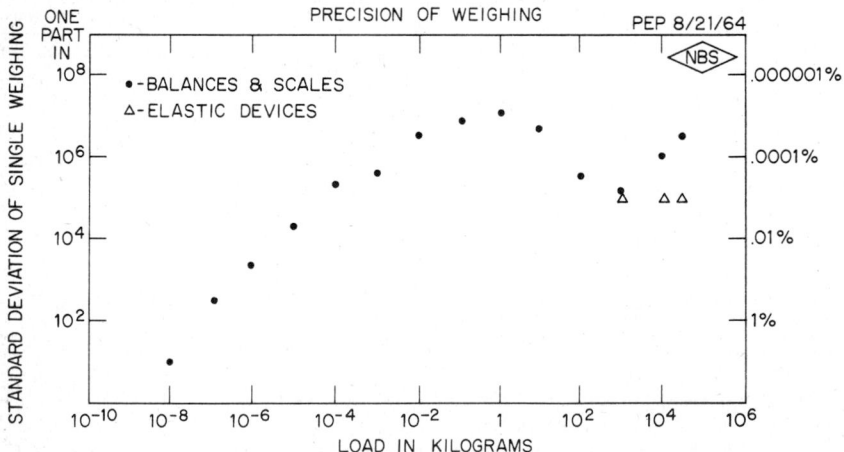

FIG. 18.5   Precision of weighing.

attained by the U.S. National Bureau of Standards when weighing loads across the spectrum of 10^{-10} to 10^6 (National Bureau of Standards, 1965).

At the base of the hierarchy, the precision of measurement is determined by the needs of fitness for use as reflected by the product and process tolerances. While some specialists urge that the test equipment be able to "divide the tolerance into tenths," this ideal is by no means always attained in practice. However, the tolerances themselves have been drastically tightened over the centuries, and this tightening has generally paralleled the advances made in the state of the art. For example, accuracy of measurement of a meter of length has progressed from an error of 1000 per million (at the end of the fifteenth century) to an error of 0.001 per million late in the twentieth century (see Loxham, 1967).

Allocation of measurement errors among the working and transfer standards has been widely discussed but has not been well standardized. The precision gap between primary reference standards and product test equipment may be anywhere from one to several orders of magnitude. This gap must then be allocated among the number of levels of standards and laboratories (transfer plus working) prevailing in any given situation. (Some models have been worked out to show the interrelation among the cost of developing greater precision in the primary reference standard, cost of attaining precision at each level of transfer laboratory, and number of laboratories at each level. See, for example, Crow, 1966.) When this problem of allocation was first faced, there was a tendency to conclude that each level should have a precision 10 times greater than the level it was checking. More recently, there has been growing awareness of how multiple levels of precision combine: i.e., their composite is better represented by the square root of the sum of the squares rather than by the arithmetic sum. This new awareness has caused many practitioners to accept a ratio of 5 to 1 rather than 10 to 1 for precision of working standards to product tolerances. This same ratio has also been tolerated among transfer standards as well.

ERROR OF MEASUREMENT

Product and process conformance are determined by measurements made by the test equipment at the bottom of the hierarchy of standards. Obviously, any error in these measurements has a direct bearing on the ability to judge conformance. On examination, the nature of measurement error is quite complex; even the terminology is confused. A clear understanding of the meaning of the measurements requires a minimal degree of understanding of the nature of measurement error. The starting point is to understand the nature of accuracy and precision. Figure 18.6 shows the meanings of these terms, by example and by analogy. See, in this connection, ASTM 177-71 (listed in Appendix III) on use of the terms "precision" and "accuracy" as applied to measurement of the properties of materials. See also Mathur, 1974, for a discussion on the influence of measurement variation in mass production of parts.

Accuracy. Suppose that we make numerous measurements on a single unit of product and that we then compute the average of these measurements. The extent to which this average agrees with the "true" value of that unit of product is called the accuracy of the instrument or measurement system which was employed. The difference between the average and the true value is called the "error" (also "systematic error," "bias," or "inaccuracy") and is the extent to which the instrument is out of calibration. The error can be positive or negative. The "correction" needed to put the instrument in calibration is of the same magnitude as the error

Measurements on One Unit of Product by Three Instruments

	Readings				Frequency Distribution of Readings	Target Analogy

Instrument A

.014	.015	.015	.017	.015
.015	.016	.014	.016	.015
.016	.016	.015	.016	.016
.017	.017	.016	.014	.016
.015	.015	.016	.014	.017

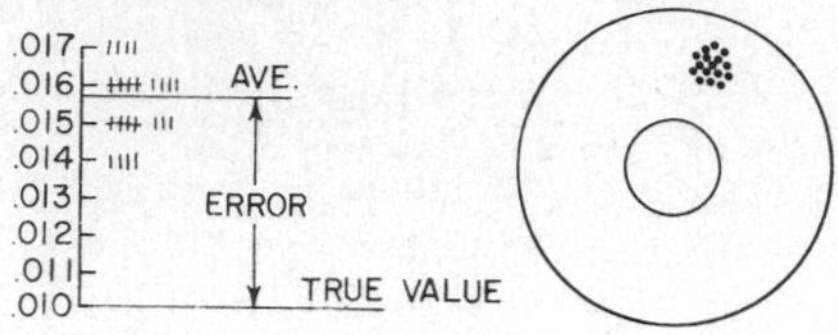

```
.017 ┌ ////
.016 ├ //// ////    AVE.
.015 ├ //// ///       ▲
.014 ├ ////           │
.013 ├          ERROR │
.012 ├               │
.011 ├               │
.010 └               ▼ TRUE VALUE
```

Precise, but Not Accurate

Instrument B

.009	.011	.008	:007	.011
.009	.011	.009	.016	.012
.008	.012	.014	.008	.011
.010	.013	.014	.011	.012
.010	.013	.015	.010	.013

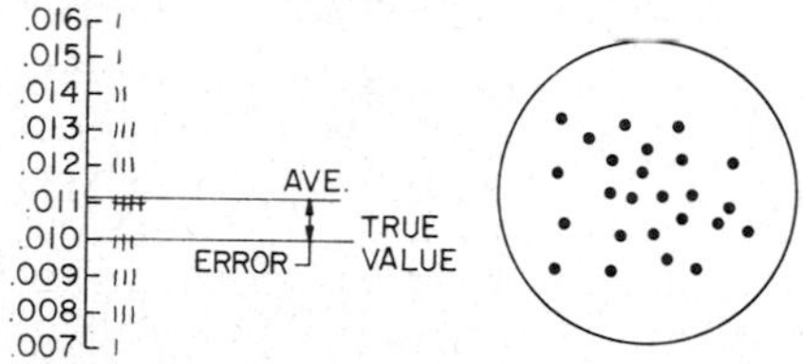

```
.016 ┌ /
.015 ├ /
.014 ├ //
.013 ├ ///
.012 ├ ///
.011 ├ ////       AVE.
.010 ├ ///        ┬ TRUE
.009 ├ ///   ERROR┘ VALUE
.008 ├ ///
.007 └ /
```

Accurate, but Not Precise

Instrument C

.009	.010	.010	.010	.009
.009	.010	.011	.011	.010
.009	.009	.011	.011	.009
.010	.011	.010	.011	.010
.010	.009	.011	.010	.010

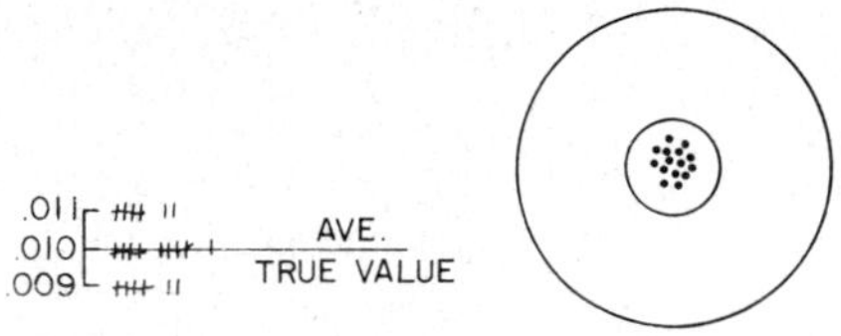

```
.011 ┌ //// //        AVE.
.010 ├ //// //// /
.009 └ //// //     TRUE VALUE
```

Accurate and Precise

FIG. 18.6   Accuracy and precision.

but opposite in sign. The instrument is still considered "accurate" if the error is less than the "tolerance" or maximum error allowable for that grade of instrument.

Accuracy and error are quantified as a difference between (1) the average of multiple measurements and (2) the true value. As will be seen, each of these is surrounded by a fringe of doubt. In consequence, the expression of accuracy must show the extent of these doubts if the full meaning of the numbers is to be conveyed.

Precision.   Irrespective of accuracy of calibration, an instrument will not give identical readings even when making a series of measurements on one single unit of product. Instead, the measurements scatter about the average, as exemplified in Figure 18.6. The ability of the instrument to reproduce its own measurements is called its "precision," and this varies inversely with the dispersion of the multiple ("replicated") measurements.

Experience has shown that any measurement system has an inherent dispersion which is itself reproducible, measurable, and therefore (once known) predictable. This inherent precision of measurement parallels the inherent process capability of a machine tool. (The parallel extends to the requirement that the system be in a state of statistical control.)

Quantification of precision is in terms of the standard deviation of replicated measurements, and is expressed by σ, the statistical symbol for standard deviation of a population.

Normally, recalibration can improve the accuracy of an instrument by reducing its error. However, recalibration normally does not improve the precision of the instrument, as this precision remains relatively constant over the working range. See Gantt (1959) for a discussion on the relation of instrument precision to product tolerance, using the ratio "repeatability."

Sources of Error.   Systematic error and dispersion of measurements have their origin in several well-known components of measurement error. (In some industries, e.g., chemical process, the measurement problems are so severe that development of valid test procedures is a major step in the launching of a new product or process.)

Within-Operator Variation.   The same operator, inspector, or technician, even when using the same measuring system on the same unit of product, will nevertheless come up with a dispersion of readings. This variation is usually referred to as "within-operator" variation.

Between-Operators Variation.   When two operators use the same measuring system on the same products, they will usually exhibit differences traceable to differences in operator technique. These differences are called "between-operators" variation and can be exhibited both as systematic error and as differences in dispersion.

Materials Variation.   In many cases it is not feasible to conduct replicated tests on the same "unit of product"; i.e., the product is changed or destroyed by testing. In other cases, the standard itself is consumable (e.g., hardness test blocks), so that material variation affects the standard as well. In these cases, where replicate testing is not feasible, the variations due to operator, equipment, and test method are composited with the materials variation. Sometimes it is feasible to resolve these composites into their components and sometimes it is not. A further complication is the case of perishable materials, which may require use of calibrations which relate time elapsed to degradation suffered.

Test Equipment Variation.   Instruments are subject to numerous sources of error, both within a single instrument and between instruments: nonlinearity, hysteresis (e.g., gear backlash), drift due to temperature rise, sensitivity to extraneous "noise" (e.g., magnetic, thermal, electrical fields). Each technology is subject to its own unique array of troubles. These instrument troubles are multiplied by the "fixturing" troubles of connecting the instruments into the larger test equipment units and of connecting the test specimens for tests. These fixturing troubles include such problems as making good electrical connections, fastening mechanical linkages, locating probes precisely, etc.

Test Procedure Variation.   In those cases where more than one test procedure is available to conduct measurement, it is essential to determine the relative variations, since these are one of the criteria for judging the adequacy of the procedure.

Between-Laboratories Variation.   This is a major problem both within companies and between companies. Some major programs must await resolution of this problem before they can be concluded, e.g., industry standardization of materials, test equipment, and test procedures. In like manner, variation between vendor and buyer laboratories may be at the root of a major quality problem. So extensive is the need to reduce between-laboratories variation that standard procedures have been evolved for the purpose (see under Interlaboratory Test Programs).

Composite Errors. The observed measurements are, of course, a resultant of the contributing variations. Generally this resultant or composite is related to the component variables in accordance with the formula:

$$\sigma^2_{obs} = \sigma^2_w + \sigma^2_b + \sigma^2_m + \sigma^2_e + \sigma^2_p + \text{etc.}$$

where σ_{obs} is the standard deviation of the observed measurements and where σ_w, σ_b, σ_m, σ_e, σ_p, etc., are the standard deviations reflecting the size of the variables which affect precision, i.e., within operator, between operators, material used, test equipment, test procedure, etc., respectively.

This relationship is valid provided the variables are independent of each other, which they often are. Where two or more of the variables are interrelated, then the equation must be modified. If for example, variables A and B are interrelated, then:

$$\sigma^2_T = \sigma^2_A + \sigma^2_B + \rho_{AB}\sigma_A\sigma_B$$

where σ^2_T = total variance
$\quad \sigma^2_A$ = variance of A
$\quad \sigma^2_B$ = variance of B
$\quad \rho_{AB}$ = the correlation coefficient (ρ) of A and B

In many cases it is feasible to quantify the effect of some component sources of variation by simple designs of experiment. When an instrument measures a series of different units of product, the resulting observations will have a scatter which is a composite of (1) the variation in the system of measurement and (2) the variation in the product itself. This relationship can be expressed as:

$$\sigma_{obs} = \sqrt{\sigma^2_{prod} + \sigma^2_{meas}}$$

where σ_{obs} = σ of the observed data
$\quad \sigma_{prod}$ = σ of the product
$\quad \sigma_{meas}$ = σ of the measuring method

Now solving for σ_{prod},

$$\sigma_{prod} = \sqrt{\sigma^2_{obs} - \sigma^2_{meas}}$$

It is readily seen that if σ_{meas} is less than one-tenth σ_{obs}, then the effect upon σ_{prod} will be less than 1 percent. This is the basis of the rule of thumb that the instrument should be able to divide the tolerance into about 10 parts.

To illustrate, in one shop the validity of a new type of instrument was questioned on the ground that it lacked adequate precision. The observed variation σ_{obs} was 11 (coded). An experiment was conducted by having the instrument make replicate checks on the same units of product. The σ_{means} was figured out to be 2. Then, since

$$\sigma^2_{prod} = \sigma^2_{obs} - \sigma^2_{meas}$$

$$\sigma_{prod} = \sqrt{121 - 4} = \sqrt{117} = 10.8$$

This was convincing proof that the instrument variation did not significantly inflate the product variation.

In another instance, involving the efficiency of an air-cooling mechanism, the observed variation σ_{obs} was 23, and the variation on retests, σ_{meas}, was 16. Thereupon

$$\sigma_{prod} = \sqrt{23^2 - 16^2} = \sqrt{529 - 256} = \sqrt{273} = 16 +$$

This showed that the measurement variation was as great as the product variation. Further study disclosed that the measurement variation could be resolved into

Variable	σ of that variable	σ^2
A	14	196
B	5	25
All other	7+	52
		273

It became clear that real progress could be made only by improving variable A, and the engineers took steps accordingly.

To quantify the individual components of variation requires still more elaborate analysis, usually through a special design of experiment (see Section 26, Design and Analysis of Experiments). (See also McCaslin and Gruska, 1976, for a discussion on an attribute gage study procedure; and Ezer, 1979, for statistical models for testing vial-to-vial variation in medical laboratories.)

Statement of Error. In publishing results it is necessary to make clear the extent of error in those results. Lacking clear conventions or statements, those who review the results simply do not know how to evaluate the validity of the data presented. To make clear the extent of error present in the data, metrologists have adopted some guidelines which are ever more widely used.

Effect of Reference Standards. Accuracy of an instrument is expressed as the difference between T, the "true" value, and $\overline{X}_m$, the average of the replicated measurements. The reference standard used is *assumed* to be the true value, but of course this is not fully valid, i.e., the standards laboratory is able to make only a close approximation. In theory, the true value cannot be attained. However, the extent of error can be ascertained through the use of replication and other statistical devices. As long as the systematic error of the standard is small in relation to the error of the instrument under calibration (the usual situation), the error of the standard is ignored. If there is some need to refer to the error of the standard, the published measurements may include a reference to the standard in a form similar to "as maintained at the National Bureau of Standards."

Effect of Significant Systematic Error. When the systematic error is large enough to require explanation, the approved forms of explanation consist of sentences appended to the data, stating (for example), "This value is accurate within $\pm x$ units," or "This value is accurate within $\pm y$ percent." [See National Bureau of Standards (1966).]

If necessary, these statements may be further qualified by stating the conditions under which they are valid, e.g., temperature range.

It is a mistake to show a result in the form "$a \pm b$" with no further explanation. Such a form fails to make clear whether "b" is a measure of systematic error or is an expression of standard deviation of replicate measurements or an expression of probable error, etc.

Effect of Imprecision. The quantification of precision is through the standard error (standard deviation), which is the major method in use for measuring dispersion. In publishing the standard error of a set of data, care must be taken to clear up what are otherwise confusions in the interpretation:

1. Does the standard error apply to individual observations or to the average of the observations? Unless otherwise stated, it should be the practice to relate the published standard error to the published average, citing the number of observations in the average.
2. If uncertainty is expressed as a multiple of the standard error, how many multiples are used? An approved form of expression is: " . . . with an overall uncertainty of ±4.5 km/s derived from a standard error of 1.5 km/s."
3. Is the standard error based solely on the data presented or on a broader history of data? To clarify this requires still more intricate wording, since a dispersion based solely on the current data is itself uncertain. (See Eisenhart, 1968.)

Effect of Combined Systematic Error and Imprecision. In these cases the expression of the published result must make clear that both types of error are present and significant. Eisenhart (1968) recommends a phraseology such as " . . . with an overall uncertainty of ±3 percent based on a standard error of 0.5 percent and an allowance of ±1.5 percent for systematic error."

Errors Negligible. Results may also be published in such a way that the significant figures themselves reflect the extent of the uncertainty. For example, in the statement, "The resistance is 3942.1 Ω, correct to five significant figures," the conventional meaning is that the "true" value lies between the stated value ±0.05 Ω.

Effect of Measurement Error on Acceptance Decisions. Two types of errors can occur in the classification of a product: (1) a nonconforming unit can be accepted (the consumer's risk) and (2) a conforming unit can be rejected (the producer's risk). In a classic paper Eagle (1954) shows the effect of precision on each of these errors (for variable measurement). McCaslin and Gruska (1976) discuss measurement error for attributes gages. These and other investigations have concluded that measurement error can be a serious problem. Greb (1976) presents a contrasting view and discusses the conditions that must occur before the problem becomes serious.

Programs to Reduce Error. As noted above in Sources of Error, there are a number of sources of variation which combine to produce the composite error. Each major variation is in turn a composite of multiple subvariations. Reducing the overall error usually involves two related programs:

1. Quantifying the components of error. These components are not equally important; they follow the Pareto principle, so that one or a very few are of greater influence than all the rest put together. Through statistical design of experiment, it is feasible to quantify the main components contributing to error. This statistical design follows the basic approach set out in Section 26, and the reader is referred to that section for a full discussion. (See also Schumacher, 1981, for a discussion on "random errors" and "systematic errors," and Abernethy et al., 1979, for a tutorial on measurement error.)
2. Finding ways to reduce the major variations through improved technique or new technology. While the major variable is usually "worker technique," this finding usually concludes also that the test has not been sufficiently engineered and that new technology is needed to minimize the variations due to worker technique (see Pipkin and Ritter, 1983).

This overall approach has much in common with that discussed in detail in Section 22 for improving quality generally.

Interlaboratory Test Programs. The most complex problem of reducing error is that involving multiple laboratories. In such cases, the approach used may be an interlaboratory test program, which is also used for some other important purposes such as:

Development of a new test method

Comparison of results of alternative test methods

Standardization of samples

Resolution of conflicts

Solution. Several hundred independent, commercial scientific inspection/test laboratories are in operation in the United States. A very useful guide to the available services is provided by the American Council of Independent Laboratories (Karasek, 1975). Selecting a capable laboratory is the most effective way to reduce the probability of error (see also Tustin, 1980).

So extensive is the need for interlaboratory test programs that the approach has been subjected to some standardization and control.

Techniques. A number of tools and techniques for monitoring laboratories have been evaluated. A general use standard is available from ASTM (1963) and a discussion of techniques from ASQC (1978).

Accreditation. Numerous accreditation programs of commercial testing laboratories have been developed to assure the accuracy of test/inspection results (see Hyer, 1979). Many accreditation programs are more familiarly known under terms such as laboratory approval, acceptance, recognition, listing, authorization, certification, endorsement, or registration programs.

Quality Assurance. Programs defining quality assurance standards for testing laboratories have also been developed and are available from ASTM (1984). See Provost and Elder (1983) for a discussion of cost-effective laboratory quality control; see also Schumacher (1976) for a discussion of methods for measuring compliance with calibration requirements.

MEASUREMENT TECHNOLOGY

While measurement technology is beyond the scope of this handbook, it is useful to note some of the aspects of this technology as they affect measurement generally. To this end, a brief look will be taken at trends in technology with respect to (1) measurement of length and (2) nondestructive testing. This is a small sample indeed.

Measurement of Length. Except for visual inspection, measurement of length is the oldest form of measurement and occupies more laboratory and inspection time than measurement for any other quality. Yet this old form of measurement has undergone several revolutions during the twentieth century alone. These revolutions include:

Obsolescence of Fixed-Limit Gages. Early in the century, product tolerances for metal cutting were generally of the order of 0.005 to 0.010 in, or about 0.10 to 0.25 mm. With such tolerances, the fixed-limit gages, despite their error of "feel" and despite the purely "good or bad" information they provided, were an adequate, inexpensive, and swift means for product inspection. In consequence, the preponderance of gages were of the fixed-limit type. While "variable" gages were available (i.e., dial gages, verniers, etc.), the fixed-limit gages dominated gage usage and the gage budgets. Still more precise measurement forms were also available, but these were usually carried out in the precision laboratories rather than on the shop floor.

Within several decades, the usual tolerances for metal cutting had been reduced by an order of magnitude or more, making the fixed-limit gage largely obsolete due to (1) the high error of "feel" in relation to the new level of tolerances and (2) the inadequacy of "good or bad" information for purposes of process control.

New Technological Principles. The early methods for measuring length all employed mechanical principles. To measure the numerous special configurations, e.g., inside diameters, depths, tapers, etc., many special tools were evolved: surface plates, scales, verniers, micrometers, dial mechanisms, amplification linkages, gage blocks. These were brought to higher and higher levels of mechanical precision. Finally, the economics of continuing to improve precision through extension of mechanical principles reached its limit and it became necessary to use other principles, mainly electronic, pneumatic, and optical.

Electronic Measurement. A usual form is built around a balanced Wheatstone bridge circuit. The gaging head or probe is used as a comparator, first resting on a known buildup of gage blocks and then on the specimen. The difference in vertical positions of this gaging head actuates a linear-variable-differential transformer which in turn unbalances the Wheatstone bridge. The amount of unbalance can be amplified by various orders of magnitude and then read on the scale, which is calibrated in units of length. Amplifications can exceed $5000\times$.

Pneumatic Measurement. The pneumatic family of instruments operates on the principle that the volume of air flowing through a gap varies with the size of the gap. In some configurations this variation is virtually linear and hence permits ready calibration. The amplification factor of these systems is surprisingly high, extending comfortably to over $10,000\times$; i.e., a product variation of 0.001 in (0.0254 mm) would show up on the scale as 10 in (or 254 mm).

Optical Measurement. There are various ways of using optical magnification for measuring length. The most precise makes use of the well-known phenomenon of "interference fringes," resulting when waves of light in the visible spectrum are alternately in and out of phase. A count of these fringes becomes a count of wavelengths of light. These distances are tiny—there are over a million wavelengths of visible light in each meter. The resulting precision permits magnifications of over a million in measuring with interference fringes. So precise is the method of using optical interference that the length of the meter, once defined as the length of a certain metal bar housed in the International Bureau of Weights and Measures (Paris), is now defined as 1,650,763.73 wavelengths of the orange-red line in the spectrum of krypton-86.

Still other means are available for measuring length: time (see Robinson, 1983), laser beams, holography, radiation, ultrasonics, eddy current, etc. (also see Abbe and O'Brian, 1972). In addition, research laboratories continue to work out new principles or new applications of old principles.

Nondestructive Testing. This broad term describes testing done to (1) detect flaws in materials and components and (2) measure physical properties such as dimensions, hardness, conductivity, composition, magnetic and elastic constants.

This testing is done without impairing the subsequent usefulness of the product, hence the name "nondestructive testing," or NDT. (Visual inspection is the oldest form of NDT.)

There is no single technique that will effectively do all the jobs required for nondestructive examination; rather each method supplements or complements the other. There are about a dozen basic technological principles which underlie the principal NDT methods (see Buckrop, 1976). These basic methods—along with their applications, advantages, and limitations—are set out in Table 18.17. Variations in technique have multiplied the dozen basic methods several times over, and this proliferation continues. (See Turner, 1974, for a discussion on emerging techniques.)

The versatility of NDT systems may be seen from Table 18.18 which shows the kinds of purposes or functions served by NDT systems in a great variety of test situations.

A likely moving force in the growing use of NDT is the need for greater assurance on matters of product safety, product liability, and government regulation. These forces stimulate not only testing but also formality of test programs. (ASTM has numerous standards on nondestructive testing, and the field is very active.) Increasingly there are demands for certification of test equipment and of the technicians who conduct the tests; i.e., the tests are not accepted as valid unless the technicians are formally qualified to conduct the tests and interpret the results.

In addition, the technology is itself tending to become "professionalized." Here and there an engineer specialist is designated as nondestructive-test engineer. An American Society for Nondestructive Testing has been in existence since 1941. Under the auspices of the society there was prepared the *Nondestructive Testing Handbook* (McMaster, 1959).

Section 27 under Computer-Aided Inspection (particularly Table 27.8) shows potential applications for automating various types of inspection.

Emergence of New Functions Associated with Measurement. The early gages were designed to classify product into good or bad. The hierarchy of standards and of laboratories served to assure that these classifying gages did an accurate job of classifying. Since then, the emphasis on defect prevention and on quality planning has demanded that the shop test equipment be usable for additional functions, mainly:

1. *Indicating:* The gages must show the "reading" along a scale of measurement. (The dial gage was the symbol of the indicating instrument until the advent of electronic readouts.) These readings become the feedback to operators for process control and to inspectors for product conformance decisions.

2. *Regulating:* In some applications it is economic to feed the measurements directly into the process so that the gage closes the loop to make the process self-regulating. See Section 16, under Automatic Process Regulation.

3. *Recording:* Increasingly, the burden of recording measurement data is being shifted from workers and inspectors to instruments specially designed to record data. These records are not merely a series of readings expressed in numbers. They include charts showing the data in time progression and related to tolerances or to control limits.

TABLE 18.17 Nondestructive Testing Comparison Table

Type	Applications	Advantages	Limitations
Eddy current	Checks for variation in wall thickness, conductivity, metallurgical properties, coating thickness, detection of incorrect material, seams, pits, porosity, surface finish, discontinuities.	Adapts to high-speed testing without probe contact. Excellent sensitivity to such defects as pinhole leakers, stitching, and hook cracks. Operates in poor optical environment and in presence of nonconductive contaminants.	Used only in conjunction with conductive materials. Alloy and hardness dependent and affected by temperature and magnetic fields. Cannot give absolute measurement, only qualitative comparison. Sensitivity of ID defects dependent on total wall thickness and depth of defect in terms of percent of wall thickness.
X-ray	Detects internal defects in welds, slag inclusion, penetration, lack of bond, thickness variations, cavities, metal inclusions, cracks, foreign particles.	Shows size and nature of hidden flaws or discontinuities in different thicknesses of metal. Gives permanent graphic record of defects. Radiation source can be turned off when not in use. Short time exposure. Unaffected by temperature changes or contaminants.	Has higher initial cost than gamma ray, requires power source, and has radiation hazard. Results not immediately known—requires trained technicians. Not sensitive to defects less than 2% thickness of total metal. Size and weight are generally larger than gamma. Depends on alloy uniformity.
Gamma ray	Detects interior flaws, cracks, seams, porosity, holes, inclusions, weld defects. Checks for thickness variations, integrity of assemblies.	Shows size and nature of hidden flaws or discontinuities in different thicknesses of metal. Needs no electrical power source nor oil or water cooling. Provides permanent record. Lower initial cost than x-ray.	Energy cannot be adjusted. Isotope must be chosen to meet sensitivity requirements and thickness of material. Sensitivity is not as great as x-ray. Trained technicians are needed. Results not immediately known.
Magnetic particle test	Detects surface and subsurface flaws that result from fatigue, thermal stresses, gas pockets,	Offers positive and simple method for finding cracklike defects at or close to the surface. Method is flexible	Limited to ferromagnetic material. No indications apparent for cracks parallel to the magnetic field, so

Method	Applications	Advantages	Limitations
	lack of fusion, slag inclusions, corrosion and grinding in ferromagnetic material. Locates cracks, seams, porosity, holes, inclusions.	and economical. Portable equipment is available. Immediate results.	magnetism in two directions is needed to find all discontinuities. Surfaces must be clean and dry.
Penetrant dye	Detects all defects open to the surface. (Cracks, seams, porosity, laps, cold shuts, leaks, weld defects, fatigue cracks, processing cracks.) Used in production dip tanks or with portable units.	Detects minute cracks and leaks. Dye penetrant appears as a deep red glow on white background. Fluorescent penetrant shows under ultraviolet. Simple to apply. Accurate, fast, low initial cost and per-test cost.	Limited to surface defects. Surface must be free from oil and grease. A semidarkened area is necessary for ultraviolet inspection.
Ultrasonic: Resonance	Gages thickness of materials with relatively smooth and parallel or concentric surfaces and some moderately rough corroded surfaces.	Displays instantly size, location, orientation and degree of flaw. Accuracy not affected by temperature or pressure—2% of thickness on rough surfaces, and up to 1% on smooth surfaces. Portable units enable field testing.	Must use a couplant (oil, grease, water, glycerine) or pressure to introduce the sound into the material under test. Rough surfaces and complex geometries complicate tests. Requires trained technicians.
Pulse echo	Locates case inclusions, internal ruptures, flaws, cracks, etc. Thickness gaging.		
Capacitive	Metallic or nonmetallic thickness and displacement gages. Dynamic vibration and high-speed inspection.	Good for both metals and nonmetals and temperature stable. Calibration relatively easy and has short response time. Readily adaptable to various configurations.	Does not work in liquid environments, and metal parts must be grounded to system.
Fiber optical	Displacement, flaw detection, and overall dimensions.	High speed and not affected by type of material or magnetic fields.	Dependent on surface optical properties and affected by ambient light. Subject to contamination.

TABLE 18.18   Functional and Situational Applications of Nondestructive Testing

Type of situation to be tested	Function or purpose of the nondestructive testing											
	Analysis	Detection*	Examination	Evaluation	Imaging	Identification	Inspection, checking	Location*	Maintenance (preventive)	Measurement*	Searching*	Testing*
Bonded areas							X					
Brazed areas							X					
Casting defects								X				
Cracks								X				
Defects, general		X					X	X				
Equipment				X			X					
Fabricating discontinuities								X				
Failure	X				X							
Fluid flow		X			X			X				
Foreign objects		X	X	X	X	X		X		X	X	
General	X		X	X		X	X	X	X	X	X	
Inclusions in castings												X

Internal parts of
hardware
systems

Internal organs,
etc., of animals

Laminar defects

Material types

Particles

Ruptures, internal

Stress—internal,
residual,
vibration

Surfaces—external,
internal, hidden

Thickness, general

Wall thickness:
corrosion wall
thinning

Welds

Weld defects

*Functions followed with an asterisk often can be performed on an automatic or semiautomatic basis instead of manually.

Source: Courtesy Lloyd B. Wilson.

4. *Computing, summarizing, and reporting:* A further step is to feed the data into computers. Some of these computers are used to figure averages and standard deviations. Others summarize data and prepare reports for supervisory and managerial review. These new and multiple functions have given rise to the name "quality information equipment" to emphasize that the dominant role is to provide information. For further discussion, especially as to the planning aspects, see Section 16, under Quality Information Equipment. See generally Section 27 (also Guest, 1981).

Collectively, these and related new functions associated with measurement have revolutionized the nature of the equipment and thereby the problems of keeping everything in calibration. It is no longer enough to assure that the mechanism which senses length remains in calibration. In addition, the entire train of attachments which indicate control, record, compute, etc., must likewise remain in calibration. All this has greatly expanded the role of the metrologists and their supporting technicians (also see Hunter, 1980).

CALIBRATION CONTROL

Measurement standards deteriorate in accuracy (and in precision) during use, and, to a lesser degree, during storage. To maintain accuracy requires a continuing system of calibration control. The elements of this system are well known and are set out below.

(The terminology associated with "calibration control" is not yet standardized. To put an instrument into a state of accuracy requires first that it be tested to see if it is within its calibration limits. This test is often referred to as "checking" the instrument. If, upon check, the instrument is found to be out of calibration, then a rectification or adjustment must be made. This adjustment is called variously "calibration," "recalibration," or "reconditioning." In some dialects, the word "calibration" is used to designate the combination of checking the instrument and adjusting it to bring it within its tolerances for accuracy.)

While the same system can be applied to all levels of standards, as well as to test equipment, there are some significant differences in detail of application. Transfer standards are exclusively under the control of standards laboratories staffed by technicians whose major interest is maintaining the accuracy of calibration. In contrast, test equipment and, to some extent, working standards are in the hands of those production, inspection, and test personnel whose major interest is product and process control. This difference in outlook affects the response of these people to the demands of the control system and requires appropriate safeguards in the design and administration of the system.

New-Equipment Control. The control system regularly receives new elements in the form of additional standards, new units of test equipment, and expendable materials. These elements should be of proved accuracy before they are allowed to enter the system. The approach varies depending on the nature of the new item:

1. *Purchased precision standards:* These include high-accuracy gage blocks, standard cells, etc. Control is based on the supplier's calibration data and on his or her certification that the calibration is traceable to the National Bureau of Standards. Where such purchased standards represent the highest level of accuracy in the buyer's company, any subsequent recalibration must be performed by an outside laboratory, i.e., the supplier, an independent laboratory, or the National Bureau of Standards.

2. *Purchased working standards:* These are subjected to "incoming inspection" by the buying company unless the demonstrated performance of the supplier merits use of "audit of decisions" (see Section 15).

3. *New test equipment:* This equipment is intended for use in checking products and processes. However, it usually embodies measuring instruments of various sorts and may well include working standards as well, i.e., test pieces ("masters" for in-place check of calibration). Such new test equipment should be checked out for calibration before being put into use. (Refer to Figure 18.7, from Meckley, 1955; in addition, there are various usage criteria, as discussed in Section 16, under Quality Information Equipment.)

4. *Test materials:* These include consumable standards as well as expandable supplies such as reagents or photographic film. Variability in such materials can directly affect the associated measurements and calibrations.

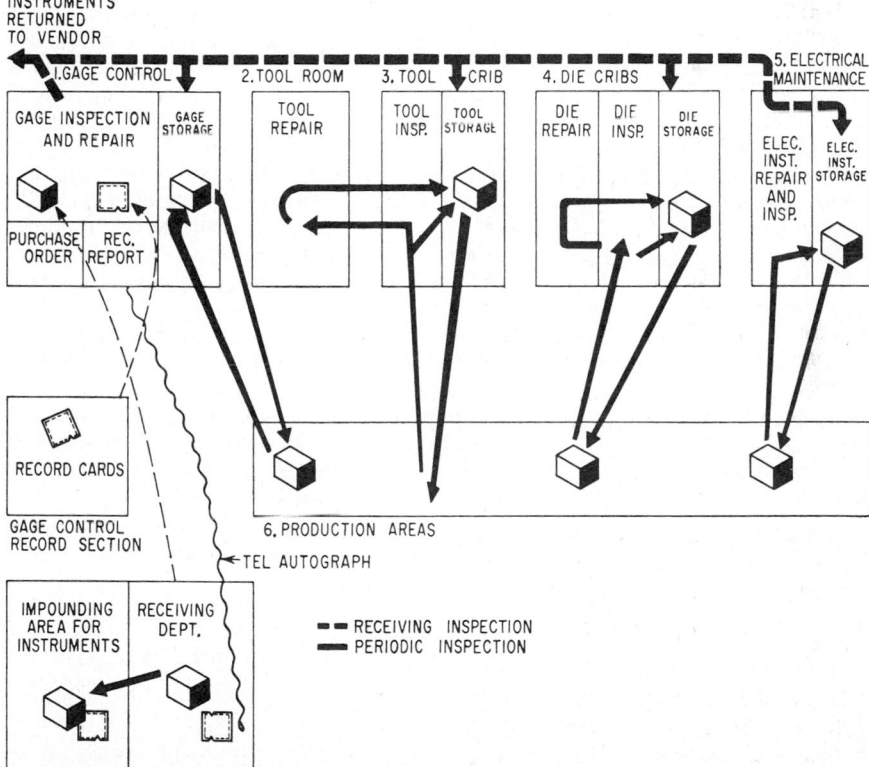

FIG. 18.7 Flow diagram for gage control. Daily: Repair orders and inspection reports sent to Gage Record Section by areas 1, 2, 3, 4, and 5. Weekly: Lists sent to gage control for periodic inspection of instruments in areas 1, 2, 3, 4, and 6. Area 5 is handled by electrical maintenance. (*From Meckley, 1955.*)

For example, a manufacturer of sandpaper needed a uniform material on which to test the abrasive qualities of the sandpaper. He investigated the possibility of using plastic blocks and found that the plastics manufacturer was using the same sandpaper as a means of testing the toughness of the plastic.

For some of these materials, the suppliers can provide data on variability. For the rest, it is necessary to discover the variability through analysis, as discussed above under Error of Measurement.

Inventory and Classification.   A systematic approach to calibration control starts with a physical inventory of all standards, instruments, and test equipment. (Where tooling is used as one of the means of product inspection, such tooling is commonly included within the list of items to be systematically controlled for accuracy.)

For each item which is to enter the system, a record card is made out. This card shows the historical origin of the item, its assigned serial number, the checking schedule, and related information. The card also provides space to record the results of checking and the repairs needed (see also Woods, 1978).

The physical test equipment is also marked with an assigned serial number for identification and traceability in the system.

Calibration Schedules.   These are established by class of equipment and are varied to reflect precision, nature, and extent of use and still other factors. At the outset, these schedules are established by judgment and bargaining. Later, as data become available on the results of checking, it becomes feasible to change the schedules in the interest of greater effectiveness and economy.

The broad intent of calibration schedules is to detect deterioration beyond tolerable levels of accuracy. This deterioration takes place primarily through usage and secondarily through the passing of time. As a result, the calibration schedules describe the extent of usage or of elapsed time in several ways:

1. *Elapsed calendar time:*   This method is in widest use. It establishes a fixed calendar time, e.g., 3 months, as a checking interval. At the end of the 3 months, steps are taken to check the equipment in accordance with schedule.

2. *Actual amount of usage:*   This is based on counting the actual usage, e.g., number of units of product checked by the equipment. The count may be made (*a*) manually, by the inspectors, (*b*) through automatic counters installed in the equipment, or (*c*) by programming the computers to show the amount of testing performed based on production schedules.

3. *Metering of actual operating hours:*   For electrical equipments it is feasible to meter the actual time that the equipment is drawing power. A simple device for this purpose is a direct reading coulometer (Figure 18.8). The heart of this device is a capillary tube filled with two columns of mercury separated by an electrolyte. Passage of direct currents results in transfer of mercury from one column to the other. The electrolytic gap moves as a result and serves as an indicator to measure cumulative current (and hence cumulative hours of use) on a calibrated scale (see Marwell, 1966).

4. *Test accuracy ratio (TAR) control.*   This is a systems approach that analyzes the degree to which interrelated parameters are identified and controlled within a *traceability cone.* Minimum TARs for each traceable parameter are measured and controlled. (See also Tobey, 1979.)

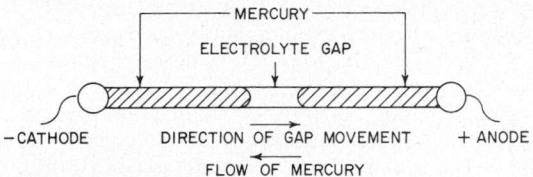

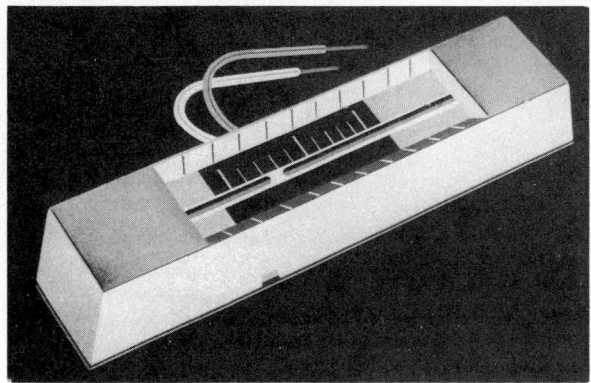

FIG. 18.8 Coulometer for recording instrument usage.

Adherence to Schedule.   This vital detail makes or breaks the entire system of calibration control.

Generally, the transfer standards and most working standards pose no problem of adherence to schedule, since they are in the custody of a few standards laboratories and a relatively few associated technicians. In contrast, the test equipment (and some working standards) are widely scattered over numerous locations and are in the custody of thousands of workers, inspectors, and testers. Some of these individuals can be relied on to see that the checking schedule is followed, but many cannot.

In part, the problem is one of lack of knowledge of when the recalibration is due. The shop personnel require the aid of a memory system if they are to know which piece of equipment is due to be checked that day. They may recall what the checking intervals for each class of equipment are, but they cannot recall what the date of the last calibration was.

Some systems for adherence to schedule make use of ingenious color codes or labels which mark on each unit of equipment the date it was put back into service. (These codes are often extended to identify the grades of the standards themselves, whether primary, secondary, etc.) For large units, the expiration date is entered on a maintenance card which is attached to the unit. Such dates are an aid to the personnel for adhering to the checking schedule.

However, an added problem is that of motivation. The numerous users of test equipment are quite concerned with recalibration when trouble is encountered but less concerned when things seem to be going smoothly. In these latter cases, interruptions for calibration can even be a nuisance.

The solution is to give responsibility (for adherence to schedule) to the standards laboratory rather than to the production, inspection, and test personnel. When this proposal is made to practicing managers, they seldom accept it purely on grounds of theory of organization. However, when it is proposed that a sample of instruments be taken at random and checked for calibration (as a test of the existing "system" of calibration control), these same managers are quite willing to conduct such a test. The resulting disclosure of the actual state of calibration of the sample (of 25 to 100 instruments) is then decisive in convincing the managers of the need for a revision in the system of adherence to schedule. Under this assignment, the laboratory organizes a plan of checking which will keep up with the scheduled load. (See also Gebhardt, 1982.)

In administering the checking plan, manual record cards may be used to identify the calibration dates. For example, in the time-interval system, the record card carries a calendar printed at the top. A "flag" is clipped to the card at the place representing the recalibration date. On that date, all cards so marked will have moved to the front of the pack. Alternatively, the system may use a computer to provide a runoff showing which standards and equipments are due to be checked in the forthcoming week.

Calibration Practice.   To assure accuracy and to establish traceability, control laboratories have evolved some widely used procedures.

Individual responsibility is established by requiring that all concerned sign for their actions. The equipment record cards carry these signatures, as do the labels on the equipment.

Dates are recorded for all actions in view of the role of elapsed time in the calibration procedures.

Manuals of practice are established, including tolerances for accuracy, and methods to be used in calibration. In some types of test, these methods must be spelled out in detail, e.g., temperature or humidity controls, time cycle, human technique, etc. (Witness the detail of some of the ASTM standards on test method.)

Training programs are established for personnel, including (in some cases) formal qualification certificates to attest to proficiency.

Equipment is tamperproofed through sealing the adjusting screws. (The seals are then imprinted with the stamp of the laboratory.) In like manner, panels and drawers of test equipments are lock-wired, and the wires are lead-sealed together. (The laboratory takes no responsibility when seals are broken, and the company takes stern measures against tampering with the seals.)

As a means of assisting enforcement, quality assurance audits are conducted to review the calibration control procedures.

Record and Analysis of Results.   It is most useful to keep a record of the results of checking calibration and of the extent of work done to restore accuracy. Typically such a record lists:

Observed deficiencies in the equipment

Causes of out-of-calibration conditions

Repair time and recalibration time

Periodic analysis of these data then becomes the basis for:

1. Reducing checking for equipment shown to be stable
2. Redesigning equipment to eliminate causes of repetitive failure

Organization for Calibration Control.   In small companies, the control laboratory carries out the multiple functions of:

1. Establishment of a system for maintaining calibration of standards and test equipment
2. Issuance, calibration, and custody in accordance with the established system

As the company grows, the standards laboratory decentralizes, partly for reasons of geography and partly for specialization in technology.

When multiple plants are located in different cities, the need for some geographical decentralization is obvious. Even in single large plants, the problems of checking test equipment may be simplified through decentralization, including the concept of mobile laboratories. For mechanical work, these take the form of the traveling gage cart equipped with surface plates, master gages, and accessories as well as an inventory of working gages. (See "Portable Gage Lab Provides Flexibility and Minimizes Downtime," 1971).

In addition, the cart carries a file drawer of gage records to aid in adhering to checking schedules. An extension of the mobile gage cart is the truck or van which is equipped as a mechanical or electrical laboratory and travels from factory to factory within the same metropolitan area.

Still another form of decentralization is the "in-place" calibration. Under this concept, a working "master" is provided to simulate product or process conditions of various kinds. The test equipment must "pass an examination" by properly classifying the masters. These masters are kept physically at the test station until they are recalled for recalibration of their own accuracy.

Physical design of the laboratory workplace has been greatly complicated by the proliferation of many varieties of specialized testing: ultrasonic, x-ray, vibration, shock, acceleration, heat, humidity, etc. The details of these designs are beyond the scope of this handbook. The practitioner must consult with the available experts: equipment manufacturers, researchers, metrologists, and still others. This must be a continuing process, since there is continuing progress in development of new tests and standards.

HUMAN FACTORS IN INSPECTION

A myriad of factors can influence inspector behavior; they are summarized by Baker (1975), as shown in Table 18.19. One factor, visual acuity or sight, is the dominant sense in human beings, and great reliance is placed upon it in inspection tasks. The effectiveness of the use of sight depends largely on eye movements which bring the images of significant features of the material being inspected to the most sensitive part of the retina. However, experience and studies have shown that the other factors in Table 18.19 have an interrelated effect on the effectiveness, productivity, reliability, and accuracy of the inspector. (See Megaw, 1978, for related studies carried out in a textile factory.)

A detailed discussion of inspector errors below follows the discussion on human factors; however, it appears appropriate to first discuss the techniques and measurements developed to improve the reliability of the inspection function.

Machine Vision.   The term "machine vision," or noncontact inspection, is applied to a wide range of electrooptical sensing techniques, from relatively sim-

TABLE 18.19   Variables Influencing Inspector Behavior

1. Individual abilities
    a. Visual activity
    b. General intelligence and comprehension
    c. Method of inspection
2. Task
    a. Defect probability
    b. Fault type
    c. Number of faults occurring simultaneously
    d. Time allowed for inspection
    e. Frequency of rest periods
    f. Illumination
    g. Time of day
    h. Objectivity of conformance standards
    i. Inspection station layout
3. Organizational and social
    a. Training
    b. Peer standards
    c. Management standards
    d. Knowledge of operator or group producing the item
    e. Proximity of inspectors
    f. Reinspection versus immediate shipping procedures

Source: Baker, 1975, p. 62.

ple triangulation and profiling to three-dimensional object recognition and bin picking, techniques based on sophisticated computerized image-analysis routines still under development. The applications are broad, ranging from relatively simple detection and measuring tasks to full-blown robot control. (See Schaffer, 1984, for a comprehensive report on machine-vision techniques.) The machine-vision industry is expected to grow by more than 50 percent a year through 1987, and annual industry sales are expected to reach $1 billion before 1990 and $10 to $20 billion by the turn of the century. Current machine-vision applications are summarized in Table 18.20.

The incentive to introduce machine-based systems, e.g., robots, is obvious—to eliminate human error. (See Spow, 1984, for a discussion of robots in an automatic assembly application.) The key influences behind the growth of the machine-vision industry also include inspector capability, inspector productivity, and inspection costs. (See also Nelson, 1984, for a review of machine-vision equipment, some designed to eliminate process contamination, in addition to human error.) Table 18.21 discusses these factors as they relate to inspecting printed circuit boards. [See Ken, 1984, for a detailed discussion of automated optical inspection (AOI) of printed circuit boards (PCB); also Denker, 1984, for a detailed discussion on justifying investments in automatic visual PCB testing.]

Vision-based systems—human or machine—involve an inspection procedure: the examination of a scene. The examination, in turn, can lead to recognition of an object or feature, to a quality decision, or to the control of a complex mechanism (Schaffer, 1984).

When the human inspector is involved, human judgment and perception have an influence on the quality assessment process. These result in two problems:

Vigilance Problem.   In highly repetitive subjective inspection (e.g., inspecting parts on an automated paint line), the process of perceiving can become numbed

TABLE 18.20 Machine-Vision Applications

1. Inspection
   a. Dimensional accuracy
   b. Hole location and accuracy
   c. Component verification
   d. Component defects
   e. Surface flaws
   f. Surface-contour accuracy
2. Part identification
   a. Part sorting
   b. Palletizing
   c. Character recognition
   d. Inventory monitoring
   e. Conveyer picking (overlap, no overlap)
   f. Bin picking
3. Guidance and control
   a. Seam-weld tracking
   b. Part positioning
   c. Processing/machining
   d. Fastening/assembly
   e. Collision avoidance

or hypnotized by the sheer monotony of repetition. In some way the scanning process and the model became disconnected, and the observer sees only what he or she expects to see, but does not see anything not actively expected. According to Thomas (1978) this happens in spite of the apparent activity of the perceptual scanning apparatus. This is called a "vigilance" problem. The known remedies are:

Break up the benumbing rhythm with pauses.

Introduce greater variety into the job.

Increase the noticeability of the faults through enhancing.

Provide background and context cues.

Arrange for frequent job rotation.

Vigilance becomes a big problem when faults are obvious and therefore serious, but infrequent and unpredictable.

TABLE 18.21 Selected Example of Factors and Effect of AOI on Printed Circuit Board

Manufacturing inspection costs	Inspection accounts for up to 30 percent of the manufacturing costs of complex double-sided and multilayer boards.
Inspection capability	Human inspection capability decreases well before 5 mil because of fatigue.
Inspection productivity	AOI reduces the number of inspections from 30 to 7 per shift while obtaining a 1 percent yield improvement and fivefold increase in inspection speeds.

Drift Problem. The second problem characteristic of the human vision-based system, discussed by Thomas (1978), is that subjective standards appear to drift over time. Thus products which would have been rejected at one time are accepted at another.

Continuous experiences of either exceptionally high-quality or low-quality product will modify the inspector's model, leading him or her to raise or lower standards. The inspector is also influenced by the comments and actions of colleagues.

INSPECTOR ERRORS

The inspector, as the human element in the inspection process, contributes importantly to inspection errors. Inspection errors due to the inspector, called "inspector errors," are discussed here. We have previously discussed the reliability of the human inspector under human factors (as opposed to noncontract machine inspection or machine-vision system). Other sources of inspection error, e.g., vague specifications, lack of standards, inaccurate instruments, etc., are discussed elsewhere in this handbook. (*Note:* The problem of human error is common to operators, inspectors, and anyone else. For an extensive discussion of problems of worker error, see Section 22, under Test of Theories of Worker-Controllable Problems, et seq.)

Inspector errors are of several categories:

Technique errors

Inadvertent errors

Conscious errors

Each of these categories has its own unique causes and remedies. Collectively, these inspector errors result in a performance of about 80 percent accuracy in finding defects, i.e., inspectors find about 80 percent of the defects actually present in the product and miss the remaining 20 percent. [*Note by the editor (Juran):* Numerous studies in various countries have yielded the 80 to 20 ratio as a broad measure of quantified inspector accuracy. For example, Konz et al. (1981) found that inspectors were only catching about 80 percent of the defects in glass subassemblies.]

However, little is known about the relative importance of each category of inspector error (e.g., lack of technique, inadvertence, conscious). For further discussion, see Tawara (1980).

Technique Errors. Into this category are grouped several subcategories: lack of capacity for the job, e.g., color blindness; lack of knowledge due to insufficient education or job training; lack of "skill," whether due to lack of natural aptitude or to ignorance of the knack for doing the job. Technique errors can be identified in any of several ways:

Check Inspection. A check inspector reexamines work performed by the inspector, both the accepted and rejected product. Figure 18.9 shows an example of the results of such check inspection of the work of several inspectors. It is evident that inspectors C and F operate to loose standards while inspector B operates to tight standards. Inspector E shows poor discrimination in both directions.

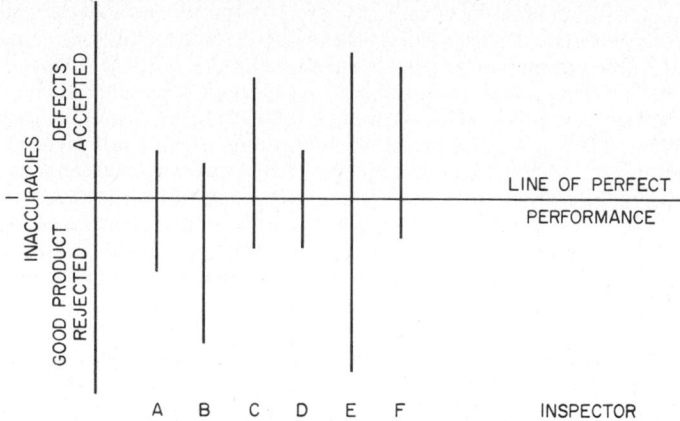

FIG. 18.9   Analysis of inspection errors.

Round-Robin Inspections.   In this analysis, the same product is independently inspected by multiple inspectors. The resulting data, when arrayed in a matrix (usually with defect type along one axis and the inspectors along the other axis), shows the defects found by each inspector in relation to the inspectors as a group.

Repeat Inspections.   In this method, the inspector repeats his or her own inspection of the product without knowledge of his or her own prior results. The analysis of the resulting data discloses the extent of the consistency or lack of consistency of the inspector's judgments.

Standard Sample Array.   In this method the inspector takes an "examination" by inspecting a prefabricated mixture of product consisting of good units plus various kinds of defects. The standard sample array is known by various names, including "job sample." For added discussion, refer to Harris and Chaney (1969). All units were previously carefully graded by a team of experts and numbered for ready analysis of results. The inspector's score and his pattern of errors all point to the need, if any, for further training or other remedial steps. (In effect, the check inspection is conducted before the inspection.)

For example, in a company making glass bottles, an attempt was made to correlate process variables with the frequency and type of defects found by inspectors stationed at the cold end of the annealing lehr. The experiment failed because inspector variability from shift to shift exceeded product variability. This also threw suspicion on the accuracy of the inspection performed by the final product sorters at the end of the line. A standard sample array of 500 bottles was created and was used to examine the inspectors. (The examinations were conducted in the Training Department, on a miniature lehr.) The suspicions turned out to be well founded. (*Note:* Consulting experience of J. M. Juran.)

Remedies for Technique Errors.   The need is to provide the missing skill or know-how and to answer the inspector's proper question, "What should I do different than I am doing now?" Unless the inspector is in a position to discover the answer for her- or himself, the answer must be provided by management. If no answer is provided, there will be no change in performance.

The various methods of analysis discussed above all can provide some clues which suggest the type of remedial action needed. In particular, use can be made of the concept of finding the "knack," as discussed in Section 10, under Technique Errors. Under this concept, the data on inspector performance are analyzed to discover which inspectors give consistently superior performances and which inferior. Next, a study is made of the work methods used by both types of inspectors to identify the differences in methods. Analysis of these differences often discovers what is the secret know-how (knack) being used to get the superior performance (or what is the secret ignorance which results in poor performance). Finally the knack can be transferred to all inspectors through retraining (Czaja and Drury, 1981, and Cooper, 1980) or through being embodied in the technology (Kusch, 1979).

Where the technique errors are the result of lack of job capacity, the foregoing may be of no avail, and the need may be to foolproof the operation (see below) or to reassign the inspector to a job for which he or she does have adequate job capacity.

Certification of Inspectors.   In critical inspections involving inspector judgment (e.g., interpreting x-rays of critical welds), it is increasingly the practice to require that the inspector be formally certified as qualified to do this job. (See Gibson, 1983, for a further discussion of inspector qualifications in offshore industries.) The qualification process follows a well-standardized series of steps:

A formal training program on how to do the job

A formal examination, including a demonstration of successful performance of the job

A formal certificate attesting to the success in the examination

A license to do the job for some designated period of time

A program of audit to review performance and to serve as a basis for renewing the license

In some companies, this concept of certification has been based on the "escape rate," i.e., the extent to which defects escape detection, as determined by subsequent check inspection. (See Measure of Inspector Accuracy, below.) When this concept is used, a limited "license" (e.g., 2 months) is given to the inspector, subject to renewal if check inspection results continue to be favorable.

Inadvertent Inspector Errors.   These errors are characterized by the fact that at the time the error is made, the inspector is not even aware he is making an error. Also, the best intentions are present—the inspector wants not to make any errors. The term "inadvertent" or "unavoidable" is used to connote the fact that the human being is simply unable to achieve perfection, no matter how good his intentions. (This topic is closely related to inadvertent worker errors. For added discussion, see Section 10, under Inadvertent Errors.)

The theory of inadvertence has wavered up and down. For years it was the sincere belief of many inspection supervisors that when product was inspected 100 percent, the inspectors would find all the defects. Numerous unpublished and published studies have since demonstrated that human inspectors do not find all defects present. By and large, the human inspector finds about 80 percent of the defects present and misses the remaining 20 percent.

While the 80 to 20 ratio is widely accepted, there are numerous aspects which are not fully researched, i.e., how this ratio changes with percent defective in the product, with types of inspection (visual, mechanical gaging, electrical testing), with product complexity, with amount of time allotted for inspection, etc. For a discussion from the viewpoint of human factors plus some supporting data (e.g., that increased product complexity results in increased inspector error), see Harris and Chaney (1969, pp. 77–85).

Inspection fallibility can easily be demonstrated in the industrial classroom. The following sentence has been used thousands of times:

> FEDERAL FUSES ARE THE RESULTS OF YEARS
> OF SCIENTIFIC STUDY COMBINED WITH
> THE EXPERIENCE OF YEARS

The sentence is flashed before the audience for 30 s or for a full minute. Each member is asked to count and record the number of times the letter F appears. When the record slips are collected and tallied, the result is invariable. Of the F's present, only about 80 percent have actually been found.

The existence of so extensive an error rate has stimulated action on several fronts:

1. *To discover why inspectors make these errors:* To date, the researches have not been adequate to provide conclusive answers, so that the industrial psychologists are not agreed on what the main causes are.

2. *To measure the extent of the errors:* Techniques for this are now available. See Measure of Inspector Accuracy, below.

3. *To reduce the extent of these errors:* There is a wide assortment of remedies, as discussed below.

Remedies for Inadvertent Inspector Errors. In the absence of convincing knowledge of the causes of these errors, managers have resorted to a variety of remedies, all involving job changes in some form. These remedies include:

Error-Proofing. There are several forms of error-proofing which are widely applicable to inspection work: redundancy, countdowns, and fail-safe methods. These are discussed in detail in Section 16, under Error-Proofing the Process. See also Inspection Planning, above.

Automation. This is really a replacement of the repetitive inspection by an automation which makes no inadvertent (or other) errors once the setup is correct and stable. The economics of automation and the state of technology impose severe limits on the application of this remedy. See Automated Inspection, above.

Sense Multipliers. Use can be made of optical magnifiers, sound amplifiers, and other devices to magnify the ability of the unaided human being to sense the defects. Development of a new instrument to do the sensing is the ultimate form of this multiplication. Evidently there is an optimum to the level of magnification, and this optimum can be discovered by experimentation. (For some industrial studies, see Harris and Chaney, 1969, pp. 124–126 and 137–142.)

Conversion to Comparison. In many types of inspection, inspectors must judge products against their memories of the standard. When such inspectors are provided with a physical standard against which to make direct comparison, their accuracy improves noticeably. For example, in the optical industry, scratches are graded by width, and tolerances for scratches vary depending on the function of the product element (lens, prism, etc.). To aid the inspectors, plates are prepared exhibiting several scratches of different measured width, so that the inspectors can compare the product to a physical standard.

Standards for comparison are in wide use: colored plastic chips, textile swatches, forging specimens, units of product exemplifying pits and other visual blemishes, etc. Sometimes photographs are used in lieu of product. There are also special optical instruments which permit dividing the field of view to permit comparison of product with standard.

In some cases it is feasible to line up units of product in a way which makes any irregularities become highly conspicuous, e.g., lining up the holes in a row. (The childhood row of tin soldiers makes it obvious which one has the broken arm.) Some practitioners advocate inspecting units of product in pairs, to utilize the comparison principle. See Shainin (1972) for further discussion.

Templates.   These are a combination gage, magnifier, and mask. An example is the cardboard template placed over terminal boards. Holes in the template mate with the projecting terminals and serve as a gage for size. Any extra or misplaced terminal will prevent the template from seating properly. Missing terminals become evident because the associated hole is empty.

Masks.   These are used to blot out the inspector's view of characteristics for which she is not responsible so she can concentrate on her real responsibility. Some psychologists contend that when the number of characteristics to be inspected rises to large numbers, the inspector error rate also rises.

Overlay.   These are visual aids in the form of transparent sheets on which guidelines or tolerance lines are drawn. The inspector's task of judging the size or location of product elements is greatly simplified by such guidelines, since they present the inspector with an easy comparison for judging sizes and locations.

Checklists.   These may be as simple as a grocery shopping list used to verify that you purchased all the items you originally planned to buy. On the other extreme a checklist may consist of the countdown for the lofting of a new space shuttle. (See Walsmann, 1981, for a discussion of the purpose, advantages, and drawbacks as well as the development and implementation of various checklists.)

Reorganization of Work.   One of the theories of cause of inadvertent inspector errors is fatigue, due to inability to maintain concentration for long periods of time. Responses to this theory have been to break up these long periods in any of several ways: rest periods; rotation to other inspection operations, several times a day; job enlargement, e.g., a wider assortment of duties, greater responsibility. Some behavioral scientists urge reorganization of work on the broader ground of motivation theory, and they offer data to support this theory (see generally Harris and Chaney, 1969, pp. 201–229). However, to date, there is no conclusive evidence that in Western culture, reorganization of work (to provide greater participation, etc.) will give measurably superior results in work accomplishments. (See, in this connection, Section 10, under Processing System Design.)

Product Redesign.   In some instances the product design is such that inspection access is difficult or that needless burdens are placed on inspectors. In such cases, product redesign can help to reduce inspector errors as well as operator errors.

For some examples, see Section 16, under Error-Proofing the Process. (See also Smith and Duvier, 1984.)

Errorless Proofreading. Beyond the techniques described in Section 16, under Error-Proofing the Process, there are special problems of error-proofing in inspection work. A major form of this is proofreading of text of a highly critical nature, i.e., critical to human safety and health. In such cases the low tolerance for error has driven many companies to use redundant checking, despite which some errors still get through.

A closer look makes it clear that proofreading is of two very different kinds:

1. *Passive proofreading:* Here the proofreader takes no overt action. For example, he silently reads the copy while someone else reads the master aloud. Alternatively, he silently reads both documents and compares them. In such cases it is quite possible for extraneous matters to intrude on him and dominate his attention temporarily.

2. *Active proofreading:* Here the proofreader must taken an overt action, e.g., she reads aloud, performs a calculation, etc. Such positive actions dominate her attention and minimize the chance of error.

For a second example, in blood donor centers it is usual to centrifuge the whole blood, remove the plasma, and then return the red blood cells to the donor. This return demands absolute assurance that the cells are being returned to that donor and to no one else. The system in use involves piping both the donation and the return through tubing on which there are repeats of 10-digit numbers. The tubing is cut when the donation goes to the centrifuge. Prior to return of the cells, two technicians check to compare the two 10-digit numbers on the two ends of the cut tubing. One technician actively reads the number on the tubing end attached to the donor. The other technician passively listens while comparing the number he or she hears with the number seen on the end of the tubing which is attached to the bag of blood cells.

It is feasible to make both technicians "active." For example, each is required to tap out on a keyboard the number he or she sees. These signals go to a computer which compares to the two numbers and signals either a go-ahead or an alarm. This same principle of comparing two independent active sets of signals can be extended to any problem in proofreading.

While the foregoing are listed as remedies for inadvertent inspector errors, most of them can also be used to reduce errors due to lack of skill or errors of a willful nature.

Procedural Errors. Aside from inadvertent failures to find defects, there are inadvertent errors in shipment of uninspected product or even shipment of rejected product. These errors are usually the result of loose shipping procedures. For example, a container full of uninspected product may inadvertently be moved in with the inspected product; a container full of defectives may inadvertently be moved into the shipping area.

Such errors can be reduced by error-proofing the identification and shipping routines:

1. The inspector must *mark the product* at the time of inspection. Sometimes the inspector places the good in one box and the bad in another, or places the good lengthwise and the bad crosswise. Lacking the markings, there is always the

risk that between shifts, during rest periods, etc., the unmarked product will go to the wrong destination.

2. The product markings should be so distinctive that the product "screams its identity" to packers and shippers. Bar codes should be used where appropriate.

3. The colors used for markers which identify good product should be used for no other purpose. These markers should be attached only when the inspector finds there remains nothing to be done but ship the product.

4. Issuance of markers used to identify good product should be restricted to specially chosen personnel.(These markers are a form of company seal.) For products of substantial value, serial numbers may be used as a further control.

5. The markers should provide inspector identity. In some companies the system of identification includes the operators and packers.

6. Shipping personnel should be held responsible for any shipment of goods failing to bear an inspector's approval.

Conscious Inspector Errors: Management-Initiated.   The distinguishing features of the willful inspector error are that the inspector knows he or she is committing the error and intends to keep it up. These willful errors may be initiated by management, by the inspector, or by a combination of both. However, with few exceptions, the major notorious quality errors and blunders have been traceable to the decisions of managers and engineers rather than to those of the inspectors at the bottom of the hierarchy. Management-initiated errors take several forms, all resulting in willful inspector errors:

Conflicting Management Priorities.   Management's priorities for its multiple standards (quality, cost, delivery, etc.) vary with the state of the economic cycle. When the state of management priorities is such that conformance to quality standards is subordinated to the need for meeting other standards, the inspectors' actions are inevitably affected, since they also are given multiple standards to meet.

Management Enforcement of Specifications.   When management fails to act on evidence of nonconformance and on cause of defects, the inspectors properly judge management's real interest in quality from these deeds rather than from the propaganda. For example, if the supervision or the Material Review Board consistently accepts a chronic nonconformance condition as fit for use, the inspectors tend to quit reporting these defects, since they will be accepted anyhow.

Management Apathy.   When management makes no firm response to suggestions on quality or to inspector complaints about vague information, inadequate instruments, etc., the inspectors again conclude that management's real interests are elsewhere. In consequence, the inspectors do the best they can with information and facilities which they believe to be deficient.

Management Fraud.   Periodically a company manager attempts to deceive customers (or the regulators, etc.) through fictitious or deceitful records on quality. Seldom can a manager acting alone perpetrate such a fraud. The manager requires confederates who submit themselves to orders, usually in a way which makes clear to them the real character of what is going on. An inspector who is a willing accomplice (e.g., for a bribe) shares in the legal responsibility. However, the inspector may also be a most reluctant accomplice, e.g., an immediate superior gives orders to prepare nonfactual reports or to take actions clearly contrary to regulations. In such cases the inspector cannot escape taking some kind of risk, i.e., participation in a conspiracy versus the threat of reprisal if he or she fails to participate.

These management-initiated errors parallel closely those associated with conscious worker errors. See Section 22, under Test of Theories of Worker-Controllable Problems.

Conscious Inspector Errors: Inspector-Initiated.   These errors likewise take multiple forms, and some take place for "good" reasons. It is important to understand the distinctions among these forms, since any misunderstandings are a breeding ground for poor industrial relations.

Inspector Fraud.   The inspector is subjected to a variety of pressures. The most rudimentary forms are those by production supervisors and operators pleading for a "break." Sometimes this extends to a collusion where piecework payments are involved, both for quality and for quantity certification. At higher levels are cases in which an inspector is exposed to suppliers who have a good deal at stake in the lot of product in question. Even a situation in which inspectors dealing directly with production supervisors who outrank them involve substantial pressures to which inspectors should not be subjected.

Another form of inspector fraud consists of reporting false results solely to improve the outward evidence of his or her own efficiency or to make life more convenient. For example, Figure 18.10 shows the results reported by an inspector after taking a sample of n pieces from each of 49 lots. There is a large predominance of three defects per lot reported in the sample (exactly the maximum allowable number). The reason was found to be the inspector's reluctance to do the paperwork involved in a lot rejection.

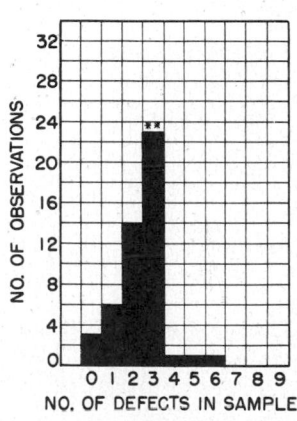

FIG. 18.10   Inspector error made for personal convenience.

In the example of Figure 18.11, the inspector was to take a sample of 100 pieces from each lot, with no defects allowable. If one or more pieces were defective, an added sample of 165 pieces was to be taken, with a total of three defects allowed in the combined sample of 265. It is seen that the inspector reported defects in virtually every first sample of 100 pieces.

However, no defects were reported in most of the second (larger) samples. It was found that the inspector could improve personal efficiency by taking second samples, since the time allowance for taking the second samples was liberal. Inspector fraud can be minimized by:

1. Filling inspection jobs only with persons of proved integrity
2. Restricting the down-the-line inspector to the job of fact finding, and reserving to the inspection supervision the job of negotiating and bargaining with other supervisors or executives

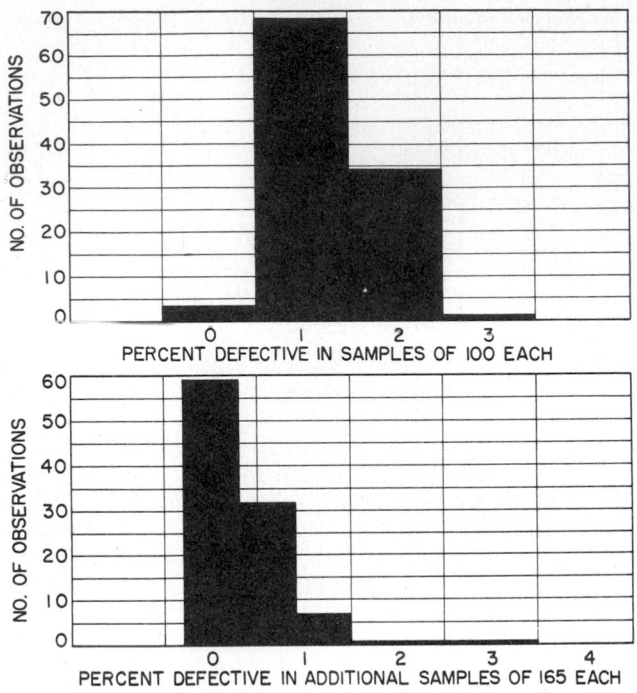

FIG. 18.11 Inspector error made to improve personal efficiency.

3. Rotating inspectors and workers to have both employee categories evaluate first hand the consequence of actions and decisions

4. Including inspectors in customer presentations or visits.

5. Conducting regular check inspections and periodic independent audits to detect fraud

6. Taking prompt action when fraud is discovered

Inspector Shortcuts. These may be unauthorized omissions of operations which the inspector has reason to believe are of dubious usefulness; e.g., accidental omissions had failed to give evidence of trouble. In some cases there is a shared blame, i.e., management has imposed a highly disagreeable task. For example, in a company making "tin cans," one inspection involved cutting up a can with hand-held tin shears, submerging the pieces in chloroform to remove the enamel, and measuring the thickness of the bare pieces with a micrometer. The cutting process was tedious and the chloroform was irritating to the skin, so the inspectors avoided the operation as much as possible. When better cutting tools and a different solvent were provided, the problem became minimal.

Flinching. This is the tendency of inspectors to falsify the results of inspection of borderline product. Flinching is actually widespread among all persons who report on performance versus goals, and especially when it is their own performance. Figure 18.12 shows a frequency distribution of measurement on volume efficiency of electronic receivers. There is an "excess" of readings at the specification maximum of 30, and there are no readings at all at 31, 32, or 33. Retest showed that the inspector recorded these "slightly over" units of product as 30.

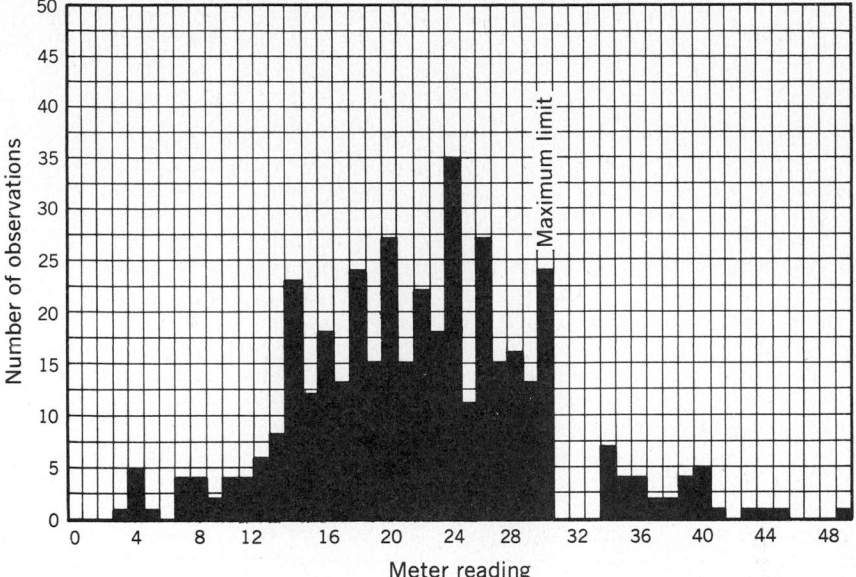

FIG. 18.12 How inspector flinches at design limit.

By this flinching, the inspector, in effect, changed the specification maximum from 30 to 33. This is a serious error (Juran, 1935).

Flinching during variables measurements is easy to detect by check inspection, which is also conducted on a variables basis. Analysis of the inspector's variables data will likewise detect flinching (as in the above example).

The remedy for flinching is an atmosphere of respect for the facts as the ethical foundation of the Inspection Department. The main means for achieving this are examples set by the Inspection supervisors.

One way *not* to deal with flinching is to criticize the inspector on the basis that the pattern of readings does not follow the laws of chance. Such criticism can be interpreted as being aimed at the symptom (the unnatural pattern of reading) rather than the disease (recording fictitious instead of factual readings). The risk is that inspectors will try to meet such criticisms by trying to make the false results look more natural, hence eliminating the symptom but not the disease.

Flinching also takes place during attribute inspection. Numerous studies have shown that inspector errors in rejecting good product outnumber the errors of accepting bad product. In part this arises because the good product outnumbers the bad and hence affords greater opportunity for error. But it also arises in part from the fact that acceptance of defects often comes dramatically to the attention of higher management, whereas rejection of good product seldom does so.

These same studies show that when check inspection is introduced and check is made both of product rejected and product accepted, the rejection of good product is reduced without affecting the acceptance of bad product.

Another form of flinching is to modify the inspection results to conform to the results which the inspector expects. For example, a visual inspection was being performed following a specified lapping operation.

An experiment to omit the lapping operations, conducted without inspector awareness of omission of the operation, resulted in rejection of less than a third of unlapped product.

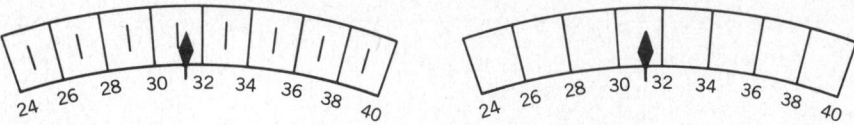

FIG. 18.13 Rounding off. The needle is in the same location on both charts. The charts are likely to be read as 31 and 32, left and right, respectively.

In some cases, flinching by inspectors is actually management-initiated through manager pressures which seem to the inspectors to leave no alternative. In one company, the inspectors making hardness tests were discovered to be flinching to an astonishing degree. This practice had been going on for years. It developed that the manufacturing vice president had designed this hardening process himself when he was the process engineer. At the time, he had deluded himself as to its capabilities and thereby had been the author of this long-standing practice (Juran, early consulting experience).

Rounding Off.   The process of dispensing with unneeded accuracy is generally referred to as "rounding off." Inspectors commonly round off their meter readings to the nearest scale division, as shown in Figure 18.13. The effect of rounding off is seen in the "picket fence" frequency distribution of Figure 18.12.

Rounding off is easy to detect from analysis of inspection data. A good analyst can, from the data alone, reconstruct the pattern of scale markings of an instrument without ever having seen the scale itself.

Rounding off is often a good thing, since it avoids undue attention to individual readings. But sometimes the need for precision on individual readings is great enough that rounding off should not be practiced. The planner and inspection supervisor should be on the alert to identify situations in which rounding off is not tolerable, and they should provide accordingly.

Instruments and gages should be properly selected for the application. (Churchill, 1956, gives a quantitative discussion on scale interval length and pointer clearance.) One practice is to require "readings to be recorded to the nearest. . . . "

Measures of Inspector Accuracy.   The collective effect of inspector errors, from all causes, is so extensive that there is need for measuring the extent of errors and for use of the data in controlling the effectiveness of inspectors. If this measurement is made only occasionally, use can be made of standard sample arrays (see above, under Technique Errors) and cross-check among inspectors, as well as check inspection. If the measurement is to be conducted regularly so as to discover trends in performance, then check inspection is necessary.

In conventional check inspection, a second inspector, i.e., a check inspector, reviews the decisions of the inspector by reexamining the product after it has been inspected. For an early example, refer to Taylor (1911). The best practice is to reexamine the rejected product as well as the accepted product.

Inspector errors may consist of accepting defective units of product or rejecting good units of product. If, in addition, the check inspection reviews the procedure followed by the inspector, other errors may be found, e.g., use of wrong issue of the specification, wrong instrument, improper filling out of documents, etc.

The conventional use of check inspection data to quantify inspector accuracy is to count the errors, to assign weights, and to use the composite of errors as an index of accuracy (of inaccuracy, usually). (See, for example, Gilman, 1963.) In some schemes, the errors discovered in later operations or in customer complaints are included in the data. The composite of errors may be expressed in terms of percent defective (found to exist in the inspected product) or in terms of demerits per unit. (Refer to Weaver, 1975, which reports on a study of inspector accuracy during the production process, based on accept/reject decisions involving the product currently produced.) Either way, the scoring system is open to the objection that the inspector's accuracy depends, to an important degree, on the quality of the product submitted to him by the process; i.e., the more defects submitted the greater is the chance of missing some.

A plan for measuring inspectors' accuracy in a way which is independent of incoming quality is that evolved in 1928 by J. M. Juran and C. A. Melsheimer. (See Juran, 1935, for the original published description of this plan.) Under this plan the check inspector, as usual, reexamines the inspected product, both the accepted and the rejected units.

In addition, the check inspector secures the inspector's own data on the original makeup of the lot, i.e., total units, total good, total defective. From these data, the following formulas emerge as applied to a single lot which has been check inspected:

$$\text{Accuracy of inspector} = \text{percent of defects correctly identified}$$

$$= \frac{d - k}{d - k + b}$$

where d = defects reported by the inspector
$\quad k$ = number of defects reported by the inspector, but determined by the check inspector not to be defects
$d - k$ = true defects found by the inspector
$\quad b$ = defects missed by the inspector, as determined by check inspection
$d - k + b$ = true defects originally in the product

Figure 18.14 illustrates how the percentage of accuracy is determined. The number of defects reported by the inspector, d, is 45. Of these, 5 were found by the check inspector to be good; that is, $k = 5$. Hence $d - k$ is 40, the true number of defects found by the inspector. However, the inspector missed 10 defects; that is, $b = 10$. Hence the original number of defects, $d - k + b$ is 50, that is, the 40 found by the inspector plus the 10 missed. Hence,

$$\text{Percentage of accuracy} = \frac{d - k}{d - k + b} = \frac{45 - 5}{45 - 5 + 10} = 80\%$$

In application of the plan, periodic check inspection is made of the inspector's work. Data on d, k, and b are accumulated over a period of months to summarize the inspector's accuracy, as for example:

Job no.	Total pieces	d	b	k
3	1000	10	0	0
19	50	3	1	0
42	150	5	1	0
48	5000	10	4	0
Total		200	30	0

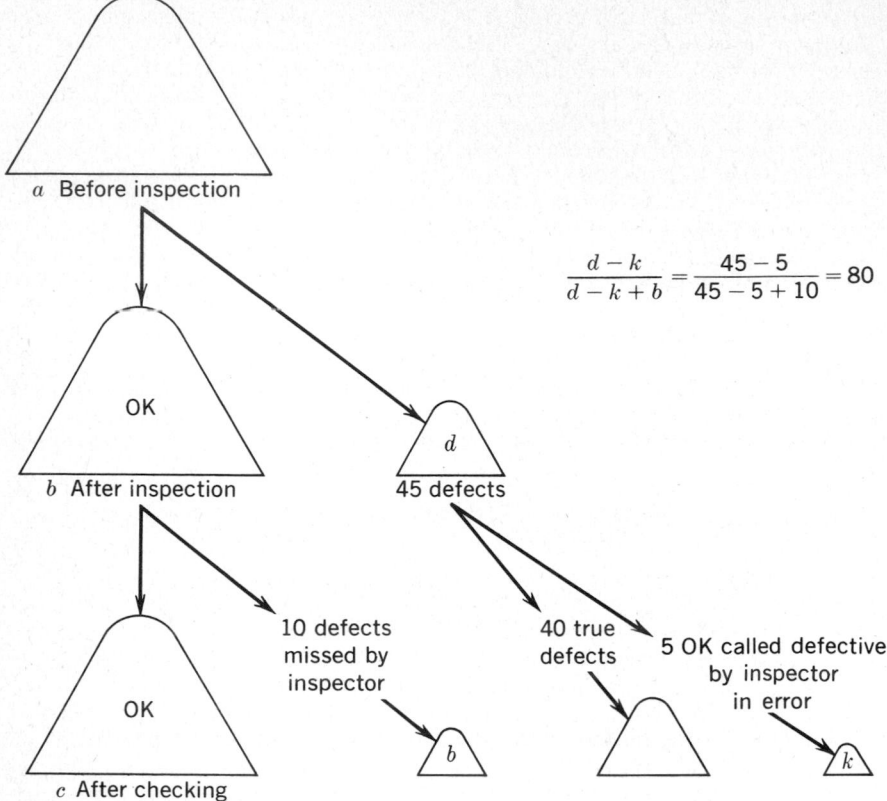

$$\frac{d-k}{d-k+b} = \frac{45-5}{45-5+10} = 80$$

FIG. 18.14 Process for determining accuracy of inspectors.

The totals give, for percent accuracy:

$$\frac{d}{d+b} = \frac{200}{230} = 87\%$$

As is evident, the plan lends itself to simple cumulation of data. However, some compromise is made with theory to avoid undue emphasis on any one lot checked. Over a 6-month period, where the cumulative checks may reach 50 or more, the need for such compromise or weighting is diminished.

The check inspector also makes errors. However, these have only a secondary effect on the inspector's accuracy. In the above example, if the check inspector were only 90 percent accurate, only 27 of the 30 defects missed by the inspector would be found. The inspector's accuracy would become:

$$\frac{200}{227} = 88.1\% \text{ instead of } 87.0\%$$

In some situations, k is small and may be ignored. However, in other situations, notably for sensory qualities, the inspector may have a bias for rejecting borderline work. In such cases, it is feasible to use, as an added measure, the inspector's accuracy due to rejection of good pieces. This has been termed "waste." Under the terminology used here:

$$\text{Waste} = \text{percent of good pieces rejected} = \frac{k}{n - d - b + k}$$

where n = total pieces inspected.

The "percent accuracy" is also equal to the percent of material correctly inspected. This feature permits use of the plan in the pay formula of the inspector.

Some investigators have developed variations on the foregoing measures of inspector accuracy as applied to visual inspection. These include measures based on probability theory (Wang, 1975), and the on use of signal-detection theory in the analysis of industrial inspection (Ainsworth, 1980).

The proportion of correct decisions made by the inspector is an intuitively good index of the inspector's efficiency when the costs of rejecting a good item and accepting a bad item are equal.

The two measures for evaluating inspector's efficiency, introduced by Wang (1975) are:

$$N_\alpha = \frac{\text{number of true defects detected by the inspector}}{\text{number of true defects}}$$

$$N_\beta = \frac{\text{number of true defects detected by the inspector}}{\text{number of all defects detected by the inspector}}$$

If the two costs are not equal, the theory of signal detectability (TSD) provides a better measure for analyzing an inspector's performance. However, the use of TSD requires assumptions about normal and equal variant population distributions, and the probability density functions for the "good" and "defective" populations must be calculated. See Johnson and Funke (1980) for a discussion of the advantages and disadvantages of a number of human performance measures, including Wang's (1975) approach.

In the application of any plan to check the accuracy of inspectors, it is essential that the checks be at random. Neither the inspector nor the check inspector should know the schedule in advance. Random dice, cards from a pack, etc., should be used. It is also essential that the responsibility be clear. The inspector who has accepted defects under orders or through inaccurate instruments, etc., cannot be held responsible for the results.

FEEDBACK OF INSPECTION DATA

Inspection generates data in profusion, and these data are widely used. Virtually all sections of this handbook involve some degree of reliance on inspection data, and for some sections this reliance is extensive. Table 18.22 lists the sections which make such extensive use of inspection data, along with the principal purpose served. In addition, Sections 23 through 26 deal with methods of data analysis; and Section 27 deals with use of computers.

Feedback to Production.   This is the most extensive inspection feedback judged by volume of data and by worker-hours consumed. The feedbacks serve mainly as alarm signals to identify out-of-control processes and to urge corrective action. In addition, to assist Production in problem identification, summaries are prepared by department, process, product, operator, etc., using the Pareto prin-

TABLE 18.22 Uses of Inspection Data

Section number and title	Inspection data used extensively
4 Quality Costs	As inputs to quality cost estimates
16 Manufacturing Planning	For process capability determination
15 Supplier Relations	As feedback to suppliers
17 Production	As feedback to production
18 Inspection and Test	To judge product instrument conformance
19 Marketing	To provide "feedforward" for customer relations
20 Customer Service	To improve field service
22 Quality Improvement	To remedy chronic defects
10 Managing Human Performance	To improve human performance
13 Product Development	To identify and certify products
8 Upper Management and Quality	To prepare executive reports on quality

ciple to focus on the vital few problems. The detailed methods, along with the nature of Inspection relations with Production, are discussed in Section 17, under Inspection Feedback to Production, as is the problem of corrective action.

Data Feedback to Management. A second extensive use of inspection data is to provide company managers with the summaries and analyses needed as part of the system of managerial control of the quality function. See Section 8 for details, including discussion of means for auditing the system of data feedback.

Feedback to Inspection. An often neglected use of inspector data is feedback to the inspector(s). Quality information feedback and the visual display of inspector data has both a positive human factors impact in reducing inspector error and an effect on improving inspector productivity (Coleman, 1982).

Data "Feedforward" to the Market. A fourth major use of inspection data is to identify the product, provide certificates of analysis, and otherwise to provide product information to consumers, marketers, regulators, etc. A great deal of this is on a "to whom it may concern" basis through use of product markings, tags, certificates, circulars, instructions, cautions, etc.

Data System. To provide data to meet these and other needs (Table 18.22), planners evolve a whole system of documentation such as is elaborated in Section 13. Briefly, this system provides:

Record forms and data sheets to secure the basic data.

A system of defect codes to simplify data recording and subsequent data processing.

Provision for data processing, whether manually or by computer (Section 27). (See also Wurster, 1980.)

ORGANIZATION FOR INSPECTION AND TEST

Prior to the industrial revolution, manufacturing industries consisted largely of small shops, each dominated by a master. The master trained the apprentices and supervised their work in various ways, including a form of quality control. This consisted of process surveillance and product inspection conducted until such time as the apprentice demonstrated the capability of repeatedly turning out quality products.

Emergence of the Inspector.   As the shops grew larger, they outgrew the ability of the master to direct all affairs personally. Therefore specialized departments were created and assistants appointed to supervise these departments. One of these assistants, the shop supervisor, took over supervision of the workers and continued the tradition of personally exercising the quality controls.

In due course the number of workers grew to an extent that exceeded the capacity of the shop foreman to exercise the quality controls. This problem was solved by creating the post of inspector and delegating to the inspector the job of judging fitness for use or conformance to specification. The earliest form of this was probably in the large construction projects of antiquity. Figure 18.15 shows an inspector using a string to measure the flatness of stone blocks while a worker is engaged in dressing the stone. The date is 1450 B.C.

FIG. 18.15 Ancient construction inspector. *(From C. Singer et al., A History of Technology, Oxford University Press, 1957, vol. 1, fig. 313.)*

The industrial revolution resulted in the growth of large manufacturing companies which included multiple production shops (foundry, lathe, etc.). The tradition of shop inspectors reporting to the foreman was carried over, so that the organization for inspection resembled that shown in Figure 18.16.

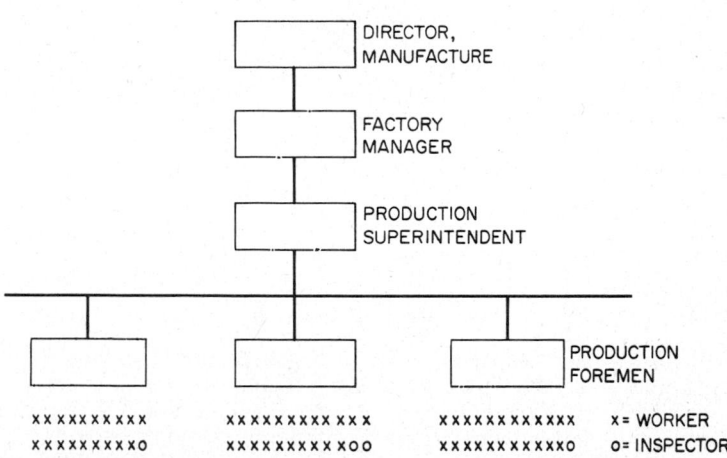

FIG. 18.16 Organization for inspection, early factories.

The supervisors of those shops had virtually no technical education. Their job knowledge was derived from long association with materials, processes, and products which had remained largely static over the years. When World War I required these shops to take on products new to them, many foremen were in deep trouble. They knew from experience how far they safely could go in overruling their inspectors on the old products. But in regard to the new products, this experience was of little help; in addition, the foremen lacked the technical education which might have qualified them to make a swift transition. In consequence, there were many serious quality failures and scandals.

Emergence of the Central Inspection Department. Following these catastrophes, and under the urging of the Taylor System advocates, the companies now accepted the advice of those who had long been calling for making the inspectors independent of the production foremen. The companies took the inspectors away from the production foremen and made them responsible to full-time inspection foremen instead. Then, to provide adequate supervision for these inspectors, a new office, that of chief inspector, was created. Figure 18.17 shows the resulting organization form in contrast to the prior form (Figure 18.16).

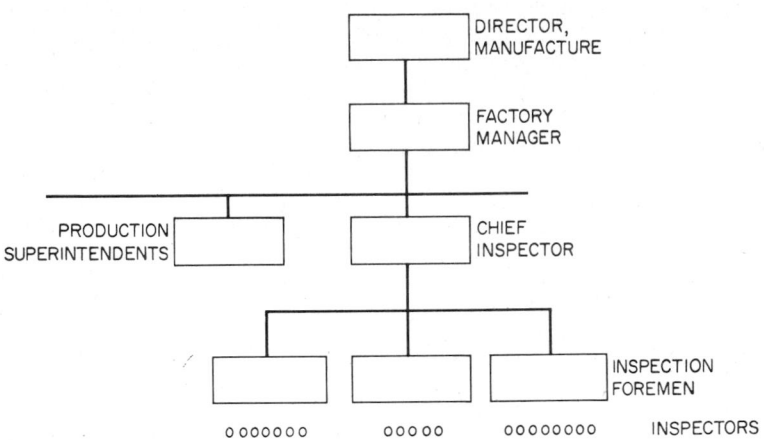

FIG. 18.17   Creation of central inspection department.

(*Note:* Frederick W. Taylor and his school of "Scientific Management" advocated creation of specialized departments to conduct various activities—manufacturing planning, cost accounting, maintenance, inspection, etc., previously responsible to the foreman. See Section 10, under Role of Motivation: The Taylor System.)

Inspection Department Structure. The early inspection departments generally took a form similar to that shown in Figure 18.18. In due course, further developments followed, as discussed below.

Purchased Material Inspection. All inspectors engaged in this work were brought together in a single organization section for some logical, compelling reasons. Incoming material was received at a central receiving station, requiring also a centralized inspection station. The purchasing routines could better be enforced by a single supplier inspection section. The problems of dealing with suppliers

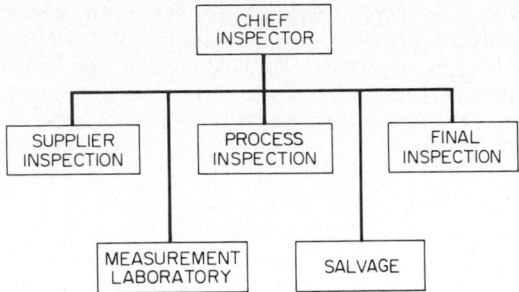

FIG. 18.18   Early central inspection department.

were special, requiring a standard supplier inspection procedure. To a very high degree, these reasons still prevail, though new concepts of supplier relations are now needed to deal with modern subcontracting. (See generally Section 15.)

Process Inspection.   The process inspectors were widely dispersed among the production processing departments. The first centralizing step was to make these inspectors responsible to a chief process inspector while remaining geographically dispersed. As the plants grew, multiple process inspection departments were organized to parallel the associated production departments, as shown in Figure 18.19.

Finished Goods Inspection.   This is also called "final inspection," "test," etc. While this has long been a separate department, there have been variations in the manner of connecting this activity into the overall organization chart.

In the mechanical and electronic industries, the usual pattern has been to make finished goods inspection responsible to the chief inspector (Figure 18.18). An alternative form has been a separation of the functional testing from the remain-

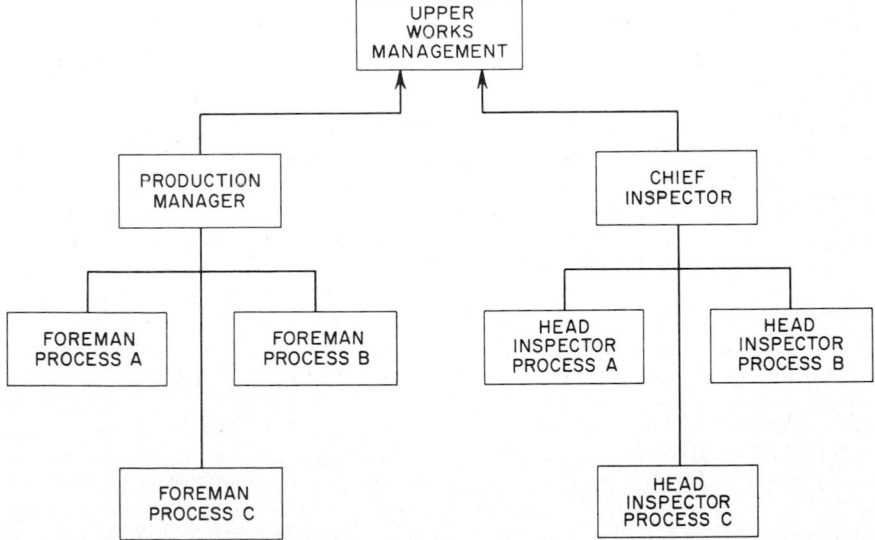

FIG. 18.19   Organization of process inspection in large plants.

ing inspection (visual, gaging, etc.). Under such an arrangement, the testing is made responsible to the Technical Department, while the remaining inspection reports to the chief inspector (Figure 18.20). Generally, the more critical the product in terms of human safety, the more likely it is that the functional testing reports to upper management, either directly or through some channel other than Manufacture.

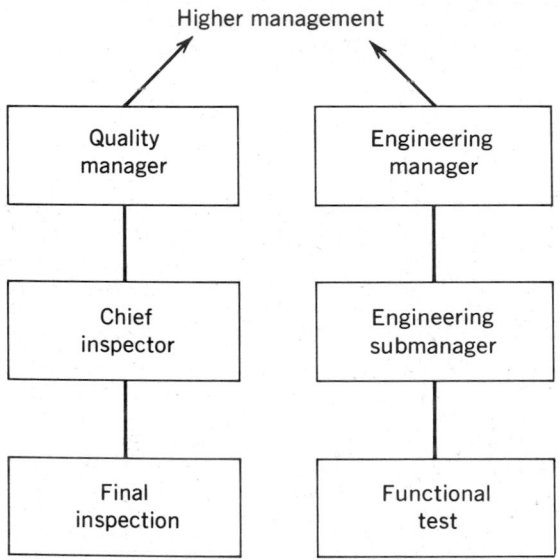

FIG. 18.20   Separation of functional test from inspection.

In the process industries, there has long been a separation of critical testing (for safety, structural integrity, and functional performance) from the inspection for esthetic and noncritical qualities. The critical testing was the responsibility of the laboratory, which reported to the technical manager. The noncritical inspection was performed by inspectors responsible to Production (Figure 18.21). To a high degree, this arrangement has persisted. In most process industries, the inspectors (for noncritical properties) are brought together in a separate department which reports to a production manager. However, in some process industries these inspectors remain dispersed organizationally and are responsible to the departmental production foremen.

In multiproduct plants there are alternatives for organizing the process and final inspection. One form is to create separate hierarchies for process and final inspectors (Figure 18.22). Another form is to create product hierarchies, each of which includes both process and final inspectors (Figure 18.23). The choice depends largely on the extent to which the processes are unique to particular products. The plan of Figure 18.23 permits better coordination if the processes are largely unique to the associated products.

Creation of the central Inspection Department also created a new organizational problem: To whom should the chief inspector report? This problem is discussed in Section 7, under Evolution of the Quality Control Hierarchy.

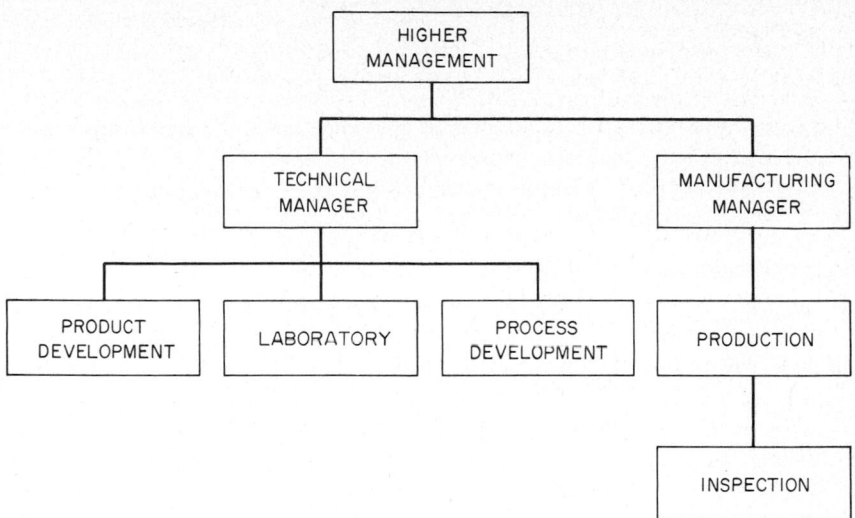

FIG. 18.21 Organization form, process industries, single plant.

Evolution of Inspection Support Activities. The formation of central inspection departments enabled the new chief inspectors to tend to some matters which had previously received scant attention. These included the following:

Metrology. Laboratories were created for calibrating, protecting, storing, issuing, and otherwise regulating the precision of measuring instruments. In addition, new skills were evolved for design of better instruments and test equipment and for planning instrumentation as part of the design of the production process and of the inspection stations. See generally Sections 16 and 18.

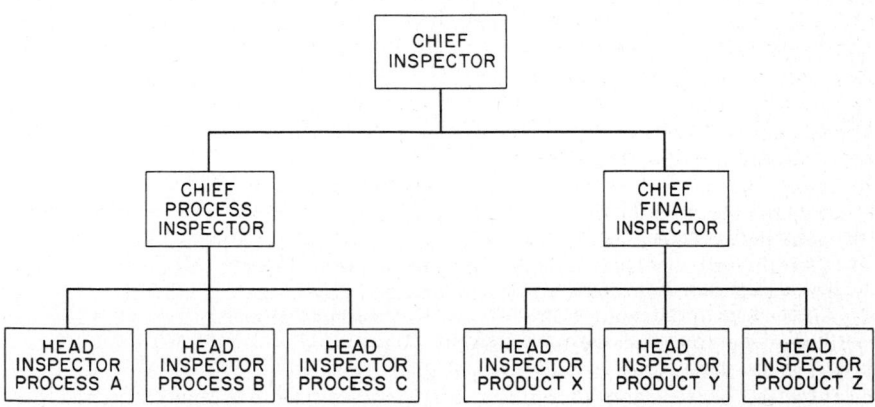

FIG. 18.22 Inspection organized by function.

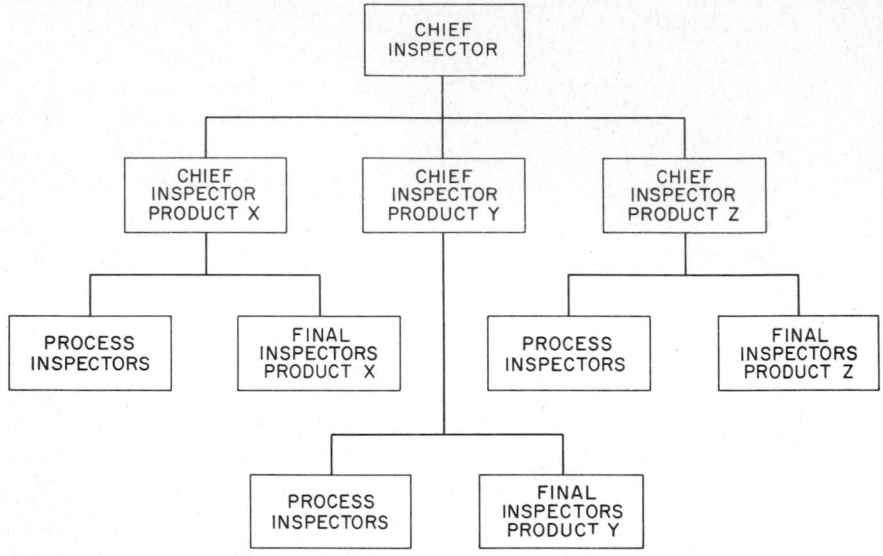

FIG. 18.23   Inspection organized by product.

Inspection Planning.   The full-time inspection supervisors evolved the concept of planning the inspection job. Inspection methods sheets were designed to list the inspection operations to be performed, sample sizes, allowable defects, instruments, standards, and other criteria needed by the inspectors. See Inspection Planning, above.

Inspector Selection, Training.   The full-time inspection supervisors felt keenly the need for well-selected, trained inspection personnel and began to evolve the means for reaching this goal. See generally Section 10.

Salvage.   The ministerial work associated with disposition of nonconforming product was gradually assigned to the chief inspector. It includes identification, segregation, custody, documentation, and still other activities. It may involve sorting the product and planning repairs or other salvage forms.

Noninspection Operations Performed by Inspectors.   In many companies there are forces which try to confine work assignments to strict jurisdictional lines; i.e., inspectors should do nothing but inspection work. (A common spur to strict enforcement of jurisdictional boundaries is management pressure on departmental budgets.) However, the increasing complexity of the quality function has weakened these boundaries. The trends appear in several forms including the counting, weighing, and packing of product.

Some assignment of noninspection work to inspectors has been on economic grounds, i.e., since the inspector handles the product anyhow, why require still another person to rehandle the product just to count it? Many other examples exist. It is evident that the planning of inspection work must be done with flexible concepts of jurisdiction. Failing this, the rigid enforcement of jurisdictional lines will lead to absurd duplications of work.

INSPECTION DEPARTMENT MANAGEMENT

Managing the Inspection Department is usually accomplished through a hierarchy of supervisors whose duties have much in common. A typical list of these common duties includes the following:

Participate in inspection planning; approve all manuals and procedures to be used by the inspectors

Approve product and process standards supplemental to engineering specifications

Prepare the departmental budget for personnel, facilities, and supplies

Participate in design of the inspection workplace, in choice of facilities and instruments, and in design of work methods; approve the final design

Recruit and train inspectors; assign work to the inspectors; supervise and evaluate their performance; motivate inspectors to meet standards of quality and efficiency

Collaborate with other departments in investigation and solution of quality problems and in other interdepartmental activities

Review the condition of products found to be nonconforming; participate in the studies leading to disposition

Review the condition of processes for which there is evidence of nonconformance to specification; collaborate in the steps needed to restore control

Prepare and approve necessary documentation on quality

Develop the potentialities of subordinates

Keep informed on new industrial developments in facilities, instrumentation, inspection methods and practices; adapt for company use as appropriate

These duties vary in detail with the specialties of the various inspection departments. The chief inspector (or equivalent title) carries, in addition, the broader duties of participating in discussion of numerous higher-level quality problems.

Laboratory Management.   This activity involves several special problems in inspection management.

Interlaboratory Comparisons.   Despite extensive standardization of test methods, it is still necessary to conduct periodic interlaboratory comparisons among companies, between division and plant laboratories, between central and branch laboratories, etc. (See also Section 26 under Planning Interlaboratory Tests for methods of graphical diagnosis, especially Youden two sample plots in Figure 26.20.)

Decentralizing the Laboratory.   It is usually not feasible to centralize all test facilities in one laboratory. The usual forms of decentralizing are:

1. *Branch laboratories:*   Branch laboratories serve to simplify the transport of samples and to provide more prompt feedback of the resulting data. The branch laboratory may consist of:

    a. A laboratory staffed full time by Inspection but located physically amid the production areas which require test service.

b. A traveling laboratory which moves from department to department according to a schedule. A common form is the gage cart or other traveling metrology laboratory used to maintain accuracy of measuring instruments.

c. A laboratory staffed part time by Production to provide prompt service without the need for requisitions and other paperwork. Such laboratories, restricted to routine testing, are located on the Production floor.

2. *Independent laboratories:* These can be a useful adjunct to the company's laboratory for reasons of cost, scarce facilities, peak loads, specialized personnel, customer relations, and still other considerations. Inspection managers are well advised to keep informed on the services offered by independent laboratories and to use these as the occasion warrants. (See Maass, 1970, for a discussion of pros and cons.)

Multiple Laboratory Functions. In many companies the Inspection laboratory is the company's sole facility for making such tests. In consequence, the laboratory will be asked to make tests for a variety of purposes:

As a service to Production, which uses the data to make process control decisions

As a service to research, which lacks a facility for making such tests

As a basis for product conformance decisions, for which the laboratory itself has the responsibility

In such cases the laboratory is "selling" test results to multiple clients, including itself. Numerous questions of schedule priority, cost allocation, etc., arise and require that the laboratory managers make these allocations by balancing the interests of all clients rather than on the basis of departmental biases. (See Burgess, 1983, for further elaboration.)

Inspection by Production Departments. There are three varieties of this, and care must be taken to identify which one is the subject under discussion:

1. Inspection conducted part time by production operators to determine whether the process should run or stop. This is a widespread form of process control and is discussed in Section 17 under Concept of Controllability.

2. Inspection conducted part time by production workers to make decisions on product conformance. This is discussed in Section 17, under Self-Inspection.

3. Inspection (product acceptance) conducted by full-time inspectors who report not to the Inspection Department but to the Production Department. This will now be discussed.

Most chief inspectors take a dim view of any arrangement in which full-time inspectors engaged in product acceptance report to anyone other than the Inspection Department. The usual reasons advanced emphasize the needs for professional inspection planning, special recruitment and training for inspectors, establishing a career pattern, unbiased judgment, etc. The real reason may be cultural resistance, but the asserted reasons have validity. However, use of modern staff concepts makes it possible to meet most of the objections by use of a well-known formula for delegation:

Activity	Responsibility assigned to	
	Production	Quality Control
Prepare and approve the inspection plan	X	X
Execute the plan	X	
Audit to see that the execution follows the plan		X

The contents of the "audit" vary depending on circumstances. For example, if the inspectors (in Production) sort or test the product 100 percent, a check inspection may be set up to follow this (Figure 18.24).

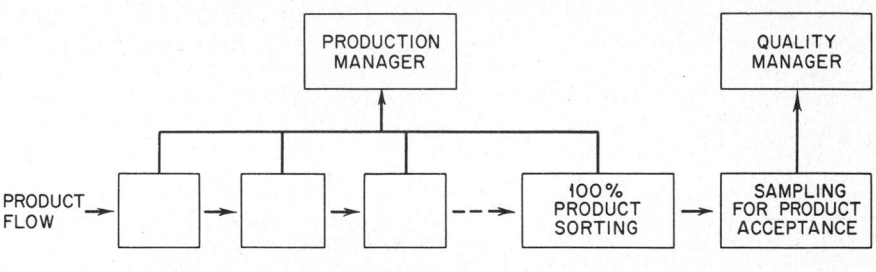

FIG. 18.24 Organization for sorting by production, with subsequent acceptance sampling.

Short-term economics are not noticeably affected by transferring full-time inspectors from Inspection to Production or vice versa. After the change, the same people perform the same duties as before. The really big effect on short-term economics is to abolish full-time inspectors by instituting "product acceptance by operators," as described in Section 17 under that heading.

The "laborpower" aspects of Inspection Department management (e.g., inspector selection, training, compensation) are discussed in Section 10, as are motivational aspects. (See also Gittler, 1973, and Carter and Carter, 1983.)

INSPECTION PERSONNEL MANAGEMENT

The effective management of Inspection personnel is an important factor in controlling the frequency and impact of inspector errors, and in improving inspector productivity (both topics discussed in this section). To be effective, management must address the following areas (see Gittler, 1973):

- Select and keep good inspectors
- Determine who is a good inspector and who is a poor one
- Know whether or not an inspector or group of inspectors are performing their jobs to expected standards
- Measure the impact inspectors have on the product and on costs

Inspection personnel must also be managed in a manner that maintains credibility with the total company (See Jaehn, 1982). There are three areas of opportunity for inspection to maintain credibility:

1. Provide adequate instructions
2. Assure the integrity of the quality measurement system
3. Monitor performance and audit compliance to the specified procedures

PRODUCTIVITY IN INSPECTION AND TEST

As the costs of quality are managed down, the ability to produce more or serve more frequently increases, resulting in increased productivity. It is also true that as internal costs or appraisal costs are decreased, the productivity of inspectors and the inspection process improves.

Loss Productivity Factors.   One of the objectives of the Quality Management Department is to optimize the effectiveness of the Inspection Department by removing any factors which decrease productivity. Some of these factors are internal while others are external to the quality function. (See Thomas, 1977, and Minor, 1981, for further discussion on factors.) Some of these factors have been discussed under other topics in this section. They include:

Employee selection

Clear information/direction

Physical layout

Efficient tools/instruments

Proper training

Effective information feedback

Motivation and incentives

Appropriate compensation and recognition

Adequate supervision

Measuring Inspectors' Productivity.   Productivity is the measure of the effectiveness of the utilization (conversion process) of allocated resources (input) to accomplish specific goals and results (output). The inspection process is also a traditional conversion process. Where inputs (items to be inspected), subject to an inspection conversion (accept/reject), result in an output (data). Therefore,the inspection process can be measured for the productivity of the inspection process and the impact of the inspector. (See Goldbeck, 1981, and Ulla, 1982 for discussion and examples.) Traditionally, the measurement or productivity metric is: units per worker-hour for month x.

BUDGETING FOR INSPECTION

An invariable responsibility of inspection supervisors is to run the department at minimal cost. This they do through the common sequence of (1) establishing efficient methods, (2) setting standards for quality and quantity of work, (3) selecting and training inspectors to be able to meet these standards, and (4) motivating them to do so. This responsibility for cost control is usually formalized into the company's system of budgetary control (see also Section 4, Quality Costs).

The inspection budget deals with the first two elements of the above sequence. These may be restated as (1) inspection cost reduction and (2) setting standards of inspection cost performance. Both these activities are concerned with doing deeds, though these deeds must be translated into the common language of money to meet the needs of management budgetary review.

Inspection Cost Reduction.   Because a budget becomes the goal to be met, it should reflect good practice, not poor practice. For this reason, inspection cost reduction should precede setting standards. There are several approaches available to achieve inspection cost reduction:

Defect Prevention. High defect levels are the most widespread single reason for high inspection costs. In consequence, a usual prerequisite for major reductions of inspection costs is to reduce the major reasons for these costs, i.e., high defect levels. (See generally Section 22.) After the causes of defects have been identified and removed, inspection costs can be reduced. The reduction in costs takes several forms including:

1. Use sampling instead of sorting (see generally Section 25).
2. Transfer inspection to the production operators while retaining an audit. (See Section 17 under Self-Inspection.)
3. Use test data from suppliers to abolish incoming inspection. Assurance is provided by an audit. (See Section 15 under Audit of Decisions.)

Census of Inspection Costs. In this census, all inspection work is identified, whether done by employees of Inspection departments, of Production departments, of Laboratory departments, etc. The decisive feature for entering the census is not the titles of the people or the names of the departments to whom they report, but the deeds they perform; i.e., do they examine product, compare the results to a specification, and make judgments of conformance?

Commonly the census is conducted to determine, for each department involved:

The number of equivalent full-time inspectors, and their pay

The type of work they do (sorting, sampling, etc.)., the job grade, and the approach to selection and training of inspectors

Other costs, e.g., facilities, supplies

The inspection plans used, the acceptance criteria, the procedures and other routines

The methods of supervision, both in setting up the inspection plan and in seeing that the execution follows the plan

The measures of performance for accuracy and efficiency

The census is not merely a questionnaire; it includes visits to all the areas to see the manner of conducting the work. Work sampling is used to help identify the nature of the jobs being done. The census may well be part of the study of quality costs, as discussed in Section 4.

The summary of the census shows the total inspection cost, which is an index of the importance of the problem in relation to other management problems. The summary also shows where these costs are concentrated, suggesting the choice of areas for more detailed study.

Contract Inspection. Service organizations, serving both private and industrial sectors, are growing in numbers and influence. (See Karabatsos, 1983, and Garfinkel and Clodfelter, 1984.) Their greatest benefit is cost savings, and therefore they provide a cost management option. Typical services offered:

Failure analysis/product liability

Materials evaluation—metallurgy

Microscopy

Nondestructive testing

Analytical laboratories

High reliability component testing

Nuclear plant inspections

Supplier surveillance

Machine/instrument calibration

First-article inspection

Statistical services

Personnel training

Consulting services

The forms of these service organizations range from "job shops" (Wood, 1979) to organizations that provide part-time inspectors ("Where Quality Control Is a Part Time Job," 1979).

Industrial Engineering Studies. These have wide application to inspection work. (See Williams, 1981, for a detailed plan for in-depth evaluation of all phases of the quality control operation.)

Methods study can be used to improve the design of workplaces. Work standards can be applied to repetitive jobs. Work simplification can be used to analyze principal operations. One plan is as follows (Barry, 1959):

1. Choose one of the more troublesome inspection operations for study.
2. Consider eliminating the operation entirely.
3. Failing this, break the job down as follows:
   a. List the work elements.
   b. List the equipment used.
   c. Prepare flow diagrams and workplace sketches.
   d. Discuss the job with the inspector to get his or her ideas.
   e. Question every detail (a checklist of 33 questions is provided).
4. Prepare a new method as the result of the study.
5. Install the new method and follow up.

Work sampling is a further industrial engineering tool available for study of the nature and content of inspection jobs (Kay, 1972).

Quality Engineering Studies. These aim at a wide variety of improvements:

1. Coordinated inspection planning is used to minimize duplication of work between Inspection and Production, or between inspection departments. Also, it may be easier to transport inspectors to the Production Department rather than move the product from Production to the Inspection Department.
2. Automated testing is developed to replace highly repetitive manual testing.
3. Sampling is used to replace detail inspection.
4. Sampling costs are reduced by use of other available knowledge about product conformance, process capability, and the sequence of manufacture (see How Much Inspection? above).

5. Economic inspection intervals are established in proportion to the potential for loss from out-of-control manufacturing processes (see "A Management Standard for Economical Inspection," 1976).

6. Documentation is reduced. One manager reduced the documentation for good product (the great majority of all orders) by imprinting the production order with a stamp which provided space for the minimal data needed for approved lots. The conventional documentation was retained for defective material. Other records of inspection can be designed for maximum utility (see Stalker, 1980), and ink stamps for efficiency (see "Inspection Can Make an Impression with a Saving," 1976).

7. Documentation is turned over to noninspectors so that the inspector can concentrate on product inspection. One form of this is to assign a separate individual to collect the papers needed by the inspector and to deliver this package to the inspector.

8. Perfectionism is reduced by studying the cost of finding a defect compared to the cost of (a) not finding it, (b) the selling price of a unit, or (c) the cost of a service call.

Interdepartmental Studies. While means are available for reducing inspection costs by purely departmental study and action, the main opportunities are through joint study with other departments. The principal forms of this study consist of:

1. Defect prevention to reduce the need for inspection (see above).

2. Collaboration with Production to determine process capability and to preserve the order of manufacture so that the information needed for decisions on conformance is not restricted to the data derived from inspection and test (see How Much Inspection? above; also Section 17, under Product and Process Relationship).

3. Collaboration with Production to transfer the inspection to production operators and to regulate this through audit of decisions (see Section 17, under Product Acceptance by Operators).

4. Challenging the standards, especially on sensory qualities. One approach is described above under Providing Standards for Sensory Qualities.

The Budgetary Process. The Inspection budget is only one of numerous departmental budgets. These must all be prepared under a common format, and in a common language, to permit summary and review at higher and higher levels until finally approved by top management. Because the common language is money, all the deeds must be restated in terms of money to make these summaries and reviews possible.

The common budgetary format is devised by the company's finance and accounting specialists. This format features several universals employed in the budgetary process.

Cost Centers. These are logical subdivisions of inspection activity, chosen to fix responsibility and to provide a basis for collecting data on actual costs. The cost centers usually follow organization boundaries, since responsibility becomes very clear thereby.

Activity Index. Most inspection costs vary with the amount of plant activity. Sound budgeting requires that there be discovered, for each cost center, an activity index, i.e., an expression of the relationship between plant activity and budgeted inspection costs. For different kinds of inspection, the budget will vary in different ways:

Type of inspection	*Budget varies with*
Receiving inspection	Number of lots
	Value of purchased goods
Process inspection	Hours of direct production labor
	Dollars of direct production labor
	Number of projects serviced
Final inspection	Units of product inspected
	Value of product inspected
	Hours of direct production labor
	Dollars of direct production labor
Test laboratory	Number of requisitions (sometimes there is a standard time for each type of test)
Instrument laboratory	Number of active instruments in use

There are added variables which affect budgeting in all activities and which may be of major effect in some activities. These variables include:

1. *Lot size:* Inspection costs per lot do not vary greatly with lot size. However, variation in lot size can cause great variation in inspection cost per unit of product or per dollar value of product.
2. *Product mix:* Budgeting is often done on the basis of a historical product mix. When this mix changes, the costs may change either way.
3. *Flow of material:* The most exaggerated form of this takes place when much or even most of the product is presented for inspection in the last few days of the month.

Historical Standards. A budget for cost control is a standard for expenditures. This standard may be established in a number of ways, the most prevalent being the historical standard; i.e., we will be guided by how much we used to spend.

An example of evolution of an historical standard is seen in Figure 18.25. In this example, it had been determined that the best activity index was direct shop labor costs. Data for the last 18 months were plotted in Figure 18.25, resulting in a correlation scatter of inspection labor costs to direct shop labor costs. A line fitted to the points resulted in the relationship of a budget of $8.80 inspection labor per every $100 of direct shop labor. Costs of the supervisory and clerical force were regarded as "constant" over a wide range of activity and these were added to the variable costs shown in Figure 18.25.

On a more sophisticated level, one company identified 11 "factors" which influence the extent of inspection needed, e.g., type of product, identity of customer, degree of "black-box" subcontracting, etc. For each factor, there were several degrees or levels of influence. From a study of eight prior projects, weights were assigned to each degree of each factor. These weights were then used to analyze new contract proposals to arrive at an estimate of the inspection personnel levels needed (see Hutter, 1966).

Standards for Projects. Another form of standard is "the plan"; i.e., spending in accordance with a prearranged plan for a project. This device is most common

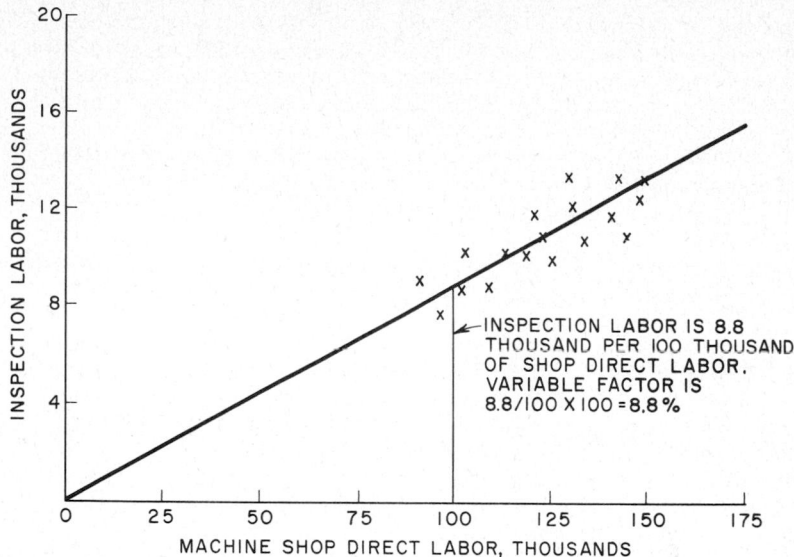

FIG. 18.25 Ratio of inspection labor costs to shop labor costs.

when the company has secured a contract based on a bid price and now faces the problem of holding its various components of cost within the respective components of the bid.

Seldom does a company use only one form of standard for costs. The cost centers are unlike, and it is common to find different forms of cost standards used in different cost centers. Moreover, there is a measure of judgment exercised in any event. None of the methods of setting standards are precise enough to be used automatically as a basis for judging future performance.

Measure of Actual Costs. The establishment of cost centers, activity indexes, and standards provides a measure of what costs should be. It remains to establish means for measuring what costs actually are. This requires added tools:

An adequate timekeeping system: Inspectors must be provided with account numbers and forms for charging their time to proper account numbers.

A system for computing expenses: In like manner, there must be account numbers, requisitions, and other means for charging supplies and services to the proper accounts.

Data-processing systems: Means must be available (manual or otherwise) for processing the basic time and expense data into prompt summaries and reports for the various cost centers.

A budget office: Coordination of the activities of budgeting and reporting requires that administration of the system be a separate responsibility, clearly assigned to specific persons.

When a company embarks for the first time on formal budgeting, it is well to go through a trial period for "debugging." During the trial period, minds are open for constructive change. Lacking a trial period, minds may close and the entire project may face defeat.

Review of Cost Performance. Reports on costs versus budgets are prepared and distributed by the budget office on a regular schedule, usually weekly or monthly. Supervisory review is concentrated on significant departure from standard. This review is often conducted as a scheduled group review of performance against budget, since there is much interrelation between causes in one department and effects in another. At these review sessions, alternative courses of action are proposed and considered.

The very act of systematically reviewing performance and questioning variances is a main factor in holding costs to standard. If variances are sure to be questioned, supervisors do their utmost to prevent variances in the first place. If there is laxity in the review, performance will soon become lax as well.

Other Cost-Control Devices. Whether inspection is budgeted or not, there are available various special tools for controlling inspection costs. These special tools use physical units rather than money. Some of these tools do not require use of the company's financial accounting system, though the clerks of the Accounting Department may process the special data prepared.

For example, it is usually feasible to establish a ratio indicating the number of inspection hours required as compared with the number of productive machine hours (or operator hours) spent producing the product. This ratio can then be built into the form of a variable budget. Within normal variations in volume of operation, as production hours change, inspection hours will change in the same proportion.

In some companies, data are available through history, or through industrial-engineering study, of expected inspection costs. The simplest form is associated with products made in discrete units—so many coils, condensers, tubes. Here the data are in terms of inspection hours per 100 units, or per 100 lb, and future estimates can be based on knowledge of the future production schedule.

Slightly more complicated is the case where there is a line of product sufficiently varied so that the hours per 100 differ somewhat for the different types in the line. Inspection for the 1A gadget may require 13.2 h per 100 as against 14.7 h for the 2A gadget and 16.8 h for the 3A gadget. Here, knowledge of the detailed production schedule or "mix" will permit an estimate. If details are not known, an estimate can still be made if there is no reason to believe that the mix has changed as compared with previous history.

This ratio of hours to hours or to units has the advantage of simplicity and ease of preparation. The main disadvantage is that only labor costs are considered, with the effect of other expenses, facility improvements, and other realities omitted.

A less precise measure is the ratio of inspectors to production workers. Beyond the deficiencies of the hours-to-hours measure, this ratio fails to consider inequalities in hours worked, absenteeism, overtime, etc.

SUMMARY

The foregoing brief look at inspection, test, and measurement systems and technologies makes it clear that revolutionary changes have been extensive. The growth of new technology can properly be called explosive. Technological breakthroughs in semiconductors, microprocessors, and computers are making 100 percent inspection and noncontact (visual) inspection applications practical and cost effective.

The growth in components and systems areas will require a much heavier demand for test and measurement instrumentation at all levels: R & D, production, manufacturing, quality control, calibration, maintenance, and so forth. It is estimated that by the end of this decade the measurement manufacturing industry will serve a market worth almost $5000 million in the United States and about $8400 million in the Free World. Refer to Figure 18.26. (See also "Test and Measurement," 1984.)

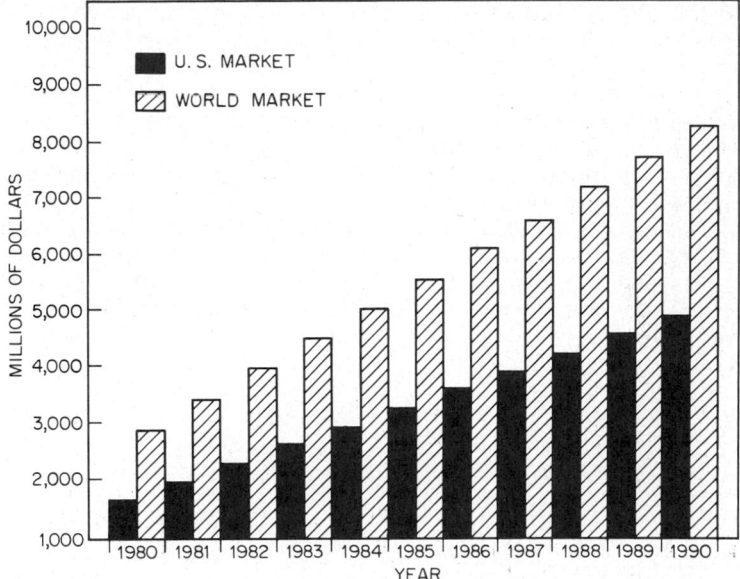

FIG. 18.26 The test and measurement equipment market, current and future estimated.

Developments such as these make clear that much effort is needed, on a continuing basis, to keep inspection and test departments, their laboratories and equipment, and above all, their personnel up to date with current developments and in a state of preparation for future developments.

Acknowledgment. The author gratefully acknowledges the assistance of Lloyd B. Wilson, then Measurement Consultant, Sperry Gyroscope Division, Sperry Rand Corporation, in preparing the material on measurements used in both the Third and current Editions.

REFERENCES

Abbe, R. C. and O'Brian, M. (1972). "A Brief Report on Non-Contact Gaging." *Quality Management and Engineering,* May, pp. 16–19.

Abernethy, R. B. et al. (1979). "Tutorial, Test Measurement Accuracy." *ISA,* ISBN 87664-453-3, pp. 1–11.

Ainsworth, L. (1980). "The Use of Signal-Detection Theory in the Analysis of Industrial Inspection." *Quality Assurance,* vol. 6, no. 3, September, pp. 63–68.

Alaimo, A. P. (1969). "A Total Inspection System." *ASQC Technical Conference Transactions,* Los Angeles, pp. 71–78.

Allen, P. E. (1959). "Evaluating Inspection Costs." *ASQC National Convention Transactions,* pp. 585–596.

"A Management Standard for Economical Inspection" (1976). *Quality,* vol. 15, no. 1, January, pp. 28–30.

American Society for Quality Control (1978). *Chemical Division Technical Supplement, Interlaboratory Testing Techniques,* Milwaukee.

American Society for Quality Control and American National Standards Institute (1984). *Guide to Inspection Planning.* ANSI/ASQC Publication E-2, Milwaukee.

American Society for Testing and Materials (1984). *Standard Guide for Establishing a Quality Assurance Program for Analytical Chemistry Laboratories.* ASTM Publication C1009-83, Annual Book of ASTM Standards, vol. 12.01, Philadelphia.

American Society for Testing and Materials (1963). *Manual for Conducting an Interlaboratory Study of a Test Method.* ASTM Special Technical Publication 335, Philadelphia.

"An Outlook for 3D Vision" (1984). *American Machinist, Quality Assurance,* November, p. 59.

"ASD's Quality Assurance Program Rates in Top 10" (1984). *Assembly Engineering, Newsline,* August, p. 6.

Babcombe, P. (1970). "Quality Control for the Very Small Batch." *Quality Engineer,* vol. 34, no. 1, January-February, pp. 19–22.

Bader, M. E. (1980). "Quality Assurance and Quality Control. Part 1: Specifications." *Chemical Engineering,* vol. 83, no. 3, Feb. 11, pp. 92–96.

Baker, E. M. (1975). "Signal Detection Theory Analysis of Quality Control Inspector Performance." *Journal of Quality Technology,* vol. 7, no. 2, April, pp. 62–71.

Ballou, D. P. and Pazer, H. L. (1982). "The Impact of Inspector Fallibility on the Inspection Policy in Serial Production Systems." *Management Science,* vol. 28, no. 4, April, pp. 387–399.

Barry, E. N. (1959). "Work Simplification Applied to Inspection." *Industrial Quality Control,* May, pp. 56–58; also June, pp. 19–20.

Blaufuss, Jo (1972). "Metric Memo." *Quality Management and Engineering,* June, p. 40.

Bond, T. P. (1983). "Basics of an MRB." *Quality,* November, p. 48.

Brandt, D. A. (1963). "When the Swallows Come Home." *ASQC Transactions of the Fifth Annual All-Day Conference, Akron-Canton Section.*

Buckrop, R. L. (1976). "Nondestructive Testing Overview." *Quality Progress,* June, pp. 26–29.

Burgess, J. A. (1983). "Quality Assurance in Testing." *Quality,* January, pp. 36–37.

Carter, C. L. and Carter, G. M. (1983). "A Motivation Program for Inspectors." *ASQC Quality Congress Transactions,* Boston, pp. 525–528.

Chebookjian, S. L. (1980). "The Inspector Is Human." *ASQC Technical Conference Transactions,* Milwaukee, p. 365.

Churchill, A. V. (1956). "The Effect of Scale Interval Length and Pointer Clearance on Speed and Accuracy of Interpolation." *Journal of Applied Psychology,* vol 40, December, pp. 358–361.

Coleman, L. R. (1982). "Detailed Defect Reporting—A Key to Productivity." *ASQC Quality Congress Transactions,* Detroit, pp. 574–579.

Cooper, J. E. (1977). "Patrol Inspection: Guide to Productivity & Profit." *ASQC Technical Conference Transactions,* Philadelphia, pp. 50–52.

Cooper, J. E. (1980). "The Care and Training of Your Inspectors." *ASQC Technical Conference Transactions,* Milwaukee, pp. 674–676.

Crow, E. L. (1966). "Optimum Allocation of Calibration Errors." *Industrial Quality Control,* November, pp. 215–219.

Czaja, S. J. and Drury, C. G. (1981). "Training Programs for Inspectors." *Human Factors,* vol. 23, no. 4, pp. 473–484.

Darby, G. R. (1970). "The Metric System—Practical Implementation." *Quality Engineer,* vol. 34, no. 4, July–August, pp. 8–10.

Davidson, D. (1982). "The Eye of the Beholder." *Quality,* vol. 21, no. 4, April, pp. 38–39.

De Simone, Daniel V. (1971). *A Metric America: A Decision Whose Time Has Come.* National Bureau of Standards Special Publication 345, July, Washington, DC; SD Catalog No. 13.10:345.

De Simone, Daniel V. (1972). "Moving to Metric Makes Dollars and Sense." *Harvard Business Review,* January–February, pp. 100–111.

Denker, S. P. (1984). "Justifying Your Investment in Automatic Visual PCB Testing." *Circuits Manufacturing,* October, pp. 56, 58, 60, 62.

Dodds, L. B. (1967). "Workmanships." *ASQC Technical Conference Transactions,* Chicago, pp. 249–252.

Dodge, H. F. (1928). *A Method of Rating Manufactured Product.* Reprint B-315, May, Bell Telephone Laboratories.

Dodge, H. F. and Torrey, M. N. (1956). "A Check Inspection and Demerit Rating Plan." *Industrial Quality Control,* vol. 13, no. 1, July, pp. 5–12.

Eagle, A. R. (1954). "A Method for Handling Errors in Testing and Measuring." *Industrial Quality Control,* March, pp. 10–14.

Eisenhart, C. (1968). "Expression of the Uncertainties of Final Results." *Science,* June 14, pp. 1201–1204.

El Gabry, A. A. (1972). "Inter-Relation of Quality Characteristics." *ASQC Technical Conference Transactions,* Chicago, pp. 422–428.

Eppen, G. D. and Hurst, E. G., Jr. (1974). "Optimal Location of Inspection Stations in a Multistage Production Process." *Management Science,* vol. 20, no. 8, April, pp. 1194–1200.

Ezer, S. (1979). "Statistical Models for Proficiency Testing." *ASQC Technical Conference Transactions,* Houston, pp. 448–457.

Fagan, M. E. (1976). "Design and Code Inspections to Reduce Errors in Program Development." *IBM Systems Journal.* Also Chapter 7 in Yourdon, Edward (ed.). *Writings of the Revolution,* pp. 123–148.

Fortuin, G. J. and Van Beek, A. (1960). "A Flavor Trial." *Statistical Nederlandica,* vol. 14, no. 2, pp. 175–185 (in Dutch).

Gantt, J. S. (1959). "Let's Take the Guesswork out of Inspection." *American Machinist,* March 9, 1959, pp. 1–6.

Garfinkel, D. and Clodfelter, S. (1984). "Contract Inspection Comes into Its Own." *American Machinist,* October, pp. 90–92.

Gebhardt, C. (1982). "Color Me Calibrated." *Quality,* March, pp. 62–63.

Geidel, H. (1978). "Statistical Evaluation of Sensory Tests." *Qualitat und Zuverlassigkeit,* vol. 23, no. 7, July, pp. 176–178 (in German).

Gibson, J. D. (1983). "How Do You Recognize a Qualified Inspector?" *Quality Assurance for the Offshore Industry (London),* April, pp. 55–56.

Gilman, J. R. (1963). "Quality Reports to Management." *Industrial Quality Control,* May, pp. 15–17. [In this demerit scheme of check inspecting the work of inspectors (who are paid by piece work), the accuracy is expressed in a form equivalent to the number of demerits found per lot checked.]

Gittler, H. (1973). "Why Not Put Inspectors on Incentive?" *Quality Management and Engineering,* December, pp. 22–24.

Goldbeck, J. M. (1981). "Measuring Inspector's Productivity." *ASQC Quality Congress Transactions,* San Francisco, pp. 343–347.

Greb, D. J. (1976). "Does Bad Test Equipment Accept Bad Product?—A Quantitative Analysis." *ASQC Technical Conference Transactions,* Milwaukee, pp. 389–391.

Griffin, R. J. (1980). "Aerospace and Defense Metric System Impact." *ASQC Technical Conference Transactions,* Atlanta, pp. 606–609.

Guest, R. (1981). "Gauging: The Next Five Years" *Quality Assurance,* vol. 7, no. 4, December, pp. 113–115.

Gunter, B. (1983). "The Fallacy of 100% Inspection." *ASQC Statistical Division Newsletter,* vol. 5, no. 1, September, pp. 1–2.

Hains, R. W. (1978). "Measurement of Subjective Variables." *ASQC Technical Conference Transactions,* Chicago, pp. 237–244.

Harris, D. H. and Chaney, F. B. (1969). *Human Factors in Quality Assurance.* John Wiley & Sons, New York, pp. 107–113.

Helm, E. and Trolle, B. (1946). "Selection of a Test Panel." *Wallerstein Laboratories Communications,* vol. 9, no. 28, pp. 181–194.

Holmes, H. (1974). "Computer Assisted Inspection." *The Quality Engineer,* vol. 38, no. 9, September, pp. 211–213.

Hunter, J. S. (1980). "The National System of Scientific Measurement." *Science,* vol. 210, Nov. 21, pp. 869–874.

Hutter, R. G. (1966). "Inspection Manpower Planning." *Industrial Quality Control,* April, pp. 521–523.

Hyer, C. W. (1979). *Principal Aspects of U.S. Laboratory Accreditation Program.* The Marley Organization, Ridgefield, CT, Jan. 24.

"Inspection Can Make an Impression with a Saving" (1975). *Quality,* vol. 15, no. 9, September, p. 37.

Jaehm, A. H. (1982). "Maintaining the Credibility of Your Quality Control Department." *TAPPI,* vol. 65, no. 5, May, p. 187.

Johnson, S. L. and Funke, D. J. (1980). "An Analysis of Human Reliability Measure in Visual Inspection." *Journal of Quality Technology,* vol. 12, no. 2, April, pp. 71–74.

Juran, J. M. (1935). "Inspector's Errors in Quality Control." *Mechanical Engineering,* vol. 59, no. 10, October, pp. 643–644.

Juran, J. M. (1945). *Management of Inspection and Quality Control.* Harper & Brothers, New York.

Juran, J. M. (1952). "Is Your Product Too Fussy?" *Factory Management and Maintenance,* vol. 110, no. 8, August, pp. 125–128.

Juran, J. M. (1969). "Mobilizing for the 1970s." *Quality Progress,* August.

Juran, J. M. (1970). "Consumerism and Product Quality." *Quality Progress,* July.

Juran, J. M. and Gryna, F. M., Jr. (1980). *Quality Planning and Analysis from Product Development through Use.* McGraw-Hill, New York, pp. 357, 360–361.

Karabatsos, N. (1983a). "Serving Quality." *Quality,* vol. 22, no. 9, September, pp. 65–68.

Karabatsos, N. (1983b). "Update on Coordinate Measuring Machines." *Quality,* vol. 22, no. 12, December, pp. 23–28, 30, 32, 34.

Karasek, F. W. (1975). "Analytical Service Laboratories." *Research/Development,* vol. 26, no. 4, April, pp. 32, 34, 36.

Kay, T. G. (1972). "Timeless Work Sampling." *Journal of Industrial Engineering,* vol. 4, no. 6, June, pp. 30–33.

Keller, T. A. et al. (1975). "Inspection by Exception through Automated Video Techniques." *ASQC Technical Conference Transactions,* San Diego, pp. 1–7.

Ken, J. (1984). "The (Artificial) Eyes Have It." *Electronic Business,* Sept. 1, pp. 154–162.

Kirwan, M. S. (1972). "Guaranteed Accurate Numerical Tapes." *Mechanical Engineering,* August, pp. 13–17.

Konz, S., Peterson, G., and Joshi, A. (1981). "Reducing Inspector Errors." *Quality Progress,* vol. 14, no. 7, July, pp. 24–26.

Kramer, A. (1952). "The Problem of Developing Grades and Standards of Quality." *Food Drug Cosmetic Law Journal*, January, pp. 23–30.

Kusch, J. (1979). "Robots and Their Advantage in Inspection." *Proceedings, Society of Photo-Optical Instrumentation Engineers*, vol. 170, *Optics in Quality Assurance, II*, pp. 40–42.

Leek, J. W. (1975). "See It as It Really Is." *ASQC Technical Conference Transactions*, San Diego, pp. 41–43.

Leek, J. W. (1976). "Benefits from Visual Standards." *Quality Progress*, December, pp. 16–18.

Linn, R. D. (1981). "Computer Aided Inspection—Its Time Has Come." *ASQC Quality Congress Transactions*, San Francisco, pp. 599–602.

Louis, A. M. (1981). "Schlitz's Crafty Taste Test." *Fortune*, Jan. 26, 1981, pp. 32–34.

Loxham, J. (1967). "From Science to Technology." *Quality Engineer*, January–February, pp. 16–26.

Maass, R. A. (1970). "The Independent Test Lab." *Quality Assurance*, Part I: April, pp. 24–29; also Part II: May, pp. 43–46.

Marwell, E. M. (1966). "Calibration by Use." *Instruments and Control Systems*, January.

Mathur, C. P. (1974). "The Influence of Measurement Variation in Mass Production of Precision Parts." *Q.R. Journal*, January, pp. 1–5.

McCaslin, J.. A. and Gruska, G. F. (1976). "Analysis of Attribute Gage Systems." *ASQC Technical Conference Transactions*, Toronto, pp. 392–400.

McMaster, R. C. (1959). *Nondestructive Testing Handbook*. Ronald Press, New York.

Measurements and Calibrations. Technical Note 252, U.S. Government Printing Office, Washington, DC, p. 4.

Meckley, D. G., III (1955). "How to Set Up a Gaging Policy and Procedure. *American Machinist*, vol. 99, no. 6, Mar. 14, p. 133.

Megaw, E. D. (1978). "Eye Movements in Visual Inspection Tasks." *Quality Assurance*, vol. 4, no. 4, December, pp. 121–125.

Miller, E. M. (1975). "Test Methods and Specification Requirements." *ASQC Technical Conference Transactions*, San Diego, pp. 229–230.

Minor, G. W. (1981). "An Approach to Inspector Productivity." *ASQC Quality Congress Transactions*, San Francisco, pp. 975–979.

Moburg, K. W. (1968). "Defect Management by Exception." *ASQC Technical Conference Transactions*, Philadelphia, pp. 685–690.

Montville, V. L. (1983). "Color Control from Start to Finish." *Quality*, March, pp. 36–38.

National Bureau of Standards (1965). *Accuracy in Measurements and Calibrations*. NBS Technical Note 262, U.S. Government Printing Office, Washington, DC, p. 4.

National Bureau of Standards (1966). "Expression of the Uncertainties of Final Results." Chapter 23 in *Experimental Statistics*. NBS Handbook 91, U.S. Government Printing Office, Washington, DC.

Nelson, A. V. (1984). "Machine Vision: Tomorrow's Inspections with Today's Equipment." *Evaluation Engineer*, vol. 23, no. 9, October, pp. 21, 24, 26, 29, 30, 34, 37.

Nygaard, G. M. (1981). "Why 100 Percent Inspection?" *Quality*, October, pp. 38–39.

Ohta, H. and Kase, S. (1980). "Evaluation of Inspectors in Sensory Tests—Qualification by Geometrical Methods and Classification by Bayesian Diagnosis Rule." *Journal of Quality Technology*, vol. 12, no. 1, January, pp. 19–24.

Papadopoulos, N. (1983). "Instrumental Color Control—Where to Start." *Quality*, December, pp. 44–46.

Paul, B. (1982). "Chance of Deadly Bridge Collapse Growing as Quality Deteriorates, Safety Critics Say." *Wall Street Journal*, Dec. 29.

Peacox, E. F. (1970). "Rating Inspectors and Evaluating Inspection." *ASQC Technical Conference Transactions*, Pittsburg, pp. 263–271.

Peryam, D. R. (1950). "Quality Control in the Production of Blended Whesday." *Industrial Quality Control,* vol. 7, no. 3, November, pp. 17–21.

Pipkin, F. M. and Ritter, R. C. (1983). "Precision Measurements and Fundamental Constants." *Science,* vol. 219, Feb. 25, pp. 913–921.

"Portable Gage Lab Provides Flexibility and Minimizes Downtime" (1971). *Quality Management and Engineering,* November, p. 23.

Provost, L. P. and Elder, R. S. (1983). "Cost-Effective Laboratory Quality Control." *ASQC Quality Congress Transactions,* Boston, pp. 496–502.

Ramaswamy, C. V. (1981). "How Good Are You as a Fabrication Inspector?" *BHEL,* January, pp. 8–10.

Riley, F. D. (1979). "Visual Inspection—Time and Distance Method." *ASQC Technical Conference Transactions,* Houston, pp. 483–490.

Robinson, A. L. (1983). "Using Time to Measure Length." *Science,* vol. 220, June 24, p. 1367.

Schaffer, G. (1984). "Machine Vision: A Sense for CIM." *American Machinist,* Special Report 767, June, pp. 101–120.

Scheffe, H. (1952). "An Analysis of Variance for Paired Comparisons." *Journal of the American Statistical Association,* vol. 47, pp. 381–400.

Schumacher, R. B. F. (1976). "Quality Control in a Calibration Laboratory." *Quality Progress,* Part I: vol. 9, no. 1, January, pp. 25–28; Part II; vol. 9, no. 2, February, pp. 16–20.

Schumacher, R. B. F. (1981). "Systematic Measurement Errors." *Journal of Quality Technology,* vol. 13, no. 1, January, pp. 10–24.

Schweber, W. (1982). "Programming for Control—Computerizing Measurement and Control." *Quality,* March, pp. 38–42.

Sears, J. A. (1982). "Changing Role of the Quality Inspection Function." *ASQC Quality Congress Transactions,* Detroit, pp. 506–512.

Shainin, D. (1972). "Unusual Practices for Defect Control." *Quality Management and Engineering,* February, pp. 8, 9, 30.

Sharp, D. B. (1976). "Inching toward the Metric System." *ASQC Technical Conference Transactions,* Toronto, pp. 381–388.

Shimoda, Y. and Miyazaki, H. (1981). "The Selection of Inspectors for Sensory Tests." *ASQC Quality Congress Transactions,* San Francisco, pp. 884–891.

"SI—Systeme International Rationale" (1972). *Quality Progress,* January, pp. 15–18.

Smith, J. R. and Duvier, H., III (1984). "Effect of Inspector Error on Inspection Strategies." *ASQC Quality Congress Transactions,* Chicago, pp. 146–151.

Spow, E. E. (1984). "Automatic Assembly." *Tooling and Production,* October, pp. 46–47.

Stalker, A. H. (1980). "The Inspection Record." *Quality,* vol. 19, no. 8, August, p. 33.

Taguchi, G. (1970). "Quality Assurance and Design of Inspection During Production—2." *Reports of Statistical Applications and Research,* Japanese Union of Scientists and Engineers, vol. 17, no. 1.

"Tape Controlled Machines at Sunstrand Aviation" (1970). *Quality Assurance,* June, pp. 30–34.

Tawara, N. (1980). "A Case Study on Measuring Inspection Performance for Inspection Job Design." *International Journal of Production Research,* vol. 18, no. 3, May–June, pp. 343–353.

Taylor, F. W. (1911). *Principles of Scientific Management.* Harper & Brothers, New York, pp. 80–96 for a discussion on inspection of ball bearings.

"Test and Measurement" (1984). *Microwave System News,* vol. 14, Nov. 12, pp. 108–188.

Thomas, J. H. (1977). "Productivity in the Quality Control Department." *ASQC Inspection Division Newsletter,* vol. 8, no. 3, March, pp. 2–3.

Thomas, L. (1978). "Human Judgement and Perceiving the Complexity of Quality." *Quality Assurance,* vol. 4, no. 4, December, pp. 116–120.

Thompson, H. A. and Reynolds, E. A. (1964). "Inspection and Testing as a Problem in Man–Machine Systems Control Engineering." *Industrial Quality Control,* July, pp. 21–23.

Tobey, D. (1979). "Metrology = Calibration." *ASQC Technical Conference Transactions,* Houston, pp. 513–520.

Trippi, R. R. (1975). "The Warehouse Location Formulation as a Special Type of Inspection Problem." *Management Science,* vol. 21, no. 9, May, pp. 986–988.

Turner, R. E. (1974). "Today and Tomorrow for NDT." *"Quality Management and Engineering,"* December, pp. 36–41.

Tustin, W. (1980). "Selecting a Testing Laboratory." *Quality,* June, pp. 24–26.

Ulla, F. M. (1982). "Productivity Measurements of Inspectors." *ASQC Quality Congress Transactions,* Detroit, pp. 108–117.

"Voice Entry System Gives Quality Inspectors a Hand" (1973). *Quality Progress,* vol. 6, no. 7, July, pp. 12–14.

Walsh, L. (1974). "Back to One Hundred Percent Inspection??" Editorial Comment, *Quality Management and Engineering,* March, p. 9.

Walsh, L. et al. (1976). "100% Inspection at Production Line Rates." *Quality,* November, pp. 30–31.

Walsh, L. et al. (1978). "Steel Wheel Maker Tests Hardness 100%." *Quality,* November, p. 37.

Walsh, L. et al. (1979a). "Can 100% Testing Be Eliminated?" *Quality,* May, pp. 42–43.

Walsh, L. et al. (1979b). "100% Inspection Plus." *Quality,* September, pp. 102, 104.

Walsmann, M. R. (1981). "The Check List—A Powerful Inspection Tool." *ASQC Technical Conference Transactions,* pp. 348–351.

Wambach, G. W. and Raymond, A. S. (1977). "The Optimum Sampling Plan." *ASQC Technical Conference Transactions,* Philadelphia, pp. 574–578.

Wang, S. C. (1975). "Human Reliability in Visual Inspection." *Quality,* September, pp. 24–25.

Wang, S. H. S. et al. (1981). "A System Simulation for Inspection Planning." *ASQC Quality Congress Transactions,* San Francisco, pp. 769–776.

Weaver, L. A. (1975). "Inspection Accuracy Sampling Plans." *ASQC Technical Conference Transactions,* San Diego, pp. 34–39.

"Where Quality Control is a Part Time Job" (1979). *Business Week,* Nov. 26, p. 44F.

Williams, C. D. (1981). "How You Can Optimize the QC Function in Your Firm." *Inspection Engineering,* March, pp. 48, 50–51.

Wood, N. (1979). "Contract Inspection Service." *Quality,* vol. 18, no. 5, May, pp. 13–14.

Woods, K. C. (1978). "Calibration System for Measuring and Testing Equipment." *Quality Progress,* March, pp. 20–21.

Woods, D. G. and Zeiss, C. (1981). "Coordinate Measuring and Finite Metrology." *ASQC Quality Congress Transactions,* San Francisco, pp. 232–237.

Wurster (ed.) (1980). "A Data Acquisition Overview." *Quality,* May, pp. 47–51.

SECTION 19
MARKETING[1]

Frank M. Gryna

INTRODUCTION **19.1**
Advertising of Quality . . . 19.2
Government Regulation of
Advertising 19.4
Assistance to Customers in
Product Selection 19.4
THE SALES CONTRACT **19.6**
Incentive Provisions on
Quality and Reliability . 19.7
ROLE OF THE MARKETING
DEPARTMENT DURING THE
LAUNCHING OF NEW
PRODUCTS **19.7**
WARRANTY OF QUALITY . . . **19.8**
Warranty: Industrial
Products 19.9
Warranty: Consumer
Products 19.9
Consequential Damage . . 19.11

GOVERNMENT REGULATION OF
WARRANTIES **19.12**
BUSINESS OPPORTUNITIES
THROUGH WARRANTIES . . . **19.12**
Product Redesign 19.12
Competition in Warranties 19.12
Extended Warranties . . . 19.13
Reliability Improvement
Warranties 19.13
LABELING **19.14**
Product Labeling 19.14
Product Grading 19.15
Brand Labeling 19.15
Certification Labeling . . . 19.17
THE MERCHANT AND QUALITY **19.18**
Quality Activities 19.18
REFERENCES **19.18**

INTRODUCTION

This step on the Spiral of Progress (see Figure 2.2 in Section 2) concerns the process of persuading customers to buy products for reasons related to product quality. This process is part of a broader marketing activity which impacts all steps on the Spiral. Some of this activity takes place before production of the product. (See Section 3, Quality and Income; also Section 12, Field Intelligence.) Still other

---

[1] In the Third Edition, this section was prepared by J. M. Juran.

marketing activity takes place after sale to customers. (See Section 20, Customer Service.) Some policy matters with respect to marketing are discussed in Section 5, Quality Policies and Objectives.

Advertising of Quality.   The process of disseminating commercial information is called "advertising." The purpose of advertising is to enlarge the sales income of the advertiser, either through (1) product advertising, which aims to induce people to buy the product, or (2) institutional advertising, which aims to create a favorable image of the company. An important adjunct to these purposes is to provide information to the customer to help in making purchasing decisions.

The concept of product advertising is that human beings harbor powerful drives, needs, and wants and that through application of relatively small stimuli, these drives can be converted into decisions to buy. Under this concept, the advertiser is then faced with the dual problems of:

1. Discovering and presenting the stimuli which can best translate these human forces into action to buy. These stimuli are appeals to animal senses and to emotions.
2. Demonstrating that the product is superior to other products for meeting the human wants. This demonstration takes the form of communicating information on quality or fitness for use and is mainly an appeal to logic and reason.

In practice, many advertisements contain appeals to both emotion and reason. However, centuries of advertising have demonstrated that when human beings are buying for their own needs, appeals to emotion generate more action than appeals to reason.

Emotional Stimuli.   These are widely used to advertise consumer products and, to a degree, industrial products as well. As they appeal to emotion, their effects are subjective and not susceptible of objective verification. They take numerous forms:

Attention getters of all sorts—singing, dancing, humor, unorthodox behavior

Product names, package colors, surrounding decor, etc., which are believed to induce a favorable response from potential buyers

A vision of the well-being which, by implication, results from purchase of the product—health, safety, comfort, social success

An aura of company competence: the record of innovation "firsts" of the company; the prizes its products have won in competitions

A display of "seals" from so-called "independent" laboratories

Asserted secret ingredients, or ingredients bearing a fanciful name for which there is no standard definition

Pseudoscientific explanations: cartoons depicting aches, pains, and their implied disappearance; staged laboratories and "scientists"

Challenges to competitors to meet performance or reliability levels

Emphasis on a high price as an indicator of better quality

Such stimuli, however, do not constitute objective evidence of fitness for use. Some of the facts stated (e.g., a list of company innovations in products generally) may warrant broad inferences about the specific product being advertised. But any idea that advertisers should replace emotional stimuli with objective evidence runs into some hard realities as applied to consumers:

1. The great majority of quality characteristics cannot be sensed by the consumer.

2. The great majority of factual explanations of the technological properties of products cannot be understood by the consumer.

The advertising managers have concluded, with much justification, that the emotional stimuli are an essential element of advertising of consumer products and a useful adjunct to the advertising of commercial products.

Objective Evidence. Advertising based on objective product and quality data is widely used for industrial products and, to some degree, for consumer products as well. These objective presentations likewise take numerous forms:

Laboratory and inspection test results: tensile strength, frequency distribution, Weibull plots, safety ratings, tar and nicotine content

Usage data: mean time between failures of 10,000 h; fuel consumption of 35 mi/gal; cost per unit product, e.g., copies from a copier machine; lower frequency of adjustments, replacements, service

Listing of features possessed by the product (often to show that competitors lack these features)

Warranty provided (see below under Warranty of Quality)

Demonstrations of product usage by a series of still pictures or on television

Evidence of user satisfaction: testimonials from named users; data on share of market, e.g., "more than all other makes combined"

Results of tests by independent test laboratories: marks or certifications from such independent laboratories

Advertising which compares product features with those of competitors has a long history. However such advertising has traditionally avoided naming the competitors in question. More recently there has been a dramatic increase in the frequency of naming the competitors. Some of these advertisements have stimulated competitors to complain to government regulators who then demand objective proof of the claims made in the advertisement. Alternatively, the competitors file legal actions to recover damages. In the face of such threats, advertisers are well advised to assure that the claims made in the advertising are based on objective test data. (See "Should an Ad Identify Brand X?" 1979.)

The benefits and problems of comparative advertising are being studied, and advertising specialists are divided on the subject. (See Wilkie and Farris, 1975.)

Despite the excesses and abuses of advertising, the movement has brought extensive benefits to consumers. The urge to develop quality reputations has stimulated manufacturers to develop product quality and quality controls to levels which can back up the advertising.

Use of distinctive packaging has improved packaging generally and has greatly simplified distribution (but at the cost of disposal of the packages). Even the propaganda, being competitive, has contributed materially to the education of consumers.

In many countries the public is skeptical about the truthfulness of advertising. One survey (Schutz and Casey, 1981) revealed that over half of those sampled believed "most" or "all" mail and telephone advertising to be misleading; 38 percent felt the same about television advertising. In another survey ("America's Search for Quality," 1983), only 6 percent of the respondents viewed advertising as the most trustworthy source of consumer information. (For a discussion of quality and the media, see Taylor, 1981.)

Puffing.   The practice of exaggerating the properties of the advertised product is known as "puffing," i.e., a self-serving exaggerated praise. Expressions like "none better," "your best buy," etc., are examples of puffing.

Puffing and caveat emptor (let the buyer beware) are now largely obsolete for industrial products and are becoming obsolete for many consumer products. (See Juran, 1970.)

The increased scrutiny of advertising (by consumer organizations, government regulators, and competitors) has stimulated the growth of internal controls. In many companies the advertising copy is reviewed by cognizant functions (e.g., legal, product development, quality) as a check on the validity of the claims. Of special importance is the potential use of the advertisement in a product liability suit. A pertinent question to raise during a review is, "How would this phrase sound in court?"

Government Regulation of Advertising.

The obsolescence of caveat emptor makes necessary a considerable change in advertising practice. Some manufacturers and merchants have already taken major steps in the direction of strict objectivity. Most of them have not, however, and this has led to demands for increasing government regulation. Examples of claims made in advertisements that have been challenged by government regulators include:

Products are superior to other brands (effectiveness of aspirin, taste of wine, on-time performance of airlines).

Specialists prefer brand X (technicians prefer a certain microwave oven, clerks are unable to assist consumers on loss of certain brands of traveler's checks).

A product contains preferred ingredients ("natural" ingredients of beer, soups with more solid ingredients).

A product promotes health (a remedy prevents colds or sore throats, a bread builds strong bodies).

Faulty performance of a product requires the replacement of a certain component (the failure of a car to start requires the replacement of the spark plugs).

An important byproduct of regulation of advertising is the fact that the government is empowered to act against the offender. In the absence of regulation, the deceived buyer must proceed directly against the advertiser, a costly, time-consuming procedure.

Some proponents of advertising contend that advertised brands tend to be of higher quality. The evidence is not strong. One study (Rotfeld and Rotzoll, 1976) examined 13 categories of consumer products for the relationship between advertising expenditures and product quality. The conclusion: No broad generalizations can be made.

Assistance to Customers in Product Selection.

Sale of manufactured products takes place through a chain of intermediate, independent merchants. (A small minority of manufacturing companies sell directly to the consumer, either through captive retail shops or through door-to-door selling by salespeople who are manufacturing-company employees.) Depending on the nature of the product and the identity of the customer, the merchant's influence on quality varies widely. To sell technological products to industrial companies requires a high level of knowledge of the product, including some capacity to provide technical assistance. At the other extreme is self-service. The selling is done by display of the product plus prior propaganda. Between these extremes are numerous situations in which the tools and the techniques of selling play an important role in the customer's decision of which competing product to buy or whether to buy at all.

Industrial Products.   The concept of technical service involves the use of technically trained intermediaries between the company and its clients. The "applications engineer" is knowledgeable in the performance capabilities of the company's products. By studying the client's needs, the engineer assists the client in choosing that product design which best suits the application. Alternatively the applications engineer proposes design modifications to adapt standard designs to the client's special needs. By having knowledge in both fields (the capabilities of the designs and the needs of the users), the engineer is helpful in bringing the two together.

For some materials and components there are hundreds or thousands of potential applications. It is impractical to establish separate product types or specifications for each application. The applications engineering concept makes it possible to offer a limited number of standard product types and yet serve a wide spectrum of applications.

It is useful for the customer to be aware of alternative products or product models that can satisfy customer needs. Sometimes the customer can become overwhelmed with information on the array of alternatives. A useful technique in these cases is multiattribute rating. (See Section 12 under Competitive Evaluations by Field Studies.) By showing how to identify quality and other important attributes, establish a relative importance rating, and score the alternatives, an applications engineer can help a customer reach a decision.

A different approach applies in situations where the industrial customer modifies the product or combines it with other products before reselling it. Many industrial customers are, in a sense, intermediaries, i.e., distributors and/or processors of the products they buy. In such capacities they may benefit by assistance from the prior manufacturer (or supplier) in making the ultimate user aware of the virtues of both the intermediate and the final product. A cooperative effort is inherent in such cases, and it can lead to increased sales for both. An important element of such arrangements is explanation of the quality features. Such explanation is usually best done by the manufacturer of those features rather than by subsequent processors. (See Fuss, 1973.)

Consumer Products.   Decision making on the selection of consumer products involves many links in the marketing chain, and is often less structured than that for industrial products.

The manufacturer of branded products faces the problem of carrying the influence of the product brand through the entire merchant chain right to the point of sale. A major tool for doing this is a good reputation, derived from prior performance of the products, for providing predictable fitness for use. Additionally, the manufacturer propagandizes the product directly to consumers through advertising and brand labeling (see under Advertising of Quality and under Labeling, respectively, in this section). Tools to aid the merchant and salespeople in selling the product, e.g., product information literature, samples, demonstration kits, prepared sales training aids, etc., can also be provided. Some manufacturers do a superlative job of aiding merchants and customers through such means. Particularly when the product possesses superior fitness for use, the manufacturer finds ways to sensitize the salespeople to this fact so that the prospective customer can, in turn, be sensitized.

In one example (van Leer, 1976), a manufacturer of latex material wished to convince consumers that latex paint outlasted oil-based paint. The latex manufacturer developed a scrubber device to demonstrate the latex property, then provided the device to paint manufacturers (the customers for the latex). The paint manufacturers demonstrated the scrubber to paint store clerks for use with customers.

In many competitive situations, there is no clear superiority in fitness for use. What is decisive in selling products in such cases is the marketing tools: prior reputation, attractive packaging, appealing propaganda, personable salespeople. In such cases, appeals to emotion prevail over appeals to precise reasoning. Since the manufacturer is competing with other manufacturers for the attention and support of the merchant and salespeople, some of the manufacturer's energies must be directed to "selling" these salespeople. In part, the manufacturer does this through favorable contract terms. In part, the manufacturer uses tools similar to those used in selling the product to the customer: prior reputation, attractive packaging, appealing propaganda, personable salespeople.

Consumer information on quality is available to merchants and consumers from several sources—manufacturers, private organizations, and government agencies. (See Section 3 under Degrees of User Knowledge.)

THE SALES CONTRACT

The sales contract often contains provisions on quality. For consumer products, these provisions may simply be a statement of the product warranty. (A discussion of warranties is provided later in this section.)

For industrial products, the sales contract may contain extensive provisions on quality such as:

1. Requirements on the product.
   a. Performance requirements. This may include highly detailed performance specifications on the product.
   b. Specific technical requirements, e.g., composition of raw material.
   c. Requirements on the "level" of quality of delivered product, e.g., number of defects per million, percent defective, mean time between failures.
2. Requirements on execution of the contract. For critical products these requirements may include:
   a. A quality plan prepared by the manufacturer to itemize the specific activities that will be conducted from design through field use.
   b. Reliability analyses (e.g., reliability predictions, failure mode, effect, and criticality analyses) and test data (e.g., inspection results, reliability test data).
   c. Product design and manufacture in accordance with other industry or government specifications; e.g., a product must comply to the specifications of the Occupational Safety and Health Administration (OSHA).
   d. Prior customer notification of changes in material or in the method of manufacture.

e. Purchase from specified suppliers of certain components going into the final product.

f. Formal approval, by the customer, of specified documentation. For example, a customer may reserve final approval of product designs before they are released for manufacturing. In another example, a purchaser of machine tools may require that a demonstration of process capability be made at the supplier's plant before the machine tool can be shipped.

g. Special warranties, such as reliability improvement, may be required along with standard warranty provisions.

Increasingly, contracts are being written on industrial products to permit certain actions by customers if a specified quality level is not met. For example, one purchaser of electronic parts reserves the right to cancel the remaining production under a contract if the quality level does not meet the requirement. Such provisions reflect the desire of industrial purchasers to eliminate incoming inspection, so that the product can be shipped directly to the manufacturing line.

Incentive Provisions on Quality and Reliability.   Manufacturers and customers of military products have experimented with contract provisions to provide monetary incentives and penalties based on product performance. An early application involved the airplane. The Wright brothers made their first sale to the Signal Corps under an incentive penalty contract. The contract called for payment of $25,000 for a "flying machine" that would achieve 40 mi/h, with a payment of $5000 extra if the machine did 2 mi/h more. If it did 2 mi/h less, the payment would be reduced by $5000. The Wrights collected the incentive (*Newsweek,* June 9, 1969).

In a more recent example involving a medium range air-to-air missile (Wood, 1982), four parameters were identified as the ones most essential for mission success. The parameters and the approach to incentives were:

Parameter	*Incentive approach*
Storage reliability	Based on tests conducted; missile has been in storage
Captive carry reliability	Reliability demonstration program
Missile on aircraft test	Award fee panel evaluates progress on mission dependability, costs, and program milestones
Free flight reliability	Award panel evaluates progress on mission dependability, costs, and program milestones

ROLE OF THE MARKETING DEPARTMENT DURING THE LAUNCHING OF NEW PRODUCTS

A key factor in launching new products is the fit of the product with market needs. The importance of field intelligence to identify market needs is discussed in Section 12.

Even with superior field intelligence and product development, the final test of the new product can be made only in the marketplace. Before mass producing and distributing the product on a nationwide basis, many companies use the concept of a "test market." In a test market, the product is sold on a limited basis for the purpose of:

1. Measuring the potential sales performance in order to decide whether or not to go ahead with full-scale marketing
2. Identifying weaknesses in the product
3. Identifying weaknesses in the marketing plan (product name, packaging, advertisements)

Conducting a test market can be expensive, and generally this step is taken only after pretesting has shown that the product will likely be a winner in the marketplace.

As in the collection of field intelligence prior to the start of product development, it is essential that a team of people from marketing, product development, manufacturing, and other departments decide what questions need to be answered by the test market. After such agreement, the marketing department (with the aid of others, if necessary) collects the information in the marketplace. The mechanisms for collecting the information can include questionnaires, phone calls, focus groups, and other marketing research techniques (see Section 12 under Some Simple Tools for Collecting Field Intelligence).

The decision of whether or not to use a test market requires a comparison of the costs and risks. The costs include not only the expenses for data collection but also the income lost by delaying a full-scale market introduction. The key risk is introducing a product that fails. Even though prior marketing research has been conducted, weaknesses in a new product are sometimes not revealed until the product lives in the marketplace environment. Examples of product weaknesses that did not show up until the marketplace are (Klompmaker et al., 1976):

1. Because packages would not stack, the scouring pads fell off the shelf.
2. A dog food discolored on the store shelves.
3. Because of insufficient glue, over half of the packages came apart during transit.

Use of test marketing can help to prevent such disasters.

The process of launching new products is an example of an activity that is worthy of review by upper management (See Section 8 under Quality Audits by Upper Managers).

WARRANTY OF QUALITY

A warranty is a form of assurance that products are fit for use or, if defective, that the customer will receive some extent of compensation. From a legal point of view, there are several types of warranties:

Implied Warranties. Warranties by the seller may be implied from actions, under the provisions of the Uniform Commercial Code (which governs contracts of sale in virtually all states of the United States). Under these provisions, the seller, by the mere act of sale, makes two implied warranties:

1. A general warranty of fitness for use ("merchantability" is the legal term) for the purposes for which such products are customarily used

2. An added special warranty of fitness for the special uses to which the user will put it, provided the seller knows these special conditions

Express Warranties. Here the seller goes beyond the mere act of sale and makes some representations about the product, i.e., properties it possesses (or lacks). The representations may take various forms: oral promises to the buyer; display of a sample of the product; descriptions of the product in specifications, catalogs, and circulars; claims made in advertising; markings on the product itself; or written statements of guarantee.

Written guarantees can be especially helpful to the parties by making clear what otherwise is usually not well understood. When stated clearly, these written guarantees serve two basic, useful purposes:

1. They protect the buyer by spelling out the seller's obligations to the buyer.

2. They protect the seller by spelling out the limit of the seller's obligation.

The discussion which follows under the various "Warranty" headings deals with matters of money but not with human health and safety. For the latter, see Section 34 under Product Liability.

Warranty: Industrial Products. Parties to a sale of industrial products are knowledgeable in contract relations and they tend to draft a purchase contract to embody their known needs and to cover contingencies experienced under previous contract arrangements. The resulting written contracts reflect mutual agreement on various pertinent matters including the warranty.

Warranties on industrial products are created uniquely for each product or type of product. For many commodity items, the warranty calls for compliance to specifications, and the warranty extends to survive "acceptance" of the item by the customer. Usually, no time period is specified. For other industrial products, the warranty often includes a time period and special provisions covering consequential damages. In some cases the warranty concept is extended to place predictable limits on users' costs. For example, a manufacturer of electrical generating equipment warrants to its industrial clients that the cost of power generated will be no higher than the cost of purchased power. If it is higher, the manufacturer agrees to pay the difference.

Warranty: Consumer Products. In contrast to the tailor-made warranties which are written into large industrial contracts, warranties for consumer products are relatively standardized. Usually printed on good quality paper with an artwork border, these warranties look like, and are, legal certificates. A preamble is included stating the good intentions and care supplied by the manufacturer. Specific statements of the manufacturer's written responsibility then follow.

Consumer product warranties are either "full" or "limited." The term "full warranty" refers to the consumer's rights, not to the portion of the physical product that is covered by the warranty; i.e., it does not have to cover the entire product. A full warranty means:

1. The manufacturer will fix or replace any defective product free of charge.

2. The warranty is not limited in time.

3. The warranty does not exclude or limit payment for consequential damages (see below).

4. If the manufacturer has been unable to make an adequate repair, the consumer may choose between a refund and a replacement.

5. The manufacturer cannot impose unreasonable duties on the consumer. For example, the warranty cannot require the consumer to ship a piano to the factory (one manufacturer listed such a condition).

6. The manufacturer is not responsible if the damage to the product was caused by unreasonable use.

The full warranty also provides that not only the original purchaser but any subsequent owners of the product during the warranty period are entitled to make claims.

A limited warranty is a warranty that does not meet the requirements for a full warranty. Typically, the limited warranty may exclude labor costs, may require the purchaser to pay for transportation charges, and may also be limited to the original purchaser of the product. As a practical matter, most warranties on consumer products are limited warranties and must be so labeled.

Duration of Warranty. This is always spelled out and may be nonuniform as to different features of the product. For example, a 1-year warranty on a product may include a 5-year warranty on certain components, while holding the warranty on finish to 30 days. Here is an actual wording:

> *During the first year* after purchase we provide home service (parts and labor) to repair any defect except surface finishes, which are guaranteed for thirty days. *During the second year* we provide replacement parts; labor is extra. *During the third, fourth, and fifth years* we provide replacement parts to repair the washer transmission; labor is extra.

A short warranty period has a subtle disadvantage for the manufacturer. Important field intelligence on the frequency and type of problems after the warranty period is not routinely collected.

Sometimes the manufacturer extends the original warranty. In one example, a heat pump experienced field failures after the warranty period. A government agency concluded that at the time of sale, the pumps had a defect resulting in the field problems. The agency obtained a "restitution for defects" by having the manufacturer agree to extend the warranty period and pay for the repairs. In another example, an automobile manufacturer extended the car warranty to cover rust problems but allegedly provided the coverage only to favored customers. A consumer group then accused the manufacturer of having a "secret" warranty program.

An example of a lengthy warranty is the 10-year warranty on homes. Originally started in Great Britain, the system was set up in the United States by the National Association of Home Builders. It is a voluntary program for builders and provides for the builder to pay for claims during the early portion of the warranty. Claims made during the remainder of the 10-year period are covered by an insurance policy paid for by the builder. The state of New Jersey has a requirement for a 10-year warranty. A few warranties have an unlimited duration. Examples include hand tools, pens, and the stainless steel tub in an automatic washing machine.

Disclaimers. Warranties also list various conditions under which the warranty is *not* to apply, e.g., use of a home laundry machine for commercial duty, or service by unauthorized personnel. There may be specific disclaimers on incidental damage, e.g., food spoiled during nonoperation of a freezer. Some disclaimers are probably of no legal effect; they are usually ruled by the courts to be contrary to public policy. Other disclaimers are probably unnecessary because they only restate the manufacturers' legal rights. However, some manufacturers use these disclaimers to discourage lawsuits or related actions.

Consumer Reactions to Warranty Provisions.   Some consumers are not satisfied with warranties, and the dissatisfaction takes several forms:

1. The warranty provisions are too complicated.
2. The length of the warranty period is too short. A typical warranty on a consumer appliance provides 1 year of free parts and labor although such appliances have an expected life of 10 years or longer. Thus the consumer usually pays more for repairs than does the manufacturer. Some research on washing machines shows that the consumer's cost for repairs is 2 to 7 times greater than that of the manufacturer's (Gryna, 1971).
3. Inadequate repairs are made during the warranty period and later.

Consequential Damage.   Users' costs associated with product failures can go well beyond the cost of parts and service labor. Additional costs can include:

Productivity losses (e.g., idle direct labor)

Extra capacity maintained because of expected failures (e.g., equipment, labor)

Damages caused by a failed item (e.g., injuries to personnel, damage to other items)

Lost income (e.g., profit on lost production, penalties due to missed schedules)

Although they can be quite substantial, consequential damage costs are seldom as well tracked as warranty period costs. (For a discussion and application of these additional costs, see Gryna, 1972 and 1977.)

Consequential, pyramiding costs are normally not implied in the warranties and are borne by the seller only if the contract says so. Some sellers try to protect themselves further by writing a disclaimer into the warranty.

There *are* instances in which contracts will specifically provide payment for consequential damage. For example, if hard castings cause tool breakage and shutdown of an automatic transfer line, the foundry pays for the broken tools and the downtime. If breaks in paper rolls require a new setup on rotary printing presses, the paper company pays for the downtime. If breaks in beams of yarn cause downtime on textile machinery, the yarn maker pays for the downtime.

Generally disclaimers in matters of injury to human beings are held by the courts to be contrary to public policy, and hence are not enforced. However, disclaimers on consequential money damages not involving human safety are generally upheld.

The service industry provides an unusual example of redress given consumers. For long-time customers who are members of a special club, a major hotel chain guarantees reservations made for a room. If the hotel is unable to honor the reservation, the hotel:

1. Finds a nearby hotel room for the guest and pays for the room
2. Gives free additional nights at any one of its hotels in the future
3. Gives the consumer $200 as a form of atonement for the inconvenience caused

GOVERNMENT REGULATION OF WARRANTIES

The Magnuson-Moss Warranty Act of 1974 was created to provide minimum warranty protection for consumer products. As originally written, it applied to consumer products which cost more than $5.00. But in implementing the act, the Federal Trade Commission adopted regulations covering only those products that cost more than $15.00.

Under the act, the warranty must be available to the consumer in written form before the sale and must contain the following information:

1. The persons who are entitled to make use of the warranty. It must be clear whether the warranty applies only to the original customer or to any subsequent owners of the product during the period of the warranty.

2. A description of the products covered by the warranty and of any product excluded from the warranty.

3. A statement detailing the items or services that will be paid for if the product does not meet the warranty.

4. The duration of the warranty and the time that the warranty begins.

5. An explanation of how to obtain warranty service and information about the handling of disputes.

6. Limitations on the duration of the warranties and any exclusions such as consequential damages.

7. A statement that the consumer has rights both under the warranty and additional rights that may vary from state to state.

8. A statement declaring the warranty to be full or limited.

The act provides basic guidelines to be implemented by the Federal Trade Commission. (For futher discussion, see Lusk et al., 1982, pp. 1063–1065.)

BUSINESS OPPORTUNITIES THROUGH WARRANTIES

Because the warranty period covers only a portion of the product life, users must contend with any service needs that arise during the remainder of the item's life. Recognizing this as a business opportunity, manufacturers are responding in several ways:

Product Redesign. If the manufacturer can create a design with few problems for the user throughout the complete product life, a competitive advantage will be gained. Though the product may have a higher initial cost, there are customers who are willing to pay the price to obtain higher reliability. Some manufacturers of both consumer and industrial products have clearly aimed at this market segment and have created a market penetration with a premium-priced product. Ironically, the warranty period maintained is the same as that of competitors with lower-priced products. Some dealers do, however, extend the duration of the warranty because the product is relatively failure-free.

Competition in Warranties. With such products as automobiles and appliances, the warranty can serve as a competitive tool. The competition usually centers around the duration of the warranty period and the extent of coverage (e.g., parts only, or parts and labor).

Extended Warranties.   For some products, the customer is offered, at extra cost, an extended warranty which covers the cost of repairs after the conventional warranty period. This is similar to a service contract. But there is a legal distinction between warranties and service contracts. A warranty is provided by the manufacturer at the time of purchase at no cost beyond the purchase price. A service contract is provided either by the original manufacturer or by some other party, at any time during the life of the product but a fee is charged for this. Extended warranties and service contracts can be a source of income for the organization offering them. The value of these contracts from the viewpoint of the customer varies with the amount and kind of use. For some customers, those who encounter frequent repairs due to heavy use, the agreements are a worthwhile investment. However, studies made on appliances and automobiles have concluded that the cost of the agreement is often larger than the probable cost of repairs. (See "Are Repair Contracts Worth It?" 1981; and "The Trouble with Auto Warranties," 1979.) An extended warranty or service contract is really a form of insurance. For some customers it is worth the cost; for others, it is not.

Reliability Improvement Warranties.   In a reliability improvement warranty, the manufacturer agrees to perform repair services on products at a previously established price for a stated period of time. The objectives are threefold:

1. Minimize the total life cycle cost for the customer.
2. Provide an incentive for the manufacturer to initially build in high reliability and to improve the reliability over time.
3. Encourage cooperation between the manufacturer and the customer to improve reliability.

A summary of some of the benefits and risks is given in Table 19.1.
From the manufacturer's point of view, a reliability improvement warranty

TABLE 19.1   Benefits and Risks of Reliability Improvement Warranties

Benefits	
Manufacturer	Customer
Potential source of profits	Potential source of cost savings
Improve sales of future products	Can foster reliability improvements at no cost to customer
Obtain field reliability data and intelligence on reliability problems and needs	Provides assurance of specified level of reliability in field
Fosters cooperation with customer	Fosters cooperation with manufacturer
Risks	
Difficulties of estimating future repair costs (number of failures, inflation, etc.)	Total cost may be higher than with conventional contracting
Product may encounter unexpected environments, misuse, etc.	Dependence on manufacturer for support of product
May result in reduction in income from spare parts	Seller may optimize design to meet seller's needs

provides an additional opportunity for profit. The manufacturer proposes a fixed price for the repair services based on an estimate of the number of repairs and unit repair costs. The manufacturer agrees to make all repairs for the period of the contract but receives the fixed price regardless of the actual number of repairs. Types of repairs for which the manufacturer is responsible are defined in the contract. Thus, if the actual number of repairs is less than that predicted, the manufacturer makes an additional profit; if the number of repairs is more than that predicted, the manufacturer does not gain the extra profit and may incur a loss. Under the concept, the manufacturer can propose changes to improve product reliability on a "no-cost" basis to the customer. Such changes, if approved and implemented, benefit the customer in terms of higher reliability and benefit the manufacturer in the form of lower repair costs. As the manufacturer performs the repairs, important field intelligence is collected about product failures for use with both the present and future products. All such proposals, of course, must compete against those from other manufacturers.

From the customer's point of view, the incentive given to the manufacturer to improve reliability tends to assure a higher level of reliability. Part of the contract can also contain a requirement on mean time between failures. If the requirement is not met, the manufacturer must provide sufficient spare parts to the customer to meet the mean time between failures. Thus, the customer has assurance that a specified mean time between failures will be met. (For a discussion from the viewpoint of the buyer, see Markowitz, 1975; the seller viewpoints are presented by Rosenthal, 1975.)

Experience with such contracts indicates that they are applicable only in certain situations. Some formal application criteria have been developed (see Balaban, 1978).

The overall results of reliability improvement contracting are encouraging and may provide a means of going further into life cycle costing.

LABELING

The term "labeling" refers to actions taken by manufacturers, or merchants, to provide users with information about the product. An early example goes back to about 1400 B.C. Inscriptions on wine jars included the year of pressing, the geographical area, the owner of the vineyard, and the chief vintner. Of 22 inscribed jars, one included the phrase "wine of good quality" ("The Pharaoh's Wine Cellar," 1978). As labeling has evolved it has taken multiple, overlapping forms.

Product Labeling.   This refers to information about the inherent nature of the product, e.g., the net weight of the package contents, the ingredients used, instructions for operation and maintenance, and warnings of danger. The information is often placed on a small tag or label, hence the term "labeling," However, the information may also be placed directly on the product, the wrapper, the container, an accompanying circular, or a manual, etc.

For most products, the extent of product labeling is determined by the manufacturer. In consequence, the "labels" (meaning any of the means to convey the information) are a mixture of product information and advertising. However, there are statutes on the books requiring that the product actually conform to the label. Generally there is good adherence to these statutes as applied to the intrinsic properties of the product. Proper labeling is essential in connection with minimizing product liability risks. (See "Lucid Labeling Lessens Liability," 1978.)

For some products, certain labeling is required by law. For example, all food packages are required by law to state the net contents and the list of ingredients. All poisonous products are required by law to be so labeled.

The Fair Packaging and Labeling Act (administered by the Federal Trade Commission) includes general provisions as to the identity of the product, identity of manufacturer (or distributor), quantity of the contents, terminology, etc. In addition, there are provisions specific to certain products. Still other provisions relate to pricing practices and promotions (Federal Trade Commission). A recent addition to the labels of many grocery products is the "bar code." Each prepackaged item for sale is coded with a set of vertical lines that represent numbers or letters. When the checkout clerk passes a wand across the code, both the price and quantity of the product are automatically entered into the cash register. This simplifies checkout procedures, reduces pricing errors, and simplifies inventory control. The bar coding concept seems destined to be extended to many kinds of products (see "Bar Codes in Industry," 1983).

On occasion, the material included on labels leads to disputes. For example, a label described a new product as "potato chips." Competing manufacturers objected. They felt that the product did not conform to the dictionary definition of a potato chip, i.e., a thin slice of raw potato, fried crisp and then salted. Instead the new "potato chip" was first dehydrated, then turned into a mush, and finally pressed and fried. A regulatory agency ruled that the manufacturer's new product could be referred to as potato chips. Subsequently, competitors came out with similar products and even packaged them in a look-alike container. ("Pringle's vs. the Real Thing," 1975.)

Product Grading.   A second form of product information is *grade* or quality of design. For manufactured products, the grade designations are based on various contrasting intrinsic qualities, which are usually measurable. When individual units of product involve substantial prices, the grade distinctions are often made in the form of model names or numbers to simplify user recognition. When the units of the product are low in price, the grading may be done in broad classes. For example, one large merchant company uses three grade designations (good, better, best) to designate differences in quality for the same functional use.

Some grade designations have led to controversies. All automobile tires sold in the United States were required, by government regulation, to have grades assigned in three performance areas—traction, heat resistance, and tread life. The grades were intended to help consumers to compare types and brands of tires. Disputes developed about the validity of the three areas as measures of performance, and it was decided to delete the grading on tread life. (For discussion, see "U.S. Punctures Tire Grading," 1983, and Endres, 1979.) The disputes occurred not only between the regulators and manufacturers but among the manufacturers themselves.

Brand Labeling.   Many companies try to build a quality reputation around a distinctive name or brand. Efforts are exerted to assure that products sold under this brand name are of sufficient quality to earn a good reputation. Use of advertising is made to promote both familiarity and confidence in the brand name. The concept dates back to Rōman pottery manufacturers in 35 B.C., and the process, application of a brand name to products, is known as brand labeling. Varied forms of such labeling are in use.

Manufacturer's Brands.   Many manufacturers market their products under their own name, which then also becomes the brand name. Other companies market the products under noncompany names (e.g., Maxwell House Coffee marketed by General Foods Corporation) or under fanciful names chosen to arrest public attention and cling to memory. In any case, the product advertising and promotion is built around the brand name.

Manufacturers protect the integrity of their branded products through conventional systems of quality controls, as described throughout this handbook.

In some cases, use of the manufacturer's brand is complicated because of intermediate manufacturers. For example, the major chemical companies have created certain materials, e.g., synthetic fibers, with special properties useful to consumers. These materials are given brand names, and these brands are propagandized by advertising aimed at consumers, including guarantees which the chemical companies make *direct to these consumers*. However, the chemical companies sell these materials not to consumers, but to the first links in the chain of yarn makers, cloth weavers, fabricators of end products (e.g., garments, blankets, carpets), retailers, and consumers. (The same applies to some industrial products, e.g., polypropylene pipe.) Hence the chemical companies conduct these sales under a license arrangement which requires that the subsequent fabricators adhere to certain essential quality standards. The terms of the license permit the chemical companies to establish controls which will safeguard the brand names.

Brand names may be so valuable that they invite the production of counterfeit merchandise. Here a manufacturer produces an item, illegally attaches a label with a brand name of another manufacturer, then sells the product for the brand-name price. Examples have been reported on consumer goods such as clothing, luggage, and beverages (see "A Crackdown on Fake Brand Name Products," 1978). If a brand name commands great respect in the marketplace, competitors may choose a similar name. Again there are disputes (see "Corporate Shoot-Outs over Brand Names," 1978). For example, a manufacturer of beer created a product that was lower in calories than the standard beer. The brand name chosen was "Lite." Because "Lite" was a success, competitors introduced similar products and included the words "light beer" on the label. A suit against the competitors for use of the term "light" was filed by the manufacturer of "Lite." The courts ruled that the competitors were allowed to describe their beer as "light beer." Even though the word was spelled differently, the manufacturer of "Lite" would not be given a trademark on a commonly used word. Other commonly used words, "aspirin" and "cellophane," for example, were originally regarded as brand names but have become part of the language and can be used by all manufacturers.

A recent development is the concept of "generic" products. Here merchants contract with the manufacturer to produce merchandise without a brand name. It is claimed that these products provide equivalent quality at a lower price than the branded products because the generic products do not incur such costs as product development, advertising, and promotion. The concept has been widely applied to consumer goods such as foods.

Merchants' Brands.   Merchants sell products both under manufacturers' brands and under their own brands. In the latter case, the merchant's source of supply is either a captive (owned) manufacturing source or a product bought from an independent manufacturer, who agrees to apply the merchant's brand to the product. Such products are known as "private label." Often these products are bought under functional specifications, leaving it to the manufacturer to prepare the detailed design.

Large merchants who market extensively under their private label make use of the tools of quality control to protect their label. Qualification testing of new designs is extensively used, as is supplier surveillance. Regular inspection for lot acceptance is highly selective, depending on the nature of the product and the record of the supplier. In addition, effort is exerted to use information on product failures and on user dissatisfaction to take remedial steps, both as to product and supplier.

Franchise and Chain Brands. Some large manufacturing and service organizations operate on a basis of a "chain" of numerous local markets, plants, restaurants, motels, etc. Some of these local units may be owned by the chain; others may be franchised under an agreement which permits them to use the brand name. The use of this brand name greatly aids the marketing efforts of the local unit.

In such chain operations the company regulations or the franchise agreements spell out the criteria under which the brand name may be used. In addition, there is provision for inspection and surveillance by a designated laboratory. This laboratory may be a corporate quality control service or even a subsidiary.

Industry Association Brands. These are the creations of industry associations. Under the concept, a number of manufacturers collectively agree on a brand which includes minimum product quality standards. The brand is then promoted by the association to achieve public knowledge and acceptance. Manufacturers who meet the standards may then use the brand and gain the marketing value it provides.

The product known as Harris Tweed is defined as "made from 100 percent pure virgin wool produced in Scotland, spun, dyed, and finished in the Outer Hebrides, and handwoven by the islanders at their own home" (Thomas, 1966). Inspection is by the Harris Tweed Association, which authorizes use of the brand.

Once more there are cases of disputes. For centuries, natives working in limestone caves in the town of Roquefort, France, have produced a cheese, and the townspeople have formed a trade group called the "Community of Roquefort." A cheese made in Italy and Hungary was marketed as "imported Roquefort cheese" in 1966 in the United States. The people from Roquefort, France, appealed to the American courts, claiming that the use of the term "Roquefort" should be restricted to cheese made in that region. The courts agreed. The judge concluded that the cheese in France was made in accordance with "ingredients, technology, and environment that no region could duplicate. Geography is one of those ingredients" ("Corporate Shoot-Outs over Brand Names," 1978).

Certification Labeling. "Certification" as used here is a form of product assurance centered around a formal document or certificate. The certificate always represents the product as either conforming to specification or as fit for use. It may or may not include test data, and it may be issued either by the manufacturer or by a separate testing service. For a detailed discussion of these differences, see Section 15 under Certification. Certification is not to be confused with conventional testing services by independent laboratories. Such laboratories provide test services to a company under a variety of conditions: The company lacks a certain instrument; the company's laboratory is momentarily overloaded; the company wants to conduct a check on its own accuracy.

In those cases where a manufacturer is "licensed" to apply an independent mark (by a government regulator or by an independent laboratory), the application of the mark is likewise a form of certification, the mark being a shorthand form of certificate; e.g., the "UL" mark for Underwriters' Laboratories, Inc., or the "©" which is the shorthand statement of "copyrighted."

It should be noted than an independent laboratory which certifies products as fit for use (or as conforming to standard) assumes some legal responsibilities. A user who relies on such certification and is damaged has the right to proceed against the independent laboratory as well as against some of the other parties directly involved.

THE MERCHANT AND QUALITY

Quality Activities. The giant merchant companies are extensively involved in all aspects of product quality. They have technical departments to establish specifications and to conduct product qualification tests. Their central purchasing departments carry out supplier selection and qualification. Their quality control departments carry out supplier surveillance and incoming inspection as required by the merchandise managers. (For a discussion of one program, see Koch, 1974.)

The small merchant (retailer) lacks technical or quality control departments. However, he or she carries out some activities which do influence quality: unpacking, handling, display, repacking, transportation. These activities afford some opportunities to find defective product, and, even more, to create new quality problems due to product damage, confusion in identity, and misplacement of components. Storage is a further source of risk, e.g., proper stock rotation (perishable products) or proper environment (temperature of frozen foods).

Much can be done by manufacturers to minimize these risks through product design or systems redesign. As to the residue of risk, the manufacturer can provide clear information on how to care for the product, establish standards to be observed, and offer assistance in training the merchant's personnel.

In addition, manufacturers are well advised to institute audits to determine how well the merchant chain conforms to standards in matters of product quality. These audits can provide a vital input to manufacturers in their efforts to attain fitness for use. At the retail store level, the large merchant also carries out these activities. See also, in this connection, the related discussions in Section 20 on merchant roles in product repairs and the handling of complaints.

REFERENCES

"A Crackdown on Fake Brand Name Products" (1978). *Business Week,* Oct. 23, pp. 53–54.

"America's Search for Quality" (1983). Whirlpool Corporation, Benton Harbor, MI.

"Are Repair Contracts Worth It?" (1981). *New York Times,* Dec. 26, p. 28.

Balaban, Harold S. (1978). "Reliability Improvement by Profit Incentive." *Quality,* November, pp. 22–28.

"Bar Codes in Industry" (1983). *Quality,* October, pp. 14–15.

"Corporate Shoot-Outs over Brand Names" (1978). *New York Times,* Jan. 22, p. 2.

Endres, David A. (1979). "Whatever Became of Performance and Safety Labeling?" *Quality Progress,* November, pp. 34–37.

Fuss, Normam H., Jr. (1973). "Pull through Marketing for Industrial Marketers." *Management Review,* April, pp. 9–18.

Gryna, Frank M. (1971). "Three Creators of Consumer Quality Problems." *ASQC Technical Conference Transactions,* Milwaukee, pp. 303–308.

Gryna, Frank M. (1977). "Quality Costs: User vs Manufacturer." *Quality Progress,* June, pp. 10–13.

Gryna, Frank M. (1972). "User Quality Costs." *Quality Progress,* November, pp. 18–21.

Juran, J. M. (1970). "Consumerism and Product Quality." *Quality Progress,* July, pp. 18–27.

Klompmaker, Jay E., Hughes, G. David, and Haley, Russell I. (1976). "Test Marketing in New Product Development." *Harvard Business Review,* May–June, pp. 128–138.

Koch, Richard A. (1974). "Consumer Product Reliability—The Role of the Retailer." *Proceedings, Annual Reliability and Maintainability Symposium.* IEEE, New York, pp. 27–29.

Lusk, Harold F., Hewitt, Charles M., Donnell, John D., and Barnes, A. James (1982). *Business Law and the Regulatory Environment: Concepts and Cases.* Richard D. Irwin, Homewood, IL.

"Lucid Labeling Lessens Liability" (1978). *Quality,* February, pp. 18–20.

Markowitz, Oscar (1975). "Failure Free Warranty/Reliability Improvement Warranty, Buyer Viewpoints." *ASQC Technical Conference Transactions,* Milwaukee, pp. 18–97.

"Pharaoh's Wine Cellar, The" (1978). *Scientific American,* March, p. 74.

"Pringle's vs the Real Thing" (1975). *New York Times,* November 30, pp. 8, 9.

Rosenthal, Sanford T. (1975). "Failure Free Warranty/Reliability Improvement Warranty—Seller Viewpoints." *ASQC Technical Conference Transactions,* Milwaukee, pp. 80–86.

Rotfeld, Herbert J. and Rotzoll, Kim B. (1976). "Advertising and Product Quality: Are Heavily Advertised Products Better?" *Journal of Consumer Affairs,* Summer, pp. 33–47.

Schutz, Howard G. and Casey, Marianne (1981). "Consumer Perceptions of Advertising as Misleading." *Journal of Consumer Affairs,* Winter, pp. 340–357.

"Should an Ad Identify Brand X?" (1979). *Media and Advertising,* Sept. 24, pp. 156–161.

Taylor, Ervin F. (1981). "Product Quality and the Media," *ASQC Quality Congress Transactions,* Milwaukee, pp. 825–830.

Thomas, Veronica (1966). "The Wizard of Plockropool." *Atlantic Monthly,* July, pp. 124–126.

"Trouble with Auto Warranties, The" (1979). *Consumer Reports,* October, pp. 598–601.

"US Punctures Tire Grading" (1983). *Consumer Reports,* April, p. 166.

van Leer, R. Karl (1976). "Industrial Marketing with a Flair." *Harvard Business Review,* November–December, pp. 117–124.

Wilkie, William L. and Farris, Paul W. (1975). "Comparison Advertising: Problems and Potential." *Journal of Marketing,* vol. 39, October, pp. 7–15.

Wood, Buddy B. (1982). "Development of the Reliability Program for the Advanced Medium Range Air to Air Missile (AMRAAM)." *Proceedings, Annual Reliability and Maintainability Symposium.* IEEE, New York, pp. 510–514.

SECTION 20
CUSTOMER SERVICE[1]

Frank M. Gryna

INTRODUCTION **20.2**

PACKAGING, TRANSPORT, AND
STORAGE **20.2**

    The Sequence of Activities
      for Packaging 20.2

    Transportation 20.3

    Storage 20.4

    Provision for Audit 20.5

INSTALLATION **20.5**

    Processing during
      Distribution 20.5

    On-Site Installation by
      Specialists 20.5

    Installation by User 20.6

USE **20.6**

    Configuration Management 20.8

FIELD SERVICE **20.8**

    Repair Service Centers . . 20.9

    Maintenance 20.10

    Service Improvement . . . 20.13

QUALITY COMPLAINTS:
GENERAL **20.14**

    Underreported Complaints 20.15

    Overreported Complaints . 20.15

SIGNIFICANCE OF FIELD
COMPLAINTS **20.16**

    Effect of Time on the
      Complaint Rate 20.17

    Effect of Word-of-Mouth
      Transmission by
      Consumers 20.18

    Field Failures versus
      Factory Rejects 20.18

PROCESSING OF COMPLAINTS **20.19**

    Sources of Complaints:
      Registration 20.19

    Programs of Action 20.20

    Satisfying the Complainant 20.20

    Identifying the "Vital Few" 20.21

DATA ANALYSIS TECHNIQUES **20.24**

    Basic Time-Related Plotting
      Techniques 20.24

    Use of Probability Paper for
      Predicting Complaint
      Level 20.25

    Effect of Time Lag 20.27

IMPROVING FIELD FEEDBACK . . **20.28**

EXECUTIVE REPORTS ON FIELD
PERFORMANCE **20.30**

    Control Subjects and Units
      of Measure 20.30

    Failures as Seen by the User 20.31

PRODUCT RECALLS **20.32**

REFERENCES **20.34**

---

[1]In the Third Edition, the section on Field Performance was prepared by J. M. Juran and Robert W.
Peach.

INTRODUCTION

This step on the Spiral for attaining quality concerns activities after a sale is made. Discussions in several other sections of this handbook are closely related. Section 3 discusses the broad aspects of quality and sales income; Section 5 discusses some policy issues concerning customer service; Section 9 identifies some areas of audit; Section 12 covers the marketing research needed to gather field intelligence on user needs; Section 19 examines the quality issues in marketing to achieve a sale.

The act of final product acceptance may be regarded as terminating the manufacturing phase. Following this act, and before customer use of the product, a number of preuse phases take place: packing, shipping, receiving, and storage. Finally, there are the use phases: installation, checkout, operation, and maintenance.

As product complexity grows, the extent of field problems increases. Field factors cause 20 to 30 percent of problems concerning fitness for use on long life products of moderate to high complexity.

Those who do quality planning for service activities can learn much from the experience of formalizing quality planning in design and manufacturing. Those who perform service activities that affect quality often believe that their current activities are sufficient to provide a quality service. In cases where service is in fact deficient, there is often need to revise the service plan as it relates to the topics discussed below. Such planning must show, explicitly, what to do differently. Generalities are unacceptable.

The degree of excellence provided in customer service clearly affects the buyer's choice on the next purchasing decision. To maintain satisfied customers, sellers must achieve a constructive relationship with buyers. Levitt (1983) offers suggestions on how sellers can maintain a useful interaction with buyers throughout the service phase of the product life cycle.

PACKAGING, TRANSPORT, AND STORAGE

One major department store found that more customer complaints were caused by store activities in packaging, storage, and delivering the product than were caused by the original manufacturing.

All products are subject to deterioration in quality due to damage during the activities following manufacture, inspection, and test. Some of the deterioration is due to inherent instability, e.g., progressive biological activity, evaporation of solvents, crystallization of metals. Control of the environment can accelerate or retard the effects of such instability. Proper quality planning and control can go far to minimize damage and ensure that the product conforms closely to that which left the factory test station.

The Sequence of Activities for Packaging.   Packaging requires a sequence of activities similar to those used to achieve fitness for use for the product itself. These activities include package design and the purchasing, manufacturing, and testing of packaging materials.

Package Design.   Designing the package and the product simultaneously is the ideal approach. Sometimes a minor alteration in product design can strengthen the product and thereby eliminate the need for extensive packaging materials.

This simultaneous approach requires that packaging design start during the product design stage rather than after manufacture begins. If little or no product information is available to the packaging engineer, the result may be a package that either underprotects or overprotects the product. Design of packaging calls for laboratory testing (e.g., impact, vibration, compression, and drop tests) and field testing of materials.

Especially for products that undergo numerous or critical handlings, it becomes important to look at handling and packaging from a systems viewpoint as opposed to numerous department viewpoints. The extent of handling during production, packaging, and transportation can be surprising. In one survey reported by Amrine (1975) handling costs were 22 percent of manufacturing costs. Some estimates run as high as 60 to 80 percent. A system review can identify opportunities to improve the overall handling by methods such as:

1. Modifying supplier packaging. Some electronic components are blister-packaged in a way that allows testing without unpacking.

2. Starting unitized and other containerization at early operations or even at the supplier's location. For example, the drug industry has evolved unitized packaging of dosages in which the identity of the dose (and even its own environment) are designed into the unit package and carry through to the patient.

3. Designing racks, trays, bins, tote boxes, etc., to provide optimal service to all companies and departments involved rather than to require added handling and repacking for some.

The systems concept includes the adaptation of the product and the package to each other. Fiedler (1978) described how a company that analyzed the interaction of their cartons (products) and cases (packages) determined the combined maximum compression resistance. The analysis led to a design that saved $50,000 annually in materials while increasing the compression resistance of the product/package system.

Purchasing, Manufacturing, and Testing of Packaging Materials. The techniques described in other sections of this handbook for manufacturing and test of the product apply equally to the packaging material. In many cases, the packaging material is obtained for a supplier, and thus the elements of a supplier quality program are applicable.

1. Suppliers are asked to submit samples of product which is intended to meet the design requirements.

2. The samples are tested and evaluated against requirements. If necessary, the production capabilities of the supplier are evaluated through the use of supplier surveys.

3. Contracts are awarded to suppliers. (Sometimes packaging costs more than the product itself.)

4. Initial production samples are obtained from the suppliers and evaluated.

5. Means are set up for periodically monitoring the quality of product received from suppliers.

The variety of packaging has grown to such an extent as to stimulate attempts at standardization (see Canut, 1975).

Transportation. Handling and transport introduce many perils to the product. Some are fully predictable: climatic temperature, humidity, vibration, and shock. Others are the result of ignorance, carelessness, blunder, and even sabotage. For some of these perils the product is in greater danger from handling and transport than from use. Fiedler (1978) recommends a seven-step program for protecting a product during transportation:

1. Define the packaging objectives.
2. Determine the method of shipment. Most manufacturers' products are handled by just a few modes of shipment. The packaging engineer can examine the vital few modes and determine the typical environmental hazards. For example, in truck shipment the hazards include loading, moving, and storing pallets, movement of the truck, and mechanical or manual handling when the load is broken into smaller quantities.
3. Conduct tests to learn how the product will react to the transportation hazards. Tests can be run to simulate shock, vibration, and other transport damage. (The stresses are measured in terms of cycles per second, "g levels" of deceleration, pulse shapes, and still other quantified measures.) The experience gained finds its way into specifications for packaging and vehicle loading.
4. Analyze the test data to decide if the product can withstand the predicted environmental hazards.
5. Decide on a course of action. Choose a packaging material or some other course of action (e.g., modify the product or change the distribution methods).
6. Select a packaging material.
7. Combine the package with the product, and together subject them to final testing. This can be done by trial shipment or simulated laboratory testing.

Damage claims on products amount to about $4 billion per year (Fiedler, 1978). Methods of prevention are clearly justified.

Storage.   Immense quantities of raw materials, components, and finished products are constantly in storage, awaiting further processing, sale, or use. To minimize deterioration and degradation, actions can be taken beyond those discussed above.

1. Establish the "shelf life" of the product based on laboratory and field data.
2. Establish standards to place limits on time in storage.
3. Date the product conspicuously to make it easy to identify the age of the product in stock.
4. Design the package and control the environment to minimize expected and unexpected degradation.

A common weakness in these programs is the failure to "date" the product conspicuously. Sometimes this failure is due to technical reasons or marketing decisions. These reasons are obsolete. Conspicuous dating on outer cartons as well as on unit packages aid in traceability as well as in stock rotation and in establishing the ages of inventories.

Where product is deliberately stockpiled for use at some unknown time, special controls are needed, notably periodic reevaluations of actual quality of the stored products. The effects of long-term storage on system reliability can become a serious matter. In one study (based on over one million hours of storage data), the expected failure rates of four classes of complex systems were determined for a 5-year period. In two of the four systems, less than 20 percent of the product was expected to be available for operation after 5 years of storage (see Cherkasky,

1970). The major factors that affected the nonoperating failure rate were the parts count, parts class, parts screening, temperature stress, parts application, mechanical stress during fabrication, humidity effects, electrical stress, variation of operating environment, check-out capability, nature of duty cycle, time between check-outs, built-in test equipment, reliability scoring, and radiation effects.

Provision for Audit. The manufacturer whose brand name is identified with the product is inevitably regarded by the user as responsible for any failures, no matter how caused. Consequently, such manufacturers are faced with the need for auditing specification conformance in packaging, transport, and storage.

The general approach to auditing is set out in Section 9 under Planning and Performing Audits. Application of this general approach to the operations of packaging, transport, and storage runs into some special problems, especially with the activities conducted by independent carriers and merchants. Common interest in reducing claims and improving customer relations is usually adequate to assure good collaboration.

INSTALLATION

Before the packaged product is put into use, it undergoes additional processing during distribution, assembly, installation and checkout, etc. These operations are as much a part of the product's progression as are design or manufacture. Thus, they demand corresponding controls.

Processing during Distribution. The distribution process carries out operations such as breaking bulk, readjusting, adding reagents, touching up finishes, repackaging, etc. Errors can be made in any of these activities, and thus planning should be embodied in specifications with provisions for an independent audit. Some of the causes of errors are "unusual," e.g., international problems of language or culture; small retailers lacking in technological skills. For such cases the need is for a systems redesign which eliminates the necessity for technological skills or even for the operations. These problems can be at their worst when the operations are to be performed by the ultimate user. (See below, under Installation by User.) Serious errors can also occur in the filling of orders.

On-Site Installation by Specialists. This is the assembly setup which is conducted at the user's premises to put the product in a state of readiness to operate plus installation "in place" at the site. Some products such as an elevator involve a complex erection; products such as a word processor may require special hookups with utilities; a simple consumer product may only need plugging in to an outlet.

On-site installation may require:

1. Special facilities to house the product (plus its auxiliary equipment), including means for controlling the environment.
2. Special tools and instruments. All too often these are not as completely engineered as are the corresponding facilities in the factory.
3. Special instructions. These are increasingly needed for complex products. The opportunities for errors and omissions are now so numerous that the instructions are needed for errorproofing as well as for information. There is still need

for reliance on skilled installers to carry out these instructions and to meet those job problems which differ from one user location to another.

Installation by User. Often products are installed by users—either a consumer or an employee of the client. Even with clear, well-illustrated instructions, there remain a distressing number of users who are seemingly unable to follow them. (A manufacturer of kitchen faucets provides an audio recording describing how the installation should be made.)

Richardson (1981) discusses some of the issues involved in designing for customer setup on computers and terminals:

1. The setup must be simple enough to be accomplished by inexperienced people without using *any* tools.

2. The instructions must be errorproof. Photographs and exploded drawings are superior to wordy descriptions.

3. The design and manufacturing of the product should be such to prevent connections from becoming loose during shipment.

4. Customer education and telephone hotlines should be provided.

5. Translation of written instructions into foreign languages must be verified to assure that the translation is clear.

6. Each step of the instructions should contain only one task and if possible provide positive feedback (e.g., an indicator light) upon successful completion of the task.

7. When the product is available with options, instructions become more complicated to write because they must address the different combinations of features possible. One approach may be to modularize the instructions.

8. Additional testing is needed to reduce susceptibility to shipping damage on customer setup products.

USE

Some field problems can be traced to improper operation of the product. LaSala and Siegel (1983) describe several studies made to quantify the extent and effect of human error on product reliability and maintainability. In one study, about 50 percent of the failures in major systems were due to human errors. The errors were sorted into five types: procedural, incorrect diagnosis, misinterpretation of communications, inadequate support of environment, and insufficient attention or caution.

As products become increasingly complex, the problem of human error during operation of the equipment becomes more critical to address.

Manufacturers have done much to prepare an operating manual or other instructions for proper use and maintenance. These manuals are rudimentary for simple products and grow to elaborate handbooks for complex products. An intermediate example is the "owners' manual" for owners of automobiles.

Of special importance are the safety warnings that must be included with many products. It is not sufficient to include these warnings in the operating instructions. They must be placed in a prominent location to assure that the user will see them. The warnings must take into account the problems of multiple languages including braille, and the messages on these notices should be user tested for complete understanding. Sometimes, changes in a product design can elimi-nate the safety hazard altogether. If this is not possible, the publication of the warning becomes critical.

While installation and use by specialists tends to become rather professional, use by consumers is characterized by much ignorance in several ways:

1. *Failure to allow sufficient time for training and learning the operation of new complex products:* The recent advances in word-processing equipment pro-vide an example. The amazing capabilities of such equipment can only be real-ized when the personnel are thoroughly trained and given sufficient time to practice. The capabilities of the equipment have tended to overshadow the importance of learning time and practice.

2. *Failure to use available information:* For example, a vacuum cleaner rotary brush encounters an obstruction and stops rotating. The owner's manual states clearly what to do: remove the obstruction and reset the little red button. The user does not know this, because the owner's manual is lost, or it is simpler to have the unit serviced.

3. *Use under environments never contemplated:* For example, a householder finds an automobile door locked frozen on a subzero day. A portable hair drier is used to thaw out the lock. The drier fails because it was not designed to operate in subzero temperatures.

4. *Application of stresses never contemplated:* For example, a householder stands on a washing machine to paint the overhead ceiling.

5. *Failure to maintain:* Consumers are notoriously lax in following prescribed schedules for lubrication, cleaning, replacement of expendables, etc.

Of paramount importance is the need for the manufacturer to find out the actual use which takes place. As this knowledge becomes available—through field observation, complaint analysis, etc.—the manufacturer has a wide variety of options for improving use: consumer education, product redesign, systems rede-sign, etc.

In many cases, the prevention of human errors during use requires changes in the product design. In one study of a printing press (LaSala and Siegel, 1983), the distribution of operating problems was as follows:

Difficulty in extracting a component	71 percent
Difficulty in positioning a component	14 percent
Extended inspection	6 percent
Difficulty in grasping a component	5 percent
Adjusting/greasing	4 percent

An analysis concluded that most of the problems could have been anticipated and prevented during product design.

Interaction of the worker and the product is important. Factors involved can be the anatomical dimensions of the worker; placement on products of push but-tons and switches; physical loads imposed on the worker by the product; monot-ony or other psychological effects of the product operation; environmental effects produced by the product, such as noise and vibration; and workplace design, such as lighting and space.

Collectively, such matters are called "ergonomics" and need to be considered during the product design (see Section 13 under Planning for Human Factors: Ergonomics).

As human performance always will be less than perfect, methodology has been developed to quantify it. Meister (1978) discusses various methods.

Configuration Management. Configuration refers to the physical and functional characteristics of a product, including both hardware and software. Ideally, a complex product is thoroughly evaluated and changes are made during design and development so that the design (configuration) released to production is "frozen." In practice, additional changes are made after production has started. If there are many changes, and if most of them are to be made to units already in the field, the customer is confronted with a maze of questions:

1. Can or should all units in the field receive the change from an engineering point of view?
2. What are the maintenance problems involved in making the change in the field (personnel, facilities, time, etc.)?
3. How should changes in operating and maintenance instructions be made?
4. What should be done with spare parts that become obsolete by the change?
5. Will the change require any retraining of workers or other personnel?

The collection of activities needed to accomplish these changes is called configuration management. A program usually has three elements:

1. *Configuration identification:* This is the process of defining and identifying every element of the product, and is discussed in Section 13 under Configuration Identification.
2. *Configuration control:* This series of actions manages the design change from the time of the original proposal for change through the implementation of approved changes. This is also discussed in Section 13 under Configuration Control.
3. *Configuration accounting:* This is the process of recording the status of proposed changes and the implementation status of approved changes. From an engineering point of view, every change must be compatible with existing hardware. In deciding which units will receive the change, the "configuration" of each unit of hardware must be recorded and reviewed. As changes may continually be made, a large but necessary, formal accounting-type system is required. The major role of verifying that the changes have been made and documentation completed is usually performed by the Quality Department.

One important adjunct to configuration management is "product traceability." This is discussed later in this section under Product Recall.

FIELD SERVICE

Many field service activities are bound up with field quality performance. The activities include:

1. Operation of owned repair service centers and franchising of independent repair shops.
2. Administration of service contracts with users. (These contracts are discussed in Section 19 under Business Opportunities through Warranties.)

3. Training of merchants, maintenance and repair personnel, users, and others with respect to quality.

4. Technical assistance throughout all phases of customer relations.

The scorecard on adequacy of services for consumer products is not strong. In a survey sponsored by the Whirlpool Corporation (1983), 998 consumers were asked how satisfied they were with customer service in general. (The survey did not address itself to Whirlpool's service.) The responses showed that 18 percent reported being "just barely satisfied" or worse; 17 percent believed that service had deteriorated in recent years.

It is valuable to analyze the factors that influence customer perception of quality after the purchase of the product. Takeuchi and Quelch (1983) show these factors for three points in time: before the purchase, at the point of purchase, and after the purchase (see Table 20.1). Note that some of the service factors that are important after the purchase are dependent on the design of the product.

Repair Service Centers. Service shop performance in the United States has been severely criticized for several reasons: incompetent mechanics, lack of prompt response, high prices, and dishonesty. Manufacturers and merchants have, to a degree, responded to these criticisms by:

1. Increasing the use of owned repair shops versus independents.

2. Reducing the list of independent shops to whom they referred user complaints.

3. Extending the use of franchise agreements and imposing standards for adequacy of repair work.

4. Extending the use of audit, in franchised shops as well as in owned shops.

5. Improving the inherent effectiveness of the service shop through improved engineering and management: design of superior facilities, diagnostic instruments, and repair tools; establishment of good systems for maintaining inventories of spare parts; training of mechanics and other personnel, etc.

6. Providing guarantees on service work. For example, a major automobile manufacturer has advertised a lifetime guarantee on the repair service provided.

It is difficult to provide up-to-date, technically superior service and high productivity in the form of small, independent shops. A revolution may be required

TABLE 20.1   Factors Influencing Customer Perception of Quality*

Before purchase	At point of purchase	After purchase
Company's brand name and image	Performance specifications	Ease of installation and use
Previous experience	Comments of salespeople	Handling of repairs, claims, warranty
Opinions of friends	Warranty provisions	Spare parts availability
Store reputation	Service and repair policies	Service effectiveness
Published test results	Support programs	Reliability
Advertised price for performance	Quoted price for performance	Comparative performance

*Not necessarily in order of importance.
Source: Takeuchi and Quelch, 1983, p. 142.

to create chains of service shops. This would enable the local manager to do a superlative job by having the resources of the chain providing basic support. The situation resembles the progressive replacement of the corner grocery store with chain food stores. The Center for Policy Alternatives (1974) has conducted research on the productivity of providing service on consumer durable products such as television sets and refrigerators. Of the service agencies, 76 percent were one-person operations. One of the conclusions from the research was that it would be difficult to obtain a substantial improvement in productivity in these operations.

Maintenance.   Maintenance includes:

Scheduled inspections, tests, and overhauls

Scheduled servicing, e.g., cleaning, lubrication, replacement of consumables

Unscheduled servicing, i.e., diagnosis of failures, and repairs to remedy the failures.

Scheduled Inspection and Test.   These scheduled activities are planned by service and quality control specialists. The planned approach is similar to that discussed in Section 18, under Inspection Planning.

Scheduled Servicing.   This is also planned by specialists as to timetables and work to be performed. It includes replacement of components either on a planned basis or as dictated by the findings of the scheduled inspections. In addition, it includes cleaning, adjustment, lubrication, replacement of filters, etc. It may include a check-out of operation following the servicing.

An important development is the concept of "reliability centered maintenance," also called "on condition maintenance." This concept grew out of an analysis of engine maintenance made by commercial airlines and is described by Nowlan and Heap (1978). Four types of preventive maintenance tasks are identified:

On condition tasks: Inspect an item at specified intervals to find and correct potential failures.

Scheduled rework tasks: Rework an item before a specified age to reduce the likelihood of failure.

Scheduled discard tasks: Discard an item before a specified age to reduce the likelihood of failure.

Scheduled failure-finding tasks: Inspect a hidden function item at specified intervals to find an actual failure that was not evident to the operating crew.

Research was conducted on previous maintenance practices to establish patterns of operating age and reliability. Surprisingly, for 89 percent of the items there was no decrease in reliability with age and therefore reliability could not be improved by imposing an age limitation on the items. Such a finding was significant because traditional maintenance concepts required that an item be replaced after it had accumulated x hours of operation.

This led to a new approach:

1. Identify those items whose failure is significant at the airplane level.
2. For each significant item, evaluate the consequences of a failure. Four types of consequences are identified: safety, economic (operational and nonoperational) and hidden failure. For each of these consequences, the appropriateness

of an on condition, rework, or discard maintenance task is considered. If none of these three tasks meets defined criteria for applicability and effectiveness and if a failed item would be evident, then the conclusion is that the item would not benefit from scheduled maintenance. If the item has a hidden function, and a failure would not be evident, then a scheduled failure-finding maintenance task must be performed.

3. When appropriate information or experience is not available, then a "default strategy" is employed. This strategy gives a conservative initial decision on maintenance that is revised as additional information becomes available.

The concept of "reliability centered maintenance" can result in significantly lower maintenance costs. One airline reported 66,000 maintenance hours on major structural inspections on a plane before establishing an initial inspection interval of 20,000 h. Traditional maintenance policies on a smaller and less complex plane required 54 million maintenance hours before the same interval (Nowlan, 1980).

An extensive form of scheduled servicing is the "overhaul," which requires removing the unit from service while major scheduled servicing is performed (or scheduling the overhaul during some shutdown). As products have become more complex, the overhaul of a product comes closer to requiring the same kinds of manufacturing skills and controls as were present in the original manufacture of the product. Some manufacturers provide technical assistance to dealers to develop quality programs for repairs and overhaul services. One such program (Caterpillar Tractor Factory, 1978) identifies the following areas that must be explicitly planned for by the dealer:

1. Identification of critical rebuild operations
2. Inspection and approval of these operations
3. Formal specifications for critical rebuild operations
4. Tools and gauges for accurate measurement
5. Systems for identifying the responsibility of service persons and recording their performance during critical repair procedures
6. Calibration schedules to ensure the accuracy of tools and gauges
7. Reporting systems to provide dealer management with progress reports on service quality levels

One agency that was responsible for reconditioning electronic gear encountered a basic issue: Should the reconditioning be done to the original product specifications? For many applications, the original specifications were unnecessarily strict. Making judgments in matters like this requires knowledge of the costs involved and the fitness-for-use needs.

Unscheduled Servicing. This category includes diagnosis and repair of the numerous failures which put users out of service and for which they demand prompt restoration.

For simple products, a product malfunction can often be corrected by replacing the defective unit. As products become more complex, the process of finding and correcting becomes more difficult. The usual steps are shown in Figure 20.1 (Juran and Gryna, 1980).

Training. The principles of training discussed in Section 11 are fully applicable to the training of maintenance personnel and are in fact applied in large manufacturing companies.

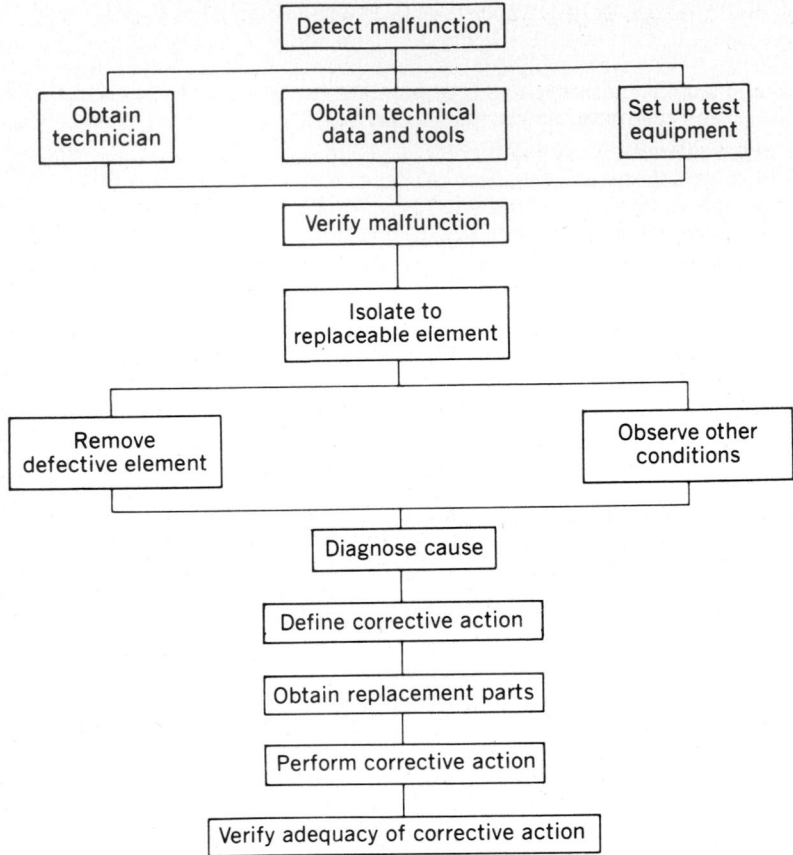

FIG. 20.1   Steps in correcting a malfunction.

Manufacturers have gone far to help small service centers by establishing training courses which the technicians may attend. Even more widespread is the preparation of special service manuals for use by service centers. These manuals provide well-designed aids for diagnosis and repair, including:

Exploded views and diagrams to show the structure of the product

Lists of parts used for various products

Color codes for wiring, and components to simplify diagnosis and repair

Detailed instruction for repair, i.e., sequence of operations, tools to be used, etc.

Multinational companies prepare these manuals in various languages. Some industries (e.g., automobile repairs) now use the concept of formal certification of technicians.

Spare Parts.   Spare parts provisioning has two major aspects: providing adequate quantities, and assuring the quality of the spare parts. Rosenthal (1983)

describes a program for provision of spare parts for a family of personal computers:

1. A maintenance strategy was based on the assumption that customers would install and maintain the computers themselves.
2. Design engineers were given specific requirements. For example, the system had to be able to self-diagnose faults down to the spare parts level. The user then had to be able to remove the part and install the replacement without being concerned about compatibility or the need for adjustments.
3. Manufacturing had to be able to produce the spare parts at high-quality levels.
4. The packaging, stocking, and distribution of the spare parts had to be properly executed, because customers were performing more of the maintenance themselves. This meant that spares had to be available to customers at many locations. That in turn increased the transportation and handling by individuals unfamiliar with electronic components and thereby increased the risks of damage.

A further problem that arises with spare parts concerns the completeness of testing. For some electronic products, the system does not provide for full interchangeability or compatibility of the subsystems. Hence the practice is to assemble the system and test it as a system before shipment, even if this means reassembly and retesting in the field. For such products, when subsystems are shipped out as spares, those subsystems have not undergone a system assembly and system test. There is no easy solution. Of course the fundamental solution is a system design which does provide full interchangeability.

Assuring the Adequacy of Maintenance Services. Maintenance itself can be a cause of failures in the field. Horn and Hall (1983) discuss techniques for estimating the extent of the maintenance contribution to field failures and also techniques for identifying maintenance-induced failures and their causes. On some Air Force activities, maintenance-induced failures varied from 2 to 48 percent of the total failures, depending on the type of equipment. Das, Hendry, and Hong (1980) have developed quantitative relationships for estimating the effect of imperfect repair on reliability.

Quality control of repair work is a troublesome problem for the service center. The great majority of shops are small, and the tradition has been self-inspection by the mechanic, with only sporadic review by the service manager. Some organizations establish standards of performance for service centers and provide audit and certification to assure that these standards are met. The Chevrolet Division of General Motors identifies 22 areas that are essential to total service satisfaction (e.g., quality, facilities, personnel, etc.). For each of these 22 areas, specific "evaluators" help to determine if the dealer conforms to the standards. The quality parameter has 15 evaluators, e.g., "inspection procedures are available." Technical assistance is provided by Chevrolet to enable the dealers to achieve certification. Certification involves both a review of the dealer's procedures and facilities and formal feedback from customers on the performance of the dealer. The program also provides for periodic recertification of the dealers.

Service Improvement. Good service is a moving target due to continuing changes in the marketplace. To keep up with competition requires continuing improvement of service. Because improvement takes place project by project, it is necessary to agree on specific needed improvements and then to organize to carry out the resulting improvement projects.

TABLE 20.2   Alternative Strategies for a Tractor

Key	Strategy
A	Improve fill rate for parts from 91% to 95%
B	Improve mean time between failures from 350 to 450 h
C	Develop and install microprocessor-based diagnostic capability in each tractor
D	Provide faster parts service using parts vans
E	Redesign tractor to permit faster modular exchange of electrical and hydraulic components
F	Provide users with tractors on loan during serious failures
G	Redesign tractor for modular exchange of electrical, hydraulic, and engine-driven train components
H	Redesign tractor as in strategy E and provide loaners
I	Redesign tractor as in strategy G and provide loaners
J	Redesign tractor as in strategy C; provide loaners and built-in diagnostics

Source: Lele and Karmarkar, 1983, p. 130.

An example of an approach to such improvement is seen in Lele and Karmarkar (1983). They use the term "support strategies"in the sense of nominations for service improvement projects. In their definition, the term "strategy" means a collection of activities used to satisfy customer service needs. A strategy can vary from one market segment to another and can change with conditions in the marketplace. A company must choose a strategy, evaluate their own and competitors' relative positions and determine when customer needs or competitive pressures require that the strategy be changed. For example, Table 20.2 shows 10 alternative strategies for an industrial tractor.

These alternative strategies were identified after investigations revealed that customers were concerned about the downtime per product failure and the total downtime. A computer simulation was run to duplicate the effect of using a strategy (or combination of strategies) in terms of downtime and operational availability. The life cycle cost of each alternative was also calculated. Additional information resulting from the simulation included the effects of improving part availability, built-in diagnostics, making loans of equipment and modular exchange. The simulation showed that there were three stages, each requiring different strategies: from 50 to 30 h of downtime, from 30 to 20 h, and 20 to 10 h. Management decided to:

1. Improve the reliability of the existing design
2. Introduce equipment on loan (strategy F) in the mid-1980s, or earlier if competitive pressures demanded it
3. Change the design to allow progressive modularization of key components
4. Switch to a combination of modular exchange and loans (strategies H and I) in the late 1980s

The simulation provided conclusions that ordinarily would not be available until many months of experience had been accumulated.

QUALITY COMPLAINTS: GENERAL

As used in this handbook, the term "complaint" is an assertion of the quality deficiency. The complaint may concern the product or it may concern other activities such as incorrect invoicing or shipment of incorrect goods. In the discussion which follows, the term "complaint" refers to the product.

Underreported Complaints.   For the most part, complaints are underreported. This is particularly true for products of low unit price, where the time and effort required to complain are large in relation to the amount at stake. Underreporting also happens for other reasons:

Shortages of Goods.   During times of shortage, merchants and users take what they can get.

Contract Limitations.   Goods sold under a limited time warranty will generate no complaints at all during the great majority of their service life.

Futility.   Users who are unable to get redress finally stop complaining to the manufacturer. Instead, they complain to their friends and become sales advocates for competitor's products.

Research performed by Andreasen and Best (1977) revealed that consumers complained about only 42.3 percent of nonprice problems. During the research, consumers were also asked questions going beyond their voiced complaints. One of the conclusions from this "probe" was that consumers do not complain about the design of products or the design of a service. The consumer tends to complain about product breakage or failure, but apparently thinks that nothing can be done about the design of the product.

Overreported Complaints

User Mistake.   Perhaps a third of the service calls made during the warranty period find nothing wrong with the product; the consumer misused the product, misread the instructions, or mislaid the instructions. In an unusual case involving a "walkie-talkie" communication set, a large number of sets that were returned as "inoperative" were found to operate perfectly. Investigation revealed that most users expected certain sounds to be audible when the set was turned on. However, the set had been designed to be free of such sounds. The quietness was interpreted by users as a defect.

Returned Spare Parts.   Sometimes a maintenance technician who is diagnosing a product failure misjudges the cause. A suspect component is replaced but the failure remains in evidence. Now the technician has a surplus component, and returns it as "defective." In some cases, from 35 to 85 percent of the components returned as defective are in fact good product.

Some servicing policies resulted in a bias of data. Under a new policy, a manufacturer refused to pay charges for a component replaced during the warranty period unless the failure was verified by the manufacturer. Suddenly, the manufacturer received a large proportion of failed components that were destroyed. This made it impossible to perform a failed parts analysis to determine the cause. An investigation revealed that dealers applied a voltage across the electronic components to destroy the component and thereby assure payment of the claim.

Subterfuge.   Some sales organizations follow a practice of leaving muiltiple models with prospective buyers who can not make up their minds. Those models which are not purchased are then returned for credit as defective. A similar situation exists when a buyer receives a product in perfect operating condition, then decides that the product is undesirable for other reasons. The sales force accepts the returned product and may classify it as defective in order to expedite acceptance of the return by the company. Companies who encourage this practice as a sales device are well aware that the complaint rate is inflated. In companies where such practices are sanctioned, it is easy for managers to be misled by the reports.

SIGNIFICANCE OF FIELD COMPLAINTS

In many product lines the levels of warranty charges, complaints, and returns are low, e.g., under 1 percent of sales. Some managers of such product lines conclude that their product has a high quality reputation in the marketplace. They reason that if no one is dissatisfied, then everyone must be satisfied. The fallacy is a subtle one: product dissatisfaction and product satisfaction are not opposites. Product satisfaction is why clients buy the product. Product dissatisfaction has its origin in product failures. Customers buy products because of a positive attitude that they have toward the product. Complaints and other measures of dissatisfaction do shed some useful light on field performance but such data must be supplemented by marketing research to draw conclusions about customer satisfaction. (See Section 12, Field Intelligence.)

Field complaints are a poor measure of product performance. Some users complain despite the fact that the product is fit for use. Other users do not complain, despite the fact that the product is not fit for use. In addition, there are some broad influences which affect entire classes of products and users:

1. *The economic climate:* Complaints fall in a seller's market and rise in a buyer's market, even for the same product. A manufacturer of photographic film noticed that when silver prices rose complaints also rose. A manufacturer of pet food learned that when postal rates increase, there is a temporary drop in complaints on small unit price packages. Also, the degree of competition appears to influence complaints. A company having an essential monopoly tends to hear fewer complaints, apparently because people view the complaint process as futile.

2. *The age, affluence, technological skills, etc., of users:* For example, complaints on breakfast foods usually involve more complaints on the toys that are included with the package than on the food itself. To the child, the toy is a high priority. There seems to be conflicting research on the influence of economic status on complaints. Some studies have found that persons of an affluent background tend to be the most active complainers. Other studies have found that this is not as important as the product involved or the nature of the problem. (See Andreasen and Best, 1977).

TARP (1976) conducted research on complaint-handling procedures used by consumers. The results included:

32 percent of the households questioned were able to recall consumer problems in the past year.

As household income increases, the propensity to have a consumer problem increases significantly.

Over age 25, as age increases, the propensity to have a consumer problem also increases.

Race, region of the country, and urban versus rural status were not associated with significant differences in the proportion of households with problems.

3. *The unit price of the product:*   Complaint rates are strongly influenced by the unit price of the product. Figure 20.2 shows graphically that the complaint rate can understate by several orders of magnitude the extent of product inadequacy.

Numerous approaches are effective for determining the ratio of complaints to defects:

1. Company employees are given the product and asked to keep detailed records of performance. The employee data is then compared to complaints received from regular customers.

2. Create an arrangement with one or several large users of the product to buy their data. This requires an agreed-upon plan of data recording.

3. Use results from product audit. (See Section 9 under Product Audit.) Product audits can be made internally before the product is shipped, or externally through a sampling of dealers paid for conducting the audit. To establish a complaint ratio, the audit results can be compared to the regular complaints received from customers. One example involves some glassware selling at a unit price of $2.00. The results of a product audit in the warehouse on breakage was 7 percent defective. This compared to a regular customer complaint rate on breakage of 1.5 percent. The ratio of complaints to actual failures then was 0.2 (1.5 percent divided by 7.0 percent).

Effect of Time on the Complaint Rate.   For long-life products, time to first failure is a major variable determining the complaint rate. Products which "wear out," i.e., fail in "old age" after giving an acceptable service life, do not generate complaints. In contrast, "infant mortality" failures are highly complaint-prone. Intermediate random failures decrease in complaint rate as the extent of failure-free operation increases. (For an elaboration of the concept of infant mortality,

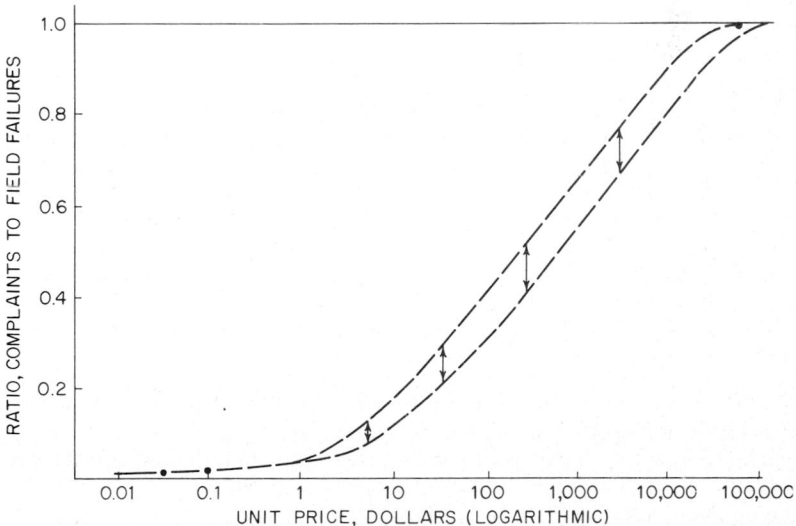

FIG. 20.2   Effect of unit price on complaint rate.

random failures, and wear-out, see Section 23 under Failure Patterns for Complex Products.)

The great importance of time to first failure requires that the product be "dated." The most useful date is that of the product's start into active service. If it cannot be secured conveniently, it can be approximated from the date of manufacture or from the date of sale. With ingenuity, it is possible to secure one of these dates at nominal cost.

Date of manufacture is marked on the product through a coded serial number or other means.

As the date of sale is difficult to record for 100 percent of the product, sampling techniques are generally used. For example, if the product is serially numbered, arrangements can be worked out with selected dealers to record the date of sale on enough product to establish the interval between date of manufacture and date of sale.

Date of actually going into service is normally available only for large units of product, in which case the date is secured from the attending service person or from the guarantee contract. For smaller units of product, resort must be had to sampling methods.

The analysis of field data from product which is dated is discussed below under Data Analysis Techniques.

Collectively, the above influences make the complaint rate a poor index of product quality especially for low-price products. However, the complaint rate is an index of user dissatisfaction, and this alone is enough to require that the complaint rate be measured and watched closely.

Effect of Word-of-Mouth Transmission by Consumers. In addition to recorded complaints received by companies, there is transmission of information by consumers through conversations with friends. Research by the Coca-Cola Company (1981) included the following findings:

> Consumers who felt their complaint had not been satisfactorily resolved told a median of 9 to 10 people about their negative experience.

> Consumers who were completely satisfied with the response from the Company told a median of 4 to 5 people about their positive experience.

> More than 12 percent of the complainants told more than 20 people about the response they received from the Company.

The research further established the effect of the process on the purchase of future products:

> Nearly 10 percent of those consumers who were completely satisfied with the response from the Company now buy more products of the Company.

> More than 30 percent of the consumers who felt their complaints had not been satisfactorily resolved said they no longer buy the products of the Company; nearly 45 percent of these dissatisfied complainants claim they now buy products of the Company less often.

Research reported by Goodman and Yates (1982) discusses the relationship between complaining and making a decision to repurchase the offending product or service. As might be expected, a decision to repurchase depends on the financial loss and the resolution of the complaint (see Table 20.3).

Field Failures versus Factory Rejects. It is illuminating to compare the list of principal field failures with the list of principal factory rejects. For example, in

TABLE 20.3   Percent Repurchase Based on Handling of Complaints

	Potential financial loss	
	$1 to $5	More than $100
Complaint satisfactorily resolved	70.0%	54.3%
Complaint unsatisfactorily resolved	46.2	19.0
Did not complain	36.8	9.5

a company making rubber products, there was a drop in the sales of a major product type. The sales force blamed the drop on poor quality, whereupon the president ordered an improvement in quality. The factory complied by tightening up on quality standards, resulting in higher shop rejections (and higher costs) for dirt, discoloration, and other factory defects. Actually, the field problems were different, as listed in Table 20.4. The factory "improvement" had no significant effect on the real quality problems of the user.

TABLE 20.4   Field Returns and Factory Rejections

Principal reasons for field returns	Percent of all field returns	Principal factory defects	Percent of all factory rejections
Product has odor	78	Dirt	46
Product crumbles	15	Discoloration	22
Product tears in use	6	Nicked	12
All other	1	All other	20

In another example, in a line of ophthalmic products, a continuing product audit regularly disclosed 65 percent of outgoing product to have minor appearance faults. But there had never been a field return for these faults. Instead, 81 percent of the field returns were for breakage, for which the product audit had no systematic test.

Comparison of the two lists can help to identify:

1. Lack of audit tests for potential field failures
2. Unjustified perfectionism in audit standards

PROCESSING OF COMPLAINTS

In small companies involved in few field complaints, there is little need for a systematic approach to complaint analysis. As the number of complaints increases, the need for a systematic approach increases. In some large companies, lack of an organized approach has been a serious obstacle to sound customer relations.

Sources of Complaints: Registration.   Complaints flow in to the manufacturer from a wide variety of sources: consumers, merchants, service shops, industrial users, regulators, consumer advocates, stockholders, etc. The channels of communication are also diverse: letters, telephone calls, personal visits, newspapers accounts. The complaints may also be addressed to various departments in the company: Sales, Service, Quality, any manager (especially the president), etc. Some companies have established a 24-h "hotline" telephone service to answer inquiries from customers.

To avoid confusion it is useful to set up a "registration desk" and to instruct all concerned to send a copy of the complaint to the desk, which will:

Register all complaints, no matter by whom received.

Assign a serial number to permit tracing progress.

Route the complaint to that department best qualified to conduct the analysis.

Assist in identifying complaint cases requiring fundamental study.

Follow up to assure that adequate analyses and dispositions are made.

Assist in summarized reporting.

The registration desk may be located in any of several departments—Complaint Bureau, Quality, Sales, or Service—depending on the organizational structure of the company.

All complaints require an immediate acknowledgment, whether or not a full response can be given at that time. The form of acknowledging a complaint and preparing further written follow-up with the customer is also important. One insurance company conducted an image study of its operations and learned that many customers felt that written communications from the company were stilted, legalistic, and difficult to understand. The company then established a unit with the responsibility for putting all correspondence into simple language.

Programs of Action.   Complaints require several different programs of action:

1. *Satisfying the complainant:*   As this program is oriented to the complainant, it is needed in virtually every case of complaint.

2. *Identifying those "vital few" serious complaints:*   Studies must be made in depth to discover the basic causes.

3. *Analysis in depth to discover the basic causes of the complaint:*   This action is oriented to the product and is especially needed in those vital few cases which are responsible for the bulk of the failures.

4. *Further analysis:*   To discover and apply remedies for the basic causes.

5. *Preventing a recurrence of isolated complaints:*   Isolated complaints are brought to the attention of those who are suspected of having caused them. It becomes their responsibility to take action to prevent a recurrence.

Satisfying the Complainant.   Typically, the manufacturer must meet three needs of the complainant:

1. *Restoration of service:*   The complainant is lacking service and needs a repair or replacement. Action must be prompt, and often the need is acute.

2. *Claim adjustment:*   Often the complainant is out of pocket because of the failure, and wants compensation.

3. *Restoration of goodwill:*   Even after service is restored and the claim is paid, there remains a residue of irritation due to annoyance and frustration. A proper complaint adjustment includes added effort to calm the ruffled feelings of the complainant. Some automobile dealers have a program of periodically calling a sample of customers to verify that a repair has been satisfactory.

Even with procedures set up to handle complaints, the response record is far from perfect. In a national survey of consumers, TARP (1976) found the following:

30 percent of the households who contacted a first source felt that the second source had to be contacted in order to resolve their problem.

27 percent of those who contacted a second source found it necessary to contact a third source.

Some organizations have set up a consumer affairs office as part of the corporate organization to assure adequate resolution of complaints. One automobile company has experimented with an approach that involves third-party arbitration. The consumer first contacts the local dealer to register the complaint. If the response is not satisfactory, the consumer then contacts the zone office of the manufacturer. If the consumer is still dissatisfied, then an arbitrator from the Better Business Bureau can be requested, with the understanding that the findings of the arbitrator are binding on both the manufacturer and the consumer. In the appliance industry the Major Appliance Consumer Action Panel (MACAP) is a recourse available to consumers who feel that a complaint has not been answered adequately. The panel consists of a group of people from the areas of law, economics, engineering, minority representation, education, and communications. Although the recommendations of the panel are not binding on the manufacturer they are regarded with great credibility.

Identifying the "Vital Few." Figure 20.3 is a flow diagram showing how one large company selects problems for resolution and then solves the selected problems. As the causes and remedies may involve many departments, a "corrective action group" is often formed with representatives from Design, Manufacturing, Purchasing, Quality, and Field Service. The group jointly analyzes the data to select the vital few problems, conducts an initial investigation to prepare a thorough problem statement, and assigns responsibility for determining a remedy.

The group meets regularly to review all new complaints and to review progress on current problems. A problem agenda is sent out by the chairperson several days ahead of the meeting date. Minutes of the meetings, including a problem-status log, are formally recorded, and actions to be taken are documented and distributed to all concerned. This log summarizes each problem before the committee. It also shows the scheduled start and completion of activity, assigns responsibility, and lists action taken. It gives Project Management an indication of major problems and the status of corrective efforts. Additional effort may then be placed on troublesome areas as deemed necessary.

Discovery of Causes. The process starts with a review of the individual and summarized field data in order to select potential problems. Techniques such as defect matrices and Pareto analyses (see Section 22 under Diagnosis) are directly applicable to field data.

Some organizations have created extensive data collection and summarization systems for repairs made in the field. A manufacturer of heavy equipment has a computer terminal system that transmits details on every repair made at dealerships throughout the country to the manufacturer. The data are continuously updated and eight different summaries provided using a Pareto ranking of defect types by serial number, model, component, part, and dealer.

This system has reduced the data collection time, because the old manual system required complex warranty forms which not only took a long time to complete but required additional time for transmission and recording into the system.

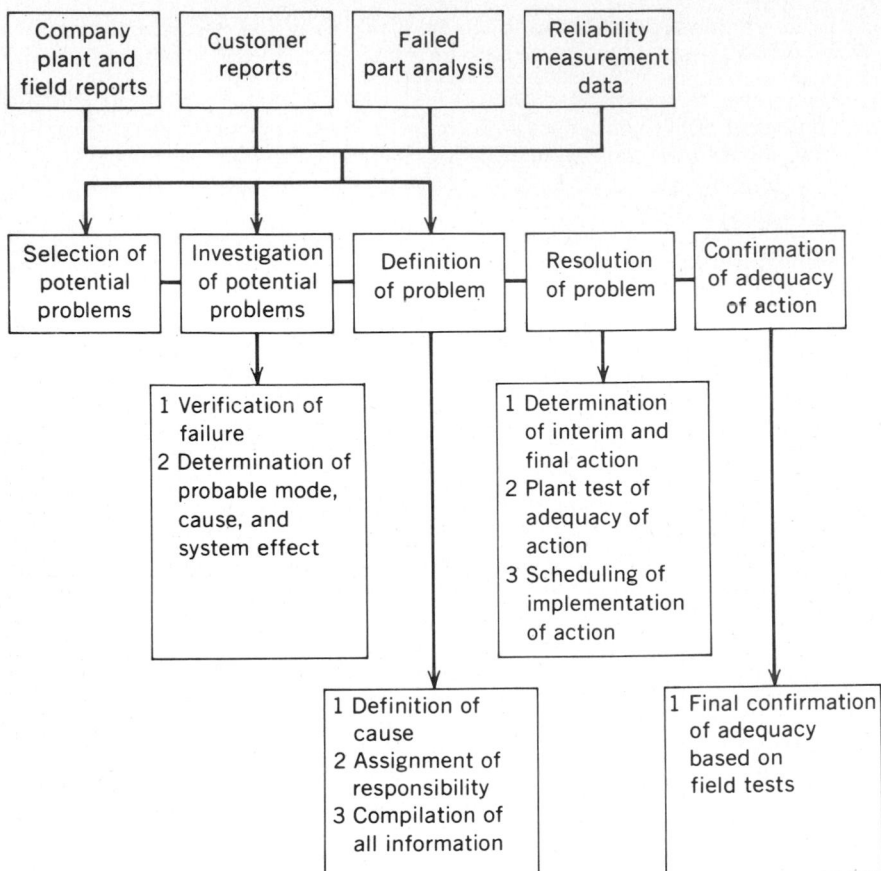

FIG. 20.3 Corrective action system.

Problem identification occurs much faster because of the Pareto analyses that are available and continually updated. Under this system, the manufacturer knows what some of the major problems are before they are apparent to all of the dealers. In many cases, the corrective action can be developed before a problem becomes widespread. The system also makes it easier to identify problems by generic part type even though individual part numbers may not have a high frequency of occurrence.

The investigation of problems often involves obtaining the physical part that failed and conducting a failed parts analysis by disassembly and/or additional laboratory tests. (One of the confusing aspects of failure analysis is that often the "failed" part works perfectly.) When a problem is determined to be real and of significant enough consequence to require follow-up, then a detailed failure analysis may be needed. Dobbins (1977) provides an excellent checklist for a failure analysis program.

Some industries have taken the progressive step of establishing special instrumentation and data systems needed to correlate product and operating variables with field failures and even incipient field failures. A large manufacturer of synthetic fibers collaborated with a textile mill to evolve a correlation of yarn breaks with causes. This was done through:

1. Equipping the process with scanners and working up a process history of each package of yarn (about 1000 lb)
2. Securing the history of the field performance of these packages, including capture of the broken yarns, through the field service personnel
3. Correlating textile mill results with chemical process variables

The resulting correlations permitted remedial steps to be taken much earlier than they could have been by accumulating failure data in the absence of planned causation data.

Instrumentation for field failure analysis is increasingly specially designed. For example, the application of computerized diagnostic tools has been applied in a wide variety of products ranging from aircraft engines and automobiles to telephone subscriber lines. Also, the application of fiber optic concepts has been applied to analysis of bearing failures (Philips and Hirschfeld, 1980).

In some cases it is necessary to study the mechanism of failure under field conditions. In one example, a bus company spent 6 months on laboratory analyses to learn the causes of failure of alternators, with no conclusions. Then an engineer noticed that the alternators were located in an area of the bus that was prone to corrosion due to the environment. It had been assumed that the alternators were in an engine compartment where the effect of corrosion would be minimal. The study concluded that the alternators were failing due to corrosion that came from the salt spray on the roads. This had not been clear from the laboratory analysis.

In some industries the problems of failure analysis are so demanding that special failure analysis laboratories and organizations are created to do the job. Such laboratories must sometimes be equipped with special facilities and a variety of technical skills. The equipment, skills, and time for failure analysis are often underestimated.

Discovery of Remedies. The complaint bureau or other investigative body can establish the cause of the product deficiency, but it cannot provide a remedy. Instead, based on the analysis for cause, the matter is referred to that department which can remedy the known cause, e.g., Design or Manufacture.

However, the investigative bureau should be a party to the tryout of the remedy to verify that the design change (or whatever) provides a "fix" which is effective under operating conditions. In addition, provisions must be made for proper disposition of shop and field inventories which have been under "hold" pending the discovery of a remedy.

Preventing Recurrence of Isolated Complaints. Under the Pareto principle, a few types of failures account for the bulk of the field performance problems. It is these "vital few" which deserve and usually receive the bulk of the investigative effort. On purely economic grounds, this discrimination against the remaining defects is fully warranted. For many of them the cure may cost more than the disease. However, for some products and applications, infrequent defects cannot be ignored merely because they are infrequent. The most obvious examples are defects which are critical to the safety of human beings. A single instance of such a defect dictates that it becomes part of the "vital few" for investigation.

In some situations, the collective volume of symptoms occurring at a low frequency overwhelms those occurring at a higher frequency. For example, on one product about 75 percent of all warranty claims involved defects occurring at a low frequency. This 75 percent overshadowed the amount of defect reduction achieved by identifying and correcting the high-frequency defects.

Isolated complaints are usually the result of inadvertent mistakes, carelessness, errors in judgment, unusual environmental conditions, etc. The error has usually taken place weeks or even months before the failure takes place, so that the fundamental cause is difficult to establish, whether by a trained investigator from a central bureau or by a departmental supervisor. A useful approach to diagnosis of isolated complaints is discussed in Section 22 under Troubleshooting.

DATA ANALYSIS TECHNIQUES

Quality-related data on field performance includes not only complaints but also basic performance data on the pattern of failures over time, data on repair frequency and repair time, data on repair costs, and still other useful field data. The analyses of such data range from simple summaries to complex statistical analyses. These analyses are used to provide measures of field performance, to help determine causes of problems, and to predict the rate at which future problems will occur. The following paragraphs describe some analytical and graphical approaches, starting with the simple and proceeding to the complex.

Basic Time-Related Plotting Techniques.   A simple plot of data over time (e.g., number of premature removals of an aircraft engine) is a useful way to start. The data for individual months are plotted, and then a moving average of the data is updated each month to indicate an underlying trend.

Another useful technique is cumulative complaint analysis. This requires that the product be "dated" to show when it was made, sold, or installed. The various dates are useful in disposing of complaints and claims for product of a slowly perishable character (candy, photographic film, etc.). They also can help in predicting the failure rate of various product designs.

An example of the cumulative data analysis technique involves women's clothing. Certain articles were tearing in service, and some were being returned. When the products made during one specific month were code dated, the cumulative returns reached 2 percent within 2 years after the date of manufacture. The resulting cumulative curve is shown on Figure 20.4. This 2 percent was regarded as tolerable. (At the unit price level of the product, it was likely that about 20 percent of the product was actually tearing in service.)

Meanwhile, the research department evolved a new product which possessed new, useful sales features that were unrelated to the problem of tearing. This new product then went into full-scale production 14 months after the "specific month" noted above. The cumulative returns for the new product are also charted on Figure 20.4. Note that by use of a horizontal time scale based on "months following manufacture," the two curves both start at the origin and hence can readily be compared with each other. By such analysis the company could be informed within the first few months of the life of the new design that the new design had, as to the problem of tearing, made the situation much worse.

Johnson (1975) describes the cumulative analysis approach as applied to data on tractors.

A technique for predicting future performance is the concept of growth curves. The concept assumes that the product involved is one that is undergoing continuous improvements in design and manufacturing, and refinements in field pro-

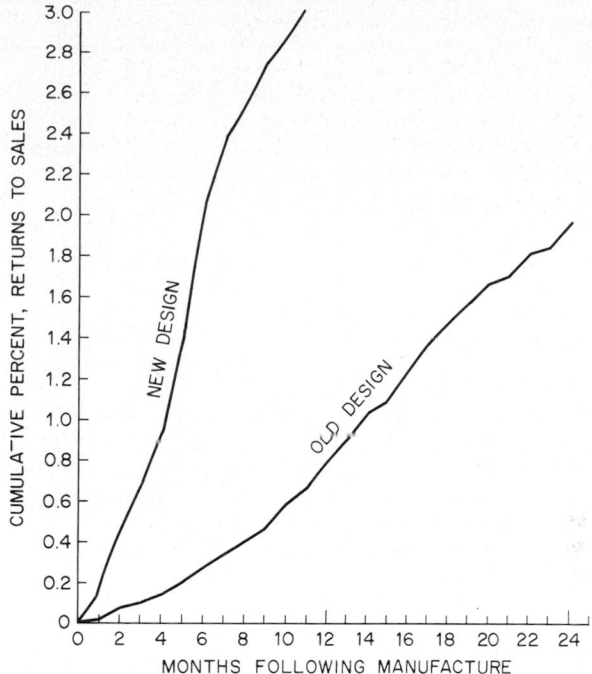

FIG. 20.4 Comparison of cumulative returns for two designs, by month, following month of manufacture.

cedures. Thus the product performance will improve ("grow") with time. The concept is discussed in Section 13 under Reliability Growth.

Use of Probability Paper for Predicting Complaint Level. Weibull probability paper (see Section 23) can be used to analyze early field data on warranty claims. Through such analysis it is possible to predict what will be the cumulative claims at the end of the warranty period.

Repair information on an electrical subassembly is collected (Ford, 1972). The cumulative repairs per 100 units is interpreted as a cumulative failure rate in percent. These data are summarized from a large number of warranty reports.

The Weibull plot is shown in Figure 20.5. The 8 months of data have been plotted and a line drawn through the points. This line has been extended, and it predicts the repair rate at the end of the 12-month warranty period to be 2.6 repairs per 100 units.

Note that this Weibull paper includes a scale for estimating the Weibull slope or shape parameter (see Section 23). The slope can be found by drawing a line parallel to the line of best fit and through the point circled on the vertical scale. Here, the slope is read as 0.7. This defines the shape of the failure distribution and can aid in problem definition.

For slopes < 1, the distribution is exponential and generally means that the failures are early failures due to manufacturing or assembly deficiencies.

For slopes > 1, the distribution is skewed or approximately normal and generally means that the failures are due to wear-out or fatigue, especially for higher slopes.

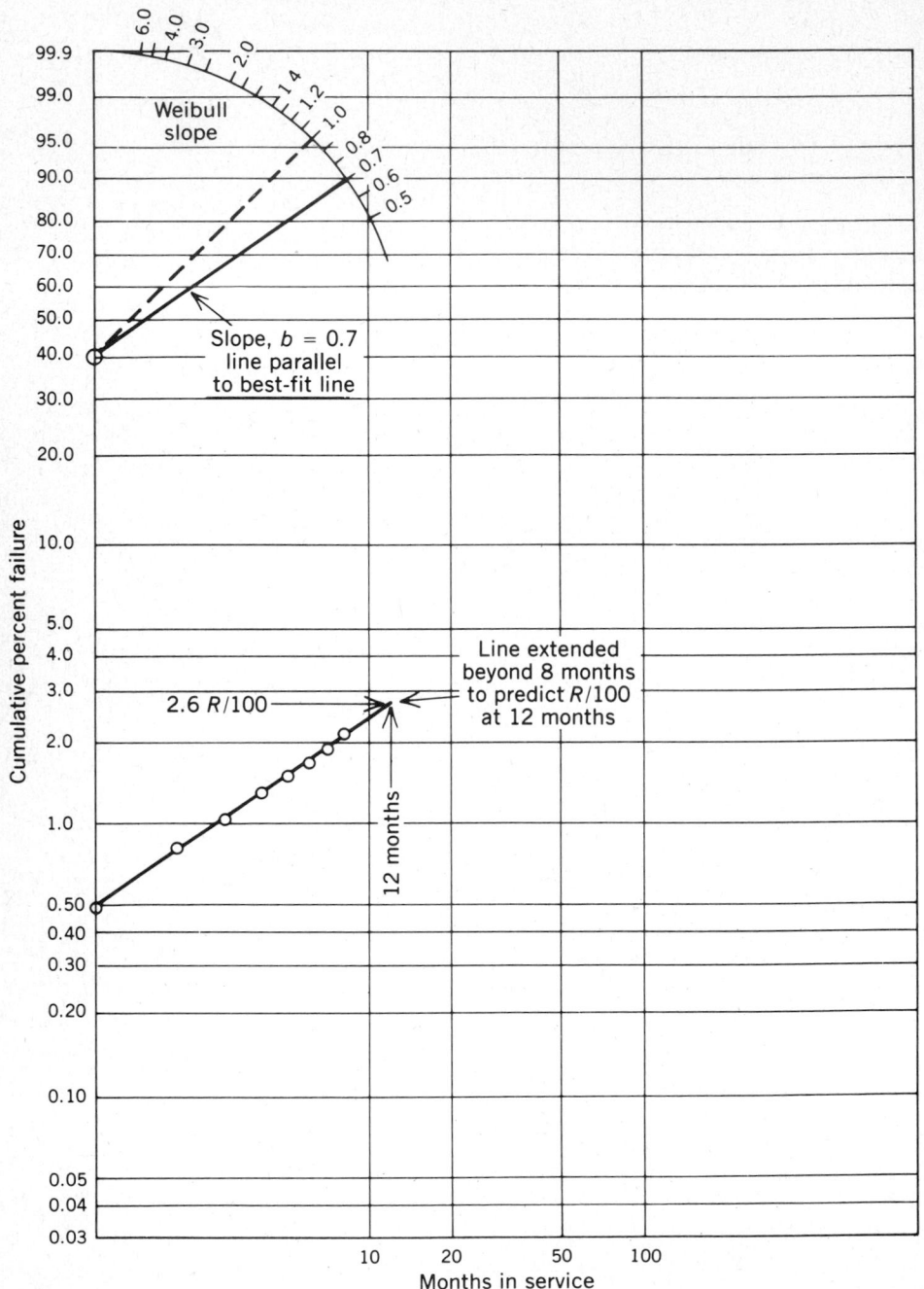

FIG. 20.5 Warranty data plot.

Extrapolation beyond the limits of actual data is always questionable. However, when extrapolated performance has been confirmed by actual performance on similar product lines, the approach may be justified. Although the approach suggested here is not rigorous, it is a major step beyond intuitive decisions.

A special case of analysis involves units in the field that have been placed in service at different dates. Some of the units have failed after having accumulated various lengths of time in service. Other units are still in operation, also with various accumulations of time in service. This type of data can be handled with "hazard plotting paper" for the Weibull or other distributions. King (1971) describes the mechanics of analysis and the application to service and warranty problems. An associated problem involves changes in the size of a warranty population. This occurs in any time interval in which the number of product units entering the warranty period differs. Alternative methods for handling this situation are discussed by Nelson (1982).

Effect of Time Lag.   Differences between usage dates, dates of sale, and dates of manufacture can create important errors in judging performance trends and in correlating cause (design and manufacturing variables) with effect (failure during usage).

For industrial apparatus, dates of installation can usually be obtained, but the lag time between the date that a failure occurs and the date that is reported to the manufacturer can be large.

For consumer products, Powell (1970) found a time lag between date of manufacture and receipt of failure reports of 6 to 32 weeks, as shown in Table 20.5.

Delays distort the reported failure rate when based purely on date of manufacture or date of sale. For a new model, the reports will, at the outset, greatly understate the failure rates, since the shipments are substantial whereas the reported failures are few due to the time lag. In contrast, when the failure reports all come in weeks or months later, the reported rate will exaggerate the actual failure rate of the units. To eliminate these exaggerations, practitioners have evolved methods for correcting failure rate data based on quantifying the time lag. (See Powell, 1970.)

A related problem is the movement of sold products into and out of the guarantee period. One measure of failure rate is the number of failures (reported during the guarantee period) per 100 units under guarantee. There are difficulties with this measure because failure rates (and hence guarantee charges) are not uniform over the guarantee period, plus the fact that the population of units covered by the guarantee period is rarely spread evenly, month by month, over the guarantee period. Sandholm (1965) and Robertson (1969) describe approaches for handling such data.

TABLE 20.5   Distribution of Time Lag

	Time elapsed, weeks	
Status	During this state	Cumulative
In manufacturer's inventory	1–12	1–12
In transit to dealer	1–2	2–14
In dealer inventory	1–8	3–22
In use	1–4	4–26
Undergoing service	1–3	5–29
Being reported	1–3	6–32

IMPROVING FIELD FEEDBACK

Improving the quality and promptness of field feedback requires a variety of actions:

1. *Provide personnel with well-designed data sheets:* This is intended to facilitate easy, accurate recording. The design of forms is not a matter that can be left to amateurs.

An important basic form is the service report. This fundamental document is originated for each service call made or each failure reported. Such forms should be designed not only to record basic information for warranty payment and analysis purposes, but also to provide information for diagnosis of the cause. Among the items that should be included are identification of the product (model number, system, assembly, subassembly, component, and part); the geographical location at which the failure occurred; operating time on the product; description of the symptom; immediate action taken to place the product back in operating condition; action taken on the failed item; and total amount of downtime, broken down into diagnosis, obtaining a replacement part, installing the replacement part, adjusting, and checking out the system.

Some open space should be left on the form for additional items of information required in the future.

2. *Provide incentives to encourage adequate feedback:* Payment on a warranty failure can be withheld until the information describing the failure is complete and in the form desired by the company.

3. *Provide a glossary of terms to improve communication and a mnemonic code number to simplify the data entry and analysis:* Words have different meanings to different people. For example, a steel company received a number of complaints of "bad coating" on wire. The company interpreted this to mean that their steel was bad and that the coating had become flakey. After much futile discussion it was finally discovered that the customer's meaning of "bad coating" was that the coating had oxidized. In another example, "fit of doors" meant dimensional problems to an automobile manufacturer. The customers meant that unless the doors were pushed shut with great effort they did not close completely. A glossary provides a written list of key words along with definitions. Personnel are then trained to use these definitions.

4. *Provide training in the how and why:* Show how the data are used. Service personnel view their primary job as repair and maintenance of a product, and not one of filling out forms and doing other paperwork. Also, many of them believe that no use is made of their reports. In order to be encouraged to provide adequate feedback, they need to be reminded how the data will be used.

5. *Conduct audits of the data feedback process:* This is intended to discover deficiencies and to demonstrate management's concern for good data. A sample of the routine reports provided can be evaluated in terms of the adequacy of information provided ("adequate, marginal, and unsatisfactory"). A summary can be given to the field personnel along with examples of both good and bad reports.

6. *Make use of modern technology to collect the field information:* An electronics company recently developed and provided each repair person with a simple recording system so that they could dictate the details of the repair instead of filling out a form. In another example, dealers selling earth-moving equipment now have computer terminals to report back daily to the factory every service operation performed.

7. *Make use of modern methods of analysis to provide managers with valid* *summaries for decision making:* McClure (1976) describes an automated data system that makes use of quality assurance indicators covering both in-plant and field performance. This information is made continuously available through computer terminals not only for the manufacturer but also for the customer. Both groups have identical access to outputs of the system. This provides a demonstration of the contractor's integrity in disclosing performance information and saves time in responding to customer requests for information.

8. *Minimize the number of data relay stations:* Each adds delay and possible noise to the signals.

9. *Make use of the sample concept:* A sample of data with precise, detailed information is more valuable than a large quantity of superficial information.

10. *Obtain the operations log:* Normally the log, which is kept on certain kinds of systems, includes records of significant phenomena observed, stoppages encountered, action taken to restore operations, proposals for improvement, and other information deemed necessary to provide a complete history.

11. *Buy the data:* It may be better to purchase the data from a customer who is keeping detailed records.

12. *Make use of the concept of controlled usage:* Here the product is used by employees or some other special group, and they provide detailed feedback on the performance of the product. In turn these users are either paid for their services or receive use of the product free of charge.

With the best of data systems it may be necessary to provide for supplementary data collection. Takeuchi and Quelch (1983) list the elements of "customer-driven" quality programs for a mail-order firm and an earth-moving equipment manufacturer (see Table 20.6). Note that in each case provisions are made for

TABLE 20.6 Customer-Driven Quality Programs

Mail-order apparel company	Equipment manufacturer
Conducting regular customer satisfaction surveys and sample group interviews to track customer and noncustomer perceptions of the quality of its own and its competitors' products and services	Conducting two customer satisfaction surveys following each purchase, one after 300 h of product use and the second after 500 h of use
Tracking on its computer all customer inquiries and complaints and updating the file daily	Maintaining a centrally managed list of product problems as identified by customers from around the world
Guaranteeing all its products to be 100% satisfactory and providing a full cash refund, if requested, on any returns	Analyzing warranty and service reports submitted by dealers, as part of a product improvement program
Asking customers to fill out a short, coded questionnaire and explain their reasons for returning the merchandise	Asking dealers to conduct a quality audit as soon as the products are received and to attribute defects to either assembly errors or shipping damages
Performing extensive field tests on any new outdoor equipment before listing it in the company's catalogs	Guaranteeing 48-h delivery of any part to any customer in the world
Even stocking extra buttons for most of the apparel items carried years ago, just in case a customer needs one	Encouraging dealers to establish side businesses in rebuilding parts to reduce costs and increase the speed of repairs

obtaining special field intelligence from customers. Smith (1979) describes the routine data system and supplementary information collected by an automobile manufacturer.

EXECUTIVE REPORTS ON FIELD PERFORMANCE

In the absence of regular reports on field performance upper managers can be stampeded by individual, isolated cases, so that they misdirect company resources for the improvement of field performance. This makes it essential that the executive instrument panel include information on the overall status on field performance.

The general concept of executive reports on quality is discussed in Section 8 under Executive Reports on Quality. The application of the concept to field performance is discussed below.

Control Subjects and Units of Measure. For field performance, the most widely used control subjects and units of measure are those shown in Table 20.7.

Beyond the control subjects listed in Table 20.7, the executive reports may include:

Breakdown of important control subjects by subcategories such as product type, subsystems, department responsibile, etc.

Lists of vital few problems and status of solution

TABLE 20.7 Control Subjects and Units of Measure for Field Performance

Control subject	Units of measure in use
Complaints	Total number of complaints Number of complaints per $1 million of sales Number of complaints per million units of product Value of material under complaint per $100 of sales for such products
Returns	Value of material returned per $100 of sales
Claims	Cost of claims paid Cost of claims per $1 million of sales
Failures	Mean time between failures (MTBF) Mean usage between failures, e.g., cycles, miles Mean time between repair calls Failures per 1000 units under warranty
Shipments	Amount of product shipped that did not meet specifications
Maintainability	Mean time to repair (MTTR) Mean downtime Number of repeat service calls for same complaint
Service cost	Ratio of maintenance hours to operating hours Repair cost per unit under warranty Cost per service call

Additional control subjects or added detail demanded by the special nature of the company's product

A composite index which reflects the collective effect of a variety of control subjects

Status information about the Complaint Bureau (or Service Department, etc.): complaints received, closed, on hand; time required to close complaints; important unresolved cases in order of age; productivity of complaint analysis

Complaint indices of various types are the most frequently used forms of field performance measure. Sasaki et al. (1978) performed a research on the complaint indices being used by companies in Japan. Twenty types of complaint indices were identified. The four must commonly used were:

1. The number of complaints
2. The loss in money by complaints
3. Comparison of the number of complaints for each product type
4. The number of complaints compared to the amount of production

The absolute number of complaints can be misleading because of the difference in seriousness of different defects. McRobb (1982) reports on comparing five measures to summarize customer perceived quality levels. A composite complaint measure was selected for reporting to management. Three categories of complaints were identified and weighting factors were assigned based on seriousness.

In one application of this system, two models of product were compared. The general impression throughout the factory was that the two models were about equal on quality. When the complaint data were summarized and a composite quality index was prepared, the index for the first model was 3000; the index for the second model was 500.

This example illustrated that the prevailing method of judging market acceptability could lead to erroneous results.

Failures as Seen By the User. Usually, the manufacturer measures repair costs only during the warranty period. The user is concerned with repair costs for the entire service life. Also, the user is concerned with various added costs caused by failures but which are divided into five categories:

R = repair cost
E = effectiveness loss (e.g., idle labor)
C = extra capacity required because of product downtime
D = damages caused by failure
I = lost income (e.g., profit)

If the categories applicable for a specific product are measured each year over the life (n) of the product and if i is the yearly interest rate, the total user failure cost (C_f) is:

$$\sum_{j=1}^{n} \frac{1}{(1 + i)^j} (R_j + E_j + C_j + D_j + I_j)$$

This model collects all the costs associated with failures over the product life and takes into account the time value of money (Gryna, 1977).

Users' costs are enormous. Studies of life cycle costs show that for consumer products the costs of failures often exceed the purchase price; for military products the *annual* maintenance cost may exceed the purchase price (see Section 13 under Planning for Maintainability). The manufacturer who is unaware of these costs may be unwittingly losing sales. In addition, the manufacturer remains unaware of the business opportunities that such knowledge would reveal.

PRODUCT RECALLS

"Product recall" is a term used to describe the actions taken due to deficiencies in products which have already been shipped to users. The actions may consist of corrections made in the field. The actions may also consist of removing the product from the field.

The most highly publicized recalls are those which pose a threat to human safety or health. Other important recalls are those which involve extensive economic loss to users.

Recalled products have spanned a broad spectrum including automobiles, toys, computers, appliances, food, and medical devices. The reasons for recall range from minor to serious. In food products, the deficiency may be as minor as a deterioration in flavor or as serious as a highly toxic contamination. In electronics, defects may range from calculators that do not work to harmful radiation emitted from television sets.

When a recall must be made the costs involved can be considerable. Jacobs and Mundel (1975) have identified the cost elements of a product recall.

For a recall to be effective it is essential that the procedures for the recall be in place before there is any need for the recall. In this sense a recall plan is similar to a will—it evokes little interest but it is necessary that the document be completed before the event takes place. Unless the recall procedures are ready for use when the recall decision is made, valuable time is lost in making the recall.

ASQC (1981) lists the key steps for implementing and evaluating a recall:

1. Initial activities to implement a recall
    a. Establishment of a management control center
    b. Description of the product, features, problem
    c. Identification of products
    d. Definition of product groups to be recalled
    e. Data on population of products
    f. Planning and designing reporting forms
    g. Estimating, ordering, and distributing replacement parts
2. Release of recall information
    a. Preparation of notification information
    b. Special news releases
    c. Notification to customers and users
    d. Internal employee information
    e. Timing
3. Field Response
    a. Response from the field
    b. Collection of internal and field cost information

  c. Parts usage traceability
  d. Field data reporting
    i. Periodic reporting
   ii. Summary reports
4. Monitoring activity
  a. Audit of field corrective action
  b. Data verification and correlation
5. Management evaluation, program completion
  a. Project review on periodic basis
  b. Success level evaluation

The quantity of product that must be recalled can be minimized if the suspect product units can be identified separately from other production. This separation is simplified if a system of "traceability" has been established. Once a recall is required, it is of critical importance not only to know where to locate the product in general, but also to be able to identify the specific suspect units quickly.

The factors to be considered in setting up a traceability program have been summarized by ASQC (1981) as follows:

1. *Product category:*   A unique designation such as a part name or part number is required.

2. *Product life:*   The longer the product life, the greater the number of similar items that are present in the field. Also, as modifications are made in design or manufacturing, the traceability plan must be able to identify which units of product embody which changes.

3. *Unit cost:*   The greater the unit cost, the greater the incentive to recall only the most important problem items.

4. *Recall or modify in the field:*   If the product is repairable, then a decision must be made whether to (*a*) bring the product in from the field and have it corrected by the manufacturer; (*b*) send a manufacturer's representative to the field to correct the problem; or (*c*) provide the user with parts and instructions to make the necessary modification.

5. *Product complexity:*   If a design consists of many components, then a decision must be made to determine how far down the product hierarchy to extend the traceability.

6. *Level of downstream traceability:*   This refers to the reason for recall. For each failure mode, it must be decided what level of traceability is needed to segregate the suspect items from the total product population. For example, if a recall results from a manufacturing problem, then the manufacturing date, facility, lot identification, etc., may be required.

7. *Documents providing traceability:*   An analysis of the failure modes will indicate the types of information necessary.

8. *Type of identification:*   The cost of identification should be consistent with the product price. For expensive products, serial numbers are often used; for lower priced products, dates are used.

9. *Should identification be coded or uncoded?*   An uncoded identification may have an adverse effect on sales, but it makes it easier to identify the defective product and thereby to finish the recall sooner.

10. *Method of identification:*   This includes tags, name plates, ink stamps, and other means.

Consideration must also be given to the need for the traceability program extending back through the vendor's organization. This is sometimes called second-tier traceability. Jacobs and Mundel (1975) discuss the elements of a program for the supplier's organization.

Even with thorough recall programs, it has not been possible to recover all of the products that are in the field. Some consumers simply do not return the product even if they are aware of the recall. Much depends on the cost of the product and other factors. Evaluating the effectiveness of the recall is part of the overall recall process.

The U.S. Consumer Product Safety Commission (1978) studied the effectiveness of some recalls. Half of the 245 recall cases studied resulted in 80 percent or more of the suspected products being examined and corrected where necessary. Seven variables were identified as having strong relationships with recall effectiveness: product price, product life, number of units, time in distribution, percent of unit in consumers' hands, recall action, and level of direct consumer notification.

For example, it was estimated that recalls will probably be less than 50 percent effective when any of the following conditions occur: the product price is less than $25; the average life is less than 6 years; the number of units is over 10,000; over two-thirds of the total units have been purchased by consumers.

One study (Food and Drug Administration, 1978) evaluated the effectiveness of seven methods of contacting customers. The conclusion was that mail with telephone follow-up was the most efficient method.

REFERENCES

American Society for Quality Control (1981). *Product Recall Planning Guide.* Milwaukee.

Andreasen, Alan R. and Best, Arthur (1977). "Consumers Complain—Does Business Respond?" *Harvard Business Review,* July–August, pp. 124–132.

Amrine, Harold, Ritchey, John A., and Hulley, Oliver S. (1975). *Manufacturing Organization and Management,* 3rd ed. Prentice-Hall, Englewood Cliffs, NJ.

Canut, Luis Sicre (1975). "Standardization of Packaging—A Survey with Examples from Western Europe." *EOQC Quality,* vol. XIX, no. 1, pp. 10–15.

Caterpillar Tractor Company (1978). *Service Quality Guide.* Peoria, IL.

The Center for Policy Alternatives, Massachusetts Institute of Technology and Charles Stark Draper Laboratory, Inc. (1974). *The Productivity of Servicing Consumer Durable Products.* Report 74-4, Cambridge, MA.

Cherkasky, Stanley M. (1970). "Long-Term Storage and System Reliability." *Proceedings, Annual Reliability and Maintainability, Symposium.* IEEE, New York, pp. 120–127.

Coca-Cola Company (1981). *Measuring the Grapevine-Consumer Response and Word of Mouth.* Atlanta, GA.

Das, S., Hendry, A., and Hong, S. (1980). "The Impact of Imperfect Repair on System Reliability." *Proceedings, Annual Reliability and Maintainability Symposium.* IEEE, New York, pp. 393–402.

Dobbins, Richard K. (1977). "A Dollars and Cents Approach to Failure Analysis." *ASQC Technical Conference Transactions,* Milwaukee, pp. 230–235.

Duane, J. T. (1964). "Learning Curve Approach to Reliability Monitoring." *IEEE Transactions on Aerospace,* vol. 2, no. 2, pp. 563–566.

Fiedler, Robert M. (1978). "Portal to Portal Product Protection." *Quality,* May, pp. 12–14.

Food and Drug Administration (1978). *Checking the Effectiveness of Recalls—A Cost-Effectiveness Study.* Publication PB-277 174, Washington, DC.

Ford Motor Company (1972). *Reliability Methods, Module No. XII.* Dearborn, MI, pp. 11–13.

Goodman, John and Yates, Jane (1982). "Economic Aspects of Quality Controlled Decisions—Development of a Market-Driven Quality Assurance System." *ASQC Conference on Statistical Control in Good Manufacturing Practice,* New Brunswick, NJ, Oct. 5. ASQC, Milwaukee, pp. 1–19.

Gryna, Frank M., Jr. (1977). "Quality Costs: User vs. Manufacturer." *Quality Progress,* June pp. 10–15.

Horn, Roy L. and Hall, Fred M. (1983). "Maintenance-Centered Reliability." *Proceedings, Annual Reliability and Maintainability Symposium.* IEEE, New York, pp. 197–204.

Jacobs, R. M. and Mundel, A. B. (1975). "Quality Tasks in Product Recall." *Quality Progress,* June, pp. 16–19.

Jayachandran, Toke and Moore, Louis R. (1976). "A Comparison of Reliability Growth Models." *IEEE Transactions on Reliability,* vol. R-25, no. 1, pp. 49–51.

Johnson, D. A. (1975). "Product Problem Control through Warranty Analysis—Ford's Approach." *ASQC Automotive Division Second Annual Agricultural, Industrial, and Construction Equipment Conference.* ASQC, Milwaukee.

Juran, J. M. and Gryna, Frank M. (1980). *Quality Planning and Analysis,* 2nd ed. McGraw-Hill, New York, p. 474.

King, James R. (1971). *Probability Charts for Decision Making.* Industrial Press, New York.

LaSala, Kenneth P. and Siegel, Arthur I. (1983). "Improved R & M in Productivity by Designs for People." *Proceedings Annual Reliability and Maintainability Symposium.* IEEE, New York, pp. 494–500.

Lele, Milind and Karmarkar, Uday S. (1983). "Good Product Support is Smart Marketing." *Harvard Business Review,* November–December, pp. 124–132.

Levitt, Theodore (1983). "After the Sale is Over." *Harvard Business Review,* September–October, pp. 87–93.

McClure, J. Y. (1976). "The Role of Automated Data in Maintaining Optimum Customer Relations."*ASQC Technical Conference Transactions,* Milwaukee, pp. 375–380.

McRobb, R. M. (1982). "Customer-Perceived Quality Levels." *ASQC Quality Congress Transactions,* Milwaukee, pp. 428–432.

Meister, David (1978). "Subjective Data in Human Reliability Estimated." *Proceedings, Annual Reliability and Maintainability Symposium.* IEEE, New York, pp. 380–384.

Nelson, Wayne (1982). *Applied Life Data Analysis.* John Wiley & Sons, New York.

Nowlan, F. S. (1980). "Reliability Centered Maintenance." *Symposium on Design to Cost and Life Cycle Cost.* North Atlantic Treaty Organization, Amsterdam, Netherlands.

Nowlan, F. Stanley and Heap, Howard F. (1978). *Reliability Centered Maintenance.* Document ADA066579, Defense Documentation Center, Alexandria, VA.

Peacore, E. J. (1975). "Reliability Developments—AWACS." *Proceedings, Annual Reliability and Maintainability Symposium.* IEEE, New York, pp. 383–389.

Phillips, G. J. and Hirschfeld, Fritz (1980). "Rotating Machinery Bearing Analysis." *Mechanical Engineering,* July, pp. 28–33.

Powell, Richard F. (1970). "Analyzing and Interpreting Field Failure Data." *Proceedings, Annual Symposium on Reliability and Maintainability.* IEEE, New York, pp. 94–100.

Richardson, Hugh W. (1981). "Designing for Customer Setup." *Quality,* October, pp. 62–65.

Robertson, James A. (1969). "Analyzing Field Failure." *Quality Progress,* January, pp. 12–13.

Rosenthal, Robert (1983). "Spare Part Quality Assurance." *Quality Progress,* May, pp. 24–27.

Sandholm, L. (1965). "Improving Quality Assurance." *Proceedings, IXth EOQC Conference, European Organization for Quality Control,* Rotterdam, pp. 186–203.

Sasaki, Osamu, Ohfuju, Tadashi, and Naoi, Tomoyoshi (1978). "The Quality Complaint

Index Being Used by Companies in Japan." *Proceedings of the International Conference on Quality Control,* Tokyo, pp. C1-17, C1-22.

Smith, R. P. (1979). "Research and Other Data in the Monitoring of Product Quality." *Journal of the Market Research Society, Great Britain,* vol. 21, no. 3, pp. 189–205.

Takeuchi, Hirotaka and Quelch, John A. (1983). "Quality is More than Making a Good Product." *Harvard Business Review,* July–August, pp. 139–145.

TARP (Technical Assistance Research Programs) (1976). *A National Survey of the Complaint/Handling Procedures Used by Consumers.* TARP, Washington, DC.

U.S. Consumer Product Safety Commission (1978). *Recall Effectiveness Study.* May, Washington, DC.

Whirlpool Corporation (1983). *America's Search for Quality.* Benton Harbor, MI, pp. 7–9.

SECTION 21

ADMINISTRATIVE AND SUPPORT OPERATIONS[1]

Frank M. Gryna

INTRODUCTION **21.2**

Historical Perspective . . . 21.2

Error Rates in
Administrative and
Support Activities 21.3

Relation to Other Sections
of this Handbook 21.3

Defining Quality
Responsibilities for
Administrative and
Support Activities 21.4

QUALITY PLANNING FOR
ADMINISTRATIVE AND
SUPPORT ACTIVITIES **21.7**

Identify the Customers . . 21.7

Discover the Needs of
Customers 21.9

Translation of Customer
Needs 21.10

Establish Measurement . . 21.10

Product Development . . . 21.11

Optimize Product Design . 21.11

Process Development . . . 21.11

Transfer to Operations . . 21.12

QUALITY CONTROL FOR
ADMINISTRATIVE AND
SUPPORT ACTIVITIES **21.14**

The Feedback Loop 21.14

Control Subjects 21.14

Evaluation of
Performance 21.14

QUALITY IMPROVEMENT IN
ADMINISTRATIVE AND
SUPPORT ACTIVITIES **21.15**

Tools of Diagnosis 21.16

ORGANIZING THE
ADMINISTRATIVE AND
SUPPORT QUALITY
ACTIVITIES **21.21**

Participation in Planning . 21.22

Provision for Diagnosis . . 21.22

REFERENCES **21.22**

---

[1]In the Third Edition, the section on support operations was prepared by S. P. Zobel.

INTRODUCTION

The quality function involves numerous activities through which we achieve fitness for use. Those activities which directly influence the nature of the product (e.g., design, purchase of materials, fabrication, inspection) have received much attention from the quality "movement." However, there are other activities which, though indirectly influencing quality of product, have largely escaped the attention of the quality movement. This section examines the ways in which the quality concepts can be applied to these activities.

The literature has not created a generic term which can embrace all of these activities. In this handbook, the term "administrative and support operations" will be used to designate these activities. Administrative activities encompass operations required for the organization to complete its overall mission. Examples include finance (billing, accounts payable, accounts receivable, corporate accounting, etc.), personnel (recruiting, training, etc.), security, data processing and computers, plant engineering (preventive maintenance, building services, new construction, etc.), legal, general publications, and other activities. Support activities are those indirect activities which have some effect on the product itself, e.g., shipping, receiving, material, in-process and finished goods storage, traffic, product publications, advertising, and order filling.

Historical Perspective.   The manufacturing company's mission is to produce a product which is fit for use, can create a market, and can thereby generate the company's income. Awareness of the interrelation between fitness for use and income has led the companies to the familiar product quality controls. These controls have been most highly developed on those aspects of product progression which are obvious to the user, i.e., materials, processes, products. The effect of the administrative and support operations on fitness for use has been less obvious, and may account for the underdevelopment of quality controls in these "indirect" activities.

This split in emphasis extends to the study of the performance of the human beings as well. Traditionally, the most intense studies of quality performance and of motivation for quality have been devoted to those people who have an obvious connection with the physical product, i.e., the inspectors and the production operators. Extension of this study to the "indirect" personnel has been a comparatively recent phenomenon. The number (and variety) of these personnel is considerable. Improvement of their contribution to the company's overall quality mission is a major opportunity which in most companies is still waiting to be realized. Taking action on the opportunity requires a better understanding of the effect on fitness for use.

People readily understand the importance of quality in manufacturing, research and development, and other technologically oriented functions. With the increased emphasis on a companywide approach to quality, personnel in administrative and support operations are wondering what quality means in their activities and "what they must do that is different." In administrative activities, the situation is not as clear. Some errors (e.g., a mistake in billing a customer for a product) can have a direct effect on the customer even though the error may not affect the physical product. Other errors (e.g., an error in a company newspaper or an error in the security activity) do not necessarily affect the product or the customer. For support operations, one can point to the effect that errors have on the product provided to the customer. For example, an error in the filling of orders for spare parts can result in the customer receiving the wrong spare parts.

However, errors in any activity usually must be corrected, and the corrective action requires additional effort analogous to rework in manufacturing. Even if no correction is made, the consequences of the errors represent a loss to someone.

The boundary line between "direct" and other quality activities has undergone considerable change in the twentieth century. The Chief Inspectors who emerged in the reorganizations following World War I tended to regard inspection, test, and metrology as the core quality activities. The rise of the Quality Engineer expanded this core through the concept of organized quality planning and defect prevention. The rise of the Reliability Engineer expanded the core further to include some vital activities inherent in the launching of new designs. In some industries (e.g., drug, food) the core now includes product packaging and storage. In all regulated industries the core now includes much of the documentation activity.

These changes underscore the dynamic nature of the boundary between direct quality activities and administrative and support quality activities. However, the direction of change has been essentially one way. The core has kept increasing, so that the administrative and support quality activities of today are all candidates to become the direct quality activities of tomorrow. At the same time, the growing complexity of industry has been creating new support activities which require new plans and controls to make them effective in control of quality.

The support activities are not unique to manufacturing industries. The service industries (see Section 33) likewise employ a wide array of administrative and support quality activities, many of which are identical to those used in the manufacturing industries. The tasks, the operations, and the tools are largely alike; what is different is the application and the emphasis.

Error Rates in Administrative and Support Activities. The potential for errors exists in *all* activities. A study made in an electronics organization identified these examples:

Fifty percent of time cards were in error.

Forty percent of all travel reservations made in one month were changed; two of them were changed nine times.

Ten percent of performance appraisals that were sampled in one month were returned because of lack of signatures.

Ten to fifteen percent of employee profiles required phone call follow up by the salary administration function.

Twenty to thirty percent of consignments to suppliers were in error.

Little work has been done to quantify the extent and cost of errors in support operations or administrative operations. It is the author's belief that the cost of poor quality for these activities is as great as the cost of poor quality directly associated with the product.

Relation to Other Sections of this Handbook. The sections on Field Intelligence, Supplier Relations, Marketing, and Customer Service discuss topics that are related to administrative and support operations. In addition, the section on Service Industries provides an additional reference because those industries use many administrative type activities. Finally, the concepts of quality planning, quality control, and quality improvement are discussed throughout this handbook, mainly as applied to the direct activities in an organization. These same three concepts apply fully to the administrative and support functions.

Defining Quality Responsibilities for Administrative and Support Activities. The concept of fitness for use can be a starting point in defining these responsibilities. At the outset, it is essential to identify the *users* or customers of the outputs. Table 21.1 shows examples of possible users for several support activities. Note that users can be internal as well as external to the company.

A further aid in defining quality responsibilities is the concept of the the three roles of each organization (see Section 6 under The Triple Role Concept). Every administrative and support activity plays the roles of user, processor, and supplier. Table 21.2 applies the concept to the personnel, finance, and warehouse and shipping. The entries in the table provide examples of activities pertinent to the three roles.

One of the units of IBM Corporation uses a "department activity analysis" which focuses on the following questions (IBM, 1984):

1. What functions or tasks does my department perform?

2. What are the key external interfaces (input/output)?

3. Have the requirements across those interfaces been clearly established?

TABLE 21.1   Examples of Multiple Users of Support Activities

Warehouse and shipping function	Finance function	Personnel function
Production withdraws raw material.	*Customers* receive invoices.	*Applicant* receives company information.
Production stores finished product.	*Suppliers* receive payments.	*Managers* receive information for hiring process.
Suppliers require documentation on deliveries.	*Employees* receive salary payments.	*Employees* receive training.
Purchasing Department requires documentation on receipts.	*Middle managers* receive cost reports.	*Government agencies* receive information on employees.
Finance Department requires documentation for invoices.	*Upper managers* receive financial reports and budgetary information.	*Outside agencies* receive information for recruiting.
	Stockholders receive financial information.	
	Government agencies receive financial information on the company and employees.	

TABLE 21.2 Examples of Triple Roles of Customer/User, Processor, and Supplier

Customer/user	Processor	Supplier
	Personnel (recruitment) function	
Receive requisitions from interested customers	Review, critique job descriptions	Supply recruits to internal customers
Receive job descriptions	Publish information on job openings	Provide associated documentation
Receive feedback from interviews	Interview, screen job applicants	Provide induction to recruits when hired
	Conduct checks on references	
	Finance (financial data) function	
Receive basic data from various sources	Establish data processing system	Publish reports
Receive feedbacks from published reports	Process data into summaries	Disseminate to internal and external customers
	Analyze data, prepare reports	
	Warehouse and shipping function	
Acquire equipment needed to conduct operations	Store goods	Ship goods to destinations
Receive goods from production areas	Select goods to fill orders	Provide shipping documents, inventory data
	Package, ship	
Receive requisitions, customers' orders to be filled	Maintain inventory status	Respond to inquiries, feedback
Receive feedback from customers	Maintain equipment	

4. Have measurements been established to verify and track the quality of input, activity, output?

Three steps are used in the analysis:

1. List all major activities. For example, the list for one finance department is:
   a. Inventory analysis and review.
   b. Supplier sourcing decisions.
   c. Equipment justifications.
   d. Payroll processing.

e. Pay adjustments.
f. Banking activities.
g. Billing.
h. Variance report.
i. Supplier payment.
j. Special checks.
k. Acceptance/rejection invoices.
l. Rejected purchase report.

2. For *each* activity (Figure 21.1):
   a. List the inputs—What? From where?
   b. Analyze the work—Why do it? What is the value? Suppose it is not done?
   c. List the outputs—What? Who receives them?
3. For each activity (Figure 21.2):
   a. Meet with the supplier and agree on the requirements.
   b. Meet with the customer and agree on the requirements.
   c. Define the measurements that will evaluate output against requirements.

Of course, the supplier and customer may be internal or external to the company.

Melan (1985) discusses techniques of process management in service and administrative operations at IBM. See also Section 10 under Team Performance: A Processing System Viewpoint.

Activity:	Dept.	Date:	Prepared By:

Input

What:
From:

Value Added — Work Accomplished in Dept.

Why Do:
Value Added:
Impact If Not Done:

Output

What:
To:

FIG. 21.1 Activity analysis for input and output (one sheet for each major activity).

Activity:	Dept.	Date:	Prepared By:

What are the input requirements that you and your supplier have agreed to?
-
-
-
-

What are the output requirements that you and your customer have agreed to?
-
-
-
-

What are the quality measurements that will show if your output meets requirements?
-
-
-
-

FIG. 21.2 Supplier and customer analysis.

QUALITY PLANNING FOR ADMINISTRATIVE AND SUPPORT ACTIVITIES

The general approach to quality planning (see Section 6, Companywide Planning for Quality) applies fully to quality planning for administrative and support activities.

Identify the Customers. The starting point is to identify the customers or users of the service provided by the administrative or support activities. This identification is aided by constructing a flow diagram to show the progression of the activities and thereby to see who is impacted. Figure 21.3 is an example of such a flow diagram (International Paper Company, 1984).

External Customers. Those who are impacted, but are not within the same company as the administrative and support departments, are external customers. External customers include:

1. *Clients:* They buy products (goods and services); they receive products and product information; they receive invoices; they receive requests for feedback of data.
2. *Regulatory agencies:* They monitor products and product information; they issue regulations and receive requests for interpretation.
3. *The public:* Members of the public may be impacted due to the effect of products on human safety, health, or on the environment.
4. *The community:* It may be impacted by numerous practices relative to: employee relations; neighborhood noise, odors, congestion; participation in community affairs; payment of community taxes.

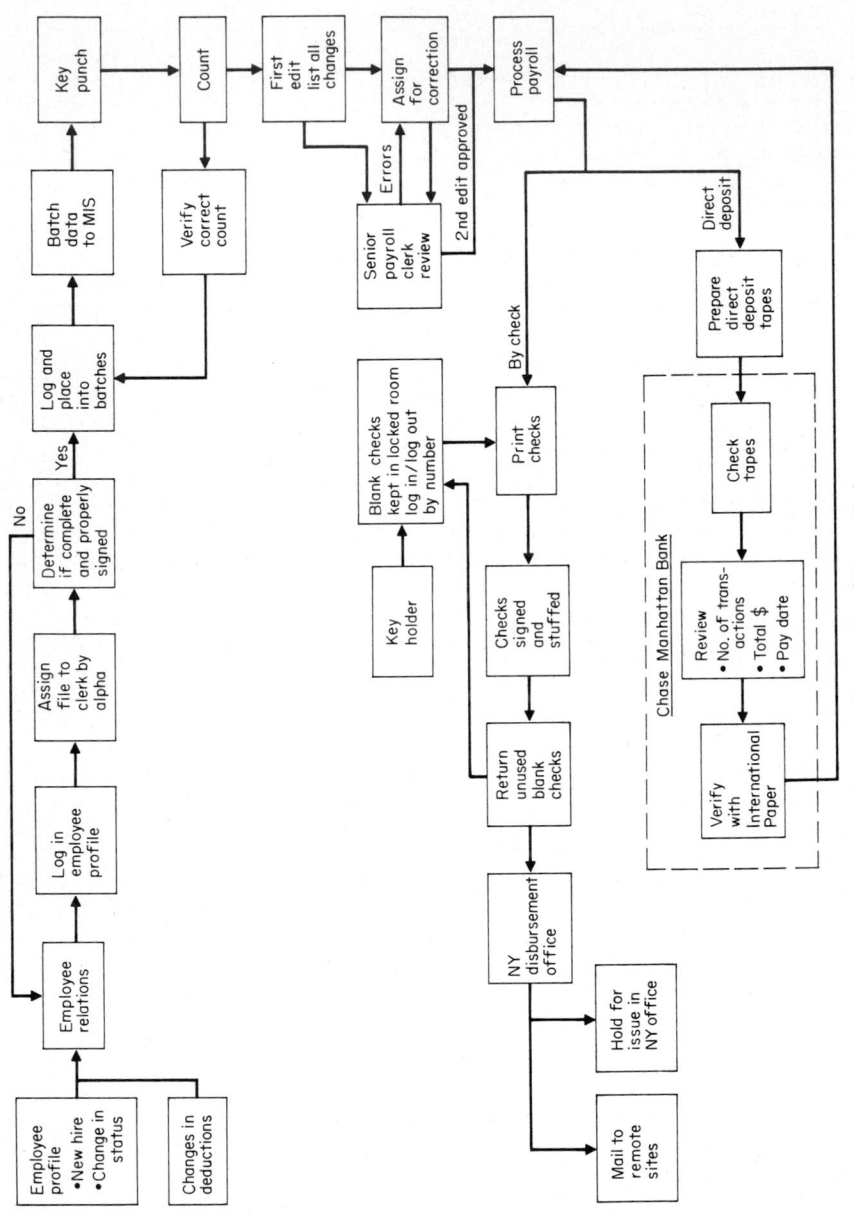

FIG. 21.3 Flow chart for payroll changes. *(Courtesy International Paper Co.)*

Internal Customers. Within any company, each internal department supplies products to other internal departments. For example:

Supplying departments	Major products	Some internal customers
Finance	Financial statements	Managers
Employment	Recruits	All departments
Order editing	Edited orders	Operations
Office services	Office space, supplies, maintenance	All office departments
Legal	Legal advice	All departments

Vital Few Customers. Customers are not equally important. Their importance follows the Pareto principle: a relative few of the customers absorb most of the impact. The planning process requires that these vital few customers be identified so that their needs will become known and met.

Discover the Needs of Customers.

Customer needs consist primarily of (*a*) product satisfaction and (*b*) freedom from product dissatisfaction. While such are the primary needs, discovery of those needs requires some looking below the surface.

Stated Needs and Real Needs. Customer's stated needs often differ from the real needs. For example, an internal department asks the finance office for a change in some cost standard. The real reason may be to avoid criticism for cost overruns.

Difference in Perceptions. Customers' perceptions often differ from those of suppliers. For example, a personnel office perceives the need to train the work force in some specialty. However, the line managers do not perceive such training as helping their departments meet departmental goals. In like manner, a budget office may propose a new procedure which will reduce the amount of work in the budget office. However, the line departments may resist the proposal because their work is increased.

Cultural Needs. The needs of customers, especially internal customers, go beyond products and processes. They include needs for job security, self-respect, respect of others, continuity of habit patterns, and still other elements of what is broadly called cultural values. While such needs are real they are seldom stated openly. Instead they are stated in disguised form.

A widespread example is "turf," i.e., the "ownership" of some area of responsibility, expertise, etc. Such ownership confers status; a threat to the ownership is a threat to that status.

Strategies for Determining Customer Needs. To learn about customer needs in adequate detail, suppliers make use of multiple strategies.

Be a Customer. Here the supplier carries out some activities similar to those carried out by customers. For example, some departments, e.g., office service, supply service to themselves as well as to other departments. A second form of "be a customer" is to provide the supplier personnel with training—to assign them to conducting the activities carried out by customers.

Communicate with Customers.   This is the most widely used form of discovering customers' needs. Some of it is initiated by customers who have endured product dissatisfactions. Some is initiated by suppliers who are conducting researches on product satisfaction. In too many companies the emphasis on external customers is so dominant that the needs of internal customers suffer from inattention.

Simulation.   Simulation is a further way of identifying needs of customers, in administrative and support activities as well as in model shops and pilot plants. A well-known example is training in simulated environments. In selected cases the concept offers cost-effective ways of reducing risks. However, the concept is itself subject to risks. Chief of these is the "two worlds" phenomenon—the world of the laboratory and the world of operations. These two worlds can differ widely in their mission, scale of operations, technology, and personnel. These differences demand that any extrapolation from laboratory findings be based on inputs from both worlds.

Tools for Determining Customer Needs.   The principal tools include

The flow diagram: See above, under Identify the Customers.

The spreadsheet: In cases involving many customers and needs it is useful to organize the information in the form of a spreadsheet (table, matrix). Then, as the planning progresses further, additional entries are made. The spreadsheet provides an orderly means for assuring that essential tasks are carried out. For examples of a planning spreadsheet, see Section 13, Figures 13.2 and 13.3.

Marketing research: The tools of marketing research are used especially to determine customer needs for product performance. This applies to internal customers as well as to external customers. For a discussion of marketing research as applied to quality, see Section 12, under Some Simple Tools for Collecting Field Intelligence and under Competitive Evaluations.

Translation of Customer Needs.   Customer needs may be stated in any of several languages:

The customer's language

The supplier's language

A common language

When customer needs are stated in the customer's language it becomes necessary to translate such needs into either the supplier's language or a common language. This necessity applies to internal customers as well as to external customers.

Beyond sheer differences in language, translation may be required due to vague terminology and to local dialects peculiar to specific functions, companies, industries, and countries. The remedies include a glossary of meanings of key terms; physical samples; use of special departments to provide translation, e.g., Order Editing; standardization; and establishment of measurement. (See below.)

Establish Measurement.   A major aid for determining customer needs is some means of expressing those needs in numbers, i.e., measurement. If such means can be made available they will also be major aids throughout the entire quality planning process.

Units of Measure and Sensors.   To "say it in numbers" requires a system of measurement consisting of

> *A unit of measure:*   A defined amount of some quality features which permits evaluation of that feature in numbers
>
> *A sensor:*   A method or instrument which can carry out the evaluation, and state the findings in numbers, in terms of the unit of measure

In the case of physical goods, the unit of measure is often technological in nature—millimeters, grams, amperes, hours. The associated sensors are technological instruments—calipers, scales, ammeters, clocks. For products from administrative and support activities, the units of measure are often statistical and financial in nature—percent of on-time deliveries, percent errors in billing (or transportation, warehousing, etc). The associated sensors are the basic documents—clock cards, material requisitions, etc.—as well as the data systems which summarize the information for use by the various customers. Figure 6.10 in Section 6 depicts how the various units of measure constitute a sort of pyramid of measure.

For added discussion of units of measure, see Section 18.

Human Sensing.   Human sensing takes place at all levels of the hierarchy of measurement. At the basic data level human beings must decide: which accounts should be charged with these hours of time; which of several tasks has top priority. At higher levels, similar questions arise with respect to use of summaries, indexes, etc. In addition, human sensing is subject to various sources of error. A discussion of Evaluation of Performance later in this section includes a listing of some of the common types of error along with the usual remedial steps.

Product Development.   In administrative and support activities, "products" consist mainly of services of various kinds. Typical examples for various functions are as follows:

Function	*Products*
Controller	Budget, controls, financial reports
Personnel	Courses, employment candidates
Purchasing	Supplier list, purchase contracts
Materials handling	Packaging, transport, storage

The purpose of these products is to meet customer needs. The building block of product design is the *product feature.* Each specific customer need is met through development of some product feature which responds to that specific need. (See Section 13 for discussion of product development tasks.)

Optimize Product Design.   Application of product development tasks to administrative and support activities requires extensive collaboration with customers. These customers are primarily internal customers, so that there is great need for participation. Such participation is needed to assure that the products meet the needs of the customers and that the product designs will optimize company performance, not departmental performance. For elaboration see Section 6 under Optimizing Product Design.

Process Development.   The purpose of this step in the planning sequence is to provide a process which is capable of producing the product features. In administrative and support activities, such processes are called systems, procedures, routines, etc. Specific process features must correspond to specific product features, just as specific product features must correspond to specific customer needs.

Section 16, Manufacturing Planning, deals with process development as applied to production of goods. The same concepts are fully applicable to the administrative and support activities for producing services. A major difference is the greater impact of the latter on internal customers. This difference in turn requires that developers of processes for producing administrative and support services establish close collaboration with the line departments to assure product fitness for use and optimal cost performance.

Process Capability.   An essential requirement of any process is that it should be capable of meeting the product goals under operating conditions. To a degree this capability can be quantified sufficiently to be used in the planning process. This concept of process capability is widely used in administrative and support activities as well as in manufacturing processes. Examples include the following:

Function	Subject of process capability information
Purchasing	Credit worthiness of suppliers
Certification of suppliers as to quality	Product quality of suppliers
Sales potential of various territories	Marketing
Certification of workers as to qualification to perform critical tasks	Personnel

Transfer to Operations.   This final step in the planning process is often carried out with formality since there is a shift of responsibility from the planning forces to the operating forces. Prior to this shift of responsibility, steps should have been taken to:

Prove Process Capability.   The process should be able to meet the product goals under operating conditions. This proof may be established in various ways: quantify process capability as discussed in Section 16 under Process Capability Measurements; conduct pilot tests under operating conditions; conduct tests under simulated operating conditions.

In one company (IBM, 1984) process capability was approached through a concept of certifying "key business processes." In one area, key processes included contract management, billing, accounts receivable, order entry, backlog, sales compensation, software, spare parts, inventory, payment generation, accounting, and materials management.

To apply the certification concept, an "owner" is designated for each key business process. For a functional process, the functional manager is the owner. For a cross-functional process, the manager of one of the key functions is designated as owner.

The key processes are then "rated" on a scale of 1 (best) to 5 for several features: control of the process, adequacy of quality management, and progress on quality improvement. Criteria are established for each level of rating, and the owner of the process is made responsible for bringing the process up to the targeted levels of rating.

Latzko (1985) presents a procedure for quantifying capability in administrative activities using attribute data on error rates. Dmytrow (1985) shows the role of control charts in evaluating capability for data collection and review processes.

Prove Process Controllability.   Here the purpose is to establish that the operating forces have been put into a state of self-control with respect to the process. Such a state of self-control requires providing the operating forces with:

1. Means of knowing what are the product and process goals
2. Means of evaluating actual performance and comparing actual to goals
3. Means to take action on the difference

Table 21.3 consists of a list of questions which are pertinent to determining whether a state of self-control has been established. The list makes clear that a good deal of thought and analysis can be involved in attaining such a state.

Transfer Know-How.   The minimal information transfer consists of the product and process specification plus the associated procedures manuals. However the planners invariably possess additional know-how which can be of value to the operating forces. Transfer of this added know-how requires special steps to be taken: briefing meetings; on-the-job training in which the planners participate as instructors; formal training courses. A widespread example of transfer of such additional know-how has been in the area of introducing word processors into administrative and support activities.

TABLE 21.3   Questions for Analyzing Self-Control

---

1. Have personnel been provided with the means of knowing what they are supposed to do?
   a. Have written policies, guidelines or procedures been developed?
   b. Have quality standards been developed?
   c. Do personnel have ready access to *a* and *b*?
   d. Do they fully understand *a* and *b* and use them?
   e. Do they know whom to consult to interpret *a* and *b*?
   f. Do they know how the results of their activity will be used?
   g. Do they know the consequences to the user of a failure to meet the requirements in *a* and *b*?
   h. Are changes in *a* and *b* transmitted rapidly to personnel affected?
   i. Do personnel know what to do when inputs to them contain errors or omissions?
2. Have personnel been provided with the means of knowing what they are doing?
   a. Are personnel provided with some means of evaluating the adequacy and completeness of their work, e.g., quality standards, checklists, etc.?
   b. Are they told how often to sample their work? Is time allowed to do the checking?
   c. Are they required to record the results of checking of their work?
   d. Is there any independent check of the work?
   e. Are personnel provided with feedback on the quality of their work?
   f. Are there provisions for periodically checking the accuracy of records prepared by support and administrative personnel?
   g. Do supervisors have a record of performance of individual personnel?
3. Have personnel been provided with the means of regulating their work?
   a. Has the quality capability of the activity been evaluated in quantitative terms and compared to the goal?
   b. Do personnel have criteria for defining when their activity requires correction?
   c. Do personnel know what to do when the criteria for action are exceeded?
   d. Have the actions which cause errors been diagnosed and told to personnel?
   e. Have the actions which prevent errors been diagnosed and told to personnel?

QUALITY CONTROL FOR ADMINISTRATIVE AND SUPPORT ACTIVITIES

As used in this handbook, quality control consists essentially of:

Evaluating actual quality performance

Comparing actual performance to quality goals

Taking action on the difference

Quality control has long been practiced in administrative and support activities. In fact, the bulk of the literature in this area deals with quality control and the associated statistical tools.

The Feedback Loop. The conceptual approach behind quality control is the feedback loop. Many sections of the handbook discuss application of the feedback loop to specific functional areas. In addition, some sections deal with the general-use tools through which the feedback loop is applied, e.g., Section 24 on Statistical Process Control. To avoid duplication, this Section 21 will give some examples of application of elements of the feedback loop to administrative and support activities, along with examples of use of specific tools.

Control Subjects. Each feedback loop is centered on a control subject which is a goal of some sort, e.g., a product goal, a process goal. For example, in the personnel recruitment area, control subjects consist of such matters as:

Adequacy of job descriptions

Effectiveness of interviews

Effectiveness of reference checks

Time required to complete the recruitment

Quality of applicants

Yield of the recruitment process

Performance of persons after hiring

Accuracy of documentation

Evaluation of Performance. Conceptually, evaluation for administrative and support activities is identical with that used for product-related activities. However, the units of measure and the associated sensors are mainly financial and statistical rather than technological. In addition, evaluation for these activities tends to require human sensing to a significant degree. Because of error-proneness of human sensing, special precautions should be taken, as set out in Table 21.4.

The administrative and support departments have made extensive use of measures of performance. Mainly these have related to cost and productivity but there are measures of quality as well. The two most widely used have been:

1. *Error rate:* Here the measure consists of a fraction in which the numerator is the number of errors, and the denominator is the number of opportunities for error. Through data summaries this fraction can be applied at any level of organization.

2. *Promptness of service:* The usual units of measure have been either (*a*) time required to provide service, or (*b*) percent of delivery promises met. (To a recipient of service, promptness is a major quality requirement.)

TABLE 21.4 Human Error Types and Remedies

Error types	Remedies
Misinterpretation	Precise definition; glossary Check lists Examples
Inadvertent errors	Aptitude testing Reorganization of work to reduce fatigue and monotony Fail-safe designs Redundancy Foolproofing (error-proofing) Automation, robotics
Lack of technique	Discovery of knack of successful workers Revision of technology to incorporate the knack Retraining
Conscious errors: coloration, bias, futility	Design review of data collection plan Remove atmosphere of blame Act on reports, or give explanation for no action Depersonalize the orders Establish accountability Provide balanced emphasis on goals Conduct quality audits Create competition, incentives Reassign the work

There is considerable need for development of further units of measure in the administrative and support area. Generally the approach is to ask those who will be impacted to propose nominations on how to measure quality. Reports are then prepared and published in response to the nominations. Those reports which seem to be useful are retained and improved. The rest are discarded.

QUALITY IMPROVEMENT IN ADMINISTRATIVE AND SUPPORT ACTIVITIES

The general approach to quality improvement is set out in Section 22, Quality Improvement. This approach is fully applicable to administrative and support activities.

Historically, most quality improvement was directed at product-related activities. However, with the emergence of the quality crisis in the late 1970s, many companies began to expand their efforts to improve quality. This expansion was at first limited to product-related activities. It has since been extended to include administrative and support activities as well. This trend seems to be irreversible.

Two examples of application can be seen in the materials handling function.

1. An apparatus manufacturer used a large amount of steel. Because of a shortage of covered storage space, much steel was stored in an uncovered yard. Before

being placed in open storage, the steel was treated with a rust preservative. However, there was much rusting since the materials handlers had no way of applying a first-in, first-out method of stock rotation. The support department (Materials Management) met all criticisms with a demand for more covered storage space. However, a quality improvement project uncovered an alternative solution by periodically changing the color of the rust preservative to enable the materials handlers to rotate the stock.

2. A team study of causes of poor customer service established that a prime cause was loss of product identification which in turn was caused by the pulling off, in transit, of the tickets which were wired to the pans. Following tryout of several alternatives, this long-standing method was replaced by use of self-adhesive clear plastic envelopes.

The action needed is an application of the breakthrough sequence (see Section 22 under The Universal Sequence for Breakthrough). It is particularly important to establish proof of the need for quality improvement. A useful starting point is to estimate the cost of poor quality in the administrative and support activities. Higgins and Dice (1984) describe a computer-assisted technique for analyzing and quantifying the time spent in administrative activities. Such analysis can help to estimate the cost of poor quality.

Tools of Diagnosis.   Reported case examples of quality improvement in administrative and support areas show that the tools of diagnosis are identical with those used in product-oriented quality improvement projects.

Pareto Analysis.   The Pareto concept is discussed in Section 22 under The Project Concept. Table 21.5 shows an analysis of the time spent performing various tasks in a finance function (Witterick, 1983). The Pareto analysis shows that of the 15 tasks, the top four account for 48 percent of the total time spent. (These tasks then become candidates for automation.) Surprisingly, the traditional function of typing consumed the least amount of personal time.

Another application of the Pareto concept comes from a study of paperwork problems in a receiving department. The Pareto analysis appears in graphic form

TABLE 21.5   Functional Analysis

Task	Percent of personal time	Cumulative percent
Forms and invoices	19	19
Planning	11	30
Writing	9	39
Arithmetic	9	48
Informal discussion	8	56
Reading	8	64
Local telephone calls	6	70
Data entry	5	75
Filing	5	80
Remote telephone calls	5	85
Formal meetings	5	90
Systems activity	4	94
Word processing	3	97
Photocopying	2	99
Typing	1	100

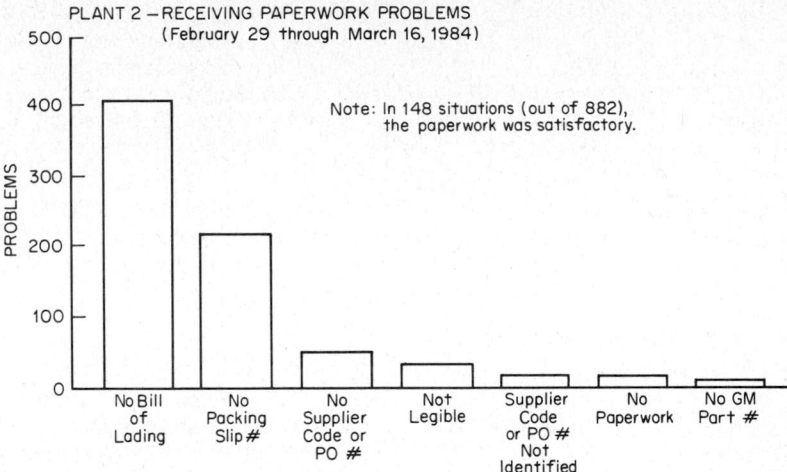

FIG. 21.4 Pareto chart. *(Courtesy General Motors.)*

in Figure 21.4 (General Motors, 1984). Missing bill of lading and packing slips are the main symptoms.

Cause-and-Effect Diagram. The cause-and-effect diagram is described in Section 22 under Generation of Theories. Figure 21.5 shows the cause-and-effect diagram for the problem of analyzing delays in filling open personnel requisitions. This diagram helped to raise a question about the time taken by hiring managers to review and return resumés. Data collection and dissection of the process

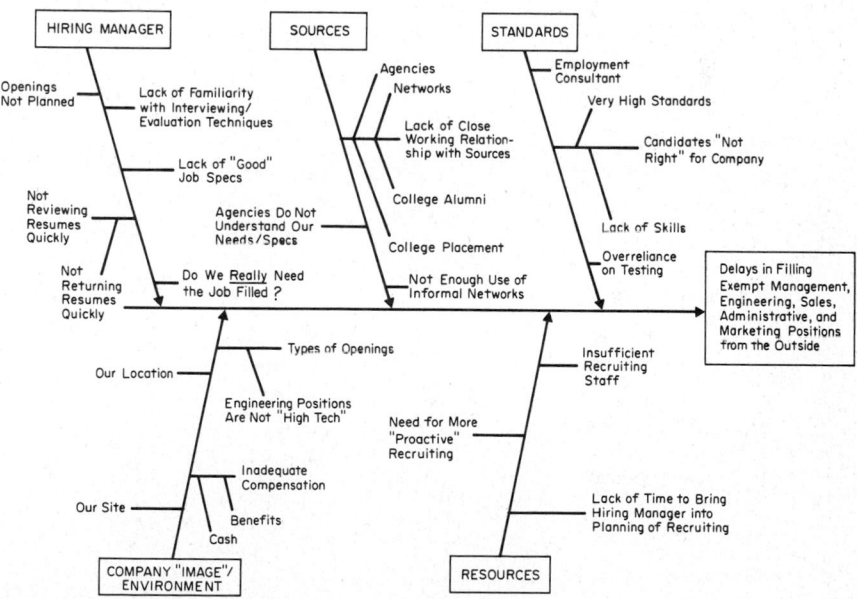

FIG. 21.5 Cause-and-effect diagram for filling positions.

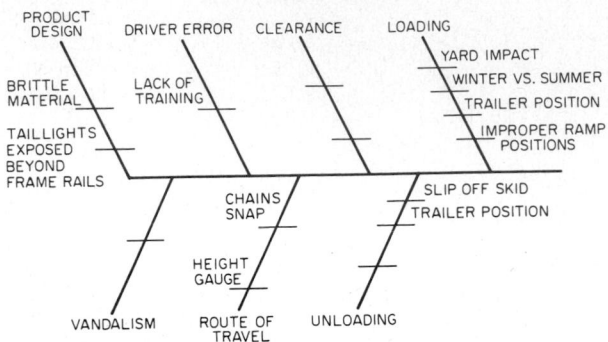

VEHICLE TRANSPORTATION DAMAGE
SOURCES OF PROBLEMS
1-TON TAILLIGHT DAMAGE

FIG. 21.6 Cause-and-effect diagram for transportation damage. *(Courtesy General Motors.)*

answered the question. Also, the diagram made clear that the process included a variety of inputs and the existence of subjective elements such as standards, applicant's perception of the company image, and the organizational environment or climate.

Another example (General Motors, 1984) of a cause-and-effect diagram is related to the transportation of product from the plant to the customer (Figure 21.6). The problem was damage to taillights during transportation of 1-ton trucks. Of course the theories shown in the diagram remain to be tested through data collection and analysis.

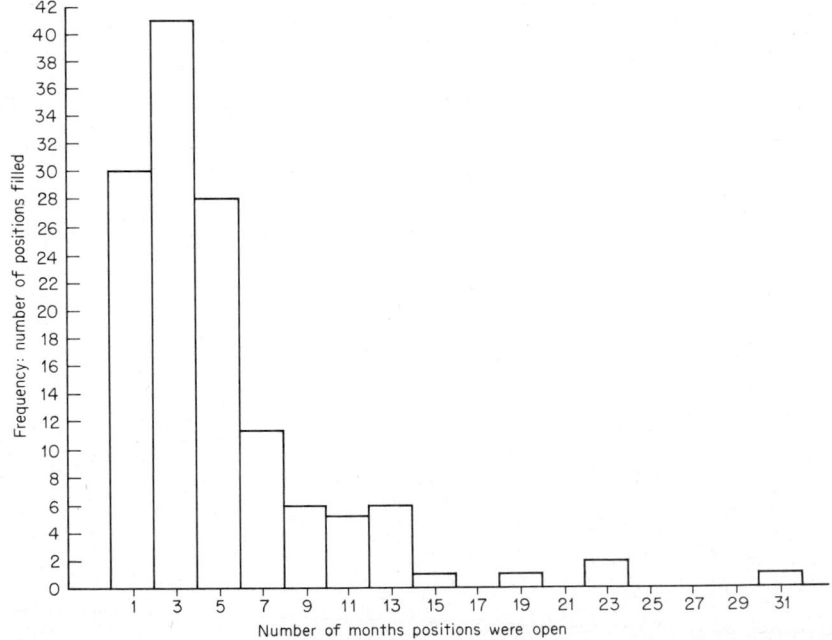

FIG. 21.7   Histogram of time to fill positions.   *(From Leonard, p. 13.)*

Frequency Distribution and Histogram. Section 23 under Descriptive Statistics for Summarizing Data discusses the Frequency Distribution and Histogram. In an application to a personnel function, data collected on the time required to fill open personnel requisitions were summarized in a histogram (Figure 21.7). Analysis showed that the average time was about 5 months, the range was about 30 months, and 75 percent of the 132 filled positions were filled within 6 months or less.

Dissection of a Process. Dissection of a process into steps is presented in Section 22 under Product and Process Dissection. Applying this concept to the study of the time required to fill personnel requisitions resulted in some surprises. In Figure 21.8, a sample of data for 24 hirees is analyzed by breaking the total processing

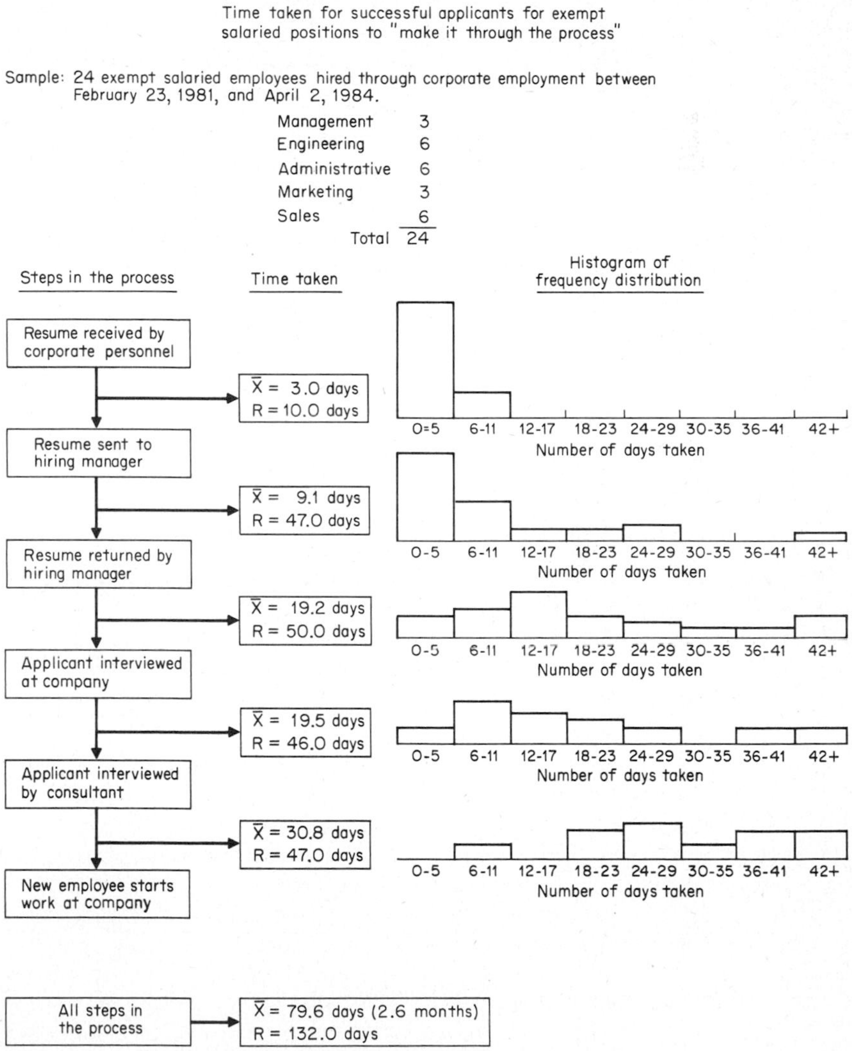

FIG. 21.8 Dissection of process for filling positions. *(From Leonard, p. 15.)*

time down into its component steps. This dissection of the total time led to several important conclusions:

1. Of the total time to fill requisitions (an average of 5.02 months), more than half (2.6 months) is spent moving the successful applicant through the *internal* company process of interviewing and decision making. Thus, to reduce the overall time to fill positions, two problems had to be addressed—the time to find the right resumé or person, and the time to move that person through the rest of the process.

2. The 30.8 days average time between the consultant interview and a new employee starting work is misleading. This number includes time over which the company had no control, i.e., the notice that people give to a former employer before leaving, and vacation time between jobs.

3. Some people take significantly longer than others to make it through the process.

Dissection of the problem into steps and the quantification at each step provided constructive information to replace the unsubstantiated beliefs, some of which turned out to be false.

Statistical Control Chart.   Section 24, Statistical Process Control, explains the concept of the control chart. Baker and Artinian (1985) describe how control charts analyzed a system for auditing freight bills and making payments to the external carrier. Audits of freight bills revealed many errors which then caused delays in making payments. As one part of a study, data were collected on the time from receipt of a freight invoice to issuance of the check to the carrier. An average and range chart (Figure 21.9) showed the system to be in statistical con-

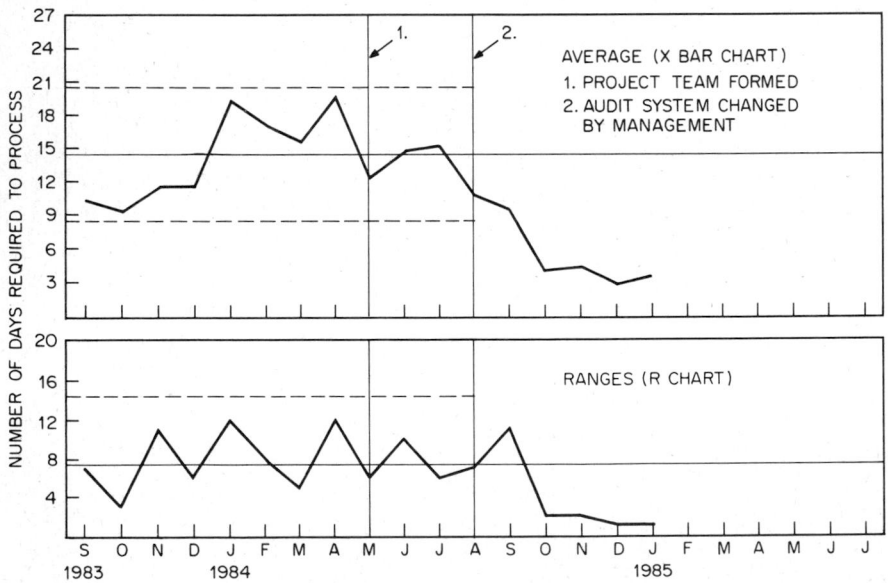

FIG. 21.9 Control charts for time required to process bills. *(Courtesy Baker and Artinian, 1985.)*

trol but at a level that was too high—an average of about 14 days. (When combined with mail delays and other factors, some carriers would wait for at least 35 days for payment.)

With the knowledge that the process was in statistical control, attention was directed to analyzing the system itself. Using a cause-and-effect diagram, the major reasons for rejection of freight bills were identified. Further analysis resulted in changes in the steps to audit bills and make payments. Results were dramatic: Bills rejected were reduced from 34 percent to under 1 percent; time required to process bills dropped from an average of 15 days to 6 days with an associated reduction in variation (Figure 21.9).

McCabe (1985) presents applications of control charts to employee communications, employee medical examinations, purchase orders, and office rearrangements. Control charts as an aid in improving the quality of data collection and review for price index preparation is discussed by Dmytrow (1985).

Sampling. Sampling is widely employed in administrative and support activities. The resulting data are used in all managerial processes, quality planning, control, and improvement. Great strides have been made in conducting sampling in accordance with valid statistical methodology as discussed in Sections 23, 24, and 25 of this handbook.

Glasser (1985) provides a detailed discussion of statistical sampling concepts applied to paperwork operations. The American Institute of Certified Public Accountants (1986) provides step-by-step procedures for financial auditing.

Reliability Engineering Tools. A collection of reliability engineering tools, both quantitative and qualitative, is presented in this handbook. (See Section 13 under Planning for Time-Oriented Performance and Section 23 under Reliability.) These tools were originally developed to evaluate reliability during design and to measure reliability during use by the customer.

A major application to administrative and support activities is in the area of facilities maintenance. Nowlan and Heap (1978) present an uncommonly comprehensive discussion of use of reliability models and other tools to improve quality and productivity in aircraft maintenance. The concepts are applicable to maintenance of any type of product or facility.

Another application is in purchase of facilities. Administrative and support areas are purchasers and users of a variety of equipment including plant facilities, materials handling equipment, computers, and office equipment. Many of these items are relatively complex and involve a considerable investment. Opportunities exist to apply reliability engineering methods during the selection, specification, and usage phases for these equipments.

ORGANIZING THE ADMINISTRATIVE AND SUPPORT QUALITY ACTIVITIES

Administrative and support quality activities are carried out by a variety of company departments, outside suppliers, and after-sales service companies. These organizations pursue their departmental or company goals, including quality goals. However, they are often handicapped in meeting their goals because of limitations in organization structure. A widespread such limitation relates to participation in broad quality planning.

Participation in Planning. Administrative and support activities do conduct departmental planning for their assigned functions. However, because of their seeming detachment from the "mainstream" of product-oriented operations, there is often a failure to plan for the interaction of administrative and support activities with the activities of other departments. For example, during the launching of a new product the Customer Service Department may be brought into the picture only after the product and process have been designed, and production has commenced. In such cases the failure to provide Customer Service with participation in the planning will result in a failure to provide early warning of problems ahead. The resulting quality problems become after-the-fact crises.

An organized approach to orchestration can consist of:

1. Identification of those aspects of the work of administrative and support operations which significantly affect product quality. This identification can logically be done by a study team which includes the support department and the Quality Department.
2. Coordination of these significant operations through a well-known table of delegation:

Activity	Role of support organization	Role of quality department
Quality planning	X	X
Execution of plan	X	
Audit of execution versus plan		X

Such an approach retains for the administrative and support activities their jurisdiction over their day-to-day operations. Orchestration is provided through the joint planning and through the audit.

Provision for Diagnosis. The administrative and support departments commonly lack specialists in problem analysis. Hence, this analysis must be done by the supervision or by outside staff specialists. A progressive step is to enlist the service of the quality staff specialists for diagnosis of chronic quality troubles.

REFERENCES

American Institute of Certified Public Accountants (1986). *Codification of Statements on Auditing Standards.* AICPA, New York.

Baker, Edward M. and Artinian, Harry L. (1985). "The Deming Philosophy of Continuing Improvement in a Service Organization: The Case of Windsor Export Supply." *Quality Progress,* June, pp. 61–69.

Dmytrow, Eric D. (1985). "Process Capability in the Service Sector." *The Juran Report,* no. 5, summer, pp. 31–37.

General Motors Corporation (1984). Internal document of Truck and Bus Division.

Glasser, Gerald J. (1985). "Quality Audits of Paperwork Operations—The First Step toward Quality Control." *Journal of Quality Technology,* vol. 17, no. 2, April, pp. 100–107.

Higgins, Brian K. and Dice, Christopher, M. (1984). "Quantifying White Collar Functions." *National Productivity Review,* summer, pp. 288–302.

IBM Corporation (1984). *IBM FSD Owego Excellence Plus Manual.* Owego, NY, pp. VIII–9 to 15.

International Paper Company (1984). *Quality Management Concepts,* section on CTQ Flow Charting. IPCO, New York.

Latzko, William J. (1985). "Process Capability in Administrative Applications." *ASQC Quality Congress Transactions,* Milwaukee, pp. 168–173.

McCabe, William J. (1985). "A Service Organization Improved Quality and Cut Costs at the Same Time." *Quality Progress,* June, pp. 85–89.

Melan, E. H. (1985). "Process Management in Service and Administrative Operations." *Quality Progress,* June, pp. 52–59.

Nowlan, F. Stanley and Heap, Howard F. (1978). *Reliability-Centered Maintenance.* Catalog no. ADA 066579, National Technical Information Service, Springfield, VA 22161.

Witterick, Leonard W. (1983). "Juran Training in the Financial Area." *The Juran Report,* no. 2, November, pp. 82–86.

SECTION 22
QUALITY IMPROVEMENT[1]

Frank M. Gryna

INTRODUCTION **22.2**

Fire Fighting versus
Improvement 22.3

EXPERIENCE WITH PRIOR
IMPROVEMENT PROGRAMS . . **22.4**

"Here Comes Another
One" 22.4

Lack of Upper Management
Involvement 22.5

No Organized Approach . . 22.5

Increased Workload . . . 22.5

No Provision for Reward . 22.5

SPORADIC AND CHRONIC
PROBLEMS **22.5**

THE PHASED APPROACH . . . **22.6**

Awareness 22.6

Setting Goals 22.7

Organizing the Overall
Program 22.7

Training 22.9

Projects 22.9

Progress Reports 22.9

Recognition 22.10

Communication 22.10

Scoreboards 22.10

Institutionalizing the
Annual Improvement
Process 22.10

Alternative Approaches to
Improvement 22.11

THE UNIVERSAL SEQUENCE FOR
BREAKTHROUGH **22.12**

PROOF OF THE NEED **22.13**

A Potential or Real Loss in
Sales Revenue 22.13

Opportunity for Major Cost
Savings 22.14

Other Forms of Proof of the
Need 22.18

THE PROJECT CONCEPT . . . **22.18**

The Pareto Principle . . . 22.19

Nominations for
Projects 22.22

Screening Nominations
and Establishing
Priorities 22.23

The Number of Projects in
a Quality Improvement
Program 22.26

ORGANIZING FOR PROJECTS . **22.26**

The Project Team 22.26

Principal Roles on Project
Teams 22.28

Responsibility for
Diagnosis 22.29

Responsibility for
Troubleshooting 22.31

---

[1]In the Third Edition, the section on Quality Improvement was prepared by J. M. Juran.

DIAGNOSIS—GENERAL 22.31

Diagnosis of Failures in
Broad Systems 22.32

Diagnosis for Improvement
Projects 22.33

ANALYSIS OF SYMPTOMS . . .**22.35**

Description of Symptoms . 22.35

Autopsies 22.35

Data Recording Methods . 22.35

Quantification of
Symptoms 22.35

FORMULATION OF THEORIES . .**22.36**

Generation of Theories . . 22.36

Arrangement of Theories . 22.37

Choosing Theories to be
Tested 22.40

**TEST OF THEORIES OF
MANAGEMENT-CONTROLLABLE
PROBLEMS** **22.40**

Product and Process
Dissection 22.41

Test of Theories by
Collection of New Data
("Cutting New Windows
in a Process") 22.50

Diagnosis through
Experiment 22.51

Measurement for Diagnosis 22.52

**TEST OF THEORIES OF
WORKER-CONTROLLABLE
PROBLEMS** **22.53**

Tools of Analysis 22.54

Inadvertent Errors 22.55

Technique Errors 22.56

Conscious Errors 22.59

DEVELOPMENT OF REMEDIES .**22.61**

Choice of Alternatives . . . 22.61

Remedial Action 22.62

PROOF OF THE REMEDIES . . .**22.65**

RESISTANCE TO CHANGE . . .**22.65**

Cultural Patterns 22.65

Analyzing the Impact of
Change 22.66

Rules of the Road for
Introducing Change . . . 22.66

Resolving Differences . . . 22.68

**CONTROL AT THE NEW
LEVEL** **22.68**

Transfer from "Laboratory"
to Operations 22.68

Concept of Control 22.69

TROUBLESHOOTING **22.70**

Product Comparisons
to Discover the
Change 22.70

Reconstructing the
Chronology 22.70

Testing the Theories . . . 22.70

Structured Procedure for
Troubleshooting 22.71

Corrective Action 22.71

REFERENCES **22.72**

INTRODUCTION

"Improvement" as used in this section is the attainment of a new level of performance that is superior to any previous level. This superiority is attained by applying the breakthrough concept to problems of quality.

Other sections of the handbook provide important supplementary material for this section. For example, see all of the sections presenting statistical concepts (particularly Section 23, Basic Statistical Methods); Section 10, Managing Human Performance (especially discussions of the human aspects of achieving change); and Section 6, Companywide Planning for Quality, on the elements of the feedback loop that is basic to the control process. Elaboration of the role of upper management in quality improvement is covered in Section 5 under Policies on Improvement and in Section 8 under Participation by Upper Management and also under Quality Audits by Upper Managers.

Quality improvement encompasses both improving fitness for use and reducing the level of defects or errors. Both of these activities apply to all customers— internal and external. Improving fitness for use can have some important benefits:

Better quality for the users

Higher market share for the manufacturer

Premium price for the manufacturer

Status in the marketplace for the manufacturer

Reducing the level of defects and errors also provides multiple benefits:

Lower costs and fewer irritations for users

Dramatically lower costs for the manufacturer

Improved productivity; more useable product is produced with the same resources

Reduction in inventories to assist the just-in-time concept

These benefits are further supplemented by improved teamwork resulting from the project team concept and opportunities for worker participation on improvement projects.

Despite these obvious benefits, most organizations have traditionally conducted their affairs with limited priority on improvement. During periods of economic growth, products are saleable if they are generally competitive as to quality. The costs due to poor quality are passed on to customers in the form of higher prices.

Wolf (1983) itemizes how the advantages of improved quality, cost reduction, and improved productivity came about on 10 pilot quality improvement projects. Lossin (1983) discusses some of the side benefits of a quality improvement program.

Fire Fighting versus Improvement. "Improvement" as defined above in the introduction relates to the chronic level of poor quality as shown in Figure 22.1.

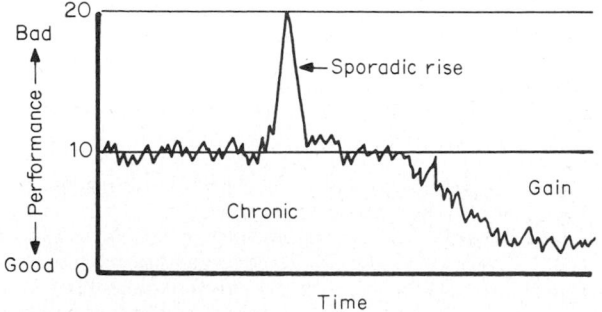

FIG. 22.1 Relation of chronic level improvement.

Figure 22.1 illustrates what is meant by quality improvement. It also brings out the critical distinction between chronic and sporadic quality problems. The figure shows one process for which the defect level regularly runs at about 10 percent. This 10 percent is the area marked "chronic." This chronic defect level goes on and on until some specific action is taken to change it—the action called quality improvement. Thus, quality improvement refers to a change in the *level* of quality.

Figure 22.1 also shows a sporadic departure from the historic level—a "spike" on the chart. This spike is the result of some sudden change in the process. The sudden rise triggers off various alarm signals. In response, the company personnel take "corrective action" to "put out the fire."

In many organizations, the word "improvement" has been considered as synonymous with "corrective action," meaning fire fighting such as getting rid of that sporadic "spike" in Figure 22.1.

EXPERIENCE WITH PRIOR IMPROVEMENT PROGRAMS

A major requirement for a quality improvement program is that it be well received by those impacted—the managers, supervisors, and the work force. This receptivity depends greatly on the history of prior programs of improvement.

Most organizations make use of periodic (annual or so) programs or drives to improve their performance. These programs aim at various targets: quality, productivity, safety, etc. When teams of managers are asked to review and critique the history of a number of such prior programs, they usually arrive at conclusions similar to those set out in Table 22.1. Peters (1983) discusses some of the reasons for success and potential weaknesses in a quality improvement program in a plant manufacturing an automobile component. Holm (1984) presents some "dos" and "don'ts" based on experiences in a quality improvement program at a petroleum equipment manufacturing organization.

The critiques listed in Table 22.1 point to some obstacles to achieving quality improvement.

"Here Comes Another One."   Any new "program," "drive," etc., is suspect. In all companies the personnel have seen a procession of improvement programs come and go. The subject matter has varied (e.g., safety, costs, morale, quality),

TABLE 22.1   Usual Strengths and Weaknesses of Prior Improvement Programs

Strengths	Weaknesses
Upper management was involved at the launching	Upper management did not stay involved
The visibility of the subject matter was raised	More work was demanded of all: attendance at meetings, filling out questionnaires, etc.
Educational materials and training were provided	No provision was made for doing the added work
A coordinator was appointed	The results were not as good as the advocates had promised
Means were provided for recognition	The program did not last. It was pushed aside to make room for the next program

but the features of the programs were alike. Some of the features were positive, but others were negative.

The results fell short of the promises of the advocates, and each program was pushed off center stage by the next program.

These and other negatives create an ever-growing crust of skepticism, so that a new program may be greeted with a cynical "Here comes another one." At the outset the new program is suspected of guilt by association.

Lack of Upper Management Involvement.   Upper managers would like to avoid getting deeply involved into yet another problem. Hence they are tempted to delegate quality improvement to subordinates. However, the subordinate managers are guided more by the actions of upper managers than by their words. If the upper managers do not become actively involved, the subordinates conclude that upper management does not give high priority to quality improvement.

No Organized Approach.   Most companies do not realize that to attain annual quality improvement requires a comprehensive and organized approach. Lacking that knowledge, they conclude that one or another of the roads (see below) constitutes a total solution.

Increased Workload.   To secure annual improvement at a revolutionary pace adds to every participant's workload. The return on investment is remarkable. (It also will in due course reduce the time spent in fire fighting.) However, the investment in added work must precede the return on investment. Persuading upper managers to make that investment has been a serious obstacle.

No Provision for Reward.   All operating managers have long had clear responsibility for meeting *operating* goals, including quality goals but not including quality *improvement* goals. The resulting legitimacy gives those operating goals a first claim on the time of the operating managers. The prevailing reward systems make little or no provision for rewarding efforts devoted to annual quality improvement.

SPORADIC AND CHRONIC PROBLEMS

Basic to the success of a quality improvement program is the distinction between chronic and sporadic quality problems (see Figure 22.1). Most of the time, the quality performance stays within a rather narrow range. However, occasionally the performance departs greatly from the historic level and results in a spike on the chart. These occasional departures from the usual level are "sporadic" quality problems. For example, if the percent defective has been averaging about 10 percent and suddenly jumps to 20 percent, a variety of alarm signals go off. In response, the supervision converges on the scene, investigates, finds out what has changed, and restores performance to the regular 10 percent. The names given to this action are "fire fighting" or "troubleshooting." This activity of restoring the status quo is not the basic kind of improvement to be emphasized in this section. (It will, however, be mentioned later in the section.)

Suppose it is desired to reduce the regular level of 10 percent defective down to 3 percent. This is a "chronic" quality problem because the 10 percent level has existed for a long time. Changing the chronic level of quality *is* the object of this section.

The action taken on the chronic problem is different from that taken on the sporadic. Because the chronic problem has existed for some time, it is often concluded, with reluctance, that the 10 percent level must be lived with and accepted. Several actions may be taken to condone and make this level legitimate: e.g., order an extra 10 percent of material so that despite the 10 percent waste enough good product will be available to meet delivery schedules.

The "regular" continuing 10 percent defect level involves far more money than the amount under the spike. Why is it then that industrial companies do not attack these chronic losses? The reasons are usually because:

1. The chronic losses do not sound any alarms; the alarm signals were disconnected long ago by building waste allowances into cost and other standards.
2. The competitors are usually also enduring the same losses. When such is the case, it is feasible to price the product so as to cover the losses.
3. Managers are unaware that solutions to chronic problems require a special series of managerial actions, each series centered around a specific improvement project. The project approach (discussed below) requires an investment of the time of management and professional personnel. Lacking such an investment, no improvement will happen; the chronic losses will go on and on.

In most companies the response to sporadic quality problems is excellent. Managers and specialists are experienced, effective fire fighters. What is missing is fire prevention—an attack on the chronic levels of waste. These two activities— fire fighting and fire prevention—are remarkably different in their nature. That difference requires a fundamentally different approach to tackle the major opportunity for improvement, i.e., chronic problems.

THE PHASED APPROACH

This "phased approach" describes the sequence of activities (phases) evolved by those companies who have made the most progress toward annual quality improvement.

Awareness. Awareness is the phase of convincing managers that there is a need to do something different with respect to quality. This conviction is secured by a mixture of:

Citing case examples of loss of sales due to poor quality

Citing case examples in which quality improvement also resulted in cost reduction, improved on-time delivery, higher productivity, etc.

Estimating the cost of poor quality to dramatize the opportunities for further cost reduction

Explaining the opportunities for increasing share of market, or for securing premium prices through quality leadership

Dramatizing the crisis atmosphere resulting from foreign competition

(Further elaboration relative to this phase is provided below under Proof of the Need.)

Setting Goals. The actual goals chosen by companies vary widely. Here are some of the more popular goals:

Quality is number one: There are meanings lurking behind this popular statement. Quite often the number one priority in the company has not been quality; it has been delivery date, or whatever. A major reason behind publicizing "quality is number one" is to announce a change in priority without admitting that it is a change.

Cut the cost of poor quality: This popular goal is sometimes quantified, e.g., "We will cut the cost of poor quality by 50 percent in the next 3 years."

Quality leadership in the marketplace: This is also a frequent goal. It is worded variously. An example from the electronics industry is: "New products may be put on the market only if their reliability is superior to that of competition."

Not limited to manufacture: We are in the early stages of a healthy movement to extend the concept of quality improvement to all the company's functions—not just manufacture. Some of the wordings of goals provide for this extension, e.g., "Quality applies to everything we do—to all of our functions and to every person's job."

No goals: An astonishing number of companies do not set out specific quality goals to be reached. Instead, they adopt some new approach in the hope that it will take them to better results. Most of the time, such hopes are not realized.

Organizing the Overall Program. The project-by-project approach to improvement requires not only the support but the involvement (through hands-on leadership) of upper management. A major form of this involvement is through a "quality improvement council."

Quality Improvement Council. A quality improvement council is a group of upper managers appointed to guide, support, and coordinate the overall program. Such councils may be established at several levels—corporate, division, function, plant. Examples are discussed by Douglas (1984), Noakes (1984), and Woodward (1984). For any level, membership consists of upper managers—the manager in charge plus selected line and staff managers.

Each such council should prepare a mission statement to define its responsibilities. The following list combines extracts from various published mission statements:

Formulate quality policy: For example, quality has top priority; we must improve annually; all must participate; quality will affect merit rating.

Estimate major dimensions: For example, quality versus competition, cost of poor quality, effectiveness of new product launchings, return on investment from prior improvements.

Establish a project system: Solicit nominations; screen; choose projects; appoint project teams. Set responsibilities for carrying out projects: define team charter; assign responsibility for appointing facilitators, team members, and team leaders.

Identify needs for training: For example, in the improvement process, problem solving, team building, group dynamics, participation, others.

Identify the trainees: Facilitators, team leaders, team members, others.

Plan the training: Curricula, course modules, sources of materials, sources of trainers, budget, schedule.

Establish support for teams: Time to work on projects, diagnostic "leg work," staff diagnostic support, facilities for tryouts, facilities for test, help over obstacles.

Provide for coordination: Meetings of facilitators, meetings of team leaders, project progress reports, reviews by higher levels.

Establish new measures: For progress on improvement, product performance, managers' performance.

Revise merit rating for managers to reflect: Quality of operations, improvement in quality.

Design plan for recognition: Establish recognition for assignments carried out, completion of training, service as facilitator, completion of improvement project.

Establish plan for publicity using various media: Bulletin boards, TV, and radio.

Recommended roles for upper management: Recommendations have included some or many of the following:

Review, approve policy.

Authorize the infrastructure: quality councils, project system, assignment of roles and responsibilities, training program, support for improvement teams, plan for coordination, plan for publicity.

Review and approve revisions in scoreboards on quality and in the merit rating system.

Review progress reports.

Hear final project team reports.

Participate in improvement projects.

Participate in training.

Each company must prepare its own list or lists. (The items on the above list would typically require two or more councils at different levels.)

Upper Management Leadership.   There is unanimous agreement that a company's approach to annual quality improvement is greatly aided if upper management is "involved." Here is a summary of experience with the principal forms of upper management involvement.

Approve the Phased Approach.   All upper managers want the benefits of annual quality improvement. However, not all of them are convinced that this or that road will lead them to those benefits. All can point to past experiences in which equally plausible proposals have ended in failure. The resulting skepticism makes upper managers reluctant to make broad commitments until they are convinced that the proposed road really leads to good results. To provide that conviction prior to proof of good results requires "selling" through means such as were discussed above under the heading Awareness.

Provide Support.   Feedback from companies have made it clear that in approving a broad, phased approach, upper managers are selective in their support for the individual activities. The most ready approval is for those activities which can be carried out without adding people to the payroll. Support for training programs also tends to be positive.

To go fully to annual improvement adds from 5 to 10 percent to the workload of all members of the management team. This means that priorities on other activities must be changed or people must be added to the payroll.

Serve on Councils.   In a gratifying number of companies the upper managers do serve on the high-level councils. There should be no hesitancy in proposing to upper managers that they preside over the high-level quality councils. The wide prevalence of this arrangement suggests that most of such proposals meet with a favorable reception.

Serve on the Project Teams.   The benefits are:

1. Setting an example for others to follow. A project team consisting of upper managers working on a problem appropriate for their level provides strong evidence of their committment to the improvement process.

2. Enabling upper managers to learn what the realities faced by subordinates are when *they* tackle projects: the added workload; the calendar time required to complete a project (about 4 to 6 months); the ingredients of project completion—persistent analysis and work, not slogans and exhortation.

3. Creating a capacity for solving those projects which cannot be solved without upper management participation. An example is a revision of quality policy on relations with suppliers.

Review Progress.   Through such reviews upper management can remain informed as to progress on quality improvement, and can take action as needed. Such reviews also show the rest of the organization that upper management places a high priority on quality.

Revise the Merit Rating System.   Merit rating of operating managers has traditionally been keyed to performance against cost and schedule goals. When a company introduces the concept of annual quality improvement, the scoreboards for evaluating managers must be changed to eliminate any doubt about the relative priority on quality.

Training.   To go into annual quality improvement is to create a new function in the company. This function assigns new roles to every member of the management team, roles such as member of a quality council; project team chairman, secretary, or member; and facilitator. To carry out these new roles requires training in concepts, skills, and tools such as the quality improvement process, the special tools of quality analysis, team building, etc. See, in this connection, Section 11 under Training for Quality Improvement.

Projects.   A structured project approach for pursuing the chronic quality problems is discussed later in this section.

Progress Reports.   During the progression of any improvement project it is important to maintain a discipline—a form of neat housekeeping—by preparing regular written progress reports. These reports serve several essential purposes:

To assure that within the project team itself there is really a meeting of the minds as to what has happened and as to the plans for the future

To keep other managers informed—those managers who are not part of the project team but who "have a need to know"; e.g., they are being asked to act on a recommendation, they are in a position to help the project get over an obstacle, etc.

To provide input to the overall evaluation of the company's approach to annual quality improvement, in order to enable the upper managers to judge effectiveness and to make revisions

The project reports are normally drafted by the project team secretary and are reviewed by the project team chair before publication.

Recognition.   Companies have evolved numerous forms of recognition to provide incentives and rewards for activities related to annual quality improvement. For example:

Certificates, placques, etc., are awarded for service as facilitator, completion of training courses, service on project teams.

Project teams present their final report in the office of the ranking local manager.

Project summaries are published in the company news media, along with team pictures.

Dinners are held to honor project teams.

These and other forms of recognition supply "reinforcement" to all.

Communication.   Good communication is another essential aspect of annual quality improvement. The most common subjects of communication used by participating companies include:

Summaries of completed projects: These have a profound impact. Their flavor of reality adds credibility to the training materials and to the associated improvement goals.

Human interest stories: These deal with the individuals behind the projects, their families, their work environment. Photos are welcomed.

News: This covers a wide range: letters from clients, visits from important personages, activities in progress, scoreboards.

The media of communication are varied and include newsletters, bulletin boards, the local press, letters to employee homes, posters, and video cassettes.

Scoreboards.   Scoreboards take several forms:

1. Progress on *individual* improvement projects.
2. Progress on projects *collectively.*
3. *Merit rating of individuals* with respect to quality improvement. There is no debate on the need for revising the merit rating system to include performance on quality improvement. Failure to do so seriously weakens the priority of quality improvement.

Companywide measures on quality performance include in-house technological measures (yield, percent defective), cost of poor quality, field performance of products, quality versus competition, and quality of nonmanufacturing processes. For an elaboration, see Section 6, particularly Table 6.4.

Institutionalizing the Annual Improvement Process.   Many companies have for years conducted annual improvement programs. Examples of such programs are new product development, cost reduction, and productivity improvement.

All of these have featured formal projects, goals, budgets, reviews, and rewards based on the merit rating. This formality has been embodied into business planning. Based on this history, institutionalizing quality improvement requires similar features.

All companies encounter difficulties when they try to institutionalize quality improvement so that it goes on year after year. The main difficulty is that the work needed to make quality improvements interferes with the "regular" job of managers (to meet the current goals for quality, cost, schedule, etc.). The solution is to make quality improvement a part of the regular job of the managers. Various methods have been tested for doing this. The most effective has been to include quality improvement in the annual business plan. Another method is to revise the system of merit rating of managers to put high priority on quality improvement.

A realization of the need to integrate quality improvement into annual business planning is described by a vice-president of manufacturing for an electronics company. Each year, he personally chairs a meeting to discuss next year's cost-reduction program. Potential cost-reduction projects for achieving labor savings are evaluated by discussing both the expected savings and the resources required. By the end of the meeting, he has decided which projects will be pursued, assigned resources to each project, and identified an individual to oversee each project. This is a routine meeting that is part of the overall business planning for the manufacturing function. In contrast, he admitted that no such meeting is held with respect to tackling the chronic quality problems. (It will in the future.)

The foregoing phased approach outlines the broad steps that must be taken to achieve a breakthrough in quality. Fundamental to the approach is the use of projects that are pursued in an organized series of steps (see below under The Universal Sequence for Breakthrough). But first we will consider some alternative approaches to the improvement process.

Alternative Approaches to Improvement. Companies have been testing out a wide variety of roads to quality improvement.

Quality Circles. The concept is one of setting up and training voluntary teams of workers to solve problems within their own department (see Section 10 under Quality Circles: Processes, Tools, Administration). Successful circles have done just that and have improved human relations as well. Circles alone cannot possibly solve the company's quality problems, since the major problems are multidepartmental and require the participation of management and professional personnel. (Of course, workers have an essential role in achieving quality objectives. This role includes handling much of the troubleshooting for processes, helping to identify chronic problems, participating in project teams, and reviewing proposed process plans.)

Statistical Quality Control (SQC). The concept here is to employ the tools of statistics to solve quality problems. A subspecies of SQC—"statistical process control" (SPC)—has been intensely applied in certain industries and clearly has made a significant contribution. (See Section 24, Statistical Process Control.) However, many managers feel that preoccupation with the tools is leading into uneconomic applications and is diverting attention from the major goals. (This actually happened in an earlier wave of SQC during the 1950s and 1960s.)

Exhortation. Many upper managers have opted for a road which can properly be called "exhortation only." This road consists of using skillful propaganda to arouse awareness among subordinates that quality is important. This is an important first step in a program, but it does not provide organizational machinery to tackle the long-standing complex quality problems. Further, it does not provide a specific answer to the questions "What do you want me to do differently?"

Some upper managers embrace the exhortation approach because of their lack of experience in quality matters. Further, any approach that avoids adding to their own workload is attractive.

Whatever the reasons, the upper managers are generally unaware of how the exhortation approach is perceived by those on the receiving end. Many of those perceptions are not at all flattering. Upper managers are well advised to take soundings on such perceptions before going into the exhortation approach.

Quantify Quality Costs. This concept is one of expanding the company's accounting system so that it regularly quantifies the cost of poor quality, plus other quality-related costs (see Section 4, Quality Costs). To carry out this expansion takes from 1 to 3 years, and a good deal of effort. The final result is a useful aid to problem identification and managerial decision making, but it is not indispensable. It is possible, by estimates, to get adequate information in much shorter time and with much less effort. In any event, the reporting of quality costs is not sufficient. What is also necessary is the machinery to diagnose and find remedies for the problems identified.

Job Self-Analysis. In this approach, employees (in many functions and many levels) undertake to identify their own customers both outside and inside the company. An analysis then determines if the customer needs are being met. The opportunity for problem identification is obvious; the means for remedy is less obvious. In addition, job self-analysis is inherently limited to analysis of intradepartmental problems. Experience with this approach has been insufficient to support any firm conclusions.

Every one of the roads discussed above (and others) can make a useful contribution to quality improvement. The fatal mistake, however, is to assume that one of these alternatives by itself can achieve a major and lasting change in the level of quality. The project-by-project approach to improvement (discussed below) incorporates most of these alternatives (and others) and has shown the most promise. Doran (1985) describes how an electronics manufacturing facility combined the project approach with statistical quality control, quality circles, process analysis, and departmental analysis to achieve a fivefold improvement in output quality over 4 years.

THE UNIVERSAL SEQUENCE FOR BREAKTHROUGH

Study of numerous cases of breakthrough has disclosed that they follow a universal sequence of events:

Proof of the need
Project identification
Organization to guide the projects
Organization for diagnosis—for analysis of projects
Diagnosis—to find the causes
Development of remedies—based on knowledge of the causes
Proof of the remedies—under operating conditions
Dealing with the cultural resistance to change
Control at the new level

TABLE 22.2 Census of Company Practices in Quality Improvement (United States)

Elements of quality improvement	Percent of responses			
	Strong	Adequate	Weak	No opinion
Atmosphere for breakthrough activity	26	41	32	1
Proof of the need	22	48	29	1
Use of the language of management	16	47	35	2
Use of Pareto analysis	16	31	49	4
Establishment of clear priorities for projects	10	39	50	1
Clear responsibility for guiding projects	11	39	49	1
Clear responsibility for diagnosis	7	33	58	2
Use of controllability concept	6	31	56	7
Diagnostic competence	13	48	37	2
Overcoming resistance to change	8	44	47	1
Action on the findings	12	47	40	1
Control at the new level	7	46	42	5

To most people the steps in the breakthrough sequence seem obvious and logical. When they are asked, however, to critically evaluate the adequacy of execution of these steps in their organization, then the effectiveness of various companies is decidedly uneven. Table 22.2 shows the results of censuses taken in the early 1980s during courses on the management of quality control. The responses, from managers in hundreds of companies, are shown as percentages of all responses. For many of these "logical" steps the actual execution is far from satisfactory. Notice that the responses to the first three elements are more positive than the responses to the other elements. (These first three elements are concerned with developing an attitude of awareness; the remaining elements provide the machinery to solve the problems.) This suggests that for many companies, steps have been taken to create *awareness* of the quality problem, but the *machinery* to carry out a program is missing.

PROOF OF THE NEED

This step consists of convincing management that the quality problem is significant enough to require a new approach to improvement.

Experience with quality improvement programs indicates that upper management typically responds well to certain major threats and opportunities.

A Potential or Real Loss in Sales Revenue. Studies of competition with respect to quality can reveal an actual or impending disaster in the marketplace. Table 22.3 identifies, for four models of product, the suppliers to a major customer. In 1980, manufacturer G was the supplier for two of the models. By 1983,

TABLE 22.3 Suppliers to a Major Customer

Model number	1980	1981	1982	1983
1	G	G	R	R
2	R	R	R	R
3	G	G	G	R
4	T	R	R	R

its position had eroded and a competitor R had gained all of the business with that customer. Manufacturer G *was competitive* on price, delivery schedules, and product features; it was *demonstrably inferior* on quality.

An important input for proof of the need is a marketing research study to determine quality status in the marketplace *relative to competition.* See Section 12 under Competitive Evaluation by Field Studies for examples.

Opportunity for Major Cost Savings.   The costs associated with poor quality are often remarkably high and present an opportunity for major savings along with a reduction in defects sent to customers. To explain this requires talking the language of money.

The Language of Money.   The approach is to use the language of money to bring the chronic quality problems out of their hiding place and convert them into alarm signals that will stimulate action.

Table 22.4 summarizes a study on the costs of poor quality for a process industry plant. Notice how much is disclosed by this study.

TABLE 22.4 Cost of Poor Quality

Category	Amount, $	Percent of total
Internal failures	7,279,000	79.4
External failures	283,000	3.1
Appraisal	1,430,000	15.6
Prevention	170,000	1.9
	9,162,000	100.0

Order of Magnitude.   The size of the quality problem is indicated as $9.2 million per year. For this plant, that sum represented a major opportunity. (For many companies all of these costs have never before been brought together into one overall figure and been expressed on an annual basis. When this is done the result typically is a number much larger than anyone would have expected.)

The Big Chunks.   The table is dominated by the costs of internal failures— 79 percent of the total. Any major reduction in costs requires action on the internal failures.

The Modest Prevention Effort.   The tiny prevention effort (1.9 percent) reveals an opportunity. An investment in additional prevention effort directed at reducing the internal failures can yield a large return on investment in the form of lower internal failure costs.

Use of a Bellwether Project.   An even more effective way to achieve a break-through in the attitude of management is to couple the study on the cost of poor quality with a case example of a successful quality improvement project within the company. This is illustrated in the approach taken by the ABC electronics company.

The order of magnitude of some essential financial data was (in millions) as follows:

Sales	$1000
Profit	100
Stockholder's investment	500
Cost of poor quality	200

A notorious quality problem was scrap for a certain major electronic compo-nent. This scrap ran to about $9 million per year. The principal defect type was defect X, and it was costing about $3 million per year.

The company took on a project to reduce the incidence of defect X. The project was a stunning success. The cost of defect X was cut from $3 million to $1 mil-lion—an annual profit improvement of $2 million.

The investment needed to make this improvement was modest—about $0.25 million (to fine-tune the process and its controls).

Then followed an exciting extrapolation and contrast. It was estimated that extension of the improvement to the entire $200 million (cost of poor quality) could cut the total in two—a profit improvement of $100 million annually. This was 50 times the savings associated with defect X. It was further estimated that this extension would require an investment of about $20 million.

An alternative way to increase profit by $100 million was through increase in sales. This would require added sales of $1000 million, i.e., doubling the size of the company. In turn such a growth in sales would require doubling the size of the investment, i.e., an added $500 million in investment.

The contrast in investment—$500 million versus $20 million—was decisive in securing credibility for the program. The upper management proceeded to give support to expanding the program. They set up an organized approach to carry out, every year, a number of projects similar to the Bellwether Project.

The defect X project proved to the ABC company managers that they could get a big return on investment by improving quality. "It happened right here in our company." This in-house project was more convincing to results-oriented managers than any amount of lectures, books, or success stories about other companies.

Every Company Has a Bellwether Project.   In every company it is possible to identify past projects involving quality improvement and cost reduction. Some of these can serve as bellwether projects. It is also feasible to estimate the "before and after" costs for these projects. It then becomes feasible to extrapolate so as to estimate the improvement potential for the entire company. This potential can then be related to the opportunities available through alternative allocations of assets, e.g., growth in sales. Indeed, such comparisons can show that investing in quality improvement projects is the *best* business to be in.

The Several Languages of Management.   In achieving a breakthrough in attitude to establish proof of the need, we may need to present information in different languages for different levels of management. Consider the pyramid of Figure

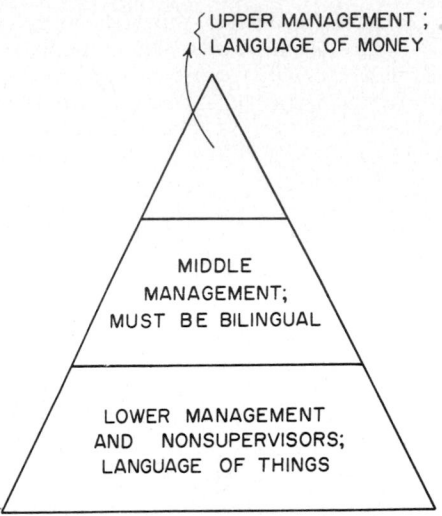

FIG. 22.2   Common languages in the company.

22.2. At the apex is the upper management—usually the general manager and the top management team. At the base are the first-line supervisors and the work force. In between are the middle managers and the specialists.

These segments of the organization use different languages, and the proof of the need must reflect this. The middle managers (and specialists) should of course understand their respective local dialects. But that is not enough. They should, in addition, understand both of the standard languages of things and money. As to these standard languages, the *middle managers should be bilingual.*

Table 22.5 shows examples of statements in money and other languages. In dealing with upper management, useful advice can be obtained from those who regularly meet with upper management on financial matters. For example, in one

TABLE 22.5   Languages of Management

Money (annual cost of poor quality)
24% of sales revenue
15% of manufacturing cost
13 cents per share of common stock
$7.5 million per year for scrap and rework compared to a profit of $1.5 million per year
$176 million per year
40% of the operating cost of a department

Other languages
The equivalent of one plant in the company making 100% defective work all year
32% of engineering resources spent in finding and correcting design weaknesses
25% of manufacturing capacity devoted to correcting quality problems
13% of sales orders canceled
70% of inventory carried attributed to poor quality levels
25% of manufacturing personnel assigned to correcting quality problems

chemical company the controller provided the key. A large part of the cost of poor quality was due to having to rework 40 percent of the batches every year. The controller reasoned as follows: If the rework could be reduced from 40 percent to 10 percent (by means of quality improvement), this would make available production capacity that was no longer needed for rework. This was significant because each year the capital budget included funds to expand the plant production capacity by about 15 percent. With a reduction in rework the controller determined that the capital expenditure for plant capacity could be completely *eliminated for a period of 2 years.* That "language" convinced management to pursue a formal program to reduce rework.

Getting the Cost Figures. The details of identifying the categories of the cost of poor quality are presented in Section 4, Quality Costs. Collecting the data takes two broad approaches.

By Estimate. This is the "quick and dirty" approach. It involves only a modest amount of effort. It can, in a few days or weeks, find out enough about quality related costs to tell us:

Whether we have a major cost reduction opportunity or not

Where this opportunity is concentrated

By Enlarging the Accounting System. This is a more elaborate approach. It requires a lot of effort from various departments, especially Accounting and Quality Control. It also takes a lot of time, running into months and even years.

In the early stages of the breakthrough sequence the estimates are good enough. They certainly involve *less work* and they provide answers in far *less time.* But how about *accuracy?*

The accuracy needed at this stage is that required for a *managerial decision:* Should we or should we not embark on a program of quality improvement and cost reduction? For such a decision the standards of accuracy are fairly loose. To illustrate, recall the process plant figure of $9.2 million of quality-related costs. That figure was an estimate. The real figure might have been as high as $11.0 million or as low as $7.5 million. Had the accuracy of the estimates been challenged, the managers' response would have been: "Every one of those three figures is too high, so let's go after the cost reduction." In other words, even over a wide range of estimate, *the managerial decisions would have been identical.*

An accuracy of ± 20 percent is adequate for such decisions.

Making Presentations to Upper Management. Experience has evolved some useful dos and don'ts:

1. *Do* summarize the total of the estimated quality costs. This summary makes clear that the total is big enough to command upper management attention.

2. *Do* show the subtotals for the broad major groupings of quality costs, where these are available. A helpful grouping is by the "categories" commonly used in "quality cost accounting" (see Table 22.4).

Note how this table shows the *fallacy of trying to start quality cost reduction by reducing inspection and test.* Typically (as in this case) most of the quality costs are associated with failures, internal and external. The proper sequence is to reduce the failure costs first. Then as the defect levels come down, we can follow through and cut the inspection costs as well.

3. *Do* describe the projects which constitute the heart of the proposed program. For such projects it is important to be bilingual—to use upper management's language of money and also the nonfinancial language of things.

4. *Do* estimate how much is to be saved by the proposed program. This estimate is mainly a buildup of the separate estimates associated with the individual projects. If the company has never before undertaken an organized program to reduce quality-related costs, then *a reasonable goal is to cut these costs in two,* within a space of 5 years.

One of the main figures in estimates of savings is return on investment. Most improvement projects involve little in costly facilities. Their investment is mainly in *analysis*. The resulting return on investment typically runs into hundreds of percent per year!

5. *Do* have the figures reviewed in advance by those people in Finance and elsewhere to whom upper management looks when questions are raised as to the validity of the numbers. It is good practice to bring such people into the estimates from the outset.

There are also some "don'ts" to be observed.

1. *Don't* inflate the present costs by including debatable or borderline items. The risk is that the decisive review meetings will get bogged down in debating the validity of the figures without ever getting to discuss the merits of the proposals for cost reduction.

2. *Don't* imply that the total quality costs can be reduced to zero. Any such implication will likewise attract the wrong kind of attention.

3. *Don't* force the first few projects on managers who are not really sold on them, or on unions that are going to oppose them. Instead, make the climate of receptivity a major parameter in choice of the first projects. It is the results obtained in the first few projects which decide whether the overall program will thrive or die.

Other Forms of Proof of the Need.   Proof of the need may also come from awareness of *new forces* which have an impact on quality. Recent examples have included product liability decisions, the consumerism movement, foreign competition, and legislation of all sorts—product safety, energy conservation, the environment.

Irrespective of the origin of the proof of the need, the approach to solution is the same—through the same universal sequence for breakthrough.

Usually the costs of poor quality *are* shockingly high. Usually something should be done about reducing them and usually it is *not* possible to reduce costs generally; we must be much more specific.

In order to become specific we make use of the project concept—identifying and tackling the specific projects which are to be the subject of the cost reduction. Project identification is the second step in the breakthrough sequence.

THE PROJECT CONCEPT

A *project* is a problem chosen for a solution; it is also a way of managerial life:

An agreed-upon project is also a legitimate project. This legitimacy puts the project on the official priority list. It helps to secure the needed budgets, facilities, and personnel. It also helps those guiding the project to secure attendance at scheduled meetings, to acquire requested data, to secure permission to conduct experiments, etc.

The project provides a forum of converting an atmosphere of defensiveness or blame into one of constructive action.

Participation in a project increases the likelihood that the participant will act on the findings.

All breakthrough is achieved *project by project,* and in no other way.

Reflections after a successful project completion often result in the question, "Why did we not solve this problem 10 years ago?" Experience suggests that the missing ingredients were the machinery for nominating and selecting projects and establishing responsibility for the diagnostic and remedial journeys (for an example, see Nester and Staal, 1986).

The Pareto Principle. As applied to the cost of poor quality, the Pareto principle states that a *few* contributors to the cost are responsible for *the bulk* of the cost. These vital few contributors need to be identified so that quality improvement resources can be concentrated in those areas.

A study of quality-related costs at a paper mill showed a total of $9,070,000 (Table 22.6a). The category called "broke" amounts to $5,560,000 or 61 percent of the quality costs. Clearly there will be no major improvement in these costs unless there is a successful attack on the broke—that is where the money is concentrated. ("Broke" is paper mill dialect for paper so defective that it is returned to the beaters for reprocessing.)

In that paper mill they make 53 types of paper. When the broke is allocated among the various types of paper, the Pareto principle is again in evidence (Table 22.6b). Six of the product types account for $4,480,000, which is 80 percent of the $5,560,000. There will be no major improvement in broke unless there is a successful attack on these six types of paper. Studying 12 percent (6 types out of 53) of the problem results in attacking 80 percent of the broke.

Finally, it is helpful to look at what kinds of defects are being encountered in these six types of paper, and how much are the associated costs for broke. The matrix of Table 22.6c show this analysis. There are numerous defect types, but five of them dominate. In addition, the cost figures in the table also follow the

TABLE 22.6a Pareto Analysis by Accounts—Quality Losses in a Paper Mill

Accounting category	Annual quality loss,* $ Thousands	Percent of total quality loss	
		This category	Cumulative
Broke	5560	61	61
Customer claim	1220	14	75
Odd lot	780	9	84
High material cost	670	7	91
Downtime	370	4	95
Excess inspection	280	3	98
High testing cost	190	2	100
Total	9070		

*Adjusted for estimated inflation since time of original study.

TABLE 22.6*b*   Pareto Analysis by Products—"Broke" Losses in a Paper Mill

Product type	Annual "broke" loss,* $ Thousands	Percent of "broke" loss	Cumulative percent "broke" loss
A	1320	24	24
B	960	17	41
C	720	13	54
D	680	12	66
E	470	8	74
F	330 (4480)	6	80
47 other types	1080	20	100
Total 53 types	5560	100	

*Adjusted for estimated inflation since time of original study.

TABLE 22.6*c*   Matrix of Quality Costs*

Type	Trim, $ thousands	Visual defects,† $ thousands	Caliper, $ thousands	Tear, $ thousands	Porosity, $ thousands	All other causes, $ thousands	Total, $ thousands
A	270	94	None‡	162	430	364	1320
B	120	33	None‡	612	58	137	960
C	95	78	380	31	74	62	720
D	82	103	None‡	90	297	108	680
E	54	108	None‡	246	None‡	62	470
F	51	49	39	16	33	142	330
Total	672	465	419	1157	892	875	4480

*Adjusted for estimated inflation since time of original study.
†Slime spots, holes, wrinkles, etc.
‡Not a specified requirement for this type.

Pareto principle. The largest numer is $612,000 for "tear" on paper type B. Then comes $430,000 for "porosity" on paper type A, and so on. It is easy to visualize how this series of analyses would be helpful to a team of managers who are trying to nominate projects for cost reduction.

In a Pareto analysis, there is an endless variety of sources to consider as "contributors." Thus the Pareto breakdown can be by organization (division, plant, etc.), by person (operators), by function (product development, manufacturing, etc.), by type of defect, by process, etc. For example, in the manufacture of an electromechanical detection device, failures can occur at any of five sources (Figure 22.3). About 50 percent of the cost of poor quality occurs at one source, component manufacturing (Betker, 1985a). See also below under Test of Theories of Worker-Controllable Problems for another graphic presentation to dramatize the Pareto principle.

The utter simplicity of the Pareto concept makes it prone to be underestimated as a key tool for quality improvement.

Generally, people hold strong opinions on what are the important areas requiring attention, but these opinions are often not shared by others. The Pareto con-

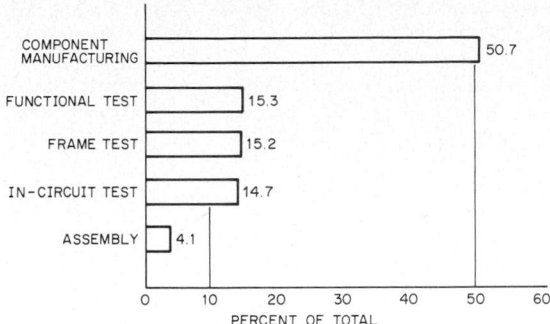

FIG. 22.3   Pareto analysis of percent total annualized failure costs.

cept helps to achieve agreement by collecting facts and summarizing them in a form that shows where most of the problem is concentrated.

The ranking of problem areas using a Pareto analysis of course depends on the criterion used. Tables 22.7a and 22.7b show an example of Pareto ranking using two different criteria (adapted from Selwitchka, 1980). Using "error frequency" and "cost" results in different rankings.

Sometimes it is useful to make Pareto analyses at higher levels as a summary of Pareto analyses made at lower levels. For example, in one large corporation, each plant routinely prepared Pareto analyses of field problems and used the results to direct plant quality improvement programs. In a special study, data from all plants were integrated. A Pareto analysis showed that 3 part types out of 200 accounted for an overwhelming part of the corporate problem. These same three part types were among the vital few at each of the plants. This higher-level Pareto analysis resulted in a corporate-directed effort on the three parts.

Occasionally, a Pareto study fails to reveal vital few contributors. For example, "83 percent of the defects were of a one-of-a-kind nature." In such cases, finding the vital few may require a different form of analysis. Instead of using *type* of defect, try making the analysis by potential *cause* of the defect (material, machine,

TABLE 22.7a   Errors Ranked by Frequency of Occurrence

Analysis 1

Type of error	Error frequency	Error proportion, %	Cumulative, Σ%	Rank
A	960	32	32	1
B	870	29	61	2
C	420	14	75	3
D	210	7	82	4
E	180	6	88	5
F	180	6	94	6
G	60	2	96	7
H	60	2	98	8
I	30	1	99	9
J	30	1	100	10

Source: Adapted from Selwitchka, 1980, pp. 3–7.

TABLE 22.7*b*   Errors Ranked by Cost

Analysis 2

Error type	Error frequency	Add. costs per annum, DM	Costs proportion, %	Proportion cumulative, %	Rank by Frequency	Cost
C	420	375,000	53.0	53.0	3	1
E	180	124,300	17.6	70.6	5	2
G	60	77,800	11.0	81.6	7	3
D	210	42,000	5.9	87.5	4	4
B	870	28,460	4.0	91.5	2	5
A	960	20,000	2.8	94.3	1	6
H	60	12,125	1.7	96.0	8	7
J	30	9,125	1.4	97.4	10	8
F	180	9,000	1.3	98.7	6	9
I	30	9,000	1.3	100.0	9	10
		706,810				

Source: Adapted from Selwitchka, 1980, pp. 3–7.

specification, etc.) or one of the other sources of contributors previously mentioned.

Nominations for Projects.   Nominations come from several sources:

1. The Pareto analysis of the quality-oriented costs.

2. The Pareto analysis of field complaints, returns claims, warranty charges, etc.

3. Analysis of other field intelligence, e.g., reports from the sales force or actions taken by competitors.

4. Emerging developments arising from the impact of product quality on society, e.g., new legislation, extension of government regulation, growth of product liability lawsuits.

5. Needs which relate to managerial processes and industrial relations, e.g., organization for quality, training programs, motivation for quality.

6. The management hierarchy, i.e., managers, supervisors, professional specialists, project teams.

7. Goal-setting processes, e.g., the annual budget, management by objectives.

8. The marketplace, as relayed by Sales, Customer Service, Technical Service, and others.

9. The work force, through informal ideas presented to supervisors, formal suggestions, ideas from quality circles, and so forth.

One structured approach for obtaining participation of workers is the error cause removed (ECR) system (Halpin, 1966). ECR forms are submitted to the supervisor with a copy to an ECR administrator who has the job of assuring that the proposal is acknowledged, analyzed, and acted upon by the supervisor or referred to other sources. (The administrator is aided by a pledge from top management that ECRs will receive prompt, serious attention.) Some of the problems documented on ECR forms become project nominations for quality improvement teams.

10. "Making the rounds," i.e., visits made by specialists (quality engineers, industrial engineers) to solicit nominations from various departments.

A description of projects from both the manufacturing and nonmanufacturing areas of a wide variety of industries will be found in *The Juran Report,* no. 2, November 1983 (pp. 52–94), *The Juran Report,* no. 2, winter 1985 (pp. 28–45 and 160–179), and *The Juran Report,* no. 6, winter 1986 (pp. 27–40 and 165–180).

An example of a large nonfactory project is cancellation of sales contracts. In one large electronics company it was found that 20 percent of all sales contracts ended up being cancelled. The cancellations were for many reasons: sale for the wrong application, failure to deliver on time, product failed to perform per contract, product not compatible with other elements of the client's system, etc. The numerous reasons followed the Pareto principle—a few of the reasons accounted for most of the cancellations. This led to revisions in the sales procedures and significant reductions in the percent of cancellations.

Screening Nominations and Establishing Priorities.   This screening or review process is typically set up at two levels—middle and upper management.

Review by Middle Management.   The project nomination should describe (1) the scope and (2) the return on investment. The scope includes the purpose of the project, the activities required to carry it out, personnel and physical facilities required, responsibility (who is to do what), time schedule, and the results expected, tangible and intangible.

Some companies use a standardized form to summarize the facts behind a proposal for a project. McGrath (1985) presents an example of such a form for an electronics company (Figure 22.4).

The explanation of return on investment shows the present costs; the estimated reduction in costs or other benefits; and the estimated investment needed in facilities, salaries, and expenses. These inputs are summarized by calculating the return on investment or, alternatively, the time required to recover the investment.

As managers review the nominations based on the foregoing kinds of information they arrive at priorities by weighing such factors as return on investment, amount of potential improvement, urgency, ease of technological solution, and likely reception of the project.

Some organizations formalize the evaluation of projects. In one approach, 10 criteria are evaluated in terms of yes, no, or uncertain answer. This is illustrated in Figure 22.5 (McGrath, 1985).

Hartman (1983) describes an approach that makes use of a "Pareto priority index" (PPI) to evaluate each project. The index is:

$$\text{PPI} = \frac{\text{savings} \times \text{probability of success}}{\text{cost} \times \text{time to completion (years)}}$$

Table 22.8 shows the application of this index to evaluate five potential projects. High PPI values suggest high priority. Note how the ranking of projects A and C is affected when the criterion is changed from savings alone to the index covering the four factors. (Other indices can be created to reflect a different set of factors.)

Obviously, no individual middle manager can supply the facts or make the

Project Title *Parts Handling Improvements*   Organization _____   Leader/Mgr. *Beth Duffy*

Symptoms: *Parts that don't meet specs. Not fit for use.*

Statement of Problem: *Damage to component parts due to handling. A total impact of $150,000.*

Possible Causes: *Handling & packaging*

Overall Objective(s): *"Receive good parts" - have a 95% improvement.*

Approach/Technique Proposed: *Analyze methods of handling and packaging. Also, analyze incoming parts.*

Project Leader Proposed: _____

Resources Required: *Study Phase*   *Implementation*

Funds   *$1100*   *$42,000*

Time   *60 hours*   *6 months*

Personnel   *Engr. 2 techs*

Product Value/Urgency _____

Productivity Increase From _____ *75%* _____ to _ *95%*

due to less incoming inspection.

Reliability Increase From _____ *75%* _____ to _ *95%*

_____

Cost Reduction From _ *$150,000* _ to _____

_____

Net Economic Impact Statement *Customer satisfaction*

Estimated Net Saving _ *$100,000*
($, ROI or Payback)

FIG. 22.4 Quality improvement project. *(From McGrath, 1984.)*

judgment as to which projects should get the highest priority. Managers from all key departments should participate in choice of the projects. Such a *jury of opinion* reduces the likelihood that the extreme optimism or pessimism of one individual will decide the fate of a project.

The result of the review by middle management is a recommended list of projects. Typically, a responsibility of an upper management quality council is to review the recommendations or create the organizational machinery for review and final approval.

Selection of Initial Projects. "The first project should be a winner." A successful project is a form of evidence to the project team members that the improvement process does lead to useful results. That same success is also a source of stimulation to do more of the same. The publicity given to the successful project conveys this stimulus to others in the company. In contrast, if the first project fails, the fact of failure is a source of discouragement and of reduced confidence in the com-

```
┌─────────────────────────────────────────────────────────────────┐
│                                                                   │
│   PROJECT SELECTION LIST                          YES  NO    ?     │
│                                                                   │
│    1.  Does the project have a measurable outcome?  ___  ___  ___  │
│                                                                   │
│    2.  Does the outcome assist in meeting unit targets? ___ ___ ___│
│                                                                   │
│          ...for QUALITY PERFORMANCE INCREASES?     ___  ___  ___   │
│          ...for PRODUCT RELIABILITY INCREASES?     ___  ___  ___   │
│          ...for QUALITY COST REDUCTIONS?           ___  ___  ___   │
│                                                                   │
│    3.  Does the proposed approach use an already existing         │
│        technology?                                 ___  ___  ___   │
│                                                                   │
│    4.  In light of all organizational financial constraints, do we │
│        presently possess the required resources to implement this │
│        project...                                                 │
│                                  FUNDS?            ___  ___  ___   │
│                                  PERSONNEL?        ___  ___  ___   │
│                                  MATERIALS?        ___  ___  ___   │
│                                  SPACE?            ___  ___  ___   │
│                                                                   │
│    5.  Are the estimated net cost savings substantial?___ ___ ___ │
│                                                                   │
│    6.  Can the project be completed or a benchmark met in 90      │
│        days?                                       ___  ___  ___   │
│                                                                   │
│    7.  Will this project be readily accepted by other departments? ___ ___ ___ │
│                                                                   │
│    8.  Can this project be done without extensive cooperation and │
│        coordination with other units?             ___  ___  ___   │
│                                                                   │
│    9.  Will this project be seen as a priority task by the people │
│        doing the work?                            ___  ___  ___   │
│                                                                   │
│   10.  Does top management see the benefits of this specific      │
│        project? Will they suport it fully?        ___  ___  ___   │
│                                                                   │
│                                       TOTALS      ═══  ═══  ═══    │
│                                                                   │
│        ┌─────────────────────────────────────────┐              │
│        │  Mostly  ? — Need more information        │              │
│        │  Mostly No — May not be a good choice     │              │
│        │  Mostly Yes— Preferred  choice            │              │
│        └─────────────────────────────────────────┘              │
│                                                                   │
└─────────────────────────────────────────────────────────────────┘
```

FIG. 22.5 Selection criteria for quality improvement projects. *(From McGrath, 1985.)*

TABLE 22.8 Ranking by Use of Pareto Priority Index (PPI)

Project	Savings, $ thousands	Probability	Cost, $ thousands	Time, years	PPI
A	100	0.7	10.0	2.0	3.5
B	50	0.7	2.0	1.0	17.5
C	30	0.8	1.6	0.25	60.0
D	10	0.9	0.5	0.50	36.0
E	1.5	0.6	1.0	0.10	9.0

pany's direction. Such discouragement and reduced confidence also become publicized and thereby have an impact outside of the project team directly involved.
    Ideally:

> The project should deal with a *chronic* problem—one which has been awaiting solution for a long time.

> The project should be feasible, i.e., have a good likelihood of bringing it to a successful conclusion within a few months.

> The project should be *significant.* The end result should be sufficiently useful to merit attention and recognition.

> The results should be *measurable* in money as well as in technological terms.

> The project should serve as a *learning experience* for the process of problem solving.

The Number of Projects in a Quality Improvement Program.   The number of projects required to achieve a significant improvement in quality is surprisingly large. Means are emerging for estimating the number of projects needed for planned results. The two cardinal figures required for making the estimates are:

1. The average amount of cost reduction achieved per project. A growing data base (Juran, 1985) indicates that for large companies (sales over $1000 million per year), the average annual cost reduction is about $100,000 per project. (Individual project savings range from over $1 million to a loss.)
2. The cost reduction goal to be reached. For example, many companies have a cost of poor quality in excess of 20 percent of sales, of $200 million per year. To reduce this cost by 50 percent would mean a goal of $100 million cost reduction. At an average of $100,000 per project, it would take 1000 projects to reach this goal!

    In the above example, if the goal were to make the cost reduction over a 5-year period, the company would need to complete 200 projects per year. That is a number far greater than the actual number of projects carried out by most companies of that size. To assure that a sufficient number of projects are identified and executed requires a methodical approach to organizing.

ORGANIZING FOR PROJECTS

The in-depth investigations needed to solve most chronic quality problems involve two journeys:

1. A journey from symptom to cause (diagnosis)
2. A journey from cause to remedy

    Table 22.9 contrasts these two journeys.
    The difficult journey is from symptom to cause. Two reasons account for the difficulty: the responsibility for diagnosis is vague, and the needed skills are not always available. These obstacles can be overcome by using a project team.

The Project Team.   The project team consists (usually) of about six to eight persons drawn from multiple company departments. Their job is to bring the project to a successful conclusion.

TABLE 22.9 Contrast of the Diagnostic and Remedial Journeys

	Diagnostic	Remedial
Responsibility	Vague	Clear
Skills needed	Quality disciplines	Technological
Skills present	Sometimes	Usually
Obstacles	Organizational training	Resistance to change

Although there is a "project chairperson" (leader, etc.; see below), the team has no "boss" in a personal sense. Instead there is an impersonal boss—the "charter" given to each project team. The team has two basic responsibilities: (1) Guide the project to a successful conclusion; (2) conduct or oversee the diagnostic work.

A typical charter gives the team the right and duty to:

Analyze the project to understand the symptoms of the problem.

Theorize as to what might be the cause(s) of the symptoms.

Arrange to test the theories to discover the cause(s).

Recommend remedial action to those organizations who are in a position to provide remedies.

Follow up and stimulate remedial action.

Prove the adequacy of the remedies under operating conditions.

Establish controls to hold the gains.

Evaluate and publish the results achieved.

Lounds and Pearson (1985) show a project charter for office automation. Dymtrow (1985) discusses a charter for a service project.

In forming the project teams, several matters must be resolved:

1. *Membership; mandatory or voluntary?* To remain competitive in quality and to reduce the cost of poor quality requires the participation of all members of the management team. Membership on project teams should be mandatory.

2. *Horizontal or vertical?* Project team membership should usually be horizontal, i.e., members are drawn from multiple functions. This approach is compatible with the reality that virtually all major chronic quality problems are multidepartmental in scope.

3. *At what level?* Project teams should be set up at all levels because such is the mixture of projects. Solution of some projects (e.g., reducing the error rate in invoices, or reducing the defect rate in gear cutting) requires team members who understand the details of the respective processes. Such team members are usually first-line supervisors and professional specialists and the work force. (Upper managers should keep out of such projects.) Other projects require extensive experience and training in managerial matters. For such projects, the membership should come from the managerial levels. An example of an upper management project is the reward and recognition process for quality.

4. *The appointment process:* Based on the nature of the project selected, the council (or subcouncil) identifies who are the organization units who should be represented on the project team. It is essential that team membership include the units that are likely to be involved in the remedial changes. The

council then contacts the heads of those organization units to secure their nominations of persons to be team members. Negotiations then take place to reach agreement on the precise makeup of the team.

5. *Team members from nontechnological functions:* Experience has shown that team members from nontechnological functions can be useful members of project teams. They are able to identify and deal with nontechnological matters such as lack of organization for improvement, or suboptimizing, i.e., meeting departmental goals at the expense of company performance. Wolf (1983) shows the constituency of project teams for ten pilot projects.

Project Teams versus Quality Circles.   There are important differences between the two types of groups (see Table 22.10).

Principal Roles on Project Teams.   The project team consists of the chairperson, secretary, and other team members.

Project Team Chairperson.   The project team chairperson (or leader) leads the team in its responsibility of carrying out the project. Successful leadership requires knowledge of the project area and skills in getting cooperation from team members from several functional areas to work as a team. It is often useful that the team chairperson come from the organizational unit most impacted by the problem.

Project Secretary.   Each team requires a project secretary to handle documentation: publish agendas, minutes, reports, etc. The secretary is preferably a member of the project team.

Project Team Members.   Team membership draws upon all of the skills and knowledge necessary for the project. For chronic problems, the teams are usually cross-functional and consist of middle management, professional, and work force personnel. Surprisingly, some projects are relatively easy and can be handled with a minimum of skills and knowledge. (Such projects are often the result of a previous lack of the project approach.) Other projects are complex and require more depth in team membership, perhaps even supplemented by consulting specialists (see below).

Supplementing the formal team membership may be two additional parties:

Facilitator.   Many companies have adopted the concept of using a "facilitator" to help project teams carry out their first project. Although not a member of the

TABLE 22.10   Comparison: Quality Circles and Project Teams

Feature	Quality circles	Project teams
Scope of project	Within a single department	Multidepartmental
Size of project	One of the useful many	One of the vital few
Members come from:	A single department	Multiple departments
Basis of membership	Voluntary	Mandatory
Composition of membership	Work force	Mostly middle management and specialists
Continuity	Circle remains intact, project after project	Team is ad hoc, disbands after project is completed

team, the facilitator can play an important role. The role of the facilitator consists of a selection from the following:

Explaining the company's approach to quality improvement and how it differs from prior efforts at quality improvement

Providing assistance in team building

Assisting in the training of project teams

Assisting the project team leader in solving human relations problems among team members

Helping the team avoid a poor choice of project

Reporting progress of projects to management

The Facilitator: Selection and Training.   For the most part, companies use part-time rather than full-time facilitators. These part-time facilitators are usually drawn from the ranks of local managers and supervisors at the various sites.

In the case of full-time facilitators, the most frequent source is the human relations organization. Such individuals typically have a background in the behavioral sciences, enabling them to contribute usefully to training and to team building.

Additional sources of facilitators include former quality circle facilitators, qualified retirees who are recalled on a temporary basis, and experienced project team chairpersons who have demonstrated an aptitude for carrying out the roles of facilitators.

Training for facilitators includes indoctrination in the company's mission with respect to annual quality improvement and the associated role of the facilitator. The indoctrination is then followed by training in the project approach, problem-solving tools, and group dynamics.

A small minority of companies have bypassed the use of facilitators. For example, one large electronics company assigned to each of its general managers the job of leading subordinates through a project. In turn, each subordinate then did the same. The roles of the facilitator were of course still there, but they were carried out by the operating managers.

McGrath (1985) discusses the development of team leaders and facilitators.

Consulting Specialist(s).   For some team meetings it may be useful to invite in a specialist who is knowledgeable in specific disciplines required by the project, e.g., metallurgy or computer software reliability engineering.

Responsibility for Diagnosis.   Lack of clear responsibility for diagnosis is the main reason for failure to make the journey from symptom to cause. This problem is solved by making the project team responsible for diagnosis.

In some projects the work of diagnosis is not extensive. In such cases the project team personally does the diagnosis.

In other projects the work of diagnosis becomes quite burdensome, due to the need for extensive data collection and analysis. In such cases the team may decide to delegate part of the work of diagnosis. The alternatives for such delegation include:

1. The team secures assistance from line or staff departments. For example: collection of new data may be done by line manufacturing personnel; planning and analysis of special experiments may be done by engineers in Quality Engineering.

2. A full-time diagnostic department is created to do the work associated with data collection and analysis.

Full-Time Diagnosticians: Centralized or Scattered? Full-time diagnosticians can be located on the organization chart in several ways (Figure 22.6.) They can be assigned as follows:

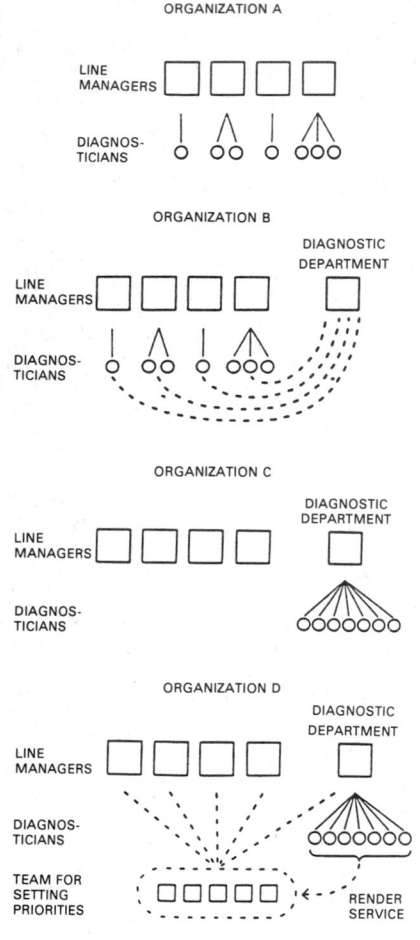

1. To the various line managers in proportion to the needs of the respective line departments.

This arrangement is preferred by most line managers. In practice, many of these arrangements have ended up with the diagnosticians being assigned to help the line manager in meeting current goals, in fire fighting, etc. Such assignments then take priority over the big, interdepartmental chronic quality problems.

2. To the various line managers [as in (1), above], but with a "dotted line" running to a central diagnostic department (e.g., Quality Engineering).

This arrangement is an improvement from the standpoint of training of diagnosticians, offering them an obvious career road and providing them with consulting assistance. However, the arrangement does not necessarily solve the problem of priorities, i.e., on which projects should the diagnosticians be working.

3. To a central diagnostic department (e.g., Quality Engineering).

This arrangement makes it possible for the diagnosticians to be assigned either to interdepartmental or intradepartmental projects. It also increases the likelihood that interdepartmental projects will have higher priority. In addition, it simplifies the provision of training and consulting assistance for diagnosticians. However, it makes no specific provision for line manager par-

FIG. 22.6 Organizing the diagnostic function.

ticipation in choice of projects or in setting up priorities. Such an omission can be fatal to results.

4. To a central diagnostic department [as in (3), above], but with a structured participation by the line managers.

In effect, a team of line managers chooses the projects and establishes the priorities. The diagnostic department assigns the diagnosticians in response to these priorities. It also provides training, consulting service, and other assistance to the diagnosticians. This arrangement is widely used and has demonstrated its ability to adapt to a wide variety of company situations.

The choice among these (and other) alternatives will depend on many factors which differ from one company to another.

Responsibility for Troubleshooting. In many companies the diagnosticians who are assigned to quality improvement teams may also be assigned to assist in troubleshooting to solve the sporadic problems. (See Section 17 under Troubleshooting.) Such multiple assignments complicate the problems of setting priorities and defining responsibilities.

Moehlenbrock (1985) describes how a capacitor manufacturer organized for quality improvement based on the distinction between chronic and sporadic problems. This led to two types of teams: control teams made of local manufacturing personnel to pursue sporadic problems and breakthrough teams made up of interdepartmental personnel to take on the chronic problems.

DIAGNOSIS—GENERAL

Certain key words relating to diagnosis are defined as follows:

A "defect" is any state of unfitness for use, or nonconformance to specification, e.g., oversize, low mean time between failures, illegible invoice. A defect also goes by other names, e.g., error, discrepancy, nonconformance.

A "project" is a problem scheduled for solution.

A "symptom" is an observable phenomenon arising from and accompanying a defect. Sometimes, but not always, the same word is used both as a defect description and as a symptom description, e.g., "open circuit." More usually, a defect will have multiple symptoms; e.g., "insufficient torque" may include the symptoms of vibration, overheating, erratic function, etc.

A "theory" is an unproved assertion as to reasons for the existence of defects and symptoms. Usually, multiple theories are advanced to explain the presence of the observed phenomena.

A "cause" is a proved reason for the existence of the defect. Often there are multiple causes, in which case they follow the Pareto principle; i.e., the vital few causes will dominate all the rest.

A "dominant cause" is a major contributor to the existence of defects and one which must be remedied before there can be an adequate solution.

"Diagnosis" is the process of studying symptoms, theorizing as to causes, testing theories, and discovering causes.

A "remedy" is a change that can successfully eliminate or neutralize a cause of defects.

Two journeys are required for quality improvement: the diagnostic journey from symptom to cause, and the remedial journey from cause to remedy. This distinction is critical. To illustrate, three supervisors were faced with a problem of burrs on screws at final assembly of kitchen stoves. In their haste to act, they skipped the diagnostic journey and concluded that better screws were needed (a remedy). Fortunately, a diagnostician interceded. He pointed out that three separate assembly lines were feeding product into one inspection station, and he suggested that the data be segregated by assembly line. The data revealed that the burrs occurred only on line 3. Further diagnosis based on data led to agreement that the true cause was an improperly trained assembler. Then, the remedy came easily.

Sometimes these two journeys must be repeated before a problem is permanently solved. For an example from a continuous chemical process, see Nester and Staal (1986).

Many managers harbor deep-seated beliefs that most defects are caused during manufacture and specifically are due to worker errors, i.e., that defects are mainly worker-controllable. The facts seldom bear this out, but the belief persists. To deal with such deep-seated beliefs it can be useful to conduct studies to separate defects into broad categories of responsibility. The more frequent of such studies include:

1. A study to determine the origin of the defects in the design, manufacture, etc. Such a study to determine the distribution of causes over functional areas often has some surprising results. In a classic study, Greenridge (1953) examined 850 failures of electronic products supplied by a number of companies. The results showed that 43 percent of the failures were caused by the product design, 30 percent by field operation conditions, 20 percent by manufacturing, and the remaining 7 percent by miscellaneous causes. For products of moderately high technology it is not unusual that about 40 percent of field problems can be traced to the product design.

2. A study to determine whether defects are primarily management-controllable or worker-controllable. ("Management" here includes not only people in supervisory positions but also others who influence quality, e.g., design engineers, process engineers, buyers, etc.) An example of a controllability study is given in Section 17 under Concept of Controllability (see Table 17.2). In general, defects are over 80 percent management-controllable and under 20 percent worker-controllable. Some authors use the term "system-controllable" for "management-controllable."

Such broad studies provide important guidance for improvement.

Diagnosis of Failures in Broad Systems.   It is beneficial to examine a broad approach to diagnosis based on a review of history. In this "historical review" approach, the objective is not to improve the quality of a specific product; the objective is to improve some segment of the systematic approach used to attain quality in the first place. The segment can be a major activity such as product development, manufacturing planning, or supplier relations.

Historical review is based on analysis of a number of past problems; i.e., some skeletons are dissected. Based on interviews, each problem is documented as follows:

1. A brief description of the problem
2. The stage at which the problem was first observed (field, final inspection, prototype test)
3. The earliest stage at which the problem could have been discovered
4. The reasons for not having discovered the problem at that earlier stage
5. What could have been done to have found the problem earlier (or to have avoided the problem altogether)

For example, a historical review of past product development problems reveals that a failure mode, effect, and criticality analysis (see Section 13 under Failure Mode, Effect, and Criticality Analysis) would have identified many of the

Date of problem observed	Symptoms	Damages	Could have been found earlier?	Reasons for not finding earlier
July 9, 1984, 10:00	High readings, all East Coast machines	$2,000 loss	Yes	No incoming inspection
July 15, 1984	Added function to the frame	Lost orders	Yes	No status meetings

FIG. 22.7 Problem log.

problems much earlier. This suggests that the product development system should be changed to require such an analysis for all or selected future products.

Ingram (1984) discusses the historical review technique as applied to specific product problems (see the problem log, Figure 22.7). Kano (1984) describes the application of this concept in new-product development.

In conducting a historical review it is essential to avoid controversy about the causes of the problem. The emphasis must be on discovering potential problems early enough to prevent them from happening.

Another form of historical review is made from established documentation. For example, a sample of 24 engineering change notices were analyzed with the following results:

1. Only one problem was found during development testing; the remaining 23 surfaced later during the production phase.

2. In all 24 cases, the engineers who originally created the design were told of the problem, but the "lessons learned" were not disseminated to other engineers.

3. Of the 24 problems, 11 were associated with performance, reliability, or safety, 8 with "administrative" matters, and 5 with manufacturing.

Many file cabinets are laden with similar collective histories of important knowledge for diagnosis.

From the historical review approach aimed at broad segments of activity, we next discuss diagnosis for specific improvement projects.

Diagnosis for Improvement Projects.   Results come solely from work done on specific improvement projects. This work begins with the diagnostic journey.

The diagnostic journey consists of:

1. Study of the symptoms surrounding the defects to serve as a basis for theorizing about causes

2. Theorizing on the causes of these symptoms

3. Data collection and analysis to test the theories and thereby determine the causes

When the defects can be "switched on or off" at will, the diagnostic journey is over. Table 22.11 lists specific diagnostic techniques and their likely application during the three phases of diagnosis. (Some of these techniques can also be helpful during the remedial journey.)

Nothing is more fundamental to diagnosis than the need to replace conjecture with the authority of fact. The starting point is a clear understanding of symptoms.

TABLE 22.11 Guide to Diagnostic Techniques

Phase of diagnosis	Technique	Reference pages
Study of symptoms	Check sheet	22.35, 22,36
	Autopsies	22.35
	Glossary	22.35
	Pareto analysis	22.19–22.22
Theorizing on causes	Brainstorming	22.36
	Nominal group technique	22.36
	Storyboarding	22.36–22.37
	Tabular arrangement	22.37
	Cause-and-effect diagram	22.37–22.39
	Force field analysis	22.39
	Affinity diagram	22.39
	Structure tree	22.39, 22.40
	Why-why diagram	22.40
	Interrelationship digraph	22.40
	Program decision process chart	22.40
	Matrix	22.40
	Check sheet	22.35, 22.36
	Pareto analysis	22.19–22.22
Data collection and analysis	Historical review	22.32–22.33
	Check sheet	22.35, 22.36
	Pareto analysis	22.19–22.22
	Flow diagram	22.41
	Arrow diagram	22.41
	Process capability analysis	16.14–16.35
	Stream-to-stream analysis	22.41
	Time-to-time analysis	22.41, 22.42
	Cumulative data plots	22.42, 22.44
	Probability paper	23.35–23.42
	Control charts	Section 24
	Piece-to-piece analysis	22.44
	Within piece-to-piece analysis	22.44–22.48
	Multi-Vari diagram	22.45
	Defect concentration diagram	22.45, 22.46
	Interrelation of variables	22.47
	Correlation	22.48
	Ranking	22.48, 22.49
	Matrix	22.49, 22.50
	Measurements at intermediate stages	22.50
	Measurements following noncontrolled operations	22.50
	Measurement of additional properties	22.50, 22.51
	Study of worker methods	22.53–22.59
	Formal experiments	22.51, Section 26
	Other statistical techniques	Section 23
	Measurement for diagnosis	22.52, 22.53

ANALYSIS OF SYMPTOMS

Evidence of defects and errors comes in two forms:

1. The words used in written documentation or oral comments describing the problem
2. The "autopsies" conducted to measure and examine the defects.

Description of Symptoms.   Understanding of symptoms is often hindered because some key word or phrase has multiple meanings.

In a plant making rubber products by the latex dip process, the word "tears" was used on the data sheets to describe torn products. One important manager regarded "tears" as worker-controllable and urged a remedy through motivational and disciplinary measures.

Actually there were three species of tears: "strip tears" from a stripping operation, "click tears" from a press operation, and "assembly tears" from an assembly operation.

Only one of these species was worker controllable, and overall extent of worker controllability was only 15 percent. Progress became possible only after the terminology had been made clear and the controllability had been quantified.

In another example, a Pareto analysis of inspection data in a wire mill indicated a high percentage of defects due to "contamination." Various remedies were tried to prevent the contamination. All were unsuccessful. In desperation the investigators spoke with the inspectors to learn more about the contamination. The inspectors explained that there were 12 defect categories on the inspection form. If the observed defect did not fit any of the categories they would report the defect as "contamination."

Imprecise wording also occurs due to use of generic terminology. For example, a software problem is described in a discrepancy report as a "coding error." Such a description is useless for analysis because there are many types of coding errors, e.g., undefined variables, violation of language rules, and violation of programming standards.

A way out of such semantic tangles is to think through the meanings of the words used, reach an agreement, and record the agreement in the form of a *glossary*. Once published, the glossary simplifies the subsequent analysis.

Autopsies.   The autopsy determines that the product unit classified as having an "electrical" defect actually exhibits the symptom of open circuit, or short circuit, or dead battery.

Using a wide variety of instruments, today's scientific autopsies furnish extensive objective knowledge about the symptoms, and thereby supplement or override the information contained in the written reports.

Data Recording Methods.   Data recording methods range from extremely simple to extremely complex. Figure 22.8 shows a simple data recording device known as a check sheet (G.O.A.L., 1985.) All forms of data recording are designed to test specific theories. For example, a concentration diagram (discussed later in this section) provides excellent input for testing a theory that defects tend to concentrate at one location on a product.

Quantification of Symptoms.   The frequency and intensity of symptoms is of great significance in pointing to directions for analysis. The Pareto principle,

Mistake		March		Total
	1	2	3	
Centering	11	111	111	8
Spelling	ЦНᵀ1 11	ЦНᵀ ЦНᵀ 1	ЦНᵀ	23
Punctuation	ЦНᵀ1 ЦНᵀ1 ЦНᵀ1	ЦНᵀ1 ЦНᵀ1	ЦНᵀ1 ЦНᵀ ЦНᵀ1	40
Missed paragraph	11	1	1	4
Wrong numbers	111	1111	111	10
Wrong page numbers	1	1	11	4
Tables	1111	ЦНᵀ1	1111	13
Total	34	35	33	102

FIG. 22.8 Checksheet of typing mistakes in Department A.

when applied to records of past performance, can help in quantifying the symptom pattern. (See above under The Pareto Principle.) The Pareto principle applies to several levels of diagnosis: finding the vital few defects, finding the vital few symptoms of a defect, and finding the vital few causes for one symptom.

FORMULATION OF THEORIES

All progress in diagnosis is made theory by theory, i.e., by affirming or denying the validity of the theories about causes. The process consists of three steps: generation of theories, arrangement of theories, and choosing theories to be tested.

Generation of Theories. Securing the theories is a serious matter and should be done systematically. The best sources of theories are the line managers, the technologists, the line supervisors, and the work force. Normally the list of theories is extensive, 20 or more. If only three or four theories have been proposed, it usually means that the theorizing process has been inadequate.

A systematic way to generate theories is the brainstorming technique. Persons who are potential contributors are assembled for the purpose of generating theories. Creative thinking is encouraged by asking each person, in turn, to propose a theory. No criticism or discussion of ideas is allowed, and all ideas are recorded. The end result is a list of theories which, after the brainstorming session is completed, are critically reviewed.

The nominal group technique is similar to brainstorming. Participants generate their ideas silently, in writing. Each then offers one idea for recording on a chart. After all ideas are recorded, they are discussed. Finally, the group votes to prioritize the ideas.

A useful supplement to the brainstorming technique is "storyboarding." Each theory proposed is recorded on an index card. The cards are appropriately arranged on a board to form a visual display of the theories. Storyboarding provides a visual system for organizing theories and planning subsequent evaluation of these theories. Betker (1986b) describes the use of storyboarding in an electronics company.

Theories should include those for systematic causes as well as those for causes which relate to specific products or processes. For example, a manager observes, "In the last 6 weeks we have lost four needed batches of unrelated products due to four different instruments being out of calibration. This shows that we should review our *system* for maintaining the accuracy of our instruments."

Arrangement of Theories. An orderly arrangement of theories is essential to help all concerned to visualize the interrelation of the theories. In addition, an orderly arrangement is an essential aid to choosing which theories to test. The orderly arrangement can be done in several forms.

Tabular Arrangement. The brainstorming process provides a helter-skelter list of theories. Brainstorming for theories can have a useful effect on a highly opinionated person. Such a person will list a belief as a theory, and realize it is only a theory. This list is then rearranged to show a logical listing: theories, sub-theories, sub-sub-theories, etc. Table 22.12 is an example as applied to yield of fine powder chemicals.

TABLE 22.12   Orderly Arrangement of Theories

Raw material	Moisture content
Shortage of weight	Charging speed of wet powder
Method of discharge	Dryer, rpm
Catalyzer	Temperature
Types	Steam pressure
Quantity	Steam flow
Quality	Overweight of package
Reaction	Type of balance
Solution and concentration	Accuracy of balance
B solution temperature	Maintenance of balance
Solution and pouring	Method of weighing
speed	Operator
pH	Transporation
Stirrer, rpm	Road
Time	Cover
Crystallization	Spill
Temperature	Container
Time	
Concentration	
Mother crystal	
Weight	
Size	

Cause-and-Effect Diagram. This diagram (also known as the Ishikawa diagram or the fishbone diagram) was developed in 1950 by Professor Kaoru Ishikawa. To create the diagram, the effect (symptom) is written at the head of the arrow. Potential causes (theories) are then added to complete the diagram. A common set of major categories for causes consists of personnel, work methods, materials, and equipment. Figure 22.9 shows the cause and effect diagram as prepared for the

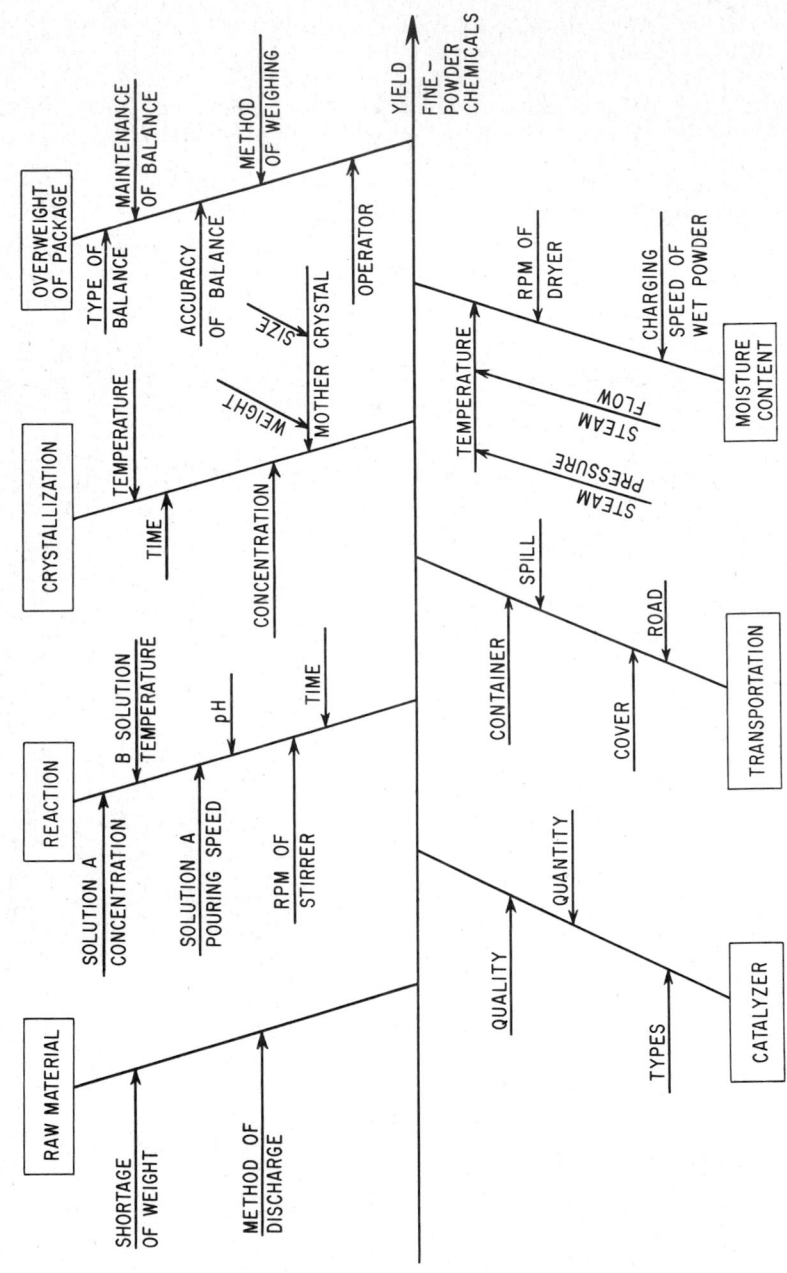

FIG. 22.9 Ishikawa cause-and-effect diagram.

same list of theories as was arranged in Table 22.12. Note how the diagram aids in identifying possible interrelationships among theories.

Betker (1983) presents both the cause-and-effect diagram and a tabular listing of theories to analyze solder defects on printed circuit board assemblies.

Some organizations use the cause-and-effect diagram to continually collect and display information on the important variables in a process. Section 16 under Initial Planning for Quality describes this simple but effective system.

Cause-and-effect diagrams can also be prepared for broad systems of accomplishing work. In one example, a group of electrical engineers employed the diagram to analyze a weak design review system. Also, see Section 21 under Cause-and-Effect Diagram for examples applied to nonmanufacturing activities.

A cause-and-effect diagram can be combined with a force field analysis (see Stratton, 1987). The team identifies the situations and events that contribute to the problem (these are the "restraining forces"). The actions necessary to counter the restraining forces are then identified (those actions are the "driving forces"). A diagram combining the restraining and driving forces is prepared to assist in diagnosis. The approach is similar to the barriers and aids analysis described below under Resistance to Change.

G.O.A.L. (1985a) describes the use of an affinity diagram for organizing facts, opinions, and issues into natural groupings as an aid to diagnosis on a complex problem. Inputs from knowledgeable people are listed on cards which are then rearranged until useful groups are identified.

Structure Trees. A structure tree is a diagram that starts with the problem, breaks it down into "subproblems," and then theorizes possible causes. An example from Florida Power and Light Company (1984, p. 44) is given in Figure 22.10.

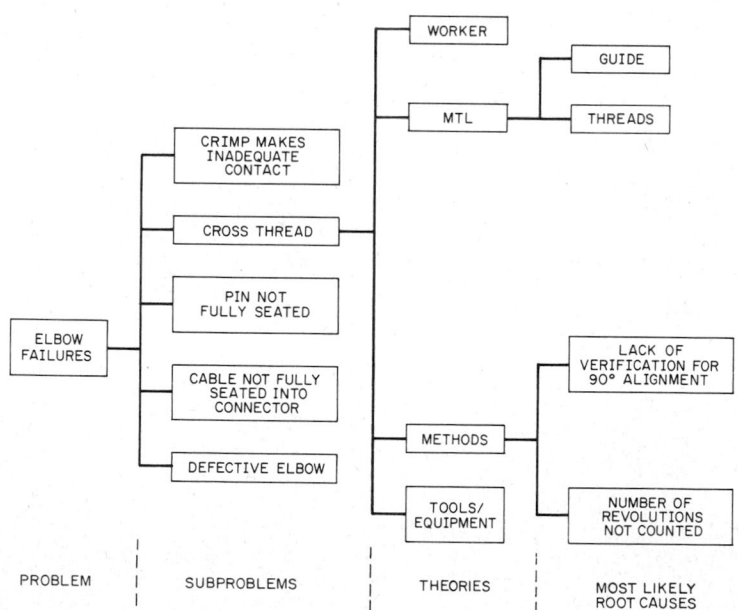

FIG. 22.10 Structure tree example. *(Adapted from Florida Power & Light Co., 1984, p. 44.)*

POTENTIAL ROOT CAUSE	ROOT CAUSE OR SYMPTOM	CAUSES 00% OF PROBLEM	ACTIONABLE (DUG DEEPLY ENOUGH TO LEAD TO CORRECTIVE ACTION) YES/NO	HOW VERIFY	SYSTEM RELATED YES/NO	OTHER
#1	Root Cause	High	Yes	Test	Yes	
#2	Symptom	Low	Yes	Check Procedures	No	
#3	Root Cause	High	Yes	Defect Rate	Yes	
#4	Root Cause	High	No	Analyse New Data	Yes	

FIG. 22.11   Root cause evaluation matrix.

In a similar approach, Bailie (1985) explains how a "why-why diagram" develops a network of reasons for the original problem. End points on the diagram represent root causes for branches of the problem.

G.O.A.L. (1985b) explains how to construct an interrelationship diagraph to help identify key factors for inclusion in a tree diagram. Information is arranged in a diagram to generate ideas and map out logical links among related items. An extension of a tree diagram is the program decision process chart (G.O.A.L., 1986b). For each branch in the tree, the question asked is "What could go wrong at this step?"

Choosing Theories to be Tested.   Priorities must be established for testing the theories. Prioritizing of various theories can be aided by a simple matrix (Figure 22.11). Each potential cause (a theory) is qualitatively evaluated for the five factors listed. These evaluations aid the project team to prioritize these causes for further study.

Gust (1985) describes an example of prioritizing theories based on interviewing people and converting the responses to a quantitative score for each theory.

Whether to test just one theory at a time, one group of interrelated theories at a time, or all theories simultaneously requires a judgment by the improvement team. Usually the experience and creativity of the team clear away much of the fog.

TEST OF THEORIES OF MANAGEMENT-CONTROLLABLE PROBLEMS

Numerous diagnostic methods and tools have been evolved to test theories. Those frequently used are set out and exemplified below. Still other methods abound in the literature. In addition, new situations keep arising, requiring modifications to standard diagnostic tools. Ishikawa (1976) provides additional discussion for many of the diagnostic techniques discussed below.

Product and Process Dissection. Some products are produced by a "procession" type of process, i.e., a series of sequential operations. At the end of the series the product is found to be defective, but it is not known which operation did the damage. In some of these cases it is feasible to "dissect" the process, i.e., make measurements at intermediate steps in the process to discover at which step the defect appears. Such discovery, if successful, can drastically reduce the subsequent effort in testing theories.

Flow Diagram. Dissection of a process is aided by constructing a flow diagram showing the various steps in the process. Engle and Ball (1986) explain the role of a flow diagram in reducing the time required for handling special customer orders. A quality improvement team discovered that no one was able to describe the special order process. To understand the process they were trying to improve, the team created a flow diagram. Examples of several types of diagrams for understanding a process are given in Section 16 under Initial Planning for Quality.

An arrow network diagram can be useful in analyzing and replanning the schedule for a complex task that can be divided into subtasks (Riggs, 1981, pp. 206–218). The arrow diagram is a simpler version of the critical path method (CPM) and program evaluation review technique (PERT).

Process Capability Analysis. One of the theories most widely encountered is: "The process can't hold the tolerances." To test this theory, measurements from the process must be taken and analyzed to determine the amount of variability inherent in the process. This variability is then compared to the specification limits. Those steps are performed in a "process-capability" study. Process capability is discussed in Section 16 under Process Capability. Process capability in administrative and support operations is covered in Section 21 under Process Capability.

Stream-to-Stream Analysis. In order to meet production volume requirements, several sources of production ("streams") are often necessary. Streams take the form of different machines, operators, shifts, suppliers, etc. Although the streams may seem to be identical, the resulting products may not be. Stream-to-stream analysis consists of recording and examining data separately for each stream. One example was the diagnosis for burrs on kitchen stoves (see above under Diagnosis—General).

Another example (Payne, 1984) comes from a glass tube cutting machine. Glass tubing was cut into small glass rings. The weight of the rings was the critical element in determining the properties of the finished glass product. A sample of data (Figure 22.12*a*) apparently confirmed a theory that the machine was not capable. However, the machine contained four heads. Data collected separately from each head (stream) revealed that there was nothing wrong with heads 2, 3, or 4—except for the need to recenter their position (Figure 22.12*b*). There was something wrong with head 1. Ultimately, the remedy was proper maintenance of the machine rather than a redesign of the machine as was originally contemplated based on Figure 22.12*a*.

Time-to-Time Analysis. Time-to-time analyses include (1) a simple plot of data on a time scale, (2) analysis of the time between abnormalities or problems, (3) analysis of rate of change, or "drift" of a characteristic, and (4) the use of cumulative data techniques with respect to time. Examples are given below.

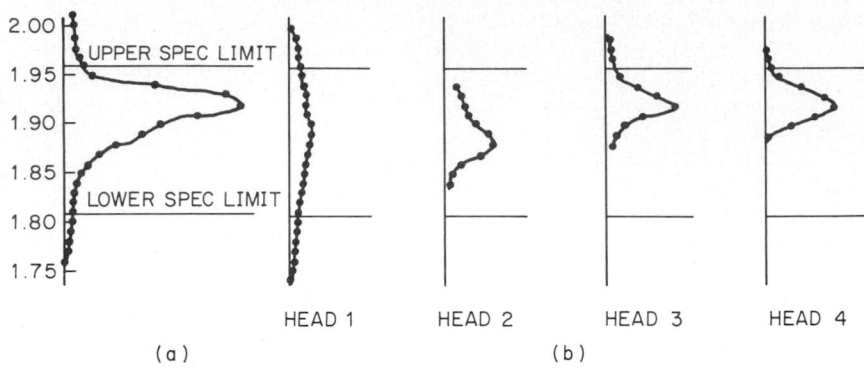

FIG. 22.12   Distribution of glass bead weights. (*a*) Sum of four heads. (*b*) Weight distribution on each of the four heads.   *(Adapted from Payne, 1984, pp. 30–31.)*

In trying to improve the uptime of production equipment, data were recorded on the amount and reasons for downtime for each machine (Payne, 1984). A superficial analysis led to a costly remedy and unsatisfactory results. Next came some real diagnosis. Data were collected for one week by machine and by time of day (Figure 22.13). Analysis of this almanac revealed:

1. Downtime in the morning is twice as much as the afternoon.
2. Much downtime occurs at the beginning of each shift.
3. Some machines perform significantly worse than others.
4. The distribution of fault types is not uniform from machine to machine.

These facts provided a whole new perspective on improving uptime.

In another example, field failures of oil coolers were assumed to be due to manufacturing. A parade of remedies (skipping the journey from symptom to cause) resulted in zero improvement. An engineer decided to plot the frequency of failures by month of the year, and this led to an important discovery. Of 70 failures over a 9-month period, 44 occurred during January, February, and March. These facts shifted the search to other causes such as winter climatic conditions. Subsequent diagnosis revealed the cause to be in design rather than manufacturing.

In analyzing time-to-time variations, the length of time between abnormalities can be a major clue to the cause. In a textile carding operation, there was a cyclic rise and fall of yarn weights, the cycle being about 12 min in length (Figure 22.14). The reaction of the production superintendent was immediate: "The only thing we do every 12 min or so is to stuff that feed box." In like manner, a process for making asbestos roofing shingles was found to produce abnormal weights every 6 min, on a precise timetable. Six minutes was also the interval for dumping a new load of material into the machine.

Within many streams, there is a time-to-time "drift"; e.g., the processing solution gradually becomes more dilute, the tools gradually wear, the worker becomes fatigued. Such drifts can often be quantified to determine the magnitude of the effect.

Cumulative plots of data can help to discover differences that are hidden when the data are in noncumulative form. Figure 22.15 compares a histogram (noncu-

TIME M/C STOPS	MACHINE 1	2	3		NUMBER 16	17	18	TOTAL
0600-0659	x	xxx	x			xxxxx	x	18
0700-0759		xx				xxxx	x	10
0800-0859			x		xx		x	6
0900-0959			x		x	xx	xxx	14
1000-1059	x				x	xx	x	9
1100-1159		xx	x		xx			11
1200-1259	xxx				x	x	xx	15
1300-1359		x	x			x		6
1400-1459	x	x	xx			xx		15
1500-1559						xx		5
1600-1659		x	x		x	x		4
1700-1759	x		x				x	6
1800-1859			x		x	x		5
1900-1959		x				x		4
2000-2059			x			x		5
2100-2159		x						1
Fault Type								
1	x	x	x		x	xx		8
2			x		x	xxx	x	9
3		x	x			xx	xx	10
4	xx	xx	xx		x	xxx	x	21
5	xx	xxx			x		xxx	16
6		x	x		x	x		10
7	x	x	x		xx	xxxxx		17
8	x	x	x			xxx	x	12
9		x	xx			xxxx	x	20
10	x	x	x		x	x	x	11

FIG. 22.13 Matrix for machine stop-time analysis. *(Adapted from Payne, 1984, p. 28.)*

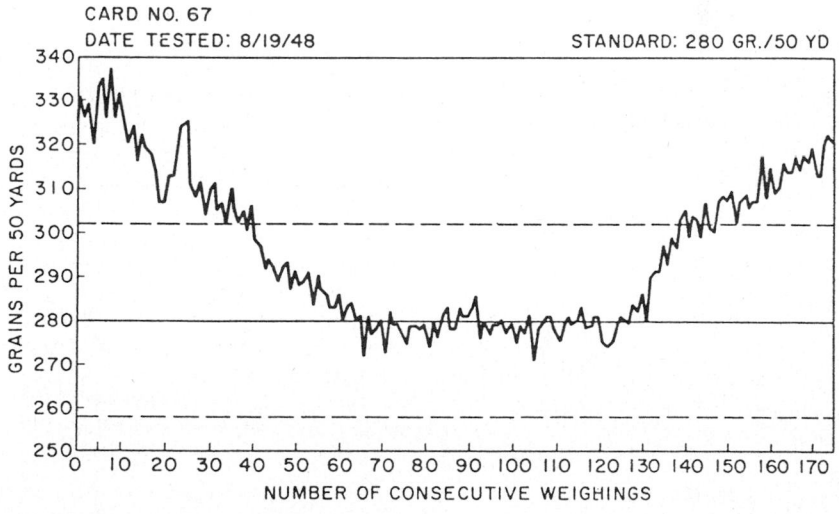

CARD NO. 67
DATE TESTED: 8/19/48   STANDARD: 280 GR./50 YD

FIG. 22.14 Consecutive weighings of card yarn.

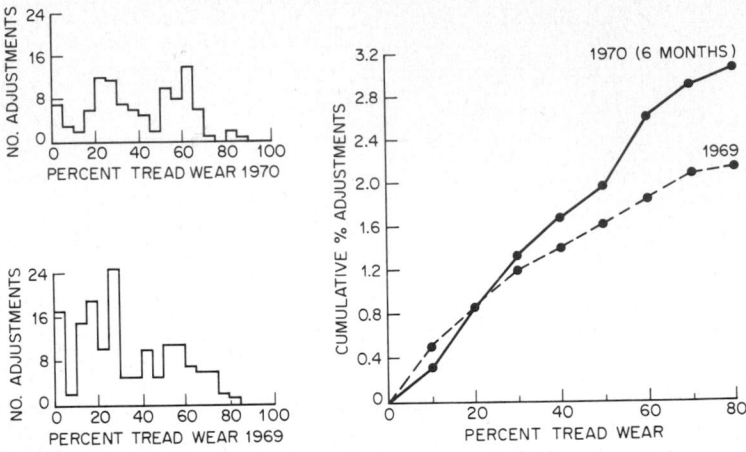

FIG. 22.15   Comparison of histograms and cumulative plots.

mulative) and cumulative plots for data from two separate years. A difference in adjustments for 1970 versus 1969 is apparent from the cumulative plot but is hidden in the histogram.

In investigating lost or diluted brine in a chemical plant, a simple plot of drops in brine concentration over the course of a 24-h production day revealed that only 2 percent differences in concentration were happening during the last 4 h of a shift. This knowledge led to the development of a new theory for test. (See Nester and Staal, 1986.)

Analysis of time-oriented data can often be made more discriminating by plotting the data on probability paper (see Section 23 under The Normal Distribution).

Control charts are a powerful tool of diagnosis. Data are plotted chronologically, and the chart then determines whether the variability from sample to sample is due to chance or assignable causes of variation. Detection of assignable causes of variation can be the link to discovering the cause of a problem. See Section 23, Statistical Process Control.

Piece-to-Piece Analysis.   Products also exhibit piece-to-piece variation, which is quite independent of variations resulting from mixture of streams or from time-to-time drift. Usually, measurement of this variation is done by the familiar techniques such as the frequency distribution. (See Section 23 under Frequency Distribution.)

Beyond conventional statistical analysis, there is room for much creativity in discovering causes of piece-to-piece variation. For example, in a stack casting operation, one theory was that the bottom castings in the stack caused far greater scrap than the remaining castings. When the castings were processed with knowledge of their prior position in the casting stack, the theory was confirmed.

Within-Piece Analysis.   In some cases, what turns out to be decisive is the variation within individual units of product. A useful charting course technique for

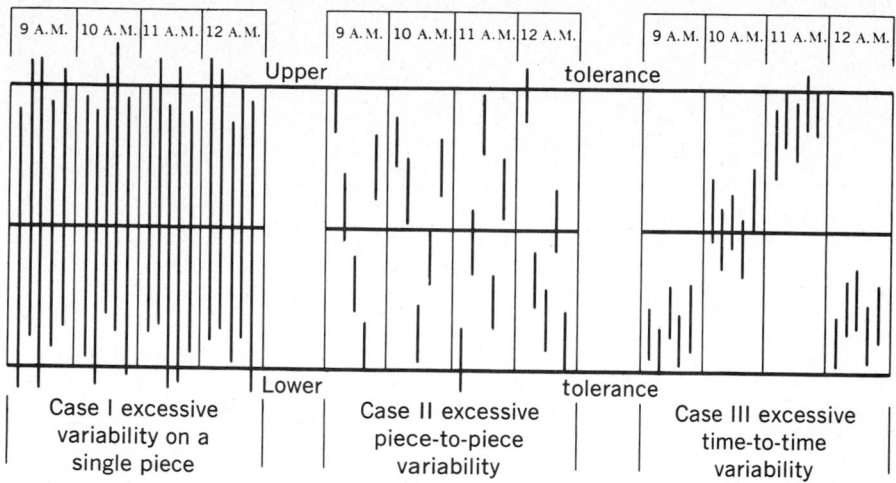

FIG. 22.16 Multi-Vari chart.

comparing within-piece variability to other sources of variability is the Multi-Vari chart.

Multi-Vari Chart.[2] In this chart, a vertical line depicts the range of variation within a single piece of product. Figure 22.16 depicts three different examples of the relationship of product variation to tolerance limits. The left-hand case is one in which the within-piece variation alone is too great in relation to the tolerance. Hence no solution is possible unless within-piece variation is reduced. The middle example is a case in which within-piece variation is comfortable, occupying only about 20 percent of the tolerance. The problem is piece-to-piece variation. In the right-hand example, the problem is excess time-to-time variability. Traver (1983) presents additional examples of Multi-Vari charts.

Defect Concentration Analysis. A "defect concentration diagram" plots attribute defect data according to the location on the product. The purpose is to discover whether defects are located in the same physical area.

Figure 22.17 shows a concentration diagram for the location of defects on an office reproduction product. The circled numbers indicate various locations on the equipment; the numbers adjacent to the circles indicate the number of defects found. An accompanying Pareto diagram of all of the locations made it clear that locations number 24 and 2 accounted for about 40 percent of the defects.

Often diagnostic tools must be combined to identify the cause of a problem. In diagnosing the cause of polishing defects on brass pieces, a combination of stream-to-stream analysis and a concentration diagram led to success. The polishing operation was performed by an endless chain of 138 "identical" holding fixtures, each fixture carrying one brass piece past the polishing wheels. A sample of

---

[2]The name "Multi-Vari" was given to this form of analysis by L. A. Seder in his classic paper "Diagnosis with Diagrams," which appeared in *Industrial Quality Control* in January and March 1950. The concept of the basic vertical line (Figure 22.16) had previously been employed by J. M. Juran (and possibly others), who derived it from the method long used by financial editors for showing stock market prices.

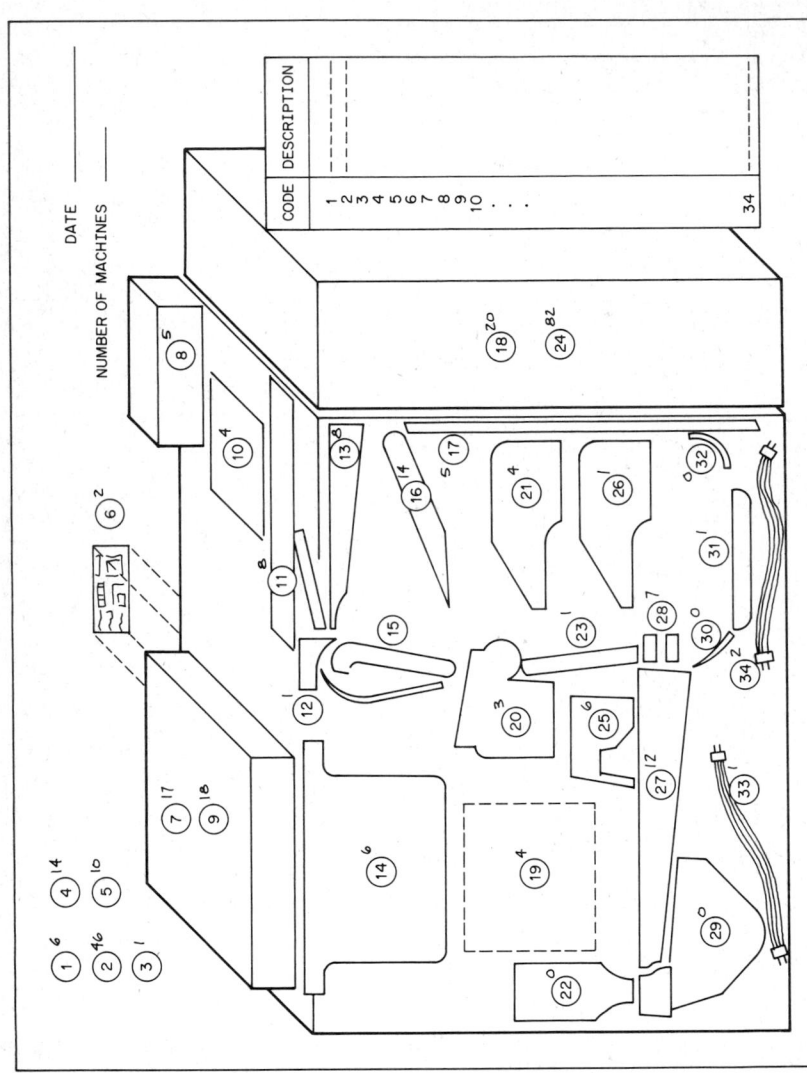

FIG. 22.17 Concentration diagram.

pieces selected at random from all fixtures showed defects occurring at different locations on the pieces. Diagnosis commenced by collecting data separately for each fixture—138 streams! Several consecutive pieces were examined from each stream, and the location of the defect was noted for each piece on a concentration diagram. This special collection of data by fixture revealed that pieces from the same fixture had defects concentrated at one location of the piece. The diagrams revealed that the location of the defect was directly related to the wear pattern on the holding fixture involved; the stream-to-stream analysis revealed that the 138 fixtures were not identical and had to be treated as 138 separate machines. Making adjustments unique to each fixture based on the direction given by the concentration diagrams proved to be an effective remedy.

Interrelation of Variables. Variables under study are often multiple in nature and are present in combination form. While they can be studied singly, there are many instances in which the need is to study them in combination. The aim of such studies is to quantify the size of the components of variation and to discover the extent to which they interact with each other. The generalized methods for such combination studies are discussed in Section 26, Design and Analysis of Experiments. However, simplified forms of analysis are available for problems which do not demand the use of sophisticated tools. One such form of analysis is the Multi-Vari chart discussed above. Other forms of such analyses are discussed below.

Simple Vectorial Resolution. Whenever the interaction among variables is negligible, the composite of multiple variations can be expressed by the relationship

$$\sigma^2_{comp} = \sigma^2_a + \sigma^2_b + \sigma^2_c + \cdots$$

where σ_{comp} = standard deviation of the composite
σ_a = standard deviation of variable a etc.

What is decisive about the size of variables in their contribution to the composite is not the standard deviation, but the square of the standard deviation! The relationship is of great practical value in affirming or denying theories and especially in establishing priorities for mounting an attack on the critical variables.

For example, three of the operations contributing to the thickness variation of optical lenses are blocking, milling, and grinding. On one set of processes the following data were secured:

Operation	σ	σ^2
Block	1.7	2.9
Mill	1.9	3.6
Grind	2.8	7.8
Sum of squares		14.3

The grinding, while seemingly a minor part of the variation when judged by the values of σ, accounts for more than half the sum of the squares.

Even more dramatic is the following synthetic example, which has numerous counterparts in the world of reality.

Six variables exhibit the following values of σ:

Variable	Original σ	Original σ^2	Improved σ	Improved σ^2
A	9	81	6	36
B	5	25	5	25
C	3	9	3	9
D	2	4	2	4
E	1	1	1	1
F	1	1	1	1
Total squares		121		76

Under a state of complete independence, the σ of composite becomes $\sqrt{121}$ = 11.

If the variability of A is now reduced from 9 to 6, the total of the squares will reduce to 76 (right-hand column) and the composite σ will reduce from 11 to 8.7.

If however, the variability of A remains constant and the variability of all the others is reduced to zero, the composite σ will become 9 (the value of A). In this synthetic example, a modest improvement in the variability of the dominant variable does more good than achievement of perfection in all other variables.

SPAN Plan. This is a structured approach to analysis of composite variations, and employs standardized data collection and analysis sheets to permit successive separation of observed total product variability into five recognized stages: lot-to-lot, stream-to-stream, time-to-time, within-piece (or positional), and error of measurement.

The plan is set out in "cookbook" fashion, so that a practitioner can collect the prescribed data, fill in the forms, and get the answer. Being a standardized procedure, the method can be used by the untrained practitioner.

Association Searches. Sometimes diagnosis can be advanced by analyzing data relating symptoms of the problem to some theory of causation pinpointing process, tools, workers, or design. Possible relationships can be examined using various statistical tools such as correlation, ranking, and matrixes.

Correlation. In this approach, data are plotted relating the incidence of symptoms of the problem to values of a potential causal variable. In some cases the analysis can be done with a simple diagram (Figure 22.18); other cases require regression and correlation analysis (see Section 23 under Regression Analysis).

In one case, the symptom was yarn breakage on weaving machines. One theory was "handling damages to the board bobbin." (The spinning mill supplied the yarn reeled into a board bobbin.) A plot of amount of damage against the number of yarn breakages clearly revealed a relationship between reels with heavy damage and subsequent yarn breakage. Further investigation showed that the corregated paper board plates used to protect the bobbins were inadequate. An investment of a few hundred dollars resulted in a cost reduction of $10,000 per year because of the yarn breakages (Bergstrom, 1985).

Ranking. In this technique, data are summarized by ranking the occurrence of the defect according to some source such as product model, machine, or operator. In one case involving 23 types of torque tubes, a ranking procedure showed that the amount of dynamic unbalance ranged form 52.3 percent defective to 12.3

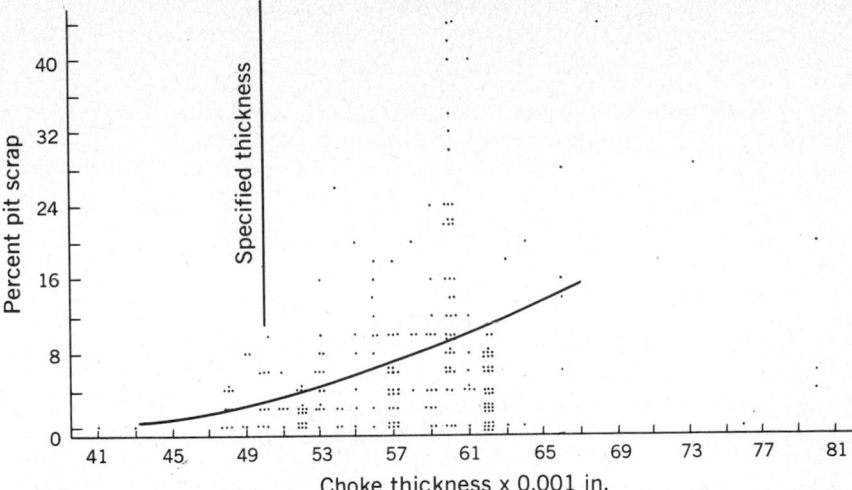

FIG. 22.18   Test of theories by correlation.

percent defective, the average being 22.1 percent. One of the theories advanced that a swaging operation was a dominant cause of dynamic unbalance. A data table (Table 22.13) showed the various types of torque tubes in decreasing order of dynamic unbalance. For each type, the table indicated whether or not a swaging operation was involved. The result was dramatic—the worst seven types were all swaged; the best seven were all unswaged. This led to a closer examination of the swaging process which in turn led to an examination of the specification. There was no requirement in the specification to hold a close coaxial relationship between the swaged and the unswaged diameters and this lack of close relationship is what led to the dynamic unbalance.

  Matrix.   In this approach, past or current data are collected on two or more variables of a problem and summarized in a table to see if any pattern exists (e.g., see Table 22.13). Additional examples are presented later in this section under

TABLE 22.13   Test of Theories by Ranking

Type	% defective	Swaged (marked ✕)	Type	% defective	Swaged (marked ✕)
A	52.3	✕	M	19.2	✕
B	36.7	✕	N	18.0	✕
C	30.8	✕	O	17.3	
D	29.9	✕	P	16.9	✕
E	25.3	✕	Q	15.8	
F	23.3	✕	R	15.3	
G	23.1	✕	S	14.9	
H	22.5		T	14.7	
I	21.8	✕	U	14.2	
J	21.7	✕	V	13.5	
K	20.7	✕	W	12.3	
L	20.3				

Test of Theories of Worker-Controllable Problems. G.O.A.L. (1986*a*) explains various adaptations of the matrix concept to include two or three sets of interrelated items.

Test of Theories by Collection of New Data ("Cutting New Windows in a Process"). In some cases the discovery of causes requires careful examination of additional stages in the process. This cutting of new windows can take several forms:

1. *Measurements at intermediate stages of a process:* Sometimes the symptom of a quality problem is not observed until after several operations have been performed, i.e., a specification applies to a finished characteristic that requires several manufacturing steps. In diagnosing some quality problems, it is necessary to go back into the previous steps and make observations there in order to evaluate theories.

An example involves the welding of large joints in critical pressure vessels. The weld is made by running a welding "bead" helically around the joint until the welding rod is consumed. A second bead follows the first, then a third, creating layer upon layer of weld material until the joint is completely built up. When the finished joint is x-rayed, any voids are identified.

The project team considered variations from a number of sources: worker, time to time, joint to joint, layer to layer, wtihin layer, and within bead. Prior test data were available to permit analysis of the first three of these theories. The remaining three could not be analyzed, since the x-ray test was performed only when a joint was completely finished. It was necessary to "dissect the process" on some joints by making an x-ray after each bead. This established that the main variable was within bead variation and that the problem was concentrated at the start of the bead.

Cutting new windows is also helpful in the diagnosis of nondissectible characteristics. A characteristic is "dissectible" if it is measurable during the process of manufacutre, e.g., the viscosity of a resinous material as it is processed into a varnish. A characteristic is "nondissectible" if it cannot be measured during such progression, e.g., the tensile strength of a casting. (Many nondissectible characteristics first come into existence at the conclusion of all manufacturing steps.) For diagnosis, it is useful in such cases to measure a related but dissectible property, e.g., hardness of the casting.

An example from a personnel process concerns the time required for hiring new engineers. Measurements taken at six steps in the overall process formed the basis for diagnosis (see Section 21 under Dissection of a Process).

2. *Measurement following noncontrolled operations:* Here, diagnosis includes the collection of additional information at individual steps in a process. Marquez (1985) describes the diagnosis of excessive shutdown time to remove a hot mold from a molding machine. The process of shutdown was divided into 11 steps and measurements taken to estimate the time required for each step. Two of the eleven steps accounted for 62 percent of the shutdown time. This Pareto effect was important in further diagnosis.

An example from a manufacturing area involves the time required to process customer returns and make a claims payment (Gust, 1985). Diagnosis was based on dissection of the overall process into five major steps. This additional information formed a basis for further diagnosis.

3. *Measurement of additional or related properties on the product or process:* Diagnosis sometimes requires measurements on characteristics other than those for which the specification is not being met. Mizell and Strattner (1981) discuss a high incidence of failures in a pressure test on automotive radiators. Effort focused on the heat treating and drying operations which occurred inside a closed assembly line braze oven. To measure accurately what was happening inside the oven, an insulated box—about the size of a radiator—was designed to hold a 10 channel data logger. Thermocouples were mounted on the outside of the box to measure temperature data and feed it to the data logger. The box was placed on the assembly line along with the radiators and sent through the oven on a normal brazing cycle. Data were recorded and transferred to a printer which showed the temperature and time. These data were used to modify the temperature profile inside the oven. Down went the failure rate.

In the manufacture of phonograph records the symptom was a high percent of records with surface defects. Automatic timers controlled the pressing cycle. Diagnosis revealed that the times for various steps should *not* be fixed but should be determined based on additional measurements periodically taken. The remedy was to monitor pressure, temperature, viscosity, and other factors. An on-line computer evaluates these data for each disk, and decides the optimum molding conditions. Only then, and no sooner, does the press create the product.

4. *Study of worker methods:* In some situations there are consistent differences in the defect levels coming from various workers. Month after month, some workers produce more "good" product than others. In such situations, there must be a cause for this consistent difference in observed performance. Diagnosis for problems related to human performance is discussed later in this section.

Diagnosis through Experiment. "Experiment" as used here means mainly creation and processing of trial lots to test the validity of theories about causes of quality deficiencies. The experiment may be conducted either in a laboratory or in the outside world, e.g., the factory, warehouse, or users' premises.

It is easy enough to put down the minimal criteria to be met by an experiment. It should:

Test the theories under study without being confused by extraneous variables

Discover the existence of major causes even if these were not advanced as theories

Be economic in relation to the amounts at stake

Provide reliable answers

To meet these criteria requires inputs from several sources. The *managers* must identify the questions that the experiment should answer; the *technologists* must select and set priorities on the proper variables to be investigated; the *diagnosticians* provide the methods for planning the experimental design and analyzing the resulting data.

Types of Experiments for Diagnosis. Section 26 presents a variety of designs of experiments, from the simple to the complex, that can be useful in diagnosing quality problems. Experimentation for diagnosis is not a matter to be left to the amateur. Although there are many forms of experimental designs, they can be broadly classified into the rifleshot experiment and the unbridled experiment.

The Rifleshot Experiment. In many projects, the analysis of available data may point strongly to only one or two suspect variables. In such cases it is common to avoid elaborate exploratory experiments and instead to conduct narrow experiments to test only the effect of the one or two suspects. Such studies are known as rifleshot experiments.

In its simplest form, the rifleshot experiment identifies, by use of the split-lot technique, which of two suspected variables is the cause. For example, for a batch of homogeneous material, half is sent through process A and the other half through process B. If the material is also a main suspect, two lots of material are split, and each is sent through both processes A and B, creating a two-by-two design of experiment. If three variables are involved, more combinations are needed; but now the technique of design of experiments enters to simplify the procedure.

The Unbridled Experiment. In the absence of strong suspicions as to one or several variables being dominant, the trial-lot approach may take the form of the "unbridled" experiment. In this form, a lot (or lots) of product is followed through the successive processes under a plan which provides for making measurements of many of the suspected variables of the materials and processes. The resulting product characteristics are also measured. The hope is that the subsequent analysis will disclose all significant correlations between causes and effects.

The unbridled experiment is so much in the nature of a fishing expedition that it should be based on a written plan to assure that it is understood and that it represents a meeting of the minds. With careful planning, a well-organized unbridled experiment has a high probability of identifying the dominant causes of variability. The disadvantage is the associated high cost and long time interval to get answers.

Statisticians have developed some remarkably useful tools for getting rid of unwanted variables through "randomizing"; for minimizing the amount of experimentation through skillful use of factorial, blocked, nested, and still other designs; and for reading the meaning out of complex data. See Section 26, Design and Analysis of Experiments.

Measurement for Diagnosis. A roadblock to diagnosis is the use of shop instruments to make the measurements. These instruments were never intended for diagnosis. They were provided for entirely different purposes—i.e., process regulation and product test. There are several principal categories of cases in which measurement for diagnosis must be different from measurement for control. These cases include:

1. *Measurement by variables instead of attributes:* Process capability studies usually demand this type of measurement.

2. *Measurement with a precision superior to that of the shop instruments:* In some cases imprecise shop instruments are the dominant cause of the quality problem.

3. *Measurements at new "windows" cut into the process:* An example is the welding bead case discussed above under Test of Theories by Collection of New Data.

4. *Measurement of properties not in the specification:* The causes of the symptom may often involve a process parameter such as temperature or pressure that is not a product specification or even defined in the manufacturing procedure.

5. *Developing means to summarize sensory test results:* For example, in the optical industry, the extent of scratches on precise components is a major problem affecting process yields and product quality. It is comparatively easy to judge one component for product acceptance purposes. However, for judging process capability, one company developed a "scratch index" which was expressed roughly as the ratio of the scratched area to the total area.

The foregoing paragraphs have described diagnostic techniques for management-controllable problems. Worker-controllable problems can involve additional diagnostic techniques.

TEST OF THEORIES OF WORKER-CONTROLLABLE PROBLEMS

A casual review of errors made by humans can lead to a conclusion that the basic cause is lack of motivation on quality. The facts refute this. Diagnosis of human errors reveals that there are "multiple species" of error and that lack of motivation is only one of the causes. To illustrate these species, Table 22.14 shows the distribution of 80 errors made by six office workers engaged in preparing insurance policy contracts.

TABLE 22.14 Matrix of Errors by Insurance Policy Writers

Error type	Policy writer						Total
	A	B	C	D	E	F	
1	0	0	1	0	2	1	4
2	1	0	0	0	1	0	2
3	0	(16)	1	0	2	0	(19)
4	0	0	0	0	1	0	1
5	2	1	3	1	4	2	(13)
6	0	0	0	0	3	0	3
27							
28							
29							
Total	6	(20)	8	3	(36)	7	80

There were 29 types of errors and they follow the Pareto principle. Notice the data for error type 3. There were 19 of these, and worker B made 16 of the 19. The table also shows the rest of the work done by worker B. Except for error type 3, B makes few errors. There is nothing basically wrong with the job specification or the method, since five workers had little or no trouble with error type 3. There is nothing basically wrong with worker B, except for defect type 3. It follows that worker B and no one else is misinterpreting some instruction, resulting in that cluster of 16 errors of type 3.

Error type 5 is of a different species. There is a cluster of 13 of these, and all the workers make this error, more or less uniformly. This suggests some difference in approach between all the workers on the one hand and the inspector on the other. Such a difference is usually of management-controllable origin, but the realities can soon be established by interviews with the respective employees.

Notice also the column of numbers associated with worker E. The total is 36 errors and is the largest cluster in the table. Worker E made nearly half the errors for the entire team and that worker made them in virtually all error type categories. Why did worker E make so many errors? It might be any of a variety of reasons, e.g., inadequate training, lack the capacity to do such exacting work, etc. Further study is needed, but it might be easier to go from symptom directly to remedy—find a less demanding job for that worker.

Thus, this one table of data shows the presence of multiple species of worker error. The remedy is not as simplistic as "motivate the worker." Understanding these species through diagnosis is important in identifying causes. See also Section 10 under Diagnosing Worker Performance.

Tools of Analysis.   The diagnostic tools include:

1. *The matrix:* An example is the above case of insurance policy errors. The matrix showed the performance of multiple workers with respect to multiple error types.
2. *The Pareto analysis (see above under Pareto Principle):* Figure 22.19 shows the distribution of imperfects for 15 weavers in a textile department. Three of the weavers account for 74 percent of the total imperfects.

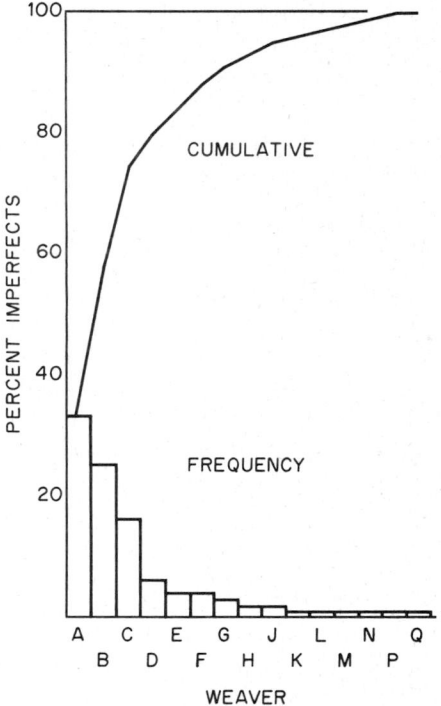

FIG. **22.19** Pareto analysis of weaving imperfects.

3. *The time-to-time analysis:* An example below (The Gun Assembly Case) shows how such an analysis establishes the presence of "consistency."

By using these tools of analysis, it soon emerges that the great majority of worker errors fall into three species: inadvertent, technique, and conscious. Table

TABLE 22.15 Interrelation among Error Pattern, Likely Subspecies of Worker Error, and Likely Solution

Pattern disclosed by analysis of worker error	Likely subspecies of error causing this pattern	Likely solution
On certain defects, no one is error-prone; defect pattern is random.	Errors are due to inadvertence.	Error-proof the process.
On certain defects, some workers are consistently error-prone while others are consistently "good."	Errors are due to lack of technique (ability, know-how, etc.). Lack of technique may take the form of secret ignorance. Technique may consist of known knack or of secret knowledge.	Discovery and propagation of knack. Discovery and elimination of secret ignorance.
Some workers are consistently error-prone over a wide range of defects.	There are several potential causes: Conscious failure to comply to standards Inherent incapacity to perform this task Lack of training	Solution follows the cause: Motivation Transfer worker Supply training.
On certain defects, all workers are error-prone.	Errors are management controllable.	Meet the criteria for self-control.

22.15 shows the interrelations among the errors pattern, the likely subspecies, and the likely remedies. The three species are examined below.

Inadvertent Errors.   Inadvertent errors are those which workers are unable to avoid because of human inability to maintain attention. Centuries of experience have demonstrated that human beings are simply unable to maintain continuing attention. (If the "not paying attention" is deliberate, the resulting errors are conscious rather than inadvertent.)

The usual examples involve a component omitted from an assembly, or a process adjustment that is set incorrectly. Unusual examples also occur. Some stock brokerage companies maintain a special account to cover expenses in connection with errors made in trading stock, e.g., the purchase of the wrong stock because of a similarity in the acronyms used to identify companies. In the athletic arena, a football game is lost because, on a key play near the end of the game, a player mistakenly hears a play called as "green" instead of "three." He misses his defensive assignment and the opposing team scores a touchdown (Anderson, 1982).

Diagnosis to identify errors as inadvertent is aided by understanding their distinguishing features. They are:

Unintentional: The worker does not want to make errors.

Unwitting: At the time of making an error, the worker is unaware of having made it.

Unpredictable: There is nothing systematic as to when an error will be made, what type of error will be made, or which worker will make the error. As a consequence of this unpredictability, the error pattern exhibits *randomness.* Conversely, *a set of data which shows a random pattern of worker error suggests that the errors are inadvertent.* The randomness of the data may apply to the types of error, to the persons who make errors, and to the time when the errors are made.

The evident "cause" of inadvertent defects is inattention. But what causes inattention? The search for an answer leads us into the complexities of psychological (e.g., monotony) and physiological (e.g., fatigue) phenomena—complexities which are not fully understood even by the experts. To explore these complexities in depth means going deeper and deeper into an endless swamp. It is simpler to go around the swamp—to go direct from symptom to remedy.

Remedies for inadvertent errors involve two approaches:

1. Reducing the extent of dependence on human attention. The tools used here are all of the error-proofing type: fail-safe designs, validation of processes, countdowns, redundant verifications, cutoffs, interlocks, alarm signals, automation, robots. Large reduction in errors can result from the use of bar codes to help identify items.

2. Making it easier for the human beings to remain attentive. Reorganization of work to reduce fatigue and monotony, job rotation, sense multipliers, templates, masks, and overlays are examples of remedies.

Technique Errors. These errors arise because the worker lacks some essential technique, skill, or knowledge needed to prevent the error from happening. Diagnosis to identify errors due to technique is aided by understanding their features. They are:

Unintentional: The worker does not want to make errors.

Specific: Technique errors are unique to certain defect types—those types for which the missing technique is essential.

Consistent: Workers who lack the essential technique consistently make more defects than workers who possess the technique. This consistency is readily evident from data on worker errors.

Unavoidable: The inferior workers are unable to match the performance of the superior workers because they (the inferior workers) do not know "what to do differently."

Discovery of the existence of technique errors makes use of the diagnostic tools for worker errors, as illustrated below in the assembly of shotguns.

The Gun Assembly Case. Guns were assembled by 22 skilled craft workers, each of whom assembled a complete gun from bits and pieces. After a safety test, about 10 percent of the guns could not be opened up to remove the spent cartridge—a defect known as "open hard after fire." For such defects it was necessary to disassemble the gun and then reassemble, requiring about 2 hours per defective gun—a significant waste.

After an agony of fruitless discussion, it was clear that the missing element was factual information. Data, already in the files, by assembler and time, were collected and arranged in a matrix (Table 22.16). Some helpful information became evident.

1. There was a wide month-to-month *departmental* variation in the defect rate, ranging from a low of 1.8 percent in January to a high of 22.6 percent in Feb-

TABLE 22.16 Matrix Analysis

Assembly operator rank	Nov.	Dec.	Jan.	Feb.	Mar.	Apr.	Total
1	4	1	0	0	0	0	5
2	1	2	0	5	1	0	9
3	3	1	0	3	0	3	10
4	1	1	0	2	2	4	10
5	0	1	0	10	2	1	14
6	2	1	0	2	2	15	22
17	18	8	3	37	9	23	98
18	16	17	0	22	36	11	102
19	27	13	4	62	4	14	124
20	6	5	2	61	22	29	125
21	39	10	2	45	20	14	130
22	26	17	4	75	31	35	188
Total	234	146	34	496	239	241	1390
% defective	10.6	6.6	1.8	22.6	10.9	11.0	10.5
5 best	9	6	0	20	5	8	48
5 worst	114	62	12	265	113	103	669
Ratio	13	10	∞	13	23	13	14

ruary. Since all workers seemed to be affected, this variation had its cause outside of the department. (Subsequent analysis confirmed this.)

2. The ratio of the five best performances to the five worst showed *a stunning consistency.* In each of the 6 months, the five worst performances add up to an error rate which is at least 10 times as great as the sum of the five best performances. There must be a reason for such a consistent difference, and it can be found by studying the work methods—the technique used by the respective workers.

The Knack.   The study of work methods showed that the superior performers used a file to cut down one of the dimensions on a complex component; the inferior performers did not file that component. This filing constituted the *"knack"*—a small difference in method which accounts for a large difference in results. (Until the diagnosis was made, the superior assemblers did not realize that the filing greatly reduced the incidence of defects.)

Usually the difference in worker performance is traceable to some superior knack used by the successful performers to benefit the product. In the case of the gun assemblers, the knack consisted of filing that component. In some cases, however, the difference in worker performance is due to unwitting *damage* done to the product (by the inferior performers). For example, the weavers who accounted for most of the imperfects (Figure 22.19) were unwittingly damaging the product—a sort of negative "knack."

There is a useful rule for predicting whether the difference in worker performance is due to a beneficial knack or to a negative knack. Who are in the minority? If the superior performers are in the minority, the difference is probably due to a beneficial knack. If the inferior performers are in the minority, the difference in performance is likely due to a negative knack.

Hiding the Knack. Occasionally, a worker knows the superior knack but chooses to hide the information. Why? Perhaps to avoid admitting that prescribed procedures are not being followed; perhaps to retain a superiority of performance over the other workers. Often the reason is never known.

Sometimes, the causes of technique errors have their origin in a condition that is management-controllable.

1. In reviewing the frequency of damage to crankshafts, an analysis by individual workers showed that only one worker's product was damaged. Observation revealed that the worker sometimes bumped a crankshaft into a nearby conveyor. Why? Because the worker was left-handed and the workplace layout was inconvenient for a left-handed person.

2. In an aircraft assembly operation, data analysis by individual workers revealed that one worker met the production quota consistently while others did not. The worker explained that he had taken his powered screwdriver home and rebuilt the motor. The company replaced all the motors with a resulting increase in productivity and quality.

A Trap for Managers. Cases such as the gun assembly situation make clear the dangers of assuming that some workers are able to do good work and others not, and therefore the remedy is to motivate the inferior workers. Such an assumption has no validity as applied to technique errors. The entire category of technique errors is doomed to go on and on until someone is able to provide the inferior workers with an answer to the question, "What should I do differently than I am doing now?"

How is this question to be answered? Sometimes the workers are able to find the answers by themselves. This is especially true if teams of workers have been trained in problem solving and are given the time to analyze problems. More usually the workers cannot find the answers by themselves. In consequence they will keep on doing what they have been doing and hence will keep on making the same defects. This will go on and on until they get the needed help from management.

Summary for Technique Errors. The sequence of events to identify, analyze, and remedy technique errors is:

1. For the defect types under study, create and collect data which can disclose any significant worker-to-worker differences.

2. Analyze the data on a time-to-time basis to discover whether consistency is present.

3. Identify the consistently best and consistently worst performers.

4. Study the work methods used by the best and worst performers to identify their differences in technique.

5. Study these differences further so as to discover the beneficial knack which produces superior results (or the negative knack which is damaging the product).

6. Bring everyone up to the level of the best through appropriate remedial action such as:

   a. Train inferior performers in use of the knack or in avoidance of damage.

   b. Change the technology so that the process embodies the knack.

   c. Error-proof the process in ways which require use of the knack or which prohibit the technique which is damaging to the product.

Conscious Errors.   Diagnosis to identify errors as conscious is aided by understanding their features. They are:

Witting: At the time of making an error the worker is aware of it.

Intentional: The error is the result of a deliberate intention on the part of the worker.

Persistent: The worker who makes the error usually intends to keep it up.

The outward evidences of conscious errors are likewise unique. Whereas inadvertent errors exhibit randomness, conscious errors exhibit consistency, i.e., some workers consistently make more errors than others. However, whereas technique errors are typically restricted to those defect types which require some special knack, conscious errors tend to cover a wider spectrum of defect types. Knowing these types is helpful in diagnosing errors as conscious.

Management-Initiated Conscious Errors.   Many "conscious" errors are management-initiated. The most common examples arise from the multiple standards which all managers must meet—cost, delivery, productivity, as well as quality. Due to changes in the marketplace, the managers keep shifting their priorities; e.g., in a sellers' market, delivery schedules will prevail over some quality standards. The pressures on the managers are then transmitted to the work force and can similarly result in conscious violation of one standard in order to meet another.

A second major source of management-initiated conscious errors is an atmosphere of blame. In such an atmosphere, workers consciously violate company rules by hiding the scrap, failing to make out the rework tickets, etc.

There are also other examples. As part of a drive to catch up on late deliveries, management posts a new scoreboard to show progress of delivery against schedules. There are no such scoreboards showing performance against quality standards. The work force concludes that mangement is more interested in quantity than quality.

Some well-intentioned actions by management can, instead, have a tragic effect. For example, the managers launch a poster campaign to urge everyone to do better work. However, while the bulk of the defects are management-controllable, the campaign makes no provision to improve quality of purchased materials, process capability, machine maintenance. To the workers it would look like a case of "Do as we say, not as we do."

Worker-Initiated Conscious Errors.   Some conscious errors are worker-initiated. Workers may have real or fancied grievances against the boss or the company. They get their revenge by not meeting standards. A few become rebels against the whole social system and they use sabotage to show their resentment. Some of the instances encountered are so obviously antisocial that no one—not the fellow employees, not the union—will defend the actions.

Some conscious errors *seem* to be worker-initiated but have their origin in inadequate communication by management. For example, three product batches fail to conform to quality characteristic X. In each case the inspector places a hold on the batch. In each case the Material Review Board concludes the batch is fit for use and releases it for delivery. However, neither the production worker nor the inspector is told the reason. Not knowing the reason, these workers may conclude that characteristic X is unimportant. That sets the stage for unauthorized actions.

Complexity of Causes.   Most conscious errors involve complexity: multiple and conflicting standards to be met, foggy communications, shared responsibilities. This complexity has its effect on the journey from symptom to cause. As with the case of inadvertent errors, the journey leads into a swamp. Going into the swamp can be avoided. Even if the causes are unknown, some broad-spectrum remedies for conscious errors are known if the symptoms are understood.

Remedies for Conscious Errors. Generally, the remedies listed here emphasize securing changes in behavior but without special effort to secure a prior change in attitude. Either way, *the approach is oriented primarily to the persons* rather than to the "system"— the managerial or technological aspects of the job.

Depersonalize the Order. In one textile plant, spinners were failing to tie the correct knots ("weaver's knots") when joining two ends of yarn together. The pleas and threats of the supervisor were of no avail. The spinners disliked the supervisor and they resented the company's poor responses to their grievances. The problem was solved when the personnel manager took the informal leader of the spinners *to the weaving department* to show her how the weavers were having trouble because of wrong knots.

The principal involved here is "depersonalizing the order."

One *person* should not give orders to another *person*. Both should take their orders from the "law of the situation" a phrase coined by Mark Parker Follett (see Metcalf and Urwick, 1941.) The situation in the weaving department required that weaver's knots be tied. Hence that situation is binding on the president, the managers, the supervisors, the spinners.

Establish Accountability (Traceability). To illustrate, in one company the final product was packaged in bulky bales which were transported by conventional fork lift trucks. Periodically, a prong of a fork would pierce a bale and do a lot of damage. But there was no way of knowing which trucker moved which bale. When the company introduced a simple means of *identifying which trucker moved which bale,* the amount of damage dropped dramatically.

Provide Balanced Emphasis. The worker discovers the company's priority on multiple standards (quality, productivity, delivery) from the behavior of management. For example, scoreboards on productivity and delivery rates must be supplemented with one on quality to provide evidence of a balanced emphasis.

Conduct Periodic Quality Audits. Systems of continuing traceability or scorekeeping are not always cost-effective. Quality audits can be designed to provide, on a sampling basis, information of an accountability and scorekeeping nature.

Provide Assistance to Workers. Visual reminders to help prevent defects can be useful. For example, a "que" card is a wall poster listing the four or five principal worker-controllable defects for a specific process. Opposite each such defect is a narrative description of the knack which could avoid the defect. Supplemental posters explain the knacks by the use of diagrams.

Improve Communications. Most companies do a good job of communicating essential quality information to workers on matters such as specifications, standards, procedures, methods. But other communication is vital to foster a positive claim for quality. For example, management should:

1. Provide means for workers to communicate their views and ideas
2. Explain to workers those management actions which, on their face, are antagonistic to quality

Assuring that managers do communicate to workers is a problem. A widely prevalent example is the case of nonconforming lots which are sent out as being fit for use, but without telling the workers why they were sent out. Virtually no company makes provision in the "hold" documents to require that managers face the question: "What shall we communicate to the work force?" Lacking such a provision the matter is seldom considered, and hence by default there is no communication.

Communication via Quality Circle Projects.   To carry out such projects, workers and managers must communicate on a variety of topics as the project progresses to a conclusion: agreement on which projects to tackle; securing essential data from other departments; securing special tools, instruments, etc., for try-out ideas; securing consulting assistance from company specialists; getting recommendations accepted.

Create Competition, Incentives.   These devices have potential value provided they are not misused. Competitions among workers and teams must be designed to be in good humor and on a friendly level, such as prevails among the interdepartmental sport or bridge competitions.

Financial incentives are deceptively attractive. They look good while pay is going up—during the part of the cycle when they are "bonuses" for good work. However, during a spate of poor work, removal of the bonuses converts the "incentives" into "penalties," with all the associated arguments about who is responsible.

Nonfinancial incentives avoid the pitfall of bonuses becoming penalties, but they must be kept above the gimmickry level.

Error-Proof the Operation.   The concept of error-proofing has wide application to conscious errors. (See Section 16 under Error-Proofing the Process.)

Reassign the Work.   An option usually available to managers is selective assignment, i.e., assign the most demanding work to the workers with the best quality record. Application of this remedy may require redesign of jobs—separation of critical work from the rest so that selective assignment becomes feasible.

Use the Tools of Motivation.   This is the eleventh form of remedy for conscious errors. The subject is discussed in Section 10, Managing Human Performance.

The foregoing list of remedies helps to solve most conscious errors, but a study of the symptoms and surrounding circumstances is essential in order to choose the most effective remedy.

Next, we consider the development of remedies in general, for both management-controllable and worker-controllable problems.

DEVELOPMENT OF REMEDIES

Following diagnosis to determine the cause, the next step in the breakthrough process is to choose a remedy. Although remedies must be unquie for each problem, some examples have already been presented for management-controllable problems and for the several subspecies of worker-controllable problems.

Choice of Alternatives.   The diagnostic journey may lead to a wide variety of dominant causes of the symptoms: weakness in the design, inadequacy in a production process, lack of precision in a measuring instrument, lack of technique by a worker. Direct remedial action means revising the design, process, instrument, or technique in response to the findings of the diagnosis. An essential criterion is that company costs and customer costs be optimized.

In quantifying company costs the cost impact on a companywide basis (not departmental) should be calculated for each alternative. Included should be the impact on the cost of poor quality, materials usage, facilities usage, productivity, energy consumption, etc. The project team, rather than one department, is best suited to make this evaluation.

Similarly for the customer, the impact on the customers' costs and well-being should be evaluated for each alternative remedy. (Section 3 under Quality and Share of Market discusses the influence of competitive differences on the customer.) Of particular concern is a remedy that results in perfectionism, i.e., adding costs without adding value. Section 3 under Perfectionism discusses perfectionism.)

In order to provide a methodical study of alternatives, a solution selection matrix is helpful (see Figure 22.20 for an example from the Florida Power and Light Company). Such a matrix assures that criteria are defined and applied to each alternative.

Remedial Action.   Once the alternatives have been weighed, the project team makes its recommendation to that line department whose responsibilities include taking the type of action recommended. This line department then embarks on the action. It is usual, however, for the project team to keep the topic on its books until the action has been taken and it has been confirmed that the remedy solves the problem. Also of importance is to verify that the remedy does not create a new problem. For example, a ceramic seal ring for a pump had a chronic "pull-out" problem. Changing the firing ridge was confirmed as a remedy for the pull-out problem, but later experience showed that the remedy introduced a new problem in which parts would stick.

Occasionally, remedies can be remarkable. In a plant making chips for integrated circuits, a vibration problem caused by a nearby railroad was solved by constructing a swimming pool between the plant and the railroad. Another problem was caused by cement dust from an adjacent concrete mixing plant. The remedy: buy the plant and destroy it.

Usually remedial actions proceed smoothly once the agreements have been reached. There are, however, some special situations which are discussed below.

Revisions in Systematic Approach.   Many remedies are primarily of a technological nature—a change in some design, tool, or instrument. However, many remedies involve changes of a systematic sort—changes in policies, goals, plans, organization, standards, procedures, or emphasis. Such remedies are typically of an

POSSIBLE SOLUTIONS	TEAM CAN IMPLEMENT	COST HIGH/LOW	MANAGEMENT RECEPTIVITY	FIXES SEVERAL ROOT CAUSES	CREATES NEW PROBLEMS	OTHER
#1	Yes	High	High	Yes	No	
#2	No	Low	High	Yes	No	
#3	Yes	Low	Low	No	?	
#4	Yes	High	Low	Yes	Yes	
#5	No	Low	High	No	No	

FIG. 22.20   Solution selection matrix.

interdepartmental character and are often identified by the project team with its broad representation. In addition, such remedies can go well beyond the specific project under study, since policies, plans, procedures, etc., are usually designed to cover wider areas of operations. Examples of the many systematic remedies are formal design review and supplier certification. These and other systematic remedies are discussed in the other sections of this handbook.

Rare but Critical Defects. Some defects or errors occur in low frequency but have a serious effect when they do occur. These "rare but critical" defects demand special approaches, several of which are discussed below.

Increased Design Margins. Some product failures are traceable to inadequate margins of safety between the capability of the design and the use to which it is put. This inadequacy can arise in various ways: sale for the wrong application, misuse by the user, cost pressures on the designer, designers' errors, or inadequate testing of models. One potential remedy common to all these causes is to increase the margin of safety.

There are multiple ways to increase the margin of safety: provide more structural material, use more exotic materials, design for misuse rather than intended use, "derate" (specify for use at lower levels of stress), and apply fail-safe and error-proof concepts to the design. Virtually all of these ways involve increase in costs.

Improved Model Testing. One of the limitations of model construction and test is the small number of model units tested relative to the subsequent large number of product units. If the product failure rates are low, it is unlikely that such failures will be present during model testing at normal conditions of use.

By increasing the severity of test conditions and properly correlating the test results with normal test data, the predictions made by model testing can be significantly improved. However, care must be taken not to increase test severity to a degree which introduces new failure modes—failure modes not encountered in actual practice.

Improved Process Capability. Some rare but critical defects have their origin in the manufacturing process: the process dispersion is too wide, the process is periodically misdirected, the workers made errors. The needed corrective actions may be in such forms as reducing process variability, improving precision of setup, providing automatic warnings or cutoffs, and error-proofing against human error.

Automated 100 Percent Inspection. This concept has been widely applied in recent decades, especially with respect to (1) safety-oriented defects and (2) screening of components which would otherwise cause defects in final products. Application of the concept has been supported by a remarkable growth in the associated technology: nondestructive test methods, automated testing devices, and computerized controls.

Redundant 100 Percent Inspection. Where automated testing is not feasible, human beings must perform the inspection. Particularly when the inspection is monotonous, 100 percent inspection by humans is error-prone; i.e., some defects will be missed. Multiple inspectors can reduce the effect of human errors. Suppose that two inspectors are used and that each finds 80 percent of the defects submitted. The first inspector will find 80 percent and hence will miss 20 percent; the second inspector will find 80 percent of the 20 percent, or 16 percent. A cumulative result of 4 percent of the original defects will be missed.

The Useful Many Defects. Identification of the vital few defects is an important step in the breakthrough process. The remaining "useful many" defects, however, collectively may still represent a sizable amount of quality deficiency.

Two general approaches are used for the useful many defects:

1. Attack on the useful many *collectively*
2. Attack on the useful many *individually,* on a project-by-project basis

Attacking the useful many *collectively* is feasible by identifying some basis which is common to the numerous "different" product types or defect types. For example, the same chemical process produces many catalog items of paint, each "different" in color. The same electrochemical process is used to produce numerous varieties of semiconducting chips, each "different" in its circuitry.

If defect data on paint is organized by paint catalog number, then the numerous small volume catalog items will likely result in low frequency of defects, and therefore none will qualify for the vital few. If the same data are organized collectively for that one chemical process, then the total defects may be able to compete for a place among the vital few.

To cite another example, in job shop work one of the main sources of product defects is order editing errors. The documents must identify with precision the way in which this order differs from all previous orders. The outward evidence of order editing errors is a long list of many minor product defects. However, the *order-editing process* is common to all of these defects and hence may qualify as one of the vital few projects.

A search for a common basis need not be restricted to a common manufacturing process. Other bases for collective grouping of data include *broader* grouping of data by source of causes, i.e., design, supplier, field conditions, etc. In the other direction, grouping can focus on a *narrower* source of causes, i.e., unanticipated environmental conditions, wrong sequence of manufacturing steps, inadequate maintenance of measuring equipment, etc.

Attacking the useful many *individually,* on a project-by-project basis, is a totally different matter. If any are critical, then the approaches for the "rare but critical defects" apply. For the remainder, the cost of assigning managers and engineers cannot ordinarily be justified by the potential cost reduction. One solution is to tap the great potential of the work force through such means as quality circles (see Section 10 under Quality Circles).

It may also be possible to create a new generic remedy which applies to a wide assortment of error types. For example, office work has long had the annoying problem of misspelled words. Most of these misspellings are inadvertent errors scattered over a wide assortment of different words. Now, some word processing programs include a dictionary in their memory as a means of detecting misspelled words. The planners found a way to deal with numerous error types, each of which is comparatively rare.

Replication of Remedies. A remedy on one project may also apply to the same or similar quality problems throughout an organization. It is useful, therefore, to set up a means of communicating the remedy to others. One method (employed by the Florida Power and Light Company) is to establish a center to track, summarize, and broadcast the remedies. The remedy is entered into a data base that can be easily examined by means of key words, and the information is disseminated to other teams working on similar problems. In addition, those who review proposed remedies on projects are responsible for recommending where else in the organization a remedy could also be helpful.

Reducing the Cost of Inspection. The obvious benefits of identifying and removing the causes of defects can be supplemented by another benefit: Inspection can be reduced. Several avenues are possible, and these are discussed in Section 18 under Defect Prevention.

PROOF OF THE REMEDIES

Before a remedy is finally adopted, it must be proven effective under operating conditions. In practice, two steps are frequently involved:

1. Preliminary evaluation of the remedy under conditions that imitate the real world ("simulation")
2. Final evaluation under complete conditions of the real world

Examples of a preliminary evaluation of a design change can start with a reliability prediction based on a mathematical model and then proceed to testing of a prototype. The evaluation of a change in a manufacturing process can employ a dry run or a pilot plant.

Preliminary evaluations have limitations. The list is unending: The reliability prediction model is based on assumptions that are never fully met; the prototype test unit is made in the engineering shop rather than the production environment; the testing is done with a small sample size and limited test conditions; the dry run for the revised manufacturing process is conducted by the best workers using the best material and watched over by supervisors and engineers who are determined to make the remedy work, etc.

There is no substitute for the remedies in the real world. If the remedy is a design change on a component, the final evaluation must be a test of the redesigned component operating in the complete system under field conditions; if the remedy is a change in a manufacturing procedure, the new procedure must be tried under typical (not ideal) factory conditions; if the remedy is a change in a maintenance procedure, the effectiveness must be demonstrated in the field environment by personnel with representative skill levels.

The issues involved in proving remedies under typical operating conditions have many similarities to those which arise in the transfer of plans to operations (see Section 6 under Transfer to Operations.)

RESISTANCE TO CHANGE

Once a remedy has been determined, then on the face of it all that remains is to apply that remedy. Not so. Instead, various objections to the remedy are voiced by different parties, e.g., delaying tactics or outright rejection of the remedy by a manager, the work force, the union. "Resistance to change" is the popular name for these obstacles. This step in the universal sequence addresses the issue of making a breakthrough in the cultural resistance to change.

Cultural Patterns.   Change consists of two parts:

1. A *technological* change
2. A *social consequence* of the technological change

The social consequence consists of the impact of the technological change on the "cultural pattern" of the human beings involved, i.e., their beliefs, habits, traditions, practices, status symbols, etc. This social consequence is the root source of the resistance to change. To make matters more complex, those who resist change often state their reasons as technological objections, whereas their real reasons relate to the social consequences. As a result, the attempts to overcome the resistance are thwarted by not knowing the true reason for the resistance.

Illustrations come from all levels:

1. A worker objects to a revised work method claiming that the flow of work will result in less, not more, productivity. Analysis revealed another, but unstated, reason—a desire for recognition. (Under the present method, finished product is stored temporarily at the machine; under the new method, the product is moved out immediately. Hence, front office personnel no longer stop at the machine to admire the superior quality.)

2. Management resists a remedy which involves purchasing new gages externally rather than making them internally. An unstated reason is pride. Management will not admit that an external supplier is a superior gage maker.

3. Some design engineers resist the use of computer-aided design (CAD), claiming that the technology is not as effective as design analysis by a human being. In the case of older designers, the real reasons may include the fear that they will have more difficulty adapting to CAD than their younger rivals.

Analyzing the Impact of Change. Unfortunately, many advocates of change do not address themselves to a key question: "What threats will this change pose to the cultural pattern of this society?" Many of these advocates are *not even aware of the existence* of the cultural pattern, let alone its detailed makeup. Awareness of the existence, while necessary, is not sufficient. The advocates of change should in addition try to discover precisely what will their proposals threaten—which habits, whose status, what beliefs.

One aid to a study of resistance to change is a *barriers and aids analysis.* With this technique, strategies can be developed to overcome inherent barriers to change and make maximum use of available aids. In applying the technique at a utility organization (Florida Power and Light Co., 1984), five factors are considered: people, environment, hardware, time, and money. The steps in the analysis are:

1. Brainstorm a list of barriers (forces pushing against change).
2. Brainstorm a list of aids (forces pushing for change).
3. Rank all listed items as high, medium, or low.
4. Identify aids which balance or overcome barriers.
5. List matching barriers and aids on a chart.
6. List nonmatching barriers and identify (brainstorm) any offsetting aids.
7. List nonmatching aids and identify any offsetting barriers.
8. Identify items needing team action using the rankings of high, medium, or low.
9. Develop an action plan.

An example of the first two steps is shown in Figure 22.21. A similar technique is "forced field analysis" (see above under Structure Trees; see also Poza, 1983).

Rules of the Road for Introducing Change. Important among these are:

1. *Provide participation:* This is the single most important rule for introducing change. To do it effectively means that those who are likely to be affected by the change should be members of the project team in order to participate in both diagnosis and remedy. Lack of participation leads to resentment which can harden into a rock of resistance.

Forces pushing against quality improvement	Forces pushing for quality improvement
• Lack of dollars	• Team
• People shortage	• Personal commitment
• Vested interest/old attitude	• Management support
• Would the team stay together	• Support of line manager
• Other priorities	• Communications
• Time	• Within team
• Maintain work flow	• Outside team
• Complicatd techniques	• New techniques
	• Increasing cost of failure
	• Good planning
	• Specific goals

FIG. 22.21 Barriers and aids.

2. *Provide enough time:* How long does it take the members of a culture to accept a change? They must take enough time to evaluate the impact of the change and find an accommodation with the advocates of the change. Providing enough time takes various forms:

   a. Start small: Conducting a small-scale tryout before going "all out" reduces the risks, for the advocates as well as for the members of the culture.

   b. Avoid surprises: A major benefit of the cultural pattern is its predictability. A surprise is a shock to this predictability and a disturber of the peace.

   c. Choose the right year: There are right and wrong years—even decades— for timing a change.

3. *Keep the proposals free of excess baggage:* Avoid cluttering the proposals with extraneous matters not closely concerned with getting the results. The risk is that the debates will get off the main subject and into side issues.

4. *Work with the recognized leadership of the culture:* The culture is best understood by its members. They have their own leadership and this is often informal. Convincing the leadership is a significant step in getting the change accepted.

5. *Treat the people with dignity:* The classic example is that of the relay assemblers in the "Hawthorne experiments." Their productivity kept rising, under good illumination or poor, because in the "laboratory" they were being treated with dignity. See Section 10 under Process Management and Worker Self-Control.

6. *Reverse the positions:* Ask the question: What position would I take if I were a member of the culture? It is even useful to go into role playing to stimulate understanding of the other person's position.

7. *Deal directly with the resistance:* There are many ways of dealing directly with resistance to change:

   a. Try a program of persuasion.

   b. Offer a quid pro quo—something for something.

   c. Change the proposals to meet specific objections.

   d. Change the social climate in ways which will make the change more acceptable.

   e. Forget it. There are cases in which the correct alternative is to drop the proposal. We simply do not know how to plan so as to be 100 percent successful.

Resolving Differences.   Sometimes the resistance to implementation of a remedy can reach an impasse. To avoid this, a structured process for resolving differences is helpful. Coonley and Agnew (1941) describe such a process and how it was used to establish quality standards on cast iron pipe. The process is based on three conditions which those in disagreement must meet:

1. They must identify their areas of agreement and their areas of disagreement. "That is, they must first agree upon the exact point at which the road began to fork." When this was done it was found that a major point of disagreement concerned the validity of a certain formula.
2. "They must agree on why they disagreed." They concluded that the known facts were inadequate to decide whether the formula was valid or not.
3. "They must decide what they were going to do about it." The decision was to raise a fund to conduct the research needed to establish the necessary facts. "With the facts at hand, the controversies disappeared."

This was essentially the approach taken by the supervisors to resolve disagreements on the causes of the burrs on screws (see the example earlier under Diagnosis—General).

Ackoff (1978) describes a six-step procedure for resolving disagreements. To start, each participant must state the other (opposing) position in a way that is acceptable to the other person. This helps to ensure that the opposing positions are clearly understood. The process continues until the participants can agree on a course of action that has the least serious error associated with it.

Kotter (1985), Argyris (1985), and Kanter (1983) elaborate on resistance to change in the industrial environment. Two classic references by Coch and French (1948) and Lawrence (1969) present the results of research based on industrial examples.

CONTROL AT THE NEW LEVEL

The final step in the breakthrough sequence is holding the gains so that the benefits of the breakthrough will continue on and on. To enable the operating forces to hold the gains requires (1) a successful transfer of the remedy from "laboratory" conditions to operating conditions and (2) a systematic means of holding the gains—the control process. Failure to meet both of these requirements can result in failure to hold the gains.

Transfer from "Laboratory" to Operations.   Three steps are essential:

1. Provide the operating forces with a process capable of holding the gains. Sometimes, this involves minimal change; other times, the process change may be complex. To the extent which is economic, the process changes should be designed to be *irreversible.*

An improvement study in a foundry illustrates two types of remedies. One remedy (irreversible) involved the replacement of old spouts with larger-diameter spouts. The old spouts were destroyed. Another remedy (reversible) required melters to use scales to accurately weigh the amount of metal to be poured. Some melters did not continue to use the scales; they went right back to estimating by eye and feel.

From another industry, changing from hand insertion of components into printed circuit boards to automatic insertion by programmed tape rolls illustrates an irreversible remedy. In wave soldering, requiring a different specific gravity for flux could be reversible because contamination or other factors could result in the previously unacceptable specific gravity.

The test of the revised process is really two tests, at different stages:

a. Under the "laboratory" conditions provided by the remedial department

b. Under operating conditions

The project is not complete until satisfactory results have been produced under operating conditions.

2. Establish operating standards and procedures to serve as a basis for training, control, and audit. Operating standards and procedures tend to be well defined with respect to input materials which are to enter the process; equipment, tools, and measuring instruments; and levels at which to set the critical process variables, e.g., temperature, pressure. In contrast, procedures are often vague or silent on matters such as why the criteria should be met; what can happen if they are not met; standards for esthetic qualities; equipment maintenance; and worker technique. Failure to deal with these latter areas will commonly show up in due course as failures to hold the gains.

3. Train the operating forces to use the procedures and to meet the standards. Changes in standards and procedures clearly require training of the operating forces with respect to the impacts of those changes. The operating forces should be trained to understand: (*a*) Just what has been changed. (*b*) The new product and process standards to be met. (*c*) What new decisions and actions will be required to make the changes effective. (*d*) Who has the responsibility to make these decisions and take these actions. (*e*) How to use the new equipment, tools, and instruments. (*f*) What the techniques are which have been demonstrated to secure the best results. (*g*) What the consequences are of deviating from the specified standards and procedures.

In conducting this training it is well to make use of information collected during diagnosis to help explain the reasons for the changes.

Concept of Control. A good transition enables the operating forces to secure the benefits of the breakthrough. However, these benefits will not be permanent because many forces lie in wait to erode them, including equipment deterioration and breakdown, material shortages and deficiencies, and human backsliding and error. Faced with such future erosion, good managers do not just walk away once the transition has been made. What the managers do is to provide a systematic means for holding the gains—something called control.

Control during operations is done through use of the feedback loop—a cyclical activity involving evaluation of actual performance, comparison with the standard of performance, and action on the difference. Elaboration of the concept of control is discussed in Section 6, under Planning for Control. Section 24, Statistical Process Control, presents a collection of statistical process control techniques for the detection of out-of-control conditions. Section 17, under Audit of Production Quality, describes process audits as a means of verifying that the required process conditions and actions continue in place.

TROUBLESHOOTING

Troubleshooting (fire fighting) is diagnosis and remedial action applied to sporadic troubles (not chronic). Ineffective troubleshooting can result in failure to hold the gains. The same "two journeys" are needed but each is much simpler than for chronic troubles. The sporadic trouble is the result of some adverse change, so the diagnostic journey is one of discovering "What was the adverse change?" The remedial journey removes the discovered adverse change so as to restore the status quo.

Product Comparisons to Discover the Change.   As with chronic troubles, there is need to clarify the symptoms, conduct autopsies, theorize, test the theories, etc. To discover what has changed, however, requires some comparisons, mainly:

> Comparison of features exhibited by products made prior to the trouble with features of products made since the trouble set in.
>
> Comparison of symptoms exhibited by defective units with features of good units, both having been made since the trouble set in.

Along with these comparisons, a chronology of events is needed.

Reconstructing the Chronology.   By definition, a sporadic trouble is the result of some change—an adverse change. During operations, changes are constantly taking place: old material batches are consumed and new material batches come in; the day shift goes out and the night shift comes in; a filling line is cleaned out to make ready for a different size of bottle.

Which of these changes might be related to the sporadic trouble? A time-log chart can be prepared showing the exact time of known changes along with product identification (serial numbers, batch records, etc.) This provides a chronological history of product and process changes. Analysis of this log will then support some theories and will deny others.

Testing the Theories.   Because of the intermittent nature of sporadic problems, some theories disappear early. "The new supplier has nothing to do with it. His material came in two days after the trouble started." As these obvious cases are cleared away, the need may arise to create new information, to use stream-to-stream analysis, time-to-time analysis, process dissection, and other tools of diagnosis. Supervisors who will be called upon to do troubleshooting should be trained in use of the necessary tools and techniques.

At company X, an unusual separation into streams helped to solve an outbreak of field complaints on elastic breaking and vinyl cracking in baby pants. Tests on competing products showed them to be free of such problems. Next, opinions focused on inferior raw material from the two suppliers. Both suppliers rejected this belief. One of them said, "What we are sending you is *better* than what we send your competitors." (That implied that the cause was during the processing at X.) To prove the claim, the supplier sent to company X a batch of material being furnished to the competitors and suggested that tests be made to compare that material with material currently in use by company X. Tests were conducted and, to the surprise of the supplier, the results showed that the material going to the competitors was superior, not inferior as claimed. The supplier reacted, "It can't be." Next, both batches of material were carefully inspected and tested. The supplier noticed that some of the "oils" in the elastic sent to company X had dried up; the condition was not present in the sample of material for the competitors. Further investigation unraveled the mystery. A buyer at company X had mistakenly ordered raw material for 2 years, instead of for 1 month. Because the material then sat in storage for many months, the oils dried up and subsequently caused the breaking and cracking problems.

Structured Procedure for Troubleshooting.   Monsanto (undated) describes a step-by-step approach for finding the cause of deviations between expected and actual performance. The approach first describes the deviation, searches for possible causes, and then determines the true cause. Seven steps are involved:

1. State the deviation. Questions are posed to identify a single effect and a single object or group of related objects. What object (or group of related objects) is involved? What's the effect? Does anyone know the cause of this deviation?
2. Specify the deviation. The nature of the deviation is described in terms of *what is involved* with the deviation and *what is not involved*. Questions about the deviation involve what, where, when, and how much?
3. Identify the unique characteristics of the deviation. This is done through use of a matrix (Figure 22.22).
4. Search for changes. The matrix is used and the question is asked, "What, if anything, has changed in, around, or about this unique characteristic?" Answers are listed in the "changes" column.
5. Develop possible causes. For each change the question is asked "How could this change have caused the deviation?"
6. Test the possible causes against the specification. Compare each possible cause to the information in the "is involved" and "is not involved" description and see if the cause is consistent with the information.
7. Verify the cause, attempt to reproduce the deviation using the most probable cause, or eliminate the deviation by correcting the most probable cause.

Operating personnel can be trained to use this type of approach to do their own troubleshooting. An elaboration of this approach is presented by Kepner and Tregoe (1981).

Corrective Action.   Once the cause of the sporadic trouble is known, the worst is over. For the great majority of sporadic troubles the remedy involves going back to what was done before. This is a return to the familiar, not a journey into the unknown (as is often the case when dealing with chronic troubles). The needed technology is usually known to the local people, and they can take the necessary action to restore the status quo. Cultural resistance is minimal.

	Is involved	*Is not involved	Unique characteristics (of "is involved")	Changes
What?				
Where?				
When?				
How much?				

FIG. 22.22   Deviation analysis.

Sometimes the local people can do better than merely restoring the status quo. They can use their ingenuity to find preventive ways to reduce repetition of the sporadic troubles and associated troubleshooting.

REFERENCES

Ackoff, Russell L. (1978). *The Art of Problem Solving.* John Wiley & Sons, New York, pp. 45–47.

Anderson, Dave (1982). "When 3 Meant 6." *New York Times,* Dec. 27, pp. C1, C3.

Argyris, Chris (1985). *Strategy, Change, and Defensive Routines.* Pitman, Boston.

Benedict, Ruth (1946). *Patterns of Culture.* Mentor Books, New American Library of World Literature, New York. Originally published by Houghton Mifflin, Boston, 1934.

Bergstrom, Sigvard (1985). "Quality Improvement by Problem Solving Groups." *Proceedings, EOQC Conference,* vol. 2, pp. 327–333.

Betker, Harry A. (1983). "Quality Improvement Program: Reducing Solder Defects on Printed Circuit Board Assembly." *The Juran Report,* no. 2, November, pp. 53–58.

Betker, Harry A. (1985*a*). "Quality Improvement Program Project to Identify and Correct All Known Problems on an Electro-Mechanical Detection Device." *The Juran Report,* no. 4, winter, pp. 70–76.

Betker, Harry A. (1985*b*). "Storyboarding: It's No Mickey Mouse Technique." *The Juran Report,* no. 5, summer, pp. 25–30.

Coch, Lester and French, John R. P., Jr. (1948). "Overcoming Resistance to Change." *Human Relations,* August, pp. 512–532.

Coonley, Howard and Agnew, P. G. (1941). *The Role of Standards in the System of Free Enterprise.* American National Standards Institute, New York.

Doran, P. K. (1985). "A Total Quality Improvement Programme." *International Journal of Quality and Reliability Management,* vol. 2, no. 3, pp. 18–36.

Douglas, R. D. (1983). "Now What Do We Do?" *The Juran Report,* no. 3, November, pp. 100–105.

Dymtrow, Eric D. (1985). "Quality Improvement in Information Processing." *The Juran Report,* no. 4, winter, pp. 134–139.

Florida Power and Light Company (1984). *FPL Quality Improvement Program, Guidebook and Roadmap.* Miami, FL, p. 44.

G.O.A.L., Growth Opportunity Alliance of Greater Lawrence (1985*a*). *The Memory Jogger.* p. 12.

G.O.A.L. (1985*b*). "Interrelationship Diagraph." *G.O.A.L. Newsletter,* November–December, pp. 3–4.

G.O.A.L. (1986*a*). "Matrix Diagram." *G.O.A.L. Newsletter,* March–April, pp. 3–5; May–June, pp. 3–4.

G.O.A.L. (1986*b*). "Program Decision Process Chart (PDPC)." *G.O.A.L. Newsletter,* July–August, pp. 3–4.

Greenridge, R. M. C. (1953). "The Case of Reliability vs. Defective Components et al." *Electronic Applications Reliability Review,* no. 1, p. 12.

Gust, Lawrence J. (1985). "Non-Manufacturing Quality Improvement." *The Juran Report,* no. 4, winter, pp. 112–120.

Halpin, J. F. (1966). *Zero Defects.* McGraw-Hill, New York.

Hartman, Bob (1983). "Implementing Quality Improvement." *The Juran Report,* no. 2, November, pp. 124–131.

Holm, Robert A. (1985). "Quality Improvement in the Oil Patch." *The Juran Report,* no. 4, winter, pp. 47–51.

Ingram, Gary E. (1984). "Historical Processes for Quality Project Management." *Project Management Institute Proceedings,* Philadelphia, pp. 1–3.

Ishikawa, Kaoru (1976). *Guide to Quality Control.* Asian Productivity Organization. Publication obtainable from the American Society for Quality Control, Milwaukee.

Juran, J. M. (1985). "Charting the Quality Course." *The Juran Report,* no. 5, summer, pp. 10-15.

Kano, Noriaki (1984). "Problem Solving in New Product Development—Application of T-Typed Matrix." *Proceedings, World Quality Congress.* European Organization for Quality Control, Berne, Switzerland, vol. 3, pp. 45-55.

Kanter, R. M. (1983). *The Change Masters.* Simon and Schuster, New York.

Kato, Osamu, Sakai, Yosho, and Sasaki, Katsuo (1981). "Improvement of the Rust Preventive Method for the Body Panel of a Motor Vehicle." *Reports of Statistical Applications and Research,* Japanese Union of Scientists and Engineers, vol. 28, no. 1, March, C section, pp. 40-55.

Kepner, Charles H. and Tregoe, Benjamin B. (1981). *The New Rational Manager.* Princeton Research Press, Princeton, NJ.

Kotter, J. P. (1985). *Power and Influence.* Macmillan Free Press, New York.

Kurland, Leonard T. and Molgaard, Craig A. (1981). "The Patient Record in Epidemiology." *Scientific American,* October, pp. 54-63.

Lawrence, Paul R. (1969). "How to Deal with Resistance to Change." *Harvard Business Review,* January–February, pp. 4-12ff.

Leonard, James F. (1986). "Quality Improvement in Recruiting and Employment." *The Juran Report,* no. 6, pp. 111-118.

Lossin, Richard D. (1983). "Quality Improvement at Westinghouse Furniture Systems." *The Juran Report,* no. 2, November, pp. 31-34.

Lounds, Andrew C. and Pearson, Larry G. (1985). "A Team Project for Improving Office Productivity and Communication." *The Juran Report,* no. 4, winter, pp. 40-45.

Marquez, Manuel (1985). "Quality Improvement at Challenger Caribbean Corporation." *The Juran Report,* no. 4, pp. 52-56.

McGrath, James H. (1985). "Preparation of Improvement Team Leaders and Facilitators." *The Juran Report,* no. 4, winter, pp. 95-101.

Mead, Margaret (ed.) (1955). *Cultural Patterns and Technical Change.* Mentor Books, New American Library of World Literature, New York; also published by UNESCO, Paris, 1951.

Metcalf, Henry C. and Urwick, L. (ed.) (1941). *Dynamic Administration.* Harper and Row, New York.

Mizell, Michael and Strattner, Lawrence (1981). "Diagnostic Measuring in Manufacturing." *Quality,* September, pp. 29-32.

Moehlenbrock, Maxine (1985). "Control Teams Contrasted with Breakthrough Teams." *The Juran Report,* no. 4, winter, pp. 175-179.

Monsanto (undated). *Managerial Analytics Pocket Manual.* Monsanto Company, Corporate Management Development, St. Louis, MO.

Nester, Donald and Staal, Rolf (1986). "The Universal Sequence of Events on the Production Floor of AHC." *The Juran Report,* no. 6, winter, pp. 99-105.

Noakes, Merle E. (1985). "The Three-Level Quality Council." *The Juran Report,* no. 4, winter, pp. 92-94.

Payne, B. J. (1984). "Statistical Techniques in the Management of Quality Improvement." *International Journal of Quality and Reliability Management,* vol. 1, no. 3, pp. 24-35.

Peters, Peter E. (1983). "Axle Plant Jura System and Example of Solving a Non-Quality Problem." *The Juran Report,* no. 2, November, pp. 77-81.

Poza, Ernesto J. (1983). "A Do It Yourself Guide to Group Problem Solving." *Personnel,* March–April, pp. 69-77.

Riggs, James L. (1981). *Production Systems: Planning, Analysis, and Control,* 3rd ed. John Wiley & Sons, New York.

Selwitchka, R. (1980). "The Priority List on Measures for Reducing Quality Related Costs." *EOQC Quality,* vol. 24, no. 5, pp. 3-7.

Stratton, Donald A. (1987). "Force Field Analysis: A Powerful Tool for Facilitators." *The Juran Report,* no. 8, winter, pp. 105–111.

Traver, Robert W. (1983). "Locating the Key Variables." *ASQC Quality Congress Transactions,* Milwaukee, pp. 231–237.

Wachniak, Raymond (1983). "Development and Implementation of a Project Support Review Program." *The Juran Report,* no. 1, pp. 87–90.

Wolf, John D. (1983). "Quality is Management at McDonnell Douglas." *The Juran Report,* no. 2, pp. 116–123.

Woodward, James D. (1985). "Not Just Another Training Program." *The Juran Report,* no. 4, winter, pp. 24–27.

SECTION 23
BASIC STATISTICAL METHODS[1]

Edward J. Dudewicz, Ph.D.

THE STATISTICAL TOOL KIT . . **23.2**

*SOURCES AND
SUMMARIZATION OF DATA* . . **23.3**

Planning for Collection and
Analysis of Data 23.3

Historical Data, Their Uses,
and Caveats 23.6

Data from Planned
Experimentation 23.8

Data Screening 23.9

Descriptive Statistics for
Summarizing Data . . . 23.11

Accurate Calculation of
Descriptive Statistics . . 23.19

*PROBABILITY MODELS FOR
EXPERIMENTS* **23.21**

Sample Space 23.21

Events 23.23

Rules of Probability,
Combinatorics 23.24

Conditional Probability;
Bayes' Theorem 23.25

*DISCRETE PROBABILITY
DISTRIBUTIONS* **23.26**

The Discrete Uniform
Distribution 23.27

The Binomial
Distribution 23.27

The Hypergeometric
Distribution 23.28

The Poisson Distribution . 23.29

The Negative Binomial
Distribution 23.29

The Multinomial
Distribution 23.30

Selecting a Discrete
Distribution 23.32

*CONTINUOUS PROBABILITY
DISTRIBUTIONS* **23.32**

The Continuous Uniform
Distribution 23.33

The Exponential
Distribution 23.33

The Weibull Distribution . 23.34

The Normal Distribution . 23.37

The Lognormal
Distribution 23.41

Mixture Distributions . . . 23.41

The Multinormal
Distribution 23.43

Selecting a Continuous
Distribution 23.44

---

[1]In the Third Edition, the section on Basic Statistical Methods was prepared by Frank M. Gryna; the section on Regression Analysis was prepared by John S. Ramberg. Portions of the present text make use of examples and illustrations from the Third Edition.

STATISTICAL ESTIMATION . . **23.45**
Point Estimates 23.46
Confidence Interval
Estimates 23.46
Prediction Intervals 23.51
Tolerance Intervals 23.52
Bayesian Estimates 23.59

**STATISTICAL TESTS OF
HYPOTHESES** **23.60**
Basic Concepts, Types of
Errors 23.60
Use of the Operating
Characteristic Curve in
Selecting an Acceptance
Region 23.63
Testing a Hypothesis When
the Sample Size Is Fixed
in Advance 23.64
Drawing Conclusions from
Tests of Hypotheses . . . 23.76
Determining the Sample
Size Required for Testing
a Hypothesis 23.78
Relation to Confidence
Intervals 23.78
Standard Cases 23.79
Statistical Significance
versus Practical
Significance 23.80

RELIABILITY **23.81**
Basic Concepts 23.81
Failure Rate 23.81
The Distribution of "Time
between Failures" 23.82
The Exponential Formula
for Reliability 23.82

The Meaning of "Mean
Time between
Failures" 23.85
Predicting Reliability Based
on the Exponential
Distribution 23.86
Predicting Reliability
during Design Based
on the Weibull
Distribution 23.86
Reliability as a Function of
Applied Stress and
Strength 23.87
The Relationship between
Part and System
Reliability 23.90
Redundancy 23.90

**ADDITIONAL STATISTICAL
TOOLS** **23.91**
Transformations of Data . 23.91
Monte Carlo Sampling
Methods 23.94
Clustering and
Discrimination 23.94

**REGRESSION AND
CORRELATION ANALYSIS** . . . **23.96**
Simple Linear Regression 23.100
Residuals, Outliers,
Confidence and
Prediction Bands,
Extrapolation; Lack of
Fit—Replicated
Observations 23.105
Confidence Intervals . . 23.107
Multiple Regression . . . 23.108

REFERENCES **23.118**

THE STATISTICAL TOOL KIT

Most decision making in quality control, as in most other areas of modern human endeavor (e.g., evaluation of new medical treatments and scanning machines, planning of scientific polling, and marketing and investment strategies to name a few) rests on a base of statistics—defined narrowly as the collection, analysis, and interpretation of data, or more broadly as "the science of decision making under uncertainty." For the practitioner, "statistics" can be thought of as a kit of tools which helps to solve problems. The statistical tool kit shown in Table 23.1 lists problems to be solved, applicable statistical tools, and where in this handbook the tool is to be found.

Examples of actual practice will be used as extensively as the space allocated to it allows, to provide the reader with both a model for solution and a data set with correct analysis which can be used to verify the accuracy of local computer software. Annotated computer program output from such packages as SAS, BMDP, STATPRO, and LABONE will be used in many of these examples.

In addition to the basic statistical methods discussed in this section, three other sections cover specific areas—Section 24 on Statistical Process Control, Section 25 on Acceptance Sampling, and Section 26 on Design and Analysis of Experiments. Many other sections include additional applications. Also, Appendix III, Selected Quality Standards, Specifications, and Related Documents, includes documents on statistical techniques and procedures.

SOURCES AND SUMMARIZATION OF DATA

The source of a set of data which we desire to analyze to solve a problem is a very important consideration. The two sources we will address and which are the most common are "historical data" and "data from planned experimentation." Investigators using historical data are like blind people probing an elephant, for reasons discussed below under Historical Data, Its Uses, and Caveats, and under Data from Planned Experimentation. Note that all data need careful review, as discussed in Data Screening, below.

Planning for Collection and Analysis of Data. The tools cited in Table 23.1 must be used in an effective manner in order to yield a return appropriate for the cost of using them. To achieve this return, it is not sufficient to plug numbers into formulas. The full process must include careful planning of data collection, analysis of the data to draw statistical conclusions, and making the transition to answer the original technical problem. A checklist of some of the key steps in achieving this is:

1. Collect sufficient background information to translate the engineering problem statement into a specific statement that can be evaluated by statistical methods.
2. Plan the collection of data.
   a. Determine the type of data needed. Variables data (readings on a scale of measurement) may be more expensive than attributes data (go or no-go data), but the information is much more useful.
   b. Determine if any past data are available that are applicable to the present problem; however, bear in mind the hazards of historical data sets.
   c. If the problem requires an evaluation of several alternative decisions, obtain information on the economic consequences of a wrong decision.
   d. If the problem requires the estimation of a parameter, define the precision needed for the estimate.

TABLE 23.1   The Statistical Tool Kit

Problem	Statistical tool	Reference pages or sections
Planning a statistical investigation	Planning and analyzing data for solving specific problems	23.3–23.6
Summarizing data	Frequency distributions, histograms, and indices	23.11–23.21
Predicting future results from a sample	Probability distributions	23.26–23.45
Determining a probability involving several events	Basic theorems of probability	23.21–23.26
Predicting performance without failure (reliability)	Reliability prediction and analysis	23.81–23.91
Determining the significance of difference between two sets of data or between a set of data and a standard value	Tests of hypotheses	23.60–23.81
Determining the sample size required for testing a hypothesis	Sample size determination for hypothesis testing	23.78
Determining the ability of a sample result to estimate a true value	Confidence limits	23.45–23.50
Determining the sample size required to estimate a true value	Sample size determination for estimation	23.50–23.51
Determining tolerance limits on single characteristics	Statistical tolerance limits	23.52–23.56
Determining tolerance limits for interacting dimensions	Tolerance limits for interacting dimensions	23.56–23.59
Incorporating past information in predicting future events	Bayes' theorem	23.25–23.26 23.59–23.60
Incorporating economic consequences in defining decision rules	Statistical decision theory	23.26
Converting data to meet statistical assumptions	Transformations of data	23.91–23.94
Evaluating the relationship between two or more variables by determining an equation to estimate one variable from knowledge of the other variables	Regression analysis	23.96–23.118

TABLE 23.1 The Statistical Tool Kit (*Continued*)

Problem	Statistical tool	Reference pages or sections
Controlling process quality by early detection of process changes:		
1. Using measurements data	Variables control charts	Sec. 24
2. Using go no-go measurements data	Attributes control charts	Sec. 24
Evaluating quality of lots to a previously defined quality level:		
1. Quality measured on a go no-go basis	Attributes sampling plans	Sec. 25
2. Quality measured on a variables basis	Variables sampling plans	Sec. 25
3. Sampling to determine reliability	Reliability sampling plans	Sec. 25
4. Bulk product	Bulk sampling plans	Sec. 25
Planning and analyzing experiments:		
1. Investigating the effect of varying one factor	One-factor experiment	Sec. 26
2. Investigating the effect of varying two or more factors	Designs for two or more factors	Sec. 26
3. Investigating the variability of laboratory measurements	Interlaboratory tests	Sec. 26
4. Experimenting under process conditions to determine optimum settings of variables	Evolutionary operation (EVOP)	Sec. 26
5. Determining the optimum set of values of a group of variables that affect a response variable	Response surface methodology (RSM)	Sec. 26

e. Determine if the error of measurement is large enough to influence the sample size or the method of data analysis; laboratory error can often dwarf experimental variability.

f. Define the assumptions needed to calculate the required sample size.

g. Calculate the required sample size considering the desired precision of the result, statistical risk, variability of the data, measurement error, and other factors.

   h. Define any requirements for preserving the order of measurements when time is a key parameter.

   i. Determine any requirements for collecting data in groups defined so as to reflect the different conditions which are to be evaluated.

   j. Define the method of data analysis and any assumptions required.

   k. Define requirements for any computer programs which will be needed.

3. Collect the data.

   a. Use methods to assure that the sample is selected in a random manner.

   b. Record the data and also all conditions present at the time of each observation.

   c. Examine the sample data to assure that the process shows sufficient stability to make predictions valid for the future.

4. Analyze the data.

   a. Screen the data.

   b. Evaluate the assumptions previously stated for determining the sample size and for analyzing the data. Take corrective steps (including additional observations) if required.

   c. Apply statistical techniques to evaluate the original problem.

   d. Determine if further data and analysis are needed.

   e. Conduct "sensitivity analyses" by varying key sample estimates and other factors in the analysis and noting the effect on final conclusions.

5. Review the conclusions of the data analysis to determine if the original technical problem has been evaluated or if it has been changed to fit the statistical methods.

6. Present the results.

   a. State the conclusions in meaningful form by emphasizing results in terms of the original problem rather than the statistical indices used in the analysis.

   b. Present the results in graphical form where appropriate. Use simple statistical methods in the body of a report and place complicated analyses in an appendix.

7. Determine if the conclusions of the specific problem apply to other problems or if the data and calculations could be a useful input to other problems.

Historical Data, Their Uses, and Caveats. "Historical data" are data which we already have and which may seem to be relevant to a question or problem which has arisen. Such data are also called "existing data sets." Often data are saved during the production process, for example. If a satisfactory process goes out of control after some years of operation, it is often suggested that it would save both time and expense to statistically analyze the historical data, rather than perform a planned experiment to obtain data which could lead to process correction. Thus, we have available data which may consist of measurements Y (such as a process yield, e.g., the strength of a material produced) and associated process variables $x_1, x_2, \ldots, x_k$ (such as x_1 = pressure and x_2 = acid concentration, with $k = 2$).

This situation is extremely different from that where experiments have been run at each of a number of settings of $x_1, \ldots, x_k$ which were selected in advance by statistical design criteria, and often little can be learned from such data even with the most thorough statistical analysis. Some of the reasons for this are:

The x's may be highly correlated with each other, hence, it may not be possible to separate an effect as due to (for example) x_1 or x_2.

The x's may have been manipulated in order to try to control the output Y of the process (some of them perhaps even in directions which move the output in directions which are not that which is desired); hence, giving spurious indications of directions of effects when analyzed.

The x's may cover a very small part of the possible operating range, so small that any indications of changes in Y attributable to changes in the x's may be overwhelmed by the size of the variability of the process (measured by "standard deviation," discussed below).

Other variables which affect the output of the process (e.g., time of day, atmospheric conditions, operator running the process, etc.) may not have been held constant, and may in fact be the real causes of changes observed in the process (while an analysis conducted based only on the x's may erroneously conclude a model which has no basis in reality).

For these and other reasons, much more information can generally be obtained from a carefully designed experiment than from extensive analysis of historical data sets collected in uncontrolled circumstances. The best one can usually hope for from such historical data set analysis is an indication of the most important variables to include in the designed experiment.

As an example of one of the failings described above, suppose that a historical data set consists of a yield Y at each of the five (x_1, x_2) pairs given in Table 23.2. We see that there is what appears to be a good spread on the x_1 (acid concentration) values, from 80 to 110, and also a good spread on the x_2 (pressure) values, from 105 to 144. However, a plot of the data points (x_1, x_2), as shown in Figure 23.1, shows that in fact all five of the data points lie on a straight line. Thus, there is no hope of any analysis of this data telling us whether any effect we see is due to x_1 or to x_2. The points do not "cover" the space of x_1 between 80 and 110, and x_2 between 105 and 144, well at all. Also, to solve the production problem it may be desirable to explore outside of this space of historical operation, and that is not allowed for in the historical data set.

A problem such as that shown in Figure 23.1 is called "multicollinearity" of the data points, i.e., of the sets of $(x_1, \ldots, x_k)$ which we have available for anal-

TABLE 23.2   Historical Data Set

Data point	x_1 (Acid concentration)	x_2 (Pressure)
1	100	131.0
2	90	118.0
3	105	137.5
4	110	144.0
5	80	105.0

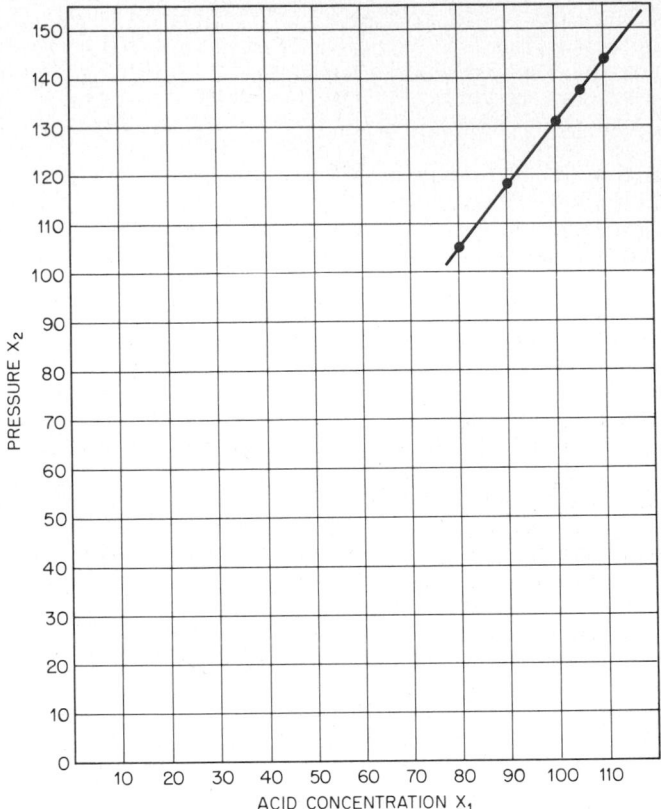

FIG. 23.1   Plot of (x_1, x_2) in a historical data set. Five data points have been plotted, and a straight line has been drawn through them.

ysis. With $k = 2$, such a problem is easy to detect by a graph such as that in Figure 23.1, and such a graph should always be made. With $k = 3$ it may be possible to detect such a situation graphically using computer graphics packages. Often, however, k is much larger than 2 or 3, and then statistical analysis is needed to detect multicollinearity. Near multicollinearity (that is, when the points almost fall on a line when $k = 2$, on a plane when $k = 3$, or on what is called a $k - 1$ dimensional hyperplane when k is larger than 3) is just as much of a problem, and is much harder to detect. For an extensive bibliography and comments on computer routines for this problem, see Hoerl and Kennard (1981).

Data from Planned Experimentation.   Data from planned experimentation are data gathered in an attempt to study the production or other problem which has arisen or is contemplated. Such data are gathered at various settings of the variables felt to be of importance $(x_1, \ldots, x_k)$, while holding constant (if possible, and recording the values of in any case) all other variables which could conceivably have an effect on the output $(x_{k+1}, \ldots, x_m)$—for example, atmospheric pressure may not be able to be controlled in most circumstances, but should be monitored and recorded in every experiment if it is felt beforehand that it might have an effect on the output. (If it is irrelevant, it can be disregarded later; if it is relevant but not recorded, we will not be able to detect that relevance.) Details of designs to use, i.e., how to choose the values of $(x_1, \ldots, x_k)$ for the experiments once the variables to be varied have been chosen, are considered in Section 26, Design and Analysis of Experiments, and in Dudewicz and Karian (1985).

Data Screening.   Once the data specified in the above Checklist for Planned Experimentation, step 2, has been collected (step 3), the first step in its analysis (step 4a) is to screen the data. We will now discuss the need for this critical (and often omitted) step, some common methods of screening, and a very commonly used method which has some great dangers.

The Need for Data Screening.   A data set which contains no instances of incorrectly transcribed values; contains no values which are technically correct but where the experiment went awry for some reason (such as equipment malfunction); and where the basic model does not change its form over the region of experimentation, is called a "clean" data set. Such data sets are commonly expected to be obtained by experimenters who exercise care in their experimental conduct and recording. However, contrary to this expectation of the experimenters, few statisticians have ever seen a clean data set (despite many years of studying many data sets arising in many areas). It follows then that all data sets need, as a first stage of analysis, to be examined for values which may cause invalid inferences to be made if those values are left in the data set. Procedures for performing this examination are called "data screening methods." Among the most powerful such methods are those which are used on the results of a regression analysis (studied later in this section).

There are also a number of methods which can and should be used at the outset, before any regression analyses are performed, with the goal of detecting "outliers," that is, observations (or groups of observations) which deviate markedly from the other available data. Numerous tests are available for detecting outliers (see Sheesley, 1977, for some of these). One simple rule calls an observation an outlier if it lies 2.5, 3, or 4 standard deviations or further from the mean (Draper and Smith, 1981). This is discussed further below.

Methods of Data Screening.   One of the most common methods of data screening is to classify observations as outliers if they are outside an interval of L multiples of the standard deviation about the mean. (Standard deviation is discussed below under Sample Characteristics.) The number L is commonly taken to be 2.5, 3, or 4. The larger L is, the less likely it is that outliers will be detected, while the smaller L is, the more good observations one will detect as potential outliers. For example, from Table B in Appendix II, we see that if $L = 3$ then $(100) (.0027) = 0.27$ percent of the observations will be further than 3 standard deviations from the mean even if there are no outliers in the data set; this assumes a normal distribution for the observations. Thus, if one uses $L = 3$, one expects to find about 3 possible outliers in a data set of 1000 data points (since 0.27 percent of 1000 is 2.7, i.e., roughly 3). As the data set being considered becomes larger, the more possible outliers one will identify even if there are no problems with the data (which is quite unlikely). For this reason:

Outliers should be deleted from the analysis only if they can be traced to specific causes (such as recording errors, experimental errors, and the like).

Typically one takes L to depend on the size of the data set to be screened; with $n = 1000$ points, $L = 3$ is reasonable; with $n = 100$, $L = 2.5$ can be used and only (100) (0.0124) = 1.24 outliers will be expected to be found if the data have no problems.

After bad data are deleted or replaced (this is desirable if the experiment can be rerun under comparable conditions to those specified in the experimental plan), the data should be screened again: With the "worst" points removed/corrected, less extreme cases may come to be identified as possible outliers.

Another commonly used method, that of crossplots, is discussed below.

Crossplots and Their Hazards. In crossplots (also called "scatter-plots"), one simply plots each pair of variables in the data set on a set of axes. For example, in the example of Table 23.2, one would plot Y versus x_1, Y versus x_2, and x_1 versus x_2. The last of these plots was given in Figure 23.1 (and showed some problems with the data which have already been discussed). Note that when using this technique, one uses all variables which were measured (and not just the variables which are thought to be of primary interest; see Nelson, 1979, Section 4).

Such plots must be used with great caution. While points which seem odd (away from the majority of the data points, for example) should be subjected to examination to see if there are problems with them, one should not use such plots to conclude relationships of the yield with x_1 and/or x_2. For example, suppose one has the data set of Table 23.3. Then from crossplots of Y versus x_1 and Y

TABLE 23.3 Data Set A for Crossplots Example

Data point	x_1	x_2	Y
1	−2	1	10
2	−1	−2	5
3	0	−5	0

versus x_2 (see Figure 23.2), one would be tempted to conclude that Y is a decreasing function of x_1 and an increasing function of x_2 (and so, in attempting to maximize yield, might set x_1 as low as possible, and x_2 as high as possible). However, as can easily be verified, the data in Table 23.3 came exactly from the relationship (model) $Y = 10 + x_1 + 2x_2$. Thus, in fact Y is an increasing function of x_1 (not a decreasing function as the crossplot had suggested). Daniel (1977) has suggested the data set of Table 23.4 may give additional insight here. Crossplots for that data set are given in Figure 23.3. Thus, one sees that even with a strong true relationship (here $Y = 10 + x_1 + 2x_2$ is used again), the crossplots may yield no

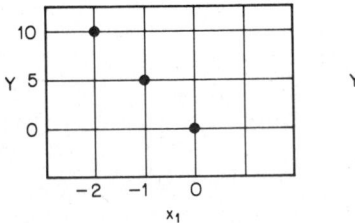 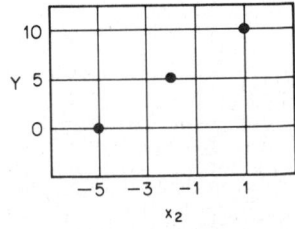

FIG. 23.2 Crossplots of Y versus x_1, and of Y versus x_2, for data set A of Table 23.3.

insight at all. Even worse, clearly by choosing the points (x_1, x_2) one may give the Y versus x_1 relationship any slope (negative, as with Table 23.3 and Figure 23.2; zero; or positive), or the relationshp can be smoothly curved in any direction or degree of complexity. (Note that the regression methods given later in this section would not be fooled by the relationships in the data of Table 23.4: They would give the true relationships.) Thus, crossplots are useful for detection of possible outliers; however, they are not a substitute for regression, and can easily be misused.

TABLE 23.4 Data Set B for Crossplots Example

Data point	x_1	x_2	Y
1	-2	1	10
2	-1	-2	5
3	0	0	10
4	1	2	15
5	2	-1	10

Descriptive Statistics for Summarizing Data.   Many of the most practical methods of summarizing data are quite simple in concept. Depending on the goals of the data summarization, sometimes one method will provide a useful and complete summarization. More often, two or more methods will be used to attain the clarity of description which is desired. Several key methods are plots versus time order of data, frequency distributions and histograms, sample characteristics (mean, median, mode, variance, standard deviation, and percentiles), measures of central tendency/location, and measures of dispersion.

Plots versus Time Order of Data.   After a data set has been obtained, it is very instructive in many situations to plot the output Y against the time order in which the experiments were run (which is essentially a crossplot of Y versus time t).

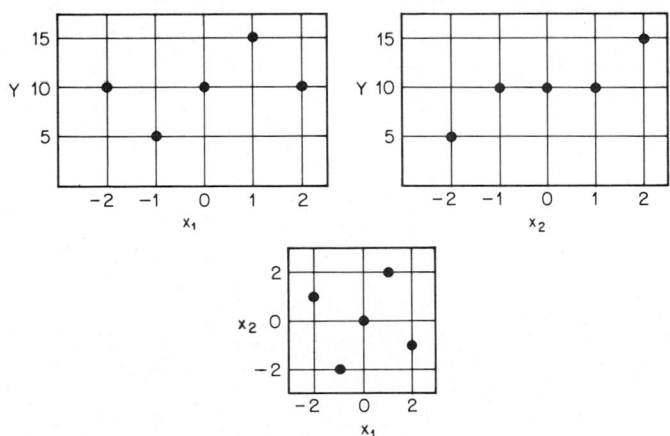

FIG. 23.3   Crossplots for data set B of Table 23.4.

Among the possible phenomena which may come to our attention from such a plot are these:

A few observations, often at the start of the experimentation, are far from the others; this often represents a learning curve of the experimenters with the experimental situation, and those experiments should be repeated if possible.

There are trends within each day (or within each week, etc.); this may represent such phenomena as warming of a machine or process, operator fatigue, or similar time-related trends.

Variability decreases (or, increases) with time; this may be due to a learning curve, or raw material characteristics (as when one lot of material is used up, and the next lot has less or greater heterogeneity).

While the above trends may be apparent even in a plot of the original observations Y versus time, they are often more easily spotted in plots of the residuals of the observations (difference between the observed and predicted value) after a regression analysis. See later in this section under Regression Analysis.

Frequency Histograms.   The frequency histogram (or, distribution) is a statistical tool for presenting numerous data in a form which makes clearer the central tendency and the dispersion along the scale of measurement, as well as the relative frequency of occurrence of the various values.

Table 23.5 shows "raw data" representing measurements of electrical resistance of 100 coils. A practitioner scanning these 100 numbers has difficulty in grasping their meaning.

Table 23.6 shows the same data after tabulation. Note how the analyst's tallies in the column "Tabulation" make more evident where the central tendency is and what the dispersion is. The column "Frequency" is merely a recorded count of these same tallies. The column "Cumulative Frequency" shows the number of coils with resistance equal to or greater than the associated resistance value.

Table 23.6 exhibits a range of values from 3.44 to 3.27, or 17 intervals of 0.01 Ω each. When it is desired to reduce the number of such intervals, the data are grouped into "cells." Table 23.7 shows the same data grouped into a frequency distribution of only six cells, each 0.03 ohms wide. Grouping the data into cells simplifies presentation and study of the distribution but loses some of the detail. (However, one can always go back to the original data if necessary.)

The following are the steps taken to construct a frequency distribution:

1. Decide on the number of cells. Table 23.8 provides guidelines which are adequate for most cases encountered. These guidelines are not rigid and should

TABLE 23.5   Resistance (Ohms) of 100 Coils

3.37	3.34	3.38	3.32	3.33	3.28	3.34	3.31	3.33	3.34
3.29	3.36	3.30	3.31	3.33	3.34	3.34	3.36	3.39	3.34
3.35	3.36	3.30	3.32	3.33	3.35	3.35	3.34	3.32	3.38
3.32	3.37	3.34	3.38	3.36	3.37	3.36	3.31	3.33	3.30
3.35	3.33	3.38	3.37	3.44	3.32	3.36	3.32	3.29	3.35
3.38	3.39	3.34	3.32	3.30	3.39	3.36	3.40	3.32	3.33
3.29	3.41	3.27	3.36	3.41	3.37	3.36	3.37	3.33	3.36
3.31	3.33	3.35	3.34	3.35	3.34	3.31	3.36	3.37	3.35
3.40	3.35	3.37	3.32	3.35	3.36	3.38	3.35	3.31	3.34
3.35	3.36	3.39	3.31	3.31	3.30	3.35	3.33	3.35	3.31

TABLE 23.6 Tally of Resistance Values of 100 Coils

Resistance, ohms	Tabulation	Frequency	Cumulative frequency
3.45			
3.44	|	1	1
3.43			
3.42			
3.41	||	2	3
3.40	||	2	5
3.39	||||	4	9
3.38	⊞⊞ |	6	15
3.37	⊞⊞ |||	8	23
3.36	⊞⊞ ⊞⊞ |||	13	36
3.35	⊞⊞ ⊞⊞ ||||	14	50
3.34	⊞⊞ ⊞⊞ ||	12	62
3.33	⊞⊞ ⊞⊞	10	72
3.32	⊞⊞ ||||	9	81
3.31	⊞⊞ ||||	9	90
3.30	⊞⊞	5	95
3.29	|||	3	98
3.28	|	1	99
3.27	|	1	100
3.26			
Total		100	

TABLE 23.7 Frequency Distribution of Resistance Values

Resistance, ohms		Frequency	Cumulative frequency
Boundaries	Midpoints		
3.415–3.445	3.43	1	1
3.385–3.415	3.40	8	9
3.355–3.385	3.37	27	36
3.325–3.355	3.34	36	72
3.295–3.325	3.31	23	95
3.265–3.295	3.28	5	100
		100	

TABLE 23.8 Number of Cells in Frequency Distribution

Number of observations	Recommended number of cells
20–50	6
51–100	7
101–200	8
201–500	9
501–1000	10
Over 1000	11–20

be adjusted when necessary; their aim is not only to provide a clear data summary, but also to reveal any underlying pattern in the data.

2. Calculate the approximate cell interval i. The cell interval equals the largest observation minus the smallest observation divided by the number of cells. Round this result to some convenient number.

3. Construct the cells by listing cell boundaries. As an aid to later calculation:

   a. The cell boundaries should be to one more decimal place than the actual data and should end in a 5.

   b. The cell interval should be constant throughout the entire frequency distribution.

4. Tally each observation into the appropriate cell and then list the total frequency f for each cell.

There are several ways of showing a frequency distribution in graphic form. The most popular is the frequency histogram. Figure 23.4 shows the electrical resistance data of Table 23.7 depicted in histogram form. The diagram is so easy to construct and interpret that it is widely used in elementary analysis of data.

One example of wide, effective use of frequency histograms is comparison of process capabilities with tolerance limits. The histogram of Figure 23.5 shows a process which is inherently capable of holding the tolerances drawn on the same figure. The high degree of defectives being produced is the result of running this process at a setting which does not locate its central tendency near the midpoint of the tolerance range. (See Section 16, under Process Capability Analysis, for other examples.)

Analyses of histograms to draw conclusions beyond the sample data should be based on at least 50 measurements.

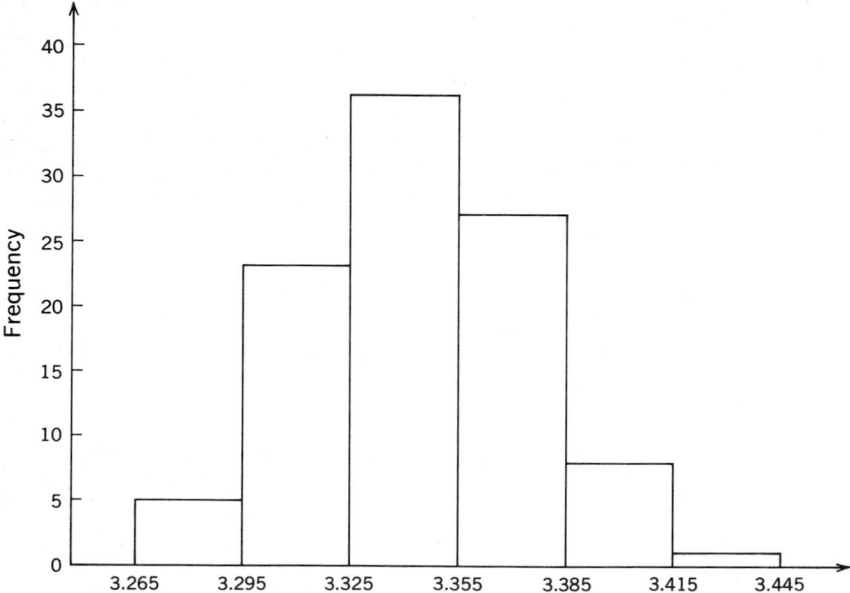

FIG. 23.4 Histogram of resistance.

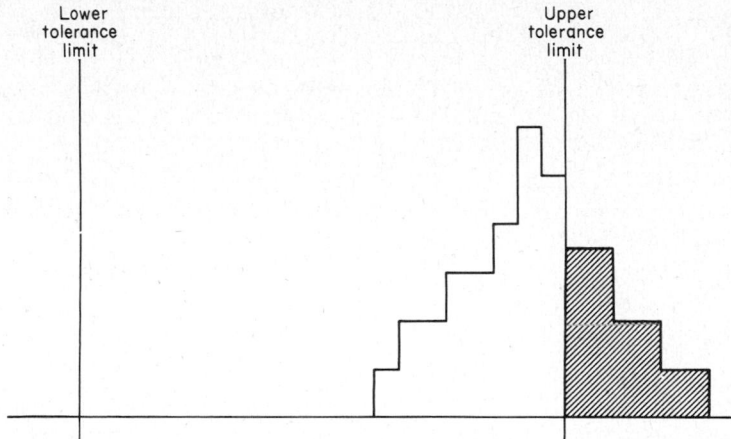

FIG. 23.5 Histogram of a process.

Sample Characteristics: Mean, Median, Mode, Variance, Standard Deviation, Percentiles. Faced with a large data set, *descriptive statistics* furnish a simple method of extracting information from what often seems at first glance to be a mass of numbers without rhyme or reason to it. These characteristics of the data may relate to a "typical (or central) value" (mean, median, mode), a measure of how much variability is present (variance, standard deviation), or a measure of frequency (percentiles). The first two types of characteristics (typical value, and variability) will be discussed below, but first we will present the concept of percentiles.

A percentile curve is a plot of the percentile rank of the data against the data values. For example, for the data of resistance of 100 coils given in Table 23.6, 1 percent are at or below resistance 3.27, 2 percent are at or below 3.28, 5 percent are at or below 3.29, and so on as given in Table 23.9. The percentile rank plot (or percentile curve) for this data is given in Figure 23.6. Note that while the data will result in a "rough" curve (since the percentile curve of the data will jump at each data point, and remain constant between actual data points), a smooth curve drawn through the data will be a better representation of reality; this is the dashed curve drawn in Figure 23.6. (Thus, while values 3.42 and 3.43 did not occur in

TABLE 23.9 Percentile Rank of Resistance Values in Table 23.6

Resistance (x)	3.27	3.28	3.29	3.30	3.31	3.32	3.33	3.34
Percentile rank (y)	1	2	5	10	19	28	38	50
	3.35	3.36	3.37	3.38	3.39	3.40	3.41	3.42
	64	77	85	91	95	97	99	99
	3.43	3.44						
	99	100						

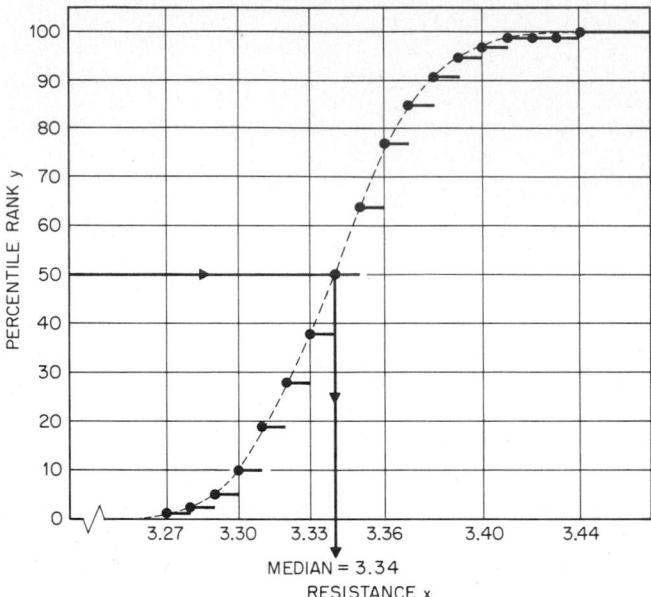

FIG. 23.6   Percentile curve of a data set.

our sample, we expect they would in a larger sample; hence the smooth curve is the one we would utilize to assess their chances of occurring.) Note that no data are discarded (or grouped) in making the percentile curve of a data set; in this sense this is a more precise process than construction of a histogram of the data (as no information is "lost" in the process). Most statistical work uses the percentile curve, under the name *distribution function* of the data. (In early papers, this was called the "cumulative" distribution function.) Since the distribution gives the proportion of the data falling at or below each value, the graph and curve are the same, only the scale on the vertical axis is changed to read from 0 to 1 (since 0 to 100, divided by 100, runs from 0 to 1).

Measures of Central Tendency/Location.   Most frequency distributions exhibit a "central tendency," i.e., a shape such that the bulk of the observations pile up in the area between the two extremes. Central tendency is one of the two most fundamental concepts in all statistical analysis.

There are three principal measures of central tendency: arithmetic mean, median, and mode.

The *arithmetic mean* (the ordinary "average") is used for symmetrical or near symmetrical distributions, or for distributions which lack a clearly dominant single peak.

The arithmetic mean X is the most generally used measure in quality work. It is employed so often to report average size, average yield, average percent of defectives, etc., that control charts have been devised to analyze and keep track of it. Such control charts can give the earliest obtainable warning of significant changes in the central value (see Section 24, Statistical Process Control).

The mean is calculated by adding the observations and dividing by the number of observations. A short method for calculating the mean is given in a subsequent example under Measures of Dispersion.

The *median* (the middle value when the figures are arranged according to size) is used for reducing the effects of extreme values, or for data which can be ranked but are not economically measurable (shades of color, visual appearance, odors) or for special testing situations. If, for example, the average of five parts tested is used to decide whether a life test requirement has been met, then the lifetime of the third part to fail can sometimes serve to predict the average of all five, and thereby the decision of the test can be made much sooner. As shown on Figure 23.6, the median is simply the horizontal scale value where the percentile curve reaches the height 50 percent.

The *mode* (the value which occurs most often in data) is used for severely skewed distributions, describing an irregular situation where two peaks are found, or for eliminating the effects of extreme values.

The statistical "efficiency" of these measures varies. See Dixon and Massey (1969, chap. 9) or Dudewicz (1976, pp. 221–222) for elaboration.

Measures of Dispersion.   Data are always scattered around the zone of central tendency, and the extent of this scatter is called dispersion or variation. A measure of dispersion is the second of the two most fundamental measures in all statistical analysis.

There are several measures of dispersion. The simplest is the range, which is the difference between the maximum and minimum values in the data. As the range is based on only two values, it is most useful when the number of observations is small (about 10 or fewer).

The most important measure of variation is the *standard deviation*. The definition of the sample standard deviation is:

$$s = \sqrt{\frac{\Sigma(X - \overline{X})^2}{n - 1}}$$

where s = sample standard deviation
   Σ = "sum of"
   X = observed values
   $\overline{X}$ = arithmetic mean
   n = numer of observations

For calculation purposes, an equivalent formula is

$$s = \sqrt{\frac{n\Sigma(X^2) - (\Sigma X)^2}{n(n - 1)}}$$

The square of the standard deviation is called the "variance." There is also a measure called "covariance," which gives information on the relationship between pairs of observations on characteristics X and Y. This is defined as

$$s_{XY} = \frac{\Sigma[(X - \overline{X})(Y - \overline{Y})]}{n - 1}$$

Further discussion of the relationship between two or more variables is given later in this section under Regression and Correlation Analysis.

With data in frequency distribution form, shortcut calculations can simplify

TABLE 23.10 Calculation of Average and Standard Deviation

Midpoint (1)	Frequency f (2)	d' (3)	fd' (4)	$f(d')^2$ (5)
3.43	1	+2	2	4
3.40	8	+1	8	8
3.37	27	0	0	0
3.34	36	−1	−36	36
3.31	23	−2	−46	92
3.28	5	−3	−15	45
	$\Sigma = 100$		$\Sigma = -87$	$\Sigma = 185$

finding the average and the standard deviation. This is illustrated in Table 23.10. To start, an arbitrary origin A is assumed as 3.37.

A zero is arbitrarily placed on this line in the d' column. The other figures in this column indicate how many cells the entry is above or below the arbitrary zero. Minus signs are attached when the entry is smaller than the assumed value, 3.37. The fd' values in column (4) are found by multiplying together the entries in columns (2) and (3). Similarly $f(d')^2$ is found by multiplying the figures in columns (3) and (4). Note that the totals in the last two columns are identified in the formulas as $\Sigma fd'$ and $\Sigma f(d')^2$, respectively, and i is the cell interval. As the multiplications are small enough to be carried out mentally, the complete table can be made quickly.

$$\overline{X} = A + \left(\frac{\Sigma fd'}{n}\right) i = 3.37 + \left(\frac{-87}{100}\right) 0.03 = 3.344$$

$$s = i \sqrt{\frac{n\Sigma f(d')^2 - (\Sigma fd')^2}{n(n-1)}}$$

$$s = 0.03 \sqrt{\frac{100(185) - (-87)^2}{100(99)}} = 0.031$$

For sample sizes of about 10 or fewer observations, the standard deviation can be approximated from the range by calculating R/d_2, where d_2 is a factor in Appendix II, Table A. For example, suppose the first column of values in Table 23.5 represents a sample of 10. The range is 3.40 − 3.29, or 0.11. From Table A in Appendix II, $d_2 = 3.078$. The estimate of the standard deviation is therefore 0.11/3.078 = 0.036. This is much simpler than calculating the standard deviation directly. Subsequent topics in this section further illustrate this feature of the range. Dixon and Massey (1969, pp. 136–140) furnish procedures and tables for a variety of applications of the range.

A final measure of variation is the "coefficient of variation." This is defined as the standard deviation divided by the mean and is thus a relative measure of variation. It can be helpful in comparing several sets of similar data that differ in mean value but may have some commonality in *relative* variation.

The methods of summarizing data covered in the previous paragraphs can be performed on a computer, as discussed below. (Also see Section 27 in general for additional information on computer programs for quality control.)

Accurate Calculation of Descriptive Statistics. Accurate calculation of even simple descriptive statistics is not as easy a task as it might seem at first, as the example in the paragraph on coding of data below shows. In particular:

Calcuation by hand is an error-prone process, especially if there are 10 or more data points.

Construction of computer programs to perform the calculations is a task which requires knowledge of both statistics and numerical analysis as well as computer programming; hence it is inadvisable to "roll your own" in most cases.

Many of the computer software routines which come with computers (especially microcomputers) are not of high quality.

In light of the above, it is recommended that a high-quality package of computer routines for statistics be obtained and used for all such analyses. In particular, the author suggests packages called SAS, BMDP, STATPRO, and LABONE. These are high quality and among them cover a wide variety of computers on which they will run (including IBM and Data General mainframe computers, APPLE and IBM PC microcomputers, and a variety of minicomputers).

For details of SAS, see SAS Institute Inc. (1982). For BMDP, see Dixon (1983). For STATPRO, see Pinsky (1983). For LABONE, see Levy and Dumoulin (1984). In each case, a telephone call will bring current information about which computers the package is available for, as well as licensing information.

Section 27 under Statistical Analysis presents additional information on statistical packages. The graphics available with these packages (such as SAS/GRAPH with SAS) are of such a quality that they would often justify the expenditure for the package to management. The American Society for Quality Control annually publishes a "Directory of Software for Quality Assurance and Quality Control" (see, for example, ASQC, 1987).

Coding of Data. Suppose that we have five observations $X_1, \ldots, X_5$ as in Table 23.11, and wish to compute the mean and standard deviation. Then on a pocket calculator (such as the Texas Instruments TI-55) or on a mainframe computer, we find

$$\sum_{i=1}^{5} X_1 = 49345 \qquad \sum_{i=1}^{5} X_i^2 = 4.8698581 \times 10^8$$

$$\overline{X} = 9869 \qquad s^2 = 0.985 \qquad s = 0.992$$

The only problem with these answers is that they are *wrong*. For example, 9869 is less than all of the observations; hence it cannot be the mean. And, the standard deviation is a measure of the spread in the data; that spread from largest to smallest is 0.00008; hence 0.992 is much too large. The problem that has led to this

TABLE 23.11 Five Data Points

$X_1 = 9869.00013$
$X_2 = 9869.00007$
$X_3 = 9869.00015$
$X_4 = 9869.00008$
$X_5 = 9869.00009$

inaccuracy is that the computers used keep only about eight decimal places of accuracy, and that results in discarding digits which are needed for accurate calculation. If it can be so troublesome to calculate the mean and standard deviation of five numbers accurately, clearly problems of meaningful size require careful analysis of numerical inaccuracy, as discussed above, and for this reason software should not be trusted without a careful analysis of its capabilities. The four packages suggested are of high quality.

If one must use untested software, it is recommended that one *code* the data; that is, calculate using $Y_1, \ldots, Y_5$ where $Y_i = a(X_i + b)$ for some a and b. For example, if we choose $a = 10^5$ and $b = 9869$, we will have $Y_1 = 13$, $Y_2 = 7$, $Y_3 = 15$, $Y_4 = 8$, and $Y_5 = 9$. For these we calculate (on the same computers)

$$\sum_{i=1}^{5} Y_i = 52 \qquad \sum_{i=1}^{5} Y_i^2 = 588 \qquad \overline{Y} = 10.4 \qquad s_Y^2 = 11.8 \qquad s_Y = 3.4351$$

which are exactly correct. Now it can be shown that the relation between $\overline{X}$, s_X^2 and $\overline{Y}$, s_Y^2 is

$$\overline{X} = \frac{1}{a}\overline{Y} - b \qquad s_X^2 = \frac{1}{a^2} s_Y^2$$

Hence we find (exactly again)

$$\overline{X} = 10.4 \times 10^{-5} + 9869 = 9869.000104$$

$$s_X^2 = 11.8 \times 10^{-10} \text{ (hence } s_X = 0.000034)$$

This method of *coding the data* will preserve accuracy in many other, more complex, statistical calculations (such as regression), and is in fact done internally by many of the high-quality statistical computer packages. Thus, it should be used whenever you are using a package other than one of the high-quality ones listed above. In addition, many absurd results from inaccurate software will be detected early if one observes the cardinal rule of statistics, namely, "look at the data." (It is all too common to have the data gathered and analyzed via computer without a careful look at them with the measures recommended in this section, and that has led to many costly problems for many companies.)

In terms of the choice of a and b for the coding, the best values to use are $a = 1/s_X$ and $b = -\overline{X}$. If those values cannot be calculated in a trustworthy manner by the software, the simple estimates of the next paragraph may be used instead.

Simple Estimates of Location and Dispersion.   Simple estimates of the center and the spread of a set of data are often desired (for example, for use in coding of data as discussed above, and also for rapid analysis of a data set under time pressure). Two simple measures for the center are: the median (X); and the midrange, expressed as

$$\frac{\text{Maximum } (X) + \text{minimum } (X)}{2}$$

A simple measure for the variability is

$$\frac{\text{Maximum } (X) - \text{minimum } (X)}{4}$$

For the data of Table 23.11, the true value was $\overline{X} = 9860.000104$. The two simple methods yield 9869.00009 and 9869.000110, respectively. Similarly, the true value of the standard deviation was $s_X = 0.000034$, and the simple estimate yields 0.000020. (If we use Table A in Appendix II and take the range divided by d_2 instead of the range divided by 4, we will have a better estimate. With five data points, $d_2 = 2.326$, so our estimate of s_X is then $0.000080/2.326 = 0.000034$.)

PROBABILITY MODELS FOR EXPERIMENTS

A distinction is made between a sample and a population (or "universe"). A "sample" is a limited number of measurements taken from a larger source. A "population" is a large source of measurements from which the sample is taken. (Note that a population may physically exist, such as all stereo sets in a certain lot. It may also be conceptual, as all experiments which might be run.)

A "probability distribution" is a mathematical formula which relates the values of the characteristic with their probability of occurrence in the population. Figure 23.7 summarizes some distributions. When the characteristic being measured can take on any value (subject to the fineness of the measuring process), its probability distribution is called a "continuous" probability distribution. For example, the probability distribution for the resistance data of Table 23.7 is an example of a continuous probability distribution because the resistance could have any value, limited only by the fineness of the measuring instrument. Experience has shown that most continuous characteristics either follow one of several common probability distributions, the "normal" distribution, the "exponential" distribution, and the "Weibull" distribution, or can be fitted with an empirical estimate as discussed later in this section. These distributions find the probabilities associated with occurrences of the actual values of the characteristic. Other continuous distributions (e.g., t, F, and chi square) are important in data analysis but do not provide probabilities of occurrence of actual values.

When the characteristic being measured can take on only certain specific values (e.g., integers 0, 1, 2, 3, etc.), its probability distribution is called a "discrete" probability distribution. For example, the distribution for the number of defectives r in a sample of five items is a discrete probability distribution because r can only be 0, 1, 2, 3, 4, or 5. The common discrete distributions are the Poisson, binomial, negative binomial, and hypergeometric (see Figure 23.7).

The following paragraphs explain how probability distributions can be used with a sample of observations to make predictions about the larger population.

Sample Space.   Statistics deals with the *outcomes* of *experiments*. When an experiment is performed, some outcome results; let us denote a typical outcome by the symbol e. Such an outcome is called a "simple event." If we list all of the possible outcomes of the experiment of interest to us, that set is called the "sample space" of the experiment.

As an example, if we perform the experiment of tossing three coins and observing for each coin whether it lands heads (H) or tails (T), the sample space will contain the eight possible outcomes

HHH   HHT   HTH   THH   HTT   THT   TTH   TTT

For simplicity of notation, let us denote these simple outcomes, respectively, by $e_1, e_2, e_3, e_4, e_5, e_6, e_7, e_8$.

We associate a number called "probability" with each of the simple events. We think of this number as representing the proportion of times each simple event would occur in a very large number of experiments of this type. For exam-

DISTRIBUTION	FORM	PROBABILITY FUNCTION	COMMENTS ON APPLICATION
NORMAL		$$y = \frac{1}{\sigma\sqrt{2\pi}}\, e^{-\frac{(X-\mu)^2}{2\sigma^2}}$$ μ = Mean σ = Standard deviation	Applicable when there is a concentration of observations about the average and it is equally likely that observations will occur above and below the average. Variation in observations is usually the result of many small causes.
EXPONENTIAL		$$y = \frac{1}{\mu}\, e^{-\frac{x}{\mu}}$$	Applicable when it is likely that more observations will occur below the average than above.
WEIBULL		$$y = \alpha\beta\,(X-\gamma)^{\beta-1} e^{-\alpha(x-\gamma)^\beta}$$ α = Scale parameter β = Shape parameter γ = Location parameter	Applicable in describing a wide variety of patterns of variation, including departures from the normal and exponential.
POISSON*		$$y = \frac{(np)^r e^{-np}}{r!}$$ n = Number of trials r = Number of occurrences p = Probability of occurrence	Same as binomial but particularly applicable when there are many opportunities for occurrence of an event, but a low probability (less than 0.10) on each trial.
BINOMIAL*		$$y = \frac{n!}{r!(n-r)!}\, p^r q^{n-r}$$ n Number of trials r = Number of occurrences p = Probability of occurrence q = 1-p	Applicable in defining the probability of r occurrences in n trials of an event which has a probability of occurrence of p on each trial.
NEGATIVE BINOMIAL*		$$y = \frac{(r+s-1)!}{(r-1)!(s!)}\, p^r q^s$$ r = Number of occurrences s = Difference between number of trials and number of occurrences p = probability of occurrence q = 1-p	Applicable in defining the probability that r occurrences will require a total of r + s trials of an event which has a probability of occurrence of p on each trial. (Note that the total number of trials n is r + s.)
HYPERGEOMETRIC*		$$y = \frac{\binom{d}{r}\binom{N-d}{n-r}}{\binom{N}{n}}$$	Applicable in defining the probability of r occurrences in n trials of an event when there are a total of d occurrences in a population of N.

FIG. 23.7   Summary of common univariate probability distributions. (Asterisks indicate that these are discrete distributions, but the curves are shown as continuous for ease of comparison with the continuous distributions.)

ple, the probability of HHH in our experiment of tossing three coins is usually taken to be $\frac{1}{8} = 0.125$ since it typically occurs in about $\frac{1}{8}$th of a large number of experiments where three coins are tossed. We denote the probability of a simple event e by $P(e)$; thus, we usually have $P(\text{HHH}) = \frac{1}{8}$.

Since some outcome occurs in each experiment, when we add up the proportion of times that each e in the sample space occurred, we must obtain a sum of 1. Since probabilities represent what those proportions would be in a large number of experiments, we must also have *probabilities* which *sum to 1 when all outcomes are accounted for.* For example, in our example with three coins

$$P(e_1) + P(e_2) + P(e_3) + P(e_4) + P(e_5) + P(e_6) + P(e_7) + P(e_8) = 1$$

Events.   Very often, we are interested not in a simple event, but a combination of them, called a "composite event." For example, the event "more heads than tails" occurs if and only if one of the simple events e_1, e_2, e_3, e_4 (i.e., the simple events HHH, HHT, HTH, THH) occurs in our example of tossing three coins. The frequency with which we find "more heads than tails" will be the sum of the relative frequencies of e_1, e_2, e_3, and e_4. Thus, we say the probability of the event "more heads than tails" is the sum of the probabilities of the simple events which comprise the event "more heads than tails":

$$P \text{ (more heads than tails)} = P(e_1) + P(e_2) + P(e_3) + P(e_4)$$

To make this simpler to write, we often denote the event of interest by a symbol, such as A for the event "more heads than tails." Then

$$P(A) = P(e_1) + P(e_2) + P(e_3) + P(e_4)$$

Thus, *the probability of a composite event is the sum of the probabilities of all the simple events which comprise it.* Since in the example with three coins we have $P(e_1) = P(e_2) = \cdots = P(e_8) = \frac{1}{8}$, we find

$$P(A) = \frac{1}{8} + \frac{1}{8} + \frac{1}{8} + \frac{1}{8} = \frac{1}{2}$$

i.e., we expect to find more heads than tails (when three coins are tossed) in about 50 percent of such experiments.

In the example with three coins, we have *equally likely simple events,* i.e., $P(e_i) = P(e_j) + P(e_j)$ for all i,j. When this is true, it follows that for any composite event A we have

$$P(A) = \frac{\text{number of simple events in } A}{\text{number of points in the sample space}}$$

In the case of the three coins, this yields the same answer obtained before, namely $P(A) = \frac{4}{8} = \frac{1}{2}$.

We say two composite events A_1 and A_2 are *mutually exclusive* if no e_i is in both A_1 and A_2. For example, if A_1 is the event "2 heads" and A_2 is the event "more tails than heads" then A_1 and A_2 are mutually exclusive since $A_1 = \{e_2, e_3, e_4\}$ and $A_2 = \{e_5, e_6, e_7, e_8\}$ have no point in common. We often express the fact that A_1 and A_2 are mutually exclusive in shorthand by writing

$$A_1 A_2 = \phi$$

If A_1 and A_2 are mutually exclusive, then for the event "A_1 or A_2" (which occurs if and only if at least one of A_1, A_2 occurs) *we have*

$$P(A_1 \text{ or } A_2) = P(A_1) + P(A_2)$$

This follows since $P(A_1$ or $A_2)$ equals the number of e_i in either A_1 or A_2 divided by the total number of simple events; since there are no points in both A_1 and A_2, this is the same as taking the number of points in A_1 and adding to it the number in A_2, then dividing by the total number of simple events. In our example, $P(A_1$ or $A_2) = P(A_1) + P(A_2) = \% + \% = \%$.

In our example so far, we have discussed the events

A: "more heads than tails"

A_1: "2 heads"

A_2: "more tails than heads"

These are shown on the sample space in Figure 23.8. Here A and A_1 are not mutually exclusive, so the simple addition of the probabilities does not hold for them, since $P(A) + P(A_2) = \% + \% = \%$ counts the points e_2, e_3, e_4 twice as to their probabilities. Thus, we see that a correct equation for $P(A$ or $A_1)$ will need

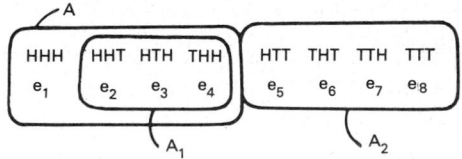

FIG. 23.8   Events and sample space, experiment of tossing 3 coins.

to subtract this overcounting part, which is $P(A$ and $A_1)$, i.e., the probability that we have an experimental outcome where both A *and* A_1 occur, which is $P(A$ and $A_1) = \%$ in this example. Thus, we have reasoned to the fact that *for any events A and A_1 the Addition Rule is:*

$$P(A \text{ or } A_1) = P(A) + P(A_1) - P(A \text{ and } A_1)$$

For mutually exclusive events the $P(A$ and $A_1)$ would be 0, so that this would reduce to 2-additivity in that case.

Rules of Probability, Combinatorics.   Probability theory underlies all decisions which are based on sampling. As we have seen, probability is expressed as a number which lies between 1.0 (certainty that an event will occur) and 0.0 (impossibility of occurrence), and the most intuitive definition of probability is one based on a frequency interpretation. In the simple case when an event A can occur in s cases out of a total of n possible and equally probable cases, then the probability that the event will occur is

$$P(A) = \frac{s}{n} = \frac{\text{number of successful cases}}{\text{total number of possible cases}}$$

Counting s and n can be complex, in which case it is called a problem of "combinatorics."

Example: A lot consists of 100 parts. A single part is selected at random, and thus, each of the 100 parts has an equal chance of being selected. Suppose a lot contains a total of 8 nonconforming parts. Then the probability of drawing a single part that is nonconforming is 8/100, or 0.08.

The following theorems are useful in solving problems involving probability:

Theorem 1: If $P(A)$ is the probability that an event A will occur, then the probability that A will not occur is $1 - P(A)$.

Theorem 2: If A and B are two events, then the probability that either A or B occurs is

$$P(A \text{ or } B) = P(A) + P(B) - P(A \text{ and } B)$$

A special case of this theorem occurs when A and B cannot occur simultaneously (i.e., A and B are "mutually exclusive"). Then the probability that either A or B occurs is

$$P(A \text{ or } B) = P(A) + P(B)$$

Example: The probabilities of r defectives in a sample of six units from a 5 percent defective lot are found below by the binomial. The probability of zero defectives is 0.7351; the probability of one defective is 0.2321. The probability of zero or one defective is then $0.7351 + 0.2321$, or 0.9672.

Theorem 3: If A and B are two events, then the probability of the joint occurrence of both A and B is

$$P(A \text{ and } B) = P(A) \times P(B|A)$$

where $P(B|A) =$ probability that B will occur assuming A has already occurred.
A special case of this theorem occurs when the two events are *independent,* i.e., when the occurrence of one event has no influence on the probability of the other event. If A and B are independent, then the probability of both A and B occurring is

$$P(A \text{ and } B) = P(A) \times P(B)$$

Example: A complex system consists of two major subsystems. The probability of successful performance of the first subsystem is 0.95; the corresponding probability for the second subsystem is 0.90. Both subsystems must operate successfully in order to achieve total system success. The probability of the successful operation of the total system is therefore $0.95 \times 0.90 = 0.855$.
The theorems above have been stated in terms of two events but can be expanded for any number of events.

Conditional Probability; Bayes' Theorem. In "conditional probability" we seek an answer to such questions as "If I know that A_2 has occurred, then on those trials of the experiment where A_2 has occurred, how often does A_1 occur?" We use a special shorthand symbol for this *conditional probability,*

$$P(A_1|A_2)$$

which is read as "the probability of A_1, given that A_2 is known to have occurred" and is calculated from the formula

$$P(A_1|A_2) = \frac{P(A_1 \text{ and } A_2)}{P(A_2)}$$

If $P(A_1 | A_2) > P(A_1)$, we say A_2 carries "positive information" about A_1.

If $P(A_1 | A_2) < P(A_1)$, we say A_2 carries "negative information" about A_1.

If $P(A_1 | A_2) = P(A_1)$, we say A_2 carries no information about A_1, or that A_1 and A_2 are "independent events." In this last case, knowing that A_2 has (or, has not) occurred does not change the chances of A_1 occurring.

The powerful *conditional probability reversal formula*

$$P(A_1 | A_2)P(A_2) = P(A_1 \text{ and } A_2) = P(A_2 \text{ and } A_1) = P(A_2 | A_1)P(A_1)$$

is the basis of Bayes' theorem. In the simplest setting, this states that

$$P(A_2 | A_1) = \frac{P(A_1 | A_2)P(A_2)}{P(A_1 | A_2)P(A_2) + P(A_1 | \text{not } A_2)P(\text{not } A_2)}$$

(Here, "not A_2" is the event that A_2 does not occur.) For worked solutions of problems in probability, see Dudewicz (1980).

The techniques presented under Tests of Hypotheses in this section consist of analyzing a sample of observations and reaching a conclusion (with defined sampling risks) to accept or reject a hypothesis. The experimenter considers the consequences of drawing incorrect conclusions and, to a lesser degree, the likelihood that extreme values of the population parameter will occur. However, this is usually done on a qualitative basis and involves judgment. In practice, a sample size is limited by economics and the experimenter defines the type I error (usually 0.05 or 0.01) in numerical terms and then must accept the type II error that results with the sample size fixed by economics. There is a methodical way of defining the consequences of the type I and type II errors and the likelihood of extreme values. The approach involves Bayes' theorem and statistical decision theory.

Statistical Decision Theory.   This concept requires two items of information not formally used in classical analysis:

1. The economic consequences of making type I or type II errors.
2. The probabilities that different values of the population parameter will occur. (The classical approach has no assumption concerning different values of the population parameter.)

Statistical tables and sampling plans based on Bayes' theorem or statistical decision concepts are not common, but the concepts can have a significant effect, and therefore development work seems imminent and worthwhile. Oliver and Springer (1972) give an example of Bayesian acceptance sampling tables. Hadley (1967) provides background material including examples on tests of hypotheses, confidence limits, and acceptance sampling plans. Lenz and Rendtel (1984) compare the performance of MIL-STD-105D, Skip Lot, and Bayesian sampling plans. See also the discussion in Section 25 under Bayesian Procedures.

DISCRETE PROBABILITY DISTRIBUTIONS

Discrete probability distributions are used to model situations where the outcome of interest can take on only a few discrete values (such as 0 or 1 for failure or success, or 0, 1, 2, 3, . . . as a number of occurrences of some event of interest). Below we give the model leading to the most commonly occurring such distributions, consider where one can obtain numerical values of their probabilities, and their uses in quality control.

The Discrete Uniform Distribution.   If each of the values $x_1, \ldots, x_n$ is equally likely to occur as the result of an experiment, then we say the value obtained has the uniform distribution on the set of values $x_1, \ldots, x_n$. In this case the probability of x_i is $1/n$. Since the probabilities are so simple, no special tables are needed.

Model Leading to a Uniform Distribution.   The model leading to a uniform distribution is random selection from a finite population in which each value occurs the same number of times. (This makes values equally likely to occur in the sample.)

Uses of Random Choices.   Random choices are often used in sampling inspection. For example, suppose that a lot of 1000 items is sequentially numbered from 500 through 1499. Then the chance that an item selected at random from the lot will have number i is (for any i between 500 and 1499) $1/1000 = 0.001$. The probability that such an item will have a serial number at least 1400 is $100/1000 = 0.01$.

The Binomial Distribution.   If the probability of occurrence p of an event is constant on each of n independent trials of the event, then the probability of r occurrences in n trials is

$$\frac{n!}{r!(n-r)!} \, p^r q^{n-r}$$

where $q = 1 - p$.

In practice, the assumption of a constant probability of occurrence is considered reasonable when the population size is at least 10 times the sample size (under this circumstance, the change in probability from one trial to the next due to depletion of the population is negligible). (Note that the binomial has fewer assumptions than the Poisson.)

Table F in Appendix II provides partial tables for the binomial and gives references for more complete tables. King (1971, chaps. 20 through 22) discusses binomial probability paper.

Model Leading to a Binomial Distribution.   When n independent trials of an experiment each have a constant probability p of occurrence of an event of interest (commonly termed a "success"), then the number of occurrences follows a binomial distribution. The name comes from the fact that the factor

$$\frac{n!}{r!(n-r)!}$$

in the probabilities is called a "binomial coefficient" in mathematics.

Binomial Probabilities and Uses.   A lot of 100 units of product is submitted by a vendor whose past quality has been about 5 percent nonconforming. A random sample of six units is selected from the lot. The probabilities of various sample results are given in Table 23.12.

In using the formula, note that $0! = 1$. Table F in Appendix II lists binomial probabilities in cumulative form, i.e., the probability of r or fewer occurrences in

TABLE 23.12   Table of Binomial
Probabilities

r	P (exactly r defectives in 6)= $[6!/r! (6-r)!](0.05)^r(0.95)^{6-r}$
0	0.7351
1	0.2321
2	0.0306
3	0.0021
4	0.0001
5	0.0000
6	0.0000

n trials. For the above example, the probability of 1 or fewer nonconforming items in a sample of 6 can be read from the table as 0.9672. Note that this is the sum of the probabilities for $r = 0$ and $r = 1$, i.e., $0.7351 + 0.2321 = 0.9672$.

The Hypergeometric Distribution.   Occasionally, the assumptions of the Poisson (see below) or binomial cannot be met even approximately. Subject only to the assumption of a random sample, the hypergeometric gives the probability of exactly r occurrences in n trials from a lot of N items having d defectives as

$$\frac{\binom{d}{r}\binom{N-d}{n-r}}{\binom{N}{n}}$$

where $\binom{N}{n}$ is the "combinations" of N items taken n at a time and is equal to $N!/$ $[n!(N-n)!]$, where $N! = [N(N-1)(N-2)\cdots 1]$ and $0! = 1$. The calculations can be avoided by using tables such as those prepared by Lieberman and Owen (1961). Duncan (1974) compares the results of Poisson, binomial, and hypergeometric distributions.

Model Leading to a Hypergeometric Distribution.   The hypergeometric distribution is appropriate when independent trials are conducted, but the probability of occurrence of the event of interest changes from trial to trial because of depletion of a finite population. Because of their simpler form, in this situation one often uses the binomial or Poisson distributions if their assumptions are approximately met.

Hypergeometric Probabilities and Uses.   A lot of 100 units is submitted by a vendor whose past quality has been about 5 percent nonconforming. A random sample of 20 units is selected from the lot. To calculate the probability of 0 nonconforming in 20, note that the lot has 5 nonconforming items and 95 conforming. Then:

$$P(0 \text{ in } 20) = \frac{\binom{5}{0}\binom{95}{20}}{\binom{100}{20}} = \frac{\left[\dfrac{5!}{0!(5-0)!}\right]\left[\dfrac{95!}{20!(95-20)!}\right]}{\dfrac{100!}{20!(100-20)!}} = 0.319$$

Repeat substitutions into the formula are made to find $P(r$ in 20), where r in this example is 0, 1, 2, 3, 4, and 5.

The Poisson Distribution. In practice, the most important discrete distribution is the Poisson. It is an approximation to more exact distributions and applies when the sample size is at least 16, the population size is at least 10 times the sample size, and the probability of occurrence p on each trial is less than 0.1. (These conditions are often met.)

Figure 23.7 states the Poisson probability function, but the real work is done by cumulative probability tables.

Model Leading to a Poisson Distribution. As well as being an approximation to more exact distributions, the Poisson is the exact distribution when certain assumptions are met. These assumptions are: that events occur at random (in time, or in space, or in location for example) with a probability of occurrence roughly proportional to the length of time (or volume of space, or area), and that there is no "clumping." (For details, see Dudewicz, 1976, Section 3.2.) For example, if a target 0.1 mi^2 in size is known to be contained in an area 10 mi^2 in size, and this area is shelled at random (one shell at a time so there will be no clumping), the probability of a hit will be 0.1/10 = 0.01. The number of hits will follow a Poisson distribution, and the number of shells fired may be set so the probability of eight or more hits on the target will be at least 0.95; this is often done in practice when it is known that eight or more hits will effectively destroy the target and a 95 percent kill probability is desired.

Poisson Probabilities and Uses. A lot of 300 units of product is submitted by a supplier whose past quality has been about 2 percent nonconforming. A random sample of 40 units is selected from the lot. Table E in Appendix II provides the probability of r or fewer defectives in a sample of n units. (The application of these probabilities is explained in Section 25, under Operating Characteristic, OC, Curve.) Entering the table with a value of np equal to 40 (0.02), or 0.8, gives Table 23.13. Individual probabilities can be found by subtracting cumulative probabilities. Thus, the probability of exactly two defectives is 0.953 − 0.809, or 0.144.

The Negative Binomial Distribution. The negative binomial distribution is one of the most commonly occurring distributions in situations where the sample size is not set in advance, but rather is determined as the experiment proceeds.

Model Leading to a Negative Binomial Distribution. If the probability of occurrence of an event is constant from trial to trial, and we make trials until we find

TABLE 23.13   Table of Poisson Probabilities

r	Probability of r or fewer in sample
0	0.449
1	0.809
2	0.953
3	0.991
4	0.999
5	1.000

m occurrences, then the probability that r trials will be needed is

$$\frac{(r-1)!}{(m-1)!(r-m)!}\,p^m(1-p)^{r-m}$$

where r can be m, $m + 1$, $m + 2$, ... This equation is equivalent to the more complex one listed in Figure 23.7. Other situations leading to a negative binomial distribution are discussed in Chapter 5 of Johnson and Kotz (1969). Tables are available in Williamson and Bretherton (1963) in case direct calculation is burdensome; Johnson and Kotz (1969) give references to additional tables.

Negative Binomial Probabilities and Uses.   A large lot is inspected until the first defective ($m = 1$) is found; if that occurs in the first five trials, the lot is rejected. Hence the lot will be accepted if no defective is found in the first five trials (and thus trials 6, 7, . . . need not be performed—we will never inspect more than five items with this scheme). If the lot is 10 percent nonconforming, then from Table 23.14 we see that the probability the lot is accepted is $1 - (0.10 + 0.09 + 0.081 + 0.0729 + 0.06561) = 0.59049$.

TABLE 23.14   Table of Negative Binomial Probabilities ($m = 1$, $p = 0.10$)

r	Probability r trials are needed to find $m = 1$ defectives
1	0.10
2	0.09
3	0.081
4	0.0729
5	0.06561
6	0.059049
7	0.053144
8	0.047830

The Multinomial Distribution.   The discrete probability distributions discussed up to this point (the uniform, binomial, hypergeometric, Poisson, and negative binomial) all relate to situations which are "univariate," that is, where the outcome of interest relates to one variable's value (such as the number of defectives in a sample of size n in the binomial case). However, there are important cases where the outcome is "multivariate." One such example is that where in a sample of size n one observes both the number needing rework and the number to be scrapped; since there are two quantities, this is called a "bivariate" situation. The multinomial distribution can be used when there are any number of categories into which the items may be classified.

Model Leading to a Multinomial Distribution.   If exactly one of the events E_1, . . . , E_k occurs on each of n independent trials, and the probabilities of occurrence of the events are respectively p_1, . . . , p_k (with $p_1 + \cdots + p_k = 1$, so that one of them must occur), then the probability that E_1 occurs x_1 times, and E_2 occurs x_2 times, . . . , and E_k occurs x_k times (where $x_1 + x_2 + \cdots + x_k = n$ since there are n trials and one of $E_1, \ldots, E_k$ must occur on each trial) is

$$\frac{n!}{x_1! x_2! \cdots x_k!} \, p_1^{x_1} p_2^{x_2} \cdots p_k^{x_k}$$

Tables are not widely available, and calculations are usually done directly from the probability formula, or (if n is large) the multivariate normal distribution (a continuous multivariate distribution discussed later in this section) is used as an approximation.

Multinomial Probabilities and Uses. Suppose that $n = 5$ large assemblies are manufactured and inspected each day. The results of each inspection are either PASS, REWORK, or SCRAP. Past results have shown that 80 percent pass, 15 percent need rework, and 5 percent need to be scrapped. What are the probabilities of the various possible outcomes of one day's output?

In Figure 23.9 we show the probabilities of the outcomes, calculated directly from the basic formula. Note that once the number to be reworked (e.g., 1) and the number to be scrapped (e.g., 0) are specified, the number passed is determined (e.g., $5 - 1 - 0 = 4$). We have had to use the multinomial probability distribu-

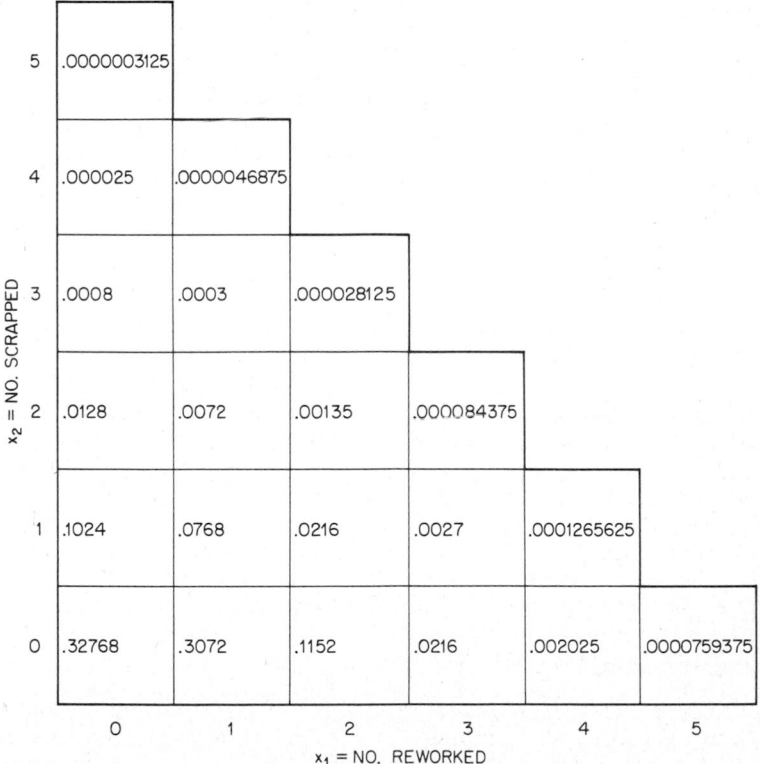

FIG. 23.9 Table of multinomial probabilities, $k = 3$ Categories, $n = 5$, $p_1 = P(\text{Rework}) = 0.15$, $p_2 = P(\text{Scrap}) = 0.05$, $p_3 = P(\text{Pass}) = 0.80$.

tion since the categories are not independent (an item cannot be both passed and scrapped).

Selecting a Discrete Distribution.   Selection of which discrete distribution to use is usually made either by knowledge of the underlying sitaution or by fitting a model from relative frequency probability. In either case, a test of the model selected is desirable to check its validity.

Selection from a Model of Reality.   In many cases one will know (or assume) that the model which leads to one of the distributions we have discussed underlies the practical situation. For example, if one draws 50 items at random from a large lot with $100p$ percent defective, one will assume the binomial model with $n = 50$ and probability p of a defective on each trial.

(Chi Square) Test of Model Validity.   To test the validity of an assumed discrete model, where cell i should occur with probability p_i, one compares the observed cell totals with those predicted by the model using the chi square test discussed later (Test 12b). Such a confirmatory test can be omitted only if one is willing to run the risk of assuming a model which in fact may have little basis in reality. (See Section 9.12 of Dudewicz and Mishra, 1988, and especially Problem 9.12.2 on p. 532.)

Empirical Models via Relative Frequency Probability.   If there is little or no reason to lead to the adoption of one of the specific models discussed, a model can be fitted to the data using the relative frequencies observed in the past. For example, if one has observed that in 100 items produced in the past there have been blemishes present in the numbers given in Table 23.15, one would estimate the probability of r blemishes as its relative frequency in the past work, i.e., as in Table 23.16. Such a model should be tested by taking a new sample and performing a chi square test as previously discussed.

TABLE 23.15   Blemishes per Item in Past Work

No. of blemishes	No. of occurrences
0	50
1	25
2	25

TABLE 23.16   Blemish Probabilities via Relative Frequency Estimation

No. of blemishes	Probability
0	.50
1	.25
2	.25

CONTINUOUS PROBABILITY DISTRIBUTIONS

Continuous probability distributions are used to model situations where the outcome of interest can take on values in a continuous range (such as all values greater than zero for the failure time of a motor which is run continuously). Below we give the model leading to the most commonly occurring such distributions, consider where one can obtain numerical values of their probabilities, and their uses in quality control.

The Continuous Uniform Distribution.   If all values between a and b ($a < b$) are possible, and the chances of the value being in a subinterval are proportional to its length, then the uniform distribution is appropriate. The probability function is flat over the interval (a,b), where $y = 1/(b - a)$. Thus, the probability the value is in a subinterval of length c is $c/(b - a)$. Since the probabilities are so simple, no special tables are needed.

Model Leading to a Uniform Distribution.   The model leading to a continuous uniform distribution over the range (a,b) is random selection of a value between a and b. For example, if a valve on a water line is spun at random between pressure 0 lb/in^2 (closed) and 100 lb/in^2 (fully open), then the resulting pressure will be a uniform random variable on (0,100).

Uses of Random Numbers.   Uniform random variables on the range (0,1) are called "random numbers." Such variables are often used to drive digital computer simulation models, and are of great importance in simulation studies of quality systems. Full details on sources of high-quality random numbers may be found in Dudewicz and Ralley (1981). Special considerations for simulation uses on microcomputers are given in Dudewicz, Karian, and Marshall (1985).

The Exponential Distribution.   The exponential probability function is

$$y = \frac{1}{\mu} e^{-X/\mu}$$

Figure 23.7 shows the shape of an exponential distribution curve. Note that the normal and exponential distributions have distinctly different shapes. An examination of the tables of areas shows that 50 percent of a normally distributed population occurs above the average value and 50 percent below it. In an exponential population, 36.8 percent are above the average and 63.2 percent below the average. (This refutes the intuitive idea that the average is always the 50 percent point.) The property of a higher percentage below the average sometimes helps to indicate applications of the exponential. For example, the exponential describes the loading pattern for some structural members because smaller loads are more numerous than larger loads. The exponential is also useful in describing the distribution of failure times of certain complex equipment.

Model Leading to an Exponential Distribution.   It can be shown that the exponential distribution of failure times arises when failures occur "at random" (and are not due to wearout, but to such items as random shocks). In fact, the exponential distribution is characterized as the only continuous distribution with the "lack of memory property" that the chances of the item living an additional t_0 time units depend only on the length t_0 and not on how long the item has already been in use (see Dudewicz, 1976, pp. 88, 106, for details).

Predictions with Exponential Distributions.   Predictions based on an exponentially distributed population require only an estimate of the population average. For example, the time between successive failures of a complex piece of equipment is measured and the resulting histogram is found to resemble the exponential probability curve. The results of a sample of measurements indicate that the average time between failures (commonly called MTBF or mean time between failures) is 100 h. What is the probability that the time between two successive failures of this equipment will be at least 20 h?

The problem is one of finding the area under the curve beyond 20 h (Figure 23.10). Table C in Appendix II gives the area under the curve beyond any particular ratio X/μ. In this problem,

$$\frac{X}{\mu} = \frac{20}{100} = 0.20$$

and from Table C in Appendix II the area under the curve beyond 20 h is thus 0.8187. The probability that the time between two successive failures is greater than 20 h is 0.8187; i.e., there is about an 82 percent chance that the equipment will operate without failure continuously for 20 or more hours. Similar calculations would give a probability of 0.9048 for 10 or more hours. Later in this section, this probability is calculated for the specified "mission time" of a product, and the result is called "reliability." These analyses could also be made using exponential probability paper.

The Weibull Distribution.   The Weibull distribution is a family of distributions having the general density function

$$y = \alpha\beta(X - \gamma)^{\beta-1}\, e^{-\alpha(X-\gamma)^{\beta}}$$

where α = scale parameter, β = shape parameter, and γ = location parameter.

The curve of the function (Figure 23.7) varies greatly depending on the numerical values of the parameters. Most important is the shape parameter β, which reflects the pattern of the curve. Note that when β is 1.0, the Weibull function reduces to the exponential and that when β is about 3.5 (and $\alpha = 1$ and $\gamma = 0$), the Weibull closely approximates the normal distribution. In practice, β varies from about ⅛ to 5. The scale parameter α is related to the peakedness of the curve; i.e., as α changes, the curve becomes flatter or more peaked.

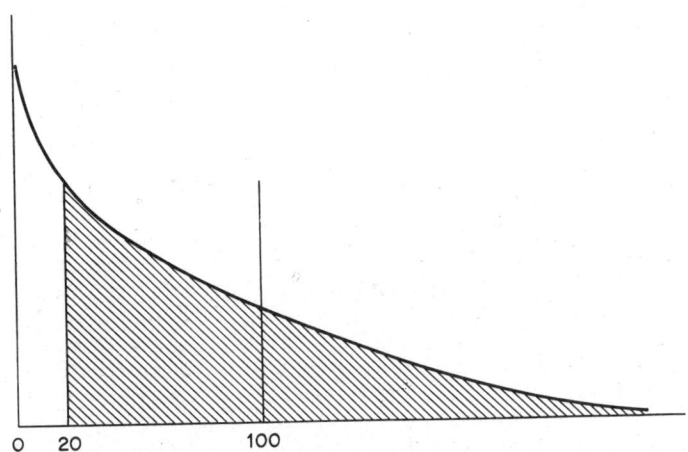

FIG. 23.10   Distribution of time between failures.

The location parameter γ is the smallest possible value of X. This is often assumed to be zero, thereby simplifying the equation. It is often unnecessary to determine the values of these parameters because predictions are made directly from Weibull probability paper. King (1971, pp. 136–140) gives procedures for graphically finding α, β, and γ.

The Weibull covers many shapes of distributions. This makes it popular in practice because it reduces the problem of examining a set of data and deciding which of the common distributions (e.g., normal or exponential) fits best. In particular, both IFR (increasing failure rate) and DFR (decreasing failure rate) cases are included, respectively, with $\beta > 1$ and $\beta < 1$ (see Dudewicz, 1976, pp. 88–89).

Model Leading to a Weibull Distribution   It can be shown that a Weibull distribution arises if an exponential variable is raised to a power, i.e., if Y is exponential then $Y^{1/\beta}$ has a Weibull distribution (Dudewicz, 1976, p. 89).

Predictions with Weibull Distributions   An analytical approach for the Weibull distribution (even with tables) is cumbersome, and the predictions are usually made with Weibull probability paper. For example, five heat-treated shafts were stress-tested until each of them failed. The fatigue life (in terms of number of cycles to failure) is:

10,263

12,187

16,908

18,042

23,271

The problem is to predict the percentage failure of the population for various values of fatigue life. The solution is to plot the data on Weibull paper, observe if the points fall approximately in a straight line, and if so, read the probability predictions (percentage failure) from the graph.

Although Weibull plotting can follow the mean rank procedure of normal probability paper (see below under Predictions with Normal Distributions), much of the literature on Weibull applications uses "median ranks." Table D in Appendix II gives, for various sample sizes, the values of the median rank. (Note that the mean rank procedure does not require a table.) The median ranks necessary for this particular example are based on a sample size of five failures and are as shown in Table 23.17. (The mean rank estimates are shown for comparison.) The

TABLE 23.17   Table of Median and Mean Ranks

Failure number i	Median rank	Mean rank $= \dfrac{i}{5 + 1}$
1	0.1294	0.1667
2	0.3147	0.3333
3	0.5000	0.5000
4	0.6853	0.6667
5	0.8706	0.8333

cycles to failure are now plotted on the Weibull graph paper against the corresponding values of the median rank (see Figure 23.11). These points fall approximately in a straight line (King, 1971, pp. 126–128, describes how to modify a plot to help obtain a straight line), so it is assumed that the Weibull distribution applies. The vertical axis gives the cumulative percent of failures in the population corresponding to the fatigue life shown on the horizontal axis. For example, about 50 percent of the population of shafts will fail in less than 17,000 cycles. About 90 percent of the population will fail in less than 24,000 cycles. By appropriate subtractions, predictions can be made of the percent of failures between any two fatigue life limits.

It is tempting to extrapolate on probability paper, particularly to predict life. For example, suppose the minimum fatigue life were specified as 8000 cycles and the five measurements above were from tests conducted to evaluate the ability of the design to meet 8000 cycles. As all five tests exceeded 8000 cycles, the design seems adequate and therefore should be released for production. However, extrapolation on the Weibull paper predicts that about 8 percent of the *population* of shafts would fail in less than 8000 cycles. This suggests a review of the design before release to production. Thus, the small *sample* (all *within* specifications) gave a deceiving result.

Extrapolation can go in the other direction. Note that a probability plot of life test data does not require that all tests be completed before the plotting starts. As each unit fails, the failure time can be plotted against the median rank. If the early points appear to be following a straight line, then it is tempting to draw in the line *before* all tests are finished. The line can then be extrapolated beyond the actual test data and life predictions can be made without accumulating a large amount of test time. The approach has been applied to predicting, *early in a warranty period,* the "vital few" components of a complex product which will be most trou-

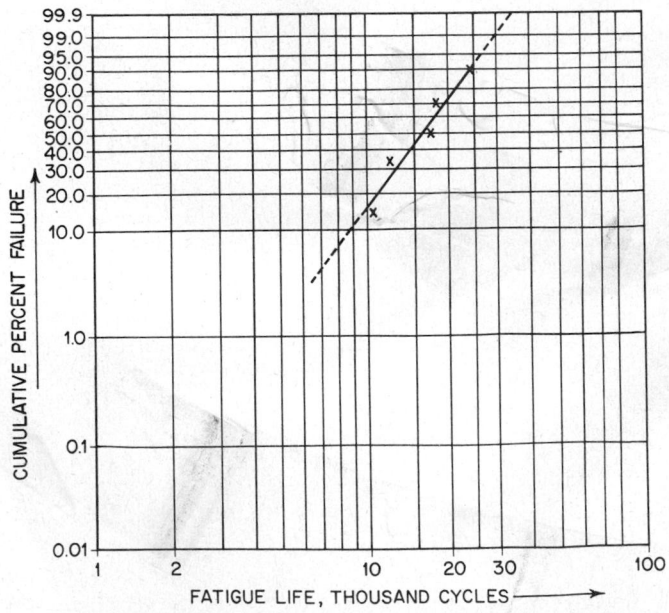

FIG. 23.11 Distribution of fatigue life on Weibull probability paper.

blesome. However, extrapolation has dangers. It requires the judicious melding of statistical theory and engineering experience and judgment.

Moult (1963) describes the use of a Weibull plot in comparing the suitability of two types of steel for use in bearings. The plot is shown in Figure 23.12.

Nelson (1982) discusses Weibull paper. Probability graph paper is available for the normal, exponential, Weibull, and other probability distributions. (A source is TEAM, Technical and Engineering Aids for Management, Box 25, Tamworth, New Hampshire 03886.) Although the mathematical functions and tables provide the same information, the graph paper reveals *relationships* between probabilities and values of X that are not readily apparent from the calculations. For example, the reduction in percent defective in a population as a function of wider and wider tolerance limits can be easily portrayed by the graph paper.

The Normal Distribution. Many engineering characteristics can be approximated by the normal distribution

$$y = \frac{1}{\sigma\sqrt{2\pi}}\, e^{-(X-\mu)^2/2\sigma^2}$$

where $e = 2.718$, $\pi = 3.141$, μ = population average, σ = population standard deviation.

Problems are solved with a table, but note that the distribution requires estimates of only the average μ and standard deviation σ of the population (unless otherwise indicated, Greek symbols will be used for population values and Roman symbols for sample values) in order to make predictions about the population. The curve for the normal probability distribution is related to a frequency distribution and its histogram. As the sample becomes larger and larger, and the width of each cell becomes smaller and smaller, the histogram approaches a smooth curve. If the entire population (in practice, the population is usually considered infinite, e.g., the potential production from a process) were measured, and if it were normally distributed, the result would be as shown in Figure 23.7. Thus,

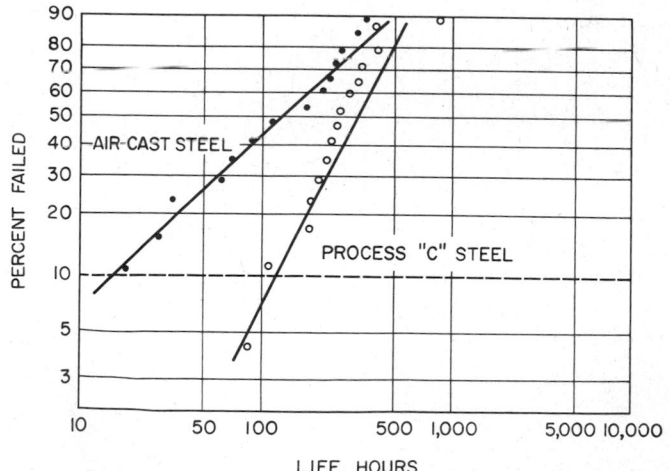

FIG. 23.12 Composite fatigue endurance—process "C" vacuum degassing versus air cast AISI 8620.

the shape of a histogram of sample data provides some indication of the probability distribution for the population. If the histogram resembles the "bell" shape shown in Figure 23.7, this is a basis for assuming that the population follows a normal probability distribution. (It is not necessary that the sample histogram be perfectly normal—the assumption of normality is applied only to the population, and small deviations from normality are expected in random samples.) Hahn (1971) gives a practical discussion of assuming normality. (The name "normal" distribution dates back to a time when all other distributions were erroneously thought to be abnormal. Today, some prefer the name "Gaussian" distribution.)

Model Leading to a Normal Distribution (Additive Errors, Central Limit Theorem). It can be shown that if a variable Y is the result of adding many other variables, and those variables are not highly dependent on each other, then Y will have approximately a normal distribution. (This result is called the Central Limit Theorem; see Dudewicz, 1976, p. 149.) Statisticians usually recommend that 10 or more terms be added before this result is relied on to produce normality; however, a number of applied studies have shown good results with as few as three terms being added.

Predictions with Normal Distributions. Predictions require just two estimates and a table. The estimates are:

$$\text{Estimate of } \mu = \overline{X} \quad \text{and} \quad \text{estimate of } \sigma = s$$

The calculations of the sample $\overline{X}$ and s are made by one of the methods previously discussed.

For example, from past experience, a manufacturer concludes that the burnout time of a particular light bulb it manufactures is normally distributed. A sample of 50 bulbs has been tested and the average life found to be 60 days, with a standard deviation of 20 days. How many bulbs in the entire population of light bulbs can be expected to be still working after 100 days of life?

The problem is to find the area under the curve beyond 100 days (see Figure 23.13). The area under a distribution curve between two stated limits represents

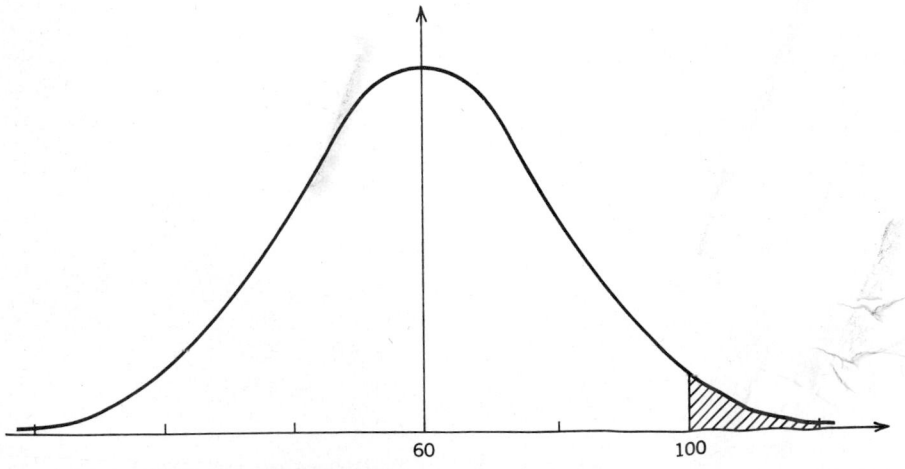

FIG. 23.13   Distribution of light bulb life.

the probability of occurrence. Therefore, the area beyond 100 days is the probability that a bulb will last more than 100 days. To find the area, calculate the difference between a particular value X and the average of the curve in units of standard deviation:

$$K = \frac{X - \mu}{\sigma}$$

In this problem, $K = (100 - 60) \div 20 = + 2.0$. Table B in Appendix II shows, for $K = 2$, a probability of 0.9773. Applied to this problem, the probability that a bulb will last 100 days or less is 0.9773. The normal curve is symmetrical about the average and the total area is 1.000. The probability of a bulb's lasting more than 100 days then is $1.0000 - 0.9773$, or 0.0227, or 2.27 percent of the bulbs in the population will still be working after 100 days.

Similarly, if a characteristic is normally distributed and if estimates of the average and standard deviation of the population are obtained, this method can estimate the total percent of production that will fall within engineering specification limits.

Figure 23.14 shows representative areas under the normal distribution curve (these can be derived from Table B in Appendix II). Thus 68.26 percent of the *population* will fall between the average of the population plus or minus 1 standard deviation of the population, 95.46 percent of the population will fall between the average $\pm 2\sigma$, and finally $\pm 3\sigma$ will include 99.73 percent of the population. The percentage of a *sample* within a set of limits can be quite different from the percentage within the same limits in the population. This important fact is crucial in testing hypotheses (covered later in this section).

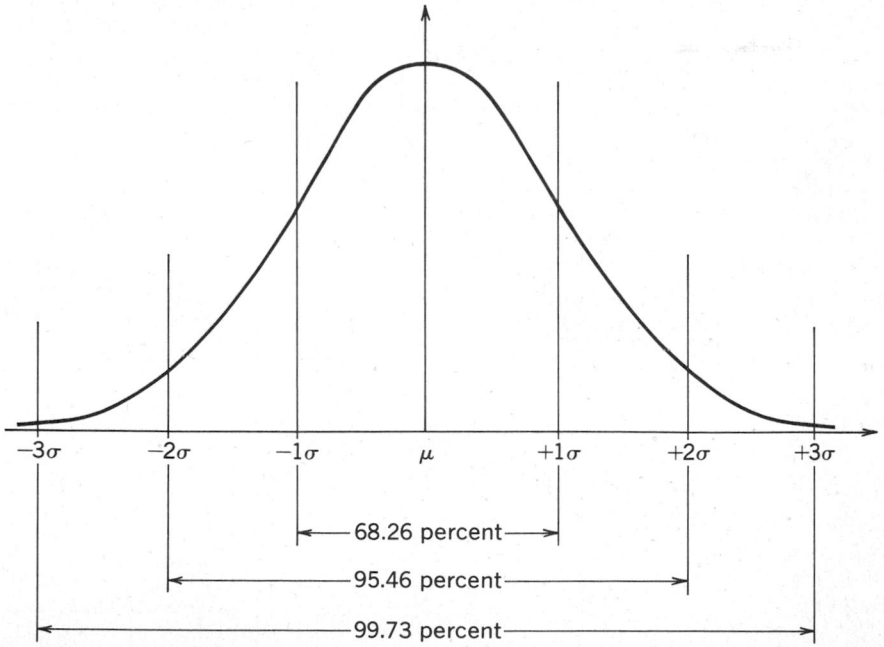

FIG. 23.14   Areas of a normal curve.

Another way of making predictions based on a normal distribution employs probability paper. Probability paper is so constructed that data from a particular kind of distribution plots as a straight line, i.e., a sample of data from a normally distributed population plots approximately as a straight line on normal probability paper. (Small deviations from a straight line are expected because the data represent a *sample* of the population.) The following are the steps taken to plot data on probability paper:

1. Arrange the observations in ascending values. The smallest value is given a rank i of 1 and the largest value a rank of n.

2. For each value, calculate the cumulative frequency.

3. For each value, calculate

$$\frac{\text{Cumulative frequency}}{n + 1} \times 100$$

This provides the mean rank probability estimate, in percent, for plotting the data.

4. Plot the observed values against their mean rank probability estimate.

If the observations are in frequency distribution form, the procedure is the same, except that instead of using the observed values the probability estimates are plotted against the cell boundaries. This is illustrated for the resistance data (see Table 23.18).

The plot is shown in Figure 23.15. Lower cell boundaries are plotted against the last column of Table 23.18 using the upper (Percent Over) scale. The line has been drawn in by eye, and the fit appears reasonable. This line represents an estimate of the population, and predictions like those obtained from the normal probability table can be read directly from the graph. For example, 5 percent of the population of coils will have resistance values greater than about 3.39. Also, 95 percent will have values greater than about 3.29. (Therefore, 95 − 5, or 90 percent, will have values between 3.29 and 3.39.)

Figure 23.16 shows a form which incorporates probability paper plotting with further analysis such as confidence limits and control limits. (This type of form was originally developed by E. F. Taylor.)

King (1971) gives a practical description of probability paper procedures for the normal and other important distributions. While fit is often evaluated by eye when we have clearly good fit (as in Figure 23.15), statistical tests are available and should be used in cases which are not so clearcut; see Iman (1982) for details and graphs on which this analysis can be performed.

TABLE 23.18 Resistance Data

Cell boundaries	Frequency	Cumulative frequency	$\dfrac{\text{Cumulative frequency}}{100 + 1}$ (100)
3.415–3.445	1	1	0.99%
3.385–3.415	8	9	8.90
3.355–3.385	27	36	35.60
3.325–3.355	36	72	71.30
3.295–3.325	23	95	94.10
3.265–3.295	5	100	99.00
	100		

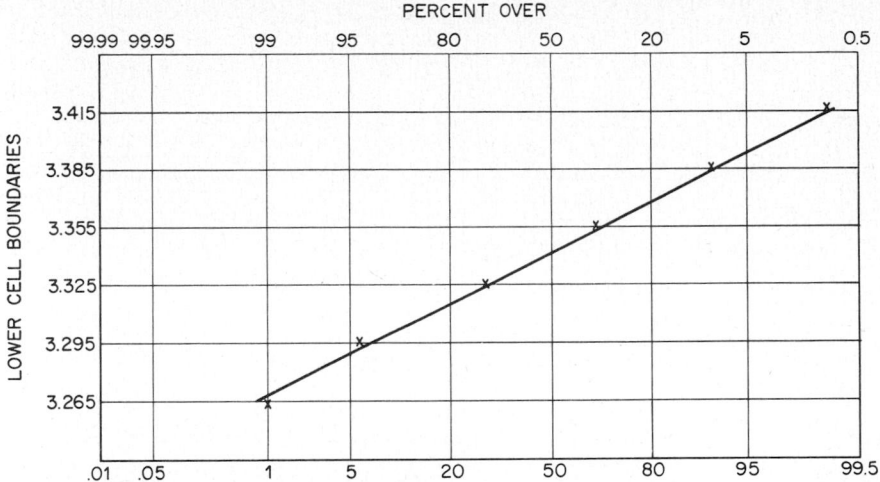

FIG. 23.15 Cumulative probability plot of Table 23.18.

The Lognormal Distribution. If $Y = e^Z$ where Z has a normal distribution, Y is said to have a lognormal distribution (since the logarithm of Y has a normal distribution).

Model Leading to a Lognormal Distribution (Multiplicative or Percentage Effects). Lognormal variables arise when effects are percentages or multiplicative, which is common in biological and many other applications. For example, if a random percent of a stock of items goes bad each time period, the percentage still good after a large number (10 or more) of time periods will be lognormally distributed. (This result follows from the Central Limit Theorem already discussed when considering the normal distribution, since the logarithm of a product is the sum of the logarithms of the items in the product.)

Predictions with Lognormal Distributions. As with the normal distribution, predictions require two estimates. For details, see Cohen and Whitten (1981). Note that the lognormal distribution is positively skewed, and is widely employed as a model for distribution of life spans, reaction times, income distributions, and other economic data.

Often the mean, standard deviation, and probabilities of the lognormal variable Y itself are of basic interest; thus, while one can easily estimate these for Z (the logarithm of $Y = e^Z$), that does not answer the real problem. For example, if Y is the lifetime of some system, one may want to estimate the average life of the system—not the mean of the logarithm of Y. This is why the special methods referred to above have been developed for this distribution.

Mixture Distributions. Y is said to have a mixture distribution if Y results from source i $100p_i$ percent of the time ($i = 1, 2, \ldots$).

Model Leading to a Mixture Distribution. When output from several sources is mixed (for example, output from several suppliers, several plants, several machines, several workers, and so on), the quality characteristics of the resulting mix have mixture distributions. If each of the components coming into the mix

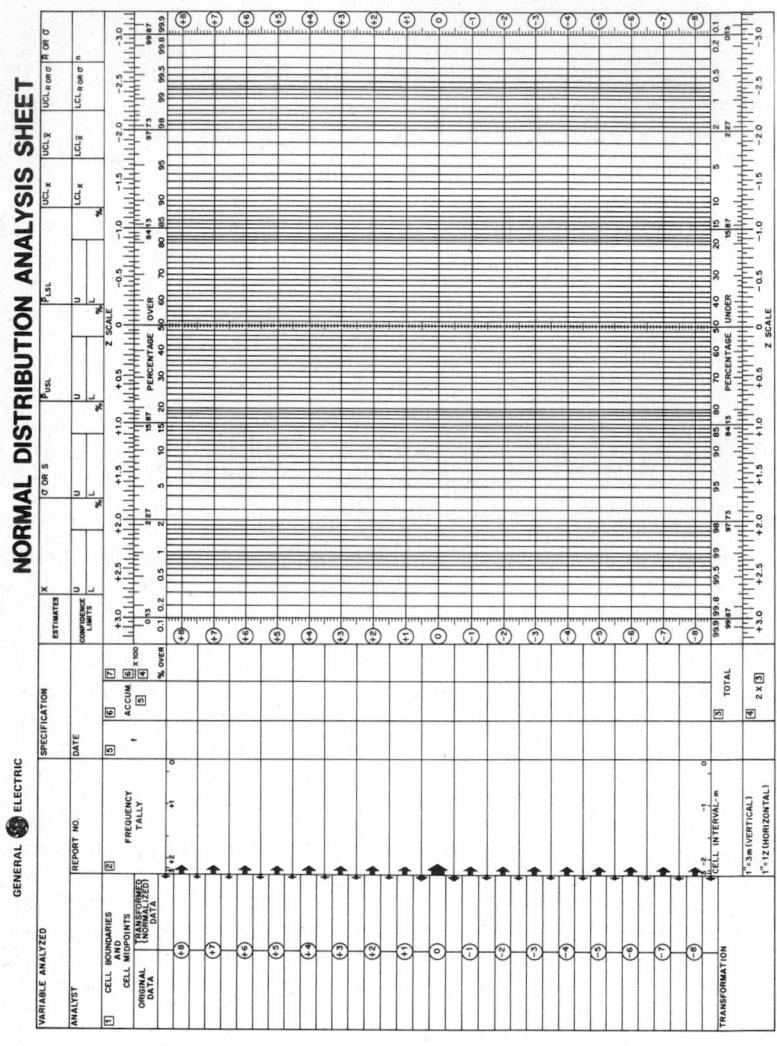

FIG. 23.16 Normal distribution analysis sheet.

has *exactly* the same distribution, then the mix will also have that distribution. However, if the components coming into the mix have different distributions, then the mix will have a "mixture distribution."

Fitting of Mixtures. As can be seen from Figure 23.7, the distributions we have considered so far are unimodal (have one peak). When in practice one sees two or more peaks in the histogram, one suspects a mixture underlies the data. In some cases, this itself leads to a study of the items coming into the mix, often to find a problem in one of the streams of what should be homogeneous product.

In other cases, the streams coming into the mix cannot be separated (or it is not desired to separate them), but rather one wishes to fit the density of Y as $p_1 f(Z_1) + p_2 f(Z_2) + \cdots + p_k f(Z_k)$ for some k (2 or more). Here the p_i's add to 1 (100 percent of the mix), and often the Z_i's are known to be normal. To fit the distribution of the Y, one must then select $k - 1$ p's (since they add to 1, the last one is then determined), k means, and k variances. This process requires use of modern computer software such as LABONE. As an example, consider the data of Table 23.19. A histogram of this data (computed as was Figure 23.4 for a similar but different data set) shows that a mixture (of two terms, since there are two peaks) may be involved. The distributions seem to the eye to be normal. Using LABONE Expert Statistical Programs (ESP), we are able to easily fit a mixture of normal distributions.

TABLE 23.19 Data for Mixture Analysis

3.37	3.34	3.48	3.32	3.33	3.38	3.34	3.31	3.43	3.34
3.29	3.46	3.30	3.31	3.43	3.34	3.34	3.46	3.39	3.34
3.45	3.36	3.30	3.42	3.33	3.35	3.45	3.34	3.32	3.48
3.32	3.37	3.44	3.38	3.36	3.47	3.36	3.31	3.43	3.30
3.35	3.43	3.38	3.37	3.54	3.32	3.36	3.42	3.29	3.35
3.48	3.39	3.34	3.42	3.30	3.39	3.46	3.40	3.32	3.43
3.29	3.41	3.37	3.36	3.41	3.47	3.36	3.37	3.43	3.36
3.31	3.43	3.35	3.34	3.45	3.34	3.31	3.46	3.37	3.35
3.50	3.35	3.37	3.42	3.35	3.36	3.48	3.35	3.31	3.44
3.35	3.36	3.49	3.31	3.31	3.40	3.35	3.33	3.45	3.31

The Multinormal Distribution. The continuous probability distributions discussed up to this point (the uniform, exponential, Weibull, normal, lognormal, and mixture) all relate to situations which are *univariate,* that is, where the outcome of interest has one component (such as lifetime). If there are additional components of interest (such as weight and height), then the outcome is *multivariate* (in this case of three, *trivariate*). The multinormal distribution is appropriate when each of the components has a normal distribution, and is the most widely used continuous multivariate distribution.

Model Leading to a Multinormal Distribution. The same sort of additive process which leads to a univariate normal distribution, leads to a multivariate normal distribution when more than one component is being measured.

Predictions with Multinormal Distributions. Predictions with multinormal distributions require computer packages in most cases. The details, with computer code and examples, are discussed by Siotani, Hayakawa, and Fujikoshi (1985).

Selecting a Continuous Distribution.   Selection of which continuous distribution to use is usually made by either knowledge of the underlying situation, or by fitting a model to the histogram (often via plots on probability papers of the most usual distributions). In either case a test of the model selected is desirable to check its validity.

Selection from a Model of Reality.   In many cases one will know (or assume) that the model which leads to one of the distributions we have discussed underlies the practical situation. For example, if the life distribution of the equipment under study has, in the past, always been adequately fitted by a Weibull model (though with parameters which change from application to application), one will usually start with a Weibull assumption.

Testing Distributional Assumptions (Probability Plotting, Tests for Specific Distributions).   In practice, a distribution is assumed by evaluating a sample of data. Often, it is sufficient to evaluate the shape of the histogram or the degree to which a plot on probability paper follows a straight line. These convenient methods do require judgment (e.g., how "straight" must the line be?) because the sample is never a perfect fit; quantitative tests for probability plots should be used (see Iman, 1982). Be suspicious of the data if the fit is "perfect." "Goodness of fit" tests (see Tests of Hypotheses later in this section) evaluate any distribution assumption using quantitative criteria.

Fitting Empirical Probability Distributions.   If there is little or no reason to suggest one of the specific models discussed, or if they are rejected (e.g., because of a poor probability paper fit), an alternative is to fit an empirical model. Such models can adapt to a wide range of distributional shapes, including many of those of the specific models discussed above. One of the most widely used empirical families is the *generalized lambda distribution* family *(GLD)*.

As an example, in Table 23.20 we have data (from p. 219 of Hahn and Shapiro, 1967) on the coefficient of friction of a metal in 250 samples. Using procedures and tables given in Ramberg, Dudewicz, Tadikamalla, and Mykytka (1979), a probability function can be developed.

As a check on the goodness of the fit, it is recommended that the probability

TABLE 23.20   Coefficient-of-Friction Data

Range	Frequency
Less than .015	1
0.015–0.020	9
0.020–0.025	30
0.025–0.030	44
0.030–0.035	58
0.035–0.040	45
0.040–0.045	29
0.045–0.050	17
0.050–0.055	9
0.055–0.060	4
More than 0.060	4
Total	250

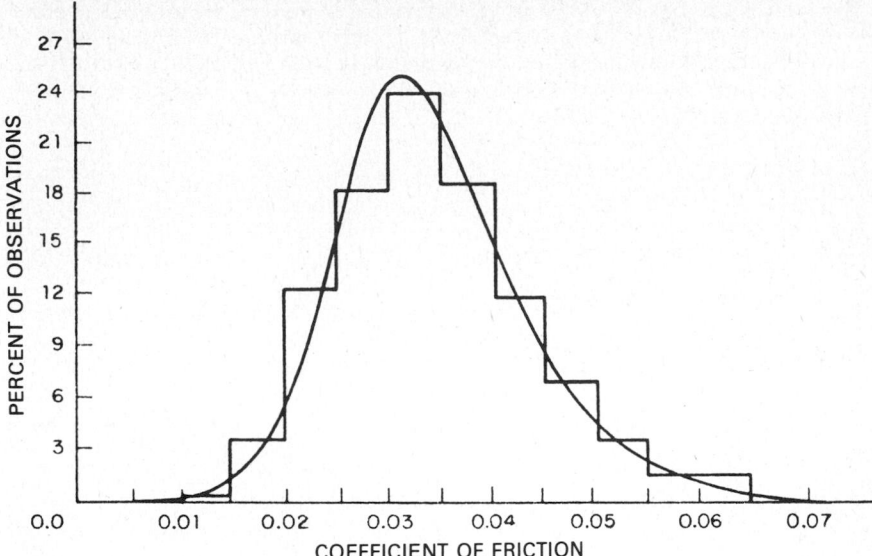

FIG. 23.17 Coefficient of friction relative frequency histogram and the fitted distribution.

function always be plotted on the same graph as the histogram for a visual assessment of the fit (which can be supplemented by a chi square test if desired). This is done in Figure 23.17, and we see that the fit is excellent (a chi square test comes to the same conclusion).

STATISTICAL ESTIMATION

In statistical estimation, we make inferences about parameters of a population from data on a sample. For example, if we have a random sample of 100 items from a large lot, information on the sample can be used to infer information about the proportion of defectives p in the lot. This inference takes the form of either a single number (a "point estimate") or a pair of numbers (an "interval estimate"); there are several types of interval estimates, depending on our goals. If we found that 15 of the 100 items in the sample were defective, we would estimate p as being $15/100 = 0.15$ (point estimate); a typical interval would be to state that we are 95 percent confident that p is between 0.08 and 0.22 (confidence interval estimate). Thus, a "confidence interval" sets limits on the unknown parameter, here the proportion p. Two other types of intervals often needed are "prediction intervals" and "tolerance intervals." Let X denote the number of defectives in a future sample; a prediction interval sets limits on X, such as

$$P[L_1 \leq X \leq U_1] = 0.95$$

In this example, a "prediction interval" would state that X would be between 5 and 25; these are limits within which one could be 95% sure the number of defectives in a future sample of 100 items would lie. A "tolerance interval" sets limits

(L, U) such that one can be 95 percent sure that at least 99 percent of the population will be included within these limits. In this example, the population is all lots of 100 items drawn from the same process; at least 99 percent of the lots will have a proportion of defectives between $L = 0.05$ and $U = 0.25$. These items are discussed in more detail below.

Point Estimates. Point estimates are customarily the points at which the interval estimates are centered. In many cases, it is preferable to give an interval estimate, since that estimate tells us how much uncertainty is associated with the estimate. For example, if we observe 15 of 100 items chosen at random from a very large lot are defective, then we will estimate the proportion of defectives in the lot as $15/100 = 0.15$. Similarly if we observe three defectives in a sample of 20 items we will estimate the proportion of defectives as $3/20 = 0.15$. However, in the first case the interval estimate (at 95 percent confidence) will be that p is between 0.08 and 0.22, while in the latter case the interval estimate (at 95 percent confidence) will be that p is between 0.00 and 0.31. In either case, if forced to estimate proportion defective in the lot by a single number, that number would be 0.15; however, the uncertainty in that estimate is much greater with the smaller sample size (where as much as 31 percent of the population might be defective) than with the larger sample size (where as much as 22 percent of the population might be defective).

The typical point estimates are covered below, as the centers of the respective intervals.

Confidence Interval Estimates. Estimation is the process of analyzing a sample result in order to predict the corresponding value of the population parameter. For example, a sample of 12 insulators has an average impact strength of 4.952 ft·lb (6.7149 N·m). If this is a representative sample from the process, what estimate can be made of the true average impact strength of the entire population of insulators?

1. The "point estimate" is a single value used to estimate the population parameter. For example, 4.952 ft·lb (6.7149 N·m) is the point estimate of the average strength of the population.

2. The "confidence interval" is a range of values which includes (with a preassigned probability called "confidence level") the true value of a population parameter. "Confidence limits" are the upper and lower boundaries of the confidence interval. Confidence level is the probability that an assertion about the value of a population parameter is correct.

Duncan (1974) provides a thorough discussion of confidence limits. The explanation here indicates the concept behind the calculations.

If the population mean is μ, the probability that the sample mean will lie between

$$\mu \pm 1.96 \frac{\sigma}{\sqrt{n}}$$

is equal to 0.95:

$$P\left(\mu - 1.96 \frac{\sigma}{\sqrt{n}} \leq \overline{X} \leq \mu + 1.96 \frac{\sigma}{\sqrt{n}}\right) = 0.95$$

This is algebraically equivalent to saying that the sample mean plus 1.96 standard deviations of means lies above μ and the sample mean minus 1.96 standard deviations of means lies below μ:

$$P\left(\mu \leq \overline{X} + 1.96\,\frac{\sigma}{\sqrt{n}} \text{ and } \overline{X} - 1.96\,\frac{\sigma}{\sqrt{n}} \leq \mu\right) = 0.95$$

or

$$P\left(\overline{X} - 1.96\,\frac{\sigma}{\sqrt{n}} \leq \mu \leq \overline{X} + 1.96\,\frac{\sigma}{\sqrt{n}}\right) = 0.95$$

Or the 95 percent confidence interval on μ is $\overline{X} \pm 1.96\,(\sigma/\sqrt{n})$. This interval has a 0.95 probability of including the population value: 95 percent of the sets of such intervals would include the population value. In practice, this is interpreted to mean that there is a 95 percent "confidence" that the limits based on one sample will include the true value.

For the sample of 12 insulators suppose $\sigma = 0.25$. Then, the 95 percent confidence limits are

$$\overline{X} \pm 1.96\,\frac{\sigma}{\sqrt{n}} = 4.952 \pm 1.96\,\frac{(0.25)}{\sqrt{12}} = 4.811 \text{ and } 5.093$$

This is interpreted to mean that there is 95 percent confidence that μ is between 4.811 and 5.093. The 95 percent is the confidence level (confidence levels of 90, 95, or 99 percent are usually assumed in practice, and some statisticians call these the "holy" numbers) and 4.811 and 5.093 are the limits of the confidence interval. A confidence level is associated with an assertion based on actual measurements and measures the probability that the assertion is true. Confidence limits are limits which include the true value with a preassigned degree of confidence (the confidence level).

Table 23.21 summarizes confidence limit formulas for common parameters. The following examples illustrate some of these formulas.

Example: Sixty-one specimens of brass have a mean hardness of 54.62 and an estimated standard deviation of 5.34. Determine the 95 percent confidence limits on the mean.

Solution:

$$\text{Confidence limits} = \overline{X} \pm t\,\frac{s}{\sqrt{n}}$$

$$= 54.62 \pm 2.00\,\frac{5.34}{\sqrt{61}}$$

$$= 53.25 \text{ and } 55.99$$

There is 95 percent confidence that the true mean hardness of the brass is between 53.25 and 55.99.

Example: A radar system has been operated for 1200 h, during which time eight failures occurred. What are the 90 percent confidence limits on the mean time between failures for the system?

TABLE 23.21   Summary of Confidence Limit Formulas and Graphs

Parameters	Formulas
1. Mean of a normal population (standard deviation known)	$\overline{X} \pm K_{\alpha/2} \dfrac{\sigma}{\sqrt{n}}$ where $\overline{X}$ = sample average K = normal distribution coefficient (see Appendix II, Table B) σ = standard deviation of population n = sample size
2. Mean of a normal population (standard deviation unknown)	$\overline{X} \pm t_{\alpha/2} \dfrac{s}{\sqrt{n}}$ where t = Student's distribution coefficient (with n − 1 degrees of freedom) (see Appendix II, Table G) s = estimated σ

3. Standard deviation of a normal population
  a. Using sample standard deviation
  b. Using sample range
	Upper confidence limit = $B_U s$
	Lower confidence limit = $B_L s$
	where B_U and B_L are numerical factors given in Natrella (1963, p. T-34), Dixon and Massey (1969, p. 140)

4. Population fraction defective based on attribute data (fraction defective in sample)	See Appendix II, Chart N
5. Population fraction defective based on variables data ($\overline{X}$ and s in sample)	See Kirkpatrick (1970)
6. Difference between the means of two normal populations (standard deviations σ_1 and σ_2 known)	$(\overline{X}_1 - \overline{X}_2) \pm K_{\alpha/2} \sqrt{\dfrac{\sigma_1^2}{n_1} + \dfrac{\sigma_2^2}{n_2}}$ where K = normal distribution coefficient (see Appendix II, Table B)
7. Difference between the means of two normal populations ($\sigma_1 = \sigma_2$ but unknown)	$(\overline{X}_1 - \overline{X}_2) \pm t_{\alpha/2} \sqrt{\dfrac{1}{n_1} + \dfrac{1}{n_2}}$ $\times \sqrt{\dfrac{\sum (X - \overline{X}_1)^2 + \sum (X - \overline{X}_2)^2}{n_1 + n_2 - 2}}$ where t = Student's distribution coefficient (with degrees of freedom = $n_1 + n_2 - 2$)(see Appendix II, Table G)
8. Difference between the means of two normal populations (σ_1 and σ_2 both unknown)	$(\overline{X}_1 - \overline{X}_2) \pm t_{\alpha/2}^* \sqrt{\dfrac{\sum (X - \overline{X}_1)^2}{n_1(n_1 - 1)} + \dfrac{\sum (X - \overline{X}_2)^2}{n_2(n_2 - 1)}}$ where t^* = Student's distribution coefficient (with the smaller of $n_1 - 1$ and $n_2 - 1$ as degrees of freedom)

TABLE 23.21 Summary of Confidence Limit Formulas and Graphs (*Continued*)

Parameters	Formulas
9. Mean time between failures (based on an exponential population of time between failures)	Upper confidence limit $= 2T/\chi^2_{\alpha/2}$ Lower confidence limit $= 2T/\chi^2_{1-\alpha/2}$ where T = total test time on all units and DF $= 2r$, where r is a preassigned number of failures and where χ^2 = chi square distribution coefficient (see Appendix II, Table L)
10. Reliability (based on a Weibull population)	See Thoman, Bain, and Antle (1970)
11. Availability (based on an exponential population of time between failures and log normal population of repair time)	See Gray and Lewis (1967)

Solution:

$$\text{Estimated } m = \frac{1200}{8} = 150 \text{ h}$$

$$\text{Upper confidence limit} = \frac{2(1200)}{7.962} = 301.4$$

$$\text{Lower confidence limit} = \frac{2(1200)}{26.296} = 91.3$$

There is 90 percent confidence that the true mean time between failures is between 91.3 and 301.4 h. (Epstein, 1960, discusses several cases of making estimates from life test data.)

Confusion has arisen on the application of the term "confidence level" to a reliability index such as mean time between failures. Using a different example, suppose the numerical portion of a reliability requirement reads as follows: "The MTBF shall be at least 100 h at the 90 percent confidence level." This means:

1. The minimum MTBF must be 100 h.
2. Actual tests shall be conducted on the product to demonstrate with 90 percent confidence that the 100-h MTBF has been met.
3. The test data shall be analyzed by calculating the observed MTBF and the lower one-sided 90 percent confidence limit on MTBF.
4. The lower one-sided confidence limit must be $\geq$ 100 h.

The term "confidence level," from a statistical viewpoint, has great implications on a test program. Note that the observed MTBF must be *greater* than 100 if the lower confidence limit is to be $\geq$ 100. Confidence level means that sufficient tests must be conducted to demonstrate, with statistical validity, that a requirement has been met. Confidence level does *not* refer to the qualitative opinion about meeting a requirement. Also, confidence level does *not* lower a requirement; i.e., a 100-h MTBF at a 90 percent confidence level does not mean that 100 h is desired but that 0.90×100, or 90 h, is acceptable. Such serious misunderstandings have occurred. When the term is used, a clear understanding should be verified and not assumed.

Determination of the Sample Size Required to Achieve a Specified Precision in an Estimate. Additional tests will increase the precision of the estimates obtained from a test program. The increase in precision usually does not vary linearly with the number of tests—doubling the number of tests usually does not double the precision (even approximately). Further, if the sample is selected randomly and if the sample size is less than 10 percent of the population size, then precision depends primarily on the absolute size of the sample rather than the sample size expressed as a percent of the population size. Thus a sample size which is 1 percent of a population of 100,000 may be more precise than a 10 percent sample from a population of 1000 (see Hahn, 1972).

The cost of additional tests must be evaluated against the value of the additional precision. Confidence limits can help to determine the size of test program required to estimate a product characteristic within a specified precision. Suppose it is desired to estimate the true mean life of a battery. The estimate must be within 2.0 h of the true mean if the estimate is to be of any value. The variability is known as $\sigma = 10.0$. A 95 percent confidence level is desired on the confidence statement. The 2.0 h is the desired confidence interval half-width, so

$$2.0 = \frac{(1.96)(10)}{\sqrt{n}} \qquad n = 96$$

A sample of 96 batteries will provide a mean which is within 2.0 h of the true mean (with 95 percent confidence). Notice the type of information required: (1) desired width of the confidence interval (the precision desired in the estimate), (2) confidence level desired, (3) variability of the characteristic under investigation. The number of tests required cannot be determined until the engineer furnishes these items of information.

Table 23.22 summarizes formulas and graphs useful in determining the sample size required to estimate a population parameter with a specified precision. The following examples illustrate some of the formulas.

Example: A sample must be selected to estimate the population mean length of a part. It appears reasonable to assume that length is normally distributed. An estimate of the standard deviation is not available, but process knowledge suggests that "almost all" production falls between 2.009 and 2.027 in. As a first approximation, the standard deviation is estimated as $(2.027 - 2.009)$ divided by 6, or 0.003 in. It is desired that the estimate of μ be within 0.001 in of the true μ and that the estimation statement be made at the 95 percent confidence level. Referring to Appendix II, Chart S, $E/s = 0.001/0.003 = 0.33$, and the required sample size is about 37. It is instructive to calculate n for other values of E and s (see Table 23.23). Such a "sensitivity analysis" is helpful in evaluating the cost of extra tests against the value of extra precision.

Example: It is desired to estimate the standard deviation σ of a population within 20 percent of the true value at the 95 percent confidence level. Referring to Appendix II, Chart T, the required degrees of freedom is about 46 and, therefore, the sample size is $46 + 1$, or 47.

TABLE 23.22 Summary of Sample Size Formulas and Graphs

Parameters	Formulas
1. Mean of a normal population (σ known)	$n = \dfrac{K_{\alpha/2}^2 \sigma^2}{E^2}$ where K = normal distribution coefficient E = maximum allowable error in estimate (desired precision)
2. Mean of a normal population (σ estimated)	See Appendix II, Chart S
3. Standard deviation of a normal population	See Appendix II, Chart T
4. Fraction defective of a population	$n = p\,(1 - p)\left(\dfrac{K_{\alpha/2}}{E}\right)^2$ where p = estimate of the population fraction defective. If no estimate of p is available, assume "worst case" of $p = 0.5$

TABLE 23.23 Effect of E and s on n

Maximum error E	Standard deviation s		
	0.002	0.003	0.004
0.0008	27	56	98
0.0010	18	37	64
0.0020	7	12	18

Prediction Intervals. A prediction interval is used when the desire is not an estimate of population characteristics directly, but rather a prediction of what we will find when we take a future item from the population. For example, in the example of $n = 61$ specimens of brass with a mean hardness of 54.62 and an estimated standard deviation of 5.34, we previously found that 95 percent confidence limits on the mean were

$$\overline{X} \pm t\,\frac{s}{\sqrt{n}} = 53.25 \text{ and } 55.99$$

Now we ask: What limits can we be 95 percent sure the next item sampled will have its hardness within? The appropriate interval here is

$$\overline{X} \pm t\,s\sqrt{1 + \frac{1}{n}} = 54.62 \pm (2.00)(5.34)(1.0082)$$

$$= 43.85 \text{ and } 65.39$$

For further considerations and tables, see Hahn (1970).

Tolerance Intervals. "Statistical tolerance limits" are similar to "process capability," i.e., they show the practical boundaries of process variability (see Section 16, under Process Capability), and therefore can be a valuable input in the determination of engineering tolerance limits (which specify the allowable limits for product acceptance). Methods for calculating statistical tolerance limits are of two types—those which assume a normal distribution and those which do not require any distributional assumption. Table 23.24 summarizes these methods.

Table 23.25 shows data we will use to illustrate these methods. Five samples of four each were taken and an outside dimension of a cathode pole recorded.

A confidence level of 95 percent and a population percentage of 99 percent have been chosen.

Using method 1 and the standard deviation s, the statistical tolerance limits are

$$\overline{X} \pm Ks = 1.00287 \pm 3.615(0.00034) = 1.00164 \text{ and } 1.00410$$

Using method 2 and the overall range R of the combined data, the limits are

$$\overline{X} \pm K_1 R = 1.00287 \pm 1.005(0.00134) = 1.00152 \text{ and } 1.00422$$

Using method 3 and the average of the ranges R, the limits are

$$\overline{X} \pm K_2 R = 1.00287 \pm 1.783(0.00078) = 1.00148 \text{ and } 1.00426$$

These methods assume that the characteristic is normally distributed. Method 4 is "distribution-free" and assumes only that the distribution is continuous and the sample is a random one (these assumptions apply to all methods). The statistical tolerance limits by this method are simply the extreme observations in the combined sample, i.e., 1.00231 and 1.00365. Appendix II, Table W indicates that at least 78.4 percent of the population will be included within these limits. (Note that Appendix II, Table X provides the sample size required to include 99 percent of the population; i.e., a sample of 473 is needed to be 95 percent confident that the sample extremes would include 99 percent of the population.)

When it is feasible to assume a normal distribution, method 1 is preferred because it usually provides the narrowest set of limits while recognizing the variation in the sample. Methods 2 and 3 are good approximations. If normality cannot be assumed, then method 4 is appropriate but at the cost of a larger sample size. In practice, a partial sample can first be obtained to evaluate the assumption of normality. If normality can be assumed, the partial sample is then used to determine statistical tolerance limits. Otherwise, the full sample should be taken and the distribution-free approach (method 4) applied to determine the limits.

Tolerance intervals have also been developed for other cases, such as where the distribution is exponential. Ranganathan and Kale (1983) give such intervals which are resistant to the presence of an outlier in the observations. Their Section 5 includes an example with data on reliability of air conditioning on a Boeing 727 jet aircraft.

All the above methods involve two probabilities, i.e., a confidence level γ and the probability P of falling within limits. This is confusing, but these two probabilities are needed to obtain a mathematically correct statement concerning the limits. An approximation uses the sample average $\overline{X}$ and standard deviation s and regards these as highly reliable estimates of μ and σ. If normality is assumed, then 99 percent statistical tolerance limits are calculated as

$$\overline{X} \pm 2.56s$$

TABLE 23.24 Methods for Calculating Statistical Tolerance Limits

Method	Distribution assumption	Formula for limits	Source of factor
1. Measure a sample of n items and calculate the average $\overline{X}$ and standard deviation s	Normal	Two-sided limits: $\overline{X} \pm Ks$ One-sided limit: $\overline{X} + Ks$ or $\overline{X} - Ks$	Appendix II, Table V Appendix II, Table V
2. Measure a sample of n items and calculate the average $\overline{X}$ and range R	Normal	Two-sided limits: $\overline{X} \pm K_1 R$	Appendix II, Table U
3. Measure N samples of n items each and calculate the grand average $\overline{\overline{X}}$ and average range $\overline{R}$	Normal	Two-sided limits: $\overline{\overline{X}} \pm K_2 \overline{R}$	Bingham (1962, p. 37)
4. Define the population percentage P which must be included between the tolerance limits. Measure a sample of n and observe the largest and smallest values	None	Two-sided limits: The probability is γ that at least P % of the population will be between the sample extremes. One-sided limit: The probability is γ that at least P % of the population will be less than the largest value in the sample (or greater than the smallest value).	Appendix II, Table W Natrella (1963, p. T-76)

TABLE 23.25 Data on Cathode Pole Dimension

	Sample 1	Sample 2	Sample 3	Sample 4	Sample 5	
	1.00263	1.00306	1.00293	1.00291	1.00310	
	1.00298	1.00328	1.00343	1.00247	1.00281	$\overline{X} = 1.00287$
	1.00293	1.00274	1.00239	1.00268	1.00256	$s = 0.00034$ (standard deviation of the
	1.00285	1.00303	1.00274	1.00365	1.00231	20 observations about $\overline{X}$)
$\overline{X}$	1.00285	1.00303	1.00287	1.00293	1.00269	$\overline{R} = 0.00078$
R	0.00035	0.00054	0.00104	0.00118	0.00079	$R = 0.00134$

where the value of 2.56 is obtained from the normal distribution table (Appendix II, Table B):

$$\overline{X} \pm 2.56s = 1.00287 \pm 2.56(0.000274)$$

$$= 1.00217 \text{ and } 1.00357$$

These limits are then interpreted to mean that 99 percent of the population is within 1.00217 and 1.00357. Another approach sets the limits at simply $\overline{X} \pm 3s$. At best, these are only approximate because $\overline{X}$ and s are not exactly equal to μ and σ. Bingham (1962) discusses the $X \pm 3s$ approximation. (Confidence limit calculations could indicate the size of the possible error.)

Another approach to simplify the probability statement uses the Chebyshev inequality theorem, which holds for any continuous distribution. The theorem states that the probability of obtaining a value which deviates from μ by more than k standard deviations is less than $1/k^2$. For the limits to include 99 percent,

$$0.01 = \frac{1}{k^2}$$

or

$$k = 10$$

The 99 percent limits would be calculated as $\overline{X} \pm 10s$. These limits are distribution-free and the prediction statement is simple; i.e., at least 99 percent of the population is within $\overline{X} \pm 10s$. However, the multiple of 10 is highly conservative and results in limits much wider than any of the other methods.

For the methods listed in Table 23.24, no provision is made for the division of the remaining $100(1 - P)$ percent between the upper and lower tails of the distribution. Owen and Frawley (1971) give a procedure and tables for setting limits which do provide for controlling the percentage outside each of the two limits.

Statistical tolerance limits are sometimes confused wtih other limits used in engineering and statistics. Table 23.26 summarizes the distinctions among five types of limits. Hahn (1970) gives an excellent discussion with examples and

TABLE 23.26   Distinction among Limits

Name of limits	Meaning
Tolerance limits	Set by the engineering design function to define the minimum and maximum values allowable for the product to work properly.
Statistical tolerance limits	Calculated from process data to define the amount of variation that the process exhibits. These limits will contain a specified proportion of the total population.
Prediction limits	Calculated from process data to define the limits which will contain all of k future observations.
Confidence limits	Calculated from data to define an interval within which a population parameter lies.
Control limits	Calculated from process data to define the limits of chance (random) variation around some central value.

tables to illustrate the differences among several types of limits. Also see Harter (1983) under "Tolerance Limits."

Tolerance Limits for Interacting Dimensions. Interacting dimensions are those which mate or merge with other dimensions to create a final result. Setting tolerance limits on such dimensions is discussed in the following paragraphs. Setting tolerance limits on noninteracting dimensions makes use of the methods presented under Statistical Tolerance Limits in this section and in Section 13 (see especially Fig. 13.14 and associated discussion).

Conventional Method Relating Tolerances on Interacting Dimensions. Consider the simple mechanical assembly shown in Figure 23.18. The lengths of components *A*, *B*, and *C* are interacting dimensions because they determine the overall assembly length.

The conventional method of relating interacting dimensions is simple addition. For the example of Figure 23.18,

$$\text{Nominal value of the result} = \text{nominal value}_A + \text{nominal value}_B + \text{nominal value}_C$$

$$\text{Tolerance } T \text{ of the result} = T_A + T_B + T_C$$

$$\text{Nominal value of assembly length} = 1.000 + 0.500 + 2.000 = 3.500$$

$$\text{Tolerance of assembly length} = 0.0010 + 0.0005 + 0.0020 = \pm 0.0035$$

This method assumes 100 percent interchangeability of components making up the assembly. If the component tolerances are met, then all assemblies will meet the assembly tolerance determined by the simple arithmetic addition.

The approach of adding component tolerances is mathematically correct, but often too conservative. Suppose that about 1 percent of the pieces of component *A* are expected to be below the lower tolerance limit for component *A* and suppose the same for components *B* and *C*. If a component *A* is selected at random, there is on the average 1 chance in 100 that it will be on the low side, and similarly for components *B* and *C*. They key point is this: If assemblies are made at random and if the components are manufactured independently, then the chance that an assembly will have all three components simultaneously below the lower tolerance limit is

$$\frac{1}{100} \times \frac{1}{100} \times \frac{1}{100} = \frac{1}{1,000,000}$$

There is thus only about one chance in a million that all three components will be too small, resulting in a small assembly. Thus, setting component and assem-

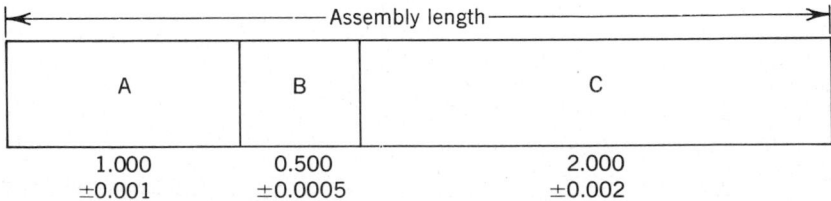

FIG. 23.18 Mechanical assembly.

bly tolerances based on the simple addition formula is conservative in that it fails to recognize the extremely low probability of an assembly containing all low (or all high) components.

Statistical Method of Relating Tolerances on Interacting Dimensions. This method states for the example Figure 23.18:

Nominal value of the result

$$= \text{nominal value}_A + \text{nominal value}_B + \text{nominal value}_C$$

Tolerance of the result $= \sqrt{T_A^2 + T_B^2 + T_C^2}$

Then:

Nominal value of the assembly $= 1.000 + 0.500 + 2.000 = 3.500$

T of the assembly $= \sqrt{(0.001)^2 + (0.0005)^2 + (0.002)^2} = \pm 0.0023$

Practically all (but not 100 percent) of the assemblies will fall within 3.500 ± 0.0023. This is narrower than 3.500 ± 0.0035 (the result by the arithmetic method).

In practice, the problem often is to start with a defined end result (e.g., assembly length specification) and set tolerances on the parts. Suppose the assembly tolerance was desired to be ± 0.0035. Listed in Table 23.27 are two possible sets of component tolerances which when used with the quadratic formula will yield an assembly tolerance equal to ± 0.0035. The tolerance set using the conventional formula is also shown.

TABLE 23.27   Comparison of Statistical and Conventional Methods

Component	Statistical		Conventional
	Alternative 1	Alternative 2	
A	± 0.002	± 0.001	± 0.0010
B	± 0.002	± 0.001	± 0.0005
C	± 0.002	± 0.003	± 0.0020

The advantage of the statistical formula is larger component tolerances. With alternative 1, the tolerance for component A has been doubled, the tolerance for component B has been quadrupled, and the tolerance for component C has been kept the same as the original component based on the simple addition approach. If alternative 2 is chosen, similar significant increases in the component tolerances may be achieved. This formula, then, may result in a larger component tolerance with no change in the manufacturing processes and no change in the assembly tolerance. Note that the *largest single* tolerance has the greatest effect on the overall result.

The disadvantage of the quadratic formula is that it involves several assumptions which, even if met, will still result in a small percent (theoretically 0.27 percent) of results not conforming to the limits set by the formula. The assumptions are:

1. The component dimensions are independent and the components are assembled randomly. This assumption is usually met in practice.

2. Each component dimension should be normally distributed. Some departure from this assumption is permissible.
3. The actual average for each component is equal to the nominal value stated in the specification. For the original assembly example, the actual averages for components *A, B,* and *C* must be 1.000, 0.500, and 2.000, respectively. Otherwise, the nominal value of 3.500 will not be achieved for the assembly, and tolerance limits set about 3.500 will not be realistic. Thus, it is important to control the *average* value for interacting dimensions. This means that process control techniques are needed using variables measurement rather than go, no-go measurement.

A summary of the two methods of tolerance is given in Table 23.28.

The statistical tolerancing formula applies both to assemblies made up of physically separate components and to a chain of several interacting dimensions within one physical item. Further, the result of the interacting dimensions can be an outside dimension (assembly length) or an internal result (clearance between a shaft and hole).

Further Applications of Statistical Tolerancing. It is easy to be deceived into concluding that the statistical method of tolerancing is merely a change from an expression of tolerances in the form of limits on each component to a form of:

1. Upper and lower limits on the average $\overline{X}$ of the mass of components.
2. An upper limit to the scatter σ of the components.

The change is much more profound than mere form of the specification. It affects the entire cycle of manufacturing planning, production, inspection, quality control, service, etc. It is, in effect, *a new philosophy of manufacture.*

The first published example of a *large-scale application* of statistical toleranc-

TABLE 23.28   Comparison of Conventional and Statistical Tolerancing

Factor	Conventional	Statistical
Risk of items not interacting properly	No risk; 100% interchangeability of items	Small percent of final results will fall outside limits (but these can sometimes be corrected with selective assembly)
Utilization of full tolerance range	Method is conservative; tolerances on interacting dimensions are smaller than necessary	Permits larger tolerances on interacting dimensions
Special process control techniques	None	Average of each interacting dimension must be controlled using variables measurement
Statistical assumptions	None	Interacting dimensions must be independent and each must be normally distributed
Lot size for components	Any size	Lot size should be moderately large (to assure balancing effect on extreme interacting dimensions)

ing appears to be that of the L-3 coaxial system (a broad-band transmission system for multiple telephone or television channels). Dodge, Kinsburg, and Kruger (1953) discuss the application.

The general plan was:

1. Discovery of the key quality characteristics of each component element of the system.
2. Determination of the precision of measurement, to separate measurement variability from process and product variability.
3. Collection of data on process capability for the key qualities, to aid in establishing realistic tolerances.

The foregoing were preliminary to:

4. Establishment of tolerances for the key quality characteristics in the dual form of a maximum on the standard deviation σ and limits on the average $\overline{X}$. The limits on X were established as $\pm$ ⅛ σ around the nominal.
5. Establishment of control procedures.

It was recognized that the limits on σ and $\overline{X}$ required further interpretation if the intent of the designers was to be carried out by the manufacturers. To this end, three forms of product acceptance were established.

1. *Control charts:* Shewhart control charts for $\overline{X}$ and σ could be used for product acceptance, provided "eligibility" was established (seven consecutive subgroups, of five pieces each, all met the control limits for X and σ) and provided subsequent statistical control was maintained (based on chart results plus absence of major changes in process).
2. *Batch control:* This was based on examination of a sample of (normally) 50 pieces by variables measurements, with limits on $\overline{X}$ and σ appropriate to the sample size of 50. Each batch stood or fell on its own measurements.
3. *Detailed classification:* Product which did not qualify under 1 or 2 was measured in detail. The resulting conforming units were classified into one of three variable classes. The packaging was then done by selecting classified units in such a way that each package contained an assortment of product which conformed to the intent of the design as to $\overline{X}$ and σ.

Grant and Leavenworth (1980) discuss statistical tolerancing including an application to shafts and holes. The Western Electric Company, Inc. (1982) in its *Statistical Quality Control Handbook* (pp. 122–127) presents examples and discusses the assumptions. Peters (1970) discusses statistical tolerancing, including a method for recognizing cost differences among components. Choksi (1971) discusses the use of computer simulation to determine optimum tolerances.

The concept may be applied to several interacting variables in an engineering relationship. The nature of the relationship need *not* be additive (assembly example) or subtractive (shaft and hole example). The formula can be adapted to predict the variation of results that are the product and/or the division of several variables. Mouradian (1966) discusses these applications.

Bayesian Estimates.   Bayesian estimation can be used when the parameter to be estimated can be considered to be a random variable for which we know the distribution. For example, in sampling inspection, if a manufacturer has a stable production process, then the proportion of defectives p in a lot may be a random variable about which we can fit a distribution by our sampling inspection over time. If so, then in the future that information can be used to provide quality assurance with less sampling; e.g., see Lenz and Rendtel (1984).

When it is not possible to cumulate information about a stable process, some have proposed that we use our "feelings" about the parameter to choose a statistical distribution for it, and then proceed as if the parameter were a random variable with that distribution. This is called the "personal probability" approach, and those who use it are called "Bayesians." Some of the proponents of this approach say it is the only method which any sensible person should use, and this has been cause for bitter debates and ill-will. In our view, while a person in a management position might find this a reasonable way to express his or her insights quantitatively, in most cases this will be an unscientific way of simply incorporating prejudices into the decision process, resulting in costly errors. This approach is of some use in general statistical decision theory (see Chapter 12 of Dudewicz, 1976), but there it is used to generate a set of decision rules which contains all good rules, not just one rule based on one's "feelings." The Bayesian approach should be considered whenever information can be gathered over time on a stable process.

STATISTICAL TESTS OF HYPOTHESES

A statistical hypothesis is an assertion about a population, often about some parameter of a population. Tests of hypotheses (also called "tests of significance") were designed so that experimenters would not ascribe causes to variations in data which were in fact due simply to random variation (and thus did not need a cause to explain them). Thus, statistical hypothesis testing is a modern day version of the medieval Occam's razor principle that "one should not multiply causes without reason." (William of Occam was an English Franciscan philosopher who died about 1349.) For example, if a process has a mean weight of 14.90 lb per item produced, a change is made with a view to increasing the weight per item produced, and a sample of 10 items (taken after the process change) has a mean weight of 15.10 lb, this *does not* necessarily mean that the process mean has been shifted up: It could be that it has remained the same (or has even decreased) and that we are simply seeing the results of the randomness of the process. Making correct inferences in the face of such possibilities is the gist of the area of hypothesis testing.

Basic Concepts, Types of Errors. "Hypothesis" as used here is an assertion made about a population. Usually the assertion concerns the numerical value of some parameter of the population. For example, a hypothesis might state that the mean life of a population of batteries equals 30.0, written as $H{:}\mu_0 = 30.0$. This assertion may or may not be correct. A "hypothesis test" is a test of the validity of the assertion, and is carried out by analysis of a sample of data.

There are two reasons why sample results must be carefully evaluated. First, there are many other samples which, by chance alone, could be drawn from the population. Second, the numerical results in the sample actually selected can easily be compatible with several different hypotheses. These points are handled by recognizing two types of error which can be made in evaluating a hypothesis:

1. *Reject* the hypothesis when it is *true.* This is called the "type I error"; its probability is called the "level of significance" and is denoted by α.

2. *Accept* the hypothesis when it is *false*. This is called the "type II error"; its probability is usually denoted by β (though some authors call it $1 - \beta$).

These error probabilities can be controlled to desired values.

The type I error is shown graphically in Figure 23.19 for the hypothesis H:μ_0 = 30.0. The area between the vertical lines represents the "acceptance region" for the hypothesis test: If the sample result falls within the acceptance region, the hypothesis is accepted. Otherwise, it is rejected. Notice that there is a small portion of the curve which falls outside the acceptance region. This portion (α) represents the probability of obtaining a sample result outside the acceptance region, even though the hypothesis is correct.

Suppose it has been decided that the type I error must not exceed 5 percent. This is the probability of rejecting the hypothesis when, in truth, the true average life is 30.0. The acceptance region can be obtained by locating values of average life which have only a 5 percent chance of being exceeded when the true average life is 30.0. Further, suppose a sample n of four measurements is taken and $\sigma = 10.0$.

Remember that the curve represents a population of sample averages because the decision will be made on the basis of a sample average. Sample averages vary less than individual measurements according to the relationship $\sigma_{\bar{x}} = \sigma/\sqrt{n}$.

Further, the distribution of sample averages is approximately normal even if the distribution of the individual measurements (going into the averages) is not normal (see Grant and Leavenworth, 1972, pp. 69–71). The approximation holds best for large values of n but is adequate for n as low as 4.

Table B in Appendix II shows that a 2.5 percent area in each tail is at a limit which is 1.96 standard deviations from 30.0. Then under the hypothesis that μ_0 = 30.0, 95 percent of sample averages will fall within $\pm 1.96\sigma_{\bar{x}}$ of 30.0, or

$$\text{Upper limit} = 30.0 + 1.96\,\frac{10}{\sqrt{4}} = 39.8$$

$$\text{Lower limit} = 30.0 - 1.96\,\frac{10}{\sqrt{4}} = 20.2$$

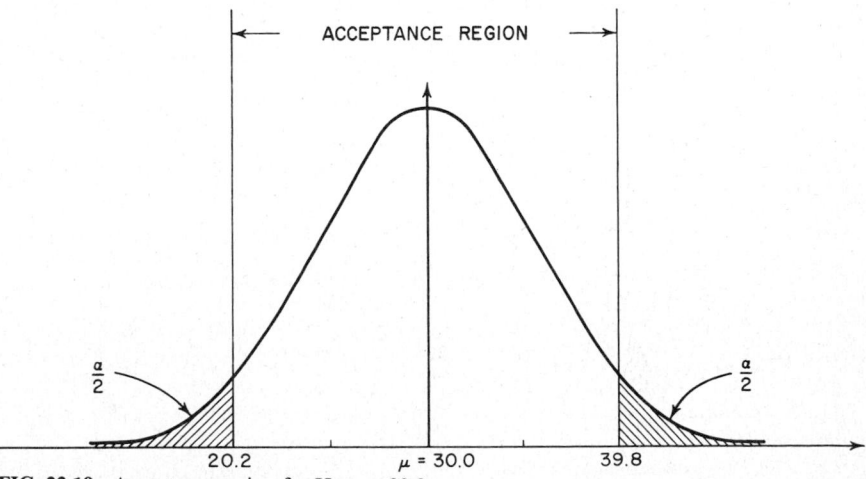

FIG. 23.19 Acceptance region for H:$\mu_0 = 30.0$.

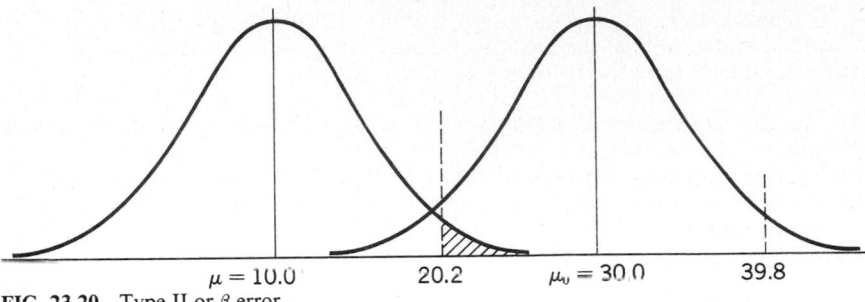

$\mu = 10.0$ 20.2 $\mu_0 = 30.0$ 39.8

FIG. 23.20 Type II or β error.

The acceptance region is thereby defined as 20.2 to 39.8. If the average of a random sample of four batteries is within this acceptance region, the hypothesis is accepted. If the average falls outside the acceptance region, the hypothesis is rejected. This decision rule provides a type I error of 0.05.

The type II or β error, the probability of accepting a hypothesis when it is false, is shown in Figure 23.20 as the shaded area. Notice it is possible to obtain a sample result within the acceptance region, even though the population has a true average which is not equal to the average stated in the hypothesis. The numerical value of β depends on the true value of the population average (and also on n, σ, and α). This is depicted by an "operating characteristic" (OC) curve.

The problem now is to construct an operating characteristic curve to assess the magnitude of the type II (β) error. As β is the probability of *accepting* the original hypothesis ($\mu_0 = 30.0$) when it is *false*, the probability that a sample average will fall between 20.2 and 39.8 must be found when the true average of the population is something other than 30.0. This has been done for many values of the true average, and the result is shown in Figure 23.21. [This curve should not be confused with that of a normal distribution of measurements. In some cases the shape is similar, but the meanings of an OC curve and a distribution curve are entirely different; Juran and Gryna (1980, pp. 410–412) give the detailed calculations; also

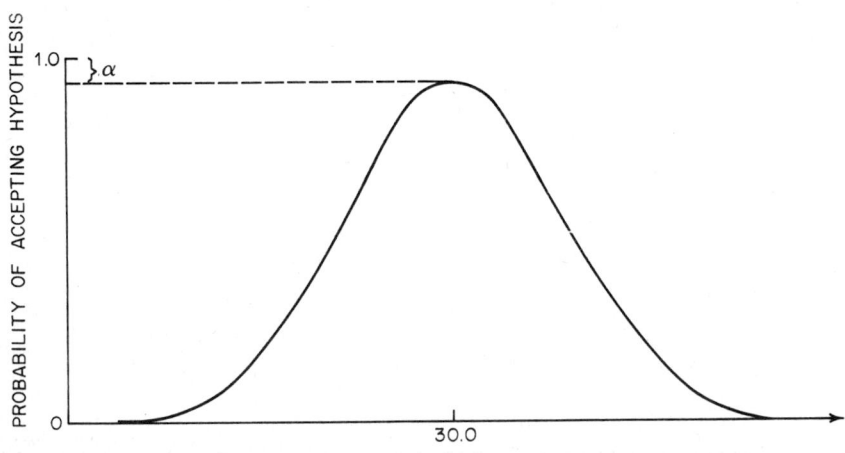

FIG. 23.21 Operating characteristic curve.

see Dudewicz, 1976, pp. 272–275.] Thus, the OC curve is a plot of the probability of accepting the original hypothesis as a function of the true value of the population parameter (and the given values of n, σ, and α).

Use of the Operating Characteristic Curve in Selecting an Acceptance Region.

The acceptance region was determined by dividing the 5 percent allowable α error into equal parts (see Figure 23.19). This is called a "two-tailed test." The entire 5 percent could also be placed at either the left or the right tail of the distribution curve (Figure 23.22). These are "one-tailed tests."

Operating characteristic curves for tests having these one-tailed acceptance regions can be developed following the approach used for the two-tailed region. Although the α error is the same, the β error varies for the three tests. (See Figure 9.2-2 on p. 275 of Dudewicz, 1976.)

In some problems, knowledge is available to indicate that if the true average of the population is *not* equal to the hypothesis value, then it is on one side of the hypothesis value. For example, a new material of supposedly higher average strength will have an average equal to or *greater than* that of the present material. Such information will help select a one-tailed or two-tailed test to make the β

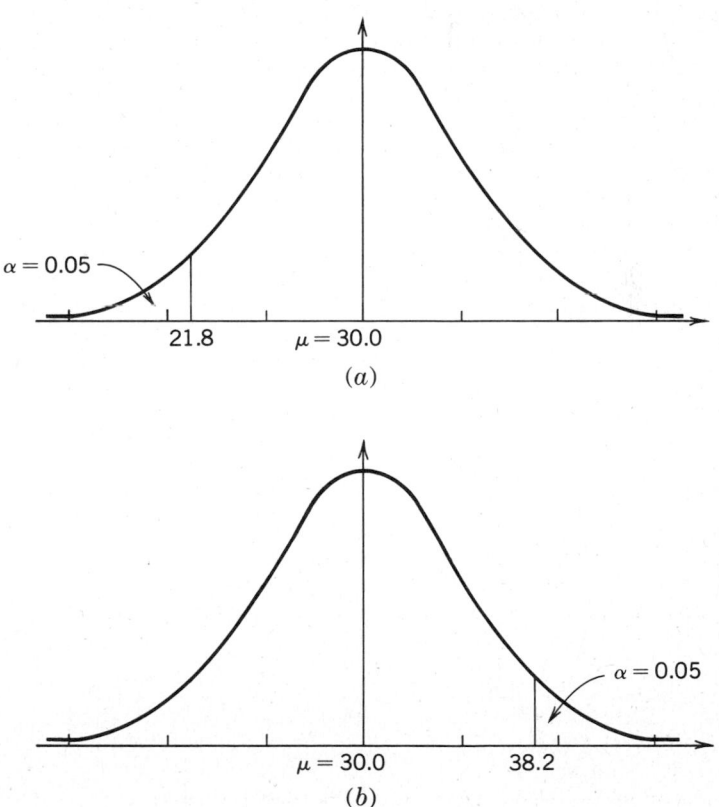

FIG. 23.22.   (*a*) Entire 5 percent error on left tail. (*b*) Entire 5 percent on right tail.

error as small as possible. The following guidelines are based on the analysis of OC curves:

Use a one-tailed test with the entire α risk on the right tail if (1) it is known that (if μ_0 is not true) the true mean is $> \mu_0$ or (2) values of the population mean $< \mu_0$ are acceptable and we are interested only in detecting a population mean $> \mu_0$.

Use a two-tailed test if (1) there is no prior knowledge on the location of the true population mean or (2) we are interested in detecting a true population mean $<$ or $>$ the μ_0 stated in the original hypothesis. (With a two-tailed test, the hypothesis is sometimes stated as the original hypothesis $H_0:\mu_0 = 30.0$ against the alternative hypothesis $H_1:\mu_0 \neq 30.0$. With a one-tailed test, $H_0:\mu_0 = 30.0$ against the alternative $H_1:\mu_1 < 30.0$ if α is placed in the left tail or $H_1:\mu_1 > 30.0$ if α is placed in the right tail.)

Every test of hypothesis has an OC curve. Duncan (1974) and Natrella (1963) are good sources of OC curves. [Some references present "power" curves, but power is simply $1 -$ (the probability of acceptance) $= 1 - \beta$.]

With this background, our discussion now proceeds to the steps for testing a hypothesis.

Testing a Hypothesis When the Sample Size is Fixed in Advance.   Ideally, desired values for the type I and type II errors are defined in advance and the required sample size determined (see later discussion on Determining the Sample Size Required for Testing a Hypothesis). If the sample size is fixed in advance because of cost or time limitations, then usually the desired type I error is defined and the following procedure is followed:

1. State the hypothesis.
2. Choose the type I error. Common values are 0.01, 0.05, or 0.10.
3. Choose the test statistic for testing the hypothesis.
4. Determine the acceptance region for the test, i.e., the range of values of the test statistic which result in a decision to accept the hypothesis.
5. Obtain the sample of observations, compute the test statistic, and compare the value to the acceptance region to make a decision to accept or reject the hypothesis.
6. Draw an engineering conclusion.

Table 23.29 summarizes some common tests of hypotheses. (These are tests commonly mentioned in the literature and used in practice. A number of them assume a normal distribution. Harter and Dubey, 1967, define tests for the mean and variance but assuming a Weibull distribution—which really covers a family of distributions.) The procedure is illustrated through the following examples. Further examples and elaboration of the procedure are provided in Dixon and Massey (1969), Johnson and Leone (1964), Duncan (1974), Dudewicz (1976), and Natrella (1963). Table 23.29 lists a few unique or additional references for certain tests. For nonparametric tests, see especially Gibbons (1985).

Example.   Tests on eight units of an experimental engine showed that they operated, respectively, for 28, 26, 31, 29, 25, 27, 28, and 27 min with 1 liter of a certain kind of fuel. A proposed specification states that the engine must operate for an average of at least 30 min. Does the engine meet the requirement? Assume a 5 percent significance level.

TABLE 23.29 Summary Table of Tests of Hypotheses

Test statistic and its distribution	Assumptions	Remarks
	Test 1. The mean of a population is equal to μ_0 ($H: \mu = \mu_0$).	
(a) $U = \dfrac{\overline{X} - \mu_0}{\sigma/\sqrt{n}}$ Normal distribution (Appendix II, Table B)	X is distribution-free but should be continuous and have only one mode.	Standard deviation of population is known.
(b) $t = \dfrac{\overline{X} - \mu_0}{s/\sqrt{n}}$ t distribution with DF $= n - 1$ (Appendix II, Table G)	X is normally distributed.	Standard deviation of population is estimated by sample s.
(c) $\tau_1 = \dfrac{\overline{X} - \mu_0}{R}$ τ_1 distribution (Appendix II, Table H)	X is normally distributed.	Dispersion of the population is estimated from sample range.
(d) $r =$ number of occurrences of less frequent sign for a two-tail test (or number of positive or negative signs for a one-tail test) Distribution of r (Appendix II, Table I)	Distribution-free but population should be continuous and symmetrical.	Data are analyzed by evaluating signs of $(X_i - \mu_0)$. (This is a "sign" test; see Gibbons, 1985, p. 106.)

TABLE 23.29 Summary Table of Tests of Hypotheses (*Continued*)

Test statistic and its distribution	Assumptions	Remarks
	Test 2. The means of two populations are equal ($H: \mu_1 = \mu_2$).	
(a) $U = \dfrac{\overline{X}_1 - \overline{X}_2}{\sqrt{\sigma_1^2/n_1 + \sigma_2^2/n_2}}$ Normal distribution (Appendix II, Table B)	X_1 and X_2 are distribution-free but should be continuous and have only one mode. If the populations are not normally distributed, sample sizes n_1 and n_2 should be large so that sampling distribution of U is approximately normal.	Standard deviations of populations are known.
(b) $t = \dfrac{\overline{X}_1 - \overline{X}_2}{\sqrt{\dfrac{1}{n_1} + \dfrac{1}{n_2}} \sqrt{\dfrac{[(n_1 - 1)s_1^2 + (n_2 - 1)s_2^2]}{n_1 + n_2 - 2}}}$ t distribution with DF $= n_1 + n_2 - 2$ (Appendix II, Table G)	$\sigma_1 = \sigma_2$. X_1 and X_2 are normally distributed.	Standard deviations of populations are estimated by sample s_1 and s_2.
(c) $\tau_d = \dfrac{\overline{X}_1 - \overline{X}_2}{0.5(R_1 + R_2)}$ Distribution of τ_d (Appendix II, Table J)	X_1 and X_2 are normally distributed.	Dispersions of populations are estimated by sample ranges.

Test	Condition	Remarks
(d) $t' = \dfrac{\bar{X}_1 - \bar{X}_2}{\sqrt{s_1^2/n_1 + s_2^2/n_2}}$ t distribution with DF = min($n_1 - 1$, $n_2 - 1$) (Appendix II, Table G)	X_1 and X_2 are normally distributed.	Standard deviations of populations are estimated by sample s_1 and s_2 (no assumption that $\sigma_1 = \sigma_2$).
(e) $t = \dfrac{\bar{d}}{s_d/\sqrt{n}}$ t distribution with DF = number of pairs − 1 (Appendix II, Table G)	Populations are normally distributed.	Data are taken in n pairs, and difference d within each pair is calculated.
(f) r = number of occurrences of less frequent sign for a two-tail test (or number of positive or negative signs for a one-tail test) Distribution of r (Appendix II, Table I)	n_1 and n_2 each ≥ 6. Populations must be continuous and symmetrical; each of the two observations in a pair has been obtained under similar conditions.	Data are analyzed by evaluating signs of ($X_1 - X_2$). (This is a "sign" test.) Distribution of r (Appendix II, Table I)

Test 3. Two characteristics on one product have specified population means (H:$\mu_X = \mu_{X0}$ and $\mu_Y = \mu_{Y0}$) (Johnson and Leone, 1964).

$$T^2 = \frac{s_Y^2}{s_X^2 s_Y^2 - s_{XY}}(X - \mu_{X0})^2 - \frac{2s_{XY}}{s_X^2 s_Y^2 - s_{XY}}(X - \mu_{X0})(Y - \mu_{Y0}) + \frac{s_X^2}{s_X^2 s_Y^2 - s_{XY}}(Y - \mu_{Y0})^2$$

where $s_{XY} = \dfrac{n\Sigma(XY) - \Sigma X\Sigma Y}{n(n-1)}$

where critical value for $T^2 = \dfrac{2(n-1)F}{n-2}$

and where the F distribution has DF$_1$ = 2; DF$_2$ = $n - 2$ (Appendix II, Table K)

Condition	Remarks
Bivariate normal distribution.	Population standard deviations are estimated by s_X and s_Y (T^2 is called Hotelling's T^2).

23.67

TABLE 23.29 Summary Table of Tests of Hypotheses (*Continued*)

Test statistic and its distribution	Assumptions	Remarks

Test 4. The standard deviation of a population is equal to σ_0 (H:$\sigma = \sigma_0$).

| $\chi^2 = \dfrac{(n-1)s^2}{\sigma_0^2}$

 Chi-square distribution with DF $= n - 1$ (Appendix II, Table L) | Population is normally distributed. | Standard deviation of population is estimated by sample s. |

Test 5. The standard deviations of two populations are equal (H:$\sigma_1^2 = \sigma_2^2$).

| (a) $F = \dfrac{s_1^2}{s_2^2}$

 F distribution with $\mathrm{DF}_1 = n_1 - 1$ and $\mathrm{DF}_2 = n_2 - 1$ (Appendix II, Table K) | Populations are normally distributed. | Standard deviations of populations are estimated by sample s_1 and s_2. |
| (b) $F' = \dfrac{R_1}{R_2}$

 Distribution of F' (Appendix II, Table M) | Distribution-free but X_1 and X_2 should be continuous. | Dispersions of populations are estimated by sample ranges. |

Test 6. The proportion of a population exhibiting a certain characteristic is p_0 (H:$p = p_0$).

| (a) $U = \dfrac{X - np_0}{\sqrt{np_0(1 - p_0)}}$

 Normal distribution (Appendix II, Table B) | $n \geq 100$. Only for large sample sizes. | Proportion of population is estimated by sample proportion. |
| (b) Determine confidence limits (Appendix II, Table N) and observe if p_0 falls within the limits | | Proportion of population is estimated by sample proportion (useful when $n < 100$). |

Test 7. The proportions in two populations are equal (H:$p_1 = p_2$).

$$U = \frac{X_1/n_1 - X_2/n_2}{\sqrt{\hat{p}(1 - \hat{p})(1/n_1 + 1/n_2)}} \quad \text{where } \hat{p} = \frac{X_1 + X_2}{n_1 + n_2}$$

Normal distribution (Appendix II, Table B)

$np > 5$ for each population. Sample sizes n_1 and n_2 must be large so that sampling distribution of U is approximately normal.

Proportions in populations are estimated by sample proportions.

Test 8. Proportion of correct decisions on a sensory evaluation is p_0 (H:$p = p_0$).

(a) $U = \dfrac{X/n - 0.50}{\sqrt{0.25/n}}$

Normal distribution (Appendix II, Table B)

$p = 0.5$, n should be $>$ 30.

Judge is asked to identify which of two specimens is the same as a control specimen originally given to him or her. (This is a "duo-trio" test.)

(b) $U = \dfrac{X/n - 0.33}{\sqrt{0.22/n}}$

Normal distribution (Appendix II, Table B)

$p = 0.33$, n should be $>$ 30.

Judge is asked to identify which of three specimens is different from the other two. (This is a "triangle" test.)

23.69

TABLE 23.29 Summary Table of Tests of Hypotheses (*Continued*)

Test statistic and its distribution	Assumptions	Remarks

Test 9. Samples are from identically distributed populations [H: $F(X_1) = F(X_2)$ where $F(X)$ = distribution function] [Johnson and Leone, 1964].

Test statistic and its distribution	Assumptions	Remarks
(*a*) For evaluation of means T' = sum of ranks in smaller sample Distribution of T' (Appendix II, Table O)	Distribution-free; if $n_1 > 8$ and $n_2 > 8$, the distribution of statistic T' can be closely approximated by normal.	Data are evaluated by ranking the combined observations from the two samples (1 for the smallest, 2 for the next smallest, etc.). Then calculate the sum of the ranks in the smaller sample. A rejected hypothesis leads to the conclusion that the means are different. (This is a "rank sum" test.)
(*b*) For evaluation of standard deviations T' = sum of ranks in smaller sample Distribution of T' (Appendix II, Table O)	Distribution-free; if $n_1 > 8$, and $n_2 > 8$, the distribution of statistic T' can be closely approximated by normal.	Data are evaluated by ranking the combined observations but ranking assigns 1 to smallest observation, 2 to largest observation, 3 to next smallest, etc. The sum of the ranks for the smaller sample is calculated. A rejected hypothesis means that the standard deviations are different. (This is a "rank sum" test.)

Test 10. The observations in a sample have been randomly drawn from a single population (Bennett and Franklin, 1954, and Dixon and Massey, 1969).

(a) u = number of runs
Distribution of runs (Appendix II, Table P)

$n_1 \geq 10$, $n_2 \geq 10$.

Data are evaluated in terms of number of sequences or "runs" above and below the median. (This is a "runs" test.)

(b) $M = \dfrac{\sum\limits_{i=1}^{n-1}(X_{i+1} - X_i)^2}{\Sigma(X_i - \overline{X})^2}$

$U = \dfrac{1 - M/2}{\sqrt{(n-2)/[(n-1)(n+1)]}}$

Normal distribution (Appendix II, Table B)

1. $n \geq 4$.
2. Normal population.

Data are evaluated in terms of differences between successive observations in a sequence $(X_{i+1} - X_i)$. (This is the "mean square successive difference, M, test.")

Test 11. An observation does belong to the same population as the other observations in a sample (Dixon and Massey, 1969; Grubbs, 1969).

Both X_1 and X_2 are to be evaluated if extreme observations in either direction are undesirable.

X is normally distributed. Population mean and standard deviation are unknown.

Data are evaluated by arranging data in order of magnitude and comparing the distance of one extreme observation from other observations with a measure of variability.

n	r
$3 \leq n \leq 7$	$r_{10} = \dfrac{X_2 - X_1}{X_n - X_1}$
$8 \leq n \leq 10$	$r_{11} = \dfrac{X_2 - X_1}{X_{n-1} - X_1}$
$11 \leq n \leq 13$	$r_{21} = \dfrac{X_3 - X_1}{X_{n-1} - X_1}$
$14 \leq n \leq 25$	$r_{22} = \dfrac{X_3 - X_1}{X_{n-2} - X_1}$

Distribution of r (Appendix II, Table Q)

23.71

TABLE 23.29 Summary Table of Tests of Hypotheses (*Continued*)

Test statistic and its distribution	Assumptions	Remarks

Test 12. A sample of data comes from a population with the specified probability function.

Test statistic and its distribution	Assumptions	Remarks
(*a*) *D* = largest deviation of actual % cumulative frequency from theoretical % cumulative frequency. Distribution of *D* (Miller and Freund, 1965, p. 409; or Gibbons, 1985, Table C)	Distribution should be continuous.	Data are evaluated by first plotting on probability paper. The largest deviation of a plotted point from a straight line is then evaluated. This test applies particularly where $n < 30$. (This is the "Kolmogorov-Smirnov test.")
(*b*) $\chi^2 = \Sigma \dfrac{(f_a - f_e)^2}{f_e}$	$n > 30$ and preferably > 100.	Data are evaluated by first constructing a frequency distribution. Theoretical frequencies (based on the distribution assumption) are calculated for each cell. The actual (f_a) and theoretical (f_e) frequencies are then compared. This test can be used for continuous and discrete distributions. If any theoretical frequency is less than 5, the cell involved should be combined with one or more adjacent cells.

Distribution	DF
Normal	Number of cells minus 3
Exponential	Number of cells minus 2
Weibull	Number of cells minus 4
Poisson	Number of cells minus 2
Binomial	Number of cells minus 2

Test statistics for all distributions follow the chi square distribution (Appendix II, Table L)

Solution: Using Test 1*b* of Table 23.29,

$$H{:}\mu_0 = 30.0$$

Test statistic:

$$\tau_1 = \frac{\overline{X} - \mu_0}{R}$$

Acceptance region:

Degrees of freedom DF $= 8 - 1 = 7$

$$t \geq -1.895$$

A mathematical derivation of "degrees of freedom" is beyond the scope of this handbook, but the underlying concept can be stated. "Degrees of freedom" is a measure of the assurance involved when a sample standard deviation is used to estimate the true standard deviation of a universe. When the true standard deviation is known, DF $= \infty$. More generally, DF equals the number of measurements used to determine the sample standard deviation minus the number of constants estimated from the data in order to compute the standard deviation. In this example, it was necessary to establish only one constant (the sample average) in order to compute the standard deviation, therefore DF $= 8 - 1$.
Analysis:

$$\overline{X} = 27.6 \qquad s = 1.86$$

$$t = \frac{27.6 - 30.0}{\dfrac{1.86}{\sqrt{8}}} = -3.68$$

Conclusion: Reject the hypothesis. There is sufficient evidence to conclude that the engine does not meet the requirement.

Example: Solve the previous example using the range instead of the standard deviation.

Solution: Using Test 1*c* of Table 23.29,

$$H{:}\mu_0 = 30.0$$

Test statistic:

$$\tau_1 = \frac{\overline{X} - \mu_0}{R}$$

Acceptance region:

$$\tau_1 \geq -0.388$$

Analysis:

$$\tau_1 = \frac{27.6 - 30.0}{6} = -0.40$$

Conclusion: Reject the hypothesis. There is sufficient evidence to conclude that the engine does not meet the requirement.

Example: Solve the previous example using the sign test.

Solution: Using Test 1*d* of Table 23.29,

$$H:\mu_0 = 30$$

Test statistic: Number of positive signs *r*.
Acceptance region:

$$r = 1 \text{ (one-tailed test)}$$

Analysis:

$\underline{X}$	$X - \mu_0$	
28	$-$	
26	$-$	
31	$+$	
29	$-$	$r = 1$
25	$-$	
27	$-$	
28	$-$	
27	$-$	

Conclusion: Reject the hypothesis. There is sufficient evidence to conclude that the engine does not meet the requirement.

Example: Five batches of rubber were made by each of two recipes and tested for tensile strength with the following results:

Recipe 1	Recipe 2
3067	3200
2730	2777
2840	2623
2913	3044
2789	2834

Test the hypothesis that average strength is the same for the two recipes. Assume a 5 percent significance level.

Solution: First, Test 5*a* of Table 23.29 tests the assumption of equal variances. The outcome of this is used to decide whether to use Test 2*b* or 2*d* to evaluate the question about average strength.

$$H:\sigma_1^2 = \sigma_2^2$$

Test statistic:

$$DF_1 = 5 - 1 = 4, \qquad DF_2 = 5 - 1 = 4$$

$$F = \frac{(s_1)^2}{(s_2)^2}$$

Acceptance region:

$$\frac{1}{9.60} \le F \le 9.60$$

Analysis:

$$s_1^2 = 16,923.7$$

$$s_2^2 = 51,713.3$$

$$F = \frac{16,923.7}{51,713.3} = 0.33$$

Conclusion: Accept the hypothesis. This is used to satisfy the assumption of equal variances in the following test of hypothesis. Now, using Test 2*b*,

$$H{:}\mu_1 = \mu_2$$

Test statistic:

$$t = \frac{\overline{X}_1 - \overline{X}_2}{\sqrt{\dfrac{1}{n_1} + \dfrac{1}{n_2}} \sqrt{\dfrac{[(n_1-1)s_1^2 + (n_2-1)s_2^2]}{n_1 + n_2 - 2}}}$$

Acceptance region:

$$DF = 5 + 5 - 2 = 8$$

$$-2.306 \le t \le +2.306$$

Analysis:

$$t = \frac{2867.8 - 2895.6}{\sqrt{\dfrac{1}{5} + \dfrac{1}{5}} \sqrt{\dfrac{(5-1)16,923.7 + (5-1)51,713.3}{5 + 5 - 2}}} = -0.24$$

Conclusion: Accept the hypothesis. There is insufficient evidence to conclude that the recipes differ in average strength.

Example: Solve the previous example using ranges instead of standard deviations.

Solution: First, Test 5*b* of Table 23.29 tests the assumption of equal variances.

$$H{:}\sigma_1^2 = \sigma_2^2$$

Test statistic:

$$F' = \frac{R_1}{R_2}$$

Acceptance region:

$$0.32 < F' < 3.2$$

Analysis:

$$R_1 = 3067 - 2730 = 337$$

$$R_2 = 3200 = 2623 = 577$$

$$F' = \frac{337}{577} = 0.58$$

Conclusion: Accept the hypothesis. This is used to satisfy the assumption of equal variances in the following test of hypothesis. Now, using Test 2c,

$$H{:}\mu_1 = \mu_2$$

Test statistic:

$$\tau_d = \frac{\overline{X}_1 - \overline{X}_2}{0.5(R_1 + R_2)}$$

Acceptance region:

$$-0.493 \le \tau_d \le +0.493$$

$$R_1 = 3,067 - 2,730 = 337$$

$$R_2 = 3,200 - 2,623 = 577$$

Analysis:

$$\tau_d = \frac{2867.8 - 2895.6}{0.5(337 + 577)} = -0.061$$

Conclusion: Accept the hypothesis. There is insufficient evidence to conclude that the recipes differ in average strength.

Drawing Conclusions from Tests of Hypotheses. The payoff for these tests of hypotheses comes from reaching useful conclusions. The meaning of "Reject the hypothesis" or "Accept the hypothesis" is shown in Table 23.30 along with some analogies to explain subtleties of the meanings.

When a hypothesis is rejected, the practical conclusion is "the parameter value specified in the hypothesis is wrong." This conclusion is made with strong conviction—roughly speaking at a confidence level of $100 (1 - \alpha)$ percent. The key question then is: Just what is a good estimate of the value of the parameter for the population? Help can be provided on this question by calculating the "confidence limits" for the parameter discussed under Statistical Estimation: Confidence Interval Estimates.

When a hypothesis is accepted, the numerical value of the parameter stated in the hypothesis has not been proved, but it has not been disproved. It is *not* correct to say that the hypothesis has been proved as correct at the $100 (1 - \alpha)$ percent confidence level. Many other hypotheses could be accepted for the given sample of observations and yet only one hypothesis can be true. Therefore, an acceptance does *not* mean a high probability of proof that a specific hypothesis is correct. (All other factors being equal, the smaller the sample size, the more likely it is that the hypothesis will be accepted. Less evidence certainly does not imply proof.) For this reason often today the wording used is "the hypothesis was not rejected at level of significance α" rather than "the hypothesis was accepted at level α."

TABLE 23.30   The Meaning of a Conclusion from Tests of Hypotheses

	If hypothesis is rejected	If hypothesis is accepted
Adequacy of evidence in the sample of observations	Sufficient to conclude that hypothesis is false	Not sufficient to conclude that hypothesis is false; hypothesis is a reasonable one but has *not* been proved to be true
Difference between sample result (e.g., $\overline{X}$) and hypothesis value (e.g., μ_0)	Unlikely that difference was due to chance (sampling) variation	Difference could easily have been due to chance (sampling) variation
Analogy of guilt or innocence in a court of law	Guilt has been established beyond a reasonable doubt	Have not established guilt beyond a reasonable doubt
Analogy of a batting average in baseball	If player got 300 base hits out of 1000 times at bat, this is sufficient to conclude that the overall batting average is about 0.300	If player got 3 hits in 10 times, this is not sufficient to conclude that the overall average is about 0.300

With an acceptance of a hypothesis, a key question then is: What conclusion, if any, can be drawn about the parameter value in the hypothesis? Two approaches are suggested:

1. Calculate confidence limits on the sample result (see the previous topic of Statistical Estimation). These confidence limits define an interval within which the true population parameter lies. If this interval is small, then an acceptance decision on the test of hypothesis means that the true population value is either equal to or close to the value stated in the hypothesis. Then, it is reasonable to act as if the parameter value specified in the hypothesis is in fact correct. If the confidence interval is relatively wide, then this is a stern warning that the value stated in the hypothesis has not been proved and that the true value of the population might be far different from that specified in the hypothesis.

2. Construct and review the operating characteristic curve for the test of hypothesis. This defines the probability that other possible values of the population parameter could have been accepted by the test. Knowing these probabilities for values relatively close to the original hypothesis can help draw further conclusions about the acceptance of the original hypothesis. For example, Figure 23.21 shows the OC curve for a hypothesis which specified that the population mean is 30.0. Note that the probability of accepting the hypothesis when the population mean μ is 30.0 is 0.95 (or $1 - \alpha$). But also note that if μ really is 35.0, then the probability of accepting $\mu = 30.0$ is still high (about 0.83). If μ really is 42.0, the probability of accepting $\mu = 30.0$ is only about 0.33.

Care must always be taken in drawing engineering conclusions from the statistical conclusions, particularly when a hypothesis is accepted. (Rutherford, 1971, discusses a procedure for drawing conclusions which requires that a choice be made between two policies for drawing conclusions, i.e., conservative and liberal.)

Determining the Sample Size Required for Testing a Hypothesis. The previous sections assumed that the sample size was fixed by nonstatistical reasons and that the type I error only was predefined for the test. The ideal procedure is to predefine the desired type I and type II errors and calculate the sample size required to cover both types of errors.

The sample size required will depend on (1) the sampling risks desired (α and β), (2) the size of the smallest true difference that is to be detected, and (3) the variation in the characteristic being measured. The sample size can be determined by using the "operating characteristic" curve for the test. Table 23.31 summarizes methods useful in determining the sample size required for two-sided tests of certain hypotheses. (Further sources of OC curves are Duncan, 1974, and Natrella, 1963.)

Suppose it were important to detect the fact that the average life of the batteries cited previously was 35.0. Specifically, be 80 percent sure of detecting this change ($\beta = 0.2$). Further, if the true average was 30.0 (as stated in the hypothesis), there should be only a 5 percent risk of rejecting the hypothesis ($\alpha = 0.05$). In using Appendix II, Chart R, d is defined as

$$d = \frac{\mu - \mu_0}{\sigma} = \frac{35.0 - 30.0}{10} = 0.5$$

Entering with $d = 0.5$ and $P_a = 0.2$ (the β risk), the curves indicate that a sample size of about 30 is required.

Duncan (1974) discusses the calculation of the sample size required to meet the type I and II errors. In practice, however, one is often not sure of desired values of these errors. Reviewing the operating characteristic curves for various sample sizes can help to arrive at a decision on the sample size required to reflect the relative importance of both risks. It is especially important to consider β as well as α, lest meaningless results be obtained. (Note that randomizing so as to reject H_0 100α percent of the time yields a test with level of significance α. That in itself, without consideration of β, is trivial.)

Relation to Confidence Intervals. Confidence limits provide a set of limits within which a population parameter lies (with specified probability). Tests of hypotheses evaluate a specific statement about a population parameter. These procedures are related, and most hypothesis tests can also be made using confidence limit calculations.

TABLE 23.31   Summary of Sample Size Graphs and Tables

Hypothesis	Graph or table
1. Mean of a population $= \mu_0$ (σ known)	Appendix II, Chart R
2. Mean of a population $= \mu_0$ (σ estimated by s)	Duncan (1974, p. 539)
3. Means of two populations are equal (σ_1 and σ_2 known)	Natrella (1963, pp. T-16, T-17)
4. Means of two populations are equal ($\sigma_1 = \sigma_2$ but estimated by s_1 and s_2)	Natrella (1963, pp. T-16, T-17)
5. Standard deviation of a population $= \sigma_0$	Duncan (1974, p. 324)
6. Standard deviations of two populations are equal	Duncan (1974, p. 572)

Example: A sample of 12 insulators has an average strength of 4.95 ft·lb (6.7149 N·M). The standard deviation of the population is known to be 0.25 ft·lb (0.34 N·M). It is desired to test the hypothesis that the population mean is 5.15 ft·lb (6.9834 N·M).

Solution using tests of hypotheses: Table 23.29 defines the test statistic $1a$ as $U = (\overline{X} - \mu_0)/(\sigma/\sqrt{n})$, and U is normally distributed. If $\alpha = 0.05$, the acceptance region is a U between ± 1.96.
   Then

$$H{:}\mu = \mu_0 = 5.15$$

$$U = \frac{4.95 - 5.15}{0.25/\sqrt{12}} = -2.75$$

As the sample index is outside the acceptance region, the hypothesis is rejected. The procedure using confidence limits is:

1. State the hypothesis concerning the value of a population parameter.
2. Obtain a sample of data and calculate confidence limits for the population parameter.
3. If the hypothesis value falls within the confidence limits, accept the hypothesis. If the hypothesis value falls outside the confidence limits, reject the hypothesis.

Solution using confidence limits:

$$H{:}\mu = \mu_0 = 5.15$$

From Table 23.21, parameter 1, the confidence limits are

$$\overline{X} \pm K_{\alpha/2} \frac{\sigma}{\sqrt{n}}$$

The 95 percent confidence limits are $4.95 \pm 1.96\,(0.25/\sqrt{12}) = 4.81$ and 5.09. As the hypothesis value falls outside the confidence limits, the hypothesis is rejected. This is the same conclusion reached by using the hypothesis testing procedure.
   Confidence limit concepts and tests of hypotheses are therefore alternative approaches to evaluating a hypothesis. [For certain hypotheses, these two approaches will result in slightly different type I errors (see Barr, 1969).] As discussed under Drawing Conclusions from Tests of Hypotheses, confidence limits are a valuable supplement to the test of hypothesis procedure. For example, in the above example, not only do confidence limits tell us that μ is not 5.15, they also tell us that μ is between 4.81 and 5.09.

Standard Cases. Some of the most important practical cases have been covered in Table 23.29, namely:

Binomial proportion	Tests 6, 8
Two binomial proportions	Test 7
Normal mean	Test 1
Two means	Test 2
Bivariate normal mean	Test 3
One normal standard deviation	Test 4

Two standard deviations	Test 5
Two distributions are equal	Test 9
Random order of observations	Test 10
Test for outliers	Test 11

Many of these problems can also be solved using sequential tests. There, the sample size is not set in advance, but based on the data we decide how many observations are needed. For example, if one decided to inspect a fixed number of items such as 100 items, and reject the lot if 15 or more defectives were found, clearly one could stop sampling as soon as the fifteenth defective were found. Similar ideas allow savings in numbers of observations in most of the standard cases listed above, and are especially important when sampling is costly or time-consuming. For details, see Govindarajulu (1981).

Paired versus Unpaired Data. In Test 2*e* of Table 23.29, a test is given which is appropriate when data are taken in pairs and the difference within each pair is used as the basic data. This procedure is often used in order to "wash out" the effects of variables which are believed to have effects, but whose effects we do not wish to study.

For example, suppose that there is an effect of the operator of the machine, and we wish to compare two types of operation on that machine—but do not wish to evaluate the size of the operator effect. Then by letting each operator perform each operation and taking the difference, we wash out the effect of the operator. (Whereas, if one operator performed all of one procedure, and another operator performed all of the other procedure, differences observed might be due not to the procedures, but to the operators.)

As another example, in testing of mailing lists to evaluate competing advertising copy, for example, often an "A/B split" is used. That is, one type of copy goes to names 1, 3, 5, 7, . . . on the list, while the other type goes to names 2, 4, 6, ... Since (on zip-code-ordered lists) adjacent listings may be expected to be more similar than entries far apart, this is an appropriate pairing.

This technique of pairing is *not* used when there is no advance pairing of the data. For example, it is an error to pair items by their sequence in a data listing (where often they may be sorted by some other characteristic).

Statistical Significance versus Practical Significance. Suppose we are using Test 1*a* of Table 23.29 to test the hypothesis that the mean is 30, and wish a two-tailed test with level of significance 0.05. Then we will reject H if U is outside the interval $(-1.96, 1.96)$. If we find $U = 3.15$, one way of reporting the result of the test is to state that H was rejected at level 0.05.

Another way of reporting is to find for which level of significance the acceptance interval would be $(-3.15, 3.15)$. From Table B in Appendix II we see that level is (2) (0.00082) = 0 00164. This is called the "significance probability" of the test we have conducted. It is the smallest level of significance at which we would reject H for the data we observed.

One advantage of the significance probability is that if we use it, then we can report the significance probability as 0.00164 without choosing a level of significance. Anyone reading our report can use the level of significance he or she believes is appropriate: If theirs is less than 0.00164 they do not reject, while if theirs is equal to or greater than 0.00164 they do reject the hypothesis.

One disadvantage of the significance probability is that it can be very small (indicating, one would think, a "very significant" result) even when the true mean is close to 30. For example, $U = 3.15$ when $\overline{X} = 33.15$ and $\sigma/\sqrt{n} = 1.00$; $U = 3.15$ also when $\overline{X} = 30.0315$ and $\sigma/\sqrt{n} = 0.01$. In each case the significance probability is 0.00164 (i.e., 0.164 percent). In the first case, the confidence interval on the mean at 95 percent confidence runs over (31.19,35.11), while in the second the interval runs over (30.0119,30.0511). In terms of *practical significance,* the latter is much more likely to be a trivial difference to the practitioner than is the former. However, there is no way to tell these two situations apart by using the significance probability. For this reason, it is recommended that this concept not be used, but that instead confidence intervals be computed and presented in all cases.

RELIABILITY

The term "reliability" is used in a general sense to express a degree of confidence that a part or system will successfully function in a certain environment during a specified time period. It is also used specifically to mean the probability of failure-free operation for a time period at least a specified t_0, in which case it is denoted $R(t_0)$.

Basic Concepts. The most basic concepts of reliability are those of reliability $R(t_0)$ as a function of time already defined, failure rate, time between failures (TBF), and average (or mean) time between failures (MTBF), which are discussed below.

Failure Rate. Complex products often follow a familiar pattern of failure. Consider the data in Table 23.32. Assume that one unit was started on test and the time when it failed was recorded. The unit was repaired, again placed on test, and the time of the next failure recorded. The "failure rate" for the unit can be calculated for equal time intervals as the number of failures per unit time. (Some applications require the use of a "hazard rate" instead of "failure rate." See Section 25, under Reliability Sampling.) When the failure rate is plotted against a continuous time scale, the resulting chart (Figure 23.23), known as the "bathtub curve," exhibits three distinct periods or zones. These zones differ from each other in frequency of failure and in the failure causation pattern as follows:

   1. *The infant mortality period:* This is characterized by high failure rates which show up early in usage. Commonly these failures are the result of blunders in design, manufacture, or usage or of misapplication and other identifiable causes. Sometimes it is possible to "debug" the product by simulated use test or by overstressing (in electronics this is known as "burn-in"). The weak units still fail, but the failure takes place in the test rig rather than in service.

   2. *The constant failure rate period:* Here the failures result from the limitations inherent in the design plus accidents caused by usage or poor maintenance. The latter can be held down by good control on operating and maintenance procedures. However, a reduction in the basic failure rate requires a basic redesign.

   3. *The wear-out period:* These are failures due to old age; e.g., the metal becomes embrittled or the insulation dries out. A reduction in failure rates requires preventive replacement of these dying components before they result in catastrophic failure.

TABLE 23.32 Failure History for a Unit of Electronic Ground Support Equipment

Time of failure, infant mortality period		Time of failure, constant failure rate period		Time of failure, wear-out period	
1	7.2	28.1	60.2	100.8	125.8
1.2	7.9	28.2	63.7	102.6	126.6
1.3	8.3	29.0	64.6	103.2	127.7
2.0	8.7	29.9	65.3	104.0	128.4
2.4	9.2	30.6	66.2	104.3	129.2
2.9	9.8	32.4	70.1	105.0	
3.0	10.2	33.0	71.0	105.8	
3.1	10.4	35.3	75.1	106.5	
3.3	11.9	36.1	75.6	110.7	
3.5	13.8	40.1	78.4	112.6	
3.8	14.4	42.8	79.2	113.5	
4.3	15.6	43.7	84.1	114.8	
4.6	16.2	44.5	86.0	115.1	
4.7	17.0	50.4	87.9	117.4	
4.8	17.5	51.2	88.4	118.3	
5.2	19.2	52.0	89.9	119.7	
5.4		53.3	90.8	120.6	
5.9		54.2	91.1	121.0	
6.4		55.6	91.5	122.9	
6.8		56.4	92.1	123.3	
6.9		58.3	97.9	124.5	

The top portion of Figure 23.23 shows the corresponding Weibull plot when a $\gamma = 2.6$ was applied to the original data. The values of the shape parameter β were approximately 0.5, 1.0, and 6.0, respectively. A shape parameter of less than 1.0 indicates a decreasing failure rate, a value of 1.0 a constant failure rate, and a value greater than 1.0 an increasing failure rate (see Figure 23.23).

The Distribution of "Time Between Failures."   Users are concerned with the length of time that a product will run without failure. For repairable products, this means that the "time between failures," or TBF, is a critical characteristic. The corresponding characteristic for nonrepairable products is usually called the "time to failure." The variation in time between failures can be studied statistically (Figure 23.24).

When the failure rate is constant, the distribution of time between failures is distributed exponentially. Consider the 42 failure times in the constant failure rate portion of Table 23.32. The time between failures for successive failures can be tallied, and the 41 resulting TBFs can then be formed into the frequncy distribution shown in Figure 23.24. The distribution is roughly exponential in shape, indicating that when the failure rate is constant the distribution of time between failures (not mean time between failures) is exponential. This is the basis of the exponential formula for reliability.

The Exponential Formula for Reliability.   The distribution of time between failures indicates the chance of failure-free operation for the specified time period. The chance of obtaining failure-free operation for a specified time period or longer

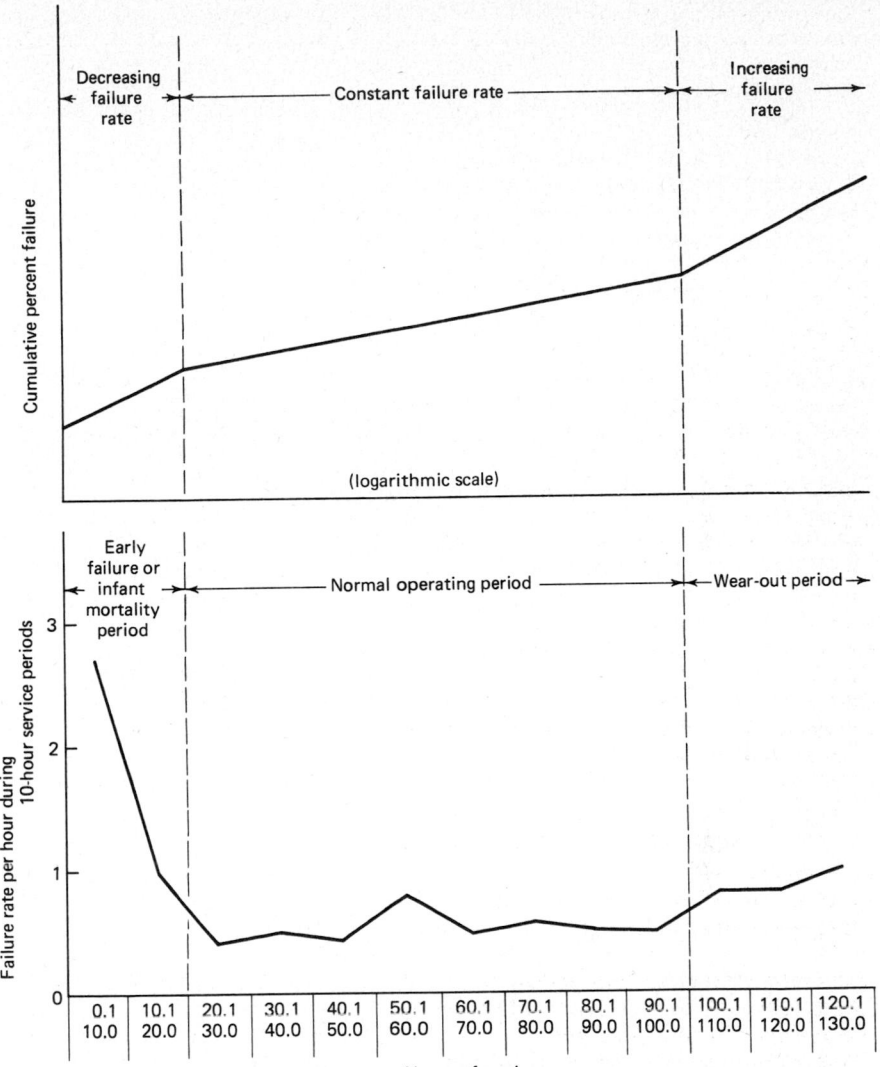

FIG. 23.23 Failure rate versus time.

can be shown by changing the TBF distribution to a distribution showing the number of intervals equal to or greater than a specified time length (Figure 23.24). If the frequencies are expressed as relative frequencies, they become estimates of the probability of survival. When the failure rate is constant, the probability of survival (or reliability) is

$$P_s = R = e^{-t/\mu} = e^{-t\lambda}$$

where $P_s = R =$ probability of failure-free operation for a time period equal to
　　　　　 or greater than t
　　　 $e = 2.718$
　　　 $t =$ a specified period of failure-free operation

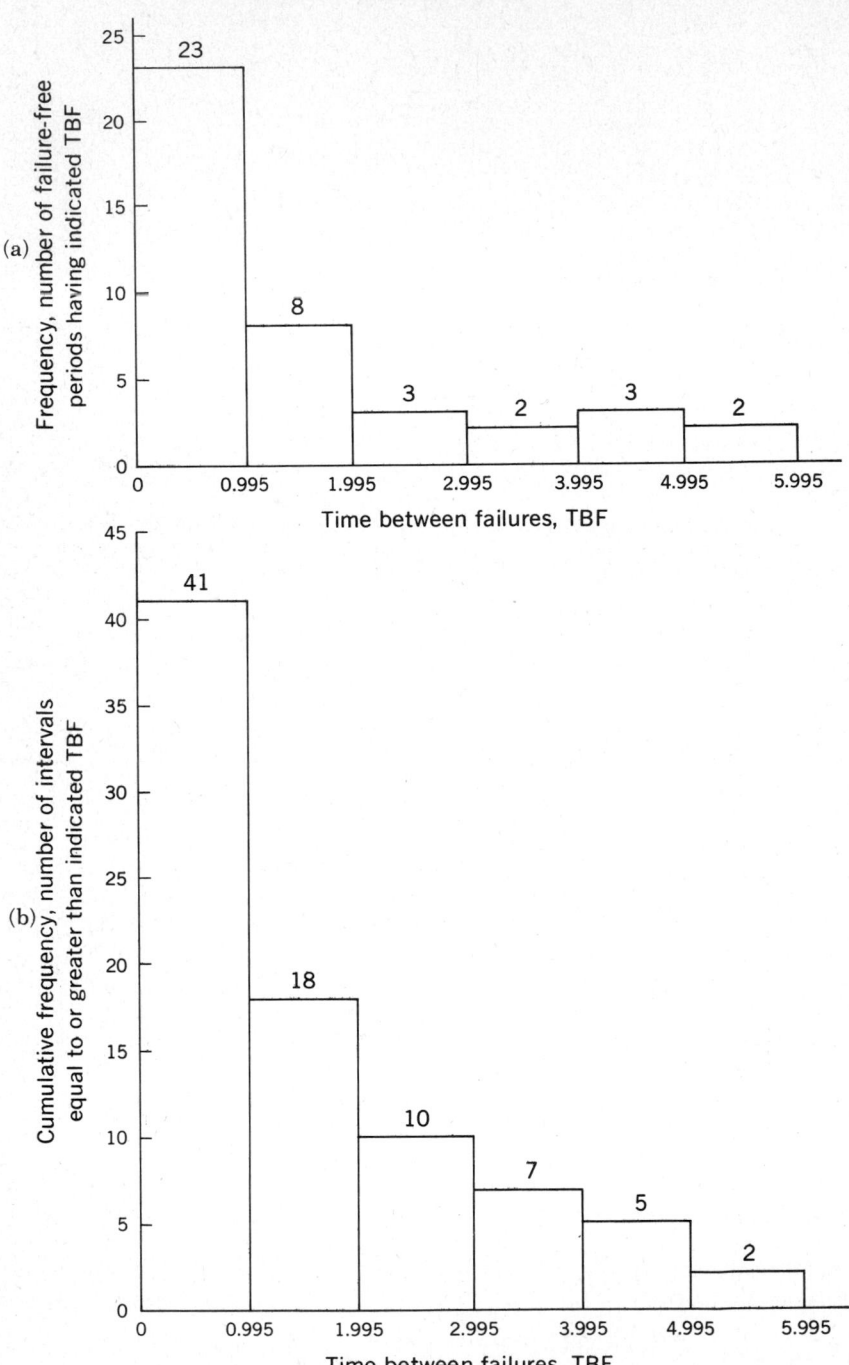

FIG. 23.24 (*a*) Histogram of time between failures. (*b*) Cumulative histogram of time between failures.

μ = mean time between failures, or MTBF (the mean of the TBF distribution)

λ = failure rate (the reciprocal of μ)

Note that this formula is simply the exponential probability distribution rewritten in terms of reliability.

Example: Previous experience shows that the mean time between failures of a radar set is 240 h. Assuming a constant failure rate, what is the chance of running the set for 24 h without failure?

$$R = e^{-t/\mu}$$

$$R = e^{-24/240} = 0.90$$

There is a 90 percent chance of obtaining 24 h or more of failure-free operation.

The assumption of a constant failure rate is rightly questioned. However, experience suggests that the assumption is often a fair one to make. (More fundamental than arguing the validity of the assumption is the need to take design actions to yield a constant failure rate. For example, the careful determination of burn-in periods and replacement periods for both parts and systems is good design practice that will help achieve a constant failure rate.)

The Meaning of "Mean Time between Failures." Confusion surrounds the meaning of "mean time between failures" (MTBF). Further explanation is warranted.

1. The MTBF is the mean (or average) time between successive failures of a product. This definition assumes that the product in question can be repaired and placed back in operation after each failure. These conditions are not always met. Furthermore, the MTBF is not always the most appropriate index for a product. For example, some other index such as percent uptime (uptime is equivalent to percent operative, as contrasted with downtime) is more pertinent when a product operates continuously as compared with the product needed for specific mission times (e.g., petroleum refinery equipment versus a guidance system for a missile).

2. If the failure rate is constant, the probability that a product will operate without failure for a time equal to or greater than its MTBF is only 37 percent. (R is equal to 0.37 when t is equal to the MTBF.) This is contrary to the intuitive feeling that there is a 50–50 chance of exceeding an MTBF.

3. MTBF is not the same as "operating life," "service life," or other indices which generally connote overhaul or replacement time. In Figure 23.23, "life" is the *length* of the constant failure rate period while MTBF is the reciprocal of the failure rate (*height* of the bathtub curve).

4. An increase in an MTBF does not result in a proportional increase in reliability (the probability of survival). If $t = 1$ h, the following table shows the mean time between failures required in order to obtain various reliabilities:

MTBF, h	R, %
5	0.82
10	0.90
20	0.95
100	0.99

A fivefold increase in MTBF from 20 to 100 h is necessary to increase the reliability by 4 percentage points as compared with a doubling of the MTBF from 5 to 10 h to get 8 percentage points increase in reliability. This is important because MTBF is often used as the criterion for making important decisions affecting reliability, whereas the probability of survival for a specified time t may be the more important index to the user.

Alternative methods (also see Section 13, Table 13.5) of denoting reliability are sometimes used to avoid the serious consequences of misinterpreting the meaning of MTBF. One alternative is the reciprocal of MTBF, i.e., the *failure rate*. This eliminates the confusion with "service life" or "operating life." Another recognizes that MTBF is really just a substitute for the reliability percent R and its associated time t. Reliability is then stated as (1) the percent reliability required and (2) the mission time, instead of condensing these two numbers into one number (MTBF).

Predicting Reliability Based on the Exponential Distributiion.   Section 13, under Reliability Analysis and Prediction, presents a procedure for reliability prediction based on the exponential distribution. The extensive use of the exponential reliability function warrants further discussion.

The mechanism underlying the exponential is that of random or chance failures which are independent of accumulated life and consequently are individually unpredictable. The justification of this type of "failure law" involves several conditions.

1. Many forces can act upon the product and produce failure. For example, various deterioration mechanisms, part failure rates, and environmental conditions often result in stress-strength combinations that produce failures randomly in time.

2. A constant failure rate often occurs for the total product regardless of the failure pattern of individual parts. This is a result of the mixing of ages of parts by replacement or repair of parts. (This concept is called the "approach to a stable state.")

3. Many parts have multiple failure modes. For example, a resistor may open or a lead may break off; a transistor may go outside tolerance limits or it may abort. For some parts, the failure modes representing random catastrophic failures are likely to occur before wear-out characteristics become evident. For other parts, catastrophic failures are not likely. However, tolerance failures—which are usually associated with wear-out—can be induced both by time and by environmental conditions. The question then is whether a tolerance failure is more likely to result from wear-out or from environmental peaks. The latter case often leads to a constant failure rate.

Because of the simplicity of the exponential function, it has been used extensively in reliability work. However, the assumption is valid only if supported [for testing the assumption with data, see Test 12*b* (Table 23.29) under the previous discussion of Tests of Hypotheses] by the failure data collected. For noncomplex products when the principal failure mechanism is wear-out, the exponential assumption is not valid.

Predicting Reliability during Design Based on the Weibull Distribution.
Prediction of overall reliability based on the simple addition of component failure rates is valid only if the failure rate is constant. When this assumption cannot be made, an alternative approach, based on the Weibull distribution, can be used.

1. Graphically or analytically use the Weibull distribution to predict the reliability R for the time period specified. Do this for each component.
2. Combine the component reliabilities using the product rule and/or redundancy formulas to obtain the prediction of system reliability.

Rich, Smith, and Korte (1967) give an example of predicting the reliability of a tractor pump for a 500-h period and a 1500-h period (see Table 23.33). The first analysis was on a proposed design. Note how the prediction highlights the "vital few" parts such as the oil seal and control valve. The analysis after some design changes on these parts shows a significant increase in reliability and decrease in failure cost per tractor. (Table 23.33 lists data for important items only and then summarizes reliability and cost for the complete assembly of 68 parts.)

Reliability as a Function of Applied Stress and Strength. In some situations, an individual component is satisfactory if its strength is greater than the stress applied to it. For the same design, strength will vary from component to component. The applied stress will also vary. The variation in each of the two parameters is depicted in Figure 23.25. Consider the difference between strength and applied stress in a given instance. The probability of successful performance ("reliability") is the probability that this difference is greater than zero. Figure 23.26 shows a distribution of the difference between strength and stress. Assuming independence of strength and stress:

$$\mu_{difference} = \mu_{strength} - \mu_{stress}$$

$$\sigma_{difference} = \sqrt{\sigma_{strength}^2 + \sigma_{stress}^2}$$

If normality is assumed, the probability of a difference greater than 0 can be estimated by finding the area under the curve.

TABLE 23.33 Reliability Prediction for a 1.38-in^3/revolution Variable Displacement Pump

Part name (only parts with significant percent failure are listed)	First analysis			Analysis after changes		
	% failure at		$/tractor at 500 h	% failure at		$/tractor at 500 h
	500 h	1500 h		500 h	1500 h	
Pump drive coupling special screws	0.6	3.0	0.21	0.2	1.0	0.07
Pump drive coupling	0.07	0.8	0.01	0.07	0.8	0.01
Hydraulic pump shaft	0.02	0.06	0.01	0.02	0.06	0.01
Pump shaft oil seal	3.7	20.0	0.41	1.0	5.0	0.10
Pump shaft bushing	0.75	2.25	0.30	0.25	0.75	0.10
O-ring packings (11) (evaluated separately)	0.63	2.10	0.08	0.63	2.10	0.08
Stroke control valve	13.0	38.0	0.77	0.05	0.15	0.02
Assembly reliability (68 parts):						
At 500 h		80%			97.3%	
At 1500 h		49%			92.0%	
Cost at 500 h			2.18			0.77

Example: Suppose the following estimates apply to a part:

	Strength, lb/in^2	Applied stress, lb/in^2
Average	60,000	46,000
Standard deviation	3,000	5,500

Then average difference = 60,000 − 46,000 = 14,000, and

$$\sigma_{\text{difference}} = \sqrt{(3000)^2 + (5500)^2} = 6260$$

$$K = \frac{0 - 14{,}000}{6260} = -2.24$$

From Table B in Appendix II, the area greater than zero is 0.9875; i.e., the reliability is 98.75 percent.

This discussion has been simplified in order to stress a basic concept. The key point is that *variation* in addition to average value must be considered in design. Designers have always recognized the existence of variation by using a "safety factor" in design. However, safety factor is often defined as the ratio of average strength to the worst stress expected. (Kececioglu and Cormier, 1964, discuss various definitions.)

Lusser (1958) proposed the use of safety margins in specifications for critical products such as guided missiles (Figure 23.27). He suggested safety margins for strength and stress. Specifically, the reliability boundary (maximum stress) was to be defined as 6 standard deviations (of stress) above the average stress. The aver-

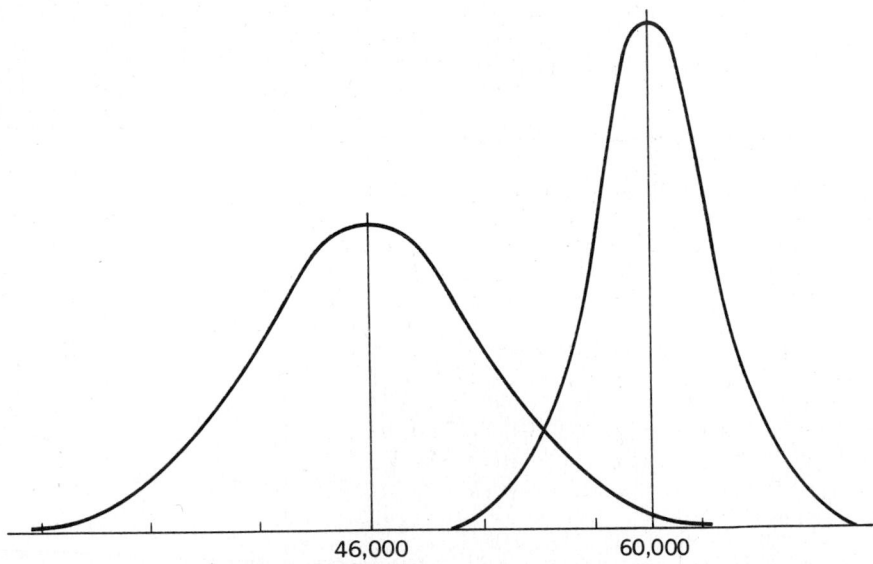

FIG. 23.25 Stress and strength distributions.

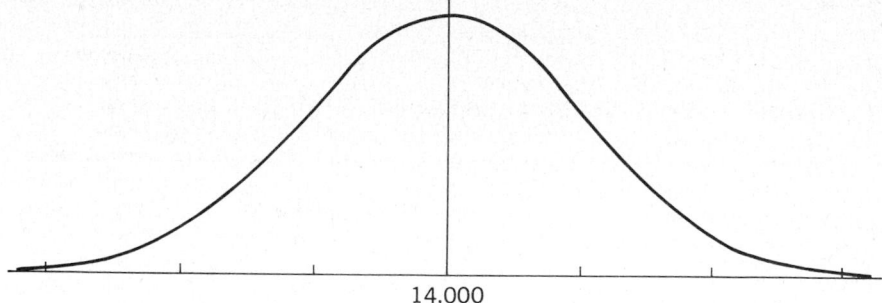

FIG. 23.26 Distribution of (strength-stress).

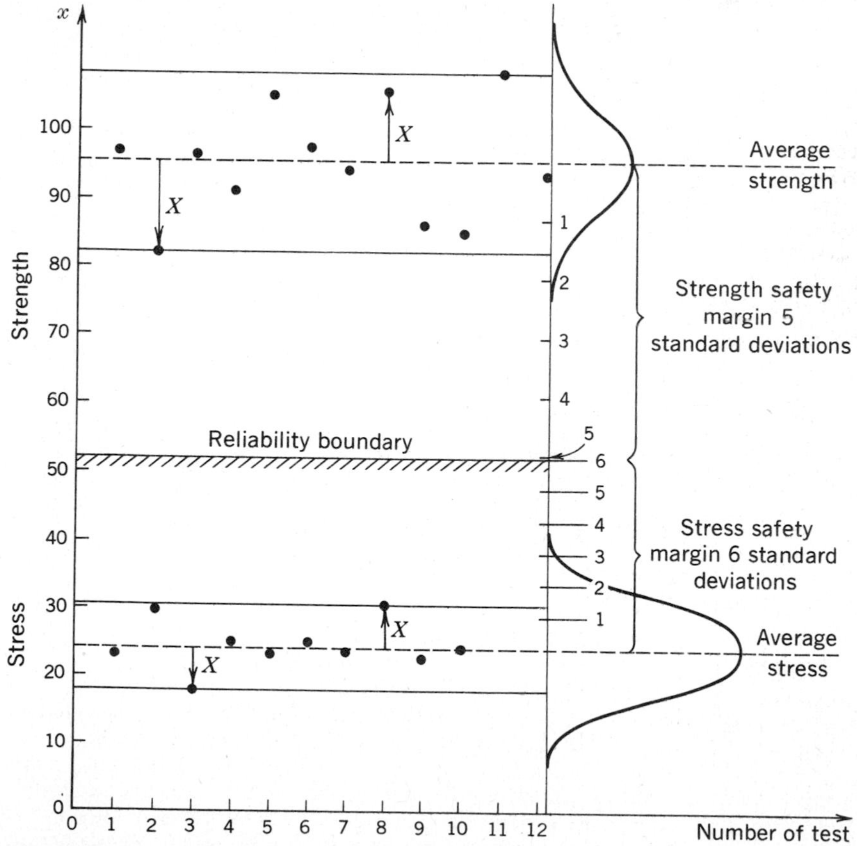

FIG. 23.27 Illustrating how scatterbands of stresses and strengths shall be separated by a reliability boundary.

age strength would have to be at least 5 standard deviations (of strength) above the reliability boundary. These minimum values of safety margin were suggested for products requiring extremely high reliability.

The Relationship between Part and System Reliability. It is often assumed that system reliability (i.e., probability of survival P_s) is the product of the individual reliabilities of the n parts within the system: $P_s = P_1 P_2 \cdots P_n$. This is known as the "product rule." The formula assumes (1) that the failures of any part will cause failure of the system and (2) that the reliabilities of the parts are independent of each other, i.e., that the reliability of one part is not dependent on the reliability of another part. (Evans, 1966, gives a good discussion of this and other assumptions in reliability calculations.) A set of lights in series on a Christmas tree demonstrates the product rule. These assumptions are usually not 100 percent correct. However, the formula is a convenient approximation that should be refined as information becomes available on the interrelationships of parts and their relationship to the system. [The redundancy formula (see below under Redundancy) is an example of this.] The following illustrates the product rule:

Example: The following reliability requirements have been set on the subsystems of a communications system:

Subsystem	Reliability (for a 4-h period), %
Receiver	0.970
Control system	0.989
Power supply	0.995
Antenna	0.996

What is the expected reliability of the overall system if the above requirements are met?

$$P_s = (0.970)(0.989)(0.995)(0.996) = 0.951$$

The chance that the overall system will perform its function without failure for a 4-h period is 95 percent.

If it can be assumed that each part follows the exponential distribution, then

$$P_s = e^{-t_1 \lambda_1} e^{-t_2 \lambda_2} \cdots e^{-t_n \lambda_n}$$

Further, if t is the same for each part,

$$P_s = e^{-t \Sigma \lambda}$$

Thus, when the failure rate is constant (and therefore the exponential distribution applies), a "reliability prediction" of a system can be made based on the addition of the part failure rates. This is illustrated in Section 13 under Reliability.

Redundancy. A number of system designs have been devised which attempt to increase system reliability by introducing redundancy. The simplest such system is the *parallel system,* which operates if at least one of its components operates.

If each component has reliability $R(t_0)$, then the parallel system consisting of m components has reliability equal to (see Dudewicz, 1976, p. 39):

$$1 - [1 - R(t_0)]^m$$

which is greater than $R(t_0)$.

Many other designs have been introduced, with a view both to reliability and cost, such as the k-out-of-n systems. For details on these and other aspects of reliability, see Zacks (1983), Ireson (1982), and Lloyd and Lipow (1982).

ADDITIONAL STATISTICAL TOOLS

Today, a large number of statistical tools are used in quality control. The statistical tool kit (see Table 23.1) stresses the statistical base of collection, analysis, and interpretation of data. "Transformations," discussed below, are a method often used to assure that data will meet the assumptions of statistical procedures, while "Monte Carlo sampling methods" and "clustering and discrimination procedures" are powerful methods whose use in quality control is now growing. They allow analysis with minimal assumptions, and analysis of multivariate characteristics, respectively.

Transformations of Data.   Most of the statistical methodology presented in this section assumes that the quality characteristic follows a known probability distribution. The analysis and conclusions that result are, of course, valid only to the extent that the distribution assumption is correct. Under Tests of Hypotheses, a "goodness of fit" test was presented for quantitatively evaluating a set of data to judge the validity of a distributional asumption. Moderate deviations of a sample of observations from a theoretical population assumption are to be expected because of sampling variation. The goodness-of-fit test determines whether the deviation of the sample from a theoretical assumption is likely to have been due to sampling variation. If it turns out as unlikely, then it is concluded that the assumption is wrong.

Sometimes a set of data does not fit one of the standard distributions such as the normal distribution. One approach uses "distribution-free" statistical methods for further analysis. Some of these were listed under Tests of Hypotheses, and Natrella (1963) and Gibbons (1985) present further material. However, these methods often require larger sample sizes than conventional methods for equivalent statistical risks. Some other approaches to analysis are:

1. Examine the data to see if there is a nonstatistical explanation for the unusual distributional pattern. For example, the output of each of several supposedly identical machines may be normally distributed. If the machines have different means or standard deviations, then the combined output probably has an unusual distribution pattern such as the mixture distribution already discussed in this section. In this case, separate analyses could be made for each machine.

2. Analyze the data in terms of averages instead of individual values. As stated under the Two Types of Sampling Error, sample averages closely follow a normal probability distribution even if the population of individual values from which the sample averages came is not normally distributed. If it is sufficient to draw a final conclusion on a characteristic in terms of the average value, the normal distribution assumption can be applied. However, the conclusions apply only to the average value and not to the individual values in the population. (Predicting the percent of a population falling outside engineering limits illustrates the situation where analysis in terms of the average would not be sufficient because engineering limits refer to individual values rather than averages.)

3. Use the Weibull probability distribution. The Weibull distribution is really a group of many continuous distributions with each distribution uniquely defined by numerical values of the parameters of the Weibull probability function (e.g., a beta value of 1.0 indicates an exponential distribution). If a set of data yields an approximate straight-line plot on Weibull paper, the straight line then directly provides estimates of the probabilities for the population. Whether the exact form of the probability distribution is normal, or exponential, or another distribution, becomes somewhat secondary because the straight-line plot provides the needed probability estimates.

4. Make a transformation of the original characteristic to a new characteristic that is normally distributed. Figure 23.28 summarizes several of these mathematical transformations. These transformations are useful for (a) achieving normality of measured results, (b) satisfying the assumption of equal population variances required in certain tests, and (c) satisfying the assumption of additivity of effects required in certain tests. Natrella (1963) discusses transformations for all these uses.

The most common transformations for achieving normality are

$$\xi_1(X_1) = \sqrt{X_1 - a}$$

$$\xi_2(X_1) = X_1^{1/3}$$

$$\xi_3(X_1) = \log_{10}(X_1)$$

$$\xi_4(X_1) = \arcsin \sqrt{X_1}$$

$$\xi_5(X_1) = \sinh^{-1} \sqrt{X_1}$$

If one of these, say $\xi(X_1)$, is normally distributed, the mean and variance of $Y_i = \xi(X_i)$ may be estimated by

$$\overline{Y} = \sum_{j=1}^{n} \frac{Y_j}{n} \qquad s_Y^2 = \sum_{j=1}^{n} \frac{(Y_j - \overline{Y})^2}{(n-1)}$$

However, interest in many cases is not in the expected value $E\xi(X_1)$, and the variance, $\text{Var} \, \xi(X_1)$, but in the original problem units, EX_1 and $\text{Var}(X_1)$. Simply using the inverse transformation—for example to estimate EX_1 by $\overline{Y}^2 + a$ in the case of ξ_1—results in a biased estimate. Good estimators for the mean of the X's are given in Table 23.34. Good estimators of the variance of the X's allows us to find approximate 95 percent confidence intervals for the mean of the X's; such estimates are given in Table 23.35. For example, when using $\sqrt{X_1 - a}$, a 95 percent confidence interval for the mean of the X's is

$$\overline{Y}^2 + a + \left(1 - \frac{1}{n}\right) s_Y^2 \pm 2\sqrt{\lambda}$$

where

$$\lambda = \frac{4}{n} s_Y^2 \overline{Y}^2 + s_Y^4 \left\{ \left(1 - \frac{1}{n}\right)^2 - \frac{n-1}{n+1} \left[1 - 2\left(1 - \frac{1}{n}\right)^2 + 3\left(1 - \frac{1}{n}\right)^4\right] \right\}$$

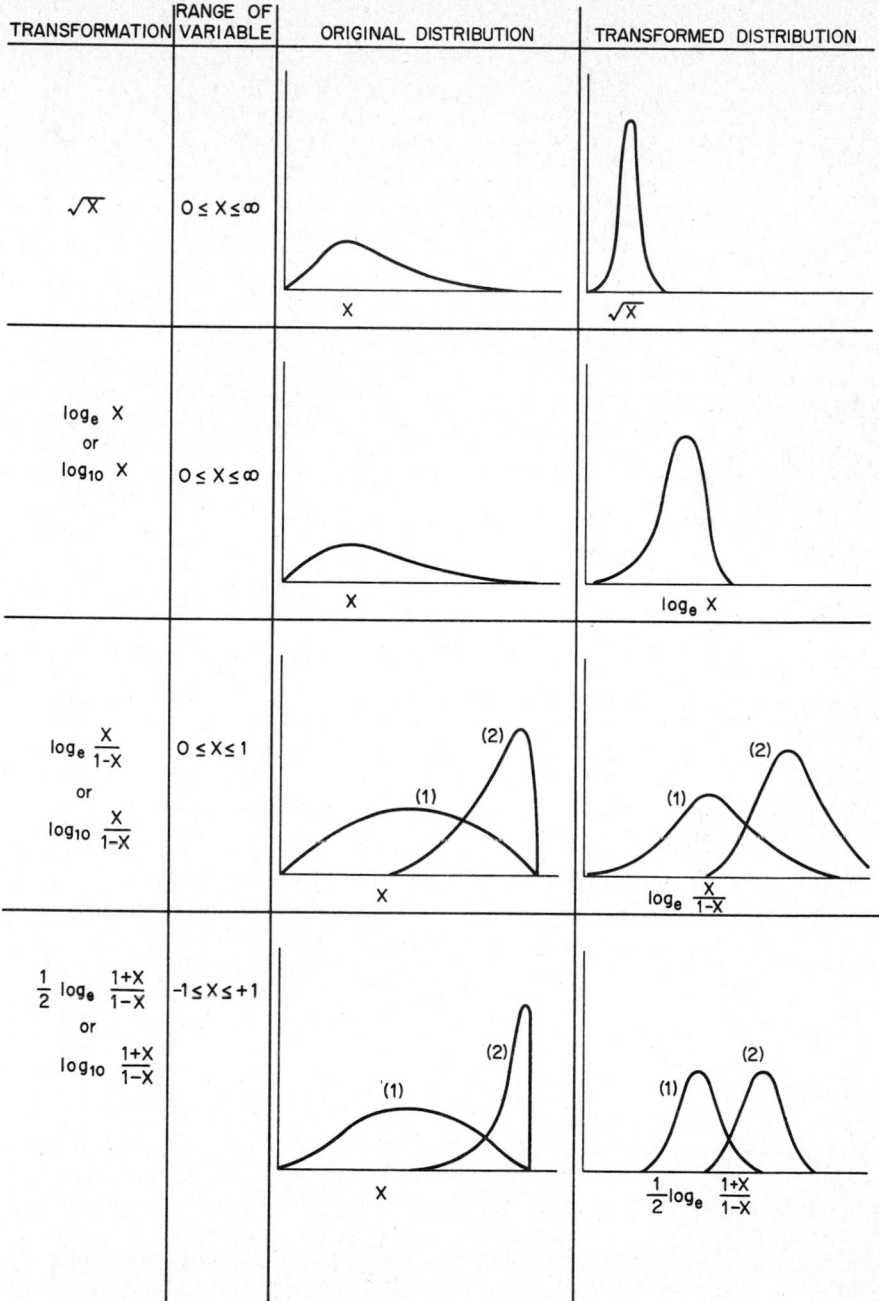

TRANSFORMATION	RANGE OF VARIABLE	ORIGINAL DISTRIBUTION	TRANSFORMED DISTRIBUTION
$\sqrt{X}$	$0 \leq X \leq \infty$	X	$\sqrt{X}$
$\log_e X$ or $\log_{10} X$	$0 \leq X \leq \infty$	X	$\log_e X$
$\log_e \frac{X}{1-X}$ or $\log_{10} \frac{X}{1-X}$	$0 \leq X \leq 1$	X	$\log_e \frac{X}{1-X}$
$\frac{1}{2} \log_e \frac{1+X}{1-X}$ or $\log_{10} \frac{1+X}{1-X}$	$-1 \leq X \leq +1$	X	$\frac{1}{2}\log_e \frac{1+X}{1-X}$

FIG. 23.28 Summary of some transformations.

TABLE 23.34 Transformations and Estimators of $E(X_1)$†

$\xi(X_1)$	Estimator of $E(X_1)$
$\sqrt{X_1 - a}$	$\overline{Y}^2 + a + \left(1 - \dfrac{1}{n}\right) s_Y^2$

†For estimators in the cases $\log_{10}(X_1)$, arcsin $\sqrt{X_1}$, and $\sinh^{-1}\sqrt{X_1}$, see Dudewicz (1983).

TABLE 23.35 Estimators of Variances of Estimators of $E(X_1)$†

$\xi(X_1)$	Estimator of variance of estimator of $E(X_1)$
$\sqrt{X_1 - a}$	$\dfrac{4}{n}s_Y^2\,\overline{Y}^2 + s_Y^4\left\{\left(1 - \dfrac{1}{n}\right)^2 - \dfrac{n-1}{n+1}\left[1 - 2\left(1 - \dfrac{1}{n}\right)^2 + 3\left(1 - \dfrac{1}{n}\right)^4\right]\right\}$

†For estimators in the cases $\log_{10}(X_1)$, arcsin $\sqrt{X_1}$, and $\sinh^{-1}\sqrt{X_1}$, see Dudewicz (1983).

Full references are given by Dudewicz (1983), which also covers procedures for dealing with cases where variances are unequal and data is normal. It is standard to recommend that equality of variability should be investigated, even when data is normal; for example, see Section 26 under General Remarks on Analysis of Data. Procedures for dealing with variance inequality when it is found had not been available until recent years. Recently, Dudewicz and Dalal (1983) showed how to compare several new processes with a standard process in this setting; their paper also includes consideration of nonnormality and a data set (their Section 5) with numerical details and normal probability plots for an example arising with solvents.

Monte Carlo Sampling Methods.   Monte Carlo sampling methods are finding increasing and important uses in quality control. For example, Gutt and Gruska (1977) use it to predict quality problems which may result from variation in manufacturing and assembly operations. This method is based on fitting distributions to data (such as the GLD distribution discussed above under Continuous Probability Distributions), and sampling from it using random numbers (also discussed previously), using the resulting data to assess the performance of the simulated system (which allows optimization of the system before it is built or modified). Other uses occur in optimization (Golden, Assad, and Zanakis, 1984).

Clustering and Discrimination.   *Clustering and discrimination* methods are a part of the area of statistics called *multivariate analysis* (Siotani, Hayakawa, and Fujikoshi, 1985). A typical type of problem where these methods are used in quality control is when several different kinds of malfunctions within a production facility cause product to fall outside of engineering limits. It is often difficult to determine the causes of the malfunction in any one case. Then, clustering a number of cases may reveal causal links via common factors over the clusters. (That is, this method allows one to ask, "What do the cases with malfunctions of each type have in common?")

As an example of the power of the "discrimination" method, Fisher (1936)

TABLE 23.36 Two Length (L_1, L_2) and Two Width (W_1, W_2) Measurements on 150 Individuals (50 from Each of Types T = 1, 2, 3), in 0.01-cm. Units*

L_1	W_1	L_2	W_2	T
50	33	14	02	1
64	28	56	22	3
65	28	46	15	2
67	31	56	24	3
63	28	51	15	3
46	34	14	03	1
69	31	51	23	3
62	22	45	15	2
59	32	48	18	2
46	36	10	02	1
61	30	46	14	2
60	27	51	16	2
65	30	52	20	3
56	25	39	11	2
65	30	55	18	3
⋮	⋮	⋮	⋮	⋮

*To save space, only the first 15 individuals' measurements are shown.

gave the data excerpted in Table 23.36. (A convenient source of the full data set is Dixon, 1983, p. 520.) This consists of two length and two width measurements on each of three distinct varieties which might be found in the same location. We wish to know: How well can the varieties (which can be classified by a more involved analysis without error) be classified by just use of the two length and two width measurements? After these data are entered into a computer, program 7M of the BMDP set of programs (Dixon, 1983) may be used to answer this question. The program code is given in Figure 23.29. From the resulting output, of key interest are the so-called *canonical variables,* which are the linear combinations of L_1, L_2, W_1, and W_2 which best discriminate among the three groups. In this example, these turn out to be

$$V_1 = 2.10510 + 0.82938L_1 + 1.53447W_1 - 2.20121L_2 - 2.81046W_2$$

$$V_2 = -6.66147 + 0.02410L_1 + 2.16452W_1 - 0.93192L_2 + 2.83919W_2$$

```
//  EXEC    BIMED, PROG =BMDP7M
/problem title is 'fisher data'.
/input variables are 5. format is '(4f3.1, f3.0)'.
/variable names are L1, w1, L2, w2, t.
grouping is t.
/group codes(5) are 1 to 3.
names(5) are set, ver, vir.
/end
```

FIG. 23.29 BMDP 7M program for dataset analysis.

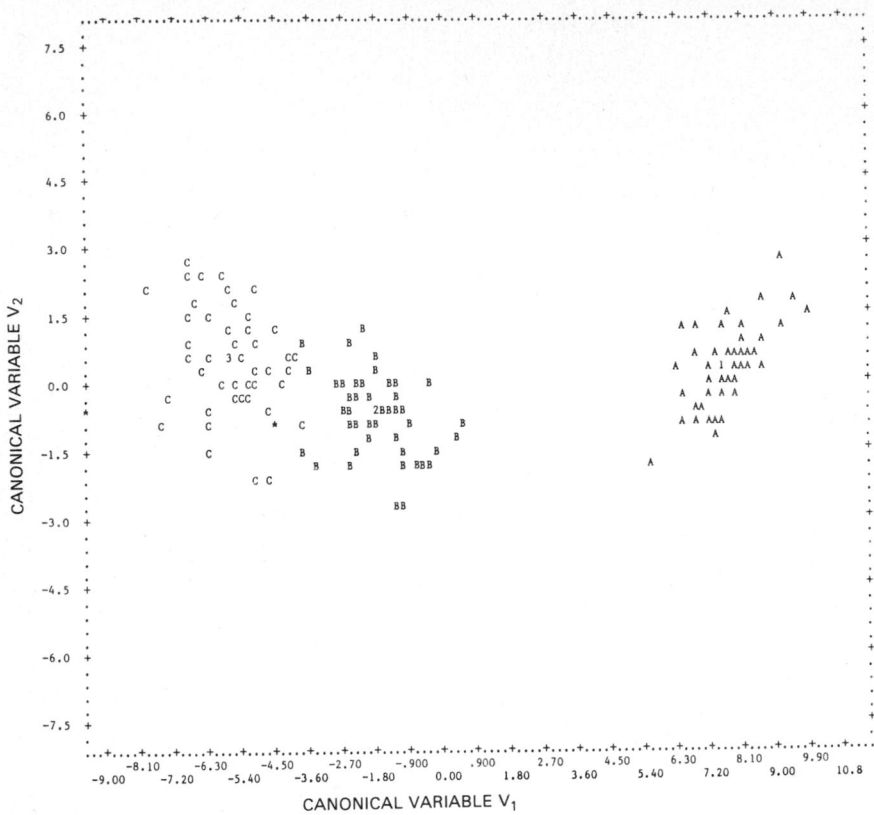

FIG. 23.30 Plot showing groups (*A, B, C*) discriminated by "canonical variables" V_1 and V_2. Overlap of different groups is indicated by *.

A plot of the (V_1, V_2) values for the 150 data points is given in Figure 23.30, with $T = 1, 2, 3$ cases labeled *A, B, C*, respectively, and shows the excellent results obtained. These results are deemed excellent since they allow us to classify a future observation into the correct group with high probability of being correct. For example, if we find $V_1 = 7.20$ and $V_2 = 1.00$, we are virtually certain group *A* is involved. (This plot is produced by program 7M.)

REGRESSION AND CORRELATION ANALYSIS

Many quality control problems require estimation of the relationship between two or more variables. Often interest centers on finding an equation relating one particular variable to a set of one or more variables. For example, how does the life of a tool vary with cutting speed? Or how does the octane number of a gasoline vary with its percentage purity?

Regression analysis is a statistical technique for estimating the parameters of an equation relating a particular variable to a set of variables. (Some authors refer

TABLE 23.37 Tool Life (Y in Minutes) versus Cutting Speed (X in Feet per Minute)

Y	X
41	90
43	90
35	90
32	90
22	100
35	100
29	100
18	100
21	105
13	105
18	105
20	105
15	110
11	110
6	110
10	110

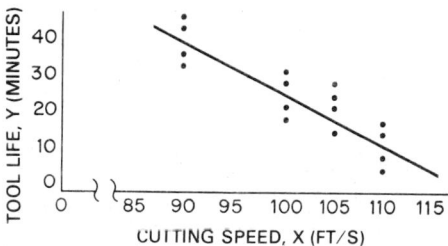

FIG. 23.31 Tool life Y versus cutting speed X.

to this as "least squares" or "curve" fitting.) The resulting equation is called a "regression equation."

Some experimental data for the tool life example are given in Table 23.37 (from Johnson and Leone, 1964, p. 380) and plotted in Figure 23.31. Tool life is the "response variable" (also called the "dependent variable" or the "predictand") and cutting speed is the "independent variable" (also called the "predictor variable"). In this case, the independent variable is controllable; i.e., it is fixed by the experimenter or the operator of the machine. In the second example, both the octane number and the percentage purity are random. The data for this example (from Volk, 1956) are given in Table 23.38 and plotted in Figure 23.32. Since the goal is to predict the octane number, it is regarded as the dependent variable, and the percentage purity is considered as the independent variable. (In many problems there are a number of independent variables, and in some cases this set of independent variables includes both random and controllable variables.)

The computations for two-variable regression problems can be done quite easily on a desk calculator, but when there are many variables, the number of com-

TABLE 23.38   Octane Number Y versus
Percentage Purity X

Y	X
88.6	99.8
86.4	99.7
87.2	99.6
88.4	99.5
87.2	99.4
86.8	99.3
86.1	99.2
87.3	99.1
86.4	99.0
86.6	98.9
87.1	98.8

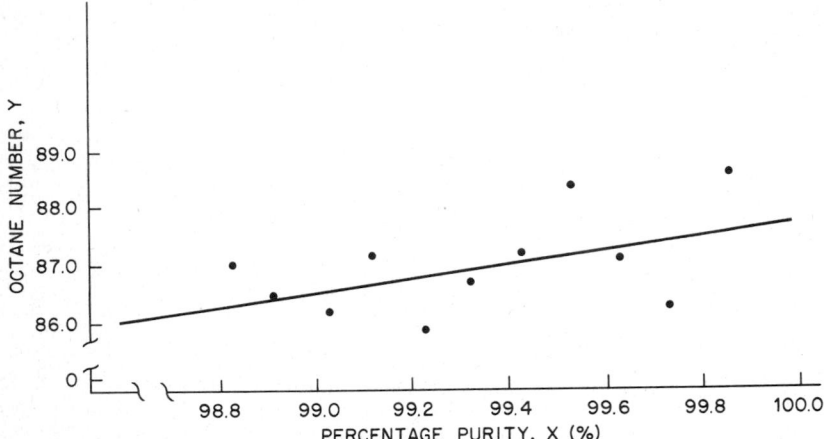

FIG. 23.32   Octane number versus percentage purity.

putations becomes overwhelming. (Even in the two-variable case, many of the computer programs available fail to provide numerically accurate calculations. It is strongly recommended that one *not* write one's own regression program, and that only major tested software packages such as SAS, BMDP, and the like be utilized.) With modern digital computer multiple regression programs, the number of variables is not a restriction. To understand and interpret the results of multidimensional problems, a thorough knowledge of the two and three variable cases is necessary.

There are many reasons for constructing regression equations. Although the motives do not affect the calculations, they do affect the interpretation of the results. In some cases, regression analysis is used to describe the nature of a relationship in a quantitative manner. Often, the *goals* are more specific. In the first example, where the cutting speed is controllable, the objective might be to find the particular value of cutting speed which minimizes tool wear or some cost function based on tool wear. Least squares regression can also be used to determine the important independent variables in a process, e.g., whether process variables such as moisture, pressure, or temperature affect a quality characteristic of the product such as strength.

In other problems, where the independent variable is not controllable, the goal may be to predict the value of the dependent or response variable. This might be done because the independent variable is easier to measure than the dependent variable. Or the independent variable may be available before the dependent variable, and hence it would be desirable to forecast the value of the dependent variable before it occurs. In still other cases it might allow a destructive test to be replaced by a nondestructive test.

The following list includes a number of *uses of regression equations:*

1. Forecasting and prediction
2. Quantitatively describing the relationship between a particular variable and another set of variables
3. Interpolating between values of a function
4. Determining the important independent variables
5. Locating the optimum operating conditions
6. Discriminating between alternative models
7. Estimating particular regression coefficients

For any of the goals stated above, the *basic steps in a regression study* are those of the Checklist for Planned Experimentation given at the beginning of this section. A summary, specifically relating the steps to regression, is:

1. Obtain a clear statement of the objectives of the study. Determine which variable is to be the response variable and which variables can be included as independent variables. In addition, obtain some measure of the precision of the results required—not necessarily in statistical terminology. (It is important to have a thorough understanding of what use will be made of the regression equation, since this may preclude the use of certain variables in the equation and will also help to give an understanding as to how much effort and money should be devoted to the project.)

2., 3. Specify collection procedures for the data. Collect the data. (The end results can only be as good as the data upon which they are based. Careful planning at this stage is of considerable importance and can also simplify the analysis of the data.)

4. Prepare crossplots (plots of one variable versus another) of the data to obtain information about the relationships between the variables; screen the data; calculate the regression equation; and evaluate how well it fits the data (including looking at transformations of variables for a better fit, or the removal of variables from an equation if they do not improve the prediction). Give measures of the precision of the equation and any procedure for using the equation. Also specify procedures for updating the equation and checks to determine whether it is still applicable, including control charts for the residuals (observed value–predicted value). (Section 24, Statistical Process Control, discusses control charts.)

5., 6., 7. As in the Checklist for Planned Experimentation.

A number of texts have been written on regression, including Daniel and Wood (1971) and Draper and Smith (1981). These include computer programs and output. Dudewicz and Karian (1985) also discuss design questions in detail. In addition to regression, other techniques have been devised for the analysis of multivariate data; see Kramer and Jensen (1969, 1970) and Siotani (1985) for details. (One of these techniques is discriminant and cluster analysis, already discussed in this section.)

Our discussion of regression begins with a single predictor problem, then proceeds to problems with more than one predictor variable and a discussion of computer programs and outputs, with their interpretation. While many texts emphasize advanced mathematical aspects of regression, this is not needed for a practical understanding now that high-quality software is available; hence we find no need for such mathematics. This makes this important subject accessible to most quality practitioners.

Simple Linear Regression.   Many problems involve only a single predictor variable X. (The dependent variable Y is often related to other predictor variables, which have either been held constant during the experiment or their effects judged to be much smaller than that of X.) These problems are often referred to as ones of "simple linear regression."

Graphing the Data.   A first step in any study of relationships between variables is to plot a graph of the data (often called a "scatter diagram"). The convention is to plot the response variable on the vertical axis and the independent variable on the horizontal axis. A graph can provide a great deal of information concerning the relationship between variables and often suggests possible models for the data. The data plotted in Figure 23.31 suggests that Y is linearly related to X over the range of this experiment. (If this were not the case, various transformations of the data as well as curvilinear relationships could also be considered. Often the relationship can be "linearized" by taking the logarithm of one or both of the variables.)

A graph can also indicate whether any of the observations are outliers, i.e., observations which deviate substantially from the rest of the data. (Outliers may be due to measurement errors or recording errors, in which case they should be corrected or deleted. They may be due to process changes or other causes, and the investigation of these changes or causes may provide more information than the analysis of the rest of the data.) No outliers are apparent in Figure 23.31.

A closer inspection of the graph can give an indication of the variability of Y for fixed X. In addition, it may show that this variability remains constant over all X or that it changes with X. In the latter case the method of weighted least squares (see Draper and Smith, 1981) may be preferred to the standard least squares technique discussed here.

The Model.   After graphing the data, we want to obtain an equation relating Y to X. To do this, a model for the data must be postulated. (We emphasize that the proposed model may be modified during the course of the study and is just a starting point.)

A possible model for the data in Figure 23.31 is

$$Y = \beta_0 + \beta_1 X + \epsilon$$

where β_0 and β_1 are the unknown intercept and slope, respectively, of the regression line. The model assumes that Y is a linear function of X plus a random error term, denoted by ϵ. This random error may be due to errors in the measurement of Y and/or to the effects of variables not included in the model, which is called

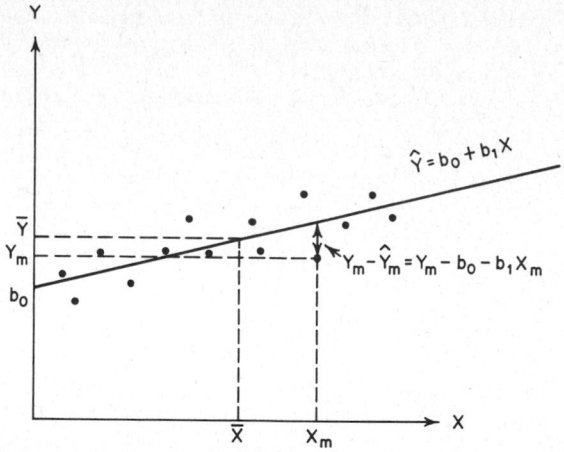

FIG. 23.33   Least squares.

"equation error." The X's are assumed to be measured with negligible error. For the data in Figure 23.31, the X's are fixed; however the same model can be used when the X's are random as in Figure 23.32.

Estimating the Prediction Equation.   The objective is to find estimates (b_0, b_1) of the unknown parameters (β_0, β_1) and thus obtain a prediction equation

$$\hat{Y} = b_0 + b_1 X$$

where $\hat{Y}$ is the predicted value of Y for a given value of X.

Least squares provides a method for finding estimates of these parameters from a set of N observations $(Y_1, X_1), \ldots, (Y_N, X_N)$. The estimates are called "least squares estimates" because they minimize the sum of the squared deviations between the observed and predicted values of the response variable $\Sigma(Y_m - \hat{Y}_m)^2 = \Sigma(Y_m - b_0 - b_1 X_m)^2$. These ideas are illustrated in Figure 23.33. (For a mathematical derivation of the estimates, see any of the texts mentioned in the introduction.)

If (1) the observations are independent, (2) the variance of the errors is constant over these observations, and (3) the linear model postulated is correct, the least squares estimates are the "best linear unbiased estimates": In the class of linear unbiased estimates of the parameters, the least squares estimates have the smallest variance. (Even if these conditions are not satisfied, the least squares technique can be used, although modifications or other methods may provide better estimates.) Note that no assumption has been made concerning the distribution of the random error, and in particular a normal distribution is not assumed: No assumption on this error term will be required until confidence intervals and tests of hypotheses are constructed.

The least squares estimates for the parameters of the linear model $Y = \beta_0 + \beta_1 X + \epsilon$ are

$$b_1 = \frac{\Sigma(X_m - \overline{X})(Y_m - \overline{Y})}{\Sigma(X_m - \overline{X})^2}$$

$$b_0 = \overline{Y} - b_1 \overline{X}$$

where $\overline{X} = \Sigma X_m/N$ and $\overline{Y} = \Sigma Y_m/N$ are sample averages. All these summations range from $m = 1$ to $m = N$. (Except where needed, the additional notation will be omitted for typographical simplicity.)

As can be seen, b_1 is related to the sample correlation coefficient

$$r = \frac{\Sigma(X_m - \overline{X})(Y_m - \overline{Y})}{\sqrt{\Sigma(X_m - \overline{X})^2\Sigma(Y_m - \overline{Y})^2}}$$

by

$$b_1 = r\sqrt{\frac{\Sigma(Y_m - \overline{Y})^2}{\Sigma(X_m - \overline{X})^2}}$$

However, the concept of correlation is meaningful only when both the variables are random, whereas b_1, the least squares estimate of the rate of change of Y per unit change in X has meaning for both the case of random X and controllable or fixed X.

The sums, sums of squares, and sum of cross-products for the data ($N = 16$) given in Table 23.37 are

$$\Sigma X_m = 90 + 90 + \cdots + 110 = 1620$$

$$\Sigma Y_m = 41 + 43 + \cdots + 10 = 369$$

$$\Sigma X_m^2 = 8100 + 8100 + \cdots + 12,000 = 164,900$$

$$\Sigma Y_m^2 = 1681 + 1849 + \cdots + 100 = 10,469$$

$$\Sigma X_m Y_m = 3690 + 3870 + \cdots + 1100 = 36,170$$

(Note that calculations for regression are very susceptible to both human and numerical error because of their complexity. Hence good software should be used. The numerical examples in this section can be used both to test one's understanding of that software and to test its accuracy.)

The summary statistics are computed using the following computational formulas:

$$\overline{X} = \frac{\Sigma X_m}{N} = 101.25 \qquad \overline{Y} = \frac{\Sigma Y_m}{N} = 23.06$$

$$\Sigma(X_m - \overline{X})^2 = \Sigma X_m^2 - \frac{(\Sigma X_m)^2}{N} = 164,900 - \frac{(1,620)^2}{16} = 875.00$$

$$\Sigma(Y_m - \overline{Y})^2 = \Sigma Y_m^2 - \frac{(\Sigma Y_m)^2}{N} = 10,469 - \frac{(369)^2}{16} = 1958.94$$

$$\Sigma(X_m - \overline{X})(Y_m - \overline{Y}) = \Sigma X_m Y_m - \frac{\Sigma X_m \Sigma Y_m}{N}$$

$$= 36,170 - \frac{(1620)(369)}{16}$$

$$= -1191.25$$

From these results the least squares estimates can be calculated as

$$b_1 = \frac{-1191.25}{875} = -1.3614$$

$$b_0 = 23.06 - (-1.3614)(101.25) = 160.9018$$

and hence the prediction equation is

$$\hat{Y} = 160.90 - 1.3614X$$

The prediction equation is sometimes written in terms of deviations from averages, i.e., $\hat{Y} = \overline{Y} + b_1 (X - \overline{X})$, which for this example becomes

$$\hat{Y} = 23.06 - 1.3614(X - 101.25)$$

Examining the Prediction Equation. After estimating the coefficients of the prediction equation, the equation should be plotted over the data to check for gross calculation errors. Roughly half the data points should be above the line and half below it. In addition, the equation should pass exactly through the point $(\overline{X}, \overline{Y})$

A number of criteria exist for judging the adequacy of the prediction equation. One common measure of the adequacy of the prediction equation is the proportion of variation R^2 explained. To compute R^2, the sum of the squared deviations of the Y_m about $\overline{Y}$ is partitioned into two parts, the sum of squares due to regression and the residual sum of squares:

$$\Sigma(Y_m - \overline{Y})^2 = \text{SS(REG)} + \text{SS(RES)}$$

$$= \Sigma(\hat{Y}_m - \overline{Y})^2 + \Sigma(Y_m - \hat{Y}_m)^2$$

$$= b_1\Sigma(X_m - \overline{X})(Y_m - \overline{Y}) + \Sigma(Y_m - \hat{Y}_m)^2$$

From this, the proportion of the variation $\Sigma(Y_m - \overline{Y})^2$ explained by the regression is computed as

$$R^2 = \frac{\text{SS(REG)}}{\Sigma(Y_m - \overline{Y})^2}$$

$$= \frac{b_1\Sigma(X_m - \overline{X})(Y_m - \overline{Y})}{\Sigma(Y_m - \overline{Y})^2}$$

$$= \frac{(-1.3614)(-1191.25)}{1958.94} = 0.828$$

Thus, in this example the prediction equation explains 82.8 percent of the variation of the tool life.

Another interpretation of R^2 (when both the independent and the dependent variables are random) is as the square of the sample multiple correlation coefficient. When there is only one independent variable, this reduces to the square of the sample correlation coefficient r defined earlier.

Although R^2 is a useful measure of the adequacy of the prediction equation,, an estimate of the variability of the Y's about the regression equation is usually more important. Either the sample variance s^2 or its square root s, called the "standard error of the estimate," can be used. The latter is often preferred, because it is measured in the same units as Y. Both of these, as well as other results, can be obtained from the analysis of variance (ANOVA) given in Table 23.39.

The corrected total sum of squares (some authors include the total sum of squares, uncorrected, in the ANOVA table, partitioning it into two parts—the corrected sum of squares and the sum of squares due to $\overline{Y}$ (or b_0); see Draper and Smith, 1981) and the regression sum of squares are calculated from the summary statistics and the estimate of the regression coefficient. Although the residual sum of squares can be calculated directly, it is more easily obtained as the difference between the corrected total sum of squares and the sum of squares due to regression. Each of these sums of squares has an associated degrees of freedom (see Testing a Hypothesis When the Sample Size is Fixed in Advance). The corrected total sum of squares has $N - 1$ degrees of freedom, since one degree of freedom is used in estimating the mean. For this *one* variable model, there is *one* degree of freedom associated with the regression sum of squares, leaving $(N - 1) - 1 = N - 2$ degrees of freedom associated with the residual sum of squares. The mean squares (MS) are calculated by dividing the sum of squares by their associated degrees of freedom. The estimate of the variance of Y about the regression line is s^2 = MS(RES); hence the standard error of the estimate is $s = \sqrt{\text{MS(RES)}}$.

From the mean squares an F statistic can be calculated as

$$F_{\text{CALC}} = \frac{\text{MS(REG)}}{\text{MS(RES)}}$$

If (1) the ϵ's in the original model are normally distributed with a common variance, (2) the observations are independent, and (3) the postulated linear model is correct, then the regression can be tested for significance, i.e., the statistical hypothesis

$$H_0:\beta_1 = 0$$

can be tested against the alternative hypothesis

$$H_1:\beta_1 \neq 0$$

by comparing F_{CALC} with the tabulated F at an appropriate level of significance α. If $F_{\text{CALC}} > F_{\text{TAB}}$, we conclude that the regression is significant and that the prediction equation is a better predictor of Y than $\overline{Y}$. Although it is difficult to

TABLE 23.39 ANOVA Table (Linear Model)

Source	Sum of squares	Degrees of freedom	Mean square
1. Due to regression (b_1)	$b_1\Sigma(X_m - \overline{X})(Y_m - \overline{Y})$	1	MS (REG) = SS(REG)/1
2. Residual	$\Sigma(Y_m - \hat{Y}_m)^2$†	$N - 2$	MS (RES) = SS(RES)/$(N - 2)$
3. Total corrected for the mean	$\Sigma(Y_m - \overline{Y})^2$	$N - 1$	

†Obtained by subtracting (1) from (3).

TABLE 23.40   ANOVA Example

Source	Sum of squares	Degrees of freedom	Mean square	F_{CALC}
1. Due to regression	1621.80	1	1621.80	67.35
2. Residual	337.14	14	24.08	
3. Total corrected for the mean	1958.94	15		

check the assumptions stated above, the test is not extremely sensitive to departures in the distribution of ϵ from normality if the number of observations is relatively large. If the X's are random, this test must be interpreted in a conditional sense, i.e., given the values of the X's.

For the example, the analysis of variance (ANOVA) table is given in Table 23.40. (See Section 26, under Completely Randomized Design—A Simple One Factor Experiment.) The regression is significant at an $\alpha = 0.01$ level ($F_{\text{TAB}} = 8.86$) and $s = \sqrt{24.08} = 4.91$.

It is important to note that even when the regression is significant, the unexplained variability can still be large, and the prediction equation may not be of any value.

Residuals, Outliers, Confidence and Prediction Bands, Extrapolation; Lack of Fit—Replicated Observations.   If it is feasible to replicate, i.e., take more than one observation on Y at one or more values of X, the adequacy of the model can also be tested. (An estimate of the pure error may sometimes be available from sources outside the immediate experiment.) In this case the SS(RES) can be partitioned into two parts—that due to pure error, SS(PE), and that due to lack of fit, SS(LF).

Suppose that there are N_m readings $Y_{m1}, Y_{m2}, \ldots, Y_{mN_m}$ at x_m, where $m = 1, 2, \ldots, k$. The contribution to the sum of squares due to pure error for X_m is

$$\sum_{j=1}^{N_m} (\hat{Y}_{mj} - \overline{Y}_m)^2 = \sum_{j=1}^{N_m} Y_{mj}^2 - \frac{\left(\sum_{j=1}^{N_m} Y_{mj}\right)^2}{N_m}$$

and the associated degrees of freedom is $N_m = 1$. The SS(PE) is just the sum of these k contributions and the associated degrees of freedom (DF) is

$$\sum_{m=1}^{k} (N_m - 1) = \sum_{m=1}^{k} N_m - k$$

For the example given in Table 23.37:

X_m		SS(PE)	DF
90	$41^2 + 43^2 + 35^2 + 32^2 - (151)^2/4 =$	78.75	3
100	$22^2 + 35^2 + 29^2 + 18^2 - (104)^2/4 =$	170.00	3
105	$21^2 + 13^2 + 18^2 + 20^2 - (72)^2/4 =$	38.00	3
110	$15^2 + 16^2 + 6^2 + 10^2 - (42)^2/4 =$	41.00	3
	Total	327.75	12

The SS(LF) is found by subtraction as

$$SS(LF) = SS(RES) - SS(PE) = 337.14 - 327.75 = 9.39$$

and the lack of fit degrees of freedom is obtained in a similar manner as $14 - 12 = 2$. The mean squares are then found by dividing the sum of squares by the appropriate degrees of freedom and

$$F_{CALC} = \frac{MS(LF)}{MS(PE)}$$

If the F_{CALC} is greater than the tabled F, the lack of fit is "significant" and a better or more complete model is needed (e.g., $Y = \beta_0 + \beta_1 X + \beta_2 X^2$). Plots of the residuals ($Y_m - \hat{Y}_m$) versus X_m are particularly helpful in suggesting alternative models. Some examples are given in Figure 23.34. (Daniel and Wood, 1971, pp. 19–24, present graphs of a number of nonlinear functions and give transformations which "linearize" them.) In each case the model $Y = \beta_0 + \beta_1 X$ was postulated and the plots are of the resulting residuals.

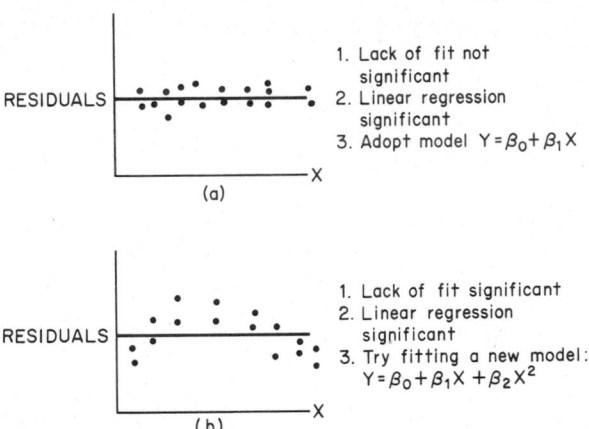

FIG. 23.34   Residuals and lack of fit.

If F_{CALC} is less than the tabled F, the model is accepted. This does not mean that other variables should not be considered in the model, but only that the form of X in the model is adequate.

The calculations for our example are summarized in Table 23.41. The lack of fit is judged not significant at an α level of 0.05 ($F_{TAB} = 3.89$). Hence, the pos-

TABLE 23.41   ANOVA Lack of Fit Example

Source	Sum of squares	Degrees of freedom	Mean square	F_{CALC}
Lack of fit	9.39*	2	4.695	0.172
Pure error	327.75	12	27.3125	

*Obtained by subtracting SS(PE) and SS(RES).

tulated model is accepted and the residual mean square is used as the estimate of the variance.

If replication is not possible, e.g., X is random rather than controllable, the Y values corresponding to X values which are close together can be used to obtain an estimate of the variability and hence judge the lack of fit. (See pp. 123–125 of Daniel and Wood, 1971.)

Confidence Intervals. Both R^2 and s^2 provide measures of the reliability or adequacy of a prediction equation. Confidence intervals provide another measure of the reliability of the various estimates. All these confidence intervals are based on the square root of the residual mean square. A $(1 - \alpha)$ two-sided confidence interval for the slope β_1 is given by

$$b_1 \pm \frac{ts}{\sqrt{\Sigma(X_m - \overline{X})^2}}$$

where the value t is obtained from Appendix II, Table G, with $N - 2$ degrees of freedom. The term in the denominator plays the role that $n^{1/2}$ plays in confidence intervals on population means. For the example, the 0.95 confidence interval on β_1 is

$$-1.36 \pm \frac{(2.145)(4.91)}{\sqrt{875}} = -1.36 \pm 0.356$$

The term $s/\sqrt{\Sigma(X_m - \overline{X})^2}$ is often called the standard error of the regression coefficient.

In addition to the confidence interval on β_1, more importantly *confidence intervals* can also be constructed *for the mean of Y at a given value of X*. The $(1 - \alpha)$ confidence interval on the mean of Y at X (or equivalently on $\beta_0 + \beta_1 X$) is

$$b_0 + b_1 X \pm ts \sqrt{\frac{1}{N} + \frac{(X - \overline{X})^2}{\Sigma(X_m - \overline{X})^2}}$$

where X is the value at which the confidence interval is being constructed and t again has $N - 2$ degrees of freedom. (By letting $X = 0$, a confidence level for β_0 is obtained.)

In addition to the assumptions previously stated, these confidence intervals also require (1) that the independent variable is fixed rather than random and (2) that the errors are normally distributed. However, if the X's are random, confidence intervals can still be calculated, but they must be interpreted in a conditional sense. Confidence intervals are not sensitive to departures from normality if the sample size is reasonably large. This is not the case for the following interval, which is very sensitive to the normality assumption. *Least absolute value* (LAV) and *Chebyshev estimation* are two possible alternatives to least squares estimation, which are less sensitive to model departures than is least squares. For sources of efficient computer algorithms, with a detailed numerical example, see Dielman and Pfaffenberger (1984).

In addition to a confidence interval on the expected value of Y at a given X, there may be a need for *an interval estimate for a future individual observation on Y at X*. (A more complete discussion of confidence intervals is given in Draper and Smith, 1981. See Daniel and Wood, 1971, for a confidence interval which simultaneously includes the whole line. See Dudewicz, 1976, p. 427, for a plot of the interval for all X, called a *prediction band,* and its uses.) In this case the interval must also take into account the variability of Y about $\beta_0 + \beta_1 X$, and the result is

$$b_0 + b_1 X \pm ts \sqrt{1 + \frac{1}{N} + \frac{(X - \overline{X})^2}{\Sigma(X_m - \overline{X})^2}}$$

where t has $N - 2$ degrees of freedom. Computations of these intervals for various values of X are given in Table 23.42.

Multiple Regression. Although there are many problems involving single predictor variables, more often there are many predictor variables. A generalization of the least squares technique, previously discussed, can be used to estimate the coefficients of the multivariable prediction equation. This problem is called multiple regression.

The General Model. For a problem with k predictor variables, the model can be written as

$$Y = \beta_0 + \beta_1 X_1 + \cdots + \beta_k X_k + \epsilon$$

where the β's are unknown parameters and ϵ is the random error. These variables may be transformations of the original data. For example, in predicting gasoline yields from data on the specific gravity and vapor pressure of crude oil, Y may be the log of the gasoline yield, X_1 the crude oil specific gravity, X_2 the crude oil vapor pressure, and X_3 the product of the crude oil specific gravity with its vapor pressure.

The general model includes polynomial models in one or more variables, such as

$$Y = \beta_0 + \beta_1 X_1 + \beta_2 X_2 + \beta_3 X_1^2 + \beta_4 X_2^2 + \beta_5 X_1 X_2 + \epsilon$$

(which is called the *full quadratic model* of Y on X_1 and X_2, and is of great use in designed experiments; see Dudewicz and Karian, 1985). This is still a linear model, since the term "linear model" means that the model is linear in the β's. (See Draper and Smith, 1981, for a discussion of models which are nonlinear.)

Estimating the Prediction Equation. The objective now is to find the least squares estimates $(b_0, b_1, \ldots, b_k)$ of the unknown parameters $(\beta_0, \beta_1, \ldots, \beta_k)$ and obtain a prediction equation

$$\hat{Y} = b_0 + b_1 X_1 + \cdots + b_k X_k$$

where $\hat{Y}$ is the predicted value of Y for the given values of $X_1, \ldots, X_k$. Letting $x_i = X_i - \overline{X}_i$ and using the fact that

$$b_0 = \overline{Y} - b_1 \overline{X}_1 - \cdots - b_k \overline{X}_k$$

this prediction equation can be expressed in the alternative form:

$$\hat{Y} = \overline{Y} + b_1 x_1 + \cdots + b_k x_k$$

To simplify the formulas, the observations can also be expressed as deviations from their sample averages; i.e., for the mth observation $x_{im} = X_{im} - \overline{X}_i$ and $y_m = Y_m - \overline{Y}$. Then the least squares estimates of the $k + 1$ parameters of the

TABLE 23.42 Computation of Confidence Limits

X (1)	$b_0 + b_1 X$ (2)	$\dfrac{(X - \bar{X})^2}{\Sigma(X_m - \bar{X})^2}$ (3)	$\sqrt{\dfrac{1}{N} + (3)}$ (4)	$ts \times (4)$ (5)	90% confidence limits on the mean of Y at X		$\sqrt{1 + \dfrac{1}{N} + (3)}$ (8)	$ts \times (8)$ (9)	90% prediction limits on Y at X	
					Lower (2) − (5) (6)	Upper (2) + (5) (7)			Lower (2) − (9) (10)	Upper (2) + (9) (11)
90	38.37	0.14464	0.4551	3.94	34.43	42.31	1.0987	9.50	28.87	47.87
100	24.76	0.00179	0.2535	2.20	22.56	26.96	1.0316	8.92	15.84	33.68
($\bar{X}$) 101.5	($\bar{Y}$) 23.06	0.0	0.2550	2.17	20.89	25.23	1.0308	8.91	14.15	31.97
110	11.15	0.08750	0.3870	3.36	7.79	14.51	1.0724	9.27	1.88	20.42

Note: Numbers in parentheses are column numbers. $t_{14,0.95} = 1.761$.

multivariable linear model $Y = \beta_0 + \beta_1 X_1 + \cdots + \beta_k X_k + \epsilon$ can be obtained by solving the set of $k + 1$ linear equations:

$$b_1 \Sigma x_{1m}^2 \quad + b_2 \Sigma x_{1m} x_{2m} + \cdots + b_k \Sigma x_{1m} x_{km} = \Sigma x_{1m} y_m$$

$$b_1 \Sigma x_{1m} x_{2m} + \quad b_2 \Sigma x_{2m}^2 \quad + \cdots + b_k \Sigma x_{2m} x_{km} = \Sigma x_{2m} y_m$$

$$\vdots \qquad\qquad\qquad\qquad\qquad \vdots$$

$$b_1 \Sigma x_{1m} x_{km} + b_2 \Sigma x_{2m} x_{km} + \cdots + \quad b_k \Sigma x_{km}^2 \quad = \Sigma x_{km} y_m$$

$$b_0 = \overline{Y} - b_1 \overline{X}_1 - b_2 \overline{X}_2 - \cdots - b_k \overline{X}_k$$

(All the above summations are on m and range from 1 to N.)

Solving these "reduced normal" equations simultaneously can be tedious, is error prone, and involves matrix algebra. Many reference works emphasize how to perform these calculations accurately. To the user of modern accurate statistical software, these calculations are of no direct importance: That user can trust they are being done accurately, and concentrate on statistical aspects of model adequacy, interpretation, and use.

Examining the Prediction Equation. After obtaining $(b_0, b_1, \ldots, b_k)$, an ANOVA table can be constructed and the adequacy of the prediction equation evaluated by a number of criteria. The ANOVA table, which is a generalization of that derived for the single predictor variable, is given in Table 23.43. The third row in Table 23.43 is the same as in Table 23.39. Note that the expressions in the first row reduce to those in the first row of Table 23.39 when $k = 1$.

Since there are k variables in the model, the sum of squares due to regression has k degrees of freedom associated with it. In addition since k coefficients and one intercept have been estimated, the residual sum of squares has $N - (k + 1)$ $= N - k - 1$ degrees of freedom associated with it. The F statistic is calculated as before—i.e., $F = \text{MS(REG)}/\text{MS(RES)}$—and $s = \sqrt{\text{SS(RES)}/(N - k - 1)}$. In this case the F statistic can be used to test the statistical hypothesis

$$H_0 : \beta_i = 0 \qquad (i = 1, 2, \ldots, k)$$

TABLE 23.43   ANOVA Table (Linear Model)

Source	Sum of squares	Degrees of freedom	Mean square
1. Due to regression	$b'a$†	k	$\text{MS(REG)} = \text{SS(REG)}/k$
2. Residual	$\Sigma(\overline{Y}_m - \hat{Y}_m)^2$‡	$N - k - 1$	$\text{MS(RES)} = \text{SS(RES)}/$ $(N - k - 1)$
3. Total corrected for the mean	$\Sigma(Y_m - \overline{Y}_m)^2$	$N - 1$	

†The sum of squares due to regression can be written as $b'a = b_1 \Sigma x_{1m} y_m + b_2 \Sigma x_{2m} y_m + \cdots + b_k \Sigma x_{km} y_m$. [Note that b' is the transpose of the b vector, i.e., $b' = (b_1 \; b_2 \cdots b_k)$. Those not familiar with vector notation can regard $b'a$ as a shorthand for the sum given in this footnote. Since computations are usually done with computer software, details of vector notation are not given and will not be needed by most readers.]

‡Obtained by subtracting (1) from (3).

against the alternative statistical hypothesis

$$H_1: \text{Some } \beta_i \neq 0 \qquad (i = 1, 2, \ldots, k)$$

The only change is in the degrees of freedom used to look up the F_{TAB} ($k, n - k - 1$ versus $1, n - 2$).

The proportion of variation explained by the equation (R^2) can be obtained from the ANOVA table. Note that R^2 does not depend on the number of variables in the equation, but s^2 does. In fact, if a new variable is added to the model (and the least squares estimates and ANOVA table are recomputed), the value of R^2 *cannot decrease.* However, s^2 can either increase or decrease, since it depends on the residual degrees of freedom in addition to the residual sum of squares, which decreases by one when a new variable is added.

Confidence Intervals. Confidence intervals for individual β's can be developed, as

$$b_i \pm ts \sqrt{c_{ii}}$$

where t has $(N - k - 1)$ degrees of freedom, and c_{ii} is defined below. However, since the b_i ($i = 1, \ldots, k$) have a joint distribution and are in general not uncorrelated, care must be taken in the interpretation of sets of these confidence intervals (see, for example, Draper and Smith, 1981).

More usefully, a confidence interval on the regression equation at a point $x = (x_1, \ldots, x_k)$ where $x_i = X_i - \overline{X}_i$ is given by

$$\overline{Y} + b_1 x_1 + \cdots + b_k x_k \pm ts \left(\frac{1}{N} + x'Cx \right)^{1/2}$$

where t has $N - k - 1$ degrees of freedom and $x'Cx$ is a quadratic form which takes into account the covariances and variances of the b's. (Here C is as defined in the next paragraph.)

In a similar manner an interval for a future Y at X is given by

$$\overline{Y} + b_1 x_1 + \cdots + b_k x_k \pm ts \left(1 + \frac{1}{N} + x'Cx \right)^{1/2}$$

where t has $N - k - 1$ degrees of freedom. (Here $C = S^{-1}$, where S is the $k \times k$ matrix whose entry in row i and column j is $\Sigma x_{im} x_{jm}$. In practice, as we will see, these matrix calculations are done by the computer and the user need not bother with them—or even understand the concept of a "matrix" and its "inverse.")

An example: The methods discussed can now be illustrated by an example furnished by Mason E. Wescott (example 5 from *Mimeo Notes,* Mason E. Wescott, Rochester Institute of Technology, Rochester, NY) with $k = 2$ predictor variables. The problem is to relate the green strength (flexural strength before baking) of electric circuit breaker arc chutes to the hydraulic pressure used in forming them and the acid concentration. The data are given in Table 23.44, with hydraulic pressure and green strength given in units of 10 lb/in^2 and the acid concentration given as a percent of the nominal rate for 20 observations. Two-variable plots of the data are given in Figures 23.35, 23.36, and 23.37. Summary statistics including sums, sums of squares, and cross products, both raw and corrected, as well as the sample means, are given in Table 23.45.

TABLE 23.44 Arc Chute Data

Green strength Y in units of 10 lb/in^2	Hydraulic pressure X_1 in units of 10 lb/in^2	Acid concentration X_2, as % of nominal rate
665	110	116
618	119	104
620	138	94
578	130	86
682	143	110
594	133	87
722	147	114
700	142	106
681	125	107
695	135	106
664	152	98
548	118	86
620	155	87
595	128	96
740	146	120
670	132	108
640	130	104
590	112	91
570	113	92
640	120	100

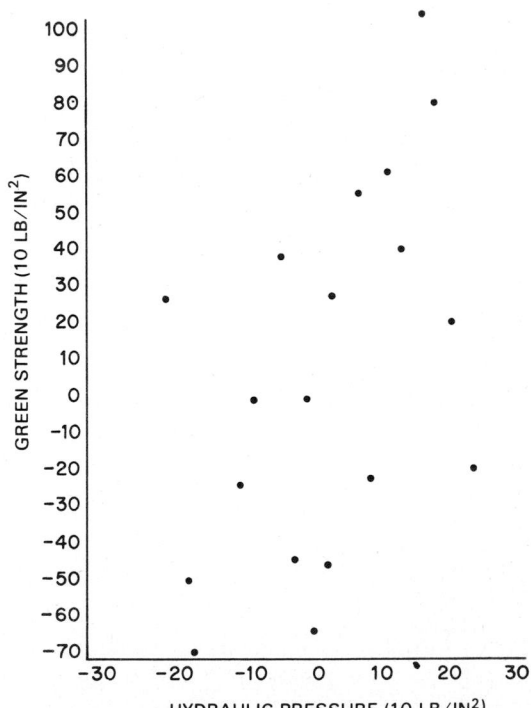

FIG. 23.35 Green strength versus hydraulic pressure (deviations from averages).

23.112

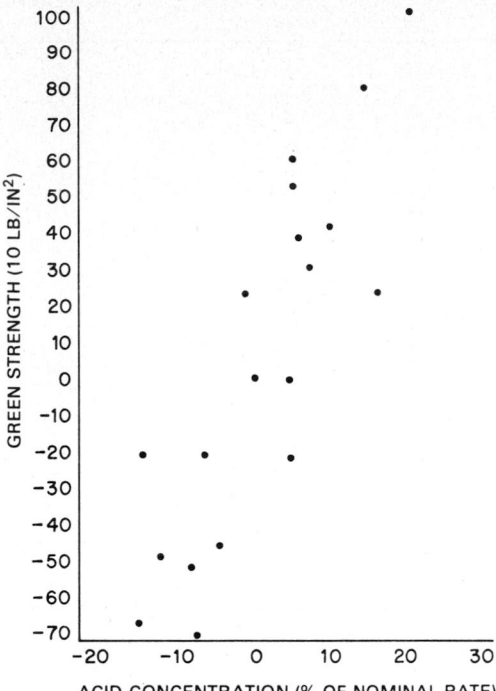

FIG. 23.36   Green strength versus acid concentration (deviations from averages).

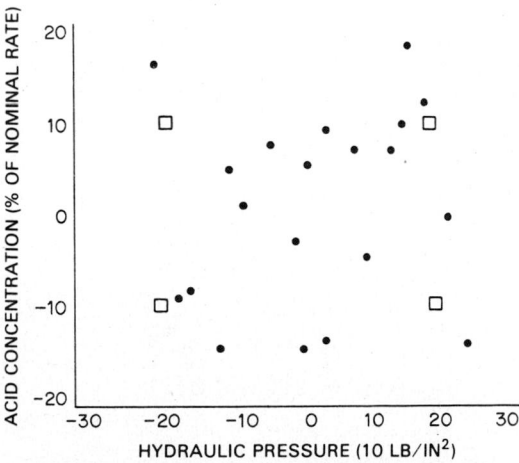

FIG. 23.37   Acid concentration versus hydraulic pressure (deviations from averages). Rectangles indicate points at which confidence intervals have been calculated.

TABLE 23.45 Summary Statistics

$N = 20$		
$\Sigma Y_m = 12{,}832$	$\Sigma X_{1m} = 2628$	$\Sigma X_{2m} = 2012$
$\Sigma Y_m^2 = 8{,}286{,}988$	$\Sigma X_{1m}^2 = 348{,}756$	$\Sigma X_{2m}^2 = 204{,}500$
$\Sigma X_{1m}Y_m = 1{,}693{,}226$	$\Sigma X_{2m}Y_m = 1{,}300{,}253$	$\Sigma X_{1m}X_{2m} = 264{,}785$
$\overline{Y} = 641.6$	$\overline{X}_1 = 131.4$	$\overline{X}_2 = 100.6$

	S	a
$s_{11} = 3436.8$	$s_{12} = 408.2*$	$a_1 = 7{,}101.2\dagger$
$s_{21} = 408.2$	$s_{22} = 2092.8$	$a_2 = 9{,}353.8$

$*s_{12} = \Sigma x_{1m} x_{2m} = \Sigma X_{1m} X_{2m} - (\Sigma X_{1m}\Sigma X_{2m}/N) = 264{,}785 - [(2628)(2012)/20] = 408.2.$
$\dagger a_1 = \Sigma x_{1m}y_m = \Sigma X_{1m}Y_m - (\Sigma X_{1m}\Sigma Y_m/N) = 1{,}693{,}226 - [(2628)(12{,}832)/20] = 7101.2.$

The estimates are:

$$b_2 = 4.162940$$

$$b_1 = 1.571779$$

$$b_0 = \overline{Y} - b_1\overline{X}_1 - b_2\overline{X}_2 = 16.27475$$

The C matrix is:

$$c_{22} = 0.00048916$$

$$c_{12}(= c_{21}) = -0.000058099$$

$$c_{11} = 0.00029787$$

and hence

$$C = \begin{vmatrix} 297.869 & -58.099 \\ -58.099 & 489.160 \end{vmatrix} \times 10^{-6}$$

The prediction equations can be calculated as

$$\hat{Y} = 16.277 + 1.572X_1 + 4.163X_2$$

$$\hat{Y} = 641.600 + 1.572(X_1 - 131.400) + 4.163(X_2 - 100.600)$$

(The latter form will be used in the remaining computations.)

The ANOVA table (Table 23.46) for the example follows directly from the summary statistics of Table 23.45 and from Table 23.43. The residual mean square error is 228.0, and hence the standard deviation s is 15.100.

The 95 percent confidence intervals on β_1 and β_2 are obtained as

$$1.572 \pm 2.110 \times 15.100 \times \sqrt{297.869} \times 10^{-3}$$

$$= 1.572 \pm 0.550 = 1.02 \text{ and } 2.12$$

and

$$4.163 \pm 2.110 \times 15.0997 \times \sqrt{489.16} \times 10^{-3}$$

$$= 4.163 \pm 0.705 = 3.46 \text{ and } 4.87$$

TABLE 23.46 ANOVA Example

Source	Sum of squares	Degrees of freedom	Mean square
1. Due to regression	50,100.8*	2	25,050.40
2. Residual	3,876.0†	17	228.0
3. Total corrected for the mean	53,976.8	19	

*(1.571779)(7101.2) + (4.16294)(9353.8) = 50,100.825.
†By subtraction.

Confidence intervals for $\beta_0 + \beta_1 X_1 + \beta_2 X_2$ and for a future observation of Y, at five combinations of X_1 and X_2, are given in Table 23.47. (The five points at which the confidence intervals are computed are also indicated in Figure 23.37.)

Computer Programs. Because of the widespread popularity of regression, almost every computer facility has at least one and most have many regression programs. These programs may have been locally written, or they may have been obtained from other sources. In the latter case, the program usually has been modified in some manner, so that it can be run on the local computer system and satisfy the needs of the local users.

Studies by Longley (1967) and Wampler (1970) indicate that the user should *strongly* prefer software such as that of SAS and BMDP. One should not presume that the program has been checked, just because a sample data problem is given in the program manual. Unfortunately a number of the algorithms used in these programs are often taken directly from desk calculator instructions. These algorithms are often not good, and can produce numerically inaccurate results, even in double precision. For example, Longley found that many of the programs computed the squared deviations of a variable about its mean by the computational formula $\Sigma X_m^2 - (\Sigma X_m)^2/N$, rather than by $\Sigma(X_m - \overline{X})^2$. Since these quantities arc the base for most of the regression calculations, numerical errors may be present in all the results.

Since the user may not be able (or simply does not want to invest the time) to check a program, a few simple checks for this purpose are given below. These can be used to gain some idea of the limitations of a program; however, we again strongly recommend against "rolling your own" when SAS, BMDP, and (perhaps) other excellent software is available at reasonable prices, and is kept up to date with advances in statistics.

1. Add the residuals about the regression line. They should sum to zero, within rounding error.
2. If the residuals sum to zero, make additional runs of the problem after adding 10, 100, 1000, 10,000 etc., to each variable. The coefficients will begin to change at a point where round-off error occurs.
3. As a check on the accuracy of the inversion routine, run a problem with two variables X_1 and X_2. Then make another run with the same response variable but two new independent variables $X_1^* = X_1 + X_2$ and $X_2^* = X_1 - X_2$. The following results should hold: $b_1 = b_1^* + b_2^*$ and $b_2 = b_1^* - b_2^*$.

Longley (1967) gives some additional checks, and Wampler (1970) lists results on many regression programs.

TABLE 23.47 Computation of Confidence Intervals

X_1 (1)	X_2 (2)	$\hat{Y}$ (3)	$(x'Cx)$ (4)	$\sqrt{\dfrac{1}{N}+(4)}$ (5)	$ts \times (5)$† (6)	95% confidence limits on the mean of Y at X_1,X_2		$\sqrt{1+\dfrac{1}{N}+(4)}$ (9)	$ts \times (9)$ (10)	95% prediction limits on Y at X_1,X_2	
						Lower (3) − (6) (7)	Upper (3) + (6) (8)			Lower (3) − (10) (11)	Upper (3) + (10) (12)
111.4	90.6	568.53	0.1457*	0.4424	14.10	554.43	582.63	1.0935	34.84	533.69	603.37
111.4	110.6	651.79	0.1922	0.4921	15.68	636.11	667.47	1.1145	35.51	616.28	687.30
131.4	100.6	641.60	0.0	0.2236	7.12	634.48	648.72	1.0247	32.65	608.95	674.25
151.4	90.6	631.41	0.1922	0.4921	15.68	615.73	647.09	1.1145	35.51	595.90	666.92
151.4	110.6	714.67	0.1457	0.4424	14.10	700.57	728.77	1.0935	34.85	679.82	749.52

Note: Numbers in parentheses are column numbers.

*Since $x' = (111.4 - 131.4, 90.6 - 100.6) = (-20, -10)$, then

$$x'Cx = (-20,-10)\begin{bmatrix} 297.869 & -58.099 \\ -58.099 & 498.160 \end{bmatrix} \times 10^{-6}\begin{bmatrix} -20 \\ -10 \end{bmatrix} = (-5,376.39, -3,819.62) \times 10^{-6}\begin{bmatrix} -20 \\ -10 \end{bmatrix} = 0.1457.$$

†t_{TAB} with 17 degrees of freedom is 2.110, $s = 15.100$.

23.116

A write-up is usually available with regression programs; it should include a complete discussion of the *input* required and an explanation of the *output* and *options* available, as well as a complete statement of the calculation formulas and a sample problem. (Although documenting a program is a difficult task, poorly written documentation is often a warning of a poorly or improperly written computer program.)

While the input formats of regression programs vary, most programs have an option which allows the user to specify a variety of transformations of the data, such as logs, powers, and cross products. Typical regression outputs include ANOVA tables, residuals plots, and other statistics, in addition to the estimates of the regression coefficients. Although often omitted, an "echo-check," i.e., a printout of the original and transformed data, is essential. Often "strange" regression results can be traced to a misplaced decimal point in an observation, the wrong variables being read in, or incorrect use of the transformation option. (If this is not available in a program, ask the computer center to modify the program so that it is automatically printed out unless the user deletes it.)

R^2 and C_p Criteria for Model Choice.

In many situations there are a large number of possible variables for a model and the problem is to select the "vital few" from these "useful many," instead of obtaining the complete regression equation. There are many reasons for not using all the variables. For example, a subset of variables can provide a better prediction equation than the full set, even though the full set has a higher R, since the full set will also include more variability. In addition, equations with fewer variables are easier to understand, and hence more likely to gain acceptance and be used.

Unless the data come from a properly designed experiment, there is no simple test for significant variables. Since there are $2^k - 1$ possible prediction equations to evaluate, for large k it is obvious that a brute force approach is not feasible (for example, if $k = 20$, then $2^k - 1 = 1,048,575$).

"Stepwise regression" is a heuristic technique for avoiding this computational problem. It begins by selecting the single independent variable which is the "best" predictor in the sense that it maximizes R^2. Then it adds variables to the equation in a sequential manner, in order of importance. At each step the variable added is the one which increases the sum of squares (and hence R^2) or equivalently reduces the residual sum of squares by the largest amount. This procedure not only selects variables, but deletes variables previously selected, if at some point they no longer appear important.

Stepwise regression does not guarantee that the "best" set of variables will be included in the final equation. However, it does provide an efficient method for reducing the number of variables k to a manageable size; e.g., if $k = 100$ then stepwise regression can be used to select the best 25 or fewer for more exhaustive study. Stepwise regression programs are widely available; see Draper and Smith (1981).

In addition to stepwise regression, numerous other techniques have been developed. One which seems to have great potential was developed by Hocking and Leslie (1967) and improved by LaMotte and Hocking (1970). Their algorithm finds the "best" subset of variables of size 1, 2, . . . , k where k is the total number of variables submitted. Although the computations require more time than the stepwise procedure, this procedure guarantees the best subset in the R^2 sense and in addition gives a number of the "contending" subsets. (Of course, if the number of variables is small, we could compute all regressions.) These "best" regression algorithms are available in BMDP, and can handle k up to 20 or 25 without computer time problems.

The set of possible variables should be selected on the basis of preliminary investigations of the factors which influence the response variables. The indiscriminate use of regression analysis to "find" relationships, where no facts suggest the existence of a relationship, often leads to nonsensical results. Unfortunately, this is usually discovered after the prediction equation fails miserably in predicting future observations.

If a large amount of data is available, one portion of it can be used for selecting variables and estimating coefficients, saving the remainder of the data for testing the derived equations. In any case, the equation should be periodically reviewed as new data become available.

A powerful tool in modern regression analysis is the C_p statistic (see, e.g., Dudewicz and Karian, 1985, pp. 236, 413). While R^2 measures the goodness of the regression equation in predicting the data points in the data set one is using to develop a model, C_p estimates the variance of future predictions made using the model. While adding a variable will increase the R^2 (even if that variable is totally unrelated to what we are trying to predict), C_p typically decreases as variables are added to the model, then increases. Thus, searching for the minimal C_p statistic in all possible regressions is a reasonable approach—though if a large gain in R^2 can be obtained with a modest increase in C_p, it should be taken.

REFERENCES

ASQC (1987). "QA/QC Software Directory." *Quality Progress,* March, pp. 33–66.

Barr, Donald R. (1969). "Using Confidence Intervals to Test Hypotheses." *Journal of Quality Technology,* vol. 1, no. 4, pp. 256–258.

Bennett, Carl A. and Franklin, Norman L. (1954). *Statistical Analysis in Chemistry and the Chemical Industry.* John Wiley & Sons, New York, chap. 11.

Bingham, R. S., Jr. (1962). "Tolerance Limits and Process Capability Studies." *Industrial Quality Control,* vol. XIX, no. 1, pp. 36–40.

Choksi, Suresh (1971). "Computer Can Optimize Manufacturing Tolerances for an Economical Design." *ASQC Technical Conference Transactions,* Milwaukee, pp. 323–330.

Cohen, A. Clifford and Whitten, Betty Jones (1981). "Estimation of Lognormal Distributions." *American Journal of Mathematical and Management Sciences,* vol. 1, no. 2, pp. 139–153.

Daniel, Cuthbert (1977). Personal Communication. August.

———— and Wood, Fred S. (1971). *Fitting Equations to Data.* John Wiley & Sons, New York.

Dielman, Terry E. and Pfaffenberger, Roger C. (1984). "Computational Algorithms for Calculating Least Absolute Value and Chebyshev Estimates for Multiple Regression." *American Journal of Mathematical and Management Sciences,* vol. 4, nos. 1 and 2, pp. 169–197.

Dixon, W. J. (1983). *BMDP Statistical Software, 1983 Printing with Additions.* University of California Press, Berkeley, CA.

———— and Massey, Frank J., Jr. (1969). *Introduction to Statistical Analysis,* 3rd ed., McGraw-Hill, New York.

Dodge, H. F., Kinsburg, B. J., and Kruger, M. K. (1953). "The L3 Coaxial System—Quality Control Requirements." *Bell System Technical Journal,* vol. 32, pp. 943–1005.

Draper, N. R. and Smith, H. (1981). *Applied Regression Analysis,* 2nd ed., John Wiley & Sons, New York.

Dudewicz, Edward J. (1976). *Introduction to Statistics and Probability.* Holt, Rinehart and Winston, New York. (Currently published by American Sciences Press, Columbus, OH. Address: P.O. Box 21161, Columbus 43221-0161.)

————— (1980). *Solutions in Statistics and Probability,* American Sciences Press, Columbus, OH.

————— (1983). "Heteroscedasticity." In N. L. Johnson, S. Kotz, and C. B. Read (eds.), *Encyclopedia of Statistical Sciences, Volume 3.* John Wiley & Sons, New York, pp. 611–619.

————— and Dalal, Siddhartha R. (1983). "Multiple-Comparisons with a Control when Variances Are Unknown and Unequal." *American Journal of Mathematical and Management Sciences,* vol. 3, no. 4, pp. 275–295.

————— and Karian, Zaven A. (1985). *Modern Design and Analysis of Discrete-Event Computer Simulations.* IEEE Computer Society Press, Los Angeles, CA. (Address is P.O. Box 80452, Worldway Postal Center, Los Angeles 90080; Order No. CN597.)

————— and Mishra, S. N. (1988). *Modern Mathematical Statistics.* John Wiley, New York.

————— and Ralley, Thomas G. (1981). *The Handbook of Random Number Generation and Testing with TESTRAND Computer Code,* American Sciences Press, Columbus, OH.

————— Karian, Zaven A. and Marshall, Rudolph James III (1985). "Random Number Generation on Microcomputers." *Proceedings of the Conference on Simulation on Microcomputers.* The Society for Computer Simulation (Simulation Councils, Inc.), La Jolla, CA. (Address: P.O. Box 2228, La Jolla, 92038.)

Duncan, Acheson J. (1974). *Quality Control and Industrial Statistics,* 4th ed., Richard D. Irwin, Homewood, IL.

Epstein, Benjamin (1960). "Estimation from Life Test Data." *Technometrics,* vol. 2, no. 4, pp. 447–454.

Evans, Ralph A. (1966). "Problems in Probability." *Proceedings of the Annual Symposium on Reliability,* IEEE, New York, pp. 347–353.

Fisher, R. A. (1936). "The Use of Multiple Measurements in Taxonomic Problems." *Annals of Eugenics,* vol. 7, pp. 179–188.

Gibbons, Jean Dickinson (1985). *Nonparametric Methods for Quantitative Analysis,* 2nd ed. American Sciences Press, Columbus, OH.

Golden, Bruce, L., Assad, Arjang A. and Zanakis, Stelios H. (eds.) (1984). *Statistics and Optimization: The Interface.* American Sciences Press, Columbus, OH.

Govindarajulu, Z. (1981). *The Sequential Statistical Analysis of Hypothesis Testing, Point and Interval Estimation, and Decision Theory.* American Sciences Press, Columbus, OH.

Grant, E. L. and Leavenworth, R. S. (1980). *Statistical Quality Control,* 5th ed., McGraw-Hill, New York.

Gray, H. L. and Lewis, Truman (1967). "A Confidence Interval for the Availability Ratio." *Technometrics,* vol. 9, no. 3, pp. 465–471.

Grubbs, Frank E. (1969). "Procedures for Detecting Outlying Observations in Samples." *Technometrics,* vol. 11, no. 1, pp. 1–21.

Gutt, J. D. and Gruska, G. F. (1977). "Variation Simulation." *ASQC Technical Conference Transactions,* Milwaukee, pp. 557–563.

Hadley, G. (1967). *Introduction to Probability and Statistical Decision Theory.* Holden-Day, San Francisco.

Hahn, G. J. (1970a). "Additional Factors for Calculating Prediction Intervals for Samples from a Normal Distribution." *Journal of the American Statistical Association,* vol. 65, no. 332, pp. 1668–1676.

————— (1970b). "Statistical Intervals for a Normal Population, Part I, Tables, Examples and Applications; Part II, Formulas, Assumptions, Some Derivations." *Journal of Quality Technology,* vol. 2, no. 3, pp. 115–125; vol. 2, no. 4, pp. 195–206.

————— (1971). "How Abnormal is Normality?" *Journal of Quality Technology,* vol. 3, no. 1, pp. 18–22.

————— (1972). "The Absolute Sample Size is What Counts." *Quality Progress,* vol. V, no. 5, pp. 18–19.

————— and Shapiro, S. S. (1967). *Statistical Models in Engineering.* John Wiley & Sons, New York.

Harter, H. Leon (1983). *The Chronological Annotated Bibliography of Order Statistics, Volume II: 1950–1959.* American Sciences Press, Columbus, OH.

————— and Dubey, Satya D. (1967). *Theory and Tables for Tests of Hypotheses concerning the Mean and the Variance of a Weibull Population.* Document AD 653593, Clearinghouse for Federal Scientific and Technical Information, U.S. Department of Commerce, Washington, DC.

Hocking, R. R. and Leslie, R. N. (1967). "Selection of the Best Subset in Regression Analysis." *Technometrics,* vol. 9, no. 4, pp. 531–540.

Hoerl, Arthur E. and Kennard, Robert W. (1981). "Ridge Regression—1980, Advances, Algorithms, and Applications." *American Journal of Mathematical and Management Sciences,* vol. 1, no. 1, pp. 5–83.

Iman, Ronald L. (1982). "Graphs for Use with the Lillefors Test for Normal and Exponential Distributions." *The American Statistician,* vol. 36, no. 2, pp. 109–112.

Ireson, W. Grant (ed.) (1982). *Reliability Handbook.* McGraw-Hill, New York.

Johnson, Norman L. and Kotz, Samuel (1969). *Discrete Distributions.* Houghton Mifflin, Boston.

Johnson, Norman L. and Leone, Fred C. (1964). *Statistics and Experimental Design, Vol. I.* John Wiley & Sons, New York.

Juran, J. M. and Gryna, Frank M., Jr. (1980). *Quality Planning and Analysis,* 2nd ed. McGraw-Hill, New York.

Kececioglu, D. and Cormier, D. (1964). "Designing a Specified Reliability into a Component." *Proceedings of the Third Annual Aerospace Reliability and Maintainability Conference.* Society of Automotive Engineers, Washington, DC, p. 546.

King, James R. (1971). *Probability Charts for Decision Making.* The Industrial Press, New York.

Kirkpatrick, R. L. (1970). "Confidence Limits on a Percent Defective Characterized by Two Specification Limits." *Journal of Quality Technology,* vol. 2, no. 3, pp. 150–155.

Kramer, C. Y. and Jensen, D. R. (1969, 1970). "Fundamentals of Multivariate Analysis." *Journal of Quality Technology,* vol. 1, no. 2, pp. 120–133, no. 3, pp. 189–204, no. 4, pp. 264–276; vol. 2, no. 1, pp. 32–40.

LaMotte, L. R. and Hocking, R. R. (1970). "Computational Efficiency in the Selection of Regression Variables." *Technometrics,* vol. 12, no. 1, pp. 83–93.

Lenz, H.-J. and Rendtel, U. (1984). "Performance Evaluation of the MIL-STD-105 D, Skip-Lot Sampling Plans, and Bayesian Single Sampling Plans." In Lenz, H.-J., Wetherill, G. B., and Wilrich, P.-Th. (eds.), *Frontiers in Statistical Quality Control 2.* Physica-Verlag, Rudolf Liebing GmbH & Co., Würzburg, W. Germany, pp. 92–106.

Levy, George C. and Dumoulin, Charles L. (1984). *The LAB ONE NMR1 Spectroscopic Data Analysis Software System, Revision 2.00 User's Manual.* Department of Chemistry, Syracuse University, Syracuse, NY. (Address: Dept. of Chemistry, Browne Hall, Syracuse University, Syracuse 13244.)

Lieberman, G. J. and Owen, D. B. (1961). *Tables of the Hypergeometric Probability Distribution.* Stanford University Press, Stanford, CA.

Lloyd, David K. and Lipow, Myron (1982). *Reliability: Management, Methods and Mathematics,* 2nd ed. Prentice-Hall, Englewood Cliffs, NJ.

Longley, J. W. (1967). "An appraisal of Least Squares Programs for the Electronic Computer from the Point of View of the User." *Journal of the American Statistical Association,* vol. 62, no. 319, pp. 819–841.

Lusser, R. (1958). *Reliability through Safety Margins.* United States Army Ordnance Missile Command, Redstone Arsenal, AL.

Martin Marietta Corp. (1966). *Reliability for the Engineer, Book 5: Testing for Reliability.* Martin Marietta, Orlando, FL, pp. 29–31.

Moult, John F. (1963). "Critical Agents in Bearing Fatigue Testing." *Lubrication Engineering,* December, pp. 503–511.

Mouradian, G. (1966). "Tolerance Limits for Assemblies and Engineering Relationships." *ASQC Technical Conference Transactions,* Milwaukee, pp. 598–606.

Natrella, Mary G. (1963). *Experimental Statistics, National Bureau of Standards Handbook 91.* Government Printing Office, Washington, DC.

Nelson, Wayne (1979). *How to Analyze Data with Simple Plots.* Volume 1 of Dudewicz, E. J. (ed.), *The ASQC Basic References in Quality Control: Statistical Techniques.* American Society for Quality Control, Milwaukee.

———— (1982). *Applied Life Data Analysis.* John Wiley & Sons, New York.

Oliver, Larry R. and Springer, Melvin D. (1972). "A General Set of Bayesian Attribute Acceptance Sampling Plans." *Technical Papers of the 1972 Conference, American Institute of Industrial Engineers,* pp. 443–455.

Owen, D. B. and Frawley, W. H. (1971). "Factors for Tolerance Limits which Control Both Tails of the Normal Distribution." *Journal of Quality Technology,* vol. 3, no. 2, pp. 69–79. See also Frawley, W. H., Kapadia, C. H., Rao, J. N. K., and Owen, D. B. (1971). "Tolerance Limits Based on Range and Mean Range." *Technometrics,* vol. 13, no. 3, pp. 651–656.

Peters, J. (1970). "Tolerancing the Components of an Assembly for Minimum Cost." ASME Paper 70-Prod.-9, *Transactions of the ASME Journal of Engineering for Industry,* American Society of Mechanical Engineers, New York.

Pinsky, Paul D. (1983). *Statpro, The Statistics and Graphics Database Workstation, Statistics User's Guide.* Wadsworth Electronic Publishing Company, Boston. (Address: Statler Office Building, 20 Park Plaza, Boston 02116.)

Ramberg, John S., Dudewicz, Edward J., Tadikamalla, Pandu R., and Mykytka, Edward F. (1979). "A Probability Distribution and its Uses in Fitting Data." *Technometrics,* vol. 21, no. 2, pp. 201–214.

Ranganathan, J. and Kale, B. K. (1983). "Outlier-Resistant Tolerance Intervals for Exponential Distributions." *American Journal of Mathematical and Management Sciences,* vol. 3, no. 1, pp. 5–25.

Rich, Barrett G., Smith, O. A., and Korte, Lee (1967). *Experience with a Formal Reliability Program.* SAE Paper 670731, Farm, Construction and Industrial Machinery Meeting, Society of Automotive Engineers, Warrendale, PA.

Rutherford, John R. (1971). "A Logic Structure for Experimental Development Programs." *Chemical Technology,* March, pp. 159–164.

SAS Institute Inc. (1982). *SAS User's Guide: Basics, 1982 Edition.* SAS Institute, Cary, NC. (Address: P.O. Box 8000, Cary 27511.)

Sheesley, J. H. (1977). "Tests for Outlying Observations." *Journal of Quality Technology,* vol. 9, no. 1, pp. 38–41.

Siotani, Minoru, Hayakawa, T., and Fujikoshi, Y. (1985). *Modern Multivariate Statistical Analysis: A Graduate Course and Handbook.* American Sciences Press, Columbus, OH.

Thoman, D. R., Bain, L. J., and Antle, C. E. (1970). "Maximum Likelihood Estimation, Exact Confidence Intervals for Reliability and Tolerance Limits in the Weibull Distribution." *Technometrics,* vol. 12, no. 2, pp. 363–371.

Volk, William (1956). "Industrial Statistics." *Chemical Engineering,* March, pp. 165–190.

Wampler, R. H. (1970). "On the Accuracy of Least Squares Computer Programs." *Journal of the American Statistical Association,* vol. 65, no. 330, pp. 549–565.

Wescott, M. E. *Mimeo Notes.* Rochester Institute of Technology, Rochester, NY.

Western Electric Company, Inc. (1982). *Statistical Quality Control Handbook.* American Society for Quality Control, Milwaukee.

Williamson, E. and Bretherton, M. H. (1963). *Tables of the Negative Binomial Probability Distribution.* John Wiley & Sons, New York.

Zacks, Shelemyahu (1983). *Workshop on Statistical Methods of Reliability Analysis for Engineers.* Center for Statistics, Quality Control, and Design, State University of New York, Binghamton, NY.

SECTION 24
STATISTICAL PROCESS CONTROL[1]

Dorian Shainin, CMC
Peter D. Shainin, PE

DEFINITIONS **24.2**

NOTATION **24.2**

SPC THEORY **24.3**
Control Charts 24.3
PRE-Control 24.4
New Developments in
Diagnostic Techniques . 24.5
Random Cause, Pareto, and
the Red X 24.5

CONTROL CHARTS **24.7**
Uses of Control Charts . . 24.7
Basic Concepts of Control
Charts 24.8
Steps in Setting Up Control
Charts 24.12

TYPES OF CONTROL CHARTS . **24.14**
Variables versus Attributes
Data 24.14
Variables Data 24.14
Attributes Data 24.20

Cumulative Sum Control
Charts 24.26
Constructing a Control
Chart for Maintaining
Control in the Future
(Control with Standard
Given) 24.29
Special Control Charts . . . 24.31

PRE-CONTROL **24.31**
PRE-Control Theory . . . 24.31
Requirements for Use . . . 24.33
Setting Up PRE-Control . 24.33
Using PRE-Control 24.34
Risk 24.35
Implementation 24.36
Comparison of $\overline{X}$, R Charts
and PRE-Control 24.36

*STATISTICAL CONTROL OF
AUTOMATED PROCESSES* . . . **24.36**
Software for Statistical
Process Control 24.38

REFERENCES **24.39**

---

[1]In the Third Edition, the section on Process Control by Statistical Methods was prepared by C. A. Bicking and Frank M. Gryna.

This section of the handbook is concerned with those statistical tools which have been evolved to quantify the elements of the feedback loop and to put process controls on a quantified basis. Other aspects of process control are discussed elsewhere in the handbook, and include:

Topic	*Discussed in*
Management universals of the feedback loop	Section 6 under The Feedback Loop
Ability of process to meet standards	Section 16 under Process Capability
Control system for dominant process variables	Section 16 under Planning Process Controls
Product acceptance	Section 25, Acceptance Sampling
Attainment of Optimum Process Conditions	Section 26 under Evolutionary Operations and Response Surface Methodology
Role of process control personnel in closing the loop	Section 17 under Concept of Self-Control

Appendix III, Selected Quality Standards, Specifications, and Related Documents, includes documents on control charts.

We start with some definitions and notation.

DEFINITIONS

Process: Any specific combination of machines, tools, methods, materials and/or people employed to attain specific qualitites in a product or service. A change in any one of these constituents results in a *new* process. These qualities (a dimension, material property, appearance, etc.) will be called "quality characteristics" to avoid confusion with levels of quality. Some processes are manufacturing processes; some are service processes; still others are support operations common to both manufacturing and service industries.

Control: The control process is a feedback loop through which we measure actual performance, compare it with standard, and act on the difference. The quicker the response to deviation from the standard, the more uniform the produced quality.

Statistical process control (SPC): The application of statistical techniques for measuring and analyzing the variation in processes.

Statistical quality control (SQC): The application of statistical techniques for measuring and improving the quality of processes. SQC includes SPC, diagnostic tools, sampling plans, and other statistical techniques.

NOTATION

In mathematics, causes are traditionally x's, and effects, y's. We will refer to the features which affect customer enthusiasm as y's and the specific quality characteristics which cause them to vary as x's. The variables which control the x's will be A's, B's, C's, etc. Cutting oil temperature on a lathe, variable A, will affect the diameter of a pump shaft cut on that lathe, quality characteristic x_1, which in turn affects the hydraulic leakage past a shaft seal, feature y_1.

Observed data are samples coming from unknown populations. In keeping with the convention of ANSI/ASQC (1985), population parameters will be represented by Greek letters and sample data by Roman letters. An overbar represents an average. A double overbar represents an average of averages (see Appendix I, Glossary of Symbols).

SPC THEORY

Control Charts. Dr. Walter A. Shewhart, of Bell Telephone Laboratories, developed a theory of statistical quality control in the second half of the 1920s. He analyzed many different processes and concluded: All manufacturing processes display variation. He identified two components: a steady component which appeared to be inherent in the process, and an intermittent component. Shewhart attributed inherent variation, currently called *random*[2] variation, to chance and undiscoverable causes, and intermittent variation to *assignable* causes. He concluded that assignable causes could be economically discovered and removed with a tenacious diagnostic program, but that random causes could not be economically discovered and could not be removed without making basic changes in the process.

The variation of any particular quality characteristic can be quantified by sampling the output of the process and estimating the parameters of its statistical distribution. Changes in the distribution can be revealed by plotting these parameters versus time. Samples usually consist of more than one individual measurement, and so are called "subgroups." Charts for variables are usually based on a subgroup size of 4 to 10 individuals, charts for attributes on a minimum of 50 and often several hundred individuals. Twenty-five subgroups are measured. For $\overline{X}$ and R charts, the most common type, the quality characteristic, X, is measured for each individual. The average, $\overline{X}$, and range, R, are calculated for each subgroup and plotted *in order of production* on separate charts. A central line is drawn on each chart at the grand average, $\overline{\overline{X}}$ and at the average range, $\overline{R}$. Control limits are established at the average ± 3 standard deviations. These are the upper control limit (UCL) and lower control limit (LCL). An example is shown in Figure 24.1 (Kukunaris, 1985).

The band between the control limits defines the random variation in the process. Points outside of the control limits indicate one or more assignable causes of variation. A process with only random causes present is said to be in "statistical control." Its output is considered to be as uniform as economically feasible.

After an assignable cause of variation is discovered and removed, new control limits calculated from 25 new subgroup averages and ranges often give a substantially narrower process capability. Under control chart theory this new process capability becomes the economic limit to improvement.

---

[2]*Random* in this sense means of unknown and insignificant cause, as distinguished from the mathematical definition of random—without cause. For a complete discussion, see Wadsworth and Bryan (1974), p. 40.

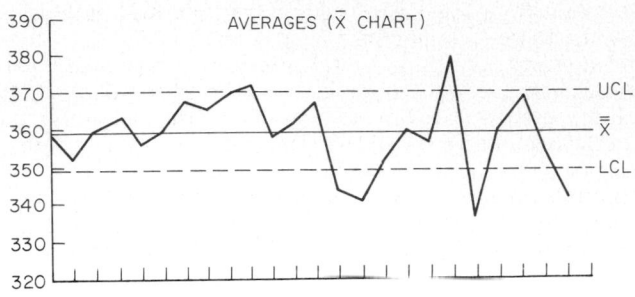

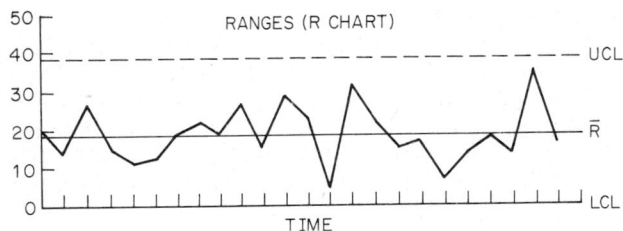

FIG. 24.1   Control chart for linewidth—proximity print photoresist process.

Shewhart organized his research material for a course at Bell Telephone Laboratories, then presented his theory to the outside world in a series of lectures at Stevens Institute of Technology. This lecture material became his well-known book, *Economic Control of Quality of Manufactured Product* (1931).

Shewhart's charts came into wide use in the 1940s as a result of war production efforts. Those who used them realized substantial gains in quality and productivity but also had difficulties in performing the required calculations and interpreting the charts. In the late 1940s and early 1950s there were many attempts to simplify the calculations and broaden the applicability of Shewhart's methods. In 1953 a team[3] from Rath & Strong, Inc., Management Consultants of Boston, MA, under contract to Jones & Lamson Machine Co. of Springfield, VT, developed PRE-Control. It was first published in 1954 and its first extensive production use was by J & L's customer, IBM, at Endicott, NY, in 1954.

PRE-Control.   PRE-Control is a simple algorithm which gives the worker direct control of his or her process. The tolerance band is divided into three zones, a target zone bounded by two cautionary zones. The worker measures a pair of individuals periodically. If both fall in the cautionary zones or either falls outside the tolerance, the operator adjusts the process immediately. Otherwise, the process is left alone. The subgroup of two does not attempt to estimate the distribution parameters, only to sense whether the distribution is safely within the tolerance or has either moved toward a tolerance limit or grown wider than the tolerance.

---

[3]The team consisted of Warren R. Purcell, Franklin E. Satterthwaite, C. W. (Bill) Carter, and Dorian Shainin.

This rapid warning allows the worker to adjust before nonconforming work is produced; thus, the name "PRE-Control."

Both $\overline{X}$ and R charts and PRE-Control enjoy wide usage today. Many of the calculation and charting difficulties associated with $\overline{X}$ and R charts have been overcome with computers. PRE-Control requires no calculations or charting. A later portion of this section presents procedures for using PRE-Control.

New Developments in Diagnostic Techniques. Since the introduction of Shewhart's theory, great strides have been made in statistics and their applications to quality control. Sir Ronald Fisher developed factorial experiments and his principles of replication, randomization, and balance (Fisher, 1935). Dr. Frank Yates (1937) published his algorithm for analyzing factorial experiments (see Section 26 under Factorial Experiments with k Factors). Leonard Seder developed Multi-Vari (see Section 22 under Diagnosis of Management-Controllable Problems), an effective charting method for analyzing variation in a process (Seder, 1950); and J. M. Juran generalized Pareto's principle: Most of the trouble comes from a few of the causes (Juran, 1950; see Section 22 under Pareto Concept). These techniques, used together, have proved to be very powerful. With them we can economically reduce variation to levels well below those of Shewhart's time. There is still a minimum level; but as our tools get better, that level gets lower. An optimist would conclude that in the next 60 years we will be able to reduce variation to levels that are inconceivable today.

Random Cause, Pareto, and the Red X. The variation described by the statistical distribution of a quality characteristic has many separate causes. The Pareto principle tells us that a few of these causes will have a major effect on the total variation. A few more will have a somewhat lesser effect. Most will have a very small effect.

Figure 24.2 illustrates the relative magnitude of effect of each of the many causes of variation. But each cause itself varies and can be described as a statistical distribution. This is illustrated in Figure 24.3.

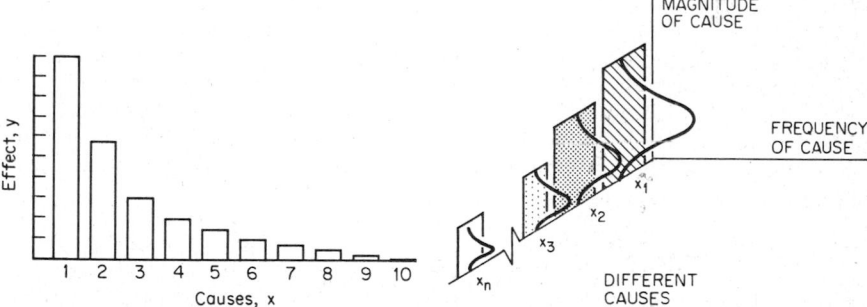

FIG. 24.2 Pareto curve.   FIG. 24.3 Distribution of causes.

Some x's are causing the quality characteristic y to move in one direction while others are causing it to move in the opposite direction and by different amounts at each different point in time. The dispersion of each of these distributions is measured by its standard deviation σ. Independent standard deviations add by the square root of the sum of the squares rule. The total variation of a quality characteristic, $\Delta x = (x_1^2 + x_2^2 + x_3^2 + x_4^2 + \cdots + x_n^2)^{1/2}$. If $x_1 = 5$ and $x_4 = 1$, then $x_1^2 = 25$ while $x_4^2 = 1$. The total effect of x_1 on variation will be 25 times the effect of x_4 even though it is only 5 times larger! This largest cause is called the "red X." The second largest is a "pink X." The shade becomes lighter as the cause becomes more minor.

Normal distributions are the result of many approximately equal causes of variation. The Pareto principle would lead us to expect that most distributions of quality characteristics would not be quite normal. Both Shewhart's and the authors' experience confirm this.

A red X will cause a distribution of *individuals* to be nonnormal, but a subgroup size of four is large enough to cause the distribution of *averages* to be very close to normal. Thus, virtually all of the averages will fall within the ± 3 standard deviation control limits. A large, steady red X will increase the dispersion of subgroup averages and/or change the location of the overall average, but it will not usually show up as an assignable cause. Assignable causes result from one or more transient red X's.

If 25 subgroups are taken to establish control limits for a new process and the process is affected by one or more transient causes during the sample period, the distribution of subgroup averages which is estimated by these 25 subgroups is an average of the different distributions of subgroup averages which existed at each different time that subgroups were taken. Subgroup averages outside of these control limits indicate that the distribution which existed at the time of the out-of-limit subgroups were taken is probably different from the "average" distribution for which the control limits were calculated.

Shewhart's assignable cause was a transient red X. His random causes were the minor X's. As each minor X was found and eliminated, it made hardly any difference at all in the process output. No wonder Shewhart thought it was not economically feasible to reduce variation below this "random" level. Unfortunately, a consistent red X will appear on a control chart as part of the random variation, and a consistent red X is the rule rather than the exception in the authors' experience. With the diagnostic techniques mentioned above, we can usually find that red X.

When Shewhart developed his theory, the concept of statistically analyzing the variation of a process in order to improve quality was unheard of. His work was truly pioneering. He intended his book as a prospectus of the future in quality control. The preface states, "This book constitutes a record of progress and an indication of the direction in which future developments may be expected to take place" (p. vii). Unfortunately, as is often the case in such matters, Shewhart's prospectus has become orthodoxy for many of today's quality control practitioners.

The concepts of improving a process by analyzing its variation and of a continuous and tenacious program to attack variation, as given to us by Shewhart, remain central to modern statistical quality control methods. The concept of dividing the causes of variation into assignable and chance catagories is of less practical use today. Processes which are running within correctly determined tolerances should be left alone. Processes which are displaying excessive variation (not running within tolerance all the time) should be investigated and improved using Multi-Vari and Factorial experiments. There are circumstances in which product uniformity around a target value is more important than the percent of product that meets specifications. See Section 16 under Process Capability; the Concept. See also Section 17 under Ability to Regulate (particularly Table 17.6) for a discussion of action to be taken considering both statistical control limits and product tolerances.

Marketing people must determine which features are important to customers and the range of each required to evoke enthusiasm. The engineering people must determine which quality characteristic(s) causes each feature and the critical range of each. This quality characteristic range becomes the manufacturing tolerance.

Many manuals on control charts suggest that if a process capability is wider than a tolerance, consideration should be given to expanding the tolerance. If the tolerance was set by an engineering guess, a common occurrence, process capability might be as good a reason as any to change it. But if the tolerance was set correctly, the tolerance must stay where it is and the process capability must be improved. If one does not find the red X, but a competitor does, one's market will be gone before one knows it.

CONTROL CHARTS

Uses of Control Charts.   Control charts are commonly used to:

1. Attain a state of statistical control (all subgroup averages and ranges within control limits; therefore, no assignable causes of variation present).
2. Monitor a process.
3. Determine process capability. *After* the process is in control, the limits of process variation can be determined. Since the control limits are established for averages, they must be multiplied by $\sqrt{n}$ (n = subgroup size) before they can be compared to tolerances. (See Section 16 under Process Capability Measurement for further discussion.)

A surprising number of companies try to use $\overline{X}$ and R for product acceptance purposes. They form subgroups by taking individuals at random from the entire lot. This is an incorrect procedure. Subgroups must be formed in production sequence.

Control charts can have an important role in product acceptance. Processes that are capable of meeting specifications and are in statistical control are prime candidates for auditing by acceptance sampling. Statistical control verifies the stability of the process and homogeneity of the product. Then a variety of sampling procedures (or no sampling at all) can be effectively applied. One of those procedures makes use of subgroups and simple statistical limits (see Section 25 under Variables Sampling; Lot Plot).

Attaining a State of Control.   Construct a control chart to attain a state of statistical control by:

1. Take 25 subgroups. The subgroup size will depend on the type of chart. Charts for variables data typically use four or five measurements; charts for attributes data employ subgroup sizes that depend on the specific type of chart.
2. Keep a log of any process changes (material, worker, tool, etc.) during the collection of these data.
3. Compute trial control limits from these data (see specific chart type for instructions).
4. Chart the data for each subgroup on their respective charts. If all points are within the control limits, the process is in statistical control. If any points fall outside the control limits, the process is not in statistical control. Find the assignable cause of this excessive variation and eliminate it. Retest as above to ensure that no assignable causes remain.

Most industrial processes are not in control when first analyzed; many points outside of control limits are common. The reasons for these assignable causes can be discovered and removed (Section 22 under Diagnosis). Mark explanations found for points out of control right on the chart. As remedies are made to the process, new data should be collected, control limits recalculated, and the new data plotted against the revised limits. Control is often attained by degrees. Removing assignable cause and recalculating control limits can be an iterative process. For an example, see Juran and Gryna (1980).

When it is difficult to collect new data, it is common practice to remove the out-of-control subgroups and recalculate the limits from the remaining data. But if new data are not taken, there is no way to be sure all assignable causes have been removed. Control limits and central lines calculated with new data will often be different than those calculated by modifying original data.

Control limits calculated from 10 rather than 25 subgroups are common practice, especially where production runs are short. Unfortunately, their proper location is known with considerably less precision.

Even if no process changes have consciously been made, it is a good idea to recalculate central lines for every 25 subgroups. In practice the old and new central lines are usually compared without any formal test. The procedures in Section 23 under Tests of Hypotheses could also be used.

Monitoring a Process. Control charts can monitor the aim and variability and thereby continually check the *stability* of the process. This check of stability in turn helps to assure that the statistical distribution of the product characteristic is consistent with quality requirements. For parts per million defect levels, tight process control procedures are the key answer to the high sample sizes that would be necessary with acceptance sampling procedures.

Basic Concepts of Control Charts

Estimating the Mean, μ. Shewhart investigated both the subgroup median and the subgroup mean as estimators of μ. He concluded that the mean, $\overline{X}$, was a more sensitive estimator. The mean of a subgroup is the sum of all of the individual points in that subgroup divided by the number of points in that subgroup. $\overline{X} = \Sigma X_i / n$.

Estimating the Standard Deviation σ. Subgroup range R is commonly used to estimate the standard deviation of the distribution of X's, σ_x. For subgroup size n of 2, R is as efficient an estimator of σ_x as the standard deviation of the subgroups s. Both statistics use all of the available data. For $n = 3$, s becomes a more efficient statistic. s uses all three of the data points in each subgroup. R uses only the two end points and thus ignores the information contained in the center point. For hand calculation and small n's, the ease of use and reduced possibility of error make R a better choice than s. Tippet (1950) recommends R for $n \leq 20$. ANSI/ASQC (1985) recommends R for manual calculation and $n \leq 10$.

$$\sigma_X \simeq \overline{R}/d_2 \simeq \overline{s}/c_2 \qquad s_X = \sqrt{\Sigma(X - \overline{X})^2/(n - 1)}$$

$$R = X_{\text{LARGEST}} - X_{\text{SMALLEST}} \qquad \overline{R} = \frac{\Sigma R}{N}$$

d_2 and c_2 are functions of subgroup size and may be found in Table A, Appendix II. Both R and s are valid estimators of σ_X only if the subgroups are taken at random from a stable population (Tippett, 1950, pp. 9–10). Since it is common practice to take subgroups periodically rather than at random, there is a risk that the frequency of sampling will align with the action of some unknown variable and produce a range or standard deviation out of proportion to σ_X.

Control Limits.   Control limits based on the statistical variation of the process can be established at the mean ± 3 standard deviations of the parameter. If the parameter being charted is distributed normally, about 99.73 percent of all values will fall within the control limits. Therefore, if a point falls outside the control limits, there are only 27 chances in 10,000 that the distribution has not changed. A red X probably caused the distribution to shift, grow wider, or both. The chance of a false out-of-control signal for control limits set at other multiples of σ_X can be found in a table of areas under the normal curve (Table B, Appendix II). The distribution of $\overline{X}$ will always be very close to normal for $n \geq 4$. The distribution of X may or may not be normal. See the specific chart types below for the formulas and factors used to calculate control limits.

The control limits for R will be too wide if the distribution of X's is skewed or leptokurtic (more pointed top and longer, thinner tails than normal); too narrow if the distribution of X's is platykurtic (flatter top than normal). If the value of $\overline{X}$ changes within the subgroups while the subgroups for setting control limits are being taken, the control limits for R will be too wide. Trending factors such as tool wear or temperature increase are a common cause of this malady. Subgroups taken too far apart will make this situation worse. Too small a number of subgroups can give an inaccurate $\overline{R}$ and thus incorrect control limits for both $\overline{X}$ and R. If the control limits for $\overline{X}$ and R are too wide, the risk of missing a signal for action (β risk) increases. If the control limits for R are too narrow, the risk of getting a false out-of-control signal (α risk) increases.

Control limits can also be calculated to include a preassigned percentage (e.g., 99.0 percent) of the charted values when the process is in statistical control. For formulas and factors, see ANSI/ASQC (1985).

A note of caution: A state of "statistical control" merely means that only random causes are present. It does not necessarily mean that the product meets specifications. Conversely, a process which is not in statistical control may still be producing product which conforms to specification. Action on such a process should have a much lower priority than action on processes which are producing nonconforming product.

Subgroup Size, n.   Since $\sigma_{\overline{X}} = \sigma_X / \sqrt{n}$, the larger the subgroup size, n, the smaller the standard deviation of the distribution of averages, $\sigma_{\overline{X}}$, the tighter the 3σ control limits, and the more sensitive the chart for $\overline{X}$. However, as n gets larger, the time required to obtain and plot the data gets longer. Transient red X's can do substantial damage before they are discovered. The sensitivity of a chart for detecting process changes with different subgroup sizes can be defined by an operating characteristic curve. An example is given below. Subgroups are normally of equal size. Grant and Leavenworth (1980) give procedures for unequal subgroups. Four and five are common subgroup sizes for variable data.

See Control Charts for Fraction Nonconforming, below, for a discussion of subgroup size when charting attribute data.

Rational Subgrouping.   Each subgroup must come from a single distinct population. A subgroup of consecutively produced individuals taken from the same die cavity of a multiple-cavity mold is appropriate.

Improper or irrational choice of subgroups can be visually detected on a plotted $\overline{X}$ and R chart. Two examples are:

1. The $\overline{X}$ points clustered close to the $\overline{\overline{X}}$ line, not filling out the space between the upper and lower control limits

2. The $\overline{X}$ points beyond both control limits most of the time

In both cases the range points nicely fill out the space between their control limits.

The first condition is caused by using items from different die cavities on a multicavity mold in the same subgroup. R is a function of cavity-to-cavity differences rather than of the time-to-time differences on which the charts are based. $\Delta \overline{X}$ is a function of time-to-time differences. Since time-to-time differences are usually much smaller than cavity-to-cavity differences, R and the resulting control limits are inflated relative to $\overline{X}$.

The second condition is caused by taking all of the individuals in one subgroup from the same die cavity but taking successive subgroups from different die cavities. Now R is smaller but $\overline{X}$ is inflated by the cavity-to-cavity differences. In this case R is a function of time but $\Delta \overline{X}$ is a function of cavity geometry.

As a general rule, a separate die cavity must be treated as a separate machine and plotted on a separate set of charts. The same logic holds for any multiple-position machine.

Some authorities recommend taking successive subgroups from different die cavities when monitoring a process that has already been shown to be in control. This would seem to allow one set of charts to do the work of several. If the die cavity numbers are noted with the subgroup average on the chart, cavity-to-cavity variation will be revealed. This is similar to Multi-Vari, but the use of averages makes it less informative.

Why Use Averages? Averages are more sensitive to change than individuals (Figure 24.4). Consider a process in which σ for individual items is 50 and the average of individuals is 1000; therefore, the limit lines will be $1000 + 150 = 1150$ and $1000 - 150 = 850$. A change in process from 1000 to 1100 will change the 3σ limit lines to 1250 and 950. The chance of an individual from the changed process falling outside the first limit lines is about 16 in 100. Detecting the change with a certainty of 99 in 100 will require, on the average, 27 subgroups of one individual each.

If subgroups of four are used, the limit lines will be $1000 \pm 3\sigma/\sqrt{n} = 1000 \pm$ (3×50)/2, 1075 and 925. For the same change in average, from 1000 to 1100, the chance of the average of the subgroup of four falling outside the first limit lines is about 84 in 100. Now to detect the change with a certainty of 99 in 100 will require, on the average, only *two* or *three* subgroups. The risk of not detecting the change is $(0.16)^2 = 0.026$ for two subgroups and $(0.16)^3 = 0.004$ for three subgroups.

Operating Characteristics Curve for a Control Chart. The operating characteristic (OC) curve is a plot of the true value of a process parameter, e.g., the average, against the probability that a single sample will fall within the control limits. It shows the ability of the chart to detect process changes. Figure 24.5 is an OC curve for an $\overline{X}$ control chart with a true average $\mu_X = 45.8$, standard deviation $\sigma_X = 2.9$, and subgroup size $n = 4$. This curve should not be confused with a normal distribution of measurements. In some cases the shape is similar but the meanings are entirely different.

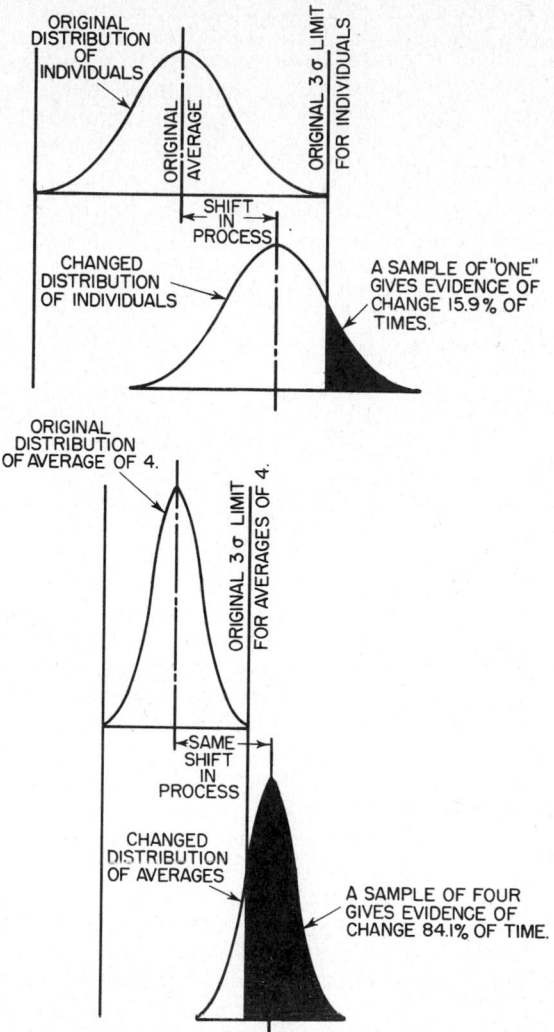

FIG. 24.4 How averages are more sensitive to detecting change than individuals.

If μ_X shifts from 45.8 to 40.0, the probability that a single subgroup average $\overline{X}$ will fall within control limits is about 0.16; there is only a 16 percent chance that a change of this magnitude will be undetected. If the process average shifted only to 43.0, the probability that a single $\overline{X}$ will fall within control limits is about 0.84. It is unlikely this shift would go undetected very long. The probability that it will be undetected after five subgroups is $(0.84)^5 = 0.418$.

The OC curve is a function of the subgroup size n, width of control limits $t\sigma$ (e.g., 1.5σ, 2σ, 3σ), and standard deviation σ. By evaluating the OC curves for various subgroup sizes and control limits, a chart can be designed for unique problems with the best compromise between n and t. Duncan (1974) has excellent discussions on the methods of constructing OC curves for $\overline{X}$, R, p, and c control charts and on the conclusions which can be drawn from these curves. Krishnamoorthi (1985) discusses sensitivity of control charts and presents the concept of customizing a chart to be most economical for the process.

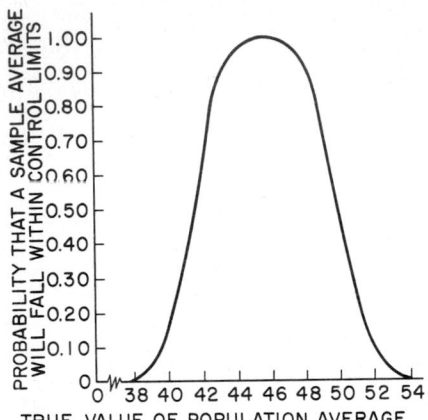

FIG. 24.5 Operating characteristic curve for a control chart.

Steps in Setting Up Control Charts

1. Choose the characteristic to be charted. This is a matter of judgment, but use the following guides:

   a. Give high priority to characteristics that are running defective and where adjustment controls are available to the worker. A Pareto analysis (see Section 22 under The Project Concept) can establish priorities.

   b. Identify the process variables and conditions contributing to end product characteristics. For example, pH, salt concentration, and temperature of plating solution are process variables which could contribute to plating smoothness. A word of warning: The selection of such variables is usually subjective and quite opinionated. Objectivity is needed. A useful step is to make a scatter plot of data on suspected variables versus the end product characteristic for at least 30 items produced at different times.

   c. Choose characteristics which will provide the kind of data needed for diagnosis of problems. Attribute data (e.g., percent defective) provide summary information but may need to be supplemented by variables data (e.g., numerical diameter of individual pieces) to diagnose causes and determine action.

   d. Determine the earliest point in the production process at which testing can be done to get information on assignable causes so that the chart can serve as an effective early warning device to prevent nonconformities.

2. Choose the type of control chart. Table 24.1 compares several basic control charts. The objective is to make items which conform to specifications. The proper use of p, np, u, and c charts should lead to their extinction.

3. Decide the central line to be used and the basis of calculating the control limits. The central line may be the average of past data, or may be a desired average (i.e., a standard value). The limits are usually set at $\pm 3\sigma$, but other multiples may be chosen for different statistical risks. $\pm 3\sigma$ limits involve a very small risk of looking for trouble that does not exist (α or type I risk), but a larger risk of failing to detect trouble when it does exist (β or type II risk). See Section 23 under Statistical Tests of Hypotheses. When the control plan incorporates a statistically determined frequency of taking subgroups, the two types of risk can be balanced. Limits set at $\pm 2\sigma$ would have a large α risk but a smaller β risk. These risks depend on the sample size and other factors. A study by Duncan (1974) found that charts using 2σ or even 1.5σ limits are more economical than charts using the conventional 3σ limits. This is true if it is possible to

TABLE 24.1 Guide to Control Charts Discussed in Section 24

Data type	Parameters plotted	Typical use	Advantages	Disadvantages	Comments
Variables					
$\overline{X}$ and R/s	Subgroup average and range or standard deviation	Machine-dominant processes	A good window into the statistical variation of a process.	Complex calculations; slow response; indirect relationship between control limits and tolerance.	Select subgroup size, frequency and number of subgroups used to set and reset control limits carefully.
X and R	Individual and subgroup range	Where only one observation per lot is available	Quicker, easier to plot and explain. Compares directly to tolerance.	Not as sensitive as $\overline{X}$ and R chart.	
CumSum	Cumulative sum of deviation of subgroup averages from a reference value	High cost product or test where 0.5σ to 2σ shift is common	Faster response to an abrupt shift in mean than $\overline{X}$ and R chart.	Complex, hard to explain.	PRE-Control is faster and simpler.
Attributes					
p	Fraction nonconforming	Only attribute data available or to monitor quality of a complex unit with more than one characteristic of interest	Data is usually easier to obtain than variable data. Calculations are easier than $\overline{X}$ charts.	Attribute data is not as useful for diagnostic work as variable data.	As quality gets better, subgroups get bigger. Eventually, all attribute charts should make themselves obsolete.
np	Number nonconforming				
u	Nonconformities per unit				
c	Number of nonconformities				

decide very quickly and inexpensively that nothing is wrong with the process when a point (just by chance) happens to fall outside the control limits; i.e., when the cost of looking for trouble when none exists is low. Contrariwise, it will be more economical to use charts with 3.5σ to 4σ limits if the cost of looking for trouble is very high.

4. Choose the rational subgroup (see Rational Subgrouping, above).

5. Choose the frequency of subgroups (individuals within a subgroup should be consecutive if possible). The rate of change in the process (tool wear or deterioration of a chemical solution) will determine the maximum time to allow between subgroups. Sample a new process frequently until the data indicate the frequency can be reduced.

6. Choose the subgroup size (see Subgroup Size, above).

7. Provide the system for collecting data. If the control chart is to serve as a day-to-day shop tool, it must be made simple and convenient to use. A shop awash with cutting oil won't do well with ordinary pencil and paper. Special covers, paper, and crayons can help. Measurement must be kept simple and error-free. Instruments must give prompt reliable readings. Direct recording instruments are best. If control charts are being used to monitor a process, data must be plotted and the results given to the worker immediately. Any delay, such as waiting until the end of the day to plot the date, will negate the value of the charts.

8. Calculate the control limits and provide specific instructions on interpretation of results and action to be taken. Ford Motor Company (1984) has prepared a useful guide giving detailed procedures and forms for applying the basic types of control charts. Vance (1983) provides an extensive bibliography of articles classified by type of control chart technique.

TYPES OF CONTROL CHARTS

Variables versus Attributes Data.   Charts for variables data require measurements on a continuous scale such as length, weight, pH, or resistance. Charts for attributes data require only a count of discrete measurements such as good or bad. Variables data include more information than attributes data, thus are preferred for SPC and essential for diagnosis.

Charts for attributes will be useful provided the defective rate is high enough to show on the chart with a reasonable subgroup size. Current competitive quality requirements in many industries are so high that attributes charts are not useful.

Variables Data

Control Chart for Average and Range, $\overline{X}$ and R.   This chart is particularly helpful for machine-dominant processes. Take 25 subgroups of four or five individuals each. Calculate the average, $\overline{X}$, and range, R, of each subgroup. Calculate the average of all subgroups, $\overline{\overline{X}}$, and the average range $\overline{R}$. Calculate the 3σ control limits using:

$$\text{Central line} = \overline{\overline{X}}$$

$$\text{Upper control limit for } \overline{X} = \overline{\overline{X}} + A_2\overline{R}$$

$$\text{Lower control limit for } \overline{X} = \overline{\overline{X}} - A_2\overline{R}$$

$$\text{Central line} = \overline{R}$$

$$\text{Upper control limit for } R = D_4\overline{R}$$

$$\text{Lower control limit for } R = D_3\overline{R}$$

For subgroup size, $n > 10$, use standard deviation σ instead of range (see above under Subgroup Size). Calculate the 3σ control limits using:

$$\text{Central line} = \overline{\overline{X}}$$

$$\text{Upper control limit for } \overline{X} = \overline{\overline{X}} + A_1\overline{s}$$

$$\text{Lower control limit for } \overline{X} = \overline{\overline{X}} - A_1\overline{s}$$

$$\text{Central line} = \overline{s}$$

$$\text{Upper control limit for } s = B_4\overline{s}$$

$$\text{Lower control limit for } s = B_3\overline{s}$$

The values of the A, B, and D factors depend on subgroup size, n, and are given in Table A, Appendix II. Draw the control limits, the $\overline{\overline{X}}$ and $\overline{R}$ or $\overline{s}$ lines, and plot $\overline{X}$ and R or s on their respective charts.

The control chart factors assume a normal population of individuals; moderate deviations are acceptable. Examples of a data sheet and control chart for $\overline{X}$ and R are shown in Figures 24.6 and 24.7.

Interpretation of Charts. Place the charts for $\overline{X}$ and R (or s) one above the other so the average and range for any one subgroup are on the same vertical line. Observe whether either or both indicate lack of control for that subgroup.

$\overline{X}$'s outside the control limits are evidence of a general change affecting all pieces after the first subgroup out of limits. Study the log kept during data collection, the operation of the process, and the worker's experience attempting to discover a variable which could have caused the out-of-control subgroups. Typical causes are a change in material, personnel, machine setting, tool wear, temperature, or vibration.

R's outside control limits are evidence that the uniformity of the process has changed. Typical causes are a change in personnel, increased variability of material, or excessive wear in the process machinery. In one case a sudden increase in R warned of an impending machine accident.

A single R out of control can be caused by a shift in the process which occurred while the subgroup was being taken.

Look for unusual patterns, nonrandomness. Nelson (1984 and 1985) provides eight tests to detect such patterns on control charts using 3σ control limits (Figure 24.8). Each of the zones shown is 1σ wide. (Note that test 2 in Figure 24.8 requires nine points in a row; other authors suggest seven or eight points in a row; see Nelson, 1985, for elaboration.) AT&T (1984) is another excellent reference for control chart patterns.

Compare the process data with specification limits. See Section 16 under Process Capability Measurement.

DATE	6/8			6/9				6/10				6/11				6/12				6/15				6/16	
TIME	8	10	12	2	8	10	12	2	8	10	12	2	8	10	12	2	8	10	12	2	8	10	12	2	8
R E A D I N G S — 1	.65	.75	.75	.60	.70	.60	.75	.60	.65	.60	.80	.85	.70	.65	.90	.75	.75	.75	.65	.60	.50	.60	.80	.65	.65
2	.70	.85	.80	.70	.75	.75	.80	.70	.80	.70	.75	.75	.70	.70	.80	.80	.70	.70	.65	.60	.55	.80	.65	.60	.70
3	.65	.75	.80	.70	.65	.75	.65	.80	.85	.60	.90	.85	.75	.85	.80	.75	.85	.60	.85	.65	.65	.65	.75	.65	.70
4	.65	.85	.70	.75	.85	.85	.75	.75	.85	.80	.50	.65	.75	.75	.75	.80	.70	.70	.65	.60	.80	.65	.65	.60	.60
5	.85	.65	.75	.65	.80	.70	.70	.75	.75	.65	.80	.70	.70	.60	.85	.65	.80	.60	.70	.65	.80	.75	.65	.70	.65
SUM	3.50	3.85	3.80	3.40	3.75	3.65	3.65	3.60	3.90	3.35	3.75	3.80	3.60	3.55	4.10	3.75	3.80	3.35	3.50	3.10	3.30	3.45	3.50	3.20	3.30
$\overline{X} = \dfrac{\text{SUM}}{\text{NO. OF READINGS}}$	.70	.77	.76	.68	.75	.73	.73	.72	.78	.67	.75	.76	.72	.71	.82	.75	.76	.67	.70	.62	.66	.69	.70	.64	.66
$R = $ HIGHEST − LOWEST	.20	.20	.10	.15	.20	.25	.15	.20	.20	.20	.40	.20	.05	.25	.15	.15	.15	.15	.20	.05	.30	.20	.15	.10	.10

FIG. 24.6 Data sheet for $\overline{X}$ and R control chart.

CONTROL CHARTS — APPLYING TO WEIGHT OF EXPLOSIVE CHARGE in Grains

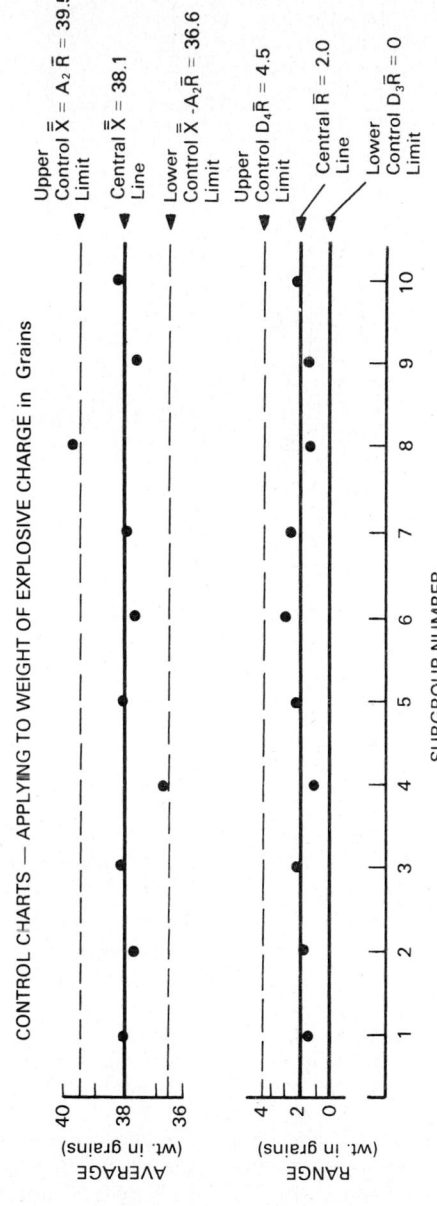

FIG. 24.7 Example of $\overline{X}$ and R control chart

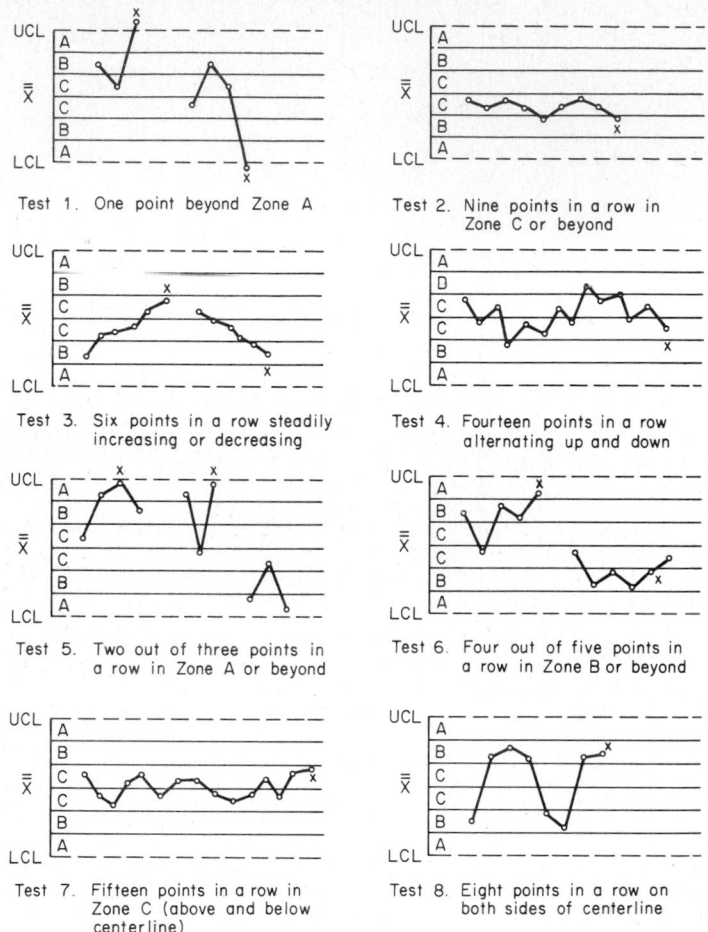

FIG. 24.8 Illustrations of tests for special causes applied to $\overline{X}$ control charts. *(From Nelson, 1984.)*

To illustrate the technical investigations that accompany a control chart, Flynn and Bolcar (1984) present a variety of examples and the lessons learned from each. Ott (1975) presents an extensive collection of cases with innovative statistical analysis conducted after the initial control charts. For an example showing how basic diagnostic tools such as Pareto analysis and the cause and effect diagram are used in conjunction with control charts, see Corbi, Nay, and Belt (1986).

Control Chart for Individuals X, and Range R. This is a plot of individual observations and is useful when only one observation per lot or batch is available. It is not as sensitive as the $\overline{X}$ chart (see Why Use Averages? above). For this reason 2σ control limits are often used. Unlike control limits for averages, control limits for individuals can be directly compared to tolerance limits.

Take a minimum of 30 individuals in subgroups of at least 2. Calculate the average of all 30 individuals, $\overline{X}$, the range of each subgroup, R, and the average of the ranges, $\overline{R}$. Calculate the 3σ control limits using:

$$\text{Central line} = \overline{X}$$

$$\text{Upper control limit for } X = \overline{X} + E_2\overline{R}$$

$$\text{Lower control limit for } X = \overline{X} - E_2\overline{R}$$

$$\text{Central line} = \overline{R}$$

$$\text{Upper control limit for } R = D_4\overline{R}$$

$$\text{Lower control limit for } R = D_3\overline{R}$$

2σ control limits are calculated by using two-thirds of the 3σ band:

$$\text{Upper control limit for } X = \overline{X} + \tfrac{2}{3} E_2\overline{R}$$

$$\text{Lower control limit for } X = \overline{X} - \tfrac{2}{3} E_2\overline{R}$$

The values of the E_2 and D factors depend on subgroup size n, and are given in Tables Y and A, respectively, Appendix II. Draw the control limits, the $\overline{X}$ and $\overline{R}$ lines, and plot X and R on their respective charts.

The control chart factors assume a normal population of individuals; moderate deviations are acceptable.

Example of a Control Chart for X and R. A batch-type manufacturing process is controlled by measurements of the flow point. Two batches are made per day, so that a daily subgroup of two is a rational one. It is desirable to examine the results for possible corrective action batch by batch. A control chart for individual batches is indicated. Data are given in Table 24.2.

TABLE 24.2 Flow Point of Resin

| | Measurements | | Range |
Subgroup	X_1	X_2	R
1	133.5	117.5	16.0
2	124.0	126.5	2.5
3	132.5	130.5	2.0
4	118.0	126.5	8.5
5	127.5	133.5	6.0
6	131.5	128.5	3.0
7	124.0	124.0	0
8	137.0	143.5	6.5
9	132.5	133.5	1.0
10	133.0	126.5	6.5
11	126.0	135.5	9.5
12	121.5	131.0	9.5
13	135.5	131.5	4.0
14	136.0	128.0	8.0
15	127.5	126.0	1.5
16	125.0	123.5	1.5
17	130.0	130.0	0
Totals		4391.0	86.0
Averages		129.15	5.06

For the X chart:

$$\text{Central line} = \overline{X} = 129.15$$

$$\text{Control limits} = \overline{X} \pm E_2\overline{R} = 129.15 \pm 2.660 \times 5.06$$

$$= 142.61 \text{ and } 115.69$$

For the R chart:

$$\text{Central line} = \overline{R} = 5.06$$

$$\text{Control limits} = D_4\overline{R} \text{ and } D_3\overline{R} = 3.27 \times 5.06 \text{ and } 0 \times 5.06$$

$$= 16.6 \text{ and } 0$$

These limits are drawn on the charts for X and R, and individual batch results and ranges are plotted. The charts are not shown, but we can see from Table 24.2 that the second batch on the eighth day is out of control. All ranges are in control. The reason for the out-of-control points should be investigated and discovered.

Unfortunately, this information came to light too late. We did not have 30 individual points on which to base the control limits until the end of day 15 which was 7 days after the out-of-control point. PRE-Control would have avoided this delay (see PRE-Control, below).

Attributes Data

Control Charts for Fraction Nonconforming. Fraction nonconforming, p, is the ratio of nonconforming items to the total number of items in a subgroup. It may describe a single quality characteristic or two or more characteristics considered collectively. A distinction is made between a nonconformity (e.g., a defect) and a nonconforming unit (e.g., a defective). A *nonconformity* is a single instance of nonconformance to some requirement; a *nonconforming unit* is a single item containing one or more nonconformities. Set up separate charts for each characteristic, if possible. Grouping nonconformities resulting from several different causes can make meaningful interpretation of the chart very difficult.

Subgroup size n is a function of the nonconformity rate. The better the quality, the larger the subgroup size needed to detect lack of control. ANSI/ASQC (1985) recommends at least one nonconforming item per subgroup. Ford (1985) recommends $n\overline{p} > 5$. n is almost always greater than 50 and $n = 400$ to 600 is not uncommon. Small subgroup sizes will give wide control limits and cause a poor process to be in control. As the nonconformity rate gets smaller and subgroup size gets larger, the time required to obtain each point gets longer and the chart's response time increases. With continuous use, all charts for attributes should make themselves obsolete for control purposes.

Subgroups should be of equal size if possible. If individual subgroups do not vary from the average subgroup size $\overline{n}$ by more than 25 percent use $\overline{n}$ rather than n to calculate the control limits. Individual subgroups varying from the average by more than 25 percent require their own separate set of control limits, calculated for each subgroup, using its particular size n. Varying control limits can be difficult to explain to both operators and management.

Take 25 subgroups. Calculate each subgroup's fraction nonconforming, p, and the average fraction nonconforming of all subgroups, $\overline{p}$. Calculate the 3σ control limits using:

$$\text{Central line} = \bar{p}$$

$$\text{Upper control limit for } p = \bar{p} + 3\sqrt{\bar{p}(1 - \bar{p})/n}$$

$$\text{Lower control limit for } p = \bar{p} - 3\sqrt{\bar{p}(1 - \bar{p})/n}$$

(For $\bar{p} < 0.10$, the control limit formula may be simplified to $\bar{p} \pm 3\sqrt{\bar{p}/n}$.) Draw the central line and the upper and lower control limits. Plot the fraction nonconforming, p, for each subgroup.

Example of Control Chart for p.   Table 24.3 shows the results of final testing and inspection, during a period of 5 months, of certain permanent magnets used in electrical relays. The total number of magnets tested was 14,091: The total number found to be nonconforming was 1030. The average sample size was

$$\bar{n} = \frac{14,091}{19} = 741.6$$

The average fraction nonconforming was

$$\bar{p} = \frac{1,030}{14,091} = 0.073$$

TABLE 24.3 p Chart Data

Subgroup: Production during week. Inspected at: Final assembly and test			
Week no.	Week ending	No. magnets inspected	No. nonconforming magnets	Fraction nonconforming, p
1	12/3	724	48	0.067
2	12/10	763	83	0.109
3	12/17	748	70	0.094
4	12/31	748	85	0.114
5	1/7	724	45	0.062
6	1/14	727	56	0.077
7	1/21	726	48	0.066
8	1/28	719	67	0.093
9	2/4	759	37	0.049
10	2/11	745	52	0.070
11	2/18	736	47	0.064
12	2/25	739	50	0.068
13	3/4	723	47	0.065
14	3/11	748	57	0.076
15	3/18	770	51	0.066
16	3/25	756	71	0.094
17	4/1	719	53	0.074
18	4/8	757	34	0.045
19	4/15	760	29	0.038
Totals		14,091	1030	
Averages		741.6	54.2	0.073

Control limits for the chart were placed at

$$\bar{p} \pm 3\sigma_p = \bar{p} \pm 3 \sqrt{\frac{\bar{p}(1-\bar{p})}{n}} = 0.073 \pm 3 \sqrt{\frac{0.073(1-0.073)}{741.6}}$$

$$= 0.073 \pm 0.0287 = 0.102 \text{ and } 0.044$$

The value 0.0287 is found either by direct calculation or by referring to Chart Z (in Appendix II). To use the graph, find the sample size on the lower scale, move upward to the intersection with the solid diagonal line at $\bar{p}$ (interpolate to find 0.073). Then move to the left-hand scale to obtain the value of $3\sigma_p$, which is given there as 0.029. The upper limit for p is thus $\text{UCL}_p = 0.073 + 0.029 = 0.102$, and the lower limit is $\text{LCL}_p = 0.073 - 0.029 = 0.044$. The resulting control chart is shown in Figure 24.9. Note that the last sample is below the lower control limit, indicating a significantly low fraction nonconforming. Although this might mean that there is some assignable cause resulting in better quality, such points can also be due to an inspector's accepting some nonconforming units in error.

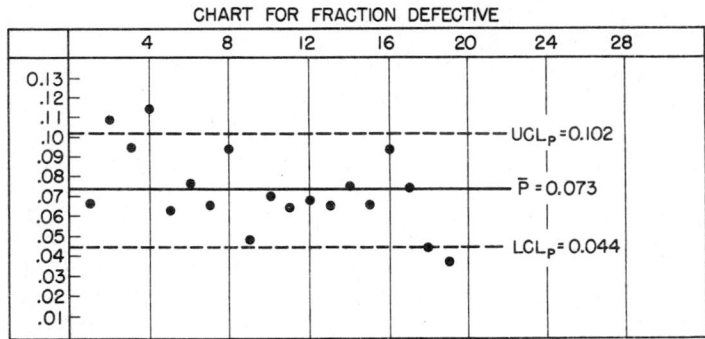

FIG. 24.9 *p* chart for permanent magnets.

The lower p may have began during week 9. The 3σ control limits can have a large β risk, thus failing to detect a change when it does exist. Grant and Leavenworth (1980) give additional examples.

Control Charts for Number Nonconforming, np. *np* is a direct count of the number of nonconforming in a subgroup. The directions and cautions for an *np* chart are the same as those for a *p* chart except all subgroup sizes must be the same.

Take 25 subgroups. Count the number nonconforming, *np*, in each subgroup. Calculate the average number nonconforming of all subgroups, $n\bar{p}$. Calculate the 3σ control limits using:

$$\text{Central line} = n\bar{p}$$

$$\text{Upper control limit for } p = n\bar{p} + 3\sqrt{n\bar{p}(1-\bar{p})}$$

$$\text{Lower control limit for } p = n\bar{p} - 3\sqrt{n\bar{p}(1-\bar{p})}$$

(For $\bar{p} < 0.10$, the control limit formula may be simplified to $n\bar{p} \pm 3\sqrt{n\bar{p}}$.) Draw the central line and the upper and lower control limits. Plot the number nonconforming, *np*, for each subgroup.

Example of Control Chart for np.   For the example in Table 24.3:

$$\text{Center line} = n\bar{p} = 54.2$$

$$\text{Control limits} = n\bar{p} \pm 3\sqrt{n\bar{p}} = 54.2 \pm 3\sqrt{54.2}$$

$$= 54.2 \pm 22.1 = 76.3 \text{ and } 32.1$$

The simplified formula is used because $\bar{p}$ is less than 0.10. The same subgroups are out of control on this basis as in the control chart for p (Figure 24.9). The charts are identical except for the vertical scale; so the np chart has not been reproduced. The sample sizes in this example vary slightly but are sufficiently similar to be treated as equal.

Control Chart for Nonconformities per Unit *u.*   The control chart for u is most useful when several independent nonconformities (they must be independent) may occur in one unit of product. This is likely to happen in complex assemblies.
   The control chart lines for sample size n are:

$$\text{Central line} = \bar{u}$$

$$\text{Upper control limit} = \bar{u} + 3\sqrt{\bar{u}/n}$$

$$\text{Lower control limit} = \bar{u} - 3\sqrt{\bar{u}/n}$$

where $\bar{u}$ is the total number of nonconformities in all samples divided by the total number of units in all samples, that is, the nonconformities per unit in the complete set of test results. For samples of unequal size, control limits are computed for each size separately, using a pooled value of $\bar{u}$.
   Example of Control Chart for u.   Table 24.4 gives inspection results for 25 consecutive lots of a product. The lot size was essentially constant; so a constant sample size ($n = 10$) was used. All nonconformities were counted because two or more nonconformities of the same or different kinds could occur on each item. The nonconformities per unit are found by dividing the number of nonconformities found by the sample size.
   Then, for the control chart for u,

$$\text{Central line} = \bar{u} = \frac{37.5}{25} = 1.5$$

$$\text{Control limits} = \bar{u} \pm 3\sqrt{\frac{\bar{u}}{n}} = 1.50 \pm 3\sqrt{\frac{1.50}{10}}$$

$$= 1.50 \pm 1.16 = 2.66 \text{ and } 0.34$$

The control chart is given in Figure 24.10. The ninth sample is out of control. An investigation is in order. Grant and Leavenworth (1980) provide additional examples.

Control Chart for Number of Nonconformities *c.*   A control chart for number of nonconformities in a sample is the equivalent of the control chart for u. It is a practical alternative when all samples are of the same size n. It is particularly effective when the number of nonconformities *possible* on a unit is large but the percentage for any single nonconformity is small. Examples are physical nonconformities such as surface irregularities, flaws, or pinholes on continuous or exten-

TABLE 24.4 Number of Nonconformities

Sample no.	Total nonconformities in sample c	Nonconformities per unit u
1	17	1.7
2	14	1.4
3	6	0.6
4	23	2.3
5	5	0.5
6	7	0.7
7	10	1.0
8	19	1.9
9	29	2.9
10	18	1.8
11	25	2.5
12	5	0.5
13	8	0.8
14	11	1.1
15	18	1.8
16	13	1.3
17	22	2.2
18	6	0.6
19	23	2.3
20	22	2.2
21	9	0.9
22	15	1.5
23	20	2.0
24	6	0.6
25	24	2.4
Total	375	37.5

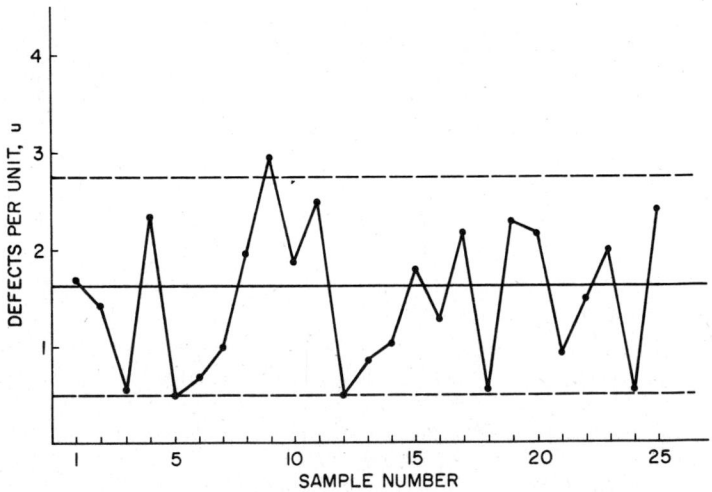

FIG. 24.10 Control chart for u.

sive products such as yarn, wire, paper, textiles, or other sheeted materials. The chance of a nonconformity occurring at any one spot may be small, but the overall opportunity for nonconformities may be great.

The chart for c makes direct use of the count of defects. See the column headed "Total Nonconformities in Sample c" in Table 24.4.

Formulas for control chart lines are

$$\text{Central line} = \bar{c}$$

$$\text{Upper control limit} = \bar{c} + 3\sqrt{\bar{c}}$$

$$\text{Lower control limit} = \bar{c} - 3\sqrt{\bar{c}}$$

where $\bar{c}$ is the total number of nonconformities in all samples divided by the number of samples, that is, the average number of nonconformities per sample.

Examples of Control Charts for c. For the examples in Table 24.4,

$$\text{Central line} = \bar{c} = \frac{375}{25} = 15.0$$

$$\text{Control limits} = \bar{c} \pm 3\sqrt{\bar{c}} = 15.0 \pm 3\sqrt{15.0}$$

$$= 15.0 \pm 11.6 = 26.6 \text{ and } 3.4$$

The same sample, no. 9, is out of control on this chart as in the control chart for u. The charts are identical except for the vertical scale; so the c chart has not been reproduced.

An example of the control chart for c to control nonconformities of a sheeted material follows. Table 24.5 shows the results of a series of pinhole tests of paper intended to be impervious to oils. Specimen sheets 11×17 in in size were taken from production at intervals, and colored ink was applied to one side of the sheet. Each individual inkblot which appeared on the other side of the sheet within 5 min was counted as a nonconformity.

The center line of the chart is located at $\bar{c} = 200/25 = 8.0$ nonconformities per sheet. Control limits, which are at $8.0 \pm 3\sqrt{8.0}$, may be computed directly or

TABLE 24.5 c Chart Data

Sheet no.	No. of pinholes	Sheet no.	No. of pinholes
1	8	14	6
2	9	15	14
3	5	16	6
4	8	17	4
5	5	18	11
6	9	19	7
7	9	20	8
8	11	21	18
9	8	22	6
10	7	23	9
11	6	24	10
12	4	25	5
13	7		
		Total	200

found from Chart AA (in Appendix II). The average value, 8.0, is located at either the upper or lower edge of this chart. The points at which the vertical line through 8.0 crosses the solid curves are noted. The corresponding limits are found at the side of the chart. In this case, the upper 3σ limit is found at 16.5 and the lower 3σ limit at zero. The resulting c chart is pictured in Figure 24.11. Grant and Leavenworth (1980) provide additional examples.

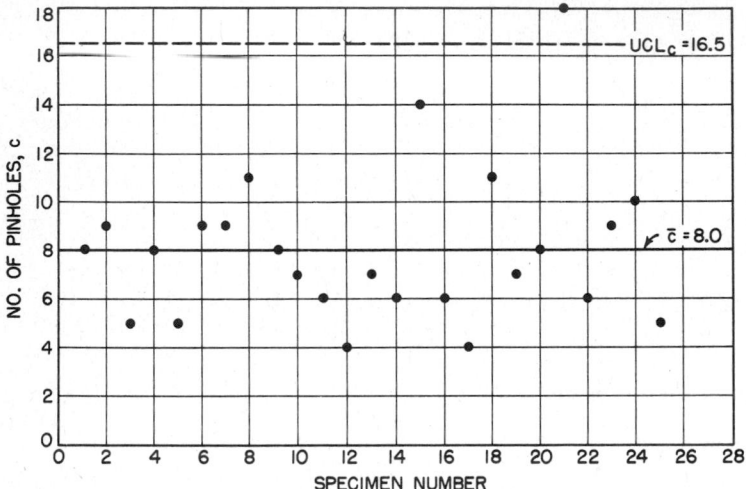

FIG. 24.11 c chart for pinholes in paper.

Cumulative Sum Control Charts.   A plot of the cumulative sum of deviations of subgroup averages from a reference value is particularly good at detecting abrupt shifts of the mean ($0.5\sigma_{\overline{X}}$ to $2.0\sigma_{\overline{X}}$) which remain with the process for at least five subgroups. Each point contains information from all observations up to and including itself. Usually, each point equals the preceding point plus the value of a statistic computed from the last subgroup.

Cumulative sum control charts (CSCC), like the other control charts discussed here, are interpreted by comparing the plotted values to critical limits. But the critical limits for a CSCC are neither parallel nor fixed. A mask in the shape of a V is usually constructed. It is laid over the chart with its origin over the last plotted point. Points covered by the mask are an indication that the process has shifted.

To Plot a CSCC

1. Obtain an estimate of $\sigma_{\overline{X}}$. (From $\overline{X}$ and R data, the estimate is $(\overline{R}/d_2)/\sqrt{n}$.)
2. Determine the least amount of change D in the average that it is desired to detect, and calculate $\delta = D/\sigma_{\overline{X}}$.
3. Determine the probability level at which decisions are to be made. For limits equivalent to standard control limits, $\alpha = 0.00135$.
4. Define k as the scale factor which is the *numerical* change in the value of the variable (vertical scale) per one unit change in *distance* (between two tick marks) in the horizontal scale. (The horizontal scale represents the subgroup

sample number.) Ewan (1963) recommends that k be chosen to be between $1\sigma_{\overline{X}}$ and $2\sigma_{\overline{X}}$, but preferably closer to $2\sigma_{\overline{X}}$.

5. To obtain the lead distance d, enter Table BB of Appendix II with $\delta = D/\sigma_{\overline{X}}$.

6. To obtain the mask angle θ, calculate D/k (recall that k is the scaling factor from step 4). Substituting D/k for δ, enter Table BB and read (or interpolate for) θ at the "δ" row corresponding to D/k.

7. Using d and θ construct the mask to define the control limits.

Subgroup Number. The guidelines for $\overline{X}$ and R charts apply, but for best results Ewan (1963) suggests:

$$n = \frac{2.25s^2}{D}$$

(where s is an estimate of the population standard deviation) and an interval between subgroups of $T/6$ where T is the permissible average time before the shift of D is detected.

Some Common Patterns of Plots. The mask is placed over the last point plotted. If any of the previous points are covered by the mask, a process shift has occurred (the process is "out of control"). Points covered by the top of the mask means a decrease in the average; the bottom of the mask detects an increase. The first point covered by the mask indicates the time at which the shift in average started. If all the points are exposed by the mask, the process is considered in control.

Some Cautions:

1. Periodically check with an R chart to see if the standard deviation is constant before drawing conclusions on the average.

2. Watch for *gradual* changes in the process average or changes that enter and leave the process (say in less than five sampling intervals). These conditions are not as apparent on a cumulative sum chart as on an $\overline{X}$ chart.

Statistical Distribution Assumption. The population of individual measurements is distributed normally.

Example of a CSCC. The data in Table 24.6 summarizes measurements from 20 subgroups of four each on the percent of water absorption in common building brick. The reference value R_0 was 10.0. To illustrate the CSCC, the original data were modified to introduce a decrease in the overall average of 2.0 percent starting with subgroup 11.

1. $\sigma_{\overline{X}}$ is estimated by $\overline{R}/d_2\sqrt{n} = 8.08/2.059\sqrt{4} = 1.96$.

2. We wish to detect a shift $D = 1\sigma_{\overline{X}}$; therefore $\partial = 1.96/1.96 = 1.0$.

3. We will use $\alpha = 0.00135$, the value for a standard $\overline{X}$ chart.

4. The scale factor $k = 2\sigma_{\overline{X}} = 2 \times 1.96 = 3.92 \approx 4$.

5. From Table BB, Appendix II, the lead distance of the mask, $d = 13.2$.

6. Substituting $D/k \approx 2/4 \approx 0.5$ for a "δ" value in Table BB of Appendix II, $\theta = 14°$.

Figure 24.12 shows the CSCC with the mask located at subgroup 17. The mask was moved from left to right with the zero point on the mask placed over each

TABLE 24.6 Data on Percent Water Absorption

Subgroup no.	$\overline{X}$	$\overline{X} - 10.0$	$\Sigma(\overline{X} - 10.0)$
1	15.1	5.1	5.1
2	12.3	2.3	7.4
3	7.4	−2.6	4.8
4	8.7	−1.3	3.5
5	8.8	−1.2	2.3
6	11.7	1.7	4.0
7	10.2	0.2	4.2
8	11.5	1.5	5.7
9	11.2	1.2	6.9
10	10.2	0.2	7.1
11	7.6	−2.4	4.7
12	6.2	−3.8	0.9
13	8.2	−1.8	−0.9
14	7.8	−2.2	−3.1
15	6.8	−3.2	−6.3
16	6.1	−3.9	−10.2
17	4.3	−5.7	−15.9
18	8.5	−1.5	−17.4
19	7.7	−2.3	−19.7
20	9.7	−0.3	−20.0

Note: $\overline{R}$ = 8.08.

plotted point. For the first 16 points, the mask did not cover any of the plotted points. This meant no shift in process level. At point 17, the mask detected the shift and indicated that the shift started at about the time subgroup 10 was taken (it really started at subgroup 11).

Figure 24.12 also shows the standard $\overline{X}$ chart. It would not have detected the shift on the basis of an $\overline{X}$ beyond the $\pm 3\sigma_{\overline{X}}$ control limits. However, note that by subgroup 17 the shift would be detected by four out of five successive points in zone B or beyond (Figure 24.8, Test 6).

A comparison of the cumulative sum chart and the standard $\overline{X}$ chart involves the concept of average run length (ARL).[4] The ARL is the average number of sample points plotted at a specified quality level before the chart detects a shift from a previous level. Ewan (1963) compares the ARL for the two charts for various amounts of shift in a process average. For shifts between about $0.5\sigma_{\overline{X}}$ and $2\sigma_{\overline{X}}$, the cumulative sum chart detects the shift with roughly half the number of subgroups as the standard $\overline{X}$ chart,[5] limiting the delay for action to that number of periods. The standard $\overline{X}$ chart works better for shifts on both sides of this range.

Johnson and Leone (1964, pp. 320–340) provide a thorough discussion and procedures (including scale values, lead distance, and mask angle) for applying CSCC to sample ranges, variances, number of defectives, fraction defective, and

---

[4]The procedure for determining d and θ can reflect desired values of the average run length. See Ewan (1963) and Bowker and Lieberman (1972), pp. 495–478.

[5]The comparison gets involved because there are modifications to the standard $\overline{X}$ chart that are pertinent (Ewan, 1963). Also the cumulative sum chart is superior only for certain significance levels (Johnson and Leone, 1964, pp. 340–342).

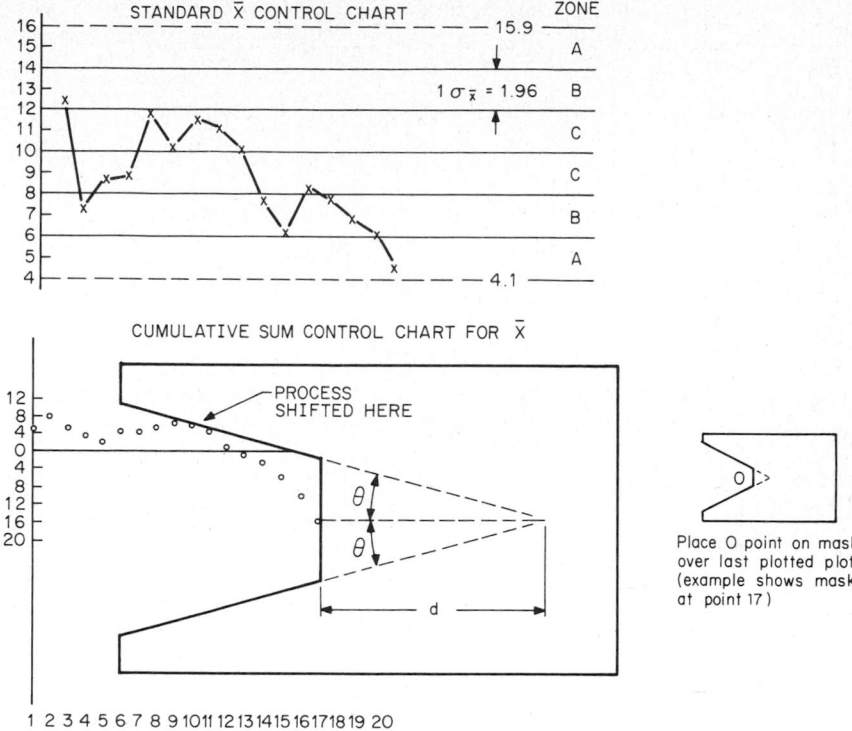

FIG. 24.12 Comparison of cumulative sum and $\overline{X}$ and R charts.

number of defects. Lucas (1985) discusses cumulative sum schemes for counts (attributes).

Constructing a Control Chart for Maintaining Control in the Future (Control with Standard Given). As a process is brought into control, data become available as to what is the expected level of the process and what is the expected dispersion. From these data it is possible to establish the expected range of variation for the process. This expected range of variation then becomes the standard against which subsequent samples are compared to detect the entry of significant causes of variation.

Use of the expected range of variation as a standard will detect significant changes in the process. Whether these changes would cause defects or not is quite another matter and depends on the relation of the product specification limits to the control limits.

The data from the process are the actual average values and are so designated, as

$$\text{Grand average} = \overline{\overline{X}}$$

$$\text{Average fraction nonconforming} = \overline{p}$$

$$\text{Average number of nonconformities} = \overline{c}$$

$$\text{etc.}$$

If these factors are used to specify the expected future values from the process, then the same quantities are simply redesignated, as "standard" values, by substituting the subscript "$_0$" symbol for the bar, so that

$$\text{Expected or "standard" average} = \overline{X}_0$$

$$\text{Expected or standard fraction nonconforming} = p_0$$

$$\text{Expected or standard number of nonconformities} = c_0$$

If the past data are not precisely the same as the desired standard, control limits based on the desired standard can still be set up, but only if there is evidence or real reason to believe the standard value can be achieved.

These standard values are for the entire volume of material to be manufactured; i.e., they are desired population values. Since the range theoretically expected in a normal population is infinitely wide, it is necessary to adopt some other measure as the standard for dispersion. The measure σ_0, which is equal to $\overline{R}/d_2$ or $\overline{s}/c_2$, is customarily used.

Control limits are calculated as follows:

Averages:

$$\text{Central line} = \overline{X}_0$$

$$\text{Upper control limit} = \overline{X}_0 + A\sigma_0 \text{ or } \overline{X}_0 + A_2 R_0$$

$$\text{Lower control limit} = \overline{X}_0 - A\sigma_0 \text{ or } \overline{X}_0 - A_2 R_0$$

Ranges:

$$\text{Central line} = R_0 \text{ or } d_2\sigma_0$$

$$\text{Upper control limit} = D_2\sigma_0$$

$$\text{Lower control limit} = D_1\sigma_0$$

Standard deviation:

$$\text{Central line} = s_0 \text{ or } c_2\sigma_0$$

$$\text{Upper control limit} = B_6\sigma_0$$

$$\text{Lower control limit} = B_5\sigma_0$$

Fraction nonconforming:

$$\text{Central line} = p_0$$

$$\text{Upper control limit} = p_0 + 3\sqrt{p_0(1 - p_0)/n}$$

$$\text{Lower control limit} = p_0 - 3\sqrt{p_0(1 - p_0)/n}$$

Number of nonconforming units:

$$\text{Central line} = np_0$$

$$\text{Upper control limit} = np_0 + 3\sqrt{np_0(1 - p_0)}$$

$$\text{Lower control limit} = np_0 - 3\sqrt{np_0(1 - p_0)}$$

Number of nonconformities per unit:

$$\text{Central line} = u_0$$

$$\text{Upper control limit} = u_0 + 3\sqrt{u_0/n}$$

$$\text{Lower control limit} = u_0 - 3\sqrt{u_0/n}$$

Values of the numerical factors are given in Appendix II, Table A. See ANSI/ASQC Z1.3 (1985) for further discussion.

Standard values may also be calculated from some criteria unrelated to the actual statistical variation of the process such as tolerance limits. The nominal may be used for $\overline{X}_0$. Upper and lower control limits will be the extreme tolerance minus the nominal all divided by $\sqrt{n}$. For a subgroup size of four the distance between the upper and lower control limits will be half the tolerance. Terms such as "modified control limits," "reject limits," and "narrow limit gaging" are associated with this approach. For an example, see Yu and Case (1984).

Control limits set without regard to the actual statistical variation of the specific group of raw materials, machines, and people employed to manufacture the product may bear little relationship to that variation. A process can be within such control limits but actually be operating out of *statistical* control. The presence of an assignable cause does not have to result in rejected work. On the other hand, a process operating in statistical control will produce a large quantity of rejects if the process capability, adjusted for sample size, is appreciably wider than the tolerance.

Correct tolerances are set by their ability to create customer enthusiasm. Customers have little interest in the statistical variation experienced by a manufacturer. It makes more sense to base limits for monitoring a process on the tolerance than on the $\pm 3\sigma$ limits of random variation of the process.

Special Control Charts.   Some of the standard control charts assume normality. When measurements are distributed nonnormally, they can sometimes be "transformed" mathematically, and the transformed measurements can then be treated by standard control limit formulas. See Section 23 under Additional Statistical Tools. Be particularly careful of special types of data such as ranks or ratios of two characteristics. Rank data are usually nonnormal. Ratios are sometimes normal but must be carefully analyzed from the viewpoint of statistical control because of possible interacting conditions between the two characteristics comprising the ratio.

Table 24.7 summarizes some special control charts not discussed above and gives references to detailed instructions for their construction and use.

PRE-CONTROL

PRE-Control Theory.   PRE-Control is a simple algorithm for controlling a process based on the tolerances. It assumes the process is producing product with a measurable and adjustable quality characteristic which varies according to some distribution. It makes no assumptions concerning the actual shape and stability of the distribution. Cautionary zones are designated just inside each tolerance extreme.

A new process (new setup, raw material, worker, etc.) is qualified by taking consecutive samples of individuals until five in a row fall within the central (non-

TABLE 24.7 Special Control Charts not Discussed in Section 24

Name of chart	Feature	Reference
Median	No arithmetic computations when subgroup size is odd	Grant and Leavenworth (1980), pp. 287–289
Moving average and moving range	Has smoothing effect to emphasize trends: new average plotted with each individual measurement	Grant and Leavenworth (1980), pp. 293–298
Geometric moving average: exponentially smoothed average	Combines successive measurements: effective in detecting small process shifts	Wortham and Heinrich (1972)
Demerits	Permits weighting of defects by degree of seriousness	Grant and Leavenworth (1980), pp. 269–271; see also Section 8 under Product Auditing
Adaptive	Evaluates process data against predicted value and quantifies adjustment needed	Section 28, under Adaptive Control
τ^2	One chart evaluates two or more related variables that have a joint effect on a quality characteristic	Montgomery and Wadsworth (1972); Hunter (1984)

cautionary) zone before two in a row fall in the cautionary zones. This ensures that the distribution is narrow enough and close enough to center to produce product within the tolerance limits. This is not statistical control; it is capability control; the process is now known to be capable of producing product within tolerance. If the process can not be qualified, diagnostic work to identify and control the red X must begin immediately.

Once the process is qualified, it is monitored by taking periodic samples consisting of two individuals each (called an A,B pair). This small subgroup size and the immediate information it provides directly to the process worker constitutes a very tight, quick feedback loop. Action is taken only if both A and B are in the cautionary zone. (For a reprint of a classic paper on adjusting processes, see Grubbs, 1983.)

The statistical power of PRE-Control resides in the rule of the product of independent probabilities: $P(A,B) = P(A) \times P(B)$. Thus the risk of a false signal is dramatically reduced by using a sample size of two. The actual probabilities are a function of the width of the cautionary zones. See α Risk, below. The probability of missing out-of-tolerance work is controlled by the size of the cautionary zones and frequency of taking samples. See β Risk, below.

The rules concerning setup, sample size, and frequency of sampling have been developed both mathematically and through operating experience (Shainin, 1984). Because the PRE-Control rules are so simple, users often conclude they are arbitrary and change them in an effort to improve PRE-Control. The sample size (two) is a compromise between lowering the risk of a false signal and waiting too long to take action. The width of the cautionary zones is a compromise between sensitivity and hunting. With the cautionary zones set as shown below, hunting is a sign that the actual distribution is wider than the tolerance. The process must be repaired. The frequency of sampling is a compromise between the cost and effort of more frequent samples and the risk of producing out-of-tolerance work. The original PRE-Control calculations indicated a frequency of 25 *A,B* pairs between typical process adjustments would ensure an average of 1 percent or less, out-of-tolerance production. Most processes require periodic adjustments to remain within specifications. Subsequent experience has shown that the currently recommended frequency of six *A,B* pairs between adjustments is sufficient to provide virtually no out-of-tolerance work. See β Risk, below. Brown (1966) reports on an application where 30,000,000 pieces were produced without a single reject. Changing the already optimized zone and subgroup size rules will result in less effective process control.

Requirements for Use. PRE-Control is effective for *any* process where the worker can measure a quality characteristic of interest (dimension, color, strength, etc.) and can adjust the process to change that characteristic, and where the process has either a continuous output (i.e., paper) or a discrete output (i.e., machine parts) with a total production run of three or more pieces.

Although PRE-Control requires a minimum of five items to qualify a setup, it is actually controlling the process while those five items are being produced. If the first two items are yellow, adjust the process *before* making the third! The qualifying count must start over, but we have already prevented possible nonconforming product. If the total production run is only three items, PRE-Control can provide valuable information before the third item is produced.

There are *no* additional requirements and *no* underlying assumptions concerning process capability or the frequency distribution of the quality characteristic. (The population of individuals need not be normal and the process need not be in statistical control.)

Setting Up PRE-Control

Two-Sided Tolerance. Place reference lines at nominal $+\frac{1}{4}$ tolerance range and nominal $-\frac{1}{4}$ tolerance range. Color the areas: between the reference lines (half the total tolerance) green, between each reference line and the adjacent tolerance limit yellow, and outside the tolerance limits red. See Figure 24.13.

One-Sided Tolerance, Total Indicator Reading (Flatness or Concentricity). Place one reference line at half the tolerance from the maximum limit toward zero. Color the areas: between zero and the reference green, between the reference and the maximum limit yellow, and above the maximum red. See Figure 24.14

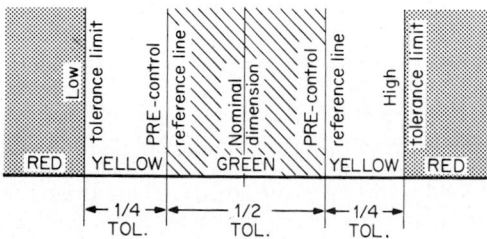

FIG. 24.13 PRE-Control lines for two-sided tolerance.

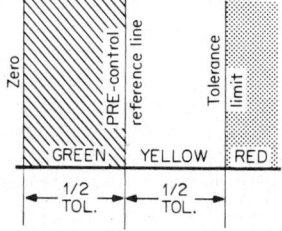

FIG. 24.14 PRE-Control lines for a one-sided tolerance, total indicator reading.

One-Sided Tolerance, Minimum or Maximum (Yield Strength).   Place one reference line a quarter of the way from the tolerance limit toward the best sample produced during past operations. Color the areas: from the reference line to beyond the best piece green, from the reference line to the tolerance limit yellow, and beyond the tolerance limit red. See Figure 24.15

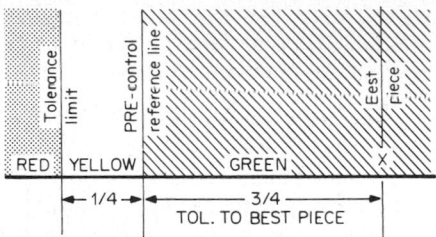

FIG. 24.15   PRE-Control lines for a one-sided tolerance, minimum and maximum.

Provide the process operator with means of measuring the characteristic, and color the instrument face green (good), yellow (caution), and red (stop) according to the rules given above.

Using PRE-Control

Qualify the Setup.   Measure every piece produced until you obtain five greens in a row. If one yellow is encountered, restart the count. If two yellows in a row or any reds are encountered, adjust the process and restart the count. This step replaces first piece inspection.

Run.   Measure two consecutive pieces periodically (called an A,B pair). If both are yellow on the same side, adjust. If yellow on opposite sides, call for help (this condition usually requires a more sophisticated correction). If either are red, adjust. In the case of two yellows, the adjustment must be made immediately to prevent nonconforming work. In the case of red, stop; nonconforming work is already being produced! Do not put the red piece in with previous parts.

Frequency of Measuring.   Measure six A,B pairs on average between each required process adjustment. Since there are 60 min in an hour, this rule conveniently reduces to: time between measurements in minutes = time between adjustments in hours $\times$ 10:

Time between adjustments, h	Time between measurements, min
1	10
2	20
3	30
4	40
etc.	

For an instructive case history on the use of PRE-Control and results obtained, see Brown (1966).

Risk. All techniques for analyzing process variation involve two risks. Section 23 under Statistical Tests of Hypotheses discusses these risks as the type I (or α) risk and the type II (or β) risk. These risks also apply to PRE-Control.

α *Risk.* The risk of a false alarm at a specific operating condition. The risk of a double yellow signal when the process should not be adjusted.

β *Risk.* The risk of a miss at a specific operating condition. The risk of producing out-of-tolerance work and not getting a double yellow or red signal.

The worst practical operating condition for α risk is a normal frequency distribution of the quality characteristic with its mean μ at the nominal (center of the tolerance) and $\pm 3\sigma$ right on the upper and lower tolerance limits, respectively (Figure 24.16). Reference to a table of areas under the normal curve (Appendix II, Table B) will show that the green zone ($\pm 1.5\sigma$) contains 86 percent of the area, leaving 7 percent for each of the yellow tails. There are nine possible permutations of A,B pairs (see Fig. 24.16). Since the probability of each is the product of the probabilities of its component events, the probability of obtaining any permutation of A and B is the proportion of area under the normal curve which will give a particular A times the proportion of area which will give a particular B. There are four permutations of A and B which will constitute a false alarm (see under "Help" and "Adjust" in Figure 24.16). The probability of each permutation is $\frac{1}{14} \times \frac{1}{14} = \frac{1}{196}$. The probability of all four permutations is therefore $\frac{4}{196} \approx 2$ percent.

In the worst likely case, an worker using PRE-Control will get a signal to adjust the process when it should not be adjusted 2 percent of the time. When the worker adjusts the process and tries to requalify the setup, probably two consecutive yellows will occur before five greens. This second double yellow signals to adjust the

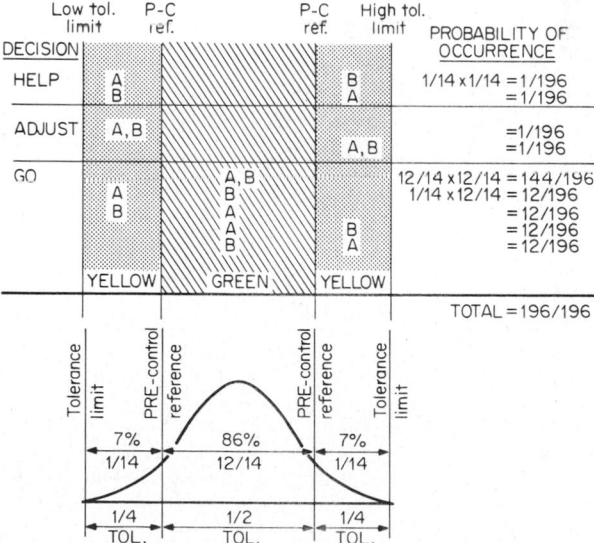

FIG. 24.16   PRE-control α risk calculation.

process back toward its original position. The result of this false signal is a sequence of two unnecessary adjustments—one as a result of the false signal and one to correct it. It does not result in the production of any nonconforming product.

The worst practical operating condition for β risk is the same normal distribution with $\pm 3\sigma$ equal to the full tolerance used above, but with its mean μ displaced from the nominal by 0.85σ. In this case the out-of-tolerance work produced will not exceed an average of 1 percent. The calculation is somewhat more complex than that for α risk. For a complete discussion of PRE-Control β risk, see Shainin (1984).

Implementation.   PRE-Control was designed to be used by the production worker as an integral part of the production process. Implementation requires his or her cooperation. Let PRE-Control sell itself. Ask for a volunteer to conduct a 2-week experiment. Explain PRE-Control and provide the volunteer with colored gages and a written set of PRE-Control rules. The faces may be colored with nail polish for this initial "experiment." Check periodically for the first couple of days to answer any questions. At the end of the 2 weeks, tell the worker the experiment is over, and offer to take the gages away. The authors' experience is that the worker will not want the gages removed. The word will already have been passed to the rest of the shop about how much more control the worker has with PRE-Control. It is not uncommon for other workers to request PRE-Control before the initial 2-week experiment is completed. Implement PRE-Control on each operation as the worker on that operation requests it. It may take 6 months before the whole shop is using it, but they will be using it effectively.

Do not provide special inspectors to measure the samples from each process and do not ask the workers to make charts or tally sheets of their measuring results. The purpose of PRE-Control, like the purpose of the shop, is to make good product, not charts or any other kind of record. PRE-Control's effectiveness can be audited with an appropriate sampling inspection plan (see Section 25, Acceptance Sampling).

Comparison of $\overline{X}$, R Charts and PRE-Control.   A comparison of $\overline{X}$ and R charts with PRE-Control is given in Table 24.8. Sinbaldi (1985) describes simulations run to compare the two techniques.

STATISTICAL CONTROL OF AUTOMATED PROCESSES

Section 16, under Automated Manufacturing, defines some of the basic approaches used in automating manufacturing processes. Section 27, Computers and Quality, discusses the role of computers in both automated and nonautomated processes.

From the viewpoint of data analysis in process control, the march toward automation has sparked some innovations:

1. Continuous reading instrumentation which yields large amounts of data on process variables and quality characteristics.

2. Automation of statistical analysis (e.g., calculation of means, standard deviation, control limits). This is discussed below under Software for Statistical Process Control.

TABLE 24.8 Comparison of $\overline{X}$ and R Control Charts and PRE-Control

Item	$\overline{X}$ and R charts	PRE-Control
Purpose	Discover amount of variation caused by "random" and assignable causes Detect time of assignable cause Provide record of SPC	Prevent manufacture of defects
Decision rules	Subgroup $\overline{X}$ beyond control limit 9 subgroup $\overline{X}$'s on same side of $\overline{\overline{X}}$ Subgroup R beyond control limit	2 consecutive yellows on same side of target zone 2 consecutive yellows on opposite sides of target zone
Subgroup size	≥ 2, usually 4 or 5	Always 2
Effect of x's distribution shape	For subgroup size ≥ 4, not significant	Not significant; controls by the size of the cautionary zones, not by the target zone
To improve statistical sensitivity	Increase subgroup size	Optimized by setting the sum of the cautionary zones equal to half the tolerance
To reduce detection time	Decrease subgroup size More frequent subgroups Speed up calculations	Take more A,B pairs between typical process adjustments
To qualify a process	Take 25 subgroups, compute control limits, demonstrate state of statistical control Common practice to take 10 subgroups and disregard 1 or 2 out-of-control points or to use old control limits after eliminating an assignable cause	Run of 5 greens in a row before 2 yellows in a row
Effect of process capability greater than tolerance	None, unless $\overline{X}$ control limits are compared with tolerance (control limit $\times$ square root of subgroup size is comparable to tolerance)	2 yellows will occur on opposite sides of target zone before a run of 5 greens, or 2 yellows on one side of target zone will switch to the other side with only a small process adjustment; therefore, stop!
Effect of one out-of-tolerance individual in a subgroup	None, as long as $\overline{X}$ is within the control limits; theory says the process cannot be economically improved, i.e., zero defects are not economically possible	Out-of-tolerance is red, therefore stop!

TABLE 24.8 Comparison of $\overline{X}$ and R Control Charts and PRE-Control (*Continued*)

Item	$\overline{X}$ and R charts	PRE-Control
α Risk, (probability of hunting)	For control limits @ $\pm 3\sigma$ = 0.0027; for control limits @ $\pm 2\sigma$ = 0.05	0.00 to 0.02
β Risk (probability of missing out-of-tolerance work)	Not usually considered but often very large (depends on frequency of subgroups and relationship between tolerance and control limits); out-of-tolerance rates of 2% not uncommon; irrational subgrouping and failure to calculate new control limits after changing the process can make this rate much worse	Depends on frequency of sampling; out-of-tolerance work theoretically will not exceed 1% for six pairs between typical adjustments; actual experience indicates rate is 0%

3. Comparison of process results with preset numerical standards. This comparison may result in

   a. The generation of a document or other form of alert giving pertinent information on a nonstandard condition.

   b. The generation of an error signal that automatically makes a process adjustment. The authors have been impressed with the improvement in recent years of "size control" devices. While an item is being ground, a measuring pair of contacts monitors the change in size and electronically instructs the grinding wheel to prepare to stop removing material as the desired size is being approached.

Software for Statistical Process Control.   Many mini and personal computer programs are available for statistical analysis of data including virtually all types of control charts. Gages with direct digital outputs can be plugged into hand-held data collection devices. These devices will store the gage readings collected on the shop floor and will download them to a personal computer in the office. As an alternative, gage readings may be entered into the collection device with its keyboard.

The software will calculate the sample parameters, initial control limits, and the control chart. Of course, control limits may be easily recalculated periodically, and $\pm 2\sigma$ limits can be calculated as an additional guide. Most software will provide additional summaries and analyses such as listings of the raw data, out-of-specification values, histograms, checks for runs and other patterns within control limits, tests for normality, process capability calculations, Pareto analyses, and trend analyses.

The relatively low cost of personal computers and the availability of software have contributed substantially to the renewed interest in $\overline{X}$ and R charts. This computer-software combination has also made it practical to collect large quantities of data and subject it to various and complex forms of analysis. However, process improvement still requires the identification of the vital few and often unexpected variables causing excess variation. Computer analysis is no substitute for such tools as Multi-Vari (Section 22 under Test of Theories of Management-Controllable Problems) or factorial experiments (Section 26 under Factorial Experiments). Computers are most helpful when the diagnostician has created a template for a spreadsheet program and least helpful when a prepackaged statistical analysis program is used. Users are rarely familiar with the detailed logic of the prepackaged programs and can be led to erroneous conclusions.

The American Society for Quality Control annually publishes a directory of software for process control and other areas of quality assurance (ASQC, 1986). In addition, the *Journal of Quality Technology* (ASQC) and *Quality* (Hitchcock Publishing Co.) have computer columns describing programs for process control.

REFERENCES

American Telephone and Telegraph (AT&T) (1984). *Statistical Quality Control Handbook,* 2nd ed., 10th printing. Delmar Printing Company, Charlotte, NC.

ANSI/ASQC (1985). Z1.1, *Guide for Quality Control Charts;* Z1.2, *Control Chart Method for Analyzing Data;* and Z1.3, *Control Chart Method of Controlling Quality during Production.* American Society for Quality Control, Milwaukee.

ASQC (1987). "QA/QC Software Director." *Quality Progress,* March, pp. 33–66.

Bowker, Albert H. and Lieberman, Gerald J. (1972). *Engineering Statistics,* 2nd ed. Prentice-Hall, Englewood Cliffs, N.J.

Brown, N. Raymond, Jr. (1966). "Zero Defects the Easy Way with Target Area Control." *Modern Machine Shop,* July.

Corbi, Jean-Claude, Nay, Michael J., and Belt, Philip Brown (1986). "Statistical Quality Control in the Bleach Plant." *TAPPI Journal,* February, pp. 60–66.

Duncan, Acheson J. (1974). *Quality Control and Industrial Statistics,* 4th ed. Richard D. Irwin, Homewood, IL.

Ewan, W. D. (1963). "When and How to Use Cu-Sum Charts." *Technometrics,* February, pp. 1–22.

Fisher, Ronald A. (1935). *The Design of Experiments.* Oliver and Boyd, London.

Flynn, Michael F. and Bolcar, John A. (1984). "The Road to Hell." *ASQC Quality Congress Transactions,* Milwaukee, pp. 192–196.

Ford Motor Company (1984). *Continuing Process Control and Process Capability Improvement.* Ford Motor Company, Statistical Methods Publications, P.O. Box 1000, Plymouth, MI 48170.

Grant, E. L. and Leavenworth, R. S. (1980). *Statistical Quality Control,* 5th ed. McGraw-Hill, New York.

Grubbs, Frank E. (1983). "An Optimum Procedure for Setting Machines or Adjusting Processes." *Journal of Quality Technology,* October, pp. 186–189.

Hunter, J. S. (1984). "The Status of U.S. Quality." *Quality,* January, p. 52.

Johnson, Norman L. and Leone, Fred C. (1964). *Statistics and Experimental Design,* vol. 1. John Wiley & Sons, New York.

Juran, J. M. (1951). *Quality Control Handbook,* 1st ed. McGraw-Hill, New York.

Juran, J. M. and Gryna, Frank M., Jr. (1980). *Quality Planning and Analysis,* 2nd ed. McGraw-Hill, New York.

Krishnamoorthi, K. S. (1985). *Why the Control Chart Ticks?* Paper 8515-001, Metals/Material Technology Series, American Society for Metals, Metals Park, OH 44073.

Lucas, James M. (1985). "Cumulative Sum (Cusum) Control Schemes." *ASQC Quality Congress Transactions,* Milwaukee, pp. 367–372.

Montgomery, Douglas C. and Wadsworth, Harrison M., Jr. (1972). "Some Techniques for Multivariate Quality Control Applications." *ASQC Technical Conference Transactions,* Milwaukee, pp. 427–435.

Nelson, Loyd S. (1984). "The Shewhart Control Chart—Tests for Special Causes." *Journal of Quality Technology,* vol. 16, no. 4, October, pp. 237–239.

Nelson, Loyd S. (1985). "Interpreting Shewhart $\overline{X}$ Control Charts." *Journal of Quality Technology,* vol. 17, no. 2, April, pp. 114–116.

Ott, Ellis R. (1975). *Process Quality Control.* McGraw-Hill, New York.

Seder, Leonard A. (1950). "Diagnosis with Diagrams." *Industrial Quality Control,* January.

Shainin, Dorian (1984), "Better than Good Old $\overline{X}$ and R Charts Asked by Vendees." *ASQC Quality Congress Transactions,* Milwaukee, pp. 302–307.

Shewhart, Walter A. (1931). *Economic Control of Quality of Manufactured Product.* D. Van Nostrand, New York.

Sinbaldi, Frank J. (1985). "PRE-Control; Does It Really Work with Non-Normality?" *ASQC Quality Congress Transactions,* Milwaukee, pp. 428–433.

Tippett, L. H. C. (1950). *Technological Applications of Statistics.* John Wiley & Sons, New York.

Vance, Lonnie C. (1983). "A Bibliography of Statistical Quality Control Chart Techniques, 1970–1980." *Journal of Quality Technology,* vol. 15, no. 2, April, pp. 59–62.

Wadsworth, G. P. and Bryan, J. G. (1974). *Applications of Probability and Random Variables.* McGraw-Hill, New York.

Wortham, A. W. and Heinrich, G. F. (1972). "Control Charts Using Exponential Smoothing Techniques." *ASQC Technical Conference Transactions,* Milwaukee, pp. 451–458.

Yates, Frank (1937). *The Design and Analysis of Factorial Experiments.* Technical Communication 35, Imperial Bureau of Soil Science, Rothamsted, Harpenden, UK.

Yu, Shawn S. and Case, Kenneth E. (1984). "An Updated Look at NLG for Process Control." *ASQC Quality Congress Transactions,* Milwaukee, pp. 308–314.

SECTION 25
ACCEPTANCE SAMPLING[1]

Edward G. Schilling
Dan J. Sommers

INTRODUCTION **25.2**

Acceptance Sampling—
General 25.2

Types of Sampling 25.4

Terminology of Acceptance
Sampling 25.4

Acceptance Sampling
Procedures 25.5

Published Tables and
Procedures 25.8

Acceptance Control and
Acceptance Sampling . . 25.9

*SAMPLING RISKS AND
PARAMETERS* **25.9**

Risks 25.9

Operating Characteristic
Curve 25.10

Average Sample Number
Curve 25.12

Average Outgoing Quality
Limit 25.12

Average Outgoing Quality
Curve 25.13

Average Total Inspection . 25.13

Minimum Total Inspection 25.14

Selection of a Numerical
Value of the Quality
Index 25.16

*IMPLEMENTATION OF AN
ACCEPTANCE SAMPLING
PROCEDURE* **25.18**

Assumptions Made in
Sampling Plans 25.18

Lot Formation 25.19

Random Sampling 25.20

Stratified Sampling 25.20

ATTRIBUTES SAMPLING **25.21**

Overview of Single, Double,
Multiple, and Sequential
Plans 25.21

Selecting Sampling Plans . 25.23

Single Sampling 25.23

Double Sampling 25.23

Multiple Sampling 25.23

Sequential Sampling . . . 25.23

Rectification Schemes . . . 25.26

Continuous Sampling . . . 25.28

Skip-Lot Schemes 25.33

Chain-Sampling 25.37

[1]In the Third Edition, material on sampling was prepared by several authors: attributes sampling by J. M. Wiesen, variables sampling by Edward G. Schilling, and bulk sampling by Acheson J. Duncan.

Cumulative Sum Sampling
Plans 25.39

Published Tables and
Procedures 25.41

VARIABLES SAMPLING . . . **25.51**

Overview 25.51

Sampling for Percent
Nonconforming 25.51

Single Sampling 25.54

Two-Point Variables Plans
for Percent
Nonconforming 25.56

Narrow-Limit Gaging for
Percent Nonconforming   25.57

Lot Plot 25.58

Grand Lot Schemes 25.58

Sampling for Process
Parameter 25.60

Published Tables and
Procedures 25.62

Mixed Plans 25.68

RELIABILITY SAMPLING . . . **25.68**

Overview 25.68

Relation of Life
Characteristics 25.73

Exponential Distribution:
H108 . . . . 25.73

Exponential Distribution:
Other Plans (MIL-STD-
690B, MIL-STD-781C) . 25.79

Weibull Distribution: TR-3,
TR-4, TR-6 . . . . . . 25.82

BULK SAMPLING **25.84**

Objectives of Bulk
Sampling 25.84

Special Terms and
Concepts 25.84

Determination of the
Amount of Sampling   25.87

Models and Their Use . . . 25.87

Models for Distinctly
Segmented Bulk Material
("Within and Between"
Models) 25.87

Models for Bulk Material
Moving in a Stream . . . 25.88

Obtaining the Test-Units . 25.88

Tests of Homogeneity . . . 25.89

BAYESIAN PROCEDURES **25.89**

**HOW TO SELECT THE PROPER
SAMPLING PROCEDURES** . . . **25.91**

**COMPUTER PROGRAMS FOR
ACCEPTANCE SAMPLING** . . . **25.92**

**CONCLUSION—MOVING FROM
ACCEPTANCE SAMPLING TO
ACCEPTANCE CONTROL** **25.97**

REFERENCES **25.99**

INTRODUCTION

Acceptance Sampling—General. The disposition of a lot can be determined by inspecting every unit ("100 percent inspection") or by inspecting a sample or portion of the lot. Economy is the key advantage of acceptance sampling as compared with 100 percent inspection. However, sampling has additional advantages:

1. Economy due to inspecting only part of the product
2. Less handling damage during inspection
3. Fewer inspectors, thereby simplifying the recruiting and training problem

4. Upgrading the inspection job from monotonous piece-by-piece decisions to lot-by-lot decisions

5. Applicability to destructive testing, with a quantified level of assurance of lot quality

6. Rejections on suppliers or shop departments of entire lots rather than mere return of the defectives, thereby providing stronger motivation for improvement

Sampling also has some inherent disadvantages:

1. There are risks of accepting "bad" lots and of rejecting "good" lots.

2. There is added planning and documentation.

3. The sample usually provides less information about the product than does 100 percent inspection.

Why is Sampling Valid? The broad scheme of use of sampling is shown in Fig. 25.1*a*. It is universally realized that inspection of a sample gives information then and there about the quality of the pieces in the lot. But that is only the beginning. Beyond this, a vast area of knowledge is unfolded because *the product can tell on the process.*

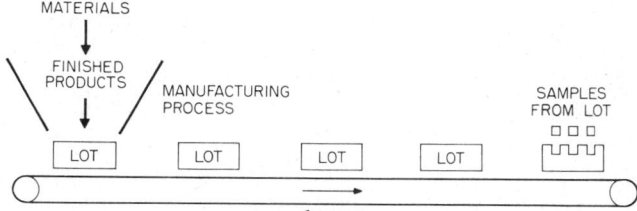

FIG. 25.1a Measurement of sample tells (1) whether the pieces in the sample are good or bad; (2) whether the process, at the time the samples were made, was doing good work or bad; (3) whether the uninspected pieces made at the same time by the same process are good or bad (principle of sampling inspection); (4) whether the process is stable; (5) whether the unmanufactured pieces are going to be good or bad (control inspection).

The sample, being the result of the variables present in the process at the time of manufacture, can give evidence as to those variables. Thereby it is possible to draw conclusions as to whether the process was doing good work or bad at the time it produced the samples.

From these conclusions about the process, it is then possible to reverse the reasoning, so that the known *process now can tell on the product.* We already know about the inspected product, but the knowledge of the process gives information about the uninspected pieces. In this way acceptance sampling of a lot is valid not only because the uninspected pieces are neighbors of the inspected pieces; acceptance sampling is also valid because the uninspected pieces may be derived from the same process which the inspected pieces have labeled as "good."

When we go a step further, and examine a series of samples, we learn whether the process is stable or not. Once the series of samples tells on the process by certifying stability, we can use this knowledge of stability to predict the quality of unmanufactured product.

Cowden (1957) has summarized the characteristics of a good acceptance plan. It will:

1. Protect the producer against having lots rejected when the product is in a state of control, and satisfactory as to level and uniformity
2. Protect the consumer against the acceptance of bad lots
3. Provide long-run protection to the consumer
4. Encourage the producer to keep the process in control
5. Minimize sampling costs, inspection, and administration
6. Provide information concerning product quality

Types of Sampling.   Any acceptance sampling application must distinguish whether the purpose is to accumulate information on the immediate *product* being sampled or on the *process* which produced the immediate lot at hand. Accordingly, two types of sampling have been distinguished:

Type A: Sampling to accept or reject the immediate lot of product at hand

Type B: Sampling to determine if the process which produced the product at hand was within acceptable limits

The type of sampling will determine the appropriate probability distribution to be used in characterizing the performance of the plan. In addition, the type of data generated will also play a role. In acceptance sampling, data can be of these types:

Attributes—go no-go information

Defectives—usually measured in proportion or percent defective. This refers to the acceptability of units of product for a wide range of characteristics.

Defects—usually measured by actual count or as a ratio of defects per unit. This refers to number of defects found in the units inspected, and hence can be more than the number of units inspected.

Variables—measurement information

Variables—usually measured by the mean and standard deviation. This refers to the distribution of a specific measurable characteristic of the product inspected.

Terminology of Acceptance Sampling.   The terminology of acceptance sampling has evolved over the years into a precise and well-directed set of terms defining various properties of acceptance sampling plans and procedures. These are clearly described in the national standard ANSI/ASQC A2 (1987), *Terms, Symbols and Definitions for Acceptance Sampling.*

It is important to distinguish between product which is not fit for use and product which does not meet specification requirements. This is done in ANSI/ASQC A2 (1978), which uses the term "defect" in relation to the former and "nonconformity" in relation to the latter. These are defined as:

Defect.   A departure of a quality characteristic from its intended level or state that occurs with a severity sufficient to cause an associated product not to satisfy intended normal, or reasonably foreseeable, usage requirements.

Nonconformity. A departure of a quality characteristic from its intended level or state that occurs with a severity sufficient to cause an associated product or service not to meet a specification requirement.

Clearly, a unit of product containing one or more defects or nonconformities is a "defective" or a "nonconforming unit."

Since acceptance sampling plans usually relate to requirements imposed by the customer (internal or external), the terms "defect" and "defective" will be generally used here. Furthermore, in referring to the literature of acceptance sampling, the terms "defect" and "defective" will be commonly found. However, in appropriate instances in this section such as variables sampling plans which compare measurements to specifications, the terms "nonconformity" and "nonconforming unit" will be used.

Acceptance Sampling Procedures

Forms of Sampling. Sampling plans can be classified in two categories: attributes plans and variables plans.

Attributes Plans. In these plans, a sample is taken from the lot and each unit classified as conforming or nonconforming. The number nonconforming is then compared with the acceptance number stated in the plan and a decision is made to accept or reject the lot. Attributes plans can further be classified by one of the two basic criteria:

1. Plans which meet specified sampling risks provide protection on a lot-by-lot basis. Such risks are:
   a. A specified quality level for each lot (in terms of percent defective) having a selected risk (say 0.10) of being accepted by the consumer. The specified quality level is known as the lot tolerance percent defective (p_2); the selected risk is known as the consumer's risk (β).
   b. A specified quality level for each lot such that the sampling plan will accept a stated percentage (say 95 percent) of submitted lots having this quality level. This specified quality level is termed the acceptable quality level (AQL). The risk of rejecting a lot of AQL quality (p_1) is known as the producer's risk (α).
2. Plans which provide a limiting average percentage of defective items for the long run. This is known as the average outgoing quality level (AOQL).

Variables Plans. In these plans, a sample is taken and a measurement of a specified quality characteristic is made on each unit. These measurements are then summarized into a simple statistic (e.g., sample mean) and the observed value compared with an allowable value defined in the plan. A decision is then made to accept or reject the lot. When applicable, variables plans provide the same degree of consumer protection as attributes plans while using considerably smaller samples.

Attributes plans are generally applied on a percent defective basis. That is, the plan is instituted to control the proportion of accepted product which is defective or out of specification. Variables plans for percent defective are also used in this way. Such plans provide a sensitivity greater than attributes but require that the shape of the distribution of individual measurements must be known and stable. The shape of the distribution is used to translate the proportion defective into specific values of process parameters (mean, standard deviation) which are then controlled.

Variables plans can also be used to control process parameters to given levels when specifications are directed toward the process average or process variability and not specifically to percent defective. These variables plans for process parameter do not necessarily require detailed knowledge of the shape of the underlying distribution of individual measurements.

Sampling plans used in reliability and in the sampling of bulk product are generally of this type. Published plans in the reliability area, however, usually require detailed knowledge of the shape of the distribution of lifetimes. Some of the important features of attributes and variables plans for percent defective are compared in Table 25.1.

The principal advantage of variables plans for percent defective over corresponding attributes plans is a reduction in the sample size needed to obtain a given degree of protection. Table 25.2 shows a comparison of variables sample sizes necessary to achieve the same protection as the attributes plan: $n = 125$, $c = 3$ (sample size of 125 units, allowable number of defectives of 3).

Probably the most important consideration in the application of variables sampling plans is the requirement that the shape of the underlying distribution of

TABLE 25.1   Comparison of Attributes and Variables Sampling Plans for Percent Defective

Feature	Attributes	Variables
Inspection	Each item classified as defective or nondefective. Go no-go gages may be employed.	Each item measured. Inspection more sophisticated. Higher inspection and clerical cost.
Distribution of individual measurements	Need not be known.	*Must* be known (normal usually assumed).
Type of defect	Any number of defect types can be assessed by one plan.	Separate plan required for each type of defect.
Sample size	Depends on protection required.	Smaller sample size for same protection as attributes (at least 30% smaller*).
Process information	Percent defective.	Percent defective plus valuable information on process average and variability for corrective action.
Severity	Weights all defectives of a given kind equally.	Weights each unit inspected by its proximity to specifications.
Evidence to supplier	Defectives available as evidence.	Possible for lot to be rejected on sample containing no defectives.
Measurement errors	Measurements not recorded.	Measurements available for review.
Screened lots	No effect on performance of plan.	Screened lots may be rejected in error even though they contain no defectives.

*Bowker and Goode (1952), pp. 32–33. Assumes single sample of one characteristic.

TABLE 25.2 Comparison of Variables and Attributes
Sample Sizes*

$p_1 = 0.0109; \alpha = 0.05; p_2 = 0.0535; \beta = 0.10$

Plan	Sample size
Single-sampling attributes	125
Variables:	
σ known	19
σ unknown (s)	52
σ unknown ($\overline{R}$ of groups of 5)	75
Sequential sampling, σ known (ASN at p_1)	10.3

*Specifications assumed to be $> 6\sigma$ apart if two-sided.
Source: MIL-STD-105D, Code K, 1% AQL.

measurements to which the plan is to be applied must be known. For example, if the diameters of individual units of product are to be inspected, those diameters must be distributed in a known pattern. This means that statistical tests on past data must show that the distribution of the measurements involved is actually that assumed by the plan. Control chart evidence is also desirable to indicate process stability. This point cannot be overemphasized since a principal use of the distributional assumption in variables acceptance sampling for percent defective is with regard to individual units and not sample means, which can usually be assumed to be normally distributed. While it has been argued that variables plans may be roughly correct when applied to distributions other than the distribution assumed, judicious application requires confirmation that the underlying distribution of the process to which the plan is applied is actually that assumed by the plan.

Since some fundamental knowledge of the process producing the product is required for proper application of variables sampling plans for percent defective, a natural area of application of such plans is to in-house inspection, e.g., process control or final inspection. Use of these plans in incoming inspection should be restricted to product from known and trusted suppliers with a confirmed history of a reasonably stable process steadily producing product with a known shape of distribution. Process history should be initially developed under an attributes sampling plan. A switch to variables may be considered after a plot on probability paper or a goodness-of-fit test (see Section 23 under Selecting a Continuous Distribution) indicates that the distribution of product is as assumed. A control chart for at least 20 lots is useful to confirm process stability. There are times when the inspection situation demands the use of fewer lots. In such situations, appropriate limits for a 10-lot control chart have been developed by Hillier (1969). Variables plans are inappropriate for inspection of single lots unless the sample size is large enough to allow for meaningful goodness-of-fit tests to confirm that the shape of the underlying distribution of measurements is as assumed.

Variables plans for process parameter may be used whenever specifications are stated in terms of process mean or standard deviation. While control charts assess the consistency of process levels, acceptance sampling plans should be used to determine conformance to specifications. This is important, since both consumer and producer risks should be considered in acceptance sampling, while conventional Shewhart control charts consider only the producer's risk at one specified level ($\alpha = 0.003$).

In applying variables plans, it is advantageous to use a "known standard deviation" plan whenever possible. This usually requires a control chart, in control, with about 20 or more samples plotted to assure a stable level of standard deviation. The chart is maintained as long as the known standard deviation plan is being used. In the absence of such a chart, unknown standard deviation plans may be used, although knowledge of the shape of the distribution is still required for variables plans for percent defective. The construction and use of control charts are discussed in Section 24, Statistical Process Control.

Types of Sampling Plans. In single-sampling plans, the decision to accept or reject a lot is based on the results of inspection of a single group of units drawn from the lot. In double-sampling plans, a smaller initial sample is usually drawn, and a decision to accept or reject is reached on the basis of this smaller first sample if the number of defectives is either quite large or quite small. A second sample is taken if the results of the first are not decisive. Since it is necessary to draw and inspect the second sample only in borderline cases, the average number of pieces inspected per lot is generally smaller with double sampling. In multiple-sampling plans, one, or two, or several still smaller samples of n individual items are taken (usually truncated after some number of samples) until a decision to accept or reject is obtained. The term "sequential-sampling plan" is generally used when a decision is possible after each individual unit has been inspected.

Sampling Schemes and Systems. While simple sampling plans are often employed solely in sentencing individual lots, sampling schemes and systems are generally used in acceptance control applications involving a steady flow of product from the producer. The ANSI/ASQC Standard A2 (1987) defines a sampling plan as "a specific plan that states the sample size or sizes to be used, and the associated acceptance and nonacceptance criteria," and a sampling scheme as "a specific set of procedures which usually consists of acceptance sampling plans in which lot sizes, sample sizes, and acceptance criteria, or the amount of 100 percent inspection and sampling are related." The Definitions and Nomenclature Subcommittee of the ANSI Z-1 Committee on Quality Assurance defined a sampling system as a "unified collection of one or more sampling schemes." Thus, $n = 134$, $c = 3$ is a sampling plan; Code J, 1.0 percent AQL is a sampling scheme; and MIL-STD-105D, or its civilian version ANSI/ASQC Z1.4, is a sampling system.

The selection of a given sampling procedure depends upon the extent and nature of quality history. Thus, with a supplier having average quality history, it may be well to start with a single sampling plan and switch to an AQL scheme after moderate quality history has been obtained and then to skip-lot, supplier certification, or control chart procedures when extensive excellent history has been generated.

Published Tables and Procedures. From the point of view of ease of negotiation between the producer and the consumer, it is usually best to use published procedures and standards. This avoids problems of credibility created when one party or the other generates its own sampling plan. Also, the legal implications of using plans which appear in the litrature (such as Dodge-Romig plans) or have been subjected to national consensus review (such as ANSI/ASQC Z1.4, 1981) are obvious. Unique plans, specifically generated for a given application are probably best used internally.

Acceptance Control and Acceptance Sampling. Acceptance sampling refers to the application of specific sampling plans to a designated lot or sequence of lots. Acceptance sampling procedures can, however, be used in a program of *acceptance control* to achieve better quality at lower cost, improved control, and increased productivity. This involves the selection of sampling procedures to continually match operating conditions in terms of quality history and sampling results. In this way the plans and procedures of acceptance sampling can be used in an evolutionary manner to supplement each other in a continuing program of acceptance control for quality improvement with reduced inspection. It is the objective of acceptance control in any application to eventually phase out acceptance sampling in favor of supplier certification and process control. After explaining a variety of specific sampling procedures, this section concludes with suggestions on how and when to progress from sampling inspection toward reliance on process control and check inspection and eventually to no inspection at all, depending on the stage of the life cycle of the product and the state of control.

SAMPLING RISKS AND PARAMETERS

Risks. When acceptance sampling is conducted, the real parties of interest are the producer (supplier or Production Department) and the consumer, i.e., the company which buys from the supplier or the department which is to use the product. Since sampling carries the risk of rejecting "good" lots and of accepting "bad" lots, with associated serious consequences, producers and consumers have gone far to standardize the concepts of what constitutes good and bad lots, and to standardize also the risks associated with sampling. These risks are stated in conjunction with one or more parameters, i.e., quality indices for the plan. These indices are as follows.

Producer's Risk. The producer's risk α is the probability that a "good" lot will be rejected by the sampling plan. In some plans, this risk is fixed at 0.05; in other plans, it varies from about 0.01 to 0.10. The risk is stated in conjunction with a numerical definition of the maximum quality level that may pass through the plan, often called the acceptable quality level.

Acceptable Quality Level. As defined by MIL-STD-105D (1963), the acceptable quality level (AQL) is the maximum percent defective (or maximum number of defects per hundred units) that, for the purpose of sampling inspection, can be considered satisfactory as a process average. A sampling plan should have a low producer's risk for quality which is equal to or better than the AQL.

Consumer's Risk. The consumer's risk β is the probability that a "bad" lot will be accepted by the sampling plan. The risk is stated in conjunction with a numerical definition of rejectable quality such as a lot tolerance percent defective.

Lot Tolerance Percent Defective. The lot tolerance percent defective (LTPD) is the level of quality that is unsatisfactory and therefore should be rejected by the sampling plan. A consumer's risk of 0.10 is common and LTPD has been defined as the lot quality for which the probability of acceptance is 0.10; i.e., only 10 percent of such lots will be accepted. (LTPD is a special case of the concept of limiting quality, LQ, or rejectable quality level, RQL. The latter terms are used in tables that provide plans for several values of the consumer's risk as contrasted to a value of 0.10 for the LTPD.)

A third type of quality index, average outgoing quality limit, is used with 100 percent inspection of rejected lots and will be discussed later in this section.

The producer's and consumer's risks and associated AQL and LTPD are summarized graphically by an operating characteristic curve.

Operating Characteristic Curve.   The Operating Characteristic (OC) curve is a graph of lot fraction defective versus the probability that the sampling plan will accept the lot.

Figure 25.1*b* shows an ideal OC curve for a case where it is desired to accept all lots 3 percent defective or less and reject all lots having a quality level greater than 3 percent defective. Note that all lots less than 3 percent defective have a probability of acceptance of 1.0 (certainty); all lots greater than 3 percent defective have a probability of acceptance of zero. Actually, however, no sampling plan exists that can discriminate perfectly; there always remains some risk that a "good" lot will be rejected or that a "bad" lot will be accepted. The best that can be achieved in practice is to control these risks.

Figure 25.1*c* shows the curve of behavior that would be obtained if an inspector were instructed to take a sample of 150 pieces from a large lot and to accept the lot if no more than four defective pieces were found. Such curves can be constructed from the appropriate probability distribution. For example, using the Poisson table (Appendix II, Table E), we find that for a sample size of 150 ($n = 150$) and 2 percent defective ($p = 0.02$) we would expect $np = 3.0$ defectives in the sample. The table shows for $r = 4$ and $np = 3.0$, the probability of acceptance (for four or fewer defectives) is 0.815.

It is seen from this curve that a lot 3 percent defective has one chance in two of being accepted. However, a lot 3.5 percent defective, though technically a "bad" lot, has 39 chances in 100 of being accepted. In like manner, a lot 2.5 percent defective, though technically a good lot, has 34 chances in 100 of not being accepted.

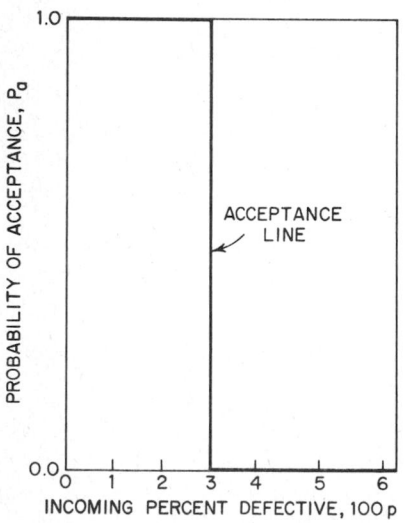

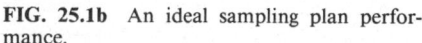

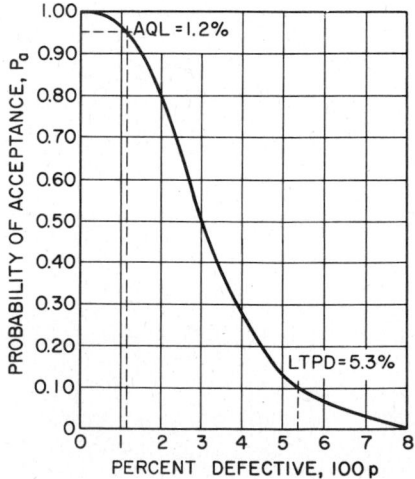

FIG. 25.1b   An ideal sampling plan performance.

FIG. 25.1c   An actual sampling plan performance.

Actually the lack of a sharp distinction may not be too serious. Economically, it may be a matter of indifference whether a lot 3 percent defective is accepted or sorted. In the case of lots 2.5 or 3.5 percent defective it makes a difference, but the difference may not be great in relation to the cost of trying for greater precision, and in view of the imponderables which are still present in computing break-even points.

The effect of parameters of the sampling plan on the shape of the OC curve is demonstrated in Figure 25.2, where the curve for perfect discrimination is given along with the curves for three particular acceptance sampling plans. The following statements summarize the effects:

1. When the sample size approaches the lot size or, in fact, approaches a large percentage of the lot size, and the acceptance number is chosen appropriately, the OC curve approaches the perfect OC curve (the rectangle at p_1).

2. When the acceptance number is zero, the OC curve is exponential in shape, concave upward (see curves 2 and 3).

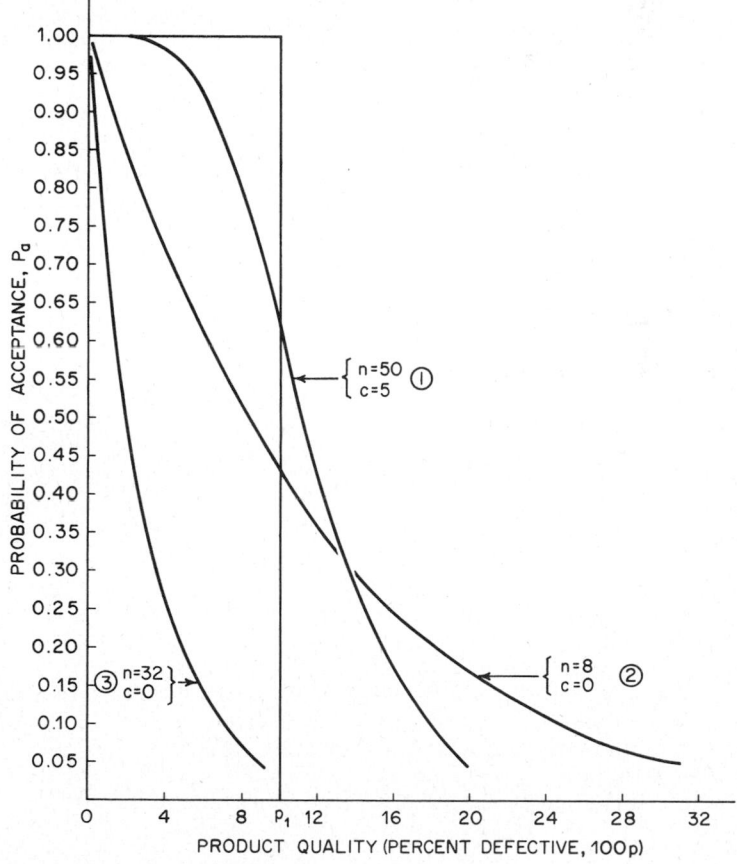

FIG. 25.2 Shape of the OC curve.

3. As the acceptance number increases, the OC curve is pushed up, so to speak, for low values of p, and the probability of acceptance for these quality levels is increased, with a point of inflection at some larger value of p (see curve 1).

4. Increasing the sample size and the acceptance number together gives the closest approach to the perfect discrimination OC curve (see curve 1).

It is sometimes useful to distinguish between type A and type B OC curves (see Dodge and Romig, 1959, pp. 56–59). Type A curves give the probability of acceptance for an individual lot that comes from finite production conditions that cannot be assumed to continue in the future. Type B curves assume that each lot is one of an infinite number of lots produced under essentially the same production conditions. In practice, most OC curves are viewed as type B. With the few exceptions noted, this section assumes type B OC curves.

Average Sample Number Curve.   The average sample number (ASN) is the average number of units inspected per lot in sampling inspection ignoring any 100 percent inspection of rejected lots. In single-sampling inspection the ASN is equal to n, the sample size. However, in double- and multiple-sampling plans the probability of not reaching a decision on the initial sample, and consequently being forced to inspect a second, third, etc., sample must be considered. For a double-sampling plan with sample sizes n_1 and n_2, the average sample number, ASN is simply

$$\text{ASN} = n_1 + (1 - P_{a_1})\, n_2$$

where P_{a_1}, is the probability of acceptance on the first sample. The ASN for multiple sampling is more complicated to calculate; see Schilling (1982).

A comparison of ASN for some specific plans is shown in Figure 25.3. (The calculations assume that all samples selected are completely inspected.) As indicated, double and multiple sampling generally lead to economies over single sampling when quality is either very good or very poor.

Average Outgoing Quality Limit.   The acceptable quality level (AQL) and lot tolerance percent defective (LTPD) have been cited as two common quality indices for sampling plans. A third commonly used index is the average outgoing quality limit (AOQL). The AOQL is the upper limit of average quality of outgoing product from accepted lots and from rejected lots which have been screened.

The AOQL concept stems from the relationship between the fraction defective before inspection (incoming quality) and the fraction defective after inspection (outgoing quality) when inspection is nondestructive and rejected lots are screened. When incoming quality is perfect, outgoing quality must likewise be perfect. However, when incoming quality is very bad, outgoing quality will also be near perfect, because the sampling plan will cause most lots to be rejected and 100 percent inspected. Thus, at either extreme—incoming quality very good or very bad—the outgoing quality will tend to be very good. It follows that between these extremes is the point at which the percent defective in the outgoing material will reach its maximum. This point is known as the AOQL.

If p is incoming quality, P_r is the probability of lot rejection, and all rejected lots are screened and made free of defects (i.e., 0 percent), then

$$\text{AOQ} = (p)P_a + (0)P_r = (p)P_a$$

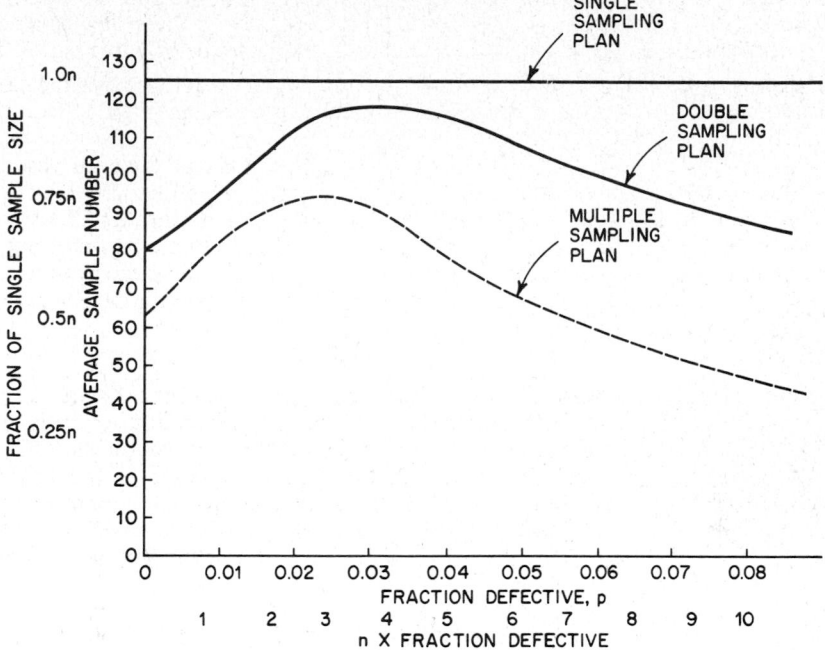

FIG. 25.3 Average sample number vs. fraction defective.

This calculation is approximate in that it does not account for the small effect of 100 percent inspection of the units in the samples from accepted lots. Taking this into account:

$$AOQ = pP_a \left(1 - \frac{n}{N} \right)$$

for sample size n and lot size N.

Average Outgoing Quality Curve. An example of the calculation for the AOQL and a plot of the average outgoing quality (AOQ) curve is shown in Table 25.3 and Figure 25.4. Schilling (1982) has indicated that for acceptance numbers of five or less

$$AOQL \simeq \frac{0.4}{n} (1.25c + 1)$$

Average Total Inspection. The average total inspection (ATI) takes into account the likelihood of 100 percent inspection of rejected lots when this is possible; i.e., inspection is nondestructive. The lot size N must now be taken into account. Again with single-sampling plans with sample size n, lot size N, probability of acceptance P_a, and probability of rejection P_r,

$$ATI = P_a n + P_r N$$

TABLE 25.3 Computations for Average Outgoing Quality Limit (AOQL); for this Example, $n = 78$, $c = 1$

Incoming quality fraction defective = p	np	Probability of acceptance = P_a	Average outgoing quality (AOQ) = $p \times P_a$
0.005	0.39	0.940	0.00470
0.010	0.78	0.820	0.00820
0.015	1.17	0.680	0.01020
0.020	1.56	0.550	0.01100*
0.025	1.95	0.430	0.01075
0.030	2.34	0.330	0.00990
0.035	2.73	0.250	0.00875
0.040	3.12	0.190	0.00760
0.045	3.51	0.140	0.00630
0.050	3.90	0.100	0.00500
0.055	4.29	0.075	0.00402
0.060	4.68	0.050	0.00300

*AOQL $\cong$ maximum AOQ $\cong$ 0.01100 = 1.1%.

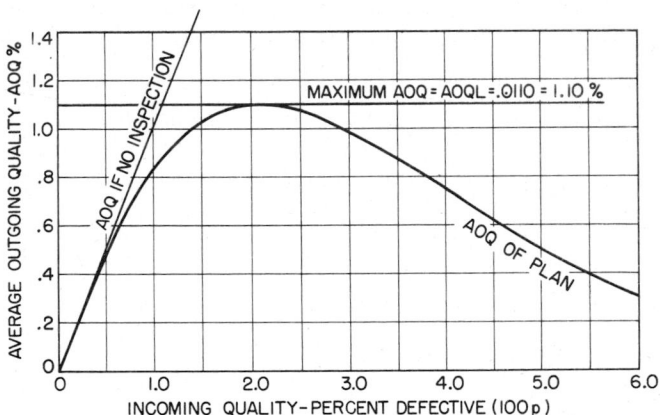

FIG. 25.4 AOQ curve and AOQL for a typical sampling plan.

An extension to double sampling is simply

$$\text{ATI} = n_1 + (1 - P_{a_1})n_2 + (N - n_1 - n_2)(1 - P_a)$$

where P_{a_1}, is the probability of acceptance on the first sample. Extension to multiple-sampling plans of k levels is straightforward and will not be derived here. See Schilling (1982).

Minimum Total Inspection. Minimum inspection per lot, for a given type of protection, can be illustrated by the following example.

Assume that a consumer establishes acceptance criteria as an LTPD of 5 percent. A great many sampling plans meet this criterion. Some of these plans are:

Take from each lot a sample n of	Accept the lot if the number of defectives does not exceed the maximum acceptance number c
46	0
78	1
106	2
134	3
160	4

Figure 25.5 shows the corresponding operating characteristic curves. Each plan has an LTPD of 5 percent; i.e., the probability of acceptance of a submitted inspection lot with fraction defective of 0.05 is 0.10. Which plan should be used? One logical basis for choosing among these plans is to use that one which gives the least inspection per lot.

The total number of units inspected consists of (1) the sample which is inspected for each lot and (2) the remaining units which must be inspected in those lots which are rejected by the sampling inspection. The number of lots

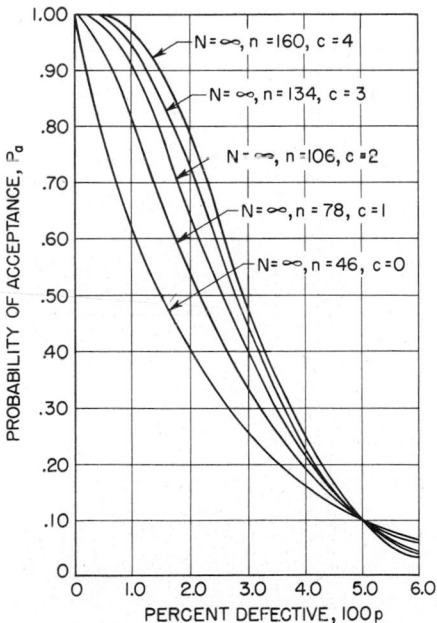

FIG. 25.5 Family of sampling plans each having LTPD = 0.05.

rejected in turn depends on the normal level of defectives in the product so that minimum inspection is a function of incoming quality.

A sample computation of minimum inspection per lot is shown in Table 25.4. It is assumed that rejected lots are detail (100 percent) inspected. For small acceptance numbers the total inspection is high because many lots need to be detailed. For large acceptance numbers the total is again high, this time because of the large size of samples. The minimum sum occurs at a point between these extremes.

From the foregoing it is seen that for any specified conditions of

Lot tolerance percent defective

Consumer's risk

Lot size

Process average

it becomes possible to derive the values of

$$n = \text{sample size}$$

to obtain $c = \text{allowable number of defectives in the sample}$

$$I_m = \text{minimum inspection per lot}$$

Similar reasoning may be applied in making a selection from a group of sampling plans designed to give the same average outgoing quality limit (AOQL).

Complete tables for sampling have been derived for minimum inspection per lot for a variety of $\bar{p}$, LTPD, and AOQL values (e.g., Dodge and Romig, 1959). These will be described later.

Selection of a Numerical Value of the Quality Index.   There are three alternatives for evaluating lots: no inspection, inspect a sample, 100 percent inspection (or more). An economic evaluation of these alternatives requires a comparison of *total* costs under each of the alternatives.

TABLE 25.4 Computation of Minimum Inspection per Lot for 5 Alternative *n-c* Combinations Appropriate to Lots of $N = 1000$ Articles

All plans have the same lot tolerance percent defective. Incoming material has a process average percent defective, $\bar{p} = 0.5\%$.

				Average no. pieces inspected		
Sample size n	Allowable number of defects c	Probability of acceptance by sampling P_a	Probability of inspecting residue of lot $1 - P_a$	In sample* n	In rest of lot† $(N - n) \times (1 - P_a)$	Total inspected per lot
46	0	0.795	0.205	46	196	242
78	1	0.940	0.060	78	55	133
106	2	0.983	0.017	106	15	121‡
134	3	0.995	0.005	134	4	138
160	4	0.998	0.002	160	2	162

*The sample size indicates the number inspected from each lot.
†The size of the uninspected residue of the lot, multiplied by the probability that it will have to be inspected because of rejection of the sample.
‡This is the minimum sought.

Enell (1954) has suggested that a break-even point be used in the selection of a quality index:

$$p_b = \frac{I}{A}$$

where I = inspection cost per item
$\quad A$ = damage cost incurred if a defective slips through inspection

If it is thought that the lot quality p is less than p_b, the total cost will be lowest with sampling inspection or no inspection. If p is greater than p_b, 100 percent inspection is best. If p is unknown, it may be best to sample using an appropriate sampling plan such as an AOQL scheme.

For example, a microcomputer device costs $0.50 per unit to inspect. A damage cost of $10.00 is incurred if a defective device is installed in the larger system. Therefore,

$$p_b = \frac{0.50}{10.00} = 0.05 = 5.0 \text{ percent}$$

If it is expected that the percent defective will be greater than 5 percent, then 100 percent inspection should be used. Otherwise, use sampling or no inspection.

The formula assumes that the sample size is small compared to the lot size, the cost to replace a defective found in inspection is borne by the producer or is small compared to the damage or inconvenience caused by a defective, and no inspection errors occur.

As a 5 percent defective quality level is the break-even point between sorting and sampling, the appropriate sampling plan should provide for a lot to have a 50 percent probability of being sorted or sampled; i.e., the probability of acceptance for the plan should be 0.50 at a 5 percent defective quality level. The operating characteristic curves in a set of sampling tables such as MIL-STD-105D can now be examined to determine an AQL. For example, suppose that the device is inspected in lots of 3000 pieces. The operating characteristic curves for this case (code letter K) are shown in MIL-STD-105D. The plan closest to having a P_a of 0.50 for a 5 percent level is the plan for an AQL of 1.5 percent. Therefore, this is the plan to adopt.

Some plans (for example, MIL-STD-105D) include a classification of defects to help determine the numerical value of the AQL. Defects are first classified as critical, major, or minor, according to definitions provided in the standard. Different AQLs may be designated for groups of defects considered collectively, or for individual defects. Critical defects may have a 0 percent AQL while major defects might be assigned a low AQL, say 1 percent, and minor defects a higher AQL, say 4 percent. Some manufacturers of complex products specify quality in terms of number of defects per million parts.

The variability in quality from lot to lot is important. If past history shows that the quality level is much better than the break-even point and is stable from lot to lot, little if any inspection may be needed. If the level is much worse than the break-even point, and consistently so, it will usually be cheaper to use 100 percent inspection (or change suppliers) rather than sample. If the quality is at neither of these extremes, a detailed economic comparison of no inspection, sampling, and 100 percent inspection should be made. Sampling is usually best when the product is a mixture of high-quality lots and low-quality lots, or when the producer's process is not in a state of statistical control.

The high costs associated with component failures in complex electronic equipment coupled with the development of automatic testing equipment for components has resulted in the economic justification of 100 percent inspection for some electronic components. The cost of finding and correcting a defective can increase by a ratio of 10 for each major stage that the product moves from production to the customer; i.e., if it costs $1 at incoming inspection the cost increases to $10 at the printed circuit board stage, $100 at the system level, and $1000 in the field (Wescom, 1978).

In practice, the quantification of the quality index is a matter of judgment based on the following factors:

1. Past performance on quality
2. Effect of nonconforming product on later production steps
3. Effect of nonconforming product on fitness for use
4. Urgency of delivery requirements
5. Cost to achieve the specified quality level

IMPLEMENTATION OF AN ACCEPTANCE SAMPLING PROCEDURE

Assumptions Made in Sampling Plans

Inspection Error.   In implementing acceptance sampling plans, it is commonly assumed that:

1. The inspectors follow the prescribed sampling plan.
2. The inspection is made without error; i.e., no human or equipment mistakes are made in measurement or in judging conformance.

In practice, these assumptions are not fully valid. See Section 18, under Inspector Errors.

Units of Product.   These may consist of (1) discrete pieces or (2) specimens from bulk material. The criteria used for judging the conformance of a single unit of product to standard are somewhat different for these two categories. The criteria used for judging lot conformance differ even more widely.

Seriousness Classification of Defects.   Many sampling plans set up their criteria for judging lot conformance in terms of an allowable number of defects in the sample. Since defects differ greatly in seriousness, the sampling plans must somehow take these differences into account.

Where there exists a formal plan for seriousness classification of defects, the sampling plans may be structured so that:

1. A separate sampling plan is used for each seriousness class, e.g., large sample sizes for critical defects, small sample sizes for minor defects.
2. A common sampling plan is used, but the allowable number of defects varies for each class; e.g., no critical defects are allowed, but some minor defects are allowed.
3. The criteria may be established in terms of defects per hundred units, the allowable number being different for each class.

4. The criteria may be based on demerits per unit; i.e., all defects found are converted to a scale of demerits based on the classification system.

In the absence of a formal system of seriousness classification, all defects are considered equally important during the sampling inspection. However, when nonconforming lots are subsequently reviewed to judge fitness for use, the review board gives consideration to the seriousness of the defects.

Lot Formation. The general approach to lot formation is discussed in Section 18, under the Nature of Lots of Product. While most acceptance sampling plans can be validly applied regardless of how lots are formed (skip-lot plans are an exception), the economics of inspection and the quality of the accepted product are greatly influenced by the manner of lot formation.

The interrelation of lot formation to economics of inspection is discussed in Section 18, under How Much Inspection? and will not be elaborated here. The interrelation of lot formation to quality of accepted product can be seen from a single example.

Ten machines are producing the same product. Nine of these produce perfect product. The tenth machine produces 100 percent defectives. If lots consist of product from single machines, the defective product from the tenth machine will always be detected by sampling. If, however, the lots are formed by mixing up the work from all machines, then it is inevitable that some defects will get through the sampling plan.

The fact that lot formation so strongly influences outgoing quality and inspection economics has led to some guidelines for lot formation:

1. Do not mix product from different sources (processes, production shifts, input materials, etc.) unless there is evidence that the lot-to-lot variation is small enough to be ignored.

2. Do not accumulate product over extensive periods of time (for lot formation).

3. Do make use of extraneous information (process capability, prior inspections, etc.) in lot formation. Such extraneous information is especially useful when product is submitted in isolated lots, or in very small lots. In such cases the extraneous information may provide better knowledge on which to base an acceptance decision than the sampling data.

4. Do make lots as large as possible consistent with the above to take advantage of low proportionate sampling costs. (Sample sizes do not increase greatly despite large increases in lot sizes.)

When production is continuous (e.g., the assembly line) so that the "lot" is necessarily arbitrary, the sampling plans used are themselves designed to be of a "continuous" nature. These continuous sampling plans are discussed later in this section.

Lot-by-Lot Inspection. When product is submitted in a series of lots (termed "lot-by-lot"), the acceptance sampling plans are defined in terms of

N = lot size
n = sample size
c = acceptance number, i.e., the allowable number of defects in the sample
r = rejection number

When more than one sample per lot is specified, the successive sample sizes are designated as n_1, n_2, n_3, etc. The successive acceptance numbers are c_1, c_2, c_3, etc. The successive rejection numbers are r_1, r_2, r_3, etc.

Selecting the Sample. The results of sampling are greatly influenced by the method of selecting the sample. In acceptance sampling, the sample should be representative of the lot. In those cases where the inspector has knowledge of how the lot was formed, this knowledge can be used in selecting the sample by stratification (see below). Lacking this knowledge, the correct approach is to use random sampling.

Random Sampling. All published sampling tables are prepared on the assumption that samples are drawn at random; i.e., at any one time each of the remaining uninspected units of product has an equal chance of being the next unit selected for the sample. To conduct random sampling requires that (1) random numbers be generated and (2) these random numbers be applied to the product at hand.

Random numbers are available in prefabricated form in tables of random numbers (Appendix II, Table CC). One uses such a table by entering it at random (without "looking") and then proceeding in some chosen direction (up, down, right, left, etc.) to obtain random numbers for use. Numbers which cannot be applied to the product arrangement are discarded.

Random numbers may also be generated by various devices. These include:

1. *Calculators or computers:* Many calculators are available with random-number routines built in. Computers are, of course, an excellent source of random numbers. Statistical software often has random numbers built in.

2. *A bowl of numbered chips or marbles:* After mixing, one is withdrawn and its number recorded. It is then replaced and the bowl is again mixed before the next number is withdrawn.

3. *Random number dice:* One form is the icosahedron (20-sided) dice. There are three of these, each of a different color, one for units, one for tens, and one for hundreds. (Each die has the numbers from 0 to 9 appearing twice.) Hence one throw of the three dice displays a random number within 000 to 999.

Once the random numbers are available, they must be adapted to the form in which the product is submitted. For systematically packed material, the container system can be numbered to correspond to the system of random numbers. For example, a lot might be submitted in 8 trays, each of which has 10 rows and 7 columns. In such a case, the trays might be numbered from 0 to 7, the rows from 0 to 9, and the columns from 0 to 6. Then, using three-digit random numbers, the digits are assigned to trays, rows, and columns, respectively.

For bulk packed materials, other practical procedures may be used. In the case of small parts, they may be strewn onto a flat surface which is marked with grid lines in a 10×10 arrangement. Based on two-digit random numbers, the cell at the intersection of these digits is identified. Within the cell, further positional identity can be determined with a third digit.

For fluid or well-mixed bulk products, the fluidity obviates the need for random numbers, and the samples may be taken from "here and there."

Stratified Sampling. When the "lots" are known to come from different machines, production shifts, operators, etc., the product is actually multiple lots which have been arbitrarily combined. In such cases, the sampling is deliberately stratified; i.e., an attempt is made to draw the sample proportionately from each true lot. However, within each lot, randomness is still the appropriate basis for sampling.

A further departure from randomness may be due to the economics of opening containers, i.e., whether to open few containers and examine a few pieces from each.

Sampling Bias.   Unless rigorous procedures are set up for sampling at random and/or by stratification, the sampling can deteriorate into a variety of biases which are detrimental to good decision making. The more usual biases consist of:

1. Sampling from the same location in all containers, racks, or bins
2. Previewing the product and selecting only those units which appear to be defective (or nondefective)
3. Ignoring those portions of the lot which are inconvenient to sample
4. Deciding on a pattern of stratification in the absence of knowledge of how the lot was made up

Sampling by Attributes.   The classical example is the legendary inspector who always took samples from the four corners and center of each tray and the legendary production worker who very carefully filled these same spots with perfect product.

Because the structured sampling plans do assume randomness, and because some forms of sampling bias can significantly distort the product acceptance decisions, all concerned should be alert to plan the sampling to minimize these biases. Thereafter, supervision and auditing should be alert to assure that the actual sampling conforms to these plans.

ATTRIBUTES SAMPLING

Overview of Single, Double, Multiple, and Sequential Plans.   In general, all four sampling plans can be planned to give lots of specified qualities nearly the same chance of being accepted; i.e., the operating-characteristic curves can be made quite similar (matched) if desired. However, the best type of plan for one producer or product is not necessarily best for another. The suitability of a plan can be judged by considering the following factors:

1. Average number of parts inspected
2. Cost of administration
3. Information obtained as to lot quality
4. Acceptability of plan to producers

The advantages and disadvantages of the four forms of sampling plans are tabulated in Table 25.5. The average number of parts that need to be inspected to arrive at a decision varies according to the plan and the quality of the material submitted. In cases where the cost of inspection of each piece is substantial, the reduction in number of pieces inspected may justify use of sequential sampling despite its greater complexity and higher administrative costs. On the other hand, where it is not practicable to hold the entire lot of parts while sampling and inspection are going on, it becomes necessary to set aside the full number of items that may need to be inspected before inspection even begins. In these circum-

TABLE 25.5 Comparative Advantages and Disadvantages of Single, Double, and Multiple Sampling

Feature	Single sampling	Double sampling	Multiple sampling	Sequential
Acceptability to producer	Psychologically poor to give only one chance of passing the lot	Psychologically adequate	Psychologically open to criticism as being indecisive	Psychologically open to criticism as being more indecisive than multiple
Number of pieces inspected per lot*	Generally greatest	Usually (but not always) 10 to 50% less than single sampling	Generally (but not always) less than double sampling by amounts of the order of 30%	Minimum over all attributes plans
Administration cost in training, personnel, records, drawing and identifying samples, etc.	Lowest	Greater than single sample	Greater	Greatest
Information about prevailing level of quality in each lot	Most	Less than single sample	Less than double	Least

*This is not to be confused with total cost of inspection, which includes administration cost of the plan.

stances single sampling may be preferable if the cost of selecting, unpacking, and handling parts is appreciable. It is of course simplest to train personnel, set up records, and administer a single-sampling plan. A crew of inspectors hastily thrown together cannot easily be taught all the intricacies of the more elaborate plans. However, double-sampling plans have been demonstrated to be simple to use in a wide variety of conditions, economical in total cost, and acceptable psychologically to both producer and consumer.

Selecting Sampling Plans. Sampling plans are often specified by choosing two points on the OC curve: the AQL denoted by p_1 and the LTPD symbolized by p_2. Tables have been developed to facilitate the selection process by using unity (np) values from the Poisson distribution. See Cameron (1952), Duncan (1974), and Schilling and Johnson (1980). Such tables use the operating ratio, $R = p_2/p_1$, in conjunction with the unity value of (np_1) or (np_2) to obtain the sample size and acceptance number(s) for the plan whose OC curve passes through the points specified. Often other unity values are provided which assess other properties of the plan. Such tables are illustrated below by the Schilling-Johnson (1980) table, reproduced in part as Table 25.6, which uses producer risk $\alpha = 0.05$ and consumer risk $\beta = 0.10$ with equal sample sizes at each stage of a double or multiple sampling plan. The table provides matched sets of single, double, and multiple sampling plans, such that their OC curves are roughly equivalent. For example, if $p_1 = 0.012$ and $p_2 = 0.053$ then $R = 4.4$. The closest value given under the column for R is 4.058, corresponding to an acceptance number of 4. The sample size is then found to be $n = 7.994 \div 0.053 = 150.8$, which would usually be taken to be 150. The operating characteristic curve for the plan can be seen in Figure 25.1c.

Single Sampling. In single sampling by attributes, the decision to accept or reject the lot is based on the results of inspection of a single sample selected from the lot. The operation of a single-sampling plan by attributes is given in Figure 25.6. The characteristics of an attributes sampling plan are given in Table 25.7.

Double Sampling. In double sampling by attributes, an initial sample is taken, and a decision to accept or reject the lot is reached on the basis of this first sample if the number of nonconforming units is either quite small or quite large. A second sample is taken if the results of the first sample are not decisive. The operation of an attributes double-sampling plan is given in Figure 25.7. The characteristics of an attributes double-sampling plan are given in Table 25.8.

Multiple Sampling. In multiple sampling by attributes, more than two samples can be taken in order to reach a decision to accept or reject the lot. The chief advantage of multiple sampling plans is a reduction in sample size for the same protection. The operation of multiple sampling by attributes is given in Figure 25.8. The characteristics of a multiple sampling plan are given in Table 25.9.

Sequential Sampling. In sequential sampling, each item is treated as a sample of size one, and a determination to accept, reject, or continue sampling is made after inspection of each item. The major advantage of sequential sampling plans is that these plans offer the opportunity for achieving the minimum sample size for a given protection. The operation of sequential sampling by attributes is given in Figure 25.9. The characteristics of a sequential sampling plan are given in Table 25.10.

TABLE 25.6 Unity Values for Construction and Evaluation of Single, Double, and Multiple Sampling Plans

($n_1 = n_2 = \cdots = n_k$; # indicates acceptance not allowed at a given stage)

Plan	Acceptance numbers	$R=p_2/p_1$	np_2		.99	.95	.90	.75	.50	.25	.10	.05	.01	.005	.001	.0005	.0001
																	Probability of acceptance
OS	Ac = 0 Re = 1	44.893	2.303	np ASN n_1	.0101 1	.0513 1	.105 1	.288 1	.693 1	1.386 1	2.303 1	2.996 1	4.605 1	5.298 1	6.908 1	7.601 1	9.206 1
1S	Ac = 1 Re = 2	10.958	3.890	np ASN n_1	.149 1	.355 1	.532 1	.961 1	1.678 1	2.693 1	3.890 1	4.744 1	6.638 1	7.430 1	9.234 1	10.000 1	11.759 1
1D	Ac = 0 1 Re = 2 2	12.029	2.490	np ASN n_1	.0860 1.079	.207 1.168	.310 1.228	.566 1.321	1.006 1.368	1.661 1.316	2.490 1.206	3.124 1.137	4.649 1.045	5.324 1.026	6.914 1.007	7.604 1.004	9.209 1.001
1M	Ac = # # 0 0 1 1 2 Re = 2 2 2 3 3 3 3	8.903	.917	np ASN n_1	.0459 3.254	.103 3.501	.148 3.637	.252 3.774	.416 3.640	.643 3.169	.917 2.601	1.121 2.270	1.602 1.761	1.815 1.618	2.325 1.388	2.549 1.319	3.075 1.205
2S	Ac = 2 Re = 3	6.506	5.322	np ASN n_1	.436 1	.818 1	1.102 1	1.727 1	2.674 1	3.920 1	5.322 1	6.296 1	8.406 1	9.274 1	11.230 1	12.053 1	13.934 1
2D	Ac = 0 3 Re = 3 4	5.357	3.402	np ASN n_1	.363 1.298	.635 1.443	.827 1.511	1.231 1.581	1.816 1.564	2.566 1.450	3.402 1.306	3.986 1.222	5.290 1.097	5.852 1.066	7.201 1.025	7.810 1.016	9.295 1.005
2M	Ac = 0 0 1 2 3 4 Re = 2 3 3 4 5 5	6.244	1.355	np ASN n_1	.111 2.432	.217 2.789	.293 2.983	.451 3.207	.683 3.165	.988 2.776	1.355 2.261	1.635 1.950	2.343 1.470	2.671 1.344	3.458 1.167	3.803 1.122	4.602 1.060

Plan	Ac	Re	Row	A	B	1	2	3	4	5	6	7	8	9	10	11	12	13
3S	3	4	np	4.891	6.681	.823	1.366	1.745	2.535	3.672	5.109	6.681	7.754	10.045	10.978	13.062	13.935	15.922
			ASN			1	1	1	1	1	1	1	1	1	1	1	1	1
			n_1															
3D	1 4	4 5	np	4.398	4.398	.635	1.000	1.246	1.750	2.465	3.373	4.398	5.130	6.808	7.542	9.270	10.019	11.757
			ASN			1.130	1.245	1.316	1.421	1.470	1.414	1.293	1.211	1.084	1.053	1.017	1.010	1.003
			n_1															
3M	# 0 1 2 3 4 6	3 3 4 5 6 6 7	np	4.672	1.626	.200	.348	.446	.642	.910	1.246	1.626	1.901	2.553	2.848	3.566	3.887	4.650
			ASN			2.461	2.820	3.026	3.286	3.288	2.935	2.450	2.156	1.693	1.559	1.340	1.274	1.163
			n_1															
4S	4	5	np	4.058	7.994	1.279	1.970	2.433	3.369	4.671	6.274	7.994	9.154	11.605	12.594	14.795	15.711	17.792
			ASN			1	1	1	1	1	1	1	1	1	1	1	1	1
			n_1															
4D	3 5	6 6	np	4.102	6.699	1.099	1.633	1.992	2.728	3.789	5.162	6.699	7.762	10.047	10.978	13.062	13.933	15.909
			ASN			1.025	1.077	1.125	1.233	1.341	1.345	1.242	1.164	1.055	1.033	1.009	1.005	1.001
			n_1															
4M	# 1 2 3 4 5 6	3 3 4 6 6 7 7	np	4.814	2.118	.266	.440	.558	.798	1.141	1.591	2.118	2.502	3.385	3.763	4.640	5.016	5.884
			ASN			2.128	2.300	2.417	2.590	2.618	2.384	2.021	1.792	1.427	1.326	1.174	1.132	1.070
			n_1															
5S	5	6	np	3.550	9.275	1.785	2.613	3.152	4.219	5.670	7.423	9.275	10.513	13.109	14.150	16.455	17.411	19.578
			ASN			1	1	1	1	1	1	1	1	1	1	1	1	1
			n_1															
5D	2 6	5 7	np	3.547	5.781	1.116	1.630	1.959	2.607	3.490	4.579	5.781	6.627	8.537	9.357	11.253	12.066	13.928
			ASN			1.097	1.199	1.263	1.360	1.405	1.352	1.243	1.171	1.064	1.039	1.012	1.007	1.002
			n_1															
5M	#1 2 3 5 7 9	4 5 6 7 8 9 10	np	3.243	2.270	.490	.700	.830	1.079	1.410	1.814	2.270	2.604	3.411	3.776	4.642	5.017	5.884
			ASN			2.496	2.906	3.143	3.459	3.516	3.188	2.677	2.347	1.791	1.628	1.367	1.292	1.171
			n_1															

Source: Schilling and Johnson, 1980, p. 221.

SCHEMATIC OPERATION OF SINGLE SAMPLING

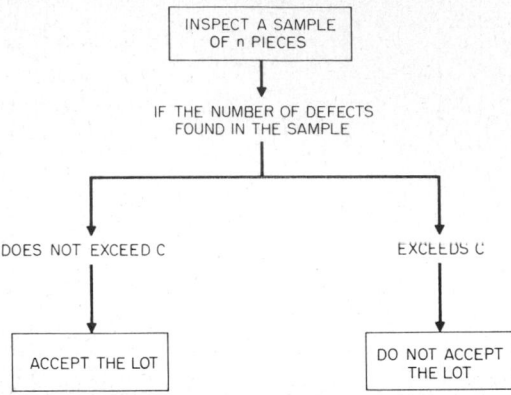

FIG. 25.6 Schematic operation of single sampling. In practice, the lot not to be accepted may be repaired, junked, etc. Sampling tables usually assume that the lot is detail-inspected and the defective pieces all repaired or replaced by good pieces.

Rectification Schemes. Rectification schemes are used when it is desired to ensure that the average outgoing quality level of a series of lots will not exceed specified levels. Such schemes employ 100 percent inspection (screening), with nonconforming items replaced by conforming items.

There are two basic types of rectification schemes: LTPD schemes and AOQL schemes. LTPD schemes ensure consumer quality level protection for each lot, while AOQL schemes ensure AOQL protection for a series of lots. Both types of schemes minimize ATI at the projected process average percent nonconforming. See Dodge and Romig (1959).

TABLE 25.7 Single Sampling by Attributes

Example: Determine a plan which will have AQL = 100 p_1 = 1.0% with producer risk α = 0.05 and LTPD = $100p_2$ = 5.0% with consumer risk β = 0.10. Suppose a sample is taken from a lot of N = 500 and four nonconforming units are found.

Summary of plan	Calculations
I. Restrictions: Random sample of dichotomous data	

II. Necessary information
    A. Producer quality level, p_1
    B. Producer risk, α
    C. Consumer quality level, p_2
    D. Consumer risk, β
	II.
	    A. p_1 = 0.01
	    B. α = 0.05
	    C. p_2 = 0.05
	    D. β = 0.10

III. Selection of plan (using Table 25.6)
    A. Calculate operating ratio
 	
        $R = p_2 \,/\, p_1$
	III.
	    A. R = 0.05/0.01
	
	        = 5

TABLE 25.7 Single Sampling by Attributes (*Continued*)

Summary of plan	Calculations
B. Choose single sampling plan (S) from Table 25.6 which shows $R \leq$ the value calculated	B. Choose Plan 3S since R shown is 4.891
C. Acceptance and rejection numbers are given	C. Ac = 3 Re = 4
D. Determine sample size from value of (np_2) shown for the plan as $n = (np_2)/p_2$; round up	D. $n = \dfrac{6.681}{0.05}$

IV. Elements

Summary of plan	Calculations
A. Sample size: See III above	IV. A. $n = 134$
B. Statistic: d = number nonconforming in sample	B. $d = 4$

C. Decision criteria:
  1. Accept if $d \leq c$
  2. Reject if $d > c$
	C. $4 > 3$, reject

V. Action:
Dispose of lot as indicated by decision rules.

V. Reject

VI. Measures (using Table 25.6)

Summary of plan	Calculations

A. Probability of acceptance (OC curve)
  1. Under each value of probability of acceptance listed across top of table, there corresponds a value of np shown for the plan
	VI.
	A.
	  1. $P_a = 0.50$ corresponds to $np = 3.672$

2. Divide the values of np by sample size n to get p	2. $p = \dfrac{3.672}{134}$ $= 0.027$
3. Draw OC curve from corresponding values of p and P_a	3. $p = 0.027$ $P_a = 0.50$

B. Average sample number (ASN curve)
  1. Calculate p from P_a as above
	B.
	  1. $P_a = 0.50$
	   $p = 0.027$

2. Under the value np from which p was calculated is listed a value of ASN/n_1	2. $ASN/n_1 = 1$
3. Multiply ASN/n_1 by n to obtain ASN corresponding to p	3. $(1)(134) = 134$
4. Draw ASN curve from corresponding values of p and P_a	4. $p = 0.027$ $ASN = 134$

C. Average outgoing quality
  1. Use formula
   $$AOQ \simeq p\,P_a$$
	C.
	  1. at $p = 0.027$,
	   $AOQ = 0.027\,(0.50)$
	   $= 0.014$

D. Average outgoing quality limit
   $$AOQL \simeq \frac{0.4}{n}(1.25c + 1) \text{ for } c \leq 5$$
	D.
	  1. $AOQL \simeq$
	   $\dfrac{0.4}{134}[1.25(3)+1] \simeq 0.019$

E. Average total inspection
   $ATI = n\,P_a + N(1 - P_a)$
	E. at $p = 0.027$
	   $ATI = 134(0.5) + 500(0.5)$
	   $= 317$

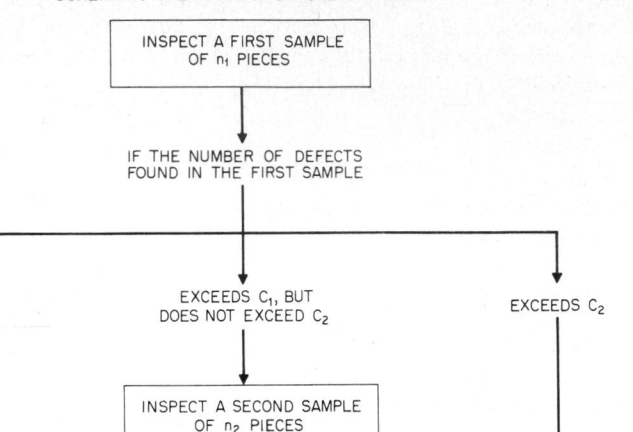

FIG. 25.7 Schematic operation of double sampling. In regard to the lot not to be accepted, inspect the remainder of the pieces, replacing or repairing those defective.

Continuous Sampling.   Some production processes deliver product in a continuous stream rather than on a lot-by-lot basis. Separate plans have been developed for such continuous production based on the AOQL concept. These plans generally start with 100 percent inspection until some consecutive number of units free of defects is found and then provide for inspection on a sampling basis until a specified number of defective units is found. One hundred percent inspection is then instituted again until a specified number of consecutive good pieces is found, at which time sampling is reinstituted. Continuous sampling plans have been proposed by Harold F. Dodge and modifications developed by Dodge and Torrey (1951). Dodge (1970) recounts these and other developments in the evolution of continuous sampling plans. MIL-STD-1235 B (1981) provides a tabulation of continuous sampling plans.

The following are prerequisites for application of the single-level continuous sampling plans:

1. The inspection must involve "moving product," i.e., product which is flowing past the inspection station, e.g., on a conveyor belt.

2. Rapid 100 percent inspection must be feasible.

TABLE 25.8 Double Sampling by Attributes

Example: Determine a double sampling plan which will have AQL = $100p_1$ = 1.0% with producer risk α = 0.05 and LTPD = $100p_2$ = 5.0% with consumer risk β = 0.10. Suppose a sample is taken from a lot of N = 500 and four non-conforming units are found.

Summary of plan	Calculations

I. Restrictions:
    Random sample of dichotomous data

II. Necessary information
    A. Producer quality level, p_1
    B. Producer risk, α
    C. Consumer quality level, p_2
    D. Consumer risk, β

II.
    A. p_1 = 0.01
    B. α = 0.05
    C. p_2 = 0.05
    D. β = 0.10

III. Selection of plan (using Table 25.6)
    A. Calculate operating ratio

$$R = p_2 / p_1$$

    B. Choose double sampling plan (D) from Table 25.6 which shows $R \le$ the value calculated
    C. Acceptance (a) and rejection (r) numbers are given as Ac and Re

    D. Determine first sample size from value of (np_2) shown for the plan as $n = (np_2)/p_2$ This is sample size of each of the double samples

III.
    A. R = 0.05/0.01
        = 5
    B. Choose plan 3D since R shown is 4.398

    C. First sample
        a_1 = 1, r_1 = 4
        Second sample
        a_2 = 4, r_2 = 5
    D. n = 4.398/0.05
        = 88

IV. Elements
    A. Sample size: See III above

    B. Statistic: d_1 = number nonconforming in first sample; d_2 = number nonconforming in second sample
    C. Decision criteria
        1. Accept on first sample if $d_1 \le a_1$
        2. Reject on first sample if $d_1 \ge r_1$
        3. Take a second sample if $a_1 < d_1 < r_1$
        4. Accept on second sample if $d_1 + d_2 \le a_2$
        5. Reject on second sample if $d_1 + d_2 \ge r_2$

IV.
    A. n_1 = 88
        n_2 = 88
    B. d_1 = 4

    C.
        1. 4 not $\le$ 1
        2. 4 $\ge$ 4, reject

V. Action:
    Dispose of lot as indicated by decision rules.

V.
    Reject

VI. Measures (using Table 25.6)
    A. Probability of acceptance (OC curve)
        1. Under each value of probability of acceptance listed across the top of table, there corresponds a value of np shown for the plan
        2. Divide the values of np by sample size n to get p

VI.
    A.
        1. P_a = 0.50 corresponds to np = 2.465

        2. p = $\dfrac{2.465}{88}$
            = 0.028

25.29

TABLE 25.8 Double Sampling by Attributes (*Continued*)

Summary of plan	Calculations
3. Draw OC curve from corresponding values of p and P_a	3. $p = 0.028$ $P_a = 0.50$
B. Average sample number (ASN curve)	B.
1. Calculate p from P_a as above	1. $P_a = 0.50$ $p = 0.028$
2. Under the value np from which p was calculated is listed a value of ASN/n_1	2. $ASN/n_1 = 1.470$
3. Multiply ASN/n_1 by n_1 to obtain ASN corresponding to p	3. $1.470(88)$ $= 129.4$
4. Draw ASN curve from corresponding values of p and P_a	4. $p = 0.028$ $ASN = 129.4$
C. Average outgoing quality	C.
1. Use formula $$AOQ \simeq p\,P_a$$	1. at $p = 0.028$ $AOQ = 0.028(.5)$ $= 0.014$
D. Average outgoing quality limit	D.
1. AOQL = maximum of AOQ curve	1. $AOQL = 0.0151$ at $p = 0.022$
E. Average total inspection $ATI = n_1 + n_2(1 - P_{a_1}) + (N - n_1 - n_2)(1 - P_a)$ where P_{a_1} is probability of acceptance on first sample	E. P_{a_1} = probability no more than one defective in 88 $P_{a_1} = 0.29$ $ATI = 88 + 88\,(0.71) +$ $324(0.50)$ $= 312.5$

3. The inspection must be relatively easy.
4. The product must be homogeneous.

CSP-1 Plans. CSP-1 plans use 100 percent inspection at the start. When i successive units are found to be acceptable and when there is assurance that the process is producing homogeneous product, 100 percent inspection is discontinued and sampling is instituted to the extent of a fraction f of the units. The sampling is continued until a defective unit is found. One hundred percent inspection is then reinstated and the procedure is repeated. Dodge (1943) has provided graphs which can be used to select such plans based on the AOQL desired. See also Schilling (1982).

For example, consider the plan $i = 35, f = \frac{1}{10}$. One hundred percent inspection is used until 35 successive units are found nondefective. Sampling, at the rate of 1 unit in 10, is then instituted. If a defective is found, 100 percent inspection is reinstituted and continued until 35 successive units are found nondefective, at which time sampling is reinstituted.

CSP-2 Plans. CSP-2 plans were developed to permit sampling to continue even if a single defective is found. Again, 100 percent inspection is used at the start until i successive units are found free of defects. When sampling is in effect and a defective is found, 100 percent inspection is instituted only if a second defective occurs in the next i or fewer sample units inspected. Details on the selection of such plans will be found in Dodge and Torrey (1951) or in Schilling (1982).

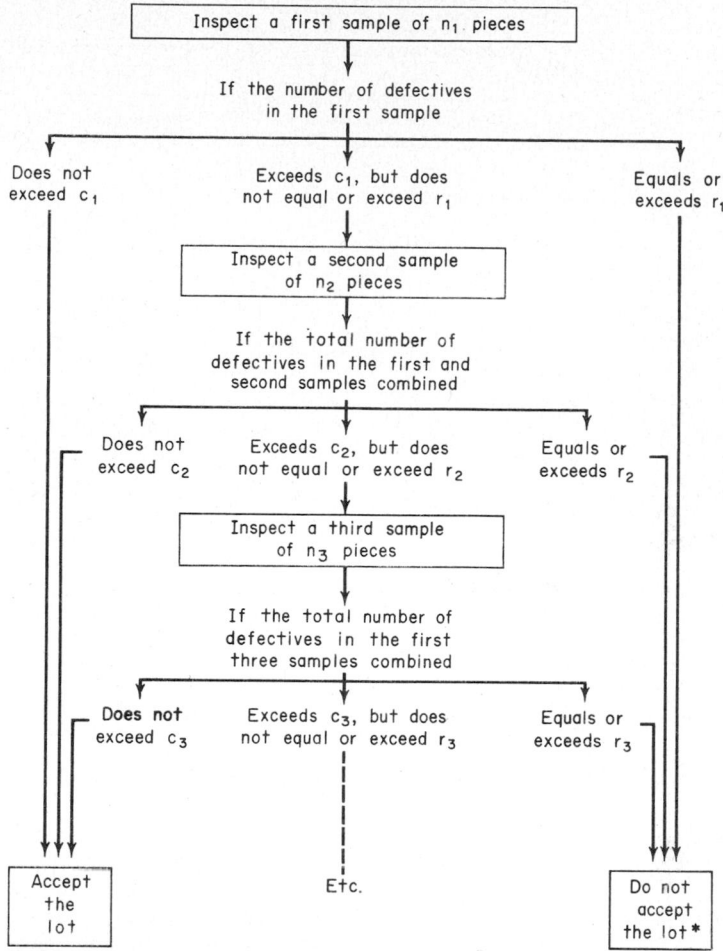

FIG. 25.8 Schematic operation of multiple sampling. Asterisk means some of these plans continue to the "bitter end," i.e., the taking of samples continues if necessary until the lot is fully inspected, unless the plan has meanwhile "made up its mind." Other plans, described as "truncated," are designed to force a decision after a certain number of inconclusive samples have been examined.

Stopping Rules.   Murphy (1959) has investigated four different "stopping rules" for use with CSP-1 plans. He concludes that a useful rule is to stop when a specified number of defectives is found during any one sequence of 100 percent inspection.

Multilevel Continuous Sampling.   Continuous sampling plans have been developed by Lieberman and Solomon (1955) and others which reduce the sampling rate beyond that of other continuous plans when the quality level is better than a defined AOQL. In addition, sudden changes in the amount of inspection are avoided by providing for several "levels" of inspection. Figure 25.10 outlines the procedure for using the plan. The procedure provides for reducing the sampling

TABLE 25.9 Multiple Sampling by Attributes

Example: Determine a multiple sampling plan which will have AQL $= 100p_1$ $= 1.0\%$ with producer risk $\alpha = 0.05$ and LTPD $= 100p_2 = 5.0\%$ with consumer risk $\beta = 0.10$. Suppose a sample is taken from a lot of $N = 500$ and four nonconforming units are found.

Summary of plan	Calculations

I. Restrictions:
Random sample from dichotomous
population

II. Necessary information
A. Producer quality level, p_1
B. Producer risk, α
C. Consumer quality level, p_2
D. Consumer risk, β

II.
A. $p_1 = 0.01$
B. $\alpha = 0.05$
C. $p_2 = 0.05$
D. $\beta = 0.10$

III. Selection of plan (Table 25.6)

A. Calculate operating ratio
$$R = p_2/p_1$$
B. Choose multiple sampling plan (M)
from Table 25.6 which shows $R \le$ the
value calculated
C. Acceptance (a) and rejection (r)
numbers are given as Ac and Re; note
# indicates acceptance is not possible
at that sample

D. Determine first sample size from value
of (np_2) shown for the plan as
$$n = (np_2)/p_2$$
This is sample size of each of the
multiple samples

III.
A. $R = 0.05/0.01 = 5$

B. Choose plan 3M since R
shows 4.672

C.
Ac = #, 0, 1, 2, 3, 4, 6
Re = 3, 3, 4, 5, 6, 6, 7

D. $n = 1.626/0.05$
$= 33$

IV. Elements
A. Sample size: See III above
B. Statistic: $\sum_{i=1}^{k} d_i =$ total number
nonconforming up to kth sample
C. Decision Criteria
1. Accept on kth sample if
$$\sum_{i=1}^{k} d_i \le a_k$$
2. Reject on kth sample if
$$\sum_{i=1}^{k} d_i \ge r_k$$
3. Continue sampling if
$$a_k < \sum_{i=1}^{k} d_i < r_k$$

IV.
A. $n = 33$
B. $\sum_{i=1}^{1} d_i = 4$

C.
1. # indicates cannot accept

2. $4 \ge 3$, reject on first
sample

V. Action
Dispose of lot as indicated by decision
rules

V. Reject

VI. Measures (using Table 25.6)
A. Probability of acceptance (OC curve)
1. Under each value of probability of
acceptance listed across the top of
the table, there corresponds a value
of np shown for the plan

VI.
A.
1. $P_a = 0.50$ corresponds to
$np = 0.910$

25.32

TABLE 25.9 Multiple Sampling by Attributes (*Continued*)

Summary of plan	Calculations
2. Divide the values of np by sample size n to get p	2. $p = \dfrac{0.910}{33} = 0.028$
3. Draw OC curve from corresponding values of p and P_a	3. $p = 0.028$ $P_a = 0.50$
B. Average sample number (ASN curve) 1. Calculate p from P_a as above	B. 1. $P_a = 0.50$ $p = 0.028$
2. Under the value np from which p was calculated is listed a value of ASN/n_1	2. $\mathrm{ASN}/n_1 = 3.288$
3. Multiply ASN/n_1 by n to obtain ASN corresponding to p	3. $\mathrm{ASN} = 3.288(33)$ $= 108.5$
4. Draw ASN curve from corresponding values of p and P_a	4. $p = 0.028$ $\mathrm{ASN} = 108.5$
C. Average outgoing quality 1. Use formula $\mathrm{AOQ} \simeq p\,P_a$	C. 1. at $p = 0.028$ $\mathrm{AOQ} \simeq 0.028(.5)$ $= 0.014$
D. Average outgoing quality limit $\mathrm{AOQL} = $ maximum of AOQ curve	D. $\mathrm{AOQL} = 0.0148$ at $p = 0.022$
E. Average total inspection (approximate) $\mathrm{ATI} \approx \mathrm{ASN}\,(P_a) + N(1 - P_a)$	E. $\mathrm{ATI} \simeq 108.5(0.5) + 500(0.5)$ $\simeq 304$

rate each time i successive units are found to be free of defects. The first sampling rate after leaving 100 percent inspection is f, and each succeeding sampling rate is f raised to one larger power. The number of sampling levels is k. Thus, if $f = \frac{1}{2}$ and $k = 3$, the successive sampling rates are $\frac{1}{2}$, $\frac{1}{4}$, and $\frac{1}{8}$.

Notice that all the continuous plans discussed so far are based on the AOQL concept, i.e., requiring periods of 100 percent inspection during which only non-defective product is accepted. This action controls the average defectiveness of accepted product at some predetermined level. In all these cases, inspection must be nondestructive to employ the AOQL principle.

Additional detail on continuous sampling plans will be found in Stephens (1979).

Skip-Lot Schemes. Skip-lot sampling plans are used when there is a strong desire to reduce the total amount of inspection. The approach is to require some initial criterion be satisfied, such as 10 or so consecutively accepted lots, and then determine what

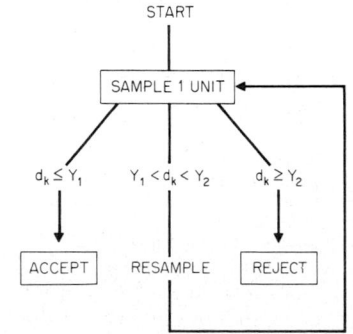

FIG. 25.9 Schematic operation of sequential sampling. *(From Schilling, 1982, p. 156.)*

TABLE 25.10 Sequential Sampling by Attributes

Example: Determine a sequential sampling plan which will have AQL $= 100p_1$ $= 1\%$ with producer risk $\alpha = 0.05$ and LTPD $= 100p_2 = 5\%$ with consumer risk $\beta = 0.10$. Suppose all the samples taken from a lot of 500 are defective.

Summary of plan	Calculations
I. Restrictions Random sample of dichotomous data	
II. Necessary information A. Producer quality level, p_1 B. Producer risk, α C. Consumer quality level, p_2 D. Consumer risk, β	II. A. $p_1 = 0.01$ B. $\alpha = 0.05$ C. $p_2 = 0.05$ D. $\beta = 0.10$

III. Selection of plan
A. Parameters
  1. $h_1 = \log [(1 - \alpha)/\beta] / \{\log (p_2/p_1) + \log [(1 - p_1)/(1 - p_2)]\}$
  2. $h_2 = \log [(1 - \beta)/\alpha] / \{\log (p_2/p_1) + \log [(1 - p_1)/(1 - p_2)]\}$
  3. $s = \log [(1 - p_1)/(1 - p_2)] / \{\log (p_2/p_1) + \log [(1 - p_1)/(1 - p_2)]\}$
 	
B. Acceptance criteria
  1. Acceptance line
    $y_1 = sk - h_1$
  2. Rejection line
    $y_2 = sk + h_2$
 	
  3. $k =$ number of samples taken
	III.
	A.
	  1. $h_1 = 1.3639$
	
	  2. $h_2 = 1.7510$
	
	  3. $s = 0.02499$
	
	B.
	  1. $y_1 = 0.02499k$
	    $- 1.3639$
	  2. $y_2 = 0.02499k$
	    $+ 1.7510$
	
	  3. Take $k = 2$

IV. Elements
A. Sample size
Not definite since samples are taken one at a time
B. Statistic
  $d_k =$ cumulative number nonconforming by the kth sample
C. Decision criteria
  1. Accept if $d_k \le y_1 = sk - h_1$
 	
  2. Reject if $d_k \ge y_2 = sk + h_2$
  3. Continue sampling if $y_1 < d_k < y_2$
	IV.
	A.
	
	B. At $k = 2$
	  $d_2 = 2$
	
	C.
	  1. 2 not ≤ -1.31, cannot accept
	  2. $2 \ge 1.8$, reject
	  3. Discontinue sampling

V. Action: Dispose of lot as indicated by the decision rule	V. Reject

VI. Measures
A. Probability of acceptance (OC curve)
  1. Pick arbitrary value of h
  2. Then
  $$p = \frac{1 - [(1 - p_2)/(1 - p_1)]^h}{(p_2/p_1)^h - [(1 - p_2)/(1 - p_1)]^h}$$
  and
  $$P_a = \frac{[(1 - \beta)/\alpha]^h - 1}{[(1 - \beta)/\alpha]^h - [\beta/(1 - \alpha)]^h}$$
	VI.
	A.
	  1. $h = 1$
	  2. $p = 0.01$
	    $P_a = 0.95$

TABLE 25.10 Sequential Sampling by Attributes (*Continued*)

Summary of plan	Calculations

B. Average sample number (ASN curve)
  1. Calculate p and P_a as above
 	
  2. Then
	B.
	  1. $p = 0.01$
	    $P_a = 0.95$
	  2. ASN = 81

$$\text{ASN} = \frac{\left\{ \begin{array}{l} P_a \log\left[(\beta/(1-\alpha)\right] + \\ (1-P_a)\log\left[(1-\beta)/\alpha\right] \end{array} \right\}}{\left\{ \begin{array}{l} p \log (p_2/p_1) + (1-p) \\ \log\left[(1-p_2)/(1-p_1)\right] \end{array} \right\}}$$

C. Average outgoing quality (AOQ curve)
  1. Use approximate formula
        $\text{AOQ} \simeq p\,P_a$
	C.
	  1. At $p = 0.01$
	      $\text{AOQ} \simeq 0.01(0.95)$
	           $= 0.0095$

D. Average outgoing quality limit
     AOQL = maximum of AOQ curve
E. Average total inspection (approximate)
     $\text{ATI} \approx \text{ASN}\,(P_a) + N(1-P_a)$
	D. AOQL = 0.0145 at
	      $p = 0.021$
	E. At $p = 0.01$
	     $\text{ATI} \approx 81(.95) + 500$
	          (0.05)
	       $\simeq 102$

fraction of lots will be inspected. Given this fraction, the lots to be inspected are chosen using some random selection procedure. The assumptions on which the use of skip-lot plans are based are much like those for chain-sampling plans (see below). OC curves for the entire skip-lot sampling scheme can be derived, and an AOQL concept does apply. Strong dependence is made on the constancy of production and consistency of process quality as well as faith in the producer and inspector. The skip-lot sampling scheme was devised by Dodge (1955a) and is, in essence, an extension of continuous sampling acceptance plans with parameters i and f. He designated the initial scheme as SkSP-1.

Here, a single determination of acceptability was made from a sample of size $n = 1$ from each lot. Lots found defective under sampling were 100 percent inspected or replaced with good lots. The AOQL then was in terms of the long term average proportion of defective *lots* that would reach the customer. This is called AOQL-2. Later, Dodge and Perry (1971) incorporated the use of a "reference" sampling plan to determine whether a lot is acceptable or rejectable. Such skip-lot plans are designated SkSP-2 and require 100 percent inspection of rejected lots. The resulting AOQL is in terms of the long-term average proportion of individual product *units* that would reach the customer. This is called AOQL-1.

The application of skip-lot sampling should be confined to those instances where a continuous supply of product is obtained from a reasonably stable and continuous process.

The parameters of the SkSP-2 plan (in terms of continuous sampling) are:

i = number of successive lots to be found conforming to qualify for skipping lots either at the start or after detecting a nonconforming lot

f = fraction of lots to be inspected after the initial criteria have been satisfied

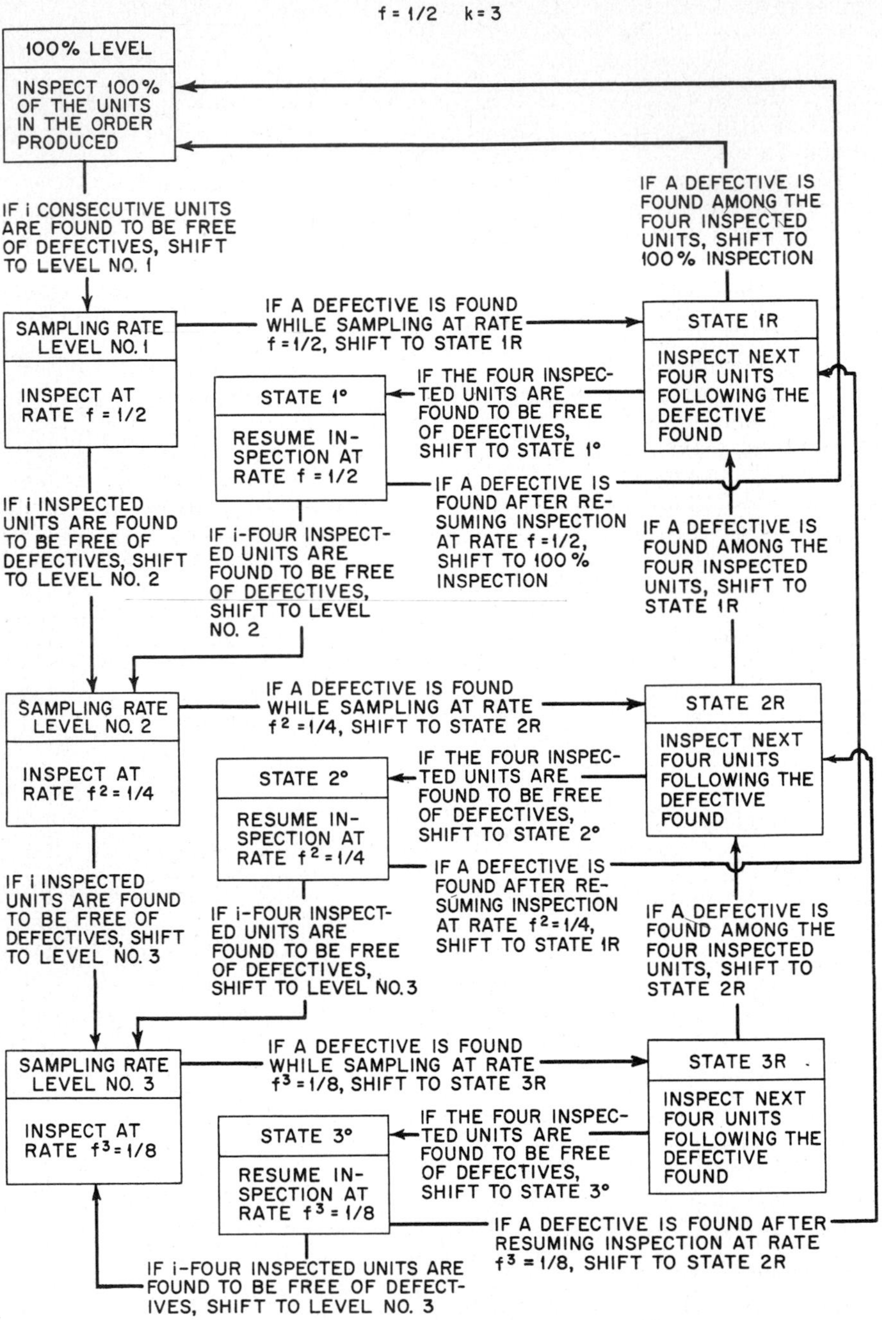

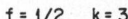
$f = 1/2 \quad k = 3$

100% LEVEL

INSPECT 100% OF THE UNITS IN THE ORDER PRODUCED

IF i CONSECUTIVE UNITS ARE FOUND TO BE FREE OF DEFECTIVES, SHIFT TO LEVEL NO. 1

IF A DEFECTIVE IS FOUND AMONG THE FOUR INSPECTED UNITS, SHIFT TO 100% INSPECTION

SAMPLING RATE LEVEL NO. 1

INSPECT AT RATE $f = 1/2$

IF A DEFECTIVE IS FOUND WHILE SAMPLING AT RATE $f = 1/2$, SHIFT TO STATE 1R

STATE 1R

INSPECT NEXT FOUR UNITS FOLLOWING THE DEFECTIVE FOUND

STATE 1°

RESUME INSPECTION AT RATE $f = 1/2$

IF THE FOUR INSPECTED UNITS ARE FOUND TO BE FREE OF DEFECTIVES, SHIFT TO STATE 1°

IF i INSPECTED UNITS ARE FOUND TO BE FREE OF DEFECTIVES, SHIFT TO LEVEL NO. 2

IF i-FOUR INSPECTED UNITS ARE FOUND TO BE FREE OF DEFECTIVES, SHIFT TO LEVEL NO. 2

IF A DEFECTIVE IS FOUND AFTER RESUMING INSPECTION AT RATE $f = 1/2$, SHIFT TO 100% INSPECTION

IF A DEFECTIVE IS FOUND AMONG THE FOUR INSPECTED UNITS, SHIFT TO STATE 1R

SAMPLING RATE LEVEL NO. 2

INSPECT AT RATE $f^2 = 1/4$

IF A DEFECTIVE IS FOUND WHILE SAMPLING AT RATE $f^2 = 1/4$, SHIFT TO STATE 2R

STATE 2R

INSPECT NEXT FOUR UNITS FOLLOWING THE DEFECTIVE FOUND

STATE 2°

RESUME INSPECTION AT RATE $f^2 = 1/4$

IF THE FOUR INSPECTED UNITS ARE FOUND TO BE FREE OF DEFECTIVES, SHIFT TO STATE 2°

IF i INSPECTED UNITS ARE FOUND TO BE FREE OF DEFECTIVES, SHIFT TO LEVEL NO. 3

IF i-FOUR INSPECTED UNITS ARE FOUND TO BE FREE OF DEFECTIVES, SHIFT TO LEVEL NO. 3

IF A DEFECTIVE IS FOUND AFTER RESUMING INSPECTION AT RATE $f^2 = 1/4$, SHIFT TO STATE 1R

IF A DEFECTIVE IS FOUND AMONG THE FOUR INSPECTED UNITS, SHIFT TO STATE 2R

SAMPLING RATE LEVEL NO. 3

INSPECT AT RATE $f^3 = 1/8$

IF A DEFECTIVE IS FOUND WHILE SAMPLING AT RATE $f^3 = 1/8$, SHIFT TO STATE 3R

STATE 3R

INSPECT NEXT FOUR UNITS FOLLOWING THE DEFECTIVE FOUND

STATE 3°

RESUME INSPECTION AT RATE $f^3 = 1/8$

IF THE FOUR INSPECTED UNITS ARE FOUND TO BE FREE OF DEFECTIVES, SHIFT TO STATE 3°

IF A DEFECTIVE IS FOUND AFTER RESUMING INSPECTION AT RATE $f^3 = 1/8$, SHIFT TO STATE 2R

IF i-FOUR INSPECTED UNITS ARE FOUND TO BE FREE OF DEFECTIVES, SHIFT TO LEVEL NO. 3

FIG. 25.10 Procedure for multilevel continuous sampling.

n = sample size per inspected lot
c = acceptance number for each inspected lot

For example, if $i = 15$, $f = \frac{1}{3}$, $n = 10$, $c = 0$, the plan is to inspect 10 units from each lot submitted until 15 consecutive lots are found conforming, i.e., have no defective in the sample. Then one-third of the submitted lots are chosen at random for inspection and inspected to the same n and c. As long as all lots are found to be conforming, the f-rate applies. When a nonconforming lot is identified, reversion to inspection of all lots occurs until again 15 consecutive lots are found to be conforming, and then skipping is permissible again.

Many values of f and i are possible. For SkSP-1 these may be obtained from the Basic Curves for Plan CSP-1. See Dodge (1955a.) In using SkSP-2, unity values for selection of a plan having a designated operating ratio will be found in Dodge and Perry (1971). See also Schilling (1982).

One further consideration is whether to apply the skip-lot procedure to only one characteristic of a product, to all characteristics simultaneously, or just to some. The plan is obvious and straightforward when applied only to one product characteristic, perhaps a particularly expensive one in time or dollars. If applied to several characteristics, it might be best to inspect the f fraction for these characteristics on each lot. For example, if 6 characteristics are candidates for skip-lot sampling and $f = \frac{1}{3}$, perhaps 2 of these would be examined on one lot, two on another, and two on the third, again in some random fashion, so that all lots receive some inspection. Of course, if the most expensive part of the sampling scheme were forming the lot, sampling from it, and keeping records, the choice might be to inspect all characteristics on the same sample units. This argument may be extended to the case where all inspection characteristics are on a skip-lot basis; but if inspection is very complex, this is difficult to visualize.

Perry (1973) has extended skip-lot plans in many ways including the incorporation of multi-level plans. See Perry (1973a). Skip-lot plans are described in detail by Stephens (1982).

Chain-Sampling. Chain-sampling plans utilize information over a series of lots. The original plans by Dodge (1955), called ChSP-1, utilized single sampling on an attributes basis with n small and $c = 0$. The distinguishing feature is that the current lot under inspection can also be accepted if one defective unit is observed in the sample provided that no other defective units were found in the samples from the immediately preceding i lots, i.e., the chain. Dodge and Stephens (1965, 1966) derived some two-stage chain-sampling plans which make use of cumulative inspection results from several samples and are generalizations and extensions of ChSP-1. Conversely, ChSP-1 is a subset of the new plans, and the discussion here will be in terms of the two-stage plans.

Before discussing the details of the plans, the general characteristics of chain sampling are described. Chain-sampling plans, in comparison with single-sampling plans, have the characteristic of "bowing up" the OC curve for small fractions defective while having little effect on the end of the curve associated with higher fractions defective. The effectiveness of chain-sampling plans strongly depends upon the assumptions on which the plans are based, namely:

1. Production is steady, as a continuing process.
2. Lot submittal is in the order of production.
3. Attributes sampling is done where the fraction defective p is binomially distributed.

4. A fixed sample size from each lot is assumed.

5. There is confidence in the supplier to the extent that lots are expected to be of essentially the same quality.

Chain-sampling plans are particularly useful where inspection is costly and sample sizes are relatively small. However, they may also be found useful with large sample sizes. The advantage over double-sampling plans is the fixed sample size. The disadvantage is that moderate changes in quality are not easily detected. However, major changes in quality are detected as easily with chain-sampling plans having much smaller sample sizes as with single-sampling with the same AQL.

The two-stage chain-sampling plans have acceptance based on cumulation of defectives in each stage separately and are defined by the parameters and designators:

n = sample size, constant over all samples
k_1 = maximum number of samples for cumulation of defectives in the first stage
k_2 = maximum number of samples for cumulation of defectives in the second stage and in the "normal" period following the second stage
C_1 = allowable number of defectives in the cumulative results of k_1 or fewer samples in the first stage
C_2 = allowable number of defectives in the cumulative results of $k_1 + 1$ to k_2 or fewer samples, or the last k_2 samples
d = number of defectives in a sample
d_i = number of defective units in the ith sample
D = cumulative number of defectives in a series of samples
D_i = cumulative number of defective units at the ith sample with cumulation performed according to the plan

The acceptance criterion is a cumulative results criterion (CRC). At the start (initial application of the plan) and at a restart, the CRC for k_1 must be satisfied. To establish the normal acceptance period, the CRC for k_2 must be satisfied, and the normal period continues as long as the CRC is satisfied for the last k_2 lots. Restart occurs whenever the CRC is not satisfied. The flow chart for the plan, reproduced from Dodge and Stephens (1966), is given in Figure 25.11.

Dodge and Stephens adopt the designation ChSP-0, 2, e.g, to designate a two-stage sampling plan with $C_1 = 0$, $C_2 = 2$, and n, k_1, k_2 as unspecified or open parameters. A plan with $n = 10$, $k_1 = 1$, $k_2 = 3$, $C_1 = 0$, $C_2 = 2$ would be a particular plan in ChSP-0, 2. Additional sets of plans would then be designated by ChSP-0, 1; CHSP-1, 2; etc.

The original ChSP-1 plans had $k_1 = k_2 - 1$ and k_1 was designated as i. The plan is to inspect a sample of n units from a lot, accept the lot if zero defectives were found in the n units, or accept the lot if one defective were found in the sample and no defectives were found in the samples from the immediately preceding i lots. Thus for ChSP-1 comparison with ChSP-0, 1; $n = n$, $k_1 = k_2 - 1 = i$, $k_2 = i + 1$, $C_1 = 0$, $C_2 = 1$, and ChSP-1 is a subset of the two-stage plans.

Formulas for the OC curves for ChSP-0, 1; ChSp-0, 2 and several OC curves for various values of n, k_1, and k_2 are given by Dodge and Stephens (1965, 1966). All are based on the type B sampling situation. Soundararajan (1978) has prepared tables of unity values for selection of chain-sampling plans from various criteria. Stephens (1982) provides additional detail on implementing chain plans.

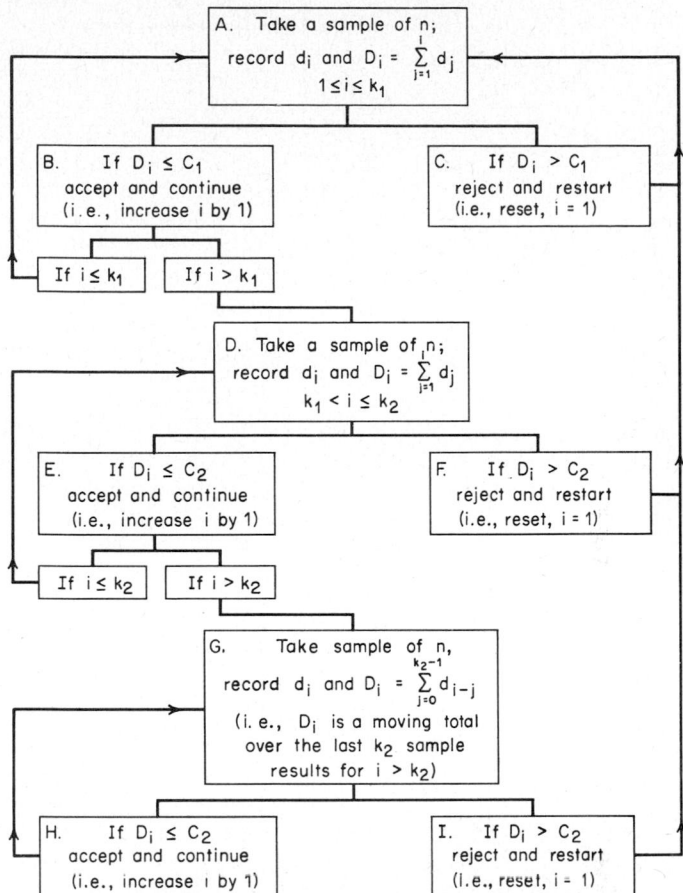

A. Take a sample of n;
record d_i and $D_i = \sum_{j=1}^{i} d_j$
$1 \le i \le k_1$

B.   If $D_i \le C_1$
accept and continue
(i.e., increase i by 1)

C.   If $D_i > C_1$
reject and restart
(i.e., reset, i = 1)

If $i \le k_1$ If $i > k_1$

D. Take a sample of n;
record d_i and $D_i = \sum_{j=1}^{i} d_j$
$k_1 < i \le k_2$

E.   If $D_i \le C_2$
accept and continue
(i.e., increase i by 1)

F.   If $D_i > C_2$
reject and restart
(i.e., reset, i = 1)

If $i \le k_2$ If $i > k_2$

G.   Take sample of n,
record d_i and $D_i = \sum_{j=0}^{k_2-1} d_{i-j}$
(i.e., D_i is a moving total
over the last k_2 sample
results for $i > k_2$)

H.   If $D_i \le C_2$
accept and continue
(i.e., increase i by 1)

I.   If $D_i > C_2$
reject and restart
(i.e., reset, i = 1)

FIG. 25.11 Flow chart of operations, two-stage chain-sampling scheme.

Cumultive Sum Sampling Plans.   A scheme has been devised by Beattie (1962) whereby the continuous inspection approach may be employed when inspection is destructive. Acceptance or rejection of the continuously produced product is based on the cumulation of the observed number of defectives. In addition, it is possible to discriminate between two levels of quality, an acceptable quality level (AQL) and rejectable quality level (RQL).

Prior to the development of continuous and cumulative sum plans, the following situation frequently occurred when inspection was destructive. Since production was continuous, usually there was no technically rational procedure for defining lots. A common procedure was to accumulate product until a lot was formed, but then the time delay in making a decision on the product was often too long, and a few short periods of bad production could cause a large quantity of good product to be rejected. Various approaches to lessening this jeopardy were used, all with some logical or practical drawback.

The procedure of Beattie (1962) establishes two zones, an accept zone and a reject zone, and product is accepted or rejected according to the cumulative sum

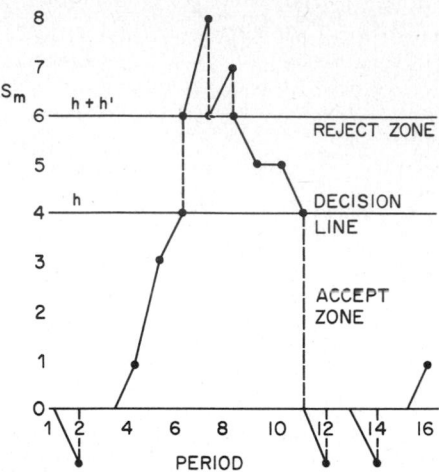

FIG. 25.12 Form of chart for acceptance under cumulative sum sampling plans.

of defectives observed. Figure 25.12 illustrates the plan. To implement the procedure, a sample of size n is chosen at regular intervals from production. The units are inspected and the number of defective units d_i in the ith sample recorded. Then,

$$S_m = \sum_{i=1}^{m} (d_i - k)$$

is accumulated, where k is a parameter of the scheme and S_m is computed and plotted according to the following rules:

1. Start the cumulation, S_m, at zero.

2. Accept product as long as $S_m < h$, where h is a second parameter of the scheme. When $S_m < 0$, return the cumulation to zero.

3. When h is crossed or reached from below, reject product and restart the cumulation at $h + h'$ (h' is a third parameter of the plan).

4. Continue rejecting product as long as $S_m > h$. When $S_m > h + h'$, return calculation to $h + h'$ and continue rejecting product until $S_m < h$.

5. When h is crossed or reached from above, accept product and restart cumulation at zero.

The discriminatory capability of the plans is controlled through the choice of k, h, and h' and their combinations. In familiar terms, k is akin to an acceptance number and h defines how far one is willing to deviate from this number over a long run and still accept product. The quantity h' is essentially how much evidence is required to be assured the process has been corrected.

The protection offered by this type of plan, which is similar to a type B acceptance situation, is defined by an OC curve which is determined by the ratio of the average run length (ARL) in the accept zone to the sum of the ARL in the accept and reject zones. An example, taken from Prarie and Zimmer (1973), follows.

A production situation exists where thermal batteries are produced at the rate of 50 per day. Testing is destructive, and a suitable number for testing is five per day. Based upon the reliability requirements of the system for which the battery is a component, a sampling plan with $P_a \approx 0.95$ at $p_1 = 0.025$ (AQL = 2.5 percent) and $P_a \approx 0.10$ at $P_2 = 0.15$ (LTPD = 15 percent) was appropriate.

On the basis of the desired AQL and LTPD, two comparable plans were suggested: (1) a conventional single-sampling plan with $n = 35$, $c = 2$, and (2) a cumulative sum plan with $n = 10$, $h = 1$, $h' = 2$, $k = 1$. The OC curves of these two plans coincide.

The two plans were compared during a period of 70 days production of 50 batteries per day. For Plan 1, a sample was generated by taking five batteries per day for 7 days, and from this sample the total number of defective batteries was recorded. If there were two or fewer observed defective batteries, the 7 day's production was accepted; otherwise it was rejected.

For Plan 2, a sample was formed by taking five batteries per day for 2 days, and from this sample the total number of defective batteries was recorded. The cumulative sum $\Sigma\,(d - 1)$, since $k = 1$, was then plotted for each 2-day period, and the decision to reject or accept these periods of production was based on the value of $\Sigma\,(d - 1)$.

The results of the comparison showed that 21 days' production with three observed defectives was accepted by the single-sampling plan and 30 days' production with four observed defectives was accepted by the cumulative sum plan. Thus, the cumulative sum plan provided a 42 percent greater yield of batteries with the same protection and approximately the same (0.027 versus 0.028) estimated quality of accepted product.

The above example points up the weakness of using a conventional single-sampling plan when the quality is spotty where just a few isolated days of bad product can cause several days' production to be rejected. Conversely, the cumulative sum procedure was able to adapt to the sporadic quality and appears to be well suited for such a process.

Published Tables and Procedures.   Table 25.11 summarizes the principal published attributes sampling tables showing, for each, its area of application, main features, and quality index.

The published plans cover three quality indices: AQL, LTPD, and AOQL.

AQL Plans.   Sampling schemes indexed by AQL are designed to give high assurance for type B situations (that is, sampling from a process) and give high assurance of lot acceptance when process quality is equal to or better than the specified AQL; i.e., the process fraction defective is less than or equal to that AQL. These plans are devised for producer's protection or to keep the producer's risk small. Consideration is given to what might be called the other end of the plan, the consumer's risk through the switching rules. If there is interest in controlling both producer's risk and consumer's risk with the use of schemes indexed by AQL values, the best approach is to study the scheme OC curves and choose the plan which provides adequate protection against both types of risks. See Schilling and Sheesley (1978); also Schilling and Johnson (1980).

MIL-STD-105D is the best-known sampling scheme indexed by AQL. The AQLs presented in this standard form a sequence which is evident in the standard. The sequence chosen, while arbitrary, does provide a sensible grouping and indexing of plans for use.

LTPD Plans.   Sampling schemes indexed by LTPD or other values of limiting quality (LQ) are designed for type A situations and are essentially the mirror

TABLE 25.11 Summary of Published Attributes Sampling Plans for Lot-by-Lot Inspection

Name of plan	Type of sampling	Type of application	Key features
MIL-STD-105D and ANSI/ ASQC Z1.4 (1981)	Single, double and multiple	General application whether or not rejected lots can be 100% inspected	Maintains average quality at a specified level or better. Aims to minimize rejection of good lots. Also provides single-sampling plans for fixed consumer risks and average quality levels in the long run. Tables and mechanics of operation are simplified to minimize training required to use plan.
Dodge-Romig	Single and double	General application where rejected lots can be 100% inspected	One type of plan has a consumer's risk of 0.10 of accepting bad quality. A second type of plan limits the average quality level in the long run. Protection is provided with minimum inspection per lot.
Chain sampling	Single- and two-stage	Particularly useful when inspection involves destructive or costly tests	Aims to minimize sample sizes without a large risk of rejection of good lots. Occurrence of a single defective does not necessarily cause rejection of lot.
Bayesian plans	Generally single	General application where probability of occurrence of defective lots can be estimated a priori	Smaller sample size required as compared with standard attribute schemes.
Skip-lot sampling plans	Single	Particularly useful when indicated quality level is high and inspection involves costly or destructive tests	Aims to minimize inspection with adequate protection against major degradation in quality.
MIL-STD-1235B	Continuous	General application when production is truly continuous and inspection is nondestructive	Although plans are indexed by AQL, plans actually limit the average quality in the long run.

TABLE 25.11 Summary of Published Attributes Sampling Plans for Lot-by-Lot Inspection (*Continued*)

Name of plan	Type of sampling	Type of application	Key features
Cumulative sum	Continuous	General application when production is truly continuous and no restriction on the nature of inspection	Plans limit the average quality in the long run but in sense different from above.

image of plans indexed by AQL. That is, the plans are chosen such that the consumer's risk of accepting a submitted lot of product with quality equal to or worse than the LQ is equal to or less than some specified value. Specifically, LTPD plans provide a 10 percent probability of accepting lots of the listed LTPD quality. The Dodge-Romig sampling scheme is the best-known set of plans indexed by LTPD. MIL-STD-105D also provides some LQ plans. Schilling (1978) has developed a set of lot sensitive plans with $c = 0$ which are selected directly from the lot size and the LTPD using a simple table.

AOQL Plans. Sampling schemes indexed by AOQL are derived to provide assurance that the long-run average of accepted quality, given screening of rejected lots, will be no worse than the indexed AOQL value. The Dodge-Romig (1959) plans provide the best available tables of sampling plans indexed by AOQL.

The steps to be applied in any lot-by-lot sampling acceptance procedure are summarized in Table 25.12.

TABLE 25.12 Summary of Lot-by-Lot Sampling Procedure

Establishment of standards (by inspection executive):
 Decide what shall be a unit of product.
 Classify the quality characteristics for seriousness.
 Fix an acceptable quality level for each class.
 Fix an inspection level for the product.
Installation of procedure (by inspection supervisor):
 Arrange for formation of inspection lots.
 Decide what type of sampling shall be used (single, double, multiple).
 Choose sampling plan from tables.
Operation of procedure (by line inspector):
 Draw sample units from each inspection lot.
 Inspect each sample unit.
 Determine whether to accept or reject the inspection lot (if sampling for acceptance) or whether to urge action on the process (if sampling for control).
Review of past results (by inspection supervisor):
 Maintain a record of lot acceptance experience and cumulative defects by successive lots.
 Determine whether to tighten or reduce inspection on future lots.

MIL-STD-105D Sampling Tables. MIL-STD-105 was first issued in 1950 as MIL-STD-105A with the current issue, MIL-STD-105D (1963), published April 29, 1963. The current issue includes many important improvements over previous issues and will be the only one discussed here. Pabst (1963) describes the theoretical aspects and characteristics of issue D. The reader interested in these matters, as well as comparison of issue D with important aspects of previous issues, should study that reference.

The quality index in MIL-STD-105D and its civilian version ANSI/ASQC Z1.4 (1981) is the acceptable quality level (AQL):

• A choice of 26 AQL values is available ranging from 0.010 to 1000.0. (Values of 10.0 or less may be interpreted as percent defective or defects per hundred units. Values above 10.0 must be interpreted as defects per hundred units.)

• The probability of accepting at AQL quality varies from 89 to 99.5 percent.

• Defects are classified as critical, major, or minor.

• The purchaser may, at its option, specify separate AQLs for each class or specify an AQL for each kind of defect which a product may show.

The purchaser also specifies the relative amount of inspection or inspection level to be used. For general applications there are three levels, and level II is regarded as normal. The three levels involve inspection in amounts roughly in the ratio of 1 to 2.5 to 4. Level II is generally used unless factors such as the simplicity and cost of the item, inspection cost, destructiveness of inspection, quality, consistency between lots, or other factors make it appropriate to use another level. The standard also contains special procedures for "small-sample inspection" where small sample sizes are either desirable or necessitated by some aspects of inspection. Four additional inspection levels (S1 through S4) are provided in these special procedures.

The procedure for choice of plan from the tables is outlined below.

1. The following information must be known:
   a. Acceptable quality level.
   b. Lot size.
   c. Type of sampling (single, double, or multiple).
   d. Inspection level (usually level II).
2. Knowing the lot size and inspection level, obtain a code letter from Table 25.13.
3. Knowing the code letter, AQL, and type of sampling, read the sampling plan from one of the nine master tables (Table 25.14 is for single-sampling normal inspection; the standard also provides tables for double and multiple sampling).

For example, suppose that a purchasing agency has contracted for a 1 percent AQL for a certain characteristic. Suppose also that the parts are bought in lots of 1500 pieces. From the table of sample size code letters (Table 25.13), it is found that letter K plans are required for inspection level II, the one normally used. Then the plan to be used initially with normal inspection would be found in Table 25.14 in row K. The sample size is 125. For AQL = 1.0, the acceptance number is given as 3 and the rejection number as 4. This means that the entire lot of 1500 units may be accepted if 3 or fewer defective units are found in the sample of 125,

TABLE 25.13   Sample Size Code Letters*

Lot or batch size		General inspection levels		
		I	II	III
2 to	8	A	A	B
9 to	15	A	B	C
16 to	25	B	C	D
26 to	50	C	D	E
51 to	90	C	E	F
91 to	150	D	F	G
151 to	280	E	G	H
281 to	500	F	H	J
501 to	1,200	G	J	K
1,201 to	3,200	H	K	L
3,201 to	10,000	J	L	M
10,001 to	35,000	K	M	N
35,001 to	150,000	L	N	P
150,001 to	500,000	M	P	Q
500,001 and over		N	Q	R

*Sample size code letters given in body of table are applicable when the indicated inspection levels are to be used. The Standard includes an added table of code letters for small-sample inspection.

but must be rejected if 4 or more are found. Where an AQL is expressed in terms of "defects per hundred units," this term may be substituted for "defective articles" throughout. Corresponding tables are provided in the standard for tightened and reduced inspection.

The system for choosing the initial sampling plan takes account of the quality of product actually submitted only in the limited sense that the AQL is thought to be attainable. When the material later submitted is of generally high quality, the functions of inspection emphasized are somewhat different from those when submitted material is of generally poor quality. If the average quality is high, sampling gives information on the prevailing quality level and provides some assurance that any sudden deterioration in quality will be detected and the resulting low-quality lots rejected. The functions of sorting good lots from bad and of applying pressure to cause the supplier to improve quality are less important. Moreover, poor or borderline material is seldom submitted for inspection (because it is usually detected by the producer in the inspection), so a relatively small amount of inspection is all that is economically justified.

If the quality of product submitted is consistently poor, most lots will be rejected. Also, it is unfortunate but true that the few inspection lots accepted in these circumstances will not be appreciably better than those rejected. If the AQL were properly chosen and is one that can or has been met by this or other suppliers, it becomes necessary to apply greater pressure to bring the supplier's quality into line. In addition, the sampling inspection has greater need for sharp discrimination between good and bad material in order to reduce the consumer's risk. Accordingly, the standard provides two variations in sampling severity from that chosen as normal, the choice of reduced or tightened inspection.

TABLE 25.14 MIL-STD-105D Master Table for Normal Inspection (Single Sampling)

Acceptable Quality Levels (normal inspection)

(Each cell gives the Acceptance number and Rejection number "Ac Re". ↓ = use first sampling plan below arrow; ↑ = use first sampling plan above arrow.)

Code	Sample size	0.010	0.015	0.025	0.040	0.065	0.10	0.15	0.25	0.40	0.65	1.0	1.5	2.5	4.0	6.5	10	15	25	40	65	100	150	250	400	650	1000
A	2	↓	↓	↓	↓	↓	↓	↓	↓	↓	↓	↓	↓	↓	↓	↓	↓	0 1	1 2	2 3	3 4	5 6	7 8	10 11	14 15	21 22	30 31
B	3	↓	↓	↓	↓	↓	↓	↓	↓	↓	↓	↓	↓	↓	↓	↓	0 1	1 2	2 3	3 4	5 6	7 8	10 11	14 15	21 22	30 31	44 45
C	5	↓	↓	↓	↓	↓	↓	↓	↓	↓	↓	↓	↓	↓	↓	0 1	1 2	2 3	3 4	5 6	7 8	10 11	14 15	21 22	30 31	44 45	↑
D	8	↓	↓	↓	↓	↓	↓	↓	↓	↓	↓	↓	↓	↓	0 1	1 2	2 3	3 4	5 6	7 8	10 11	14 15	21 22	30 31	44 45	↑	↑
E	13	↓	↓	↓	↓	↓	↓	↓	↓	↓	↓	↓	↓	0 1	1 2	2 3	3 4	5 6	7 8	10 11	14 15	21 22	30 31	44 45	↑	↑	↑
F	20	↓	↓	↓	↓	↓	↓	↓	↓	↓	↓	↓	0 1	1 2	2 3	3 4	5 6	7 8	10 11	14 15	21 22	30 31	44 45	↑	↑	↑	↑
G	32	↓	↓	↓	↓	↓	↓	↓	↓	↓	↓	0 1	1 2	2 3	3 4	5 6	7 8	10 11	14 15	21 22	30 31	44 45	↑	↑	↑	↑	↑
H	50	↓	↓	↓	↓	↓	↓	↓	↓	↓	0 1	1 2	2 3	3 4	5 6	7 8	10 11	14 15	21 22	30 31	44 45	↑	↑	↑	↑	↑	↑
J	80	↓	↓	↓	↓	↓	↓	↓	↓	0 1	1 2	2 3	3 4	5 6	7 8	10 11	14 15	21 22	30 31	44 45	↑	↑	↑	↑	↑	↑	↑
K	125	↓	↓	↓	↓	↓	↓	↓	0 1	1 2	2 3	3 4	5 6	7 8	10 11	14 15	21 22	30 31	44 45	↑	↑	↑	↑	↑	↑	↑	↑
L	200	↓	↓	↓	↓	↓	↓	0 1	1 2	2 3	3 4	5 6	7 8	10 11	14 15	21 22	30 31	44 45	↑	↑	↑	↑	↑	↑	↑	↑	↑
M	315	↓	↓	↓	↓	↓	0 1	1 2	2 3	3 4	5 6	7 8	10 11	14 15	21 22	30 31	44 45	↑	↑	↑	↑	↑	↑	↑	↑	↑	↑
N	500	↓	↓	↓	↓	0 1	1 2	2 3	3 4	5 6	7 8	10 11	14 15	21 22	30 31	44 45	↑	↑	↑	↑	↑	↑	↑	↑	↑	↑	↑
P	800	↓	↓	↓	0 1	1 2	2 3	3 4	5 6	7 8	10 11	14 15	21 22	30 31	44 45	↑	↑	↑	↑	↑	↑	↑	↑	↑	↑	↑	↑
Q	1250	↓	↓	0 1	1 2	2 3	3 4	5 6	7 8	10 11	14 15	21 22	30 31	44 45	↑	↑	↑	↑	↑	↑	↑	↑	↑	↑	↑	↑	↑
R	2000	↓	0 1	1 2	2 3	3 4	5 6	7 8	10 11	14 15	21 22	30 31	44 45	↑	↑	↑	↑	↑	↑	↑	↑	↑	↑	↑	↑	↑	↑

⇩ = Use first sampling plan below arrow. If sample size equals, or exceeds, lot or batch size, do 100 percent inspection.

⇧ = Use first sampling plan above arrow.

Ac = Acceptance number.

Re = Rejection number.

Inspection Severity—Definitions and General Rules for Changing Levels. The commonly used attributes acceptance sampling plans make provision for shifting the amount of inspection and/or the acceptance number as experience indicates. If many consecutive lots of submitted product are accepted by an existing sampling plan, the quality of submitted product must exceed that specified as necessary for acceptance. This makes it desirable to reduce the amount and cost of inspection (with a subsequent higher risk of accepting an occasional lot of lesser quality) simply because the quality level is good. On the other hand, if more than an occasional lot is rejected by the existing sampling plan, the quality level is either consistently lower than desired or the quality level fluctuates excessively among submitted lots. In either case it is desirable to increase the sampling rate and/or reduce the acceptance number to provide greater discrimination between lots of adequate and inadequate quality.

Three severities of inspection are provided: normal, tightened, and reduced. All changes between severities are governed by rules associated with the sampling scheme. Normal inspection is adopted at the beginning of a sampling procedure and continued until evidence of either lower or higher quality than that specified exists. Schematically, the rules for switching severities specified in MIL-STD-105D and ANSI/ASQC Z1.4 (1981) are given in Figure 25.13.

From the schematic it can be seen that the criteria for change from normal to tightened and back to normal are simple and straightforward. (This is a vast improvement over past issues of MIL-STD-105.) Again, the change from reduced to normal is straightforward and occurs with the first indication that quality has slipped. Considerably more evidence is required to change from normal to reduced.

In using schemes like MIL-STD-105D or ANSI/ASQC Z1.4 (1981), the customer assumes that the changes from normal to tightened and reduced to normal are a necessary part of the scheme. (Recall that such AQL plans provide primarily producer's assurance that quality at the AQL level will be accepted.) The change from normal to tightened or reduced to normal occurs when evidence exists that quality level has deteriorated. In this way the consumer's protection is maintained.

On the other hand, the supplier is interested in keeping inspection costs as low as possible consistent with the demands placed upon it. Certainly it is desirable to change from tightened to normal inspection when conditions warrant. Generally it would be economic to change from normal to reduced except in those cases where record-keeping costs or bother exceed the saving in reduced sampling effort. The initiative for these types of change generally rests with the supplier; only in those instances where an economic advantage exists would a customer insist on reduced inspection. This might occur, e.g., when the customer is using these sampling plans, where inspection is destructive or degrading, or when the psychological impact on the supplier makes reduced inspection a motivational force.

The case could arise where a complex item is being inspected for many characteristics, some of which are classified as critical, some major, and some minor. A different sampling plan could be in effect for each class. It is also possible on this same product to have reached the situation where, for example, reduced inspection could be in effect for critical defects, tightened inspection for major defects, and normal inspection for minor defects. The bookkeeping involved with complete flexibility of sampling plan choice by classification of characteristic and inspection severity can be enormous. On the other hand, the savings involved with lower inspection rates, especially with destructive inspection, could be sizable. Inspection cost and convenience, along with the consequences of the error of

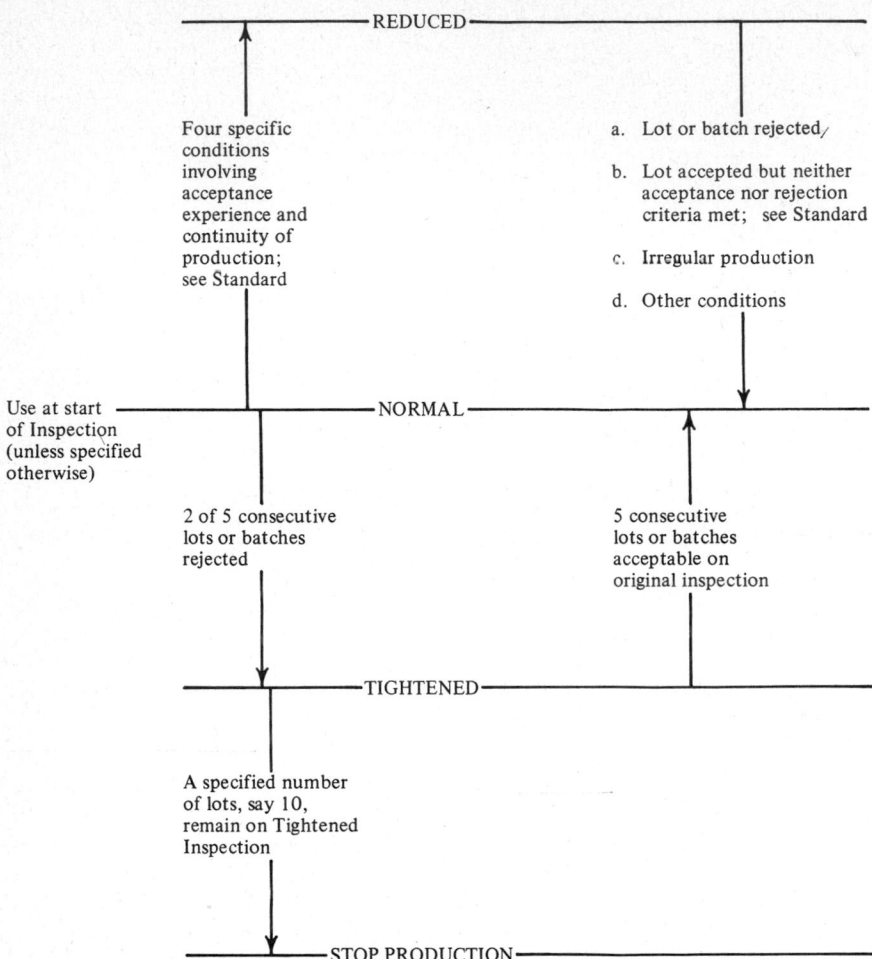

FIG. 25.13   Rules for switching inspection severity, MIL-STD-105D.

applying an improper sampling plan, are the main determinants in any decision to use anything but the highest sampling rate associated with all defect classifications and whether to take advantage of reduced inspection for one or more defect classes when allowed. Of course, when tightened inspection is dictated by sampling experience, there is no recourse but to adopt it for at least that classificaton or characteristic, other than to discontinue acceptance inspection of submitted product.

The standard also provides limiting quality (LQ) single-sampling plans with a consumer's risk of 10 percent (LTPD) and 5 percent for use in isolated lot acceptance inspection. If other levels of LQ are desired, the individual OC curves can be examined to adopt an appropriate plan.

Finally, a table of AOQL values is provided for each of the single-sampling plans for normal and tightened inspection. These may also be used as rough guides for corresponding double- and multiple-sampling plans.

The sampling plans in MIL-STD-105D and ANSI/ASQC Z1.4 are sufficiently varied in type (single, double, multiple), amount of inspection, etc., to be useful in a great number of situations. The inclusion of operating characteristic curves and average sample size curves for most of the plans is a noteworthy advantage of the standard. The reader is also referred to the excellent supplementary publication, H-53 (1965), which discusses and provides recommendations on many of the practical problems that arise during the day-to-day application of the standard.

Dodge-Romig Sampling Tables.   Dodge and Romig (1959) provide four different sets of tables:

1. Single-sampling lot tolerance tables (SL)
2. Double-sampling lot tolerance tables (DL)
3. Single-sampling AOQL tables (SA)
4. Double-sampling AOQL tables (DA)

All four types of plans were constructed to give minimum total inspection for product of a given process average. All lots rejected are assumed to be screened, and both the sampling and the expected amount of 100 percent inspection were considered in deriving the plan which would give minimum inspection per lot. This is a particularly appropriate approach for a manufacturer's inspection of its own product as when the product of one department is examined prior to use in another. Practically, it may be reasonable to use the same theory even when the sampling is done by the purchasing company and the detailing of rejected material is done by the supplying company, since in the long run all the supplier's costs to provide material of a specified quality are reflected in the price.

The first and second sets of tables are classified according to lot tolerance percent defective at a constant consumer's risk of 0.10. Available lot tolerance plans range from 0.5 to 10.0 percent defective. In contrast, the third and fourth sets of tables are classified according to the average outgoing quality limit (AOQL) which they assure. Available AOQL values range from 0.1 to 10.0 percent. Lot tolerance plans emphasize a constant low consumer's risk (with varying AOQLs). In other words, they are intended to give considerable assurance that individual lots of poor material will seldom be accepted. The AOQL plans emphasize the limit on poor quality in the long run, but do not attempt to offer uniform assurance that individual lots of low quality will not get through. The relative importance of these two objectives will guide the choice of types.

Table 25.15 shows a representative Dodge-Romig table for single sampling on the lot tolerance basis. All the plans listed in this table have the same risk (0.10) of accepting submitted lots that contain exactly 5 percent of defective units. The table has six columns. Each of these lists a set of plans appropriate to a specified average value of incoming quality. For example, if the estimated process average percent defective is between 2.01 and 2.50 percent, the last column at the right gives the plans that will provide the minimum inspection per lot. However, the assurance that a lot of quality 5 percent defective will be rejected is the same for all columns, so an initial incorrect estimate of the process average would have little effect except to increase somewhat the total number of pieces inspected per lot. The selection of a plan from this table thus requires only two items of information: the size of the lot to be sampled and the prevailing average quality of the supplier for the product in question. If the process average is unknown, the table is entered at the highest value of process average shown.

TABLE 25.15 Dodge-Romig Table* for Lot Tolerance Single Sampling

Lot tolerance percent defective = 5.0%

Lot size	Process average %																	
	0–0.5			0.06–0.50			0.51–1.00			1.01–1.50			1.51–2.00			2.01–2.50		
	n*	c*	AOQL* %	n	c	AOQL %	n	c	AOQL %	n	c	AOQL %	n	c	AOQL %	n	c	AOQL %
1–30	All	0	0	All	0	0	All	0	0	All	0	0	All	0	0	All	0	0
31–50	30	0	0.49	30	0	0.49	30	0	0.49	30	0	0.49	30	0	0.49	30	0	0.49
51–100	37	0	0.63	37	0	0.63	37	0	0.63	37	0	0.63	37	0	0.63	37	0	0.63
101–200	40	0	0.74	40	0	0.74	40	0	0.74	40	0	0.74	40	0	0.74	40	0	0.74
201–300	43	0	0.74	43	0	0.74	70	1	0.92	70	1	0.92	95	2	0.99	95	2	0.99
301–400	44	0	0.74	44	0	0.74	70	1	0.99	100	2	1.0	120	3	1.1	145	4	1.1
401–500	45	0	0.75	75	1	0.95	100	2	1.1	100	2	1.1	125	3	1.2	150	4	1.2
501–600	45	0	0.76	75	1	0.98	100	2	1.1	125	3	1.1	150	4	1.3	175	5	1.3
601–800	45	0	0.77	75	1	1.0	100	2	1.2	130	3	1.2	175	5	1.4	200	6	1.4
801–1,000	45	0	0.78	75	1	1.0	105	2	1.2	155	4	1.4	180	5	1.4	225	7	1.5
1,001–2,000	45	0	0.80	75	1	1.0	130	3	1.4	180	4	1.6	230	7	1.7	280	9	1.8
2,001–3,000	75	1	1.1	105	2	1.3	135	3	1.4	210	6	1.7	280	9	1.9	370	13	2.1
3,001–4,000	75	1	1.1	105	2	1.3	160	4	1.5	210	6	1.7	305	10	2.0	420	15	2.2
4,001–5,000	75	1	1.1	105	2	1.3	160	4	1.5	235	7	1.8	330	11	2.0	440	16	2.2
5,001–7,000	75	1	1.1	105	2	1.3	185	5	1.7	260	8	1.9	350	12	2.2	490	18	2.4
7,001–10,000	75	1	1.1	105	2	1.3	185	5	1.7	260	8	1.9	380	13	2.2	535	20	2.5
10,001–20,000	75	1	1.1	135	3	1.4	210	6	1.8	285	9	2.0	425	15	2.3	610	23	2.6
20,001–50,000	75	1	1.1	135	3	1.4	235	7	1.9	305	10	2.1	470	17	2.4	700	27	2.7
50,001–100,000	75	1	1.1	160	4	1.6	235	7	1.9	355	12	2.2	515	19	2.5	770	30	2.8

Note: n = size of sample; entry of "All" indicates that each piece in lot is to be inspected.
    c = allowable defect number for sample.
    AOQL = average outgoing quality limit.

Source: Reproduced from Dodge and Romig (1959) by permission of the publisher and of Bell Telephone Laboratories, Inc.

Process average is determined from control charts and past records, modified by any supplemental knowledge useful for predicting the expected level of defects. The following are suggested as useful rules for determining process average:

1. Compute from the first samples[2] taken on about 25 lots, the total inspected, the total defects found, and the resultant average fraction defective $\bar{p}$.
2. Eliminate any samples from "abnormal" lots. This is done by plotting a control chart to find any instances in which the fraction defective for one sample exceeds the average fraction defective $\bar{p}$ by any amount greater than $3\sqrt{\bar{p}(1-\bar{p})/n}$, where n is the size of the sample for the lot under suspicion. (Dodge and Romig (1959) recommend that these abnormal samples be not eliminated but rather corrected through equating them to $\bar{p} \pm 2\sqrt{\bar{p}(1-\bar{p})/n}$ depending on the direction of the abnormality.)
3. Recompute $\bar{p}$ with the abnormal cases eliminated (or corrected by the Dodge-Romig method). The new value of $\bar{p}$ is to be used as process average $\bar{p}$.

VARIABLES SAMPLING

Overview.   In using variables plans, a sample is taken and a measurement of a specified quality characteristic is made on each unit. These measurements are then summarized into a simple statistic (e.g., sample mean) and the observed value is compared with an allowable value defined in the plan. A decision is then made to accept or reject the lot. When applicable, variables plans provide the same degree of consumer protection as attributes plans while using considerably smaller samples.

Table 25.16 summarizes various types of variables plans showing, for each, the assumed distribution, the criteria specified, and special features.

Sampling for Percent Nonconforming.   When interest is centered on the proportion of product outside measurement specifications, and when the underlying distribution of individual measurements is known, variables plans for percent nonconforming may be used. These plans relate the proportion of individual units outside specification limits to the population mean through appropriate probability theory. The sample mean, usually converted to a test statistic, is then used to test for the position of the population mean.

Assume the distribution of individual measurements is known to be normal and a plan is desired such that the OC curve will pass through the two points (p_1, $1 - \alpha$) and (p_2, β) where

$$p_1 = \text{acceptable quality level}$$
$$1 - \alpha = \text{probability of acceptance at } p_1$$
$$p_2 = \text{rejectable quality level}$$
$$\beta = \text{probability of acceptance at } p_2$$

The OC curve should appear as indicated in Figure 25.14. Some important plans of this type are described below.

---

[2]If this computation is made from all samples in double sampling, the results will be biased, since second samples are taken only from lots of borderline quality.

TABLE 25.16 Summary of Variables Sampling Plans

Type of plan	Plan	Assumed distribution	Criteria specified	Features
	Single-sampling variables plan	Normal	Acceptable and rejectable percent nonconforming	Formulas for determining sample size and acceptance criteria to meet defined risks.
	Double-sampling variables plan	Normal	Acceptable and rejectable percent nonconforming	Tables for determining sample size and acceptance criteria to meet defined risks.
Percent nonconforming	Narrow-limit gauging	Normal	Acceptable and rejectable percent nonconforming	Tables for determining sample size and acceptance criteria to meet defined risks.
	Lot plot	None	Allowable percent nonconforming	Requires 50 measurements. Simple calculations and graphical procedure used to evaluate lot.

	Test of hypothesis	Appropriate for test	Mean or standard deviation	
Lot or process parameter—general		Appropriate for test	Mean or standard deviation	Formulas for determining sample size and acceptance criteria to meet defined risks.
	Acceptance control chart	Appropriate for determining acceptable and rejectable values of mean	Mean	Graphical procedure to determine if mean falls within defined limits.
	Sequential sampling	Normal	Mean or standard deviation	Procedures for evaluating one measurement at a time to determine if mean falls within defined limits. Complex but total sample size lower than with other plans.
Published plans for percent nonconforming	MIL-STD-414	Normal	Acceptable quality level (percent defective)	Tables and procedures for lot evaluation to a specified AQL. Requires tightened and reduced inspection. OC curves given. Includes mixed plans for use when lots have been screened before submission to sampling inspection.
Lot or process parameter—bulk sampling	Specific bulk sampling models	Appropriate for test	Mean	Formulas for determining sample size to estimate mean with specified confidence interval. Applicable for gaseous, liquid, or solid products which occur in nondiscrete units.

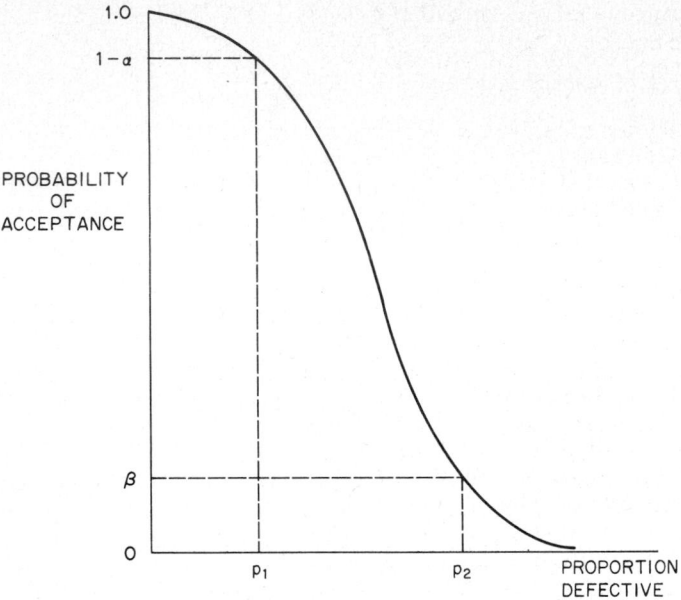

FIG. 25.14   Operating characteristic curve.

Single Sampling.   The rationale for variables sampling plans for percent non-conforming is illustrated in Figure 25.15, which assumes the underlying distribution of measurements to be normal with standard deviation σ known.

Suppose the following sampling plan is used to test against an upper specification limit U:

1. Sample n items from the lot and determine the sample mean $\overline{X}$.

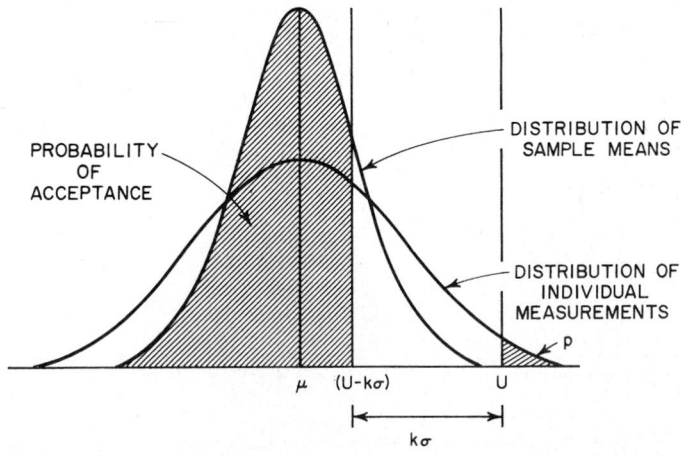

FIG. 25.15 $(U - k\sigma)$ method.

2. Test against an acceptance limit $(U - k\sigma)$, k standard deviation units inside the specification.

3. If $\overline{X} \leq (U - k\sigma)$, accept the product; otherwise reject the product.

If the distribution of individual measurements is normal, as shown, a proportion p of the product above the specification limit U implies the mean of the distribution must be fixed at the position indicated by μ. Means of samples of size n are, then, distributed about μ, as shown; so the probability of obtaining an $\overline{X}$ not greater than $(U - k\sigma)$ is indicated by the shaded area of the distribution of sample means. This shaded area is the probability of acceptance when the fraction nonconforming in the process is p. Note that the normal shape supplies the necessary connection between the distribution of the sample means and the proportion of product nonconforming. While, for reasonable sample sizes, the distribution of sample means will be normal, regardless of the shape of the underlying distribution of individual measurements, it is the underlying distribution of measurements itself that determines the relationship of μ and p. Hence, the plan will be quite sensitive to departures from normality.

Since $\overline{X} \leq U - k\sigma$ is equivalent to $\overline{X} + k\sigma \leq U$, the above sampling plan may be expressed as follows:

1. Sample n items from the lot and determine the sample mean $\overline{X}$.

2. If $\overline{X} + k\sigma \leq U$, accept the product; otherwise reject the product.

This is the method used to specify variables sampling plans in MIL-STD-414 (1957) and its civilian version ANSI/ASQC Z1.9 (1980). Diagrammatically, this second method of specifying a sampling plan is indicated in Figure 25.16. Adding $k\sigma$ to each $\overline{X}$ moves the distribution of the sample means to the right a distance $k\sigma$, so that the upper specification limit U plays the role of the acceptance limit. This can be seen by comparing Figure 25.15 with Figure 25.16.

Using Figure 25.15 or Figure 25.16 and normal probability theory, it is possible to calculate the probability of acceptance P_a for various possible values of p, the proportion defective. A graph of P_a versus p traces the operating characteristic curve of the acceptance sampling plan. Figure 25.17 shows the operating charac-

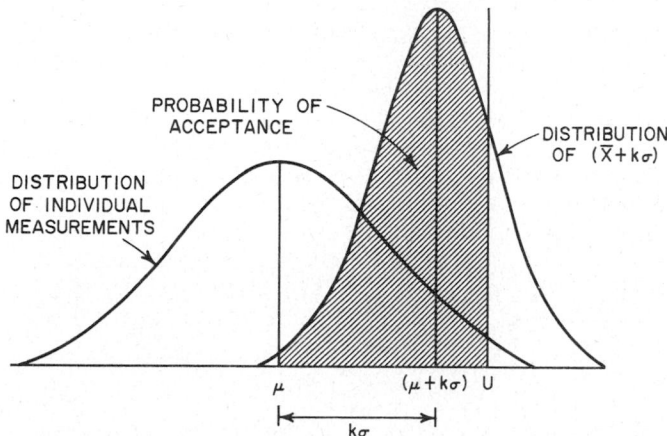

FIG. 25.16 $(\overline{X} + k\sigma)$ method.

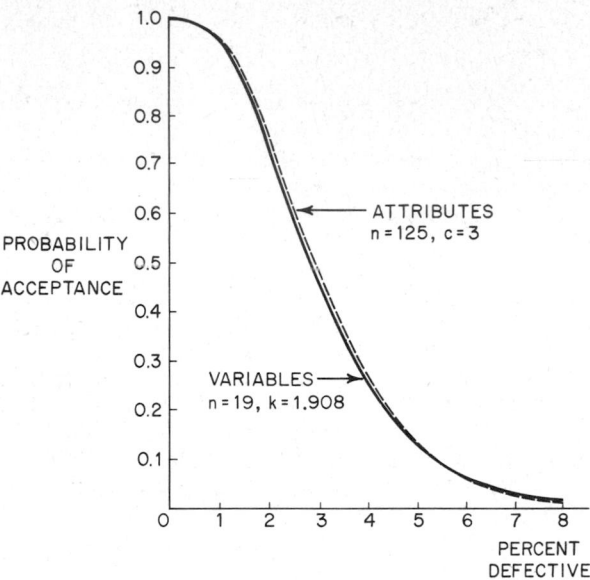

FIG. 25.17   Operating characteristic curve.

teristic curve of the variables plan $n = 19$, $k = 1.908$, testing against a single-sided specification limit with known standard deviation. For comparative purposes, the OC curve of the attributes plan $n = 125$, $c = 3$ is also given. Note that the OC curves intersect at about $p = 0.01$ and $p = 0.05$, indicating roughly equivalent protection at these fractions defective.

Probability theory appropriate to other methods of specifying variables plans (e.g., standard deviation unknown, double specification limits) can be used to give the OC curves and other properties of these procedures. Formulas for determining plans to meet specific prescribed conditions can also be derived. Note that the OC curves of variables plans are generally considered to be type B. That is, they are regarded as sampling from the process producing the items inspected, rather than the immediate lot of material involved.

Two-Point Variables Plans for Percent Nonconforming.   Two-point single-sampling plans for variables inspection can be readily obtained using an approximation derived by Wallis. For example, a two-point plan testing against a single specification limit, incorporating producer's quality level p_1 and consumer's quality level p_2 with producer's and consumer's risks fixed at $\alpha = 0.05$ and $\beta = 0.10$ may be found using

$$k = 0.438Z_1 + 0.562Z_2$$

$$n_\sigma = \frac{8.567}{(Z_1 - Z_2)^2}$$

or

$$n_s = \left(1 + \frac{k^2}{2}\right) n_\sigma$$

Here Z_1 is the standard normal deviate corresponding to an upper tail area of p_1, and Z_2 is the standard normal deviate corresponding to an upper tail area of p_2. Use n_σ or n_s depending on whether the standard deviation is known or unknown. For other risks or double specification limits more detailed procedures are necessary. See Duncan (1974).

As an example of the use of the procedure, consider $p_1 = 0.01$, $p_2 = 0.05$, $\alpha = 0.05$, $\beta = 0.10$. Application of the formulas with $Z_1 = 2.326$ and $Z_2 = 1.645$ gives $k = 1.94$, $n_\sigma = 18.5 \sim 19$ and $n_s = 53.3 \sim 54$. This plan matches the attributes plan $n = 131$, $c = 3$.

A procedure for applying double-sampling variables plans was first presented by Bowker and Goode (1952). Tables to expedite the selection and application of these plans are given by Sommers (1981). Double sampling by variables can account for about a 20 percent reduction in average sample numbers from single sampling. For example, the plan matching the single-sampling plan derived above would have average sample size 14.9 for the known standard deviation plan and 41.5 when the standard deviation is unknown. The application of double-sampling by variables is analogous to double sampling by attributes.

The relative efficiency of two-point variables plans over the matched variables plans varies with k. Hamaker (1979) has shown that

$$\frac{n_a}{n_\sigma} = 2\pi p_k \, (1 - p_k) \, e^{k^2}$$

where p_k is the upper tail normal area corresponding to the standard normal deviate $Z = k$ and n_a is the attributes sample size. For the example above, $k = 1.94$ so $p_k = .0262$ and $n_a/n_\sigma = 6.9$ and we observe that $131/19 = 6.9$.

Narrow-Limit Gaging for Percent Nonconforming. Narrow- (or compressed-) limit gaging plans bridge the gap between variables and attributes inspection by combining the ease of attributes inspection with the power of variables inspection to reduce sample size. An artificial specification limit is set inside the specification limit. Samples are selected and gaged against this artificial "narrow limit." The narrow limit is set using the properties of the normal distribution, to which the product is assumed to conform. A standard attributes sampling plan is applied to the results of gaging to the narrow limit and the lot is sentenced accordingly.

The criteria for the narrow-limit gaging plan are, then, as follows

n = sample size
c = acceptance number
t = number of standard deviation units the narrow-limit gage is set inside the specification limit

The standard deviation σ is assumed to be known.

A set of two-point plans having minimum sample size for selected values of producer's and consumer's quality levels with $\alpha = 0.05$ and $\beta = 0.10$ has been given by Schilling and Sommers (1981). They have also compiled a complete set of narrow-limit plans matching MIL-STD-105D.

Consider the plan having producer's and consumer's quality levels $p_1 = .01$ and $p_2 = 0.05$ with $\alpha = 0.05$ and $\beta = 0.10$. The appropriate plan given in the Schilling-Sommers tables is $n = 28$, $c = 14$, $t = 1.99$. A narrow-limit gage is set 1.99σ inside the specification limit. A sample of 28 is taken and gaged against the limit. If 15 or more units fail the narrow limit, the lot is rejected. Otherwise, it is accepted.

A good approximation to the optimum narrow limit plan can be constructed from the corresponding known standard deviation variables plan (n_σ, k) as follows:

$$n = \frac{3n_\sigma}{2}$$

$$t = k$$

$$c - \frac{3n_\sigma}{4} - \frac{2}{3}$$

For the example, we have seen that $n_\sigma = 18.5$ and $k = 1.94$

$$n = 27.8 \sim 28$$

$$t = 1.94$$

$$c = 13.2 \sim 14$$

Narrow-limit plans have had many successful applications and are readily accepted by inspectors because of the ease with which they can be applied.

Lot Plot. Probably no variables acceptance sampling plan matches the natural inclination of the inspector better than the lot plot method developed by Dorian Shainin (1950) at the Hamilton Standard Division of United Aircraft Co. The procedure employs a histogram and rough estimates of the extremes of the distribution of product to determine lot acceptance or rejection. A standard sample size of 50 observations is maintained.

The method is useful as a tool for acceptance sampling in situations where more sophisticated methods may be inappropriate or not well received by the parties involved. The lot plot plan is especially useful in introducing statistical methods. The subjective aspects of the plan (classification of frequency distributions, their construction, etc.) and its fixed sample size suggest the use of more objective procedures in critical applications. The wide initial acceptance of Shainin's (1952) work attests to its appeal to inspection personnel. The lot plot method is outlined in Table 25.17. See Grant and Leavenworth (1979) for details. For a critical review, see Moses (1956).

A special lot plot card is helpful in simplifying some of the calculations. Figure 25.18 shows the form filled out for the example given in Table 25.17.

Grand Lot Schemes. Acceptance inspection and compliance testing often require levels of protection for both the consumer and the producer that make for large sample size relative to lot size. A given sample size can, however, be made to apply to several lots jointly if the lots can be shown to be homogeneous. This reduces the economic impact of a necessarily large sample size. Grand lot schemes, as introduced by L. E. Simon (1941), can be used to effect such a reduction. Application of the grand lot scheme has been greatly simplified by incorporating graphical analysis of means procedures in verifying the homogeneity of a grand lot. In this way individual sublots are subjected to control chart analysis for uniformity in level and variation before they are combined into a grand lot. The resulting approach can be applied to attributes or variables data, is easy to use, provides high levels of protection economically, and can reduce sample size by as much as 80 percent. It may be applied to unique "one-off" lots, isolated lots

TABLE 25.17   Variables Plans for Percent Defective Lot Plot

Example: A lot plot is to be used in inspecting the width of caps. A sample of 50 is taken in 10 subgroups of 5 with the following results:

1	2	3	4	5	6	7	8	9	10
0.2538	0.2581	0.2556	0.2531	0.2501	0.2521	0.2541	0.2555	0.2489	0.2529
0.2519	0.2571	0.2542	0.2566	0.2506	0.2557	0.2499	0.2569	0.2557	0.2579
0.2508	0.2521	0.2521	0.2534	0.2534	0.2569	0.2514	0.2553	0.2542	0.2565
0.2537	0.2545	0.2521	0.2557	0.2516	0.2541	0.2536	0.2496	0.2529	0.2577
0.2529	0.2563	0.2518	0.2519	0.2559	0.2524	0.2492	0.2512	0.2546	0.2541

These data are shown analyzed in Fig. 25.18. Should the lot be accepted?

Summary of plan	Calculations

I.   Restrictions: None.

II.   Necessary information: Specification limits.

III.   Selection of plan.
   A. Plan is constant lot to lot.
   B. A special form (Fig. 25.18) is used to apply plan.

IV.   Elements
   A. Sample size: A random sample of 50 pieces is taken from the lot in 10 subsamples of 5 each. Subsample identification is maintained.

   B. Statistic (for symmetric distribution).
      1. Statistic is $\overline{\overline{X}} \pm 3\hat{\sigma}$ calculated as follows:
         a. Construct cells for frequency distribution on chart.
            (1) Determine mean $\overline{X}_1$ and range R_1 for the first subgroup
            (2) Position $\overline{X}_1$ at line number 0 on lot plot form
            (3) Set cell width w so that $w \simeq R_1/4$
            (4) Fill in lot plot form with cell midpoints
         b. Tally measurements for frequency distribution using subsample number as tally mark. Tally marks form a histogram.
         c. Record range of each subsample on form in terms of number of cells between lowest and highest tally mark for each subgroup.
         d. Calculate grand mean $\overline{\overline{X}}$ from frequency distribution in terms of line numbers above ($+$) and below ($-$) arbitrary origin taken as the zero cell.

B.

1a. $\overline{X}_1 = 0.2526$, $R_1 = 0.003$

$\overline{X}_1 \sim 0.253$ at 0

$w \simeq \dfrac{0.003}{4} = 0.00075$

take $w = 0.001$

1b.   See Fig. 25.18

1c.   See Fig. 25.18 under "range" on right side

1d.   Zero cell shown as arrow in Fig. 25.18 $\overline{\overline{X}} = +0.14$

25.59

Table 25.17 Variables Plans for Percent Defective Lot Plot (*Continued*)

Summary of plan	Calculations
e. Draw $\overline{\overline{X}}$ on chart in terms of line numbers.	1*e.* $\overline{\overline{X}}$ drawn 0.14 cell widths above middle of zero cell
f. Estimate 3σ of line numbers from average of subsample ranges $3\hat{\sigma} = 3\overline{R}/d_2 = 1.29\,\overline{R}$	1*f.* $3\hat{\sigma} = 1.29\left(\dfrac{51}{10}\right) = 6.6$
g. Label $\overline{\overline{X}} \pm 3\sigma$ in terms of line numbers as (1) ULL = Upper Lot Limit $(\overline{\overline{X}} + 3\hat{\sigma})$ (2) LLL = Lower Lot Limit $(\overline{\overline{X}} - 3\hat{\sigma})$	1*g.* See Fig. 25.18 marked ULL and LLL
h. Draw specification limits on chart.	1*h.* See Fig. 25.18 marked SPEC

   C. Decision criteria.
      1. Acceptance criterion.
        a. Symmetric distribution well within specification limits—accept automatically.
        b. Symmetric distribution other than above:
          (1) Lot limits within specification—accept.
          (2) Lot limits outside specification—estimate proportion of product outside specification with special technique using code strip. If less than allowable value—accept. See reference below.
        c. Nonsymmetric, bimodal distributions, etc. Special technique provided for estimating proportion out of specification using code strip. See reference below. If less than allowable value—accept.
      2. Rejection criterion: Reject otherwise.

V. Action: Dispose of lot as indicated. The Lot plot form provides a useful communication device with vendor.	V. Reject the lot

VI. Characteristics: See source reference below.

VII. Reference: Shainin, 1950.

---

from a continuing series, an isolated sequence of lots, or to a continuing series of lots. The procedure has been described in depth by Schilling (1979).

Sampling for Process Parameter. When process parameters are specified, sampling plans can be developed from analogous tests of significance with cor-

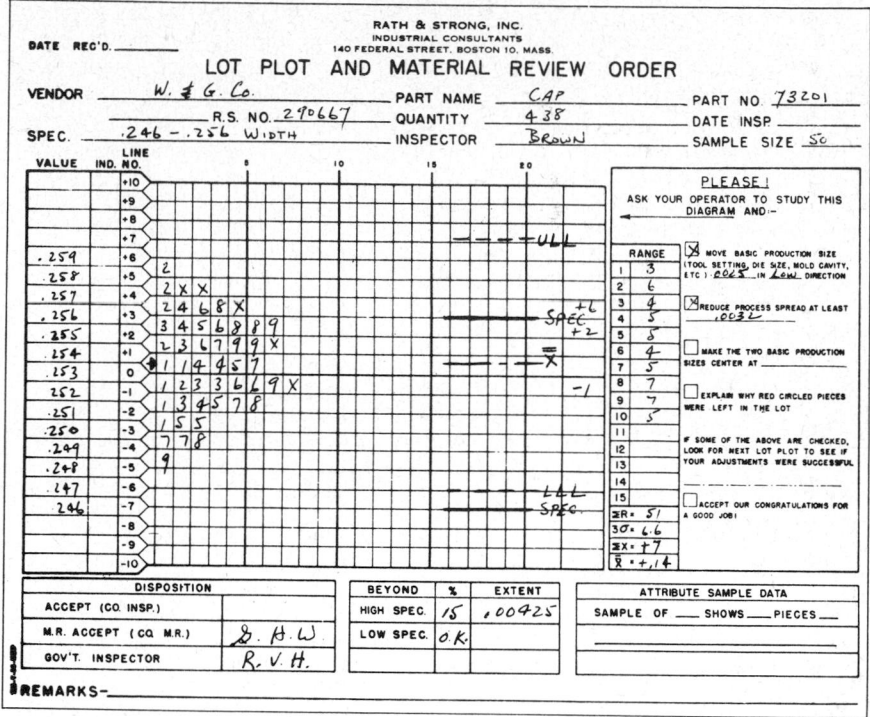

FIG. 25.18 Illustration of lot plot method.

responding OC curves. These plans do not require percent nonconforming to be related to the process mean, since the specifications to which they are applied are not in terms of percent nonconforming. This means that assumptions of process distribution may not need to be as rigorously held as in variables plans for percent nonconforming.

With specifications stated in terms of process location or variability, as measured by specific values of the mean μ or the process standard deviation σ, interest is centered not on fraction defective, but rather on controlling the parameters of the distribution of product to specified levels. From specifications of this type, it is usually possible to distinguish two process levels which may be used as bench marks as conceived by Freund (1957):

1. APL = acceptable process level—a process level which is acceptable and should be accepted most of the time by the plan.
2. RPL = rejectable process level—a process level which is rejectable and should be rejected most of the time by the plan.

The probability of acceptance for each of these process levels is usually specified as:

$$1 - \alpha = \text{probability of acceptance at the APL}$$

$$\beta = \text{probability of acceptance at the RPL}$$

where α = producer's risk, β = consumer's risk.

Variables plans appropriate for this type of specification can be derived from the operating characteristic curves of appropriate tests of hypotheses. This is the case for single-sampling plans for process parameter which are, simply, appropriately constructed tests of hypotheses, e.g., testing the hypotheses that μ equals a specific value, against a one- or two-sided alternative. Thus, the statistical tests presented in Section 23 under Statistical Tests of Hypotheses can be used for this type of acceptance sampling plan.

Sequential sampling procedures have been developed which are particularly useful when levels of process parameter are specified. They usually offer a substantial decrease in sample size over competing procedures, although they may be difficult to administer. To use sequential sampling:

1. Take a sample of one measurement at a time.
2. Plot the cumulative sum T of an appropriate statistic against the sample number n.
3. Draw two lines

$$T = h_2 + sn$$

$$T = -h_1 + sn$$

where the intercepts h_1 and h_2 are values associated with the plan used and the symbol s is not a standard deviaton but is a constant computed from the values of the acceptable process level (APL) and the rejectable process level (RPL). The use of s here corresponds to its use in the literature of sequential sampling plans.

4. Continue to sample if the cumulative sum lies between these lines, and take the appropriate action indicated if the plot moves outside the lines.

Procedures for constructing such plans and determining appropriate values of h_1, h_2, and s are given in detail in Duncan (1974).

Acceptance control charts offer a unique answer to the problem of sampling for process parameter and can be used to implement such plans when an acceptable process level and rejectable process level are defined in terms of the mean value. They satisfy the natural desire of inspection personnel to observe quality trends and to look upon sampling as a continuing process.

These charts incorporate predetermined values of consumer and producer risk in the limits and so provide the balanced protection for the interested parties that is often lacking in the use of a conventional control chart for product acceptance.

It is not necessary that the population of individual measurements be normally distributed. The distribution must be known so that acceptable and rejectable values of the mean can be calculated. The procedure then uses the normal distribution in the analysis of the sample mean because the distribution of sample means of samples of reasonable size may be regarded as normal for any distribution of individual measurements.

The procedure for implementing this technique is shown in Table 25.18. The acceptance control chart concept is shown in Figure 25.19, and an acceptance control chart example is shown in Figure 25.20. See Freund (1957) for additional details.

Published Tables and Procedures. There is often much more involved in acceptance sampling than simple tests of hypotheses. Sampling plans applied individually to guard against an occasional discrepant lot can be reduced to

TABLE 25.18 Variables Plans for Process Parameter—Acceptance Control Charts

Example: The specification limits for electrical resistance are 620 and 680, the AQL 2.5%, and the standard deviation 13. Assuming a normal distribution of individual measurements, the mean may be as low as $620 + 1.96 (13)$, or 646, or as high as $680 - 1.96 (13)$, or 654. This pair of values represents the range of the acceptable process level (APL). It was decided that the rejectable process level would occur when 14% was beyond a specification limit. Thus, the range of RPL was $620 + 1.08 (13)$ and $680 - 1.08 (13)$, or 634 and 666. Should the lot be accepted if $\overline{X} = 647$?

Summary of plan	Calculations
I. Restrictions: None	
II. Necessary information (single-sided specification)	II.
A. σ = known standard deviation	A. $\sigma = 13$
B. μ_1 = APL (acceptable process level) with $P_a = 1 - a$	B. $\mu_1 = 654$, $P_a = 0.95$
C. μ_2 = RPL (rejectable process level) with $P_a = \beta$	C. $\mu_2 = 666$, $P_a = 0.10$
III. Selection of plan: See below	
IV. Elements	IV.
A. Sample size $$n = \left[\frac{(z\alpha + z\beta)\,\sigma}{\mu_2 - \mu_1} \right]^2$$ where z_p cuts off upper tail area of p in standard normal curve	A. $n =$ $$\left[\frac{(1.645 + 1.282)(13)}{12} \right]^2$$ $n = 10.06 \sim 10$
B. Statistic: $\overline{X}$ = mean of sample of n	B. $\overline{X} = 647$
C. Decision criteria	C. $d =$
1. Compute: $$d = \frac{z_\alpha}{z_\alpha + z_\beta} |\mu_2 - \mu_1|$$ and set the acceptance control limit, ACL, a distance d from APL in the direction of the RPL. Sign of $|\mu_2 - \mu_1|$ ignored.	$\left(\dfrac{1.645}{1.645 + 1.282} \right)(12)$ $= 6.74$ Upper ACL = $654 + 6.74$ $= 660.74$ By symmetry Lower ACL = $646 - 6.74$ $= 639.26$
2. Construct an acceptance control chart (Fig. 25.19) and accept if $\overline{X}$ falls within acceptance control limits; reject otherwise. Double-sided specification chart shown (see remarks below). Use appropriate half of chart for single-sided specification.	Plot as in Fig. 25.20
V. Action: Single lot disposed of as indicated by chart	V. Accept the lot
VI. Characteristics: Two points originally specified give indication of OC curve	

TABLE 25.18   Variables Plans for Process Parameter—Acceptance Control Charts
(*Continued*)

Summary of plan	Calculations
VII. Reference:	Freund, 1957.
VIII. Remarks	VIII.
A. Above formulas are for single upper or single lower process limits, or for both if (Upper ACL − Lower ACL) $\geq k\sigma / \sqrt{n}$ where:	A. Can use both upper and lower limits since $(660.74 - 639.26) >$ $\dfrac{(5)(13)}{\sqrt{10}}$ $21.48 > 20.56$

$$\begin{array}{c|c} \alpha & k \\ \hline 0.05 & 5 \\ 0.01 & 6 \\ 0.001 & 7 \end{array}$$

If (Upper ACL − Lower ACL) $< k\sigma / \sqrt{n}$, see above reference for appropriate factors

B. If standard deviation is estimated from control chart, see reference above for appropriate limits

C. Advisable to run range chart with acceptance control chart to ensure stability of variation

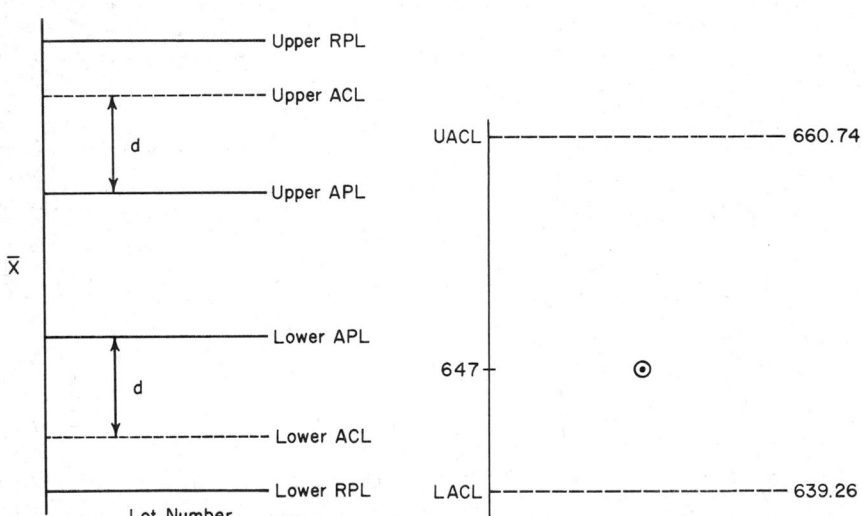

FIG. 25.19 Acceptance control chart concept.   **FIG. 25.20**   Acceptance control chart example.

hypothesis tests. Sampling plans, however, may be combined into sampling schemes, intended to achieve a predetermined objective. Sampling schemes, as overall strategies using one or more sampling plans, have their own measures such as AOQ (average outgoing quality) or ATI (average total inspection), not to be found in hypothesis testing. Thus, MIL-STD-105D (1963) and its civilian version ANSI/ASQC Z1.4 (1981) together with their variables counterpart MIL-STD-414 (1957) and its modified civilian version ANSI/ASQC Z1.9 (1980) are sampling schemes which specify the use of various sampling plans under well-defined rules.

Military Standard 414 (1957) and the modernized version ANSI/ASQC Z1.9 (1980) are AQL-type sampling schemes which assume the individual measurements to which they are applied to be normally distributed.

These standards allow for the use of three alternative measures of variability: known standard deviation σ, estimated standard deviation s, or average range $(\overline{R})$. If the variability of the process producing the product is known and stable as verified by a control chart, it is profitable to use σ. The choice between s and $\overline{R}$, when σ is unknown, is an economic one. The range requires larger sample sizes but is easier to compute. The operating characteristic curves given in the standards are based on the use of s, the σ and $\overline{R}$ plans having been matched, as closely as possible, to those using s.

MIL-STD-414 and ANSI/ASQC Z1.9 (1980) offer two alternative procedures. In addition to the method using an acceptance constant k, each standard also presents a procedure for estimating the proportion defective in the lot from the variables evidence. The former method is called Form 1; the latter is called Form 2. Form 2 is the preferred procedure in MIL-STD-414 since the switching rules for reduced and tightened inspection cannot be applied unless the fraction defective of each lot is estimated from the sample. The switching rules of ANSI/ASQC Z1.9 are patterned after MIL-STD-105D and can be used with Form 1 or Form 2.

These two forms can be compared with equivalent forms of attributes sampling. One possibility is to compare the number of defectives found in the sample d with an acceptance number c. Alternatively, the proportion defective in the population could be estimated from the proportion defective in the sample, and that estimate then compared with some acceptance limit (M). These possibilities are compared with their variables counterparts in Figure 25.21.

	Attributes	Variables
Form 1	$d \leq c$	$z = \dfrac{U - \overline{X}}{s} \geq k$
Form 2	$p = \dfrac{d}{n} \leq \dfrac{c}{n} = M$	$Q = \dfrac{U - \overline{X}}{s}$ is used to estimate p
		$p \leq M$

FIG. 25.21 Criteria for acceptance (sample of n).

The standards are composed of sections indexed by measure of variability, type of specification (single or double), and form of the acceptance procedure. Only Form 2 is officially available for the case of double specification limits; however, factors are provided for application of Form 1 if desired. The structure of these standards is shown in Figure 25.22. Table 25.19 contrasts MIL-STD-414 and ANSI/ASQC Z1.9.

Application of these variables schemes follows the pattern of MIL-STD-105D, which is also an AQL sampling scheme. Sample sizes are determined from lot size, and after choosing the measure of variability to be used and the Form of the acceptance procedure, appropriate acceptance limits are obtained from the standard. As in MIL-STD-105D, operating characteristic curves are included in MIL-

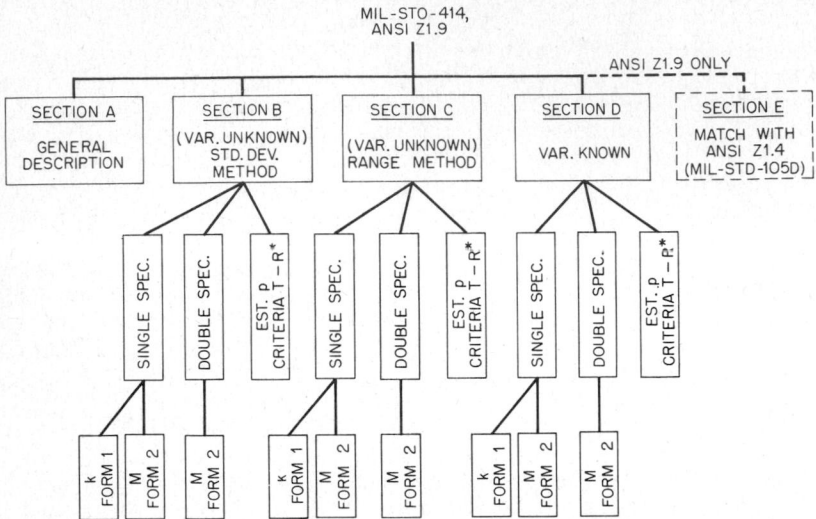

FIG. 25.22   Structure of MIL-STD-414 and ANSI/ASQC Z1.9-1980.   *(From E. G. Schilling (1981). "ANSI/ASQC Z1.9(1980)—A Modernization of MIL-STD-414." Quality Progress, March, p. 28.)*

TABLE 25.19   Comparison of ANSI Z1.9-1980 and MIL-STD-414

	ANSI Z1.9-1980	MIL-STD-414
Switching rules	Same as MIL-STD-105D; Figure 25.13	Unique; Figure 25.23
Inspection levels and sample size code letters	Same as MIL-STD-105D; Table 25.13	Unique; Table 25.21
Plans	Matched to MIL-STD-105D	Unique

STD-414 and ANSI/ASQC Z1.9. These should be consulted before a specific plan is instituted. Note that the plans contained in MIL-STD-414 and MIL-STD-105D do not match; however, the plans in ANSI Z1.9 are matched to MIL-STD-105D and ANSI/ASQC Z1.4.

Since it is an AQL scheme, MIL-STD-414 and its civilian counterpart are based on an overall strategy which incorporates switching rules to move from normal to tightened or reduced inspection and return depending on the quality observed in the previous 10 lots. These switching rules are indicated in Figure 25.23 for MIL-STD-414 and should be used if the standard is to be properly applied. The switching rules for ANSI/ASQC Z1.9 (1980) are the same as those of MIL-STD-105D and ANSI/ASQC Z1.4 (1981) except that the limit numbers for reduced inspection have been eliminated. This allows these standards to be readily interchanged.

A check sequence for application of MIL-STD-414 and ANSI/ASQC Z1.9 (1980) is given in Figure 25.24. Tables 25.20 to 25.25 show the specific steps involved in application of the two forms using the sample standard deviation as a measure of variability. Although the procedures of ANSI/ASQC Z1.9 (1980) are

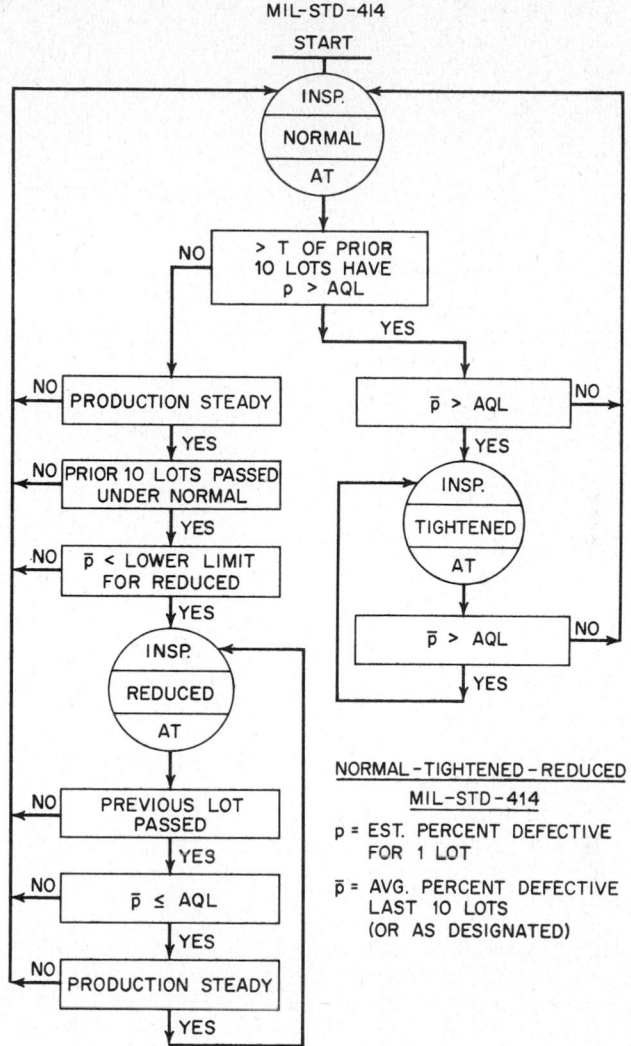

FIG. 25.23 Switching rules for MIL-STD-414 only. *(From Schilling, 1970.)*

analogous, it should be noted that the ranges, inspection levels, and tables of plans are different in the two standards, since Z1.9 has been revised to match MIL-STD-105D and ANSI/ASQC Z1.4 (1981). Procedures for upper, lower, and double specification limits are indicated in these tables together with appropriate references to the standard and an illustrative example. Modifications to the procedure, necessary when variability is measured by average range or a known standard deviation, are described. Table 25.26 shows the relationship of the statistics and procedures used under the various measures of variability allowed, for each of the forms.

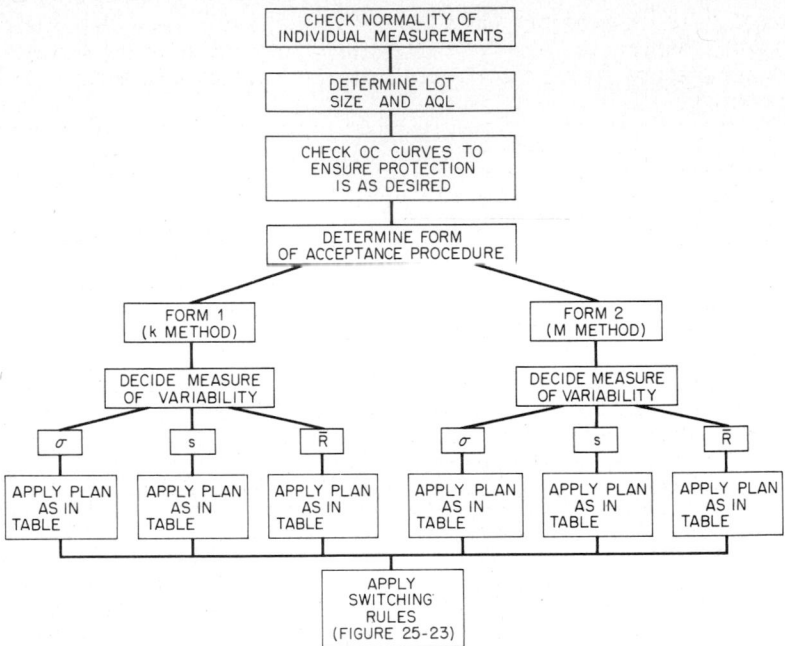

FIG. 25.24   Check sequence for MIL-STD-414 and ANSI/ASQC Z1.9-1980.

MIL-STD-414 has a liberal supply of excellent examples. The reader is referred to the standard for more detailed examples of its applications.

Mixed Plans.   One disadvantage of variables plans is the fact that screened lots may at times be rejected by a sample $\overline{X}$ or s indicating percent defective to be high when, actually, the discrepant material has been eliminated. To prevent rejection of screened lots, double-sampling plans have been developed which use a variables criterion on the first sample and attributes on the second sample. Lots are accepted if they pass variables inspection; however, if they do not pass, a second sample is taken and the results are judged by an attributes criterion. In this way screened lots will not be rejected, since rejections are made only under the attributes part of the plan. This type of plan was proposed by Dodge (1932). The procedure has been discussed in some detail by Bowker and Goode (1952), Gregory and Resnikoff (1955), and Schilling and Dodge (1969). MIL-STD-414 and ANSI/ASQC Z1.9 (1980) allow for the use of such procedures, although only ANSI/ASQC Z1.9 (1980) is properly matched to MIL-STD-105D or ANSI/ASQC Z1.4 (1981) to allow for proper use of mixed plans. The steps involved are shown in Table 25.27.

RELIABILITY SAMPLING

Overview.   Sampling plans for life and reliability testing are similar in concept and operation to the variables plans previously described. They differ to the

TABLE 25.20 MIL-STD-414 (1957) and ANSI/ASQC Z1.9 (1980), Variability Unknown, Standard Deviation Method, Form 1

Example: The specification for electrical resistance of a certain component is 620 to 680 ohms. A lot of 100 is submitted for inspection, inspection level IV, normal inspection, with AQL = 2.5 percent. Should the lot be accepted if $\overline{X}$ = 647 and s = 17.22?

Summary of plan	Calculations
1. Restrictions: Individual measurements normally distributed	
II. Necessary information	II.
A. Lot size	*A.* Lot size = 100
B. AQL	*B.* AQL = 2.5%
C. Severity of inspection: normal, tightened, reduced	*C.* Normal inspection
III. Selection of plan	III.
A. Determine code letter (Table 25.21 for MIL-STD-414 only) from lot size and inspection level [normally, inspection level IV is used in MIL-STD-414 and inspection level II in ANSI/ASQC Z1.9 (1980)]	*A.* Code F
B. From code letter and AQL, determine (Table 25.22 for MIL-STD-414 only)	*B.*
1. Sample size = n	n = 10
2. Acceptance constant = k	k = 1.41
C. Double specification limits: obtain MSD = $F(U - L)$, where F is obtained from appropriate table in the Standard	*C.* MSD = 0.298(680 − 620) = 17.88
IV. Elements	IV.
A. Sample size: See above	*A.* n = 10
B. Statistic	*B.* T_U = (680 − 647)/ 17.22 = 1.92
1. Upper specification: $T_U = (U - \overline{X})/s$	
2. Lower specification: $T_L = (\overline{X} - L)/s$	
3. Double specification: T_U and T_L	
C. Decision Criteria	*C.*
1. Acceptance criterion	
a. Upper specification: $T_U \geq k$	1.92 > 1.41
b. Lower specification: $T_L \geq k$	1.57 > 1.41
c. Double specification: $T_U \geq k$, $T_L \geq k$, and $s \leq$ MSD	17.22 < 17.88
2. Rejection criterion: Reject otherwise	
V. Action: Dispose of lot as indicated and refer to switching rules for next lot; see Figure 25.23	V. Accept the lot
VI. Characteristics: OC curves given	
VII. Reference: 1957 version of MIL-STD-414 and ANSI/ASQC Z1.9 (1980).	
VIII. Remarks (use appropriate tables from Standard)	
A. Range method	
1. Use $\overline{R}$ of subsamples of 5 if $n \geq 10$; use $\overline{R}$ if $n < 10$	
2. Substitute $\overline{R}$ for s in statistics	
3. Double specifications—use values of f (for MAR) in place of F (for MSD), where MAR is the maximum allowable range	
B. Variability known: Substitute σ for s in statistics	

TABLE 25.21   MIL-STD-414 Sample Size Code Letters*

	Inspection levels				
Lot size	I	II	III	IV	V
3–8	B	B	B	B	C
9–15	B	B	B	B	D
16–25	B	B	B	C	E
26–40	B	B	B	D	F
41–65	B	B	C	E	G
66–110	B	B	D	F	H
111–180	B	C	E	G	I
181–300	B	D	F	H	J
301–500	C	E	G	I	K
501–800	D	F	H	J	L
801–1,300	E	G	I	K	L
1,301–3,200	F	H	J	L	M
3,201–8,000	G	I	L	M	N
8,001–22,000	H	J	M	N	O
22,001–110,000	I	K	N	O	P
110,001–550,000	I	K	O	P	Q
550,001 and over	I	K	P	Q	Q

*Sample size code letters given in body of table are applicable when the indicated inspection levels are to be used.

extent that, when units are not all run to failure, the length of the test becomes an important parameter determining the characteristics of the procedure. Further, time to failure tends to conform naturally to skewed distributions such as the exponential or as approximated by the Weibull. Accordingly, many life test plans are based on these distributions. When time to failure is normally distributed and all units tested are run to failure, the variables plans assuming normality, discussed above, apply; attributes plans such as MIL-STD-105D may also be used.

Life tests, terminated before all units have failed, may be:

1. Failure terminated—a given sample size n is tested until the rth failure occurs. The test is then terminated.
2. Time terminated—a given sample size n is tested until a preassigned termination time T is reached. The test is then terminated.

Furthermore, these tests may be based upon specifications written in terms of one of the following characteristics:

1. Mean life—the mean life of the product
2. Hazard rate—instantaneous failure rate at some specified time t
3. Reliable life—the life beyond which some specified proportion of items in the lot or population will survive
4. Failure rate (FR or λ)—the percentage of failures per unit time (say 1000 hours of test)

Several sets of plans are available for the testing of life and reliability. Table 25.28 summarizes some of these plans. Nelson (1983) provides considerable insight into the analysis of reliability data.

TABLE 25.22 MIL-STD-414 Master Table for Normal and Tightened Inspection for Plans Based on Variability Unknown, Standard Deviation Method

(Single specification limit, form 1)

Sample size code letter	Sample size	Acceptable quality levels (normal inspection)													
		0.04	0.065	0.10	0.15	0.25	0.40	0.65	1.00	1.50	2.50	4.00	6.50	10.00	15.00
		k	k	k	k	k	k	k	k	k	k	k	k	k	k
B	3	↓	↓	↓	↓	↓	↓	↓	↓	↓	1.12	0.958	0.765	0.566	0.341
C	4								1.45	1.34	1.17	1.01	0.814	0.617	0.393
D	5	↓	↓			2.00	1.88	1.65	1.53	1.40	1.24	1.07	0.874	0.675	0.455
E	7							1.75	1.62	1.50	1.33	1.15	0.955	0.755	0.536
F	10				2.24	2.11	1.98	1.84	1.72	1.58	1.41	1.23	1.03	0.828	0.611
G	15	2.64	2.53	2.42	2.32	2.20	2.06	1.91	1.79	1.65	1.47	1.30	1.09	0.886	0.664
H	20	2.69	2.58	2.47	2.36	2.24	2.11	1.96	1.82	1.69	1.51	1.33	1.12	0.917	0.695
I	25	2.72	2.61	2.50	2.40	2.26	2.14	1.98	1.85	1.72	1.53	1.35	1.14	0.936	0.712
J	30	2.73	2.61	2.51	2.41	2.28	2.15	2.00	1.86	1.73	1.55	1.36	1.15	0.946	0.723
K	35	2.77	2.65	2.54	2.45	2.31	2.18	2.03	1.89	1.76	1.57	1.39	1.18	0.969	0.745
L	40	2.77	2.66	2.55	2.44	2.31	2.18	2.03	1.89	1.76	1.58	1.39	1.18	0.971	0.746
M	50	2.83	2.71	2.60	2.50	2.35	2.22	2.08	1.93	1.80	1.61	1.42	1.21	1.00	0.774
N	75	2.90	2.77	2.66	2.55	2.41	2.27	2.12	1.98	1.84	1.65	1.46	1.24	1.03	0.804
O	100	2.92	2.80	2.69	2.58	2.43	2.29	2.14	2.00	1.86	1.67	1.48	1.26	1.05	0.819
P	150	2.96	2.84	2.73	2.61	2.47	2.33	2.18	2.03	1.89	1.70	1.51	1.29	1.07	0.841
Q	200	2.97	2.85	2.73	2.62	2.47	2.33	2.18	2.04	1.89	1.70	1.51	1.29	1.07	0.845
		0.065	0.10	0.15	0.25	0.40	0.65	1.00	1.50	2.50	4.00	6.50	10.00	15.00	
		Acceptable quality levels (tightened inspection)													

Note: All AQL values are in percent defective.

↓ Use first sampling plan below arrow, that is, both sample size as well as k value. When sample size equals or exceeds lot size, every item in the lot must be inspected.

Source: 1957 version of MIL-STD-414.

25.71

TABLE 25.23 MIL-STD-414 and ANSI/ASQC Z1.9 (1980), Variability Unknown, Standard Deviation Method, Form 2

Example: The specification for electrical resistance of a certain electrical component is 620 to 680 ohms. A lot of 100 is submitted for inspection, inspection level IV, normal inspection, with AQL = 2.5 percent. Should the lot be accepted if $\overline{X}$ = 647 and s = 17.22?

Summary of plan	Calculations
I. Restrictions: Individual measurements normally distributed	
II. Necessary information	II.
A. Lot size	A. Lot size = 100
B. AQL	B. AQL = 2.5%
C. Severity of inspection: normal, tightened, reduced	C. Normal inspection
III. Selection of plan	III.
A. Determine (Table 25.21 for MIL-STD-414 only) code letter from lot size and inspection level (usually, inspection Level IV is used in MIL-STD-414 and inspection Level II in ANSI/ASQC Z1.9)	A. Code F
B. From code letter and AQL, determine (Table 25.24 for MIL-STD-414 only)	B.
1. Sample size = n	n = 10
2. Value of M	M = 7.29
IV. Elements	IV.
A. Sample size: See above	A. n = 10
B. Statistic	B.
1. Upper specification: $Q_U = (U - \overline{X})/s$	Q_U = (680 − 647)/17.22 = 1.92
2. Lower specification: $Q_L = (\overline{X} - L)/s$	Q_L = (647 − 620)/17.22 = 1.57
3. Double specification: Q_U and Q_L	
C. Estimate Percent Defective from Table 25.25	C.
1. Upper specification: estimate p_U (%) from Q_U and n	p_U (%) = 1.68
2. Lower specification: estimate p_L (%) from Q_L and n	p_L(%) = 4.92
3. Double specification: estimate p (%) = p_U (%) + p_L(%)	p(%) = 6.60
D. Decision criteria	D.
1. Acceptance criterion	
a. Upper specification: p_U (%) < M	
b. Lower specification: p_L(%) < M	
c. Double specification: p(%) < M	6.60 < 7.29
Note: if AQLs not equal on upper and lower specifications, obtain M for each and apply a, b, c, above, using larger of two M values in c	

TABLE 25.23   MIL-STD-414 and ANSI/ASQC Z1.9 (1980), Variability Unknown, Standard Deviation Method, Form 2 (*Continued*)

Summary of plan	Calculations
2. Rejection criterion: Reject otherwise	
V. Action: Dispose of lot as indicated and refer to switching rules for next lot; see Figure 25.23	V. Accept the lot
VI. Characteristics: OC curves given	
VII. Reference: 1957 version of MIL-STD-414 and ANSI/ASQC Z1.9 (1980).	

VII. Remarks (use appropriate tables from Standard)
  A. Range method—similar except:
    1. Use $\overline{R}$ of subsamples of 5 if $n \geq$ 10; use R if $n < 10$
    2. Substitute $\overline{R}/c$ for s in statistics, where c is a scale factor given with n and M in the Standard
  B. Variability known—similar except:
    1. Substitute σ/v for s in statistics, where v factor is given with n and M in the Standard	

Relation of Life Characteristics.   Specification and test of various life characteristics are intimately related. Tables 25.29 and 25.30 will be found useful in converting life test characteristics. Formulas for various characteristics are shown in terms of mean life μ. Thus, using the tables, it will be found that a specification of mean life $\mu = 1000$ hours for a Weibull distribution with $\beta = 2$ is equivalent to a hazard rate of 0.000157 at 100 hours or to a reliable life of 99.22 percent surviving at 100 hours.

Exponential Distribution: H108.   *Quality Control and Reliability Handbook,* H108 (1960), presents a set of life test and reliability plans based on the exponential model for time to failure. The plans contained therein are intended for use when mean time to failure β is specified[3] in terms of acceptable mean life β_0 and unacceptable mean life β_1. Testing may be conducted:

With replacement: Units replaced when failure occurs. Test time continues to be accumulated on replacement unit.

Without replacement: Units not replaced upon failure.

The handbook contains three types of plans:

1. *Life tests terminated upon occurrence of a preassigned number of failures:*   Here, n units are tested until r failures occur. The average life is calculated and compared with an acceptable value defined by the plan, and a decision is made.

---

[3]Note that elsewhere in this handbook the mean value is described by the symbol μ.

TABLE 25.24 MIL-STD-414, Master Table for Normal and Tightened Inspection for Plans Based on Variability Unknown, Standard Deviation Method

(Double specification limit and form 2, single specification limit)

Sample size code letter	Sample size	Acceptable quality levels (normal inspection)													
		0.04	0.065	0.10	0.15	0.25	0.40	0.65	1.00	1.50	2.50	4.00	6.50	10.00	15.00
		M	M	M	M	M	M	M	M	M	M	M	M	M	M
B	3								→	↓	7.59	18.86	26.94	33.69	40.47
C	4							→	1.53	5.50	10.92	16.45	22.86	29.45	36.90
D	5					→	1.06	1.33	3.32	5.83	9.80	14.39	20.19	26.56	33.99
E	7				→	0.422	1.06	2.14	3.55	5.35	8.40	12.20	17.35	23.29	30.50
F	10			→	0.349	0.716	1.30	2.17	3.26	4.77	7.29	10.54	15.17	20.74	27.57
G	15	0.099	0.186	0.312	0.503	0.818	1.31	2.11	3.05	4.31	6.56	9.46	13.71	18.94	25.61
H	20	0.135	0.228	0.365	0.544	0.846	1.29	2.05	2.95	4.09	6.17	8.92	12.99	18.03	24.53
I	25	0.155	0.250	0.380	0.551	0.877	1.29	2.00	2.86	3.97	5.97	8.63	12.57	17.51	23.97
J	30	0.179	0.280	0.413	0.581	0.879	1.29	1.98	2.83	3.91	5.86	8.47	12.36	17.24	23.58
K	35	0.170	0.264	0.388	0.535	0.847	1.23	1.87	2.68	3.70	5.57	8.10	11.87	16.65	22.91
L	40	0.179	0.275	0.401	0.566	0.873	1.26	1.88	2.71	3.72	5.58	8.09	11.85	16.61	22.86
M	50	0.163	0.250	0.363	0.503	0.789	1.17	1.71	2.49	3.45	5.20	7.61	11.23	15.87	22.00
N	75	0.147	0.228	0.330	0.467	0.720	1.07	1.60	2.29	3.20	4.87	7.15	10.63	15.13	21.11
O	100	0.145	0.220	0.317	0.447	0.689	1.02	1.53	2.20	3.07	4.69	6.91	10.32	14.75	20.66
P	150	0.134	0.203	0.293	0.413	0.638	0.949	1.43	2.05	2.89	4.43	6.57	9.88	14.20	20.02
Q	200	0.135	0.204	0.294	0.414	0.637	0.945	1.42	2.04	2.87	4.40	6.53	9.81	14.12	19.92
		0.065	0.10	0.15	0.25	0.40	0.65	1.00	1.50	2.50	4.00	6.50	10.00	15.00	
		Acceptable quality levels (tightened inspection)													

Note: All AQL and table values are in percent defective.

↓ Use first sampling plan below arrow, that is, both sample size as well as M value. When sample size equals or exceeds lot size, every item in the lot must be inspected.

Source: 1957 version of MIL-STD-414.

TABLE 25.25 Table for Estimating the Lot Percent Defective Using Standard Deviation Method

Q_U or Q_L								Sample sizes									
	3	4	5	7	10	15	20	25	30	35	40	50	75	100	150	200
0.1	47.2	46.7	46.4	46.3	46.2	46.1	46.1	46.1	46.0	46.0	46.0	46.0	46.0	46.0	46.0	46.0
0.2	44.5	43.3	42.9	42.5	42.4	42.2	42.2	42.2	42.2	42.1	42.1	42.1	42.1	42.1	42.1	42.1
0.3	41.6	40.0	39.4	38.9	38.6	38.4	38.4	38.3	38.3	38.3	38.3	38.3	38.2	38.2	38.2	38.2
0.4	38.7	36.7	35.9	35.3	34.9	34.7	34.6	34.6	34.6	34.6	34.5	34.5	34.5	34.5	34.5	34.5
0.5	38.8	33.3	32.4	31.7	31.4	31.2	31.1	31.0	31.0	31.0	31.0	30.9	30.9	30.9	30.9	30.9
0.6	32.6	30.0	29.0	28.3	27.9	27.7	27.6	27.6	27.6	27.5	27.5	27.5	27.5	27.5	27.4	27.4
0.7	29.3	26.7	25.7	25.0	24.7	24.5	24.4	24.3	24.3	24.3	24.3	24.3	24.2	24.2	24.2	24.2
0.8	25.6	23.3	22.5	21.9	21.6	21.4	21.3	21.3	21.3	21.3	21.2	21.2	21.2	21.2	21.2	21.2
0.9	21.6	20.0	19.4	18.9	18.7	18.5	18.5	18.5	18.5	18.4	18.4	18.4	18.4	18.4	18.4	18.4
1.0	16.7	16.7	16.4	16.1	16.0	15.9	15.9	15.9	15.9	15.9	15.9	15.9	15.9	15.9	15.9	15.9
1.1	9.8	13.3	13.5	13.5	13.5	13.5	13.5	13.5	13.5	13.5	13.5	13.5	13.6	13.6	13.6	13.6
1.2	0	10.0	10.8	11.1	11.2	11.3	11.4	11.4	11.4	11.4	11.4	11.5	11.5	11.5	11.5	11.5
1.3	0	6.7	8.2	8.9	9.2	9.4	9.5	9.5	9.6	9.6	9.6	9.6	9.6	9.6	9.6	9.7
1.4	0	3.3	5.9	7.0	7.4	7.7	7.8	7.9	7.9	7.9	7.9	8.0	8.0	8.0	8.0	8.0
1.5	0	0	3.8	5.3	5.9	6.2	6.3	6.4	6.5	6.5	6.5	6.6	6.6	6.6	6.6	6.6

TABLE 25.25 Table for Estimating the Lot Percent Defective Using Standard Deviation Method (Continued)

Q_U or Q_L	Sample sizes															
	3	4	5	7	10	15	20	25	30	35	40	50	75	100	150	200
1.6	0	0	2.0	3.8	4.5	4.9	5.1	5.2	5.2	5.3	5.3	5.3	5.4	5.4	5.4	5.4
1.7	0	0	0.7	2.6	3.4	3.8	4.0	4.1	4.2	4.2	4.2	4.3	4.4	4.4	4.4	4.4
1.8	0	0	0	1.6	2.5	2.9	3.1	3.2	3.3	3.4	3.4	3.4	3.5	3.5	3.5	3.6
1.9	0	0	0	0.9	1.8	2.2	2.4	2.5	2.6	2.6	2.6	2.7	2.8	2.8	2.8	2.8
2.0	0	0	0	0.4	1.2	1.6	1.8	1.9	2.0	2.0	2.1	2.1	2.2	2.2	2.2	2.2
2.1	0	0	0	0.1	0.7	1.2	1.3	1.4	1.5	1.5	1.6	1.6	1.7	1.7	1.7	1.8
2.2	0	0	0	0	0.4	0.8	1.0	1.1	1.1	1.2	1.2	1.2	1.3	1.3	1.3	1.4
2.4	0	0	0	0	0.1	0.3	0.5	0.5	0.6	0.6	0.7	0.7	0.7	0.8	0.8	0.7
2.6	0	0	0	0	0	0.1	0.2	0.3	0.3	0.3	0.3	0.4	0.4	0.4	0.4	0.4
2.8	0	0	0	0	0	0	0.1	0.1	0.1	0.1	0.2	0.2	0.2	0.2	0.2	0.2
3.0	0	0	0	0	0	0	0	0	0.1	0.2	0.1	0.1	0.1	0.1	0.1	0.1

Source: 1957 version of MIL-STD-414.

TABLE 25.26 Application of MIL-STD-414 and ANSI/ASQC Z1.9 (1980)

Step	Section	Form 1	Form 2
Preparatory		Obtain k and n from appropriate tables	Obtain M and n from appropriate tables
Determine criteria	Section B (s)	$T_U = \dfrac{U - \overline{X}}{s}$ $T_L = \dfrac{\overline{X} - L}{s}$	$Q_U = \dfrac{U - \overline{X}}{s}$ $Q_L = \dfrac{\overline{X} - L}{s}$
	Section C ($\overline{R}$)	$T_U = \dfrac{U - \overline{X}}{\overline{R}}$ $T_L = \dfrac{\overline{X} - L}{\overline{R}}$	$Q_U = \dfrac{(U - \overline{X})c}{\overline{R}}$ $Q_L = \dfrac{(\overline{X} - L)c}{\overline{R}}$
	Section D (σ)	$T_U = \dfrac{U - \overline{X}}{\sigma}$ $T_L = \dfrac{\overline{X} - L}{\sigma}$	$Q_U = \dfrac{(U - \overline{X})v}{\sigma}$ $Q_L = \dfrac{(\overline{X} - L)v}{\sigma}$
Estimation			Enter table with n and Q_U or Q_L to get p_U or p_L
Action	Single specification	Accept if $T_U \geq k$ or $T_L \geq k$	Accept if $p_U \leq M$ or $p_L \leq M$
	Double specification	Accept if* $T_U \geq k$, $T_L \geq k$ and $s <$ MSD or $\overline{R} <$ MAR	Accept if $p_U + p_L \leq M$

Note:
$$c = \text{scale factor}$$
$$v = \sqrt{\dfrac{n}{n - 1}}$$

*Not official procedure.
Source: Schilling, 1970, p. 175.

2. *Life tests terminated at a preassigned time:* Here, n units are tested for a specified length of time T. If T is reached before r failures occur, the test is stopped and the lot accepted. If r failures occur before T is reached, the test is stopped and the lot rejected.

3. *Sequential life testing plans:* Here n units are placed on test and time, and failures are recorded until sufficient data are accumulated to reach a decision at specified risk levels. Periodically throughout the test, the time accumulated on all units is calculated and compared with the acceptable amount of time for the total number of failures accumulated up to the time of observation. If the total time exceeds the limit for acceptance, the lot is accepted; if the total time

TABLE 25.27 Variables Plans for Percent Defective, Mixed Variables—Attributes, ANSI/ASQC Z1.9 (1980)

Example: The specification for electrical resistance of a certain component is 620 to 680 ohms. A lot of 100 is submitted for inspection, inspection level IV, normal inspection, with AQL = 2.5 percent. Should the lot be accepted if $\overline{X}$ = 647 and s = 17.22?

Summary of plan	Calculations
I. Restrictions: Measurements normally distributed	
II. Necessary information	II.
A. Lot size	*A.* Lot size = 100
B. AQL	*B.* AQL = 2.5%
III. Selection of plan	III.
A. Using AQL and Lot Size, select appropriate variables plan from ANSI/ASQC Z1.9—1980, Normal Inspection	*A.* $n = 10$ $M = 7.29$

B. Using AQL and Lot Size, select single-sampling attributes plan from MIL-STD-105 or ANSI/ASQC Z1.4—1981 using Tightened Inspection	*B.* MIL-STD-105D gives Code F
	      $n = 32$
	      $c = 1$

IV. Elements	IV.

A. Sample size: See above; use items drawn in first sample as part of second sample	*A.* First sample: $n = 10$
	      Second sample:
	      $n = (32 - 10)$
	      $n = 22$

B. Statistic: Use appropriate statistics from ANSI/ASQC Z1.9 (1980) and MIL-STD-105 or ANSI/ASQC Z1.4 (1981) as indicated in each standard	

C. Decision criteria
     1. Apply ANSI/ASQC Z1.9 (1980) plan
       a. Accept lot if plan accepts
       b. Otherwise, apply MIL-STD-105 or ANSI/ASQC Z1.4 (1981) plan, taking additional samples to satisfy sample size requirements
     2. Apply MIL-STD-105 or ANSI/ASQC Z1.4 (1981) plan if necessary
       a. Accept lot if plan accepts
       b. Otherwise reject lot
	C. Table 25.23 indicates ANSI/ASQC Z1.9 (1980) plan accepts; if the plan rejected the lot, an additional 22 samples would be drawn and the MIL-STD-105D or ANSI/ASQC Z1.4 (1981) plan applied to the number of defectives in the combined sample of 32

V. Action
   A. Dispose of lot as indicated
   B. Switching rules not applicable to mixed variables-attributes inspection
	V. Accept the lot

TABLE 25.27   Variables Plans for Percent Defective, Mixed Variables—Attributes, ANSI/ASQC Z1.9 (1980) (*Continued*)

Summary of plan	Calculations

VI. Characteristics
   A. Since the procedure outlined in MIL-STD-414 is a "dependent" mixed plan, see the following references:
    1. σ known: Schilling and Dodge (1969)
    2. σ unknown: Gregory and Resnikoff (1955)
    3. Approximation for σ unknown: Bowker and Goode (1952)	

Source: ANSI/ASQC Z1.9 (1980).

exceeds the limit for rejection, the lot is rejected. If the total time falls between the two limits, the test is continued.

Plans are given for various values of the consumer and producer risks, and operating characteristic curves are provided for life tests terminated at a preassigned number of failures or preassigned time. Special tables are also included showing the expected saving in test time by increasing the sample size or by testing with replacement of failed units.

Exponential Distribution: Other Plans (MIL-STD-690B, MIL-STD-781C). MIL-STD-690B (1960) is a military standard concerned primarily with "process qualification," i.e., an explicit decision on the process rather than the lot. The standard provides plans that evaluate the ability of the process to produce electronic parts that meet a specified failure rate requirement. It presents three sets of plans (Tables I, II, and IV of the standard), based on failure rate (FR) levels expressed in percent failures per 1000 hours of operation (%/1000 hours). The standard is intended as a tool for the assessment of:

1. Qualification of the process at the initial FR level

2. Extension of qualification to lower FR levels

3. Maintenance of FR level qualification

4. Lot conformance FR inspection

Operating characteristic curves for the qualifying plans are provided, and confidence levels are also specified. The plans involved are similar in operation to the time terminated sampling plans of H108, which are presented in that handbook in terms of mean life (ML). Note that

$$ML = \frac{1,000,000}{\%/1000\ h} = \frac{100,000}{FR}$$

An excellent discussion of MIL-STD-690B is given by Grubman, Martin, and Pabst (1969).

MIL-STD-781C (1977) provides a standard set of acceptance testing plans for both preproduction reliability qualification and reliability acceptance testing in production. This standard was developed for electronic equipment as contrasted

TABLE 25.28 Summary of Some Life Testing and Reliability Plans

Document*	Basic distribution and type of plan	Plans in terms of				Type of test		
		Mean life	Hazard rate	Reliable life	Failure rate (FR)	Failure terminated	Time terminated	Sequential
MIL-HDBK 108	Exponential, Lot by Lot	X			X	X	X	X
MIL-STD 690B	Exponential, Lot by Lot				X		X	
MIL-STD-781B	Exponential, Sampling Scheme	X					X	X
TR-3	Weibull, Lot by Lot	X					X	
TR-4	Weibull, Lot by Lot		X				X	
TR-6	Weibull, Lot by Lot			X			X	
TR-7	Weibull, (Lot by Lot, converts MIL-STD-105D)	X	X	X			X	

*See References for this section for complete publication information on documents cited.

TABLE 25.29 Life Characteristics for Two Failure Distributions

$$\text{Exponential } f(t) = \frac{1}{\mu} e^{-t/\mu}$$

$$\text{Weibull*} f(t) = \frac{\beta t^{\beta-1}}{\eta^\beta} e^{-(t/\eta)^\beta} \text{ where } \mu = \eta \Gamma \left(1 + \frac{1}{\beta}\right)$$

Life characteristic	Exponential	Weibull
Proportion $F(t)$ failing before time t	$F(t) = 1 - e^{-t/\mu}$	$F(t) = 1 - e^{-g(t/\mu)^\beta}$
Proportion $R(t)$ of population surviving to time t	$R(t) = e^{-t/\mu}$	$R(t) = e^{-g(t/\mu)^\beta}$
Mean life, ML or mean time between failures	μ	μ
Hazard rate, $Z(t)$, instantaneous failure rate at time t	$Z(t) = \frac{1}{\mu}$	$Z(t) = \frac{\beta g t^{\beta-1}}{\mu^\beta}$
Cumulative hazard rate $M(t)$ for period 0 to t	$M(t) = \frac{t}{\mu}$	$M(t) = \frac{g t^\beta}{\mu^\beta}$
Failure rate λ or average hazard rate period 0 to t, $m(t)$	$\lambda = \frac{1}{\mu}$	$m(t) = \frac{g t^{\beta-1}}{\mu^\beta}$

*Weibull parameters explained in discussion of TR-3. The formulas given here are those of H108 (exponential) and TR-3 (Weibull).

to MIL-STD-690B developed for electronic parts. Much of the standard is devoted to test conditions and procedural considerations. The sampling plans given are expressed in terms of mean time between failures (MTBF). Appendix C of the standard presents the following plans:

1. Fixed-length test plans
2. Probability ratio sequential tests (PRST)

TABLE 25.30 Values of $g = [\Gamma(1 + 1/\beta)]^\beta$ for Weibull Distribution*

β	0.0	0.1	0.2	0.3	0.4	0.5	0.6	0.7	0.8	0.9
0.0	· · ·	4.5287	2.6052	1.9498	1.6167	1.4142	1.2778	1.1794	1.1051	1.0468
1.0	1.0000	0.9615	0.9292	0.9018	0.8782	0.8577	0.8397	0.8238	0.8096	0.7969
2.0	0.7854	0.7750	0.7655	0.7568	0.7489	0.7415	0.7348	0.7285	0.7226	0.7172
3.0	0.7121	0.7073	0.7028	0.6986	0.6947	0.6909	0.6874	0.6840	0.6809	0.6778

β	0.33	0.67	1.33	1.67	3.33	4.00	5.00
g	1.8171	1.2090	0.8936	0.8289	0.6973	0.6750	0.6525

*The columns of this table are subdivisions of the rows. Thus when $\beta = 1.2$, the value of g is 0.9292.

3. Short-run, high-risk PRST plans
4. All-equipment reliability test

Expected test time (ETT) curves are given for the PRST plans.

The sequential tests operate in a manner analogous to those presented in H108. The fixed length tests are also similar to the time terminated tests of H108; however, no specific sample size is set, much in the manner of the failure terminated plans of H108. Note that MTBF in MIL-STD-781C is analogous to ML in H108. The plans given in MIL-STD-781C are indexed by producer's risk α, consumer's risk β, and discrimination ratio θ_0/θ_1. OC curves are given for the sequential tests, all-equipment, and fixed-length tests. Methods for construction of confidence intervals on MTBF are also provided for application after a fixed-length test. Schmee (1980) describes MIL-STD-781C and shows how appropriate confidence intervals can be constructed for the PRST plans.

Weibull Distribution: TR-3, TR-4, TR-6.   Defense Department quality control and reliability technical reports TR-3 (1961), TR-4 (1962), TR-6 (1963) present sampling plans based on an underlying Weibull distribution of individual measurement t. The cumulative probability distribution function at time t_0 is

$$F(t_0) = p' = P(t \le t_0) = 1 - \exp\left[-\left(\frac{t_0 - \gamma}{\eta}\right)^\beta \right]$$

with density function

$$f(t) = \frac{\beta(t - \gamma)^{\beta} - 1}{\eta\beta} \exp\left[-\left(\frac{t - \gamma}{\eta}\right)^\beta \right] \qquad t \ge \gamma$$

The symbol p' is used for cumulative probability in the technical reports. The three reports provide plans for reliability criteria developed from the following relationships:

$$\mu = \gamma + \eta\Gamma\left(1 + \frac{1}{\beta}\right)$$

where Γ is the gamma function. A table giving values of gamma will be found in Burrington and May (1970).

$$Z(t) = \frac{\beta}{\eta}\left(\frac{t - \gamma}{\eta}\right)^\beta - 1$$

$$P_r = \gamma + \eta(- \ln r)^{1/\beta}$$

where γ = location (or threshold) parameter
β = shape parameter
η = scale parameter (characteristic life)
μ = mean life
$Z(t)$ = hazard rate—instantaneous failure rate
P_r = reliable life—life beyond which some specified proportion r of the items will survive

In general the location parameter γ is taken to be zero. If it is not zero, say $\gamma = \gamma_0$, then the observations t are adjusted to $t' = t - \gamma_0$; so accordingly $\mu' = \mu -$

γ_0, and the analysis proceeds in terms of t' and μ'. Then the final results are reported in terms of t and μ by reversing the process, so that

$$t = t' + \gamma_0$$

$$\mu = \mu' + \gamma_0$$

for final results t' and μ'.

Plots on probability paper or goodness-of-fit tests must be used to assure that individual measurements are distributed according to the Weibull model. When this distribution is found to be an appropriate approximation to the failure distribution, methods are available to characterize a product or a process in terms of the three parameters of the Weibull distribution (see Section 23 under The Weibull Distribution). These include probability plots and also point and interval estimates. Sampling plans are available for use with the Weibull approximation, which assumes β and γ to be known. The plans are given in the technical reports mentioned above and are based on the following criteria:

1. Mean life criterion (TR-3)
2. Hazard rate criterion (TR-4)
3. Reliable life criterion (TR-6)

The tables cover a wide range of the family of Weibull distributions by providing plans for shape parameter β from ⅓ to 5. The technical reports abound in excellent examples and detailed descriptions of the methods involved.

Technical report TR-3 provides plans and procedures for developing and applying Weibull plans using mean life μ as the criterion for acceptance. The dimensionless ratio t/μ is related to the cumulative probability p'. Values of t or μ can easily be determined for either of the constituents of the ratio t/μ once the other is specified. Since p' is the proportion of product failing before time t, it can be used in the role of "percent defective" in any attributes plan. The relationship of p' to t/μ then, ties the "percent defective" to specified values of test time t and mean life μ. Seven tables, using this relationship, present factors and classifications useful in designing life test plans when the underlying distribution is Weibull. Each is indexed by various values of the shape parameter β. The tables included in TR-3 are:

Table 1: Values of $(t/\mu) \times 100$ indexed by p' (%)

Table 2: Values of p' (%) indexed by $(t/\mu) \times 100$

Table 3: Values of sample size n and $(t/\mu) \times 100$ for which $P_a \geq 0.95$ (shown in parentheses) indexed by acceptance number c and $(t/\mu) \times 100$ for which $P_a \leq 0.10$

Table 4: Values of the discrimination ratio $\mu_{0.95}/\mu_{0.10}$ indexed by acceptance number c

Table 5: Conversions of MIL-STD-105B to Weibull life test; values of $(t/\mu) \times 100$ for which $P_a \leq 0.10$ indexed by AQL and related $(t/\mu) \times 100$ and also by sample size code letter

Table 6: Values of $(t/\mu) \times 100$ indexed by related AQL values

Table 7: Single-sampling acceptance criteria for MIL-STD-105B (1958)

Tables 1 and 2 allow the direct conversion of any attributes plan to a Weibull life test. Tables 5 and 7 give factors to convert MIL-STD-105B. Tables 3 and 4 provide for the construction of Weibull life tests on the basis of the discrimination ratio $\mu_{0.95}/\mu_{0.10}$.

TR-4 is patterned after TR-3, using the product $tZ(t) \times 100$ in place of the dimensionless ratio $(t/\mu) \times 100$. Note that the value of t given is the termination time of the test. If hazard rates are specified for other times, tables are provided which convert the hazard rate specified into a corresponding hazard rate at the termination time of the test. The cumulative probability p' is related to $tZ(t) \times 100$. Resulting values and classifications useful in converting any attributes plan to a Weibull life test, where hazard rate is specified, are presented in seven tables, each indexed by various values of the shape parameter β. These tables are analogous to those found in TR-3. The use of Tables 3 and 4 in TR-4 corresponds to Tables 3 and 4 in TR-3.

Technical report TR-6 is also patterned somewhat after its predecessors, TR-3 and TR-4, but uses the reliable life (p) criterion. It uses the dimensionless quantity $(t/p) \times 100$ in the manner of $(t/\mu) \times 100$ and $tZ(t) \times 100$ in the previous reports. The cumulative probability p' is related to $(t/p) \times 100$, and resulting values and classifications useful in converting any attributes plan to a Weibull life test where reliable life is specified are presented in six tables, each indexed by various values of the shape parameter β. Plans are provided for values of reliable life of 0.50, 0.90, and 0.99. These tables are similar to those given in the previous two technical reports.

Technical report TR-7 (1965) provides factors and procedures for adapting MIL-STD-105D plans to life and reliability testing when a Weibull distribution of failure times can be assumed. Tables of the appropriate conversion factors are provided for the following criteria:

Table	Criterion	Conversion factor
1	Mean life	$(t/\mu) \times 100$
2	Hazard rate	$tZ(t) \times 100$
3	Reliable life $(r = 0.90)$	$(t/p) \times 100$
4.	Reliable life $(r = 0.99)$	$(t/p) \times 100$

Each table is presented in three parts, each of which is indexed by 10 values of $\beta(\beta = \frac{1}{3}, \frac{1}{2}, \frac{2}{3}, 1, 1\frac{1}{3}, 1\frac{2}{3}, 2, 2\frac{1}{2}, 3\frac{1}{3}, 4)$. TR-7 is used in a manner analogous to the three technical reports.

BULK SAMPLING [4]

Bulk material may be of gaseous, liquid, or solid form. Usually it is sampled by taking increments of the material, blending these increments into a single composite sample, and then, if necessary, reducing this gross sample to a size suitable for laboratory testing.

If bulk material is packaged or comes in clearly demarked segments, if it is for all practical purposes uniform within the packages, but varying between packages,

---

[4]This section is condensed from Section 25A of the third edition of this handbook, prepared by Acheson J. Duncan.

and if the quality of each package in the sample is measured, then the sampling theory developed for discrete units may be employed.

A special theoretical discussion is necessary for the sampling of bulk material:

1. If the packages are uniform but the increments from individual packages are not tested separately; instead they are physically composited, in part at least, to form one or more composite samples that are tested separately

2. If the contents of the packages are not uniform so that the question of sampling error arises with respect to the increments taken from the packages

3. If the bulk material is not packaged and sample increments have to be taken from a pile, a truck, a railroad car, or a conveyor belt

In the above circumstances, the special aspects that make bulk sampling different from the sampling of discrete indivisible units are:

1. The possibility of physical compositing and the subsequent physical reduction (or subsampling) that is generally necessary.

2. The need in many cases to use a mechanical sampling device to attain the increments that are taken into the sample. In this case the increments are likely to be "created" by the use of the sampling device and cannot be viewed as preexisting.

Objectives of Bulk Sampling. In most cases the objective of sampling bulk material is to determine its mean quality. This may be for the purpose of pricing the material or for levying custom duties or other taxes, or for controlling a manufacturing process in which the bulk material may be used. It is conceivable that interest in bulk material may also at times center on the variability of the material; or, if it is packaged, on the percent defective; or on the extreme value attained by a segment or package, as described in ASTM (1968). In view of the limited space that is available, the discussion will be restricted to estimation of the mean quality of a material.

Special Terms and Concepts. A number of special terms and concepts are used in the sampling of bulk material. These are:

1. *Lot:* The mass of bulk material the quality of which is under study—not to be confused with a statistical population.

2. *Segment:* Any specifically demarked portion of the lot, actual or hypothetical.

3. *Strata:* Segments of the lot that are likely to be differentiated with respect to the quality characteristic under study.

4. *Increment:* Any portion of the lot, generally smaller than a segment.

5. *Sample increments:* Those portions of the lot initially taken into the sample.

6. *Gross sample:* The totality of sample increments taken from the lot.

7. *Composite sample:* A mixture of two or more sample increments.

8. *Laboratory sample:* That part of a larger sample which is sent to the laboratory for test.

9. *Reduction:* The process by which the laboratory sample is obtained from a composite sample. It is a method of sampling the composite sample. It may take the form of hand-quartering or riffling or the like.

10. *Test-unit:* That quantity of the material which is of just sufficient size to make a measurement of the given quality characteristic.

11. *Quality of a test-unit:* The expected value of the hypothetically infinite number of given measurements that might be made on the test-unit. Any single measurement is a random sample of one from this infinite set. The analytical variance is the variance of such measurements on the infinite set.

12. *Mean of a lot:* If a lot is exhaustively divided into a set of M test-units, the mean of the qualities of these M test-units is designated the mean of the lot. It is postulated that this mean will be the same no matter how the M test-units are obtained. This assumes that there is no physical interaction between the quality of test-units and the method of division. See item 16 below.

13. *Mean of a segment (stratum, increment, composite sample, or laboratory sample):* Defined in a manner similar to that used to define the mean of a lot. It is assumed that the segment is so large relative to the size of a test-unit that any excess over the integral number of test-units contained in the segment can be theoretically ignored. If this is not true, then the quality of the fraction of a test-unit remaining is arbitrarily taken to be the quality of the mean of the segment minus this fraction.

14. *Uniformity:* A segment of bulk material will be said to be uniform if there is no variation in the segment. If, for example, every cubic centimeter of a material contains exactly the same number of "foreign particles," the density of these particles would be said to be uniform throughout the segment. See the note under item 15, however.

15. *Homogeneous:* A segment of bulk material will be said to be homogeneous with respect to a given quality characteristic if that characteristic is randomly distributed throughout the segment.

    Note: The character of being uniform or homogeneous is not independent of the size of the units considered. The number of foreign particles may be the same for every cubic meter of a material, and with respect to this size unit the material will be said to be uniform. For units of size 1 cubic centimeter, however, there may be considerable variation in the number of foreign particles, and for this size of unit the material would not be judged to be uniform. The same considerations are involved in the definition of homogeneity. The number of foreign particles per cubic meter could vary randomly from one cubic meter to the next, but within each cubic meter there might be considerable (intraclass) correlation between the number of foreign particles in the cubic centimeters that make up the cubic meter.

16. *Systematic physical bias:* If the property of the material is physically affected by the sampling device or method of sampling employed, the results will have a systematic bias. A boring or cutting device, for example, might generate sufficient heat to cause loss of moisture.

17. *Physical selection bias:* If a bulk material is a mixture of particles of different size, the sampling device may tend to select more of one size particle than another. This means that if a segment was exhaustively sampled by such a device, early samples would tend to have relatively more of certain size particles than later samples.

18. *Statistical bias:* A function of the observations that is used to estimate a characteristic of a lot, e.g., its mean, is termed a "statistic." A statistic is statistically biased if in many samples its mean value is not equal to the lot characteristic it is used to estimate.

Determination of the Amount of Sampling. Since the variance of a sample mean $\sigma_{\overline{X}}^2$ is a function of the amount of sampling, say the number of increments taken, then once a model has been adopted and a formula obtained for $\sigma_{\overline{X}}^2$, it becomes possible to determine the amount of sampling required to attain a confidence interval of a given width or to attain a specified probability of making a correct decision.

A similar approach is involved in determining the amount of sampling to get a desired set of risks for lot acceptance and rejection.

Models and Their Use. Sampling plans for discrete product have been cataloged in a number of tables. This has not yet been possible for bulk sampling, and instead, a "sampling model" must be created for each type of bulk material and the model used to determine the sample size and acceptance criteria for specific applications.

A bulk sampling model consists of a set of assumptions regarding the statistical properties of the material to be sampled plus a prescribed procedure for carrying out the sampling. A very simple model, for example, would be one in which it is assumed that the quality characteristics of the test-units in a lot are normally distributed and simple random sampling is used.

With the establishment of a model, a formula can generally be derived for the sampling variance of an estimate of the mean of a given lot. This must be uniquely derived based on the type of product, lot formation, and other factors. The reader is urged to consult the references for specific formulas (see especially Duncan, 1962). From an estimate of this sampling variance, confidence limits can be established for the lot mean, and/or a decision with given risk can be made about the acceptability of the lot.

Let the variance of a sample mean be denoted as $\sigma_{\overline{X}}^2$ and its estimate as $s_{\overline{X}}^2$. Then "0.95 confidence limits" for the mean of the lot will be given by

$$0.95 \text{ confidence limits for } \mu = \overline{X} \pm t_{0.025} s_{\overline{X}}$$

where μ is the mean of the lot, $\overline{X}$ is the sample mean, and $t_{0.025}$ is the 0.025 point of a t-distribution for the degrees of freedom involved in the determination of $s_{\overline{X}}^2$.

If a decision is to be made on the acceptability of a lot, a criterion for acceptability will take some such form as

$$\text{Accept if } t = \frac{\overline{X} - L}{s_{\overline{X}}} \text{ is positive or if it has a}$$

negative value numerically less than $t_{0.025}$

where L is the lower specification limit on the product and $t_{0.025}$ is the 0.025 point of a t-distribution for the degrees of freedom involved in the determination of $s_{\overline{X}}^2$. See Grubbs and Coon (1954).

Models for Distinctly Segmented Bulk Material ("Within and Between" Models). Much bulk material comes in distinctly segmented form. It may be packaged in bags, bales, or cans, for example, or may come in carloads or truckloads.

For distinctly segmented material it can be established that the overall variance of individual test-units is, for a large number of segments each with a large number of test-units, approximately equal to the sum of the variance between segments and the average variance within segments. In what follows, the variance within segments is assumed the same for all segments.

Model 1A. Isolated Lots, Nonstratified Segments.   For an isolated lot of distinctly segmented material, the sampling procedure will be to take an increment of m test-units from each of n segments, reduce each increment to a laboratory sample, and measure its quality X. The mean of the n test-units is taken as an estimate of the mean of the lot.

Model 1B. One of a Series of Lots.   Suppose the current lot is one of a series of lots of distinctly segmented material and that estimates of the between and within variances have been made in a pilot study, together with estimates of the reduction variance and test variance. It will be assumed that the reduction variance yielded by the pilot study is valid for larger amounts than that used in the study.

With the given prior information, an estimate of the sampling variance for the current sample estimate of mean lot quality can be based on the pilot study, and there is need only for a current check on the continued validity of this study. Consequently, composite samples can be used requiring only a few measurements, and the cost of inspection of the current lot may be considerably curtailed.

The "Within and Between" Models: Stratified Segments.   In some situations the quality characteristic of the bulk material may be stratified in that in each segment it may vary from layer to layer and is not randomly distributed throughout the segment. Difficulties in formulating a model for stratified segments of this kind can be overcome if the strata are reasonably parallel and if the increments taken from the sample segments are taken perpendicular to the strata and penetrate all strata. In taking a sample from a bale of wool, for example, a thief could cut a sample running vertically from top to bottom of the bale.

Models for Bulk Material Moving in a Stream.   In many instances the bulk material to be sampled is moving in a stream, say on a conveyer belt. In such instances it is the common practice to take increments systematically from the stream, the increment being taken across the full width of the stream.

Isolated Lots.   If increments are taken at random from the stream, we would have a simple random sample from the lot, and we could proceed much as indicated for isolated lots of distinctly segmented material.

Model 2A. A Stream of Lots: A Segregation Model.   When a stream of bulk material persists for some time, with possible interruptions, determinations of quality and/or action decisions may have to be made for a number of lots. Here, a pilot study might be profitable.

The kind of pilot study needed will depend on the assumptions about the statistical properties of the material in the stream. If the quality of the material varies randomly in the stream, then a pilot study based on a number of randomly or systematically taken increments would be sufficient to determine the variance of the material, and this could be used to set up confidence limits for the means of subsequent lots or make decisions as to their acceptability, even though in each of these lots a single composite sample was taken.

Obtaining the Test-Units.   Three factors are important in obtaining the test-units.

1. *The models discussed above assume random sampling:* Either the increments are picked at random (using, preferably, random numbers if the units can be identified) or the increments are selected systematically from material that is itself random. Random sampling may have to be undertaken while the material is in motion or being moved. If random sampling cannot be used, special efforts should be made to get a representative picture of a lot, noting strata and the like. Some element of randomness must be present in a sampling procedure to yield a formula for sampling variance.

2. *Grinding and mixing:* In the processing of bulk material and in the formation of composite samples, grinding and/or mixing may be employed in an attempt to attain homogeneity or at least to reduce the variability of the material.

If a material can be made homogeneous for the size increment that is to be used in subsequent sampling, then an increment of that size can be viewed as a random sample of the material. The attainment of homogeneity of bulk material in bags, cartons, barrels, etc., is thus a worthy objective when the contents of these containers are to be sampled by a thief or other sampling instruments. However, random sampling does not guarantee minimum sampling variation, and grinding and mixing may lead to a reduction in overall sampling variation without attaining homogeneity. See Cochran (1977).

Although grinding and mixing are aimed at reducing variability, these operations may in some circumstances cause segregation and thus increase variability.

3. *Reduction of a sample to test-units:* Measurements often may be made directly on the sample itself. However, sometimes a portion of the sample must be carefully reduced in either particle size or physical quantity to facilitate laboratory testing. The unreduced portion of the sample may be retained for subsequent reference for legal purposes or verification of results. An example of a technique is coning and quartering. The material is first crushed and placed in a conical pile, which is then flattened. The material is then separated into quarters and opposite quarters selected for further quartering or as the final test-units.

Bicking (1967) and Bicking, Donovan, Sosnowski, and Bicking (1967) provide unique details on obtaining test-units for a large variety of specific bulk products.

Tests of Homogeneity. The homogeneity of bulk material may be tested by $\bar{X}$-charts and c-charts. For mixtures of particles that can be identified, local homogeneity may be tested by running a χ^2 short-distance test. See Shinner and Naor (1961).

BAYESIAN PROCEDURES

The concept that experience or analytical studies can yield prior frequency distributions of the quality of submitted lots and that these "prior" distributions can in turn be used to derive lot-by-lot sampling plans has gained some popularity in recent years. This is generally termed the "Bayesian approach." Bayes' theorem and the Bayesian decision theory concept are discussed in Section 23, Basic Statistical Methods. The general concept of the use of prior information is discussed in Section 18, under How Much Inspection?

Considerable literature exists on Bayesian sampling. However, a very limited number of sampling tables based on particular prior distributions of lot quality are available. Calvin (1984) provides procedures and tables for implementing

Bayesian plans. Another example is the set of tables by Oliver and Springer (1972), which are based on the assumption of a Beta prior distribution with specific posterior risk to achieve minimum sample size. This avoids the problem of estimating cost parameters. It is generally true that a Bayesian plan requires a smaller sample size than does a conventional sampling plan with the same consumer's and producer's risk. Among others, Schafer (1967) discusses single sampling plans by attributes using three prior distributions of lot quality. Given specified risks α and β, sampling plans which satisfied these risks and which minimized sample size were determined. For example, with a particular prior distribution, $n = 6$ and $c = 0$ gave protection equivalent to a conventional sampling plan with $n = 34$, $c = 0$.

Advantages similar to those quoted above are usually cited. However, one prime factor is frequently ignored: How good is the assumption on the prior distribution? Hald (1960) gives an extensive account of sampling plans based on discrete prior distributions of product quality. Hald also employs a simple economic model along with the discrete prior distribution and the hypergeometric sampling distribution to answer a number of basic questions on costs, relationship between sample size and lot size, etc. Schafer (1964) also considers the Bayesian operating characteristic curve. Hald (1981) has also provided an excellent comparison of classical and Bayesian theory and methodology for attributes acceptance sampling. The Bayesian approach to sequential and nonsequential acceptance sampling has been described by Grimlin and Breipohl (1972). Most such plans incorporate cost data reflecting losses involved in the decision making process to which the plan is to be applied. An excellent review of Bayesian and non-Bayesian plans has been given by Wetherill and Chin (1975).

While the explicit specification of a prior distribution is characteristic of the classical Bayes approach, procedures have been developed to incorporate much of the philosophy and approach of Bayes without explicit specification of a prior distribution. These methods are based on the incorporation of past data into an empirical estimate of the prior, and hence the approach is called "empirical Bayes." An excellent description of this method of estimation has been presented by Krutchkoff (1972). Application of the empirical Bayes methodology to attributes sampling has been given by Martz (1975). Craig and Bland (1981) show how it can be used in variables sampling.

These ideas have been further extended by the application of shrinkage estimators to the empirical Bayes problem as described by Morris (1983). One outstanding application of such procedures is in the so-called "universal sampling plan" utilized in the quality measurement plan (QMP) of American Telephone and Telegraph. Audit sample sizes are based on historical process control, economics, quality standards, and the heterogeneity of audit clusters as described by Hoadley (1981). Strictly speaking, the weights for the Stein shrinkage estimators utilized in the procedure are developed through a classical Bayes approach, and so this application is more properly viewed as Bayes empirical Bayes methodology.

Application of Bayesian methods has been hindered by the difficulty involved in correct assessment of the necessary prior distributions and in collecting and keeping current the required cost information. Clearly, greater reliance on prior empirical information and the potential of the computer for generating cost information should be helpful in this regard. Pitfalls in the selection of a prior distribution have been pointed out by Case and Keats (1982).

While studies have indicated that Bayesian schemes may be quite robust to errors in the prior distributions and loss functions, they nevertheless assume the prior to be stationary in the long-term sense (i.e. a process in control). Classical methods do not make this assumption. Bayesian plans are, in fact, quite application-specific, requiring extensive information and update for proper application, and like variables sampling, they are applied one characteristic at a time. Nevertheless, where appropriate, they provide yet another tool for economic sampling.

HOW TO SELECT THE PROPER SAMPLING PROCEDURES

The methods of acceptance sampling are many and varied. It is essential to select a sampling procedure appropriate to the acceptance sampling situation to which it is to be applied. This will depend upon the nature of the application itself, on quality history, and the extent of knowledge of the process and the producer. Indeed, according to Dodge (1950, p. 8):

> A product with a history of consistently good quality requires less inspection than one with no history or a history of erratic quality. Accordingly, it is good practice to include in inspection procedures provisions for reducing or increasing the amount of inspection, depending on the character and quantity of evidence at hand regarding the level of quality and the degree of control shown.

This will be discussed further in the Conclusion, below.

The steps involved in the selection and application of a sampling procedure are shown in Figure 25.25 taken from Schilling (1982). Emphasis here is on the feedback of information necessary for the proper application, modification, and evolution of sampling. As Ott (1975, pp. 181–182) has pointed out:

> There are two standard procedures that, though often good in themselves, can serve to postpone careful analysis of the production process:
>
> 1. On-line inspection stations (100% screening). These can become a way of life.
>
> 2. On-line acceptance sampling plans which prevent excessively defective lots from proceeding on down the production line, but have no feedback procedure included.
>
> These procedures become bad when they allow or encourage carelessness in production. It gets easy for production to shrug off responsibility for quality and criticize inspection for letting bad quality proceed.

It is therefore necessary for sampling to be constantly subject to modification in a system of acceptance control. Each plan has a specific purpose for which it is to be applied. Table 25.31 shows the relation of plan and purpose for some of the plans which have been discussed. Those not discussed here will be found described in detail in Schilling (1982). These plans then are the elements involved in a system of acceptance control. Their effective use in a continuing effort to provide protection while reducing inspection and moving to process control is a function of the ingenuity, integrity, and industry of the user.

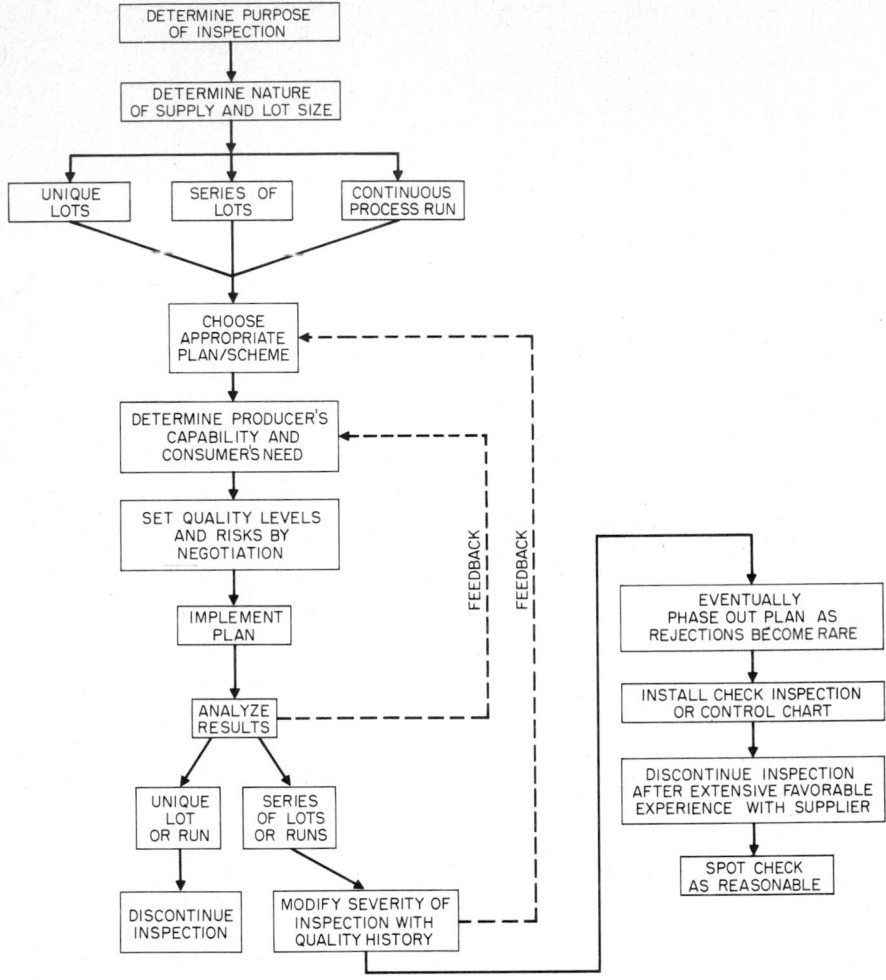

FIG. 25.25   Check sequence for implementation of sampling procedure.

COMPUTER PROGRAMS FOR ACCEPTANCE SAMPLING

A variety of computer programs have become available for application of specific sampling plans. Some of these are listed in Table 25.32. They will become increasingly important, particularly in the application of selected plans and in the development of plans for specific applications. It should be noted, however, that it is unlikely that these programs will ever replace hard copy procedures and standards which play a vital role in the negotiations between producer and consumer and which are immediately available for in-plant meetings and discussions at any location.

TABLE 25.31 Selection of Plan

Purpose	Supply	Attributes	Variables
Simple guarantee of producer's and consumer's quality levels at stated risks	Unique lot	Two-point plan (type A)	Two-point plan (type B)
	Series of lots	Dodge-Romig LTPD Two-point plan (type B)	Two-point plan (type B)
Maintain level of submitted quality at AQL or better	Series of lots	MIL-STD-105D QSS plan	MIL-STD-414 No calc. plan
Rectification guaranteeing AOQL to consumer	Series of lots	Dodge-Romig AOQL Anscombe plan CSP-1, 2, 3 Multilevel plan MIL-STD-1235A Wald-Wolfowitz Girschik	Romig variables plans
	Flow of individual units		Use measurements as go–no go
	Flow of segments of production		Use measurements as go–no go
Reduced inspection after good history	Series of lots	Skip-lot Chain Deferred sentencing	Lot plot Mixed variables-attributes Narrow-limit gaging

TABLE 25.31 Selection of Plan (*Continued*)

Purpose	Supply	Attributes	Variables
Check Inspection	Series of lots	Demerit rating	Acceptance control chart
Compliance to mandatory standards	Unique lot	Lot-sensitive plan	Mixed variables-attributes with $c = 0$
	Series of lots	TNT plan	Simon grand lot plan
Reliability sampling	Unique lot	Two-point plan (type B)	MIL–HDBK-108 TR 7
	Series of lots	LTPD plan QSS system CRC plan	TR-7 using MIL-STD-105D switching rules
Check accuracy of inspection	Series of lots	MIL–HDBK-109	Use measurements as go–no go

Source: Schilling, 1982, p. 569.

TABLE 25.32 Computer Programs for Acceptance Sampling (Optional Input/Output in Brackets)

Purpose	Input	Output	Reference
Single sampling—derivation	p_1, p_2, α, β, (lot size, p)	Plan (ATI at p, AOQL)	Snyder and Storer, 1972
Double sampling—derivation	AQL, LTPD (lot size) (assumes $\alpha = 0.05$, $\beta = 0.10$)	Plans for $n_2 = n_1$ and $n_2 = 2n_1$ with AOQL (p, P_a, AOQ, ATI, ASN)	Chow, Dickinson, and Hughes, 1973 and 1975
Multiple sampling—derivation	AQL, LTPD (lot size) (assumes $\alpha = 0.05$, $\beta = 0.10$)	Plans for equal n with AOQL (p, P_a, AOQ, ATI, ASN)	Hughes, Dickinson, and Chow, 1973
Single, double, multiple sampling—evaluation (P_a given p or p given P_a) (hypergeometric, binomial Poisson, normal)	Distribution, sample sizes, acceptance/rejection numbers, fractions defective to be evaluated, probabilities of acceptance to be determined (lot size)	Plan control table, p, P_a ASM, AOQ, ATI	Schilling, Sheesley, and Nelson, 1978

TABLE 25.32 Computer Programs for Acceptance Sampling (Optional Input/Output in Brackets) (*Continued*)

Purpose	Input	Output	Reference
Dodge continuous sampling—evaluation CSP-1, 2, 3	Fractions defective, index of plan (1, 2, 3). f, i, k	p, F, P_a, AOQ	Sheesley, 1975
MIL-STD-414—implementation acceptance/rejection Decision given data	Number lots, type inspection (T, N, R), measure of variability, lot size, specification limits, AQL, data	Plan $\hat{p}, M$, accept or reject	Nelson, 1977

Snyder, D. C. and Storer, R. F. (1972). "Single Sampling Plans Given an AQL, LTPD, Producer and Consumer Risks." *Journal of Quality Technology*, vol. 4, no. 3, July 1972, pp. 168–171.

Chow, B., Dickinson, P. C., and Hughes, H. (1973). "A Computer Program for the Solution of Double Sampling Plans." *Journal of Quality Technology*, vol. 4, no. 4, October 1973, pp. 205–209; also, *Journal of Quality Technology*, vol. 5, no. 4, October 1975, p. 166.

Hughes, H., Dickinson, P. C., and Chow, B. (1973). "A Computer Program for the Solutions of Multiple Sampling Plans." *Journal of Quality Technology*, vol. 5, no. 1, January 1973, pp. 39–42.

Schilling, E. G., Sheesley, J. H., and Nelson, P. R. (1978). "GRASP: A General Routine for Attribute Sampling Plan Evaluation." *Journal of Quality Technology*, vol. 10, no. 3, July 1978, pp. 125–130.

Sheesley, J. H. (1975). "A Computer Program to Evaluate Dodge's Continuous Sampling Plans." *Journal of Quality Technology*, vol. 7, no. 1, January 1975, pp. 43–45.

Nelson, P. R. (1977). "A Computer Program for Military Standard 414: Sampling Procedures and Inspection by Variables for Percent Defective." *Journal of Quality Technology*. vol. 9, no. 2, April 1977, pp. 82–86.

Source: Schilling, 1982, p. 587.

CONCLUSION—MOVING FROM ACCEPTANCE SAMPLING TO ACCEPTANCE CONTROL

There is little control of quality in the application of a sampling plan to an individual lot. Such an occurrence is static, whereas control implies movement and direction. When used in a system of *acceptance control,* over the life of the product, however, the plan can provide:

Protection for the consumer

Protection for the producer

Accumulation of quality history

Feedback for process control

Pressure on the producer to improve the process

Acceptance control involves adjusting the acceptance sampling procedure to match existing conditions with the objective of eventually phasing out the inspection altogether. This is much as the old-time inspector varied the inspection depending on quality history. Thus, acceptance control is "a continuing strategy of selection, application and modification of acceptance sampling procedures to a changing inspection environment" (see Schilling, 1982, p. 564). This involves a progression of sampling procedures applied as shown in Table 25.33.

These procedures are applied as appropriate over the lifetime of the product in a manner consistent with the improvement of quality and the reduction and elimination of inspection. This can be seen in Table 25.34.

Modern manufacturing is not static. It involves the development, manufacture, and marketing of new products as well as an atmosphere of continuing cost reduction, process modification, and other forms of quality improvement. Changes are continually introduced into the production process which are delib-

TABLE 25.33   Progression of Attribute Sampling Procedures

Past results	Quality history			Criterion
	Little	Moderate	Extensive	
Excellent	AQL plan	Cumulative results plan	Demerit rating or remove inspection	Almost no (<1%) lots rejected
Average	Rectification or LTPD plan	AQL plan	Cumulative results plan	Few (<10%) lots rejected
Poor	100% inspection	Rectification or LTPD plan with cumulative results criterion	Discontinue acceptance	Many (≥10%) lots rejected
Amount	Fewer than 10 lots	10–50 lots	More than 50 lots	

Source: Schilling, 1982, p. 565.

TABLE 25.34 Life Cycle of Acceptance Control Application

Stage	Step	Method
Preparatory	Choose plan appropriate to purpose	Analysis of quality system to define the exact need for the procedure
	Determine producer capability	Process performance evaluation using control charts
	Determine consumer needs	Process capability study using control charts
	Set quality levels and risks	Economic analysis and negotiation
	Determine plan	Standard procedures if possible
Initiation	Train inspector	Include plan, procedure, records, and action
	Apply plan properly	Ensure random sampling
	Analyze results	Keep records and control charts
Operational	Assess protection	Periodically check quality history and OC curves
	Adjust plan	When possible change severity to reflect quality history and cost
	Decrease sample size if warranted	Modify to use appropriate sampling plans taking advantage of credibility of supplier with cumulative results
Phase out	Eliminate inspection effort where possible	Use demerit rating or check inspection procedures when quality is consistently good. Keep control charts
Elimination	Spot check only	Remove all inspection when warranted by extensive favorable history

Source: Schilling, 1982, p. 566.

erate, or unexpected from an unknown source. When this happens, acceptance sampling is necessary to provide protection for the producer and the consumer until the process can be brought into control. This may take days, months, or years. Under these circumstances, the inspection involved should be systematically reduced in a system of acceptance control which will reduce inspection reciprocally with the increase of the learning curve in the specific application. This can provide the protection necessary for the implementation of proper process control in a manner protrayed roughly in Figure 25.26. Acceptance control and process control are synergistic in the sense that one supports proper use of the other. As Dodge (1969, p. 156) has pointed out:

The "acceptance quality control system" . . . encompassed the concept of protecting the consumer from getting unacceptable defective material and encouraging

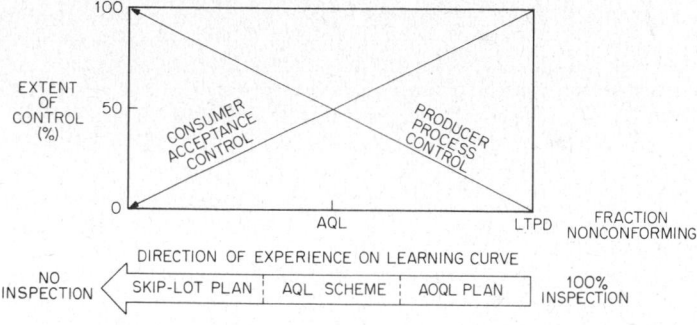

FIG. 25.26 Synergy between Acceptance Control and Process Control. *(From Schilling, 1982, p. 570.)*

the producer in the use of process quality control by: varying the quantity and severity of acceptance inspections in direct relation to the importance of the characteristics inspected, and in inverse relation to the goodness of the quality level as indicated by these inspections.

It is in this sense that acceptance control is an essential part of the quality system.

REFERENCES

ANSI/ASQC A2 (1987). *Terms, Symbols and Definitions for Acceptance Sampling.* American Society for Quality Control, Milwaukee.

ANSI/ASQC Z1.9 (1980). *Sampling Procedures and Tables for Inspection by Variables for Percent Nonconforming.* American Society for Quality Control, Milwaukee.

ANSI/ASQC Z1.4 (1981). *Sampling Procedures and Tables for Inspection by Attributes.* American Society for Quality Control, Milwaukee.

ASTM (1968). *Standard Methods of Test for Sampling Coal* (D2234-68). American Society for Testing and Materials, Philadelphia.

ASTM (1981). *Recommended Practice for Sampling Industrial Chemicals* (E 300-73). American Society for Testing and Materials, Philadelphia.

Beattie, D. W. (1962). "Continuous Acceptance Sampling Procedure Based upon a Cumulative Sum Chart for the Number of Defectives." *Applied Statistics,* vol. 11, no. 3, November, pp. 137–147.

Bicking, C. A. (1967). "The Sampling of Bulk Materials." *Materials Research and Standards,* March, pp. 95–116.

Bicking, C. A., Donovan, T. A., Sosnowski, T. S., and Bicking, C. M. (1967). *Bibliography on Precision Bulk Sampling and Related Applications of Statistics—Supplement.* CA Report 10, Technical Association of the Pulp and Paper Industry.

Bowker, A. H. and Goode, H. P. (1952). *Sampling Inspection by Variables.* McGraw-Hill, New York.

Burington, R. S. and May, D. C. (1970). *Handbook of Probability and Statistics with Tables,* 2nd ed. McGraw-Hill, New York.

Calvin, T. W. (1984). *How and When to Perform Bayesian Acceptance Sampling.* American Society for Quality Control, Milwaukee.

Cameron, J. M. (1952). "Tables for Constructing and for Computing the Operating Characteristics of Single Sampling Plans." *Industrial Quality Control,* vol. 9, no. 1, July, pp. 37–39.

Case, K., and Keats, J. B. (1982). "On the Selection of a Prior Distribution in Bayesian Acceptance Sampling." *Journal of Quality Technology,* vol. 14, no. 1, January, pp. 10–18.

Cochran, W. G. (1977). *Sampling Techniques,* 3rd ed. John Wiley & Sons, New York.

Cowden, D. J. (1957). *Statistical Methods in Quality Control.* Prentice-Hall, Englewood Cliffs, NJ, pp. 489–490.

Craig, J. A., Jr. and Bland, R. P. (1981). "An Empirical Bayes Approach to a Variables Acceptance Sampling Plan Problem." *Communication in Statistics—Theory, Methods,* vol. A10, no. 23, pp. 2399–2410.

Dodge, H. F. (1932). "Statistical Control on Sampling Inspection." *American Machinist,* October, pp. 1085–1088.

Dodge, H. F. (1943). "A Sampling Plan for Continuous Production." *Annals of Mathematical Statistics,* vol. 14, no. 3, pp. 264–279.

Dodge, H. F. (1950). "Inspection for Quality Assurance." *Industrial Quality Control,* vol. 7, no. 1, June, p. 8.

Dodge, H. F. (1955). "Chain Sampling Inspection Plan." *Industrial Quality Control,* vol. 11, no. 4, January, pp. 10–13.

Dodge, H. F. (1955a). "Skip-lot Sampling Plans." *Industrial Quality Control,* vol. 11, no. 5, February, pp. 3–5.

Dodge, H. F. (1969). "Notes on the Evolution of Acceptance Sampling Plans, Part II." *Journal of Quality Technology,* vol. 1, no. 3, July, p. 156.

Dodge, H. F. (1970). "Notes on the Evolution of Acceptance Sampling Plans, Part IV." *Journal of Quality Technology,* vol. 2, no. 1, January, pp. 1–8.

Dodge, H. F. and Perry, R. L. (1971). "A System of Skip-Lot Plans for Lot-by-Lot Inspection." *ASQC Technical Conference Transactions,* Milwaukee, pp. 469–477.

Dodge, H. F. and Romig, H. G. (1959). *Sampling Inspection Tables,* 2nd ed. John Wiley & Sons, New York.

Dodge, H. F. and Stephens, K. S. (1965). "Some New Chain Sampling Inspection Plans." *ASQC Technical Conference Transactions,* Milwaukee, pp. 8–17.

Dodge, H. F. and Stephens, K. S. (1966). "Some New Chain Sampling Inspection Plans." *Industrial Quality Control,* vol. 23, no. 2, August, pp. 61–67.

Dodge, H. F. and Torrey, M. N. (1951). "Additional Continuous Sampling Inspection Plans." *Industrial Quality Control,* vol. 7, no. 5, March, pp. 7–12.

Duncan, A. J. (1962). "Bulk Sampling Problems and Lines of Attack." *Technometrics,* vol. 4, no. 3, August, pp. 319–344.

Duncan, A. J. (1974). *Quality Control and Industrial Statistics.* Richard D. Irwin, Homewood, IL.

Enell, J. W. (1954). "What Sampling Plan Shall I Choose?" *Industrial Quality Control,* vol. 10, no. 6, May, pp. 96–100.

Freund, R. A. (1957). "Acceptance Control Charts." *Industrial Quality Control,* vol. 14, no. 4. October, pp. 13–23.

Grant, E. L. and Leavenworth, R. S. (1979). *Statistical Quality Control,* 5th ed. McGraw-Hill, New York.

Gregory, G. and Resnikoff, G. J. (1955). *Some Notes on Mixed Variables and Attributes Sampling Plans.* Technical Report 10, Applied Mathematics and Statistics Laboratory, Stanford University, Stanford, CA.

Grimlin, D. R. and Breipohl, A. M. (1972). "Bayesian Acceptance Sampling." *IEEE Transactions on Reliability,* vol. R-21, no. 3, August pp. 176–180.

Grubbs, F. E. and Coon, H. J. (1954). "On Setting Testing Limits Relative to Specification Limits." *Industrial Quality Control,* vol. 10, no. 5, March, pp. 15–20.

Grubman, S., Martin, C. A., and Pabst, W. R., Jr. (1969). "MIL-STD-690B Failure Rate Sampling Plans and Procedures." *Journal of Quality Technology,* vol. 1, no. 3, July, pp. 205–216.

MIL-HDBK-53 (1965). *Guide for Sampling Inspection.* Government Printing Office, Washington, DC, June 30.

MIL-HDBK-108 (1960). *Sampling Procedures and Tables for Life and Reliability Testing (Based on Exponential Distribution).* Quality Control and Reliability Handbook, U.S. Department of Defense, Government Printing Office, Washington, D.C.

Hald, A. (1960). "The Compound Hypergeometric Distribution and a System of Single Sampling Inspection Plans Based on Prior Distributions and Costs." *Technometrics,* vol. 2, no. 3, August, pp. 275–340.

Hald, A. (1981). *Statistical Theory of Sampling Inspection by Attributes.* Academic Press, New York, pp. 532.

Hamaker, H. C. (1979). "Acceptance Sampling for Percent Defective by Variables and by Attributes." *Journal of Quality Technology,* vol. 11, no. 3, July, pp. 139–148.

Hillier, F. S. (1969). "$\overline{X}$ and R—Chart Control Limits Based on a Small Number of Subgroups." *Journal of Quality Technology,* vol. 1, no. 1, January, pp. 17–26.

Hoadley, B. (1981). "The Universal Sampling Plan." *ASQC Quality Congress Transactions,* Milwaukee, pp. 80–87.

Krutchkoff, R. G. (1972). "Empirical Bayes Estimation." *The American Statistician,* vol. 26, no. 5, December, pp. 14–16.

Lieberman, G. J. and Solomon, H. (1955). "Multi-Level Continuous Sampling Plans." *Annals of Mathematical Statistics,* vol. 26, no. 4, pp. 686–704.

Martz, H. F. (1975). "Empirical Bayes Single Sampling Plans for Specified Posterior Consumer and Producer Risks." *Naval Research Logistic Quarterly,* vol. 22, no. 4, December, pp. 651–665.

MIL-STD-105B (1958). *Sampling Procedures and Tables for Inspection by Attributes.* Government Printing Office, Washington, DC.

MIL-STD-105D (1964). *Sampling Procedures and Tables for Inspection by Attributes.* Government Printing Office, Washington, DC.

MIL-STD-414 (1968). *Sampling Procedures and Tables for Inspection by Variables for Percent Defective.* Military Standard, U.S. Department of Defense, Government Printing Office, Washington, DC.

MIL-STD-690B (1960). *Failure Rate Sampling Plans and Procedures,* Military Standard, U.S. Department of Defense, Government Printing Office, Washington, DC.

MIL-STD-781C (1977). *Reliability Tests: Exponential Distribution.* Military Standard, U.S. Department of Defense, Government Printing Office, Washington, DC.

MIL-STD-1235B (1981). *Continuous Sampling Procedures and Tables for Inspection by Attributes.* Government Printing Office, Washington, DC.

Morris, C. N. (1983). "Parametric Empirical Bayes Inference: Theory and Applications." *Journal of the American Statistical Association,* vol. 78, no. 131, March, pp. 47–55.

Moses, L. E. (1956). "Some Theoretical Aspects of the Lot Plot Sampling Inspection Plan." *Journal of the American Statistical Association,* vol. 51, no. 273, pp. 84–107.

Murphy, R. B. (1959). "Stopping Rules with CSP-1 Sampling Inspection Plans in Continuous Production." *Industrial Quality Control,* vol. 16, no. 5, November, pp. 10–16.

Nelson, W. (1983). *How to Analyze Reliability Data.* American Society for Quality Control, Milwaukee.

Oliver, L. R. and Springer, M. D. (1972). *A General Set of Bayesian Attribute Acceptance Plans.* American Institute of Industrial Engineers, Norcross, GA.

Ott, E. R. (1975). *Process Quality Control,* McGraw-Hill, New York, pp. 181–182.

Pabst, W. R., Jr. (1963). "MIL-STD-105D." *Industrial Quality Control,* vol. 20, no. 5, November, pp. 4–9.

Perry, R. L. (1973). "Skip-Lot Sampling Plans." *Journal of Quality Technology,* vol. 5, no. 3, July, pp. 123–130.

Perry, R. L. (1973a). "Two-Level Skip-Lot Sampling Plans—Operating Characteristic Properties." *Journal of Quality Technology,* vol. 5, no. 4, October, pp. 160–166.

Prairie, R. R. and Zimmer, W. J. (1973). "Graphs, Tables, and Discussion to Aid in the

Design and Evaluation of an Acceptance Sampling Procedure Based on Cumulative Sums." *Journal of Quality Technology,* vol. 5, no. 2, April, pp. 58–66.

Schafer, R. E. (1964). "Bayesian Operating Characteristic Curves for Reliability and Quality Sampling Plans." *Industrial Quality Control,* vol. 21, no. 3, September, pp. 118–122.

Schafer, R. E. (1967). "Bayes Single Sampling Plans by Attributes Based on the Posterior Risk." *Naval Research Logistics Quarterly,* vol. A, no. 1, March, pp. 81–88.

Schilling, E. G. (1970). "Variables Sampling and MIL-STD-414." *Transactions of 26th Quality Control Conference of the Rochester Society for Quality Control,* March 30, pp. 175–188.

Schilling, E. G. (1978). "A Lot Sensitive Sampling Plan for Compliance Testing and Acceptance Inspection." *Journal of Quality Technology,* vol. 10, no. 2, April, pp. 47–51.

Schilling, E. G. (1979). "A Simplified Graphical Grand Lot Acceptance Sampling Procedure." *Journal of Quality Technology,* vol. 11, no. 3, July, pp. 116–127.

Schilling, E. G. (1982). *Acceptance Sampling in Quality Control.* Marcel Dekker, New York and Basel.

Schilling, E. G. and Dodge, H. F. (1969). "Procedures and Tables for Evaluating Dependent Mixed Acceptance Sampling Plans." *Technometrics,* vol. 11, no. 2, May, pp. 341–372.

Schilling, E. G. and Johnson, L. I. (1980). "Tables for the Construction of Matched Single, Double and Multiple Sampling Plans with Application to MIL-STD-105D." *Journal of Quality Technology,* vol. 12, no. 4, October, pp. 220–229.

Schilling, E. G. and Sheesley, J. H. (1978). "The Performance of MIL-STD-105D under the Switching Rules." *Journal of Quality Technology,* Part 1: vol. 10, no. 2, April, pp. 76–83; Part 2: vol. 10, no. 3, July, pp. 104–124.

Schilling, E. G. and Sommers D. J. (1981). "Two-Point Optimal Narrow Limit Plans with Applications to MIL-STD-105D." *Journal of Quality Technology,* vol. 13, no. 2, April, pp. 83–92.

Schmee, J. (1980). "MIL-STD-781C and Confidence Intervals." *Journal of Quality Technology,* vol. 12, no. 3, April, pp. 98–105.

Shainin, D. (1950). "The Hamilton Standard Lot Plot Method of Acceptance Sampling by Variables." *Industrial Quality Control,* vol. 7, no. 1, July, pp. 15–34.

Shainin, D. (1952). "Recent Lot Plot Experiences around the Country." *Industrial Quality Control,* vol. 8, no. 5, March, pp. 20–29.

Shinner R. and Naor, P. (1961). "A Test of Randomness for Solid-Solid Mixtures." *Chemical Engineering Science,* vol. 15, no. 3/4, pp. 220–229.

Simon, L. E. (1941). *An Engineer's Manual of Statistical Methods.* John Wiley & Sons, New York.

Sommers, D. J. (1981). "Two-Point Double Variables Sampling Plans." *Journal of Quality Technology,* vol. 13, no. 1, January, pp. 25–30.

Soundararajan, V. (1978). "Procedures and Tables for Construction and Selection of Chain Sampling Plans (ChSP-1)." *Journal of Quality Technology,* Part 1: vol. 10, no. 2, April, pp. 56–60; Part 2: vol. 10, no. 3, July, pp. 99–103.

Stephens, K. S. (1979). *How to Perform Continuous Sampling (CSP).* American Society for Quality Control, Milwaukee.

Stephens, K. S. (1982). *How to Perform Skip-Lot and Chain Sampling.* American Society for Quality Control, Milwaukee.

TR-3 (1961). *Sampling Procedures and Tables for Life and Reliability Testing Based on the Weibull Distribution (Mean Life Criterion).* Quality Control and Reliability Technical Report, U.S. Department of Defense, Government Printing Office, Washington, DC.

TR-4 (1962). *Sampling Procedures and Tables for Life and Reliability Testing Based on the Weibull Distribution (Hazard Rate Criterion).* Quality Control and Reliability Technical Report, U.S. Department of Defense, Government Printing Office, Washington, DC.

TR-6 (1963). *Sampling Procedures and Tables for Life and Reliability Testing Based on the Weibull Distribution (Reliable Life Criterion).* Quality Control and Reliability Technical Report, U.S. Department of Defense, Government Printing Office, Washington, DC.

TR-7 (1965). *Factors and Procedures for Applying MIL-STD-105D Sampling Plans to Life and Reliability Testing.* Quality Control and Reliability Technical Report, U.S. Department of Defense, Government Printing Office, Washington, DC.

"Wescom, Inc.—A Study in Telecommunications Quality." (1978). *Quality,* August, p. 30.

Wetherill, G. B. and Chin, W. K. (1975). "A Review of Acceptance Sampling Schemes with Emphasis on the Economic Input." *International Statistical Review,* vol. 43, no. 2, pp. 191–209.

SECTION 26

DESIGN AND ANALYSIS OF EXPERIMENTS[1]

J. Stuart Hunter

*with Mary G. Natrella, E. Harvey Barnett,
William G. Hunter, and Truman L. Koehler*

INTRODUCTION 26.2
    Basic Definitions 26.3
    Some Tools for Good
      Experimentation 26.4

CLASSIFICATION OF
EXPERIMENTAL DESIGNS . . . 26.6

COMPLETELY RANDOMIZED
DESIGN—A ONE-FACTOR
EXPERIMENT 26.10
    Example 26.10
    Analysis 26.10

GENERAL COMMENTS ON A
COMPLETELY RANDOMIZED
DESIGN 26.14
    One-Way Analysis of
      Variance—Models . . 26.14

FACTORIAL EXPERIMENTS—
GENERAL 26.16

EXAMPLE OF A FACTORIAL
EXPERIMENT WITH TWO
FACTORS 26.17
    Analysis 26.18

FACTORIAL EXPERIMENTS
WITH k FACTORS (EACH
FACTOR AT TWO LEVELS) . . . 26.22
    Symbols 26.22
    Example 26.23
    Estimation of Main Effects
      and Interactions 26.24
    Testing Main Effects and
      Interactions 26.27
    Collapsing 2^k Factorials . . 26.29
    Half-Normal Plots 26.29
    Detection of "Wild Values" 26.29

EVOP: EVOLUTIONARY
OPERATION 26.29
    Response Surface 26.30
    EVOP Technique 26.30

BLOCKING THE 2^k FACTORIALS 26.36

FRACTIONAL FACTORIAL
EXPERIMENTS (EACH FACTOR
AT TWO LEVELS) 26.38
    Confounding (Aliasing,
      Biasing) 26.38

[1]This section borrows extensively from the Third Edition, in which Mary Natrella prepared the section on design and analysis of experiments; E. Harvey Barnett prepared the section on evolutionary operation; and William G. Hunter and Truman L. Koehler prepared the section on response surface methodology. The present author, J. Stuart Hunter, gratefully acknowledges this earlier work and takes full responsibility for all changes in organization and emphasis.

DESIGNING A FRACTIONAL
FACTORIAL DESIGN 26.39
   Example 26.39
   Identifying the Estimates . 26.40
   Additional Fractional
     Designs 26.42

ADDITIONAL COMMENTS ON
FACTORIAL EXPERIMENTS   26.42
   Internal Estimates of
   Error 26.43
   Estimates of Variance from
     Past Experience 26.43
   Orthogonal Arrays 26.43
   Multilevel Fractionals . . . 26.44
   Screening Experimentation 26.44
   Off-Line Quality Control . 26.44

RESPONSE SURFACE DESIGNS . 26.45
   Weakness of One-Variable-
     at-a-Time Approach . . . 26.47
   Example 26.47
   Respone Surface 26.47
   Beginning of Program . . . 26.48
   First-Order Strategy 26.49
   Second-Order Strategy . . 26.53

BLOCK DESIGNS 26.54

RANDOMIZED BLOCK DESIGN . 26.55
   Example 26.56
   Analysis 26.56

Analysis of the Treatment
   Effects 26.57
Analysis of the Block
   Effects 26.59

BALANCED INCOMPLETE BLOCK
DESIGNS 26.59
   General Comments on
     Block Designs 26.60
   Covariance Analysis . . . 26.62

LATIN SQUARE DESIGNS 26.62

YOUDEN SQUARE DESIGNS . 26.64

NESTED DESIGNS 26.64

MIXTURE DESIGNS 26.66

GROUP SCREENING DESIGNS . .26.69

PLANNING INTERLABORATORY
TESTS 26.70
   A Rank Sum Test for
     Laboratories 26.71
   Youden Two-Sample Plan 26.71

PLANNING THE SIZE OF THE
EXPERIMENT 26.73
   Example 26.74

GENERAL REMARKS ON
ANALYSIS OF DATA 26.76
   Remarks on Computing . . 26.76
   Missing Values 26.76

DEVELOPMENTS IN
EXPERIMENTAL DESIGN 26.77

REFERENCES 26.77

INTRODUCTION

An experiment has been defined, in the most general sense, as a "considered course of action aimed at answering one or more carefully framed questions." This section discusses a more restricted kind of experiment, in which the experimenter chooses certain factors for study, deliberately varies those factors in a controlled fashion, and then observes the effect of such action. In addition, this section discusses how to design such experiments and how to interpret the resulting data.

The section is organized into three subdivisions:

1. An introduction, which provides those basic definitions that are essential to the understanding of problems in experimental design and analysis. Other definitions are provided later as needed.

2. A series of typical problems in design and analysis of experiments, starting with the simplest and increasing in complexity. For each of these problems the method of structuring the experiment and analyzing the resulting data is presented. General comments on each design are also presented.

3. A discussion of the size of the experiment, assumptions, and other matters pertinent to all designs, plus reference to other works.

Basic Definitions. Several fundamental terms are widely used throughout this section. They may be defined as follows:

Factor. A "factor" is one of the controlled or uncontrolled variables whose influence upon a response is being studied in the experiment. A factor may be quantitative, e.g., temperature in degrees, time in seconds. A factor may also be qualitative, e.g., different machines, different operators, switch on or off.

Level (Version). The "levels" ("versions") of a factor are the values of the factor being examined in the experiment. For quantitative factors, each chosen value becomes a level, e.g., if the experiment is to be conducted at four different temperatures, then the factor "temperature" has four "levels." In the case of qualitative factors, "switch on or off" becomes two levels (versions) for the switch factor; if six machines are run by three operators, the factor "machine" has six levels (versions) while the factor "operator" has three levels (versions).

Treatment. A "treatment" is a single level (version) assigned to a single factor during an experimental run, e.g., temperature at 800 degrees. A "treatment combination" is the set of levels for all factors in a given experimental run. For example, an experimental run using an 800-degree temperature, machine 3, operator A, and switch off would constitute one treatment combination.

Experimental Units. The "experimental units" consist of the objects, materials, or units to which treatments are being applied. They may be biological entities, natural materials, fabricated products, etc.

Experimental Environment. The "experimental environment" comprises the surrounding conditions that may influence the results of the experiment in known or unknown ways.

Block. A factor in an experimental program that has influence as a source of variability is called a "block." The word is derived from early agricultural usage, in which blocks of land were the sources of variability. A block is a portion of the experimental material or of the experimental environment that is likely to be more homogeneous within itself than between different portions. For example, specimens from a single batch of material are likely to be more uniform than specimens from different batches. A group of specimens from such a single batch would be regarded as a block. Observations taken within a day are likely to be more homogeneous (to have smaller variance) than observations taken across days. "Days" then becomes a block factor.

Experimental Design. The formal plan for conducting the experiment is called the "experimental design" (also the "experimental pattern"). It includes the choice of the responses, factors, levels, blocks, and treatments and the use of certain tools called planned grouping, randomization, and replication.

Some Tools for Good Experimentation. Good experimentation is an art and depends heavily upon the prior knowledge and abilities of the experimenter. Some tools of experimentation of importance in the statistical aspects of experimental planning and design follow.

Planned Grouping or Blocking. Beyond the factors selected for study, there are other "background" variables that may affect the outcome of the experiment. When the experimenter is aware of these variables, it is often possible to plan the experiment so that:

1. Possible influences due to background variables do not affect information obtained about the factors of primary interest.
2. Some information about the effects of the background variables can be obtained.

In designing experiments wide use is made of the uniformity within blocks in order to minimize the effect of unwanted variables and to accentuate the effect of the factors under study. Designs that make use of this uniformity within blocks are called "block designs," and the process is called "planned grouping."

Randomization. The sequence of experiments and/or the assignment of specimens to various treatment combinations in a purely chance manner is called "randomization." Such assignment increases the likelihood that the effect of uncontrolled variables will balance out. It also improves the validity of estimates of experimental error variance and makes possible the application of statistical tests of significance and the construction of confidence intervals. Whenever possible, randomization is part of the experimental program.

Replication. "Replication" is the repetition of an observation or measurement in order to increase precision or to provide the means for measuring precision. A single replicate consists of a single observation or experimental run. Replication provides an opportunity for the effects of uncontrolled factors or factors unknown to the experimenter to balance out and thus, with randomization, acts as a bias-decreasing tool. Replication also helps to detect gross errors in the measurements. In replications of groups of experiments, different randomizations should apply to each group.

Table 26.1 lists some requisites for sound experimentation and shows the way in which these tools contribute to meeting the requisites. A checklist that should be helpful in all phases of an experiment is given in Table 26.2; see Bicking, 1954.

TABLE 26.1 Some Requisites and Tools for Sound Experimentation

Requisites	Tools
1. The experiment should have carefully defined objectives. See Table 26.2.	1. The definition of objectives requires all the specialized subject matter knowledge of the experimenter, and involves such things as: *a.* Choice of factors, including their range *b.* Choice of experimental materials, procedures, and equipment *c.* Choice of the metric for the factors (e.g., temperature or log

TABLE 26.1 Some Requisites and Tools for Sound Experimentation (*Continued*)

Requisites	Tools
	temperature) and method of measurement
2. As far as possible, effects of factors should not be obscured by other variables.	2. The use of an appropriate experimental pattern helps to free the comparisons of interest from the effects of uncontrolled variables and simplifies the analysis of results.
3. As far as possible, the experiment should be free from bias, conscious or unconscious.	3. Some variables may be taken into account by planned grouping. Use randomization. Replication helps randomization to do a better job.
4. Experiments should provide a measure of experimental error variance (precision).	4. Replication provides the measure of variance and randomization ensures its validity.
5. Precision of experiment should be sufficient to meet objectives set forth in requisite 1.	5. Greater precision may be achieved by: refinements of measurement and experimental technique, experimental pattern (including planned grouping), replication.

TABLE 26.2 Checklist for Planning Test Programs

A. Obtain a clear statement of the problem.
   1. Identify the problem area in quantitative terms.
   2. Identify the response(s) to be measured, the factors that may be varied, the factors to be held constant, and the factors that cannot be controlled.
   3. Identify the ranges or limitations of the measurements and of the experimental factors.
B. Collect available background information.
   1. Investigate all available sources of information.
   2. Tabulate data pertinent to planning the experimental program.
   3. Be quantitative.
C. Design the experimental program.
   1. Hold a conference of all parties concerned.
      a. State the propositions to be explored.
      b. Agree on magnitude of differences in the response considered worthwhile.
      c. Outline possible alternative outcomes.
      d. Choose the factors to be studied.
      e. Determine practical range of factors and specify levels.
      f. Choose the measurements and methods of measurement.
      g. Consider the effect of sampling variability and of precision of the measurement methods.
      h. Consider possible interrelationships (interactions) of the factors.
      j. Determine influences of time, cost, materials, manpower, instrumentation, and other facilities and of extraneous conditions such as weather.
      k. Consider personnel and human relations requirements of the program.
   2. Design the experimental program in preliminary form.
      a. Prepare a systematic and inclusive schedule, which includes the randomization pattern.
      b. Provide for stepwise performance or adaptation of schedule if necessary.

TABLE 26.2   Checklist for Planning Test Programs   (*Continued*)

> *c.* Eliminate effect of variables not under study by controlling, balancing, or randomization.
> *d.* Minimize the number of experimental runs consistent with objectives.
> *e.* Choose the method of statistical analysis.
> *f.* Arrange for orderly accumulation of data.
> 3. Review the experimental design program with all concerned.
>   *a.* Adjust the program as required.
>   *h.* Spell out the steps to be followed in unmistakable terms.
> D. Plan and carry out the experimental work.
>   1. Develop methods, materials, and equipment.
>   2. Carry out the experimental design in some random order.
>   3. Record ancillary data.
>   4. Record any modifications of the experimental design.
>   5. Take precautions in the collection and recording of data, especially data from extra experiments and missing experiments.
>   6. Record progress of the program by date, run number, and other ancillary data.
> E. Analyze the data.
>   1. Review the data with attention to recording errors, omissions, etc.
>   2. Use graphics: plot the data, plot averages, plot simple graphs.
>   3. Apply appropriate statistical techniques.
> F. Interpret the results.
>   1. Consider all the observed data.
>   2. Confine initial conclusions to strict deductions from the experimental evidence at hand.
>   3. Elucidate the analysis in both graphical and numerical terms.
>   4. State results in terms of verifiable probabilities.
>   5. Arrive at conclusions as to the technical meaning of results as well as their statistical significance.
>   6. Point out implications of the findings for application and for further work.
>   7. Account for any limitations imposed by the data or by the methods of analysis used.
> G. Prepare the report.
>   1. Describe work clearly, giving background, pertinence of problems, meaning of results.
>   2. Use tabular and graphic methods of presenting data, and consider their possible future use.
>   3. Supply sufficient information to permit readers to verify results and to draw their own conclusions.
>   4. Limit conclusions to objective summary of evidence.

CLASSIFICATION OF EXPERIMENTAL DESIGNS

Statisticians by themselves do not design experiments, but they have developed a number of structured schedules called "experimental designs," which they recommend for the taking of measurements. These designs have certain rational relationships to the purposes, needs, and physical limitations of experiments. Designs also offer certain advantages in economy of experimentation and provide straightforward estimates of experimental effects and valid estimates of variance. There are a number of ways in which experiment designs might be classified, for example, the following:

1. By the number of experimental factors to be investigated (e.g., single-factor versus multifactor designs)

2. By the structure of the experimental design (e.g., blocked, factorial, nested, or response-surface design)
3. By the kind of information the experiment is primarily intended to provide (e.g., estimates of effects, estimates of variance, or empirical mappings)

Some of the common statistical experimental designs are summarized in Table 26.3. Basic features of the designs are summarized in terms of these criteria of classification and the details of design and analysis are given under the topics that follow. The analysis for observed responses is always based on a statistical model unique to the specific design.

TABLE 26.3 Classification of Designs

Design	Type of application	Structure	Information sought
Completely randomized	Appropriate when only one experimental factor is being investigated.	Basic: One factor is investigated by allocating experimental units at random to treatments (levels of the factor). Blocking: none.	1. Estimate and compare treatment effects. 2. Estimate variance.
Factorial	Appropriate when several factors are to be investigated at two or more levels and interaction of factors may be important.	Basic: Several factors are investigated at several levels by running all combinations of factors and levels. Blocking: none.	1. Estimate and compare effects of several factors. 2. Estimate possible interaction effects. 3. Estimate variance.
Blocked factorial	Appropriate when number of runs required for factorial is too large to be carried out under homogeneous conditions.	Basic: Full set of combinations of factors and levels is divided into subsets so that some high-order interactions are equated to blocks. Each subset constitutes a block. All blocks are run. Blocking: Blocks are usually units in space or time. Estimates of certain interactions are sacrificed to provide blocking.	1. Same as factorial except that certain high-order interactions cannot be estimated.

TABLE 26.3 Classification of Designs *(Continued)*

Design	Type of application	Structure	Information sought
Fractional factorial	Appropriate when there are many factors and levels and it is impractical to run all combinations.	Basic: Several factors are investigated at several levels but only a subset of the full factorial is run. Blocking: Sometimes possible.	1. Estimate and compare effects of several factors. 2. Estimate certain interaction effects (some may not be estimable). 3. Certain small fractional factorial designs may not provide sufficient information for estimating the variance.
Randomized block	Appropriate when one factor is being investigated and experimental material or environment can be divided into blocks or homogeneous groups.	Basic: Each treatment or level of factor is run in each block. Blocking: Usually with respect to only one variable.	1. Estimate and compare effects of treatments free of block effects. 2. Estimate block effects. 3. Estimate variance.
Balanced incomplete block	Appropriate when all the treatments cannot be accommodated in a block.	Basic: Prescribed assignments of treatments to blocks are made. Every pair of treatments will appear at least once in the experimental design, but each block will contain only a subset of pairs.	1. Same as randomized block design. All treatment effects are estimated with equal precision. Treatment averages must be adjusted for blocks.
Partially balanced incomplete block	Appropriate if a balanced incomplete block requires a larger number of blocks than is practical.	Basic: Prescribed assignments of treatments to blocks are made.	1. Same as randomized block design but all treatments are not estimated with equal precision.

TABLE 26.3 Classification of Designs *(Continued)*

Design	Type of application	Structure	Information sought
Latin square	Appropriate when one primary factor is under investigation and results may be affected by two other experimental variables or by two sources of nonhomogeneity. It is assumed that no interactions exist.	Basic: Two cross groupings of the experimental units are made corresponding to the columns and rows of a square. Each treatment occurs once in every row and once in every column. Number of treatments must equal number of rows and number of columns Blocking: With respect to two other variables in a two-way layout.	1. Estimate and compare treatment effects, free of effects of the two blocked variables. 2. Estimate and compare effects of the two blocked variables. 3. Estimate variance.
Youden square	Same as Latin square but number of rows, columns, and treatments need not be the same.	Basic: Each treatment occurs once in every row. Number of treatments must equal number of columns. Blocking: With respect to other variables in a two-way layout.	1. Same as Latin square.
Nested	Appropriate when objective is to study relative variability instead of mean effect of sources of variation (e.g., variance of tests on the same sample and variance of different samples).	Basic: Factors are strata in some hierarchical structure; units are tested from each stratum.	1. Relative variation in various strata, components of variance.

TABLE 26.3 Classification of Designs (*Continued*)

Design	Type of application	Structure	Information sought
Response surface	Objective is to provide empirical maps (contour diagrams) illustrative of how factors under the experimenter's control influence the response.	Factor settings are viewed as defining points in the factor space (may be multidimensional) at which the response will be recorded	Maps illustrating the nature of the response surface
Mixture designs	Same as factorial designs.	Many unique arrays. Factor settings are constrained. Factor levels are often percentages that must sum to 100%. Other factor level constraints are possible.	Same as factorial

COMPLETELY RANDOMIZED DESIGN—A ONE-FACTOR EXPERIMENT

The completely randomized design is appropriate when a total of N experimental units are available for the experiment and there are k treatments (or levels of the factor) to be investigated. Of the total number N, it is usual to assign *randomly* an equal number n to each of the k treatments.

Example. A study was made to investigate the effect of three different conditioning methods on the breaking strength T (in pounds per square inch) of cement briquettes. Fifteen briquettes were available from one batch and were assigned at random to the three methods. The results are summarized in Table 26.4. The purpose of the experiment was to investigate the effect of conditioning methods on breaking strength, and the analysis was designed to answer the question: Do the mean breaking strengths differ for the different conditioning methods?

This is an example of a randomized one-factor experiment. Only one experimental factor (method of conditioning) is under study. There are three methods, i.e., the number of treatments k equals 3. The number of units n assigned at random to each treatment is 5. The total number of experimental units N is 15.

Analysis. The analysis of these data begins with a plot of the three treatment averages, as shown in Figure 26.1. The reference distribution plotted above the averages will be explained later. The average responses are obviously different. The key question is whether the observed differences between the averages is due

TABLE 26.4   Breaking Strength T of Cement Briquettes, lb/in^2

	Method 1	Method 2	Method 3
	553	553	492
	550	599	530
	568	579	528
	541	545	510
	537	540	571
Total T	2749	2816	2631
n	5	5	5
Average $\overline{y}$	549.8	563.2	526.2
Estimate of variance s^2	145.7	626.2	864.2
Degrees of freedom	4	4	4

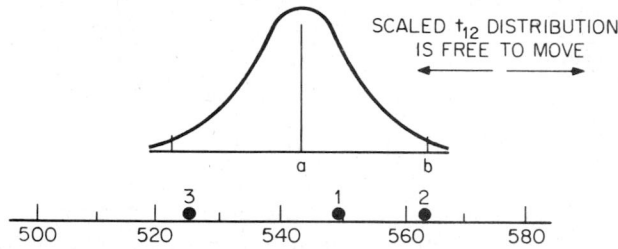

FIG. 26.1   Plot of treatment averages and their reference t-distribution. (Distance from a to $b = t_{\nu,\ \alpha/2}\sqrt{s^2/n} = t_{12,\ 0.025}\sqrt{s^2/n} = 2.179\sqrt{545.4/5} = 22.8$.)

solely to the inherent variability of the observations or is caused by this variability plus real differences between the treatment means. (In this section on experimental design the word "mean" is used to connote the *expected value* of an average, that is, the value an average would take if an infinite number of observations were made.) The analysis of variance (ANOVA) is a basic statistical technique in the analysis of such data and is illustrated for the data in Table 26.5.

Analysis of Variance.   Referring to Table 26.4, the total T is:

$$T = 8196 \qquad N = 15 \qquad n_i = 5 \qquad i = 1,2,3$$

TABLE 26.5   Analysis of Variance for a One-Factor Experiment

Source of variation	Sum of squares	Degrees of freedom	Mean square
Between treatments	SSB = 3,509.2	$(k - 1) = 2$	MSB = SSB/$(k - 1)$ MSB = 3509.2/2 = 1754.6
Within treatments	SSW = 6,544.4	$k(n - 1) = 12$	MSW = SSW/$k(n - 1)$ MSW = 6544.4/12 = 545.4
Total	TSS = 10,053.6	$(N - 1) = 14$	

Calculate the following:

The *uncorrected* total sum of squares $\Sigma y^2 = 4{,}488{,}348$

$$C = \text{correction factor (a special constant)} = \frac{T^2}{N} = \frac{(8196)^2}{15} = 4{,}478{,}294.4$$

$\text{TSS} = corrected \text{ total sum of squares } \sum y^2 - C$

$$= 4{,}488{,}348 - 4{,}478{,}294.4 = 10{,}053.6$$

$$\text{SSB} = \text{between-treatments sum of squares} = \sum_i \frac{T_i^2}{n} - C = \frac{22{,}409{,}018}{5} - C$$

$$= 4{,}481{,}803.6 - 4{,}478{,}294.4 = 3509.2$$

$\text{SSW} = \text{within-treatments sum of squares} = \text{TSS} - \text{SSB}$

$$= 10{,}053.6 - 3{,}509.2 = 6{,}544.4$$

(SSW is here obtained by subtraction. It may be obtained directly for the special case of the completely randomized design by calculating $\Sigma y^2 - [(\Sigma y)^2/n]$ for each treatment and summing for all treatments.)

The corrected total sum of squares TSS has $N - 1$ degrees of freedom (DF), the between-treatments sum of squares SSB has $(k - 1)$ degress of freedom, and the within-treatments sum of squares SSW has $(N - k)$ degrees of freedom.

The mean-square column in the table is computed as follows:

$$\text{Mean square between treatments MSB} = \frac{\text{SSB}}{k - 1}$$

$$\text{Mean square within treatments MSW} = \frac{\text{SSW}}{N - k}$$

These calculated quantities are inserted in Table 26.5.

Calculate $F = \text{MSB/MSW} = 1754.6/545.5 = 3.22$. Choose α, the significance level of the test. If the calculated F exceeds $F_{1-\alpha}$ from Appendix II, Table K, for $(k - 1)$ and $k (n - 1)$ degrees of freedom, conclude that there are differences among treatment means. For example, $\alpha = 0.05$ level, $F_{0.95}$ for (2,12) degrees of freedom $= 3.89$; the calculated F does not exceed this value, and we may conclude that the mean breaking strength is not different for the different conditioning methods. The differences between the treatment averages are thus assumed to be due to the error variance. Had the hypothesis that there are no treatment effects been rejected by the F test, then one could conclude that at least one of the mean breaking strengths differs from the others. The formal issue of comparing treatment means, the problem of "multiple comparisons," is discussed in Montgomery (1976).

In this example the n_i are all equal. Designs that have an equal number of observations in each treatment are generally to be preferred. Such designs provide each treatment with an equal opportunity for comparison against all other treatments. On rare occasions, as when one of the treatments is a standard against which all other treatments are to be compared, more observations are placed in the standard treatment than in the alternatives. When the n_i are not all equal, use the following formula for the between-treatments sum of squares:

$$\text{SSB} = \frac{T_1^2}{n_1} + \frac{T_2^2}{n_2} + \cdots + \frac{T_k^2}{n_k} - C$$

Here SSW = TSS − SSB and MSW = SSW/$(N - k)$ as before. The MSW (the overall estimate of variance) can also be obtained by estimating the variance within each treatment and pooling these estimates. The pooled estimate has $N - k$ degrees of freedom.

Graphical Analysis. An approximate graphical analysis of these data is provided by sketching an appropriate "reference" distribution for the average, as illustrated in Figure 26.1. When σ^2 (the population variance) or, equivalently, σ (the population standard deviation) is known, averages may be referred to a normal distribution with standard error $\sigma/\sqrt{n}$. Here σ^2 is unknown, and its estimate s^2 must be determined from the data. Averages must be referred to a student's t-distribution, suitably scaled by $s/\sqrt{n}$. The number of degrees of freedom in t is equal to the number of degrees of freedom in s^2. The estimate of σ^2 is obtained from the analysis of variance table (s^2 = MSW) or by pooling the separate estimates of variance obtained from within each treatment classification. The pooled estimate of variance is given by the weighted average of the individual estimates, the weights being their degrees of freedom. Thus

$$s^2 = \sum_i \frac{(n_i - 1)s_i^2}{N - k}$$

$$= \frac{4(145.7) + 4(626.2) + 4(864.2)}{16} = 545.5$$

$$s = 23.34 \text{ with 12 degrees of freedom}$$

A sketch of the appropriately scaled t distribution appears in Figure 26.1. The distance from the center of the distribution to each extremal point equals $t_{12,\ 0.025}s/\sqrt{n} = 2.18(23.35)/\sqrt{5} = 22.8$, and 95 percent of the distribution falls within the range $2(22.8) = 45.6$. The distribution is easily sketched; there is no need for great precision in its shape save that it look reasonably normal. The distribution can be moved back and forth, and has been located in this instance so that it just fits over the three averages. Thus, based upon this graphical evidence, the suggestion that all three averages could have come from the same parent distribution and hence could be estimates of the identical mean seems reasonable.

This graphical interpretation is verified by using the F test in the analysis of variance table; that is, the computed F ratio was not statistically significant. When averages do not fit reasonably under the distribution, the graphical analysis suggests that the differences between the treatment averages reflect real differences between the treatment means. Such graphical evidence could, of course, be verified by an F test. The scaled reference distribution can be of great value in interpreting treatment averages. Often, although it is technically possible to place the reference distribution over all the averages and simultaneously to obtain a nonsignificant F test, interesting differences between groups of the averages may become clear. The F test does not consider patterns among the averages, a factor that can be of great importance to the analyst (see Box, Hunter, and Hunter,

1978). Alternative approximate analysis techniques, in particular those based upon the use of the range statistic in place of the estimated standard deviation, are available (see the papers by Kurtz et al., 1965, and by Sheesley, 1980).

GENERAL COMMENTS ON A COMPLETELY RANDOMIZED DESIGN

The completely randomized design is simple to organize and analyze and may be the best choice when the experimental material is homogeneous and when background conditions can be well controlled during the experiment.

The advantages of the design are:

1. Complete flexibility in terms of number of treatments and number of units assigned to a treatment
2. Simple analysis
3. No difficulty with lost or missing data

In planning the experiment, n units are assigned at random to each of the k treatments. When the data have been taken, the results are set out as in Table 26.6.

Displayed this way, the results of experiments are indistinguishable from a situation in which there has been no design and no allocation at all but in which several different samples have been tested from each of several different sources of material or several observations have been made under each of several different conditions. Whether the observations come from units randomly allocated to several different treatments or from units obtained from several different sources, the data table looks the same, and in fact the analysis will be essentially the same.

This simple one-factor design is called "completely randomized" to distinguish it from other experiment designs in which either randomization is constrained or the principle of "blocking," or planned grouping, has been made part of the structure.

One-Way Analysis of Variance—Models.   The results of an experiment run according to a completely randomized design are summarized in a one-way table such as Table 26.6. The completely randomized design is called a "one-way" clas-

TABLE 26.6   Completely Randomized Design

Observations within treatments*	Treatments				
	1	2	3	$\cdots$	k
1	y_{11}	y_{12}	y_{13}	$\cdots$	y_{1k}
2	y_{21}	y_{22}	y_{23}	$\cdots$	y_{1k}
3	y_{31}	y_{32}	y_{33}	$\cdots$	y_{3k}
.	.	.	.		.
.	.	.	.		.
.	.	.	.		.
n	y_{n1}	y_{n2}	y_{n3}	$\cdots$	y_{nk}

*The entire nk observations are recorded in random order *without* regard to the treatment classifications.

sification of data, whether or not the data came from a designed experiment. To discuss the associated analysis of variance, statisticians require "models" for the data. In the case of a one-way classification analysis of variance, the most appropriate model is determined by answering the question: Do the several groups (into which the data are classified) represent unique groups of interest to the experimenter? If they do, the model is called "Model I," the "Fixed Effects Model." If, on the other hand, the groups are considered to be a random sample from some population made up of many such groups, the model is called "Model II," the "Random Effects Model." For example, suppose that the data in Table 26.4 were not from a completely randomized design in which 15 briquettes were allocated at random to three unique conditioning treatments of interest to the experimenter. Suppose instead the column headings were "Batch 1," "Batch 2," "Batch 3," where the "batches" represented some convenient grouping of briquettes so that five briquettes were tested per batch. In the original experimental program, in which the three conditioning treatments of the designed experiment were the unique treatments of interest to the experimenter, the data may be represented by the Fixed Effects Model (Model I), whereas in the second program the three batches presumably were a random sample of batches, and hence these data are represented by the Random Effects Model (Model II).

For both Model I and Model II, the experimenter is trying to determine whether the three groups are different in mean value. For Model II the experimenter may also be interested in knowing about the "components of variance"; that is, the variance between samples from the same batch and the variance existing between batches. Knowledge of the variability of different samples within a batch and between different batches is helpful in planning how many samples to test in future experiments.

Data obtained from a designed experiment, as described for this completely randomized design, are usually considered to be represented by Model I, since presumably the experimenter includes the treatments of interest. If the data correspond to Model II, the analysis of variance table and F test are used with one extra step, which requires adding an extra column labeled "Expected Mean Square," to Table 26.5.

	Expected mean square
Between groups	$\sigma_w^2 + n\sigma_b^2$
Within groups	σ_w^2

For the data in Table 26.5, we have:

	Mean square	Expected mean square
Between groups	MSB = 1754.6	$\sigma_w^2 + 5\sigma_b^2$
Within groups	MSW = 545.4	σ_w^2

The quantity σ_b^2 is called the "between component of variance," and σ_w^2 is called the "within component of variance"; MSB is an estimate of the "Expected Between-Groups Mean Square"; and MSW is an estimate of the "Expected

Within-Groups Mean Square." Estimates of s_b^2 and s_w^2 or σ_b^2 and σ_w^2 can be obtained as follows:

MSB is set equal to $s_w^2 + ns_b^2$ and MSW is set equal to s_w^2:

$$s_w^2 = 545.4$$

$$s_b^2 = \frac{1754.6 - 545.4}{5} = \frac{1209.2}{5} = 241.8$$

The total variance assignable to a single observation from one randomly chosen batch and a single briquette is estimated as:

$$s^2 = s_b^2 + s_w^2$$

FACTORIAL EXPERIMENTS—GENERAL

Factorial designs are most frequently employed in engineering and manufacturing experiments. In a factorial experiment several factors are controlled, and their effects upon some response are investigated at each of two or more levels. The experimental plan consists of taking an observation at each of all possible combinations of levels that can be formed from the different factors. Each different combination of factor levels is called a "treatment combination."

Suppose that an experimenter is interested in investigating the effect of the two factors amperage (current) level and force upon the response y, which equals the measured resistivity of silicon wafers. In the past, one common experimental approach has been the so-called "one-factor-at-a-time" approach. This experimental strategy studies the effect of first varying amperage levels at some constant force and then applying different force levels at some constant level of amperage. The two factors would thus be varied one at a time with all other conceivable factors held as constant as possible. The results of such an experiment are fragmentary in the sense that we learn about the effect of different amperage levels only at one force level and the effect of different force levels at only one amperage level. The effects of one factor are conditional on the chosen level of the second factor. The measured resistivity of the wafer at different current levels may, of course, be different when a different force level has been chosen. Similarly, any observed relation of resistivity to force level might be quite different at other amperage levels. In statistical language, there may be an "interaction effect" between the two factors over the range of interest, and the one-at-a-time procedure does not enable the experimenter to detect the interaction.

In a factorial experiment, the levels of each factor are chosen, and a measurement is made at each of all possible combinations of levels of the factors. Suppose that five levels of amperage and four levels of force are chosen. There would thus be 20 possible combinations of amperage and force, and the factorial experiment would consist of 20 trials. In this example, the term "level" is used in connection with quantitative factors, but the same term is also used when the factors are qualitative.

In the analysis of factorial experiments, one speaks of "main effects" and "interaction effects" (or simply "interactions"). Estimated main effects of a given factor are always functions of the average yield response at the various levels of the factor. When a factor has two levels, the estimated main effect is the difference between the average responses at the two levels, i.e., the averages computed over all levels of the other factors. In the case in which the factor has more than two levels, there are several main effect components (linear, quadratic, cubic, etc.), the number of estimable main effect components being one less than the number of levels.

When the factors are qualitative, other comparisons, called treatment "contrasts," are possible. If the difference in the expected response between two levels of factor A remains constant over the levels of factor B (except for experimental error), there is no interaction between A and B; that is, the AB interaction is zero. Figure 26.2 shows two examples of response, or yield, curves; one example shows the presence of an interaction and the other shows no interaction. If there are two levels each of the factors A and B, then the AB interaction (neglecting experimental error) is the difference in the average yields of A at the second level of B minus the difference in the average yields of A at the first level of B. If there are more than two levels of either A or B, then the AB interaction can be composed of more than one component. If we have a levels of the factor A and b levels of the factor B, then the AB interaction has $(a - 1)(b - 1)$ independent components. A two-factor interaction (e.g., AB) is also called a "second-order" effect or "coupled" effect.

For factorial experiments with three or more factors, interactions can also be defined. For example, the ABC interaction is the interaction between the factor C and the AB interaction (or, equivalently, between the factor B and the AC interaction or between A and the BC interaction). A three-factor interaction (e.g., ABC) is a "third-order" effect.

EXAMPLE OF A FACTORIAL EXPERIMENT WITH TWO FACTORS

A two-factor experiment is the simplest kind of multifactor experiment, i.e., all possible combinations of the levels of the two factors are run. For example, mea-

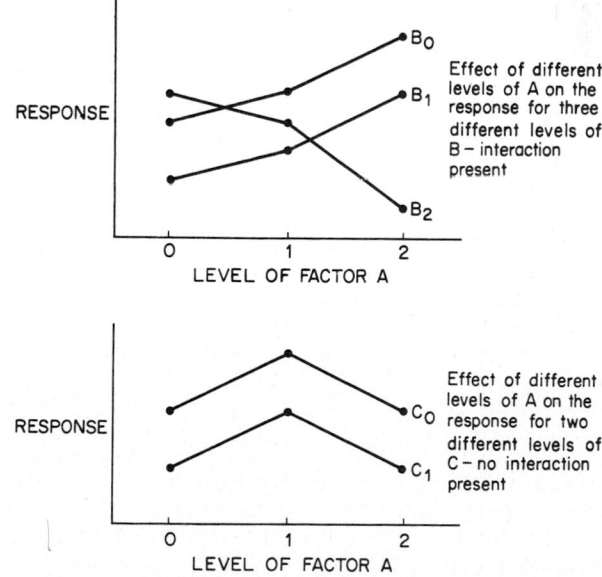

FIG. 26.2 Response curves showing presence or absence of interaction.

surements of the response resistivity of a silicon wafer are usually made at a standard amperage level while using 150 g of force. Let us consider an investigation in progress to see what happens when other values of force and amperage are employed. Four values of force are to be investigated (25, 50, 100, 150 g), along with five levels of amperage (levels 1, 2, 3, 4, and 5, where level 3 is the standard level). An experimental trial is made at each of the $4 \times 5 = 20$ possible combinations. The data can be displayed in a two-way array, as in Table 26.7. This is an unreplicated two-factor multilevel factorial experiment. Some textbooks will describe it as having two "crossed" factors.

Analysis. The first stage of the analysis is to compute, plot, and review both the column and row averages shown in Table 26.8.

Plots of the response versus the factor levels are always useful; in this case they would point up the noticeably higher resistivity values at amperage level 5 and the apparent changes in the resistivity with increasing force, particularly at the outer values of amperage. When the factors are quantitative and the levels equally spaced, there are simple methods to check on various types of trends (linear, quadratic, etc.) in the response measurements as a function of varying levels of a factor (see Hicks, 1982).

The analysis of variance can be used to test two hypotheses: (1) the mean resistivity at all levels of force is the same; and (2) the mean resistivity at all levels of amperage is the same.

The construction of the analysis of variance table would proceed as follows:

$$r = \text{number of rows} = 4$$

$$c = \text{number of columns} = 5$$

$$T = \text{grand total} = \sum_j C_j = \sum_i R_i = 236.77$$

$$N = \text{total number of observations} = r \times c = 20$$

$$C = \text{the correction factor} = \frac{T^2}{N} = 2803.001645$$

$$\text{SSR} = \text{row sum of squares} = \frac{\sum_i R_i^2}{r} - C = 0.014855$$

$$\text{SSC} = \text{column sum of squares} = \frac{\sum_j C_j^2}{r} - C = 0.021430$$

$$\text{TSS} = \text{total corrected sum of squares}$$

$$= (\text{all observations squared}) - C$$

$$= 2803.043500 - 2803.001645 = 0.041855$$

$$\text{SSE} = \text{error (or residual) sum of squares}$$

$$= \text{TSS} - \text{SSR} - \text{SSC} = 0.005570$$

The analysis of variance table for this (unreplicated) two-factor crossed factorial is shown in Table 26.9. Tests of hypotheses that no treatment effects exist are now possible. For rows conclude that statistically significant effects exist between rows

TABLE 26.7 Resistivity Measurements

Force, g	Current level					Row totals R_i
	1	2	3	4	5	
25	11.84	11.83	11.84	11.81	11.96	$R_1 = 59.28$
50	11.84	11.88	11.88	11.87	11.90	$R_2 = 59.37$
100	11.77	11.80	11.80	11.81	11.88	$R_3 = 59.06$
150	11.79	11.80	11.80	11.80	11.87	$R_4 = 59.06$
Column totals C_j	$C_1 = 47.24$	$C_2 = 47.31$	$C_3 = 47.32$	$C_4 = 47.29$	$C_5 = 47.61$	$T = 236.77$

TABLE 26.8 Table of Averages and Effects

Row number	Row average	Row effect
1	11.8560	0.0175
2	11.8740	0.0355
3	11.8120	−0.0265
4	11.8120	−0.0265

Column number	Column average	Column effect
1	11.8100	−0.0285
2	11.8275	−0.0110
3	11.8300	−0.0085
4	11.8225	−0.0160
5	11.9025	0.0640

TABLE 26.9 Analysis of Variance of Resistivity Measurements given in Table 26.7

Source of variation	Sum of squares (SS)	Degrees of freedom (DF)	Mean square = SS/DF	F*
Rows (force)	0.014855	$(r - 1) = 3$	0.004952	10.67†
Columns (current)	0.021430	$(c - 1) = 4$	0.005358	11.54†
Error	0.005570	$(r - 1)(c - 1) = 12$	0.000464	
Total	0.041855	$(rc - 1) = 19$		

*F = mean square (source)/mean square (error).
†Significant at the 1% level.

TABLE 26.10 Residuals, Row and Column Effects, Grand Average

Force, g	Amperage, A					Force effects
	Level 1	Level 2	Level 3	Level 4	Level 5	
25	0.0125	−0.0150	−0.0075	−0.0300	0.0400	0.0175
50	−0.0055	0.0170	0.0145	0.0120	−0.0380	0.0355
100	−0.0135	−0.0010	−0.0035	0.0140	0.0040	−0.0265
150	0.0065	−0.0010	−0.0035	0.0040	−0.0060	−0.0265
Current effects	−0.0285	−0.0110	−0.0085	−0.0160	0.0640	$11.8385 = \bar{y}$

TABLE 26.11 Analysis of Variance Table for Two-Factor Factorial (k Replicates per Cell)

Source of variation	Sum of squares	Degrees of freedom	Mean square	F
Rows	SSR	$r - 1$	$SSR/(r - 1) = MSR$	MSR/MSE
Columns	SSC	$c - 1$	$SSR/(c - 1) = MSC$	MSC/MSE
Interaction	SSI	$(r - 1)(c - 1)$	$SSI/(r - 1)(c - 1) = MSI$	MSI/MSE
Error	SSE	$rc(k - 1)$	$SSE/rc(k - 1) = MSE$	
Total	SST	$krc - 1$		

if $F =$ (row mean square)/(error mean square) is greater than $F_{1-\alpha}$ for $(r - 1)$ and $(r - 1)(c - 1)$ degrees of freedom (from Appendix II, Table K). Similarly, for columns conclude that statistically significant effects exist if $F =$ (column mean square)/(error mean square) is greater than the tabulated value of F for $(c - 1)$ and $(r - 1)(c - 1)$ degrees of freedom. In this example both F tests reject the hypothesis that no effects exist.

The analysis of variance table and its associated tests of hypotheses are only one part of the analysis of data from a factorial design. The model postulated for the data assumes that the force and amperage factor effects are additive. Thus there can be no interactions; that is, the effects of force upon resistivity remain unchanged whatever the levels of the second factor. One way to check this assumption is to compute Tukey's one-degree-of-freedom test for nonadditivity (see Snedecor and Cochran, 1967, or Box, Hunter, and Hunter, 1978). The test for nonadditivity here proved to be nonsignificant.

Table 26.8 has been extended to include the estimated row and column *effects* (the estimated row effect is the row average minus the grand average; the estimated column effect is the column average minus grand average). The row and column effects can then be used to make a two-way table of "residuals," in which the residual for the cell in the ith row and jth column is equal to the observation in that cell minus the sum of the grand average, the ith row effect, and the jth column effect. The table of residuals, Table 26.10, is examined for individual large values (indicating a possibly erroneous observation) and for unusual patterns in sign and size (indicating possible interaction effects). The residuals should be plotted in the time order in which the treatment combinations were run; any indication of trends indicative of other factors disturbs the response. The residuals can also be plotted on normal probability paper as a check on the normality assumption.

The discussion thus far assumes that only one determination per cell was made. To obtain a truly valid estimate of the error variance from this experiment, the cell's observations must be replicated. When experiments are replicated (ideally with each cell containing the same number of observations), it is useful to have a table similar to Table 26.7, where now in each cell both the average and the estimate of variance are recorded. Homogeniety of variance tests may be made (see Snedecor and Cochran, 1967, or Duncan, 1974), although it is well to remember that such tests require near exact normality if they are to be useful. The analysis of variance assumes these variance estimates to be homogeneous and pools them.

A plot of each cell average versus cell estimate of variance (or standard deviation) is often revealing. Individual outlying points or a pattern of dependence of variability on average value should be looked for. (In the latter case, the need for a transformation of the data should be considered; see Box, Hunter, and Hunter, 1978.)

In this experiment replicate measurements were made in each cell of the table since the investigator was interested in finding out about possible interactions and whether the variance of the resistivity measurements would be constant at the extreme values of the factors. In this original experiment, no significant interactions were found, nor was the variance nonhomogeneous.

The analysis of variance of a replicated two-factor crossed factorial design experiment is easily modified from that of the unreplicated one. The procedure is to calculate the following quantities and insert them in Table 26.11:

$$r = \text{number of rows}$$

$$c = \text{number of columns}$$

k = number of determinations per cell

N = total number of observations = krc

T = grand total

$C = T^2/N$

$$\text{SSR} = \text{row sum of squares} = \frac{\sum_i R_i^2}{kc} - C$$

$$\text{SSC} = \text{column sum of squares} = \frac{\sum_j C_j^2}{kr} - C$$

SSI = Interaction sum of squares

$$= \frac{(\text{cell}_{ij} \text{ total})^2}{k} - \text{SSR} - \text{SSC} - C$$

$$\text{TSS} = \text{total sum of squares} = \Sigma y^2 - C$$

$$\text{SSE} = \text{error sum of squares} = \text{TSS} - \text{SSR} - \text{SSC} - \text{SSI}$$

The foregoing instructions will fill in all the cells in the "Sum of squares" column of the analysis of variance table (Table 26.11), but the similarities to Table 26.5 should be noted. The value of the mean square error (MSE) in Table 26.11 can also be obtained by pooling the ($r \times c$) estimates of the within-cell variances.

FACTORIAL EXPERIMENTS WITH k FACTORS (EACH FACTOR AT TWO LEVELS)

The 2^k factorial designs have widespread industrial applicability. The designs permit the separate estimation of the individual effects and the interaction effects of the k factors in an experimental program in which all k factors are varied simultaneously in a carefully organized pattern of trials.

Symbols. A factorial experiment with k factors, each at two levels, is known as a 2^k factorial experiment. The experiment consists of 2^k trials, one trial at each combination of levels of the factors. To identify the individual trials, different notations are used, as illustrated in Table 26.12. One convention is to label each factor by a letter (or numeral) and then to denote the two levels (versions) of each factor by a plus ($+$) and a minus ($-$) sign. Commonly the minus sign refers to the lower level, the standard condition, or the absence of the factor. Thus, if there are three factors labeled A, B, and C, the eight trials comprising the 2^3 factorial design are as shown in Table 26.12. The ($+$, $-$) notation is sometimes referred to as "geometric." For example, the eight ($\pm, \pm, \pm$) factor settings for the 2^3 design may be interpreted as giving the ($\pm 1, \pm 1, \pm 1$) coordinates of the eight vertices of a cube. Alternative notations are to employ 0 and 1, respectively, or, following the Japanese tradition earlier established by Taguchi, 1 and 2 for the two versions of each factor. The classical convention is to denote the two versions of each lettered factor by the presence and absence of its corresponding lowercase

TABLE 26.12 Different Notations for the 2^3 Factorial Design

Run no.	Geometric notation			Alternative notation			Japanese notation			Classical notation		
	A	B	C	A	B	C	A	B	C	A	B	C
1	−	−	−	0	0	0	1	1	1	1		
2	+	−	−	1	0	0	2	1	1	a		
3	−	+	−	0	1	0	1	2	1	b		
4	+	+	−	1	1	0	2	2	1	ab		
5	−	−	+	0	0	1	1	1	2	c		
6	+	−	+	1	0	1	2	1	2	ac		
7	−	+	+	0	1	1	1	2	2	bc		
8	+	+	+	1	1	1	2	2	2	abc		

letter, as is also illustrated in Table 26.12. Here the trial in which all factors are at their "low" level is denoted by a 1. The sequence of trials in Table 26.12 is written in standard or "Yates" order. The trials would, of course, be run in random order.

Example. The data in Table 26.13 are taken from a larger experiment on fire-retardant treatments for fabrics. The excerpted data are intended only to provide an example for demonstrating the technique of analysis. The experiment has four

TABLE 26.13 Results of Flame Test of Fire-Retardant Treatments (a 2^4 Factorial Experiment)

Treatment combinations					Response yield, inches burned
Geometric notation				Classical notation	
A	B	C	D		
−	−	−	−	1	4.2
+	−	−	−	a	3.1
−	+	−	−	b	4.5
+	+	−	−	ab	2.9
−	−	+	−	c	3.9
+	−	+	−	ac	2.8
−	+	+	−	bc	4.6
+	+	+	−	abc	3.2
−	−	−	+	d	4.0
+	−	−	+	ad	3.0
−	+	−	+	bd	5.0
+	+	−	+	abd	2.5
−	−	+	+	cd	4.0
+	−	+	+	acd	2.5
−	+	+	+	bcd	5.0
+	+	+	+	abcd	2.3

factors, each at two levels, i.e., it is a 2^4 factorial. Note that all factors are qualitative in this experiment. The experimental factors and levels (versions) are:

Factors	Levels
A—Fabric	− Sateen
	+ Monk's Cloth
B—Treatment	− Treatment x
	+ Treatment y
C—Laundering	− Before laundering
	+ After one laundering
D—Direction	− Warp
	+ Fill

The observations reported in Table 26.13 are inches burned, measured on a standard-sized sample after a flame test. For convenience, alternative design notations representing the treatment combinations appear beside the resulting observation.

Estimation of Main Effects and Interactions.   The 2^k factorial designs permit the estimation of all k main effects (first-order effects), all $k(k-1)/2$ two-factor interactions, all $k(k-1)(k-2)/3!$ three-factor interactions, etc. Each estimated effect is a statistic of the form $\bar{y}_+ - \bar{y}_-$, that is, it is expressed by the difference between two averages, each containing 2^{k-1} observations. For a 2^k design the analyst would thus be able to estimate, in addition to the grand average, four main effects, six two-factor interactions, four three-factor interactions, and a single four-factor interaction, giving a total of 16 statistics. Remarkably, all these statistics are "clear" (orthogonal) of one another, that is, the magnitudes and signs of each statistic are in no manner influenced by the magnitude and sign of any other.

The question as to which observations go into which average for each estimated effect is determined from the k columns of + and − signs that together form the experimental design (the design column "vectors"). Additional column vectors of + and − signs are then constructed for each interaction, as illustrated in Table 26.14. For example, the vector of signs labeled AB is obtained by algebraically multiplying, for each row, the + or − sign found in column A by the + or − sign found in column B.

Table 26.14 also contains the column of observations. To estimate the AB interaction effect, all the observations carrying a + sign in the AB column are placed in $\bar{y}_+$ and those with a minus sign in $\bar{y}_-$. The estimated AB interaction effect $(\bar{y}_+ - \bar{y}_-)$ is therefore:

$$\frac{4.2 + 2.9 + \cdots + 2.3}{8} - \frac{3.1 + 4.5 + \cdots + 5.0}{8}$$

$$= \frac{27.0}{8} - \frac{30.5}{8} = \frac{-3.5}{8} = -0.4375$$

Yates' Algorithm.   An alternative and more rapid method for obtaining estimates of main effects and interactions for two-level factorials, called "Yates' algorithm," applies to all two-level factorials and fractional factorials. The first step

TABLE 26.14 Table of Signs for Calculating Effects for a 2^4 Factorial

A	B	C	D	AB	AC	AD	BC	BD	CD	ABC	ABD	ACD	BCD	ABCD	Obs.*
−	−	−	−	+	+	+	+	+	+	−	−	−	−	+	4.2
+	−	−	−	−	−	−	+	+	+	+	+	+	−	−	3.1
−	+	−	−	−	+	+	−	−	+	+	+	−	+	−	4.5
+	+	−	−	+	−	−	−	−	+	−	−	+	+	+	2.9
−	−	+	−	+	−	+	−	+	−	+	−	+	+	−	3.9
+	−	+	−	−	+	−	−	+	−	−	+	−	+	+	2.8
−	+	+	−	−	−	+	+	−	−	−	+	+	−	+	4.6
+	+	+	−	+	+	−	+	−	−	+	−	−	−	−	3.2
−	−	−	+	+	+	−	+	−	−	−	+	+	+	−	4.0
+	−	−	+	−	−	+	+	−	−	+	−	−	+	+	3.0
−	+	−	+	−	+	−	−	+	−	+	−	+	−	+	5.0
+	+	−	+	+	−	+	−	+	−	−	+	−	−	−	2.5
−	−	+	+	+	−	−	−	−	+	+	+	−	−	+	4.0
+	−	+	+	−	+	+	−	−	+	−	−	+	−	−	2.5
−	+	+	+	−	−	−	+	+	+	−	−	−	+	−	5.0
+	+	+	+	+	+	+	+	+	+	+	+	+	+	+	2.3

*Obs. = observations.

26.25

in Yates' algorithm is to list the observed data in Yates order, as illustrated in Table 26.15. The generation of the values in Table 26.15 proceeds as follows:

1. A two-level factorial with r replicates contains $N = r2^k$ runs. The associated Yates' algorithm table will have $k + 2$ columns, the first of which contains the experimental design, i.e., the 2^k treatment combinations in standard (Yates) order.

2. In column 2 enter the observed yield corresponding to each treatment combination listed in column 1. If the design is replicated, enter the total for each treatment combination.

3. In the top half of column 3 enter, in order, the sums of consecutive *pairs* of entries in column 2, i.e., the first plus the second, the third plus the fourth, and so on. In the bottom half of column 3 enter, in order, the differences between the same consecutive pairs of entries, i.e., second entry minus first entry, fourth entry minus third entry, etc. Change the sign of the top (first of the pair) and algebraically add.

4. Obtain columns 4, 5, ..., $k + 2$, in the same manner as column 3, i.e., by obtaining in each case the sums and differences of the pairs in the preceding column in the manner described in step 3.

5. The entries in the last column (column $k + 2$) are labeled $g(T)$, $g(A)$, $g(B)$, $g(AB)$, etc. The letters in the parentheses correspond to the + signs in the geometric notation. The first value $g(T)$ is divided by N to give the grand average. Estimates of the remaining main effects and interactions are obtained by dividing each $g(\cdot \cdot \cdot)$ by $N/2$. (*Note:* The remaining steps of this procedure are checks on the computations.)

6. The sum of all the individual responses (column 2) should equal the total given in the first entry of column 6, i.e., $g(T)$ must equal the grand total.

TABLE 26.15 Yates' Method of Analysis Using Data of Table 26.13

A B C D	2	3	4	5	6		Estimated effects	
− − − −	4.2	7.3	14.7	29.2	57.5 =	$g(T)$	Average =	3.5938
+ − − −	3.1	7.4	14.5	28.3	−12.9 =	$g(A)$	A =	−1.6125
− + − −	4.5	6.7	14.5	−5.2	2.5 =	$g(B)$	B =	0.3125
+ + − −	2.9	7.8	13.8	−7.7	− 3.5 =	$g(AB)$	AB =	−0.4375
− − + −	3.9	7.0	−2.7	1.2	− 0.9 =	$g(C)$	C =	−0.1125
+ − + −	2.8	7.5	−2.5	1.3	− 0.5 =	$g(AC)$	AC =	−0.0625
− + + −	4.6	6.5	−3.5	−0.8	1.3 =	$g(BC)$	BC =	0.1625
+ + + −	3.2	7.3	−4.2	−2.7	0.5 =	$g(ABC)$	ABC =	0.0625
− − − +	4.0	−1.1	0.1	−0.2	− 0.9 =	$g(D)$	D =	−0.1125
+ − − +	3.0	−1.6	1.1	−0.7	− 2.5 =	$g(AD)$	AD =	−0.3125
− + − +	5.0	−1.1	0.5	0.2	0.1 =	$g(BD)$	BD =	0.0125
+ + − +	2.5	−1.4	0.8	−0.7	− 1.9 =	$g(ABD)$	ABD =	−0.2375
− − + +	4.0	−1.0	−0.5	1.0	− 0.5 =	$g(CD)$	CD =	−0.0625
+ − + +	2.5	−2.5	−0.3	0.3	− 0.9 =	$g(ACD)$	ACD =	−0.1125
− + + +	5.0	−1.5	−1.5	0.2	− 0.7 =	$g(BCD)$	BCD =	−0.0875
+ + + +	2.3	−2.7	−1.2	0.3	0.1 =	$g(ABCD)$	$ABCD$ =	0.0125
Total	57.5							

Sum of squares 219.15   3506.40

7. The sum of the squares of the quantities in column 2 should equal the sum of the squares of the entries in column $(k + 2)$ divided by 2^k.

8. Each $g(\cdot \cdot \cdot)$ in the last column equals the sum of observations carrying a $+$ sign minus the sum of observations carrying a $-$ sign when the columns of signs displayed in Table 26.14 are employed. The corresponding estimated effects are given by $g(\cdot \cdot \cdot)/(N/2)$. The algorithm is best explained with an example.

Example: The example shown in Table 26.13 has 2^4 runs. Thus the associated Yates algorithm will have six columns, as shown in Table 26.15. The grand average is $\bar{y} = 57.5/16 = 3.5938$. The next entry in column 6 is $g(A) = -12.9$. The estimated main effect of factor A is then:

$$A \text{ effect} = \frac{-12.9}{8} = -1.6125$$

The estimate of the main effect of A can be checked by taking the average of the responses recorded on the high $(+)$ side of the factor A and subtracting the average response on the low $(-)$ side to give $\bar{y}_+ - \bar{y}_- = 22.3/8 - 35.2/8 = -12.9/8 = -1.6125$.

The remaining effects are similarly computed. Thus the estimated AD interaction effect $= -2.5/8 = -0.3125$.

The following steps are checks on the computations in Table 26.15:

6. The sum of column 2 equals $g(T)$.

7. The sum of squares of the entries in column 2 equals 219.5. The sum of squares in column 6 divided by $2^4 = 3506.4/16 = 219.5$.

Testing Main Effects and Interactions. The following steps are used for testing the statistical significance of main effects and interactions.

1. Choose α, the level of significance.

2. If there is no available estimate of the variance due to experimental error, one way to proceed is to use the sum of squares associated with interactions of three or more factors. The sum of squares with one degree of freedom associated with a two-level factorial effect is given by:

$$\frac{N(\text{effect})^2}{4}$$

for all replicated or nonreplicated two-level factorial and fractional factorial designs; N is always the total number of observations.

3. To obtain s^2, divide the total of the sum of squares obtained in step 2 by e, where e is the number of interaction effects contributing to the total. In a 2^k factorial, the number of third- and higher-order interactions will be $2^k - (k^2 + k + 2)/2$. If an independent estimate of error variance is available, use this s^2.

4. Look up $t_{\alpha/2}$ for e degrees of freedom in Appendix II, Table G. If an independent estimate s^2 is used, e equals the degrees of freedom associated with this estimate.

5. The standard error (SE) for each estimated effect is given by:

$$\text{SE(estimated effect)} = \text{SE}(\bar{y}_+ - \bar{y}_-) = \frac{2s}{\sqrt{N}}$$

and the $100(1 - \alpha)$ percent confidence limits by:

$$\text{Effect} \pm t_{\alpha/2}[\text{ SE(effect)}]$$

6. For any estimated main effect or interaction, if the absolute value of an estimated effect is greater than the $t \cdot \text{SE(effect)}$, conclude that the difference of true effect from zero is statistically significant.

Example:

1. Let $\alpha = 0.05$
2. Using Table 26.15, the sum of squares equals:

$$\frac{16[(ABC)^2 + (ABD)^2 + \cdots + (ABCD)^2]}{4}$$

$$= \frac{16[(0.0625)^2 + (-0.2375)^2 + \cdots + (0.0125)^2]}{4} = 0.3231$$

3. We have

$$e = 5 \text{ DF}$$

$$s^2 = \frac{0.3231}{5} = 0.0646 \quad \text{and} \quad s = 0.254$$

4. We also have

$$t_{1-\alpha/2} \text{ for 5 DF} = 2.571$$

5. Then

$$\text{Standard error (effect)} = \frac{2(0.254)}{\sqrt{16}} = 0.1270$$

$$\text{Effect 95\% confidence limits} = \pm 2.571(0.1270) = \pm 0.3265$$

6. Only the main effect of A and the AB interaction are greater than 0.3265; therefore, the main effect of A and the interaction effect AB are declared to be statistically significant.

TABLE 26.16   Collapsed 2^4 Giving a Replicated 2^3

A B D	Responses	Difference	
− − −	4.2, 3.9	0.3	
+ − −	3.1, 2.8	0.3	
− + −	4.5, 4.6	−0.1	
+ + −	2.9, 3.2	−0.3	$s^2 = \Sigma d^2/2n_d$
− − +	4.0, 4.0	0	
+ − +	3.0, 2.5	0.5	$s^2 = 0.57/2(8)$
− + +	5.0, 5.0	0	$= 0.03560$
+ + +	2.5, 2.3	0.2	

Collapsing 2^k Factorials.   An alternative method for obtaining an estimate of variance from an unreplicated 2^k factorial (or 2^{k-p} fractional factorial) requires the analyst to identify the largest estimated effects without regard to sign and then to note whether any of the k studied factors are absent. In this example, the largest estimated effects are, in order, A, AB, B, and AD. Factor C appears to have no great influence upon the response. If the analyst now assumes that factor C has no effect or effects so small as to be readily shrouded by error, then the 2^4 design collapses into a replicated 2^3 design in the effective factors A, B, and D. The collapsed design is displayed in Table 26.16.

The estimated effects for factors A, B, and D remain unchanged. An estimate of variance can now be obtained from the repeated runs. When there are pairs of observations, a shortcut computation for s^2 is given by:

$$s^2 = \frac{\sum_i d_i^2}{2n_d}$$

where the d_i are the differences between the $i = 1, 2, \ldots, d$ pairs of observations and n_d is the number of differences. This estimate of variance has $e = n_d$ degrees of freedom. Thus, for this example:

$$s^2 = \frac{0.57}{(2)(8)} = 0.0356$$

with $e = 8$ degrees of freedom and $s = 0.1887$. The standard error of each effect (excluding all those carrying the label C, of course), is

$$\text{SE(effect)} \frac{2s}{\sqrt{N}} = \frac{2(0.1887)}{\sqrt{16}} = 0.0943$$

Using t with $e = 8$ degrees of freedom, the 95 percent confidence limits for the estimated effects are given by

$$(t_{\alpha/2})\text{SE(effect)} = \pm 2.306(0.0943) = \pm 0.2175$$

Half-Normal Plots.   Daniel (1959) proposed a simple and effective technique for use in the interpretation of data from factorial experiments with all factors at two levels. This technique, called "half-normal plots," helps one to study the magnitude of the effects, identify which main effects and interactions can reasonably be assumed to be zero, and detect wild observations. It may also give evidence that the conditions of the actual experiment have inadvertently departed from the assumptions usually made in the analysis.

Detection of "Wild Values."   Half-normal plots can be used to detect an aberrant value. Hunter (1966) proposed a method which reverses the procedure of Yates' algorithm, using significant coefficients only, to obtain predicted values for each treatment combination. Residuals (differences between observed values and predicted values) are then obtained and examined. Large residuals may indicate aberrant observations and should be investigated.

EVOP: EVOLUTIONARY OPERATION

An important application of experimental design in the production environment was proposed by Box (1957). Essentially, a simple experimental design, run repeatedly, provides a routine of small systematic changes in a production process. The objective is to force the process to produce information about itself while simultaneously producing product to standards. Only small changes in the process factors are allowed, and the consequences of these changes must be detected in the presence of the many natural variabilities that surround the process. The repetition of an experimental design, commonly a 2^2 factorial with center point, permits the blocking of many of the disturbances that commonly influence production. Through the process of replication, the design provides steadily improving estimates of the main effects and interactions of the studied factors.

Response Surface.   A response surface is the mathematical or graphical representation of the connection between important independent variables, controlled factors, and a dependent variable. (An independent variable is a factor that is, or conceivably could be, controlled. Examples are flow rate and temperature. The value of a dependent variable is the result of the settings of one or more independent variables.) Most processes have several dependent variables, such as yield, impurities, and pounds per hour of a byproduct. These responses are usually smooth and may be graduated approximately by simple contours such as a family of circles or of parabolas. We ordinarily work on processes that have unknown response surfaces—if they were known, the work would not be necessary.

A response surface for a process might look like the one in Figure 26.3, which shows the yield of a catalytic oxidation as a function of temperature and feed rate of hydrocarbon. If this information were known, the pounds per hour of product could be determined and better operating conditions selected for any desired production rate. The response surface is initially unknown, but improvement can be made if we only find out which way is up. Multiple regression can be used to approximate the response contours (see Section 23, under Multiple Regression).

EVOP Technique.   The problem, then, is to increase profit in an operating plant with minimum work and risk and without upsetting the plant. These are the steps:

1. Survey company reports and open literature on the process. Study cost, yield, and production records.

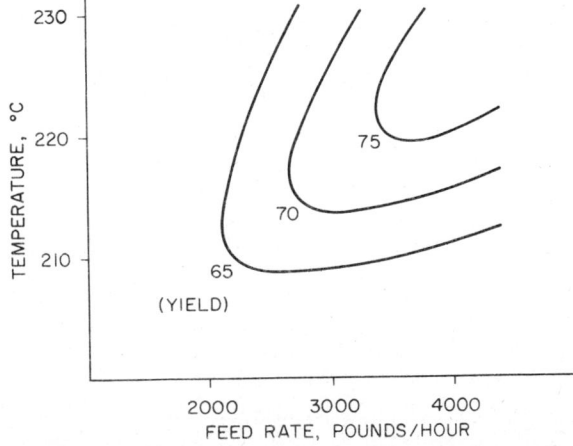

FIG. 26.3   Typical response surface: yield as a function of feed rate and temperature for a catalytic reactor.

2. Study this section on EVOP and preferably the definitive text (Box and Draper, 1969).

3. Obtain agreement and support from production management. Hold training sessions.

4. Select two or three controllable factors that are likely to influence the most important response.

5. Change these factors in small steps according to a plan.

6. After the second repetition of the plan (Cycle 2) and each succeeding cycle, estimate the effects.

7. When one or more of the effects is significant, move to the indicated better operating conditions and start a new EVOP program, perhaps with new ranges or new factors.

8. After eight cycles, if no factor has been shown to be effective, change the ranges or select new variables (Box and Draper, 1967).

9. Continue moving the midpoint of the EVOP plan and adjust the ranges as necessary.

10. When a maximum has been obtained, or the rate of gain is too slow, drop the current factors from the plan and run a new plan with different factors.

The following topics explain these steps in detail.

Literature Search. Sources of information include the process instructions, company reports, manufacturers' literature, patents, textbooks, and encyclopedias of technology. Do not neglect people. Company personnel, consultants, and operators can all contribute. Search for information on:

1. Important independent variables
2. Test methods for intermediate and final results
3. Recommended procedures
4. Records of good and bad results and their causes
5. Long-term history of results; plant production rate and yield by week or month and similar data; effect of past changes in equipment and conditions

When information is contradictory, an EVOP program is an ideal strategy for resolving the conflict.

Always consider the physical and chemical principles that apply.

The EVOP Design. EVOP uses planned runs that are repeated over and over (replicated). One plan in wide use is the two-level complete factorial. There are important reasons to maintain observations on a known set of conditions, called a "reference point." For simplicity in the present discussion, let this point be the center of the square formed by the vertices of the factorial.

Example: This example shows coded data from an actual EVOP program (Barnett, 1960). The problem involved a batch organic reaction, and after the steps above were followed, the two factors and their ranges were selected as shown in Figure 26.4. The response Y is a coded yield in pounds per batch and should be maximized. In this diagram, the reference run (batch) was made at 130°C for 3½ h. The next batch was made at 120°C for 3 h, and so on. The first *cycle* contains five runs, one at each of the conditions. Samples were taken from each batch and analyses were obtained.

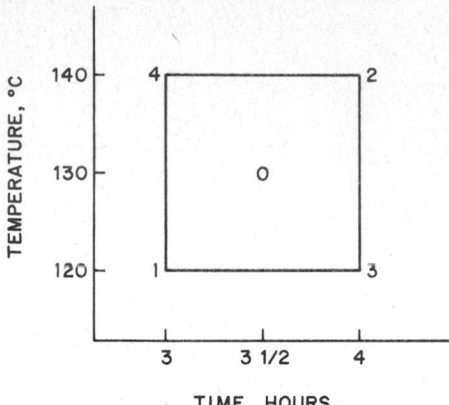

FIG. 26.4 An EVOP plan. Numbers are in run order; 0 is the reference run.

If the process were continuous, it would be allowed to stabilize after each change of conditions, perhaps by waiting for three residence times or preferably by determining the actual time to equilibrium by a test. (Residence time is volume of the vessel divided by the flow rate in appropriate units.)

Warning: It is not unusual to have difficulty in obtaining a representative sample. Procedures and tests are discussed in Sections 23 and 25.

Effects can be estimated at the end of Cycle 1, but in the absence of repeated trials, no estimate of error variance is available. At the conclusion of Cycle 2 both estimated effects and error variance are possible. The estimated effects and their confidence intervals may be computed on a form such as Figure 26.5, which shows this example. The form helps reduce the work and minimizes mistakes. Instructions should be printed on the reverse side (see Figure 26.6).

Here, the error term that puts the magnitude of effects into perspective is obtained from the range by use of factor K first derived by Box and Hunter (1959). The uncertainty in estimating the effects is stated as a confidence interval and the Change-in-mean effect (CIM) is calculated by comparing the results at the outer four corners with the result in the center. The use of this last information is discussed below.

A "phase" is defined as all the cycles that use the same settings of the same factors. The phase average shows the general level of the response and can be used to compare different phases.

The left part of the form is used to record data and estimate effects. It also has the scaled diagram of the phase. The right third is used to determine the error limits of effects and corner averages. The error limits are called "2 S.E." for "two standard errors." The estimated effect ± 2 S.E. covers the usual 95 percent confidence region. Caution should be exercised in claiming statistical significance until after two or three cycles.

For the present example, at the end of Cycle 2 the A effect (time) is estimated as 66 ± 166; it lies somewhere between -100 and $+232$. Thus, the true value of this effect could be negative, positive, or nil. The B (temperature) effect, however, is estimated to be 174 ± 166, or in the range $+8$ to 340. Technically, it is likely to be a positive real effect. The interaction AB is small, and so is the change in mean. Since the confidence region for B is so close to zero and following the

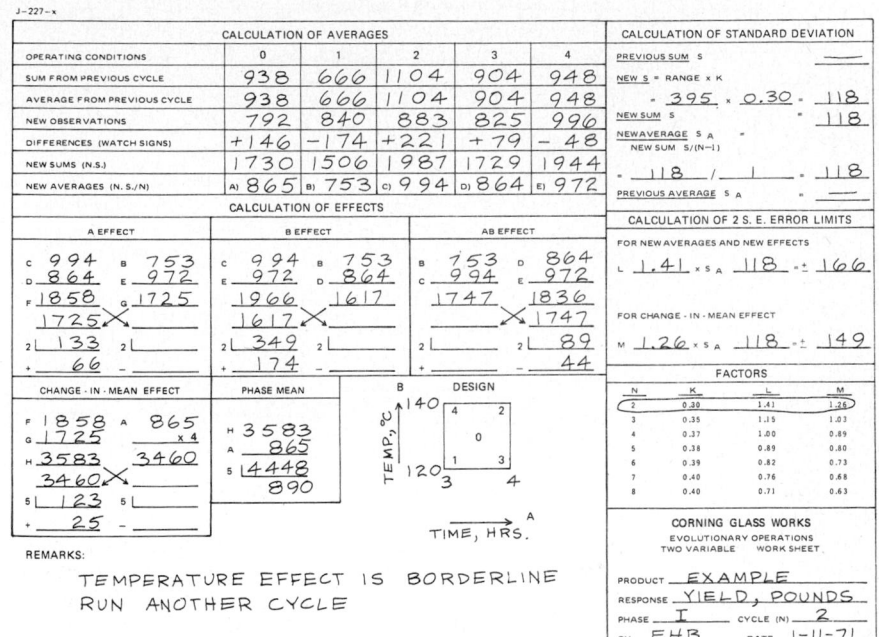

FIG. 26.5 Calculation form at the end of Cycle 2. *(Modified from Barnett, 1960.)*

Differences	Subtract new observations from old averages. Note the algebraic sign of the difference. (938 − 792 = 146)
New Sums	Add the new observations to the old sums. (938 + 792 = 1,730)
New Averages	Divide the new sums by N, the number of the cycle. (1730/2 = 865)
Calculation of Effects	(For example, the A effect) Write the new averages for operating conditions 2 and 3 opposite (C) and (D). Add these two to get the number in space (F). Carry out corresponding operations to get the number for space (G). The next operation is subtraction. If (F) is larger than (G), recopy (G) under (F) and subtract (G) from (F). If (G) is larger than (F), recopy (F) under (G) and subtract (F) from (G). In either case divide by 2 and the sign of quotient is shown on the form. (The A effect is +66.)
Change-in-mean effect	Copy (F) and (G) as shown and add these two. (A) is multiplied by 4. The next operation is subtraction as above. Divide by 5. (The Change-in-mean effect is +25.)
Average phase	Copy (H) and (A) from Change-in-mean box, add them, and divide by 5. (The phase mean is 890.)
Calculation of Standard Deviation	Range. The range is the algebraic difference between the most positive and most negative differences. The range is always positive. (The range of +146, −174, +221, +79, and −48 is 395.) The standard deviation is estimated by taking the range times K.
Constants	Read K, L, and M factors from the table.
Note:	The numerical illustrations apply to the data of Fig. 26.5.

FIG. 26.6 Instructions for EVOP form.

J-227-x'

CALCULATION OF AVERAGES						CALCULATION OF STANDARD DEVIATION		
OPERATING CONDITIONS	0	1	2	3	4	PREVIOUS SUM S		118
SUM FROM PREVIOUS CYCLE	1730	1506	1987	1729	1944	NEW S = RANGE × K		
AVERAGE FROM PREVIOUS CYCLE	865	753	994	864	972	= 119 × 0.35 = 42		
NEW OBSERVATIONS	934	853	1066	852	953	NEW SUM S = 160		
DIFFERENCES (WATCH SIGNS)	-69	-100	-72	+12	+19	NEW AVERAGE S_A = NEW SUM S/(N-1)		
NEW SUMS (N.S.)	2664	2359	3053	2581	2897	= 160 / 2 = 80		
NEW AVERAGES (N.S./N)	A) 888	B) 786	C) 1018	D) 860	E) 966	PREVIOUS AVERAGE S_A = 118		

CALCULATION OF EFFECTS

A EFFECT
c 1018   B 786
D 860   E 966
F 1878   G 1752
   1752 ✕
2 126   2 ___
+ 63   − ___

B EFFECT
c 1018   B 786
E 966   D 860
  1984   1646
   1646 ✕
2 338   2 ___
+ 169   − ___

AB EFFECT
B 786   D 860
c 1018   E 966
  1804   1826
     1804 ✕
2 ___   2 22
+ ___   − 11

CALCULATION OF 2 S. E. ERROR LIMITS

FOR NEW AVERAGES AND NEW EFFECTS
L 1.15 × S_A 80 = ± 92

FOR CHANGE - IN - MEAN EFFECT
M 1.03 × S_A 80 = ± 82

CHANGE - IN - MEAN EFFECT
F 1878   A 888
G 1752   × 4
H 3630   3552
  3552 ✕
5 78   5 ___
+ 16   − ___

PHASE MEAN
H 3630
A 888
5 4518
  904

	FACTORS		
N	K	L	M
2	0.30	1.41	1.26
3	0.35	1.15	1.03
4	0.37	1.00	0.89
5	0.38	0.89	0.80
6	0.39	0.82	0.73
7	0.40	0.76	0.68
8	0.40	0.71	0.63

B DESIGN
TEMP, °C
140   4   2
    0
120   1   3
   3   4
→ A
TIME, HRS.

REMARKS:

TEMPERATURE EFFECT IS +77 ⟶ +261
INCREASE TEMPERATURE & START PHASE II

CORNING GLASS WORKS
EVOLUTIONARY OPERATIONS
TWO VARIABLE   WORK SHEET

PRODUCT EXAMPLE
RESPONSE YIELD, POUNDS
PHASE I   CYCLE (N) 3
BY EHB   DATE 1-12-71

MANUFACTURING AND ENGINEERING DIVISION

FIG. 26.7 Calculation form after Cycle 3.

advice above to be cautious at Cycle 2, another cycle is run. Its results are shown in Figure 26.7.

After Cycle 3, the B effect (temperature) was declared statistically significant, since its likely values fall in the range of 169 ± 92, or +77 to +261. It does not appear that data from more cycles would change the conclusion that temperature should be increased to increase the response y.

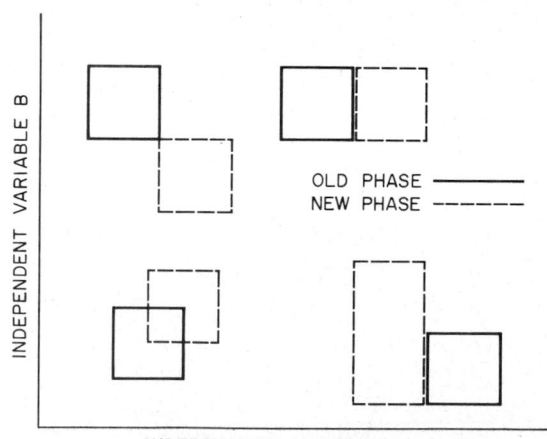

INDEPENDENT VARIABLE B

OLD PHASE ⎯⎯⎯
NEW PHASE - - - - -

INDEPENDENT VARIABLE A

FIG. 26.8 Possible relations of old phase and new phase.

When statistical significance is found for one factor but not for the other, *move* the plan in the desirable direction for the "discovered" important factor and increase the range for the second (nonsignificant) one. Possible old and new phases of an EVOP program are shown in Figure 26.8. When significance is found for both variables, the center of the plan is moved in both directions in proportion to the size of the effects. This is the direction of steepest ascent (see below, under Determine Direction of Steepest Ascent). Whenever the plan is changed, a new *phase* is started. During the second and later phases, the previous estimate of standard deviation is often used since it was obtained under the current operating method.

Moves.   To be conservative, as EVOP should be, moves are contiguous; i.e., one or more of the points in the old phase and new phase coincide. This limits the moves to those types shown in Figure 26.8.

There is nothing "magic" about drawing these plans as squares—1 h does not equal 20°C anyway. A particularly strong signal may justify a move to a plan that does not adjoin the previous one.

Change-in-Mean.   The Change-in-mean effect is the difference between the results at the center point and the average of the other four peripheral points. It is therefore a signal of curvature as shown in Figure 26.9. It is used in conjunction with the effects to indicate when a maximum (or a minimum) has been reached and to indicate the sensitivity of the response to changes in the independent factors. In rare cases it may happen that the first phase is located symmetrically about the maximum with respect to the two independent factors chosen. In this case the factors should be nonsignificant but the Change-in-mean may be significant.

Blocking.   A process response ordinarily changes slightly with time, reflecting changes in sources of raw material, changes in air temperature from day to night, and so on.

Runs made close together in time are expected to be more nearly alike than those over a longer interval. Blocking is used to minimize the trouble caused by

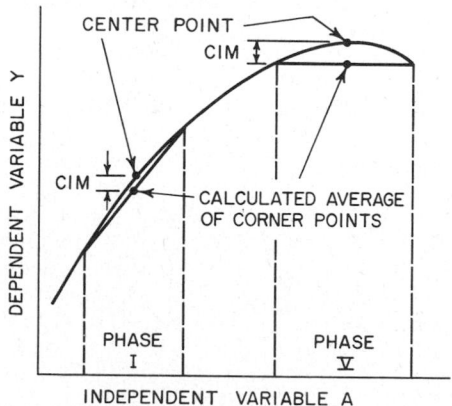

FIG. 26.9   Cross section through a response surface. CIM indicates curvature.

temporal changes of this type. For the EVOP calculations shown here, a block is one cycle. Changes in average level that occur between cycles are completely eliminated from the estimated effects, as can be seen by adding a constant to the five runs of Cycle 3 and recalculating the effects. (The phase average is changed, of course.)

Multiple Dependent Responses. So far the explanation has been in terms of a single dependent response. This is rather unrealistic, except for the profit variable. Most processes have several dependent responses that must be measured or calculated, such as yield, production rate, percent impurity, or pounds of by-product. A calculation sheet is made for each dependent response, and statistical significance may be noted on one dependent sheet but not on others. In this case, it may be well to run another cycle or two to get more information on the other dependent responses before a move is made.

The most troublesome case occurs when the indicated directions for improvement of two responses (say production rate and percent impurity) do not agree. The EVOP program has brought information from the production process. Decisions as to what to do next now rest upon information supplied by the EVOP program coupled with information to be supplied by the subject matter experts.

BLOCKING THE 2^k FACTORIALS

Experimenters often find difficulty in maintaining a homogeneous experimental environment for all the experiments required in a 2^k factorial. For example, an experimenter might need 2 days to run the eight trials required in a 2^3 factorial. The question is how to choose the trials to be run each day so as not to disturb the estimates of the major effects of the three factors, i.e., how to best "block" the design into two blocks of four runs each. Here blocking is accomplished by sacrificing the interaction estimate of least concern, i.e., the three-factor interaction. The procedure to be followed is illustrated in Table 26.17, part *a*, for a 2^3 factorial. First, the plus and minus signs of the 2^3 design are written down. Next, the columns of plus and minus signs commonly used to estimate the *ABC* interaction is constructed and labeled the block "generator." Those runs carrying a plus sign in the block generator column form the first block; those carrying a minus sign form the second block.

When this design is employed, the estimate of the three-factor interaction (abbreviated 3fi) cannot be distinguished from the block effect; the block effect and 3fi effect are "confounded." All other estimated effects are clear of the block effect.

To partition the design into four blocks of two runs each, the proper block generators are provided by the two columns of plus and minus signs associated with the interactions *AB* and *BC* as illustrated in Table 26.17, part *b*. Note that the generators produce four combinations of minus and plus signs, each combination identifying a block of two runs. In this particular design all 2fi (two-factor interactions) are confounded with blocks.

The block generators must be carefully chosen. The blocking arrangements for the 2^3, 2^4, and 2^5 designs appear in Table 26.18. A more complete table and description of factorial design blocking appears in Box, Hunter, and Hunter (1978).

TABLE 26.17 Partitioning the 2^3 Factorial Design

a. Partitioning the 2^3 into two blocks of four runs

2^3		2^3 in two blocks	
	ABC = block	(+) Block	(−) Block
A B C	generator	A B C	A B C
− − −	−	+ − −	− − −
+ − −	+	− + −	+ + −
− + −	+	− − +	+ − +
+ + −	−	+ + +	− + +
− − +	+		
+ − +	−		
− + +	−		
+ + +	+		

b. Partitioning the 2^3 into four blocks of two runs

2^3	Block generators	
A B C	AB	BC
− − −	+	+
+ − −	−	+
− + −	−	−
+ + −	+	−
− − +	+	−
+ − +	−	−
− + +	−	+
+ + +	+	+

++ Block	−+ Block	+− block	−− Block
A B C	A B C	A B C	A B C
− − −	+ − −	+ + −	− + −
+ + +	− + +	− − +	+ − +

TABLE 26.18 Blocking Arrangements for the 2^k Factorials

k = number of factors	Block size	Block generators	Interactions confounded with blocks
3	4	ABC	ABC
	2	AB,BC	AB,BC,AC
4	8	$ABCD$	$ABCD$
	4	ABC, ACD	ABC, ACD,BD
	2	AB,BC,CD	all 2fi and 4fi
5	16	$ABCDE$	$ABCDE$
	8	ABC,CDE	$ABC,CDE, ABDE$
	4	ABC,BCD,CDE	$ABC,BCD,CDE, AD, ABDE, BE, ACE$
	2	AB,BC,CD,DE	all 2fi and 4fi

FRACTIONAL FACTORIAL EXPERIMENTS (EACH FACTOR AT TWO LEVELS)

If there are many factors, a complete factorial experiment, requiring all possible combinations of the levels of the factors, involves a large number of tests—even when only two levels of each factor are being investigated. In these cases, it is useful to have a plan that requires fewer tests than the complete factorial experiment. The fraction is a carefully prescribed subset of all possible combinations. The analysis of fractional factorials is relatively straightforward, and the use of a fractional factorial does not preclude the possibility of later completion of the full factorial experiment.

Confounding (Aliasing, Biasing).   In a complete factorial experiment we have 2^k experimental trials. In the analysis of a complete factorial, we have the grand average, k main effects, $2^k - k - 1$ interaction effects. The 2^k experiments can be used to give independent estimates of all 2^k effects. In a fractional factorial (say the fraction $1/2^p$) there will be only 2^{k-p} experiments, and therefore only 2^{k-p} independent estimates are possible. In designing the fractional plans (i.e., in selecting an optimum subset of the 2^k total combinations), the goal is to keep each of the 2^{k-p} estimates as unbiased or "clear" as possible, i.e., to keep the estimates of main effects and if possible second-order interactions mutually unbiased, or nearly so.

To explain, consider the following 2^{3-1} fractional:

A B C	Observed
− − +	$y_1 = 8$
+ − −	$y_2 = 11$
− + −	$y_3 = 9$
+ + +	$y_4 = 14$

The main effects are given by the statistics $\bar{y}_+ - \bar{y}_-$, where once again the plus and minus subscripts of each letter in the design identify the observations entering each average. Thus, the main effect of A is estimated to be $(11 + 14)/2 - (8 + 9)/2 = 4.0$. The main effects of B and C are, respectively, $(9 + 14)/2 - (8 + 11)/2 = 2$ and $(8 + 14)/2 - (11 + 9)/2 = 1.0$. Now consider the estimate of the two-factor interaction AB. The analyst will find that the signs required to estimate the AB interaction are identical to those already employed to estimate the main effect of C. The main effect of C and the two-factor interaction AB are confounded. Said another way, the statistic $\bar{y}_+ - \bar{y}_- = 1.0$ has an "alias" structure, that is, the statistic may be identified as either C or AB. In fact, the expected value of the statistic equals $C + AB$, the sum of the two effects, and in the absence of clear information on the main effect of C, we cannot tell whether the AB effect is plus, minus, large, or small. The reader will note that estimate A is confounded with BC, as is B with AC.

When some or all main effects are confounded with two-factor interactions, the fractional factorial design is said to be of "Resolution III." When one or more of the main effects are confounded with (at least) three-factor interactions, the fractional is said to be a "Resolution IV" design. Fractionals with main effects confounded with (at least) four-factor interactions are of "Resolution V," etc. (See Box and Hunter, 1959.)

DESIGNING A FRACTIONAL FACTORIAL DESIGN

Let N equal the number of runs and k the number of factors to be investigated. When $N = 2^k$, we have a full factorial design. When $N = 2^{k-p}$, we have a $(\frac{1}{2})^p$ replicate of the 2^k factorial; for example, a 2^{7-3} is a one-eighth replicate of a 2^7 factorial and contains 16 runs.

To design a one-half replicate design in N runs, first write down (Yates order is best) the full factorial design in $(k - 1)$ factors. Next write down the column of signs associated with the highest-order interaction. These signs are now used to define the versions of the kth factor. For example, to construct the 2^{4-1} design, begin with a 2^3 factorial in factors A, B, and C as illustrated in Table 26.19. Next to the columns for A, B, and C write down the column of signs associated with the ABC interaction. Use these signs to identify the two versions of factor D. (The other one-half fraction is obtained by reversing the signs of the column ABC.)

To construct a one-quarter replicate design, two columns of signs are required in addition to the standard factorial in N runs; the one-eighth replicate design requires three additional columns, etc. The columns of signs to be used must be carefully chosen; they are listed in Table 26.20 for designs up to $k = 7$ factors. Table 26.20 is an adaptation of a much more extensive table given in Box, Hunter, and Hunter (1978). Extensive listings of fractional factorial designs can also be found in Diamond (1981).

Example.   To construct a fractional factorial design for $k = 6$ factors in $N = 16$ runs, first write down the full factorial 2^4 design in factors A, B, C, and D. Consulting Table 26.20, the vectors of plus and minus signs associated with the interaction ABC are now used to define the versions of factor E. The signs of the BCD interaction are similarly used to define the versions of factor F. The completed

TABLE 26.19   Constructing the 2^{4-1} Fractional Factorial*

Generator		Principal design	Alternative design†
$A\ B\ C$	$ABC = D$	$A\ B\ C\ D$	$A\ B\ C\ D$
− − −	−	− − − −	− − − +
+ − −	+	+ − − +	+ − − −
− + −	+	− + − +	− + − −
+ + −	−	+ + − −	+ + − +
− − +	+	− − + +	− − + −
+ − +	−	+ − + −	+ − + +
− + +	−	− + + −	− + + +
+ + +	+	+ + + +	+ + + −

*Example run: Run no. 2 requires the experimenter to hold factor A at +, factor B at −, factor C at −, and factor D at +.

†The alternative fraction is obtained by reversing the signs of the ABC vector, that is, by setting $D = -ABC$.

TABLE 26.20   Vectors Used for the Construction of Fractionals

Number of runs N	Number of factors k				
	3	4	5	6	7
4	2^{3-1} $\pm AB = C$	NA	NA	NA	NA
8		2^{4-1} $\pm ABC = D$	2^{5-2} $\pm AB = D$ $\pm AC = E$	2^{6-3} $\pm AB = D$ $\pm AC = E$ $\pm BC = F$	2^{7-4} $\pm AB = D$ $\pm AC = E$ $\pm BC = F$ $\pm ABC = G$
16			2^{5-1} $\pm ABCD = E$	2^{6-2} $\pm ABC = E$ $\pm BCD = F$	2^{7-3} $\pm ABC = E$ $\pm BCD = F$ $\pm ACD = G$
32				2^{6-1} $\pm ABCDE = F$	2^{7-2} $\pm ABCD = F$ $\pm ABDE = G$
64					2^{7-1} $\pm ABCDEF = G$

2^{6-2} design is displayed in Table 26.21 along with observed responses, Yates' algorithm, and identified effects.

Identifying the Estimates.   The 2^{6-2} design was generated by setting $E = ABC$ and $F = BCD$. A simple procedure for identifying the biases (aliases) of the effects estimable from this design is as follows. Multiply the expression $E = ABC$ by E and the expression $F = BCD$ by F. This gives $E^2 = ABCE$ and $F^2 = BCDF$. Now adopt the rule that whenever a symbol appears squared, it is replaced by an I, the "identity," a symbol equivalent to the numeral 1. We now have for the design "generators" $I = ABCE$ and $I = BCDF$. Multiplying the generators together gives the "defining relation" $I = ABCE = BCDF = AB^2C^2DEF$, which reduces to $I = ABCE = BCDF = ADEF$.

When Yates' algorithm is applied to the 16 runs of the 2^{6-2}, the algorithm estimates 15 effects and provides each with its initial name, as illustrated in Table 26.21. The defining relation is now employed to determine the additional names (aliases or biases) of each of these statistics. Thus, the statistic labeled the "main effect" of A actually equals $A = BCE = ABCDF = DEF$, an expression obtained by multiplying through the defining relation by the symbol A. Similarly, the statistic initially called the "ABC interaction" actually estimates $ABC = E = ADF = BCDEF$. The estimates and their full names are given in Table 26.21.

Five of the estimates appear unusually large and are good candidates for measured phenomena distinguishable from natural variability (noise). Using only their first- and second-order names we have: -17.375 estimates $AB + CE$, 11.625 estimates C, 21.125 estimates E, 16.375 estimates D, and 15.375 estimates $DE + AF$. A reasonable interpretation of these statistics is that factors C, D, and E have detectable important influences upon the response over their studied ranges, while factors A and B do not. This conclusion obviously needs confirmation, but

TABLE 26.21 A 2^{6-2} Resolution IV Fractional Factorial and Associated Yates Analysis

Generators: $E = ABC$ and $F = BCD$
Defining relation: $I + ABCE + BCDF + ADEF$

A B C D E F	Obs.*	Yates algorithm				Effects	Identification
							Average
$-\ -\ -\ -\ -\ -$	124	271	541	1137	2405	150.3125	
$+\ -\ -\ -\ +\ -$	147	270	596	1268	11	1.375	$A + BCE + ABCDF + DEF$
$-\ +\ -\ +\ +\ -$	145	284	615	-1	35	4.375	$B + ACE + CDF + ABDEF$
$+\ +\ -\ +\ -\ -$	125	312	653	12	-139	-17.375	$AB + CE + ACDF + BDEF$
$-\ -\ +\ +\ -\ +$	138	307	3	27	93	11.625	$C + ABE + BDF + ACDEF$
$+\ -\ +\ +\ +\ +$	146	308	-4	8	-1	-0.125	$AC + BE + ABDF + CDEF$
$-\ +\ +\ -\ +\ +$	162	323	3	-63	35	4.375	$BC + AE + DF + ABCDEF$
$+\ +\ +\ -\ -\ +$	150	330	9	-76	169	21.125	$ABC + E + ADF + BCDEF$
$-\ -\ -\ +\ -\ -$	125	23	-1	55	131	16.375	$D + ABCDE + BCF + AEF$
$+\ -\ -\ +\ +\ +$	182	-20	28	38	13	1.625	$AD + BCDE + ABCF + EF$
$-\ +\ -\ -\ +\ -$	181	8	1	-7	-19	-2.375	$BD + ACDE + CF + ABEF$
$+\ +\ -\ -\ -\ -$	127	-12	7	6	-13	-1.625	$ABD + CDE + ACF + BEF$
$-\ -\ +\ +\ -\ +$	168	57	-43	29	-17	-2.125	$CD + ABDE + BF + ACEF$
$+\ -\ +\ -\ +\ +$	155	-54	-20	6	13	1.625	$ACD + BDE + ABF + CEF$
$-\ +\ +\ +\ +\ +$	154	-13	-111	23	-23	-2.875	$BCD + ADE + F + ABCEF$
$+\ +\ +\ +\ -\ +$	176	22	35	146	123	15.375	$ABCD + DE + AF + BCEF$

*Obs. = observations.

it represents a good first guess. The 2^{6-2} design now collapses into a 2^3 factorial repeated in factors C, D, and E.

Additional Fractional Designs.   There have been many developments in fractional factorial designs. For estimating missing values in unreplicated two-level factorial and fractional factorial designs, see Draper and Stoneman (1964). For methods of construction of fractional replicate plans for mixed-level fractionals, see Addelman (1961, 1962, and 1963). For methods of partial duplication, augmentation, and sequencing of fractional factorial designs, see Patel (1963), Daniel (1962, 1966), John (1966), and Addelman (1969). For an example of Yates' method and inverse Yates' method in a metallurgical context, see Duckworth (1965). An unusually extensive listing of the designs is given by Diamond (1981).

ADDITIONAL COMMENTS ON FACTORIAL EXPERIMENTS

The analyses presented above apply only to a two-level factorial design in which every level of one factor can be combined with every level of the other factors. Sometimes a table of data will appear to represent a factorial design, but information on the experimental conditions will reveal that the design was not a factorial. Consider the following experiment, which could be summarized by the two-way Table 26.22. This design is not a factorial experiment. Three batches of *each* of three types of cement have been made and some property of each has been measured. Batch 1 from cement type 1 is unique to cement 1 and has nothing in common with batch 1 from type 2 or type 3. Thus, there is no overall batch effect and no interaction between types and batches. The two factors, types and batches, are said to be "nested"; i.e., the levels of one factor (batches) exist only within the levels of the other factor (types). This is a hierarchical experiment to investigate differences between types and between batches within types (possibly between samples within batches, etc.). (See Nested Designs, later in this section.)

The example of cement types and batches might not cause trouble, since this is so clearly a nested design, but let us consider the two-way table displayed in Table 26.23. It is not obvious from Table 26.23 whether the data form a factorial experiment or not—one must know how the experiment was run. If in fact the same three heads were used on each machine, the design is a factorial design, i.e., the two classifications, heads and machines, are crossed. If, on the other hand, a different set of three heads was used on each machine, the design is nested.

TABLE 26.22   A Plan That Is *Not* a Factorial, but Nested

Batch	Cement type		
	1	2	3
1	y_{11}	y_{12}	y_{13}
2	y_{21}	y_{22}	y_{23}
3	y_{31}	y_{32}	y_{33}

TABLE 26.23   A Plan That *May* Be a
Factorial, i.e., Crossed

	Machine		
Head	1	2	3
1	y_{11}	y_{12}	y_{13}
2	y_{21}	y_{22}	y_{23}
3	y_{31}	y_{32}	y_{33}

Internal Estimates of Error.   As in any experiment, a measure of experimental error variance is required for judging the significance of the observed differences in treatment averages. The best estimate of experimental error variance comes from repeated random trials, but repeated trials are not always possible in the larger factorial designs. However, estimates of higher-order interactions will be available, and, as a working rule, estimates of third- and higher-order interactions are generally viewed as manifestations of error. Their associated sums of squares, $N(\text{effect})^2/4$, and degrees of freedom are then used to estimate variance. This does not imply that third-order interactions are always nonexistent. Occasionally a large three-factor interaction will occur, but fortunately such occurrences are infrequent. As always, the judgment of the experimenter becomes crucial. For a very small factorial design, e.g., 2^3 or smaller, the experiments should be replicated (repeated) in order to obtain an estimate of the error variance.

In blocked factorial designs, some of the higher-order interactions are confounded with blocks and are not available as estimates of error. When a 2^3 factorial is arranged in two blocks of four observations, the single third-order interaction provides the blocking (the means of subdividing the experiment into homogeneous groups). Here again it may be necessary to replicate the experiment or at least part of it in order to have an estimate of experimental error.

Estimates of Variance from Past Experience.   In those cases in which the experimental design does not provide an adequate estimate of the error variance, an estimate based upon past experience with the experimental and measurement process is sometimes used. In many laboratory and industrial situations, this information is often at hand.

Other Two-Level Fractionals.   Although the 2^{k-p} fractional factorial designs are frequently used, many other fractional factorials exist. For example, the 2^{k-p} designs are part of the larger family of Plackett and Burman (1946) designs, which are fractionals with N a multiple of 4, for example, the $k = 11$, $N = 12$ design found in Table 26.24.

Orthogonal Arrays.   Experimenters often want to study factors at three levels. Rather than run the full 3^k factorial, they can choose many different fractions. Most of these fractions of the 3^k design are constructed from designs of the Latin square variety and are called "orthogonal arrays." In general, all the two- and three-level designs described thus far may be considered orthogonal arrays. This terminology, used extensively by Japanese quality engineers, recognizes the geometric multidimensional nature of the designs; that is, in the k-dimensional space of the factors, the vectors comprising the design are all mutually perpendicular,

TABLE 26.24 A Plackett and Burman Design
(k = 11 factors, N = 12 runs)

A	B	C	D	E	F	G	H	I	J	K
+	−	+	−	−	−	+	+	+	−	+
+	+	−	+	−	−	−	+	+	+	−
−	+	+	−	+	−	−	−	+	+	+
+	−	+	+	−	+	−	−	−	+	+
+	+	−	+	+	−	+	−	−	−	+
+	+	+	−	+	+	−	+	−	−	−
−	+	+	+	−	+	+	−	+	−	−
−	−	+	+	+	−	+	+	−	+	−
−	−	−	+	+	+	−	+	+	−	+
+	−	−	−	+	+	+	−	+	+	−
−	+	−	−	−	+	+	+	−	+	+
−	−	−	−	−	−	−	−	−	−	−

and hence the designs are orthogonal arrays. Fractional factorial designs constructed from Latin square designs are also referred to as "main effect clear" designs. Most of the Latin square variety of fractional factorials do *not* allow for estimation of interactions, which is an undesirable quality in the minds of many experimenters. An example employing these designs is given in Phadke et al. (1983). A critique of the applications of three-level orthogonal arrays is found in Hunter (1985). The Box-Behnken (1960) designs form novel fractions of the three-level designs.

Multilevel Fractionals.   The 2^k and 3^k factorials and fractional factorials can be used to generate designs of more than two or three versions (see Addelman, 1962). Many novel fractionals have been published: Webb (1968a,b), Margolin (1969), Anderson and Thomas (1979), and Rechtschaffner (1967). The subject of fractional factorials has generated a vast and growing literature. Significant textbooks are by Box, Hunter, and Hunter (1978); Diamond (1981); and Raktoe, Hedayat, and Federer (1981).

Screening Experimentation.   The 2^{k-p} designs and the fractions of the 3^k designs for $k > 4$ are commonly used as "screening" designs, that is, the designs are used to determine which few factors from a large host of candidate factors have the greatest influence upon the measured response. Experimentally, the objective is to identify the "vital few," and ideally, a cause-and-effect diagram associating many factors with the response under study will have been made. The most important subset is then subjectively selected, the ranges, or versions, of these factors are chosen for study and used to derive a fractional factorial design. Experiments are then performed and analyzed to effectively provide the experimenter with information on those vital few factors having the most important influence upon the response. Remaining factors found to have little detectable influence over the ranges varied can, in future trials, either be explored over wider ranges or be fixed at levels considered most economical.

Off-Line Quality Control.   An adaptation of experimental design to product design in the assembly industries has been developed by Taguchi (see Taguchi and Wu, 1978). The methodology is similar to that performed in the process industries for determining optimum operating conditions in pilot-plant and continuous production processes, i.e., the strategy begins with the identification of those factors having the greatest influence upon the response. The Taguchi approach considers engineering design and cost factors simultaneously with environmental factors that may later influence the use of the assembled product.

Phadke et al. (1983) describe an application of the Taguchi approach to the manufacturing planning for integrated circuits. The example concerns the dimensions of contact windows on an integrated chip. Windows that are not open or are too small result in loss of contact, while excessively large windows lead to shorted devices. Nine critical factors were selected, six at three levels and three at two levels, and an 18-run fractional factorial design was employed. Three dimensions were measured on each window. The problem was to determine the factor levels that would yield the least variability in window dimensions while simultaneously keeping the mean dimension on target. Taguchi calls factors that have a significant effect on process variability relative to mean performance "control" factors. Other factors that influence only mean performance are termed "signal" factors. The discovered control factors are placed at their optimum settings, and the discovered signal factors are employed to force the response to be on target. In the Phadke example, six factors were found to be control factors and one a signal factor. The resulting benefits were a 50 percent reduction in the standard deviation of window dimensions and a 40 percent reduction in visual defects. (A further discussion of this example is found in Section 16 under Application of Experimental Design to Optimize Process Variables.)

Inner and Outer Arrays.   As part of the Taguchi approach to product design, two experimental designs are run simultaneously in a split-plot fashion. One design, called the inner array, is used to identify those factors with the greatest and least influence upon both the mean and variance. To get an estimate of the variance at each experimental trial of the inner array, a second, outer array design is used in which minor modifications are made in selected factors to simulate the kinds of variability these factors may produce when the finished product is in the consumer's hands. Most or all of the k factors in the inner array may also be present in the outer array, along with still other environmental factors. Thus, an inner array might consist of a 2^{8-4} fractional design while the outer array consists of a 3^{4-2} design. The total number of experiments would then equal $(16)(9) = 144$.

RESPONSE SURFACE DESIGNS

Response Surface Methodology (RSM) has been successfully used to optimize many different kinds of industrial units, processes, and systems. It is an experimental approach and has been applied in research and development laboratories and sometimes on actual plant equipment itself. In the latter situation, however, Evolutionary Operation is often more appropriate. Evolutionary Operation is a gentle form of RSM that is useful for both objectives of screening and optimizing.

With RSM, selected important factors influencing the process are varied in a carefully chosen way, measurements are made on the operating capabilities of the process, and these data are analyzed to indicate in what ways the factors should be adjusted to improve performance. These steps may be repeated as often as is required. It is not necessary to be a statistician or mathematician to use these ideas. Quality control engineers can easily learn the fundamental principles and put them to use.

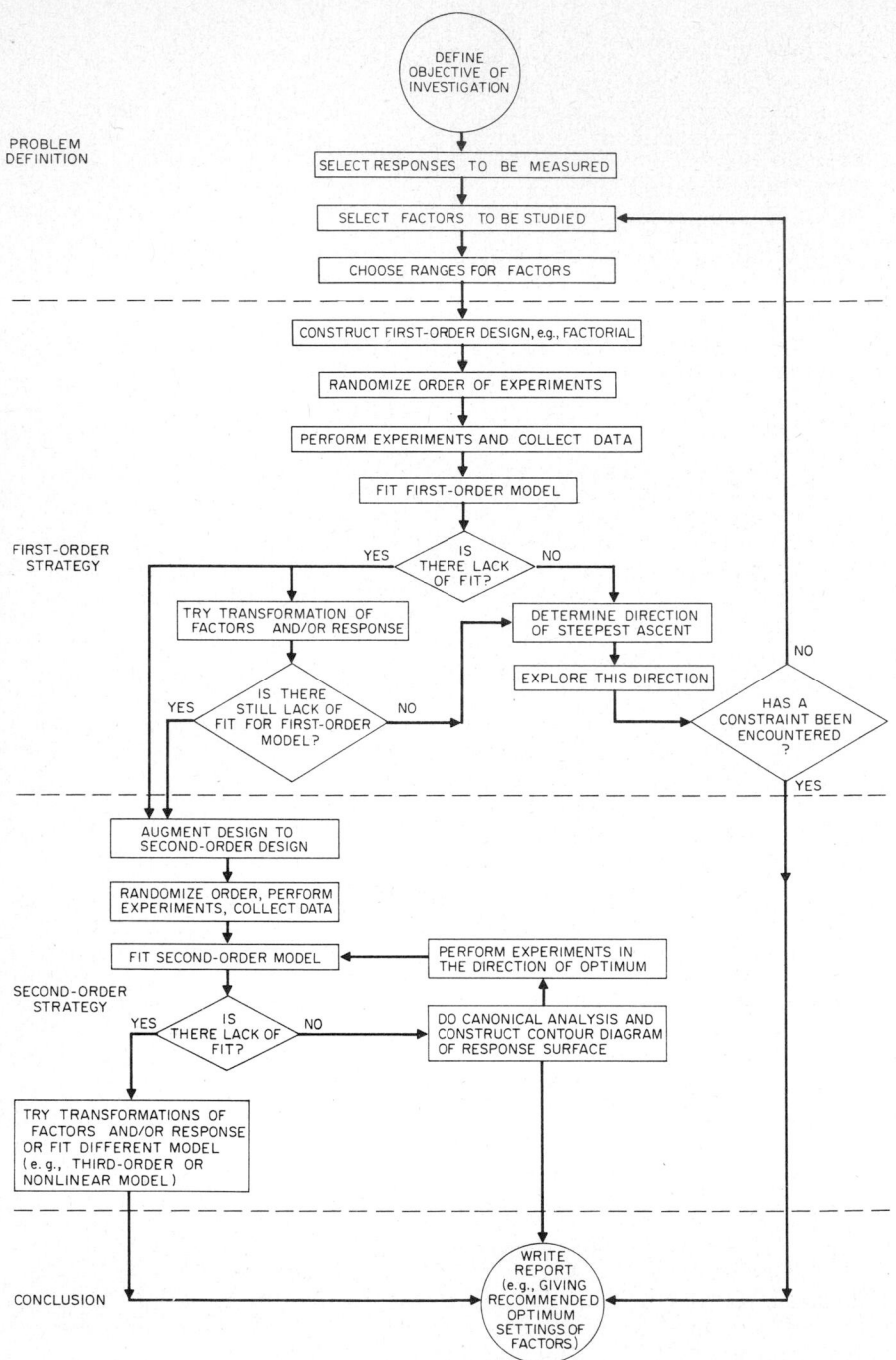

FIG. 26.10 Outline of main ideas of Response Surface Methodology.

In implementing RSM, a number of statistical procedures discussed in other sections of this Handbook are used. The concept of RSM was first developed and described by Box and Wilson (1951). At first RSM was used primarily as an experimental optimization technique in the chemical industry. Since then, however, it has found application in many other fields (see Hill and Hunter, 1966).

RSM can be usefully regarded as consisting of two stages:

1. First-order stage, in which a first-order mathematical model is contemplated, a factorial or other first-order design performed, the data fitted, the contours of the response surface drawn, and the direction of steepest ascent determined and pursued

2. Second-order stage, in which a second-order mathematical model is contemplated, a central-composite or other second-order design performed, the data fitted, the contours drawn, a canonical analysis performed, and an optimum located

Response Surface Methodology is actually more flexible than these brief definitions indicate. A skeletal outline, which shows some of the possible paths through an RSM study, is given in flow-diagram form in Figure 26.10.

Weakness of One-Variable-at-a-Time Approach. A popular method of experimentation is the one-factor-at-a-time approach. Each factor, in turn, is varied while all the rest of the factors are held at some fixed, constant levels. One trouble with this approach is that a false optimum can be reached. Consider the following hypothetical illustration.

Example. Under study is a chemical reaction in which there are two factors of interest, the concentration of one of the reactants and the time reaction. What settings for these two factors will maximize the yield? The best known settings, at the outset of the investigation, are a concentration of 25 percent and a time of 1 h.

Following a one-factor-at-a-time approach, the engineer first runs a series of experiments by varying the time, while holding the concentration at 25 percent. The results show that a maximum yield of about 65 percent is obtained when the time is 1.9 h. Holding the time fixed at this value, varying concentration, and obtaining a maximum at 25 percent, the engineer reaches the conclusion that the maximum yield (65 percent) is achieved when the concentration is 25 percent and the time is 1.9 h. This conclusion, however, is incorrect.

Response Surface. The actual situation, unknown to the experimenter, is shown in Figure 26.11. Here the yield is shown as a function of both concentration and time. The solid curved lines in the figure are contour lines of constant yield. For example, there is an entire set of conditions of concentration and time that give an 80 percent yield. The contour surface can be viewed as a mountain; the peak of the mountain is the point *P*. The contours of 90, 80, and so forth, can be viewed as altitudes. These numbers represent the percentage yields.

The engineer's objective was to find those settings for the concentration and time that would give the maximum yield. Viewed geometrically, what the engineer was trying to do was to climb to the highest point on the mountain. The attempt failed for a fairly simple reason.

Figuratively speaking, by varying time, the engineer first traversed the hill going along a path from point *A* to point *B* (see Figure 26.11). Between *A* and *E* the path led up the mountain, but then at point *E* it started to go down the other

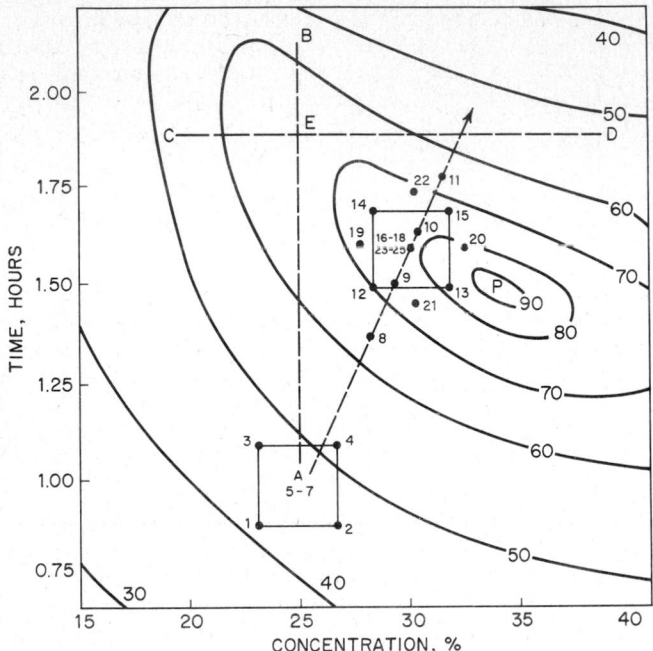

FIG. 26.11   Response surface showing yield of a chemical reaction as a function of concentration and time.

side. From point E to point B the engineer was walking down the other side of the hill. The traverse for varying concentration (C to E to D) is shown.

The experimenter has achieved a yield of only 65 percent (at E), whereas a yield in excess of 90 percent (at P) is possible. This higher yield can be achieved by *simultaneously* increasing concentration and decreasing time from the experimenter's reported "optimum" values.

If the contours of the hill were circular and there were no experimental error, this one-at-a-time-procedure would have taken the engineer to the highest point on the hill. In general, the contours of real response surfaces are not circular or spherical, and thus what is needed is a more sophisticated experimental strategy such as RSM.

Beginning of Program.   The RSM approach (see Figure 26.10) will now be applied to the example of maximizing the yield.

Define Objective of Investigation.   It is of the utmost importance to define clearly the objective of the study to be undertaken. It is surprising how often in practice this step is either ignored or not given the careful attention it deserves. This often leads to difficulties later on. In the present example the objective is to maximize the yield. The objective, in general, may involve multiple criteria.

Select Factors and Ranges.   The next step is to select the factors to be studied together with the ranges over which they are to be studied. It is necessary to understand the technical aspects of the experimental situation for this to be done intelligently. The specific *scale* over which each factor is to be studied must also be chosen. For example, instead of varying time linearly in units of hours, the experimenter might choose the basic scale to be the logarithm of the number of hours. In the present example, the variables concentration and time are selected. Initially, it is decided to vary concentration from 23 to 27 percent and time from 0.9 to 1.1.

First-Order Strategy

Construct Design and Collect Data. The 2^2 factorial design with three center points, shown in Table 26.25, is constructed. (Further discussion of the number of center points and other matters on setting up the design is given in Cochran and Cox, 1957, and Hunter, 1959.) The order of the seven runs is randomized,

TABLE 26.25   Results of First-Order Design

Run number	X_1 = concentration %	X_1 = concentration Coded units	X_2 = time Hours	X_2 = time Coded units	Y = yield %
1	23	-1	0.9	-1	43.7
2	27	$+1$	0.9	-1	44.5
3	23	-1	1.1	$+1$	47.2
4	27	$+1$	1.1	$+1$	51.8
5	25	0	1.0	0	46.8
6	25	0	1.0	0	45.9
7	25	0	1.0	0	45.3

Calculation of main effects

Concentration: $(-Y_1 + Y_2 - Y_3 + Y_4)/2 = (-43.7 + 44.5 - 47.2 + 51.8)/2 = 2.7$
Time: $(-Y_1 - Y_2 + Y_3 + Y_4)/2 = (-43.7 - 44.5 + 47.2 + 51.8)/2 = 5.4$
Interaction: $(+Y_1 - Y_2 - Y_3 + Y_4)/2 = (43.7 - 44.5 - 47.2 + 51.8)/2 = 1.9$
Curvature: $(+Y_1 + Y_2 + Y_3 + Y_4)/4 - (Y_5 + Y_6 + Y_7)/3 = 46.8 - 46.0 = 0.8$

Calculation of confidence intervals

Concentration: $\pm 2ts/\sqrt{n} = \pm 2(4.30)(0.755)/\sqrt{4} = \pm 3.25$
Time: $\pm 2ts/\sqrt{n} = \pm 2(4.30)(0.755)/\sqrt{4} = \pm 3.25$
Interaction: $\pm 2ts/\sqrt{n} = \pm 2(4.30)(0.755)/\sqrt{4} = \pm 3.25$
Curvature: $\pm ts\sqrt{(1/n) + (1/n_0)} = \pm (4.30)(0.755)\sqrt{(\frac{1}{4}) + (\frac{1}{3})}$
$= \pm 2.48$

Effects	Calculated 95% confidence interval, % yield
Concentration	2.7 ± 3.25
Time	5.4 ± 3.25
Interaction	1.9 ± 3.25
Curvature	0.8 ± 2.48

the experiments are performed, and the results shown in Table 26.25 are obtained. (Assume that, unknown to the engineer, the true relationship between X_1 and X_2 and the yield of product are given by the response surface shown in Figure 26.11.) The results are also shown in Figure 26.12.

Fit First-Order Model and Check for Lack of Fit. The analysis of these results can be carried out in either one of two equivalent ways. The effects and interaction of the factorial design can be calculated with their associated 95 percent confidence intervals, as is also shown in Table 26.25.

In addition, Table 26.25 shows how these confidence intervals were calculated. (The concept of confidence intervals is discussed in Section 23, under Statistical Estimation: Confidence Limits.) Note that Y_i is the yield for run number i, n is the number of runs in the factorial design (in this case four), n_0 is the number of center points (in this case three), and t is the appropriate t value for a 95 percent confidence interval. The quantity s is the square root of

$$s^2 = \frac{\displaystyle\sum_{i=5}^{7} (Y_i - \overline{Y}_0)^2}{n_0 - 1}$$

where $\overline{Y}_0$ is the average of the center points Y_5, Y_6, and Y_7. Of course, confidence intervals at levels different from 95 percent may be calculated. A curvature effect has been calculated, which is the difference between the average of the factorial design points (runs 1 to 4) and $\overline{Y}_0$ the average of the center points (runs 5 to 7).

As the center-point conditions have been repeated three times, an estimate of the variance can be readily obtained. (If repeat runs have not been performed, it might be possible to obtain an appropriate estimate in some other way, for example, from some external source, past experience, or from a technique like half-

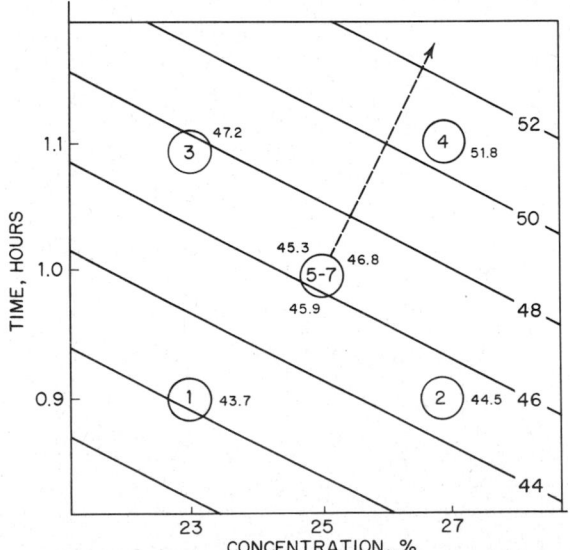

FIG. 26.12 Results of first-order design with fitted first-order (planar) response surface.

normal plots; see Daniel, 1959.) With the three values 46.8, 45.9, and 45.3, $s^2 =$ 0.57 is calculated as an estimate of the variance of an individual observation with two degrees of freedom.

These intervals suggest first that, since the statistics measuring second-order effects (interaction and curvature) are small, the relationship between time, concentration, and yield may be described geometrically as a plane. That is, there is no apparent lack of fit of the first-order model. Second, it appears that time is clearly important. The data suggest that longer time and perhaps higher concentration produce increased yield. A more precise analysis can be made using the equation

$$Y = \beta_0 + \beta_1 X_1 + \beta_2 X_2 + \epsilon$$

where the β's are constants whose values we can estimate from the data, Y is the measured value of the response (the yield), ϵ the random error, and

$$X_1 = \frac{\text{concentration}(\%) - 25}{5}$$

$$X_2 = \frac{\text{time(h)} - 1.0}{0.1}$$

The formulas for X_1 and X_2 code the original values of the settings, i.e., +1 for the high level, 0 for the middle level, and −1 for the low level (see Table 26.25). From our data, the fitted first-order model becomes

$$\hat{Y} = 46.46 + 1.35 X_1 + 2.70 X_2$$

which is a regression equation the coefficients of which can be obtained by standard regression techniques. (See Section 23.) Alternatively, in this case since a factorial design has been employed, the constant term can be obtained by calculating the average, that is, $\overline{Y} = 46.46$, and the other two values can be obtained by calculating ½ concentration effect = ½(2.7) = 1.35 and ½ time effect = ½(5.4) = 2.70.

A second method for evaluating the fit is to use the analysis of variance. The resulting ANOVA table (Table 26.26) indicates that the first-order model (above equation) adequately fits the data. (See Section 23; also Draper and Smith, 1981.) The ratio of the lack of fit mean square divided by the pure error mean square is 4.13, and since this value is less than $F_{2,2}(0.95) = 19.0$, there is no evidence of

TABLE 26.26   ANOVA Table: First-Order Model, First Design*

Source	Sum of squares	Degrees of freedom	Mean square
Mean b_0	15,107.86	1	
b_1	7.29	1	7.29
b_2	29.16	1	29.16
Lack of fit	4.71	2	2.36
Pure error	1.14	2	0.57
Total	15,150.16	7	

*In the literature of response surface methodology, it is customary that the ANOVA table include a term for the sum of squares for the mean. In other uses of ANOVA, some authors exclude the sum of squares for the mean.

TABLE 26.27 Results of Second-Order Design

Run number	Concentration (coded units)X_1	Time (coded units)X_2	Yield Y, %
	First-order design		
12	-1	-1	69.3
13	$+1$	-1	85.1
14	-1	$+1$	72.8
15	$+1$	$+1$	73.6
16	0	0	80.9
17	0	0	78.4
18	0	0	80.4
	Augmenting runs		
19	$-\sqrt{2}$	0	71.4
20	$+\sqrt{2}$	0	78.9
21	0	$-\sqrt{2}$	73.9
22	0	$+\sqrt{2}$	69.1
23	0	0	76.4
24	0	0	78.5
25	0	0	76.3

lack of fit of the first-order model. Since there is no evident lack of fit, it is reasonable to study the implications of the fitted first-order model (above equation). The plane described by this equation is represented in Figure 26.12 by the straight contour lines.

Determine Direction of Steepest Ascent. The direction of steepest ascent is indicated in Figure 26.12. (For further details on direction of steepest ascent, see Cochran and Cox, 1957, p. 357, and Davies, 1954, chap. 11.) It is perpendicular to the contour lines. Four experiments (numbers 8 to 11) in this direction indicate that the center of a second design should be approximately at a concentration of 31 percent and a time of 1.6 h. The design employed and the data obtained after performing the runs in random order are shown in Table 26.27 as runs 12 to 18. An analysis of the data shows apparent lack of fit (Table 26.28). The ratio of the

TABLE 26.28 ANOVA Table: First-Order Model, Second Design

Source	Sum of squares	Degrees of freedom	Mean square
Mean b_0	41,734.32	1	
b_1	68.89	1	68.89
b_2	16.00	1	16.00
Lack of fit	94.12	2	47.06
Pure error	3.50	2	1.75
Total	41,916.83	7	

lack of fit mean square divided by the pure error mean square is 26.8, and since this value is greater than $F_{2,2}(0.95) = 19.0$, there is evidence of lack of fit of the first-order model.

Second-Order Strategy

Construct Design and Collect Data. Since lack of fit is detected, the design is augmented by adding runs 19 to 25 to form the second-order (central composite) design shown in Table 26.27. (In general, if a model does not fit, it may be advantageous, instead of immediately considering a higher-order model, to consider transformations of the factors and/or the responses. See Box and Cox, 1964, Box and Tidwell, 1962, and Draper and Hunter, 1967.)

Fit Second-Order Model and Check for Lack of Fit. The fitted second-order equation obtained by least squares is

$$\hat{Y} = 78.50 + 3.40X_1 - 1.85X_2 - 3.75X_1X_2 - 1.21X_1^2 - 3.03X_2^2$$

The contours of this equation are shown in Figure 26.13 with the second-order design results. No lack of fit is evident from either visual inspection or statistical calculation (see Table 26.29). The form of the above equation can be simplified so the shape of the response surface can be better appreciated. It is difficult to visualize the surface from the equation because it contains six constants. A canonical analysis, which involves a translation and rotation of the coordinates from

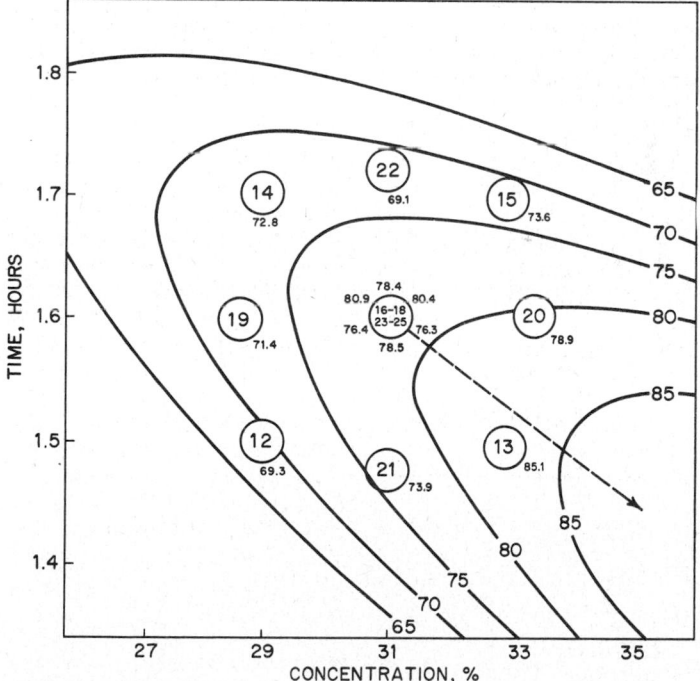

FIG. 26.13 Results of second-order design with fitted second-order (non-planar) response surface.

TABLE 26.29   ANOVA Table: Second-Order Model

Source	Sum of squares	Degrees of freedom	Mean square
Mean b_0	81,016.07	1	
First-order b_i	119.87	2	59.94
Pure second-order b_{ii}	80.73	2	40.37
Mixed second-order b_{ij}	56.25	1	56.25
Lack of fit	2.23	3	0.74
Pure error	21.77	5	4.35
Total	81,296.92	14	

Note: The ratio of the lack of fit mean square divided by the pure error mean square is 0.17, and since this value is less than $F_{0.95}$ for 3, 5 degrees of freedom (5.41), there is no evidence of lack of fit of the second-order model.

the original (X_1, X_2) axes to the new (Z_1, Z_2) axes, gives an equation containing only three constants:

$$Y - 173.83 = -0.0332Z_1^2 - 8.4075Z_2^2$$

This equation indicates that because of the negative coefficients for Z_1^2 and Z_2^2, the fitted response surface has a maximum point. A direction in which to proceed at the next stage to search for the maximum is indicated by the arrow in Figure 26.13. The arrow points toward the "top of the mountain." The investigation might terminate after experimenting in this direction, perhaps with a few added points in the vicinity of the maximum. In some situations it may be useful to perform a full second-order design near the final optimum. (For further details on canonical analysis and RSM in general, see Davies, 1954, Myers, 1971, or Box and Draper, 1987.)

BLOCK DESIGNS

The several levels, or versions, of a studied factor or group of studied factors are called "treatments," and the major objective of an experimenter is to study the influences of these different treatment levels upon some response. Often all the levels of the studied factors are repeated on another day or with a different operator, machine, supply of raw materials, etc. Each complete replication of the set of treatments is called a "block." The experimenter should plan the treatments so as to prevent differences between the blocks from influencing the comparisons between the treatments. For example, if the blocks in the experiment are time periods, the first aim of the experiment is to evaluate the effects of the studied factors free of the effects of time-caused differences. A secondary aim might actually be to measure the effects of the time periods to help in planning future experiments. In blocked designs it is generally assumed that blocking factors do not interact with studied factors. In the simplest block designs the data, when taken, can be summarized in a two-way table, as illustrated in Table 26.30. Note that this design is *not* a factorial design. In a factorial design all the factors (here rows and columns) are studied factors whereas in the design under consideration here, the blocking factor is not under the control of the experimenter. The block-

TABLE 26.30 Schematic for a Simple Block Design

	Treatments			
	1	2	$\cdots$	k
Block 1	y_{11}	y_{12}	$\cdots$	y_{1k}
Block 2	y_{21}	y_{22}	$\cdots$	y_{2k}
.	.	.	.	.
.	.	.	.	.
.	.	.	.	.
Block b	y_{b1}	y_{b2}	$\cdots$	y_{bk}

ing factor is, however, recognized as capable of influencing the response. The experimenter's objective is to remove from the influences of the studied factors any possible contributions to the response that are provided by the blocking factors. Blocking factors are commonly environmental phenomena outside the control of the experimenter.

The interest in the factor called blocks has several objectives. Some of these are:

1. The aim of the experimenter is to estimate effects of treatments free of block effects; numerical estimates of block effects are not particularly needed. For example, if blocks are days, day-to-day differences should be eliminated as sources of variability and are of no particular interest in themselves.

2. The primary aim is to estimate effects of the treatments (the studied factors) and secondarily to have estimates of block effects.

3. Sometimes the treatment effects and the block effects are of almost equal interest. In this case a "block design" is analogous to a "two-factor experiment," but the experimenter must be sure that the studied and blocking factors do not interact before using a block design data analysis. If interaction between factors exists or is suspected, the design and analysis for a factorial experiment must then be used.

A block design (with one-way blocking) can be considered as a one-factor design or a two-factor-no-interaction design. The simplest design with one-way blocking is the "randomized block design."

RANDOMIZED BLOCK DESIGN

In comparing a number of treatments, it is clearly desirable that all other conditions be kept as nearly constant as possible. Unfortunately, the required number of tests is often too large to be carried out under similar conditions. In such cases, the experimenter may be able to divide the experiment into blocks, or planned homogeneous groups. When each such group in the experiment contains exactly one observation on every treatment, the experimental plan is called a randomized block plan. The treatments are run *in a random order* within the blocks.

There are many situations in which a randomized block plan can be profitably utilized. For example, a comparison of several levels of some factor may take several days to complete. If we anticipate that the different days may also have an influence upon the response, then we might plan to observe each of the factor levels on each day. A day would then represent a block. In another situation, several operators may be conducting the tests, and differences between operators may be expected. The tests or observations made by a given operator can be considered to represent a block. The size of a block—that is, the number of tests contained within the block—may be restricted by physical considerations. In general, a randomized block plan is one in which each of the treatments appears exactly once in every block. The treatments are allocated to experimental units at random within a given block. The results of a randomized block experiment can be exhibited in a two-way table such as Table 26.31, in which we have $b = 4$ blocks and $k = 6$ treatments. Since each treatment occurs exactly once in every block, the treatment totals or averages are directly comparable without adjustment.

Example. The data in Table 26.31 represent the conversion gain of four resistors measured under six different conditions. The response, conversion gain, is defined as the ratio of available current-noise power to applied dc power expressed in decibel units and is a measure of the efficiency with which a resistor converts dc power to available current-noise power. Each test condition involves the same four resistors. The experimenter is interested in comparing differences between conditions (the studied factor) clear of possible influences due to the resistors (the blocking factor). A quick review of Table 26.31 indicates large differences between the resistors, i.e., between the block averages. The key question is whether, with this resistor variability eliminated, the experimenter can now detect real differences between the test conditions since the differences between the observed test condition averages are small and may merely reflect experimental error.

Analysis. The analysis of a randomized block experiment depends on a number of assumptions. We assume that each of the observations is the sum of four components. If we let y_{ij} be the observation on the ith treatment in the jth block, then

$$y_{ij} = \eta + \phi_i + \beta_j + \epsilon_{ij}$$

The term η is the grand mean, ϕ_i is the effect of treatment i, β_j the effect of block j, and ϵ_{ij} the experimental error associated with the measurement y_{ij}. (The sub-

TABLE 26.31 Randomized Block Design Response: Conversion Gain of Resistors

Resistor (blocks)	Test set (treatments)						Row total	Row average
	1	2	3	4	5	6		
1	138.0	141.6	137.5	141.8	138.6	139.6	$B_1 = 837.1$	$b_1 = 139.52$
2	152.2	152.2	152.1	152.2	152.0	152.8	$B_2 = 913.5$	$b_2 = 152.25$
3	153.6	154.0	153.8	153.6	153.2	153.6	$B_3 = 921.8$	$b_3 = 153.63$
4	141.4	141.5	142.6	142.2	141.1	141.9	$B_4 = 850.7$	$b_4 = 141.78$

Column totals

$T_1 = 585.2$ $T_2 = 589.3$ $T_3 = 586.0$ $T_4 = 589.8$ $T_5 = 584.9$ $T_6 = 587.9$ Grand total $G = 3523.1$

Column averages

$\bar{y}_1 = 146.30$ $\bar{y}_2 = 147.32$ $\bar{y}_3 = 146.50$ $\bar{y}_4 = 147.45$ $\bar{y}_5 = 146.22$ $\bar{y}_6 = 146.98$

scripts $i = 1, 2, \ldots, k$ and $j = 1, 2, \ldots, b$.) The mean for the ith treatment equals $\eta + \phi_i$, and the mean for the jth block equals $\eta + \beta_j$. The terms ϕ_i and β_j represent, respectively, the unique contributions (effects) of treatments and blocks. The estimate of the mean η is given by $\bar{y}$, the grand average. Letting $\bar{y}_i$ equal the average for the ith treatment, the estimate of treatment effect ϕ_i is $\bar{y}_i - \bar{y}$. Similarly, $\bar{y}_j - \bar{y}$ estimates the block effect β_j.

In order to make interval estimates for or tests of hypotheses on the treatment or block contributions, we assume that the values of the experimental error ϵ_{ij} are independently and normally distributed with constant variance. If the experiment is randomized properly, failure of these assumptions will, in general, not cause serious difficulty.

A more serious difficulty occurs when count data are recorded. Count data are frequently Poisson-distributed, and hence the variance of the observations is linked directly to their mean. In such circumstances, it is best first to take the square roots of the count data and then to proceed with the estimation of effects and the analysis of variance.

Analysis of the Treatment Effects.   The plot of the $k = 6$ treatment averages is displayed in Figure 26.14.

To construct an appropriate reference distribution for these averages or to test hypotheses concerning the treatment effects, an estimate of σ^2 is required. Using the model, the associated analysis of variance table can now be constructed. The procedure is:

1. Compute the corrected sum of squares (TSS)

$$\text{TSS} = \sum_i \sum_j y_{ij}^2 - \frac{G^2}{kb}$$

i.e., compute the sum of the squares of all the observations and subtract G^2/kb, where $G = \sum_i \sum_j y_{ij}$ is the grand total.

2. Compute the sum of squares of the b blocks (SSB)

$$\text{SSB} = \frac{B_1^2 + B_2^2 + \cdots + B_b^2}{k} - \frac{G^2}{kb}$$

3. Compute the sum of squares of the t treatments (SST)

$$\text{SST} = \frac{T_1^2 + T_2^2 + \cdots + T_k^2}{b} - \frac{G^2}{kb}$$

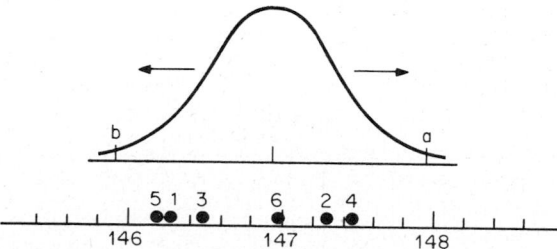

FIG. 26.14   Plot of $k = 6$ treatment averages and their reference t-distribution. (Distance from a to $b = 2ts/\sqrt{b} = 2.02$.) Numbers above scale are treatment numbers from Table 26.31.

4. Compute the estimate of the variance

$$s^2 = \frac{\text{TSS} - \text{SSB} - \text{SST}}{(b-1)(k-1)}$$

This estimate has $v = (b-1)(k-1)$ degrees of freedom.

5. Compute $t_{v,\alpha/2}s/\sqrt{b}$ (there are b observations in each treatment average), and construct a reference distribution such that 95 percent of the area lies within $\pm ts/\sqrt{b}$, where t has $v = (k-1)(b-1)$ degrees of freedom.

6. To test the hypothesis that the treatment effects equal zero (or equivalently that all treatment means are equal), select a level of significance α for the test. Commonly, the level of α is equal to that used in Step 5 above.

7. Compute the F ratio, where $F_{v_1, v_2} = [\text{SST}/(k-1)]/s^2$ and where the degrees of freedom are $v_1 = (k-1)$ and $v_2 = (t-1)(b-1)$. If this computed F is greater than that given in Appendix II, Table K, reject the hypothesis that all treatment effects are zero.

Example. Use the data in Table 26.31 with $b = 4$, $k = 6$.

1. TSS $= 518,123.130 - 517,176.40 = 946.730$

2. SSB $= 518,104,065 - 517,176.40 = 927.665$

3. SST $= 517,181.998 - 517,176.40 = 5.598$

4. $s^2 = 13.467/15 = 0.8978$; $s = 0.9478$; $v = 15$.

5. $2ts/\sqrt{b} = 2(2.13)(0.9478)/\sqrt{4} = 2.02$. See Figure 26.14.

6. $\alpha = 0.05$

7. $F_{5,15} = 1.196/0.8978 = 1.2470$. The critical value of $F_{5,15} = 2.90$. We cannot reject the hypothesis that the treatment effects are zero.

Comment. Figure 26.14 displays the reference distribution for the $k = 6$ treatment averages. The figure, a bell-shaped curve such that 95 percent of its area is contained within $2ts/\sqrt{b}$ (here a total distance of 2.02), can be sketched in by hand. More exact constructions require the ordinates of the t distribution. Graphical imagery is the objective here, and great precision in drawing the bell-shaped t distribution is not essential for a reasonable analysis. The six averages do appear, reasonably, all to have come from a single distribution with a fixed but unknown mean n. The experimenter may thus conclude that there are no differences between the treatment averages over and beyond those caused by random error variations. Each of the averages is but an estimate of the same population mean.

The graphical interpretation using the reference distribution is supported by the exact F test. However, other inferences come quickly to mind upon viewing Figure 26.14. For example, the analyst might note that if the reference distribution is placed over averages 1, 3, and 5, then the averages 2, 4, and 6 do not appear as reasonable events drawn from that distribution. Or if the distribution is placed over averages 2 and 4, then the averages 1 and 5 or 1, 5, and 3 appear as outliers. The analyst is now faced with the problem of *multiple comparisons.*

An extensive literature exists on the topic of multiple comparisons; the question concerns how best to make reasonable comparisons between k treatment means and maintain a fixed α risk (see Duncan, 1955, Tukey, 1949, Scheffe, 1953, Keuls, 1952, and Box, Hunter, and Hunter, 1978). Good practice requires that the analyst not try to test every hypothesis imaginable but rather only those few

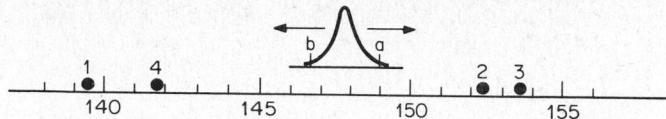

FIG. 26.15 Plot of b = 4 block averages from Table 26.31 and their reference t-distribution. (Distance from a to b = $2ts/\sqrt{k}$ = 1.65.)

hypotheses that appear reasonable in the light of information from outside the data.

Analysis of the Block Effects. The plot of the $b = 4$ block averages appears in Figure 26.15. The block computations are similar to those completed earlier for the treatments.

8. The interval containing 95 percent of the appropriate t reference distribution is given by $\pm t_\nu s/\sqrt{k}$ (there are k observations in each block average), $\nu = (k - 1)(b - 1)$.

9. Using the same α level as in Step 6, to test the hypothesis that the block effects β_j equal zero, compute the F ratio $F_{\nu_1,\nu_2} = [SSB/(b - 1)]/s^2$ where the number of degrees of freedom $\nu_1 = (b - 1)$ and $\nu_2 = (k - 1)(b - 1)$. If this computed F_{ν_1,ν_2} is greater than that given in Appendix II, Table K, reject the hypothesis that all block effects are zero.

Example

8. Calculate $2ts/\sqrt{k} = 2(2.13)(0.9478)/\sqrt{6} = 1.65$. This scaled t distribution is plotted in Figure 26.14.

9. With $\alpha = 0.05$, $F_{3,15} = (927.605/3)/0.8968 = 344.81$. The critical value of $F_{3,15} = 3.29$. The observed F is very unusual, and the analyst rejects the hypothesis that the block effects are zero.

Comment. On viewing Figure 26.15 it is obvious that the reference distribution, wherever located, cannot reasonably account for the four averages. Further, it is clear that block averages 1 and 4 are distinctly separable from block averages 2 and 3, and if the analyst slides the reference distribution to the vicinity of averages 1 and 4, we may even suspect that these two averages are also unlikely to be events from some single distribution. The graphical display does, however, suggest that block averages 2 and 3 may indeed be from a single distribution.

A plot of the averages along with their appropriate t reference distribution, coupled with the notion that the reference distribution may be slid back and forth, provides a powerful *approximate graphical* tool for the analysis of experimental data. When required, detailed arithmetical analyses can always be devised to test more precisely the hypotheses suggested by the graphical display. An alternative approximate graphical analysis is provided by the "analysis of means" which employs a Shewhart chart to distinguish meaningful effects. See Ott, 1975.

BALANCED INCOMPLETE BLOCK DESIGNS

In an incomplete block design, all the treatments cannot be accommodated within a single block. To illustrate, consider a production manager who wishes to study the differences between the products supplied by six different suppliers. Unfortunately, personnel and equipment limit the number of suppliers that can be studied to three a day. The production manager is concerned that day-to-day differences might upset comparisons between suppliers and wishes to block the contributions of days, but the individual blocks are not large enough to encompass all six treatments. The appropriate experimental design to use is a "balanced incomplete block design," as illustrated in Table 26.32. The six suppliers (treatments) labeled A, B, C, D, E, and F are then studied in groups of three within each day (block). The blocks and the sequence of trials within the blocks are to be chosen in some random order.

Note that in the design displayed in Table 26.32 every letter supplier is tested the same number of times and every pair of letters appears within a block the same number of times. Another design appropriate to the case of six treatments constrained to be studied three at a time is the "combinatoric" design, that is, a design consisting of all combinations of six things taken three at a time. The combinatoric balanced incomplete block would have required 20 blocks; the design illustrated in Table 26.32 requires only 10.

One consequence of using an incomplete block design is that each treatment average must be adjusted for the blocks in which it appears and the differences between the *adjusted* treatment averages appraised. The computations are straightforward but go beyond what can be accommodated in this handbook. Interested readers are referred to Cochran and Cox (1957) or Natrella (1963).

To enumerate the situations in which it is possible to construct a balanced incomplete block design, the quantities r, b, t, k, L, E, and N are defined as follows:

r = number of replications (the number of times a treatment appears)

b = number of blocks in the plan

t = number of treatments

k = block size, i.e., the number of treatments that can appear in each block

L = number of blocks in which a given treatment pair appears: $L = r(k - 1)/(t - 1)$

E = a constant used in the analysis: $E = tL/rk$

N = total number of observations: $N = tr = bk$

Plans are indexed in Table 26.33 for $4 < t < 10$ and $r < 10$. For an extensive listing of the designs and many worked examples see Cochran and Cox (1957) and Natrella (1963).

General Comments on Block Designs. In the simplest type of block design, Randomized Blocks, each block is large enough to accommodate all the treatments one wishes to test. In Incomplete Block Designs, the block size is not large enough for all treatments to be tested in every block. In Balanced Incomplete Block Designs, treatments are assigned to blocks that lead to equal precision in the estimation of differences between treatments.

If Randomized Block and Balanced Incomplete Block Designs do not meet the needs of the experimenter with regard to number of blocks, size of blocks, number of treatments, etc., other kinds of plans are available, for example, *partially* balanced incomplete block designs (Clatworthy, 1973), and "chain block" designs, which are useful whenever observations are expensive and the experimental error is small. (See Mandel, 1954, and Natrella, 1963, for the structure and details of analysis.)

TABLE 26.32 A Balanced Incomplete Block Design

Days	Before randomization	After randomization	Six treatments A B C D E F
1	ABE	DBC	t = 6 treatments
2	ABF	CDA	b = 10 blocks
3	ACD	FBD	k = 3 treatments/block
4	ACF	CEB	r = 5 replicates/treatment
5	ADE	DEF	L = 2, i.e., each
6	BCD	EBA	treatment pair
7	BCE	AFB	appears twice
8	BDF	DEA	
9	CEF	FCE	
10	DEF	CFA	

TABLE 26.33 Balanced Incomplete Block Plans ($4 < t < 10$ and $r < 10$)

t	k	r	b	L	E^*	Plan†
4	2	3	6	1	2/3	1
	3	3	4	2	8/9	Comb‡
5	2	4	10	1	5/8	2
	3	6	10	3	5/6	Comb
	4	4	5	3	15/16	Comb
6	2	5	15	1	3/5	3
	3	5	10	2	4/5	4
	3	10	20	4	4/6	5
	4	10	15	6	9/10	6
	5	5	6	4	24/25	Comb
7	2	6	21	1	7/12	Comb
	3	3	7	1	7/9	7
	4	4	7	2	7/8	8
	6	6	7	5	35/36	Comb
8	2	7	28	1	4/7	9
	4	7	14	3	6/7	10
	7	7	8	6	48/49	Comb
9	2	8	36	1	9/16	Comb
	3	4	12	1	3/4	11
	4	8	18	3	27/32	12
	5	10	18	5	9/10	13
	6	8	12	15	15/16	14
	8	8	9	7	63/64	Comb
10	2	9	45	1	5/9	15
	3	9	30	2	20/27	16
	4	6	15	2	5/6	17
	5	9	18	4	8/9	18
	6	9	15	5	25/27	19
	9	9	10	18	80/81	Comb

*The constant $E = tL/rk$ is used in this analysis.
†For the plan classification number see Clatworthy (1973).
‡"Comb" indicates plans constructed by taking all possible combinations of t treatments in groups (block size) of k.

Covariance Analysis. On some occasions the phenomenon to be blocked is not a simple aggregate, such as a day or a machine operator, but a continuous phenomenon such as a time trend, a temperature gradient, or the age of each test item. On these occasions, if both the response observed and its associated covariate measurement are recorded, a statistical analysis procedure called "covariance analysis" can eliminate the effect of the covariate both from the estimate of variance and from the estimated effects of the studied treatments. The computations can become difficult, and the services of a professional experimental statistician should be evoked. A good reference is Cochran and Cox (1957).

LATIN SQUARE DESIGNS

A Latin square plan (or a Youden square plan, described later) is useful when it is necessary to investigate the effects of different levels of a studied factor while simultaneously allowing for two specific sources of variability or nonhomogeneity in the conditions affecting test results, i.e., two different blocking variables. Such designs were originally applied in agricultural experimentation when the sources of nonhomogeneity in fertility were simply the two directions on the field, and the "square" was literally a square plot of ground. Its usage has been extended to many other applications in which there are two sources of nonhomogeneity (two blocking variables) that may affect experimental results—for example, machines and positions or operators and days. The studied variable, the experimental treatment, is then associated with the two blocking variables in a prescribed fashion. The use of Latin squares is restricted by two conditions:

1. The number of rows, columns, and treatments must all be equal.
2. There must be no interactions between the row, the column, and the studied factors (see Factorial Experiments—General, for discussion of interaction).

Youden square plans are less restrictive than Latin squares: the number of rows, columns, and treatments need not be the same, but only certain numbers of combinations are possible.

As an example of a Latin square, suppose we wish to compare four materials with regard to their wearing qualities. Suppose further that we have a wear-testing machine that can handle four samples simultaneously. The two blocking variables might be the variations from run to run and the variations among the four positions on the wear machine. A 4 × 4 Latin square will allow for both sources of

TABLE 26.34 A 4 × 4 Latin Square

Run	Position number			
	1	2	3	4
1	A	B	C	D
2	B	C	D	A
3	C	D	A	B
4	D	A	B	C

inhomogeneity. The Latin square plan is as shown in Table 26.34 (the four materials are labeled *A*, *B*, *C*, *D*).

Examples of Latin squares from size 3×3 to 7×7 are given in Table 26.35. In the case of the 4×4 Latin square, four different squares are given. One of the four should be selected at random. The procedure to be followed in using a given Latin square is as follows:

1. Permute the columns at random.
2. Permute the rows at random.
3. Assign letters randomly to the treatments.

If squares of 5×5 and higher are used, then, strictly speaking, each time we use one we should choose a square at random from the set of all possible squares. The Fisher and Yates tables (1964) give complete representations of the squares from 4×4 to 6×6 and sample squares up to 12×12.

The results of a Latin square experiment are recorded in a two-way table similar to the plan itself. The treatment totals and the row and column totals of the Latin square plan are each directly comparable without adjustment.

The analysis of the Latin square design is discussed in many textbooks; see the references at the end of this section. The reader is warned that the mathematical model underlying the analysis of the Latin square designs assumes that no interactions exist between rows, columns, and treatments. Failure to meet these assumptions leads to biased estimates of the treatment effects and, what is equally serious, to a biased estimate of the variance. The Latin square is *not* a factorial design, i.e., an experimental program that allows interactions between the separate factors comprising the design. Some of the difficulties with analysis can be avoided either by fully repeating the design or through partial replication (see Youden and Hunter, 1955).

The Latin square designs can be modified to include additional blocking factors. The Greco-Latin square and hyper-Greco-Latin square designs are also described in the Fisher and Yates tables (1964) and in many texts.

TABLE 26.35   Selected Latin Squares

		4×4		
3×3	1	2	3	4
A B C	A B C D	A B C D	A B C D	A B C D
B C A	B A D C	B C D A	B D A C	B A D C
C A B	C D B A	C D A B	C A D B	C D A B
	D C A B	D A B C	D C B A	D C B A

5×5	6×6	7×7
A B C D E	A B C D E F	A B C D E F G
B A E C D	B F D C A E	B C D E F G A
C D A E B	C D E F B A	C D E F G A B
D E B A C	D A F E C B	D E F G A B C
E C D B A	E C A B F D	E F G A B C D
	F E B A D C	F G A B C D E
		G A B C D E F

YOUDEN SQUARE DESIGNS

The Youden square, like the Latin square, allows for two experimental sources of inhomogeneity. The conditions for the use of the Youden square, however, are less restrictive than those for the Latin square. The use of Latin square plans is restricted by the fact that the number of rows, columns, and treatments must all be the same. Youden squares have the same number of columns and treatments, but a fairly wide choice in the number of rows is possible. We use the following notation:

t = number of treatments to be compared

b = number of levels of one blocking variable (columns)

k = number of levels of another blocking variable (rows)

r = number of replications of each treatment

L = number of times that two treatments occur in the same block

In a Youden square, $t = b$ and $k = r$.

Some Youden square plans are given in Table 26.36. The analysis of the Youden squares must be carefully handled; in particular, the treatment averages must be adjusted for the rows in which they appear *before* they can be compared. Further, the standard error of the adjusted averages requires special computation. Reference should be made to the textbooks listed at the end of this section for the numerical details.

NESTED DESIGNS

Most experimental designs are primarily intended to provide estimates of the means and differences between the means of experimental treatments or factors.

TABLE 26.36 Youden Square Arrangements

$t = 3$	$t = 4$	$t = 5$
A B	A B C	A B C D
B C	B A D	B A E C
C A	C D B	C D A E
	D C A	D E B A
		E C D B

$t = 6$	$t = 7$	or	$t = 7$
A B C D E	A B D		A C D E
B F D C A	B C E		B D E F
C D E F B	C D F		C E F G
D A F E C	D E G		D F G A
E C A B F	E F A		E G A B
F E B A D	F G B		F A B C
	G A C		G B C D

However, in many sampling studies and in investigations of test methods, the studied factors may be sources of variation and the primary information sought is knowledge of the relative variability of the sources, that is, the "components of variance" assignable to the sources. Designs intended to provide this information—i.e., estimates of variance at various stages of a sampling scheme or analytical test method—are called "nested" or "hierarchical" designs. In experiments that are not components of variance studies but in which some experimental factors are "nested" rather than "crossed" (see Two-Factor Experiments), similar information is sought for some factors, e.g., the variability among levels of one factor *nested* within another factor. A simple example of a nested design is shown in Figure 26.16, where two samples are taken and duplicate tests made on each sample.

The primary information sought is estimates of the variability of tests made on the same sample and the variability of tests across the different samples. This is a two-stage balanced nested design; if the same number of subunits is taken from each unit at any stage, the design is called "balanced." Figure 26.17 shows balanced three-, four-, and five-stage nested designs, with one unit at the primary stage A.

When a separate experimental design is run to discover the influence of additional factors *within* a block, the resulting configuration is called a "split-plot" design. The estimation of the main plot (block) and within-plot effects and, more particularly, the determination of the appropriate variance of each effect must be carefully handled. The analysis of balanced completely nested designs and split-plot designs may be found in many standard textbooks; see Appendix 6B of Davies (1954), Montgomery (1976), or Snedecor and Cochran (1980). For the analysis of a two-stage nested design, see the analysis of variance for Completely Randomized Design, given above, and calculate the components of variance as described for the Random Effects Model under One-way Analysis of Variance—Models. For the more complicated "nested factorials," where some factors are crossed and some are nested, see Hicks (1982), Steel and Torrie (1962), or Snedecor and Cochran (1980). Some useful rules for determining the expected mean squares in the analysis of variance are given by Lenter (1965). A Bayesian method for estimating variance components is given in Box and Tiao (1973).

In Figure 26.17, at each stage only two subunits of each unit are taken, but the total number of tests multiplies rapidly as the number of stages increases. Because of the rapidly increasing total number of tests, only a few units are usually used at the top levels. In other words, balanced nested designs tend to provide too little information on the upper levels (the initial stages, or factors A and B) and often provide more than enough information at the bottom levels (factors E, for example). Bainbridge (1965) has considered alternative "unbalanced" nested designs with a fixed total number of tests. He prefers a design, which he calls a "staggered nested design," that is easy to administer and provides about the same number of degrees of freedom for each factor. Bainbridge shows staggered nested designs

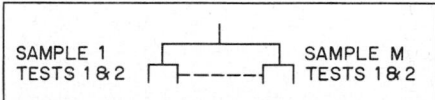

FIG. 26.16 A two-stage balanced nested design. *(Reprinted with permission from Bainbridge, 1965.)*

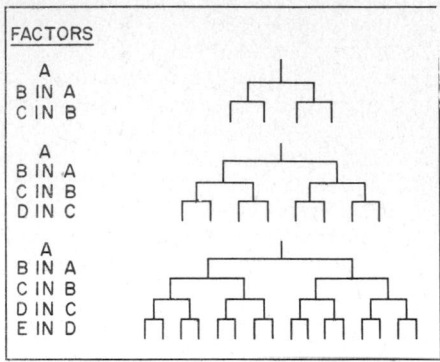

FIG. 26.17   Balanced nested designs for three, four, and five factors. *(Reprinted with permission from Bainbridge, 1965.)*

for three, four, five, and six factors (see Figure 26.18 for the designs and their analysis).

MIXTURE DESIGNS

In some experiments with mixtures, the property of interest depends on the proportions of the mixture components and not on the amounts (volume or weight) of the individual components. For example, stainless steel is a mixture of different metals, and its tensile strength depends on the proportions of the metallic elements present; gasoline is ordinarily a blend of various stocks, and the octane rating of the final blend depends on the proportions going into the blend. The proportions of the components of a mixture must add up to unity, and in the most general case the proportion of any component may range from zero to unity.

In the design of mixtures, the factor space available for experimentation is constrained, since the proportions used must sum to unity. It has been shown that if the number of components in the mixture is q, the available factor space becomes a regular $(q - 1)$-dimensional simplex (e.g., a triangle for $q = 3$, a tetrahedron for $q = 4$).

A natural approach would be to take a uniformly spaced distribution of experimental points over the available factor space. This results in the simplex lattice designs proposed by Scheffé (1958). A (q, m) lattice, for example, is a lattice for q components, where the proportions for each component have $m + 1$ equally spaced values from 0 to 1, i.e., the values 0, $1/m$, $2/m$, etc. For three components, the proportions of each component would be 0, ½, 1 when $m = 2$; and 0, ⅓, ⅔, 1 when $m = 3$. The lattice resulting when $m = 2$ is called the quadratic lattice, the lattice resulting when $m = 3$ is called the cubic lattice, etc. (see Figure 26.19).

In addition, modified lattices can be made by adding center points to the two-dimensional face or faces of the quadratic lattice. This provides a useful design called the "special cubic lattice."

The number of points k required for any lattice except the special cubic is found by using the formula

$$k = \frac{(m + q - 1)!}{m!(q - 1)!}$$

Sources of Variance	Sums of Squares	Degrees of Freedom	Expectations of Mean Squares	Format of A–Units
A	$(5) - CF$	$m-1$	$\sigma_c^2 + 1\frac{2}{3}\sigma_b^2 + 3\sigma_a^2$	
B in A	$(3) + (4) - (5)$	m	$\sigma_c^2 + 1\frac{1}{3}\sigma_b^2$	
C in B	$(1) + (2) - (3)$	m	σ_c^2	
Total	$(1) + (2) + (4) - CF$	$3m-1$	4A Three Factors	a b c
A	$(7) - CF$	$m-1$	$\sigma_d^2 + 1\frac{1}{2}\sigma_c^2 + 2\frac{1}{2}\sigma_b^2 + 4\sigma_a^2$	
B in A	$(5) + (6) - (7)$	m	$\sigma_d^2 + 1\frac{1}{6}\sigma_c^2 + 1\frac{1}{2}\sigma_b^2$	
C in B	$(3) + (4) - (5)$	m	$\sigma_d^2 + 1\frac{1}{3}\sigma_c^2$	
D in C	$(1) + (2) - (3)$	m	σ_d^2	
Total	$(1) + (2) + (4) + (6) - CF$	$4m-1$	4B Four Factors	a b c d
A	$(9) - CF$	$m-1$	$\sigma_e^2 + 1\frac{2}{5}\sigma_d^2 + 2\frac{1}{5}\sigma_c^2 + 3\frac{2}{5}\sigma_b^2 + 5\sigma_a^2$	
B in A	$(7) + (8) - (9)$	m	$\sigma_e^2 + 1\frac{1}{10}\sigma_d^2 + 1\frac{3}{10}\sigma_c^2 + 1\frac{3}{5}\sigma_b^2$	
C in B	$(5) + (6) - (7)$	m	$\sigma_e^2 + 1\frac{1}{6}\sigma_d^2 + 1\frac{1}{2}\sigma_c^2$	
D in C	$(3) + (4) - (5)$	m	$\sigma_e^2 + 1\frac{1}{3}\sigma_d^2$	
E in D	$(1) + (2) - (3)$	m	σ_e^2	
Total	$(1) + (2) + (4) + (6) + (8) - CF$	$5m-1$	4C Five Factors	a b c d e
A	$(11) - CF$	$m-1$	$\sigma_f^2 + 1\frac{1}{3}\sigma_e^2 + 2\sigma_d^2 + 3\sigma_c^2 + 4\frac{1}{3}\sigma_b^2 + 6\sigma_a^2$	
B in A	$(9) + (10) - (11)$	m	$\sigma_f^2 + 1\frac{1}{15}\sigma_e^2 + 1\frac{1}{5}\sigma_d^2 + 1\frac{2}{5}\sigma_c^2 + 1\frac{2}{3}\sigma_b^2$	
C in B	$(7) + (8) - (9)$	m	$\sigma_f^2 + 1\frac{1}{10}\sigma_e^2 + 1\frac{3}{10}\sigma_d^2 + 1\frac{3}{5}\sigma_c^2$	
D in C	$(5) + (6) - (7)$	m	$\sigma_f^2 + 1\frac{1}{6}\sigma_e^2 + 1\frac{1}{2}\sigma_d^2$	
E in D	$(3) + (4) - (5)$	m	$\sigma_f^2 + 1\frac{1}{3}\sigma_e^2$	
F in E	$(1) + (2) - (3)$	m	σ_f^2	
Total	$(1) + (2) + (4) + (6) + (8) + (10) - CF$	$6m-1$	4D Six Factors	a b c d e f

TOTALS NEEDED TO GET SUMS OF SQUARES

$(1) = \Sigma a^2$

$(2) = \Sigma b^2$

$(3) = \dfrac{\Sigma (a + b)^2}{2}$

$(4) = \Sigma c^2$

$(5) = \dfrac{\Sigma (a + b + c)^2}{3}$

$(6) = \Sigma d^2$

$(7) = \dfrac{\Sigma (a + b + c + d)^2}{4}$

$(8) = \Sigma e^2$

$(9) = \dfrac{\Sigma (a + b + c + d + e)^2}{5}$

$(10) = \Sigma f^2$

$(11) = \dfrac{\Sigma (a + b + c + d + e + f)^2}{6}$

$CF = \dfrac{(\text{Grand Total})^2}{\text{Total No. of Tests}}$

FIG. 26.18 Staggered nested designs for three, four, five, and six factors. *(Reprinted with permission from Bainbridge, 1965.)*

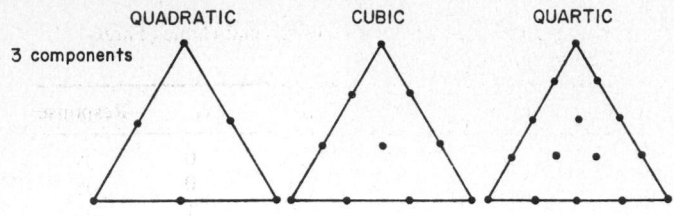

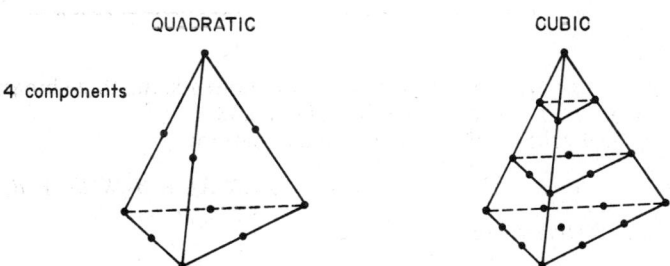

FIG. 26.19 Lattice designs for three- and four-component mixtures. *(Reprinted with permission from Gorman and Hinman, 1962.)*

The number of points required for the special cubic is

$$k = \frac{q(q+1)}{2} + \frac{q(q-1)(q-2)}{6}$$

The number of points required for several values of m and q is given in Table 26.37.

The property of interest is measured at each of the design points (corresponding to mixtures of different proportions). Simplified polynomials are used to relate the response variable y to the various mixture proportions used.

Another useful design called the "special cubic" by Scheffé (1958) requires seven points for three-component mixtures—the six points of a ($q = 3$, $m = 2$) lattice plus a seventh point at $X_1 = \frac{1}{3}$, $X_2 = \frac{1}{3}$, $X_3 = \frac{1}{3}$.

TABLE 26.37 Number of Points Required for Lattice Designs

Number of components q	Type of lattice			
	Quadratic, $m = 2$	Special cubic, $m = 2$	Cubic, $m = 3$	Quartic, $m = 4$
3	6	7	10	15
4	10	14	20	35
5	15	25	35	70
6	21	41	56	126
8	36	92	120	330

TABLE 26.38 Design Points for Special Cubic (Three-Component Mixture)

Point number	x_1	x_2	x_3	Response
1	1	0	0	y_1
2	0	1	0	y_2
3	0	0	1	y_3
4	½	½	0	y_4
5	½	0	½	y_5
6	0	½	½	y_6
7	⅓	⅓	⅓	y_7

The seven mixtures are the three pure components, the three binary mixtures, and the ternary mixture, as shown in Table 26.38.

The "special cubic" corresponds to the equation:

$$y = B_1X_1 + B_2X_2 + B_3X_3 + B_{12}X_1X_2 + B_{13}X_1X_3 + B_{23}X_2X_3 + B_{123}X_1X_2X_3$$

The computed coefficients are:

$$b_1 = y_1 \qquad b_2 = y_2 \qquad b_3 = y_3$$

$$b_{12} = 4y_4 - 2(y_1 + y_2)$$

$$b_{13} = 4y_5 - 2(y_1 + y_3)$$

$$b_{23} = 4y_6 - 2(y_2 + y_3)$$

$$b_{123} = 27y_7 - 12(y_4 + y_5 + y_6) + 3(y_1 + y_2 + y_3)$$

The subject of mixture designs has a vast literature. The reader is referred to the textbook by John A. Cornell (1981) for further details, and to the papers by Snee (1973, 1979), Crosier (1984), and Peipel and Cornell (1985). An early excellent discussion of such designs is found in an article by Gorman and Hinman (1962). An adaptation of mixture designs and response surface methods is given in Thompson and Myers (1968).

GROUP SCREENING DESIGNS

Novel experimental designs for finding the few effective factors out of a very large number of possible factors have been called "group screening designs." These designs have the following structure: groups are formed, each containing several factors; the groups are tested; and individual factors of the groups that prove to contain significant factors are then separately tested. Such designs, proposed by Connor (1961) and further studied by Watson (1961), are intended to minimize the amount of experimentation required.

The experimental variables are divided into groups, and each group is treated as a single variable until an effect on the response variable is shown.

The following assumptions are made:

1. All factors initially have the same probability of being effective.
2. The factors do not interact.

3. The directions of effects, if they exist, are known.

The number of factors is $f = gk$, where g = number of groups and k = number of factors per group. For example, consider an experiment with nine factors, which are divided into three groups of three factors each (i.e., $g = 3$, $k = 3$). The upper and lower levels of the groups are defined as follows:

1. Group factor X consists of factors A, B, C.
Level 1: All three factors at lower level (0, 0, 0)
Level x: All three factors at upper level (1, 1, 1)

2. Group factor Y consists of factors D, E, F.
Level 1: All three factors at lower level (0, 0, 0)
Level y: All three factors at upper level (1, 1, 1)

3. Group factor Z consists of factors G, H, I.
Level 1: All factors at lower level (0, 0, 0)
Level z: All factors at upper level (1, 1, 1)

The first-stage design studies the *group* factors, as for example by using a half-replicate of a 2^3 factorial. This requires the four group treatment combinations x, y, z, and xyz corresponding to treatment combinations for the nine factors as follows:

$$x(1,1,1 \ 0,0,0 \ 0,0,0)$$

$$y(0,0,0 \ 1,1,1 \ 0,0,0)$$

$$z(0,0,0 \ 0,0,0 \ 1,1,1)$$

$$xyz(1,1,1 \ 1,1,1 \ 1,1,1)$$

The results of the first-stage experiment will indicate which group factors contain at least one effective factor. A second-stage experiment, which may consist of a half-replicate of a 2^3, will then be run on each effective group factor to determine which of the individual factors are effective. For further details, see Watson (1961). Patel (1962) gives detailed procedures for two-, three-, and four-stage screening tests.

The application of group screening designs that has been discussed here is to the identification of effective experimental factors, but there is extensive literature relating to the screening of effective responses, e.g., to compounds and drugs, and to the group testing of individuals. Papers of interest are by Ehrenfeld (1972), Pocock (1977), Mundel (1984), Hwang (1984), and Hayre (1985).

PLANNING INTERLABORATORY TESTS

Here we present a few simple techniques that are useful in planning and analyzing the results of interlaboratory (or round-robin) tests. The article by Wernimont (1951) is a good introduction to the general problem. More specific techniques of analysis, some of which are given here, may be found in Youden (1967), Mandel (1964), and many publications of the American Society for Testing and Materials (ASTM) and the International Standards Organization (ISO). An excellent early compilation of published papers on statistical concepts and procedures, including eight articles on interlaboratory tests, can be found in Ku (1969).

A Rank Sum Test for Laboratories.   In almost any set of interlaboratory test data, some of the reported results fall so far out from the main body of results that there is a real question as to whether these data should be omitted in order to avoid distortion of the true picture. It is always a difficult problem to decide whether or not outlying results should be screened. One does not wish to discard a laboratory's results without good reason; on the other hand, if a laboratory is careless or not competent, one does not wish to "punish" the test method. A ranking test for laboratories due to Youden (1963), reprinted in Ku (1969), is described here. This is only one of several nonparametric ranking procedures that may be of interest to the reader. Excellent references on these nonparametric approaches are the texts by Hollander and Wolfe (1973) and Noether (1967).

An interlaboratory test usually involves sending several materials containing some particular chemical element or compound or possessing some physical quality to each of several laboratories. The ranking test for laboratories uses the recorded measured responses of the materials to rank the laboratories. The data from the interlaboratory test are summarized in a two-way table with materials as rows and laboratories as columns (or vice versa).

For each material, the laboratory having the largest result is given rank 1, the next largest rank 2, etc. (Tied values are treated as is usual in ranking procedures, each tied value being given the average of those ranks that would have been assigned if the values had differed.)

For each laboratory, the assigned ranks are summed over all materials. A laboratory that is consistently high in its ability to measure the response will show a lower rank sum, and a laboratory that is consistently low will show a higher rank sum than the average or expected rank sum. The question is whether such rank sums are excessively high or excessively low. To decide this, tables have been provided (see Table 26.39).

A Ruggedness Test for Use by the Initiating Laboratory.   Very often a test method is judged to have acceptable precision by the original laboratory, but when the test is performed by several laboratories, the results are disappointing. The reason is usually that the original laboratory has carefully controlled conditions and equipment and that the operating conditions in other laboratories are slightly different. (There are always slight deviations, which are permissible within the instructions contained in the standard procedure for the test method.) Youden (1967) proposed that the initiating laboratory investigate the effects of such deviations by deliberately introducing small variations in the method, a "ruggedness test," so as to be prepared for the variations resulting when the test is used by other laboratories. In order to minimize the extra work required for the original laboratory, he proposed that the Plackett-Burman designs for 7, 11, 15 factors be used to detect such effects. If significant effects result from such variations of conditions in a single laboratory, the method needs further refinement before interlaboratory tests are run.

Youden Two-Sample Plan.   A simple plan to investigate the performance of laboratories and of the test procedure itself was suggested by Youden (1959) and reprinted in Ku (1969). Samples of two materials (A and B) are sent to each laboratory in the program. The two materials should be similar in kind and in the value of the property to be measured. The laboratories should have the same internal precision. The pairs of results are used to plot a graph on which the x and y scales are equal and each laboratory is represented by one point. A laboratory's result on sample A is the x coordinate and its result on sample B is the y coordinate of that point. There will be as many points as there are laboratories.

TABLE 26.39   Approximate 5% Limits for Ranking Scores

Number of laboratories participating	Numbers of materials									
	3	4	5	6	7	8	9	10	11	12
3	· · ·	4	5	7	8	10	12	13	15	17
	· · ·	12	15	17	20	22	24	27	29	31
4	· · ·	4	6	8	10	12	14	16	18	20
	· · ·	16	19	22	25	28	31	34	37	40
5	· · ·	5	7	9	11	13	16	18	21	23
	· · ·	19	23	27	31	35	38	42	45	49
6	3	5	7	10	12	15	18	21	23	26
	18	23	28	32	37	41	45	49	54	58
7	3	5	8	11	14	17	20	23	26	29
	21	27	32	37	42	47	52	57	62	67
8	3	6	9	12	15	18	22	25	29	32
	24	30	36	42	48	54	59	65	70	76
9	3	6	9	13	16	20	24	27	31	35
	27	34	41	47	54	60	73	79	85	91
10	4	7	10	14	17	21	26	30	34	38
	29	37	45	52	60	67	73	80	87	94
11	4	7	11	15	19	23	27	32	36	41
	32	41	49	57	65	73	81	88	96	103
12	4	7	11	15	20	24	29	34	39	44
	35	45	54	63	71	80	88	96	104	112

Note: Let L laboratories test each of M materials. Assign ranks 1 to L for each material. Sum the ranks to get the score for each laboratory. The mean score is $M(L + 1)/2$. The entries are lower and upper limits that are included in the approximate 5% critical region.

For graphical diagnosis, a vertical line is drawn through the median of all points in the x direction and a horizontal line through the median of all points in the y direction. The lines could be drawn through the x and y averages just as well, but the medians are convenient for quick graphical analysis.

Individual points that are very far removed from the main body of the results indicate laboratories that should probably be screened from the analysis. The two intersecting median lines divide the space into four quadrants, and the first (and often revealing) step in the analysis is to look at the distribution of points among the quadrants. If only random errors of measurement were operating, there would be a circular scatter of points with roughly equal numbers in each quadrant. The plots of most real-life interlaboratory data, however, show concentrations in the upper right and lower left quadrants (see Figure 26.20). If a laboratory is high on both samples, its point will lie in the upper right; if a laboratory is low on both samples, its point will lie in the lower left. Being high (or low) on both samples is an indication that a laboratory has somehow put its own stamp on the procedure, i.e., that there are systematic differences between the laboratories. Where these systematic differences exist, the points will tend to lie along a long, narrow ellipse. Assuming that the two materials are similar in kind and in value of the property measured, as prescribed, and that the scatter in results for sample A does turn out to be approximately the same as the scatter for sample B, we can calculate an estimate of the standard deviation of a single result as follows:

1. Calculate the "signed differences" $d = A - B$ for each laboratory, that is, compute the difference and keep the sign (for the ith laboratory $d_i = A_i - B_i$).

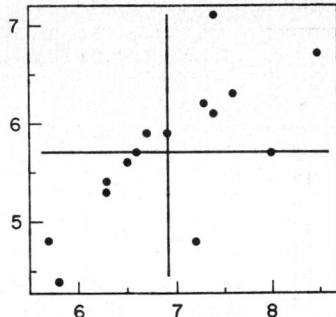

FIG. 26.20 Percent phthalic anhydride in two paint samples—Youden plot showing systematic differences.

2. Calculate $\overline{d}$, the algebraic average of the d's.

3. Calculate $d'_i = d_i - \overline{d}$.

4. Take the absolute d' values and calculate their average; that is, drop the signs before averaging.

5. Multiply this value by 0.886 to get an estimate s of the standard deviation of a single result. (The value 0.886 is $1/d_2$, Appendix II, Table A, for $n = 2$.)

A circle can now be drawn that is expected to contain any stated percentage of the points. The circle is centered at the median point and its radius (for the stated percentage to be contained within it) is obtained by multiplying s (from Step 5) by the factor given in Table 26.40.

Points lying outside the circle usually indicate laboratories with systematic differences. Further deductions are possible from such plots (see Youden, 1959); they have been used in a wide variety of applications, including chemical and engineering tests and standards comparisons.

TABLE 26.40   Radius of Circle on Youden Plot in Terms of Multiples of the Standard Deviation

Percent of points within circle	Multiple of the standard deviation
90	2.146
95	2.448
99	3.035

PLANNING THE SIZE OF THE EXPERIMENT

Methods for determining the number of observations required for estimating the mean and variance with certain precision, or for comparing two sets of data with regard to mean and variance with certain risks of error, are given in Section 23,

Basic Statistical Methods. A method for determining the number of observations required when comparing several groups is given here.

For example, the analysis of variance F test (see Completely Randomized Design) is designed to test the hypothesis that all group means are the same, i.e., $\eta_1 = \eta_2 \cdots \eta_k = \eta$. The corresponding averages $\bar{y}_1, \bar{y}_2, \ldots, \bar{y}_k$ computed from the recorded data will, of course, be different. The outcome of the test of hypothesis depends on the significance level α at which the test is performed, the true variability of individual observations, the number of observations per average, and the size of the true difference (if any) between group means. When planning experiments, if there are no restrictions on the number of observations that can be made, one should specify the size of those differences in means that are considered important from a practical standpoint. When the significance level at which the test is to be made is also specified, existing tables or charts can be used to determine the necessary sample size (number of observations per average) for achieving a stated probability $(1 - \beta)$ of detecting differences between the means of the required size. To use such tables, we compute a quantity

$$\phi^2 = \frac{n \sum_i (\eta_i - \eta)^2}{k\sigma^2} = \frac{n\delta_i^2}{k\sigma^2}$$

where n = number of observations per group (to be determined)
k = number of groups
σ^2 = true value of within-group variance (assumed same for all groups; can be estimated from previous similar work)
η_i = mean for ith group
η = grand mean

Let $(\eta_i - \eta) = \delta_i$. The sum of the δ_i values must equal zero.

Appendix II, Table DD gives values ϕ^2 for $\alpha = 0.01$ and $\beta = 0.2$, $(1 - \beta = 0.80)$, and DF_1 and DF_2 degrees of freedom. In the simple case used in the example, $DF_1 = k - 1$ and $DF_2 = k(n - 1)$. Other charts and tables are available in slightly different form and for additional values of α and β. See, for example, Dixon and Massey (1969) or Owen's tables (1962).

Example. Consider the experiment shown in Table 26.4. Suppose that another experiment is to be run and that we wish to determine beforehand how many briquettes to test using each method in order to achieve a certain discrimination between the means for the three methods. If the statistical test is to be done at the $\alpha = 0.01$ level and if we want the probability of detecting the postulated differences to be at least 0.8, we can use Appendix II, Table DD. Assume $\sigma^2 = 545$, an estimate of the variance determined from the previous experiment. Suppose the following differences between the means are considered practically important:

$$\delta_1 = \eta_1 - \eta = -30$$

$$\delta_2 = \eta_2 - \eta = +20$$

$$\delta_3 = \eta_3 - \eta = +10$$

(Obviously, many different values for the δ's will yield the same value for $\Sigma\delta^2$ and therefore the same ϕ^2.)

The δ's chosen should be meaningful for each experimental situation. Here we have postulated three particular differences; in other situations the pattern of the differences might take on special meanings. For example, if the groups were

increasing levels of a quantitative variable such as temperature, a meaningful pattern for the d's might be a constant change in mean from one level to the next higher one. (Remember that the δ_i's must sum to zero.)
Calculate:

$$\phi^2 = \frac{n\Sigma\delta_i^2}{k\sigma^2}$$

$$\phi^2 = \frac{n(1400)}{3(545)} = \frac{1400n}{1635} = 0.86n$$

$$DF_1 = k - 1 = 3 - 1 = 2$$

$$DF_2 = k(n - 1) = 3n - 3$$

Using Appendix II, Table DD, we must find two values of n, one that gives ϕ^2 larger than required and one that gives a smaller value than required:

n	$DF_2 = 3n - 3$	Tabled ϕ^2	Desired ϕ^2 = 0.86n
7	18	6.05	6.02
8	21	5.83	6.88

The "tabled ϕ^2" for $n = 8$ was obtained by linear interpolation. The solution lies between $n = 7$ and $n = 8$, and we take the larger n. Eight observations per group will give us an 80 percent chance of detecting the postulated differences when we do an F test at the $\alpha = 0.01$ level.

This method may be used for multifactor experiments provided the proper values for DF_1 and DF_2 are used. It is used when the purpose of the experiment is to compare group averages, and it works for any number of groups provided the number of observations per group is large enough. In this case and in the case described below, equal numbers of observations should be taken in each group.

For another kind of experiment, in which the purpose is to compare the between-group variance with the within-group variance (see discussion of Model II, Random Effects Model, under One-way Analysis of Variance—Models), a *minimum* number of *groups* is required to achieve desired discrimination in terms of the relative variability. For example, see Table 26.41, where α and β are

TABLE 26.41 Minimum Number of Groups—Random Effects Model

	$\alpha = \beta = 0.05$		$\alpha = \beta = 0.01$
δ_1/δ_0	Minimum number of groups	δ_1/δ_0	Minimum number of groups
1.5	35	1.5	68
2.0	14	2.0	25
2.5	9	2.5	16
3.0	7	3.0	12

the risks of the two kinds of error, δ_0 is an "acceptably small" value of the ratio σ_b/σ_w (large enough to achieve a significant result), and δ_1 is an unacceptably large value for σ_b/σ_w.

Useful discussions on determining the number of observations are given in the texts by Cochran and Cox (1957) and Cox (1958). Extensive tables are given in the papers by Kastenbaum, Hoel, and Bowman (1970a and b).

GENERAL REMARKS ON ANALYSIS OF DATA

Usual analysis assumes that observations are normally distributed and that the variability of results within a treatment is the same for every treatment. Where there is serious doubt about normality, the use of a transformation should be considered. For the simple, completely randomized designs a special analysis using ranks and not requiring the assumption of normality is available.

The assumption of equal variance should be investigated. If there are more than a few treatments, plot each treatment average versus a measure of the variability within a treatment (i.e., range or estimated standard deviation). If the plot shows that the estimates of the variances and the averages tend to covary, the data should be transformed and the analysis performed on the transformed data (see Box, Hunter, and Hunter, 1978, for further exposition and an example). In addition to a rough graphical check of this sort, there are tests of homogeneity of a set of variance estimates (see Snedecor and Cochran, 1980, or Duncan, 1974). These tests are, unfortunately, more sensitive to departures from normality than are the tests used to compare means. The experimenter's own feelings about whether the variability should be the same in different groups should not be ignored. However, the experimenter should also remember that quite large variations in s^2 can occur when σ^2 is constant, particularly when the number of degrees of freedom in s^2 is small.

The most important assumption underlying all the statistical techniques thus far described is that of the *independence* of the observations. The act the experimenter must perform to guarantee this essential assumption is *randomization*. Some aspect of randomization must be part of every experimental program that plans to use the statistical tools of hypothesis testing and interval estimation. In the absence of independence, concerns about normality and homogeneous variance are almost frivolous.

Remarks on Computing.   The methods of analysis given here, and those found in most textbooks, are methods intended for hand or desk calculators. There now exists much activity in the development and merchandising of packaged computer programs to do various kinds of analyses and statistical computations. Two general cautions are in order: (1) the computing methods given in this section should not be literally translated into a computer program—they could be very inefficient as programming instructions; and (2) the user of packaged statistical programs should be as critical a consumer of programs as of everything else. Information on software for statistical purposes is provided in Section 27 under Statistical Analysis.

Missing Values.   If there are missing values in the data from a designed experiment (observations lost, not completed, etc.) consult Cochran and Cox (1957) or Davies (1954) for the details appropriate to each kind of design. Rules are given for supplying one or a few missing values so that the analysis can be done in the regular way. The experimenter may wish to simply insert the average of all the recorded results, or some value representing a good guess, for the missing observation. Seldom do the inferences obtained from the analyzed design change profoundly when such approximate missing data replacements are used.

DEVELOPMENTS IN EXPERIMENTAL DESIGN

An article by Herzberg and Cox (1969) reviews early developments and includes a bibliography of about 800 articles. Ostle (1967) gives a review of articles on the statistical design of experiments that have appeared in *Industrial Quality Control* and *Technometrics*. A recent paper reviewing experimental design developments of particular interest to industrial experimenters is by Steinberg and Hunter (1984).

REFERENCES

Addelman, Sidney (1961). "Irregular Fractions of the $2n$ Factorial Experiments." *Technometrics,* vol. 3, no. 4, pp. 479–496.

Addelman, Sidney (1962). "Symmetrical and Asymmetrical Fractional Factorial Plans." *Technometrics,* vol. 4, no. 1, pp. 47–58.

Addelman, Sidney (1963). "Techniques for Constructing Fractional Replicate Plans." *Journal of the American Statistical Association,* vol. 58, no. 301, pp. 45–71.

Addelman, Sidney (1969). "Sequences of Two-Level Fractional Factorial Plans." *Technometrics,* vol. 11, no. 3, pp. 477–509.

Anderson, D. A. and Thomas, A. M. (1978). "Resolution IV Fractional Factorial Designs for the General Asymmetrical Factorial." *Communications in Statistics,* vol. A8, pp. 931–943.

ASTM Manual for Conducting an Interlaboratory Study of a Test Method (1981). ASTM Special Publication 335, American Society for Testing and Materials, Philadelphia.

Bainbridge, T. R. (1965). "Staggered, Nested Designs for Estimating Variance Components." *Industrial Quality Control,* vol. 22, no. 1, pp. 12–20.

Barbeson, R. A. et al. (1970). "Picking Optimization Methods." *Chemical Engineering,* vol. 77, pp. 32–142.

Barnett, E. H. (1960). "Introduction to Evolutionary Operation." *Industrial and Engineering Chemistry,* vol. 52, pp. 500–503.

Bicking, C. A. (1954), "Some Uses of Statistics in the Planning of Experiments." *Industrial Quality Control,* vol. 10, pp. 23–31.

Bingham, R. S. (1963). "EVOP for Systematic Improvement." *Industrial Quality Control,* vol. 20, no. 3, pp. 17–23.

Box, G. E. P. (1954). "The Exploration and Exploitation of Response Surfaces: Some General Considerations and Examples." *Biometrics,* vol. 10, p. 16.

Box, G. E. P. (1966). "A Simple System of Evolutionary Operation Subject to Empirical Feedback." *Technometrics,* vol. 9, pp. 10–26.

Box, G. E. P. and Behnken, D. W. (1960). "Some New Three Level Designs for the Study of Quantitative Variables." *Technometrics,* vol. 2, pp. 477–482.

Box, G. E. P. and Cox, D. R. (1964). "An Analysis of Transformations." *Journal of the Royal Statistical Society,* series B, vol. 26, p. 211.

Box, G. E. P. and Draper, N. R. (1969). "Isn't My Process Too Variable for EVOP?" *Technometrics,* vol. 10, pp. 439–444.

Box, G. E. P. and Draper, N. R. (1987). *Empirical Model Building with Response Surfaces.* John Wiley & Sons, New York.

Box, G. E. P. and Hunter, J. S. (1959). "Condensed Calculation for Evolutionary Operation Programs." *Technometrics,* vol. 1, pp. 77–95.

Box, G. E. P., Hunter, W. G., and Hunter, J. S. (1978). *Statistics for Experimenters.* John Wiley & Sons, New York.

Box, G. E. P. and Tiao, George C. (1973). *Bayesian Inference in Statistical Analysis.* Addison-Wesley, Reading, MA.

Box, G. E. P. and Tidwell, P. W. (1962). "Transformation of the Independent Variable." *Technometrics,* vol. 4, p. 531.

Box, G. E. P. and Wilson, K. B. (1951). "On the Experimental Attainment of Optimum Conditions." *Journal of the Royal Statistical Society,* series B, vol. 13, p. 1.

Box, G. E. P. and Youle, P. V. (1955). "The Exploration and Exploitation of Response Surfaces: An Example of the Link between the Fitted Surface and the Basic Mechanism of the System." *Biometrics,* vol. 11, p. 287.

Carr, Jesse M., and McCracken, E. A. (1960). "Statistical Program Planning for Process Development." *Chemical Engineering Progress,* vol. 56, no. 11, pp. 56–61.

Chew, Victor (ed.) (1964). *Experimental Designs in Industry.* John Wiley & Sons, Inc., New York.

Clatworthy, W. H. (1973). *Tables of the Two-Associate-Class Partially Balanced Designs.* National Bureau of Standards Applied Mathematics Services Publication 63, U.S. Government Printing Office, Washington, DC.

Cochran, William G., and Cox, Gertrude M. (1957). *Experimental Designs,* 2d ed. John Wiley & Sons, New York.

Connor, W. S. (1961). "Group Screening Designs." *Industrial and Engineering Chemistry,* vol. 53, pp. 69A–70A.

Cooper, B. E. (1968). "The Extension of Yates' $2n$ Algorithm to any Complete Factorial Experiment." *Technometrics,* vol. 10, pp. 575–577.

Cornell, J. A. (1981). *Experiments with Mixtures.* John Wiley & Sons, New York.

Cox, D. R. (1958). *Planning of Experiments.* John Wiley & Sons, New York.

Croisier, R. B. (1984). "Mixture Experiments: Geometry and Pseudocomponents." *Technometrics,* vol. 26, pp. 209–216.

Current Index to Statistics: Applications, Methods and Theory (1976–1984). Vols. 1–10. American Statistical Association and Institute of Mathematical Statistics, Washington, DC.

Daniel, C. (1959). "Use of Half-Normal Plots for Interpreting Factorial Two-Level Experiments." *Technometrics,* vol. 1, pp. 311–341.

Daniel, Cuthbert (1962). "Sequences of Fractional Replicates in the 2p-q Series." *Journal of the American Statistical Association,* vol. 57, no. 298, pp. 403–429.

Daniel, Cuthbert (1966). "Parallel Fractional Replicates." *Technometrics,* vol. 8, no. 2, pp. 469–480.

Daniel, C. (1976). *Applications of Statistics in Industrial Experimentation.* John Wiley & Sons, New York.

Davies, O. L. and Hay, W. A. (1950). "Construction and Use of Fractional Factorial Designs in Industrial Research." *Biometrics,* vol. 6, p. 233.

Davies, O. L. (ed.) (1954). *The Design and Analysis of Industrial Experiments.* Hafner, New York.

DeBusk, R. E. (1962). "Evolutionary Operation at the Tennessee Eastman Company." *Industrial Quality Control,* vol. 19, pp. 15–21.

Diamond, W. (1981). *Practical Experimental Designs.* Wadsworth, Belmont, CA.

Dixon, Wilfred J. and Massey, Frank J., Jr. (1969). *Introduction to Statistical Analysis,* 3d ed. McGraw-Hill, New York.

Draper, Norman R. and Stoneman, David N. (1964). "Estimating Missing Values in Unreplicated Two-Level Factorial and Fractional Factorial Designs." *Biometrics,* vol. 20, no. 3, pp. 443–458.

Draper, N. R. and Hunter, W. G. (1967). "Transformations, Some Examples Revisited." *Technometrics,* vol. 11, p. 23.

Draper, N. R. and Smith, H., Jr. (1981). *Applied Regression Analysis,* 2d ed. John Wiley & Sons, New York.

Duckworth, W. E. (1965). "Statistical Method in Metallurgical Development." *The Statistician,* vol. 15, pp. 7–30.

Duncan, Acheson J. (1974). *Quality Control and Industrial Statistics,* 4th ed. Richard D. Irwin, Homewood, IL.

Duncan, D. B. (1955). "Multiple Range and Multiple F Tests." *Biometrics,* vol. 11, p. 1.

Dunnett, C. W. (1964). "New Tables for Multiple Comparisons with a Control." *Biometrics,* vol. 20, p. 482.

Ehrenfeld, S. (1972). "On Group Sequential Sampling." *Technometrics,* vol. 14, pp. 167–174.

Fisher, R. A., and Yates, F. (1964). *Statistical Tables for Biological, Agricultural and Medical Research Workers,* 6th ed. Stechert-Hafner, New York.

Gorman, J. W., and Hinman, J. E. (1962). "Simplex Lattice Designs for Multicomponent Systems." *Technometrics,* vol. 4, no. 4, pp. 463–487.

Hayre, L. S. (1985). "Group Sequential Sampling with Variable Group Sizes." *Journal of the Royal Statistical Society,* series B, vol. 47, pp. 90–97.

Hertzberg, Agnes M. and Cox, D. R. (1969). "Recent Work on the Design of Experiments: A Bibliography and a Review." *Journal of the Royal Statistical Society,* series A, vol. 132, pt. 1, pp. 29–67.

Hicks, Charles R. (1982). *Fundamental Concepts in the Design of Experiments,* 3d ed. Holt, Rinehart & Winston, New York.

Hill, W. J. and Hunter, W. G. (1966). "A Review of Response Surface Methodology: A Literature Survey." *Technometrics,* vol. 8, pp. 571–590.

Himmelblau, D. M. (1970). *Process Analysis by Statistical Methods.* John Wiley & Sons, New York.

Hollander, Myles and Wolfe, Douglas (1973). *Nonparametric Statistical Methods.* John Wiley & Sons, New York.

Hunter, J. S. (1959). "Determination of Optimum Operating Conditions by Experimental Methods, Parts I, II, and III." *Industrial Quality Control,* December 1958, January and February 1959.

Hunter, J. S. (1966). "The Inverse Yates Algorithm. *Technometrics,* vol. 8, no. 1, pp. 177–183.

Hunter, J. S. (1985). "Statistical Design Applied to Product Design." *Journal of Quality Technology,* vol. 17, pp. 210–221.

Hunter, W. G. and Kitrell, J. R. (1966). "Evolutionary Operation: A Review." *Technometrics,* vol. 8, pp. 389–397.

Hwang, F. K. (1984). "Robust Group Testing." *Journal of Quality Technology,* vol. 16, pp. 189–195.

International Standards Organization (1981). *International Standard 5725-1981, Precision of Test Methods—Determination of Repeatability and Reproducibility by Interlaboratory Tests.* Geneva, Switzerland.

John, Peter W. M. (1966). "Augmenting $2n$-1 Designs." *Technometrics,* vol. 8, no. 3, pp. 469–480.

Kastenbaum, M. A., Hoel, D. G., and Bowman, K. O. (1970a). "Sample Size Requirements: One-Way Analysis of Variance." *Biometrika,* vol. 57, pp. 421–430.

Kastenbaum, M. A., Hoel, D. G., and Bowman, K. O. (1970b). "Sample Size Requirements: Randomized Block Designs." *Biometrika,* vol. 57, pp. 573–578.

Keuls, M. (1952). "The Use of the Studentized Range in Connection with an Analysis of Variance." *Euphytica,* vol. 1, p. 112.

Koehler, T. L. (1959). "Evolutionary Operation." *Chemical Engineering Progress,* vol. 55, pp. 76–79.

Ku, Harry H. (ed.) (1969). *Precision Measurement and Calibration—Statistical Concepts and Procedures.* National Bureau of Standards Special Publication 300, vol. 1, U.S. Government Printing Office, Washington, DC.

Kurtz, T. E., Link, B. F., Tukey, J. W., and Wallace, D. L. (1965). "Short-cut Multiple Comparisons for Balanced Single and Double Classifications." *Technometrics,* vol. 7, no. 2, pp. 95–165.

Lenter, M. M. (1965). "Listing Expected Mean Square Components." *Biometrics,* vol. 21, no. 2, pp. 459–466.

Mandel, John (1954). "Chain Block Designs with Two-Way Elimination of Heterogeneity." *Biometrics,* vol. 10, no. 2, pp. 251–272.

Mandel, John (1964). *Statistical Analysis of Experimental Data.* John Wiley & Sons, New York.

Margolin, B. H. (1969). "Results on Factorial Designs of Resolution IV for the $2n$ and $2n3m$ Series." *Technometrics,* vol. 11, pp. 431–444.

Mead, R. and Pike, D. J. (1975). "A Review of Response Surface Methodology from a Biometric Point of View." *Biometrics,* vol. 31, p. 803.

Moder, J. J. (1956). "A Teaching Aid of Regression, Correlation, Analysis of Variance, and Other Statistical Techniques." *Industrial Quality Control,* vol. 13, pp. 16–21.

Montgomery, D. C. (1976). *Design and Analysis of Experiments.* John Wiley & Sons, New York.

Mount-Campbell, C. A. and Neuhardt, J. B. (1980). "Selecting Cost-Optimal Main Effects Fractions of $3n$ Factorials." *AIEE Transactions,* vol. 12, pp. 80–86.

Mundel, A. (1984). "Group Testing." *Journal of Quality Technology,* vol. 16, pp. 181–188.

Myers, R. H. (1971). *Response Surface Methodology.* Allyn & Bacon, Boston.

Natrella, Mary G. (1963). *Experimental Statistics.* National Bureau of Standards Handbook 91, U.S. Government Printing Office, Washington, DC.

Neuhardt, J. B. and Mount-Campbell, C. A. (1978). "Selection of Cost-Optimal 2k-p Fractional Factorials." In *Communications in Statistics—Simulation and Computation,* vol. B7, pp. 369–383.

Neuman, D. (1939). "The Distribution of the Range in Samples from a Normal Population Expressed in Terms of an Independent Estimate of the Standard Deviation." *Biometrika,* vol. 31, p. 20.

Noether, Gottfried E. (1967). *Elements of Non-Parametric Statistics.* John Wiley & Sons, New York.

Ostle, Bernard (1967). "Industry Use of Statistical Test Design." *Industrial Quality Control,* vol. 24, no. 1, pp. 24–33.

Ott, E. R. (1975). *Process Quality Control.* McGraw-Hill, New York.

Owen, D. B. (1962). *Handbook of Statistical Tables.* Addison-Wesley, Reading, MA.

Patel, M. S. (1962). "Group Screening with More than Two Stages." *Technometrics,* vol. 4, no. 2, pp. 209–217.

Patel, M. S. (1963). "Partially Duplicated Fractional Factorial Designs." *Technometrics,* vol. 5, pp. 71–83.

Phadke, M. S., Kacker, R. N., Speeney, D. V., and Grieco, M. J. (1983). "Off-Line Quality Control in Integrated Circuit Fabrication Using Experimental Design." *Bell System Technical Journal,* vol. 62, pp. 1273–1309.

Piepel, G. F. and Cornell, J. A. (1985). "Models for Mixture Experiments when the Response Depends on the Total Amount." *Technometrics,* vol. 27, pp. 219–227.

Plackett, R. L. and Burnam, J. P. (1946). "The Design of Optimum Multifactorial Experiments." *Biometrika,* vol. 33, p. 305.

Pocock, S. J. (1977). "Group Sequential Methods in the Design and Analysis of Clinical Trials." *Biometrika,* vol. 64, pp. 191–199.

Raktoe, B. L., Hedayat, A., and Federer, W. T. (1981). *Factorial Designs.* John Wiley, New York.

Rechtschaffner, R. (1967). "Saturated Fractions of the $2n$ and $3n$ Factorial Designs." *Technometrics,* vol. 9, pp. 569–575.

Russell, E. R. and Stephens, K. S. (1970). "An EVOP Teaching Game Using a Simulated Process." *Journals of Quality Technology,* vol. 2, no. 2, pp. 61–66.

Scheffé, H. (1953). "A Method for Judging All Contrasts in an Analysis of Variance." *Biometrika,* vol. 40, p. 87.

Scheffé, H. (1958). "Experiments with Mixtures." *Journal of the Royal Statistical Society,* series B, vol. 20, pp. 344–360.

Scheffé, H. (1963). "The Simplex Centroid Design for Experiments with Mixtures." *Journal of the Royal Statistical Society,* series B, vol. 25, pp. 235–251.

Sheesley, J. H. (1980). "Attributes Comparison of k Samples Involving Variables or Data Using the Analysis of Means." *Journal of Quality Technology,* vol. 12, pp. 47–52.

Snedecor, George W. and Cochran, William G. (1980). *Statistical Methods.* The Iowa State University Press, Ames.

Snee, R. D. (1973). "Design and Analysis of Mixture Experiments." *Journal of Quality Technology,* vol. 3, pp. 159–169.

Snee, R. D. (1979). "Experimental Design for Mixture Systems with Multicomponent Constraints." *Communications in Statistics,* vol. A8, pp. 303–326.

Spendley, W., Hext, G. R., and Himsworth, F. R. (1962). "Sequential Application of Simplex Designs in Optimization and Evolutionary Operation." *Technometrics,* vol. 4, pp. 441–461.

Steel, Robert G. D. and Torrie, James H. (1962). *Principles and Procedures of Statistics.* McGraw-Hill, New York.

Steinberg, D. M. and Hunter, W. G. (1984). "Experimental Design: Review and Comment." *Technometrics,* vol. 26, no. 2, pp. 71–97.

Taguchi, G. and Wu, Y. (1978). *Introduction to Off-Line Quality Control.* Central Japan Quality Control Association (available from The American Supplier Institute, Detroit).

Thompson, William O. and Myers, Raymond H. (1968). "Response Surface Designs for Mixture Problems." *Technometrics,* vol. 10, no. 4, pp. 739–756.

Tukey, J. W. (1949). "Comparing Individual Means in the Analysis of Variance." *Biometrics,* vol. 5, p. 99.

Watson, G. S. (1961). "A Study of the Group Screening Method." *Technometrics,* vol. 3, no. 3, pp. 371–388.

Webb, S. R. (1968a). "Non-Orthogonal Designs of Even Resolution." *Technometrics,* vol. 10, pp. 291–299.

Webb, S. R. (1968b). "Saturated Sequential Factorial Design." *Technometrics,* vol. 10, pp. 535–550.

Wernimont, Grant (1951). "Design and Interpretation of Interlaboratory Studies of Test Methods." *Analytical Chemistry,* vol. 23, p. 1572.

Yates, F. (1937). *The Design and Analysis of Factorial Experiments.* Imperial Bureau of Soil Sciences, Harpenden, England.

Youden, W. J. (1951). *Statistics for Chemists.* John Wiley & Sons, New York.

Youden, W. J. (1959a). "Graphical Diagnosis of Interlaboratory Tests." *Industrial Quality Control,* vol. 15, no. 11, pp. 1–5.

Youden, W. J. (1959b). "Evaluation of Chemical Analyses on Two Rocks." *Technometrics,* vol. 1, no. 4, pp. 409–417.

Youden, W. J. (1963). "Ranking Laboratories by Round Robin Tests." *Materials Research and Standards,* vol. 3, pp. 9–13.

Youden, W. J. (1967). *Statistical Techniques for Collaborative Tests.* Association of Official Analytical Chemists, Washington, DC.

Youden, W. J. and Hunter, J. S. (1955). "Partially Replicated Latin Squares." *Biometrics,* vol. 5, pp. 99–104.

SECTION 27

COMPUTERS AND QUALITY[1]

Fredric I. Orkin

INTRODUCTION **27.2**

TYPES OF COMPUTERS **27.2**

    Mainframe Computers . . 27.2

    Minicomputers 27.3

    Microcomputers 27.3

    Getting Started with a
    Personal Computer . . . 27.3

TYPES OF SOFTWARE **27.3**

    Machine Language 27.3

    Assembly Language 27.5

    High-Level Programming
    Languages 27.5

APPLICATIONS SOFTWARE . . **27.5**

    Expert Systems 27.6

    Software Quality 27.6

MANAGING COMPUTER
PROJECTS **27.7**

    Planning the Program . . . 27.7

    Organizing the Project
    Team 27.8

    Integrating the Effort . . . 27.9

    Measuring Progress and
    Performance 27.11

NEW-PRODUCT QUALITY
DESIGN REVIEW **27.11**

NEW-PROCESS QUALITY . . . **27.12**

    Large-Scale Plant-Wide
    Systems 27.13

    Large-Scale System
    Example 27.15

    Small-Scale System
    Example 27.16

INSPECTION **27.17**

    Computer-Aided Inspection 27.17

    In-Cycle Gaging 27.17

POST-PRODUCTION QUALITY . **27.23**

STATISTICAL ANALYSIS **27.24**

    Sources of Statistical
    Software 27.24

    Microcomputers 27.25

    Mainframe Computers . . 27.25

COMPUTER INTEGRATION INTO
PRODUCT DESIGN **27.25**

    Product Reliability and
    Safety 27.25

    Microprocessor Reliability
    and Quality 27.30

---

[1]In the Third Edition, the section on computers in quality control was prepared by J. E. Blum and R. S. Bingham, Jr.

Software Reliability and
Quality 27.30
System Fail-Safe Design
Quality Using
Microprocessors 27.31
The Reliability and Fail-
Safe Design Program . . 27.32

QUALITY IN THE FUTURE . . . 27.33
Near Term 27.33
Long Range 27.36
ACKNOWLEDGMENTS 27.36
REFERENCES 27.37

INTRODUCTION

The exponential growth of computers into every phase of quality will make most professionals uncomfortable at best, obsolete at worst. Management and practitioners alike need to supplement a basic understanding with frequent reviews of state-of-the-art technology to maintain their skills and competitive position. Breakthrough technology can be expected to totally transform quality aspects of our business system, product, and process design by the turn of the century.

Personal computers, or microcomputers, are gaining rapid popularity with quality professionals.

This section will include: (1) an introduction to computer terms and concepts; (2) a discussion of computer projects; (3) use of computers in several functional activities; (4) statistical applications; and (5) a discussion of the quality aspects of integrating computers into product design.

Examples and checklists are provided to assist the reader in the application of computer technology. The contributions of computers to quality-related activities are presented throughout this handbook. See particularly Section 14, Software Development; Section 16, under Automated Manufacturing and under Computer Simulation of Process Capability; Section 23 under Descriptive Statistics for Summarizing Data and under Multiple Regression; Section 24 under Software for Statistical Process Control; Section 25 under Computer Programs for Acceptance Sampling; and Section 26 under Remarks on Computing. Appendix III, Selected Quality Standards, Specifications, and Related Documents, includes documents on computer software.

TYPES OF COMPUTERS

Computers fall into one of three general categories. Costs (as of 1986) are $1 million or more for mainframe computers, $10,000 to $100,000 for minicomputers, and $1000 to $10,000 for microcomputers.

Mainframe Computers. A "mainframe" is a large-scale, general-purpose computer system. The architecture is designed around a 32-bit word size, which allows rapid access to an extremely large memory space. These computers usually have significant on-line storage, which is readily accessible by the computer without human intervention. Machines are generally housed in specially constructed facilities for security reasons and because they require special environmental conditions.

The architecture of a computer is designated in terms of word size. Word size is the fixed number of "bits" (binary digits, i.e., 1s or 0s) that serves as the basic logical unit of information. Normally called a "byte," a machine's word size defines the amount of information handled in one machine execution cycle and the number of memory cells available to store data.

Minicomputers. A "minicomputer" is a general-purpose computer that is very similar to a mainframe. It is usually smaller in physical size, memory space, and cost. Minicomputers are designed around a 16-bit word size, which distinguishes them from larger machines.

Microcomputers. The wide variety of computers that fall into the category of "microcomputer" makes this the most diverse classification. It generally includes systems built around an 8-bit or 16-bit architecture with wide-ranging power capabilities. Personal computers and home computers are included in this category.

Because of the low cost and limited capacity of most microcomputers, they are often dedicated to a single user or a single application. Yet microcomputers can handle a wide variety of applications, including small numerical analyses, data bases, graphics, word processing, and data acquisition.

An interesting application of microcomputers allows them to function as the primary user interface into a computer network. It allows the user the luxury of off-line computing power while retaining the ability to connect into a more powerful minicomputer or mainframe. This allows a more effective use of both the mainframe and the minicomputer.

Getting Started with a Personal Computer. Contrary to the advice of many sales personnel, purchasing a minimally outfitted personal computer for professional use with the plan of future expansion is not recommended. "For features as cheap as memory and input/output ports, install as much as the computer will take; the modest additional cost outweighs the problems created when you run out of computing power" (Lu, 1984, p. 30). By using application-specific circuit boards in the expansion slots of the personal computer, significant increases in productivity can be achieved.

TYPES OF SOFTWARE

Machine Language. Machine language is the only language a computer can understand. All other languages must be translated into machine language by programs. A "program" is a sequence of instructions given to the computer to perform specific functions or tasks. These programs, which act as translators to machine language, are called "compilers" or "interpreters."

Machine language consists of binary strings of 1s and 0s, which the computer processes as commands and variables. There are no variable names or command names in machine language.

Machine language is machine-dependent. Programs cannot be transferred between computers manufactured by different suppliers and in many cases cannot be transferred between various models of computers manufactured by a single supplier.

TABLE 27.1 High-Level Programming Languages

Acronym	Full name	Major fields of use	Comments
BASIC	Beginner's All-purpose Symbolic Instructional Code	Commercial	1. "Built-in" language for many microcomputers 2. Interpreted rather than compiled* 3. Easy to learn
FORTRAN	FORmula TRANslator	Scientific Mathematics Engineering	1. Not as rigorously structured as BASIC† 2. Preferred by many engineers and statisticians
COBOL	COmmon Business Oriented Language	Business	1. Handles file management and text quickly and efficiently 2. English-like self-documenting feature‡ 3. Ease of output format
PL/1	Programming Language number 1	Scientific Business	1. Powerful language that supports structured programming techniques§ 2. Highly disciplined approach to programming
C		Scientific Business	1. Derived from PL/1¶ 2. Compilers now available for microcomputers
PASCAL	Named after mathematician Blaise Pascal	Scientific Business	1. Highly disciplined approach to programming, like PL/1 2. Reliable/efficient 3. Often used to teach programming

*BASIC is interpreted instead of compiled. This means that BASIC instructions are translated into machine code and executed one instruction at a time before the next instruction is processed. Other high-level languages translate all the instructions at once and store them in a file for later execution. This feature makes BASIC programs execute more slowly than compiled high-level language programs.

†The American National Standards Institute has standardized FORTRAN in an attempt to organize the many versions on the market.

‡COBOL is available for use on computers from many different suppliers and, over time, it has undergone numerous refinements. A standard COBOL has been developed and has been approved by the American National Standards Institute. COBOL is widely used in the business world today and probably will remain popular owing to the tremendous amount of existing software written in COBOL for numerous business applications.

§PL/1 has been standardized by the American National Standards Institute, so that when a program is written in ANSI PL/1, the source code can be transferred to another computer without changing the program.

¶Like PL/1, C has been standardized so that it can run without change on many computers (is very portable) and features economy of expression.

Assembly Language. "Assembly language" was developed for programmers who liked the power of machine language but did not like the binary string syntax of 0s and 1s. Assembly language uses symbolic names for memory addresses and instructions and has to be translated into machine language by a program called the "assembler." Unlike other languages, which must be compiled, each assembly language instruction corresponds to exactly one machine language instruction.

Very little programming in assembly language is currently performed in business applications, since newer high-level languages are more efficient. Assembly language is still often used as a subroutine of a larger program when response time of the program requires optimized use of machine cycles.

High-Level Programming Languages. When compared with assembly or machine language, high-level languages (Table 27.1) can increase programming productivity by orders of magnitude in every field. They are easier to learn and easier to use. Productivity is gained at the expense of machine memory requirements and processing speed. Since computer hardware technology has so significantly reduced memory cost and processing time since the mid-1970s, these issues seldom influence language selection decisions.

APPLICATIONS SOFTWARE

Use of the computer as a utility to process and communicate general business and technical data has begun to revolutionize offices and laboratories. Applications software packages are available in any size and price range for the applications listed in Table 27.2.

TABLE 27.2 Application Software Packages

Word processing
Data base management
Integrated spreadsheets
Financial
Graphics
Project management
Accounting systems
Desktop environments
Communications/productivity tools
Statistics
Network applications
Language utilities

Applications software adapted to the quality function is becoming more sophisticated and broader in scope. "Packaged software enjoys a ten- or twenty-to-one price advantage over a custom system and provides the invaluable benefit of experience" (Keane, 1981, p. 629).

Each March *Quality Progress* lists an updated directory of applications software specific to the quality function. The directory includes price information, purchasing data, computer requirements, and a program description. An excellent introduction to the use of a spreadsheet for quality analysis in given in the Qualityware section of the May, June, and September issues of *Quality Progress* (Clements, 1985).

Expert Systems. Expert systems, sometimes called "artificial intelligence," are being developed to transform computers into machines that can draw conclusions from huge stores of data. What best differentiates the operation of an expert system from conventional software is flexibility. While standard programs specify precisely how all the operations must be performed, expert systems tell the computer what to do without specifying how to do it. "This is achieved by using special computer languages such as LISP or PROLOG, that allow a computer to manipulate symbols rather than numbers. Moreover, the programs are divided so the decision-making rules and the knowledge used to reach a conclusion are separate ("Artificial Intelligence," 1984)

Application of expert systems to aspects of quality control can be expected early in their development. Systems that predict equipment failure from large manufacturing and product service data bases are already in use. "American Telephone and Telegraph Company's ACE system . . . quickly locates faults in telephone cables. It does in an hour a job that previously took a team of technicians a week to accomplish" ("Artificial Intelligence," 1984).

Software Quality. Regardless of language, program size, complexity, or use, the software quality factors listed in Table 27.3 will generally apply. Preventive action in software development requires early definition of requirements by quality professionals from the using organization.

The steps necessary to acquire an application program package and the pitfalls associated with supplier packages are shown in Tables 27.4 and 27.5, respectively. A complete guide to the purchase of software is provided in Glaushenner (1984).

Selection of the software package is only the beginning. Management of the specific application development process is the most time-consuming and most important aspect of a large project.

TABLE 27.3 Definition of Software Quality Factors*

Correctness	Extent to which a program satisfies its specifications and fulfills the user's mission objectives
Reliability	Extent to which a program can be expected to perform its intended function with required precision
Efficiency	Amount of computing resources and code required by a program to perform a function
Integrity	Extent to which access to software or data by unauthorized persons can be controlled
Usability	Effort required to learn, operate, prepare input of, and interpret output of a program
Maintainability	Effort required to locate and fix an error in an operational program
Testability	Effort required to test a program to ensure that it performs its intended function
Flexibility	Effort required to modify an operational program.
Portability	Effort required to transfer a program from one hardware configuration and/or software system environment to another
Reusability	Extent to which a program can be used in other applications—related to the packaging and scope of the functions that programs perform
Interoperability	Effort required to couple one system with another

*Adapted from McCall et al. (1977).

TABLE 27.4 Steps in Acquiring an Application Package*

---

1. List present and future requirements of the application in detail.
2. Survey all available packages for that application.
3. Examine package documentation and user manuals.
4. Check whether the package has sufficient application parameters.
5. Check whether the package has adequate aids to maintenance.
6. Draw up a short list of suitable packages.
7. Try out each package with corporate data, if possible.
8. Determine whether the package can link into the corporate data base plans.
9. Conduct benchmarks (comparison trials) if performance is critical.
10. Allow end users to implement them on a temporary basis if the end user interface is critical.
11. Negotiate and write an appropriate contract.

---

*Adapted from Martin and McClure (1983).

TABLE 27.5 Pitfalls of Application Packages*

---

1. The package does not fully adapt to changes in requirements.
2. The data processing department must modify the package when it is installed, and subsequent maintenance becomes almost as expensive as in-house application programs.
3. Expensive maintenance becomes necessary later when the hardware, operating system, terminals, network, or user requirements are changed.
4. The package is hard to maintain owing to poor documentation, no provision for user-created code, poor structure, absence of source code, excessive complexity, low-level languages, or poor-quality coding.
5. The package has been made difficult to maintain because it has been tinkered with in-house and modifications have been made that are ill documented and difficult for others to understand.
6. The package does not fit with the corporate data base implementation and strategy.
7. The software house that owns the package ceases operations.

---

*Adapted from Martin and McClure (1983).

MANAGING COMPUTER PROJECTS

Planning the Program. Implementing a program to automate manual quality functions or processes begins with planning. An initial study helps to define current and future information needs and capabilities, to define specific projects to meet these needs, and to rank these projects in order of importance. The result of this effort is a plan outlining an integrated approach to computer applications that is consistent with the quality organization's functional objectives.

When potential projects have been identified in a high-level plan, a specific project is chosen for implementation based on its importance, cost, and other relevant factors. Once selected, specific project-related planning is conducted to produce (1) a statement of the scope and objectives; (2) a definition of the nature of the tasks required to meet these objectives; (3) an assessment of the skills required to complete these tasks; and (4) a project schedule and proposed method of controlling the project. The remainder of this section concentrates on the planning activities required at the project level.

"Project management" approaches provide a framework within which project-specific planning takes place. Project management views a project as consisting of generally sequential phases, each with specific end products and management review points. Regardless of the terminology used, all project-management approaches contain project phases concerned with the following activities:

Defining project requirements

Designing a system to meet these requirements

Implementing the system

Maintaining the system

Though similar, every approach to project management provides a slightly different description of the phases involved.

The nature of the work performed in each of these phases and their specific products are discussed below under Integrating the Effort.

What are the advantages of a project-management approach to you as the user of a computer system? Some major advantages are outlined below.

First, *this approach allows you to retain control of the project.* The temptation for some is to hand the problem to the Data Processing Department or consultants and let them design a solution. When such an approach is taken, the product delivered is rarely what the user really wanted. The user involvement inherent in the project-management approach ensures that you, as the user of the system, retain control of your operations and your new computer system.

Project management facilitates communication between the user and the computer professionals designing the system. The documentation produced throughout the project is reviewed and approved by the user group at each project phase. This provides a record of the decision-making process.

Formal project management adds continuity to the project. Long-term projects frequently experience the loss of key personnel, within either the user function or the data processing function. New project team members have a written record of the development of the project, which facilitates their integration into the project effort.

Problems are more readily identified and resolved. Continuous involvement in the project means that the users can quickly see if the project is straying from their requirements. Also, having a member of the user function involved in the project gives the data processing personnel someone to contact when problems do occur.

Organizing the Project Team. *The most important member of the project team is the project manager.* The project manager has responsibility for organizing the project, assigning tasks, tracking the progress of the project, and reporting problems. In most cases, the project manager with senior management support will select the other members of the team.

The project manager may come from either the user function or the data processing function. In either case, the project manager is responsible to the management of both groups for the duration of the project. The person assigned to be the project manager does not necessarily have to possess detailed technical computer skills but must be familiar enough with computer technology and the user function to communicate effectively with project team members and the management of both the user and data processing areas.

At least one person from the user function should be a member of the project team during all phases. Depending on the nature of the project, a different individual may be involved at different phases of the project. In a large complex project involving the automation of several operations or functions, representatives from each of the different functions should participate on the project team.

Assembling the right project team in terms of skills and numbers is vital to the ultimate success of the project.

Integrating the Effort.   The project management approach defines a project in terms of several phases. (See Planning the Program, above.)

While it is convenient to discuss each of these phases separately and consider them as sequential, there is a great deal of overlap between the phases. Some activities span only a few phases while others occur throughout the project. The products of each phase provide the basis for the activities in the following phase.

This section discusses in detail the phases of integrated project management as they apply to a computer project. Much of this information is based on "Method/1" (1984), Archibald (1976), Bingham and Davies (1978), Keryner (1979), and Martin (1976).

Defining Project Requirements.   Defining the quality project requirements in terms of scope and objectives is the true starting point for the computer project. The project manager uses the project definition to determine the general approach to project completion, the skills required by the project team members, and the complexity of the project. The project definition provides a basis for determination of anticipated project costs and benefits. Assembly of the project team begins during the project definition phase.

A clear statement of the user's requirements for the project and its expected outcome provides the basis for the project effort. In particular, the products of the project definition phase include:

- A clear description of the scope and objectives of the project
- An overall project approach
- An estimate of time and skills required
- Anticipated costs and benefits

Many project teams find that classification of requirements into "musts" and "wants" aids in the early prioritization and sets limits on project scope. Every nontrivial project should have a basis for trade-off decisions of function, cost, and schedule.

System Design.   During the system design phase of the project the team begins to address the requirements outlined in the previous phase. The specifics of the design, both technical and functional, are outlined. The requirements previously defined are expanded into detailed descriptions of current functions and required changes. The project team moves from addressing the "what" of the project into "how" the project will be completed. This includes selecting the hardware and software that will form the basis of the system and the way in which the users will interact with the system. A timetable for implementation is developed on the basis of the more detailed description of the user's requirements.

User participation during the system design phase is crucial. The requirements outlined in the project definition are expanded and refined. In addition to the primary user, recipients of reports or other data should be interviewed to ensure that their needs are also considered. As with all phases of a project, the primary responsibility for the tasks in the system design phase lies with the project manager.

The products of this phase include reports addressing the technical, functional, and management aspects of the system. Specific topics include:

- Details of the user functions addressed by the system
- Input and output information
- The information the system will contain and process
- The technical aspects of the system design
- Hardware and software recommendations
- A timetable for project completion
- Costs and benefits of the system

An important product of the system design phase is an understanding by the users and an agreement by management as to what the system will and will not do. Producing written reports facilitates this understanding and provides a basis for management approval. The products of the design phase provide the basis for the next project phase, system implementation.

System Implementation.   During the system implementation phase, the project is defined in enough detail to guide the programming effort, the actual programming is performed, and the system is installed. The work in this phase integrates the information needs outlined in the previous phases with the technical abilities of the project team members. This phase may be thought of as the actual "work" phase of the project. Until now most of the activity has involved planning and defining requirements but in this phase the necessary hardware is installed, the users are trained, and the system is tested and accepted for use.

During the system implementation phase, there is usually a clearer definition of areas of responsibility than in the previous phases. For example, data processing specialists will be involved in the actual programming effort, and the users will be involved in producing a user's manual.

It is particularly important that detailed design specifications produced by the data processing specialists be reviewed by the user(s) on the project team before programming begins.

It is the author's experience that review by the users at this time can prevent major disappointments and changes due to incorrect assumptions. The difficulty in reviewing a technical document can be overcome if a project team member from the user area "walks through" an oral review of the specification with the data processing specialist.

Another critical area of user involvement is the system test. After the individual programs have been written and "debugged" by the data processing personnel, the system must be tested as a whole. Ideally, the system test involves using the system under all possible conditions and with all possible data. Unless there are only a very limited and easily defined number of conditions for use of the system, this approach to testing is not practical. For this reason testing of a computer system relies on the development of test cases that represent as many conditions and as much data as possible. User input is necessary in the development of these test cases to ensure an accurate representation of the actual operating environment.

Two other tasks occurring during the system implementation phase are production of the user's manual and training. A user's manual is absolutely necessary both as a training tool and as an operational reference. The document should be developed by the users because it gives them the opportunity to explain the system in their particular functional terms. The manual describes the nonautomated as well as the automated procedures necessary to use the system and should be produced in a manner that allows for configuration management and updating.

The approach to training depends on the complexity and scope of the system. Training is generally undertaken as a joint effort between the users and the data processing personnel.

The main product of the system implementation phase is the actual system, accepted and formally approved. Other products of this phase are:

- Fully documented programs and specifications
- Trained users
- A manual outlining user procedures
- Documentation required for maintaining the system

System Maintenance. The final phase of a project is system maintenance. This phase continues for as long as the system is in use and provides a formal means by which the users can request changes or modifications in the system. It often also includes a schedule for assessing the actual performance of the system after it has been in place and operating error-free for some period of time. This periodic assessment of system performance monitors user satisfaction, actual costs and benefits, and the number of changes or enhancements required. No system has an infinite life, and the data obtained through periodic audits of the system in use will provide information for developing the requirements for a replacement system.

Measuring Progress and Performance. Project management provides a means of tracking the progress of a project. Techniques such as bar charts, the Critical Path Method (CPM), and the Program Evaluation Review Technique (PERT) are usually employed. Work breakdown structures and similar tools are also available for creating and revising schedule and cost estimates over the life of the project. Frequently, this emphasis on budget and schedule overshadows the importance of measuring how well the system delivered to the users actually meets the requirements and objectives agreed upon by management. Failure in either area marks a project as unsuccessful.

Paragraphs that follow deal with potential quality applications during a product life cycle.

NEW-PRODUCT QUALITY DESIGN REVIEW

To capture and record the "corporate experience" of past problems solved has been a universal goal. If known past problems can be kept out of new designs, productivity and effectiveness within the product development cycle can be greatly enhanced. Designers can focus on the new, innovative, state-of-the-art aspects of a design. As reported by Hitachi (Nitta et al., 1980, p. 152): " . . . results of practical use [of their computer-aided design review program] indicate that more than 30% of product failures due to misdesign [have] been prevented." This effort was not without early problems. Hitachi reports over 20 years of unsuccessful earlier activity due to the following major factors:

1. Disorganized indexing systems
2. Troublesome data maintenance
3. Insufficient connection with design reviews

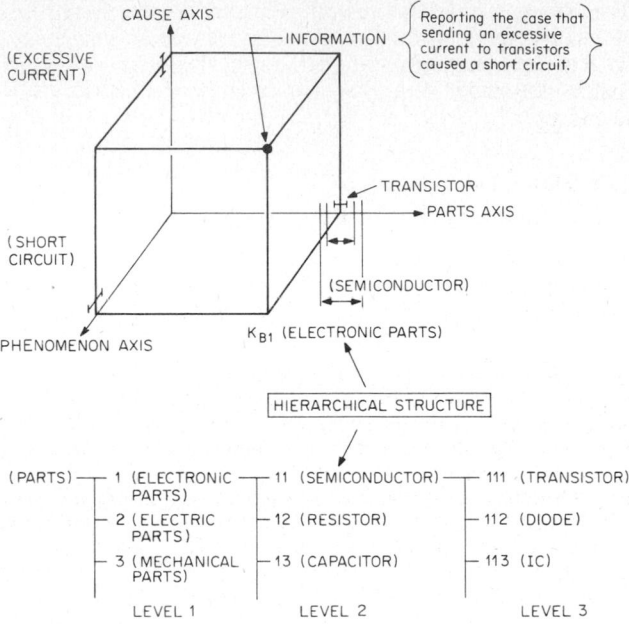

FIG. 27.1 Conceptual thesaurus structure. *(Adapted from Nitta et al., 1980, p. 154. © IEEE. Used with permission.)*

These problems can be reduced by automating the capture, recording, and retrieval of past experiences. The Hitachi Design Review System includes key word features, a computer-assisted thesaurus, an interactive retrieval mode, and an information manager for systems support and maintenance.

In the Hitachi three-axis hierarchical structure, each axis is a collection of key words that share common attributes or concepts. With a phenomenon axis, parts axis, and cause axis, we see the information location reporting excessive current (cause) sent to transistors (parts), which resulted in a short circuit (phenomenon) (Figure 27.1). Each axis in turn has a hierarchical structure, which lists key words according to relationship, i.e., transistor-semiconductor-electronic part (Figure 27.1). Standardization of key words and careful selection of axes have permitted the companywide system to operate on approximately 3000 or fewer key words (Nitta et al., 1980).

Retrieval results are displayed on a computer screen for titles, abstracts, and key words. Primary source data are provided through a microfiche retrieval system, which supplies photographed documents.

NEW-PROCESS QUALITY

Major advances in instrumentation, automation, and computer technology have built new industries focused on process control. These activities, generally called "computer-integrated manufacturing" (CIM) or "computer-aided manufacturing" (CAM), can range from continuous process plants such as oil refineries and paper mills to fabrication and assembly operations. Replacing small quality and/ or manufacturing staffs, automation has focused large numbers of diverse technical staffs on process control. In addition to control aspects, quality assurance in many industries has provided an integration and coordination role. For a discussion of the concepts involved, see Section 16 under Automated Manufacturing.

Large-Scale Plant-Wide Systems

Computer-Aided Process Planning. Computer-Aided Process Planning involves selection of a cost-effective sequence of operations for manufacturing, inspection, and testing of a product under prescribed conditions. The "variant" and "generative" approaches are the primary types of computerized process planning.

> In the variant approach, the standard process plan for a given parts family is retrieved using a parts classification and coding technique. The standard process plan is then modified for the specific or new part. This approach partially automates the manual procedure by using existing process planning information to produce a new plan for an existing or new part.
>
> In the generative approach, the idea is to provide the computer with enough intelligence about machining and manufacturing operations to allow it to generate a sequence of operations and a detailed operational plan. This kind of system requires detailed input about part design and drawing features. Also, the machining and manufacturing logic must be captured into the data base (Tipnis, 1980, pp. 129–130).

At Baxter Healthcare Corp., the variant approach is used to plan assembly operations by grouping product specifications and process plans into families of similar products. New assembled products can be introduced by modifications and expansion of existing documentation.

Conversely, the generative approach is used to plan new molded parts. Computer-aided drafting systems allow the part design to drive the automatic generation of the following outputs:

1. Mold drawings
2. Inspection and test fixture drawings
3. Optimized tool path
4. Numerical controlled machine instruction programs

Process planning must also consider aspects of process control.

Hierarchical Systems. A basic computer-assisted process control system involves the use of a widely distributed set of isolated control functions carried out by small and inexpensive microcomputers. These systems may be highly redundant to preserve the integrity of the total control system in the face of possible failure of any one unit. In turn, their work is coordinated by a set of successively higher-level computers connected to each other and to the distributed remote control computers by an extensive plant communication system (Williams, 1976).

The benefits of such a hierarchical system are shown in Table 27.6. The hardware and software specific to individual control functions and the communication system that links them is called a "computer network." "The network is a collection of nodes, each having different functions and capabilities, and interconnected by data links" (Bizarro, 1976, p. 151).

TABLE 27.6 Benefits of a Hierarchical System*

1. Flexible system configuration—distributed subsystems may be modified, replaced, or deleted without upsetting the rest of the system.
2. Graceful degradation—failure in one or more components or subsystems does not cause the entire system to fail.
3. High system reliability due to redundant systems and error detection codes.
4. Simplified lower-cost systems, allowing multiple use of standard components, standard software, and incremental design and installation.

*Adapted from Williams (1976).

The mesh network consists of a random net of connections, built up as the need for them emerges, which may open up several alternative data routes between participating devices.

Hierarchical control involves partitioning control functions into tiers, with responsibilities corresponding to levels of scope or authority in the organizations. Typically, the lowest tier includes computers and/or smart controllers that monitor and control specific pieces of equipment. These machines are accessible to operators (and inspectors) on the plant floor. [For design of operator/inspector interface, see Table 27.7.] The next higher tiers involve computers to analyze operating data and management instructions from points throughout the plant. The highest tiers are reserved for plant-wide tasks such as systems development, production planning, and monitoring overall efficiencies. (Bizzaro, 1976, p. 155)

TABLE 27.7 Operator-Inspector Interface Design*

1. Avoid parallel displays mounted on extended panels since they contain more information than a human operator can observe simultaneously.
2. Process operation information should be displayed on an exception basis.
3. Compact indication of process performance or status should take advantage of pattern recognition display techniques.
4. Data should be grouped to convey knowledge of the operations of natural subsystems.
5. Alarms should be hierarchical, being selectively suppressed as a function of operating state.
6. Manual operation of most control valves should be possible as a redundant feature. [When designing automated valving systems, catastrophic system failure can often be avoided by purchasing valves that are wired to indicate their state (open or closed) at both ends rather than depending on spring-loaded devices that have only one indicator state and assume proper spring operation.]
7. History and trends in data should be available for operator guidance.
8. Analog displays should be used for qualitative information, digital displays for quantitative information. These two forms can be mixed as required.
9. Available derived variables (efficiency, quality, etc.) should be used as performance indicators rather than simple variables (temperature, viscosity, etc.).
10. A single interface should be provided with all of the functions and information available at any one location.
11. Interfaces should not be compromised to support other functions such as maintenance and management. (Separate hardware should be provided to accomplish these functions.)

*Adapted from Williams (1976).

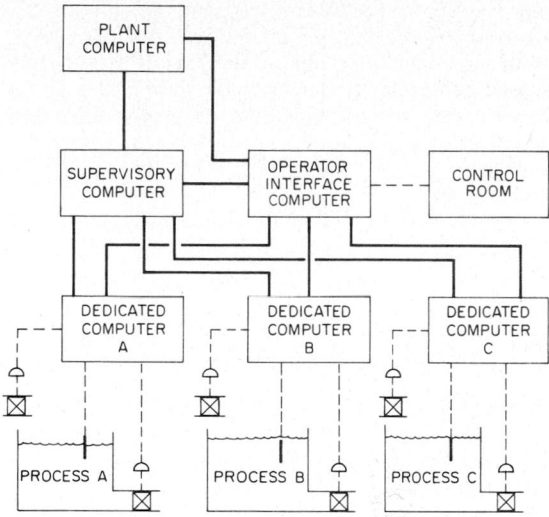

FIG. 27.2 Network used for distributed control in a chemical blending plant. *(Excerpted by special permission from Chemical Engineering, vol. 83, no. 26, December 1976, p. 154. © 1979, McGraw-Hill, Inc.)*

An example of this type of networking is shown in Figure 27.2. Industrial examples of both large- and small-scale systems illustrate practical applications of hierarchical process design.

Large-Scale System Example.   Properly designed, automated test systems can provide significant benefits in addition to improvement in test productivity. Additional design objectives typically are the following:

- To provide more positive and constant control over test processes
- To provide more reliable and positive indicators of early-stage malfunctions
- To improve data availability and report preparation
- To improve accuracy and repeatability of test parameter measurement and recording
- To provide closed-loop calibrations
- To provide closed-loop feedback control

The "computer-controlled gas turbine engine package system" provides a model for a large scale, multiunit system[2] (Gellagher and Ball, 1976).

Prior to entering the test cell complex, a pretest area is utilized to provide for electrical, electronic, pneumatic, and hydraulic-type hookup. The preassembly of test system cables results in maximum computer system utility. As preparation can typically consume 30 to 50 percent of the calendar time associated with a large-scale integrated test, the reader is advised to devote significant attention to

---

[2]The system described in this example was designed by Digital Equipment Corp. and installed at Solar Turbines International, San Diego.

the planning and design of the pretest hookup and instrumentation activities. As noted earlier in this section, deliverable equipment design requirements must include the access to equipment controls, as well as quick hookup and disconnect.

Special test connectors are the preferred method of design so that internal connections need not be broken when testing deliverable product. The obvious needs restatement: automated testing should be done on equipment that is as close to deliverable configuration as possible under conditions that simulate the customer's use as closely as possible.

A 13-cell test complex is divided into three major modules. The first consists of the test cell itself and the unit undergoing test. The second is the test control room, where the test operator actually controls and monitors the test. The third is the computer room, which includes a host computer and three satellite computer systems. Each satellite system is responsible for the test process in four test cells, and all computer systems may operate simultaneously and independently (see Hierarchical Systems, above).

Located in each control room is an operator-controlled console, which provides the means of communicating with the computer and the test unit, a printer, facility and computer junction boxes, and a special pressure test system that allows sequential multiplexing of pressure signals as well as calibration pressures.

Human engineering at the operator control console is especially critical. Control and display units at this console provide the operator with the capability of monitoring and controlling the power and stimuli to operate the test unit and to measure and evaluate its performance. Although the computers perform the operational tasks, the test operator in this system need not be directly concerned with the computer or its programming.

This computer test system is a quality control tool that operates in real time. After programming and under minimum operator control, it is the computer that (1) applies or enables the application of test stimuli, (2) measures test response, and (3) outputs test results. Capability also includes complete computerized control of the test sequence and actual test events.

Availability of off-line systems that support development of application software and data base preparation is vital to a continuing operation of any major installation. Change is inevitable, and application software is necessary to implement this change. Design of systems that do not allocate off-line support for application program development are forced to trade off important productivity and test utilization time for application development.

Small-Scale System Example.   As discussed by Stubin (1978), a real-time process monitoring and control system was developed for chemical tank temperatures. By using the resources already available and by incorporating a standard microprocessor, personnel and technical expertise requirements to implement the project were significantly minimized. This project monitors 15 chemical tank temperatures critical to the plating of multilayer printed wiring boards.

Hardware selected included temperature indicator instrumentation. A microcomputer, keyboard, and printer complete the stand-alone system. Capability to transmit biweekly historical data to a host computer is also provided.

Microcomputer operating systems software, including editor/debug commands and real-time clock, were coupled with the following microcomputer applications software to control the system:

- *Temperature monitoring system program:*   a sensor scanning subroutine
- *Limit alarm:*   a program to print out a warning when specification or preferred range is exceeded and to extrapolate trend readings

- *Down load program:* a program to load data from memory to the host computer system

Improved process quality as well as system payback is achieved by continuous control and digital display of chemical tank temperatures. The actual record lists the indicator number and the corresponding temperature. Any temperature that is out of specification or out of preferred range is immediately printed out on an interrupt basis as a warning. A record is also provided to show that chemical processes are performed per specification. Operator awareness of chemical solutions is improved, with corresponding reduction in operator error, decreased rework, and increased yield (Stubin, 1978).

INSPECTION

Computer-Aided Inspection. Rapid breakthroughs in computer-aided design (CAD) and computer-aided manufacturing are providing the data base and information structure for the introduction of computer-aided inspection and computer-aided test. Cost incentives are also expected to accelerate the development of inspection and test automation to keep pace with major gains in manufacturing automation. Many manufacturers are reporting inspection costs significantly rising as a percentage of total manufacturing costs. This dramatic increase is largely attributable to inspection techniques being outstripped by manufacturing automation (see New-Process Quality, above).

Achievement of defect levels in the parts per million range also requires breakthrough technology. All industries are increasingly accepting on-machine automated 100 percent inspection and testing.

As reported by Scott (1982), although automated inspection has existed in many forms over a number of years, the development of microprocessors has greatly expanded the potential number of applications. The microprocessor can deal with large quantities of information and very rapidly produce a go–no go decision. "The decision taken by the system will contain a known basis for the judgment, unlike the human inspector whose performance and judgment can vary depending on what sort of a day the inspector has had already on the shop floor" (Scott, 1982, p. 2).

Generally, automatic inspection will couple a transducer to a computer. Transducers can take the form of dimensional position indicators or indicators of physical effects such as force, flow, vibration, electrical properties, or magnetic properties.

The multitude of potential applications for automated inspection and the computer functions are detailed in Table 27.8. This table, developed by the author, should prove useful as a checklist for potential project ideas.

In-Cycle Gaging. The use of touch trigger probes to take measurements during a numerically controlled machine tool cycle is called "in-cycle gaging." As reported by Roe (1982), recent developments in this technology have led to the availability of new techniques that can compensate for machine thermal movement, setup tolerances, and the wear of tools. Software is now widely available to enable users to employ these techniques.

Yee (1982) describes a system for predicting when the failure of a rotating machine tool or part is imminent or when a tool is worn. Drill wear and breakage prediction is implemented by applying time-domain analysis on a signal from an

TABLE 27.8 Potential Applications for Automated Inspection

Industry applications	Equipment type	Transducer type	Computer type	Computer function
Dimensional gaging	Automatic high-speed, noncontact video inspection, and optical comparators	Optical, laser, video, solid-state camera	Micro, mini	Video image processing; auto-focus; mass storage for uninterrupted cycle execution; part and table multiple-axis servo positioning; inspection of unaligned parts
	Coordinate measurement machine	Touch probe	Micro, mini	Geometrical tolerance programming, tolerance analysis, data handling, multiple probe calibration, laser calibration, math processing, contouring, operator prompting, editing, feedback, accept/reject decision
	Computer-assisted gaging (lab)	Touch probe, electronic, air	Micro, mini	Supervised prompting, automatic mastering, magnification set, zeroing display, statistics, counting, spec comparison, diagnostic testing Off-line programming, CAD/CAM compatibility
	Electronic gages and measuring systems with computer interface	Calipers, micrometers, snap gages, bore gages, indicator probes, height gages, air gages, ultrasonic gages, magnetic gages, etc.	Micro	Direct digital output, gages to host computer through interface
	In-cycle gaging on numerical-controlled (NC) machines	Touch probe	Micro, mini	On machine measurements, tool wear compensation, temperature compensation, automatic check of tool offset, work location, table and spindle relationship

Category	Item	Type	Computer	Application
	Bench laser micrometer	Laser	Micro	Automatic laser scan, data handling, statistical dimension calculations, part sorting, accept/reject decision
	Holography	Laser	Micro	Automatic stress, strain, displacement, image processing
	Laser interferometer	Laser	Micro	Automatic temperature and humidity compensation, data handling and storage, math processing
	3-D Theodolite, coordinate, measurement	Optical	Micro	Interactive operator prompting, automatic angular measurement, data handling
	Scanning laser acoustic microscope (SLAM)	Laser, acoustic	Micro	Beam scanning, data processing
Electrical and electronic instrumentation	Temperature measurement	Thermocouple, thermistor, resistance temperature detector (RTD)	Micro, mini	Calibration, data acquisition analysis and processing
	Robotic-printed circuit board test	Electronic	Mini	Robot control, fully automatic board test
	Weight and balance, filling and packaging, inspection	Electronic	Micro	Automatic tare, statistical processing, data recording
	Circuit analyzers	Electronic	Micro, mini	Special-purpose test systems
	Automatic test equipment functional testers	All	Micro, mini, mainframe	Special-purpose test systems with complete real-time input, processing and output data
	Cable testers	Electrical	Micro	Automated harness continuity and high-potential testing
	Semiconductor testers		Micro	Automated test of standard and special-purpose chips

TABLE 27.8 Potential Applications for Automated Inspection (*Continued*)

Industry applications	Equipment type	Transducer type	Computer type	Computer function
Lab devices and equipment	Chromatographs	Optical	Mini	Fully automatic preprogrammed sampling and data recording
	Strength of materials	Probe, force, displacement, strain gage	Micro	Preprogrammed cycle operation, data, chart and graphic output records, multichannel recording, on-line data processing
	Hardness testing	Probe	Micro	Robotic, fully automatic testing and recording, results analysis, and prediction
	Analyzers	All	Micro, mini	Automatic calibration, testing, and recording
	Electron microscopes	Electromagnetic	Micro, mini	Cathode ray tube (CRT) processing and materials analysis preprogrammed for failure analysis
Optical imaging	Video borescope, fiberoptic inspection	Optical	Micro	Digital data image processing documentation
	Photographic	Optical	Micro	Fully automatic strobe, photographic sequencing and processing
	Video microscopes	Optical	Micro	Video image processing data documentation
	High-speed video recording	Optical	Micro	Automatic 200–12,000 frames per second stop-motion recording of machine and manual processes; motion analysis; data processing
Environmental and functional test equipment	Test chamber controls	Temperature, humidity, altitude	Micro	Preprogrammed cycle controls, time and data records

Leak detection	Vacuum, gas, acoustic	Micro	Automatic zeroing, built-in calibration, automatic sequencing, tolerance checking, data processing and display
Shock and vibration testing	Accelerometer	Mini	Automatic cycle control, built-in calibration, data logging and display
Built-in equipment	Electrical, electronic	Micro, mini	Preprogrammed part and system functional and environmental cycling, recording
EMI measurement	Electronic, magnetic	Mini	Data processing, math analysis, recording
Data acquisition systems	All	Mini, mainframe	Complete data acquisition and processing
Materials testing equipment			
Surface and roughness measurement	Stylus follower, air flow	Micro	Operator prompting, data analysis
Coating thickness, sheeting thickness	Electronic, video, ultrasonic, beta backscatter	Micro	Calculation and math processing; display; self-calibration; automatic filter changing and positioning; prompting self-diagnostics; feedback; accept/reject decision
Paper, plastic, and coated product process inspection for holes, particulates, streaks, thickness	Laser	Micro, mini	Automatic high-speed processing, feedback controls, data analysis and alarms
Nondestructive test equipment			
Magnetic particle, eddy current	Probe	Micro	Self-regulations, calibration, data handling, defect recognition
Ultrasonic flaw detection	Sonic, vibration	Micro, mini	Automated quantitive analysis, curve matching, automated procedures, graphics data acquisition and storage

TABLE 27.8 Potential Applications for Automated Inspection (*Continued*)

Industry applications	Equipment type	Transducer type	Computer type	Computer function
Nondestructive test equipment (*continued*)	Scanning laser acoustic microscope (SLAM) flaw detection	Laser, acoustic	Micro	Beam scanning, data processing, flow detection
	X-ray, fluoroscopic	Optical, electronic	Micro	Automatic calibration, operator prompting, data handling, statistics, stored programming, defect recognition
	Acoustic emission	Acoustic	Micro	Independent channel monitoring and display, linear, zone location, tolerance comparison, preprogrammed tests, graphics output, triangulation, source location
	Infrared test systems	Optical, video	Micro	Calibration, system control
	Radiographic, gamma	Optical, gamma	Micro	Programmable, automatic, self-diagnostic, safety malfunction interrupts, automatic defect recognition, robotic part handling, automatic detection of missing parts
	Computer-aided tomography (CAT) scanner	X-ray	Mini	Data acquisition, processing, interpretation and imaging
	Nuclear magnetic resonance (NMR) scanner	Magnetic	Mini	Data acquisition, processing, interpretation and imaging

accelerometer mounted on the work piece. This analysis is performed by a single-chip microcomputer. It is reported that in 49 of 50 cases the system predicted that the drill would fail 2 to 20 holes before actual failure. The system includes a transducer for producing an output related to the work piece vibrations of the machine tool. It also contains an analog comparator, which measures this output against a threshold signal related to the normal operation of the tool. Levels established by a microcomputer determine whether signals that exceed the threshold are produced during each of a predetermined number of subsequent time intervals related to the rotational speed of the tool. If so, a "failure" signal is produced, which may be used, for example, to cause retraction of the tool.

POST-PRODUCTION QUALITY

Computer systems allow quality personnel to collect data on industrial products during their operation in the field. An example of such a system, as described in Figure 27.3, shows the utility of a central Reliability Data Center managed by the Quality Assurance Department.

A Reliability Data Center is established and operated to collect, analyze, measure, and report data pertaining to part and system operating history. These data are summarized periodically and used as product reliability indicators. In this

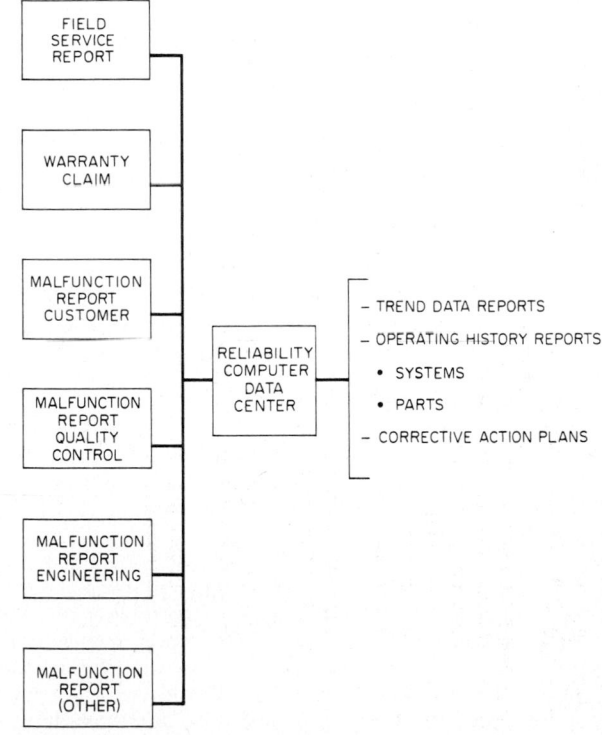

FIG. 27.3 Reliability data center.

example, the Reliability Data Center is concerned with product design problems as distinct from quality problems encountered in production. Examples of integrated systems are available in the literature.

Failure and defect statistics continue to be reported for review until trend data reach a predetermined level established by Reliability Engineering.

As seen in the system flow chart (Figure 27.3), data can enter the system from six independent sources. Telephone conversations, memoranda, and other direct communications are also documented.

An important lesson learned is that to ensure routine input of primary field service report data, the field service expense report should be incorporated on the back of the Reliability Data Reporting Form.

STATISTICAL ANALYSIS

One of the first and still important uses of the computer in quality control is for statistical analysis (see Besterfield, 1979). Most statistical techniques discussed in this handbook may be programmed by using one of the programming languages discussed under Types of Software and Applications, above. Computers are proving useful in the design of experiments as well as in the analysis of data (Snee, 1985). The advantages of programmed statistical software techniques are:

1. Time-consuming manual calculations are eliminated.
2. Timely and accurate analyses may be performed to diagnose one-time problems or maintain process control.
3. Many researchers and engineers with only limited knowledge or training in statistics can now perform their own statistical analyses (Francis, 1981).

Three types of computers are popular in statistical quality control: pocket programmable calculators, microcomputers, and main frames.

"The Shewhart Chart is a child of the precomputer age, when all recordkeeping was done manually. With today's off-the-shelf computing capabilities, the total technology system needed can readily be put together" (Marquardt, 1984, p. 12).

Sources of Statistical Software.   An important key to the success of programming devices is availability of effective user-oriented software or computer programs: " . . . most users do not really want to become skilled programmers; thus, the successful use of the device depends on what applicable software can be found" (Berger and Hale, 1980, p. 2).

Quality control and statistical software is an undefined market, which was estimated at $135 million sales in 1982 and is growing at 25 percent per year (Bernstein, 1984). Many companies enter and exit annually, and software suppliers should be evaluated on their ability to support their products over the long range.

Pocket programmable calculators are versatile, inexpensive, and easy to use in all physical environments. Preprogrammed memory modules are available that contain standard calculations widely used in a particular field, e.g., quality control, business mathematics, and electrical engineering (Berger and Hale, 1980).

Program-listing booklets that contain specialized program listings are also available. These programs must be keyed into the calculator manually and stored on magnetic cards if desired. There are usually 10 to 20 programs per booklet. Common subjects shown in a statistics program booklet include sampling, tests of significance, analysis of variance, control charting, etc.

Microcomputers. The availability of statistical software for microcomputers is increasing at a very rapid rate. In addition to packages available from the manufacturer and published as user guides or manuals, other sources of software are found in technical journals, computer magazines, and catalogs.

Commercial packages that are approaching the power of mainframes are rapidly entering the market. They deal with specific solutions (e.g., sampling or control charts) or general statistics and sell for under $1000.

Statistical software sources for microcomputers are discussed in detail in *Directory of Statistical Microcomputer Software* (Woodward et al., 1985).

Mainframe Computers. Extensive statistical software for mainframe computers is published in the form of statistical packages. An excellent reference, *Statistical Software, A Comparative Review* (Francis, 1981) provides a comparison of the capabilities, portability, ease of learning and using, reliability, and maintenance of over 100 statistical packages.

Table 27.9 provides information on 11 general statistical packages, including Developer and Distributor Addresses, Computer Makes, Operating Systems, Interfacing Systems, and Source Language. The programs are "uniformly strong in most aspects of statistical analysis . . . Many of them also have capabilities for data management and tabulation" (Francis, 1981).

Journals are another source of software. Both the *Journal of Quality Technology* and *Quality Progress* provide periodic quality-related software directories.

COMPUTER INTEGRATION INTO PRODUCT DESIGN

An increasing number of commercial, industrial, and military systems are employing some form of microprocessor as an integral part of the product design. A "microprocessor" is a central processing unit consisting of an arithmetic logic unit and a control unit organized on one or more chips by means of large-scale integration technology. A microprocessor is used as the central processing unit of a microcomputer system.

Microprocessors are now inexpensive enough for thousands of applications, and as costs decrease, capabilities are increasing. Examples range from watches, appliances, and automobiles to complex medical and aerospace equipment.

The microprocessors of today are superior in most aspects to the major processors of a dozen or more years ago. The decrease in size and cost of processors has correspondingly increased the range of their practical applications by several orders of magnitude.

The incorporation of a microprocessor in the product design also includes some distinct technical advantages:

1. Increased control over the function of the product
2. Ease in making changes in software as compared with hardware redesign
3. Ease of incorporating fail-safe design features such as self-test, internal diagnostics, and condition monitoring
4. Increased functions without proportional increases in physical size or complexity of operation and without sacrifice of reliability

Product Reliability and Safety. The incorporation of microprocessors changes the way in which the quality, reliability, and safety design objectives are defined, managed, and analyzed.

TABLE 27.9 General Statistical Software Packages

Statistical package	Developer	Distributor	Computer makes	Operating systems*	Interfaced systems†	Source language
1. Consistent System (CS)	Laboratory of Architecture Room 4-209 Massachusetts Institute of Technology Cambridge, MA 02139	Renaissance Computing, Inc. P.O. Box 699 Cambridge, MA 02139 (617)491-0900	Honeywell Multics	DPS-68 or equivalent	BMDP-79, IMSL	PL/1
2. Statistical Analysis System (SAS)	SAS Institute, Inc. Box 8000, SAS Circle Cary, NC 27511	Same	IBM 360/370/403X 43XX Series, Amdahl, Itel, National, Two Pi, Magnuson, Hitachi, Nanodata	OS, OS/VS, VM/CMS, MFT, MVT, VSI, VS2, SVS, MVS		PL/1, Assembly
3. Omnitab	Dr. David Hogben, Mrs. Sally T. Peavy National Bureau of Stds. Room A337, Bldg. 101 Washington, DC 20234	Mrs. Alice Dugan National Bureau of Stds. A323, Physics Bldg. Washington, DC 20234	Univac-1108-1110, IBM-4331, CDC-Cyber 173, HP3000, IBM-158, DEC-PDP10, CDC-6600	UNIVAC-EXE8, IBM-VM/CMS CDC-NOS 1.4, MPE III, IBM-OS/VS1, TOPS-10, KRONOS 2.1		FORTRAN
4. HP Stat Packs	T.J. Boardman Statistical Laboratory Colorado State University Fort Collins, CO 80523	David Deane, Marketing Hewlett-Packard, D.C.D. 3400 East Harmony Rd. Fort Collins, CO 80525	Hewlett-Packard 9845 Desktop Computer	System 45		BASIC
5. Minitab— Version 80	Minitab Project 215 Pond Laboratory University Park, PA 16802 (814) 865-1595	Same	Amdahl (All); Buroughs 4000, 5000, 6000, 7000; CDC (All); Data Gen. Eclipse; Dec 10,20; Harris (All);	AOS		FORTRAN

Package	Contact		Machines	Operating Systems		Language
6. BMDP	BMDP Statistical Software Dept. of Biomathematics University of California Los Angeles, CA 90024 (213)825-5940	Same	Hewlett-Packard HP 3000; Honeywell 6000; IBM360, Models 40+; IBM370, Models 115+; IBM4300, IBM3030; PDP-11 11/03+; PRIME 150, 250,350+; Tandem 16; Texas Instr. TI990; UNIVAC 70, 80, 90 1100; VAX; Xerox Sigma	Multics, GCOS, DTSS; VS, VM, TSO, CMS, DOS VS, OS; RSTS, RSX11, RT11, IAS; VMS, UNIX	P-STAT, SAS, SIR	FORTRAN
7. New Interactive Statistical Analysis Package (NISAN)	Dr. Chooichiro Asano Research Institute of Fundamental Information Science Kyushu University 33 Fukuoka 812, Japan	Same	Amdahl; Burroughs; CDC6000; Cyber; Data General; DEC 10/20; Facom; Hitac; Honeywell; HP 3000; IBM; ICL 2900/System 4; Interdata; Itel PDPII/LSI-11; Prime; Siemens; Telefunken TR440; Univac 1108, 1110; VAX 11/780; Xerox Sigma 7; FACOM, IBM 370	IBM/OS, VS, TSO, VM/CMS, DOS/VOS (many others); FACOM M-190, FACOM M-200, OS, MVT/TSO		FORTRAN

TABLE 27.9 General Statistical Software Packages (*Continued*)

Statistical package	Developer	Distributor	Computer makes	Operating systems*	Interfaced systems†	Source language
8. General Statistical Program (GENSTAT)	Statistics Dept. Rothamsted Experimental Station Harpenden, Herts., UK	Statistical Pkg. Coordinator NAG Central Office 7 Banbury Road Oxford OX2 6NN, UK	Burroughs 6700 CDC 6000 Series Cyber Series 7600 DEC System 10,20 Honeywell IBM 360, 370 ICL 1900 Series ICL 2900 Series ICL 4-70/75 Prime 400+ SIEMENS Univac 1100 Series VAX	MCP NOS Scope 2.0 TOPS 10, 20 GCOS OS George 2, 3 EMAS, VME, B, K Multijob Primos BS2000 EXEC 8 VMS		FORTRAN
9. Speakeasy III	Speakeasy Computing Corp. 222 West Adams Street Chicago, IL 60606 (312)346-2745	Same	IBM360; 370 Fujitsu M Series Burroughs 6700	IBM/OS, VS, TSO, VM/CMS NCSS, Burroughs 6700		FORTRAN
10. TROLL	Center for Computational Research Economics & Mgmt. Science Massachusetts Institute of Technology 292 Main Street Room E38-200 Cambridge, MA 02139	Same	IBM 370	IBM/OS, VS, MVS/TSO, VM/CMS, DOS, MTS		FORTRAN, Assembly

| 11. Interactive Data Analysis & Forecasting System (IDA) | Robert F. Ling
Dept. of Mathematical Sciences
0-104 Martin Hall
Clemson University,
Clemson, SC 29631

Harry V. Roberts
Graduate School of Business
University of Chicago
1101 East 58th Street
Chicago, IL 60637 | SPSS, Inc.
444 N. Michigan Ave.
Chicago, IL 60611 | IBM 360, 370
DEC System 10, 20
HP-3000
Data General Eclipse/
Nova
MV-8000
Prime
Honeywell (CP-6)
VAX 11/780, 11/750 | TSO, VM/CMS
VMS, TOPS-10, TOP S-20,
AOS, RDOS | FORTRAN |

*Operating system: The software that runs the system and performs functions necessary to control system operations. It is the control system under which all other software functions.
†Interfaced system: Application software that shades into system software. Software that enhances the computer's basic information processing abilities in ways that seem to be system-based rather than applications-based.

The level and degree of product quality, reliability, and safety must first be established by a quality systems analysis and incorporated into the Requirements Definition for the product (see Managing Computer Projects, above).

In analyzing the quality, reliability, and safety goals, any product can be viewed as a collection of electronic, electromechanical, and mechanical components.

Products that utilize microprocessors require an additional category consisting of program software, which adds a unique dimension to the problem of design analysis. While methods have evolved to analyze, predict, and control the reliability of conventional systems, software as an entity has an altogether different character, presents greater difficulties, and must be treated separately.

Even though the software aspect of the microprocessor is more difficult to analyze, the product fail-safe design and self-test objectives are easier to achieve when the design involves the use of microprocessors. Some products, because of the type of application for which they will be used, have higher criticality than do others. The level of design effort that goes into each type of product must be commensurate with the application.

The following discussion focuses on the reliability and quality of the microprocessor itself as an electronic device, the reliability of the software program associated with the processor, and the design advantages that the microprocessor allows.

Microprocessor Reliability and Quality.   Microprocessors and peripheral devices are supplied by many manufacturers. Typical device costs vary with the number of instructions, execution time, and underlying technology. The quality level of these hardware devices has a direct effect on the reliability of the computer system. They can be procured at specified levels of quality as defined by MIL-M-38510D and MIL-STD-883C, which are keyed to the models for predicting reliability failure rate that are given in MIL-HDBK-217D.[3] These specifications define levels of qualification testing, screening tests, and burn-in.

Commercial types have also demonstrated excellent performance, but testing is not documented. However, as a minimum, they generally undergo visual inspection and electrical parameter testing.

Software Reliability and Quality.   Built-in software is an element of the total product that governs computational or control functions. Once established, a microcomputer program will not be changed for most applications. Consequently the programs for microcomputers are normally stored in ROM or EPROM rather than in RAM.

ROM (Read Only Memory): A permanent memory circuit written during manufacture, which cannot be altered by a user.

EPROM (Erasable Programmable Read Only Memory): A programmable memory, which can only be read and normally not changed. By using special hardware, an EPROM can be erased with ultraviolet light and reprogrammed.

RAM (Random Access Memory): A memory storage area within the microcomputer for programs and data. Information in RAM is not retained when power is lost.

---

[3]See References at end of this section for full publication data of these standards and sources where they can be obtained. See also Appendix III, Selected Quality Standards, Specifications, and Related Documents.

The basic program instructions for ROM and EPROM are generally referred to as "firmware."

Regardless of the memory type, the task of developing the program is the same, i.e., the translation of instructions ultimately into binary machine language. Developing the program, in general, involves the same steps described in Managing Computer Applications, above.

Each step of the program development process is inherently error-prone. Errors can be introduced from misinterpretation, mistakes in translation, or mistakes in coding. Unless special attention is given to each step, a large number of errors could be introduced. It is most cost-effective to detect and eliminate errors as early in the program development process as possible.

Figure 27.4 shows the cost of correcting an error relative to the phase in which the error is detected. The figure indicates that an error corrected during operation can cost over 75 times as much as if it had been corrected during preliminary design (Anderson and Martin, 1982).

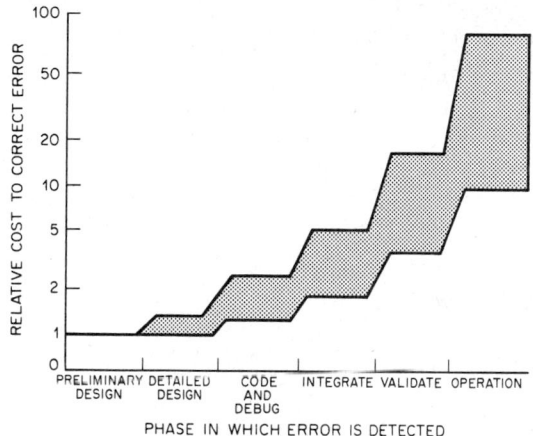

FIG. 27.4 Software error correction cost. *(Adapted from Anderson and Martin, 1982, p. 8.)*

To ensure high reliability in software programs, the development phase should provide for initial analysis and testing of sections or modules of the total software package. Interfaces between tested modules can then be analyzed and tested in subsequent steps. Basic procedures that improve the opportunities for reliable software are discussed in Managing Computer Projects, above.

After software has been integrated with the hardware system, testing procedures will exercise the functions of the software. They should include the testing of boundary conditions and simulation of both legitimate and illegitimate input combinations to assess the system response. The use of fault generators at the inputs of built-in microcomputer systems has been demonstrated to test hardware-software interfaces with significant saving of analysis time (Kenyon and Newell, 1982).

System Fail-Safe Design Quality Using Microprocessors. The incorporation of a microprocessor into the design of a product permits greater freedom in designing the system. Failures of single circuit components can be detected before the effects of those failures produce a hazard to the user.

Quality analysis techniques such as Hazards Analysis and Failure Mode, Effect, and Criticality Analysis (FMECA) are important "preventive" tools (see Section 13, Product Development).

Although somewhat tedious, it is also possible to verify, through test of the final design, that certain undesirable failure modes cannot produce a hazardous result. Such test methods involve the systematic simulation of an internal fault and observation of the response of the system.

Electronic systems including microprocessors are susceptible to *environmental* threats, which require different types of protection. Electromagnetic interference (EMI) and radio frequency interference (RFI) are present in most operating environments. These effects are not always easy to measure and trace to their source. Both EMI and RFI can produce transient, unpredictable behavior, which even the most thorough fail-safe circuit design cannot manage. Forethought must be given to the methods by which the system will be shielded and protected from these effects.

Because of the often nonreproducible nature of EMI/RFI-induced failures, such problems could easily be thought to exist in the software logic of the microprocessor. Therefore, EMI/RFI must be ruled out before an unrewarding search through the software is begun. Electrostatic discharge, temperature, humidity, and vibration also need to be considered.

The Reliability and Fail-Safe Design Program.   The amount of effort that goes into a product to ensure that it is fail-safe and reliable depends on the criticality of its use and its inherent complexity. A product can be graded into four categories, as shown in Figure 27.5.

At the low end of the product scale are devices that are relatively simple and noncritical in terms of their application. Many simple commercial products fall into this category.

At the high end of the scale are microprocessor systems used in aircraft control systems and patient-connected medical devices. These types of device are both

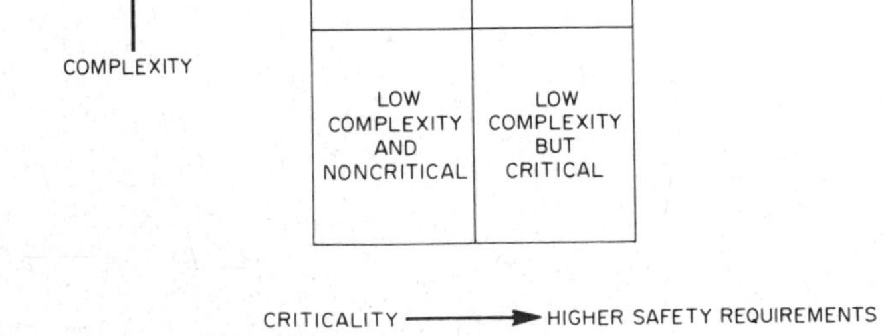

FIG. 27.5   Product criticality and complexity.

complex and critical, and their development requires a great deal more attention to the details of design and the procedures by which the designs are brought forward. For products that are both complex and critical in operation, the use of a microprocessor simplifies some problems but introduces others in the validation of the software.

For systems that have high complexity and low criticality, emphasis must be placed on ensuring that the reliability is sufficient to the needs of the application. The reliability emphasis for complex systems is due to the inverse relationship between complexity and reliability. Unless adequate reliability procedures and programs are followed, complex systems are likely to be disappointing in their mean-time-between-failure performance.

Table 27.10 displays a matrix of program approaches and procedures that can be applied to achieve a given desired level of reliability and/or fail-safe operation for the four categories of complexity and criticality. (Note that Table 27.10 is divided into the same four categories as Figure 27.5.) These procedures can be applied more or less stringently and in appropriate combinations in order to meet the development effort objectives.

Three phases of design are described:

1. Design approach
2. Design analysis
3. Test requirements

Each of these categories contains specific elements applicable to the hardware, software, and system. The menu presented within each matrix cell provides a checklist or guide to the level and type of effort that will be required to achieve the desired level of reliability and safety.

Human communication is also an essential design issue when faced with trade-off decisions on display, alarms, and shutdown routines.

Software recovery techniques for responding to an unsafe state are classified as "backward" or "forward." Backward recovery returns the system to an earlier state with instructions to proceed using an alternate block of coded instructions. "Forward recovery" utilizes predetermined logic to correct the faulty state, return it to a safe state, or proceed to an alternate mode (Leveson, 1984).

QUALITY IN THE FUTURE

With computer applications still in their infancy in quality control and with the knowledge that we face an exponential growth pattern in this field, it is difficult to comprehend, let alone define, the changes in store over the next 20 years. A study of the literature does offer some clues to their direction.

Near Term.   Quality will be attained by monitoring the system, the process, and the machines to ensure quality of output (McKee, 1983). At the 1986 Quality Expo trade show, 26 percent of the exhibits involved computers and related material, and an additional 31 percent involved electrical and electronic instrumentation, including automated test equipment ("Problem/Solution," 1986).

Traditional concepts of sampling inspection will increasingly be replaced by automated 100 percent inspections whose output would be used more frequently for feedforward data support for selective assembly than for feedback data for corrective action (McKee, 1983). Monitoring of the process conditions will also

TABLE 27.10 Matrix of Program Approaches and Procedures

HIGH COMPLEXITY/LOW CRITICALITY

	System	Hardware	Software

DA
E P
S P
I R
GO
NA
C
H
	• Requirements definition
	• Environmental hardening
	• Integrated design
	• High-reliability design
	• Maintainability
		• High-reliability design
		  –Derating
		  –High-reliability
		    components
		  –Proven technology
		  –Simplification
			• Requirements
			• Structured logic
			• Flow chart logic network
			• Testability
			• Use proven routines

DA **E N** **S A** **I L** **GY** **NS** **I** **S**	• Systems design review • Reliability prediction/ allocation analysis • Maintainability	• Design review • Reliability prediction	• Analyze logic • Structured walkthrough • Peer review

T
E
S
T
	• Design qualification testing
	• Environmental stress
	• Quality acceptance test
	• Reliability growth
	• Maintainability
	  demonstration
	• Field test
		• Developmental testing
		• Subsystem testing
		• Systems integration and
		  functional testing
			• Integrate into system and
			  test
			  –Functional
			  –Boundary conditions test
			  –Simulation testing

LOW COMPLEXITY/LOW CRITICALITY

	System	Hardware	Software
DA **E P** **S P** **I R** **GO** **NA** **C** **H**	• Requirements definition • Environmental hardening	• Standard design practice	• Requirements • Structured logic • Flow chart logic network
DA **E N** **S A** **I L.** **G** **N**	• System design review	• Design review	• Analyze logic
T **E** **S** **T**	• Design qualification testing • Environmental stress test • Quality acceptance testing	• Developmental testing	• System integration and functional test

HIGH COMPLEXITY/HIGH CRITICALITY

	System	Hardware	Software

DESIGN APPROACH	● Requirements Definition
	● Environmental hardening
	● Integrated design
	● Failsafe design
	● High-reliability design
	● Maintainability
		● Failsafe Design
		  –Condition monitoring
		  –Self-diagnosis
		  –Alarms
		  –Failed state control
		● High-reliability design
		  –Derating
		  –High reliability
		    components
		  –Proven technology
		  –Simplification
			● Requirements
			● Structured logic
			● Flow chart logic network
			● Testability
			● Use proven routines
			● Redundant programs

DESIGN ANALYSIS	● Systems design review ● Systems hazards analysis ● Reliability prediction/ allocation analysis ● Systems FMECA ● Fault tree analysis ● Functional flow analysis	● Design reviews ● Reliability prediction ● FMECA ● Sneak path circuit analysis	● Analyze logic ● Structured walkthrough ● Peer review ● Sneak path analysis

TEST	● Design qualification testing
	● Environmental stress
	● Fault simulation
	● Reliability growth
	● Maintainability
	  demonstration
	● Test data review
	● Quality acceptance test
	● Field test
		● Developmental testing
		● Subsystem testing
		● Fault simulation testing
		● Systems integration and
		  functional testing
			● Modular test
			● Integrate into system and
			  test
			  –Functional test
			  –Boundary conditions test
			  –Simulation testing

LOW COMPLEXITY/HIGH CRITICALITY

	System	Hardware	Software

DESIGN APPROACH	● Requirements definition
	● Environmental hardening
	● Failsafe design
		● Failsafe design
		  –Condition monitoring
		  –Self-diagnostics
		  –Alarms
		  –Failed state control
		● High-reliability design
		  –Derating
		  –High reliability
		    components
		  –Proven technology
			● Requirements
			● Structured logic
			● Flow chart logic network
			● Testability
			● Use proven routines
			● Redundant programs

DESIGN ANALYSIS	● System design reviews ● System hazards analysis ● System FMECA	● Design reviews ● FMECA ● Sneak path circuit analysis	● Analyze logic ● Structured walkthrough ● Peer review

TEST	● Design qualification testing
	● Environmental stress
	● Quality acceptance test
	● Fault simulation
	● Test data review
	● Field test
		● Developmental testing
		● Fault simulation testing
		● Systems integration and
		  functional testing
			● Integrate into system and
			  test
			  –Functional test
			  –Boundary conditions test
			  –Simulation testing

be mandatory in the automated factory. Control of environmental factors, chemical processes, and tool wear will all shape the quality of the future product. Computer-aided design is evolving at a rapid pace and will provide the central data base for the evolution of computer-integrated manufacturing, test, and inspection (McKee, 1983, and Langevin, 1979).

A major primary new role of quality will be software quality assurance. Beyond control of the software itself will be issues of configuration interfaces and computer-related change controls (Langevin, 1979). The paperless factory and laboratory are also quickly evolving. Computers have the capacity to replace all manually generated forms and to report decision data to the quality unit for management control. Paperless factories will allow design data to be entered into a common data base, placed under configuration control, and made available for use by all functional organizations (Caine, Nolan, and Poyer, 1982). Computerized industrial tomography with x-ray techniques coupled to powerful programs to provide three-dimensional cross-sectional slices of internal structures and assemblies will lead us to a new era of nondestructive tests (Lampe, 1983).

It can be expected that microcomputers will evolve as control devices that substitute for manual work and make possible previously impossible tasks (Ishihara,1979). Smaller, dedicated minicomputers will serve as work stations for individuals. Large general-purpose computers will control the major quality data base systems and, when equipped with large-system software, will provide for general-purpose development (Ishihara, 1979).

When computers are equipped with Compact Disk Memories (CD-ROM), multiple data bases, each with 550 megabytes (275,000 pages) of information, will be instantly available at every desk. In both industrial and social environments, "CD-ROM's will change the whole nature of scholarship.... By the year 2000 anyone who seriously wanted to would be able to get the answer to any answerable question" (Pournille, 1986, p. 290).

The evolution of high-speed telecommunications will provide the link between the major data banks and the individual user's needs (Ishihara, 1979).

Long Range. As reported by Simon (1977), computer intelligence is constrained only by the limits of human intelligence. The elementary processes underlying human thinking are essentially the same as the computer's elementary information processes. Research into artificial intelligence suggests that through a process of selective search and under the guidance of program strategies, it is entirely possible for programs to modify themselves—that is, to learn (Simon, 1977). Thus, computers will be used to model and simulate real world conditions and optimize product and process designs before the commitment of major resources. Computers can provide not only the information on which decisions are made but also the decisions themselves (Simon, 1977).

Process control computers have led the way and provide a glimpse into the future of decision-making machines. Their programs are decision strategies, which, as the systems variables change from moment to moment, retain control over the ongoing process (Simon, 1977). Control of the computer and its software is the primary challenge for the quality professional in the next decade.

ACKNOWLEDGMENTS

This section represents the work of many contributors at Baxter Healthcare Corp. Authorship by Section included:

Managing Computer Projects	Susan Lynch
Statistical Analysis	Gerald Phillips
Computer Integration into Product Design	James Wingfield

The support of Louis X. Ball in supplying the large-system test example and the editorial assistance of Robert Machalski, Kenneth S. Orkin, and Anne Dinklenburg are also recognized and appreciated.

REFERENCES

Anderson, R. T. and Martin, T. L. (1982). *Guidebook for Management of Software Quality.* Reliability Technology Associates, Lockport, IL, p. 8.

Archibald, Russel D. (1976). *Managing High-Technology Programs and Projects.* John Wiley & Sons, New York.

"Artificial Intelligence Is Here." (1984). *Business Week,* July 9, p. 57.

Berger, R. and Hale, M. (1980). "Programmable Calculators in Quality Control—Tutorial." *34th Annual Technical Conference Transactions,* Atlanta, pp. 1–10.

Bernstein, Amy (1984). "A Case for Quality." *Business Computer Systems,* March, pp. 48–58.

Besterfield, Dale H. (1979). *Quality Control.* Prentice-Hall, Englewood Cliffs, NJ.

Bingham, John E. and Davies, Garth W. P. (1978). *A Handbook of Systems Analysis.* The Macmillan Press, London.

Bizarro, L. A. (1976). "Networking Computers for Process Control." *Chemical Engineering,* vol. 83, no. 26, December, pp. 151–156.

Caine, R., Nolan, T., and Poyer, T. (1982). "Toward a Paperless Factory." *ASQC Quality Congress Transactions,* Milwaukee, pp. 584–591.

Clements, John (1985). "One-Two-Three-Go." *Quality Progress,* Part 1: vol. 18, no. 6, p. 92; Part 2: vol. 18, no. 7, pp. 48–50; Part 3: vol. 18, no. 8, p. 54.

Francis Ivor (1981). *Statistical Software: A Comparative Review.* Elsevier North Holland, New York.

Gellagher, B. M. and Ball, L. X. (1976). "Productivity Jumps with Computer-Controlled Engine Test." *Quality,* vol. 15, no. 10, October, p. 12.

Glaushenner, A. (1984). *How to Buy Software.* St. Martin's Press, New York.

Ishihara, Z. (1979). "Where Should Management and Computer Applications Go from Here?" *Management Japan,* vol. 12, no. 1, spring, pp. 14–21.

Keane, John (1981). "Computers and Quality," *AQSC Quality Congress Transactions,* Milwaukee, pp. 625–631.

Kenyon, Richard L. and Newell, Richard J. (1982). "FMEA Technique for Microcomputer Assemblies." *Proceedings, Annual Reliability and Maintainability Symposium.* Institute of Electrical and Electronic Engineers, New York, pp. 117–120.

Keryner, Harold (1979). *Project Management: A Systems Approach to Planning, Scheduling, and Controlling.* Van Nostrand Reinhold, New York.

Lampe, David (1983). "CIT Scanners—Industry's New See through Anything Eyes." *Popular Science,* vol. 223, no. 3, September, pp. 52–56.

Langevin, Roger (1979). "What's Ahead for Quality Control in the 1980's." *Quality Progress,* vol. 12, no. 10, October, pp. 11–16.

Leveson, Nancy G. (1984). "Software Safety in Computer Controlled Systems." *Computer IEEE,* vol. 17, no. 2, February, p. 53.

Lu, Cary (1984). "Putting a PC to Work—A Guide to Assuring an Effective Computer." *High Technology,* vol. 4, no. 10, October, pp. 30–33.

Marquardt, D. (1984). "New Technical and Educational Directions for Managing Product Quality." *The American Statistician,* vol. 38, no. 1, February, pp. 8–13.

Martin, Charles C. (1976). *Project Management: How to Make It Work.* AMACOM (Division of American Management Assn.), New York.

Martin, J. and McClure, C. (1983). "Buying Software off the Rack." *Harvard Business Review,* vol. 61, no. 6, November–December, p. 40.

McCall, J., Richards, P., and Walters, G. (1977). *Factors in Software Quality—Concepts and Definitions of Software Quality.* Joint General Electric-U.S. Air Force Report No. RADC-TR-77-369, vol. 1, November, pp. 3–5.

McKee, Keith E. (1983). "Quality in the 21st Century." *Quality Progress,* vol. 16, no 6, June, pp. 16–20.

"Method/1: An Information Systems Methodology." (1984). Arthur Anderson & Co., Chicago.

MIL-HNDBK-217D (1982). *Reliability Prediction for Electronic Equipment.* U.S. Department of Defense, Washington, DC. Available from Dept. of Defense and NASA, Washington, DC 20301.

MIL-M-38510D (1977). *General Specifications for Microcircuits.* U.S. Department of Defense, Washington, DC. Available from Dept. of Defense and NASA, Washington, DC 20301.

MIL-STD-883C (1983). *Test Methods and Procedures for Microelectronics.* U.S. Department of Defense, Washington, DC. Available from Dept. of Defense and NASA, Washington, DC 20201.

Nitta, Y., Nukada, K., Mori, K., and Ohkawa, M. (1980). "Information Retrieval for Design Review Support." *Proceedings, Annual Reliability and Maintainability Symposium,* Institute of Electrical and Electronic Engineers, New York, pp. 152–157.

Pournille, Jerry (1986). "The Information Revolution." *Byte,* vol. 2, no. 4, April, p. 290.

"Problem/Solution Cross Reference." (1986). *Quality,* vol. 25, April, pp. 15-Q to 25-Q.

Roe, J. (1982). "In-Cycle Gauging—a New Concept in Component Size Control." *6th International Conference on Automated Inspection and Product Control.* IFS Publications, Kempston, Bedford, England, April, pp. 17–28.

Scott, A. J. (1982). "Why Should I Use Automated Inspection?" *6th International Conference on Automated Inspection and Product Control.* IFS Publications, Kempston, Bedford, England, April, pp. 1–5.

Simon, Herbert (1977). "What Computers Mean for Man and Society." *Science,* vol. 195, March 18, pp. 1186–1192.

Snee, Ronald D. (1985). "Computer-Aided Design of Experiments—Some Practical Experiences." *Journal of Quality Technology,* vol. 17, no. 4, October, pp. 222–236.

Stubin, Robert J. (1978). "Temperature Monitoring and Control System for MLB's." *ASQC Technical Conference Transactions,* Milwaukee, pp. 273–278.

Tipnis, V. A. (1980). "Computer Aided Process Planning." *ASQC Technical Conference Transactions,* Milwaukee, pp. 129–134.

Williams, T. J. (1976). "Trends in the Development of Process Control Computer Systems." *Journal of Quality Technology,* vol. 2, no. 2, April, pp. 63–73.

Woodward, W. A., Elliott, A. C,. and Gray, H. L. (1985). *Directory of Statistical Microcomputer Software.* Marcel Dekker, New York.

Yee, Kenneth W. (1982a). *Rotating Tool Wear Monitoring Apparatus.* U.S. Department of Commerce, Washington, DC. Corp. Source Codes: 001948000.

Yee, Kenneth W. (1982b). *An On-Line Method of Determining Tool Wear by Time-Domain Analysis.* Society of Manufacturing Engineers Technical Paper MR82-901. Corp. Source Codes: 004692000.

SECTION 28
PROCESS INDUSTRIES[1]

R. S. Bingham, Jr.
Clyde H. Walden, Ph.D.

INTRODUCTION **28.2**

General Background . . . 28.2

Nature of the Processes . . 28.4

CHEMICAL INDUSTRY **28.4**

Organization for Quality . . 28.4

QUALITY IN PRODUCT
PLANNING—CHEMICALS . . . **28.6**

The New Product Cycle . . 28.6

Formulation and
Methodology 28.6

Laboratory Scale
Evaluation 28.6

Field Trials and Customer
Feedback 28.7

DESIGN OF PROCESS—
RESEARCH AND DEVELOPMENT
PHASE **28.7**

Initial Experimentation . . 28.7

Optimization of Process
Conditions 28.8

Definition of Raw Material
Quality Required 28.8

Tentative Process or
Tentative Operating
Procedure 28.8

DESIGN OF PROCESS—PILOT
PLANT OR INTERIM
PRODUCTION PHASE **28.9**

Need for Partial Scale-Up . 28.9

Process Simulation and
Reaction Kinetics 28.9

Validating Empirical
Equations 28.9

Material for Field Trials . . 28.9

MANUFACTURE OF
COMMERCIAL PRODUCT—
QUALITY ORGANIZATION AND
RESPONSIBILITIES **28.9**

Research and Development 28.9

The Analytical or Control
Laboratory 28.10

Need for Understanding
Analytical Method . . . 28.19

Control of Product Quality 28.21

---

[1]Portions of this section were prepared in earlier editions by C. A. Bicking, J. D. Hinchen, and the authors.

THE MANUFACTURING
DEPARTMENT 28.22
    Raw Material Acceptance . 28.22
    Process Control. 28.22

UNIT OPERATIONS 28.23
    Solvent Extraction 28.23

UNIT PROCESSES 28.25
    Polymerization 28.25

ANALYSIS OF FINISHED
PRODUCT QUALITY 28.30
    Classification of Product . . 28.30

QUALITY IMPROVEMENT—
CHEMICALS 28.30
    Evolutionary Operation . . 28.31
    Adaptive Control 28.31
    Plant Experimentation . . 28.35
    Process Automation. . . . 28.36
    Data Banks 28.36
    Quality Motivation
        Programs 28.36

PLANNING FOR FUTURE
NEEDS 28.37
    Research. 28.37
    Analytical Laboratory . . . 28.37
    Manufacturing
        Department 28.37

METALS INDUSTRY 28.38

QUALITY IN PRODUCT
PLANNING—METALS 28.40
    Customer Relations 28.41
    New Products Controls . . 28.44
    Raw Material Controls . . 28.47
    Process Controls 28.47
    Product Controls 28.49
    Standards and
        Specifications. 28.51

QUALITY IMPROVEMENT—
METALS 28.52
    The Climate for
        Improvement 28.52
    Project Identification . . . 28.53
    Organizing for Quality
        Improvement 28.54
    Special Problems 28.55
    Cultural Problems 28.55
    The Role of Statistics in
        Improvement 28.56
    Results 28.57

MEASURES OF PERFORMANCE 28.57
    Measures in Current Use . 28.57

QUALITY PROBLEMS 28.58
    Current Problems 28.58

ACKNOWLEDGMENT 28.59

REFERENCES 28.59

FURTHER READING 28.63

INTRODUCTION

General Background. The process industries generally are engaged in performing physical and chemical changes on materials. The starting materials may be "raw," e.g., ore, sand, clay, rosin, wood chips, air, water. They may also be products of other operations such as coke manufacturing, oil cracking, or metal smelting. Or they may be plants, animal glands, or mold spores. Broadly, the process industries include rubber, food, beverages, heavy chemicals, pharmaceuticals, petroleum, plastics, refractories, wood products, and metals.

To build the desired properties, performance characteristics and economics into the finished product, the processes must be controlled. Important to this control are the properties of the raw materials, the characteristics of the unit processes and operations required, residence time under specified temperatures, pressures, and concentrations, and the methods of measurement employed.

In addition to conventional quality problems, the process industries face other problems which differ from the conventional:

1. The measurement methods may in themselves be miniature chemical, physical, or biological processes requiring control. (See Wernimont, 1957.)

2. Reaction kinetics continue with time, making it necessary to protect samples from delay in delivery, contamination with air, freezing, container contamination, etc.

3. In-process samples may differ markedly in composition from the finished product.

4. Control of isomers of the desired product may be difficult.

5. Testing time may be relatively long compared with batch reaction time, requiring control decisions to be anticipated.

6. Product specifications may not fully define performance under widely varying customer conditions.

7. The product may have to be packaged for single-dose usage, to prevent tampering, and still be attractive during its shelf life. In some instances, the packaging must protect the product from the environment until used. In other cases, the package itself must be free from toxic components.

In these industries the same materials are often applied to multiple customer uses. In consequence, the quality controls must achieve the dual purposes of:

1. Assuring that the materials produced possess the correct properties whether physical, chemical, metallurgical, or biological.

2. Assuring that the materials will perform satisfactorily in the customer's process and product. For example, a polyvinyl chloride resin must be readily processable in a floor tile plant, and must also impart good wear characteristics and soil resistance in the finished floor tile.

The process industries share with all industries the problems of rapid product obsolescence and the need for prompt conversion of research effort into profitable production. In particular, the quality needs of the marketplace change rapidly and, often, unpredictably. To illustrate, concern with ecology and consumer safety may require: development of different fuels and lubricants for automobile engines; flame-retardant paints and textiles; biodegradable detergents, fertilizers, weed killers, and insecticides.

While the ultimate purpose of all this change is superior fitness for the user, the industry must learn, with precision, just what the effects of raw material quality and process conditions are on product properties and performance. To learn all this, the industry must also continually develop new tests which simulate usage but can be conducted in the laboratory. In addition, as specifications for chemical purity become more stringent, more sensitive and precise methods of determining trace impurities are needed. Developing such new tests and precisions requires extensive collaboration among suppliers and users, new technology in testing procedures, correlation of chemical and physical tests with use-type tests, and finally, correlation of all these with field performance.

Since some of its end products, in particular drugs and food, are directly consumed, the process industries have become further involved in how products from one sector (e.g., growth stimulants, fertilizers, pesticides) influence the composition and properties of products in another sector (foods, drugs). Further, the ability to measure minute quantities has raised questions about the effect of pesticide residues accumulating in fish or in drinking water from surface water runoff of fertilized fields. (See Gushue and Shashidhara, 1986.)

Last, human response to materials, either in process or as finished goods, varies widely both in its intended usage or in accidental exposure. This necessitates extensive toxicity studies and clinical trials which are time consuming, expensive, and frequently complex. Statistically designed experiments are usually the order of the day.

Nature of the Processes. There is a great deal of similarity of the control procedures required by all of the process industries. Moreover, in most process industries, there are two distinctly different manufacturing missions. One mission is the conversion of basic raw materials such as ore, crude oil, etc., into refined materials directly usable (e.g., gasoline, paint, salts, antifreezes, etc.) or suitable for subsequent fabrication into finished products. The second mission is accomplished with a variety of mechanical processes designed to fabricate finished products. There are some very basic differences between the conversion and fabrication processes that require different quality procedures. The variety of processes found in the process industries is shown in Table 28.1.

TABLE 28.1   Unit Operations of the Process Industries

Process industry	Conversion process	Fabrication process
1. Metals	Ore refining, smelting	Ingot casting, rolling extrusion, forging, etc.
2. Chemical	Refining, extraction, polymerization, etc.	Formulation, pelletizing
3. Plastics	Compounding, blending	Extrusion, coating, molding, laminating
4. Refractories	Sizing, blending, drying	Molding, casting, firing
5. Petroleum	Refining, separation, blending	Container filling
6. Pulp and Paper	Log debarking, chipping, pulping	Paper forming, coating, container manufacturing
7. Tires	Compounding	Calendering, extrusion, tire building, curing

As it can be seen, there are a host of different processes and it is not feasible to treat each of them. To illustrate the types of quality procedures employed in the process industries, we have focused on the practices of the chemical and metal industries. The chemical industry provides a comprehensive coverage of quality methods in the conversion type of processes, while the metals industry is illustrative of both conversion and fabrication processes.

CHEMICAL INDUSTRY

Organization for Quality.   Traditionally, responsibility for achieving quality controls has been concentrated in three broad areas as discussed below.

The Research and Development Laboratory.   This unit has basic responsibility for:

Inventing the product

Defining the technology for making it

Identifying competing reactions causing reduced yield or substandard quality

Providing sufficient data to design the plant

Pinpointing from theoretical considerations when, where, and how process control should be exercised

The most economic quality control is achieved by building the right conditions into processes before they commence full-scale manufacture. Changing a going process is enormously costly compared with *controlling research* on how to design the process originally. The key is not necessarily to spend more time in the process development and pilot plant stages, but to structure the best possible *design of experiment* during those stages. The special methods of experiment design and statistical analysis now available are of paramount importance in learning the most from a minimum amount of information. (See Section 26.) The research and development laboratory is expected to use all techniques available to it. (Throughout this section the authors have recommended, wherever possible, the most appropriate statistical procedures which have been practically used. As many of the examples show, the $\overline{X}$ or range control chart is frequently suitable for the task. However, many problems are more rapidly solved by what may *appear* to be unnecessarily complex methods. See Wernimont, 1967, for a problem requiring characteristic vector analysis for its solution; anything less skirts the real problem. See also Polymerization, in this section—a typical case history using control charts and regression analysis for problem definition. Control charts provide operator control.)

The Analytical or Control Laboratory.   Laboratory measurements are the bases for acceptance of raw materials, manufacturing process decisions, and release of outgoing product. Also, they are the means for product uniformity improvement through assessment of how process variables affect equipment behavior and operating procedures. Quantitative knowledge of the extent of variation due to sampling and to the accuracy and precision of the analytical test is essential to the most effective use of laboratory measurements. Activities and methods for obtaining such knowledge are normally the responsibility of the analytical or control laboratory.

The Manufacturing Plant.   Prime responsibility for delivering on time according to specifications lies here. Except in drug and food companies, commonly Manufacturing decides whether to ship, reblend, rework, or scrap. When it cannot meet its specifications (whether they be yield, cost, quality, or safety), it calls for Research and Development or Engineering assistance and advises the Sales Department of possible impact on customers.

The plant also enhances major process improvements by close attention to process behavior (See Carpenter, 1982.) Opportunities abound in the process industries to obtain higher conversions, larger yields, less scrap or waste, and fewer recycles for reworking through improved manufacturing control. Success in achieving these goals lies in being able to discover the specific influence of the important process variables on the product characteristics and to devise the routine control procedures for steadily maintaining these variables at the desired levels. The process industries look to the manufacturing plants to take the initiative in making these improvements.

Segments of the process industries involved with product conversion or fabrication typically have a staff quality engineering group. These groups design, help install, and audit the use of quality controls, including automatic process gauging and inspection methods throughout the fabrication operations. Examples include papermaking, plastic film, and metals fabrication. Drugs packaging is a special case.

The functions of these three major centers are elaborated here and there in the remainder of this section.

QUALITY IN PRODUCT PLANNING—CHEMICALS

The New Product Cycle. The process industries follow conventional practice in discovering market needs and in mobilizing technological and managerial resources to respond to those needs. The general industrial approach (Section 6, under The Quality Planning Road Map) is largely applicable to the process industries. In like manner, field trials and customer feedback largely follow conventional practice (see Section 12 under Analysis of Available Field Intelligence). However, in the initial project formulation stages, the process industries face an "experimental space" which is uncommonly broad and multidimensional. Extensive literature searching of patents, technical journals, and company reports via computer indexing and information retrieval methods serves to limit the "space" to be explored. This essential first step is rarely omitted.

Formulation and Methodology. Many variables need to be considered in the laboratory, and the experiment designs will usually be of a screening type. The fractional factorial, primarily the 2^n series (see Section 26), is of considerable value to screen out the less important variables and to retain those which appear to have the greatest effects on the desired properties. The screening designs may be followed by simplex or central composite designs to optimize. Analysis of variance and multiple regression are the statistical techniques principally employed. (See Section 26.)

If the product is to be a blend of several ingredients, and the properties will blend linearly (in direct proportion to the amounts of each component present), then linear programming techniques can be used. These procedures permit the researcher to obtain a minimum cost formulation consistent with the product specifications. If the properties do *not* blend linearly, a combination of linear and nonlinear multiple regression techniques can be employed to obtain a best fit via computer to a set of desired properties (one of which may be cost). Harrington's (1965) *desirability function* is such an approach.

Laboratory Scale Evaluation. The candidate product is evaluated in the research laboratory on the basis of its chemical, physical, metallurgical, electrical, and biological properties as well as prototype performance tests. In addition, the product will be checked against industry standard tests, and for conformance to government and other specifications, e.g., Underwriters' Laboratories, FDA, SAE, and specific customer requirements. During this phase of product design, it is advisable to seek out, whenever possible, theoretical relationships among various measurable characteristics, each generally giving insight into its successor:

Molecular structure $\rightarrow$ chemical properties $\rightarrow$

physical properties $\rightarrow$ performance tests

Based on this work, a product is eventually selected for field trial. Quantities of the product may be synthesized on a laboratory scale, and shipped to potential customers' plants for field evaluation. These tests may result in tentative acceptance by the customer, or feedback of information for product modification.

Field Trials and Customer Feedback.   In addition to following conventional practice as described in Section 12, Field Intelligence, process industries must face several additional problems:

At the development stage only small quantities are available for customer evaluation.

Most customers are industrial users who further process the new product prior to consumer testing (performance both in-plant and at consumer level is important).

This may require "fine-tuning" customer process equipment thereby entailing delay, added cost, and uncertainty. Where the product has been fabricated to customer specifications (as to shape, form, structure, density, etc.), it is especially important that appraisal trials be carefully planned.

Many products require lengthy field evaluation of shelf life (see Chaisson and Sue-Ho, 1984), weathering, aging, degradation under environmental exposure, etc. under different climatic conditions (relative humidity, temperature, ozone, salt spray, etc.).

Technical data describing typical properties, toxicity, safe handling practices, preferred storage, etc., take time to develop, especially when the new product is an ingredient (and frequently only a minor one) in many other products.

The customer may also be a competitor and may deny observation of the new product in its plant, making informed comparison of old and new product sketchy.

Wherever possible, time and effort can be saved by suitable choice of statistical designs. (See Section 26. Latin square, incomplete block, and factorial designs can usually be constructed to meet the need; see Cornell, 1983, where mixtures are involved in formulating the final composition.) These can be used to develop technical data to introduce the product and to assist the customer in an evaluation. (See Bingham, 1961, on the impact of testing and manufacturing variation relative to the amount of testing necessary in a customer's plant.) In any event, field trials and customer acceptance are key steps in establishing quality controls.

DESIGN OF PROCESS—RESEARCH AND DEVELOPMENT PHASE

Initial Experimentation.   Process design presents separate problems from product design (although sometimes handled concurrently). With an understanding of product requirements, the research effort is directed toward finding the best way to make it. (See Bobis and Andersen, 1970.) To be considered are raw material quality, the process type (continuous versus batch), equipment to be used, variables to be studied, unit processes and unit operations required, number of process stages, variables at each stage and their effects on subsequent stages, etc. All these things and more ideally should be tied down before the process is turned over to the manufacturing department.

Once the process type and equipment decision has been made, prototype equipment (glassware, small-scale reactors, etc.) is set up and the task of quantifying process variables begins. After a few feasibility experiments, the experimenter may use screening designs such as the Plackett and Burman series (1946) or other fractional factorial designs. (See also Daniel, 1963.) These experiments are to pick out the *important* process variables and decide which will be held constant, which deliberately varied, which will be allowed to vary but will be recorded, etc. (See Section 26 for a more complete discussion.)

Optimization of Process Conditions.   Once important variables have been selected, optimizing processing conditions is next. The experimenter using reaction kinetics, if they are known, will use experiment designs to calculate rate constants. Physical and chemical characteristics of the process may enter into this phase. See Atkinson and Hunter (1968) (may be useful for nonlinear-type experiment design).

If the reactions are numerous and complex, or if the kinetic models are not known, an empirical approach to optimization via a central composite or 3^n factorial design is often used. Data analysis frequently calls for multiple regression allowing the desired equation to be examined analytically for optima, areas of constant results, etc.

Definition of Raw Material Quality Required.   One of the elements to be considered in the optimization step is the quality of the raw materials used. These may be materials purchased from another company, and in such situations, a quality specification may already exist. On the other hand, the starting raw material may be an in-house product or intermediate, or even a by-product of another process. In such cases, variability from lot to lot may be large, and it is the function of Research to define the limits within which the raw material must be maintained to produce a satisfactory process. (See Bingham, 1965; also Bingham, Gioele, and Shelburne, 1959, who describe sampling and testing as they relate to vendor comparisons and specification.) This information can then be included in a formal raw material specification and used for supplier negotiations on price and quality.

Tentative Process or Tentative Operating Procedure.   From the process definition, a tentative process procedure is written prior to turning it over to manufacturing or pilot plant personnel. This document contains pertinent information on how the process is to be operated, subject to demonstration of its feasibility. It commonly includes sections called introduction, synopsis of process, flow sheet, equipment required, bill of materials, process detail, discussion of important variables, raw material specifications, finished material specifications, analytical methods, toxicity and hazards, and pollution abatement. This document is read and approved by the departments concerned prior to the next stage, scale-up to larger equipment.

DESIGN OF PROCESS—PILOT PLANT OR INTERIM
PRODUCTION PHASE

Need for Partial Scale-Up.   In scaling up a process from the laboratory to the manufacturing plant, there is often an intermediate or *pilot plant,* stage. Usually, this is a manufacturing unit, larger than laboratory-scale equipment, but smaller than the ultimate commercial manufacturing unit. Manufacturing the new product on this intermediate scale provides a better look at problems which may occur in the final plant, especially in cases where a new plant is being built. The pilot plant stage provides:

Solution of scale-up problems

Sufficient material for long-term testing or large-scale trial run at customers' plants

Development of standard operating procedures (see Setzer, 1986)

Process Simulation and Reaction Kinetics.   Ideally, scaling up a process to larger equipment, whether pilot plant or full-scale manufacturing plant, uses all available technology. This includes reaction kinetics and the mechanisms for agitation, heat transfer, and other physical phenomena. This information can be scaled up theoretically to the dimensions of the larger equipment. Simulating the process on a computer is becoming more prevalent. If this is done, by varying the computer conditions one may predict (subject to verification) what can be expected in plant-scale equipment.

Validating Empirical Equations.   When the process information consists primarily of empirical equations developed on the laboratory scale, the scale-up operation can be aided by selected sequential experimentation in the pilot plant. Using this technique, a single experiment is substituted for one of those made in the laboratory scale equipment, the regression is run again, and any changes in fit or in coefficients are noted. This procedure is iterated until the coefficients stabilize, or until sufficient evidence is uncovered that the operations are essentially the same.

Material for Field Trials.   The pilot plant also aids in the development of a quality product by providing sufficient material to permit definitive field trials by a large number of customers. Information fed back can be used to revise the process and product if required. If the full-scale manufacturing plant is not ready, interim production to obtain and hold new markets can be carried out in the pilot plant.

MANUFACTURE OF COMMERCIAL PRODUCT—
QUALITY ORGANIZATION AND RESPONSIBILITIES

Research and Development.   This group is responsible for three tasks related to manufacturing:

Process demonstration

Major process modifications

Approval of tentative procedures, specifications, and process changes

Each is discussed below.

The Research Department is commonly called upon to demonstrate the new process prior to its being accepted by Manufacturing. A series of plant runs in full-scale production equipment is made, supervised by the technical team[2] responsible for the process and product development. During this period, operating and quality difficulties are ironed out. If these are not readily surmountable, the responsibility for further work remains with Research. Normally, once a predetermined amount of product or number of runs are made without mishap, the process is accepted for regular production by the Manufacturing Department.

If for any reason, after a long period of successful operation, the process changes or ceases to produce the desired quality and yield, Technical may be called in to ascertain the reasons and to assist Manufacturing in correcting the situation. This can occur if unforeseen variables enter the picture, such as changes in raw materials source, customer requirements, or competitive action. Transfer of process responsibility back to Research is negotiated between Manufacturing and Technical.

Sometimes continuous experience with a process will identify operating improvements to increase profitability or obtain better quality. Amendments to tentative process procedures, standard operating procedures, or finished material specifications when required are usually subject to the approval of the Technical Department.

The Analytical or Control Laboratory.   A major key to successful manufacture of a quality chemical is to have valid, pertinent analytical methods to monitor product quality. In many situations, standard test methods already exist in the literature. Adaptation of these methods to the particular product or process is the responsibility of the Analytical or Control Laboratory. It may also be asked to develop new tests relating to customer performance requirements. In filling these various needs it is responsible for selecting testing methods whose accuracy, precision, reliability, and pertinence match the particular need. (See McFarren et al., 1970; Mandel, 1976; Lentzen et al., 1982; and Provost and Elder, 1983.) Whether the new tests are passed on to the Analytical Laboratory from Research, or the new development takes place completely in the Analytical Laboratory, control charts, experiment design, and regression analysis are very helpful. (See Hill and Brown, 1966, 1968, for two review articles covering significant papers in the areas of statistical and quality control methods, models and design of experiments, precision, interlaboratory studies, analytical methods, chemical processes, optimization, kinetics, and regression. See also Bingham, 1976, pp. 127–253, for 245 references pertinent to quality control in analytical chemistry.)

Intelligent interpretation of process data—whether from the manufacturing or pilot plant—requires an exact knowledge of the degree to which the sample represents the product, and the accuracy and precision of the test methods. (See Bicking, 1957; Sinibaldi, 1983; and Bingham and Jaehn, 1986.) Quantitative deter-

---

[2]Typically, the team has chemists, metallurgists, or biologists from the central R&D staff. They are complemented by engineers or technologists from the Technical Department of the operating plant. The latter inherit operating support responsibility. Once the process becomes operational, the Technical Department of Manufacturing assumes process change approval authority. Its process engineering staff works closely with the Quality Control staff. See also Bingham, R. S. (1976). "Development and Utilization of a Quality Control Program." In I. M. Kolthoff and P. J. Elving (eds.), *Treatise on Analytical Chemistry,* part III, vol. 3, sec. C, pp. 144–145, Interscience Publishers, a division of John Wiley & Sons, New York, for detailed discussion of quality engineering and processing engineering roles.

mination of these variabilities rests primarily on obtaining valid data, statistically analyzing the data, and expressing the results in a meaningful form. Almost inevitably, such quantitative determination leads to reduction in *overall* variation, once the major sources of excessive variability have been disclosed. Thus, time is usually well spent in studying laboratory test methods.

Test Method Development—Satisfying Multiple Criteria. In developing a new test method, the analytical chemist will search for equipment, techniques, and conditions to determine the desired property as accurately and precisely as needed. Costs, difficulty of operation, or time required to obtain a result may be among the many criteria for deciding which of many possible methods is the best. (See Lawton and Sylvestre, 1971, and Mandel and McCrackin, 1963, for aids when the response is a curve.)

Suppose an analyst is interested in measuring the amount of by-product A in a sample of finished product from a manufacturing process. The nature of A is such that to measure its concentration, it must be converted to compound B which can be titrated directly. Conversion requires heating A in the presence of a catalyst for a period of time. Some B may be lost at extreme conditions. The analyst is searching for the combination of time, temperature, and catalyst concentration to produce the *maximum* amount of B, and the combination which produces the *most consistent amounts* of B. The hope is that these conditions will be the same.

In light of the optimization objectives, a three-factor central composite experiment design is chosen. (See Section 26 for details of this design.) Temperature is varied over the range of 105 to 125°C, reaction time from 15 to 75 min, and catalyst concentration from 0.1 to 0.5 percent. Using a large uniform sample of

TABLE 28.2 Test Method Development—Experimental Conditions

Condition no.	X_1, Time, min	X_2, Temp., °C	X_3, Catalyst, %	Yield of B (3 runs) Avg.	Range
1	30	110	0.2	15.4	0.48
2	30	110	0.4	17.4	0.45
3	30	120	0.2	17.7	0.49
4	30	120	0.4	20.7	0.46
5	60	110	0.2	19.7	0.39
6	60	110	0.4	21.7	0.36
7	60	120	0.2	20.9	0.40
8	60	120	0.4	23.9	0.37
9	15	115	0.3	14.6	0.51
10	75	115	0.3	22.1	0.33
11	45	105	0.3	15.6	0.41
12	45	125	0.3	20.1	0.43
13	45	115	0.1	15.3	0.46
14	45	115	0.5	20.3	0.39
15	45	115	0.3	24.7	0.42

Note: X_1 = time − 45 min
      X_2 = temperature − 115°C
      X_3 = catalyst − 0.3%

Material A, the reaction to produce B is run at 15 different experimental conditions, each repeated 3 times. The order of the 45 runs is a random sequence. The experimental conditions and the amount of B determined are shown in Table 28.2.

To obtain an estimate of the conditions producing the highest *yield* of B and the smallest variability, the data are fitted to a second-order equation as a first approximation. (See Section 23, under Regression Analysis, for details on empirical curve fitting for optimizing-type models.)

The same model is also used to determine the equation for the *range*, and also for the *ratio* of the range to the *average yield*. The equations obtained by computer using the backward regression method are:

$$\text{Yield} = 24.67 + 0.125\ X_1 + 0.225\ X_2 + 12.50X_3 - 0.007X_1^2 - 0.0683X_2^2$$

$$- 170.833X_3^2 - 0.00333X_1X_2 + 0.50X_2X_3$$

$$\text{Range} = 0.422 - 0.003X_1 + 0.001X_2 - 0.1625X_3 + 0.1163X_3^2$$

$$\text{Range/yield} = 0.0171 - 0.00032X_1 - 0.00023X_2 - 0.0242X_3 + 0.000008X_1^2$$

$$+0.000066X_2^2 + 0.1795X_3^2 + 0.000008X_1X_2 + 0.000387X_1X_3$$

These equations can be solved for maxima or minima by differentiation, and the optimum conditions for each obtained. However, it may be more useful to place certain restrictions on the results, such as "the test method is to have minimum error and still report 25 percent recovery of compound B."

Figure 28.1 shows the contour plot[3] of range/yield versus time and temperature, at a catalyst concentration of 0.3 percent. The ratio appears to have a minimum value near 65 min and 116°. (The area surrounded by the contour line symbolized by "O" will give ratios of less than 0.0150). Figure 28.2 shows that the area of maximum yield is found near 55 min and 116°. The yield will be 25 percent or more within the area symbolized by the *"A"* contour line. Optimum conditions for both error and yield occur where these two areas (minimum ratio and maximum yield) overlap.

Test Method Development—Comparison of Equipment and Techniques. In developing test methods, the interest may not be in optimizing a reaction as part of the experimental procedure. The problem may be one of deciding which piece of equipment, sample size, or operating technique might optimize the recovery and error in measuring a particular component in a sample. In gas-liquid chromatography (GLC) studies, for example, the variables might be column-detector combinations, methods of integration, and sample size for analysis of several different classes of material. One experiment design useful in a study of this type is shown

---

[3]Contour plots (plots of equal response Y) may be obtained, once the coefficients have been estimated, by setting the response Y and all but one of the X's to selected values, and solving the equation for the unspecified X. A new level of one X is taken and the process repeated until the values of X of interest have been evaluated. The Y value is changed and the process repeated. Most computer programs restrict evaluation to the levels of the experiment design but permit selecting many levels for the response. Figure 28.1 has 11 levels for the range/yield response.

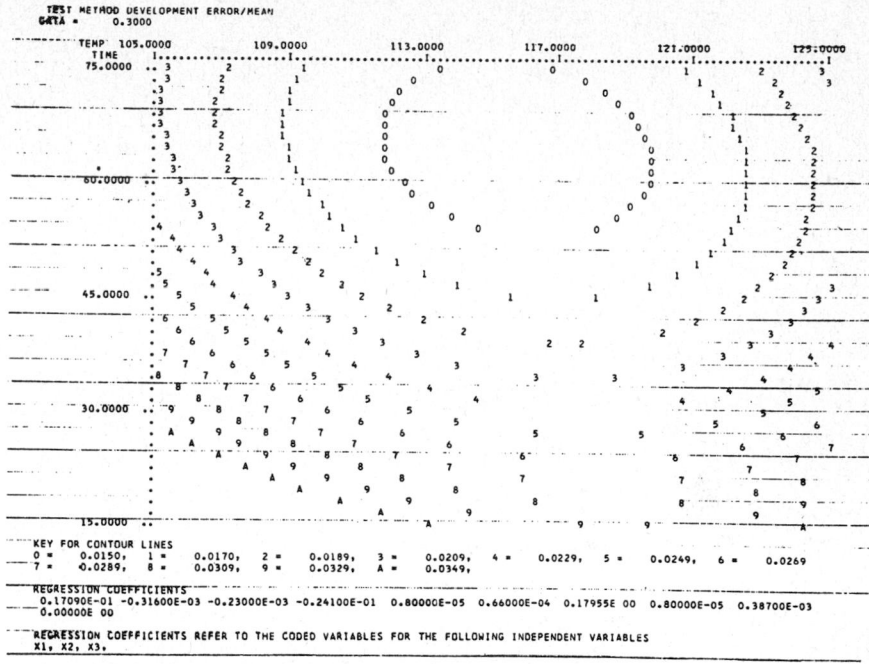

FIG. 28.1 Contour plot—test method development (range/yields).

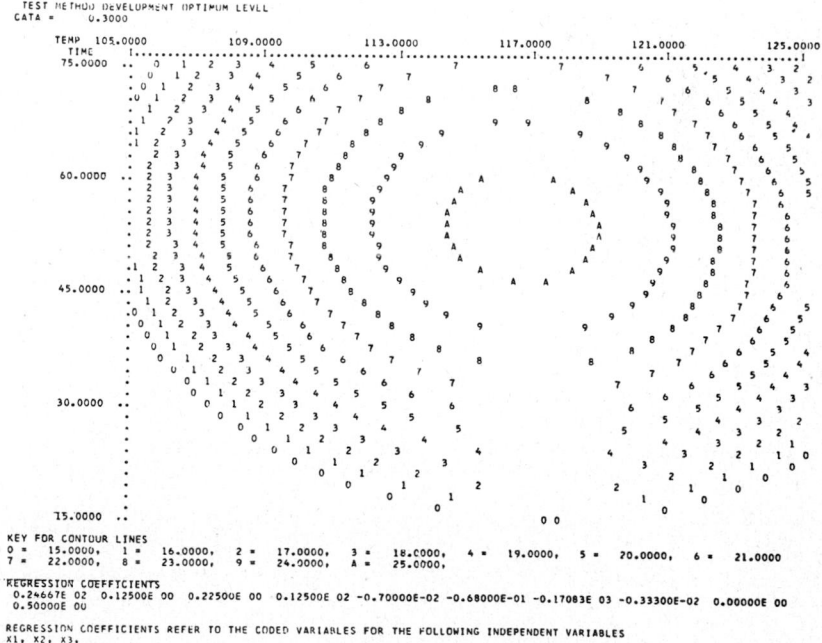

FIG. 28.2 Contour plot—test method development (yield).

TABLE 28.3 Experiment Design for Chromatography Study

Column type		I		II		III		IV	
Sample size		Small	Large	Small	Large	Small	Large	Small	Large
Material	Integration								
A	1								
	2								
	3								
B	1								
	2								
	3								
C	1								
	2								
	3								
D	1								
	2								
	3								

Note: Column types:
   I—packed column, hot wire
   II—packed column, thermistor
   III—packed column, flame ionization
   IV—capillary column, flame ionization

Integrators:
   1—digital
   2—disk
   3—peak height

Materials:
   A—gas mixture
   B—low-boiling liquid
   C—medium-boiling liquid
   D—high-boiling liquid

TABLE 28.4 Precision Study Results, Sample Type and Component Concentration Comparison

Sample mixture	Digital integrator areas relative 2s in parts per hundred
Gas	1.11
Low-boiling liquid	0.67
Medium-boiling liquid	1.14
High-boiling liquid	1.15
Component concentration:	
10%	1.34
30%	0.95
60%	0.60

in Table 28.3. Three observations were taken on each combination of these factors. By analysis of variance, it was possible to select a column-detector combination, sample size, and integration technique to minimize error and bias on each of the sample types tested. (More details are given in Emery, 1967.) As shown in Table 28.4, more precise results were generally obtainable at higher component concentrations, the digital integrator gave better results than the disk integrator or peak height (see Table 28.5), and only the thermistor detector was poorer in precision than the other techniques studied (see Table 28.6).

Once the pertinent method has been selected, its long-term reliability may be determined. (See also Tingey, 1972, Mandel, 1976, for other examples of test method development.)

TABLE 28.5 Precision Study Results, Integrator and Sample Size Comparisons

Normalized peak values	Relative 2s in parts per hundred*	
	Small sample	Large sample
Digital integrator	1.17	0.73
Disk integrator	2.00	1.69
Peak height	1.54	1.77

*Relative 2s = two standard deviations as percent of mean value.

TABLE 28.6 Precision Study Results, Column-Detector Comparison

Combination	Digital integrator areas relative 2s in parts per hundred
Packed column, hot wire	0.93
Packed column, thermistor	1.23
Packed column, flame ionization	0.80
Capillary column, flame ionization	0.89

Determining Test Method Reliability. In examining the reliability of a chemical method, "nested" classifications provide measures of variation between duplicates run on the same sample, between replicates analyzed on the same shift or day, or between samples from various parts of a boxcar. Knowledge of these variations permits optimum construction of a sampling schedule to meet a given precision requirement. A sampling and analysis plan similar to that shown in Figure 28.3 allows comparison of two laboratory methods, each on several days while assessing the size of sample-to-sample fluctuations and duplicate repeatability. The plan can be enlarged to include comparisons of analysts or equipment, but in new-methods development it is frequently advantageous to limit the work to one analyst until the method is pretty well defined; then its reliability can be tested by other chemists or technicians. (See Marcuse, 1949, and Mitchell, 1947. Nested

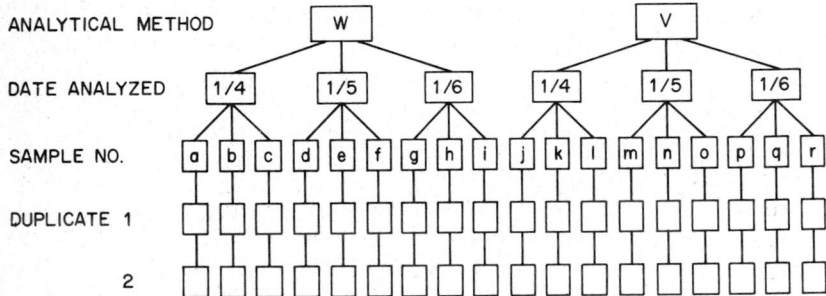

FIG. 28.3   Test layout in analytical method development.

TABLE 28.7   Development of a Test Method to a Given Precision

Method	Weight								
Days	¼			⅕			⅙		
Sample	a	b	c	d	e	f	g	h	i
Duplicates:									
1	62	44	45	48	54	48	81	52	60
2	64	44	42	42	50	44	78	52	61
Average	63.0	44.0	43.5	45.0	52.0	46.0	79.5	52.0	60.5
Day average	⋯	⋯	50.2	⋯	⋯	47.7	⋯	⋯	64.0
Method	Volumetric								
Days	¼			⅕			⅙		
Sample	j	k	l	m	n	o	p	q	r
Duplicates:									
1	35	42	44	52	58	48	79	50	58
2	37	42	40	45	54	43	77	50	59
Average	36.0	42.0	42.0	48.5	56.0	45.5	78.0	50.0	58.5
Day average	⋯	⋯	40.0	⋯	⋯	50.0	⋯	⋯	62.2

Note: Data shown are coded (-15.00, $\times\ 100$).

TABLE 28.8 Analysis of Variance*

Source	Degrees of freedom	Sums of squares	Mean squares	F ratio	Expected mean squares† (EMS)
Methods	1	93.44	93.44	<1	$\sigma_d^2 + l\sigma_S^2 + jkl\sigma_M^2$
Days	2	2164.50	1082.25	5.6[a]	$\sigma_d^2 + l\sigma_S^2 + ikl\sigma_D^2$
					$\sigma_d^2 + l\sigma_S^2 + kl\sigma_{DM}^2$
Days × methods	2	243.06	121.53	<1	
Sample (within days)	12	2334.00	194.50	34.0[b]	$\sigma_d^2 + l\sigma_S^2$
Duplicates (within samples)	18	103.00	5.72	· · ·	σ_d^2
Total	35	4938.00			

*Significant at 0.05 ([a]) and 0.001 ([b]) levels.
†Mathematical model:
$$y_{ijkl} = \mu + M_i^F + D_j^F + (DM)_{ij}^F + S_{k(ij)}^R + d_{l(ijk)}^R$$
where M = methods (i = 1, 2; 1 = weight; 2 = volumetric)
   D = days (j = 1, 2, 3)
  DM = method × day interaction
   S = samples within days and methods (k = 1, 2, 3)
   d = duplicates within samples, days, and methods (l = 1, 2)
   F = fixed factor, R = random factor

Set EMS = mean squares and solve; that is, σ_d^2 = 5.72; = $\sigma_d^2 + 2\sigma_S^2$ = 194.50; σ_S^2 = 94.39.

and staggered nested designs are further explained in Section 26; see Bainbridge, 1965, and Goldsmith and Gaylor, 1970.)

In this example, prior to the analysis, a carboy of solution was prepared and well agitated. Pint samples were withdrawn and labeled. One-half the bottles were chosen at random for analysis by each of the methods, and the order of analysis as well as method (weight or volumetric) was decided by lot also. Only the last stage of analysis, titration, was duplicated on an aliquot of the sample. Statistical analysis of the data in Table 28.7 is shown in Table 28.8. Comparing differences between samples with differences between duplicates, it is evident that the latter severely underestimates the variability of both the methods. Failure of the day-method interaction to reach significance signifies that, whatever the day-to-day effects are, they are uniform in their action on all samples. Since the methods do not differ, the volumetric, being quicker, was chosen.

Confidence Limits for Single Determinations. From the components of variance, confidence limits can be estimated for the analytical differences on samples. The methods for making these estimates are discussed in detail, with examples, in Section 23, under Statistical Estimation.

$$\sigma_{\text{duplicates}}^2 + 2\sigma_{\text{samples}}^2 = 194.50$$

σ_{dup}^2 = 5.72   (from data)

σ_{sam}^2 = 94.39   (by solving above equation)

σ_{total}^2 = 100.11

σ_{total} = 10.0

$\sigma_{T(\text{decoded})}$ = 0.10

For the 12 degrees of freedom available,[4] $t = 2.18$. Hence, 95 percent confidence limits for a *single* sample analyzed *once* on a given day are $\pm L = t\sigma_T = 2.18 \times 0.10 = 0.218$. Inasmuch as the existing specification range was only 0.50 percent, neither method was adequate. Solution temperature control eliminated the day effect and additional analysts were trained in the volumetric method before the tests shown in Table 28.9 were made. The statistical analysis (Table 28.10) verified that differences among analysts compared with the replicate sample variance were no larger than could be expected by chance alone. Hence, the precision of the laboratory method was calculated from the total sum of squares, resulting in a standard deviation of 0.0235, only one-fourth as large as earlier obtained, and significantly smaller at the 0.02 level as judged by an F test[5]:

$$F = \left(\frac{0.100}{0.0235} \right)^2 = 18.1; \; F(0.02; 12, 9) = 5.1$$

Number of Samples to Analyze. In deciding whether several samples[6] should be analyzed and the results averaged to improve precision of the estimate, the following approach can be taken. If precision is wanted such that only 10 percent of the specification range is consumed by the measuring method, the number of samples needed can be calculated directly from the specifications. Given a specification of 16.00 ± 0.25 percent, the uncertainty of any reported analysis should

TABLE 28.9 Test of Modified Method by Several Analysts

Replicate sample no.	Analyst identification*				
	A	B	C	D	E
1	9	8	6	8	6
2	3	4	6	8	2
Average	6	6	6	8	4

*Data coded $(-15.00, \times 100)$(one test per sample).

---

[4]A rule of thumb to use here is: "When the mean squares are significantly different (or do not estimate the same variance) use the degrees of freedom of the biggest variance." (See Satterthwaite, 1946; see also Davies, 1957b, for procedures for confidence limits *for individual components of variance;* 95 percent limits for σ of samples are 0.0558 and 0.130.)

[5]A double-tailed test was used since it was unknown a priori which variance would be least.

[6]*Samples* are to be replicated here since $\sigma = 0.0235$ represents variation due to *both* sample-to-sample difference and analytical-test-method variation. A preferred way is to use a nested design, as in Fig. 28.3, but with *analyses* replicated (in the sense of Fig. 28.5). See Section 25 for more details. Also see Bicking, 1967.

TABLE 28.10   Analysis of Variance

Source	Degrees of freedom	Sums of squares	Mean squares	F ratio
Analysts	4	16	4.0	<1
Sample replicates	5	34	6.8	
Total	9	50		

not exceed ± 0.025 percent. The number of samples n to be analyzed and averaged is

$$n = \left(\frac{t\sigma}{\pm L} \right)^2 = \left(\frac{2.26 \times 0.0235}{\pm 0.025} \right)^2 = 4.52 \text{ or } 5$$

using $t = 2.26$ based on 9 degrees of freedom and 95 percent confidence limits.

Control samples (five randomly taken at a time) submitted for analysis would be judged acceptable or not as the average of the five determinations fell within control limits for an average chart.[7]

$$\overline{X}_0 \pm \frac{2\sigma_0}{\sqrt{n}} = 16.00 \pm \frac{2 \times 0.0235}{\sqrt{5}} = 16.00 \pm 0.021$$
$$UCL = 16.021\%$$
$$\overline{X}_0 = 16.000\%$$
$$LCL = 15.979\%$$

Cumulative Average Chart.   An alternative technique, sequential in nature, compares successive cumulative averages based on one, two, three, etc., tests until it truncates at a given number, with appropriate limits, as shown in Figure 28.4. Note that additional analysis is called for in certain cases when even though the average lies within specifications it falls within the no-decision zone. The cumulative average limits represent the test error divided by the square root of cumulative sample size.

Relation of Test Limits and Specification Limits.   A third method is to establish a predetermined relationship between test limits and specification limits. (See Grubbs and Coon, 1954; see also Eagle, 1954.)

Control Chart to Check Test Method.   Range control charts are commonly used to monitor the analytical process. See Section 24, under Basic Concepts of Control Chart, et seq.

Need for Understanding Analytical Method.   An important consideration in establishing test limits or charts for controlling accuracy or precision of laboratory methods is proper identification of the testing scheme. (See Wernimont, 1957.) Since precision of an average is improved only if the average represents two or

---

[7]See Section 24, under Control Charts for Average and Range; note that the average of five analyses will show as an out-of-control point about 6 times in 10 if the process average has shifted more than 0.025 percent from the nominal, or about 99 times in 100 if it has shifted more than 0.050 percent from the nominal.

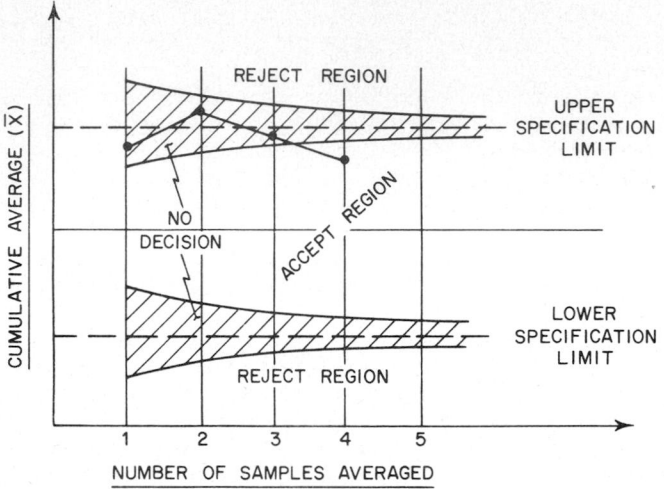

FIG. 28.4 Test on cumulative average.

more *independent* results, it is usually rewarding to draw the flow sheet of the testing process. Method A of Figure 28.5 represents the typical "duplicate" analysis, where only the titration repeatability is checked; no measure of precision of steps 1 through 3 is available in the differences between the titrated results. Method B represents the true independent "replicate," in which each stage is performed independently of any previous weighing. Note that weighing in step 1 is *not* carried out first for replicate 1 then 2; but preferably all of replicate 1 is completed prior to starting replicate 2. This is not always feasible, and different-sized samples, clearing the balance pan of weights, and other complete "startover" methods can be used. (See also Calder, 1964, Higgins, 1964, and Hsi, 1966.)

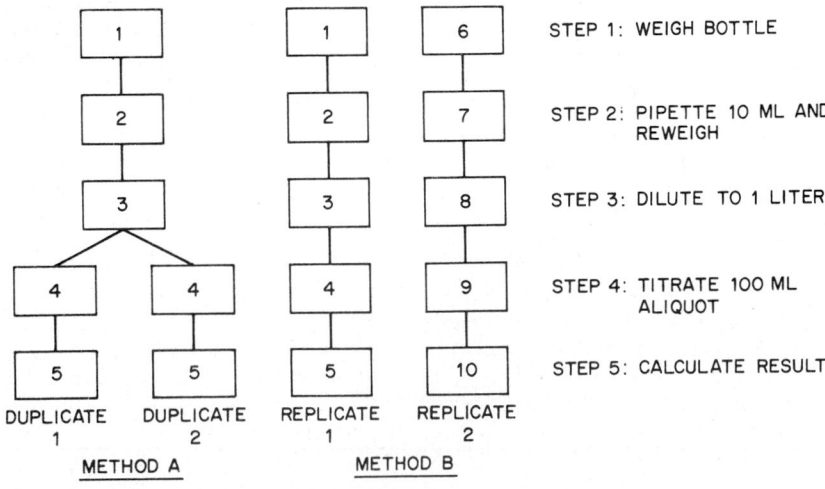

FIG. 28.5 Relation of duplicates and replicates.

Control of Product Quality.   This requires sampling and testing of raw materials, analysis of samples during manufacture, and analysis of finished products. Each is discussed below.

Most *raw materials* for chemical processes are purchased on the basis of chemical analysis, with standard specifications typical. (See Patek, 1968, for detailed discussion pertinent to this industry.) The methods and philosophy of sampling and testing depend upon the nature of the material (bulk solids, bulk liquids, type of packaging, etc.). (See Section 25.) Once a supplier's quality has been established as acceptable and uniform, the raw material may be accepted on the basis of the vendor's analysis. Control charts or certification of statistical control of the vendor's process may accompany the invoice. (See also Section 15 under Improvement of Supplier Quality.)

Process control of product quality on the basis of tests *after* the product is made may be too little and too late. Instead, samples are taken during the operation, and based on the results, process adjustments made. The tentative process as received from Research usually specifies the control points and action to be taken, but the initiative of the control chemist is required when problems arise. Regression studies are useful in determining the relationship between control test results and finished product properties. Many companies beneficially use continuous sampling devices to provide continuous control and avoid blending composite grab samples. Connected to gas-liquid chromatographs and other instruments, they provide continuous monitoring of the process stream. These automatic instruments may in turn be connected to a digital computer so sample composition can be calculated immediately. Open-loop control, subject to operator action, predominates currently, but closed-loop computer control is rapidly replacing obsolete instruments.

When chemical control tests are run by operators at plant test stations, commonly the analytical laboratory maintains the equipment, standardizes test solutions, and occasionally checks operator results. (See Mitchell, 1947.)

Finished product testing is done by the Analytical Laboratory to determine specification conformance and the state of process control. Normally, the sample is delivered to the laboratory by the manufacturing personnel responsible for the process. Occasionally the laboratory will actually obtain a sample of the finished material. Responsibility for maintaining the accuracy and precision of the tests belongs to the laboratory, and based on the results, material is accepted or rejected. *Disposition* of rejected finished product is not a laboratory function. Manufacturing usually decides how the rejected product is to be modified (blended, treated, recycled, scrapped, etc.). The Sales Department is notified if customer specifications cannot be met.

The finished product results are reported to manufacturing as each batch or lot is tested. Results are also recorded in a permanent ledger and are available for statistical analysis. (See Bingham, 1957*a*, for a description of an application of Dodge's CSP-3 plan to multiple attributes of an organic product.)

Control Charting and Reporting of Results.   In many laboratories it is the practice to maintain control charts, either in the laboratory or preferably adjacent to process units in the plant. Laboratory personnel monitor these charts on a day-to-day basis, and call production personnel's attention to trends, shifts in level, out of control points, etc., as they occur whether the individual lots remain in specification or not. The charts also can be reviewed periodically with Production Supervision, Marketing, Technical Service personnel, and Quality engineers. In this way they form a basis, together with field performance information, for periodic quality audits for each product.

Modifications of the standard Shewhart control chart are quite common in chemical process quality control. These include cumulative sum charts which are very sensitive to shifts in level, narrower control chart limits (2σ versus 3σ), individual charts and moving-range charts. (See Section 24 for details; see also Goodman, 1982.) For process use, careful weighing of the risks involved has often resulted in the use of 2σ limits and even in some unusual instances of 1.5 or 1σ limits. For average charts, the narrowed limits are directly proportional to the reduced number of standard deviations. (See Section 24 for the increase in "power" afforded.)

Individual measurement and moving-range charts are particularly suited for study of batch-type processes. The individual measurement chart may be used with average and range charts or alone. Since, characteristically, data accumulate slowly in batch operations, it is often advantageous to use the moving-range method of calculating control chart limits for the individual measurements. This consists of averaging the differences between consecutive pairs of measurements, i.e., between 1 and 2, 2 and 3, etc. (see Section 24, Statistical Process Control, on the number of observations to establish "state of control"), and substituting constants in the following formula for 2σ limits:

$$\overline{\overline{X}} \pm 2/3 \, (1.88 \, \overline{R} \sqrt{2})$$

which reduces to $\overline{\overline{X}} \pm 1.77 \, \overline{R}$.

THE MANUFACTURING DEPARTMENT

Raw Material Acceptance.   In many companies, the responsibility for acceptance of raw material lies with the Manufacturing Department. If all specifications are met, or if the supplier has certified that the material is of standard quality, there is no problem. However, if one or more properties deviate from standard, and it is judged that by process modification, satisfactory product can be made from the raw material, Manufacturing management may exercise the prerogative of accepting the material. In such cases, the material will be used under a limited procedure, which is subject to the review and approval of the Research Department, as well as several responsible individuals in manufacturing. The supplier, of course, is notified of the discrepancy in raw material quality. (See Mitchell, 1947.)

Process Control.   Control of quality during manufacturing rests with the Manufacturing Department. This includes preparation of standard operating procedures, Operating Instructions for process operators, and taking specific action based on control test results. Production Supervision is responsible for recognizing and correcting unusual situations, and has the sole responsibility for shutting down a line that is producing off-quality product.

In many instances exceptionally fine control of quality is unnecessary because of the ease of blending, reworking, or making alternate classification of materials of variable qualities. However, the prevalence of these practices often affords an opportunity for substantial cost reduction by careful process control. Every such instance should be examined on its merits.

In batch-type operations, in particular, the control of processing time is often the most important source of saving in processing costs as well as a means of improving quality level and uniformity. A great deal about effect on quality of formulations, operating conditions, and personnel performance can be learned by intelligent use of a combination of charts on processing time and quality measurements. (See Traylor, 1948, for a noteworthy paper.)

Much of the effectiveness of quality control and especially of the use of control charts is their psychological effect. In many instances, major improvements in quality level and uniformity have come about almost immediately upon installation of charts in operating areas. Removal of the charts has resulted in poorer quality performance. The same kind of thing is probably present, to some degree, in all parts of the effort to improve quality. (See Section 10, Managing Human Performance.) The human aspects of application of the scientific method are always as important as its technical phases. The supervisor or chemist using the techniques must learn to accept a way of thinking which is often contrary to academic training. (See Hampton, Summer, and Webber, 1968, especially pp. 413–425, "Innovation and Conflict in Industrial Engineering," and pp. 273–355, "The Impact of Informal Organization: Social Factors in Organizational Behavior.") A new generation of scientific and engineering personnel may well come into industry better equipped originally for the job of quality control.

In any application of industrial statistics, no matter what the industry, the general form of the statistical method applying to a particular kind of problem is essentially the same. The general forms of the most widely applicable techniques have been set forth in Sections 23 through 26 of this handbook. For the process industries at least, greatest interest is likely to center on the manner of approaching the solution of a series of typical problems rather than a rigorous development of the statistical methods used. The general outline of what follows is to state the problem as clearly as possible; provide a background of general information to orient the reader; describe in some detail the preparation made for the work, and the psychological and technical approach followed; indicate with tables or charts the principal steps in the statistical analysis of the data; and finally, point out the results of the work done. (See Bennett and Franklin, 1954, and Davies, 1957a, for additional examples amplifying these points.) The following examples of unit operations and unit processes are typical of those met in process control and quality improvement efforts.

UNIT OPERATIONS

Solvent Extraction.   Solvent extraction consists of the physical separation of two or more materials which have been in close association. It may separate a soluble from an insoluble material by a solvent under heat and pressure, or separate two liquids by means of a solvent in which the liquids are unequally soluble, as in countercurrent extraction. Typical products of processes in which solvent extraction is involved are coal gas, insecticides, perfumes, oils, acetic acid, rosin, and lubricating oils.

The example describes a process in which a shredded raw material is subjected to alternate periods of solvent pumping and steam heating under pressure. The extractors are arranged in a battery so that, as a new charge is placed in the cycle, an exhausted charge is removed. At this stage, the process continues intermittently, although preparation of the raw material, evaporation, and subsequent finishing operations are continuous. Figure 28.6 gives a simplified diagram of the extraction operation.

The raw material contains approximately 20 percent of extractable materials. All but a fraction of 1 percent of these extractable substances are readily removed.

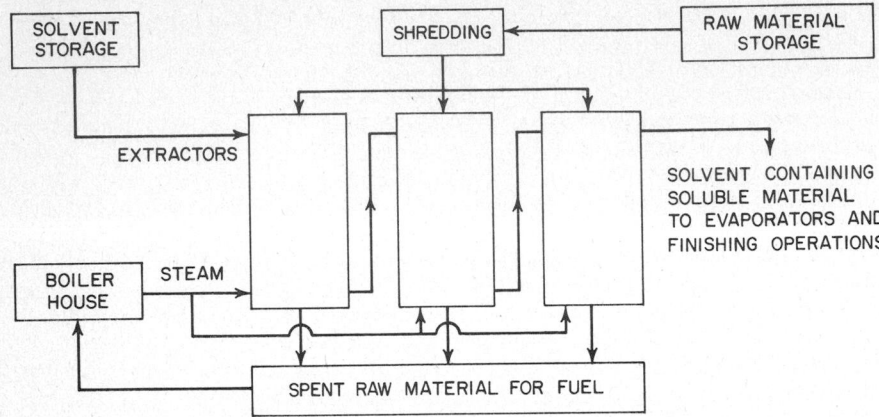

FIG. 28.6 Simplified flow sheet for solvent-extraction operation.

However, the tonnage handled is so great that extraction of an additional 0.05 percent would increase the value of product by about $1670 per day. Very close control and lowest possible level of extractable material remaining in the spent charge is desirable. As a means of analyzing existing efficiency and of readily following the effect of changes, a control chart like the one in Figure 28.7 is effective. Weekly average values are plotted on this chart because of the greater precision of averages of a test which is not highly reproducible. The control limits are based on the average range of weekly subgroups made up of seven daily test values. (See also Vance, 1966, for an alternative approach to setting limits.)

A number of long-term factors affect extraction efficiency. Their influence is so gradual that, though they may be control charted, the charts are not effective as a direct means of process control. Two of these basic factors are the amount of raw material processed and seasonal factors (the latter is concerned with methods of handling and storing the raw material; each can modify its moisture content). Also, over a period of years, a change in the quality of the raw material may become apparent. The relative importance of these factors may be tested by correlation studies of monthly or quarterly averages. The correction of their effects usually involves major equipment changes, such as the addition of more extractors to the battery, decreasing rate of production by lengthening the extraction cycle, location of a higher grade of raw material, or bulk drying of the raw material before extracting it.

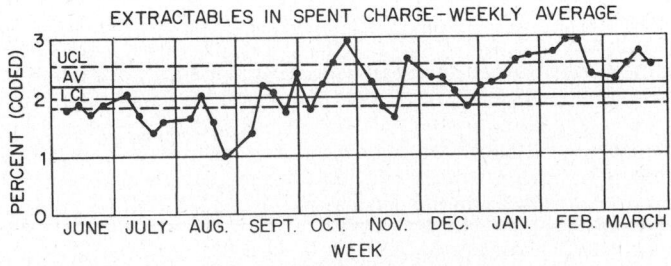

FIG. 28.7 Solvent-extraction efficiency.

After the long-term factors have been taken into account, something can be done by the operators in the extraction area to reduce the extractables in the spent material. Their efforts may be guided by control charts to follow variations in the critical operating conditions.

Fourteen processing measurements are regularly made and recorded in the processing log. With this many variables affecting efficiency, it is difficult for the operator to know what to do when in trouble. Even if all 14 factors were control charted, it would be difficult because little is known of the *combination* of factors or interactions which may affect the result. What is required before the operator can change the controls with beneficial effect is to pinpoint attention on the few most critical points of control.

All 14 factors were studied by multiple regression, and 11 were eliminated successively until only three factors remained. The outcome was to ask the operators to keep three control charts and take action when control limits were exceeded on:

1. Quality of the solvent
2. Concentration of the extractable in the solvent at the end of the cycle
3. Size of shreds

The quality of the solvent can be controlled by greater attention in the solvent-recovery procedure, the concentration by varying the rate of pumping of solvent, and the size of shreds by screening and reshredding when necessary. Figure 28.8 shows diagrammatically the direct relationships among the principal processing factors. The high residual extractables at *A* are explained by a peak in the curve of solvent quality and in the concentration curve. Similarly, peak *B* is explained by large-sized shreds and high concentration. Finally, the low residual at *C* is based on unusually good solvent quality and low concentrations.

These charts are scaleless, but the extent of departure from control limits is in proper proportion in each instance. The correspondence of shaded areas in the three lower charts with shaded areas in the upper chart leads to the conclusion that often lack of control in one or another of the three critical processing factors will reflect in lack of control in efficiency. It follows that action to correct for lack of control in the process control charts (or to reproduce exceptional conditions in the more favorable direction) will improve control of efficiency.

The action charts to be used for control of solvent quality, concentration of solvent, and size of shreds will be similar to Figure 28.7, except that the limits should be changed to limits for daily measurements and daily results plotted as they are obtained. [Alternatives for closer process control include moving average charts, cumulative sum charts (see Section 24) or Adaptive Control (see below). The choice in part is determined by individual preference. However, for the results to be meaningful, they must reflect process response time (to adjustments) and test variability.] The charts should be kept in the operating area where the area superintendent, shift supervisors, and operators may follow them continually. Charting may be done by control-laboratory personnel, a records clerk, or the operator, depending on plant preference.

UNIT PROCESSES

Polymerization. Polymerization is used in the petroleum industry and in manufacture of synthetic rubber and of many organic materials. In polymerization, a reaction occurs in which two or more molecules of the same substance combine

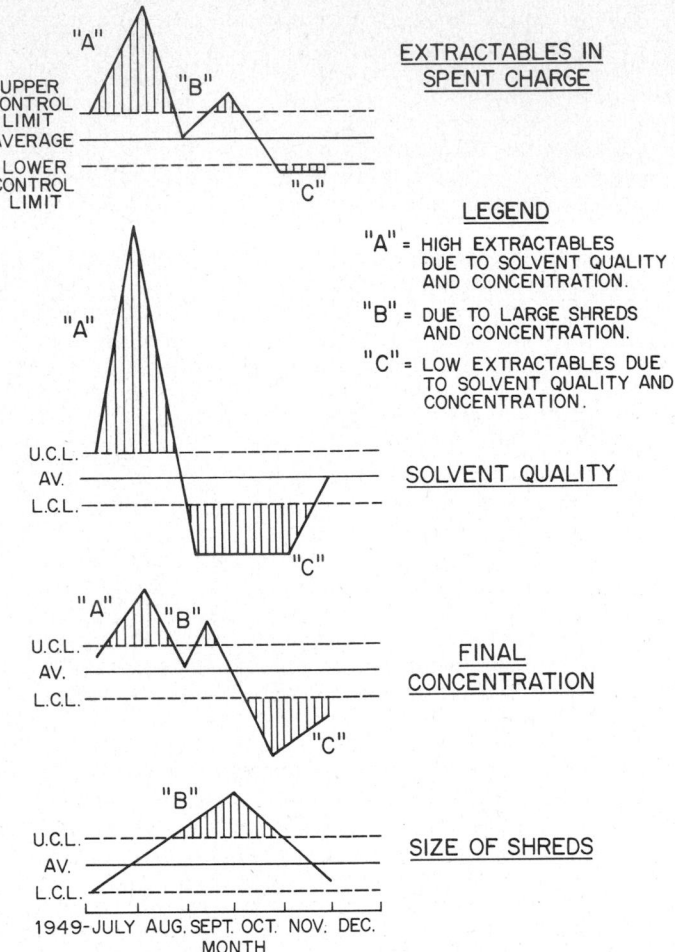

FIG. 28.8 Solvent-extraction efficiency compared with process variables.

to form a compound from which the original substance may or may not be regenerated.

An example from a polymerization process illustrates the condition common to the more involved reactions. (See also Bingham, 1957*b* and 1957*c*, for examples of countercurrent, multistage operations.) Rather complete statistical analysis of all the measurable variables in the process precedes the use of any simple method to assist control. The step-by-step approach described provides a pattern for handling many other processes of similar complexity.

The first step by the quality engineer was to assemble as much information as possible about the process, including process control and final quality measurements over a period long enough to permit analysis. The type of generalized information needed is shown in the simplified flow sheet in Figure 28.9.

The first control chart was based on previous final quality measurements from the process. About 25 subgroups of four hourly measurements each were taken

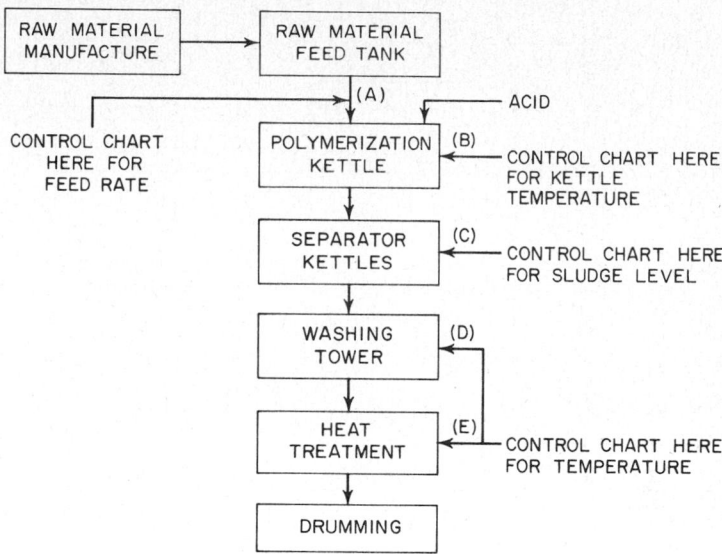

FIG. 28.9 Simplified flow sheet for polymerization process.

from a past period of acceptable operation to be used as a standard against which to compare future results. The original limits for the three principal quality measurements are given in the left half of the charts in Figure 28.10. A typical series of hourly readings from the normal period before starting the statistical study is plotted between the limits. These provide what is known as a master control chart, or an overall picture of quality results. It is suitable for keeping in the operating area so that the operators and quality engineer may see the results of their joint efforts to improve quality.

Lack of control occurs frequently on the original charts. If possible, action should be taken to adjust the process on the basis of lack of control. An operator closely following a process may be able to identify on the charts results of some of the adjustments and thus receive direct assistance in future handling of the process. It is more likely, however, that this master control chart will portray results based on more detailed process studies. These studies may use special statistical analyses or action-control charts spaced at strategic spots in the process.

When the process was initially surveyed, it was realized that before charts could be placed, an analysis of several variables had to be made. Variables affecting softening point of the product were studied first by multiple regression: feed rate, polymerizer temperature, and sludge levels in the separator kettles. The regression showed all three factors significantly affected softening point. Together they accounted for 78 percent of the total product variation. Past performance for these three variables was then plotted on action-control charts. Corrective action for each is different and is described in turn.

Fluctuations in the *feed rate,* which sent its action chart out of control so often, were beyond the power of the polymerization-area operators to regulate. The production area supplying the raw material for polymerization frequently reduced production rate or diverted the supply to other finishing areas. Naturally, lack of control occurred on those occasions on the action chart, and the effect could even be traced to fluctuations in the product quality as portrayed in the master control

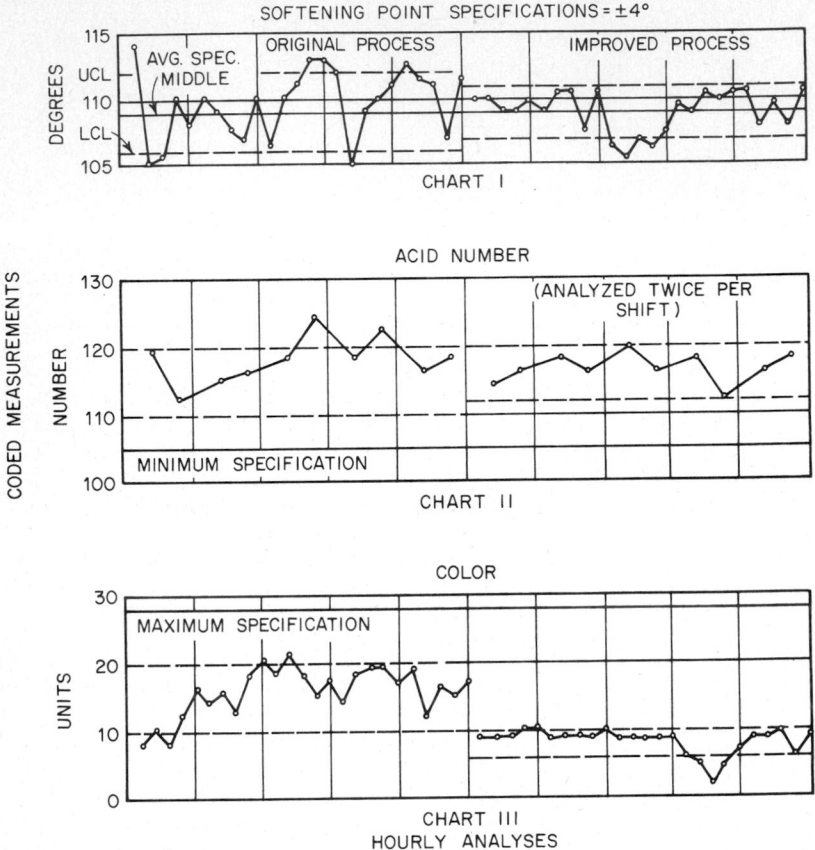

FIG. 28.10 Master control chart—polymerization.

chart. Once identified, remedial action was justified. A large storage tank was installed so raw material could be accumulated during periods of high availability. This evened out the flow rate to such an extent that good control was obtained and maintained on the first action chart. Charting of feed rate was then discontinued.

A new multiple regression was then made of the three variables mentioned earlier: feed rate, temperature, and sludge level against softening point. This time the *flow rate* turned out to be *nonsignificant* while the other two significant factors continued to account for about the same proportion of the total variation in softening point as they originally did (see Table 28.11).

While the feed rate work was going on, sludge levels were studied by a second action chart chalked on a blackboard in the operating area. This was a real action chart because the start and end of pumping periods were determined by float bob position with respect to the control limits. As long as the operators maintained close watch over the positions of the bobs, good control was maintained. However, though reduced slightly from the start, the limits were still wide. Also, as shown in Table 28.11, the variance due to sludge levels was still significant.

Once again it was time for action. This time only part of the engineering action

TABLE 28.11 Regression Analysis—Softening Point of Polymerization
Product

Source	Sums of squares	Degrees of freedom	Mean squares	F ratio	Probability of significance, %
Temperature	19.48	1	19.48	32.5	99.9
Sludge level	13.77	1	13.77	23.0	99.9
Feed rate	0.37	1	0.37	$\cdots$	None
Residual	12.63	21	0.60		
Totals	46.25	24			

decided on was taken initially on a trial basis. Automatic sludge-level controllers
were installed on part of the kettles. Regression of the data from the controlled
kettles showed the effect of sludge levels had disappeared[8] (see Table 28.12).

Subsequently, all kettles were equipped with automatic controls, and temperature was left as the sole significant source of variation measured. The cost of
automatic feed and acid rate control was then investigated to determine the feasibility of further reducing quality variation by a third process adaptation. (This
step had not been taken at the time represented by the right half of the control
charts in Figure 28.10. It will be seen from the chart that the softening point had
become better controlled within a more uniform range.)

So far, the charts spotted at points A, B, and C in Figure 28.9 have been discussed. Much the same procedure was carried out in setting up charts at B, D,
and E for color improvement.

A regression of feed color, bleaching property of the feed, and heat-treatment
temperature showed that the first and last significantly accounted for 46.5 percent
of the product color variation. Nothing could be done immediately about the feed
color. However, other variables could be studied to identify causes of a larger
proportion than 46.5 percent of the total variation. Accordingly, kettle temperatures, wash-tower temperature, sludge levels, solution concentration, contamination of feed, and acidity of wash water were added to the regression. The first two
were found to be additional significant factors which brought the accounted-for
variation to a satisfactory total.

---

[8]See Hinchen (1970). He outlines the errors in interpretation possibly resulting when specific degrees
of correlation among the independent variables exist.

TABLE 28.12 Regression Analysis—Softening Point of Polymerized Product, Partial
Sludge-Level Control

Source	Sums of squares	Degrees of freedom	Mean squares	F ratio	Probability of significance, %
Temperatures	19.48	1	19.48	16.1	99.9
Sludge level	0.12	1	0.12	$\cdots$	None
Residual	26.65	22	1.21		
Totals	46.25	24			

Control on polymerizer kettle temperature had already been arranged because of its effect on softening point. Action charts were prepared for installation at the washing tower and at the heat-treater as shown on the flow sheet. The resulting improvement in product color is shown vividly in the right-hand portion of the master control chart (Figure 28.10). [See also Pasteelnick and Leder, 1957, for further information on polymerizer control. An alternative procedure when two or more attributes are correlated uses multivariate control charts (Hotelling's T^2). See Johnson and Leone, 1964; see also Hicks, 1955, Jackson, 1956, and DeBaun and Schneider, 1957.]

ANALYSIS OF FINISHED PRODUCT QUALITY

Classification of Product.   One of the incentives for producing a product "right the first time" is the classification of substandard product at a lower valuation than first quality product. Correction of this situation then becomes economically desirable to the manufacturing supervisor. Charts on "percent right first time" maintained in the operating area, and competition between various crews often results in improved quality. Since the process capability versus specification range may vary from product to product, quality *percentage* standards are set up for individual products, with the goal being to exceed the standard.

Substandard product may be reworked, blended off, scrapped, or sold at reduced price or occasionally at full price with customer and Marketing Department approval.

Determination of Causes of Off-Grade Production.   The process industries have their share of instances in which off-grade materials are produced. The reasons are numerous: lapses in control, changes in raw material lots, catalyst degradation, equipment wear, etc.

However, there are some good means for dealing with these instances. The data system is usually well developed and includes records of operating conditions, material batch numbers, and logs of difficult or unusual occurrences. In addition, the companies are usually self-sufficient in the availability of engineers to analyze and solve problems. The methods of analysis follow conventional practice for the most part (see Section 22). However, there are many pitfalls, since operating variables are interrelated and time lags exist between a variable change and the resultant product property change. (See Hinchen, 1968, Draper and Smith, 1981, and Section 23, under Regression and Correlation Analysis.)

Investigation of Customer Complaints and Returned Goods Reports.   This follows conventional practice as described in Section 20, under Processing of Complaints.

QUALITY IMPROVEMENT—CHEMICALS

Much of the conventional approach to quality improvement (see Section 22) is directly applicable to the process industries. However, the tools of analysis often must be quite sensitive, since many industry products are high-volume, low-profit (commodity) materials. In such cases, large sums of money rest on small differences in yield. The tools of analysis needed to deal with such small differences must be flexible enough to accommodate numerous variables, many of which are nonlinear, and which may interact with other variables. Such tools do exist, and the industry has made much progress in applying them to improve yields and controls. (Some additional examples are given in Bingham, 1962b, and in Bingham and Gioele, 1959, 1961, and 1962.)

Evolutionary Operation. This technique, developed by G. E. P. Box, was pioneered in the chemical industry and applied profitably in hundreds of process operations. (See Section 26 for full discussion, examples, and extensive references, most relating to process industry application.)

Adaptive Control. Control charts as described in Section 24 are designed to detect shifts in process level, increases or decreases in process variability, or non-randomness (as typified by trends, cycles, etc.). As such, control charts "call for action." The *kind* or *amount* of action is not always clear.

Adaptive control, a technique developed by Box and Jenkins (1970), aims to improve process control and thereby outgoing product by "anticipating" where the process will wander if left unadjusted. Furthermore, it describes *when* action is called for and the *amount* of correction. The aim is to eliminate all but random variation in the quality or composition of products. The procedure is appropriate when:

There is a "dead time" or delay before the adjustment takes effect.

The adjustment begins to take effect immediately, but the full effect of the change is not felt for some period of time.

Improper choice of either the *amount* of correction or the *timing* of the correction may cause the process to oscillate, overshoot the desired target, or undershoot the target.

It is not possible to control one or more inputs to the process, but the effect of variation in these inputs can be measured and correction taken to offset them (i.e., the process adjustments minimize the effect of the input upsets on the output quality).

Changes in the process level are selected from time to time (e.g., to make different "grades" of a product) and it is desired to get from one process level to another in the shortest time or with minimum "off grade" product made.

The benefits likely to be achieved from using adaptive control include:

Faster response to unexpected disturbances

Closer match of process level to process set point

Elimination of overcontrol

Faster startup

The technique is ideally suited to the process industries because it permits optimal process control as well as process optimization. As indicated earlier, in the process design stage the plant process equipment, piping, storage tanks, mixers, towers, etc., are sized to match plant capacity specifications. At this time, valves are selected, tower packing chosen, etc., to acknowledge reaction kinetics and transport phenomena. In these engineering calculations, commonly analog or digital computer models of the proposed process are utilized. By doing so, expected process upsets and dynamics can be superimposed on the plant design to determine the appropriate method for process control.

When the process is unusually complex, or the reaction kinetics unknown, empirical approaches as described earlier and in Section 26 can be used to approximate reaction kinetics. Furthermore, the plant typically finds after startup that the process is not "tuned" for optimum operating conditions. In actual plant practice, competing reactions may have modified the kinetics, the piping may have been rerouted, valve action rendered sluggish, mixing effectiveness reduced, catalyst activity degraded, tower packing fouled, or flow turbulence reduced. Under such conditions, the appropriate control action may be quite different from that taken to meet "theory" or from that taken immediately after startup or a "piping boilout."

Essentially, Box and Jenkins have built on the practices of control engineers who typically have designed into the mechanical or electronic linkages of automatic controllers *derivative, proportional,* and *integral* action. Their procedure uses mathematical equations or charts whose parameters can be changed instead of changing the controller mechanism.

The following steps are common to the procedure:

1. *Process identification:* Determine the nature of disturbances commonly seen by the process, including estimates of process variance.
2. *Process prediction:* Derive an equation for predicting where the process level would be if unadjusted, when disturbed as in step 1 above. (The equation may include the latest measurement, the differences between successive measurements, and the cumulative algebraic sum of the deviations of a series of measurements from their predicted value.)
3. *Process correction:* Derive an adjustment equation including measures of "process gain"—the change in the "output" (response) variable to adjustment of an "input" or control variable. (This equation takes into account process dynamics including lags between the time an adjustment is made and the time the effect is observed *at the sampling point.*)
4. *Chart control:* Construct charts to be used by the operator to simplify the prediction and calculation of adjustments. (In closed loop computer control, automatic adjustment would replace operator correction.)

Viscosity Control by Adaptive Control—An Example. The following example (modified from Box and Jenkins, 1970) illustrates the elements of the technique but is not meant to be all-inclusive. It concerns viscosity control of a process in which gas is injected into a liquid in a continuous reactor. Twenty-five of some 200 observations available are shown in Table 28.13.

1. *Process identification.*
Process objective: Resultant mixture viscosity is to be between 86 and 98 centipoise with 92 the target.
Process disturbance: The incoming gas composition varied within commercially acceptable limits but with substantial impact on the mixture viscosity.
Process adjustment: Reaction control was achieved by feeding in more or less gas.
Process gain: Experimentally, it was observed that a change in gas rate of 50 lb/min eventually produced a viscosity change of 10 centipoise, i.e., $g = 10/50 = 0.2$.
Process dynamics: The viscosity change was observed to be exponential[9] with time; half of the expected change occurred in 1 h. Over a period in which *no* adjustments were made, changes in viscosity level appeared to occur stepwise.

---

[9]Fraction changed $(y/x) = 1 - \exp(-x)$. $x = T/TC$, where T = time in hours, TC = time constant in hours. See Harrison and Bollinger, 1966.

TABLE 28.13 Adaptive Control—
Viscosity of Product of Gas Reactor

Hour	Viscosity	Hour	Viscosity
1	90	14	92
2	94	15	93
3	94	16	96
4	95	17	90
5	98	18	88
6	90	19	93
7	92	20	87
8	89	21	90
9	93	22	91
10	94	23	95
11	91	24	91
12	95	25	97
13	91		

(The inference is that gas composition varied stepwise and shifted the viscosity to higher or lower levels rather than trending upward or downward.)

2. *Process prediction:* To predict[10] the next viscosity result ($\hat{z}_{p+1}$), the optimal predictor would be the previous result (z_p), that is, $\hat{z}_{p+1} = z_p$.

3. *Process correction:* In light of the step function disturbance, and the exponential process dynamics,[11] the appropriate corrective adjustment uses the change in error Δe_p plus the latest error e_p. Algebraically, this becomes twice the current difference from set point minus the previous difference from set point.

$$\text{Correction } (X_{p+1}) = \frac{-1}{g(\Delta e_p + e_p)} = \frac{-1}{g(2e_p - e_{p-1})}$$

This should be intuitively satisfying, since only one half of the corrective effect is felt by the time the next sample is taken.

4. *Chart control:* The charts to control the process are shown in Figure 28.11. The proportional (P) chart is a plot of the hourly readings from Table 28.13. The horizontal line is drawn at the target value, 92. The second scale shows the deviations from target value and represents e_p in the correction equation.

On the difference chart (D), the difference between successive readings is plotted. (For example, the first point is the difference between hour 2 and hour 1, 94 − 90 = +4. The second point, 94 − 94 = 0, etc.) These differences are plotted about a horizontal line at zero. They represent Δe_p in the correction equation.

The third chart is the action (A) chart. On this chart the sums of the deviations on charts P and D are plotted. (For hour 2, 2 + 4 = 6; for hour 3, 2 + 0 = 2, etc.) Hence chart A represents $\Delta e_p + e_p$. The action chart is plotted on a scale

---

[10]Box and Jenkins (1962*a* and 1962*b*) describe several methods for theoretically and empirically determining the appropriate predictor and correction equations, e.g., when the disturbance is not approximated by a step function or the process dynamics by an exponential function. One trial-and-error method evaluates, over limited ranges within a so-called "stability region," choices of three parameters having similar effect as the "derivative, proportional, and integral" control action used by control engineers.

[11]$\Delta e_p = e_p - e_{p-1}$, where e_p = deviation of latest reading from the process target or set point.

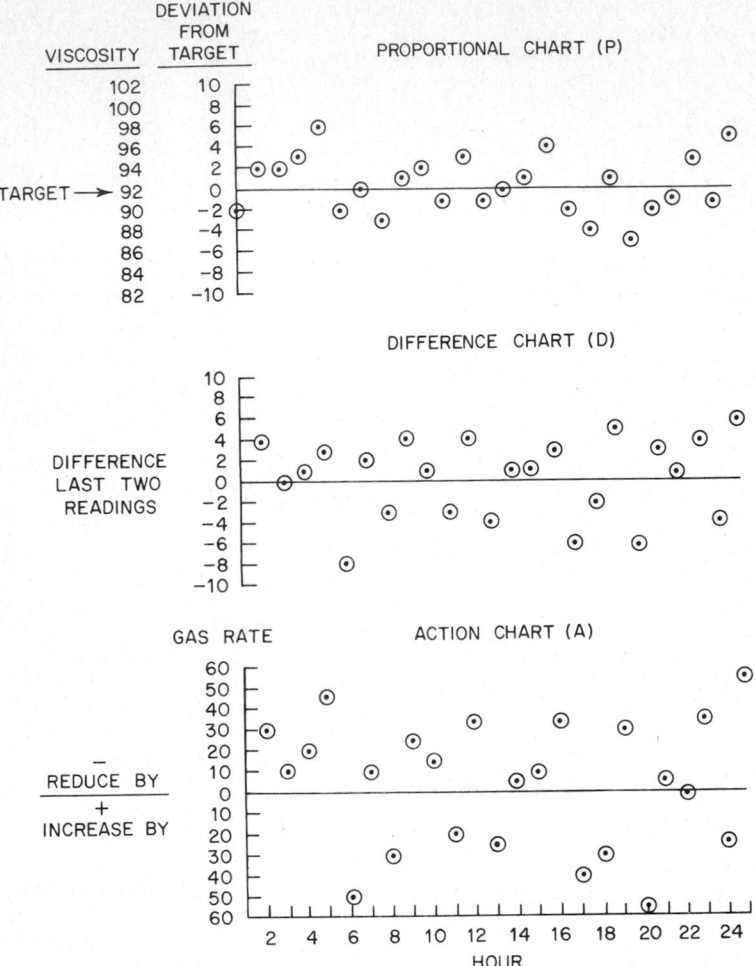

FIG. 28.11 Adaptive quality control charts.

$(-1/g$ times the sum of the deviations) which shows directly the adjustment required.

Each hour, the operator enters the viscosity result on the P chart, calculates and plots D, then adds the deviations on P and D to get A. The appropriate correction is read from the A scale and the required adjustment to the gas rate is made.

Extensions of Adaptive Control. The adaptive control charts can be modified to take care of lags through a process, i.e., elapse of time before an adjustment takes effect. Also, there can be large changes in the prediction and correction equation weighting factors, (G0, G1, GM1)[12] without much effect on the efficiency of the

---

[12]Box and Jenkins (1962*a* and 1962*b*) use γ_0, γ_1, and γ_{-1} where G0, G1, and GM1 are used here.

technique. In other words, the dynamics do not need to be exactly represented. Box and Jenkins (1962) have shown "the choice of the coefficients is not very critical; a sum of squares slightly greater than the smallest value can be obtained over a fairly wide area of the (G0, G1, GM1) parameter space."[13]

Box and Jenkins have also described:

"Zone adjustment" in which the action chart (A of Figure 28.11) is marked off into bands with one corrective adjustment made for all points falling within a band.

"Constrained" correction procedures which limit the variance of the controlled variable (gas flow in this example). They give methods for calculating the increase in output variance (viscosity in the example) due to less than full correction.

Forecasts and their variances more than one observation ahead.

Using *iterative* steps in process identification, prediction, and correction modeling, the technique provides control adaptive to a wide range of process industry disturbances and dynamics.

Plant Experimentation. Ideally, experimentation in the factory aimed at improving quality, yield, and throughput will make full use of experiment designs. Because of the large number of variables commonly present in industrial plants, more use is apt to be made of the screening designs described by Plackett and Burman (1946), or fractional factorials listed by Hunter and others. To make optimum use of data as obtained, sequential experimentation may be used.

Process optimization is frequently the goal of plant experimentation. The central composite designs of Box (see Box, 1954, and Box and Youle, 1955) and Hunter (see Section 28, and Box and Hunter, 1961a and 1961b) are very useful, combined with multiple regression and response surface plotting. These designs may be used sequentially to seek an optimum under various strategies. (See Marquardt, 1970, and Hoerl and Kennard, 1970a and 1970b.)

One of the dangers in plant experimentation is that the pressures for output and quality may not permit running all the planned experiments. In one such example, a 2^6 factorial design was set up to study the factors affecting product quality. Gathering information took several weeks, during which all shifts were involved. After 96 runs had been made, only 33 were found to be a part of the original design. The other 63 runs were repeats of some of the design; others were

---

[13]Here e is defined as "predicted value—observed value" or $e_p = \hat{z}_p - z_p$. The computing procedure for a chosen set of G0, G1, GM1 starts by setting $\hat{z}_1 = z_1$ so that $e_1 = 0$, $\Delta e_0 = 0$, $Se_1 = 0$. Then $\hat{z}_2$ is predicted by substituting z_1, e_1, Δe_1, Se_1 in the equation

$$\hat{z}_{p+1} = z_p + G0e_p + G1Se_p + GM1\Delta e_p$$

From the new $\hat{z}$, e, Δe, and Se are calculated and the process repeated. The "sum of squares" (SSE) being minimized is

$$e_1^2 + e_2^2 + e_3^2 + \cdots + e_n^2$$

$(Se_p = e_1 + e_2 + e_3 + \cdots + e_p. \ \Delta e_p = e_p - e_{p-1})$

Within the stability region described by Box and Jenkins, the combination explored covered the range of GM1 from -0.80 to 0.80 in steps of 0.20 [that is, -0.80 (0.20) 0.80]. Likewise G0 and G1 ranged 0.0 (0.2) 4.0 as appropriate.

Box and Jenkins suggest procedures for testing adequacy of the prediction and correction models. They recommend 200 to 400 points rather than the 25 used for illustration here.

points not originally planned. It was possible to analyze the data using multiple regression. However, many of the interactions of interest were not measurable, with considerable information lost.

Multiple regression is valuable in plant experimentation and in analyzing data which may be produced as a byproduct of normal operation. (See Draper and Smith, 1981, on advantages and pitfalls of this approach; see also Section 23.)

Process Automation.   One of the keys to building better quality into industrial products is adequate control of the operating variables. The old days when an operator could stick a thumb into the product and "adjust" the quality level are fast disappearing. Instead, continuous viscometers, continuous samplers, on-line gas-liquid chromatographic analyzers, etc., are being installed by many companies. These techniques give instantaneous pictures of how the process is doing. In addition, automatic controls on temperature, pressure, product feed rate, etc., permit restraint of these variables within very narrow limits. Control engineers have developed computer-monitored open- and closed-loop systems. In some of these, all sampling, analysis, calculation of results, and corrective signal to the controlling device are coordinated by the computer. (See Section 27 under New Process Quality.)

Data Banks.   A relatively new computer-aided approach to quality improvement is the data bank concept. Operating information from a process is taken continuously on magnetic tape. Periodically, the information is plotted out on a computer in the form of cumulative sum charts, together with the quality information stored. Comparisons can then be made over a period of time and action taken on those conditions which appear difficult to control. As described in Section 27, via multiple regression the same information may give clues as to why some conditions vary. (See also Wetzstein, 1982.)

Quality Motivation Programs.   In the process industries, the managers are quite aware that control over product quality is primarily in the hands of the technical specialists rather than the work force. In consequence, the industry has generally avoided undue enthusiasm for structured motivation programs. (See generally Section 10.) However, the industry makes wide use of some elements of quality motivation:

> Employee training (see Bingham, 1962a) includes information on what happens to the product when standard procedures are not followed. (This is extended to explain how and why processes work, how instruments, controllers, and computers control, etc.)

> Examples are used to show how customer problems are related to the measured chemical and physical properties of the product. These examples underscore the importance of the job of controlling those properties.

> Display racks may be set up to contrast good with poor product, and to publicize the relation of control testing to product quality.

The "employees" who can affect quality adversely include auxiliary personnel as well as operators. Products can be contaminated when lines and tanks are used for more than one product if the auxiliary personnel fail to clean the containers properly. In such cases, foolproofing and redundancy can be of help to all: special fittings, color coding, tags, etc.

PLANNING FOR FUTURE NEEDS

The process industries use conventional means to discover the changing needs of the market: competitive analysis, customer contact, and still others as discussed in Section 12. The evaluations require conventional collaboration between Marketing, Research, and Analytical Laboratories. Membership and active participation in technical society and industry committees provides added opportunities for keeping ahead of changing quality needs and even for guiding their direction. The ideal feedback is quantified data on future market demands, but soundly based opinions can be helpful in providing Research with directions for product improvement work and new product developments.

Research.   The bulk of research is directed to product and process improvement. (Ideally, a small but consistent portion of resources should be expended in fundamental research to answer basic questions of "why and how," and in the hope of being rewarded by an occasional fundamental discovery.) It focuses on existing products and processes, investigating new raw material sources, improving yields, comparing batch- and continuous-type processes, seeking better methods of control, etc. These defensive strategies aim to offset future quality problems.

When a new product is developed to fit an existing or new need, the prudent research manager may often continue the research effort, and come up with the so-called second-generation or third-generation product. These anticipate the projected requirements two or three years hence. The ability to pull a new product off the shelf as required often permits a company to get the jump on competition, or at least have an answer ready if competition moves first.

Analytical Laboratory.   The analytical laboratory can prepare for future quality problems by being alert to new testing needs and by improving existing methods and equipment. Continual monitoring of test accuracy and precision directed toward definite improvement goals will permit acceptance of tighter test precision standards when such needs arrive. (Within-company laboratory comparisons are commonly made. Further, cooperative, "round robin" or interlaboratory "programs" are effective in deriving standardized test methods of known accuracy and precision traceable to the National Bureau of Standards. See Lashof, 1964, Wernimont, 1950 and 1967, and Youden, 1963 and 1967, for classical descriptions of test techniques. See also Section 26 under Planning Interlaboratory Tests.)

If existing equipment and methodology fail to provide desired and foreseen test reliability, it is the responsibility of the analytical laboratory to investigate, purchase, and check out newly developed testing equipment.

One of the foreseen problems resulting from changing quality requirements may be the need for increasing test load from time to time. Automation of testing equipment and computerizing test calculations may alleviate the situation. Some companies already have interfaced gas-liquid chromatography and Instron testing equipment to provide input to computers for computation. Any equipment where large numbers of repetitive tests are run is fair game for this approach. (See Secrest, 1968, for papers on automation of analytical testing methods and uses of computers in the analytical laboratory. See also Section 26.)

Manufacturing Department.   The Manufacturing Department investigates, purchases, and installs new equipment to increase yield, productivity, and quality. Better instrumentation can help in process studies aimed at determining the effects of operating conditions on product quality and in developing controls which keep the process on target. New equipment and instrumentation can lead to automatically controlled plants in which a computer becomes part of the control loop, providing information for operator control, or even sending impulses to the operating equipment to regulate the process.

Interfacing of process instrumentation, automatic sample analyzers, and the computer has been successfully accomplished and data logging used for process improvement and control. (See Bicking, Bingham, and Weiss, 1963; see also ISA, 1986, for review articles on more recent practice.) In highly interacting processes where corrective adjustment to one portion of the process results in a disturbance elsewhere, it is necessary to look at everything at once, which the operator is unable to do. But this is just what a computer does well, and a description of such a plant is given by Shah and Stillman, 1970 (see also Section 27).

It is also important to improve packaging and storage techniques in anticipation of changing market needs. For example, if a customer formerly purchased material in drums and now wants truck or tank-car shipments, the quality of the material must be protected in storage and in transit. The Manufacturing Department may often maintain a staff of packaging and shipping experts whose function is to solve these problems. In addition, packaging changes may be needed to stay abreast of or anticipate competitive action.

METALS INDUSTRY

The modern metals industry produces over thirty *basic* types of metals in a wide diversity of alloys and grades. This spectrum is then processed into a wide variety of forms such as sheet, coil, wire, ingot, and billet, each with its own quality problems. Despite the myriad of permutations of metals and shapes, there is much commonality in the underlying quality principles employed to meet the needs of fitness for use and to do so economically. This commonality is well exemplified by the problems and practices of the steel and aluminum industries. It is these industries (with which the author has some degree of familiarity) which will mainly be discussed in this part of this section. In like manner, the following material will concentrate on those aspects of quality management which are widely prevalent in the industry and can therefore be regarded as a main road amid a bewildering array of side roads.

The metals industry has exhibited an impressive pace of improving technology and adopting new concepts of process control. There was a day, not too long ago, when most metals processes were governed by the state of the art, and were heavily dependent upon operator skill. Computer control is now becoming commonplace, the tools of the applied statistician are being put to use, and it is a safe prediction that by the end of the 1980s, the industry will be highly automated and will have assimilated the most advanced of quality techniques. (See Table 28.14.)

Economic factors have a direct bearing upon the type of quality problems as well as upon the attempts to resolve these problems. The industry is closely coupled to its source of raw material, the ore body, and this places restrictions upon its flexibility to adopt new processes. On the other hand, as the older ore bodies are depleted, the basic smelting processes must be modified to consume new ore sources. These new sources usually present new and often more difficult processing problems. The metals processes must accommodate to the raw material that is available, and there is only limited ability to select ores that are optimum for the process. This limitation on the availability of a variety of ores also pertains to the supplementary raw materials such as coal, coke, pitch, and limestone. These materials constitute very significant cost factors and are used in large quantities. Hence, the economic concerns are often more determinative in the selection of raw materials than are the quality factors. These economic realities have had an influence on the extent of the quality effort directed to raw materials. Still another economic characteristic is that expansion of production capability requires immense outlays of capital funds. Prudence dictates that these funds be directed to proved processes, and there is necessarily a reluctance to make process changes which would obsolete existing investments. This provides an inertia working against rapid changes in processes and equipment.

The subject matter will be treated under three main topics. *Quality in Product Planning* will treat the subjects related to controlling an existing process in order to achieve maximum product quality at minimum cost. *Quality Improvement* will be directed to those techniques which will yield breakthrough in technology,

TABLE 28.14   Effect of Anatomy of Metals Processes on Plans of Process Control

Anatomy of process	Type I	Type II	Type III	Type IV
Process and product characteristics	Single product Single process Continuous operation One or few large production units	Single product Single process Continuous operation Numerous small production units	Multiple products Batch process	Multiple products Multiple processes
Plan of control emphasizes	Control of input raw materials Rigid control of process variables Control of important process parameters	Signals to indicate process upsets Prompt response to nonconforming units Reliance on operator skills Product inspection after completion	Means for making incremental adjustments to variables in input materials and in process conditions	Clear understanding of customer requirements Formal procedures for filling customer orders Process modifications to meet customer needs Reliance on operator of equipment with minimal process surveillance Process inspection between operations Final product inspection

equipment, and controls that will permit operating at new, higher levels of quality that are so important for an industry to remain competitive and forge ahead. *Measures of Performance* is directed to techniques for guiding the quality improvement effort, for determining that the control plan is working and that the gains predicted from quality improvement activities are realized.

QUALITY IN PRODUCT PLANNING—METALS

The quality plan for a specific metals process depends upon a number of basic considerations. Of prime concern is the nature of the product and its quality requirements. The design of the plan also depends upon the volume of metal being processed and the anatomy of the process. Process anatomy is the functional structure of the total process and can best be explained by referencing some representative metals processes.

1. Figure 28.12 illustrates in schematic form the flow diagram of the process of manufacturing steel mill products from the basic raw materials of iron ore, limestone, and coal. That portion of the total operation concerned with the smelting of iron ore to iron is concerned with a single process and a single product and is categorized here as a Type I process. This Type I process has its counterpart in aluminum, where bauxite ore is converted to refined aluminum oxide. The types of controls employed in this type of process, as well as the approach one takes to quality improvement, will differ from other types of processes concerned with a variety of products and/or a variety of processes.

The Type I process concerned with a single process and a single product allows for the concentration of quality effort to be directed to a rigid control of process variables. Little, if any, effort is directed to customer contacts or to developing new products. Quality of raw materials is an important consideration for quality and cost. Since process efficiency depends heavily upon continuous operation, a concerted effort is made to provide a preventive "front-end" type of control over this type of process. The term "front-end" refers here to a type of control plan that is directed to the control of important process parameters as opposed to a "back-end" control that is geared to react in a compensative fashion when the process output is nonconforming.

2. Figure 28.13 illustrates in schematic form a process of a different anatomy calling for a different logic of control. It depicts the process for converting aluminum oxide into molten aluminum metal. It employs a multitude of individual electrolytic reduction cells each producing the same product but operating almost completely independently of each other. This type of process will be referred to as a Type II process. It has its counterpart in the chemical industry wherein chlorine and caustic are produced from sodium chloride in banks of individual electrolytic cells. The unique feature of this type of operation is the large number of units which are operated in an almost independent manner. It is common for the number of individual units to number in the hundreds.

The Type II process differs from a Type I process in that it is concerned with a multitude of small identical processes producing a single product. For economic reasons, the total process control effort is likely to be spread lightly over a host of production units with considerable reliance for quality being placed upon "operator skill." Should process upsets occur in a few of the units, it would have a relatively small impact upon the whole plant, and as a result, one is likely to drift into a posture of "back-end" control. The principal control effort is then directed to finding the process upsets and restoring control by compensative corrective action.

3. In Figure 28.12, the basic oxygen furnace unit operating on a batch basis represents a third type of process that will be referred to as a Type III process. It has its counterpart in the casting of aluminum alloys by increments of individual heats.

A Type III process is generally referred to as a batch process. The logic of control here is directed to controlling on an incremental basis with provisions made for process adjustments on a batch basis. Quality problems are readily detected and defective product can be easily isolated. The exposure to major process upsets is at a minimum. Less emphasis is required on controlling the inputs when the opportunities exist for correction.

4. Figure 28.14 illustrates in schematic form the anatomy of the process for converting aluminum metal into the variety of mill products needed to satisfy the requirements of a wide range of customers and end uses. It is being designated as a Type IV process and is also illustrated by the steel fabrication operations shown in Figure 28.12. It is a multiunit, multiproduct type of process that requires increased emphasis on individual customer requirements. This type of process can be likened to a large job shop.

A Type IV process presents a formidable control problem. It requires that a major effort be directed to customer relations and it calls for frequent process modifications in order to satisfy a range of customer requirements. Operating procedures must be rather formal and complex in order to convey the exact production practices for each product. The inspection function must be extensive, since it is directed to a large number of products and customers. Reliance must be placed upon the equipment operator to control the process, and only a minimum amount of quality control surveillance over the process is economically feasible. Since the material progresses through a number of operations, there are opportunities for in-process inspection that prove useful for detecting processing problems prior to final inspection.

The above is intended to give the reader some appreciation of the factors that go into developing a control plan for a specific metals process.

The remaining discussion of the control plan will cover the control techniques and problems for the entire sequence of activities through which the products are designed, manufactured, marketed, used, and serviced. The treatment will start with an understanding of those customer relations aspects which influence the selection of the type of controls to be employed. It will then consider the types of controls that are exercised over new products and the special problems experienced in the metals industry. The manufacturing control plan will then treat the three basic elements of control: (1) *raw material control,* (2) *process control,* and (3) *product control.* Emphasis will be placed on those elements of control which appear to be common to the industry.

Table 28.14 summarizes the effect of the anatomy of metals processes on the control plan.

Customer Relations

Identification of Customer Requirements. A large volume of metal products is sold to customers whose end-use requirements are well understood and whose

The raw materials of steelmaking must be brought together, often from hundreds of miles away, and smelted in a blast furnace to produce most of the iron that goes into steelmaking furnaces. Air and oxygen are among the most important raw materials in iron and steelmaking.

PELLETS

IRON ORE

SINTER

LIMESTONE

CRUSHING

COAL

COKE OVENS

COKE OVEN BY-PRODUCTS

BLAST FURNACE

SCRAP OR PREREDUCED ORE

MOLTEN IRON TRANSFER CAR

SLAG

CASTING PIG IRON

MIXER

BASIC OXYGEN FURNACE

OPEN HEARTH FURNACE

ELECTRIC FURNACE

A FLOWLINE ON STEELMAKING

This is a simplified road map through the complex world of steelmaking. Each stop along the routes from raw materials to mill products contained in this chart can itself be charted. From this overall view, one major point emerges: Many operations—involving much equipment and large numbers of men—are required to produce civilization's principal and least expensive metal.

FIG. 28.12 Flow diagram of steelmaking. *(American Iron and Steel Institute.)*

basic quality requirements are stated in the standards and codes published by ASTM, various trade associations, or governmental agencies. These basic requirements, in most instances, have to be augmented by individual customer requirements that make the product amenable to specific end uses. It is a common practice for the customer to reference the standard and then add to this any special requirements. Orders for new customers and new products are commonly reviewed by quality control and/or metallurgical personnel before the order is approved for manufacture.

In addition to the large quantity of standard products sold, a variety of products are sold that are not adequately described in existing and recognized standards. The customer has a specific end use but may lack sufficient knowledge to state exact needs in terms of alloy, temper, and functional requirements. The product is being ordered on a fitness-for-use basis, and it is left up to the metal

Molten steel must solidify before it can be made into
finished products by the industry's rolling mills and forging presses. The metal is usually formed first at high
temperature, after which it may be cold-formed into
additional products.

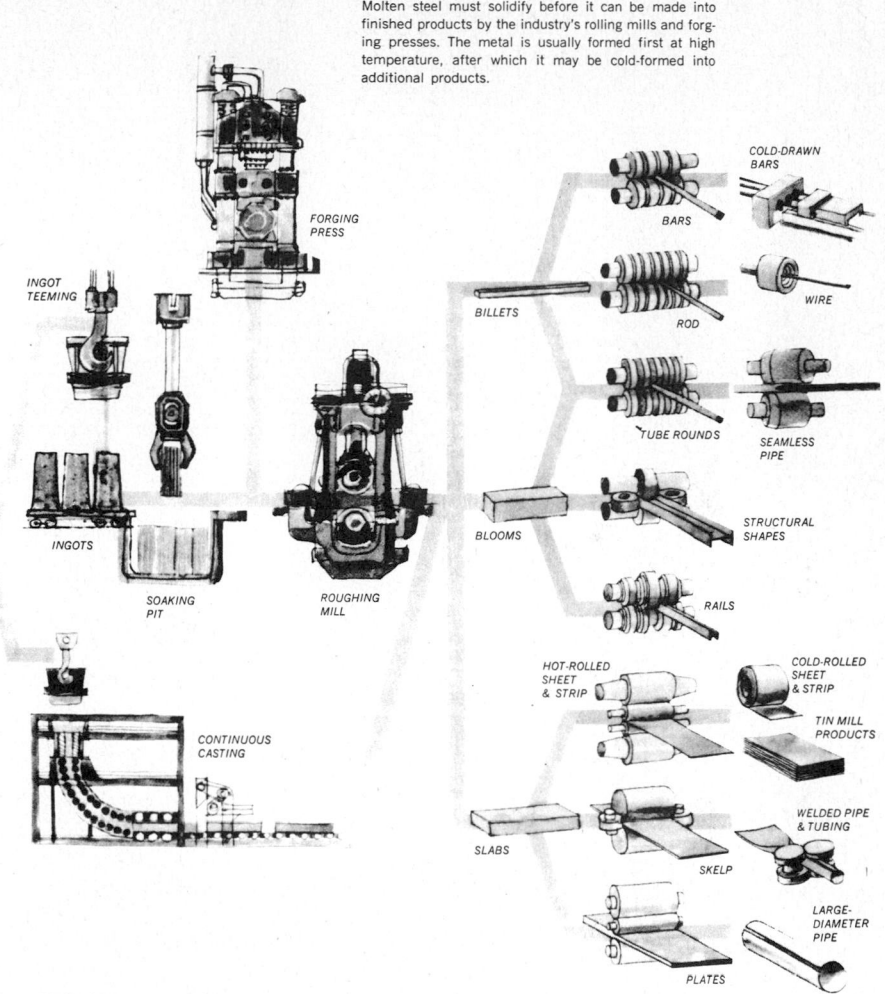

FIG. 28.12 (*Continued*)

producer to gain an understanding of the customer's requirements and to produce
to meet these needs. The metals industry has recognized this need to assist the
customer in determining quality requirements and has developed technical specialists who work directly with the customer in determining any unique requirements. The lack of complete product specifications can and does lead to misunderstandings with the customers and, at times, to monetary losses for both the
metal producer and the customer.

The above remarks are addressed to the broad subject of product specification
and customer requirements, and do not apply to the chemical composition of
metals and their alloys. The metals industry has a very keen appreciation of the
importance of chemical composition in determining metal performance. Alloy
designation and composition limits are very carefully defined and rigidly adhered
to in the quality control of the product.

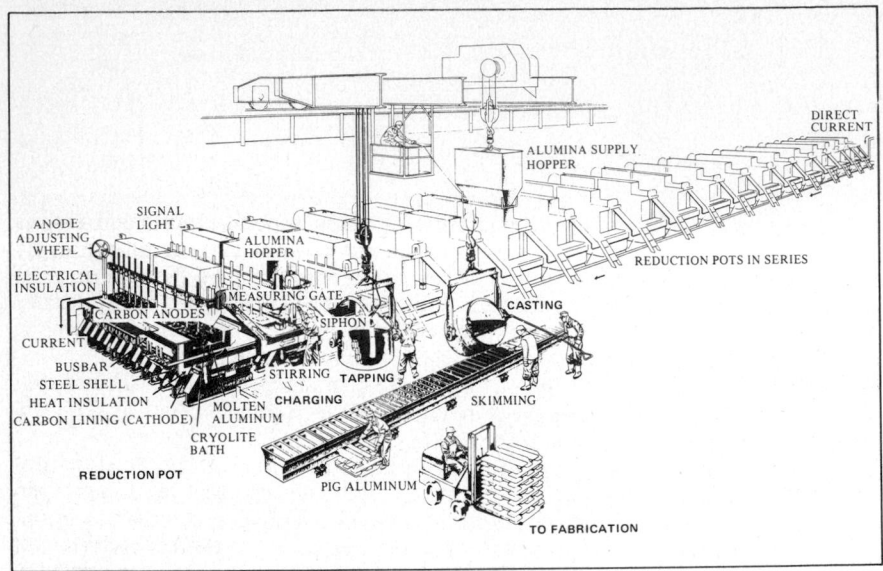

FIG. 28.13 Flow diagram of aluminum reduction. *(Metals Engineering Institute–American Society of Metals.)*

Another type of customer relation is the sale of metal through distributors. The distributor may handle a number of different metals and stock a variety of alloys, compositions, and physical shapes. These are products that have general use but usually in quantities which would not warrant the customer placing an order directly to a metal producer. There is the added advantage to the customer of generally receiving prompt delivery. The customer relations responsibility at the metals plant may then take on a dual character, with the principal responsibility and contact being to and with the distributor but still maintaining a secondary responsibility to the ultimate customer.

Information Feedback from the Customer. A vital part of the producer-consumer relationship is a system for providing prompt and accurate feedback of information to the mill should the customer experience quality problems.

The Sales Department is usually the first to hear of customer quality problems, and accepts the prime responsibility for the initial inquiry and investigation. It is a common and recommended practice that the salesman immediately notify the Quality Department at the producing mill of any quality problem so that immediate action can be taken on any additional orders for this product which might be in the process of being manufactured. Should the Quality or Metallurgical Departments sense a serious problem, they may elect, on their initiative, to visit the customer's plant, but in most cases the problems can be resolved by telephone calls, samples, and correspondence. In some instances the customer will request technical assistance from the metal producer in order to help in fabricating the metal or in more clearly defining the product requirements.

New Products Controls. The metals industry as treated within the scope of this section is not called upon to produce a host of new products each year in order to maintain market position. Since the products are for the most part standard

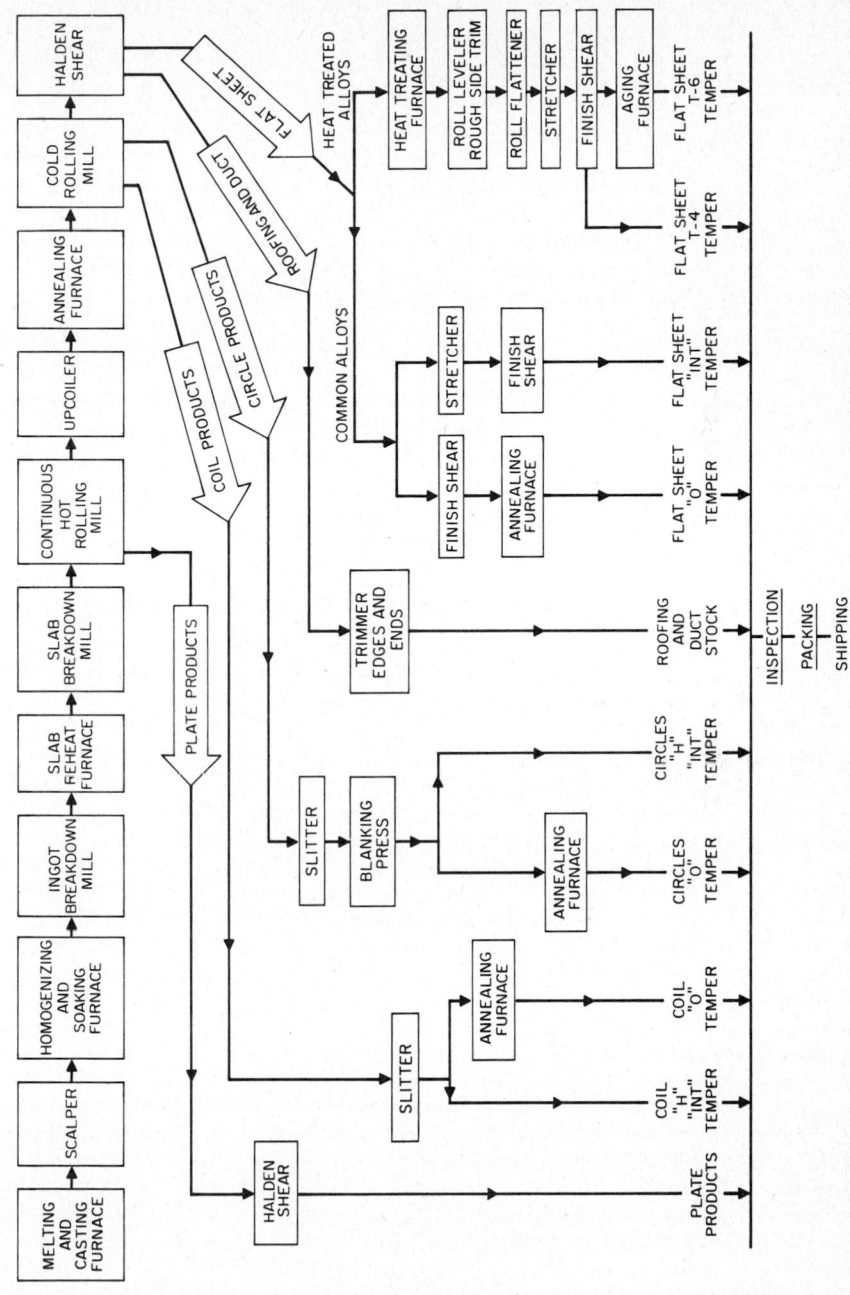

FIG. 28.14 Flow diagram for aluminum conversion. *(Metals Engineering Institute–American Society of Metals.)*

mill products that are used as raw materials for subsequent processing, they are not as subject to frequent redesign as are those which are manufactured for the customer market. As a result, there is a relatively high degree of stability of the basic design characteristics of standard mill products.

There are a number of new product controls which are somewhat unique to the metals industry and merit some discussion.

The Trial Order. It is usual for orders placed for mill products to run into thousands of pounds. When such an order fails to perform, financial claims of major magnitude arise. For this reason, it is common and recommended practice for a metals plant to first undertake the production of a new product (or an old product for a new use) on the basis of a small trial order, with the major production quantities to be produced only after the trial order material had been successfully utilized by the customer. This approach has merit on a number of counts:

1. It affords the opportunity for close surveillance by Quality and/or Metallurgy of the actual manufacture of the trial order. This is helpful in validating the manufacturing procedures and assures that the trial order material will be representative of the normal production product.

2. By working with the customer on the basis of a trial order, it is possible to avoid many misunderstandings. The customer is aware that the product is being manufactured on a trial basis. Should the trial order fail to perform, the producer's quality image is not damaged, and avenues are left open for subsequent trial orders.

3. It is common practice for the Quality and/or Metallurgical representative from the mill to be present during the processing of the trial order in the customer's plant. This provides an excellent opportunity for the producing mill to understand more completely the manner in which its product will be used and to observe the product's shortcomings should it fail to perform.

New Product Availability. The manufacture of mill products, from a quality viewpoint, can often be likened to a large job shop. The basic metal can be manufactured in a myriad of final mill products which vary by composition, by temper, by physical shape, or by surface condition. It is a common practice for the metal companies to publish sales data sheets describing their available standard products, but it is understood that additional products can be made available upon inquiry. Requests for new-product availability go to the Quality Department as well as other interested departments before a determination can be made as to whether or not the mill has the capability of producing the product in a profitable manner.

Qualification Tests for New Products. A great many of the new products generated by the metals industry concern only minor adaptations to standard products in order to meet the specific processing requirements of individual customers, but there are still others that represent very significant changes in composition, physical properties, and end-use application. The latter category requires more rigid controls.

Products that are associated with major changes in metal composition and basic manufacturing methods are generally the result of a company's Research and Development Program and are directed to specific new needs in the marketplace. The basic development work, along with the attendant product testing, is often done in a research environment and then, when feasibility has been demonstrated, it is programmed for mill production. These new products often require new equipment or complete new facilities and must be manufactured in accordance with new standard operating procedures. They also require new methods of quality assurance.

The routine product acceptance testing will seldom suffice for determining that a new product will perform as intended. The development work associated with these major changes in product design must be supported by tests that will serve to predict reliability in service, and they must be broad enough in scope to detect the unexpected modes of failure.

Raw Material Controls.   The metals industry has some unique problems associated with the control of raw material quality. The principal raw material is the ore, which usually comes from a predetermined source. Variations in the processing quality characteristics of the ore can have a profound influence upon the quality of the metal as well as the efficiency of the process. It is a common practice to blend ores from various mining areas in order to achieve a more uniform feed to the smelting operation. In the aluminum operation the bauxite ore undergoes a chemical processing operation that converts it to a purified aluminum oxide before it is consigned to the smelting operation for conversion to metal. In some metals industries there are often types of ore beneficiation operations which are directed to the task of concentration, removal of harmful impurities, and achieving greater uniformity. In many instances the metals process must be made to conform to the quality of the ore available.

Other basic raw materials such as coal, coke, pitch, limestone, and recycle metal are, for economic reasons, subject to much the same types of limitation in respect to assuring uniformity. There are, however, lesser quantities of raw materials such as alloying components, chemicals, rolling mill coolants, and refractories which are used in the metals industry and are amenable to formal vendor controls.

It is a common practice in the metals industry for the responsibility of evaluating raw material quality to be assigned to the Metallurgical Department with little or no involvement on the part of the Quality Department. It is the opinion of the author that raw material control systems as we now know them in the metals industry would improve if the task of controlling to a quality level were considered a quality control function.

The problem of controlling the quality of raw material from the smelter to the casting and fabrication operation is usually one of internal quality controls. The molten metal is sampled, analyzed, and graded, and this system serves the industry well in controlling the quality of the composition of the metal. This control point will take on increased importance as the metals industry moves more and more to continuous types of process.

Process Controls.   The process control plans employed in the metals industry are so many and varied that only two basic operations will be considered:

1. Ore smelting
2. Metal fabrication

Ore Smelting.   At the smelting stage of a metals process, the raw materials represent the major input to the process, and hence, the process control plan should be addressed to their control. The plan should contain provisions for either controlling the uniformity of raw material quality or detecting shifts in quality and altering the process to cope with these shifts. This is not a simple task. For many of the metals processes, consideration of the cost and availability of raw materials overshadow the concerns about their quality characteristics. Coal, limestone, and metal-bearing ores are naturally occurring materials, do not possess the uniformity of manufactured materials, and present problems in obtaining a representative sample. Seldom are alternative sources of supply readily available. Despite these formidable problems, process control plans can accomplish a great deal in smoothing out the variations. Most smelting processes have flexibility for operating efficiently with varying grades of raw materials if the changes can be anticipated. An adequate knowledge of raw material quality presents opportunities for the blending of materials possessing wide variations in quality into a uniform feed to the smelting process.

After due consideration of the control of raw materials, the process control plan must treat the important operating variables such as raw material feed rates, energy inputs, and reaction times. These vary from process to process depending upon the chemistry of the process as well as equipment design. Some of these variables are amenable to instrumented control, but many depend upon operator skill and attention.

The process control plan for a smelting operation must also address itself to the quality of the metal produced. It requires a regimen for collecting metal samples and submitting these to chemical testing. These tests are directed to metal purity and are usually carried out by instrumented x-ray or spectrographic methods that provide for a rapid feedback of data to the smelter.

Metal Fabrication.   The process control plan for a metal fabrication process is directed to the product attributes that are of importance to the customer. We will consider three principal types of product characteristics.

1. *Metallurgical characteristics:*   The metals industry has developed sophisticated controls for both process inputs and product outputs related to strength and function. In addition to effective control of metal composition as described above, fabrication practices are designed to achieve the correct balance of properties to satisfy both the strength and the function requirements for the product.

These fabrication practices are concerned with the heat treating and rolling of the metal. Heat treating procedures are defined in detailed operating practices, and the accuracy and uniformity of the equipment used for these operations is closely monitored. The sequence of operations during fabrication is important to the control of metallurgical characteristics and this is defined in operating practices.

In order to be assured that the fabrication practices are followed, some form of auditing is employed. In many instances this is the informal auditing carried on during routine supervision. However, a more formal and documented audit plan provides greater assurance.

2. *Thickness:*   Thickness control is achieved either by operator skill or, increasingly, through a closed-loop computer control system. In either case, the final result is recorded in chart form by a continuous thickness measuring device, and the operator has a continuous display of actual strip thickness available to read.

3. *Surface appearance:*   While audits of roll conditions, tensions, speeds, etc., are employed in an effort to control appearance, the fundamental approach in rolling is still to examine one end of some predetermined fraction of the coils produced, such as every fourth or fifth coil, and to take corrective action if defects are found. In slitting, sheeting, and leveling operations, operators examine the

sheet as it passes at operating speeds, which presents some obvious control limitations.

Product Controls. In the metals industry, product assurance controls can be logically grouped into the following three categories:

1. Control of metal composition
2. Control of mechanical properties
3. Control of dimensional and visual characteristics

There are, however, a number of inspection and testing problems which are unique to the metals industry.

Control of Metal Composition. The control of metal composition starts at the smelting operation, at which time a level of metal purity is established. A subsequent control at the time of casting is directed to the chemical composition of the metal alloy or grade of metal as well as to the extent of the nonmetallics such as oxides, carbides, and dissolved gases.

The procedures for sampling molten metal and for performing the chemical analysis are well developed and are generally carried out in accordance with ASTM approved procedures.

The metals industry generally uses melt or heat numbers that are associated with specific casts of metals, and these numbers follow the product no matter how often the lot is divided. This practice has served the industry well in relating metal composition to problems encountered in end use.

The control of nonmetallics is dependent upon a rigid adherence to casting practices that have been designed to scavenge these impurities from the metal. It proves difficult to sample and verify by analytical techniques that this control has been completely achieved. Process audits provide an adequate degree of product assurance for most products, but when it is critical that the level of nonmetallics be maintained at a very low level, the ultrasonic, nondestructive testing technique is employed. (See Krautkramer and Krautkramer, 1961, pp. 279–411.)

Control of Mechanical Properties. Mechanical properties of metals include such attributes as tensile strength, yield strength, percent elongation, electrical conductivity, resistance to stress corrosion, forming ability, and hardness.

These quality characteristics are built into the product by control of metal composition as well as by the in-process controls exercised during fabrication. These controls relate to casting conditions, ingot preheat, rolling techniques, heat treating, etc. The proper sequencing of the operation as well as the control of the operating parameters in each operation are required in order to develop the required properties. These are specified in operating practices and are incorporated into the manufacturing procedures for each product.

An assurance of these controls is obtained by sampling each lot of material after fabrication and performing on this sample the various standard tests that have been developed by ASTM, the industry, or the customer.

For metal products used in critical end-use application, it is a common practice for the customer to require a certification of test results. These are typed listings of chemical and mechanical properties and are attested to by a Quality or Metallurgical representative before forwarding to the customer. (It is questionable how well it serves to add to the reliability of metal products, since the metals industry has long recognized its reponsibility to supply products that conform to chemical and mechanical properties and has developed the internal controls that provide a high degree of product assurance.)

Control of Dimensional and Visual Characteristics.   Metal products are produced in all manner of physical shapes and sizes, and with a wide range of permissible variations in dimensional tolerances and visual characteristics. The dimensions and the visual appearance are determined during the fabrication operations, and in-process controls are exercised by the operational personnel at each step of the operation. The product assurance controls for dimensional and visual characteristics are exercised either at the time of the final operation or by inspection carried out in an inspection area.

A number of specific problems associated with the inspection of dimensional and visual characteristics in the metals industry merit some discussion here.

1. *Coil inspection:*   The inspection of metal products produced in a coil form presents a difficult problem. For the most part, the equipment operator has to be looked upon as an inspector for coil products, since it is not feasible to recoil and inspect the product independently of the final operation. The operator is called upon to inspect a moving strip and often at speeds that make it difficult to detect all the visual flaws or problems relating to lack of flatness. Special auxiliary techniques such as the use of strobe lights or the introduction of slack loops in the moving strip are sometimes employed to increase the effectiveness of this inspection.

Samples, several feet in length, are removed from the ends of the coiled product, and these have been found to correlate amazingly well with the material in the center of the coil. These samples provide an opportunity to verify width of the coil as well as the thickness as it occurs at either end of the coil. When thickness uniformity throughout the coil is critical, use is made of continuous recording gages at the final operation.

2. *Problems of visual standards:*   Aside from the problem of visual inspection on a coiled product, there is a more general problem of establishing adequate standards of visual quality. The industry often falls back upon what is referred to as a standard of commercial quality. This is not a well-defined standard and it must be defined for each type of product, giving proper consideration to the end use and the customer's stated requirements. This still leaves much to be desired. There are varying degrees of severity for each type of visual defect, and it proves difficult to express these in written form. In addition to the categories of visual discontinuities termed defects, there is another type of discontinuity which is referred to as a "condition," meaning that the visual discontinuity is an inherent result of the manufacturing process and is not a cause for rejection.

3. *Problems of flatness standards:*   There is an expressed or an implied requirement for adequate flatness in all metal products sold in either sheet or coil form. To achieve adequate flatness requires extremely close control of the rolling operation and often corrective measures after rolling. As a result of the customer concern and the production problems associated with flatness, a significant amount of the product inspection effort is being directed to the flatness quality characteristic. Despite this concern for flatness, the industry lacks well-defined standards for flatness. This aspect of product quality, like that of visual appearance, is scarcely treated in the industry product standards, and when it is treated, it fails to cover the subject adequately.

It is quite difficult to express the degree of flatness in a simple quantitative fashion. Conventionally, out-of-flat conditions have been expressed as height of waves on specified center-to-center of adjacent waves. For example, the tolerance might be expressed as ½-in wave on 2-ft wave centers. These waves do not occur with any sort of regularity, and this type of tolerance is difficult to apply in inspections.

Supplementary Product Controls.   It is a common practice to have operating personnel inspect cast ingots before they are sent to rolling. This inspection is for the purpose of sorting out ingots which are obviously defective because of cracks and other surface conditions.

The visual inspection of metal as it moves from step to step in the metals process is commonly a part of the operator's responsibility. This in-process inspection serves to detect manufacturing problems as well as to avoid the application of more work to an already defective product.

Another type of supplementary product control that is gaining some acceptance in the metals industry is that of product auditing. These audits represent a second inspection performed on a small sample of the product by a representative of the Quality Department, conducted independently from the routine inspection. The merits of product audits are presented in Section 21 of this handbook and are treated in detail by Woltz (1963). This approach has some special implications in the metals industry.

1. *Control of visual standards:*   Because of the difficulty of defining visual standards of quality, a great deal of reliance has to be placed upon the experience and skill of the inspector to make correct decisions concerning visual quality. By and large, the training provided these inspectors proves effective, but many metals plants are faced with changes in job assignments which can leave the task of visual inspection in the hands of inspectors with relatively little experience. The audit proves useful in assuring that the eyes of the inspector are in constant calibration with the eyes of the product specialist in quality control who is fully versed as to the customer's requirements.

2. *Control of special customer requirements:*   Quite often a metals plant is called upon to produce a wide variety of products to the specific requirements of a large number of customers. These specific requirements cover product quality, packaging requirements, product identification, and restrictions on the size of lots or items. While systems are established for conveying these requirements through the operation, it presents opportunities for oversights and errors. A product audit system proves effective in reducing such errors.

A third type of supplementary control that is gaining some acceptance in the metals industry is that of process audits. (See Walden and Widener, 1967, pp. 23–24.) These audits are directed to the critical process parameters known to influence the quality of the product. The audits serve the dual purpose of increasing the reliability of the process and of assuring greater product uniformity. The observations may be carried out by technicians operating under the control of the Metallurgical or Quality Department, or they may be the accepted responsibility of the Production supervision. The process audits relate to product control insofar as they provide assurance that the product has been manufactured in accordance with design and that quality has hence been "built into" the product.

Standards and Specifications.   Many of the standards and specifications associated with metal products had their origin in governmental requirements but are still basic to the industry. The ASTM has played a significant role in developing specifications, and the various trade associations of the metals industry have assumed a responsibility for developing the more universal standards which treat commercially available products. (The publication *Aluminum Standards and Data Mill Products,* issued by the Aluminum Association, is an excellent source of standards for aluminum products.) ASTM has also played a very significant role in standardizing sampling and testing procedures. Technical societies (for example, ASME Boiler and Pressure Vessel Code, The American Society of Mechanical Engineers, New York 10017) representing the consumers of metals products have developed standards which are germane to their field of interest. The large aerospace and defense-related contractors have seen the need to super-impose their own requirements on those of governmental and trade associations. The entire subject of standards and specifications in the metals industry is extremely complex, and most metals companies find the need for employing one or more specification engineers, assigned to the task of keeping abreast of the sub-ject matter and providing an information service to Sales, Development, Manu-facturing, and Quality. These specialists are called upon to interpret the complex requirements and to ferret out any conflicts which may exist between the custom-ers' requirements and the product capabilities. These standards and specifications concern themselves with product characteristics, test methods, and even the ele-ments of the quality system used in the producing plant. The requirements fre-quently change, and individuals must be sure that they are referencing the most recent amendment of the specification. Many customers' orders make reference to specification documents, and a plant order entry system must be capable of reviewing the requirements of the referenced specification before the order is accepted for fabrication.

QUALITY IMPROVEMENT—METALS

The metals industry in its early beginnings started on the basis of art rather than science, but even in these early years it made rapid improvements in product quality that were sufficient to support the metals requirements of the industrial revolution. It offered products of unique but at the same time versatile character-istics that led to breakthroughs in effort to master the environment. Each suc-ceeding decade has seen new advances that have included new metals as well as improvements in the quality of older metals. The great wonder of these quality improvements is that they have been accompanied by parallel improvements in the efficiencies of the process.

Much of the credit for these successes should be given to the profession of metallurgy, which has developed the metals process into a true science. Metals processes have been developed which are capable of fabricating metal products with a tremendous range in properties and which demonstrate a high degree of reliability. The physical metallurgist has developed the skills of alloying and fab-rication while the extractive metallurgist, the chemist, and the engineer have pro-vided continual improvements in the treatment of ore and its conversion to high-grade metal. Many of the basic metals processes that started on the basis of art have now become sciences.

The Climate for Improvement.   Many factors have worked in a positive man-ner to hasten quality and process improvements and a few have, at times, worked in opposition to change. The metals industry is one of the largest industries in our total economy and thus has been able to attract high-caliber personnel to develop new processes and products. Competition has always been keen within each segment of the industry, and quality improvements that have filled new requirements have always yielded market share improvement.

Defense industries and space exploration have offered great challenges to the metals industry. The response has doubtless contributed very significantly to improvements in technology and product quality.

The industry's high capital investments as well as very significant operating costs have spurred the search for newer and more efficient processes. High capital investment has also acted to retard rapid innovation when it called for replacing costly existing processes. It is not uncommon to see the same product made in one plant by an old process and in a new plant by the most modern of processes. The significance of this reluctance to replace the older and inefficient processes was vividly displayed after World War II when the war-torn countries of Europe and Japan rebuilt their metals industry with new processes which have produced major breakthroughs in product quality and manufacturing costs.

The climate for applying the best quality practices toward the goals of quality improvement has not been consistently good in the metals industry. Only in most recent years do we see the acceptance of the concepts of modern quality control. Quality has generally grown as an arm of the Metallurgical Department, and many of the tasks normally assigned to the Quality Department remain within the province of the metallurgist. The net result has been a slow acceptance, by the metals industry, of the quality methodology that can contribute to product improvement. In addition, the main thrust of the Metallurgical Department has been toward the metallurgical aspects of the operation with lesser emphasis placed on the nonmetallurgical aspects of fabrication. The Quality Department, working with the metallurgist, has, however, played a very significant role in achieving quality improvement through its customer contacts and identification of the product characteristics that required improvement.

Project Identification.   In the metals industry, there are a number of sources of information that are useful for identifying areas for quality improvement. The most common sources relate to the following:

Yield or recovery information

Customer claims and complaints

Promised delivery performance

Raw material cost variances

Information of competitors' quality

(The term "recovery" is often used in preference to yield.)

From such a range of source information, it is not difficult to identify potential quality improvement projects, but the question does arise as to the relative priority of projects. How do we pick the vital few and avoid the pitfall of working on projects of marginal value? The priority of many products can be determined by their obvious economic significance but, in other instances, must be based upon judgment.

Some quality improvement projects specific, if not unique, to the metals industry warrant some elaboration.

Yield Improvement Projects.   It is common practice in the metals industry to use the process yield as one of the principal measures of manufacturing efficiency.

Many of the causes of low yield are quality related and are therefore appropriate targets for quality improvement. (See Rosenzweig, 1968.) Quality problems can reduce process yields either in the form of defective finished product or in the more usual form of in-process scrap. For this reason, the percentage of nonconforming finished product cannot be used as the exclusive index of relative importance of quality improvement projects; i.e., the main losses may have been experienced during processing. In addition, a distinction must be made between:

1. "Quality" losses due to failures of conformance.
2. Other scrap losses considered to be inherent in the processes, e.g., the trim removed from the sides of rolled coils because of the invariable irregularities at these edges. These "inherent" losses are sometimes called "natural waste."

The metals industry can recycle much of the metal that is scrapped during fabrication, but nevertheless the recycling costs represent a major cost factor and hence an opportunity for process and quality improvement.

It is useful to supplement these yield data with a system of scrap identification and nomenclature which describes the observed defects ("symptoms") in precise enough language to provide clues to the causes of the defects. The Pareto principle of identifying and working on the vital few can best be applied when scrap is properly categorized in the above manner.

Customer Claims and Complaints.   The metals industry has its share of dissatisfied customers. In the case of large shipments, the customer will not only complain if inadequate quality exists, but will also ask for a refund and will want to return the material. In many instances, the product in question may be found in accord with commercial standards as well as the stated customer requirements but still fails to perform in the customer's plant. In other words, it is not fit for the customer's intended use. If the claim is significant in size and the reason is not readily obvious, a product engineer or a metallurgist most familiar with the type of product in question is usually dispatched to the customer's plant in order to identify the product quality deficiency and to decide upon the validity of the claim. This customer contact activity often yields information that can focus attention on the need for some basic quality improvements if this market is to be satisfactorily serviced.

Promised Delivery Performance.   For mills producing products to customer orders rather than carrying warehouse inventories of standard items, there is always a problem of producing and shipping promptly in accordance with a promised date for shipment or delivery. Since most customers desire to carry a minimum-sized inventory, the shorter lead times become a sales asset, while failure to meet promises on delivery can erode customer relations.

The manufacturing problem of failing to meet promised delivery dates may seem unrelated to the need for quality improvement, but upon close examination one finds that quality problems relate to an appreciable number of missed promises. The reasons for missed promises can be analyzed and can lead to the identification of the main needs for quality improvement.

Organizing for Quality Improvement.   In most metals plants, the quality function reports to the same department head as the process engineer and/or metallurgist. This department may be designated as the Technical Department or, at times, the Metallurgical Department.

One distinct advantage of this organizational setup is that the quality engineer can work closely with those individuals who are responsible for technology, when the quality engineer is called upon to work on quality improvement projects. A disadvantage is that the quality effort is slow to adopt new quality methodology and that the quality function seldom achieves the organizational stature required.

The quality engineer makes the greatest contribution to the quality improvement effort by collecting and analyzing the facts and steering the work clear of the pitfall of acting on the basis of opinion.

Special Problems.   The metals industry is faced with a number of problems which work against achieving rapid and permanent quality improvements.

Plant Experimentation.   Many quality improvement projects call for some form of experimentation in the plant. At best, these experiments interfere with the production activity. They may also create inordinate amounts of scrap. Primary metals products are produced by processes which are massive in size, often continuous in nature, and hence not readily amenable to plant experimentation. An alternative course is to develop pilot plant equipment, but this, too, is expensive and often yields results that are not predictive of full-scale production operation.

All the above problems emphasize the necessity for well-designed experiments. The statistically designed approach to experimentation will yield the maximum information with the least cost.

Holding the Gain in Quality Improvement.   A quality improvement project also provides increased knowledge of the process. If this increased knowledge can be consistently applied to the process, the resulting quality improvement can also be retained. This calls for revised manufacturing practices and greater attention to one or more of the manufacturing variables. For metals operations that rely on written operating practices and formal methods of process control, this prevents very few problems. However, for processes that rely principally upon the knowledge and the skill of the production operator, there are serious problems of making sure that the new knowledge is put to use.

Wide Range of Product Types.   Most metals operations produce a wide range of products which are, in turn, sold to a large number of customers having a variety of requirements. When quality problems arise, they often appear as being related to a single product rather than to a basic process deficiency. In the face of marketing a host of products with a variety of quality problems, it is difficult to select the area for improvement which will yield the most results.

Cultural Problems.   It is to be expected that an industry as old as the metals industry will experience some cultural resistance in adopting the changes in operating practices required for achieving a breakthrough in quality improvement. In the metals industry, this cultural resistance is greatly influenced by two long-standing practices:

Technical Organization.   Usually the technical organization in a metals plant is headed by a chief metallurgist. The evolution of this metallurgical-centered type of organization is understandable, since over the years, the science of metallurgy has been the main contributor to the basic technology of the industry. The metallurgists responsible for these advances have properly gained the respect of other departments, and have been awarded high organization status for their contributions.

A subtle byproduct of this organization form has been the equating of the metallurgical function to the total technical function. This has often resulted in two failures to balance priorities:

1. Nonmetallurgical technology (e.g., chemical analysis, mechanical equipment) has received less emphasis than metallurgy.

2. The concepts of a quality function, and of nonmetallurgical skills for solving quality problems, e.g., quality planning, statistical methods, motivation, and quality costs, have not been fully grasped or aggressively utilized.

Aside from the plant chemist, charged with directing the chemical analysis, it is not uncommon to find the entire technical staff possessing a metallurgical education. Certainly, some of these individuals broaden their field of technical knowledge and demonstrate capabilities for making contributions beyond the limits of metallurgical phenomena, but the strong metallurgical connotation has resulted in technical organizations having a narrow charter in respect to the entire technology of the process.

Operator Cognizance. In its infancy, the metals industry depended almost entirely upon the skill of the equipment operator to achieve good processing results in both smelting and fabrication. It took some time to convince the melter in the steel industry that a laboratory analysis might yield a processing decision which excelled visual skill for determining the quality of a heat. The aluminum industry still depends a great deal upon operator skill for the operation of electrolytic reduction cells. The skill required to operate a large rolling mill was long considered to be the epitome of craftsmanship. As a result of this heritage, many metallurgical processes operate based on operator skill and under operator cognizance. This condition has changed rapidly with the advent of new equipment, computer controls, and increased technology.

The Role of Statistics in Improvement. The metals industry explored the use of statistical tools for quality control long before it considered the broader concepts of quality control. Two European authors[14] appear to have been the first to use statistical methods for analyzing variables in the steel industry. However, the technique was slow in spreading. Such success as was achieved was the result of individual effort rather than a general acceptance of the discipline.

While the present author can report that use of statistical methods is on the increase, the metals industry cannot yet be regarded as one of the leaders in applying statistics. The opportunities afforded by experimentation using techniques of factorial designed experiments and EVOP will likely await the general acceptance of statistical methodology as an essential part of the metallurgical curriculum or until the methods gain acceptance for plant use after their worth has been demonstrated in the research and development laboratories.

Statistics has played a role in steering the quality improvement efforts in the metals industry. The use of capability studies has resulted in attention being focused on process deficiencies and this, in turn, has resulted in a direction of technical effort to those areas requiring improved capability. The basic statistical techniques such as the control chart and the histogram have been used to identify the nature of process control problems.

---

[14]The first published paper appears to have been "Metallurgy and Probability" by A. Jude, delivered in 1922 and published in the *Journal of the Birmingham Metallurgical Society,* vol. VIII, no. 8, pp. 309 et seq. A portion of this paper was reproduced in *Quality (Journal of European Organization for Quality Control),* vol. 15, no. 1, pp. 19–22. More widely known is the 1923 paper by Dr. Karl H. Daeves, *Stahl und Eisen,* vol. 43, no. 14, pp. 462–466 (in German).

Results. The industry has been seriously challenged by imports, by competition from plastics and other competing materials, by problems of oversupply, and by the escalating cost of new process facilities. All these challenges plus the universal problem of rising labor costs have placed increased emphasis on the need for new technology. The basic oxygen furnace process has revolutionized the manufacture of steel. Modern gage instrumentation and computers have allowed an increase of rolling speeds as well as increased capability for holding a close tolerance on gage and flatness.

Specific quality problems in which the industry has been able to achieve significant improvements include the following.

Improvement in Thickness Control. Thickness control is essential at each step of metal rolling. The product must be thick enough to provide structural integrity for the intended use. However, excess thickness is an economic loss. Hence customers have continually demanded closer tolerances on thickness, and these demands have required control over both the nominal and the range of thickness throughout the product.

The metals industry has responded to these needs by constantly improving its ability to roll a strip to closer thickness tolerances. More recently this improvement has come from application of improved measuring devices such as x-ray and nuclear gages to the computer controls of rolling mills.

Flatness of Sheet and Coil. A prerequisite for achieving flatness is uniform thickness of the input material. In addition, the reduction during rolling must be uniform across the width of the strip. Nonuniform rolling may be caused by such variables as deflection of mill work rolls, nonuniform heat buildup in the rolls, or use of the same roll contour for a variety of widths.

Significant improvements in thickness measurement have been realized by employing x-ray and nuclear gages. The rolling equipment has been improved, and fine adjustments can now be made by means of computer controls, all of which result in improved flatness. Coincidentally with these advances, there has been the development of a whole new generation of leveling equipment that is capable of reworking a strip until it is flat.

MEASURES OF PERFORMANCE

The metals industry makes use of several measures of quality performance, as set out in Table 28.15. Despite the value of these measures, further work remains to be done to evolve a method of expressing quality performance in simple terms understandable by upper management as well as by managers in Technical, Production, and Sales. Lacking an adequate measure, quality performance is commonly equated with the cost of customer claims or with percent scrap. Such indicators fall short of presenting an overall picture, and are not adequate to relate quality to income and profit.

Measures in Current Use. Metals plant operation generates a great deal of information needed for process regulation and for making decisions on product conformance. These data serve their intended purpose but are not easily reduced to a form which permits measuring quality performance. Hayter (1961) and Rogers (1962) reported on the type of quality performance data available in a steel mill and how they are used to improve quality and productivity. Teschner (1968) reports on the use of computers for informational control.

TABLE 28.15 Measures of Performance

Application	Control subject	Unit of measure
Metals industry generally	Customer claims	Percent of claims to sales
Metals industry generally	Process yield	Percent acceptable product to material input
Ore smelting	Raw material usage	Usage versus standard
Aluminum reduction	Power consumption	Ratio of power used in reduction to total power consumption
Metals industry generally (recent)	Quality losses	Losses versus standards

Turning to the measure of quality performance listed in Table 28.15, cost of customer claims does provide some index of customer satisfaction and hence has gained acceptance. It has limitations since it is an after-the-fact measure, provides no early alert to unfavorable trends, and fails to reflect internal plant losses due to poor quality.

Process yield (or percent recovery) expresses the "survival rate," i.e., the percentage of material (introduced into an operation) which emerges as acceptable product. This yield does bear a relation to product quality but is usually considered as a measure of manufacturing efficiency rather than of quality performance.

Some metals companies have recently established procedures for expressing their quality performance in terms of the total economic loss attributable to poor quality and have coupled this with the cost of quality appraisal to arrive at a measure of quality performance in terms of dollars. (See Burtenshaw and Klein, 1969, Dunn, 1966, and Hains, 1969.) A new approach to this problem was developed by the author and is reported upon by Burtenshaw and Klein (1969). This method makes use of indicators which have been developed on the basis of establishing standards of quality performance and then measuring and reporting conformance to these standards.

QUALITY PROBLEMS

The summary which follows discusses some principal current and future quality problems of the metals industry. Because these problems are inherent to the manufacturing processes employed, they are representative of the industry.

Current Problems

Surface Appearance. This is a major reason for product rejection and customer dissatisfaction. This deficiency may be merely a matter of a nonuniform surface texture, or it may involve measurable surface flaws imparted by the fabrication equipment. Many metal products such as those manufactured from aluminum are designed to be used with the natural mill surface finish or, at most, with a thin coating. The customer expects a product having a uniform, eye-pleasing appearance, but to achieve such a product consistently requires rigorous controls at each operation and an effective method for inspecting and sorting the product.

Many factors in a metal operation work in opposition to achieving a uniform surface. Metallic oxides introduced in the rolling operation erode the surface, and the mechanical operations inherent to the rolling process take their toll. The product experiences handling damage in the plant and is subjected to further damage during shipping and exposure to the elements.

Flatness. In recent years significant progress has been made in improving the flatness of sheet and coil products, but the lack of adequate flatness remains as one of the principal problems of the industry.

Yield Improvement. The metals industry recognizes the need to increase its process yield if it is to increase its profit and minimize the need for capital expenditures. There are many factors which detract from high yields. Some of these relate to process design, but others are attributable to chronic and sporadic quality problems that require indentification and resolution.

Thickness Control. Major improvements have been made in the metals industry's ability to achieve tighter tolerance for the thickness of its rolled products. These improvements have resulted from improvements in rolling mill equipment, gage instrumentation, and computer controls. These improvements have been significant, but the problem remains paramount as the customer continues to demand ever tighter tolerances. The uniformity of thickness relates to the product processing characteristics in the customers' plants.

ACKNOWLEDGMENT

To Aleta Korslin goes our endless thanks for the especially careful job she did in revising the footnotes, references, and manuscript.

REFERENCES

Atkinson, A. C. and Hunter, W. G. (1968). "Design of Experiments for Parameter Estimation." *Technometrics,* vol. 10, no. 2 (May), pp. 271–290.

Bainbridge, T. R. (1965). "Staggered Nested Designs for Estimating Variance Components." *Industrial Quality Control,* vol. 22, July, pp. 12–20.

Bennett, C. A. and Franklin, N. L. (1954). *Statistical Analysis in Chemistry and the Chemical Industry.* John Wiley & Sons, New York.

Bicking, C. A. (1957). "A Statistical Approach to the Study of Test Precision, I, Defining Precision Standards." *TAPPI,* vol. 40, no. 3 (March), pp. 191–192.

Bicking, C. A. (1967). "The Sampling of Bulk Material." *Materials Research and Standards,* vol. 7, March, pp. 95–116.

Bicking, C. A., Bingham, R. S., Jr., and Weiss, R. L. (1963). "Automatic Data Logging for Experimentation and Quality Control." *Industrial Quality Control,* vol. 20, no. 6 (December), pp. 12–16.

Bingham, R. S., Jr. (1957a). "An Application of Continuous Sampling Plans for Chemical Acceptance and Control." *Transactions, Statistical Methods in the Chemical Industry,* Jan. 12, pp. 67–85. Published by American Society for Quality Control, Chemical Division, Hoboken, NJ.

Bingham, R. S., Jr. (1957b). "Control Charts in Multi-Stage Batch Processes." *Industrial Quality Control,* vol. 13, no. 12 (June), pp. 21–26.

Bingham, R. S., Jr. (1957c). "Practical Chemical Process Control." *Industrial Quality Control,* vol. 13, no. 11 (May), pp. 46–56.

Bingham, R. S., Jr. (1961). "Ten Minutes with Top Management." *Industrial Quality Control,* vol. 18, no. 4 (October), pp. 5–8.

Bingham, R. S., Jr. (1962*a*). "Chalk Dust and Chemicals—S.Q.C. Training for the Chemical Industry." *Industrial Quality Control,* vol. 18, no. 10 (April), pp. 15–18.

Bingham, R. S., Jr. (1962*b*). "Quality Control Applications in the Coated Abrasive Industry." *Industrial Quality Control,* vol. 19, no. 5 (November), pp. 5–12.

Bingham, R. S., Jr. (1965). "A Program for Controlling Incoming Chemical Quality." *Chemical Purchasing,* vol. 1, no. 1 (January–February), pp. 14–16.

Bingham, R. S., Jr. (1976). "Development and Utilization of a Quality Control Program." In Kolthoff, I. M. and Elving, P. J. (eds.), *Treatise on Analytical Chemistry,* part III, vol. 3, sec. C. Interscience, a division of John Wiley & Sons, New York.

Bingham, R. S., Jr., and Gioele, J. L. (1959). "Statistical Methods for Ceramic Process Control and Experiment Planning." *Journal of the Canadian Ceramic Society,* vol. 28, pp. 46–49.

Bingham, R. S., Jr., and Gioele, J. L. (1961). "Statistical Methods for Ceramic Process Control and Experiment Planning (Addendum)." *Journal of the Canadian Ceramic Society,* vol. 30, p. 135.

Bingham, R. S., Jr., and Gioele, J. L. (1962). "Ceramic Pressing—Optimization of Equipment Effectiveness through Experimental Design." *Transactions, 14th Annual All Day Conference on Quality Control,* New Brunswick, NJ, Sept. 8, pp. 61–77.

Bingham, R. S., Jr., Gioele, J. L., and Shelburne, V. B. (1959). "Studies in Ore Car and Abrasive Grain Sampling Variation." *ASTM Symposium on Bulk Sampling,* Special Technical Publication 242, Philadelphia, May, pp. 45–56.

Bingham, R. S., Jr. and Jaehn, A. H. (1986). "What Management Expects from a Quality Control Testing Program." *TAPPI,* vol. 69, no. 6 (June), pp. 38–42.

Bobis, A. H. and Andersen, L. E. (1970). "An Approach for Economic Discrimination between Alternative Chemical Syntheses." *Technometrics,* vol. 12, no. 3 (August), pp. 439–456.

Box, G. E. P. (1954). "Exploration and Exploitation of Response Surfaces." *Biometrics,* vol. 10, no. 1 (March).

Box, G. E. P. and Hunter, J. S. (1961*a*). "The 2^{k-p} Fractional Factorial Designs—Part I." *Technometrics,* vol. 3, no. 3 (August).

Box, G. E. P. and Hunter, J. S. (1961*b*). "The 2^{k-p} Fractional Factorial Designs—Part II." *Technometrics,* vol. 3, no. 4 (November).

Box, G. E. P. and Jenkins, G. M. (1962*a*). "Some Statistical Aspects of Adaptive Optimization and Control." *Journal of the Royal Statistical Society,* no. 2, pp. 297–333.

Box, G. E. P. and Jenkins, G. M. (1962*b*). *Some Statistical Aspects of Adaptive Optimization and Control.* Technical Report 8, NSF-G14768, University of Wisconsin, May.

Box, G. E. P. and Jenkins, G. M. (1970). *Time Series Analysis, Forecasting and Control,* Holden-Day, San Francisco.

Box, G. E. P and Youle, P. V. (1955). "The Exploration and Exploitation of Response Surfaces. II. An Example of the Link between the Fitted Surface and the Basic Mechanism of the System." *Biometrics,* vol 11, pp. 287–323.

Burtenshaw, O. L. and Klein, N. A. (1969). "Let's Put Quality Control in Its Place." *ASQC Technical Conference Transactions,* Milwaukee, pp. 417–418.

Calder, A. B. (1964). "Statistical Approach in Analytical Chemistry: Why It Is Important." *Analytical Chemistry,* vol. 36 (August), pp. 25A–34A.

Carpenter, Ben H. (1982). "Control of Copper Ore Roasting Exit Gas Quality." *ASQC Quality Congress Transactions,* Milwaukee pp. 748–755.

Chaisson, Donald A. and Sue-Ho, William M. (1984). "Reliability Concepts in Drug Stability Studies." *ASQC Quality Congress Transactions,* Milwaukee, pp. 414–419.

Cornell, John A. (1983). "How to Run Mixture Experiments for Product Quality." *ASQC Quality Congress Transactions,* Milwaukee, pp. 1–6.

Daniel, C. (1963). "Factor Screening in Process Development." *Industrial and Engineering Chemistry,* vol. 55, no. 5 (May), p. 5.

Davies, O. L. (ed.) (1957a). *Design and Analysis of Industrial Experiments,* 3rd ed. rev. Oliver & Boyd, Edinburgh.

Davies, O. L. (ed.) (1957b). *Statistical Methods in Research and Production,* 3rd ed. rev. Oliver & Boyd, Edinburgh, pp. 144–149.

DeBaun R. M. and Schneider, A. M. (1957). "Some Examples of Multivariate Analyses." *Mid-Atlantic Conference Transactions,* American Society for Quality Control, Milwaukee, pp. 19–26.

Draper, N. and Smith, H. (1981). *Applied Regression Analysis,* 2nd ed. John Wiley & Sons, New York.

Dunn, D. S. (1966). "Quality Control for Profit Improvement in the Specialty Steel Industry." *ASQC Technical Conference Transactions,* Milwaukee, pp. 152–155.

Eagle, Alan R. (1954). "A Method for Handling Errors in Testing and Measuring." *Industrial Quality Control,* vol. 10, no. 5 (March), pp. 10–15.

Emery, E. M. (1967). "The Role of Quantitation in Gas Chromatography." *Journal of Gas Chromatography* (December).

Ferris, C. D., Grubbs, F. E., and Weaver, C. L. (1946). "Operating Characteristics for the Common Statistical Tests of Significance." *Annals of Mathematical Statistics,* vol. 17, pp. 178–192.

Goldsmith, C. H. and Gaylor, D. W. (1970). "Three Stage Nested Designs for Estimating Variance Components." *Technometrics,* vol. 12, no. 3 (August), pp. 487–498.

Goodman, Alan L. (1982). "Cumulative Sum Control and Continuous Processes." *ASQC Quality Congress Transactions,* Milwaukee, pp. 270–274.

Grubbs, F. and Coon, H. (1954). "On Setting Test Limits Relative to Specification Limits." *Industrial Quality Control,* vol. 10, no. 5 (March), pp. 15–20.

Gushue, John M. and Shashidhara, N. S. (1986). "Quality Assurance for Hazardous Waste Management." *ASQC Quality Congress Transactions,* Milwaukee, pp. 492–498.

Hains, R. W. (1969). "Economics of Quality." *ASQC Technical Conference Transactions,* Milwaukee, pp. 439–443.

Hampton, D. R., Summer, C. E., and Webber, R. A. (1968). *Organizational Behavior and the Practice of Management.* Scott, Foresman, Glenview, IL.

Harrington, E. C., Jr. (1965). "The Desirability Function." *Industrial Quality Control,* vol. 21, April, p. 10.

Harrison, H. L. and Bollinger, J. G. (1966). *Introduction to Automatic Controls,* 3rd printing. International Textbook, Scranton, PA, pp. 66–67.

Hayter, W. T. (1961). "Process and Quality Control for Management." *ASQC Technical Conference Transactions,* Milwaukee, pp. 61–66.

Hicks, C. R. (1955). "Some Applications of Hotelling's *T.*" *Industrial Quality Control,* vol. 11, no. 9 (June), pp. 23–26.

Hayter, W. T. (1961). "Process and Quality Control for Management." *ASQC Technical Conference Transactions,* Milwaukee, pp. 61–66.

Higgins, J. (1964). "Subtracting the Blank Value." *Analyst,* vol. 89, pp. 211–215.

Hill, H. M. and Brown, R. H. (1966). "Statistical Methods in Chemistry." *Analytical Chemistry,* vol. 38, no. 5 (April), pp. 440R–442R.

Hill, H. M. and Brown, R. H. (1968). "Statistical Methods in Chemistry." *Analytical Chemistry,* vol. 40, no. 5 (April), pp. 376R–380R.

Hinchen, J. D. (1968). "Multiple Regression in Process Development." *Technometrics,* vol. 10, no. 2 (May), pp. 257–269.

Hinchen, J. D. (1970). "Multiple Regression with Unbalanced Data." *Journal of Quality Technology,* vol. 12, no. 1 (January), pp. 22–29.

Hoerl, A. E. and Kennard, R. W. (1970a). "Ridge Regression—Application to Nonorthogonal Problems." *Technometrics,* vol. 12, no. 1 (February), pp. 69–82.

Hoerl, A. E. and Kennard, R. W. (1970b). "Ridge Regression—Biased Estimation for Non-orthogonal Problems." *Technometrics,* vol. 12, no. 1 (February), pp. 55–68.

Hsi, B. P. (1966). "Optimization of Quality Control in the Chemical Laboratory." *Technometrics,* vol. 8, August, pp. 519–534.

ISA, Instrument Society of America (1986). *Instrumentation in the Chemical and Petroleum Industries, vol. 17: Smarter Projects—From Concept to Implementation, Proceedings of the 1985 Spring Symposium.* ISA, Research Triangle Park, NC.

Jackson, J. E. (1956). "Quality Control Methods for Two Related Variables." *Industrial Quality Control,* vol. 12, no. 7 (January), pp. 4–8.

Johnson, N. L. and Leone, F. C. (1964). *Statistics and Experimental Design.* John Wiley & Sons, New York, vol. 1, pp. 347–348.

Krautkramer, J. and Krautkramer, H. (1961). *Ultrasonic Testing of Materials.* Springer-Verlag, New York.

Lashof, T. W. (1964). "Ranking Laboratories and Evaluating Methods of Measurement in Round Robin Tests." *Materials Research and Standards,* vol. 4, August, pp. 397–407.

Lawton, W. H. and Sylvestre, E. A. (1971). "Self Modeling Curve Resolution." *Technometrics,* vol. 13, no. 3 (August), pp. 617–634.

Lentzen, Donald E. et al. (1982). "Methods and QA for Asbestos Measurements." *ASQC Quality Congress Transactions,* Milwaukee, pp. 760–766.

Mandel, J. (1976). "Statistical Methods in Analytical Chemistry." In Kolthoff, I. M. and Elving, P. J. (eds.), *Treatise on Analytical Chemistry,* part III, vol. 3. Interscience, a division of John Wiley & Sons, New York, pp. 79–125.

Mandel, J. and McCrackin, F. L. (1963). "Analysis of Families of Curves." *Journal of Research of the National Bureau of Standards,* vol. 67A, no. 3, p. 259.

Marcuse, S. (1949). "Optimum Allocation and Variance Components in Nested Sampling with an Application to Chemical Analysis." *Biometrics,* September, pp. 189–206.

Marquardt, D. W. (1970). "Generalized Inverses, Ridge Regression, Biased Linear Estimation and Nonlinear Estimation." *Technometrics,* vol. 12, no. 3 (August), pp. 591–612.

McFarren et al. (1970). "Criteria for Judging Acceptability of Analytical Methods." *Analytical Chemistry,* March, p. 358.

Mitchell, J. A. (1947). "Control of the Accuracy and Precision of Industrial Tests and Analyses." *Analytical Chemistry* (formerly *Industrial and Engineering Chemistry. Analytical Edition*), vol. 19, no. 12 (December), pp. 961–967.

Pasteelnick, L. A. and Leder, W. B. (1957). "Statistical Analysis in a Polymerization Process." *Chemical Engineering Progress,* vol. 53, no. 8 (August), pp. 392–395.

Patek, J. M. (1968). "Specifications." In Kolthoff, I. M. and Elving, P. J. (eds.), *Treatise on Analytical Chemistry,* part III, vol. 1. Interscience, a division of John Wiley & Sons, New York.

Plackett, R. L. and Burman, J. P. (1946). "The Design of Optimum Multifactorial Experiments." *Biometrika,* vol. 33, pp. 305–325.

Provost, Lloyd P. and Elder, Robert S. (1983). "Cost-Effective Laboratory Quality Control." *ASQC Quality Congress Transactions,* Milwaukee, pp. 496–502.

Rogers, W. T. (1962). "Total Quality Control in an Integrated Steel Plant." *ASQC Technical Conference Transaction,* Milwaukee, pp. 481–491.

Rosenzweig, G. (1968). " 'Less Steel in the Scrap Bucket,' Yield Improvement Program in a Rolling Mill." *ASQC Technical Conference Transactions,* Milwaukee, pp. 217–221.

Satterthwaite, F. E. (1946). "An Approximate Distribution of Estimates of Variance Components." *Biometrics Bulletin,* vol. 2, pp. 110–114.

Secrest, D. (1968). "Time Sharing Experimental Control on a Small Computer." *Industrial and Engineering Chemistry,* vol. 60, no. 9 (September), p. 9.

Setzer, Susan R. (1986). "Quality Assurance for Scrubber Operations R&D." *ASQC Quality Congress Transactions,* Milwaukee, pp. 484–491.

Shah, M. J. and Stillman, R. E. (1970). "Computer Control and Optimization of a Large Methanol Plant." *Industrial and Engineering Chemistry,* vol. 62, no. 12 (December), p. 12.

Sinibaldi, Frank J. (1983). "Nested Designs in Process Variation Studies." *ASQC Quality Congress Transactions,* Milwaukee, pp. 484–491.

Teshner, H. G. (1968). "Controlling Data Flow in a Steel Mill." *Control Engineering,* vol. 15, no. 4 (April), pp. 76–80.

Tingey, F. H. (1972). "Design of Experiments in Analytical Chemistry Investigation." In Kolthoff, I. M. and Elving, P. J. (eds.), *Treatise on Analytical Chemistry,* part I, vol. 10. Interscience, a division of John Wiley & Sons, New York, pp. 6405–6493.

Traylor, W. S. (1948). "Use of Statistical Methods for Time Study of Batch Processes." *Industrial Quality Control,* vol. 4, no. 4 (January).

Vance, F. P. (1966). "An Economic Basis for Setting Confidence Limits." *Industrial and Engineering Chemistry,* vol. 58, February, p. 2.

Walden, C. H. and Widener, P. L. (1967). "Quality Control of an Aluminum Sheet Mill." *ASQC Technical Conference Transactions,* Milwaukee, pp. 23–24.

Wernimont, G. (1950). "Precision and Accuracy of Test Methods." *ASTM Symposium on Applications of Statistics,* Special Technical Publication 103, pp. 13–26.

Wernimont, G. (1957). "The Basis for Interpreting Results from a Testing Process." *Experientia Supplementum,* vol. 5.

Wernimont, G. (1967). "Evaluation of Laboratory Performance of Spectrophotometers." *Analytical Chemistry,* May, p. 554.

Wetzstein, Carl (1982). "Take the Hassle out of Managing Experimental Data." *ASQC Quality Congress Transactions,* Milwaukee, pp. 254–261.

Woltz, J. R. (1963). "Product Quality Audit System." *ASQC Technical Conference Transactions,* Milwaukee, pp. 291–295.

Youden, W. J. (1963). "Ranking Laboratories by Round Robin Tests." *Materials Research and Standards,* January, pp. 9–13.

Youden, W. J. (1967). *Statistical Techniques for Collaborative Tests.* Association of Official Agricultural Chemists (now Association of Official Analytical Chemists), Washington, DC.

FURTHER READING

Dux, James P. (1986). *Handbook of Quality Assurance for the Analytical Chemistry Laboratory.* Van Nostrand Reinhold, New York.

Hinchen, J. D. (1966). *Practical Statistics for Chemical Research.* Methuen & Co., London.

Johnson, N. L. and Leone, F. C. (1964). *Statistics and Experimental Design in Engineering and the Physical Sciences,* 2 vols. John Wiley & Sons, New York.

Youden, W. J. (1951). *Statistical Methods for Chemists.* John Wiley & Sons, New York.

SECTION 29

ELECTRONIC COMPONENTS INDUSTRIES[1]

A. Blanton Godfrey, Ph.D.
Robert E. Kerwin, Ph.D.

INTRODUCTION **29.1**

QUALITY MANAGEMENT IN
ELECTRONIC COMPONENTS
INDUSTRIES **29.5**

    Development Program . . 29.6

    Initial Production 29.7

    Mass Production 29.8

PRODUCT DESIGN AND
DEVELOPMENT **29.8**

TESTING AND INSPECTION . . **.29.10**

    The Functions of Testing . 29.10

    Determining What to Test 29.11

    Automated Testing 29.11

PROCESS DESIGN **29.11**

RELIABILITY **29.14**

    Reliability Prediction for
      Components 29.15

    Reliability in the
      Manufacturing Cycle . . 29.17

PROGNOSIS **29.17**

REFERENCES **29.18**

INTRODUCTION

Components are the basic building blocks of manufacturing processes. Electronic components include simple items such as resistors and capacitors and semiconductor devices and complex items such as very-large-scale-integration (VLSI) devices, lasers, and hybrid integrated circuits. Despite the wide variety of components and design and manufacturing processes used, there is a commonality of quality and reliability principles used in all components industries. These principles are applied throughout the industry by the leading companies and form the basis for this section. Our experiences and expertise lie mainly in the electronics industry, and all the examples in this section come from this area. Except for

[1] In the Third Edition, the section on electronic components was prepared by Edwin S. Shecter.

specific fabrication and test methods, measurements and analyses which are not covered here in any case, the quality and reliability principles apply to a wide range of components.

There are several characteristics of components. For the most part, they are produced in highly automated plants or sections of plants in very large quantities. They are measured, handled, tested, and packaged in highly automated processes. They are often 100 percent tested, sometimes several times during the manufacturing process. Since many components constitute the critical building blocks of complex systems (e.g., microprocessors used in personal computers), samples of components are often selected for life tests, stress tests, humidity tests, vibration tests, and accelerated life tests.

Although the quality and reliability of components are often the critical determinants of the quality and reliability of the final system, components are often purchased from outside suppliers, manufactured in different manufacturing plants or company divisions, or manufactured in separate sections of assembly plants. Supplier quality control is essential for component quality and reliability. Specific procedures must be carefully developed for quality reporting, sharing test and inspection results, and tracking quality and reliability performance.

As the complexity of products and systems increases, the need for high-quality, high-reliability components increases dramatically. This can be readily seen in Figure 29.1, where we have plotted the impact of defective components on the quality of circuit packs. Three curves are shown. The first curve shows the impact of circuit packs containing 50 components. The second curve shows the impact when the circuit pack contains 100 components, and the third curve shows the impact when the circuit pack contains 200 components. The points plotted on the curve for 100 components per circuit pack show that the quality of components must be close to 0.1 percent defective [1000 parts per million (ppm)] for even a 90 percent yield at circuit pack assembly. For a 95 percent yield, the component quality must be close to 0.05 percent defective (500 ppm).

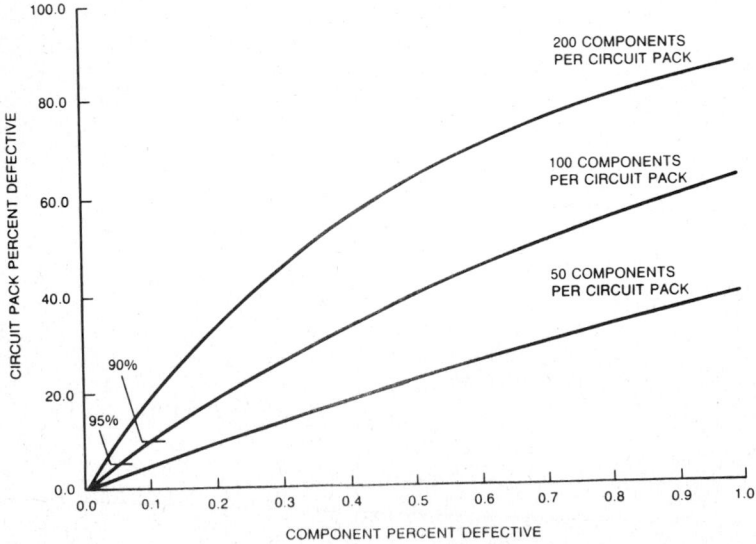

FIG. 29.1   Impact of component defects on circuit pack assembly.

Two distinct trends in the quality and reliability of components have become apparent in the 1980s. The quality levels of components have been improving dramatically. Component qualities are now commonly measured in parts per million (ppm) defective whereas only a few years ago percent defective was the accepted norm. In Figures 29.2, 29.3, 29.4, and 29.5 we show how rapidly component qualities have improved in the last few years. In Figure 29.2 the quality of metal film resistors is plotted at 6-month intervals for the years 1983 to 1985. The quality has improved from almost 500 to 100 ppm. In Figure 29.3 we can see that multilayer capacitors have improved from almost 200 ppm to under 20 ppm in the same year interval. The quality of semiprecision resistors has improved even more dramatically. In Figure 29.4 we see a sharp decline from around 850 ppm in 1983 to almost 100 ppm in 1985. The quality of integrated

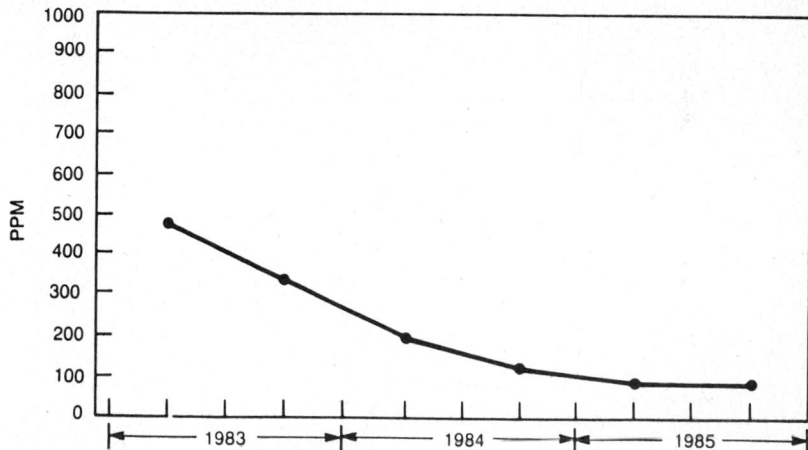

FIG. 29.2   Parts per million quality—metal film resistors.

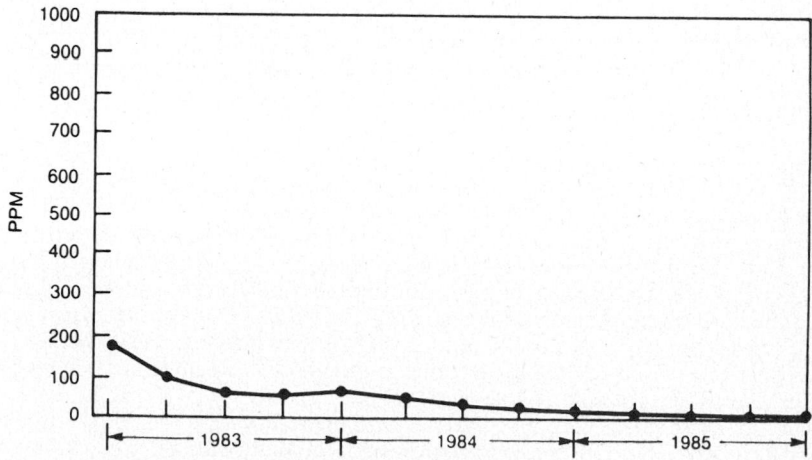

FIG. 29.3   Parts per million quality—multilayer capacitors.

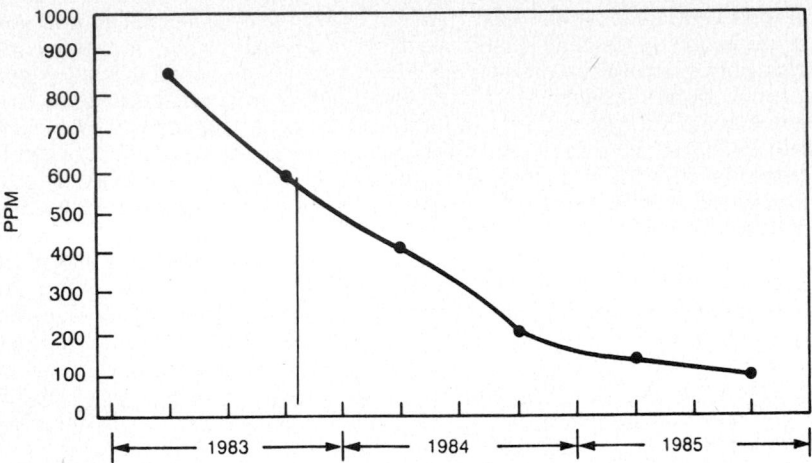

FIG. 29.4 Parts per million quality—semiprecision resistors.

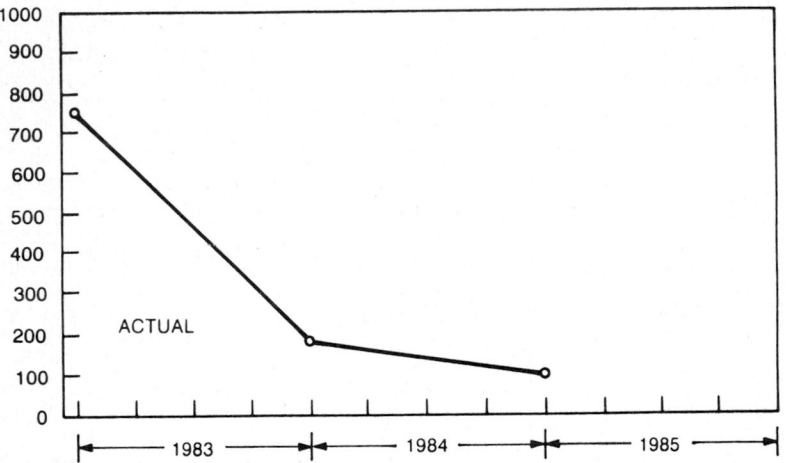

FIG. 29.5 Parts per million quality—integrated circuits.

circuits is also improving rapidly. In Figure 29.5, results from 1983 and 1984 show a decline from 750 ppm to just above 100 ppm.

Component reliabilities have also improved dramatically, often by orders of magnitude. With these improvements have come new quality challenges. Measuring component qualities in parts per million is extremely difficult. The classical acceptance sampling procedures are no longer adequate. Measuring component reliabilities when lifetimes may be tens of years is also difficult. New methods for accelerated life testing are being used, and methods for using degradation results rather than times to failure are being developed.

A major challenge in component design and manufacture is process yields. The automated testing and inspection procedures, although complex and difficult to implement and maintain, are so effective that many leading component suppliers are shipping components in the parts per million defect range. What distinguishes the suppliers in the marketplace and often means the difference in a company's success or failure is the process yields. The process yields, especially in the competitive electronics markets, are major determinants in the manufacturing costs. These costs are a major factor in determining the prices a company can charge. Improving yields, the percent of components passing all tests with no adjustment or repair, is the critical challenge of the modern component quality systems. These yields especially for complex electronic integrated circuits, are often only a few percent during the first weeks of full production. Intensive quality improvement programs, often involving designed experiments, are used to rapidly increase the yields.

Another major challenge in component manufacture, especially for electronic components, is early-life reliability or "infant mortality." Many electronic components either fail early in life, in the first 6 months or 1 year, or last a very long time. Measuring early-life reliability, applying screening methods for identifying early-life failures, and removing the causes of these failures are all characteristic activities in a well-run component quality program.

The subject matter in this section will be treated in six parts. Quality Management in Electronic Components Industries will cover the means used for establishing and achieving standards in the entire sequence of activities through which the components are designed, produced, marketed and shipped, and used. Product Design and Development covers the steps necessary for developing high-quality, high-reliability components. Testing and Inspection covers a function which is especially critical for component manufacture. Process Design explains some of the important considerations in designing high-yield component manufacturing processes. Reliability is covered as a separate topic since component reliability is such a key part of any quality program. The usual ways in which reliability is estimated, including life testing, accelerated life testing, operational life testing, and field tracking, are described. Failure mode, effect, and criticality analysis (FMECA), an extremely important area of reliability, is covered in Section 13 under Planning for Time-Oriented Performance and under Planning for Maintainability. Finally, we present a Prognosis of the future including our view of the unsolved problems facing us today and the challenges facing us in the future.

QUALITY MANAGEMENT IN ELECTRONIC COMPONENTS INDUSTRIES

Quality management for components depends on the specific steps to be taken in the design, manufacture, and delivery of the particular type of component. Figure 29.6 illustrates the flow diagram and responsibilities of quality and reliability management for semiconductor memory devices.

The planning process begins with the marketing organization understanding the customer needs and clearly defining the customer requirements. The design organization translates the customer requirements into detailed design specifications. The reliability engineering organization (sometimes part of the design organization) develops clear reliability objectives. In developing the reliability objectives, reliability engineering takes into account the current reliability performance of existing products, including the major competitors' performance, the needs of the customers, and the capabilities of different designs and processes. Reliability objectives for components are often stated in terms of early-life reliability (3 months, 6 months, or 1 year) and steady-state or long-term reliability. Objectives

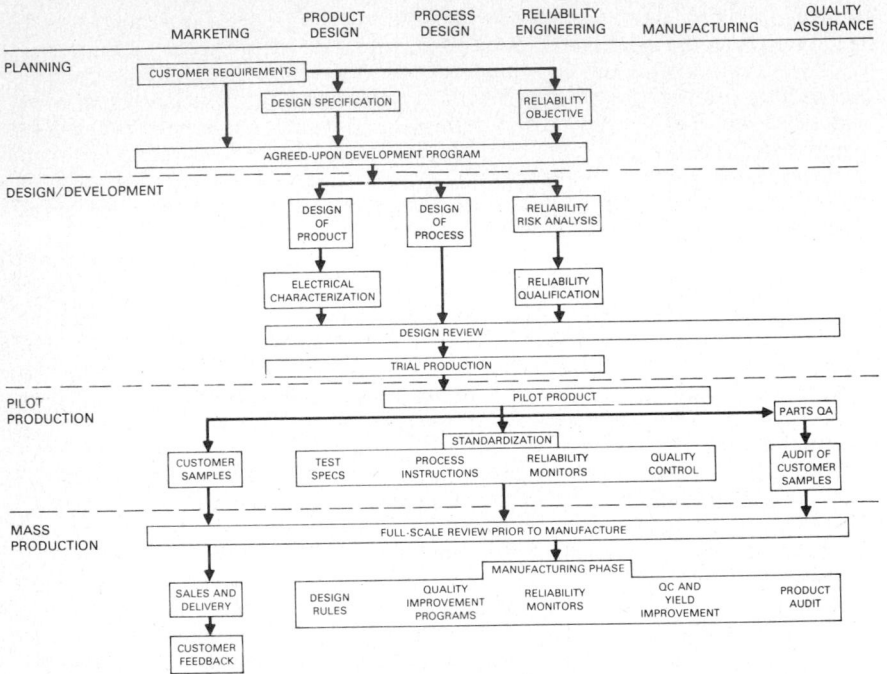

FIG. 29.6 Quality and reliability management—semiconductor manufacture.

may be stated in terms of failure rates or mean time to failure. These objectives may be derived from the "reliability budget" for the entire system. For example, the new transatlantic telecommunications system AT&T is installing (a complex submarine lightguide system) has a reliability objective of no more than three ship failures in 20 years. (Ship failures are those which require the repair ship to be dispatched.) System reliability models were then used to determine reliability objectives for each of the thousands of components to be used in the system.

Development Program. After these steps are complete, the marketing, product design, process design, and reliability engineering organizations produce and agree on a development program. A design review is recommended at this stage to review requirements, specifications, and objectives prior to beginning the product or process design.

The design-development phase begins with the acceptance of the development program, the design specifications, and the reliability objectives. The electrical and physical designs for the product are developed, and the manufacturing process design is begun. The product designers specify the materials to be used and the test requirements and physical dimensions and layouts of the product, and the process designers specify the manufacturing and testing steps and the types of equipment that will be used in the manufacturing processes. At this time the reliability engineers perform the reliability risk analysis. Early tests of materials and processes are often performed at this time also. The process designers identify the process controls to be used and the locations in the manufacturing process where these controls are to be placed. Test procedures, analysis techniques, and reporting procedures are clearly defined.

The next steps in the design-development phase for semiconductors are the electrical characterization and reliability qualification tests. Full functional and parametric testing is performed on early models of the device. This testing is performed iteratively with design and process changes to ensure device characteristics which are consistent with customer requirements and the device data sheet. A narrower spectrum of cost-effective production tests is then defined with tight control limits to assure that all devices shipped will meet the published data sheet specifications. Complete reliability qualification testing is performed on a large sample of production devices prior to any shipment to customers, and small sample periodic reliability monitoring is specified.

After the electrical characterizations and reliability qualifications are completed, a formal design review is held. At this design review the review team (usually consisting of designers, manufacturing engineers, operating personnel, quality engineers, and reliability engineers) studies the results of the electrical characterizations and reliability qualifications; reviews the product and process designs, the test plans and inspection-test points, and the manufacturing layouts; and reviews the entire quality plan and management system.

Initial Production. For semiconductor devices, trial production is usually performed by product and process engineers in a manufacturing plant where subsequent mass production will take place. During the trial production run the product and process designers identify problems and eliminate the causes.

After the trial production, pilot production begins. During the pilot production runs, the product and process designers, operating personnel, and process engineers complete and standardize test specifications, process instructions, quality control processes and reports, and reliability monitoring procedures. Quality assurance engineers complete the planning and development of the quality assurance audit procedures and test these procedures during the pilot production. Marketing receives the first customer samples, reviews the samples with respect to the original customer requirements, and shares the samples with leading customers to gain further information as to how closely the customers' needs are being met. Quality Assurance and Reliability Engineering Departments obtain early production samples for life testing and accelerated life testing.

At the completion of the pilot production runs, a full-scale review is held prior to production. The review team at this stage usually includes members from Marketing, Product Design, Process Design, Manufacturing Engineering, Reliability Engineering, Manufacturing Quality Control, and Quality Assurance Departments. The team reviews all problems discovered during the pilot production and the changes made to the test specifications, process instructions, reliability monitors, and quality control procedures. The team reviews the results of inspections, quality control checks, and the quality assurance audits. The team also reviews the results of the process capability studies and the process control plans, procedures, and the charts that will be used in mass production. The process control plans, procedures, and charts are often described in a manufacturing layout or quality manual. The control tools for each quality or reliability characteristic are described or referenced, and sampling frequencies, measurement methods, and charting procedures are specified. Detailed corrective action and feedback procedures for continuous quality and reliability improvement are also provided. Marketing personnel share with the team early feedback from the customers receiving the pilot production samples. Quality Assurance and Reliability Engineering

Department members share the preliminary results of the life test and accelerated life tests.

Mass Production.   During the mass production phase the marketing organization monitors the sales and delivery processes and implements the customer feedback system. Information on customer complaints, customer suggestions for design changes or improvements, and results of comparisons with competing products are shared with the product and process designers, manufacturing managers and operators, reliability engineers, and quality control and quality assurance personnel. The product designers revise the design requirements and make necessary changes to the product design to increase customer satisfaction or to improve manufacturability. Quality improvement teams are formed and begin to address the most important issues. Quality Control provides quick feedback for timely correction of out-of-control processes and begins work with the quality improvement teams on yield improvement. The reliability engineers monitor product reliability and collect information to (1) help identify problem areas and (2) provide details on the symptoms associated with these problem areas. Such information is used by product and process engineers to guide the reliability growth program in order to assure that reliability objectives are met. Quality Assurance provides product and process audit results to management and operating personnel to continuously monitor the quality and reliability of products and processes.

PRODUCT DESIGN AND DEVELOPMENT

The basic principles of quality in the product development phase are well covered in Section 13. These principles apply in general to components, but components have many special characteristics that make tight controls in product design and development even more critical than for other products. The extremely high volumes of production, the high reliability requirements, the difficulties of adequately testing for function and reliability, and the difficulty (or impracticality) of repairs are all contributing factors in the importance of product design and development for component quality and reliability.

Goksel, Sekino, and Troutman (1986) give an excellent overview of the tools and techniques for assuring the quality of VLSI circuits. VLSI chips now being designed and manufactured with more than 170,000 transistors match the complexity of mainframe computers of less than two decades ago. Those authors describe eight levels in the design process: architectural, functional, logic, circuit-timing, layout, wafer-chip, integration-system, and product engineering. We show their levels, models, tools, and methods of quality assurance as Table 29.1.

After extensive discussions with customers, the product designers set product features in computer-aided design (CAD) tools. Extensive design reviews of each feature are held by the architects, developers, verifiers, and customers to determine the importance and priority of each feature. Often the features are simulated to determine the performance and advantages of each feature. Design verification tests are generated from a test specification document, and the test results are verified through a list of expected results. During the design review, the tests, test results, and test specifications are thoroughly reviewed.

During the functional design, the features created in the architectural design are specified in logical entity subdivisions known as "blocks." A computer simulation is run to study the functional specification. This functional simulator is

TABLE 29.1   VLSI Design Process and Design Verification

Design phase	Model	Tool	Quality assurance
Architectural	Behavioral simulator	C language	Tests, reviews, analysis
Functional	Functional simulator	C, AIDE, PLA tools, checker	Tests, reviews, regression
Logic	Logic model	LAMP, DRAW, checker	Tests, synthesis, regression
Circuit and timing	Circuit model	MOTIS, ADVICE, checker	Tests, regression, analysis, synthesis
Layout	Layout model	Circuit extractor, LTX, CTL-LCC	Analysis
Wafer and chip	Wafer	Test machine	Tests, fault analysis
Integration and system certification	Chip	Test facilities	Tests, regression
Product engineering	Chip	Test machine	Tests, analysis, parametric characterization

Source: Goksel, Sekino, and Troutman, 1986.

verified by regressing it against the architectural simulator and comparing results of identical tests. During this phase, the product designer regularly conducts test reviews and inspections and has a means of automatically checking simulation results.

In logic design, quality assurance is accomplished through test, regression, and synthesis. Each logic block is placed in the corresponding function block in the functional simulator, and the results of the tests are compared to objectives.

The performance times of the functions are very important and are verified through analysis, regression, and synthesis. Multilevel timing simulators and circuit simulators are used to test timing paths and locate suspected slow paths. The product designer also uses graphical layout editors for circuit verification.

Layout design provides the detailed circuit information required to write the mask used to fabricate the chip. The designer uses various CAD tools to check violations of design requirements for manufacturability and test ability. A layout verification software tool is used to verify layout design against logic design.

At this time we are ready to leave the software models and go to a physical product. The chip-on-wafer phase is the first realization of a physical product. The designers run many tests on each operational chip. These tests are designed to cover as many possible faults as possible.

During the integration–system certification phase, chip models are tested exhaustively. Millions of tests are used to stress all aspects of each chip. System test is the final certification of the chip before it is committed to full-scale manufacturing. Chips are tested in customerlike environments where the chips are subjected to system loads and stress loads.

Extensive characterizations of the chip are accumulated during product engineering to assure economic manufacturability. Large samples of the wafers are tested, and results of the tests are studied to determine whether production yields are sensitive to fabrication variations. After the manufacturability of the design is proved, the chip is transferred into full production.

A general discussion of quality in the development process is given by Pettijohn (1986). Pettijohn begins with a review of the definition of quality and a discussion of how to determine whether product *is fit for use*. Pettijohn also presents an excellent discussion of design quality appraisal.

TESTING AND INSPECTION

Testing and inspection are especially critical functions in component manufacture. The extremely high manufacturing volumes, tight tolerances, multiple quality characteristics, and importance of reliability make testing and inspection difficult. The cost of testing can easily exceed other manufacturing costs. Teradyne (1974) provides a guide to high-volume testing for electronic device users and presents several simple cost models for calculation of the cost of testing versus the cost of not testing. Testing and inspection should be done as early in the production cycle as possible. Waiting until a product is almost ready for shipment before discovering failures can be very expensive. Costs can vary considerably according to a wide range of factors, but the cost of finding a bad component roughly increases by an order of magnitude at every level of testing, where level refers to wafer, packaged chip, circuit pack, or system level manufacture. When we also consider the growing complexity of circuit packs and systems, we can understand the strong demand for constantly increasing component quality and reliability. The costs also increase dramatically for testing and repair for multiple faults (two or more bad components on one circuit pack or in a system) and for intermittent failures.

The Functions of Testing.   We must also consider the different functions of testing. Teradyne (1974) identifies five separate functions of component testing: inspection, classification, evaluation, diagnosis, and physical adjustment. Inspection usually refers to a pass-fail or go no-go tests where components are subjected to a fast sequence of individual tests, each of which must be passed. "Inspections" can be simple visual tests where an inspector or process checker examines each component for a certain physical characteristic, mechanical go no-go tests where each fabricated device or component is checked for a physical dimension using a two-sided measuring device, or very sophisticated computer-controlled electrical tests where each device is subjected to literally a million electrical tests.

"Classification" is when inspection results are used to establish the appropriate category or bin for each component. Components may be graded in several ways for future use. A simple example is the testing of resistors and classifying each resistor according to predetermined tolerance limits.

"Evaluation" usually refers to studies of the characteristics of a single device or of a single lot of devices for quality control purposes. Many different variables may be measured and recorded. These results may be used to change the component design, the production process, or the materials used.

"Diagnosis" is the testing operation used to attempt to determine the cause of failure or the exact location of failure. This information aids in the repair of the component and helps in developing preventive measures to reduce future failures. The diagnosis function is becoming very sophisticated in modern component manufacture with x-ray machines, scanning electron microscopes, and computer-driven test facilities being widely used.

"Physical adjustment" refers to the test function where results are used to change the component to meet requirements and specifications. Electromechanical components can frequently be adjusted as can many mechanical components to meet the design and manufacturing specifications.

Determining What to Test. The most difficult part of creating a test plan is determining what to test. We must decide not only whether to sample or to 100 percent test all components but also which characteristics to test. We must also decide whether to test each characteristic once, to test several times to check for intermittent failures, or to test over a period of time to estimate reliability. It is almost impossible to create a complete characterization of all the failure modes for any component that covers all possible applications of that component. What is important is that we understand the basic failure modes and characteristics of a given component and the general range of applications of that component.

For each type of component, there are distinctive characteristics and recommended tests. For example, Teradyne (1974) describes the basic test characteristics and failure modes separately for digital integrated circuits, linear integrated circuits, transistors, diodes, zener diodes, relays, resistors, and capacitors. Iwasaki (1974) gives an excellent discussion of inspection and test planning for mechanical components with an example of welding testing.

Takanashi (1978) gives an excellent example of quality assurance for semiconductors and the test functions performed at different stages. In Figures 29.7 and 29.8 we reproduce his figures showing Toshiba's qualification test system and a mapping of failure modes to corrective actions. In Figure 29.7 we can see what tests and measurements are done at each stage of manufacturing. Takanashi stresses the importance of assuring the quality of materials and parts and a thorough and active process control system. This includes establishing quality control standards, thorough corrective measures for process abnormalities, thorough equipment and test instrument control, and feedback of failure information.

In Figure 29.8 Takanashi maps the failure modes observed to failure mechanisms to corrective actions. The use of the historical review concept is recommended here to capture this information in rules for future design (see Section 22, under Diagnosis—General; Diagnosis of Failures in Broad Systems).

Automated Testing. Today much testing and inspection in component manufacture is automated. Automated test equipment (ATE) has the ability to perform a sequence of preprogrammed tests without operator intervention. ATE is usually controlled by stored computer programs, but ATE controlled by digit switches, program cards, and paper tapes is still in use. New ATE is including visual test capabilities, sound sensing (e.g., for stress cracks in welding), and test functions integrated with robotics. Some manufacturing robots now test components as they handle them and will assemble only good components.

PROCESS DESIGN

The key elements of process design are covered in Section 16, Manufacturing Planning. A major new idea is emerging in component manufacturing processes: robust process design. Kackar and Shoemaker (1986) give an excellent discussion of the main concepts and illustrate the application of these ideas. They point out that a main cause of poor yield in manufacturing processes is manufacturing variation. The main objective of robust process design is to provide a sophisticated statistical experiment to identify process control parameter settings that reduce the sensitivity of a process to this manufacturing variation (see Section 16, under

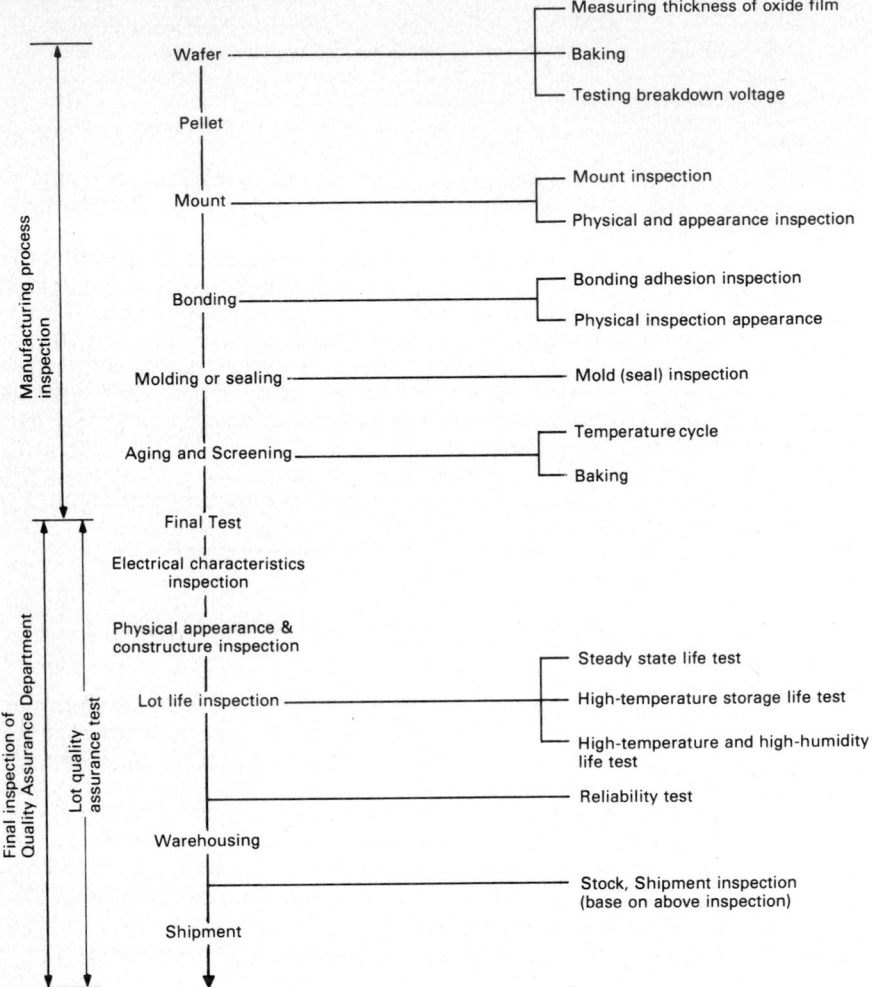

FIG. 29.7 Toshiba's qualification test system. *(From Takanashi, 1978.)*

Process Capability Measurement; Application of Experimental Design to Optimize Process Variables). Kackar and Shoemaker illustrate these ideas with an example showing how robust process design was used to improve the process for making optical filters. These filters consist of a quartz substrate coated with a thin layer of titanium dioxide and silicon dioxide.

Two important quality characteristics of the optical filter are the index of refraction and the absorption. Kackar and Shoemaker wanted to reduce the variation of these characteristics as much as possible. Two variables affect these quality characteristics: control parameters and sources of noise. The control parameters are the controllable process variables. In this example control parameters included the temperature of the substrates during deposition and the method of

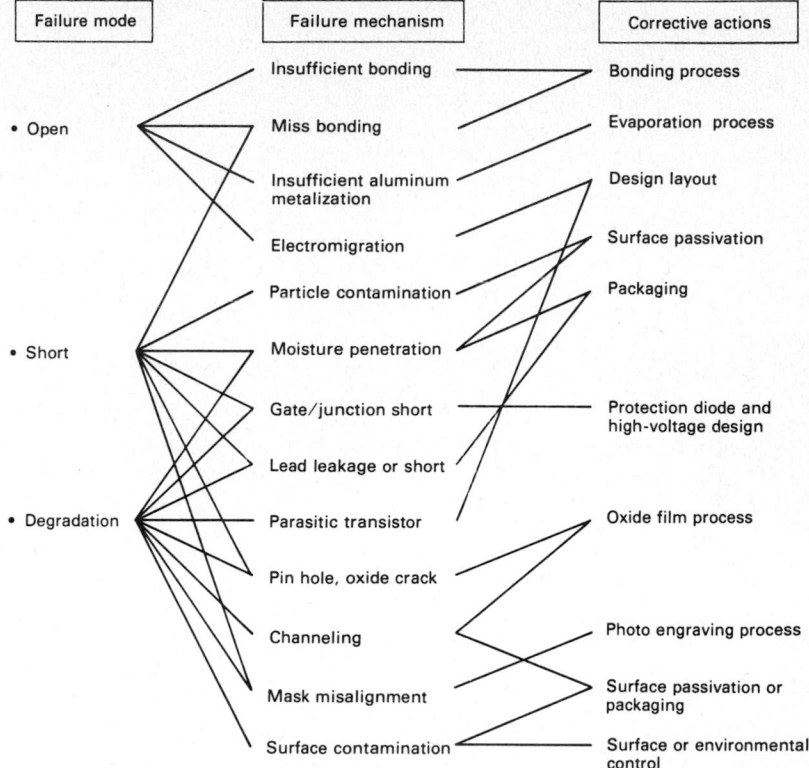

FIG. 29.8 Mapping of failure modes to corrective actions.   *(From Takanashi, 1978.)*

cleaning the substrates. The sources of noise are those variables which are expensive (or sometimes impossible) to control. Examples of noise variables include ambient conditions, variations in raw materials, and drifts in process control parameters.

There are four basic steps in robust process design: list the important quality characteristics, control parameters, and sources of noise; plan the experiment for an optimized set of tests defining how and which control parameters will be varied and how the effects of the noise will be measured; run the experiment and identify the critical control parameters and the best settings; and run a confirmation experiment using these settings and verify the results.

Kackar and Shoemaker (1986) illustrate each of these steps for the process of growing epitaxial layers on polished silicon wafers. Other examples are given in Phadke, Kackar, Speeney, and Grieco (1983); Taguchi and Wu (1979); and Phadke (1986). A general overview of robust design methods is given in Godfrey, Phadke, and Shoemaker (1986). Kackar (1985) gives a more thorough discussion of the statistical methods. An introduction to the design and analysis of experiments is in Section 26 of this handbook; see also Chapter 17 of Wadsworth, Stephens, and Godfrey (1986). A thorough treatment of experimental design is the book by Box, Hunter, and Hunter (1978).

RELIABILITY

Since components are the basic building blocks of systems, the reliability of the system is determined in large part by the reliability of the components. Performance and life testing of systems and completed products is difficult, very time consuming, and expensive. For these reasons, component reliability information is critical in modern quality systems. Components are functionally tested, accelerated life tested, operational life tested, and burned in at many stress levels. Reliability estimates for components are carefully calculated and catalogued in reference books or databases. Designers use these estimates with systems reliability models to predict system reliability early in the design process. When these predictions indicate that the system may not meet its reliability estimates, the designers may choose different components, add redundancy to the system, use components at less than full rated values, burn-in the critical components to improve reliability, or use other approaches (see Section 13, under Reliability Improvement).

Figure 29.9 shows a typical systems reliability assurance program. The importance of component reliability is evident. Early in the design planning, reliability objectives are determined. The designers select components and obtain information on the cost, availability, quality, and reliability of the components. They then predict system reliability using accepted reliability modeling techniques and

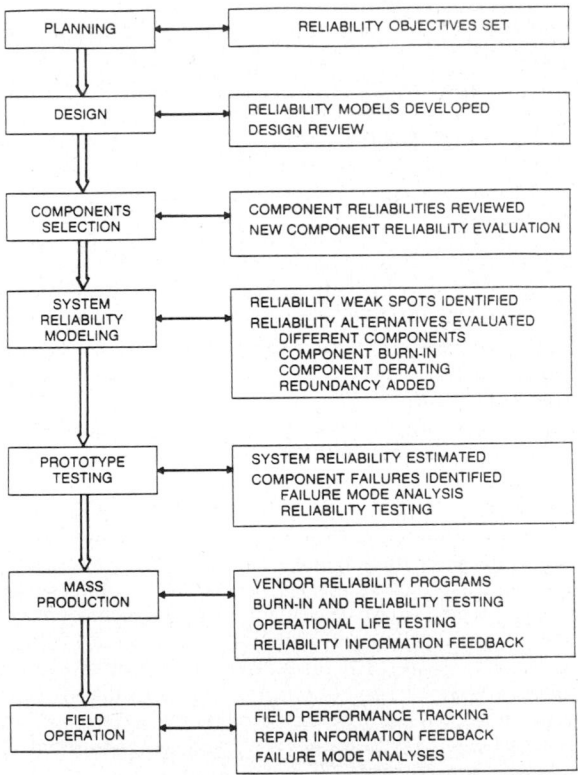

FIG. 29.9 Reliability assurance program.

look for weak spots in the system's reliability. Life tests and accelerated life tests are often used to refine the reliability estimates for the selected components. As indicated in Figure 29.9, the systems designer has several options available to assure that components have the required reliability. When necessary, the designer may require burn-in of certain components to eliminate early-life reliability failures. The designer may require reliability qualifications of critical components. During prototype testing, the designers are able to estimate system reliability and evaluate the system reliability predictions and the component reliability estimates. At this time they may decide to develop special supplier reliability requirements and reliability assurance programs. They may require incoming component burn-in or reliability testing or operational life testing. They may also improve the reliability performance of key components by making changes in the manufacturing process. During mass production the reliability assurance programs are applied to assure that components continue to meet reliability objectives. The reliability information system provides feedback on reliability problems and improved component reliability estimates for use in new designs. The performance of the system in use in the customers' environment provides extremely useful reliability information. Component reliability information is collected through field performance tracking studies and through repair studies. Failure-mode analyses (sometimes called "failed-part analyses") are used extensively to determine causes of component failures and remove these causes out of the design-manufacturing process.

Reliability Prediction for Components.   The fundamental concepts and methods of reliability are covered in Section 13. The reliability methods used for components are very similar, and here we will cover only some of the specific differences. Healy (1986) gives an excellent discussion of modeling integrated circuit failure rates. Models are necessary for estimating component failure rates because no database will contain information on the reliability of every component that may be selected, since leading-edge designs will utilize unproved devices. Interpolation using the models permits predictions of failure rates not given in the tables and allows extrapolations to components beyond the ranges of the tables. The most frequently used models for predicting component reliabilities are those in *Military Handbook 217D* (Department of Defense, 1982). Although these models have been used for years and give excellent reliability predictions for military applications, Healy (1986) and Spencer (1986) show that these models far underestimate reliability for integrated circuits used in other applications such as telecommunications.

Most companies have reliability information databases containing reliability estimates for the most frequently used components and models for predicting the reliabilities of components not in the database and new components. Many of these models are based on *Military Handbook 217D*, but many other models have been developed for electronic components, mechanical components, castings, and metal fabrications. We shall use Healy's (1986) models as an example of how component reliability prediction models are used. Table 29.2 reproduces Healy's summary of his integrated circuit failure rate models. In his models, F is the failure rate in FITS [failures in ten-to-the-ninth (i.e., one billion) hours], B is the number of kilobits, T is the number of transistors, and G is the number of gates. Healy gives a simple example to show how easy it is to use his models. To obtain the failure rate of 1K nonhermetic n-channel metal-oxide semiconductor (NMOS) static random-access memory (RAM), one uses the formula

$$F = 69(1 + 0.25)^{0.72} = 81 \text{ FITS}$$

TABLE 29.2   IC Failure-Rate Models

	Hermetic	Nonhermetic
Dynamic RAM		
MOS	$F = 33(B + 0.25)^{0.60}$	$F = 45(B + 0.25)^{0.60}$
Static RAM		
NMOS-PMOS	$F = 39(B + 0.25)^{0.72}$	$F = 69(B + 0.25)^{0.72}$
CMOS	$F = 89(B + 0.25)^{0.75}$	$F = 163(B + 0.25)^{0.75}$
RAM		
Bipolar	$F = 60(B + 0.25)^{0.79}$	$F = 83(B + 0.25)^{0.79}$
ROM		
NMOS-PMOS	$F = 24(B + 0.25)^{0.66}$	$F = 37(B + 0.25)^{0.66}$
CMOS	$F = 40(B + 0.25)^{0.64}$	$F = 79(B + 0.25)^{0.64}$
Bipolar	$F = 22(B + 1)^{0.84}$	$F = 32(B + 1)^{0.84}$
PROM		
Bipolar	$F = 23(B + 1)^{0.95}$	$F = 35(B + 1)^{0.95}$
EPROM, EEPROM		
NMOS-PMOS	$F = 29(B + 0.25)^{0.65}$	$F = 44(B + 0.25)^{0.65}$
CMOS	$F = 42(B + 0.25)^{0.71}$	$F = 76(B + 0.25)^{0.71}$
Linear		
Bipolar	$F = 2(T)^{0.78}$	$F = 3(T)^{0.78}$
Digital Logic		
Bipolar	$F = 0.15(G + 100)^{0.96}$	$F = 0.19(G + 100)^{0.96}$
NMOS-PMOS	$F = 0.15(G + 100)^{0.96}$	$F = 0.25(G + 100)^{0.96}$
CMOS	$F = 0.14(G + 100)^{0.99}$	$F = 0.22(G + 100)^{0.99}$

Source: Healy, 1986.

Spencer (1986) demonstrates how critical accurate component reliability predictions are for developing useful system reliability predictions. He reviews the component reliability prediction procedures of some of the leading telecommunications companies, including Bell Communications Research (Bellcore), British Telecom (BT), the French Centre National d'Etudes des Telecommunications (CNET), and Nippon Telegraph and Telephone (NTT). He compares the component reliability predictions obtained by their models with those obtained using *Military Handbook 217D.* (His comparisons are presented in Table 29.3.) He then calculates the reliability of a memory board with 70 plastic encapsulated 64K dynamic random-access memory chips (DRAMs). He finds a wide range of pre-

TABLE 29.3   Predicted Failure Rates for Hermetic NMOS SRAMS

Component complexity	Reliability prediction model				
	BT	NTT	CNET	Bellcore	*217D*
256 bits	8	26	35	24	67
1K	8	42	67	46	176
4K	10	69	140	120	518
16K	15	271	282	290	1563
64K	25	638	665	790	4734

Source: Spencer, 1986.

dicted reliability ranging from 700 FITS (0.6 percent board replacements per year) to 4,240,460 FITS (3,713 percent board replacements per year). He then calculates the reliability of a hypothetical board with 52 components of eight different types. By creating this standard board, Spencer was able to remove some of the exaggeration of differences in circuit board reliability prediction inherent in his memory board example. His predictions ranged from 1258 FITS (about 1 percent of the circuit boards failing per year) to 715,784 FITS (over 600 percent). These examples (summarized in Table 29.4) show how component reliability predictions vary greatly with the reliability prediction model used.

TABLE 29.4   Predicted Reliabilities, in FITS, of Circuit Boards Using Different Component Reliability Prediction Models

Circuit board	Reliability prediction model				
	BT	NTT	CNET	Bellcore	*217D*
Memory board	700	37,940	37,870	38,500	4,240,460
Hypothetical board	1,258	9,525	16,714	12,502	715,784

Source: Spencer, 1986.

Reliability in the Manufacturing Cycle.   Reliability is usually considered to be determined by the design to a great extent, but there are many manufacturing steps that affect reliability. The integrity of solder joints and welds, electrostatic discharge (ESD) latent effects, rework, and repair can all have significant impact on component reliabilities. DesPlas (1986) discusses several ways companies are building in reliability. Solder joints are automatically inspected by means of laser inspection systems. Studies have shown this system can improve quality and long-term reliability. Temperature testing (both hot and cold) of integrated circuits can improve system quality and reliability and significantly reduce total test costs. Electrostatic discharge controls are extremely important for assuring electronic component reliability.

PROGNOSIS

The electronics industry is faced with ever-increasing complexity at system, subsystem, and component levels, the rapid introduction of new technologies, and the shortening of product life cycles.

Increasing complexity at the system and subsystem levels leads to the necessity of the incorporation of self-testing and diagnostics at the design stage, and the requirement for extremely high levels of component quality and reliability. The high-quality levels require, in turn, the development of new supplier and user quality programs and measurement and information systems to replace traditional acceptable quality level (AQL) and average outgoing quality limit (AOQL) sampling plans and incoming inspection programs. Subsystem level complexity leads to an increased emphasis on the understanding, measurement, and control of the quality and reliability of interconnection processes. At the component level, increased complexity, as represented by VLSI circuits, coupled with relatively smaller production runs, as represented by application-specific integrated circuits, lead to the necessity for built-in self-testing at the device level, statistically meaningful fractional test coverage, and a dependence on robust process line quality and reliability controls in addition to inspection and testing.

The rapid introduction of new technologies based on increasingly fine dimensional controls, (e.g., fractional micron dimensions in VLSI circuits), calls for an increased sensitivity to reliability problems. Every decrease in metallization linewidths and insulator thicknesses leads to increased wear-out mechanisms such as electromigration, electrostatic discharge, and hot-electron effects. New reliability models, measures, and control systems will be needed.

The shortening of product life cycles implies that both quality and reliability measures must be developed and in place on "immature" product lines. We no longer have the luxury of long learning curves during production buildup. This product life cycle acceleration necessitates early focus on robust designs and robust manufacturing processes using the most sophisticated experimental design procedures to establish these. We also no longer have the luxury of very-long-term reliability test programs; thus we must learn to derive reliability indicator information from degradation studies and process monitors.

Increasing demands on component quality and reliability require increased emphasis on the research and development of quality technology and tools.

REFERENCES

Amster, S. J. and Hooper, J. H. (1986). "Statistical Methods for Reliability Improvement." *AT&T Technical Journal,* vol. 65, no. 2, March-April, pp. 69–76.

Amster, S. J. and Hooper, J. H. (1983). "Accelerated Life Tests with Measured Degradation Data and Growth Curve Models." *American Statistical Association Annual Meeting, Program and Abstracts*, p. 124.

Amster, S. J., Brush, G. G., and Saperstein, B. (1982). "Planning and Conducting Field-Tracking Studies." *Bell System Technical Journal,* vol. 61, no. 9, pp. 2333–2364.

Bell Communications Research (1984). *Reliability Prediction Procedures for Electronic Equipment.* Bellcore Technical Advisory TA-000-23620-84-01, Bellcore Communications Research, Red Bank, N. J.

Box, G. E. P., Hunter, W. G., and Hunter, J. S. (1978). *Statistics for Experimenters—An Introduction to Design, Data Analysis and Model Building.* John Wiley & Sons, New York.

Department of Defense (1977). *Reliability Design Qualification and Production Acceptance Tests: Exponential Distribution.* Defense Document Distribution Center, Washington, DC. August, p. 116.

DesPlas, Edward P. (1986). "Reliability in the Manufacturing Cycle." *Proceedings, Annual Reliability and Maintainability Symposium.* IEEE, New York, pp. 139–144.

Godfrey, A. B., Phadke, M. S., and Shoemaker, A. C. (1986). "The Development & Application of Robust Design—Taguchi's Impact in the United States." *Journal of the Japanese Society for Quality Control,* April, pp. 145–153.

Goksel, A. K., Sekino, W. T., and Troutman, W. W. (1986). "Tools and Techniques for VLSI Quality." *AT&T Technical Journal,* vol. 65, no. 2, March-April, pp. 77–84.

Healy, John (1986). "Modeling IC Failure Rates." *Proceedings, Annual Reliability and Maintainability Symposium.* IEEE, New York, pp. 307–311.

Iwasaki, Iwao (1974). "Mechanical Components." Chapter 37 in Juran, J. M. (ed.), *Quality Control Handbook,* 3rd ed. McGraw-Hill, New York.

Juran, J. M. (ed.), Gryna, F. M., Jr., and Bingham, R. S., Jr. (assoc eds.) (1974). *Quality Control Handbook.* 3rd ed. McGraw-Hill, New York.

Kackar, R. N. (1985). "Off-line Quality Control, Parameter Design and the Taguchi Method." *Journal of Quality Technology,* vol. 17, October, pp. 176–209.

Kackar, R. N. and Shoemaker, A. C. (1986). "Robust Design: A Cost-Effective Method for Improving Manufacturing Processes." *AT&T Technical Journal,* vol. 65, no. 2, March-April, pp. 39–50.

Lawless, J. F. (1982). *Statistical Models and Methods for Lifetime Data.* John Wiley & Sons, New York.

MIL-HDBK-217D (1982). *Reliability Prediction of Electronic Equipment.* Department of Defense; available from Defense Document Distribution Center, Washington, DC.

Pettijohn, C. L. (1986). "Achieving Quality in the Development Process." *AT&T Technical Journal,* vol. 65, no. 2, March-April, pp. 85–93.

Phadke, M. S., Kackar, R. N., Speeney, D. V., and Grieco, M. J. (1983). "Off Line Quality Control in Integrated Circuit Fabrication Using Experimental Design." *Bell System Technical Journal,* May-June, pp. 1273–1309.

Phadke, M. S. (1986). "Design Optimization Case Studies." *AT&T Technical Journal,* vol. 65, no. 2, March-April, pp. 51–68.

Phadke, M. S. (1982), "Quality Engineering Using Design Experiments." *Proceedings of the American Statistical Association,* Section on Statistical Education, Cincinnati, August, pp. 11–20.

Phadke, M. S. and Taguchi, G. (1984). "Quality Engineering through Design Optimization." *Proceedings of the IEEE Communications Society, GLOBECOM 84.* IEEE, New York.

Spencer, James L. (1986). "The Highs and Lows of Reliability Predictions." *Proceedings, Annual Reliability and Maintainability Symposium.* IEEE, New York, pp. 156–162.

Taguchi, G. and Wu, Yu-In (1979). *Introduction to Off-Line Quality Control.* Central Japan Quality Control Association, Meieki Nakamura-Ku, Nagaya, Japan (available in English through the American Supplier Institute).

Takanashi, Masahide (1978). "Quality Assurance System for the Integrated Circuit." *ICQC '78-Tokyo.* Japanese Union of Scientists and Engineers, Tokyo, pp. C1-51–C1-56.

Teradyne, Inc. (1974). *High-Volume Testing for Electronic Device Users.* Teradyne, Boston.

Wadsworth, H. M., Stephens, K. S., and Godfrey, A. B. (1986). *Modern Methods for Quality Control and Improvement.* John Wiley & Sons, New York.

SECTION 30
ASSEMBLY INDUSTRIES[1]

J. Douglas Ekings

INTRODUCTION **30.2**
The Assembly Process . . . 30.2
Business Pressures on
Quality 30.3

**QUALITY MANAGEMENT IN
ASSEMBLY INDUSTRIES** **30.4**
Corporate Level—Strategic
Business Statement . . . 30.4
The Quality System 30.5
Total Organization
Involvement in Quality . 30.6
Product Development
Strategy 30.6
Product Development
Cycle 30.7
Typical Production Process
in an Assembly Company 30.8
Pilot Plant Production . . . 30.8
Customer-Supplied
Specifications 30.10

NEW-PRODUCT CONTROLS . . **30.11**
Preventive versus
Corrective Action 30.11
Quality Planning during
Design and Development 30.11
Consideration of
Production and Service
Needs 30.14
Overall Evaluation 30.16

Production as Part of the
Product Delivery Team . 30.16

PLANNING FOR PRODUCTION . . **30.17**
Production Plan 30.17
Production Flow 30.17
Support Functions 30.17

WORKING WITH SUPPLIERS . . **30.18**
Supplier Certification . . . 30.18
Supplier Recognition
Programs 30.21

PRODUCTION **30.21**
The Major Functions . . . 30.21
In-Process Controls 30.24
Process Capability Studies 30.24
Quality Growth 30.24
Product Screens 30.24
Corrective Action Systems 30.26

CRITERIA FOR QUALITY . . . **30.27**
Product Release Criteria . . 30.28
Competitive Benchmarking 30.28
Production Process
Instructions 30.29
Inspection Instructions . . 30.29
Requirements for Line
Operators 30.29
Tool Tryout Assessment . . 30.29

---

[1] In the Third Edition, this section was prepared by A. J. Hitzelberger. Some material, primarily several tables and figures, is from the Third Edition's section on automotive industry, by Soichiro Toyoda, and the section on household appliances, by Lennart Sandholm.

ASSEMBLY PROCESS AND
CONTROLS **30.30**

   Product Flow 30.30

   Quality Objectives 30.30

   Quality Targets 30.30

   Quality Feedback 30.31

   Customer Service Support 30.33

   Service Support in the
      Appliance Industry . . . 30.35

RESPONSIBILITY PATTERNS . . **30.36**

   Responsibility for Quality . 30.36

   Quality Activities 30.36

DATA PLAN **30.37**

   Internal Systems 30.37

   External Systems 30.40

   Customer Feedback
      Systems/Surveys 30.41

   Plant Visitation Programs . 30.44

   Reporting of Field Failures 30.44

AUDIT PLAN **30.45**

   Quality Audit Process . . . 30.45

   Quality Systems Audit . . . 30.45

   Product Audit 30.46

QUALITY IMPROVEMENT . . . **30.47**

SUMMARY AND OUTLOOK . . . **30.48**

ACKNOWLEDGMENTS **30.49**

REFERENCES **30.49**

INTRODUCTION

This section of the handbook deals with quality in the assembly industry and covers the major elements of quality management common to companies in this industry. The basic quality activities used during the design, development, production, and customer use phases of these companies will be addressed.

The history, the methodology, and the detailed how-to's of these quality activities are covered elsewhere in the handbook and will only be referenced in this section.

The Assembly Process.   A typical assembly company forms components into subassemblies, subassemblies into major assemblies, and major assemblies into systems ranging from simple products (i.e., appliances) to complex systems (e.g., automobiles, computers, copiers, and communication systems).

Assembly companies generally have a product design and development phase and a production phase. They acquire piece parts—either as discrete units (semiconductors, integrated circuits, and memory devices) or as functional modules (clutches, power supplies, and fans). The quality mission of the company (through specification, design, procurement, testing, and the assembly sequence) is to deliver a product or system that meets the customer's explicit or implicit quality requirements (i.e., fitness for use). To do this, the product assembler must rely on numerous suppliers—from those supplying raw materials to those supplying the components or modules used in final product assembly. The diversity of raw materials ranges from rubber compounds and molded parts to sheet metal and materials that form an integral part of internally fabricated subassemblies and/or subassemblies, which are procured on a contract basis. When assembling, for example, a complex digital communication system for the customer, the system assembly firm may procure major subassemblies designed primarily for commercial use (e.g., page printers, card readers, and other data processing subassemblies). Although these subassemblies may have already met one set of quality requirements, the assembly firm must also ensure that their customer's quality and reliability requirements are satisfied. These requirements, combined with the growth of industrial and consumer expectations for product quality and reliability, have resulted in increased demands on the manufacturer of the "as delivered assembly." As a result, the need for careful product definition, specification, procurements, subassembly, inspection, test, and quality improvement continues to dramatically increase.

Business Pressures on Quality. A classic example of business pressures on quality is illustrated in the relationship among product cost, delivery schedule, and quality (Figure 30.1). Improved quality of conformance can reduce product cost and can support the achievement of required delivery schedules. However, one pressure that has decreased the emphasis on acceptable product quality at the customer site has been the "strong emphasis on shipments and short-term sales." Another pressure, which runs in about a 10-year cycle, is an overemphasis on product cost at the expense of inherent product quality and reliability. Another negative pressure on product quality results from the divergent objectives of the various departments of the assembly company. Each department focuses on its own objectives, instead of its contribution to the overall objectives of the company. Thus the company's resources are not fully united toward the primary goal of high product quality. One example of such conflicting departmental objectives is shown in Figure 30.2.

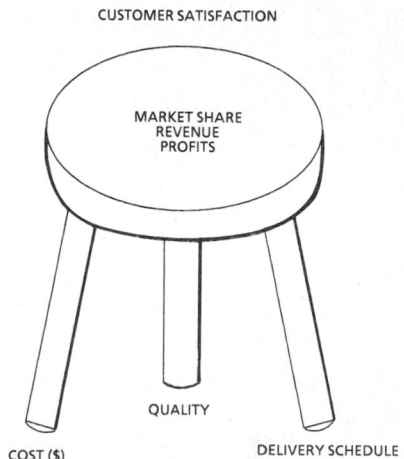

FIG. 30.1 Relationship between product cost, delivery schedule, and quality.

In some companies, for example, the Design Department might focus its priorities and resources on new product features, lighter materials, miniaturization, cost-reduced subassemblies, and design documentation. This focus sometimes does not make the Manufacturing Department's job easier because, at the same time, the Manufacturing Department may be focusing on the introduction of new processes and automation to reduce the cost of production. More importantly, neither department has time to focus on external customer needs or on advances of the competition.

Pressures outside the assembly firm have also caused product quality to decrease. Sellers' markets in the past have left customers with little ability to show their distress with poor workmanship or reliability. Inordinate emphasis on delivery schedule imposes a negative pressure on achieving high product quality. As a result, products are placed in the market that do not completely meet the customer's requirements. For example, companies that produce copiers, computers, or aircraft may have products that work smoothly until delivered to the customer. Once the customer becomes dissatisfied, the company implements recovery programs. These programs range from massive product recall to field retrofit programs that upgrade design shortfalls and manufacturing defects. Such actions

```
•• DESIGN DEPARTMENT
    –   NEW FEATURES
    –   RELIABILITY
    –   TOTAL PRODUCT COST [UNIT MANUFACTURING COST (UMC) AND
        FIELD COST]
    –   NEW TECHNOLOGY


•• MANUFACTURING DEPARTMENT
    –   NEW PROCESSES
    –   COMMON STANDARD ("OLD") PARTS
    –   OUTGOING QUALITY
    –   SUPPLIER QUALITY
    –   PRODUCT COST [UNIT MANUFACTURING COST (UMC)]
    –   DELIVERY DATES


•• BOTH DEPARTMENTS
    –   NOT FULLY SENSITIVE TO CUSTOMER NEEDS
    –   NOT FULLY AWARE OF COMPETITOR'S PERFORMANCE
```

FIG. 30.2   An example of conflicting departmental objectives.

incur significant costs of nonconformance for the assembly firm on a short-term basis, place a long-term stain on their reputation for quality, and also decrease profit (i.e., lost opportunity).

The secondary role of quality has begun to change. For example, Juran (1979b) described why a U.S. television manufacturer changed its priority on the importance of quality in the marketplace. The reversal was triggered as foreign competitors began to erode the U.S. and worldwide television markets with higher-quality and lower-cost products. This erosion of the television market marked the start of the impact of foreign competition on U.S. markets. It affected products ranging from automobiles to medical drugs to copiers and included about every high labor content product that formerly enabled U.S. industries to dominate worldwide markets. As an example, Xerox Corporation, through its patented xerographic copiers, dominated the market in 1970. Ten years later, after the Xerox patents expired, this market share had been substantially reduced, because of aggressive competition from Japan and other U.S. "blue chip" companies which capitalized on the use of their newly acquired access to xerographic technology.

QUALITY MANAGEMENT IN ASSEMBLY INDUSTRIES

Assembly industries are moving from broad statements of quality policy (Figure 30.3) to more specific statements of strategy for a product (Figure 30.4).

Corporate Level—Strategic Business Statement.   Increasingly, many companies' long-range plans now state that "We will achieve quality parity with competition in the year 1986," or that "We will surpass the competition and become a worldwide leader in quality by 1988." Any quality strategy must be an integral

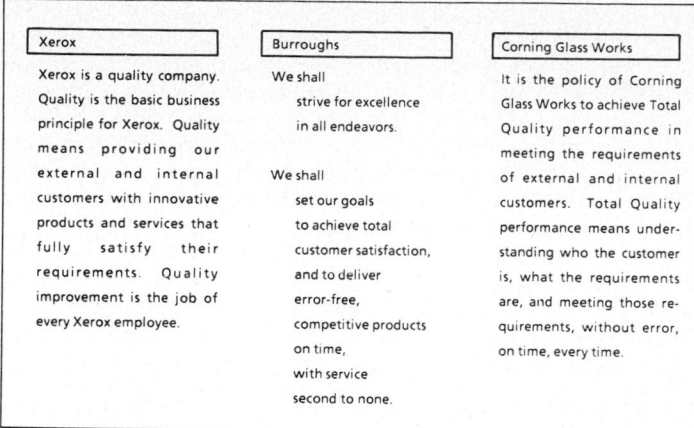

FIG. 30.3 Typical corporate quality policies.

part of a company's business strategy if the firm wants to achieve a total approach to quality. For example, if a procurement policy is defined independently of the quality policy, then several mutually exclusive policies and strategies might result so that actions to improve quality will not be realized.

The Quality System. In large companies, a standard quality system generally identifies the various production segments and control points that are the basis for doing business. If there are unique customer requirements, operations, or technology, the quality plan must also address these requirements.

The total time required to design, develop, and produce a product as complex as an automobile, a copier, or a radio set can range from 2 to 7 years. Various external and/or internal forces can lengthen or shorten this time frame. Japanese manufacturing firms have been able to design and develop a new technology product in 2 years. In many U.S. companies, the design and development of the same technology to produce the same complex product would take roughly twice as long. The full development cycle is proportionally shorter for a new model copier or for an automobile that is a modification of the original model. A new design requires the full design and development period, whereas the modifications (minor or major changes to the original design) can be introduced to the market in a much shorter time. The degree of depth and resources of the quality program required to assure customer satisfaction are directly related to the amount of new design and must be fully integrated with all activities of the design and development phase.

> • MATURE PRODUCT QUALITY WILL BE ACHIEVED AT LINE BALANCE.
>
> • MONTH ONE RELIABILITY OF THE NEW PRODUCT WILL BE
>   EQUAL (OR BETTER) TO THE DEMONSTRATED MONTH ONE RELIABILITY OF THE PRODUCT
>   BEING REPLACED.

FIG. 30.4 Quality strategy for a typical product.

Assembly companies now use statistical quality control and other quality improvement techniques that focus on assemblies, processes, and tooling to make it possible to provide consistently defect-free assemblies to the customer. These techniques are used extensively by the automotive and copier companies. Before such in-depth data collection and data analysis programs, the tendency was to assume that the production workers generally were not motivated or had no interest in achieving error-free workmanship. However, many analyses showed that the tools and/or equipment provided to the workers prevented them from achieving a defect-free product. Teamwork programs, such as the *quality of work life* and *employee involvement programs* used at Xerox, do consider the motivation and behavior of the individuals. Working either individually or in a team using different, newly acquired behavioral skills has become increasingly important within the assembly companies.

Total Organization Involvement in Quality. A total quality program has the quality functions of *each* of the company's departments incorporated into the total company quality plan. Defining these departmental quality functions is important when determining quality objectives, allocating company resources, and translating the results of the marketing department market research, for example, into meaningful specifications for the product design team to translate into product service and support for the delivered product. The outline of a quality program developed during the design and development phase is outlined in Figure 30.5 and shows the involvement of all of the departments of the company.

PROGRAM TARGETS	DISTRIBUTION & SERVICE	
PRODUCT PLANNING	–	SERVICE AND LOGISTICS STRATEGIES
DESIGN	–	SERVICE COST
MANUFACTURING	–	CONFIGURATION MANAGEMENT
– MATERIALS	–	FIELD SPARES, EQUIPMENT HANDLING
– ASSEMBLY	–	SERVICE PUBLICATIONS, SERVICE TRAINING
– FINAL PRODUCT	–	INSTALLATION PROCEDURES
– TRAINING	–	CUSTOMER TRAINING
– SAFETY	–	CUSTOMER ACCEPTANCE TEST (CAT)
MARKETING & SALES	–	LAUNCH

FIG. 30.5 Quality program.

Product Development Strategy. Strategy and direction are defined for the development of a product from 2 to 7 years before the customer sees the product. This defining is an ongoing process because as the initial performance specification is formulated, many support functions (such as logistics, spares, and maintenance concepts) must be also clarified with regard to the characteristics associated with or described within the performance specifications. During the design and development phases, information must be acquired from representative customers to assure that the characteristics defined are truly those that will make the new product a success in the marketplace.

Once the strategic business objectives are defined, a complex, synergistic process marries the marketing requirements to the technological capability of the company. A typical product development process is shown in Figure 30.6. This

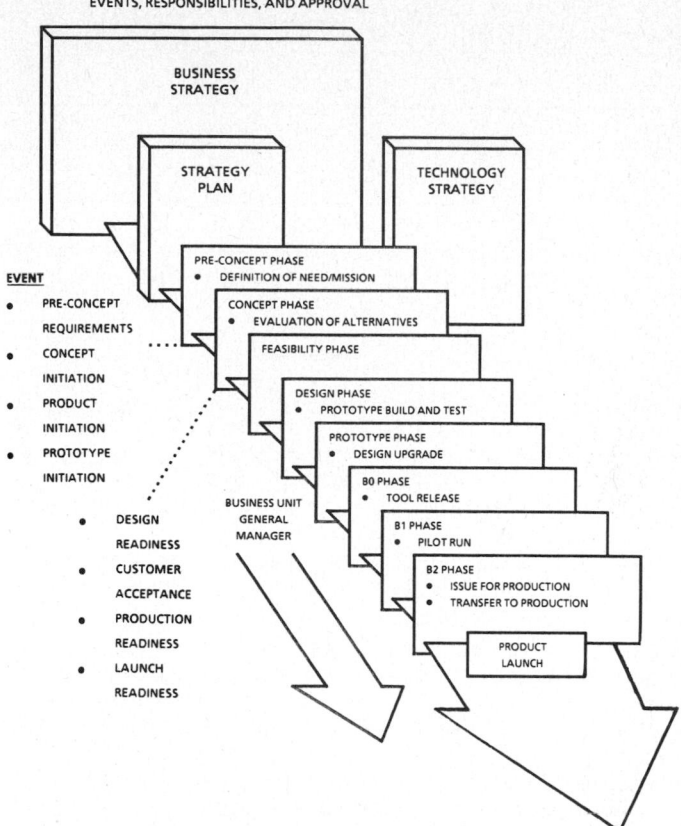

FIG. 30.6 Product development process.

figure also shows the operational events associated with product development, production, and the field use phases.

Product Development Cycle. All assembly companies use a fairly consistent product development cycle to advance a product from the preconcept phase through the design and development phase, the production phase, and ultimately to the field (i.e., customer site). Figure 30.7 shows the product development phases, originally defined in the aerospace industry, that, with minor variations,

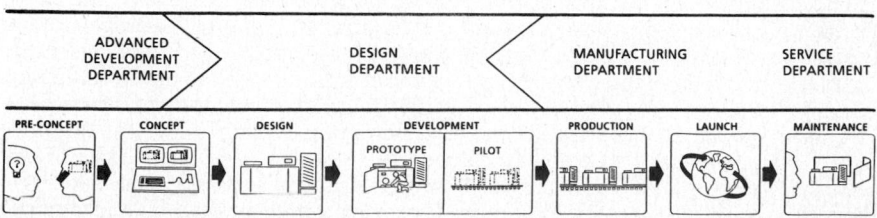

FIG. 30.7 Typical program phases.

	PHASES						
	I	II	III	IV	V	VI	VII
PHASE NAME	Preconcept	Concept	Design	Development	Production	△ Launch	Market Assessment
PHASE OBJECTIVE	Commit Development Funds to a Project	Product Strategy	Demonstrate Design Intent Meets Goals	Release for Manufacturing Qualification of Product	First Customer Ship	First Customer Placements	Evaluate Customer Satisfaction Achievement of Business Objectives

FIG. 30.8 Typical product development cycle objectives.

have been used by many assembly firms. A series of checkpoints and objectives should be associated with each of the product phases, as shown in Figure 30.8.

Typical Production Process in an Assembly Company. An example of a production process is shown in Figure 30.9. Production starts as purchased material is received at the dock of the assembly firm and continues to the minor and major subassembly, inspection, and test areas (including final test), then is delivered to the customer's site. Many companies, such as Xerox and IBM, have manufacturing facilities throughout the world where the use of a common quality system is all the more important. At product introduction, there might only be a single manufacturing site. Later on, other manufacturing sites will be added to assemble the product for delivery to the different international markets (operating companies). As a result, corporate quality guidelines outline the minimum quality activities that are required within each manufacturing site. The corporate quality manual should include the policies and detailed operating procedures for each manufacturing facility, as well as standards for each production function within the manufacturing department. The elements of a quality system for an assembly company are described in this section. Another useful reference is Caplan (1980). He identifies 100 elements that comprise a quality system for a small, medium, or large company.

Pilot Plant Production. Many companies use a pilot plant operation to develop the manufacturing processes and inspection instructions and to train the production personnel after the definition of the design configuration. Concurrent with design planning is planning for mass production. In some car companies, this planning centers on a pilot production plant that assembles only a few cars daily. The pilot production lines, which start up about 9 months before mass production begins, are closely observed by the Design, Methods, Quality, and Production Departments to identify the problems inherent in scaling up to full production. The pilot plant also enables the company to evaluate tooling and processing adequacy and to train key supervisors from the assembly plants. These supervisors then train the remaining assembly supervisors in their respective plants.

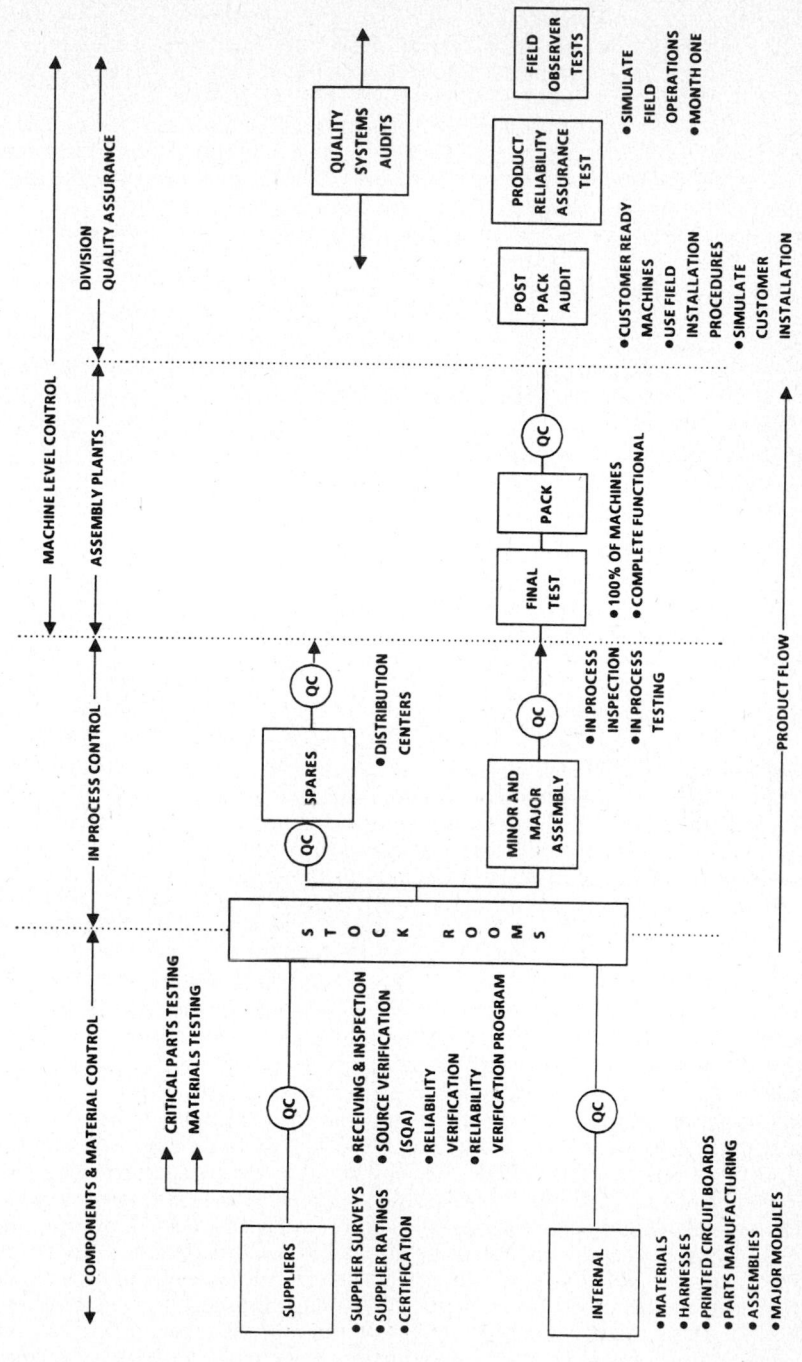

FIG. 30.9 Production process.

The pilot plant also assembles many of the engineering prototypes, which again enables production personnel to identify potential tooling, production, and quality problems at an early date. During design and development, a series of product assessments takes place. These assessments include design analysis, design reviews, and informal and formal tests and evaluations. These activities occur during the design phase and are used to qualify the design intent to the performance specification and to determine the readiness of the design for release to production and subsequent market introduction. The assessments focus on those design parameters (mean time between failures, paper handling, copy quality, and operability) that are important to achieving customer satisfaction. The product's capability to be built to an assembly process, to be inspected to final inspection instructions, and to conform consistently to design requirements can be evaluated on products assembled using the manufacturing process, and occurs during initial production build. This can be done on a simple basis by effectively planning a physically identifiable pilot plant or through the pilot phase. However, it is still the responsibility of the Design Department to build a quantity of systems; assess them in detail for conformance to the system performance specification, subassembly, and component specifications; and to determine that the design is capable of being assembled consistently in accordance with the manufacturing process.

Customer-Supplied Specifications. Compared to the consumer or industrial market, military contracting practices over the last 20 years have been fairly straightforward. A military agency (for example, the Air Force) develops its own performance specifications for the product. These specifications are definitive and are included in a request for proposal (RFP) or some other fairly definitive set of procurement requirements. Predominant performance parameters (failure rate or mean time between failures, quality requirements, error rate requirements, size, weight, shape, and other operational features) are clearly defined. In many cases, logistic support requirements for each *market segment* are also included. Within the performance specification, the operating parameters—that is, the parameters of the system as perceived by the customer—are determined by negotiation between the marketing organization and the design and development organization. The range of manufacturer interfaces with the customer again is quite varied. The interfaces will range from no customer contact at all to in-depth discussions of requirements, approaches, and quality assurance programs with the military customer after the request for proposal is submitted.

Customer requirements for an industrial market segment are difficult to describe until the assembly firm's marketing organization develops a representation of the market needs for a new product. Selectively, clients that have been satisfied or those who are responsive to new-product development can be used as new-product consultants, and in some cases, specifications can be given to decision makers at these companies for assessment and feedback to the manufacturer.

Even in the early product planning stages it is necessary to set out, in a preliminary product specification, the essential requirements of performance, use, safety, appearance, etc. Some firms create a special document (usually called a "product specification") containing these requirements. As design and development proceed, it becomes necessary to change the product specification. By the time production starts, it has been finalized and becomes the authoritative statement of design requirements. This product specification should be prepared in a systematic, comprehensive manner. It should reference all essential codes, standards, test methods, etc., required by internal policies, including pertinent national and international standards. Figure 30.10 contains an example of the

1. Applicable documents
   a. Internal: Main drawing. Packaging drawing. Component specifications
   b. External: Rules and standards (e.g., UL, AGA)
2. Product description
   a. General features
   b. Variants
3. Product provisions
   a. Function: General data. Operating characteristics. Acceptable noise level.
      Reliability (mean life, guarantee service rate)
   b. Materials and workmanship
   c. Grounding and insulation (safety requirements)
   d. Dimensions
   e. Finish: Appearance. Corrosion resistance
   f. Marking (contents and location of data plate)
4. Manufacture
   a. Fabrication
   b. Painting
   c. Assembly
5. Shipping
   a. Packaging: Requirements. Tests
   b. Marking (contents and location of labels)
6. Inspection

FIG. 30.10   Contents of product specification.

format for an appliance product specification. This same format is used when specifying requirements for critical components, such as thermostats, timers, compressors, switches, and electric motors.

NEW-PRODUCT CONTROLS

Preventive versus Corrective Action.   One of the current emphases in U.S. industry is to implement preventive actions during design and development and early production phases so that the product is provided to internal and external customers at a relatively mature level.

Extensive quality planning in the early phases of copier design and development, appliance design, and automotive design is becoming the standard for the assembly industry. This early quality program ensures that production is not adversely affected by continual changes in design, materials, or suppliers when trying to meet tight schedules at extremely high production rates.

Quality Planning during Design and Development.   Most firms that have developed assembly products in the last 20 years use some formal approach to develop a quality plan. In these firms, there has been a continuing evolution toward implementing quality control activities in the product design and development phases (see Feigenbaum, 1986). (See Section 13 under The Phase Concept of Product Development for the description of the product development cycle.) Once the product has gone through the design phase, a decision is required for the development phase to begin, followed by the subsequent production and market placement of the product. Many organizations establish major checkpoints (or phase gates) throughout this product cycle. At these checkpoints, the capability of the technology, design, and, as appropriate, manufacturing processes, to conform to established practices, criteria, and customer requirements is evaluated by independent teams composed of senior design and manufacturing personnel. Copier manufacturing companies, such as Xerox, have a similar review cycle with various checkpoints. Figure 30.11 illustrates the responsibilities of the design and the

EVENT	DESIGN DEPARTMENT	PRODUCTION DEPARTMENT
Model build to pilot plant	Responsible	Not directly involved
Pilot plant to production start-up	Responsible	Concurrence
Production start-up to full scale production	Responsible	Approval

FIG. 30.11 Transition from design to production.

production departments in the transfer of the product to the production plant. The criteria for moving from the design to the initial product building phase are shown in Figure 30.12. Figure 30.13 shows the criteria used when going from pilot plant to production startup.

Typical major tests during product development and production are shown in Figure 30.14. These tests are generally design and development tests to see if the design intent has been satisfied, followed by a field readiness qualification test of production systems. In subsequent tests, the product should be evaluated against requirements that simulate customer expectations in the field. Assuming the existence of meaningful subsystem or module specifications for the product, an extensive amount of formal testing of the product subsystems and systems also takes place (Figure 30.14).

	METRIC	PERFORMANCE LEVEL	MEASUREMENT POINT	ACCOUNTABILITY
QUALITY	LOT ACCEPTANCE	X	RI & SQA	CHIEF ENGINEER
	DPHM	X	PPA	CHIEF ENGINEER
	% PROBLEM FREE MONTH 1 RELIABILITY	X	PPA	CHIEF ENGINEER
	UMs/MACHINE	X	PST	CHIEF ENGINEER
	UMs/MACHINE	X	FRT	CHIEF ENGINEER
	UMs/MACHINE	X	PRAT	CHIEF ENGINEER
COST	PRODUCT COST	X	BU FINANCIAL CONTROL	CHIEF ENGINEER

DPHM:	Defects per Hundred Machines
UMs:	Unscheduled Maintenance Actions
PPA:	Post Pack Audit
RI:	Receiving Inspection
SQA:	Supplier Quality Assurance
BU:	Business Unit
PRAT:	Product Reliability Assurance Test
PST:	Process Stabilization Test
FRT:	Field Readiness Test

FIG. 30.12 Typical transfer criteria—design to production.

	METRIC	PERFORMANCE LEVEL*	MEASUREMENT POINT	ACCOUNTABILITY
	PPM	Y	LINE	CHIEF ENGINEER
	DPHM	Y	PPA	CHIEF ENGINEER
QUALITY	% PROBLEM FREE	Y	PPA	CHIEF ENGINEER
	% PROBLEM FREE	Y	FIELD	CHIEF ENGINEER
	MONTH 1 RELIABILITY			
	UMs/MACHINE	Y	FRT	CHIEF ENGINEER
	UMs/MACHINE	Y	PRAT	CHIEF ENGINEER
	PWBA % DEFECTIVE	Y*	LINE	CHIEF ENGINEER
	PRODUCT COST	Y		CHIEF ENGINEER
COST	MATERIAL	Y	TBD	CHIEF ENGINEER
	LABOR	Y		CHIEF ENGINEER
	OVERHEAD	Y		CHIEF ENGINEER
CONTINUITY OF SUPPLY	MONTHS OF SUPPLY	Y	LINE	MANUFACTURING PROGRAM MGR
	SPARES DELIVERY	Y	FIELD	MATERIALS MANAGEMENT

*THREE CONSECUTIVE MONTHS

PPM:	Parts Per Million
DPHM:	Defects Per Hundred Machines
PWBA:	Printed Wiring Board Assembly
PPA:	Post Pack Audit
FRT:	Field Readiness Test
PRAT:	Product Reliability Assurance Test
UM:	Unscheduled Maintenance Action

FIG. 30.13 Typical transfer criteria—pilot plant to production startup.

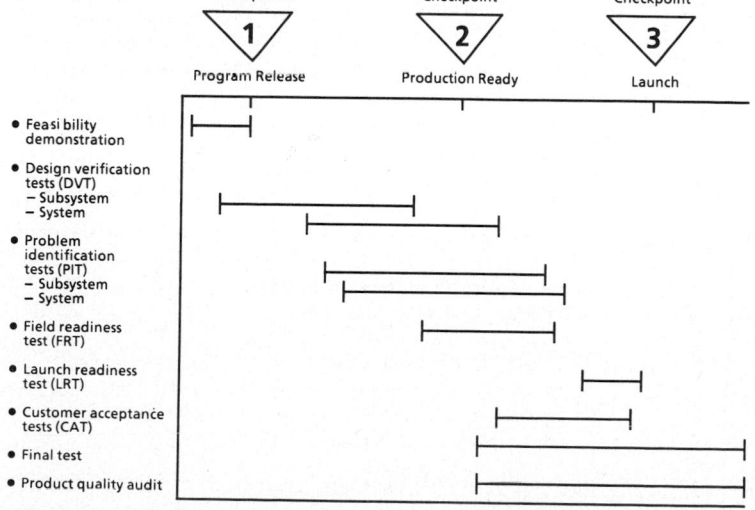

FIG. 30.14 Major tests—product development and production.

Subsystems. Subsystem tests can be static and/or dynamic and should include some measure of reliability characteristics. A materials evaluation test should be done, particularly for consumables (toners and belts in a copier, for example). Test results are used to quantitatively compare the significant performance parameters of the product to the performance specification. This comparison also allows problems that require corrective actions to be identified. These assessments are planned before each major checkpoint during design and development. Figure 30.15 identifies the major tasks that are recommended for a useful reliability engineering program. The quality program for the design and development phases includes reliability as well as quality activities.

- Specification of Reliability Requirements
- Reliability Program Plan
- Components Reliability Program
- Developmental and Qualification Test Program
- Reliability Measurement Program
- Reliability Screens
- Data Collection, Analysis, and Corrective Action Program
- Reliability Improvement Programs

FIG. 30.15   Minimum engineering reliability tasks.

Consideration of Production and Service Needs.

The marketing of assembled products usually requires that dealers be provided with stocks of finished units before the sales campaign is launched. Providing these stocks requires the production of thousands of units before consumers can use them and discover any previously overlooked defects. To prevent unpleasant surprises, manufacturers use various forms of early warning reviews and tests. These early warning events are set up at various checkpoints in the manner shown in Table 30.1

Some of these early warning tests are derived from past or current experience with similar products. Previous designs, components, or materials may have created quality problems in production, field failures, high cost of quality, frequent service calls, or difficult repairs. Data reflecting these experiences are an essential input to the new designs and to the parameters of the new products. As the early warning reviews and tests listed in Table 30.1 are conducted, they provide information essential to achieving a high level of product quality. The relationship between early warning events and product characteristics is shown in Table 30.2.

TABLE 30.1   Plan of Early Warning*

Checkpoint	Design review	Laboratory testing	Field testing	Transport testing	Pilot production
Design concept	XX				
Components used	XX	XX			
Prototypes	XX	XX		X	
Prepilot runs		XX	XX	XX	XX
Pilot runs		XX	XX	XX	XX
Limited production runs		X	X	X	XX

*XX = primary; X = secondary.

TABLE 30.2 Relation of Early Warning Events to Product Quality Characteristics*

Characteristic	Design review	Laboratory testing	Field testing	Transport testing	Pilot production
Performance	XX	XX	XX		
Reliability	XX	XX	XX	XX	
Safety	XX	XX	X	X	
Maintainability	XX		XX		
Producibility	XX				XX
Controllability	XX				XX
Usability	XX	X	XX		

*XX = primary; X = secondary.

In all assembly companies—whether the company is making connectors, single sideband radios, computers, copiers, or automobiles—a certain point is reached at which the Design Department feels that they have satisfied their requirements and the product is ready for transfer to the Production Department. At this time, jurisdictional disputes between the two departments may arise. Some of these disputes arise because the objectives of the design engineer differ from those of the production engineer, even though they work for the same company. The design engineer's primary objective is usually to issue drawings, while the production engineer's primary objective is to establish the production process. If the production engineer works directly with the design engineer before a design is issued, their joint efforts will achieve much better continuity from the design phase to the production phase. In the last 10 years, many companies have made great progress toward getting the Design and Production Departments to direct their united efforts to a common goal. The need to design a high-quality product that can be economically produced necessarily places a requirement on both the design and production departments to work together to achieve this common business objective.

Three ways for uniting these two departments have been used by assembly companies:

- Have the manufacturing department provide the criteria to the design department and then sign off each drawing denoting approval/concurrence.

- Include the manufacturing department on the same team as the design department (i.e., product development team and product delivery team).

- Train the design engineers so that they have the skills to design a high-quality product that can be economically produced and serviced.

An example of how the design and manufacturing departments worked together effectively during the design phase of the Ford Taurus automobile is described by Veraldi (1985).

Design Evaluation by Use. In any product, the ultimate test of design is use. The ultimate test of the design of a car is in driving the vehicle under actual road conditions. For this reason, most automobile companies (and some tire companies) maintain test tracks that simulate a wide spectrum of road surfaces and driving conditions. The test track is an elaborate and expensive facility used to evaluate a wide variety of vehicle and component performances. Another evaluation by use is by collaboration with vehicle fleets. For example, one automobile manufacturer, which wanted to provide a 5-year warranty on transmissions, arranged to install transmission prototypes in New York City taxicabs to obtain data on use under severe operating conditions.

Safety and Health Evaluation. Test facilities for accident prevention include a psychological laboratory and a driving simulator room for physical and psychological evaluation of driver response to disturbance, visual range, comfort, fatigue, and ease of use of various switches and levers. Exhaust emissions are analyzed and measured by chassis dynamometer, engine dynamometer, exhaust gas analyzer, and blow-by gas measuring devices. The results are combined and analyzed by computer. A test of exhaust emission from an engine itself is conducted in another test room. The safety of cars on impact is evaluated at an outdoor test ground equipped with test facilities to measure the effects of head-on collisions, barrier collisions, and vehicle rollover. Laboratory facilities include an impact simulator for reproducing collision phenomena indoors, analyzing driver and passenger behavior, and confirming whether the car is responsive to users' complaints and service needs and whether the model has remedied various quality problems prevailing in existing models. Other impact tests evaluate the safety of parts. From these evaluations and from those of pilot production line performance, the Product Planning Department determines the extent to which the attainment of planned goals for quality, cost, and production capacity permit the project to proceed to mass production and marketing.

Overall Evaluation. The results of design review, laboratory testing, use testing, and customer evaluations are constantly fed back to the Product Design and Product Planning Departments. In addition, overall evaluations are conducted to see how well the model compares with the competition and whether the production processes are compatible with the design characteristics. These evaluations are used as a checkpoint before production is started. This preproduction phase is critical with regard to resolving variations from the product performance specification, proofing the production process and inspection instructions, and providing the production workers with hands-on training on the design configuration to be produced.

The Design Department must finalize the design configuration and documentation to conform to the performance specification. The plan for material flow and continuity of supply to the production line must also be finalized along with the readiness of the Manufacturing Department with regard to hard tooling, the final production assembly processes, worker training, and final inspection instructions. These major items need to be addressed if the transition from the design phase to the production phase is to be successful and provide continuity of support to production of the product.

Figure 30.16 illustrates the production assembly criteria for actions to be either completed or planned before beginning to assemble a new product. These criteria are applicable throughout the latter phases of assembly in the pilot plant and early production in the assembly plant.

Production as Part of the Product Delivery Team. The product delivery team is responsible for the design of the product, the selection of components, the design drawings, and the production engineering skills required to prepare the manufacturing and assembly processes for the assembly plant. The team is grouped into several major skill areas: design engineering, component engineering, reliability, human factors engineering, industrial design engineering, and value analysis. The production organization includes production engineers, production control and operations personnel, and quality engineers. Many firms use

• Engineering model build, included in initial production build	• Quality-sensitive parts plans in place
• Configuration Control	• Material replenishment and control in place
• Process Availability	• Safety requirements
• Plant Facilities	• Central corrective action
• Material Handling	• Product packaging
• Tools/gages/test equipment	• Quality information system
• Labor Plans	• Audit procedure issued
• Training plans in place	• Process analysis studies planned/completed
• Tryout schedule complete	• Controlled build planned/scheduled

FIG. 30.16 Production assembly criteria.

these quality engineers to interface with the design engineer to specify inspection tooling, gauging, and development of the inspection instructions concurrently with the development of the design documentation.

PLANNING FOR PRODUCTION

Production Plan. The manufacturing team is normally an integral part of the product delivery team during the early design phase. At this point, production plans are developed to identify resources for the production phase of the product. The production plan should include:

1. The site and facility that will initially produce the product.
2. The location of multiple sites (as in multinational production) required for concurrent production of the primary assembly. *(The plan should define location of major modules production sites.)*
3. The capital equipment requirements, the tooling budget, the quality plan, and the materials acquisition plan.
4. The development of the rolling production plan. (This plan connects the requirement for product placement in the market to the design release cycle and serves as the basis for developing the production delivery schedule.)

Production Flow. The production process (Figure 30.5) shows the flow of material from external and internal suppliers into the firm, the flow of material from the dock to stocking areas for support of field spares and major line assemblies, and the flow through some form of a progressive production line into an assembled configuration and then to final test.

Support Functions. Materials management, procurement, and quality personnel who work directly with suppliers are sometimes grouped into a separate organization supporting the product delivery team. For example, the materials management organization supports the product delivery team when they are responsible for obtaining suppliers capable of providing materials or components that satisfy program needs. Thus, the commodity manager would be part of the development team. We see an increasing focus both on management responsibility for quality being transferred to the procurement buyers and on an earlier involvement of suppliers with the design, procurement, and quality personnel. This involvement is designed to promote better understanding between both suppliers and the assembly firm personnel. Various elements of this early supplier involvement (ESI) program and early supplier commitment (ESC) are shown in Figure 30.17.

Critical parts lists are used to focus on the critical areas, both for procured components and for internally produced components. The ranked critical parts represent 2 to 3 percent of the total assembly parts in a product. The criteria for ranking these items are quality, reliability, and cost of quality. Listing of materials for first article inspection and visits of supplier quality assurance personnel to manufacturing sites are initiated by the critical parts program.

WORKING WITH SUPPLIERS

Manufacturers of assembled products generally use the methods of dealing with suppliers described in Section 15, Supplier Relations. For example, the Xerox early supplier involvement (ESI) program was started in the early 1980s. Various elements of these programs are shown in Figure 30.17. Once the initial characteristics of the design were known, potential suppliers were invited to review the design intent and the planned production assembly process with the firm's design, procurement, and quality representatives. These reviews required suppliers to describe the capability of their material and processes to conform to the design specifications, past quality histories of similar materials or components, and a review of the inspection, test, and measurement equipment used by the supplier to evaluate material to specifications.

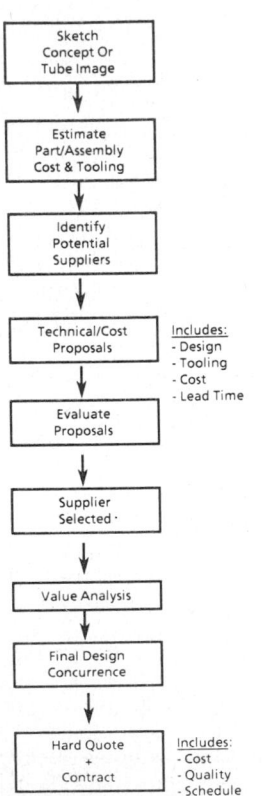

FIG. 30.17 Early supplier involvement/early supplier committment program.

Supplier Certification. In the early 1980s, many equipment assembly firms had *thousands* of active suppliers. This large supplier base diffused the amount of attention that could be placed on the material quality and continuity of supply; therefore, a new philosophy was developed to reduce the supplier base. The premise was that by dealing with a smaller supplier base (instead of many suppliers with qualities ranging from excellent to marginal), the results achieved from the supplier base could be improved. The assembly firm could better monitor the supplier's process and shift the responsibility for producing defect-free material to the supplier. Programs were developed by many automotive, copier, and computer companies to train suppliers to share in the benefits of longer relationships and in the reduction in costs associated with poor quality products. The assembly firms trained the supplier's personnel in the principles and techniques of statistical process control.

The transition to establish the "certification" of suppliers is now being effected. This certification requires that inspection data, histograms, and control charts be submitted with shipments of materials so that the material can be moved directly into stock or into the production line without inspection. In some cases, the cost of defining the commodities that fall into this program, training personnel, developing measurement systems, and streamlining quality evaluation procedures amounted to more than half a million dollars before the first supplier part was certified. And, this cost was only the tip of the investment required. The supplier who is able to apply this knowledge throughout a plant can effect significant cost savings by reducing scrap and rework. Procurement usually administers the statistical process control training program, and it usually consists of a training program for internal personnel and for supplier personnel. A typical curriculum used at Xerox is shown in Figure 30.18 (Madigan, 1981). Personnel within the firm (procurement buyers, procurement managers, quality engineers, supplier quality assurance personnel, and design engineers) are trained concurrently with the training of suppliers. The certification program consists of a series of elements as illustrated in Figure 30.19.

SESSION	TOPIC
1	Introduction-terminology. The histogram and its use.
2	The indispensable statistics, X_{bar} and sigma. The calculation for grouped and ungrouped data. The use of the computer for this analysis. Examples of actual studies using only a histogram.
3/4	Variables data continued. X_{bar} and R charts, plotting, interpretation, satisfactory versus statistical control. Lab session 1.
5/6	X_{bar} and R charts continued. Rational subgroups, plotting, interpretation, satisfactory versus statistical control. Lab session 1.
7	Special process control techniques, process versus product control, additive and mating tolerances. Lab session 2.
8	Trend charts and simple linear regression using only a calculator. Summary of the techniques for variable data. Brief introduction to attributes data analysis. The P, C, NP, and U chart.
9	Completion of attributes data. The Pareto principle. Examples of computer analysis of attributes data. Lab session 3.
10	Introduction to acceptance sampling as it is currently applied for use at Xerox. The $N = 20$, $C = 0$; and $N = 10$, $C = 0$ plans and the operating characteristics (OC) curves.

FIG. 30.18 Statistical process control training outline. *(Madigan, 1981).*

- Supplier quality audit conducted; approval granted.
- Quality plan approved.
- Production process submitted.
- Process capability report submitted.
- Corrective actions completed to assure
  process compatible to requirements (Critical Characteristics).
- Part number certified.

FIG. 30.19 Elements for part certification.

The types of supplier surveys are as follows:

1. Quality surveys at the supplier's plant.

2. Source inspection and acceptance at site and revisits to the supplier to review corrective action plans for problems found during assembly at the production site.

3. Certification of suppliers only for specific part numbers. This certification is based on evaluation of important dimensional, visual, and functional characteristics in the receiving inspection department of the assembly firm or, more effectively, on demonstrated process capability of the supplier's output.

Measurement of Supplier Quality Performance. Parts per million (PPM) measurement systems for the overall mix of commodities and material flow are applied, and annual quality targets are issued. A typical report assessing quality performance for components/materials is shown in Figure 30.20. Displays of defect data by commodity identify those components and supplies that represent the largest opportunity for process as well as product improvement. Certain techniques, such as mold approval and first-piece-first article inspection, are used where there are critical processes. These techniques have been used for more than 30 years where molded parts, rubber parts, or plastic parts are used.

Initial pieces are fabricated and a small number of samples is subjected to an extensive inspection of all dimensions, critical characteristics, and functional requirements before the process is certified. Monitoring techniques, such as control charts at key process steps, are used to assure that shifts in the production process are detected and appropriate corrective actions taken to achieve the nominal specification. The Burndy Corporation used this technique on molded parts and assemblies associated with military connectors (Shahnazarian, 1964). Quality requirements for modules from suppliers (i.e., printed wiring board assemblies) including special screening programs, such as a 100 percent functional test or a 100 percent dynamic test in systems, were used at Xerox to protect the assembly

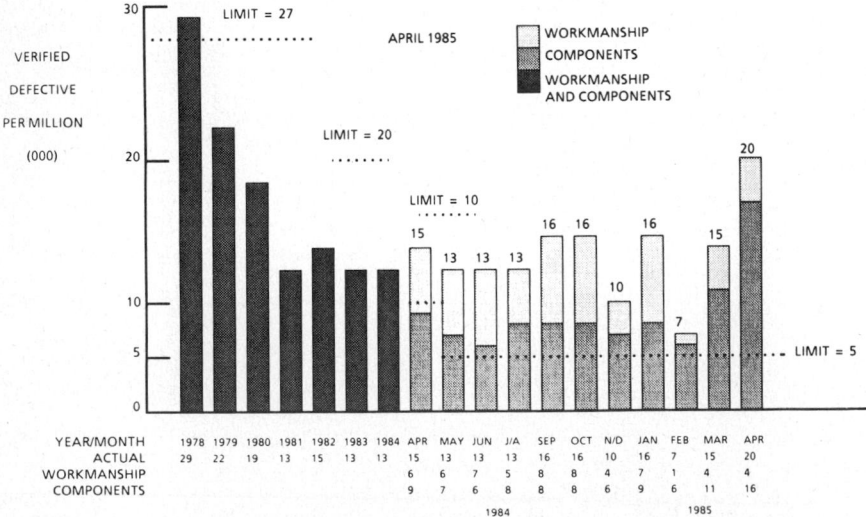

FIG. 30.20 Component/material quality assessment report measured on system production line.

plant from having excessive defect levels on the production line. Typically 40 to 50 different modules (part numbers) of varying complexities (i.e., 30 to over 200 active semiconductor devices) were subjected to a screening program to assure that each module would meet the product assemblers' quality requirements. Initially, all spare electronic modules were 100 percent tested in line stations on the manufacturing floor. Ultimately, electronic simulators that simulated the static and dynamic functions of the module in the final product were used for tests at the supplier's plant. Quality criteria were also established to provide a maximum acceptable defect level for field spares. A defective spare found in the supplier screen eliminated a "dead-on-arrival" spare when they were required by customer service engineers to replace failed modules. Spares could then be directly shipped from the supplier to the field. (These 100 percent screens were over and above other test/burn-in requirements.)

Supplier Recognition Programs. Typical criteria on which supplier recognition programs are based are shown in Table 30.3. The criteria include quality, conformance to price, and delivery. Many assembly firms hold an annual supplier

TABLE 30.3 Criteria of Supplier Recognition Programs

Quality performance	50%
Conformance to price	20%
On-time delivery	30%

recognition and awards banquet. At this time, the top 50 or 60 suppliers are recognized by the assembly firm's management and are given an award to signify the appreciation that the firm has for the suppliers' adherence to quality, price, and delivery schedule.

PRODUCTION

The Major Functions. The production process of the assembly firm consists of six broad functions: (1) receipt of materials and components, (2) in-process material flow, (3) assembly of minor and major subassemblies, (4) final assembly, (5) tests and/or screens, and (6) assessments of product quality. The production process consists of the timely scheduling and delivery of materials to a series of work stations, shown in Figure 30.21, that compose manual, progressive, or automated production lines. The control process uses quality tools, such as control charts and defect listings, at each work station. There are many possible causes for defects that are identified by the quality system during the production phase. Business factors, such as continuity of supply, design changes, change of suppliers, unsuccessful tool tryouts, removal of defective material from the production line, and personnel movement, all tend to disrupt the production process and create defects during production, which are discovered as defects in the product as well as significant degradations to a stabilized manufacturing process.

By establishing quality measures that separate the effects of material, personnel, equipment, and design changes, the factors specifically affecting product quality can be identified. Once the relationship or significance of the individual factors

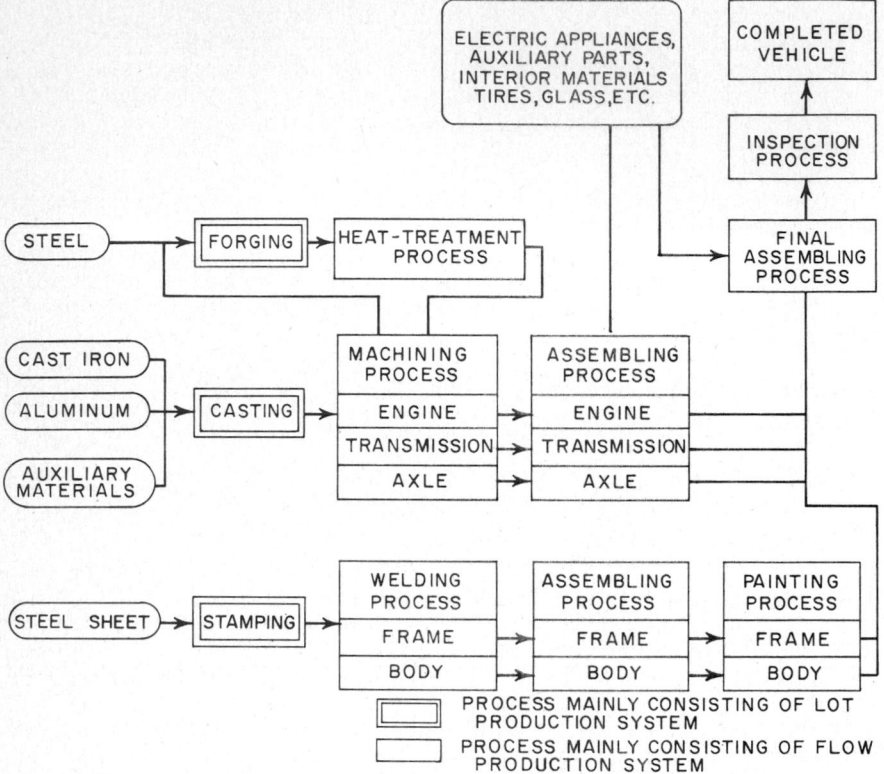

FIG. 30.21 Flow of production process in the automotive industry.

is determined, criteria for a quality process can be established in advance. A typical set of metrics is shown in Figure 30.22. A recommended approach for use of these metrics is to conduct investigations to identify the most significant production factors that degrade product quality. By following this quality-improvement process, continual quality growth is realized. Figure 30.23 shows the results of

METRIC	SOURCE OF DATA
• Defects per hundred machines	Post Pack Audit
• Defects per hundred machines	Final Test
• Line fallout PPM. Supplier responsibility	Assembly Line
• Line fallout. Sub-assembly responsibility	Assembly Line
• Cost of internal failure	Control
• Line purges	Manufacturing Operations
• Part certification status	Materials QC
• Line interruptions - material	Manufacturing Operations
• Line interruptions - hours/incidence	Manufacturing Operations
• Daily critical shortages	Manufacturing Eng.
• Design change tryouts	Manufacturing Eng.
• Personnel moves	Manufacturing Operations

FIG. 30.22 Product quality metrics.

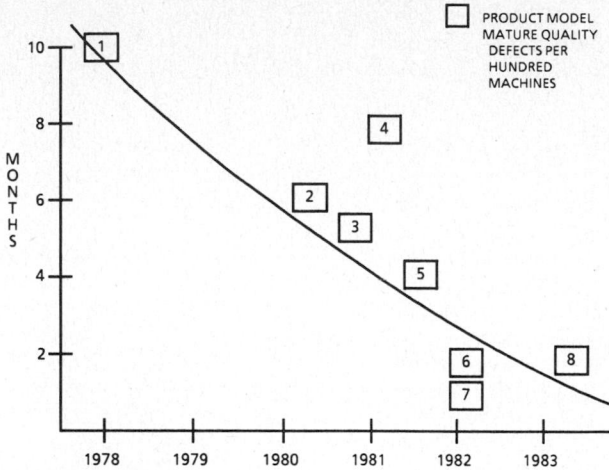

FIG. 30.23 Months to achieve mature quality.

such a quality improvement process. The amount of time to achieve the mature and acceptable quality level is continually reduced. Another example is shown in Figure 30.24, which displays the defects per hundred machines (DPHM) for a series of products manufactured by Fuji Xerox over a 6-year period. Note that the time required to reach a mature quality level (DPHM) decreases as a result of ongoing quality improvement actions. Also the quality level of each successive program improves as a result of the quality improvement actions. (Ekings and Hill, 1983.)

By using metrics, such as monthly line fallout, cost of scrap and rework levels, or line interruptions, criteria for process quality can be defined so that with time,

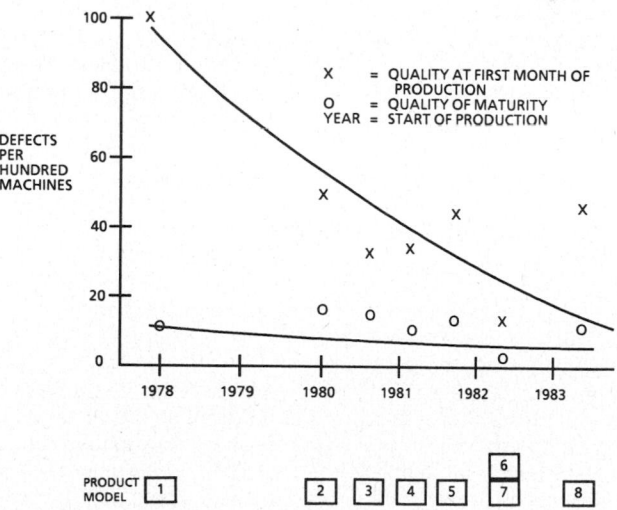

FIG. 30.24 Quality growth process—Fuji Xerox. *(Courtesy Fuji Xerox.)*

improvements can be realized in the assembly process. The results of these process improvements will show in the higher levels of product quality. These new levels can then be used as the criteria for the production of the next generation of products.

In-Process Controls.   There are a variety of in-process controls that can be included in the production process and in the support tooling and test equipment required for production. A series of controls for copiers is used as part of the production process prior to product shipment. These controls range from 100 percent final test to manufacturing verification tests, which evaluate 100 percent of the product after final test. For example, special electrical tests are often required by company policy or by federal law. These special tests are typically high pot (flash) test and electromagnetic emissions (conducted and/or radiated noise). One hundred percent screening or burn-in programs should be applied to major components that can exhibit infant mortality problems at the customer's site. The cost of these tests can be justified by the reduction in the cost of external failure (i.e., service cost) for electromechanical and electronic assemblies, (i.e., power supplies, printed wiring board assemblies, etc.) and should be included in the quality plan.

Process Capability Studies.   Process capability studies (see Section 16 under Process Capability) based on attributes or variables are used to good advantage by equipment assembly companies. Tooling tryouts have been examined from an attribute viewpoint: Can the product be assembled with the applicable tooling, using some formalized degree of an assembly process? For example, tooling process qualification was developed at a copier manufacturing site. Each of the key tools required to assemble a major new product was evaluated on five sets of assemblies.

Quality Growth.   Classic learning curves apply wherever there is a product with a high labor content, such as in a production or a service organization. The quality or reliability of the product will improve due to a learning effect of experience. In many companies, quality objectives based on performance to a percent problem-free level or defect level are 10 to 20 percent better than the previous year. This type of management by objectives and "top down" objective setting is used to forecast the expected product quality performance during the production and use phases.

Product Screens.   Various run-in and burn-in techniques (or screens) for products such as copiers, computers, and subassemblies are described in the literature. (See Ekings and Sweetland, 1983.) A simple screening method was used when the Eastman Kodak Company developed the disk camera. Both the major camera subassembly and the final assembly were operated at each of the in-process subassembly and final process steps. As data were collected and analyzed, infant mortality problems were corrected. This screen or burn-in step was then eliminated from the manufacturing process plan.

   One hundred percent burn-in of electronic modules was used at Xerox to protect the customer from early failures. The original standard for all complex electronic modules was to burn-in under a profile that required 96 h of operation and an 8-h thermal excursion ranging from 25 to 70°C with power applied to the module. Significant capital equipment was acquired to equip the internal source plant with the necessary test equipment and tooling to conform to this particular requirement. The second key objective was to eliminate or reduce problems that caused the need to implement the very costly burn-in program. The key ingredients of this effort were to collect data (difficult to do in a production environment dedicated to throughput), define the problems, and implement corrective action so that (1) incremental capital equipment and tooling would not be required, (2) the module's inherent reliability characteristics could be upgraded, and (3) production throughput would be improved (Sie, 1983). This was not easily done. On one program, which had a mix of 12 to 14 very complex assemblies, experiments were conducted over 18 months to assess the shape of the "bathtub curve" (the problems that contributed failures within each 24-h interval of the 96-h burn-in period). Corrective actions were then implemented, which resulted in the reduction of burn-in from the 96 h to 72 h to 48 h and, ultimately, to zero hours (no burn-in) for some modules.

The same approach should be applied where there is need for an initial assembly level burn-in (i.e., run-in) to simulate some period of product operation at the customers' site.

Figure 30.25 shows an example of a reliability improvement program. A key element of this improvement program was the simulation of 1 month's operation on 100 percent of the product (i.e., burn-in) during the early production start-up phase. This simulation had the benefits of (1) rapidly building a large data base to supplement design phase fixture and equipment testing, (2) providing a screen, particularly to prevent production-controllable defects from occurring after the product was delivered, and (3) more clearly defining design characteristics that appeared only at the system level.

The "base case target" (Figure 30.25) was the expected outcome with no reliability improvement program. The "improvement target" was the reliability level expected with a reliability improvement program. The measured results (X's) indicated the reliability level that was achieved. The four actions shown under "improvement actions" (Figure 30.25) formed the basis of the reliability improvement program for this equipment. This test procedure permitted a product to be shipped only if there were a specified number of failure-free hours for each indi-

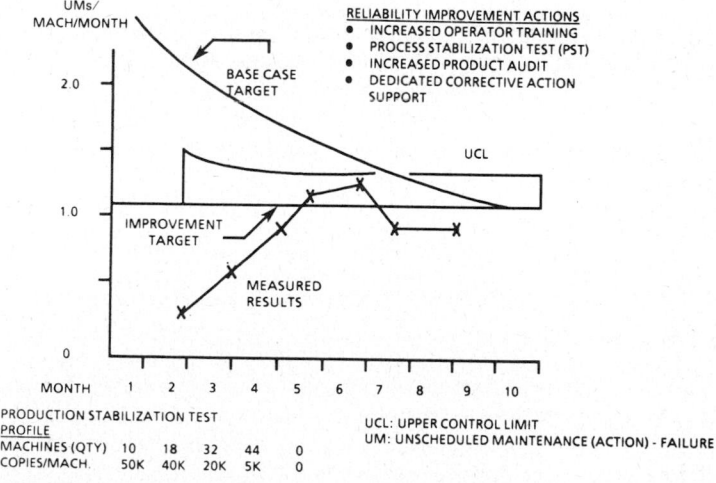

FIG. 30.25 Manufacturing reliability program (typical).

vidual equipment serial number. If the criteria for acceptable failures were exceeded, this product would be recycled, reexamined, repaired, and resubmitted for final test.

The Advisory Group on the Reliability of Electronic Equipment (AGREE) Reliability Program has been one of the most rigorous and expensive programs to qualify a product to an acceptable reliability requirement (e.g., mean time between failures). The program is based on a series of nine procedures issued to define, measure, and improve the reliability of military electronic equipment. These procedures were issued by the Advisory Group from 1956 through 1958 (AGREE, 1958). Users of the AGREE program have generally been prime contractors or Department of Defense contractors. For example, Hughes Aircraft Corporation contracted with the Electronics Division of General Dynamics and Collins Radio for airborne electronics for the F106 aircraft. The F106 product subsystems to which all AGREE procedures were applied were the high frequency radio system and the tactical air navigation (TACAN) systems. The full reliability program was used: specification of reliability requirements, reliability allocation, circuit analysis, reliability prediction, and design reviews in addition to reliability qualification testing. This reliability program also included a preproduction evaluation of models from production build to design drawings. Extensive burn-in programs were required—from device screens and dynamic burn-in to burn-in of major modules of the system—before the product was subjected to the qualification test program. This program was intended to qualify the design before it was released for production. Bimonthly reliability sampling tests were conducted over the duration of production to ensure that the production processes or the accumulated design changes had not degraded the product's reliability.

Corrective Action Systems. The corrective action system should involve the entire product development team: design engineers, production engineers, and line workers. Corrective action meetings should generally be chaired by quality engineering personnel or by quality managers.

There are many types of corrective action systems. Seven typical corrective action systems are as follows:

1. *Centralized assembly plant corrective action system:* This system includes representatives from all program organizations and deals with assembly, workmanship, and design problems associated with the product (Figure 30.26).

2. *Supplies and materials corrective action system:* This includes representatives from each functional organization of this major business unit (BU).

3. *Sunrise meetings system:* It focuses more on short-term actions. The meetings are attended by engineering and production personnel and are held daily at sunrise.

4. *Work grid system:* It combines the knowledge of the design and production engineer with the knowledge and experience of the production worker.

5. *Discrepant material control process system:* Often referred to as part of the hidden factory, this system assigns responsibility for corrective action. These responsibilities link procurement with design and not with the supplier's corrective action system.

6. *Integrated corrective action system:* It can put all elements of the quality program together to meet business needs. For example, a four-level corrective action system was developed at the Rank Xerox Mitcheldean facility. This sys-

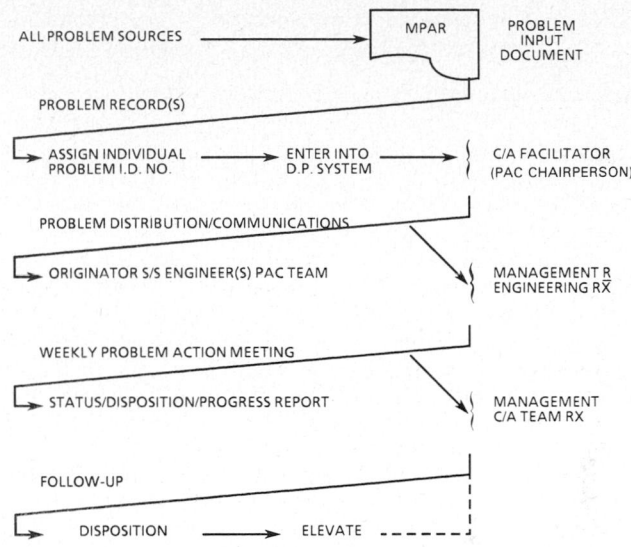

FIG. 30.26 Centralized assembly plant corrective action system; MPAR = Manufacturing problem analysis report.

tem integrated the corrective action systems of the day-to-day operations with the second level (line supervisors), who focused on the significant problems, i.e., design; the third level (middle management), who served as further resources and analysts of generic problems; and the top (corporate) level, who made the business decisions needed to implement the corrective action system. (See "Excellence in England," 1985.)

7. *Corrective action system:* This is a system for field problems (see below under Reporting of Field Failures).

CRITERIA FOR QUALITY

Assembly companies use a broad range of quality criteria. Measurement of actual performance compared to these preestablished criteria provide important information about the readiness of the production system as well as the readiness of the new product for the marketplace. These criteria include quantitative criteria to determine if a product is ready for transfer from the design phase to the production phase.

Some typical criteria used in an assembly plant are:

1. Product release criteria
2. Transfer criteria
3. Competitive benchmark levels [i.e., estimated competitive levels (ECLs) for quality]
4. Line quality targets (i.e., parts per million)
5. Production process and inspection instructions

6. Work criteria for the line worker and inspectors

7. Tooling tryouts assessment (i.e., criteria for successful tooling tryouts)

A brief description of some of these criteria follows.

Product Release Criteria. Release criteria describe the performance criteria and levels that must be achieved before a product is released to the field. It is essential, particularly for companies introducing the same product (assembled at several manufacturing sites) to numerous business markets, that the original quality strategy includes the release criteria. Some examples of such release criteria for quality would be defects per hundred machines (DPHM) and percent problem-free levels. Products ready for delivery are evaluated internally to these criteria by the *product quality audit program.* The measured results are used as leading indicators of quality performance, which can be expected to be seen as the products are installed at the customer's site. The criteria "percent problem-free" is the quality metric used to evaluate the quality of the product installation at the customer's site.

An important set of quality criteria used to establish product quality objectives are referred to (at Xerox) as estimated competitive levels (ECLs) for quality. Figure 30.27 illustrates a typical quality criteria, defects per hundred machines (DPHM). The lower dashed line represents the best knowledge of competitive quality performance (as a function of complexity). To achieve parity with that competitor, internal quality targets need to be issued at these values.

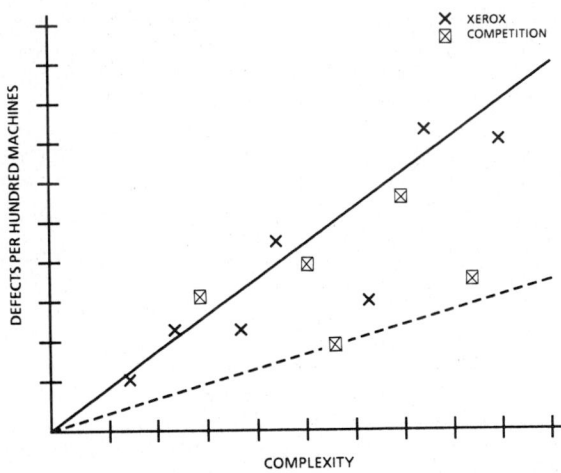

FIG. 30.27 Estimated competitive levels (ECLs) of quality.

Competitive Benchmarking. "Competitive benchmarking" at Xerox is "the continuous process of measuring our products, services, and practices against our toughest competitors or those companies renowned as the leaders." Competitive benchmarking is a relatively new concept. However, many companies have previously used elements of benchmarking, such as measures of product cost, delivery, and quality (including customer satisfaction), to set long-range objectives and to establish the basis for quality improvement programs designed to achieve either parity with or an advantage over the competition. A significant amount of information is available from newsletters that rank industrial products by customer satisfaction, reliability, and features. Other organizations, such as Consumers Union, provide evaluations of products, particularly appliances and automobiles. Many automotive publications, such as *Car and Driver,* evaluate various U.S. automobile models against each other and against their foreign counterparts. This information is important for an objective assessment of product features, which, in a large part, generate a customer's perception of good quality. Selected customers evaluate the features and benefits of the developed product well before the product is introduced to the market. Of course, after this evaluation, the development phase must be able to accommodate the changes obtained from this customer evaluation. The assessment of market and customer needs is described in Section 12, Field Intelligence.

Production Process Instructions.   The production documentation referred to as the "production process instructions" includes the inspection points, the characteristics for inspection, and data recording procedures. Various systems have been used to automatically record and process data, perform fairly sophisticated statistical analysis, and provide visual displays of data (control charts). Several automotive industries and suppliers of automotive components (such as carburetors) have used automatic assembly and data processing and recording systems for many years. These data processing and recording terminals and work stations should be an integral part of the assembly process, and the worker and supervisor should be trained in data analysis techniques as well as in simple trend analysis. Other key inspection steps are generally incorporated into the final test procedures, which are performed on 100 percent of the outgoing products. Future objectives are to achieve such a state of total production process stability and control that economies can be effected simply by sampling (i.e., audit), and the need for a final test station can be eliminated.

Inspection Instructions.   These criteria are normally contained in a written manufacturing process document used by the worker and/or by in-process inspectors. The inspection instructions are developed by quality engineers, based on dimensions specified on the product design drawings and on historical product and processing problems. In high-volume assembly industries, these instructions are an integral part of the semiautomated assembly process. In the automotive and copier industries, inspection checks have been incorporated into the robotic or automated assembly methods used on the production line.

Requirements for Line Workers.   Another class of criteria includes the job requirements for production workers and inspectors. Job descriptions (requirements) are developed and production workers are trained in classrooms, laboratories (product training), and at work stations. This training should take place *before* they are assigned to the production line or reassigned to a production line for a different product model.

Tool Tryout Assessment.   Line tooling tryouts establish the capability of the production phase tooling to provide stable dimensions and to establish what the variation from required tolerances will be. Management of tooling tryouts is a continuous process from the issuance of soft tooling to the acquisition of hard tooling that supports the high-volume production phase. Tooling tryouts should be handled just as carefully with regard to data collection, evaluation, and corrective action as the initial design phase because these tryouts have the most impact on subassembly integrity. Statistical process control studies have been run by both automotive and copier manufacturers on their tooling to provide information on dimensions and variations from them so that they can be fully assured of a work station that will support production requirements. If the source of supply changes from a certified supplier to a new supplier, this change can also affect the assembly process. The new supplier's capability must be assessed before a full cut-in of the new material is accomplished.

ASSEMBLY PROCESS AND CONTROLS

Product Flow.   The assembly process is remarkably similar across different assembly firms. Copier manufacturers, electronic equipment firms, and automobile companies all use progressive assembly lines where material is either kitted or produced in bulk and then sent through a progressive line.

Production volume must be considered early in the development of the program's manufacturing plan; however, it is not constant and is subject to adjustment during production. For example, when market requirements increase, expansion from single- to double- or triple-shift operations must be considered and planned for in advance. Often production facilities constrain the optimum balance of line stations. Figures 30.22 to 30.24 show a singular work flow uniting a series of work stations and inspection stations. The stations range from simple operations on minor assemblies to major module assembly and final system integration. The assembly process work flow should be defined early because the relationship of production standards to inspection points, worker group training, and worker assignment depend on this particular flow. The layout of major assembly and inspection equipment is also dependent on the flow of the line. Responsibilities for developing the work flow fall, in many cases, to the production and industrial engineering personnel.

Quality Objectives.   Long-range objectives should be primarily qualitative; for example, the XYZ Company will have the highest perceived image of product quality of all producers of word processing equipment in the international market. Short-range (i.e., annual, quarterly) objectives can also be qualitative, but should primarily be quantitative objectives that have a clearly defined method for measurement. For example:

- All products from the Northern Division will demonstrate a 40 percent reduction in defects per hundred machines when measured by product quality audit.
- The number of design changes from the Antisubmarine Warfare Design Department will be less than 1.5 per original drawing.
- All airborne electronics products will have at least a 25 percent increase in mean time between failures (MTBF) by year end.

Quality Targets.   Many copier firms use three units of measure for defining quantitative quality targets:

1. *Percent problem-free:* Measured before product delivery via the post pack audit procedure. It is also used to measure quality during the installation of the product in customer facilities.
2. *Defects per hundred machines:* Measured internally via the post pack audit procedure.

3. *Parts per million:* Quality of supplier components/material as evaluated during use on the production line.

The first two criteria, "percent problem-free" and "defects per hundred machines," are related in terms of defects observed (i.e., a defect is a problem). The strategy for establishing quality targets can range from setting progressively tighter levels—yearly levels of improvement—to using competitive product quality data (estimated competitive levels) and establishing quality levels based on what the competition has achieved. "Parts per million" has been used both to eliminate the psychological impact of sampling inspection and to define the degree of unacceptable defect levels. Percent defective levels or percent acceptable quality levels (AQLs) often led production firms to assume that material quality levels were adequate. One of the main reasons was a fairly common misunderstanding of the use of AQLs for sampling plan selections compared to the actual incoming and outgoing quality levels. The criterion of parts per million can be used to target and measure the quality of all commodities and materials—regardless of type—as these materials are used in the assembly operations. This criterion reflects the amount of noncomforming material as a percentage of the total amount of material required to support the production line.

Quality Feedback. For many years, major critical modules (e.g., printed wiring board assemblies) were measured against percent defective targets (i.e., 2.7 percent defective)—the expected and allowable quality defect level for a commodity from a supplier. Figure 30.28 shows a numerical display, in terms of parts per million by commodity and by supplier, that was used to focus attention on the need for corrective action based on the quality performance of an electronic/electromechanical commodity during system assembly operations. This system, however, did not apply to all types of mechanical parts and subassemblies. The parts per million criterion is a more comprehensive method used to establish annual quality objectives and to create opportunities for the identification of products, processes, or suppliers in need of quality improvement. The reasons are primarily that it provides a more universally understood language of quality levels than process averages and better describes the impact of defects on the company.

Another form of quality measurement became fairly prevalent in the early

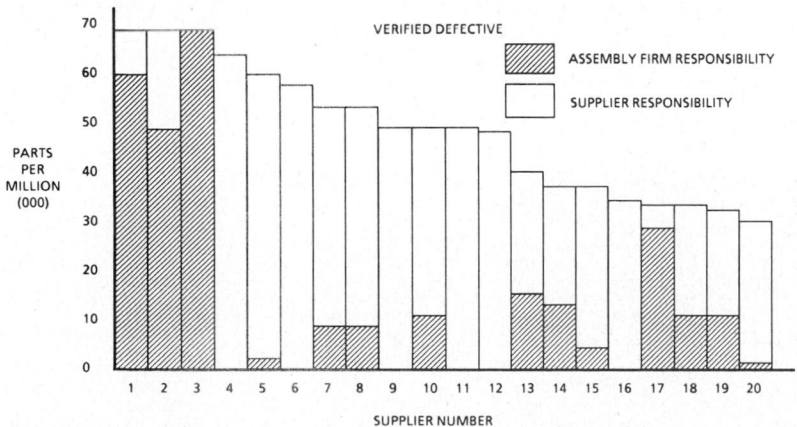

FIG. 30.28 Quality summary electronic/electromechanical components.

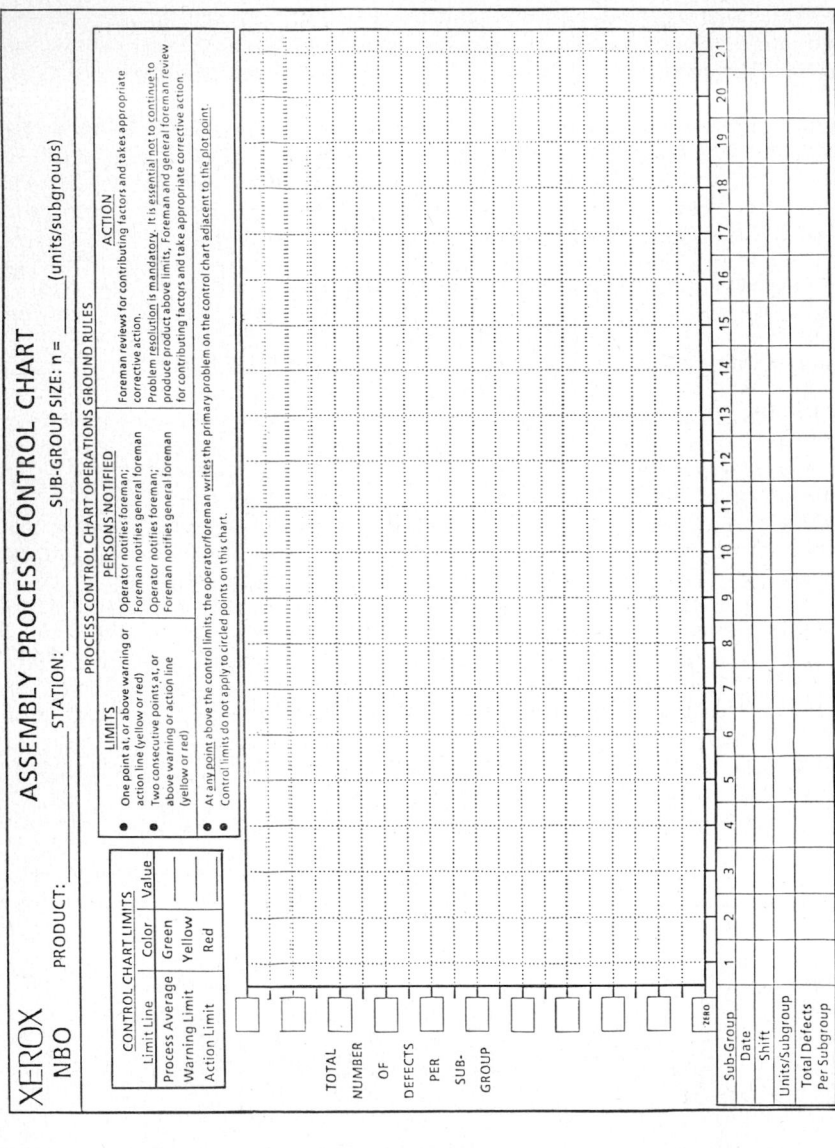

FIG. 30.29 Assembly process control chart.

1980s—the use of process control charts at each applicable line station. Many variations in these charts have been used, but one of the more effective types is the chart of defects per lot (i.e., 20 subassemblies) against preestablished control limits. A listing of the defects found by type could be recorded by the production operator at the work station. A typical display of this type is shown in Figure 30.29. In-line final test defect records are used to collect an extensive amount of information. Collection of in-line defect data by sophisticated automatic measurment and recording systems is described in Section 27 under New Process Quality. Analyses by laboratory and specially skilled personnel verify the causes of product nonconformance to specification and determine whether the defects are a function of the design, the assembly process, or other factors. Failure analysis laboratories, which also employ highly skilled personnel, are necessary to identify mechanisms of failure in components. These laboratories are an integral part of the analytical system that support the data collection process. Data summaries and analyses provide the basis for input to a corrective action system. Different forms of corrective action systems used by equipment assembly companies are summarized above under Corrective Action Systems.

Customer Service Support. Markets for assembly industries can be divided into at least four major segments. One segment is the government, such as an agency of the Department of Defense (the Army, the Navy, or the Air Force). A second segment, defined as original equipment manufacturers (OEMs), is a defined set of companies (i.e., customers). A third segment is a potentially very broad market, the private sector or industrial or direct customers of the product. The fourth segment is an industrial market of corporations that have specific industrial needs, such as the data processing industries, the banking industries, or insurance and financial planning organizations. A fifth external market is that of distributors. This market is really not independent, but provides products to most of the first four markets just mentioned.

Sales to OEMs and the Government.   Figure 30.30 shows the seven major channels of sale for most assembled products. Sales in channels 1 and 2 often undergo

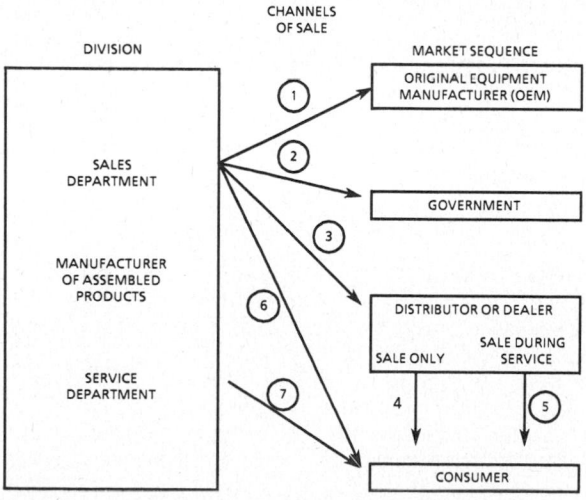

FIG. 30.30   Channels of distribution, sales, agents, lease.

a degree of preacceptance inspection, so that feedback data are usually available and prompt. In contrast, sales through the remaining channels do not automatically yield such data, so special provisions must be made to collect such data, over and above in-house quality and reliability testing programs.

Sales to Distributors. See Figure 30.30, channel 3. Some distributors (and dealers) purchase products in large volume. One method for securing feedback from their customers is for the assembly firm to select certain service distributors as special data sources. A joint program is worked out, and the distributors are given extra compensation to provide the data needed by the assembly firm. A further approach, used with selected distributors who have product test facilities, is a program of "open and test." This is done on a sampling basis related to quantities purchased, in collaboration with the assembly firm's field representatives. Data such as these serve two main purposes:

1. As a prompt feedback of troubles encountered
2. As a source of analysis and of correlation with other data

Sales to Consumers. See Figure 30.30, channels 4 through 7. These sales are made one at a time to customers who, though they certainly lack test facilities and may even lack technical knowledge of the product, are able to respond in other ways.

For example, car sales are seldom direct from the assembly firm to the user; they usually take place through intermediate distributors and dealers. Because the car is a long-life product, the manufacturer's continuing obligations for product performance and reliability are also transmitted through this distribution chain, which includes the dealers, garages or speciality shops, and local service stations.

Role of the Dealer. The dealer's contract with the car manufacturers imposes various obligations on that dealer for product quality. The dealer's role is not only to sell cars, but also to:

1. Deliver the vehicle in good condition and transmit the manufacturer's information (on vehicle care, etc.).
2. Maintain good customer relations, including repair service, facilitation of recalls, and claim adjustment.
3. Provide the manufacturer with data on customer experience, vehicle performance, and defective parts as feedback for improving present products and for planning new products.
4. Accept used vehicles as trade-ins on new cars.

The Vehicle Service System. Cars are driven over long distances and in many geographical areas. During operation, they require local sources of fuel, other supplies, inspection services, and repair services. To meet these needs, a system of vehicle service has evolved.

During the warranty period, car dealers provide this service. After the warranty expires, the customer has a range of choices, including the car dealer shops. Local service stations can make the more frequent minor repairs and replacements. More extensive repairs usually require the services of garages or specialty shops.

Service Support in the Appliance Industry. The marketing of household appliances follows two main routes: bulk sales to, for example, building contractors, laundromats, caravan manufacturers, etc., and sales to individual customers through intermediate appliance dealers, department stores, and discount houses. Service facilities are provided in several different ways: factory-owned service companies, franchised service companies, distributor service departments, selling dealers, utility companies, independent service centers, and self-maintenance (by large users, e.g., laundromats). The most common market is through a combination of selling dealers and independent service centers.

An effective repair/service program is needed for these markets. Effective repair service requires good original design for maintainability, trained repairpersons, and a supply of spare parts. The growing complexity of appliances has required the use of training courses, service repair manuals, parts lists, "exploded" views, and other aids to improve the skills and competence of the repairperson. The supply of spare parts has likewise become complex to the point that original planning for a new model must include provisions for having spare parts available once the model goes on sale. Neglect of such planning (and weak inventory controls) has caused long delays for some customers. Discontinuing a model does not abolish the need for spare parts, because appliances still in use will need spares for years to come. Reputable manufacturers usually stock spare parts for about 10 years after discontinuing the model. In widespread marketing areas, especially in international distribution, these parts stocks are difficult to maintain.

As many as 30 to 50 percent of all service calls could be avoided if customers followed the provisions of the "use and care" manuals provided by manufacturers. However, surveys have shown that these manuals are seldom read and are often merely put aside or discarded once the appliance has been unpacked or installed. Some manufacturers try to overcome this by permanently attaching the essential information to the product. Government surveys show that unsatisfactory service is the biggest single source of customer complaints about appliances. (See U.S. Department of Commerce, 1974.) One study included an analysis of 415 letters containing approximately 1000 complaints about appliances. Complaints predominantly concerned service (lack of competent repairpersons and the unavailability of service or parts) and design and production (burned-out motors, broken plastic parts, clogging disposers, "sweating" freezers, faulty timers, corroding ovens and other types of product failures). Customers also complained about the nonfulfillment and inadequacy of warranties; e.g., the most frequent breakdowns were the most expensive, but the least often covered by guarantee.

Poor quality household appliances are understandably one of the focal points of the consumer movement. At the very outset, when consumers are considering purchase, they are confronted with numerous choices of brands and models. Yet they usually lack the objective information needed to choose what best meets their needs, despite the fact that the appliance may be a major expenditure. As noted, any failure disturbs the orderly daily life the consumer has built on the assumption that the appliance will continue to work. The real difficulties of securing satisfaction on the warranties—and of securing service after the warranty period—have aggravated matters further. It is therefore not surprising that appliance users have been among the most vocal in their complaints. In addition, having concluded that many manufacturers are not responsive to the complaints of individual consumers, appliance users have turned to alternative sources of product information and alternative organizations in an attempt to get satisfaction.

These alternatives extend to independent laboratories, consumer unions, government agencies, standardization bodies, etc. (See Section 3, under Consumer Products.)

RESPONSIBILITY PATTERNS

Responsibility for Quality.   A belief has existed, particularly in the design and production departments, that they alone are responsible for the design, build, and ship functions and that the quality organization alone is responsible for quality. This feeling has lead to many problems, typified by the following statements:

- "Inspection makes the product better."
- "Let's let the inspection department inspect the quality in."
- "Let's use as is."
- "Hire more inspectors because the material coming into receiving inspection has a high defect level."
- "If we eliminate half of the inspectors, the quality level will improve."

Companywide quality control (CWQC) or total quality control (TQC) programs emphasize that quality is a result of action by *all* departments and personnel. Sections 12 through 21 describe the tasks in various functional departments that will lead to achieving fitness for use.

Crosby (1979) gives the following good advice to the quality manager. Identify the name or cause of each quality problem: "We have a design problem"; "The supplier's process is unstable"; or "The cause of the covers falling off is due to poor welding." In this way, the resources of the responsible organization can be applied to eliminate the customer's complaint. Identification of all customer problems as quality problems only indicates that the Quality Department has done an inadequate inspection, measurement, or audit, and considerably shortens the tenure of the incumbent quality manager. A typical example, described below, is of a photocopy machine manufacturer whose machine showed unsatisfactory copy quality, leading to a perception of poor product quality. There are a number of causes for unacceptable copy quality. Two examples will suffice to illustrate the diversity of responsibility required to solve this quality problem.

The first example is that of a transfer subsystem design that results in copy streaking, and the second is that of an improper assembly of the toner (dry ink) that causes excessive toner to be deposited on the copy. In the first case, a design change is needed to eliminate the streaking problem. In the second case, the process and (possibly) operations require a change (and workers trained for that change) in the inspection sequence so that overtoning is eliminated. In the first example, it is the responsibility of the design department to eliminate the "quality problem." In the second example, it is the responsibility of production operations with the support of line quality control, and possibly design engineering assistance, to eliminate the "quality problem."

Quality Activities.   To establish the quality budget, identification of the quality activities is essential. In its simplest form, the formation of the quality organization is the meaningful grouping of quality activities into functions. These functions are then organized by department to allow the resources (i.e., personnel,

TABLE 30.4 Typical Quality Activities

1. Review customer/contract requirements	26. Corrective action system
2. Prepare quality plans	27. Quality reporting and measurement
3. Preparation of quality policies, and procedures	28. Purchased material inspection
4. Training	29. Supplier source inspection
5. Issue quality manual	30. Supplier rating system
6. Standards of workmanship	31. Discrepant supplier list
7. Procurement quality planning	32. Electrical test process certification
8. Supplier surveys	33. Configuration verification
9. Supplier quality requirements	34. Visual inspection
10. Inspection planning	35. Production tool inspection
11. Environmental test planning	36. Mechanical inspection
12. Quality assurance coordination	37. Packaging inspection
13. Drawing/specification review	38. Product audit
14. Engineering data conformance	39. Qualification test
15. Change control board	40. Environmental test
16. Process specification review	41. Reliability measurement and demonstration
17. First article approval	42. Interchangeability
18. Engineering product acceptance	43. Materials review
19. Systems audit	44. Records
20. Process certification and control	45. Integrated test planning
21. Data collection	46. Component screening
22. Data analysis	47. Process detail review
23. Measurement standards	48. Maintainability demonstration
24. Gage control	49. Reliability assurance
25. Budgets and cost control	50. Product safety assurance

expense, and capital costs) to be optimized with regard to services rendered to the organization. Table 30.4 illustrates typical quality activities of either a large or small assembly company. Table 30.5 illustrates the responsibilities for the major quality activities by functional department.

DATA PLAN

Internal Systems. This information covers supplier activity, receiving inspection, in-process line stations, and final test. An internal quality reporting system consists of at least four prime sources. The data from each source supplier (supplier plant or assembly plant receiving inspection), in process line station, final test, and quality audit have two major uses. The first is to define the major problems associated with the hardware found at each source. The second, and most important, is to identify the corrective action required throughout the entire production process.

1. *Supplier site:*   This information includes final inspection results and certified data on components, materials, and process capability.
2. *In-process inspection:*   In-process inspection information includes various types of control charts and tabulations of defects, which reflect repetitive problems requiring corrective action somewhere within the production process.

TABLE 30.5 Table of Responsibility*

Activity	Functions or departments available for participation								
	Market research	Marketing	Service	Product development and design	Manufacturing planning	Purchasing	Production	Inspection	Quality control
Definition stage:									
Identification of customer quality needs	XX	X		X					
Definition of new product in terms of product specification	X	X		XX					
Preliminary design stage:									
Judging and testing components				XX					
Making prototypes				XX					
Testing and analysis of prototypes				XX					X
Design review			X	XX	X	X			X
Final design stage:									
Testing components				XX					X
Testing and analysis of prototypes				XX					
Establishing tolerances and classification of characteristics				XX					
Establishing visual standards for appearance	X	X		XX					
Preparation of component specifications				XX					
Design review			X	XX	X	X			X
Pilot production stage:									
Planning of manufacturing setup				X	XX		X		XX
Design, ordering, and tryout of tools and other equipment					XX		X		XX
Design and ordering of quality information equipment				X	X		X	X	XX
Selection of suppliers				X		XX	X		X

Activity								
Evaluation of new suppliers (in respect to quality)			X	X		X		XX
Planning of process inspection and final inspection			X	X		X	X	XX
Planning of receiving inspection				X			X	XX
Initial sample inspection			X	X			X	XX
Evaluation of parts to be used in prepilot and pilot runs			X	X			X	XX
Prepilot and pilot runs			X	XX		X		X
Testing and evaluation of units produced in prepilot and pilot runs				X		X	X	XX
Prepilot and pilot run review			XX	X		X		X
Planning of maintenance and calibration of quality information equipment			X	X		X		XX
Preparation of service manuals and spare parts lists		XX	X					
Preparation of use and care manuals	XX	X						
Production stage:								
Operating processes as specified				X		XX		X
Executing inspection as specified			X	X		X	XX	XX
Disposition of parts and materials not meeting the specifications					X		X	X
Reporting and analysis of internal failures				X		X	X	XX
Quality rating of outgoing product			X					XX
Life testing			X					XX
Use stage:								
Reporting and analysis of external failures	X	XX	X	X		X	X	X
Meetings for solving quality problems		X	X			X		XX
Reporting quality costs								XX

*XX = primary, X = secondary.

3. *Final test:*   Defect data collected during final test typically are grouped by assembly, design and components, as shown in Figure 30.31.

4. *Post-pack audit:*   In post-pack audit, the data system is one of a defect base (or demerits or service cost). Data are used both to identify problems in the production process and to measure outgoing product quality.

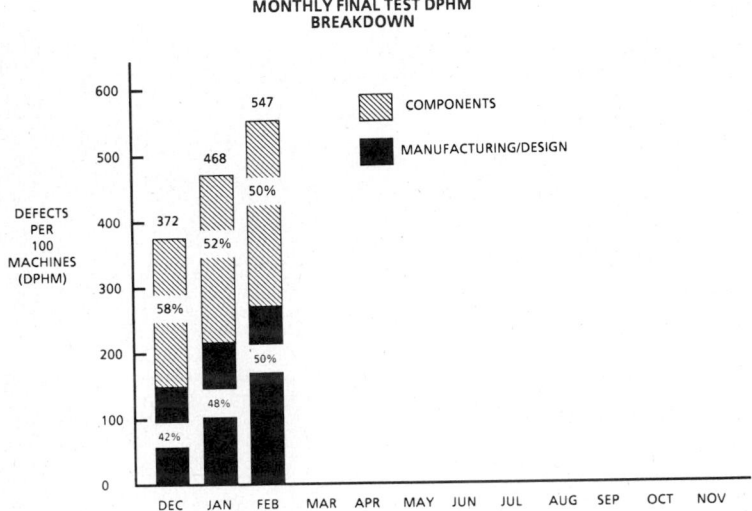

FIG. 30.31   Quality defect summary—by responsibility.

If there are numerous plants within each of several divisions within a business group, quality reports should be designed to follow the organizational structure of the company. This will dictate the form of the reporting system for the applicable levels of management. The first level includes the in-plant records maintained for measurement and identification of problems with received materials and assembled equipment (Figure 30.32). The second level provides an evaluation of actual quality results against quality objectives. An example of this style is shown in Figure 30.33. At the third or group level, major monthly summaries are distributed (Figure 30.34). Sometimes, it is important to provide the top executive with frequent status reports (Figure 30.35).

Where specific and complex commodities are obtained from suppliers (i.e., internal sources or subcontractors), reporting systems should be customized to measure the quality of these complex modules. In this way, quality trends can be measured over time. Subassemblies that do not conform to the quality objectives can be identified, reasons for nonconformity can be investigated, and corrective action plans can be developed. Expensive or critical commodities (such as motors, blowers, fans, or power supplies) obtained from external suppliers are generally tracked also to identify opportunities for quality improvement.

External Systems.   Most service companies have elaborate field data systems to collect and process information, return defective parts for analysis, and provide measures of reliability, service cost, and quality improvement opportunities.

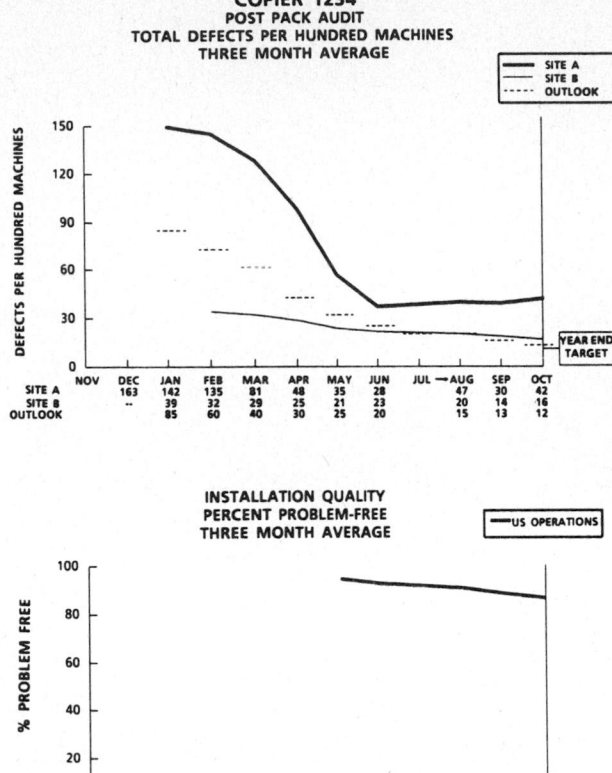

COPIER 1234
POST PACK AUDIT
TOTAL DEFECTS PER HUNDRED MACHINES
THREE MONTH AVERAGE

	NOV	DEC	JAN	FEB	MAR	APR	MAY	JUN	JUL — AUG	SEP	OCT
SITE A		163	142	135	81	48	35	28	47	30	42
SITE B		--	39	32	29	25	21	23	20	14	16
OUTLOOK			85	60	40	30	25	20	15	13	12

INSTALLATION QUALITY
PERCENT PROBLEM-FREE
THREE MONTH AVERAGE

MONTH	NOV	DEC	JAN	FEB	MAR	APR	MAY	JUN	JUL	AUG	SEP	OCT
US OPERATIONS							95	93	90	91	86	83

FIG. 30.32 Quality performance summary.

Table 30.6 illustrates the types of data collection systems used during the introduction of a new product design to the field. The field service reporting system provides measures of the key business variables associated with customer satisfaction and service costs. Typical variables are response time, call duration, emergency order rates, reliability rates, customer service engineer visits per machine per month, installation time, and various forms of service labor and defective material measures such as percent of calls terminated because of defective or missing parts or percent of calls terminated for reasons including parts and other customer service engineer demand factors (i.e., different customer requires service call).

Customer Feedback Systems/Surveys. The customer satisfaction management system of the Xerox Corporation includes the use of a survey questionnaire with 25 questions grouped in four categories: equipment, service, sales, and administration. Quantitative measurements of customer satisfaction with these product and support functions are used to summarize the responses.

Monthly sampling of each product's customer satisfaction level is done to obtain a continual evaluation of trends. Response rates are a minimum of 40 per-

COPIER 1234
POST PACK AUDIT
SITE A

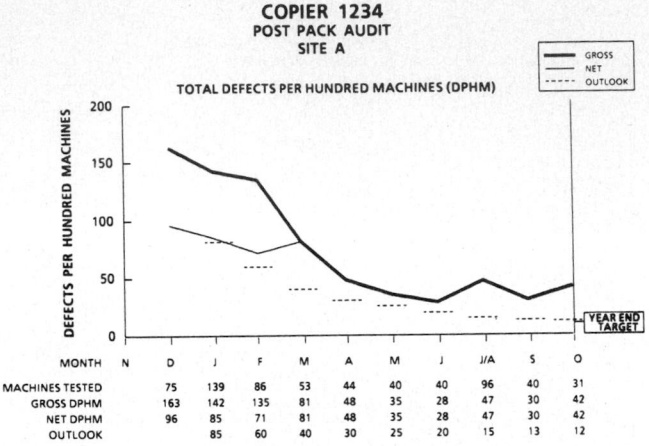

TOTAL DEFECTS PER HUNDRED MACHINES (DPHM)

MONTH	N	D	J	F	M	A	M	J	J/A	S	O
MACHINES TESTED		75	139	86	53	44	40	40	96	40	31
GROSS DPHM		163	142	135	81	48	35	28	47	30	42
NET DPHM		96	85	71	81	48	35	28	47	30	42
OUTLOOK			85	60	40	30	25	20	15	13	12

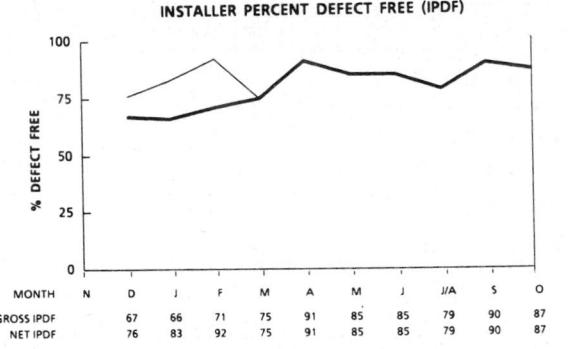

INSTALLER PERCENT DEFECT FREE (IPDF)

MONTH	N	D	J	F	M	A	M	J	J/A	S	O
GROSS IPDF		67	66	71	75	91	85	85	79	90	87
NET IPDF		76	83	92	75	91	85	85	79	90	87

EXECUTIVE SUMMARY

<u>Post Pack Audit (Quality)</u>
- Monthly Performance:
  Total defects per hundred machines met target.

  Total percent Problem-Free three-month average
  unfavorable to target.

- <u>Significant Problems:</u> Defect levels decreased in both
  functional and nonfunctional categories this month. The only
  problem this month (misadjusted paper feed solenoid) was
  allocated to design.

FIG. 30.33 Typical display of quality performance.

REPROGRAPHICS MANUFACTURING OPERATIONS
MAY 1985
QUALITY PERFORMANCE

XEROX - INTERNAL

	DEFECTS PER HUNDRED MACHINES			% PROBLEM FREE		
		3 MO.	MAY		3 MONTH	MAY
	TARGET	ACTUAL	ACTUAL	TARGET	ACTUAL	ACTUAL
SYSTEM A	26	14	--	90%	90%	--
SYSTEM B	28	36	--	89%	79%	--
PRODUCTION SITE A						
INPUT DEVICE #1	3	4	0	99%	76%	100%
INPUT DEVICE #2	4	11	11	98%	96%	98%
PRODUCTION SITE B						
PROCESSOR	20	6	--	92%	97%	--
OUTPUT DEVICE #1	3	4	--	99%	96%	--
OUTPUT DEVICE #2	4	19	43	99%	85%	60%

INSTALLATION (US OPERATIONS)	91%

MANUFACTURING STATUS
PRODUCTION SITE A
- INPUT DEVICE #1 EXHIBITED SECOND MONTH OF DEFECT FREE AUDITS.

- INPUT DEVICE #2 DEGRADED WITH FIVE NON-REPETITIVE ASSEMBLY DEFECTS. CORRECTIVE ACTION INCLUDES LINE, PARTS PURGES, OPERATOR RETRAINING AND ADDITIONAL ASSEMBLY SCREENS.

PRODUCTION SITE B
- OUTPUT DEVICE #2 PRODUCTION NOW ON HOLD PENDING RESOLUTION OF TWO DESIGN PROBLEMS. IT IS EXPECTED THAT THE PROCESSOR/OUTPUT DEVICE #2 HEIGHT MISALIGNMENT PROBLEM WILL BE ADDRESSED AS PART OF OUTPUT DEVICE #2 FIELD INSTALLATION. THE SECOND, TRAY JAMS, WILL BE SOLVED BY RETURN TO AN EARLIER OUTPUT DEVICE #2 CONFIGURATION. RESOLUTION OF BOTH PROBLEMS IS EXPECTED BY 6/15.

FIG. 30.34 Quality performance summary.

To	From
Chief Executive	Quality Office

Subject	Date
Quality Results	June 12, 1985

The Product Quality Audit and installation (field) quality results for the week ending June 7, 1985 are:

	SAMPLE SIZE (WEEK)	DEFECTS PER HUNDRED MACHINES			PROBLEM-FREE		
			4-WEEK	WEEK		4-WEEK	WEEK
		TARGET	AVERAGE	ACTUAL	TARGET	AVERAGE	ACTUAL
AUDIT							
SYSTEM							
A	--	28	--	--	89%	--	--
B	--	25	--	--	91%	--	--
PROD. SITE A (US)							
INPUT DEVICE #1	0	3	--	--	99%	--	--
INPUT DEVICE #2	0	6	--	--	97%	--	--
PROD. SITE B (EUROPE)							
PROCESSOR	13	19	10	8	93%	94%	92%
OUTPUT DEVICE #1	0	3	--	--	99%	--	--
OUTPUT DEVICE #2	0	3	--	--	99%	--	--

INSTALLATION (US OPERATIONS)

- Processor continued to essentially achieve quality targets.

- Output Device #2 production on hold pending resolution of two design problems. It is expected that the height misalignment problem will be corrected by 9/15. The second problem, tray jams, will be solved by return to an earlier configuration. Action will be completed by 6/15.

FIG. 30.35 Quality summary—management.

TABLE 30.6 External Data Sources

Focus group interviews/discussions
User's tests _____
    Customer acceptance test (CAT)
      Internal and external

Product launch _____
    Product launch reporting system

Product installation and ongoing support _____
    Installation quality reporting: Field work support system

Customer satisfaction measurement system (CSMS)
    Customer satisfaction surveys: 100%—after initial installs
                           Sampling—continuous
                           Telephone surveys—periodic

cent per month for each product line and business segment samples (i.e., regional sales and service area). (See Ekings, 1986.)

Other forms of surveys used by the assembly industry are telephone surveys and third party surveys of competitive products. In telephone surveys, a team of personnel, each using the same form, talks directly to the consumer to better understand the reason for customer dissatisfaction. Many companies use telephone "hot lines" to encourage communications from the field service organizations or from customers directly to the quality executive. The service organization in many companies has teams of highly skilled engineers (i.e., tiger teams), sensitive to both service and product problems. These personnel back up the field service organizations and apply higher diagnostic skills to complex problems that cause customer dissatisfaction. These service organizations generally are separate from the organizations that provide the large amount of statistical and historical data referred to previously and are a useful resource when developing quality and reliability improvement programs. They have direct contact with the customer or dealer and, thus, can provide a perception of the customer's dissatisfaction and very detailed cause and effect information on the type of problems experienced by the customers.

Plant Visitation Programs. Xerox uses a plant visitation program to communicate to customer service engineers the corrective actions taken or planned on product problems within the control of the manufacturing organization. This visitation program is repeated quarterly at major production sites and is a key to developing a feeling of mutual support on field problems between the field operations and the assembly plant. Other support problems, such as lack of spares and timely, functional documentation and training, are outside the scope of the responsibilities of the production department, but need to be dealt with to improve support from the headquarters service groups.

Reporting of Field Failures. A key element of a field failure reporting system, whether the reports go to the production plant, or to the director of quality assurance, or to a centralized staff field engineering organization, is a form of documented feedback of corrective action to the field personnel. Such documentation stimulates the customer service engineer to take the time to report and to measure the effectiveness of the data reporting and corrective action system. Figure 30.36 illustrates a closed loop field problem reporting and corrective action system. The corrective actions incorporated by the various departments of the assembly plant are included in a monthly field service publication, which maintains a strong link between the field service and support organizations and the assembly plant.

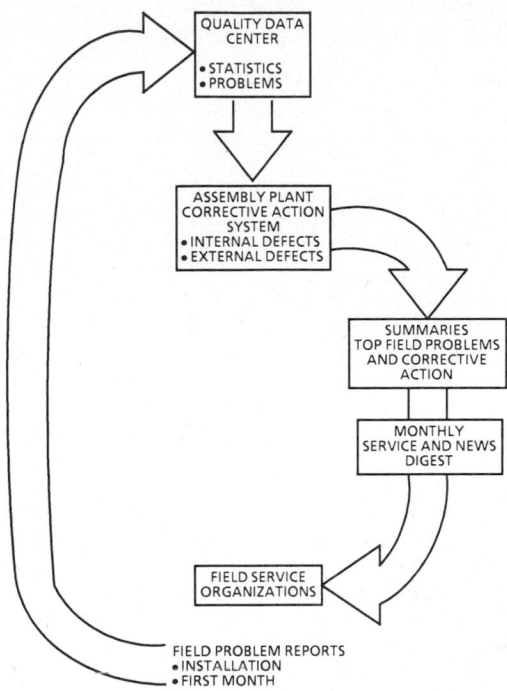

FIG.   30.36 Corrective   action   feedback—field problems.

AUDIT PLAN

Quality Audit Process.   Assembly companies use a variety of audit processes. Three major types of audits can be identified: quality systems audit, product audit, and supplier quality audit (or survey). Supplier quality audit is discussed in Section 15 under Evaluating Supplier Capability.

Quality Systems Audit.   The quality systems audit provides a review of an activity that influences quality. See Section 9 under Quality Audit for the approach used. The audit, as used by companies such as Xerox and Motorola, is accomplished by an independent organization (with no vested interest in the outcome) composed of senior professional quality personnel. Larger companies have a corporate staff that conducts quality systems audits, just as a financial audit would be accomplished by an independent or consulting organization. The systems audit can also be used within major business groups of an enterprise or within divisions of a business enterprise. The primary style, which has been used ever since the audit philosophy was developed by Western Electric, is an audit by skilled personnel. These personnel may also be part of the line organization. The audit team conducts an in-depth review of the organization to determine whether the policies and procedures in the quality manual are, in fact, practiced in the production facilities.

Various measurements or assessments of conformance or nonconformance with the elements of the quality system are used. With the integration of the Design and Manufacturing Departments in recent years, technical audits accomplished by independent teams within the design department have been incorporated with the assessment of the state of readiness of the design as of the production department to build products to a defined production schedule.

Product Audit. Product audits are generally those audit programs done on samples of product ready to be shipped to the customer (see Section 9 under Product Audit). The purpose of product audits is to (1) provide a measurement against preestablished quality objectives, (2) record defect data used to define problems within the design or production process, and (3) identify areas of opportunity for corrective action (Radigan and Zeccardi, 1976). The prime responsibility for detailed investigation and definition of corrective action rests with the program's corrective action team. The information about the source of problems obtained from the audit is invaluable. Product audits are designed to simulate product installation at the customer's site. In the case of copiers, for example, auditors are trained as service engineers. The quality auditors use the documentation and tools of the service engineer. The manner in which the machine is tested and the supplies used are derived from the product performance specification. Correlation of outgoing quality is accomplished by comparing the product audit data to the field quality reporting system data and identifying the variances. Certain problems, such as damage due to shipping or handling, or improper installation or use at the customer account, cannot be detected by the internal product audit. Separate test and evaluation programs are required.

Module and Product System Audit. Some assembly products consist of modules assembled at production sites many thousands of miles apart. An ongoing product audit of the full system is conducted to evaluate interface problems. Using various forms of slave subsystems and test equipment, or simply conducting the audit on the production hardware produced at the manufacturing site, has resulted in system interface problems occurring in the field. The preferred method is to conduct the audit at the facility with primary design and production responsibility. This primary organization is responsible for acquiring and auditing representative production units from nonprimary (module) manufacturing sites and then conducting an audit on the complete product system to assure the quality of the system as it will be configured at the customer's facility.

Product Audit—Reliability. Product audits assess the outgong product's reliability. Common forms are the product reliability assurance tests (PRAT) and the periodic sample reliability tests (i.e., quarterly reliability qualification tests and bi-monthly reliability sampling tests). Product reliability assurance tests are generally a simulation of the product right after installation (i.e., over the first month). The purpose of the test is to detect significant problems; it is not used to statistically measure performance. It can be used to make shipping decisions. Quarterly reliability qualification tests are a shortened version of the original reliability qualification test and are used to detect major changes in the manufacturing process, as well as to assure that the design integrity of the as-built configuration is maintained throughout production. Bimonthly reliability sampling tests are similar to quarterly tests, but are frequently used to make shipping decisions.

QUALITY IMPROVEMENT

Projects for quality improvement are identified by applying the Pareto principle to the summaries of field failures, quality rating of outgoing products, quality costs, etc. Discovering the causes for chronic defects usually requires in-depth statistical and operational analysis. The wide geographic dispersion of use and the difficulties of transportation add to the complexity of the problems and, thereby, to the need for competent analyses.

Appliance assembly companies often make special arrangements with a few selected service shops to obtain all replaced parts and the related repair information for the type of defect being studied. This information may be supplemented by special questionnaires or report forms filled out by repairpersons. These forms are especially useful in studying damage caused in transit. Such forms can show the nature and location of the damage to the appliance and the location of the damaged appliance in the transport vehicle.

Remedies for chronic defects follow conventional practices (see Section 22, Quality Improvement). As a follow-up to see if the changes have produced the desired improvement, dates of manufacture are used to compare the performance of units made before and after the change. Organization for quality improvement almost always requires an interdepartmental approach, though the degree of formality varies. Some firms use formal teams, with members from Design, Production, Quality, Sales, and Service. These teams are given wide latitude for guiding projects and stimulating corrective actions. As in other industries, the causes of most problems can be controlled by management.

Extensive training in quality improvement programs has occurred since 1980 in all assembly industries for all personnel. Many firms have developed problem-solving or quality-improvement processes. One such quality-improvement process is used by the Xerox Corporation. Xerox Corporation's Leadership Through Quality strategy has, as part of its initial phase, a 40-h training module that *all* company personnel attend—from the CEO on down. The Nine-Step Quality Improvement Process is part of this training (Figure 30.37). This quality improvement process has been used effectively in many ways, from redesigning staff meetings to addressing technical problems associated with limited photoreceptor life in the field.

Equipment assembly firms have extended training in quality improvement to their suppliers. These programs were developed (1) to make suppliers an integral part of the organization, (2) to achieve volume pricing advantages in product cost, and (3) to achieve a 100 percent defect-free product, which avoids line outages due to the loss of continuity of supply of materials to the line. These programs required extensive strategic planning, increased resources to train the trainers, and an allocation of time for training both the suppliers and the internal departments. The ultimate goal is to focus on the processing of materials and components so that a greater compatibility can be achieved between the design requirements of the component and the capability of the process and supplier to achieve a consistently defect-free product. The incidences of material outages, defective materials, and poor product quality have decreased dramatically, and the morale of the production workers has greatly increased.

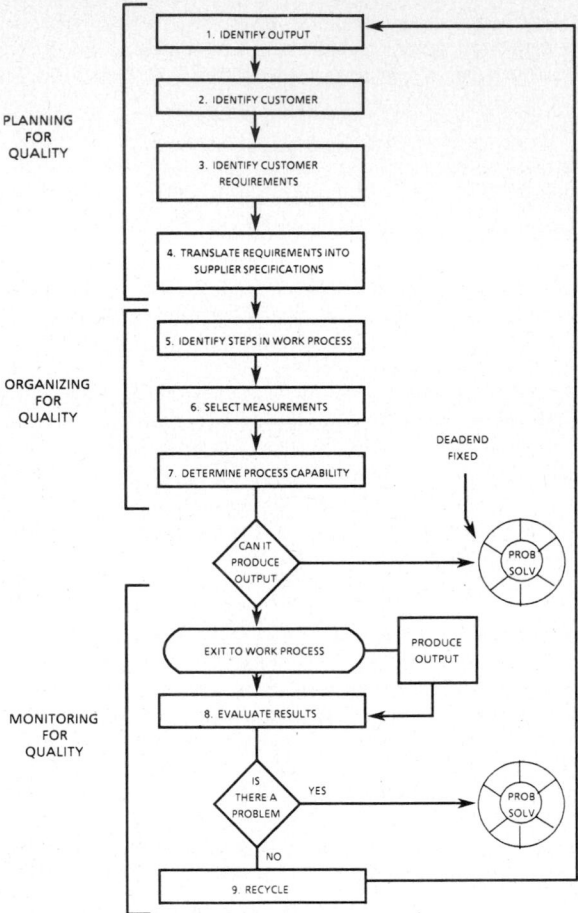

FIG. 30.37   Quality improvement process—nine steps.

SUMMARY AND OUTLOOK

The quality system described and illustrated in this section must, of course, be an integral part of the design, development, and production processes, not an after-the-fact overlay. It is hoped that the reader using this section will be able to clearly discern the difference between corrective actions that improve the quality of the design and production processes and corrective actions that improve the product hardware. This is a critical distinction.

Quality is the No. 1 business issue in the United States today (Gallup Survey, 1987). In particular, the senior managers of U.S. assembly firms recognize that a company with a quality strategy has the foundation for market growth (or survival) over the next decade. All major assembly firms are defining and implementing quality management processes for all organizations.

The American Society for Quality Control refers to the "quality professional." Yesterday's quality professional worked in the Quality Control, Inspection, or

Reliability Departments. However, if the manufacturing firms of the assembly industry are to improve quality, reduce the cost of quality, and reduce product-development delivery time, then each employee must become a quality professional.

ACKNOWLEDGMENTS

I would like to recognize the very significant editorial support of Ms. Diane Barr and members of her staff of Xerox Corporation. The secretarial support of C. Castell, B. Lanham, and Sue Szczepanski is also very much appreciated. The explicit contributions of P. Russo, R. W. Sweetland, and R. Sholts of Xerox were very helpful. The implicit help of nearly all the individuals noted in the References and, of course, of many others has enabled me to write this section as well as to succeed in the quality profession.

REFERENCES

AGREE, Advisory Group on Reliability of Electronic Equipment (1958). *Reliability of Military Electronic Equipment.* Office of Assistant Secretary of Defense, Washington, DC.

Caplan, F. (1980). *The Quality System.* Chilton, Radnor, PA.

Crosby, P. B. (1979). *Quality is Free: The Art of Making Quality Certain.* McGraw-Hill, New York.

Ekings, J. D. (1986). "A Nine-Step Quality Improvement Process to Improve Customer Satisfaction." *Transactions of the 30th European Organization for Quality Control,* Stockholm, June, pp. 323–328.

Ekings, J. D. and Hill, T. D. (1982). "MTBF Requirements—Nice or Competitive." *Reliability Review,* vol. 2, no. 4, pp. 51–52.

Ekings, J. D. and Sweetland, R. L. (1978). "Burn-In Forever: There Must Be a Better Way!" *Proceedings, Annual Reliability and Maintainability Symposium.* IEEE, New York, pp. 286–293.

Ekings, J. D. (1976). "Profit and Customer Satisfaction Equals the Specification for Commercial Reliability Programs." *Proceedings, Annual Reliability and Maintainability Symposium.* IEEE, New York.

"Excellence in England." (1985). *Quality Progress,* September, pp. 19–24.

Feigenbaum, A. V. (1986). *Total Quality Control,* 3rd ed. McGraw-Hill, New York.

Gallup Survey (1987). *Executives Perceptions concerning the Quality of American Products and Services.* Gallup Organization, Princeton, NJ.

Juran, J. M. (1979a). *Managerial Breakthrough.* McGraw-Hill, New York.

Juran, J. M. (1979b). "Japanese and Western Quality—A Contrast." *Quality,* January and February.

Madigan, M. J. (1981). *Introduction to Statistical Quality Control.* Xerox training manual.

Radigan, R. A. and Zeccardi, J. J. (1976). "Auditing Systems which Affect Product Quality." *ASQC Quality Congress Transactions,* Milwaukee, pp. 323–329.

Shahnazarian, T. (1964). (Private letter, Nov. 10, 1986.)

Sie, C. (1981). (Private letter, Jan. 17, 1987.)

U.S. Department of Commerce (1974). *Report of the Task Force on Appliance Warranties and Service.* Washington, DC, p. 166.

Veraldi, L. C. (1985). *The Team Taurus Story.* Paper presented at the MIT Conference, Chicago, Aug. 22.

SECTION 31
COMPLEX INDUSTRIES[1]

H. Dean Voegtlen

INTRODUCTION 31.1

A MESSAGE FROM THE TOP . . 31.2

The Staircase of Quality
Improvement 31.3

Management Establishes
the Quality Climate . . . 31.3

QUALITY MANAGEMENT
MODEL 31.4

Definitions 31.6

General Requirements . . . 31.7

Critical Tasks 31.7

Responsibilities 31.8

ACHIEVING PRODUCT QUALITY
ATTRIBUTES—THE RELIABILITY
EXAMPLE 31.9

Reliability Engineering
Management 31.9

THE PROGRAM MANAGEMENT
FUNCTION 31.11

Development Risk
Control 31.12

The Transition from
Development to
Production 31.13

APPLYING THE LESSONS
LEARNED 31.19

THE QUALITY/VALUE
RELATIONSHIP 31.20

The Value Engineering
Process 31.20

Quality Enhancement . . . 31.22

A Team Approach 31.23

REFERENCES 31.24

INTRODUCTION

Complex industries are generally characterized by both the nature of their products and their organizational structures. The products are complex, consisting of tens of thousands to millions of discrete parts and including assemblies, units, equipment, subsystems, and complete systems. Typical of such products are com-

---

[1] In the Third Edition, this section was prepared by Dr. Leslie W. Ball.

mercial and military satellites, radar systems, missiles, telecommunication centers, navigational systems, aerospace equipment, and mainframe computers, to name just a few. The products involve many technologies in the physical, chemical, electronic, and mechanical sciences, each of which is moving forward at an ever-increasing pace. New knowledge emerges and is applied in prototype development, tested, and incorporated into new or upgraded product. These complex products each have an array of quality characteristics all of which are important, in one way or another, to the customer. For example, the primary functional requirements of range, speed, accuracy, power output, memory, lethality, etc., are augmented by characteristics such as reliability, maintainability, safety, availability, flexibility, and reusability. Furthermore, many of these products contain a large amount of computer software, which frequently serves as the brain of the system—the executive function that programs and directs its operations.

As the products are complex, so also are the companies that create them, and frequently, the organizations that buy them and use them—the customers. Most manufacturers of complex products employ hundreds of subcontractors and suppliers. The integration of these outside sources of product elements together with the internal portion constitutes a development-systems engineering-production-human resources and capital management challenge of considerable complexity. It is inevitable that such organizations follow a policy of decentralization and delegation of work and that specialization within many technical and management fields is essential.

How then does the quality message get through to this very large constituency that makes up the typical complex product producer? Certainly the sections in this handbook dealing with managerial and statistical concepts contain relevant information applicable in a large measure to the complex industries' quality task. In this section we will look briefly at several topics, which although not exclusively limited to the complex product arena, embody practices frequently followed in the attainment of quality in these industries. The topics to be discussed are:

1. A message from the top
2. A quality management model
3. Achieving quality attributes
4. The program management function
5. Applying the lessons learned
6. The quality-value relationship

A MESSAGE FROM THE TOP

Serving the needs of others is the only legitimate business in the world today.[2]

The mid-1980s has witnessed the beginnings of a revolution in quality awareness and purpose. Throughout the world, consumers are demanding better quality, and companies are mounting major quality improvement efforts. This trend has special meaning in the complex product area. Organizations are large, and the quality message is difficult to send clearly and meaningfully down through the hierarchy.

---

[2]A. P. Giannini (1870–1949)—founder of the Bank of America.

Many companies are adopting the principle that every part of the organization, every department, every operation, indeed, every individual has a customer with legitimate quality requirements to be met. Quality goals, including criteria and methods of measurement, are being established throughout entire organizations. Teamwork across organizational boundaries to solve quality problems or achieve higher quality levels is becoming common practice in some more enlightened companies.

The Staircase of Quality Improvement. The quality improvement trend is effectively described by Hayes (1985) in an article on today's management challenge. Figure 31.1 shows successive levels of increasing quality awareness and the resultant actions within an organization. This hierarchy provides an indication of a company's cultural climate, management's prevailing philosophy about running the company, and steps that may be taken to improve quality and productivity.

Most companies in the complex product field will range across the spectrum from Stage 1 to Stage 5 in Figure 31.1. Portions of the organization will be trapped in the past practices that once worked for them but are characteristic of the turmoil and coercive management of Stages 1 and 2. Other portions will operate in the Stage 3 and 4 modes, while some elements of the company may be moving into the truly team effort approach of Stage 5. Juran (1985) believes that exhortation and excessive absorption in statistical methods for their own sake instead of as the means to an end, are giving way to strategic quality planning, project-by-project quality improvement, and hands-on leadership by upper management.

Management Establishes the Quality Climate A number of forward-looking companies in the high-tech complex product field are making fundamental changes in their policies and practices, which address quality excellence head on.

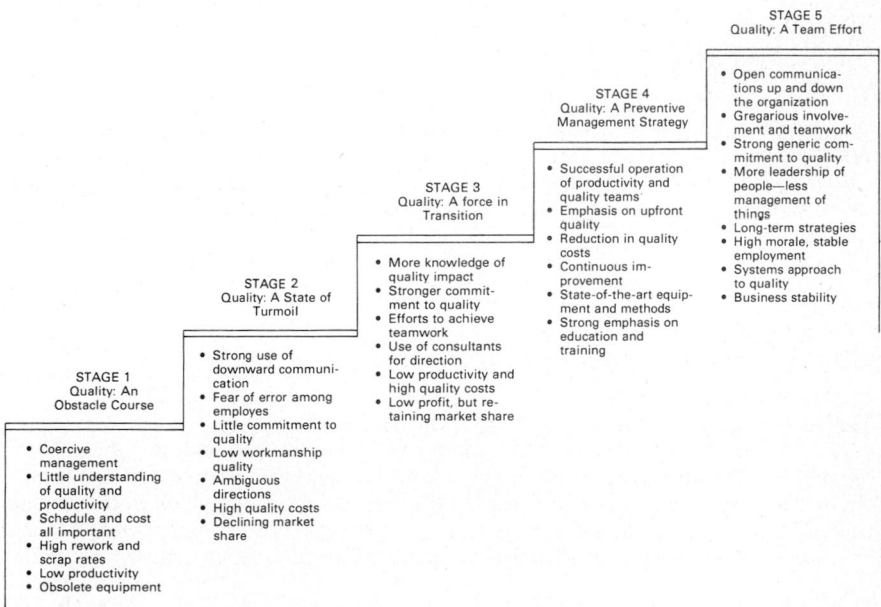

FIG. 31.1 Up the staircase to quality and productivity improvement.

A major corporation in the commercial product field has enunciated the following principles:

1. Quality is the basic principle for us to continue to be a leadership company.
2. We will understand our customer's existing and latent requirements.
3. We will provide all our external and internal customers with products and services that meet their requirements.
4. Employee involvement through participative problem solving is essential to improve quality.
5. Error-free work is the most cost-effective way to improve quality.

A major defense contractor has identified six major goals of which product quality is key:

- To delivery quality products and services in a timely manner and provide complete support of these products
- To maintain a highly motivated employee population with the highest standards of integrity, professionalism, and competence
- To continually improve productivity through emphasis on quality and effective interaction of technology, capital, and human resources
- To attain earnings necessary to provide investment for human resources, research and development, facilities, working capital, and corporate obligations
- To explore and expand the frontiers of the company's technologies and seek useful applications in defense, space, and industrial markets
- To conduct business in a manner that fully meets corporate responsibility to society

This company has further developed a quality strategy, as shown in Figure 31.2. All 60,000 employees have received parchment renditions of these documents sent to their home addresses.

The Department of Defense, a principal customer of the aerospace and electronics firms, has developed a number of initiatives under the broad banner of quality, as shown in Table 31.1.

These top-level pronouncements from industry and customers are indicative of fundamental changes in quality consciousness. Major organizations are establishing senior quality councils, setting quality goals, and establishing measurement and reporting systems and are beginning to see encouraging results.

QUALITY MANAGEMENT MODEL

In today's environment of total quality awareness, the axiom "quality is everyone's business" is heard over and over again. But what does it really mean? It is true that in the past quality tasks were frequently delegated to the Quality Department or Inspection function. Today, however, the quality job is being spread appropriately to all organizations within the company, with clearly defined tasks, measurement criteria, and methods to ensure that prescribed quality levels are achieved.

Figure 31.3 presents a typical description of a quality program that is characteristic of complex industries. For simplicity, the model is restricted to product-

Our Objective: Superior Products
The objective of the Hughes Aircraft Company is to serve our Nation and the World at the forefront of technology by creating and providing affordable products of superior quality, reliability and performance.

Our Strategy: Quality First
Our central stragegy for achieving this objective is to make quality of products and operations our primary focus and our number one operating priority. This strategy incorporates the following principles: • The ultimate measure of the quality of our products is the degree to which they satisfy the needs of our customers   • No operating decision will be allowed to impact negatively the quality of our products and operations.   We are convinced that unequivocal concentration on quality will not only provide better products and better value to our customers, but also will cause other traditional business objectives to follow successfully.

Our Implementation: Total Quality
Our primary thrust for implementing the quality-first strategy is Companywide adoption of the Total Quality approach, comprising: • Assumption by each individual of responsibility for the quality of his/her own effort and output.   • Assumption by management of responsibility to provide systems and training so each indiviudal can perform to his/her highest capability.   • Recognition that each individual has one or more customers, and that the quality of his/her output is measured by the degree to which that output satisfies the needs of those customers.   • Concentration on error and defect prevention in all activities through careful workmanship and process measurement and control, as contrasted with after-the-fact error and defect detection.   Each operating organization will generate and operate to a plan to achieve Total Quality objectives. Achievement will be assessed by checking progress toward measurable goals.

FIG. 31.2 Company quality strategy. *(Courtesy Hughes Aircraft Company.)*

TABLE 31.1 Department of Defense Quality Excellence Program*

Initiative	Focus
1. "Design/build quality in"	Improve the technical disciplines of engineering/manufacturing
2. Award contracts based on quality	Ensure that contracts are not awarded to contractors with poor quality history
3. Streamline contract requirements	Focus on high-priority contract requirements; eliminate unnecessary requirements that serve to diffuse attention
4. Modernize factories	Improve process control and automatic inspection
5. Provide incentives for employees to reduce scrap/rework/repair	Investigate use of gain-sharing in defense industry
6. Increase and improve training/communication in the quality discipline	Assist academe and industry in development of quality improvement programs
7. Implement guarantees	Ensure design and manufacturing to specified performance requirements, free from defects in material and workmanship
8. Minimize use of specification/source control drawings	Eliminate unnecessary testing requirement by using standard parts
9. Improve prime contractor discipline over subcontractors	Reemphasize prime contractor's audit and surveillance over subcontractors or vendors
10. Tighten quality surveillance and investigate fraud and abuse, when indicated	Ensure contract compliance

*Developed by the Office of the Assistant Secretary of Defense for Acquisition and Logistics, the Pentagon, Washington, DC.

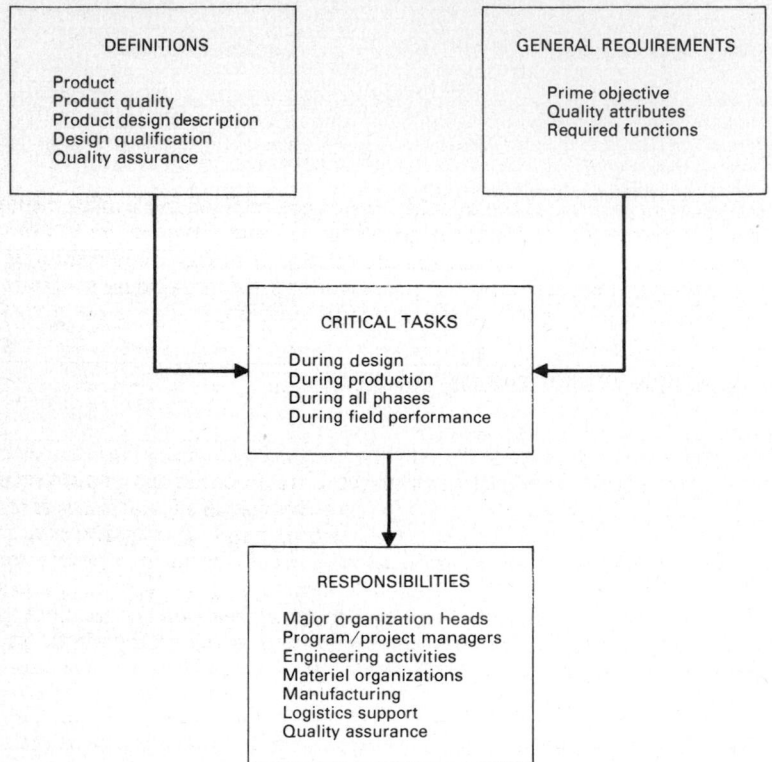

FIG. 31.3 A quality management model.

related functions and does not include such elements of an organization as finance, legal, or personnel, although their presence and interaction are clearly implied. Following is a description of specific requirements, tasks, and responsibilities that are represented in Figure 31.3.

Definitions

Product: An item produced for a customer or in support of a contract or company-defined effort, which may be in the form of hardware, software, firmware, handbooks, data, documentation, or any combination thereof.

Product quality: The presence in a product of the composite of attributes necessary to satisfy the customer's stated requirements and any applicable company requirements.

Product design description: The technical description of a product as set forth in drawings and specifications and documentation provided therein, plus applicable general manufacturing instructions from which the product is to be manufactured. The technical description includes specification of critical manufacturing processes and of the parameters to be verified for product acceptance.

Design qualification: The objective verification that a product built in accordance with the product design description satisfies the qualification test and other specified requirements.

Quality assurance: The objective verification that (1) design qualification is accomplished in accordance with specified requirements; (2) the procurement, fabrication, assembly, processing, and test operations are capable of producing a quality product; and (3) the manufactured product meets established workmanship standards and conforms to the product design description.

General Requirements

1. A prime objective of the company is to provide its customers with affordable products of superior quality, reliability, and performance. This objective is pursued through companywide implementation of total quality and the competent and integrated application of appropriate engineering, manufacturing, materiel, quality assurance, logistics support, and program management disciplines.

2. The attributes of quality products include reliability, performance, affordability, maintainability, safety, and others, depending upon product type and user requirements. The disciplines for achieving quality products include the technical and managerial techniques and controls for developing product designs having the desired attributes and for manufacturing products in assured conformance with those designs.

3. The functions required to ensure product quality are performed by Program/ Product Line Management, Engineering, Manufacturing, Materiel, Quality Assurance and Logistics Support organizations. Quality staff organizations provide assistance within the areas of their expertise to the above listed organizations and also provide overall assessment of organizational operations and interfaces relative to product quality.

Critical Tasks

During Design

1. Engineering activities apply design disciplines and criteria as necessary to ensure that the resulting product design fulfills customer and company requirements and standards. To ensure that the reliability and system safety inherent in the design will be realized in production, the product design description includes call-out of any uniquely required component acceptance tests, stress screening, process controls, and system safety controls to be applied during production.

2. Manufacturing and Materiel activities assist Engineering to achieve product designs that are producible economically and with high quality.

3. Logistics Support activities assist Engineering to achieve product designs that will be effectively supportable in the field.

4. Quality Assurance activities assist Engineering and Program Management in the design, design management, and design review processes, and may provide specialized analytical and other technical resources.

5. Quality Assurance activities verify that design qualification is accomplished in accordance with specified requirements.

During Production

6. Manufacturing and Materiel activities ensure and Quality Assurance activities verify that products meet workmanship standards and conform to the product design description.

7. Engineering activities assist Manufacturing and Program Management through: (1) review of the manufacturing planning and the processes called out therein to ensure that they adequately reflect the intent of the product design description; (2) investigation of producibility problems; (3) participation in review and disposition of nonconforming materiel; (4) failure analysis; and (5) generation of corrective or product improvement design changes.

8. Quality Assurance activities review the manufacturing planning and monitor, before and during production, appropriate procurement, fabrication, assembly, processing, and test operations to ensure that these are capable of producing a quality product within the scope of the product design description.

9. Manufacturing, Test, and Quality Assurance activities ensure that the delivered product conforms to customer and company requirements as verified by inspection, test, and data analysis.

During All Phases

10. Program instructions relative to specific contract requirements are authorized by cognizant program management. In case of conflict between such contract requirements and company product requirements or company practices, the contract requirements govern.

11. Program and functional organizational planning and budgeting provide for attaining quality, reliability, maintainability, system safety, and other product attributes as required by the contract and company standards.

12. Program Management ensures the adequacy of configuration management and, in particular, conducts the function of engineering change management. Quality Assurance verifies change incorporation at specified effectivities and the accuracy of configuration accounting and participates, along with Engineering, Manufacturing, Materiel, and Logistics Support, in the evaluation of proposed changes.

During Field Performance

13. The effectiveness of products in the field is monitored by designated activities, which ensure that operational and maintenance data are analyzed and that necessary corrective actions and product improvements are pursued to an extent commensurate with contract and company requirements.

Responsibilities

1. *Major organization heads:* They provide the manpower, organizational relationships, and facilities necessary to perform product-related functions.

2. *Program or project managers:* They assure that the product-related functions are defined that are to be performed as a part of their program or project in accordance with customer and company requirements, including services to be supplied by specialized technology groups and supporting organizations. Program managers also conduct engineering change management.

3. *Engineering activities:* These apply design disciplines and criteria as necessary for developing a product design description that achieves the required

product attributes; for qualification of the design; and for reviewing manufacturing planning and the processes called out therein to ensure that they adequately reflect the intent of the product design description.

4. *Materiel organizations:*   They procure parts, materials, and subcontract items in accordance with the design description, test, and other requirements of the prime contract flow-down and applicable company standards.

5. *Manufacturing:*   This department economically produces products that meet established workmanship standards and conform to the product design description. Manufacturing reviews product design descriptions for producibility.

6. *Logisitics Support:*   This department provides Engineering with design criteria for achieving effective supportability of products in the field.

7. *Quality Assurance:*   This department verifies that design qualification has been accomplished, that the manufactured product meets established workmanship standards and conforms to the product design description, and that quality assurance and manufacturing process data are analyzed to uncover needs for corrective action.

ACHIEVING PRODUCT QUALITY ATTRIBUTES—THE RELIABILITY EXAMPLE

The quality management model just described covers the broad quality program requirements of an organization, with emphasis on the responsibilities and roles of specific players (Program Management, Engineering, Manufacturing, Quality Assurance, etc.). Quality has been defined as "the presence in a product of the composite of attributes necessary to satisfy the customer's stated requirements. . . ." These product attributes include performance, reliability, affordability, maintainability, safety, and others, depending on the product type and user requirements. Each must be inherent in the basic design of the product. One of these attributes is reliability. We will now examine the engineering/management process essential for the achievement of reliability. To define it: Reliability engineering is the determination and application of appropriate reliability tasks and criteria during the design, development, manufacture, test, and support of a product that will result in the achievement of the specified product reliability.

Reliability Engineering Management.   The following is a description of 10 basic reliability engineering management actions, which experience on many complex products has shown to be necessary.

1. *Mission needs and reliability requirements:*   These are analyzed for new or anticipated procurements in consultation with prospective customers whenever possible.

2. *Reliability goals or requirements:*   These are specified in quantitative terms to assist in determining the selection and level of application of the appropriate reliability engineering tasks and to evaluate the achievement of reliability performance.

3. *Specific tasks:*   Each task listed in Table 31.2 is considered for appropriateness and level of application for a particular program. Such selection takes account of the following factors:

TABLE 31.2 Potential Reliability Engineering Tasks

Program Direction and Coordination:
  Definition of requirements/goals
  Reliability program planning
  Proposal inputs and negotiations
  Program instructions
  Design standards/criteria

Numerical analyses:
  Reliability modeling
  Reliability prediction and allocation
  Reliability assessment
  Reliability growth

Design analyses:
  Derating
  Thermal analysis
  Electrical analysis
  Failure modes, effects, and criticality
    analysis
  Electrostatic discharge analysis
  Radiation effects analysis
  Electromagnetic effects analysis
  Mechanical analysis
  Risk analysis
  Parts application review
  Functional/design/program reviews
  Change analysis/review

Parts, materials, and processes (PMP) control:
  PMP standardization
  PMP selection
  Nonpreferred PMP
  Prohibited PMP
  PMP control board
  Parameter drift screening
  Process controls
  Process baseline definition/controls
  PMP specification controls
  Critical item controls
  Part qualification program
  Material and process qualification

Testing:
  Qualification testing
  Test, analyze, and fix
  Demonstration testing
  Acceptance testing
  Life testing

Environmental stress screening:
  Incoming tests/screens
  Burn-in
  Subassembly conditioning
  Stress screens

Failure reporting, analysis and
    corrective action:
  Data collection
  Failure reporting
  Yield analyses
  Failure review board
  Corrective action board
  Field data analysis

a. Cost and funding to perform the task and its contribution to the attainment of customer-and company-specified reliability requirements and/or goals

b. Support of the maintenance philosophy/concept, including such factors as skill levels and personnel levels assigned to perform the maintenance, equipment availability for maintenance, and the role of built-in test capability

c. System/equipment complexity and technology level and the risks associated with these factors

d. Mission profile and environmental conditions for usage

    e. Program phase, e.g., conceptual, development, production, or operational deployment

4. *A reliability program plan:* This is prepared to identify the level of application of the reliability engineering tasks selected (from Table 31.2), how they are to be implemented, and their integration with other engineering, manufacturing, and support disciplines.

5. *Reliability design guidelines and criteria:* These cover items such as parts derating and maximum junction temperature levels and are developed, maintained, and implemented in a manner consistent with the results of design trade-off analyses and/or contractual requirements.

6. *Manufacturing capability:* This is evaluated to ensure that design reliability is not degraded by the production process. The evaluation covers such areas as procurement practices, facilities and equipment, manufacturing processes, operator and inspection capabilities, storage and handling operations and includes the procedures and instructions used in each of these areas.

7. *Appropriate controls:* These are applied to minimize the potential negative impact of critical reliability issues.

8. *Supplier reliability requirements, controls, and verification methods:* These are specified in procurement or work transfer documents. Suppliers are monitored and evaluated to verify compliance with specified procedures, controls, and performance requirements.

9. *Environmental stress screening:* This is an essential element of the hardware development and production processes. Stress screening is selectively applied to developmental and prototype hardware. A cost-effective screening program is included in all proposals for or leading to production. The proposed screening program may be refined during the design/development phase and is fully specified in the product design description.

10. *Inspection, stress screening, test, and other failure data:* These are acquired and analyzed to the degree necessary to identify failure trends and to serve as a basis for problem investigation, corrective action, and feedback for future designs.

    The above reliability engineering tasks and management actions provide a brief overview of the treatment of one major quality attribute, reliability. Emphasis was placed on "what to do," not "how to do it." Section 13, Product Development, discusses reliability engineering concepts and techniques. Lamberson (1985) provides an excellent tutorial on reliability engineering practices, including the "how-to" for a number of the tasks listed in Table 31.2. Lloyd and Lipow (1962) and Kapur and Lamberson (1977) have published authoritative textbooks on the subject, both of which provide in-depth treatment of the Table 31.2 tasks.

THE PROGRAM MANAGEMENT FUNCTION

Having briefly outlined the function of quality management for a complex product and looked at the more detailed treatment of a specific quality attribute, it is now appropriate that we consider the major task of program management. It is through this function that quality is "designed in" and "built in" to the product. Ball (1974) discusses two types of organization for carrying out program management. One of these types is exemplified by a company that produces domestic appliances. In that company, the person who was made responsible for developing a new dishwasher would be called the "Model X Project Engineer." Within the company there might have been a dozen such project engineers, all of whom accomplished their new product development responsibilities through the existing functionally oriented organizational structure.

For most complex products, however, it has become customary to establish a "program" type of organization. The program manager is appointed by top management and is given the responsibility and line authority for all program objectives, i.e., cost, schedule, and technical performance, for one major product and perhaps for one customer. Personnel for the program are drawn from the functional departments (e.g., engineering, manufacturing) in much the same way that a building contractor hires architects, carpenters, plumbers, and electricians and directs their work until a new building is designed and its construction is finished. When a development program is finished, the people who have been reporting to the program manager return to their "home" departments. Thus the program has the flexibility to draw upon a reserve of specialists as they are needed and also to achieve a transfer of knowledge and experience between programs. In some cases in which the product development extends over many years and goes through a series of upgrades, the program organization will assume more and more of the "doing" functions previously performed by outside elements of the company that were funded by the program manager.

Quite often dominant customers, such as government agencies or commercial airlines, will request that a program type of organization be established. Their reasons for doing so include the belief that the centralization of responsibility and authority will provide for rapid development of the new system and for good communication between contractor and customer personnel.

It is often said that the essence of program management is the effective management of change. Although a great deal of planning is done, a program manager is continuously reviewing previous decisions on assignments of budgets, schedules, and technical requirements and is continuously adjusting these assignments on the basis of the most recent project status data. A program type of organization greatly facilitates the required rapid and economical management of change.

Potential compromises of performance objectives resulting from program managers' decisions are subject to the checks and balances provided by routine contact with the functional organizations from which program personnel were borrowed. Conflicts do arise, but when all concerned have experience with this form of organization, the conflicts are viewed as a normal element of operation, which helps to provide balance among cost, schedule, and performance. Gutman (1984) provides an excellent analysis of matrix organizations, which combine functional and program management styles. He points out the limitations and strengths of each style and indicates how (ideally) they should work together. In summary, the program manager decides what and when, and the functional manager decides how and with whom.

Development Risk Control.   A narrow interpretation of the term "fitness for use" might limit the scope of assurance objectives to cover only assurance that a complex system would perform its mission or satisfy its markets, irrespective of development cost or development schedule. Obviously, this would be an unwarranted interpretation, because a product that the customer cannot afford or that is not developed when it is needed does not really provide fitness for use. Consequently, total quality control in the development of complex systems must address itself to the following three types of development risk:

1. *Cost risk:*   This is the risk that technical success will be achieved within schedule but at a development or production cost far in excess of that which was predicted at the beginning of the development.
2. *Schedule risk:*   This type of risk covers technical success within development costs but with serious schedule delay.
3. *Technical risk:*   This type of risk covers failure to achieve one or more of the vital system performance characteristics.

It is grave concern with controlling these development risks that has driven many companies to adopt the line program management type of organization for developing complex systems and to place upon the shoulders of the program manager the primary responsibility for controlling cost, schedule, and technical risks.

The Transition from Development to Production

Too often in the past, when faced with funding and schedule constraints, we have compromised the technical integrity of our programs by deleting or deferring vital program elements that contribute to system performance, producibility, and supportability. We have added unintentionally to the life cycle cost and postponed effective operational capability dates by pursuing development programs which do not yield producible designs and supportable configurations in a timely manner. (Weinberger, 1984, p. 1.)

In response to the above widely perceived feeling, especially among certain members of the U.S. Congress, the Defense Science Board established a special task force on Transitioning from Development to Production. The task force was composed of very senior executives from Lockheed, Boeing, General Dynamics, Litton, Raytheon, Westinghouse, Bell Labs, McDonnell Douglas, Texas Instruments, Honeywell, Hughes, Gould, and Northrop and included a senior officer from each of the three armed services.

It was the dominant conclusion of the task force that the fundamental disciplines of *design, test,* and *production* needed to be improved. Current Department of Defense (DOD) systems acquisition policies do not take into account the fact that systems acquisition must interface basically and primarily with an industrial process. The structure, organization, and operation of an industrial process bear no similarity whatsoever to the DOD systems acquisition process as it is conventionally described. The industrial process is a technical process focused on the design, test, and productin of a product. It will either fail or falter if these process steps are not performed in a disciplined manner, because design, test, and production are a continuum of interrelated and interdependent disciplines. A failure to perform well in one area will result in failure to do well in all areas. When this happens—as it does all too often—the result is a high-risk program whose equipment is fielded later and at far greater cost than planned.

The major thrust is directed toward the identification and establishment of *critical engineering processes* and their control methods. This will lead to a more organized accomplishment of these activities and will place on them greater significance and accountability. In order do to this, the Defense Science Task Force generated a matrix of the most critical events in the design, test, and production elements of the industrial process. These events were then transformed into what are referred to as "templates" (Defense Science Board, 1983). Figure 31.4 describes the perspective and approach identified by the task group and the action level on which the needed disciplines are applied.

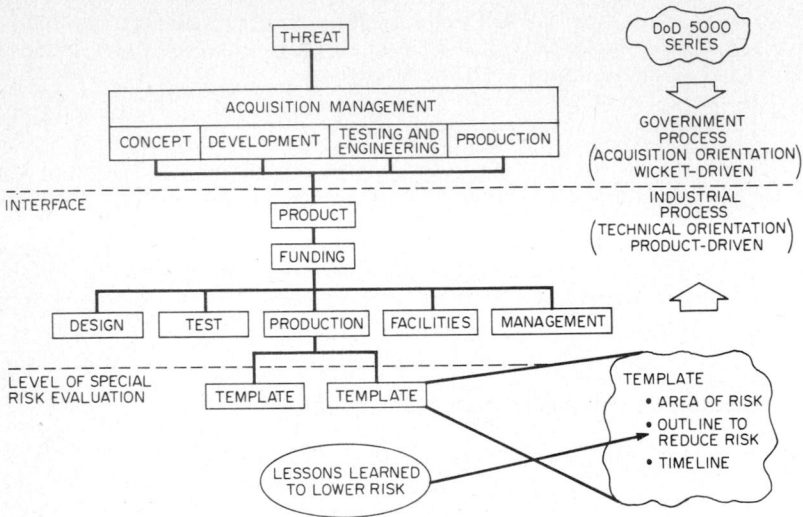

FIG. 31.4 Perspective and action to lower product transition risk.

Specific attributes overrride all detail requirements. These are: (1) assurance of design maturity, (2) measurement of test stability, and (3) certification of manufacturing processes. Design maturity is a qualitative assessment of the implementation of contractor design policy. Test stability is the absence or near absence of failures in development testing. Certification of the manufacturing processes implies (1) design for production and (2) proof of process, which occurs during pilot production.

Each of the above attributes is a function of the proper applicaton of all of the templates identified in the design, test, and production functions. Figure 31.5 identifies the entire network of critical tasks that have been found to be necessary to adequately control the schedule, cost, and technical risks of a complex program. The templates represent the distillation of a wealth of experience across many programs and years. Owing to space limitations, only three of the templates are described here: Design analysis, Failure Reporting System, and Manufacturing Screening. The reader will note the parallel and complementary fit with other portions of this section of the handbook.

Design Analysis Template

Area of Risk. Engineering design involves many specialized analyses, most of which are oriented toward meeting desired performance specifications. There are also specialized analyses oriented toward proofing design risk, but they are not widely practiced. When they are accomplished, it is often by personnel other than the design engineers most familiar with the product design. These analyses are critical to assuring a low-risk design.

Outline for Reducing Risk

- Stress and stress versus strength analyses are performed by the design engineers to ensure that for all parameters specified in the derating, margin of safety, and safety factor criteria for all component parts and materials, the applied values meet those criteria.

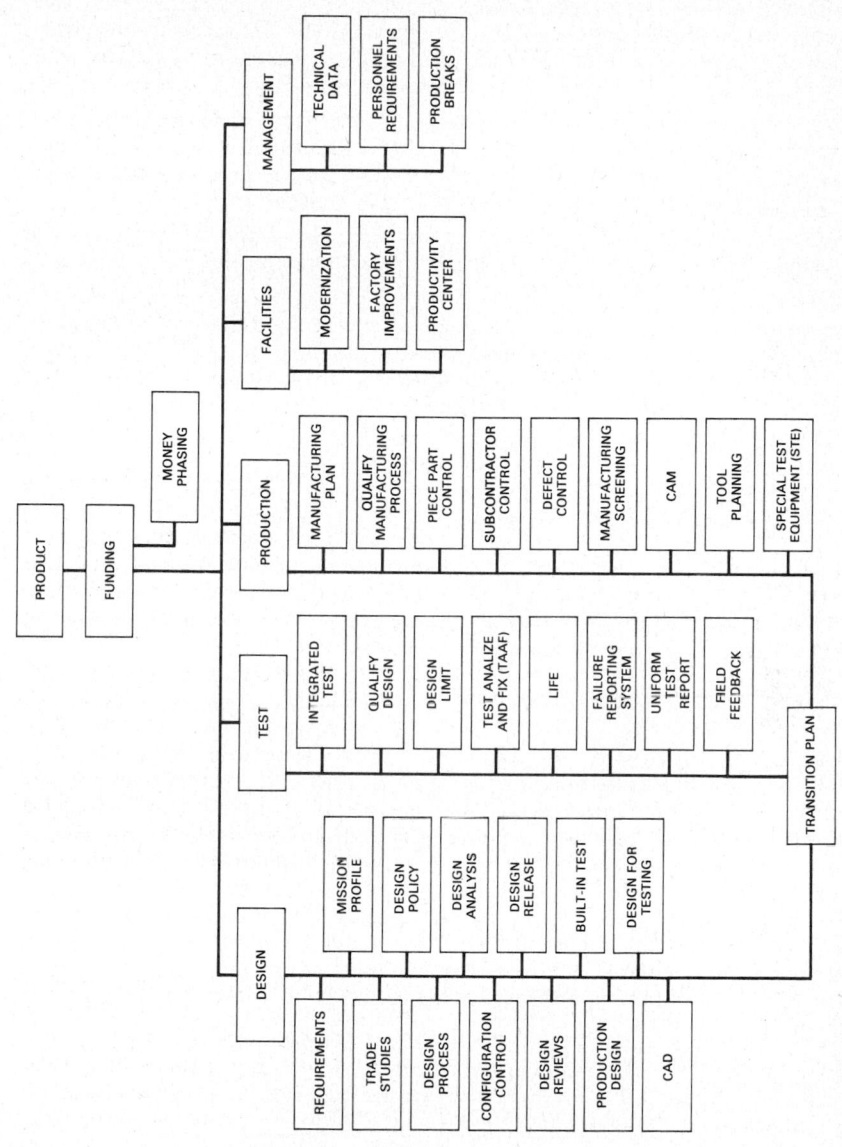

FIG. 31.5 Critical path templates.

- Worst-case tolerance analyses are performed by the design engineers to ensure that the system design performance will remain within specified limits for any combination of component part parameters within the limits of their own allowable tolerances.

- Sneak circuit analyses are performed by the design engineers to detect such unexpected failure modes as those caused by latent circuit paths, timing errors, or obscure cause-and-effect relations, which may trigger unintended actions or block desired ones without any part failures having occurred.

- Analyses of failure modes and effects analyses are performed by the design engineers in order to understand the effect on overall design performance of each component part failure in any predictable manner or mode so that these effects may be reduced to a minimum through design changes.

- A thermal survey is conducted on electronic systems to validate the accuracy of the thermal stress analysis, which is then revised as indicated by the survey to yield more accurate detailed results.

- The results of these analyses are utilized to revise the design as necessary to reduce design risk, and the analyses are also updated as necessary to reflect changes in the design. Design risk analyses are not performed simply for the sake of meeting contract data requirements.

- Computer-aided design techniques are developed or acquired as necessary to perform these analyses to the maximum extent possible, both to achieve potential savings in engineering time and cost and in the interest of improved and more consistent analytical accuracy.

Design analysis policies are developed and proved prior to full-scale development but may be updated and otherwise refined as experience is gained during development. Their use is largely completed, except for engineering changes to correct failures, at the conclusion of the design process.

Failure Reporting System Template

Area of Risk. Although there are several military standards (MIL-STD-785B, MIL-STD-781C) that require failure reporting, analysis, and corrective action systems, the implementation of these requirements in many instances has been poorly managed, not properly defined, and undisciplined. The flow-down of requirments from prime contractor to subcontractors has not been uniform, analysis of all failures has not been required, the timely close-out of failure reports has been overlooked and systems for alerting higher management to problem areas have been missing. Figure 31.6 and the following outline show the essential elements of a system for failure reporting, analysis, and corrective action system, which will aid in minimizing the risk of transition from known failure modes to production.

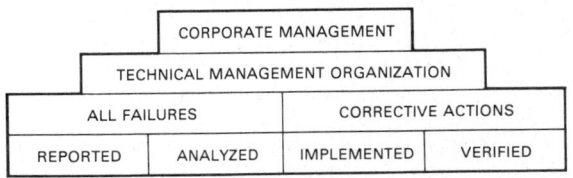

FIG. 31.6 Outline for reducing risk.

Outline for Reducing Risk

• A central technical organization is responsible for implementation and monitoring.

• Failure reporting, analysis, and corrective action are initiated with the start of subsystem testing.

• Uniform requirements are imposed on subcontractors, prime contractors, and government activities.

• All failures are reported.

• All failures are analyzed in sufficient depth to identify failure cause and necessary corrective actions.

• All failure analysis reports are closed out within 30 days of failure occurrence or rationale is provided for any extensions.

• Corporate management is automatically alerted to failures exceeding close-out criteria.

• Corporate management is automatically alerted to ineffective corrective actions.

• Small subcontractors lacking facilities for in-depth failure analysis arrange for the use of prime contractor, government, or independent laboratory facilities to perform such analyses.

The failure reporting system should be initiated with the start of the test program and should continue through the early stages of deployment.

Manufacturing Screening Template

Area of Risk. Environmental stress screening (ESS) is a manufacturing *process* for inducing parts and workmanship defects in electronic assemblies and units. Although ESS has been proved to reduce field failure rates by 20 to 90 percent (reducing life cycle costs) and to reduce in-plant failure rates by as much as 75 percent (reducing production costs), its use is still not universally accepted by many contractors as a standard part of their manufacturing process. When ESS is performed during development, it helps ensure that the electronics hardware performs on demand, that the most effective screening levels are determined before high-rate production, and that possible part type and vendor problems are discovered early. One should not confuse ESS with environmental qualification testing (which is designed to demonstrate design maturity). Analysis of failures experienced on unscreened developmental systems indicates that:

60 percent are due to workmanship

30 percent are due to bad parts

10 percent are due to design problems

The percentages cited above are not typical of mature equipment operating in the user's environment. As a program proceeds through development and into high-rate production, the manufacturing learning curve will account for correction of many workmanship errors. Other persistent, so-called workmanship problems may ultimately dictate design change because of unrealistic expectations of manufacturing capability. Repeated product testing during development, production buildup, and final acceptance will remove many workmanship errors. In the operating environment, failures are more likely to indicate inherent design/reliability problems, which manifest themselves over time.

Outline for Reducing Risk

- Environmental stress screening is designed during development.
- Temperature cycling and random vibration are the most efficient environmental stress screens and are performed on 100 percent of military electronic hardware.
- The predominant factors in temperature cycling are:

    Rate of change of temperature

    Number of cycles

    Minimum/maximum range of temperature

    Level of assembly on which performed
- The predominant factors in random vibration are:

    Spectral density (in g^2/Hz or grms)

    Axis of stimulation

    Duration of screen
- Random vibration stimulates more defects than fixed or swept-sine vibration at similar levels of excitation.
- Recommended starting regimens are:

Random vibration	*Temperature cycling*
Duration: 10 min per axis	Temp. range: -40 to $+95°C$
2 axes	Temp. rate: 15°C/min
Accel. spectrum: 0.04 g^2/Hz	No. of cycles: 10 (last failure free)
Power on	Power: on (except cool down)

- The ESS process is not used to identify design defects.
- The manufacturing process is adjusted to minimize recurrence of defects found during ESS, thus reducing costs to produce.
- The ESS program is a dynamic one, adjusting procedures as indicated by the defect data to maximize efficient finding of defects.
- The ESS process is not done on a sample basis; it is done on 100 percent of electronics hardware delivered.
- Appropriate screening for manufacturing defects as an acceptance test is developed for all product types.
- Environmental stress screens are designed and proofed during development and adjusted as appropriate during production.

The reader is urged to acquire the complete report containing all the critical path templates (Defense Science Board, 1983). It is available as a DOD manual, which is listed as a reference at the end of this section. The critical paths and tasks to be considered for reducing the risks constitute a recipe for quality improvement that merits careful examination and application. While the templates address specifically the design, test, and manufacturing functions, the roles of the other principal players identified in an earlier portion of this section under Quality Management Model, are clearly evident. The role of the Quality Assurance

Department is to make certain that these tasks are performed or that the rationale for their modification or deletion is documented.

APPLYING THE LESSONS LEARNED

Since most complex products are developed and produced in organizations in which both program and project teams operate in limited time frames together with functional or more permanent elements of the organizations, it is useful to consider the interrelationships of these two groups. Figure 31.7 provides a perspective from which to examine the two complementary roles. On the upper half of the figure are those activities typical of a program or project; on the lower half appear those activities characteristic of functional organizations. The experience gained on programs (Steps 4, 5, and 6) provides a rich source of information, knowledge, and lessons learned to be codified by the functional organizations in terms of experience retention. This experience, together with that from other programs, forms the basis for identification of needed disciplines, technique development, and training (Steps 1, 2, and 3) to be applied as resources for application to the next major program or project.

For example, many important techniques, such as electronic stress analysis, design review, or production environmental testing, start out by being actually performed by competent people as required to support a particular project. Temporary technical excellence may be developed by such effort, but this is not enough. In order to ensure repetition of successes and avoid repetition of failures and in order to spread technical excellence throughout the company, it is neces-

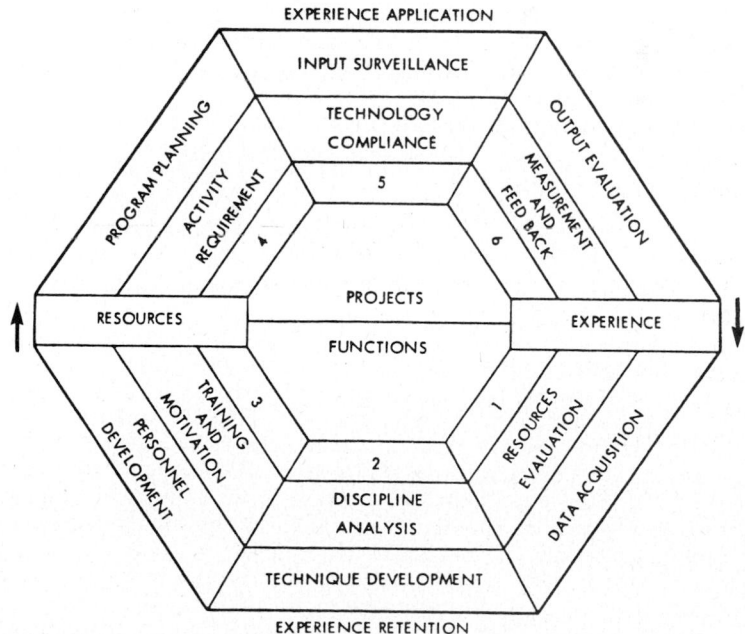

FIG. 31.7 Applying the lessons learned.

sary to document the technology. Such documentation covers lessons learned on all projects and thereby represents the best of which the company is capable. Documented technology does not of itself achieve results—people must be taught the technology and be motivated to use it. Such people then constitute the primary resources for successful execution of new projects.

Thus the critical tasks identified earlier in this section are in a constant state of refinement and development as new technology becomes available and recent experience is analyzed for application to the next project. Section 13 under Design Experience Retention discusses several tools for applying the lessons learned. Section 27 under New Product Quality Design Review shows a system of automating the recording and retrieval of past experiences.

THE QUALITY-VALUE RELATIONSHIP

The economic dimension in quality is well recognized today, as worldwide competition for markets has placed a premium on quality of products or services. Maurer (1982) provides two useful equations that include the economic dimension:

$$\text{Value} = \underbrace{\frac{\text{Satisfaction of customer desires}}{\text{selling price}}}_{\textit{Market definition}} = \underbrace{\frac{\text{Functional requirements and quality specifications}}{\text{cost to produce}}}_{\textit{In-house definition}}$$

Section 13, under Planning to Minimize Cost, defines "value engineering" as a technique for evaluating the design to ensure that essential functions are provided at minimum cost. Such a systematic effort is based on an analysis of the functional requirements of systems, equipment, facilities, procedures, and supplies to achieve essential functions at the lowest total cost consistent with needed performance, reliability, safety, etc.

Clearly, in the equations above value may be increased by raising the levels of the numerator, by reducing the denominator, or by doing both at the same time. The similarity of concept between quality and value engineering (VE) is obvious. Both efforts are aimed at meeting customer requirements at least cost. While the quality program is committed to preservation of acceptable standards, the VE program is continually probing to find out how these standards can be met at a lower cost. The tools of VE are thus a powerful means to help achieve quality objectives.

The Value Engineering Process. Most complex products have hundreds of requirements, from the top level functional specifications on down through the tiers of detailed requirements for equipment, assemblies, and parts. Requirements, practices, and processes tend to become codified—after all, if it worked before, why change? Yet the cardinal principle of VE is to challenge everything. Kaufman (1981) provides an excellent diagram of VE as shown in Figure 31.8. The steps in a VE study and some tools of analysis are discussed in Section 13 under Value Engineering.

Because of its simplicity, this powerful technique is often mistakenly perceived as superficial. Its value arises from the clarity with which it identifies cost problems by freeing the mind from inhibitions, false constraints, specific configurations, and preconceived ideas. It facilitates comparisons that reveal unnecessary

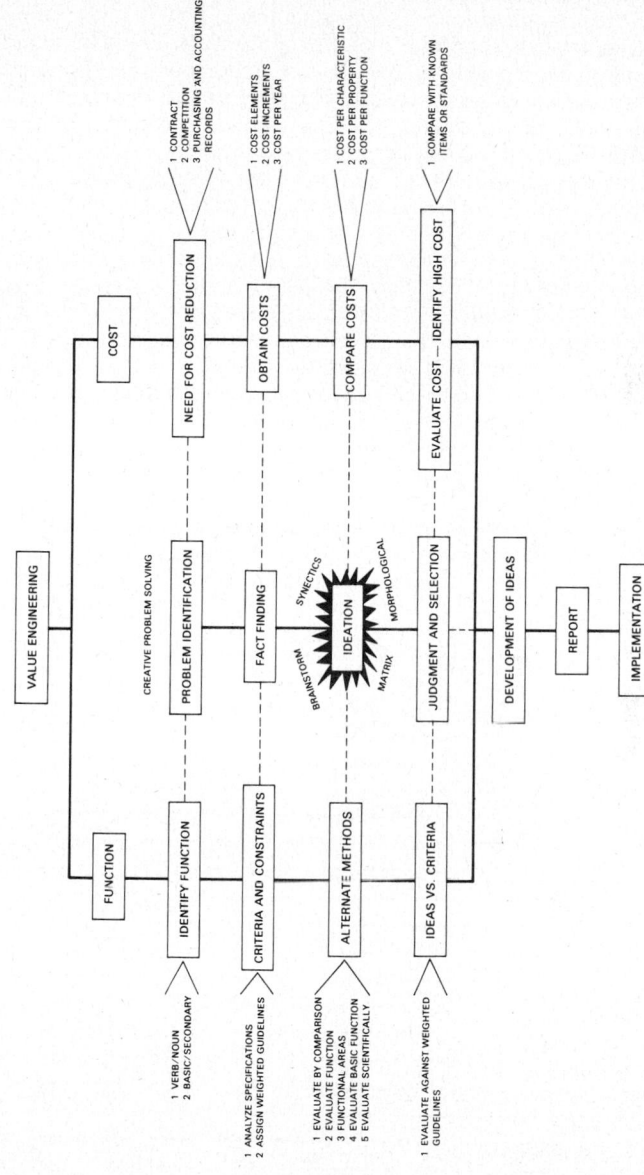

FIG. 31.8 The value engineering process.

costs and releases creativity that results in less costly ways to accomplish the functions. It is the *focus on function* that sets value engineering apart from all other cost reduction methods.

After the cost problem has thus been identified, and only thereafter, creative problem-solving techniques are used to create alternative ways of accomplishing the functions. In practice, creativity is a matter of: careful investigation and observation of a clearly defined problem; making new associations between ideas; and, probably most important, recognizing and working around the perceptual, emotional, cultural, and habitual roadblocks that inhibit the generation and acceptance of new ideas in ourselves and others.

To get around these roadblocks, a number of aids and techniques have been devised. Since the mind is both creative and judgmental, the most important technique in individual or group creativity is to re-release the natural creativity and to defer judgment because new ideas are fragile and need nurturing and building up rather than criticism. Checklists that list attributes and suggest questions that can open up new viewpoints are useful. Brainstorming by teams that bring together people of wide and varied experience is a potent technique.

When the search for new ideas is exhausted, the selection phase takes place. The best ideas that meet the objectives of lowest cost with required performance of the functions are combined. In the final phase, good human relations techniques are used to overcome reluctance to accept new ideas on the part of the people who must approve the proposal.

Quality Enhancement. Most value studies result in product simplification. Design complexity is reduced, fewer parts are used, reliability is increased, weight is reduced, etc. Figure 31.9 summarizes the field analysis of several hundred value

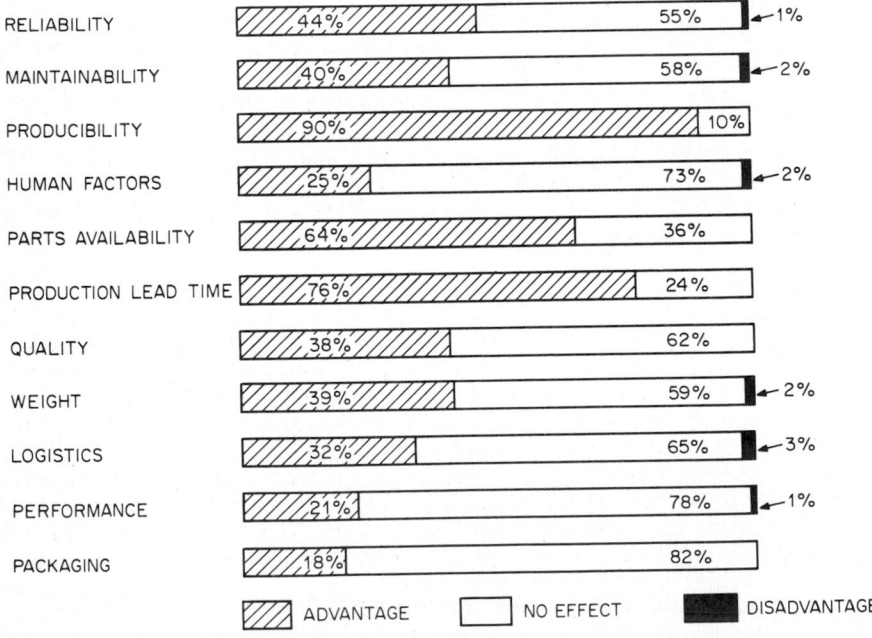

FIG. 31.9 The multiple benefits of value engineering.

THE IMPROVEMENTS

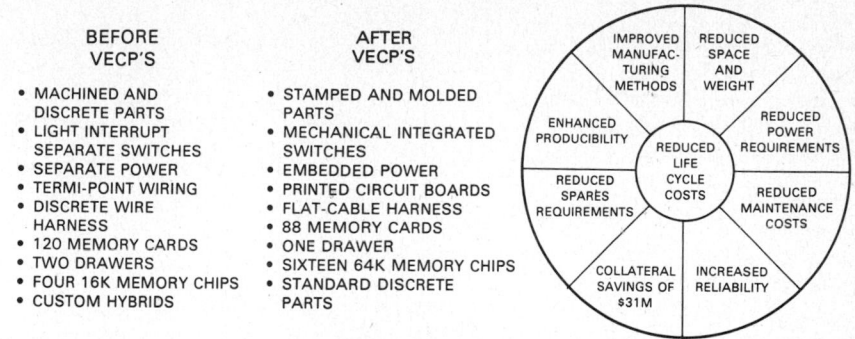

BEFORE VECP'S	AFTER VECP'S
• MACHINED AND DISCRETE PARTS	• STAMPED AND MOLDED PARTS
• LIGHT INTERRUPT SEPARATE SWITCHES	• MECHANICAL INTEGRATED SWITCHES
• SEPARATE POWER	• EMBEDDED POWER
• TERMI-POINT WIRING	• PRINTED CIRCUIT BOARDS
• DISCRETE WIRE HARNESS	• FLAT-CABLE HARNESS
• 120 MEMORY CARDS	• 88 MEMORY CARDS
• TWO DRAWERS	• ONE DRAWER
• FOUR 16K MEMORY CHIPS	• SIXTEEN 64K MEMORY CHIPS
• CUSTOM HYBRIDS	• STANDARD DISCRETE PARTS

Circle diagram segments: IMPROVED MANUFACTURING METHODS; REDUCED SPACE AND WEIGHT; ENHANCED PRODUCIBILITY; REDUCED POWER REQUIREMENTS; REDUCED LIFE CYCLE COSTS (center); REDUCED SPARES REQUIREMENTS; REDUCED MAINTENANCE COSTS; COLLATERAL SAVINGS OF $31M; INCREASED RELIABILITY

TOTAL SAVINGS OVER PRODUCTION QUANTITIES

$40,796,600.00

FIG. 31.10   The resultant quality enhancement.   *(Courtesy Hughes Aircraft Co.)*

engineering changes incorporated into products. The study was made by a task group of the American Ordnance Association (now known as the American Defense Preparedness Association).

The benefits identified in the above study were achieved on relatively mature designs, where "before" and "after" field performance data were available to determine the effect of the change. However, the earlier in the development phase that VE changes can be incorporated, the less disruptive the changes and the greater the return on the study dollars invested.

A value engineering study was completed on the Standard Data Display System, manufactured for the U.S. Navy by Hughes Aircraft Company. Nine Value Engineering Change Proposals (VECPs) were implemented to improve the design and manufacturing techniques. The improvements reduced mean time between failures and mean time to repair, and simplified built-in test features. Subcontractor participation was increased. Figure 31.10 illustrates the power of the VE methods when applied early in the design prototype phase. Design simplification and technology advances were incorporated during the design process by using knowledge that was not available when the original development contract was signed.

A Team Approach.   A typical VE study involves participation of individuals from Engineering, Manufacturing, Materiel, Quality, Marketing, and the program office. The interdisciplinary approach across organizational lines provides a depth of focus and a variety of viewpoints that enrich the process. It is interesting to note that project teams (see Section 22 under Organizing for Projects), small group activities, circles, and other temporary groupings of specialists and generalists, organized to solve a specific problem, are becoming more and more prevalent on the industrial scene. Fraser and Talbot (1974) have eloquently addressed this growing trend, and characterize the resultant "ad-hocracies" as essential ingredients in casting off those bureaucratic practices that immobilize an organization and render it less responsive to change.

Thus, the quest for improved product value can be effectively addressed through the leadership and teaming roles of quality engineering and VE practitioners.

REFERENCES

Ball, L. W. (1974). "Complex Systems." Section 44 in *Quality Control Handbook,* 3rd ed. McGraw-Hill, New York, pp. 44-1 through 44-19.

Defense Science Board (1983). *Solving the Risk in Transitioning from Development to Production.* DOD 4245.7-M (Manual), Department of Defense, Technical Information Center, Cameron Station, Alexandria, VA.

Fraser, R. A. and Talbert, J. E. (1974). "Preparation for *Change* in Management of the Future Industrial Complex." *Proceedings of the 1974 SAVE Conference.* Society of American Value Engineers, Chicago, pp. 108–115.

Gutman, N. (1984). "The Matrix Management." Chapter 9 in *How to Keep Product Costs in Line.* Marcel Dekker, New York, pp. 139–150.

Hayes, G. E. (1985). "Quality and Productivity: Challenges for Management." *Quality Progress,* October, pp. 42–46.

Juran, J. M. (1985). "Catching Up: How Is the West Doing?" *Quality Progress,* November, pp. 18–22.

Kapur, K. C. and Lamberson, L. R. (1977). *Reliability in Engineering Design.* John Wiley & Sons, New York.

Kaufman, J. J. (1981). *Value Engineering: An Executive Overview.* Cooper Industries, Houston.

Lamberson, L. R. (1985). "Reliability Tutorial." *ASQC Quality Congress Transactions,* Milwaukee, pp. 88–99.

Lloyd, D. K. and Lipow, M. (1962). *Reliability: Management, Methods, and Mathematics.* Prentice-Hall, Englewood Cliffs, NJ.

Maurer, J. H. (1982). "The Quality Side of Value." *Proceedings of the 1982 SAVE Conference.* Society of American Value Engineers, Chicago, IL, pp. 108–115.

MIL-STD-781C (1981). *Reliability Design Qualification and Production Acceptance Tests: Exponential Distribution.* U.S. Department of Defense, Technical Information Center, Alexandria, VA.

MIL-STD-785B (1986). *Reliability Program for Systems and Equipment Development and Production.* U.S. Department of Defense, Technical Information Center, Alexandria, VA.

Weinberger, C. W. (1984). Memorandum to Secretaries of the Military Departments. Subject: DOD Directive 4245.7, "Transition from Development to Production." Department of Defense, Technical Information Center, Alexandria, VA.

SECTION 32

JOB SHOP INDUSTRIES

Leonard A. Seder

WHAT IS A JOB SHOP? **32.1**

THE JOB SHOP QUALITY
PROGRAM **32.5**

THE JOB NUMERICS **32.6**

JOB PLANNING **32.8**

  Organizing for Job Planning   32.8

  Detecting and Correcting
    Job Planning Errors 32.10

  Improving Job Planning . . . 32.11

JOB SHOP CONTROL **32.11**

  Overall Control System . . . 32.11

  Data Feedback and
    Corrective Action 32.12

  The Current Job Approach   32.12

  The Repeat Job Approach   32.15

IMPACT OF ADVANCES IN
METALWORKING TECHNOLOGY **32.18**

  New Developments 32.18

  Effect of Developments . . 32.19

Job Planning and
  Controlling 32.19

QUALITY IMPROVEMENT . . . **32.19**

  The Chronic Offenders
    Approach 32.20

  The Product Family
    Approach 32.22

  The Non-Job Approach . . 32.22

  Diagnostic Techniques . . 32.26

REMEDIES FOR JOB SHOP
PROBLEMS **32.27**

  Challenging the Basic
    Premises 32.27

THE SMALL JOB SHOP **32.29**

REFERENCES **32.30**

WHAT IS A JOB SHOP?

The terms "job shop" and "mass production shop," though widely used, are loosely defined. Managers who use these terms are well aware that industrial life as lived in the job shop differs considerably from that prevailing in the mass production shop. This difference extends to the problems of creating, controlling, and improving quality. This section undertakes to define the nature of the job shop and to explain the methods in use for dealing with job shop quality.

There is no single parameter which distinguishes the job shop from the mass production shop. Job shops vary in size from very small to very large. Some are captive; others are independent. Some serve sophisticated industrial customers; others serve relatively naive consumers. Their products range from one-of-a-kind nonrepeating items to large lots of frequently reordered stock items. Some make proprietary products of their own design. Others develop designs jointly with customers' design. Many cannot even be classified neatly in the foregoing terms, since their product mix spreads across the whole spectrum of customer sophistication, design responsibility, lot sizes, repeat rate, etc.

Despite this difficulty of classification, it is possible to identify certain basic common types of job shops and to recognize among them differences and commonality that affect the fashioning of a quality control program to suit their individual needs. Table 32.1 identifies four common types of job shop, and shows some typical products or operations which exemplify each type.

TABLE 32.1   Types of Job Shops

		Typical products—or operations	
Type	Description	Percent repeat jobs low to moderate	Percent repeat jobs moderate to high
I	Large complex equipment	Locomotives Chemical Plants Buildings Automated production equipment Radar sets	Farm equipment Aircraft Machine tools Printing presses
II	Small, simple end products and components	Fashion fabrics Industrial adhesives Circuit boards Fabricated metals Books	Tires Shoes Garments Wall covering Small appliances Metal shapes Automotive components Electronic components Private-label foods Furniture
III	Custom parts	Machined parts Forgings Weldments	Stampings Castings Molded plastics Screw-machine parts Molded rubber parts Extruded parts Containers
IV	Subcontracted services	Toolmaking Diemaking Moldmaking Printing Machining Testing	Heat treating Welding Plating Packaging Electropolishing

Percent Repeat Jobs. The term "percent repeat jobs," which appears in the headings of Table 32.1, is one of the universal parameters of job shop operation. Percent repeat jobs is defined as the percentage of the total number of jobs in the factory in any one month that are identical repeats of job orders run previously.

The classification of low, moderate, and high percent repeat jobs have the following approximate values: "low" = under 35 percent; "moderate" = 35 to 80 percent; "high" = over 80 percent.

Large Complex Equipment. Companies in Type I (Table 32.1) produce large complex units, each made up of thousands of different parts and components, each of these in turn being defined by its own "drawing number." These companies call themselves job shops because an individual job order or contract usually calls for a very small number of such large units, often only one. Only if the percent repeat jobs is moderate to high are they able to justify manufacturing these units as stock items and making (or buying) the input parts in economic quantities. Lacking a stock of finished units or components, it is necessary to produce from "scratch," and the time pressure becomes severe.

Small End Products and Components. The Type II companies usually produce large quantities on any one order. However, they regard themselves as job shops because of the endless variations of size, shape, color, style, or configuration typically involved in their product lines. Even those with "standard" product lines frequently show hundreds of different "model numbers" in their catalogs. Those who make "specials" for the various customers' unique requirements have thousands of drawing numbers in their engineering files.

Custom Parts. These Type III companies are mainly in business as suppliers to Type I and II companies. They specialize in one or more of the processes listed and fill their shops with customer-designed parts of thousands of different configurations and compositions. Often they can satisfy a customer's annual requirements for a particular part number in just a few hours of production running time. The nature of the problems of such a job shop has been well portrayed by Furukawa, Kogure, and Ishizu (1981), as shown in Figure 32.1.

Subcontracted Services. Type IV companies differ from Type III only in that they tend to be small, independent shops specializing in particular operations, often working on customer-furnished material. Captive shops of this type are often in-house departments within a large Type I, II, or III company. Variety of jobs is again the rule, each job usually requiring only a few hours of production time.

Jobs per Worker per Week. All four types of job shops exhibit two recurring themes of commonality:

1. *Wide variety of designs* (due to a myriad of different configurations, options, colors, sizes, shapes, models)
2. *Short production time* for any individual production task on any one "job"

These two factors may be conveniently combined into a single parameter of "jobs per worker per week," reflecting the average number of different orders, or different setups, or setup changes that will be handled by each worker over a week's time. (As more and more of the worker skills, memories, and decisions associated with setup changes are replaced by computers and automated setup

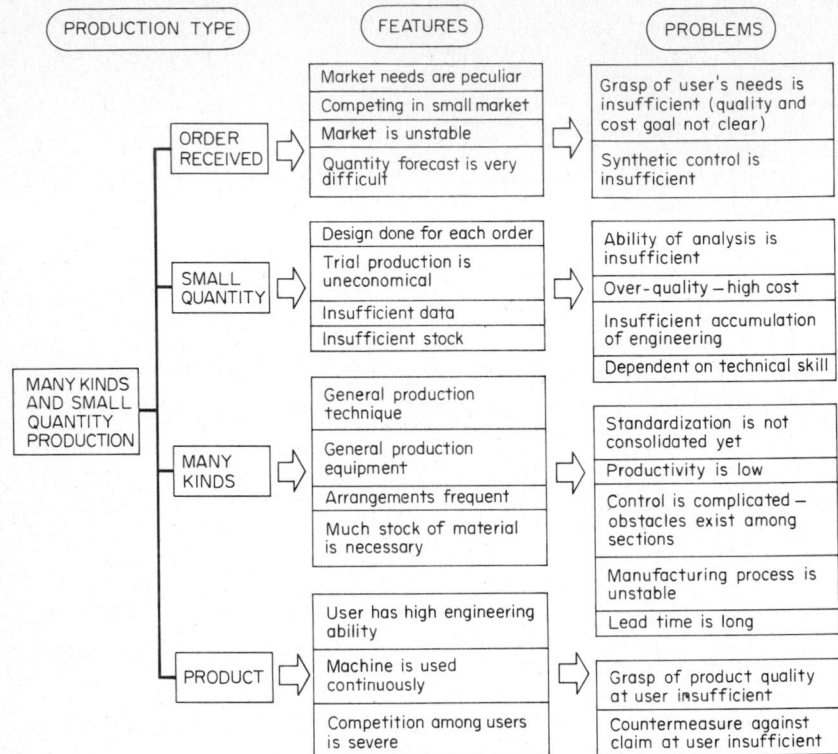

FIG. 32.1   Problems of quality control at a plant producing to customer order.

changers, the name of this parameter will have to change to "jobs per machine per week.") Whatever the type of job shop, this number is generally much higher in the job shop than in the mass production shop. This fact has a direct bearing on the nature of the job shop quality program.

The percent repeat jobs (defined above) also varies in size among job shop types and within types. However, the percent repeat jobs is generally much lower for job shops as a class than for mass production shops. As implied in Table 32.1, the percent repeat jobs tends to be higher for some job shop types than others, e.g., Type II versus Type I. However, the rate varies over the whole range and for individual shops within one type.

Job Shop Grid.   When the two parameters of jobs per worker per week and percent repeat jobs are related to each other on the same diagram, there emerges a convenient way to quantify the distinction between the production shop and the job shop. The "job shop grid" in Figure 32.2 is designed to show this relationship.

The job shop grid opens the way to design and apply quality control methods which are keyed to the quantified parameters. At the outset it is evident that production shops are generally those with a small number of jobs per worker per week and a high percentage of repeat jobs. Above the level of 20 jobs per worker per week, we consider it a job shop regardless of the percentage of repeat jobs. Also, below a 50 percent repeat job rate, we consider it a job shop even though the number of jobs per worker per week is low.

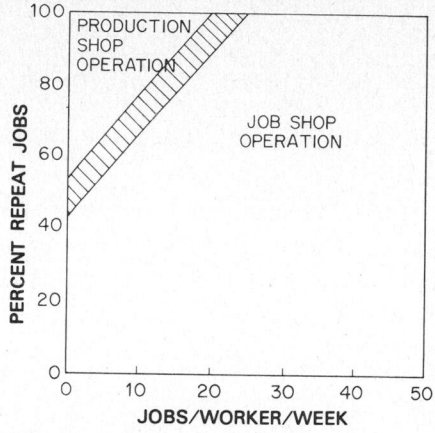

FIG. 32.2 The job shop grid.

THE JOB SHOP QUALITY PROGRAM

In a broad sense, the problems of job shop quality management are the same as for any other shop:

1. Planning of quality for new or modified products and processes
2. Controlling the quality during manufacture
3. Improving quality levels to reduce quality losses

Similarly, in a broad sense, the concepts and principles of solution of quality problems are the same as presented elsewhere in this handbook, i.e., Planning, Sections 6, 13, and 16; Controlling, Sections 17 and 24; Improving, Sections 22 and 10. However, the numerous job orders (which create high jobs per worker per week and low percent repeat jobs) greatly influence the job shop approach to quality.

The impact of these numerous job orders is not on the materials, processes, or people; these generally remain common to all jobs. Neither is the impact on the systems, practices, and procedures; these likewise remain common to all jobs. (These common "ingredients" may, however, contain the root cause of chronic quality problems.) Rather, the impact is similar to that involved in launching many "new products" every week. For each of these "new products" there is need to discover (1) what is "new," (2) how this affects product design, plan of manufacture, special tools, quality requirements, etc., and (3) what needs to be done to assure that the "newness" is correctly identified and complied with by all departments.

Stated another way, the impact of the numerous job orders is primarily on pre-production planning, and especially on *manufacturing planning.* This planning creates a considerable problem of communicating to all concerned what is "different" about each order so that responsive action can be taken. The amount of such communication can rise to enormous proportions because of the multiplying effect of (1) the number of job orders, (2) the number of ways in which each order is different, and (3) the number of processes, tools, etc., affected by each of these differences. A consequence of this great volume of communication is that the problem of quality control is a problem in *quality of communication* as much as a problem in conventional process and product quality control. As a corollary, when product nonconformance is detected, the correction to be made is very frequently in some detail of the job plan rather than in the product or manufacturing process.

In the light of the foregoing, the quality program for the job shop must include special provisions for:

Planning to communicate essential quality information to all concerned

Controlling the errors and inadequacies in this communication

Improving not merely the processes and products but also the planning and communication

THE JOB NUMERICS

As noted, preproduction planning is a major job shop activity, and involves every job. Since each job differs from all others in *design*, each requires its own *product specifications*, spelling out in detail the materials, formulation, configuration, end-product physical properties, quality and reliability requirements, and the rest. (Simplification is often possible in instances in which a single specification can be used to specify a whole "family" of items largely resembling each other but differing only in specific detail of size or color, etc.)

Since jobs also differ in the exact manufacturing process to be followed, each requires its own *manufacturing plan,* to communicate to Production and Inspection the necessary details of input materials, operation sequence, inspection or laboratory release points, special or unique tooling, in-process properties required, mandatory processing restrictions, and the like.

There appears to be no accepted generic term to represent, for a specific job order, all the details of product and manufacturing process. "Job documentation" comes close, but it sometimes is used to include the recorded quality data, which are not part of our definition. Hence the author has coined the term "primary job numerics" to serve as such a generic term. Table 32.2 summarizes and gives typical examples of these primary job numerics. Obviously, mass production shops must also have these same numerics. However, in the mass production shop the numerics are few in number, tend to become stabilized, and are easily remembered by shop personnel. In the job shop they are many in number, are frequently changed, and require constant reference to the written documents.

Not all job shops have responsibility for preparing the numerics to define *both* product and manufacturing plan. Types II and IV (Table 32.1) ordinarily receive product specifications from their customers and hence prepare only the manufacturing plan. Types I and II prepare both sets of numerics for their own products, but only product specifications for those materials and components which they purchase.

The primary job numerics have long been recognized as essential and have found expression in various types of "legitimate" documentation in the shop. The product specification, manufacturing drawing, material specification, formulation or batching sheet, tool drawings, exploded assembly view, route card, operation sheet, inspection detail sheet, test procedure, and job order card are the more common names for the various means of communicating the needed numerics to shop personnel.

TABLE 32.2 Primary Job Numerics

Aspect of definition	Typical examples
To define the product	
Materials	Material specification numbers for metals, chemicals, agricultural products, etc.
Formulation	Specific proportions of various materials to be used
Configuration	Drawing or sketch showing dimensions, component parts, assembly details, etc.
End-product acceptability	Dimensional, physical, chemical, optical, metallurgical, electrical, visual, etc., tolerances
	Functional test requirements
Reliability	Maximum failure rate, or degree of degradation in specified endurance test
To define the manufacturing plan	
Input materials	Sources, subcontractors
Operation sequence	Exact order of primary, secondary, finishing, packaging, etc., operations
	Specific machines, baths, ovens (when restricted)
Inspection points	Location of inspection stations or laboratory release points
Unique tooling	Design of specific form tools, molds, dies, assembly fixtures, artwork, etc.
In-process properties	Dimensions, thicknesses, densities, colors, electrical outputs, chemical values, strengths, etc., needed at specific operations
Mandatory processing restrictions	Temperatures and times for bakes, heat treatments, reactions, drying, curing, pasteurizing, etc.
	Hold times between operations

The primary job numerics outlined in Table 32.2 are the minimum details necessary to define and make the product. However, they are seldom sufficient to assure the quality of the end product or to attain economic operation. To make up for these deficiencies, there are additional numerics which provide the added information needed to minimize product deficiencies, rejections, repairs, yield losses, and customer complaints.

Some of these "supplementary job numerics" are shown in Table 32.3. For each aspect of product and process definition, there are special details, unique to the individual job, that are of value to the shop personnel. Communicating these details to the shop personnel (through the documentation) provides the advance knowledge that can often spell the difference between success and failure to meet end-product requirements or between high and low "quality costs." It is probably no exaggeration to say that the key to preventing product deficiencies in the job shop lies in perfecting the knowledge of how to store and retrieve the supplementary job numerics. Computers obviously can make a major contribution here. Not all these supplementary job numerics are needed for all jobs. Indeed, one of the real dilemmas faced by job shop managers is the decision of how far to go in this direction (see below).

TABLE 32.3 Supplementary Job Numerics (to Prevent Product Deficiencies and Losses)

Aspect of definition	Typical examples
Materials	Special supplier requirements for process control
	Special gages or test methods
	Packaging requirements
	Classification of characteristics
	Acceptable quality levels
	Certifications required
Operation sequence	Special work instructions
	Exact details of important hand operations
	Permissible deviations from sequence
Inspection points	Special gages or test methods
	Classification of characteristics
	Acceptable quality levels
Unique tooling	Identification numbers
	Tool inspection details
	Permissible tool deviations
In-process properties	Optimum settings of process variables
	Special gages or test methods
	Plans of control for operations with setup approval criteria, running approval criteria
	Statistical control plans to be used
Mandatory processing	Tolerances for times, temperatures, etc.
	Certifications required
End-product acceptability	Special gages or test methods
	Special customer "idiosyncrasies"
	Classification of characteristics
	Acceptable quality levels
	Customer data submittals or certifications
	Visible defect acceptability limits
	Customer sampling plan impositions
Reliability	Testing details

JOB PLANNING

To generate, communicate, and comply with all these job numerics requires that a major element of the job shop quality program must be concerned with individual job planning. This involves (1) organizing for job planning, (2) detecting and correcting job planning errors, (3) improving the job planning.

Organizing for Job Planning. A major question is how far to go in completeness of planning. It is usual to carry out planning of the *primary* job numerics in total (or to leave only minor details to be worked out during the production run). However, the *supplementary* job numerics present a problem in striking the proper balance between overplanning and underplanning. Establishment of the numerics beforehand will work to avoid errors and misjudgments during the production run. However, the volume of detail and the lack of adequate information of some aspects (e.g., the expected rate of occurrence of specific defects, sequence deviations, or tool deviations; knowledge of the optimum settings of process variables, etc.) make it uneconomic or impossible to fill in all the details.

A major consideration in this decision is the "percent repeat jobs." A shop with a low percent repeat jobs must necessarily devote a major effort to planning the supplementary job numerics, since there is no "second chance." A shop with a high percent repeat jobs can place its major effort in control, at the sacrifice of planning, since the control activities will, over a period of time, influence the evolution of the correct numerics. Figure 32.3 shows this contrast diagrammatically.

A further consideration in extent of planning is the time schedule. Planning can be less than complete when the manufacturing cycle permits a trial lot to be piloted through ahead of the job order (to pin down many of the supplementary job numerics) or when the job running time is long enough to use data feedback and corrective action for the same purpose. (See Job Shop Control, below.)

Responsibility for job planning varies widely among job shops. In all but the smallest shops, the primary numerics are commonly developed and issued by a staff group, separate from line production. This group is variously designated as Research and Development, Engineering or Technical (especially when definition of product is part of the work), or as Manufacturing Engineering, Process Engineering, Production Engineering, Estimating, Planning or Industrial Engineering (when the planning is most limited to definition of manufacturing plan). However, there is no universal pattern of responsibility for generating the supplementary numerics. In some instances, staff quality engineers or process engineers have this responsibility. In other shops, line supervisors, inspection supervisors, and even workers and inspectors have the assignment. In still other cases, the supplementary inspection numerics are prepared by staff specialists, while the supervisor is left to his or her own devices to develop and convey information on tools, setups, settings of process variables, etc.

As is usual in matters of organizing, it is more important to be clear than to be logical or uniform. There is a need for providing the supplementary numerics, and the responsibility for doing so should be clear. The job shop which has left this question vague would do well to face it cleanly. As a general rule, if the generation and maintenance of any portion of the supplementary job numerics is to be delegated to Production, the responsibility and method should be made clear. Otherwise, in the author's experience, it tends to be neglected, poorly maintained, and ineffective.

Often the variety of work makes it necessary and possible to do the planning

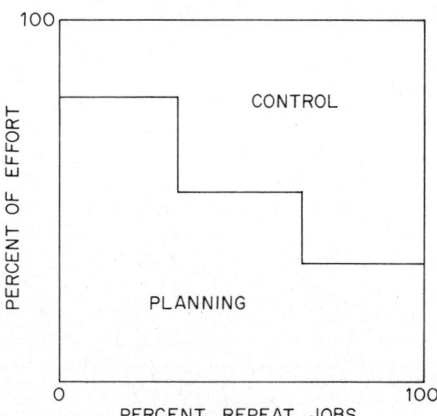

FIG. 32.3 Effect of percent repeat jobs on allocation of planning effort.

selectively based on the size or complexity of the job. Jobs over a certain size, or involving new manufacturing techniques, or expected to become new standard products, are planned by the staff group, whereas small jobs, or those which involve only minor changes from "standard items" or previously run jobs, are planned by the line production people.

Detecting and Correcting Job Planning Errors. The sheer number of details involved in the primary and supplementary numerics makes it inevitable that errors will occur in job planning. Some will be the inadvertent errors of misplaced decimal points, transposed digits, incorrect arithmetic, and the like. Others will arise from lack of sufficient knowledge, by the planner, of processes, economics of manufacture, capabilities, and reliabiities.

To minimize planning errors, it is useful to review the planning in some appropriate way. For large jobs, this review tends to be elaborate and formal. The planning documents are circulated to the key departments, after which there is a formal review meeting. This meeting not only goes over errors and refinements; it also identifies possible problem areas. In addition, it may determine whether there is need to provide "sample" or "trial lot" evaluation before full production. The review meeting also may establish the guidelines for delegating development of the supplementary numerics to lower levels of organization.

For smaller, low repeat rate jobs, the planning documents are likewise circulated to the key departments. However, the review and sign-off usually take place without formal review meetings.

Enlisting the participation of workers in identification of errors has been a goal of many quality programs. Schafer (1978) describes a successful program for error identification in a machine shop. "Job check" cards (see Figure 32.4) were developed for machining, welding, assembly, electrical, paint, packaging, and crating to aid workers in performing a systematic review. When errors were found, workers filled out a problem report, which was circulated to the planners for corrective action.

MACHINING JOB CHEC

PRINT/PROCESS REVIEW		MACHINE REVIEW	
●Blueprint Correct & Clear	●Information Adequate	●Correct Speed	●Correct Horizontal Setting
●Process Correct	●Unknowns / Problems	●Correct Feed	●Machine Functioning **OK**
●Process=Print	●Areas to Machine	●Correct Vertical Setting	●Machine Capable
TOOLS/FIXTURES/LOCATION REVIEW		**MATERIAL/PARTS REVIEW**	
●Tools Correct & Sharp	●Inspection Tools	●Correct Material	●Correct Prior Operations
●Correct Fixture	●Locating Surfaces **OK**	●Correct Size & Shape	●Part Complete
●Fixture Capable, Complete	●Holding Method for Machining	●Material Condition **OK**	●Appearance **OK**
1st PIECE SAMPLE CHECK		**IN PROCESS SAMPLE CHECK**	
●Part to Print	●Part Damage	●Part to Print	●Part Moving Location
●Part Usable	●Machining Acceptable	●Machine Drifting	●Machine Settings **OK**
●Off Specifications **OK'd**	●Appearance Acceptable	●Tool Dull	●Every 10th Piece **OK**

E. J. Buska Printing   Q-10 10/77

FIG. 32.4 "Job check" card for operator detection of errors.

For high percent repeat jobs, reliance is more heavily placed on the control system (see Job Shop Control, below).

Improving Job Planning.   Improvement of this planning, as applied to manufacture, involves preparation and use of machine and process capability knowledge in establishing tolerances, choosing processes, classifying characteristics, etc. The approach which is generally conventional, is discussed in Section 16.

A concept known as "group technology" involves planning of jobbing work by identifying "families" of parts based on commonality of operations. This commonality then is used as a basis for standardization of drawings, tooling, etc., with an obvious residual effect on quality planning. The group technology idea extends beyond planning to machine layout, product flow, cellular and flexible manufacturing systems, and production scheduling. Abou-Zeid (1975) describes several methods of grouping parts and components. See also Section 16 under Group Technology.

JOB SHOP CONTROL

The "jobbing" nature of the job shop is derived from the diversity of products. However, the manufacturing processes which turn out these diverse products exhibit a high degree of commonality in materials, machines, instruments, and people. As a result, the job shop systems for quality control of manufacture closely parallel the systems in use in the mass production shops, but scaled to the size and needs of the particular job shop. In addition, the large number of jobs per worker per week and the mass of detail contained in the job numerics make it important to have special approaches to data feedback and corrective action.

Overall Control System.   Those minimal job shop systems that parallel the mass production systems are listed below, including references to the handbook sections that discuss conventional approaches:

Control system	Section reference
Supplier material	15
Identity and flow	17, 21
Process control decision making	17
Tool and equipment qualification and maintenance	16, 17
Calibration and maintenance of measuring equipment	18
Disposition of rejected material	18
Analysis and followup of customer complaints	12

To formalize these systems, it is convenient to document them in a quality control manual which is then distributed to those concerned (see Section 6, under Quality Manual).

In the job shop it is uncommonly important to provide a sound plan for making decisions on whether the process should run or stop, and to make clear delegation of responsibility for decision making on the factory floor (see Section 17 under Quality Responsibilities on the Factory Floor). With limited workforce to spread over a multitude of jobs, it is also important that the job shop understand and make use of the concept of dominance (see Section 16 under Control Systems and the Concept of Dominance) in order to maximize the effectiveness of that laborpower. Setup dominance is the prevailing mode for most quality characteristics in the small-lot job shop, especially those of Types III and IV. The main reason is that the running time is usually so short that the "time-to-time" variation of the process is minimal. (Another reason is the prevalence of special tooling.) Hence "if the setup is right, the lot is right." Accordingly, the job setup is a vital control station, and demands use of statistically valid plans for setup approval, e.g., narrow limit gaging, precontrol, control charts, etc. (see Section 24 under the respective headings). These plans are needed whether the setup approval decision is assigned to operators or to inspectors.

Because of the importance of the setup, many job shops have made use of redundancy in the setup approval by requiring inspectors to check the setup before the lot is run off. This has not been merely a check on the operator (or setup person); it has also been a means of checking against vague specifications, special measuring equipment, etc. However, as skills have been upgraded and statistical plans have gained wider acceptance, there has been a trend toward establishing a state of self-control by the operator to whom the setup acceptance is then turned over. (See generally Section 17 under Self-Inspection.)

In one machine tool company where machine shop lot quantities were normally 15 pieces or less, the setup acceptance responsibility was transferred from inspectors to experienced operators. Following the changeover, inspectors performed random audits of completed lots and reported the results for immediate manufacturing action. In addition, the summarized data were fed back in chart form to "rate" the various departments (lathe, milling, grinding, etc.). See Ingle (1968).

Data Feedback and Corrective Action.   Many job shop managers have fallen into the trap of believing that once they have established an inspection system (even if, in a small shop, it means the hiring of the first inspector), they now have "quality control" and can relax. Now "quality control" will protect them against bad purchased materials, stop defects from being manufactured, and guard the outgoing product. It may well do these things, but an essential added need is to use the *information* gained from performing the inspection to *improve* quality. It can do this in several ways if appropriate feedback mechanisms are established:

1. For preventing defects in the unmanufactured portion of a job
2. For preventing defects in repeat orders of a job
3. For preventing defects in future orders for other jobs in the same "family"
4. For correcting problems in the "ingredients" (i.e., policies, systems, procedures, practices) common to all jobs

The extent of these benefits available to a particular job shop depends on the "jobs per workers per week," the "percent repeat jobs," and other factors. Consideration of these factors leads to the "current job approach" and the "repeat job approach" as two basic ways of achieving feedback and corrective action.

The Current Job Approach.   This is a means of preventing defects in the unmanufactured portion of a job through feedback of information from the manufactured portion of the same job. It can be used whenever the running time of the job is longer than the time necessary to give the feedback signal, diagnose the cause, and determine and implement the corrective action. See, schematically, the

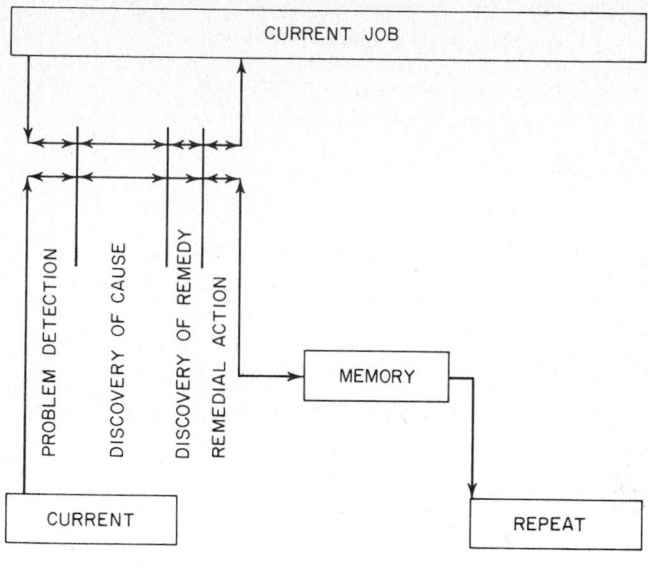

TIME ⟶

FIG. 32.5 Current job versus repeat job correction.

top part of Figure 32.5. The value of such prevention is so obvious as to provide an incentive to prompt feedback of data on quality troubles, and prompt corrective action on the feedback.

Figure 32.6 shows the mechanism used in one electronics assembly plant to secure such prompt feedback and corrective action. The results of subunit, unit, and systems test are recorded by serial number as to the item and the nature of the discrepancy. Copies of the test records are reviewed daily by a quality control engineer who determines the nature of each deficiency and initiates a "corrective-action request" (Figure 32.6) to the design engineer, manufacturing engineer, components engineer, test supervisor, test-set maintenance person, supplier liaison person, or other individual who can take the necessary action. The quality engineer follows up each of the requests and the associated replies until the matter is disposed of by action, or by decision that no action is necessary.

Corrective action that will benefit the unmanufactured product may either involve a change in the *job numerics* or correction of an error in *complying* with the job numerics.

This current job approach is most applicable when the following combination of circumstances is present:

1. The economic gain through preventing defects in the unmanufactured units is obviously greater than the cost of the feedback and prevention machinery, i.e., large lots or expensive items are involved.

2. The causes of the defects are obvious enough to permit prompt diagnosis.

3. The organization for feedback and follow-up can be kept simple, e.g., one employee with a clear assignment.

INSPECTION REPORT		INSTRUMENT DEVELOPMENT LABORATORIES, INC. 67 MECHANIC ST., ATTLEBORO, MASS.					REPORT NUMBER	
FORM #164 REV.							DATE:	
LOT QUANTITY		PART NUMBER:		DESCRIPTION:			VENDOR:	
154		401185		Barrel			IDL	

ACC.	REJ.	INSPECTOR	P.O.	R.R.	W.O.	A.O.	DATE REC'D IN INSP.
0	All	J. Couchie	⋈ ⋈ ⋈	⋈ ⋈ ⋈	0801B	0502	

CERTIFICATION REQUIRED OPERATION NO. 150 – Complete

CLASS	A. Q. L.	SAMPLE SIZE	REJECTION NO.	NO. IN SAMPLE DEFECTIVE	ACCEPTED PCS. RECEIVED BY:
					M. Taylor – Stockroom
MAJOR	1.5%	35	2	2	DATE:
					REJECTED PCS. RECEIVED BY:
MINOR	4.0%	25	3	4	W. Pendergast – Prod. Control
OTHER					DATE:

REJECTIONS | **DISPOSITION**

REASONS FOR:	LIST BY ITEM:
1. 1.595 + 001 is 1.5947 to 1.5956	1. Sort for undersize 1.595 diameter and
−000	return defectives for rework
2. 0.125 ± 005 holes are 0.126 − 0.133	2. Defective 0.125 hole sizes do not affect
	function or fit – accept as is.
	Results of sorting: 143 accepted
	11 rejected.

CORRECTIVE ACTION

Tooling correction promised by Industrial
Engineering.
File for follow - up on 12/2

MATERIAL REVIEW BOARD

QUALITY CONTROL:	DATE:
W. Wold	
PRODUCT ENGINEER:	DATE:
C. Logan	
GOVERNMENT:	DATE:
L. Thuotte - AFQCR	

FIG. 32.6 Typical rejection, disposition, and corrective action scheme.

In the job shop with a low percentage repeat job rate it is often desirable to create deliberately the opportunity to use the current job approach even when the normal running time would be too short to use it. Instead of processing the entire order as a lot, a small "pilot" lot or single item precedes the main lot, and time is allowed for the feedback and correction to take place.

The pilot lot idea has long been used in job shops. However, in its early form the pilot lot was processed like any other lot. Then the final results were scanned, and if no trouble was reported in production, everything was assumed to be satisfactory, i.e., the tentative job numerics could be made permanent. Often the pilot lot was considered to be solely the means of making samples for customer approval. Experience has shown that there is much value in expending extra effort in planning the trial lot, collecting special data, analyzing the data, and using the results to modify the job numerics.

For example, when a mechanical piecepart moves through a series of operations, all of which can influence a critical dimension, the fact that 9 of the 10 pieces in the pilot lot conform to final specifications might seem to be adequate to firm up the numerics; yet the full job order could easily run 30 percent defective as a result of inadequate process capability or wrong process centering. By requiring measurements of the 10 pieces after each operation, and treating the means and ranges statistically, the alert analyst would easily discover the problem and, moreover, would be able to identify the operation responsible, thus preventing a large loss when the remainder of the order is run.

The Repeat Job Approach.   For many jobs the running time is so short that the job is completed before the sequence of "analysis, feedback, and corrective action" can be completed. In such cases, the knowledge gained from the analysis cannot be put to use on the "current" job. However, this same knowledge can be put to use on a repeat order *provided there is a memory system* which can:

1. Store the knowledge
2. Provide ready recall when repeat orders are received

The lower half of Figure 32.5 shows diagrammatically the time relationship that permits this "repeat job approach" to give to future orders the benefit of the knowledge gained from previous orders. Since this approach involves the costs of maintaining a memory system, it is most applicable when the percent repeat jobs is relatively high, of the order of 75 percent or more. It probably cannot be justified economically if the percent is low, say 25 percent or lower. In between, the economics of the specific situation must be examined to determine whether it is less costly to provide protection for all potential repeat orders or suffer the losses of repeating the error for that smaller number of jobs that will be reordered. In addition, there are special situations that may warrant a memory system, as in the case of small first runs of development work on complex equipment, for it is generally important to "debug" the job numerics in the event that production orders are received later.

Memory Systems for Job Numerics.   An astonishing variety of memory systems have been invented in different job shops to utilize this approach. In a medium-sized plant manufacturing custom aircraft parts (Type III), a "job history file" is maintained on each job by the manufacturing planning staff group. Into this file go the specifications, the job order copy, the job numerics, in-process and final inspection data on each run, comments on problems encountered and actions taken, results of troubleshooter's investigations, recommendations, and any formal change requests. When a repeat order is received, the planner must refer to this file to obtain the drawings, operation sequence, and other numerics. Thereby the planner "automatically" reviews the data and notes before issuing the new manufacturing order. Similar planning memories are in use in other plants with respect to items purchased from suppliers, or for subcontracted operations. In other instances, designers maintain job files to accumulate suggested and/or confirmed design changes. Upon receipt of a repeat order, the designer is able to incorporate the accumulation into a reissue of the specifications.

Such memory systems for designers and planners often contain a mixture of raw quality data, unconfirmed "theories" as to the reasons for production diffi-culties, suggested changes in the job numerics, results of actual on-the-spot inves-tigations, and solidly confirmed corrective actions. Experience has shown that these bits and pieces should be "digested," and that a plan of corrective action should be prepared during or immediately after the completion of the current job.If preparation of the plan of corrective action is delayed until the arrival of the repeat order, it is commonly found that the "undigested" information has deteriorated badly with the passing of time (since it relies so heavily on the fallible memories of human beings). In addition, the arrival of the new order is com-monly accompanied by such considerable time pressure that digestion and anal-ysis may be bypassed. However, while preparation of a plan of correction action should not be delayed, making the corrective changes effective can properly be delayed until the reorder has in fact been received from the customer. Such is the usual practice in the Type III shops. On the other hand, Type II shops usually issue the changes for standard items as soon as the analysis is complete.

"Digestion" requires establishing the discipline of corrective action investiga-tion and follow-up, *even though the current job may already be completed.* The organization for investigation may, as in the case of the current job approach, be limited to one analyst when simple technology is involved. However, where the causes of defects and the needed corrections are not obvious, more talents are needed. In any event, responsibility for the investigation and decision should be clearly allocated. It may be a material review board, corrective action board, fac-tory service group, quality engineering, or other specially designated team. The agreed-on corrective actions are ordinarily recorded, and the responsible depart-ment designated, together with the expected date of accomplishment (see Figure 32.6). Diligent followup by a systematic routine is then needed to assure that these intentions are executed during the interval between orders. Someone must there-fore be given the job of "keeping a book" on pending corrective actions until completion. (See, for example, Section 17 under Knowledge of "Is Doing.")

Memory Systems for Manufacture.   These systems are created, usually by pro-duction departments, to alert personnel to the hazards of known prior errors of execution, and to evolve more optimum supplementary numerics. For worker-controllable defects, for example, special "warning" or "caution" slips are often attached to the blueprints or instructions in the job file maintained in the factory. The worker assigned to the repeat order is thereby "flagged" to exercise special care on a particular job. An example is seen in the "pitfall sheet" shown in Figure 32.7, which is used in a large job shop described by Fletcher and Novy (1972).

A further example is the job "setup card" file maintained for some processes. Each card is a record for a single job order. On the card are posted the conditions which prevailed in the process while that job was being run, as well as the results of inspection and test. For example, in calendering plastic film, the setup involves such numerics as roll speeds, roll temperatures, roll spacing, material feed rate, and many others. Often some of these are altered (and duly recorded) during the run to improve the quality of film being produced, based on the judgment of the supervisor. The subsequent inspection and test results are likewise posted to the card.

When this same plastic film is reordered, the setup person consults the card file to identify the lots which showed the best test results. He or she then tries to reproduce the process conditions which prevailed during the manufacture of this best product.

As the card file builds up, a further step can be taken by analyzing the data through more sophisticated statistical methods, e.g., regression analysis (see Sec-tion 23).

PITFALL SHEET

DR # _____   CONT # [   ]

DATE _____

W/O REF _____   ED _____   OPS _____   CC _____

PREVIOUS PARTS REJECTED FOR:

_____

_____

_____

_____

_____

_____

REMARKS _____

_____

_____

_____

P/N

FOLLOW UP

NEXT LOT   [   ]   [   ]

                    YES   NO

_____   _____

   PROD SUPV DATE   INSP SUPV DATE

PITFALL SHEET

FIG. 32.7   Memory system "flag" for operators.

Memory Systems for Inspection.   Such memory systems usually consist of job history cards to which inspection results are posted. The resulting knowledge of job quality levels and frequencies of specific defects can be used for a variety of improvement purposes. It can warn of inspection errors, lead to revision of defect classifications and acceptable quality levels (AQLs), promote changes in inspection or test methods or gages, provide additional supplier instructions or notifications, furnish Pareto summaries of the vital few defects of each job, identify jobs where inspection or testing can be reduced, etc.

In addition, the memory system concept offers the job shop a way to diagnose the causes of "mysterious" defects, to determine process capabilities, to discover dominance, and to perform other statistical analyses. For example, in mass production, a few days or even hours may produce enough defects to provide the data needed for conclusive analysis. Job shop managers ordinarily are envious at these opportunities to collect and analyze data in such short order, and they often give up trying to apply such techniques to jobbing work. However, repeated small lots, plus a memory system, plus patience, will likewise furnish the data, analyses, and solutions. When the data are organized by machine center rather than by defect type,the economics of analysis may be more favorable.

Computer Memory Systems.   It is obvious that computerization of such memory systems can provide much more effective and efficient accumulation of and real time access by production personnel to the needed job numerics and useful information. At the same time, the stored data can be readily manipulated to prepare Pareto analyses and to perform the more sophisticated analyses referred to above. Rapid analyses made possible by the computer will go a long way in diagnosing job shop quality improvement problems, hitherto felt to be too complicated and time-consuming to pursue.

However, it is not obvious that computers will be dedicated to these memory systems unless the significance of the foregoing descriptions of the spontaneous and "unofficial" memory systems is recognized. They were the primitive responses to a real need; that need must now be satisfied by a well-planned "official" system.

The literature contains some references to the development of such computerized systems for recording, processing, and utilizing job shop data. One such is known as the automated process audit and certification system (APAC) and was developed by Swaton and Green (1973) at the Martin-Marietta Corp. The system utilizes the generated data from in-process testing to control the process, determine process capability, provide a record for verification of process inspection/ test, and provide data for regression analysis. The primary benefits realized by utilization of APAC, according to the authors, are reduction of costs, information for correct decision making, and additional information for a more detailed analysis. It was estimated that the application of APAC would result in a reduction of about 80 percent of manual operation.

IMPACT OF ADVANCES IN METALWORKING TECHNOLOGY

Advances in metalworking production technology over the past decade are having a major impact on job shops engaged in the fabrication of metal parts. While most of these developments have been aimed at increasing productivity, they are dramatically altering the basic worker-machine relationships that have characterized small batch production of metal parts (estimated, in 1983, at 50 to 75 percent of the national outlay for parts manufacturing).

New Developments.   The thrust of the new developments, from the quality standpoint, has been to improve process capability in a number of ways and reduce the dependence on worker judgment for process control decisions. Among the developments have been:

* Improved tooling, fixturing, and work movement methods, such as pneumatic and hydrostatic holding devices (see "Quality in the Manufacturing Cycle," 1973; Carter, 1975; and "Mass-Producing Gas Turbines," 1973)
* Numerically controlled machine tools, in which punched tapes or computers establish and set machine operating speeds, feeds, and other cutting conditions

- Automatic selection of proper tools, from a carousel holding as many as 60, and their insertion into the machine chucks, which sharply reduces job setup time and makes small lot production even smaller
- Computer control of the motions of the machine to execute the desired functions from simple hole drilling to very complex contouring (see Cook, 1975, for a lucid explanation of computer-managed parts manufacture)
- Production of a variety of goods from a single set of tools and equipment by means of programmable automation (see Blumenthal and Dray, 1985)
- Use of sophisticated robots for assembly operations and inspection of dimensions of parts (see Blumenthal and Dray, 1985)

Effect of Developments. The main effect of these developments has been to increase radically the amount of job planning and reduce, though by no means eliminate, the amount of job controlling in the traditional sense. In terms of the earlier discussion in this section, many of the supplementary numerics have had to be thought out and incorporated into the computer program. While such a move is to be applauded, it brings on new needs for controlling:

> The programmer typically works in an office away from the factory floor. Only a few are experienced machinists . . . Programs often have mistakes . . . A misoriented tool can drill a hole in the wrong place or become chipped . . . and debugging takes anywhere from two hours to two weeks. (Blumenthal and Dray, 1985, p. 34)

> The machinist must still set up the workpiece to be cut, make adjustments to correct for tool wear and stop the machine if anything goes wrong. (Shaiken, 1985, p. 18)

> An operator may find that the rough casting to be machined is larger than the programmer expected and thus requires more cutting. An alloy may turn out to be harder than expected, in which case the part must be fed more slowly into the cutting tool. (Shaiken, 1985, p. 19)

Job Planning and Controlling. Most of these developments make the need for detecting and correcting job planning errors even more of a necessity than before. Software development and quality assurance, discussed in Section 14, becomes a new routine operation in shops that adopt the new technology.

A second necessity is validation of the correctness of all the planning details, including the software, by thorough setup acceptance of the very first pieces from the automated process. This should include determination of process capability, both for validation purposes and for establishment of a benchmark against which to judge later repeat runs.

Regular setup acceptance at the time of each subsequent job order can thus be reduced to a simple determination that no change has taken place since the validation, i.e., tool sharpness has been maintained, work placement is correct, feeds and speeds are optimum for *this* lot of material, etc.

QUALITY IMPROVEMENT

To remain competitive the job shop must constantly engage in improvement or "breakthrough," quite aside from its day-to-day problems of enforcing quality compliance. The mass production shop must likewise engage in breakthrough, and the conceptual approach to breakthrough is identical for these two forms of industrial organization. Where they differ is mainly in the nature of the improvement "project." Because of sheer volume, the mass production shop quality improvement project usually involves a specific defect on a specific product, e.g., the 3KL cylinders are out of round on the 2.500-in (63.5-mm) dimension. In contrast, the job shop quality improvement project is usually concerned with remedy of some common cause which cuts across a variety of jobs.

(These "usual" projects are not universal. A mass production shop may have an ineffective system of maintaining instrument accuracy, so that many products are affected. In like manner, a job shop project may involve some high-volume production and numerous low-volume jobs.)

The preoccupation with individual jobs is often a detriment to organizing for job shop improvement. A given common cause may adversely affect, say 25 percent of the jobs (see, for example, the case of "inductance out of specification" below). Preoccupation with looking for "blame" or for the "corrective action" in each of the jobs affected may blind the managers to the existence of a common cause, and thereby to the opportunity for leveraged improvement.

Identification of logical job shop improvement projects is largely a matter of ingenious use of the Pareto principle (see Section 22 under Pareto Principle). The need is to identify those common causes which are at the root of the greatest amount of job shop trouble, and thereby will result in the greatest value of improvement for the least cost of analysis. Once a project has been chosen, the usual limitation to solution is more a matter of management than technology; someone must be liberated from the daily, job-to-job problems and given a license to diagnose the improvement projects.

Three approaches for project identification in job shops are presented below:

The chronic offenders approach

The product family approach

The non-job approach

The Chronic Offenders Approach.   In this approach, the Pareto analysis is first one of identifying the few jobs that result in the bulk of the quality losses. (The term "chronic offenders" refers to these few jobs.)

For example, a manufacturer of a line of floor polishers found that punch-press scrap was an important quality cost. A Pareto analysis of this scrap by part number (Figure 32.8) established that five of the parts accounted for half of the punch-press scrap. It became a logical project to reduce scrap on these chronic offenders, since the "percent repeat jobs" was high. (The detailed approach to analysis of causes and discovery of remedy is discussed in Section 22, Quality Improvement).

In the complex assembly job shop, interest centers on individual assembly defects rather than on jobs per se. Defects may be so numerous and varied on each job that corrective action must be concentrated on those recurring defects which account for the greatest dollar loss, or are the most serious to the customer, or both. A "chronic offender" chart is then made for each major job, indicating the predominant defects. When high losses and seriousness are both involved, the list can be a composite of "five top dollar-loss defects," plus all the serious ones.

Corrective action for chronic offenders follows the general methods discussed under the Repeat Job Approach, above. In addition, the list of chronic offenders is publicized for the attention and priority of all—managers, supervisors, analysts, production workers, inspectors, etc. (In one plant in which the defects were

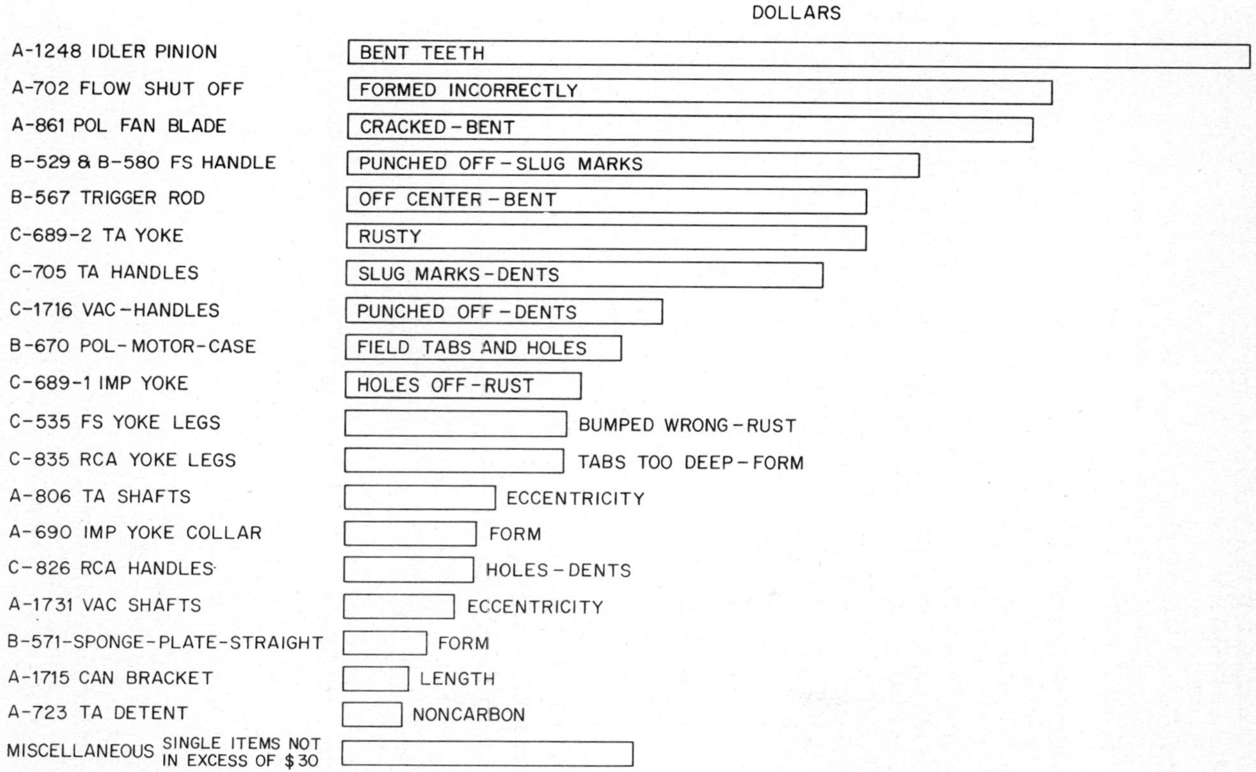

FIG. 32.8 Pareto analysis by part number.

mainly worker-controllable, good results were achieved by posting the chronic offenders list in each production department.) Along with this, the plant manager received a weekly bulletin of progress in tackling these high dollar-loss items.

The chronic offenders list is never static. Some projects are removed from the list because they have been solved. New projects are added to the list as the result of new customer demands or competitor practice. Accordingly, it is necessary to revise the list of the "worst" offenders periodically (in the same manner that law enforcement officers revise the list of the ten most wanted criminals).

The Product Family Approach.   This approach utilizes the fact that all jobs in a product family have similar customer requirements, design specifications, sequence of operations, process variables, inspection instructions, or other job numerics. Under such conditions, any job is a repeat for any other job in the same product family. Through this relationship, the percent repeat jobs is greatly increased. In consequence, the effort of diagnosis and remedy is amortized over a greater number of jobs. This amortization tends to make this approach economic for moderate and even low percent repeat job rates.

The instances of "families" are legion. Tire manufacturers have hundreds of job specifications to cover all permutations of brand, size, fabric, construction, grade, wall color, tread design, etc. Yet, most of the numerics for, say, a four-ply nylon tire are alike (allowing for size scaling) for all members of that family. In the calendered vinyl plastics business, myriads of artistic printing and embossing patterns are applied to only a dozen or so basic families of laminated, unsupported, or coated films. Again, the job numerics for each of these families prior to printing and embossing are largely alike. In machine shops, the family concept has led to the group technology approach of identifying operations, sizes, materials, etc. that are common to a whole group of parts and restructuring the plan of manufacture.

The product family approach directs its efforts toward improving the job numerics for the entire family. This may come about in several ways:

1. By extending to all members of the family the knowledge gained when using the "current job" control plan. Once corrective action has become known for one job, such knowledge can be used to benefit other members of the family.

2. By utilizing the product family concept in setting up the memory system for the "repeat job" approach. Such usage supplies more data in a shorter time, and facilitates the identification of chronic offenders or defect concentrations. In turn, diagnosis of these "vital few" family problems leads to remedies which can be extended to the whole family.

3. By setting up a special project, in the absence of a memory system, to furnish the information in item 2 above and tackle the "vital few."

The Non-Job Approach.   "Non-job" is used here in the sense of an approach to chronic defect reduction through discovery and elimination of common causes that are not job-related, i.e., the causes that cut across many jobs. Because the causes common to many jobs are quite numerous, the first step in the non-job approach is to use the Pareto analysis to identify those common causes that might warrant further analysis. The Pareto study is conducted in various ways—by defect type, failure mode, process, department, discrepancy, "basic cause," etc. Out of these studies emerges the most promising avenue for further study, usually that Pareto distribution in which the fewest number of defects types (or whatever) account for the greatest proportion of the trouble.

The usual starting point is to study the distribution of rejects or losses by *common symptoms,* on the normally valid premise that common symptoms will be found to have common causes when further analyzed. For example, an electronics assembly shop found (at subassembly) that a Pareto distribution by defect provided a good basis for further study, since one defect (solder) accounted for about 37 percent of all defects (Figure 32.9). Studies by failure mode, error type, discrepancy, etc., are similar in nature.

For many products, the study can usefully go one step further, even at the exploratory stage. Whenever the causes for the principle symptoms categories are "obvious" (i.e., all knowledgeable hands agree) from the nature of the symptoms, then an analysis can be made by *basic cause categories.* (Such obvious causes are so well recognized that they often find their way into the very name of the defect, such as "toolmarks," "incompletely lapped," "undercured," or "double-knurled.")

In an automobile tire plant, a Pareto distribution by defects was of no avail, since there was not sufficient concentration among the 85 identifiable defect types to justify study projects for each of about 20 principal defects. However, by regrouping the 85 defect types into 7 basic cause categories (Figure 32.10), it became evident that one operation (curing) required better control systems, while another operation (finishing) needed improved attention to setups. It also became evident that the relationship of ply angle to width required a more complete planning of the supplementary job numerics by Engineering.

In still other cases in which causes are not obvious and defects might be the result of any of several possible causes, it is nevertheless instructive to attempt to classify by basic cause categories in the job shop. This can be done by setting up a special study for a limited period (e.g., a week or a month), during which time

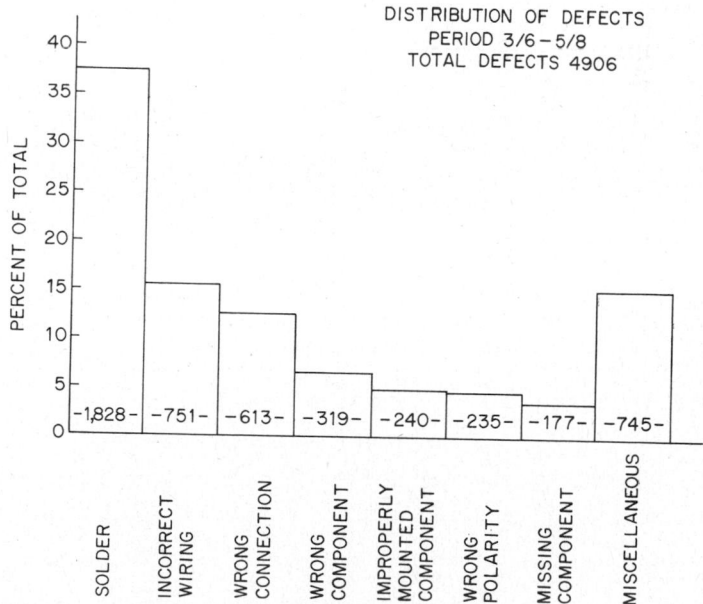

FIG. 32.9 Pareto analysis by common symptoms.

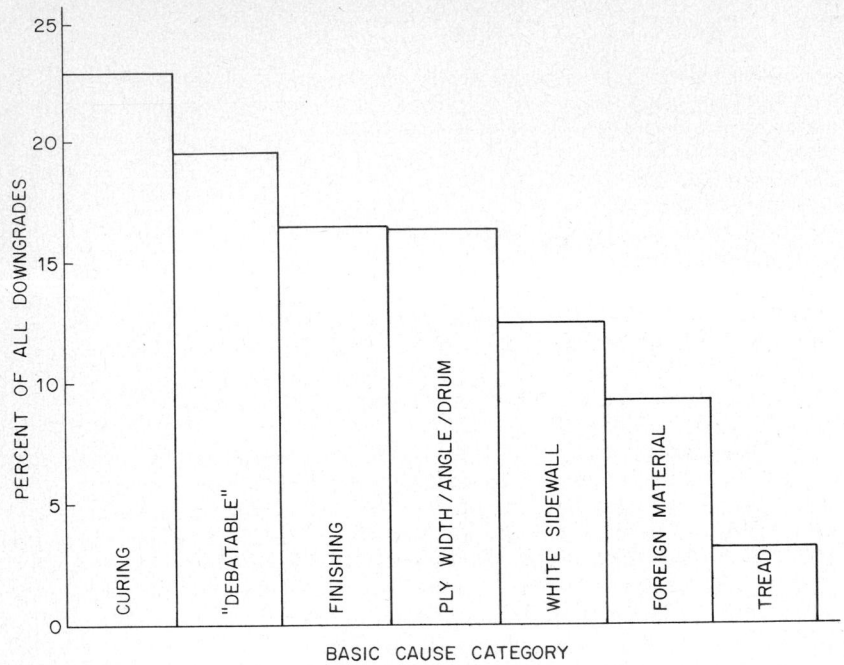

FIG. 32.10 Pareto analysis of auto tire downgrades by basic causes.

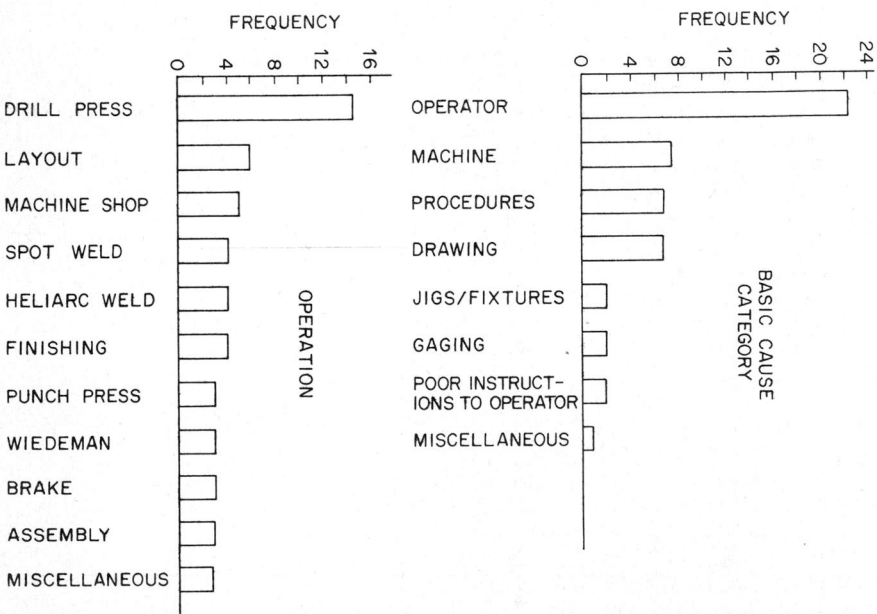

FIG. 32.11 Two-way Pareto analysis by operation and basic cause category.

each rejection or error is carefully traced to its origin by a task force representing Engineering, Production, and Inspection. Based on the facts unearthed, they try to agree on the cause classification.

For example, a sheet metal fabricating shop studied its rejections in this way and obtained the Pareto distributions shown in Figure 32.11. The most promising direction for study was the basic cause category "operator error," since operator errors (acknowledged as such by the operator in each case) were by a wide margin the biggest single class.

One machine tool builder prepared a check sheet to assist supervisors in analysis of causes of defects. The check sheet required each foreman to:

Describe the defect in terms of the specification, and of the effect on assembly or customer

Identify the source of process dominance (see Section 16 under Planning Process Controls)

Identify the plan in use for detecting nonconformance

Identify where the defect occurred and where it was found

Determine the extent to which worker self-control was present (see Section 17 under Concept of Controllability)

Determine the basic cause for the defect (Figure 32.12) (see section 22 under Diagnosis)

The resulting data offered many possible useful Pareto analyses.

In a company making electrical inductors, "inductance out of specification" was by far the most frequent defect. Frequency distributions of a dozen high-reject lots showed two different symptoms patterns:

1. Some lots had adequate within-lot variability, but had poor centering of the mean of the distribution, resulting in rejects all beyond one of the limits.

WHAT WAS THE BASIC CAUSE FOR THE DEFECT ?

____ SPECIFICATION NOT CLEAR	____ TOOL WEAR
____ SPEC MISINTERPRETED BY OPERATOR	____ OPERATOR LOADING WRONG
____ ROUTING ERROR	____ OPERATOR REPEATABILITY
____ MACHINING SKETCH ERROR	____ MACHINE REPEATABILITY
____ TAPE ERROR	____ MEASUREMENT METHOD
____ TOOLING ERROR	____ MEASUREMENT ERROR
____ FIXTURE WRONG	____ DEVIATION FROM ROUTING SEQUENCE
____ OPERATOR SET UP ERROR	____ SUPPLIER MATERIAL DEFECTIVE
____ LAYOUT ERROR	____ MACHINE MALFUNCTION
____ PRIOR OPERATION WRONG	____ WRONG FEEDS & SPEEDS
____ OTHER (DESCRIBE BELOW)	____ OPERATOR INATTENTION

FIG. 32.12 Check sheet for basic cause analysis in a machine shop.

2. Other lots had excessive within-lot variability, resulting in defects outside of both limits.

The common cause in this case was in the Engineering Department "sample shop," which established product tolerances (e.g., inductance, resistance) as well as manufacturing instructions for wire size and number of turns. The practice of the sample shop was to make a single trial coil to meet the customer's electrical requirements. Then, the wire size and number of turns that had been used to make this trial coil were incorporated in the manufacturing instructions. The system was defective because it failed to consider the effect of production variability from coil to coil. The results of one trial coil provided no information on natural coil-to-coil variability from which to establish the tolerance width, nor was the sample coil necessarily at the center of the tolerance range, as assumed by the Engineering Department—hence the observed symptoms when the Production Department followed the manufacturing instructions for wire size and number of turns. When the sample shop procedure was changed to making three coils, with calculated consideration for expected variability, there soon was a substantial reduction in the rejections.

It is evident from such cases, especially the last one, that job shop quality improvement is not confined to changing the job numerics or to providing a warning to Production the next time the job is run. The "common cause" often interacts randomly with jobs; it can affect any job at any time. Once tracking of such a common cause gets under way, the diagnostic trail frequently leads back to the fundamentals of the very system of preparing specifications, of assigning tolerances, of bidding or estimating, of controlling processes, etc.

Diagnostic Techniques. The techniques for diagnosis and remedy of the chronic problems in the job shop are similar to those in any shop; they are covered in detail in Section 22, Quality Improvement. However, the job shop diagnostician is seldom able to collect large quantities of data at will; lot sizes are too small. This calls for ingenuity by the diagnostician in collecting the needed data from repeat orders of a job or from several members of a family. Often a variant of the "memory system" (see under The Repeat Job Approach, above) provides the answer by accumulating the data gradually over a period of time.

For example, machine capabilities in a job shop can be determined from an accumulation of measurements of 5 to 10 pieces per job over a series of jobs. As the data accumulate, a statistically adequate basis for estimating machine capability emerges from the "within-job range. (See Section 16, under Process Capability.)

Similarly, dominance can be identified by recording 5 or 10 "first piece" and "last piece" measurements on a series of jobs in the memory system. If for a given machine or process the series of jobs show no significant change between the two sets of measurements, setup dominance is indicated; otherwise, time dominance. In the latter event, the accumulated data give important quantified information on whether the time-to-time variation is steady or erratic from run to run. Recording of worker identity is the key to identifying worker dominance.

Even "within-piece" or positional concentration of defects can be discovered by accumulation of data from small lots. In a plant making large castings for pumps and air compressors, a condition of leaks in castings was remedied only after patient recording of the location of the leaks, month by month. In this case the castings were made a few at a time, repaired, and shipped out. The memory device was a drawing copy on which the diagnostician accumulated all leak locations.

REMEDIES FOR JOB SHOP PROBLEMS

When the identified problems are job-related, so are the remedies. In the chronic offenders and product family approaches, the remedies indicated by the diagnoses are usually changes in the job numerics. When the identified problems are not job-related, as in the non-job approach, the remedies must go deeper, e.g., modification of the overall system of specification, planning, and control.

Challenging the Basic Premises.   The most difficult remedies are those for which it is necessary to question the basic premises or axioms underlying management thinking. These premises are often of such long standing that little effort is being devoted toward changing them or even questioning them. These premises are further entrenched because their effect is interdepartmental, i.e., several major company departments are involved. In consequence, a change requires acquiescence or formal approval from the upper management of the company.

Some widespread examples of need for challenging basic premises are listed below. In studying these examples, it is well to keep in mind that these premises were very likely well founded in years gone by but have meanwhile become obsolete by the slow, undetected movement of events.

Unrealistic Specifications.   The large number of jobs per worker per week (so usual in the job shop) exposes the production and inspection personnel to a very large number of quality characteristics. Under such conditions, systems of "unrealistic specifications loosely enforced" become unmanageable because the shop people must carry in their heads so much detail of how loosely to enforce the specifications.

For job shops engaged in custom work, the way to avoid recurring violation of specifications (by workers who conclude that the tolerance is unrealistic or unimportant) seems, on the face of it, to give binding force to the specifications. However, no amount of criticizing, threatening, or pleading will assure compliance if the process capability is inadequate. The trouble is that the system is founded on a defective premise. The remedy lies not in more intense use of the present system; the remedy lies in change of the basic system.

This is not as easy as it sounds, since the system is logical once the basic premise is accepted. It is common to discuss enforcement of tolerances without questioning the basic premise itself. Such discussions may settle the specific instance without settling the broad question. It is only when the question "tight tolerances loosely enforced versus realistic tolerances rigidly enforced" appears on some important agenda as a topic in its own right that the question has been brought out in the open. (See generally Section 13, under Planning for Manufacturing.)

Informal Communication.   In very small model shops and specialty shops the communication from designer and planner to mechanic is highly informal and includes much oral communication. As the shop grows, this close relationship is gradually eroded by sheer size and complexity, and the need is for greater formality and greater reliance on written communication. However, in some job shops this communication retains many aspects of the informality of the model shop or speciality shop despite the fact that these have long since been outgrown. As discussed under Job Numerics, above, the communication of the supplementary job numerics is a necessary response in the modern industrial world of multiplicity of requirements.

Quotation Review. The prevailing practice in quoting prices to customers is to base them on cost estimates prepared by an estimator who makes use of cost standards based on historical data.

In some types of product, the precision demanded has become such that the decisive factor in meeting cost and delivery standards is the ability to hold tolerances. Yet seldom is the estimator provided with adequate standard data (on the cost of precision) to come up with quotations which reflect the realities of holding the precision demanded.

Of course, adequate standard data should be prepared and made available to the estimators, who in turn should be trained in how to use them. Until this is done, the job shop is well advised to bring the Quality Department into the quotation procedure so that available quality capability knowledge is utilized. Use of this knowledge can aid in identifying unrealistic tolerances, predicting costs, anticipating gaging problems, defining vague characteristics, and improving inspection planning.

The basic premise here is that the estimator should be able to prepare the quotation. The premise is sound only if the estimator is equipped with the data on which a sound quotation can be built up.

Quality Planning. The "basic premise" question here is primarily one of separation of planning from execution. However, the question extends to numerous facets—choice of methods, tool control, gage control, definition of responsibilities, feedback systems, etc. The really decisive question is whether to formalize or not. Once there is a decision to formalize, the people involved can usually find ways appropriate to their needs.

An example of combined quality planning and execution is the Engineering Department model shop. These shops are manned by skilled model makers working directly with the engineering designers. The atmosphere is highly informal, with little reliance on drawings, tolerances, methods sheets, or other written communication. The model maker is expected to make the model by utilizing general-use machinery, to create ingenious setups so as to avoid expenditure for tools, to consult freely with the designer on open questions, and even to contribute ideas to the design itself. In such an organization form, reliance for quality is on the model maker rather than on some formal system.

As the job shop grows, the need arises for a greater degree of separation of planning from execution. This need is met by the creation of separate planners and a Planning Department. (The quality counterpart of this is separate quality engineers and a Quality Engineering Department.) The planners soon find (as did the model makers before them) that the planning should not be uniformly applied to all jobs or functions. Some jobs are more defect-prone, more expensive, more unstable than others. Hence there arises the need for a rationale or logic to determine which part of the planning is to be done by the planners and which is to remain with the shop personnel.

Outdated Factory Organization. Many job shops organize their machinery on the colony plan, e.g., all lathes are in one room, all presses in another, etc. The intention is to reduce investment in machinery and to develop skills in the respective processes. This colony form of machine organization multiplies greatly the problem of preparing the job numerics and increases the opportunities for error. (It also increases process inventories, overall manufacturing intervals, and the complexities of process control.)

Here the basic premise is that as the job shop grows, the colony organization must be retained. This premise has been questioned on the grounds that growth should be through creation of "cellular" groupings, which use special machine designs to minimize the preparation of extensive job numerics, increase machine utilization, improve coordination, etc. Highly automated forms of such cellular groupings, known as "flexible manufacturing systems," are in use, which can significantly lower production and quality costs. A good description has been given by Black (1983).

For example, a manufacturer of cigarette making machinery (Williamson, 1968) embarked on a program of:

1. Use of light alloys to increase speed of metal cutting
2. Design of special machines on the Numerical Control principle to perform multiple operations during a single setup
3. Design of special inspection machines to verify the setups
4. Organization of the shop into small, compact crews (see the discussion of "Group Technology" under Improving Job Planning, above)

Multiple Suppliers.   For the small job shop, material usage is so modest that when an adequate source of supply has been established for any specific material, there is little point looking for a second source. As the shop grows, material usage grows with it, and there may be a need to shift from single to multiple suppliers for some materials. However, the basic premise of single suppliers may meanwhile have become so rooted that it blocks consideration of multiple suppliers (see Section 15 under Multiple Suppliers versus Single Source).

Worker Motivation.   The economics of job shop planning favor a higher degree of delegation to the work force than is readily feasible in the mass production shop. This delegation reduces the prevalence of worker monotony and boredom, but also increases the extent of worker controllability of defects. (See generally Section 10 and especially under Worker Participation in Process Management. See also Section 17 under Concept of Controllability.) As these defects are brought to light, the managers conclude that since worker inattention, blunder, etc., created these defects (which is often true), it follows that better worker attention, etc., will eliminate all defects. An extension of this logic is that the way to improve quality is to penalize workers for defects. However, the logic is based on a defective premise, since even if worker errors can be eliminated, there still remain the management controllable defects (which usually are about 80 percent of all defects).

Actually, the wide delegation of duties to shop personnel, so prevalent in job shops, creates a favorable climate for new approaches to increasing job interest and improving worker motivation. The job shop is thereby a good laboratory for testing out some of the modern ways being evolved to improve motivation (see Section 10 under Job Enlargement).

THE SMALL JOB SHOP

The approaches discussed in this section for planning, controlling, and improving quality require much technique and effort beyond that needed for the basic "line" activities of designing and producing the product. In the large job shop this additional work is mostly performed by staff specialists in a "Quality Engineering" department. However, the small job shop seldom can justify use of such full-time

TABLE 32.4 Assignment of Quality Tasks in a Small Job Shop

Tasks	Assigned to
Receiving inspection, in process inspection and test	Line inspectors and testers
Gage control and gage procurement	One full-time technician
Reliability test and evaluation, inspection planning, test equipment design, statistical methods	One quality engineer
Quality laboratory, special process controls	One laboratory technician
Supplier control, troubleshooting	Laboratory technician and quality manager
New design review	Quality manager
Command of the department	Quality manager

Source: Kilduff, 1965, p. 20.

specialists. Neither can this small shop endure high quality losses. The answer to this dilemma is universal for all small enterprises: everyone wears several hats. The necessary quality "staff" activities do get carried out, but as part-time tasks for someone who is busy with many other part-time tasks.

For example, in one small job shop a wide array of quality tasks was assigned as shown in Table 32.4.

REFERENCES

Abou-Zeid, Mohammad Raafat (1975). "Group Technology." *Industrial Engineering*, May, pp. 32–39.

Black, J. T. (1983). "Cellular Manufacturing Systems Reduce Setup Time, Make Small Lot Production Economical." *Industrial Engineering*, November, pp. 36–48.

Blumenthal, Marjory and Dray, Jim (1985). "The Automated Factory: Vision and Reality." *Technology Review*, vol. 88, no. 1, January, pp. 30–37.

Carter, Bob (1975). "Simplifying NC Fixtures." *Industrial Engineering*, July, pp. 40–41.

Cook, Nathan (1975). "Computer-Managed Parts Manufacture." *Scientific American*, February, pp. 23–29.

Fletcher, O. L. and Novy, E. (1972). "Application of Hypergeometric Sampling Plans in a Large Job Shop." *ASQC Technical Conference Transactions*, Milwaukee, pp. 489–500.

Furukawa, O., Kogure, M., and Ishizu, S. (1981). "Systems Approach to QC System of Job Production." *ASQC Quality Congress Transactions*, Milwaukee, pp. 225–262.

Groover, M. P. and Zimmers, E. W. (1980) "Energy Constraints and Computer Power Will Greatly Impact Automated Factories in the Year 2000." *Industrial Engineering*, November, pp. 34–43.

Ingle, Sudhaker R. (1968). "Job Shop Sampling." *Quality Assurance*, September, pp. 28–30.

Kilduff, Francis B. (1965). "For Small Shops: Low Cost Q.C." *Quality Assurance*, March, p. 20.

"Mass-Producing Gas Turbines for Megawatts." (1973). *Mechanical Engineering*, June, pp. 35–41.

"Quality in the Manufacturing Cycle Means Quality in Westinghouse Gas Turbines." (1973). *Quality Management and Engineering*, June, pp. 20–23.

Schafer, Reed (1978). "Error Reduction in the Job Shop." *ASQC Technical Conference Transactions*, Milwaukee, pp. 162–166.

Shaiken, H. (1985). "The Automated Factory: The View from the Shop Floor." *Technology Review*, vol. 88, no. 1, January, pp. 17–24.

Swaton, Lawrence E. and Green, Carl P., Jr. (1973). "Automated Process Audit and Certification Program." *Quality Management and Engineering*, vol. 12, no. 3, March, pp. 24–28.

Williamson, D. T. N. (1968). "A Better Way of Doing Things." *Science Journal*, June, pp. 53–59.

SECTION 33
SERVICE INDUSTRIES[1]

Charles D. Zimmerman, III
John W. Enell

INTRODUCTION **33.2**
What Is "Service?" 33.2
The Service Industries . . . 33.2
Characteristics of a Service
Company 33.3
WHAT IS SERVICE QUALITY? . **33.6**
Quality Characteristics . . 33.7
SERVICE QUALITY DESIGN . . . **33.7**
Design for Many Customers 33.7
Time as a Service
Parameter 33.8
Design for Consumer
"Well-Being" 33.9
Design for Continuity of
Service 33.10
*THE SERVICE QUALITY
PROGRAM* **33.11**
What a Service Quality
Program Involves 33.11
What a Quality Program
Does 33.12
Scope of Application . . . 33.12
Components of Service
Quality Programs 33.13

Establishing Service
Standards 33.13
Measuring Conformance . . 33.16
Analyzing Results 33.18
Taking Corrective Action . 33.19
Quality Improvement . . . 33.20
Monitoring Progress . . . 33.21
*DEVELOPING SERVICE QUALITY
PROGRAMS* **33.22**
Earning the Support of
Upper Managers 33.22
Creating the Quality
Department 33.23
Creating the Quality
Program 33.25
Setting the Quality
Standards 33.25
Testing/Measuring
Conformance 33.31
Analysis 33.35
Corrective Action 33.37
*IMPLEMENTING A SERVICE
QUALITY PROGRAM* **33.41**
Education and Training . . 33.41

[1]In the third edition, this section was prepared by J. M. Juran and R. S. Bingham, Jr.

Motivation 33.42

Installation 33.42

**THE SERVICE QUALITY
PROGRAM IN OPERATION** . . . **33.42**

Quality Audits 33.43

Who Audits 33.45

When Quality Audits Are
Conducted 33.45

How Quality Audits Are
Conducted 33.45

How Quality Audits Are
Used 33.46

**EXTENDING THE SERVICE
QUALITY PROGRAM** **33.47**

Supplier Quality 33.48

Other Company Functions 33.48

SERVICE INDUSTRY CASES . . **33.49**

Insurance Quality 33.49

Control of Hospital
Medication Errors . . . 33.56

Bank Quality 33.64

Airline Quality 33.70

REFERENCES **33.71**

INTRODUCTION

This section describes approaches used in the service industries. From studies of methods used to carry out quality missions in a number of these industries and from other experience, the authors have drawn a number of principles applicable to service industries generally.

The provider of a service wishes it to be "fit for use," just as the provider of a physical product does. There are parallels between the quality assurance techniques of service industries and manufacturing industries, but also distinctions.

An appreciation of the special characteristics of service is essential to understanding the special modifications of quality principles needed to fit them to the service industries. This section therefore begins with some definitions and distinctions, moves on to offer a number of universal principles, and then turns to a series of service industry cases.

What Is "Service?"   Service is work performed for someone else. The service may be provided to a consumer (e.g., haircutting), to an institution (e.g., computer leasing), or to both (e.g., energy service).

Service work exists because it can outperform the clients in meeting their own needs. For some of these needs (e.g., distant voice communication) only large centralized organizations are able to assemble the technology and investment required. Without them the needs would not be met at all. Other service work exists because it offers alternatives that are superior to self-service in cost, time, convenience, etc. (e.g., the checking account service of a bank). Still other service work exists to meet a wide variety of human psychological and physiological needs: amusement, freedom from disagreeable chores, opportunity for learning and for creativity.

The Service Industries.   Conventional classification of a national economy into "industries" begins with a subdivision into:

1. Manufacture, meaning mainly the processing of materials into finished durable and nondurable goods

2. Nonmanufacture, which is all other industry and which in turn is divided into:

a. Service industries (see below)

b. Nonservice industries such as mining, agriculture, and construction

From a quality viewpoint, the nonservice industries have much in common with manufacture, as they engage in processing of materials and (often) produce finished products.

The category "service industries" includes principally:

Transportation (railroads, airlines, bus lines, subways, common carrier trucking, pipelines)

Public utilities (telephone communication, energy services, sanitation services)

Marketing (retail food, apparel, automotive, wholesale trade, department stores)

Finance (banks, insurance, sales finance, investment)

Real estate

Restaurants, hotels, and motels

News media

Business services (advertising, credit services, computer services)

Health services (nursing, hospitals, medical laboratories)

Personal services (amusements, laundry and cleaning, barber and beauty shops)

Professional services (lawyers, doctors)

Repair services (garages, television and home repairs)

Government (defense, health, education, welfare, municipal services)

It is evident that the term "service industry" may be given multiple meanings, such as nonmanufacture, utilities, or personal services. The meaning used by the authors is an industry that generally meets the criteria set out below under Characteristics of a Service Company.

Collectively, the service industries account for two-thirds of the national economy and employment of the United States, as indicated in Figure 33.1 and Table 33.1. Some of the service industries are highly automated, e.g., electrical power supply; however, many are labor-intensive (e.g., restaurants). For such industries, wages may represent about 70 percent of total costs, as compared with 30 percent for manufacture. These labor-intensive industries face severe problems in recruitment, training, and motivation of employees, as well as intense pressures to increase their (usually) low wages. A major consequence is a trend toward increased use of new technology to improve both productivity and quality.

Characteristics of a Service Company. A "service company" is an organized system of special skills and facilities. (The term "company" is used here in a generic sense; it includes governmental bodies and other nonprofit organizations created for service, as well as business firms.) It offers the benefits of its system to its clients in a variety of forms, for example:

Use of facilities, e.g., bus rides, telephone calls

Lease of facilities, e.g., rental automobiles, apartments

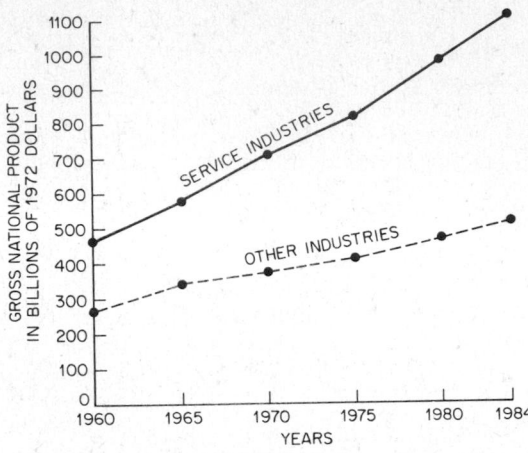

FIG. 33.1 Relative contributions of service and nonservice industries in the United States, 1960–1984. Service industries include transportation, communication, and other utilities; wholesale and retail trade; finance; insurance; real estate; business, personal, and professional services; education; and government. Other industries include manufacturing, agriculture, mining, and construction. *(From Statistical Abstract of the U.S., 1986, Table 722.)*

TABLE 33.1 Employment in Service and Tangible-Product Industries Compared

Industry	1984 Employment, millions
Tangible-product industries	28.7
Manufacturing	21.0
Construction	6.7
Mining	1.0
Service-producing industries	73.2
Services (health service, business services, personal services, hotels, education, welfare, etc.)	32.2
Wholesale and retail trade	22.0
Transportation, communication, and other public utilities	7.4
Finance, insurance, and real estate	6.8
Public administration	4.8
Total nonagricultural employment	101.9

Source: Statistical Abstract of the United States, 1986, Table 682.

Professional advice, e.g., medical, legal

Health maintenance, e.g., hospitals, medical laboratories

Product maintenance, e.g., automobile repairs

Viewing or hearing performances, e.g., theater, television, radio

Delivery of knowledge, e.g., courses, training

Relief from self-service, e.g., restaurant service

Service companies generally share the characteristics discussed below.

Direct Sales.   The service company normally sells direct to the user. This is true for small users as well as large industrial users. In this respect, the service company differs sharply from most manufacturing companies.

There are some exceptions. Airlines and insurance companies, for example, sell extensively through independent agents. Some manufacturing companies sell direct to the consumer, e.g., through mail orders or through house-to-house selling. But the service companies as a group make a high proportion of their sales direct to the consumer, while manufacturing companies as a group make a low proportion of direct sales.

Direct Contacts with Users.   In carrying out its mission, the service company has many contacts with its customers. For example, a number of hotel representatives may be in touch with the traveler: a reservation clerk, courtesy car driver, doorman, reception clerk, bellhop, dining room or room service personnel, housekeeper, and cashier. The telephone company has contacts with all its customers through service representatives, installers, operators, directory assistance personnel, billing service, repair service, and repair technicians. Each of these contacts provides an opportunity for either good or bad quality of service.

These multiple contacts give rise to huge numbers of individual transactions. An electric power company serving a million customers may send out over 5 million invoices annually, receive over 1 million telephone calls, and be involved in hundreds of thousands of moves made by these customers. All these transactions have their impacts on human beings, many highly articulate.

A favorable aspect of these direct contacts with the consumer is the opportunity for good feedback as to fitness for use. In this respect, the service company has an easier job than the manufacturing company, which is comparatively insulated from the customer and must resort to special studies to secure adequate feedback.

The extensive personal contact also sets up some relationships that are inherently uncomfortable for the customer. To secure some services, the customer surrenders property into the custody of the service company, e.g., baggage for transport or an automobile to be repaired. The service company holds this property in captivity, and a failure or delay in returning it can greatly inconvenience the customer. In other cases it is the customer personally who feels held captive. The most usual example of this is waiting in line or waiting for service to be performed when there is no practical alternative.

Benefit Provided on Demand.   The service company has to be prepared to provide its service when the user needs it. If one airline has flights at inconvenient times, the traveler will use another. If one supermarket frequently has long lines at its checkout counters, the customer will turn to another. Customers consider timely availability of service to be an element of quality.

Completion Time Important. The service company also has to complete its assignment within the period desired by the customer. If one airline offers to transport a passenger to a specified city in 4 hours while another can do it in 3 hours, many travelers will select the second airline. If one painter promises to complete the painting of a house within 4 weeks while another says in about 3 months, the first will have a competitive edge.

Work Not Storable or Transportable. In most of the service industries, benefits can be made available to customers only at the rate they can be created currently. The telephone company cannot draw on yesterday's idle time to handle a rush of calls today. Many restaurants cannot seat diners until tables are available. Idle hotel rooms in one city cannot be made available to travelers in another city. Unlike physical products, which can, for example, be manufactured in the summer for Christmas sales, services normally have to be generated at the time the customer wants to receive them. Moreover, the service usually has to be created or given in the customer's locale.

Output Created as It Is Delivered. A closely linked feature is that much service is produced as it is provided. A physician diagnoses, gives advice, and prescribes medication as he or she examines the patient. A gasoline station attendant fills the gas tank while the customer waits. A bank teller discusses the depositor's needs and then cashes a check. In these and many other service transactions, the thinking, speaking, calculating, or other service activity is performed on the spot in the presence of the customer. There is no opportunity in these cases for an inspector to examine an individual unit of service, or for someone to "repair" an imperfect service, before it is delivered to the customer. This fact deserves special consideration in planning for service quality control.

Primary Benefit Not a Physical Product. Many services deliver no tangible product at all (e.g., transportation companies, hospitals, barbers). Others provide a tangible item but only incidentally to the service given to the client. An insurance company issues an insurance policy, but the primary benefit of the insurance service is security against financial loss. An auto repair shop may install spark plugs in the course of its work to carry out the owner's order to make the car's motor operate smoothly. A restaurant may supply veal and mushrooms, but the diner is chiefly interested in the restaurant's ability to combine a number of ingredients into a tasty meal served pleasantly and promptly in attractive surroundings.

WHAT IS SERVICE QUALITY?

As in the case of *product* quality, the concept of *service* quality starts with "fitness for use." Service firms—banks, insurance companies, transportation companies, hospitals and other organizations—are all engaged in serving human beings. The relationship is constructive only if the services respond to the needs of the client in price, delivery time, and suitability for the client's purpose. The extent to which the service successfully satisfies the needs of the client as it is rendered is called "fitness for use."

Fitness for use is determined by those features of the service that the client recognizes as beneficial, e.g., *timeliness* of airline flight arrivals, *courtesy* of store clerks, *consistency* of flavor of food on successive visits to a restaurant, easy *acces-*

sibility (nearness) of service stations, *noise-free transmission* of telephone conversations, *numerical accuracy* of transactions in a bank, *cleanliness* of bathrooms in a hotel. The judge of fitness for use is the client, not the airline, bank, hotel, or repair shop.

Quality Characteristics. The basic building blocks of fitness for use are the "quality characteristics." These are the identifiable features or attributes of a service that are needed to achieve fitness for use. There are several subfeatures:

Psychological, e.g., beauty of surroundings, comfort, recognition of regular customers

Time-oriented, e.g., queuing time, repair time

Contractual, e.g., guarantee of satisfactory service

Ethical, e.g., honesty of service shops, principled and courteous conduct of personnel, truth in advertising

Technological, e.g., clarity of cable television picture

While the service industries have quality characteristics in all the above categories, the psychological, time-oriented, and ethical characteristics appear to be especially important to their customers.

Once a service company has identified the quality characteristics most valued by its clients, it proceeds to plan for its quality of design and quality of conformance. The broad approach is described in Section 6 under The Quality Planning Roadmap.

SERVICE QUALITY DESIGN

In establishing their quality of design, the service industries are bound by the same broad considerations that apply to the manufacturing companies: identification of what constitutes fitness for use, choice of a design concept that is responsive to the identified needs of the user, and translation of this concept into specifications.

Design for Many Customers. Beyond these basic needs, the service industries must give special emphasis to several added aspects of design, which are inherent in dealing with a large clientele.

"Made to Order" Designs. Individuals exhibit a wide spectrum of needs and likes, all stemming from differences in status, personal taste, etc. The service industries respond to this spectrum by such methods as:

Creating a range of choice for the client, e.g., the restaurant menu.

Providing a modular system design, which permits the user to direct the system in accordance with his or her special needs. The classic example is the automated telephone system, which permits the customer to reach millions of destinations unaided by human intervention. The humble vending machine is another example.

Providing assistance to meet that residue of "to order" needs that the engineered system cannot provide directly to the customer. Examples are variations in cooking of meals to personal taste or setting up conference telephone calls.

While these made-to-order designs are an essential aspect of service quality design, they are also a breeding ground for errors, i.e., in interpreting the special needs and in conforming to them. In addition, the special designs require special pricing, which again multiplies the chances of error.

Technical Assistance. The customer has extensive need for technological assistance. In some cases the technological ignorance of the customer requires that qualified specialists be available to diagnose these needs, e.g., human illness or a television set that is out of service. In other cases the need is mainly for explanation, e.g., insurance policy provisions or airline timetables.

Simplicity. In offering a design of service to thousands or millions of clients, the need for simplicity is absolute. Many customers are unable to understand complex rules, variations, effects, etc. Still more customers are unwilling to take the time to learn. (The unwillingness of customers to read the "fine print" gets some of them into trouble.)

Auxiliary Services. The service industries teem with "free" services, which are provided to clients as part of the quality of design. An automobile service station may clean the client's windshield and check the status of oil, batteries, and tires while the pump is filling the gasoline tank. It also provides washroom facilities for the travelers. Some motel chains offer free calls to a distant city to provide reservations for a future night's lodging. Airlines provide reading material for travelers who desire it. Fuel oil companies provide free oil burner inspection during the summer to avoid emergency calls during the busy winter heating season.

These auxiliary services are designed partly to meet competition and partly to meet a special need of consumers for "well-being" (see below).

Time as a Service Parameter. A striking feature of the service industries is that the time required to obtain service is regarded as an element of quality. Although in manufacturing companies delivery time is certainly regarded as a vital parameter of customer relations, it is not regarded as part of "quality"; it is a wholly separate parameter. The organizational structure reflects this—a separate department (Production Control, Materials Management, etc.) is designated to establish standards (schedules), measure performance, and report on results.

Some service industries distinguish sharply among different subdivisions of time:

1. *Access time:* This is the length of time that elapses from the client's first effort to gain the service company's attention until the effort succeeds. The standard for this "accessibility" is expressed, for example, in the form: "At least 80 percent of the incoming telephone calls are to be answered within 15 seconds after the first ring."

2. *Queuing time:* Some services involve a queuing of clients due to variable loads or to considerations of economy. In such cases the customer is concerned with:

   a. The length of the queue, which determines the waiting time. The service company is in a position to plan this on the basis of past history and probability considerations ("queuing theory").

   b. The integrity of the queue, i.e., adherence to the principle of first come, first served. Some companies organize this by use of assigned serial numbers. This also permits the clients to sit while they wait and to occupy themselves with reading material provided for the purpose. This arrangement may be embellished by a playroom and toys for children.

3. *Action time:* This is commonly defined as the interval between taking the customer's order and providing the service requested.

In designing the time aspect of service, it is important to stress the *customer's viewpoint* of elapsed time. For a railroad or an airline, the emphasis on travel time may be from terminal to terminal, and this is clearly important. For the shipper or passenger, the emphasis is from dock to dock or from point of origin to point of final destination. The customer will make decisions on this point-to-point basis, no matter what the carrier thinks.

In many situations the time taken to provide service is the decisive factor in marketing that service. One category of such cases arises from the limited time available to the client. The segment of the food service industry known as "fast food" has emerged to meet just such a need.

A second major reason for the critical importance of service time is the cumulative effect of delays. A byproduct of organizing human affairs around complex systems is that when those systems fail, a great deal of human activity is disrupted. For example, consider a situation in which a vital machine tool is delayed 8 days during railroad shipment. Because the machine is critical to a factory production line, the entire factory operation is delayed for 8 days. Some or all of this delay may extend to the factory's customers and to *their* customers, and so on down the line.

As a corollary of the critical nature of service time, the service industries generally need to:

1. Establish standards for the various components of service time and set up controls to enforce these standards
2. Improve present service time by studying enough cases of service to find out just where the time is being consumed (see below, under Quality Improvement)
3. Make service time a major parameter in design of future systems.

To illustrate the last point, through design of special pallets and support equipment the air freight industry has reduced to 30 minutes the time required to load 40 tons of cargo on a jet airplane (Cornwall, 1964). In like manner, car rental companies have shortened the time required to serve "regular" customers. This is done by conducting a credit investigation of these customers and creating a special computerized file on their wishes regarding car rentals so that they may bypass future credit checks and paper work.

Design for Consumer "Well-Being." A further parameter of service quality is consumer well-being. This parameter is difficult to define, but some examples will make clear what is meant:

1. A service technician repairs a household appliance, promptly and with competence, for a fair charge. What the homeowner remembers is that the person tracked mud into the kitchen and smoked a vile-smelling cigar.
2. A cardholder phones a credit card company to question an entry on a monthly invoice. The service clerk straightens it out to the customer's satisfaction. What the cardholder tells friends is that the service clerk was rude.

The service industries recognize that there are positive and negative aspects that affect customer well-being. On the positive side are matters such as those discussed below.

Atmosphere.   Some service industries take active steps to create an "atmosphere" that will meet the tastes of their clientele. Obvious examples are seen in the industries devoted to travel, leisure, and entertainment. The clients may be predominantly commercial travelers, senior citizens, young unmarrieds, couples with young children, etc. These categories differ in their tastes to such an extent that the service industries design differences in, for example, ambiance, furnishings, refreshments, music, and provisions for leisure time.

Feeling of Importance.   Because service is work done for someone else, many consumers view the relationship between client and service company as one akin to that between master and servant. This viewpoint is flattering to the ego of the customer and leads him or her to expect attention, courtesy, respect, and still other elements common to a master-servant relationship.

Service companies are well aware of this viewpoint and stress to their employees the importance of courtesy and pleasing the customer. Some go further and design into their plan of customer relations some elements that reinforce the customer's feeling of importance, such as formal "welcome" symbols, use of the customer's name, various forms of continuing attention, free souvenirs, and "thank you" letters.

Information.   Still another element of well-being depends on knowing what to expect. For example, when a train is late, the passengers waiting in the station to board that train want to be informed of the expected departure time. This "need to know" is not for the purpose of enabling the traveler to change plans depending on the length of delay—unless the delay is overwhelming, virtually all the passengers will wait it out anyway. Instead, the need to know is based on an instinctive human desire for mastery over the environment. The customers who know what to expect derive a feeling of well-being from this knowledge, since they have the information needed for predictability and, at their option, for choosing of alternatives. Lacking knowledge of what to expect, they are at the mercy of rumors and surprises, with the result that anxiety rises.

Increasingly, service companies are showing awareness of the customer's need to know and are making provision, in their system design, to keep consumers informed on matters they regard as important to well-being.

Safety.   Because the user entrusts his or her person, property, and well-being to the custody of the service industries, "service safety" becomes as vital as product safety. Hotels, restaurants, carriers, and other services all have responsibilities for this safety, and these responsibilities were on the statute books for centuries before the current wave of activity in product liability.

The discussion of product liability, in Section 34 under Product Safety and Product Liability, has a good deal of application to the service industries, and the reader is urged to study the material presented.

Design for Continuity of Service.   Many designs include provisions for maintaining continuity of service despite failures. Telephone companies and airlines make use of alternative routings in the event of unavailability of standard routings. Professional services groups (physicians, lawyers) organize their work in a way that permits continuity in the absence of any member. Sometimes the alternative is provided through upgrading, e.g., a hotel or car rental service will meet the client's guaranteed reservation by providing a normally more expensive room or car at the guaranteed price. Still another form is that used by those repair shops that lend a piece of equipment while the client's equipment is undergoing repair.

THE SERVICE QUALITY PROGRAM

What a Service Quality Program Involves. To control the quality of service, it is necessary to specify the acceptable level of each needed quality characteristic, measure actual performance, note deviations from targets, and seek out and correct their causes. See Section 6 under The Feedback Loop.

The ingredients of a service quality program are similar to those in a manufacturing environment:

1. *Design and specification of services:* To meet the client's fitness-for-use requirements and to make day-to-day conformance to specifications feasible

2. *Establishment of control points in the process:* To ascertain if the services are being rendered in a correct, consistent, and timely fashion

3. *Process control:* To monitor and adjust the service process so that output will conform to requirements

4. *System for identification and correction of sporadic errors:* To uncover, investigate the causes of, and eliminate spurts in service defects

5. *Collection of statistical data:* To document the accuracy of the process or service itself and its fitness for use

6. *Correction process:* To prevent the performance of services that are not fit for customer needs or to provide recourse to the customer after nonconforming service has been rendered

7. *Feedback:* To adjust the process or specifications to keep them in tune with the customer's requirements

8. *Quality improvement:* To provide training, tools, and organizational arrangements for identifying important chronic problems, finding their causes, and eliminating them. See Section 22, Quality Improvement.

The accepted principles and practices of quality control have been applied effectively by enough service companies to give convincing evidence that they work in the service industries as well as in the manufacturing industries. To date, however, organized systems of quality control have not been as universally employed in the service industries as in the manufacturing industries. Several reasons for this have been suggested.

1. Many of the service industries are composed of large numbers of small organizations, which have little internal staff and are obliged to use simple systems for most of their functions (e.g., marketing, accounting, personnel administration).

2. Much of the "product" of the service industries is created on the spot by individual employees working in the field on a decentralized basis, which poses some extra problems for inspection and control.

3. The units of measure for the fitness-for-use descriptors of manufactured products are relatively well established (e.g., weights in grams, tire life in kilome-

ters, loudness of sounds in decibels). The fitness-for-use descriptors for many services are newer or still being developed (e.g., appropriate measures for courtesy, completeness of information received, feeling of security, recognition of regular customers).

4. The individual service industries (e.g., hospitals, repair services, chain stores, telephone companies) have not shared their experiences and techniques with other service industries to the extent that the various manufacturing industries have shared theirs.

These impediments have slowed the adoption of organized quality control systems in service industries. The percent of service firms with quality control or quality assurance departments is as yet lower than that of manufacturing companies. The supply of quality managers with service industry experience is lower than the supply with manufacturing experience. Training courses oriented to service quality are fewer.

Nevertheless, the benefits of quality programs have been substantial in those service industries in which they have been introduced. In the opinion of the authors, service companies generally would do well to adopt such programs.

What a Quality Program Does. Increasingly, service companies are adopting formal service quality programs—planned, ongoing systems for achieving fitness for use of the organization's services. The program is *planned* in order to address the philosophical aims of the service organization and ensure that the efforts of all units of the organization affecting quality are coordinated. It is *ongoing* in order to develop a body of data on the best achieved levels of service performance quality against which to compare current levels of performance and also in order to identify trends.

The quality program quantifies and records deviations from service performance standards. It provides for analyzing data on service performance, taking into account the analysis that is anticipated, since the choice and format of data to be collected will depend on the uses to which the data are to be put. Ideally, it collects data in a manner that will permit future enhancement of analysis techniques. It provides for utilizing the results of analysis as the basis for periodic reevaluation of service standards, direct service processes, and support functions. The quality program is placed in an administrative or organizational framework that makes it possible for reevaluations to result in concrete changes in standards, processes, and support activities as found desirable to increase the quality of service.

An effective quality program also has the visible support of top management, a permanent place in the business plans of the service organization, a prominent position in the hierarchy of corporate goals and objectives, and an orientation and training schedule that ensures companywide dissemination of quality principles and techniques.

Scope of Application. A quality program can be used to measure external, internal, and regulated service. Applied to external service, the program can measure and control the incidence of nonconforming service encounters with consumers as they occur. Applied internally, the program can measure and control the conformance of internal processes and administrative functions vital to providing good external service. A formalized quality program can also be used to provide data on the conformance of the service organization to regulatory requirements.

Components of Service Quality Programs. Study of well-regarded service firms discloses a shared feature—they have put in place six essential components in their quality programs:

1. Service performance standards
2. A system to measure conformance to those standards
3. Analytical procedures to determine the causes of deviations from standard performance
4. A corrective action program to eliminate the causes of nonconformance
5. A program for making improvements (breakthroughs) to levels of quality above those traditionally achieved
6. A control function to ensure that the program for service quality improvement is ongoing

Establishing Service Standards. The first step toward attaining quality is defining what constitutes fitness for use. It is in this first step that service industries differ most dramatically from other industries. It may be the inherent difficulty of defining "fit-for-use service" that has caused the service industries to lag behind manufacturing in developing true quality control programs. The extent to which service fulfills its intent cannot be simply weighed, measured in millimeters, or x-rayed. Because service industries are traditionally human-labor- and human-contact-intensive, creating a measurable template of the standard service encounter has proved bewildering, if not impossible, at times as it depends on many subjective factors.

It might be sufficient, for instance, to develop a checklist of activities that all service station attendants must perform in order to complete a sale of gasoline if a once-in-a-lifetime sale to each potential consumer is all the service station hopes to accomplish. If repeat sales are the goal, however, the standards for service must include other parameters: speed of the transaction, courtesy of the attendant, accessibility and cleanliness of auxiliary facilities such as rest rooms or vending machines, and overall appearance and attractiveness of the service station premises.

Creating scales or measurements of the quality parameters—timeliness, integrity, consistency, customer satisfaction—is a matter of carefully investigating and defining the needs and desires of the relevant segment of the service-buying public.

As they set about defining their quality standards, companies in the service industries thus normally need to consult the public to obtain data on the relative importance of various aspects of service to customers and on the levels of service desired. They also need to study the performance of their competitors in the course of arriving at their own standards.

The service standards established normally fall under one of the four service quality categories of timeliness, integrity, predictability, and customer-satisfaction, as discussed below.

Timeliness. "A distinguishing feature of most services is the time spent by the customer in getting the service, otherwise known as service time" (Troxell, 1981, p. 35). The time necessary to complete a service can be measured on an individual service transaction basis.

A service transaction consists of the series of elements necessary from the origin of demand to completion of service so that a reasonable measure of satisfaction is obtained. In some cases (e.g., taking the order and supplying the food at a fast-food counter) it may be sufficient to establish a time standard for the complete transaction. In other situations it may be desirable to set separate standards for the component steps that make up the total transaction. For example, the process of getting an automobile repaired may involve blocks of time for the following steps: (1) getting through to the service desk by telephone (line may be busy, etc.) to make an appointment; (2) waiting until the appointment date; (3) on the appointed day, waiting for a mechanic to become available; (4) diagnosis of cause of trouble; (5) waiting for replacement parts to be secured; (6) making the repair; (7) testing the repaired car.

The customer may be particularly intolerant of time consumed by some of these elements, such as items 2, 3, and 5, above. Thus it may be desirable to have separate standards for the time required for the elements most critical to customer satisfaction.

The appropriate time to be set as a standard is determined by what the customer considers "reasonable." The cutomer's concept of "reasonable" is influenced by such factors as the urgency of his or her need for the service, the relative price level of the supplier's service, and the speed of service given by competitors. For a fast-food establishment, acceptable service with respect to time might be provided by filling the order within 5 minutes of the customer's arrival at the counter. In a four-star restaurant, a good rating for timeliness might involve allowing 10 to 15 minutes between courses. The markets for the two service establishments are different, so the timeliness standards are different.

Integrity.   Integrity refers to completeness of service. Standards of service integrity spell out all the elements that need to be included if a particular type of service transaction is to be considered complete and well handled. A preliminary checklist of elements may be assembled from study of current transactions and from employees' suggestions. This is tested by obtaining views of customers (e.g., through rating sheets, questionnaires, or interviews) and examining practices of competitors.

Predictability.   (Predictability is sometimes termed "reliability" in the service industries. In this handbook the term "reliability" has been reserved for the probability of a product performing without failure for a given period of time.)

As a service characteristic, predictability has two aspects. One is *consistency*, the uniformity of successive service transactions (achieved, for example by an airline reservation clerk always giving information on schedules cheerfully whenever a customer calls or by servings of corned beef hash in a restaurant having the same flavor and texture on different days). The second is *persistence*—the frequency of demand for a service (e.g., hourly, daily, monthly) (Troxell, 1981). This in turn has implications for the desirable frequency of availability of the service (e.g., how often the bus comes).

Standards for predictability identify the proper processes or procedures that need to be followed (e.g., broiling filet mignon for 8 minutes) to ensure that the end service received by the customer will be error-free and otherwise satisfying. They may include standards for availability of people, materials and equipment, and schedules of operation.

Customer Satisfaction.   Standards for customer satisfaction set targets for favorable customer reactions to services of the organization. These may be in terms of the organization's standing on a particular rating scale or its relative ranking among competitors providing a specified service.

The advantages of treating these various performance standards or specifications as laws (to be enforced to the letter, with no deviation allowed) are uniformity and consistency in processes and outcomes. True control over the service or product becomes possible, as well as accurate determination of the cost of poor service quality. Seven possible difficulties in establishing performance standards as *laws* are discussed below.

1. *Performance standards may be regarded as desired by the quality control department only:* Performance specifications must be conceived and communicated as company policy, that is, an outline of service activities and accompanying quality standards for each must be provided that best describe and demonstrate the proper service level in light of customer demands and competitors' offerings. Quality performance specifications that are viewed as suggestions or unattainable ideals or as arbitrary requirements of one department cannot function successfully as standards of expected performance.

2. *Specifications may be put into effect without accompanying justification:* This impediment to gaining support of performance specifications is particularly applicable to the service industries. In a human-contact-intensive environment, the support of the employees expected to follow the specifications is essential. In the service industries, we deal with people, not machines. Most people want to understand the purpose of a performance standard before making a commitment to it.

3. *Performance standards may be interpreted inconsistently:* Traditionally, members of the quality control staff have been burdened with the responsibility of articulating the meaning and application of specifications in case of a dispute. From an administrative standpoint, this may seem simpler than putting more exact statements into the written specifications. Unfortunately, the lack of clear standards sometimes leads to as many different levels of performance as there are performers of the functions. Such a situation calls for clarification of the performance standard and perhaps demonstrations of the desired service technique for training purposes. Various functions in the service company can be involved not only in setting and improving standards of performance but also in clarifying whether they have or have not been met.

4. *Specification bending may have informal approval:* When a specification or standard of performance becomes outdated, there is sometimes an off-the-record closing of eyes to a deviation. In time, the specification may not be taken seriously. The best practice is to compare experience with requirements periodically and update any requirements that have become obsolete.

5. *Standards may sometimes be unrealistic:* Performance specifications are workable when they describe achievable performance rather than unattainable perfection. Unrealistic or unobtainable performance goals create frustration and, eventually, casual disregard. When everyone involved in providing service "knows" that a published standard is impossible to meet, the machinery designed to measure and enforce performance falters. A specification review mechanism is needed.

6. *Specifications, when treated as laws, will be ignored in the same way that laws are broken:* Many human beings are tempted to break, or at least bend, the laws. Laws represent a constraint on individual freedom, the reasons for laws and specifications are not always immediately apparent, and the lack of consistent enforcement of laws and specifications sometimes communicates a lack of justice.

7. *Correction of deviations from standards or specifications may require* *changes in people's behavior:* This impediment also poses extra problems in the service environment. In manufacturing, corrective action most often means adjustments to machines or changes in materials. In the service environment corrective action most often requires changes in human actions and involves coaching, counseling, or reprimands. The provider of service is a human being, and if service is not executed in an acceptable manner, it is the human being's behavior that needs to be suitably altered. Stress may be involved in seeking to bring this about. (Pitt, 1981.)

The foregoing difficulties illustrate the problems in adhering to performance standards rigorously, i.e., in treating them as laws. However, the other side of the coin is more disturbing for a service industry. Treating specifications as guidelines only—flexible, amenable to interpretation and on-the-spot amendment—leads to other difficulties:

1. *Lack of uniformity and consistency in service:* Integrity and predictability are two of four universal parameters of service performance. If these can be dispensed with or defined at will, only two categories of standards remain—timeliness (which tells us nothing about the true quality of the central element of service provided) and customer satisfaction. Anyone who has worked in a public-contact position knows that customer satisfaction is variable and ephemeral; it is influenced not only by the service itself but also by the state of mind of the customer at the moment. Thus it is risky to judge satisfaction (and in turn, quality of service) on the basis of complaints or compliments alone.

2. *Loss of control and discipline:* When treated as guidelines only, specifications soon become mere artifacts. Each provider of service interprets the guidelines in his or her own way, employees do not know what to expect or deliver, and customers soon come to realize that they cannot count on consistent service.

3. *Undocumented procedures and results:* Without firm conformance to specifications, it becomes impossible to say just what type and level of service was rendered at any particular time, present or past. One cannot put any dependence on what the specifications called for at the time.

4. *Eventual deterioration of the ability to judge which specifications are realistic:* If the service is allowed to be performed in an inconsistent fashion so that it may vary along all four parameters each time it is performed, any feedback on performance is of doubtful value. Because a strict effort to conform to specifications is not made, it is often not possible to tell whether the specifications would be attainable under conditions of control.

For all the difficulties that specifications treated as laws present, they have the clear value of providing a template for service performance. This is not to say that human deviation from these standards cannot be treated on a humane level or that good management of the providers of service should be discarded in favor of cold-blooded measurement and punishment when specifications are not followed. Managers, however, need concrete data upon which to base their decisions about the performance of their subordinates. A service industry needs concrete data on which to base its diagnosis of the industry's health. Without standards clearly expressed and communicated as laws, such concrete information is unobtainable.

Measuring Conformance. Established service standards of performance provide a template against which each service encounter can be measured. Ongoing measurement of service encounters against established standards is the second component of a service quality control program. Testing and measurement provide an evaluation or score for each service encounter. Once tests and measurements have been made and recorded, the results are available for diverse uses, even if use of only a few specific analysis techniques is planned initially; as a quality program evolves, more sophisticated techniques can be applied. It is desirable to retain measurement data in form that makes it possible to apply a variety of analysis techniques.

Timeliness. Measurement of telephone answering time can be made automatic. Transactions entered into a computer or modern cash register can show the time. Times for some other service activities may be gleaned from records already kept. For example, in an automobile service shop the mechanics may routinely clock in and out for each customer's job.

In many other kinds of service activity, special random-sampling studies need to be made to obtain data on actual transaction times and waiting-line situations so that performance can be compared with standards.

Integrity. Some services by their nature generate a record of each step or phase in the service encounter. For such services, service integrity can be measured by sampling past service transactions on a random basis to verify that all steps or phases were complete.

For service encounters that do not create such documentation as a byproduct, observation of randomly selected service encounters can provide the same type of information. Some airlines and hotel, restaurant, and store chains, for example, employ full-time evaluators to sample the services at their various locations and compare them with carefully prepared checklists. Where use of a full-time observer would be too costly, such sampling may be part of the assignment of a manager, quality assurance person, etc., who also has other duties.

Some of the techniques used to establish performance standards can also be adapted to measure service performance. Questionnaires can be distributed to random consumers, asking them to indicate whether or not individual services were actually performed as part of their service encounter. In addition, complaints can be organized and analyzed to determine if a particular component of service has been omitted frequently.

Predictability. Consistency may be assessed by sampling the service at random intervals or by questioning repeat customers. Persistence is often evaluated by studying the waiting lines that result from various rates of demand for the service.

Customer Satisfaction. Much useful information on customer satisfaction can be obtained through market surveys, questionnaires, and observation.

An obvious source of data on satisfaction and failures in service is the cross section of customer complaints and claims. These reactions do not reflect the full frequency of annoyance suffered by customers, however, since most of the annoyed customers will not take the trouble to complain but will just look for another source of service (see Section 20 under Quality Complaints). However, the complaints received do represent a sample of the *types* of annoyance to which customers are subject.

In income-producing organizations, another indicator of customer satisfaction is profitability. Such organizations, service or otherwise, normally make analyses of profits and losses. Trends in profitability, market share, and demand for services are an indication not only of economic health but of quality performance. It has been found useful in service firms to put profit and loss information in a form that can be matched to quality measurements. For instance, if a service organization serves several different types of markets, profit and loss information on these various services and populations can be maintained separately and studied to see if trends differ from one to another. If individual services or populations do indeed show differing trends, the other quality factors can then be studied in more detail to see if there is a connection between satisfaction, timeliness, integrity, or consistency and the financial indicators.

Analyzing Results. The purpose of measurement and analysis of service activities is to identify concentrations of faulty service transactions or encounters and to track down their origins. There are two basic approaches to analyzing results of service performance measurement, subjective and statistical. The approach selected will depend, in large part, on the measurement technique used.

Subjective. Subjective analysis involves extensive review of customer complaints or responses to questionnaires and surveys, careful cataloging and summarization of consumer feedback, and creative interpretation. Because subjective measurement is susceptible to a wide range of interpretations, it can be advantageous to communicate the results of customer feedback to a wide network of individuals involved in dispensing the service being measured. The feedback is circulated in an unedited and raw form to those whose functions and experience might provide additional insight into the causes of complaints or negative survey results.

Once the "feedback loop" has been completed, the results and interpretations are again catalogued, analyzed, and summarized and used as the basis for recommended corrective action.

Statistical. The timeliness and integrity parameters lend themselves to quantitative measurement and statistical analysis. The measurement of service encounters against these parameters results in data on the number of service encounters that took place during a given time, the number of those encounters that met or failed to meet performance standards, and, for those that failed to meet standards, the degree to which they were defective. Data on the incidence of defects are then organized in order of importance (Pareto analysis) or frequency over time (trend analysis).

Because of the human-contact-intensive nature of the service industries, Pareto analysis is performed both on an organization-wide and on an employee-by-employee basis. The latter enables managers to determine whether a faulty service is caused by a flaw in the process as a whole or in the work of just a few out of many employees. Figure 33.2 illustrates the way in which such analysis can point out the "vital few" individuals contributing to certain service failures (see Section 22 under The Project Concept; Pareto Principle).

Because of the cyclical nature of many service industries, trend analysis is performed to isolate "peak times," i.e., error-prone periods, in defective service performance. Figure 33.3 illustrates the month-by-month pattern of certain service followup failures. Where measurements are recorded in sufficient detail, trend analysis can also reveal peak times of poor service on a daily or hourly basis. For example, First Tennessee Bank studied tellers and waiting lines and found regular, predictable patterns of bank traffic. These were accommodated by rearranging staffing patterns. Some part-time assignments were added, some full-time assignments were discontinued, and cross-training was given to provide more flexibility for handling peaks. Without any layoffs, over $1 million a year was saved and maximum waiting time was reduced by 80 percent.

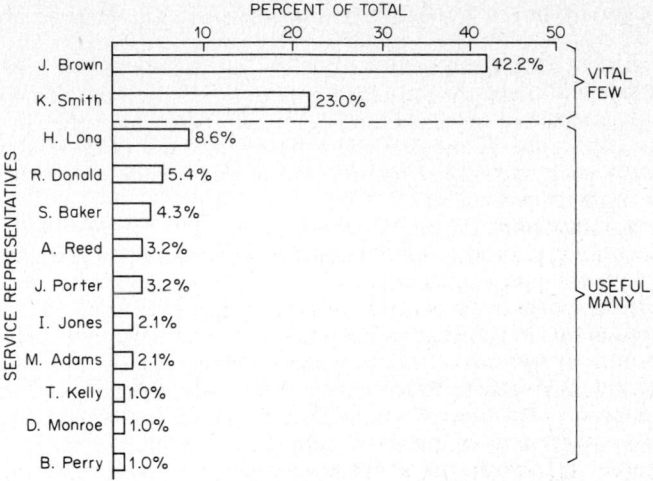

FIG. 33.2 Pareto analysis of service follow-up failures.

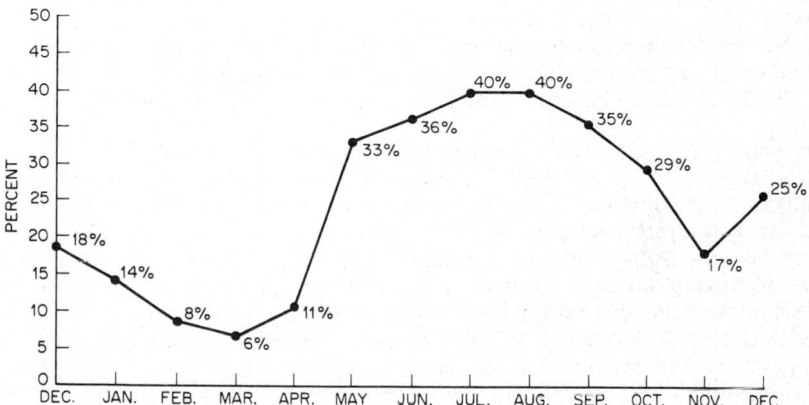

FIG. 33.3 Trend analysis of service follow-up failures.

Taking Corrective Action.   Once the origins and times of faulty service events
have been identified, corrective action is mapped out and taken as soon as possible, and plans are developed to attack the root causes of defective service
encounters.

A total corrective-action program may have as its first goal the correction of
an immediate, specific outbreak of trouble. A second important part of a corrective-action program is, however, development of a plan to eliminate the potential
for repetition of the problem. Even when service defects arise as a consequence
of unexpected events, the corrective-action program seeks to develop plans to
cope with similar situations in the future. For example, an electric utility that has
had frequent outages caused by tree limbs falling on its lines in storms might
undertake a program of trimming overhanging branches. When a service firm is

providing specialized expertise to the consumer, the firm must be prepared to provide that service even under adverse conditions.

A third part of a corrective-action program is planning for any assistance that it may be feasible to give to customers who have received a specified kind of unsatisfactory service. In the manufacturing environment, a defective product can be replaced. In the service environment, the customer is offered some appropriate resource if the service encounter proves to be defective. For example, many stores offer a "raincheck" if they run out of an advertised item on the day of the sale; an association presenting management courses offers free attendance at an alternate course, or a cash refund, if a registrant reports that a course was not up to his or her expectations.

The internal portion of a corrective-action program may be directed toward the service process itself or toward individual service workers. Both areas, process and individual, are carefully considered in designing corrective action programs. The diagnostic journey (see Section 22) will normally tell which should receive the main attention.

Corrective-action programs aimed at the process may include any of the following remedies: reevaluation of standards; changes in service tools, such as checklists, forms, telephone networks, interactive computer systems, facilities, office supplies, furniture, and signs and advertisements; adjustment of the total service system including but not limited to the reporting structure, and assignment of personnel to locations based on service volume; hours of operation; employee shift times and rotations; and quality circles.

Corrective-action programs oriented toward individual employees ordinarily include some or all of the following techniques: training; retraining; individual coaching or counseling; employee bulletins or newsletters; awareness incentive programs; career path orientation; reassignment to less demanding tasks; and probation and/or termination in the case of chronic performance problems.

Quality Improvement.   The service industries abound in chronic quality problems and thereby in opportunities for quality improvement. While routine corrective-action systems overcome sporadic upsurges in the number of errors or other service faults, quality improvement programs attack chronic problems and seek to reduce service faults to low levels not previously reached. The general approach to such improvement, as set out in Section 22, can be applied to the service industries.

The Florida Power and Light Company (FPL), for example, is a service organization with top-management commitment to quality, giving training in quality improvement techniques and utilizing project teams to solve problems (McDonald, 1984). This company has a quality council composed of senior managers, who oversee an organized quality improvement program. The company has trained a large number of employees in improvement methods and has over 1000 teams of employees (60 percent volunteers) at work on quality problems. Managers throughout FPL set priorities for "critical to quality" operations, establish goals, and measure progress toward the goals. Documented savings through 1984 have approached $50 million.

The Bureau of Labor Statistics (BLS), U.S. Department of Labor, provides another illustration of a service organization that uses a team approach and guidance from a quality assurance unit for problem identification and resolution (Dmytrow, 1984). Among the tools used in problem solving are:

Pareto analysis

Frequency distributions and plots

Sampling techniques

Regression analysis and other statistical tools

Ishikawa (fishbone) diagrams

Brainstorming and other group techniques

The BLS improvement teams have, for example, sharply reduced the error rate in "data capture" for its price index program and improved control of its process for printing and stuffing massive quantities of envelopes for its surveys.

Many of the service industries are not well organized to attack chronic quality problems through use of systematic analysis to make breakthroughs to higher levels of quality. These weaknesses in organization form do not preclude quality improvements if top management provides the leadership. For example, the Howard Johnson restaurant chain has engaged in massive programs for improving quality through:

1. Transferring much of the food processing to centralized plants
2. Shifting from franchised restaurants to owned restaurants

Additional improvement projects are the result of supplier initiative. Equipment manufacturers and material suppliers are active in studying the problems of the service industries as a source of ideas for new equipment or materials that will improve productivity, quality, etc. Purchase of such new equipment usually involves substantial investments for the new service company and thereby requires the approval of top management.

Large service companies maintain staffs of full-time technologists, particularly with respect to facilities and equipment. These technologists are active in studying ways to improve productivity, quality, etc., through changes in facilities and equipment.

Where top management does not provide the leadership for quality improvement, the initiative, if any, must come from middle managers. However, in the absence of a manager devoted full-time to the quality function, it is difficult and unusual for line managers to evolve programs for quality improvement.

Monitoring Progress. Service quality control is an ongoing, continuous activity. As service encounters are being measured, analysis is being performed on a set of data collected during previous measurements. While one body of data is being analyzed, corrective-action programs are being developed to alleviate problems discovered through prior analysis. As corrective-action programs are implemented, testing of service performance continues so that improvements in the trend of service performance are measured. Where a system for reporting the cost of poor quality is in place, progress in the reduction of such costs is seen. By its very nature, a quality control program provides feedback on the efficacy of corrective-action programs.

The program itself is also monitored to ensure that it continues to function as designed at all levels at which it has been installed. This can be accomplished through remote reporting and program audits (see Quality Audits, below). The design for ongoing monitoring is normally mapped out at the same time that the program itself is designed. An important component of ongoing monitoring for the service industries is feedback from employees. Service people are in the best position to identify service problems as they occur and are often the best source of suggestions on corrective actions that will be effective in solving sporadic or chronic problems.

DEVELOPING SERVICE QUALITY PROGRAMS

With adequate planning, the development of an active quality program and its integration into the service environment are not difficult when managerial personnel understand the concepts of quality. However, one of the problems in the service industries' early attempts at quality management is that responsibility for quality has commonly been left to line personnel with little or no exposure to concepts of quality planning, control, and improvement.

Earning the Support of Upper Managers.   One of the needs of service-industry quality personnel is to attract the proper attention from upper managers. Without such attention, quality efforts frequently begin, and sometimes stay, at low levels in the organization in small, segmented subdivisions. Some quality managers are unsuccessful in gaining the support of upper managers. Yet the principles of quality presentations, well tested in the manufacturing industries, also apply to presentations to upper managers in the service industries.

It is persuasive for the quality manager to discuss the specific benefits, particularly the financial benefits, that improved quality offers to the company.

The benefits fall into seven categories:

Reduced expenses: Less redoing of work and less need to make adjustments for dissatisfied customers means lower human and material costs.

Higher productivity: Quality improvement increases output by reducing rework and also the wasted effort that goes into multistep tasks after an error has been made in an early step.

Improved image: Greater consistency of good service improves the organization's reputation.

Improved marketability: Better image and lower costs give advantages over competitors, thereby increasing sales.

Improved employee environment: Clarified standards and better training reduce employee frustration.

Proactive stance: Organized improvement planning allows concentrating efforts on solving the most important problems and progressively reduces "firefighting."

Improved profits: The efforts listed above add up to improved profits (Scanlon and Hagan, 1983).

One reason that the quality manager often has not become "one among equals" within the corporate structure is that quality professionals have not yet been able to establish their proper role as financial contributors within the corporation's operational and fiscal structure. Reducing errors is not good enough by itself; reduced errors need to be translated into some financial context so that the returns from effort and money invested in quality control can be compared with returns from other kinds of investments.

If the focus of upper managers is on return on investment, for example, it is advisable for the quality manager to translate quality benefits (e.g., reduced errors, fewer delays in serving customers) into return-on-investment language. If the upper managers concentrate on bottom-line results, then it is desirable to show them how quality efforts bring about improved bottom-line results and what the dollar amounts are.

An approach that has been successful in many companies is to do such a good job in the area of original responsibility that upper managers will seek expansion of the quality program throughout the company. To do this, the quality professionals need both to bring about improvements and to gather data on costs of poor quality so that improvements can be documented. (The elements of quality cost and the means of gathering data or estimates are discussed in Section 4, Quality Costs.)

Results of bellweather quality improvement projects can be put in dollar terms and communicated upward to management in the financial format familiar at the corporate level. Discussions with financial officers may help with the gathering of data and shaping of presentations to demonstrate the gains from quality activities effectively.

It can be helpful to upper managers, for example, to discuss and disprove the idea that "we don't have enough people to do the quality job correctly." Most companies have adequate staff to handle defective service encounters (scrap, redoing of work). Investment of some dollars in preventive activities has repeatedly been shown to reduce scrap and rework costs by a much larger amount. Real savings, in dollars and staff, can attract the attention of any level of management.

Managers of departments that feel the consequences of imperfect quality (e.g., the Sales Department) may also be enlisted to aid in convincing upper management that quality improvement will increase sales, reduce costs, speed service, etc.

Persuasive arguments can be made by providing to upper managers details of the benefits other companies have gained through quality improvements and by familiarizing them with concepts of quality assurance. This approach can be made by encouraging them to join with other upper managers in suitable seminars or, over time, by one-on-one discussions with individual managers.

Creating the Quality Department.   Because of the scarcity of experienced quality professionals in most service industries, responsibility for running a newly established quality department is often bestowed upon an individual who has established a good record in some other function of the organization. Such an individual may not have had previous formal training in quality concepts and may have had little or no exposure to organized quality control practices. A quality manager needs specific, structured training in quality concepts and applications, just as do professionals in accounting, engineering, or other fields. The nature and sources of such training are described in Section 11, Training for Quality.

In the service industries, it has not been unusual for the quality responsibility to be assigned to an individual as an extra function in addition to normal line responsibilities. The quality responsibilities then compete or even conflict with performance of the manager's original line duties. In the authors' experience, the quality program within a company is much more likely to be successful when its head performs no other functions and is able to concentrate on quality matters. When an individual is given quality responsibilities as a secondary function rather than as a full responsibility, it is difficult to apply the full range of quality concepts. For example, it may limit involvement in areas apart from the person's line responsibilities, such as gathering data from customers or designing and planning for the quality of services.

In those service organizations in which the quality function has made a major contribution to the company structure, the head of the quality department usually devotes full time to quality education, application, implementation, audit, and assurance at all levels of the organization. The broader the charter of the quality department, the greater the opportunity for success. It is an advantage for the department to be independent and to have a charter that gives it broad-ranging freedom to cross over organizational lines throughout the company without fear of retaliation from operating departments.

Planning.   Focusing of the quality department's efforts is aided by setting long-range, attainable goals as well as short-term targets. The goals are based on data showing where the quality levels and program stand and where the company wishes them to be in the future. Without systematic planning involving all pertinent disciplines within the company, it is difficult to make the quality program successful.

Early identification of areas where cost-effective quality improvement efforts can be fruitfully made is especially important in the initial stages of development. The department needs to achieve a track record of positive performance while projecting a professional attitude to earn credibility throughout the company. Goals need to be attainable by steps within practical reach so that the quality department is in control of its destiny. This is best accomplished by thoughtful and detailed planning.

The Departmental Franchise.   Since the establishment of a quality unit within a service industry frequently marks a new beginning for a company's emphasis on quality, the chief executive officer's (CEO's) active support can make a significant difference. If upper managers give quality the emphasis and resources it needs throughout the corporation, the whole work force will note the new aims and structure and see that positive change is expected in the way the company does business.

To this end, before creating a quality department it is desirable for the CEO to hold discussions with other upper managers to agree on the mission of the department and to establish its goals. It has been found helpful in a number of companies for the CEO to issue a charter for the quality department and circulate it among the company's managers. The following is an example of such a charter:

Quality Assurance Charter

The Quality Control program as described in the Quality Control Manual has the absolute and unqualified support of the Chair of the Board and Chief Executive Officer.

The company's deep sense of responsibility for the assurance of corporate quality goals must be understood by all employees. The requirements for control and documentation procedures to assure the quality of our products and services are of constant concern to executive management.

The company has established a Quality Assurance Department responsible for development of the company Quality Control Program, including the establishment of the company Quality Control Manual.

The Quality Assurance Department has been assigned the responsibility of enforcing the Quality Control Program within the company and has the authority to define quality problems and initiate corrective action as necessary. There will be freedom to make decisions without hint of pressure or bias.

The program, as described in the Quality Control Manual, provides for procedural controls, documentation, and your individual responsibilities.

It should be recognized that quality control is an interdisciplinary function involving all of our organizational components and is not the sole domain of our Quality Assurance Department. Ultimately, the achievement of our quality objectives can only be attained by each individual performing assigned work in strict compliance with standards outlined in both Operational and Quality Control Manuals.

The Company Quality Control Program Charter is hereby approved and accepted for use by all personnel.

_____   _____

Chair of the Board   Date

_____   _____

Chief Executive Officer   Date

While it is not an absolute that a charter be obtained, a charter helps to gain acceptance for strengthened quality activities. It also gives the Quality Assurance/ Control Department the freedom to move throughout the corporation in the course of its efforts to find solutions to quality problems and to strengthen problem prevention processes.

Creating the Quality Program.   Once the responsibility for the quality program has been established, the planning and design of the program begins. Each component—established standards, measurement, analysis, corrective action, quality improvement, and monitoring—is investigated and tested. Extensive input and feedback on quality goals from all levels of the organization are solicited. Careful review of the entire quality system ensures that the feedback of design review, inspection, and other quality information leads to corrective action and that the quality system has become part of the ongoing process of each department.

Setting the Quality Standards.   An early task for the quality program to address is the establishment or clarification of service standards. In a number of service industries, standards for service have not been explicitly set in the past, as have standards (specifications, drawings, test requirements) for manufactured products. Such standards are best based on research and analysis so that the company's target will meet the expectations of consumers. Their development can be carried out through a combination of internal analysis and field research on the actual expectation levels of prospective recipients.

Companies in the service industries resort both to soul-searching and to market study in the course of establishing service standards. A logical starting point for a service company is to reexamine its reason for being, its economic goals and objective, and its philosophical basis as a first step in establishing service standards. It then looks into the attitudes and actions of those who purchase or may purchase its service. It also studies the response of the public to various grades of service offered by competitive organizations to round out its view of the environment within which it is setting its own service standards.

Existing Guidelines

What service standards are already in place?

Which of these standards have been clearly communicated to all facilitators of the service?

Which of these standards have also been communicated to the public at large?

How successful has the company been in meeting these existing standards?

Have any of these standards outlived their usefulness?

Which of these standards are important but require refinement?

Intent

What is the final result of the service provided?

What should it ideally be?

The service company is delving into its management and values at this point. Whatever the original purpose of the organization, it certainly has an ultimate goal and it is helpful to articulate this on an individual customer basis before specific service standards are created. For example, an establishment offering a dry cleaning service might select as its goal the return to its customers within 48 hours, in thoroughly cleaned and pressed condition, of all the garments they delivered for servicing. Statements of service intent are necessarily rather broad and all-encompassing. Such a statement of philosophical intent is needed, however, before more specific performance standards can be established.

Quality Factors.   What aspects or components of the service affect its quality? In this phase, the detailed specifications are developed. Beginning with the broad parameters of timeliness, integrity, consistency, and customer satisfaction, the service organization must ask itself very specific questions about each parameter. The company can begin to set specifications from within but must continue its search for acceptable standards by consulting potential consumers and analyzing the service and price levels of its competitors.

Timeliness

What is the maximum access time (e.g., time on line at a bank teller's window) that a patron will tolerate without feeling inconvenienced?

How long should it take to perform the service itself?

What is the minimum time in which the service can *possibly* be performed?

What is the maximum time for completion of service before the customer's view of the service is negatively affected?

During which phase of the service performance is timeliness most crucial?

When do we consider that the service begins and what is used as an indicator of completion of the service?

How many different people must deal with the consumer in completing the service?

How many different phases or steps make up the complete service?

How long should or must each of these phases take?

Can the organization itself signal the end of the service, or is customer input required before it is considered complete?

Flowcharting the steps in the performance of a service can be extremely useful in identifying where and when each step occurs and how long it takes. Program Evaluation Review Technique (PERT) charts provide an additional dimension by illustrating which chain of events constitutes the "critical part" of activities, i.e., those which, if performed in their correct order, take the longest amount of time. Once the critical path of the PERT chart is established, the organization can see where to concentrate its efforts if the overall time spent in performing the service is unacceptable.

Integrity. Since it is unacceptable to perform some parts of the service and not others, the organization must determine:

The components that are essential

Those that are desirable but not essential

Those that represent potentially superfluous activity

Even activity that initially appears to be superfluous must be subjected to close scrutiny. During the soul-searching phase, the organization needs only to establish those components of service that are essential to address the customer's request or desire fully and completely. If steps that appear to be superfluous or unnecessary are identified, they can be analyzed in the light of customer opinion to determine whether or not they can be eliminated.

Integrity of service often requires establishment of record-keeping systems that enable the organization to trace or follow up on service encounters. It may require the creation of checklists that prompt the service employee to perform diagnostic or maintenance activities beyond those specifically requested by the customer. While the customer generally knows a great deal about what can be reasonably expected, in some cases the customer may overlook or be unable to observe absent components of services. For example, if in the 10,000-mile servicing of an automobile at a garage the mechanic neglects to lubricate the engine fan, the bearing may later suffer an untimely failure.

Consistency

What components or aspects of service *must* be controlled to deliver a service encounter of equal quality each time it occurs?

Which components can differ from encounter to encounter while still leading to a total service encounter that meets standards?

Over what time period or number of encounters must service be identical?

How frequently can the organization change standards without damaging its public image?

What products that affect its service performance does a service organization obtain from other sources?

Once supplier impact is identified, the company faces an important decision: How far must the service quality control program be expanded in order to ensure that incoming materials or support services are of a quality sufficient to guarantee the success of the overall service encounter?

Customer Satisfaction

How large is the potential market for the service?

What percentage of that market must be satisfied in order for the company to realize a profit?

How important is continued use of the service?

Is the organization essentially a problem-solving organization?

These last two questions are among the most important that a company must ask itself. If the service organization has the function of solving acute problems (as do, for example, lawyers, doctors, hospitals, and automotive and appliance repair services), the potential client approaches the service encounter in an already disturbed state of mind. Such a service organization's performance standards must address the heightened sensitivity on the part of its clients.

If the service is regarded as a necessity (e.g., heating oil delivery or electrical power), potential customers may have less patience with deviations from acceptable standards than if it is elective or nonessential. The customer may view services that fulfill basic survival needs or alleviate serious problems as a right. These services are needed for the consumer's resumed or continued well-being. The gratification of a luxury or psychological need may not be, in the consumer's mind, as pressing.

In a highly developed country such as the United States, more and more service functions are perceived by the consumer as "survival" needs. For instance, efficient and extensive banking service ceases to be regarded as a luxury. Maximum return on investment becomes a requisite for the consumer's well-being. A society that relies on the automobile as its primary mode of transportation no longer regards efficient automotive service as a luxury; one's automobile can very well be the means to one's livelihood.

The nature of the service and its market demographics determine to a large extent whether or not the service will be perceived as a luxury or necessity by that market. Certainly few Americans would now consider telephone service a luxury, and some segments of the American service-buying public may very well consider legal or travel agency service a necessity.

Regulatory Requirements.   What is the service that the organization is required to provide under federal, state, or local law?

Service industries range from those that are highly controlled and regulated, such as banking, to those that are regulated only to the extent that poor or injurious service may be subject to redress under common law. Regulatory requirements must be met if the service organization is to remain viable in the marketplace. If the service organization is not large enough to employ full-time legal counsel, it certainly must consult with attorneys well versed in the appropriate legislation to identify service standards mandated by law or administrative regulations.

Market Feedback.   Once the service organization has established what it considers to be the parameters and standards of quality service performance, it must make sure that its standards and those of the service-buying public are consistent. This is usually accomplished by the use of one or more of the methods discussed below. (See also Section 12, Field Intelligence.)

Market Surveys: Market surveys may be conducted by the organization itself or by an established marketing survey organization. The Gallup poll is a classic example of a survey used as a measurement of consumer satisfaction with service. The media, the public, and politicians all study Gallup poll results to arrive at judgments of the efficacy and perceived acceptability of decisions made by the political leaders whose "image" is being studied.

Questionnaires: Questionnaires are often distributed for completion at the end of a service encounter. The consumer is asked to comment on and rate the quality of the service, usually divided into several components. Consumers are also often asked whether or not they would purchase the service again.

Complaints: Complaints can be handled in any of several ways. The organization can establish formal complaint logging procedures and study these periodically. It can establish a formal complaint desk or department, which then logs, handles, and follows up on all complaints received by the organization. In small organizations, the owners or executives may receive and handle many of the complaints directly. The degree of detail in complaint records varies tremendously, from a file of complaint letters to detailed analytical worksheets designed to record specific comments on various aspects of the service. Followup procedures also vary, from one-time handling of the specific complaint to followup by appointed service representatives anywhere from a number of days to months or sometimes even years after the complaint is received.

In establishing specifications and measurement standards, the service company returns once again to its soul-searching phase and asks again how important consistency and customer satisfaction are to the continued existence and health of the organization.

Observation. Observation of service transactions as a means of determining or measuring client satisfaction with service varies in frequency and sophistication from one service organization to another. It is sometimes done on a sampling basis, with a checklist used to record certain customer behavior following service encounters during predetermined periods of time or at specific locations. These sampled encounters are then rated and measured against the total number of encounters observed to arrive at a percentage of acceptable service performance. Observations can be conducted by managerial personnel on an informal basis or by specially trained observers as part of the overall quality program. The inherent subjectivity of the observer and the difficulty in reading or interpreting customer behavior as an indication of satisfaction or dissatisfaction are the main drawbacks of observation.

Combination Techniques. It is sometimes useful to combine observation and questionnaire techniques. Essentially, the observer selects and identifies specific customers and, following completion of the service encounter, requests that they answer a questionnaire. Customers chosen to complete questionnaires at this point are most likely to be those who, during or following the service encounter, exhibited clear or exaggerated responses to the service encounter. The questionnaire follow-up to observation can be used either to confirm observation or to gain more detail about the reasons for the customer's particular behavior.

Purpose of Consumer Research. The primary use of consumer research is to feed consumer reactions back into the design of the service. Such research allows management to sense changing demands and requirements and redesign the service accordingly. "Consumer research takes the pulse of the consumer's reactions and demands, and seeks explanations for the findings" (Deming, 1982).

Airline Example. Shephard (1975) tells how Qantas Airways made a thorough review of the organization's thinking on quality standards. The managers started by reexamining such questions as: What is service? What are the parameters of quality of service? Why does scheduled air transport exist? They concluded that it would be appropriate to make their targets for service more explicit—to spell out their customer service standards. As they proceeded to set standards, they based individual standards on some or all of the following:

Historical records of (actual) performance

Standards set by other airlines

Individual experience or judgment by staff in the field as to what the customer needs

Complaint records—types and levels

Passenger surveys

Through a survey of 2500 passengers Qantas found the relative rankings given to more than 50 elements of customer service. Table 33.2 shows the rankings of 22 service elements that passengers rated as "essential." While the 22 items were not unexpected, the rankings held some surprises. For instance, on-time arrivals and departures ranked well below careful and prompt baggage service, comfort items, quality meals, friendly staff, and other items. If standards had been set mainly on the basis of history, practices of other airlines, and opinion of staff without study of survey and complaint data, emphasis might easily have been out of step with customer wishes.

Since customer satisfaction—the public's perception of the quality of service provided—is so essential to the setting of adequate and specific service performance standards, it is important for a service organization to devote as much creativity and energy to this effort as to any other portion of its total quality control program.

In the authors' opinion, other novel approaches to consumer surveys, such as the cable television customer survey in Figure 33.4, are worth pursuing.

Just as the service industries have been adapting traditional quality principles to their use, they can cull from the available literature on human relations and organization psychology various tools and techniques to help them obtain a better reading of the needs and desires of present and potential customers in their target markets. The emerging field of organizational psychology has made extensive use

TABLE 33.2   Rankings Given by Qantas Airways Passengers to Various Services and Amenities Termed "Essential"

---

1. No lost baggage
2. No damaged baggage
3. Clean toilets
4. Comfortable seats
5. Prompt baggage delivery
6. Ample leg room
7. Good-quality meals
8. Prompt reservation service
9. Friendly/efficient cabin crew
10. Clean and tidy cabin
11. Comfortable cabin temperature/humidity
12. Assistance with connections
13. Being kept informed of delays
14. Transport from airports to cities
15. Accurate arrival information to relatives/friends
16. Well-organized boarding
17. Quick/friendly airport check-in
18. Self-service baggage trolleys
19. On-time arrival
20. Provision of pillows/rugs
21. Assistance with customs/immigration
22. On-time departures

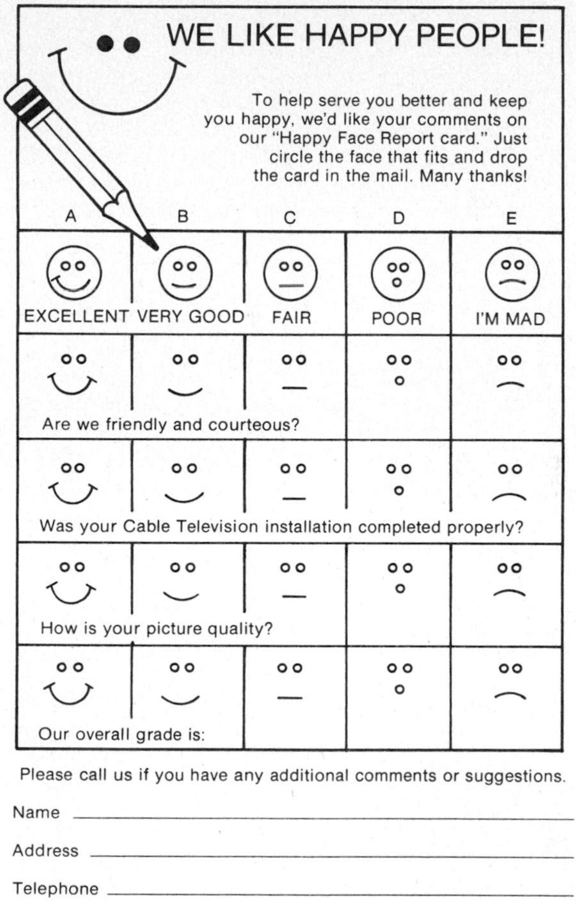

FIG. 33.4 Example of a consumer questionnaire.

of psychological tests to obtain subjective, but very telling, information on employee and customer impressions and perceptions. Such tests sometimes involve the use of photographs to prompt the subject to invent a scenario of which the photograph might be illustrative. Similarly, silent video tapes could show the service encounters, which customers or potential customers would then describe. Such customer feedback on staged service encounters of various quality levels might provide very useful insights into the aspects of the service encounter that are most important to the customer.

Testing/Measuring Conformance. To keep track of service performance, it has been found useful to develop a measurement system that will provide documented, historical data. Once historical data have been collected, it is then possible to analyze the data in conjunction with survey data and arrive at reasonable target levels for individual service employees and for the service organization as a whole. The first goal of testing and measurement, however, is to measure present levels of performance. Under an ongoing quality control program, it is not necessary to measure and record the quality of each separate service encountered. It is sufficient to set up a random sampling program based upon the desired degree of protection, using as a base an existing sampling program, such as that covered by MIL-STD-105D. A sampling program can reduce the total amount of paperwork required and provide an accurate indication of the quality of all service encounters. In any event, 100 percent inspection has been found to be only about 85 percent effective. (Sampling is discussed in more detail in Section 25, Acceptance Sampling. The accuracy of inspection is examined under Inspector Errors in Section 18.)

Once the sampling procedure has been determined, actual testing and measurement takes the form of evaluation for timeliness, integrity, consistency, or customer satisfaction.

Timeliness.   A service transaction is the sum of the operations necessary from the origin of demand for the service to the time that a reasonable measure of satisfaction is attained. A transaction is made up of one or more individual services, each of which is performed in an essentially uninterrupted time period. Service can be classified in two ways:

1. *Duration:*   This is the duration of an individual service, ranging from fractions of a second to continuous years. Five basic classes of duration are minutes, hours, days, weeks, and months.

2. *Persistence:*   Persistence can be defined as "the frequency of occurrence of a situation creating demand for the service" (Troxell, 1981, p. 35).

Queuing theory, one of the tools of operations research, explains the behavior of waiting lines. Queue parameters can be used to specify the degree of timeliness and to measure the conformance of individual service encounters to the service time standards. The standards for persistence and duration of a service can be established from historical data or from results of a survey of patron requirements or may be based on the inherent capacity of the service organization. The conformance of individual service encounters to the duration and persistence standards can be measured by one or more of the methods listed below:

Work sampling: Independent observers can be trained to select service encounters at appropriate sampling intervals, properly document the encounter for identification purposes (location, time, name of service person, nature of service rendered), time the service encounter with a stopwatch, and record the time for future use in analysis.

Survey: Service buyers can be given questionnaires or survey forms requesting information on the time required to secure individual services and their persistence in using this particular service.

Computers: If a service involves the use of an interactive computer terminal, the system can be programmed to provide data on the duration of computer access time and the persistence of an individual client in purchasing the service.

Mechanical devices: If the service involves actual queues, then electric eyes, treadles, or turnstiles can be used to record the number of customers who pass through a given point in the line. This will provide information on volume and (in a sophisticated environment, where two electric eyes, treadles, or turnstiles are used) can even record the duration of the service.

Logs: Record-keeping systems can be designed for service encounters to make the summarization and analysis of information on service persistence readily available.

Audits: In establishments that take in customers' goods to be serviced and returned within a specified time, periodic on-site audits can be conducted to determine the number of items taken in on a given date, the number of items processed within the specified time, and the number of items still requiring work after the return time. The "nonconforming" items (those remaining on the premises longer than the specified time) can then be arranged in groups by time categories.

Integrity. Many of the techniques used to establish integrity standards can be used to measure the conformance of service encounters to these standards. (1) In one approach service transactions are sampled on a random basis, and an observer, using a checklist, records the steps or phases completed. (2) Questionnaires can be distributed to random customers requesting information on the individual services received. (3) The complaint file can be analyzed to discover patterns or trends in missing service components.

Consistency. Studies of complaint files and consumer questionnaires are the most effective means of determining the conformance of service encounters to established consistency standards.

Questionnaires or surveys are designed to provide repeat customers with an opportunity to evaluate subsequent service transactions against initial transactions. The format and distribution of questionnaires and surveys can be based on existing records that provide clear identification of service location, time, and individual service person. (Consumer responses that cannot be traced to specific locations and employees are of little value in later analysis.)

Samples for consistency are taken separately for each logical unit of service provision. Such a service subcategory may be a location, person, flight route, appointment time, geographic region, or other unit that allows the Quality Department to group or compare the results of like service units constructively (e.g., for Pareto analysis).

In some industries (e.g., fast-food chains), the consistency of service at individual service locations depends significantly on suppliers or subcontractors (e.g., for freshness and flavor of ground beef). If the service organization allows local managers to select their own suppliers, it is appropriate to analyze results of quality measurements to determine if supplier quality has affected service quality. (See Supplier Quality, below.)

Customer Satisfaction. For business organizations, sales volume and profitability provide overall indications of customer satisfaction. The relative demand for service (e.g., the ridership of competing airlines on a given route, the per capita circulation of a public library) is also a general indicator of satisfaction. The proportion of repeat business or reuse of service is another indicator of satisfaction with performance. The same subdivision of service providers into logical units that is used for consistency testing may also be appropriate for analysis of customer satisfaction. This allows the service organization to compare and study the volumes or profitabilities of its various units. Demand and profit are of interest as general indicators of customer satisfaction. However, they do not tell whether the customer is mainly pleased with accessibility, caliber of the service, friendliness, speed of service, price, or other aspects of service.

A more detailed picture of customer satisfaction can be obtained through the use of surveys and questionnaires, on-site interviews of customers by trained personnel, maintenance of a well-planned and organized complaint file, and market surveys. Examples of consumer comment forms are shown in Figures 33.5 and 33.6.

	Yes	No
Was your reservation handled courteously?	☐	☐
On your arrival, did you receive friendly courteous service from		
Doorman	☐	☐
Reservation clerk	☐	☐
Bellman	☐	☐
During your stay, did you receive friendly courteous service from		
Maid	☐	☐
Telephone operator	☐	☐
Room service	☐	☐
Valet service	☐	☐
Cashier	☐	☐

FIG. 33.5 Typical consumer comment form—hotel.

	Yes	No
Was the food quality satisfactory?	☐	☐
Was the service prompt?	☐	☐
Was the service friendly?	☐	☐
Were the prices reasonable?	☐	☐
Was the restaurant clean?	☐	☐
Was the washroom clean?	☐	☐

FIG. 33.6 Typical consumer comment form—restaurant.

Planning for Measurement. From experience with the development of testing and measurement systems for service quality programs, the authors suggest the following guidelines:

1. Design the measurement systems to be natural outgrowths or enhancements of existing record-keeping or data-gathering systems, if possible.
2. If existing systems do not provide adequate quality performance data, plan the measurement system to follow the format of existing systems or forms as closely as possible. This simplifies the training process and allows a closer correlation of quality and nonquality data for analysis.
3. Make the data collection as simple and routine as possible.
4. Plan to capture data on process *and* human conformance to standards.
5. When human conformance to standards is involved, plan for use of measures in conjunction with normal performance appraisals of individual employees.
6. Announce and clearly explain new fact gathering and measures to all employees who may be subject to measurement. The known introduction of a measurement system will usually stimulate an increase in employee quality and productivity. However, like a "Radar in Use" sign along a highway, the short-term "Hawthorne effect" of the new measurement systems is no substitute for an ongoing system that provides data actually used for analysis and corrective action.

7. Communicate results of measurement to all employees periodically, preferably on a service unit basis. Whenever possible, provide information on quality levels actually achieved—both the average for the company and specific features for individual organizational units or individual people—so employees of individual units can judge for themselves where their performance falls in relation to the standard.

Analysis. Analysis of service performance can be *subjective* or *quantitative*. Subjective analysis has great relevance to the service industries. Customer satisfaction is in itself a largely subjective quality parameter. Subjective data, feelings, and impressions of the service organization can be summarized to provide the entire organization with feedback on how the service given conforms to standards.

Subjective Analysis. Well-designed surveys and questions used in measuring service performance are developed with future analysis in mind. Essentially, this requires that questions be phrased and grouped in a way that allows a variety of later uses. The questionnaire or survey is divided into sections, which deal with specific quality parameters. Results from all questionnaires can then be combined to provide indicators of service timeliness, integrity, consistency, and customer satisfaction on an organizationwide basis.

If sufficient identifying information is incorporated in surveys and questionnaires (e.g., name or location, person, nature of service provided), service performance comments and ratings can be sorted and reported on a unit-by-unit basis. It is often difficult to judge before reviewing responses what classifications will best accommodate the range of replies. However, after a representative sample has been reviewed, broad categories usually begin to emerge. Responses to surveys and questionnaires can be grouped initially into favorable versus unfavorable. These two groups can then be further divided into more specific categories of complaint or compliment.

Statistical conclusions can be drawn from the results of sorting and grouping subjective responses. It is possible to prepare reports that indicate the number of surveys or questionnaires completed, the number generally positive, the number generally negative, the number of specific types of positive or negative comments, and the percentage that each category represents of the total population of responses.

Parcto analysis can be used to identify the leading causes of nonconforming service performance. Once the signficant few factors have been isolated, these can be studied for potential causes. If the responses have been grouped by service unit, it may be possible to determine the location or individual involved most frequently in nonconforming encounters. Further study of data on these locations or individuals may disclose that nonquality indicators are also below standards. For instance, a service location with an above-average number of customer complaints may also prove to be one that often runs over budget, or an individual employee with a poor quality record may also have a record of other performance problems.

The analysis of service performance required to discover the "why" of survey and questionnaire results can become very sophisticated. Among the factors to be considered in evaluating the reasons for poor service performance are:

Individual employees: Time on job; time in industry; educational level; training completed; training record; attendance record; prior experience in other industry; job grade or level; time in job grade or level; productivity ratings

Location, division, department, or other physical basis: Size of unit; number of personnel assigned to unit; experience of personnel; nature and age of equipment; geographic indicators; demographics of geographic location; supervision; time in existence; type of suppliers; customer; budget; profit margin; business plans or operational goals

Design of service: Completeness, grade, and timeliness of service in relation to the cost or effort required of the patron

Environment: Availability of alternative kinds and levels of service from competitors; prevailing economic climate

The quality analyst then looks for relationships between quality indicators and these factors. If low quality ratings are found to be associated with low time in job and low training, for example, this may lead to a theory (still to be tested at this point) that suitable training would yield higher customer satisfaction.

The subjective portions of observers' findings and the data available in complaint files or logs can be analyzed in much the same manner as the results of surveys and questionnaires.

Quantitative Analysis.   Timeliness and persistence parameters lend themselves to quantitative analysis. It is fairly simple to time individual services or service transactions. Deviations from the time standards can then be identified, summarized, and analyzed. Persistence can be evaluated by comparing the number of return or repeat patrons with a preestablished standard of expected repeated use. Individual customers who use the service less frequently than the standard would suggest can be counted and the data on them summarized and analyzed.

Based on sampling, a periodic report of measurements of timeliness and persistence can show:

Number and percentage of nonconforming encounters

Number and percentage of conforming encounters

Actual average access or service times for key service elements

Actual percentages of repeat patrons for specified services

Trends in conformance or nonconformance over time or among locations and individual facilitators

Degree of nonconformance (categories of excessive access or service times)

Frequency of nonconformance for each appropriate duration class

These quantitative analyses can be performed on an individual or physical unit basis.

Companies find it desirable to maintain statistical results at two levels: (1) the administrative or professional level, where detailed figures are needed for use in management decisions; and (2) at the line employee level, where summaries, in graphic form if possible, are most useful.

As with the raw results of measurement, companies find it beneficial to communicate the result of analysis rather widely throughout the organization. This enables individual employees to assess their own performance against the performance of others. It also provides information that makes suggestions for corrective action possible. Because wide distribution requires that results be understandable at various levels, graphics (histograms, charts, graphs) are helpful as a means of portraying analysis results simply and concisely.

Corrective Action. An important purpose of standard-setting, measurement, and analysis is to draw attention to deviations from standards and provide clues that make it possible to design appropriate *corrective action.* Corrective actions must be as varied as the circumstances of nonconformance that require them. One way of viewing corrective action, however, is to note that it can be applied to the *process* or to *individuals.* Figure 33.7 illustrates the separation of a number of kinds of data processing problems into individual ("coder") and process ("management") categories.

Corrective action programs designed to alleviate *process* defects may be aimed at any or all of the following areas:

1. Organizational structure
2. Reporting structure (span of control of an individual superior, line of command for service decisions, communication network)
3. Service design
   a. Individual services (steps required to complete, number of employees required to complete, tools used in completion, documentation maintained on indivdiual services)
   b. Service transactions (the number of individual services required to complete, nature of individual services required to complete, number of persons required to complete, standard duration and pesistence of transactions)
4. Physical facilities (number of locations, sites of locations, size of buildings or offices, furniture, equipment, accessibility, hours)

Corrective-action programs aimed at *individuals* usually utilize personnel management tools and techniques common to all industries. Service quality

PROBLEM-SOLVING RESPONSIBILITY MATRIX

ERROR	CONTROLLABLE BY		
	CODER	MANAGEMENT	UNCONTROLLABLE
CODING FORM DESIGN		X	
TRAINING		X	
KEY ENTRY ERRORS	X		
STAT PLAN CHANGE		X	X
CODING OMISSION	X		
LINE CODES	X		
MANUAL INTERPRETATION	X	X	
GOVERNMENTAL REGULATIONS			X
TERRITORY CODES	X		

FIG. 33.7 Analysis of responsibility for corrective actions.

guidelines for individual employees start with complete and detailed descriptions of job duties and performance requirements. These are communicated to each employee early in the training process. Employee conformance to these standards of performance is measured periodically to provide supervisors with feedback necessary to evaluate and suitably reward or adjust performance.

Pareto analysis of errors, omissions, slow service, incidents of discourtesy, etc. may show that certain of these occur most often with one or a few out of a number of employees doing like work. If the reason is apparent, coaching or training may be appropriate. If the reason is not known, careful comparison of the techniques of the more successful and the less successful employees may disclose that some have a special knack or skill, which can be shown to others.

One notable difference between the analysis and corrective-action steps used for quality control purposes and the routine employee performance review for salary administration purposes is that analysis sometimes uncovers a weakness in the established standards for employee performance. In such a case, corrective action needs to be directed to the duty descriptions or instructions that are unrealistic or counterproductive rather than to the skills or behavior of the individual.

A relatively random spread of defects over the performance of a number of employees doing like work points the search toward the system within which they work. Among possible causes for faults that are rather evenly spread among employees are unclear standards for the work, incomplete instructions, insufficient training, lack of checklists, equipment that does not function consistently or is hard for the employee to use (e.g., computer terminals with eye-straining displays), and unfavorable job design.

Telephone Company Example. The compiling of directories is a large-volume clerical operation involving many employees and opportunities for error. Ford (1979) reports that the Indiana Bell Telephone Company, for instance, had 33 clerks compiling all the directories for the state. Their work, divided into 21 steps, passed from clerk to clerk in production-line style. Employees found the work uninspiring, and turnover was severe. Accuracy and productivity were less than desired. Indiana Bell made a succession of improvements in the employees' work assignments. Initially, supervisors identified the most competent employees. They asked them if they felt they could do error-free work so that it would not be necessary for other clerks to check their work. The employees agreed that they could and expanded their jobs by doing their own checking. This reduced the number of steps to 14. Later, the supervisors invited each of several employees to take on all 14 steps for a small complete telephone book—to "own" his or her book. This worked well, so the supervisors offered each employee working on a large-city book the opportunity to handle all 14 steps for certain letters of the alphabet. Overall, the job redesign was strikingly successful in raising productivity, accuracy, and morale while reducing turnover.

Many units of the American Telephone and Telegraph Company have had good results in situations in which they have given each employee such a "natural area of responsibility." The company seeks to create "wholeness" in jobs. The supervisors bring together related slices of work to build one of the following entities for an employee (Ford, 1973):

1. A customer for his or her work (usually someone outside the company)

2. A client (usually someone inside the business, helping the employee to serve the customer)

3. A task (where, ideally, the individual employee produces complete items)

Another example illustrates the differences between actions with regard to the process, actions with regard to individual employees, and actions to improve standards.

Travel Agency Example.   Travel agencies provide a variety of services to the public through employees working in offices where customers can walk in or make an appointment. Travel agencies also transact business over the phone and use computer systems to access transportation information. A vacationer can purchase a broad spectrum of services from a travel agency, from airline tickets to a fully planned and guided vacation. One total payment is delivered to the agency and all the services covered by that fee are then dispensed according to the terms of the package.

One travel agency, as a result of an ongoing quality program, determined that several of its locations had an excessively high rate of defective service encounters. Analysis identified three factors contributing to many customer complaints and to a reduction in repeat business at those locations. These factors were:

1. *Process:*   The agency had designed an air travel tour package to Europe that automatically included guided tours. Many customers requested packages consisting of travel arrangements, accommodations, and land transport *without* guided tours. The inclusion of guided tours built up the cost of the packages and limited the market for the travel agency's European packages.

2. *Performance of individuals:*   A large number of customers had complained about several employees at the locations under study. They specified inaccessibility of staff, abrasive behavior, and absence of followup services such as reminder phone calls or letters. Analysis indicated that three employees in particular had been cited over the past several months for brusque and argumentative behavior.

3. *Standard practices for individuals:*   The problem locations had experienced an increased rate of turnover in the previous several months, and the results of a recent employee survey indicated that job satisfaction had declined. Further review showed that a recent change in service practices had decreased the operational responsibility of individual employees and removed several items from the checklist of service activities to be performed for each transaction.

In an effort to improve the performance of the locations under study, the travel agency took the following corrective steps:

1. *Process:*   Current packages were further subdivided to provide customers with an option to purchase travel arrangements and accommodations alone; travel arrangements, accommodations, and land transport; or a total package that included guided tours. Appropriate pricing adjustments were made to reflect the reduced service required of the travel agency, and a limited marketing campaign was designed to advertise and promote the new "menu" system.

2. *Performance of individuals:*   Individuals at the problem locations whose records had indicated performance weaknesses were interviewed and counseled. Careful records of the counseling process were created and maintained for future reference. In one case, it was discovered through the counseling interviews that the employee and his supervisor were experiencing a personality conflict. A transfer to another location was arranged for this employee. In another case, it was discovered that the employee had been hired on the basis of prior experience in

another agency with entirely different standards of performance and significantly different marketing strategies. Remedial training was arranged for this employee. In still another case, later measurement indicated a further decline in performance and after several months, this employee was terminated.

3. *Standard practices for individuals:* A new employee survey was conducted at the problem locations, with questions geared specifically toward discovering employee perception of the recently revised standards. The results were significant enough to warrant an expansion of the survey to all agency locations. After the results of the survey were summarized, management created a task force to study the current checklist of service activities. Activities that had been deleted, such as followup phone calls, were reinstituted. An appointment schedule was created, and specific hours of each day were set aside for customers without appointments. This allowed the staff to control schedules better and provide more personalized service to each customer.

The above example illustrates the way that corrective action can be tailored to the specific service defect. In the cases described, applying punitive measures to employees whose performance had deteriorated as a result of inadequate service standards would have been inappropriate. On the other hand, attempting to revise service standards to accommodate the employees whose performance continued to decline would have been equally inappropriate.

Although corrective action programs are highly individualized and problem-specific, the design of an effective corrective action plan will be aided by following several guidelines:

1. Involve joint efforts of all levels in the organization. Corrective action is a basic responsibility of the line organization, not the exclusive purview of a Quality Department. It is usually best brought about through the cooperation of management, marketing, supervision, and functional staff.

2. Plan corrective actions fully, with schedules and records so that followup testing and measurement will clearly reflect any positive changes and results. It is especially important that corrective action procedures be fully described and the date of implementation reported.

3. Usually, introduce the corrective actions in stages or phases. Sweeping changes in standards and procedures, even when implemented with the intent of improving operations, will have an initial negative effect on operations. Any change in standards and procedures requires training and reorientation and can result in a short-term decline in productivity.

4. Clearly communicate the reasons for corrective actions to all members of the organization. If a change in procedures is introduced to correct specific problems, the problems and the expected results of the change should be explained. The best-planned and executed corrective action program will fail if it does not have the support of the employees responsible for implementing it.

5. When incidents involving customer dissatisfaction have been found, plan for immediate remedial action as a first step in a long-term effort. If customer complaints have triggered a corrective action effort, it may be necessary to follow up with individual customers to provide immediate recourse. In the example above, the customers who had expressed an interest in reduced-rate, limited travel packages could be contacted and advised that such packages are now available. Remedial action and customer recourse can satisfy individual consumers and demonstrate to a larger segment of the service's market that customer feedback is important and that the service organization will make good-faith efforts to meet customer needs.

IMPLEMENTING A SERVICE QUALITY PROGRAM

Education and Training. When a service organization embarks on a comprehensive quality effort, each step in the process of designing and developing a quality program needs to be communicated widely. All employees are informed about the purposes of and need for quality control, and their individual roles in the effort are defined. Figure 33.8 shows a portion of an orientation brochure for new employees of a company.

USF&G, Quality, and You

These are the ingredients in our "Performance Recipe" and *You* are the most important one. Only *You* can ensure that the recipe is a success every time. The *Quality* work *You* produce is the backbone of *USF&G's* service and reputation.

Here's a page from our "Quality Cookbook," so you can always reach for the right ingredients.

Quality

Quality starts as an attitude. A *Quality Attitude* is a way of looking at yourself and anything you're responsible for that gets the job done right, the first time and every time. A *Quality Attitude* lets you approach your job with the expectation that you can *do it right the first time*, with "*Zero Errors*." A goal of "*Zero Errors*" is the heart of the *Quality Attitude*.

But, is it reasonable to expect to achieve "*Zero Errors*" in your work? Let's look at the consequences of accepting anything but the best. If you assume that a goal of 90% accuracy from all areas of USF&G is reasonable, you might also assume that other companies and their employees will accept the same "reasonable" goal.

Would you be willing to accept:
- 10% of the food you buy being spoiled?
- The bank failing to record your deposits 10% of the time?
- A TV repairman fixing 90% of the problems in your TV, and then the TV still doesn't work?
- Your USF&G paycheck having too much withheld 10% of the time?

Of course you wouldn't! But that's exactly what a 90% accuracy goal means. Obviously you expect, even demand, perfection from people who supply goods and services to you. And "*Zero Errors*" is just another way of saying, "*demand of yourself what you demand from others.*"

The Cost of the Lack of Quality

Sometimes it's hard in a company as large as USF&G to see how your job fits into the overall scope of a major insurance company. That's why it may be difficult to recognize the impact of an error, even a "small" one. In reality, there are no such things as "small" errors. The cost of any error may be as much as three times the cost of "getting it right the first time." *Every* error costs us, in time alone:

(1) The time taken to do it the first time.
(2) The time taken to correct the error.

(3) The time lost which could have been spent on a new task.

At USF&G, time *is* money, because prompt, reliable service to our customers is the most important part of the insurance we sell.

You

Just as there are no such things as "small" errors, there are no small jobs at USF&G. The work you do affects the overall success of the corporation. The work you do has to be done in the most efficient manner possible. There may be other people who could learn to do your job, but only *you* can add your special, personal touch — your *mark of Quality*.

Caring about your job is what *Quality* at *USF&G* is all about. In your dealings with our customers, you represent *USF&G*. You can help make sure that the products and service you provide meet the needs of our customers.

At *USF&G*, *Quality* is doing your job, whatever that job may be, right — the first time. This means following instructions carefully and asking questions when you don't understand.

FIG. 33.8 Orientation brochure. *(Courtesy United States Fidelity & Guaranty Company, Quality Assurance Dept., Baltimore, MD.)*

Many organizations conduct miniseminars or briefings for all employees to provide basic background in quality principles and to give specifics on the service organization's own quality program. A modified quality circle approach can have long-term benefits for the organization. Early understanding and support of all employees is critical to the success of the program.

As the program develops, written bulletins or newsletters on progress can provide interim information to employees on each step in the design and development of the program. Of special significance are any refinements made in design or development as a result of employee feedback. Such changes are reported, and credit is given to individual employees. Proper information and training enable employees to pick up and use quality principles early in the effort. A broad base of training in quality principles for all employees makes it possible for them to work together on quality matters on a continuing basis.

Motivation. Quality efforts are often enhanced by an incentive awareness program aimed at individual providers of service. Quality goals are as important as productivity goals. Letters of compliment from customers, outstanding records of quality service performance, and educational achievements of individual employees provide the achievers with incentives to continue their efforts. The quality achievements of peers can provide additional motivation for every employee. Incentive awareness or incentive assessment programs can include financial rewards for outstanding achievements, although recognition properly given can be as great a motivator as money.

Many organizations have discovered that a cumulative effect is achieved if rewards are given to operating units as contrasted with individuals. By making the basis for incentive rewards a department, office, or location, the organization is encouraging the cooperative efforts of all employees in that unit. The resulting peer pressure can often do more than any supervisor's effort to motivate an individual employee.

Installation. The startup date for the quality program should be advertised well in advance. It is often useful to mark the introduction of a quality effort. Clear, attainable interim goals are set at the outset, and feedback is given to all employees at regular intervals on the success of the program. Written instructions, whether they be checklists, quality manuals, or operational manuals, are set down in simple style and illustrated with examples. Such material on quality is widely distributed.

If the commitment of upper management has been well established, a copy of the quality policy or charter or an official communique from a prominent corporate officer is distributed to all supervisors or to all employees. It is essential that everyone involved in the quality effort understand the scope and importance of the effort. If the quality program is clearly identified as one of the essential components of the overall business plan, it will receive the same attention and support as any other business goal.

It can be useful to introduce an employee feedback system along with the program. Employees can be encouraged to comment on the program and offer suggestions at any time. If an employee's suggestion system already exists, the same channels can be used for quality suggestions. If no such suggestion program exists, its installation along with the quality program can lead to an influx of line employees' suggestions for cost-effective changes in the organization. By implementing a suggestion program as part of a quality control program, the concepts of quality and productivity can be linked in the minds of all members of the organization.

THE SERVICE QUALITY PROGRAM IN OPERATION

One of the first results of a quality program is the discovery, by the organization, of the "hidden office." Almost every service organization has an underground system for dealing with defective service encounters. The hidden office may be limited to a few individual employees who have learned how to deal with inadequate standards, tools, and procedures or may represent a complete subculture of service defect correction. This is indeed a hidden office; an effort as large and pervasive as that conducted to provide the original service may be required to correct faults in it and continue to do business.

The hidden office checks to prevent the release of defective service, corrects internal defects (due to clerical mistakes, incorrect decisions, improper use of equipment, etc.), fixes defects that have directly affected customers, makes adjustments, and calms ruffled customers.

It is hard to separate the productivity goals of a company from its quality goals. In some companies, operations to meet these goals have been merged into one to provide an improvement in productivity and a corresponding improvement in quality. Quality and productivity are complementary. Any improvement in initial quality that also maintains the original productivity level results in a productivity gain. It is not necessary to adjust service that was handled properly the first time.

There are many instances in which companies have embarked upon separate productivity gain programs and have totally overlooked the impact on the quality of the service being dispensed. This approach to productivity leads to more and more defects. When people are being paid on the basis of quantity rather than quality, there is a long-term downslide in quality and financial benefits once the short-term gain has been realized.

In any business environment, it is important to maintain or improve productivity if the business is to survive. However, complementing that desire must also be the desire to reduce overall defect rates wherever possible, so that defects are not released and do not have to be corrected.

Quality Audits. A "quality audit" is an independent review conducted to compare some aspect of quality performance with a standard for that performance. An audit may cover both internal and external systems for achieving quality of services. (See also Section 9, Quality Assurance.)

Internal Quality Audits. These reviews have three basic functions: auditing the quality program; auditing for conformance to quality requirements; and auditing for effectiveness.

Auditing the Program. Once a company has established a formalized quality program, it is advisable to build a monitoring device into the management activity. Program audits provide assurance that the quality program, i.e., the process or system and procedures, is in place in a department or location, is functioning as planned, and is totally understood. This type of audit can be beneficial in two ways: (1) it can provide a systematic evaluation of the process itself and identify weaknesses in the quality program throughout the company; and (2) the visit by quality auditors, properly conducted, can be an additional educational experience for all employees involved in the quality program.

The role of the auditor in the service industries is that of a professional, providing constructive input, guidance, and continued emphasis on the concept of quality to all within the organization. Without this educational component, the quality audit takes on the traditional role of audit only, which is frequently perceived as negative or even punitive. If the quality audit is used as an educational tool and an enhancement to the total management of a company, the benefits are more far-reaching and the quality program can grow.

Auditing for Conformance. A second function of the internal quality audit is to ensure that the company's services are being rendered in accordance with predetermined, quantifiable, and measurable standards of conformance. This presupposes the development of a quality program that provides the basis for evaluation. An auditable quality program is one in which procedures and specifications are identified, conformance is measured, and a scale of conformance to these specifications is established. Table 33.3 shows a portion of one section of a list of questions used in a hospital quality audit.

TABLE 33.3 Questions Used in One Part of a Hospital Quality Audit

1. Are drug storage and preparation areas within the pharmacy under the supervision of a pharmacist?
2. Are all drugs, chemicals, and biologicals clearly, accurately, and appropriately labeled?
3. Are unconfirmed drug orders stamped with "unconfirmed" stamp?
4. Is all intravenous work done 6 inches or more inside an intravenous laminar flow hood?
5. Are applicable intravenous solutions stored under refrigeration prior to delivery?

The audit procedure itself is communicated to those who are audited at all levels. Audits frequently involve a multiple-level evaluation. For example, in a service with four or five separate departments or locations under the leadership of one manager, each of the five units needs to have specific, identifiable, attainable quality responsibilities, goals, and objectives. Each individual is accountable for the performance of quality efforts in his or her domain. The quality scores of individuals are sometimes combined to provide the manager's evaluation. If the quality program is to be effective, quality results become part of the performance appraisal of each individual employee and manager.

The quality goals and objectives are discussed with the manager at the beginning of the evaluation period. The performance during that period is then summarized to develop, in effect, a quality score, which becomes a part of the individual's evaluation.

Auditing for Effectiveness. The discussion above has dealt with checking for existence of the accepted components of the quality program and evaluating the performance of individuals under that program. It is also necessary to assess the results achieved with the program and process. For example, it is possible to have a quality program that is in complete compliance with procedures and working from a process standpoint. However, if this process has not resulted in an improvement in the services themselves, the process is ineffective. Such a situation would indicate that:

1. The process for quality planning or control needs reexamination.
2. If the program is at fault, changes to quality planning or control procedures need to be made.
3. If the program in place is in the intended form, renewed emphasis needs to be placed on the results of the quality improvement program.

External Quality Audits. *External quality audits* in the service industries fall into two general categories: auditing the supplier and auditing the user.

Auditing the Supplier. In the service industries, as in manufacturing, it is important that the quality audit address the goods and services received from other companies, e.g., suppliers of printed materials, equipment, computer and copier expendables, or training. Service industries, as a group, are probably the largest users of other service industry goods and products. It is important that the service industries have supplier quality programs in place so that they get what they are paying for.

Auditing the User. In auditing the user, the service organization is determining whether the intended levels of timeliness and other service elements are being provided to the ultimate user. Actual performance is checked, usually by sampling, for comparison with predetermined standards for timeliness, integrity, and consistency and for ongoing redefinition of consumer needs.

Who Audits.   Internal quality audits—of program procedures, of conformance of overall service to corporate standards, of program effectiveness—are normally conducted by quality assurance personnel. All three types of internal audits are conducted to evaluate the proper functioning of the quality program and its effect on overall service quality levels. A high level of training in quality matters is needed to conduct well-informed, objective audits. The quality assurance department is in the best position to plan and conduct internal audits efficiently and effectively.

External quality audits—of both suppliers and users—can be conducted either by a centralized quality department or by individual service units. It is sometimes beneficial to have individual service units control the quality of suppliers, particularly if service units purchase independently from the suppliers. Also, it may be most feasible from a procedural and records standpoint for individual service units to monitor the views of their own users. Individual service units usually maintain the highest level on user records. These service units are in a good position to determine a sample for audit and can greatly reduce the workloads of quality assurance personnel by collecting data at individual service locations.

It is advisable, however, for the quality assurance department to be responsible for review of external audit procedures and results. This ensures that reasonable uniformity of practices and reporting is maintained among service units so that the audit results of one service unit can be compared with those of another.

When Quality Audits Are Conducted.   The frequency of quality audits, both internal and external, is a function of the purpose and use of audit results.

Internal audits for procedural integrity, conformance to corporate standards, and program effectiveness are often used as parts of the company's overall evaluation of individual service units. For this reason, the timing of internal audits may be dependent on an established evaluation cycle.

External audits are scheduled to capture data on suppliers and users at intervals that allow corrective action to be designed, taken, and evaluated. Supplier audits can be timed to correspond with billing cycles or shipping cycles. User audits can be conducted to coincide with seasonal peaks in service use or with accounting cycles.

One of the purposes of an external audit is to detect changes brought about by corrective action taken as a result of a prior audit. It may be desirable to allow enough time between audits for the effect of such corrective action to have taken place. It is appropriate to adjust audit methodology to reflect changes in service performance and also to concentrate on areas that continue to have the highest incidence of defective service encounters.

How Quality Audits Are Conducted.   The *internal* quality audit provides a "snapshot" view of the quality control program in operation and of its effect on service. For this reason, audits are designed to incorporate an evalaution of as much historical data as it is feasible to collect and review. Auditing on a one-time basis can be misleading. Employee awareness that an audit is in prospect or in progress can lead to temporary changes of practice that bias the results. If an observation approach is adopted, it is best to balance it with an evaluation of quality record keeping, maintenance of quality manuals, past quality reporting, records of corrective action taken, and objective measures of service performance.

When auditing for conformance of service to corporate service standards, the same techniques used to test and measure individual service encounters can be applied to a larger sample and compared with a population average. The results of the audit are then compared with ongoing quality control results. This will indicate whether or not the ongoing program, especially if conducted at service unit locations, is performing its proper role of documenting defect information continuously.

Internal quality audits to measure actual service performance should be conducted similarly to audits for conformance to corporate goals. The essential difference between conformance and effectiveness audits is that conformance audits are used in an effort to bring *standards* into line with the overall quality goals of the organization, whereas effectiveness audits are used to quantify individual unit service performance for comparison with organization or industry performance. Results of conformance audits are used to adjust individual unit standards. Results of effectiveness audits are used as indicators of actual service quality levels of individual service units and of the organization as a whole.

Internal audit design includes design of the feedback mechanism that will be used to advise individual service units of audit results. Feedback may take the form of a score, a narrative evaluation, or specific recommendations for quality control program revisions. It is desirable for feedback to all service units to be given on a consistent basis. Audit results are recorded and maintained so that future audits can be compared and improvement or decline can be measured.

External supplier audits can often be designed to include the supplier's personnel in the audit and evaluation process. Checklists can be designed to allow the supplier routinely to review and record the quality of goods and services provided. The individual service unit can periodically review supplier audit results and conduct less frequent, on-site audits of the supplier. Standards for supplier performance need to be clearly communicated to suppliers as a standard practice—in any case, well in advance of an audit. Scoring procedures and consequences of various scores are also defined in advance.

An important goal of supplier audits is the improvement of supplier services, if defective, or, failing improvement, discontinuation of use. The supplier needs to understand this, and if audit results indicate consistent failure to provide the quality of goods and services required, it is important that the promised consequences take effect. The supplier audit is useless if it does not ensure that future supplier service will enhance the operations of the service organization.

External user audits follow the standard format for other testing and measurement devices, except that they are conducted on a larger population at less frequent intervals. Surveys, questionnaires, observation, complaints, etc. are summarized and analyzed. Where user satisfaction is tested and measured on a large scale, the authors recommend that results of the audit be communicated to the users. Such communication may take the form of a newsletter or report to customers and, if indicated, may outline the corrective action the service organization plans to take as a result of negative audit feedback.

How Quality Audits Are Used.   Audits measure actual performance, both past and current, against broad standards: quality control program procedures, corporate goals, organization or industry achievements, supplier requirements, and consumer needs and expectations. Good practice is for the audits to:

1. Be paced to allow gradual improvement over the course of a series of audits
2. Serve as a basis for planning future quality assurance activities and goals for the entire organization
3. Provide a history of quality progress

Audits, like ongoing quality control inspections, lead to corrective action and, normally, to an improvement in service performance. Adjustments in quality goals resulting from audits may focus on the process, on individuals, or on standards. Although audits may be used immediately as part of a service unit's or service employee's evaluation, audits aim to lead ultimately to long-term improvements in the quality system and in the quality of service to customers. By providing a comparison between the independent review and normal reports of the branch or location, audits also improve the accuracy of internal reporting on inspection within the company. Figure 33.9 gives an example of a chart of audit results.

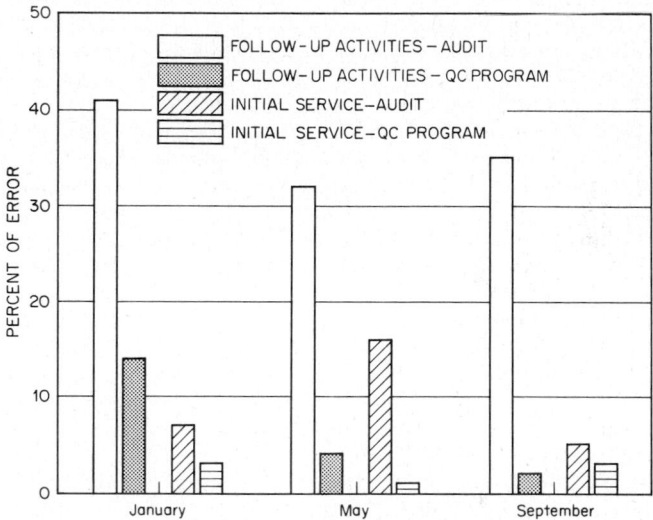

FIG. 33.9 Comparison of audit and other data.

EXTENDING THE SERVICE QUALITY PROGRAM

A service quality program is an integral part of the organization. Because of established feedback loops and ongoing inspection and audit, the service organization's environment can be studied and improvements in existing quality procedures can be planned. In addition to serving for the present, quality programs need to be readied for future needs. The quality program can never be considered a static process; it must develop continuously and change to meet evolving needs of the service organization.

The quality program is reevaluated periodically in light of audit results, ongoing inspection results, changing market conditions, changes or expansions of service, changes in the economy, and, in the case of regulated services, changing regulatory requirements.

As problem areas are brought under control, the standards of the service organization are reassessed. Quality programs are aimed at bringing the overall service organization's performance into line with customer expectations. As expectations are met in one area, the program is altered or expanded to address other, unmet needs.

Several areas are appropriate candidates for application of quality concepts as soon as basic service processes are brought into conformance with established standards.

Supplier Quality.   The quality of services and products purchased from suppliers (e.g., meals to be served in flight by an airline) is often important both to the quality reputation and the efficiency of a service company. The quality systems and capabilities of prospective suppliers of critical services or products can be assessed by a survey team from the purchasing organization before contracts are signed and samples can be evaluated. The supplier's quality practices can be reviewed periodically through quality audits while the contract is in force.

Basic responsibility for meeting the purchaser's quality standards rests with the supplier organization. However, the survey or audit of observed quality of services or products delivered may reveal weaknesses in the supplier's quality systems. Cooperative efforts are useful in identifying and overcoming such weaknesses. Service companies with significant purchases normally assign responsibility for matters pertaining to supplier quality to specific quality professionals in their organizations.

The components, design, and development of a supplier quality program are similar to those of the service organization's own program. Quality standards are established, by consensus of supplier and purchaser; a system of measurement is designed and established; defects are routinely analyzed to determine their causes; corrective action is planned and implemented to eliminate or minimize the causes of defects; ongoing monitoring is conducted to ensure that gains are maintained. For elaboration, see Section 15, Supplier Relations.

A major difference between a supplier's quality program and the service organization's own internal quality program is that the supplier's program is sometimes confined to a specific sector of the supplier's operations—the sector supplying the purchaser who has insisted that the supplier introduce a quality program. In some cases one supplier who serves several manufacturing and service organizations will have several different quality control procedures in place. This may make it difficult to elicit complete cooperation from the supplier, especially if the purchaser is not one of the supplier's larger customers. However, attempts should be made to exert control over quality procedures in as much as possible of that part of the supplier's operation that affects the service organization. If the supplier provides a critical product or service, it may be necessary for the purchasing organization to make an established quality program a contract requirement. Supplier quality records need to be maintained so that the service organization's representatives can review them as necessary.

Because of the complexities of the supplier quality program and the possible reluctance on the part of the supplier to institute one, it may be necessary for the service organization to demonstrate first that such a program is necessary. A limited supplier's inspection activity can be established within the service organization itself. Goods and services can be inspected on a sampling basis as they are received. If testing and inspection results indicate that recurring or significant problems exist, such data can provide the evidence and impetus necessary to involve the supplier in a quality control program. If the service organization chooses to inspect suppliers' goods internally at first, the standards developed can then be relayed to the suppliers for their in-house use. This eliminates the need to develop an additional, separate quality program for the supplier.

Other Company Functions.   If a service company's quality program is initially directed to specific functions or areas, it can be expanded progressively to incorporate inspection, documentation, analysis, corrective action, and prevention in other areas. Planning for future expansion is a normal part of the initial quality effort. Section 21, Administrative and Support Operations, provides examples.

If a centralized quality department is established in an organization that already has fragmented quality activities, the existing efforts need to be reevaluated; steps will then usually need to be taken to integrate and extend these activities to bring about "total quality control" encompassing all aspects of enhancement of customer services and reduction of the costs of poor quality.

One of the normal pursuits of the quality professional is watching for additional areas in which the costs of poor quality may be high. A well-planned quality approach with expansion over time into such areas will pay its own way and provide the quality professional with opportunities to extend the benefits of a quality program. But this will not happen unless homework is done, cost dollars are identified, and savings are evident. During the early stages of development of a quality program in a service industry, it is useful to introduce the quality cost study as a means of identifying the true benefits of the quality effort. Cost records can be valuable in showing the benefits of defect prevention, reduced redoing of work, reduced waste of materials, etc.

Computer Services.   Computer processing of information is one of the fastest-growing services, both internally and as a purchased service. In some service industries, material printed out by computer (e.g., insurance policies, bank statements, air travel tickets) is a tangible part of the company's service to customers. In many others the computer provides support services, keeping vital records and performing important detail work behind the scenes (e.g., airline reservations, accounting, records of credit card transactions, mailing lists). Organizations do well to examine the quality and accuracy of such data. The process begins with an organized examination of data collection, of software, and of output products. The steps toward improvement of data quality are generally along the lines of those already discussed for other areas of quality improvement. However, specialized literature on data-processing quality is beginning to appear (see, for example, Burrell and Ellsworth, 1982). In addition, Appendix III, Selected Quality Standards, Specifications, and Related Documents, includes a list of documents on software quality system and program requirements.

Customer Billing.   In the service industries, it is common to bill customers, often by computer, on a monthly, installment, or other schedule. Companies are finding it profitable to put quality programs in place to ensure that collection of data and of incoming money is carried out smoothly and rapidly. Many use full quality programs involving performance standards, inspection, measurement, monitoring, and reporting. The increase in cash flow brought about by such a quality program can be a noteworthy point in a management presentation on results of the quality control program.

SERVICE INDUSTRY CASES

The remainder of this section is devoted to a series of examples of the application of quality control concepts in specific service industries.

Insurance Quality.   The insurance industry provides illustrations of methods used to maintain and improve quality of service.

Insurance companies exhibit much commonality in their processes for issuing insurance policies. An individual contacts an insurance agent to obtain insurance protection (life, health, automobile, home, or commercial coverage). Together the customer and agent complete a policy application, which is sent to the company to issue an insurance policy. At this point, the company must provide the customer with timely and accurate service.

Many insurance companies have introduced quality controls to monitor and control the timeliness, accuracy, and service being provided to the customer.

To measure the timeliness of policy issuance, companies closely monitor the "turnaround time." Turnaround time is the period between receipt of the application by the company and delivery of a policy to the insured. Performance is measured against preestablished service targets for turnaround time. Figure 33.10 is an example of a service report comparing actual performance with targeted times.

Four times a year supervisors categorize each item of work in the department, compare actual turnaround time with its target, and tally it as meeting or not meeting the target. The results of their checks are shown separately for each type of policy processed. Supervisors and managers can see from the quarterly report whether or not actual processing times for various types of policies are exceeding targeted times. They can also see whether their departments are gaining or losing in timeliness, as the report compares results of current and previous quarters for each policy type. Such a monitoring system enables a company to keep track of the promptness of service to the customer. It alerts supervisors to situations in which reallocation of resources or other action may be needed.

Controlling the accuracy of insurance policy rating, typing, and other internal functions can be more complex. For these operations insurance companies have developed quality programs modeled after typical manufacturing quality assurance operations. The processing of an insurance application and preparation of a policy can be viewed as taking place in a "paper factory." Many parallels can be drawn between the clerical activities in an insurance company and the operations of a factory assembly line. The paper moves from work station to station, and the quality of the final product must be controlled.

Most of the information on an application for insurance is translated into computer-readable code. This coded application information is collected and used for management decisions and rate making. The coded information collected is commonly subject to quality control inspections. The information, generally referred to in the insurance industry as "statistics," includes such elements as:

State	Policy term
Territory	Premium amount
Risk classification	Loss amount
Exposure	Type of loss
Policy limits	Deductible

United States Fidelity & Guaranty Company (USF&G), for example, has taken a series of special steps to ensure that it is producing accurate and timely statistical data. Its goals are to provide data and service of high quality at the lowest possible cost. In the belief that this will provide maximum profits for the company, USF&G strives to achieve these goals through:

1. Employee education and participation
2. A coordinated and well-documented quality program

In order to control the accuracy of the statistical data, the company has established an error identification system. This system pinpoints promptly for supervisors the types and quantities of errors that occur. It also provides immediate feedback to individuals who have made errors.

USF&G CASUALTY DEPARTMENT
INSURANCE **QUARTERLY SERVICE REPORT**

| | BRANCH OFFICE | COMPLETED BY | DATE COMPLETED | PERIOD ENDING |

POLICY TYPE		TOTAL NO. ITEMS IN DEPT.	CURRENT QUARTER								% INCREASE OR DECREASE (+% OR - %)
			NO. ITEMS WHICH DO NOT MEET PRE-ESTABLISHED TARGETS						TOTAL NO. ITEMS BELOW TARGET	% OF ITEMS BELOW TARGET	
			NEW	RENEWAL	ENDORSE-MENT	CANCEL-LATION	TOTAL NO. ITEMS BELOW TARGET	% OF ITEMS BELOW TARGET			
Commercial Automobile											
Private Passenger	Machine										
	Manual										
General Liability Monoline											
Packages											
Workers Comp.	Machine										
	Manual										
Audits/ Interim Statements	Machine										
	Manual										
Umbrella CEP-PEP											
TOTALS											

Are Commercial policies renewed automatically? ☐ Yes ☐ No
If "Yes", indicate cycle: ☐ 30 ☐ 60 ☐ Other

FIG. 33.10 Quarterly report on service quality. *(Courtesy United States Fidelity & Guaranty Company, Quality Assurance Dept., Baltimore, MD.)*

The quality control program at USF&G consists of four separate functions:

1. *Error identification:*　Errors are identified through inspection, and the inspection results are recorded.
2. *Error analysis:*　After errors have been identified, they are analyzed in order to ascertain their cause(s).
3. *Corrective action/prevention:*　Once the cause(s) of errors has been determined, necessary steps are taken to eliminate them.
4. *Control:*　The program is monitored to ensure that it is working properly, i.e., that errors are being identified and analyzed and that effective corrective action is being taken to eliminate cause(s).

The quality control program requires:

1. Separating a portion (a sample) of the items produced by a department each day (or as often as the item is produced)
2. Inspecting the selected items for accuracy
3. Documenting the results of the inspection
4. Returning any item in error to the person who made the error(s) for correction
5. Ensuring that the correction(s) to the item has been made properly

The number of items to be inspected is determined from a sample of the total items produced each day, with use of the sampling procedures and tables found in MIL-STD-105D.

Inspecting Sampled Items.　The inspection is to determine the accuracy of the documents that have been produced. The standard with which the document is compared depends on the department or function being inspected. For example, if computer coding is being inspected, the coded information is compared with worksheets and information provided by the insured and the agent. Inspectors are instructed to refer to procedural manuals instead of relying on memory for procedures and standards.

Documenting Results and Analysis.　When the inspection reveals an error, the inspector prepares a three-part error memorandum that describes the error. One copy of the memorandum remains in a log book for use in documenting the program results; a second copy is attached to the nonconforming item for audit purposes and becomes a permanent part of the file; and the third copy is given for information and action to the person who made the error.

The person who made the error corrects it and returns the document to the inspector for verification and eventual release to the next step in processing.

The results of inspection of each employee's output are summarized on an "individual daily performance sheet" (Figure 33.11). This accumulates the person's record of accuracy or errors for the month. The report is given to supervisory personnel at the end of the month for analysis of quality levels and for corrective action.

The individual daily performance sheet shows the supervisor the numbers and types of errors discovered in the work samples of a specific employee. It summarizes the errors for each day, week, and month. The report points up for the supervisor the leading types of errors being discovered in the work of the employee—this is thus a form of Pareto analysis. If the employee's overall results are unsatisfactory, the supervisor can see what types of problems the individual is having and can decide what corrective action is appropriate.

INDIVIDUAL DAILY PERFORMANCE

INDIVIDUAL: Jack Kye
LINE OF BUSINESS: Homeowners
MONTH/YEAR: Feb. /83

	M	T	W	TH	F	WEEK	M	T	W	TH	F	WEEK	M	T	W	TH	F	WEEK	M	T	W	TH	F	WEEK	M	T	W	TH	F	WEEK	TOTAL
DATE (DAY)	1	2	3	4			7	8	9	10	11		14	15	16	17	18		21	22	23	24	25		28	29					
NO. OF ITEMS INSPECTED	6	5	7	2		20	4	9	7	7	7	34	8	3	1	0	6	18	12	9	2	10	6	39	9	6				15	126
NO. OF ITEMS IN ERROR	1	0	2	2		5	0	0	0	0	0	0	0	7	1	1	2	11	0	2	2	1	3	8	1	0				1	25
TOTAL NO. OF ERRORS	1	0	3	8		12	0	0	0	0	0	0	0	7	1	1	3	12	0	2	4	3	3	12	1	0				1	37

TYPE OF ERROR

	M	T	W	TH	F	WEEK	M	T	W	TH	F	WEEK	M	T	W	TH	F	WEEK	M	T	W	TH	F	WEEK	M	T	W	TH	F	WEEK	TOTAL
State Code	1	1				2					1	1	1	7			2			1	1		1		1					1	11
Line Code		1	6			7					1	1		1			1	3		1	1	2		3							11
Address		1				1				1	1		1					3													5
Insured's Name		2	2			2					1	1	2	2			2	6	1	1	2	2			1					1	10

PREPARED BY: Mary Carter

USF&G ® INSURANCE

FIG. 33.11 Individual daily performance sheet. *(Courtesy United States Fidelity & Guaranty Company, Quality Assurance Dept., Baltimore, MD.)*

33.53

The "quality control weekly summary" (Figure 33.12) gives the supervisor a weekly view of quality results for a cluster of as many as five employees. It shows what kinds of errors have been made most frequently by the group as a whole and compares the error rates of individual employees.

Comparison of the results of several people performing similar work may

QUALITY CONTROL WEEKLY									LINE OF BUSINESS Auto - Claims	PERIOD March 25, 1983
	INDIVIDUAL NAMES									
	Jim Mosely	Tina Fuller	Liz Lombardo	Jake Arcadia						TOTAL
NO. OF ITEMS INSPECTED	62	25	89	41						217
NO. OF ITEMS IN ERROR	3	12	2	9						26
TOTAL NO. OF ERRORS	19	36	2	16						73
PERCENT OF ITEMS IN ERROR	5	48	2	22						12

TYPE OF ERROR											PERCENT OF TOTAL NO. OF ERRORS
State Code	2	6	1	16						25	34
Draft Amount	3	6								9	12
Insured's Name		5								5	7
Claimant's Address		2								2	3
Payment Code	13	8								21	29
Class Code	1	9	1							11	15

USF&G INSURANCE

PREPARED BY *Sam Pratt*

FIG. 33.12 Quality Control weekly summary. *(Courtesy United States Fidelity & Guaranty Company, Quality Assurance Dept., Baltimore, MD.)*

point to one or another as appearing to need special coaching, counseling, or other attention. In other cases it may single out a person whose record is so favorable as to indicate a special knack or special skill or knowledge, which can be identified and provided to others.

The "quality control monthly performance report" provides a means for the home office Quality Assurance Department to review the progress of branch office quality programs and the quality of the data being produced. Filing of this report with the home office Quality Assurance Department within 10 days after the end of each month is mandatory. The report summarizes the results of the individual branch office department's quality control program for a series of insurance lines. Such reports allow study of month-to-month error trends and comparisons of error rates of various offices. They show the number of items inspected, by line of business; the number of items containing errors; the total number of errors identified; and the percentage of items containing errors.

"Quarterly performance charts" are completed by supervisory personnel as a means of watching for error trends in their departments. These charts show a plot of percent of error by week for each line of business.

Program Audits.   An audit of the quality control program is conducted annually at each USF&G location once such a program has been instituted. The audit examines practices and procedures in order to determine whether sampling, error identification, documentation, and analysis procedures are being conducted in accordance with program specifications.

The quality control audit team conducts an on-site inspection and evaluation of the quality control program at each location. Members of the team interview employees who are responsible for the program administration and employees who are being monitored. They observe the program in operation and examine completed documentation to evaluate the department or branch office against program standards. The results of the audit indicate either conformance to program procedures or potential problems and discrepancies that should be corrected. If the quality control program is functioning properly, significant problems will be prevented.

A numerical score for quality control is calculated for each department and each branch office. This score becomes part of the annual performance evaluations of supervisory personnel.

Statistical Audits.   In addition, audits of the statistical data of each branch are conducted approximately three times a year by the Quality Assurance Department. The statistical audit is performed to determine the accuracy of coded data generated during a 1-month period. The home office personnel use sampling and error identification techniques similar to those required for branch offices—they are simply making an objective, third-party check. Branch offices are instructed to compare statistical audit results with their own results to see if there are variances. If the home office audit uncovers significantly more errors than the branch office inspection during the same month, the branch office inspection is most probably flawed and failing in its purpose of discovering errors for analysis.

A statistical audit is launched with a memorandum from the home office to the target branch approximately 1 month before the audit is to begin. Such a memorandum specifies the period to be covered by the audit and reminds the branch of the procedures to be followed in submitting work to be audited.

During the audit month, the target office(s) submit copies of all the statistics they have created in that month and corresponding source documentation. Source documents may be applications, printed or typed policies, endorsements, or other paper that would normally be considered an external product. Quality assurance personnel then independently code these documents and record any variations from coding manual and source document information. The errors are identified specifically by policy so the branch office can examine and correct its entries.

Error results are also summarized by line of business and error type. This provides the branch with detailed information on error concentrations and trends for more detailed analysis. Figure 33.13 illustrates a completed line-of-business "Departmental Results" summary.

The individual correction listings, summaries, and a cover report are forwarded to the branch within 2 to 3 weeks after the audit month ends. Home office Quality Assurance personnel also receive copies of the final report to assist in ongoing monitoring and analysis of branch office programs.

Computers: Uses and Misuses. Advances in computer technology now allow insurance companies to produce automatically and overnight insurance policies that once took days or weeks to produce manually. To ensure that proper data are being entered into the computer, companies have developed sophisticated editing programs, which validate information as it is entered.

This computer editing can check whether input information conforms to pre-established values and relationships. Edit tables are constructed with preestablished values for various parameters; for information to be accepted, it must fall within an acceptable value range. To take a simple example, if the edit is constructed to accept only a two-digit numerical character, an entry of three alpha characters would be rejected as being invalid and in error.

Each state has a two-digit numerical value. Therefore if an individual is translating this information into a computer-acceptable format, the value must fall within the range of codes available. The editing program will accept any one of the codes on the list. However, if a code is entered that does not fall within this range, the editing program will reject it as being invalid.

One of the myths of computer editing is that it can control the accuracy of coding. While an edit can eliminate much invalid information, it cannot guarantee the accuracy of the information it accepts. For example, the state of Alabama carries a code of 01. If the person making this translation incorrectly codes the state of Alabama as code 10 and enters it into the computer, the computer edit will not reject the information as being invalid or incorrect, since code 10 is acceptable as the code for the state of Georgia. However, if the individual coding Alabama uses 00 or 76 or ALA as a code, it would be rejected by the computer edit since this code is not within the acceptable range.

While computer editing programs provide assistance in improving the quality of data, data accuracy can only be tested through some form of information recheck. Although USF&G policy-writing computer systems are programmed with validity edits, computer-produced policies still require quality control inspection at the branch office level.

Control of Hospital Medication Errors. During the last several centuries, the health industry has been spectacularly successful in increasing the human life span. Maintaining the benefits of this breakthrough has required setting up numerous quality controls on a wide variety of activities, products, and systems, all relating to human health. One of these systems is that of providing medication to sick people.

Outside the hospital the procedure for medication is comparatively simple and direct:

The physician prescribes the medication by writing out a prescription in longhand and giving it to the patient.

QUALITY ASSURANCE — QUALITY REVIEW UNIT

DEPARTMENTAL RESULTS
FMML — COMMERCIAL LINES (CSP)

PERIOD COVERED BY REVIEW		REVIEWED BY	DATE REVIEW COMPLETED	BRANCH OFFICE
FROM	TO			

THE FOLLOWING SECTIONS ILLUSTRATE THE BREAKDOWN, BY NUMBER & TYPE, OF CODING ERRORS THAT WERE FOUND DURING THIS REVIEW

SECTION I — STATISTICAL CODING ERRORS FOUND ON PREMIUM STAT CODING VERIFICATION SHEET.

A LINE OF BUSINESS	LINE	STATE	TERR.	SUB-LINE	POL. TYPE LIAB. LIM.	CLASS	FORM COV.	CONSTR.	RATE GROUP	PROT. DEV. RATE ID.	NO. STOR.	DED. PREM.	O. PREM.	F.D.	STAT. RATING DATE MO. YR	RATE MOD.	RATE DEP.	ZIP AREA NO. RATING BASIS	COMM. SPEC. EXP.	NO. EMP.	BOND AMOUNT	(a) TOTAL NO. OF STATISTICAL ERRORS
BUSINESSOWNERS																						
SMP																						
OTHER																						
▶ MULTIPERIL ⑧																						
BOILER & MACHINERY																						
BURGLARY																						
EARTHQUAKE																						
FIRE & ALLIED																						
GLASS																						
INLAND MARINE																						
OCEAN MARINE																						
PACKAGE POLICIES																						
▶ COMM. LINES ALL OTHER ⑨																						
TOTALS ▶																						

SECTION II — POLICY & ACCOUNTING INFORMATION ERRORS FOUND ON PREMIUM STAT CODING VERIFICATION SHEET.

A LINE OF BUSINESS	TRANS. TRANS. CODE MO./DA./YR.	CO.	B.O.	AGENT	PKG. CODE	POLICY PERIOD ISSUE MO./DA./YR.	EXP. MO./DA./YR.	H.O. EVIDENCE NOT STAMPED	POLICY NO.	INS. NAME	TERM IN MONTHS COMM.	OTHER	(b) TOTAL NO. OF POL. & ACCNTG. INFO. ERRORS
BUSINESSOWNERS													
SMP													
OTHER													
▶ MULTIPERIL ⑧													
BOILER & MACHINERY													
BURGLARY													
EARTHQUAKE													
FIRE & ALLIED													
GLASS													
INLAND MARINE													
OCEAN MARINE													
PACKAGE POLICIES													
▶ COMM. LINES ALL OTHER ⑨													
TOTALS ▶													

SECTION III — ANALYSIS

A LINE OF BUSINESS	B NO. OF POLICIES REVIEWED	C NO. OF POLICIES MISCODED	D TOTAL NO. OF ERRORS	E PERCENT OF POLICIES MISCODED [(C ÷ B) × 100]	AVERAGE NO. OF ERRORS PER POLICY MISCODED

FIG. 33.13 Departmental coding error summary. (Courtesy United States Fidelity & Guaranty Company, Quality Assurance Dept., Baltimore, MD.)

The patient takes the prescription to a pharmacist, who dispenses the medication, i.e., gives the patient the pills, capsules, etc., called for by the prescription. The pharmacist also labels the container with a reference number and with the physician's instructions as to dose size and frequency.

The patient administers the medication himself or herself and so bears the responsibility for following the medication program.

This procedure involves minimal record keeping. The original longhand prescription is filed by the pharmacist. The pharmacist assigns a serial number and also imprints this serial number on the label attached to the container given to the patient. If the pharmacist encounters problems in interpreting the prescription (e.g., legibility, abbreviations, units of measure), he or she contacts the physician directly.

The Hospital Procedure.   In the hospital, the medication procedure becomes far more complex, partly because of sheer size and partly because of addition of the nurse to the chain of communication and action. The traditional procedure has involved the following basic steps:

The physician writes out an order for a medication program (along with other orders) for the patient. The nurse transcribes this order onto a form, a copy of which goes to the pharmacist.

The pharmacist dispenses the drugs, which are then delivered to the nurse.

The nurse administers the medication to the patient.

In a large hospital the resulting procedural network becomes formidable. The "pharmacist" becomes a central pharmacy with several branches. The "nurse" becomes numerous people in many departments, including nursing supervisors, floor clerks, etc. The "drug" is not necessarily a simple pill, which a patient can take unaided; it now often involves specialized techniques for dilutions, measurement, injection, intravenous administration, etc. The need to keep adequate histories and to fix responsibility creates added paperwork. In due course the "system" reaches such a state of size and complexity that in itself it becomes part of the problem.

Attempts to change this procedure must take account of the vested interest of the "professional" groups involved. Each has jurisdictional rights, which are rooted in tradition and backed up by legislation: The physician may prescribe, dispense, and administer; the pharmacist may only dispense; and the nurse may only administer.

The Medication Error.   Hospitals define a medication error as "a deviation from the physician's order." In quality control jargon, such an error is a "nonconformance," i.e., a failure to conform to specification.

It does not follow that in the absence of medication errors (as defined above) the medication will be fit for use. From the patient's viewpoint, an error is any state of affairs in which he or she is not cured, whether the medication does or does not conform to the physician's order. The patient's viewpoint broadens the concept of error to include "quality of design," i.e., the validity of the physician's order. This in turn depends on such factors as the adequacy of the diagnostic equipment, the competence of the physician, and the completeness of the research program behind the development of the prescribed drugs.

In the following discussion, the studies of "medication error" have been limited to studies of nonconformance, i.e., the hospital's definition.

The Extent of Medication Errors. The annual number of medications ("dosages") administered to patients is fantastically high. Yet until the 1960s there existed only misinformation on how many of these medications were failing to conform to the orders of the physicians. The reasons behind this misinformation are informative in themselves.

1. Some medication errors are inadvertent and undiscovered, i.e., their existence is not known to the persons who made the errors. Most of these errors go undetected because the adverse effect falls on hospitalized sick people. The "alarm signal" created by the adverse effect cannot readily be recognized; it is drowned out by other alarms already present. The person most qualified to detect the new alarms is the physician, who is seldom there.

2. Other errors are detected by the persons committing them, who likely will be reluctant to report them to the hospital authorities, since historically the response of these authorities has often been one of criticism rather than one of analysis to look for ways of minimizing the error rate through foolproofing the system.

3. Even when errors are detected by persons other than those who committed them, hospitals have traditionally been reluctant to put the incidents on record for fear of publicity or of lawsuits. (Thereafter, in the absence of such records, analysis for repetitive causes is effectively blocked.)

The foregoing (and other) forces had long combined to create a false sense of security concerning possible medication errors. Occasional checks "showed" that these errors were rare occurrences. Some practitioners were openly skeptical of these findings but lacked the data to make an adequate challenge.

A breakthrough came with the "disguised observation technique" developed by Kenneth N. Barker (Barker, 1961; Barker and McConnell, 1962). This technique involves observation of hospital personnel and of the circumstances involved in medication in a way that reconstructs (1) what should have happened and (2) what did happen. The disguised aspect of the observation lies in the fact that some subterfuge is used. The hospital personnel are given a plausible reason for the need for a team of observers during the period of study. However, the main reason is to study the error rate.

The first such study, conducted at the University of Florida Teaching Hospital, secured data on 572 doses administered by nine nurses. It was found that one dose in every six involved some kind of error. This incidence was remarkably higher than that suggested by earlier studies purporting to be quantitative.

An elaboration of the disguised observation technique was the classic study by Barker, Kimbrough, and Heller (1966), which will be referred to here as the BKH study. This study was made at a nonuniversity hospital to see whether such a service-oriented hospital was as subject to error as a university hospital, with its strong orientation to teaching and research.

The BKH study confirmed the results of earlier disguised observation studies. In 9789 "opportunities for error" (defined as doses ordered and administered plus doses ordered but not administered), a total of 1461 actual errors were detected. This is one error for every 6.7 opportunities; it also averages out to about one error per patient-day. Table 33.4 shows the error pattern in detail.

Further Studies. Davis and Cohen (1981) have summarized the results of similar studies of medication errors in five Kentucky and Ohio hospitals using conventional drug distribution systems. While the error categories and methods in these studies were not identical, the results confirmed that there were medication

TABLE 33.4 Medication Errors in a Hospital

Error type	No. of errors	Percent Of opportunities for errors	Of all errors
Dose administered at wrong time	808	8.3	55
Wrong amount administered	253	2.6	17
Dose omitted	188	1.9	13
Extra dose	113	1.2	8
Unordered drug	88	0.9	6
Wrong dosage form	11	0.1	1
Totals	1461	15.0	100

error rates of 5.33, 8.34, 9.90, 11.45, and 20.56, respectively, in the five hospitals even after eliminating the "wrong time" category.

Causes of Medication Errors.   The BKH study undertook also to analyze causes of the observed errors. To a surprising extent, the study found that procedural and technological problems were the leading error causes.

Dose Administered at Wrong Time.   Of the 808 "wrong time" errors, only 15 were categorized as "cause probably found." The real problem seemed to be one of "unrealistic tolerances loosely enforced."

To elaborate, the hospital establishes standard schedules for administering drugs. For example, drugs to be given four times each day may be scheduled for 9 a.m., 12 noon, 3 p.m., and 6 p.m. These published schedules, though uniform within one department, can vary from one department to another. However, the tolerances around these standards schedules are not clear. The BKH investigators established an arbitrary tolerance of 30 minutes, but found that the schedules were not being followed with any precision.

There is evidence that the standardized schedule is regarded not as a firm specification but rather as a target. It is obvious that some tolerance is needed around the schedule time in any event because it is clearly impossible for the nurses to give all the medications at precisely the time scheduled. However, the tolerance as evolved by the nurses and the supervision appears to be much wider than that regarded as reasonable by a set of investigators. For this reason, many of the 808 "wrong time" errors listed by the investigators would probably not be regarded as a serious matter by the hospital staff.

Wrong Amount Administered.   The BKH study found 153 instances of "wrong dose." By a wide margin, the "outstanding characteristic" behind the error was determined to be "nurse mismeasured or miscalculated"; 150 of the 153 errors were categorized in this way. However, a look at the details of the "mismeasured or miscalculated" soon makes clear that both calculation and measurement involve some technical obstacles. Only 15 of the 150 errors in this category involved simple count of capsules or tablets; the rest required various manipulations, e.g., dilution, measurement, or injection.

Calculation consists of simple arithmetic, but this is complicated by multiple units of measure. Young physicians prescribe in metric units, but some older physicians retain the apothecary units, which affords obvious opportunities for error. An official teaspoon is 5 mL; however, physicians commonly use the apothecary notation for 1 dram to prescribe 1 teaspoonful. The *U.S. Pharmacopeia* equates

1 dram with 3.7 mL, but this may be rounded off to 4.0 mL. Less frequent is the problem posed by the use of Fahrenheit and Celsius scales for temperature.

Measurement seems simple on the face of it, but on the nursing floor it is complicated by the variables inherent in the materials, tools, and measuring instruments used. In theory, the nurse/administrator has the last chance to avoid the error, or to make up, by human resourcefulness, for the deficiencies in the engineering of the system. Some nurses do exactly that. However, others are defeated by problems such as how to get the right number of drops (again, how to measure a "drop") into a wriggling patient's nose; by liquids that are viscous or that foam; or by the need to measure 8 mL with a cup that has graduations marked only at 5 and 10 mL.

Unordered Drug; Omission. The BKH study reported 188 omissions and 88 instances of unordered drug. In the former cases, the patient failed to receive an ordered drug; in the latter, the patient received a drug not ordered by the physician. Both these errors can and do occur in cases described by "Nurse Selected and Used Wrong Drug," i.e., the nurse omitted the right drug and administered an unordered drug.

Of the 66 such cases, involving 91 errors, a majority (52 of the 91 errors) involved the phenomenon of similarity in names of drugs. An example (involving nine cases) is a group of drugs all containing the name Darvon (the generic word is propoxyphene). At the time of the BKH study the manufacturer had four forms on the market:

Name	*Contents*
Darvon	Propoxyphene 32 mg
Darvon 65	Propoxyphene 65 mg
Darvon Compound	Propoxyphene 32 mg in combination with aspirin, phenacetin, and caffeine
Darvon Compound-65	Propoxyphene 65 mg in combination with aspirin, phenacetin, and caffeine

In like manner there are many other drugs involving variations on some basic name, e.g., Hystadyl and Hystadyl EC; Lextron and Lextron Ferrous; Dimetane Expectorant and Dimetane Expectorant DC. So long as such similarities prevail, the nurses have the responsibility of keeping the distinction clear. However, the question may be asked: Why should the industry endure a system of names that, on the record, makes confusion easy?

Extra Dose. There were 113 extra doses given in the BKH study. In 75 of these cases the investigators found evidence of the cause; and of these cases 53 resulted from resumption of medication after surgery in the absence of known orders. A major contributing factor was the widespread confusion owing to the simultaneous presence of:

Published hospital procedure relative to automatic stopping of medication for patients "going to surgery"

Vague definitions of what constitutes "surgery" (e.g., is removal of a cast in the category of surgery?)

Physicians' "standing verbal orders" countermanding the hospitals' published procedures

Inconsistencies in practice among hospital departments and from physician to physician

Controllability of Medication Errors.   The foregoing analysis makes clear that the hospital medication system has quite a distance to go if it is to put the nurse in a state of self-control. To be in a state of self-control, the nurse (or anyone else) must have knowledge of what he or she is supposed to do; knowledge of what he or she is doing; means to regulate what he or she is doing (see Section 17, under Concept of Self-Control). None of the criteria for self-control is fully met, so the system abounds in "management controllability."

Knowledge of "Supposed to Do."   The basic "specification" is the physician's order for medication, and the prime job of the nurse is to assist the physician by executing that order. The nurse must interpret and (usually) copy the order despite problems of handwriting legibility, abbreviations, private shorthand systems, etc. (Of course, it all should be standardized, but it is not standardized.)

Moreover, the nurse receives orders from a number of other sources:

1. Impersonal orders on medication in the hospital procedural manual (e.g., automatic stop orders for patients going to surgery or after 72 hours)

2. Jurisdictional rules governing interfacing with the other professions and skills assembled in the hospital

3. Overriding legislation on some matters, e.g., handling of narcotics

4. An extensive workload, including activities not related to medication and having standards of their own, which compete for the time and attention of the nurse

5. The special cultural pattern, unique to each hospital, which as a continuing human community evolves its own regulations, habits, jargon, etc. (making it necessary for a nurse moving from one hospital to another to have time to assimilate the local rules and jargon)

These multiple sources of orders converging on the nurse are obvious breeding grounds for "error."

Knowledge of "Is Doing."   The nurse has a good deal of this knowledge through direct observation, supplemented by some instrumentation, although, as noted above, there remains a residue of unsolved problems in measurement. However, as compared with the factory worker, the nurse gets only limited "feedback" from the patient to whom the medication is administered. A medication error may not produce a perceptible warning sign, especially in the short term.

Ability to "Regulate."   This criterion requires that the nurse be able to take some remedial action in the event that the medication or equipment available does not seem to permit conformance to specifications. The nurse has access to the physician or to a supervisor to secure answers to conflicts in orders, to get action on inadequate instruments, etc. In practice, the nurse makes good use of these sources of assistance and reference. But there are also numerous situations in which the workloads, the congestion, the emergencies, the oral orders, and the need for decisiveness in times of stress may force the nurse to act promptly because there seems to be no time to investigate or no one available to consult.

Reduction of Medication Error Rate.   The incidence of hospital medication errors is simply shocking. In the experience of the authors, no other industry so critical to human life and under the supervision of professionals exhibits so high an error rate. Only the error rate for outpatients is worse (and it is much worse; see Latiolais and Berry, 1969).

Successful reduction of this error rate has involved programs that require contributions from all the disciplines present in the hospital, including administration.

The Team Approach. All the comprehensive studies of medication error have made clear that the root causes of most errors go beyond the simplistic tendency to blame this or that department. In consequence, an interdepartmental study has been resorted to. To this end, a team is organized that consists of key people from the cognizant hospital departments, with perhaps a respected outsider or two. This team identifies all activities involved in the medication procedure and structures a flow diagram to aid all members in understanding the overall procedure. As the team broadens its understanding, it identifies "trouble spots," and these become the focal points for joint effort at improvement. (For an excellent discussion, see Conley, 1969/1970.)

Quantifying the Error Rates. This fundamental step not only establishes the overall frequency of error; it also identifies the main components of the error rate, i.e., the vital few types of error that result in the bulk of the overall problem. In the absence of knowledge as to what these vital few types of error are, the remedial steps are like blind therapy: a remedy is applied without knowledge of the precise nature of the disease. The methodology exemplified in the BKH study is a proved way of quantifying the error rates.

Hill and Wigmore (1967) report on a similar approach used by a British study team, which also quantified the prevailing error rates and the main contributing components. The overall error rate was comparable with that found in the BKH study.

Remedying the Major Causes of Error. As the team identifies the vital few causes of error, it also develops potential solutions. These can then be tested to see whether the error rate actually declines.

The British team structured several experiments to test various potential improvements. (For example, in one experiment, physicians were asked to prescribe in metric units, using only official or approved names, writing in block capitals, and abandoning most abbreviations, Latin, and ambiguous directions.) Some drastic reductions in error rate were observed, e.g., from 15.3 percent to 4.2 percent.

To an increasing extent the teams can find assistance from the results of studies reported in the literature (see, for instance, Davis and Cohen, 1981). For example, the nurse's transcription of the physician's order is a breeding ground for errors, and there is a broad school of thought that proposes to abolish this transcription. A related school of thought proposes to restore the direct linkage between physician and pharmacist on the ground that the pharmacist is professionally qualified to interpret the physician's order, whereas the nurses, aides, clerks, and other paramedical personnel assigned to transcription lack this qualification in varying degrees. Practitioners have found ways to meet both these needs by providing the pharmacist with a copy of the prescription in the physician's own handwriting (Dimmit and Lantos, 1967).

Restructuring the Hospitals' Internal Procedures. Restructuring of internal procedures is needed to hold the gains resulting from the team efforts and to guard against sporadic errors. It is essential that this restructuring likewise be done by a team rather than being left for "each department on its own" because of the high degree of mutual interdependence.

Some of the restructuring consists of clarifying long-standing ambiguities and tightening up loose practices (Eckel, 1968). Mainly, however, the restructuring relates to ensuring that the new practices designed to minimize the major causes of error are actually made effective and that they will remain in effect.

A mistake to be avoided is that of restructuring the procedure in the absence of quantified knowledge of what the main error types are. Without such knowledge any revision of procedures may reduce only the minor causes of error and may actually "lock in" some of the major causes.

Broad "Systems Revision."   Remedies for causes of error are in some cases beyond the ability of the hospital "industry" alone. In such cases the hospital must enlist the aid of the support industries that collaborate in the overall objective health. In many instances, it is these support industries that have taken the initiative (e.g., development of new drugs, instruments, and equipment).

An example closely related to medication error is the development of the "unit-dose" concept. Under this concept, drugs are identified at the factory in a way that preserves their identity until they reach the bedside, i.e., the dosages are individually packaged and labeled with the drug name, dosage, and expiration date. While there are variations in details, the American Society of Hospital Pharmacists points out four common elements of unit-dose systems: (1) Medications are contained in, and administered from, single-dose or unit-dose packages; (2) medications are dispensed in ready-to-administer form to the extent possible; (3) for most medications, not more than a 24-h supply of doses is provided to or available at the patient care area at any time; and (4) a patient medication profile is concurrently maintained in the pharmacy for each patient (American Society of Hospital Pharmacists, 1980). Davis and Cohen (1981) report that studies of medication in three hospitals using the unit-dose system (not counting wrong-time errors) found error rates of 3.5, 1.9, and 0.64 percent, respectively—a major step forward.

In other respects, the need to reduce hospital medication errors is in conflict with vested interests of support industries or disciplines. Older physicians cling to their habitual use of antiquated units of measure and terminology. Drug manufacturers may well resist eliminating "similar name" drugs (some of these have their origin in the marketing technique of deliberately using similar names to secure an association with an already accepted product).

In such cases of cultural or economic resistance, the hospital may choose to be circumspect, but it has a good deal of economic power that it can bring to bear, and this power is on the increase.

Bank Quality.   The quality needs of banks are dictated by a host of governmental regulations, by customers' expectations of fault-free service, and by the mechanization of vast numbers of banking transactions. In recent years, a growing number of banks have recognized an increased need for quality and have been adopting modern control procedures to match the advances made by computerization of bank services.

A joint committee of the Bank Administration Institute and the American Society for Quality Control's Banking Committee sent questionnaires on the quality control state of the art to the 200 largest U.S. commercial banks in 1982. The survey found that there were quality control programs in 39 percent of the banks responding, including some 76 percent of the very largest banks responding (those with more than 3000 employees), 39 percent of those with 1000 to 3000 employees, and 25 percent of those with less than 1000 employees (Henke, 1982).

Detailed records of the cost of poor quality (as discussed in Section 4, Quality Costs) do not appear to be kept in the majority of banks. A few banks have worked out definitions and instructions, in banking terminology, for collecting data on the four categories of cost: appraisal, internal failure, external failure, and prevention (Aubrey and Zimbler, 1983). One major bank, which has compiled such cost data carefully in 19 divisions, found that these quality-associated costs came to 37 percent of total operating expense. Of this total cost, 59 percent was for appraisal costs, 20 percent for external failure costs, 13 percent for internal failure costs, and 8 percent for preventive work (Eldridge and Aubrey, 1983).

In banking, as in manufacturing, attention has been given both to design quality and to production quality. "Design quality" is the level of service specified to meet the customers' requirements, explicit or implicit—the fitness-for-use concept as applied to services. Examples are specifications for speed of service at tellers' windows and freedom from errors in monthly statements. "Production quality" is the quality of work as it is actually produced. Lack of production quality takes such forms as errors in calculations, checks charged to the wrong account, or excessive handling time.

Bank operations include both mass-production machine operations (e.g., imprinting checks with magnetic characters or making computer runs to prepare statements of customers' accounts) and large-scale human brain operations (teller transactions, loan application processing, clerical work).

While nearly all methods of quality management are applicable to banking, three are especially pertinent: process control, analytical studies, and acceptance sampling.

"Process control" is accomplished by collecting data, analyzing the data to determine the process capability of the system and using information on deviations from process capability to signal a need for correction where necessary. Statistical process control systems are particularly applicable in the check-processing and microfilming areas.

"Analytical studies" are conducted to solve specific problems. Teller queueing, testing of new equipment for reliability, and sampling a data file for operating information are a few examples of these techniques.

"Acceptance sampling" involves the drawing of a sample of materials used in performing bank functions, testing the sample, and maintaining records of the quality level of the materials tested.

Control of Machine Processes. A number of the mechanized processes in banks (e.g., check processing and microfilming) lend themselves to use of quality methods similar to those used in manufacturing (identification of key quality characteristics, establishment of control points, sampling for control purposes, separation of outputs of like machines, Pareto analysis, etc.)

For example, the banking industry depends on magnetic ink character recognition (MICR) symbols to process checks, deposit tickets, and internal documents mechanically. These small numbers, found at the bottom of each check, are usually both preprinted and encoded by the bank of first deposit. Normally, the preprinting is applied when the check is originally manufactured.

If any of the magnetic characters do not conform to American National Standards Institute (ANSI) specifications (ANSI X3.2 and ANSI X3.3), either in the way the character is formed, in its magnetic strength, or in its placement, the check is rejected by the reader/sorter machine. This results in an out-of-balance condition in the automatic check processing and requires a process called "reconcilement" to enter the data into the computer system correctly.

The cost of correcting each rejected check ranges from $0.35 to $1.00 (Latzko, 1978). A modest-sized bank, processing an average of 500,000 checks a day, spends $400,000 per year for each 1 percent of rejects. Since the national average for rejects as reported by the Bank Administration Institute is between 2 and 4 percent, the average bank spends about $1 million per year on such rejects. While not all of the cost is avoidable, substantial savings are possible with MICR Quality Control.

A major source of MICR rejects is the printer of the original checks. While there is a group of printers who specialize in MICR printing and have very low defect rates (about 0.25 to 0.5 percent), other printers contribute greatly to the reject rate by improper MICR printing. Whatever the reason—inexperience or inattention—the effect is costly. Not only does it cost the bank money for reconcilement, but the user of the check stands a risk that it will be classed as not being a "cash item" (not processable) by the Federal Reserve System. When that happens the "check" becomes a "collection item" subject to a collection fee.

While checks are rarely declared to be noncash items, this has occurred. A major firm issued a series of dividend checks with very defective MICR symbols. A midwestern Federal Reserve bank returned these items to the depositing banks, which in turn returned them to their depositors. The depositors, who were stockholders, called the firm wanting to know if they were on the brink of bankruptcy. It took a lot of explaining on the part of the firm's treasurer, as well as a reissue of checks, to clear up the problem. To avoid problems with checks, many banks have established testing centers. Printers send a specified sample of the checks to these centers before shipping the lot. If the checks meet the specifications, the lot is shipped and used; otherwise the lot is reprinted. This method is called "predelivery sampling" (PDS). It has been the experience of a number of banks that for nonpersonal check orders 1 lot in 10 requires reprinting. Personal check orders have a very fine record of quality.

In practice, most commercial checks are ordered by the user firm directly from the printer. The buying firm has no way of judging the quality of the magnetic ink characters.

A large customer of a major New York bank received delivery of several hundred thousand payroll checks. The total order was for 2 million checks, a 2-year supply. The customer sent a sample to this bank. Some 35 percent of the checks were defective. A sample from the remainder of the order showed the same percentage defective. The printer visited the bank and was shown the checks being tested on the banks's modern test equipment. He immediately indicated that the wrong paper had been used in the printing, causing the problem.

New paper was ordered for a reprint. Owing to a paper shortage, delivery was very slow. Some time later, the bank noted that the company's payroll checks were being rejected in such massive numbers that the bank could not perform the check reconcilement service the customer required. It turned out that the customer's company had run out of the old stock of checks. A payroll must be met, so, in desperation, the company had used the defective checks. The customer agreed to pay all the extra charges for the extra handling. These amounted to more than $25,000 before new, adequate checks were furnished by the printer. As a result of such experiences, a number of banks now require that all check orders be tested before use. Some banks have developed a list of approved printers who agree to this testing procedure. Customers may also submit names of their printers for addition to the approved list.

Banks themselves add MICR impressions to their depositors' checks—for example, to translate the handwritten or typewritten money amounts into machine-readable form. While there are various methods for applying MICR to bank paper, one important technique is the use of "encoders," some of which are called "inscribers." They range from relatively simple, small devices, which are operated manually, to sophisticated computer-driven models with built-in logic capable of handling thousands of documents per hour. The four most common problems found in such machines are: (1) wrong placement of MICR; (2) wrong use (or absence) of symbols; (3) embossment; and (4) extraneous ink arising from ribbon flaking. Apart from elementary corrective steps (such as moving the encoding to a central encoding unit with better equipment than is available at branches), it has been found advisable to test each encoder at the start of each shift by passing a number of specially designed test documents through the machine. This test serves not only to check the quality of the encoding but also to clean the hammers of any extraneous ink that might have accumulated owing to the failure of a document to pass through the transport.

The test documents are examined as soon as they are produced. The shift supervisor checks line placement with a Glardon gage and examines the MICR line visually. If voids due to extraneous ink or embossment can be seen by the naked eye, they probably exceed the ANSI standards. More sophisticated devices can be used to confirm suspected deviations from standard. If the test documents are defective, the machine is taken out of service until repaired by a mechanic.

It is advisable to maintain a record of the number of checks processed between failures by machine. Since, except for random fluctuations, the machine should have a stable process rate between failures, a record disclosing a lower-than-expected process rate is a signal of the start of a major problem with the machine.

Control of Work Force Processes.   Quality improvement in banking depends to an important degree on bringing the quality of human operations to a high level. The daily volume of transactions handled individually by bank personnel is immense. Even with heavy use of computers as an operating tool, banks still depend essentially on people for inputs and decisions. Verification, signing of documents, checking, etc., are still widely practiced. In spite of this effort, mistakes and delays still occur.

A newer approach used by banks to improve these operations can be illustrated by describing the system used by the Irving Trust Company (Latzko, 1975, 1978, and 1982). The Irving Quality Improvement Program (QUIP) involves supervisor participation, separate measurement of the error rates of individuals, determination of achievable process capability, and problem-solving help given in a supportive way to individuals who are not reaching this level of correctness of work.

In the bank's Money Transfer Department, the basic operation consists of receiving fund transfer instructions, which are edited and checked for balance adequacy. If these are approved, the necessary paperwork is typed from the edited instructions and then sent to be verified. If satisfactory, the documents are sent for signature, a second verification, and release to the next processing department. While this procedure has now been automated, the essential work flow remains the same.

In the QUIP approach, the first step consists of determining what makes each operation correct. That becomes the operational definition of each job step. To assemble this information, the verifiers are asked to list what they are checking on each document. This list is compared with what management thinks is being checked. Important differences of omission and commission are noted and reconciled. The result is a work list, which for the first time tells all the operators what is expected of them. The list has been found to be very useful in training both clerks and verifiers.

The next step is for the supervisor to spend 1.5 h a day in 10-min segments going from clerk to clerk and examining the last piece of work completed. The results of these examinations, both good and bad, are recorded on individual records for each clerk. The weekly records are summarized and processed as described below.

A supervisor who comes across an error asks the operator why the work was performed in that particular manner. Responses have been found to fall into three categories:

1. *Improper training:*   The operator says, "Isn't that the way it should be done?"

In such a case, the supervisor coaches the clerk on the proper way to do the job.

2. *Systems problems:* If, for example, the typewriter does not always function or the carbon paper in a form does not extend fully, causing lost dollar data, the supervisor moves the operator to good equipment or initiates whatever steps are needed to fix the system.

3. *Operator failure:* The operator has made a mistake. The supervisor's action in this case depends on whether this is the first or the nth occurrence of the mistake, which can only be determined with the summary information described next.

The weekly summary of each operator's data is analyzed by statistical methods. The cumulative results of several weeks of data are usually sufficiently reliable to determine not only the process average but the process capability and to identify any clerk with excess errors. A computerized output is shown in Figure 33.14. Clerks with error rates outside normal limits (2σ is suggested) are noted. It must be determined that the input data for Figure 33.14 are correct and that any clerk noted as out of control is doing work similar to the others.

The supervisor works with any clerk whose error rate is out of control to determine the cause and to help the clerk obtain better results. In the money transfer operation, several clerks showed out-of-control error rates. It was found that some needed glasses or new prescriptions. One verifier was found to be taking tranquilizers to help lower his recently developed high blood pressure. This clerk was transferred to an equivalent but less demanding task.

As a result of using the QUIP approach, the overall error rate of the operation has been cut in half. Workers are happier because they realize that they and man-

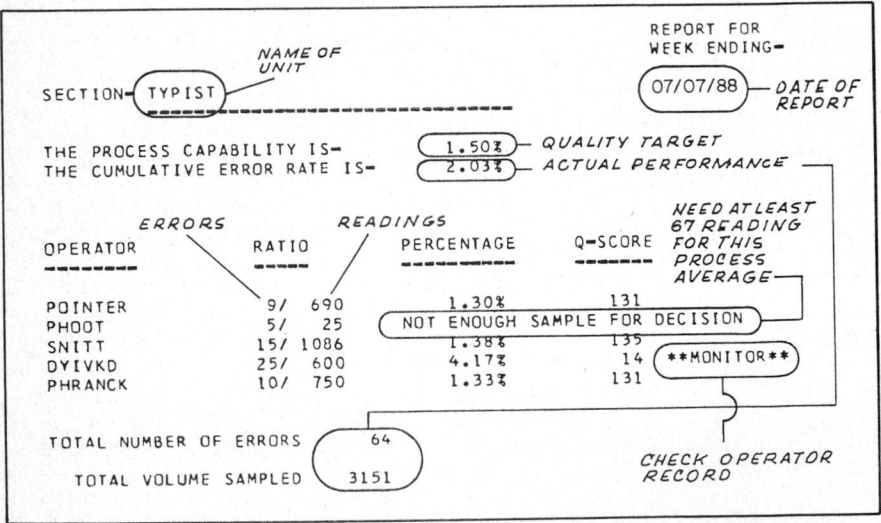

FIG. 33.14 Bank supervisor's inspection record. The analysis includes the individual operator's name, ratio, percentage, and Q-score, for which 100 is arbitrarily set as the average. On the basis of input data, the system not only determines the individual's Q-score but indicates situations in which there is "not enough sample for decision" and individuals who are recommended for "monitor." (Latzko, 1986, p. 77.)

agement are on the same side and that they can count on fair help. Work attitudes have improved. And in spite of an increase in volume, penalty payments were several hundred thousand dollars less in the year after QUIP was introduced.

The QUIP system is based on four principles:

1. Gather data on accuracy/errors on a current basis, and separately for each person or other source.
2. Determine the level of accuracy that is achievable (process capability) by studying the records of effective employees.
3. Gain active participation of supervisors in data collection, searches for causes of problems, and corrective steps.
4. "Fix the problem, not the blame."

While the quality of the work flow of a department can be measured at several different points in the process, it is most informative to measure at the sources. If several clerks are doing like work, for example, one may be producing substantially more errors than the others. The combined stream of work will show an error rate (process average) higher than the error rate of the more successful employees (process capability). Study of accuracy/errors at the sources shows what is achievable.

The QUIP system analyzes current work on an ongoing basis. The item reviewed by the supervisor has just been completed. The transaction is still fresh in the employee's mind. In banks that, in contrast, seek to identify causes of errors mainly by studying items returned by other departments or by customers, the work may have been done days or even months earlier. The clerk may not be able to remember the circumstances of the particular transaction. Such a follow-up long after the fact has less chance of uncovering a causal factor.

Supportive participation by supervisors is essential because:

1. It emphasizes that quality, not just quantity, is important and that the supervisor is committed to working to achieve it.
2. It brings to bear the supervisor's ability to solve problems and eliminate error causes that are beyond the individual employee's control.
3. A climate of support rather than blame helps in finding solutions.

Team Efforts. After identifying prevalent types of errors through Pareto-type analysis of inspection records, banks rely to a large extent on the ability of individual supervisors to find and eliminate causes. Help is given by quality specialists in banks that have such positions. In some banks, problem-solving teams are set up to develop ways to prevent errors found to occur frequently (Bureau of Business Practice, 1968).

Continental Illinois National Bank (Chicago) reports good success with more than 100 quality circles, organized to help with this task (Aubrey and Eldridge, 1981; Aubrey and Fend, 1982). Continental established departmental steering committees, composed of managers, to plan for the circles and establish policies and procedures. Part-time facilitators have been appointed and trained to assist and coordinate quality circles. Membership in circles is on a volunteer basis, with a wide cross section of employees being offered briefing on circles and some training in specific techniques before committing to circle involvement. Those who become circle members are given training in eight techniques used by circles, with examples from bank operations. Techniques include Pareto analysis and cause-and-effect analysis. The bank has professional circles, clerical circles, management circles, and facilitator's circles. These address different types of problems selected to fit their varying skill and experience.

Airline Quality.   A major airline conducted studies at 16 airports to determine customers' expectations of airline service. This FOCUS Program ("Focus on Customer Service") also provided a comparison of the airline's actual performance against standards based on customer's expectations. It was initially designed to measure passenger service, ramp service, and aircraft appearance standards. The basic program had the capability of being expanded into additional areas such as reservations, dining service, in-flight service, air freight, and cabin service—in essence, to cover all areas involving direct contact with the customer.

Measurement was obtained through observation. Consistency in measurements and reports was obtained through training of observers. The results were used by each station, region, and division, although the service measurements were defined in terms of group rather than individual performance. Evaluations of the latter remained under local supervision.

The major objectives of the FOCUS program were:

1. To provide factual, objective measurements and reports
2. To provide contributions to problem solving through analysis of causes and formulation of corrective action
3. To provide recognition of achievement above, as well as below, performance expectations
4. To provide performance levels that are competitive when compared with the performance of other carriers
5. To provide clarification of service goals using input from the field, regional, and divisional levels
6. To provide cost-service relationships between personnel and service, adjusted or relocated volumes of passengers and cargo, and service priorities
7. To introduce service-level goals into the personnel planning system

The FOCUS program was administered by each division office, with technical and functional direction provided by the Industrial Engineering Department. Actual observation and evaluation were performed at the regional level. Daily worksheets were filed for review by all station personnel, with a monthly summary provided to each departmental manager and station operations manager. Statistical performance results were also provided to each region and division as well as to the Industrial Engineering Division. The Industrial Engineering Division prepared system performance reports, which were published in an established newsletter the second week of each month.

Measurements were presented in three sections:

Airport arrival and departure

Aircraft interior and exterior appearance

Additional miscellaneous measurement categories of proven value in evaluating station performance

Each section was further subdivided into broad categories of performance.

Examples of standards for aircraft arrival and departure (Section 1), are shown in Table 33.5 (United Air Lines, 1973).

TABLE 33.5 Examples of Airline Arrival/Departure Standards
Section 1

Category	Goal
I. People	Of public contact transactions, 95% are positive overall.
II. Skycap availability	A skycap is available at curbside within 1 minute 90% of the time.
III. Ticketing	Line waits of not more than 5 minutes for 80% of all passengers.
IV. Baggage check-in	Line waits of not more than 3 minutes for 90% of all passengers.
V. Baggage delivery	Narrow body: 90% of the flights have all the baggage delivered to the Claim Area within 20 min of block arrival.
	Wide body: 90% of the flights have all the baggage delivered to the Claim Area within 25 min of block arrival.

REFERENCES

American Society of Hospital Pharmacists (1980). *ASHP Guidelines on Hospital Drug Administration and Control.*

ARA Services, Inc. (1980). *ARA Performance Incentive Operational Manual.* Paper PPM D10.15.16. Philadelphia.

Aubrey, Charles A., II (1985). *Quality Management in Financial Services.* ASQC Quality Press, Milwaukee.

Aubrey, Charles A. II and Eldridge, L. A. (1981). "Banking on High Quality." *Quality Progress*, December, pp. 14–19.

Aubrey, Charles A. II and Fend, W. C. (1982). "Management, Professional and Clerical Quality Circles." *ASQC Quality Congress Transactions*, Milwaukee, pp. 1–11.

Barker, Kenneth N. (1969). "The Effects of an Experimental Medication System on Medication Errors and Costs." *American Journal of Hospital Pharmacy*, June-July, pp. 324–333.

Barker, Kenneth N. (1961). "A Study of the Problem of Detecting Medication Errors in a Hospital." Master's thesis, University of Florida, Gainesville.

Barker, Kenneth N., Kimbrough, W. W., and Heller, W. M. (1966). *A Study of Medication Errors in a Hospital.* Original publication printed by University of Arkansas Press. Reprinted, University of Mississippi Press, 1968.

Barker, Kenneth N. and McConnell, W. (1962). "How to Detect Medication Errors." *Modern Hospital*, July, pp. 95–105.

Bureau of Business Practice, Inc. National Foreman's Institute, Waterford, CT (1968). "Participation Teams Help You Bank on Quality." *Quality Control Supervisor's Bulletin*, April 25, pp. 1–4.

Burrell, Claude W. and Ellsworth, L. W. (1982). *Quality Data Processing: The Profit Potential for the 80s.* Burrell-Ellsworth Associates, Tenafly, NJ.

Conley, Dean (1969–1970). "A Management Team Approach to Hospital Systems Analysis." *Hospital Administration,* Winter, pp. 1–21.

Cornwall, L. P. (1964). *Quality Control in International Air Freight.* Railroad Systems and Management Association, Chicago.

Davis, Neill M. and Cohen, M. R. (1981). *Medication Errors: Causes and Prevention.* George F. Stickley Co., Philadelphia.

Deming, W. Edwards (1982). *Quality, Productivity and Competitive Position.* Massachusetts Institute of Technology, Cambridge, MA, p. 226.

Dimmit, Deanna M. and Lantos, R. L. (1967). "Development of a Revised Manual Medication System in a Community Hospital." *American Journal of Hospital Pharmacy,* November, pp. 617–24.

Dmytrow, Eric D. (1984). "Quality Control in the Calculation of Price Indexes." *ASQC Quality Congress Transactions,* Milwaukee.

Dunn, Robert and Ullman, Richard (1982). *Quality Assurance for Computer Software.* McGraw-Hill, New York.

Eckel, Fred M. (1968). "Ten Traps in Drug Systems Cause Most Medication Errors." *Modern Hospital,* November, pp. 104, 106, 108.

Eldridge, L. A. and Aubrey, C. A. II (1983) "Stressing Quality—The Path to Productivity." *Bank Administration,* June, p. 2024.

Ford, Robert N. (1973). "Job Enrichment Lessons from AT&T." *Harvard Business Review,* January-February.

Ford, Robert N. (1979). *Why Jobs Die and What to Do about It.* AMACOM, New York.

Henke, John A. (1982). "Quality State of the Art in Banking—Survey Results." *ASQC Quality Congress Transactions,* Milwaukee, pp. 202–205.

Hill, Peter A. and Wigmore, H. M. (1967). "Measurement and Control of Drug Administration Incidents." *The Lancet,* March 25, pp. 671–674.

Latiolais, C. J. and Berry, C. C. (1969). "Misuse of Prescription Medications by Outpatients." *Drug Intelligence and Clinical Pharmacy,* October, pp. 270–277.

Latzko, William J. (1986). *Quality and Productivity for Bankers and Financial Managers.* ASQC Quality Press, Milwaukee.

Main, Jeremy (1981). "Toward Service without a Snarl." *Fortune,* March 23, pp. 59–66.

McDonald, Marshall (1984). "Commitment to Success at FPL." *Quality Progress,* January, pp. 26–28.

Pitt, Hy (1981). "Specifications: Laws or Guidelines?" *Quality Progress,* July pp. 15–18.

Rosander, A. C. (1985). *Applications of Quality Control in the Service Industries.* ASQC Quality Press, Milwaukee.

Rosenzweig, George (1978). "Cost of Quality in the Service Industries." *ASQC Technical Conference Transactions,* Milwaukee, pp. 321–325.

Sasser, W. E., Olsen, R. P., and Wyckoff, D. D. (1978). *Management of Service Operations.* Allyn & Bacon, Boston, pp. 58–72.

Scanlon, Frank and Hagan, J. T. (1983). "Quality Management for the Service Industries." *Quality Progress,* May and June.

Shephard, K. L. (1975). "Quality Control of Service in Air Transportation." *Australian Organization for Quality Control National Seminar,* September.

Thorner, M. E. and Manning, P. B. (1983). *Quality Control in Foodservice.* Avi Publishing Co., Westport, CT.

Townsend, Patrick and Gebhardt, J. E. (1986). *Commit to Quality.* ASQC Quality Press, Milwaukee.

Troxell, Joseph R. (1981). "Service Time Quality Standards." *Quality Progress,* September, pp. 35–36.

United Air Lines, Inc. (1973). *FOCUS Familiarization Manual.* Chicago.

SECTION 34
QUALITY AND SOCIETY

J. M. Juran

THE BACKGROUND **34.1**

CONSUMERISM **34.2**

Researches on Consumer
  Grievances 34.3

Consumer Problems . . . 34.3

Consumer Perceptions . . . 34.3

Remedial Proposals 34.4

Remedies before the Fact . 34.4

Consumer Test Services . . 34.6

Remedies after the Fact . . 34.9

No Remedy 34.12

Consumer Organizations . 34.12

Perceptions of the
  Consumer Movement . . 34.12

GOVERNMENT REGULATION OF
QUALITY **34.13**

Bases for Regulation . . . 34.13

The Plan of Regulation . . 34.14

Effectiveness of
  Regulation 34.15

PRODUCT SAFETY AND
PRODUCT LIABILITY **34.19**

Defensive Action 34.19

Defense against Lawsuits . 34.21

Insurance 34.21

Prognosis 34.21

Personal Liability 34.21

REFERENCES **34.22**

THE BACKGROUND

Human society has depended on quality since the dawn of history.

In primitive societies this dependence has been on quality of natural goods and "services." Human life can exist only within rather narrow limits of climatic temperature, air quality, food quality, etc. For most primitive societies, life even within these narrow limits was marginal, despite extensive use of the human mental and physical faculties.

Human adaptation to the natural environment has been based on two major areas of response:

1. *Human sensing:* The human senses are used to judge the quality of natural goods and services. The result is a form of "incoming inspection" prior to use.

2. *Lessons learned:* The experience of the past is condensed into lessons learned (e.g., when to plant crops; which berries are poisonous). These lessons learned are handed down from generation to generation.

34.1

Despite these responses, human beings in most primitive societies have lived precariously. Hours of work were often long and exhausting. Life spans were shortened by malnutrition, disease, natural disasters, etc.

To protect themselves against these risks, primitive societies created nonnatural aids to their mental and physical capabilities, aids such as:

Division of labor

Community forms, e.g., villages

Artificial shelter, e.g., houses

Processing of natural materials to produce nonnatural goods, e.g., pottery, textiles

Tools, weapons

The subsequent growth of commerce and of science and technology greatly expanded the extent and variety of these nonnatural goods and services.

As a result human beings in many modern industrial societies live longer and more varied lives. They are also largely shielded from the perils which their ancestors faced. However, all those nonnatural goods and services have created new dependencies, and therefore new perils. Instead of being largely subject to the perils of natural forces, human beings are now largely subject to risks resulting from their own ingenuity:

1. Sometimes those goods and services fail. The resulting breaks in continuity are costly and annoying.
2. Some of those goods and services contain threats to human safety and health, and to the environment.

The extent of such product failures and threats to human well-being depends on the quality built into those nonnatural goods and services. Years ago the author coined the phrase "Life behind the Quality Dikes" to designate these risks. For elaboration, see Section 3, under Major Economic Influences; Life Behind the Quality Dikes.

The ability to cope with breaks in the quality dikes varies remarkably among human beings. Large organizations (e.g., industrial companies, governments) can employ technologists or otherwise use their economic and political strengths to plan, control, and improve quality. In contrast, the individuals (consumers, the citizenry) find themselves pitted against forces which to them seem quite as overpowering and mysterious as the natural forces seemed to their primitive ancestors.

Any one individual has only a very limited capacity to deal with these forces. However, these individuals are very numerous. Collectively their powers, economic and political, are formidable. These powers have emerged in a movement generally called "consumerism." This movement, though loosely organized, has been influential in providing individual members of society with protection and recourse relative to breaks in the quality dikes.

CONSUMERISM

Consumer grievances have existed throughout recorded history. Whether the grievance rate (the ratio of grievances to consumer transactions) has over the decades been getting better or worse is not known with any precision. However the absolute number of consumer grievances has risen to huge proportions. A major reason is growing affluence, which results in more and larger consumer transactions. This large number of consumer grievances has generated much publicity—grievances are inherently newsworthy. In recent decades these grievances and the associated publicity have stimulated consumers toward some sort of collective action. The terms "consumerism" and "consumer movement" have emerged as popular names for a collective effort to help consumers secure redress for their grievances and (better yet) to shut off the root causes of the grievances. (See Juran, 1970, also Sentry, 1976, pp. 36, 37.)

Researches on Consumer Grievances.   The number of consumer grievances is known to be huge. However, until the 1970s there had been little systematic quantification of the extent and kind of these grievances, or of the trends. Numerous individual investigators had conducted and published researches and pseudoresearches on various aspects of the problems of consumers. Generally these publications dramatized selected instances of asserted company and industry responsibility for consumer troubles and then generalized from these instances to make public attacks on the competence and integrity of the companies.

The published attacks were successful in attracting a large following among the public, the press, and legislators. Lacking scoreboards and other accepted indexes, the companies and industries were unable to make a successful defense, so they lost the initiative for action. The resulting vacuum attracted numerous contenders for leadership of the consumerism movement: government agencies, politicians, social reformers, consumer advocates ("consumerists"), consumer associations, standardization organizations, independent test laboratories, and still others. A serious risk arose that a bargaining agent would intervene between industrial companies and their customers.

Starting in the 1970s some well-structured researches were undertaken and published. These researches identified the dominant prevailing problems as well as the perceptions among the various interested groups: consumers, consumer organizations, government, business, insurance, etc.

Consumer Problems.   The major quality-oriented problems are listed in Table 34.1 (derived from Sentry, 1976, p. 5).

TABLE 34.1   Major Consumer Quality-Oriented Problems

Poor quality of many products
Failure to live up to advertising claims
Poor quality of after-sales service and repairs
Misleading packaging or labeling
Futility of making complaints; nothing substantial will be done
Inadequate guarantees or warranties
Failure of companies to handle complaints properly
Too many dangerous products
The absence of reliable information about the different goods and services
Not knowing what to do when something goes wrong with a purchased product
The difficulty of choosing which of the competing products to buy

---

Consumer Perceptions.   Consumer expectations sometimes rise faster than the market rate of improvement (Sentry, 1976, p. 3). In addition, consumer perceptions can differ from the realities. For example, it has been widely believed by consumers that quality of product has been getting worse; that "products do not last as long as they used to." Yet study of specific product lines almost always finds that quality has kept improving. (It is not clear whether this is also true of after-sale service.)

This widespread perception may well be the result of the growth of the *number* of consumer grievances and the associated growth in publicity. An obvious parallel is seen in human mortality statistics. More people are dying than ever before. Yet the human life span is longer than ever before. The explanation is that the human population is larger than ever before.

Even though some consumer perceptions differ from the realities, the perceptions are important in their own right. People act on their perceptions of the realities. In consequence it is quite important to understand what are the perceptions of consumers.

For some additional findings on consumer perceptions relative to product quality, see the study sponsored by the American Society for Quality Control (ASQC, 1980).

Perceptions on Self-Help. Consumers generally felt that there was much they could do to help themselves relative to quality. They generally felt that the necessary product information was available but that the information was not being used by consumers. They had similar views with respect to product safety. They generally felt that most products were safe if used properly; also that many product safety problems arose because of failure to read the instructions properly (Sentry, 1976, pp. 9, 10).

Remedial Proposals. There are a number of these, amid much difference of opinion. The differences arise in part because of the impact on costs and prices (see below). In addition there are differences due to a contest for power. Various organizations—consumer activists, government departments, etc.—feel that they should play larger roles and that certain traditional powers of business should be restricted.

Remedies before the Fact. Ideally, the remedies should eliminate the causes of consumer problems at their source. The consumerism movement has been skeptical that such prevention will take place at the initiative of the industrial companies. Hence the main proposals have related to establishing ways to enable consumers to judge beforehand whether they are about to buy trouble.

Data Banks on Product Performance. It would be most helpful for consumers to have access to data on product tests and field performance. The bulk of these data are in the possession of the manufacturers. They regard such information as proprietary. They do disclose selected portions, but mainly to aid in sale of the product. The risk of bias is obvious.

There have been some proposals to establish quality information centers, i.e., data banks on actual product performance, quality failures, consumer complaints, and other evidence relating to product fitness for use. The data bank would process the data and publish the results, so that consumers could inform themselves on the quality performance of competing products before making their purchases.

Under this concept, industrial companies would be required to disclose their test data, complaint data, etc., to the data bank. The bank would also collect data from the users as to product performance, service effectiveness, company response to failures, etc. In addition, the bank would acquire data from other sources which had useful data to contribute, e.g., government regulatory agencies.

A long-standing parallel for such data banks is the finance (credit) data bank of Dun & Bradstreet, Inc. However, manufacturers and merchants in the capitalistic economies have successfully resisted establishing such data banks on quality. Since this resistance was successful during the decades when the political climate was favorable to the consumerism movement, there is little likelihood that such data banks will be established in the near future.

Independent Certification. Under this concept, products are required by law to be independently approved for adequacy before they may be sold to the public. This concept is already widely applied to specific product categories (e.g., pharmaceuticals, foods) in various countries. Generally, the market-based economies have avoided such mandatory independent certification for consumer products and have relied on the competitive forces of the marketplace to contest for the favor of the consumers, in quality as well as in other matters. In contrast, the planned economies, as exemplified by the Soviet Union, have gone heavily into the setting of standards for consumer products and the use of independent laboratories to enforce compliance to these standards (which have the force of law).

Data Banks on Business Practices. Many consumer complaints are traceable to company business practices, e.g., evasiveness in meeting the provisions of the guarantee rather than product failures in the technological sense. As always, the Pareto principle holds, i.e., a comparatively few companies engage in business practices which create the bulk of the consumer problems. Under this principle, a data bank on company business practices can serve to identify the vital few "bad guys" and aid in removing their influence.

The organizations known as Better Business Bureaus (BBBs) have been a step in the direction of creating such data banks. A BBB receives consumer complaints (among others) on unethical business practices, and endeavors as an ombudsman (see below) to get these practices changed. When citizens call a BBB, they are able to learn whether the company under inquiry has a record of complaints lodged against it.

As in the case of product data banks, there exists a cultural resistance to publicizing the names of companies. Even highly ethical companies exhibit such resistance, one major reason being the belief that the information will be seized on by publicists, muckrakers, and political demagogues to make unwarranted attacks and smears. (On the record, there is much evidence to support this belief.)

Consumer Education. Beyond the above forms of data banks, still other kinds of independent before-the-fact information are available to consumers. The more well known include the product test reports published in *Consumer Reports* by Consumers Union (see below). Various government departments publish information describing the merits (or lack of merits) of products and product features in general. However, the most often used source of product information is advice from friends and relatives. Consumers regard this advice as reliable, along with information from independent test results and Better Business Bureaus (Sentry, 1976, p. 55).

The limiting factors in the use of the available independent data sources are the consumers and their education. Subscribers to *Consumer Reports* run to less than 10 percent of U.S. families. The lack of use of other available independent information (much of which is available free of charge) may well have its origin in a school system which makes little provision to educate children in one of the major roles they will play as adults—the role of consumer.

Better Business Bureaus.   A good description of who BBBs are and what they do, is the following quotation from *Consumer's Resource Handbook* (1980, p. 4):

> What They Are: BBBs are non-profit organizations sponsored by private businesses. There are 147 BBB locations across the U.S. today, sponsored by local and national business. While BBBs vary from place to place, most offer a variety of basic services. These include: general information on products or services, reliability reports, background information on local businesses and organizations, and records of companies' complaint handling performances. Depending on the policy of the individual BBB, it may or may not tell you the nature of the complaint registered against a business. BBBs accept written complaints, and will contact a firm on your behalf.
>
> What They Do: BBBs attempt to settle consumer complaints against local business firms. A BBB considers a consumer complaint settled when:
>
> 1. The customer receives satisfaction.
> 2. The customer receives a reasonable adjustment—in other words, gets what was paid for.
> 3. The company provides proof that the customer's demands are unreasonable or unwarranted.
>
> The BBB does not: judge individual products or brands, handle complaints concerning the prices of goods or services, or give legal advice.
>
> More than 100 of the 147 BBBs offer binding arbitration to those who ask for it, and others are beginning programs. Arbitration is a way for people to settle a dispute by having an impartial person or board (people who have nothing to gain or lose from the decision) decide the outcome of the dispute. In arbitration, parties are bound by the decision, and it can be enforced by the courts. Do not enter arbitration lightly since you must follow the decision that is made.
>
> BBBs also handle false advertising cases. Your local BBB looks into local advertising, while the BBBs' National Advertising Division (NAD) checks out complaints about national advertising.
>
> How to Reach Them: To find a BBB, check your local phone book, local consumer office, or library.

Some observers explain "unwise" consumer behavior on grounds other than lack of education. They note that many consumers spend money on narcotic drugs, alcohol, or tobacco; kill themselves (and others) by driving in a drunken state; eat "junk" food; gamble their money away. It is understandable that some skeptics conclude that consumers who are gullible or stupid will learn only from their mistakes.

Consumer organizations are quite aware that "most consumers do not use the information available about different products in order to decide to buy one of them" (Sentry, 1976, p. 10). However, consumer organizations never characterize consumers (their clientele) as being gullible or stupid ("Laetrile," 1977).

Consumer Test Services.   An alternative source of data banks on product quality is through the use of test laboratories which are independent of the companies which make and sell the products. Under this concept a competent laboratory makes an expert, independent evaluation of product quality so that consumers can obtain the unbiased information needed to make sound purchasing judgments.

Adequate consumer test services involve professionals and skilled technicians, well-equipped test laboratories, acquisition of products for test, and dissemination of the resulting information. Financing of all these needs becomes so severe a problem that the method of financing determines the organizational form and the policies of the test service.

Consumer-Financed Tests.   In this form the test laboratory derives its income by publication of test results, usually in the form of a monthly journal plus an annual compendium. Consumers are urged to subscribe to the journal on the ground that they will save money by acquiring superior knowledge of product values thereby. The advertising by the test laboratory stresses the question, "Would you pay $100 for an appliance when independent tests show that a $75 appliance is just as good?"

In their operation, these consumer-financed test laboratories buy and test competitive products, evaluate their failures and their fitness for use, compare these evaluations with the product prices, and rate the products according to some scale of relative value, e.g., best value, good value, poor value. The ratings, test result summaries, descriptions of tests conducted, etc., are published in the journals. Manufacturers play no role in the testing and evaluation, although they may be consulted on market information. In addition, manufacturers are not permitted to quote the ratings, test results, or other material published in the journals.

It can be seen that the service offered to consumers consists of:

1. Laboratory test results which are commonly objective and unbiased.
2. Judgments of values which are subjective and carry a risk of bias, i.e., the stress of the advertising (showing the consumer that lower-priced products are as good as higher-priced products) creates a bias against higher-priced products. More importantly, the judgments are not necessarily typical of consumer judgments.

Despite the obvious problems of financing a test service out of numerous small subscription prices, there are many such services in existence in affluent and even developing countries. In the United States the most widely known source of such tests is Consumers Union. The test results are published in the journal *Consumer Reports.*

Manufacturer-Financed Tests.   In this form, the income of the test service is derived from fees paid by manufacturers who seek the mark (seal, label) of the testing service as an aid to marketing the product. These test services vary widely in their purpose and especially in their objectivity.

Mandatory Marks.   An obvious example is the mark needed for export of products from those countries which impose controls of export quality. The laboratories are financed out of fees paid by the exporters, and the exporters must pay the fees if they wish to market their products abroad.

Closely related is the example of Underwriters' Laboratories (UL). Originally created by the National Board of Fire Underwriters to aid in fire prevention, UL (now independent) is involved in the general field of fire protection, burglary protection, hazardous chemicals, and still other matters of safety. Its activities include:

Developing and publishing standards for materials, products, and systems.

Testing manufacturers' products for compliance with these standards (or with other recognized standards).

Awarding the UL mark to products which comply. This is known as "listing" the products.

Numerous other laboratories are similarly involved in safety matters, e.g., steam boilers, marine safety.

In some of these safety categories it is unlawful to market the products without the certificate of the testing service. In other cases it is lawful, but the testing is mandatory for economic reasons; e.g., the insurance companies will demand extraordinarily high premiums or will not provide insurance at all. Because of these legal or economic imperatives, the laboratories (which often have achieved a status that confers a monopoly for that type of testing) are generally able to support themselves out of the fees paid for testing.

Voluntary Marks. These forms of testing service are built around the same elements as the mandatory mark:

1. Developing and publishing standards
2. Testing products for conformance
3. Awarding a mark to conforming products

The distinguishing feature of the voluntary mark is that the manufacturer is under no compelling legal (e.g., export control) or economic (e.g., insurance) imperative to obtain the mark. Lacking these imperatives, the manufacturer is interested in the mark solely as a device for competitive marketing. Understandably, manufacturers vary in their views on the value of the mark. Generally, powerful companies tend to feel their own brand or mark carries greater prestige than that of the testing laboratory, which, according to them, has value only for less prestigious companies.

In some countries the voluntary mark is offered by organizations whose independent status is beyond question since they are the official national standardization bodies, e.g., Japan Standards Association or the French AFNOR. Companies that wish to use the JIS mark (Japan Industrial Standards) or the NF mark (Normale Français) must first submit their products to independent test and must pay for these tests. If the products qualify, the manufacturers are granted the right to use the mark.

Government-Subsidized Tests. In this form, neither the consumer nor the manufacturer pays for the standardization and testing, the concept being that the costs should be borne by the public generally. The concept is widely used in the Eastern European countries.

An example in a market-based country was the Teltag scheme administered by the British Consumer Council. Under this scheme, the Council, in consultation with interested groups, decided what data were needed by consumers for various consumer products. The Teltags were designed to provide these needed data on the basis of tests and verifications made by the Council.

Any manufacturer could then voluntarily apply for a license to use the tags on its products. To secure the license, the manufacturer had to submit its product, factory operations, and plan of quality control to examination by the Council, a nonprofit organization qualified under Board of Trade regulations governing independent laboratories. If the license was issued, the manufacturer could attach the Teltags to the product and could refer to the fact of certification in any advertising. The Council derived its income partly from license fees and the sale of the tags but largely from a government subsidy. When the government withdrew the subsidy, the scheme was no longer financially viable.

Standards for Consumer Products. Award of a seal or mark presupposes some standard against which the product can be tested on an objective basis. Providing such standards for consumer products has not received the priorities given to standards for metrology, basic materials, and other technological and industrial needs. However, the consumerism movement has very likely stimulated the pace of developing these standards. Industry associations especially have been stimulated to undertake more of this type of activity.

A continuing need for consumer standards is in the definition of key words. When the same word has both a technical meaning and a common dictionary meaning, this difference may become critical in consumer products. For example, one measure of the quality of watches has been the number of jewels. When some manufacturers began to include nonfunctional jewels to provide a basis for labeling the watch to imply higher quality, it became necessary to create a precise definition of what constitutes a jewel.

A serious limitation on creating standards for consumer products is the pace of product obsolescence versus the time required to set standards. Usually, it takes years to evolve a standard owing to the need for securing a broad base of agreement. For comparatively stable subjects such as metrology or basic materials and tests, these standards, once approved, will have a very long life. However, for consumer products the life is limited by the rate of obsolescence, and for many products the life of the standard becomes so short as to raise serious questions about the economics of doing it at all.

A further problem in standards for consumer products is that the traditional emphasis of the standardization bodies has been on quality of design. The resulting tests and marks have also emphasized quality of design.

However, many of the consumer problems are traceable to deficiencies with respect to other parameters—quality of conformance, the "abilities," quality of field service. (See, generally, Juran, 1970.) The test laboratories have generally not been involved in these matters and have only recently begun to respond to them.

Generally the laboratories are not able to certify quality of conformance. Many of the certification agreements do contain language authorizing the laboratories to sample the flow of production or to visit the manufacturing premises for surveillance. In practice, the authority is seldom used because the tradition and the fee structure are against it.

In the case of the "abilities," we are only in the early stages of being able to use the concept of a mark. Standards are either in rudimentary form or nonexistent. The ratios between laboratory test results and usage results are similarly in early stages of development.

In postsale service, the situation is at its worst. Here the laboratory and its equipment are academic matters in relation to the problem, since the standards needed are for the competence, promptness, and integrity of the service organizations.

The Standardization Organizations. There are many of these, but those of greatest importance to consumers are:

1. Leading manufacturers and merchants, whose standards exert wide influence on suppliers and competitors

2. Industry bodies such as the American Gas Association or the Association of Home Appliance Manufacturers

3. Professional organizations such as the American Society for Testing and Materials or the Society of Automotive Engineers

4. Independent agencies such as Underwriters' Laboratories

5. The American National Standards Institute (ANSI), which is a recognized clearinghouse for committees engaged in setting national standards and is the official publisher of the approved standards

6. The National Bureau of Standards, the government agency which establishes and maintains standards for metrology

Objectivity of Test Services.   Unless the testing service is objective, consumers may be misled by the very organization on which they thought they could rely. The criteria for objectivity include:

Financial Independence.   This requires that the income of the test service be unrelated to the test results. The best form of this independence exists when the income is derived from sources other than the manufacturer whose products are under test. Failing this, the payments by the manufacturer should be solely for the test service and in no way contingent on the test results.

One example of a failure to meet these criteria is the organization which carries on the dual activities of (1) conducting a labeling scheme based on product test and approval and (2) publishing a journal of general circulation in which manufacturers who apply for the label must also be advertisers in the journal.

In such arrangements, the risk of conflict of interest is very high, and consumers should be cautious about giving credence to such marks.

Organizational Independence.   The personnel of the test service should not be subordinate to the companies whose products are undergoing test.

Objective Standards.   In the absence of standards, the test facility is placed in the position of simultaneously setting standards and testing conformance. Long experience has confirmed the need for separating these very different functions.

Technological Capability.   This obvious need includes a qualified professional staff, appropriate test equipment, and competent management. Whether the managers should judge these capabilities of their own organization is open to serious question.

So important is the question of objectivity that in cases of mandated testing it is usual to write into the statute the need for defining criteria of what constitutes an appropriate laboratory. The administrator of the act is then responsible for determining qualifications of laboratories against these criteria.

The Resulting Information.   Consumer test services provide a wide range of information. The principal forms include:

1. Comparative data on competitive products for (*a*) price and (*b*) fitness for use, plus a judgment of comparative value. In this form, the information is also a recommendation for action.

2. Comparative data on competitive products for conformance to standard. In this form, consumers are thrown on their own to discover competitive prices and to make a judgment on comparative fitness. For many consumers, it is a considerable burden to acquire this added information.

3. Evidence of single product conformance to standard (through the seal or mark). Here the consumer is largely asked to equate the standard with fitness for use and to use other means to discover competitive differences and competitive prices.

While conformance to standard serves many useful purposes for industrial buyers, it is very doubtful that this information, by itself, is of great intrinsic value to consumers. For them the optimum information consists of comparative data on fitness for use plus comparative data on cost of usage.

Remedies after the Fact.   Consumers who encounter product quality problems during the warranty period are faced with a choice of alternatives. They may be able to resolve the problem unaided; i.e., they study the product information and then apply their skills and ingenuity. More usually they must turn to one of the companies directly in interest: the merchant who sold them the product, or the manufacturer who made the product. If none of these organizations provides satisfaction, the consumers have still other alternatives for assistance (see below).

Warranties. Quality warranties are a major after-the-fact aid to consumers. However, many consumers feel that warranties are not understandable. In addition, most consumers feel that warranties are written mainly to protect manufacturers rather than consumers. Nevertheless, consumers are increasingly making the warranty an input to their buying decisions. This means also that warranties are increasingly important as marketing tools (Sentry, 1976, pp. 14, 15).

Complaints—to Whom? By a wide margin, consumers complain to the merchant (store, dealer) rather than to the manufacturer. A third choice is to complain to the Better Business Bureau (Sentry, 1976, p. 15).

The Ombudsman. This is a Swedish word used to designate an official whose job is to receive citizens' complaints and to help them secure action from the government bureaucracy. The ombudsman is familiar with government organizational channels and is able to find the government official who has the authority or the duty to act. The ombudsman has no authority to compel action, but has the power to publicize failures to act.

The concept of the ombudsman has been applied to problems in product quality. Some companies have created an in-house ombudsman and have publicized the name and telephone number. Consumers can phone (free of charge) to air grievances and to secure information. In the United States a more usual title is Manager (Director), Consumer Affairs (Relations). Such a manager usually carries added responsibilities for stimulating changes to improve relations with consumers on a broad basis. In one company these efforts resulted in programs to effectuate a consumer "bill of rights"—rights to safety, to information, to choice, to be heard, to redress. For elaboration, see Peterson (1974).

Another form is the industry ombudsman. An example is the Major Appliance Consumer Action Panel (a group of independent consumer experts) created by the Association of Home Appliance Manufacturers to receive complaints from consumers who have not been able to secure satisfaction locally.

Still another form is the Joint Industry-Consumer Complaint Board. Examples are the government-funded boards which mediate and adjudicate consumer disputes in some Scandinavian industries. The boards have no power to enforce their awards other than to publicize unsatisfied awards. Yet they have met with wide acceptance by and cooperation from the business community.

The concept of the ombudsman is fundamentally sound. It is widely supported by consumers and regulators as well as by a strong minority of business managers (Sentry, 1976, p. 77). Some newspapers provide an ombudsman service as part of their department of Letters to the Editor.

Mediation. Under this concept, a third party—the mediator—helps the contestants to work out a settlement. The mediator lacks the power of enforcement—there is no binding agreement to abide by the opinion of the mediator. Nevertheless mediation stimulates settlements. Best (1981) reports that the New York City Department of Human Affairs achieved a 60 percent settlement rate during 1977 and 1978.

The mediation process helps to open up channels of communication and thereby to clear up misunderstandings. In addition, an experienced mediator exerts a moderating influence which encourages a search for a solution.

Arbitration.   Under this concept the parties agree to be bound by the decision of a third party. Arbitration is an attractive form of resolving differences because it avoids the high costs and long delays inherent in most lawsuits. In the great majority of consumer claims the cost of a lawsuit is far greater than the amount of the claim. Nevertheless there are obstacles to use of the arbitration process. Both parties must agree to binding arbitration. There is a need to establish local, low-cost arbitration centers and to secure the services of volunteer arbitrators at nominal fees or no fees. These obstacles have limited the growth of use of arbitration for consumer complaints.

No Remedy.   Under the prevailing free enterprise, competitive market system, many valid consumer complaints result in no satisfaction to the consumer. Nevertheless the system includes some built-in stabilizers. Companies which fail to provide such satisfaction also fail to attract repeat business. In due course they mend their ways or lose out to companies which have a better record of providing satisfaction. In the experience of the author every other system is worse.

Consumer Organizations.   These exist in a wide variety of forms. Some are product- or service-oriented, e.g., automotive safety, truth in lending. Others are adjuncts of broader organizations, e.g., departments of test laboratories, labor unions, or farm cooperatives. Still others are specially organized to deal broadly with consumer problems. In addition, there are broader federations, national and international, which endeavor to find ways of improving the collective strength of all local and specialized consumer groups.

Government Agencies.   These exist at national, state, and local levels of government. All invite consumers to bring unresolved complaints to them as well as to report instances of business malpractice. These complaints aid the agency in identifying widespread problems, which, in turn, become the basis for:

1. Conducting investigations in depth
2. Proposing new legislation
3. Issuing new administrative regulations

The agencies also try to help the complaining consumers, either in an ombudsman role or by threat of legal action.

Testing Organizations.   These offer to the consumer a form of independent product knowledge, through either of the following:

1. A combination of product standard plus test of conformance and a label or seal attesting to conformance
2. A test of fitness for use plus a judgment of value

See Consumer Test Services, above, for details of these approaches.

Perceptions of the Consumer Movement.   There is wide agreement, including among business managers, that "the consumer movement has kept industry and business on their toes." There is also wide agreement that the consumer movement's demands have "resulted in higher prices." Despite this, most of the public feels that the "changes are generally worth the extra cost." Consumers feel strongly that the consumer advocates should consider the costs of their proposals. However, a significant minority of the consumers believe that the advocates do not consider the costs involved (Sentry, 1976, pp. 39, 40, 42, 47).

GOVERNMENT REGULATION OF QUALITY

From time immemorial, "governments" have established and enforced standards of quality. Some of these governments have been political—national, provincial, local. Others have been nonpolitical: Professional Societies, Industry Associations, Standardization Organizations, Independent Laboratories, etc. Whether through delegation of political power or through long custom, these governing bodies have attained a status which enables them to carry out programs of regulation as discussed below.

Bases for Regulation.   Regulation of quality has evolved to serve a wide variety of purposes:

Metrology.   All organized human activity, and especially technological activity, involves standardized units of measure for time, mass, and other fundamental constants. So basic are these standards that they are now international in scope.

Interchangeability.   A second level of standards has brought order out of chaos in such day-to-day matters as household voltages and interchangeability of myriads of the bits and pieces of an industrial society. Compliance is an economic necessity.

Technological Definition.   A third array of standards has been prepared to define numerous materials, processes, products, tests, etc. These standards are developed by committees drawn from the various interested segments of society. While compliance is usually voluntary, the economic imperatives result in a high degree of acceptance and use of these standards.

Beyond the foregoing bases, which are all related to standardization, and encounter little resistance to compliance, there are other bases which involve enforcement as well as standardization.

Safety and Health of the Citizenry.   The main emphasis of political government regulation has been at this level. There are laws which prescribe and enforce safety standards for building construction, oceangoing ships, mines, aircraft, bridges, and many other structures and habitations. Other laws are aimed at hazards which have their origins in fire, food, drugs, dangerous chemicals, etc. Still other laws regulate who may perform certain activities essential to public safety and health, e.g., licensing of professional engineers, physicians, airline pilots. Most recently these laws have proliferated extensively into the areas of: consumer product safety, environmental protection, occupational safety and health. (Some of the standards for safety are established and enforced by nonpolitical government.)

Safety and Health of the State.   In addition to protecting their military safety, governments have developed standards and regulation to protect their economic health. Integrity of the coinage is one example. (Political governments have a monopoly on the right to debase the currency.) Laws regulating the quality of exports are of ancient origin and are for the purpose of protecting a nation's reputation for quality from the carelessness or greed of individual manufacturers. In those cases where the government is a purchaser (defense weapons, public utility facilities), the basis of government regulation includes the normal rights of a purchaser to ascertain fitness for use.

Economics of the Citizenry. This category of government regulation is highly controversial in the market-based societies. Some of the resistance is on ideological grounds—the competitive marketplace is asserted to be a far better regulator than a government bureau. Other resistance is based on the known deficiencies of the administration of government regulation (see below). Some of the growth of this category of regulation has been stimulated by the consumerism movement.

Volume of Legislation. The volume of all this legislation has grown to formidable proportions. A desk reference book (Kolb and Ross, 1980) includes lists (in fine print) of appendices as follows:

21 pages of exposure limits for toxic substances

93 pages of hazardous materials and the associated criteria for transportation

24 pages of American National Standards for safety and health

36 pages of Federal record-retention requirements

38 pages of standards-setting organizations

Much of this legislation is within the scope of the Federal Trade Commission, which exercises a degree of oversight relative to "unfair or deceptive practices in commerce." That scope has led to specific legislation or administrative action relative to: product warranties, packaging and labeling, truth in lending, etc.

In a sense these actions all relate to "advertising," i.e., representations made by sellers to consumers. In its oversight the Federal Trade Commission stresses two major requirements:

1. The advertising, labeling, and other product information must be clear and unequivocal as to what is meant by the seller's representation.
2. The product must comply with the representation.

These forms of government regulation are a sharp break from the centuries-old rule of *caveat emptor* (let the buyer beware). That rule was (and is) quite sensible as applied to conditions in the village market places of developing countries. However it is not appropriate to the conditions prevailing in industrialized, developed countries. For elaboration, see Juran (1970).

The Plan of Regulation. Once it has been determined that there shall be regulation in some new matter involving quality, the approach follows a well-beaten path. The sequence of events listed below, while described in the language of regulation by political government, applies to nonpolitical government as well.

The Statute. An enabling act defines the purpose of the regulation and especially the products to be regulated. It establishes the "rules of the game" and creates an agency to administer the act.

The Administrator. The Administrator is given powers to establish standards and to see that they are enforced. To this end he or she is armed with the means for making awards and applying sanctions on matters of great importance to the regulated industries.

The Standards. The Administrator has the power to set standards and may exercise this power by adopting existing industry standards. These standards are not limited to products; they may deal with materials, processes, tests, descriptive literature, advertising, qualifications of personnel, etc.

Test Laboratories. The Administrator has the power to establish criteria to be used for judging the qualifications of "independent" test laboratories. Once these criteria are established, he or she also may have the power to issue certificates of qualification to laboratories which meet the criteria. In some cases Administrators have the power to establish their own test laboratories.

Test and Evaluation. Here there is great variation. For some undertakings, prior test and evaluation are a prerequisite to the right to market, e.g., new drug applications or plans for the operation and maintenance of a new fleet of airplanes. Some agencies put much stress on surveillance, i.e., review of the manufacturer's control plan and adherence to that plan. Other agencies emphasize final product sampling and test.

The Seal or Mark. Regulated products are frequently required to display a seal or mark to attest to the fact of compliance with the regulations. Where the regulating agency does the actual testing, it affixes the mark; e.g., government meat inspectors physically stamp the carcasses.

More usually, the agency does not test and stamp the product. Instead, it determines, by test, that the product design is adequate. It also determines, by surveillance, that the manufacturer's system of control is adequate. Having made these determinations, it authorizes the manufacturer to affix the seal or mark. The statutes always provide for penalties for unauthorized use of the mark.

Sanctions. The regulatory agency has wide powers of enforcement, such as the right to:

Investigate product failures and user complaints

Inspect the manufacturer's processes and system of controls

Test products in all stages of distribution

Recall products already sold to users

Revoke the manufacturer's right to sell, or to apply the mark

Inform users of deficiencies

Issue cease-and-desist orders

Effectiveness of Regulation. Regulators face the difficult problem of balance—protecting consumer interests while avoiding creation of burdens which in the end are damaging to consumer interests. In part the difficulty is inherent because of the conflicting interests of the parties. However, much of the difficulty is traceable to deficiencies in the regulatory agencies' policies and practices in carrying out the regulatory process. These deficiencies relate mainly to the conceptual approach; setting standards, the enforcement process, and cost of regulation.

The Conceptual Approach. An example is seen in the policies employed by the National Highway Traffic Safety Administration (NHTSA) for administering two laws enacted in 1966:

1. The National Traffic and Motor Vehicle Safety Act, directed primarily at the vehicle

2. The Highway Safety Act, directed primarily at the motorist and the driving environment

Even prior to 1966, the automobile makers, road builders, etc., had improved technology to an extent which provided the motorist with the means of avoiding the "first crash," i.e., accidents due to collisions, running off the road, etc. The mandated provision of seat belts then provided the motorist with greatly improved means of protection against the "second crash." This crash takes place when the deceleration due to a collision hurls the occupants against the steering wheel, windshield, etc.

The U.S. traffic fatality rate was in fact the lowest among all industrialized countries.

At the time of the creation of NHTSA it was known, from overwhelming arrays of data, that the motorist was the limiting factor in traffic safety:

Alcohol was involved in about half of all fatal accidents.

Young drivers (under age 24) constituted 22 percent of the driver population but were involved in 39 percent of the accidents.

Excessive speed and other forms of "improper" driving were reported as factors in about 75 percent of the accidents. (During the oil crisis in 1974 the mandated reduction of highway speeds resulted in a 15 percent reduction in traffic fatalities, without any change in vehicles.)

Most motorists did not buy safety belts when they were optional, and most did not wear them when they were provided as standard equipment.

In the face of this overwhelming evidence NHTSA paid little attention to the main problem—improving the performance of the motorists. Instead, NHTSA concentrated on setting numerous standards for vehicle design. These standards did provide some gains in safety with respect to the second crash. However the gains were minor, while the added costs ran to billions of dollars—to be paid for by consumers in the form of higher prices for vehicles.

The policy can be seen to have been one of dealing strictly with a highly visible political target—the automobile maker—while avoiding any confrontation with a large body of voters. It was safe politically but it did little for safety.

For elaboration, see Juran (1977).

Setting Standards. An example of a major problem faced by regulators is whether to establish design standards or performance standards. These alternatives were examined by a Presidential task force assigned to review the safety regulations of the Occupational Safety and Health Administration.

Design standards admit of precise definition, but they have serious disadvantages. Their nature and numbers are such that they often lack flexibility, are difficult to understand, become very numerous, and become prohibitive to keep up to date.

Performance standards are generally free from the above disadvantages. However, they place on the employer the added burden of determining how to meet the performance standard, i.e., the burden of creating or acquiring a design. Performance standards also demand the use of compliance officers who have the levels of education, experience, and training needed to make the subjective judgments as to whether the standard has been met.

The recommendation of the task force was to go to a "performance/hazard" concept. Under that concept, the standard "would codify into a requirement the fact that a safe workplace can be achieved only by ensuring that employees are not exposed to the hazards associated with the use of machines. Under this standard, the employer would be free to determine the most appropriate manner in which to guard against any hazard which is presented, but his compliance with the requirement is objectively measurable by determining whether or not an employee is exposed to the hazard.

For elaboration, see the complete *OSHA Safety Regulation* report, 1977.

The Enforcement Process. A major deficiency in the regulatory process is the failure to concentrate on the vital few problems. Regulatory agencies receive a barrage of alerts: consumer complaints, reports of injuries, accusations directed at specific products, etc. Collectively the numbers are overwhelming. There is no possibility of dealing thoroughly with each and every case. Agencies which have tried to do so have become hopelessly bogged down. The resulting paralysis then became a target for critics, with associated threats to the tenure of the Administrator, or even to the continued existence of the agency.

The Occupational Safety and Health Administration faced just such a threat in the mid-1970s. In response it undertook to establish a classification for its cases based on the seriousness of the threats to safety and health. It also recalled about 1000 safety regulations which were under attack for adding much to industry costs and little to worker safety.

With experience, the agencies tend to adopt the Pareto principle of vital few and useful many. This enables them to concentrate their resources and to produce visible results.

Choice of the vital few is sometimes based on quantitative data: frequency of injuries, frequency of consumer complaints. However, subjective judgment plays an important role, and this enables influential special pleaders to secure high priority for their cases.

How to deal with the "useful many" needs for assistance has been a perplexing problem for all agencies. The most practical solution seems to have been to make clear that the agency is in no position to resolve such problems. Instead it provides consumers with information and educational material of a self-help nature: where to apply for assistance; how to apply for assistance; what the rights of the consumer are; what to do and not to do. See, for example, *Consumer's Source Handbook,* 1980.

The failure of regulators to deal forthrightly with such consumer problems has no doubt contributed to the mediocre status given to regulators by the public, in response to the question, "Which [of four options] would you like to be primarily responsible for the job of seeing that consumers get a fair deal?"

For elaboration, see Sentry, 1976, p. 70.

A Rule for Choosing the Vital Few. In 1972 the author proposed the following as a quantitative basis for separating the vital few from the rest, on matters of safety:

Any hour of human life should be as safe as any other hour.

To effectuate such a policy it is first necessary to quantify safety nationally, on some common basis such as injuries per million worker hours of exposure. In general, the data for such quantification are already available, though some conversions are needed to arrive at a common unit of measure. For example, statistics on safety at school are computed based on injuries per 100,000 student-days; motor vehicle statistics are on a per 100 million miles of travel basis; etc.

The resulting national average will contain relatively few situations which are well above the average and a great many which are below. Those above the average are automatically nominated to membership in the vital few. Those below the average are not so nominated; the burden of proof is on any special pleader to show why something below the national average should take priority ahead of the obvious vital few.

For elaboration, see Juran (1972).

The Costs and Values of Regulation.　　The costs consist largely of two major components:

1. The costs of running the regulatory agencies. These are known with precision, and have risen to many billions of dollars per year. The costs are paid for by consumers, in the form of taxes which are then used to fund the regulatory agencies.

2. The costs of complying with the regulations. These costs are not known with precision, but they are reliably estimated to be many times the costs of running the regulatory agencies. These costs are in the first instance paid for by the industrial companies, and ultimately by consumers in the form of higher prices.

For an example of a study of industry costs, see The Business Roundtable, 1978.

The value of all this regulation is difficult to estimate. Safety, health, and a clean environment are widely believed to be enormously valuable. Providing consumers with honest information and prompt redress is likewise regarded as enormously valuable. However such general agreements provide no guidelines for what to do in specific instances. Ideally, each instance should be examined as to its cost-value relationship. Yet the statutes have not required the regulators to do so. The regulators have generally avoided facing up to the question of the costs.

The support for studying the cost-value relationships has come mainly from the industrial companies. For example, a study of mandated vehicle safety systems (Crain, 1980) found that:

" . . . states which employ mandatory periodic inspection programs do not have lower accident rates than those states without such requirements." (p. 36)

" . . . only a relatively small portion of highway accidents—some 2 to 6 percent—are conclusively attributable to mechanical defects." (p. 37)

" . . . human factors (such as excess speeds) are far more important causes of highway accidents than vehicle condition." (p. 38)

For elaboration see the Crain article.

The indifference of regulators to costs inevitably creates regulations and a rigidity of enforcement so absurd that in due course they become the means for securing a change in policy. The companies call such absurdities to the attention of the media, who relish publicizing them. (The media have little interest in scholarly studies.) The resulting publicity then puts the regulators on the defensive while stimulating the legislators to hold hearings. During such hearings (and depending on the political climate) the way is open to securing a better cost-value balance. Such a scenario has been followed in a number of regulatory situations.

The political climate is an important variable in securing attention to cost-versus-value considerations. During the 1960s and 1970s the U.S. political climate was generally favorable to regulatory legislation. Then during the 1980s the climate changed, and with it a trend toward requiring cost justifications.

PRODUCT SAFETY AND PRODUCT LIABILITY

Until the early twentieth century it was comparatively rare for users to file lawsuits based on injuries resulting from use of manufactured products. Since then, the growth in the number of these lawsuits in the United States has been remarkable. By the mid-1960s they were estimated to have reached over 60,000 annually and by the 1970s to over 100,000 per year (most are settled out of court). This growth in number of lawsuits has been accompanied by an equally remarkable growth in the size of individual claims and verdicts. From figures measured in thousands of dollars, individual verdicts have grown to a point where awards in excess of $100,000 are frequent. Awards in excess of $1,000,000 are no longer a rarity.

Several factors have combined to bring about these conditions:

1. "Population explosion" of products. The industrial society has placed large numbers of manufactured products in the hands of amateurs. Some of these products are inherently dangerous. Others are misused. While the injury rate (injuries per million hours of usage) has probably been declining sharply, the total number of injuries has been rising, thereby also creating a rise in total number of lawsuits.

2. Erosion of manufacturers' defenses. As these lawsuits came to trial, the courts proceeded to erode the former legal defenses available to manufacturers. Formerly, a plaintiff's right to sue a manufacturer rested on one of two main grounds:

   a. A contract for sale of product, with an actual or implied warranty of freedom from hazards. Being based on the contract relationship, the plaintiff had to establish "privity," i.e., that he or she was a party to the contract. The courts have in effect abolished the need for privity by taking the position that there is an implied representation that the product is safe and that this implication follows the product around, irrespective of who the user is.

   b. Negligence by the manufacturer. In such cases the burden of proof was on the plaintiff to show that the manufacturer was negligent. The courts have tended to adopt the principle of "strict liability" on the ground that the costs of injuries resulting from defective products should be borne "by the manufacturers that put such products on the market rather than by the injured persons who are powerless to protect themselves." (Sometimes the injured persons are not powerless; they may contribute to their own injuries. However, juries are notoriously sympathetic to injured plaintiffs.)

Manufacturers' disclaimers (published announcements of nonliability) have, with respect to product safety, generally been held to be contrary to public policy.

Defensive Action.   The basic defense against liability is to eliminate the causes of injuries at their source. Analysis soon shows that all company levels and functions are able to contribute to making products safer and to improving the company's defenses in the event of lawsuits. The respective contributions are about as follows:

Top Management. Promulgate a policy on product safety and product recalls; structure an organized approach through product safety committees and formal programs; demand dating of the product and good traceability; set up an audit of the entire program; support industry programs which go beyond the capacity of the unaided company.

To this list should be added a scoreboard, i.e., a measure of the injury rate of the company's products relative to some reference level. A useful unit of measure is the number of injuries per million worker-hours of usage, since some major data banks on injuries are already expressed in this form or are convertible to this form.

Design. Adopt product safety as a design parameter; adopt a fail-safe philosophy of design; organize formal design reviews; follow the established codes; secure listings from the established laboratories; publish the ratings; utilize modern tools of design technique.

Manufacture. Establish a sound quality control program to include systems and procedures for foolproofing matters of product safety; train supervisors and operators in use of the product as part of the motivation plan; open up suggestion plans to ideas on product safety; set up the documentation needed to provide traceability and historical evidence.

Marketing. Provide product labeling for warnings, dangers, antidotes; train the field force in contract provisions; supply safety information to distributors and dealers; set up exhibits on safety procedures; conduct tests after installation, and train users in safety; publish the list of do's and don'ts which contribute to safety; maintain a climate of customer relations which minimizes animosity and claims.

Contracts should be drawn to avoid unrealistic commitments and unrealistic guarantees. Judicious disclaimers should be included, again to discourage unjustified claims.

Advertising. Set up secure technological and legal review of copy; propagandize product safety through education and warnings. The practice of "puffing" can backfire in liability suits, e.g., if a product is advertised as "absolutely safe." During advertising review, one of the questions should be, "How would this phrase sound in court?"

Customer Service. Observe use of the product; discover hazards inherent in this use; feed the information back to all concerned, including users, who should be warned and trained.

Consumers exhibit a wide range of intelligence, including the lowest. In consequence, actual use of the product can differ significantly from the intended use. For example, some stepladders include a light platform which is intended to hold tools or materials (e.g., paint) but is not intended to carry the weight of the user. However, some users nevertheless do stand on these platforms with resulting injury to themselves. The philosophy of the consumerists and regulators is clearly that products should be designed to stand up under actual usage and not merely intended usage.

There are also additional activities, which involve joint responsibilities resulting from multiple functions.

Documentation.   The growth of safety legislation and product liability has enormously increased the need for documentation. A great deal of this documentation is mandated by legislation, along with retention periods. (For a compilation, see Kolb and Ross, 1980, pp. 547–584.)

Defense against Lawsuits.   The necessary preparation includes reconstruction of the events which led up to the injury. This involves: study of the relevant documents—specifications, manuals, procedures, correspondence, reports; analysis of internal performance records for products and processes; analysis of field performance information; physical examination of the pertinent facilities; study of the failed hardware. All this should be done promptly, by qualified experts, and with early notification to the insurance company. For elaboration, see Gray et al. (1975), pages 67–93; also Kolb (1980), pages 275–286.

Whether and how to go to trial involves a great deal of special knowledge and experience. See generally, Gray et al. (1975); see also Kolb (1980), pp. 275–286.

Insurance.   This defense is widely used, but the costs have escalated severely, again because of the growing number of lawsuits and size of awards. In some fields the insurance rates have become major factors in the cost of operations. For elaboration, see *Interagency Task Force on Product Liability; Final Report* (1978), chapter III. See also Kolb (1980), pp. 287–327.

Prognosis.   As of the late 1980s there remained some formidable unsolved problems in the area of liability. To many observers the legal system for resolving the issues contained some serious deficiencies:

Lay juries lack the technological literacy needed to determine liability in a technological society.

Lay juries are too easily swayed emotionally to determine the size of awards.

The "punitive damages" concept along with "pain and suffering" contribute to inflated awards.

Lawyers are permitted to work on a contingency fee basis, which assertedly stimulates lawsuits.

The adversary system of conducting trials places the emphasis on winning rather than on doing justice.

Only a minority of the award money goes to the injured parties. The majority goes to pay lawyers and administrative expenses.

The legal system which endures these deficiencies is deeply rooted in U.S. culture. It is therefore speculative whether the system will undergo dramatic change. The major obstacle appears to be the lawyers. They have strong vested interests in the present system, both financial and cultural. In addition, they are very influential in the legislative process—many legislators are members of the legal profession.

The European legal system for dealing with liability is quite different, and is generally free from the above asserted deficiencies.

Personal Liability.   The overwhelming majority of product liability lawsuits have been aimed at industrial companies; they and their insurers have the greatest capacity to pay. As a corollary, such civil lawsuits are rarely aimed at individuals, e.g., design managers or quality managers. These individuals have little cause for concern with respect to civil liability. They are not immune from lawsuits but they are essentially immune from payment of damages.

Criminal liability is something else. Now the offense (if any) is against the state, and the state is the plaintiff. Until the 1960s, prosecution for criminal liability in product injury cases was directed almost exclusively at the corporations rather than the managers. During the 1960s and the 1970s the public prosecutors became more aggressive with respect to the persons involved. The specific targets were usually the heads of the companies but sometimes included selected subordinate managers such as those in charge of product development or quality.

A contributing factor has been an earlier provision of the Food, Drug, and Cosmetic Act making it a crime to ship adulterated or misbranded drugs. This provision was interpreted by the Supreme Court to be applicable to the head of a company despite the fact that he or she had not participated in the events and even had no knowledge of the goings-on. For an analysis, see O'Keefe and Shapiro (1975). Also see O'Keefe and Isley (1976).

For the great majority of industrial managers the threat of criminal liability is remote. Before there can be such liability, the manager must be found guilty of (1) having *knowingly* carried out illegal actions or (2) having been grossly negligent in his or her duties. These things must be proved to a jury beyond a reasonable doubt. It is a difficult proof. (Many real criminals escape conviction because of this difficulty.)

REFERENCES

ASQC (1980). *Consumer Attitudes on Quality in the United States, 1980.* American Society for Quality Control, 310 West Wisconsin Ave., Milwaukee, WI 53203.

Best, Arthur (1981). *When Consumers Complain.* Columbia University Press, New York.

The Business Roundtable (1978). *Cost of Government Regulation Study for the Business Roundtable.* This is a study of the direct incremental costs incurred by 48 companies in complying with the regulations of six federal agencies during 1977. Available from The Business Roundtable, 200 Park Ave., New York, NY 10166.

Consumer's Resource Handbook (1980). A publication of the U.S. Office of Consumer Affairs. Includes: a "complaint handling primer"; where to go for assistance; functions, services, and information available from federal offices; directories of federal, state, and local offices. Available from Consumer Information Center, Dept. 532G, Pueblo, CO 81009.

Crain, W. Mark (1980). *Vehicle Safety Inspection Systems. How Effective?* American Enterprise Institute for Public Policy Research, Washington, DC.

Gray, I., Bases, A. L., Martin, C. H., and Sternberg, A. (1975). *Product Liability: A Management Response.* American Management Association, New York. (Emphasis is on defense against product liability suits.)

Interagency Task Force on Product Liability; Final Report. (Undated; about 1978). Distributed by National Technical Information Service, Springfield, VA 22161. (A comprehensive study on product liability, including the impact, the legal implications, the insurance problems, and especially, the merits of various proposals for remedy.)

Juran, J. M. (1970). "Consumerism and Product Quality." *Quality Progress,* July, pp. 18–27.

Juran, J. M. (1972). "Product Safety." *Quality Progress,* July, pp. 30–32.

Juran, J. M. (1977). "Auto Safety, A Decade Later." *Quality,* October, pp. 26–32; November, pp. 54–60; December, pp. 18–21. Originally presented at the 1976 European Organization for Quality Conference (Copenhagen).

Kolb, John and Ross, Steven S. (1980). *Product Safety and Liability—A Desk Reference.* McGraw Hill, New York. (A comprehensive reference treatise: attaining safety throughout the product life cycle; defenses against lawsuits; insurance; reference tables.)

"Laetrile, the Political Success of a Scientific Failure." (1977). *Consumer Reports,* August, pp. 444–447.

National Business Council for Consumer Affairs (1973). *Safety in the Market Place.* Available from Superintendent of Documents, Washington, DC, Stock No. 5274-00009. Makes 14 recommendations, along with details for implementation.

O'Keefe, Daniel F., Jr. and Shapiro, M. H. (1975). "Personal Criminal Liability under the Federal Food, Drug and Cosmetic Act—The Dotterweich Doctrine." *Food-Drug-Cosmetic Law Journal,* vol. 30, no. 5, January.

O'Keefe, Daniel F., Jr. and Isley, C. Willard (1976). "Dotterweich Revisited—Criminal Liability Under the Federal Food, Drug, and Cosmetic Act." *Food-Drug-Cosmetic Law Journal,* vol. 31, no. 2, February.

OSHA Safety Regulation (1977). American Enterprise Institute for Public Policy Research, Washington, DC. This is the report of a Presidential task force assigned to review the safety regulatory practices of the Occupational Safety and Health Administration.

Peterson, Esther (1974). "Consumerism as a Retailer's Asset." *Harvard Business Review,* May–June, pp. 91–101.

Sentry Insurance (1976). *Consumerism at the Crossroads.* Sentry Insurance Co., Stevens Points, WI. Results of a national opinion research survey on the subject.

Travelers Insurance Co. (1972). *The Act and Its Principal Features.* The Travelers Insurance Companies. An explanation of the Consumer Product Safety Act.

Travelers Insurance Co. (1973). *A Management Guide to Protect Quality & Safety.* The Travelers Insurance Companies. Sets out contributions and responsibilities of various company functions, relative to product safety.

SECTION 35A

QUALITY AND THE NATIONAL CULTURE

J. M. Juran

INTRODUCTION 35A.1

QUALITY IN CAPITALISTIC
ECONOMIES 35A.2

   Competition in Quality . . .35A.2

   Direct Access to
     Marketplace Feedback . . 35A.3

CULTURAL DIFFERENCES . . .35A.3

MULTINATIONAL
COLLABORATION 35A.4

REFERENCES 35A.5

INTRODUCTION

The goal of high quality is common to all countries. This common goal must compete with other national goals amid the massive national forces—political, economic, and social—which determine the national priorities. This section examines these national forces and their effects on the problems of attaining quality.

The growth of international trade and of multinational companies has required that attention be directed to understanding the impact of national culture on managing for quality. To aid in this understanding, the subject is organized under the following general subdivisions:

Developing economies: The special problems of managing for quality in such economies are discussed in Section 35B.

Capitalistic developed economies: Several of the sections discuss the problems of managing for quality in specific economies:

   Section 35C: Quality in France

   Section 35D: Quality in the Federal Republic of Germany

   Section 35E: Quality in Great Britain

   Section 35F: Quality in Japan

   Section 35G: Quality in the United States

Socialist economies: Managing for quality is discussed in Section 35H.

In all types of national economy there are natural resources and limitations which influence the priority of goals. However, an even greater force is that of human leadership and determination. Historically, these human forces have been more significant than natural resources in determining whether goals are attained.

The words "capitalistic," "socialistic," and "developing" are simple labels for some very complex concepts. The broad definition of "capitalism" is private ownership of the means of production and distribution, as contrasted with state ownership under socialism. Yet all self-styled capitalistic countries include a degree of state ownership, e.g., in matters of health, education, transport, and communication. Similarly, the self-styled socialistic countries contain, in varying degrees, some private ownership of enterprises for production of goods and services. In like manner, countries which are "developing" in the industrial sense may be highly developed in terms of other aspects of national maturity, e.g., political or social. The reader is urged to keep in mind that the words "capitalistic," "socialistic," and "developing" are used in a relative sense and cannot be considered as absolutes.

The subject matter of this section and of the companion Sections 35B through 35H are of obvious interest and importance to those engaged (or contemplating engagement) in operations of an international nature. Such operations are becoming ever more extensive as trade barriers are progressively removed. However, removal of governmental barriers has little effect on cultural barriers. These remain as a continuing problem until the cultural patterns (and the reasons behind them) are understood, appreciated, and taken into account.

In the economic sense, the capitalistic developed countries are the "vital few." The developing countries are the most numerous, occupy most of the land surface, and include most of the human population. However, it is the capitalistic developed countries which produce the bulk of the world's goods and services. This great importance (in the economic sense) suggests that those who engage in international trade should acquire a working knowledge of the forces which operate in these countries.

QUALITY IN CAPITALISTIC ECONOMIES

All capitalistic economies exhibit some basic similarities which influence the importance of quality in relation to other goals in the economy.

Competition in Quality. Capitalistic societies permit and even encourage competition among enterprises. One form of this competition is in quality. This competition in quality takes several different forms:

Creation of New Enterprises. A frequent reason for the birth of new enterprises is poor quality of goods or services. For example, a neighborhood has outgrown the capacity of the local food shop or restaurant; so the clients must wait in long queues before they can receive service. In such cases, entrepreneurs will sense a market opportunity and will create a new enterprise which attracts clients by offering superior service.

The ease of creating new enterprises is a far greater force in quality improvement than is generally realized. All economies, whether capitalistic or socialistic, suffer poor quality during shortages of goods. Creation of new enterprises is one means of alleviating shortages, and thereby of eliminating an invariable cause of poor quality.

Product Improvement. A very common form of competition in quality is through improving products so that they have more appeal to the users and can therefore be sold successfully in the face of competition from existing products. These product improvements come mainly from internal product development carried on by existing companies. In addition, some product improvements are made by independents who either launch new enterprises or sell their ideas to existing companies.

New Products. These may be "products" or even new systems approaches, e.g., designs which minimize user maintenance. The industrial giants of today include many members founded on new systems concepts. As with product improvements, the new products may originate through development from within or through acquisition from without.

Competition in quality results in duplication of products and facilities. Such duplication is regarded as wasteful by some economists. However, the general effect has been to stimulate producers to outdo each other, with resulting benefit to users.

Direct Access to Marketplace Feedback.

In the capitalistic economies, the income of the enterprise is determined by its ability to sell its products, whether directly to users or through an intermediate merchant chain. If poor quality results in excessive returns, claims, or inability to sell the product, the manufacturers are provided with the warning signals which are a prerequisite to remedial action.

This severe and direct impact of poor quality on the manufacturers' income has the useful byproduct of forcing manufacturers to keep improving their market research and systems of early warning signals, so as to be able to respond promptly in case of trouble.

Direct access to the marketplace is not merely a matter of receiving complaints and other information about bad quality, important though that is. Even more important is the access to the marketplace *before* products are launched and sales programs are prepared. In the capitalistic economies, the autonomous companies all make their own forecasts on how much they expect to sell. Their ability to thrive depends on how well they are able to realize their forecasts. The potential benefits and detriments force the companies to pay careful attention to the needs of the marketplace, which is the source of their income.

Protection of Society. The autonomy of the capitalist enterprises makes it possible for them to misrepresent their products, sell unsafe products, damage the environment, fail to live up to their product warranties, etc. The extent of such bad practice is small relative to the total economy. However, the total has been large enough to generate extensive preventive legislation. See generally, Section 34, Impact of Quality on Society.

CULTURAL DIFFERENCES

There are many of these. Even the vital few seem numerous. They include:

Language: This is basic—a serious barrier to communication. (Many countries harbor multiple languages and numerous dialects.)

Customs and traditions: These and related elements of the culture provide the precedents and premises which are decisive for setting priorities, judging what is "logical," etc.

Ownership of the companies: The pattern of ownership determines the strategy of short term versus long term, as well as the motivations of owners versus nonowners.

The methods used for managing operations: These are determined by numerous factors such as: reliance on system versus people; extent of professional training for managers; extent of separation of planning from execution; careers within a single company versus mobile careers.

Suspicions: In some countries the prior history of hostilities and subjugations generates suspicions which are handed down to subsequent generations.

These and still other elements of national cultures make clear the importance of learning about the nature of a culture before negotiating with members of that culture. To a considerable extent, companies expose their personnel to such training prior to assigning them to foreign countries. Similarly, when companies establish foreign subsidiaries, it is common practice to train local nationals to qualify for the senior posts.

MULTINATIONAL COLLABORATION

Collaboration across cultures is a many-faceted problem. For example, a system may be designed in country A but the subsystem designs may come from other countries. In like manner, companies from multiple countries may supply components, carry out manufacture, marketing, installation, maintenance, etc.

Numerous methodologies have been evolved to help coordinate such multinational activities. Those widely used include:

Standardization: This is achieved through organizations such as the International Organization for Standardization (ISO) and the International Electrotechnical Commission (IEC). A special application is the Allied Quality Assurance Publication (AQAP) standards widely used by the North Atlantic Treaty Organization countries for multinational contracting. Some of the standards available from these and other organizations are listed in Appendix III, Selected Quality Standards, Specifications, and Related Documents.

The consortium: This form involves creating an association of companies from various countries. The consortium is usually dedicated to a specific project, e.g., the Airbus. See Debout (1978) for elaboration.

Contract management: In many cases the prime contractor provides a coordinating service for the subcontractors (who may include a consortium). See McClure (1979) relative to the F16 aircraft; see also McClure (1976).

Technology transfer: This is carried out in numerous well-known ways: international professional societies and their committees; conferences; exchange visits; training courses and seminars. In large multinational companies such activities are carried out within the companies as well. For an example involving the use of multinational quality councils, see Groocock (1978).

REFERENCES

Debout, E. (1978). "European Aerospace Cooperation and Quality." *International Conference on Quality Control,* Tokyo, pp. A1–11 to A1–16.

Groocock, J. M. (1978). "Quality Councils—A Means for International Cooperation." *International Conference on Quality Control,* Tokyo, pp. A1–17 to A1–22.

McClure, J. Y. (1976). "Quality—A Common International Goal." *ASQC Technical Conference Transactions,* Milwaukee, pp. 459–466.

McClure, J. Y. (1979). "Procurement Quality Control within the International Environment." *ASQC Technical Conference Transactions,* Milwaukee, pp. 643–649.

SECTION 35B

QUALITY IN DEVELOPING COUNTRIES

Lennart Sandholm

A HETEROGENEOUS GROUP OF COUNTRIES **35B.2**

THE LIMA TARGET **35B.2**

TECHNOLOGY IN DEVELOPING COUNTRIES **35B.3**

Appropriate Technology . . 35B.4

FACTORS IMPEDING PRODUCT QUALITY IMPROVEMENT . . . **35B.4**

Shortage of Goods and Absence of Competition 35B.5

Foreign Exchange Constraints 35B.5

Incomplete Infrastructure . 35B.5

Inadequate Knowledge . . 35B.5

INDUSTRIAL DEVELOPMENT AND QUALITY **35B.5**

Phase I. Subsistence Economy 35B.5

Phase II. Export of Natural Materials 35B.5

Phase III. Export of Processed Materials . . . 35B.5

Phase IV. Integrated Manufacture for Domestic Use 35B.6

Phase V. Export of Manufactured Product . 35B.6

QUALITY ACTIVITIES **35B.6**

NATIONAL EFFORTS FOR QUALITY **35B.7**

STANDARDIZATION **35B.8**

CERTIFICATION **35B.10**

EXPORT INSPECTION **35B.14**

LEGISLATION **35B.16**

NATIONAL PROMOTION . . . **35B.16**

EDUCATION AND TRAINING . **35B.18**

National Level 35B.18

International Level . . . 35B.19

EXTERNAL ASSISTANCE . . . **35B.22**

INSTITUTIONAL INFRASTRUCTURE **35B.23**

NATIONAL QUALITY CONTROL SOCIETY **35B.24**

CONCLUSION **35B.25**

ACKNOWLEDGMENTS **35B.25**

REFERENCES **35B.25**

A HETEROGENEOUS GROUP OF COUNTRIES

Countries are often classified as "developing" or "developed." This terminology is not very good, as countries that are classified as "developing" could in many respects be more advanced than some so-called developed countries, for example, when such facets of human life as morale, culture, social relations, democratic rights, and equal opportunities are taken into consideration.

A clearer grouping would be into "industrialized" versus the "less industrialized" countries. This is, in fact, what is usually meant by the "developed" versus "developing" classification.

Neither developing nor developed countries can be treated as forming a homogeneous group; they show differences in terms of industrial development, natural resources, size, economic strength, access to markets, national policy, human resources, etc.

A comparison of the industrial structures of developing countries with each other can be made by comparing them individually with the typical structure of a developed market economy. A measure used for this purpose is the "coefficient of similarity" (*World Industry,* 1979, p. 72), which for developing countries ranges from 0.06 (almost no resemblance to the developed economy) to 0.95 (almost identical with the developed economy). This range clearly reflects the degree of heterogeneity among the developing countries.

By considering the ratios between the shares of various branches of industry in developing countries and the corresponding shares in developed countries, some indication of areas of relative specialization in the two groupings can be obtained (*World Industry,* 1979, p. 73). The branches in which the developing countries appear to have specialized are petroleum refining and basic consumer industries such as food, beverages, and tobacco. Branches in which the developing countries are relatively underrepresented are those (other than petroleum refining) mainly concerned with engineering activities, such as machinery, iron and steel, transport equipment, and professional and scientific equipment. There are differences between individual countries. For example, in the least developed countries the share of the food industry is about 50 percent. In semi-industrialized countries such as Algeria, Argentina, Brazil, India, Mexico, and the Republic of Korea, the share of the food industry is less than 20 percent.

There are several stages in industrial processing: raw material, processed raw material, semiprocessed product, first-stage (or raw) finished product, second-stage (or simple) finished product, and complex finished product. The developing countries have a relative specialization in the earlier processing stages. Export of raw materials is much more important among developing countries, while export of complex finished products stands out among developed countries (*World Industry,* 1979, p. 188).

THE LIMA TARGET

The Second General Conference of the United Nations Industrial Development Organization (UNIDO) was held in Lima, Peru, in 1975. At this conference, The Lima Declaration on Industrial Development and Cooperation was adopted. The declaration includes policy guidelines and recommendations for industrial development, as well as a target for industrial production in developing countries. To meet this target (often referred to as the "Lima target"), the share of developing countries "should be increased to the maximum possible extent and as far as possible to at least 25 percent of total world industrial production by the year 2000, while making every endeavor to ensure that the industrial growth so achieved is distributed among the developing countries as evenly as possible" (*Lima Declaration,* 1975).

The developing countries' share of world production was 8.6 percent by 1975 (the year in which the Lima target was set). A continuation of each country's growth at rates identical to those attained for 1960 to 1975 will give a share of only 13.9 percent by the year 2000 (*World Industry,* 1979, pp. 51–59). In 1982, the developing countries accounted for 11 percent of the world's manufacturing output and 66 percent of its population. It has been estimated by UNIDO that those countries may cxpcct to produce 14.9 percent of manufacturing output in the year 2000 while accounting for 72 percent of the world's population (*Industry in a Changing World,* 1983, p.1).

From these figures it is seen that the Lima target requires a fundamental change in world industrial production, which has implications for investment, consumption, the structure of world trade, etc.

Also, the uneven contribution of the individual countries should be considered: 10 countries account for 70 percent of the total manufacturing value added of all the developing countries (see Table 35B.1).

TABLE 35B.1   The Ten Developing Countries with the Largest Share in the Manufacturing Value Added of their Economic Grouping, 1980

Country	Share percentage
Brazil	22.66
Mexico	10.85
Argentina	9.86
India	8.27
Republic of Korea	4.46
Turkey	3.73
Iran	3.02
Venezuela	2.61
Philippines	2.51
Thailand	2.01
Total	69.98

Source: Industry in a Changing World (1983), p. 35.

TECHNOLOGY IN DEVELOPING COUNTRIES

In many developing countries the manufacturing sector may be divided into a modern component, a modernizing component and a nonmodern component, which utilize different technology.

Modern component: This component consists of the largest industrial enterprises, which are located mainly in urban areas where infrastructure and an adequate work force, including skilled workers, are available and which use comparatively modern technology.

Modernizing component: This component includes mainly small to medium-sized industrial enterprises, located mostly in urban areas but also in some rural areas, in which various intermediate levels of technology are used.

Nonmodern component: This consists of small industrial enterprises and artisan workshops, located largely in rural but also in urban areas, which use traditional and upgraded traditional technologies.

Appropriate Technology. Discussions of the technological basis for industrial development in developing countries are often focused on the choice of appropriate technologies and their development, transfer, and adoption.

The term "appropriate technology" for developing countries is often thought to mean simple and labor-intensive technology. The concept is based on the observations that industrial technologies are designed in the developed countries and that conditions in these countries are quite different from those in the developing countries. Technologies that are more suitable to conditions in developing countries are needed.

The concept of appropriate technology includes factors other than economic efficiency and growth, for example, employment, working conditions, and provision of basic needs. This means that appropriate technologies will differ from country to country depending on the different weights given to these various factors.

There are several factors inhibiting the use of appropriate technologies (Bos, 1977):

1. Incorrect factor and product prices, which tend to bias the choice of technology in favor of capital-intensive projects
2. Lack of or incomplete information about available technologies
3. Dependence on suppliers of equipment designed for use in industrialized countries
4. Policies of some foreign firms operating in developing countries
5. Choice of technology based on engineering preferences instead of on economic or developmental considerations
6. Preference for superficially attractive projects and for the latest technology because of the bias that the latest will be the best; prejudice, not based on proper and specific analysis, against small-scale, labor-intensive technologies or against the use of second-hand equipment; or investments based on hasty critical decisions
7. Neglect of basic development objectives
8. Policies of some donor governments, for example, through the tying of aid to political or other conditions

FACTORS IMPEDING PRODUCT QUALITY IMPROVEMENT

Developing countries face several problems with regard to product quality. The nature of these problems differs depending on the phase of development the country is in. Consequently, the solutions to the problems also differ.

Discussions that the author has had with many representatives of developing countries show that there are several factors impeding improvement of quality in developing countries, of which the four major seem to be shortage of goods, constraints on foreign exchange, incomplete infrastructure, and inadequate knowledge.

Shortage of Goods and Absence of Competition.   The shortage of goods provides some guarantee to the manufacturers that everything produced will be sold; they then show very little interest in quality. Restrictions on the importation of goods protect locally produced goods against competition from goods produced in more industrialized countries.

Foreign Exchange Constraints.   Most developing countries have a shortage of foreign exchange, and the industrial sector of the economy has to compete with other sectors for the inadequate amount available. This leads to obsolete technology, inadequate machinery, and poor material, all of which have a negative effect on quality.

Incomplete Infrastructure.   The infrastructure is not satisfactory; services in areas such as standardization, testing, training, and consulting are not adequate for the needs of the manufacturers.

Inadequate Knowledge.   The managerial as well as technical knowledge of personnel in industry is in general limited. The high illiteracy rate in many developing countries adds to the problem.

INDUSTRIAL DEVELOPMENT AND QUALITY

Industrial development usually follows some recognizable phases, from a primitive, agricultural subsistence economy to a sophisticated one producing manufactured goods for export. Five phases of development can be defined (Juran, 1975, pp. 4, 5), as described below.

Phase I. Subsistence Economy.   Economic activity consists mainly of the production of subsistence goods for local consumption (agriculture, fishing, etc.). Quality is low—there is a lack of quality standards, technology, test facilities, etc. Quality control takes place mainly by consumer inspection of products in the village marketplace.

Phase II. Export of Natural Materials.   In this phase the economy undertakes export of natural materials such as fruits, fibers, minerals. Selling these goods in the international market requires adherence to international quality standards, which are usually higher than domestic standards. Quality therefore has to be improved. The contracts for export normally include the quality specifications to be met, the tests to be used, and the sampling procedures to be followed, which requires test laboratories, instruments, and appropriate knowledge. In order to provide for the necessary services, a national standards institute evolves.

Phase III. Export of Processed Materials.   Local processing of materials is started, and the economy shifts to export of processed rather than raw materials, e.g., metals instead of ore, plywood instead of logs, canned instead of raw fruit. The economy must now include the acquisition, operation, and maintenance of technological processes. International quality standards for processed products have to be met, and process controls have to be introduced. Supplier relationships concerning quality have to be developed, since packaging materials, raw materials, etc. will be supplied from external sources within the country. The traditional work of the standards institute will be expanded. In addition, new needs will arise as tools from the modern quality control profession (statistical methodology, quality planning, supplier quality activities, organization for quality, etc.) are introduced. This requires training and consulting services.

Phase IV. Integrated Manufacture for Domestic Use. In this phase the economy undertakes integrated manufacture of modern industrial and consumer products for domestic use. The industries now have to control quality in all stages of industrial production, from determining the market need through product development, design, manufacture, and marketing. This requires not just training and consulting services but also professional development through research work, conferences and seminars, publications, quality control society activities, exchange of views with colleagues, etc.

Phase V. Export of Manufactured Product. Finally the manufactured products are sold in the international market, where they have to compete with products from other countries that have fully developed industrial economies.

QUALITY ACTIVITIES

The different phases of industrial development require various activities to attain and control quality. In a subsistence economy these consist primarily of inspection by consumers.

During the early stages of industrialization there is an increasing need for standardization activities, such as preparation of standards covering specifications, testing methods, sampling methods, etc. It is also necessary to develop applied and legal metrology, as well as a national testing capability. A certification scheme for selected products is sometimes introduced. All these tasks are usually given to the national standards institute.

As industrialization continues, there arise new needs, which cannot be met by traditional standardization activities on a national level. These new needs have to be met primarily by in-company quality activities, e.g., quality planning, design reviews, new-product testing, supplier surveys and controls, process capability analyses, inspection planning, quality audits, quality data feedback, quality cost analyses, quality improvement programs, quality policies and objectives, and organizational development. There must be knowledge about these activities and the appropriate tools (under the designation of quality management) in industry, which creates needs for education and training, development of quality specialists and managers, consulting assistance, etc. These needs are met by means that may include training courses, conferences and seminars, research committees, publications, and/or quality control societies.

Consequently, there is a wide range of quality activities the importance of which depends on the stage of industrial development. Basically the activities can be grouped as follows:

Inspection by consumers: Inspection of products in the marketplace

Standardization: National standards on terminology, sampling methods, testing methods, specifications, and codes of practice; applied and legal metrology, national testing facilities, certification, legislation

Quality management: Application of managerial tools to plan for quality, attain and control quality, follow up and improve quality, as well as to organize for quality and to develop a work force

Figure 35B.1 shows the growth of the total quality effort in the industrial development. Figure 35B.2 shows the importance of the activities on a relative basis. It is clear that the dominance is shifting from inspection by consumers to standardization and from standardization to quality management.

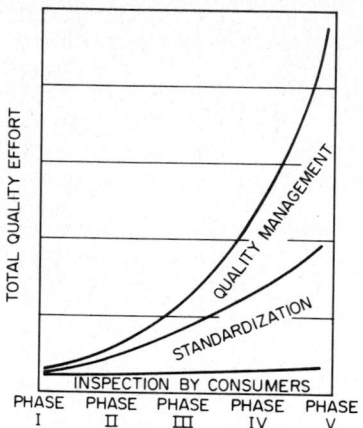

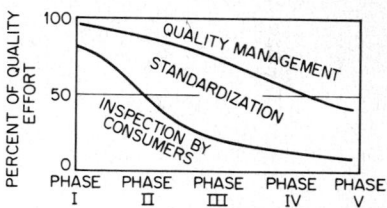

FIG. 35B.1 The growth of total quality effort in industrial development. *(Based on Juran, 1975, pp. 4–5.)*

FIG. 35B.2 The relative importance of the quality activities. *(Based on Juran, 1975, pp. 4–5.)*

NATIONAL EFFORTS FOR QUALITY

The problems related to product quality in developing countries are of such a nature that they cannot be solved on a company level. Instead, efforts on a national level are necessary, and these depend largely on the national policy of the country. In some countries, government is ahead in developing means for a good quality control program. National efforts include:

Standardization: Preparation of national standards covering terminology, sampling methods, testing methods, specifications, and codes of practice

Certification: To attest that products comply with standards

Export inspection: Ensuring quality of certain products for export through preshipment inspection

Legislation: Enforcement of standardization, certification, export inspection, etc. through acts of parliaments and legislatures

National promotion: National programs to promote a general awareness of quality

Education and training: Development of the necessary knowledge and skills, as well as exertion of influence on attitudes

External assistance:　Assistance from multinational organizations, bilateral aid programs, foreign manufacturers, etc., to cut short the development process

Institutional infrastructure:　Services by institutions in the areas of standardization, certification, testing, metrology, quality planning, and training

National quality control society:　To develop the competence of quality control professionals and practitioners

The steps to be taken on a national level are determined mainly by the governments of the respective developing countries. The way this is done depends on the policy of the government. In many developing countries there is a centrally planned economy, and in these we will often find a strong reliance on governmental institutions and legislation. In other countries only some basic needs (e.g., standardization, education) are satisfied by the government.

STANDARDIZATION

Standardization plays an important part in the industrial development of a country. This statement has to be viewed in a broad context, which means that it is not just a matter of preparing national standards covering terminology, sampling methods, testing methods, specifications, and codes of practice; the necessary infrastructure of applied and legal metrology must also be provided as well as the necessary testing facilities.

Standards from other countries and international standards are useful sources of information for developing countries in preparing their own standards. Of course, adaptation to the local situation is necessary—in dealing with indigenous products, it is also necessary to undertake some research.

Standards can be mandatory or voluntary. Mandatory standards are found in countries with a centrally controlled economy, while countries with a free enterprise economy normally have voluntary standards. Standards dealing with safety and health, however, are in most cases mandatory in any type of economy. Mandatory standards are used for some consumer products in order to ensure a minimum quality level. This is an important reason, because in most developing countries competition in the marketplace is lacking and goods are scarce.

Standardization activities on a national level are dealt with by a national standards institute. This body, carrying full government recognition (in many countries through legislation), is responsible for the development and publication of national standards, as well as for keeping them up to date. In preparing standards, the institute calls upon the knowledge and experience of manufacturers, users, government departments, universities, etc. This is normally done by setting up technical committees with this wide representation.

As an example of standards preparation, the procedure used in Thailand may be cited. The national body for standardization in this country is the Thai Industrial Standards Institute (TISI), which is a government department under the Ministry of Industry.

The procedure under which standards are selected, discussed, and ratified in Thailand is shown in Figure 35B.3. The following steps are involved (Stephens, 1979, pp. 14–17):

1. A request for a standard may be received from any authoritative source, such as an industry, commerce, academic, or consumer group.

2. The Standards Council agrees that the standard be placed on the work schedule and may even assign it a higher priority than others. Alternatively, it rejects the request for technical or other reasons.

3. If the proposal is accepted, a technical committee is formed at the invitation of the Minister of Industry, and a chairman is selected. The committee is chosen for competence and direct association with the subject matter of the standard.

4. The technical committee, served by a secretary—a technically competent officer from the TISI staff—holds a series of meetings to reach agreement on the standard specification. In this step the library of other national and international standards, maintained by TISI, is a valuable resource. Copies of relevant standards or sections thereof are prepared for discussion and included in the minutes.

5. A draft standard is finally agreed upon, and this is circulated widely outside the committee for comment.

6. At the conclusion of the comment period, the committee meets to discuss any suggested amendments. Some may be accepted and the draft revised accordingly; others may be rejected for various reasons.

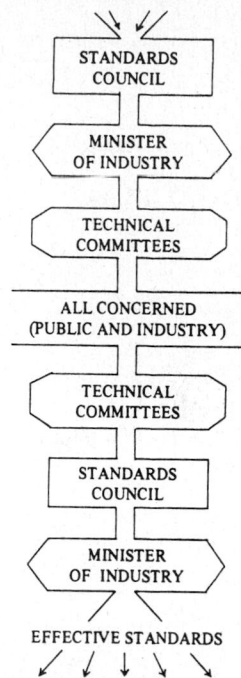

REQUEST FOR PRODUCTS TO
BE CONSIDERED FOR
SELECTION FOR STANDARDIZATION

FIG. **35B.3** Standardization procedure in Thailand. *(From Stephens, 1979, p. 15.)*

7. The final draft is then presented first to the Standards Council and, if approved, to the Minister of Industry for ratification.

8. Publication in the *Government Gazette* makes the standard official.

9. Publication in booklet form by TISI makes the standard available for distribution and use, including certification and license to use the TISI quality mark.

The procedure used by the Indian Standards Institution is shown in Figure 35B.4.

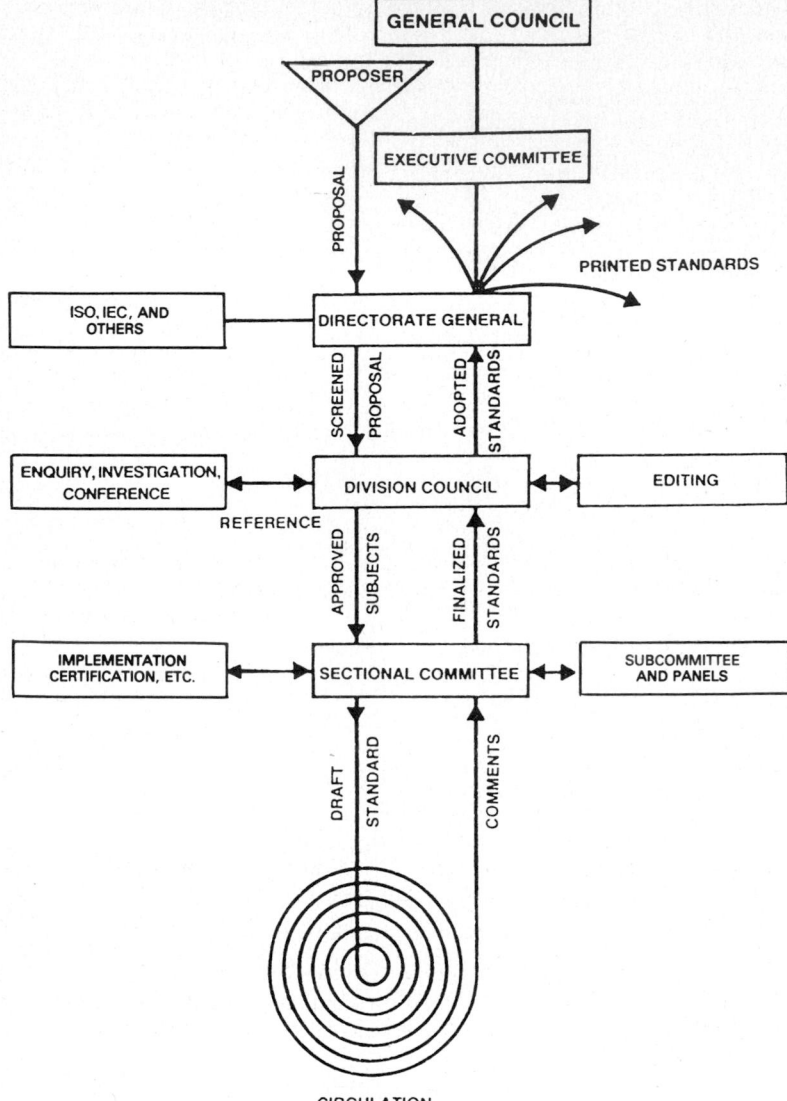

FIG. 35B.4 Standardization procedure in India. Amended and/or revised when and as needed. Reviewed every 5 years to keep pace with technological developments. *(Courtesy Indian Standards Institution.)*

CERTIFICATION

Standardization is very often combined with a certification program, which involves checking and certifying that products comply with the standards. Such products are given a certification mark. Licenses can even be given to manufacturers having certain quality control activities.

The purpose of a certification program is to give the buyer confidence that the product is of a certain quality or that it meets quality requirements. Such certification goes beyond the seller's assurances that the product conforms to the requirements and beyond the buyer's own verification—instead, systems operated by impartial bodies are used (third-party certification). The impartial certification body can be a governmental or nongovernmental organization; in developing countries the national standards institute normally assumes this responsibility.

In developing countries there are various reasons for having a third party certification program. One is to upgrade quality in the domestic market. Owing to shortages of goods and the absence of competition, which very often prevail in developing economies, product quality is likely to be poor, and a mandatory certification system can provide for a minimum quality level. A second reason is to promote exports. A certification system can be an important factor in enabling developing countries to secure access to foreign markets. A third reason is to prevent importation of products of inferior quality. Some developing countries have had the misfortune to be used as dumping grounds for unscrupulous foreign manufacturers.

A third-party certification can take various forms:

Type testing: A sample of the product is tested according to a test specification in order to verify conformance with certain specified quality requirements. The testing is done by the certification body or by a recognized testing institute or laboratory.

Audit testing: In order to provide for a subsequent assurance, the type testing can be followed by an audit testing of samples purchased in the marketplace or selected from the manufacturer's production before shipment.

Assessment: Specialists visit the manufacturer's factory in order to find out how the quality control activities are performed.

These forms can be combined into certification systems (see Table 35B.2).

Products that are under a certification program and have been found to comply with the standards are marked with a certification mark upon grant of a license issued by the certification body (in most cases the national standards institute). Some examples of certification marks are shown in Figure 36B.5.

Within the International Organization for Standardization (ISO) there is a specialized Certification Committee (CERTICO). According to the terms of reference, ISO/CERTICO has:

> To study means of securing greater mutual acceptance of the validity of national and regional certification marks, as ensuring conformity with standards specifying the functions and properties of products, particularly when safety, health, or environmental factors are involved; and the definition of the rules and procedures necessary for securing a widening matrix of such agreements, recognizing that the use of national certification systems and marks as a protective measure will thereby be reduced. (ISO/ITC, 1980, p. 95).

The International Organization for Standardization and the International Trade Center provide developing countries with advice and guidance in establishing and adapting certification programs (see ISO/ITC, 1980).

TABLE 35B.2 Certification Systems

Certification system	Description	Advantages	Disadvantages
System 1. Type Testing	Type testing is a method under which a sample of the product is tested according to a prescribed test method in order to verify the compliance of a model with a specification.	For each model or type of product only one set of tests is required. The manufacturer can claim that the product has been independently shown to comply with the specification. The costs are minimal.	Only the prototype, or sample of the actual model, is tested for compliance with the specification. There is no follow-up by the approval authority and therefore no knowledge of whether subsequent production of the same model complies with the specification. The model tested may be specially produced and no evidence is available that the manufacturer has the capability for continuing compliance. Factory quality control is not considered.
System 2. Type testing followed by subsequent surveillance through audit testing of samples purchased on the open market	This is a system based on type testing but with some follow-up action to check that subsequent production is in conformity. Open-market audit testing means random audit testing of the type-tested model from distributors' or retailers' stock.	Some check on continuing conformity is provided at small cost. Continuing supervision of the manufacturer's production standards by the approval authority is provided for. The information obtained also covers the influence of the distribution channel and the conditions under which the final purchaser receives the product.	The cost to the manufacturer is greater than for type testing. An inspection staff to cover the market outlets to the extent required to produce worthwhile results may not be easy to establish. Action by the approval authority if noncompliance is discovered is not preventive in character. Withdrawal of a type testing certificate based on a single check of a multiproduced item is impractical and illogical. Factory quality control is not considered.

System	Description	Advantages	Disadvantages
System 3. Type testing followed by subsequent surveillance through audit testing of factory samples	This is a system based on type testing but with some follow-up action to check that subsequent output conforms. Audit testing of factory samples involves a regular check of samples of type-tested models selected from the manufacturer's production before dispatch.	Some check on continuing conformity is provided at small cost. Continuing supervision of the manufacturer's production standards by the approval authority is provided for. The manufacturer's own test facilities can be assessed and test results checked. Factory sample testing may provide an opportunity for some preventive action on nonconformity.	The cost to the manufacturer is greater than for type testing alone. An inspection staff is required for the collection of samples in addition to the test work.
System 4. Type testing followed by subsequent surveillance through audit testing of samples from both the open market and the factory	This is a system based on type testing but with follow-up action to check that subsequent production conforms, since audit testing is done of both factory and open-market samples.	Depending on the number of samples tested, this system should combine the advantages of systems Nos. 2 and 3. Open-market sample testing is to a certain extent an audit of the testing done on the factory samples.	Open-market testing needs a larger or more widely distributed inspection staff to cover purchasing in a multitude of trade outlets, whereas factory samples can be collected with a smaller staff. The cost to the manufacturer is greater than for type testing alone. An inspection staff is required for the collection of both factory and open-market samples.
System 5. Type testing and assessment of factory quality control and its acceptance, followed by surveillance that takes into account the audit	This is a system based on type testing with assessment and approval of the manufacturer's quality control arrangements, followed by regular surveillance through	A reliable and thorough-going system is provided for verification that continuous production is in conformity.	This system is more complex and costly than the foregoing. Distance from an inspection staff employed for surveillance of quality control can be a disadvantage.

TABLE 35B.2 Certification Systems (*Continued*)

Certification system	Description	Advantages	Disadvantages
of factory quality control and the testing of samples from the factory and the open market	inspection of factory quality control and audit testing of samples from both the open market and the factory.		
System 6. Factory quality control assessment and its acceptance only	This is a system under which the manufacturer's capability to produce a product in accordance with the required specification, including manufacturing methods, quality control organization, and type and routine testing facilities is assessed and approved, with respect to a specific technology. This system can be applied particularly where the specification covers a type of manufacture, possibly a material, but the end product may take a variety of forms for which there are no particular specifications.	The capability of the manufacturer is approved or authorized and the manufacturer can use this approval in claiming general manufacturing competence for a specified range of end products. The approval authority exercises supervision over the manufacturer's quality control. The system is widely used by government organizations.	The end product cannot be certified by the certification body as complying with the specification.

Source: Based on ISO/ITC (1980).

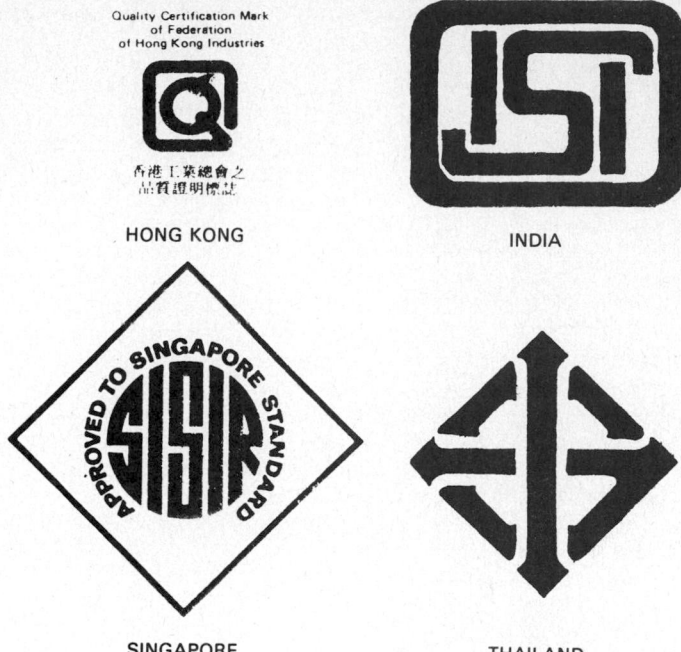

FIG. 35B.5 Quality marks used for certified products in several countries.

EXPORT INSPECTION

In assuring foreign buyers goods of an acceptable quality, plans for preshipment inspection of products for export can be used. Some countries have legislation dealing with export inspection; these include the People's Republic of China, India, Kenya, the Republic of Korea, Sudan, and Thailand. The legislation generally applies to specific commodities that are of key importance for the national economy (coconut, coffee, cocoa, fruit, jute, rice, rubber, timber, etc.).

An example of such legislation is the law on export inspection in India. This law vests the government with the power to:

1. Indicate commodities that shall be subject to inspection prior to export
2. Specify the type of inspection to be applied to an indicated commodity
3. Establish, adopt, or recognize one or more standard specifications for an indicated commodity
4. Prohibit the export in the course of international trade of an indicated commodity unless it either is accompanied by a certificate stating that the commodity satisfies the conditions relating to inspection or has affixed or applied to it a mark or seal recognized by the government as indicating that it conforms to the standard specifications.

The Indian law also provides for an Export Inspection Council to advise the government on measures for the enforcement of preshipment inspection. The council consists of eminent representatives of government organizations, trade, and industry. The work of compulsory preshipment inspection is performed by five export inspection agencies with about 300 officers at more than 50 offices all over India.

There is in the Indian system a provision for appeal against a decision of the inspectorate. Whenever a disagreement occurs between an exporter and the inspection staff, the former can appeal to a panel consisting of experts from industry and government organizations. The representatives from industry have a two-thirds majority. This procedure is said to have created confidence among exporters, as they can obtain a just and unbiased treatment in case of dispute. There have been, however, very few cases in which the exporters have had to appeal to the panel.

In some countries (e.g., Bangladesh, Ethiopia, Ghana, Jamaica, Mauritius, Sri Lanka), the national standards institute is authorized to conduct preshipment inspection of selected items for export. Also, institutions specialized in certain commodities (e.g., foods, drugs, textiles) can be engaged in export inspection. The items inspected often come under a certification procedure.

In many developing countries there is no national framework for export inspection, which instead must be provided by the producer, the exporter, or the importer. Usually, the importers require inspection and certification through recognized commercial agencies operating on an international level.

Developing countries can get assistance in setting up export inspection programs through the International Trade Center, United Nations Conference on Trade and Development/General Agreement on Tariffs and Trade (ITC, UNCTAD/GATT), which is the United Nations unit for trade promotion. Since 1980 ITC has provided advisory services in export quality control with the aim of helping developing countries to establish appropriate policies, legislation, organizations, and services for securing acceptable quality levels for export products.[1] (See International Trade Center, 1982; and Sierra, 1983.)

LEGISLATION

Standards organizations in developing countries have been established by acts of parliaments or legislatures. Such acts, normally called "standards acts," stipulate the role of the national standards institute in promoting standardization throughout the country. An outline of such an act is given in Table 35B.3. Provisions related to the enforcement of standards are sometimes incorporated into some of these laws, for example, foods acts or certification mark acts.

The standards act may also deal with weights and measures. In some countries such standards are covered by a separate weights and measures act, which also deals with the testing of weighing and measuring equipment to ensure that it is fit for use in trade. Most developing countries are in the process of metrication.

There may also be legislation on export inspection, which is the case for certain items in some developing countries.

NATIONAL PROMOTION

In some developing countries, national programs for promoting a general awareness of quality have been launched with the involvement of government agencies and trade and consumer organizations. The national programs usually have the following components:

---

[1]As a service to exporters and industries in developing countries, ITC publishes a newsletter, *Export Quality Control.* This is available through Mr. E. Sierra, Adviser on Export Quality Control, International Trade Center UNCTAD/GATT, Palais des Nations, CH-1211 Geneva 10, Switzerland.

1. Short title

Part I. Establishment, Objects, and Powers of the Sri Lanka Standards Institution
2. Establishment of the Sri Lanka Standards Institution
3. Objects of the Institution
4. Powers of the Institution
5. General or special directions by the Minister
6. Vesting of the powers, duties, and functions of the Institution in the Council and constitution of the Council
7. The Chairman of the Council
8. Disqualification from being a Council member
9. Term of office of Council members
10. Removal of member of Council other than the Vice-Chairperson
11. Eligibility for reappointment
12. Remuneration of members
13. Meetings of the Council
14. Seal
15. Delegation of powers and duties of the Council
16. Establishment of committees

Part II. Certification Marks
17. Certification marks
18. Prohibition of registration of marks identical with certification marks as trade marks
19. Certification marks not to be applied to commodities or products unless authorized by permits or otherwise than in accordance with this section
20. Power of Minister by order to declare compulsory certification marks
21. Notice of intention to make an order under Section 20.
22. Appeals
23. Sale of a commodity or product to which Section 20 applies prohibited except under a permit and unless the commodity or product complies with the specification, etc.
24. Issuance of permits

Part III. Staff of the Institution
25. Appointment of Director-General of the Institution
26. Appointment of other officers and servants of the Institution
27. Power of the Council to exercise disciplinary control over officers and servants of the Institution
28. Delegation of powers of the Council
29. Appointment of inspectors
30. Powers of inspectors
31. Pension scheme for the staff of the Institution

Part IV. Finance and Accounts of the Institution
32. Accumulated fund
33. Revenue and the running expenses of the Institution
34. Budget of the Institution
35. Charging fees for services rendered and disposal of income derived therefrom
36. Donations and contributions made to the Institution
37. Financial year and the audit of accounts

Part V. General
38. Protection of Council and members thereof
39. Secrecy
40. Rights to discoveries, inventions, and improvements made by any member of the staff of the Institution to vest in the Institution
41. State property to be made available to the Institution
42. Exemption from taxes and duties
43. The use by any person carrying on any activity, business, trade, or occupation of certain words
44. Duty of persons to whom permits have been issued to transmit samples of commodities or products or furnish information relating to commodities or products whenever required to do so
45. Offenses
46. Penalties
47. Offenses by bodies of persons
48. Regulations
49. Repeal and savings
50. Interpretation

High-level recognition: Support from ministries and important national organizations is granted. Even the head of state may be involved.

Publicity: Public media such as newspapers, magazines, radio, and television are used.

Conferences, seminars, and other meetings: Speeches are given by political leaders, industrialists, quality professionals, etc.

Slogans: Slogans such as "Quality first" are disseminated through posters, pamphlets, stickers, badges, etc.

Logotype: The campaign has a common emblem, displayed on posters, flags, pamphlets, etc.

Awards: Deserving companies and individuals are recognized through awards, which are presented with great publicity.

Quality month: The promotional activities may be concentrated in a particular month (e.g., September in the People's Republic of China).

A national program for promoting awareness of quality was held in Singapore in 1973. The program, called the "Prosperity through Quality and Reliability" (PQR) campaign, included many activities on a national level:

Training courses for workers at all levels in quality control concepts and techniques

An essay competition for preuniversity students

A science and industry quiz for secondary schools

Worker-of-the-month competitions in factories participating in the campaign

A national PQR stamp selection contest

Public lectures and talks on quality to manufacturers and workers

Distribution of PQR flags and posters to participating organizations

Presentation of worker-of-the-month certificates and awards to deserving workers

Awards of citations to companies active in promoting the PQR ideals

The PQR campaign was planned and carried out with participation from various organizations, e.g., the National Trade Union Congress, the Singapore Manufacturers' Association, the Singapore Institute of Standards and Industrial Research, and the Consumers' Association of Singapore.

In 1982 a second quality campaign was held in Singapore. The name of this campaign was "Productivity through Quality and Reliability." The emphasis was to increase public awareness of the concepts of productivity and quality through better teamwork.

EDUCATION AND TRAINING

A key to quality upgrading is education and training, which involve developing necessary knowledge and skills, as well as influencing attitudes. In developing countries, it is necessary to direct activities of this kind not only toward producers but also toward consumers; consequently, the activities are very far-reaching. The difficulties are aggravated by the normally high illiteracy rate in these countries.

National Level. Education and training in the quality field can be dealt with in different ways within a developing country (Sandholm, 1981):

Educational Institutions. Courses on quality control are, with the exception of a few countries, not available in educational institutions such as universities and technical institutions. The few courses offered deal mainly with statistical techniques, taught by professors of statistics who have little experience in industry. More practically oriented courses taught by lecturers with experience in industrial quality control are rare. Locally developed training texts are usually not available.

Courses and Seminars Offered by Associations, Institutes, and Other Organizations. In countries that have reached a higher level of industrialization, courses and seminars are offered by national institutions for standardization, productivity, etc. and by professional associations (e.g., manufacturers' associations, national quality control societies), as well as by consultants. Some countries are very active in inviting foreign lecturers (e.g., the People's Republic of China, Malaysia, Singapore).

Meetings and Conferences. An important activity of a national quality control organization is to hold meetings and conferences at which practitioners can exchange ideas and experiences. Countries with a more developed industrial sector generally have a quality control association that is active in this way. Such organizations are the China Quality Control Association, the Colombian Association of Quality Control, the Indian Association for Quality and Reliability, the Philippine Society for Quality Control, and the Singapore Quality Reliability Association.

Self-Instruction. Independent study of books and journals can provide considerable knowledge in the quality control field, particularly for managers and engineers. In many developing countries there is, however, a shortage of such literature, owing to lack of foreign exchange, a national language with limited readership, etc. Some national quality control organizations publish a journal or newsletter, which is a means of promoting the professional development of the members. Such organizations include for example, those mentioned above in connection with meetings.

In-Company Training Programs. In-company training programs are rare in developing countries, with the exception of some larger enterprises. The quality circle movement[2] has, however, led to such in-company training. Companies that have gone into quality circle activities have given the involved workers some training in the usual quality diagnosis tools (Pareto analysis, Ishikawa diagram, etc.) Unfortunately, the training of other categories (managers, designers, manufacturing engineers, etc.) is generally meager in these enterprises. An exception is the in-company training program shown in Table 35B.4 (Dandekar et al., 1984).

On-the-Job Training. On-the-job training is the principal method of training inspectors, even in developing countries. Instructions are given by the supervisor or a more experienced inspector. The result depends on both the technical ability and the instructional and motivational ability of the instructor. In general, these abilities vary more in countries having a limited industrial tradition.

International Level. Developing countries also have opportunities for training on the international level by sending trainees to more industrialized countries.

---

[2]There seems to be great interest in quality circles in some developing countries, particularly in Asia and Latin America. Of the 66 papers presented at the International Convention on QC Circles held in Tokyo in 1985, 43 were presented by speakers from developing countries. The proceedings are available from the Union of Japanese Scientists and Engineers (JUSE), QC Circle Headquarters, 5-10-11 Sendagaya, Shibuya-ku, Tokyo 151, Japan.

TABLE 35B.4 Training Program in Jysti, Ltd., India

Training Program	No. of batches*	Total no. of participants*	Personnel trained
1. Upper Management and Quality	1	6	General Managers
2. Quality Management and Quality Circles	18	464	General managers, managers, senior engineers
3. Quality Management (Quality Circles in Gujarati)	3	59	Engineers, foremen
4. Faculty Development Training Program (to train operators)	3	51	Senior engineers and managers
5. Quality Concepts in Design & Development	6	137	Product development managers and senior engineers in R&D
6. Applied Statistics and Industrial Experimentation	1	22	Senior engineers (R&D, PEG)
7. Quality in Support Services—Purchase, Commercial, Finance, Personnel, Administration	8	133	General managers, managers, senior officers
8. Quality Circles	34	624	Operators
9. Creativity Program for Operators' QC Group Leaders	1	20	QC Leaders
Totals	75	1516	

*Figures from July 1981 to December 1983.
Source: Dandekar et al. (1984), pp. 498–506.

International organizations such as UNIDO, the ISO, and the Asian Productivity Organization (APO) organize quality control courses for developing countries.

The Swedish government sponsors a 10-week training course entitled "Quality Control in Industry." The course, which has been given annually in Sweden since 1973, was organized by UNIDO during the years 1973 to 1980. Since 1981, because of a change in the policy of the sponsoring government, the course is organized by the Swedish Agency for International Technical and Economic Cooperation, which is a governmental body.[3] The course includes 8 weeks of theoretical training (divided into three parts lasting 4, 2, and 2 weeks) and 2 weeks of practical training in industry (see Sandholm, 1981). The content of the theoretical training sessions is listed in Table 35B.5.

---

[3] The author is responsible for the course, which is administered by the Swedish Management Group of the Swedish Employers' Confederation. Information is available from Bjorklund and Sandholm AB, P.O. Box 28, S-182 51 Djursholm, Sweden.

TABLE 35B.5   Topics Covered in the Course "Quality Control in Industry," Given Annually in Sweden

Theoretical part 1

Basic concepts: Quality; the quality function; terms used in quality control; development in quality control

Companywide quality control: Company functions affecting quality; coordination of quality activities; quality assurance; life cycle of a product

Statistical tools in quality control: Basic concepts; the statistical tool kit; methods of summarizing data; probability distributions; process studies; control charts; acceptance sampling; confidence limits; tests of hypothesis; design of experiments

Metrology: Measurement technology; error of measurement; calibration control

Inspection: The nature of inspection; statistical tools in inspection; automated inspection; inspection accuracy; inspection workplace; inspection feedback; inspection by operator; inspection planning (general); planning of incoming inspection; planning of process inspection; planning of final inspection

Reliability: Definitions, concepts, and goals; maintainability and logistic support; life distributions and underlying failure mechanisms; reliability prediction; redundancy; failure mode analysis and safety analysis; reliability and environmental testing

Theoretical part 2

New-product quality: Product phases and development programs; design reviews; definition phase; preliminary design phase; final design phase; pilot production phase; production and use phases; management

Quality specifications: Purpose and content; setting requirements; standards

Supplier activities: Supplier-purchaser relationships; purchase documents; supplier selection; joint quality planning; activities in the supplier's plant; incoming inspection; supplier surveillance; supplier certification; rejections

Manufacture of quality: Manufacturing planning; nature of process; capable process; capable instruments; process control; feedback to production

Customer relations: Market quality; field performance, consumerism; product liability; guarantees

Quality audit: Quality audit concept; product quality audit; process quality audit; systems quality audit

Economics of quality: Optimum; users' costs; life cycle costing; quality costs

Quality data: Concepts, paperwork tools, in-plant data; usage data; quality costs; executive reports; computers

Improving quality: Concepts; need for a program; identifying projects; diagnosis; remedy; organizing for improvement

Theoretical part 3

Human factors in quality control: Controllability; theories of motivation; motivational programs; quality motivation for managers; training; inspection accuracy; inspector selection

Quality policy and objectives: Quality policy; quality objectives; responsibility in formulating quality policy and objectives; the annual quality program

Quality system: Quality control work elements; the systems concept; systems requirements and standards; the quality manual

Organizing for quality: Concepts; quality control work elements; evolution of the quality control organization; organization for acceptance; organization for prevention; organization for improvement; organization for coordination; organization for assurance

Quality consulting: Efficiency of the quality work; procedure; analysis; reporting; case study

Getting started: Introducing change; selling quality control to top management; developments in quality control; national approaches to quality; quality control associations and organizations

Developing countries and quality control: Phases in industrial development; situation in developing countries; national plan for quality control

The participants in this course have degrees in engineering (or the equivalent). In their own countries they occupy positions related to quality control in manufacturing industries or in organizations providing assistance to industry and to standards institutes. About 60 countries in Africa, Asia, Europe, and Latin America have been represented.

Based on the replies to a questionnaire sent to governments, organizations, and other bodies concerned with industrial training, UNIDO has since 1972 been publishing an annual guide to training opportunities for personnel from developing countries. The 1984 edition (United Nations Industrial Development Organization, 1984) has approximately 400 entries covering more than 3000 training courses. The section dealing with courses organized by bodies other than UNIDO, lists 21 courses under the heading of Quality Control and Standardization, of which the majority deal with standardization, certification, and metrology.

Another UNIDO activity is to award fellowships for individual studies. A major advantage of such fellowships is the possibility of designing and implementing a training program tailored to the needs and wishes of the candidate and his or her country.

EXTERNAL ASSISTANCE

External assistance plays a significant role in the industrial and economic growth of developing countries by making it possible to shorten the process of development. There are various forms of assistance.

Of great importance to developing countries is assistance from UNIDO, which was set up in 1967 to promote and accelerate their industrial growth and to coordinate the efforts of all United Nations agencies in this field. Most of the money for well over 2000 projects a year in more than 120 countries comes from the United Nations Development Program (UNDP), the world's largest multilateral source of technical aid. To these projects, UNIDO contributes expert advice, equipment, and training facilities. The recipient countries themselves shoulder the major cost of the projects, making their contribution in the form of land, buildings, services, staff, and cash.

In the field of quality control, UNIDO has provided assistance in the form of foreign experts, most of whom are attached to projects on standardization. Examples of countries in which quality control experts have been working are Bangladesh, Barbados, Brazil, Chile, Ecuador, Ethiopia, Ghana, Hong Kong, Indonesia, Iran, Iraq, Jordan, Mauritius, Nigeria, Saudi Arabia, Singapore, Thailand, and Turkey. The majority of the quality control experts do not, however, assist industrial enterprises in setting up quality control programs. They are more concerned with quality control on a national level, which means dealing with certification schemes, national testing facilities, and metrology. Another UNIDO activity is to conduct symposia, seminars, workshops, and training programs.[4]

Other international organizations providing assistance to developing countries in the field of quality control are the Food and Agriculture Organization of the United Nations (FAO), ITC, ISO, APO, and Commonwealth Science Council.

---

[4]The monthly *UNIDO Newsletter* gives information on current activities of UNIDO. Published in English, French, and Spanish, it can be ordered free of charge from United Nations Industrial Development Organization, P.O. Box 300, A-1400 Vienna, Austria.

A great deal of the external assistance to developing countries is through bilateral aid from industrialized countries. In this way, experts on quality control have assisted in various developing programs. External assistance may also take the form of collaboration with foreign manufacturers to obtain benefits such as technical know-how in joint ventures, import of plants and equipment, or consultant service. This kind of assistance is vital to developing countries.

INSTITUTIONAL INFRASTRUCTURE

Industrial enterprises require access to an infrastructure of institutions able to render a wide range of services for instance, in the areas of standardization, certification, testing, metrology, quality control consulting, and training. Developing countries that are in the process of industrializing must also provide for development of such an institutional infrastructure.

In most developing countries, a national standards institute is in operation primarily to provide services in standardization, certification, testing, and metrology. Unlike standards institutes in most industrialized countries, the national standards institute in a developing country is usually a governmental body under the ministry of industry.

The tasks of national standards institutes usually are:

Preparation and implementation of national standards

Testing compliance with standards

Certification of goods that are manufactured in accordance with standards

Provision of a national calibration service for testing and calibration of measuring instruments

National metrology service, including provision and maintenance of primary standards of units of measure

The national standards institutes normally do not provide any service to industry in the fields of quality consulting and training.

The standards institutes are in most countries governed by a council, which is responsible for the overall policy on standardization, as well as for the approval of standards and certification marks. The drafting of standards is supervised by technical committees representing manufacturers, users, university-affiliated institutions, research centers, etc. Usually, there are technical committees in particular fields, such as electrical, mechanical, civil, chemical, and textiles.

The staff of a national standards institute is usually headed by a director, who is usually in charge of departments for standardization, certification (sometimes called quality control or quality assurance), metrology, laboratory services, information, and administration.

In some developing countries, a specialized body has been set up on a national level to work for improved industrial productivity. The tasks of some of these national productivity institutes include assisting industry by providing consultation and training in quality. This is the case, for example, with the National Productivity Council in India and the National Productivity Board in Singapore. The latter body is very active in the promotion of quality circles and also serves as the national registration center for quality circles in Singapore.

NATIONAL QUALITY CONTROL SOCIETY

A national quality control society can play an important role in promoting quality control nationwide, in developing as well as in developed countries. Quality control societies are being formed in an increasing number of countries. Some of the national societies offer individual membership only and some offer institutional membership only, but most offer both.

Some societies are very active, for example, the Argentine Institute of Quality Control, the Brazilian Association of Quality Control, the China Quality Control Association, the Colombian Association of Quality Control, the Indian Association for Quality and Reliability, the Institute of Quality Control Malaysia, the Philippine Society for Quality Control, and the Singapore Quality Reliability Association. These societies organize conferences and seminars, conduct training programs, and distribute information (newsletters, journals, etc.).

A case in point is the Singapore Quality Reliability Association (SQRA), formed in 1971. At the end of 1980 it had 600 individual members and 89 organizational members (in a country with a population of 2 million). The objectives of SQRA are, according to the constitution:

To promote nationally an appreciation of the importance of quality and reliability in Singapore products and services and to foster and, where necessary, initiate ways of attaining these

To correlate the quality and reliability activities of all members of the association

To provide the means for interchange of information among individuals and organizations concerned with quality and reliability

To assist all individual and organizational members in correlating their quality and reliability activities

To act as a central source of information about activities for advancing the study and promotion of quality and reliability

To promote training and education in the field of quality and reliability

The association is managed by an executive committee consisting of 10 elected members and 5 advisory members (nominated) representing the Singapore Institute of Standards and Industrial Research, the National Trade Union Congress, the Singapore Manufacturers' Association, the National Productivity Board, and the Consumers' Association of Singapore. Thus, SQRA has the backing of important organizations in the country.

One SQRA function is to organize training courses, seminars, and evening talks (often with foreign experts as lecturers). The first national quality congress was held in 1982. Factory visits and social gatherings are other activities of SQRA. Study missions to Japan have been arranged.

As a member service, SQRA has videocassettes, slides, and literature for loan, as well as books and posters that are available for sale. It also publishes a bimonthly journal (*QC Focus*), which contains articles on quality control topics, announcements, book reviews, etc.

Because of an affiliated society agreement with the American Society for Quality Control (ASQC), members of SQRA can obtain ASQC certification under the programs for certified quality engineer, certified reliability engineer, and certified quality technician. The examinations are held in Singapore.

CONCLUSION

The so-called developing countries are in various phases of industrial development—some have just started with manufacture, whereas others are almost fully industrialized. No matter which phase a country is in, the quality of the products that it manufactures is important to its economic growth. Quality control in a broad sense will ensure the fitness of goods for domestic use, reduce the waste of scarce resources, and facilitate the export of national products.

It is of great importance to developing countries to use appropriate methods in quality control work. Simple basic techniques will in most cases give a better result than currently fashionable methods (to which too much attention is often paid). Before methods are selected, true needs have to be determined. This seemingly obvious point, however, is often overlooked. The focus should be shifted from a method-oriented to a more problem-oriented approach, with increased emphasis placed on studies of established facts. Such an approach will provide a better basis for successful development.

There is an obvious need for extensive studies on how to deal with quality control in developing countries on both a national and a company level and on the relations between the two levels. Models and plans for different levels of industrial development, different industrial structures, different branches of industry, etc. should be worked out. This is an important international undertaking.

ACKNOWLEDGMENT

Thanks are due to Dr. Noriaki Kano (professor at the Science University of Tokyo, Japan), Mr. Enrique Sierra (Senior Advisor on Export Quality Control, International Trade Center UNCTAD/GATT, Geneva, Switzerland), and Dr. Kenneth S. Stephens (UNIDO Senior Industrial Adviser, Beijing, Peoples Republic of China), who have given the author useful information by sharing with him their great experience of quality control in developing countries. In his work in developing countries, the author has had the privilege of meeting many dedicated persons, both as colleagues and as students, who are too numerous to be mentioned by name. Their contributions are highly appreciated.

REFERENCES

Bos, H. C. (1977). "The Use of Appropriate Technology: A Survey." *Equality of Opportunity within and among Nations.* Praeger, New York.

Dandekar, A. V. et al. (1984). "Group Motivation and Management—an Indian Experience." *Proceedings, World Quality Congress,* Brighton, England, pp. 498–506.

Industry in a Changing World (1983). United Nations, New York.

International Organization for Standardization (ISO) and International Trade Center, UNCTAD/GATT (ITC) (joint publication) (1980). *Certification—Principles and Practice.* ISO and ITC UNCTAD/GATT, Geneva. (See also *General Terms and their Definitions Concerning Standardization and Certification,* ISO Guide 2-1983; *Code of Principles on Third Party Certification Systems and Related Standards,* ISO/IEC Guide 16-1978; *Guidelines for the Acceptance of Testing and Inspection Agencies by Certification Bodies,* ISO

Guide 24-1978; *General Requirements for the Acceptance of Certification Bodies,* ISO Guide 40-1983. ISO, Geneva.)

International Trade Center UNCTAD/GATT (1982). *Advisory Services of ITC in Export Quality Control.* ITC/DIP/INF/11, Apr. 28, Geneva.

Juran, J. M. (1975). "Standardization and Quality." *Quality Progress,* February, pp. 4–5.

Lima Declaration and Plan of Action on Industrial Development and Co-Operation. (1975). United Nations Industrial Development Organization, Vienna.

Sandholm, Lennart (1981). "Education and Training in Developing Countries." *ASQC Quality Congress Transactions,* Milwaukee, pp. 862–868.

Sierra, E. (1983). "Quality Control Systems in Developing Contries: Some Experiences of the International Trade Center UNCTAD/GATT (ITC)." *Proceedings, 27th EOQC Conference,* Madrid. EOQC, Berne.

Stephens, K. S. (1979). *Preparing for Standardization, Certification and Quality Control.* Asian Productivity Organization, Tokyo.

United Nations Industrial Development Organization (UNIDO) (1984). *Guide to Training Opportunities for Industrial Development,* 13th issue. UNIDO, Vienna.

World Industry since 1960: Progress and Prospects. (1979). United Nations, New York.

SECTION 35C
QUALITY IN FRANCE

Jean-Marie Gogue

HISTORY 35C.1

ECONOMIC DATA 35C.4

MANAGERS 35C.4

TRADE UNIONS 35C.6

QUALITY CONTROL WITHIN
FRENCH INDUSTRY 35C.6

ASSOCIATIONS DEVOTED TO
QUALITY CONTROL 35C.7

FRENCH CONSUMERISM 35C.8

GOVERNMENT AGENCIES FOR
QUALITY CONTROL 35C.8

QUALITY CONTROL EDUCATION
AND TRAINING 35C.9

REFERENCES 35C.9

HISTORY

French industry is about 400 years old, except for the handicrafts, which are obviously much older. The first prominent factories were textile mills in Lyons, steel mills in Saint-Etienne, and paper mills in Annonay. During the seventeenth century silks from Lyons attained a worldwide reputation for high quality.

To understand the evolution of French industry, it is first necessary to understand that France has had a long history of strong central government. King Louis XI (1423–1483) was the first sovereign to centralize national powers. He strengthened the king's power at the expense of the power of political bodies and of the clergy and promoted economic growth throughout the kingdom, particularly in the Lyons area.

State ownership (nationalization) of some factories, which is widespread in France today, has been practiced to some extent since the seventeenth century. In fact, Jean-Baptiste Colbert, the Minister of Finance under Louis XIV, founded the famous Sèvres and Gobelins state factories, which made luxury products such as porcelain, tapestry, and furniture. Colbert established steel mills, shipyards, and many processing industries as well.

Colbert's awareness of the importance of quality appears in a report to the king (dated August 3, 1664): "If our factories, through careful work, assure the quality of our products, it will be to the foreigners' interest to get supplies from us, and their money will flow into the kingdom."

The French government regulated privately owned factories as well as the nationalized ones. We can see a good example of the role of government in the case of the paper industry, of which the Bureau of Commerce (an agency within the Ministry of Finance) made a survey in 1769. Admitting that Dutch paper was of better quality than French, they addressed a questionnnaire to most of the leading manufacturers, one of whom was Etienne de Montgolfier (the man who invented ballooning), who ran a paper mill in Annonay with his brothers Pierre and Joseph. Pierre replied to the questionnaire, and a fruitful cooperation started between the Montgolfiers and Nicolas Desmarest, a government official who had visited Dutch paper mills. Desmarest made a survey of the Annonay plant and helped the Montgolfiers to improve their process.

An interesting letter in the Montgolfier files illustrates the supplier-purchaser relations during this period (Gillispie, 1983). A man named Jean-Baptiste Réveillon was a well-known wallpaper manufacturer in Paris. The Montgolfier company was his main supplier, and Réveillon became one of the few friends to share real intimacy with Etienne. Réveillon was the decorator of the first Montgolfier balloons, which were launched in the presence of King Louis XVI.

In June 1785 Réveillon wrote a regretful letter, telling his old friend that the last shipment of paper was of such inferior quality that it should never have come out of the Montgolfier vats. Only 12 reams out of 67 were passable, and only 4 were close to what they should have been although even so not quite up to standard. He was so astonished that he showed samples to Etienne's uncle, who confirmed his judgment. Etienne de Montgolfier, according to Desmarest's advice, implemented the Dutch process with funds from the provincial authorities. But the superiority of the Dutch lay not just in their machines but also in their management. Entrepreneurs in the Netherlands had developed labor-saving machinery and had learned to substitute it, wherever possible, for human labor, instead of being dominated by custom and therefore allowing their workers to impede efficient utilization of machinery. Ignorance and routine were the enemy in France, being evidenced by inertia among manufacturers and resistance among workers.

An imaginative concept was the creation of a workshop in which the most efficient processes and machines would be in use. Such a workshop would then be open to observation and study by any manufacturers who wished to keep themselves informed about the operation of these processes. Workers would then be trained to operate the new equipment. However, in the summer of 1780 a climate of hostility developed between the managers and the work force, and labor troubles continued for several years.

At about the same time, another French government official developed the principle of interchangeability, which is of great importance in modern manufacturing. Vaquette de Gribeauval, the Inspector General of Artillery, published the first mechanical engineering rules, which were based on:

Limiting the dimensions on the specifications to a set of standard sizes

Determining the tolerances assigned to these sizes

Using a conformance control system, implementing gauges, and adequate instruments (Cave, 1970, p. 409)

In 1794, during the French Revolution, the French government created a workshop for manufacturing all gauges and inspection tools used in the national munitions factories. (The workshop was installed in a house that, before the revolution, had been the Jacobin convent in Paris.) These general principles and the establishment of this workshop allowed the French army to achieve interchangeability of guns and ammunition. (Later on, with the development of automobiles, standardization was extended to all mechanized industries. But early in 1796, thanks to standardization, French artillery outperformed enemy forces and greatly contributed to Napoleon's victories.)

To an important extent modern industry started with the invention of the steam engine and the railroad. The Montgolfier family largely contributed to the development of this new technology. In fact, Marc Séguin, the inventor of the tubular boiler, the heart of all steam locomotives, was Etienne de Montgolfier's great-nephew. His first engine went into service on the Saint-Etienne to Lyons railway in 1832, 3 years after the opening of the Liverpool and Manchester railway in England.

Séguin was ahead of many inventors of his times by his quality-of-design awareness. For example, the tubular boiler patent points out that the main object is to improve the efficiency of heat transfer. He was a pioneer in the field of steam engines, railroads, and suspension bridges, and his success was undoubtedly due to his determination to achieve practical utility for his designs. But he often had to defend himself against some pseudo-scientists and higher officials who did not accept his ideas.

During World War I increased national productivity was urgently needed. In 1916 Henri Fayol, a French industrialist who successfully managed the Commentry iron works, wrote a digest of his experience in management (Fayol, 1981). According to his theory, management operations can be broken down into five stages:

1. Forecasting
2. Organizing
3. Commanding
4. Coordinating
5. Controlling

Fayol's short book strongly influenced French industry for over 20 years. Many of Fayol's ideas are still valid, but his concept of "controlling" is ambiguous, and it prompted most managers to mistake product inspection for quality control.

French economic policy until World War II was based on protectionist principles—heavy duties were imposed on foreign goods. On the other hand, the export trade remained at a low level. This policy resulted in a relative steadiness of French industry during and after the Wall Street crash in 1929. In 1935, the French government was faced with an economic crisis because of the flight of capital abroad. To counteract this, the government took strong deflationist measures in the industrial field: public works planning, cuts in wages, and prohibition of new investments in flour milling, sugar refining, and boot and shoe manufacturing. In the following year, the unpopularity of these measures brought about the election of a socialist majority ("front populaire"). However, the new government, in spite of an economic revival, did not succeed in bringing about recovery from the economic crisis.

During all this time, French industry maintained a tradition of quality, especially in furniture, automobiles, clothes, and food. Quality was synonymous with good reputation, but also with high prices. Factories employed many inspectors.

It was clear in the manager's mind that product cost was increasing with conformance level. The French industrialist was proud of his first-rate quality and did not worry much about prices.

After World War II, western European countries gradually set up the European Economic Community (EEC), defined in 1957 by the Rome Treaty. All French industry prepared to meet the international competition. It was a new and exciting challenge.

In 1947 the United States offered the Europeans economic assistance in order to quickly restore a proper standard of living. Sixteen countries accepted the proposal, known as the Marshall Plan, in which France received a total of $2 billion. However, the government was aware that these funds could be properly used only with management improvements. Emphasis was placed on productivity, and a bureau for productivity growth was created in 1950.

As early as 1951, some French engineers discovered the quality control (QC) concept in America and became convinced that quality management would be a trump card in international competition. However, officials and industrialists continued to mistake product inspection for quality control. The French quality control association (Association Française pour le Contrôle Industriel et la Qualité, or AFCIQ) was formed by these engineers in 1957. In the same year similar associations were formed in Germany, Italy, the Netherlands, and the United Kingdom. These five associations founded the European Organization for Quality Control (EOQC), which was later expanded to include 25 countries.

In 1974 an economic crisis severely affected the whole spectrum of processing industries. Steel, engineering, textiles, and plastics suffered from competition from the Far East. In many companies, the loss of orders was the warning that motivated the chief executive to take an interest in quality control.

ECONOMIC DATA

French economic activity is equally divided among agriculture, industry, and trade. The 1980 figures were published in a report by the Ministry of Industry (1982). The most interesting data are shown in Table 35C.1.

Most of the largest French companies are nationalized. The state became the owner of some of them, such as Renault Motors Company, in 1945. Another important nationalization program took place in 1982. The nationalized companies account for 35 percent of industrial sales, and their assets amount to 44 percent of total industrial assets.

There are two kinds of state-owned enterprises, the public services companies and the oligopolistic companies. The former (telephone, electricity, railways) have no competition and no profit objectives. The latter (automobile, aircraft, electronics) have competition and must be profitable. In these companies, the government behaves as an ordinary shareholder, and they compete with private French and foreign companies.

MANAGERS

French universities do not attempt to train personnel for managerial and other company staff positions; they concentrate on education of teachers and research

TABLE 35C.1   Selected Data on French Economic Activity

Population	People, thousands
Inhabitants	53,700
Working population	21,683
Working in industry	5,026

Economic indicators	Dollars, billions
Gross national product	313.5
Industry added value	86.4
Capital expenditure	15.8
Export sales	48.1
Import purchases	62.5

Company size, employees	Industry total, percent	
	People	Sales
20-49	9.4	6.3
50–99	7.5	5.5
100–199	9.0	6.6
200–499	13.7	11.0
500 and more	56.4	67.0

Industry type	Industry total, percent	
	People	Sales
Power plants	5.8	20.6
Foundries	9.3	10.6
Chemical plants	13.8	16.1
Rolling mills	8.8	5.5
Mechanics	10.7	8.3
Electronics	12.1	9.3
Transport equipment	14.9	13.6
Textile	10.8	5.9
Paper mills	6.1	5.5

Source: Ministère de l'Industrie (1982). *Données Économiques.* La Documentation Française, p. 27.

workers. In addition to the universities, the *grande école* system at present provides an educational channel for managers. There are two types of grande école:

1. Scientific schools, e.g., Ecoles Polytechniques

2. Management schools, e.g., Ecoles des Hautes Etudes Commerciales (HECs)

Graduation from grande école depends on government authorization. There are 160 grandes écoles, which graduate 11,000 students per year. Admission is based on a rigorous examination, but nearly all students who are admitted graduate. The main problem for the young man or woman is not graduation but admission. Competence in mathematics is important. In large companies, 80 percent of the managers are grande école graduates, but in the small ones the proportion drops to 40 percent.

Management knowledge can be improved by seminars held in training institutes (e.g., INSEAD, Fontainebleau). The fees are usually paid by the company hiring the student. The largest companies (e.g., Renault) have their own management training centers.

Most company leaders have combined into a powerful association, the Conseil National du Patronat Français (CNPF). The CNPF has 6000 members, who have responsibility for 1 million workers, and its annual income is about $10 million. The organization is divided into 87 technological federations (e.g., chemistry, glass, electronic components).

TRADE UNIONS

The organization of French labor unions is very unusual compared with those in most industrial countries. Most of the unions belong to large federations, and three national confederations represent 80 percent of all union members. They are:

Confédération Générale du Travail (CGT)

Confédération Française Démocratique du Travail (CFDT)

Force Ouvrière (FO)

Membership in French labor unions is not very high. Only 20 percent of the workers regularly pay union dues. However, the workers have another opportunity to be represented by a union, the elections for the joint factory committees. In 1982, 81.6 percent of elected members were union members. In fact, the results were:

CGT	32.3%
CFDT	22.8%
FO	11.7%
Other unions	14.8%
Nonunion workers	18.4%

The trade union leaders negotiate the workers' wages and rights at a national level with the CNPF and the government. In every company the union representatives negotiate only local agreements, in accordance with the nationwide labor union policy.

QUALITY CONTROL WITHIN FRENCH INDUSTRY

Until 1970, inspection and testing were the only quality control activities in most French companies. This situation has gradually changed, and since 1980 about 30 percent of companies employing more than 100 people have had a quality control department.

Public utilities (railroads, telephone) or ministries (defense, agriculture) have their own quality audit and inspection departments. Their former practice was to inspect products and penalize the supplier in case of poor quality. Now, however, they require a QC management system in the supplier's company by contracts, and they regularly audit this system.

The Surveillance Industrielle de l'Armement (SIAR), which is the QC Department of the Ministry of Defense, has contributed greatly to the growth of quality management among its suppliers. At the same time Electricité de France (EDF) began to require QC departments and manuals, not only from its suppliers but also from its suppliers' suppliers and subcontractors.

Nevertheless, a quality assurance contract is not enough to promulgate good practices in all companies if top management is not aware of the benefit of a comprehensive QC system. This is why the Ministry of Industry in 1981 made a sample survey of the cost of failure to control quality. The cost nationwide was estimated at $20 billion, i.e., 10 percent of industrial sales.

Immediately, the CNPF began to take an interest in this money-saving approach. In 1982 the president of the CNPF declared in front of his colleagues, "Let's sweep up our front door. We cannot ask for tax reduction as long as French industry is so wasteful." Since this statement was issued, many new QC managers have been appointed. Statistics obtained from newspaper advertisements indicate an increase of 50 percent in 1983.

As early as 1978, French industrialists and staff managers toured Japan in order to study the basis of Japanese productivity. They were impressed by the widespread existence of QC circles, and on their return they decided to initiate a French quality circle movement. An organization AFCERQ Services was founded in 1981 in order to help French companies to develop quality circles. In 1983 about 360 companies were members and 5000 circles were registered. Most AFCERQ leaders are staff managers in large companies. They provide the circles with motivational techniques and start them off independently of any QC system.

Newspapers have given much attention to quality circles. The proponents have said they signalled a new start in many companies, and the opponents have called them a weapon against trade unions. In any case, the quality circles provided some "fresh hand" consultants.

The government did not adopt a definite position regarding the matter. The CNPF declared in favor of the quality circles, and the trade unions declared against them.

ASSOCIATIONS DEVOTED TO QUALITY CONTROL

French laws make it easy for anyone to establish an association—in fact, the number of registered associations is about 100,000. Several of them deal with some aspects of QC. But if we consider only the public utility associations, to which a higher status has been granted by the Council of State, their number is 2000. The only public utility association devoted to quality control is the Association Française pour le Contrôle Industriel et la Qualité (AFCIQ).

Founded in 1957, AFCIQ includes 1500 individual members and 140 companies. The headquarters are located in Paris. Eight regional sections, covering the territory, have their secretariats in Bordeaux, Lille, Lyons, Montpellier, Nancy, Nantes, Paris, and Toulon. Six professional sections and nine working groups improve QC methods and implement them throughout French industry. The parent organization is a member of EOQC, and its professional sections and working groups keep in close contact with EOQC committees and sections.

Every year since 1980 AFCIQ has awarded a national prize to companies for their good quality management, *le prix industrie et qualité*. Only two companies win the prize every year, a large one with more than 500 employees and a smaller company. Any producer of goods or services can compete for the prize. A preliminary selection of 12 companies is made after examination of dossiers, and the final selection is made after an audit in the field. Experts are appointed by AFCIQ from among retired QC managers and a selection committee is appointed from among leading scientists and industrialists. The prize is given in November jointly by the Minister of Industry and the CNPF president. About 1000 high-level officials attend the ceremony. The weekly magazine *L'Usine Nouvelle* is associated with AFCIQ and handles public relations concerning the prize.

Since 1984 AFCIQ has also awarded a national prize for individuals, *la médaille Georges Borel*. The selection committee includes the AFCIQ president and four past presidents. Its purpose is to recognize employees at any level in the industry for outstanding contributions to quality improvement in their firms. There are two winners per year. Georges Borel, who died in 1982, was a French pioneer of companywide quality control.

FRENCH CONSUMERISM

French consumers are protected against fraud or product liability by three acts of the French parliament known as:

Loi sur la répression des fraudes (1905)

Loi Royer (1973)

Loi Scrivener (1978)

A number of products are certified as safe and in conformity with national standards by the *marque NF*. This label is given by the Association Française de Normalisation (AFNOR), the French standards association, which is a member of the International Organization for Standardization (ISO). The producers are subjected to an audit and their products are tested. AFNOR uses various testing laboratories, associated with a national product testing network (Réseau National d'Essais).

Many associations contribute to the consumers' rights movement, most of which are associated with the *Union Fédérale des Consommateurs*. They perform comparative tests and publish the resulting ratings in their monthly magazines. They can also institute proceedings on behalf of their members.

GOVERNMENT AGENCIES FOR QUALITY CONTROL

Several government bureaus deal with quality, namely:

Ministry of Defense: Direction de la surveillance industrielle de l'armement

Ministry of Agriculture: Direction de la qualité

Ministry of Industry: Direction de la qualité

Ministry for Consumer Affairs

Treasury: Institut National de la Consommation

The oldest such bureau, the *Service de la répression des fraudes*, was founded in 1947 within the Ministry of Agriculture. All these bodies now aim at promoting quality control, but they have kept the power to penalize producers, especially for failures relative to product safety.

Since 1976 the *Institut National de la Consommation,* a department of the Ministry of Finance, has been broadcasting an 18-minute weekly program with the object of alerting the public to product quality.

QUALITY CONTROL EDUCATION AND TRAINING

Since 1980 some *grandes écoles* have included QC courses in their curriculum, namely:

Université de Technologie de Compiègnc (UTC)

Ecole Spéciale des Travaux Publics

Ecole des Hautes Etudes Commerciales (HEC)

Ecole Supérieure de Commerce de Paris

The UTC grants a QC engineer's degree after 3 years of study. Sixty students graduate every year. The HEC offers 32 hours of lecture for one term, at the end of which the students receive grades for making a QC survey of a company.

For many years, postgraduate QC training has been sponsored jointly by AFCIQ and AFNOR. It includes lectures on quality of design, quality of production, etc., given for 2, 3, and 5 days. Since 1970 under this joint sponsorship, J. M. Juran has conducted annual 3-day courses on quality control management. By the end of 1983, a cumulative total of over 1500 managers and engineers had participated in these courses. In 1982 the joint sponsors inaugurated annual 1-day seminars on the subject of upper management and quality. These likewise have been well attended.

Some large companies have set up their own QC training programs. For example, Citroën Motor Company has a 40-hour quality course for engineers; 300 people take the course every year.

Currently quality management is giving French industry a great opportunity for significant cultural change. In 1936, the philosopher Simone Weil predicted "By aiming at increasing production, the employers weakened their ascendancy over labor. But what was lost on this side we shall recover by noble motives, such as professional pride, fondness for work, interest in achieving one's task, sense of responsibility" (Weil, 1964, p. 281).

REFERENCES

Cave, René (1970). *Le Contrôle Statistique des Fabrications,* 4th ed. Eyrolles éditeur, Paris.

Fayol, Henri (1981). *Administration Industrielle,* 8th ed. Dunod éditeur, Paris.

Gillispie, Charles Coulston (1983). *The Montgolfier Brothers and the Invention of Aviation.* Princeton University Press, Princeton, NJ, pp. 17–19, 127.

Ministère de l'Industrie (1982). *Les Chiffres Clés.* Dunod éditeur, Paris.

Weil, Simone (1964). *La Condition Ouvrière,* 2nd ed. NRF Gallimard, Paris.

SECTION 35D
QUALITY IN THE FEDERAL REPUBLIC OF GERMANY

Dipl.-Ing. Ernst Schlötel

ECONOMY OF THE FEDERAL REPUBLIC OF GERMANY **35D.1**

Structure 35D.1

Guilds in Germany and Origin of Quality Assurance 35D.2

QUALITY ASSURANCE IN THE GERMAN ECONOMY **35D.3**

Statistical Methods and Quality Management . .35D.3

Activities of DGQ 35D.4

Training and Education in Quality 35D.5

CONSUMERS AND QUALITY . **35D.5**

Quality Marks; Trade Marks 35D.6

Legal Aspects of Quality; Product Liability in Germany 35D.6

REFERENCES **35D.7**

ECONOMY OF THE FEDERAL REPUBLIC OF GERMANY

Germany has a high population density but only limited natural resources. To import such resources the economy has been oriented toward export. German manufactured goods—mechanical, optical, chemical, electronic—have been sold worldwide, along with technology and services.

The competitive nature of international export has required extensive innovations and inventions. In addition, methods developed in other countries have been adapted to some extent, but only in their broad outlines; their application was in most cases preceded by modifications resulting in better products. In addition, such methods, e.g., the Taylor system, were applied only after adapting them to German conditions and culture. As a consequence, German methodology has changed slowly, in an evolutionary manner. The older concepts, e.g., guilds and craftsmanship, remain very much in evidence.

Structure. *Large enterprises* (more than 500 employees) account for only about 25 percent of the employed work force. However, these enterprises are world-renowned, and capital invested in them is broadly based. *Medium-sized enter-*

prises are those that employ between about 10 and 499 people. These enterprises employ nearly 59 percent of the work force, account for about 50 percent of the gross national product, train nearly 45 percent of all apprentices, and account for a considerable share of German exports. *Craft enterprises* account for about 12 percent of the gross national income, but they employ about 16 percent of shop workers and train about 41 percent of all apprentices. These enterprises are organized into handicraft specialties, much as were the guilds that preceded them. Their statutes have their roots in the statutes of the guilds. Overall, in the Federal Republic of Germany there are over 25 million employed persons and 1.7 million trainee positions.

A recent development in ownership of enterprises may turn out to be an influential quality-motivating force. This is the concept of "Vermögensbildung" (asset formation), under which part of workers' wages goes into savings deposits or into purchase of company shares. The workers earn, first, pay in the form of additional savings ("Arbeitnehmersparzulage") and, second, interest or dividends on these funds. In turn, the company is able to use the money in the savings accounts or to borrow against the shares to finance company operations. This is a significant help, since German firms are self-financed to a lesser extent than American companies. A further result is that the workers become owners of the firms for which they work; they share in the earnings but also in the losses.

Guilds in Germany and the Origin of Quality Assurance. The eleventh century saw a growth of population in Germany. Because of the decline of chivalry, some other form of protection was needed. That encouraged the founding of large settlements—the towns. Since the towns required extensive division of labor, the need arose for the services of artisans (free persons, not serfs) to provide the inhabitants with bread, meat, cloth, shoes, etc.

In turn, these artisans took steps to ensure their livelihood by incorporating into guilds, one for each product type. These guilds became monopolies, and they enacted statutes that regulated professional conduct and even social affairs. The principal features embodied in these statutes included the following:

1. Each craftsman (master) within the community had to be a member of the appropriate guild to be allowed to practice his profession.

2. Guilds were autonomous; each had jurisdiction in professional matters and in discipline.

3. Guild members engaged actively in social pursuits, both religious and secular. Their frequent meetings gave rise to the well-known taprooms (Trinkstuben).

4. Only a limited number of journeymen, often only one, could be hired.

5. The training of apprentices lasted 3 or more years.

6. A candidate to become a master could be approved only after successfully completing an apprenticeship and then, in addition, traveling for 3 to 5 years as a journeyman (in order to complete his training outside of his own community). The decision to approve rested with the guild members, who gave this approval only if there was enough work in the community.

7. The guild determined the kind and amount of material to be used, working methods, amount to be produced, wages, and prices of manufactured products (if not fixed by the authority, as they were especially in later years).

8. Chosen guild elders tested the quality.

9. Trading of a guild member's own products was allowed only at the marketplace, where all guild members offered their qualified goods.

10. Offenses against the rules, especially poor quality, were mostly cruelly punished.

11. The members were obligated to be members of the guild's levy (*aufgebot*) for the town's defenses.

The main purpose of incorporating into guilds and enacting such statutes was to ensure the livelihood of each guild member. Hence, no one was allowed to produce in any way other than specified. (In effect, the quality mission consisted of conformance to rather static product specifications and manufacturing methods rather than making the best product for the changing needs of consumers.) One result was that progress was stopped for centuries. Competition was nearly prevented by the statutes, by the limitations imposed, and by the qualification practiced.

Evaluation of quality under the guilds included most of the concepts of modern quality assurance. The craftsmen themselves had to test the work of their journeymen as well as their own work. The chosen guild elders acted much like quality auditors. They conducted:

Unannounced product audits in the marketplace or in the workshops, with signing of approved work

Workshop audits to ensure that input materials were of proper quality and that specified procedures were followed

Metrology calibration, originally a part of the workshop audit but later taken over by the community to ensure independence and also to collect the associated revenue

The guild structure was influential in Europe, and especially in Germany, for centuries, until mechanization and industrialization brought changes. However, the structure of craft work in Germany retains to this day many of the features of the guild structure, notably those corresponding to items 1, 2, and 5, plus (in part) 3 and 6, of the above list. In recent years some craft associations have created arbitration committees, which provide a form of added consumer protection, similar to that of item 8. Training of apprentices will remain the task of the craft system, as a means of providing a supply of skilled workers (see Hoffmann, 1979; Lentze, 1964; Wissel, 1974; and *Politik in Zahlen '83*).

QUALITY ASSURANCE IN THE GERMAN ECONOMY

The historical craft tradition with its associated quality tradition established a sound basis for quality assurance during the subsequent growth of industrialization and mechanization. There was no need for a fundamental change in the basic approach to quality. Use of more progressive methods did evolve, however, but often these methods were introduced only after hesitation.

Statistical Methods and Quality Management. The normal, or gaussian (after K. F. Gauss), probability distribution is known everywhere. In 1913 Spieker, Lubberger, Holm, and Rückle used the methods of probability theory to investigate the number of transmission lines needed for telephones. Application of statistical methods to process control and research was described by K. Daeves in his March 1922 article in the American periodical *Testing*. (Some of this work was cited by W. A. Shewhart in his papers on control charts and sampling.) In 1928 to 1929 a group of engineers and scientists held a conference on statistical methods in process control. Similar studies took place in several other European countries as well, but they did not lead to broad application.

In German industry at that time, product quality was assured by employment of *skilled* workers, well trained and not too specialized, and by inspectors who represented management.

Widespread application of modern statistical methods began in the 1950s. Previously, U. Graf and H. J. Henning, in cooperation with the textile industry, had tested new types of control charts using original data despite the possible absence of a normal population distribution. Their experience was that these charts did work in practice. In 1952 they published the first book in the German language on statistical methods in textile research *(Statistische Methoden bei textilen Untersuchungen),* which described comprehensively all statistical methods for production, investigation, and research work.

A stimulus to broader activity was given by a small group of engineers and scientists, who founded a subcommittee on statistics in technology (Technische Statistik, TESTA) within the Ausschuss für wirtschaftliche Fertigung (AWF) (Committee for Economical Manufacture). In 1953 the European Productivity Agency (EPA) promoted lectures by W. E. Deming, followed by the lectures of Professor Paul Clifford in 1954 and 1955. In the meantime, members of the TESTA committee formed regional groups to exchange experiences.

The year 1956 brought organizational changes. The TESTA committee became the Arbeitsgemeinschaft für Statistische Qualitâtskontrolle im AWF (ASQ) (Committee for Statistical Quality), internationally better known under its present name, Deutsche Gesellschaft für Qualität (DGQ) (German Society for Quality). In Paris the same year saw the founding of the European Organization for Quality Control (EOQC), whose first president was W. Masing of Germany.

In Germany modern quality concepts were promoted by individuals—by idealists—who elaborated or adapted methods learned mainly through the activities of DGQ (ASQ). They became the experts who introduced the methods to industry. Because of the initiatives and activities of these same experts, some industry branches, e.g., electronics, textiles, steel, aeronautics, and automotive, achieved notably high quality standards.

German industry made only limited use of the practice of sharply separating production planning from actual production, which has been so widely adopted in the United States. A major reason was the aforementioned high availability of skilled workers. In addition, procedures developed in other countries were used only after they had been adapted to the German cultural pattern.

Activities of DGQ.   Modern quality methods have been promoted mainly by DGQ and its members. In 1983 DGQ had 1100 individual and 470 institutional members. The activities of DGQ include the following:

Committees are formed to solve specific problems, to devise methods and procedures, and to prepare training materials. In 1983 there were 11 such committees. The results of their investigations are commonly published in brochure form.

Fifty such brochures have been published by DGQ, some of which have been issued in several revised editions. Currently, 27 remain up to date.

Twenty-seven regional groups meet periodically to exchange experiences.

A scientific advisory board develops new scientific methods pertaining to quality.

Cooperative arrangements have been made with quality-oriented organizations in Switzerland and Austria and with the quality section of the German Automotive Association (VDA). Cooperative efforts with these groups have resulted in five joint publications of common interest.

Additional Cooperative arrangements include those with the Association for Techniques of Measurement and Control (GMR), the Central Association of the Electrical Industry (ZVEI), and of course the German Standards Institute (DIN). (See Strauch, 1961; Graf, 1952; Altenkirch, 1959 and 1972; and DGQ, 1983.)

Training and Education in Quality.   The DGQ plays a major role in training activities. Each year about 4000 persons participate in courses and seminars such as:

1. Courses in statistical methods for quality control, conducted at different levels, i.e., for quality inspectors, supervisors, technicians, and engineers. In 1983, 98 such courses were given, with 2073 participants. In addition 68 in-house courses, involving 1143 participants, were licensed.
2. Special courses on statistical methods for research and development engineers.
3. Seminars on quality assurance for managers.
4. Seminars on quality assurance and quality control for quality managers.
5. Seminars for instructors to enable them to give in-house courses.

The courses are taught by 50 practitioners, and 20 quality experts guide the participants in the seminars.

The technical academies in Wuppertal and Esslingen have organized many lectures and courses, including lectures by Professors Deming and Clifford of the United States. Increasingly, the technical institutes (technische Hochschulen) and universities are training students in scientific methods of quality assurance and quality control.

Unique and successful are the activities of the Berufsförderungswerk der Stiftung Rehabilitation (occupational therapy unit of the Rehabilitation Foundation). There, disabled persons (including those with congenital or accidentally incurred disabilities) are taught inspection theory and practice, as well as testing and quality control methods. Those who pass the training are thereby enabled to work and to earn their own livelihoods (see Methner, 1980).

CONSUMERS AND QUALITY

In Germany there has never been a strong need for national legislation to protect consumers against poor quality. In earlier centuries the guilds and/or the local municipalities assumed this responsibility. A similar approach has been adopted by industry associations, for example, the Verein Deutscher Elektrotechniker (VDE) (Association of German Electrical Engineers) has developed regulations for electrical equipment. Another example is in the area of product liability: German industrial, commercial, and retail trade associations signed a declaration in 1978 to the effect that their member companies would ensure that deficient technical equipment would be returned to the producer rather than being shipped to consumers.

Quality Marks: Trade Marks.   During the age of the guilds, trading was permitted only in designated marketplaces; direct sales from workshops to consumers were forbidden. In the marketplaces all competitors displayed their goods, and consumers could observe differences in quality.

An added aid to consumers was the quality mark. Chosen senior craftsmen tested the products and signed those of proper quality. For products whose quality was not verifiable by consumers, e.g., the purity of gold or silver, some guilds required the artisan to sign his products as a guarantee. Signatures used for these or other reasons tended to become quality marks. For example, large trading enterprises, such as Fugger or Welser, signed the goods they sold, which were then accepted without any further inspection. In 1887 the British Parliament revised the Merchandise Marks Act to protect its domestic market by requiring all foreign products to be identified by the country of origin. The designation "Made in Germany" soon became recognized as a trademark for quality applicable to all goods and services coming from Germany.

Today, quality marks and trademarks abound. For example, the grade classification (three to five classes) of certain special characteristics of food products must be shown on the package.

Ever since 1925 an association for terms of delivery and quality assurance (RAL) has initiated quality marks (Gütezeichen). This association is directed by representatives from all groups that influence public life: consumer associations, industry, craft workers, commerce, retail trade, government departments, unions, etc. These quality marks are not mandated by law but are voluntarily initiated by specific branches of industry that submit products and provide specifications.

Yet another form of consumer protection is the testing conducted and published by the Stiftung Warentest (Product Testing Foundation). The concept is that publication of inspection and test results on competing consumer products aids consumers in deciding which products to buy. This approach has been used since 1961.

Under this concept, any consumer product may be selected to undergo comparative testing. A special advisory committee of 5 to 10 experts (from consumer, producer, and retail sales organizations) is formed to design an appropriate test program. Up to 20 competing models are acquired and tested according to the program. The results were orginially published in the periodical *DM* and since 1961 have been published in the magazine *Test*.

Nearly 70 such test programs, covering samples of about 1500 products, are carried out annually. The test results are further disseminated by the press, television, and radio, as well as by advertising. Such extensive publicity brings the results forcibly to the attention of consumers, retail merchants, and, especially, producers. The effect on consumer product quality is significant. (See Fuhr, 1980; Schirmer, 1980; and Hüttenrauch, 1980.)

Legal Aspects of Quality: Product Liability in Germany.   As in all economies, calibration of certain measurement systems, e.g., weighing scales or volumetric measure, is mandated by law and enforced by regulatory bodies.

The use of prepackaging in retail trade has deprived consumers of the opportunity to observe the measurement process in the retail shops. In consequence, a law on gaging and calibration was enacted in 1969. This law established mean values and tolerances relative to label claims. Also, the law required statistical methods of evaluation, including control of the production process by the use of control charts. Such requirements for use of statistical methods had never before appeared in a legislative document.

Another worldwide legal problem is that of product liability. All industrialized economies have a need to protect consumers and the public against injury from unsafe equipment. However, there are differences in the extent of protection, depending mainly on the nature of the laws and the jurisdiction.

Germany uses the system of "Roman jurisdiction," meaning that judges issue verdicts according to written laws or precedents. The public prosecutor and the defense attorney propose which laws, edicts, or precedents are applicable to the case under trial.

According to the edict on liability, as stated in paragraph 823 of the Bürgerliches Gesetzbuch (BGB) (Civil Law Book), one party has a liability claim against a second party when:

There has been damage to body, health, life, freedom, or property

The damage was contrary to law

The damage was caused by the action or product of the second party

The damage was done "in a guilty way"

Guilt must be proved by the party who sustained the damage.

As a result of the increasing use of complicated industrial equipment by unskilled persons, the law on Industrial Equipment, today called the Gerätesicherheitsgesetz (GSG) (Tools Safety law), was enacted in 1968. The aim was to reduce the risk of accidents during use of technical tools. GSG states:

Tools must be designed and produced in accordance with the common technical standards (those of the International Organization for Standards, German Standards Institute, Association of German Electrical Engineers, etc.).

Clear instructions must be provided on how to use the tools under realistic conditions.

If a tool causes death, injury or impaired health, the manufacturer or importer is liable.

Guilt is presumed.

The presumption of guilt means that the injured party is not required to prove guilt. This represents a considerable change in the adjudication of liability. The reason for the change is that in a complex technological society it is nearly impossible for an injured person to furnish evidence of the guilt of a manufacturer. Under the edict on liability, the injured party must establish that:

There was damage.

The damage was caused by the product.

The judge accepts such evidence as establishing a presumption of guilt. The burden of proof is then on the manufacturing company to establish its innocence by proving that everything possible was done to prevent the damage. This is difficult to prove. However, "strict liability" as practiced in some countries is not applied in Germany (see Bundesverband der deutschen Industrie (BDI), and Schlötel, 1972).

REFERENCES

Altenkirch, F. (1959). "Entwicklung und Stand der Statistischen Qualitätskontrolle (SQK) in der Bundesrepublik." *Qualitätskontrolle,* vol. 4, no. 8/9, pp. 87–89.

Altenkirch, F. (1972). "20 Jahre ASQ-Rückblick und Ausblick." *Qualität und Zuverlässigkeit,* vol. 17, no. 9, pp. 180–182.

Bundesverband der Deutschen Industrie (BDI) (1978). *Merkblatt zur "Gemeinsamen Erklärung" der Spitzenorganisationen von Industrie und Handel zur Anwendung des Gesetzes über technische Arbeitsmittel (Gerätesicherheitsgesetz—GSG).* BDI, Cologne.

Deutsche Gesellschaft für Qualität (DGQ) (1983). *Tätigkeits und Finanzbericht 1982.* DGQ, Frankfurt-am-Main.

Fuhr, H. (1980). "Warenkennzeichnung." In Masing, W. (ed.), *Handbuch der Qualitätssicherung.* Carl Hanser Verlag, Munich and Vienna.

Graf, K. and Henning, H. J. (1952). *Statistische Methoden bei textilen Untersuchungen,* Springer Verlag, Berlin.

Hoffman, J. G. (1979). *Das Interesse des Menschen und Bürgers bei den bestehenden Zunftverfassungen.* (Königsberg 1803) Kronberg.

Hüttenrauch, R. (1980). "Gebrauchstauglichkeit." In Masing, W. (ed.), *Handbuch der Qualitätssicherung.* Carl Hanser Verlag, Munich and Vienna.

Lentze, H. (1964). *Der Kaiser und die Zunftverfassung.* Scientia Verlag, Aalen.

Methner, H. (1980). "Aus- und Weiterbildung auf dem Gebiet der Qualitätssicherung." In Masing, W. (ed.), *Handbuch der Qualitätssicherung.* Carl Hanser Verlag, Munich and Vienna.

Politik in Zahlen '83 (1983). Verlag Information für die Wirtschaft, Bonn.

Schirmer, W. (1980). "Gütegemeinschaften im RAL." In Masing, W. (ed.), *Handbuch der Qualitätssicherung.* Carl Hanser Verlag, Munich and Vienna.

Schlötel, E. (1972). "Schadensersatzhaftung—Produzentenhaftung." *Qualitätskontrolle Informationen,* vol. 9, pp. 1–7.

Strauch, H. (1961). "Die Anwendung der statistischen Methoden in der modernen wissenschaftlichen Betriebsführung." *Qualitätskontrolle,* vol. 6, no. 7, pp. 72–77.

Wissell, R. (1974). *Des Alten Handwerks Recht und Gewohnheit.* Colloquium Verlag, Berlin.

SECTION 35E
QUALITY IN GREAT BRITAIN

Wilfred R. Thoday, Ph.D.

TERMINOLOGY **35E.1**

ATTITUDES AND INFLUENCES . **35E.2**

Professional 35E.3

Industrial 35E.5

Commercial 35E.6

REFERENCES **35E.6**

TERMINOLOGY

A recognition of international differences in the meanings of words we use in quality control is essential in literature that is available worldwide and in communications.

In Britain and other West European countries over the past two decades, there has been evolution and change even in meanings of fundamental terms. Close liaison is maintained with the Glossary Committee of the European Organization for Quality Control (EOQC), of which the basic working language is English, to ensure international compatibility in successive editions of the EOQC (1981) *Glossary*. The glossary now includes 17 translations of the English terms.

The EOQC Glossary Committee has been granted the status of Delegated Authority by the United Nations agency Infoterm, which is administered by the Austrian Standards Institution. Infoterm's international lexicographers are the accepted authority for all specialized terminology.

In Britain and Western Europe, the overall term used to refer to the management of quality is "quality assurance," although it is recognized that in some other parts of the world "quality control" is used as the all-embracing label. In 1972 the former term was adopted in the title of the British professional body in this field, the Institute of Quality Assurance.

The term "quality assurance" is used by the North Atlantic Treaty Organization (NATO), where key defenses documentation has the title *Allied Quality Assurance Procedures* (AQAPs). These procedures are very comprehensive, and in them quality assurance is thus regarded as all-embracing.

The British use the word "quality" in four main areas: quality of products, quality of services, quality of environment, and quality of people. While the widest internationally agreed-on definition of "quality" has the fundamental meaning of "what kind of" product or service, many other meanings are applied. These include:

Quality as a degree of excellence

Quality as fitness for purpose, used in the sense of a comparative element or sales aid

Quality as conformance to requirements, including regulations, legislation, and safety

Quality as an economic factor, the most profitable or best return on investment

For *products* the quality elements include design, manufacture, availability, and satisfaction of the need of the product. *Services* quality generally includes wherewithal and features the aspects of comfort and well-being. *Environmental quality* concerns pollution, which offends our senses, affects our health, and also wastes resources. *Quality of people* is about personal conduct but includes education, health, wealth, and the elements of so-called quality of life.

Analysis of the elements of quality reveals those that determine the quality achieved and the measures by which such achievement is recognized. Thus, the prime determinant is the user's needs, which lead to a specification and a design intended to meet them. In products, the manufacturing materials and processes are also determinants. The measures of quality are in the realms of *conformance,* that is, how well the specification and design are matched by the achievement at the conclusion of the manufacturing processes; and *performance,* or how well the user's needs and expectations are met during the life of the product.

Note that quality can only be controlled from the input side, that is, by ensuring that the determinants are correct and, if not, by making suitable adjustments or amendments. The measures, in themselves, do not control; they merely show whether control is in effect or not.

The initial achievements of quality control in Britain have been in the application of statistical techniques and, more recently, in the standardization of quality-management systems. Earlier differences between Britain, Europe, and the United States have practically disappeared. The methods and techniques of quality control and management do not differ significantly from those in other progressive Western countries. The growth of influence of multinational companies, greater ease of communication and travel, and increased competitiveness on industrial and national levels have led to uniformity of aims and methods of achievement. When unique new techniques are introduced or exotic changes are observed, they are soon absorbed by others and modified for universal application.

Most of the areas and elements of the determinants of quality are under some degree of regulation by various bodies having authority or influence.

ATTITUDES AND INFLUENCES

The principal determinants of quality are created by people, particularly their attitudes, policies, and actions generated toward quality. Also, feedback information from user complaints, guarantees and warranties, spares usage, and criticisms and compliments have their effects on quality aims. The attitudes and influences affect the determinants in various ways. For example, there are a number of consumer advisory organizations that affect the choices exercised by consumers, and therefore the "user's need" may be changed. The realms of safety and hazard have an effect on product specification, whether voluntarily or by regulation or legislation.

Production and marketing aspects have recently taken account of possible product liability litigation, with consequent influence on design and material usage. Marketeers and economists try to ensure that the quality achieved reflects value for money and adequate return on investments.

The people who create the determinants of quality are generally members of groups or bodies that fall into three main classifications: professional, industrial, and commercial.

Professional.   The professionals start with Her Majesty's Government. From the Prime Minister and through the Cabinet Office, directions are given to ministers in matters concerning the national image and performance in quality. The general intentions in the past decade seem to have been very similar despite diametrically opposite political viewpoints of those in power.

The Chancellor of the Exchequer periodically arranges "working breakfasts" for fellow ministers, with a keynote subject affecting the national economy. In early 1983 the subject was Quality and Quality Assurance, and the ministers were expected to make themselves sufficiently knowledgeable to discuss the subject effectively.

The outcome of top-level actions is the generation of legislation that affects quality practice—for example, the legal aspects of fair trading and laws on consumer protection and value for money.

There exists a Parliamentary and Scientific Committee consisting of Members of Parliament, both Commons and Lords, and representatives of institutions and industry. (The author is a member representing the Institute of Quality Assurance.) The purpose is discussion of scientific matters, which involves dialogue between Parliament and industry as to what is desirable and what is possible from both points of view.

The Ministries.   The influences arising concern various ministries, for example, the Department of Trade and Industry (formerly separate ministries and now combined). The control and encouragement on the creative side in industry and performance are seen in gross trade figures for the nation. The gross trade figures, particularly the overseas balance of payments, are regarded as a prime measure of the well-being of the national economy.

Discussion papers, in the form of ministerial white papers and green papers, are circulated to all areas concerned; they focus attention on and gather knowledge of capabilities.

In recent times promotional campaigns have been launched in the quailty sphere under the broad banner of "competitiveness." The campaign is supported by much advertising, distribution of literature, organization of seminars, and funding of specific projects, such as the establishment of a National Quality Information Centre to be undertaken by the Institute of Quality Assurance (IQA).

The government influence on the determinant side of quality is very wide. The measures of quality are reflected in the protective legislation, much of which is regulated through offices of fair trading, with final dissatisfied consumer appeals to an ombudsman. Legislation to control the broad aspects of product liability has been in preparation for many years. When enacted, it will have to at least match other European laws. Other areas of legislation that impinge on quality are those dealing with import and export controls.

Among the ministries' responsibilities are the procurement and purchasing functions, which are the largest in Britain. These include requirements for education, health, and the civil service. Further, particular ministries are effective in their special areas—for example, the Ministry of Defence in the quality control of the vast budget of armaments and the matching of NATO procedures in procurement requirements.

The structure of defense quality assurance in the United Kingdom was discussed by Harry Drew, CB, Chief Executive, Defence Quality Assurance Board, in his paper at the ASQC Conference in Washington, DC (Drew, 1972). A further paper in this area, entitled "Quality—Common International Goal—The U.K. Approach," was given by Phil Corner, Director General, Quality Assurance, of the Ministry of Defence, at the ASQC Conference in Toronto (Corner, 1976). These writers emphasize the significant influence that the high-spending government departments have on quality.

The Ministry of Education and Science not only regulates the availability of academic studies but, where necessary, makes available funds for research and development. At least two levels are promoted: the fundamental research for unique and novel ideas, and the ongoing evolution of existing ones. The motivation for much of the research is quality; for example, the work of the Transport and Road Research Laboratory has led to findings regarding safety and pollution that directly infuence future vehicle (and road) designs to improve quality in these and other characteristics. The academic establishments provide not only the educational material but also the qualifying examinations for those professionals seeking to manage the quality aspects of manufacture. In 1983 the Department of Trade and Industry published a *Directory of Quality Training and Education in the U.K.* There are 173 educational bodies listed, with details of their course offerings and qualifying examinations. (See References at end of this section.)

The Institutions.   Other professionals in quality are found in the institutions, particularly the Institute of Quality Assurance (IQA), founded in 1919, which provides the syllabus, examination, and qualification of its individual professional members. The IQA also has another division for corporate members, the British Quality Association (BQA), to provide information and service to those firms seeking knowledge of quality aims and management techniques. Other institutions, such as the Institution of Mechanical Engineers, the City and Guilds of London, and the Institution of Production Engineers, have special sections dealing with the interests and qualification of quality professionals.

Another group dealing with the training and educational aspects of quality management is the consultants. In 1983 the Department of Trade and Industry published a *Directory of Quality Assurance Consultants in the U.K.* The directory lists 213 consultants; there are four categories of organization, covering 30 different industrial specialties and 25 areas of consultancy expertise. (See References at end of this section.)

There are several major organizations whose activities bridge both the professional and industrial aspects of influence on those factors that determine quality.

The Design Council.   The Design Council, a body supported by public funds, has the basic object of encouraging improvement of designs in the United Kingdom. The improvements reflect customer appeal, safety, ease of manufacture, conservation of materials, and various other factors generally regarded as good quality.

The encouragement to better quality is general and specific. As part of its general activities, every month the Design Council selects about 100 products as the latest examples of good design, and these items are displayed at the Design

Centre. The products are selected by a panel of independent specialists from the fields of design, manufacturing, marketing, and retailing and are judged by stringent criteria covering all aspects of design, including fitness for purpose, ease of use, ease of maintenance, good appearance, and value for money. The manufacturers of the products selected by the Design Council are entitled to mark their product with a distinctive label indicating Design Centre approval.

The Design Council also publishes a list of specific design problems. Prizes are awarded for the best solutions to these problems.

The overall activity of the Design Council has a beneficial effect on the work of designers, thus contributing to the general improvement of quality.

Confederation of British Industry, British Institute of Management, and Institute of Directors. The Confederation of British Industry has a large membership of corporations in the manufacturing field and of trade associations, while membership in the British Institute of Management and the Institute of Directors is for individuals, mainly in the senior management sector of industry. Although there has been much criticism in the past that the achievement of quality has been delegated to a manager of a Quality Department, there are indications that exhortations from the Department of Trade and Industry, the three bodies mentioned above, and the British Quality Association are actively encouraging chief executives in quality leadership.

The British Standards Institution. The British Standards Institution (BSI) has made a significant contribution to quality assurance since its founding in 1901. Its work is in two divisions, under the Standards Councils and under the Quality Assurance Council.

Since the first Standard on Quality Control, BS.600 (1935), *Industrial Standardisation and Quality Control,* the Quality Assurance Council, through more than 20 committees, has produced a most comprehensive range of publications on management of quality. These publications are listed in the BSI's (1982) *Sectional List of British Standards,* SL44, which lists 30 standards in quality assurance systems. "The Role of Standards in Quality Assurance" was the title of the Fourth John Loxham lecture delivered by G. B. R. Feilden (Feilden, 1978).

The BSI also operates a supplier-assessment scheme using the Standard BS.5750, parts 1 to 6, whereby approved firms can appear on a register published by the Department of Trade and Industry. W. R. Thoday (1983) described the application of this scheme in his paper "Supplier Assessment," given at the ASQC Conference in Boston.

Product certification is also undertaken by the BSI, which issues approval marks or labels.

Industrial. Manufacturers vary in their responsibility for quality. Large corporations—and very small ones—have quality achievement vested in the top management. Medium-sized firms still largely delegate the quality function to a middle-management department. Despite much coercion from institutions, the transition to companywide quality control is very slow.

Few companies have a policy of annual improvement. Usually an improvement drive is sponsored, and once some benefit has been achieved, it is assumed that this is the limit, and the drive is ended. The large firms and the multinationals are more sophisticated, with designers responsible for failure mode and effect analysis, and Production Engineering making process capability studies to ensure minimum variability in production.

The aspects of metrology are well taken care of. An efficient British Calibration

Service operates in accordance with the national Basic Standards of the National Physical Laboratory. Independent test houses and laboratories, organized and approved under a ministry scheme, are available for control purposes.

Commercial.   The commercial interests in quality are vested in chambers of commerce, with membership of local productivity associations, trade associations, and marketing and retailing representations. The Consumers' Association regularly publishes the results of comparative product testing in their magazine *Which?* Marketing is affected by competitive advertising and public opinion expressed through the media and through selling pressures.

The area of quality is important as an economic factor in trading. Business owners, as well as financial institutions as investors, endeavor to see that quality is such as to produce best return on investment. The economic measures of quality are based on satisfaction both of the user and the producer with money judgments and with value as expressed by the equation:

$$\text{Value} = \frac{\text{quality}}{\text{cost}}$$

The professional, industrial, and commercial interests all have some particular viewpoint in quality and how it affects the volume and efficiency of their trading. They tend to act collectively to regulate quality features to their best advantage. The trade unions cover the interests of the workers and are concerned with the impact of quality matters, particularly where motivation and participation are considered, as, for example, in the work of quality circles.

The many factors involved do not all work in the same direction. Adjustment, compromise, and agreement have to be negotiated to obtain the best overall situation for each level of interest, whether nationally or individually and whether as an investor, manufacturer, or consumer.

In the United Kingdom, manufactured products already account for less than 50 percent and services for more than 50 percent of the total gross national product (GNP)—which, in financial terms, is all that we create and supply. The trend to a diminishing proportion of production and increasing proportion of services has continued over the past decade. Although this trend to predominance of services has been apparent for some time, only very recently has there been any collective attempt to organize systematic quality control techniques in this area.

Overall, one sees that quality assurance, or the control of quality, is being treated less and less as a *separate* regulatory function. The management of quality is becoming increasingly professional, and the focus on quality is being more and more integrated into the design and production functions.

REFERENCES

British Standards Institution (1982). *Sectional List of British Standards,* SL44. BSI, London. Covers general management, quality assurance, quality control, and statistics.

Corner, P. (1976). "Quality—A Common International Goal." *ASQC Technical Conference Transactions,* Toronto, pp. 432–436.

Department of Trade and Industry (1983). *Directory of Quality Assurance Consultants in the U.K.* DTI, London.

Department of Trade and Industry (1983). *Directory of Quality Training and Education in the U.K.* DTI, London.

Drew, H. E. (1972). "Defence Quality Assurance in the United Kingdom." *ASQC Technical Conference Transactions,* Washington, DC., pp. 21–28.

European Organization for Quality Control (1981). *Glossary of Terms Used in Quality Control,* 5th ed. EOQC, Bern, Switzerland.

Feilden, G. B. R. (1978). "The Role of Standards in Quality Assurance." *Quality Assurance,* vol. 4 no. 1, September.

Thoday, W. R. (1983). "Supplier Assessment." *ASQC Technical Conference Transactions,* Boston.

SECTION 35F
QUALITY IN JAPAN

Yoshio Kondo

DEVELOPMENT OF MODERN
QUALITY CONTROL IN
JAPAN . 35F.1

Introduction of Modern
Quality Control from the
United States 35F.1

Establishment of JUSE . . 35F.2

Deming Prizes 35F.2

Development of the QC
Concept into
Companywide QC . . . 35F.3

QC Circle Activities 35F.4

Quality Revolution in
Japanese Industries . . . 35F.6

COMPANYWIDE QUALITY
CONTROL IN JAPAN 35F.8

Two Basic Features of
Japanese Companywide
QC 35F.8

Companywide QC
Education and Training   35F.9

Self-control 35F.11

Policy Control ("Hoshin
Kanri") in Japanese
Companies 35F.12

Internal QC Audit by Top
Management 35F.15

QUALITY ASSURANCE AND
AND NEW-PRODUCT
DEVELOPMENT 35F.18

Customer-Oriented
Concept 35F.18

"Backward" and "Forward"
Quality 35F.19

"Fitness for Use and
Environment" and
"Surplus Quality" . . . 35F.19

Teamwork Relationship
among Departments   . 35F.20

Teamwork Relationship
with Relatively Few
Suppliers 35F.20

Quality Information—
Quality Complaints
versus Systematic and
Positive Collection of
Quality Information . . 35F.22

New-Product Development
and QC 35F.23

REFERENCES 35F.29

DEVELOPMENT OF MODERN QUALITY CONTROL IN JAPAN

Introduction of Modern Quality Control from the United States. Prior to World War II, Japanese research on and application of modern quality control

(QC) were limited. Japanese product quality was poor relative to international standards. These poor products were sold only at ridiculously low prices, but it was difficult to secure repeat sales. Among the exceptions were some Japanese companies that made high-technology products primarily for military use, but without successful application of mass production techniques.

The concepts and techniques of mdoern quality control were introduced from the United States in 1945 immediately after World War II: The first 1-week seminar on quality control was held toward the end of 1945 by W. G. Magil, Civil Information Division, General Headquarters (GHQ) of the Allied Occupation Forces, for the managers and engineers of Japanese telecommunication industries (Ishikawa, 1962). Presumably the GHQ of the Allied Forces intended to improve the quality of telecommunication service in Japan, which was indispensable for the military administration.

It was thought then that the statistical methods used in the quality control activities were very helpful, and indeed indispensable, for the reconstruction and development of Japanese industries. It should be noted that during World War II Japanese industries were almost completely destroyed. Since Japan lacks abundant natural resources and has virtually the highest population density of any country in the world, it became an overriding national priority to design and manufacture industrial products of superior quality and export them to foreign countries. Modern quality control is the most important and indispensable tool for improving and maintaining the quality of manufactured products.

Establishment of the Japanese Union of Scientists and Engineers. The Japanese Union of Scientists and Engineers (JUSE) was established in 1946 and has been at the very core of quality control activities in Japan (Kondo, 1978). This nonprofit organization, which neither receives financial support from nor is controlled by the government, was established "to contribute to human prosperity through industrial development, achieved by creating, applying, and promoting advanced science and technology." To achieve this aim, close cooperation between scientists and engineers has been emphasized, as reflected in the name of the organization [which was selected by the late Ken-ichi Koyanagi, JUSE's first managing director and the American Society for Quality Control (ASQC) Edwards medalist in 1963].

Among JUSE's early activities was the formation of the QC Research Group in 1949, which included Professors Asaka, Ishikawa, Kogure, Mizuno, Moriguchi, etc., many of whom became Deming medalists and members of the International Academy for Quality (IAQ). With these people on the teaching staff, JUSE opened a 6-month basic QC course in 1949. The course was since held 147 times through April 1983 and was attended by 18,127 engineers, who went on to provide the nucleus of QC activities in their respective companies.

A famous American, W. E. Deming, accepted the invitation of JUSE to visit Japan in 1950. He lectured at JUSE's 8-day QC courses and QC seminars for top management held in several large cities in Japan. His lectures at these seminars helped the Japanese participants to understand the importance of statistical quality control in manufacturing industries (Deming, 1982).

Deming Prizes. In recognition of Deming's friendship and contributions to Japan, the Deming Prizes were established in 1951, and JUSE serves as secretariat to the awarding committee. The Deming Prizes include the Deming Prize itself and the Deming Application Prizes. The former is awarded every year to a person whose contribution is judged outstanding in theoretical research work and in the practical application of statistical methods. Those who promote increased use of statistical methods in the industries are also eligible.

The Deming Application Prizes are awarded every year to the companies (including public enterprises) that have achieved outstanding improvement in their quality control activities by applying the concept and methods of statistical quality control. This prize also includes the prizes awarded to medium-sized and small companies and to the divisions within a company (Deming Application Prizes for Medium and Small Enterprises and for Divisions, respectively). The Deming Application Prizes provide a powerful incentive for Japanese companies to promote and achieve their quality control activities. Since their inception, the prizes have been awarded to 84 companies and three divisions. JUSE's managing director is responsible for the procedures of awarding the various Deming prizes.

In 1954, the Nippon Keizai Shimbun Co. (Japanese Economic Newspaper Co.) established the Nikkei QC Literature Prize as an award for excellent papers on statistical quality control. Award of the prize is entrusted to the Deming Prize Award Committee, and it is presented as a part of the Deming Prize award ceremony in November, which is quality month in Japan, every year.

Development of the QC Concept into Companywide QC. Statistical methods were found by Japanese engineers to be very effective for assigning causes of variation in manufacturing processes, clarifying the correlation between manufacturing conditions and product quality, reducing the work force needed for inspection by introducing sampling inspection techniques, etc. However, during the first decade after their introduction from the United States in 1945, the application of these methods was limited to the fields of manufacturing and inspection.

During this early decade, engineers in the metallurgical and chemical industries showed a keen interest in applying statistical methods to their manufacturing processes. In contrast, engineers in the mechanical, electrical, and construction industries were rather indifferent to the activities of statistical quality control. In fact, the winners of the Deming Application Prizes in this early period were steel, pharmaceutical, chemical, and other such companies.

Although the application of statistical methods to manufacturing and inspection processes yielded remarkable results in the decade following World War II, many Japanese managers and engineers started to feel that they were reaching a dead end and that a breakthrough was needed. J. M. Juran visited Japan in 1954, when JUSE held QC courses for top and middle management personnel. His lectures in these courses stimulated and accelerated the expansion of the QC concept from the above-mentioned narrow fields of manufacturing and inspection operations to operations in almost all branches of the company. Following the path shown in Juran's courses, JUSE created the QC middle management course in 1955 and the QC top management course in 1957. These courses have continued very successfully (see Ishikawa and Kondo, 1969, and Mizuno and Kume, 1978).

Teijin Co. (a synthetic fiber manufacturer) and Sumitomo Electric Industries Co. won the Deming Application Prizes in 1961 and 1962, respectively. In these companies, the quality control activities were defined broadly to include marketing, design, manufacturing, inspection, sales, and administration departments and subsidiaries; the companies achieved outstanding—even epoch-making—results, for which the prizes were awarded. Their success stimulated other Japanese companies, providing them with a very powerful incentive to broaden their quality control activities.

It is well known that the majority of customer complaints in home electric appliances, for example, are due to the defects in design and in the components.

Activities in marketing, designing, and purchasing from suppliers should be improved in order to obtain customer satisfaction. The internal quality control audit by top management started in many companies in the latter part of the 1950s, was also found to be very effective for promoting and improving companywide quality control activities.

QC Circle Activities.   The importance of the role of first-line workers has been recognized along with the progress of companywide QC; without the daily efforts of those workers, the quality of conformance of manufactured products cannot be achieved. To offer training to the workers, a 13-week short-wave radio series, "QC for the First-Line Supervisors," was planned and broadcast from October to December 1956, and it was continued by NHK (the Japan Broadcasting Corp.) until 1962. During the first year about 100,000 transcripts of the radio broadcast text were sold at newsstands. In 1959 a weekly television series on quality control was initiated. *QC Text for Foremen,* edited by K. Ishikawa, was published by JUSE in 1960, and 200,000 copies were sold before the end of 1967. Thus the education and training of supervisors and first-line workers were carried out very enthusiastically. This provided the most important basis for the birth of the QC circle movement.

In 1962, JUSE began publishing the monthly magazine *Gemba-to-QC (Quality Control for Foremen)* as a sister magazine of *Hinshitsu Kanri (Statistical Quality Control),* which began publication in 1950. This new publication aimed at:

1. Education and training, in addition to dissemination of statistical methods among the supervisors and workers
2. Formation of QC circles
3. Application of the workers' knowledge to their own daily jobs, attainment of the set target, and elevation of their own capability

To implement the second of these purposes, the QC circle members study QC activities on the shop floor by using the magazine as a textbook, and they thus become the core of the activities. The QC circle activities are the QC activities of the first-line workers on the shop floor, who are responsible for attainment of the design quality of manufactured products. A QC circle consists of a group of workers and a supervisor who voluntarily meet to solve job-oriented quality problems. These activities are intended to be tightly linked with companywide QC activities.

In May 1962, the first QC circle was registered at the QC Circle Headquarters of JUSE in Tokyo, and thereafter the number of QC circles and the number of members have been increasing year after year. The number of registered QC circles at the end of November 1982 was 148,106; registered members numbered 1,305,780.

Recognition of the daily efforts of QC circle members is important, and JUSE undertook to organize QC circle conferences for presentation of the members' case histories. The first Foremen's QC Conference was held in Tokyo in November 1962, which was the third nationwide Quality Month; 12 papers were presented and 235 foremen attended. In parallel with this annual conference, the first nationwide QC Circle Conference was held in May 1963, where 19 papers were read and 193 people attended. These conferences and local QC circle meetings have continued with great success. Mutual visits and discussions among QC circle members from different companies were also revealed to be very effective in motivating the workers and broadening their viewpoints. These visits were started in March 1963, and JUSE assists in arranging them when its services are requested.

According to the *QC Circle Koryo (General Principles of the QC Circles)*, published by JUSE in 1970, the major purposes of the QC circle movement are:

1. To improve the leadership and management abilities of the foremen and first-line supervisors in the workshop and to encourage improvement by self-development

2. To increase employee morale and simultaneously create an environment in which everyone is more conscious of quality problems and the need for improvement

3. To function as a nucleus for companywide quality control (CWQC) at the workshop level

The basic goals behind these immediate purposes are

1. To contribute to the improvement and development of the enterprise

2. To develop respect for humanity and build a happy, bright workshop, which is meaningful to work in

3. To display human capabilities fully and eventually to draw out unlimited possibilities

As recommended by Juran, JUSE has been sending foremen's QC teams composed of QC circle leaders and members abroad every year since 1968. They visit various plants in foreign countries and present papers on their own case studies in the workshop at various conferences and meetings. The QC Circle Cruising Seminar was also started in 1971; the members spend 2 weeks on a boat trip and attend seminars and discussion meetings held on the boat. They visit various countries in southeast Asia during the trip.

Regarding the major effects of QC circle activities, it can be said in the first place that the willingness, creativity, and viewpoints of first-line workers are enhanced or broadened, which results in the formation of centers of QC activities in the manufacturing process. The elevation of morale and the improvement of human relations among workers are clear. The reduction of manufacturing defects is always evident, and this brings out the elevated level of quality assurance. Thus the engineers and staff personnel can, without any worry, entrust to the supervisors and workers the greatest part of their daily duties as troubleshooters in the manufacturing line, and they can concentrate their efforts on their own proper duties (development of new products and techniques, etc.)

The present QC circle activities are further marked by the following features (Kondo, 1976, pp 71–81):

1. *Division of a QC circle into "subcircles" and "minicircles":* As study among workers progresses and their capabilities are enhanced, the QC circles are often divided into smaller circles. Some workers become the leaders of these smaller circles, to which the supervisors who were the former leaders of the larger QC circles serve as advisors and promoters.

2. *Formation of joint QC circles:* Joint QC circles are also often organized by combining QC circles along manufacturing lines or QC circles of manufacturing and inspection, etc. These joint QC circles are effective in finding and solving new quality problems.

3. *Service of workers as QC circle leaders:* Formerly, it was the custom for the supervisor to be elected as the QC circle leader. However, as the QC circle

members progressed in their studies, many of them assumed prominent leadership roles in QC circles. In many Japanese companies it became customary to rotate the leadership among the QC circle members.

4. *Establishment of autonomous administrative systems in QC circle activities:* Conferences and meetings of QC circles are always conducted by the attending members who were assigned as the session moderators. The company staff members and university professors serve only as the advisors.

5. *Expansion of QC circle themes:* The themes being chosen include not only the reduction of defects, elevation of productivity, and reduction of manufacturing and inspection costs, but also improvements in preventive maintenance jobs, the manufacturing schedule, and other aspects of production.

6. *Improvement of techniques employed:* The elementary statistical tools—stratification of samples, Pareto diagrams, checksheets, histogram, cause-and-effect diagram, graphs such as control charts, and scatter diagrams—are called the "seven tools" in QC circle activities. In addition, techniques such as regression analysis, process capability studies, analysis of variance, and value analysis are being used.

7. *QC circle activities in supporting operations:* QC circles are being formed, and their activities are becoming broader, not only in manufacturing and inspection workshops but also in supporting services such as warehousing, transportation, purchasing, administration, reception, and telephone operation. The above-mentioned statistical methods are also helpful and effective in QC circles in these areas.

8. *QC circle activities in subsidiary companies:* QC circle activities in subsidiaries that make parts and components or carry out an intermediate manufacturing process are recognized to be very important, in fact indispensable, for ensuring product quality, and parent companies are encouraging the formation of QC circles in their subsidiaries. Mutual visits and discussion among QC circle members from the parent company and from its subsidiaries are always effective in identifying and solving quality problems.

Along with the expansion of companywide quality control activities in the service industries in Japan, QC circles are becoming active and effective in companies that operate hotels, restaurants, banks, department stores, supermarkets, retail stores, etc.

Quality Revolution in Japanese Industries. Before World War II, many Japanese products had a reputation abroad for uncertain and poor quality. Today, in contrast, many Japanese products are winning a reputation for high and dependable quality and reliability. In domestic and foreign markets, it is this assured quality rather than their price that make Japanese products so competitive.

At the end of World War II, the former Japanese military and political leaders were no longer in power, having been replaced in large part by relatively young industrialists, who wanted Japan to advance as an industrialized country and not to fall back into the old agricultural economy of the type prevalent in some parts of Asia. After this decision was made, they faced a difficult road. Poor product quality was a principal obstacle; no one wanted to repeatedly buy such low-quality goods. For a country so lacking in raw materials, the inability to sell finished goods for export also meant an inability to earn foreign exchange and hence an inability to buy the materials needed to create an upward spiral of industrial development. Thus a revolution in product quality became essential (see Juran, 1981).

This quality revolution has been taking place in Japan since the early 1950s as the result of efforts to apply the concepts and techniques of statistical quality control on a companywide scale. It may be said that the Japanese cultural environment is rather favorable to the adoption and development of quality control. This can be summarized as follows.

1. The adaptability of Japanese people to foreign culture is fairly high. For example, Buddhism and Chinese characters were transplanted from mainland China more than 1000 years ago, and the Japanese modified them to fit the original Japanese culture. This adaptability has also been fully displayed in the introduction of Western culture.

2. Japan's population density is virtually the highest in the world, and the competition among companies has been intense in both domestic and international markets. Japanese managers are aware of the importance of product quality and reliability in satisfying customers and coping with this competition.

3. Japanese society is rather homogeneous, with the same race and language, and the mobility of employees is relatively low; the custom of lifetime employment is still widely prevalent. In these circumstances, Japanese companies are very enthusiastic about the education and training of employees (see Ishikawa and Kondo, 1969, and Mizuno and Kume, 1978).

4. The labor market in Japanese industries became increasingly tight in the late 1960s and early 1970s. Compared with the United States, for example, the mobility of Japanese workers has been low. Rising educational levels in Japan, furthermore, led to an increasing proportion of new labor force entrants who were unwilling to accept the least demanding jobs. Instead, the workers wanted jobs that would allow them to develop their abilities and talents. The idea of increasing job attractiveness through introduction of modern quality control and creation of participative work structures appeared to management to be one reasonable strategy that merited investment of money and efforts (Cole and Walder, 1981, p. 28).

5. The kind of professionalism that is prevalent in the Western countries has not yet been fully established in Japan. The Japanese companies needed to promote "companywide quality control," in which all employees participate (see Juran, 1978), rather than providing a large central quality department with numerous centralized functions of quality planning, coordination, and auditing. Most of these quality-oriented functions are carried out in Japanese companies by the line personnel, who have the necessary education and training for such functions. (Japanese companies have quality departments, but they are small in terms of personnel and they perform a limited array of functions, such as broad planning, audit, and consulting services.)

The First International Conference on Quality Control (ICQC) was held in 1969 in Tokyo. At this Conference, J. M. Juran delivered the following message:

It is the Japanese who have demonstrated to the world that determined people can revolutionize their quality performance, even out of the ashes of war, and can do so within the life span of a single generation. The Japanese are to be congratulated on having created this first worldwide QC Conference. By any measure, it reaches a new level of QC attainment. Never before has so distinguished an assemblage of QC experts been drawn from so many national origins to discuss so vital a range of QC subject matter. Those of us who have the good fortune to attend this historic conference are most grateful to our Japanese hosts. ICQC '69 is a monument to their vision and courage in undertaking so bold a concept, and to their competence and dedication in bringing this concept to fruition. (Chapman, 1969, pp. 28–31)

Juran (1981) summarized three features of quality control activities in Japanese industries that created the revolution in quality:

1. A massive quality-related training program
2. Annual programs of quality improvement
3. Upper management leadership of the quality function

COMPANYWIDE QUALITY CONTROL IN JAPAN

Two Basic Features of Japanese Companywide QC.   Japanese quality control activities have been gradually broadened from the narrow fields of manufacturing and inspection to almost all branches of the company. It became widely known that achievement of "fitness for use and environment" is important to ensure product quality and to secure customer satisfaction and that it is realized by improving not only the quality of conformance but also the quality of design.

The Deming Application Prizes award committee for example, defined the performance of statistical quality control as follows:

> It is the activities of designing, manufacturing and supplying the manufactured products and related service at an economic level, through which the demands of customers are satisfied, in addition to paying keen attention to public welfare. The aim of the company is to be achieved through the repetition of planning, execution, evaluation, and corrective actions by applying the statistical concept and methods to activities of survey, research, designing, purchasing, manufacturing, inspection, sales, etc., and the related activities in the inside and outside of the company.

The subjects of investigation by the committee on the candidate companies cover the activities of new-product development, basic and applied research, control of raw materials and parts, facility maintenance, management of subcontractors, education and training of employees, etc.

Quality control activities in Japanese industries were expanded in the 1960s (Ishikawa, 1965) to:

1. Establishing the top management policy on quality and the long-term QC plan of the entire company to realize the policy
2. Introducing the QC concept and techniques into new-product development
3. Establishing the quality assurance system, which covers the whole company
4. Conducting QC audits
5. Expanding QC activities to include the sales and marketing activities of the agents, the trading firms, the stores and shops, etc.

A second feature of Japanese QC is the willingness of employees to participate in the QC activities of the company. For example, the QC circle movement, discussed above, came from this idea. In Japanese companies QC activities are not restricted to QC staff but include all employees of the company, from the president to the factory workers and the salespersons. Among them, the leadership of top management is indispensable for launching and continuing the activities.

Thus the QC activities in Japanese companies, which we call "companywide QC," is a movement that involves the entire company.

Companywide QC Education and Training.   Study of and education in modern quality control were started in Japan in 1949. It was a prevailing thought then among the members of the QC Research Group in JUSE that a Japanese model of quality control should be established because of differences in background and cultural pattern between Japan and Western countries (see Ishikawa, 1972). For example, companywide quality control, in which all company employees participate, is a specifically Japanese approach; the concept of professionalism, which is rather widespread in Western countries, had not yet been established in Japan as of 1949.

Introduction and promotion of companywide quality control led to a revolution in management philosophy, which required lengthy, persevering efforts in education and training. Thus, since the early 1950's education and training in quality control have been continued for everyone from top management to first-line workers in each and every department, including research and development, designing, manufacturing, inspection, purchasing, marketing, sales, and administration. As an example, training courses that have been held by JUSE are summarized in Table 35F.1.

Currently there are more than 40 quality control training courses of different kinds, which are held regularly by nonprofit organizations such as JUSE and the Japanese Standards Association (JSA). (See Section 11, Table 11.18, for a more recent list of JUSE courses.)

Furthermore, many Japanese companies are enthusiastic about quality control education for the employees of both the parent company and the subsidiaries. Many subsidiaries have their own training programs. Education and training in companywide quality control usually start with top management and are then extended to middle management, supervisors, and first-line workers. It is often emphasized that the progress of companywide quality control exactly reflects the leadership of the company's top management.

On-the-job training is also emphasized. One example is the training that results from internal QC audits by top management, which are effective in obtaining the facts within the company and lead to appropriate corrective actions. Another example is the on-the-job training of engineers. Concerning the training of engineers who design color television sets, Juran (1978, pp. 10–18) commented as follows:

A second aspect of training of designers is "practical experience." One major area for such experience is in the production shop, to give the designer an awareness of some of the realities faced by the production personnel and thereby to give him a better understanding of how to design for "producibility." A second major area for designer experience acquisition is in field service work. Through such experience, the designer learns much about the conditions of use, the problems of diagnosing field failures, the difficulties of making repairs, etc. As a result, he understands better how to design for reliability and maintainability.

With respect to such "training by practical experience," there are wide differences between Japan and the West. It is common, though not invariable, for Japanese companies to require that designers acquire such shop and field experience before being assigned to key responsibilities in product design. In the West the requirement for such experience is unusual.

A third area of designer training is in the quality control disciplines—variation, sampling, reliability analysis, design of experiment and analysis of variance, Weibull analysis, etc. In Japan it is the rule that designers must receive such training. In one published account (Ishikawa, 1969), the training courses for those in charge of design and research add up to 144 hours in length. In the West such training programs are

TABLE 35F.1 Education and Training Courses of JUSE

Title	Term	Frequency per year	Number of attendants (cumulative to March 1978)	Date established
Quality control				
Top Management Course	4 days	2 courses	1,357	1957
Executive Course	5 days	2 courses	1,706	1962
Middle Management Course	12 days	6 courses	14,350	1955
Basic Course	30 days	4 courses	14,625	1949
Elementary Course	8 days	6 courses	13,335	1956
TQC Instructor Course	6 days	1 course	103	1976
Course for Sales Dept.	15 days	1 course	563	1968
Elementary Course for Sales	4 days	2 courses	503	1974
Course for Procurement Dept.	15 days	1 course	331	1970
Basic Course for Foremen	6 days	10 courses	14,426	1967
Basic Course for Group Leaders	3 days	5 courses	574	1974
Top Management Course on QC Circles	2 days	2 courses	262	1973
QC Circle Instructor Course	6 days	4 courses	1,393	1972
Correspondence Course	6 months	2 courses	24,514	1971
QC Circle Cruising Seminar	15 days	1 course	2,044	1971
Product Liability Prevention Seminar	4 days	1 course	151	1973
Computer application				
Computer Programming Seminar	9 days	1 course	1,200	1959
Reliability Management Course	4 days	1 course	610	1966
Basic Course	15 days	2 courses	1,805	1960
Elementary Course	4 days	2 courses	1,573	1962
Design of experiment				
DE Seminar	30 days	2 courses	2,795	1955
Elementary Course	8 days	2 courses	2,099	1961
Multivariate Analysis	6 days	2 courses	673	1970
Sensory Test Seminar	11 days	1 course	1,132	1963
Statistical Methods Course for Clinical Test	7 days	1 course	433	1972
Operations research (OR)				
Management Course	8 days	1 course	1,611	1962
OR Seminar	30 days	2 courses	4,832	1953
Market research (MR)				
MR Seminar	17 days	1 course	1,203	1951
Industrial engineering (IE)				
E Seminar	16 days	1 course	685	1963
Basic Course for Foremen	6 days	4 courses	1,331	1971

available but are rarely mandated. Some companies provide a climate which is favorable for designers to take such courses, but progress has been slow. In fact, many designers whose skills lie in the scientific and engineering disciplines remain scornful of the statistical discipline.

For the above-mentioned purposes of broadening the viewpoint of designers and engineers, job rotation of employees is also emphasized in Japanese companies. The lack of established professionalism in Japanese society is thought favorable for this rotation.

The large-scale and intensive training of supervisors and workers was an indispensable prerequisite for the birth and development of the QC circle movement in Japan, as mentioned earlier. In addition, the managers actively support QC circle activities in the company by providing the place and time for QC circle meetings, the required budget, etc., as well as by explaining the top policy on companywide QC, including QC circle activities.

It was reported (Kondo, 1976) that a top manager of an automobile company in Japan always accompanied the workers of his company to QC circle conferences. In addition, he stayed in the same accommodations as the workers during the conferences and discussed very frankly with them their present quality problems, his own intentions with regard to the future of the company, etc. It goes without saying that his positive attitude motivated the workers immensely.

Self-Control.   It is widely accepted in Japanese industries that the control process follows the so-called Deming's cycle, which is composed of the four steps plan, do, check, and act, as shown in Figure 35F.1a. The objective (or standard) and the process should be established before doing the work. The results are then checked by comparing them with the standard. Corrective actions are taken when any significant difference is found after evaluation. By following this plan-do-check-act (PDCA) cycle, it is expected that not only the results obtained but also the process itself will be improved in an upward spiral. This leads to improvement and strengthening of the company structure.

In some forms of manufacturing planning, the quality standard and operations manual are established by the engineering staff and management, and the workers are only requested to perform their jobs in accordance with the established manual. Thus the planning and execution are separated.

In such cases, if manufactured products are found to be defective, the supervisor may seek the causes and reproach a worker. The worker may then reply, "I

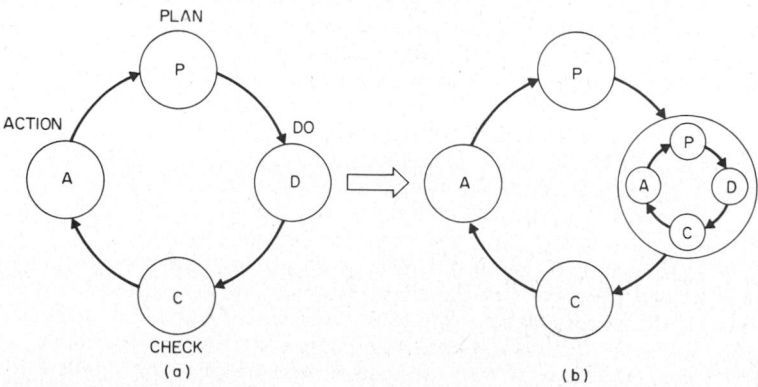

FIG. 35F.1   Deming's cycle.

am not responsible for the defect. I honestly followed the operation manual that you gave me. You are responsible for the result." It is clear that when workers are responsible only for following the established manual, their responsibility for quality becomes obscure. Such vague responsibility is detrimental to high quaility of conformance, which is achieved only if the workers are conscious of quality and have a keen sense of responsibility.

It is true that the workers are assigned to perform the manufacturing job. However, this job performance is also composed of a plan-do-check-act cycle, as shown in Figure 35F.1*b*. The extent to which Deming's cycle is followed in this portion of the overall job is considered to reflect the self-control of workers. Everyone is in a state of self-control to a greater or lesser extent. Thanks to this ability of self-control, we humans can enjoy our lives, including sports and leisure. Of course, education and training are to a certain extent necessary to cultivate the self-control capacity of the workers. The criteria for self-control are discussed elsewhere in this handbook. See Section 17 under Concept of Controllability.

Policy Control ("Hoshin Kanri") in Japanese Companies.   Quality control activity in Japanese industries is companywide, and top management personnel are in the position of leading and promoting the quality control activities of their companies. They are responsible for deciding top policy on quality of manufactured products and service and for establishing the long-term plan of companywide quality control in order to realize that policy. In addition, they evaluate whether the policy and the plan are being realized on schedule and whether any corrective actions need to be taken by top management. These activities are a form of companywide Deming's cycle and are called "policy control" ("hoshin kanri") in Japanese industries. Internal quality control audits by top management, which will be described later, are an effective way to evaluate the results as a basis for appropriate corrective actions. (This concept of policy control is followed in many but not all Japanese companies.)

Recently, many Japanese companies have undertaken to investigate and decide at the start of every fiscal year what their long-term plans and targets will be for the coming 3 to 5 years, the plan and target for the first year being set to coincide with the present fiscal year. In this way, long-term plans are taken into consideration in establishing each annual or semiannual plan and target.

It is widely understood that planning should be results-oriented rather than procedure-oriented. For example, a plan to extend standardization might at the end of the year have produced 100 new procedure manuals. If all this effort failed to improve operating results, this would be evidence that the plan had been procedure-oriented.

At the investigation and discussion stage of the draft annual plan, the persons concerned are encouraged to offer many alternative proposals. It is of great importance at this stage to discuss thoroughly the true aim of the proposals and to clarify the "resultant present problem." The above-mentioned extension of standardization is merely a procedure. The high percentage of defects and rework, low productivity and yield, etc., are the resultant present problems. After the resultant problems become clear, data are collected and analyzed. The "vital few" problems can be further determined with a Pareto diagram. Two-stage Pareto analysis always makes the problems and the corrective actions clearer.

Goals should be inspiring; if not, people do not give them serious attention, and they are not achieved. Two Japanese examples are given here.

At the Car Radio Division of Matsushita Electric Industries Co., engineers and staff personnel up to the division manager were discussing an unattained goal of 10 percent cost reduction for a car radio as requested by an automobile company.

When former President Matsushita visited the division, he was told of the situation. He said, "You should consider 15 percent cost reduction when you are requested by a customer to reduce the cost by 10 percent." Because he was the founder of the company and is esteemed as a "godfather" by all employees, they started to investigate cost reduction possibilities more thoroughly and finally achieved a 13 percent reduction. After hearing of this success, Mr. Matsushita visited the automobile company and expressed his appreciation by saying, "Thanks to your request for a 10 percent cost reduction, we have succeeded in achieving a 13 percent cost reduction. Thank you very much for that."

At the Nankai Plant of Bando Chemical Co. near Osaka, where V-shaped belts are manufactured, it was previously the custom for the plant manager to announce the monthly production target and to urge the supervisors and workers to achieve this target. However, the target was never achieved even though the employees exerted all possible efforts, especially toward the end of every month. On the advice of an outside consultant, the plant management changed the procedure for determining the monthly target by having the plant manager prepare a draft target and ask the supervisors and workers in every workshop to thoroughly investigate the possibility and the ways and means of attaining the target. In the early stage of this revised procedure, the sum of the individual targets proposed by the supervisors was more demanding than the draft target indicated by the manager. The plant manager, however, established the supervisors' proposals as the targets of the month because they were the result of their thorough investigations. Interestingly, the supervisors always achieved their targets. Moreover, a few months later the overall target proposed by the supervisors and employees started to rise month after month, and in half a year or so it even exceeded the previously unmet target of the manager.

There are two ways of determining the target, from the top down and from the bottom up. The example of Matsushita is top-down, and the case of Bando is bottom-up. Both of these were very successful. Top management is always concerned about the future of the company, and the top-down target is usually determined from the company's needs. On the other hand, the employees usually investigate the draft target indicated by the top management from the viewpoint of feasibility. If the draft target is not investigated thoroughly by the employees, they easily find their own good excuses when it is not achieved.

Many Japanese companies, during annual or semiannual planning, adopt a combination of top-down and bottom-up approaches. Top management prepares a draft plan, which then is discussed, for example, among the top managers and the division managers. From this discussion the draft plans of each division are made. The draft plan of each division is then further discussed among the divisional and lower managers and finally among the supervisors and the QC circle leaders. After these investigations and discussions, the detailed draft plans are formulated. They are brought to the top management, which decides on the final annual plan of the company. This procedure of diffusing the annual or semiannual planning throughout the company is called "playing catch" in Japanese companies. The procedure is believed to be effective in establishing the annual plan, although it is somewhat time-consuming. Through this procedure, what was a norm enforced by top management is revised to become the voluntary target of each employee. This revision is extremely important for motivation.

The establishment of results-oriented plans makes evaluation easier, the characteristics used in the targets become the basis for review by the respective managers. Corrective actions are cooperative. When it becomes clear that a target will not be achieved, for example, companies often assign an additional budget, work force, etc. in order to attain the target within the time limit. Although this may be called a type of corrective action, it is actually a superficial countermeasure, or adjustment. A matter of greater importance is to detect the assignable causes by which failures, defects, rework, delays, etc. are created and to remove them from the process. This is the action of "cause removal," which is essential for improving the basic process.

An example of the breakdown of a broad goal into subgoals is that of Komatsu Ltd., a manufacturer of construction machinery. This company originated the "flag diagram" by skillfully combining the Pareto and Ishikawa diagrams (see Kondo, 1977). An example is shown in Figure 35F.2. This diagram shows

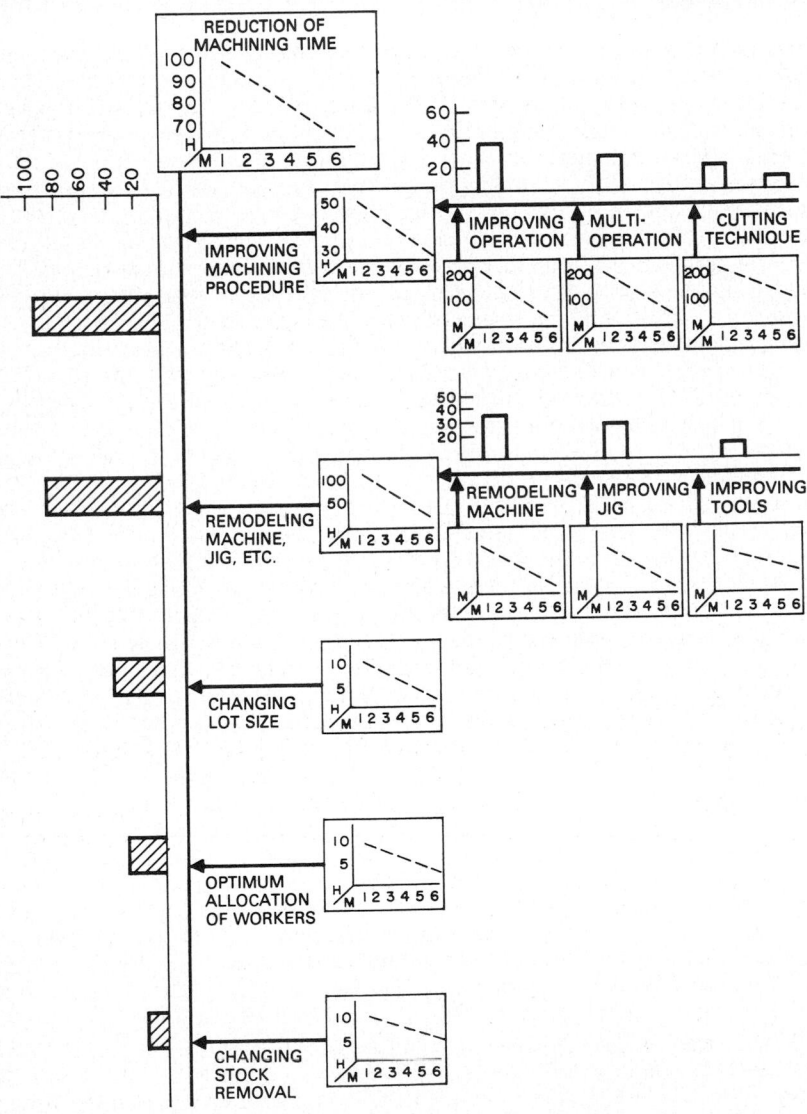

FIG. 35F.2 An example of a "flag diagram."

machining time classified into several major items according to the Pareto principle. Each item is further broken down into the respective secondary items. The target line is drawn in the diagram of each item. The subsequent performance is also plotted in the same diagram and compared with the respective target. Each diagram becomes an item for review by the responsible manager and for appropriate corrective action in the event of significant deviations in performance. Such diagrams make it easier for all employees involved to understand their own situations, the roles of their colleagues, and the interrelationship among them. Such understanding contributes to the common interest. New and worthwhile ideas are born from discussions among employees who have common interests and yet can see the problems from different viewpoints.

Internal QC Audit by Top Management.   Internal QC audit by top management is one of the outstanding features of Japanese companywide quality control (Kondo, 1969). It is carried out in ways similar to the activities of checking and taking corrective actions in the policy control discussed above. The aim of this internal QC audit differs from that of the external audit—it is not merely for the employees "to pass the examination" but to stimulate mutual discussion between the auditors and the people involved in order to find ways and means to improve the present situation. Corrective actions on both sides are required. Thus the internal audit is educational in character, involving on-the-job training as well as the survey itself. It may be defined as follows: Internal QC audit is a study of the present situation regarding the system of companywide QC and the quality functions of the whole processes in order to find and take the necessary corrective actions. This is the reason why many Japanese companies prefer to call the internal QC audit the QC "diagnosis" or the "discussion meeting of [those performing] QC activities with top management."

The procedure of carrying out the internal audit is not fixed, but is flexible according to the situation of the division, the department, the plant, or the branch office audited. It is also flexible according to the kind of internal audit being undertaken in the company; usually a company has a few kinds of audit at different levels, as will be mentioned below.

The top managers of a Japanese company are in the position of leading and promoting the company's QC activities. They are responsible for determining the top policy on the quality of products and services and also for establishing the long-term QC plan in order to realize that policy. The aim of the internal audit is to determine whether the policy and the plan are being realized and attained on schedule and whether any corrective actions by top management are needed.

Mizuno (1967, pp. 835–839) explained the aim of the audit as follows:

> It is essentially desirable in the QC function that effective daily checks be made and that the important quality problems in the company be pinpointed in order to take corrective actions. However, it is embarrassing for a company to remain unaware of the problems involved. The aim of the internal audit is to investigate and analyze systematically the hidden causes of those quality problems that cannot be detected by daily checking. Because the audit in any form is an energy-consuming job, it is a must for the auditors and the coordinators to pursue resultant benefits that are worthy of the input energy.

The educational character of the audit is considerable. The audit offers the best chance for top management to grasp systematically those facts that may reflect on themselves. The employees audited are also given opportunities to examine and to rearrange their daily work. Moreover, the internal audit contributes to the improvement of mutual understanding and human relations among the employees. Such an opportunity can hardly be obtained through the daily meetings and reports. For these reasons, it is often effective to announce beforehand the audit theme and the checklist being used in the audit.

The audit is usually carried out in either of the following ways: In some companies the audit is done by the president and by the members of the board of directors separately; in other companies it is done by a top management team that includes the president. In the audit by the directors, the emphasis is usually laid on the general management of the company. In the audit by the management team, there is usually more emphasis on specifics than in the audit by the directors. The two audits are planned to be correlated with each other. Usually, the auditors are accompanied by QC staff members and sometimes by a university professor as a third party. The audit is done either with or without a predetermined theme. When the theme of the audit is not determined beforehand, it usually covers a wide range of items.

At Toshiba Electric Company, for example, it was reported (Sugimoto, 1968, pp. 1136–1140) that the following items were checked by the president during the plant tour:

1. Putting the shop in order—its cleanliness and working environment
2. Layout of the shop and the machines
3. Flow of materials and the line balance
4. Material handling
5. Operation standards
6. Efficient use of jigs and tools, mechanization, and automation
7. Maintenance of machines and measuring instruments
8. Inventories of on-line stocks, materials, and parts
9. Attitude and motivation of workers
10. Administration of storehouse
11. Reducing the number of slips and chits
12. Content and worker-hours of indirect work
13. Production control
14. Quality assurance
15. Supervision of subcontractors
16. Maintenance of buildings, roads, and incidental facilities

During the discussion after the plant tour, the following items were considered:

1. Profit and loss in production operations
2. Cost reduction in production operations
3. Productivity per worker and number of direct and indirect employees
4. Improving productivity
5. Value added in the manufacturing process
6. Dependence on subcontractors
7. Amount of inventory
8. Investment for manufacturing facilities

   9. Reduction of defects
   10. Development of new products and techniques
   11. Mechanization and automation
   12. Standardization
   13. Actual planning for realizing items 1 to 12

The discussion was concentrated on how to double productivity within 5 years.

When experienced auditors are not available, an audit covering such a wide range of topics tends to become a loose and formalistic one, which cannot be effective. This is why the audit with a predetermined theme is preferred in many companies; these audits become more intensive. There is also a prevailing tendency for the audit to develop from a departmental one into a functional one, with emphasis being given to the functional interrelationship among departments.

Usually the internal QC audit is done once or twice a year. This is because it is related to annual or semiannual planning of the company ("policy control"); the schedule of the audit parallels that of the planning.

The auditors often request a short report explaining the current situation of the department that is to undergo audit. This report enables the reporters ("auditees") to rearrange their ideas in a proper form. Although a checklist is sometimes prepared, the audit items do not always follow it. Since this checklist summarizes the ideas and the points of the audit, it is often effective to announce it before the audit.

Although the way of carrying out the audit is flexible, it usually includes a plant tour and a roundtable discussion, which takes place after presentation of the report about the current situation of the department. It is essential during the plant tour for the members of the auditing team to be very observant in order not to miss any details. To walk through the entire manufacturing process, from the storehouse to the final inspection, for example, is an effective way to locate and "shoot" the troubles. It is also important for the top managers to talk to the supervisors and workers to encourage and motivate them; the audit offers a golden opportunity for conversation between them, which can hardly occur in the course of daily work. Sugimoto (1968) reported that a young worker at Toshiba Electric Company wrote a letter to the president after an audit saying that she would welcome him to her workshop again because she sincerely wished to have a chance to talk to him.

Concerning the short report that is read before the discussion, it is advisable to review the actions taken by the department on comments and recommendations made at the preceding audits. The discussion based on the report and on the facts observed during the plant tour is the most important part of the audit.

After the discussion, comments and recommendations are summarized and announced by the leader of the auditing team. The consultant (often a university professor) also contributes suggestions. In addition to the recommendations that the department take corrective actions, the statement should include the recommendations made for actions by the auditors. It is also important to include not only the faults but also the merits in the performance of the department under audit. Of course, the recommendations made should be seriously considered by the department audited, and the results should be checked at subsequent audits (Itoh, 1974).

A study in one company reported that the content of 90 percent of the comments was in line with the opinions of the workers audited and that of the remaining 10 percent was different. Two-thirds of the employees welcomed the audit, while the others felt that the audit was troublesome although necessary (Murata, 1968). These figures, of course, are merely from one example.

The effectiveness of the internal QC audit should be evaluated from the standpoint of whether the aim of the audit is accomplished or not. That aim is to see whether the top policy on quality is being disseminated and the long-term QC plan realized; whether the attitude of top management toward the QC concept and function penetrates the minds of all employees; and whether the concept and policies of top management are adequate or not. It is also imperative for top management to take corrective actions based on the results of the audit.

It is difficult to evaluate independently the effectiveness of the internal QC audit. However, the number of Japanese companies using the internal audit has increased in the last 20 years, and the way of conducting the audit is continually being improved.

Comments on the internal QC audit are cited from an issue of *Hinshitsu Kanri (Statistical Quality Control),* published by JUSE (Murata, 1968, p. 300).

1. By doing the internal audit, the communication and the cooperation between top and bottom and between departments of the company are improved. The policies become consistent.

2. Troubles remaining unsolved between departments are taken up and pursued in the audit, and cooperation is improved.

3. Internal QC audit offers both to top management and to employees a chance to examine their own daily work.

4. Members of the board of directors can observe the stiuation throughout the company and they are offered a chance to establish direct contact with the workers.

5. Internal QC audit contributes greatly to the management of the company. It can be said that the audit is a part of the management process.

6. Employee morale is improved by the audit.

The audit is also effective for improving human relations within the company.

On the other hand, the audit may become superficial and lapse into some mere formality if it tends to be rigid and routine. Recommendations to avoid this are:

Modify the manner of doing the audit.

Do the audit on a predetermined theme.

Rotate the members of the audit team.

It sometimes happens in the report that the department manager tends to "blow his own horn." The audit teams should avoid being overinfluenced by this; they should base their report on the facts. The audit may also contribute to a breakthrough in performance, since new facts that may be uncovered often point the way.

QUALITY ASSURANCE AND NEW-PRODUCT DEVELOPMENT

Customer-Oriented Concept.   Quality assurance is the most important companywide quality control activity in Japanese companies. The general concept and activities of quality assurance are discussed in Section 9 of this handbook. Several features of the Japanese approach are discussed below.

The first Japanese emphasis is on the requirement that the activities of quality assurance be customer-oriented. While this concept is well known, it is quite common for companies to judge the adequacy of their quality assurance by the amount paid out as a result of customer complaints. In effect, that consists of judging the adequacy of quality assurance by the cost to the company rather than the cost to the customer.

The "user's quality cost," as discussed by Gryna (1976), was introduced and evaluated by a few home electric appliance companies in Japan. The user's quality cost takes account of customer demand and is based on a customer-oriented approach. However, although this user's cost concept is useful, it fails to take account of certain other aspects of customer satisfaction which are not quantifiable in monetary terms but are nevertheless influential in creating customer confidence.

"Backward" and "Forward" Quality.   Ishikawa (1978) prefers to classify product quality as "backward" and "forward" quality. In the evolution of modern quality assurance methods, the early practice of 100 percent inspection gave way to process improvements to avoid manufacture of defective products in the first place. If this reduces defect levels to zero, it solves the problem of short-term customer dissatisfaction but not necessarily the problem of customer satisfaction, i.e., fitness for use. Solution of this problem requires market surveys to obtain the facts from the users.

Takenaka Komuten, a Japanese construction company, made extensive process improvements and succeeded in greatly reducing defects such as cracks in concrete or water leaks. They raised the question: Is this enough to satisfy our customers? To learn the answer, they visited and surveyed the hospitals they had designed and built. During these interviews, they learned for the first time, for example, that nurses encountered daily troubles with the hospital facilities; that patients on the window side complained of the traffic noise and wished to be moved to quieter rooms; and that serious problems with maintenance of air conditioners were found early every summer. (All this had been going on despite the fact that the hospital director and some physicians were very satisfied with the building and facilities.) The findings were promptly reported to the design department, which took action to revise the design manuals and checklists. This in turn resulted in a remarkable increase in the company's share of the hospital construction market.

"Fitness for Use and Environment" and "Surplus Quality."   In Japan the concept of fitness for use is enlarged to include fitness for the environment. For example, room air conditioners are used extensively in the densely populated Japanese cities. Beyond the need for comfortable temperature and humidity are the requirements of quiet operation and low consumption of electricity. Some of the complaints about air conditioners come from neighbors who are disturbed by the noise.

Another problem is that of "surplus quality," which is associated with higher quality of design. A delicate balance must be struck between achievement of higher quality and the associated costs. Thus, conflicting pressures result from the desire to reduce costs and the desire to elevate the technological level of the company and its associated capability for new-product development.

During the 1970s, Japanese television makers requested the manufacturers of electronic components to reduce defect levels below 10 per million. It took a great deal of effort to meet this request, but the result has been beautiful pictures on Japanese television sets, which are extremely reliable.

Teamwork Relationship among Departments.   In order to achieve the goal of quality assurance, it is important, even indispensable, first to improve the quality of design to meet the target of fitness for use and environment. Second, the quality of manufactured products should be in conformance with this quality of design.

Although this procedure for assuring product quality is accepted, another general rule emphasized in Japan is teamwork among all departments. In other words, the cycle of plan-do-check-act should be rotated to involve marketing, design, manufacture, inspection, and sales. A slogan to the effect that the successive processes are the "guest customers" prevails in Japanese industries. It can be said, in line with this slogan, that not only are the customers of the design department the final customers in the market but so are the personnel in the successive processes of manufacturing, inspection, transportation, distribution, sales, etc.

The feedback of data from these processes to the design department and their utilization for the improvement of design quality are indispensable for achievement of customer satisfaction in the successive processes. For example, studies of process capability in the manufacturing processes and feedback of the data obtained to the design department are of basic importance. When process capability is inadequate relative to design tolerances, either the manufacturing process itself should be improved or the quality specification should be carefully reexamined and investigated as to whether or not it can be broadened to meet customer demand for product quality and reliability.

Teamwork Relationship with Relatively Few Suppliers.   The quality and reliability of modern complex products depend heavily on the quality and reliability of components and parts. This product quality cannot be assured solely by 100 percent inspection. Japanese manufacturers have been trying to establish and maintain a cooperative relationship with their suppliers in order to improve and assure component quality.

The establishment of teamwork relationships starts with the selection of suppliers. Questionnaires are distributed and visits made, and the suppliers are screened on the basis of financial status, facilities, basic ideas and policies of top management, enthusiasm for quality improvement, level of education and training of employees, etc. Large Japanese companies usually have an established procedure for this selection and a standardized checklist.

Good teamwork relationships with suppliers is based on mutual trust and confidence and cannot usually be established in the short term; it takes at least a few years. Importance is attached to the basic philosophy and the enthusiasm of the top management personnel. Because of the smaller size of the supplier companies, QC activities and product quality and reliability are rather rapidly improved under the positive leadership of their top management. Independent ideas and attitudes of the suppliers are emphasized, rather than a dependent relationship to the purchasing company. Positive guidance and QC educational services are made unsparingly available by the company on the understanding that voluntary efforts will be made by the suppliers. The importance of education and training—which become more effective in the relatively long term—is emphasized.

There is a recent trend in Japan for smaller manufacturers of components and parts to have their own test laboratories for these components so as to ensure that their quality and reliability are adequate before permitting the design department of the purchaser to specify them for use in the final manufactured products. Such test laboratory activities by the parts manufacturers are also effective in the development of new products of their own. It is fairly common in Japan for data on process capability index and manufacturing process control charts in supplier organizations to be sent to the purchasing company and utilized in the manufacturing, inspection, and design departments in addition to the QC department. Internal QC audit by top management is voluntarily carried out by the suppliers. In this audit, appropriate representatives of the purchasing company as an outside authority are sometimes invited to attend the audit and express comments.

In Japanese industries, parts per million (ppm) is often used as a unit of measure for product quality. In such cases, application of the acceptable quality level (AQL) concept is useless. Instead, quality and reliability tests (such as overstressing or environmental testing) are made in the design qualification stages in order to reveal component weaknesses and defects. Furthermore, the failure modes are thoroughly investigated so that remedial action by cause removal can be taken. During manufacturing, freedom from defects can be assured down to the parts per million level by the very high process capability index, and defects can be detected by automated sorting.

"Ten Principles for Vendee-Vendor Relations from the Standpoint of Quality Control" were established in 1966 and presented by Ishikawa (1969*b*) at ICQC 1969 Tokyo as follows:

Preface: Both vendee and vendor should have mutual confidence, cooperation, and high resolve of "live and let live" based on the responsibilities of enterprises for the public. Following the above spirit, both parties should sincerely practice the following "Ten Principles."

Principle 1: Both vendee and vendor are fully responsible for Quality Control application with mutual understanding and cooperation on their Quality Control systems.

Principle 2: Both vendee and vendor should be independent of each other, and esteem the independence of the other party.

Principle 3: Vendee is responsible to bring clear and adequate information and requirements to the vendor, so that the vendor can understand what he should manufacture.

Principle 4: Both vendee and vendor, before entering into business transactions, should conclude a rational contract between them in respect of quality, quantity, price, delivery term, and terms of payment.

Principle 5: Vendor is responsible for the assurance of quality that will give full satisfaction to vendee. And he is also responsible for submitting necessary and actual data upon the vendee's request, if necessary.

Principle 6: Both vendee and vendor should decide the evaluation method of various items beforehand, which will be admitted as satisfactory to both parties.

Principle 7: Both vendee and vendor should establish in their contract the systems and procedures through which they can reach amicable settlement of disputes whenever any problems occur.

Principle 8: Both vendee and vendor, taking into consideration the other party's standing, should exchange information necessary to carry out better Quality Control.

Principle 9: Both vendee and vendor should always perform control business activities sufficiently, such as on ordering, production and inventory planning, clerical work, and systems, so that their relationship is maintained upon an amicable and satisfactory basis.

Principle 10: Both vendee and vendor, when dealing with business transactions, should always take full account of consumer's interest.

These principles were formulated through enthusiastic cooperation and thorough discussions among purchasers and suppliers. Their meaning is obvious, although they have not always been adhered to. It is hoped that they will further be utilized as much as possible as a basic guideline for improving the purchaser-supplier relationship.

Quality Information—Quality Complaint versus Systematic and Positive Collection of Quality Information.   In a paper on quality design, Aiba (1966) emphasized the importance of securing external quality information from customers in the marketplace. Such raw information is then converted into measurable quality characteristics.

In this connection, external quality complaints, while demanding prompt and remedial action, are collectively a poor index of quality. They reflect "backward" quality—the negative quality of product dissatisfaction. The need is to go further and to collect positive information on the following:

1. Customer demands, i.e., how the commodities are used by the customers and the conditions of use

2. Quality of similar commodities manufactured by competitors

3. Actual conditions of transportation and storage by distributors' channel and retailers

4. Present and future market trends

At the Cotton Underwear Division of Gunze Co., Japan, the division director received a letter from an elderly male customer expressing his hearty appreciation for the excellent quality and durability of Gunze cotton underwear, of which he had been wearing the same articles for more than 10 years. This customer also urged the director to develop new products of such high durability. The director requested a consultant's opinion about the development of such new products. The consultant asked, "How long do customers usually wear your underwear?" Since the division had not investigated the life span of the underwear, it conducted a market survey. When the results were summarized in the form of a histogram, the distribution of life span clearly was well approximated by a normal distribution curve, with a mean of about 3 years and a standard deviation of about 0.5 years. It became evident from this histogram that the number of customers who continue to wear the same underwear for longer than 4.5 years was 1 to 2 per 1000. The data suggested that the market for a new product of much higher durability was very limited.

To avoid possible adverse consequences of reacting to sporadic customer information, it is necessary to collect market quality information on a systematic basis. Such systematic collection is comparatively easy for products of high unit price, as in the case of Takenaka Komuten construction company, mentioned earlier. With products of low unit price, some ingenious methods are necessary. A questionnaire card is often enclosed with the product asking customers their reasons for purchasing, the name of the retailer, impressions of product performance, conditions of use, etc. In Japan customers usually mail this card immediately after their purchase and before using the product. Hence their comments about quality and reliability are meaningless. Furthermore, only a small proportion of the cards are usually sent back to the manufacturer. A better way is to utilize the returned cards to design followup surveys and then to apply sampling techniques based on types of customers and conditions prevailing during use. Interviews with the customers are usually far more fruitful than mailed questionnaires.

New-Product Development and QC.   In many Japanese companies new products are classified into the following groups on the basis of their novelty:

1. New in the world
2. New in Japan
3. New in the company
4. Model change of a current product, etc.

Such a classification is effective for determining the steps and stresses in new product development. For a new product of class 1, the quality, including safety, and the reliability should be most strictly assured even though time and money are needed. The new users of these products should also be broadly pursued and developed. In contrast, for new products of classes 3 and 4, the emphasis is on promptness, so that product development cycle time can be shortened in order to cope with competition in the market.

During quality design, there is a need for conversion of true quality characteristics requested by customers into measurable substitute characteristics. The quality table (Takayanagi, 1973) was developed for this purpose and is being widely used in Japan. This is a diagram that illustrates the relationship between true quality characteristics and measurable substitute characteristics. An example is shown in Figure 35F.3. After converting the true quality characteristics (level 1) into the measurable substitute characteristics (levels 3 and 4), it becomes easier to determine the quality specifications for each item. The quality table has been further expanded to the quality conversion table, in which both the true quality characteristics and the measurable substitute characteristics are presented and correlated with each other in a two-dimensional matrix. An example is shown in Figure 35F.4.

The measurable substitute characteristics that evolve (from the true quality characteristics demanded by the customers) become the focus of various checkpoints in the manufacturing and inspection processes. During the design and pilot stages of the manufacturing process, a "QC process chart" is established for assurance of quality in the manufacturing process. Figure 35F.5 shows an example of such a process chart, which, as may be seen, uses the substitute characteristics. Thus the quality function is implemented throughout the whole company (see Kogure and Akao, 1983).

The steps in new-product development are roughly as follows:

1. Market research
2. Conceptualization
3. Experiments, market research
4. Application for patent
5. Quality design
6. Pilot-scale manufacturing and qualification testing
7. Process design
8. Full-scale production testing and test sales
9. Mass production

These steps and the company departments involved may be summarized by a chart of the quality assurance system, an example of which is shown in Figure 35F.6. This chart will vary with the novelty of the products.

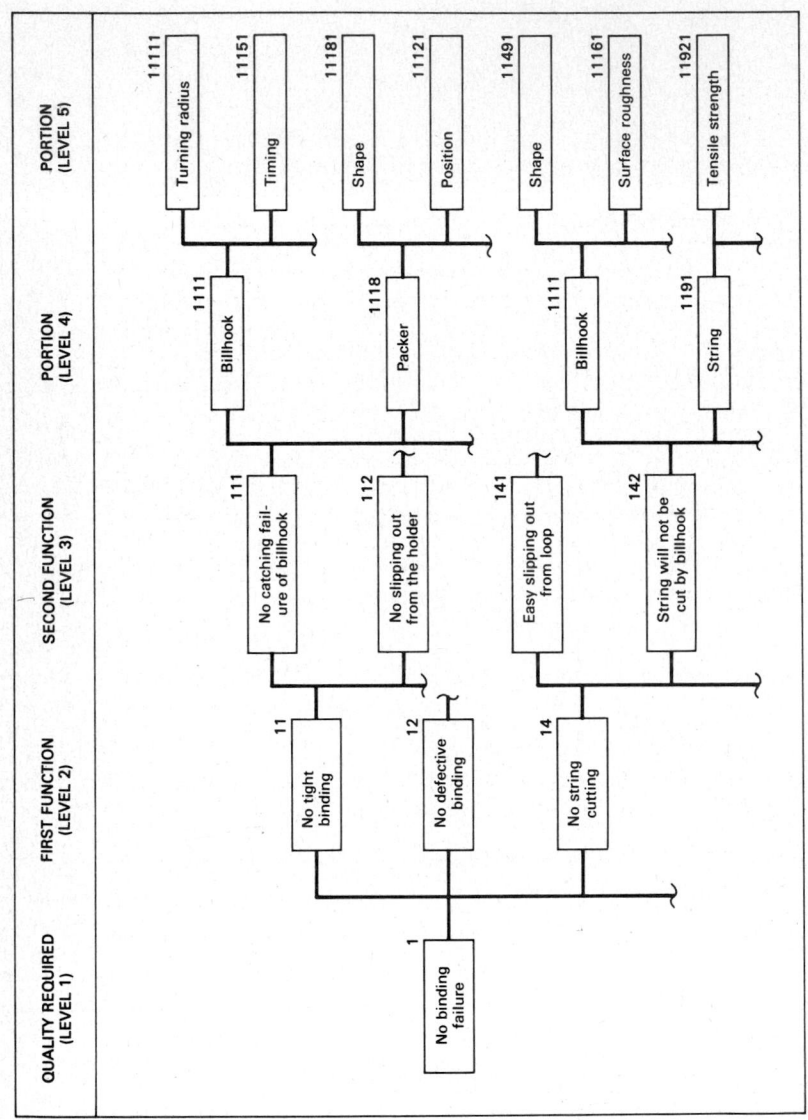

FIG. 35F.3 A quality table.

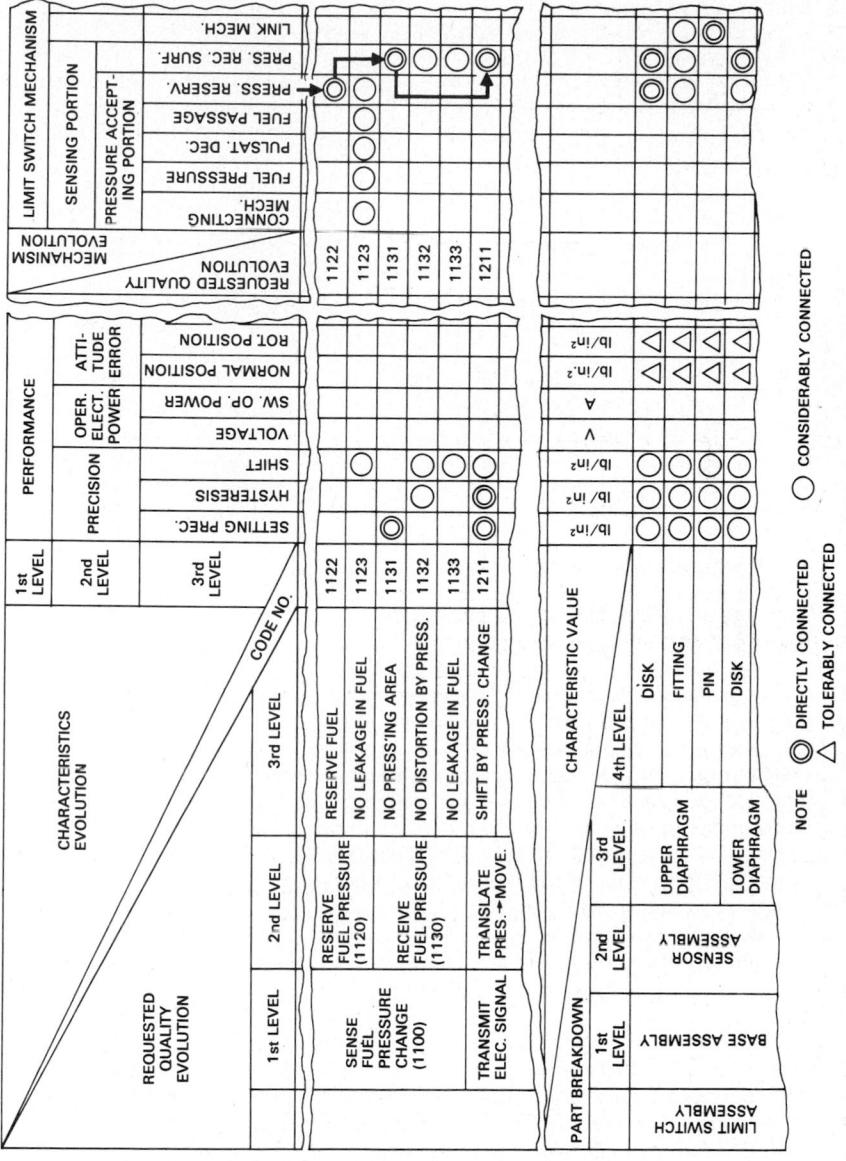

FIG. 35F.4 Quality conversion table for a limit switch. *(Kamizawa, Ishizuka, and Akao, 1978.)*

NAME OF PART	FLOW CHART MATERIAL PROCESS	FLOW CHART MAIN PROCESS	NAME OF PROCESS	OPERATION MANUAL	ITEM	METHOD	PERSON	SAMPLING	MEASUREMENT
Lead chip			Preforming	32-2-RC-1	T.W.	$\bar{X}$-R chart	Mr. F	Every lot, random $n = 5$	Autobalance
				22-RCG -005 -006	T. dia. / Appearance / Temperature / Speed constancy	Check sheet / p-Chart	Mr. F / Mr. F / Mr. F / Mr. F	Every lot, random $n = 10$ / Every lot, total $n = 300$ / Twice a day / Twice a day	Gauge / Eyes / Drum
			Preheat		Temperature	Check sheet	Mr. S	Twice a day	
			Forming	222-RCG	L-dimension / Temperature / Pressure	$\bar{X}$-R chart / Check sheet / Check Sheet	Mr. S / Mr. S / Mr. S	Every lot, random $n = 5$ / Once a day / Once a day	Slide calipers
			Aging	222-RCG 6-1	Temperature	Check sheet	Mr. S	Once a day	

FIG. 35F.5 A QC process chart for a solid resistor. *(Ishiwara, 1975.)*

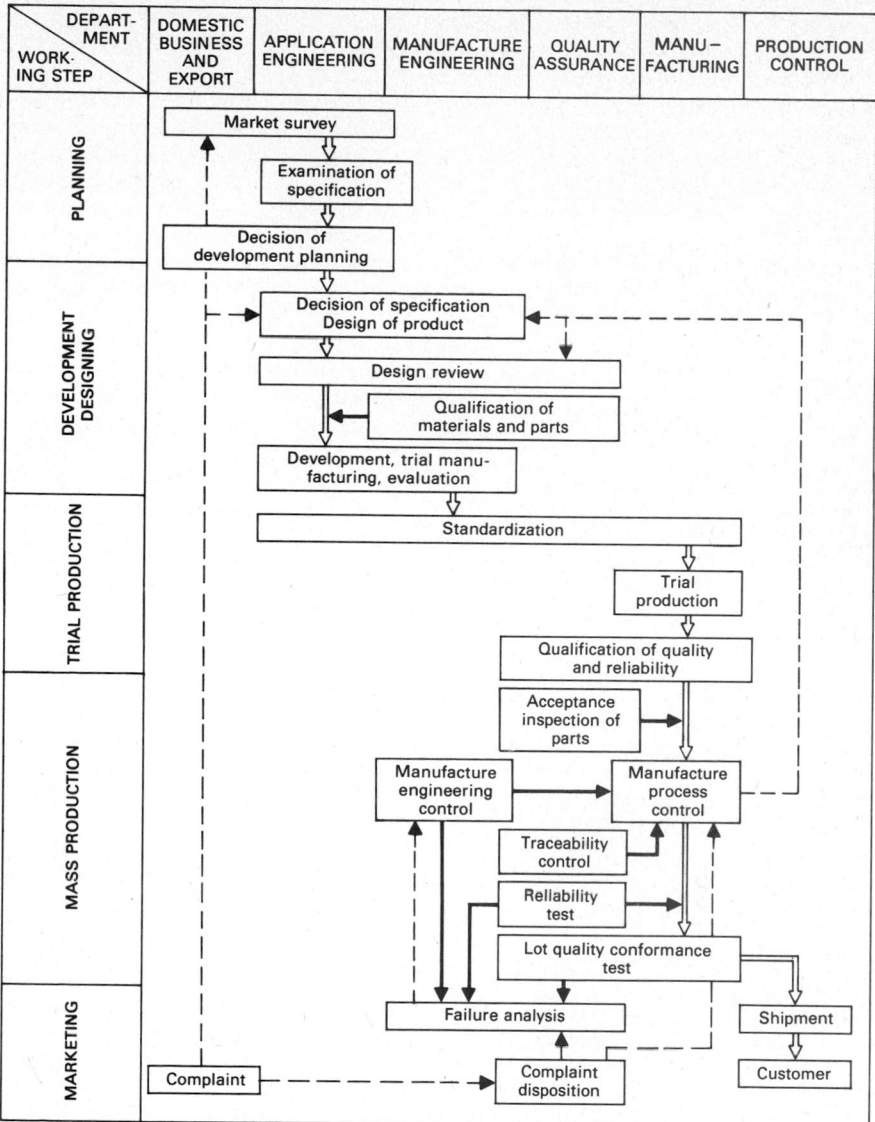

FIG. 35F.6 Chart of quality assurance system. *(Takanashi, 1978.)*

Development of new products is usually a time-consuming undertaking, involving many trial-and-error procedures. However, the procedures of evaluation, qualification, review, etc. carried out during the various steps can be standardized, which becomes the first step in introducing QC to new-product development.

Two stages of market research are shown in the above-listed steps of new-product development (steps 1 and 3). The preliminary market research is rather general in character and may lead to an idea for a new product. The later market research is to confirm the effectiveness of this idea.

For example, in the late 1960s (Yoneyama, 1969), the half-size camera was becoming popular in Japan. The first manufacturer was company X. At company Y, there was discussion among top managers about developing a new half-size camera to compete with that of company X. Mr. A was appointed a senior member of the development team. First, he collected statistics on monthly camera sales from the relevant government report and classified them into sales of half-size and full-size cameras. He found that total sales were rising mainly because of the increased sales of half-size cameras. From this study, top management decided to develop a new camera.

The second market research program (step 3) was then launched. This company Y was also selling color film, which was ultimately developed at the company's central laboratory. It was found from the analysis of developed film that the pictures taken indoors by half-size cameras were often blurred. It was decided on the basis of this fact that the new camera should be equipped with a brighter lens.

Mr. A went out every Sunday with two counters in his pockets. He strolled in downtown Tokyo and then in suburban resorts and counted the number of people who carried a camera; he pushed one counter for each full-size camera and pushed the other counter for each half-size camera. He found that the ratio of half-size to full-size cameras was lower downtown than in the suburbs. It became clear that the customers were buying the carrying convenience and light weight of a half-size camera. It was then further decided that the new camera should be lighter than the camera of company X.

These two features of company Y's new half-size camera became very profitable sales points. It should be noted that the ideas conceived in step 2 above need to be examined and confirmed in the market research of step 3. Systematic and positive collection of quality information from the market is also important for determining test conditions in qualification and for improving the items subject to design evaluation and review in the intermediate stages.

Design review, evaluation, and qualification done at proper stages of development, such as steps 5, 6, and 8, are prevalent in Japanese companies. These evaluations aim at determining:

1. Whether the quality of design was appropriate or not
2. Whether the design or the foregoing procedures were adequate or not

With regard to exported goods, quality information from foreign markets is extremely important because environmental conditions (temperature, humidity, dust, etc.), laws, weights and measures, customs, conditions of use, physical constitution of customers, etc., are quite different as compared with the domestic market. Although these data in foreign markets could not be anticipated in the earlier stages of foreign trade, records of previous failures of various kinds were accumulated and utilized as much as possible to prevent recurrences. Those corrective actions that improve the design, testing, and evaluation procedures are most effective.

The aim of the full-scale test (or trial), which is the final stage of new-product development, is not always clear. It is often carried out by the skilled workers, with quite satisfactory results. When mass production starts, however, the manufacturing department is always worried about problems in the manufacturing process. The reasons are clear: They reflect the differences in skill of the workers engaged in the full-scale test run and in mass production. The distribution of the quality of components and parts is also sometimes different. The true aim of the full-scale test should then be clearly defined and achieved. One of its most important purposes is to thoroughly squeeze "pus" out of manufacturing and take corrective actions before the start of mass production.

An "idea bank" system is provided in many Japanese companies in the process of new-product development. As mentioned before, new-product development is a procedure in which many trials and errors are made. Many new ideas fail, and many prototypes are unsuccessful. The reports of these failures are filed in the idea bank. It is always important to utilize the "bank deposit" easily and fully by considering and rearranging the file index. It frequently happens that a new product fails because the timing is too early.

REFERENCES

Aiba, K. (1966). "Significance of Quality Designing." *Hinshitsu Kanri (Statistical Quality Control)*, vol. 17, pp. 88–89 (Japanese).

Chapman, M. K. (1969). "The World Prosperity through Quality." *Quality Assurance,* December, pp. 28–31.

Cole, R. E. and Walder, A. G. (1981). "Structural Diffusion: The Politics of Participative Work Structures in China, Japan, Sweden, and the United States." CRSO Working Paper No. 226, University of Michigan, February, p. 28.

Deming, W. E. (1982). *Quality, Productivity, and Competitive Position.* Massachusetts Institute of Technology, Center for Advanced Engineering Study, Cambridge, MA.

Gryna, Frank, M. (1977). "Quality Costs: User vs. Manufacturer." *Quality Progress,* June, pp. 10–13.

Ishikawa, K. (1962). *Kanrizu-ho (Control Chart).* Japanese Union of Scientists and Engineers, Tokyo, p. 10 (in Japanese).

Ishikawa, K. (1965). "Recent Trend of Quality Control." *Reports of Statistical Applications and Research,* Japanese Union of Scientists and Engineers, vol. 12, no. 1, pp. 1–17.

Ishikawa, K. (1969a). "Education for Quality Control in Japanese Industry." *Reports of Statistical Applications and Research,* Japanese Union of Scientists and Engineers, vol. 16, no. 3, pp. 21–40.

Ishikawa, K. (1969b). "Ten Principles of Vendee-Vendor Relations from the Standpoint of Quality Control." *Proceedings, International Conference on Quality Control.* Japanese Union of Scientists and Engineers, Tokyo, pp. 333–336.

Ishikawa, K. (1972). "Quality Control Starts and Ends with Education." *Quality Progress,* August, p. 18.

Ishikawa, K. (1978). "QC Specialists and Standardization." *Proceedings, International Conference on Quality Control.* Japanese Union of Scientists and Engineers, Tokyo, pp. A6-5 through A6-10.

Ishikawa, K. and Kondo, K. (1969). "Education and Training for Quality Control in Japanese Industry." *Quality,* no. 4, pp. 90–96.

Ishiwara, K. (1975). "Process Flow Chart for Management." *Hinshitsu Kanri (Statistical Quality Control),* vol. 26, pp. 332–333 (Japanese).

Itoh, S. (1974). "Executive Reports on Quality: Audit Reports and Quality Reports." *Reports on Statistical Applied Research,* vol. 21, no. 3, pp. 65–77.

Juran, J. M. (1978). "Japanese and Western Quality—A Contrast." *Quality Progress,* December, pp. 10–18.

Juran, J. M. (1981). "Product Quailty—A Prescription for the West." *Proceedings, 25th Conference EOQC,* Paris, June, vol. 3, pp. 221–242.

Kamizawa, N., Ishizuka, N., and Akao, Y. (1978). "Quality Evolution System and FMEA." *Proceedings, International Conference on Quality Control.* Japanese Union of Scientists and Engineers. Tokyo, pp. B4-19 through B4-28.

Kogure, M. and Akao, Y. (1983). "Quality Function Development and CWQC in Japan." *Quality Progress,* October, pp. 25–29.

Kondo, Y. (1969). "Internal QC Audit in Japanese Companies." *Quality,* no. 4, pp. 97–103.

Kondo, Y. (1976). "The Roles of Manager in QC Circle Movement." *Reports of Statistical Applications and Research,* Japanese Union of Scientists and Engineers, vol. 23, pp. 71–81.

Kondo, Y. (1977). "Creativity in Daily Work." *ASQC Technical Conference Transactions,* Milwaukee, pp. 430–439.

Kondo, Y. (1978). "JUSE—A Center of Quality Control in Japan." *Quality Progress,* August, pp. 14–15.

Mikayama, M. (1978). "Development of Quality Control in the Whole of Kubota Ltd." *Reports of Statistical Applications and Research,* Japanese Union of Scientists and Engineers, vol. 25, no. 2, pp. 54–77.

Mizuno, S. (1967). "Execution of Internal QC Audit." *Hinshitsu Kanri (Statistical Quality Control),* vol. 18, pp. 835–839 (Japanese).

Mizuno, S. and Kume, H. (1978). "Development of Education and Training in Quality Control." *Reports of Statistical Applications and Research,* Japanese Union of Scientists and Engineers, vol. 25, pp. 36–60.

Murata, T. (1968). "Internal QC Audit by the Top Management." *Hinshitsu Kanri (Statistical Quality Control),* vol. 19, pp. 300–305 (Japanese).

QC Circle Koryo (1980). QC Circle Headquarters, Japanese Union of Scientists and Engineers, Tokyo.

Sugimoto, T. (1968). "QC Audit by the Top Management." *Hinshitsu Kanri (Statistical Quailty Control),* vol. 19, pp. 1136–1140 (Japanese).

Takanashi, M. (1978). "Quality Assurance System for the Integrated Circuit." *Proceedings, International Conference on Quality Control.* Japanese Union of Scientists and Engineers, Tokyo, pp. C1-51 through C1-56.

Takayanagi, A. (1974). "Quality Control Activities at a Shipyard." *Hinshitsu Kanri (Statistical Quality Control),* vol. 24, pp. 515–519 (Japanese).

Yoneyama, T. (1969). *Hinshitsu Kanri no Hanashi (Some Topics on QC).* Japanese Union of Scientists and Engineers, Tokyo, pp. 115–118 (Japanese).

SECTION 35G
QUALITY IN THE UNITED STATES OF AMERICA

J. M. Juran

THE BACKGROUND **35G.1**

  Early Systems of Managing
    for Quality 35G.2

  The Taylor System and Its
    Impact on Managing for
    Quality 35G.2

*WORLD WAR II AND ITS
IMPACT* **35G.4**

*THE JAPANESE QUALITY
REVOLUTION AND ITS IMPACT* **35G.4**

*QUALITY INTO A POSITION OF
PROMINENCE* **35G.5**

*RESPONSE TO ''LIFE BEHIND
THE QUALITY DIKES''* **35G.5**

*RESPONSE TO THE JAPANESE
QUALITY REVOLUTION* **35G.6**

  Solution by Blocking
    Imports 35.6

  Solution by Joint Ventures 35.6

  Solution by Improving
    Quality 35G.6

LESSONS LEARNED **35G.7**

  Companywide Quality
    Management 35G.7

  Upper Management
    Participation 35G.7

  The Quality Trilogy 35G.8

  Internal Customers 35G.8

  Big Q and Little Q 35G.8

  The Significance of Cost of
    Poor Quality 35G.8

  Quality Improvement . . .35G.9

  Quality Planning 35G.9

  Quality Control 35G.10

  Training 35G.11

PROGNOSIS **35G.12**

REFERENCES **35G.13**

THE BACKGROUND

The American economy rests mainly on a base of numerous autonomous producers and marketers of goods and services. These autonomous companies are characterized by:

1. A high concentration of industry in relatively few companies; i.e., the number of manufacturing companies runs to over a million, but the top 500 manufacturing companies account for most of the national manufacture.
2. A high degree of private ownership of these large companies; i.e., normally a large company will have thousands of owners, no one of whom owns more than a few percent of the company.
3. A "professional" management; i.e., the company is run by persons who consider their lifetime careers to be that of managing. These persons become the real power in the company, since the owners are too numerous and since the established legal system of boards of directors usually results in the managers dominating those boards. The American managers and their highly developed concept of professional management are one of the main strengths of the American economy.

The features of autonomous companies and professional managers to run them have a considerable impact on the conduct of the quality function. Within the flexibility permitted by the "anarchy of the marketplace," each company determines what it will make or stop making, what quality policies it will employ, etc. Innovation plays an important role throughout, owing to the rather unique industrial history of the country.

The early European colonists in America faced the problems and opportunities associated with exploiting the immense natural resources of a large geographic area. Self-reliance and risk taking emerged as major traditions. An innovative spirit was developed in the early agricultural days and remained a driving force when the new nation undertook to industrialize. Self-reliance emerged as a major and respected tradition. This tradition in turn raised entrepeneurship and individualism to a state of respect. American companies tend to organize in ways which assign responsibility to individuals rather than to teams. The tradition of self-reliance also stimulates job mobility. American workers, engineers, and managers tend to change jobs more often than their counterparts in other countries. The concept of a lifetime career is often viewed as being associated with a trade, a union, or a profession rather than with a specific company.

Early Systems of Managing for Quality.   At the outset the manufacturing industries in the colonies followed the craftsmanship concept which prevailed in their European country of origin. Apprentices learned a trade, qualified to become craftsmen, and in due course might become masters of shops.

Achievement of quality was one of the essential skills learned by the apprentice. A major force for assuring quality of product was the village form of society in which the craftsman met face to face with the users. In a shop of any size the master carried out a form of product inspection and process audit which provided added quality assurance. Alternatively the master delegated this function to an inspector.

When the Industrial Revolution was exported from Europe to America, the colonists again followed European practice. The craftsmen became factory workers and the masters became factory foremen. Quality was assured as before—through the skills of the craftsmen supplemented by supervisory audit or by a departmental inspection.

The Taylor System and Its Impact on Managing for Quality.   Late in the nineteenth century the Americans broke sharply with European tradition by adopting the Taylor System of "Scientific Management." (For elaboration, see Section 10 under the Taylor System of Management. See also Juran, 1973).

Central to the Taylor System was the concept of separating planning from execution. This separation made possible a considerable rise in productivity. It also dealt a crippling blow to the concept of craftsmanship. In addition, the new emphasis on productivity had a negative effect on quality. To restore the balance the factory managers created a central Inspection Department headed by a Chief Inspector. The various departmental inspectors were transferred to the new department over the opposition of the production supervisors. In due course the Inspection Departments grew into broad-based organizations called variously "Quality Control," "Quality Assurance," etc. These organizations evolved into quality-oriented specialties such as quality engineering and reliability engineering. For elaboration on these trends, see Section 9, under Evolution of the Quality Management Hierarchy.

The central activity of these quality-oriented departments remained that of inspection and test—separating good product from bad. The prime benefit of this activity was to reduce the risk that defective products would be shipped to customers. However, there were serious detriments:

This central activity of the Quality Department helped to foster a widespread belief that achievement of quality was the responsibility of the Quality Department.

In turn, this belief hampered efforts at eliminating the causes of defective products—the responsibilities were confused.

As a result, failure-prone products and incapable processes remained in force and continued to generate high costs of poor quality.

What emerged *de facto* was a concept of managing for quality somewhat as follows:

Each functional department carried out its assigned function and then delivered the result to the next function in the sequence of events.

At the end, the Quality Department separated the good product from the bad.

For defective product which escaped to the customer, redress was to be provided through customer service based on warranties.

By the standards of later decades this concept of prime reliance on inspection and test was unsound. However, it was not a handicap if competitors employed the same concept, and such was usually the case. Despite the deficiencies inherent in this "concept of detection," U.S. goods came to be well regarded as to quality. In some product lines the American companies became the quality leaders. In addition, the U.S. economy grew to superpower size. Some of this growth was achieved in ways which had implications for quality:

1. The domestic economy was unified by the laws governing movement of goods in interstate commerce. These laws avoided the obstacles inherent in the national boundaries then prevailing in Western Europe.

2. Entrepreneurs were on the alert to create sales in various ways: e.g., bringing new, improved products to market; creating additional production capacity to eliminate shortages. (Elimination of shortages also eliminates an inevitable cause of poor quality.)

3. Managers were willing to invest in facilities to improve productivity. Some of these investments (e.g., in machines, tools, instruments) improved quality as well.

4. The United States became a leader in the concept of a "professional" approach to management, involving extensive training for managers and specialists.

5. The growing number of quality specialists developed numerous new methods and tools specifically oriented to managing for quality. However, utilization of these methods was limited because of the prevailing organization forms and especially upper management's limited understanding of the quality function.

WORLD WAR II AND ITS IMPACT

During World War II U.S. industry was faced with the added burden of producing enormous quantities of military products, many of which made use of new, sophisticated technology. However, the basic system of managing for quality remained unchanged. Each function carried out its responsibility and delivered the result to the next function in the sequence. At the end, inspection and test separated the good from the bad.

The military clients secured their quality assurance largely by additional inspection and test. Not until well after World War II did they evolve the concept of mandating the quality system to be followed by contractors.

A part of the grand strategy during World War II was to shut off production of many civilian products: automobiles, household appliances, entertainment products, etc. A massive shortage of goods developed amid a huge buildup of purchasing power. It took the rest of that decade (the 1940s) for supply to catch up with demand. In the interim the manufacturing companies gave top priority to meeting delivery dates, so that quality of product went down. (Quality always goes down during shortages.) The habit of giving top priority to delivery dates then persisted long after the shortages were gone.

It should be noted that during this progression of events the priority given to quality declined significantly. In addition, the leadership of the quality function became vague and confused. In the days of the craft shops, the master (then also the chief executive) participated personally in the process of managing for quality. What emerged was a concept in which upper management became detached from the process of managing for quality.

THE JAPANESE QUALITY REVOLUTION AND ITS IMPACT

Following World War II the Japanese embarked on a course of reaching national goals by trade rather than by military means. The major manufacturers, who had been largely involved in military production, were faced with converting to civilian products. A major obstacle to selling these products in international markets was a national reputation for shoddy goods created by the export of poor quality goods prior to World War II.

The Japanese adopted a variety of strategies for improving their quality. (See, generally, Section 35F, Quality in Japan.) In the judgment of the author, several of those strategies were decisive in creating a successful revolution in quality:

1. The upper managers personally took charge of leading the revolution.

2. All levels and functions underwent training in managing for quality.

3. Quality improvement was undertaken at a continuing, revolutionary pace.

In the early postwar period the impacted U.S. companies logically considered Japanese competition to be in regard to price rather than quality. Their response was to shift the manufacture of labor-intensive products to low-labor-cost areas, often offshore. Then, as the years unfolded, price competition declined while quality competition increased. However, the U.S. companies generally failed to recognize these trends or to heed the warning signals. In 1966 the author sounded the following alarm at the European Organization for Quality Control Conference (for the full text, see Juran, 1967):

> The Japanese are headed for world quality leadership and will attain it in the next two decades because no one else is moving there at the same pace.

During the 1960s and 1970s numerous Japanese manufacturers greatly increased their share of the U.S. market. A major reason was superior quality. Numerous industries were impacted: consumer electronics, automobiles, steel, machine tools, etc. Some researches quantified the quality differences. See Juran, 1979 (color television sets); also Garvin, 1983 (room air conditioners).

QUALITY INTO A POSITION OF PUBLIC PROMINENCE

A second major postwar phenomenon was the rise of product quality to a position of prominence in the public mind. This growth in prominence was the result of the convergence of multiple trends:

Growing concern about damage to the environment

Action by the courts to impose strict liability

Fear of major disasters and near disasters

Pressure from consumer organizations for better quality and more responsive redress

Growing public awareness of the role of quality in international competition, e.g., in trade, weapons

Collectively these trends are the phenomenon of "Life Behind the Quality Dikes." For elaboration, see Section 34, Quality and Society.

RESPONSE TO "LIFE BEHIND THE QUALITY DIKES"

The U.S. companies' responses were generally specific. Many companies created high-level committees to establish policies, goals, and action plans with respect to product safety, environmental damage, and consumer complaints. In some cases new corporate departments were created to help develop these plans and to audit the subsequent conformance to goals.

RESPONSE TO THE JAPANESE QUALITY REVOLUTION

The most obvious effect of the Japanese quality revolution was a massive export of goods to the United States. The impact on the United States was considerable, especially in certain sensitive areas:

The impacted manufacturing companies were damaged by the resulting loss of sales.

The work force and their unions were damaged by the resulting "export of jobs."

The national economy was damaged by the resulting unfavorable trade balance.

The responses took many directions, some of which bore no relation to improving U.S. competitiveness.

Solution by Blocking Imports.   Many of those impacted tried to solve their problem by reducing or eliminating the imports. They urged legislation which would establish restrictive import quotas and tariffs. They urged criminal prosecutions on the grounds of violation of laws against "dumping," (selling below cost, or at "less than fair value"). They filed civil lawsuits on the grounds of unfair trade practices. They appealed to the citizenry to "Buy American."

These responses did not arouse much sympathy among the buying public. Influential journals, economists, legislators, etc. pointed out that restriction of imports generated serious side effects: Buyers are deprived of better values; restriction invites retaliatory restriction; companies have no incentive to become more competitive, etc. For some case examples in which import restrictions damaged the industries they were intended to protect, see Levinson (1987).

Solution by Joint Ventures.   A relatively few companies took steps to join the Japanese rather than to oppose them. These joint ventures took various forms, but usually gave the Japanese partner the dominant manufacturing role while the U.S. partner retained the major marketing role.

In general, companies which established such joint ventures fared better than those which tried to exclude Japanese imports.

Solution by Improving Quality.   Many upper managers recognized that the soundest response to a competitive challenge was to become more competitive. Not being trained or experienced in managing for quality, these same upper managers sought advice from the experts, internal and external. It turned out that the various experts proposed numerous strategies, including:

Motivation of the work force

Quality circles

Statistical process control

Awareness for managers and supervisors

Computation of cost of quality

Project-by-project improvement

Complete manuals of procedure

Revision of organization structure

Incentives for quality

Automated inspection and test

Robotics

Everyone of those (and other) directions has merit under appropriate conditions. The upper managers were then faced with selecting one or more of the available strategies as the basis for a plan of action. They were experienced managers but not in managing for quality. Generally they opted for "action now," i.e., do something plausible promptly rather than endure delay.

The results were generally less than satisfactory. In some cases the strategies selected (e.g., statistical process control, project-by-project improvement) were effective for specific major quality needs, with resulting significant gains. More usually the strategies chosen had little relation to the companies' major quality problems.

The fundamental reason for these unsatisfactory experiences was the lack of diagnosis of what were the companies' needs before applying the remedies. In a sense the companies went directly from symptom to remedy without knowing what was the disease.

For some observations comparing Japanese and Western practices, see Kano (1978).

LESSONS LEARNED

The experiences of all those companies have provided feedback—a body of lessons learned: which strategies produced useful results, and why; which strategies failed, and why. Some of those lessons learned apply so widely that they become a vital input to future grand strategy.

Companywide Quality Management.   It has become evident that quality competitiveness in the twenty-first century will not be achieved by adding specific new methods or tools to the traditional approach. Instead, a new basic approach must be designed. Generally the new approach takes the form of enlarging the strategic business plan to include quality goals. Plans for meeting these quality goals then parallel the plans long used for meeting traditional goals in the areas of sales, product development, profit, etc. See, generally, Section 6, under Companywide Quality Management.

Upper Management Participation.   One element present in all successes, and absent in most failures, has been the personal involvement of upper managers in managing for quality. This involvement has consisted of some very specific roles for upper managers, including:

Serving on the Quality Committee (Quality Council, etc.)

Establishing quality goals

Providing the needed resources

Providing quality-oriented training

Stimulating quality improvement

Serving on quality improvement teams

Reviewing progress

Giving recognition

Revising the reward system

For elaboration see Section 8, Upper Management and Quality, under Participation by Upper Management.

The feedback of experience has also shown that many upper managers have resisted such extensive additions to their own workload. Their preference has been to establish broad goals and then urge their subordinates to meet the goals. However, there is abundant evidence that a major revision in the approach to managing for quality is *not highly delegable*. The upper managers must participate throughout.

For elaboration see Section 8, Upper Management and Quality, under Upper Management Resistance to Participation.

The Quality Trilogy.   As upper managers have become more closely involved with managing for quality, they have been helped by the financial analogy. Both financial management and managing for quality make use of three basic managerial processes:

Planning

Control

Improvement

Upper managers are generally quite experienced in using these processes as applied to management of finance. This experience makes it easy for them to accept the same trilogy as a basis for managing for quality.

For elaboration, see Section 2, The Quality Function, under How to Think About Quality.

Internal Customers.   The concept that customers are internal as well as external is not new. However, the recent exposures of upper managers to the problems of managing for quality have emphasized the importance of the concept. Upper managers have widely recognized that many quality problems of the past were traceable to failure to meet the needs of internal customers. (A widespread example has been product designs which designers "threw over the wall" to be made by the manufacturing department.) This new emphasis has in turn led to broader acceptance of the concept of participation; i.e., internal customers should participate in those planning activities which relate to their operations.

Big Q and Little Q.   An important concept grasped by upper managers has been that managing for quality should not be limited to factory goods and factory processes. Instead it should extend to all products and processes. Obvious examples are the numerous business processes and their products: invoicing and invoices, order entry and edited orders, etc. Many of these processes are error-prone. They delay service to customers, require costly rework, damage the company's image as a "quality house," etc.

In the interest of precise communication some companies refer to this broader concept as "Big Q" in contrast to the traditional concept which is referred to as "Little Q."

The Significance of Cost of Poor Quality.   Upper management's exposure to managing for quality has taught such managers a good deal about the cost of poor quality. Some of the lessons learned have come as surprises.

Cost of poor quality relates to Big Q: Many upper managers had assumed that cost of poor quality consisted of the cost of running the Quality Department, or alternatively, the costs traceable to deficient factory goods and processes. It is now widely accepted that cost of poor quality should include the costs traceable to deficiencies anywhere, i.e., deficiencies in Big Q.

Costs of poor quality are huge: Available estimates suggest that, depending on the nature of the industry, these costs consume between 20 percent and 40 percent of the effort expended by the enterprises. In the aggregate, close to one-third of what is done in the United States consists of redoing what had been done before. Translated into financial terms, the sums are staggering. Translated into other terms, the effects are equally staggering: the delays in getting new products to market or in providing service; the damage done to customer relations; the damage to internal harmony, etc.

Higher quality costs less: Many upper managers have long held the view that to improve quality requires an increase in costs. For some of these managers the premise was that the road to higher quality is through more inspection and test. Under that premise it is of course logical to conclude that higher quality produces higher costs. Other upper managers interpreted "quality" as meaning those product features which make the product salable. Under that meaning higher quality usually does cost more.

The deeper involvement in managing for quality provided new insights for such managers. They came to realize that the high cost of poor quality presented an opportunity for cost reductions at a higher return on investment than virtually any other managerial activity.

For additional discussion see generally Section 4, Quality Costs.

Quality Improvement.   The feedback has increased upper management's awareness of opportunities for improving quality. These opportunities go beyond reducing the cost of poor quality; they extend to making products more salable by means such as: improved design processes; improved manufacturing planning; improved business processes, etc. In addition, the upper managers have been exposed to some of the basic concepts and realities which are fundamental to establishing a revolutionary rate of quality improvement:

All quality improvement takes place project by project; there is no such thing as improvement in general.

Major quality problems are multifunctional in nature. It takes multifunctional teams to dispose of them.

There has been no clear responsibility for making quality improvements.

The accumulated projects waiting for solution are very numerous.

To establish quality improvement at a revolutionary pace and on a continuing basis requires a structured approach.

For elaboration, see Section 22, Quality Improvement.

Quality Planning.   The feedback from completed quality improvement projects has established that many of the remedies consisted of replanning for the products and/or processes. This in turn pointed to quality planning as a cause—a hatchery—of chronic quality problems. It became evident that the quality planning process itself required improvement.

For elaboration, see generally Section 6, especially under Lessons Learned.

Quality Control.   One of the most popular directions chosen by companies was statistical process control (SPC). These companies trained managers, supervisors, specialists, and work force members in basic statistical tools and how to apply those tools to specific quality problems. In many of these companies the training then led to better collection and analysis of data on quality of products and processes. In turn these analyses led to improvements in the control process through such means as:

> Earlier detection of adverse changes in products and processes
>
> Better discrimination between real changes and apparent changes
>
> Earlier discovery of relationships between process variables and product results
>
> Improvements in process capabilities

Some large companies, having gained such benefits from SPC, have mandated that their suppliers undertake training in SPC and make certain minimal applications in their operations. Compliance with this mandate then became one of the criteria for judging supplier performance.

The emphasis on extending the use of SPC has tended to underemphasize certain other essential aspects of quality control. These include:

Self-control: That is, satisfying the conditions which enable a worker to meet the operating goals. For elaboration, see Section 13 under Improving the Effectiveness of Product Development and Section 17 under Concept of Controllability.

Clear responsibility: "Responsibility for quality" is vague until it is defined in terms of responsibility for the specific decisions and actions which are vital to quality control.

Establishing such definitions is an essential part of planning the quality controls. For an example, see Section 17 under Quality Responsibilities on the Factory Floor.

Multifunctional coordination: Major processes (e.g., filling customers' orders) are usually multifunctional in nature. They progress sequentially, step by step, through multiple functional departments. The responsibility for each step is clear and personal. The responsibility for coordinating the overall process is usually done impersonally, through written procedure. This form of coordination is quite useful for routine events and unchanging conditions. However, conditions do keep changing, and nonroutine events do occur. Adaptation to such changes requires the intervention of flexible human intelligence. The responsibility for such intervention is clear in the case of any functional department; it is vague for the overall process.

Various means have been evolved to provide the missing coordination:

Committees: They are most effective if the committee members also have "line" jurisdiction over the respective functional departments.

Matrix organizations: They superimpose a team culture on the functional departments.

"Owners" or "Champions":   They are functional department heads who are specially designated to coordinate overall processes.

For elaboration, see Section 7, Organizing for Quality, under Coordination of the Quality Function.

Training. Until the 1980s, training in managing for quality was largely concentrated in the Quality Departments. As a result, most quality planning was being done by persons whose prime responsibility was something else. This "quality planning by experienced amateurs" took place at all levels and in all functions. The major deficiencies included:

Lack of participation by internal customers

Lack of a systematic approach

Lack of use of modern methods and tools

When the companies set out to raise their quality competitiveness, they soon discovered additional gaps in training. For example, companies which tried to go into large-scale quality improvement found that their managers lacked training in how to organize for improvement, to choose projects, to build teams, to conduct diagnosis, etc. (See, generally, Section 22, Quality Improvement.) Still other training gaps became evident with respect to the quality control process.

During the 1980s U.S. companies became quite active in providing quality-oriented training to various levels of personnel. The dominant areas of subject matter included: problem-solving tools, quality awareness, quality improvement, managing for quality.

Although much training was done, a major weakness was widespread. The hope had been that once trained, the managers and work force would proceed to make the companies fully competitive in quality. There were in fact widespread gains. Most were modest; some were outstanding. Overall, the results fell far short of bringing the companies fully up to competitive levels. The principal reasons were:

1. The quality gap had already become so wide that the effort required to "catch up" was much greater than had been realized.

2. Meanwhile, the competitors were continuing to improve; in some cases the gap was actually widening.

3. The companies had been unrealistic in believing that they could achieve competitiveness solely by subjecting the personnel to training. The training could not provide answers to the question "What should I do different?" because of lack of a coherent approach consisting of specific goals, deployment, plans, resources, reviews, recognition, rewards, etc. This lack was in turn traceable to upper managers' lack of training and experience in managing for quality.

As of the late 1980s there had emerged no consensus on how companies should structure their training in how to manage for quality. In the judgment of the author, the most impressive results had been achieved by companies which carried out a phased sequence somewhat as follows:

1. A "pilot test" of project-by-project quality improvement using the methods, tools, and training described in Section 22, Quality Improvement.

2. Extension of project-by-project improvement throughout the company by enlarging the business plan to include quality improvement. This phase includes training in such subject matter as Companywide Quality Management (see generally Section 6 under that heading).

3. Improving quality planning, based on lessons learned. For this phase the training includes subject matter such as:

   Fundamental concepts (see Section 2)

   Quality planning road map (see Section 6)

   Effect of quality on company economics (see Sections 3 and 4) and on society (see Section 34)

   The managerial processes through which quality is attained (Sections 5 through 11)

4. Improving quality controls through the self-control concept. For this phase the training includes subject matter such as:

   The feedback loop (Section 6)

   Statistical tools (Sections 23 through 26)

   Application of computers (Section 27)

   The activities carried out by the functional departments (Sections 12 through 21)

PROGNOSIS

The late 1980s found many U.S. industries on the defensive with respect to product quality. Foreign competitors had successfully invaded the U.S. market with products which offered superior quality and value. The resulting public perception then became a force in its own right.

During the 1980s many U.S. managers sharpened their awareness of this state of affairs. They also tried various strategies in an effort to become fully competitive. Generally they exceeded their own historical performance but failed to close the gap in the marketplace. Their pace of quality improvement remained well below that of their foreign competitors.

The key to competitiveness in quality is the pace of quality improvement. As of the late 1980s U.S. companies had not achieved either the pace or the habit of quality improvement needed to close the gap. Their rate of improvement remained much lower than that of their foreign competitors. U.S. companies still faced a huge backlog of needed improvements in product performance, cost of poor quality, and quality planning and controls. For those companies to become fully competitive in quality they needed to increase their pace of quality improvement dramatically. This could not come about without the personal participation of upper management in the forms set out in Section 8, Upper Management and Quality, under Participation by Upper Management.

It should be noted that even with full upper management participation it takes years for a company to attain the habit of annual quality improvement at a revolutionary pace. It takes several years to conduct the pilot test, review the results, and extend the concept companywide. It then takes years of project-by-project improvement to shrink down the longstanding accumulation of chronic quality problems. Additional years are then needed to evaluate the lessons learned and to improve the quality planning process.

Meanwhile other powerful forces are at work. Foreign competitors do not stand still. The demands of the marketplace are a moving target. Additional developing countries keep entering the international market; some are emerging as formidable competitors.

Still another new force is the entry of foreign-owned companies to conduct manufacturing in the United States. There has always been a degree of foreign ownership of U.S. businesses. What is different now is that the recent entries have emphasized quality from the outset. The new factories are designed to use the very means of managing for quality which so successfully gained market leadership for the prior imports from the parent company.

All in all the prognosis is a gloomy one. It is unlikely that U.S. companies will, in the aggregate, achieve full quality competitiveness before the twenty-first century.

REFERENCES

Garvin, David A. (1983). "Quality on the Line." *Harvard Business Review,* September–October, pp. 64–75.

Juran, J. M. (1967). "The QC Circle Phenomenon." *Industrial Quality Control,* January, p. 336.

Juran, J. M. (1973). "The Taylor System and Quality Control." A series of articles in *Quality Progress,* May through December (listed under "Management Interface").

Juran, J. M. (1979). "Japanese and Western Quality—A Contrast." *Quality,* January and February. Also published under the same title, in *Proceedings of the International Conference on Quality Control.* Japanese Union of Scientists and Engineers, Tokyo, 1978, pp. A3-11 to A3-25.

Kano, Noriaki (1978). "Comparison of the background of Quality between Japan and the West." *International Conference on Quality Control.* Japanese Union of Scientists and Engineers, Tokyo, pages C3-1 to C3-8.

Levinson, Marc (1987). "Asking for Protection Is Asking for Trouble." *Harvard Business Review,* July–August, pp. 42–47.

SECTION 35H
QUALITY IN SOCIALIST COUNTRIES

Professor F. Egermayer, RN Dr., Dr. Sc.

RELEVANCY OF QUALITY FOR
SOCIALIST COUNTRIES 35H.1

STATE QUALITY CONTROL . . 35H.2

PRODUCT CERTIFICATION . . . 35H.4

INTEGRATED QUALITY
CONTROL 35H.7

QUALITY INFORMATION 35H.9

QUALITY MOTIVATION 35H.9

QUALITY EDUCATION AND
TRAINING 35H.11

REFERENCES 35H.13

RELEVANCY OF QUALITY FOR SOCIALIST COUNTRIES

All industrially developed countries, irrespective of their social systems, place major emphasis on the problem of product quality. For the socialist countries, acting jointly within the Council for Mutual Economic Assistance (CMEA),[1] quality is a determining element of the effectiveness of their national economies. The central planning system, characteristic for socialist countries, includes special provisions for the growth of quality. Planning must balance the contending needs of an economy, and the priorities must be shifted as required. In the national economies of socialist countries, product quality is just as relevant as product volume, price, and delivery time. There is also awareness that improvement in product quality means as much as increase in volume of production and leads to savings in production capacity. Thus, product quality improvement represents a significant reserve for increase in productivity and in national income.

Since the 1960s, the CMEA countries have been carrying out economic

---

[1] The CMEA includes seven European countries (USSR, GDR, Poland, Czechoslovakia, Hungary, Bulgaria, and Rumania) and three non-European countries (Mongolia, Cuba, Vietnam). In addition, Yugoslavia cooperates with the CMEA (Sütö, 1978).

reforms aimed at increasing the management effectiveness of the national economies and especially of the central planning methods. The reform process has devoted attention to planning mechanisms, to reducing undue rigidity in the role of directive economic indexes, and to extending the competence, responsibility, and material interests of industrial enterprises. The resulting reforms emphasize the continuing role of the central political and economic authorities in conceptual decisions on economic policies while providing more favorable conditions for industrial enterprises and their production activity. The reforms are also directed toward support of the state policy concerning technical progress, including product quality improvement, since product quality is a limiting factor in modern development.

An important role in product quality improvement in socialist countries is played by the CMEA, which for the period from 1971 to 1980 adopted a complex program of economic integration. This program elaborates fundamental principles for integrated international standardization (CMEA standards), short of the introduction of modern methods of quality control on different levels of management. To cope with this problem, a Permanent Committee for Standardization was established, which includes a working group for quality in which experts of the CMEA member countries are active. The working group prepares proposals for measures to increase product quality, including: prediction and planning of quality; improvement of product reliability; quality control systems, especially quality information systems; standardization of principles, methods, and requirements for certification of products; development of statistical quality control (QC) standards; economic and moral incentives for quality; education and training programs for quality; and others (Linczenyi, 1978).

STATE QUALITY CONTROL

Contemporary quality control in the CMEA member countries is based on the concept of a Unified (uniform) System of State Quality Control (USSQC), which means state management of quality control. This system is of many years' standing and has recently accelerated development of quality control in countries with central planning of the national economy (Glichev, 1978). The fundamental principles of the system were formulated in the USSR in 1978 by a decree of the State Committee for Standards (Gosstandart USSR) in cooperation with the USSR State Planning Committee and the State Committee for Science and Technology. These principles have been gradually applied in all the CMEA member countries.

The main objective of the system is to activate all necessary technical, production, economic, social, and organizational resources in order to achieve and maintain a high rate of quality improvement in all important types of products. The system itself is a complex of measures, methods, and means for ensuring coordinated activities of all interested management systems, with the aim of achieving the above-mentioned objectives. The USSQC is an inherent part of managing the national economy on all its levels—interindustrial, branch, and company levels—as well as in its regional organizations. It includes all aspects of production of materials in various phases of the product life cycle.

The highest-level managing body is, as a rule, a government presidium (Council of Ministers). This provides a direct method of management, involving mainly managerial actions based on top political decisions. This is the first area of management aimed at product quality. Special professional problems of quality control, common to all branches of production, are handled by specialized bodies of the state center. This is an indirect method of management, using mainly economic mechanisms to influence the managed production sphere (companies and "concerns") of industrial ministries. In addition, producing units are placed under the influence of regional, social, and special-interest organizations. This again represents indirect management. The final area on which direct quality control is concentrated (management objective) is composed of producing units with characteristic pyramidal arrangements on various management levels: company-concern (trust)-industrial ministry.

Specialized organizations of state administration, to which belong various nonindustrial ministries, central agencies, and state committees, as well as regional (republic, district, city), social, and special-interest organizations (e.g., trade unions), provide means of indirectly influencing decision processes in direct management. This takes the form of rules and regulations of technical and mainly economic nature. This is the way the state exercises its influence on product quality, which is the essence of the USSQC.

The organizational and technical basis of the system is provided by state standardization in a broad sense of the word, with three characteristic elements: technical normalization, metrology, and state testing of product quality. The development of standardization is managed with the help of standardization plans, which are part of the national economic plan and with which compliance is assured by specialized state bodies for standardization. Standardization in the CMEA countries has been developing vigorously, and CMEA's activities have broadened considerably, so that CMEA has become a decisive element in USSQC development. The leading role in this sense belongs to the Gosstandart USSR, which is a model for state standardization boards in the CMEA countries.

A special role played by standardization can be seen in an organic link of technical standards and metrology with product quality, which enables the countries to balance demands and needs concerning the chief parameters of product quality and to lay down uniform methods of measuring and testing product quality. With this aim the Soviet standardization system has elaborated new methods of helping to improve product quality. Among them should be mentioned complex[2] and perspective[3] standards, as well as the creation of large interbranch systems of normalization, such as uniform systems for technical documentation, for technological provision of production, or for certification (attestation) of product quality.

An important element of the Gosstandart USSR is its scientific and research basis, with a number of institutes aiding in the development of scientific principles and methods of standardization. Among the most important of them is the All-Union Research Institute for Standardization, which has elaborated and experimentally verified the principles of the Integrated Quality Control System (IQCS) in industrial companies as an integral part of the USSQC. Standardization, with its methods and orientation facilitates exercise of quality control on practically all levels of the national economy.

In their concept and place within the framework of the USSQC, various organizations and institutions of state standardization in the CMEA countries are close to the Gosstandart USSR. Most of them also have their origin in boards or offices for standardization and metrology, and their scope as applied to the tasks of quality control has gradually broadened.

---

[2]The term "complex" is used to describe efforts to coordinate the interests of manufacturers and consumers through optimizing standards for related semifinished and finished products.

[3]The term "perspective" refers to multiple grades within a standard, grades being associated with a special target date for accomplishment. The intention is to avoid the static character of standards by building into them a dynamic rate of improvement. Perspective standards take into consideration future changes of product quality parameters brought about by technological progress (Tkachenko, 1973).

A strong influence on this development is exercised by the CMEA—namely by its Permanent Committee for Standardization, with a working group for quality—by means of CMEA standards and methodological recommendations in the field of quality control. This is ultimately reflected by unification of the organizational structure of state standardization.

As early as 1973 in the GDR, the German Board for Measuring and Product Testing (DAMW) and the Office for Normalization merged into the Office for Standardization, Metrology, and Quality Control (ASMW), the activities of which very closely resemble the functions of the Gosstandart USSR. Similarly, in Poland the National Board for Quality and Measures (CUJM) was replaced by the State Committee for Standards, Measures, and Quality (PKNMiQ), which occupies a central place in the USSQC. The same trend can be observed in Bulgaria, Czechoslovakia, and Hungary and, since 1981, also in Cuba, where this function is assumed by a State Committee for Standardization; in Rumania it is the General Inspectorate for Quality Control. The statutes of such organizations differ, but they are mostly subordinated to the Council of Ministers (presidium of the government).

In addition to the above-mentioned central authorities for standardization, some other organizations are active in USSQC. These are mainly state inspection boards—organizations concerned with quality control of exported goods, which is carried out within the ministry of foreign trade. Similarly the state inspection system operates in the areas of domestic trade, food and agricultural products, energy, etc.

PRODUCT CERTIFICATION

The most widely practiced function of state QC systems in socialist countries is product certification (attestation), according to three quality categories (quality degrees or grades). Certified products of high quality are given special quality marks. Product certification consists of attestation of selected products based on comparisons of their properties with the properties of analogous products of top domestic or foreign manufacturers.

Attestation of certified products, as a rule, is compulsory. It applies to products that are important in satisfying the needs of the national economy of a country that influence the standard of living of its inhabitants, or that are of importance for competition on foreign markets. At the same time, certified products should be economically advantageous for customers. Products subject to compulsory attestation are registered in special lists, and their manufacturers apply to have them evaluated for attestation.

Product certification appeared in the CMEA member countries as early as the 1960s, and since then its practice has gradually expanded. Up to now, however, its implementation in the CMEA countries is not uniform, and certification results are not internationally valid. Product certification in a most detailed form was elaborated in the USSR, where it is based on theoretical results of "qualimetry" as a branch of science dealing with quality estimation (Glichev, 1972; Azgaldov, 1982).

In 1972 the Gosstandart USSR adopted directives on a Uniform System of Product Quality Certification (ESAKP), according to which certified products are classified into one of three quality categories (degrees, grades): highest, first, and second. To the highest-quality category belong products whose parameters reach or surpass the highest quality level of comparable domestic or foreign products. Such products can be granted a quality mark. Products classified in the first-quality category are those whose characteristics satisfy the requirements of currently valid technical standards. The second-quality category consists of products whose characteristics do not satisfy current requirements and that are of poor quality.

Certified products in the highest- and first-quality categories are launched into full-scale production. Products of the second-quality category should be improved and eventually withdrawn from production if they are manufactured, or new technical standards should be developed.

The certifications of products in the highest- or first-quality categories are valid for 1 to 3 years according to their intended use. State product certification is preceded by careful adjustment of manufacturing units to the necessary production conditions. All needed information and documentation are given on the units' own preliminary "home" attestation.

The state certification is carried out by certification commissions of respective industrial ministries, composed of representatives of producer and customer departments, the Gosstandart USSR, research institutes, and other selected experts. Decisions of certification commissions concerning products of the highest quality category are registered in the Gosstandart USSR. The producing department performs regular and random inspections in order to verify if the full-scale manufactured products satisfy all the certification requirements. Periodic inspections are also carried out by the Gosstandart, which is entitled to withdraw the quality mark in case of infringement of the terms of certification.

In the GDR product certification is currently carried out in conformity with a decree of the Council of Ministers from 1983. Products of highest quality can be granted a quality mark "Q." Products that, by their characteristics, do not satisfy the requirements of technical standards but whose production continues for economic reasons, e.g., according to the requirements of a foreign customer, are produced with special permission of ASMW. ASMW's approval is requested for products from the point of view of technical regulations.

In Czechoslovakia, manufacturers apply for registration of their products subject to compulsory attestation by state testing laboratories. Newly developed products subject to attestation are obligatorily registered for attestation in the preproduction stage. Certified products are classified into one of three quality grades: "1" (product of excellent quality), "2" (product of good quality), and "3" (all other products, of poor quality). If the product grossly fails in its functional properties, a state testing laboratory refuses to classify it into any quality degree. (Starting in 1987, three quality categories—Q, 1, 2 instead of 1, 2, 3—are being applied in Czechoslovakia.)

Manufacturers of products classified into the first or second quality grade are granted the right to use the quality mark by a state testing laboratory if the laboratory is convinced that the manufacturer is able to produce products with properties required by attestation. The validity of certification extends no more than 3 years for grade Q and 5 years for grade 1. As far as the third quality grade (2) is concerned, attestation must be repeated after no more than 2 years.

Selected products suspected of endangering the life or health of users or of causing great losses to the national economy are subject to compulsory approval in state testing laboratories. Nonapproved products must not be distributed. Approved products must be identified with an approval mark.

State testing laboratories perform random tests and inspections of the properties of attested or approved products. If it is established that a product does not satisfy the terms of attestation, the product is reclassified into a lower-quality grade or eventually may be deprived of its quality or approval mark.

In addition to product certification performed by state testing laboratories, in Czechoslovakia so-called "technical progressivity" or obsolescence of products is evaluated. The evaluation is performed by the State Committee for Technical Development and Investments, and it concerns mainly new products resulting from projects of the state plan of scientific and technical development. Such products are no longer subject to certification by state testing laboratories. This evaluation also classifies products into three grades, which depend on the technical and economic longevity of the products.

In other CMEA member countries, there exist product certification systems analogous to that in the USSR, although, naturally, with a number of individual features resulting from the historical and on-going development of product certification. Unification of product certification methodology represents one of the important tasks of further economic integration of the CMEA countries.

Data on certification of products subject to obligatory attestation provide a basis for planning industrial production levels (in physical and monetary units) according to various quality categories. The share of attested products in the production volume is mainly planned and supervised. In 1979 this share constituted 54 percent in the GDR. In Czechoslovakia it increased from 26 to 31 percent from 1976 to 1980. In 1979 products of highest quality accounted for 13.3 percent of the total production volume in the USSR and 11 percent in the GDR.

Table 35H.1 gives an idea of the distribution structure of attested products among different quality grades in Czechoslovakia from 1975 to 1981. It shows that the proportion of highest-quality products has regularly increased since 1975, reaching approximately one-quarter of all attested products in 1981, while the proportion of poor-quality products decreased to 3.3 percent in 1981.

On the basis of the data on state product certification, indexes important for quality planning are calculated. For example, in Czechoslovakia from 1978 to 1982 experimental indexes were devised to quantify the trends of such phenomena as: the proportion of products reaching the highest level of quality; the number of certificates issued for technological progress in total production volume; and the proportion of products of highest quality among those product categories attested at state testing laboratories. These and other indexes based on results of state product certification were then evaluated for the 5-year plan covering the period 1981 to 1985.

Product certification serves as an economic motivation for high-quality production. Material incentives for high product quality are based, first of all, on motivation for higher product prices and consequently for higher profits. Manufacturing companies are given price preferences for products of highest quality, for example, in the form of an increase of the basic wholesale price of such prod-

TABLE 35H.1   Products Rated by Quality Grade, Czechoslovakia, 1975–1981

Year	Number of estimated products	Quality grades, %			% not classified
		1	2	3	
1975	7616	12.0	77.4	9.9	0.7
1976	7658	14.4	73.4	11.5	0.7
1977	6482	16.9	70.3	11.9	0.9
1978	8536	20.7	71.0	7.8	0.5
1979	6811	24.6	68.6	5.9	0.9
1980	8733	22.1	72.2	5.3	0.4
1981	8991	25.8	70.2	3.3	0.7

Source: Reports of the Czechoslovak Office for Standards and Measurements.

ucts; in contrast, a price penalty in the form of a decrease of the basic wholesale price is applied to products of poor quality.

In Czechoslovakia, price preferences for products of highest quality and those for technically improved products are fixed in conformity with 1978 price regulations in the form of a premium of 25 percent added to the wholesale price when the economic benefit has been proved (otherwise it is only 15 percent). On the other hand, products of poor quality (third quality grade), as well as technologically obsolete products are subject to a price penalty in the form of a 15 percent reduction from the basic wholesale price of equivalent products (such a reduction may be increased to 30 percent as a result of repeated certification). The effective term of price premiums and penalties corresponds to the term of validity of respective quality grades.

Price premiums and penalties for attested products provide an effective economic incentive for manufacturing companies and their employees because they increase or decrease company funds. Such funds, which contribute to material incentives, include: first, a fund for cultural and social needs; also a development fund; and finally a fund for employees' compensation and bonuses, the amount of which is increased by income resulting from price premiums and decreased by price penalties on attested products. Such methods provide strong material incentives and promote the interests of manufacturers in the results of product certification and product quality.

The product certification system also includes evaluations of cultural and aesthetic properties and of industrial design of selected products. In the GDR, the Board of Industrial Design confers predicates (SL) of excellent design. In Czechoslovakia, the Institute of Industrial Design confers an award for excellent design each year to selected products of optimum quality.

INTEGRATED QUALITY CONTROL

The most important element of USSQC is the direct quality control in the producing sphere in which the product quality originates. Quality control, which, in producing units, originally included only limited aspects of management (mainly measuring, inspection, and testing) has in addition acquired the nature of a complex system with all management components. This universal development of QC manifested itself in countries with central planning in the form of the so-called integrated quality control system (the previously cited IQCS), which nowadays is the prevailing form of quality control in socialist industrial companies on the management axis company-concern (trust)-ministry. (In some respects, it resembles the Japanese "companywide" or "total" QC system.)

The IQCS is a complex of technological, organizational, economic, and social measures, which includes all factors and conditions influencing product quality, thus ensuring the possibility of reaching a planned level of quality. The complex nature of IQCS is also seen from the fact that quality can be controlled at all stages of the product life cycle—i.e., at the stage of research, design, development, and initial production of a new product; at the stage of full-scale production; and at the stage of storage, transportation, sale, and product usage (Glichev, 1978; Udovichenko, 1977).

The IQCS is based on company standards elaborated in full conformity with state and branch standards and other regulations. The methodology of IQCS is a combination of goal-oriented and functional approaches. In accordance with this, quality control functions are established and assigned to management bodies and departments within industrial companies. General management of IQCS is exercised by company directors and their deputies.

In the IQCS the following main functions are carried out (Glichev, 1981, pp. 17–18):

- Forecasting of needs, engineering level, and product quality. The forecast results represent initial data for planning quality enhancement. This function should be carried out by the Chief Designer's Department or Reliability Section, with the participation of the Chief Engineer's Department and the Planning and Economic Departments. The Chief Designer's Department should also specify and standardize quality requirements.

- Product certification (attestation) according to three quality categories, which is performed jointly by the Chief Designer's, Chief Engineer's, and Inspection Departments.

- Development and initial production of products, i.e., creation of design documents and prototype models, which are carried out jointly by the Chief Designer's and the Chief Engineer's Departments.

- Engineering provisions for production, which means services and production facilities, should be made available for the manufacturing process, responsibility for which lies jointly with the Departments of the Chief Engineer, Production Controller, Capital Construction, Chief Mechanical Engineer, and Chief Power Engineer.

- Material and equipment supply, i.e., provision of a company with raw materials, semifinished items, production equipment, and other materials, for which the Purchasing Department is responsible.

- Assurance of a stable quality level, which should be a result of joint efforts of the Production, the Chief Mechanical Engineer's, and Power Engineer's Departments.

- Storing, handling, assembling, service, and repairs, which should be the function of the Sales Department with specialized sections in cooperation with the Chief Designer's Department.

- Technical inspection and testing of products, which should be carried out by the Inspection Department.

- Metrological provisions ensuring the uniformity and accuracy of measurement related to product quality, for which the Mechanial Engineer's Department, together with the central laboratory, are responsible.

- Promotion of quality enhancement through material and moral incentives, which is the responsibility of the Labor and Wages Department.

- Selection, education, and training of personnel, for which the Personnel Department is responsible.

- Legal and judicial assurance of quality in strict conformity with legislation is performed by the Legal Department.

- Provision of all required information related to product quality, for which the Information Department and data processing center are responsible.

A special role in IQCS is played by the Quality Control Department. According to the Soviet concept (Glichev, 1981), as a rule a specialized QC section coordinates the activities of all departments in performing QC functions, i.e., auditing, analyzing, and reporting on their quality activities.

However, in a number of the CMEA countries this role is taken over by Quality Control Departments with far wider responsibilities. In addition to coordinating functions in the IQCS, they exert direct responsibilities, especially defect prevention activities (quality engineering) by use of progressive statistical and computer techniques, inspection, tests and their planning, quality training, and other methods. This is also the case with industrial companies in Czechoslovakia (Egermayer, 1983) and in the GDR (Lilie, 1979). The organizational structure and the number of employees in Quality Control Departments depend on the size of a company as well as on the nature and complexity of production. The company QC Department manager is subordinated directly to the company director.

In addition, there exist small QC Departments within concerns (trusts) of companies as well as in the respective ministries, which methodically guide company QC Departments. Similar relations are also valid for other functions in the IQCS on the management axis company-concern-ministry. At present the IQCS has also been implemented in various modifications in the other CMEA countries (Vecsenyi, 1977a; Mladjov, 1977).

QUALITY INFORMATION

For carrying out decisions, appropriate information on product quality as the most important element of the management process in the QC systems is necessary. The information system is a basis for creating an IQCS on all management levels. It unites companies, concerns (trusts), industrial ministries, and other central bodies, enabling them to coordinate with the USSQC (Egermayer, 1978; Ganushkin, 1980).

One of the most important areas of quality information is that concerning the quality properties of currently manufactured and newly developed products. It is information of a technical nature, which directly indicates product quality. Its primary source is the basic records of product quality (quality cards, test reports, data from market research). The majority of data come from internal (company) records, but some are obtained from external sources (suppliers and subsuppliers, testing laboratories, and domestic and foreign trade). The data are processed and summarized in records and surveys, mainly for the use of higher management levels.

Other quality information provides an indirect quality evaluation—these data concern the quality of the entire output of a production unit. This information relates especially to losses connected with poor product quality (internal and external failures).

Other important sources of information on quality are data from state and branch certification of products, which are of a technical and economic nature. They are data on the classification of products by quality grades and on their inspection. The data are summarized in records and surveys necessary for higher-level management units. Data from state and branch certification provide a starting point for the construction of indexes, which are used in quality plans and serve as economic motivators of companies and their employees for quality.

Quality data are also used for the calculation of indexes of economic effectiveness of the implementation of the IQCS (Egermayer, 1979). In 1978 the Gosstandart USSR elaborated special systematic instructions for this purpose.

QUALITY MOTIVATION

Quality motivation as a process of stimulating people (operators, supervisors, managers, QC specialists) to take action to reduce errors that lead to poor quality has always played an important role in quality improvement. This has also been confirmed in socialist countries. In the Soviet Union the Saratov system of defect-free manufacture of products appeared as early as 1955. (It is necessary to distinguish this sytem from the zero-defects system, which appeared in the early 1960s in the United States and was based on different motivational principles.) The Saratov system is based on the following principles:

The majority of errors committed by an employee on the job can be prevented.

Every employee is responsible for the quality of work done and therefore is obliged to control it. (This is the principle of so-called self-control.)

Every employee should know the exact job duties and must be given all facilities to accomplish them.

The system may include only such kinds of work as can be objectively controlled and estimated.

Originally, the Saratov system was aimed at estimating the quality of operators' work (operator-controllable errors) in piece and small-scale production, with work results (parts, components, assemblies) submitted in separate lots. It was only later that the system was enlarged to also cover other operators' jobs and production.

The main feature of the Saratov system is work performance, with the results being turned in right the first time. Defective products must be separated by the worker from products without defects, which are then turned over to inspection. The finding of even one defect is reason for returning the lot to the worker for correction. This procedure can be repeated during the second or further submittals of the lot to inspection, but always with consent of the supervisor. This method of submitting the work has also changed the nature of inspectors' jobs.

The procedure corresponds to the prime quantitative measure of worker performance in terms of percentage of products that are right the first time. In addition, the Saratov system naturally makes use of other indexes—e.g., amount and costs of scrap and rework, percentage of claims and complaints—which, however, are only supplementary in this system.

Another characteristic feature of the system is the institution of self-inspectors. Workers whose percentages of work performed correctly the first time are persistently high are given the authority to inspect their own work. For this purpose, the worker receives a personal inspection stamp with which to mark products no longer submitted to technical inspection. Attainment of this license not only qualifies the worker to a special bonus, but it is also of a high morale value. Before being granted the right to be a self-inspector, a worker must perform work without defects during a period of at least 6 months. The rate of defective products scrapped by the worker must not exceed a given limit, and the worker is expected to fulfill at least 100 percent of the production quota. Technical inspection of the work of self-inspectors is performed only randomly. If work deteriorates, the worker loses the right to be a self-inspector and consequently also loses the personal inspection stamp.

The percentage of work done correctly the first time also provides a basis for financial incentives on a graduated scale of bonuses, not only for individual workers and groups but also for an entire plant.

Because of its simplicity, the Saratov system has spread to a great number of Soviet industrial enterprises which, owing to the functioning of this system, have achieved impressive economic results, especially in decreases of rejects, rework, and product claims.

The Saratov system has also been extended to other socialist countries. In the GDR, performance according to the Saratov system ("fehlerfreie Arbeit") has become a prerequisite for the creation of the IQCS (Lilie, 1979). In Poland, the Saratov system has become one of the elements of the DO-RO system (DO-RO means "good work"), based on the principles of good work elaborated by T. Kotarbiński. The DO-RO system represents a continuous motivational campaign aimed at product quality enhancement and at improvement of the quality control level. In the period from 1968 to 1979, several thousands of Polish industrial companies took part in it in the framework of an all-state competition (Khojecki, 1974; Gwiazdecki, 1978). The Saratov system also took deep roots in Bulgaria and Czechoslovakia in the 1960s and became a starting point for the creation of the IQCS.

The Saratov system enabled, first of all, improvement of the quality of work performed by direct production operators. This has led to reduction of operator-controllable errors, which represent less than 20 percent of all errors. The planned product quality, however, cannot be achieved except by reducing both operator- and management-controllable errors. In the 1970s a new variant of defect-free work was introduced, which was capable of eliminating the limitations of the Saratov system and including work evaluations for all categories of workers, including managers. The new system was elaborated in industrial enterprises of the Lvov area and soon it spread widely not only in the Soviet Union, but also in other socialist countries.

The main indicator of work quality in the Lvov system of defect-free work has become a "work quality factor," which quantitatively expressed the quality of work of all employees involved in the production process (Glichev, 1978). This factor has the form of a coefficient, consisting of a base value (1 is usually chosen) from which are subtracted numerical values that are assigned by a special classifier to errors committed by individual employees in their work performance, and to which are added numerical values assigned to better than expected work—e.g., decreased percentage of rejects, rework, and claims (Udovichenko, 1977; Artamonov, 1977).

The work quality factor can be calculated for individual workers or for groups of workers, as well as for a whole plant. It permits comparison of work of different departments and units and may be used in incentive plans for quality. Owing to its universal nature, the work quality factor can be used for work evaluation not only in industrial enterprises but also in research and engineering institutes.

In socialist countries, so-called quality control circles have begun to be used as a labor motivational technique aimed at defect-free work (Zipfel, 1983; Nagy, 1983). A consultation center for quality control circles was established in the GDR in 1983.

QUALITY EDUCATION AND TRAINING

Qualification of employees is one of the main conditions for successful adaptation and implementation of the IQCS. The IQCS brings about special emphasis on education and training of employees active in the framework of this system in specific enterprises as well as in the organizations (suppliers, customers, testing laboratories, research institutes, etc.) that deal with these enterprises. From this also results a need for education in schools at all levels. Coincidental with such needs, education and training programs have been developed in all European socialist countries.

The largest and most detailed quality education and training system was developed in the 1970s in the Soviet Union in the framework of the Gosstandart activity. In this respect it influences the whole system of education, and its functioning is closely involved with that of social organizations. It is necessary, however, to recall once again that in the USSR quality control problems are always integrally connected with standardization. The same is also true of the field of quality education and training.

In the USSR the central body responsible for the methodology of quality education and training is the All-Union Research Institute for Standardization (VNIIS Gosstandart). This institute has developed basic education and training programs not only for training Gosstandart employees but also for employees of companies in all branches of industry and even for quality education in schools. The VNIIS also guides the education of scientific workers in the field of QC (Soviet as well as foreign citizens).

In 1978 the VNIIS worked out a detailed educational package called "Recommendations for QC Training of Employees in Industrial Companies," which includes methodological principles, forms and organization of instruction, and, particularly, examples of training programs for various categories of employees. The VNIIS has also built a model visual aids laboratory and consultation center, with audio equipment designed for group instruction as well as film projectors, videorecorders, and television sets. The center is used by managers and QC specialists from industrial companies (25 to 30 persons), who take part in 1- or 2-day seminars on specific subjects (Ogryzkov, 1979).

The main training center of the Gosstandart is the All-Union Upgrading Institute for Standardization, Quality Control, and Metrology (VISM), with several departments (Artes, 1977). This unique postgraduate institute admits some 20,000 trainees per year for studies of various lengths. Specialists from company technical inspection staffs and QC departments take part in 2 months of full-time training and in a 6-month course of studies while working, at the conclusion of which they receive a certificate. Similar training is organized for QC managers and chief inspectors. Specific courses are reserved for managers of other departments.

On behalf of the United Nations Industrial Development Organization (UNIDO), the VISM also organizes a 4-month course for industrial quality instructors from developing countries, in which the medium of instruction is English. The VISM has carried out some training programs in Cuba and Bulgaria. Large companies (such as the Likhachev automotive works) organize quaity training programs for their own employees at their own training institutes.

Problems of QC are also included in the curricula of several Soviet technical colleges and universities (e.g., at the Moscow Automobile and Road Construction Institute) or at technical secondary schools (e.g., the Vocational School of the Gosstandart for training of standardization specialists and metrologists in Odessa).

The Gosstandart also organizes QC training on a broad basis in so-called people's universities with the help of its local bodies (laboratories of state inspection).

Social organizations are an important factor in quality education and training in the Soviet Union. The National Council of Technological Societies (NTO) and the Society for Propagation of Political and Scientific Knowledge (Znanye), together with the Gosstandart in the Polytechnic Museum of Moscow, have founded the so-called Reliability Study ("Cabinet"), which, through seminars, lessons, consultations, and publications, propagates new knowledge among a large public of specialists. Similar "cabinets" can be found in a number of Soviet cities and industrial centers.

Objectives and activities in quality education and training similar to those in the Soviet Union can be found also in other socialist countries, with the obvious difference that these do not have such specialized institutes as the VNIIS and the VISM. For this reason, mutual cooperation between educational and social organizations is even more important.

In the GDR, great progress has been achieved in establishing quality education and training for preparation of QC and inspection engineers and technicians at the Technical University in Karl-Marx-Stadt (Chemnitz), GDR, in cooperation with the ASMW and the Chamber of Technology (Kammer der Technik) (KdT) (Trumpold, 1976). An active part in organization of postgraduate studies for QC personnel has also been taken by technical colleges and universities in the other CMEA countries, for instance, in Czechoslovakia (Egermayer, 1976), Hungary (Makay and Tarnoy, 1977), Bulgaria (Atanasov, 1977), and Poland (Khwialkowski, 1980).

Social organizations of the CMEA countries, mainly scientific and technological associations, have also created favorable conditions for quality education and training. In this sense so-called quality centers ("cabinets"), which are very active in the field of large-scale and systematic education and training for quality in Bulgaria, are remarkable (Dikov, 1977).

Recently, as a result of the development of the IQCS in the CMEA countries, there has been an increasing tendency to create global (integrated) programs of education and training for quality for all categories of employees active in the IQCS in various branches of industry. This is of special importance for managers. Such practices can be seen, for example, in mechanical engineering (Valenta, 1977), in the chemical industry (Lishka, 1977), in light industry (Farkas, 1973), in the construction industry (Vecsenyi, 1977), and in other industries.

An important role in promoting the integration of activities in quality education and training in the CMEA countries was played by a seminar organized by the EOQC Educational and Training Committee (ETC) in Odessa in 1977. All the CMEA countries take an active part in the activities of this committee.

REFERENCES

Artamonov, V. P. (1977). *Quality of Work.* Gosstandart, Moscow (in Russian).

Artes, A. E. (1977). "Up-grading of Specialists in Products Quality Control through VISM." *Proceedings EOQC ETC Seminar,* Odessa. EOQC, Bern, p. 59.

Atanasov, A. (1977). "Initial Criteria and Basic Factors Underlying the Level of Postgraduate Education and Training of QC Specialists." *Proceedings EOQC ETC Seminar,* Odessa. EOQC, Bern, p. 67.

Azgaldov, G. G. (1977). *Theory and Practice of Estimation of Product Quality.* Ekonomika, Moscow (in Russian).

Dikov, D. (1977). "Experience Gained by the Quality Centres in Bulgaria." *Proceedings EOQC ETC Seminar,* Odessa. EOQC, Bern, p. 125.

Egermayer, F. (1976). "Education and Training Programme for QC." *Proceedings 20th EOQC Conference,* Copenhagen. EOQC, Bern, vol. B, p. 91.

Egermayer, F. (1978). "Quality Information System in Integrated Quality Control." *Quality and Reliability,* vol. 24, no. 8, p. 127 (in German).

Egermayer, F. (1979). "Estimation of Economic Effect of Quality Control System." *Proceedings 23rd EOQC Conference,* Budapest. EOQC, Bern, vol. 5, p. 133.

Egermayer, F. (1983). *Quality Control in Mechanical Engineering Works.* University Press, Prague (in Czech).

Farkas, A. (1973). "Some Practical Aspects of Education and Training for Quality in Light Industry." *Proceedings 17th EOQC Conference,* 3rd section, Belgrade. EOQC, Bern, p. 127.

Ganushkin, V. V. (1980). "Information Supply of Quality Management System in the Ministry of Electronics and Electrical Engineering in Bulgaria." *Proceedings 24th EOQC Conference,* Warsaw. EOQC, Bern, vol. 3, p. 409.

Glichev, A. V. (1972). "Objectives of Qualimetry Estimation of Quality with Quantitative Methods." *Proceedings 15th EOQC Conference,* session 2, Moscow. EOQC, Bern, p. 3.

Glichev, A. V. (1977). "Quality Control and Personnel Training." *Proceedings EOQC ETC Seminar,* Odessa. EOQC, Bern, p. 21.

Glichev, A. V. (1978). "Quality Improvement and Efficiency of Social Production." *Proceedings International QC Conference,* A3, Tokyo, p. 7.

Glichev, A. V. (1981). "The Soviet QC Experience." *Quality Progress,* vol. 14, no. 10, p. 16.

Gwiazdecki, M. (1978). "Good Work Competition—Essential Element of Quality Policy in Poland." *Proceedings 22nd EOQC Conference,* vol. 1, Dresden. EOQC, Bern, p. 150 (in German).

Khojecki, H. (1974). *Quality Optimization—Psychological Methods.* PWE, Warsaw (in Polish).

Khwialkowski, H. (1980). "New Form of Education and Training of the Managerial Staff in the Field of QC in Poland." *Proceedings 24th EOQC Conference,* Warsaw. EOQC, Bern, vol. 1, p. 93.

Lilie, H. (ed.) (1979). *Quality Control and Standardization Handbook.* Die Wirtschaft (publishing house), Berlin.

Linczenyi, A. (1978). "International Collaboration in the Domain of QC in the C.M.E.A. Countries." *Proceedings International Conference QC,* JUSE, Tokyo, vol. A1, p. 5.

Lishka, K. (1977). "Training and Upgrading of Top Management of Chemical and Light Industries in QC." *Proceedings EOQC ETC Seminar,* Odessa. EOQC, Bern, p. 99.

Makay, G. and Tarnoy, E. (1977). "A Complex Method for Teaching QC in the Engineering Industry in Hungary." *Proceedings EOQC ETC Seminar,* Odessa. EOQC, Bern, p. 28.

Mladjov, L. A. (1977). "Bulgarian Variants of the Integrated QC System on the Basis of Standardization." *Proceedings 21st EOQC Conference,* Varna. EOQC, Bern, vol. 1, p. 214.

Nagy, E. (1983). "Methodological Problems of the Implementation of QC Circles." *Proceedings 27th EOQC Conference,* Madrid. EOQC, Bern, Appendix.

Ogryzkov, V. M. (1979). "Quality Training of Industrial Workers by Means of Technical Aids." *Proceedings EOQC ETC Seminar,* Heidelberg. EOQC, Bern, p. 78.

Sütö, K. (1978). "Standardization in the CMEA and its Realization in Hungary." *Proceedings International QC Conference,* vol. A6, Tokyo. EOQC, Bern, p. 7.

Tkachenko, V. V. (ed.) (1973). *Principles of Standardization and Quality Control.* Gosstandart, Moscow (in Russian).

Trumpold, H. (1976). "Experience with Education and Training of Mechanical Engineers in QC." *Proceedings 20th EOQC Conference,* Copenhagen. EOQC, Bern, vol. B, p. 91 (in German).

Udovichenko, E. J. (ed.) (1977). *Integrated System of Quality Control.* Publishing House of Technology, Kiev (in Russian).

Valenta, B. (1977). "System of Training and Education in QC of Top Workers in CSSR Engineering." *Proceedings EOQC ETC Seminar,* Odessa. EOQC, Bern, p. 49.

Vecsenyi, J. (1977*a*). "Implementation of Quality Control Systems by the Provizorg Method." *Proceedings 21st EOQC Conference,* Varna. EOQC, Bern, vol. 1, p. 290.

Vecsenyi, J. (1977*b*). "Postgraduate Training for QC Specialists in the Building Industry." *Proceedings EOQC ETC Seminar,* Odessa. EOQC, Bern, p. 92.

Zipfel, H. J. (1983). "Quality Control Circles—an Efficient Instrument for Enhancement of Product Quality." *Standardization and Quality,* vol. 29, no. 2, p. 52 (in German).

APPENDIX I
GLOSSARY OF SYMBOLS

a = combination of factors A, B, C, ... , n in a 2^n experiment in which only A occurs at the high level; similarly for b, c, ... , n.

A = unit cost of acceptance (damage done by a defective piece which slips through inspection).

A = a multiplier of σ_0 used to locate the 3-sigma control limits above and below the central line on an X chart.

A = in maintenance time prediction, a rating for product design features.

A_1 = a multiplier of $\bar{s}$ used to locate the 3-sigma control limits above and below the central line on an $\bar{X}$ chart.

A_2 = a multiplier of $\bar{R}$ used to locate the 3-sigma control limits above and below the control line of an $\bar{X}$ chart.

A_c = in sampling acceptance schemes, the acceptance number, i.e., the maximum allowable number of defective pieces in a sample of size n.

A_i = intrinsic availability.

A_o = operational availability.

ACL = acceptance control limit, i.e., a distance d from APL in the direction of the RPL.

ANOVA = analysis of variance.

AOQ = average outgoing quality, i.e., the quality of product leaving the inspection department after acceptance sampling and any detailing found necessary.

AOQL = average outgoing quality limit, i.e., the worst quality, on the average, after acceptance sampling and any detailing found necessary.

APL = acceptance process level, i.e., a process level which is acceptable and should be accepted most of the time by the plan.

AQL = acceptable quality level, i.e., a specified quality level for each lot such that the sampling plan will accept a stated percentage (say 95 percent) of submitted lots having this quality level.

ARL = average run length.

ASN = average sample number, i.e., the average number of units inspected per lot in sampling inspection, ignoring the 100 percent inspection of rejected lots.

ATI = average total inspection, i.e., average number of items inspected in a lot under a specified acceptance procedure.

b = number of blocks in a randomized block experimental design.

b = number of good units rejected by the inspector.

$b_1, b_2, \ldots$ = estimates of regression coefficients $\beta_1, \beta_2, \ldots$.

b_{10}, b_{50} = life by which 10 percent (or 50 percent) of a population would have failed.

B = in maintenance time prediction, a rating for design dictates for maintenance personnel.

B_3 = a multiplier of $\bar{s}$ used to locate the 3-sigma lower control limit on a chart for σ.

B_4 = a multiplier of $\bar{s}$ used to locate the 3-sigma upper control limit on a chart for σ.

B_5 = a multiplier of σ_0 used to locate the 3-sigma lower control limit on a chart for σ.

B_6 = a multiplier of σ_0 used to locate the 3-sigma upper control limit on a chart for σ.

c = number of defects, usually in a sample of stated size.

c = in sampling acceptance schemes, the acceptance number, i.e., the maximum allowable number of defective pieces in a sample of size n. (In government sampling tables the symbol Ac is used.)

c = a scale factor given in MIL-STD-414.

c = number of columns in an experimental design.

$\bar{c}$ = average number of defects per sample in a series of samples.

c_0 = standard or aimed-at average number of defects in a sample of stated size. c_0 may also refer to the population average number of defects per sample.

c_2 = ratio between the expected value of $\bar{\sigma}$ in a long series of samples and the σ of the population from which they were drawn. $c_2 = \dfrac{\sqrt{2}}{n}\left(\dfrac{n-2}{2}\right)!\left(\dfrac{n-3}{2}\right)!$

c_{ii} = element in the ith row and ith column of a matrix C.

C = cost of repairing or replacing a defective once found.

C = extra capacity required.

C = correction factor, constant.

C_1 = the allowable number of defectives in the cumulative results of k_1 or fewer samples in the first stage.

C_2 = the allowable number of defectives in the cumulative results of $k_1 + 1$ to k_2 or fewer samples or the last k_2 samples.

C_f = total user failure cost.

C_p = variance of regression predictions.

C_{pk} = performance index.

$\hat{C}_{pk}$ = estimate of C_{pk}.

ChSP = chain sampling plan.

CIM = change-in-mean-effect in Evolutionary Operations.

CRC = cumulative results criterion in acceptance sampling.

CSCC = cumulative sum control chart.

CSP = continuous sampling plan.

d = ratio of the difference to be detected in a test divided by the measure of variability.

d = the difference in readings in a paired sample.

d = the number of defectives in a sample.

d = number of defects reported by the inspector.

d_i = number of defective units in ith sample.

d_i = the signed differences in a Youden two-sample interlaboratory test.

$\bar{d}$ = the average difference in readings in a paired sample.

d' = deviation, in cells, from the assumed origin of a frequency distribution.

d_2 = ratio of the expected value of $\bar{R}$ (in samples of size n) to the s of the population.

D = the cumulative number of defectives in a series of samples.

D = largest deviation of actual percent cumulative frequency from theoretical percent cumulative frequency.

D = in a cumulative sum control chart, the least amount of change in the average that it is desired to detect.

D = damages caused by failure.

D_1 = a multiplier of σ_0 used to locate the 3-sigma lower control limit on a chart for R.

D_2 = a multiplier of σ_0 used to locate the 3-sigma upper control limit on a chart for R.

D_3 = a multiplier of $\bar{R}$ used to locate the 3-sigma lower control limit on a chart for R.

D_4 = a multiplier of $\bar{R}$ used to locate the 3-sigma upper control limit on a chart for R.

D_i = cumulative number of defective units at the ith sample.

DA = double sampling AOQL tables of the Dodge-Romig sampling tables.

DF = degrees of freedom, the number of independent comparisons possible with a given set of observations (also called f).

DL = double sampling lot tolerance of the Dodge-Romig sampling tables.

DPU = defects per unit.

$e =$ the constant 2.71828+.

$e_{ij} =$ the experimental error associated with the measurement Y_{ij}.

$E =$ maximum allowable error in estimate (desired precision).

$E =$ the effect being estimated (difference between averages).

$E =$ effectiveness loss.

$E_2 =$ a multiplier of $\overline{R}$ to determine the 3-sigma control limits on a chart for individuals.

ETT = expected test time.

EVOP = evolutionary operation.

$f =$ frequency; generally, the number of observed values in a given cell of a frequency distribution.

$f =$ sampling rate in continuous sampling.

$f =$ in Skip Lot sampling, the fraction of lots to be inspected after the initial criteria have been satisfied.

$f =$ degrees of freedom, the number of independent comparisons possible with a given set of observations (also called DF).

$f =$ severity effect of the occurrence of an unsafe event.

$F =$ ratio of two estimates of variance or the distribution of this ratio.

$F =$ number of failures.

$F_{CALC} =$ calculated value of F.

$F_{TAB} =$ tabulated value of F.

$F' =$ ratio of two sample ranges or the distribution of this ratio.

$F(t) =$ proportion of population failing before time t.

FITS = failures in ten to the ninth (i.e., one billion) hours.

FR = failure rate, i.e., the percentage of failures per unit time.

$g =$ number of groups in a group screening experimental design.

$g =$ a numerical factor used in calculations for the Weibull distribution.

GLD = generalized lambda distribution.

$h =$ a parameter of cumulative sum sampling plans.

$h' =$ a parameter of cumulative sum sampling plans.

$h_1, h_2 =$ intercept values in a sequential sampling plan for process parameter.

$H =$ an index calculated in the Kruskal-Wallis ranks test.

H: = hypothesis.

$i =$ cell interval; for grouped data, the distance from a point in one cell to a similar point in the next cell.

$i =$ in Skip Lot sampling, the number of successive lots to be found conforming to qualify for skipping lots either at the start or after detecting a nonconforming lot.

$i =$ number of successive acceptable units in continuous sampling.

I = cost of inspecting one piece.

I = lost income.

I_m = minimum inspection per lot.

I = the square identity matrix.

k = number of sampling levels in continuous sampling plans.

k = a parameter of cumulative sum sampling plans.

k = number of treatments or levels of the factor to be investigated.

k = number of good units rejected by the inspector.

k_1 = the maximum number of samples for cumulation of defectives in the first stage.

k_2 = the maximum number of samples for cumulation of defectives in the second stage and in the "normal" period following the second stage.

K = the difference between a particular value and the average of the curve in units of standard deviation. $K = \dfrac{X - \mu}{\sigma}$. Also called z.

K = in Evolutionary Operation, a factor used in determining the error term. Converts range into estimated standard deviation.

L = a numerical factor used in calculations for Evolutionary Operations.

L = loss function.

L = multiples of the standard deviation.

L = lack of fit.

LACL = in variables sampling plans, the lower acceptance control limit.

LAV = least absolute value.

LCL = lower control limit on a control chart.

LQ = limiting quality.

LTPD = lot tolerance percent defective, i.e., the level of defectiveness that is unsatisfactory and therefore should be rejected by the sampling plan.

m = number of occurrences.

M = in MIL-STD-414, an acceptance limit.

M = a numerical factor used in calculations for Evolutionary Operation.

MAR = maximum allowable range.

ML = mean life.

MS = mean square.

MSB = mean square between treatments.

MSE = error mean square.

MSW = mean square within treatments.

MTBF = mean time between failures.

MTTR = mean time to repair.

$M(t)$ = cumulative hazard rate for period 0 to t.

n = number of articles or observed values in a sample or subgroup. Also, the number of trials of some event.

n = number assigned to each treatment.

n_0 = in a response surface experimental design, the number of center points.

n_1 = in double sampling, the number of pieces in the first sample.

n_2 = in double sampling, the number of pieces in the second sample.

n_a = attributes sample size.

$\bar{n}$ = average sample size.

$n!$ = $n(n-1)(n-2)\ldots$

np = number of defective articles in a sample of size n.

$n\bar{p}$ = average value of np in a set of sample size n.

N = number of articles in a lot or population.

N = number of subgroups.

$N_\alpha N_\beta$ = measures for evaluating inspector efficiency.

OC = operating characteristic, a plot describing the risks in a sampling plan.

p = fraction nonconforming, i.e., the ratio of the number of nonconforming units to the total number of nonconforming and conforming units.

p = probability of occurrence of an unsafe event.

p = in sensory tests, the fraction correct identification of the unknown with standard.

p = fraction correct identification of unknown with standard (in sensory test).

p = incoming quality.

p_1 = in variables sampling plans, the acceptable fraction nonconforming.

p_2 = in variables sampling plans, the rejectable fraction nonconforming.

p_0 = aimed-at or standard values of the fraction of nonconforming articles; also, the true value of p in a lot or population being sampled.

$\bar{p}$ = average fraction nonconforming, i.e., the total number of nonconforming units found in a set of samples divided by the total number of units in the samples.

p_b = break-even value of fraction nonconforming for which cost of inspection of $1/p_b$ units is equal to cost of damage done by one nonconforming.

p_b = break-even value of p.

$p_L(\%)$ = in variables sampling plans, estimate of percent defective below the lower specification limit.

$p_U(\%)$ = in variables sampling plans, estimate of percent defective.

P = the population percentage included between statistical tolerance limits.

P_a = probability of accepting a given lot. Also, the probability of accepting a hypothesis.

$P(A)$ = probability of occurrence of event A.

$P_0, P_1, P_2, \ldots$ = probability of finding exactly 0, 1, 2, ... defectives in a sample.

P_i = reliability of individual elements in a redundancy.

P_r = reliable life.

P_r = the probability of lot rejection.

PC = PRE-Control.

PE = pure error.

PRST = probability ratio sequential test.

P_s = reliability of system.

P_s = probability of survival. The probability of failure-free operation for a time period equal to or greater than t. (This is identical with R, reliability.)

q = $1 - p$, the probability that a particular event will not happen in a single trial.

q = in experimental design, number of components in a mixture.

Q_L, Q_U = quality indices used in MIL-STD-414.

r = the number of occurrences of some event, e.g., the number of defectives in a sample, the number of occurrences of the less frequent sign in a test of hypothesis. Also, the distribution of this statistic.

r = the sample correlation coefficient.

$r!$ = $r(r - 1)(r - 2) \ldots$.

R = range of a set of n numbers, i.e., the difference between the largest number and the smallest number.

R = reliability. The probability of failure-free operation for a time period equal to or greater than t. (This is identical with P_s, the probability of survival.)

R = unit cost of rejection (cost of finding a defective in a rejected lot, plus expense of correcting it).

$\overline{R}$ = mean of several ranges.

R_e = the rejection number, i.e., the number of defective pieces in a sample of size n which causes rejection of the lot.

$R(t)$ = proportion of population surviving to time t.

REG = regression.

RES = residual.

RL = reference level or reference quality level, i.e., engineering estimate of what the quality at delivery should be.

RPL = rejectable process level, i.e., a process level which is rejectable and should be rejected most of the time by the plan.

RQL = rejectable quality level.

RSM = response surface methodology, an experimental approach
used to optimize many different kinds of industrial unit processes, and systems.

R^2 = the proportion of variation explained by a regression model.
Also the square of the sample multiple correlation
coefficient.

s = sample estimate of σ (standard deviation of population); e.g.,
s is the sample estimate of the standard deviation of individual values, $s_{\overline{X}}$ is the sample estimate of the standard
deviation of sample means. Also called $\hat{\sigma}$.

s = in sequential sampling plans, a constant computed from the
values of the APL and the RPL.

s = for the negative binomial, the difference between number of
trials and number of occurrences.

s^2 = sample estimate of σ^2 (variance of a population); e.g., s^2 is
the sample estimate of the variance of individual values,
$s_{\overline{X}}^2$ is the sample estimate of the variance of sample means.

S = safeness of the system.

S_m = test statistic in cumulative sum sampling plans.

SA = single-sampling AOQL tables of the Dodge-Romig tables.

SE = standard error.

SKSP = Skip Lot sampling plan.

SPC = statistical process control.

SL = single-sampling lot tolerance tables of Dodge-Romig tables.

SS = sum of squares; e.g., SSE is sum of squares for error.

SSB = between-treatments sum of squares.

SSC = column sum of squares.

SSE = error sum of squares.

SSI = interaction sum of squares.

SSR = row sum of squares.

SSW = within-treatments sum of squares.

t = a specified period of failure-free operation.

t = treatment in a randomized block design.

t = statistic used to compare sample means or the distribution
of the statistic.

t' = statistic used to compare sample means when the population
standard deviations cannot be assumed equal. $t' =$
$$\frac{\overline{X}_1 - \overline{X}_2}{\sqrt{s_1^2/n_1 + s_2^2/n_2}}$$

t = number of standard deviation units.

t_0 = number of time units.

T = in sequential sampling, the cumulative sum of an appropriate statistic against the sample number n.

T = in cumulative sum control charts, the permissible average time before a process shift of D is detected.

T = tolerance.

T_L = $(\overline{X} - L)/s$, a statistic used in MIL-STD-414.

T_U = $(U - \overline{X})/s$, a statistic used in MIL-STD-414.

T^2 = a statistic used to test population means on two characteristics (called Hotelling's T^2).

TBF = time between failures.

TSS = corrected total sum of squares.

u = defects per unit.

$\bar{u}$ = total number of nonconformities in all samples divided by the total number of units in all samples, i.e., the nonconformities per unit.

U = symbol used for statistics (for testing hypotheses) that follow a normal distribution.

U = upper specification limit for a quality characteristic X.

UCL = upper control limit on a control chart.

w = the ranges of the n observations on each treatment.

W = importance weights.

x = a vector of elements.

x' = the transpose of the x vector.

$X_1, X_2, \ldots$ = observed value of some variable, usually a quality characteristic.

$\overline{X}$ = arithmetic mean, the average of a set of numbers $X_1, X_2, X_3, \ldots, X_n$ is the sum of the numbers divided by n.

$\overline{X}_0$ = an aimed-at or standard value of a quality characteristic. Also used to represent the true but often unknown mean of a universe being sampled.

$\overline{\overline{X}}$ = mean of several $\overline{X}$ values. Often called the grand average.

$\overline{X}_c(h)$ = the mean of the h composite measurements.

X_p = control variable.

X = a matrix of elements.

$\tilde{X}$ = median value of X.

Y = response characteristic.

Y = observed value of a variable.

Y_i = the yield for run number i.

Y_{ij} = the observation on the ith treatment in the jth block.

$\overline{Y}$ = average of values of Y variable.

$\overline{Y}_0$ = in response surface methodology, the average of the center points.

$\hat{Y}$ = the predicted value for Y.

Z = logarithm of $Y = e^z$.

Z = normal distribution coefficient.

Z_i = the ith values after a canonical analysis of the original X_i axis.

$Z(t)$ = hazard rate, i.e., instantaneous failure rate at time t.

α (alpha) = probability of rejecting the hypothesis under test when it is true. (Called the type I error or level of significance.) In acceptance sampling, α = the producer's risk.

α = scaling parameter of the Weibull distribution.

α = level of significance.

β (beta) = probability of accepting the hypothesis under test when it is false. (Called the type II error.) In acceptance sampling, β is the consumer's risk.

$\beta_1, \beta_2, \ldots$ = in regression the unknown parameters of the model.

β = shaping parameter of the Weibull distribution.

β_i = a term peculiar to a given block. It is the amount by which the response of a given treatment in the ith block differs from the response of the same treatment averaged over all blocks, assuming no experimental error.

γ (gamma) = confidence level.

γ = location parameter of the Weibull distribution.

Γ (gamma) = the gamma function.

δ (delta) = width of confidence interval.

σ_0 = in analysis of variance, an acceptably small value of the ratio σ_b/σ_w, the ratio of between-group variability to within-group variability.

σ_1 = in analysis of variance, an unacceptably large value for the ratio σ_b/σ_w, the ratio of between-group variability to within-group variability.

σ_i = differences between means.

Δ = total variation of.

ϵ (epsilon) = a random error term of a linear function.

η (eta) = scale parameter of the Weibull distribution.

η = group means, grand mean.

θ = in reliability, mean life.

θ = in cumulative sum control charts, an angle on the mask used in the chart.

λ (lambda) = failure rate, i.e., the percentage of failures per unit time.

λ_t = accumulative failure rate.

μ (mu) = the population mean (average), e.g., the mean of a lot, the mean time between failures, or the mean life. (μ_0 is the acceptable mean life and μ_1 is the unacceptable mean life.)

ξ (xi) = transformation value.

π (pi) = the constant $3.14159+$.

σ (sigma) = the population standard deviation; e.g., σ is the standard deviation of individual values, $\sigma_{\overline{X}}$ is the standard deviation of sample means. (Some literature uses σ' in place of σ.)

$\bar{\sigma}$ = mean of several standard deviations.

Σ (sigma) = a mathematical sign meaning "take the algebraic sum of the quantities which follow."

τ_d (tau$_d$) = $\dfrac{\overline{X}_1 - \overline{X}_2}{\frac{1}{2}(R_1 + R_2)}$, a statistic used to test the hypothesis about μ_1 and μ_2. Also, the distribution of the statistic.

τ_1 = $\dfrac{\overline{X} - \mu_0}{R}$, a statistic used to test the hypothesis about μ_0. Also the distribution of the statistic.

ϕ (phi) = mutually exclusive.

ϕ_i = in a randomized block experimental design, a term peculiar to the ith treatment, constant for all blocks regardless of the block in which the treatment occurs.

Φ (p) = distribution function of process average.

χ^2 (chi^2) = ratio of $\dfrac{(n-1)s^2}{\sigma_0^2}$ or the distribution of this ratio.

! = factorial sign $n!$ means "take the product of the integers from 1 through n." (Note: either 0! or 1! = 1.)

∞ = infinity.

See Appendix III for a listing of standards covering symbols and other matters.

APPENDIX II
TABLES AND CHARTS

TABLE A. FACTORS FOR COMPUTING CONTROL CHART LINES AII.3

TABLE B. NORMAL DISTRIBUTION AII.5

TABLE C. EXPONENTIAL DISTRIBUTION AII.8

TABLE D. MEDIAN RANKS . . . AII.9

TABLE E. POISSON DISTRIBUTION AII.10

TABLE F. BINOMIAL DISTRIBUTION AII.14

TABLE G. DISTRIBUTION OF t . . AII.16

TABLE H. PERCENTILES FOR
$$\tau_d = \frac{\overline{X} - \mu_0}{R}$$ AII.17

TABLE I. CRITICAL VALUES OF r FOR THE SIGN TEST AII.18

TABLE J. PRECENTILES FOR
$$\tau_d = \frac{\overline{X}_1 - \overline{X}_2}{\frac{1}{2}(R_1 + R_2)}$$ AII.19

TABLE K. DISTRIBUTION OF F . AII.20

TABLE L. DISTRIBUTION OF χ^2 . AII.26

TABLE M. PERCENTILES OF
$$F' = \frac{R_1}{R_2}$$ AII.27

CHART N. CONFIDENCE LIMITS FOR FRACTION DEFECTIVE . . . AII.28

TABLE O. CRITICAL VALUES OF SMALLER RANK SUM FOR THE WILCOXON-MANN-WHITNEY TEST AII.29

TABLE P. LIMITING VALUES FOR NUMBER OF RUNS ABOVE AND BELOW THE MEDIAN OF A SET OF VALUES AII.30

TABLE Q. CRITERIA FOR TESTING FOR EXTREME MEAN   AII.31

CHART R. OPERATING CHARACTERISTICS OF THE TWO-SIDED NORMAL TEST FOR A LEVEL OF SIGNIFICANCE EQUAL TO 0.05 . . . . AII.32

CHART S. SIZE OF SAMPLE FOR ARITHMETIC MEAN WHEN σ IS UNKNOWN AII.33

CHART T. NUMBER OF DEGREES OF FREEDOM REQUIRED TO ESTIMATE THE STANDARD DEVIATION WITHIN $P\%$ OF ITS TRUE VALUE WITH CONFIDENCE COEFFICIENT γ . . AII.34

TABLE U. TOLERANCE FACTORS FOR NORMAL DISTRIBUTION AII.35

TABLE V. ONE-SIDED AND TWO-SIDED STATISTICAL TOLERANCE LIMIT FACTORS k FOR A NORMAL DISTRIBUTION   AII.36

TABLE W. P FOR INTERVAL BETWEEN SAMPLE EXTREMES   AII.38

TABLE X. N FOR INTERVAL BETWEEN SAMPLE EXTREMES   AII.38

TABLE Y. E_2 FACTORS FOR CONTROL CHARTS AII.39

CHART Z. CONTROL LIMITS FOR p CHARTS AII.39

CHART AA. CONTROL LIMITS
FOR c, NUMBER OF DEFECTS
PER SAMPLE AII.40

TABLE BB. FACTORS FOR
CUMULATIVE SUM CONTROL
CHART AII.40

TABLE CC. RANDOM NUMBERS AII.41

TABLE DD. VALUES OF ϕ^2 FOR
DETERMINING SAMPLE SIZE IN
ANALYSIS OF VARIANCE . . . AII.42

For more extensive tables see Owen, D. B. (1962). *Handbook of Statistical Tables.* Addison-Wesley, Reading, MA. 1962.

TABLE A Factors for Computing Control Chart Lines*

Observations in Sample, n	Chart for averages — Factors for control limits			Chart for standard deviations — Factors for central line		Chart for standard deviations — Factors for control limits				Chart for ranges — Factors for central line			Chart for ranges — Factors for control limits			
	A	A_2	A_3	c_4	$1/c_4$	B_3	B_4	B_5	B_6	d_2	$1/d_2$	d_3	D_1	D_2	D_3	D_4
2	2.121	1.880	2.659	0.7979	1.2533	0	3.267	0	2.606	1.128	0.8865	0.853	0	3.686	0	3.267
3	1.732	1.023	1.954	0.8862	1.1284	0	2.568	0	2.276	1.693	0.5907	0.888	0	4.358	0	2.574
4	1.500	0.729	1.628	0.9213	1.0854	0	2.266	0	2.088	2.059	0.4857	0.880	0	4.698	0	2.282
5	1.342	0.577	1.427	0.9400	1.0638	0	2.089	0	1.964	2.326	0.4299	0.864	0	4.918	0	2.114
6	1.225	0.483	1.287	0.9515	1.0510	0.030	1.970	0.029	1.874	2.534	0.3946	0.848	0	5.078	0	2.004
7	1.134	0.419	1.182	0.9594	1.0423	0.118	1.882	0.113	1.806	2.704	0.3698	0.833	0.204	5.204	0.076	1.924
8	1.061	0.373	1.099	0.9650	1.0363	0.185	1.815	0.179	1.751	2.847	0.3512	0.820	0.388	5.306	0.136	1.864
9	1.000	0.337	1.032	0.9693	1.0317	0.239	1.761	0.232	1.707	2.970	0.3367	0.808	0.547	5.393	0.184	1.816
10	0.949	0.308	0.975	0.9727	1.0281	0.284	1.716	0.276	1.669	3.078	0.3249	0.797	0.687	5.469	0.223	1.777
11	0.905	0.285	0.927	0.9754	1.0252	0.321	1.679	0.313	1.637	3.173	0.3152	0.787	0.811	5.535	0.256	1.744
12	0.866	0.266	0.886	0.9776	1.0229	0.354	1.646	0.346	1.610	3.258	0.3069	0.778	0.922	5.594	0.283	1.717
13	0.832	0.249	0.850	0.9794	1.0210	0.382	1.618	0.374	1.585	3.336	0.2998	0.770	1.025	5.647	0.307	1.693
14	0.802	0.235	0.817	0.9810	1.0194	0.406	1.594	0.399	1.563	3.407	0.2935	0.763	1.118	5.696	0.328	1.672
15	0.775	0.223	0.789	0.9823	1.0180	0.428	1.572	0.421	1.544	3.472	0.2880	0.756	1.203	5.741	0.347	1.653
16	0.750	0.212	0.763	0.9835	1.0168	0.448	1.552	0.440	1.526	3.532	0.2831	0.750	1.282	5.782	0.363	1.637
17	0.728	0.203	0.739	0.9845	1.0157	0.466	1.534	0.458	1.511	3.588	0.2787	0.744	1.356	5.820	0.378	1.622
18	0.707	0.194	0.718	0.9854	1.0148	0.482	1.518	0.475	1.496	3.640	0.2747	0.739	1.424	5.856	0.391	1.608
19	0.688	0.187	0.698	0.9862	1.0140	0.497	1.503	0.490	1.483	3.689	0.2711	0.734	1.487	5.891	0.403	1.597
20	0.671	0.180	0.680	0.9869	1.0133	0.510	1.490	0.504	1.470	3.735	0.2677	0.729	1.549	5.921	0.415	1.585
21	0.655	0.173	0.663	0.9876	1.0126	0.523	1.477	0.516	1.459	3.778	0.2647	0.724	1.605	5.951	0.425	1.575
22	0.640	0.167	0.647	0.9882	1.0119	0.534	1.466	0.528	1.448	3.819	0.2618	0.720	1.659	5.979	0.434	1.566
23	0.626	0.162	0.633	0.9887	1.0114	0.545	1.455	0.539	1.438	3.858	0.2592	0.716	1.710	6.006	0.443	1.557
24	0.612	0.157	0.619	0.9892	1.0109	0.555	1.445	0.549	1.429	3.895	0.2567	0.712	1.759	6.031	0.451	1.548
25	0.600	0.153	0.606	0.9896	1.0105	0.565	1.435	0.559	1.420	3.931	0.2544	0.708	1.806	6.056	0.459	1.541

*The above table is a copy of Table 27 in *ASTM Manual on Presentation of Data and Control Chart Analysis.* (1976). ASTM Publication STP15D, American Society for Testing and Materials, Philadelphia, pp. 134–135. Used with permission.

Notes: For $n > 25$, $A = 3/\sqrt{n}$, $A_2 = 3/c_4\sqrt{n}$, $A_3 = 3/c_4\sqrt{n}$, $c_4 \approx 4(n-1)/(4n-3)$; $B_3 = 1 - 3/c_4\sqrt{2(n-1)}$, $B_4 = 1 + 3/c_4\sqrt{2(n-1)}$,

$$B_5 = c_4 - 3/\sqrt{2(n-1)}, \quad B_6 = c_4 + 3/\sqrt{2(n-1)}$$

FORMULAS

Purpose of chart	Chart for	Central line	3-Sigma control limits
For analyzing past inspection data for control ($\overline{\overline{X}}$, $\overline{s}$, $\overline{R}$ are average values for the data being analyzed)	Averages	$\overline{\overline{X}}$	$\overline{\overline{X}} \pm A_3\overline{s}$, or $\overline{\overline{X}} \pm A_2\overline{R}$
	Standard deviations	$\overline{s}$	$B_3\overline{s}$ and $B_4\overline{s}$
	Ranges	$\overline{R}$	$D_3\overline{R}$ and $D_4\overline{R}$
For controlling quality during production ($\overline{X}_0$, σ_0, R_0, are selected standard values; $R_0 = d_2\sigma_0$ for samples of size n)	Averages	$\overline{X}_0$	$\overline{X}_0 \pm A\sigma_0$ or $\overline{X}_0 \pm A_2R_0$
	Standard deviations	s_0 or $c_4\sigma_0$	$B_5\sigma_0$ and $B_6\sigma_0$
	Ranges	R_0 or $d_2\sigma_0$	$D_1\sigma_0$ and $D_2\sigma_0$

TABLE B Normal Distribution*

Proportion of total area under the curve from $-\infty$ to $K = \dfrac{X - \mu}{\sigma}$. To illustrate: when $K = +2.0$, the probability is 0.9773 of obtaining a value equal to or less than X.

K	0.09	0.08	0.07	0.06	0.05	0.04	0.03	0.02	0.01	0.00
−3.5	0.00017	0.00017	0.00018	0.00019	0.00019	0.00020	0.00021	0.00022	0.00022	0.00023
−3.4	0.00024	0.00025	0.00026	0.00027	0.00028	0.00029	0.00030	0.00031	0.00033	0.00034
−3.3	0.00035	0.00036	0.00038	0.00039	0.00040	0.00042	0.00043	0.00045	0.00047	0.00048
−3.2	0.00050	0.00052	0.00054	0.00056	0.00058	0.00060	0.00062	0.00064	0.00066	0.00069
−3.1	0.00071	0.00074	0.00076	0.00079	0.00082	0.00085	0.00087	0.00090	0.00094	0.00097
−3.0	0.00100	0.00104	0.00107	0.00111	0.00114	0.00118	0.00122	0.00126	0.00131	0.00135
−2.9	0.0014	0.0014	0.0015	0.0015	0.0016	0.0016	0.0017	0.0017	0.0018	0.0019
−2.8	0.0019	0.0020	0.0021	0.0021	0.0022	0.0023	0.0023	0.0024	0.0025	0.0026
−2.7	0.0026	0.0027	0.0028	0.0029	0.0030	0.0031	0.0032	0.0033	0.0034	0.0035
−2.6	0.0036	0.0037	0.0038	0.0039	0.0040	0.0041	0.0043	0.0044	0.0045	0.0047
−2.5	0.0048	0.0049	0.0051	0.0052	0.0054	0.0055	0.0057	0.0059	0.0060	0.0062
−2.4	0.0064	0.0066	0.0068	0.0069	0.0071	0.0073	0.0075	0.0078	0.0080	0.0082
−2.3	0.0084	0.0087	0.0089	0.0091	0.0094	0.0096	0.0099	0.0102	0.0104	0.0107
−2.2	0.0110	0.0113	0.0116	0.0119	0.0122	0.0125	0.0129	0.0132	0.0136	0.0139
−2.1	0.0143	0.0146	0.0150	0.0154	0.0158	0.0162	0.0166	0.0170	0.0174	0.0179
−2.0	0.0183	0.0188	0.0192	0.0197	0.0202	0.0207	0.0212	0.0217	0.0222	0.0228
−1.9	0.0233	0.0239	0.0244	0.0250	0.0256	0.0262	0.0268	0.0274	0.0281	0.0287
−1.8	0.0294	0.0301	0.0307	0.0314	0.0322	0.0329	0.0336	0.0344	0.0351	0.0359
−1.7	0.0367	0.0375	0.0384	0.0392	0.0401	0.0409	0.0418	0.0427	0.0436	0.0446
−1.6	0.0455	0.0465	0.0475	0.0485	0.0495	0.0505	0.0516	0.0526	0.0537	0.0548
−1.5	0.0559	0.0571	0.0582	0.0594	0.0606	0.0618	0.0630	0.0643	0.0655	0.0668
−1.4	0.0681	0.0694	0.0708	0.0721	0.0735	0.0749	0.0764	0.0778	0.0793	0.0808
−1.3	0.0823	0.0838	0.0853	0.0869	0.0885	0.0901	0.0918	0.0934	0.0951	0.0968
−1.2	0.0985	0.1003	0.1020	0.1038	0.1057	0.1075	0.1093	0.1112	0.1131	0.1151
−1.1	0.1170	0.1190	0.1210	0.1230	0.1251	0.1271	0.1292	0.1314	0.1335	0.1357

TABLE B (*Continued*)

Negative values of K:

K	0.00	0.01	0.02	0.03	0.04	0.05	0.06	0.07	0.08	0.09
−1.0	0.1587	0.1562	0.1539	0.1515	0.1492	0.1469	0.1446	0.1423	0.1401	0.1379
−0.9	0.1841	0.1814	0.1788	0.1762	0.1736	0.1711	0.1685	0.1660	0.1635	0.1611
−0.8	0.2119	0.2090	0.2061	0.2033	0.2005	0.1977	0.1949	0.1922	0.1894	0.1867
−0.7	0.2420	0.2389	0.2358	0.2327	0.2297	0.2266	0.2236	0.2207	0.2177	0.2148
−0.6	0.2743	0.2709	0.2676	0.2643	0.2611	0.2578	0.2546	0.2514	0.2483	0.2451
−0.5	0.3085	0.3050	0.3015	0.2981	0.2946	0.2912	0.2877	0.2843	0.2810	0.2776
−0.4	0.3446	0.3409	0.3372	0.3336	0.3300	0.3264	0.3228	0.3192	0.3156	0.3121
−0.3	0.3821	0.3783	0.3745	0.3707	0.3669	0.3632	0.3594	0.3557	0.3520	0.3483
−0.2	0.4207	0.4168	0.4129	0.4090	0.4052	0.4013	0.3974	0.3936	0.3897	0.3859
−0.1	0.4602	0.4562	0.4562	0.4483	0.4443	0.4404	0.4364	0.4325	0.4286	0.4247
−0.0	0.5000	0.4960	0.4920	0.4880	0.4840	0.4801	0.4761	0.4721	0.4681	0.4641

Positive values of K:

K	0.00	0.01	0.02	0.03	0.04	0.05	0.06	0.07	0.08	0.09
+0.0	0.5000	0.5040	0.5080	0.5120	0.5160	0.5199	0.5239	0.5279	0.5319	0.5359
+0.1	0.5398	0.5438	0.5478	0.5517	0.5557	0.5596	0.5636	0.5675	0.5714	0.5753
+0.2	0.5793	0.5832	0.5871	0.5910	0.5948	0.5987	0.6026	0.6064	0.6103	0.6141
+0.3	0.6179	0.6217	0.6255	0.6293	0.6331	0.6368	0.6406	0.6443	0.6480	0.6517
+0.4	0.6554	0.6591	0.6628	0.6664	0.6700	0.6736	0.6772	0.6808	0.6844	0.6879
+0.5	0.6915	0.6950	0.6985	0.7019	0.7054	0.7088	0.7123	0.7157	0.7190	0.7224
+0.6	0.7257	0.7291	0.7324	0.7357	0.7389	0.7422	0.7454	0.7486	0.7517	0.7549
+0.7	0.7580	0.7611	0.7642	0.7673	0.7704	0.7734	0.7764	0.7794	0.7823	0.7852
+0.8	0.7881	0.7910	0.7939	0.7967	0.7995	0.8023	0.8051	0.8079	0.8106	0.8133
+0.9	0.8159	0.8186	0.8212	0.8238	0.8264	0.8289	0.8315	0.8340	0.8365	0.8389
+1.0	0.8413	0.8438	0.8461	0.8485	0.8508	0.8531	0.8554	0.8577	0.8599	0.8621
+1.1	0.8643	0.8665	0.8686	0.8708	0.8729	0.8749	0.8770	0.8790	0.8810	0.8830
+1.2	0.8849	0.8869	0.8888	0.8907	0.8925	0.8944	0.8962	0.8980	0.8997	0.9015
+1.3	0.9032	0.9049	0.9066	0.9082	0.9099	0.9115	0.9131	0.9147	0.9162	0.9177
+1.4	0.9192	0.9207	0.9222	0.9236	0.9251	0.9265	0.9279	0.9292	0.9306	0.9319
+1.5	0.9332	0.9345	0.9357	0.9370	0.9382	0.9394	0.9406	0.9418	0.9429	0.9441

z	.00	.01	.02	.03	.04	.05	.06	.07	.08	.09
+1.6	0.9452	0.9463	0.9474	0.9484	0.9495	0.9505	0.9515	0.9525	0.9535	0.9545
+1.7	0.9554	0.9564	0.9573	0.9582	0.9591	0.9599	0.9608	0.9616	0.9625	0.9633
+1.8	0.9641	0.9649	0.9656	0.9664	0.9671	0.9678	0.9686	0.9693	0.9699	0.9706
+1.9	0.9713	0.9719	0.9726	0.9732	0.9738	0.9744	0.9750	0.9756	0.9761	0.9767
+2.0	0.9773	0.9778	0.9783	0.9788	0.9793	0.9798	0.9803	0.9808	0.9812	0.9817
+2.1	0.9821	0.9826	0.9830	0.9834	0.9838	0.9842	0.9846	0.9850	0.9854	0.9857
+2.2	0.9861	0.9864	0.9868	0.9871	0.9875	0.9878	0.9881	0.9884	0.9887	0.9890
+2.3	0.9893	0.9896	0.9898	0.9901	0.9904	0.9906	0.9909	0.9911	0.9913	0.9916
+2.4	0.9918	0.9920	0.9922	0.9925	0.9927	0.9929	0.9931	0.9932	0.9934	0.9936
+2.5	0.9938	0.9940	0.9941	0.9943	0.9945	0.9946	0.9948	0.9949	0.9951	0.9952
+2.6	0.9953	0.9955	0.9956	0.9957	0.9959	0.9960	0.9961	0.9962	0.9963	0.9964
+2.7	0.9965	0.9966	0.9967	0.9968	0.9969	0.9970	0.9971	0.9972	0.9973	0.9974
+2.8	0.9974	0.9975	0.9976	0.9977	0.9977	0.9978	0.9979	0.9979	0.9980	0.9981
+2.9	0.9981	0.9982	0.9983	0.9983	0.9984	0.9984	0.9985	0.9985	0.9986	0.9986
+3.0	0.99865	0.99869	0.99874	0.99878	0.99882	0.99886	0.99889	0.99893	0.99896	0.99900
+3.1	0.99903	0.99906	0.99910	0.99913	0.99915	0.99918	0.99921	0.99924	0.99926	0.99929
+3.2	0.99931	0.99934	0.99936	0.99938	0.99940	0.99942	0.99944	0.99946	0.99948	0.99950
+3.3	0.99952	0.99953	0.99955	0.99957	0.99958	0.99960	0.99961	0.99962	0.99964	0.99965
+3.4	0.99966	0.99967	0.99969	0.99970	0.99971	0.99972	0.99973	0.99974	0.99975	0.99976
+3.5	0.99977	0.99978	0.99978	0.99979	0.99980	0.99981	0.99981	0.99982	0.99983	0.99983

*Adapted with permission from Grant, Eugene L. and Leavenworth, Richard S. (1972). *Statistical Quality Control*, 4th ed. McGraw-Hill, New York, pp. 642–643.

TABLE C   Exponential Distribution*

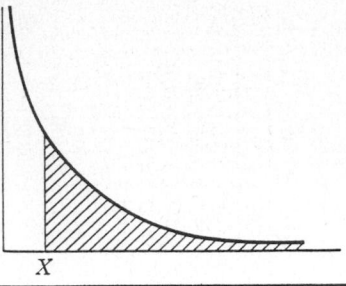

$\dfrac{X}{\mu}$	0.00	0.01	0.02	0.03	0.04	0.05	0.06	0.07	0.08	0.09
0.0	1.000	0.9900	0.9802	0.9704	0.9608	0.9512	0.9418	0.9324	0.9231	0.9139
0.1	0.9048	0.8958	0.8860	0.8781	0.8694	0.8607	0.8521	0.8437	0.8353	0.8270
0.2	0.8187	0.8106	0.8025	0.7945	0.7866	0.7788	0.7711	0.7634	0.7758	0.7483
0.3	0.7408	0.7334	0.7261	0.7189	0.7118	0.7047	0.6977	0.6907	0.6839	0.6771
0.4	0.6703	0.6637	0.6570	0.6505	0.6440	0.6376	0.6313	0.6250	0.6188	0.6126
0.5	0.6065	0.6005	0.5945	0.5886	0.5827	0.5769	0.5712	0.5655	0.5599	0.5543
0.6	0.5488	0.5434	0.5379	0.5326	0.5273	0.5220	0.5169	0.5117	0.5066	0.5016
0.7	0.4966	0.4916	0.4868	0.4819	0.4771	0.4724	0.4677	0.4630	0.4584	0.4538
0.8	0.4493	0.4449	0.4404	0.4360	0.4317	0.4274	0.4232	0.4190	0.4148	0.4107
0.9	0.4066	0.4025	0.3985	0.3946	0.3906	0.3867	0.3829	0.3791	0.3753	0.3716
	0.0	0.1	0.2	0.3	0.4	0.5	0.6	0.7	0.8	0.9
1.0	0.3679	0.3329	0.3012	0.2725	0.2466	0.2231	0.2019	0.1827	0.1653	0.1496
2.0	0.1353	0.1225	0.1108	0.1003	0.0907	0.0821	0.0743	0.0672	0.0608	0.0550
3.0	0.0498	0.0450	0.0408	0.0369	0.0334	0.0302	0.0273	0.0247	0.0224	0.0202
4.0	0.0183	0.0166	0.0150	0.0130	0.0123	0.0111	0.0101	0.0091	0.0082	0.0074
5.0	0.0067	0.0061	0.0055	0.0050	0.0045	0.0041	0.0037	0.0033	0.0030	0.0027
6.0	0.0025	0.0022	0.0020	0.0018	0.0017	0.0015	0.0014	0.0012	0.0011	0.0010

*Adapted with permission from Selby, S. M. (ed.) (1969). *CRC Standard Mathematical Tables,* 17th ed. The Chemical Rubber Co., pp. 201–207.

TABLE D Median Ranks*

Sample size = n

	1	2	3	4	5	6	7	8	9	10	11	12	13	14	15	16	17	18	19	20
1	.5000	.2929	.2063	.1591	.1294	.1091	.0943	.0830	.0741	.0670	.0611	.0561	.0519	.0483	.0452	.0424	.0400	.0378	.0358	.0341
2		.7071	.5000	.3864	.3147	.2655	.2295	.2021	.1806	.1632	.1489	.1368	.1266	.1178	.1101	.1034	.0975	.0922	.0874	.0831
3			.7937	.6136	.5000	.4218	.3648	.3213	.2871	.2594	.2366	.2175	.2013	.1873	.1751	.1644	.1550	.1465	.1390	.1322
4				.8409	.6853	.5782	.5000	.4404	.3935	.3557	.3244	.2982	.2760	.2568	.2401	.2254	.2125	.2009	.1905	.1812
5					.8706	.7345	.6352	.5596	.5000	.4519	.4122	.3789	.3506	.3263	.3051	.2865	.2700	.2553	.2421	.2302
6						.8909	.7705	.6787	.6065	.5481	.5000	.4596	.4253	.3958	.3700	.3475	.3275	.3097	.2937	.2793
7							.9057	.7979	.7129	.6443	.5878	.5404	.5000	.4653	.4350	.4085	.3850	.3641	.3453	.3283
8								.9170	.8194	.7406	.6756	.6211	.5747	.5347	.5000	.4695	.4425	.4184	.3968	.3774
9									.9259	.8368	.7634	.7018	.6494	.6042	.5650	.5305	.5000	.4728	.4484	.4264
10										.9330	.8511	.7825	.7240	.6737	.6300	.5915	.5575	.5272	.5000	.4755
11											.9389	.8632	.7987	.7432	.6949	.6525	.6150	.5816	.5516	.5245
12												.9439	.8734	.8127	.7599	.7135	.6725	.6359	.6032	.5736
13													.9481	.8822	.8249	.7746	.7300	.6903	.6547	.6226
14														.9517	.8899	.8356	.7875	.7447	.7063	.6717
15															.9548	.8966	.8450	.7991	.7579	.7207
16																.9576	.9025	.8535	.8095	.7698
17																	.9600	.9078	.8610	.8188
18																		.9622	.9126	.8678
19																			.9642	.9169
20																				.9659

*Adapted with permission from "The Table of Median Ranks of Sample Values on Their Population with an Application to Certain Fatigue Studies." (1951). *Industrial Mathematics*, no. 2, p. 7.

TABLE E Poisson Distribution*

1000 × probability of r or fewer occurrences of event that has average number of occurrences equal to np.

np \ r	0	1	2	3	4	5	6	7	8	9
0.02	980	1,000								
0.04	961	999	1,000							
0.06	942	998	1,000							
0.08	923	997	1,000							
0.10	905	995	1,000							
0.15	861	990	999	1,000						
0.20	819	982	999	1,000						
0.25	779	974	998	1,000						
0.30	741	963	996	1,000						
0.35	705	951	994	1,000						
0.40	670	938	992	999	1,000					
0.45	638	925	989	999	1,000					
0.50	607	910	986	998	1,000					
0.55	577	894	982	998	1,000					
0.60	549	878	977	997	1,000					
0.65	522	861	972	996	999	1,000				
0.70	497	844	966	994	999	1,000				
0.75	472	827	959	993	999	1,000				
0.80	449	809	953	991	999	1,000				
0.85	427	791	945	989	998	1,000				
0.90	407	772	937	987	998	1,000				
0.95	387	754	929	984	997	1,000				
1.00	368	736	920	981	996	999	1,000			
1.1	333	699	900	974	995	999	1,000			
1.2	301	663	879	966	992	998	1,000			
1.3	273	627	857	957	989	998	1,000			
1.4	247	592	833	946	986	997	999	1,000		
1.5	223	558	809	934	981	996	999	1,000		
1.6	202	525	783	921	976	994	999	1,000		
1.7	183	493	757	907	970	992	998	1,000		
1.8	165	463	731	891	964	990	997	999	1,000	
1.9	150	434	704	875	956	987	997	999	1,000	
2.0	135	406	677	857	947	983	995	999	1,000	

r np	0	1	2	3	4	5	6	7	8	9
2.2	111	355	623	819	928	975	993	998	1,000	
2.4	091	308	570	779	904	964	988	997	999	1,000
2.6	074	267	518	736	877	951	983	995	999	1,000
2.8	061	231	469	692	848	935	976	992	998	999
3.0	050	199	423	647	815	916	966	988	996	999
3.2	041	171	380	603	781	895	955	983	994	998
3.4	033	147	340	558	744	871	942	977	992	997
3.6	027	126	303	515	706	844	927	969	988	996
3.8	022	107	269	473	668	816	909	960	984	994
4.0	018	092	238	433	629	785	889	949	979	992
4.2	015	078	210	395	590	753	867	936	972	989
4.4	012	066	185	359	551	720	844	921	964	985
4.6	010	056	163	326	513	686	818	905	955	980
4.8	008	048	143	294	476	651	791	887	944	975
5.0	007	040	125	265	440	616	762	867	932	968
5.2	006	034	109	238	406	581	732	845	918	960
5.4	005	029	095	213	373	546	702	822	903	951
5.6	004	024	082	191	342	512	670	797	886	941
5.8	003	021	072	170	313	478	638	771	867	929
6.0	002	017	062	151	285	446	606	744	847	916

	10	11	12	13	14	15	16
2.8	1,000						
3.0	1,000						
3.2	1,000						
3.4	999	1,000					
3.6	999	1,000					
3.8	998	999	1,000				
4.0	997	999	1,000				
4.2	996	999	1,000				
4.4	994	998	999	1,000			
4.6	992	997	999	1,000			
4.8	990	996	999	1,000			
5.0	986	995	998	999	1,000		
5.2	982	993	997	999	1,000		
5.4	977	990	996	999	1,000		
5.6	972	988	995	998	999	1,000	
5.8	965	984	993	997	999	1,000	
6.0	957	980	991	996	999	999	1,000

TABLE E (*Continued*)

np \ r	0	1	2	3	4	5	6	7	8	9
6.2	002	015	054	134	259	414	574	716	826	902
6.4	002	012	046	119	235	384	542	687	803	886
6.6	001	010	040	105	213	355	511	658	780	869
6.8	001	009	034	093	192	327	480	628	755	850
7.0	001	007	030	082	173	301	450	599	729	830
7.2	001	006	025	072	156	276	420	569	703	810
7.4	001	005	022	063	140	253	392	539	676	788
7.6	001	004	019	055	125	231	365	510	648	765
7.8	000	004	016	048	112	210	338	481	620	741
8.0	000	003	014	042	100	191	313	453	593	717
8.5	000	002	009	030	074	150	256	386	523	653
9.0	000	001	006	021	055	116	207	324	456	587
9.5	000	001	004	015	040	089	165	269	392	522
10.0	000	000	003	010	029	067	130	220	333	458

	10	11	12	13	14	15	16	17	18	19
6.2	949	975	989	995	998	999	1,000			
6.4	939	969	986	994	997	999	1,000			
6.6	927	963	982	992	997	999	999	1,000		
6.8	915	955	978	990	996	998	999	1,000		
7.0	901	947	973	987	994	998	999	1,000		
7.2	887	937	967	984	993	997	999	999	1,000	
7.4	871	926	961	980	991	996	998	999	1,000	
7.6	854	915	954	976	989	995	998	999	1,000	
7.8	835	902	945	971	986	993	997	999	1,000	
8.0	816	888	936	966	983	992	996	998	999	1,000
8.5	763	849	909	949	973	986	993	997	999	999
9.0	706	803	876	926	959	978	989	995	998	999
9.5	645	752	836	898	940	967	982	991	996	998
10.0	583	697	792	864	917	951	973	986	993	997

	20	21	22
8.5	1,000		
9.0	1,000		
9.5	999	1,000	
10.0	998	999	1,000

r np	0	1	2	3	4	5	6	7	8	9
10.5	000	000	002	007	021	050	102	179	279	397
11.0	000	000	001	005	015	038	079	143	232	341
11.5	000	000	001	003	011	028	060	114	191	289
12.0	000	000	001	002	008	020	046	090	155	242
12.5	000	000	000	002	005	015	035	070	125	201
13.0	000	000	000	001	004	011	026	054	100	166
13.5	000	000	000	001	003	008	019	041	079	135
14.0	000	000	000	000	002	006	014	032	062	109
14.5	000	000	000	000	001	004	010	024	048	088
15.0	000	000	000	000	001	003	008	018	037	070

	10	11	12	13	14	15	16	17	18	19
10.5	521	639	742	825	888	932	960	978	988	994
11.0	460	579	689	781	854	907	944	968	982	991
11.5	402	520	633	733	815	878	924	954	974	986
12.0	347	462	576	682	772	844	899	937	963	979
12.5	297	406	519	628	725	806	869	916	948	969
13.0	252	353	463	573	675	764	835	890	930	957
13.5	211	304	409	518	623	718	798	861	908	942
14.0	176	260	358	464	570	669	756	827	883	923
14.5	145	220	311	413	518	619	711	790	853	901
15.0	118	185	268	363	466	568	664	749	819	875

	20	21	22	23	24	25	26	27	28	29
10.5	997	999	999	1,000						
11.0	995	998	999	1,000						
11.5	992	996	998	999	1,000					
12.0	988	994	997	999	999	1,000				
12.5	983	991	995	998	999	999	1,000			
13.0	975	986	992	996	998	999	1,000			
13.5	965	980	989	994	997	998	999	1,000		
14.0	952	971	983	991	995	997	999	999	1,000	
14.5	936	960	976	986	992	996	998	999	999	1,000
15.0	917	947	967	981	989	994	997	998	999	1,000

*Adapted with permission from Grant, E. L. and Leavenworth, Richard S. (1972). *Statistical Quality Control,* 4th ed. McGraw-Hill, New York.

TABLE F Binomial Distribution*

Probability of r or fewer occurrences of an event in n trials, where p is the probability of occurrence on each trial.

n	r	p 0.05	0.10	0.15	0.20	0.25	0.30	0.35	0.40	0.45	0.50
2	0	0.9025	0.8100	0.7225	0.6400	0.5625	0.4900	0.4225	0.3600	0.3025	0.2500
	1	0.9975	0.9900	0.9775	0.9600	0.9375	0.9100	0.8775	0.8400	0.7975	0.7500
3	0	0.8574	0.7290	0.6141	0.5120	0.4219	0.3430	0.2746	0.2160	0.1664	0.1250
	1	0.9928	0.9720	0.9392	0.8960	0.8438	0.7840	0.7182	0.6480	0.5748	0.5000
	2	0.9999	0.9990	0.9966	0.9920	0.9844	0.9730	0.9571	0.9360	0.9089	0.8750
4	0	0.8145	0.6561	0.5220	0.4096	0.3164	0.2401	0.1785	0.1296	0.0915	0.0625
	1	0.9860	0.9477	0.8905	0.8192	0.7383	0.6517	0.5630	0.4752	0.3910	0.3125
	2	0.9995	0.9963	0.9880	0.9728	0.9492	0.9163	0.8735	0.8208	0.7585	0.6875
	3	1.0000	0.9999	0.9995	0.9984	0.9961	0.9919	0.9850	0.9744	0.9590	0.9375
5	0	0.7738	0.5905	0.4437	0.3277	0.2373	0.1681	0.1160	0.0778	0.0503	0.0312
	1	0.9774	0.9185	0.8352	0.7373	0.6328	0.5282	0.4284	0.3370	0.2562	0.1875
	2	0.9988	0.9914	0.9734	0.9421	0.8965	0.8369	0.7648	0.6826	0.5931	0.5000
	3	1.0000	0.9995	0.9978	0.9933	0.9844	0.9692	0.9460	0.9130	0.8688	0.8125
	4	1.0000	1.0000	0.9999	0.9997	0.9990	0.9976	0.9947	0.9898	0.9815	0.9688
6	0	0.7351	0.5314	0.3771	0.2621	0.1780	0.1176	0.0754	0.0467	0.0277	0.0156
	1	0.9672	0.8857	0.7765	0.6554	0.5339	0.4202	0.3191	0.2333	0.1636	0.1094
	2	0.9978	0.9842	0.9527	0.9011	0.8306	0.7443	0.6471	0.5443	0.4415	0.3438
	3	0.9999	0.9987	0.9941	0.9830	0.9624	0.9295	0.8826	0.8208	0.7447	0.6562
	4	1.0000	0.9999	0.9996	0.9984	0.9954	0.9891	0.9777	0.9590	0.9308	0.8906
	5	1.0000	1.0000	1.0000	0.9999	0.9998	0.9993	0.9982	0.9959	0.9917	0.9844
7	0	0.6983	0.4783	0.3206	0.2097	0.1335	0.0824	0.0490	0.0280	0.0152	0.0078
	1	0.9556	0.8503	0.7166	0.5767	0.4449	0.3294	0.2338	0.1586	0.1024	0.0625
	2	0.9962	0.9743	0.9262	0.8520	0.7564	0.6471	0.5323	0.4199	0.3164	0.2266
	3	0.9998	0.9973	0.9879	0.9667	0.9294	0.8740	0.8002	0.7102	0.6083	0.5000
	4	1.0000	0.9998	0.9988	0.9953	0.9871	0.9712	0.9444	0.9037	0.8471	0.7734
	5	1.0000	1.0000	0.9999	0.9996	0.9987	0.9962	0.9910	0.9812	0.9643	0.9375

n	x										
6		0.9922	0.9963	0.9984	0.9994	0.9998	0.9999	1.0000	1.0000	1.0000	1.0000
8	0	0.0039	0.0084	0.0168	0.0319	0.0576	0.1001	0.1678	0.2725	0.4305	0.6634
	1	0.0352	0.0632	0.1064	0.1691	0.2553	0.3671	0.5033	0.6572	0.8131	0.9428
	2	0.1445	0.2201	0.3154	0.4278	0.5518	0.6785	0.7969	0.8948	0.9619	0.9942
	3	0.3633	0.4770	0.5941	0.7064	0.8059	0.8862	0.9437	0.9786	0.9950	0.9996
	4	0.6367	0.7396	0.8263	0.8939	0.9420	0.9727	0.9896	0.9971	0.9996	1.0000
	5	0.8555	0.9115	0.9502	0.9747	0.9887	0.9958	0.9988	0.9998	1.0000	1.0000
	6	0.9648	0.9819	0.9915	0.9964	0.9987	0.9996	0.9999	1.0000	1.0000	1.0000
	7	0.9961	0.9983	0.9993	0.9998	0.9999	1.0000	1.0000	1.0000	1.0000	1.0000
9	0	0.0020	0.0046	0.0101	0.0207	0.0404	0.0751	0.1342	0.2316	0.3874	0.6302
	1	0.0195	0.0385	0.0705	0.1211	0.1960	0.3003	0.4362	0.5995	0.7748	0.9288
	2	0.0898	0.1495	0.2318	0.3373	0.4628	0.6007	0.7382	0.8591	0.9470	0.9916
	3	0.2539	0.3614	0.4826	0.6089	0.7297	0.8343	0.9144	0.9661	0.9917	0.9994
	4	0.5000	0.6214	0.7334	0.8283	0.9012	0.9511	0.9804	0.9944	0.9991	1.0000
	5	0.7461	0.8342	0.9006	0.9464	0.9747	0.9900	0.9969	0.9994	0.9999	1.0000
	6	0.9102	0.9502	0.9750	0.9888	0.9957	0.9987	0.9997	1.0000	1.0000	1.0000
	7	0.9805	0.9909	0.9962	0.9986	0.9996	0.9999	1.0000	1.0000	1.0000	1.0000
	8	0.9980	0.9992	0.9997	0.9999	1.0000	1.0000	1.0000	1.0000	1.0000	1.0000
10	0	0.0010	0.0025	0.0060	0.0135	0.0282	0.0563	0.1074	0.1969	0.3487	0.5987
	1	0.0107	0.0232	0.0464	0.0860	0.1493	0.2440	0.3758	0.5443	0.7361	0.9139
	2	0.0547	0.0996	0.1673	0.2616	0.3828	0.5256	0.6778	0.8202	0.9298	0.9885
	3	0.1719	0.2660	0.3823	0.5138	0.6496	0.7759	0.8791	0.9500	0.9872	0.9990
	4	0.3770	0.5044	0.6331	0.7515	0.8497	0.9219	0.9672	0.9901	0.9984	0.9999
	5	0.6230	0.7384	0.8338	0.9051	0.9527	0.9803	0.9936	0.9986	0.9999	1.0000
	6	0.8281	0.8980	0.9452	0.9740	0.9894	0.9965	0.9991	0.9999	1.0000	1.0000
	7	0.9453	0.9726	0.9877	0.9952	0.9984	0.9996	0.9999	1.0000	1.0000	1.0000
	8	0.9893	0.9955	0.9983	0.9995	0.9999	1.0000	1.0000	1.0000	1.0000	1.0000
	9	0.9990	0.9997	0.9999	1.0000	1.0000	1.0000	1.0000	1.0000	1.0000	1.0000

*Adapted with permission from Miller, Irwin and Freund, John E. (1965). *Probability and Statistics for Engineers*. Prentice-Hall, Englewood Cliffs, NJ, pp. 388–389.

For more extensive tables see The Staff of Harvard University Computation Laboratory (1955). *Tables of Cumulative Binomial Probability Distribution*. Harvard University Press, Cambridge, MA. See also Robertson, W. H. (1960). *Tables of the Binomial Distribution Function for Small Values of p*. Sandia Corp. Monograph, available from the Office of Technical Services, Department of Commerce, Washington, DC.

TABLE G* Distribution of t

Value of t corresponding to certain selected probabilities (i.e. tail areas under the curve). To illustrate: The probability is 0.975 that a sample with 20 degrees of freedom would have $t = +2.086$ or smaller.

DF	$t_{.60}$	$t_{.70}$	$t_{.80}$	$t_{.90}$	$t_{.95}$	$t_{.975}$	$t_{.99}$	$t_{.995}$
1	0.325	0.727	1.376	3.078	6.314	12.706	31.821	63.657
2	0.289	0.617	1.061	1.886	2.920	4.303	6.965	9.925
3	0.277	0.584	0.978	1.638	2.353	3.182	4.541	5.841
4	0.271	0.569	0.941	1.533	2.132	2.776	3.747	4.604
5	0.267	0.559	0.920	1.476	2.015	2.571	3.365	4.032
6	0.265	0.553	0.906	1.440	1.943	2.447	3.143	3.707
7	0.263	0.549	0.896	1.415	1.895	2.365	2.998	3.499
8	0.262	0.546	0.889	1.397	1.860	2.306	2.896	3.355
9	0.261	0.543	0.883	1.383	1.833	2.262	2.821	3.250
10	0.260	0.542	0.879	1.372	1.812	2.228	2.764	3.169
11	0.260	0.540	0.876	1.363	1.796	2.201	2.718	3.106
12	0.259	0.539	0.873	1.356	1.782	2.179	2.681	3.055
13	0.259	0.538	0.870	1.350	1.771	2.160	2.650	3.012
14	0.258	0.537	0.868	1.345	1.761	2.145	2.624	2.977
15	0.258	0.536	0.866	1.341	1.753	2.131	2.602	2.947
16	0.258	0.535	0.865	1.337	1.746	2.120	2.583	2.921
17	0.257	0.534	0.863	1.333	1.740	2.110	2.567	2.898
18	0.257	0.534	0.862	1.330	1.734	2.101	2.552	2.878
19	0.257	0.533	0.861	1.328	1.729	2.093	2.539	2.861
20	0.257	0.533	0.860	1.325	1.725	2.086	2.528	2.845
21	0.257	0.532	0.859	1.323	1.721	2.080	2.518	2.831
22	0.256	0.532	0.858	1.321	1.717	2.074	2.508	2.819
23	0.256	0.532	0.858	1.319	1.714	2.069	2.500	2.807
24	0.256	0.531	0.857	1.318	1.711	2.064	2.492	2.797
25	0.256	0.531	0.856	1.316	1.708	2.060	2.485	2.787
26	0.256	0.531	0.856	1.315	1.706	2.056	2.479	2.779
27	0.256	0.531	0.855	1.314	1.703	2.052	2.473	2.771
28	0.256	0.530	0.855	1.313	1.701	2.048	2.467	2.763
29	0.256	0.530	0.854	1.311	1.699	2.045	2.462	2.756
30	0.256	0.530	0.854	1.310	1.697	2.042	2.457	2.750
40	0.255	0.529	0.851	1.303	1.684	2.021	2.423	2.704
60	0.254	0.527	0.848	1.296	1.671	2.000	2.390	2.660
120	0.254	0.526	0.845	1.289	1.658	1.980	2.358	2.617
∞	0.253	0.524	0.842	1.282	1.645	1.960	2.326	2.576

*Adapted with permission from Dixon, W. J. and Massey, F. J., Jr. (1969). *Introduction to Statistical Analysis,* 3rd ed. McGraw-Hill, New York. Entries originally from Fisher, R. A. and Yates, F. *Statistical Tables.* Oliver & Boyd, London, Table III.

TABLE H*   Percentile for $\tau_d = \dfrac{\overline{X} - \mu_0}{R}$

Sample size	$\phi_{.95}$	$\phi_{.975}$	$\phi_{.99}$
2	3.175	6.353	15.910
3	0.885	1.304	2.111
4	0.529	0.717	1.023
5	0.388	0.507	0.685
6	0.312	0.399	0.523
7	0.263	0.333	0.429
8	0.230	0.288	0.366
9	0.205	0.255	0.322
10	0.186	0.230	0.288
11	0.170	0.210	0.262
12	0.158	0.194	0.241
13	0.147	0.181	0.224
14	0.138	0.170	0.209
15	0.131	0.160	0.197
16	0.124	0.151	0.186
17	0.118	0.144	0.177
18	0.113	0.137	0.168
19	0.108	0.131	0.161
20	0.104	0.126	0.154

*Adapted with permission from Lord, E. (1957). "The Use of the Range in Place of the Standard Deviation in the *t* Test." *Biometrika,* vol. 34.

TABLE I Critical Values of r for the Sign Test*

Percentages are values for α for a two-tail test. (Two-tail percentage points are given for the binomial for $p = 0.05$.)

N	1%	5%	10%	25%
1				
2				
3				0
4				0
5			0	0
6		0	0	1
7		0	0	1
8	0	0	1	1
9	0	1	1	2
10	0	1	1	2
11	0	1	2	3
12	1	2	2	3
13	1	2	3	3
14	1	2	3	4
15	2	3	3	4
16	2	3	4	5
17	2	4	4	5
18	3	4	5	6
19	3	4	5	6
20	3	5	5	6
21	4	5	6	7
22	4	5	6	7
23	4	6	7	8
24	5	6	7	8
25	5	7	7	9
26	6	7	8	9
27	6	7	8	10
28	6	8	9	10
29	7	8	9	10
30	7	9	10	11
31	7	9	10	11
32	8	9	10	12
33	8	10	11	12
34	9	10	11	13
35	9	11	12	13
36	9	11	12	14
37	10	12	13	14
38	10	12	13	14
39	11	12	13	15
40	11	13	14	15
41	11	13	14	16
42	12	14	15	16
43	12	14	15	17
44	13	15	16	17
45	13	15	16	18
46	13	15	16	18
47	14	16	17	19
48	14	16	17	19
49	15	17	18	19
50	15	17	18	20

*Adapted with permission from Dixon, W. J. and Massey, F. J., Jr. (1969). *Introduction to Statistical Analysis*, 3rd ed. McGraw-Hill, New York.

TABLE J* Percentiles for $\tau_d = \dfrac{\overline{X}_1 - \overline{X}_2}{\frac{1}{2}(R_1 + R_2)}$

$n = n_A = n_B$	$\phi'_{.95}$	$\phi'_{.975}$	$\phi'_{.99}$
2	2.322	3.427	5.553
3	0.974	1.272	1.715
4	0.644	0.813	1.047
5	0.493	0.613	0.772
6	0.405	0.499	0.621
7	0.347	0.426	0.525
8	0.306	0.373	0.459
9	0.275	0.334	0.409
10	0.250	0.304	0.371
11	0.233	0.280	0.340
12	0.214	0.260	0.315
13	0.201	0.243	0.294
14	0.189	0.189	0.276
15	0.179	0.216	0.261
16	0.170	0.205	0.247
17	0.162	0.195	0.236
18	0.155	0.187	0.225
19	0.149	0.179	0.216
20	0.143	0.172	0.207

*Adapted with permission from Lord, E. (1947). "The Use of the Range in Place of the Standard Deviation in the *t* Test. " *Biometrika,* vol. 34.

TABLE K* Distribution of F

Values of F corresponding to certain selected probabilities (i.e., tail areas under the curve). To illustrate: The probability is 0.05 that the ratio of two sample variances obtained with 20 and 10 degrees of freedom in numerator and denominator, respectively, would have F = 2.77 or larger. For a two-sided test, a lower limit is found by taking the reciprocal of the tabulated F value for the degrees of freedom in reverse. For the above example, with 10 and 20 degrees of freedom in numerator and denominator, respectively, F is 2.35 and 1/F is 1/2.35, or 0.43. The probability is 0.10 that F is 0.43 or smaller or 2.77 or larger.

n_2 \ n_1	1	2	3	4	5	6	7	8	9
					$F_{.95}$ (n_1, n_2)				
1	161.4	199.5	215.7	224.6	230.2	234.0	236.8	238.9	240.5
2	18.51	19.00	19.16	19.25	19.30	19.33	19.35	19.37	19.38
3	10.13	9.55	9.28	9.12	9.01	8.94	8.89	8.85	8.81
4	7.71	6.94	6.59	6.39	6.26	6.16	6.09	6.04	6.00
5	6.61	5.79	5.41	5.19	5.05	4.95	4.88	4.82	4.77
6	5.99	5.14	4.76	4.53	4.39	4.28	4.21	4.15	4.10
7	5.59	4.74	4.35	4.12	3.97	3.87	3.79	3.73	3.68
8	5.32	4.46	4.07	3.84	3.69	3.58	3.50	3.44	3.39
9	5.12	4.26	3.86	3.63	3.48	3.37	3.29	3.23	3.18
10	4.96	4.10	3.71	3.48	3.33	3.22	3.14	3.07	3.02
11	4.84	3.98	3.59	3.36	3.20	3.09	3.01	2.95	2.90
12	4.75	3.89	3.49	3.26	3.11	3.00	2.91	2.85	2.80
13	4.67	3.81	3.41	3.18	3.03	2.92	2.83	2.77	2.71
14	4.60	3.74	3.34	3.11	2.96	2.85	2.76	2.70	2.65
15	4.54	3.68	3.29	3.06	2.90	2.79	2.71	2.64	2.59
16	4.49	3.63	3.24	3.01	2.85	2.74	2.66	2.59	2.54
17	4.45	3.59	3.20	2.96	2.81	2.70	2.61	2.55	2.49
18	4.41	3.55	3.16	2.93	2.77	2.66	2.58	2.51	2.46
19	4.38	3.52	3.13	2.90	2.74	2.63	2.54	2.48	2.42
20	4.35	3.49	3.10	2.87	2.71	2.60	2.51	2.45	2.39
21	4.32	3.47	3.07	2.84	2.68	2.57	2.49	2.42	2.37
22	4.30	3.44	3.05	2.82	2.66	2.55	2.46	2.40	2.34
23	4.28	3.42	3.03	2.80	2.64	2.53	2.44	2.37	2.32
24	4.26	3.40	3.01	2.78	2.62	2.51	2.42	2.36	2.30
25	4.24	3.39	2.99	2.76	2.60	2.49	2.40	2.34	2.28
26	4.23	3.37	2.98	2.74	2.59	2.47	2.39	2.32	2.27
27	4.21	3.35	2.96	2.73	2.57	2.46	2.37	2.31	2.25
28	4.20	3.34	2.95	2.71	2.56	2.45	2.36	2.29	2.24
29	4.18	3.33	2.93	2.70	2.55	2.43	2.35	2.28	2.22
30	4.17	3.32	2.92	2.69	2.53	2.42	2.33	2.27	2.21
40	4.08	3.23	2.84	2.61	2.45	2.34	2.25	2.18	2.12
60	4.00	3.15	2.76	2.53	2.37	2.25	2.17	2.10	2.04
120	3.92	3.07	2.68	2.45	2.29	2.17	2.09	2.02	1.96
∞	3.84	3.00	2 60	2.37	2.21	2.10	2.01	1.94	1.88

*Adapted with permission from Pearson, E. S. and Hartley, H. O. (eds.) (1958). *Biometrika Tables for Statisticians*, 2nd ed. Cambridge University Press, New York, vol. I.

Note: n_1 = degrees of freedom for numerator. n_2 = degrees of freedom for denominator.

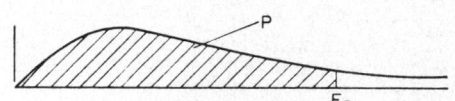

10	12	15	20	24	30	40	60	120	∞
				$F_{.95}\ (n_1,\ n_2)$					
241.9	243.9	245.9	248.0	249.1	250.1	251.1	252.2	253.3	254.3
19.40	19.41	19.43	19.45	19.45	19.46	19.47	19.48	19.49	19.50
8.79	8.74	8.70	8.66	8.64	8.62	8.59	8.57	8.55	8.53
5.96	5.91	5.86	5.80	5.77	5.75	5.72	5.69	5.66	5.63
4.74	4.68	4.62	4.56	4.53	4.50	4.46	4.43	4.40	4.36
4.06	4.00	3.94	3.87	3.84	3.81	3.77	3.74	3.70	3.67
3.64	3.57	3.51	3.44	3.41	3.38	3.34	3.30	3.27	3.23
3.35	3.28	3.22	3.15	3.12	3.08	3.04	3.01	2.97	2.93
3.14	3.07	3.01	2.94	2.90	2.86	2.83	2.79	2.75	2.71
2.98	2.91	2.85	2.77	2.74	2.70	2.66	2.62	2.58	2.54
2.85	2.79	2.72	2.65	2.61	2.57	2.53	2.49	2.45	2.40
2.75	2.69	2.62	2.54	2.51	2.47	2.43	2.38	2.34	2.30
2.67	2.60	2.53	2.46	2.42	2.38	2.34	2.30	2.25	2.21
2.60	2.53	2.46	2.39	2.35	2.31	2.27	2.22	2.18	2.13
2.54	2.48	2.40	2.33	2.29	2.25	2.20	2.16	2.11	2.07
2.49	2.42	2.35	2.28	2.24	2.19	2.15	2.11	2.06	2.01
2.45	2.38	2.31	2.23	2.19	2.15	2.10	2.06	2.01	1.96
2.41	2.34	2.27	2.19	2.15	2.11	2.06	2.02	1.97	1.92
2.38	2.31	2.23	2.16	2.11	2.07	2.03	1.98	1.93	1.88
2.35	2.28	2.20	2.12	2.08	2.04	1.99	1.95	1.90	1.84
2.32	2.25	2.18	2.10	2.05	2.01	1.96	1.92	1.87	1.81
2.30	2.23	2.15	2.07	2.03	1.98	1.94	1.89	1.84	1.78
2.27	2.20	2.13	2.05	2.01	1.96	1.91	1.86	1.81	1.76
2.25	2.18	2.11	2.03	1.98	1.94	1.89	1.84	1.79	1.73
2.24	2.16	2.09	2.01	1.96	1.92	1.87	1.82	1.77	1.71
2.22	2.15	2.07	1.99	1.95	1.90	1.85	1.80	1.75	1.69
2.20	2.13	2.06	1.97	1.93	1.88	1.84	1.79	1.73	1.67
2.19	2.12	2.04	1.96	1.91	1.87	1.82	1.77	1.71	1.65
2.18	2.10	2.03	1.94	1.90	1.85	1.81	1.75	1.70	1.64
2.16	2.09	2.01	1.93	1.89	1.84	1.79	1.74	1.68	1.62
2.08	2.00	1.92	1.84	1.79	1.74	1.69	1.64	1.58	1.51
1.99	1.92	1.84	1.75	1.70	1.65	1.59	1.53	1.47	1.39
1.91	1.83	1.75	1.66	1.61	1.55	1.50	1.43	1.35	1.25
1.83	1.75	1.67	1.57	1.52	1.46	1.39	1.32	1.22	1.00

n_2 \ n_1	1	2	3	4	5	6	7	8	9
					$F_{.975}(n_1, n_2)$				
1	647.8	799.5	864.2	899.6	921.8	937.1	948.2	956.7	963.3
2	38.51	39.00	39.17	39.25	39.30	39.33	39.36	39.37	39.39
3	17.44	16.04	15.44	15.10	14.88	14.73	14.62	14.54	14.47
4	12.22	10.65	9.98	9.60	9.36	9.20	9.07	8.98	8.90
5	10.01	8.43	7.76	7.39	7.15	6.98	6.85	6.76	6.68
6	8.81	7.26	6.60	6.23	5.99	5.82	5.70	5.60	5.52
7	8.07	6.54	5.89	5.52	5.29	5.12	4.99	4.90	4.82
8	7.57	6.06	5.42	5.05	4.82	4.65	4.53	4.43	4.36
9	7.21	5.71	5.08	4.72	4.48	4.32	4.20	4.10	4.03
10	6.94	5.46	4.83	4.47	4.24	4.07	3.95	3.85	3.78
11	6.72	5.26	4.63	4.28	4.04	3.88	3.76	3.66	3.59
12	6.55	5.10	4.47	4.12	3.89	3.73	3.61	3.51	3.44
13	6.41	4.97	4.35	4.00	3.77	3.60	3.48	3.39	3.31
14	6.30	4.86	4.24	3.89	3.66	3.50	3.38	3.29	3.21
15	6.20	4.77	4.15	3.80	3.58	3.41	3.29	3.20	3.12
16	6.12	4.69	4.08	3.73	3.50	3.34	3.22	3.12	3.05
17	6.04	4.62	4.01	3.66	3.44	3.28	3.16	3.06	2.98
18	5.98	4.56	3.95	3.61	3.38	3.22	3.10	3.01	2.93
19	5.92	4.51	3.90	3.56	3.33	3.17	3.05	2.96	2.88
20	5.87	4.46	3.86	3.51	3.29	3.13	3.01	2.91	2.84
21	5.83	4.42	3.82	3.48	3.25	3.09	2.97	2.87	2.80
22	5.79	4.38	3.78	3.44	3.22	3.05	2.93	2.84	2.76
23	5.75	4.35	3.75	3.41	3.18	3.02	2.90	2.81	2.73
24	5.72	4.32	3.72	3.38	3.15	2.99	2.87	2.78	2.70
25	5.69	4.29	3.69	3.35	3.13	2.97	2.85	2.75	2.68
26	5.66	4.27	3.67	3.33	3.10	2.94	2.82	2.73	2.65
27	5.63	4.24	3.65	3.31	3.08	2.92	2.80	2.71	2.63
28	5.61	4.22	3.63	3.29	3.06	2.90	2.78	2.69	2.61
29	5.59	4.20	3.61	3.27	3.04	2.88	2.76	2.67	2.59
30	5.57	4.18	3.59	3.25	3.03	2.87	2.75	2.65	2.57
40	5.42	4.05	3.46	3.13	2.90	2.74	2.62	2.53	2.45
60	5.29	3.93	3.34	3.01	2.79	2.63	2.51	2.41	2.33
120	5.15	3.80	3.23	2.89	2.67	2.52	2.39	2.30	2.22
∞	5.02	3.69	3.12	2.79	2.57	2.41	2.29	2.19	2.11

10	12	15	20	24	30	40	60	120	∞
				$F_{.975}(n_1, n_2)$					
968.6	976.7	984.9	993.1	997.2	1,001	1,006	1,010	1,014	1,018
39.40	39.41	39.43	39.45	39.46	39.46	39.47	39.48	39.49	39.50
14.42	14.34	14.25	14.17	14.12	14.08	14.04	13.99	13.95	13.90
8.84	8.75	8.66	8.56	8.51	8.46	8.41	8.36	8.31	8.26
6.62	6.52	6.43	6.33	6.28	6.23	6.18	6.12	6.07	6.02
5.46	5.37	5.27	5.17	5.12	5.07	5.01	4.96	4.90	4.85
4.76	4.67	4.57	4.47	4.42	4.36	4.31	4.25	4.20	4.14
4.30	4.20	4.10	4.00	3.95	3.89	3.84	3.78	3.73	3.67
3.96	3.87	3.77	3.67	3.61	3.56	3.51	3.45	3.39	3.33
3.72	3.62	3.52	3.42	3.37	3.31	3.26	3.20	3.14	3.08
3.53	3.43	3.33	3.23	3.17	3.12	3.06	3.00	2.94	2.88
3.37	3.28	3.18	3.07	3.02	2.96	2.91	2.85	2.79	2.72
3.25	3.15	3.05	2.95	2.89	2.84	2.78	2.72	2.66	2.60
3.15	3.05	2.95	2.84	2.79	2.73	2.67	2.61	2.55	2.49
3.06	2.96	2.86	2.76	2.70	2.64	2.59	2.52	2.46	2.40
2.99	2.89	2.79	2.68	2.63	2.57	2.51	2.45	2.38	2.32
2.92	2.82	2.72	2.62	2.56	2.50	2.44	2.38	2.32	2.25
2.87	2.77	2.67	2.56	2.50	2.44	2.38	2.32	2.26	2.19
2.82	2.72	2.62	2.51	2.45	2.39	2.33	2.27	2.20	2.13
2.77	2.68	2.57	2.46	2.41	2.35	2.29	2.22	2.16	2.09
2.73	2.64	2.53	2.42	2.37	2.31	2.25	2.18	2.11	2.04
2.70	2.60	2.50	2.39	2.33	2.27	2.21	2.14	2.08	2.00
2.67	2.57	2.47	2.36	2.30	2.24	2.18	2.11	2.04	1.97
2.64	2.54	2.44	2.33	2.27	2.21	2.15	2.08	2.01	1.94
2.61	2.51	2.41	2.30	2.24	2.18	2.12	2.05	1.98	1.91
2.59	2.49	2.39	2.28	2.22	2.16	2.09	2.03	1.95	1.88
2.57	2.47	2.36	2.25	2.19	2.13	2.07	2.00	1.93	1.85
2.55	2.45	2.34	2.23	2.17	2.11	2.05	1.98	1.91	1.83
2.53	2.43	2.32	2.21	2.15	2.09	2.03	1.96	1.89	1.81
2.51	2.41	2.31	2.20	2.14	2.07	2.01	1.94	1.87	1.79
2.39	2.29	2.18	2.07	2.01	1.94	1.88	1.80	1.72	1.64
2.27	2.17	2.06	1.94	1.88	1.82	1.74	1.67	1.58	1.48
2.16	2.05	1.94	1.82	1.76	1.69	1.61	1.53	1.43	1.31
2.05	1.94	1.83	1.71	1.64	1.57	1.48	1.39	1.27	1.00

n_2 \ n_1	1	2	3	4	5	6	7	8	9
					$F_{.99}(n_1, n_2)$				
1	4,052	4,999.5	5,403	5,625	5,764	5,859	5,928	5,982	6,022
2	98.50	99.00	99.17	99.25	99.30	99.33	99.36	99.37	99.39
3	34.12	30.82	29.46	28.71	28.24	27.91	27.67	27.49	27.35
4	21.20	18.00	16.69	15.98	15.52	15.21	14.98	14.80	14.66
5	16.26	13.27	12.06	11.39	10.97	10.67	10.46	10.29	10.16
6	13.75	10.92	9.78	9.15	8.75	8.47	8.26	8.10	7.98
7	12.25	9.55	8.45	7.85	7.46	7.19	6.99	6.84	6.72
8	11.26	8.65	7.59	7.01	6.63	6.37	6.18	6.03	5.91
9	10.56	8.02	6.99	6.42	6.06	5.80	5.61	5.47	5.35
10	10.04	7.56	6.55	5.99	5.64	5.39	5.20	5.06	4.94
11	9.65	7.21	6.22	5.67	5.32	5.07	4.89	4.74	4.63
12	9.33	6.93	5.95	5.41	5.06	4.82	4.64	4.50	4.39
13	9.07	6.70	5.74	5.21	4.86	4.62	4.44	4.30	4.19
14	8.86	6.51	5.56	5.04	4.69	4.46	4.28	4.14	4.03
15	8.68	6.36	5.42	4.89	4.56	4.32	4.14	4.00	3.89
16	8.53	6.23	5.29	4.77	4.44	4.20	4.03	3.89	3.78
17	8.40	6.11	5.18	4.67	4.34	4.10	3.93	3.79	3.68
18	8.29	6.01	5.09	4.58	4.25	4.01	3.84	3.71	3.60
19	8.18	5.93	5.01	4.50	4.17	3.94	3.77	3.63	3.52
20	8.10	5.85	4.94	4.43	4.10	3.87	3.70	3.56	3.46
21	8.02	5.78	4.87	4.37	4.04	3.81	3.64	3.51	3.40
22	7.95	5.72	4.82	4.31	3.99	3.76	3.59	3.45	3.35
23	7.88	5.66	4.76	4.26	3.94	3.71	3.54	3.41	3.30
24	7.82	5.61	4.72	4.22	3.90	3.67	3.50	3.36	3.26
25	7.77	5.57	4.68	4.18	3.85	3.63	3.46	3.32	3.22
26	7.72	5.53	4.64	4.14	3.82	3.59	3.42	3.29	3.18
27	7.68	5.49	4.60	4.11	3.78	3.56	3.39	3.26	3.15
28	7.64	5.45	4.57	4.07	3.75	3.53	3.36	3.23	3.12
29	7.60	5.42	4.54	4.04	3.73	3.50	3.33	3.20	3.09
30	7.56	5.39	4.51	4.02	3.70	3.47	3.30	3.17	3.07
40	7.31	5.18	4.31	3.83	3.51	3.29	3.12	2.99	2.89
60	7.08	4.98	4.13	3.65	3.34	3.12	2.95	2.82	2.72
120	6.85	4.79	3.95	3.48	3.17	2.96	2.79	2.66	2.56
∞	6.63	4.61	3.78	3.32	3.02	2.80	2.64	2.51	2.41

10	12	15	20	24	30	40	60	120	∞
				$F_{.99}$ (n_1, n_2)					
6,056	6,106	6,157	6,209	6,235	6,261	6,287	6,313	6,339	6,366
99.40	99.42	99.43	99.45	99.46	99.47	99.47	99.48	99.49	99.50
27.23	27.05	26.87	26.69	26.60	26.50	26.41	26.32	26.22	26.13
14.55	14.37	14.20	14.02	13.93	13.84	13.75	13.65	13.56	13.46
10.05	9.89	9.72	9.55	9.47	9.38	9.29	9.20	9.11	9.02
7.87	7.72	7.56	7.40	7.31	7.23	7.14	7.06	6.97	6.88
6.62	6.47	6.31	6.16	6.07	5.99	5.91	5.82	5.74	5.65
5.81	5.67	5.52	5.36	5.28	5.20	5.12	5.03	4.95	4.86
5.26	5.11	4.96	4.81	4.73	4.65	4.57	4.48	4.40	4.31
4.85	4.71	4.56	4.41	4.33	4.25	4.17	4.08	4.00	3.91
4.54	4.40	4.25	4.10	4.02	3.94	3.86	3.78	3.69	3.60
4.30	4.16	4.01	3.86	3.78	3.70	3.62	3.54	3.45	3.36
4.10	3.96	3.82	3.66	3.59	3.51	3.43	3.34	3.25	3.17
3.94	3.80	3.66	3.51	3.43	3.35	3.27	3.18	3.09	3.00
3.80	3.67	3.52	3.37	3.29	3.21	3.13	3.05	2.96	2.87
3.69	3.55	3.41	3.26	3.18	3.10	3.02	2.93	2.84	2.75
3.59	3.46	3.31	3.16	3.08	3.00	2.92	2.83	2.75	2.65
3.51	3.37	3.23	3.08	3.00	2.92	2.84	2.75	2.66	2.57
3.43	3.30	3.15	3.00	2.92	2.84	2.76	2.67	2.58	2.49
3.37	3.23	3.09	2.94	2.86	2.78	2.69	2.61	2.52	2.42
3.31	3.17	3.03	2.88	2.80	2.72	2.64	2.55	2.46	2.36
3.26	3.12	2.98	2.83	2.75	2.67	2.58	2.50	2.40	2.31
3.21	3.07	2.93	2.78	2.70	2.62	2.54	2.45	2.35	2.26
3.17	3.03	2.89	2.74	2.66	2.58	2.49	2.40	2.31	2.21
3.13	2.99	2.85	2.70	2.62	2.54	2.45	2.36	2.27	2.17
3.09	2.96	2.81	2.66	2.58	2.50	2.42	2.33	2.23	2.13
3.06	2.93	2.78	2.63	2.55	2.47	2.38	2.29	2.20	2.10
3.03	2.90	2.75	2.60	2.52	2.44	2.35	2.26	2.17	2.06
3.00	2.87	2.73	2.57	2.49	2.41	2.33	2.23	2.14	2.03
2.98	2.84	2.70	2.55	2.47	2.39	2.30	2.21	2.11	2.01
2.80	2.66	2.52	2.37	2.29	2.20	2.11	2.02	1.92	1.80
2.63	2.50	2.35	2.20	2.12	2.03	1.94	1.84	1.73	1.60
2.47	2.34	2.19	2.03	1.95	1.86	1.76	1.66	1.53	1.38
2.32	2.18	2.04	1.88	1.79	1.70	1.59	1.47	1.32	1.00

TABLE L* Distribution of χ^2

Values of χ^2 corresponding to certain selected probabilities (i.e., tail areas under the curve). To illustrate: The probability is 0.95 that a sample with 20 degrees of freedom, taken from a normal distribution, would have $\chi^2 = 31.41$ or smaller.

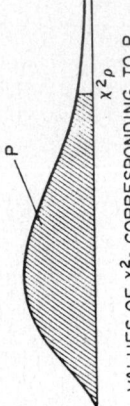

VALUES OF χ^2_P CORRESPONDING TO P

DF	$\chi^2_{.005}$	$\chi^2_{.01}$	$\chi^2_{.025}$	$\chi^2_{.05}$	$\chi^2_{.10}$	$\chi^2_{.90}$	$\chi^2_{.95}$	$\chi^2_{.975}$	$\chi^2_{.99}$	$\chi^2_{.995}$
1	.000039	0.00016	0.00098	0.0039	0.0158	2.71	3.84	5.02	6.63	7.88
2	0.0100	0.0201	0.0506	0.1026	0.2107	4.61	5.99	7.38	9.21	10.60
3	0.0717	0.115	0.216	0.352	0.584	6.25	7.81	9.35	11.34	12.84
4	0.207	0.297	0.484	0.711	1.064	7.78	9.49	11.14	13.28	14.86
5	0.412	0.554	0.831	1.15	1.61	9.24	11.07	12.83	15.09	16.75
6	0.676	0.872	1.24	1.64	2.20	10.64	12.59	14.45	16.81	18.55
7	0.989	1.24	1.69	2.17	2.83	12.02	14.07	16.01	18.48	20.28
8	1.34	1.65	2.18	2.73	3.49	13.36	15.51	17.53	20.09	21.96
9	1.73	2.09	2.70	3.33	4.17	14.68	16.92	19.02	21.67	23.59
10	2.16	2.56	3.25	3.94	4.87	15.99	18.31	20.48	23.21	25.19
11	2.60	3.05	3.82	4.57	5.58	17.28	19.68	21.92	24.73	26.76
12	3.07	3.57	4.40	5.23	6.30	18.55	21.03	23.34	26.22	28.30
13	3.57	4.11	5.01	5.89	7.04	19.81	22.36	24.74	27.69	29.82
14	4.07	4.66	5.63	6.57	7.79	21.06	23.68	26.12	29.14	31.32
15	4.60	5.23	6.26	7.26	8.55	22.31	25.00	27.49	30.58	32.80
16	5.14	5.81	6.91	7.96	9.31	23.54	26.30	28.85	32.00	34.27
18	6.26	7.01	8.23	9.39	10.86	25.99	28.87	31.53	34.81	37.16
20	7.43	8.26	9.59	10.85	12.44	28.41	31.41	34.17	37.57	40.00
24	9.89	10.86	12.40	13.85	15.66	33.20	36.42	39.36	42.98	45.56
30	13.79	14.95	16.79	18.49	20.60	40.26	43.77	46.98	50.89	53.67
40	20.71	22.16	24.43	26.51	29.05	51.81	55.76	59.34	63.69	66.77
60	35.53	37.48	40.48	43.19	46.46	74.40	79.08	83.30	88.38	91.95
120	83.85	86.92	91.58	95.70	100.62	140.23	146.57	152.21	158.95	163.64

*Adapted with permission from Dixon, W. J. and Massey, F. J., Jr. (1969). Introduction to Statistical Analysis, 3rd ed. McGraw-Hill, New York.

TABLE M* Percentiles of $F' = \dfrac{R_1}{R_2}$

Values of F' corresponding to certain selected cumulative probabilities. To illustrate: The probability is 0.95 that the ratio of sample ranges R_1/R_2 is 2.6 or less when $n_1 = n_2 = 5$.

n_2	Cumulative probability	n_1								
		2	3	4	5	6	7	8	9	10
2	0.025	0.039	0.217	0.37	0.50	0.60	0.68	0.74	0.79	0.83
	0.05	0.079	0.31	0.50	0.62	0.74	0.80	0.86	0.91	0.95
	0.95	12.7	19.1	23	26	29	30	32	34	35
	0.975	25.5	38.2	52	57	60	62	64	67	68
3	0.025	0.026	0.160	0.28	0.39	0.47	0.54	0.59	0.64	0.68
	0.05	0.052	0.23	0.37	0.49	0.57	0.64	0.70	0.75	0.80
	0.95	3.19	4.4	5.0	5.7	6.2	6.6	6.9	7.2	7.4
	0.975	4.61	6.3	7.3	8.0	8.7	9.3	9.8	10.2	10.5
4	0.025	0.019	0.137	0.25	0.34	0.42	0.48	0.53	0.57	0.61
	0.05	0.043	0.20	0.32	0.42	0.50	0.57	0.62	0.67	0.70
	0.95	2.02	2.7	3.1	3.4	3.6	3.8	4.0	4.2	4.4
	0.975	2.72	3.5	4.0	4.4	4.7	5.0	5.2	5.4	5.6
5	0.025	0.018	0.124	0.23	0.32	0.38	0.44	0.49	0.53	0.57
	0.05	0.038	0.18	0.29	0.40	0.46	0.52	0.57	0.61	0.65
	0.95	1.61	2.1	2.4	2.6	2.8	2.9	3.0	3.1	3.2
	0.975	2.01	2.6	2.9	3.2	3.4	3.6	3.7	3.8	3.9
6	0.025	0.017	0.115	0.21	0.30	0.36	0.42	0.46	0.50	0.54
	0.05	0.035	0.16	0.27	0.36	0.43	0.49	0.54	0.58	0.61
	0.95	1.36	1.8	2.0	2.2	2.3	2.4	2.5	2.6	2.7
	0.975	1.67	2.1	2.4	2.6	2.8	2.9	3.0	3.1	3.2
7	0.025	0.016	0.107	0.20	0.28	0.34	0.40	0.44	0.48	0.52
	0.05	0.032	0.15	0.26	0.35	0.41	0.47	0.51	0.55	0.59
	0.95	1.26	1.6	1.8	1.9	2.0	2.1	2.2	2.3	2.4
	0.975	1.48	1.9	2.1	2.3	2.4	2.5	2.6	2.7	2.8
8	0.025	0.016	0.102	0.19	0.27	0.33	0.38	0.43	0.47	0.50
	0.05	0.031	0.14	0.25	0.33	0.40	0.45	0.50	0.53	0.57
	0.95	1.17	1.4	1.6	1.8	1.9	1.9	2.0	2.1	2.1
	0.975	1.36	1.7	1.9	2.0	2.2	2.3	2.3	2.4	2.5
9	0.025	0.015	0.098	0.18	0.26	0.32	0.37	0.42	0.46	0.49
	0.05	0.030	0.14	0.24	0.32	0.38	0.44	0.48	0.52	0.55
	0.95	1.10	1.3	1.5	1.6	1.7	1.8	1.9	1.9	2.0
	0.975	1.27	1.6	1.8	1.9	2.0	2.1	2.1	2.2	2.3
10	0.025	0.015	0.095	0.18	0.25	0.31	0.36	0.41	0.44	0.48
	0.05	0.029	0.13	0.23	0.31	0.37	0.43	0.47	0.51	0.54
	0.95	1.05	1.3	1.4	1.5	1.6	1.7	1.8	1.8	1.9
	0.975	1.21	1.5	1.6	1.8	1.9	1.9	2.0	2.0	2.1

*Adapted with permission from Dixon, W. J. and Massey, F. J., Jr. (1969). *Introduction to Statistical Analysis,* 3rd ed. McGraw-Hill, New York.

CHART N Confidence Limits for Fraction Defective*

Enter the horizontal scale with the sample fraction defective. Rise vertically to the upper and lower curves for the stated sample size. Read the corresponding upper and lower confidence limits on the vertical scale. To illustrate: If a sample of 50 is 20% defective, the 95% confidence limits on the population fraction defective are 10 and 35%.

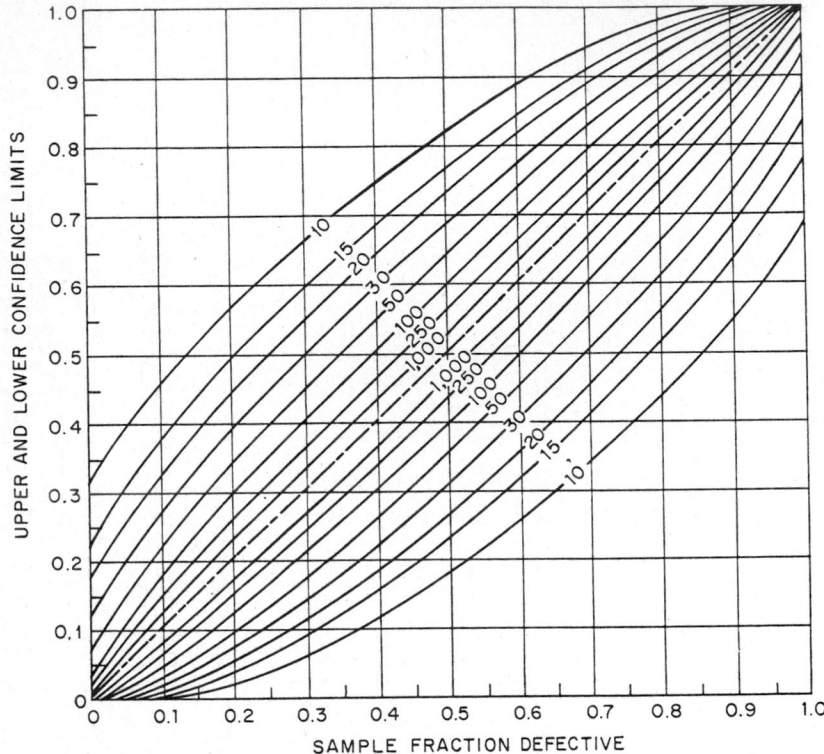

*By permission of Prof. E. S. Pearson from Clopper, C. J. and Pearson, E. S. (1934). "The Use of Confidence or Fiducial Limits Illustrated in the Case of the Binomial." *Biometrika,* vol. 26, p. 404.

TABLE O Critical Values of Smaller Rank Sum for the Wilcoxon-Mann-Whitney Test*

n_2	α for 2-sided test	α for 1-sided test	n_1 (smaller sample)											
			1	2	3	4	5	6	7	8	9	10	11	12
3	0.20	0.10		3	7									
	0.10	0.05			6									
	0.05	0.025												
	0.01	0.005												
4	0.20	0.10		3	7	13								
	0.10	0.05			6	11								
	0.05	0.025				10								
	0.01	0.005												
5	0.20	0.10		4	8	14	20							
	0.10	0.05		3	7	12	19							
	0.05	0.025			6	11	17							
	0.01	0.005					15							
6	0.20	0.10		4	9	15	22	30						
	0.10	0.05		3	8	13	20	28						
	0.05	0.025			7	12	18	26						
	0.01	0.005				10	16	23						
7	0.20	0.10		4	10	16	23	32	41					
	0.10	0.05		3	8	14	21	29	39					
	0.05	0.025			7	13	20	27	36					
	0.01	0.005				10	16	24	32					
8	0.20	0.10		5	11	17	25	34	44	55				
	0.10	0.05		4	9	15	23	31	41	51				
	0.05	0.025		3	8	14	21	29	38	49				
	0.01	0.005				11	17	25	34	43				
9	0.20	0.10	1	5	11	19	27	36	46	58	70			
	0.10	0.05		4	9	16	24	33	43	54	66			
	0.05	0.025		3	8	14	22	31	40	51	62			
	0.01	0.005			6	11	18	26	35	45	56			
10	0.20	0.10	1	6	12	20	28	38	49	60	73	87		
	0.10	0.05		4	10	17	26	35	45	56	69	82		
	0.05	0.025		3	9	15	23	32	42	53	65	78		
	0.01	0.005			6	12	19	27	37	47	58	71		
11	0.20	0.10	1	6	13	21	30	40	51	63	76	91	106	
	0.10	0.05		4	11	18	27	37	47	59	72	86	100	
	0.05	0.025		3	9	16	24	34	44	55	68	81	96	
	0.01	0.005			6	12	20	28	38	49	61	73	87	
12	0.20	0.10	1	7	14	22	32	42	54	66	80	94	110	127
	0.10	0.05		5	11	19	28	38	49	62	75	89	104	120
	0.05	0.025		4	10	17	26	35	46	58	71	84	99	115
	0.01	0.005			7	13	21	30	40	51	63	76	90	105

*Reproduced with permission from Tate, M. W. and Clelland, R. C. (1957). *Non-parametric and Shortcut Statistics*. The Interstate Printers & Publishers, Danville, IL.

TABLE P Limiting Values for Number of Runs above and below the Medi an of a Set of Values*

n_1 = number of values above the median and n_2 = number of values below the median.

$m = n_1 = n_2$	Probability of an equal or smaller number of runs		Probability of an equal or larger number of runs	
	$\alpha = 0.05$	$\alpha = 0.01$	$\alpha = 0.05$	$\alpha = 0.01$
5	3	2	9	10
6	3	2	11	12
7	4	3	12	13
8	5	4	13	14
9	6	4	14	16
10	6	5	16	17
11	7	6	17	18
12	8	7	18	19
13	9	7	19	21
14	10	8	20	22
15	11	9	21	23
16	11	10	23	24
17	12	10	24	26
18	13	11	25	27
19	14	12	26	28
20	15	13	27	29
21	16	14	28	30
22	17	14	29	32
23	17	15	31	33
24	18	16	32	34
25	19	17	33	35
26	20	18	34	36
27	21	19	35	37
28	22	19	36	39
29	23	20	37	40
30	24	21	38	41

*Reproduced with permission from Swed, Freda S. and Eisenhart, C. (1943). "Tables for Testing Randomness of Grouping in a Sequence of Alternatives." *Annals of Mathematical Statistics,* vol. XIV, pp. 66 and 87, Tables II and III.

TABLE Q Criteria for Testing for Extreme Mean*

Statistic	No. of observations	$P_{.90}$	$P_{.95}$	$P_{.98}$	$P_{.99}$
$r_{10} = \dfrac{X_2 - X_1}{X_n - X_1}$	3	0.886	0.941	0.976	0.988
	4	0.679	0.765	0.846	0.889
	5	0.557	0.642	0.729	0.780
	6	0.482	0.560	0.644	0.698
	7	0.434	0.507	0.586	0.637
$r_{11} = \dfrac{X_2 - X_1}{X_{n-1} - X_1}$	8	0.479	0.554	0.631	0.683
	9	0.441	0.512	0.587	0.635
	10	0.409	0.477	0.551	0.597
$r_{21} = \dfrac{X_3 - X_1}{X_{n-1} - X_1}$	11	0.517	0.576	0.638	0.679
	12	0.490	0.546	0.605	0.642
	13	0.467	0.521	0.578	0.615
$r_{22} = \dfrac{X_3 - X_1}{X_{n-2} - X_1}$	14	0.492	0.546	0.602	0.641
	15	0.472	0.525	0.579	0.616
	16	0.454	0.507	0.559	0.595
	17	0.438	0.490	0.542	0.577
	18	0.424	0.475	0.527	0.561
	19	0.412	0.462	0.514	0.547
	20	0.401	0.450	0.502	0.535
	21	0.391	0.440	0.491	0.524
	22	0.382	0.430	0.481	0.514
	23	0.374	0.421	0.472	0.505
	24	0.367	0.413	0.464	0.497
	25	0.360	0.406	0.457	0.489

*Adapted with permission from Dixon, W. J. and Massey, F. J., Jr. (1969). *Introduction to Statistical Analysis,* 3rd ed. McGraw-Hill, New York.

CHART R Operating Characteristics of the Two-Sided Normal Test for a Level of Significance Equal to 0.05*

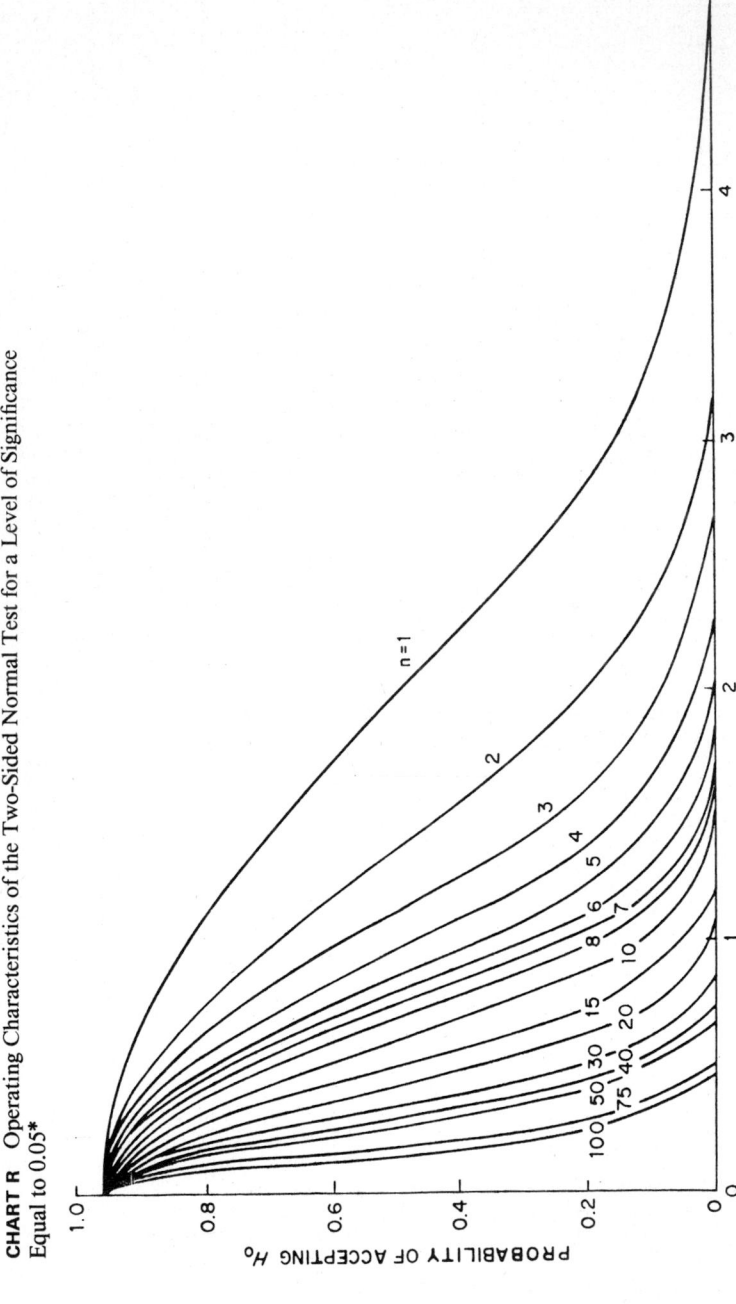

*Adapted with permission from Ferris, Charles D., Grubbs, Frank E., and Weaver, Chalmers L. (1946). "Operating Characteristics for the Common Statistical Tests of Significance." *Annals of Mathematical Statistics*, June.

CHART S Size of Sample for Arithmetic Mean When σ is Unknown*

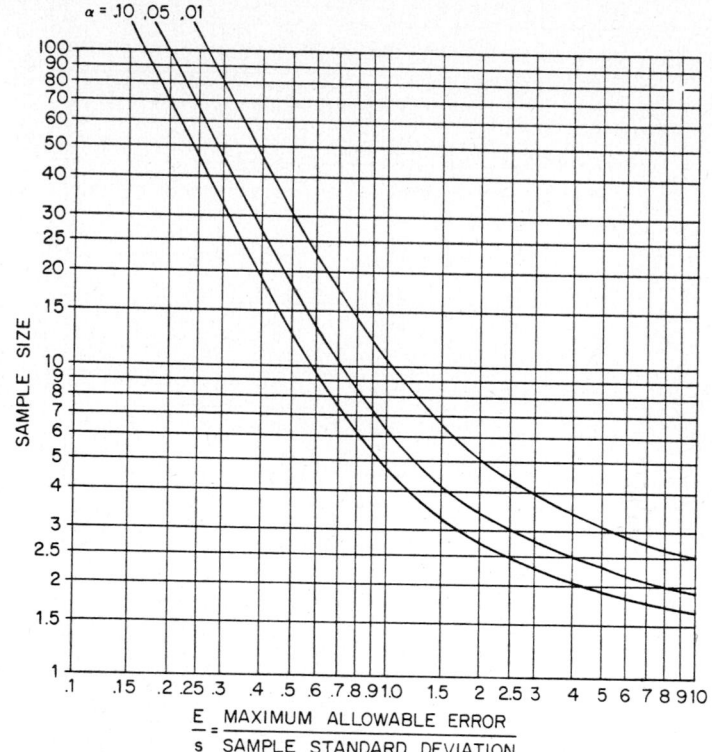

$$\frac{E}{s} = \frac{\text{MAXIMUM ALLOWABLE ERROR}}{\text{SAMPLE STANDARD DEVIATION}}$$

*Reproduced with permission from Weida, Frank M. and Lum, Mary D. (1953). *Statistical Inference, Reliability, and Significance.* WADC Technical Report 53-149, U.S. Air Force.

CHART T Number of Degrees of Freedom Required to Estimate the Standard Deviation within *P*% of Its True Value with Confidence Coefficient γ

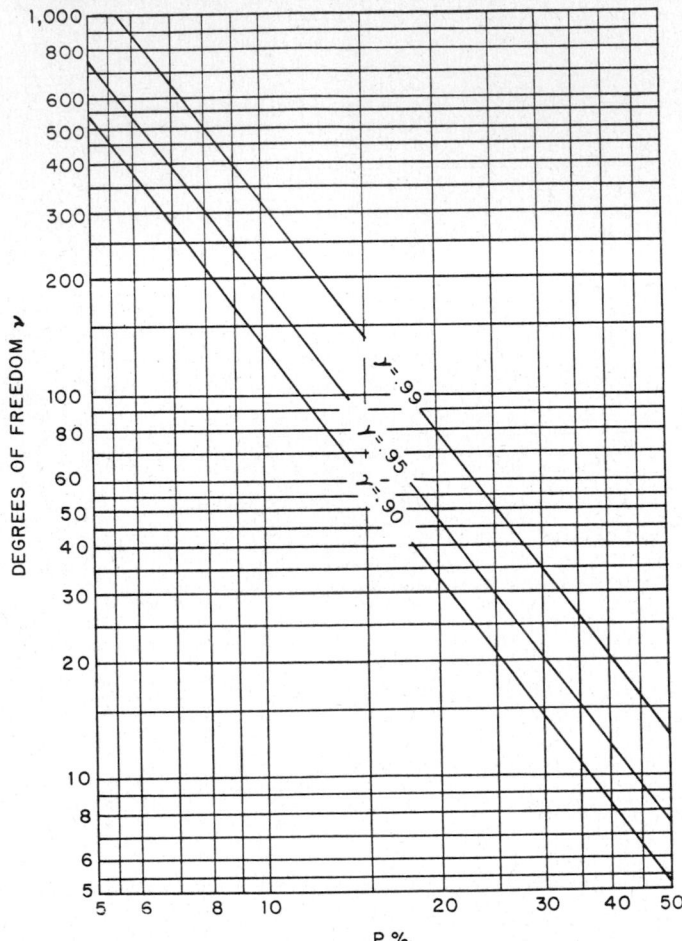

*Adapted with permission from Greenwood, J. A. and Sandomire, M. M. (1950). "Statistics Manual, Sample Size Required for Estimating the Standard Deviation as a Percent of Its True Value." *Journal of the American Statistical Association*, vol. 45, p. 258. The manner of graphing is adapted with permission from Crow, E. L., Davis, F. A., and Maxfield, M. W. (1955). *NAVORD Report 3369*. NOTS 948, U.S. Naval Ordnance Test Station, China Lake, CA. (Reprinted by Dover Publications, New York, 1960.)

TABLE U Tolerance Factors for Normal Distribution*

Factors K_r such that the probability is γ that at least a proportion P of the distribution will be included between $\overline{X} \pm K_r R$ where $\overline{X}$ is the mean and R is the range in a sample of size n.

	$\gamma = 0.90$				$\gamma = 0.95$				$\gamma = 0.99$			
P	0.90	0.95	0.99	0.999	0.90	0.95	0.99	0.999	0.90	0.95	0.99	0.999
n												
2	11.298	13.294	17.090	21.374	22.635	26.634	34.238	42.821	113.429	133.469	171.576	214.588
3	3.069	3.631	4.711	5.936	4.399	5.206	6.752	8.509	9.951	11.776	15.275	19.249
4	1.877	2.227	2.902	3.672	2.422	2.873	3.744	4.737	4.233	5.021	6.543	8.279
5	1.428	1.697	2.216	2.812	1.749	2.078	2.715	3.444	2.709	3.219	4.205	5.335
6	1.194	1.420	1.857	2.360	1.418	1.686	2.206	2.803	2.042	2.429	3.178	4.038
7	1.050	1.248	1.635	2.080	1.222	1.453	1.903	2.420	1.678	1.996	2.615	3.325
8	0.951	1.131	1.483	1.888	1.090	1.297	1.700	2.165	1.449	1.724	2.261	2.878
9	0.879	1.046	1.372	1.747	0.997	1.187	1.556	1.981	1.290	1.536	2.014	2.565
10	0.824	0.981	1.286	1.639	0.926	1.103	1.446	1.843	1.176	1.400	1.836	2.340
11	0.780	0.929	1.219	1.554	0.871	1.037	1.361	1.735	1.088	1.296	1.701	2.168
12	0.745	0.887	1.164	1.484	0.827	0.985	1.292	1.648	1.020	1.215	1.594	2.033
13	0.715	0.852	1.118	1.426	0.790	0.940	1.235	1.575	0.964	1.148	1.507	1.922
14	0.690	0.822	1.079	1.377	0.759	0.904	1.187	1.514	0.917	1.093	1.435	1.830
15	0.669	0.797	1.046	1.334	0.733	0.873	1.146	1.462	0.878	1.046	1.373	1.753
16	0.650	0.774	1.016	1.297	0.710	0.845	1.110	1.417	0.845	1.007	1.322	1.687
17	0.633	0.755	0.991	1.265	0.690	0.822	1.109	1.377	0.816	0.972	1.277	1.630
18	0.619	0.737	0.968	1.235	0.672	0.801	1.051	1.342	0.790	0.941	1.236	1.578
19	0.605	0.721	0.947	1.209	0.656	0.782	1.027	1.311	0.768	0.916	1.203	1.535
20	0.594	0.707	0.929	1.186	0.642	0.765	1.005	1.282	0.748	0.892	1.171	1.495

*Adapted with permission from Mitra, S. K. (1957). "Tables for Tolerance Limits for a Normal Population Based on Sample Mean and Range on Mean Range." *Journal of the American Statistical Association*, vol. 52, no. 277, March, p. 92.

TABLE V One-Sided and Two-sided Statistical Tolerance Limit Factors k for a Normal Distribution*

Factors k such that the probability is γ that at least a proportion P of the distribution will be less than $\bar{X} + ks$ (or greater than $\bar{X} - ks$) where $\bar{X}$ and s are estimates of the mean and standard deviation computed from a sample size of n. Two-sided factors cover $\bar{X} \pm ks$.

One-sided Factors[a]

	$\gamma = 0.90$				$\gamma = 0.95$				$\gamma = 0.99$			
n \ P	0.90	0.95	0.99	0.999	0.90	0.95	0.99	0.999	0.90	0.95	0.99	0.999
3	4.258	5.310	7.340	9.651	6.158	7.655	10.552	13.857				
4	3.187	3.957	5.437	7.128	4.163	5.145	7.042	9.215				
5	2.742	3.400	4.666	6.112	3.407	4.202	5.741	7.501				
6	2.494	3.091	4.242	5.556	3.006	3.707	5.062	6.612	4.408	5.409	7.334	9.540
7	2.333	2.894	3.972	5.201	2.755	3.399	4.641	6.061	3.856	4.730	6.411	8.348
8	2.219	2.755	3.783	4.955	2.582	3.188	4.353	5.686	3.496	4.287	5.811	7.566
9	2.133	2.649	3.641	4.772	2.454	3.031	4.143	5.414	3.242	3.971	5.389	7.014
10	2.065	2.568	3.532	4.629	2.355	2.911	3.981	5.203	3.048	3.739	5.075	6.603
11	2.012	2.503	3.444	4.515	2.275	2.815	3.852	5.036	2.897	3.557	4.828	6.284
12	1.966	2.448	3.371	4.420	2.210	2.736	3.747	4.900	2.773	3.410	4.633	6.032
13	1.928	2.403	3.310	4.341	2.155	2.670	3.659	4.787	2.677	3.290	4.472	5.826
14	1.895	2.363	3.257	4.274	2.108	2.614	3.585	4.690	2.592	3.189	4.336	5.651
15	1.866	2.329	3.212	4.215	2.068	2.566	3.520	4.607	2.521	3.102	4.224	5.507
16	1.842	2.299	3.172	4.164	2.032	2.523	3.463	4.534	2.458	3.028	4.124	5.374
17	1.820	2.272	3.136	4.118	2.001	2.486	3.415	4.471	2.405	2.962	4.038	5.268
18	1.800	2.249	3.106	4.078	1.974	2.453	3.370	4.415	2.357	2.906	3.961	5.167
19	1.781	2.228	3.078	4.041	1.949	2.423	3.331	4.364	2.315	2.855	3.893	5.078
20	1.765	2.208	3.052	4.009	1.926	2.396	3.295	4.319	2.275	2.807	3.832	5.003
21	1.750	2.190	3.028	3.979	1.905	2.371	3.262	4.276	2.241	2.768	3.776	4.932
22	1.736	2.174	3.007	3.952	1.887	2.350	3.233	4.238	2.208	2.729	3.727	4.866
23	1.724	2.159	2.987	3.927	1.869	2.329	3.206	4.204	2.179	2.693	3.680	4.806
24	1.712	2.145	2.969	3.904	1.853	2.309	3.181	4.171	2.154	2.663	3.638	4.755
25	1.702	2.132	2.952	3.882	1.838	2.292	3.158	4.143	2.129	2.632	3.601	4.706
30	1.657	2.080	2.884	3.794	1.778	2.220	3.064	4.022	2.029	2.516	3.446	4.508
35	1.623	2.041	2.833	3.730	1.732	2.166	2.994	3.934	1.957	2.431	3.334	4.364
40	1.598	2.010	2.793	3.679	1.697	2.126	2.941	3.866	1.902	2.365	3.250	4.255
45	1.577	1.986	2.762	3.638	1.669	2.092	2.897	3.811	1.857	2.313	3.181	4.168
50	1.560	1.965	2.735	3.604	1.646	2.065	2.863	3.766	1.821	2.296	3.124	4.096

n												
2	15.978	18.800	24.167	30.227	32.019	37.674	48.430	60.573	160.193	188.491	242.300	303.054
3	5.847	6.919	8.974	11.309	8.380	9.916	12.861	16.208	18.930	22.401	29.055	36.616
4	4.166	4.943	6.440	8.149	5.369	6.370	8.299	10.502	9.398	11.150	14.527	18.383
5	3.494	4.152	5.423	6.879	4.275	5.079	6.634	8.415	6.612	7.855	10.260	13.015
6	3.131	3.723	4.870	6.188	3.712	4.414	5.775	7.337	5.337	6.345	8.301	10.548
7	2.902	3.452	4.521	5.750	3.369	4.007	5.248	6.676	4.613	5.488	7.187	9.142
8	2.743	3.264	4.278	5.446	3.136	3.732	4.891	6.226	4.147	4.936	6.468	8.234
9	2.626	3.125	4.098	5.220	2.967	3.532	4.631	5.899	3.822	4.550	5.966	7.600
10	2.535	3.018	3.959	5.046	2.839	3.379	4.433	5.649	3.582	4.265	5.594	7.129
11	2.463	2.933	3.849	4.906	2.737	3.259	4.277	5.452	3.397	4.045	5.308	6.766
12	2.404	2.863	3.758	4.792	2.655	3.162	4.150	5.291	3.250	3.870	5.079	6.477
13	2.355	2.805	3.682	4.697	2.587	3.081	4.044	5.158	3.130	3.727	4.893	6.240
14	2.314	2.756	3.618	4.615	2.529	3.012	3.955	5.045	3.029	3.608	4.737	6.043
15	2.278	2.713	3.562	4.545	2.480	2.954	3.878	4.949	2.945	3.507	4.605	5.876
16	2.246	2.676	3.514	4.484	2.437	2.903	3.812	4.865	2.872	3.421	4.492	5.732
17	2.219	2.643	3.471	4.430	2.400	2.858	3.754	4.791	2.808	3.345	4.393	5.607
18	2.194	2.614	3.433	4.382	2.366	2.819	3.702	4.725	2.753	3.279	4.307	5.497
19	2.172	2.588	3.399	4.339	2.337	2.784	3.656	4.667	2.703	3.221	4.230	5.399
20	2.152	2.564	3.368	4.300	2.310	2.752	3.615	4.614	2.659	3.168	4.161	5.312
21	2.135	2.543	3.340	4.264	2.286	2.723	3.577	4.567	2.620	3.121	4.100	5.234
22	2.118	2.524	3.315	4.232	2.264	2.697	3.543	4.523	2.584	3.078	4.044	5.163
23	2.103	2.506	3.292	4.203	2.244	2.673	3.512	4.484	2.551	3.040	3.993	5.098
24	2.089	2.480	3.270	4.176	2.225	2.651	3.483	4.447	2.522	3.004	3.947	5.039
25	2.077	2.474	3.251	4.151	2.208	2.631	3.457	4.413	2.494	2.972	3.904	4.985
26	2.065	2.460	3.232	4.127	2.193	2.612	3.432	4.382	2.460	2.941	3.865	4.935
27	2.054	2.447	3.215	4.106	2.178	2.595	3.409	4.353	2.446	2.914	3.828	4.888
30	2.025	2.413	3.170	4.049	2.140	2.549	3.350	4.278	2.385	2.841	3.733	4.768
35	1.988	2.368	3.112	3.974	2.090	2.490	3.272	4.179	2.306	2.748	3.611	4.611
40	1.959	2.334	3.066	3.917	2.052	2.445	3.213	4.104	2.247	2.677	3.518	4.493
45	1.935	2.306	3.030	3.871	2.021	2.408	3.165	4.042	2.200	2.621	3.444	4.399
50	1.916	2.284	3.001	3.833	1.996	2.379	3.126	3.993	2.162	2.576	3.385	4.323

*Adapted from Lieberman, Gerald J. (1958). "Tables for One-Sided Tolerance Limits." Industrial Quality Control, vol. XIV, no. 10, April, p. 8. Adapted with permission of the American Society for Quality Control.
†Adapted with permission from Eisenhart, C., Hastay, M. W., and Wallis, W. A. (1947). Techniques of Statistical Analysis. McGraw-Hill, New York.

TABLE W   *P* for Interval between Sample Extremes*

*γ is the probability that an interval will cover a proportion
P of the population with a random sample of size N.*

N \ γ	0.5	0.7	0.9	0.95	0.99	0.995
2	0.293	0.164	0.052	0.026	0.006	0.003
4	0.615	0.492	0.321	0.249	0.141	0.111
6	0.736	0.640	0.490	0.419	0.295	0.254
10	0.838	0.774	0.664	0.606	0.496	0.456
20	0.918	0.883	0.820	0.784	0.712	0.683
40	0.959	0.941	0.907	0.887	0.846	0.829
60	0.973	0.960	0.937	0.924	0.895	0.883
80	0.980	0.970	0.953	0.943	0.920	0.911
100	0.984	0.976	0.962	0.954	0.936	0.929
150	0.990	0.984	0.975	0.969	0.957	0.952
200	0.992	0.988	0.981	0.977	0.968	0.961
500	0.997	0.996	0.993	0.991	0.987	0.986
1,000	0.999	0.998	0.997	0.996	0.994	0.993

*Adapted with permission from Dixon, W. J. and Massey, F. J.,
Jr. (1969). *Introduction to Statistical Analysis,* 3rd ed. McGraw-Hill,
New York.

TABLE X   *N* for Interval between Sample Extremes*

P \ γ	0.50	0.70	0.90	0.95	0.99	0.995
0.995	336	488	777	947	1,325	1,483
0.99	168	244	388	473	662	740
0.95	34	49	77	93	130	146
0.90	17	24	38	46	64	72
0.85	11	16	25	30	42	47
0.80	9	12	18	22	31	34
0.75	7	10	15	18	24	27
0.70	6	8	12	14	20	22
0.60	4	6	9	10	14	16
0.50	3	5	7	8	11	12

*Adapted with permission from Dixon, W. J. and Massey,
F. J., Jr. (1969). *Introduction to Statistical Analysis,* 3rd ed.
McGraw-Hill, New York.

TABLE Y E_2 Factors for Control Charts

Number of observations in subgroup	E_2
2	2.660
3	1.772
4	1.457
5	1.290
6	1.184
7	1.109
8	1.054
9	1.010
10	0.975
11	0.946
12	0.921
13	0.899
14	0.881
15	0.864

CHART Z   Control Limits of p Charts

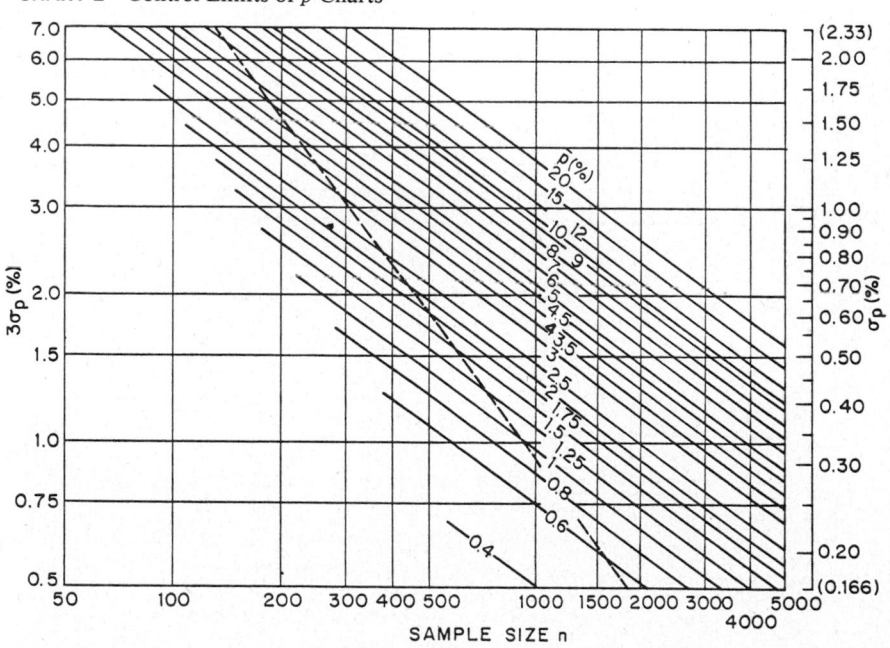

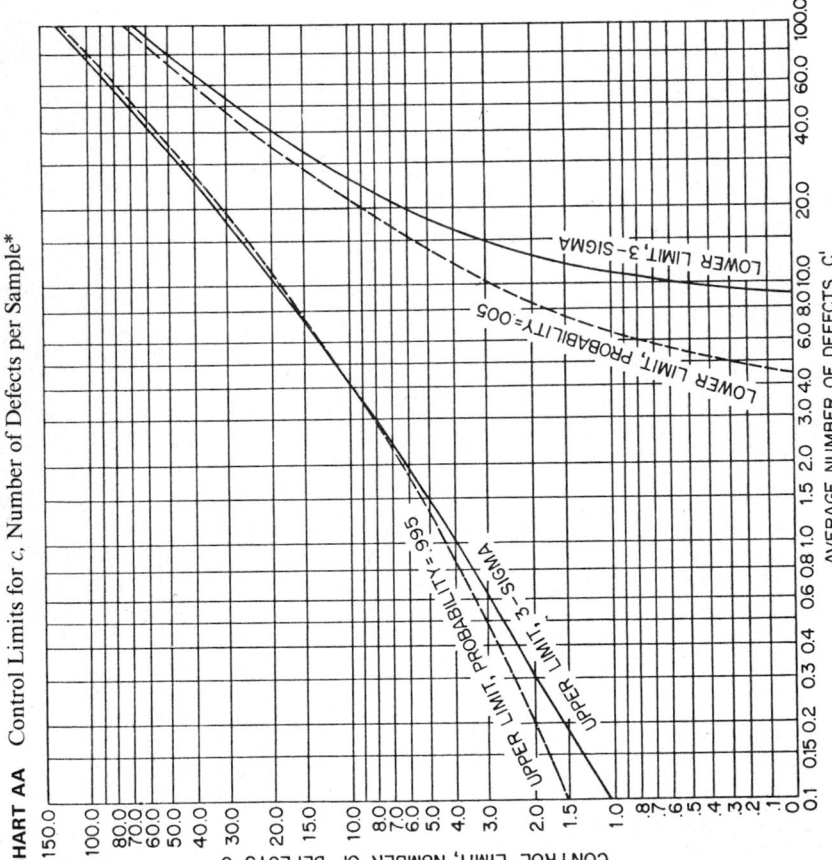

CHART AA Control Limits for c, Number of Defects per Sample*

*Reproduced by permission from American War Standard Z1.3-1942, American Standards Association, New York.

TABLE BB Factors for Cumulative Sum Control Chart*

δ	$2\alpha_0 = 0.0027$ $\alpha_0 = 0.00135$† θ	d
0.2	5°43'	330.4
0.4	11°19'	82.6
0.5	14°00'	52.9
0.6	16°42'	36.7
0.8	21°48'	20.6
1.0	26°34'	13.2
1.2	30°58'	9.2
1.3	32°59'	7.8
1.4	35°00'	6.7
1.6	38°40'	5.2
1.8	41°59'	4.1
2.0	45°00'	3.3
2.2	47°44'	2.7
2.4	50°12'	2.3
2.6	52°26'	2.0
2.8	54°28'	1.7
3.0	56°19'	1.5

*Adapted with permission from Johnson, Norman L. and Leone, Fred C. (1964). *Statistics and Experimental Design in Engineering and Physical Sciences*. John Wiley & Sons, New York, vol. I, p. 322.

†For limits comparable with the 3-sigma limits used in the Shewhart control chart.

TABLE CC   Random Numbers*

1306	1189	5731	3968	5606	5084	8947	3897	1636	7810
0422	2431	0649	8085	5053	4722	6598	5044	9040	5121
6597	2022	6168	5060	8656	6733	6364	7649	1871	4328
7965	6541	5645	6243	7658	6903	9911	5740	7824	8520
7695	6937	0406	8894	0441	8135	9797	7285	5905	9539
5160	7851	8464	6789	3938	4197	6511	0407	9239	2232
2961	0551	0539	8288	7478	7565	5581	5771	5442	8761
1428	4183	4312	5445	4854	9157	9158	5218	1464	3634
3666	5642	4539	1561	7849	7520	2547	0756	1206	2033
6543	6799	7454	9052	6689	1946	2574	9386	0304	7945
9975	6080	7423	3175	9377	6951	6519	8287	8994	5532
4866	0956	7545	7723	8085	4948	2228	9583	4415	7065
8239	7068	6694	5168	3117	1586	0237	6160	9585	1133
8722	9191	3386	3443	0434	4586	4150	1224	6204	0937
1330	9120	8785	8382	2929	7089	3109	6742	2468	7025
2296	2952	4764	9070	6356	9192	4012	0618	2219	1109
3582	7052	3132	4519	9250	2486	0830	8472	2160	7046
5872	9207	7222	6494	8973	3545	6967	8490	5264	9821
1134	6324	6201	3792	5651	0538	4676	2064	0584	7996
1403	4497	7390	8503	8239	4236	8022	2914	4368	4529
3393	7025	3381	3553	2128	1021	8353	6413	5161	8583
1137	7896	3602	0060	7850	7626	0854	6565	4260	6220
7437	5198	8772	6927	8527	6851	2709	5992	7383	1071
8414	8820	3917	7238	9821	6073	6658	1280	9643	7761
8398	5224	2749	7311	5740	9771	7826	9533	3800	4553
0995	8935	2939	3092	2496	0359	0318	4697	7181	4035
6657	0755	9685	4017	6581	7292	5643	5064	1142	1297
8875	8369	7868	0190	9278	1709	4253	9346	4335	3769
8399	6702	0586	6428	7985	2979	4513	1970	1989	3105
6703	1024	2064	0393	6815	8502	1375	4171	6970	1201
4730	1653	9032	9855	0957	7366	0325	5178	7959	5371
8400	6834	3187	8688	1079	1480	6776	9888	7585	9998
3647	8002	6726	0877	4552	3238	7542	7804	3933	9475
6789	5197	8037	2354	9262	5497	0005	3986	1767	7981
2630	2721	2810	2185	6323	5679	4931	8336	6662	3566
1374	8625	1644	3342	1587	0762	6057	8011	2666	3759
1572	7625	9110	4409	0239	7059	3415	5537	2250	7292
9678	2877	7579	4935	0449	8119	6969	5383	1717	6719
0882	6781	3538	4090	3092	2365	6001	3446	9985	6007
0006	4205	2389	4365	1981	8158	7784	6256	3842	5603
4611	9861	7916	9305	2074	9462	0254	4827	9198	3974
1093	3784	4190	6332	1175	8599	9735	8584	6581	7194
3374	3545	6865	8819	3342	1676	2264	6014	5012	2458
3650	9676	1436	4374	4716	5548	8276	6235	6742	2154
7292	5749	7977	7602	9205	3599	3880	9537	4423	2330
2353	8319	2850	4026	3027	1708	3518	7034	7132	6903
1094	2009	8919	5676	7283	4982	9642	7235	8167	3366
0568	4002	0587	7165	1094	2006	7471	0940	4366	9554
5606	4070	5233	4339	6543	6695	5799	5821	3953	9458
8285	7537	1181	2300	5294	6892	1627	3372	1952	3028

*Adapted with permission from Owen, Donald B. (1962). *Handbook of Statistical Tables.* Addison-Wesley, Reading, MA. Courtesy U.S. Atomic Energy Commission.

TABLE DD   Values of ϕ^2 for Determining Sample Size in Analysis of Variance*

$\alpha = 0.01; \beta = 0.2$

DF₁ DF₂	1	2	3	4	5	6	7	8	9	
2	80.37	106.63	119.75	127.62	132.87	136.63	139.45	141.63	143.38	
4	17.28	18.58	18.95	19.11	19.18	19.21	19.23	19.24	19.24	
6	11.36	11.12	10.77	10.49	10.27	10.11	9.97	9.86	9.77	
8	9.41	8.76	8.21	7.83	7.54	7.32	7.15	7.01	6.89	
10	8.47	7.63	7.02	6.58	6.26	6.03	5.84	5.68	5.56	
12	7.91	6.98	6.33	5.87	5.54	5.29	5.09	4.93	4.80	
14	7.55	6.56	5.88	5.41	5.07	4.81	4.61	4.45	4.31	
16	7.30	6.26	5.56	5.09	4.75	4.49	4.28	4.11	3.98	
18	7.11	6.05	5.35	4.86	4.51	4.24	4.04	3.87	3.73	
20	6.96	5.89	5.17	4.68	4.33	4.06	3.85	3.68	3.54	
24	6.76	5.66	4.93	4.41	4.08	3.80	3.57	3.42	3.28	
30	6.55	5.42	4.68	4.19	3.82	3.55	3.33	3.16	3.02	
40	6.35	5.20	4.45	3.96	3.57	3.31	3.10	2.92	2.79	
60	6.18	5.00	4.25	3.74	3.37	3.10	2.88	2.70	2.55	
80	6.10	4.88	4.16	3.65	3.28	2.99	2.76	2.59	2.43	
120	6.00	4.80	4.04	3.53	3.17	2.89	2.66	2.50	2.34	
240	5.90	4.71	3.96	3.46	3.06	2.79	2.56	2.40	2.25	
∞	5.84	4.62	3.87	3.35	2.98	2.70	2.47	2.29	2.14	

*These tables are computed from Lehmer, Emma (1944). "Inverse Tables of Probabilities of Errors of Second Kind." *Annals of Mathematical Statistics,* vol. 15, p. 390. Reproduced from Dixon, W. J. and Massey, F. J., Jr. *Introduction to Statistical Analysis,* 1st ed. McGraw-Hill, New York, p. 330.

10	12	15	20	24	30	40	60	120	∞
144.82	147.02	149.30	151.63	152.84	154.06	155.30	156.55	157.83	159.09
19.24	19.24	19.24	19.22	19.21	19.21	19.19	19.18	19.18	19.17
9.69	9.57	9.44	9.30	9.22	9.14	9.07	8.99	8.90	8.81
6.80	6.64	6.48	6.31	6.21	6.12	6.02	5.91	5.81	5.70
5.45	5.29	5.11	4.92	4.82	4.71	4.61	4.49	4.38	4.26
4.69	4.52	4.33	4.13	4.02	3.91	3.80	3.68	3.56	3.43
4.20	4.02	3.83	3.63	3.52	3.40	3.28	3.16	3.03	2.89
3.86	3.68	3.48	3.27	3.16	3.04	2.92	2.80	2.66	2.52
3.61	3.43	3.23	3.01	2.90	2.78	2.66	2.53	2.39	2.24
3.42	3.23	3.03	2.82	2.70	2.58	2.46	2.32	2.18	2.03
3.13	2.96	2.76	2.53	2.43	2.31	2.16	2.02	1.88	1.72
2.90	2.70	2.50	2.27	2.16	2.02	1.88	1.74	1.59	1.42
2.66	2.46	2.25	2.02	1.90	1.77	1.61	1.46	1.30	1.13
2.43	2.23	2.02	1.78	1.66	1.52	1.37	1.21	1.04	0.841
2.31	2.13	1.90	1.66	1.54	1.39	1.25	1.08	0.902	0.689
2.22	2.02	1.80	1.56	1.44	1.28	1.12	0.960	0.766	0.528
2.13	1.90	1.69	1.44	1.32	1.17	1.00	0.828	0.624	0.345
2.02	1.81	1.58	1.34	1.21	1.05	0.884	0.704	0.472	0.000

APPENDIX III

SELECTED QUALITY STANDARDS, SPECIFICATIONS, AND RELATED DOCUMENTS

This list is limited to documents likely to be of general interest. Of the several sources used to develop the list, special acknowledgment is given to B. A. MacDonald and M. V. Petty for their compilation "List of Quality Standards, Specifications and Related Documents," Feb. 10, 1987 (unpublished).

The list below is divided into three parts as follows:

System and Program Requirements	*Statistical Techniques and Procedures*	*Inspection and Test Methods*
Definitions	Definitions,	Definitions, units of
Quality	symbols, formulas	measurement
Reliability	Analysis of data	Inspection and Test
Maintainability	Control charts	Methods and
Software	Acceptance sampling	Requirements
Safety		Evaluation of
Certification		inspection and test
programs		systems
Other		Precision and accuracy

In some cases, the official document designation includes abbreviations or other notations:

Amd:	Amendment
Chg not:	Change Notice
Supp:	Supplement
'79:	1979

Following the complete listing, addresses are given for the organizations issuing the documents.

SYSTEM AND PROGRAM REQUIREMENTS

Definitions

ANSI/ASQC A3-1987 (Draft)	Quality Systems Terminology
ANSI/IEEE 729-1983	Software Engineering Terminology, Glossary of
IEC 271 (1974)	List of Basic Terms, Definitions and Related Mathematics for Reliability
IEC 271A (1978)	First Supplement
IEC 271B (1983)	Second Supplement
IEC 271C (1985)	Third Supplement
ISO 8402-1986	Quality—Vocabulary
MIL-STD-109B 4 Apr 69	Quality Assurance Terms and Definitions
MIL-STD-280A 7 Jul 69	Definition of Item Levels, Item Exchangeability, Models and Related Terms
MIL-STD-721C 12 Jun 81	Definitions of Terms for Reliability, Maintainability, Human Factors and Safety

Quality

ANSI/ASQC Q1-1986	Generic Guidelines for Auditing of Quality Systems
ANSI/ASQC Z1.15-1979	Generic Guidelines for Quality Systems
ANSI/ASQC Z1.8-1971	Specifications of General Requirements for a Quality Program
ANSI/ASQC 3.2-1982	Administrative Controls and Quality Assurance for the Operational Phase of Nuclear Power Plants
AQAP-1 Edition #3, 1 May 85 (NATO)	NATO Quality Control System Requirements for Industry
AQAP-2 Edition #3, 1 May 84 (NATO)	Guide for the Evaluation of a Contractor's Quality Control System for Compliance with AQAP-1
BSI Handbook 22:1981	Quality Assurance (contains 15 publications)
CAN3-Q395-81 (CSA)	Quality Audits
CAN3-Z299.1-85 (CSA)	Quality Assurance Program—Category 1
CAN3-Z299.2-85 (CSA)	Quality Assurance Program—Category 2
CAN3-Z299.3-85 (CSA)	Quality Assurance Program—Category 3
CAN3-Z299.4-85 (CSA)	Quality Assurance Program—Category 4
IEC Guide 102 (1979)	Specification Structures for the Quality Assessment of Electronic Components
IEC QC 001001 (1981)	Basic Rules of the IEC Quality Assessment System for Electronic Components (IECQ)

IEC QC 001002 (1981)	Rules of Procedure of the IEC Quality Assessment System for Electronic Components (IECQ), Section One: Clauses 1 to 8
IEC QC 001002 (1981)	Rules of Procedure of the IEC Quality Assessment System for Electronic Components (IECQ), Section Two: Clauses 9 to 14
ISO 9000 ANSI/ASQC Q90-1987	Quality Management and Quality Assurance Standards—Guidelines for Selection and Use
ISO 9001 ANSI/ASQC Q91-1987	Quality Systems—Model for Quality Assurance in Designed Development, Production, Installation, and Servicing
ISO 9002 ANSI/ASQC Q92-1987	Quality Systems—Model for Quality Assurance in Production and Installation
ISO 9003 ANSI/ASQC Q93-1987	Quality Systems—Model for Quality Assurance in Final Inspection and Test
ISO 9004 ANSI/ASQC Q94-1987	Quality Management and Quality System Elements—Guidelines
MIL-HDBK-50 23 Apr 65	Evaluation of a Contractor's Quality Program
MIL-STD-454K 14 Feb 86	Standard General Requirements—Electronic Equipment
MIL-STD-1521B Notice 1 19 Dec 85	Technical Reviews and Audits for Systems, Equipments, and Computer Software
MIL-STD-1535A 1 Feb 74	Supplier Quality Assurance Program Requirements
MIL-STD-2164 14 Apr 85	Failure Reporting, Analysis and Corrective Action System
MIL-Q-9858A Amd 2, 8 Mar 85	Quality Program Requirements
MIL-S-19500G Supp. 1 11 Mar 85	General Specification for Semiconductor Devices
MIL-T-50301 6 May 69	Quality Control System Requirements for Technical Data
NHB 5300.4(1B) Apr 69 (NASA)	Quality Program Provisions for Aeronautical and Space System Contractors
NHB 5300.4(1D-2) Oct 79 (NASA)	Safety, Reliability, Maintainability and Quality Provisions for the Space Shuttle Program
NHB 5300.4(2B-1) Jun 85 (NASA)	Quality Assurance Provisions for Government Agencies
NQA-2-1983 (ANSI/ASME)	Quality Assurance Program Requirements for Nuclear Power Plants (includes revision service)
NQA-2-1983 (ANSI/ASME)	Quality Assurance Requirements (includes revision service)
STP 616 (1977) (ASTM)	Quality Systems in the Nuclear Industry

Reliability

IEC 272 (1968)	Preliminary Reliability Considerations
IEC 300 (1984)	Reliability and Maintainability Management
IEC 319 (1978)	Presentation of Reliability Data on Electronic Components (or Parts)
IEC 362 (1971)	Guide for the Collection of Reliability, Availability, and Maintainability Data from Field Performance of Electronic Items
IEC 409 (1981)	Guide for the Inclusion of Reliability Clauses into Specifications for Components (or Parts) for Electronic Equipment
MIL-STD-756B Notice 1 31 Aug 82	Reliability Modeling and Prediction
MIL-STD-781C Chg Not 1 20 Mar 81	Reliability Design, Qualification and Production Acceptance Tests: Exponential Distribution
MIL-STD-785B Notice 1 3 Jul 86	Reliability Program for Systems and Equipment Development and Production
MIL-STD-790C Notice 1 2 Nov 79	Reliability Assurance Program for Electronic Parts Specifications
MIL-STD-1543A 25 Jun 82	Reliability Program Requirements for Space and Missile Systems
MIL-STD-1629A Chg Not 2 28 Nov 84	Procedure for Performing a Failure Mode, Effects, and Criticality Analysis
MIL-STD-1635 3 Feb 78	Reliability Growth Testing
MIL-STD-2068 21 Mar 77	Reliability Development Tests
MIL-STD-2101 15 Mar 78	Failure Classification for Reliability Testing
MIL-HDBK-189 13 Feb 81	Reliability Growth Management
MIL-HDBK-217D Chg Not 1 13 Jun 83	Reliability Prediction of Electronic Equipment
MIL-HDBK-251 19 Jan 78	Reliability/Design Thermal Applications
MIL-HDBK-338 15 Oct 84	Electronic Reliability Design Handbook, Vols. I and II
NHB 5300.4(1A) Apr 70 (NASA)	Reliability Program Provisions for Aeronautical and Space System Contractors
NHB 5300.4(1D-2) Oct 79 (NASA)	Safety, Reliability, Maintainability and Quality Provisions for the Space Shuttle Program

Maintainability

DOD-HDBK-472 Not 1 12 Jan 84	Maintainability Prediction
IEC 300 (1984)	Reliability and Maintainability Management
IEC 362 (1971)	Guide for the Collection of Reliability, Availability, and Maintainability Data from Field Performance of Electronic Items
IEC 706— 706-1(1982)	Guide on Maintainability of Equipment Part 1: Sections One, Two and Three. Introduction, Requirements and Maintainability Program
MIL-STD-470A 3 Jan 83	Requirements for Systems and Equipment
MIL-STD-471A Int. Not. 8 Dec 78	Maintainability Verification/Demonstration/ Evaluation
NHB 5300.4(1D-2) Oct 79(NASA)	Safety, Reliability, Maintainability and Quality Provisions for the Space Shuttle Program

Software

ANSI/IEEE 729-1983	Software Engineering Terminology, Glossary of
ANSI/IEEE 730-1984	Software Quality Assurance Plans
ANSI/IEEE 828-1983	Software Configuration Management Plans
ANSI/IEEE 829-1983	Software Test Documentation
ANSI/IEEE 830-1984	Software Requirements Specifications, Guide to
ANSI/IEEE 983-1986	Guide for Software Quality Assurance Planning
ANSI/IEEE MIL-S-52779A 1 Aug 79	Software Quality Assurance Program Requirements
AQAP-13-1981 (NATO)	Software Quality Control System Requirements
AQAP-14-1984 (NATO)	Guide for the Evaluation of a Contractor's Software Quality Control System for Compliance
DI-R-3521-1982 (DOD)	Software Quality Assurance Plan
DOD-STD-1467 (AR) (1985)	Military Standard Software Support Environment
DOD-STD-2167 (1985)	Military Standard Defense System Software Development
MIL-HDBK-334 15 Jul 82	Evaluation of a Contractor's Software Quality Assurance Program
MIL-STD-SQAM 1 Oct 1982 (DOD)	Software Quality Assessment and Measurement
Q396.1-1982 (CSA)	Software Quality Assurance Program, Part 1

Safety

MIL-STD-882B 30 Mar 84	System Safety Program Requirements
NHB-5300.4(ID-2) Oct 79 (NASA)	Safety, Reliability, Maintainability and Quality Provisions for the Space Shuttle Program

Certification Programs

ANSI Z34.1-1982	Certification Procedures, Practice for
ANSI Z34.2-1980	Self-Certification by Producer or Supplier
ISO/IEC Guide 7 (1st Edition-1982)	Requirements for Standards Suitable for Product Certification
ISO/IEC Guide 16 (1st Edition—1978)	Code of Principles on Third-Party Certification Systems and Related Standards
ISO/IEC Guide 22 (1st Edition—1982)	Information on Manufacturer's Declaration of Conformity with Standards or Other Technical Specifications
ISO/IEC Guide 23 (1st Edition—1982)	Methods of Indicating Conformity with Standards for Third-Party Certification Systems
ISO/IEC Guide 24 (1st Edition—1978)	Guidelines for the Acceptance of Testing and Inspection Agencies by Certification Bodies
ISO/IEC Guide 27 (1st Edition—1983)	Guidelines for Corrective Action to be Taken by a Certification Body in the Event of Either Misapplication of Its Mark of Conformity to a Product, or Products Which Bear the Mark of the Certification Body Being Found to Subject Persons or Property to Risk (Excludes Certificates of Conformity)
ISO/IEC Guide 28 (1st Edition—1982)	General Rules for a Model Third-Party Certification System for Products
ISO/IEC Guide 31 (1st Edition—1981)	Contents of Certificates of Reference Materials
ISO/IEC Guide 40 (1st Edition—1983)	General Requirements for the Acceptance of Certification Bodies
ISO/IEC Guide 42 (1st Edition—1984)	Guidelines for a Step-By-Step Approach to an International Certification System
ISO/IEC Guide 44 (1st Edition—1985)	General Rules for ISO or IEC International Third-Party Certification Schemes for Products

Other

ANSI Y14.5M-1982	Dimensioning and Tolerancing
DOD-STD-480A Notice 1 29 Dec 78	Configuration Control—Engineering Changes, Deviations and Waivers
DOD-STD-2101 10 May 79	Classification of Characteristics
FED-STD-209B Amendment 1 30 May 76	Clean Room and Work Station Requirements, Controlled Environment

ISO/IEC Guide 26 (1st Edition—1983)	Justification of Proposals for the Establishment of Standards
ISO/IEC Guide 37 (1st Edition—1983)	Instructions for Use of Products of Consumer Interest
MIL-H-46855B Amd. 2 5 Apr 84	Human Engineering Requirements for Equipment and Facilities
MIL-HDBK-727 5 Apr 84	Design Guidance for Producibility
MIL-STD-449A 1 May 74	Engineering Management
MIL-STD-481A 18 Oct 72	Configuration Control—Engineering Changes, Deviations and Waivers (Short Form)
MIL-STD-482A 1 Apr 74	Configuration Status Accounting Data Elements and Related Features
MIL-STD-483A 4 Jun 85	Configuration Management Practices for Systems, Equipment, Munitions, and Computer Programs
MIL-STD-680A 21 Oct 81	Contractor Standardization Program Requirements
MIL-STD-1246A 18 Aug 67	Product Cleanliness Levels and Contamination Control Program
MIL-STD-1472C Chg Not 2 10 May 84	Human Engineering Design Criteria for Military Systems, Equipment and Facilities
MIL-STD-1546 12 Feb 81	Parts, Material, and Processes Standardization Control and Management Programs for Spacecraft and Launch Vehicles

STATISTICAL TECHNIQUES AND PROCEDURES

Definitions, Symbols, Formulas

ANSI/ASQC A1-1987 (ANSI Z1.5)	Definitions, Symbols, Formulas and Tables for Control Charts
ANSI/ASQC A2-1987 (ANSI Z1.6)	Terms, Symbols and Definitions for Acceptance Sampling
ISO 3534-1977	Statistics—Vocabulary and Symbols
ISO 3534/3-1985	Statistics—Vocabulary and Symbols—3: Design of Experiments

Analysis of Data

ASTM E 29-67 (R1980)	Standard Recommended Practice for Indicating Which Places of Figures Are to be Considered Significant in Specified Limiting Values
ASTM E178-80	Dealing with Outlying Observations, Standard Practice for
ASTM E 678-84	Evaluation of Technical Data, Standard Practice for

IEC 493	Guide for the Statistical Analysis of Aging Test Data
IEC 493-1(1974)	Part 1: Methods Based on Mean Values of Normally Distributed Test Results
ISO 2602-1982	Statistical Interpretation of Test Results—Estimation of the Mean-Confidence Interval
ISO 2854-1976	Statistical Interpretation of Data—Techniques of Estimation and Tests Relating to Means and Variances
ISO 3207-1975	Statistical Interpretation of Data: Determination of a Statistical Tolerance Interval; also Addendum 1-1978
ISO 3301-1975	Statistical Interpretation of Data—Comparison of Two Means in the Case of Paired Observations
ISO 3494-1976	Statistical Interpretation of Data—Power of Tests Relating to Means and Variances
ISO Hndbk 3-1981	Statistical Methods
ISO/IEC Guide 45 (1st Edition—1985)	Guidelines for the Presentation of Test Data
STP 468/A (1969) (ASTM)	Evaluation of Technical Data, Standard Practice for Manual on Methods for Retrieving and Correlating Technical Data

Control Charts

ANSI/ASQC B-1, B-2, B-3 (1985) (ANSI Z1.1, Z1.2, Z1.3—1985)	Guide for Quality Control, Control Chart Method of Analyzing Data, and Control Chart Method of Controlling Quality during Production
STP 15 D (1976) (ASTM)	Manual on Presentation of Data and Control Chart Analysis

Acceptance Sampling

ANSI/ASQC Z1.4-1980	Sampling Procedures and Tables for Inspection by Attributes
ANSI/ASQC Z1.9-1980	Sampling Procedures and Tables for Inspection by Variables for Percent Nonconforming
IEC 410 (1973)	Sampling Plans and Procedures for Inspection by Attributes
IEC 419 (1973)	Guide for the Inclusion of Lot-By-Lot and Periodic Inspection Procedures in Specifications for Electronic Components (or Parts)
ISO 2859-1974	Sampling Procedures and Tables for Inspection by Attributes; also Addendum 1-1977, General Information on Sampling Inspection, and Guide to the Use of the ISO 2859 Tables
ISO 2859/2-1985	Sampling Procedures and Tables for Inspection by Attributes—Part 2: Sampling Plans Indexed by Limiting Quality (LQ) for Isolated Lot Inspection
ISO 3951-1981	Sampling Procedures and Charts for Inspection by Variables for Percent Defective

MIL-STD-105D Chg Not 2 20 Mar 64	Sampling Procedures and Tables for Inspection by Attributes
MIL-STD-414 Notice 1 8 May 68	Sampling Procedures and Tables for Inspection by Variables for Percent Defective
MIL-STD-690B Chg Not 2 1 Aug 74	Failure Rate Sampling Plans and Procedures
MIL-STD-1235B 1981	Continuous Sampling Procedures and Tables for Inspection by Attributes
FED-STD-358 10 Jan 1975	Sampling Procedures
MIL-HDBK-53/1A 30 Jun 65	Guide for Attribute Lot Sampling Inspection and MIL-STD-105
MIL-HDBK-106 31 Oct 58	Multi-Level Continuous Sampling Procedures and Table for Inspection by Attributes
MIL-HDBK-107	Single-Level Continuous Sampling Procedures and Table for Inspection by Attributes
MIL-HDBK-108 29 Apr 60	Sampling Procedures and Tables for Life and Reliabiilty Testing (Based on Exponential Distribution)
MIL-HDBK-109 6 May 60	Statistical Procedures for Determining Validity of Suppliers Attributes Inspection
TR-3 1961 (DOD)	Sampling Procedures and Tables for Life and Reliability Testing Based on the Weibull Distribution (Mean Life Criterion)
TR-4 1962 (DOD)	Sampling Procedures and Tables for Life and Reliability Testing Based on the Weibull Distribution (Hazard Rate Criterion)
TR-6 1963 (DOD)	Sampling Procedures and Tables for Life and Reliability Testing Based on the Weibull Distribution (Reliable Life Criterion)
TR-7 1965 (DOD)	Factors and Procedures for Applying MIL-STD-105D Sampling Plans to Life and Reliability Testing
Z90-1975 (CSA)	Introduction to Sampling Procedures for Materials and Manufactured Products

INSPECTION AND TEST METHODS

Definitions, Units of Measurement

ASTM E 548-84	Standard Practice for Preparation of Criteria for Use in the Evaluation of Testing Laboratories and Inspection Bodies
ASTM E 994-84	Laboratory Accreditation Systems, Standard Guide for
ASTM 03-511085-34 (1985)	ASTM Standards on Precision and Bias for Various Applications

ISO Hndbk 2-1982	Units of Measurement
ISO Guide 2 (4th Edition—1983)	General Terms and Their Definitions Concerning Standardization, Certification, and Testing Laboratory Accreditation
ISO/IEC Guide 30 (1st Edition—1981)	Terms and Definitions Used in Connection with Reference Materials
MIL-STD-1309C 18 Nov 83	Definitions of Terms for Test, Measurement, and Diagnostic Equipment

Inspection and Test Methods and Requirements

IEC 605 IEC 605-1 (1978) Amendment No. 1 (1982)	Part 1: Equipment Reliability Testing General Requirements
IEC 605-5(1982)	Part 5: Compliance Test Plans for Failure Rate and Mean Time between Failures, Assuming Constant Failure Rate
IEC 605-7 (1982)	Part 7: Compliance Test Plans for Failure Rate and Mean Time between Failures Assuming Constant Failure Rate
ISO 1-1975	Standard Reference Temperature for Industrial Length Measurements
ISO R286-1962	ISO System of Limits and Fits—Part 1: General, Tolerances, and Deviations
ISO R1938-1971	ISO System of Limits and Fits—Part II: Inspection of Plain Workpieces
ISO Guide 12 (1st Edition—1978)	Comparative Testing of Consumer Products
ISO/IEC Guide 36 (1st Edition—1982)	Preparation of Standards Methods of Measuring Performance (SMMP) of Consumer Goods
ISO/IEC Guide 39 (1st Edition—1983)	General Requirements for the Acceptance of Inspection Bodies
ISO/IEC Guide 43 (1st Edition—1984)	Development and Operation of Laboratory Proficiency Testing
MIL-STD-120 Chg Not 1 9 Sept 63	Gage Inspection
MIL-STD-202F Chg Not 7 28 Mar 85	Test Methods for Electronic and Electrical Component Parts
MIL-STD-252B 19 Jan 70	Classification of Visual and Mechanical Defects for Equipment, Electronic, Wired and Other Devices
MIL-STD-271E Notice 2 1 May 84	Nondestructive Testing Requirements for Metals
MIL-STD-415D Notice 1 8 Oct 71	Test Provisions for Electronic Systems and Associated Equipment, Design Criteria for
MIL-STD-810D 19 July 83	Environmental Test Methods and Engineering Guidelines

MIL-STD-1520C 27 Jun 86	Corrective Action and Disposition System for Nonconforming Material
MIL-STD-1540C 27 Jun 86	Test Requirements for Space Vehicles
MIL-STD-2165 14 Apr 85	Environmental Stress Screening Process for Electronic Equipment
MIL-STD-2165 26 Jan 85	Testability Program for Electronic Systems and Equipment
MIL-STD-45662 Chg Not 3 14 Dec 84	Calibration System Requirements
MIL-T-5422F 30 Nov 71	Testing, Environmental, Airborne Electronic and Associated Equipment
MIL-I-6870E 29 Aug 79	Inspection Program Requirements, Nondestructive Testing for Aircraft and Missile Materials and Parts
MIL-M-38793 1 May 69	Manuals, Technical, Calibration Procedures, Preparation of
MIL-I-45208A Amd 1 24 Jul 81	Inspection Systems Requirements
MIL-HDBK-204 16 Aug 62	Inspection Equipment Design
MIL-HDBK-333 10 Apr 74	Handbook for Standardization of Nondestructive Test Methods, Vols. I and II
NHB 5300.4(1C) Jul 71 (NASA)	Inspection System Provisions for Aeronautical and Space System Materials, Parts, Components and Services
STP 335 (1963) (ASTM)	Manual for Conducting an Interlaboratory Study of a Test Method
STP 540 (1973) (ASTM)	Sampling, Standards, and Homogeneity
STP 624 (1977) (ASTM)	Nondestructive Testing Standards—A Review

Evaluation of Inspection and Test Systems

ANSI/ASQC E2-1984	Guide to Inspection Planning
ISO/IEC Guide 25 (2nd Edition—1982)	General Requirements for the Technical Competence of Testing Laboratories
ISO/IEC Guide 38 (1st Edition—1983)	General Requirements for the Acceptance of Testing Laboratories
MIL-HDBK-51 3 Jan 67	Evaluation of a Contractor's Inspection System
MIL-HDBK-52A 17 Aug 84	Evaluation of a Contractor's Calibration System
MIL-STD-410D Notice 2 24 Sept 79	Nondestructive Testing Personnel Qualification and Certification (Eddy Current, Liquid Penetrant, Magnetic Particle, Radiographic and Ultrasonic)
STP 814 (1983) (ASTM)	Evaluation and Accreditation of Inspection and Test Activities

Precision and Accuracy

ASTM E 691-79	Conducting an Interlaboratory Test Program to Determine the Precision of Test Methods, Standard Practice for
ASTM D 2906 (1985)	Recommended Practice for Statements on Precision and Accuracy
ASTM E177-71 (1980)	Use of the Terms Precision and Accuracy as Applied to Measurement of a Property of a Material, Standard Recommended Practice for
ISO 5725-1981	Precision of Test Method—Determination of Repeatability and Reproducibility by Interlaboratory Tests

Copies of the above standards and specifications can be ordered by writing to the organizations indicated below:

ANSI Standards	American National Standards Institute 1430 Broadway New York, NY 10018
	American Society for Quality Control 310 Wisconsin Ave. Milwaukee, WI 53203
ASTM Publications	American Society for Testing and Materials 1916 Race Street Philadelphia, PA 19103
AQAP	North Atlantic Treaty Organization Autoroute De Zaventem 1110 NATO (Brussels), Belgium In the United States, contact: Naval Publications and Forms Center 5801 Tabor Avenue Philadelphia, PA 19120
BSI	British Standards Institution 101 Pentonville Road London N19ND, England
CSA	Canadian Standards Association 178 Rexdale Blvd. Rexdale (Toronto), Ontario Canada M9W 1R3
DOD	The Department of Defense The Pentagon Washington, DC 20301-1155
Federal Standards	General Services Administration Region 3, Federal Supply Service Special Programs Division Specifications Activity, Bldg. 197 Washington Navy Yard Annex Washington, DC 20407
IEC Publications	American National Standards Institute 1430 Broadway New York, NY 10018

ISO Publications   American National Standards Institute
                                  1430 Broadway
                                  New York, NY 10018

Military Handbooks   The Naval Publications and Forms Center
Military Specifications   5801 Tabor Avenue
Military Standards   Philadelphia, PA 19120

NASA Reliability,   Superintendent of Documents
Maintainability, and   U.S. Government Printing Office
Assurance Publications   Washington, DC 20402

APPENDIX IV
QUALITY SYSTEMS TERMINOLOGY

The following terms and definitions are given in the 1987 draft of ANSI/ASQC Standard A3, *Quality Systems Terminology*. The reader is urged to consult the full standard for valuable notes and comments associated with individual terms (available from American Society for Quality Control, 310 West Wisconsin Avenue, Milwaukee, WI 53203).

Accreditation: Certification by a duly recognized body of the facilities, capability, objectivity, competence, and integrity of an agency, service or operational group or individual to provide the specific service(s) or operation(s) needed.

Availability: The ability of an item to perform its designated function when required for use.

Certificate of compliance: A document signed by an authorized party affirming that the supplier of a product or service has met the requirements of the relevant specifications, contract, or regulation.

Certificate of conformance (Certificate of conformity): A document signed by an authorized party affirming that a product or service has met the requirements of the relevant specifications, contract, or regulation.

Certification: The procedure and action by a duly authorized body of determining, verifying, and attesting in writing to the qualifications of personnel, processes, procedures, or items in accordance with applicable requirements.

Compliance: An affirmative indication or judgment that the supplier of a product or service has met the requirements of the relevant specifications, contract, or regulation; also the state of meeting the requirements.

Conformance: An affirmative indication or judgment that a product or service has met the requirements of the relevant specifications, contract, or regulation; also the state of meeting the requirements.

Conformity: The fulfilling by an item or service of specification requirements.

Dependability: The state of being counted on or trusted.

Design review: A formal, documented, comprehensive, and systematic examination of a design to evaluate the design requirements and the capability of the design to meet these requirements and to identify problems and propose solutions.

Deviation permit: Written authorization, prior to production or provision of a service, to depart from specified requirements for a specified quantity or for a specified time.

Grade: An indicator of category or rank related to features or characteristics that cover different sets of needs for products or services intended for the same functional use.

Inspection: Activities, such as measuring, examining, testing, gaging one or more characteristics of a product or service, and comparing these with specified requirements to determine conformity.

Maintainability: Ability of an item under stated conditions of use to be retained in, or restored to, within a given period of time, a specified state in which it can perform its required functions when maintenance is performed under stated conditions and while using prescribed procedures and resources.

Process quality audit: An analysis of elements of a process and appraisal of completeness, correctness of conditions, and probable effectiveness.

Product liability or Service liability: A generic term used to describe the onus on a producer or others to make restitution for loss related to personal injury, property damage, or other harm caused by a product or service.

Product quality audit: A quantitative assessment of conformance to required product characteristics.

Quality: The totality of features and characteristics of a product or service that bear on its ability to satisfy stated or implied needs.

Quality, Relative: Degree of excellence of a product or service.

Quality assurance: All those planned or systematic actions necessary to provide adequate confidence that a product or service will satisfy given requirements for quality.

Quality audit: A systematic and independent examination and evaluation to determine whether quality activities and results comply with planned arrangements and whether these arrangements are implemented effectively and are suitable to achieve objectives.

Quality control: The operational techniques and the activities used to fulfill requirements of quality.

Quality engineering: That branch of engineering which deals with the principles and practice of product and service quality assurance and control.

Quality loop/Quality spiral: Conceptual model of interacting activities that influence the quality of a product or service in the various stages ranging from the identification of needs to the assessment of whether these needs have been satisfied.

Quality management: That aspect of the overall management function that determines and implements the quality policy.

Quality measure: A quantitative measure of the features and characteristics of a product or service.

Quality plan: A document setting out the specific quality practices, resources, and activities relevant to a particular product, process, service, contract, or project.

Quality policy: The overall intentions and direction of an organization as regards quality as formally expressed by top management.

Quality surveillance: The continuing monitoring and verification of the status of procedures, methods, conditions, products, processes, and services, and analysis of records in relation to stated references to ensure that requirements for quality are being met.

Quality system: The organizational structure, responsibilities, procedures, processes, and resources for implementing quality management.

Quality system audit (Quality plan audit):   A documented activity performed to verify, by examination and evaluation of objective evidence, that applicable elements of the quality system are suitable and have been developed, documented, and effectively implemented in accordance with specified requirements.

Quality system review: A formal evaluation by management of the status and adequacy of the quality system in relation to quality policy and/or new objectives resulting from changing circumstances.

Reliability: The ability of an item to perform a required function under stated conditions.

Reliability, Numerical: The probability that an item will perform a required function under stated conditions for a stated period of time.

Reliability engineering: That engineering function dealing with the principles and practices related to the design, specification, assessment, and achievement of product or system reliability requirements and involving aspects of prediction, evaluation, production, and demonstration.

Specification: The document that prescribes the requirements with which the product or service has to conform.

Statistical process control: The application of statistical techniques to the control of processes.

Statistical quality control: The application of statistical techniques to the control quality.

Testing: A means of determining the capability of an item to meet specified requirements by subjecting the item to a set of physical, chemical, environmental, or operating actions and conditions.

Traceability: The ability to trace the history, application, or location of an item or activity and like items or activities by means of recorded identification.

Verification: The act of reviewing, inspecting, testing, checking, auditing, or otherwise establishing and documenting whether items, processes, services, or documents conform to specified requirements.

Waiver: Written authorization to use or release a quantity of material, components, or stores already manufactured but not conforming to the specified requirements.

NAME INDEX

See also Glossary of Symbols, Appendix I; Subject Index

Abbe, R. C., **18.**70
Abbott, R. A., **15.**44
Abernethy, R. B., **18.**115
Aboud, G. M., **6.**46
Abou-Zeid, M. F., **32.**11
Ackoff, R. L., **22.**68
Adamek, K. C., **4.**29
Addelman, S., **26.**42, **26.**44
Agnew, P. G., **6.**14, **22.**68
Aiba, K., **35F.**29
Ainsworth, L., **18.**97
Akao, Y., **10.**42, **13.**13, **35F.**23, **35F.**25
Alaimo, A. P., **18.**38
Alberts, D. S., **14.**24
Allen, P. E., **18.**39
Altenkirch, F., **35D.**7, **35D.**8
Amrine, H., **20.**3
Amsden, D. M., **16.**23, **16.**26
Amsden, R. T., **16.**23, **16.**26
Amster, S. J., **29.**18
Andersen, L. E., **28.**8
Anderson, D., **22.**55
Anderson, D. A., **26.**44
Anderson, R. D., **14.**18
Anderson, R. T., **27.**31
Andreasen, A. R., **20.**15, **20.**16
Antle, C. E., **23.**49
Archibald, R. D., **27.**9
Argyris, C., **22.**68
Armstrong, G. R., **16.**16
Arnitz, W. E., **13.**38
Artamonov, V. P., **35H.**11
Artes, A. E., **35H.**13
Artinian, H. L., **10.**43, **21.**20
Asano, C., **27.**27
Asby, C. C., **17.**31
Assad, A. A., **23.**94
Atanasov, A., **35H.**13
Atkinson, A. C., **28.**8
Aubrey, C. A., **4.**29, **33.**64, **33.**69
Azgaldov, G. G., **35H.**4

Babcombe, P., **18.**116
Bader, M. E., **18.**38

Bailey, E., **3.**17
Bailey, R. A., **13.**34
Bain, L. S., **23.**49
Bainbridge, T. R., **26.**67, **28.**16
Bajaria, H. J., **13.**74
Baker, E. M., **10.**1, **10.**19, **10.**36, **10.**43, **18.**81, **21.**22
Balaban, H. S., **19.**18
Ball, L. W., **31.**1*n.*, **31.**11
Ball, L. X., **27.**15
Ballou, D. P., **18.**9
Barasia, R. K., **3.**21, **3.**26
Barbeson, R. A., **26.**77
Barker, K. N., **33.**59
Barnes, A. J., **19.**12
Barnett, E. H., **26.**1
Barr, D. R., **23.**79
Barra, R., **10.**46, **10.**47
Barry, E. N., **18.**110
Bases, A. L., **34.**22
Batt, W. L., Jr., **10.**13, **10.**21
Beaton, G. N., **13.**22
Beattie, D. W., **25.**39
Beeck, W. O., **13.**64
Beer, M., **10.**38
Beizer, B., **14.**24
Belbin, R. M., **13.**3
Bell, L. F., **6.**46, **16.**45
Belt, P. B., **24.**18
Bemesderfer, J. L., **6.**18, **16.**32, **16.**37, **16.**38
Bender, A., **13.**59
Bennett, C. A., **23.**118, **28.**23
Berger, R., **27.**24
Berger, R. L., **13.**31
Berger, R. W., xiii
Bergstrom, S., **22.**48
Berke, H. L., **13.**70
Berman, D. L., **10.**7, **10.**18
Berman, H. S., **9.**29, **15.**33, **15.**34
Bernstein, A., **27.**37
Berry, C. C., **33.**62
Best, A., **20.**15, **20.**16, **34.**11
Besterfield, D. H., **27.**24
Betker, H. A., **22.**37, **22.**39

1

Bhote, K. R., **6.**24
Bicking, C. A., **24.**1*n.*, **25.**89, **26.**5, **28.**1*n.*, **28.**18, **28.**38
Bingham, J. E., **27.**9
Bingham, R. S., **23.**55, **26.**77, **27.**1*n.*, **28.**1, **28.**7, **28.**8, **28.**10, **28.**21, **28.**26, **28.**31, **28.**36, **28.**38, **33.**1*n.*
Binstock, S. L., **11.**31
Bizarro, L. A., **27.**13, **27.**14
Bjorklund, O., **3.**30
Black, J. T., **32.**28
Blackburn, K., **8.**24, **9.**21
Blake, G. B., **8.**16
Blanchard, B. S., **13.**46, **13.**47
Bland, R. P., **25.**90
Blaufuss, J., **18.**58
Bluestone, I., **10.**13, **10.**19, **10.**21, **10.**39
Blum, J. E., **27.**1*n.*
Blumenthal, I. R., **17.**17
Blumenthal, M., **32.**19
Boardman, T. J., **27.**26
Bobis, A. H., **28.**8
Bodis, M., **15.**15
Bolcar, J. A., **24.**15
Bollenbacher, R. L., xiii
Bollinger, J. G., **28.**61
Bond, T. P., **18.**116
Borwick, R., xiii
Bos, H. C., **35B.**4
Boudreault, A., **15.**30
Bowers, V. L., **15.**45
Bowker, A. H., **24.**28, **25.**6
Bowman, K. O., **26.**76
Box, G. E. P., **11.**26, **26.**13, **26.**29, **26.**31, **26.**32, **26.**44, **26.**47, **26.**53, **26.**54, **26.**58, **26.**65, **26.**76, **28.**31–**28.**35, **29.**13
Brach, J. P., **13.**31
Brainard, E. H., **6.**51, **15.**16
Brandt, D. A., **18.**55
Breipohl, A. M., **25.**90
Bretherton, M. H., **23.**30
Brethower, D. M., **10.**23
Brokke, H. M., xiii
Bronson, C. S., **3.**9
Brook, C., **3.**21
Brown, A. W., **7.**31
Brown, F. X., **4.**11, **4.**29
Brown, N. R., **24.**33
Brown, R. H., **28.**10
Bruce-Briggs, B., **10.**14
Bruewer, H. F., **15.**28
Brunetti, W., **6.**51, **8.**16, **8.**23
Brush, G. G., **29.**18
Bryan, J. G., **24.**3
Bryan, N. S., **3.**26
Buchholz, R. A., **15.**44
Buckrop, R. L., **18.**71
Bullock, R. J., **10.**35
Burck, C. G., **10.**13

Burgess, J. A., **13.**11, **15.**27, **17.**17, **18.**116
Burington, R. S., **25.**99
Burke, W. W., **10.**8
Burman, J. P., **25.**43, **28.**8, **28.**35
Burr, J. T., **9.**11
Burrell, C. W., **33.**49
Burtenshaw, O. L., **28.**58
Burton, C., **10.**22
Butler, H. E., **16.**23, **16.**26
Buzzell, R. D., **3.**18
Byrne, D. M., **16.**31

Cahill, H. E., **13.**31
Caine, R., **27.**36
Calder, A. B., **28.**20
Calder, B. J., **12.**15
Calvin, T. W., **25.**89
Calvo, A. B., **3.**21
Cameron, J. M., **25.**23
Cameron, R. D., **9.**22, **9.**28
Canut, L. S., **20.**34
Caplan, F., **4.**21, **4.**29, **6.**3, **15.**42, **16.**40
Carlisle, R., **17.**31
Carlson, H. C., **10.**43
Carpenter, B. H., **16.**12, **28.**5
Carr, J. M., **26.**78
Carruba, E. R., **11.**26
Carter, B., **32.**18
Carter, C. L., **18.**107
Carter, C. W., **24.**4
Carter, G. M., **18.**107
Cary, T., **14.**24
Case, K., **25.**90
Case, K. E., **24.**31
Casey, M., **19.**3
Castagna, E., **17.**26
Caswell, A. R., **16.**57
Catlin, J. C., Sr., **3.**22
Cave, R., **35C.**2
Chaisson, D. A., **28.**7
Chaney, F. B., **10.**30, **18.**85, **18.**87–**18.**88
Chapman, M. K., **35F.**8, **35F.**29
Charbonneau, H., **11.**25
Charnoff, G., **9.**7
Chebookjian, S. L., **18.**54
Cherkasky, S. M., **20.**34
Cherry, D. H., **13.**73
Chew, V., **26.**78
Chin, W. K., **25.**90
Choksi, S., **23.**59
Christensen, K. L., **15.**33
Churchill, A. V., **18.**94
Clarke, P. C., **16.**16
Clatworthy, W. H., **26.**78
Cleland, D. I., **7.**23
Clements, J., **27.**5
Clements, J. A., **8.**17
Clodfelter, S., **18.**109
Coch, L., **22.**68

Cochran, W. G., **25**.89, **26**.21, **26**.60, **26**.65, **26**.76
Cohen, A., **23**.118
Cohen, M. R., **33**.59, **33**.63
Cohen-Rosenthal, E., **10**.22
Cole, R. E., **10**.4, **10**.7–**10**.12, **10**.15, **35F**.7
Coleman, L. R., **18**.98
Colter, M., **14**.12
Compa, L., **10**.22
Conley, D., **33**.71
Connellan, T. K., **10**.23, **10**.27, **10**.30, **10**.32, **10**.36, **10**.45
Connor, W. S., **26**.69
Constable, G. K., **11**.34
Cook, H. M., **18**.1*n*.
Cook, N., **28**.19, **32**.19
Coon, H. J., **25**.87
Coonley, H., **6**.14, **22**.68
Coop, P. G., **11**.19
Cooper, B. E., **26**.78
Cooper, J., **15**.20
Cooper, J. E., **18**.116
Corbi, J. C., **24**.18
Cormier, D., **23**.88
Cornell, J. A., **26**.69, **28**.7
Corner, P., **35E**.4
Cornish, J. W., **7**.24
Cornwall, L. P., **33**.9
Cound, D. M., **6**.3
Cowden, D. J., **25**.4
Cox, D. R., **26**.53, **26**.77
Cox, G., M., **26**.60, **26**.76
Craig, J. A., **25**.90
Crain, W. M., **34**.18
Crosby, P. B., **11**.26, **30**.36
Crosier, R. B., **26**.69
Crow, E. L., **18**.63
Cutrona, M., xiii
Czaja, S. J., **18**.117

Daeves, K. H., **28**.56
Dahl, O. J., **14**.15
Dalal, S. R., **23**.94
Dale, B. G., **4**.12
Dandekar, A. V., **35B**.19
Daniel, C., **26**.78
Daniel, C., **11**.26, **23**.100, **23**.106, **23**.107, **26**.29, **26**.42, **26**.51
Daniels, A. C., **10**.36
Darby, G. R., **18**.58
Das, S., **20**.13
Davids, R. C., **13**.31
Davidson, D., **18**.54
Davidson, W. H., **10**.43
Davies, G. W. P., **27**.9
Davies, O. L., **26**.54, **26**.65, **26**.76, **28**.18, **28**.23
Davis, L. E., **10**.13, **10**.17, **10**.40, **10**.41
Davis, N. M., **33**.59, **33**.63

Davis, S., xiii
Deane, D., **27**.26
DeBaun, R. M., **28**.30
Debout, E., **35A**.4
DeBusk, R. E., **26**.78
Dedhia, N. S., **17**.26
De Marco, T., **14**.10, **14**.11
Deming, W. E., xiii, **8**.21, **8**.24, **10**.7, **10**.9, **10**.15, **10**.19, **10**.25, **10**.27, **10**.29, **10**.34, **10**.36, **10**.42, **10**.52, **33**.29, **35F**.2
Denissoff, B. A., **17**.31
Denker, S. P., **18**.82
Derbisher, A., **8**.19
De Simone, D. V., **18**.58
DesPlas, E. P., **29**.18
Diamond, W., **26**.42, **26**.44
Dice, C. M., **21**.16
Dickson, W. J., **10**.4
Dielman, T. E., **23**.107
Diggs, E. J., **9**.29
Diggs, J., **15**.9
Dijsktra, E. W., **14**.24
Dikov, D., **35H**.13
Dimmit, D. M., **33**.63
Dinklenburg, A., **27**.37
Dixon, W. J., **23**.17, **23**.19, **23**.48, **23**.64, **23**.95, **26**.74
Dmytrow, E. D., **21**.12, **21**.21, **22**.27, **33**.20
Dobbins, R. K., **9**.17, **15**.41, **20**.22
Dodds, L. B., **18**.38
Dodge, H. F., **18**.117, **23**.59, **25**.12, **25**.28, **25**.37, **28**.21
Donnell, J. D., **19**.12
Donnelly, J. F., **10**.7
Donovan, T. A., **25**.89
Doom, I. F., **3**.30
Doran, P. K., **22**.12
Doty, A. L., **15**.26
Douglas, R. D., **22**.7
Downer, W. C., **16**.40
Draper, N. R., **23**.9, **23**.100, **23**.107, **23**.108, **23**.111, **23**.117, **26**.31, **26**.42, **26**.51, **26**.53, **28**.30, **28**.36
Dray, J., **32**.19
Drew, H. E., **35E**.4
Drury, C. G., **18**.117
Duane, J. T., **13**.40, **20**.34
Dubey, S. D., **23**.64
DuBuisson, J. C., **3**.31
Duckworth, W. E., **26**.42
Dudewicz, E. J., **23**.1, **23**.9, **23**.17, **23**.32, **23**.33, **23**.35, **23**.44, **23**.63, **23**.64, **23**.94, **23**.100, **23**.107, **23**.108, **23**.118
Dugan, A., **27**.26
Duhan, S., **3**.22
Dumoulin, C. L, **23**.19
Duncan, A. J., **11**.26, **23**.28, **23**.46, **23**.64, **23**.78, **24**.11, **25**.1*n.*, **25**.23, **25**.87, **26**.76

Duncan, D. B., **26**.21, **26**.58
Dunn, D. S., **28**.58
Dunn, R., **33**.72
Dunnett, C. W., **26**.79
Dushman, Allan, **3**.30
Dussault, H. B., **13**.75
Duvier, H., III, **18**.120

Eagle, A. R., **18**.117, **28**.19
Ebenfelt, H., **3**.21
Eckel, F. M., **33**.63
Edinburgh, B., xii
Edinburgh, O., xii
Egermayer, F., **35H**.1, **35H**.9
Ehrenfeld, S., **26**.70
Eisenhart, C., **18**.117
Ekings, J. D., xiii, **13**.39, **30**.1, **30**.23, **30**.24, **30**.44
Ekvall, D. N., xiii, **16**.1n.
Elder, R. S., **18**.69, **28**.10
Eldridge, L. A., **33**.64, **33**.69
El Gabry, A. A., **18**.39
Elliott, A. C., **27**.38
Ellsworth, L. W., **33**.49
Elving, P. J., **28**.10
Emery, E. M., **28**.15
Emmons, S. L., **17**.31
Emphrain, M., **13**.20
Endres, A. C., xiii
Endres, D. A., **19**.15
Enell, J. W., xiii, **25**.17, **33**.1
Ephlin, D. F., **10**.22
Eppen, G. D., **18**.9
Epstein, B., **23**.49
Epstein, E. **10**.15
Erhardt, C. C., **13**.75
Eustis, G. E., **3**.30
Evans, D. H., **13**.59
Evans, R. A., xii, **23**.90
Ewan, W. D., **24**.27, **24**.28
Ezer, S., **18**.117

Fabrycky, W. J., **13**.46, **13**.47
Fagan, M. E., **18**.117
Fairbank, J. A., **10**.29
Farkas, A., **35H**.14
Farris, Paul W., **19**.3
Farrow, J. H., **9**.4
Fayol, H., **35C**.3
Federer, W. T., **26**.44
Feigenbaum, A. V., **11**.25, **16**.35, **30**.11
Feilden, G. B. R., **35E**.5
Fend, W. C., **33**.71
Fennell, T. L., **13**.31
Ferris, C. D., **28**.61
Fiedler, R. M., **20**.3
Fischer, W. R., **13**.62
Fisher, B. A., **10**.45
Fisher, J. R., **17**.17

Fisher, R. A., xii, **23**.119, **24**.5, **26**.63
Fitzgibbons, R. G., **15**.1n.
Fitzsimmons, A., **14**.15
Flavell, N. L., **16**.56
Fletcher, O. L., **32**.16
Flynn, M. F., **24**.15
Fody, T. J., **3**.24
Follett, M. P., **6**.15
Follett, R., xiii
Ford, R. N., **33**.38
Fortuin, G. J., **18**.56
Fortune, P., **14**.1
Francis, I., **27**.25
Frank, N. C., **13**.36, **13**.59
Franklin, N. L., **23**.118, **28**.23
Frankovich, J., **8**.17
Fraser, R. A., **31**.23
Frawley, W. H., **23**.55
Frederiksen, L. W., **10**.36
French, J. R. P., Jr., **22**.68
Freund, J. E., **11**.26
Freund, R. A., xiii, **9**.17, **17**.31, **25**.61
Freund, W. C., **10**.15
Fry, R. E., **10**.59
Fuhr, H., **35D**.6
Fujikoshi, Y., **23**.43, **23**.100
Fukuda, R., **10**.47, **16**.9, **17**.9
Funke, D. J., **18**.97
Furukawa, O., **32**.3
Fuss, N. H., Jr., **19**.5

Gager, R., **13**.62
Gallagher, B. M., **3**.26
Gannon, J. D., **14**.24
Gansler, J. S., **3**.26
Gantt, J. S., **18**.65
Ganushkin, V. V., **35H**.9
Garfinkel, D., **18**.109
Garrick, B. J., **13**.42
Garvin, D. A., **35G**.5
Gaylor, D. W., **28**.16
Gebhardt, C., **18**.80
Gebhardt, J. E., **33**.72
Geidel, H., **18**.54
Gellagher, B. M., **27**.15
George, W. W., **6**.22
Gestwicki, C., **10**.55
Giannini, A. P., **31**.2
Gibbons, J. D., **16**.33, **23**.64, **23**.65, **23**.72, **23**.91
Gibson, J. D., **18**.117
Gibson, T. C., **8**.7
Gilbert, R. A., **13**.34
Gilbert, T. F., **10**.56
Gillispie, C. C., **35C**.2
Gilman, J. R., **18**.94
Gilmore, H. L., **4**.17
Gioele, J. L., **28**.8, **28**.31
Gittler, H., **18**.107

Glasser, G. H., **21**.22
Glaushenner, A., **27**.6
Gleason, D., **3**.30
Glichev, A. V., **8**.19, **35H**.4, **35H**.7, **35H**.8, **35H**.11
Goble, J., **12**.20
Godfrey, A. B., **29**.1, **29**.13
Gogue, J., **35C**.1
Goksel, A. K., **29**.8
Goldbeck, J. M., **18**.108
Golden, B. L., **23**.94
Golden, K. A., **10**.13
Goldhar, J. D., **16**.57
Goldsmith, C. H., **28**.16
Goldstein, R., **9**.11
Goode, H. P., **25**.6, **25**.68
Goodman, A. L., **28**.61
Goodman, J., **20**.19
Gopal, K., **11**.37
Gordon, J. J., **9**.24
Goree, P. F., **6**.29, **13**.75
Gorman, J. W., **26**.68, **26**.69
Govindarajulu, Z., **23**.80
Graf, K., **35D**.8
Grant, E. L., **11**.25, **23**.61, **24**.9, **24**.23, **24**.32, **25**.58
Gray, H. L., **23**.49, **27**.38
Gray, I., **34**.21
Greb, D. J., **18**.68
Green, C. P., Jr., **32**.18
Greenridge, R. M. C., **22**.32
Gregory, G., **25**.68
Grieco, M. J., **16**.58, **29**.13
Griffin, R. J., **18**.59
Grimlin, D. R., **25**.90
Grimm, A. F., **4**.15
Grinath, A. C., **14**.20
Grogan, J. C., **13**.75
Groocock, J. M., **2**.4, **2**.13, **4**.26, **35A**.4
Groover, M. P., **32**.30
Gross, I., **3**.12, **12**.19
Grubbs, F. E., **23**.119, **24**.32, **25**.87, **28**.19
Grubman, S., **25**.78
Gruska, G. F., **18**.67–**18**.68, **23**.119
Gryna, D., xiii
Gryna, D. S., xiii
Gryna, F. M., **3**.23, **4**.1, **4**.8, **4**.26, **4**.28, **9**.1, **10**.10, **10**.15, **10**.27, **10**.39, **10**.46, **11**.1, **12**.1, **12**.13, **12**.20, **13**.1, **13**.3, **13**.22, **13**.23, **15**.1, **16**.1, **17**.1, **18**.17, **19**.1, **19**.11, **20**.1, **20**.11, **20**.31, **21**.1, **22**.1, **23**.1, **23**.62, **24**.1, **24**.8, **29**.18
Guest, R. H., **10**.13, **18**.76
Guith, T. A., **17**.2
Gulliver, F. R., **6**.28
Gunn, T. G., **16**.56
Gunter, B., **18**.118
Gushue, J. M., **28**.4
Gust, L. J., **13**.70, **22**.40, **22**.50

Gutman, N., **31**.12
Gutt, J. D., **23**.119
Gwiazdecki, M., **35H**.11
Gyllenhammar, P. G., **10**.39

Hackman, J. R., **10**.37, **10**.39, **10**.40
Hadley, G., **23**.26
Hagan, J. T., **4**.12, **6**.3, **33**.22
Hahn, G. J., xiii, **23**.38, **23**.44, **23**.50, **23**.51, **23**.55
Hains, R. W., **18**.56, **28**.58
Hald, A., **25**.101
Hale, M., **27**.24
Haley, R. I., **19**.8
Hall, F. M., **20**.13
Halpin, J. F., **22**.22
Halstead, M. H., **14**.15
Hamaker, H. C., **25**.101
Hamilton, A. B., **13**.20
Hammel, L., **13**.6
Hammer, W., **13**.51
Hampton, D. R., **28**.23
Hanlon, M. D., **10**.22
Harrington, E. C., Jr., **28**.6
Harrington, H. A., xii
Harrington, H. J., **4**.26, **4**.29, **16**.40, **16**.44
Harrington, J., **16**.53
Harris, D. H., **18**.85, **18**.87–**18**.88
Harrison, H. L., **28**.61
Harter, H. L., **23**.56, **23**.64
Hartman, B., **22**.23
Hartz, O., **6**.51
Hauck, W. C., **10**.35
Hay, W. A., **26**.78
Hayakawa, T., **23**.43, **23**.100
Hayes, G. E., **9**.6, **11**.25, **15**.20, **31**.3
Hayre, L. S., **26**.70
Hayter, W. T., **28**.57
Healy, J., **29**.15
Heaney, D. F., **3**.18, **13**.16, **16**.9
Heap, H. F., **2**.11, **3**.25, **20**.10, **21**.21
Heckel, J., **15**.3
Hedayat, A., **26**.44
Heinrich, G. F., **24**.32
Heldt, J. J., **11**.25, **11**.34
Hellend, K. L., **13**.76
Heller, W. M., **33**.59
Helm, E., **18**.53
Henderson, J. T., **3**.30
Hendry, A., **20**.13
Henke, J.A., **33**.64
Henning, H. J., **35D**.8
Hermann, J. A., **10**.43
Herrold, G. R., **13**.38
Herzberg, A. M., **26**.77
Herzberg, F., **10**.4, **10**.8
Heskett, J. L., **6**.29
Heslop, S., **6**.27
Hewitt, C. M., **19**.12

Hext, G. R., 26.81
Hicks, C. R., 26.18, 26.65, 28.30
Higgins, B. K., 21.16
Higgins, J., 28.20
Hill, H. M., 6.21, 11.7, 28.10
Hill, J. S., 13.76
Hill, P. A., 33.63
Hill, T. D., 30.23
Hill, W. J., 26.47
Hillier, F. S., 25.7
Himsworth, F. R., 26.81
Hinchen, J. D., 28.1n., 28.29, 28.30
Hines, J. E., 17.31
Hinman, J. E., 26.68, 26.69
Hirschfield, F., 20.23
Hoadley, B., 25.90
Hoare, C. A. R., 14.24
Hocking, R. R., 23.117
Hodge, J. H., 15.43
Hoel, D. G., 26.76
Hoerl, A. E., 23.8, 28.35
Hoffman, J. G., 35D.3
Hogben, D., 27.26
Hollander, M., 26.71
Holm, R. A., 22.4
Holmes, H., 18.28
Holmes, R. K., 13.59, 16.58
Holmes, W. A., 13.75
Holt, J., 6.41
Hong, S., 20.13
Hooper, J. H., 29.18
Hopkins, D. S., 3.17
Hoppmann, W. H., 11.33
Horn, R. L., 20.13
Hotzelberger, A. J., 30.1n.
Howard, H. P., 13.6
Howard, R., 10.17
Howell, V. W., 17.7
Hoylman, F. M., 10.7, 10.19
Hromi, J. D., 11.20
Hsi, B. P., 28.20
Hsiang, T. C., 9.24
Huang, J. C., 14.16
Hughes, G. D., 19.8
Hulley, O. S., 20.34
Humble, J., 8.23
Hunter, J. S., 11.27, 18.76, 24.32, 26.1,
    26.13, 26.29, 26.32, 26.44, 26.58,
    26.63, 26.76, 28.35, 29.13
Hunter, W. G., 16.21, 26.1, 26.13, 26.44, 26.47,
    26.53, 26.58, 26.76, 26.77, 28.8, 29.13
Hurst, E. G., Jr., 18.9
Huse, E. F., 10.38
Hüttenrauch, R., 35D.6
Hutter, R. G., 18.112
Hwang, F. K., 26.70
Hyer, C. W., 18.69

Iman, R. L., 23.120

Immerwahr, J., 10.17, 10.18, 10.21
Ingle, N., 10.15
Ingle, S., 10.15, 10.46, 10.47
Ingle, S. R., 32.12
Ingram, G. E., 6.29, 13.70, 22.33
Ireson, W. G., 23.91
Ishihara, Z., 27.36
Ishikawa, K., 8.21, 8.23, 9.5, 9.28, 10.11,
    10.23, 10.26, 10.42, 10.46, 10.47, 11.6,
    11.19, 35F.2, 35F.7–35F.9, 35F.19,
    35F.21, 35F.26
Ishiwara, K., 35F.29
Ishiyama, T., 16.44
Ishizu, S., 32.3
Ishizuka, N., 35F.25
Isley, C. W., 34.22
Itoh, S., 35F.17
Itoh, W., 15.6, 15.19
Iwasaki, I., 29.18

Jackson, J. A., 28.30
Jacobs, R. M., 13.8, 20.32, 20.34
Jaehm, A. H., 18.118
Jaehn, A. H., 28.10
Jayachandran, T., 13.40, 20.34
Jefferson, G. R., 13.62, 13.76
Jelinek, M., 16.57
Jenkins, G. M., 28.31–28.35
Jenkins, L. C., 13.31
Jensen, D. R., 23.100
John, P. W. M., 26.42
Johnson, D. A., 20.24
Johnson, L. I., 25.23
Johnson, M., 4.22
Johnson, N. L., 11.26, 23.30, 23.64, 23.97,
    24.28, 28.62
Johnson, R., 15.43
Johnson, S. L., 18.97
Joshi, A., 18.118
Jude, A., 28.56
Juran, J. M., 1.1, 2.1, 2.6, 3.1, 3.4–3.6,
    3.16, 4.22, 4.26, 5.1, 6.1, 6.3, 6.23,
    6.36, 7.1, 7.9, 8.1, 8.2, 9.1, 9.21, 10.7,
    10.9, 10.10, 10.14, 10.17, 10.19, 10.23,
    10.25–10.28, 10.36, 10.39, 10.42, 10.45,
    10.48, 10.49, 11.1, 11.25, 11.26, 11.33,
    12.1, 13.3, 13.23, 15.1, 15.2, 16.1,
    16.23, 17.1, 17.17, 17.34, 17.36, 17.49,
    17.84, 17.85, 17.93–17.95, 18.1, 18.9,
    19.1, 19.4, 20.1, 20.11, 22.26, 22.45,
    23.62, 24.5, 24.8, 29.18, 30.4, 31.3,
    34.1, 34.3, 34.9, 34.14, 34.16, 34.18,
    35A.1, 35B.26, 35F.6–35F.9, 35G.1,
    35G.5
Juran, S., xiii

Kackar, R. R, 16.58
Kacker, R. N., 29.11, 29.13, 29.19
Kale, B. K., 23.52

Kamizawa, N., **35F**.25
Kane, E. J., **10**.43
Kane, R. W., **4**.11, **4**.29, **9**.5
Kane, V. E., **16**.20
Kaneko, H., **16**.57
Kano, N., **6**.29, **13**.70, **22**.33, **35G**.7
Kanter, R. M., **10**.18, **10**.43, **22**.68
Kapur, K. C., **13**.21, **31**.11
Karabatsos, N., **6**.27, **18**.28, **18**.109
Karasek, F. W., **18**.69
Karian, Z. A., **23**.9, **23**.33, **23**.100, **23**.108, **23**.118
Karmarkar, U. S., **20**.14
Kartha, C. P., **16**.21
Kase, S., **18**.54
Kassarda, J. B., **17**.18
Kast, F. E., **10**.23
Kastenbaum, M. A., **26**.76
Kaufman, J. J., **31**.20
Kaufman, R. J., **3**.25, **3**.30
Kay, T. G., **18**.110
Keane, J., xiii, **27**.5
Kearney, F. J., **16**.5
Keats, J. B., **25**.90
Kececioglu, D., **23**.88
Kegarise, R. J., **3**.31, **15**.5, **15**.36
Kegg, R. L., **16**.53
Keller, T. A., **18**.118
Ken, J., **18**.82
Kennard, R. W., **23**.8, **28**.35
Kenyon, R. L., **27**.37
Kepner, C. H., **22**.71
Kerwin, R. E., **29**.1
Keryner, H., **27**.9
Ketchum, L. D., **10**.39
Keuls, M., **26**.58
Khojecki, H., **35H**.11
Khwialkowski, H., **35H**.14
Kiang, T. D., **3**.26
Kilduff, F. B., **32**.30
Kimble, R. G., **13**.46
Kimbrough, W. W., **33**.59
King, J. R., **20**.27, **23**.36
Kinnucan, P., **16**.58
Kinsburg, B. J., **23**.59
Kirkpatrick, R. L., **23**.120
Kirwan, M. S., **18**.28
Kitrell, J. R., **26**.79
Klein, N. A., **28**.58
Klompmaker, J. E., **19**.8
Knoblock, W. H., **3**.26
Knuth, D. E., **14**.15
Kobayashi, M. K., **10**.8
Koch, R. A., **19**.19
Koehler, T. L., **26**.1
Kofoed, C. A., **6**.3
Kogure, M., **10**.23, **10**.42, **13**.13, **32**.3, **35F**.23
Kohoutek, H. J., **6**.25

Kolacek, O. G., **4**.18, **6**.3
Kolb, J., **34**.14, **34**.21
Kolinka, E., **17**.26
Kolthoff, I. M., **28**.10
Kondo, Y., **10**.8, **10**.11, **10**.26, **10**.27, **10**.29, **10**.43, **35F**.1, **35F**.2, **35F**.5, **35F**.7, **35F**.11, **35F**.14, **35F**.17
Konz, S., **18**.84
Korslin, A., **28**.59
Korte, L., **23**.87
Kotter, J. P., **10**.43, **22**.68
Kotz, S., **23**.30
Kraljic, P., **15**.4
Kramer, A., **18**.56
Kramer, C. Y., **23**.100
Kramlinger, T., **10**.33
Krautkramer, J. H., **28**.49
Krishnamoorthi, K. S., **4**.16, **24**.12
Krouse, J., **16**.58
Kruger, M. K., **23**.59
Krutchoff, R. G., **25**.90
Ku, H. H., **26**.71
Kukla, R., **12**.15
Kukunaris, **24**.3
Kume, H., **4**.21, **4**.22, **11**.36, **16**.36, **35F**.7
Kurtz, T. E., **26**.14
Kusaba, I., **10**.47
Kusch, J., **18**.119

LaForge, R. L., **11**.34, **15**.33
Lamberson, L. R., **13**.21, **31**.11
LaMotte, L. R., **23**.117
Lampe, D., **27**.37
Land, W. E., **11**.34
Lange, H. N., **6**.27
Langenborg, N. O., **18**.51
Langevin, R., **27**.36
Lantos, R. L., **33**.63
LaSala, K. P., **20**.6, **20**.7
Lashof, T. W., **28**.37
Laskin, R., **3**.26
Latham, G. P., **10**.36
Latiolais, C. J., **33**.62
Latzko, W. J., **21**.12, **33**.65, **33**.67
Lawler, E. E., **10**.13, **10**.15, **10**.23, **10**.35
Lawless, J. F., **29**.19
Lawlor, A. J., **13**.10
Lawrence, P. R., **22**.68
Lawson, G. W., **13**.43
Lawton, W. H., **28**.11
Leaman, D. C., **11**.28, **11**.34
Leavenworth, R. S., **11**.25, **23**.61, **24**.9, **24**.23, **24**.32, **25**.58
LeBarre, K. C., **15**.45
Leder, W. B., **28**.30
Leek, J. W., **10**.52, **10**.54, **18**.50
Lele, M., **20**.14
Lenter, M. M., **26**.80
Lentze, H., **35D**.3

Lentzen, D. E., **28**.10
Lenz, H. J., **23**.26, **23**.60
Leonard, **21**.19
Leonard, J. F., xiii
Leone, F. C., **11**.26, **23**.64, **23**.97, **24**.28, **28**.62
Leslie, R. N., **23**.120
Levenson, N. G., **27**.33
Levinson, M., **35G**.6
Levitt, T., **3**.6, **20**.35
Levy, G. C., **23**.19
Lewis, T., **23**.49
Lewis, W. H., **6**.3
Lieberman, G. J., **23**.28, **24**.28, **25**.101
Lilie, H., **35H**.9, **35H**.11
Linczenyi, A., **35H**.2
Lindbergh, C. A., **3**.6
Ling, R. F., **27**.29
Linn, R. D., **18**.28
Lipow, M., **23**.91, **31**.11
Lishka, K., **35H**.14
Livini, H., **6**.21
Lloyd, D. K., **23**.91, **31**.11
Locks, M. O., **13**.43
Longley, J. W., **23**.115
Loson, D. B., xiii
Lossin, R. D., **22**.3
Louis, A. M., **18**.53
Lounds, A. C., **22**.27
Love, K. S., **9**.23
Love, T., **14**.15
Lowry, D. W., **13**.76
Loxham, J., **18**.63
Lu, C., **27**.3
Lucas, J. M., **24**.29
Lunch, S., **27**.37
Lund, R. T., **3**.24
Lundvall, D. M., **4**.1*n.*
Luscher, W., xiii
Lusk, H. F., **19**.12
Lusser, R., **23**.88

Maass, R. A., **18**.119
McAfee, N. J., xii
McCabe, W. J., **21**.21
McCall, J., **27**.6
McCarthy, R., **13**.76
McCaslin, J. A., **18**.67–**18**.68
McClaskey, D. J., **11**.7
McClure, C., **27**.7
McClure, J. Y., **15**.43, **20**.29, **35A**.4
McConnell, W., **33**.59
McCormick, E. J., **10**.30, **10**.31
McCrackin, F. L., **28**.11
McCubbin, R. E., **16**.29
McDonald, M., **8**.16, **33**.20
McFarren, E. F., **28**.10
McGaughy, D. A., xiii
MacGowan, T. G., **3**.11

McGrath, J. H., **22**.23–**22**.25, **22**.29
McGregor, D. N., **10**.5, **10**.8
Machalski, R., **27**.37
McKee, K. E., **27**.33, **27**.36
McManus, J. I., **14**.19
McMaster, R. C., **18**.71
McQuade, W., **13**.76
McRobb, R. M., **20**.35
Madigan, M. J., **30**.19
Maher, J., **10**.38
Main, J., **10**.14, **33**.72
Majerus, R. E., **10**.35
Makay, G., **35H**.14
Mandel, J., **26**.60, **26**.70, **28**.10, **28**.11, **28**.15
Manning, P. B., **33**.72
Marash, S. A., **9**.29
Marcuse, S., **28**.16
Margolin, B. H., **26**.44
Marguglio, B. W., **13**.69, **13**.70, **16**.41
Markowitz, O., **19**.14
Marquardt, D. W., **6**.46, **27**.24, **28**.35
Marquez, M., **22**.50
Marshall, R. J., **23**.33
Martin, C. A., **25**.78
Martin, C. C., **27**.38
Martin, C. H., **34**.22
Martin, J., **14**.13, **27**.7
Martin, T. L., **27**.31
Martz, H. F., **25**.90
Marwell, E. M., **18**.78
Mase, H., **10**.7, **10**.18
Masing, W., **35D**.4, **35D**.8
Maslow, A. H., **10**.4, **10**.8
Mason, D. L., **6**.18
Mason, R., **14**.24
Massey, F. J., **23**.17, **23**.48, **23**.64, **26**.74
Mathur, C. P., **18**.63
Maurer, J. H., **31**.20
Mausman, B., **10**.56
May, E., **10**.28
May, R, **17**.5
Maytag, F., **6**.27
Mazzeo, J. M., xiii
Mead, R., **26**.80
Meal, H. C., **16**.3
Meckley, D. G., **18**.77
Megaw, E. D., **18**.81
Meister, D., **20**.35
Melan, E. H., **10**.43, **21**.6
Melsheimer, J. M., **18**.95
Mentch, C. C., **16**.21, **16**.25
Metcalf, H. C., **22**.60
Methner, H., **35D**.5
Michalek, J. M., **13**.59, **16**.58
Midas, M., **8**.20
Mihalasky, J., **13**.55
Mikayama, M., **35F**.30
Miles, L. D., **13**.64
Miller, E. F., **9**.17

Miller, E. M., 18.9
Miller, E. W., 13.46
Miller, G., 3.31
Miller, G. D., 3.11, 3.31, 15.5, 15.36
Miller, I., 11.26
Miller, L. M., 10.17–10.19, 10.27, 10.30,
    10.36
Minor, G. W., 18.119
Mishra, R. K., 23.32
Mitchell, J. A., 28.16, 28.21, 28.22
Mitsuya, C., 13.31
Miyazaki, H., 18.54
Mizell, M., 22.50
Mizuno, S., 9.15, 11.36, 35F.7, 35F.15
Mladjov, L. A., 35H.9
Moburg, K. W., 18.119
Moder, J. J., 26.80
Moehlenbrock, M., 10.43, 22.31
Mohrman, S. A., 10.15
Montgomery, D. C., 24.32, 26.65
Montville, V. L., 18.56
Moore, L. R., 13.40, 20.35
Mori, K., 27.38
Moroney, M. J., 11.26
Morris, C. N., 25.90
Morris, R. T., 3.9
Morris, W., 8.24, 9.21
Moses, L. E., 25.101
Mottle, N. J., 3.6
Moult, J. F., 23.37
Mount-Campbell, C. A., 26.80
Mouradian, G., 23.59
Mudge, A. E., 13.64
Müller, A., 6.21
Mulvihill, R. J., 13.42
Mundel, A. B., 11.25, 15.34, 20.32, 20.34,
    26.70
Munro, B., 8.14
Murata, T., 35F.18
Murphy, R. B., 25.31
Murray, D. J., 6.41
Musson, T. A., 6.29, 13.75
Myers, G. J., 14.16–14.18
Myers, M. S., 10.18, 10.19, 10.23, 10.27,
    10.28, 10.36, 10.38, 10.40
Myers, R. H., 26.54, 26.69
Mykytka, E. F., 23.44

Nagy, E., 35H.11
Nakajo, T., 16.36
Namiki, N., 10.59
Naoi, T., 20.35
Naor, P., 25.102
Natrella, M. G., 23.64, 23.78, 23.91, 26.1,
    26.60
Nay, M. J., 24.18
Nelson, A. V., 18.82
Nelson, L. S., xii, 11.25, 16.21, 24.15, 24.18
Nelson, W., 13.36, 20.27, 23.37, 25.70

Nester, D., 22.32, 22.44
Neuhardt, J. B., 26.80
Neuman, D., 26.80
Newell, R. J., 27.37
Nicholson, R. H., 6.46
Nickell, W. L., 4.26, 10.43
Nicolino, T. A., 13.31
Nitta, Y., 27.11
Noakes, M. E., 15.32, 22.7
Noether, G. E., 26.71
Nolan, T., 26.36
Noonon, M., 17.31
Norquist, W. E., 15.8
Norton, C. E., 6.18
Nosow, S., 10.7, 10.12, 10.14
Novy, E., 32.16
Nowlan, F. S., 2.11, 3.25, 21.21
Noyes, R. J., 8.14
Noz, W. C., 4.19
Nukada, K., 27.38
Nygaard, G. M., 18.119

O'Brian, M., 18.70
O'Brien, R. M., 10.36
O'Keefe, D. F., Jr., 34.22
Ogren, S., 3.21
Ogryzkov, V. M., 35H.14
Ohfuju, T., 20.35
Ohkawa, M., 27.38
Ohta, H., 18.54
Oldham, G. R., 10.37, 10.39, 10.40
Oliver, L. R., 23.26, 25.90
Ollson, J. R., 3.19, 3.20
Olsbro, B., 6.3
Olsen, R. P., 33.72
Onnias, A., 8.12, 8.15
Orkin, F. J., xiii, 27.1
Orkin, K. S., 27.37
Orr, K., 14.11
Ortwein, W. J., 4.22
Ostle, B., 26.80
Ott, E. R., 11.26, 24.18, 25.91, 26.59
Ouchi, W. G., 10.7, 10.14
Overbach, W., 10.58
Overturf, G., 11.20
Owen, D. B., 23.28, 23.55, 26.74
Ozley, L., 10.13

Pabst, W. R., Jr., 25.44, 25.78
Page-Jones, M., 14.13
Palmer, G., 10.58
Papadopoulos, N., 18.57
Parker, H. V., 17.13
Parsons, H. M., 10.30
Pasteelnick, L. A., 28.30
Patek, J. M., 28.21
Patel, M. S., 26.42
Paul, B., 18.14
Payne, B. J., 22.41–22.43

Pazer, H. L., **18**.9
Peach, R. W., **20**.1*n*.
Peacore, E. J., **20**.35
Peacox, E. F., **18**.119
Pearson, L. G., **22**.27
Peavy, S. T., **27**.26
Pedrick, P. C., **3**.26
Peipel, G. F., **26**.69
Peratino, G. S., **3**.26
Pereira, A. L., **9**.22
Perris, F. A., **13**.75
Perry, R. L., **25**.37
Persol, D., **10**.58
Peryam, D. R., **18**.56
Peters, J., **23**.59
Peters, P. E., **22**.4
Peters, T. J., **10**.7, **10**.14, **10**.18
Peterson, E., **34**.11
Peterson, G., **18**.118
Pettigrew, T. J., **10**.43
Pettijohn, C. L., **29**.10
Pfaffenberger, R. C., **23**.107
Phadke, M. S., **16**.31, **26**.44, **29**.13
Phelps, E. L., **3**.21
Philips, G. J., **20**.23
Phillipp, T. J., **16**.55
Phillips, G., **27**.37
Phillips, G. P., **13**.60
Pierce, R. J., **6**.1*n*.
Pignatiello, J. J., xiii
Pike, D. J., **26**.80
Pinschmidt, R. J., **11**.25
Pinsky, P. D., **23**.19
Pipkin, F. M., **18**.68
Pipp, F. J., **12**.12
Pitt, H., **33**.72
Plackett, R. L., **26**.43, **28**.8, **28**.35
Plovnick, M. S., **10**.59
Plum, K. S., **9**.5
Pocock, S. J., **26**.70
Pournille, J., **27**.36
Powell, R. F., **20**.27
Poyer, T., **27**.36
Poza, E. J., **22**.66
Prarie, R. R., **25**.40
Prince, G. M., **10**.45
Provost, L. P., **18**.69, **28**.10
Prue, D. M., **10**.29
Punkett, J. J., **4**.12
Purcell, W. R., **9**.29, **24**.4
Putnam, A. O., xii

Quelch, J. A., **20**.9, **20**.29

Radigan, R. A., **17**.31, **30**.46
Rado, L. G., **11**.13
Raheja, D., **13**.77, **16**.44
Raktoe, B. L., **26**.44
Ralley, T. G., **23**.119

Ramanujam, V., **10**.13
Ramaswamy, C. V., **18**.120
Ramberg, J. S., xii, **23**.1*n.,* **23**.44
Ranganathan, J., **23**.52
Rau, S. Y. R., **15**.21
Raymond, A. S., **18**.121
Reavey, E. P., **12**.22
Rechtschaffner, R., **26**.44
Redding, B. F., **4**.19
Rehg, V., **11**.25
Reiff, H. E., **13**.40
Reisman, B., **10**.22
Reisz, P. C., **3**.9
Remboldt, U., **16**.58
Rendtel, U., **23**.26, **23**.60
Renna, V. F., **13**.6
Rennie, D. M., **8**.24, **9**.21
Resnikoff, G. J., **25**.68
Reynolds, E. A., xii, **11**.11, **18**.15
Rich, B. G., **23**.87
Richards, P., **27**.38
Richardson, H. W., **12**.23, **20**.6
Riggs, E. J., **9**.30
Riggs, J. L., **22**.41
Riley, F. D., **18**.51
Riley, F. H., **10**.52, **10**.54
Rimondi, G., **13**.77
Ritchey, J. A., **20**.34
Ritter, R. C., **18**.68
Robert, P. A., **7**.18
Robertson, J. A., **20**.27
Robinson, A. L, **18**.120
Roche, J. G., **6**.26
Rockart, J. F., **8**.17
Roe, J., **27**.17
Roethlisberger, F. J., **10**.4
Rogers, W. T., **28**.57
Romig, H. G., **9**.6, **11**.25, **15**.20, **25**.12
Rosander, A. C., **33**.72
Rose, J., **3**.21
Rosen, T. A., **10**.36
Rosenberg, H., **3**.26
Rosenthal, R. **20**.12
Rosenthal, S. T., **19**.14
Rosenzweig, G., **28**.54, **33**.72
Rosenzweig, J. E., **10**.23
Rosow, M. P., **10**.13
Ross, S. S., **34**.14, **34**.21
Ross, T. L., **10**.35
Rotfeld, H. J., **19**.4
Rotzoll, K. B., **19**.4
Rubin, I. M., **10**.45
Rubinstein, S. P., **10**.10, **10**.13, **10**.21, **10**.22, **10**.43
Rudelius, W., **15**.44
Rummler, G. A., **10**.23
Russell, E. R., **26**.81
Rutherford, J. R., **23**.121
Ryan, J. M., **9**.30

Ryan, W. J., **3**.26

Sahrmann, H., **16**.23, **17**.19
Salvendy, G., **4**.30
Sanders, G., **17**.26
Sanders, M. S., **10**.30, **10**.31
Sandholm, L., **10**.10, **11**.36, **20**.27, **35B**.1
Saperstein, B., **29**.18
Sasaki, O., **20**.31
Sasser, W. E., **33**.72
Satterthwaite, F. E., **24**.4, **28**.18
Sayle, A. J., **9**.5, **9**.10, **9**.11
Scanlon, F., **6**.3, **33**.22
Schafer, R. E., **25**.90, **32**.10
Schaffer, G., **18**.82
Schaffer, J., **18**.78
Schalick, J. A., xiii
Schecter, E. S., **29**.1
Scheffe, H., **18**.55, **26**.58, **26**.66
Schein, E. H., **10**.7, **10**.11, **10**.17
Scherkenbach, W. W., **10**.36
Schilling, E. G., **11**.26, **18**.50, **25**.12
Schirmer, W., **35D**.6
Schlötel, E., **35D**.1, **35D**.7, **35D**.8
Schmee, J., **25**.102
Schmid, M. M., xiii
Schmidt, W. H., **10**.19
Schneider, A. M., **28**.30
Schneiderman, A. M., **4**.22
Schoeffler, S., **3**.18
Schonberger, R. J., **16**.3, **17**.4
Schrader, L. J., xiii, **4**.30, **13**.78
Schuck, J. R., **10**.36
Schulmeyer, G. G., **14**.19
Schumacher, R. B. F., **18**.68–**18**.69
Schuster, M., **10**.22
Schutz, H. G., **19**.3
Schweber, W., **18**.120
Scott, A. J., **27**.17
Sears, J. A., **7**.14, **18**.120
Secrest, D., **28**.62
Seder, L. A., **22**.45, **24**.5, **32**.1
Seghezzi, H. D., **2**.4
Sekino, W. T., **29**.8
Selwitchka, R., **22**.21, **22**.22
Seth, M. K., **16**.58
Sethi, S. P., **10**.7, **10**.9, **10**.12, **10**.14–**10**.17
Setzer, S. R., **28**.9
Shah, M. J., **28**.38
Shahnazarian, T., **30**.20
Shaiken, H., **32**.19
Shainin, D., **13**.56, **18**.88, **24**.1, **24**.4, **24**.36, **25**.58
Shainin, P. D., **24**.1
Shapiro, M. H., **34**.22
Shapiro, S. S., **23**.44
Sharp, D. B., **18**.58
Shashidhara, N. S., **28**.4
Shaw, A. C., **14**.24

Shea, G. P., **10**.46
Shecter, E. S., **29**.1n.
Sheesley, J. H., **23**.9, **25**.41, **26**.14
Sheil, J., **6**.26
Shelburne, V. B., **28**.8
Shephard, K. L, **33**.29
Sheppard, J. W., **15**.46
Sherwood, J. J., **10**.7, **10**.19, **10**.39
Shewhart, W. A., **10**.25, **10**.26, **24**.3, **28**.22
Shiah, P. M., **3**.6
Shilliff, K. A., **15**.15
Shimoda, Y., **18**.54
Shimoyamada, K., **8**.23
Shinner, R., **25**.102
Shoemaker, A. C., **29**.11
Shumaker, M. J., **3**.31
Sie, C., **30**.25
Siegel, A. I., **20**.6, **20**.7
Sierra, E., **35B**.16
Siff, W. C., **16**.9
Simmons, D. A., **11**.26
Simon, H., **27**.36
Simon, L. E., **25**.58
Sinibaldi, F. J., **24**.36, **28**.10
Sink, D. S., **10**.44
Siotani, M. **23**.43, **23**.100
Skratt, J. P., **3**.21
Small, B. B., **11**.26
Smith, H., Jr., **23**.9, **23**.100, **23**.107, **23**.108, **23**.111, **23**.117, **26**.79, **28**.30, **28**.36
Smith, J. R., **18**.120
Smith, M., **11**.26
Smith, M. R., **7**.17
Smith, O. A., **23**.87
Smith, R. M., xiii
Smith, R. P., **20**.30
Smithhisler, W. L., **3**.26
Snedecor, G. W., **26**.21**26**.65, **26**.76
Snee, R. D., xiii, **16**.29, **26**.69, **27**.38
Snyderman, B., **10**.56
Solomon, H., **25**.101
Sommers, D. J., **25**.1, **25**.57
Sorrell, D. L., **6**.21
Sosnowski, T. S., **25**.89
Soundararajian, V., **25**.38
South, S. E., **12**.24
Speeny, D. V., **16**.58, **29**.13
Spencer, J. L., **29**.15, **29**.16
Spendley, W., **26**.81
Spow, E. E., **18**.82
Springer, M. D., **23**.26, **25**.90
Staal, R., **22**.32, **22**.44
Staffiery, R. A., **16**.40
Stalker, A. H., **18**.111
Steel, R. G. D., **26**.65
Steers, R. R., **15**.33
Stehle, F. N., **3**.21
Stein, B. A., **10**.43
Steinberg, D. M., **26**.77

Stemberg, A., **34**.22
Stenecker, R. G., **9**.10
Stephens, K. S., **11**.31, **11**.37, **25**.37, **26**.81, **29**.13, **35B**.9
Sterett, W. K., **8**.16
Stevens, R. T., **13**.31, **13**.36
Still, R. R., **13**.76
Stillman, R. E., **28**.38
Stokes, R. G., **3**.21
Stone, H. D., **17**.2
Stoneman, D. N., **26**.42
Strattner, L., **22**.50
Stratton, D. A., **22**.39
Strauch, H., **35D**.8
Stubin, R. J., **27**.16, **27**.17
Sue-Ho, W. M., **28**.7
Sugimoto, T., **10**.47, **35F**.16
Sukert, A. N., **14**.24
Sullivan, K. H., **16**.20
Sullivan, L. P., **10**.42, **13**.78, **16**.58
Sullivan, R. G., **16**.54
Summer, C. E., **28**.23
Sutherland, L. A., xiii
Sütö, K., **35H**.1
Suzuki, T., **10**.23
Swanson, C. L, **10**.59
Swaton, L. E., **32**.18
Sweetland, R. L., **13**.39, **30**.24
Sylvestre, E. A., **28**.11

Tachiki, D. S., **10**.15
Tadikamalla, P. R., **23**.44
Taguchi, G. **6**.3, **16**.30, **18**.120, **26**.44, **29**.13
Taguchi, S. **16**.31, **29**.19
Takahashi, H., **11**.22
Takanashi, M., **29**.11, **35F**.27
Takayanagi, A., **35F**.23
Takeuchi, H., **20**.9, **20**.29
Takezawa, S., **10**.8
Talbot, J. E., **31**.23
Talley, D. J., **8**.16
Tannenbaum, R., **10**.19
Tarnoy, E., **35H**.14
Tarver, M. G., **16**.17
Tavazza, G., **13**.77
Tawara, N., **18**.84
Taylor, E. F., **19**.19
Taylor, F. W., **7**.9, **8**.2, **10**.3, **16**.5, **18**.94, **18**.100
Teschner, H. G., **28**.57
Thayer, S., **11**.25
Thoday, W. R., **2**.4, **15**.17, **35E**.1, **35E**.2, **35E**.5
Thoman, D. R., **23**.49
Thomas, A. M., **26**.44
Thomas, J. H., **18**.120
Thomas, L., **18**.83
Thomas, V., **19**.17
Thompson, H. A., **18**.15

Thompson, W. O., **26**.69
Thorner, M. E., **33**.72
Thresh, J. L., xiii, **9**.13, **9**.14, **9**.23, **9**.24
Tiao, G. C., **26**.65
Tichy, N. M., **10**.13, **10**.39
Tidwell, P. W., **26**.53
Tingey, F. H., **28**.15
Tipnis, V. A., **27**.13
Tippett, L. H. C., **24**.9
Tkachenko, V. V., **35H**.3
Tobey, D., **18**.78
Todt, H. C., **6**.46
Toohey, E. F., **3**.21
Torrey, M. N., **18**.117, **25**.28
Torrie, J. H., **26**.65
Townsend, P., **33**.72
Toyoda, S., **30**.1n.
Traver, R. W., **22**.45
Traylor, W. S., **28**.23
Tregoe, B. B., **22**.71
Trimble, J. M., **11**.19
Trippi, R. R., **18**.9
Trolle, B., **18**.53
Troutman, W. W., **29**.8
Troxell, J. R., **33**.13, **33**.14, **33**.32
Trulli, H. B., **9**.17. **17**.31
Trumpold, H., **35H**.14
Tsiakals, J. J., xiii, **4**.26
Tuggle, G., **10**.60
Tukey, J. W., **26**.58
Turello, U., **13**.77
Turner, R. E., **18**.71
Tustin, W., **18**.69

Udovichenko, E. J., **35H**.7, **35H**.11
Ulla, F. M., **18**.108
Ullman, R., **33**.72
Urwick, L., **22**.60
Utzig, L., **12**.17, **12**.20, **12**.24

Valenta, B., **35H**.14
Van Beek, A., **18**.56
Vance, F. P., **28**.63
Vance, L. C., **24**.14
Vanderwicken, P., **12**.24
Van Leer, R. K., **19**.6
Vaughn, T. C., **4**.14
Vecsenyi, J., **35H**.9
Venn, B., **16**.9
Veraldi, L. C., **6**.12, **13**.16, **30**.15
Vess, P. H., **14**.20
Vinson, W. D., **13**.16, **16**.9
Voegtlen, H. D., xiii, **13**.1n., **31**.1
Volk, W., **23**.97

Wachniak, R., **9**.30
Wadsworth, G. P., **24**.3
Wadsworth, H. M., xiii, **24**.32, **29**.13
Walden, C. H., **28**.1, **28**.51

Walden, J. C., **8**.16
Walder, A. G., **35F**.7
Walsh, L., **18**.121
Walsmann, M. R., **18**.121
Walters, G., **27**.38
Walton, R. E., **10**.13
Wambach, G. W., **18**.121
Wampler, R. H., **23**.115
Wang, S. C., **18**.97
Wang, S. H. S., **18**.121
Ware, P. A., **4**.19
Warren, R., xiii
Waterman, R. A., **10**.7, **10**.14, **10**.18
Watson, G. S., **26**.69
Weaver, C. L., **28**.61
Weaver, H., **15**.29
Weaver, L. A., **18**.95
Webb, S. R., **26**.44
Webber, R., **15**.43
Webber, R. A., **28**.23
Webster, G. L., **11**.25
Weil, S., **35C**.9
Weinberg, E., **10**.13, **10**.21
Weinberger, C. W., **31**.13
Weinstein, J., **16**.58
Weiss, R. L., **28**.38
Wellborn, J. M., **13**.43
Werner, G. W., **16**.48
Wernimont, G., **26**.81, **28**.3, **28**.5, **28**.19, **28**.37
Wescott, M. E., **23**.111
West, A. H., **11**.37
Wetherill, G. B., **25**.90
Wetzstein, C., **28**.36
Wexley, K. N., **10**.36
White, B., **9**.17
Whitten, B. J., **23**.118
Whittingham, P. R. B., **17**.25, **17**.26
Widener, P. L., **28**.51
Wiesen, J. M., **25**.1n.
Wigmore, H. M., **33**.63
Wilborn, W., **6**.28, **9**.30
Wilhelm, W. C., **6**.3
Wilkie, W. L., **19**.3
Willard, I. E., **13**.40
Williams, C. D., **18**.110
Williams, T. J., **27**.13, **27**.14
Williamson, D. T. N., **32**.31
Williamson, E., **23**.30
Willis, R. G., **16**.54
Wilson, K. B., **26**.47
Wilson, L. B., **18**.115
Wingfield, J., **27**.37

Wirkus, S. R., **17**.31
Wissel, R., **35D**.3
Witt, J. H., **3**.26
Witterick, L. W., **21**.16
Wolf, J. D., **22**.3, **22**.28
Wolfe, D., **26**.71
Woltz, J. R., **28**.51
Wong, H. Y. S., **9**.30
Wood, B. B., **19**.7
Wood, F. S., **23**.100, **23**.106, **23**.107
Wood, N., **18**.110
Woodman, R. W., **10**.39
Woods, D. G., **18**.28
Woods, K. C., **18**.78
Woodward, J. D., **22**.7
Woodward, W. A., **27**.25
Wortham, A. W., **24**.32
Wu, Y., **26**.44, **29**.13
Wurster, **18**.98
Wyckoff, D. D., **33**.72
Wynholds, H. W., **3**.21

Yamada, K., **13**.78
Yamamoto, M., **10**.9
Yankelovich, D., **10**.17, **10**.18, **10**.21
Yates, F., xii, **24**.5, **26**.63
Yates, J., **20**.19
Yee, K. W., **27**.17
Yoneyama, T., **35F**.30
Youden, W. J., **26**.63, **26**.70, **26**.71, **26**.73, **28**.37
Youle, P. V., **28**.35
Yu, S. S., **24**.31

Zacks, S., **23**.91
Zaludova, A. H., **2**.4, **13**.78
Zanakis, S. H., **23**.94
Zander, A., **10**.45
Zaworski, R. A., **15**.28
Zeccardi, J. J., **17**.31, **18**.1, **30**.46
Zeiss, C., **18**.28
Zelkowitz, N. V., **14**.24
Zemke, R., **10**.32
Zetzsche, E., **16**.48
Ziegler, A. H., **15**.9, **15**.43
Zimbler, D. A., **4**.29
Zimmer, J. D., **16**.57
Zimmer, W. J., **25**.40
Zimmerman, C. D., **33**.1
Zimmers, E. W., **32**.30
Zipfel, H. J., **35H**.11
Zobel, S. P., **21**.1n.

SUBJECT INDEX

See also Name Index; Glossary of Symbols, Appendix I; Quality Systems Terminology, Appendix III

Ability to regulate, 10.30, 17.18–17.21
  (*See also* Self-control)
Accelerated testing for reliability, 13.35
Acceptable process level, 25.61–25.63
Acceptable quality level (AQL):
  defined, 25.5
  interpretation by supplier, 15.23
  in MIL-STD-105, 25.41
  in MIL-STD-414, 25.65
  in selecting sampling plans, 25.16–25.18
  use in sampling table, 25.44–25.47
Acceptance control:
  concept, 25.9
  moving from acceptance sampling to,
    25.97–25.99
Acceptance inspection (*see* Inspection and test;
    Inspection planning)
Acceptance number, 25.11
Acceptance sampling:
  by attributes:
    chain-sampling, 25.37–25.39
    continuous sampling, 25.28, 25.36
    cumulative sum sampling plans,
      25.39–25.41
    Dodge-Romig plans, 25.49–25.51
    double sampling, 25.23–25.30
    multiple sampling, 25.23–25.33
    overview, 25.21, 25.22
    published tables and procedures,
      25.41–25.51
    rectification schemes, 25.26
    selecting sampling plans, 25.23
    sequential sampling, 25.23, 25.34, 25.35
    single sampling, 25.23–25.27
    skip-lot schemes, 25.33, 25.37
    summary of plans, 25.41–25.43
  basic concepts of:
    acceptance control and acceptance
      sampling, 25.9, 25.97–25.99
    acceptance sampling procedures,
      25.5–25.8
    advantages and disadvantages, 25.2–25.4
    assumptions made in sampling plans,
      25.18, 25.19

Acceptance sampling, basic concepts of
    (*Cont.*):
    average outgoing quality curve, 25.13
    average outgoing quality limit,
      25.12–25.13
    average sample number curve, 25.12
    average total inspection, 25.13–25.14
    Bayesian procedures, 25.89–25.91
    comparison of attributes and variables
      plans, 25.6
    computer programs, 25.92, 25.96
    lot formation, 25.19, 25.20
    minimum total inspection, 25.14–25.16
    operating characteristic curve,
      25.10–25.12
    published tables and procedures, 25.8
    random sampling, 25.20
    risks, 25.9–25.12
    selecting the sampling procedures,
      25.91–25.94
    selection of a numerical value of the
      quality index, 25.16–25.18
    seriousness classification of defects,
      18.41–18.45, 25.44
    stratified sampling, 25.20–25.21
    terminology of, 25.4–25.5
    types of, 25.4
  of bulk product:
    amount of sampling, 25.87
    models, 25.87–25.89
    objectives, 25.85
    obtaining test-units, 25.88–25.89
    terms and concepts, 25.85–25.86
    tests of homogeneity, 25.89
  for reliability:
    exponential distribution, 25.73–25.82
    overview, 25.68–25.71
    relation of life characteristics, 25.73
    Weibull distribution, 25.82–25.84
  of variables:
    acceptance control charts, 25.62–25.64
    grand lot schemes, 25.58
    lot plot, 25.58–25.61
    MIL-STD-414 plans, 25.62–25.77

Acceptance sampling, of variables (*Cont.*):
  mixed plans, **25**.68
  narrow-limit gaging for percent noncon-
    forming, **25**.57–**25**.58
  overview, **25**.57
  published tables and procedures,
    25.62–**25**.77
  sampling for percent nonconforming,
    25.51–**25**.58
    single sampling, **25**.54–**25**.56
    two-point variables plans for percent
      nonconforming, **25**.56–**25**.57
  sampling for process parameter,
    25.60–**25**.62
  summary of plans, **25**.51–**25**.53
Access time in service industries, **33**.8
Accreditation, **6**.46
Accuracy:
  of inspector, **18**.94–**18**.97
  of instrument, defined, **18**.63–**18**.64
Action time in service industries, **33**.9
Adaptive control, **24**.32, **28**.31–**28**.35
Administrative and support operations:
  defined, **21**.2
  defining quality responsibilities, **21**.4–
    21.7
  errors in, **21**.3, **21**.14, **21**.15
  organizing quality activities, **21**.21,
    21.22
  policies, **5**.11, **5**.12
  quality improvement in, **21**.15–**21**.21
  quality control for, **21**.14, **21**.15
  quality planning for, **21**.7–**21**.14
Admiral Corporation, **15**.41
Advertising, **19**.2–**19**.6
  by emotional stimuli, **19**.2–**19**.3
  government regulation of, **19**.4
  by objective evidence, **19**.3–**19**.4
  puffing, **19**.4
  truth in, **5**.10, **19**.4
Advisory Group on the Reliability of
    Electronic Equipment (AGREE), **2**.9,
    30.26
Advisory tolerances, **17**.9–**17**.10
AFCIQ (Association Française pour le
    Contrôle Industriel et la Qualité),
    35C.7, **35C**.8
Affinity diagram, **22**.39
AFNOR (Association Française de
    Normalisation), **34**.8
Airline service quality, **33**.29–**33**.30,
    33.70–**33**.71
ALGOL 68 (programming language), **14**.15,
    14.16
All-union Research Institute for Standardiza-
    tion, **8**.19
Allis-Chalmers Company, **4**.18, **9**.17
Allowances as quality costs, **4**.5
Aluminum Company of America, **3**.11

American Defense Preparedness Association,
    31.23
American human resource management
    practices:
  influence on motivation and quality,
    10.14–**10**.16
  transplanted from Japan, **10**.14–**10**.16
American Institute of Certified Public
    Accountants, **21**.21
American Management Association training
    courses, **1**.12
American National Standards Institute (ANSI),
    2.4, **2**.13, **18**.7, **24**.9, **27**.4, **34**.9
American Ordnance Association, **31**.23
American Society for Nondestructive Testing
    (ASNDT), **18**.71
American Society for Quality Control (ASQC),
    2.13, **4**.18, **9**.10, **12**.18, **13**.40, **15**.15,
    15.19, **18**.7, **34**.3
American Society for Testing and Materials
    (ASTM), **18**.61, **18**.69, **26**.70
American Telephone & Telegraph Company
    (AT&T), **10**.4, **10**.13, **10**.22, **11**.36,
    24.15
Analysis of variance (ANOVA):
  in completely randomized experiment,
    26.11–**26**.16
  in factorial design, **26**.18–**26**.22,
    26.24–**26**.29
  in randomized block design, **26**.57–**26**.59
  in regression, **23**.104–**23**.107, **23**.110,
    23.114, **23**.115
  in response surface design, **26**.51–**26**.54
  sample size, tables for determining,
    AII.42–**AII**.43
Anatomy of the process, **6**.16, **16**.4,
    28.39–**28**.45
Anchor Brewing Company, **6**.27
Annual quality program (*see* Companywide
    quality management)
ANSI/ASQC, **15**.9, **21**.4, **21**.9, **25**.44–**25**.49,
    25.62–**25**.77
  (*See also* MIL-STD-105D; MIL-STD-414)
ANSI/ASQC standards:
  attributes sampling plans, **25**.44–**25**.49
  selected documents, Appendix III
  terminology, Appendix IV
  variables sampling plans, **25**.62–**25**.77
AOQL (*see* Average outgoing quality limit)
Appliance industry (*see* Assembly industries)
Appraisal costs, **4**.5, **4**.6
Approved parts list, **13**.27
AQL (*see* Acceptable quality level)
Arbitration, **34**.12
ARINC Research Corporation, **13**.24
Arithmetic mean (*see* Mean)
Arrow diagram, **22**.41
ASQC (*see* American Society for Quality
    Control)

Assembly industries:
  assembly process, **30.2, 30.30–30.32**
  audit plan for, **30.45–30.47**
  competitor quality, **30.28–30.29**
  conflicting departmental objectives, **30.3–30.4**
  corrective action systems in, **30.26–30.27**
  criteria for quality, **30.27–30.30**
  customer-supplied specifications in, **30.10–30.11**
  data plan in, **30.37, 30.40–30.44**
  design evaluation by use, **30.15–30.16**
  field failures, reporting of, **30.44–30.45**
  in-process controls, **30.24**
  manufacturability, planning for, **30.15**
  new-product controls in, **30.11–30.17**
  pilot-plant production in, **30.8–30.10**
  planning for production in, **30.17–30.18**
  planning for quality in, **30.11–30.14**
  product development in, **30.5–30.8**
  product development cycle in, **30.7–30.8**
  product safety and health evaluation, **30.16**
  production process in, **30.8–30.9, 30.21–30.24**
  quality activities in, **30.37**
  quality improvement in, **30.47–30.48**
  quality management in, **30.4–30.11**
  quality policies illustrated, **30.5**
  quality system in, **30.5–30.6**
  reliability improvement in, **30.25–30.26**
  reports on quality, **30.40–30.44**
  responsibility for quality in, **30.36–30.39**
  service for products in, **30.34–30.36**
  service needs, planning for, **30.14–30.15**
  strategic business statements in, **30.4–30.5**
  suppliers, working with, **30.18–30.21**
Assembly tree, **22.39**
Assessment of quality:
  broad review, **9.15**
  self-audit, **9.11**
  summary of status, **9.20**
Assignable causes of variation vs. random causes, **24.3–24.6**
Association Française pour le Contrôle Industriel et la Qualité (AFCIQ), **35C.7–35C.8**
Assurance for quality:
  concept, **9.2–9.4**
  defined, **7.18, 9.2**
  departmental assurance activities, **9.3**
  in Japan, **35F.18–35F.22**
  personnel for, **9.27–9.29**
  product auditing (*see* Product auditing)
  quality audits (*see* Audits)
  similarity to financial audit, **9.3**
  surveys (*see* Surveys)
Attributes and variables data, defined, **25.4**
Attributes sampling demonstrator, **11.28**

Attributes sampling plans (*see* Sampling, by attributes)
Audits:
  in assembly industries, **30.45–30.47**
  categories of, **9.4, 9.5**
  of decisions, **17.26**
  distinguished from survey, **9.14, 9.15**
  of execution vs. plans, **9.6, 9.7**
    examples of deficiencies, **9.6, 9.7**
    prudence audits, **9.7**
    surveillance, **9.7**
  general, **9.5, 9.6**
  organization for, **8.23, 8.24**
  planning and performing, **9.7–9.14**
    audit completion, **9.14**
    audit implementation, **9.10**
    audit initiation, **9.7**
    audit planning, **9.7–9.10**
    audit reporting, **9.12**
  by president, **8.23**
  of production quality, **17.26**
  quality assurance of, **9.14**
  of quality plans: checklists, **9.5, 9.6**
    reference standards, **9.6**
    subject matter, **9.5, 9.6**
  in service industries, **33.43–33.47**
  subject matter, **8.21, 8.22**
  third party, **8.23, 8.24**
  by upper managers, **8.20–8.24**
  who performs, **17.27, 17.29**
  why?, **8.20–8.21**
  (*See also* Product auditing)
Automated gaging, **18.27**
Automated inspection, **18.26–18.28, 18.81–18.83, 18.87, 22.63**
Automated manufacturing:
  benefits, **16.53**
  computer integrated manufacturing, **16.54**
  flexible manufacturing system, **16.55–16.56**
  group technology, **16.54–16.55**
  quality planning for, **16.56**
Automated optical inspection, **18.82–18.83**
Automated processes, control of, **24.36–24.39**
Automated quality information, **17.17**
Automobile safety, **34.15, 34.16**
Automotive industry, (*see* Assembly industries)
Autopsies, in diagnosis, **22.35**
Availability (continuity of service):
  concept, **2.9**
  intrinsic, **13.41**
  operational, **13.41**
Average outgoing quality limit (AOQL):
  in continuous sampling plans, **25.28**
  defined, **25.12**
  in Dodge-Romig plans, **25.49**
  in skip-lot schemes, **25.35**
Average sample number (ASN), **25.12**
Average total inspection (ATI), **25.13–25.14**

Averages (*see* Mean)
Avoidable quality costs, **4.11–4.12**
  hidden in standards, **4.11**
Awards for quality motivation, **8.6–8.7**
Awareness of quality, **9.20, 22.6**

"Backward and forward quality," **35F**.19
Balanced incomplete block design of
    experiments, **26.59–26.62**
Bank of America, **31**.2
Banking industry, quality in, **33**.64–**33**.69
Bar-code, **16**.40
Base line, **13**.67
BASIC (programming language), **27**.4
Batch production:
  control concepts, **16**.39
  example of process, **28**.41, **28**.42
  traceability in, **16**.39
Bathtub curve, **23**.81, **23**.83
Baxter Healthcare Corporation, **27**.13, **27**.36
Bayes' theorem, **23**.25–**23**.26, **23**.59–**23**.60
Bayesian estimates, **23.59–23.60**
  procedure in acceptance sampling,
    25.89–25.91
  of variance components, **26**.65
Bayesian sampling plans, **25.89–25.91**
Behavioral scientists' theories of motivation,
    10.4–10.8
Bell Communications Research, **29**.16
Bell curve (*see* Normal distribution)
Bell System, **9.28, 18**.39
Bell Telephone Laboratories, **24**.3
Bellwether project, **4**.17, **22**.15
Bias:
  physical selection, **25**.89
  systematic physical, statistical, **25**.86
Bibliographies:
  in management of quality, **10.60–10.61**
  standards and specifications, **AIII**.1–**AIII**.13
  system and program requirements,
    AIII.2–AIII.7
  in training for quality, **11.25–11.28**
  (*See also* references at the end of each
    section)
Big Q, **35G**.8
Binomial probability distribution, **23.27–23.28**
  negative, **23.29–23.30**
  tables of, **AII**.14–**AII**.16
Black book, **17**.7
Blast furnace process, **28**.40
Bleaching chemicals, control of, **28**.29
Block diagram, **13**.29
  functional, **13**.24, **13**.25
  reliability, **13**.24, **13**.25
Blocked factorial experiments, **26.36–26.37**
Blocking:
  block designs, **26.54–26.62**
  in design of experiments, defined, **26**.3
  in EVOP, **26.35–26.37**

Brainstorming, **22**.36, **22**.37
Brand labeling:
  chain, **19**.17
  franchised, **19**.17
  industry association, **19**.17
  manufacturer's, **19.15–19.16**
  merchant's, **19.16–19.17**
Break-even chart, **3**.13
Breakthrough:
  defined, **5**.20
  objectives for, **5**.20
  universal sequence of steps of, **22**.12
British Consumer Council, **34**.8
British Institute of Management, **13**.3
British Petroleum, **6**.28
British Standards Institution (BSI), **9**.21,
    15.17, **15**.18
British Telecom, **29**.16
BSI (British Standards Institution), **9**.21,
    15.17, **15**.18
Budgeting for inspection and test,
    18.108–18.114
  activity index, **18**.112, **18**.113
  budgetary process, **18**.111, **18**.112
  census of inspection costs, **18**.109
  cost centers, **18**.111
  industrial engineering studies, **18**.110
  inspection cost reduction, **18**.108, **18**.109
  interdepartmental studies, **18**.111, **18**.112
  measure of actual costs, **18**.113, **18**.114
  nonfinancial controls, **18**.114
  quality engineering studies, **18**.111
  standards for cost, **18**.111, **18**.112
Budgeting for staff quality activities, **7**.31
Bulk product sampling (*see* Acceptance
    sampling, for bulk product)
Burndy Corporation, **30**.20

C (programming language), **27**.4
c chart, **24.23–24.26**
  for attaining control, **24**.7, **24**.23,
    24.25–24.26
  control limits, chart of, **AII**.41
CAD (computer-aided design), **13**.31
CAI (computer-aided inspection),
    18.26–18.28, 27.17–27.23
Calibration control, **18.76–18.81**
  coulometer in, **18**.78, **18**.79
  flow diagram for, **18**.77
  inventory needed in, **18**.78
  mobile laboratories for, **18**.81
  for new equipment, **18.76–18.77**
  organization for, **18**.81
  practice in, **18**.80
  of purchased standards, **18.76–18.77**
  records in, **18**.80
  responsibility for, **18.79–18.81**
  schedule adherence in, **18.79–18.80**
  schedules for, **18**.78

Calibration control (*Cont.*):
  terminology of, **18**.76
  for test materials, **18**.77–**18**.78
CAM (computer-aided manufacturing), **16**.53
Campaigns for quality, **10**.48–**10**.55
  budgeting for, **10**.50
  communication plan for, **10**.50
  implementation of, **10**.54–**10**.55
  launching of, **10**.53–**10**.54
  measuring results, **10**.51–**10**.52
  prelaunch planning for, **10**.49–**10**.53
  prerequisites for, **10**.48
  steering, **10**.49–**10**.50
Canonical variables, **23**.95
Capitalistic economies, quality in,
      35A.2–**35A**.3
Careers in the quality function, **11**.32–**11**.33
Carlsberg Breweries, **18**.53
Carpet yarn standard, weight example, **15**.23
Carryover of failure-prone designs, **3**.20,
      13.11
CASE (Coordinated Agency for Supplier
      Evaluation), **15**.13
Cause:
  of complaints, **2**.4, **12**.4, **20**.20, **20**.21
  confused with symptom, **22**.56
  defined, **22**.31
  dominant, **22**.31
  vs. theory, **22**.31
Cause-and-effect (Ishikawa) diagram,
      22.37–**22**.39
  in administrative and support operations,
      21.17, **21**.18
Caveat emptor, **19**.4, **34**.14
Cells, in frequency distribution:
  boundaries of, **23**.14
  intervals for, **23**.14
  number of, **23**.12, **23**.13
Central tendency, measures of, **23**.16–**23**.17
Certificate:
  of compliance, **15**.32
  of supplier qualification, **15**.32–**15**.34
  of test, **15**.32
Certification:
  accreditation, **6**.46
  audits, third-party, **8**.23–**8**.24
  for consumer products, **15**.32, **19**.17
  defined, **6**.46, **15**.32, **15**.34
  in developing countries, **35B**.10–**35B**.14
  of electronic components, **15**.33
  of inspectors, **18**.86
  labeling, **19**.17
  of quality and reliability specialists, **11**.33
  by quality survey, **9**.21
  in socialist countries, **35H**.4–**35H**.7
  in supplier relations, **15**.32–**15**.34
  of suppliers, **21**.12, **30**.18–**30**.21
  of workers, **21**.12
  (*See also* Marks for quality)

Certified Quality Engineer, **11**.33
Certified Reliability Engineer, **7**.29–**7**.30
Chain-sampling plans:
  basic description, **25**.37
  flow chart, **25**.38
  procedure for using, **25**.37–**25**.38
Chance causes of variation, **24**.3, **24**.5
Change:
  engineering, **13**.69, **22**.33
  detection by averages vs. individuals, **24**.10
  introducing, **22**.66–**22**.68
  nature of, **22**.65
  (*See also* Resistance to change)
Change-in-mean effect, in EVOP, **26**.32,
      26.35
Characteristic, quality, **2**.4, **33**.7
  dissectable and nondissectable, **22**.50
Chargeback for defects, **18**.36
Charter:
  project team, **22**.27
  quality department, **33**.24–**33**.25
Chebyshev inequality theorem, **23**.55
Check inspection:
  to identify inspector errors, **18**.84–**18**.85
  to measure inspector accuracy, **18**.94–
      18.97
  (*See also* Product auditing)
Check sheet, **22**.35, **22**.36
Checklists:
  for designers, **13**.72
  for self-control, **17**.12, **17**.18, **17**.21
Chemical industry, **28**.4–**28**.38
  analysis of finished product quality, **28**.30
  analytical or control laboratory in (*see*
      Control laboratory)
  control of product quality, **28**.21–**28**.22
  design of process, **28**.7–**28**.9
  manufacture of product, **28**.9–**28**.23
  organization for quality, **28**.4–**28**.6
  pilot plant phase, **28**.9
  planning for future needs, **28**.37, **28**.38
  process control in, **28**.22–**28**.23
  product planning for quality, **28**.6–**28**.7
  quality improvement in, **28**.30–**28**.35
  unit operations in, **28**.4, **28**.23–**28**.25
  unit processes in, **28**.25–**28**.30
  (*See also* Process industries)
Chi square (χ^2):
  distribution, table, **AII**.26
  test, defined, **23**.28, **23**.32, **23**.68, **23**.72
Chip manufacture, **16**.30–**16**.31, **26**.44–**26**.45,
      29.9
Chronic problems:
  corrective actions, **6**.38
  defined, **22**.26
  distinguished from sporadic, **22**.5–**22**.6
  identification in supplier relations,
      15.13–**15**.16
  related to objectives for breakthrough, **5**.20

CIM (computer-integrated manufacturing), **16.54**
Circles, quality:
    compared to project teams, **22.28**
    concept and application, **10.9–10.11, 10.61, 22.11**
    Japanese origins, **35F.4–35F.6**
    QC circle Koryo, **11.20**
    socialist counties, **35H.11**
Classification of characteristics, **16.6–16.8, 18.44, 18.45**
Classification of defects, **18.38–18.44**
    (*See also* Seriousness classification)
Clemson University, **27.29**
Clustering and discrimination, **23.94–23.96**
COBOL (programming language), **27.4**
Coding of data, **23.19, 23.20**
Coefficient of variation, defined, **23.18**
Colorado State University, **27.26**
Committee:
    for coordination of quality function, **7.22**
    for quality planning companywide, **6.26**
Community of Roquefort, **19.17**
Companywide planning for quality:
    application of road map, **6.19–6.23**
        to functional levels, **6.21**
        to major programs, **6.23**
        to multifunctional systems, **6.21–6.23**
        to small companies, **6.26–6.28**
        to supervisory and worker levels, **6.19–6.21**
    concept, **6.3**
    discovery of customer needs, **6.6, 6.10**
    feedback loop, **6.32–6.39**
        analysis for decision making, **6.36–6.38**
        application to upper-management control, **6.38**
        control reports, **6.38, 6.39**
        control stations, **6.34–6.35**
        control subject, **6.33–6.34**
        corrective action, **6.38**
        data collection and processing, **6.36**
        sensor, **6.35–6.36**
        unit of measure, **6.35**
    generic standards, influence of, on quality planning, **6.45–6.47**
        adaptation to diversity, **6.46**
        certification; accreditation, **6.46–6.47**
        evolution of, **6.45**
        mandated and advisory, **6.45**
        purposes of, **6.45**
    identification of customers, **6.4**
    Japanese practices in, **35F.8–35F.18**
    lessons learned, **6.28–6.30**
        application to functional processes, **6.29, 6.30**
        application to multifunctional processes, **6.28**
        forms of improvement, **6.29**
        log of problems, **6.28**

Companywide planning for quality (*Cont.*):
    optimizing product design, **6.12–6.15**
    planning for control, **6.31**
    planning for quality improvement, **6.40**
    process development, **6.15–6.17**
    product development, **6.11, 6.12**
    quality control, **6.31–6.32**
        defined, **6.31**
        on-line and off-line, **6.32**
        self-control, **6.19, 6.32**
    quality manual, **6.40–6.45**
        contents of, **6.41–6.43**
        distribution of, **6.43–6.44**
        evolution of, **6.40–6.41**
        limitations of, as predictors of good quality, **6.44–6.45**
        provision for audit, **6.44**
        terminology, **6.40**
    road map of, **6.3–6.23**
    tools for quality planners: design review, **13.7–13.11, 16.5, 16.6**
        feedback loop, **6.32–6.39**
        flow chart, **6.4, 6.6, 6.7**
        general, **6.48–6.49**
        process capability analysis, **16.14–16.35**
        project-by-project improvement, **22.18–22.36**
        quality cost analysis, **4.12–4.14**
        quality manual, **6.40–6.45**
        responsibility matrix, **7.25–7.27**
        road map, **6.5**
        spreadsheet, **6.7–6.9**
        supplier surveys, **15.12–15.18**
    training for quality planners, **6.49–6.50**
        common subject matter, **6.49**
        quality school, **6.50**
        training for clients, **6.50**
        training for suppliers, **6.50**
    transfer to operations, **6.17, 6.18**
    triple-role concept, **6.19–6.20**
    types of quality plan, **6.4**
    who plans for quality?, **6.47–6.48**
        allocation of responsibilities, **6.48**
        future trends, **6.48**
        influence of the scope of the planning, **6.47–6.48**
Companywide quality management (CWQM), **6.23–6.25**
    in assembly industries, **30.4–30.11**
    in complex industries, **31.4–31.9**
    deployment of corporate quality goals, **6.25**
    disadvantages of, **6.24**
    establishing strategic quality goals, **6.24–6.25**
    organization for, **6.26**
    participation by upper management, **8.3, 8.4, 8.10, 8.15, 8.23**
    purposes of, **6.24**
    in small companies, **6.26–6.28**

Companywide quality management (CWQM)
(*Cont.*):
in socialist countries, **35H**.7–**35H**.9
strategic business statements in, **30**.4, **30**.5
training for quality planners, specialized
subject matter, **6**.49, **6**.50
translation into suppliers' language,
6.10–**6**.11
in U.S.A., **35G**.7
upper-management role in, **8**.3, **8**.4, **8**.10,
8.15, **8**.23
Compatibility ratio, **16**.19
Competitive evaluations, **12**.16–**12**.20
Competitor quality:
in assembly industries, **30**.28, **30**.29
assessed through field studies, **12**.16–**12**.20
Compiler (interpreter) for computer, **27**.3
Complaint rate:
effect of time on, **20**.17–**20**.18
effect of unit price on, **20**.17, **20**.18
vs. failure rate, **20**.14–**20**.16, **30**.44
Complaints, **20**.14–**20**.24
action programs, **20**.20–**20**.24
consumer, **34**.11
defined, **20**.14
field, **12**.6, **12**.7
grievances, **34**.2–**34**.3
handling related to repurchase, **20**.18, **20**.19
Japanese practice, **35F**.22
over-reported, **20**.15, **20**.16
predicting level, **20**.25–**20**.27
processing of, **20**.19–**20**.24
product performance and, **20**.16–**20**.18
reports of failures, **30**.44, **30**.45, **31**.16,
31.17
satisfaction relationship, **20**.16–**20**.18
Completely randomized design of experiment,
26.5–**26**.16
(*See also* Design of experiments, completely
randomized design)
Complex industries:
defined, **31**.1
development risks in, **31**.12–**31**.13
failure reporting system, **31**.16–**31**.17
program management in, **31**.11–**31**.19
quality management model, **31**.4–**31**.9
reliability engineering in, **31**.9–**31**.11
transition from development to production,
31.13–**31**.19
value engineering in, **31**.20–**31**.23
Component dominance, **17**.21
Computer-aided design (CAD), **13**.31,
29.8–**29**.9
Computer-aided inspection (CAI),
18.26–**18**.28, **27**.17–**27**.23
Computer-aided manufacturing (CAM),
16.53–**16**.54
Computer applications:
automatic testing, **18**.26, **27**.21–**27**.22

Computer applications (*Cont.*):
design (CAD), **13**.31, **29**.8–**29**.9
data analysis, **17**.17
examples of applications, **27**.13,
27.15–**27**.17
field data analysis, post-production,
27.23–**27**.24
inspection, **18**.26–**18**.28, **27**.17–**27**.23
integration into product design, **27**.25,
27.30–**27**.33
managing projects, **27**.7–**27**.11
in manufacturing, automated, **16**.53–**16**.56
in Monte Carlo simulation, **13**.59
new process quality, **27**.12–**27**.17
new product quality design review, **27**.11,
27.12
process industries, **28**.36
process planning, **27**.13
service industries, **33**.56
statistical analysis, **23**.19, **23**.115, **26**.76,
27.24–**27**.29
table of applications, **27**.34–**27**.35
training, interactive instruction, **11**.27
Computer-integrated manufacturing (CIM),
16.53–**16**.54
Computer programming languages:
ALGOL 68, **14**.15, **14**.16
C, **27**.4
COBOL, **27**.4
FORTRAN, **14**.15, **27**.4
PASCAL, **14**.15, **27**.4
PL/1, **14**.15, **27**.4
Computer programs (*see* Software, computer)
Computer projects, managing:
integrating the effort, **27**.9–**27**.11
measuring progress and performance, **27**.11
organizing project team, **27**.8, **27**.9
planning, **27**.7, **27**.8
Computer simulation and process capability,
16.29
Computer software (*see* Software, computer)
Computer system, **14**.2
capability, **14**.3, **14**.9
complexity, **14**.4, **14**.9
components, **14**.3
defined, **14**.2
differences between hardware and software,
14.4
system size and risk, **14**.22
Computers, types of, **27**.2, **27**.3
Concept of dominance, **6**.16, **16**.50,
17.19–**17**.21
Confidence limits:
basic concept, **23**.46
in control laboratory, **28**.17–**28**.18
defined, **23**.46
example in test precision, **23**.47, **23**.49
formulas and graphs, **23**.48–**23**.49
for fraction defective, chart of, **AII**.28

Confidence limits (*Cont.*):
  for MTBF, **23.49–23.50**
  in regression analysis, 23.107–23.108
  relation to statistical tests of hypotheses,
      23.78–23.80
  sample size required, **23.50**
  for single determinations, **28.17–28.18**
Configuration:
  control, **13.67, 13.68**
  defined, **13.66–13.67**
  management, **13.66–13.70, 20.8**
    configuration identification, **13.67**
    in software development, 14.19, 14.20
Configuration Control Board, 13.68
Conformance:
  decisions, **18.32, 18.33, 18.35**
  judgment of, **18.52**
  quality of, **2.3**
  to requirements, **2.3**
  to specifications, **2.3**
  (*See also* Fitness for use)
Conscious errors, **6.37, 21.15, 22.59–22.61**
Consistency of service, 33.33
Constant failure rate period, **23.81**
Consumer:
  "bill of rights," **34.11**
  complaints, grievances, 34.2–34.4, 34.11
  defined, **18.46, 34.2–34.3**
  education, 34.5, 34.6
  movement, 34.2–34.13
    (*See also* Consumerism)
  perceptions, 34.3
  products, standards for, 34.8–34.10
  reports, **34.7**
  research, in service industries, 33.29–33.31
  and sensory characteristics, 18.46–18.49
  test services, 34.6–34.10
    (*See also* Customer)
Consumerism:
  defined, 34.3
  in France, 35C.8
  general, 34.2–34.13
  in Germany, 35D.5, 35D.6
  in Great Britain, 35E.6
  grievances, 34.3
Consumer's Resource Handbook,
      34.6, 34.17
Consumer's risk, 25.9–25.10
Consumers Union, 3.9, 3.10, 34.6, 34.7
Continuous probability distributions:
  exponential distribution, 23.33
  fitting of mixtures, 23.43
  multinomial, 23.30–23.32
  multinormal distribution, 23.43
  normal distribution, 23.37–23.43
  selecting a continuous distribution,
      23.44–23.45
  uniform distribution, 23.33
  Weibull distribution, 23.34–23.37

Continuous sampling plans, **25.28–25.36**
Contour plot, examples of, 28.13
Contract Representative Service, **15.28**
Contracts:
  sales, **19.6–19.9**
  service, **19.13–19.14, 20.8**
  supply, study of problems in, **6.30**
Control of quality:
  defined, **2.6, 6.31–6.32, 21.14, 24.2**
  formal plan, **15.22**
  planning for, 6.31
  of process, 16.49–16.51, 28.21
  pyramid, **6.33–6.34**
  self- (*see* Self-control)
  stations, **6.34–6.35**
  statistical process, **24.1–24.39**
  statistical quality, 22.11, 24.2–24.7
  subjects, 6.33
  system, in job shop industries, **32.11–32.18**
  universal steps in, 6.31
Control charts:
  adaptive, 24.32
  in administrative and support operations,
      21.14, 21.20, 21.21
  for attributes, **24.20–24.26**
  for average and range, **24.14–24.18**
  basic concepts of, **24.8–24.12**
  chance and assignable causes, 24.3
  confusion when introduced, **17.10, 17.11**
  control limits, 24.9
    average and dispersion, **AII.3–AII.4**
    for *c* charts, **AII.41**
    cumulative sum, **AII.41**
    individuals, **AII.40**
    for *p* charts, **AII.40**
  for cumulative sum, **24.26–24.29**
  for demerits, 24.32
  E_2 factors for, **AII.40**
  estimating the standard deviation, 24.8,
      24.9
  for fraction nonconforming, **24.20–24.22**
  for geometric moving averages, exponen-
      tially smoothed average, 24.32
  for individuals and ranges, **24.18–24.20**
  for maintaining control in the future,
      24.29–24.31
  for median, 24.32
  for moving average and moving range,
      24.32
  noncomformities per unit, **24.23**
  for number nonconforming, **24.22, 24.23**
  operating characteristic curve, **24.10–24.12**
  and process capability, **16.25–16.28**
  for range, **24.14–24.18**
  rational subgrouping, 24.9, 24.10
  special, 24.31, 24.32
  steps in setting up, **24.12–24.14**
  subgroup size, 24.9
  for T^2, 24.32

Control charts (*Cont.*):
  theory, **24.**3
  types of, **24.**13–**24.**32
  uses of, **24.**7, **24.**8
  for variables, **24.**14–**24.**20
  why use averages?, **24.**10
  $\bar{X}$, *R* charts and PRE-Control, **24.**36–**24.**38
Control laboratory, **28.**5, **28.**10–**28.**20
  confidence limits in, **28.**17–**28.**18
  determining test method reliability in,
    28.15–**28.**18
  number of samples to analyze, **28.**18–**28.**19
  test method development in, **28.**11–**28.**15
Control limits, **24.**3, **24.**9
Control stations, **18.**28–**18.**31
Control subjects:
  in assembly industries, **30.**37–**30.**44
  in executive reports, **8.**10, **8.**11
  in feedback loop, **6.**33
  in process industries, **28.**57, **28.**58
  in service industries, **33.**16–**33**18,
    33.31–**33.**35
Controllability, **17.**4
  (*See also* Self-control)
Coordinating Agency for Supplier Evaluation
    (CASE), **15.**13
Coordination of quality function (*see*
    Organizing for quality)
Corporate quality manager, **7.**14–**7.**21
Corporate quality staff, **7.**25, **7.**28–**7.**30
Corrective action:
  in assembly industries, **30.**26–**30.**27
  in job shop industries, **32.**12–**32.**18
  in service industries, **33.**19–**33.**20,
    33.37–**33.**40
Correlation, **22.**48
Correlation analysis (*see* Regression and
    correlation analysis)
Correlation coefficient, **23.**102, **23.**103
Cost of poor quality (quality costs):
  analyzing the categories of, **4.**18
  appraisal costs, **4.**5, **4.**6
  bases for comparison, **4.**24, **4.**25
  categories of, **4.**4–**4.**12, **22.**14
  category cautions, **4.**6, **4.**8
  collecting and summarizing the data, **4.**23,
    4.24, **22.**17
  company costs and user costs, **4.**28
  controversial cost categories, **4.**9
  cost balance different in certain circum-
    stances, **4.**21
  data collection, **4.**12–**4.**14, **4.**23–**4.**25
  defined, **4.**3
  defining the cost of poor quality, **4.**23
  discovering the optimum, **4.**17
  distribution, **4.**26
  evolution, **4.**2–**4.**4
  example, **4.**9, **22.**14
  external failure costs, **4.**5

Cost of poor quality (quality costs) (*Cont.*):
  format, **4.**25, **4.**26
  French experience, **35C.**7
  frequency of reporting, **4.**26
  gaining approval for the quality improve-
    ment program, **4.**17, **22.**14–**22.**18,
    35G.8, **35G.**9
  hidden costs, **4.**11–**4.**12
  hiding the scrap, **4.**14
  input-output analysis, **4.**14
  internal failure costs, **4.**5
  interrelation of categories, **4.**16
  issues concerning, **4.**22
  lessons learned, **4.**2
  making the initial cost study, **4.**12
  matrix, **4.**6, **4.**7
  meanings, **4.**3
  objectives of evaluation, **4.**3
  optimizing with suppliers, **15.**20
  other applications of the quality cost
    concept, **4.**26
  presentation of initial findings to manage-
    ment, **4.**14
  prevention costs, **4.**6
  rare but large cost, **4.**14
  relating the grand total to business
    measures, **4.**15
  reporting the results, **4.**25–**4.**26
  responsibility for publication, **4.**26
  road map for introducing a reporting system,
    4.28
  scoreboard, **4.**22–**4.**26
  sources of data, **4.**13, **4.**14
  special problems encountered in data
    collection, **4.**14
  two languages, **4.**15
  why quality cost programs fail, **4.**27–**4.**28
  zones of quality improvement, **4.**19, **4.**20
Cost effectiveness, **13.**63, **31.**20
Cost-savings opportunity, in quality improve-
    ment, **22.**14–**22.**15
Council, quality, **22.**7
Courses, training (*see* Training)
CPM (critical path method), **14.**19, **22.**41,
    27.11
Critical components list, **13.**28
Critical items, identification of, **16.**6
  Pareto principle in, **22.**19–**22.**22
  project concept in, **22.**18–**22.**26
  (*See also* Pareto analysis)
Critical path method (CPM), **14.**19, **22.**41,
    27.11
Crosby, Philip, Associates, **11.**12
Crossplots (scatter-plots), **23.**10, **23.**11
CSCC (cumulative sum control chart),
    24.26
CSP (*see* Continuous sampling plans)
Cultural resistance to change (*see* Resistance to
    change)

Culture:
   creating responsive corporate, **10.17–10.20**
   defining corporate, **10.17–10.20**
   national, and quality, **35A.1–35A.5**
   on production floor, **17.21–17.23**
   use of questionnaire, **9.20**
Cumulative complaint analysis, **20.24–20.27**
Cumulative data plots, **22.42, 22.44**
Cumulative sum control chart (CSCC),
      24.26–24.29
   tables of factors for, **AII.41**
Cumulative sum sampling plans, **25.39–25.41**
Customer(s):
   defined, **2.2, 2.3, 5.6, 6.4**
   external, **2.2**
   feedback from, **33.0–33.31, 33.34**
   identifying, **6.4, 21.7, 21.9**
   internal, **2.2, 6.4, 35G.8**
   needs, **2.3, 6.6–6.10, 21.9, 21.10**
   satisfaction forms, **33.34**
   and suppliers, contrasting views of, **3.1,
      3.5–3.7**
Customer relations (*see* Customer service)
Customer service:
   complaints, **20.14–20.24**
      (*See also* Complaints; *also* under
         particular industry)
   defined, **20.2**
   field failure, **20.6, 20.24–20.27**
      (*See also* Field failures)
   field performance, **20.30–20.32**
   field service (*see* Field service)
   improving feedback, **20.28–20.30**
   installation, **20.5–20.6**
   packaging, **20.2–20.3**
   policies, **5.10**
   in process industries, **28.41–28.54**
   product recalls, **20.32–20.34**
   storage, **20.4–20.5**
   transportation, **20.3–20.4**

Data analysis:
   descriptive statistics for summarizing,
      23.11–23.21
   dictionary, **14.11**
   historical data, uses and caveats, **23.6–23.8**
   in job shop industries, **32.12**
   from planned experimentation, **23.8, 23.9**
   planning for collection and, **23.3–23.6**
   sources of data, **12.9–12.12, 23.2**
   statistical, **23.1–23.121**
Data banks:
   on business practices, **34.5**
   for consumers, **34.5, 34.6**
   for process control, **28.36**
   on product design experience, **13.72**
   on product performance, **34.4, 34.5**
   for reliability, **13.37, 13.38**
   on suppliers, **15.13**

Data base management system (DBMS), **14.12**
Data dictionary, **14.11**
Data flow diagram (DFD), **14.10**
Datsun's mobile training vehicle, **11.30**
Debugging in software development, **14.18**
Decomposition, hierarchical, **14.10**
Deere and Company, **16.6**
Defect (*see also* Nonconformity):
   vs. defective, **24.20**
   defined, **22.31, 25.4–25.5**
   management-controllable and worker-
      controllable, **17.5–17.6, 18.84–18.94,
      22.40–22.61**
   vs. nonconformity, defined, **25.4–25.5**
   seriousness classification of, **18.41–18.45**
Defect concentration analysis, **22.45, 22.47**
Defect concentration diagram, **22.45, 22.46**
Defense Science Board, **31.13, 31.18**
Deficiency, product, **2.3**
Degrees of freedom, concept of, **23.73**
Delivered product, evaluation of, **15.28–15.32**
Deming Prize, **8.21–8.24, 9.15–9.16, 10.10,
      35F.2**
Demonstration tests in reliability program,
      13.34–13.36
Department activity analysis, **21.4–21.7**
Department of Defense, U.S. (DOD), **3.25,
      31.5, 31.13**
Department of Transportation, U.S. (DOT),
      3.10, 16.28
Deployment of corporate quality goals, **6.25**
Derating, in reliability program, **13.28–13.29**
Design of experiments:
   balanced incomplete block designs,
      26.59–26.62
      concept, **26.54, 26.55**
   classification of designs, completely
      randomized design: description,
      26.6–26.10
      example and analysis, **26.10–26.14**
      general comments, **26.14–26.16**
   concept, **26.29, 26.30**
   definitions, **26.3–26.4**
   developments in, **26.77**
   evolutionary operation (EVOP),
      26.29–26.36
   example and analysis, **26.38–26.54**
   example for chromatography study, **28.14**
   factorial experiments with two factors,
      26.16–26.22
   factorial experiments with *k* factors:
      blocking, **26.36, 26.37**
      detection of wild values, **26.29**
      estimates of variance from past experi-
         ence, **26.43, 26.44**
      example and analysis, **26.22–26.29**
      half-normal plots, **26.29**
      interactions, **26.27–26.28**
      multilevel fractionals, **26.44**

Design of experiments, factorial experiments
  with k factors (*Cont.*):
  offline quality control, **26.44, 26.45**
  screening experimentation, **26.44, 26.45**
  symbols, **26.22–26.23**
  fixed effects and random effects models,
    26.15
  example and analysis with two factors,
    26.17–26.22
  general, **26.16–26.17**
  interactions, **26.16–26.17**
  fractional factorial design: additional
    fractional designs, **26.42–26.45**
  concept, **26.38–26.39**
  example and analysis, **26.39–26.42**
  general remarks on analysis of data: missing
    values, **26.76–26.77**
  remarks on computing, **26.76, 26.77**
  group screening designs, **26.69–26.70**
  Latin square design of experiments,
    26.62–26.63
  mixture designs, **26.66–26.69**
  nested designs, **26.64–26.66**
  randomized block designs, **26.55–26.59**
  example and analysis, **26.56–26.59**
  requisites, **26.4–26.7**
  response surface, **26.30, 26.47–26.48**
  response surface designs, **26.45–26.54**
  weakness of one-variable-at-a-time
    approach, **26.47**
  size of experiment, **26.73–26.76**
  technique, **26.30–26.36**
  tools, **26.4, 26.5**
  Youden square designs, **26.64**
Design assurance, **13.7**
Design experience retention, **13.70, 13.72**
Design of product (*see* Product development)
Design quality index, **13.61**
Design review:
  characteristics in product development,
    13.8–13.10
  in computer applications, **27.11, 27.12**
  computer use in, **27.11, 27.12**
  early warning of problems, **13.7**
  evaluation by use, **30.15, 30.16**
  ingredients for success, **13.10, 13.11**
  for producibility, **16.5, 16.6**
  responsibilities in, **13.8–13.9**
  software development, **14.13, 14.14**
  team membership for, **13.9**
  types of, **13.9**
Design Standards Manual, **13.72**
Design-to-cost (DTC) approach, **13.66**
Designers, **13.7–13.11, 13.70–13.74**
  cultural resistance of, **13.10, 22.66**
  improving effectiveness of, **13.70–13.72**
  training for, **13.72–13.73**
Developing countries, quality in:
  awareness promotion, **35B.16, 35B.18**

Developing countries, quality in (*Cont.*):
  certification, **35B.10–35B.14**
  development phases and, **35B.5–35B.6**
  education and training, **35B.18–35B.22**
  export inspection, **35B.15–35B.17**
  external assistance, **35B.22–35B.23**
  impediments to improvement, **35B.4–35B.5**
  institutional infrastructure, **35B.23**
  national efforts for, **35B.7–35B.24**
  national quality control society, **35B.24**
  standardization, **35B.7–35.9**
  technology in, **35B.3–35B.4**
Development of product (*see* Product
  development)
DFD (data flow diagram), **14.10**
DGQ (Deutsche Gesellschaft für Qualität),
  35D.4, 35D.5
Diagnosis, **22.31–22.61**
  defined, **22.31**
  description of symptoms in, **22.35–22.36**
  diagnostic journey, **22.26**
  dissectable and nondissectable characteris-
    tics, **22.50**
  through experiment, **22.51–22.52**
  formualtion of theories in, **22.36–22.40**
  measurement for, **22.52**
  responsibility for, **22.29–22.31**
  techniques, list of, **22.34**
  test of theories in, **22.40–22.61**
    (*See also* Test of theories)
    (*See also* under Improvement of quality)
Diagnosticians, **22.30**
Digital Equipment Corporation, **27.15**
Dikes, quality, life behind, **3.3–3.4**
Disciplines, quality, defined, **11.3, 11.4**
Discrete probability distributions, **23.26**
  binomial distribution, **23.27–23.28**
    negative, **23.29–23.30**
  discrete uniform distribution, **23.27**
  hypergeometric distribution, **23.28–23.29**
  multinomial distribution, **23.30–23.32**
  negative binomial distribution, **23.29–23.30**
  Poisson distribution, **23.29**
  selecting a discrete distribution, **23.32**
Dispersion, measures of, **23.17, 23.18**
Disposition of nonconforming product,
  18.32–18.33, 18.35–18.36
Dissatisfaction and satisfaction with product,
  12.5
Dissection:
  in administrative and support operations,
    21.19
  piece-to-piece analysis, **22.44**
  for quality improvement, **22.41**
  stream-to-stream analysis, **22.41**
  time-to-time analysis, **22.41–22.44**
  within-piece analysis, **22.44–22.48**
Distribution, processing during, **20.5**
Distribution-free methods, **23.52**

Division quality manager, 7.16–7.18
DOD (U.S. Department of Defense), 3.25,
     31.5, 31.13
Dodge-Romig sampling plans, 25.49–25.51
Dominance:
  component, 16.50, 17.21
  concept of, 6.16, 16.50, 17.19–17.21
  information, 16.50, 17.21
  setup, 16.50, 17.19
  time, 16.50, 17.19–17.20
  worker, 16.50, 17.20
Dominant cause, defined, 22.31
DOT (U.S. Department of Transportation),
     3.10, 16.28
Double sampling plans, 25.23–25.30
Downtime, 2.9, 13.41, 22.42
Drives for quality (see Campaigns for quality)
DTC (design to cost), 13.66
DuPont de Nemours & Co., E. I., 3.4, 9.20

Early warning concept, 13.7
Eastman Kodak Company, 3.11, 13.55, 30.24
Echo-check, 23.117
ECN (engineering change notice), historical
     review of, 22.33
Economic models of quality conformance,
     4.19–4.22
Economics and influences on quality, 3.1–3.29
ECR (error cause removal), 22.22–22.23
Education for quality (see Training)
Effectivity of design change, 13.67
Efficiency, statistical, 23.17
Electronic components industries:
  automated testing of, 29.11
  characteristics of, 29.2
  chip development and manufacture, 29.9
  computer-aided design in, 29.8, 29.9
  design review in, 29.8
  determining what to test, 29.11
  development program, 29.6–29.10
  failure modes, 29.13
  functions of testing, 29.10–29.11
  initial production of, 29.7–29.8
  international certification for, 15.33
  mass production, 29.8
  process design, 29.11–29.13
  process yields, 29.4, 29.5, 29.11
  prognosis, 29.17, 29.18
  quality levels, 29.2–29.4
  quality management in, 29.5–29.8
  reliability, 29.14–29.17
    in manufacturing cycle, 29.17
    prediction for, 29.15–29.17
    program, 29.14, 29.15
  robust process design, 29.11
  testing and inspection, 29.10–29.11, 29.15
Emotional stimuli in advertising, 19.2–19.3
Engineering change notice (ECN), historical
     review of, 22.33

Engineering design, quality in (see Product
     development)
Engineering Index, Inc., 1.4
Engineering Societies Library, 8.17
Environmental stress screening, 13.34,
     31.17–31.19
EOQC (see European Organization for Quality
     Control)
Ergonomics (human engineering), 13.55, 20.7
Error(s):
  in administrative and support operations,
     21.14, 21.15
  human error types and remedies, 21.15
  in inspection (see Inspector errors)
  by inspector (see Inspector errors)
  of instrument, defined, 18.63
  of measurement (see Measurement error)
  rates, in administrative and support
     operations, 21.3
  worker-controllable and noncontrollable,
     17.5–17.6
  by workers, 22.55–22.61
Error cause removal (ECR), 22.22–22.23
Error-proofing:
  error-prone systems, 16.36–16.37
  in inspection planning, 18.14, 18.15
  methods of, 16.35–16.36
European Organization for Quality Control
     (EOQC), 2.4, 2.12, 11.27, 11.36,
     35D.4, 35E.1
Evolutionary operation (EVOP): 16.30,
     26.29–26.36
  background, 26.29–26.30
  design and example, 26.31–26.35
  multiple dependent variables, 26.36
  response surface, 26.30
  (See also Design of experiments, evolution-
     ary operation)
Executive reports (see Reports on quality)
Executive Sciences Institute, Inc., 1.5
Experiment:
  defined, 22.51, 26.2
  design (see Design of experiments)
  rifleshot, 22.51–22.52
  size of, 26.73–26.76
  unbridled, 22.52
Experimental design (see Design of experi-
     ments)
Experimental environment, defined, 26.3
Experimental units, defined, 26.3
Exponential formula for reliability,
     23.82–23.85
Exponential probability distribution:
  formula, 23.33
  in reliability sampling, 25.73, 25.77, 25.79,
     25.81–25.82
  table of, AII.8
Export inspection, developing countries' use of,
     35B.15–35B.16, 35B.17

External failure costs, **4.5**
(*See also* Cost of poor quality)

F distribution, tables of, **AII.21–AII.26**
F' percentiles, tables of, **AII.28**
F test:
  in analysis of variance, **26.11, 26.18**
  defined, **23.68**
  example of, **23.105**
  in regression analysis, **23.104**
  tables of, **AII.21–AII.26**
Facilitator, in quality improvement, **10.46,
    22.28–22.29**
Factor, defined, **26.3**
Factorial design of experiments, **26.16–26.22**
Factorial experiments with *k* factors,
    26.22–26.28
  (*See also* Design of experiments, factorial
    experiments with *k* factors)
Fail-safe designs, **13.54**
Failure costs:
  external, **4.5**
  internal, **4.5**
Failure mode, effect, and criticality analysis
    (FMECA), **13.28–13.30, 13.46**
  in electronic components, **29.13**
  for processes, **16.42–16.44**
Failure-prone designs, **3.20, 13.11**
Failure rate, **13.11, 20.17, 30.44**
  defined, **13.20**
  trends in electronic components, **29.3–29.5**
Failure reporting system, **31.16–31.17**
Fair Packaging and Labeling Act, **19.15**
Fault tree analysis, **13.28–13.30, 13.51–13.53**
Fayol, Henri, **35C.3**
Federal Republic of Germany, quality in,
    35D.1–35D.8
  Ausschuss für Statistische Qualität (ASQ),
    35D.4
  consumers and, **35D.5–35D.7**
  Deutsche Gesellschaft für Qualität (DGQ),
    35D.4–35D.5
  economy and, **35D.1–35D.3**
  government role in, **35D.6, 35D.7**
  guilds and history, **35D.2–35D.3**
  legal aspects, **35D.6–35D.7**
  statistical methods, growth of, **35D.3–35D.4**
  Technische Statistik, TESTA, **35D.4**
  training and education, **35D.5**
Federal Trade Commission, **19.12, 19.15, 34.14**
Feedback:
  criteria, **17.14, 17.15**
  of field data, **27.23, 27.24**
  of inspection data, **18.97–18.98**
  loop (*see* Feeback loop)
  methods, **17.13–17.14**
  of quality data in complex industries,
    30.40–30.45
  related to action, **17.15–17.16**

Feedback (*Cont.*):
  to supervisors, **17.16–17.17**
  timeliness, **17.14**
Feedback loop, **6.32–6.39, 17.13, 21.14**
  in administrative and support operations,
    6.32–6.39, 21.14
  concept, **6.32–6.39, 30.40–30.45**
  in production, **17.12–17.18**
Field data, computer analysis of, **27.23, 27.24**
Field failures:
  analysis of data on, **20.24–20.27**
  in customer service, **20.6–20.8**
  factory rejects and, **20.19**
  human error in, **20.6–20.8**
  reporting of, in assembly industries,
    30.41–30.45
  user cost model, **20.31–20.32**
Field intelligence:
  analysis of available, **12.5–12.8**
    data from customers, **12.7–12.8**
    decline in sales, **12.5**
    field complaints, **12.6**
    government reports, **12.8**
    independent laboratories, **12.8**
    sale of spare parts, **12.7**
    salesperson's reports, **12.6**
  in assembly industries, **30.40–30.45**
  competitive evaluations, **12.16–12.20**
  consumer reports, **34.7**
  customer perception of service quality, **20.9**
  data sources, **12.9–12.12**
  defined, **12.2**
  discovering marketing opportunities,
    12.20–12.24
  feedback on performance of current
    products, **12.2–12.5**
  field failure reports (*see* Field failures)
  needs and sources, **12.2, 12.3**
  organization for, **12.8–12.12**
  in process industries, **28.7**
  tools for, **12.12–12.16**
Field performance, **20.24**
  complaint significance in, **12.2, 12.4, 20.16**
  computer analysis of data, **27.23, 27.24**
  executive reports, **20.30–20.32**
  improving feedback, **20.28–20.30**
  measures of, **20.30–30.31**
  (*See also* Field failures)
Field performance measures:
  basic approach, **20.24–20.27**
  basic data analyses, **20.24–20.27**
  basic data sources, **12.2–12.8, 12.9–12.12**
  complaint analysis report, role in, **12.2,
    12.4, 20.16–20.18, 20.30**
  service report role in, **12.11–12.12**
Field service, **20.8–20.14**
  for assembly industry products, **30.34–30.36**
  consumer products, **20.9**
  customer perception of service quality, **20.9**

Field service (*Cont.*):
  design for maintainability, **13.46–13.48**
  improvement in, **20.13–20.14**
    assuming adequacy of, **20.13**
  maintenance: assuming adequacy of, **20.13**
    training and, **20.11–20.12**
  scheduled servicing, **20.10–20.11**
  service shops, **20.9**
  unscheduled servicing, **20.11**
Figures of merit:
  in maintainability, **13.44**
  in reliability, **13.20**
Finance, analogy to quality management, **2.5–2.6**
Finance function, quality in, **21.4, 21.5, 21.16**
Finished goods inspection (*see* Inspection and
    test)
Fishbone diagram, **21.17, 21.18, 22.37–22.39**
Fitness for use, **2.8, 2.11**
  activities needed, **2.11, 2.12**
  characteristics in, **2.8**
  defined, **2.8**
  and environment, **35F.19**
  judgment of, **18.31–18.38**
  user knowledge of, **3.8, 3.9**
  (*See also* Conformance)
FITS, **29.15–29.17**
Flexible manufacturing system (FMS), **16.55,
    16.56**
Florida Power and Light Company, **8.16, 10.43**
Flow diagrams (flow charts), **6.6, 6.7, 13.16,
    13.17, 22.41, 28.45**
  administrative and support operations, **21.8**
  for assembly industry control, **30.3**
  for calibration control, **18.77**
  for data, **14.10**
  for quality planning, **6.4, 6.6, 6.7**
  symbols for, **6.4, 6.7**
FMECA (Failure mode, effect, and criticality
    analysis), **13.28–13.30, 13.46,
    16.42–16.44**
FMS (flexible manufacturing system), **16.55,
    16.56**
Focus groups, **12.15, 12.16**
Food industries (*see* Process industries)
Foolproofing (*see* Error-proofing)
Force field analysis, **22.39**
Ford Motor Company, **3.4, 6.12, 10.22, 15.9,
    15.22, 16.24, 16.33, 16.42, 24.14,
    30.15**
  formal control plan, **15.22**
Formal experiments, **22.51**
  (*See also* Design of experiments)
FORTRAN (programming language), **14.15,
    27.4**
"Forward and backward quality," **35F.19**
Fractional factorial design of experiment,
    26.38–26.42
  (*See also* Design of experiments, fractional
    factorial designs)

France, quality in, **35C.1–35C.9**
  AFCIQ, **35C.7–35C.8**
  Centre National d'Etudes des Telecommuni-
    cations, **29.16**
  consumerism, **35C.8**
  education and, **35C.4–35C.6**
  government agencies, **35C.8–35C.9**
  history, **35C.1–35C.4**
  quality control since 1970, **35C.6–35C.7**
  Surveillance Industrielle de l'Armement
    (SIAR), **35C.7**
Frequency histogram (distribution) (*see*
    Histogram)
Function of product:
  assumed, **13.64–13.65**
  basic, **13.64–13.65**
  secondary, **13.64–13.65**
Function analysis system technique (FAST),
    13.65
Functional and nonfunctional characteristics,
    13.62
Functional requirements, **13.13–13.17**

Gage:
  fixed-limit, **18.69, 18.70**
  variables, **18.70**
General Dynamics Corporation, **8.15, 8.19**
General Electric Company, **11.17, 12.17**
General Foods Corporation, **19.16**
General Motors Corporation, **10.22, 21.17,
    21.18**
Generalized lambda distribution (GLD) family,
    23.44
Germany, quality in (*see* Federal Republic of
    Germany, quality in)
GIDEP (Government Industry Data Exchange
    Program), **13.38, 15.13**
Glossary:
  in analysis of symptoms, **22.35**
  EOQC, **2.4, 2.12**
  of symbols, **AI.1–AI.11**
  of terminology, quality systems,
    AIV.1–AIV.3
  (*See also* Terminology)
GMP (good manufacturing practices), **16.14**
Goals for quality (*see* Objectives for quality)
"Gold in the mine" (*see* Cost savings
    opportunity)
Good manufacturing practices (GMP),
    16.14
Goodness of fit test (of data to distribution),
    23.72
Gosstandart USSR, **35H.2**
Government Industry Data Exchange Program
    (GIDEP), **13.38, 15.13**
Government regulation:
  of advertising, **19.4**
  of quality, **34.18–34.19**
  of warranties, **19.12**

Government role in quality:
Federal Republic of Germany, **35D.6, 35D.7**
France, **35C.8–35C.9**
Great Britain, **35E.3–35E.5**
socialist countries, **35H.2–35H.4**
Grade of quality, **19.15**
in Czechoslovakia, **35H.6**
defined, **2.3**
(*See also* Certification; Marks for quality)
Grand lot schemes in acceptance sampling, **25.58**
Great Britain, quality in, **35E.1–35E.7**
attitudes and influences, **35E.2–35E.6**
British Standards Institution (BSI), **35E.5**
directory of quality assurance consultants in the U.K., **35E.4**
European Organization for Quality Control (EOQC), **35E.1**
government activities, **35E.3–35E.5**
Institute of Quality Assurance (IQA), **35E.4**
terminology in, **35E.1–35E.2**
Grid, in job shop industries. **32.4–32.5**
Group screening, design of experiments, **26.69–26.70**
Group technology, **16.54–16.55**
Guarantee (*see* Warranty of quality)

H108, reliability sampling plan, **25.73– 25.79**
Harley-Davidson Company, **11.20**
Harris Tweed Association, **19.17**
Hartford Steam Boiler Inspection and Insurance Company, **6.29**
Hawthorne plant, AT&T, **10.4, 10.13**
Hazard:
analysis, **13.51**
frequency, **13.50**
severity, **13.50**
Health and safety regulation (*see* Safety and health regulation)
Hewlett-Packard Company, **27.26**
Hidden costs of poor quality, **4.11, 4.12**
Hiding the scrap, **4.14**
Hierarchical decomposition, **14.10**
Hierarchy:
of human needs, **10.4–10.5**
of motivational needs, **10.5**
Histogram, **16.15, 16.16, 23.12–23.15**
in administrative and support operations, **21.18, 21.19**
perception of, **23.12–23.15**
use on supplier data, **15.30**
Historical review:
lessons learned, **6.28–6.30, 16.47, 16.48, 31.19, 31.20**
in quality improvement, **22.32, 22.33**
Homogeneous, in bulk sampling, defined, **25.89**

"Hoshin kanri," **35F.12**
Hospital medication errors, **33.56–33.64**
causes of, **33.60**
controllability of, **33.62**
procedures and system revision, **33.64**
Household appliances, **30.35**
How to find it (in this handbook), **1.3–1.5**
(*See also Quality Control Handbook*)
Hughes Aircraft Company, **31.5, 31.23**
Human engineering (ergonomics), **13.55**
Human errors:
in administrative and support operations, **21.14, 21.15**
in inspection. **18.84–18.97**
(*See also* Inspector errors)
in measurement, **6.36, 6.37**
worker-controllable, **17.5, 17.6, 22.53–22.61**
(*See also* Test of theories, worker-controllable problems)
Human factors, **13.55**
Human performance, managing:
American human resource practices and, **10.12–10.16**
in assembly industries, **30.4–30.11**
behavioral scientists' theories, **10.4–10.8**
consensus decision making, Japan, **10.10, 10.18–10.19**
consequences of positive and negative behavior, **10.33–10.36**
deficiencies in motivation management, **10.31–10.33**
employee orientation brochure, **33.41**
Hawthorne effect in, **10.30**
hierarchy of human needs in, **10.5**
hygiene factors in, **10.5**
Japanese and American human resource practices compared, **10.7–10.16**
Japanese human resource practices and, **10.7–10.12**
through job change, **10.37–10.41**
through job design, **10.37–10.41**
through job enlargement, **10.37–10.39**
through job enrichment, **10.37–10.40**
in job shop industries, **32.29**
management's role in, **10.16–10.21**
motivators in, **10.5**
in process industries, **28.36–28.37**
punishment of negative behavior, **10.33, 10.34**
through quality campaigns, **10.48–10.55**
(*See also* Campaigns for quality)
quality circles and, **10.9, 10.10, 10.45–10.48, 10.61**
recruitment role in, **10.16–10.21**
reinforcement of positive behavior, **10.19–10.20**
self-control and, **10.27–10.31**
in Japan, **10.10, 10.11**

Human performance, managing, self-control
and (*Cont.*):
  in processing systems, **10.28–10.30**
 in service industries, **33.22–33.23**
 social and cultural controls in Japan, **10.11**
 Socialist countries, **35H.9–35H.11**
 Taylor system of, **5.10, 10.3, 10.4, 10.27,
  10.37**
 teamwork and, **10.41–10.48**
 theories of, **10.4–10.7**
 theory X and theory Y, **10.5–10.7**
 training role in, **10.21–10.23**
 in U.S. operations of Japanese companies,
  10.12
 worker education and, **10.17**
 through worker participation in process
  management, **10.25–10.31**
 worker self-control and, **10.27–10.31**
Human resources:
 American practices transplanted from Japan,
  10.14–10.16
 management for quality, **10.1–10.61,
  11.1–11.39**
 practices: American, **10.14–10.16**
  Japanese, **10.7–10.12**
 (*See also* Human performance, managing)
Hygiene factors and motivation, **10.5**
Hypergeometric distribution, **23.28–23.29**
Hypotheses, tests of, **23.60–23.72**
 basic concepts, **23.60–23.63**
 determining sample size required, **23.78**
 drawing conclusions, **23.76–23.77**
 operating characteristic curve, use of,
  23.63–23.64
 relation to confidence intervals, **23.78–23.80**
 sample size fixed in advance, **23.64–23.76**
 statistical significance vs. practical
  significance, **23.80, 23.81**
 summary of common tests, **23.65–23.72**
Hypothesis, defined, **23.60**

IBM (*see* International Business Machines
  Corporation)
Identification of critical items, **16.6**
Import control, **35G.6**
Improvement of quality:
 in administrative and support operations,
  21.15–21.21
 alternate approaches to, **22.11, 22.12**
  exhortation, **22.11–22.12**
  quality circles, **22.11, 22.28**
  statistical quality control, **22.11**
 in assembly industries, **30.47, 30.48**
 benefits of, **22.3**
 British practice in, **35E.5**
 in chemical industries, **28.30–28.35**
 for chronic problems, **22.2, 22.5–22.6**
 control at new level in, **22.68–22.72**
 council, **22.7**

Improvement of quality (*Cont.*):
 defined, **22.2**
 development of remedies in, **22.61–22.64**
 diagnosis role in, **22.29–22.31**
 diagnostic journey in, **22.31–22.61**
  description of symptoms in, **22.35, 22.36**
  formulation of theories in, **22.36–22.40**
  test of theories, **22.40–22.61**
   (*See also* Test of theories)
 vs. fire fighting, **22.3, 22.5**
 fundamentals, **35G.9**
 in job shop industries, **32.19–32.26**
 in metals industries, **28.39–28.44**
 mission statement, **22.7, 22.8**
 obstacles to achieving, **22.4, 22.5**
 organizing for projects, **22.26, 22.31**
 Pareto concept, **22.19–22.22**
 phased approach for, **22.6–22.11**
 vs. prior improvement programs, **22.5, 22.6**
 project nominations in (*see* Project
  nominations)
 project organization in (*see* Project team
  organization)
 proof of need in (*see* Proof of need)
 proof of remedies in, **22.65**
 resistance to change in, **22.65–22.68**
 role of facilitator, **22.29**
 screening projects, **22.23–22.26**
 in service industries, **32.20, 32.21**
 sporadic vs. chronic problems, **22.5, 22.6**
 strategies attempted in U.S.A., **35G.6,
  35G.7**
 in supplier relations, **15.34–15.37**
 universal sequence for, **22.13–22.72**
Inadvertent errors, **18.86–18.89, 22.55–22.56**
Incentives for quality:
 in reliability contracts, **19.7**
 in sales contracts, **19.7**
 under Saratov system, **35H.10–35H.11**
 (*See also* Human performance, managing)
Income, quality and, **3.1–3.32**
 customer and supplier views, **3.1, 3.5–3.7**
 economic influence, **3.2–3.5**
 life cycle costing, **3.20–3.27**
  (*See also* Life cycle costing)
 perfectionism, **3.27–3.29**
  (*See also* Perfectionism)
 price and quality, **3.9–3.12, 35H.7**
 share of market, **3.12–3.17**
 strategy for quality, **3.17–3.20**
  (*See also* Companywide planning for
   quality)
 user knowledge, **3.7–3.9**
Incoming inspection, **15.29–15.32, 18.29**
Increment in bulk sampling, defined, **25.85**
India, National Productivity Council, **35B.23**
Indifference zone in quality costs, **4.20**
Indirect personnel, role of, in quality effort,
 21.1

Industry in changing world, **35B**.3
Infant mortality period in product reliability, **23**.81
Information dominance, **17**.21
Input-process-output (IPO) technique, **14**.11
Inspection and test, **18**.1–**18**.121
  automated, **18**.26–**18**.28, **22**.63
  budgeting for (see Budgeting for inspection and test)
  calibration in (see Calibration control)
  communication decision, **18**.17–**18**.19
  computer use in, **27**.17–**27**.23
  conformance decision, **18**.17–**18**.18
  criteria for judging conformance, **18**.20–**18**.23
  defined, **18**.4
  disposition of unfit product, **18**.36–**18**.37
  in electronic components industries, **29**.10–**29**.11
  feedback of inspection data, **18**.97–**18**.98
  finished goods inspection, **18**.31
  fitness-for-use decision, **18**.17–**18**.18
  how much inspection?, **18**.21–**18**.28
  human factors in, **18**.81–**18**.97
  incoming inspection, **15**.29–**15**.32, **18**.29
  at inspection stations, **18**.28–**18**.31
  inspector errors (see Inspector errors)
  judgment of fitness for use, **18**.31–**18**.38
  lots, nature of, **18**.20–**18**.23
  management of, **18**.105–**18**.107
  manuals, **18**.15–**18**.17
  measurement (see Measurement; Measurement error)
  measurement standards in (see Measurement standards)
  organization for (see Organization for inspection and test)
  patrol inspection, **18**.29–**18**.30
  personnel management, **18**.107–**18**.108
  physical control of product in, **18**.37–**18**.38
  planning (see Inspection planning)
  process inspection, **18**.29
  product, nature of, **18**.19
  product conformance, **18**.19–**18**.21
  by production departments, **18**.106–**18**.107
  productivity in, **18**.108
  purposes of, **18**.5–**18**.6
  sensory qualities, **18**.45–**18**.57
    (See also Sensory qualities; Sensory testing)
  seriousness classification of defects, **18**.39–**18**.45
  setup inspection, **18**.29
  standards, quality, **18**.38–**18**.45
  three decisions in, **18**.17
  tollgate inspection, **18**.31
  variables influencing inspector behavior, **18**.82

Inspection and test (Cont.):
  of visual characteristics (see Visual quality characteristics)
  (See also Measurement)
Inspection and test methods and requirements, selected documents, **AIII**.10–**AIII**.12
Inspection design for incoming product, **15**.29–**15**.32
Inspection level in MIL-STD-105D, **25**.44, **25**.47
Inspection manual, **18**.15–**18**.17
  (See also Manuals, quality)
Inspection planning, **18**.7–**18**.15
  errorproofing in, **18**.14, **18**.15
  extent of, **18**.14
  for finished goods acceptance, **18**.10
  flow diagram in, **18**.8, **18**.9
  foolproofing in, **18**.14, **18**.15
  for inspection data, **18**.11
  for inspection stations, **18**.8
  interpretation of specification, **18**.9, **18**.10
  list of characteristics, **18**.9
  human-machine relationship in, **18**.15, **18**.16
  for nonproduction operations, **18**.11
  overplanning in, **18**.15
  of patrol beat, **18**.10, **18**.12, **18**.13
  recognition of profound changes as need in, **18**.14
  of test procedure, **18**.10
  three decisions in, **18**.17
  who does?, **18**.7
  written inspection instructions in, **18**.10
Inspection stations:
  list of characteristics, **18**.9
  planning of, **18**.8
Inspector accuracy, measure of, **18**.94–**18**.97
Inspector errors, **18**.84–**18**.97
  categories of, **18**.84
  conscious, **18**.90–**18**.94
  due to flinching, **18**.92–**18**.94
  inadvertent, **18**.86–**18**.89
  due to inspector fraud, **18**.91–**18**.92
  due to inspector shortcuts, **18**.92
  management initiated, **18**.90, **18**.91, **18**.94
  measuring inspector accuracy, **18**.94–**18**.97
  methods for identifying, **18**.84, **18**.85, **18**.93–**18**.97
  procedural, **18**.89–**18**.90
  quantitative extent of, **18**.86, **18**.87
  remedies for, **18**.83, **18**.85–**18**.90
  due to rounding off, **18**.94
  due to technique, **18**.84–**18**.85
Installation of product (assembly and setup), **20**.5–**20**.6
Institute of Quality Assurance (IQA), **11**.27
Instructional technology:
  audiovisual systems, **11**.27
  bibliography, **11**.25–**11**.27
  computer interactive instruction, **11**.27

Instructional technology (*Cont.*):
  facilities, **11.**30
  homestudy instruction, **11.**28
  journals, **11.**26
  teaching aids, **11.**28–**11.**30
  textbooks, **11.**25–**11.**26
  training films, **11.**27–**11.**28
Instrument Society of America, **14.**15
Insurance industry, quality in, **33.**49–**33.**57
Insurance policy writers, error analysis,
    33.50–**33.**52
Interacting dimensions, simulation of, **13.**59
Interaction in design of experiments:
  and block designs, **26.**54
  defined, **26.**16–**26.**17
  in factorial experiments, **26.**27–**26.**28
  and Latin square designs, **26.**63
Interlaboratory tests, **18.**69
  design of experiment, **26.**70–**26.**73
Internal customers, **6.**4, **35G.**8
Internal failure costs, **4.**5
  (*See also* Cost of poor quality)
International Bureau for Weights and
    Measures, **18.**70
International Business Machines Corporation
    (IBM), **11.**9, **11.**14, **11.**15, **11.**36,
    14.11, **21.**12, **24.**4, **30.**8
International collaboration, **35A.**4
International Paper Company, **21.**7
International Trade Center, **35B.**16
Interrelation of variables, **22.**47
Interrelationship diagraph, **22.**40
"Is doing," knowledge of, **10.**29–**10.**30,
    17.12–**17.**18, **33.**62
  (*See also* Self-control)
Ishikawa (cause-and-effect) diagram, **21.**17,
    21.18, **22.**37–**22.**39

Japan, quality in, **35F.**1–**35F.**30
  companywide quality control: audit by top
      management, **35F.**15–**35F.**18
    defined, **35F.**8
    education and training in, **35F.**9–**35F.**11
    and Japanese origins, **35F.**15–**35F.**18
    policy control, **35F.**12–**35F.**15
    practices, **35F.**8–**35F.**18
    self-control in, **35F.**11–**35F.**12
  complaint information, **35F.**22
  cultural environment, **35F.**7, **35F.**8
  customer information, **35F.**22
  history, **35F.**1–**35F.**8
  new-product development, **35F.**23–**35F.**29
  practices, **35F.**8–**35F.**18
  quality assurance, **35F.**18–**35F.**22
    suppliers and, **35F.**20
  western influences, **10.**8–**10.**9
Japan External Trade Organization (JETO),
    10.12
Japan Industrial Standards (JIS), **34.**8

Japanese human resource management
    practices, **10.**7–**10.**12
  consensus decision making, **10.**10–**10.**11
  economic influences on workers, **10.**11
  education and training influences, **10.**11
  project teams, **10.**10
  quality circles, **10.**9–**10.**10
  social and cultural influences on workers,
      10.11
  western influences, **10.**8–**10.**9
Japanese practices relating to quality,
    35F.8–**35F.**18
  (*See also* Japan, quality in, companywide
      quality control)
Japanese Union of Scientists and Engineers
    (JUSE), **10.**47, **11.**35, **35B.**19, **35F.**2,
    35F.4, **35F.**5
Job design, **10.**37–**10.**41
Job enlargement, **10.**37–**10.**39
Job enrichment, **10.**37
Job shop industries, **32.**1–**32.**31
  control of quality in, **32.**5–**32.**6,
      32.11–**32.**18
  control system for, **32.**11–**32.**18
  corrective action for, **32.**12–**32.**18
  current job approach and, **32.**12–**32.**15
  data feedback in, **32.**12
  definition of job shop, **32.**1–**32.**4
  effect of factory organization, **32.**28,
      32.29
  grid, **32.**4, **32.**5
  impact of advances in metalworking
      technology, **32.**18–**32.**19
  job numerics in, **32.**6–**32.**8
  job planning for, **32.**8–**32.**11, **32.**19
  jobs per worker per week, **32.**3–**32.**4
  memory systems for, **32.**15–**32.**18
  parameters of, **32.**2
  percent repeat jobs in, **32.**3
  pilot lot use in, **32.**14–**32.**15
  planning for, **32.**8–**32.**11, **32.**28
  quality improvement in, **32.**19–**32.**26
    chronic offenders approach, **32.**20–**32.**22
    common cause analysis, **32.**26
    diagnostic techniques for, **32.**26
    non-job approach to, **32.**22–**32.**26
    Pareto analysis for, **32.**20–**32.**26
    product family approach in, **32.**22
    project identification in, **32.**20
    remedies in, **32.**27–**32.**29
  quality planning in, **32.**8–**32.**11, **32.**28
    detecting job planning errors,
        32.10–**32.**11
    improving job planning, **32.**11
    organizing for job planning, **32.**8–**32.**10
  quotation review and quality, **32.**28
  remedies for quality problems in,
      32.27–**32.**29
  repeat job approach in, **32.**15, **32.**16

Job shop industries (*Cont.*):
    setup dominance in, 32.29–32.30
    small job shop, 32.29–32.30
    suppliers, multiple vs. single source, 32.29
    types of, 32.2
    worker motivation in, 32.29
Johnson & Johnson Co., 5.8
Joint Industry-Consumer Complaint Board, 34.11
Joint ventures, 35G.6
Jones & Lamson Machine Co., 24.4
Jones and Laughlin Co., 16.9, 16.46
Judgment of fitness for use, 18.31–18.38
    decision making in, 18.32
    delegation of decisions, 18.33
    effect of multiple usage, 18.35–18.36
    material review board for, 18.32–18.33
Juran Institute, Inc., 11.17, 11.21
Juran Trilogy, 2.7–2.8
JUSE (*see* Japanese Union of Scientists and Engineers)

Knack of worker, 22.57–22.58
Kolmogorov-Smirnov test, 23.72
Komatsu Ltd., 8.21
Kyushu University, 27.28

Label:
    brand, 19.15–19.17
    certification, 19.17–19.18
    product, 19.14–19.15
Labor unions and quality, 10.21–10.23
Laboratories, management of, 18.105–18.106
    test, consumer-financed, 34.7
Lagging and leading indicators, 8.11, 8.12
Languages of quality, 4.15
Latin square experimental designs, 26.62-26.63
Leadership in quality, as strategy, 3.17–3.20
Leading and lagging indicators, 8.11, 8.12
Learning curve, 13.12
Least squares estimates in regression analysis, 23.101–23.103
Legal problems:
    German, 35D.6, 35D.7
    product liability, 34.19–34.22
    suppliers and, 15.43
Lessons-learned concept, 6.28, 34.1
    in complex industries, 31.19, 31.20
    in manufacturing planning, 16.47, 16.48
    in planning for quality, 6.28–6.30
    (*See also* Historical review)
Level in design of experiments, 26.3
Level version, defined, 26.3
Licensing of production workers, 21.12
Life:
    operating, 23.85
    service, 23.85

"Life behind the quality dikes," 3.3, 3.4, 34.2
Life cycle costing 3.20–3.27
    application of: to consumer products, 3.23
        to defense industries, 3.25
        to industrial products, 3.25
    breadth of application, 3.22
    contracts based on amount of use, 3.26
    cultural resistance, 3.26
    in product development, 13.66
Life testing and reliability sampling plans:
    introduction to plans, 25.68
    summary of plans, 25.80
    (*See also* Reliability)
Lighting for inspection, 18.50–18.51
Lima target, 35B.2–35B.3
Limiting quality (LQ) sampling plans, 25.41
Limits, distinction among, 23.55, 23.56
Little q, 35G.8
Lloyd's Register of Shipping, 9.21
Location parameter in Weibull distribution, 23.34–23.35
Lot:
    in bulk sampling, defined, 25.85
    formation in acceptance sampling, 25.19–25.20
    identification and traceability, 15.23
Lot plot sampling plan, 25.58–25.61
Lot tolerance percent defective (LTPD):
    in Dodge-Romig plans, 25.49, 25.50
    in selecting sampling plans, 25.9
LTPD (*see* Lot tolerance percent defective)

MACAP (Major Appliance Consumer Action Panel), 20.21, 34.11
Magnuson-Moss Warranty Act of 1974, 19.12
Maintainability:
    concepts and terms, 2.10, 2.11, 13.41
    data systems, 13.48
    defined, 2.10–2.11, 13.40–13.41
    demonstration, 13.48
    design aids, 13.46, 13.48
    figures of merit, 13.44
    measurement of, 13.46
    modeling and allocation, 13.43–13.44
    in new-product design, 13.41–13.48
    prediction, 13.44–13.47
    program, 13.43
    requirements for, 13.43–13.44
Maintenance:
    in field, 20.10–20.13
    reliability-centered, 20.11
Major Appliance Consumer Action Panel (MACAP), 34.11
Management:
    defined, 2.11
    earning support of, 33.22–33.23
    role in motivation, 10.16–10.21

Management-controllable and worker-
  controllable defects, **17.5–17.6,
  18.84–18**.94, **22.40–22.61**
Management, role of upper (*see* Upper
  management)
Mandatory tolerances, **17.9–17.10**
Manuals, quality, **6.40–6.45**
  contents of, **6.41–6.43**
  distribution of, **6.43–6.44**
  evolution of, **6.40–6.41**
  limitations as predictors of good quality,
    6.44–6.45
  provision for audit, **6.44**
  terminology, **6.40**
Manufacturability (producibility), **2.11**
  planning for, in assembly industries, **30.15,
    30**.17, **30.18**
  planning for, in product development,
    13.55–13.62
Manufacturing planning:
  in assembly industries, **30.17–30.18**
  and automated manufacturing, **16.53–16.56**
  checklist for review, **16.44–16.45**
  classification of characteristics in, **16.6–16.8**
  component dominance in, **16.50**
  computer use in, **27.12–27.17**
  corporate quality manager, **7.18–7.21**
  defined, **16.2**
  design of manufacturing process, **28.7–28.9**
  design review in, **16.5, 16.6**
  dominance concept in, **16.50**
  equipment and methods, **16.37, 16.38**
  error-proofing, **16.35–16.37**
  for evaluation of product, **16.52**
  experimental lots in, **16.42**
  importance of, **16.3**
  information equipment, **16.52**
  initial planning for, **16.9–16.14**
  for material, **16.38–16.40**
  overall review of, **16.41–16.48**
  policies, **5.9**
  for personnel requirements, **16.38**
  process capability, **16.14–16.35**
    (*See also* Process capability)
  of process controls, **16.48–16.51**
  of process environment, **16.40, 16.41**
  relative importance of characteristics,
    16.6–16.8
  responsibility for, **16.3–16.5**
  role of quality assurance, **16.45–16.46**
  seriousness classification in, **13.61,
    18.38–18.45**
    (*See also* Production)
Mark for quality, **34.7, 34.8–34.9, 35B**.15,
  35D.6
    (*See also* Grade of quality)
Market quality information:
  from alarm signals, **12.2, 12.4**
  analysis of, **12.5–12.8**

Market quality information (*Cont.*):
  from customers' data, **12.7–12.8**
  from decline in sales, **12.5**
  from field troubles, **12.6**
  from government reports, **12.8**
  from independent laboratories, **12.8**
  from salesperson's reports, **12.6–12.7**
  sources of, **12.2, 12.3**
  from spare parts sales, **12.7**
    (*See also* Customer; Field intelligence)
Market research in quality:
  organization for, **12.8–12.12**
  planning for, **12.9**
  tools for, **12.12–12.16**
    (*See also* Customer; Field intelligence)
Market share:
  and consumer preference, **3.15–3.17**
  and quality, **3.12–3.18**
Marketing:
  advertising of quality, **19.2–19.6**
  department, **19.7, 19.8**
  feedback, in service industries,
    33.28–33.31, 33.34
  labeling, **19.14–19.18**
  opportunities, discovering, **12.20–12.24**
  policies, **5.10**
  research, **12.2**
  warranty of quality, **19.8–19.14**
    (*See also* Warranty of quality)
Martin Marietta Corp., **16.8**
Massachusetts Institute of Technology, **27.26,
  27.29**
Material Review Board (MRB), **18.32–18.33**
Materials review, **18.31–18.38**
Matrix organizations, **7.23**
Mean:
  arithmetic, **23.16**
  in bulk sampling, defined, **25.86**
  calculation of, **23.16–23.18**
  chart of sample sizes for, **AII.33**
  control chart for, **24.14–24.18**
  estimating, **24.8**
  in experimental design, defined, **26.11**
  extreme, percentiles, table of, **AII.31**
  in variables sampling, **25.51**
Mean time between failures (MTBF), **2.9,
  13**.41, **23.85, 23.86**
Mean time to repair (MTTR), **2.9, 2.10, 13.41**
Measurement:
  of additional properties, **22.50, 22.51**
  in administrative and support operations,
    21.10, **21.11**
  calibration control for, **18.76–18.81**
  defined, **18.57**
  for diagnosis, **22.52, 22.53**
  error of (*see* Measurement error)
  following noncontrolled operations, **22.50**
  in hospital medication, **33.60, 33.61**
  by inspectors, **17.13–17.16**

Measurement (*Cont.*):
  interlaboratory comparisons, **18**.69
  at intermediate stages of a process, **22**.50
  of length, **18**.69, **18**.70
    electronic, **18**.70
    with fixed-limit gages, **18**.69–**18**.70
    mechanical, **18**.69, **18**.70
    optical, **18**.70
    pneumatic, **18**.70
  metrication, **18**.58–**18**.60
  new functions associated with, **18**.71, **18**.76
  by nondestructive testing, **18**.71–**18**.75
  of nonmeasurable characteristics, **18**.60
  in planning for quality, **6**.11
  precision statements for, **18**.67, **18**.68
  of process capability, **16**.25–**16**.30
  for sensory qualities, **18**.56, **18**.57
  SI system of units, **18**.58–**18**.60
  standards (*see* Measurement standards)
  technology of, **18**.69, **18**.70
  units of measure, **18**.58–**18**.60
  by workers, **17**.12–**17**.13
Measurement error, **18**.63–**18**.69
  accuracy of instrument, **18**.63–**18**.64
  between-laboratories variation, **18**.65
  between-operator variation, **18**.65
  composite, **18**.66–**18**.67
  interlaboratory comparisons, **18**.69
  precision of instrument, **18**.64–**18**.65
  reduction of, **18**.68–**18**.69
  sources of, **18**.65
  statement of, **18**.67, **18**.68
  test equipment variation, **18**.65
  test materials variation, **18**.65
  test procedure variation, **18**.65
  within-operator variation, **18**.65
Measurement standards:
  hierarchy of, **18**.61–**18**.63
  primary reference standards, **18**.60–**18**.61
  transfer standards, **18**.62, **18**.63
  working standards, **18**.62, **18**.63
Median, defined, **23**.17, **23**.20
Median ranks, table of, **AII**.9
Mediation, **34**.11–**34**.12
Medication errors (*see* Hospital medication errors)
Memory systems:
  for inspection, **18**.26–**18**.28
  for job numerics, **32**.6–**32**.8
  for job shop manufacture, **32**.15–**32**.18
  (*See also* Computer applications)
Merchant, quality activities by, **19**.18
Metals industry, **28**.38–**28**.63
  customer relations in, **28**.41–**28**.44
  measures of quality performance in, **28**.57–**28**.58
  process controls in, **28**.47–**28**.52
  product planning, **28**.39–**28**.44
  project identification in, **28**.53–**28**.55

Metals industry (*Cont.*):
  quality improvement in, **28**.52–**28**.57
  quality problems in, **28**.58–**28**.59
  raw materials controls in, **28**.47
  special problems of, **28**.55–**28**.57
  (*See also* Process industries)
Metrication, **18**.58–**18**.60
Metrology, **18**.103
  Great Britain, practice in, **35E**.5–**35E**.6
Microprocessors, **13**.54, **27**.3
Midrange, **23**.20
MIL-HDBK-189, *reliability, growth*, **13**.40
MIL-HDBK-217D, *reliability*, **13**.26
MIL-I-45208A, *Inspection Systems Requirements*, **6**.46
MIL-Q-9858A, *Quality Program Requirements*, **6**.45, **6**.46, **15**.9
MIL-S-19500, failure rates of transistors, **13**.26
MIL-STD-105D, sampling plans, basic description, **25**.44–**25**.49
MIL-STD-414, sampling plan, **25**.55–**25**.56, **25**.62–**25**.77
  basic description, **25**.55–**25**.56, **25**.65
MIL-STD-449A, design-to-cost steps, **13**.66
MIL-STD-470A, maintainability, **13**.43
MIL-STD-471A, maintainability demonstrations, **13**.48
MIL-STD-690B, reliability sampling plan, **25**.79
MIL-STD-721C, maintainability, **13**.43
MIL-STD-781C, reliability testing, **13**.34
MIL-STD-785B, reliability testing, **13**.18, **13**.31, **18**.34
MIL-STD-882, safety programs, **13**.49
MIL-STD-1629A, criticality of failure modes, **13**.28
Minicapability study, **16**.23
Minitab project, **27**.26
Mission statement, quality improvement, **22**.7–**22**.8
Mixture design, of experiments, **26**.66–**26**.69
Mode, defined, **23**.17
Modified control limits, **24**.31
Modular vs. nonmodular construction, **13**.46
Monopoly of designers, **13**.13
Monte Carlo:
  sampling methods, **23**.94
  simulation, **13**.59
Motivation (*see* Human performance, managing)
MRB (material review board), **18**.32–**18**.33
MTBF (*see* Mean time between failures)
MTTR (*see* Mean time to repair)
Multiattribute study, **12**.20
Multicollinearity, defined, **23**.7, **23**.8
Multinational collaboration, **35A**.4
Multinomial distribution, **23**.30–**23**.32
Multinormal distribution, **23**.43

Multiple acceptance sampling plans, 25.23–25.33
Multi-Vari Chart, **22.45, 24.5, 24.10**

Narrow limit gaging, **24.31**
National Association of Home Builders (NAHB), **19.10**
National Association of Purchasing Agents (NAPA), **15.46**
National Bureau of Standards (NBS), **18.61, 18.63, 18.67, 18.76, 27.26, 34.10**
National culture, quality and, **35A.1–35A.5**
  differences, **35A.3, 35A.4**
National Highway Traffic Safety Administration (NHTSA), **34.15**
NATO (North Atlantic Treaty Organization), **15.9**
Naval Air Systems Command, **13.25**
NDT (nondestructive testing), **18.71–18.75**
Negative binomial distribution, **23.29–23.30**
Nested design of experiments, **26.64–26.66**
New-product development (*see* Product development)
New-product quality (*see* Product development)
New York Stock Exchange, **10.14**
NHTSA (National Highway Traffic Safety Administration), **34.15**
Nippon Telegraph and Telephone (NTT), **29.16**
Nominal group technique, **22.36**
Nonconformity:
  control charts: fraction nonconforming, **24.20–24.22**
    nonconformities per unit, **24.23**
    number of nonconformities, **24.23–24.26**
    number nonconforming, **24.22–24.23**
  vs. defect, defined, **25.4–25.5**
  vs. nonconforming unit, **24.20**
  (*See also* Defect)
Nondestructive testing, **18.71–18.75**
Normal distribution, **23.37–23.43**
  formula for, **23.37**
  making predictions from, **23.38–23.41**
  table of, **AII.5–AII.7**
  table of statistical tolerance limit factors for, **AII.36–AII.37**
  table of tolerance factors for, **AII.35**
Normale Français, **34.8**
North Atlantic Treaty Organization (NATO), **15.9**
Northrup Corp., **18.50**
Notation, statistical process control, **24.2–24.3**
np charts, **24.22–24.23**
NTT (Nippon Telegraph and Telephone), **29.16**
Numerical control (*see* Automated manufacturing)
Numerics, job shop, **32.6–32.8**

Objectives for quality, **5.15–5.23**
  in assembly industries, **30.3–30.4**
  bases for establishing, **5.18–5.20**
  for breakthrough or control, **5.20–5.21**
  comparison of: to policies, **5.15, 5.16**
    to standards, **5.15, 5.16**
  for control, **5.22**
  criteria for, **5.17–5.18**
  defined, **5.15**
  establishing, **5.22**
  for improvement, **5.22**
  strategic, **5.22–5.23**
  subject matter of, **5.15–5.17**
  zero defects as, **5.21–5.22**
Obsolescence, voluntary and involuntary, **3.4–3.5**
OC curve (*see* Operating characteristic curve)
Occupational Safety and Health Administration (OSHA), **19.6, 34.16, 34.17**
Off-line quality control, **16.30, 26.44–26.45**
Office of Assistant Secretary of Defense, **15.33**
Oklahomians, **11.28**
Ombudsman, **34.11**
Operating characteristic (OC) curve:
  for acceptance sampling, **25.10–25.12**
  construction of, **25.10**
  for control chart, **24.10–24.12**
  defined, **25.10**
  effect of parameters, **25.11**
  ideal, **25.10**
  use in selecting acceptance region, **23.63–23.64**
Operational readiness, **2.9**
Operator-controllable errors (*see* Worker errors)
Optimum, in quality costs, **4.17–4.22**
Order of manufacture, **24.3**
Ore smelting, **28.47, 28.48**
Organization for inspection and test, **18.98–18.107**
  evolution of inspection department, **18.100–18.107**
  evolution of inspectors, **18.98–18.107**
  finished goods inspection, **18.101–18.102**
  industrial revolution form of, **18.100**
  inspection department structure, **18.100–18.104**
  inspection support activities, **18.103–18.104**
  in multiproduct plants, **18.103, 18.104**
  noninspection operations, **18.104**
  in process industries, **18.102, 18.103**
  process inspection, **18.101**
  purchased material inspection, **18.100–18.101**
Organizing for quality:
  building the structure, **7.2**
    work elements and jobs, **7.3–7.7**

Organizing for quality (*Cont.*):
  coordination of the quality function:
    committees, **7.**22
    common boss, **7.**21–**7.**25
    crisis-by-crisis coordination, **7.**23
    among divisions, **7.**24–**7.**25
    matrix organizations, **7.**23
    owner, **7.**23
    precedent, **7.**22
    project manager, **7.**23, **7.**26, **7.**28
    responsibility matrix, **7.**25–**7.**27
    self-coordination, **7.**22
    staff departments, **7.**23, **7.**30–**7.**32
    staff quality activities (*see* Staff quality
      activities)
    tools for, **7.**23
    written procedure, **7.**22
  defined, **7.**2
  evolution of quality management hierarchy,
    7.8–**7.**13
    organization for assurance, **7.**10
    organization for prevention, **7.**9
    proliferation of quality function activities,
      7.10–**7.**13
  quality manager's job, **7.**14–**7.**21, **7.**24
    corporate quality manager, **7.**18–**7.**21
    division quality manager, **7.**16–**7.**18
    plant quality manager, **7.**13–**7.**16
    why quality managers fail, **7.**21
  work elements and jobs: assignment of
    responsibility, **7.**5, **7.**6
    nontraditional work elements, **7.**7–**7.**8

p chart:
  for attaining control, **24.**20–**24.**22
  control limits, chart of, **AII.**40
Package design, **20.**2, **20.**3
Packaging in customer service, **20.**2–**20.**3
Paper industry (*see* Process industries)
Pareto analysis:
  in administrative and support operations,
    21.16, **21.**17
  in assembly industries, **30.**47
  concept of, **22.**19–**22.**21, **24.**5
  by defect types, **22.**19–**22.**21
  examples, **22.**19–**22.**22
  by operators (weavers), **22.**54
  by part number, **15.**35
  in process industries, **28.**54
  by processes, **22.**19–**22.**20
  as proof of need, **22.**19–**22.**22
  in quality improvement programs,
    22.19–**22.**22
  ranking by measure, **12.**6, **12.**7
  in service industries, **33.**35
  in statistical process control, **24.**5
  supplier improvement, use in, **15.**35
  vital few, identifying, **20.**21, **21.**9
Pareto principle, defined, **6.**20, **22.**19

Participation:
  role in introducing change, **22.**66
  role in motivation, **10.**25–**10.**31
Parts selection and control, **13.**27, **13.**28
PASCAL (programming language), **14.**15,
  27.4
Patrol inspection, **18.**10, **18.**12–**18.**13,
  18.29–**18.**30
Payroll change process, **21.**2, **21.**3
Penetrant dye testing, **18.**73
Percentiles, **23.**15–**23.**16
Perfectionism, **3.**27–**3.**29
  in the "abilities," **3.**28
  defenses against, **3.**29
  in field service, **3.**28
  by government regulators, **3.**28
  perfectionists, **3.**28
  in quality of conformance, **3.**28
  in quality of design, **3.**27
Performance Evaluation Review Technique
  (PERT), **14.**19, **27.**11
Performance index in process capability, **16.**20
Personal liability, **34.**21, **34.**22
Personnel function, quality in, **21.**4, **21.**5,
  21.17–**21.**20
Personnel management for quality,
  10.1–**10.**61, **11.**1–**11.**39
PERT (Performance Evaluation Review
  Technique), **14.**19, **27.**11
Petroleum industry (*see* Process industries)
Pharmaceutical industry (*see* Process
  industries)
Phase, in EVOP, **26.**32
Phase concept of product development,
  13.4–**13.**7
Phototyping in software development, **14.**23
Piece-to-piece analysis, **22.**44
Pilot plant production:
  in assembly industries, **30.**8–**30.**10
  in job shop industries, **32.**14–**32.**15
  in process industries, **28.**9
PIMS (profit impact of market strategies), **3.**18
PL/1 (programming language), **14.**15, **27.**4
Planning for quality:
  in administrative and support operations,
    21.7–**21.**14
  applications to various levels, **6.**21–**6.**23
  in assembly industries, **30.**11–**30.**14
  audit of, **9.**7–**9.**14
  companywide quality management,
    6.23–**6.**26
  in complex industries, **31.**4–**31.**11
  concept, **6.**3
  of control process, **6.**31, **6.**32
  customer needs, **6.**6–**6.**10
    (*See also* Field intelligence)
  in customer service (*see* Customer service)
  deployment of corporate goals, **6.**25
  discovery of customer needs, **6.**6, **6.**10

Planning for quality (*Cont.*):
  in electronic components industries,
    29.5–29.13
  feedback loop, **6**.32–**6**.39
  generic standards, **6**.45–**6**.47
  identification of customers, **6**.4
  improvement, **22**.1–**22**.74, **35G**.9
  for inspection and test, **13**.62
  in job shop industries, **32**.8–**32**.11, **32**.28
  lessons learned, **6**.28–**6**.30
  for maintainability, **13**.40–**13**.48
  for manufacturing, **13**.55
  in marketing (*see* Marketing)
  to minimize cost, **13**.63–**13**.66
  optimizing product design, **6**.12–**6**.15
  organization for CWCM, **6**.26
  for packaging, transportation, and storage,
    13.62
  of personnel requirements, **16**.38
  planning for quality control, **6**.31–**6**.39
  planning road map of steps, **6**.3–**6**.23
  process development, **6**.15–**6**.17
    (*See also* Manufacturing planning)
  in process industries, **28**.6–**28**.9
  product development, **6**.11–**6**.12, **13**.13–**13**.66
  for production in assembly industries,
    30.17, **30**.18
  for purchased product (*see* Supplier relations)
  quality manual, **6**.40–**6**.45
  for reliability, **13**.17–**13**.40
  road map for, **6**.3–**6**.5
  for safety, **13**.48–**13**.55
  in service industries, **33**.7–**33**.40
  small companies, application to, **6**.26–**6**.28
  standards, **6**.45–**6**.47
  terminology, **6**.3
  training for planners, **6**.49, **6**.50
  transfer to operations, **6**.17–**6**.18
  translation into supplier's language,
    6.10–**6**.11
  triple-role concept, **6**.19–**6**.20
  who plans?, **6**.47–**6**.48
    (*See also* Companywide planning for
    quality)
Plant quality manager, **7**.13, **7**.16
Plots of two variables, **23**.111–**23**.113
Point estimate, **23**.46
  confidence interval, defined, **23**.46
  confidence level, defined, **23**.46
  confidence limits, defined, **23**.46
  defined, **23**.46
Poisson distribution, **23**.29
  in constructing OC curves, **25**.10
  tables of, **AII**.10–**AII**.13
Policies for quality:
  adherence to, **5**.14–**5**.15
  in administrative and support functions,
    5.11–**5**.12
  advantages and disadvantages, **5**.3, **5**.4

Policies for quality (*Cont.*):
  in assembly industries, **30**.5
  audit of, **5**.15
  in complex industries, **31**.4
  corporate, **5**.4–**5**.7
  credibility of, **5**.15
  defined, **5**.2
  divisional, **5**.7–**5**.8
  formulation of, **5**.13–**5**.14
  as holy ground, **5**.14
  need for, **5**.2
  policy formulation process, **5**.13–**5**.14
  for product development, **13**.11–**13**.13
  for product safety, **5**.12
  publication of, **5**.14
  for reliability, **5**.12
  the "right" policies, **5**.13
  for specific functions, **5**.8–**5**.12
  for specific parameters, **5**.12–**5**.13
  written, **5**.2–**5**.7
Policy control, Japanese application of,
    35F.12–**35F**.15
Polymerization process, **28**.25–**28**.30
Population, defined, **23**.21
PRE-Control:
  basic concept, **24**.4–**24**.5
  comparison with $\bar{X}$ and R charts,
    24.36–**24**.38
  implementation, **24**.36
  requirements for use, **24**.33
  risk, **24**.35–**24**.36
  setting up, **24**.33–**24**.34
  theory, **24**.31–**24**.33
  using, **24**.34–**24**.36
Precision:
  cost of, **13**.61
  of instrument, **18**.64–**18**.65
  statements of, **18**.67–**18**.68
    (*See also* Measurement error)
Predicting complaint level, **20**.25–**20**.27
Prediction intervals, **23**.51
Preferred supplier program, **15**.34
Preproduction runs, **16**.42
Preproduction trials, **16**.41–**16**.42
Preserving the order of manufacture, **24**.3
President's quality audit, **8**.23
Prevention costs (*see* Cost of poor quality)
Preventive maintenance, **16**.38
Price and quality:
  bundled price, **3**.12
  in Czechoslovakia, **35H**.7
  effect on complaint rate, **20**.17, **20**.18
  interaction of, **3**.9–**3**.12
  vs. cost of usage, **3**.7
Prior franchise, **3**.16
Probability, basic concepts, **23**.21, **23**.24
Probability distributions, **23**.21–**23**.22
  defined, **23**.21
  summary of, **23**.22

Probability distributions (*Cont.*):
  types and examples, **23.26–23.45**
  (*See also* Discrete probability distributions;
    Continuous probability distributions)
Probability models for experiments,
    23.21–23.26
  Bayes' theorem, **23.25–23.26**
  combinatorics, **23.24, 23.25**
  conditional probability, **23.21**
  events, **23.23–23.24**
  rules of probability, **23.21, 23.24**
  sample space, **23.21–23.23**
Probability paper, **13.58, 16.22, 23.35–23.37,
    23.42**
Process capability:
  analysis, **16.14–16.35**
  applications: in administrative and support
      operations, **16.14–16.35**
    choice among alternative processes, **16.33**
    interrelation of sequential processes,
      16.34–16.35
    in manufacturing planning, **16.14–16.35**
    other uses, **16.35**
    purchase of machines, **16.33**
  concept of, **16.14, 21.12**
    basic definitions, **16.14–16.15**
    process patterns, **16.15–16.17**
    product mixture, **16.17**
    relation to product tolerance, **16.18–16.21**
    standardized formula, **16.17–16.18**
  data, **13.61**
    application of experimental design,
      16.30–16.31
    complex processes, **16.32**
    measuring inherent capability,
      16.25–16.30
    measuring present performance,
      16.21–16.25
    planning for, **16.32–16.33**
  defined, **16.14, 16.17, 16.21**
  performance index, **16.20**
  supplier qualification, use in, **15.13–15.14**
Process capability analysis, **16.14–16.35**
Process control(s):
  in assembly industries, **30.24**
  and concept of dominance, **16.50, 16.51**
  criteria, **16.49**
  evaluation of, **16.50, 16.52**
  relation to product controls, **16.49–16.50,
    28.21**
  statistical (*see* Statistical process control)
Process control tools, **17.19**
Process design (*see* Process development; *also*
    Manufacturing planning)
Process development:
  in administrative and support operations,
    21.11–21.12
  in assembly industries, **30.11–30.18**
  in chemical industry, **28.7–28.9**

Process development (*Cont.*):
  in complex industries, **31.13–31.19**
  for electronic components, **29.11–29.13**
  in job shop industries, **32.8–32.11, 32.20**
  in service industries, **33.7–33.11**
Process diagrams, **16.9**
Process failure analysis, **16.50**
Process industries:
  analytical or control laboratory (*see* Control
    laboratory)
  chemical industries, **28.4–28.38**
  control in, **28.22–28.23, 28.37–28.38**
  control of product quality, **28.21–28.22**
  customer relations in, **28.41–28.44**
  data banks in, **28.36**
  design of process in, **28.7–28.9**
  field trials in, **28.7**
  finished product quality, **28.30**
  future needs, planning for, **28.37**
  laboratory experimentation in, **28.11–
    28.19**
  manufacturing department, **28.22–28.23**
  measures of quality performance in,
    28.57–28.58
  metals industries, **28.38–28.59**
  plant in, **28.5–28.6**
  plant experimentation in, **28.35–28.36,
    28.55**
  process automation in, **28.36**
  product planning for quality—chemicals,
    28.6–28.7
  product planning for quality—metals,
    28.40–28.52
  quality improvement—chemicals,
    28.30–28.35
  quality improvement—metals, **28.52–28.57**
  quality motivation in, **28.36–28.37**
  raw materials controls in, **28.47**
  responsibilities of manufacturing,
    28.22–28.23
  responsibilities of R&D laboratory, **28.5,
    28.9–28.10**
  special problems of quality in, **28.3,
    28.55–28.77**
  unit operations in, **28.4, 28.23–28.25**
  unit processes in, **28.25–28.30**
Process specifications, **17.7–17.8**
Process variables, correlation of, with product
    results, **16.9–16.14**
Processing during distribution, **20.5**
Producer's risk, **25.9**
Producibility (manufacturability), **2.11**
  planning for, in assembly industries,
    30.15–30.18
  planning for, in product development,
    13.55–13.62, 16.5–16.6
Product:
  deficiency, **2.3**
  defined, **2.2**

Product (*Cont.*):
  design (*see* Product development)
  development (*see* Product development)
  features and quality characteristics, **2.2, 2.8,**
    2.9
  inspection of incoming product,
    15.29–15.32, 18.29
  liability, defensive action, **34.19–34.22**
  performance (*see* Product performance)
  recalls, **20.32–20.34**
  release criteria, **30.28**
  safety, **13.49–3.53, 30.16**
  satisfaction vs. dissatisfaction, **2.3, 2.4**
  service in field (*see* Field service)
  specification, **13.12, 17.6, 17.7**
Product acceptance:
  by control chart, **25.62–25.64**
  by operators, **17.24–17.26**
  product approval, defined, **17.3**
  (*See also* Acceptance sampling; Self-
    inspection)
Product auditing:
  action on discrepancies, **9.26–9.27**
  definition and purposes, **9.22**
  designing the audit plan, **9.23–9.24**
  effect on clarifying quality standards, **9.27**
  reporting the results of, **9.24–9.26**
  stage of evaluation, **9.22–9.23**
Product development:
  in administrative and support operations,
    21.11
  American practices, **35G.1–35G.13**
  in assembly industries, **30.5–30.8**
  in complex industries, **31.12–31.19**
  computer integration in, **27.25, 27.30–27.33**
  configuration management, **13.66–13.70**
  design assurance, **13.7**
  design review, **13.7–13.11**
  of electronic components, **29.8–29.10**
  importance of, **13.3**
  improving effectiveness, **13.70**
  Japanese practices, **35F.23–35F.29**
  marketing department role in, **19.7, 19.8**
  phase concept, **13.4–13.7**
  planning for human factors, **13.55**
  planning for inspection and test, **13.62**
  planning for maintainability, **13.40–13.48**
    (*See also* Maintainability)
  planning for manufacturing, **13.55**
  planning to minimize cost, **13.63–13.66**
  planning for packaging, transportation, and
    storage, **13.62**
  planning for safety, **13.48–13.55**
  policies, **5.8**
  policy issues, **13.11–13.13**
  in process industries, **28.6, 28.7**
  reliability, **13.18–13.27**
  self-control, **13.70, 13.71**
  staff specialist organization, **13.72, 13.74**

Product development (*Cont.*):
  testing, **13.31–13.36**
  traditional and modern products, **13.3,**
    13.4
  value engineering, **13.63–13.66**
Product liability:
  defensive action, **34.19–34.21**
    against lawsuits, **34.21**
  insurance, **34.21**
  prognosis, **34.21**
  personal liability, **34.21, 34.22**
  recalls, **20.32–20.34**
  (*See also* Safety)
Product performance, data banks, **34.4–34.5**
Production:
  in assembly industries, **30.8–30.9,**
    30.21–30.24
  audit of inspection decisions, **17.26**
  audit of systems, **17.26–17.29**
  concept of dominance, **17.19–17.21**
  controllability, **17.4–17.6**
  culture, **17.21–17.23**
  defined, **16.2, 17.2**
  policies, **5.9, 5.10**
  process control tools, **17.19**
  responsibilities, **17.2–17.4**
  self-control, **17.4–17.21**
    (*See also* Self-control)
  self-inspection, **17.24**
  specifications, **17.6–17.8**
  troubleshooting, **17.29, 17.30**
  (*See also* Manufacturing planning)
Productivity as a measure, **8.20**
Professionalism, **11.33**
Profit impact of market strategies (PIMS),
  3.18
Program, computer (*see* Software, computer)
Program decision process chart, **22.40**
Program Evaluation and Review Technique
  (PERT), **14.19, 27.11**
Program management in complex industries,
  31.11–31.19
Progress, Spiral of, **2.4, 2.5**
Project, defined, **22.31**
Project change administrator, **13.68**
Project identification, **22.22–22.26**
Project management for computer projects,
  27.8
Project nominations, **22.22–22.26**
  initial projects, **22.24–22.26**
  subsequent projects, **22.22–22.24**
Project team organization, **22.26–22.31**
  chairperson, **22.28**
  facilitators, **22.28–22.29**
  secretary, **22.28**
  team members, **22.28**
  teams, **22.26–22.28**
Project planning for new products,
  13.13–13.66

Project teams, compared to quality circles, 22.28
Proof of need, **22.13–22.18**
  cost of poor quality for, **22.14, 22.15, 22.19–22.22**
  marketing research for, **22.14–22.18**
  Pareto analyses for, **22.19–22.22**
Proofreading:
  active, **18.89**
  errorless, **18.89**
  passive, **18.89**
Pseudocode, **14.13**
Puffing, **19.4**
Punishment of negative behavior, **10.33, 10.34**
Purchased material control, **15.24–15.32, 18.29**
Purchasing (*see* Supplier relations)
Purchasing managers:
  centralization, **15.8**
  decisions by, **15.19**
  responsibilities, **15.6–15.8**

Qantas Airways, **33.29–33.30**
QC Circle Koryo, **11.20**
QC circles (*see* Circles, quality)
QIE (quality information equipment), **16.52**
Qualification test:
  in electronic components industries, **29.11, 29.12**
  in process industries, **28.46, 28.47**
  in product development, **13.31–13.36**
Qualimetry, **8.19, 8.20**
Quality, defined, **2.2, 2.3, 2.4, 2.12, 3.6, 3.7, 5.5, 6.40**
Quality and national culture:
  capitalistic economies, **35A.2, 35A.3**
  cultural differences, **35A.3–35A.4**
  multinational collaboration, **35A.4**
Quality and society:
  consumerism, **34.2–34.13**
  government regulation, **34.13–34.19**
  product safety and product liability, **34.19–34.22**
Quality assurance (*see* Assurance for quality)
Quality audit (*see* Audits)
Quality characteristic (*see* Characteristic, quality)
Quality circles (*see* Circles, quality)
Quality control (*see* Control of quality)
Quality control, defined, **6.31–6.32, 21.14**
Quality Control Handbook:
  adapting to use, **1.5**
  bibliographies, **1.4**
  citations, **1.4**
  cross-references, **1.4**
  index, use of, **1.3**
  industry sections in, **1.3**
  main road and side roads, **1.4–1.5**
  management sections in, **1.2**

Quality Control Handbook (*Cont.*):
  organization of, **1.2–1.3**
  statistical sections in, **1.3**
  tables of contents, **1.3**
  uses of, **1.2**
Quality control societies (*see* Societies centering on quality)
Quality costs (*see* Costs of poor quality)
Quality disciplines, **11.3**
Quality function:
  business, management, and technology, **2.11, 2.12**
  fitness for use, **2.8–2.11**
  how to think about quality, **2.5–2.8**
  quality defined, **2.2–2.4**
  terminology, standardization, **2.12, 2.13**
Quality function deployment, **13.13, 13.17**
  of corporate quality goals, **6.25, 8.5**
Quality goals (*see* Objectives for quality)
Quality improvement (*see* Improvement of quality)
Quality information equipment (QIE), **16.52**
Quality manager, **7.13–7.21**
Quality manuals, **6.40–6.45**
Quality mission, **22.7–22.8**
Quality objectives (*see* Objectives for quality)
Quality planning (*see* Planning for quality)
Quality policies (*see* Policies for quality)
Quality reports (*see* Reports on quality)
Quality Representative—Certified Vendor Representative, **15.28**
Quality surveys (*see* Audits; Surveys)
Quality systems terminology, **AIV.1–AIV.3**
Quality table, new-product development, use of, **35F.23–35F.25**
Quality trilogy, **2.6, 35G.8**
Queuing time, **33.8–33.9**
Quincunx, **11.29**
Quotation review and quality, **32.28**

r values, table of, **AII.18**
R&D, quality in (*see* Product development)
RADC (Rome Air Development Center), **13.51, 13.52**
Random causes of variation, **24.3, 24.5**
Random effects in experiments, **26.15–26.22**
Random numbers:
  sources and use of, **23.33**
  table of, **AII.42**
  use in sampling, **25.20**
Randomization, defined, **26.4**
Randomized block design of experiment, **26.55–26.59**
  (*See also* Design of experiments, randomized block designs)
Range (R):
  defined, **23.17**
  use in control charts, **22.7**
Ranking, **22.48, 22.49**

Rath & Strong, Inc., **24**.4
Rational subgroups:
  composition of frequency, **24**.9–**24**.10
  selection from lots, **24**.10
Realistic tolerances rigidly enforced, **13**.60
Recalls of product, **20**.32–**20**.34
Receiving inspection (*see* Incoming inspection)
Recognition for quality, **8**.6, **8**.7,
    10.33–**10**.36, **30**.21
Red X, **24**.5–**24**.6
Reduction in bulk sampling, defined, **25**.85
Redundancy, **13**.39, **23**.90–**23**.91
Regression and correlation analysis,
    23.96–**23**.118
  basic concept, **23**.96–**23**.100
  confidence intervals, **23**.107–**23**.111,
    23.114–**23**.116
  in maintainability, **13**.46
  methods of analysis, **23**.96–**23**.118
  multiple, **23**.108–**23**.117
  residuals, **23**.105–**23**.107
  sample linear regression, **23**.100–**23**.105
  studies, **13**.57
  in tolerancing, **13**.57
Regulate, ability to, **17**.18–**17**.21
  (*See also* Self-control)
Reinforcement of positive behavior,
    10.19–**10**.20
Reject limits, **24**.31
Reliability, **2**.9, **2**.10, **13**.17–**13**.27
  acceptance tests, **13**.34
  analysis, **13**.21–**13**.27
  apportionment, **13**.21
  in assembly industries, **30**.24–**30**.26
  basic concepts, **23**.81
  in complex industries, **31**.9–**31**.11
  data banks, **13**.37–**13**.38
  data systems, **13**.36, **13**.37
  defined, **13**.18
  development/growth tests, **13**.34
  distribution of time between failures, **23**.82
  of electronic components, **29**.14–**29**.17
  engineering, in complex industries,
    31.9–**31**.11
  exponential formula, **23**.82–**23**.85
  failure rate, **23**.81, **23**.82
  figures of merit, **13**.20
  goals, **13**.20
  growth, **13**.40
  improvement, **13**.38–**13**.40
  index (figures of merit), **13**.20
  intrinsic and operational, **2**.9, **2**.10
  mean time between failures, **23**.85, **23**.86
  objectives, **13**.22
  predicting based on exponential and Weibull
    distributions, **23**.86–**23**.87
  predicting based on stress and strength,
    23.87–**23**.90
  prediction, **13**.21, **23**.81, **29**.15

Reliability (*Cont.*):
  program, **13**.18–**13**.19
  qualification tests, **13**.34
  quantification, **13**.19–**13**.27
  redundancy, **23**.90, **23**.91
  relationship between part and system
    reliability, **23**.90
  requirement, **13**.19–**13**.21
  sampling plans (*see* Acceptance sampling,
    reliability)
  statistical concepts, **23**.81
  tests, **13**.34–**13**.36
Reliability engineer:
  certified, **7**.29–**7**.30
  interface with quality control engineers,
    7.29
Reliability prediction and analysis, **23**.81–**23**.91
Remedy, defined, **22**.31
Repair time:
  accessing, **33**.8
  active, **13**.41
Replication (replicate analysis), **26**.4
Reports on quality:
  in administrative and support operations,
    21.14, **21**.15
  in assembly industries, **30**.40–**30**.44
  control subjects, **8**.10
  cost of poor quality, **4**.28–**4**.29
  early executive reports, **8**.9
  executive report battery, **8**.15, **8**.16
  on field performance, **20**.30–**20**.32
  format, **8**.16, **8**.17
  interpretation, **8**.17–**8**.19
  in metals industry, **28**.57, **28**.58
  publication, **8**.17
  revisions in, **8**.9, **8**.10
  in service industries, **33**.51–**33**.58
  universal measure for quality, **8**.19
  (*See also* Audits, planning and performing)
Requirements allocation sheet, **13**.17
Research and development, quality in (*see*
    Product development)
Residuals in statistical analysis, **23**.106
Resistance to change, **22**.65–**22**.68
  analyzing impact of change, **22**.66
  cultural patterns, **22**.65, **22**.66
  introducing change, **22**.66–**22**.68
  resolving differences, **22**.68
Response surface, **26**.30, **26**.47–**26**.48
Response surface designs of experiment,
    26.45–**26**.54
  (*See also* Design of experiments, response
    surface designs)
Response surface methodology, **16**.30,
    26.45–**26**.54
Responsibility for quality:
  allocation of, in planning, **6**.48
  of analytical laboratory, **28**.5
  in assembly industries, **30**.36–**30**.39

Responsibility for quality (*Cont.*):
assignment of, in organizing, **7.5–7.7**
at control stations, **18**.28
design review team, **13**.3
on the factory floor, **17**.2–**17**.4
(*See also* Organizing for quality)
Responsibility matrix for fitness for use needs, **12**.9, **12**.10
Return on investment, **22**.23
Reversible and irreversible remedies, **22**.68, **22**.69
Rewards for quality, **8**.6, **8**.7, **10**.33–**10**.36
Rework, as quality cost, **4**.5
Risks:
in acceptance sampling, **25**.9–**25**.12
for control charts, **25**.35–**24**.36
in modern society, **34**.2
ROA Films, **11**.27
Road maps for actions:
for improvement of quality, **22**.6–**22**.11, **22**.13–**22**.72
for introducing a cost-reporting system, **4**.28
for planning quality, **6**.3–**6**.5
Robust process design, **29**.11–**29**.13
Robust product design, **13**.39
Rome Air Development Center (RADC), **13**.51, **13**.62
Root mean square deviation (*see* Standard deviation)
Roquefort, Community of, **19**.17
Running approval, **17**.3
Runs, limiting values for, table of, **AII**.31

Safety:
analysis, **13**.50–**13**.53
in assembly industries, **30**.16
automobile, **34**.15–**34**.16
improving through design, **13**.53–**13**.55
objectives, **13**.49, **13**.50
program, **13**.38, **13**.49
quantification, **13**.49–**13**.50
regulation, **34**.13–**34**.17
standards, vital few, **34**.17–**34**.18
tasks, **13**.49, **13**.50
Safety and health regulation, **34**.13–**34**.17
Safety margin in product design, **23**.88, **23**.90
Sales contract, **19**.6–**19**.9
incentive provisions, **19**.7
Sample:
in bulk sampling, defined, **25**.85
defined, **23**.21
size to achieve a specified precision, **23**.50, **23**.51
size for lot acceptance decisions (*see* Acceptance sampling)
size to test a hypothesis, **23**.78
Sample intervals, tables of extremes, **AII**.39
Sampling:
in administrative and support operations, **21**.21

Sampling (*Cont.*):
by attributes, **25**.21–**25**.51
for bulk product, **25**.85–**25**.89
demonstrators, **11**.28, **11**.29
in field intelligence, **12**.12
random, **25**.20
for reliability, **25**.73–**25**.84
stratified, **25**.20–**25**.21
by variables, **25**.51–**25**.77
Saratov system, **35H**.10–**35H**.11
SAS Institute, Inc., **23**.19, **27**.26
Satisfaction vs. dissatisfaction with product, **2**.3, **2**.4, **12**.5
Saturn Corporation, **10**.22
Scale parameter in Weibull distribution, **23**.34
Scatter diagrams (crossplots), **23**.10, **23**.11, **23**.100
Schick Co., **3**.14
Schlitz, Joseph, Brewing Co., **18**.53
Scoreboard on cost of poor quality, **4**.22–**4**.26
Scrap:
as quality cost, **4**.5
feedback on, **18**.97, **18**.98
SDLC (*see* Software development life cycle)
Seal, quality, **34**.7
Segment in bulk sampling, defined, **25**.85
Self-control, **6**.19
"ability to regulate" and, **10**.30, **17**.18–**17**.21, **32**.62
in administrative and support operations, **21**.13
application of concept in Japan, **10**.10, **10**.11, **35F**.11, **35F**.12
checklist, **17**.12, **17**.18, **17**.21
concept of, **10**.27–**10**.30, **17**.4–**17**.21
knowledge of "is doing," **10**.29, **17**.12–**17**.18, **33**.62
knowledge of "supposed to do," **10**.29, **17**.6–**17**.12, **33**.62
in manufacturing, **17**.4
in processing systems, **10**.28–**10**.30
in product development, **13**.70, **13**.71
in service industries, **33**.62
Self-inspection:
advantages, **17**.24
cautions, **17**.25
criteria, **17**.24–**17**.25
defined, **17**.23–**17**.24
results, **17**.26
sequence, **17**.25
Semiconductor manufacture, **29**.5, **29**.6
Semicontinuous process example (polymerization), **28**.25–**28**.30
Sensor, defined, **6**.35
Sensory qualities, **18**.45–**18**.57
consumer likes and dislikes, **18**.46–**18**.48
creating instruments to measure, **18**.56–**18**.57
defined, **18**.45
in fitness for use, **18**.46–**18**.49

Sensory qualities (*Cont.*):
  judgment of conformance, **18.52–18.57**
  setting standards for, **18.51, 18.52**
  standards based on consumer sensitivity,
    18.48–18.49
Sensory testing:
  analysis of test data, **18.54–18.56**
  consumer panels for, **18.52–18.53**
  design of tests, **18.54–18.56**
  environment for, **18.50, 18.51, 18.53–18.54**
  laboratory panels for, **18.53–18.54**
  panels for, **18.52–18.55**
  tables of uses for, **18.47**
  types of tests, **18.47**
Sentry Insurance Co., **34.3, 34.4, 34.6, 34.11,
    34.17**
Sequential sampling for acceptance,
    25.23–25.27
Seriousness classification, **13.61, 18.38–18.45**
  classification of characteristics, **18.44**
  defect classification, **18.41–18.45**
  definitions for classes, **18.40, 18.44**
  effect on amount of inspection, **18.38–18.39**
  in product auditing, **9.24–9.25**
  in quality audits, **9.13**
  for sampling plans, **18.41–18.45, 25.44**
Service:
  defined, **33.2**
  feedback on quality, **33.28–33.31**
  for products (*see* Field service)
Service company:
  characteristics of, **33.3–33.6**
  defined, **33.3**
Service industries:
  access time, **33.8**
  action time, **33.9**
  airlines, **33.29–33.30**
  audits, **33.43–33.47**
  characteristics of quality, **33.7**
  charter for quality department, **33.24–33.25**
  consistency of service, **33.33**
  consumer research, **33.29–33.31**
  contribution to GNP, **33.4**
  corrective action, **33.19–33.20, 33.37–33.40**
  customer satisfaction forms, **33.34**
  customers, feedback from, **33.30, 33.31,
    33.34**
  defined, **33.2–33.3**
  earning management support, **33.22–33.23**
  employee orientation brochure, **33.41**
  employment in, **33.4**
  hospital, **33.56–33.64**
  insurance company, **33.49–33.57**
  integrity of service, **33.33**
  marketing feedback, **33.28–33.31, 33.34**
  measurement of service, conformance,
    33.34, 33.35
  measuring, **33.33–33.35**
  monitoring service, **33.21**

Service industries (*Cont.*):
  quality audits in (*see* Audits)
  quality department creating, **33.23–33.25**
  quality improvement, **33.20–33.21**
  quality program (*see* Service quality,
    programs)
  quality report forms, **33.51, 33.53–33.54**
  quality standards (*see* Service standards)
  queuing time, **33.8–33.9**
  telephone company, **33.38**
  testing/measuring conformance, **33.31–33.35**
  timeliness of service, **33.32–33.33**
  travel agency, **33.39**
Service quality:
  analysis of, **33.35, 33.36**
  in assembly industries, **30.34–30.36**
  characteristics of, **33.7**
  defined, **33.6**
  design of, **33.7–33.11**
  measurement of, **33.16–33.18, 33.34–33.35**
  programs, **33.11–33.49**
    case examples, **33.11–33.49**
    description of, **33.11–33.22**
    developing, **33.22–33.40**
    extending, **33.37–33.49**
    implementing, **33.41**
    ingredients of, **33.11**
    in operation, **33.42–33.47**
  report forms, **33.51, 33.53, 33.54, 33.57,
    33.68**
Service standards:
  establishing, **33.13–33.16**
  integrity of service, **33.14, 33.17**
  measuring conformance to, **33.16–33.18,
    33.34, 33.35**
  predictability of service, **33.14, 33.17**
  satisfaction with service, **33.17–33.18**
  timeliness, **33.13–33.14, 33.17**
  treating as laws, **33.15–33.16**
Setup:
  approval, defined, **17.2**
  dominance, **16.50, 17.19, 32.29, 32.30**
  in job shops, **32.29–32.30**
  responsibility, **16.3, 16.4**
Shape parameter in Weibull distribution, **23.34**
Share of market and quality, **3.12–3.17**
Shewhart control charts (*see* Control charts)
SI measurement system, **18.58–18.60**
Sign test, **23.65, 23.67, 23.74**
Signal-to-noise ratio, **16.30**
Significance:
  practical, **23.80–23.81**
  statistical, **23.80–23.81**
    and economic, **6.36–6.38**
  test of (*see* Hypotheses, test of)
Singapore, National Productivity Board in,
    35B.23
Single sampling plans, **25.23, 25.54–25.56**
Size of designed experiment, **26.73–26.76**

Skip-lot sampling plans, **25**.33–**25**.37
Small companies, quality management in,
    6.26–**6**.28
Sneak-circuit analysis, **13**.31
Socialist countries, quality in, **35H**.1–**35H**.14
    Council for Mutual Economic Assistance
      (CMEA), **35H**.1–**35H**.2
    education and training, **35H**.11–**35H**.13
    integrated quality control, **35H**.7–**35H**.9
    Integrated Quality Control System (IQCS),
      35H.3, **35H**.7–**35H**.9
    motivation, **35H**.9–**35H**.11
    product certification, **35H**.4–**35H**.7
    Saratov system, **35H**.10–**35H**.11
    state quality control, **35H**.2–**35H**.4
    work quality factor, **35H**.11
Societies centering on quality:
    American Society for Nondestructive
      Testing (ASNDT), **18**.71
    American Society for Quality Control
      (ASQC), **2**.13, **4**.18, **9**.10, **11**.33,
      11.34, **12**.18, **15**.15, **15**.19, **18**.7,
      34.3
    American Society for Testing and Materials
      (ASTM), **18**.61, **18**.69, **26**.70
    Association Française pour le Contrôle
      Industriel et la Qualité (AFCIQ),
      35C.7–**35C**.8
    Ausschuss für Statistische Qualitätscontrolle
      (ASQ), **35D**.4
    Deutsche Gesellschaft für Qualität (DGQ),
      35D.4–**35D**.5
    in developing countries, **35B**.24
    European Organization for Quality Control
      (EOQC), **2**.4, **2**.12, **11**.27, **11**.36,
      35D.4, **35E**.1
    Institute of Quality Assurance (IQA), **11**.27
    Japanese Union of Scientists and Engineers
      (JUSE), **10**.47, **11**.35, **35B**.19, **35F**.2,
      35F.4, **35F**.5
Software, computer, **27**.3
    for acceptance sampling, **25**.92,
      25.95–**25**.96
    debugging, **14**.18
    development (*see* Software development life
      cycle)
    expert systems, **27**.6
    packages, **27**.5–**27**.7
    quality, **27**.6
    quality factors, defined, **27**.6
    for regression analysis, **23**.115, **23**.117
    reliability of, **27**.30–**27**.31
    sources of, **27**.24
    statistical, general, **27**.26–**27**.29
    for statistical process control, **24**.38–**24**.39
    types of: assembly language, **27**.5
      high-level programming language, **27**.5
      machine language, **27**.3, **27**.4
    unit of measure, **8**.10

Software development:
    basic concepts, **14**.2–**14**.5
    coding, **14**.14–**14**.16
    design, **14**.11–**14**.14
    errors, **14**.8
    life cycle (SDLC), **14**.7–**14**.19
    maintenance, **14**.18, **14**.19
    management issues, **14**.19, **14**.20
    phases, **14**.7
    prototyping, **14**.23
    requirements analysis, **14**.9–**14**.11
    resources, **14**.7, **14**.8
    test and installation, **14**.16–**14**.18
    validation, **14**.20–**14**.22
Software engineering, defined, **14**.3, **14**.6
Solar Turbines International, **27**.15
Solvent extraction process, **28**.23–**28**.25
Sorting of product, **18**.36–**18**.37
Spare parts, sale of, **12**.7
Speakeasy Computing Corporation, **27**.27
Specifications:
    conformance to, **2**.3
    and fitness for use, **2**.3, **2**.8
    process, **17**.7, **17**.8
    production, **13**.12, **17**.6–**17**.8
    standards, **AIII**.1–**AIII**.13
Spiral of progress in quality, **2**.5
Sporadic problems, **22**.5–**22**.6
SPSS, Incorporated, **27**.29
Staff quality activities:
    budgeting for, **7**.31
    examples of, **7**.25, **7**.28
    interface among staff quality specialties,
      7.29–**7**.30
    introducing change, **7**.32
    life cycle of, **7**.28
    other specialties, staff-staff conflicts, **7**.30
    other staff-line relationships, **7**.32
    perceptions, **7**.30
    police image, **7**.15
    quality control engineering, **7**.28–**7**.29
    quality manager, **7**.13–**7**.21
      (*See also* Quality manager)
    reliability engineering, **7**.29
    reports on, **7**.31–**7**.32
    transfer from staff to line, **7**.31
Stage system (*see* Phase concept of product
    development)
Standard deviation:
    of averages vs. individuals, **23**.16–**23**.17
    calculation methods, **23**.17–**23**.18
    chart of degrees of freedom for estimating,
      AII.34
    defined, **23**.17
    estimating, **24**.8
Standardization:
    of conditions of inspection, **18**.50–**18**.51
    in developing countries, **35B**.8, **35B**.9
    generic quality standards, **6**.45–**6**.46

Standardization (*Cont.*):
  organizations, **34.9–34.10, 35B**.16
  of terminology, **2**.13
  (*See also* Standards)
Standards:
  in assembly industries, **30.27–30.30**
  for executive reports, **8.14–8.15**
  in feedback loop, **6.45–6.46**
  generic quality, **6.45–6.46**
  under government regulation, **34**.8
  for inspection costs, **18.108–18.109**
  list of, **AIII.1–AIII**.13
  measurement (*see* Measurement standards)
  for product auditing, **9**.26
  for product compliance, **34.7–34.10**
  for quality surveys, **9.21–9.22**
  selected, **AIII.1–AIII**.3
  sensory, **18.48–18.52**
  (*See also* Service standards)
Statistical control of automated process,
    24.36–24.39
Statistical control charts (*see* Control charts)
Statistical decision theory, **23**.26
Statistical estimation, **23**.45
  Bayesian estimates, **23.59–23.60**
  concept, **23.45–23.46**
  confidence interval estimates, **23.46–23.51**
  point estimates, **23**.46
  prediction intervals, **23**.51
  tolerance intervals, **23.52–23.59**
Statistical methods:
  acceptance sampling, **25.1–25.103**
  analysis of development data, **13.57, 13.58**
  basic methods, **23.1–23.121**
  calculation of descriptive statistics,
    23.16–23.19
  clustering and discrimination, **23.94–23.96**
  computer use in analysis, **23.115–23.117,
    27.24–27.29**
  continuous probability distributions,
    23.32–23.45
  descriptive statistics, **23.11–23.21**
  design and analysis of experiments,
    26.1–26.77
  discrete probability distribution,
    23.26–23.32
  estimation (*see* Statistical estimation)
  measures of central tendency, **23.16–23.17**
  measures of dispersion, **23.17–23.18**
  probability models for experiments,
    23.21–23.26
  regression and correlation (*see* Regression
    and correlation analysis)
  reliability, **23.81–23.91**
  sources of data, **23.3–23.11**
  statistical process control, **24.1–24.39**
  statistical tool kit, **23.2–23.5**
  tests of hypotheses (*see* Hypotheses, tests of)
  transformation of data, **23.91–23.94**

Statistical process control (SPC):
  of automated processes, **24.36–24.39**
  control charts in (*see* Control charts)
  defined, **24**.2
  PRE-Control in (*see* PRE-Control)
  software for, **24.38–24.39, 27.26–27.29**
  theory, **24.3–24.7**
Statistical quality control (SQC), **22**.11
  defined, **24**.2
  theory, **24.3–24.7**
  (*See also* Statistical process control)
Statistical techniques and procedures, selected
    documents, **AIII.7–AIII**.9
Statistical tolerance limits, **23.52–23.56**
Statistical tolerancing, comparison of, with
    conventional, **23.58–23.59**
Statistical tool kit, **23.2–23.5**
Steelmaking process, **28.39–28.40**
Steelworkers of America, **10**.22
Steering arm (*see* Project team organizations)
Steinway & Sons Piano Co., **6**.27
Stepwise regression, **23**.117
Stevens Institute of Technology, **24**.4
Storage areas for inspection, **18.37, 18.38**
Storyboarding, **22.36–22.37**
Strata in bulk sampling, defined, **25**.85
Strategic planning for quality, **12**.24
Strategy for quality, **3.17–3.20**
  (*See also* Companywide planning for
    quality)
Stream-to-stream analysis, **22**.41
Stress testing, in software development, **14**.18
Structure tree, **22**.39
Structured product/process analysis, **13**.13
Supplier/customer network, **10.23–10.24**
Supplier part control, plan form, **15**.22
Supplier quality rating, **15.40–15.44**
  measures in use, **15.41–15.42**
  supplier data, use of, **15.42–15.43**
Supplier quality survey, **15.14–15.17**
  information collected, **15**.15
  merits and limitations, **15.16–15.17**
  scoring, **15**.15
  steps in, **15**.14
  third-party assessment, **15.17–15.18**
Supplier relations:
  activities in, **15.3–15.4**
  approved supplier lists, **15**.18
  in assembly industries, **30.18–30.21**
  audits, **15.33, 30.44, 30.46, 30.48**
  capability evaluation, **15.12–15.18**
  certificate of compliance, **15**.32
  certificate of test, **15**.32
  certification, **15.32–15.34, 30.18–30.21**
  communication in, **15.24, 15.27**
  cooperation with suppliers during execution
    of contract, **15**.25
  corrective action, **15**.27
  data banks in, **15**.13

Supplier relations (*Cont.*):
  departmental responsibilities, **15.7–15.9**
  design changes, **15.26**
  deviations, **15.26**
  early involvement of, **30.18**
  evaluating delivered product, **15.28–15.32**
  importance of, **15.2**
  improvement of quality, **15.34–15.37**
  incoming inspection, **15.29–15.32**
  in job shop industries, **32.29**
  joint economic planning, **15.20–15.21**
  joint managerial planning, **15.23–15.25**
  joint quality planning, **15.20–15.25**
  joint technological planning, **15.21–15.23**
  "just-in-time" inventory, **15.3**
  legal problems, **15.43**
  manual, **15.24–15.25**
  models for, **15.9**
  multiple vs. single-source suppliers, **15.6,
    32.29**
  objectives for, **15.3**
  organizing for, **15.7–15.9**
  part control plan form, **15.22**
  policies, **5.8–5.9**
  positive communication, **15.27**
  precontract planning, **15.9–15.12**
  preferred supplier program, **15.34**
  process capability analysis, **15.13–15.14**
  published quality policy, **15.7**
  qualification of supplier design, **15.12**
  qualification of supplier manufacturing
    process, **15.13–15.18**
  qualification process, **15.12–15.18**
  quality policy, **15.4–15.7**
  rating suppliers, **15.40–15.44, 30.20–30.21**
  recognition of suppliers, **30.21**
  responsibility, buyer vs. supplier, **15.23**
  savings from improvement, **15.37**
  single-source suppliers, **15.38**
  stimulating the supplier to take action,
    15.35
  supplier certification, **15.32, 30.18–30.21**
  supplier reliability program, **15.11**
  supplier selection, **15.18–15.20**
  supplier surveillance, **15.27–15.28**
  suppliers' views vs. customers', **3.1,
    3.5–3.7**
  survey of quality (*see* Supplier quality
    survey)
  teamwork, **15.5, 15.25, 15.36, 15.37, 15.40**
  technical assistance to the supplier,
    15.36–15.37
  third-party assessment, **15.17–15.18**
  total cost of a purchase, **15.19–15.20**
  training of suppliers, **11.22, 15.38–15.40,
    30.19**
  two-way communication in, **15.26–15.27**
  upper management, role of, **15.37**
Supplier reliability program, **15.11**

Supply sources:
  internal vs. external, **15.6**
  long-term, **15.6**
  multiple vs. single, **15.6, 32.29**
Support activities:
  defined, **21.2**
  diagnostic assistance for, **21.16–21.21**
  feedback loop for, **21.14**
  measures of quality performance,
    21.14–21.15
  Pareto analysis in, **21.16–21.17**
  quality improvement in, **21.15–21.21**
"Supposed to do," knowledge of, **10.29,
    17.6–17.12, 33.62**
"Surplus quality," **35F.19**
Surveys:
  of customers, **33.30–33.31, 33.34,
    33.70–33.71**
  distinguished from audits, **9.14–9.15**
  examples, **9.15–9.17**
  for field intelligence, **12.14–12.15**
  of product (*see* Product auditing)
  questions in companywide issues, **9.17–9.18**
    functional areas, **9.18–9.20**
  reference standards for, **9.21–9.22**
  third-party audit in, **9.20–9.21**
  (*See also* Audits)
Symbols, **Appendix I**
Symptom(s):
  analysis of, **22.35–22.36**
  confusion with cause, **22.56**
  defined, **22.31**
System and program requirements, selected
    documents, **AIII.2–AIII.7**
Systems approach to improve fitness for use,
    12.23–12.24
Systems audit, **17.26, 17.28**
  (*See also* Audits)
Systems engineering, **13.13, 14.5**
  defined, **14.4**
  process, **14.6**
  in product development, **13.13**
  in software development, **14.5–14.6**

t test:
  defined, **23.65, 23.66**
  examples, **23.64**
  table for, **AII.16**
τ_d percentiles, table of, **AII.17, AII.19**
Tables and charts, **AII.1–AII.43**
Tabular arrangement of theories, **22.37**
Taylor system, **5.10, 10.3–10.4, 10.27, 10.37,
    35G.2–35G.3**
  adverse effects of, **10.4, 10.27, 10.37**
  description of, **10.3, 10.4**
  effects of, **10.3, 10.4**
  nature of innovations in, **10.4**
  separation of planning from operation, **10.3**
  union response to, **10.4**

TBF (*see* Time between failures)
Team performance, **10.41–10.45**
Technical Engineering Aids for Management, **23.37**
Technical Assistance Research Programs (TARP), **20.16, 20.21**
Technique errors, **6.37, 22.56–22.58**
Telephone company service quality, **33.38**
Teltag, **34.8**
Tennessee Valley Authority, **3.22**
Terminology:
 in diagnosis, **22.31**
 in the quality function, **2.1–2.13**
 in the quality manual, **6.40**
 quality systems, **AIV.1–AIV.3**
 standardization of, **2.12–2.13**
 (*See also specific terms, under "defined"*)
Test of theories, **22.40–22.59**
 management-controllable problems, **22.40–22.53**
  association searches for, **22.48–22.50**
  defect concentration diagrams for, **22.45**
  designed experiments for, **22.51–22.52**
  flow diagrams for, **22.41**
  process capability studies for, **22.41**
  stream-to-stream analysis for, **22.41**
  time-to-time analysis for, **22.41–22.45**
 worker-controllable problems, **22.53–22.61**
  conscious errors, **22.59–22.61**
  inadvertent errors, **22.55–22.56**
  technique errors, **22.56–22.58**
 (*See also* Hypotheses, tests of)
Test market, **19.8**
Test methods:
 development, in chemical industry, **28.11–28.15**
 precision, in chemical industry, **28.16–28.19**
 (*See also* Inspection and test)
Test-unit in bulk sampling, defined, **25.86**
Texas Instruments, Inc., **8.12, 8.15, 23.19**
Theories of defect causation, **22.40–22.61**
 formulation of, **22.36**
 orderly arrangement of, **22.37**
  use of Ishikawa diagram for, **22.37–22.39**
 sources of, **22.36**
 test: by correlation, **22.48, 22.49**
  by "cutting new windows," **22.50**
  by matrixes, **22.49**
  by measurement of additional properties, **22.50–22.51**
Theory:
 vs. cause, **22.31**
 defined, **22.31**
Theory X and Theory Y, **10.5–10.7**
Third-party audit, **8.23–8.24**
Three Mile Island nuclear plant, **10.40**
Time between failures (TBF), **23.82–23.85**
Time-dominant operations, **16.50, 17.19–17.20**

Time-to-time analysis, **22.41–22.44**
Timeliness of service, **33.13–33.14, 33.17**
Tolerance intervals, **23.52–23.59**
Tolerances:
 advisory vs. mandatory, **17.9–17.10**
 capable process relation to, **16.18**
 cost of, **16.8**
 incompatible with process capability, **16.15–16.16**
 for interacting dimensions, **23.56–23.59**
 mandatory and advisory, **17.9–17.10**
 methods of setting, **13.56–13.61, 23.52–23.60**
 one-sided, **24.33**
 in PRE-Control **24.33–24.34**
 process control and product acceptance, **17.9**
 statistical tolerance limits, **23.52**
 two-sided, **24.34**
 unrealistic, **13.60**
 (*See also* Specifications)
Tolerancing, **13.56–13.61**
 simulator, **11.19, 11.30**
Top management (*see* Upper Management)
Total cost of purchase, categories of, **15.19**
Toyota, **10.10**
TR-3, TR-4, TR-6, and TR-7, reliability sampling plans, **25.82–25.85**
Traceability, **16.39**
Trademark, **19.16**
Training:
 American Management Association, **11.12**
 American Society for Quality Control, **11.12**
 budgets for, **11.37**
 classroom training, **11.12**
 for course leaders, **11.22–11.23**
 for designers, **13.72–13.73**
 effect of, **11.4**
 evaluation, **11.31**
 in developing countries, **35B.18–35B.22**
 for first-line supervisors, **11.19, 11.20**
 instructional technology, **11.25–11.30**
 (*See also* Instructional technology)
 Japanese companywide quality control and, **35F.9–35F.11**
 Juran Institute, **11.12**
 major issues, **11.4–11.5**
 means of providing, **11.10–11.13**
  classroom training, **11.12**
  self-instruction, **11.12**
  supplements to formal training approach, **11.12**
 methods, application to company problems, **11.24**
  case examples, **11.24–11.25**
  role playing, **11.25**
  simulation, **11.25**
 national approaches, **11.34–11.37**
 need for, **11.2**

Training (*Cont.*):
  needs analysis for, **11.9, 35G.11–35G.12**
  for nonsupervisors, **11.19, 11.20**
  for other middle managers, **11.15**
  for outsiders, **11.21–11.22**
  planning, **11.5–11.9**
    corporate plan or not?, **11.7**
    examples, **11.5–11.9**
    who plans?, **11.5, 11.7**
  premises, **11.3–11.4**
  production personnel, **17.30**
  for quality improvement, **22.9**
  for quality managers, **11.15**
  for quality planners, **6.49–6.50**
  role in motivation, **10.17**
  rotational job experience, **11.11**
  schedules for, **11.37–11.38**
  for service industries, **11.21**
  in socialist countries, **35H.11–35H.13**
  for specialists, **11.16–11.19**
  for suppliers, **6.50, 11.22, 15.38–15.40, 30.19**
  for support areas, **11.21**
  in U.S.A., **35G.11, 35G.12**
  at university level, **11.33–11.34**
  for upper management, **8.24, 11.13–11.14**
  why programs fail, **11.9–11.10**
Transfer to operations, **6.17–6.18**
  in administrative and support activities, **21.12, 21.13**
Transformations of data, **23.91–23.94**
Transportation in customer service, **20.3–20.4**
Travel agency service quality, **33.39**
Treatment in design of experiments, defined, **26.3**
Trilogy:
  Juran, **2.7–2.8**
  quality, **2.6, 35G.8**
Triple-role concept:
  applied to administrative and support operations, **21.4, 21.5**
  defined, **6.19–6.20**
Troubleshooting, **17.29–17.30, 22.70–22.72**
TRW, Inc., **11.36**
Two-sided normal test, chart of operating characteristics, curves, **AII.33**
Two-tail test vs. one-tail, **23.64**
Type A and Type B sampling, **25.4**
Type I error, **23.60–23.63**
Type II error, **23.61–23.63**

u charts, **24.23, 24.24**
Unbridled experiment, **22.52**
Underwriters' Laboratories (UL), **28.6, 34.7**
Uniform commercial code, **19.8**
Uniform distribution, **23.33**
Uniformity in bulk sampling, defined, **25.86**
Unions and quality, **10.21–10.23**
United Air Lines, **33.70–33.71**

United Auto Workers, **10.22**
United States, quality in, **35G.1–35G.13**
  early systems, **35G.2–35G.4**
  economic background, **35G.1–35G.2**
  Japanese impact, **10.14–10.16, 35G.4**
  lessons learned, **35G.7–35G.12**
  prognosis, **35G.12–35G.13**
  response to the Japanese quality revolution, **35G.6–35G.7**
  Taylor system impact, **10.3–10.4, 35G.2–35G.3**
  upper-management participation, **35G.7**
  World War II impact, **35G.4**
U.S. Department of Defense, **3.25, 31.5, 31.13**
U.S. Department of Transportation, **3.10, 16.28**
United States Fidelity & Guaranty Co., **33.50–33.57**
Units of measure, **6.35, 18.58–18.60, 21.11**
University of California, **27.27**
University of Chicago, **27.29**
Unrealistic tolerances loosely enforced, **13.60–13.61**
Upper management:
  defined, **8.2**
  evolution in managing for quality, **8.2**
  participation by, **8.3–8.7, 35G.7**
    establish quality council, **8.4**
    establish quality goals, **8.4–8.5**
    establish quality policies, **8.4**
    give recognition, **8.6–8.7**
    provide problem-oriented training, **8.5**
    provide resources, **8.5**
    resistance to participation, **8.7–8.8**
    review progress, **8.6**
    revise the reward system, **8.7**
    role in supplier relations, **15.37**
    selective participation, **8.8**
    serve on quality council, **8.4**
    serve on quality improvement teams, **8.6**
    stimulate improvement, **8.6**
  quality assurance for, **8.8**
  quality audits by, **8.20–8.24**
    (*See also* Audits)
  reports to executives on quality, **8.8–8.20**
    (*See also* Reports on quality)
  training for, **8.24**
Uptime, **2.9, 13.41, 22.42**
User:
  defined, **2.3**
  definition of quality by, **3.7–3.8**
  knowledge of fitness for use by, **3.8–3.9**
User knowledge, degrees of, **3.7–3.9**

Validation in computers, **14.5, 14.20–14.22**
Value:
  defined, **35E.6**

Value (*Cont.*):
  as measure of relative importance, **12.19**, **12.20**
  and quality, **3.10**
Value engineering (value analysis), **13.63**
  in complex industries, **31.20–31.23**
  defined, **13.63–13.66**
  steps, **13.63–13.66**
Variables, acceptance sampling of (*see* Acceptance sampling, of variables)
Variance:
  analysis of (*see* Analysis of variance)
  defined, **23.17**
  segregation, in bulk sampling, **25.88**
  test, in bulk sampling, **25.89**
Vendor relations (*see* Supplier relations)
Verification in computers, **14.5**
Very large-scale integration (VLSI) devices, **29.8**, **29.9**
Visual quality characteristics, **18.49–18.52**
  consumer sensitivity to, **18.48–18.49**
  defect grades for, **18.50**
  inspection standards for, **18.50–18.51**
  inspector judgments in, **18.49**
Vital few (*see* Pareto analysis, vital few)

Wall Street Journal, The, **13.6**
Warranty of quality, **19.8–19.14**, **34.11**
  business opportunities, **19.12–19.14**
  consequential damage, **19.11**
  consumer products, **19.9–19.10**
  consumer reactions to warranty provisions, **19.11**
  disclaimers, **19.10–19.11**
  duration of, **19.10**
  express, **19.9**
  full or limited, **19.9–19.10**
  government regulation, **19.12**
  implied, **19.8–19.9**
  industrial products, **19.9**
  period, **12.5**, **12.13**
  reliability improvement, **19.13–19.14**
  warranties and service contracts, **19.13**

Wear-out period, **23.81**
Weibull distribution, **23.34–23.37**
  in reliability testing, **13.35**, **25.82–25.84**
Western Electric Company, Inc., **23.59**
  Hawthorne plant, **10.4**, **10.13**
Westinghouse Electric Corporation, **11.3**
Why-why diagram, **22.40**
Wilcoxon-Mann-Whitney test, table of, **AII.30**
Wilson Learning Corporation, **9.20**
Within-piece-to-piece analysis, **22.44–22.48**
Worker-controllable and management-controllable defects, **17.5–17.6**, **18.84–18.94**, **22.40–22.61**
Worker-dominant operations, **16.50**, **17.20**
Worker errors:
  in administrative and support operations, **21.14–21.15**
  conscious, **22.59–22.61**
  controllable and noncontrollable, **17.5–17.6**, **18.84–18.94**
  inadvertent, **22.55–22.56**
  in inspection (*see* Inspector errors)
  remedies for, **21.15**
  technique, **22.56–22.58**
Worker methods, study of, **22.58–22.59**
Worker ownership in Germany, **35D.2**
Worker participation in process management, **10.25–10.31**
World industry, **35B.2**
Worst-case analysis, **13.31**

$\overline{X}$ charts, **24.8–24.18**
X-ray testing, **18.72**
Xerox Corp., **30.4**, **30.8**, **30.12**, **30.19**, **30.28**, **30.41**, **30.44**

Yields, process, **29.4–29.5**, **29.11**
Youden square design of experiments, **26.64**

Zero defects:
  contrasted with Saratov system, **35H.10–35H.11**
  as an objective, **5.21–5.22**

ABOUT THE EDITORS

J. M. JURAN, industrial executive, engineer, author, lecturer, and consultant for over half a century, has published the leading international reference literature and training media on quality. He and his work have received over 30 honors from some one dozen countries.

FRANK M. GRYNA, Distinguished Professor of Industrial Engineering Emeritus at Bradley University and vice president of Juran Institute, Inc., is co-author (with Dr. Juran) of *Quality Planning and Analysis* (also published by McGraw-Hill).